Britain

Ryan ver Berkmoes
Neal Bedford   Oda O'Carroll
Lou Callan   Nick Ray
Fionn Davenport   Tom Smallman

LONELY PLANET PUBLICATIONS
Melbourne • Oakland • London • Paris

BRITAIN

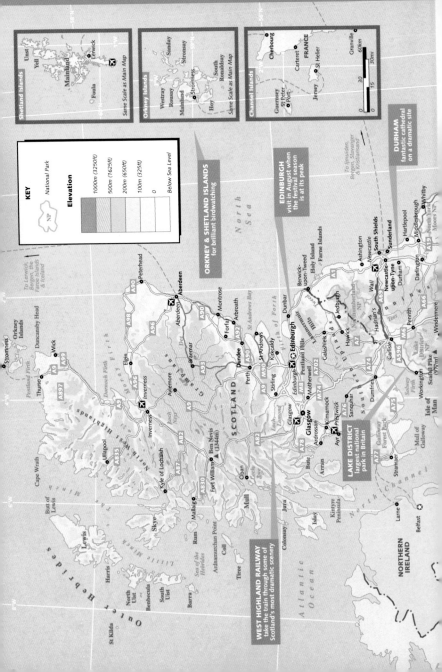

Shetland Islands
Same Scale as Main Map

Unst
Yell
Mainland
Foula
Lerwick

Orkney Islands
Same Scale as Main Map

Sanday
Stronsay
Westray
Rousay
Mainland
Stromness
South
Ronaldsay
Hoy

Channel Islands

FRANCE
Cherbourg
Carteret
St Helier
Granville
Guernsey
St Peter Port
Jersey

0   15   30m
0   30   60km

KEY

National Park

NP

Elevation

	1000m (3250ft)
	500m (1625ft)
	200m (650ft)
	100m (325ft)
	0
	Below Sea Level

ORKNEY & SHETLAND ISLANDS
for brilliant birdwatching

EDINBURGH
visit in August when
the festival season
is at its peak

DURHAM
fantastic cathedral
on a dramatic site

North
Sea

To Lewick, Bergen, the Faroe Islands & Iceland

To Ijmuiden, Bergen, Stavanger & Kristiansand

Orkney
Islands
Stromness
Duncansby Head
Thurso
Wick
A9
A99
A97

Peterhead
Aberdeen
Montrose
Arbroath
Forfar
St Andrews Bay

Elgin
A96
A98
Inverness
Aviemore
Braemar
Dundee
St Andrews
Perth
Kirkcaldy

Cape Wrath
Ullapool
A835
Kyle of Lochalsh
Loch Ness
Ben Nevis
(1344m)
Fort William
Stirling
Pentland Hills
Edinburgh
Dunbar
Berwick-upon-Tweed
Holy Island
Farne Islands

Butt of Lewis
Lewis
Harris
Skye
Rum
Mallaig
Oban
Mull
Iona
Colonsay

North Uist
Benbecula
South Uist
Barra
St Kilda

Sea of the Hebrides
Little Minch
The Minch

SCOTLAND
Grampians
North West Highlands
Moray Firth
Dornoch Firth
Pentland Firth

Glasgow
Motherwell
Kilmarnock
Ayr
Prestwick
Ardrossan
Bute
Arran
Jura
Islay
Tiree
Coll
Ardnamurchan Point
Kintyre Peninsula

Galashiels
Hawick
Jedburgh
Southern Uplands
Dumfries
Sanquhar
A76
A74
A75
Stranraer
Mull of Galloway

Newcastle upon Tyne
South Shields
Sunderland
Hartlepool
Middlesbrough
Whitby
North York Moors NP
Darlington
A19
A1
A66
Penrith
Carlisle
Hadrian's Wall
Northumberland NP
Cheviot Hills
Ashington
A69
Workington
Whitehaven
Isle of Man
Lake District NP
Scafell Pike
(977m)
Windermere
Solway Firth

WEST HIGHLAND RAILWAY
take the train through some of
Scotland's most dramatic scenery

LAKE DISTRICT
largest national
park in Britain

NORTHERN
IRELAND

Belfast
Larne

Atlantic
Ocean

North Channel

Irish Sea

Galloway
Forest Park

Outer Hebrides

LONDON

SOUTH-EASTERN ENGLAND

SOUTH-WESTERN ENGLAND

237

15

303

Contents – Text

Britain
4th edition – April 2001
First published – April 1995

Published by
Lonely Planet Publications Pty Ltd ABN 36 005 607 983
90 Maribyrnong St, Footscray, Victoria 3011, Australia

Lonely Planet Offices
Australia Locked Bag 1, Footscray, Victoria 3011
USA 150 Linden St, Oakland, CA 94607
UK 10a Spring Place, London NW5 3BH
France 1 rue du Dahomey, 75011 Paris

Photographs
Many of the images in this guide are available for licensing from
Lonely Planet Images.
email: lpi@lonelyplanet.com.au

Front cover photograph
Palace guards on duty in London (Rob Atkins, The Image Bank)

ISBN 1 86450 147 2

text & maps © Lonely Planet 2001
photos © photographers as indicated 2001

Printed by The Bookmaker International Ltd
Printed in China

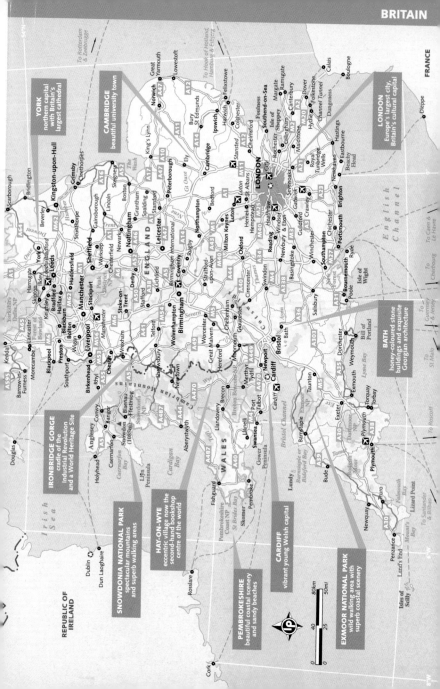

BRITAIN

YORK
northern capital with Britain's largest cathedral

CAMBRIDGE
beautiful university town

LONDON
Europe's largest city, Britain's cultural capital

BATH
honey-coloured stone buildings and exquisite Georgian architecture

IRONBRIDGE GORGE
cradle of the Industrial Revolution and a World Heritage Site

SNOWDONIA NATIONAL PARK
spectacular mountains and superb walking areas

HAY-ON-WYE
eccentric village now the second-hand bookshop centre of the world

CARDIFF
vibrant young Welsh capital

PEMBROKESHIRE
beautiful coastal scenery and sandy beaches

EXMOOR NATIONAL PARK
wild walking area with superb coastal scenery

REPUBLIC OF IRELAND

FRANCE

CENTRAL ENGLAND

EASTERN ENGLAND

FACTS ABOUT WALES

CARDIFF (CAERDYDD)

SOUTH WALES

CENTRAL WALES

NORTH WALES

Contents – Maps

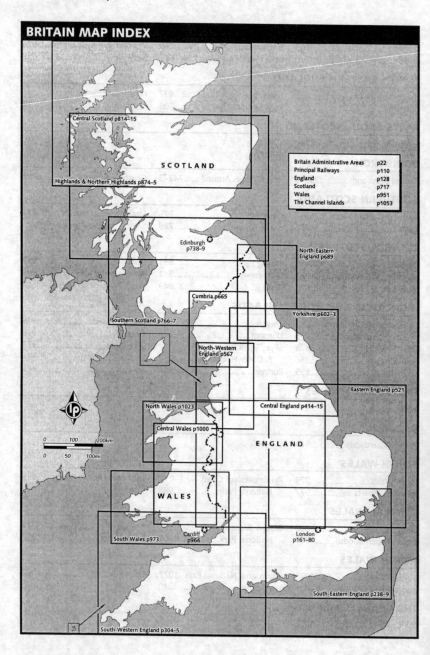

BRITAIN MAP INDEX

Central Scotland p814–15

SCOTLAND

Highlands & Northern Highlands p874–5

Britain Administrative Areas	p22
Principal Railways	p110
England	p128
Scotland	p717
Wales	p951
The Channel Islands	p1053

Edinburgh p738–9

North-Eastern England p689

Cumbria p665

Yorkshire p602–3

Southern Scotland p766–7

North-Western England p567

Eastern England p521

North Wales p1023

Central England p414–15

Central Wales p1000

ENGLAND

WALES

South Wales p973

Cardiff p964

London p161–80

South-Eastern England p238–9

South-Western England p304–5

0   100   200km
0   50   100mi

The Authors

Ryan Ver Berkmoes

Ryan was coordinating author of this book and researched and wrote the front chapters, London, Yorkshire and the Channel Islands. Ryan grew up in Santa Cruz, California, which he left aged 17 for college in the Midwest, where he discovered snow. All joy of this novelty soon wore off. His first job was in Chicago at a small muckraking publication where he had the impressive title of Managing Editor because he was second on a two-person editorial staff and the first person was called Editor. After a year of 60-hour weeks, Ryan took his first trip to Europe, which lasted seven months and confirmed his long-suspected wanderlust. Since then his by-line has appeared in scores of publications and he has covered everything from wars to bars. He definitely prefers the latter. Among his work for Lonely Planet, he is the author of *Chicago* and *Moscow*, co-wrote *Texas*, *Canada* and *Western Europe*, and coordinated *Russia, Ukraine & Belarus*, *Great Lakes*, *Out to Eat London*, *Netherlands* and *England*. In the future, Ryan hopes to add more warm-weather destinations to the list above, although covering places filled with pubs is a novelty that never wears out. He and his journalist wife Sara Marley reside in London near the point of inspiration for noted musician Nigel Tufnel.

Neal Bedford

Born in Papakura, New Zealand, Neal gave up an exciting career in accounting to experience the mundane life of a traveller. With the urge to move, travel led him through a number of countries and jobs, ranging from an au pair in Vienna, lifeguard in the USA, fruit picker in Israel and lettuce-washer at rock concerts. Deciding to give his life some direction, he well and truly got his foot stuck in the door by landing the lucrative job of book-packer in Lonely Planet's London office. One thing led to another and he managed to cross over to the mystic world of authoring.

Neal currently resides in London, but the need to move will probably soon kick in and force him to try his luck somewhere else. This is his second book for Lonely Planet.

Lou Callan

After completing a degree in languages, Lou bounced between a variety of jobs while completing further study in publishing and editing. After lots of strenuous book-launch parties as Publicity Manager at Oxford University Press Australia, she found work as a contributing editor on *Australian Bookseller & Publisher*. In 1998, after four years at Lonely Planet as Phrasebooks Editor, Lou packed up and followed her husband, Tony, to the red dunes of the United Arab Emirates for a very long, hot 2½ years. Here she wrote Lonely Planet's *Dubai City Guide* and, with Gordon Robison, *Oman & UAE* as well as an update for *Middle East*. Lou is now very nicely wedged between beaches and wineries on the Mornington Peninsula in Victoria with Tony the husband and Ziggy the cat.

Fionn Davenport

Fionn was born in and spent most of his youth in Dublin – that is, when his family wasn't moving him to Buenos Aires or Geneva or New York (all thanks to his dad, whose job took him far and wide). Infected with the travel disease, he became a nomad in his own right after graduating from Trinity College, moving first to Paris and then to New York, where he spent five years as a travel editor and sometime writer. The call of home was too much to resist, however, so armed with his portable computer, his record collection and an empty wallet he returned to Dublin where he decided to continue where he left off in New York. Only it was quieter, wetter and a hell of a lot smaller. When he's not DJing in pubs and clubs throughout the city he's writing and updating travel guides. This is his fifth book for Lonely Planet, having worked already on *Spain*, *Dublin*, *Ireland* and *Sicily*.

Oda O'Carroll

Oda updated the Welsh chapters – her first assignment with Lonely Planet. Born in Roscommon, in the windy mid-west of Ireland, she packed her knapsack for the big smoke of Dublin where she studied Communications until 1990.

Since graduating she has worked as a television researcher and writer for the independent sector in Ireland. Oda also spent some time donkey-working on film sets and made her own short film in 1998. She has travelled extensively in Europe and last summer chugged between America's coasts, with friends, in a clapped-out 1967 Cadillac (without A/C) and hopes to return soon for the northern route. She lives happily in Dublin with her husband Eoin and daughter Ésa.

Nick Ray

Nick wrote the South-Western England and Central England chapters. A Londoner of sorts, he harks from Watford, the sort of town that makes you want to travel. He studied history and politics at Warwick University and stumbled out clutching a piece of paper that said he knew stuff about things. For this guide, for once, he didn't have to travel too far, darting about the green fields of England, not to mention a few pubs along the way. Usually, he is to be found writing books in the more obscure parts of Africa or Asia, Cambodia in particular, a country he thinks of as a second home.

Tom Smallman

Tom lives in Melbourne, Australia, and had a number of jobs before joining Lonely Planet as an editor. He now works full-time as an author and has worked on Lonely Planet guides to Scotland, Edinburgh, Australia, New South Wales, Sydney, Canada, Ireland, Dublin and Pennsylvania.

FROM THE AUTHORS

Ryan Ver Berkmoes Thanks to the tourism authorities in Yorkshire, London and the rest of the country. The many stand-outs include Bill Breakell at the North York Moors National Park and Margaret Coates in Whitby. Many others were generous with their time, including Lonely Planet authors David and Corinne Else, who showed me a fine time in Sheffield and bore with grace my strained relations with the Punto.

I have a huge debt to Steve Fallon for supplying the fine text from Lonely Planet's *London* that formed the basis for my own London research. Also in London, my debts are many and include Andrew Humphreys, who always is a fount of wisdom, and Dave Moorman, Ted Allen and Barry Rice for joining me in my explorations.

It was a delight to work with the other authors, who warmed my heart with their enthusiastic response to my call for more pub recommendations.

Lonely Planet's London office proved their value in matters beyond warm beer on occasional Fridays. Kath Leck tossed the project to me in the first place (and I will forever thank her for the easy commute). Marcel Gaston and Amanda Canning were their fine professional selves and David Wenk was thoughtful in mapping matters and proved adept as a bicycle delivery service. Emma Sangster did a splendid job of coping with the entire country from her Kentish Town desk. Tom Hall hit all the right notes with his music contribution and Imogen Franks was a peach for her insider knowledge of the posh bits of Yorkshire.

Finally, many thanks to my partner in British travel and beyond, Sara Marley. Okay, next time I'll do a *warm* book...

Neal Bedford Thanks firstly go to Ryan for all the guidance I received during the research and writing. Hearty thanks to John Richards for his wisdom on Manchester, and Dawn Hedley and Nick Rowley for their northern England travel tips. Big thanks to everyone in the London Lonely Planet office, in particular for their extra special effort (which they had no choice in giving!) – Paul Bloomfield, Katrina Browning, Imogen Franks, Tom Hall, Howard Ralley, Tim Ryder, Sam Trafford, Angie Watts and Dave Wenk. And also to the ex-Planeteers – Tom Bevan, Nicky Robinson and Anna Sutton. As always, special thanks to the tourist-office staff throughout the country who made my life easier.

My gratitude and sympathy go out to those who had to put up with me on the road, the Bevan family and friends for their wonderful hospitality (the best B&B in England), Nik Pickard and Rachel Parker for being great friends and Robert Box and Claire Delamey for doing my head in!

Thanks to Tony Ludlam, part of the Dublin contingency that kept me on track. And a big bussi to Christina Tlustos for all the support and guidance.

Lou Callan Special thanks to Tony Cleaver, my darling husband and ideal travel companion; to Sarah Biggs and Nigel Biggs in the UK, who are always so generous and helpful; and to Danny Foster in the UK, thanks for the phone calls and the beers.

Fionn Davenport Thanks to everybody at the Tourist Information Centres (TICS), who were extremely friendly, courteous and helpful. A big thanks to all the folks in Cambridge; you made my stay a very pleasant one. Cheers to all the staff at The Dôme, who gave me plenty of great tips and steered me in the right direction. Lastly, thanks to Ryan and Sara for putting me up: your hospitality is greatly appreciated and I look forward to seeing you both again.

Oda O'Carroll Thanks to all the helpful staff at Cardiff TIC, the witty Nova at Porthmadog TIC, Eoin and Etain for their scintillating company on the road (and for fixing my seat), Jim & Curley (happy surfing!), Gareth & Eva Evans for the Indian and gossip, Melvyn Williams and Ynyr Williams for all their useful information, Margaret Bamford in Dolgellau, Jay Bourke and Kathryn Maguire (who almost made it).

Nick Ray Many thanks to many people, most importantly my loving girlfriend Kulikar for enriching my life, to my wonderful parents for their enduring support and to my fantastic friends, the finest around. A big thank you also to my relatives in Worcestershire for pointers in that part of the country, particularly Nick George and Sarah Barr. In Nottingham, a big hello to the Johnson brothers, Chris and Andrew, who gave me a full-on introduction to that fine city. Thanks to Brigham Whitney for hospitality in Bristol. Cheers also to the many good folk of England who helped me out in many ways and proved that, but for a few idiots, the English are generally a pretty decent bunch. In particular, thanks to the staff of numerous TICs for their insights and many of the staff at Lonely Planet's London office and my fellow authors for suggestions, advice and patience.

Tom Smallman My eternal gratitude to Sue Graefe for her patience and tolerant support; to Hugh MacKenzie Gore for his encyclopaedic knowledge; to Alistair, Elspeth and family in Kelso; to all the people in the travel industry who patiently answered my questions and to those readers who wrote in with comments on the previous edition.

This Book

This is the 4th edition of Lonely Planet's Britain. Richard Everist, Tony Wheeler and Bryn Thomas wrote the 1st edition. Bryn Thomas, Sean Sheehan and Pat Yale wrote the 2nd edition. Bryn Thomas, Tom Smallman and Pat Yale wrote the 3rd edition. Ryan Ver Berkmoes was coordinating author of this edition and also updated the London, Yorkshire, Channel Islands and introductory chapters. Lou Callan updated the South-Eastern England chapter. Nick Ray updated the South-Western and Central England chapters. Fionn Davenport updated the Eastern England chapter. Neal Bedford updated the North-Eastern England, North-Western England and Cumbria chapters. Oda O'Carroll updated the Wales chapters. And finally Tom Smallman updated the Scotland chapters.

From the Publisher

This 4th edition of Britain was produced in Lonely Planet's London office and coordinated by Emma Sangster (editing) and David Wenk (mapping and design).

Emma was assisted with editing and proofing by a team comprising Heather Dickson, Imogen Franks, Michala Green, Claire Hornshaw, Anna Jacomb-Hoods and Arabella Shepherd. Abigail Hole and Michala Green produced the index. David was assisted with the mapping by Paul Edmunds, James Ellis, Ed Pickard, Ian Stokes and James Timmins. Adam McCrow designed the front cover and Jim Miller drew the back-cover map. Jane Smith supplied the illustrations.

Thanks are also due to Paul Bloomfield, Amanda Canning, Paul Clifton, Tim Fitzgerald, Quentin Frayne, Marcel Gaston, Tom Hall, Rachel Suddart and Samantha Trafford for their expert advice.

Thanks to all the authors for their hard work and good humour, and especial gratitude to Ésa O'Carroll, who waited patiently until her mother had made the final touches to the Welsh chapters before making her entrance into the world.

Foreword

ABOUT LONELY PLANET GUIDEBOOKS

The story begins with a classic travel adventure: Tony and Maureen Wheeler's 1972 journey across Europe and Asia to Australia. Useful information about the overland trail did not exist at that time, so Tony and Maureen published the first Lonely Planet guidebook to meet a growing need.

From a kitchen table, then from a tiny office in Melbourne (Australia), Lonely Planet has become the largest independent travel publisher in the world, an international company with offices in Melbourne, Oakland (USA), London (UK) and Paris (France).

Today Lonely Planet guidebooks cover the globe. There is an ever-growing list of books and there's information in a variety of forms and media. Some things haven't changed. The main aim is still to help make it possible for adventurous travellers to get out there – to explore and better understand the world.

At Lonely Planet we believe travellers can make a positive contribution to the countries they visit – if they respect their host communities and spend their money wisely. Since 1986 a percentage of the income from each book has been donated to aid projects and human rights campaigns.

Updates Lonely Planet thoroughly updates each guidebook as often as possible. This usually means there are around two years between editions, although for more unusual or more stable destinations the gap can be longer. Check the imprint page (following the colour map at the beginning of the book) for publication dates.

Between editions up-to-date information is available in two free newsletters – the paper *Planet Talk* and email *Comet* (to subscribe, contact any Lonely Planet office) – and on our Web site at www.lonelyplanet.com. The *Upgrades* section of the Web site covers a number of important and volatile destinations and is regularly updated by Lonely Planet authors. *Scoop* covers news and current affairs relevant to travellers. And, lastly, the *Thorn Tree* bulletin board and *Postcards* section of the site carry unverified, but fascinating, reports from travellers.

Correspondence The process of creating new editions begins with the letters, postcards and emails received from travellers. This correspondence often includes suggestions, criticisms and comments about the current editions. Interesting excerpts are immediately passed on via newsletters and the Web site, and everything goes to our authors to be verified when they're researching on the road. We're keen to get more feedback from organisations or individuals who represent communities visited by travellers.

> Lonely Planet gathers information for everyone who's curious about the planet – and especially for those who explore it first-hand. Through guidebooks, phrasebooks, activity guides, maps, literature, newsletters, image library, TV series and Web site we act as an information exchange for a worldwide community of travellers.

Research Authors aim to gather sufficient practical information to enable travellers to make informed choices and to make the mechanics of a journey run smoothly. They also research historical and cultural background to help enrich the travel experience and allow travellers to understand and respond appropriately to cultural and environmental issues.

Authors don't stay in every hotel because that would mean spending a couple of months in each medium-sized city and, no, they don't eat at every restaurant because that would mean stretching belts beyond capacity. They do visit hotels and restaurants to check standards and prices, but feedback based on readers' direct experiences can be very helpful.

Many of our authors work undercover, others aren't so secretive. None of them accept freebies in exchange for positive write-ups. And none of our guidebooks contain any advertising.

Production Authors submit their raw manuscripts and maps to offices in Australia, USA, UK or France. Editors and cartographers – all experienced travellers themselves – then begin the process of assembling the pieces. When the book finally hits the shops some things are already out of date, we start getting feedback from readers, and the process begins again ...

WARNING & REQUEST

Things change – prices go up, schedules change, good places go bad and bad places go bankrupt – nothing stays the same. So, if you find things better or worse, recently opened or long since closed, please tell us and help make the next edition even more accurate and useful. We genuinely value all the feedback we receive. Julie Young coordinates a well travelled team that reads and acknowledges every letter, postcard and email and ensures that every morsel of information finds its way to the appropriate authors, editors and cartographers for verification.

Everyone who writes to us will find their name in the next edition of the appropriate guidebook. They will also receive the latest issue of *Planet Talk*, our quarterly printed newsletter, or *Comet*, our monthly email newsletter. Subscriptions to both newsletters are free. The very best contributions will be rewarded with a free guidebook.

Excerpts from your correspondence may appear in new editions of Lonely Planet guidebooks, the Lonely Planet Web site, *Planet Talk* or *Comet*, so please let us know if you *don't* want your letter published or your name acknowledged.

Send all correspondence to the Lonely Planet office closest to you:

Australia: Locked Bag 1, Footscray, Victoria 3011
USA: 150 Linden St, Oakland, CA 94607
UK: 10a Spring Place, London NW5 3BH
France: 1 rue du Dahomey, 75011 Paris

Or email us at: talk2us@lonelyplanet.com.au

For news, views and updates see our Web site: www.lonelyplanet.com

HOW TO USE A LONELY PLANET GUIDEBOOK

The best way to use a Lonely Planet guidebook is any way you choose. At Lonely Planet we believe the most memorable travel experiences are often those that are unexpected, and the finest discoveries are those you make yourself. Guidebooks are not intended to be used as if they provide a detailed set of infallible instructions!

Contents All Lonely Planet guidebooks follow roughly the same format. The Facts about the Destination chapter or section gives background information ranging from history to weather. Facts for the Visitor gives practical information on issues like visas and health. Getting There & Away gives a brief starting point for researching travel to and from the destination. Getting Around gives an overview of the transport options when you arrive.

The peculiar demands of each destination determine how subsequent chapters are broken up, but some things remain constant. We always start with background, then proceed to sights, places to stay, places to eat, entertainment, getting there and away, and getting around information – in that order.

Heading Hierarchy Lonely Planet headings are used in a strict hierarchical structure that can be visualised as a set of Russian dolls. Each heading (and its following text) is encompassed by any preceding heading that is higher on the hierarchical ladder.

Entry Points We do not assume guidebooks will be read from beginning to end, but that people will dip into them. The traditional entry points are the list of contents and the index. In addition, however, some books have a complete list of maps and an index map illustrating map coverage.

There may also be a colour map that shows highlights. These highlights are dealt with in greater detail in the Facts for the Visitor chapter, along with planning questions and suggested itineraries. Each chapter covering a geographical region usually begins with a locator map and another list of highlights. Once you find something of interest in a list of highlights, turn to the index.

Maps Maps play a crucial role in Lonely Planet guidebooks and include a huge amount of information. A legend is printed on the back page. We seek to have complete consistency between maps and text, and to have every important place in the text captured on a map. Map key numbers usually start in the top left corner.

Although inclusion in a guidebook usually implies a recommendation we cannot list every good place. Exclusion does not necessarily imply criticism. In fact there are a number of reasons why we might exclude a place – sometimes it is simply inappropriate to encourage an influx of travellers.

Introduction

At one stage of its history this small island ruled half of the world's population and had a major impact on many of the rest. For those people whose countries once lay in the shadow of its great empire, a visit to Britain may almost be a cliche but it is also essential – a peculiar mixture of homecoming and confrontation.

To the surprise of many, Britain remains one of the most beautiful islands in the world. All the words, paintings and pictures that have been produced about it are not just romantic, patriotic exaggerations.

In terms of area it is small, but the more you explore the bigger it seems to become. Visitors from the New World are often unaware of this magical expansion and try to do too much too quickly. JB Priestley observed of England, 'She is pretending to be small.' Covering it all in one trip is impossible – and that's before you start thinking of Scotland and Wales.

The United Kingdom comprises Great Britain (England, Scotland and Wales) and Northern Ireland. Its full name is the United Kingdom of Great Britain and Northern Ireland. This book confines itself to the island of Great Britain (the largest of the British Isles), the Isle of Man, the Channel Islands and Scotland's outlying islands – the Hebrides in the west and the Orkney and Shetland Islands in the north-east.

Sometimes in summer it seems like the whole world has come to Britain. Don't spend all your time in the big, tourist-ridden towns. Do pick a small area and spend at least a week or so wandering around the country lanes and villages.

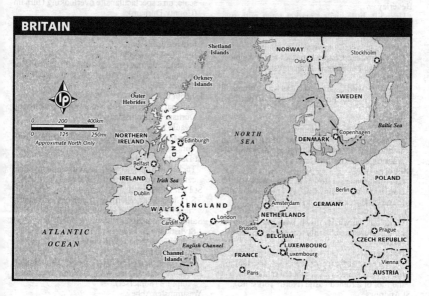

BRITAIN

19

Facts for the Visitor

HIGHLIGHTS

Planning a trip around Britain can be a little bewildering for the first-timer and is no less straightforward if you live here. The country may be small, but its long history as an influential world power has left it with a rich heritage of medieval castles and cathedrals, historic cities and towns, stately homes and elegant gardens. Added to this are the natural attractions: the national parks, beautiful coastal regions and the spectacular Highlands and islands of Scotland. Britain's highlights are so many that we've broken them down into categories.

Historic Cities & Towns

Bath
  Blessed with superb Georgian architecture, but inundated with tourists (south-western England).
Beverley
  Unspoilt, little-visited market town with two superb medieval churches (Yorkshire).
Cambridge
  Famous university town with a compact centre. King's College Chapel is one of Europe's most impressive buildings (Cambridgeshire).
Edinburgh
  One of the world's greatest cities with a dramatic site and extraordinary architectural heritage (Scotland).
Liverpool
  Once a great port and industrial city, boasting a superb legacy of Victorian and Edwardian architecture, a strong cultural identity and vibrant nightlife (north-western England).
Melrose
  Charming market town in the heart of the Borders, with a ruined abbey and good walks (Scottish Borders).
Oxford
  Gorgeous university town with evocative architecture, marred only by summer crowds (Oxfordshire).
Richmond
  On the edge of the Yorkshire Dales, overlooking the River Swale, with a cobbled marketplace at the foot of a ruined castle (North Yorkshire).
St Andrews
  Old university and golfing town, with a ruined castle and harbour, on a headland overlooking a sweeping stretch of sand (Fife, Scotland).

Shrewsbury
  Interesting town with half-timbered architecture and curious medieval streets (Shropshire).
Whitby
  Atmospheric fishing port on magnificent coastline (North Yorkshire).
Winchester
  Ancient English capital, rich in history, with a great cathedral (Hampshire).
York
  Proud city with medieval walls and a spectacular cathedral, and many excellent museums (North Yorkshire).

Cathedrals & Churches

Canterbury Cathedral
  The Church of England's most important cathedral, and crowded with ghosts of the past (Kent).
Durham Cathedral
  Monolithic Norman cathedral, overwhelming in scale, on a spectacular site overlooking Durham (County Durham).
Ely Cathedral
  Huge building looming over the fens (Cambridgeshire).
King's College Chapel
  Perpendicular masterpiece with brilliant acoustics and one of Britain's best boys' choirs (Cambridge).
Lincoln Cathedral
  Unusual cathedral with a site surpassed only by Durham (Lincolnshire).
Rievaulx Abbey
  Romantic abbey ruins on a beautiful site (North Yorkshire).
St David's Cathedral
  Tucked in a dale, a small, secretive and mystical cathedral (Pembrokeshire, Wales).
St Paul's Cathedral
  Sir Christopher Wren's masterpiece, with a great view from the dome (London).
Salisbury Cathedral
  Stylistically coherent, with Britain's tallest spire; a soaring elegance (Wiltshire).
Wells Cathedral
  Centrepiece of the best medieval cathedral precinct in Britain, with brilliant west front sculpture (Somerset).
Westminster Abbey
  Rich in history – since King Harold, almost every monarch has been crowned here – and with an excellent boys' choir (London).

Winchester Cathedral
Architectural styles from Norman to perpendicular in perfect harmony (Hampshire).

York Minster
Largest medieval church in Britain, incorporating Roman ruins and superb stained glass (North Yorkshire).

Museums & Galleries

British Museum
Great museum with comprehensive coverage of archaeology of ancient civilisations (London).

Burrell Collection
Fascinating, moderate-sized art collection made by a wealthy shipowner, housed in a superb museum in parkland (Glasgow).

HMS *Victory* and HMS *Mary Rose*
The world's oldest commissioned warship and Nelson's flagship at the Battle of Trafalgar; and King Henry VIII's flagship rescued from the mud beneath Portsmouth Harbour (Portsmouth).

Ironbridge Gorge
Birthplace of the Industrial Revolution, restored and recreated over a number of sites, including the world's first iron bridge (Shropshire).

National Gallery
National collection of European art from the 15th to the early 20th century (London).

Tate Modern
Huge new museum on the River Thames covering modern art since 1900 (London).

Victoria and Albert Museum
Bewildering array of applied and decorative arts, including furniture, paintings, woodwork, jewellery, textiles and clothing (London).

York Castle Museum
Intriguing museum of everyday life, including reconstructed streets and authentically furnished rooms from the 17th to the 20th century (York).

Historic Houses

Blenheim Palace
Enormous Baroque-style private house built by Sir John Vanbrugh in 1704, set in parkland (Oxfordshire).

Castle Howard
Another Vanbrugh masterpiece with a dramatic setting in superb landscaped gardens (North Yorkshire).

Charleston Farmhouse
Home to Vanessa Bell, Duncan Grant and David Garnett (of the Bloomsbury Group), decorated with frescoes and postimpressionist art, and with a charming garden (East Sussex).

Haddon Hall
Dating from the 12th century and added to for 500 years, one of the most complete, surviving medieval manor houses (Derbyshire).

Hampton Court Palace
Begun in 1514 and a royal residence until the 18th century, an enormous, fascinating complex surrounded by beautiful gardens (London).

Ightham Mote
Small moated manor house that has scarcely changed for 500 years (Kent).

Knole House
Enormous house dating from the 15th century and virtually untouched since the 17th century, set in parkland (Kent).

Royal Pavilion
Exotic fantasy, combining Indian, Chinese and Gothic elements, built by George IV in 1815 (Brighton).

Tenement House
Small apartment giving a vivid insight into middle-class life in the late 1800s (Glasgow).

The Queen's House
Inigo Jones masterpiece, started in 1616 but not completed until 1635 (Greenwich).

Traquair
Extraordinary building dating from the 10th century, seemingly untouched by time (Scottish Borders).

Medieval Castles

Alnwick
Dramatic castle begun in the 12th century and converted to a great house without losing its medieval character (Northumberland).

Caerlaverock
Unusual, triangular castle surrounded by a moat (Dumfries & Galloway, Scotland).

Caernarfon
After Windsor, the largest castle in England and Wales (North Wales).

Conwy
One of the most complete of the many fine castles built by Edward I to subdue the Welsh (North Wales).

Dover
Massive fortress begun shortly after the Norman conquest, but encompassing a Roman lighthouse, Saxon church and tunnels last used in WWII (Kent).

Hermitage
Brutal but romantic castle surrounded by bleakly beautiful countryside (Dumfries & Galloway, Scotland).

Leeds
Extraordinarily beautiful castle in the middle of a lake, marred by crowds (Kent).

Stirling
Favoured royal residence of the Stewarts (Central Scotland).

Tower of London
Begun in 1078, a fortress, royal residence and

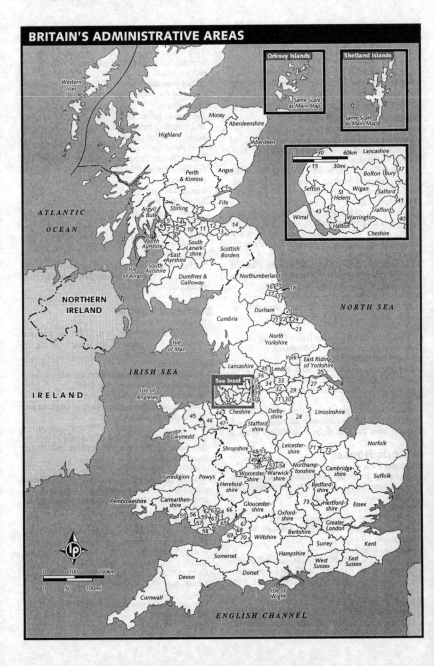

BRITAIN'S ADMINISTRATIVE AREAS

BRITAIN'S ADMINISTRATIVE AREAS

1	Dundee	26	North-East Lincolnshire	50	Sandwell
2	Clackmannanshire			51	Walsall
3	Falkirk	27	North Lincolnshire	52	Birmingham
4	East Dunbartonshire	28	Nottinghamshire	53	Solihull
5	West Dunbartonshire	29	Doncaster	54	Coventry
6	Inverclyde	30	Rotherham	55	Swansea
7	Renfrewshire	31	Sheffield	56	Neath & Port Talbot
8	East Renfrewshire	32	Barnsley	57	Bridgend
9	Glasgow	33	Wakefield	58	Vale of Glamorgan
10	North Lanarkshire	34	Kirklees	59	Rhondda Cyon Taff
11	West Lothian	35	Bradford	60	Cardiff
12	Edinburgh	36	Calderdale	61	Caerphilly
13	Mid Lothian	37	Rochdale	62	Merthyr Tydfil
14	East Lothian	38	Oldham	63	Blaenau Gwent
15	North Tyneside	39	Tameside	64	Torfaen
16	Newcastle upon Tyne	40	Stockport	65	Newport
17	Gateshead	41	Manchester	66	Monmouthshire
18	South Tyneside	42	Knowsley	67	South Gloucestershire
19	Sunderland	43	Liverpool	68	Bristol
20	Hartlepool	44	Flintshire	69	North Somerset
21	Darlington	45	Conwy	70	Bath & North-East Somerset
22	Stockton-on-Tees	46	Denbighshire		
23	Middlesbrough	47	Wrexham	71	Rutland
24	Redcar & Cleveland	48	Wolverhampton	72	Peterborough
25	Kingston-upon-Hull	49	Dudley	73	Buckinghamshire

state prison, now home to the British crown jewels (London).

Windsor
Magnificent royal residence with restored state rooms and the beautiful St George's Chapel (Berkshire).

Coast

Beachy Head
Spectacular chalk cliffs backed by rolling downland rich in wild flowers (East Sussex).

Brighton
Tacky but vibrant resort town (East Sussex).

Ilfracombe to Lynton/Lynmouth
Humpbacked cliffs overlooking the Bristol Channel and backed by the beautiful Exmoor National Park (Devon).

Land's End to St Ives
Beautiful coast and a landscape littered with historical reminders and relics (Cornwall).

Llandudno
Old-style seaside resort with great Victorian architecture and a beautiful setting (North Wales).

St David's to Cardigan
Unspoilt coastline in Pembrokeshire Coast National Park (South Wales).

St Ives
Picturesque village and artists' haunt with two excellent sandy beaches (Cornwall).

Scarborough
Classic English seaside resort with a superb location (North Yorkshire).

Scarborough to Saltburn
Unspoilt coastline with beautiful fishing villages (particularly Staithes and Robin Hood's Bay) and major cliffs, backed by the North York Moors National Park (North Yorkshire).

Scotland
The Scottish coast ranges from beautiful (Berwick-upon-Tweed in England to John o'Groats on the east coast, and Gretna to Glasgow on the west) to extraordinary (the northwest). From Oban to John o'Groats it is one of the world's greatest natural spectacles. Some of the most spectacular cliffs in Britain are to be found in Orkney and Shetland.

Tintagel
Surf-battered headland, topped by a ruined castle, believed to be King Arthur's birthplace (Cornwall).

Islands

Colonsay
Fine sandy beaches, good walks and a mild climate with only half as much rain as on the mainland (Argyll, Scotland).

Farne Islands
Tiny, rocky islands, with amazingly tame nesting

What's in a Name?

England dominates the rest of the UK in all things to such an extent that not only the English but most of the world tend to say 'England' when referring to the UK as a whole. The island of Britain (England, Scotland and Wales), together with Northern Ireland, make up the country whose official name is the United Kingdom of Great Britain and Northern Ireland.

It may seem an obvious point, but it's important to get the name of the country right. The Scots, the Welsh and the people of Northern Ireland find it deeply insulting if you tell them how much you like being 'here in England' when you're in their part of the UK.

seabirds, including puffins and Arctic terns (Northumberland).

Harris
Mountainous and spectacular, with beautiful beaches and isolated crofts (Outer Hebrides, Scotland).

Iona
Very touristy during the day, but spend the night here to experience the magic of this holy island (Argyll, Scotland).

Jura
Wild and remote, with dramatic scenery, superb walks, few people and just one road (Argyll, Scotland).

Orkney
Beautiful beaches, wild flowers and the unique Stone-Age ruins at Skara Brae (off the north coast of Scotland).

Staffa
Boat trips from Mull to see the incredible rock formations that inspired Felix Mendelssohn's *Hebridean Overture* (Argyll, Scotland).

Gardens

Bodnant Garden
Famed for its rhododendrons and camellias and with fine mountain views – particularly spectacular in spring (North Wales).

Castle Kennedy Gardens
Laid out in the 18th century around castle ruins, with formal gardens and a rhododendron collection (Dumfries & Galloway, Scotland).

Forde Abbey
Former Cistercian abbey with wide lawns, ponds, huge trees and colourful borders (Dorset).

Great Dixter
Series of gardens begun by Sir Edwin Lutyens, featuring wild flowers and brilliant spring bulbs (Kent).

Hidcote Manor Gardens
One of Britain's most famous modern gardens (Gloucestershire).

Regent's Park
Vast lawns, spectacular Queen Mary's Rose Garden with 60,000 roses, ornamental ponds and a zoo (London).

Royal Botanic Gardens, Kew
One hundred and twenty hectares of formal gardens, woods, rock gardens, conservatories and the magnificent Palm House (London).

Sissinghurst
Magical garden created by Vita Sackville-West and Harold Nicholson of the Bloomsbury Group (Kent).

Stourhead and Stourton
Two very different neighbouring gardens. Stourhead comprises superb landscaped parkland designed in the 1740s around a lake. The flower garden of Stourton House is in perfect contrast (Wiltshire).

Stowe Landscape Garden
Enormously influential garden started in the 17th century and now being restored by the National Trust (Buckinghamshire).

Studley Royal & Fountains Abbey
Superb water garden on a grand scale, framing extraordinary monastic ruins (North Yorkshire).

Trelissick Garden
Rhododendrons, magnolias, hydrangeas and sub-tropical plants thrive in this area's mild climate (Cornwall).

Prehistoric Remains

Avebury & Around
More impressive than Stonehenge; extensive remains, including a stone circle and avenue, and nearby Silbury Hill and West Kennet Long Barrow (Wiltshire).

Callanish Standing Stones
Cross-shaped avenue and circle on a dramatic site (Lewis, Scotland).

Castlerigg Stone Circle
Stone circle with a beautiful location near Keswick in the Lake District (Cumbria).

Mousa Broch
Britain's best-preserved broch, or defensive tower (Shetland).

Ring of Brodgar
Well-preserved stone circle, part of a ceremonial site that includes standing stones and a chambered tomb (Orkney).

Skara Brae
Extraordinarily well-preserved remains of a

village inhabited 5000 years ago – including dressers, fireplaces, beds and boxes all made from stone (Orkney).

Stonehenge

Extraordinary monument, but marred by crowds and nearby road (Wiltshire).

Roman Sites

Chedworth Villa

Well-preserved mosaic floors at this remote rural villa (Gloucestershire).

Fishbourne Palace

Britain's only Roman palace, with beautiful mosaics (near Chichester, West Sussex).

Hadrian's Wall

Evocative ruins of a monumental attempt to separate two countries (Northumberland/Cumbria).

Train Journeys

Ffestiniog Line

Most scenic of the 'Great Little Trains' of Wales, running 14 miles through Snowdonia National Park (North Wales).

Leeds-Settle-Carlisle Line

Spectacular engineering feat running through the beautiful Yorkshire Dales (North Yorkshire).

Snowdon Mountain Railway

The lazy way to the top of Britain's second-highest mountain (Wales).

Tarka Line

Running from Exeter to Barnstaple through classic Devon countryside (Devon).

Vale of Rheidol

Spectacular 12 mile narrow-gauge steam railway between Aberystwyth and Devil's Bridge (Wales).

West Highland Railway

Scotland's renowned railway line, with particularly dramatic sections crossing Rannoch Moor and from Fort William to Mallaig (Scotland).

SUGGESTED ITINERARIES

Depending on the time at your disposal, you might want to see and do the following:

One week

Visit London, Oxford, the Cotswolds, Bath and Wells.

Two weeks

Visit London, Salisbury, Avebury, Bath, Wells, Oxford or Cambridge, York and Edinburgh.

One month

Visit London, Cambridge, York, Edinburgh, Inverness, Isle of Skye, Fort William, Oban, Glasgow, the Lake District, Chester, the Cotswolds, Wells, Bath, Avebury, Salisbury, Oxford and Stratford-upon-Avon. You could also add in one of the excellent Welsh castles.

Two months

As for one month, but stay put for a week or so in one place. Explore Snowdonia (North Wales) and perhaps attempt a long-distance walk such as the West Highland Way.

PLANNING
When to Go

Anyone who spends any extended period of time in Britain will soon sympathise with the locals' conversational obsession with the weather – although in relative terms the climate is mild and the rainfall not spectacular (see the Climate sections in the Facts About England, Scotland and Wales chapters for more details).

Settled periods of weather – sunny or otherwise – are rare and rain is likely at any time. Even in midsummer you can go for days without seeing the sun, and showers (or worse) should be expected. To enjoy Britain it helps to convince yourself that

Whither the Weather?

It was Dr Johnson who noted that 'when two Englishmen meet, their first talk is of the weather', and over two centuries later not much has changed. According to the Meteorological Office, weather reports are the third-most-watched television broadcasts, and when a move was made to dump the shipping forecast on BBC Radio 4, there was a huge outcry from listeners, most of whom would never need to know the weather out in the North Sea.

British folklore is rich in ways of second-guessing the weather. If it snows on St Dorothea's day (6 February), we can expect no heavier snowfall. If it rains on St Swithin's day (15 July), brollies should be kept to hand for the next 40 days. The slightest tinge of evening pink and Brits are heard chanting 'A red sky at night, shepherd's delight; a red sky at morning, shepherd's warning' like a mantra.

Even so, the weather still manages to defeat us. A few weeks without rain and hosepipe (garden hose) bans are rushed in; one snowflake and the railways grind to a halt. Each winter, the railways try to explain away delays by blaming the 'wrong kind of snow'.

you *like* the rain – after all, that's what makes it so incredibly green!

The least hospitable months for visitors are November, December, January and February – it's cold and the days are short (less than eight hours of daylight in December). March is marginal – although there are 12 hours of daylight and daffodils appear in the south, it can still be very cold. October is also marginal – there are nearly 11 hours of daylight, temperatures are reasonable, and weather patterns seem to be unusually stable, which means you can get good spells of sun, or rain.

Temperatures vary around the island but, as you would expect, it's generally true that the farther north you go, the colder it gets. There's also quite a difference in the number of daylight hours. In early spring or late autumn, it's probably best to concentrate a visit in the south, especially the mild south-west.

April to September are undoubtedly the best months for all of Britain, and this is when most sights and Tourist Information Centres (TICs) are open, and when most people visit. July and August are the busiest months, and best avoided if possible. The crowds on the coast, at the national parks, in London and in popular towns such as Oxford, Bath and York have to be seen to be believed. You're just as likely to get good weather in April, May, June, September and October, although October is getting late for the Scottish Highlands.

There is so much to see and do in London that doesn't depend on the weather that the tourist season really extends year round. Besides, you're almost as likely to have a damp miserable day in June as you are in January.

In Scotland, many places close from October to March or April. In winter the weather's cold and daylight hours are short. Though travel in the Highlands can be difficult, roads are rarely closed and Scotland's five ski resorts are popular at that time. Although many facilities close, there's always one TIC open for an area (though several within that area may close). Many hostels, B&Bs and hotels stay open year round (though by no means all, especially in remoter areas). Travel in the islands can be a problem then because high winds easily disrupt ferries. Edinburgh and Glasgow are well-worth visiting any time of year.

Wales has its tourist rush in July and August. Spring and autumn are fine times to go. In winter many small places are closed and mountain passes may have snow.

What Kind of Trip

Although many people restrict their trip to Britain to a visit to London and a quick whip round the 'milk-run' towns of Oxford, Cambridge, Stratford-upon-Avon, Bath, York, Chester and Edinburgh, you'll get more out of a stay if you take the time to explore some of the less touristy towns (Glasgow, Bristol, Manchester and Leeds for example) and the wonderful countryside. The remoter parts of Wales and Scotland, in particular, are best appreciated on a longer stay. London is a great city, but it's also very expensive and unrepresentative of Britain as a whole – don't let it absorb all your time.

It's easy enough to get round the country by train or bus, although it's usually much cheaper to travel by bus than by train. Alternatively, there are plenty of coach tours, either around the whole country from London, or around specific areas. There are several hop-on, hop-off coach tours specifically designed for backpackers (see the Getting Around chapter).

Travellers who are planning to find work and long-term places to live should bear in mind that the peak tourist season generates casual jobs, which are often advertised in May and June. June can be a good time to look for housing as the universities and colleges close for summer and many students move back home; in addition, travellers pack up and move on to the Mediterranean. Everything tightens up in October and November when people return to rebuild their finances and hibernate through winter.

Maps

The best introductory map to Britain is published by the British Tourist Authority (BTA) and is widely available in TICs. The TICs usually have excellent regional maps covering their area.

If you plan to use the trains, the bad news is that you have to buy the whole hefty timetable (£9) just to get the 'free' map that goes with it. You can try asking at train stations for maps, but you're likely to get lots of little pamphlets from the Train Operating Companies (TOCs; see the Getting Around chapter), each showing just their services.

There's not much to distinguish the range of excellent road atlases in terms of accuracy or price (£7 to £10), but the graphics differ – pick the one you find easiest to read. If you plan to go off the beaten track, you'll need one that shows at least 3 miles to the inch.

The Ordnance Survey (OS) caters to walkers with a wide variety of maps at different scales. The OS Landranger maps at 1:50,000, or about 1¼ inches to the mile, are ideal (£4.95). Their Explorer and Outdoor Leisure maps have even more detail – 1:25,000 – and should satisfy the most demanding hiker or walker. These maps are for sale in book shops and TICs.

What to Bring

Since anything you think of can be bought in British cities (including Vegemite and bad peanut butter), pack light and pick up extras as you go along. Although you'll frequently find that prices are higher than they would be at home.

A travelpack – a combination of a backpack and shoulder bag – is the most popular item for carrying gear, especially if you plan to do any walking – a suitcase will probably force you to use expensive taxis. A travelpack's straps zip away inside the pack when not needed, making it easy to handle in airports and on crowded public transport. Most travelpacks have sophisticated shoulder-strap adjustment systems and can be used comfortably, even for long hikes.

If you don't plan to take your luggage with you on walks, then the always-popular small bag with built-in handle and wheels will get you through airports and train stations – although buses will be a bit tougher.

Whether you bring a tent probably depends on how enthusiastic a camper you are; the weather hardly encourages camping and long-distance walks are well served by hostels, camping barns and B&Bs. A sleeping bag is useful in hostels and when visiting friends. A sleeping sheet with pillow cover is necessary for staying in Scottish YHA hostels – if you don't bring one you'll have to hire or purchase one.

A padlock is handy for locking your bag to a train or a bus luggage rack, and may also be needed to secure your hostel locker. A Swiss Army knife (or any pocketknife that includes a bottle opener and strong corkscrew) is useful for all sorts of things. For city sightseeing, a small daypack is harder for snatch thieves to grab than a shoulder bag.

Other possibilities include a compass, an alarm clock, a torch (flashlight), an adapter plug for electrical appliances, sunglasses and an elastic clothesline.

Wet weather gear is absolutely mandatory. Whether it's waterproof outwear or an umbrella or both, bring whatever you need because you can expect rain at any time anywhere in Britain.

Toiletries are easily purchased. However, if you're heading to the Scottish Highlands in the summer (when the midges are ferocious), bring a good insect repellent. That goes for other rural areas in Britain as well, as mosquitoes can be a bother. For some reason, finding good bug goop in Britain can be hard.

Use plastic carrier bags to keep things organised, and dry, inside your bag or backpack in case it's left sitting in the rain. Airlines lose bags from time to time, but there's a much better chance of getting them back if they're tagged with your name and address *inside* as well as on the outside.

RESPONSIBLE TOURISM

Except for its remoter and more mountainous reaches, Britain is a very crowded island even before the peak tourist season brings yet more millions to the streets. Congestion on the roads is a major problem and visitors will do residents – as well as themselves! – a favour if they forgo driving in favour of using public transport.

Mountain bikers should stick to roads or designated bike tracks as cyclists have caused considerable damage to mountain paths (eg, in Snowdonia). If you are rough camping make sure you ask permission of the landowner first and take care not to damage crops or leave any litter.

TOURIST OFFICES

The British Tourist Authority (BTA; ☎ 020-8846 9000) stocks masses of information, much of it free. Its UK headquarters are at Thames Tower, Black's Rd, Hammersmith, London W6 9EL. Contact the BTA before you leave home because some discounts are only available to people who book before arriving in Britain. Travellers with special needs (be it disability, diet etc) should also contact the nearest BTA office. Its Web site is at www.bta.org.uk.

In London the British Travel Centre at 1 Regent St (see the London chapter) is a good starting point for information collecting.

Regional Tourist Boards

The English Tourism Council does not deal with the public, but rather is a group representing the interests of the regional and local tourist boards that deal with the public. Useful regional bodies are listed at the start of the relevant chapters.

The Scottish Tourist Board (STB; ☎ 0131-332 2433, fax 315 4545) has its headquarters at 23 Ravelston Terrace (PO Box 705), Edinburgh EH4 3EU. In London, contact the STB (☎ 020-7930 8661/2), 19 Cockspur St, London SW1 5BL, off Trafalgar Square, for routes, detailed information and reservations. Its Web site is at www.visitscotland.com.

The Wales Tourist Board (WTB; ☎ 029-2049 9909) has its headquarters on the 12th floor of Brunel House, 2 Fitzalan Rd, Cardiff CF2 1UY, and also operates a branch in the British Travel Centre in London (no telephone, call-in centre only). Check its Web site at www.visitwales.com.

Local Tourist Offices

Every British town (and many villages) has its own TIC, where a wide range of information is available, particularly about places within a 50-mile radius. Most also operate a local bed-booking system and a Book-A-Bed-Ahead (BABA) scheme. In addition, there are National Park Visitor Information Centres. Local libraries are also good sources of information.

Most TICs open 9 am to 5 pm Monday to Friday, although in popular tourist areas they may also open on Saturday and stay open later in the evening. In real honey pots, such as Stratford and Bath, they'll be open seven days a week throughout the year. October to March smaller TICs are often closed.

Many TICs have 24-hour computer databases that can be accessed even when the office is closed. Others put posters with basic information about accommodation and a town plan in the window.

Tourist Offices Abroad

Overseas, the BTA represents the tourist boards of England, Scotland and Wales. Addresses of some offices are as follows:

Australia
 (☎ 02-9377 4400, fax 9377 4499, @ visit britainaus@bta.org.uk) Level 16, The Gateway, 1 Macquarie Place, Circular Quay, Sydney, NSW 2000

Canada
 (☎ 888-847 4885, fax 905-405 1835) 5915 Airport Rd, Suite 120, Mississauga, Ontario L4V 1T1

France
 (☎ 01 44 51 56 20, fax 01 44 51 56 21) Maison de la Grande Bretagne, 19 Rue des Mathurins, 75009 Paris (entrance in les Rues Tronchet et Auber)

Germany
 (☎ 069-971123, fax 9711 2444, @ gbinfo@ bta.org.uk) Westendstrasse 16–22, 60325 Frankfurt

Ireland
 (☎ 01-670 8000, fax 670 8244) 18–19 College Green, Dublin 2

Netherlands
 (☎ 020-689 0002, fax 618 6868, @ britinfo .nl@bta.org.uk) Stadhouderskade 2, 1054 ES Amsterdam

New Zealand
 (☎ 09-303 1446, fax 377 6965) 17th Floor, Fay Richwhite Building, 151 Queen St, Auckland 1

USA
 Chicago: (☎ 800-462 2748, @ travelinfo@ bta.org.uk) 625 N Michigan Ave, Suite 1001, Chicago IL 60611 (personal callers only)

New York: (☎ 212-986 2200) 551 Fifth Avenue, Suite 701, New York, NY 10176

There are more than 40 BTA offices worldwide; their addresses are listed on its Web site at www.bta.org.uk.

VISAS & DOCUMENTS

Unlike many other European countries, people in the UK are not required by law to carry identification, but it's always a good idea to have your passport or some other sort of photo ID on your person. Also, with very few exceptions, London is an excellent place to gather information about visas for other countries worldwide.

Passport

Your most important travel document is a passport, which should remain valid until well after your trip; if it's just about to expire, renew it before you go. This may not be easy to do overseas, and some countries insist that your passport remains valid for a specified minimum period (usually three months) after your visit.

Applying for or renewing a passport can be an involved process taking from a few days to several months, so don't leave it till the last minute. Bureaucracy usually grinds faster if you do everything in person rather than relying on the mail or agents. First check what is required: passport photos, birth certificate, population register extract, signed statements, exact payment in cash, whatever.

Australian citizens can apply at post offices, or the passport office in their state capital; Canadians can apply at regional passport offices; New Zealanders can apply at any district office of the Department of Internal Affairs; and US citizens must apply in person (but may usually renew by mail) at a US Passport Agency office or some courthouses and post offices.

Citizens of European countries may not need a passport to travel to Britain. A national identity card can be sufficient, and usually involves less paperwork and processing time. Check with your travel agent or the British embassy.

Visas

At present, citizens of Australia, Canada, New Zealand, South Africa and the USA are given 'leave to enter' the UK at their point of arrival for up to six months, but are prohibited from working. If you're a citizen of the European Union (EU), you don't need a visa to enter the country and may live and work here freely.

Visa regulations are always subject to change, so it's essential to check with your local British embassy, high commission or consulate before leaving home.

The immigration authorities in the UK are tough; dress neatly and be able to prove that you have sufficient funds to support yourself. A credit card and/or an onward ticket will help.

Visa Extensions Tourist visas can only be extended in clear emergencies (eg, an accident). Otherwise you will have to leave the UK (perhaps going to Ireland or France) and apply for a fresh one, although this tactic will arouse suspicion after the second or third visa. To extend (or attempt to extend) your stay in the UK, contact the Home Office's Immigration & Nationality Department (☎ 020-8686 0688), Lunar House, 40 Wellesley Rd, Croydon CR2 2BY, before your existing visa expires. It opens 10 am to noon and 2 to 4 pm Monday to Friday. You can also telephone the Visa & Passport Information Line on ☎ 08706-067766.

Student Visas Nationals of EU countries can enter the country to study without any formalities. Otherwise, you need to be enrolled on a full-time course of at least 15 hours per week of weekday, daytime study at a single educational institution to be allowed to remain as a student. For further details you can consult the British embassy, high commission or consulate in your own country.

Work Permits EU nationals don't need a work permit to work in Britain, but everyone else does. If the main purpose of your visit is to work, you have to be sponsored by a British company.

However, if you're a citizen of a Commonwealth country aged between 17 and 27 inclusive, you may apply for a Working Holiday Entry Certificate, which allows you to spend up to two years in the UK and take work that is 'incidental' to a holiday. You're not allowed to engage in business, pursue a career (evidently working as a bartender is not considered a career pursuit) or provide services as a professional sportsperson or entertainer.

You must apply to the nearest UK mission overseas – Working Holiday Entry Certificates are *not* granted on arrival in Britain. It's not possible to switch from being a visitor to a working holiday-maker, nor is it possible to claim back any time spent out of the UK during the two-year period. When you apply, you must satisfy the authorities that you have the means to pay for a return or onward journey and that you will be able to maintain yourself without recourse to public funds.

Commonwealth citizens with a parent born in the UK may be eligible for a Certificate of Entitlement to the Right of Abode, which means you can live and work in Britain free of immigration control.

If you're a Commonwealth citizen with a grandparent born in the UK, or if the grandparent was born before 31 March 1922 in what is now the Republic of Ireland, you may qualify for a UK Ancestry Employment Certificate, which means you can work full time for up to four years in the UK.

Visiting students from the USA who are at least 18 years old and studying full time at a college or university can get a permit allowing them to work for six months. It costs US$200 and is available through the Council on International Educational Exchange (☎ 212-661 1414), 205 East 42nd St, New York, NY 10017. Check out its Web site at www.ciee.org. The British Universities North America Club (BUNAC; ☎ 020-7251 3472, fax 7251 0215, ⓔ enquiries@bunac.org.uk), 16 Bowling Green Lane, London EC1R 0QH, can also help you organise a permit and find employment. Its Web site is at www.bunac.org.

If you have any queries once you're in the UK, contact the Home Office's Immigration & Nationality Department (see the earlier Visa Extensions section).

Onward Tickets

Although you don't need an onward ticket to be granted 'leave to enter' on arrival (see Visas earlier), this could help if there's any doubt over whether you have sufficient funds to support yourself and purchase an onward ticket in Britain.

Travel Insurance

Whichever way you're travelling, make sure you take out a comprehensive travel insurance policy that covers you for medical expenses and luggage theft or loss, and for cancellation of or delays in your travel arrangements. Ticket loss should also be included, but make sure you have a separate record of all the details – or better still, a photocopy of the ticket. There are all sorts of policies, but the international student travel policies handled by STA Travel and other student travel organisations are usually good value. Some policies offer lower and higher medical expense options – unless you're eligible for free NHS treatment (see the Health section later in the chapter for details), go for as much as you can afford. Other policies are cheaper if you forgo cover for lost baggage.

Buy insurance as soon as possible. Otherwise you may find that you're not covered for delays to your flight caused by strikes or other industrial action. Always read the small print carefully for loopholes.

Paying for your ticket with a credit card often provides limited travel accident insurance, and you may be able to reclaim the payment if the operator doesn't deliver. In the UK, credit card providers are required by law to reimburse consumers if a company goes into liquidation and the amount in contention is more than £100.

Driving Licence & Permits

Your normal driving licence is legal for 12 months from the date you last entered the UK; you can then apply for a British licence at post offices. The International Driving Permit (IDP) is not needed in the UK.

Camping Card International

Your local automobile association also issues a Camping Card International, which is basically a camping ground ID. They're also issued by local camping federations, and sometimes on the spot at camp sites. They incorporate third party insurance for damage you may cause, and many camping grounds offer a small discount if you sign in with one. Some hostels and hotels also accept carnets for signing-in purposes, but won't give discounts.

Hostel Cards

If you're travelling on a budget, membership of the Youth Hostel Association (YHA) or Hostelling International (HI) is a must (£12 adult, £6 under-18). There are over 320 hostels in Britain and members are also eligible for all sorts of discounts. See the Accommodation section later in the chapter for more information about hostelling in Britain.

Student & Youth Cards

Most useful of these is the International Student Identity Card (ISIC), a plastic ID-style card with your photograph that costs £5 in the UK and provides cheap or free admission to museums and sights, inexpensive meals in some student restaurants and discounts on many forms of transport.

There's a worldwide industry in fake student cards, and many places now stipulate a maximum age for student discounts, or simply substitute a 'youth discount' for a 'student' one. If you're aged under 26 but not a student, you can apply for a GO25 card issued by the Federation of International Youth Travel Organisations (FIYTO), or a Euro 26 Card, which give much the same discounts for the same fee as the ISIC.

All these cards are issued by student unions, hostelling organisations and student travel agencies.

Seniors Cards

Many attractions reduce their admission cost for people aged over 60 or 65 (sometimes as low as 55 for women); it's always worth asking even if you can't see a discount listed. Discount cards for people aged over 60 are available for rail and bus travel. See the Bus Passes & Discounts and Railcards sections in the Getting Around chapter.

Other Documents

If you're visiting Britain on a Working Holiday Entry Certificate, don't forget to bring any course certificates or letters of reference that might help you find a job.

Copies

All important documents (passport data page and visa page, credit cards, travel insurance policy, air/bus/train tickets, driving licence etc) should be photocopied before you leave home. Leave one copy with someone at home and keep another with you, separate from the originals.

It's also a good idea to store details of your travel documents in Lonely Planet's free online Travel Vault in case you lose the photocopies or can't be bothered with them. Your password-protected Travel Vault is accessible online anywhere in the world – create it at www.ekno.lonelyplanet.com.

EMBASSIES & CONSULATES
British Embassies, High Commissions & Consulates

British missions overseas include those listed below. If you need the details of others, consult the Foreign & Commonwealth Office Web site at www.fco.gov.uk.

Australia
High Commission: (☎ 02-6270 6666, fax 6270 6653) Commonwealth Ave, Yarralumla, Canberra, ACT 2600
Consulate: (☎ 02-9247 7521, fax 9251 6201) Level 16, The Gateway, 1 Macquarie Place, Sydney, NSW 2000
Web site: www.uk.emb.gov.au

Canada
High Commission: (☎ 613-237 1530, fax 232 2533) 80 Elgin St, Ottawa, Ontario K1P 5K7
Consulate: (☎ 416-593 1290, fax 593 1229) Suite 2800, 777 Bay St, College Park, Toronto, Ontario M5G 2G2
Web site: www.britain-in-canada.org

France
Embassy: (☎ 01 44 51 31 00, fax 01 44 51 31 28) 35 rue du Faubourg Saint Honoré, 75008 Paris
Web site: www.amb-grandebretagne.fr

Germany
Embassy: (☎ 030-201 840, fax 201 84159)
Unter den Linden 32-34, 10117 Berlin
Web site: www.britischebotschaft.de

Ireland
Embassy: (☎ 01-205 3822, fax 205 3890)
29 Merrion Rd, Ballsbridge, Dublin 4
Web site: www.britishembassy.ie

Netherlands
Embassy: (☎ 070-427 0427, fax 427 0345)
Lange Voorhout 10, 2514 ED The Hague
Consulate: (☎ 020-676 43 43, fax 676 10 69)
Konigslaan 44, 1075 AE Amsterdam
Web site: www.britain.nl

New Zealand
High Commission: (☎ 04-472 6049, fax 471
1974) 44 Hill St, Wellington 1
Consulate: (☎ 09-303 2973, fax 303 1836)
17th floor, Fay Richwhite Building,
151 Queen St, Auckland 1
Web site: www.brithighcomm.org.nz

South Africa
High Commission: (☎ 021-461 7220, fax 461
0017) 91 Parliament St, Cape Town 8001
Consulate: (☎ 011-325 2133, fax 325 2132)
Dunkeld Corner, 275 Jan Smuts Ave,
Dunkeld West, Johannesburg 2196
Web site: www.britain.org.za

USA
Embassy: (☎ 202-588 6500, fax 588 7850)
3100 Massachusetts Ave, NW, Washington,
DC 20008
Consulate: (☎ 212-745 0200, fax 745 3062)
845 Third Ave, New York, NY 10012
Web site: www.britainusa.com/bis
/embassy/embassy.stm

Embassies & Consulates in Britain

It's important to realise what your own embassy – the embassy of the country of which you are a citizen – can and can't do to help you if you get into trouble. Generally speaking, it won't be much help in emergencies if the trouble you're in is remotely your own fault. Remember that you are bound by the laws of the country you are in. Your embassy will not be sympathetic if you end up in jail after committing a crime locally, even if such actions are legal in your own country.

In genuine emergencies you might get some assistance, but only if other channels have been exhausted. For example, if you need to get home urgently, a free ticket home is exceedingly unlikely – the embassy would

expect you to have insurance. If you have all your money and documents stolen, it might assist with getting a new passport, but a loan for onward travel is out of the question.

Some foreign missions in London include:

Australia
High Commission: (☎ 020-7379 4334, fax
7240 5333) Australia House, Strand WC2

Canada
High Commission: (☎ 020-7258 6600, fax
7258 6333) 1 Grosvenor Square W1

France
Embassy: (☎ 020-7838 2050, fax 7838 2046)
58 Knightsbridge SW1

Germany
Embassy: (☎ 020-7824 1300, fax 7824 1435)
23 Belgrave Square SW1

Ireland
Embassy: (☎ 020-7235 2171, fax 7245 6961)
17 Grosvenor Place SW1

Netherlands
Embassy: (☎ 020-7590 3200, fax 7590 3458)
38 Hyde Park Gate SW7

New Zealand
High Commission: (☎ 020-7930 8422,
fax 7839 4580) New Zealand House,
80 Haymarket SW1

South Africa
High Commission: (☎ 020-7451 7299,
fax 7451 7284) South Africa House,
Trafalgar Square WC2

USA
Embassy: (☎ 020-7499 9000, fax 7495 5012)
24 Grosvenor Square W1

Edinburgh's consulates and high commissions include:

Australia (☎ 0131-624 3333) 37 George St,
EH2 2HT
Canada (☎ 0131-220 4333) 30 Lothian Rd,
EH1 2DH
Denmark (☎ 0131-556 4263) 4 Royal Terrace,
EH7 5AB
France (☎ 0131-225 7954) 11 Randolph
Crescent, EH3 7TT
Germany (☎ 0131-337 2323) 16 Eglinton
Crescent, EH12 5DG
Italy (☎ 0131-226 3631) 32 Melville St, EH3
7HA
Netherlands (☎ 0131-220 3226) 53 George St,
EH2 2HT
Norway (☎ 0131 226 5701) 86 George Street,
EH2 3BU
Spain (☎ 0131-220 1843) 63 North Castle St,
EH2 3LJ

Signs of the times: The Punch Tavern, London; Gaelic plaque; coat of arms, Christ's College, Cambridge; commandments at the cathedral in St David's; a confusing choice at Durness; and The Old Bell, London

CHRIS MELLOR

DOUG McKINLAY

CHARLOTTE HINDLE

MANFRED GOTTSCHALK

People in action: high as a kite on Parliament Hill, London; in the saddle in Hyde Park, London; a street artist puts on an act, and his face, in Leicester Square, London; and one man and his sheep, Isle of Skye

Switzerland (☎ 0131-226 5660) 66 Hanover St, EH2 1HH
USA (☎ 0131-556 8315) 3 Regent Terrace, EH7 5BW

CUSTOMS

Entering Britain, if you have nothing to declare go through the green channel; if you may have something to declare go through the red channel. If you are arriving from an EU country, go through a third, blue, channel.

Like other EU nations, the UK has a two-tier customs system: one for goods bought duty-free and one for goods bought in another EU country where taxes and duties have already been paid.

Duty Free

Duty-free sales to those travelling from one EU country to another were abolished in 1999. For goods purchased at airports or on ferries *outside* the EU, you are allowed to import 200 cigarettes or 250g of tobacco, 2L of still wine plus 1L of spirits over 22% or another 2L of wine (sparkling or otherwise), 50g of perfume, 250cc of toilet water, and other duty-free goods (including cider and beer) to the value of £136.

Tax & Duty Paid

Although you can no longer bring in duty-free goods from another EU country, you *can* bring in goods from another EU country, where certain goods might be cheaper, if taxes have been paid on them. The items are supposed to be for individual consumption, but a thriving business has developed, with many Brits making day trips to France to load up their cars with cheap alcohol and cigarettes, which they often sell back in the UK. The savings can more than pay for the trip.

If you purchase from a normal retail outlet, customs uses the following maximum quantities as a guideline to distinguish personal imports from those on a commercial scale: 800 cigarettes, 200 cigars, 1kg of tobacco, 10L of spirits, 20L of fortified wine, 90L of wine (of which not more than 60L are sparkling) and 110L of beer.

Pets

To protect its rabies-free status, Britain has long had draconian pet quarantine policies that required any animal brought into Britain to be placed in quarantine for six months.

The rules thawed slightly in 2000, when a pilot scheme was introduced for dogs and cats only. And it's not just any pooches and pussies, but only those from certain countries: Andorra; Austria; Belgium; Denmark; Finland; France; Germany; Gibraltar; Greece; Italy; Liechtenstein; Luxembourg; Monaco; Netherlands; Norway; Portugal; San Marino; Spain; Sweden; Switzerland; and the Vatican.

In addition, there are numerous further regulations that include: the dog or cat must not have been outside of the qualifying countries in the six months before travel to Britain and the animal must have an identity microchip implanted. The animals must also have various vaccinations, tests and certifications. The process is complex, but at least it is a thaw from the previous no-exceptions policy.

If you are contemplating bringing your pet to Britain, you should contact your nearest UK embassy and consulate to find out the latest details on the pet quarantine situation.

MONEY
Currency

The British currency is the pound sterling (£), which is divided into 100 pence (p). Coins of 1p and 2p are copper; 5p, 10p, 20p and 50p coins are silver; and the bulky £1 coin is gold-coloured. The £2 coin, introduced into circulation in 1997, is gold-coloured on the edge with a silver centre.

Notes come in £5, £10, £20 and £50 denominations and vary in colour and size. The £50 notes can be difficult to change – avoid them.

You may also come across notes issued by three Scottish banks – Clydesdale Bank, Royal Bank of Scotland and Bank of Scotland – including a £1 note, which are legal tender on both sides of the border. If you have any problems getting them accepted in England and Wales, ask a bank to swap them for you.

Exchange Rates

Exchange rates at the time of going to print were:

country	unit		pounds
Australia	A$1	=	£0.37
Canada	C$1	=	£0.46
EU	€1	=	£0.59
France	10FF	=	£0.91
Germany	DM1	=	£0.31
Ireland	IR£1	=	£0.76
Japan	¥100	=	£0.64
New Zealand	NZ$1	=	£0.28
Spain	100 ptas	=	£0.35
USA	US$1	=	£0.67

Exchanging Money

By 2002, most of the EU will have a single currency called the euro. Until then, francs, Deutschmarks, pesetas and so on will remain in place or share equal status with the euro. The pound will continue to be the unit of currency in the UK as the British government has decided not to adopt the euro for the time being. You're likely to see some of the acrimonious debate on the issue in the press during your visit.

Cash Nothing beats cash for convenience – or risk. It's still a good idea, however, to travel with some cash in pounds sterling, if only to tide you over until you get to an exchange facility. There's no problem if you arrive at any of Britain's airports; they usually have good-value exchange counters open for incoming flights.

Travellers Cheques & Eurocheques

Travellers cheques offer protection from theft. Ideally your cheques should be in pounds and preferably issued by American Express (Amex) or Thomas Cook, which are widely recognised, well represented and don't charge for cashing their own cheques.

Bring most cheques in large denominations. It's only towards the end of a stay that you may want to change a small cheque to make sure you don't get left with too much local currency. Travellers cheques are rarely accepted outside banks, or used for everyday transactions in Britain, so you need to cash them in advance.

If you have a European bank account, Eurocheques, guaranteed up to a certain amount, are available. When cashing them, you'll be asked to show your Eurocheque card bearing your signature and registration number as well as your passport or ID card. Eurocheques are not as commonly used in the UK as they are in continental Europe, and many places refuse to accept them. Some people may never have seen them before.

Buying Travellers Cheques The cost of buying travellers cheques varies considerably, depending on the seller. Amex is often the cheapest, charging 1% commission with no minimum charge. Main post offices also offer very competitive rates. The banks are usually more expensive and often want advance warning: NatWest charges 1% commission for sterling travellers cheques, with a £4 minimum charge; Lloyds TSB, HSBC and Barclays all charge 1.5% commission, with a minimum charge of £3.

Lost or Stolen Travellers Cheques Keep a record of the numbers of your cheques and which cheques you have cashed, then if they're lost or stolen you will be able to tell the issuing agency exactly which cheques have gone. Keep this list separate from the cheques themselves.

As soon as you realise any cheques are missing, you should contact the issuing office or the nearest branch of the issuing agency. Amex (☎ 029-2066 6111) and Thomas Cook (☎ 01733-318950), both of which operate 24 hours a day, seven days a week, can often arrange replacement cheques within 24 hours.

ATMs Plastic cards make the perfect travelling companions – they're ideal for major purchases and let you withdraw cash from selected banks and automatic telling machines (ATMs), God's greatest gift to the travelling world since the backpack was invented. ATMs are usually linked up to international money systems such as Cirrus, Maestro or Plus, so you can enter your card, punch in your personal identification number (PIN) and get instant cash. But ATMs aren't fail-safe, especially if the card was issued outside Europe, and it's safer to go to a human teller. It can be a major headache if an ATM swallows your card.

Debit cards, which you use to withdraw money directly from your bank or savings account, are widely linked internationally – ask your bank at home for advice. Credit cards, on the other hand, may not be hooked up to ATM networks unless you specifically ask your bank to do this for you and request a PIN. However, once you've done this, you'll find most ATMs are linked to the Visa and/or MasterCard networks. Amex cards are accepted in many ATMs as well. You might also ask which UK banks' ATMs will accept your particular card, and whether you pay a fee to use them.

Credit Cards Visa, MasterCard, Amex and Diners Club cards are widely accepted in Britain, although small businesses, such as B&Bs, prefer cash. Businesses sometimes make a charge for payment by credit card so this isn't always the most economical way to go. You can get cash advances using your Visa and MasterCards at many banks. If you have an Amex card, you can cash up to £500 worth of personal cheques at Amex offices in any seven-day period.

If you plan to use a credit card, make sure you have a high-enough credit limit to cover major expenses such as car hire or airline tickets.

If you're going to rely on plastic, go for two different cards – an Amex or Diners Club with a Visa or MasterCard. Better still, combine cards and travellers cheques so you have something to fall back on if an ATM swallows your card or the bank won't accept it.

Lost or Stolen Cards If a card is lost or stolen you must inform the police and the issuing company as soon as possible – otherwise you may have to pay for the purchases that the unspeakable thief has made using your card. Here are some numbers for cancelling your cards:

Amex	☎ 01273-689955
Diners Club	☎ 01252-516261

MasterCard	☎ 01702-362988
Visa	☎ 0800 895082

International Transfers If you instruct your bank back home to send you a draft, be sure you specify the bank and the branch to which you want your money directed, or ask your home bank to tell you where a suitable one is. The whole procedure will be easier if you've authorised someone back home to access your account.

Money sent to you by telegraphic transfer should reach you within a week; by mail, allow at least two weeks. When it arrives, it will most likely be converted into local currency – you can then take it as is, or buy travellers cheques. The charge for this service is usually around £20.

You can also transfer money using Amex or Thomas Cook or by post office Money-Gram. Americans can also use Western Union (☎ 0800 833833), although it has fewer offices in Britain from which to collect and charges 10% plus commission.

Moneychangers Changing your money is never a problem in London, with banks, bureaux de change and travel agencies all competing for your business. Just make sure you are getting the best deal possible. Be particularly careful using bureaux de change; they may seem to offer good exchange rates, but frequently levy outrageous commissions (branches of Chequepoint charge up to 8% to cash a sterling travellers cheque) and fees. Check the exchange rate, the percentage commission and any minimum charge very carefully.

The exchange desks at the international airports charge less than most high-street banks and cash sterling travellers cheques for free; for other currencies they charge about 1.5% with a £3 minimum. They can also sell you up to £500 worth of most major currencies on the spot.

Other Methods Personal cheques are still widely used in the UK – a group of diners will often write separate cheques to pay for their share of a meal – and are validated by a cheque-guarantee card. Increasingly, retail outlets are linked to the Switch and Delta networks, which allow customers to use a debit card (deductions are made directly from your UK current account).

If you plan to stay a while in Britain, you may want to open a bank account, but it's no simple matter. Building societies tend to be more welcoming than banks and often have better interest rates. You'll need a permanent address in the UK, and it will smooth the way if you have a reference or introductory letter from your bank manager at home, plus bank statements for the previous year. Owning credit/charge cards also helps.

Make sure you look for a current account that pays interest (however tiny), gives you a cheque book and a cheque guarantee/debit card, and gives access to ATMs.

Security

Whichever way you decide to carry your funds, it makes sense to keep most of it out of easy reach of thieves in a money belt or something similar. It's always sensible to keep something like £50 apart from the rest of your cash for use in an emergency.

Take particular care in crowded places such as the London Underground and never leave wallets sticking out of trouser pockets or daypacks and never leave bags hanging over the back of chairs in pubs and restaurants. Also watch out on buses and around popular tourist attractions, such as the Tower of London and Stonehenge.

Costs

Britain is expensive and London is horrific. While in London you will need to budget £30 to £35 a day for bare survival. Dormitory accommodation alone will cost a minimum of £10 to £20 a night, a one-day Travelcard is £3.90 (Zones 1 and 2), and drinks and the most basic sustenance will cost you at least £8 to £10, with any sightseeing or nightlife on top. There's not much point visiting if you can't enjoy some of the city's life, so if possible add another £15 a day.

Costs will obviously be even higher if you choose to stay in a central hotel and eat restaurant meals. Hotel rates start at around £30 per person and a restaurant meal will set you back at least £10. Add a couple of pints of beer (about £2 each) and admission fees to a tourist attraction or nightclub and you could easily spend £55 per day – without being extravagant.

Once you start moving around the country, particularly if you have a transport pass, the costs will drop. Away from London, England is cheaper and Scotland and Wales are a bit cheaper yet. Fresh food costs roughly the same as in Australia and the USA. However, without including long-distance transport, and assuming you stay in hostels and an occasional cheap B&B, you'll still need at least £25 per day. A country youth hostel will cost from £8; add £5 for food, £7 for admission charges and/or local buses, and £4 for miscellaneous items such as film, shampoo, books and telephone calls.

If you hire a car or use a transport pass, stay in B&Bs, eat one sit-down meal a day and don't stint on admission fees, you'll need £50 to £60 per day (still not including long-distance transport costs). Most basic B&Bs will be from £15 to £25 per person and dinner will be from £8 to £15 (depending on whether you're eating in a restaurant or a pub and how much you drink); then add £5 for snacks and drinks, £4 for miscellaneous items and at least £7 for admission fees. If you're travelling by car you'll probably average a further £8 to £15 per day on petrol and parking (not including hire charges); if you travel using some sort of pass you'll probably average a couple of pounds a day on local transport or hiring a bike.

Train fares usually rise by around 5% every January. Bus fares usually increase by a few pence every April and October. Admission fees seem to rise by 50p or £1 a year.

Throughout this book admission costs are given as adult/child.

Tipping & Bargaining

Many restaurants now add a 'discretionary' service charge to your bill, but in places that don't you are expected to leave a 10 to 15% tip unless the service was unsatisfactory. Waiting staff are often paid derisory wages on the assumption that the money will be supplemented by tips. It's legal for restaurants to include a service charge in the bill, but this should be clearly advertised. You needn't add a further tip. And you never tip to have your pint pulled in a pub.

Taxi drivers also expect to be tipped (about 10%), especially in London. It's less usual to tip minicab drivers.

Bargaining is virtually unheard of, even at markets, although it's fine to ask if there are discounts for students, young people or youth hostel members. Some 'negotiation' is also OK if you're buying an expensive item such as a car or motorcycle.

Taxes & Refunds

Value-added tax (VAT) is a 17.5% sales tax levied on most goods and services except food and books. Restaurants must by law include VAT in their menu prices.

It is sometimes possible for visitors to claim a refund of VAT paid on goods – a considerable saving. You are eligible if you have spent fewer than 365 days out of the two years prior to making the purchase living in the UK, and if you are leaving the EU within three months of making the purchase.

Not all shops participate in the VAT refund scheme, called the Retail Export Scheme or Tax-Free Shopping, and different shops will have different minimum-purchase conditions (normally around £75 in one shop). On request, participating shops will give you a special form (VAT 407). This form must be presented with the goods and receipts to customs when you depart (VAT-free goods can't be posted or shipped home). After customs has certified the form, it should be returned to the shop for a refund (minus an administration/handling fee), which takes eight to 10 weeks to come through.

Several companies offer a centralised refunding service to shops and participating shops carry a sign in their window (eg Tax-Free Shopping). You can avoid bank charges for cashing a sterling cheque by using a credit card for purchases and asking that the VAT refund be credited to your account. Cash refunds are sometimes available at major airports.

POST & COMMUNICATIONS
Post

Although the queues in post offices can be long, the Royal Mail (☎ 0845-600 0606) delivers quite a good service. Post office hours can vary, but the majority are open 9 am to 5 pm, Monday to Friday, and 9 am to noon on Saturday. First-class mail (within the UK or the EU) is quicker and more expensive (27p per letter) than 2nd-class mail (19p).

Air-mail letters to other European countries cost 36p, to the Americas and Australasia 45/65p (up to 10/20 grams).

If you don't have a permanent address, mail can be sent to poste restante in the town or city where you are staying. American Express Travel offices will also hold card-holders' mail free of charge.

An air-mail letter generally takes less than a week to get to the USA or Canada; around a week to Australia or New Zealand.

Telephone

To call Britain from abroad, dial your country's international access code, then 44 (the UK's country code), then the area code (dropping the initial 0) followed by the phone number.

British Telecom's (BT) famous red phone-boxes survive only in conservation areas. More common these days are the glass cubicles with phones that accept coins, prepaid phonecards and/or credit cards.

All phones come with reasonably clear instructions. BT offers phonecards for £2, £5, £10 and £20 that are widely available from all sorts of retailers, including post offices and newsagents. A digital display on the telephone indicates how much credit is left on the card.

Some special phone codes worth knowing are:

☎ 0500	toll-free
☎ 0800	toll-free
☎ 0845	local call rate applies
☎ 0870	national call rate applies
☎ 0891	premium rate (49p per minute)
☎ 09064	premium rate (49p per minute)

Beware of other codes (such as six digits) that may indicate you're calling a mobile phone. This is usually considerably more expensive than calling a conventional phone.

Local & National Calls & Rates Local calls are charged by time alone; national calls are charged by both time and distance. Daytime rates apply 8 am to 6 pm Monday to Friday; the cheap rate applies 6 pm to 8 am Monday to Friday; and the cheap weekend rate applies midnight Friday to midnight Sunday. The latter two rates offer substantial savings.

For directory enquiries/information call ☎ 192. These calls are free from public phones but cost 25p if you call from a private one. To get the operator call ☎ 100.

International Calls & Rates To call someone outside the UK dial 00, then the country code, the area code (you usually drop the initial zero if there is one) and the number. International direct dialling (IDD) calls to almost anywhere in the world can be made from almost all public telephones.

To make a reverse-charge (collect) call, dial ☎ 155 for the international operator. Direct dialling is cheaper. For international directory enquiries dial ☎ 153 (50p from private phones).

For most countries (including Europe, the USA and Canada) it's cheaper to phone overseas between 8 pm and 8 am Monday to Friday and at weekends; for Australia and New Zealand, however, it's cheapest from 2.30 to 7.30 pm and from midnight to 7 am every day. The savings are considerable.

There's a wide range of local and international phonecards. Lonely Planet's eKno Communication Card is aimed specifically at independent travellers and provides budget international calls, a range of messaging services, free email and travel information – for local calls, you're usually better off with a local card. You can join on-line at www.ekno.lonelyplanet.com, or by phone from Britain by dialling ☎ 0800 376 1704. Once you have joined, to use eKno from Britain, dial ☎ 0800 169 8646 (or ☎ 0800 376 2366 from a payphone).

Check the eKno Web site for joining and access numbers from other countries and updates on local access numbers and new features.

It is also possible to undercut BT international call rates by buying a special card (usually denominated £5, £10 or £20) with a PIN that you use from any phone, even a home phone, by dialling a special access number. There are dozens of cards available – with sci-fi names such as Alpha, Omega, Phone Com, Climax, Swiftlink and America First – available from newsagents and grocers. To decide which is best you really have to compare the rate each offers for the particular country you want – posters with the rates of the various companies are often displayed in shop doors or windows.

Mobile Phones Britain uses GSM 900/1800, which is compatible with the rest of Europe and Australia but not with the North American GSM 1900 or the totally different system in Japan (though some North Americans have GSM 1900/900 phones that do work here). If you have a GSM phone, check with your service provider about using it in Britain, and beware of calls being routed internationally (very expensive for a 'local' call).

If you want the convenience of a mobile in Britain, the simplest solution may be simply to buy one of the pay-as-you-talk phones sold not only from a plethora of high-street shops, but also from supermarkets, Woolworth's and just about anywhere else.

For under £70 you get a phone with a decent amount of air time and your own telephone number. As you use up your air-time, you simply buy more. There are no contracts or billing hassles. All four main mobile phone companies in Britain – Orange, Vodaphone, One 2 One and BT Cellnet – have variations on this scheme.

Fax
Many newsagents and tobacco shops offer a fax service. Ask at a TIC or just look for the signs.

Email & Internet Access

Travelling with a portable computer is a great way to stay in touch with life back home, but unless you know what you're doing it's fraught with potential problems. If you plan to carry your notebook or palmtop computer with you, remember that the power supply voltage in the countries you visit may vary from that at home, risking damage to your equipment. The best investment is a universal AC adapter for your appliance, which will enable you to plug it in anywhere without frying the innards. You'll also need a plug adapter for each country you visit – often it's easiest to buy these before you leave home. See the Electricity section for details about British power and plugs.

Also, your PC-card modem may or may not work once you leave your home country – and you won't know for sure until you try. The safest option is to buy a reputable 'global' modem before you leave home, or buy a local PC-card modem if you're spending an extended time in any one country. Keep in mind that the telephone socket in each country you visit will probably be different from the one at home, so ensure that you have at least a US RJ-11 telephone adapter that works with your modem.

Britain uses a unique phone connector, however it's not too hard to procure an adapter that bridges the gap between British and RJ-11 modems. Hotels aimed at business travellers usually have sockets for RJ-11 plugs, while in others you can re-route the in-room telephone cord – which typically connects to the phone with an RJ-11 plug – into your modem. However, at cheaper places and B&Bs, the phone may be hard-wired or there may not be a socket of any kind and when you ask the host for help you'll be met with a wide-eyed and bewildered stare.

For more information on travelling with a portable computer, see www.teleadapt.com or www.warrior.com.

Although major Internet service providers (ISPs) such as AOL (www.aol.com), Earthlink (www.earthlink.net) and CompuServe (www.compuserve.com) have dial-in nodes in Britain, it's best to download a list of the dial-in numbers before you leave home. If you access your Internet email account at home through a smaller ISP or your office or school network, your best option is either to open an account with a global ISP, like those mentioned above, or to rely on cybercafes and other public access points to collect your mail.

If you do intend to rely on cybercafes the best thing you can do is use a Web-based email service such as Hotmail (www.hotmail.com) or Yahoo (www.yahoo.com). This lets you log on for your email from any computer with Web access. There is a free eKno email option as well (www.ekno.lonelyplanet.com).

Otherwise, if you want to use your email service from home, you'll need to carry three pieces of information with you to enable you to access your Internet mail account: your incoming (POP or IMAP) mail server name, your account name and your password. Your ISP or network supervisor will be able to give you these. Armed with this information, you should be able to access your Internet mail account from any net-connected machine in the world, provided it runs some kind of email software (remember that Netscape and Internet Explorer both have mail modules). It pays to become familiar with the process for doing this before you leave home.

Places with Internet access are common in Britain. Try libraries, hostels, cybercafes and the like; many are listed in this book. Otherwise, TICs usually know right where to send you.

INTERNET RESOURCES

Britain is second only to the USA in its number of Web sites and there are plenty of sites to interest cyber travellers. Towns, tourist boards, attractions, B&Bs, hotels and transportation companies all have Web sites. You will find many listed throughout this book. Three good places to begin are the three Web sites listed under Tourist Offices earlier in the chapter.

The Web is also a rich resource for travellers in general. You can research your trip, hunt down bargain air fares, book hotels, check on weather conditions or chat with locals and other travellers about the best places to visit (or avoid!).

There's no better place to start your Web explorations than the Lonely Planet Web site (www.lonelyplanet.com). Here you'll find succinct summaries on travelling to most places on earth, postcards from other travellers and the Thorn Tree bulletin board, where you can ask questions before you go or dispense advice when you get back. You can also find travel news and updates to many of our most popular guidebooks, and the sub-WWWay section links you to the most useful travel resources elsewhere on the Web.

BOOKS

Countless guidebooks explore Britain's every nook and cranny. The book shops listed in this book, as well as most TICs, are groaning with scores of guidebooks. The latter are good for unusual local and specialist titles.

Most books are published in different editions by different publishers in different countries. As a result, a book might be a hardcover rarity in one country, but readily available in paperback in another. Fortunately, bookshops and libraries search by title or author, so your local bookshop or library is best placed to advise you on the availability of the following recommendations.

Lonely Planet

Lonely Planet also publishes *Walking in Britain* and *Cycling Britain* that make excellent companions to this book. *Scotland, Edinburgh* and *Wales* give detailed regional and local information. *London* is a comprehensive guide to the capital while the *London Condensed Guide* provides essential information in a handy format. *Out to Eat – London* describes an enormous selection of London's best eateries, while the *London* video provides a visual complement. Lonely Planet's *Ireland* guide covers Northern Ireland and the Irish Republic. Those who want to get to grips with British English – Cockney in particular – should get hold of the Lonely Planet *British phrasebook*.

Travel Photography: A Guide to Taking Better Pictures is written by internationally renowned travel photographer, Richard I'Anson. It's full colour throughout and designed to take on the road.

Guidebooks

Numerous books list B&Bs, restaurants, hotels, country houses, camping and caravan parks, and self-catering cottages, but often their objectivity is questionable as the places they cover pay for the privilege of being included. Those published by the tourist authorities are reliable (if not comprehensive) and widely available in TICs. The *Which?* books, produced by the Consumers' Association, are good and accurate: no money changes hands for recommendations.

People of a literary bent might like to look at the *Oxford Literary Guide to Great Britain and Ireland* that details the many writers who have immortalised the towns and villages.

There are scores more specialist guidebooks; you can spend hours looking them over in larger book shops. One favourite is the annual *Good Beer Guide,* which can steer you to the best British beers and ales and the pubs that serve them.

Travel

Bill Bryson's highly entertaining and perceptive *Notes from a Small Island* is a continuous best-seller that covers Britain. *The Kingdom by the Sea,* by Paul Theroux, was written in 1982 and so is now a little dated, but nonetheless very readable. Theroux's eye is as keen and his mood just as irritable as in his other books.

Iain Sinclair walked throughout the grittier parts of the south-east in the 1990s and his reflections on where England is going form a powerful book in *Lights Out for the Territory.*

Dervla Murphy's *Tale of Two Cities,* written in 1987, offers a veteran travel writer's view of life among Britain's ethnic minorities in Bradford/Manningham and Birmingham/Handsworth.

Two of the great Scottish travelogues are *Journey to the Western Isles of Scotland* and *The Journal of a Tour to the Hebrides,* by James Boswell. These recount the journey of famous lexicographer, Samuel Johnson, and his Scottish biographer, Boswell. In 1773 they visited Skye, Coll and Mull, and met

Flora MacDonald (who helped Bonnie Prince Charlie escape after the battle of Culloden).

In Search of Scotland, by Englishman HV Morton, a journalist turned travel writer, is a humorous and lively portrait of Scotland resulting from his exploration of the country in 1929. *Scottish Journey,* by poet Edwin Muir, a contemporary of Morton, is also well worth reading though his approach was more dour.

More recently, *Native Stranger,* by Alistair Scott, recounts the efforts of a Scot, who knew 'more about the Sandinistas', to learn the realities of 1990s' Scotland by travelling throughout the country. In *Danziger's Britain,* Nick Danziger describes the grim reality of life for many marginalised people in the Highlands and Glasgow.

History & Politics

The Year 1000, by Robert Lacey and Danny Danzinger, was an unexpected best-seller and examines what life was like in England in 1000 (it was cold and damp then too).

The Other Side of the Dale, by Gervase Phinn, aims to be a repeat of James Herriot's vet adventures. Only this time the little animals are school children (is there a difference?) and the protagonist is a school inspector.

The Isles: A History, by Norman Davies, is a much-acclaimed history of the British Isles and their diverse and restive peoples.

The Course of My Life, by Edward Heath, is the autobiography by one of Britain's most important politicians and prime ministers. *Windrush – The Irresistible Rise of Multicultural Britain,* by Mike and Trevor Phillips, traces the history of black Britain and the impact of immigrants on British society.

Simon Winchester's *The Surgeon of Crowthorne* is the true story of a homicidal American lunatic and a staid Scottish scholar who, between them, were largely responsible for the creation of the *Oxford English Dictionary.*

A Short History of Scotland, by Richard Killeen, is a concise, up-to-date introduction from the Stone Age to the 1990s. Aimed at visitors to the country *A Traveller's History of Scotland,* by Andrew Fisher, covers Scottish history from ancient times to devolution in under 250 pages. *The Scottish Nation,* by TM Devine, is a vigorous examination of the role of Scotland between 1700 and the modern day in the context of British, European and world history.

To flesh out some of the great figures of Scottish history, there are many well-written biographies, including Antonia Fraser's *Mary Queen of Scots* and Fitzroy Maclean's *Bonnie Prince Charlie.* John Prebble has written several passionate accounts: *The Highland Clearances, Culloden,* the story of the battle, and *Glen Coe,* about the massacre.

General

The English, by BBC television presenter Jeremy Paxman, is as literate as one would expect from possibly the toughest interviewer on British airwaves. It's all about just what the title suggests.

The Queen and Di, by Ingrid Seward, is just one of literally hundreds of books pertaining to the royalty. But lots of people come to Britain because they're enthralled by the royalty, so there you have it.

That Was Satire, That Was, by Humphrey Carpenter, is a great look at the explosion – so to speak – of British satire beginning in the 1960s.

Gavin Maxwell wrote a trilogy of memorable books about his life in the early 1960s among otters and other wildlife in the Highlands; *Ring of Bright Water,* the first in the series, is the best known.

The naturalist, Mike Tomkies, wrote an evocative series of books, including *Last Wild Years,* about his experiences while living in a remote West Highland cottage in the 1980s; in this book, the last in the series, he describes the slow destruction of his beloved Highlands.

If you want to get to grips with Welsh mythology, the book to start with is *The Mabinogion,* a collection of tales that date back to the mystic Celtic past, but which were not actually written down until the 14th century, or translated until the 19th.

For an impressionistic and entertaining description of Wales and its history, look for Jan Morris' *The Matter of Wales,* a modern travel writer's account of her home country. John Davies' *A History of Wales* fills in the more prosaic facts and figures.

FILMS

The British film industry has been having its best years in, well, years of late. A steady stream of commercial successes has injected life and energy into the industry. *Lock Stock and Two Smoking Barrels,* a comedy of some hapless London hoods and sort of a British *Pulp Fiction,* was wildly popular with Brits.

The big hit film of 1999, *Notting Hill,* managed to bring hordes of tourists to the already-trendy neighbourhood. Previously, the 1990s were marked by several other hits. *The Full Monty,* a tale of unemployed Sheffield steelworkers turned male strippers, became the most popular British film ever. *Four Weddings and a Funeral* remains popular, especially whenever TV programmers need a 'light, romantic comedy'.

Trainspotting spawned much imitation for its tough and cynical look at the Edinburgh drug culture. Fortunately, we haven't found a toilet that bad...Less hyped but in some ways an even better film is *Brassed Off,* the sad story of a colliery band attempting to keep going while the South Yorkshire pit on which they depend for work closes down.

A world away from such gritty social realism were the spate of adaptations of Jane Austen novels that hit the screens during the 1990s. *Pride and Prejudice* was made for television, but *Emma* and *Sense and Sensibility* were feature-length films. Filming took place all round England; see if you can recognise Montacute in Somerset, Lacock in Wiltshire and Lyme Park in Cheshire.

The French Lieutenant's Woman, based on the John Fowles' novel of the same name, made great play with the landscape around Lyme Regis in Dorset. *Howard's End,* the Merchant-Ivory adaptation of the EM Foster novel, looked as if it was set in the Home Counties but actually strayed as far afield as Ludlow in Shropshire.

And if you haven't already found it on your cable movie channel, *How Green Was My Valley* is the 1941 classic about Welsh coal miners.

NEWSPAPERS & MAGAZINES
Newspapers

Breakfast need never be boring in Britain – there's a very wide range of dailies available.

The bottom end of the British newspaper market is occupied by the *Sun,* the *Mirror, Daily Star* and the *Sport.* The *Sun* is a national institution with witty headlines and nasty, mean-spirited contents. After a long period in the doldrums, the *Mirror,* once a decent paper with left-wing sympathies, has started to reposition itself slightly (very slightly) more upmarket. The *Sport* takes bad taste to the ultimate, with a steady diet of semi-naked women of improbable proportions and stories of space invaders.

The middle-market tabloids – the *Daily Mail* and *Daily Express* – are Tory strongholds, thunderously supporting the Conservatives and playing to Middle England's fears with a steady diet of crime reports bolstered by thinly veiled scare stories about threatening immigrants and homosexuals.

The broadsheets can be stuffy and self-important, but are generally stimulating and well written, although they frequently show little regard for multiple sources and other voices in their stories. The *Daily Telegraph,* or 'Torygraph', outsells its rivals and its readership remains old fogeyish despite efforts to attract a new clientele (check out the frequent spectaculars on topics such as Lady Somebody and her horse or the latest in garden party fashion, for instance). *The Times,* once Britain's finest paper, has lost ground under Murdoch's ownership, but remains conservative and influential. It has good travel pages as well. The *Independent* tries hard to live up to its title and seems to have been thrown a lifeline by the strong economy. The lively and innovative, if mildly left-wing, *Guardian* is read by the chattering classes.

The Sunday papers are essential to the British way of life. On their day of rest, the British still settle in comfy armchairs and plough their way through endless supplements; the *Sunday Times* must destroy at least one rainforest per issue. Most of the daily papers have a Sunday stablemate that shares their political views. The oldest of the Sundays, the *Observer*, is the seventh day version of the *Guardian*. What these virtual logs have in common is a lack of much news; the news sections of the Sunday papers are filled, then, with aimless musings of overseas correspondents and news features that seem sparked by press releases.

You can also buy the Paris-based *International Herald Tribune*, arguably the best brief source of international news available, and many foreign-language papers in major train stations and throughout London.

There are local and regional papers throughout England.

The Scots have published newspapers since the mid-17th century. Scotland's home-grown dailies include the *Scotsman*, a Liberal Democrat paper, and the popular tabloid *Daily Record*. The *Herald*, formerly the *Glasgow Herald*, is the oldest daily in the English-speaking world, having been founded in 1783. The *Sunday Post* is Scotland's best-selling Sunday paper. Most papers sold elsewhere in Britain are available in Scotland, some designed specifically for Scottish readership.

In Wales the *Western Mail* is a reasonable national daily, with *Wales on Sunday* taking over at weekends. In Cardiff, it's worth glancing at the *South Wales Echo*, while in Swansea you might want to pick up the *Swansea Evening Post*, not because it's a lively read (it isn't particularly), but because it's the paper on which Dylan Thomas cut his journalistic teeth.

Magazines

Walk into any high-street newsagent and you'll realise that Britain boasts a magazine for almost any interest, with whole shelves of computer magazines, trainspotting magazines, heritage magazines, even magazines devoted to such esoteric interests as feng shui and naturism.

Most big towns have a listings magazine broadly along the lines of London's *Time Out*. Some are free, although the best cost about £2 and are mentioned in the relevant chapters of this book.

Of the myriad women's magazines *Marie Claire* is probably the most stimulating and original. But in recent years the surprise growth market has been in non-porn magazines for men. Liftoff really came after the launch of *Loaded*, a raunchy magazine aimed at the so-called New Lad culture. Hot on its heels came *FHM*, *GQ* and *Esquire*.

The biweekly satirical *Private Eye* is another British institution that retains its sharp edge, even at the risk of regular run-ins with the law.

Time and *Newsweek* are readily available, but the *Economist* remains the best news weekly here or anywhere.

The monthly *Scots Magazine*, with articles on all aspects of Scottish life, has been in circulation since the 18th century.

RADIO & TV
Radio

BBC radio caters for most tastes. Radio 1 (275M/1089kHz and 285M/1053kHz MW; 98.8MHz FM), the main public pop/indie music station, has undergone a revival after some years in the doldrums. Simultaneously, Radio 2 (88–90.2MHz FM) has broadened its outlook and now plays gooey 1960s, 1970s and 1980s stuff alongside even older tracks.

Radio 3 (247M/1215kHz MW; 91.3MHz FM) sticks with classical music and plays, while Radio 4 (1500M/198kHz LW; 417M /720kHz MW; 93.5MHz FM) offers a mixture of drama, news, current affairs and talk; its *Today* programme (6 to 9 am Monday to Friday, from 7 am Saturday) is particularly popular. Radio 5 Live (463M/693kHz MW), sometimes known as 'Radio Bloke', provides a mix of sport, current affairs and talk, although the latter is downright intelligent by American standards.

The BBC World Service (463M/648kHz MW) offers brilliant news coverage and quirky bits and pieces from around the globe.

The BBC also has numerous local services scattered about the country. BBC Radio Wales offers daily news and features on Wales, while BBC Radio Cymru transmits the same in Welsh.

You'll also find a range of commercial stations with everything from pop to elevator music to classical.

Sianel Pedwar Cymru's Success

Currently receiving a subsidy of £78 million a year, making it the world's most heavily subsidised public television channel, Sianel Pedwar Cymru (S4C – Channel 4 Wales) might not sound like a success story. The benefits of this Welsh-language TV service, on the air since the early 1980s, are only now becoming obvious to its critics, who thought the money could be better spent elsewhere.

S4C came into being not through the benevolence of Whitehall, but after heavy campaigning by Cymdeithas yr Iaith Cymraeg (the Welsh Language Society), which included a hunger strike by Gwynfor Evans, the Welsh nationalist. Since then the channel has played an important part in rejuvenating the language, and it's now estimated that 32% of children in Wales can speak at least some Welsh. Accountants are no doubt pleased to see that the channel's benefits are not only cultural. S4C has been successful in selling its programs to other TV channels, and film makers from abroad are starting to choose Welsh locations and use production companies based there.

The long-running Welsh soap *Pobol y Cwm* (People of the Valley) has been transmitted with subtitles to the rest of Britain on BBC2. Other acclaimed productions have included the children's cartoon *SuperTed*. S4C's greatest success to date, however, is *Hedd Wynn*, which won an Oscar in 1994 for Best Foreign Language Film.

TV

It's probably true to say that Britain still turns out some of the world's best TV, although the increasing competition as channels proliferate is resulting in slipping standards. Recent years have seen a spate of fly-on-the-wall documentaries that simply point a camera at the run-of-the-mill (hotels, driving schools, even Lonely Planet) and leave you amused but none the wiser.

There are currently five regular TV channels – BBC1 and BBC2 are publicly funded by a TV licence and don't carry advertising; ITV and Channels 4 and 5 are commercial stations and do. Of these, Channel 4 has the most interesting programming, ITV has lots of soaps and mass-entertainment, while Channel 5 is where you go for breasts.

These stations are up against competition from Rupert Murdoch's satellite TV, BSkyB, and assorted cable channels. Cable churns out mostly missable rubbish, but Sky is slowly monopolising sports coverage and has pioneered pay-per-view screenings of the most popular events.

There are regional TV variations, and Scottish Television (STV) carries Gaelic-speaking programmes. Wales has its own alternative to Channel 4, Sianel Pedwar Cymru (S4C), that broadcasts Welsh-language (but not exclusively) programmes daily.

VIDEO SYSTEMS

With many tourist attractions now selling videos as souvenirs it's worth bearing in mind that British videos are VHS PAL format and not compatible with NTSC or SECAM.

PHOTOGRAPHY & VIDEO
Film & Equipment

Although print film is widely available, slide film can be more elusive; if there's no specialist photographic shop around, Boots, the high-street chemist chain, is the likeliest stockist. Print film (36-exposure) costs from £3.50 for ISO 100 to £5 for ISO 400.

Technical Tips

With dull, overcast conditions common, high-speed film (ISO 200 or ISO 400) is best. In summer, the best times of day for photography are usually early morning and late afternoon when the sun's glare has passed.

Lonely Planet's full-colour *Travel Photography: A Guide to Taking Better Pictures*, written by internationally renowned travel photographer Richard I'Anson, is designed to take on the road.

Restrictions

Many tourist attractions either charge for taking photos or prohibit it altogether. Use of flash is frequently forbidden to protect delicate pictures and fabrics. Video cameras are often disallowed because of the inconvenience they can cause to other visitors.

Airport Security

You will have to put your camera and film through the x-ray machine at all British airports. The machines are supposed to be film-safe, but you may feel happier if you ask for exposed films to be examined by hand.

TIME

Wherever you are in the world, the time on your watch is measured in relation to the time at Greenwich – Greenwich Mean Time (GMT) – although, strictly speaking, GMT is used only in air and sea navigation, and is otherwise referred to as Universal Time Coordinated (UTC).

Daylight-saving time (DST) muddies the water so that even Britain itself is ahead of GMT late March to late October. But to give you an idea, San Francisco is eight hours and New York five hours behind GMT, while Sydney is 10 hours ahead of GMT. Phone the international operator on ☎ 155 to find out the exact difference.

Most public-transport timetables use the 24-hour clock.

ELECTRICITY

The standard voltage throughout Britain is 240V AC, 50Hz. Plugs have three square pins and adapters are widely available.

WEIGHTS & MEASURES

In theory Britain has now moved to metric weights and measures, although non-metric equivalents are still used by much of the population. Distances continue to be given in miles, except on some Scottish islands where hostel locations are indicated in kilometres. In most cases this book uses miles to indicate distance.

Most liquids other than milk and beer are sold in litres. For conversion tables, see the inside back cover.

LAUNDRY

Every high street has its laundrette. The average cost for a single load is about £3 to wash and dry. Bring soap powder with you; it can be expensive if bought in a laundrette. They should be able to direct you to one of these fun-filled social centres from wherever you are staying.

TOILETS

Although many conveniences are still pretty grim (graffitied or rendered vandal-proof in solid stainless steel), those at train stations, bus terminals and motorway service stations are generally good, usually with facilities for disabled people and those with young children. At the London rail and coach terminals you usually have to pay 20p to use the facilities, but at least they're clean.

Elsewhere, you can try your charms on publicans or lose yourself in the anonymity of large department stores. McDonald's, a not necessarily welcome addition to every high street, almost always has clean toilets you can breeze in and use.

No Kilos Please, We're British

One of the horrors of the year 2000 for the British was supposed to be the nightmare of another EU directive, this one mandating metrification. Suddenly your pound of carrots would become a 0.45 kg of carrots.

However, the expected outrage didn't occur. This is largely because people ignored the new standard. One of the largest supermarkets – Tesco – announced that it would simply add the metric measurements to its existing imperial labels. Where the new standards were adopted, it was often with a bit of cynicism. One supermarket displayed two kinds of tomatoes: the loose ones were priced with imperial measurements, while the pre-packaged tomatoes were priced metrically. It was almost impossible to determine that the more convenient pre-packaged tomatoes did indeed cost much more.

Car salespeople – never known for candour – needn't change their spiel at all; the EU has ceded a permanent exemption for speed and distance. Pubs will be able to continue pulling pints and milkmen can go on popping a morning pint on doorsteps.

Many disabled toilets can only be opened with a special key that can be obtained from some tourist offices or by sending a cheque or postal order for £2.50 to RADAR (see the Disabled Travellers section later in the chapter), together with a brief description of your disability.

HEALTH

Travel health largely depends on predeparture preparations, day-to-day health care while travelling and how you handle any medical problem or emergency that does develop.

Britain is a healthy place to travel. Hygiene standards are high (despite what your nose tells you on a hot and crowded tube train) and there are no unusual diseases to worry about. Your biggest risks will be from over-doing it on any activities you engage in, may they be physical, chemical or other.

Predeparture planning

Immunisations No immunisations are necessary.

Health Insurance Make sure you have adequate health insurance. See Travel Insurance earlier in the chapter.

Other Preparations Make sure you're healthy before you start travelling. If you are going on a long trip make sure your teeth are OK. If you wear glasses take your prescription.

If you require medication take an adequate supply, as it may not be available locally. Take packaging showing the generic name, rather than the brand, which will make getting replacements easier. It's a good idea to have a legible prescription or letter from your doctor to show that you legally use the medication to avoid any problems.

Basic Rules

Care in what you eat and drink is the most important health rule; stomach upsets are the most likely travel health problem (between 30 and 50% of travellers in a two-week stay experience this) but the majority of these upsets will be relatively minor.

Even in Britain it doesn't pay to be complacent. Beware of dodgy street vendors selling even dodgier food, for instance.

Water

Tap water is always safe unless there's a sign to the contrary (eg on trains). Don't drink straight from a stream – you can never be certain there are no people or cattle upstream.

Environmental Hazards

Sunburn Even in Britain, and even when there's cloud cover, it's possible to get sunburned surprisingly quickly – especially if you're on water, snow or ice. Use 15+ sunscreen, wear a hat and cover up with a long-sleeved shirt and trousers.

Heat Exhaustion Again, Britain may not seem like a place to worry about heat exhaustion, but that very complacency can lead to problems. Dehydration or salt deficiency can cause heat exhaustion. In hot conditions and if you're exerting yourself make sure you get sufficient nonalcoholic liquids. Salt deficiency is characterised by fatigue, lethargy, headaches, giddiness and muscle cramps. Vomiting or diarrhoea can rapidly deplete your liquid and salt levels.

Hypothermia Too much cold can be just as dangerous as too much heat. If you are walking or trekking at high altitudes, be prepared. In much of Britain you should always be prepared for cold, wet or windy conditions, even if you're just out walking or hitching. Every year people set out for walks on mild days – especially in the Scottish Highlands – and end up in trouble after the weather suddenly changes.

Hypothermia occurs when the body loses heat faster than it can produce it and the core temperature of the body falls. It is surprisingly easy to progress from very cold to dangerously cold due to a combination of wind, wet clothing, fatigue and hunger, even if the air temperature is above freezing. It is best to dress in layers; silk, wool and some of the new artificial fibres are all good insulating materials. A hat is important as a lot of heat is lost through the head.

Medical Kit Check List

Following is a list of items you should consider including in your medical kit – consult your pharmacist for brands available in your country.

- ☐ **Aspirin** or **paracetamol** (acetaminophen in the USA) – for pain or fever
- ☐ **Antihistamine** – for allergies, eg, hay fever; to ease the itch from insect bites or stings; and to prevent motion sickness
- ☐ **Cold** and **flu tablets, throat lozenges** and **nasal decongestant**
- ☐ **Multivitamins** – consider for long trips, when dietary vitamin intake may be inadequate
- ☐ **Antibiotics** – consider including these if you're travelling well off the beaten track; see your doctor, as they must be prescribed, and carry the prescription with you
- ☐ **Loperamide** or **diphenoxylate** – 'blockers' for diarrhoea
- ☐ **Prochlorperazine** or **metaclopramide** – for nausea and vomiting
- ☐ **Rehydration mixture** – to prevent dehydration, which may occur, for example, during bouts of diarrhoea; particularly important when travelling with children
- ☐ **Insect repellent, sunscreen, lip balm** and **eye drops**
- ☐ **Calamine lotion, sting relief spray** or **aloe vera** – to ease irritation from sunburn and insect bites or stings
- ☐ **Antifungal cream** or **powder** – for fungal skin infections and thrush
- ☐ **Antiseptic** (such as povidone-iodine) – for cuts and grazes
- ☐ **Bandages, Band-Aids (plasters)** and other wound dressings
- ☐ **Water purification tablets** or **iodine**
- ☐ **Scissors, tweezers** and a **thermometer** – note that mercury thermometers are prohibited by airlines

A strong, waterproof outer layer (and a 'space' blanket for emergencies) is essential. Carry basic supplies, including food containing simple sugars to generate heat quickly and fluid to drink.

Symptoms of hypothermia are exhaustion, numb skin (particularly toes and fingers), shivering, slurred speech, irrational or violent behaviour, lethargy, stumbling, dizzy spells, muscle cramps and violent bursts of energy. Irrationality may take the form of sufferers claiming they are warm and trying to take off their clothes.

To treat mild hypothermia, first get the person out of the wind and/or rain, remove their clothing if it's wet and replace it with dry, warm clothing. Give them hot liquids – not alcohol – and some high-kilojoule, easily digestible food. Do not rub victims: instead, allow them to slowly warm themselves. This should be enough to treat the early stages of hypothermia. The early recognition and treatment of mild hypothermia is the only way to prevent severe hypothermia, which is a critical condition.

Jet Lag Probably the worst health hazard you'll face in Britain, jet lag is experienced when a person travels by air across more than three time zones (each time zone usually represents a one-hour time difference). It occurs because many of the functions of the human body (such as temperature, pulse rate and emptying of the bladder and bowels) are regulated by internal 24-hour cycles. When we travel long distances rapidly, our bodies take time to adjust to the 'new time' of our destination, and we may experience fatigue, disorientation, insomnia, anxiety, impaired concentration and loss of appetite. These effects will usually be gone within three days of arrival, but to minimise the impact of jet lag:

- Rest for a couple of days prior to departure.
- Try to select flight schedules that minimise sleep deprivation; arriving late in the day means you can go to sleep soon after you arrive. For very long flights, try to organise a stopover.
- Avoid excessive eating (which bloats the stomach) and alcohol (which causes dehydration) during the flight. Instead, drink plenty of non-carbonated, nonalcoholic drinks such as fruit juice or water.
- Avoid smoking.
- Make yourself comfortable by wearing loose-fitting clothes and perhaps bringing an eye mask and ear plugs to help you sleep.
- Try to sleep at the appropriate time for the time zone you are travelling to.

Motion Sickness Eating lightly before and during a trip will reduce the chances of motion sickness. If you are prone to motion sickness try to find a place that minimises movement – near the wing on aircraft, close to midships on boats, near the centre on buses. Fresh air usually helps; reading and cigarette smoke don't.

Commercial motion-sickness preparations, which can cause drowsiness, have to be taken before the trip commences. Ginger (available in capsule form) and peppermint (including mint-flavoured sweets) are natural preventatives. These precautions will be especially appreciated if you plan any ferry trips to the islands in the far north.

Infectious Diseases

Fungal Infections To prevent fungal infections, wear loose, comfortable clothes, wash frequently and dry carefully. Always wear flip-flops (thongs) in shared bathrooms. If you get an infection, consult a chemist. Try to expose the infected area to air or sunlight as much as possible and wash all towels and underwear in hot water as well as changing them often.

Diarrhoea Simple things like a change of water, food or climate can all cause a mild bout of diarrhoea, but a few rushed toilet trips with no other symptoms is not indicative of a major problem.

Dehydration is the main danger with any diarrhoea, particularly in children or the elderly as dehydration can occur quickly. Under all circumstances *fluid replacement* (at least equal to the volume being lost) is the most important thing to remember. Weak black tea with a little sugar, soda water, or soft drinks allowed to go flat and diluted 50% with clean water are all good. With severe diarrhoea a rehydrating solution is preferable to replace minerals and salts lost. Keep drinking small amounts often. Stick to a bland diet as you recover.

HIV & AIDS Infection with the human immuno-deficiency virus (HIV) may lead to acquired immune deficiency syndrome (AIDS), which is a fatal disease. Any exposure to blood, blood products or body fluids may put the individual at risk. The disease is often transmitted through sexual contact or dirty needles – vaccinations, acupuncture, tattooing and body piercing can be potentially as dangerous as intravenous drug use. HIV/AIDS can also be spread through infected blood transfusions; but in Britain these are screened and safe.

Sexually Transmitted Diseases HIV/AIDS and hepatitis B can be transmitted through sexual contact. Other STDs include gonorrhoea, herpes and syphilis; sores, blisters or rashes around the genitals and discharges or pain when urinating are common symptoms. In some STDs, such as wart virus or chlamydia, symptoms may be less marked or not observed at all, especially in women. Chlamydia infection can cause infertility in men and women before any symptoms have been noticed. Syphilis symptoms eventually disappear completely but the disease continues and can cause severe problems in later years. While abstinence from sexual contact is the only 100% effective prevention, using condoms is also effective. The treatment of gonorrhoea and syphilis is with antibiotics. The different STDs each require specific antibiotics.

Insect Bites & Stings Bee and wasp stings are usually painful rather than dangerous. However, in people who are allergic to them severe breathing difficulties may occur and require urgent medical care. Anti-itch creams and lotions such as Calamine will provide relief and ice packs will reduce the pain and swelling.

Midges – small bloodsucking flies – are a major problem in Scotland during summer. Bring mosquito repellent and some antihistamine if you suffer from allergies; it can help limit your body's reaction to the bite.

Women's Health

Gynaecological Problems Antibiotic use, synthetic underwear, sweating and contraceptive pills can lead to fungal vaginal infections, especially in hot climates. Fungal infections are characterised by a rash, itch and discharge and can be treated with a vinegar or lemon-juice douche, or with yogurt. Nystatin, miconazole or clotrimazole pessaries or vaginal cream are the usual treatment. Maintaining good personal hygiene and wearing loose-fitting clothes and cotton underwear may help prevent these infections.

STDs are a major cause of vaginal problems. Symptoms include a smelly discharge, painful intercourse and sometimes a burning sensation when urinating. Medical attention should be sought and male sexual partners must also be treated. For more details see the section on Sexually Transmitted Diseases earlier in the chapter. Besides abstinence, the best thing is to practise safer sex using condoms.

Medical Services

Reciprocal arrangements with the UK allow residents of Australia, New Zealand and several other countries to receive free emergency medical treatment and subsidised dental care through the National Health Service (NHS); they can use hospital emergency departments, GPs and dentists (check the *Yellow Pages* phone directory). Long-term visitors with the proper documentation will receive care under the NHS by registering with a specific practice near where they live. Again check the phone book for one close to you. EU nationals can obtain free emergency treatment on presentation of an E111 form, validated in their home country.

Travel insurance, however, is advisable as it offers greater flexibility over where and how you're treated and covers expenses for an ambulance and repatriation that won't be picked up by the NHS (see the Travel Insurance section under Documents earlier in the chapter). Regardless of nationality, anyone will receive free emergency treatment if it's a simple matter like bandaging a cut.

Chemists (Pharmacies)

Chemists can advise on minor ailments such as sore throats, coughs and earache. There's always one local chemist that's open 24 hours; other chemists should display details in their window or doorway, or look in a local newspaper. Since all medication is readily available, either over the counter or on prescription, there's no need to stock up.

WOMEN TRAVELLERS
Attitudes Towards Women

The occasional wolf-whistle and groper on the London Underground aside, women will find Britain reasonably enlightened. There's nothing to stop women going into pubs alone, although not everyone likes doing this; pairs or groups of women blend more naturally into the wallpaper. Some restaurants still persist in assigning the table by the toilet to lone female diners, but fortunately such places become fewer by the year.

Safety Precautions

Solo travellers should have few problems, although common-sense caution should be observed in big cities, especially at night. Hitching is always unwise.

While it's certainly not essential, it can help to go on a women's self-defence course before setting out on your travels, if only for the increased feeling of confidence it's likely to give you.

Condoms are now often sold in women's toilets as well as men's. Otherwise, all chemists and many service stations stock them. The contraceptive pill is only available on prescription in the UK, as is the 'morning-after' pill (actually effective for up to 72 hours after unprotected sex).

Organisations

Most big towns have a Well Woman Clinic or Centre that can advise on general health issues. Find its address in the local phone book or ask in the library. Should the worst come to the worst, Rape Crisis Centres can offer support after an attack.

If you'd like to stay with women while you're travelling it's worth joining Women Welcome Women (☎/fax 01494-465441), an organisation which exists to put women travellers in touch with potential hostesses. It's at 88 Easton St, High Wycombe, Bucks HP11 1LT.

GAY & LESBIAN TRAVELLERS

In general, Britain is tolerant of homosexuality. Certainly it's possible for people to acknowledge their homosexuality in a way that would have been unthinkable 20 years ago; there are several openly gay MPs in the present Parliament.

In a bid to attract more 'pink pound' tourists, the BTA recently launched a massive advertising campaign overseas under the slogan 'You don't know the half of it'.

That said, there remain pockets of out-and-out hostility (you only need read the *Sun, Mail* or *Telegraph* to realise the limits of toleration). On 21 June 2000, the Scottish Parliament voted to repeal the notorious Section 28, a law that forbids 'the promotion of homosexuality in schools', despite an expensive campaign to prevent its abolition waged by Brian Souter, the man behind the Stagecoach bus and train empire. In England and Wales the situation is ongoing although the government remains committed to repealing the law.

The battle by the Labour government to lower the homosexual age of consent from 18 to 16, in line with that for heterosexuals, is also telling. It passed the House of Commons but needs to pass the House of Lords. Yet the usually docile Lords have repeatedly vetoed the measure. If it finally passes, it will automatically go to the Queen for her assent.

London has a flourishing gay and lesbian scene. Manchester and Brighton also have large gay scenes and in other cities of any size you'll find a community not entirely in the closet. However overt displays of affection are not necessarily wise away from acknowledged 'gay' venues and districts.

Organisations

The Gay Men's Press has two useful pocket guides: *London Scene* and *Northern Scene*. To find out what's going on pick up a free listings magazine such as the *Pink Paper* or *Boyz*, or the *Gay Times* (£2.50), which also has listings. *Diva* (£2) is for lesbians. They're all available at Gay's The Word bookshop (☎ 020-7278 7654), 66 Marchmont St WC1, and the freebies at most gay bars, clubs and saunas.

Another useful source of information is the 24-hour Lesbian & Gay Switchboard (☎ 020-7837 7324), which can help with most enquiries, general and specific. London Lesbian Line (☎ 020-7251 6911) offers similar help but only 2 to 10 pm Monday and Friday and 7 to 10 pm Tuesday to Thursday.

DISABLED TRAVELLERS

For many disabled travellers, Britain is an odd mix of user-friendliness and unfriendliness. These days few buildings go up that are not accessible to wheelchair users; large, new hotels and modern tourist attractions are therefore usually fine. However, most B&Bs and guesthouses are in hard-to-adapt older buildings. This means that travellers with mobility problems may end up having to pay more for accommodation than their more able-bodied fellows.

It's a similar story with public transport. Newer buses sometimes have steps that lower for easier access, as do trains, but it's always wise to check before setting out. Tourist attractions sometimes reserve parking spaces near the entrance for disabled drivers.

The 1995 Disability Discrimination Act makes it illegal to discriminate against people with disabilities in employment or the provision of services. Under Part 3 of the Act, barriers to access have to be removed by 2004. This includes introducing physical features such as ramps and automatic doors, so the situation for wheelchair users should slowly improve.

Many ticket offices, banks and so on are fitted with hearing loops to assist the hearing impaired; look for the symbol of a large ear. Some tourist attractions have Braille guides or scented gardens for the visually impaired.

Organisations

If you have a physical disability, get in touch with your national support organisation and ask about the countries you plan to visit. They often have complete libraries devoted to travel, and can put you in touch with travel agents who specialise in tours for the disabled.

The Royal Association for Disability and Rehabilitation (RADAR) stocks several useful titles, including *Holidays in the British Isles: A Guide for Disabled People* (£7.50). Contact RADAR (☎ 020-7250 3222) at Unit 12, City Forum, 250 City Rd, London EC1V 8AF.

The Holiday Care Service (☎ 01293-774535), 2nd floor, Imperial Buildings, Victoria Rd, Horley, Surrey RH6 7PZ, publishes *A Guide to Accessible Accommodation and Travel* for Britain (£5.95) and can offer general advice.

Many TICs have leaflets with accessibility details for their particular area.

See the Trains section of the Getting Around chapter for details on obtaining the Disabled Persons Railcard, which gives discounts on fares.

SENIOR TRAVELLERS

Senior citizens are entitled to discounts on things such as public transport, museum admission fees etc, provided they show proof of their age. Sometimes they need a special pass. The minimum qualifying age is generally 60 to 65 for men, 55 to 65 for women. See the Trains section of the Getting Around chapter for details on obtaining the Senior Railcard, which gives discounts on fares.

Organisations

In your home country, a lower age may entitle you to special travel packages and discounts (on car hire, for instance) through organisations and travel agents that cater to senior travellers. Start hunting at your local senior citizens advice bureau.

TRAVEL WITH CHILDREN

Britain is notorious as a country whose residents prefer animals to children. Even though having babies is a trendy topic with the media, anyone travelling with children needs to be prepared for hotels that won't accept their offspring and for frosty stares if they bring them into restaurants.

That said, there are some child-friendly oases. Branches of *TGI Friday* lay on crayons and balloons for younger visitors (and, of course, McDonald's tries hard to cultivate future burger-buyers). Many pubs have given up the battle to exclude children and now lay on playgrounds and children's meals.

It never hurts to ask when making accommodation reservations if children are welcome. Modern, purpose-built hotels will almost certainly be able to rustle up a cot.

These days most supermarkets, big train and bus stations, motorway service stations, and major attractions will have toilets with baby-changing facilities. Some rail companies have also launched separate 'family carriages' – they're not all that special but it's a step in the right direction.

Breast feeding in public remains controversial. Women are fighting hard – a brave female MP even tried it in the House of Commons – but it'll be some time before the British feel relaxed about breasts displayed for any purpose other than titillation.

See Lonely Planet's *Travel with Children,* by Maureen Wheeler, for more information.

USEFUL ORGANISATIONS
Historic Organisations

Membership of National Trust (NT), English Heritage (EH), Historic Scotland (HS), the National Trust for Scotland (NTS) and Cadw, the Welsh historic monuments agency, are worth considering if you plan to travel a lot around the UK and are interested in stately homes, castles, ruined abbeys and other historical buildings. All are nonprofit organisations dedicated to the preservation of the environment, and care for hundreds of spectacular sites.

National Trust (☎ 020-8315 1111)
Most NT properties cost nonmembers up to £5.50 to enter. Membership for those aged over/under 26 is £30/15; membership for a couple is £51 and for a family is £57. It provides free admission to all the NT's English, Welsh and Northern Irish properties as well as an excellent guidebook and map. You can join at most major sites. There are reciprocal arrangements with the NT organisations in Scotland, Australia, New Zealand and Canada and the Royal Oak Foundation in the USA. In this book, National Trust properties are designated by NT after the phone number.
Web site: www.nationaltrust.org.uk

English Heritage (☎ 01793-414910)

EH properties cost nonmembers between £1.50 and £6 to visit. Adult membership costs £28, a couple pays £46 and family membership costs £49.50. Membership gives free admission to all EH properties, half-price admission to Historic Scotland and Cadw (Wales) properties during the first year (free with membership thereafter), and an excellent guidebook and map. In this book, English Heritage properties are designated by EH after the phone number.

Web site: www.english-heritage.org.uk

Tracing your Ancestors

Many visitors to Britain have ancestors who once lived in this country. Your trip would be a good chance to find out more about them and their lives; you may even discover relatives you never knew about. There is, however, no one central record office – records for England and Wales are kept in London, and those for Scotland are kept in Edinburgh.

England & Wales

Start your search with the Family Records Centre (☎ 020-8392 5300, fax 8392 5307), 1 Myddelton St, London EC1R 1UW (⊖ Angel). This office is part of the Public Records Office (PRO) and is used to dealing with people tracing their past. They have several publications they can send you outlining what you'll have to do. Their Web site is at www.pro.gov.uk/about/frc.

The office itself is very helpful and open 9 am to 5 pm weekdays (until 7 pm Tuesday and Thursday) and 9.30 am to 5 pm Saturday. Take your passport or another form of identification if you want to see original records. Remember that documents referring to individuals are closed for 100 years to safeguard personal confidentiality. It is also not possible to see documents or records until the PRO has preserved them, even though they may have been officially released.

If you'd like someone to complete the search for you (for a fee), the Association of Genealogists & Record Agents (no telephone number), 29 Badgers Close, Horsham, West Sussex RH12 5RU, can send you a list of professional record agents and researchers. The association can also supply the name of an agent who will search for living relatives. Their Web site is at www.agra.org.uk.

Scotland

If your ancestors were Scottish you should first go to the General Register Office (GRO; ☎ 0131-314 4433), New Register House, 3 West Register St, Edinburgh EH1 3YT. This office holds birth, marriage and death records since 1855, the census records and old parochial registers. Contact the GRO for leaflets giving details of its records and fees. The office opens 9 am to 4.30 pm Monday to Friday. Before you go, contact the office to reserve a search-room seat, particularly if you have limited time in Edinburgh.

Next door is part of the Scottish Record Office (☎ 0131-535 1314), HM General Register House, 2 Princes St, Edinburgh EH1 3YY. There are two search rooms: the historical search room, where you research ancestors (no charge) and the legal search room, where you can see records for legal purposes (a fee is payable). Staff will answer simple inquiries by correspondence if precise details are given. If you want further research to be carried out for you (perhaps before you come) the office can send you a list of professional searchers. All correspondence should be addressed to: The Keeper of the Records of Scotland, Scottish Record Office, and sent to the above address.

Another place to try is the Scottish Genealogy Society (☎ 0131-220 3677, ⓔ scotgensoc @sol.co.uk), 15 Victoria Terrace, Edinburgh EH1, which has a library, microfilm, microfiche and books for sale. See their Web site at www.sol.co.uk/s/scotgensoc.

Books

Never Been Here Before, by Jane Cox and Stella Colwell (£6.99), is a useful guide to the Family Records Centre. *Tracing Your Scottish Ancestors*, by Cecil Sinclair (£9.99), is also useful.

Historic Scotland (☎ 0131-668 8800)

HS manages more than 330 historic sites, including top attractions such as Edinburgh and Stirling castles. It offers short-term 'Explorer' membership – three/seven/14 days for £10/15/20. A year's membership costs £26/20 for an adult/concession, giving free admission to HS sites and half-price admission to EH properties in England, and Cadw properties in Wales. There are standard HS opening times. Properties open 9.30 am to 6.30 pm daily, April to September. They close two hours earlier October to March. Last admission is 30 minutes before closing time. In this book, the initials HS after the telephone number indicate a Historic Scotland property – and, unless indicated otherwise, standard opening times apply.

Web site: www.historic-scotland.gov.uk

National Trust for Scotland (☎ 0131-226 5922)

NTS is separate from the National Trust (England, Wales and Northern Ireland), although there are reciprocal membership agreements. The NTS cares for over 100 properties and 74,000 hectares of countryside. A year's membership of the NTS costing £27 (£12 if you're aged under 26) offers free access to all NTS and NT properties. In this book, National Trust for Scotland properties are designated by NTS after the phone number.

Web site: www.nts.org.uk

Cadw (☎ 029-2050 0200)

Cadw, the Welsh historic monuments agency, looks after most of the ruined abbeys and castles in Wales, including the group of castles (Caernarfon, Harlech, Conwy and Beaumaris) in North Wales that has been designated a UNESCO World Heritage List site. One-year membership for an adult costs £24 and gives free admission to all Cadw sites. A young person (aged from 16 to 20) can join for £15, and a child for £12. Family membership, covering two parents and children aged under 21, is excellent value at £42 (single-parent family ticket costs £28). Cadw members are also eligible for half-price admission to EH and HS sites (free in the second year of Cadw membership). Three-day/seven-day Explorer Passes are also available, costing £9/15 per adult, £16/25 for two people, £21/30 for a family. Most Cadw sites have standard opening times. The properties open 9.30 am to 6.30 pm daily April to late October. In winter they open 9.30 am to 4 pm Monday to Saturday, and 2 to 4 pm Sunday. Last admissions are 30 minutes before closing time. Occasionally, opening times may vary, so before making a long trip to a remote site, it's as well to double check. In this book a Cadw-run property is indicated by the word Cadw, usually following the phone number.

Great British Heritage Pass

This pass gives you access to almost 600 NT, EH and expensive private properties. A seven-day pass costs £32, 15 days is £45, one month is £60. It's available overseas from the BTA or from larger TICs throughout Britain. It can only be purchased by non-Brits (show your passport).

DANGERS & ANNOYANCES
Crime

Britain is a remarkably safe country considering its size and the disparities in wealth. However, city crime is certainly not unknown, so taking caution, especially at night, is necessary. Pickpockets and bag snatchers operate in crowded public places such as the London Underground and popular museums.

Take particular care at night. When travelling by tube in London, choose a carriage containing lots of other people and avoid some of the deserted suburban tube stations; a bus or cab can be a safer choice.

The most important things to guard are your passport, papers, tickets and money. It's always best to carry these items next to your skin or in a sturdy leather pouch on your belt. Carry your own padlock for hostel lockers.

Be careful even in hotels; don't leave valuables lying around in your room. Never leave valuables in a car and remove all luggage overnight. This is especially true in seemingly safe rural locations. While you're out tramping about the countryside, someone may well be tramping off with your belongings. Look for secure parking areas near TICs and national park visitor centres.

Report thefts to the police and ask for a statement, or your travel insurance company won't pay out.

Drunkenness

The sight of a bleary-eyed lad of 20 ordering four pints of beer 15 minutes before closing time is but a precursor of trouble to come. The splattered evidence all over the pavements of British cities is a Sunday morning tradition. Worse, drunken brawls are not uncommon as liquored-up lager louts are tossed out onto the streets when the pubs close. The best you can do is give these yobs a wide berth – and watch where you step.

Touts & Scams

Hotel/hostel touts descend on backpackers at underground and main-line stations such as Earl's Court, Liverpool Street and Victoria. Treat their claims with scepticism and don't accept an offer of a free lift unless you know precisely where you are going (you could end up miles away).

Never accept the offer of a ride from an unlicensed taxi driver either – they'll drive you round and round in circles, then demand an enormous sum of money. Use a metered black cab, or phone a reputable minicab company for a quote.

Cardsharping – where tourists are lured into playing a game that seems to be going all one way until they join in whereupon the luck changes sides – seems to be on the wane, but in its place have come the mock auctions that operate primarily out of London's Oxford St. You may be handed a flyer advertising an auction of electrical and other goods at unbelievably cheap prices. But watch that word 'unbelievable' because that's just what they are. At the advertised venue you'll see attractive goods on display. However, you'll be asked to bid for goods in black plastic bags that you can't remove until the show's over. When you do remove it, you'll find your wonderful bargain has turned into fool's gold.

Beggars

The big cities, particularly London, have many beggars; if you must give money, don't wave a full wallet around – carry some change in a separate pocket. All the arguments against giving to beggars in developing countries apply; it's probably better to donate something to a recognised charity than give directly. Shelter (☎ 020-7505 2000), 88 Old St, London EC1, is a charity that helps the homeless and gratefully accepts donations. Also consider buying the *Big Issue* (£1), a weekly magazine available from homeless street sellers who benefit directly from sales.

Racism

Britain is not without racial problems, particularly in some of the deprived inner cities, but in general tolerance prevails. Visitors are unlikely to have problems associated with their skin colour, but please let us know if you find otherwise.

Though few visitors will be aware of anti-English feelings, they do exist, fanned by organisations that try to dissuade the English (and other nationalities) from buying property in the Scottish Highlands. Pockets of similar attitudes exist in Wales.

Weather

Expect rain at any time and never assume that just because it's the middle of summer it will be warm and you'll do fine. It's also wise to take more serious precautions if you will be out in rural areas.

Scottish Highland hikers should be properly equipped and cautious: the weather can get vicious at any time of the year. After rain peaty soil can become boggy; always wear stout shoes and carry a change of clothing.

It's wise to treat the Brecon Beacons and Snowdonia national parks in Wales with the respect they deserve. Mists can come down with a startling suddenness and you shouldn't venture to the heights without checking weather forecasts first. Plus you should certainly make sure you're sensibly and warmly clad and shod, and that you have food, water and a compass for emergencies.

Wherever you are in Britain, ideally make sure someone knows where you're heading if it's off the beaten track or in dubious climatic conditions.

Midges

The most infuriatingly painful problem facing visitors to the west coast of Scotland and Highlands is midges. These tiny bloodsucking flies are related to mosquitoes. From late May to mid-September (especially from mid-June to mid-August) they can be prolific. It's at least partly thanks to them that much of Scotland remains a wilderness. They're at their worst in the evening or in cloudy or shady conditions.

Cover yourself up, particularly in the evening; wear light-coloured clothing (midges are attracted to dark colours); and, most importantly, buy a reliable insect repellent containing DEET or DMP.

Church Regulations

In the Scottish Highlands and islands the Free Church of Scotland (the Wee Frees) and the United Free Presbyterians, adhere so strictly to the Scriptures that in some areas on Sundays the public toilets are padlocked and ferries aren't allowed to operate.

EMERGENCIES

The national emergency services number in Britain is ☎ 999. Use it for police, fire and medical emergencies; ☎ 112, the emergency number for much of Europe, can also be used.

LEGAL MATTERS
Drugs

Illegal drugs of every type are widely available, especially in clubs. Nonetheless, all the usual dangers associated with drugs apply and there have been several high-profile deaths associated with ecstasy, the purity of which is often dubious. Possession of small quantities of cannabis usually attracts a small fine (still a criminal conviction) or a warning; other drugs are treated more seriously.

Driving Offences

The laws against drink-driving have got tougher and are treated more seriously than they used to be. Currently you're allowed to have a blood-alcohol level of 80mg/100mL but there's talk of reducing the limit. The safest approach is not to drink anything at all if you're planning to drive. For information about current speed limits and parking violations, see Car & Motorcycle in the Getting Around chapter.

Fines

In general you rarely have to cough up on the spot for an offence. The two main exceptions are trains (including those on the London Underground) and buses, where people who can't produce a valid ticket for the journey when asked to by an inspector can be fined there and then; £5 on the buses, £10 on the trains, no excuses accepted.

BUSINESS HOURS

Offices are generally open from 9 am to 5 pm, Monday to Friday. Shops may be open longer hours, and most are open on Saturday from 9 am to 5 pm. An increasing number of shops also open on Sunday, perhaps from 11 am to 4 pm. In country towns, particularly in Scotland and Wales, shops may have an early-closing day – usually Tuesday, Wednesday or Thursday afternoon. Late-night shopping is usually on Thursday or Friday.

In London and some of the other large cities there are a growing number of 24-hour stores of all kinds.

PUBLIC HOLIDAYS & SPECIAL EVENTS
Public Holidays

Most banks, businesses and some museums and other places of interest close on public holidays: New Year's Day, 2 January (Bank Holiday in Scotland), Good Friday, Easter Monday (not in Scotland), May Day Bank Holiday (first Monday in May), Spring Bank Holiday (last Monday in May), Summer Bank Holiday (first Monday in August in Scotland, last Monday in August outside Scotland), Christmas Day and Boxing Day.

There are exceptions in Scotland, however. Bank holidays there are just holidays for the banks. Scottish towns normally have a spring and autumn holiday, but the dates vary not only from year to year but also from town to town.

British museums and other attractions may well observe the Christmas Day and Boxing Day holidays, but generally stay open for the other holidays. Exceptions are those that normally close on Sunday; they're quite likely to close on bank holidays too. Some smaller museums close on Monday and/or Tuesday, and several places, including the British Museum, close on Sunday morning.

Special Events

Countless events are held around the country all year. Even small villages have weekly markets, and many still re-enact traditional customs and ceremonies, some dating back hundreds of years. Useful BTA publications include *Forthcoming Events* and *Arts Festivals,* which list a selection of the year's events and festivals with their dates.

New Year

Hogmanay – huge street party to greet New Year; Edinburgh

Mid-March

Crufts Dog Show – premier dog show; Birmingham

Cheltenham Gold Cup – horse-racing meeting; Cheltenham

Last week in March

Oxford/Cambridge University Boat Race – traditional rowing race between the two university teams; River Thames, Putney to Mortlake, London

First Saturday in April

Grand National – famous horse racing meeting; Aintree, Liverpool

Early May

FA Cup Final – deciding match in England's premier football knock-out tournament; Wembley, London

Brighton Festival – arts festival; runs for three weeks

Last week in May

Chelsea Flower Show – premier flower show; Royal Hospital, London

Bath International Festival – arts festival; runs for two weeks

First week in June

Beating Retreat – military bands and marching; Whitehall, London

Derby Week – horse racing and people watching; Epsom, Surrey

Mid-June

Trooping the Colour – the Queen's birthday parade with spectacular pageantry; Whitehall, London

Royal Ascot – more horses and hats; Ascot, Berkshire

Late June

Lawn Tennis Championships – runs for two weeks; Wimbledon, London

Henley Royal Regatta – premier rowing and social event; Henley-on-Thames, Oxfordshire

Glastonbury Festival – huge open-air festival and hippy happening; Pilton, Somerset

Royal Highland Show – Scotland's national agricultural show; Edinburgh

Mardi Gras – one of Europe's loudest and proudest gay and lesbian parades and festivals; London

Early July

Hampton Court Palace International Flower Show – London

Mid-July

Royal Welsh Show – national agricultural show; Llanelwedd, Builth Wells

Late July

Cowes Week – yachting spectacular; Isle of Wight

Farnborough International Aerospace Exhibition and Flying Display – world's largest aerospace exhibition; Farnborough, Surrey

Early August

Edinburgh Military Tattoo – pageantry and military displays; runs for three weeks

Royal National Eisteddfod of Wales – Gaelic cultural festival; alternates between sites in North and South Wales

Mid-August

Edinburgh International and Fringe Festivals – premier international arts festivals; run for three weeks

Late August (August Bank Holiday)

Notting Hill Carnival – huge Caribbean carnival; London

Reading Festival – outdoor rock and roll for three days; Reading, Berkshire

Early September

Braemar Royal Highland Gathering – kilts and cabers; Braemar, Scotland

October

Horse of the Year Show – best-known show-jumping event in Britain; Wembley, London

5 November

Guy Fawkes Day – commemorating an attempted Catholic coup; bonfires and fireworks around the country

COURSES

No matter whether you want to study sculpture or Sanskrit, circus skills or computing, somewhere in Britain there's going to be a course. Local libraries are often a good starting point for finding information.

Language

Every year thousands of people come to Britain to study English and there are centres offering tuition all around the country. The problem is to identify the reputable ones, which is where the British Council (☎ 020-7930 8466), 10 Spring Gardens, London SW1, comes in. It produces a free list of accredited colleges that meet minimum standards for facilities, qualified staff and pastoral backup. It offers general advice to overseas students on educational opportunities since many normal colleges and universities now offer courses aimed at students from abroad.

The British Council has 243 offices in 110 countries around the world that can provide the same beginners information so you don't have to wait until you get to Britain to ask for help in choosing a college. Its Web site is at www.britishcouncil.org.

The BTA also produces a brochure for people wanting to study in England.

WORK

If you're prepared to work at menial jobs and long hours for relatively low pay, you'll almost certainly find work in Britain. The trouble is that without skills, it's difficult to find a job that pays well enough to save money. You should be able to break even, but will probably be better off saving in your home country. Like millions before you, you'll probably want to start your search in London.

Traditionally, unskilled visitors have worked in pubs and restaurants and as nannies. Both jobs often provide live-in accommodation, but the hours are long, the work exhausting and the pay not so good (and then there are all those pissheads to deal with). If you live in, you'll be lucky to get £130 per week; if you have to find your own accommodation you'll be lucky to get £180. Before you accept a job, make sure you're clear about the terms and conditions, especially how many hours (and what hours) you will be expected to work. A minimum wage of £3.60 per hour (£3 for those aged 18 to 21) was introduced in 1999, but if you're working under the table no one's obliged to pay you even that.

Accountants, health professionals, journalists, computer programmers, lawyers, teachers and clerical workers with computer experience stand a better chance of finding well-paid work. Even so, you'll probably need some money to tide you over while you search. Don't forget copies of your qualifications, references (which will probably be checked) and a CV (resumé).

Teachers stand a good chance in London, where turnover can be high. You should contact the individual borough councils, which have separate education departments, although some schools recruit directly. To work as a trained nurse you have to register with the United Kingdom Central Council for Nursing which can take up to three months. The initial application fee

is £70 (for overseas-trained nurses) and once the application has been accepted, a fee of £56 is required to be admitted to the register. The registration is then renewable every three years thereafter for a fee of £36. Contact the Overseas Registration Department (☎ 020-7333 9333, fax 7636 6935, ℮ update@ukcc.org.uk), UKCCN, 23 Portland Place, London W1N 4JT. If you are not registered you can still work as an auxiliary nurse. Its Web site is at www.ukcc.org.uk.

The free *TNT Magazine* is a good starting point for jobs and agencies aimed at travellers. For au pair and nanny work buy the quaintly titled *The Lady*. Also check the London *Evening Standard,* national newspapers and the government-operated jobentres, which are scattered throughout London and other cities. They're listed under Employment Services in the *Yellow Pages*. Whatever your skills, it is definitely worth registering with several temporary agencies.

For details on all aspects of short-term work consult the excellent *Work Your Way Around the World,* by Susan Griffith. Another good source is *Working Holidays,* published by the London-based Central Bureau for Education Visits & Exchanges.

If you play a musical instrument or have other artistic talents, you could try working the streets. As every Peruvian pipe-player (and his fifth cousin once removed) knows, busking is fairly common in London. It has traditionally been banned in the Underground (£20 fine), though that has hardly stopped many musicians and there is now talk of LRT licensing buskers to play in certain stations after they have auditioned. The borough councils are also moving to license buskers at top tourist attractions and popular areas such as Covent Garden and Leicester Square. You will still be able to play elsewhere, but those areas will be off-limits to anyone without a permit.

Tax

As an official employee, you'll find income tax and National Insurance automatically deducted from your weekly pay-packet. However, the deductions will be calculated on the assumption that you're working for the entire financial year (which runs from 6 April to 5 April). If you don't work as long as that, you may be eligible for a refund. Contact the Inland Revenue or use one of the agencies that advertise in *TNT Magazine* (but check their fee or percentage charge first). Check a local telephone directory to find the closest Inland Revenue office.

ACCOMMODATION

This will almost certainly be your single greatest expense. Even camping can be expensive at official sites.

For travel on the cheap, there are two main options: youth hostels and bed & breakfasts (B&Bs), although over the past few years several independent backpackers' hostels have opened and the number is growing, particularly in popular hiking regions.

In the middle range, superior B&Bs are often in beautiful old buildings and some rooms will have private bathrooms with showers or baths. Guesthouses and small hotels are more likely to have private bathrooms, but they also tend to be less personal. If money's not a concern, there are also some superb hotels, the most interesting in converted castles and mansions.

The national tourist boards operate a classification and grading system; participating hotels, guesthouses and B&Bs have a plaque at the front door. If you want to be confident that your accommodation reaches basic standards of safety and cleanliness, the first classification is 'listed', which denotes clean and comfortable accommodation. One crown means each room will have a washbasin and its own key. Two crowns means washbasins, bedside lights and a TV in a lounge or in bedrooms. Three crowns means at least half the rooms have private bathrooms and that hot evening meals are available. And so on up to five crowns.

In addition there are also gradings ('approved', 'commended', 'highly commended' and 'deluxe'), which may actually be more significant since they reflect a judgement on quality.

In practice there's a wide range within each classification and some of the best B&Bs

don't participate at all because they have to pay to do so. A high-quality 'listed' B&B can be 20 times nicer than a low-quality 'three crown' hotel. In the end actually seeing the place, even from the outside, will give the best clue as to what to expect. Always ask to look at your room before deciding. As ever, single rooms are in short supply.

The worst value accommodation tends to be in big towns where you often pay more for inferior quality (abrupt service, chaotic decor, ropey fittings). There are rarely any really cheap B&Bs in the city centres, which means those without cars are also stuck with bus services that tail off just when they're getting ready to go out in the evening.

TIC Reservations

Most TICs will book accommodation. In England and Wales the charge is a 10% fee, which is subtracted from the nightly price. A few TICs also charge an extra fee, in these cases you should complain bitterly and point out that the 10% deposit (which they usually keep) should be sufficient.

In Scotland, the TICs don't keep the fee, and instead charge £1 or £2.

Most TICs also participate in the Book-A-Bed-Ahead (BABA) scheme that allows you to book accommodation for the next two nights anywhere in Britain. Most charge around £3 and take a 10% deposit. Outside opening hours, most TICs put a notice and map in their windows showing which local places have unoccupied beds. These services are particularly handy for big cities and over weekends and the peak summer season.

Camping

Free camping is rarely possible, except in Scotland. Camp sites vary widely in quality; most have reasonable facilities, but they're usually tricky to get to without your own transport. The RAC's *Camping & Caravanning in Britain* has extensive lists; local TICs also have details.

Those planning to camp extensively, or tour with a van, should join the Camping & Caravanning Club (☎ 02476-694995), Greenfields House, Westwood Way, Coventry CV4 8JH. The world's oldest camping and caravanning club runs many British sites, including club-owned sites, certificated sites with minimal facilities taking only five vans, and commercial sites, which range from enormous holiday parks to quiet, overnight stops for backpackers. The annual dues are £27.50 and are good for one camp site and all who use it. You also receive a guide to several thousand camping grounds in Britain and Europe and other useful services. Check out its Web site at www.campingandcaravanningclub.co.uk.

Camping is possible at some NT properties; see the earlier listing under Useful Organisations for contact details. You can also camp at Forestry Commission (☎ 0131-334 0066, ⓔ fe.holidays@forestry.gsi.gov.uk) facilities throughout Britain. Check out the Web site at www.forestry.gov.uk/recreation /holidays.html.

The tourist boards rate caravan and camp sites with one to five ticks; the more ticks, the higher the standard.

In Scotland, you can camp free on public land (unless it's specifically protected). Commercial camping grounds are geared to caravans and vary widely in quality. Most tent sites cost between £5 and £10. If you plan to use a tent regularly, invest in *Scotland: Camping & Caravan Parks,* available from most TICs.

In Wales, camp sites, too, are concentrated in the national parks and along the coast. The TICs have a free *Wales Touring Caravan and Camping* leaflet with sites graded for facilities and quality by the WTB. Expect to pay about £6 a night for a tent, although on some sites prices go much lower, especially out of the high season. Most sites only open March or April to October, so phone before going out of your way at other times.

YHA Hostels

Membership of a Youth Hostel Association (YHA) gives you access to a network of hostels throughout England, Wales and Scotland – and you don't have to be young or single to use them.

There are separate local associations for England/Wales and Scotland, and each publishes its own accommodation guide. If you plan to use hostels extensively it's wise to get hold of these as they include the often complicated opening times, as well as exact details of how to reach each place.

All the British associations are affiliated to Hostelling International (HI).

England & Wales For England and Wales the YHA head office (☎ 0870 870 8808, ⓔ customerservices@yha.org.uk) is at 8 St Stephen's Hill, St Albans, Herts AL1 2DY. Membership prices are £12 for adults, £6 for under-18s and £24 for a family. Expect to pay anywhere from £7 in the country to £23 in London for adults and £6 to £20 for under-18s. Check out the Web site at www.yha.org.uk.

Scotland The Scottish Youth Hostel Association (SYHA; ☎ 01786-891400, fax 891333, ⓔ syha@syha.org.uk), 7 Glebe Crescent, Stirling FK8 2JA, is separate from the YHA. Its hostels are generally cheaper and often better than those in England. The SYHA produces a handbook (£1.50) giving details on over 70 hostels, including transport links. In big cities or popular towns, costs are around £12.75/ 11.25 for adults/under-18s; the rest range from £6.75/6 to £9.25/8. Its Web site is at www.syha.org.uk.

Facilities All hostels have facilities for self-catering and some provide cheap meals. Advance booking is advisable, especially at weekends, bank holidays and at any time over the summer months. Booking policies vary: most hostels accept phone bookings and payment with Visa or Access (MasterCard) cards; some will accept same-day bookings, although they will usually only hold a bed until 6 pm; some participate in the BABA scheme; some work on a first come, first served basis.

The advantages of hostels are primarily price (although the difference between a cheap B&B and an expensive hostel isn't huge) and the chance to meet other travellers. The disadvantages are that some are still run dictatorially, you're usually locked out between 10 am and 5 pm, the front door is locked at 11 pm, you usually sleep in bunks in a single-sex dormitory, and many are closed during winter. Official youth hostels are rarely in town centres; fine if you're walking the countryside or have your own transport, a pain if you're not.

Throughout this book, higher hostel prices for adults are given first, followed by the reduced price for juniors.

Independent Hostels

The growing network of independent hostels offers the opportunity to escape curfews and lockouts for a price of around £9 to £18 per night. Like YHA hostels these are great places to meet other travellers, and they tend to be in town centres rather than out in the sticks, which will suit the non-walking fraternity. New places are opening fast so it's worth double-checking with the TIC.

The Scottish *Independent Hostel Guide – Backpackers Accommodation,* available from some TICs. Alternatively, send a stamped, addressed envelope to Pete Thomas, Croft Bunkhouses & Bothies, Portnalong, Isle of Skye IV47 8SL. The Web site is at www.hostel-scotland.co.uk.

Bothies, Camping Barns & Bunkhouses

Bothies are primitive shelters, often in remote Scottish places. They're not locked, there's no charge, and you can't book. Take your own cooking equipment, sleeping bag and mat. Users should stay one night only, and leave it as they find it.

A camping barn (called a *böd* in Shetland) – usually a converted farm building – is where walkers can stay for around £5 per night. Bunkhouses are a grade or two up from camping barns, have stoves for heating and cooking and may supply utensils. They may have mattresses, but you'll still need a sleeping bag. Most charge from £7.50. These can be found through the north of England and Scotland.

University Accommodation

Many British universities offer their student accommodation to visitors during the holidays: usually for three weeks over Easter and Christmas and from late June to late September. Most such rooms are comfortable, functional single bedrooms but without single supplements. Increasingly, however, there are rooms with private bathroom, twin and family units, self-contained flats and shared houses.

University catering is usually reasonable; full-board, half-board, B&B and self-catering options are available. Bed and breakfast normally costs from £18 to £25 per person. Several possibilities are listed in the London chapter. In other places, TICs invariably have details.

For more information contact British Universities Accommodation Consortium (BUAC; ☎ 0115-846 6444, fax 846 6333, ✉ buac@nottingham.ac.uk), Box No 1928, University Park, Nottingham NG7 2RD. You can visit the Web site at www.buac.co.uk.

B&Bs & Guesthouses

B&Bs are a great British institution and the cheapest private accommodation around. At the bottom end (£14 to £20 per person) you get a bedroom in a private house, a shared bathroom and an enormous cooked breakfast (juice, cereal, bacon, eggs, sausage, baked beans and toast). Small B&Bs may only have one room to let, and you can really feel like a guest of the family – they may not even have a sign.

More upmarket B&Bs have private bathrooms and TVs in each room. Traditionally the British have preferred baths to showers. In many B&Bs and private houses you may find just a bath or a highly complicated contraption that produces a thin trickle of scalding hot or freezing cold water. Get the home-owner to explain how it works if you want a half-decent shower.

Double rooms will often have two single beds (twin beds) rather than a double bed so you don't have to be lovers to share. Many B&Bs have conservative owners so it pays to be a little careful in what you say and how you act.

Guesthouses, which are often just large, converted houses with half a dozen rooms, are an extension of the B&B concept. They

British Interior Design

Visitors will gain a vivid insight into modern British interior design if they stay at B&Bs. Most feature do-it-yourself (DIY) renovation and strive for a popular style that has been described as 'cosy, with a country house, cottagey look'!

A classic example of a B&B will have embossed and flowery wallpaper, hung crookedly, and swirly-patterned, synthetic carpets, laid badly. The light fittings will be mock candelabras and fussy lamps. The furniture will be covered in orange vinyl, purple velour and lace doilies. There will be a display of porcelain figures and ashtrays, and a collection of souvenirs – including at least one miniature wooden clog and a plastic sombrero. There'll be electric or gas heating and a fake fireplace with plastic logs and orange lights. Finally, there will be at least one print of a kitten in a gilt frame.

Bryn Thomas

range from £12 to £50 a night, depending on the quality of the food and accommodation. In general, they're less personal than B&Bs, and more like small budget hotels.

More expensive B&Bs can be truly luxurious and offer a range of services and amenities for guests. At the highest end, you may even have the chance to enjoy fresh fruit instead of baked beans with your breakfast.

Hotels

The term hotel covers everything from local pubs to grand properties.

Pubs usually have a bar or two and a lounge where cheap meals are served; sometimes they'll also have a more upmarket restaurant. Increasingly in the countryside they also offer comfortable mid-range accommodation, but they can vary widely in quality. Staying in a pub can be good fun since it places you in the hub of the community, but they can be noisy and aren't always ideal for lone women travellers.

On the coast, and in other tourist-attracting areas, there are often big, old-style, residential hotels. The cheapest have sometimes

been taken over by long-term homeless families who are being 'temporarily' housed by local authorities. They're not places for foreign visitors at all…which is one reason why it's wise to stick with tourist board-approved places except in rural areas. Many others are just fine, although stay in enough old British hotels and you'll soon realise that the TV series *Fawlty Towers* was really a documentary.

More and more purpose-built chain hotels are appearing along motorways and in city centres. Most depend on business trade and offer competitive weekend rates to attract tourists; they also often have a flat rate per room (with twin or double beds and private bathroom), making them relative bargains for couples and small families.

The very best hotels are magnificent places, often with restaurants to match. Many boast fascinating histories and often have extensive grounds and other luxuries. In rural areas you'll find country-house hotels in superb settings, and castles complete with crenellated battlements, grand staircases and the obligatory rows of stags' heads. For these you can pay from around £60 to well over £100 per person.

Rental Accommodation

There has been an upsurge in the number of houses and cottages available for short-term rent. Staying in one place gives you an opportunity to get a real feel for a region and its community. Cottages for four can cost as little as £125 per week; some are even let for three days.

Outside weekends and July/August, it's not essential to book a long way ahead. You may be able to book through TICs, but there are also excellent agencies who supply glossy brochures to help the decision-making, but these typically cost more, as you have to help pay for those brochures.

Hoseasons Country Cottages (☎ 1502-501515, fax 584962), Sunway House, Lowestoft NR32 2LW, handles a huge range of cottages in all price categories. You can pay under £200 in the far-off-season but in these cases you'll want to confirm that the fireplace works. In the summer, the average weekly rate is closer to £500. But these cottages come completely equipped. Its Web site is at www.hoseasons.co.uk.

The most spectacular possibilities are offered by the Landmark Trust (☎ 01628-825925, fax 825417, 🄴 bookings@landmarktrust.co.uk), Shottesbrooke, Maidenhead, Berkshire SL6 3SW. This architectural charity was established to rescue historic buildings and is partly funded by renting the properties after they've been restored. The trust owns 164 unusual buildings, including medieval houses, castles, Napoleonic forts and bizarre 18th-century follies (including the wonderful Pineapple near Falkirk, Scotland). Its Web site is at www.landmarktrust.co.uk.

FOOD

Britain is the nation that brought us mashed potato, mushy peas and the fried Mars Bar, a cuisine so undesirable that there's no English equivalent for the French phrase *bon appétit*.

It's an image that has proved hard to shake off but, fortunately, things are improving fast, especially in the south. The use of fresh fruit and vegetables has increased immeasurably. In the main towns and cities a decent range of cuisines is available. Particularly if you like pizza, pasta and curry (and consider those a decent range of cuisines), you should be able to get a reasonable meal pretty well anywhere. Indeed, the one thing that may be hard to find (except in pubs) is traditional English cuisine – dishes like roast beef and Yorkshire pudding or steak and kidney pie.

These days you'll come across lots of restaurants serving what is called modern British cuisine, originally a term used to cover the mix-and-match use of all sorts of fresh ingredients served into continental-style dishes, but now extended to include all manner of creatively prepared foods. Even the humble bangers and mash can rise to new heights when you take handmade

---

The Chain Gangs

In high-traffic areas, such as many high streets, it may seem that the only places to eat you see are part of chains. It's a sorry development, driven by the high costs of developing new restaurants in places where expenses are high. It's much easier for a corporation to endlessly replicate a concept with food and drink that can be easily prepared by semi-skilled staff than it is to run high-quality unique restaurants with individual chefs, menus and concepts.

With the proliferation of chains in Britain, there may be times when you feel that you've no choice but to try one. Here's a run-down of some of the better options.

Cafes & Restaurants

Pret a Manger is a massive chain of sandwich outlets that provide wonderfully fresh sandwiches in innovative variations: the chicken Caesar exudes parmesan, the 'more than mozzarella' comes with basil and pine nuts. The coffees are made to order. Pret deserves credit for lifting the standards of the British takeaway lunch.

Soup Opera has a range of freshly made soups that changes daily and can include interesting items such as Tuscan bean and smoked haddock chowder.

Café Flo, **Café Rouge** and **Dôme** all try to replicate casual French brasseries. The menus are heavy with salads, omelettes, steaks and frites, frites and more frites. All three are usually bright and airy, but something else they share we've found in several visits is pokey service, possibly because the owners sit in corporate offices far away. Expect to pay between £15 and £20 each, including drinks.

Pizza Express is a quirky chain that individualises its outlets with smart, but eclectic decor. Individual pizzas (about £6) come in a panoply of flavours and are usually quite good. Some locations even have regular live jazz.

Café Pasta and **Spaghetti House** are the pick of the formula Italian joints. Both have items on the menu that go a few steps beyond spaghetti bolognaise. Expect to pay around £15 each with drinks.

thyme sausages and pair them with, say, a fennel mash. Generally modern British really just means: 'Pretty good food that's not bad like the old British.'

Vegetarianism has taken off in a big way in Britain. Most restaurants have at least a token vegetarian dish, although it's common for menus at better places to offer several choices. As anywhere, vegans will find the going tough.

Takeaways

Curries have overtaken fish and chips as Britain's most popular takeaways. Certainly they are the preferred choice of the mobs pouring out of the pubs at 11 pm.

Every high street has its complement of takeaway restaurants, from McDonald's and Pizza Hut to the ubiquitous local curry house and – especially in the north – fish and chip shops. Although there are some notable 'chippies' about, the best you can

say about these places is that they provide piles of stodge for reasonable prices.

One of the best developments in high-street cuisine has been the emergence of takeaways specialising in fresh food. Chains such as Pret a Manger sell wonderful sandwiches and salads made from fresh ingredients in innovative combinations. They have good juice too. See the boxed text 'The Chain Gangs' below.

Cafes

In the bigger towns, you will find cafes, usually referred to as caffs or greasy spoons. Although they often look pretty seedy, they're usually warm, friendly, very British places and invariably serve cheap breakfasts (eggs, bacon and baked beans) and English tea (strong, sweet and milky). They also have plain but filling lunches, usually a roast with three veg, or bangers and mash (sausages and mashed potato).

The Chain Gangs

Pubs

All Bar One apes the best of the modern local pubs in London's residential neighbourhoods: light and airy, big tables with comfortable chairs, decent beers and large plates of vaguely modern European food. Of course, these places don't capture the individual charm of the best locals.

Hogshead is notable solely for its excellent range of hard-to-find beers from some of Britain's best and smallest breweries. The food is much less interesting.

Coffee

The days of a grim cup of weak and tasteless coffee in Britain are gone. Scores of outlets sell steaming cups of coffee in a myriad of permutations and sizes. Many of the purveyors are chains, and competition is fierce for prime, high-traffic locations. Other quality coffee bars can be found in bookstores such as Borders, Books Etc and Waterstones, allowing you to ponder your pages over a frothy brew. Even train stations and other places once known for squalid joe have decent coffee outlets.

Here are the major players in Britain's coffee wars. At all you have the choice of taking your beverage with you or remaining on the premises while you sip and possibly dip into a newspaper.

Aroma has stylish locations that belie their corporate ownership by McDonald's. The coffee comes in big, primary-coloured cups and you get a little chocolate on the side.

Coffee Republic has huge easy chairs at many of its outlets as well as baked goods and cold sandwiches.

Costa adds a menu of fresh soups, bakery items and hot and cold sandwiches at many of its locations. This is the choice for people who want more sustenance than just a hot drink.

Starbuck's continues its global assault and Britain is a major front for the ubiquitous American chain. Stores tend to be large with a variety of seating that makes them good for a long stay.

Amidst all the merry camaraderie, the food is often as grim as the furnishings.

There's another form of cafe you'll likely find in tourist areas. These specialise in teas and scones amidst twee decor. You can usually buy various gift items (meaning cutesy crap) by the exit.

Pubs

These days most pubs also do food, although Sunday can be tricky. At the cheaper end pub meals are not very different from those in cafes, but at the expensive end they're closer to restaurants. Many pubs embrace both extremes with a cheap bar menu and a more formal restaurant. Chilli con carne or lasagne are often the cheapest offerings on the bar menu (and easily microwaved by the untrained staff). A filling 'ploughman's lunch' of bread, cheese and pickle rarely costs more than £4. Another ubiquitous item is the 'jacket potato', which is nothing more than a baked potato slathered with some sort of flavoured gloop. Yum.

Better bets are the growing numbers of pubs that care about their food. Many have Thai restaurants attached and the food can be fresh and good – albeit a bit odd in a pub setting. Better yet are the growing number of 'gastro-pubs', which is short for gastronomy pubs. Here the food is often the vaguely defined modern British, but it is also often inventive, good and reasonably priced.

Restaurants

There are many good and excellent restaurants in Britain. Seafood, various meats, roasts and many other dishes are often very well prepared. London has scores of restaurants that could hold their own in major cities worldwide.

That said, the entire dining experience in Britain still has major short-comings. The prices are too high and the service is not good enough. Worse, many places – often those with only adequate food but loads of customers – cheerfully expect those paying the inflated prices to suffer numerous indignities of which the worst is timed eating. You call to make a booking (almost mandatory at many places) and are given a window for your meal, usually something like 8 to 10 pm. Not finished with your coffee? Still nibbling on your dessert? Just want to sit, digest and stare into your partner's eyes? Tough. You must leave your table as the next suckers have been booked in. Oh, and that will be £100. Try this in Paris or New York and the restaurant owner would rapidly be moving back to Britain where he/she can get away with it.

Self-Catering

The cheapest way to eat in Britain is to cook for yourself. Even if you lack great culinary skills, you can buy good-quality precooked meals from the supermarkets (Marks & Spencer's are the most highly regarded).

Breakfast

If your accommodation includes breakfast, it's liable to be some combination of eggs, fatty bacon, sausages, fried mushrooms, baked beans, fried bread, toast, cereal and on and on. What you will rarely receive is any combination of the words 'fresh' and 'fruit'. Tourists tend to enjoy the traditional English breakfasts (the Scottish and Welsh variations can include such horrors as black pudding) because they don't eat such things often at home. If they did they would die.

Scottish Cuisine

If it's hard to find what was once called English cuisine in England, it is much easier to find traditional Scottish foods in Scotland.

Scotland's chefs have an enviable range of fresh meat, seafood and vegetables at their disposal. The country has gone a long way to shake off its once dismal culinary reputation. Most restaurants are reasonably good while some are internationally renowned.

The country's high rate of heart disease partly results from high consumption of alcohol and cigarettes, but also from many poorer Scots eating a less healthy diet – high on fried foods, refined sugar and white bread – than previous generations. However, restaurants don't usually serve greasy, fatty foods.

As well as ordinary scones (similar to

JON DAVISON

JULIET COOMBE

LEE FOSTER

A selection of produce: a ripened crop at harvest time, near Salisbury; a stallholder flogging his wares at Columbia Rd flower market, London; and a big cheese at one of London's many cheesemongers

Churchly scenes (clockwise from left): stained-glass window detail; a gravestone's solemn inscription; Upper Slaughter's Norman church; Whitby's 13th-century abbey ruins; a Wesleyan chapel, Heptonstall

American biscuits), Scottish bakeries usually offer milk scones, tattie scones and griddle scones.

Bannocks are a cross between scones and pancakes. Savoury pies include the *bridie* (a pie filled with meat, potatoes and sometimes other vegetables) and the Scotch pie (minced meat in a plain round pastry casing – best eaten hot). A *toastie* is a toasted sandwich.

Dundee cake, a rich fruit cake topped with almonds, is highly recommended. Black bun is another type of fruit cake, eaten over Hogmanay (New Year's Eve).

Scotch broth, made with barley, lentils and mutton stock, is highly nutritious and very good. Cock-a-leekie is a substantial soup made from a cock, or chicken, and leeks.

Steak eaters will enjoy a thick fillet of world-famous Aberdeen Angus beef, while beef from Highland cattle is much sought after. Venison, from the red deer, is leaner and appears on many menus. Both may be served with a wine-based or creamy whisky sauce. Then there's haggis, Scotland's much-maligned national dish, which really is nothing more than a sheep's stomach that's filled with various minced up organs and oatmeal and then roasted.

Scottish salmon is well known, but there's a big difference between farmed salmon and the leaner, more expensive, wild version. Both are available either smoked (served with brown bread and butter) or poached. Smoked brown trout is cheaper, and also good.

As an alternative to kippers (smoked herrings) you may be offered Arbroath smokies (lightly smoked fresh haddock), traditionally eaten cold. Herrings in oatmeal are good if you don't mind the bones. *Krappin heit* is cod's head stuffed with fish livers and oatmeal. Mackerel paté and smoked or peppered mackerel (both served cold) are also popular.

Prawns, crab, lobster, oysters, mussels and scallops are available in coastal towns and around lochs, although a lot is exported.

Welsh Cuisine

Outside Wales, it could hardly be claimed that Welsh cuisine has a high profile.

Pressed, some people might remember the lamb, the leeks and the rarebits, but that's about it.

Traditional Welsh dishes include *cawl*, a thick vegetable broth, often flavoured with meat; and laverbread, not a bread at all, but seaweed that is often served mixed up with oatmeal and bacon on toast – a surprisingly tasty combination.

Welsh rarebit is a sophisticated variation of cheese on toast, with the cheese seasoned and flavoured with butter, milk and a little beer. Rarebit is a modern name – originally it was called Welsh rabbit.

Glamorgan sausages are made from cheese, breadcrumbs, herbs and chopped leek, making them good for vegetarians. *Bara brith* is spicy fruit loaf, made with tea and marmalade as well as the more conventional ingredients, while Welsh cakes are fruity griddle scones.

DRINKS

Takeaway alcoholic drinks are sold from neighbourhood off-licences rather than pubs. Opening hours vary, but although some stay open to 9 or 10 pm, seven days a week, many keep ordinary shop hours. Alcohol can also be bought at supermarkets and the diminishing collection of corner shops.

Most restaurants are licensed and their alcoholic drinks, particularly good wines, are always expensive. There are few BYO restaurants (where you can 'bring your own' bottles). Most charge an extortionate sum for 'corkage' – opening your own bottle for you.

Pubs

Given how much pubs epitomise Britain for many visitors, it's odd how unenthusiastic the breweries seem to be about hanging onto them. Not only are the high streets vanishing beneath a plethora of brewery-owned bars and brassieres, but many of the traditional pubs are reinventing themselves as Irish theme bars (O'Neill's) or Australian theme bars (Walkabout Inns).

Simultaneously, names that have endured sometimes for centuries are being banished in favour of infantile 'brand' names (see the later boxed text 'What's in a (Pub) Name?').

What's in a (Pub) Name?

Wandering around English villages you'll come across hundreds of ancient pubs with workaday names such as The Red Lion, The King's Arms and The Royal Oak with attractive signboards to illustrate them.

But what's this in Big Town high street? Yet another pub which manages to mix together some combination of 'rat', 'carrot', 'newt', 'slug' and 'firkin' in its name. Look closely at the signs and you'll find no trace of the individuality that marked out their predecessors. Instead come cartoon characters which look to have been designed with a kindergarten rather than an adult audience in mind.

Perhaps there's no point in mourning the passing of The Queen Victoria and The Bunch of Grapes. But many old pub names are as much a part of local history as England's medieval churches.

Take Nottingham's wonderful Ye Olde Trip to Jerusalem, a name that commemorates the Crusaders as they assembled for their long journey to the Holy Land. Or The Nobody Inn at Doddiscombsleigh, near Exeter, said to recall a mix-up over a coffin. Look harder at that Royal Oak sign and you'll see the head of Charles II peeping through the oak leaves – these signs harp back to the story that the king had to hide in an oak tree at Boscobel after his defeat at the Battle of Worcester. Signs for The Five Alls regularly show the king who rules over all, the parson who prays for all, the lawyer who pleads for all, the soldier who fights for all, and John Bull who pays for all.

Finally, there's the astonishing I Am The Only Running Footman, at 5 Charles St, London W1, a reminder of the 18th-century running footmen employed by wealthy men to run in front of their carriages lighting the way and shifting any obstacles.

The trend of chain pubs with stupid names has even brought comment from the government. In 2000 a minister openly decried the loss of traditional pub names. Perhaps he was able to seek solace at the nearby Adam & Eve (81 Petty France, London SW1).

But this assault on pubs hasn't meant the death of good ones. In fact in a way the best traditional pubs have more business as patrons find their options limited. Britain still has scores of splendid pubs, many of which are covered in this book. From a charming rural pub in England to a classic Edwardian drinking palace in Edinburgh, you will find many memorable places to have a pint.

Pubs are allowed to open for any 12 hours a day Monday to Saturday. Most maintain the traditional 11 am to 11 pm hours; the bell for last orders rings out at about 10.45 pm. On Sunday most open noon to 3 pm and 7 to 10.30 pm, though many stay open all day. Moves are afoot to finally – and we mean *finally* – get rid of these silly laws, but unlike a lad intent on getting his last pint before the bell, the process is moving very slowly.

For many visitors, getting thrown out of a pub just when you are starting to relax after a gruelling day of touring is the worst aspect of a British holiday.

Nonalcoholic Drinks

The British national drink is undoubtedly tea, although coffee is now just as popular and it's perfectly easy to get a cappuccino or espresso in southern towns. You can almost measure your geographical position by the strength of the tea in cafes. From a point somewhere around Birmingham the tea gets progressively stronger (and more orange), the sort of brew you can stand your teaspoon up in, or so idiom would have it. Farther south you're as likely to be offered Earl Grey or a herbal tea as a traditional Indian or Sri Lankan brew.

Alcoholic Drinks

Beer British pubs generally serve an impressive range of beers – lagers, bitters, ales and stouts. What New Worlders know as beer is actually lager and, much to the distress of local connoisseurs, lagers (including Fosters and Budweiser) now constitute a huge chunk of the market. Fortunately, the traditional

British bitter is fighting back, thanks to the Campaign for Real Ale (CAMRA) organisation – look for its endorsement sticker on pub windows.

The wonderfully wide choice of beers ranges from very light (almost like lager) to extremely strong and treacly. They're usually served at room temperature, which may come as a shock if you've been raised on lager. But if you think of these 'beers' as something completely new, you'll discover subtle flavours that a cold, chemical lager can't match. Ales and bitters are similar; it's more a regional name difference than anything else. The best are actually hand-pumped from the cask, not carbonated and drawn under pressure. Stout is a dark, rich, foamy drink; Guinness is the most famous brand.

Beers are usually served in pints (from £1.60 to £2.50), but you can also ask for a 'half' (a half pint). The stronger 'special' or 'extra' brews vary in potency from around 2 to 8%.

Among our favourite English brews is Boddingtons from Manchester as well as anything from the Young's Brewery, London. Courage is another good brewery, as is Websters. In Scotland, look for Deuchars or Bellhaven, which can also be found in England. In Wales, Brains is a smart choice.

There are hundreds of different beers and you'll want to do your own sampling. The key is to opt only for those that are poured from hand-pulled taps, that at least guarantees you're not getting something which has a name that begins with B-U-D.

Wine Good wine is widely available. Wine bars became popular in the 1980s and, while the concept is a bit old hat now, it did force many pubs to improve their selection of wines by the glass. Restaurants tend to have decent wine lists as well and if you're looking for something for a picnic, large supermarkets have large and impressive selections, at very good prices.

Whisky First distilled in Scotland in the 15th century, whisky (spelt without an 'e' if it's Scottish) is Scotland's best-known product and biggest export; over 2000 brands are now produced.

There are two kinds of whisky: single malt, made from malted barley, and blended whisky, distilled from unmalted grain (maize) and blended with selected malts. Single malts are rarer (there are only about 100 brands) and more expensive than blended whiskies. Although distilleries exist all over the country, there are concentrations around Speyside (Aberdeenshire & Moray) and on the Isle of Islay (Inner Hebrides).

As well as blends and single malts, there are also several whisky-based liqueurs such as Drambuie. If you must mix your whisky with anything other than water try a whisky-mac (whisky with ginger wine). After a long walk in the rain there's nothing better to warm you up.

When out drinking, Scots may order a dram (measure) of whisky as a chaser to a pint of beer. Only tourists say 'Scotch' – what else would you be served in Scotland?

ENTERTAINMENT

Depending on where you're staying, you'll find a wonderful choice of concert halls, theatres, cinemas and nightclubs to fill your evenings. The world-class venues are mainly in London (see Entertainment in the London chapter) but most of the big towns have at least one good theatre and perhaps an art cinema to supplement the multiplexes. Choice is much more restricted if you're staying in the countryside.

However you budget both your time and money, make sure that you see some British theatre. It easily lives up to its reputation as the best in the world. And it's not all on the theatres of London's West End – although there can be some fine shows here. Small, yet impressive theatre companies can be found elsewhere in London and elsewhere in England, Scotland and Wales. During the summer, some of the best troupes go on the road and perform in towns throughout Britain.

For nightlife, the major cities have many choices. Perhaps its because the pubs close so early, but Britain has an excellent range of clubs. Many have DJs and theme nights that draw patrons from an entire region. Manchester, Sheffield, Leeds, Liverpool, Edinburgh, Cardiff and many more places besides London all have very active clubbing scenes.

Britain invented rock music and bands continue to emerge from all over the country, like so many mushrooms after the rain. Most hope to end up in some late-night dingy club in London as prelude to a big recording contract. But you can hear some great music in most of the same towns that have good clubbing scenes. The best way to find out who and what is hot is to ask around.

Folk music is alive and well in Scotland and Wales and you will find live performances in venues from pubs to concert halls.

The major cities throughout Britain have a good range of classical music. London's major orchestras are world renowned.

SPECTATOR SPORTS

The Brits love their games and play and watch them with fierce, competitive dedication. They've been responsible for inventing or codifying many of the world's most popular spectator sports: cricket, tennis, football (soccer) and rugby; and the Scots can claim golf. To this list add billiards and snooker, lawn bowls, boxing, darts, hockey, squash and table tennis.

The country also hosts premier events for a number of sports: Wimbledon (tennis), the FA Cup Final (football), the British Open (golf), Test Cricket, Badminton Horse Trials (equestrianism), the British Grand Prix (motor racing), the Isle of Man TT (motorcycle racing), the Derby and the Grand National (horse racing), the Henley Regatta (rowing), the Five Nations Tournament (rugby union), the Super League Final (rugby league) and the Admirals Cup (yachting).

All year round, London hosts major sporting events. If you want to see live action, consult *Time Out* for fixtures, times, venues and ticket prices. Also see Spectator Sports in the London chapter.

Football

Britain's largest spectator sport and one of the most popular participation sports is football, also known as 'soccer' to distinguish it from rugby football.

Since the introduction of the Premiership in 1992, football has become very big business in England. This elite league, for the top 20 clubs in the country, has had huge cash injections, making the league and its players much better off than before (most players now earn about £15,000 a week). The extra money is mainly generated from television deals signed with Sky, one of the world's largest and richest satellite channels. Unfortunately, few of the smaller and less successful clubs have benefited from these changes. It's a case of the big clubs getting richer and the smaller ones struggling to survive.

This reconstruction has transformed the image of the game. In the 1980s, British football was associated with hooliganism and violence. The 1990s has seen clubs trying hard to appeal to a wider range of fans, realising the importance of making football more socially acceptable. On the whole, they have succeeded. Britain even has a Minister for Sport who is a keen Arsenal fan. Being broadcast on Sky has made the games more accessible not only to people in England but around the globe. Most football grounds are now suitable places for a family day out. (Of course, all these good feelings haven't stopped English – and they are English, not British as they will scream in your face – hooligans from shaming the entire nation with their antics such as those at Euro 2000 in Belgium and the Netherlands.)

England boasts some of the best and most expensive footballers in the world.

Many of the bigger clubs have recently been floated on the stock markets and are being run as serious, money-making businesses. It has become so commercial that most clubs make as much money from selling their merchandise as from entry into the games.

The domestic football season lasts from August to May. Most matches are played at 3 pm on Saturday afternoons. Tickets cost from £12 to £40 and are usually very difficult to purchase so try to book them well in advance.

Some of the bigger clubs include Manchester United, Arsenal, Liverpool and Newcastle United. Traditionally, the English national team has played its home internationals at Wembley, which has also been the regular site of the FA Cup final each May. However, at present Wembley is undergoing a controversial reconstruction program that's set to last to 2003.

England does not have a monopoly on football fanaticism. In Scotland football is the largest spectator sport, and the Scottish Football League, which has a number of divisions, is the main national competition. The best clubs form the Scottish Premier League, which has been dominated for the last decade or so by Glasgow Rangers. Its main rival, Glasgow Celtic, was the first British club to win the European Cup (1967) and still the only Scottish club to have done so. The Scottish FA Cup is an annual knock-out competition whose final is held mid-May at Hampden Park, Glasgow. The Scottish national team also plays its home international matches at Hampden Park. The domestic football season lasts early August to May.

Football, comparatively, is a far less popular sport in Wales, although some of the bigger teams – Wrexham, Cardiff City and Swansea City – play in lower divisions of the English FA League. Although the Welsh national team has underachieved in competition in the last 10 years, quite a few well-known Welsh players, for example Ryan Giggs, play for top UK Premiership teams.

Cricket

Sometimes called the English national game, cricket is still a popular participation sport. Every summer weekend, hundreds of teams play on idyllic village greens (and city sports fields), and display all the finest English characteristics – fair play, team spirit and individual excellence (plus maiming the opposing team and abusing the umpire).

Those not familiar with the game will need someone to explain the rules, and may find it slow. But at its best, cricket is exciting, aesthetically pleasing, psychologically involving, and quintessentially English.

Several clubs founded in the 18th century still survive. The most famous and important is Marylebone Cricket Club (MCC), based at Lord's cricket ground in north London.

Every summer, the national side of at least one of the main cricket-playing countries (Australia, India, New Zealand, Pakistan, South Africa, Sri Lanka, West Indies, Zimbabwe) will tour and play a series of five-day test matches and crowd-pulling one-day matches. Tickets cost from £20 to £40 and tend to go fast. Those for county championship matches are a much more manageable £7 to £15.

Rugby

It was once said that the difference between football and rugby was that football was a gentlemen's game played by hooligans while rugby was a hooligan's game played by gentlemen. Class distinctions may have fallen away, but the hooligan element lives on. A recent report listed rugby as Britain's most dangerous sport, with four times as many serious injuries per player as football.

Rugby (aka rugby football or rugger) takes its name from Rugby school in Warwickshire where the game is supposed to have originated when William Ellis picked up the ball and ran off with it during a football match in 1823. An alternative code of the game, rugby league, is played in the north of England, and differs from the traditionally amateur game of rugby union in that the team has only 13, rather than 15, players. Rules and tactics differ slightly, most notably in that possession changes from one team to the other after five tackles.

Rugby league is primarily a summer game and the Super League final is held at Old Trafford in September. Teams to watch include St Helen's, Wigan and Warrington.

England, Scotland and Wales make up half of the annual Six Nations Rugby Union Championship with Ireland, France and Italy. The union season runs from September to May, with the big internationals starting in January.

In England, Bath and Leicester are among the better union clubs. Fans will find London the place to be, with a host of good-quality teams (including the Harlequins, Richmond and Wasps). Twickenham is the impressive national stadium and headquarters for the English game.

North of the border, rugby union football is administered by the Scottish Rugby Union based at Murrayfield, Edinburgh, where home international games are played. The most important fixture is the clash against the auld enemy, England, for the Calcutta Cup.

At club level, among the better union teams are those from the Scottish Borders such as Hawick, Kelso and Melrose. At the end of the season teams play a Rugby Sevens (seven a side) variation of the 15-player competition.

In Wales, rugby union is the national sport. It enjoys most of its support from the working class communities of the south, although the game is passionately regarded throughout the country. The most successful club sides are Cardiff, Swansea, Neath and Llanelli and you can catch their matches between September and Easter. Tickets for normal fixtures are easy to obtain at reasonable prices (around £10 to £25; ☎ 0990-582582 for details). Even if you're not a rugby zealot, it's worth catching a game for the atmosphere and singing in the terraces.

Golf

Although games that involve hitting a ball with a stick have been played in Europe since Roman times, it was the Scottish version that caught on. Apparently dating from the 15th century, golf was popularised by the Scottish monarchy and gained popularity in London after James VI of Scotland also became James I of England.

With the Royal and Ancient Golf Club (the recognised authority on the rules) and the famous Old Course both in St Andrews, this small Scottish town is known as the home of golf. London, in contrast, can boast the world's oldest golf club. James VI played on Blackheath in 1608 and London's

Royal Blackheath takes the date of its founding from this royal teeing off.

See the Activities chapter for information about playing golf in Britain.

Horse Racing

Even the Queen turns up for Royal Ascot, which takes place for a week in late June. The cheapest tickets cost £5, but to be invited into the enclosure you must be well dressed and expect to cough up around £30. Booking is essential (☎ 01344-622211).

The Derby is run at Epsom (☎ 01372-726311) on the first Saturday in June. This is traditionally popular with the masses and you won't see a tuxedo in the place – unlike Ascot.

The Grand National steeplechase at Aintree is probably the best known of all Britain's famous horse races. It's run in early April.

SHOPPING

Napoleon once dismissed the British as a nation of shopkeepers but today, as standardised chain stores sweep the high streets, it would be truer to say they're a nation of shoppers. Shopping is the country's most popular recreational activity.

Multinational capitalism being what it is, there are very few things you can buy that are unique to Britain. On the other hand, if you can't find it for sale in London it probably doesn't exist. The capital has some of the world's greatest department stores as well as oodles of specialty shops. See Shopping in the London chapter for details.

Don't bother buying anything you can also purchase at home, it's probably cheaper there. Instead, concentrate on items unique to Britain.

What to Buy in England

Books of all sorts, especially unusual out-of-print books, are some of the best purchases that can be made in England. The specialist book shops of London, such as those along Charing Cross Rd, have a range of books and titles that are unmatched anywhere else in the world.

Albums, whether vinyl or CD, are other sought-after items. Unusual and hard-to-find recordings can be found in the quirky specialist music stores of London and most other towns of any size.

Antiques – the detritus from all those centuries of history – are sold everywhere. The range and prices span the gamut and, for connoisseurs, entire holidays can be planned around antique shopping. The popularity of the BBC television series *Antiques Roadshow* is testament to the English love of all things old and collectible.

Classic clothing such as the trench coat – literally derived from the garments of hapless millions of WWI troops – and suits are much sought after. In London the custom tailors of Savile Row and the shirt-makers of Jermyn St are popular with clients worldwide.

British design has always been excellent – even if some of the cars and office blocks don't do it credit – and there's a whole range of items from the whimsical to the practical that may catch your eye.

What to Buy in Scotland

Making things to sell to tourists is big business in Scotland, and almost every visitor attraction seems to have been redesigned to funnel you through the gift shop. However, among the tourist kitsch are some good-value, high-quality goods.

Tartan, Tweed & Other Textiles Scottish textiles, particularly tartans, are popular and tartan travelling rugs or scarves are often worth buying. There are said to be over 2000 designs, some officially recognised as clan tartans. Many shops have a list and can tell you if your family belongs to a clan, but these days if you can pay for the cloth you can wear the tartan. There are some universal tartans, such as the Flower of Scotland, that aren't connected with a clan. For about £350 to £420, you can have a kilt made in your clan tartan, but this shouldn't be worn without a *sporran* (purse), which can cost from around £50 for a plain version up to £1000 for an ornate silver-dress sporran. Full kilts are traditionally worn only by men, while women wear kilted or tartan skirts.

There are mill shops in many parts of Scotland, but the best-known textile manufacturing areas are the Scottish Borders and Central regions, particularly around Stirling and Perth. Scotland is also renowned for a rough woollen cloth known as tweed – Harris tweed is world famous. There are various places on this Hebridean island where you can watch your cloth being woven.

Knitwear Scottish knitwear can be great value and is sold throughout Scotland. Shetland is most closely associated with high-quality wool, and at knitwear factory shops you can buy genuine Shetland sweaters for as little as £12. The most sought-after sweaters bear the intricate Fair Isle pattern – the genuine article from this remote island costs at least £28.

Jewellery & Glassware Silver brooches set with cairngorms (yellow or wine-coloured gems from the mountains of the same name) are popular. Jewellery decorated with Celtic designs featuring mythical creatures and intricate patterns is particularly attractive, although some pieces are actually made in Cornwall. Glassware, particularly Edinburgh crystal and Caithness glass, is another good souvenir.

Food & Drink Sweet, butter-rich Scottish shortbread makes a good gift. Look for local variations. The stuff made by Walkers, although just fine, can be purchased anywhere.

As for souvenir bottles of whisky, you're better off buying it duty-free at the airport than in high-street shops, unless it's a rare brand, though you may be able to get a good price at a distillery store. Miniature bottles make good presents.

What to Buy in Wales

The recent revival of craft industries in craft centres all over Wales has provided plentiful shopping fodder for visitors with a yen for pottery, knitwear and lovespoons. Indeed, there can be hardly a visitor attraction left

Lovespoons

All over Wales, craft shops are turning out wooden spoons with contorted handles in a variety of different designs, at a speed that would have left their original makers – village lads with their eyes on a lady – gawking in astonishment. The carving of these spoons seems to date back to the 17th century, when they were made by men to give to women to mark the start of courtship. Various symbols were carved into the spoons; their meanings are as follows:

Anchor – I want to set up home with you

Ball – child (the number of balls corresponds to the number of children desired)

Bell – wedding

Chain – forever together

Cross – faith

Double Spoon – side by side forever

Flowers – love and affection

Heart – take my heart

Horseshoe – luck

Key – my house is yours

Vine – our love is growing

Wheel – I will work for you forever

If you want to see carving in progress, the Welsh Folk Museum at St Fagans can usually oblige. Any number of shops will be happy to sell you the finished product.

that doesn't have its shop selling commemorative T-shirts, pencils, stationery, books and souvenir fudge. Even the industrial sites have got in on the act, hawking repro miner's

lamps, coal sculptures and similar artefacts. Prices are often high, and quality variable, but among the furry red dragons there are some classy items to be had.

Activities

Pursuing a favourite activity or interest is one of the best ways of escaping the beaten track. Becoming part of a country's life, and preferably an active participant, is much more rewarding than remaining an isolated spectator viewing the world through a camera lens or car window.

There's no escaping the fact that Britain is an expensive place to travel. However, many activities not only open up some of the most beautiful and fascinating corners of the island, they are also well within the reach of the tightest budget. In fact, those on a shoestring budget may find themselves hiking or cycling out of necessity. Fortunately, a walk or ride through the countryside will almost certainly be a highlight – as well as the cheapest part – of a British holiday.

At the other end of the scale, those with big budgets may want to try one of the traditional British sports which are still played with enthusiasm. These activities have many variations – often involving horses, hunting, shooting or fishing – but the constant aim is to extract money from fat wallets.

Most activities are well organised and have clubs and associations that can give visitors invaluable information and, sometimes, substantial discounts. Many of these organisations have national or international affiliations, so check with local clubs before leaving home. The British Tourist Authority (see Tourist Offices in the Facts for the Visitor chapter) has brochures on most activities, which can provide a starting point for further research.

Almost every sport, activity and hobby known to humankind has obsessive British devotees. Most are pleased to meet someone who shares their interest, and their response is often generous and hospitable to a fault.

Walking

Every weekend, millions of people take to the parks and countryside. Perhaps because Britain is such a crowded island, a high premium is placed on open space and the chance to find some fresh air. In the cities, ritual weekend expeditions to the shops and markets are very often combined with a stroll in a park, ending somewhere that sells tea or beer. And the countryside is invaded every weekend by people (and dogs) taking short walks – and ending up somewhere that sells tea or beer.

Although modern developments have had a negative impact, a surprising amount of the countryside appears frozen in time, conforming to a picture of rural Britain that every movie-goer, TV-watcher and book-reader is accustomed to.

The infrastructure for walkers is excellent. Every Tourist Information Centre (TIC) has details (free or for a nominal charge) of suggested walks that take in local points of interest. Hundreds of books are available that describe walks ranging from half-hour strolls to week-long expeditions, and these are widely available in TICs, newsagents, bookshops and outdoor-equipment shops.

Every village and town is surrounded by footpaths, so keen walkers should consider a week based in one interesting spot (perhaps in a self-catering cottage, a youth hostel or a camp site) with a view to exploring the surrounding countryside. Numerous short walks are detailed in this book.

ACCESS

Again, perhaps because Britain is such a crowded island, the rights of people to gain access to land, even privately owned land, are jealously protected. In England and Wales the countryside is crisscrossed by a network of countless 'rights of way', most of them over private land, that can be used by any member of the public. They may traverse fields, moors, woodlands and even farmhouse yards.

These public footpaths and bridleways (the latter can be used by horse riders and mountain bikers) have existed for centuries, sometimes millennia. They are marked on maps and are often signposted where they intersect with roads. Some also have special markers at strategic points along their length (yellow arrows for footpaths, blue for bridle-ways, or other special markers if they are part of a particular walk). Some, however, are completely unmarked, so a good map, and the ability to use it, can be essential. If a path is overgrown or obstructed in some way, walkers are permitted to remove enough of the obstruction to pass, and to walk carefully through a crop. Discretion is advised – no farmer will appreciate damage to property.

Some rights of way cross land that is owned by the Ministry of Defence (MOD) and used occasionally by the army. When troop manoeuvres or firing are in progress, access is denied and red flags are put up to warn walkers.

There are some areas where walkers can move freely beyond the rights of way, and these are clearly advertised. For instance, the National Trust (NT) is now one of the largest landowners in Britain and some of its properties are open to the public. However, land within national parks does not necessarily fit into this category. National parks were set up in England and Wales by the Countryside Commission to protect the finest landscapes and to provide opportunities for visitors to enjoy them, but the land remains largely privately owned and farmed so access is restricted. It is almost always necessary to get permission from a landowner before pitching a tent. In England and Wales, Areas of Outstanding Natural Beauty and Heritage Coasts are also legally protected, but again that doesn't guarantee unlimited access.

Scotland does not have a formal system of registered rights of way, but there is a tradition of relatively free access to open country, especially in mountain and moorland areas (although there may be restrictions during the grouse- and deer-hunting seasons). Nor does Scotland have national parks, although development is controlled in a number of areas that have been designated as National Scenic Areas and Nature Reserves. There are long-term plans to develop the first Scottish national park around Loch Lomond and the Trossachs.

LONG-DISTANCE WALKS

The energetic, and the impecunious, should definitely consider some long-distance multi-day walks. With the exception of parts of Scotland, civilisation is never far away so it's easy to put together walks that connect with public transport and link hostels and villages. In most cases, a tent and cooking equipment is not necessary. Warm and waterproof clothing (including a hat and gloves), sturdy footwear, lunch and some high-energy food (for emergencies), a water bottle (with purification tablets), a first-aid kit, a whistle, a torch (flashlight), and a map and compass are all you need.

The best areas for long-distance walks include the Cotswolds, the Exmoor National Park, the Dartmoor National Park, the North York Moors National Park, the Yorkshire Dales National Park, the Lake District, the Pembrokeshire Coast National Park and the Scottish islands.

There are many superb, long-distance walks in Scotland but, in general, the potential combination of isolation and severe weather mean they require a reasonably high degree of preparation.

There are now 11 long-distance paths (LDPs) called National Trails that have been developed by the Countryside Agency, a body created in 1999 by the merger of the Countryside Commission and the Rural Development Commission. Many of these are amalgamations of walks that had been developed by the Countryside Commission over the past 40 years. The National Trails offer walkers access to outstanding countryside and a number of them traverse the national parks. They follow routes that travellers have journeyed for thousands of years.

In addition, there are over 200 LDPs that are regional routes created by county councils and unofficial long-distance routes devised by individuals or groups such as the Ramblers' Association. Some are excellent, well organised and have good information available. On the other hand, all you need is a good map and you can plan your own!

Walkers may choose to walk the entire length of a long-distance trail (or *way*, as they are often called), which could be from

30 to 600 miles long, but many just choose a section that meets constraints of time and transport. City-dwelling walkers often manage to walk an entire trail over a series of weekends.

Some of the long-distance walks in England, particularly along the coast and in the Lake District and Yorkshire Dales, can be crowded on weekends and in July/August – advance bookings for accommodation can be worthwhile at these times (contact the appropriate TICs for details).

The countryside can look deceptively gentle but, especially in the hills or on the open moors, the weather can turn very nasty very quickly at any time of the year. If you're walking in upland areas, it is vital to be well equipped and to carry (and know how to use) good maps and a compass. Always leave details of your route with someone trustworthy.

Maps, Guides & Information

Lonely Planet's *Walking in Britain* not only covers the main long-distance walks but also has a good selection of day hikes.

The Countryside Agency, in conjunction with Aurum Press and the Ordnance Survey (OS), publishes excellent guides for many trails. They include detailed track notes and incorporate the relevant sections from the OS 1:25,000 Explorer maps. There are hundreds of other specialist walking guides.

The Ordnance Survey (OS) organisation publishes a wide variety of maps covering the country which are widely available. For walkers, the Landranger maps at 1:50,000 – about 1¼ inches to the mile, covering about 25 x 25 miles – are usually sufficiently detailed. In some instances, where paths are unclear, the Explorer series (which is replacing the Pathfinder series) at 1:25,000 – about 2½ inches to the mile, covering around 12½ x 12½ miles – is useful. There are Pathfinder Walking Guides (covering short walks in popular areas) and Outdoor Leisure maps (covering most national parks), both at 1:25,000. The OS Web site, www.ordsvy.gov.uk, is very useful.

Those intent on a serious walking holiday should contact the Ramblers' Association

(☎ 020-7339 8500), Camelford House, 87–90 Albert Embankment, London SE1 7TW. Its Web site, www.ramblers.org.uk, has numerous links and information on many walks. Its *Yearbook* (£4.99) is widely available and itemises the information available for each walk and the appropriate maps; it also gives a list of nearby accommodation (hostels, B&Bs and bunkhouses).

Other good sources of local information are the many outdoor-gear shops that can be found in even the smallest of towns along popular walking routes. Many are listed in this book.

Luggage Services

In recent years there has been a welcome addition to the British walking scene in the form of luggage services that allow travellers to send their luggage on ahead each day to their next stop, leaving them unencumbered and free to enjoy their walks. While purists may scoff, the services are especially good for travellers combining a long-distance walk as part of a larger walk. Rates are widely variable depending upon the services desired.

Two firms are:

The Sherpa Van Project (☎ 020-8569 4101, fax 8572 9788) that offers luggage and bicycle carriage on a number of routes including the Pennine Way, the Dales Way, the Cleveland Way and the C2C Cycle Way.
  Web site: www.sherpavan.com
The Coast to Coast Pack Horse (☎/fax 01768-371680, ✉ packhorse@cumbria.com) exclusively serves the Coast to Coast Walk from St Bees in Cumbria to Robin Hoods Bay in Yorkshire. Besides transporting luggage and gear, they will transport faltering spouses and other companions who would rather take a lift to the next stop than walk.

South West Coast Path

At slightly over 610 miles long, this is the longest long-distance walk in Britain. It follows the coast through four counties from Minehead in Somerset, around Devon and Cornwall, to Poole in Dorset. The path is also known as the South West Way and the South West Peninsula Coastal Path.

The South West Coast Path is based on the trails used by coastguards to patrol the area in search of smugglers, so it mostly sticks to the edge of the coast and a considerable amount of walking up and down hills is involved.

Few people walk the whole path in one go because this takes about six to seven weeks. The most scenic and popular part is the route that runs from Padstow to Falmouth around Land's End, a distance of 163 miles entirely within Cornwall. This section is a medium to easy walk and it can easily be done in two weeks. There's plenty to see – secret coves, wrecks, the remains of cliff castles, barrows (a heap of earth placed over prehistoric tombs), settlements, disused mines and quarries, a wide range of bird life, seals – so a pair of binoculars is a good idea.

Accommodation is not a problem; there are many hostels, camp sites, B&Bs and pubs on or very near the path.

The Aurum Press guides cover Minehead to Padstow, Padstow to Falmouth, Falmouth to Exmouth and Exmouth to Poole. A single-volume guidebook and accommodation list for the whole route is published by The South West Coast Path Association (☎ 01752-892237). There is also a useful Web site at www.swcp.org.uk.

Cotswold Way

The Cotswold Way follows the western edge of the Cotswold Hills from Chipping Campden, just south of Stratford-upon-Avon, to Bath. The countryside and Cotswold villages are a delight, but the way is also a walk through England's history, with numerous prehistoric hillforts and ancient burial barrows. There are Saxon and Civil-War battle sites, reminders of the Romans, some fine stately homes, the ruins of a magnificent medieval monastery and many other historical markers and monuments. The path itself winds through fields and woods and over hills, and through a patch of England that is at its most affluent. The pretty-as-a-picture-postcard villages exude a heady aroma of solid bank accounts and expensive public schools.

The Cotswold Way is about 100 miles long and can be done in five days, although a week is better. It was approved for National Trail status in 1998, although the official designation has yet to occur while trails and signage are upgraded.

For all information on the trail, contact the Cotswold Way National Trail Office (☎ 01452-425637, ✉ jronald@gloscc.gov.uk), Environment Dept, Shire Hall, Gloucester GL1 2TH.

The Cotswold Way is well-suited for walkers on a medium budget as pubs with rooms abound along its route. However, those on a tighter budget will find few hostels.

Cleveland Way

The 109-mile-long Cleveland Way is the second-oldest National Trail and unquestionably one of the greatest walks in Britain, showing a cross section of the best scenery in Yorkshire and a region rich in history, geology and wildlife.

It loops around the North York Moors National Park, passing through small Yorkshire villages and farmland, past the ruins of Rievaulx Abbey and over heather-covered moors. It then follows a spectacular coastline through fishing villages and seaside resorts. There is a rich assortment of relics on the way, including Bronze-Age burial sites, Iron-Age forts, Roman signal stations, medieval abbeys and castles, and industrial relics from the 17th and 18th centuries. The region is also closely associated with Captain James Cook and there are monuments and museums commemorating his life.

The full walk is undeniably challenging and takes about a week. However, the way is never more than a couple of miles from a sealed road so there are numerous potential cut-out points and many options for tackling shorter sections, especially along the coast. For a longer hike, you can add on the Wolds Way which begins at the Cleveland Way's endpoint in Filey (see the next section).

There are scores of publications on the Cleveland Way. The official *Cleveland Way – Accommodation & Information Guide* (50p) is available from visitor centres and local TICs, or free if you write to National Trails Officer (☎ 01439-770657), North

York Moors National Park, The Old Vicarage, Bondgate, Helmsley, York YO6 5BP. You could also check out the Web site at www.clevelandway.gov.uk.

Wolds Way

One of the least used of the National Trails, the Wolds Way is a delight, not just for its scenery, but for its solitude. It starts at Hessle, near Hull, on the Humber estuary and winds its way over the Yorkshire Wolds for 80 miles to Filey on the coast. Here the trail meets up with the Cleveland Way (see the previous section).

The Wolds Way is a good introduction to long-distance walking as it has few serious climbs and the path conditions are usually good through the year. The *Wolds Way National Trail Guide,* by Roger Ratcliffe, (£9.99) covers the entire trail. Contact details are the same as for the Cleveland Way. The Web site at www.woldsway.gov.uk is also useful.

Cumbria Way

The Cumbria Way is a 68-mile walk that traverses the county of Cumbria and the incomparable landscape of the Lake District, first popularised for walkers by William Wordsworth and Samuel Taylor Coleridge. Most of the way lies within the Lake District National Park, and most of it follows valleys at relatively low altitudes, so bad weather is not a major issue. However, it also traverses several high passes and gives a dramatic taste of the mountains. A number of peaks are within easy reach.

If the weather does remain good (a day or so of rain is virtually inevitable and *cannot* be considered bad weather!), it's impossible to imagine a more beautiful walk. It takes in a full cross-section of the best of the Lake District – from the little-visited southern valleys to the shores of Coniston Water, the great peaks of the Langdale Pikes, Derwent Water, the flanks of Skiddaw, and another forgotten backwater between Keswick and Carlisle. As an introduction to the Lake District it's definitely unsurpassed.

This is not a National Trail, but its popularity ensures that there are many publica-

tions available. A good Aurum Press book covering the walk is *The Cumbria Way* (£12.99), by Anthony Burton. And when the rain does hit, you might appreciate *Harvey's Cumbria Way Waterproof Map* (£7.95).

Hadrian's Wall

Hadrian's Wall runs for over 70 miles across the north of England, from Newcastle upon Tyne to Bowness-on-Solway, west of Carlisle. Much of the wall has disappeared completely or is in ruins but, in theory, the route would make an excellent long-distance trail, and an extra five miles would make it a coast-to-coast walk. Currently, however, this involves quite a bit of walking along roads and through towns – the best way to experience the wall is on a series of day hikes, totalling 27 miles. A National Trail is being developed and is due for completion in 2002.

To walk the most interesting sections of the wall you could base yourself in or around Haltwhistle, or at Once Brewed, and make use of the good local public transport system. Alternatively, there are places to stay along the route at Greenhead, Gilsland and Brampton. As well as the wall itself, this route takes in several Roman forts, including Housesteads and Vindolanda, various turrets and temples, and also passes through Northumberland National Park, where the scenery is at its finest.

Hadrian's Wall, by Mark Richards, is an excellent two-volume guide (£7.99 each), one volume describing a route that follows the wall, the other giving detours into the countryside. There are many more maps and books available. For more information, contact the National Trail Officer (☎ 0191-232 8252, ✆ david.mcglade@countryside .gov.uk), Countryside Agency North East Region, Warwick House, Grantham Rd, Newcastle upon Tyne NE2 1QF.

The Pennine Way

The 256-mile Pennine Way can claim to be the granddaddy of British long-distance walks: it was first conceived back in 1935, though it was not 'officially' recognised until the 1960s. It can be one of the toughest walks in Britain if the weather is uncooperative as it follows the mountainous spine of northern England into Scotland, often crossing long stretches of unprotected high country. Careful planning, good equipment and caution are all essential requisites for walking the Pennine Way. Completing the whole walk in two weeks is a real endurance test; allowing three weeks is far more realistic.

The walk starts at Edale, in the north of the Peak District, and immediately makes the tough climb up to the 600m-high Kinder Scout plateau. This 'in-the-deep-end' approach on the first day is followed by a long spell of 'bog hopping' across the exposed moors of the Dark Peak. Continuing north through Brontë country, the route goes right through the Yorkshire Dales National Park, then joins Hadrian's Wall for a pleasant jaunt along the most interesting section of this ancient barrier. The final stretch of the walk crosses the full length of the Northumberland National Park before bringing weary walkers to a well-earned rest at Kirk Yetholm, just over the border in Scotland.

There are numerous books on the Pennine Way, including the two-volume *Pennine Way*, by Tony Hopkins (£10.99 each). For more information, contact the Countryside Agency (☎ 0113-246 9222), Yorkshire and the Humber Region, Victoria Wharf, Embankment IV, Sovereign St, Leeds LS1 4BA. You could also check out the Web site at www.pennineway.demon.co.uk.

Peddars Way & Norfolk Coast Path

This is an undemanding 88-mile trail that follows a Roman road across the middle of Norfolk from Knettishall Heath to the beautiful north Norfolk coast at Holme-next-the-Sea. It follows this coastline through a number of attractive, untouched villages such as Wells-next-the-Sea and Cromer.

Although the trail ends at Cromer, it's possible to continue for another 40 miles to Great Yarmouth. The start of the trail (Knettishall Heath) is also the end of another path, the Icknield Way, which runs for 105 miles across England from Ivinghoe Beacon. Ivinghoe Beacon also happens to be the end of the Ridgeway (see the following

section) so these three paths could be linked together into a long march of 284 miles from Avebury to Cromer.

There are several guidebooks, including *National Trail Guide: Peddars Way & Norfolk Coast Path* (£10.99), by Bruce Robinson. For further information, contact Peddars Way and Norfolk Coast Path National Trail Office (☎ 01328-711533, @ peddars.way@ dial.pipex.com), 6 Station Rd, Wells-next-the-Sea, Norfolk NR23 1AE.

The Ridgeway

The remains of a prehistoric track that is Britain's oldest road, the Ridgeway is now a National Trail beginning near Avebury (Wiltshire) and running north-east for 85 miles to Ivinghoe Beacon near Aylesbury (Buckinghamshire). It follows the high, open ridge of the chalk downs and then descends to the Thames Valley before finally winding through the Chiltern Hills. Unfortunately, the western section is popular with suburbanites trying out their 4WD Range Rovers.

The best guide is *The Ridgeway*, written by Neil Curtis (£10.99). For more information, contact the Ridgeway National Trail Office (☎ 01865-810224), Cultural Services, Holton, Oxford OX33 1QQ. You could also visit the Web site at www.nationaltrails .gov.uk/ridgeway/rwayinto.htm.

Thames Path

The path that runs the length of the River Thames, from the river's source in Gloucestershire to the Thames Barrier in London (173 miles), was designated in 1996. This famous waterway rises at Thames Head, south of Cirencester, and flows through a varied landscape that includes quintessentially English villages, peaceful meadowland and ugly suburban sprawl around the capital.

The Thames Path – National Trail Guide, by David Sharp, (£12.99) is a good all-round source. For more information, contact the Thames Path National Trail Office (☎ 01865-810224), Cultural Services, Holton, Oxford OX33 1QQ, or visit the Web site at www.nationaltrailsgov.uk /thames/thpainto.htm.

South Downs Way

The South Downs Way National Trail is a bridleway. It covers 100 miles between the coastal resort of Eastbourne and Winchester, a cathedral city and the ancient capital of England.

It's an easy walk and readily accessible from London, so parts can be busy, especially at the weekend. It covers a beautiful cross-section of classic English landscapes, beginning with spectacular chalk cliffs at Beachy Head, then traversing an open chalk ridge (the Downs) with great views, before entering rolling, wooded country as you approach Winchester.

The chalk downs are among the longest continuously inhabited parts of the island and the way itself follows an ancient ridgeway track that dates back 4000 years. It passes numerous prehistoric remains and some charming medieval villages. You are never far from a comfortable B&B and a good pub; there are also six youth hostels on or near the way, although they are all in the section between Eastbourne and Arundel.

The way can be walked in a week. For further information, contact the National Trail Officer (☎ 01705-597618), Queen Elizabeth Country Park, Gravel Hill, Horndean, Hampshire PO8 0QE. Also worth a visit is the Web site at www.nationaltrails .gov.uk/sdowns/sdointo.htm.

Dales Way

The Dales Way links two of England's greatest national parks – the Yorkshire Dales and the Lake District – and, although it's not an official National Trail, it's a popular and well-organised route. Some parts aren't signposted, however, so you need good maps.

Officially it begins at Ilkley, accessible from Leeds by regular trains, in a densely populated corner of West Yorkshire famous for its mill towns. Alternatively, you could start at Bolton Priory or Grassington (see the Yorkshire Dales National Park in the North-Eastern England chapter), both of which are on the way. Much of the walk follows river banks through the Yorkshire Dales so the walking is easy, although there are some open expanses of moorland between one dale (valley) and the next. The walk ends with a spectacular descent to Bowness on the shores of Lake Windermere, the main town in the Lake District National Park.

There are numerous guidebooks, including *The Dales Way Route Guide*, by Arthur Gemmell and Colin Speakman (£4). The TICs at Leeds, Grassington and Windermere are all good sources of information, as is the Ramblers' Association (see the earlier Maps, Guides & Information section), which produces an accommodation brochure, the *Dales Way Handbook* (£1.50).

Coast-to-Coast Walk

The walk was devised by the creator of superb, illustrated walking guides and near-legendary walker, Alfred Wainwright. It's an unofficial trail covering 190 miles from St Bees Head on the west coast to Robin Hood's Bay on the east. It traverses three national parks – the Lake District, Yorkshire Dales and North York Moors – and covers a range of England's most spectacular scenery, from sea cliffs to mountains, dales and moors.

The walk is serviced by the innovative Coast to Coast Packhorse (see the earlier Luggage Services section).

The classic guidebook is *A Coast to Coast Walk*, by Alfred Wainwright and Michael Joseph (£10.99). The Ramblers' Association publishes the *Coast to Coast Walk Accommodation List* (£2.95).

West Highland Way

This 95-mile hike through the Scottish Highlands runs from Milngavie (pronounced 'mullguy'), seven miles from the centre of Glasgow, north along Loch Lomond to Fort William.

The route passes through a tremendous range of landscape that includes some of the most spectacular scenery in the country. It begins in the Lowlands, but the greater part of this trail is among the mountains, lochs and fast-flowing rivers of the Highlands. In the far north the route crosses wild Rannoch Moor and reaches Fort William via Glen Nevis, in the shadow of Britain's highest peak, Ben Nevis.

The path is easy to follow and it uses the old drove roads along which cattle were herded in the past, the old military road built by troops to help control the Jacobites in the 18th century, and disused railway lines.

Accommodation shouldn't be too difficult to find, though between Bridge of Orchy and Kinlochleven it's quite limited. In summer you should book B&Bs in advance. There are some youth hostels on and near the path, as well as bunkhouses. It's also possible to camp in some parts.

The Aurum Press *West Highland Way*, by Anthony Burton, (£12.99) is comprehensive. For more information, contact the Loch Lomond Park Authority (☎ 01389-758216), Balloch Castle, Balloch, Dunbartonshire G53 8LX.

Pembrokeshire Coast Path

This 186-mile cliff-top trail includes some of the finest beaches in Britain and offers the best coastal scenery in Wales.

Lying entirely within the Pembrokeshire Coast National Park in south-west Wales, the coast path passes through tiny fishing villages, skirts secluded coves and crosses some sparsely populated regions. The only towns of any size on the route are Pembroke, Milford Haven and Fishguard, but there are, nevertheless, numerous places to stay that are conveniently located along the path.

As well as being renowned for its superb coastal scenery, the area is of particular interest to bird-watchers – only parts of the Scottish coast attract more varied seabird life. Although there are a number of steep climbs and descents along its route, the path is not hard-going if you take it slowly. And there are numerous worthwhile distractions along the way: St David's (the smallest city in Britain, with its fine cathedral), several ruined castles, Iron-Age forts, beaches and nature reserves – not to mention the pubs.

Brian John's *Pembrokeshire Coast Path – National Trail Guide* (£10.99) is a good resource. For more information, contact the Pembrokeshire Coast National Park (☎ 01437-764636, ⓔ pcnp@pembrokeshire coast.org), Winch Lane, Haverfordwest, Pembrokeshire SA61 1PY.

The Offa's Dyke Path

Offa's Dyke was a grand earthwork project, conceived and executed in the 8th century by King Offa to separate his kingdom of Mercia from Wales. The English-Welsh border has been defined roughly by the dyke ever since.

The 177-mile trail runs from Chepstow in the south through the beautiful Wye Valley and Shropshire Hills to end on the north Wales coast at Prestatyn. Rather than sticking religiously to the dyke, which is overgrown in some places and built over in others, the trail makes many detours along quiet valleys and ridges. The route offers a tremendous range of scenery, possibly the most varied of any long-distance trail.

Offa's Dyke Path is a two-volume book on the northern and southern portions of the walk, written by Ernie and Kathy McKay and Mark Richards (£10.99 each). Contact the Offa's Dyke Association (☎ 01547-528753, ⓔ oda@offasdyke.demon.uk), West St, Knighton, Powys LD7 1EN, for details.

WALKING TOURS

There are scores of companies offering walking tours of Britain. A few include:

Ramblers Holidays (☎ 01707-331133, ⓔ ram hols@dial.pipex.com), Box 43, Welwyn Garden City, Herts AL8 6PQ, concentrates on the Lake District.
English Wanderer (☎ 01740-650900), 1 High St, Windermere, Cumbria LA23 1AF, arranges unescorted walks by setting up accommodation, providing maps and so on.
Highlander Mountaineering (☎ 01807-590250), Highlea, Auchnarrow, Glenlivet, Banffshire AB37 9JN, provides training in mountain walking including navigation and survival skills.

Cycling

Travelling by bicycle is an excellent way to explore Britain. Away from the motorways and busy main roads, there's a vast network of quiet country lanes leading through peaceful villages. Bring your own bike or hire one when you arrive. Cycle routes have been suggested throughout the book.

INFORMATION

Lonely Planet's new *Cycling Britain* has details of the best cycling routes, information on places to stay and eat and a handy section on bicycle maintenance.

The British Tourist Authority publishes a free booklet, *Cycling*, with some suggested routes, lists of cycle holiday companies and other helpful information. Many regional TICs have information on local cycling routes and places where you can hire bikes. They also stock cycling guides and books – look out for the range of route map/guides produced by Ordnance Survey (OS).

The Cyclists' Touring Club (CTC) (☎ 01483-417217, fax 426994, ℮ cycling@ctc.org.uk), 69 Meadrow, Godalming, Surrey GU7 3HS, is a membership organisation providing comprehensive information (free of charge to members) about cycling in Britain and overseas. It can provide suggested routes (on- and off-road), lists of local cycling contacts and clubs, recommended accommodation, organised cycling holidays, a cycle-hire directory and a mail-order service for OS maps and cycling books. Annual membership costs £25 (those aged under 26 and seniors £15). Some cycling organisations outside Britain have reciprocal membership arrangements with the CTC.

Tours

As for walking, there are many specialist tour companies catering to cyclists in Britain. Two possibilities include:

Country Lanes (☎ 01425-655022, fax 655177, ℮ bicycling@countrylanes.co.uk) 9 Shaftesbury St, Fordingbridge, Hampshire SP6 1JF. This is a small company running a range of cycling trips in the Lake District, the Cotswolds and the New Forest.
Bicycle Beano Cycle Tours (☎ 01982-560471, ℮ mail@bicycle-beano.co.uk) Erwood, Builth Wells, Powys, LD2 3PQ, Wales. This company offers tours in the English-Welsh border region; they cater to vegetarians.

Transporting your Bicycle

Air Most airlines will carry a bike free of charge as long as the bike and panniers don't exceed the per-passenger weight allowance (usually 20kg). Hefty excess-baggage charges may be incurred if you do and this applies to internal and international flights. Note that some charter-flight companies do make a charge for the carriage of bikes.

Inform the airline that you will be bringing your bike when you book your ticket. Arrive at the airport in good time to remove panniers and pedals, deflate tyres and turn handlebars around – the minimum dismantling usually required by airlines.

Train Bikes can be taken on most train journeys in Britain. However, the privatisation of rail services in Britain means that each of the 25 train companies can decide their own policy about bikes on trains.

Generally, bikes can be taken on local services free of charge on a first-come-first-served basis, though some train operating companies do not carry bikes on certain routes or during peak hours. On most long-distance routes it is necessary to make a reservation for your bike. Reservations will almost always incur a charge – usually around £3 for a single journey.

To be sure that you can take your bike you should make your reservation (and get your ticket) and check bike-carriage details at least 24 hours before travelling – this is because some trains only carry one or two bikes. You should also check if there are going to be engineering works on the line because bikes cannot be carried on replacement bus services. A good place to start with this chore is the National Rail Enquiry Service (☎ 0845 748 4950) but you should also check with the train company.

Roads, Lanes & Tracks

Bikes are not allowed on motorways, but you can cycle on all other roads (on the left!) unless the road is marked 'private'. A-roads tend to be busy and are best avoided. B-roads are usually quieter and many are pleasant for cycling.

The best roads for the cyclist are the unclassified roads, or 'lanes' as they are called. Linking small villages together, they are not numbered: you simply follow the

Sustrans & the National Cycle Network

Sustrans is a non-profit group working towards the creation of a 6500-mile network of cycle paths that will pass through the middle of most major towns and cities in Britain. In 2000, the first 5000 miles of routes were officially opened and the goal is to have the network pass within two miles of the homes of half the British population.

When Sustrans announced this objective in 1978 the charity was barely taken seriously, but the growth in popularity of bicycles, coupled with possibly terminal road congestion, has brought lots of attention to the idea of cycle paths. There's been official support of the network – including £43.5 million from the Millennium Commission. Sustrans has also benefited from some high-profile support from the government as well as big names such as Neil Kinnock (politician), Jeremy Paxman (broadcast journalist) and Richard Rogers (famous architect).

Half the network is to be on traffic-free paths (including disused railways and canalside towpaths), the rest of the system along quiet minor roads. Cyclists will share the traffic-free paths with walkers, although it will be interesting to see how this combination mixes.

The Sustrans *Official Guide to the National Network* (£9.99) details 29 one-day rides throughout the network. Maps are available for all the routes (free for the shorter paths, £3.99 to £5.99 for map-guides for the national routes). For more information contact Sustrans (☎ 0117-929 0888, ⓔ info@ nationalcyclenetwork.org.uk), 35 King Street, Bristol BS1 4DZ. Its Web site is at www.sustrans.org.uk.

---

signposts from village to village. There is a whole network of lanes throughout lowland Britain, meandering through quiet countryside via picturesque villages. Lanes are clearly shown on OS maps.

In England and Wales, cycles can be ridden on any unmade road (track) that is identified as a public right of way on OS maps. The right to cycle does not, however, usually exist on a footpath. In Scotland the rules for off-road riding are different and it's best to enquire locally whether cyclists can use a particular track. The surface condition of tracks varies considerably: some are very poor and slow going.

WHERE TO CYCLE
South-Eastern England

The south-eastern corner of England has more traffic than other parts of the country, but with careful route planning you can find quiet roads and tracks and forget how close you are to the busy city of London. Northwest of London, the Chiltern Hills offer scenic cycling. The area to the south and east of London is characterised by the North and South Downs, two ridges of higher land running east–west, and the Weald in between – undulating, often wooded terrain.

The landscape here is beautiful in places and offers plenty of opportunities for good cycling. The south coast is heavily populated so the main roads here are busy and best avoided by cyclists.

You should also avoid cycling in London if possible; traffic is heavy and road surfaces can be poor. If you must cycle in the city, contact the London Cycling Campaign (☎ 020-7928 7220, fax 7928 2318) for maps and information. Check out its Web site is at www.lcc.org.uk.

South-Western England

The counties of Somerset, Dorset and Wiltshire have a varied landscape, with a combination of easy valley routes and steeper climbs in the hill ranges. Many parts of this region are popular with cyclists. The ancient woodland and open heath of the New Forest offer easy cycling.

Cornwall and Devon, with their steep country lanes, can be challenging. In the north, the coastline is rugged and sometimes inaccessible. Small roads drop steeply to pretty fishing villages nestling in the coves along the coast. The bleak, upland landscapes of Dartmoor, Bodmin Moor and Exmoor contrast starkly with the seaside towns on the south coast of Devon. The coast enjoys the best of the British climate, but suffers its share of tourist traffic during the summer months.

Midlands

The Cotswolds area of Gloucestershire and Oxfordshire is a particularly attractive place to cycle, but there's a shortage of budget accommodation here. The dense network of motorways and heavily trafficked roads serving the industrial centres farther north means that any extensive tour of the region would require careful planning in order to avoid these busy arteries. There are pockets of quiet roads with pretty villages and some forests, lakes and canals worth exploring – Charnwood Forest, for example, and parts of Hereford and Worcester, and Northamptonshire. The land is relatively low-lying and the cycling is gentler than in the north of England.

The Peak District (in Derbyshire) is one of the most popular cycling areas and marks the southern tip of the Pennines. There's challenging terrain, steep hills, rewarding scenery and a fairly good network of quieter roads, plus some excellent cycling/walking tracks along disused railway routes.

Eastern England

This is an excellent area for a first cycling tour and for those seeking an easy-going cycling holiday. East Anglia is generally low-lying and flat, with small areas of gently undulating country and woodland, particularly in the Suffolk area. Much of the area is characterised by arable farmland dissected by rivers, lakes (broads), marshes (such as the Fens) and many small, picturesque settlements.

Norfolk and Suffolk have a good network of quiet country roads. There are, however, two things to watch out for. First, breezes off the North Sea can sometimes be strong, especially in the Fens. Second, although the area is well served with bridges, roads sometimes run parallel to a river or canal and you may have to travel a little farther than expected to find a bridge. It pays to have a good map and to plan your route in advance.

Northern England

This region offers superb cycling, much of it strenuous – especially high up in the Pennines where you're exposed to the elements.

There are some exhilarating rides in the wild North York Moors. Take plenty of warm clothes and food for these exposed areas. To the west, the Yorkshire Dales offer tough cycling over the tops of the moors and gentler riding in the valleys. The scenery is superb, there's plenty of interest and some excellent pubs.

The Lake District of Cumbria is best explored by cyclists outside the months of July and August when its limited network of roads is crammed with tourist traffic. Use the smaller roads where possible and be prepared for some steep, long climbs in this magnificent region of mountains and lakes.

The area around Manchester and Liverpool, built-up and crisscrossed with motorways and other busy roads, is far less attractive to cyclists.

In the far north of England, Northumberland has quiet roads and plenty of historical interest. There are some very attractive sections of coastline in this area. Inland, the Cheviot Hills and Kielder Forest offer many rough tracks – great for the off-road rider to explore, but it's easy to get lost. Take good maps and a compass.

Scotland

Cyclists in search of the wild and remote will enjoy north-western Scotland. Its majestic Highlands and mystical islands offer quiet pedalling through breathtaking mountains. There are fewer roads in this part of Scotland and generally less traffic. Roads are well graded but sometimes very remote so be sure to carry plenty of food with you. Of the isles, Skye has a bridge to the mainland and suffers the worst of seasonal traffic; good ferries between all the islands offer easy escape routes.

For the less intrepid cyclist, the beautiful forests, lochs, glens and hills in the central and southern areas of Scotland are more easily accessible and have a more intimate charm. Cyclists can seek out the smaller roads and tracks to avoid the traffic.

Beware of the Scottish midge, prevalent during summer and early autumn. It's a true pest.

Wales

The varied landscape of the country and the warm welcome you get from the people make Wales an excellent place to cycle.

In the north, the rugged peaks of the Snowdonia National Park rise to over 900m, providing a dramatic backdrop to any cycling trip. During the summer the main roads can get busy with holiday traffic so it's best to visit this area early or late in the season.

Alternatively, head farther east towards the Clwydian and Berwyn hills, where less rugged but more peaceful cycling can be found.

The Cambrian mountains through mid-Wales offer quiet cycling both on- and off-road. In southern Wales, the scenic Black Mountains and Brecon Beacons National Park are popular cycling areas.

Much of Wales is hilly, and some low gears will be appreciated. For a less strenuous tour, the English/Welsh border is an area of gently undulating hills. The Isle of Anglesey in the far north-west and the Pembrokeshire coast in the far south-west are also popular with cyclists seeking to avoid the hills.

SOME SUGGESTED CYCLING ROUTES

The CTC provides useful touring sheets (available to members only; free) for every cycling region in Britain with accommodation suggestions. It can also help you plan a long-distance cycling trip.

Land's End to John o'Groats

The best-known long-distance route on the island runs from the extreme south-western tip, Land's End, to the north-eastern corner, John o'Groats. Along quiet roads, this is a distance of some 1000 miles – hopefully with the wind behind you.

The ride is a classic British favourite, but not only with cyclists. Along the route you'll meet such eccentric characters as bed-pushers and three-legged pub-crawlers,

all being sponsored per mile, raising money for charitable causes.

The route is challenging and goes via the scenic western side of England, crossing to the east once in Scotland. Many cyclists do the ride in two to three weeks, following one of the CTC's recommended routes. The main road route runs via Exeter, Cheddar, Shrewsbury, Carlisle, Dumfries, Fort William and Bonar Bridge. The 14-day youth hostel route follows quiet roads via Exeter, Wells, Leominster, Chester, Slaidburn, Windermere, Dumfries, Glasgow, Loch Lomond, Fort William and Loch Ness. The B&B route also follows quiet roads through North Devon, Cheddar, Ludlow, Slaidburn, Brampton, Peebles, Edinburgh, Crieff, Dunkeld and Inverness.

Farthest East to Farthest West

This is another coast-to-coast challenge through some of the best of Britain's varied scenery. The route starts at Lowestoft Ness in Suffolk and ends at the lighthouse at Ardnamurchan Point, on the west coast of Scotland. It's worth taking two to three weeks for this 700-mile route, although the CTC has details of a 10-day trip with accommodation in youth hostels. This is an exhilarating ride through some spectacular scenery.

Other Coast-to-Coast Routes

There are many other coast-to-coast variations undertaken by cyclists. You could go from Cumbria to Whitby, staying in youth hostels; from St David's Head (southern Wales) to Great Yarmouth (Norfolk); follow the 'Opposite Diagonal' – the opposite route to Land's End–John o'Groats – from Dover (Kent) to Durness and Cape Wrath (north-western Scotland); or ride across Scotland, from Aberdeen to the Isle of Mull, and back.

Wye Valley

The River Wye meanders some 130 miles from the Welsh Cambrian Mountains to the Severn estuary. It is usually possible to follow quiet roads near the river and a week to 10 days could easily be spent exploring the area.

The southern part of the Wye Valley forms the border between the south-eastern corner of Wales and Gloucestershire in England. It is densely wooded. Chepstow, situated on the northern reaches of the Severn estuary, is an ideal and accessible starting point. The main road (A466) follows an attractive course alongside the river, but this road can be busy during the tourist season. Climb the steep valley sides onto quieter country roads and enjoy the expansive views out over the Severn estuary. It's undulating terrain with some steep hills.

A detour east into the Forest of Dean provides opportunities for family cycle rides and day excursions, many of the forest tracks being open to cyclists. Back by the River Wye, Monmouth and Ross-on-Wye are pleasant towns worth visiting.

Yorkshire Dales

A week-long cycle tour through this magnificent national park is an exhilarating experience and Skipton is a convenient starting point. Cycle north to Linton (in Wharfedale) and Hubbersholme. Climb north-west over Fleatmoss to Hawes; the roads are steep but the scenery is breathtaking. Take quiet roads eastwards along Wensleydale to Askrigg and Aysgarth, then north to Reeth.

For the intrepid, a detour over Tan Hill and back to Keld may be attempted. Alternatively, follow Swaledale westwards, then head north-west to Kirkby Stephen. From here, cycle south to Sedbergh and then through beautiful Dentdale. Head south to Horton-in-Ribblesdale, Stainforth and then east, passing Malham Tarn to Malham and back to Skipton.

This route covers about 130 miles, but there are plenty of opportunities for scenic detours.

Hebridean Islands

The Hebridean Islands off the west coast of Scotland, linked by a comprehensive ferry system, provide superb cycling opportunities. You need to allow two to three weeks to give yourself time to enjoy the scenery in this enchanting region. Interesting circular routes are possible on most islands. This route comprises some 280 miles of cycling, and any tour will need to be planned around

the timings of the ferry crossings (some are summer only).

Ardrossan, near Ayr, is a good starting point since the ferry to the Isle of Arran leaves from here. On Arran, cycle north to Lochranza for another ferry to the Kintyre peninsula. You can cycle north to Lochgilphead and Oban to catch the ferry to Tobermory on the Isle of Mull.

Mull is worth exploring before taking the ferry across to Kilchoan. Cycle eastwards along the Ardnamurchan peninsula to Salen, then north to Mallaig. Ferries leave from here to Armadale on the Isle of Skye. You can then cycle north to Uig, or follow numerous other routes around the island.

From Uig, take a ferry to Tarbert (Isle of Harris) in the Outer Hebrides. These outer isles are wild and remote places with very quiet lanes to explore. Cycle south to Benbecula and on to South Uist where you can catch the ferry back to Oban.

Golf

Britain, and in particular Scotland, is the home of golf. There are, in fact, more golf courses per capita in Scotland than in any other country in the world. The game has been played here for centuries and there are currently over 1900 courses in Britain – both private and public – with 500 in Scotland alone.

All courses are tested for their level of difficulty and most are playable year round. Some of the private clubs only admit members, friends of members and golfers who have a handicap certificate or a letter of introduction from their club, but the majority welcome visitors.

Note that most clubs give members priority in booking tee-off times; it's always advisable to book in advance. It should be easier to book a tee-off time on a public course, but weekends on all courses are usually busy (like anywhere in the world). You should also check whether there's a dress code, and whether the course has golf clubs for hire (not all do) if you don't have your own.

INFORMATION

Tourist boards have lots of information. The Scottish Tourist Board has a wealth of golf information, see the Facts for the Visitor chapter for contact details.

Two useful national amateur golf organisations are:

Scottish Golf Union (☎ 01382-549500, fax 549510, ℮ sgu@scottishgolf.com) Scottish National Golf Centre, Drumoig, Leuchars, St Andrews, Fife, KY16 0DW

English Golf Union (☎ 01526-354500, fax 01526-354020, ℮ info@englishgolfunion.org) National Golf Centre, Woodhall Spa, Lincolnshire LN10 6PU

COSTS

A round of golf on a public course will cost as much as £20 to £25. Private courses are more expensive, with green fees ranging from £20 right on up to £70 or more for championship courses (but averaging more like £35 to £40). Many clubs offer a daily or weekly ticket. It's always worth asking about passes. In addition, many hotels have arrangements for reduced fees or guaranteed tee-off times.

A set of golf clubs costs £5 to £10 (per round) to hire.

Surfing & Swimming

Most overseas visitors do not think of Britain as a place to go for a beach holiday – and there are good reasons for this, not least the climate and the water temperature. You definitely have to be hardy or equipped with a wetsuit to do anything more than take a quick dip. On the other side of the equation, Britain has some truly magnificent coastline and some wonderful sandy beaches. And the British have been taking holidays by the seaside since the 18th century so there is a fascinating, sometimes bizarre, tradition to explore.

Visiting a British seaside resort should be high on the list of priorities for anyone wishing to gain an insight into British society.

The resorts vary from staid retirement enclaves such as Eastbourne to vibrant cultural centres such as Brighton and cheerful family resorts such as Hastings. And then there's Blackpool, which pretty much defies categorisation. One thing remains common to them all, however, and that is that the fun happens on shore and it's done fully clothed!

Summer water temperatures are roughly equivalent to winter temperatures in southern Australia (approximately 13°C). Winter temperatures are about 5 or 6°C colder, giving a temperature range not dissimilar to that in northern California. So getting in the water, at least in summer, is definitely feasible if you have a wetsuit. A 3mm fullsuit (steamer) plus boots will be sufficient in summer, while winter requires a 5mm suit plus boots, hood and gloves.

The best beaches, with the best chance of sun and surf and the genuine possibility of luring you into the water, are in Cornwall and Devon. Newquay, on the west Cornish coast (five or six hours by road from London), is the capital of the British surf scene. It has a plethora of surf shops and all the appropriate paraphernalia and trappings, from Kombis to bleached hair. The boards and wetsuits sold are good quality and competitively priced in international terms.

The south-western coast of Wales also has a number of good surfing spots. From east to west, try Porthcawl, Oxwich Bay, Rhossili, Manorbier, Freshwater West and Whitesands.

The most unusual aspect of surfing in Britain is the impact of the tides. The tidal range is huge, which means there are often a completely different set of breaks at low and high tides. As is usually the case, the waves tend to be biggest and best on an incoming tide. Sadly, the waves in spring, autumn and winter tend to be bigger and more consistent than in summer. The conditions in summer are pretty unreliable.

The entire western coast of Cornwall and Devon is exposed to the Atlantic and there is a string of surf spots from Land's End to Ilfracombe. The shallow continental shelf, however, means the waves rarely get over 1.5m. Spring and autumn are the best times for a surf. There are quite a few good breaks around Newquay including Fistral, England's premier surfing beach and home to the main surfing contests. There are similar conditions on the Gower Peninsula and the south-western corner of Wales from Tenby to Fishguard.

Northern Scotland has the island's biggest and best surf, and although the outside temperatures are considerably lower than in the south, the water temperatures are only marginally lower. The entire coast has surf but it's the north, particularly around Thurso, that has outstanding world-class possibilities. The west coast is mainly sheltered by islands, and although there are no doubt untapped possibilities on the islands, they are difficult and expensive to get to. Islay is occasionally surfed. The east coast is easily accessible, but the swells are unreliable and short-lived.

There's quite a large surfing community in Thurso, thanks to several famous breaks. There are two breaks, one in front of the harbour wall with lefts and rights, known as Reef, and one at the beach. Thurso East (Castle Reef) is the big one: a huge right that works up to 4½m.

There is an excellent surfing Web site, www.britsurf.org, that has comprehensive links and surf reports from all around Britain. There is accommodation information, lively chat rooms, classified ads and much more.

Far less salubrious is the Web site maintained by Surfers Against Sewage (☎ 0845 458 3001), www.sas.org.uk, which gives full details of this group's campaign to stop just what its name implies. Although the situation is improving, many British municipalities still discharge a fair amount of crap – literally – into their nearby sea.

Fishing

Angling, as a sport and pastime, was obviously well established in England by medieval times. A *Treatyse of Fysshnge With an Angle*, published in 1496, described fishing flies that are still in use today. The 17th century saw great improvements in equipment and also brought Izaak Walton's classic book on fishing, *The Compleat Angler*.

Fishing is divided into several distinct categories, topped by dry-fly fishing, considered by its proponents to be the highest form of the sport. An artificial lure, made to imitate a small insect, must be gently dropped on the surface in order to deceive and catch the fish. Fly fishing is used for that most cautious of game fish, the trout. Fish are described as coarse fish or game fish, the latter because they vigorously struggle against capture. Curiously, fishing is an activity with widely differing vocabularies between English and American usage.

RULES & REGULATIONS

Fishing is enormously popular in Britain, but also highly regulated. Many prime stretches of river are privately owned, and fishing there can be amazingly expensive. The Environment Agency (☎ 0870 166 2662) administers licences for rod fishing in England and Wales. A one year licence (valid from 1 April to 31 March) for non-migratory trout and coarse fishing costs £19/9.50 adult/youth and senior. The price for eight days costs £6.50 (no concessions) and one day is £2.50. Prices for salmon and sea trout are roughly triple. The Environment Agency has a useful Web site, www.environment-agency.gov.uk, with all sorts of fishy details.

Rod licences are available from every post office in England and Wales, bankside agents and Environment Agency Regional Offices. Tackle shops are good places to make fishing enquiries. Before fishing anywhere in England and Wales you must have the correct licence and the permission of the owner or tenants of the fishing rights.

There is a statutory close season (15 March to 15 June) when coarse fishing is banned on all rivers and streams – different rules apply on canals, lakes, ponds and reservoirs. The actual dates for close seasons vary according to the region and need to be checked in advance – the Environment Agency will be able to advise.

The fishing situation in Scotland, where there is a dense thicket of regulations on salmon fishing, is even more complicated. Fishing in Scotland can also be very costly.

It's a good idea to ask at local TICs for details as they are aware of the multitude of individual variations in the rules.

Horse Riding & Pony Trekking

Seeing the country from the saddle is highly recommended, even if you're not an experienced rider. There are riding schools catering to all levels of proficiency, many of them in national park areas.

Pony trekking is a popular holiday activity; a half-day should cost around £10 (hard hats are included). Many pony trekkers are novice riders so most rides are at walking speed with the occasional trot. If you're an experienced rider there are numerous riding schools with horses to hire – TICs have details.

For more information contact the British Horse Society (☎ 01926-707700, ⓔ enquiry@bhs.org.uk), Stoneleigh Deer Park, Kenilworth, Warks CV8 2XZ. It publishes *Where to Ride*, which lists places throughout the UK, and can also send you lists specific to a particular area (eg the Cotswolds). Its Web site is at www.bhs.org.uk.

Canal & Waterway Travel

Britain's surprisingly extensive network of canals and waterways spread rapidly across the country at the same time as the Industrial Revolution transformed the nation. As a method of transporting freight (passengers were always secondary) they were a short-lived wonder, trimmed back by railways and killed off by modern roads. By WWII, much of the waterway system was in terminal decline; the once-bustling canals had become stagnant channels of no economic significance. Today, however, the canals are booming once again as part of the leisure industry.

Exploring Britain by canal can be immensely rewarding. Narrow boats (narrow canal boats) can be rented from numerous operators around Britain and, for a family or a group, they can provide surprisingly economical transport and accommodation. They also allow you to explore a hidden side of Britain. While travelling the waterways, it's easy to forget that the Britain of motorways and ring roads even exists. Canals lead you to a Britain of idyllic villages, pretty countryside and convenient and colourful waterside pubs. More surprisingly, they can show you a very different side of some otherwise unremarkable cities. Birmingham from its canals is quite different from Birmingham from the ring road.

The canal system is also a wonderful example of the power and vision of the Industrial Revolution's great engineers. No obstacle stood in the way of these visionaries, who threw flights of locks up steep hillsides or flung amazing aqueducts across wide valleys. They built to last as well – the lock equipment which you 'work' as you travel along the canals is often well over a century old.

The canals are not restricted to narrowboat users only. The canal towpaths have become increasingly popular routes for walkers and cyclists, who can enjoy the same hidden perspective as people actually out on the waterways. There are over 3000 miles of navigable canals and rivers in Britain, so there is plenty to explore.

HISTORY
As the Industrial Revolution swept across Britain, a growing need developed for means of transporting goods, ranging from coal and iron to fine Wedgwood pottery. The first serious canals appeared in the 1760s, led by James Brindley's Bridgewater Canal, used for conveying coal to the burgeoning factories in Manchester. The development of canal locks, enabling the canal boats to go up and down hills, facilitated the spread of canals. Thomas Telford pioneered more modern canals, which took the shortest route from A to B, even when it involved multiple locks, tunnels, embankments and other complex engineering work. The Birmingham & Liverpool Junction was an example of this more advanced type of canal.

Some of the most interesting examples of canal engineering include the nearly two-mile-long Blisworth Tunnel near Stoke Bruerne (Northamptonshire). For particularly long inclines, locks were sometimes arranged in flights, where the top gate of one lock was also the bottom gate of the next. Ingenious attempts were made to design alternatives to canal locks. The inclined plane at Foxton, near Market Harborough (Leicestershire), dating from 1900, moved boats 23 vertical metres – the equivalent of a flight of 10 locks. The 1875 Anderton Lift, near Northwich (Cheshire), simply floated the boats into a tank that was then lifted 15m. When a valley or river intervened, some canal engineers carried their canals right across in aqueducts. The most famous example of this is the 307m-long Pontcysyllte Aqueduct in Wales.

For an interesting offshoot of the canals, visit the High Peak Trail in the Peak District. This early railway line has now been recycled to become a walking and bicycle track, but it was originally constructed by canal engineers still thinking in canal terms. Instead of engineering the long gentle inclines so they would be suitable for railway engines, they built the line with short steep rises up which the trains would have to be hauled, a dry-land equivalent of a canal's lock system.

Early canal boats were pulled by horses, walking on the towpaths alongside the canals, but by the mid-19th century steam power was starting to supersede horsepower. Later, diesel power replaced steam. Modern narrow boats for cruising still follow the traditional style, but come equipped with all mod cons, from refrigerators to televisions.

Even if you don't get out on the canals, it's fascinating to visit one of the canal museums around Britain. They can be found at Stoke Bruerne near Northampton, at Devizes in Wiltshire, at Ellesmere Port near Chester.

THE WATERWAYS

Britain's boating waterways consist of natural rivers and lakes plus artificial canals. In all there are over 3000 miles of navigable waterways; about half are canals and half of those are 'narrow' canals, where the locks are just over 2m wide.

A narrow boat trip can vary from lazy relaxation to surprisingly hard work. When you're chugging down a wide river with only the occasional lock to be worked, it's the easiest means of transport imaginable. On the other hand, on a steep section of canal where one lock is followed immediately by another, narrow boat travel can be a combination of aerobics (keys to be wound, paddles to be raised and lowered), weight lifting (heavy lock gates to be pushed open and closed) and jogging (the lock crew runs on ahead to prepare the lock before the boat gets there). Canal travel is great if you have children, and they're often exhausted by the end of the day!

Locks

A lock enables boats to go up or down a hill. It's a bathtub-shaped chamber with a single door at the top end and a double door at the bottom. *Sluices* in the doors let water flow into or out of the lock when the *paddles* over the sluices are opened. A winding handle or *key* is used to open or close the paddles and this is one of the essential pieces of equipment for narrow boat travel. The process of going through a lock is known as *working* the lock.

On narrow canals the locks are usually wide enough and long enough for just one boat at a time. On rivers or wider canals they may be large enough for two or more boats. In a wider lock it's essential to keep your boat roped to the side to prevent it yawing around as the water flows in or out of the lock. But don't tie it up tightly – the ropes will need to be shortened or lengthened as the water level changes.

Narrow Boats

There are over 200 firms renting narrow boats in Britain. Typically, a narrow boat will be 12 to 21m in length and no more than 2m or so wide. Narrow boats are usually surprisingly comfortable and well equipped with bunks and double beds, kitchen and dining areas, a fridge, cooker, flush toilet, shower and other mod cons. Usually they are rented out by the week although shorter periods are sometimes available.

Narrow boats usually come so well equipped for everyday living that food supplies are all you need to worry about and there are plenty of shopping opportunities along the waterways. Alternatively, careful planning can see you moored at a riverside pub or restaurant for most meals.

Boats can accommodate from two or three people up to a party of 10 or 12. Costs vary with the size of boat, the standard of equipment and the time of year. At the height of the summer season, a boat for four can vary from around £500 to £1000 per week. Larger boats work out cheaper per person; a boat for eight might cost £1000 per week. This means canal travel can cost not much over £100 per person for a week's transport and accommodation, a terrific travel bargain. Although there are independent boat operators scattered all over the country, there are also centralised booking agencies who handle bookings for many of the individual companies. One of the biggest is Hoseasons Holidays (☎ 01502-501010, fax 514298), Sunway House, Raglan Rd, Lowestoft, Suffolk NR32 3LW. Its Web site is at www.hoseasons.co.uk.

If you only want a brief introduction to the canal system, there are over 50 firms operating day trips from various centres. A number of operators offer hotel boat trips where you simply come along for the ride.

INFORMATION
More information on the canal system is available from the Inland Waterways Association (☎ 01923-711114), PO Box 114, Rickmansworth, Herts WD3 1ZY. It publishes *The Inland Waterways Guide* (£3.25), a general guide to holiday hire with route descriptions. Its Web site is at www.waterways.org.uk.

Approximately two-thirds of the waterways in Britain are operated by the British Waterways Board (☎ 01923-226422), Willow Grange, Church Rd, Watford, Hertfordshire WD17 4QA. It publishes *The Waterways Code for Boaters*, a free, handy

booklet packed with useful information and advice. Also available is a complete list of boat-hire and hotel-boat companies.

TRAVELLING THE WATERWAYS
No particular expertise or training is needed, nor is a licence required to operate a narrow boat. You're normally given a quick once-over of the boat and an explanation of how things work, a list of rules and regulations of the waterways and a brief foray out onto the river or canal and then you're on your way. Proceed with caution at first, although you'll soon find yourself working the locks like a veteran.

Skiing

No one comes to Britain to ski. Indeed, some may be surprised to learn that there are ski resorts here. There are actually five main ski centres, all in Scotland, but the slopes are far less extensive and the weather considerably less reliable than anything you'll find in the Alps. On a sunny day, however, and with good snow, it can be very pleasant.

Scotland offers both alpine (downhill) and nordic (cross-country) skiing, as well as other snow-related sports. The high season is January to April, although it is sometimes possible to ski from as early as November to as late as May. Package holidays are available, but it's very easy to make your own arrangements, with all kinds of accommodation on offer in and around the ski centres.

INFORMATION
Contact the Scottish Tourist Board (see the Facts for the Visitor chapter) for its detailed *Ski Scotland* brochure and accommodation list. Alternatively, you can phone the skiing information centre for each area. These are: Nevis Range (☎ 01397-705825); Glencoe (☎ 01855-851226); Glenshee (☎ 01399-741320); The Lecht (☎ 01975-651440); and Cairngorm (☎ 01479-861261). There's an answering machine service for calls outside business hours.

The Ski Hotline weather report service can be useful. Phone ☎ 0891 654 followed by 654 for all centres; 660 for Nevis Range; 658 for Glencoe; 656 for Glenshee; 657 for The Lecht; and 655 for Cairngorm. For nordic skiing the number is ☎ 0891 654659. Alternatively, check the Web site at www.ski.scotland.net, which is updated daily during the ski season.

COSTS

It's easy to hire ski equipment and clothes when you arrive at the resort, but you should book lessons, if you want them, in advance. The prices vary in each centre, but on average expect to pay £13 per day for skis, sticks and boot hire, and £10 per day for ski clothes.

Lift passes cost £15 to £20 per day, or £65 to £70 for a five-day pass (photo required). In a group, ski lessons cost £15 to £24 for a day, and £60 to £75 for five days; private lessons cost around £20 per hour.

Packages including ski hire, tuition and lift-pass cost from £100 for three days (midweek). Two, four or five day, and weekend packages are also available.

Charges are lower for under-18s at Nevis Range and Cairngorm, and for under-16s at Glencoe, Glenshee and The Lecht.

RESORTS

The biggest ski centres are **Glenshee** (920m) and **Cairngorm** (1097m). Glenshee offers the largest network of lifts and selection of runs in Scotland. It also has snow machines for periods when the real thing is absent. At Cairngorm there are almost 30

The Great Little Trains of Wales

Wales' narrow-gauge steam railways are survivors from its industrial heyday when mine and quarry owners needed to move their produce more quickly than horses could manage, in terrain that defied normal standard-gauge trains. In the 20th century, as these lines gradually lost their *raison d'être*, train enthusiasts took many over and now run steam-hauled services on them – particularly in summer. Most of these lines run through glorious scenery, primarily in northern and central Wales, so they're worth checking out even if you're not a rail buff.

Schedules vary depending on the time of year. The Tourist Information Centres (TICs) usually have timetables for the routes nearest to them. Otherwise, contact any of these numbers for details: Bala Lake Railway (☎ 01678-540666); Brecon Mountain Railway (☎ 01685-722988); Ffestiniog Railway (☎ 01766-512340), Web site: www.festrail.co.uk; Llanberis Lake Railway (☎ 01286-870549); Vale of Rheidol Railway (☎ 01970-625819); Talyllyn Railway (☎ 01654-710472); Welsh Highland Railway (☎ 01766-513402); and Welshpool & Llanfair Railway (☎ 01938-810441).

JANE SMITH

Wales' steam trains were originally used to carry slate from the mines.

Wanderer tickets are available for all eight railways, April to October. A pass giving four days' travel in any eight day period costs £32/16 for adults/children; for eight days travel in any 15 days it's £42/21. Passes are sold at the main stations of the participatory railways, or write to GLTW, The Railway Station, Llanfair Caereinion, Powys SY21 0SF. Holders of some mainline rail passes may be eligible for discounts. Some of the railways operate Santa Specials over the Christmas period.

runs spread over an extensive area. Aviemore is the main town and there's a ski bus service from here and from the surrounding villages to the slopes.

Glencoe (1108m) is the oldest of the existing resorts and opens all week. The **Nevis Range** (1221m) offers the highest ski runs, the only gondola in Scotland to take you to the foot of the main skiing area, and a dry (plastic) ski slope. **The Lecht** (792m) is the most remote centre, but it's good for beginners and families, as well as for nordic skiers.

Access to the centres is probably easiest by car and there are plenty of car parks. Slopes are graded in the usual way, from green (easy) through blue and red to black (very difficult) and each centre has a ski patrol. You should ensure that your travel insurance covers you for winter sports.

All the ski resorts have facilities for snowboarding. The Lecht is best for beginners and the other four resorts are best for intermediates. They're all OK for advanced snowboarders.

Steam Railways

The invention of the steam engine and the subsequent rapid spread of the railway to almost every corner of Britain transformed life in the 19th century. The 1963 Beeching Report led to the closure of many rural lines and stations, and British Rail stopped using steam trains in 1968. For many people these two events brought the first century of rail travel to a sad end. It wasn't long, however, before rail enthusiasts reopened some of the lines and stations and restored many of the steam locomotives and rolling stock used in the proverbial 'golden age of rail'.

There are now nearly 500 private railways in Britain, many of them narrow gauge, using steam or diesel locomotives from all over the world. The main lines are detailed in the appropriate sections of this book. A useful guide to private steam railways is *Railways Restored* (£12.99) by Ian Allan Publishing (for orders ☎ 0711-027099). You can also order a copy through their Web site at www.ianallan.com.

Getting There & Away

London is a transport hub for the world and competition between airlines means that you should be able to find tickets at good prices from just about anywhere. The emergence of several discount carriers has increased competition on flights to/from Europe and Ireland – routes that were once characterised by their ridiculously high fares.

Bus travel to/from Europe and Ireland is usually the cheapest option, but it can be bone-crunching and exhausting, and the savings are not huge compared to the cheap airfares you should be able to find.

The Channel Tunnel has provided stiff competition for the multitude of ferries to/from Europe and fare wars for passengers with and without their own transport are frequent. The Eurostar train between London and Paris and Brussels also has numerous special offers throughout the year and is very convenient.

Ferries have lowered their prices and speeded up their services between Britain and Europe. Prices and times are both improved on the Ireland routes as well.

From the rest of the world to Scotland, you will usually have to fly through one of the London airports. The cost of the connecting flight adds little to the overall cost of the trip when bought in conjunction with the main ticket. However, there are times when to save the most money you may have to transfer from one London airport to another that has a low-cost carrier to Scotland, or you may have to shift to a bus or train. It's good to weigh up these inconveniences against the savings.

AIR
Airports & Airlines
London's Heathrow followed by Gatwick are the two main airports for transcontinental flights. A few of these flights – from North America and Asia – also go to Manchester. Glasgow has a few flights to/from North America.

Flights from Europe are served not only

> ## Warning
>
> The information in this chapter is particularly vulnerable to change. Prices for international travel are volatile, routes are introduced and cancelled, schedules change, special deals come and go, and rules and visa requirements are amended. Airlines and governments seem to take a perverse pleasure in making price structures and regulations as complicated as possible. You should check directly with the airline or a travel agent to make sure you understand how a fare (and ticket you may buy) works. In addition, the travel industry is highly competitive and there are many lurks and perks.
>
> The upshot of this is that you should get opinions, quotes and advice from as many airlines and travel agencies as possible before you part with your hard-earned cash. The details given in this chapter should be regarded as pointers and are not a substitute for your own careful, up-to-date research.

by London's five airports, but also scores of other airports throughout Britain. Manchester, Birmingham, Edinburgh and Glasgow all have numerous continental European and Irish flights, and many other smaller airports have services as well. Cardiff's international airport is mainly used for holiday charter flights, although there are some scheduled flights to Scotland, Ireland and Paris.

Most of the world's major airlines serve London at least. The following are telephone numbers for reservations; they can be used throughout Britain. Note that most are not free.

Aer Lingus	☎ 0845 973 7747
Aeroflot	☎ 020-7355 2233
Air Canada	☎ 0870 524 7226
Air France	☎ 0845 084 5111
Air New Zealand	☎ 020-8741 2299
Alitalia	☎ 0870 544 8259
American Airlines	☎ 0345 789789

British Airways	☎ 0345 222111
British Midland	☎ 0870 607 0555
Cathay Pacific Airways	☎ 0845 758 1581
Continental Airlines	☎ 01293-776464
Delta Air Lines	☎ 0800 414767
El Al Israel Airlines	☎ 020-7957 4100
Emirates Airlines	☎ 0870 243 2222
Iberia	☎ 0870 606 2032
KLM-Royal Dutch Airlines	☎ 0870 507 4074
Lufthansa Airlines	☎ 0845 773 7747
Olympic Airways	☎ 0870 606 0460
Qantas Airways	☎ 0845 774 7767
Sabena	☎ 0845 601 0933
Scandinavian Airlines (SAS)	☎ 0845 6072 7727
Singapore Airlines	☎ 0870 608 8886
South African Airways	☎ 0870 747 1111
TAP Air Portugal	☎ 0845 601 0932
Thai Airways International	☎ 0870 606 0911
Turkish Airlines	☎ 020-7766 9300
United Airlines	☎ 0845 844 4777
Virgin Atlantic	☎ 01293-616161

In addition, there are now several discount, no-frills airlines. They are not usually on computerised reservations systems, such as those used by travel agencies or those on Web sites such as www.travelocity.com and www.expedia.com. To check their fares you'll have to visit their Web sites (which often have extra discounts for tickets bought on the Internet) or call their reservations numbers.

Buzz (☎ 0870 240 7070)
An off-shoot of KLM, Buzz flies from London Stansted to several European destinations.
Web site: www.buzzaway.com

easyJet (☎ 0870 600 0000)
A feisty carrier with bright orange jets, easyJet flies to several European destinations from London Luton as well as Liverpool.
Web site: www.easyjet.com

Go (☎ 0845 605 4321)
An off-shoot of British Airways, Go flies from London Stansted to a variety of European destinations.
Web site: www.go-fly.com

Ryanair (☎ 0870 156 9569)
An Irish-based airline, Ryanair flies from numerous British airports to various airports in Ireland, and from London Stansted to several European destinations. However, note that some

of the European airports it flies to are secondary fields far from the cities Ryanair claims to serve. Always check where they really fly to and what transportation links there are.
Web site: www.ryanair.com

Virgin Express (☎ 020-7744 0004)
Flying to a growing number of European cities, Virgin Express offers flights from all London Stansted, Gatwick and Heathrow airports.
Web site: www.virgin-express.com

Buying Tickets

World aviation has never been so competitive, making air travel better value than ever. But you have to research the options carefully to make sure you get the best deal. The Internet is an increasingly useful resource for checking air fares.

Full-time students and those aged under 26 (under 30 in some countries) have access to better deals than other travellers. You have to show a document proving your date of birth or a valid International Student Identity Card (ISIC) when buying your ticket and boarding the plane.

Generally, there is nothing to be gained by buying a ticket direct from the airline. Discounted tickets are released to selected travel agencies and specialist discount agencies, and these are usually the cheapest deals going.

One exception to this rule is the expanding number of 'no-frills' carriers, which mostly only sell direct to travellers. Unlike the 'full-service' airlines, no-frills carriers often make one-way tickets available at around half the return fare, meaning that it is easy to put together an open-jaw ticket when you fly to one place but leave from another.

The other exception is booking on the Internet. Many airlines, full-service and no-frills, offer some excellent fares to Web surfers. They may sell seats by auction or simply cut prices to reflect the reduced cost of electronic selling.

Many travel agencies around the world have Web sites, which can make the Internet a quick and easy way to compare prices. There is also an increasing number of online agencies such as www.travelocity.co.uk and www.deckchair.com that operate only

Air Travel Glossary

Alliances Many of the world's leading airlines are now intimately involved with each other, sharing everything from reservations systems and check-in to aircraft and frequent flyer schemes. Opponents say that alliances restrict competition. Whatever the arguments, there is no doubt that big alliances are the way of the future.

Cancelling or Changing Tickets If you have to cancel or change a ticket, you need to contact the original travel agency who sold you the ticket. Airlines only issue refunds to the purchaser of a ticket – usually the travel agency who bought the ticket on your behalf. There are often heavy penalties involved; insurance can sometimes be taken out against these penalties.

Courier Fares Businesses often need to send urgent documents or freight securely and quickly. Courier companies hire people to accompany the package through customs and, in return, offer a discount ticket which is sometimes a bargain. However, you may have to surrender all your baggage allowance and take only carry-on luggage.

Fares Airlines traditionally offer 1st class (coded F), business class (coded J) and economy class (coded Y) tickets. These days there are so many promotional and discounted fares available that few passengers pay full fare.

Lost Tickets If you lose your airline ticket an airline will usually treat it like a travellers cheque and, after enquiries, issue you with another one. Legally, however, an airline is entitled to treat it like cash and if you lose it then it's gone forever. Take good care of your tickets.

Onward Tickets An entry requirement for many countries is that you have a ticket out of the country. If you're unsure of your next move, the easiest solution is to buy the cheapest onward ticket to a neighbouring country or a ticket from a reliable airline which can later be refunded if you do not use it.

Open-Jaw Tickets These are return tickets where you fly out to one place but return from another. If available, this can save you backtracking to your arrival point.

Overbooking Since every flight has some passengers who fail to show up, airlines often book more passengers than they have seats. Usually excess passengers make up for the no-shows, but occasionally somebody gets 'bumped' onto the next available flight. Guess who it is most likely to be? The passengers who check in late. If you do get 'bumped' you are normally offered some form of compensation.

Reconfirmation Some airlines require you to reconfirm your flight at least 72 hours prior to departure. Check your travel documents to see if this is the case.

Restrictions Discounted tickets often have various restrictions on them – such as needing to be paid for in advance and incurring a penalty to be altered or cancelled. Others are restrictions on the minimum and maximum period you must be away.

Round-the-World Tickets RTW tickets give you a limited period (usually a year) in which to circumnavigate the globe. You can go anywhere the carrying airlines go, as long as you don't backtrack. The number of stopovers or total number of separate flights is decided before you set off and they usually cost a bit more than a basic return flight.

Ticketless Travel Airlines are gradually waking up to the realisation that paper tickets are unnecessary encumbrances. On simple one-way or return trips, reservations details can be held on computer, and the passenger merely shows ID to claim his or her seat.

Transferred Tickets Airline tickets cannot be transferred from one person to another. Travellers sometimes try to sell the return half of their ticket, but officials can ask you to prove that you are the person named on the ticket. On an international flight tickets are always compared with passports.

on the Internet. These are examples of general online agencies. Only include agents that are relevant to your specific destination. Online ticket sales work well if you are doing a simple one-way or return trip on specified dates. However, online superfast fare generators are no substitute for a travel agency who knows all about special deals, has strategies for avoiding layovers and can offer advice on everything from which airline has the best vegetarian food to the best travel insurance to bundle with your ticket.

You may find the cheapest flights are advertised by obscure agencies. Most such firms are honest and solvent, but there are some rogue fly-by-night outfits around. Paying by credit card generally offers protection, as most card issuers provide refunds if you can prove you didn't get what you paid for. Similar protection can be obtained by buying a ticket from a bonded agency, such as one covered by the Air Travel Organiser's Licence (ATOL) scheme in the UK (more details available at www .atol.org.uk). Agents who only accept cash should hand over the tickets straight away and not tell you to 'come back tomorrow'. After you've made a booking or paid your deposit, call the airline and confirm that the booking was made. It's generally not advisable to send money (even cheques) through the post unless the agent is very well established – some travellers have reported being ripped off by fly-by-night mail-order ticket agencies.

If you purchase a ticket and later want to make changes to your route or get a refund, you need to contact the original travel agency. Airlines only issue refunds to the purchaser of a ticket – usually the travel agent who bought the ticket on your behalf. Many travellers change their routes halfway through their trips, so think carefully before you buy a ticket which is not easily refunded.

Courier Flights These are occasionally advertised in the newspapers, or you could contact air-freight companies listed in the phone book. You may even have to go to the air-freight company to get an answer – the companies aren't always keen to give out information over the phone. Travel Unlimited (PO Box 1058, Allston, MA 02134, USA) is a monthly travel newsletter based in the USA that publishes many courier flight deals from destinations worldwide. A 12-month subscription to the newsletter costs US$25, or US$35 for readers outside the USA. Another possibility (at least for US residents) is to join the International Association of Air Travel Couriers (IAATC). The membership fee of $45 gets members a bi-monthly update of air-courier offerings, access to a fax-on-demand service with daily updates of last minute specials and the bi-monthly newsletter the *Shoestring Traveler*. For more information, contact IAATC (☎ 561-582 8320) or visit its Web site, www.courier.org. However, be aware that joining this organisation does not guarantee that you'll get a courier flight.

In the UK, courier flights can often be obtained from British Airways (☎ 0870 606 1133) and ACP Express (☎ 020-8897 5133).

Travellers with Specific Needs

If they're warned early enough, airlines can often make special arrangements for travellers, such as wheelchair assistance at airports or vegetarian meals on the flight. Children under two years travel for 10% of the standard fare (or free on some airlines) as long as they don't occupy a seat. They don't receive a baggage allowance. 'Skycots', baby food and nappies should be provided by the airline if requested in advance. Children aged between two and 12 can usually occupy a seat for half to two-thirds of the full fare, and do get a baggage allowance.

The disability-friendly Web site, www .everybody.co.uk, has an airline directory that provides information on the facilities offered by various airlines.

Departure Tax

All domestic flights and those to destinations within the EU from Britain carry a £10 departure tax. For flights to other cities abroad you pay £20. This is usually built into the price of your ticket.

Ireland

Competition on the many air routes between Britain and Ireland means that you can usually get a discount ticket for as little as £50 on any of the airlines serving the routes. In addition to the main Dublin to London route, there are a number of regional services linking smaller airports in both countries.

Continental Europe

There is not much variation in air fare prices for departures from the main European cities. All the major airlines usually offer some sort of deal, and travel agencies generally have a number of deals on offer, so shop around.

Expect to pay the equivalent of about £50 to £200 on major airlines for discounted return tickets to Britain. The low-cost carriers charge about £50 to £150 to the destinations they fly to, which coincidentally are usually the most competitive markets.

Across Europe many travel agencies have ties with STA Travel, where cheap tickets can be purchased and STA-issued tickets can be altered (usually for a US$25 fee). Outlets in major cities include: Voyages Wasteels in Paris (☎ 0 803 88 70 04 – this number can only be dialled from within France – fax 01 43 25 46 25), 11 rue Dupuytren, 756006 Paris; STA Travel in Berlin (☎ 030-311 0950, fax 313 0948), Goethestrasse 73, 10625 Berlin; Passaggi in Rome (☎ 06-474 0923, fax 482 7436), Stazione Termini FS, Galleria Di Tesla, Rome; and ISYTS in Athens (☎ 01-322 1267, fax 323 3767), 11 Nikis St, Upper Floor, Syntagma Square, Athens.

France has a network of student travel agencies that can supply discount tickets to travellers of all ages. OTU Voyages (☎ 01 44 41 38 50) has a central Paris office at 39 Ave Georges Bernanos (5e) and another 42 offices around the country. Their Web site is at www .otu.fr. Acceuil des Jeunes en France (☎ 01 42 77 87 80), 119 rue Saint Martin (4e), is another popular discount travel agency.

General travel agencies in Paris that offer some of the best services and deals include Nouvelles Frontières (☎ 0 803 33 33 33), 5 Ave de l'Opéra (1er), and Voyageurs du Monde (☎ 01 42 86 16 00) at 55 rue Sainte Anne (2e). Nouvelles Frontières' Web address is www.nouvelles-frontieres.com.

Belgium, Switzerland, the Netherlands and Greece also have good agencies that sell discount air tickets. In Belgium, Acotra Student Travel Agency (☎ 02-512 86 07), rue de la Madeline, Brussels, and WATS Reizen (☎ 03-226 16 26), de Keyserlei 44, Antwerp, are both well-known agencies. In Switzerland, SSR Voyages (☎ 01-297 11 11) specialises in student, youth and budget fares. There is a branch in Zurich at Leonhardstrasse 10 and others in most major Swiss cities. Their Web site is at www.ssr.ch.

NBBS Reizen (☎ 020-624 09 89), Rokin 66, Amsterdam, is the official student travel agency in the Netherlands. There are several other agencies around the city. Another recommended agent in Amsterdam is Malibu Travel (☎ 020-626 32 30), Prinsengracht 230.

In Athens, check the many travel agencies in the backstreets between Syntagma and Omonia Squares. For student and non-concessionary fares, try Magic Bus (☎ 01-323 7471, fax 322 0219).

The USA

Since the late 1990s there has been a permanent price war between the airlines flying between the USA and London, the busiest transcontinental route in the world.

Fares on all major airlines flying from the East Coast to London have fallen as low as US$300 in winter, US$400 in spring and autumn, and US$600 in summer. From the West Coast fares are about US$100 higher. These are the same fares that were being charged about 10 years ago.

Given how low the advertised fares are, you may not need a travel agency and instead can contact the airlines directly or check their Web sites.

However, should you need an agency, Council Travel (☎ 800 226 8624), America's largest student travel organisation, has around 60 offices in the USA; its head office is 205 E 42 St, New York, NY 10017. Call for details of your local office or visit its Web site at www.ciee.org. STA Travel (☎ 800 777 0112) has offices in Boston,

Chicago, Miami, New York, Philadelphia, San Francisco and other major cities. Call the toll-free 800 number for office locations or visit its Web site at www.statravel.com.

Canada

Canada has enjoyed the same kind of discount fares to Britain as the USA (see earlier). However, now that Canadian Airways International has been gobbled up by Air Canada, it will be interesting to see if fares increase.

Canadian discount air ticket sellers are also known as consolidators, and their air fares tend to be about 10% higher than those sold in the USA. The *Globe & Mail,* the *Toronto Star,* the *Montreal Gazette* and the *Vancouver Sun* carry travel agencies' advertisements and are a good place to look for cheap fares.

Travel CUTS (☎ 800 667 2887) is Canada's national student travel agency and has offices in all major cities. Its Web site is at www.travelcuts.com.

Australia

There are a lot of competing airlines and a wide variety of air fares for flights between Europe and Australia. Round-the-world (RTW) tickets are often real bargains and, since Australia is pretty much on the other side of the world from Britain, it can sometimes work out cheaper to keep going on a RTW ticket than do a U-turn on a return ticket.

Expect to pay anywhere from A$1800 in the low season to A$3000 in the high season for return tickets from Australia to Britain.

Flights from Australia to Britain generally go via South-East Asian capitals, involving stopovers at Kuala Lumpur, Bangkok, Hong Kong or Singapore. If a long stopover between connections is necessary, transit accommodation is sometimes included in the price of the ticket. If it's at your own expense, it may be worth considering a more expensive ticket. The very cheapest flights may be on carriers, such as Emirates Airlines, which entail two stops on the way to/from Britain.

Quite a few travel offices specialise in discount air tickets. Some travel agencies, particularly smaller ones, advertise cheap air fares in the travel sections of weekend newspapers, such as the *Age* in Melbourne and the *Sydney Morning Herald.*

Two well-known agencies for cheap fares are STA Travel and Flight Centre. STA Travel (☎ 03-9349 2411) has its main office at 224 Faraday St, Carlton, VIC 3053, and offices in all major cities and on many university campuses. Call ☎ 131 776 Australia-wide for the location of your nearest branch or visit its Web site at www.statravel .com.au. Flight Centre (☎ 131 600 Australia-wide) has a central office at 82 Elizabeth St, Sydney, and dozens of offices throughout Australia. Its Web site is at www.flightcentre.com.au.

New Zealand

RTW fares for travel to or from New Zealand are usually the best value, often cheaper than a return ticket. Depending on which airline you choose, you may fly across Asia, with possible stopovers in India, Bangkok or Singapore, or across the USA, with possible stopovers in Los Angeles, Honolulu or one of the Pacific Islands.

Prices are similar to those from Australia, but the trip is even longer; about two 12-hour flights minimum.

The *New Zealand Herald* has a travel section in which travel agencies advertise fares. Flight Centre (☎ 09-309 6171) has a large central office in Auckland at National Bank Towers (on the corner of Queen St and Darby St) and many branches throughout the country. STA Travel (☎ 09-309 0458) has its main office at 10 High St, Auckland, and has other offices in Auckland and in Hamilton, Palmerston North, Wellington, Christchurch and Dunedin. For more information, check out its Web site at www.sta.travel.com.au.

Asia

Although most Asian countries now offer fairly competitive air-fare deals, Bangkok, Singapore and Hong Kong are still the best places to shop around for discount tickets. The travel market in Hong Kong can be unpredictable, but some excellent bargains are available if you are lucky.

Khao San Rd in Bangkok is the budget travellers' headquarters. Bangkok has a number of excellent travel agencies, but there are also some suspect ones; ask the advice of other travellers before handing over your cash. STA Travel (☎ 02-236 0262), 33 Surawong Rd, is a good and reliable place to start.

In Singapore, STA Travel (☎ 737 7188) in the Orchard Parade Hotel, 1 Tanglin Rd, offers competitive discount fares to Britain. Singapore, like Bangkok, has hundreds of travel agencies, so you can compare prices on flights before you buy. Chinatown Point shopping centre, on New Bridge Rd, has a good selection of travel agencies.

Hong Kong has a number of excellent, reliable travel agencies and some not-so-reliable ones. A good way to check on a travel agency is to look it up in the phone book: fly-by-night operators don't usually stay around long enough to get listed. Many travellers use the Hong Kong Student Travel Bureau (☎ 2730 3269), 8th floor, Star House, Tsimshatsui. You could also try Phoenix Services (☎ 2722 7378), 7th floor, Milton Mansion, 96 Nathan Rd, Tsimshatsui.

India Although it is possible to get cheap tickets in Mumbai (formerly Bombay) and Calcutta, Delhi is the real wheeling and dealing centre.

In Delhi there are a number of discount travel agencies around Connaught Place, but as always, be careful before handing over your cash. If you use one of these discount agents, double-check with the airline to make sure that the booking has been made. STIC Travels (☎ 011-332 5559), an agent for STA Travel, has an office in Delhi in Room 6 at the Hotel Imperial in Janpath.

In Mumbai, STIC Travels (☎ 022-218 1431) is located at 6 Maker Arcade, Cuffe Parade. Another travel agency in Mumbai that comes highly recommended is Transway International (☎ 022-262 6066), 2nd floor, Pantaky House, 8 Maruti Cross Lane, Fort. Most of the international airline offices in Mumbai are in or around Nariman Point.

Africa

Nairobi and Johannesburg are probably the best places in East and South Africa to buy tickets. Some major airlines have offices in Nairobi, which is a good place to determine the standard fare before you make the rounds of the travel agencies. Getting several quotes is a good idea as prices are always changing. Flight Centres (☎ 02-210024), in Lakhamshi House, Biashara St, has been in business for many years.

In Johannesburg, the South African Student's Travel Services (☎ 011-716 3045) has an office at the University of the Witwatersrand. STA Travel (☎ 011-447 5551) has an office in Johannesburg, on Tyrwhitt Ave in Rosebank.

The main international airports in West Africa are Abidjan, Accra, Bamako, Dakar and Lagos. There are also some regular charter flights from some European countries to Banjul (Gambia). It is usually better to buy tickets in West Africa through a travel agency rather than from the airline. Travel agencies' fares are generally the same as those offered by the airlines, but agents may be more helpful if anything goes wrong.

In Abidjan, Saga Voyages (☎ 32 98 70), is located opposite Air Afrique in Le Plateau. Haury Tours (☎ 22 16 54, fax 22 17 68, ℮ haury@africaonline.co.ci), 2nd floor, Chardy Bldg in Le Plateau, is an affiliate of the French travel group Nouvelles Frontières.

In Accra, try Expert Travel & Tours (☎ 021-775498), on Ring Rd East near the US embassy.

There are several agencies in Bamako dealing in international and regional flights. Two of the best are ATS Voyages (☎ 22 44 35), on Ave Kassa Keita, and TAM (☎ 23 92 00, ℮ tvoyage@sotelma.net), on Square Lumumba, which is open until midnight Monday to Saturday and on Sunday morning.

Agencies in Dakar include Senegal Tours (☎ 823 31 81), 5 Place de l'Indépendance, and SDV Voyages (☎ 839 00 81), 51 Ave Albert Sarraut.

In Lagos there are many travel agencies in the Race Course Rd complex on the southern side of Tafawa Balewa Square on Lagos Island. Most of the airline offices are in this area too. Try L'Aristocrate Travels & Tours (☎ 01-266 7322), on the corner of Davies St and Broad St, or Mandilas Travel (☎ 01-266 3339), on Broad St.

South America

Venezuela has the cheapest air links with Britain and Europe, and the most convenient northern gateway to Europe. TAP Air Portugal and Iberia often have the cheapest tickets to Europe.

In Caracas, IVI Tours (☎ 02-993 60 82), Residencia La Hacienda, Piso Bajo, Local 1-4-T, Final Avenida Principal de las Mercedes, is the agent for STA Travel in Venezuela and often has a range of good deals.

Rio de Janeiro is Brazil's most popular international gateway and there is no shortage of travel agencies. The Student Travel Bureau (☎ 021-259 0023), an affiliate of STA Travel, is at Rua Visconde de Piraja 550, Ipanema.

Buenos Aires Aeropuerto Internacional Ministro Pistarini has excellent air connections to the UK. ASATEJ (☎ 011-4315 14570), Argentina's nonprofit student travel agency and the agent for STA Travel, is located on the 3rd floor, Oficina 319-B, at Florida 835, Buenos Aires.

LAND
Bus

Even without using the Channel Tunnel, you can still get from/to Europe by bus with a short ferry ride as part of the deal. Eurolines (☎ 0870 514 3219), 52 Grosvenor Gardens, London SW1 (⊖ Victoria), an association of companies that together form Europe's largest international bus network, connects an enormous number of European destinations – from Ireland and Morocco to Finland and Greece. Eurolines' Web site at www.eurolines.com has links to the sites of all the national operators. Buses are slower and less comfortable than trains, but they are cheaper, especially if you qualify for the 10 to 20% discount available to people aged 13 to 25 or over 60, or take advantage of the discount fares on offer from time to time.

You can book Eurolines tickets through National Express offices, including Victoria Coach Station, and at many travel agencies.

Or visit the National Express Web site at www.gobycoach.com. Eurolines offices and affiliated companies can be found across Europe, including Amsterdam (☎ 020-560 87 87), Barcelona (☎ 93 490 4000), Berlin (☎ 030-86 0960), Brussels (☎ 02-203 0707) and Madrid (☎ 91 528 1105).

The following single/return adult fares and journey times are representative: Amsterdam £32/45 (nine hours); Barcelona £79/111 (22–24 hours); Berlin £39/65 (22½ hours); Brussels £32/45 (seven hours); Dublin £24/44 (11 hours).

At peak times in summer (when you should add between 5 and 10% to the above fares), you should make reservations a few days in advance. Also note that on trips from places such as Barcelona, you'll pay the same fare and save about 20 hours and lots of sanity by getting a discount fare with an airline such as easyJet.

Train

Eurostar The Channel Tunnel has opened up a land link between Britain and France. The Eurostar passenger train service (☎ 0870 518 6186 in the UK, or 0 836 35 35 39 in France) travels between London and Paris and London and Brussels with stops in Lille and Calais in France and Ashford in England.

The trains run around 16 times daily between Paris' Gare du Nord and London. There are around 11 daily between Brussels and London. In London, trains arrive and depart from Waterloo International Terminal. Immigration formalities are usually completed on the train, but British customs is at Waterloo.

The Paris–London journey takes three hours (which will drop to just 2½ hours when the high-speed track through Kent is *finally* completed). The journey from Brussels to London takes two hours and 40 minutes; this will be reduced to two hours and 10 minutes.

You can buy tickets from travel agencies, major train stations or by phoning Eurostar directly. The Eurostar Web site, at www.eurostar.com, often has special deals. The normal single/return fare from Paris and Brussels is an eye-opening £250. But the fare system is the same as the airlines and there are numerous special and discount fares. It's not uncommon for there to be a £79 return fare. There are also discount fares for children and those aged 12 to 25 or over 60.

Bicycles are only allowed on the Eurostar if they're collapsible; otherwise you can use the Esprit Parcel Service (☎ 01 55 31 58 31), which will take your bike for around 200FF.

There are numerous good possibilities for train connections to Eurostar in Brussels, Lille and Paris. For enquiries about European trains contact Rail Europe/Rail International on ☎ 0870 584 8848, or check on the Internet – for example, the international Deutsche Bahn site (www.bahn.de) or the Rail Europe site (www.raileurope.com).

Eurotunnel Specially designed shuttle trains run 24 hours a day, departing up to four times an hour in each direction from 6 am to 10 pm, and every hour between 10 pm and 6 am.

Eurotunnel terminals are clearly signposted and connected to motorway networks. British and French Customs and Immigration formalities are carried out before you drive onto Eurotunnel. Travel time from motorway to motorway, including loading and unloading, is one hour; the shuttle itself takes 35 minutes. This sounds impressive, but the total time by hovercraft is under two hours, and ferries only take 2½ hours.

A car and its passengers costs from £270. You can make an advance reservation (☎ 0870 535 3535) or pay by cash or credit card at a toll booth. There are also day-trip fares that cost £69 or less. Visit the Web site at www.eurotunnel.com.

Train & Ferry Connections There are still several connections to/from Europe involving trains at either end and ferries across the Channel. Rail/ferry links generally arrive at Victoria, Liverpool Street and King's Cross train stations, depending on the European departure point. There are information centres at all the main stations.

Fares to/from London depend on where you are coming from in Europe. The ferry routes with train links at both ends include:

Hook of Holland (Netherlands) to Harwich and
  London Liverpool Street Station
Ostende (Belgium) to Dover and London
  Charing Cross Station
Calais (France) to Dover and London Charing
  Cross Station
Boulogne (France) to Folkestone and London
  Charing Cross Station

See the Sea section later in this chapter for details on sailings.

Car & Motorcycle

Drivers of vehicles registered to other EU countries will find bringing a car into Britain a fairly straight-forward process. The car must have registration papers and a nationality plate. The driver must have insurance. Although the International Insurance Certificate (Green Card) is no longer required, it remains excellent proof that you are covered.

There are motorways from all the main ferry ports and the Channel Tunnel that converge on the M25 motorway around London. You can use this often clogged artery to skirt (well, maybe slog) past the city and on to other destinations.

SEA

There's a bewildering array of alternatives between Britain and mainland Europe. This chapter outlines the main alternatives, but doesn't give a complete listing.

Competition from Eurotunnel and low-fare airlines has led to mergers of once competing ferry lines, but that hasn't led to higher prices. Instead the entire market is so competitive that there are constant sales and special fares.

Services are comprehensive but complicated. The same ferry company often has a host of different prices for the same route, depending upon the time of day or year, the validity of the ticket, or the size of a vehicle. Return tickets may be much cheaper than two one-way fares; on some routes a standard five-day return is the same as a one-way ticket; and vehicle tickets may also cover a driver and passenger. There are cheap day-return tickets, but they're strictly policed.

You will definitely have to plan ahead to try to find the best deals. Because of the thicket of fares, the listings below are limited to high-season return fares for a single foot passenger, and for one car and a driver. Remember that you will often be able to beat these fares through special offers at all but the busiest times. Also, on longer ferry rides there will be options for more deluxe accommodation, including cabins. Contact information for the companies mentioned is provided in the later boxed text 'Ferry Companies'.

France

On a clear day, you can see across the Channel from England to France. A true budget traveller would obviously swim – it's only seven hours and 40 minutes if you match the record.

Dover/Folkestone/Newhaven The shortest sea link from Europe is to Dover and Folkestone from Calais and Boulogne.

Dover is the most convenient port for those who plan onward travel (in England) by bus or train. Between Calais and Dover, P&O Stena Line and Hoverspeed operate every one to two hours.

P&O Stena Line ferries take 75 minutes and cost £48/321.

Hoverspeed's Seacats (large catamarans) only take 45 minutes to cross the Channel from Dover to Calais (£48/330), and 55 minutes from Folkestone to Boulogne (£48/298).

Hoverspeed operates catamarans from late April to early September between Dieppe and Newhaven. Fares cost £56/360.

Portsmouth P&O European Ferries operates three to four ferries daily to/from Cherbourg and Le Havre. The day ferries take five to six hours and the night ferries take seven to eight hours. Fares for both cost £60/190.

Brittany Ferries has at least one sailing a day between St Malo and Portsmouth (nine hours). The fares are £75/292. There are other ferries run by other operators that travel via the Channel Islands. See the Channel Islands chapter for details.

Spain

From Plymouth, Brittany Ferries operates at least one ferry a week to Santander, on Spain's north coast. The journey time is 24 hours; fares cost £154/460.

P&O European Ferries has a twice-weekly service between Bilbao and Portsmouth (35 hours). Fares cost £100/440.

Scandinavia

Until you see the ferry possibilities, it's easy to forget how close Scandinavia and Britain are, and why the Vikings found British villages so convenient to pillage.

Aberdeen & Shetland One of the most interesting possibilities is boat between Shetland, Norway, the Faroe Islands and Iceland.

The Smyril Line operates a weekly ship late May to early September. The following fares are all for single foot passengers travelling one way, accommodation is in a berth. From Bergen, Norway to Shetland, the trip costs £40 and takes about 13 hours; you can also travel from Lerwick to the Faroes (£40, 13 hours) and from the Faroes to Seydisfjördur, Iceland (£75, 17 hours).

See the Highlands & Northern Islands chapter for details on the regular P&O Scottish Ferries from Orkney and Aberdeen in Scotland to Lerwick on Shetland.

Newcastle Norway's Fjord Line operates ferries all year to/from Stavanger (20 hours) and Bergen (27 hours) in Norway and Newcastle. The boats sail three times a week in summer and twice-weekly at other times. Fares cost £200/690 (foot passenger/car and four people sharing one cabin) between either Norwegian city and Newcastle.

DFDS Seaways operates ferries to/from Kristiansand, Norway. They depart twice weekly (£198/336, 17 hours). Fares include a berth in an economy cabin.

Harwich This is the major port linking southern England to Denmark and Northern Germany. DFDS Seaways has two to three ferries a week to Esbjerg. The fares cost £168/276 (20 hours) and include a berth in an economy cabin.

Ferry Companies

Europe to Britain

Brittany Ferries
(☎ 0870 901 2400)
www.brittany-ferries.co.uk

DFDS Seaways
(☎ 0870 533 3000)
www.dfdsseaways.co.uk

Fjord Line
(☎ 0191-296 1313)
www.fjordline.no

Hoverspeed
(☎ 0870 240 8070)
www.hoverspeed.co.uk

P&O European Ferries
(☎ 0870 242 4999)
www.poef.com

P&O North Sea Ferries
(☎ 01482-377177)
www.ponsf.com

P&O Scottish Ferries
(☎ 01224-572615)
www.poscottishferries.co.uk

P&O Stena Line
(☎ 0870 600 0600)
www.posl.com

Smyril Line (UK agent)
(☎ 01224-572615)
www.smyril-line.fo

Stena Line
(☎ 0870 570 7070)
www.stenaline.com

Ireland to Britain

Irish Ferries
(☎ 0870 517 1717)
www.irishferries.ie

P&O Irish Sea
(☎ 0870 242 4777)
www.poirishsea.com

Sea Containers Ferries
(☎ 0870 552 3523)
www.steam-packet.com

Stena Line
(☎ 0870 570 7070)
www.stenaline.com

Swansea Cork Ferries
(☎ 01792-456116)
www.swansea-cork.ie

Belgium, the Netherlands & Germany

There are two direct links with Germany but many people prefer to drive to/from the Dutch ferry ports.

Dover Hoverspeed operates Seacat catamarans to/from Ostende in Belgium and Dover. There are at least three trips daily (£28/215, two hours).

Harwich DFDS Seaways has three ferries a week to/from Hamburg and Harwich. The fare (£168/276, 19½ hours) includes a berth in an economy cabin.

Stena Line has two fast ferries daily to/from Hook of Holland, near Rotterdam in the Netherlands (£44/260, four hours).

Hull P&O North Sea Ferries has daily ferries to/from Rotterdam (13 hours) and Zeebrugge (13½ hours) and Hull. The fares on both routes cost £81/136.

Newcastle DFDS Seaways operates daily to/from Ijmuiden, near Amsterdam in the Netherlands (£118/256, 15 hours). The fare includes a berth in an economy cabin.

Ireland

There's a great variety of ferry services from Britain to Ireland using modern car ferries. Figures quoted are return fares for a single adult and for one adult with a car in the high season. There are often special deals, return fares and other money savers worth investigating and in the low season fares are significantly lower.

Want to travel free? On some routes the cost for a car includes up to four or five passengers at no additional cost. If you can hitch a ride in a less than full car, it costs the driver nothing extra.

From south to north, ferry possibilities include:

Cork to Swansea

Swansea Cork Ferries has a 10-hour crossing that costs £68/378 (for up to five people and one car). It operates several times each week mid-March to early November.

Rosslare to Fishguard and Pembroke

To/from Pembroke, Irish Ferries has two daily crossings that take just under four hours. The fares are £20/179. To/from Fishguard, Stena Line has two daily regular ferries that take 3½ hours and cost £40/179. The frequent catamaran service takes under two hours and costs £50/209.

Dublin and Dun Laoghaire to Holyhead
Irish Ferries has two daily slow ferries to/from Dublin that take a little over three hours and cost £40/189. Fast ferries travel four-times daily, take two hours, and cost £50/239. Stena Line has several slow ferries a day to/from Dublin that take 3¾ hours and cost £184 (foot passengers not accepted). Stena fast ferries go to/from Dun Laoghaire in under two hours and cost £50/229.

Dublin to Liverpool
Sea Containers runs daily (£50/249, 3¾ hours).

Belfast to Stranraer
Stena Line has several daily slow ferries (£40/189, three hours). The frequent fast ferry service (1¾ hours) costs slightly more.

Belfast to Troon
Sea Containers Ferries has several daily catamarans (£50/249, 2½ hours).

Larne to Cairnryan
P&O Irish Sea has at least two daily slow ferries (£42/238, 2¼ hours). Frequent fast ferries cost £50/290 (one hour).

Getting Around

Public transport in Britain is generally good, but it can be expensive. During most of the 1980s and 1990s government policy was openly hostile to public transportation. Car ownership was favoured and local rail and bus services suffered. The chaos-filled privatisation of British Rail is but one dismal illustration of this. The Labour government has made great promises to reverse this decline, but it will take years for the results to be felt. This is bad news for visitors without their own wheels, as transport to many national parks and small villages is poorly serviced.

It's certainly worth considering car rental for at least part of your trip. However, even if you're not driving, with a mix of local buses, the odd taxi, walking and occasionally hiring a bike, and plenty of time, you can get almost anywhere.

Buses are nearly always the cheapest way to get around. Unfortunately, they're also the slowest (sometimes by a considerable margin). With discount passes and tickets bought in advance, trains can be competitive; they're quicker and often take you through beautiful countryside relatively unspoilt by the modern age.

Ticket types and prices vary considerably. Travelling by bus and train can be as complicated as finding a cheap airline ticket. For many, the convenience of a train or bus pass will outweigh any potential savings from endlessly looking for the best deal.

See the bus and train fare tables in this chapter to get an idea of the way the different tickets stack up. If you know how far you're travelling (even if your planned journey is not specifically covered) you can get a rough idea of costs by working from the mileage columns.

AIR

Most regional centres and islands are linked to London. However, unless you're going to the outer reaches of Britain, in particular northern Scotland, planes are only marginally quicker than trains if you include the time it takes to get to/from airports. They also aren't anywhere near as scenic.

Domestic Air Services

The main operators are British Airways (BA), British Midland, easyJet, Go and Ryanair. See the Getting There & Away chapter for contact information for each of these carriers.

There are all the usual advance-purchase and discount fares available. There are also youth fares (for under-25s), but Apex and special-offer fares are usually cheaper. Depending on how flexible you are you may be able to find a ticket that compares favourably with the cheaper train fares.

Air Passes

If you're flying into the UK on BA you may be eligible for a One World Visit Europe Air Pass. This allows you to buy tickets on all UK domestic flights for an additional £59 each. This can be an excellent deal if you want to get from London to the far north and islands. However, these tickets must be arranged at least seven days prior to arrival in the UK.

BUS

Road transport in Britain is almost entirely privately owned and run. National Express (☎ 0870 580 8080) runs the largest national network – it completely dominates the market and is a sister company to Eurolines – but there are often smaller competitors on the main routes. You can visit the National Express Web site at www.gobycoach.com.

In Britain, long-distance express buses are usually referred to as coaches, and in many towns there are separate bus and coach stations. Over short distances, coaches are more expensive (though quicker) than buses. There is a web of bus companies serving England and the important ones are highlighted in each chapter.

Scotland's internal bus network has one major player, Scottish Citylink (☎ 0870 550

5050), part of the National Express group. Its Web site at www.citylink.co.uk has useful information, including sample fares and a journey planner. There are many more smaller regional operators, several forming part of the Stagecoach or First networks.

Coach/Bus Fares from London

The sample fares below are for unrestricted single and return travel from London on the National Express coach/bus system. Within each category, the first fare is available to anyone and the second fare requires one of the National Express discount cards (see Passes & Discounts under Bus later).

If you can avoid travelling on Fridays, you can save a few pounds off these fares. National Express has advance-purchase fares on many routes that also save a few pounds (although nowhere as dramatic a savings as is the case with advance-purchase train fares), so it's worth checking if your trip qualifies for such a fare. For destinations close to London there are day return fares that cost just a bit more than the regular single fare.

On some of the routes below you will have to change coaches/buses one or more times.

road mileage from London	destination	best time (hours)	single (£)	return (£)
51	Brighton	1¾	7.50/6	12.50/10
54	Cambridge	2	8/6.50	12.50/10
56	Canterbury	2	8/6.50	12.50/10
57	Oxford*	1¾	7	7.50
71	Dover	2½	9.50/7.50	15/12
83	Salisbury	2¾	12/9.50	18/14
92	Stratford	2¾	11/10	16/13
106	Bath	3	11.50/9.50	22/17
110	Birmingham	2½	10/9	15/12
115	Bristol	2¼	11/11	18/18
131	Lincoln	4¾	19.25/13.75	28.25/20.75
150	Shrewsbury	4½	12.50/10.50	18/15
155	Cardiff	3¼	14/11.50	24/19.50
172	Exeter	3¾	16.50/13.50	30/24
184	Manchester	4	15/13	25/19.50
188	York	4	18/15	28/23
193	Liverpool	4½	15/13	25/19.50
211	Aberystwyth	7¼	19.25/13.75	28.25/20.75
215	Scarborough	5¾	22/18	34/26
255	Durham	4¾	20/16	32/25
299	Carlisle	5½	22/18	33/27
375	Edinburgh	8	22/18	33/27
397	Glasgow	7	22/18	33/27
434	Dundee	8¼	26/21	41/33
450	Perth	8¼	26/21	41/33
503	Aberdeen	10½	28/22	46/37
536	Inverness	12	30/24	47/38

* Operated by Oxford Tube (☎ 01865-772250); fares are for an unrestricted single and a one-day return ticket; an open return costs £9.50.

The major operators serving Wales are Arriva Cymru for the north and west, and First Cymru in the south, both at the same centralised telephone number (☎ 0870 608 2608).

Unless otherwise stated, prices quoted in this book are for economy single tickets. See the Coach/Bus Fares table for a rough idea of long-distance coach/bus prices.

Local Buses & Information

Although local and regional buses seem to cover the lengths of Britain, they often do not do so in a way useful to the visitor. Away from cities, buses may run at times designed to serve schools and industry. Besides the fact that this means that there may be few midday services, it can mean even fewer weekend services. You might plan a spectacular hike in one of the national parks, only to find that there is no bus service at all on the day you plan to finish.

A number of counties operate telephone enquiry lines that try to explain the fast-changing and often chaotic timetables; wherever possible, these numbers have been provided. Before commencing a journey off the main routes it is wise to phone for the latest information.

An even better alternative for bus information is the National Bus Enquiry Service (☎ 0870 608 2608). A government initiative, it is meant to provide the same kind of usefulness as the National Rail Enquiry Service. However, it is in its early stages and in mid-2000 information was only available for several northern counties and parts of Wales. You should definitely try it for your own needs to see if it has been extended to cover the area you seek information about.

Bus Passes & Discounts

Besides the national passes mentioned below, there are literally scores of regional and local bus passes. Most can be bought from the driver as you board the bus. If you are going to spend any amount of time in one area, it is always worth asking what sorts of Rover or other regional passes are available.

In addition, some of the passes mentioned

later in this chapter under Rail include certain bus services.

Discount Card National Express sells discount coach cards that get 20 to 30% off standard adult fares. The cards are available to full-time students, and those aged between 16 and 25, and 50 or over. They can be purchased from all National Express agents and cost £9. A passport photo is required – ISIC cards are accepted as proof of student status, and passports for date of birth. These cards also offer a discount on all Scottish Citylink buses.

Travel Pass The National Express Travel Pass allows unlimited coach travel within a specified period. It's available to all overseas visitors, but it must be bought outside Britain, usually from a Eurolines agent.

The costs (adults/those aged under 26) of the various passes are:

5 days	£65/50
7 days	£95/75
14 days	£135/105
30 days	£185/145

Tourist Trail Pass The National Express Tourist Trail Pass can be bought by anyone in the UK and is thus the easiest pass to purchase. Over 2000 National Express ticket agents sell this family of passes, which allow for a certain number of days unlimited bus travel within a larger but limited period. The passes are sold at a discount to those aged under 16 as well as holders of any of the National Express discount cards described above. The costs (adult/discount) of the various passes are:

2 days in 3	£49/39
5 days in 10	£85/69
7 days in 21	£120/94
14 days in 30	£187/143

Backpackers Buses

The Stray Travel Network is an excellent bus service (☎ 020-7373 7737, fax 7373 7739) designed especially for those staying in hostels, but useful for all budget travellers.

Buses run on a regular circuit between London, Windsor, Bath, Manchester, Haworth, the Lake District, Glasgow, Stirling, Edinburgh, York, Nottingham, Cambridge and London, and call in on hostels. You can get on and off the bus where you like and catch another one as it comes along.

There are four ticket options:

1 day	£24
3 days in 2 months	£79
4 days in 2 months	£99
6 days in 4 months	£129

Tickets are available from branches of STA; look in the Yellow Pages for the nearest branch. You can also visit the Web site at www.straytravel.com.

The Edinburgh-based Radical Travel Network (☎ 0131-557 9393, fax 558 1177) operates several different bus services. Border Raiders tours cover the highlights of England, Scotland and Wales and offer various packages. The Full Monty covers the entire route for £129 and you can hop on and hop off. The Haggis Flexitour covers Edinburgh, Pitlochry, Inverness, Loch Ness, Ullapool, Isle of Skye, Fort William, Oban, Loch Lomond and Glasgow and costs from £69. Check out the Web site at www.radicaltravel.com.

The Backpackers Bus Company (☎ 029-2066 6900), 98 Neville Street, Riverside, Cardiff CF1 8LS, is a bus service for backpackers that offers tours and treks of Wales for four/six days for £99/119.

Postbus

Royal Mail postbuses provide a stable, reliable service to remoter areas and can be useful for walkers. For information and timetables contact the Postbus Helpline (☎ 01246-546329), or Customer Services (☎ 0845 774 0740). Postbuses take four to 10 people, but most don't carry bicycles.

Tour Buses

Several companies operate bus tours in tourist towns around England. They have regular buses circulating on a fixed route and your one-day ticket lets you get on and off the bus as many times as you like. Useful local tour companies are mentioned throughout this book.

Bushwakkers (☎ 020-8573 3330), 15 Chartwell Court, 145 Church Rd, Hayes, Middlesex UB3 2LP, is a London-based company offering weekend adventure trips to Wales by minibus. Prices are around £115, accommodation is in tents and activities include walking, mountain-biking, canoeing and horse riding. You can visit the Web site at bushwakkers.com.

TRAIN

Despite the damage wrought by privatisation, Britain still has an impressive rail service – that is if you're using the rail system as a tourist rather than a commuter. There are several particularly recommended trips on beautiful lines through sparsely populated country, the most famous being in Wales and Scotland. See the Highlights section in the Facts for the Visitor chapter for some ideas.

The main routes are served by fast trains that travel at speeds of up to 140 mph and, for example, whisk you from London to Edinburgh in just over four hours.

Privatisation

Following the privatisation of the railways, instigated by the Conservative party and inherited by the current Labour government, the rail system appears to be becoming less reliable than it was in the days when it was the single nationalised company known as British Rail. Services are provided by 25 Train Operating Companies (TOCs). A separate company, Railtrack, owns and maintains the track and the stations. For the sake of convenience, the British Rail logo and name are still used on directional signs.

What all this diversification means is that Britain's railways have become a Tower of Babel, with the different TOCs and Railtrack often not working together for the common (read: passengers') good. Amazingly, ridership is soaring with the strong economy and the system frequently threatens to come apart at the seams – or does, as with the Paddington and Hatfield disasters of 1999 and 2000. There are all sorts of plans

Rail Fares from London

The following are sample standard fares that were in effect between London and selected destinations in the summer of 2000. Single-ticket prices are for unrestricted tickets that allow for stop-overs along the journey. Day Return fares are the cheapest return tickets that have no advance purchase requirement. However, as you have to do all your travelling on the same day, these are only listed for destinations under two hours away from London. The one night or more return tickets listed are the cheapest tickets that allow you to do this. These often have advance-purchase requirements and other restrictions, but as you can see they can be quite cheap. Where there is more than one route between London and a destination, the faster route is shown, although the slower one is likely to be cheaper.

For ease of comparison, the destinations are shown in the same order as the bus fares from London, but note that there are great variations in the train mileage versus the road mileage. Also, note that the journey times are the best times possible and may involve one or more connections.

rail mileage from London	destination	best time (hours)	single (£)	day return (£)	one night or more return (£)
51	Brighton	¾	13.70	14.60	18.80
56	Cambridge	1	14.50	14.60	18.80
62	Canterbury	1½	15.90	15.40	17.10
64	Oxford	¾	15.10	14.80	18.90
77	Dover	1¼	19.80	18.30	20.60
84	Salisbury	1¼	22.50	21.90	26.70
121	Stratford	1¾	20	19.50	22.50
107	Bath	1½	34	31	25.50
110	Birmingham	1½	43.50	27	15
118	Bristol	1½	36	32	18.50
137	Lincoln	1¾	37	39	21
156	Shrewsbury	2½	55	-	18
151	Cardiff	2	43.50	-	23
174	Exeter	2	39	-	28
184	Manchester	2½	85	-	20
188	York	2	58	-	23
194	Liverpool	2½	79	-	20
237	Aberystwyth	5¼	71	-	29
230	Scarborough	2¾	60	-	29
254	Durham	2¾	74	-	23
299	Carlisle	3½	91	-	27
393	Edinburgh	4	86	-	30
402	Glasgow	5	91	-	53
452	Dundee	5¾	89	-	50
450	Perth	6	89	-	50
524	Aberdeen	6½	90	-	66
568	Inverness	8¼	91	-	50

for new and better railways, but the majority won't be executed in the near future. Still, the railways are often the best means of getting from one place to another.

The main railcards (see under Railcards later) are accepted by all the companies and travellers are still able to buy a ticket to any destination from most train stations or from

PRINCIPAL RAILWAYS

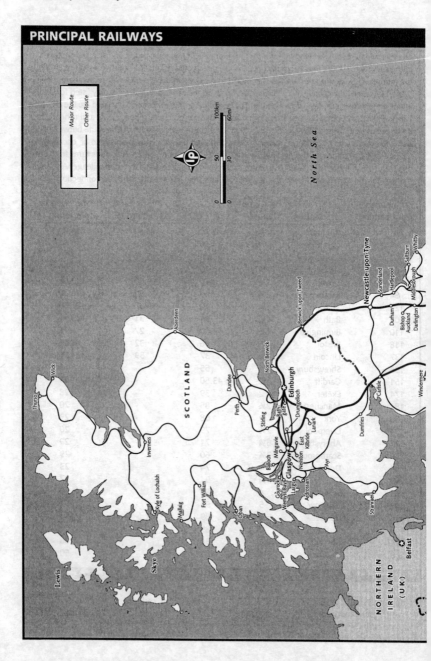

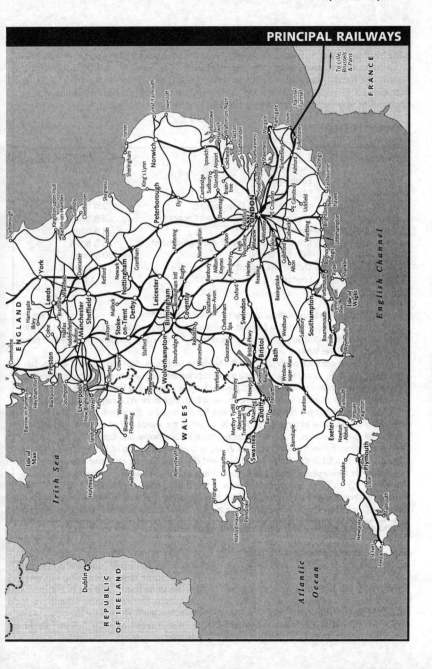

Rail Itineraries

The following itineraries include tourist highlights as well as some of the most scenic rail trips. Journey times are approximate. Most of the suggested stops are on main lines so services are fairly frequent. The National Rail Enquiry Service (☎ 08457-484950, outside the UK ☎ 44 1332-387601), the Railtrack Web site at www.railtrack.co.uk, or one of the timetable publications mentioned in the text, will be very useful in planning your schedule.

Britain (14 Days)

origin	destination	journey times
London	York	2 hours
York	Durham	50 minutes
Durham	Edinburgh	1¾ hours
Edinburgh	Glasgow	1 hour
Glasgow	Windermere (via Oxenholme)	2½ hours
Windermere	Chester (via Oxenholme and Crewe)	3½ hours
Chester	Conwy	1¼ hours
Conwy	Cheltenham (via Crewe and Birmingham)	3½ hours
Cheltenham	Bath (via Bristol)	50 minutes
Bath	Oxford (via Didcot)	1¼ hours
Oxford	London	1 hour

Route

From London's King's Cross station, it's only two hours to York. With Roman walls, medieval streets and the largest Gothic cathedral in England, York is high on every visitor's list of priorities. Under an hour to the north is Durham, tiny in comparison to York, but with a magnificent cathedral, rising high above the River Wear.

From Durham, continue north and cross the border to Edinburgh, Scotland's capital, with its famous castle and even more famous festival, the world's largest. Completely different in atmosphere, and with superb galleries and a lively arts scene, Glasgow is under one hour to the west.

To reach the Lake District from Glasgow, you need to change trains in Oxenholme. Stay two nights in Windermere so that you can spend at least one full day taking in the superb scenery that inspired Wordsworth and many other poets and artists. To get to the walled city of Chester, with its black and white Tudor buildings, you need to change trains in Oxenholme and Crewe.

From Chester, follow the north coast of Wales to Conwy to visit one of Edward I's magnificent castles, built to subdue the Welsh. Travel back and change at Chester or Crewe and again at Birmingham for Cheltenham, the grand Regency town on the edge of the Cotswolds. From Cheltenham, move on to the beautiful city of Bath, a 12-minute train journey beyond Bristol.

Bath to Oxford requires a change at Didcot. Spend two nights at Britain's oldest university town, allowing time for an excursion to nearby Blenheim Palace. The trip back to London takes only one hour.

🌴🌴🌴🌴🌴🌴🌴🌴🌴🌴🌴🌴🌴🌴🌴🌴🌴🌴🌴🌴🌴🌴🌴🌴🌴🌴🌴🌴🌴

authorised travel agents, though travel agents are not able to sell the full range of tickets.

Passengers can travel only on services provided by the company who issued their ticket and each company is able to set whatever fare it chooses. Thus, on routes served by more than one operator, passengers can choose to buy a cheaper ticket with a company offering a less frequent/direct service or pay more for a faster service. In some cases competing companies use the same route. The era of competition also means that companies often have special offers such as 'two for the price of one' or special reductions for tickets bought in advance.

Rail Itineraries

Scotland (4 Days)

origin	destination	journey times (hours)
Edinburgh	Glasgow	1
Glasgow	Fort William	3¾
Fort William	Mallaig	1½
Mallaig	Kyle of Lochalsh	2 (by boat, summer only)
Kyle of Lochalsh	Inverness	2½
Inverness	Perth	2½
Perth	Edinburgh	1½

Route

This route includes the West Highland Line, arguably the most scenic rail journey in the country, and the Kyle Line across the Highlands from Kyle of Lochalsh to Inverness. The ScotRail Flexi Rover ticket (£79) allows travel on this route for four days out of eight.

It takes less than one hour from Edinburgh to Glasgow's Central station. Nearby, from Queen St station, trains depart on the West Highland Line. The route passes Loch Lomond on the way to Crianlarich, then climbs over wild Rannoch Moor, with views of Ben Nevis, Britain's highest peak. From Fort William, the train crosses the River Lochy. There are superb views of Loch Shiel and, after Glenfinnan station, Loch Eilt. The tracks run through tunnels along the edge of the sea lochs to Arisaig, Britain's most westerly train station, then north to Morar with views across to the islands of Skye, Rhum and Eigg. The line follows the coast from Morar to Mallaig.

In the summer there are ferry services for the two-hour voyage to Kyle of Lochalsh, the terminus of the Kyle Line from Inverness. From Inverness there are frequent departures south to Perth, where it's worth stopping to see Scone Palace before continuing to Edinburgh.

Wales (3 Days)

origin	destination	journey times (hours)
Shrewsbury	Dovey Junction	1¾
Dovey Junction	Porthmadog	1½
Porthmadog	Blaenau Ffestiniog	1¼
Blaenau Ffestiniog	Llandudno Junction	1¼
Llandudno Junction (via Chester)	Shrewsbury	2

Route

Wales is known for its Great Little Trains, narrow-gauge railways passing through some spectacular countryside. This route links several of them with the mainline network to make an enjoyable three-day trip around North Wales, starting and ending in Shrewsbury (England). It might just be possible to do the whole journey in one day, but spending a couple of nights in Wales would allow time to appreciate the superb scenery of Snowdonia National Park. The North & Mid Wales Flexi Rover ticket (£26.30) allows travel anywhere on this route for three days out of seven.

From Shrewsbury you travel west to Dovey Junction to join the Cambrian coast railway that follows the coast north. You could stop at Harlech to see the 13th-century castle. From Porthmadog, the narrow-gauge Ffestiniog Railway takes you in steam-hauled carriages through Snowdonia to Blaenau Ffestiniog. Another small railway continues through Betws-y-Coed to Llandudno Junction to connect with the coastal railway. Follow the coast east back to England. Connecting trains for Shrewsbury leave from Chester.

Information

National Rail Enquiries (☎ 0845 748 4950, from outside the UK ☎ 44 1332-387601) is a much improved service that can provide all timetable and fare information. Also, it's worth visiting Railtrack's Web site at www.railtrack.co.uk for its timetable feature.

The individual TOCs publish free timetables, but collecting these is probably best left to the train spotters. The *Thomas Cook European Timetable* (£9.50) and the *OAG Rail Guide* (£7.50) list all the most important services yet manage to be reasonably svelte. Both publications can be found at larger newsstands in train stations.

See the section Buying Tickets for details of the complex procedure for buying train tickets in Britain.

Classes

There are two classes of rail travel: 1st, and what is now officially referred to as standard (although in class-conscious Britain this will always be called 2nd class). First class costs 30 to 50% more than standard and, except on very crowded trains, is not really worth the extra money. However, it can be a bargain at weekends when you can upgrade many standard-class tickets for £6 to £12.

On overnight trains (between London and Exeter, Plymouth and Penzance, and on the routes to Scotland) there are sleeping compartments with one berth in 1st class and two in standard. There's a variety of fares for these services, and at times they can work out to be better value than a night in a hotel. It's essential to reserve berths in advance.

Unless stated otherwise, prices in this book are for standard-class adult single tickets.

Train Passes

Unfortunately, Eurail passes are not recognised in Britain. However, as with bus passes, there are oodles of local and regional passes, but they aren't recognised in the rest of Europe. Many are mentioned throughout this book. If you will be spending any amount of time in one place, it is always worth checking to see if there is a local rail pass, many of which combine bus validity as well.

Holders of BritRail, Eurail and Euro passes are entitled to discounted fares on Eurostar trains (eg London to Paris or Brussels for US$79). Unfortunately, BritRail passes no longer cover the Heathrow Express trains. There is also a variant on the BritRail passes that includes Ireland for not much more. Children's passes are usually half the adult cost or less.

BritRail passes are popular with visitors, but they are *not available in Britain* and must be bought in your country of origin. Most large travel agencies will have details.

BritRail Classic There are several flavours of BritRail Classic passes, all of which are for consecutive days of travel. Prices are for adult 1st class/adult standard class/60 and over 1st class (the only option).

8 days	US$400/265/340
15 days	US$600/400/510
22 days	US$760/505/645
30 days	US$900/600/765

Anyone getting their money's worth out of the last pass should qualify for some sort of award for heroism from Railtrack.

Youth passes are good for those aged between 15 and 25, are available for standard class only and cost US$215/280/355/420 for 8/15/22/30 days.

BritRail Flexipass These passes are usually a better option for travellers as you don't have to get on a train every day and ride for hours to get full value. They are good for a certain number of days within a 60-day period. Prices are for adult 1st class/adult standard class/60 and over 1st class (the only option).

4 days	US$350/235/300
8 days	US$510/340/435
15 days	US$770/515/655

Youth passes are good for those aged between 15 and 25, are available for standard class only and cost US$185/240/360 for 4/8/15 days.

BritRail Pass 'n' Drive This combines a BritRail Flexipass with the use of a Hertz rental car for side trips. The package is available in various combinations: a three-day Flexipass plus two days car rental in one month costs US$279 for one person, or US$219 each for two people in one car. There are options that allow you to customise this pass in almost any way.

BritRail SouthEast Pass BritRail's regional SouthEast Pass covers the dense network of railways in South-Eastern England, including all the rail lines in and around London.

The passes combine a set number of days over a period of validity and are good in both standard and 1st class.

3 days in 8	US$74/105
4 days in 8	US$105/142
7 days in 15	US$142/189

Freedom of Scotland Pass The comprehensive Freedom of Scotland Pass covers all rail services in Scotland, plus those north of Berwick and Carlisle in England. It also includes CalMac ferries and Strathclyde Public Transport (SPT) ferries; a 33% discount on postbuses and selected regional bus routes with Scottish Citylink, Fife Scottish and First Edinburgh; a 33% discount on the P&O Scottish Ferries Orkney (Stromness) to Scrabster ferry; and a 20% discount on P&O's Aberdeen to Shetland and Aberdeen to Orkney ferries.

These good-value passes combine a set number of days over a period of validity and are good in standard class only.

4 days in 8	£79
8 days in 15	£109
12 days in 15	£119

These passes can be bought in Britain.

Freedom of Wales Rover This provides unlimited travel on all Welsh trains and many bus services as well. The passes are valid for eight days' travel within a 15-day period and cost £92.

Railcards

You can get discounts of up to 33% on most fares (except certain heavily discounted tickets) if you're aged between 16 and 25, over 60, studying full time, or disabled – but you must first buy the appropriate railcard. There is also a railcard for families.

The cards are valid for one year and most are available from major stations.

Young Person's Railcard
Costs £18 and gives you 33% off most tickets and some ferry services; you must be aged between 16 and 25, or a student of any age studying full time in the UK. You need proof of age, proof of student status (if necessary) and a passport-size photo.

Senior Railcard
Available to anyone over 60, this card costs £18 and gives a 33% discount. You need to have proof of age.

Family Railcard
Costs £20 and allows discounts of 33% (20% for some tickets) for up to four adults travelling together, providing a card-holder is a member of the party. Up to four accompanying children pay a flat fare of £2 each. A couple of journeys can pay for the card.

Disabled Person's Railcard
Costs £14 and gives a 33% discount to a disabled person and one person accompanying them. Pick up an application form from a station and then send it to the Disabled Person's Railcard Office, PO Box 1YT, Newcastle upon Tyne, NE99 1YT. It can take up to three weeks to process this card so you should apply early.

Network Card
If you're planning to do a lot of rail travel in the south of England, a Network card may be worth considering. This is valid for the region previously known as Network SouthEast – London and the entire south-east of England, from Dover to Weymouth, Cambridge to Oxford. It costs £20. Discounts of 33% apply to up to four adults travelling together providing a card-holder is a member of the party. Children pay a flat fare of £1. Travel is permitted after 10 am from Monday to Friday and at any time at the weekend. A couple of journeys can pay for the card.

Tickets

If the various train passes and railcards aren't complicated enough, try making sense of the different tickets.

Children under five travel free; those aged

between five and 15 pay half-price for most tickets (except for certain heavily discounted tickets). However, when travelling with children it is almost always worth buying a Family Railcard.

See the train fare table for ticket prices. The various TOCs all have their own discount schemes not unlike those of the airlines. These come and go throughout the year and at any time there may be several offers outstanding. That's why you have no choice but to shop around if you want to be sure of getting the best fares. And just like the airlines, the cheapest fares have advance-purchase and minimum-stay requirements, as well as limited seating. Many are non-refundable, so if you miss your train, you're stuck.

The following are the main classifications of fares that are not heavily discounted and have few restrictions.

Single ticket
Valid for a single journey at any time on the day specified; expensive but you can usually get on and off at several stops along the way or get one valid for several days, thus allowing you to, say, travel from Edinburgh to London via Cambridge while stopping at five or six places along the way.

Day Return ticket
Valid for a return journey at any time on the day specified; relatively expensive.

Cheap Day Return ticket
Valid for a return journey on the day specified on the ticket, but there are time restrictions such as not being allowed to travel on a train that leaves before 9.30 am, and it is usually only available for short journeys. It is often about the same price as a single, is a great deal for day-trippers and is usually good on commuter trains where there are no advance-purchase tickets.

Open Return ticket
For outward travel on a stated day and return on any day within a month.

Buying Tickets

For tickets in the categories above, as well as discounted tickets that don't require an advance purchase, your best option is to buy the tickets at a train station where the staff can usually help you find the best deal. The same advice applies if you are going to be in Britain long enough to buy an advance-purchase ticket. However, if you want an advance-purchase ticket and you won't be in Britain in time to buy it, the situation becomes rather difficult.

First, phone the National Rail Enquiry Service (☎ 0845 748 4950, from outside the UK ☎ 44 1332-387601) to get the time of your train and the price of the ticket. You'll then be given another number for one of the 25 TOCs where you can make a credit card booking for your journey. Once you've bought the ticket from the TOC, specify that you will pick up the ticket at the originating station on the day of travel. But be sure to get to the station early as queues are often quite long.

Alternatively, you can book tickets at the Web site at www.thetrainline.com run by Virgin Trains, but more often than not it insists on mailing you your tickets (and to UK addresses only), a non-starter if you're travelling, or live outside the UK. However, using this site can be useful to find out if there is a fare deal enticing enough to make the cost of the calls worthwhile.

CAR & MOTORCYCLE

Travelling by private car or motorcycle enables you to get to remote places, and to travel quickly, independently and flexibly. Unfortunately, the independence you enjoy does tend to isolate you, and cars are nearly always inconvenient in city centres.

Despite the traffic density, Britain has the safest roads in the EU. There are five grades of road. Motorways and main A-roads are triple or dual carriageways and deliver you quickly from one end of the country to another, but you miss the most interesting countryside. Be careful if you use them in foggy or wet conditions. Minor A-roads are single carriageways and are likely to be clogged with slow-moving trucks.

Life on the road is more relaxed and interesting on the B-roads and minor roads. Fenced by hedgerows, these roads wind through the countryside from village to village. You can't travel fast, but you won't want to.

Avoid bringing a car into London if you

ROAD DISTANCES (MILES)

	London	Aberystwyth	Bath	Birmingham	Cambridge	Cardiff	Dover	Edinburgh	Glasgow	Holyhead	Inverness	Manchester	Oxford	Penzance	Stranraer	Thurso	Windermere	York
London	---																	
Aberystwyth	240	---																
Bath	116	142	---															
Birmingham	117	119	97	---														
Cambridge	60	213	174	101	---													
Cardiff	155	115	56	107	213	---												
Dover	77	310	200	203	121	233	---											
Edinburgh	401	335	384	293	337	393	457	---										
Glasgow	400	331	384	291	349	393	490	45	---									
Holyhead	264	106	245	155	246	209	351	327	321	---								
Inverness	569	493	544	453	500	558	648	159	171	486	---							
Manchester	197	133	181	88	153	188	283	218	335	125	378	---						
Oxford	56	156	66	63	80	109	148	362	355	212	518	154	---					
Penzance	312	313	213	278	368	232	365	563	563	409	722	358	265	---				
Stranraer	414	346	398	304	361	406	503	133	88	334	267	226	371	576	---			
Thurso	652	626	655	590	630	685	740	290	298	585	130	300	650	858	368	---		
Windermere	259	443	251	150	248	250	350	148	145	182	310	81	220	415	163	423	---	
York	209	480	236	128	150	241	274	195	208	192	360	71	185	405	228	482	112	---

can. Traffic moves slowly and parking is expensive. Traffic wardens and wheel clampers operate with extreme efficiency and if your vehicle is towed away it'll cost you over £100 to get it back.

Driving in Scotland can be an adventure; in some areas roads are only single track, meaning just one-lane. At passing places (it's illegal to park in these places), a vehicle stops to allow oncoming cars through, or to allow someone from behind to overtake. In the same areas petrol stations are few and far between and sometimes closed on Sunday.

Getting around north and south Wales is made simple by the A55 and M4 respectively. Away from these highways, roads are still good but generally slower, especially in the mountainous areas and Central Wales. Bear in mind that some of the highest roads may be snowbound in winter. Even when the snow clears, ice can linger to make driving conditions treacherous, especially on windy, narrow mountain roads, which are often single-track affairs with passing places at intervals.

At around 99p per litre (equivalent to just under US$6 for a US gallon), petrol is expensive by American or Australian standards, and diesel is only a few pence cheaper. Distances, however, aren't great.

Road Rules

Anyone using the roads should read the *Highway Code* (often available in Tourist Information Centres; TICs). A foreign driving licence is valid in Britain for up to 12 months from the time of your last entry into the country. If you plan to bring a car from Europe make sure you're adequately insured.

Briefly, vehicles drive on the left-hand side of the road; front seat belts are compulsory and if belts are fitted in the back they must be worn; the speed limit is 30 mph (48 kph) in built-up areas, 60 mph (96 kph) on single carriageways, and 70 mph (112 kph) on dual or triple carriageways; you give way

Driving Itineraries

If you're only visiting Britain for a short holiday, you can pack a lot more in if you have your own set of wheels and plan your itinerary carefully.

On the following route around England, you could travel from the airport to London and from London to Cambridge by train or bus, pick up your rental car there, tour round the country and return the car to the airport as you leave, without going back to London.

England (12 Days)

origin	destination	road distances (miles)
London	Cambridge	61
Cambridge	Lincoln	94
Lincoln	York	81
York	Durham	75
Durham	Windermere	115
Windermere	Chester	113
Chester	Stratford-upon-Avon	65
Stratford-upon-Avon	Bath	99
Bath	Salisbury (via Avebury)	59
Salisbury	Windsor	75
Windsor	London	23

Route

Leave London on the M11 that leads directly to Cambridge. Spend the day in this ancient university town and take a punt out on the river. From Cambridge, take the A604 to Huntingdon to join the A1, stopping at Stamford for a quick look at this unspoiled old town. Continue along the A1, turning off onto the A46 for Lincoln. This old Roman city has a superb Norman cathedral and castle.

Leave Lincoln on the A15, the Roman road known as Ermine St, heading north. Join the M180 for seven miles, then take the A15 over the Humber Bridge. Immediately after crossing the bridge, take the A63 for seven miles, then the A1034 to Market Weighton, following signs for York via the A1079. York Minster is the largest Gothic cathedral in England, and York is a fascinating place.

Head west out of York on the A59 to join the A1. Leave the A1(M) and get on the A690 to Durham, an easier route than the A177. Durham is a World Heritage Site with one of the finest cathedrals in the country.

From Durham, take the A691 to Consett, and then the A692 four miles south-west to join the A68 going north. The A69 leads west through Haydon Bridge to Bardon Mill, where signposts direct you for the three-mile journey to Housesteads Fort, part of Hadrian's Wall. After stopping to see the fort, continue west along the B6318 to rejoin the A69, following signposts for Carlisle. Two miles east of Carlisle, take the M6 south to the A66, which you follow west for a mile. Turn left onto the scenic A592, which leads into the heart of the Lake District, past Ullswater to Windermere. Stay two nights in Windermere to give yourself time for a long walk in this beautiful area.

From Windermere take the A591 south-east to join the M6 south, eventually taking the M56 to Chester. Spend the night in Chester before taking the A41 and A442 south to join the M54 near Telford. You may wish to stop at nearby Ironbridge Gorge to see this cradle of the Industrial Revolution and its interesting museums, or at Warwick, south of Birmingham, to see its impressive castle.

Bypass Birmingham on the M6 and join the M40 (watch the signs as this is an easy exit to miss). Take the A3400 to Stratford-upon-Avon for a quick look at Shakespeare's birthplace and to see a

Driving Itineraries

play performed by the Royal Shakespeare Company in the evening.

The following day, visit Blenheim Palace, one of the most impressive stately homes in the country, and drive through Cotswold villages to the beautiful city of Bath. The A3400 and the A44 lead you to Woodstock, and Blenheim stands on the edge of the town.

From Blenheim, take the A4095 to Witney, the A40 to the village of Burford, the B4425 through Bibury to Cirencester, and the A433, then the A46, to Bath.

From Bath, follow the A4 to the prehistoric complex of Avebury, less well known but more atmospheric than Stonehenge. Continue east along the A4 to join the A346 and A338 south to Salisbury, well known for its cathedral.

Leave Salisbury on the A360 north to join the A303 near Stonehenge, continuing east onto the M3. At Basingstoke, take the A33 to join the M4, stopping at Windsor to see the castle. Heathrow airport is only about 10 miles from Windsor, so you could stay the night in the Windsor area and drop off your rental car at the airport as you leave.

Scotland (7 Days)

origin	destination	road distances (miles)
Edinburgh	St Andrews	58
St Andrews	Aberdeen	83
Aberdeen	Inverness	106
Inverness	Fort William	65
Fort William	Glasgow	102
Glasgow	Stirling	26
Stirling	Edinburgh	35

Route

Take the A90 out of Edinburgh over the Forth Road Bridge. The A90 becomes the M90 soon after the bridge, and you should turn onto the A91 north of Kinross, following signs to St Andrews. It's worth spending the night in this interesting seaside town, best known as the home of golf.

From St Andrews, turn off the A91 along the A919 and A92, following signs for Tay Bridge and Dundee. Stop to see Scott's Antarctic research ship *Discovery*, conveniently moored beside the bridge in Dundee. Continue on the A929 and the smaller A928 to Glamis Castle, one of the most famous of Scotland's many castles. From Glamis take the A94 to the affluent granite city of Aberdeen.

You could take one of several routes from Aberdeen to Inverness. The direct route is along the A96 via Elgin, a distance of 106 miles. Alternatively, and if you have an extra day to spare, consider taking the route through the Grampian Mountains, via the A93, A939, A95 and A9, about 150 miles. Balmoral Castle, the Queen's Scottish residence, which can be visited when the royal family is not at home, is a short distance off this route.

From Inverness, follow Loch Ness on the A92, stopping at Urquhart Castle and the nearby Loch Ness Monster Exhibition. Continue on the A82 to Fort William, leaving yourself time for an evening walk in Glen Nevis. To climb Ben Nevis, Britain's highest peak, you'd need to allow a whole day.

Take the A82 south from Fort William, stopping in Glen Coe and then continuing past Loch Lomond to Glasgow. Spend the following day in this lively city before taking the M80 to Stirling, a drive of under one hour. Look around Stirling's magnificent castle the next day before returning to Edinburgh.

Driving Itineraries

Wales (5 Days)

origin	destination	road distances (miles)
Cardiff	Brecon	35
Brecon	St David's	85
St David's	Machynlleth	77
Machynlleth	Llanberis	60
Llanberis	Llandudno (via Caernarfon)	27
Llandudno	Chester	47

Cardiff is about 30 miles from the River Severn and the border with England. Spend half a day in the Welsh capital to see the castle or the folk museum before taking the A470 north to Brecon.

After a morning's walk in the Brecon Beacons National Park, drive west on the A40 to St David's. Situated in the heart of the Pembrokeshire Coast National Park, this is Britain's smallest cathedral town.

Follow the coast road, the A487, to the seaside town of Aberystwyth and the village of Machynlleth, on the southern edge of Snowdonia National Park. Located just outside Machynlleth, the Centre for Alternative Technology is an interesting place to visit.

Get an early start the next day and take the quickest route to the foot of Mount Snowdon, the second-highest peak in Britain. From Machynlleth, follow the A487 to Dolgellau, then the A470 and A487, turning off at Penrhyndeudraeth onto the A4085 to Beddgelert. From here take the A498 and the A4086, following signs for Llanberis.

To walk up Snowdon, stop by the youth hostel on the pass before Llanberis; if you're going to cheat and take the mountain railway to the top, continue into Llanberis. There are numerous B&Bs in this area.

From Llanberis it's about seven miles to Caernarfon, a run-down town dominated by a magnificent castle. Take the A487 and A55 east to Conwy, where there's another interesting castle, and spend the night in Llandudno, four miles north. This is a classic British seaside resort with rows of welcoming B&Bs.

To return to England, the A55 provides fast access to Chester, just over an hour's drive east.

---

to your right at roundabouts (traffic already on the roundabout has the right of way); and motorcyclists must wear helmets.

See Legal Matters in the Facts for the Visitor chapter for information on drink-driving rules.

Parking

Many places in Britain, big and small, could easily be overrun by cars. As a result, there are often blanket bans on, or at least active discrimination against, bringing cars into the centre. It's a good idea to go along with it even if sometimes you'll have to walk further. The parking will be easier and you'll enjoy a place more if it's not cluttered up with cars – yours and others. This particularly applies in small villages – park in the car parks, not on the street.

In bigger cities there will often be 'short-stay' and 'long-stay' car parks. Prices will often be the same for stays of up to two or three hours, but for lengthier stays the short-stay car parks rapidly become much more expensive. The long-stay car parks may be slightly less convenient but they're much cheaper.

A yellow line painted along the edge of the road indicates there are parking restrictions. The only way to establish the exact restrictions is to find the nearby sign that spells them out. A double line means no parking at any time; a single line means no parking for at least an eight-hour period between 7 am and 7 pm; and a broken line means there are some restrictions. In some cities there are also red lines, which mean no stopping or parking.

Rental

Rates are expensive in the UK; often you will be best off making arrangements in your home country for some sort of package deal. The big international rental companies charge from around £120 per week for a small car such as a Ford Fiesta or Fiat Punto.

The main companies include:

Avis	(☎ 606 0100)
Budget	(☎ 0541-565656)
Europcar	(☎ 0870 607 5000)
Hertz	(☎ 0870 844 8844)
National Car Rental	(☎ 0870 400 4502)
Thrifty Car Rental	(☎ 01494-751600)

When visiting the Scottish and Channel islands, it's usually cheaper to rent a car locally when you reach your island rather than paying for one to be transported over on the ferry.

Purchase

If you're planning to tour around Britain you may want to buy a vehicle. It's possible to get something reasonable for around £1000. Pick up a copy of *Loot* (five times weekly in London, less often elsewhere) or *Autotrader* (every Thursday) for adverts. The monthly *Motorists' Guide* lists models and their average prices.

All cars require a Ministry of Transport (MOT) safety certificate valid for one year and issued by a licensed garage; full third-party insurance – shop around but expect to pay at least £300; a registration form signed by both the buyer and seller, with a section to be sent to the MOT; and a licence disc proving you've paid your Vehicle Excise Duty (VED), a tax of £82.25/155 for six months/one year (£55/100 for a vehicle with an engine of 1100cc or less). The discs are sold at post offices on presentation of a valid MOT certificate, registration document and proof of insurance.

You're strongly advised to buy a vehicle

with a valid MOT certificate and a VED disc; both remain with the car through a change of ownership. Third-party insurance goes with the driver rather than the car, so you'll still have to arrange this (and beware of letting others drive the car unless they are listed on the policy). For further information contact a post office or a Vehicle Registration Office for leaflet V100.

Camper Van These provide a popular method of touring around the UK and the rest of Europe, particularly for shoestring travellers. Often three or four people will band together to buy or rent a van. Look for adverts in *TNT Magazine* if you wish to form or join a group.

Both *Autotrader* and *Loot* carry adverts for vans. The Van Market, in Market Rd N7 (off Caledonian Rd) in London, is a long-running institution where private sellers congregate on a daily basis. Some second-hand dealers offer a 'buy-back' scheme for when you return, but buying and reselling privately is better if you have the time in order to avoid the profits that must be diverted to the dealer.

Vans usually feature a fixed high-top or elevating roof and from two to five bunk beds. Apart from the essential camping gas cooker, professional conversions may include a sink, a fridge and built-in cupboards. You will need to spend a minimum of £1000 to £2000 for something reliable enough to get you around.

Motorcycle Touring

Britain is made for motorcycle touring, with good quality winding roads, and stunning scenery to stimulate the senses. Just make sure your wet-weather gear is up to scratch. Crash helmets are compulsory.

The Auto-Cycle Union (☎ 01788-566400, fax 01788-573585), ACU House, Wood Street, Rugby, Warwickshire CV21 2YX, publishes a very useful booklet about motorcycle touring in Britain.

Motoring Organisations

The two largest motoring organisations in the UK, both offering 24-hour breakdown assistance, are the Automobile Association (AA; ☎ 0800 444999) and the Royal Automobile Club (RAC; ☎ 0800 550550). One year's membership starts at £44 for the AA and £39 for the RAC, and both can also extend their cover to include continental Europe. Your motoring organisation at home may have a reciprocal arrangement with the AA or RAC.

BICYCLE
See Cycling in the Activities chapter.

HITCHING
Hitching is never entirely safe in any country in the world, and we don't recommend it. Travellers who decide to hitch should understand that they are taking a small but potentially serious risk. People who do choose to hitch will be safer if they travel in pairs and let someone know where they are planning to go.

Hitching is becoming less common in England. The same mutual suspicions between hitchers and drivers that exist elsewhere are becoming the norm. Given all the potential risks it hardly seems worth it. You may travel weeks and not see anyone hitching.

It's against the law to hitch on motorways or the immediate slip roads; make a sign and use approach roads, nearby roundabouts, or the service stations.

However, as is the case with so many other things, it's all a bit different in rural Scotland. On some of the Scottish islands, where public transport is infrequent, hitching is so much a part of getting around that local drivers may stop and offer you lifts without you even asking.

WALKING
See Walking in the Activities chapter.

BOAT
Refer to the various regional chapters for local services, such as those to islands in Scotland. If you plan to set sail yourself, see Canal & Waterway Travel in the Activities chapter.

LOCAL TRANSPORT
British cities usually have good public transport. The biggest problem you'll have is sorting through it: in another one of those anti-public transport initiatives by the former Conservative government, local buses throughout Britain were privatised with often shambolic results. Local governing bodies were disbanded and companies allowed to compete willy-nilly. In many towns, no one is quite sure who's running buses where. Fortunately London managed to retain overall control of its partially privatised system. It's actually easier to find your way around London by bus than Leeds!

Taxis
See the London chapter for info on the famous London taxis and their minicab competitors. Outside London and other big cities, taxis are usually reasonably priced. In rural areas you can expect to pay around £1.40 per mile, which means they are definitely worth considering as a means of reaching an out-of-the-way hostel, sight, or the beginning of a walk. A taxi over a short distance will often be very competitive with a local bus, especially if there are three or four people to share the cost. More importantly, when it's Sunday and you find that the next bus due to visit the charming town you've hiked to is on Monday, a taxi can get you to a transport hub for a reasonable cost.

ORGANISED TOURS
General Tours
Since travel is so easy to organise in Britain, there is very little need to consider a tour. Still, if your time is limited and/or you prefer to travel in a group, there are some interesting possibilities. The British Tourist Authority (BTA) has information in this respect (see also Backpackers Buses in the Bus section earlier in this chapter).

Drifters (☎ 020-7262 1292, fax 7706 2673), 22 Craven Terrace, London W2 3QH, runs day trips from London starting from £17, and longer trips lasting up to two weeks around Britain. The trips are aimed at people in their 20s. You can visit the Web site at www.driftersclub.com.

Contiki (☎ 020-7637 0802, fax 7637 2121), Royal National Hotel, Bedford Way, London WC1 H0DG, has trips aimed at young people that last from seven to 16 days. Further details can be obtained from the Web site at www.contiki.com.

Tracks (☎ 020-7937 3028, fax 01797-344164), The Flots, Brookland, Romney Marsh, Kent TN29 9TG, specialises in budget trips. Its UK tours range from day trips to three-day breaks. Check out the Web site at www.tracks-travel.com.

Shearings Holidays (☎ 01942-824824, fax 230949), Miry Lane, Wigan, Lancashire WN3 4AG, has a very wide range of four- to eight-day coach tours covering the whole country. Most of its trips are aimed at mature travellers.

For those aged over 60, Saga Holidays (☎ 0800 300500, fax 01303-776647), Saga Building, Middleburg Square, Folkestone, Kent CT20 1AZ, offers holidays ranging from cheap coach tours and resort holidays to luxury cruises around Britain. They have a Web site at www.saga.co.uk.

Nature Tours

In the national parks you can often join nature walks led by park wardens, sometimes free of charge; enquire at information centres for details. Seashore rambles can also be an enlightening experience if led by an expert.

Several different companies offer wildlife holidays which range from weekend breaks to longer residential courses, and include various activities ranging from nature rambles to bird-, fox- and badger-watching from special hide-outs.

The following are just a few possibilities. Enquire locally at TICs for more.

Wildlife Breaks (☎/fax 01926-842413, e oaktreefarm@btinternet.com), Oaktree Farm, Buttermilk Lane, Yarningale Common, Claverdon, Warwickshire CV35 8HP, organises tours where you can seek out badgers, birds, butterflies and other winsome creatures.

In the Peak District, Peak National Park Centre (☎ 01433-620373, fax 620346), Losehill Hall, Castleton, Derbyshire S30 2WB, has tours from one to three days aimed at wildlife enthusiasts as well as nature painters and walkers. You can visit the Web site at www.peakdistrict.org.

If you would like to volunteer to work on an environmental project in Britain, contact the British Trust for Conservation Volunteers (☎ 01491-821600, fax 821603), 36 St Mary's Street, Wallingford OX10 0EU.

Facts about England

England dominates both the political entity that is the United Kingdom and the geographical entity that is the island of Great Britain. Although the Scots and Welsh made an enormous contribution to the British Empire it was, and in some ways remains, an English empire.

England's position on the edge of continental Europe, removed but in many ways an integral part, has always created unique opportunities and problems. The pendulum has swung from isolation to integration and back again a number of times. In this era of the European Union (EU) and the Channel Tunnel, England is probably more European than it has been for 700 years.

Despite this, travellers will find a country where the institutions and symbols that had such an enormous role in shaping the modern world remain cherished and intact – from the monarchy to parliament, from the British Museum to Canterbury Cathedral, from Harrods to the market at Camden Lock, from Eton College to Oxford University, from Wembley Stadium to Lord's Cricket Ground. The list goes on and on.

Perhaps its most significant contribution, however, is the English language – anyone who uses the language has England at the foundation of their consciousness. This can make England seem strangely familiar, but beyond this first impression lies a foreign country that still has the ability to bewilder.

It's an overpopulated, crowded country so day-to-day life can be difficult and intense. The country's fertility has meant that it has supported a (relatively) large population for thousands of years. Every square inch of land has, in some way, been modified or altered by human activities. The result of this collaboration between humanity and nature is often breathtakingly beautiful, although 19th- and 20th- century capitalism has also produced some pretty grim and ugly industrial and urban developments.

A remarkable proportion of the country, however, remains unspoiled. There are few more seductive sights than the English countryside on a sunny day – the vivid greens, the silky air, the wildflowers, the ballooning trees, the villages, the grand houses and the soaring church spires.

HISTORY
Celts

England had long been settled by small bands of hunters when, around 4000 BC, a new group of immigrants arrived from Europe. Using stone tools, the new arrivals were the first to leave enduring marks on the island as they farmed the chalk hills radiating from Salisbury Plain. They also began the construction of stone tombs and, around 3000 BC, the great ceremonial complexes at Avebury and Stonehenge.

The next great influx involved the Celts, a people from central Europe who had mastered the smelting of bronze and, later, of iron. They started arriving around 800 BC and brought two forms of the Celtic language: the Gaelic, which is still spoken in Ireland and Scotland, and the Brythonic, which was spoken in England and is still spoken in Wales.

Romans

Julius Caesar made investigative forays into England in 55 and 54 BC, but the real Roman invasion didn't take place until nearly 100 years later in AD 43. Quite why the Romans decided to extend their power across the English Channel is unclear. It may have been that Emperor Claudius felt the need to display his military prowess, it may have been fear of the Celts in Britain joining forces with the Gauls in France, or it may simply have been the feeling that there was money to be made in England. The latter certainly turned out to be true, but the expense of obtaining it was horrible; the British holdings of the Romans never had the desired impact on the Empire's profit and loss account.

Claudius' forces crossed the channel to

Kent and before AD 50 they controlled England all the way to the Welsh border. The 'wretched British', as a Roman note discovered near Hadrian's Wall referred to them, did not give in easily and centurions had their hands full quelling the warlike Welsh and, between AD 60 and 61, the warrior queen Boudicca (aka Boadicea), who fought her way as far as Londinium, the Roman port on the present site of London. Nevertheless, opposition was essentially random and sporadic and posed no real threat to the well-organised Roman forces. In reality, the stability and wealth the Romans brought was probably welcomed by the general population, and by around AD 80 Wales and the north of England were under Roman control.

Scotland proved more tricky, and in 122 the Emperor Hadrian decided that the barbarians to the north were a lost cause – rather than conquer them, he'd settle for simply keeping them at bay. Accordingly, he ordered a wall to be built right across the country; to the south would be civilisation and the Roman Empire, to the north would be the savages. Only 20 years later, the Romans made another attempt at bringing the unruly northerners into line and constructed the Antonine Wall, farther north. This was soon abandoned and for nearly 300 years Hadrian's Wall marked the furthermost limit of the Roman Empire. Paved roads radiated from London to important regional centres – Ermine St ran north to Lincoln, York and Hadrian's Wall, and Watling St ran northwest to Chester.

The Romans brought stability and considerable economic advancement to Britain for nearly four centuries. After it was recognised by Emperor Constantine in 313, they also brought Christianity. By this time the Empire was already in decline, but the Romans were not driven out by the British, nor did they withdraw to fight fires closer to home. Britain was simply abandoned. Money stopped coming from Rome and, although the outposts stumbled on for some time, eventually they crumbled and were deserted. The end of Roman power in Britain is generally dated at around 410.

Anglo-Saxons & Viking Invasions

As Roman power faded, England went downhill. The use of money, once supplied by Rome, dwindled. As a result, trade declined, rural areas lost their population, travel became unsafe and local fiefdoms developed. Heathen Angles, Jutes and Saxons – Teutonic tribes originating from north of the Rhine – began to move into the vacuum created by the Roman departure. During the 5th century, these tribes advanced across what had been Roman England, absorbing the Celts so thoroughly that today most place names in England have Anglo-Saxon origins.

By the end of the 6th century, England had split into a number of Anglo-Saxon kingdoms, and by the 7th century these kingdoms had come to think of themselves collectively as English. The Celts, particularly in Ireland, kept Latin and Roman Christian culture alive. Christianity, a fragile late-Roman period import, may have declined at first but the arrival of St Augustine in 597 was followed by the swift spread of Augustinian missions.

As memories of Rome faded and the Celts merged with the Anglo-Saxons, England was divided into three strong kingdoms. In the 7th century, Northumbria was the dominant kingdom, extending its power far across the border into Scotland. In the 8th century, Mercia became stronger and King Offa marked a clear border between England and Wales, delineated by Offa's Dyke. Mercia's power eventually withered, to be replaced by that of King Egbert of Wessex, who was the first to rule all England. At the same time, the fierce northern Vikings inflicted a new round of attacks on the country.

In 865 an occupying Viking army moved in to conquer the Anglo-Saxon kingdoms. The Norwegian Vikings took northern Scotland, Cumbria and Lancashire, while the Danes conquered eastern England, making York their capital. They spread across England until, in 871, they were confronted by Alfred the Great of Wessex.

England was divided between the northern Danelaw and southern Wessex, the old Roman Watling St approximating the border.

ENGLAND

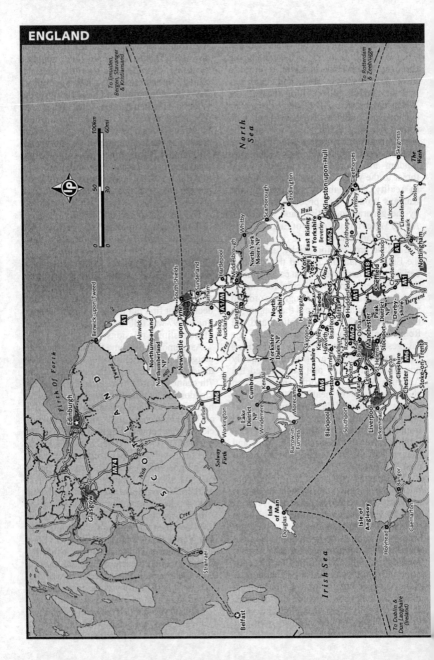

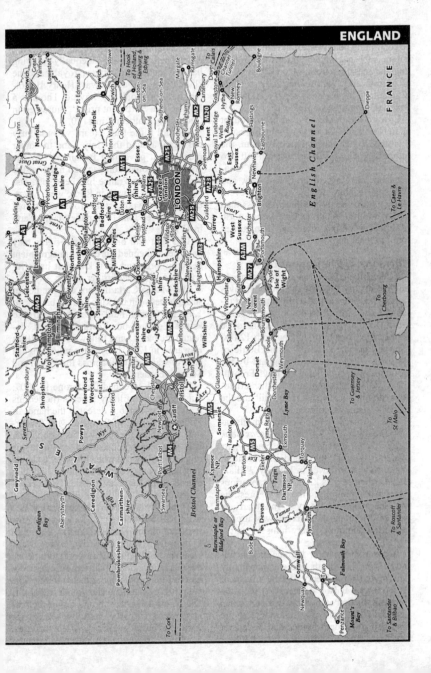

Alfred's successor, Edward the Elder, ended up controlling both Wessex and the Danelaw, but in subsequent generations control of England seesawed from Saxon (Edgar, king of Mercia and Northumberland) to Dane (Canute and his hopeless sons) and back to Saxon (Edward the Confessor).

Edward the Confessor had been brought up in Normandy – a Viking duchy in France – alongside his cousin Duke William, the future Conqueror. Edward's death left two contenders for the crown: Harold Godwineson, his English brother-in-law, and William, his Norman cousin. Harold eventually gained the throne but ruled less than a year, during which time he marched north to defeat a Viking invasion, then turned south to meet another.

Normans & Plantagenets

The year 1066 is of enormous importance in English history because the Norman invasion in that year capped a millennium of invasions and since then there have been no more. In that year William, soon to be dubbed the Conqueror, landed with 12,000 men and defeated Harold at the Battle of Hastings. The conquest of England by the Normans was completed rapidly; French-speaking Normans replaced English aristocrats, dominating castles were built and the feudal system was imposed.

The Normans were efficient administrators; already by 1085–6 the *Domesday Book* had provided a census of the country, its owners, its inhabitants and its potential. William I was followed in 1087 by William II and, when he was killed by a mysterious arrow while hunting in the New Forest, he was succeeded by Henry I. Intermarriage between Normans and Saxons was already becoming common, Henry himself marrying a Saxon princess.

A bitter struggle for the succession followed Henry I's death, and was not finally determined until Henry II (the Count of Anjou and grandson of Henry I) took the throne as the first of the Plantagenet Norman kings in 1154. Henry II had inherited more than half of modern France and his power actually surpassed that of the French king.

Not only was the enduring English habit of squabbling between royalty becoming established, but an almost equally enduring habit of squabbling between royalty and the church was also under way. Henry II blotted his copybook by having Thomas á Becket, that 'turbulent priest', murdered in Canterbury Cathedral in 1170.

Richard I, the Lion-Heart, was too busy crusading around the Holy Land to bother much about governing Britain and by the end of his brother John's reign much of the Norman land in France had been lost, disputes with the Church in Rome were never-ending and the powerful barons were so fed up they forced John to sign the Magna Carta in 1215.

This first real bill of human rights may have been intended purely as an agreement between lords and their king but its influence was to spread further afield.

The Magna Carta did not end the power struggle between the king and his barons. In 1265 the barons held both Henry III and Prince Edward, but Edward escaped, defeated the barons and followed Henry III as Edward I in 1272. During his reign English control was extended across the Welsh and Scottish borders.

Edward II ascended the throne in 1307, but his lack of military success (he led his army to a horrendous defeat at the hands of Robert the Bruce of Scotland), his favouring of personal friends over his barons and, it is said, his homosexuality brought his reign to a grisly end when his wife, Isabella, and her lover, Roger Mortimer, had him murdered in Berkeley Castle, Gloucestershire.

Things were scarcely better during Edward III's 50-year reign. His long rule saw the start of the Hundred Years' War with France in 1337 and the arrival of the Black Death in 1349. After a series of return bouts, the plague eventually carried off one and a half million people, more than a third of the country's population. The young Richard II had barely taken the throne before he was confronted with the Peasants' Revolt in 1381. Its brutal suppression led to unrest across an already deeply unsettled country.

As well as this clash between the peasantry and the ruling class, the 14th century saw considerable changes in society, exemplified by the rise of English in place of French, the language of the nobility.

In 1380, John Wycliffe made the first English translation of the Bible, but 150 years later William Tyndale was burned at the stake for daring to *print* the Bible in English.

Geoffrey Chaucer's *Canterbury Tales*, first published around 1387, was not only one of the first books to be written in English, it was also one of the first printed books.

The struggle to retain English control over territory in France was a prime cause of the Hundred Years' War, and to finance these adventures the Plantagenet kings had to concede a considerable amount of power to parliament, which jealously protected its traditional right to control taxation.

Houses of Lancaster & York

Richard II was an ineffectual king and in 1399 Henry IV seized the throne as the first king of the House of Lancaster. His father, John of Gaunt, one of the younger sons of Edward III, was not only the power behind the throne during Edward III's last years, but had also been the major influence on Richard II.

Henry IV was followed by Henry V, who decided it was time to stir up the dormant Hundred Years' War. He defeated the French at Agincourt and Shakespeare later ensured his position as one of the most popular English kings.

Henry VI ascended the throne as an infant and devoted himself to building works (King's College Chapel in Cambridge and Eton Chapel near Windsor) interspersed with bouts of insanity. When the Hundred Years' War finally ground to a halt in 1453, the English forces returned from France and threw their energies into the Wars of the Roses (the battle for control of the crown between the houses of Lancaster and York).

Once again it was a question of succession, with Henry VI represented by the red rose of Lancaster and Richard, Duke of York, by the white rose of York. Henry VI may have been helpless, but his wife, Margaret of Anjou, was made of different mettle and in 1460 her forces defeated and killed Richard, only for Richard's son Edward to turn the tables on her and her king a year later.

As Edward IV, he was the first Yorkist king, but he now had to contend with Richard Neville, the scheming earl of Warwick. Labelled 'the kingmaker', the earl teamed up with Margaret of Anjou to bring Henry VI back to the throne and shuttle Edward IV into exile in 1470. Then in 1471 Edward IV came bouncing back to defeat and kill the earl and capture Margaret and Henry. Soon after, Henry was mysteriously dispatched in the Tower of London.

Edward IV was a larger-than-life king but his 12-year-old son Edward V reigned for

Wars – a Hundred Years & the Roses

Wars are rarely what they seem. In recent times, WWI was the 'Great War' until WWII came along to give it a number. The Hundred Years' War was an on-again, off-again affair that effectively lasted for 116 years, from the first English success at Crécy to the final English realisation that they could not hold France as well as England. It's been suggested that the war was as much a French civil war as an Anglo-French conflict, but the struggle really resulted from the entangled English and French royal family lines and their conflicting spheres of control. The Black Death, shortage of funds and other 14th-century catastrophes combined to provide plentiful interruptions.

The Wars of the Roses were a similarly stop-and-start dispute, which only got their name nearly 400 years later, courtesy of romantic novelist Sir Walter Scott. It's been estimated that over the 30 years from 1455 until Henry VII grabbed the throne, actual 'war' only occupied 60 weeks. Medieval warfare was nothing like later blood-and-death struggles; damaging a rival economically by destroying villages and crops was as likely to be the policy as full-on fighting.

only two months in 1483 before being murdered, with his younger brother, in the Tower of London. Whether Richard III, their uncle and the next king, was their killer has been the subject of much conjecture, but few tears were shed when he was tumbled from the throne by Henry Tudor, first of the Tudor dynasty, in 1485.

Tudors

Henry VII, a Lancastrian descended on his mother's side from John of Gaunt, patched things up with the York side by marrying the daughter of Edward IV and arranged strategic marriages for his own children.

Matrimony may have been a more useful tool than warfare for Henry VII, but the multiple marriages of his successor, Henry VIII, were a very different story. Fathering an heir was Henry VIII's immediate problem and the church's unwillingness to cooperate with this quest led to the split with the Catholic church. Parliament made Henry the head of the Church of England and the Bible was translated into English. In 1536 Henry VIII 'dissolved' the smaller monasteries in Britain and Ireland, a blatant takeover of their land and wealth, as much as another stage in the struggle between church and state. The general populace felt little sympathy for the wealthy and often corrupt monasteries, and in 1539–40 another monastic land grab swallowed the larger ones as well. The property was sold or granted to members of the nobility, raising money for the king's military campaigns and ensuring the loyalty of his followers.

Nine-year-old Edward VI followed Henry VIII in 1547, but only ruled for six years. During his reign Catholicism declined and Protestantism grew stronger. His devoutly Catholic sister Mary I reversed that pattern, but she too only ruled for five years.

Elizabeth I, the third child of Henry VIII, seemed to have inherited a nasty mess of religious strife and divided loyalties, but her 45-year reign (1558–1603) saw a period of boundless English optimism epitomised by the defeat of the Spanish Armada, the global explorations of English seafarers, the expansion of trade, the literary endeavours of William Shakespeare and the scientific pursuits of Francis Bacon.

Stuarts & the Commonwealth Interlude

The one thing the Virgin Queen failed to provide was an heir, so she was succeeded by James I, first of the inflexible Stuart dynasty. Since he was already James VI of Scotland, he effectively united England, Scotland and Wales into one country. His attempts to smooth relations with the Catholics were set back by the anti-Catholic outcry that followed Guy Fawkes' Gunpowder Plot, an attempt to blow up parliament and king in 1605. The power struggle between monarchy and parliament became even more bitter during Charles I's reign, eventually degenerating into the Civil War which pitched the king's royalists (Cavaliers) against the parliamentarians (Roundheads). Catholics, traditionalist members of the Church of England and the old gentry supported Charles I, whose power base was the north and west. The Protestant Puritans and the new rising merchant class based in London and the towns of the south-east supported parliament.

The 1644–9 struggle resulted in victory for the parliamentary forces, the execution of Charles I and the establishment of the Commonwealth, ruled by Oliver Cromwell, the brilliant parliamentary military leader. A devastating and cruel rampage around Ireland starting in 1649 failed to exhaust his appetite for mayhem.

By 1653 he had also become fed up with parliament and as the 'Protector' assumed near dictatorial powers. Oliver Cromwell laid the foundation for the British Empire by modernising the army and navy and was followed half-heartedly by his son. But in 1660 parliament decided to re-establish the monarchy as the alternatives were proving far worse.

Charles II (the exiled son of Charles I) proved to be an able, though often utterly ruthless king who brought order out of chaos, and the Restoration foreshadowed a new burst of scientific and cultural activity after the strait-laced Puritan ethics of the

Kings & Queens

Nobody glancing at England's tempestuous story could ever claim that the country's history was dull. The position of king or queen of England (or perhaps worse, *potential* king or queen) would probably rank with being a drug dealer in a present-day American ghetto as one of history's least safe occupations. They've died in battle (an arrow through the eye for Harold II), been beheaded (Charles I), been murdered by a wicked uncle (Edward V at the age of 12) or been knocked off by their queen and her lover (Edward II, for whom a particularly horrible death was concocted as 'punishment' for his homosexuality).

The English monarchs have often been larger-than-life characters: wife abusers of the very worst kind like Henry VIII, sufferers from insanity like George III, even stutterers like George VI. And as for scandal, the current royal family's antics during the 1990s were only a fleeting shadow of what their predecessors got up

King Charles I: put on trial for treason and executed in 1649

to. Nor has it been left solely to the men. England has been led by some powerful women, from the day Queen Boudicca charged her chariot through the Romans, right down to Maggie Thatcher, who projected herself as a queen even if she wasn't one. The two most successful monarchs in English history were probably Elizabeth I and Victoria, and the hapless Henry VI was lucky to be married to Margaret of Anjou, who seemed to have a private army which she led with much greater aplomb than her husband.

Saxons & Danes
Alfred the Great 871–99
Edward the Martyr 975–9
Ethelred II (the Unready)
   979–1016
Canute 1016–35
Edward the Confessor
   1042–66
Harold II 1066

Normans
William I (the Conqueror)
   1066–87
William II (Rufus) 1087–1100
Henry I 1100–35
Stephen 1135–54

Plantagenet (Angevin)
Henry II 1154–89
Richard I (Lion-Heart) 1189–99
John 1199–1216
Henry III 1216–72
Edward I 1272–1307
Edward II 1307–27
Edward III 1327–77
Richard II 1377–99

Lancaster
Henry IV (Bolingbroke)
   1399–1413
Henry V 1413–22
Henry VI 1422–61 & 1470–71

York
Edward IV 1461–70 & 1471–83
Edward V 1483
Richard III 1483–5

Tudor
Henry VII (Tudor) 1485–1509
Henry VIII 1509–47
Edward VI 1547–53
Mary I 1553–8
Elizabeth I 1558–1603

Stuart
James I 1603–25
Charles I 1625–49

Commonwealth & Protectorate
Oliver Cromwell 1649–58
Richard Cromwell 1658–9

Restoration
Charles II 1660–85
James II 1685–8
William III (of Orange)
   1689–1702
Mary II 1689–94
Anne 1702–14

Hanover
George I 1714–27
George II 1727–60
George III 1760–1820
George IV 1820–30
William IV 1830–37
Victoria 1837–1901

Saxe-Coburg-Gotha
Edward VII 1901–10

Windsor
George V 1910–36
Edward VIII 1936
George VI 1936–52
Elizabeth II 1953–

Commonwealth. Colonies soon stretched down the American coast and the East India Company established its headquarters in Bombay.

Unfortunately, James II (1685–8) was not so far-sighted and his attempts to ease restrictive laws on Catholics ended with his defeat at the hands of William III, better known as William of Orange (the Dutch husband of Mary II, the Protestant daughter of James II). To take their joint throne, however, William and Mary had to agree to a Bill of Rights, and with the later Act of Settlement Britain was established as a constitutional monarchy with clear limits on the powers of the monarchy and a ban on any Catholic (or anyone married to a Catholic) ascending the throne.

Although William and Mary's Glorious Revolution of 1688 was relatively painless in Britain, the impact on Ireland, where the Protestant ascendancy dates from William's victory over James II at the Battle of the Boyne, laid the seeds for the troubles that have continued until now.

Mary died before William, who was followed by Anne (the second daughter of James II), but the Stuart line died with her in 1714. The throne was then passed to distant (but safely Protestant) German relatives.

Empire & Industry

In the 18th century, the Hanoverian kings increasingly relied on parliament to govern and from 1721 to 1742 Sir Robert Walpole became Britain's first prime minister in all but name. Bonnie Prince Charlie shattered this period of tranquillity in 1745, attempting to seize the throne, but this Jacobite Rebellion ended in disaster for Scotland at the Battle of Culloden.

Stronger English control over the British Isles was mirrored by even greater expansion overseas, where the British Empire absorbed more and more of America, Canada and India, and the first claims were made to Australia after Captain James Cook's epic voyage in 1768.

The Empire's first major reverse came when the American colonies won their independence in 1782. This setback led to a period of isolationism. During this time, Napoleon rose to power in France before naval hero Nelson and military hero Wellington curtailed, then ended, his expansion in 1815.

Meanwhile, at home, Britain was becoming the crucible of the Industrial Revolution. Canals (following the Bridgewater Canal in 1765), steam power (patented by James Watt in 1781), steam trains (launched by George Stephenson in 1830), the development of coal mines and water power transformed the means of production and transport and the rapidly growing towns of the Midlands became the first industrial cities.

Medical advances led to a dramatic increase in the population, but the rapid change from an agricultural to an industrial society caused great dislocation. Nevertheless, by the time Queen Victoria took the throne in 1837, Britain was the greatest power in the world. Britain's fleets dominated the seas, linking an enormous empire, and its factories dominated world trade.

Under Prime Ministers Disraeli and Gladstone, the worst excesses of the Industrial Revolution were addressed, education became universal, trade unions were legalised and the right to vote was extended to most men. Women didn't get the vote until after WWI.

Edwardian Era to WWII

Queen Victoria died in 1901 and the ever-expanding Britain of her era died with her. It wasn't immediately evident that a century of relative decline was about to commence when Edward VII, so long the king in waiting, ushered in the relaxed new Edwardian era. In 1914 Britain bumbled into the Great War (WWI), a war of stalemate and horrendous slaughter. It not only added trench warfare to the dictionary but also dug a huge trench between the ruling and working classes as thousands of ordinary men lost their lives at the behest of their commanding officers.

The old order was shattered and by the war's weary end in 1918 one million Britons had died and 15% of the country's accumulated capital had been spent. The euphoria of victory brought with it an extension of the right to vote to all men aged 21 and women aged 30 and over. It wasn't until 1928 that women were granted the same rights as men, despite Winston Churchill's opposition.

Political changes also saw the eclipse of the Liberal Party. It was replaced by the Labour Party which won power, albeit in coalition with the Liberals, for the first time in the 1923 election. James Ramsay MacDonald was the first Labour prime minister. A year later the Conservatives were back in power, but the rankling 'us and them' mistrust which had developed during the war, fertilised by soaring unemployment, flowered in the 1926 General Strike. When over half a million workers hit the streets, the heavy-handed government response included sending in the army which set the stage for the labour unrest that was to plague Britain for the next 50 years.

However, in the mid-1920s, it did look as if Britain had finally solved one centuries-old problem. The war had no sooner ended than Britain was involved in another struggle, the bitter Anglo-Irish War, that commenced in 1919 and ground to a halt in mid-1921, with Ireland finally achieving independence. Unhappily, the decision to divide the island in two was to have long-term repercussions.

The unrest of the 1920s worsened in the 1930s as the world economy slumped, ushering in a decade of misery and political upheaval. Even the royal family took a knock when Edward VIII abdicated in 1936 to marry a woman who was not only twice divorced but also American.

The less-than-charismatic George VI followed his brother Edward, but the scandal hinted at the prolonged trial by media the royal family would undergo 50 years later.

Britain dithered through the 20s and 30s with mediocre and visionless government failing to confront the country's problems. Meanwhile on the continent, the 30s saw the rise of imperial Germany under Adolf Hitler. By the time Prime Minister Neville Chamberlain returned from Munich in 1938 with a promise of 'peace in our time', the roller coaster was already rattling downhill to disaster. On 1 September 1939, Hitler invaded Poland and two days later Britain declared war.

WWII

German forces swept through France and pushed a British expeditionary force back to the beaches of Dunkirk in May/June 1940. Only an extraordinary flotilla of rescue vessels turned a disaster into a brave defeat. By mid-1940, the other countries of Europe were either ruled by or under the direct influence of the Nazis. Stalin had negotiated a peace agreement, the USA was neutral, and Britain, under Churchill's stirring leadership, was virtually isolated. Neville Chamberlain, reviled for his policy of appeasement, had stood aside to let Churchill lead a wartime national coalition government.

Between July and October 1940, the Royal Air Force withstood the Luftwaffe's bombing raids to win the Battle of Britain. Churchill's extraordinary exhortations inspired the country to resist and Hitler's invasion plans were blocked, although 60,000 civilian Britons were killed during the war.

As in WWI a stalemate ensued, although this time the English Channel was the trench between the opposing forces. But, as in

Never at a loss for words:
Sir Winston Churchill (1874–1965)

WWI, the entry of the USA into the conflict tipped the balance. In December 1941, Japanese forces invaded Malaya and just hours later, bombed the US fleet in Pearl Harbour.

The British colony of Hong Kong fell within days and Singapore fell by February, but in Europe the arrival of American forces and the bitter fighting in Russia, which Hitler had invaded in June 1941, began to change things round. In late 1942, German forces were defeated in North Africa and the 1940–41 raids on England were answered with Allied raids on Germany in 1942–3. Tragically, the Allied forces mirrored the German decision to bomb cities rather than military targets, resulting in huge civilian losses which failed to cripple Hitler's war machine.

By 1944 Germany was in retreat, the Allies had complete command of the skies and the long-awaited D-day invasion took place on the Normandy beaches in June 1944. Meanwhile, the Red Army was pushing back the Nazi forces from the east. In May 1945 it was all over for the Nazis. Hitler was dead, Germany a smoking ruin, and Europe was to suffer new divisions which would last for nearly 50 years. Three months later, two atomic bombs forced the surrender of Japan and ended WWII.

Postwar Reconstruction

Fortunately there was greater postwar wisdom in 1945 than in 1918. The Marshall Plan, which helped rebuild an economically strong Europe, stood in stark contrast to the post-WWI demands for reparations. An electorate hungry for change tumbled Churchill from power and ushered in the Labour Party's Clement Attlee.

In the 1930s the brilliant economist John Maynard Keynes had suggested that government could and should influence the economy, adding the term Keynesian Economics to the dictionary; his ideas on economics were also a factor in the much lower levels of unemployment that followed the war. Nationalisation of key industries, government manipulation of the economy and the institution of the National Health Service were all part of the creation of the post-war welfare state, but rebuilding after the damage of the war was to be a slow process.

The postwar baby boomers experienced rationing and belt-tightening for many years after hostilities ceased. Britain's depleted reserves also had to cope with the retreat from empire as one by one the colonies became independent: India in 1947, Malaya in 1957 and Kenya in 1963. In 1953 Elizabeth II became queen, she is now the world's second-longest reigning monarch.

Postwar Britain was a less powerful nation but the recovery was still sufficiently strong for Prime Minister Harold Macmillan to boast in 1957 that most people in Britain had 'never had it so good'.

Swinging 60s to the Thatcher Years

By the 1960s the wartime recovery was really complete, the last vestiges of the empire had been sloughed off and the Beatles era suddenly made grey old England a livelier place. On the surface the economy also looked stronger and more resilient, but even though Harold Wilson's Labour Party seemed to be doing the right things it was building on shaky foundations. The 1970s brought the oil crisis, inflation and increased international competition, a combination that quickly revealed the British economy's inherent weaknesses.

Everything in Britain eventually comes down to class and the long struggle between a disgruntled working class and an inept ruling class finally boiled over in the 70s.

Neither Labour, under Wilson and Jim Callaghan, nor the Conservatives, under Ted Heath, proved capable of controlling the industrial strife of 1974, and its repercussions later in the decade finally brought drastic change. In the 1979 election the 'Iron Lady', Margaret Thatcher, led the Conservatives to power and ushered in the tough new era of Thatcherism.

Her solutions were brutal and their consequences are still being debated today. British workers and their unions were obstructive and Luddite? She broke them. British companies were inefficient and unimaginative? She drove them to the wall.

The postwar nationalised companies were a mistake? Like Henry VIII dissolving the monasteries, she sold them off. To the horror of those who thought a female leader would be more pacific than a man, she led Britain into battle after Argentina invaded the Falkland Islands in 1982.

The new harder working, more competitive Britain was also a polarised Britain, with a new trench dug between the people who prospered from the Thatcher years and the many others who found themselves not only jobless but jobless in a harsher environment. Despite the evident dislike of a large slice of the population, by 1988 Thatcher was the longest serving British prime minister of the 20th century. Her repeated electoral victories were aided by the Labour Party's dark days of destructive internal struggles.

Through to the New Millennium

The unpopular flat-rate poll tax reached even her own party's limits of tolerance, and in 1990 Thatcher was dumped by her party in favour of John Major. Unfortunately for the Labour Party, the immense reserves of suspicion they had managed to bank up were enough to see Major win the 1992 election. But the end came with a vengeance in 1997 when New Labour, under Prime Minister Tony Blair, rocketed to power with a record parliamentary majority of more than 170 seats.

In its early days, the government disappointed many old Labour stalwarts by keeping a tight reign on public spending. Voters, hoping for immediate improvements in the creaking health and transportation sectors that the Tories had allowed to run down, were disappointed by a lack of progress. The Blair government also had a series of damaging miscues of which the most comic and embarrassing was their attempt to stage-manage the election for London's mayor. This back-fired horribly.

However, the government did follow through on promises to allow for constitutional reform and devolution, at least in part, in Scotland and Wales. These changes will have far-reaching effects for decades to come.

In 2000, the Blair government finally opened up the taps on public expenditure, with billions promised for health, transportation and education. With talk turning to the next election, it will remain to be seen if voters think the promised improvements are too little too late. Tony Blair could take some comfort from the fact that leader of the Conservative opposition was William Hague, a little-loved leader who tried to soften his staid image by wearing an American-style baseball cap. It didn't work.

GEOGRAPHY

Covering 50,085 square miles, England is the largest of the three political divisions within the island of Great Britain. Bound by Scotland to the north and Wales to the west, England is no more than 20 miles from France across the narrowest part of the English Channel. However, now that the Channel Tunnel has been completed, it's no longer completely cut off from mainland Europe.

Much of England is flat or low-lying. The highest point (Scafell Pike in Cumbria) is only 978m above sea level; Scotland and Wales have more mountains and higher peaks.

England can be divided into four main geographic areas. In the north of the country a ridge of limestone hills and valleys, known as the Pennines, stretches from Derbyshire 250 miles north to the border with Scotland. To the west are the Cumbrian Mountains and the Lake District, probably the best known of Britain's national parks.

South of the Pennines is the heavily populated central area known as the Midlands, the industrial heartland since the 19th century. At its centre is Birmingham, Britain's second-largest city after London. The Black Country stretches from north of Birmingham through Staffordshire to Wolverhampton.

The south-west peninsula, known as the West Country and including Cornwall, Devon, Dorset and parts of Somerset, is a plateau with granite outcrops and a rugged coastline. A high rainfall and rich pastures provide good dairy farming – Devon cream is world-famous. The numerous sheltered coves and beaches, and the mild climate make the West Country a favourite holiday destination for the British. The wild grass-covered moors of Dartmoor and Exmoor are popular with walkers.

The rest of the country is known geographically as the English Lowlands, which are a mixture of farmland, low hills, an industrial belt and densely populated cities, including the capital. The eastern part of this region, including Lincolnshire and East Anglia (Norfolk, Suffolk and Cambridgeshire), is almost entirely flat and at sea level. The Fens are the rich agricultural lands, once underwater but drained in the 18th century, that extend from Lincoln to Cambridge.

London is in the south-east of the country, on the River Thames. Farther south are hills of chalk known as downs. The North Downs stretch from the south of London to Dover where the chalk is exposed as the famous white cliffs. The South Downs run across Sussex, parallel to the south coast.

CLIMATE

Climatologists classify England's climate as temperate maritime – read mild and damp.

Despite the country being fairly far north, temperatures in England are moderated by light winds that blow in off seas warmed by the Gulf Stream. In winter, when the sea is

warmer than the land, this stops temperatures inland falling very far below 0°C. In summer, when the sea is cooler than the land, it keeps temperatures from rising much above 30°C. The average high in London from June to August is 21°C; the average low is 12°C.

Variations in the weather across England are not as great as across Britain. It tends to be colder in the north but not as cold as in Scotland. London, the south-east and the West Country are the warmest regions.

Rainfall is greatest in hilly areas (the Lake District and the Pennines) and in the West Country. Some of these areas can get up to 4500mm of rain a year. The eastern side of England gets the lowest amount of rain in the whole of the UK. Some parts of Essex and Kent have recorded an annual rainfall of less than 600mm.

You can, however, expect some cloudy weather and rain anywhere in Britain at any time. An umbrella or raincoat are recommended. A large plastic cycling cape can be useful even if you're not on a bike, since it can be worn over a backpack. Come prepared and you needn't find the weather as depressing as the locals do – the 50% of Brits who said in a recent survey that they'd emigrate if given the chance cited the climate as the main reason.

ECOLOGY & ENVIRONMENT

In a place as small as England, with its long history of human occupation, it's hardly surprising that the way the countryside looks today is largely the result of human interaction with the environment. As the population has grown, so too have the demands made upon the land to yield more food, firewood and building materials. This has led to the extinction of unknown numbers of plant and animal species.

Since WWII the pattern of land use in England has changed dramatically, with a similarly dramatic effect on wildlife. Modern farming methods have changed the lie of the land in some places from a cosy patchwork of small fields separated by thick hedgerows to vast open cultivated areas. As well as protecting fields from erosion, hedgerows

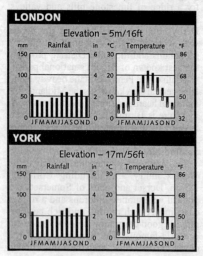

provide habitat for wildlife and shelter for other plant species. Tens of thousands of miles of hedgerows have been destroyed and their destruction continues – since 1984, over 25% of hedgerows have disappeared.

The general reduction in England's biodiversity over the last 50 years has numerous other causes, including the increased use of pesticides, blanket planting of conifers in areas such as the North York Moors National Park (see the Flora section later) and huge road-building schemes. For many years government policy favoured road over rail, allocating billions of pounds a year to new roads and encouraging private car ownership. Vehicle numbers have nearly quadrupled over the last 30 years. The problem is so bad that pressure groups have been established, dedicated to preventing new road construction and to stopping cars using existing roads.

Tourism is also taking a terrible toll on the environment. Eight million day-trippers a year flock to the New Forest in Hampshire, eroding the soil, churning up meadows and generally disturbing the wildlife. Most come by car. It's a similar story in parts of the Lake District and the Peak District, England's most visited national park. Slowly the authorities are realising that better public transport will have to be provided if these problems are to be resolved.

Despite all this bad news, large tracts of the country are also protected as nature reserves, national parks and Sites of Special Scientific Interest (SSSIs) where development is restricted.

Britain also has hundreds of wildlife and environmental groups. For more information try Greenpeace (☎ 020-7865 8100, fax 7865 8200, ✉ info@uk.greenpeace.org), Canonbury Villas, London N1 2PN. Or visit the Web site at www.greenpeace.org.uk.

Friends of the Earth (☎ 020-7490 1555, fax 7490 0881), 26–28 Underwood St, London N1 7JQ, is another good source for information and contacts. Its Web site is at www.foe.co.uk.

To find out more about the problems posed by tourism, contact Tourism Concern (☎ 020-7753 3330, fax 7753 3331), Stapleton House,

277–281 Holloway Rd, London N7 8HN. The Web address is www.tourismconcern .org.uk.

Other groups are The Royal Society for the Protection of Birds (RSPB; ☎ 01767-680551), The Lodge, Sandy, Beds SG19 2DL, and The Wildlife Trusts (☎ 01636-677711), The Kiln, Waterside, Mather Rd, Newark, Notts NG24 1WT. They have Web sites at www.rspb.org.uk and www.wildlife trust.org.uk respectively. Also, see Useful Organisations in the Facts for the Visitor chapter for details of the National Trust.

Pollution

The UK has been a perennial loser on the EU's list of countries with polluted beaches and finished 13th out of the 15 EU nations in the annual survey released in 2000. Most of the UK's polluted beaches are in England, with the EU singling out 15 in Cornwall and Devon for failing to meet minimum standards. The popular beach resort of Blackpool was on the list as well. Much of England's problems with the EU water-testers stem from the long practice of dumping raw sewage into the ocean. This practice – more commonly associated with the Third World – has been widespread in England. Only in recent years have major efforts been made to stem this flow.

More sinister than sewage (if you can imagine that!) is the waste water discharged into the Irish Sea from the nuclear fuel plant at Sellafield, on the Cumbrian coast near the Lake District. Run by British Nuclear Fuels Ltd (BNFL), a government-owned company, the complex takes nuclear fuel used by other nuclear power plants in Britain and elsewhere and reprocesses it into new fuel which can be used again. As part of the process it uses over a million gallons of water each day. This water, which becomes slightly radioactive, is then dumped back into the Irish Sea. Needless to say, the Irish aren't happy about this and have called for the plant's immediate closure. However, the British government, mindful of the huge fortune of public money that has been invested at Sellafield, will only commit to reducing the radioactivity of the discharged water to 'near to zero' by 2020.

Other problems have involved radioactive discharges into the air and in one tragic incident, it was found that pigeons roosting in abandoned but still radioactive buildings had spread radioactive contamination throughout village playgrounds where people fed them.

Elsewhere in England there are many concerns over the large number of ageing nuclear power plants, some of which have been operating for 10 or more years past their original design life.

FLORA & FAUNA
Flora
England was once almost entirely covered with woodland, but gradually tree coverage fell until it was the lowest of all European countries except Ireland. As long ago as 1919, the Forestry Commission drew up a long-term plan to plant two million hectares of trees by the year 2000, a target already achieved by the early 1980s as a result of substantial grants to landowners. Unfortunately, the trees planted were mainly fast-growing conifers instead of indigenous broadleaves. Very little can grow beneath conifers and large areas of ancient peatland were destroyed to create the plantations. These problems have now been recognised and more broadleaf woods are being planted. An ambitious programme to create forests on the perimeter of big cities is also well under way.

Apart from the vast stands of conifers (mainly in northern England, Scotland and Wales), other trees common in England include the oak, chestnut, lime (not the citrus variety), ash and beech.

Despite the continued destruction of plant habitat, there's still a wide variety of wildflowers, particularly in spring. Small white snowdrops are the first to flower, sometimes as early as February. Around Easter (late March or early April), parks around the country are bright with daffodils. In woodlands there are purple carpets of bluebells; yellow primroses, buttercups and cowslips are common in meadows. Tall purple foxgloves flower from June to September.

In summer, cultivated fields may be edged with red poppies and you can hardly fail to notice the oilseed rape crop that turns fields brilliant yellow as it flowers.

Gorse bushes, with small yellow flowers and a mass of sharp spines instead of leaves, flourish on heaths and other rough sandy places. Found in the same habitat, broom is very similar, though lacking the prickles. Fern-like bracken is also common.

The moors nurture several varieties of flowering heathers, bracken and whortleberries (also known as bilberries) growing on small shrubs. These tiny blue-black berries are good to eat when they ripen in the summer.

A classic plant identification book is *The Concise British Flora in Colour*, with 1486 beautifully accurate paintings of different species by artist-vicar William Keble Martin.

Fauna
There are over 100 protected animal species in Britain, but the once common beaver, wolf and reindeer are now extinct.

The red deer is England's largest mammal, with herds found on Exmoor and Dartmoor and in the Lake District. Fallow deer, introduced long ago by the Romans, live in small herds of 20 or so animals and can still be seen in the New Forest and Epping Forest. Roe deer are smaller, about the size of a large goat, and are quite common in forest areas where they do considerable damage to young trees. Other species that have been introduced include the Asian muntjac and the Chinese water deer. As England's forest cover is spreading, so the number of deer is increasing.

There are large numbers of foxes, especially in urban areas – they can even be found prowling in the allies of London. Although nocturnal, the fox can often be seen before dark scavenging around rubbish bins. Badgers are much more shy and although their setts (burrows) may be seen in woods, they only come out at night. Another animal that you're more likely to see as a roadside casualty is the equally nocturnal hedgehog.

The grey squirrel, introduced from North America, is very common and has almost entirely replaced the smaller red squirrel. Having escaped – or been released by

JANE SMITH

The common hedgehog: its spiny quills were used during surgery in the late 19th century

animal rights protesters – from fur farms, the foreign mink is prospering. Otter numbers are also rising as Britain's rivers are cleaned up and recently they have been spotted on the outskirts of several big cities. Once very rare, the pine marten is again being seen in some forested regions. Stoats and weasels are rarely encountered.

Rabbits are extremely common; the brown hare, with longer legs and ears, less so. Small species of rodent include the brown rat (originally from Asia), the tiny shrew and harvest mouse (once common in hedgerows) and the water vole (water rat). At dusk, bats sometimes put in an appearance in rural areas.

Two species of seal – the grey seal and the common seal, which is actually less common than the grey – frequent the English coast.

England's only venomous snake is the adder, also known as the viper, which inhabits dry and ferny places on heaths and moors; numbers had fallen from hundreds of thousands to less than 20,000 before it was added to the list of protected species. Other reptiles include the harmless grass snake, the slowworm, the common lizard, and amphibians such as frogs, toads and newts.

Among England's various fish species, the salmon and brown trout are best known. See Fishing in the Activities chapter.

Birds Bird-watching is a popular pastime in Britain where the mild climate and varied landscape support a wide variety of species.

While coastal bird species seem to be doing well, the same can't be said for inland species. Several species that were quite common only 30 years ago are rapidly dwindling as their habitats are destroyed. Endangered species now include the tree sparrow, corn bunting, yellow wagtail, turtle dove, bullfinch, song thrush and lapwing. On the other hand, goldfinches, swallows, nuthatches and greater spotted woodpeckers are making a comeback.

England's back gardens harbour the sparrow, thrush, blackbird, blue tit (yellow front, blue/white head) and the easily recognisable red-breasted robin. Pigeons are so abundant that they're now considered a pest, particularly in cities (just try eating outside the National Film Theatre in London if you don't believe this). Crows are very common, as is the black and white magpie, another member of the crow family.

Skylarks are becoming less common each year, but you can still hear them twittering high above open ground. The once common tawny owl recently joined them on the list of endangered birds.

Lakes and inland waterways support all sorts of bird life. The mute swan is Britain's biggest bird. All swans, except for two groups on the River Thames, are said to belong to the monarch. Unfortunately swans have died from lead poisoning after swallowing discarded fishing weights.

The aggressive Canada goose, introduced 300 years ago, has bred so successfully that it's now seen as a menace; large numbers of them can strip fields of crops, and that's not to mention their droppings.

Of the several species of duck, the mallard is most common. The male, with green head and narrow white collar, is easily identified.

The pheasant was introduced from Russia over 900 years ago and, while reared on large estates for shooting, now also breeds in the wild. Other game birds include the partridge and grouse.

Raptors are now rare. There are a few heavily protected golden eagles in the Lake District. Kestrels and sparrowhawks are sometimes seen hunting near motorways.

Around the coast are large populations of seagulls, terns, cormorants, gannets, shags, razorbills and guillemots. The tiny, comical puffin, with its clumsy red-and-yellow bill, is a member of the auk family. It comes to land only to breed, which it does in numerous colonies across the length of the British Isles from the Isle of Wight to the Shetland Islands.

Twitchers (or bird-watchers) should contact the Royal Society for the Protection of Birds (RSPB; ☎ 01767-680551), The Lodge, Sandy, Bedfordshire SG19 2BR, which runs over 100 reserves. It has a Web site at www .rspb.org.uk.

Membership of the Wildfowl and Wetlands Trust (☎ 01453-891900, ⓔ membership@ wwt.org.uk), Slimbridge, Gloucestershire GL2 7BT, gives free entry to its reserves. Its Web site is at www.wwt.org.uk.

Bird-watching – and not the kind discussed on *Men Behaving Badly* – is so popular in England that bookshop shelves groan under the loads of twitcher guides.

National Parks

England's national parks – Dartmoor, Exmoor, the Lake District, the Peak District, the Yorkshire Dales, the North York Moors and Northumberland – cover about 7% of the country. The New Forest and the Broads have also been given national park status.

But unlike national parks in some other countries, England's are not wilderness areas where humans have been excluded. Nor are they owned by the nation; most of the land within the national parks is privately owned or belongs to charitable trusts such as the National Trust (see Useful Organisations in the Facts for the Visitor chapter). However, they also include places of outstanding natural beauty that have been given special protection through a 1949 act of parliament.

National park status doesn't guarantee visitors any special rights of access. It does, however, mean that development is controlled through planning committees and that information centres and recreational facilities are provided for visitors.

For more information, contact the individual parks of the Association of National Park Authorities (☎ 01647-440245, fax 440187), Ponsford House, Moretonhamp-

stead, Devon TQ13 8NL. Or you could visit the Web site at www.anpa.gov.uk.

GOVERNMENT & POLITICS

At present the United Kingdom doesn't have a written constitution but operates under a mixture of parliamentary statutes, common law (a body of legal principles based on precedents dating back to Anglo-Saxon customs) and convention.

The monarch is the titular head of state, but the current queen is a mere figurehead who acts almost entirely on the advice of 'her' ministers and parliament.

Parliament is made up of three separate elements – the queen, the House of Commons and the House of Lords. In practice, the supreme body is the House of Commons, which is directly elected every five years. An earlier election can be called at the request of the party in power, or if the party in power loses a vote of confidence.

Voting is not compulsory, and candidates are elected if they win a simple majority in their constituencies (a committee is currently considering whether Britain should change to some form of proportional representation). There are 659 constituencies (seats) – 529 for England, 40 for Wales, 72 for Scotland and 18 for Northern Ireland.

The House of Lords consists of the Lords Spiritual (26 senior bishops of the Church of England) and 12 law lords who act as the UK's highest court. In addition, for a time in 2000 there were 92 hereditary peers (titles that passed from one generation to the next) as well as 10 members granted life peerages by Tony Blair. However this is an interim set-up as the government ponders reform of the House of Lords. In a dramatic move, over 1000 hereditary peers were tossed out of the House of Lords in 1999. In a compromise move, the 92 hereditary peers were allowed to remain, having been selected by the entire House of Lords before most members left for good.

The prime minister has the power to appoint lifetime peers, that is members of the House of Lords who may serve for life, but who cannot pass the privilege on. Exactly what form the next stage will take is unclear.

There is general support to make the House of Lords some sort of directly elected body, but that's as far as reform has progressed. At present it remains a deeply undemocratic body with few powers beyond the ability to hold up and amend legislation.

The prime minister is the leader of the majority party in the House of Commons and is technically appointed by the queen. All other ministers are appointed on the recommendation of the prime minister, most of them coming from the House of Commons. Ministers are responsible for government departments. The senior 20 or so ministers make up the Cabinet, which, although answerable to parliament, meets confidentially and in effect manages the government and its policies.

For the last 150 years a predominantly two-party system has operated. Since 1945 either the Conservative Party (also known as the Tory party) or the Labour Party has held power, the Conservatives drawing support mainly from the countryside and suburbia, Labour from urban industrialised areas, Scotland and Wales.

Traditionally, the Conservatives were regarded as right-wing, free-enterprise supporters, while Labour was left-wing in the social-democratic tradition. However, in the 1990s Labour shed much of its socialist credo and accepted many of the arguments of the free-marketers. The New Labour government that was elected in 1997 has proven to be quite centrist. It's adopted many of the market reforms long favoured by moderate conservatives.

Since 1972 Britain has been a member of the EU, albeit rather grudgingly. The result is that some British legislation now originates in Brussels rather than London. In general British governments have resisted moves to closer integration with Europe. The current Labour government has promised a referendum before Britain will start using the single European currency (the euro). However this is emerging as the most contentious issue in modern British politics, with the Tories engaging in all sorts of euro-scare tactics in the hope of saving the pound and thereby winning votes. Industry and business is solidly for the euro as sticking with the strong pound makes British products uneconomic to customers in euro-priced Europe.

ECONOMY

Britain dominated 19th-century world trade but when the 20th century dawned, decline was already under way. Britain had been the pioneering influence in many of the 19th century's leading engineering fields, from railways to ocean liners, but it didn't enjoy the same dominant role when it came to 20th-century developments such as automobiles and aircraft. Following WWII, much of industry was nationalised as initially railways, gas and electricity services, coal mines, steel manufacturing and shipbuilding, and later even cars, came under government control. If anything, public ownership only accelerated the decline until the worldwide upheavals in manufacturing in the 1970s and 80s turned gradual fall into precipitous drop. Meanwhile, many traditional areas of activity, such as mining and engineering, simply disappeared and only North Sea oil shielded Britain from a disastrous economic crash.

For better for worse Margaret Thatcher waged a relentless assault on the power of the trade unions and the old-school-tie brigade and their ossified work and business practices. Although huge changes and social upheavals were the result, by 1992 Britain's economy was in such poor shape that the government was forced to withdraw from the European Exchange Rate Mechanism. Politically this was a disaster, but economically it marked a turning point; exchange rates fell and exporters found business looking up again in the face of a devalued pound.

The Labour government had the good fortune to come to power at a time when the British economy was gaining strength. Although not as buoyant as the US economy across the pond, the British economy showed solid, long-term growth. Early in 2000 it was announced that the number of unemployed had fallen below one million for the first time since the boom years of 1975. Although the figure is debatable and many jobs are part-time, it still points to what in many places has become a job-seekers market. Along the M4 motorway west from London, there are towns with less than 1% unemployment. High-tech and service jobs account for much of the growth.

In the Midlands and the north of England there are still pockets of economic depression, especially in places that never recovered from the collapse of heavy industry in the 1980s. Many fear that England's southeast will continue to grow while the north stagnates.

POPULATION & PEOPLE

Britain has a population of around 60 million, or around 625 inhabitants per sq mile, making the island one of the most crowded on the planet. Most of the population is concentrated in England (which has a population of 51 million), in and around London, and in the Midlands around Birmingham, Manchester, Liverpool, Sheffield and Nottingham. To these figures you can factor in an annual influx of about 26 million tourists.

The Brits are a diverse bunch, as one would expect given the variety of peoples who have made this island their home. But in general the dominant Anglo-Saxons, as they are sometimes called, are predominantly Germanic/Scandinavian in origin.

Particularly since the Industrial Revolution, England has attracted large numbers of people from Scotland, Wales and Ireland. In the 18th, 19th and 20th centuries there were also significant influxes of refugees, most recently from troubled corners of the globe such as Somalia and eastern Turkey.

Since WWII there has also been significant immigration from many ex-colonies, especially the Caribbean, Pakistan and India. Outside London and the big Midlands cities, however, the population is overwhelmingly Anglo-Saxon, although the immigrant influence can be felt in the Chinese and Indian restaurants, found in even the smallest of towns. Recently, population growth has been virtually static, even negative, and emigrants have often outnumbered immigrants. See Society & Conduct later in the chapter.

EDUCATION

Schooling is compulsory for those aged between 5 and 16, and an increasing number of young people stay on at school (or sixth-form college or further education college) until they're 18. Education for those aged up to 18 is free. The number of people going on to university (and the number of universities) has also been growing, putting such pressure on funding that the government now expects students to pay their own tuition and living fees by taking out loans.

Despite what should sound a fairly rosy scenario, there's a widely held perception that education standards have been falling, with hotly disputed figures suggesting a rise in the number of people escaping 11 years of compulsory schooling unable to read or write properly. Along with the euro, the National Health Service and transport, education remains at the top of the English political agenda.

ARTS

The greatest artistic contributions of the English have been in theatre, literature and architecture. Although there are notable exceptions, there's not an equivalent tradition of great painters, sculptors or composers.

Perhaps the most distinctive phenomenon is the huge number of extraordinary country houses. Waited-on hand and foot, the elite of a mighty empire, the aristocrats of the 18th and 19th centuries surrounded themselves with treasures in the most beautiful houses and gardens of Europe.

Fortunately, although their successors have often inherited the arrogance intact, inheritance taxes have forced many to open their houses and priceless art collections to the public. England is a treasure house of masterpieces from every age and continent. The architectural heritage is superb but, with a few exceptions, the 20th century failed to add anything more inspiring than motorways, high-rise housing estates and tawdry suburban development.

British publishers churn out 80,000 new titles a year, and the range and quality of theatre, music, dance and art is outstanding.

Literature

Anyone who has studied 'English' literature will discover that the landscapes and people they have read about can still be found to some extent. Travelling in the footsteps of the great English, Scottish and Welsh writers, and their characters, can be one of the highlights of visiting Britain. A wealth of books capture a moment in time, a landscape, or a group of people. This guide can only make a few suggestions as to where to start.

Literature classes usually begin with *Beowulf*, the epic Anglo-Saxon poem written between the 7th and 8th centuries. A new verse translation of the struggle between the heroic Scandinavian king and the monster Grendel was published in 2000 by Seamus Heaney, the Irish Nobel Prize winner.

Geoffrey Chaucer's *Canterbury Tales* (modern translation by Neville Coghill) is another starting-off point, written in the 14th century. This book may have launched a thousand boring lectures, but in its natural environment it gives a vivid insight into medieval society, in particular into the lives of pilgrims on their way to Canterbury.

A further blight on schoolchildren's lives is the literary genius of William Shakespeare, recognised as probably the world's greatest dramatist. Many will be tempted to retrace his steps – to Stratford-upon-Avon where he lived – and to the new Globe Theatre in London, near the site where his works were originally performed.

The most vivid insight into 17th-century London life comes courtesy of Samuel Pepys' diary, which contains a complete account of the plague and the Great Fire of London. Society was satirised in works such as Alexander Pope's *Rape of the Lock* and Jonathan Swift's *Gulliver's Travels*.

The popular English novel, as we know it, only appeared in the 18th century with the growth of a literate middle class. If you plan to spend time in the Midlands, read Elizabeth Gaskell's *Mary Barton*, which paints a sympathetic picture of the plight of workers during the Industrial Revolution. This was also the milieu about which Charles Dickens wrote most powerfully.

Hard Times, set in fictional Coketown, paints a brutal picture of the capitalists who prospered in it.

Jane Austen wrote about the prosperous, provincial middle class. The intrigues and passions boiling away under the stilted constraints of 'propriety' are beautifully portrayed in *Emma* and *Pride and Prejudice*. Her grave is in Winchester Cathedral.

If you visit the Lake District, you'll find constant references to William Wordsworth, the influential poet who lived there for the first half of the 19th century. His early work saw the beginning of the Romantic movement in English poetry, conveying an exhilirating appreciation of the natural world.

More than most writers, Thomas Hardy depended on a sense of place and on the relationship between place and people. His best work is an evocative picture of Wessex, the region of England centred on Dorchester (Dorset) where he lived. *Tess of the d'Urbervilles* is one of his greatest novels.

Moving into the 20th century, DH Lawrence chronicled life in the Nottinghamshire coal-mining towns in the brilliant *Sons and Lovers*.

Written during the 1930s Depression, George Orwell's *Down and Out in Paris and London* describes the author's destitute existence as a temporary vagrant. Some travellers in the 1990s may find they can identify with him. At about the same time, Graham Greene wrote of the seedy side of Brighton in *Brighton Rock*.

Doris Lessing painted a picture of 1960s London in *The Four-Gated City*, a part of her 'Children of Violence' series. Julian Barnes deconstructed suburbia in *Metroland*.

One of the funniest and most vicious portrayals of Britain in the 1990s is by Martin Amis in *London Observed*, a collection of stories set in the capital. In other interesting perspectives, Hanef Kureishi writes about the lives of young Pakistanis in London in *The Black Album*, and Caryl Phillips describes the Caribbean immigrants' experience in *The Final Passage*.

High Fidelity, by Nick Hornby, the story of a record-shop owner in Holloway, North London, has made many a reader's top ten list. Ted Hughes, poet laureate until his death in 1999, had one of the best-selling books of poetry ever, *Birthday Letters*. It marks the first time he has written about his wife Sylvia Plath, who committed suicide in 1963.

Theatre

London is still one of the world's theatre capitals, with a historical legacy stretching back to Shakespeare and medieval times.

It is the best city in the world for live theatre, bar none. For too many tourists a night at the theatre will involve such pap as Agatha Christie's *Mousetrap*, now in its fifth decade and the longest running play in history, or Andrew Lloyd Webber's *Cats*, now into a second decade. The average issue of *Time Out* lists more than 100 different shows being staged. Some are the mass-audience musicals and feel-good fare of Lord Webber and others. More will simply be great West End drama such as the long-running *An Inspector Calls,* but many more will be innovative and interesting performances in smaller theatres all over the capital.

There is no 'Golden Age' of English theatre. Rather, the art of English drama has been one of development and evolution. Although it's easy – and usually correct – to deride the undemanding crowd-pleasers found in many West End theatres, it's also easy to forget that before the age of television, many of these theatres staged nothing but the lightest of comedies that would appeal to the masses. The coming of television took away the mass audience and forced the theatres to look for more interesting work that could be differentiated from both television and the movies. These forms of mass entertainment also had another unexpected benefit for London's theatre: they worked as a form of welfare for many veteran stage performers. One role in a Hollywood movie or TV show could bring in more money than a year's worth of performances on the stage.

In the 1950s Laurence Olivier, John Gielgud, Peggy Ashcroft and others were at their professional peak in the West End. They brought force and energy to classic productions of Shakespeare, among others. A wave of young actors in the 1960s, such as Peter O'Toole and Albert Finney, brought a gritty realism to productions that more than ever addressed the issues of the day.

During the 1970s, scores of theatres began operating away from the West End and while they tended to come and go with great rapidity, these small theatres often produced compelling work and served as a breeding ground for new talent. Cut-backs in government funding in the late 1970s caused many marginal operations to close, while others had to scramble about for corporate sponsorship.

Fuelling the English interest in theatre has been the phenomenal popularity of amateur theatre groups; some 17,000 are thought to exist. While some embody the very meaning of the word amateur, others stage productions that rival the best of the pros. Professional regional theatre has a long and proud tradition, but after the lean years of funding during the 1980s and 1990s, many excellent theatres were on life support. If the government delivers on promises for greatly increased cultural funding that were announced in 2000, it won't be a moment too soon.

In London, the National Theatre is the nation's flagship theatre and offers a cocktail of revived classics, contemporary plays and appearances by radical young companies. The Barbican in London, and Stratford-upon-Avon are home to the excellent Royal Shakespeare Company. Most regional cities have at least one world-class company and the facilities to stage major touring productions.

London's many fringe theatre productions offer an invigorating selection of the amazing, the boring, the life-changing and the downright ridiculous. On any night of the year you should also be able to watch performances of plays by great British dramatists such as Harold Pinter, John Osborne, Alan Ayckbourn, Alan Bennett, David Hare and Simon Gray. Careful perusal of the schedules in *Time Out* may also turn up opportunities to see actors of the calibre of Dame Judi Dench, Daniel Day-Lewis or Vanessa Redgrave strut their stuff.

American movie and TV stars are also treading the West End boards, from Kevin Spacey in *The Iceman Cometh* to George Wendt, Patrick Duffy and Richard Thomas in *Art* and Kathleen Turner and Jerry Hall playing a stripped-down Mrs Robinson in *The Graduate*. Perhaps they were inspired by the success of *The Blue Room*, in which Nicole Kidman 'got her kit off'.

London theatre figures to strike it big in Hollywood include Kenneth Branagh and ex-wife Emma Thompson. Sam Mendes segued from success in the intimate Donmar Warehouse to the Oscar for best director for *American Beauty*.

Cinema

Film-makers are constantly whingeing that if only there were sufficient funding and support at home, then British directors and actors (Alan Rickman, Tim Roth, Emma Thompson, Mike Figgis...) wouldn't have to move to Hollywood for work. Even filmmakers who mostly work within the country aren't always assured of support. Mike Leigh, who won the 1996 Palme d'Or at the Cannes Film Festival for *Secrets and Lies*, has made several compelling movies about contemporary Britain that never found large audiences.

It's a pity because there is a wealth of talent and tradition associated with film in England. Hollywood has always known this and saw the British film industry as an important resource long before it lured Alfred Hitchcock across the pond in the 1940s.

The 1990s saw something of a renaissance for the commercial fortunes of British cinema, which was often dismissed as being able to churn out little more in the way of hits than the biannual Bond movie. With the help of television cash from the likes of Channel Four and the BBC, films such as *Four Weddings and a Funeral* found audiences worldwide and brought in much needed revenue.

Even a primarily Hollywood movie such as *Shakespeare in Love* boasts a cast and crew who are largely English. The English film industry has definitely achieved wide respect not just from the critics but from in-

vestors as well, thanks to the success of movies such as *The Full Monty*, *Notting Hill* and Madonna beau Guy Ritchie's East-End gangster movie *Lock, Stock and Two Smoking Barrels*. See Films in the Facts for the Visitor chapter.

Classical Music & Opera

Arguably, London is Europe's classical music capital, and most of the major companies undertake country-wide tours. There are five symphony orchestras, various smaller outfits, a wonderful array of venues, reasonable prices and high standards of performance. The biggest dilemma facing concertgoers is the enviable one of picking from the embarrassment of riches on offer.

Despite this, finding home-grown classical music to listen to can be a struggle. Until this century, virtually the only truly major British composer was Henry Purcell (1659–95). But you should be able to track down concerts of music by big 20th-century names such as Edward Elgar, Ralph Vaughan Williams, Benjamin Britten or William Walton. John Tavener found a wider following after his music was played to a worldwide audience at the funeral of Diana, Princess of Wales.

London's flagship opera company, based at the Royal Opera House off Covent Garden, seemed poised to leave its contentious past behind when its grand home reopened after a long and costly renovation. Critics piled on the praise and the company began a critically acclaimed season with one sell-out after another. The Royal Opera House is also home to the Royal Ballet, which while foremost is but one of many acclaimed dance troupes in England.

Popular Music

English musicians have had an enormous impact on popular music, much greater, strangely, than their influence on 'serious' music.

We could begin a survey with Gilbert and Sullivan's light operas – but we won't. The swinging 60s produced the Beatles, the Rolling Stones, the Who and the Kinks. The late 60s and the glam years of the early

70s had such stardust-speckled heroes as David Bowie, Marc Bolan and Bryan Ferry, and bands such as Fleetwood Mac, Pink Floyd, Deep Purple, Led Zeppelin and Genesis. Punk's best-known spokesmen, the Sex Pistols and the Clash, followed.

The turbulent, ever-changing music scene of the 80s saw the new romantics, left-wing 'agitpop', and the development of a club and rave scene featuring house and techno music. Bands that made it big included the Police, the Eurythmics, Wham, Duran Duran, Dire Straits, UB40 and the Smiths.

In the early 1990s, American grunge dominated rock music. However, the late 90s brought post-grunge music and the renaissance of the quintessentially English indie pop band with the likes of Blur, Elastica, Pulp, Suede and above all Oasis.

Popular groups range from the remarkably enduring and bubble gum-snapping Spice Girls and S Club 7 to Supergrass, Gomez, Stereolab and many more.

Visual Arts

William Hogarth (1697–1764) emancipated English art from European influences with a series of paintings and engravings satirising social abuses. The most famous of these is probably *A Rake's Progress*. The founding president of the Royal Academy, Joshua Reynolds (1723–92), and his rival Thomas Gainsborough (1727–88) raised the artist to a new level of dignity in England; the former through his prodigious output and influence on men of letters such as Dr Samuel Johnson and James Boswell; the latter through his individual genius and the patronage of the royal family.

The tradition of landscape painting, which started with Gainsborough, was continued by John Constable (1776–1837) and was the inspiration for a whole generation of French impressionists. Constable's contemporary romantics, William Blake (1757–1827) and JMW Turner (1775–1851) could not have been more different. Blake used personal symbolism to express a mystical philosophy in drawings, prints and poetry – he disliked oils and canvas. Turner on the other hand, was equally at home with oils as he was with watercolours and he increasingly subordinated detail to the effects of light and colour. By the 1830s, with paintings such as *Snow Storm: Steam-boat off a Harbour's Mouth*, his compositions seemed entirely abstract and were widely vilified.

John Everett Millais (*Christ in the House of His Parents;* 1850) and William Holman Hunt (*The Scapegoat;* 1854) attempted to recapture the simplicity of early Italian art. This gave way to the pseudo-medievalism of Dante Gabriel Rossetti (*Beata Beatrix*; 1864) and his followers Edward Burne-Jones (*King Cophetua and the Beggar Maid;* 1862) and William Morris (1834–96). Morris has had a lasting influence in the design of English furniture, tapestry, stained-glass and fabrics, and his emphasis on good workmanship has been the inspiration for generations of small, craft-based workshops in England.

In the 20th century, the monumental sculptures of Henry Moore (1898–1986), the contorted, almost surreal, painting of Francis Bacon (1909–92), and David Hockney's stylish, highly representational paintings of friends, swimmers and dachshunds, have ensured the place of British art in the international arena.

Both Paul Nash (1889–1949), who was an official war artist in WWI and WWII, and Graham Sutherland (1903–80) followed in the romantic and visionary tradition of Blake, Samuel Palmer and Turner. Nash introduced surrealism to English painting and incidentally wrote *The Shell Guide to Dorset* (1936). Sutherland (also renowned as an official WWII artist) is celebrated for his paintings of ruined buildings. Moore's drawings of people sheltering from air-raids in London's underground consolidated his reputation as one of the most influential English artists of all time. He is also renowned as an official war artist.

Richard Hamilton's photomontage *Just what is it that makes today's homes so different, so appealing?* (1956) launched the pop art movement in England. Peter Blake designed the cover of the Beatles' *Sergeant Pepper's Lonely Hearts Club Band* (1967) and heralded an explosion of British popular culture.

In the seventies and eighties conceptual artists and land artists such as Richard Long competed with performance artists such as Gilbert and George. Through the Thatcher era the commercial galleries held sway until in the 1990s a number of prolific young artists working in a variety of media burst upon the scene: Rachel Whiteread's resin casts of commonplace objects, including an entire East End house, have earned her international acclaim; Damien Hirst's use of animals in his work has provoked much debate; Tracey Emin sewed the names of everyone she'd ever slept with inside a tent and then went on to display her filth-covered bed; and the Chapman brothers' gross figures with misplaced genitals have attracted the attention of censors. Chris Ofili won the 1999 Turner prize with a painting of the Virgin Mary that included elephant dung among its components. Puritanical Americans that included the mayor of New York tried to get it banned from exhibition.

The big news of 2000 was for once actually big. The new Tate Modern, a museum featuring works of art from approximately 1900 onwards, opened in a huge disused power station in Bankside.

ARCHITECTURE

England's architectural heritage reaches back more than 5000 years to the remarkable Stonehenge, and the village of Skara Brae in Orkney. Although the record is sometimes sparse, there are survivors from every period after that.

Roman and Saxon work is rare, which is not so surprising considering the Roman heyday is getting close to 2000 years old. Complete Norman buildings are also rare, but there are still many examples of 900-year-old craftsmanship in everyday use, especially in the many churches and cathedrals.

Buildings from the 16th and 17th centuries are more common, and more ordinary domestic architecture survives alongside the grand houses. Rural England is still home to a number of thatched cob cottages, many of which date back to the 17th century.

Some of the styles that can be seen in churches also appeared in the castles. While church design focused more on decorative or imaginative elements, the design of castles was based largely around their military function. The benefits of living in a large utilitarian pile of stones, however, gradually vanished as times grew more peaceful.

From the 16th century, most of the great architectural innovations were made in houses. Often the English nobility adopted, and adapted, various European styles. Sometimes castles were completely abandoned, or swallowed up by new, improved versions.

One of the most distinctive features of the English countryside and of English culture is the ongoing love affair between the rich and their enormous, and beautiful, country residences. No other country has a comparable number. Like churches, many have evolved over time and incorporate all sorts of architectural styles.

Monumental British architecture has always been outstanding and domestic vernacular architecture was certainly visually appealing up to the Industrial Revolution. But since then the guiding principle for builders and architects has often been to spend as little money as possible; aesthetic considerations were for the wealthy few. Post-WWII, much building has shown a lack of regard for the overall fabric of the cities. Prince Charles, for one, has been an outspoken advocate of a more humanistic and aesthetically sensitive architectural approach.

It's not all bad news though, and some fine new buildings do make it past the drawing board, especially in London where the Lloyd's Building is one stunning example.

Fortunately, there's also a strong campaign to protect the island's architectural heritage (thanks in particular to the National Trust and English Heritage). This nostalgic obsession is, however, sometimes carried to extremes and can encourage conservatism in modern British architecture and design.

While distinct architectural styles and periods in Britain are certainly identifiable, the categories were not always rigid: different styles often influenced each other, and certain periods partially overlapped.

The standard works of reference on British architecture are the wonderfully detailed *Buildings of Britain* books by Niko-laus Pevsner. See the Architectural Glossary at the end of the book for architectural terms.

Church Architecture

As buildings surviving from the middle ages, England's many fine medieval churches provide numerous examples of interesting and unique architecture, and attract a large number of curious visitors.

While this rich collection of churches is of great interest to history and architecture buffs, the terminology can be confusing to outsiders. You're invited to inspect ceilings in chancels, inscriptions in naves, miseri-cords in choirs, monuments in chapels, and tombs in transepts. Furthermore, the church might be Saxon or Norman, Early English or perpendicular, or more likely a combination of two or more of these styles. It may not even be a church after all, but an abbey, chapel, minster or cathedral. What does it all mean?

Basically no matter what the name, they're all places of Christian worship. Technically, a cathedral is the principal church of a diocese and contains the bishop's throne (a diocese is the district for which a bishop is responsible). In practice, a cathedral is usually larger and grander than a church, although there are some large churches and some small cathedrals. In contrast, a church is usually a more local affair; the term 'parish church' indicates that local nature. Chapels are even smaller than churches, and are often the 'churches' of Non-Conformist groups such as Methodists or Baptists.

An abbey was where a group of monks or nuns lived. The abbey church was a church intended principally for use by the monks or nuns, rather than the general population.

When Henry VIII dissolved the monasteries in the 1530s, many of the abbeys in England and Ireland were destroyed or converted into private homes, although some survived as churches. Thus there are abbey churches which were taken over by the general populace (such as Malmesbury Abbey in Wiltshire) and also stately homes which are known as abbeys (such as Beaulieu Abbey in Hampshire). A minster (such as Wimborne Minster in Dorset) refers to a church at one time connected to a monastery.

English churches are fascinating to wander around, especially once you've learned something about the various periods, styles and design elements. Very few of them are uniformly of one style. Usually a window from one period has cut into a wall from another. When decay, subsidence or an accident brought part of a church down, the reconstruction was carried out in whatever was the current style; growing congregations or increased wealth often inspired extensions or more magnificent towers or spires, inevitably in the latest style.

Political changes also affected churches and their design. For example, the Reformation of the 16th and 17th centuries saw an attack on imagery in churches and many statues and images were destroyed, particularly during the attack on 'Popish' influence during the reign of Mary I.

Although the great churches were often built using the cutting edge of building technology for their particular time, it wasn't unusual for catastrophic collapses to occur even during construction.

Architectural Styles & Periods

Neolithic & Bronze Ages The communal burial mounds of the agriculturally-based Neolithic people comprise some of the oldest surviving examples of construction in Britain. Dating from around 3500 BC, these 'barrows' are concentrated around the chalky regions of Dorset and Wiltshire.

Stonehenge, arguably Britain's most famous historical landmark, is thought to have been built by a Bronze-Age race. Construction on this mysterious monolithic circle began around 3000 BC.

Celtic & Roman The Celtic invaders began to arrive in 700 BC, ushering in the Iron Age and building a number of fortified villages and hilltop forts; Maiden Castle in Dorset is one impressive example.

The Celts were followed about 700 years later by the Roman invaders. The Roman occupation lasted 350 years and left behind an impressive architectural legacy, including the grand Fishbourne Palace in West Sussex (built around AD 75), and several Roman baths (one of which gave the town of Bath its name).

Anglo-Saxon Following the withdrawal of the Romans, the Vikings were the next invaders to set foot on English soil. England's first churches were built during this Anglo-Saxon era (from around AD 700 to 1050). Saxon churches were generally small, squat, solid and unembellished, and were characterised by round arches and square towers.

Since most Anglo-Saxon churches were built of wood, few survive. Stone churches have fared better; a notable example is St Laurence in Bradford-on-Avon, Wiltshire. All Saints at Brixworth and All Saints at Earls Barton, both near Northampton, have very clear Anglo-Saxon origins.

Norman After the Norman invasion of 1066, Saxon architecture gave way to Norman; as in Saxon churches, the architectural style was characterised by rounded arches and squat, square towers. The difference in appearance largely comes down to questions of detail and decoration.

The Norman style lasted only about a century, but surviving Norman churches are generally larger than their Saxon predecessors. 'Massive', 'thick' and 'bulky' are all adjectives applied to the Norman style.

There are no purely Norman churches left in England but Norwich, Peterborough and Durham cathedrals are all predominantly Norman.

Gothic The Gothic style developed primarily to serve the needs of the church. The period spanned almost four centuries and is

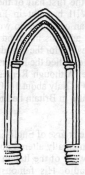

Perpendicular arch

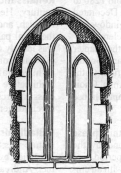

Early English window

Geometrical window

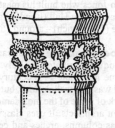

15th-century capital

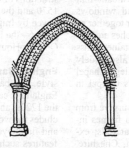

Early English arch

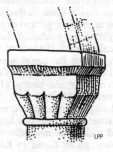

Norman capital

classified into three distinct but related styles. Gothic churches look much lighter and more delicate than their heavier predecessors.

Early English The Early English style was popular from around 1150 to 1280; this period was the first distinct phase of Gothic design, although the Gothic tag itself was not dreamt up until the 17th century. Early English churches are characterised by pointed arches, ribbed vaults and lancet windows (narrow, pointed windows used singly or in groups).

Salisbury Cathedral is the finest example of Early English; Lichfield Cathedral, and Rievaulx Abbey in Yorkshire are also mostly Early English.

Decorated The mid-Gothic, or Decorated, period followed Early English from 1280 to 1380. As the name indicates, the Decorated period was marked by ornate window tracery and other elaborate design elements.

Examples of the style include the chapter houses of Salisbury Cathedral and Southwell Minster, the naves of Lichfield Cathedral and Exeter Cathedral, the Angel Choir at Lincoln Cathedral and the chapter house of York Minster.

Perpendicular The third Gothic phase thrived between 1380 and 1550 and saw the ornate tracery of the Decorated period give way to more rectilinear designs with an emphasis on strong vertical lines. The nave of Canterbury Cathedral is a good example.

Engineering developments meant that arches could span further and windows could be much larger and closer together so many of the perpendicular churches are fantastically light and spacious. Stained glass and elaborate fan vaults were also widely featured, notably at King's College Chapel in Cambridge and Henry VII's Chapel in Westminster Abbey.

Many half-timbered houses survive from this time, their great oak beam frames infilled with brick and other materials; examples can be found in Kent, Cheshire, Hereford and Worcestershire.

Elizabethan & Jacobean During the Gothic period most domestic architecture was either very modest or primarily defensive. The terms Early English, Decorated and perpendicular are not very relevant to ruggedly constructed castles. However, by the mid-16th century domestic architecture is much more important.

After the Reformation, church architecture came to a virtual standstill for a century and, in more peaceful times, impressing the neighbours was more important than physically fighting them off.

Houses such as Hardwick Hall and Knole combine the perpendicular's large areas of glass with the beginnings of an understanding of classical architecture, both in terms of overall proportions and symmetry and in details such as columns and cornices.

Renaissance In the first half of the 16th century, Henry VIII brought in French, Flemish, and Italian craftsmen to work on the royal palaces, and this imported talent was largely responsible for the introduction of what's sometimes called the Renaissance architectural style. Although Renaissance architecture began in Italy about 1420, pure classical architecture in Britain had to wait much longer.

Palladianism The course of English architecture was fundamentally altered not once but twice by the work of the Italian architect Andrea Palladio. His famous *Four Books of Architecture,* showing his own austere buildings and his imagined reconstructions of Roman ruins, was published in 1570 and the illustrations were closely followed by Inigo Jones who built his masterpieces – the Banqueting Hall (London) and Queen's House (Greenwich) – around 1620.

English Baroque Like the Renaissance style, the baroque originated in Italy. In England it came later (late 17th century to the 1720s) and was less well defined, but includes the work of some of the most famous and flamboyant architects. It uses classical features such as columns, arches and pediments in an exuberant way with dramatic juxtapositions of forms and amazingly elaborate silhouettes.

The greatest and most influential baroque architect was Sir Christopher Wren who, in the aftermath of the Great Fire of 1666, radically changed the appearance of the City of London. His masterpiece is St Paul's Cathedral, but he was responsible for no less than 53 churches. The secular style is most famous in the work of Nicholas Hawksmoor and Sir John Vanbrugh, who collaborated on Castle Howard and Blenheim Palace.

Neo-Palladianism Lord Burlington, an aesthetically minded aristocrat, was responsible for a return to simpler classical forms after the excesses of the baroque period. In the design of his own house at Chiswick (London) he led the way with strict adherence to rules of proportion and symmetry and soon the accepted form for country houses was a central block with a columned portico and flanking wings. Holkham Hall in Norfolk (by William Kent 1734) and Prior Park in Bath (by John Wood the Elder 1735) are good examples.

The terraced houses of John Wood the Elder and John Wood the Younger in Bath, and Robert Adam in Edinburgh show the same ideals put to different use in a city context.

Neoclassicism The neoclassical style, which flourished between 1760 and 1830, was the result of a more accurate study of classical ruins, not only in Italy but in Greece and Asia Minor. A new generation of architects had a bigger vocabulary of classical motifs and felt free to assemble them as they wished.

Architect Robert Adam was a key proponent of the style, and was known for his decorative interiors; the house at No 20 Portman Square in London, is one famous example of his work.

There was little religious building during the 17th century apart from Sir Christopher Wren's magnificent St Paul's Cathedral (and other London churches), which adopted neoclassical designs copied from the continent.

Gothic & Greek Revivals The Greek Revival countered the more eclectic approach of neoclassicism with an emphasis on accurate recreations of Greek forms and aimed to replicate the heavy massing of Greek prototypes.

The British Museum, designed by Sir Robert Smirke and built between 1823 and 1846, is one notable example of this style, which started at the end of the 18th century and carried on until the 1840s.

The first phase of the Gothic Revival (1840s) was based on earnest historic research, but this was combined with a passionate belief that a return to Gothic architecture could achieve social reform and that classicism was linked to the urban depravations of industrialism.

Decorated and occasionally Early English Gothic were design sources for churches, schools and vicarages with asymetric, irregular, plans. High Victorian Gothic used a wider range of sources, including perpendicular, north Italian and French Gothic forms for all types of building. The Houses of Parliament by Augustus Pugin and Sir Charles Barry are an early example of Gothic Revival architecture, while Manchester Town Hall by Alfred Waterhouse 1868, shows how the style had moved on.

Arts and Crafts Heavy-handed Victorian church 'restorations' (often a complete rebuilding) inspired William Morris to found the Society for the Protection of Ancient Buildings in 1877. Morris' ideas, together with the writings of John Ruskin, led to an increased appreciation of craft skills in new building as well as restorations. Many very original buildings as well as new ideas about planning and layout of towns meant that Britain was very influential at this period. Foreign visitors were especially interested in the Garden City Movement of which Letchworth is the first example.

20th Century The rise of Nazism meant that many European modern-movement architects fled to Britain in the 1920s and 1930s and had a profound effect. One of the most famous and fun examples of their work is the Penguin Pool at London Zoo by Lubetkin.

Swedish modernism was also influential, evident from the huge number of postwar housing estates and public buildings, replacing bomb damage as well as slum clearance. The tough, sculptural concrete buildings in 1960s brutalist style, such as the National Theatre by Sir Denys Lasdun, are just beginning to be appreciated again (but by a few, a very, very few).

During the late 1970s and early 1980s, two distinct responses to modernism developed. Postmodern architects returned once more to traditional architectural vocabular-ies, assembling motifs from many different styles in an ironic way.

In the 1980s the redevelopment of Docklands gave the greatest scope for postmodern architecture, often by American architects, and has been severely criticised. Terry Farrell's buildings on the Thames at Charing Cross and Vauxhall are more popular.

In contrast, high-tech architecture in the 1980s and early 1990s celebrated the potential of technology usually with complex, lightweight structural skeletons, such as Stansted airport by Norman Foster, the Waterloo International train terminal by Nicholas Grimshaw and the Lloyd's Building

The Norman & Richard Show

If all the world's a stage, then front and centre for architects Norman Foster and Richard Rogers is London, with Other Bits of England serving as the wings.

These two men, who were once partners in the 1960s, have won the bulk of major architectural commissions around London and the south-east for the past 30 years.

Although both have firms that have won contracts and designed projects world-wide, London is where you will find their best as well as most controversial work.

Foster favours clean designs with flowing lines. This is reflected in his new glass roof for the Great Court of the British Museum, where the flowing lines are sinuous and definitely sensuous. The same can be said for his Millennium Bridge across the Thames (unfortunate wiggle notwithstanding – but maybe that was part of being sensuous), and his Canary Wharf station for the Jubilee Line extension is almost organic in its flow of form.

Farther afield, Foster created the Stansted airport terminal as a bold and bright exclamation point mark to a journey (or at least it was until BAA, the operators, gummed up the insides with their usual plethora of shops). He walks a real tightrope with his redevelopment plan for Wembley Stadium, which does away with the iconic twin towers.

In contrast, the work of Rogers is anything but sinuous. Rather, it is technical and intricate and often looks like the work of a mad child with a collection of building blocks.

With its spindly yellow towers and vast expanse of curving white, the Millennium Dome always provokes a reaction among those who see it. But the strongest reactions are often reserved for his 1980s Lloyds Building in the City of London. The guts of the building are all there to see on the outside, whether you want to or not. It was a natural progression from the work that put Rogers on the map, the inside-out Centre Pompidou in Paris which he designed with Renzo Piano.

But if much of the work of Foster and Rogers wins plaudits, or at least sparks strong opinions, some of it has a harder time. Rogers is the designer of a massive complex called Paddington Basin to be built near the station of the same name. It is so huge it has actually provoked fear among some residents. The components are awash with the kind of obsessive and revealing details that make the Lloyds Building just that, the Lloyds Building.

Meanwhile, Foster has won the competition to design the new headquarters for the London mayor and council, which will be built near Tower Bridge. It's a dramatic glass tube topped with an ovoid 'eye'. The new London mayor and probable future tenant, Ken Livingston, dismissed any question that Foster's sensual eye had scored here when he called it 'a glass testicle'.

in London with brilliantly coloured service pipes on the outside. Today the boundaries are harder to define, although many young architects are using restaurant and bar jobs to make a very minimal style fashionable.

Diverse, recent additions to the cityscape include the controversial Millennium Dome, by Richard Rogers, and the Millennium Bridge, by Foster. See the earlier boxed text 'The Norman & Richard Show'.

SOCIETY & CONDUCT
Traditional Culture
It's difficult to generalise about the English and their culture, but there's no doubt they're a creative, energetic and aggressive people who've had an impact on the world that's entirely out of proportion to their numbers.

Many visitors arrive with strong preconceptions about English characteristics, the most common being that the English are reserved, inhibited and stiflingly polite. The reaction to the death of Princess Diana showed just how outdated this stereotype is. Remember, however, that Britain is one of the planet's most tourist-inundated and crowded countries and that some of the famed reserve is a protective veneer developed to help deal with a constant crush of people. Remember, also, that although regional and class differences have shrunk, accents and behaviour still vary widely depending on where you are and who you're mixing with.

Terms like 'stiff-upper-lip', 'cold' and 'conservative' might apply to some sections of the middle and upper classes, but in general they don't apply to the working class, or to northerners. Visit a nightclub in one of a big city, a football match, a good local pub, or a country B&B, and other terms, such as uninhibited, tolerant, exhibitionist, passionate, aggressive, sentimental, hospitable and friendly, might spring to mind more readily.

No country in the world has more obsessive hobbyists, some of whom teeter on the edge of complete madness. Train and bus spotters, twitchers, sports fanatics, fashion victims, royalists, model-makers, egg collectors, ramblers, pet owners, gardeners, they all find a home here.

England is a country of sceptical individualists who deeply resent any intrusion into their privacy or freedom, so it's hardly surprising that their flirtation with state socialism was brief. Change happens slowly, and only after endless consultations, committee meetings, departmental get-togethers and government referrals.

Dos & Don'ts
England being the reasonably tolerant place it is, it's not particularly easy to cause offence without meaning to. That said, it's as well to be aware that most locals would no sooner speak to a stranger in the street than fly to the moon. If you're obviously a tourist battling with directions, there's no problem – but try starting a general conversation at the bus stop and you'll find people staring at you as if you're mad.

Queuing The English are notoriously addicted to queuing, and many comedy sketches depend on the audience accepting that people might actually join a queue without knowing what it's for. The order of the queue is sacrosanct – few things are more calculated to spark an outburst of tutting than an attempt to 'push in' to a queue. And make certain you stand on the right on escalators.

Clothes In some countries what you wear or don't wear in churches can get you into trouble. In general, England is as free and easy about this as it is about how you dress in the streets. Bear in mind, however, that if you go into mosques or temples you may be expected to take off your shoes and cover your arms, legs and/or head.

Some classy restaurants and many clubs operate strict dress codes. In restaurants that usually means a jacket and tie for men and no trainers for anyone; in clubs it means whatever the management and their bouncers choose it to mean and can vary from night to night.

Treatment of Animals
The English are widely believed to love their animals more than their children: the

Royal Society for the Prevention of Cruelty to Animals was established before the National Society for the Prevention of Cruelty to Children and still rakes in more donations.

Not surprisingly, fox-hunting, the ancient sport derided by Oscar Wilde as 'the unspeakable in pursuit of the inedible', has become highly controversial.

Britain's 200-odd hunts are estimated to kill about 20,000 foxes a year (another 40,000 are killed by vehicles and over 100,000 are trapped or shot). Pro-hunt campaigners argue that many foxes actually owe their existence to the hunters since fox-hunting farmers are less likely to dig up the hedgerows and small woods that provide living quarters for their prey.

Nevertheless, most people see hunting as a cruel sport, inappropriate to a 'civilised' society at the beginning of the 21st century. Anti-hunting sentiment in England runs strong and polls suggest that two-thirds to three-quarters of the population would support a ban, figures mirrored in a recent free vote on the subject in parliament. Unfortunately, the pro-hunters are a well-organised and powerful bunch; they've managed to stave off efforts to ban the hunt, despite several efforts by the government.

As often in England, hunting is tied up with class. Hunting is mainly a sport of the upper class or at least the wealthy. The famous attire, starting with a 'pink' (which in fox-hunting parlance means red!) jacket, can cost thousands from a London tailor, and that's before the fees to join a specific hunt and the cost of the horses.

Recent years have seen high-profile lobbies against factory farming and the export of live animals. Perhaps 10% of the population are vegetarians, or near vegetarians. Most supermarkets stock free-range eggs and meat supposedly from animals who have been allowed to roam free.

RELIGION

The Church of England, a Christian church that became independent of Rome in the 16th century (see the Tudors under History earlier), is the largest, wealthiest and most influential in the land. Like the Church of Scotland, it's an 'established' church, meaning that it's officially the national church, with a close relationship with the state (the queen or king appoints archbishops and bishops on the advice of the prime minister).

Although 70% of the population still claim to be Christian, the latest survey suggests that only 8.2% regularly attend church, a fall of a million people in the last 20 years. It's difficult to generalise about the form of worship that varies from the pomp and ceremony of High church, to the less traditional Low church, which has been more influenced by Protestantism and, more recently by the evangelical movement. Evangelical and charismatic churches are the only ones attracting growing congregations.

Traditionally, the Church of England has been aligned with the ruling classes but some sectors became very critical of the Conservatives in their declining years. In 1994, after many years of agonising, the first women were ordained as priests. The debate has now moved on to the rights and wrongs of gay priests.

Other significant Protestant churches with no connection to the state include Methodists, Baptists, the United Reformed Church and the Salvation Army.

At times since the 16th century, Roman Catholics have been terribly persecuted; one modern legacy is the ongoing problem of Northern Ireland. Today about one in 10 Britons considers themselves a Catholic, but over the last 20 years the number attending mass has also slumped.

Recent estimates suggest there are now well over one million Muslims, together with significant numbers of Sikhs and Hindus. Nowadays more English non-Christians visit their places of worship than do Christians.

LANGUAGE

English is probably England's most significant contribution to the modern world. The English, of every class and background, take enormous pleasure in using their language and idiom inventively (nowhere, for instance, are there more crossword fanatics).

The language continues to evolve and to be used and exploited to the full. See the Glossary at the back of the book for examples.

English English can be incomprehensible to overseas visitors – even to those who assume they've spoken it all their lives. Regional dialects may be disappearing, but significant variations, especially in accent, still flourish and some can be virtually impenetrable to outsiders. It's OK to ask someone to repeat what they've said, but laughing at them is unlikely to go down well. Besides, they probably can't quite get your oddball accent either.

London

☎ 020 • pop 12 million

What can be said about London that hasn't been said so many times before? That the weighty resonance of its very name suggests history and might? That it is the premier city in Europe in terms of size, population and per-capita wealth? That its opportunities for entertainment by day and by night go on and on and on?

London is all these things and much, much more. Not only is it home to such familiar landmarks as Big Ben, the Eros statue, Tower Bridge and the murky River Thames, it also boasts some of the greatest museums and art galleries anywhere and more lush parkland than any other world capital. It is an amazingly tolerant place for its size, its people pretty much unshockable.

Visitors are often surprised to find how multicultural the British capital is, with a quarter of all Londoners belonging to one of almost three dozen ethnic minorities, most of whom get along fairly well together.

It's a cosmopolitan mixture of the developed and developing worlds, of chauffeurs and beggars, of the establishment and the avant-garde, with seven to 12 million inhabitants (depending on where you stop counting), and almost 30 million visitors a year. London has been a major recipient of the vast sums of culture money raised by the National Lottery. With projects such as the huge new Tate Modern gallery that opened in 2000, the number of visitors to the city seems likely to grow ever more.

HISTORY

Although a Celtic community established itself around a ford across the River Thames, it was the Romans who first developed the square mile now known as the City of London. They built a bridge and an impressive city wall, and made the city an important port and the hub of their road system.

The Romans left, but trade went on. Few traces of Dark Age London can now be found, but the city survived the incursions of

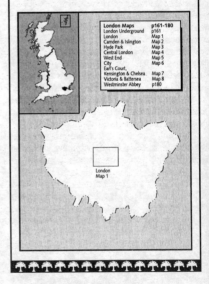

Highlights

- Walking the banks of the Thames
- Going for a spin on the London Eye
- Tossing back good ales in an old pub
- Enjoying the world's best array of live theatre
- Being perplexed by the Tate Modern's art
- Losing yourself in the Hampton Court Palace maze

London Maps	p161-180
London Underground	p161
London	Map 1
Camden & Islington	Map 2
Hyde Park	Map 3
Central London	Map 4
West End	Map 5
City	Map 6
Earl's Court, Kensington & Chelsea	Map 7
Victoria & Battersea	Map 8
Westminster Abbey	p180

the Saxons and Vikings. Fifty years before the Normans arrived, Edward the Confessor built his abbey and palace at Westminster.

William the Conqueror found a city that was, without doubt, the richest and largest in the kingdom. He raised the White Tower (part of the Tower of London) and confirmed the city's independence and right to self-government.

During the reign of Elizabeth I the capital began to expand rapidly. Unfortunately, medieval, Tudor and Jacobean London was virtually destroyed by the Great Fire of 1666. The fire gave Sir Christopher Wren the opportunity to build his famous churches, but did nothing to halt or discipline the city's growth.

By 1720 there were 750,000 people and London, as the seat of parliament and focal point for a growing empire, was becoming ever richer and more important. Georgian architects replaced the last of medieval London with their imposing symmetrical architecture and residential squares.

As a result of the Industrial Revolution and rapidly expanding commerce, the population jumped from 2.7 million in 1851 to 6.6 million in 1901 and a vast expanse of suburbs developed to accommodate them.

Georgian and Victorian London was devastated by the Luftwaffe in WWII – huge swathes of the centre and the East End were totally flattened. After the war, ugly housing and low-cost developments were thrown up on the bomb sites. The docks never recovered – shipping moved to Tilbury and the Docklands declined to the point of dereliction, until rediscovery by developers in the 1980s.

Riding on a wave of Thatcherite confidence and deregulation, London boomed in the 1980s. The new wave of property developers proved to be only marginally more discriminating than the Luftwaffe, and most think their buildings only slightly better than the eyesores of the 1950s. What the next spate of projects planned for the first years of the new millennium will bring remains to be seen.

London's government, always a bewildering array of squabbling councils, boroughs and other bodies, got its first true mayor in 2000. Feisty Ken Livingstone was elected by a large majority, not necessarily because of his liberal politics, but because most Londoners liked the fact he promised to thumb his nose at the central government at every opportunity – in the best London tradition, of course.

ORIENTATION

The city's main geographical feature is the Thames, a sufficiently deep (for anchorage) and narrow (for bridging) tidal river that enabled the Romans to build a port that was easily defended from the dangers of the North Sea. Running from west to east, it divides the city into its northern and southern halves. But because it flows in wide bends, creating peninsulas in its wake, it is not always clear on what side of the river you are – especially in the far west and east.

Despite London's great size, the Underground system (the 'tube') makes most of it easily accessible, and the official and ubiquitous – though geographically misleading – Underground map is easy to use. Most important sights, theatres, restaurants and even affordable places to stay lie within a reasonably compact rectangle formed by the tube's Circle Line (colour-coded yellow), which encircles central London just north of the river.

In this chapter, the nearest tube or train station has been given for each address; Map 1 shows the location of tube stations and the areas covered by the detailed district maps.

It's common for people to refer to areas by their postcode. The letters correspond to compass directions from the centre of London, which according to the post office must lie somewhere not too far from St Paul's Cathedral: EC means East Central, WC means West Central, W means West, NW means North West, and so on. The numbering system after the letters is less helpful: 1 is the centre of the zone, higher numbers relate to the alphabetical order of the postal-district names, which are not always in common use.

Districts and postal codes are often given on street signs, which is obviously vital when names are duplicated (there are 47 Station Roads), or cross through a number of districts. To further confuse visitors, many streets change name – Holland Park Ave becomes Nötting Hill Gate, which becomes Bayswater Rd, which becomes Oxford St...Sometimes they duck and weave like the country lanes they once were. Street numbering can also bewilder: on big streets the numbers on opposite sides can be way out of kilter (315 might be opposite 520) or, for variation, they can go up one side and down the other.

Most of London's airports lie some distance from the centre, but transport is easy (if not cheap). See the Getting Around section later in the chapter for details.

Maps

A decent map is vital. Ideally, get a single-sheet map so you can see all of central London at a glance; the Lonely Planet *London City Map* (£3.99) has three separate maps at different scales as well as an inset map of Theatreland and an index. The bound *Mini London A–Z Street Atlas & Index* (£3.75) provides comprehensive coverage of London in a discreet size. Both of these products will help you avoid standing bewildered on a corner holding some immense fold-out map that's about to be blown away by the latest rain squall.

INFORMATION

Lonely Planet has several publications with more detailed coverage of London. For comprehensive coverage, see *London* (£9.99). For colourful coverage in a handy pocket size, try *London Condensed* (£5.99), while *Out to Eat – London* (£7.99) describes an enormous selection of London's best eateries.

Time Out magazine (issued every Tuesday, £1.95) is a complete listing of everything happening and is recommended for every visitor. Another good read is the only daily newspaper that is well and truly a Londoner, the *Evening Standard* (35p). This widely read afternoon tabloid can vacillate from being right-wing to radical (usually when matters directly affecting London are concerned). Its Thursday entertainment supplement *Hot Tickets* can often be a better and more eclectic source of information than *Time Out*.

Free magazines are available from pavement bins, especially in Earl's Court, Notting Hill and Bayswater. *TNT Magazine*, *Southern Cross* and *SA Times* cover Australian, New Zealand and South African news and sports results, but are mostly invaluable for their entertainment listings, excellent travel sections and useful classifieds covering jobs, cheap tickets, shipping services and accommodation.

Loot (£1.30) is issued five times weekly and is made up of classified ads placed free by sellers. It's the best place to look for flats and house-share ads.

Tourist Offices

London is a major travel centre, so along with information on London, tourist offices can help with England, Scotland, Wales, Ireland and most countries world-wide.

Britain Visitor Centre The Britain Visitor Centre (Map 5), 1 Regent St SW1 (⊖ Piccadilly Circus), is a comprehensive information and booking centre, with the tourist boards of Wales, Scotland, Northern Ireland, the Irish Republic and Jersey as well as a map and guidebook shop on the ground floor. On the mezzanine level are a Thomas Cook outlet where you can arrange accommodation and tours as well as train, air and car travel, a theatre ticket agency, a bureau de change, international telephones and computer terminals for accessing tourist information on the Internet. It can get *very* busy but opens daily 9 am to 6.30 pm Monday to Friday and 10 am to 4 pm Saturday and Sunday (from 9 am to 5 pm Saturday late June to September). The centre deals with direct queries and walk-in customers only; there are no telephone enquiries. If you're not in the area and need information about Britain or Ireland ring the British Tourist Authority (BTA) general enquiries on ☎ 8846 9000. Check out the Web site at www.visitbritain.com.

Tourist Information Centres As well as providing information, London's main Tourist Information Centre (TIC), which is in Victoria train station (Map 8; ⊖ Victoria), handles accommodation bookings. It opens 8 am to 8 pm Monday to Saturday and to 6 pm Sunday, April to October; and 8 am to 7 pm Monday to Saturday and until 6 pm Sunday, the rest of the year. It too can get positively mobbed in the peak season.

There's also a TIC in the arrivals hall at Waterloo International Terminal (Map 4; ⊖ Waterloo), open 8.30 am to 10.30 pm daily, and one in Liverpool Street station

[continued on p181 ...]

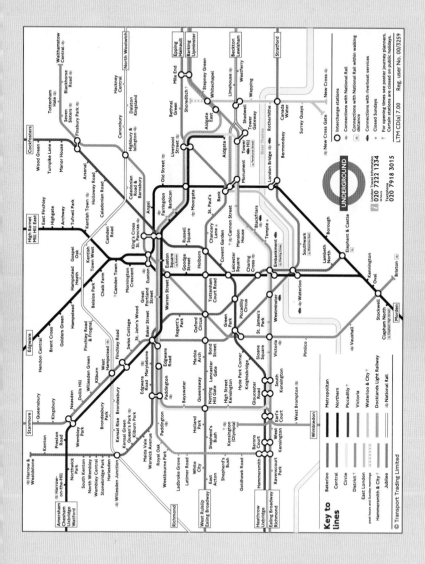

MAP 1 – CENTRAL LONDON

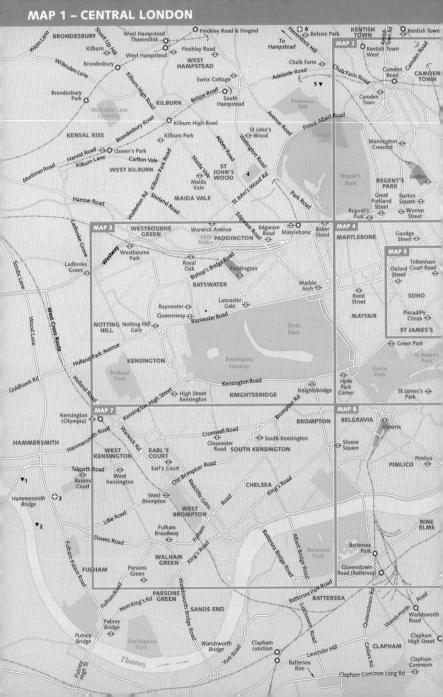

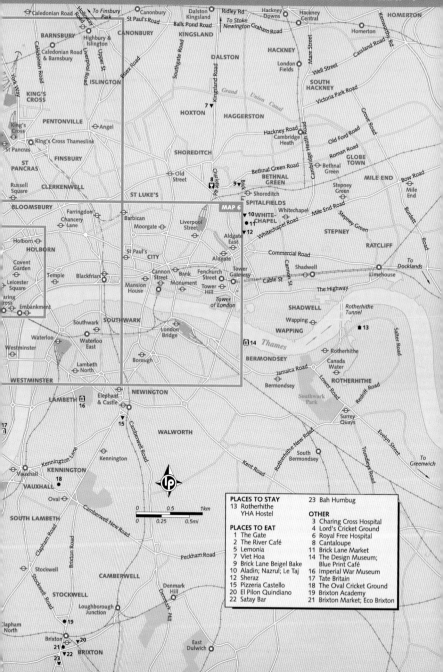

PLACES TO STAY
13 Rotherhithe
   YHA Hostel

PLACES TO EAT
1 The Gate
2 The River Café
5 Lemonia
7 Viet Hoa
9 Brick Lane Beigel Bake
10 Aladin; Nazrul; Le Taj
12 Sheraz
15 Pizzeria Castello
20 El Pilon Quindiano
22 Satay Bar

23 Bah Humbug

OTHER
3 Charing Cross Hospital
4 Lord's Cricket Ground
6 Royal Free Hospital
8 Cantaloupe
11 Brick Lane Market
14 The Design Museum;
   Blue Print Café
16 Imperial War Museum
17 Tate Britain
18 The Oval Cricket Ground
19 Brixton Academy
21 Brixton Market; Eco Brixton

MAP 2

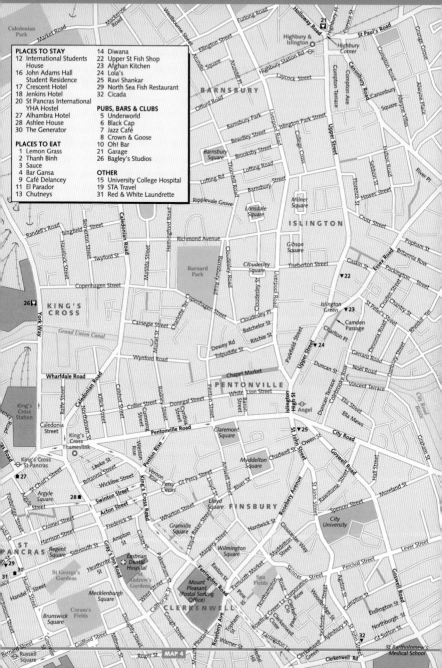

MAP 2

PLACES TO STAY
12 International Students House
16 John Adams Hall Student Residence
17 Crescent Hotel
18 Jenkins Hotel
20 St Pancras International YHA Hostel
27 Alhambra Hotel
28 Ashlee House
30 The Generator

PLACES TO EAT
1 Lemon Grass
2 Thanh Binh
3 Sauce
4 Bar Gansa
9 Café Delancey
11 El Parador
13 Chutneys
14 Diwana
22 Upper St Fish Shop
23 Afghan Kitchen
24 Lola's
25 Ravi Shankar
29 North Sea Fish Restaurant
32 Cicada

PUBS, BARS & CLUBS
5 Underworld
6 Black Cap
7 Jazz Café
8 Crown & Goose
10 Oh! Bar
21 Garage
26 Bagley's Studios

OTHER
15 University College Hospital
19 STA Travel
31 Red & White Laundrette

MAP 3

MAP 3

29

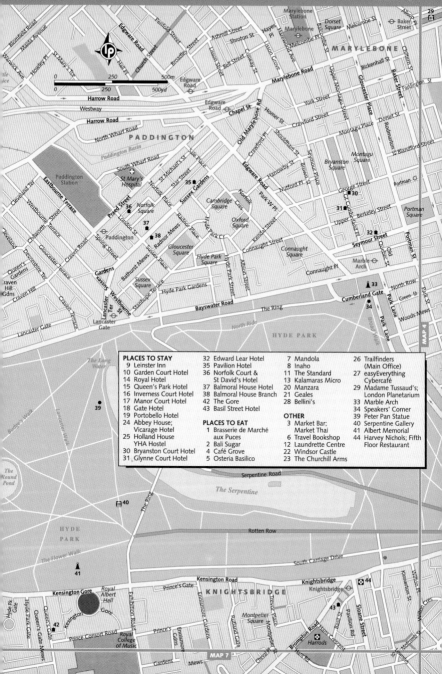

PLACES TO STAY
9 Leinster Inn
10 Garden Court Hotel
14 Royal Hotel
15 Queen's Park Hotel
16 Inverness Court Hotel
17 Manor Court Hotel
18 Gate Hotel
19 Portobello Hotel
24 Abbey House;
   Vicarage Hotel
25 Holland House
   YHA Hostel
30 Bryanston Court Hotel
31 Glynne Court Hotel

32 Edward Lear Hotel
35 Pavilion Hotel
36 Norfolk Court &
   St David's Hotel
37 Balmoral House Hotel
38 Balmoral House Branch
42 The Gore
43 Basil Street Hotel

PLACES TO EAT
1 Brasserie de Marché
   aux Puces
2 Bali Sugar
4 Café Grove
5 Osteria Basilico

7 Mandola
8 Inaho
11 The Standard
13 Kalamaras Micro
20 Manzara
21 Geales
28 Bellini's

OTHER
3 Market Bar;
   Market Thai
6 Travel Bookshop
12 Laundrette Centre
22 Windsor Castle
23 The Churchill Arms

26 Trailfinders
   (Main Office)
27 easyEverything
   Cybercafé
29 Madame Tussaud's;
   London Planetarium
33 Marble Arch
34 Speakers' Corner
39 Peter Pan Statue
40 Serpentine Gallery
41 Albert Memorial
44 Harvey Nichols; Fifth
   Floor Restaurant

MAP 4

MAP 4

MAP 2

RUSSELL SQUARE

Russell Square

Russell Square

Guilford Street

Queen Sq

14

Gt Ormond Street

Old Hall
15

Bedford Place

Southampton Row

New North St

Harpur St

Great Ormond St

Theobald's Road

Northington St

Jockey's Fields

Gray's Inn Road

Clerkenwell Road

CLERKENWELL

Hatton Wall

Leather
Lane
Market

St Cross St

Saffron Hill

Clerkenwell
Green

16

Elm Hill

Britton Street

St John's St

Farringdon
Station

17

18

19

Cowcross Street

23

Charterhouse Street

22

Smithfield
Market

20

21

Little
Britain

Bartholomew's
Hospital

Montague Street

Bloomsbury Way

Barter St

Catton St

Proctor St

High Holborn

HOLBORN

Holborn
Circus

Holborn Viaduct

Hosier La

Snow Hill

Cock La

Bloomsbury
Square

13

Red Lion Sq

Eagle St

Gray's Inn
Gardens

Gray's Inn

Gray's Inn Sq

South Sq

Chancery
Lane

Baldwin's Gdns

Greville St

24

Ely Pl

Ely
Ct

Holborn

St Andrew St

New St

Shoe Lane

Stone-
cutter
St

City
Thameslink
Station

Newgate
Street

Central
Criminal
Court

St Paul's
Cathedral

THAMES

MAP 4

Horse guard on duty in immaculate costume

Houses of Parliament, home to heated debates

MAP 5

PLACES TO STAY
14 Fielding Hotel
37 Hazlitt's Hotel
41 Oxford St YHA Hostel
59 Strand Palace

PLACES TO EAT
3 Rasa Samudra
8 Ruskins Café
9 Coffee Gallery
10 Mandeer
15 Café des Amis du Vin
16 Café Pacifico
17 Belgo Central
18 Food for Thought
19 Neal's Yard Salad Bar
20 World Food Café
21 Rock & Sole Plaice
22 Franx Snack Bar
30 Maison Bertaux
31 Pollo
32 Old Compton Café
33 Bar Italia
34 Garlic & Shots
36 Mildred's
40 Soba
42 Yo! Sushi
44 Melati
46 Spiga
48 Gopal's of Soho
49 Pâtisserie Valerie
50 Cam Phat
51 Tokyo Diner
54 Calabash
57 Orso
58 Simpson's-in-the-Strand
69 Gaby's
71 Fung Shing
72 Mr Kong
73 Gerrard's Corner
74 Wong Kei
75 Chuen Cheng Ku
79 L'Odéon

PUBS, BARS & CLUBS
2 100 Club
7 Museum Tavern
12 The End
23 First Out
24 Astoria
25 Velvet Room
27 Borderline
45 O Bar
47 Balans
53 Lamb & Flag
61 Retro Bar
62 Sherlock Holmes

OTHER
1 HMV
4 On The Beat
5 Division One
6 Virgin Megastore
11 Sir John Soane's Museum
13 Bikepark
26 Waterstone's
28 Foyle's
29 Blackwell's
35 Trax
38 Black Market Records
39 Council Travel
43 Hamleys
52 Stanford's
55 Theatre Museum
56 London Transport Museum
60 YHA Adventure Shop
63 easyEverything Cybercafé
64 Charles I Statue
65 Nelson's Column
66 St Martin-in-the-Fields;
   Café in the Crypt
67 Trafalgar Square Post Office
68 Coliseum;
   English National Opera
70 Half-Price Ticket Booth
76 Rock Circus
77 Eros Statue
78 Tower Records
80 Waterstone's
81 St James's Piccadilly
82 Britain Visitor Centre
83 American Express

Built in 1894, Tower Bridge still opens up to allow tall ships through.

LIZ BARRY

MAP 5

MAP 5

BLOOMSBURY

British Museum

7

8

9 ▼

▼ 10

12

Bloomsbury Street

Museum Street

Little Russell St.

Bloomsbury Way

Bury Place

Barter Street

Southampton Place

Southampton Row

Holborn

Procter St.

High Holborn

Great Russell Street

New Oxford Street

Shaftesbury Ave.

West Central St.

Grape Street

High Holborn

Stukeley Street

Newton Street

Macklin Street

Parker Street

Drury Lane

HOLBORN

Whetstone Park

Gate Street

Lincoln's Inn Fields

11

Bucknall Street

St Giles High Street

23

Denmark Street

New Compton Street

13 ●

Shorts Gardens

Betterton Street

Shelton Street

Great Queen Street

Wild Court

Kingsway

Lincoln's Inn Fields

Sardinia Street

Portsmouth Street

Portugal St.

Kean Street

Kemble Street

22

21 ▼

Neal's

20

19

Seven Dials

18 ▼

17 ▼

Shaftesbury Avenue

Monmouth Street

Neal Street

Endell Street

COVENT GARDEN

Earlham Street

Wild Street

Drury Lane

Broad Court

Crown Court

14

Cambridge Circus

Charing Cross Road

29 ●

Earlham Street

Mercer Street

Langley Street

16

15

Long Acre

Floral Street

Royal Opera House

Bow Street

Russell Street

55

56

Catherine Street

Tavistock Street

Wellington Street

Exeter Street

57

Aldwych

Bush House

India House

The Waldorf

Litchfield St

West Street

Upr St Martin's Lane

Long Acre

Rose St.

52

54

King Street

Central Market Hall

Covent Garden

James St.

Southampton Street

Henrietta Street

60

59

58

Strand

The Savoy

Somerset House

Newport

51

Newport Ct.

Great Newport St.

Cranbourn Street

Garrick Street

St Martin's Lane

Bedford Street

Maiden Lane

Little Newport St

Leicester Square

53

Bear Street

69

Cecil Court

New Row

Hop Gardens

St Martins Lane

May's Court

Chandos Place

61

Carting Lane

Savoy Street

Savoy Place

Lancaster Place

Waterloo Bridge

The Hampshire

Irving Street

Orange Street

68

67

William IV Street

Wyndham Lane

Adam Street

John Adam Street

Strand

Victoria Embankment

Cleopatra's Needle

National Portrait Gallery

St Martin's Place

66

Duncannon St.

National Gallery

Charing Cross

Charing Cross

Villiers Street

Craven Street

63

Trafalgar Square

65

64

Charing Cross

Northumberland Ave.

Whitehall

Northumberland St.

62

Charing Cross Station

Victoria Embankment Gardens

Embankment

Charing Cross Pier

THAMES

Waterloo Bridge

Cockspur Street

Admiralty Arch

The Mall

Spring Gardens

MAP 6

PLACES TO STAY
1 Barbican YMCA
3 Great Eastern Hotel
16 Bankside Residence Student Hall

PLACES TO EAT
2 Mesón Los Barriles
6 Sweeting's
7 Wine Library
8 Café Spice Namaste

9 Cantina del Ponte
18 Fish!

OTHER
4 Museum of London
5 WWII Monument to the People of London

10 Tower Bridge Experience
11 HMS Belfast
12 London Dungeon
13 Southwark Cathedral
14 The Anchor
15 Shakespeare's Globe
17 Vinopolis – City of Wine
19 George Inn
20 Ministry of Sound

Griffin marking the city limits

Head to Waterloo if you plan to get away by Eurostar.

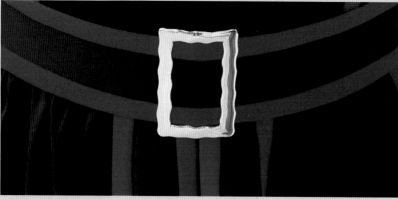

A Beefeater's buckling belly

Black cabs and red buses set London in motion.

Battersea Power Station

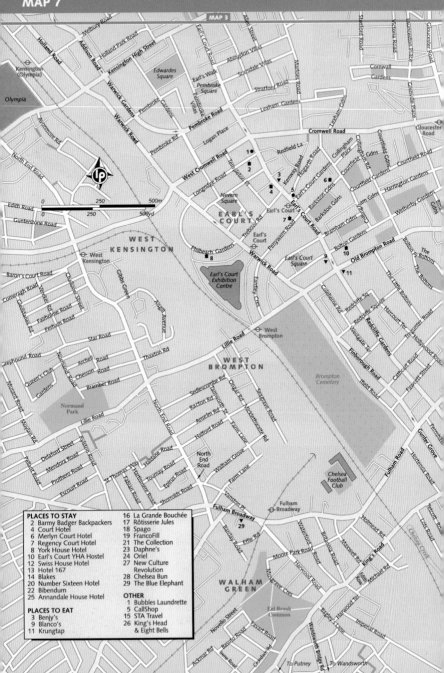

MAP 7

MAP 7

MAP 3

Queen's Gate Ter
Ilvaston Place
Imperial College Road
Science Museum
Brompton Road
Queen's
Natural History Museum
Victoria & Albert Museum
Beaufort Gdns
Brompton Square
Beauchamp Place
Ovington Square
Yeoman's Row
Hans St
Pont Street
Gardens
Cromwell Road
Thurloe Place
Thurloe Square
Egerton Terrace
Egerton Gardens
Walton Street
Ovington Street
Lennox Gardens
Clabon Mews
Cadogan Square
Cadogan Lane
Cadogan Place
Stanhope Gdns
Queen's Gate
Queensberry Place
Cromwell Place
Thurloe St
South Terrace
Dome Pl
Hasker Street
First Street
Milner Street
Moore St
Cadogan Pl
Ellis St
Harrington Road
South Kensington
Pelham Street
Draycott Avenue
Denyer St
Rawlings St
Hasker St
Cadogan Gardens
Cadogan Street
Cadogan
Sloane Ter
Stanhope Gdns
16
17
18
19
21
22
23
Moscow Road
Sumner Place
Onslow Square
Sloane Avenue
Lucan Place
Petyward St
Whitehead's Gro
Draycott Place
Peter Jones
Sloane Square
Sloane St
Olveden Place
24
SOUTH KENSINGTON
15
20
Cranley Place
Onslow Gardens
Neville St
Fulham Road
Elystan Street
Ixworth Place
Pond Place
King's Road
Duke of York's Territorial Army Headquarters
Lower Sloane St
Holbein Place
Sloane Gdns
25
12 13
14
Roland Way
Drayton Gardens
Cranley Gardens
Old Onslow Gardens
Cale Street
Sydney Street
Elystan Place
Markham Square
Cheltenham Ter
Franklin's Row
Turk's Row
Priory Walk
Evelyn Gardens
Elm Park Gardens
South Parade
Dovehouse Street
Cale Street
Britten Street
St Luke's St
Jubilee Pl
Markham St
Smith St
St Leonard's Ter
Royal Avenue
Burton's Court
Royal Hospital Road
Clifton Road
Elm Park Road
Chelsea Square
Manresa Road
CHELSEA
Smith Ter
Walpole St
Chelsea Royal Hospital
Cathcart Rd
The Vale
Carlyle Square
King's Road
Chelsea Old Town Hall
Radnor Wk
Shawfield Street
Flood Street
Tedworth Square
Ormonde Gate
West Road
National Army Museum
MAP 8
Beaufort Street
Park Walk
Chelsea Park Gardens
Old Church Street
Mallord Street
Bramerton Street
Flood St
Oakley Street
Alpha Pl
Redburn St
Christchurch St
Royal Hospital Road
Swan Walk
Tite Street
Limerston Street
Mallord Street
Upper Cheyne Row
Phene St
Cheyne Gdns
Chelsea Physic Garden
Chelsea Embankment
Gertrude Street
Lamont Road
28
27
Paultons Square
Old Church Street
Cheyne Row
26
Cheyne
Walk
Chelsea Reach
Ann Lane
Milman's Street
Beaufort Street
Cadogan Pier
Albert Bridge
The Parade
Children's Zoo
Ashburnham Rd
Cremorne Road
Cheyne Walk
Battersea Bridge
Carriage Drive North
Tadema Road
Uverdale Road
Burnaby Street
Lots Road
THAMES
Battersea Church Road
Hester Road
Antram Road
Elcho St
Parkgate Road
Albert Bridge Road
Carriage Drive West
BATTERSEA PARK
Thames Ave
Westbridge Road
Battersea Bridge Road
Worfield Street
Juer Street
Rosery Road
Carriage Drive South
Harbour Ave
Chelsea Harbour
Parkham Street
Petworth Road
Surrey Lane
Prince of Wales Drive
Cambridge Rd
Brynmaer Road
Warriner Gdns
Battersea Park Road
Orbel St
Este St
Elsley Rd
Octavia St

Olé! A vivacious mural in Waterloo

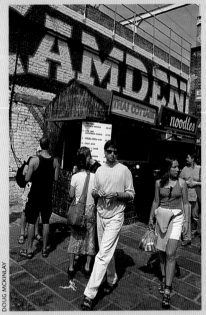

Discovering what's on the market at Camden

Brick Lane is laced with market stalls on a Sunday morning: try some classic Doc Martens for size.

MAP 8

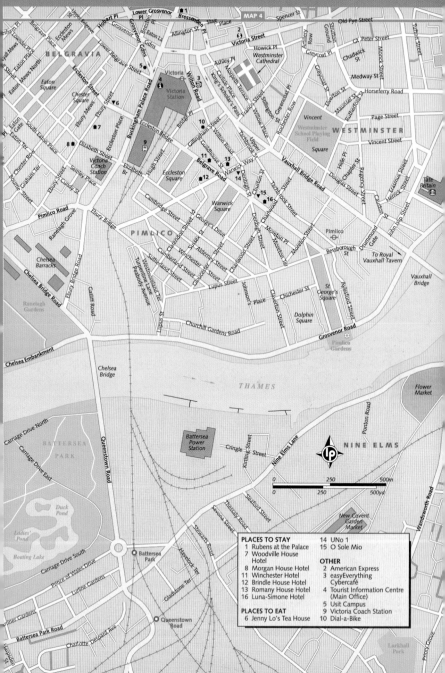

MAP 4

BELGRAVIA

WESTMINSTER

PIMLICO

THAMES

NINE ELMS

BATTERSEA PARK

Chelsea Barracks

Ranelagh Gardens

Chelsea Bridge

Battersea Power Station

New Covent Garden Market

Flower Market

Larkhall Park

PLACES TO STAY
1 Rubens at the Palace
7 Woodville House Hotel
8 Morgan House Hotel
11 Winchester Hotel
12 Brindle House Hotel
13 Romany House Hotel
16 Luna-Simone Hotel

PLACES TO EAT
6 Jenny Lo's Tea House

14 UNo 1
15 O Sole Mio

OTHER
2 American Express
3 easyEverything Cybercafé
4 Tourist Information Centre (Main Office)
5 Usit Campus
9 Victoria Coach Station
10 Dial-a-Bike

WESTMINSTER ABBEY

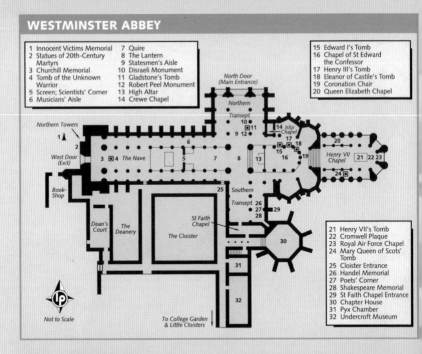

1 Innocent Victims Memorial
2 Statues of 20th-Century Martyrs
3 Churchill Memorial
4 Tomb of the Unknown Warrior
5 Screen; Scientists' Corner
6 Musicians' Aisle
7 Quire
8 The Lantern
9 Statesmen's Aisle
10 Disraeli Monument
11 Gladstone's Tomb
12 Robert Peel Monument
13 High Altar
14 Crewe Chapel
15 Edward I's Tomb
16 Chapel of St Edward the Confessor
17 Henry III's Tomb
18 Eleanor of Castile's Tomb
19 Coronation Chair
20 Queen Elizabeth Chapel

21 Henry VII's Tomb
22 Cromwell Plaque
23 Royal Air Force Chapel
24 Mary Queen of Scots' Tomb
25 Cloister Entrance
26 Handel Memorial
27 Poets' Corner
28 Shakespeare Memorial
29 St Faith Chapel Entrance
30 Chapter House
31 Pyx Chamber
32 Undercroft Museum

Something special: the beautifully restored St Pancras train station, King's Cross

ELLIOT DANIEL

[... continued from p160]

(Map 6; ⊖ Liverpool Street), open 8 am to 6 pm daily. There are TICs at Heathrow Terminal 3 (arrivals concourse), open 6 am to 11 pm daily, and in Heathrow Terminals 1, 2, 3 Underground station, open 8 am to 6 pm. Gatwick, Stansted, Luton and London City airports, Paddington train station and Victoria Coach Station have information desks too.

Written enquiries should be sent to the London Tourist Board & Convention Bureau, Glen House, Stag Place, London SW1E 5LT (or fax 7932 0222). You can also make use of their Visitorcall system. You simply dial ☎ 09064 123 and then add another three digits, depending on what information you're looking for. These are premium-rate calls costing 60p per minute and can only be dialled within the UK. You could also visit www.londontown.com.

Money

Banks and ATMs abound across central London. Whenever possible, avoid using bureaux de change such as Chequepoint to change your money. If you must use them, check their commission rates carefully first.

There are 24-hour bureaux in Heathrow Terminals 1, 3 and 4. Terminal 2's bureau opens 6 am to 11 pm daily. Thomas Cook has branches at Terminals 1, 3 and 4. There are 24-hour bureaux in Gatwick's South and North Terminals and one at Stansted. Luton and City airports have desks open during their operating hours. The airport bureaux are actually good value; they don't charge commission on sterling travellers cheques, and on other currencies it's 1.5% or £3 minimum.

The principal American Express office (Map 5; ☎ 7930 4411), 6 Haymarket SW1 (⊖ Piccadilly Circus), opens for currency exchange 9 am to 5.30 pm Monday to Friday and 9 am to 4 pm Saturday and Sunday. There are slightly longer hours June to September. There are a welter of slightly shorter hours for services such as mail. Amex has offices scattered throughout London. The one at 96 Victoria St SW1 (Map 8), near Victoria train station, opens 9 am to 5.30 pm weekdays and to 4 pm Saturday.

The main Thomas Cook office (☎ 7853 6400), 30 St James's St SW1 (⊖ Green Park), opens 9 am (10 am Wednesday) to 5.30 pm weekdays and until 4 pm Saturday. There are branches throughout central London. The one on the 1st floor of the Victoria Place shopping centre at Victoria station opens 7.30 am to 8 pm Monday to Saturday and 8 am to 6pm Sunday.

Discounts

If you plan to do a lot of sightseeing, the London GoSee card (£10/16/26 for one/three/seven days) can be purchased at and is valid for entry to 17 museums and galleries. Family cards, covering free admission for up to two adults and four children, cost £30/50 for three/seven days.

The participating museums are Apsley House (Wellington Museum), Barbican Art Gallery, BBC Experience, BFI London IMAX Cinema, Design Museum, Hayward Gallery, Imperial War Museum, London Transport Museum, Museum of London, National Maritime Museum, Natural History Museum, Royal Academy of Arts, Science Museum, Shakespeare's Globe, Theatre Museum, Tower Bridge Experience and Victoria & Albert Museum.

Post & Communications

Poste Restante Unless you (or the person writing to you) specify otherwise, poste restante mail sent to London ends up at the Trafalgar Square post office (Map 5), 24–28 William IV St, London WC2N 4DL (⊖ Charing Cross). It opens 8 am to 8 pm weekdays and 9 am to 8 pm Saturday. Mail will be held for four weeks; ID is required.

Telephone See the Facts for the Visitor chapter for details on beating BT's high prices on international calls using special cards such as Lonely Planet's eKno card.

The private company CallShop offers cheaper international calls than BT. You can find them open from 9 am to 11.30pm at 181a Earl's Court Rd SW5 (Map 7; ☎ 7390 4549; ⊖ Earl's Court). You phone from a metered booth and then pay the bill. You can also send and receive faxes.

Email & Internet Access EasyEverything, a division of no-frills airline easyJet, is opening numerous huge Internet cafes around London that are open 24 hours. Charges vary according to how busy the location is: £1 buys you from 40 minutes to six hours of access. Locations include:

Trafalgar Square
(Map 5; ☎ 7930 4094) 457-459 The Strand WC2 (⊖ Charing Cross)
Victoria
(Map 8; ☎ 7233 8456) 9–13 Wilton Road SW1 (⊖ Victoria)
Oxford St
(Map 4; ☎ 7491 8986) 358 Oxford St W1 (⊖ Bond St)
Kensington High St
(Map 3; ☎ 7938 1841) 160-166 Kensington High St W8 (⊖ High St Kensington)

Travel Agencies

London has always been a centre for cheap travel. Refer to the Sunday papers (especially the *Sunday Times*), *TNT Magazine* and *Time Out* for listings of cheap flights, but beware of sharks.

Long-standing and reliable firms include:

Council Travel
(Map 5; ☎ 7437 7767) 28a Poland St W1 (⊖ Oxford Circus).
Web site: www.counciltravel.com
STA Travel
(☎ 7361 6161 for European enquiries, ☎ 7361 6262 for world-wide enquiries, ☎ 7361 6160 for tours, accommodation, car hire or insurance) 86 Old Brompton Rd SW7 (Map 7; ⊖ South Kensington); and 117 Euston Rd NW1 (Map 2; ⊖ Euston)
Web site: www.statravel.co.uk
Trailfinders
(Map 3; ☎ 7938 3939 for long-haul travel, ☎ 7938 3444 for 1st and business class flights) 194 Kensington High St W8 (⊖ High Street Kensington) which also has a visa and passport service (☎ 7938 3848), immunisation centre (☎ 7938 3999), foreign exchange (☎ 7938 3836) and information centre (☎ 7938 3303)
Web site: www.trailfinders.com
Usit Campus
(Map 8; ☎ 7730 3402 for European travel, ☎ 7730 8111 for world-wide enquiries) 52 Grosvenor Gardens SW1 (⊖ Victoria)
Web site: www.usitcampus.co.uk

Bookshops

See Bookshops under Shopping later for bookshops in London that have good ranges of useful travel books and maps.

Laundry

Many hostels and some hotels have self-service washing machines and dryers, and virtually every high street has its own launderette – with rare exceptions, a disheartening place to spend much time. The average cost to wash and dry a single load is £2.50 to £3. Hours vary but are usually from 7 or 8 am to 8 or 9 pm daily.

The following is a selected list of laundrettes (your lodging should always be able to steer you to a local laundry):

Bloomsbury (Map 2)
Red & White Laundrette, 78 Marchmont St WC1
Earl's Court (Map 7)
Bubbles, 113 Earl's Court Rd SW5
Bayswater (Map 3)
Laundrette Centre, 5 Porchester Rd W2

Left Luggage

All the train stations and Victoria Coach Station have left-luggage offices or lockers, as do the airports (see the Getting There & Away section later in the chapter). They cost between £2 and £6 a day, depending on the size of the bag or locker.

Medical Services

For the address of a local doctor or hospital, look in the phone book or phone ☎ 100 (toll-free). The following hospitals have 24-hour accident and emergency departments:

Charing Cross Hospital
(Map 1; ☎ 8383 0000) Fulham Palace Rd W6 (⊖ Hammersmith)
Guy's Hospital
(Map 6; ☎ 7955 5000) St Thomas St SE1 (⊖ London Bridge)
Royal Free Hospital
(Map 1; ☎ 7794 0500) Pond St NW3 (⊖ Belsize Park)
University College Hospital
(Map 2; ☎ 7387 9300) Grafton Way WC1 (⊖ Euston Square)

To find an emergency dentist phone the Dental Emergency Care Service on ☎ 7955 2186 weekdays between 8.45 am and 3.30 pm or call into Eastman Dental Hospital (Map 2; ☎ 7915 1000), 256 Gray's Inn Rd WC1 (⊖ King's Cross).

The travel agency Trailfinders (☎ 7938 3999) has a clinic at 194 Kensington High St W8 with a full range of travel vaccines available. Nomad (☎ 8889 7014), 3-4 Wellington Terrace, Turnpike Lane N8 (⊖ Turnpike Lane), sells travel equipment and medical kits and gives immunisations on Thursday and Saturday evenings.

Emergency

Dial ☎ 999 (free) for fire, police or ambulance.

Dangers & Annoyances

Crime Considering its size and the disparities in wealth, London is remarkably safe; most visitors will spend their time in the capital without anything worse happening than being overcharged for an ice-cream cone. That said, you should take the usual precautionary measures against pickpockets, who operate in crowded public places such as the Underground, pubs and major tourist attractions.

Take particular care at night. When travelling by tube, choose a carriage with other people in it and avoid some of the deserted suburban stations; a bus or a taxi is a safer choice.

Terrorism London remains the occasional target of terrorists trying to make a point. There is a much higher sense of security here than in, say, Sydney or even New York, and precautions are taken regularly – and seriously. *Never* leave your bag unattended in case you trigger a security alert. If you see an unattended package, keep calm and alert those in authority and anyone nearby as quickly as possible; do *not* touch it.

Touts & Scams Hotel and hostel touts descend on backpackers at tube and main-line stations such as Earl's Court, Liverpool Street and Victoria. Treat their claims with scepticism and don't accept any free lifts unless you know exactly where you're going.

Every year foreign men are lured into Soho strip clubs and hostess bars and are efficiently separated from huge amounts of money; refuse to pay and things may rapidly turn nasty. Do yourself a favour and give them a wide berth.

Finally, when you're in high-traffic places such as Oxford St you may smell the overwhelming odour of frying onions. These emanate from one of the many unlicensed hot dog carts that lurk around London. Resist the urge (if there's one at all); the sanitary conditions are dubious.

CENTRAL LONDON
Trafalgar Square (Map 5)

At the heart of visitors' London is Trafalgar Square WC2 (⊖ Charing Cross). This is where many great marches and rallies take place, and where the new year is seen in by thousands of drunken revellers. It's also where you'll fight for space with flocks of pigeons – those dirty flying rats.

The square was designed by John Nash in the early 19th century on the site of the King's Mews and executed by Sir Charles Barry, who was also partly responsible for the Houses of Parliament. The 43.5m-high **Nelson's Column**, which incorporates granite from Cornwall to the Scottish Highlands, was completed in 1843 and commemorates Admiral Nelson's victory over Napoleon off Cape Trafalgar in Spain in 1805. The four bronze lions at its base were designed by Edwin Landseer and added in 1867. If you glance up at the statue of the good admiral, you'll see that he is facing to the south-west, surveying his fleet of ships, some say, atop the lampposts lining The Mall.

Trafalgar Square is flanked by many imposing buildings and important thoroughfares fan out from it. To the north is the **National Gallery** and behind it the **National Portrait Gallery**; Pall Mall runs south-west from the north-western corner. The church of **St Martin-in-the-Fields** is to the north-east. To the south, the square opens out and you catch glimpses down Whitehall through the traffic. To the south-west stands **Admiralty**

Arch, erected in honour of Queen Victoria in 1910, with The Mall leading to Buckingham Palace beyond it.

The traffic streaming past makes it difficult to appreciate Trafalgar Square. Plans are being considered to pedestrianise much of the square – a splendid idea.

National Gallery With some 2300 western paintings on display, the National Gallery (☎ 7747 2885), Trafalgar Square WC2, is one of the world's largest – and finest – art galleries. The lovely Sainsbury Wing on the western side was added in 1991.

The paintings in the National Gallery are hung in a continuous time-line; by starting in the Sainsbury Wing and progressing eastwards you can take in a collection of pictures painted between the mid-13th and 20th centuries in chronological order. If you're keen on the real oldies (1260–1510), head for the Sainsbury Wing; for the Renaissance (1510–1600), go to the West Wing in the museum's main building. Rubens, Rembrandt and Murillo are in the North Wing (1600–1700); if you're after Gainsborough, Constable, Turner, Hogarth and the impressionists visit the East Wing (1700–1900). For a larger collection of paintings by British artists you should visit the Tate Britain (see the following Westminster & Pimlico section) or the Tate Modern (see Southwark later).

The highlights listed in the boxed text will give you an idea of the *crème de la crème* at the gallery, but if you want to know a lot more, borrow an audioguide (contribution suggested) from the central hall. Each painting is numbered; punch this into the machine and it will skip to the appropriate place on the CD-ROM. There are also highlights audioguide tours (featuring 30 paintings) and activity sheets for kids (50p). Free one-hour guided tours, which introduce you to a manageable half-dozen paintings at a time, leave at 11.30 am and 2.30 pm on weekdays and at 2 and 3.30 pm on Saturday (additional tour at 6.30 pm on Wednesday). The Micro Gallery has interactive screens where you can plan your own tour and then print out a plan.

The National Gallery opens 10 am to 6 pm daily (until 9 pm Wednesday). Admission is free. You can visit its Web site at www.nationalgallery.org.uk.

National Portrait Gallery A visit to the National Portrait Gallery (☎ 7306 0055), St Martin's Place WC2, is not so much about art as history – to put faces to the famous and infamous names in British history from the Middle Ages to the present day. The gallery, founded in 1856, houses a primary collection of some 10,000 works on five floors, and there is no restriction on media; there are oil paintings, watercolours, drawings, miniatures, sculptures, caricatures, silhouettes, photographs and even electronic art.

The pictures are displayed roughly in chronological order, starting with the early Tudors on the top floor and descending to the late 20th century. The portraits of Elizabeth I from 1575 in all her finery and Byron in romantic oriental garb (1813) by Thomas Phillips are as wonderful as the more recent works: Elizabeth II as seen by Andy Warhol; Prince Charles posing under a banana tree; photographs of Oscar Wilde and Virginia Woolf and more.

A major revamp of the gallery opened in

National Gallery Highlights

- *Arnolfini Wedding* – Van Eyck
- *Rokeby Venus* – Velásquez
- *Wilton Diptych*
- *Bathers* – Cézanne
- *Venus & Mars* – Botticelli
- *Virgin of the Rocks* – da Vinci
- *Virgin & Child with St Anne & St John the Baptist* – da Vinci
- *Battle of San Romano* – Uccello
- *The Ambassadors* – Holbein the Younger
- *Charles I* – Van Dyck
- *Le Chapeau de Paille* – Rubens
- *The Hay-Wain* – Constable
- *Sunflowers* – Van Gogh
- *The Water Lily Pond* – Monet
- *The Fighting Temeraire* – Turner

2000. There are expanded galleries, and escalators in the new Ondaatje Wing now whisk visitors to the top floor, where any sensible tour begins and where there is a cafe with a great view.

The National Portrait Gallery opens 10 am to 6 pm Monday to Saturday (from noon Sunday). Admission is free. Check out the Web site at www.npg.org.uk.

St Martin-in-the-Fields An influential masterpiece by James Gibbs (1682–1754), the 'royal parish church' of St Martin-in-the-Fields (☎ 7930 0089), Trafalgar Square WC2, occupies a prime site at the north-eastern corner of the square. There's an adjoining craft market, and in the crypt you'll find a brass-rubbing centre (☎ 7930 9306), bookshop and popular cafe (see Trafalgar Square under Places to Eat later). The church opens 8 am to 6.30 pm daily, the brass-rubbing centre 10 am (noon on Sunday) to 6 pm.

Westminster & Pimlico (Maps 4 & 8)
While the City of London (known simply as 'the City') has always concerned itself with trade and commerce, Westminster is the centre of political power and most of its places of interest are linked with the monarchy, parliament or the Church of England.

Pimlico (Map 8), to the south and southwest, has never been as smart as, say, Belgravia, but contains some wonderful early-19th-century houses and the incomparable Tate Britain.

Whitehall Lined with government buildings, statues, monuments and other historical sights, Whitehall SW1 (Map 4; ⊖ Charing Cross or Westminster) and its extension Parliament St is the wide avenue that links Trafalgar Square with Parliament Square. The best way to take it all in is to follow the short walk described below.

Whitehall Walking Tour (Map 4) What was once the administrative heart of the British Empire remains the focal point for British government.

Start your walk at the southern end of Trafalgar Square as it leads into Whitehall. As you walk south you'll see **Admiralty Arch** (1910) and the **Old Admiralty** on the right and farther along on the left the **Ministry of Defence**.

Just in front of the latter is **Banqueting House** (☎ 7930 4179), the only surviving part of the Tudor Whitehall Palace, which once stretched most of the way along Whitehall but burned down in 1698. Designed by Inigo Jones in 1622, it was England's first purely Renaissance building. Its claim to fame is that it was on a scaffold built against a 1st-floor window that Charles I, accused of treason by Cromwell, was executed on 30 January 1649. Inside there's a video account of the house's history and on the 1st floor a huge, virtually unfurnished hall whose ceiling displays nine panels painted by Rubens in 1634. It opens 10 am to 5 pm Monday to Saturday. Admission costs £3.60/2.30.

Opposite Banqueting House is **Horse Guards Parade**, where the mounted troopers of the Household Cavalry are changed at 11 am Monday to Saturday and at 10 am Sunday, offering a more accessible version of the ceremony than the one outside Buckingham Palace.

South of Horse Guards Parade is **Downing St**. No 10 has been the site of the British prime minister's official residence since 1732 although Tony Blair and his family actually now live in the larger apartments at No 11. During Margaret Thatcher's time in office the gates were erected and the street closed off to the public for fear of IRA terrorist attacks.

A short distance farther on in the middle of Whitehall is the **Cenotaph** (Greek for 'empty tomb'), a memorial to Commonwealth citizens who were killed during the two world wars.

To the west of the Cenotaph is the **Foreign & Commonwealth Office** (FCO; 1872) restored by Sir George Gilbert Scott and Matthew Digby Wyatt.

If you walk west along King Charles St, you'll reach the **Cabinet War Rooms** (☎ 7930 6961), where the British government took refuge underground during

Lottery Bonanza

From 2000, visitors who think they know London are in for a delightful shock: the capital's cultural heritage has been almost completely revamped.

Thanks to the National Lottery, which funds cultural projects, a windfall of hundreds of millions of pounds has rained down on London, much of it tied to the millennium. This has sparked much private money to be invested as well.

Here's a list of the major projects, look for details in the text:

Tate Modern A huge new museum on the Thames dedicated to modern art
British Museum Dramatic new glass roof opens up the Great Court, plus new galleries for African art
National Portrait Gallery Expansion eases access to the wonderful galleries on higher floors
Somerset House The gleam is restored to a London gem and the Gilbert Collection opens
Science Museum The new Wellcome Wing celebrates the latest discoveries
Imperial War Museum A new permanent exhibition on the Holocaust
Wallace Collection Restoration and new galleries
Southwark Cathedral Restoration and a new visitors centre
National Maritime Museum A complete revamp, with new galleries
Millennium Bridge A new pedestrian footbridge from the Tate Modern to the City
Hungerford Bridge Smart new walkways linking the South Bank to the West End

WWII, conducting its business from beneath 3m of solid concrete. It opens 9.30 am to 6 pm daily (from 10 am October to March). Admission is £4.80/free.

Whitehall ends at **Parliament Square**, where swirling traffic makes it hard to appreciate the statues of past prime ministers such as **Winston Churchill**. To the north-east along Bridge St is the new ultramodern and ultra-expensive **Parliament Building**. You're now in place to explore the sights below.

Westminster Abbey One of the most visited churches in Christendom, Westminster Abbey (Map 4; ☎ 7222 5152), Dean's Yard SW1 (⊖ Westminster) has played a pivotal role in the history of both England and the Anglican church. With the exception of Edward V and Edward VIII, every sovereign has been crowned here since William the Conqueror in 1066. All the monarchs from Henry III (died 1272) to George II (1760) were buried here as well, but since the death of George III in 1820 they have been laid to rest in St George's Chapel in Windsor.

Its popularity means that certain areas are cordoned off to protect the floors and the

northern transept now serves as the main entrance.

The abbey, though a mixture of various architectural styles, is the finest example of Early English Gothic (1180–1280) still standing. The original church was built by the 11th-century King (later Saint) Edward the Confessor, who is buried in the chapel behind the main altar. Henry III (reigned 1216–72) began work on the new building but didn't complete it; the French Gothic nave was finished in 1388. Henry VII's huge and magnificent chapel was added in 1519.

Unlike St Paul's, Westminster Abbey has never been a cathedral but is a 'royal peculiar', administered directly by the crown.

Orientation The main entrance is through the northern door. Immediately past the barrier you come to the **Statesmen's Aisle**, where politicians and eminent public figures are commemorated. The Whig and Tory prime ministers who dominated late-Victorian politics, Gladstone (who is buried here) and Disraeli (who is not) have their monuments uncomfortably close together. Nearby is a monument to Sir Robert Peel who, as home secretary in 1829, created the metropolitan police force. Above them is a rose window designed by James Thornhill and depicting 11 of the Apostles (Judas is omitted).

On your left as you turn and walk eastwards are several small chapels with fine 16th-century monuments, including a lovely Madonna and Child in alabaster in Crewe Chapel. Opposite the Islip Chapel in the northern ambulatory are three wonderful medieval tombs. Farther on are the tombs of Edward I and Henry III.

At the eastern end of the sanctuary, opposite the entrance to the Henry VII Chapel, is the rather ordinary-looking **Coronation Chair**, upon which almost every monarch is said to have been crowned since 1066. In fact, the oaken chair dates from the late 13th century – another chair must have been used prior to this.

Up the steps in front of you and to your left is the narrow **Queen Elizabeth Chapel**. Here Elizabeth I, who gave the abbey its charter, and her half-sister 'Bloody Mary' share an elaborate tomb.

In the easternmost part of the abbey you'll find the **Henry VII Chapel**, an outstanding example of late perpendicular architecture (a variation of English Gothic) with spectacular circular vaulting on the ceiling. Behind the chapel's altar, with a 15th-century *Madonna and Child* by Vivarini, is the elaborate sarcophagus of Henry VII and his queen, Elizabeth of York. Beyond this is the **Royal Air Force Chapel** and the Battle of Britain stained-glass window. Next to it a plaque marks the spot where Oliver Cromwell's body lay until the Restoration.

The chapel's southern aisle contains the **tomb of Mary Queen of Scots** (beheaded on the orders of her cousin Elizabeth and with the acquiescence of her son, the future James I) and the stunning tomb of Lady Margaret Beaufort, mother of Henry VII. Also buried here are Charles II, William and Mary, and Queen Anne.

The **Chapel of St Edward the Confessor**, the most sacred spot in the abbey, lies just east of the sanctuary and behind the high altar; access may still be restricted to protect

the 13th-century floor. St Edward was the founder of the abbey.

Some of the surrounding tombs in the chapel – those of Henry III, Edward I, Edward III, Richard II, Henry V and four queens – are visible from the northern and southern ambulatory. **Eleanor of Castile**, the wife of Edward I, lies in one of the oldest bronze tombs. The abbey's southern transept contains **Poets' Corner**, where many of England's finest writers are buried, a precedent established with Geoffrey Chaucer.

In front of medieval wall-paintings of St Christopher and the doubting apostle St Thomas on the eastern wall stands the **William Shakespeare Memorial** (although like Byron, Tennyson, William Blake, TS Eliot and various other luminaries, he was not actually buried here). Here, too, you'll find memorials to Handel (holding a score of the *Messiah)*, Edmund Spenser and Robert Browning, as well as the graves of (or memorials to) Charles Dickens, Lewis Carroll, Rudyard Kipling and Henry James. St Faith's Chapel (entrance to the east) is reserved for private prayer.

Just north of Poet's Corner is the **Lantern**, the heart of the abbey, where coronations take place. If you face east while standing in the centre, the **sanctuary** is in front of you. The ornate **high altar** was designed in 1897. Behind you (ie, to the west) Edward Blore's mid-19th-century **quire** (or chancel) is a breathtaking structure.

The entrance to the **Cloister** dates from the 13th century. East down a passageway off the Cloister, the octagonal **Chapter House** has one of Europe's best-preserved medieval tile floors and retains traces of religious murals. The state still runs the Chapter House and the adjacent **Pyx Chamber**, once the Royal Treasury and containing the pyx, a chest with standard gold and silver pieces for testing coinage weights. It now contains the abbey's treasures and liturgical objects as well as the oldest altar in the abbey.

The **Undercroft Museum** (or the Abbey Museum) exhibits the death masks of generations of royalty as well as armour and stained glass.

To reach the 900-year-old **College Garden**, the oldest in England, enter Dean's Yard and the **Little Cloisters** off Great College St. There are free lunch-time concerts in the College Garden on Thursday in July and August.

Set in the floor at the western end of the nave is the **Tomb of the Unknown Warrior** in remembrance of those who died in WWI. Just before it is a stone commemorating **Winston Churchill**.

Straight up the aisle is the 1834 screen separating the nave from the quire. Against this stand monuments to Sir Isaac Newton, Darwin, Lord Stanhope, Michael Faraday and four Nobel laureates, including Lord Kelvin and Ernest Rutherford – a veritable **Scientists' Corner**.

The northern aisle of the nave is known as the **Musicians' Aisle**, with memorials to music-makers such as Henry Purcell who served the abbey as an organist.

The two towers above the western door, through which you exit, were completed in 1745. Just above the door, perched in 15th-century niches, are the latest sacred additions to the abbey: 10 stone statues of the **20th-century martyrs**. To the right as you exit is a memorial to victims of oppression, violence and war around the world. 'All you who pass by, is it nothing to you?' it asks poignantly.

Hours & Tickets The abbey opens 9 am to 4.45 pm weekdays and 9 am to 2.45 pm Saturday. The last admission is one hour earlier. The Chapter House opens 9.30 am to 5.30 pm April to October and until 4 pm the rest of the year. The Pyx Chamber and Undercroft Museum open 10 am to 4.30 pm daily. The College Garden opens 10 am to 6 pm Tuesday to Thursday, April to September (to 4pm the rest of the year). The Cloisters open 8 am to 6 pm daily.

Admission to Westminster Abbey costs £5/2. Admission to just the Chapter House, Pyx Chamber and Undercroft Museum costs £2.50 (£1 with an abbey ticket). Admission to the Cloisters is free.

One of the best ways to visit the abbey is to attend a service, particularly evensong (5 pm weekdays, 3 pm at weekends). Sunday Eucharist is at 11 am.

Guided Tours Guided tours (☎ 7222 7110) of the abbey cost £3 and last about 1½ hours, They depart between three and six times a day, Monday to Saturday.

Houses of Parliament Comprising the House of Commons and the House of Lords, the Houses of Parliament are in the Palace of Westminster (Map 4; ☎ 7219 4272), Parliament Square SW1 (✛ Westminster). It was built by Sir Charles Barry and Augustus Pugin in 1840 when the neo-Gothic style was all the rage, and a thorough cleaning has revealed the soft golden brilliance of the original structure. The most famous feature *outside* the palace is the Clock Tower, commonly known as **Big Ben** (the real Ben, a bell named after Benjamin Hall, who was commissioner of works when the tower was completed in 1858, hangs inside).

The **House of Commons** is where Members of Parliament (MPs) meet to propose and discuss new legislation and to question the prime minister and other ministers. Although the Commons is a national assembly of 659 MPs, the chamber has seating for only 437 of them. Government members sit to the right of the Speaker and Opposition members to the left.

Visitors are admitted to the **Strangers' Gallery** of the House of Commons via St Stephen's Entrance after 4.15 pm Monday to Thursday and from 10 am Friday; expect to queue for at least an hour. Admission is free. Parliamentary recesses (holidays) last for three months over the summer and another few weeks over Easter and Christmas, so it's best to ring in advance to check whether parliament is in session. However, an experimental opening during the summer recess in 2000 (with tours for £3.50) may become a regular event, so check. Handbags and cameras must be checked at a cloakroom before you enter the gallery, and no large suitcases or backpacks are allowed through the airport-style security gate.

Originally built in 1099, **Westminster Hall** is the oldest surviving part of the Palace of Westminster, the seat of the English monarchy from the 11th to the early-16th centuries. Added between 1394 and 1401, the roof is the earliest known example of a hammer-beam roof and has been described as 'the greatest surviving achievement of medieval English carpentry'.

Jewel Tower Once part of the Palace of Westminster, the Jewel Tower (☎ 7222 2219), an English Heritage (EH) property opposite the Houses of Parliament and beside Westminster Abbey, was built in 1365 to house Edward III's treasury. Now it houses exhibitions describing the history of parliament and showing how it works. The Jewel Tower opens 10 am to 6 pm daily April to September; 10 am to 5 pm daily in October; and 10 am to 4 pm daily, November to March. Admission costs £1.50/80p.

Westminster Cathedral Completed in 1903, Westminster Cathedral (Map 8; ☎ 7798 9064), Victoria St SW1 (✪ Victoria), is the headquarters of the Roman Catholic Church in Britain and is the only good example of neo-Byzantine architecture in London. Its distinctive candy-striped red-brick and white-stone tower features prominently on the west London skyline.

The interior is part splendid marble and mosaic and part bare brick; the money ran out and the cathedral was never completed. It features the highly regarded stone carvings of the 14 Stations of the Cross (1918) by Eric Gill. The cathedral opens 7 am to 7 pm daily. For £2 you can take a lift up the tower for panoramic views of London.

Tate Britain Built in 1897 and now with a new entrance on Atterbury St, the Tate Britain (Map 1; ☎ 7887 8008), Millbank SW1 (✪ Pimlico) has been spruced up and expanded in conjunction with the high-profile opening of its sister gallery, the Tate Modern, down the Thames at Bankside (see Southwark later). It serves as the historical archive of British art from the 16th century to the present. You'll find works by notables such as William Blake, the Hogarths, Gainsborough, Whistler, Spencer and many more. Adjoining the main building is the quirky **Clore Gallery**, where the bulk of JMW Turner's paintings can be found.

The Tate Britain opens 10 am to 5.50 pm daily and only major special exhibitions have an admission fee. Guided tours of the museum are available at 11.30 am, 2.30 pm and 3.30 pm weekdays; and at 3 pm Saturday. Its Web site is at www.tate.org.uk.

St James's & Mayfair (Map 4)

St James's is a mixture of exclusive clubs, historic shops and elegant buildings; indeed, there are some 150 historically noteworthy buildings within its 36 hectares. It has largely escaped the redevelopment that has taken place in much of London.

Mayfair is the area bordered by Oxford St to the north, Piccadilly to the south, Park Lane and Hyde Park to the west and Regent St to the east.

Institute for Contemporary Arts The Institute for Contemporary Arts (ICA; ☎ 7930 3647), The Mall SW1 (✪ Charing Cross), has a reputation for being at the cutting edge of all kinds of arts. In any given week this is the place to come for obscure films, dance, photography, art, theatre, music, lectures, multimedia works and book readings. The ICA opens noon to 7.30 pm daily. A day pass costs £1.50, £2.50 at weekends.

St James's Park & St James's Palace The neatest and most royal of London's royal parks, St James's Park, The Mall SW1 (✪ St James's Park or Charing Cross) has the best vistas, including Westminster, Buckingham Palace, St James's Palace, Carlton Terrace and Horse Guards Parade. In summer, the flower beds are sumptuous and colourful. But what makes St James's Park so particularly special is its large lake and the waterfowl that inhabit it, including a group of pelicans.

The striking Tudor gatehouse of **St James's Palace**, the only surviving part of a building initiated by the palace-mad Henry VIII in 1530, is best approached from St James's St to the north of the park. It is the residence of Prince Charles and his sons, the princes William and Harry, and is never open to the public. Foreign ambassadors to the UK are still accredited to 'the Court of

St James's'. Next door is **Clarence House** (1828), the residence of the Queen Mother.

Buckingham Palace The palace (☎ 7830 4832; ⊖ St James's Park or Victoria) is at the end of The Mall, where St James's Park and Green Park meet at a large roundabout. In the centre is the **Queen Victoria Memorial**, close to where Marble Arch stood until it was moved to its present location in 1851.

Buckingham Palace was built in 1803 for the Duke of Buckingham and has been the royal family's London home since 1837 when St James's Palace was judged too old-fashioned and insufficiently impressive. A total of 18 rooms (out of 661) are open to visitors for a brief period each year, but don't expect to see the Queen's bedroom. She and the Duke of Edinburgh share a suite of 12 rooms in the northern wing overlooking Green Park; this is a tour of the state apartments only. Many people find the visit overpriced and disappointing.

The tour includes **Queen Victoria's Picture Gallery** (a full 76.5m long, with works by Rembrandt, Van Dyck, Canaletto, Poussin and Vermeer) and the **Throne Room**, with his-and-hers pink chairs initialled 'ER' and 'P' sitting smugly under what looks like a theatre arch.

The palace opens 9.30 am to 4.30 pm daily, early August to early October and admission costs £10.50/5.

Changing of the Guard This is a London 'must see' – though you'll probably go away wondering what all the fuss was about. The old guard (Foot Guards of the Household Regiment) comes off duty to be replaced by the new guard on the forecourt of Buckingham Palace, which gives tourists a chance to gape at the bright red uniforms, bearskin hats (synthetic alternatives are being looked at), shouting and marching. The ceremony takes place at 11.30 am daily from April to June and at the same time on odd dates (eg, 1, 3, 5 July and so on) the rest of the year. For any schedule changes phone ☎ 0839-123411.

Queen's Gallery The Queen's Gallery, with its extensive Royal Collection, is closed for renovation through to 2002. Call the palace for the latest details.

Royal Mews South of the palace, the Royal Mews, Buckingham Palace Rd SW1 (⊖ Victoria), started life as a falconry but now houses the flashy vehicles the royals use for getting around on ceremonial occasions, including the stunning Gold State Coach of 1762. The Royal Mews opens noon to 4.30 pm Monday to Thursday, August and September (to 4.00 pm the rest of the year). Admission costs £4.30/2.10.

Green Park Adjoining St James's Park to the north-west across The Mall, Green Park is a less fussy, more naturally rolling park, with trees and open space, sunshine and shade. Note the serene **Memorial to Canadian War Dead** near Buckingham Palace.

Mayfair As everyone who's ever played the British version of Monopoly will know, Mayfair is one of London's most exclusive neighbourhoods. At the heart of the district is **Grosvenor Square**, dominated by the hideous US embassy on the western side and with a **memorial to Franklin D Roosevelt** in the centre.

The West End (Maps 4 & 5)

No two Londoners ever agree on the exact borders of the West End but let's just say it takes in Piccadilly Circus and Trafalgar Square to the south, Oxford St and Tottenham Court Rd to the north, Regent St to the west and Covent Garden and the Strand to the east. A heady mixture of consumerism and culture, the West End is where outstanding museums and galleries rub shoulders with tacky tourist traps.

Piccadilly Circus Piccadilly Circus (Map 5) is home to the statue of the *Angel of Christian Charity,* commonly known as **Eros** and dedicated to Lord Ashley, the Victorian Earl of Shaftesbury, who championed social and industrial reform.

Piccadilly Circus used to be the hub of London, where flower girls flogged their wares and people arranged to meet or simply bumped into each other. Nowadays it's fume-choked and pretty uninteresting, overlooked by Rock Circus and Tower Records.

Rock Circus Brought to you by the Madame Tussaud's people, the revamped Rock Circus (Map 5; ☎ 7734 7203), London Pavilion, Piccadilly Circus W1 (⊖ Piccadilly Circus), is one of the capital's most popular attractions. You're whipped back to rock's cotton-picking origins so fast you barely have time to take in what's happening, after which you're treated to a succession of animated models who lip-sync to their music while jerking their limbs around like puppets. It opens 10 am to 10 pm daily (from 11 am Tuesday). Admission costs £8.25/6.25.

London Trocadero The Trocadero (Map 5; ☎ 09068-881100), 1 Piccadilly Circus W1 (⊖ Piccadilly Circus), is a huge indoor entertainment complex on six levels with several high-tech attractions, anchored by the **Segaworld** indoor theme-park. It's a good place to take youngsters who can't be sold on London's more cultural attractions, but don't expect a peaceful – or cheap – night or day out. There's no admission charge to Segaworld, but you must pay £3 for each of the eight rides. Check for discounts on multiple ticket purchases. **Funland** has upwards of 400 video games to keep even the most hyperactive active. The centre opens 10 am until midnight daily (to 1 am Friday and Saturday).

Piccadilly Running west from Piccadilly Circus, Piccadilly (Map 5) is home to **St James's Piccadilly**, a church designed by Sir Christopher Wren after the Great Fire of 1666.

The **Royal Academy of Arts** (☎ 7300 8000), Burlington House, Piccadilly W1 (⊖ Green Park), has traditionally played poor relation to the Hayward Gallery. But in recent years exhibitions here have broken all records. Each summer, the academy holds its traditional Summer Exhibition, an open show that anyone can enter. It opens 10 am to 6 pm daily (often to 8.30 pm Friday).

Admission costs depend on what's on, but expect to pay around £6.

Regent St Elegant shop-fronts line Regent St (Map 5). Here you'll find Hamley's (☎ 7734 3161), London's premier toy and game store, and the upmarket department store Liberty. Go east along Great Marlborough St and you'll reach the northern end of **Carnaby St**, which runs parallel to Regent St. It was the street for fashion in the 'swinging London' of the 1960s, and this lives on in the Union Jack-emblazoned gewgaws it off-loads to tourists.

The BBC Experience North of Oxford Circus is **Broadcasting House** (Map 4), from which the BBC began broadcasting in 1932. The basement now houses the BBC Experience (☎ 0870 603 0304) where you can watch clips of popular BBC programmes and see the Marconi Collection of early wireless equipment. It opens 10 am (from 11 am Monday) to 5.30 pm daily. Admission costs £6.95/4.95. There's a shop stocking any number of videos, tapes and books relating to BBC programmes.

Oxford St Once London's finest shopping street, Oxford St (Maps 4 & 5) is a big disappointment for most visitors, especially if you emerge from Oxford Circus tube and head east towards Tottenham Court Rd. Things are much better if you head west towards Marble Arch; this is where you'll find the famous department stores, including Selfridges.

Soho East of Regent St and south of Oxford St, with Shaftesbury Ave and Charing Cross Rd to the south and the east, is Soho (Map 5), one of the liveliest corners of London and the place to come for fun and games after dark. A decade ago it was known mostly for strip clubs and peepshows. The sleaze is still there, of course, but these days it rubs shoulders with some of London's trendiest clubs, bars and restaurants.

Leicester Square Despite efforts to smarten it up and the presence of four huge cinemas, various nightclubs, pubs and restaurants, pedestrianised Leicester (pronounced les-ter) Square (Map 5) still feels more like a transit point between Covent Garden and Piccadilly Circus than its own world.

Chinatown Immediately north of Leicester Square are Lisle and Gerrard Sts, the heart of London's Chinatown (Map 5), where street signs are in both English and Chinese. This is the place to come for an after-hours Chinese meal (see Places to Eat later).

Covent Garden In the 1630s Inigo Jones converted something that had started life as a vegetable field belonging to Westminster Abbey into the elegant square – or piazza – at Covent Garden. But by Victorian times a fruit and vegetable market had been set up (immortalised in *My Fair Lady*, the 1964 screen adaptation of George Bernard Shaw's play *Pygmalion*). When the market was moved out in the 1980s, Covent Garden was transformed into one of central London's liveliest hubs, with shops built into the old arcades.

Covent Garden (Map 5; ⊖ Covent Garden) gets horribly overcrowded in summer but remains one of the few bits of London where pedestrians rule, and there's always a corner of relative peace where you can listen to the licensed buskers.

JANE SMITH

The usual, and the not-so-usual, busker performances entertain at Covent Garden.

Beyond the piazza are lively streets of clothes shops and bars, restaurants and designer gift shops. To the north, Floral St is where swanky designers have their outlets.

London Transport Museum Tucked into the corner of Covent Garden between the Jubilee Hall and Tutton's restaurant, the London Transport Museum (Map 5; ☎ 7836 8557) tells how London made the transition from streets choked with horse-drawn carriages to the arrival of the DLR and the modern Jubilee Line extension – a more interesting story than you might suspect. It opens 10 am to 6 pm daily (from 11 am Friday) and admission costs £5.50/2.95. There's an excellent shop with merchandise and books.

Theatre Museum A branch of the Victoria & Albert Museum, the Theatre Museum (Map 5; ☎ 7836 7891), Russell St WC2 (⊖ Covent Garden), displays costumes and artefacts relating to the history of the theatre. The museum opens 10 am to 6 pm Tuesday to Sunday. Admission is £4.50/free.

The Strand At the end of the 12th century nobles built sturdy houses of stone with gardens along the 'beach' of the Thames. The Strand (Maps 4 & 5) linked Westminster, the seat of political power, with the City, London's centre of industry and trade, and became one of the most prestigious places in London to live; in the 19th century Disraeli pronounced it the finest street in Europe. Today this three-quarters-of-a-mile thoroughfare is a hotchpotch of shops, fine hotels, theatres and offices, in whose doorways the homeless lay out their sleeping bags for the night.

Somerset House This splendid Palladian masterpiece (Map 4; ⊖ Temple), designed by William Chambers in 1775, contains two fabulous museums: the Courtauld Gallery and the new Gilbert Collection of decorative arts. In 2000 the central courtyard reopened after a long restoration that saw a car park banished and one of London's most elegant spaces restored to its former glory.

It has tables outside in the summer as well as a fountain and occasional live open-air theatre. Out the back there's a great terrace over-looking the Thames with a cafe (see Places to Eat) and tables for picnickers. In 2001, a gallery showing selected pieces from the renowned Hermitage in St Petersburg is set to open.

Courtauld Gallery Housed in the North Wing (or Strand Block), the Courtauld Gallery (☎ 7848 2526) displays some of the Courtauld Institute's marvellous collection of paintings in grand surroundings following a £25 million architectural refurbishment. Exhibits include works by Rubens, Bellini, Velásquez and Botticelli. However, for many visitors the most memorable display is of impressionist and postimpressionist art by Van Gogh, Cézanne, Rousseau, Gauguin, Toulouse-Lautrec, Manet, Pissarro, Sisley, Renoir, Degas and Monet.

The gallery opens 10 am to 6 pm daily (from noon Sunday). Admission is £4/free. On Monday between 10 am and 2 pm it's free for everyone. Joint admission with the Gilbert Collection costs £7 (see below).

Gilbert Collection One of London's newest museums, the Gilbert Collection (☎ 7240 5782) includes such treasures as European silver, gold snuffboxes and Italian mosaics bequeathed to the nation by London-born American businessman Arthur Gilbert. Worth over £100 million, the collection is housed in the vaults beneath the South Terrace. Opening hours and admission charges are the same as the Courtauld Gallery.

Bloomsbury (Maps 2 & 4)

East of Tottenham Court Rd and north of High Holborn, south of Euston Rd and to the west of Gray's Inn Rd, Bloomsbury is a peculiar mix of the University of London, the British Museum and beautiful Georgian squares. **Russell Square** (Map 4), the very heart of Bloomsbury, is London's largest square. It was laid out in 1800. At night it becomes a very busy gay cruising area.

Between the world wars these pleasant streets were colonised by a group of artists and intellectuals who became known collectively as the Bloomsbury Group. The novelists Virginia Woolf and EM Forster and the economist John Maynard Keynes are perhaps the best-known members. The centre of literary Bloomsbury was **Gordon Square** (Map 2) where many writers lived. Look for the blue plaques on the buildings. Lovely **Bedford Square** (Map 4) is the only completely Georgian square still surviving in Bloomsbury and was once home to many publishing houses.

British Museum London's most visited tourist attraction with more than six million annual visitors, the British Museum (Map 4; ☎ 7636 1555), Great Russell St WC1 (⊖ Tottenham Court Road or Russell Square) is Britain's largest museum and one of the oldest in the world. (The operators of the Millennium Dome – see Greenwich later – always hoped to attract twice the amount of visitors. Ha!)

Late in 2000, the museum's inner courtyard, hidden from the public for almost a century and a half, was due to reopen as the **Great Court**, covered with a spectacular glass and steel roof designed by Norman Foster. This grand new space, which cost almost £100 million in lottery money, is designed to open up the labyrinth that is the British Museum.

The collection is vast, diverse and amazing – so much so that it can seem pretty daunting. To make the most of the museum don't plan on seeing too much in one day; the fact that admission is still free means you can come back several times and appreciate the museum's exhibits at your leisure.

The British Museum has two entrances: the imposing Smirke-designed porticoed main entrance off Great Russell St, and a back entrance off Montague Place, which tends to be less congested.

The following are the top highlights in the museum. However, it can be equally rewarding to get away from the crowds, pick an exhibit at random and read the usually excellent explanatory material to learn all sorts of surprising things.

Room 25 has Egyptian sculptures and the **Rosetta Stone**, written in two forms of ancient Egyptian (hieroglyphics and demotic) and in Ancient Greek. The Rosetta Stone was the key to deciphering Egyptian hieroglyphics, which had stymied scholars up to that time. The famous mummies have been moved to the new Mummies Gallery on the 2nd floor.

Rooms 1 to 15 feature finds from the classical Greek, Roman and Hellenistic empires. Best known of the exhibits here are the **Elgin Marbles**, pilfered from the walls of the Parthenon on the Acropolis in Athens by Lord Elgin from 1801 to 1806. They are thought to show a great procession to the temple but have been pretty battered and beaten over the centuries (not the least by the British Museum, see the boxed text 'Hey! We Want Our Marbles Back!').

Upstairs in rooms 51 and 52 is the stunning **Oxus Treasure**, a collection of 7th- to 4th-century BC pieces of Persian gold. These artefacts are believed to date back to the third millennium BC, placing them among the oldest exhibits in the museum.

Rooms 49 and 50 contain artefacts from Roman Britain and from the Bronze Age and Celtic Europe (approximately 900 to 100 BC). This is where you'll see the stunning **Mildenhall Treasure**, a 28-piece silver dinner service dating from the 4th century.

This is also where you'll find **Lindow Man**, an Iron Age unfortunate who seems to have been struck on the head with a narrow axe (there are holes in the skull) and then garrotted.

At the heart of the museum, the **Reading Room** in the centre of the covered Great Court is the grand structure where George Bernard Shaw and Mahatma Gandhi studied and Friedrich Engels and Karl Marx wrote *The Communist Manifesto* when it was used for the British Library. The northern end of the courtyard's lower level is to house the museum's Sainsbury African Galleries and will be linked with new galleries for the American, Asian, Middle Eastern, European and Pacific ethnographical collections on the ground floor of the main hall.

Hours & Tickets The British Museum opens 10 am to 5 pm Monday to Saturday and noon to 6 pm Sunday. Admission is free.

Guided Tours The museum offers visitors free Eye Opener tours of individual galleries (eg, World of Asia and Treasures of Islam).

Hey! We Want Our Marbles Back!

Wonderful though it is, the British Museum can sometimes feel like one vast repository for stolen booty. Much of what you're looking at wasn't just 'picked up' along the way by Victorian travellers and explorers, but stolen, or purchased under dubious circumstances.

KATE NOLAN

During the 1990s, restive foreign governments occasionally popped their heads over the parapet to demand the return of 'their' property. The loudest voice was that of the Greeks calling for the return of the so-called Elgin Marbles to their original home on the Parthenon in Athens. However, successive British governments have been intransigent, possibly figuring that millions of free-spending British holiday-makers to Greece each year are payment enough.

All along, the British Museum has sniffed that the marbles were better off under its protective care. This arrogance proved tragicomic when it emerged in 1999 that earlier in the 20th century the museum had 'cleaned' the marbles using chisels and wire brushes. As a result, the finishes applied to the marbles by the ancient Greeks were destroyed.

Greece lost its Marbles to British diplomat Thomas Bruce in 1906

These last an hour and generally take place between 11 am and 3 pm Monday to Saturday and between 1 and 4 pm Sunday.

Holborn & Clerkenwell (Maps 2 & 4)

Holborn (pronounced hoe-bun; Map 4), the area north of the Strand and Fleet St and wedged between the City to the east, Covent Garden to the west and High Holborn to the north, includes several of the Inns of Court, where London's barristers practise, and the wonderful Sir John Soane's Museum. It is the smallest of London's former metropolitan boroughs and takes its name from a tributary of the River Fleet.

Immediately north-west of the City, Clerkenwell has become a very trendy corner of the capital, with the usual batch of pricey restaurants and expensive property. The area around Clerkenwell Green is very attractive.

Sir John Soane's Museum Sir John Soane's Museum (Map 5; ☎ 7405 2107), 13 Lincoln's Inn Fields WC2 (⊖ Holborn) is partly a beautiful – if quirky – house and partly a small museum representing one man's personal taste. Some visitors consider it their favourite 'small' sight in London.

Sir John Soane (1753–1837) was a leading architect who had a real passion for collecting. His eclectic acquisitions include an Egyptian sarcophagus and the original *Rake's Progress*, William Hogarth's set of cartoon caricatures of late-18th-century London lowlife. The museum opens 10 am to 5 pm Tuesday to Saturday and 6 to 9 pm on the first Tuesday of every month. Admission is free.

The City (Maps 4 & 6)

The City of London is 'the square mile' on the northern bank of the Thames where the Romans first built a walled community 2000 years ago. The boundaries of today's City haven't changed much, and you can always tell when you're within them because the Corporation of London's coat of arms appears on the street signs, and the small statue of a griffin emblazoned with the motto *Domine Dirige Nos* (God Direct Us)

marks the City's borders. This is the business heart of London where you'll find not only the Bank of England, but also the headquarters of many British and overseas banks, insurance companies and other financial institutions. Under 10,000 people actually live in the City but around 300,000 commute there to work every day.

A quiet weekend stroll when the banks and offices are closed offers a unique chance to appreciate the architectural richness of its many famous buildings and the atmospheric little alleyways that now separate futuristic office towers.

Fleet St Ever since Wynkyn de Worde moved Caxton's printing press from Westminster to a shop beside St Bride's Church in 1500, Fleet St (Map 4; ⊖ Blackfriars) has been ink-splattered. In the 20th century it earned the nickname of 'London's Street of Shame', where printing presses stoked by gossip and lies churned out their scurrilous product: the UK's tabloid newspapers. But then the mid-1980s brought Rupert Murdoch, new technology and the Docklands redevelopment and all the papers moved away.

Temple Church Just off Fleet St is Temple Church (Map 4; ☎ 7353 1736), Inner Temple, King's Bench Walk EC4 (⊖ Temple or, on Sunday, Blackfriars), under the archway beyond No 17. Duck under it and you'll find yourself in the Inner Temple, one of the Inns of Court. Temple Church was originally planned and built by the secretive Knights Templar between 1161 and 1185. They modelled it on the Church of the Holy Sepulchre in Jerusalem.

Temple Church opens 10 am to 4 pm Wednesday to Saturday. Westminster Abbey and St Paul's Cathedral aside, this is possibly London's most interesting and architecturally important church. Don't miss it.

St Bartholomew-the-Great One of London's oldest churches, St Bartholomew-the-Great (Map 4; ☎ 7606 5171), West Smithfield EC1 (⊖ Barbican), is a stone's throw from the Barbican and worth more than a fleeting visit. The authentic Norman arches and details lend this holy space an ancient calm; approaching from nearby Smithfield Market through the restored 13th-century archway is like walking back in time.

The church opens 8.30 am to 5 pm Monday to Friday, 10.30 am to 1.30 pm Saturday and 8 am to 8 pm Sunday.

Central Criminal Court (Old Bailey) All Britain's major gangsters and serial killers eventually find themselves at the Central Criminal Court, better known as the Old Bailey (Map 4) after the street on which it stands. Look up at the great copper dome and you'll see the figure of justice holding a sword and scales in her hands; oddly she is *not* blindfolded, which has sparked many a sarcastic comment from those being brought in here.

The court's public gallery (☎ 7248 3277), on Newgate St, opens 10.30 am to 1 pm and 2 to 4 pm weekdays.

St Paul's Cathedral Built, amid much controversy, between 1675 and 1710 by Sir Christopher Wren, St Paul's Cathedral (Map 6; ☎ 7236 4128; ⊖ St Paul's) stands on the site of four previous cathedrals, the first of which dated from 604.

The dome still dominates the City and the only church dome that exceeds it in size is that of St Peter's in Rome. Pictures of the cathedral miraculously surviving the devastation of WWII bombing can be seen in a glass case in the southern choir aisle and the images have become an icon of the Blitz.

Before you enter, take a moment to walk around to the north of the cathedral (that's to the left as you face the large stairway). A long overdue **monument to the people of London** – not all those warmongers, sabre-rattlers and heroes at rest in the crypt – has been unveiled in the small garden just outside the northern transept in St Paul's Churchyard. Simple, elegant, it honours the 32,000 civilians killed in London during WWII.

From the main entrance, proceed up the northern aisle, past the **Chapel of St Dunstan**, dedicated to the 10th-century archbishop of

Canterbury, and the grandiose **Duke of Wellington Memorial** (1875), until you reach the central pavement area under the dome. Some 30m above the paved area is the first of three domes – actually a dome, inside a cone, inside a dome – supported by eight massive columns. The walkway around its base is called the **Whispering Gallery**, because if you talk close to the wall it carries your words around to the opposite side 32m away.

In the northern transept chapel is Holman Hunt's celebrated painting *The Light of the World*, which depicts Christ knocking at an overgrown door that, symbolically, can only be opened from the inside. Beyond are the **quire** (or chancel), whose ceilings and arches dazzle with green, blue, red and gold mosaics, and the high altar. Walk around the altar, with its massive gilded oak canopy, to the **American Chapel**, a memorial to the 28,000 Americans based in Britain who lost their lives during WWII.

On the eastern side of the southern transept, a staircase leads down to the Crypt, Treasury and OBE Chapel, where services (weddings, funerals, etc) reserved for members of the Order of the British Empire are held. The **Crypt** has memorials to up to 300 military demigods, including Wellington, Kitchener and Nelson, who is below the dome in a black sarcophagus.

The most poignant memorial of all is to Sir Christopher himself. It is south of the **OBE Chapel** and is just a simple slab with his name, the year of his death (1723) and his age ('XCI'). The **Treasury** displays some of the cathedral's plate. There is also a cafe and a shop in the crypt open 9 am to 5 pm Monday to Saturday (from 10.30 am Sunday).

Back upstairs in the nave, the Whispering Gallery as well as the **Stone Gallery** and the **Golden Gallery** can be reached by a staircase on the western side of the southern transept. All in all there are 259 steps to the first gallery, another 116 to the Stone Gallery and 155 more steps to the top gallery; that's a total of 530 steps to climb up and down. Even if you can't make it right up to the Golden Gallery, it's worth struggling as far as the Stone Gallery for one of the best views of London.

The cathedral opens 8.30 am to 4 pm Monday to Saturday. Admission costs £5/ 2.50. Audioguide tours lasting 45 minutes are available for £3. Guided 90-minute tours (£2.50/2) leave the tour desk at 11 and 11.30 am, and 1.30 and 2 pm. There are organ concerts at St Paul's at 5 pm most Sundays. Evensong takes place at 5 pm most weekdays and at 3.15 pm Sunday.

Guildhall The Guildhall (Map 6; ☎ 7606 3030), off Gresham St EC2 (☻ Bank), which sits exactly in the centre of the square mile, has been the City's seat of government for nearly 800 years. The present building dates from the early 15th century.

Visitors can see the **Great Hall** where the mayor and sheriffs are still elected, a vast empty space with church-style monuments and the shields and banners of the 12 principal livery companies of London.

The **Guildhall Art Gallery** to the southeast in Guildhall Yard opened in 1999 and brings together the Corporation's huge art collection for the first time since WWII. Over 250 works are on display at any time.

Admission to the Guildhall's art gallery costs £2.50/1, otherwise it is free. It opens 10 am to 5 pm daily (to 4 pm Sunday), except Sunday October to April.

Barbican Tucked into a corner of the City of London where there was once a watchtower (or 'barbican'), the Barbican (Map 6; ☎ 7638 4141), Silk St EC2 (☻ Barbican or Moorgate), is a vast urban development built on a large bomb site from WWII.

The original ambitious plan was to create a terribly smart, modern complex for offices, housing and the arts. Perhaps inevitably, the result was a forbidding series of wind tunnels with a dearth of shops, plenty of expensive high-rise apartments and an enormous cultural centre lost in the middle. Here you'll find the London home of the Royal Shakespeare Company (RSC), the London Symphony Orchestra and the London Classical Orchestra. There are also smaller theatrical auditoriums, the Museum

of London and the wonderful **Barbican Art Gallery** (☎ 7588 9023) on Level 3, with among the best photographic exhibits in London. The hours vary with each exhibit, but be warned – even Londoners get to the Barbican early to make sure of finding their way to the right spot at the right time.

For details of the theatres and concert halls, see Entertainment later.

Museum of London Despite it's unprepossessing setting amid the concrete walkways of the Barbican (look for gate 7), the Museum of London (Map 6; ☎ 7600 3699, 7600 0807 for a recording), London Wall EC2 (☻ Barbican), is one of the city's finest museums, showing how the city has evolved from the Ice Age to the Internet.

The sections on Roman Britain and Roman Londinium make use of the nearby ruins of a Roman fort discovered during road construction. Otherwise, the displays work steadily through the centuries, using audiovisual materials to show such events as the Great Fire of London.

Part of the museum's collection dealing with London's port and the Thames will be transferred to a new museum in the Docklands when it opens in 2001.

The museum opens 10 am to 5.50 pm Monday to Saturday and from noon Sunday. Admission is £5/free. Tickets are valid for a year. The fine shop has a wide selection of fictional and factual accounts of London.

Tower of London One of London's three World Heritage Sites (the others are Westminster Abbey and its surrounding buildings and Maritime Greenwich), the Tower of London (Map 6; ☎ 7680 9004), Tower Hill EC3 (☻ Tower Hill), has dominated the south-eastern corner of the City of London since 1078 when William the Conqueror laid the first stone of the White Tower to replace the earth and timber castle he'd already built on the site.

In the early Middle Ages, the Tower of London acted not just as a royal residence but also as a treasury, a mint, an arsenal and a prison. After Henry VIII moved to Whitehall Palace in 1529, the Tower's role as a prison became increasingly important, with Thomas More, queens Anne Boleyn and Catherine Howard and Lady Jane Grey just some of the most famous Tudor prisoners.

These days the Tower is visited by more than two million people a year, with impressive crowds even on cold winter afternoons; however the queues move quickly.

Orientation The most striking building in the Tower is undoubtedly the huge **White Tower**, in the centre of the courtyard, with its solid Romanesque architecture and four turrets. It was whitewashed during the reign of Henry III and thus got its name. It now houses a collection from the Royal Armouries. On the 2nd floor is the **Chapel of St John the Evangelist**, which dates from 1080 and is therefore the oldest church in London.

Facing the White Tower to the north is the **Waterloo Barracks**, which now contains the Crown Jewels: orbs, sceptres and the centrepiece, the Imperial State Crown, set with diamonds (2868 of them to be exact), sapphires, emeralds, rubies and pearls.

Beside the Waterloo Barracks stands the **Chapel Royal of St Peter ad Vincula** (St Peter in Chains), which can only be visited on a group tour or after 4.30 pm. It's a rare example of ecclesiastical Tudor architecture.

What looks quite a peaceful, picturesque corner of the Tower is in fact one of its most tragic. On the small green in front of the church stood the **scaffold**, set up during Henry VIII's reign and where seven people were beheaded. On it were executed his two allegedly adulterous wives, Anne Boleyn and Catherine Howard.

Beside Wakefield Tower stands the **Bloody Tower**, probably the best-known part of the complex. On the 1st floor you can see the windlass that controlled the portcullis, the grating that could be dropped down to guard the gateway. A 17th-century wooden screen separates it from a room where Sir Walter Raleigh was imprisoned and where he wrote his *History of the World* (a copy is on display).

Once called the Garden Tower, the Bloody Tower acquired its unsavoury nickname

from the story that the 'princes in the Tower', Edward V and his younger brother, were murdered here. The blame is usually laid at the door of their uncle Richard III, but there are those who prefer to finger Henry VII for the crime.

Don't leave the Tower without taking a look at the stretch of green between the Wakefield and White towers where the Great Hall once stood. Here you'll find the Tower's famous ravens, which legend says will cause the White Tower to collapse when they leave. Their wings are clipped to avoid that problem.

Hours & Tickets The Tower opens 9 am to 6 pm Monday to Saturday and from 10 am Sunday. It closes at 5 pm November to March. Last admission is an hour before and costs £11/7.30.

Guided Tours Hugely entertaining, hour-long tours led by the Yeoman Warders, or 'Beefeaters', leave from the Middle Tower every 30 minutes from 9 am (from 10 am Sunday) to 3.30 pm daily.

Tower Bridge When it was built in 1894, London was still a thriving port and Tower Bridge (Map 6; ☎ 7378 1928; ⊖ Tower Hill) had to allow ships to pass through. The bridge's walkways afford excellent views across the City and Docklands.

For the **Tower Bridge Experience**, a lift takes you up from the modern visitors' facility in the northern tower where the story of its building is recounted. It opens 10 am to 6.30 pm daily, April to October; and 9.30 am to 6 pm daily, November to March. Admission costs £6.25/4.25.

South of the Thames

As recently as a decade ago, the southern part of central London was the city's forgotten underside – run-down, neglected and offering little for foreign visitors once they'd visited the South Bank arts venues. Recently, however, all that has changed and parts of London immediately south of the river can seem as exciting as anywhere farther north.

Bermondsey (Maps 1 & 6) Although parts of Bermondsey still look pretty dejected, there are pockets of refurbishment, even gentrification. Its main sight is the sparkling white **Design Museum** (Map 1; ☎ 7403 6933), 28 Shad Thames SE1 (✆ Tower Hill), which has displays on how product design has evolved over time and how it can make the difference between success and failure for items intended for mass production. It opens 11.30 am to 6 pm daily (from 10.30 am weekends). Admission costs £5.50/4.

Southwark (Maps 4 & 6) Originally settled by the Romans, Southwark (pronounced **suth**-erk) became an important thoroughfare for people travelling to London in the Middle Ages. For centuries London Bridge was the only place to cross the Thames.

Although Southwark is still pretty rundown it's on the up and up; some say it's London's new Left Bank. There are a slew of sights to be found along the Thames in Bankside, an area that's home to popular destinations such as the new Tate Modern gallery.

HMS Belfast The HMS *Belfast* (Map 6; ☎ 7407 6328), Morgan's Lane, Tooley St SE1 (✆ London Bridge), is a large, light cruiser built with 16 six-inch guns and launched in 1938. It saw much action during WWII. It's now preserved by the Imperial War Museum. You can visit the ship from 10 am to 6 pm daily, March to October (to 5 pm the rest of the year). Admission is £5/free.

London Dungeon Under the arches of London Bridge station, the London Dungeon (Map 6; ☎ 7403 7221), 28–34 Tooley St SE1 (✆ London Bridge), is long on gore and short on substance. The reconstruction of the French guillotine in action is gruesome but still doesn't hold a candle to the section dealing with Victorian serial killer Jack the Ripper. Kids, of course, love it.

The dungeon opens 10 am to 5.30 pm daily, October to March; 10 am to 6.30 pm daily, April to June and September; and 10 am to 9 pm daily, July and August.

Admission costs £9.95/6.50. Beware of touts selling fake tickets.

Southwark Cathedral There was already a church on this site in 1086, but it was rebuilt in 1106 and then for a third time in the 13th century. By the 1830s it had fallen into decay and much of what you see today is actually Victorian – the nave was rebuilt in 1897 – although the central tower dates from 1520 and the choir from the 13th century. In 1905 the old church became Southwark Cathedral (Map 6; ☎ 7407 3708), Montague Close SE1 (✆ London Bridge), with its own bishop. It emerged from a major clean-up during 2000, complete with a new visitors centre.

There are monuments and details galore inside and it's worth picking up one of the small guides. On the choir floor are tablets marking the **tomb of Edmond Shakespeare**, actor-brother of the Bard, who died in 1607. Along the southern aisle of the nave, stop and look at the green alabaster **monument to William Shakespeare**, whose great works were originally written for the Bankside playhouses.

The cathedral opens 8 am to 6 pm daily. Admission is free although a £2.50 donation is requested. Evensong is sung at 5.30 pm on Tuesday and Friday, 4 pm on Saturday and 3 pm on Sunday.

Vinopolis – City of Wine Vinopolis (Map 6; ☎ 0870 444 4777), 1 Bank End, Park St SE1 (✆ London Bridge), in a hectare of Victorian railway vaults in Bankside, cashes in on Londoners' love affair with things red, white and rosé. The high-tech exhibits introduce visitors to the history of wine-making and, more importantly, there are tastings of five wines as you tour. It opens 10 am to 5.30 daily (until 8 pm weekends) with last entry two hours before it closes. Admission costs £11.50/5 (children don't get any wine).

Shakespeare's Globe & Exhibition The Globe Theatre (Map 6; ☎ 7401 9919), 21 New Globe Walk SE1 (✆ London Bridge), consists of the reconstructed Globe Theatre and, beneath it, an exhibition focusing on Elizabethan London and the struggle by

American actor (later film director) Sam Wanamaker to get the theatre rebuilt.

The original Globe (known as the 'Wooden O' after its circular shape and roofless centre) was erected in 1599. It was burned down in 1613 and was immediately rebuilt. In 1642 it was finally closed by the Puritans, who regarded theatres as dreadful dens of iniquity. The new Globe opened in 1997 and is meant to replicate the original, right down to the thatched roof and lack of seats for the 500 'groundlings', who stand to watch performances.

The Globe opens to visitors 10 am to 5 pm daily. A visit to the exhibition, which also includes a guided tour of the Globe Theatre itself (except on days with a matinee performance, when tours are in the morning only), costs £7.50/5. Performances run from mid-May to late-September.

Tate Modern The vast Bankside Power Station, designed by Giles Gilbert Scott after WWII but decommissioned in 1986, is home to the Tate Modern (Maps 4 & 6; ☎ 7887 8000 for information), Queen's Walk SE1 (✆ Blackfriars or London Bridge), London's most popular new attraction. The galleries spread over five floors, all of which open onto the cavernous old **Turbine Hall**. The machinery is gone – although a piped in hum recalls it – and in its place is some rather huge works of art including a giant spider by Louise Bourgeois.

The collections cover art from 1900 in all of its many forms from paintings to videos to bits of rock piled up on the floor. The curators have wisely placed the exhibition titled 'Nude/Action/Body' on the top gallery floor, which means that salacious hordes are drawn well into the building. However, the policy of grouping the art by theme has come in for near universal criticism; the *Evening Standard's* art critic Brian Sewell called it 'shallow and capricious'.

The Tate Modern opens 10 am to 6 pm Sunday to Thursday and until 10 pm Friday and Saturday. It's free, although special exhibitions charge fees. The £1 audio guides are worthwhile for their descriptions of some of the works.

Millennium Bridge Of all the projects conceived to help usher in the third millennium, this footbridge (Map 6) over the Thames is arguably the most important to the people of London: it is beautiful and will do much to bring London back to the Thames, its birthplace, and link its two banks. Designed by the ubiquitous Norman Foster to look like a 'blade of light', it links the Tate Modern and Bankside with the City and St Paul's. That said, the opening of the bridge in June 2000 turned into the cock-up of all cock-ups when – not surprisingly – mobs arrived to try it out. As the span filled with people it began rocking to such an extent that people had to clutch the rails and each other to keep from toppling over. The hand-wringing bridge commission promptly closed it, even though it was generally agreed to be safe, just wobbly. Sadly, the bridge remained closed at the time of writing and the hand-wringing and finger-pointing continued. It should reopen in April 2001.

The South Bank (Map 4) North of Waterloo station and across the Thames from Embankment tube station, the South Bank is a labyrinth of arts venues strung out on rain-stained concrete walkways between Hungerford Railway Bridge and just beyond Waterloo Bridge. Few people have a good word to say about the ugly architecture and a complete overhaul is on the cards – expect a lot of work to be going on here.

The **Royal Festival Hall** hosts classical, opera, jazz and choral music. Alongside a range of pricey cafes and restaurants and a good music shop, it also has a foyer where free recitals take place most evenings. The smaller **Queen Elizabeth Hall** to the northeast and the **Purcell Room** host similar concerts. A full-scale refurbishment of the Royal Festival Hall began in 1999.

Tucked almost out of sight under the arches of Waterloo Bridge is the **National Film Theatre** (NFT), built in 1958 and screening some 2000 films a year. The popular **Museum of the Moving Image** is closed for redevelopment until 2003.

The **Hayward Gallery** (☎ 7928 3144), Belvedere Rd SE1 (✆ Waterloo), built in 1968, usually hosts blockbuster modern art exhibitions. Hours and prices for these vary. The **Royal National Theatre**, a love-it-or-hate-it complex of three theatres (Olivier, Lyttleton and Cottesloe), is Britain's flagship theatre.

Hungerford Bridge This once mundane railway bridge (⊖ Embankment or Charing Cross) linking Charing Cross Station with South London was due to receive a long overdue rehab. The narrow but vital pedestrian walkway on the eastern side was supposed to be replaced by two new dramatically suspended walkways on both sides of the bridge. But right after work began all sorts of engineering cock-ups occurred and as of autumn 2000, the project was postponed indefinitely. For some reason London is having problems doing what the Romans had no problem accomplishing 2000 years ago: bridging the Thames.

British Airways London Eye London's newest landmark and right on the Thames, the British Airways London Eye (⊖ Waterloo), is, at 135m tall, the world's largest sight-seeing wheel (for all sorts of technical reasons it's not a *Ferris* wheel, ok?). It is a thrilling experience to be in one of the 32 enclosed glass gondolas, enjoying views of some 25 miles (on rare clear days) across the capital; the 'Millennium Wheel' (as it's also known) takes 30 minutes to rotate completely.

The wheel operates from 9 am to 10 pm daily, April to October (10 am to 6 pm the rest of the year), but such is its popularity that the hours keep lengthening. Tickets cost £8.50/5. However, all those riders mean that you have to plan ahead. You can order tickets in advance (☎ 0870 500 0600) for a set date and time and then pick them up before your ride, or purchase the tickets in person at the wheel. However, on weekends and during summer, don't expect to just turn up and spin as the entire day is often sold out. For same-day riding you either have to show up before opening to nab some of the few same-day tickets sold or you have to avail yourself of a ticket-hawker (beware of fake tickets, huge mark-ups, etc).

London Aquarium Despite being one of the largest in Europe, the London Aquarium (☎ 7967 8000), County Hall, Westminster Bridge Rd SE1 (⊖ Westminster or Waterloo) is curiously disappointing, partly because its location on three levels in the basement is so dark but also because the fish on display are generally of the less colourful variety. The new coral-reef display, however, is not bad. It opens 10 am to 6 pm daily. Admission costs £8/5.

Lambeth (Maps 1 & 4) Lambeth is the district immediately south of Westminster Bridge.

Imperial War Museum The Imperial War Museum (Map 1; ☎ 7416 5000), Lambeth Rd SE1 (⊖ Lambeth North), is housed in a striking building dating from 1815.

Although there's still plenty of military hardware on show, these days the museum places more emphasis on the social cost of war. This point is driven home in the **Holocaust Exhibition**, a heart-breaking permanent exhibition that opened in 2000. Artefacts and survivors' recollections are used to tell the story of the Nazis and their deeds. Little is held back and it is not recommended for those aged under 14.

Other exhibits are only a bit less grim and cover topics such as the Blitz and the WWI Trench Experience, which depicts the grim day-to-day existence of a WWI infantryman in a frontline trench on the Somme. There are always several special exhibits. The museum opens 10 am to 6 pm daily. Admission costs £5.50 (free for children, and for everyone after 4.30 pm).

Chelsea, South Kensington & Earl's Court (Map 7)

Much of west London is high-class territory; indeed, Kensington & Chelsea enjoys the highest average gross income of all London boroughs (over £485 a week). Go a bit farther west, though, and you'll reach Earl's Court and Barons Court, less prosperous areas that seem to have been dropped here by accident.

Thanks to the 1851 Great Exhibition, a

huge display of technology, South Kensington is first and foremost museumland, boasting the Natural History, Science and Victoria & Albert museums all on one road.

Victoria & Albert Museum The Victoria & Albert Museum (☎ 7942 2000), Cromwell Rd SW7 (☉ South Kensington) is a vast, rambling, wonderful museum of decorative art and design, part of Prince Albert's legacy to Londoners in the aftermath of the successful Great Exhibition of 1851.

Here you can see a mixed bag of ancient Chinese ceramics and modernist architectural drawings, Korean bronze and Japanese swords, samples from William Morris' 19th-century Arts and Crafts movement, cartoons by Raphael and Asian watercolours, Rodin sculptures, gowns from the Elizabethan era and dresses straight from this year's Paris fashion shows, ancient jewellery, a 1930s wireless set, an all-wooden Frank Lloyd Wright study, and a pair of Doc Martens. Think of it as the nation's attic.

Like the British Museum, this is one that needs careful planning if you're to get the most out of your visit. As soon as you're through the turnstile look at the floor plan and decide what you're most interested in; then stick to that plan unless you want to find that the time has flown by and you're still inspecting the plaster casts of classical statues. Alternatively, take one of the free introductory guided tours. A few of the eclectic highlights include: the Music Room from Norfolk House, the Throne of Maharaja Ranjit Singh, the Becket Casket, Henry VIII's writing desk and the Ardabil Carpet.

The museum opens 10 am to 5.45 pm daily and 6.30 to 9.30 pm Wednesday. Admission costs £5/3. There are free introductory tours of the V&A lasting between one and 1½ hours to some of the museum's galleries between 10.30 am and 4.30 pm.

Natural History Museum The Natural History Museum (☎ 7938 9123), Cromwell Rd SW7 (☉ South Kensington), has collections divided between the adjoining Life and Earth Galleries. Where once the former was full of dusty glass cases of butterflies and stick insects, there are now wonderful interactive displays on themes such as Human Biology and Creepy Crawlies. Plus there's the crowd-pulling exhibition on mammals and dinosaurs, which includes animatronic movers and shakers such as the 4m-high Tyrannosaurus Rex.

In some ways, though, it's the Earth Galleries that are the most staggering. Enter from Exhibition Rd and you'll find yourself facing an escalator that slithers up and into a hollowed-out globe. Upstairs there are two main exhibits: Earthquake and the Restless Surface, which explains how wind, water, ice, gravity and life itself impact on the earth.

The museum opens 10 am to 5.50 pm daily (from 11 am Sunday). Admission costs £6.50 (free for children, and for everyone after 4.30 pm weekdays and after 5 pm weekends).

Science Museum The Science Museum (☎ 7942 4455), Exhibition Rd SW7 (☉ South Kensington), has had a complete makeover since the days when it was a rather dreary place for eggheads and reluctant school children. The ground floor looks back at the history of the Industrial Revolution via examples of its machinery and then looks forward to the exploration of space. There are interactive and fascinating exhibits on five floors dealing with aeroplanes, the impact of science on food, computers, the history of medicine and much more.

The new £50 million Wellcome Wing focuses on contemporary science, medicine and technology and includes a 450-seat IMAX cinema. The latest scientific breakthroughs will be presented and there is an on-going, on-site study involving DNA titled 'What am I?'.

It opens 10 am to 6 pm daily. Admission costs £6.95 (free for under-17s, and for everyone after 4.30 pm).

Knightsbridge & Kensington (Map 3)

Knightsbridge is where you'll find some of London's best-known department stores, including Harrods and Harvey Nichols. To the west and north-west is Kensington, another thoroughly desirable London neighbourhood where you'll not get much change from a million pounds if you want to buy a sizeable house. Its main thoroughfare, Kensington High St, is another shoppers' paradise.

Albert Memorial On the southern edge of Hyde Park facing Kensington Gore, the Albert Memorial (⊖ South Kensington or Gloucester Road) is an over-the-top monument to Queen Victoria's German husband Albert (1819–61), which was unwrapped in 1998 after an eight-year renovation costing £11 million.

Kensington Palace Sometime home to Princess Margaret and the late Diana, Princess of Wales, Kensington Palace (☎ 7937 9561), Kensington Gardens W8 (⊖ High Street Kensington) dates from 1605 when it was home to the 2nd earl of Nottingham. Hour-long tours of the palace take you round the small, wood-panelled State Apartments dating from the time of William and the much grander, more spacious apartments of the Georgian period.

The **Sunken Garden** near the palace is at its prettiest in summer. Also nearby is **The Orangery**, designed by Hawksmoor and Sir John Vanbrugh and with carvings by Grinling Gibbons. Tea here is a pricey treat.

The State Apartments open 10 am to 5 pm daily. Admission costs £9.50/7.10. The park and gardens open 5 am to 30 minutes before dusk.

Hyde Park, Notting Hill & Bayswater

The huge popularity of the Notting Hill Carnival (in late August) reflects the multicultural appeal of this area of West London. Notting Hill became a focus for immigrants from Trinidad in the 1950s. Today it's a thriving, vibrant corner of London separated from the West End by the expanse of Hyde Park. It also echoes with the footsteps of tourists drawn by the eponymous film.

Hyde Park At 145 hectares, Hyde Park (Map 3) is central London's largest open space. Expropriated from the Church by Henry VIII in 1536, it became a hunting

ground for kings and aristocrats, and then a venue for duels, executions and horse racing. In 1851 the Great Exhibition was held here and during WWII it became an enormous potato field. More recently, it has served as a concert venue. The park is a riot of colour in spring, and full of lazy, milk-white to pink sunbathers in summer. Boating on the Serpentine is an option for the relatively energetic.

Along with sculptures by Henry Moore and Jacob Epstein, and the statue of Peter Pan by George Frampton, Hyde Park boasts its own art gallery. The **Serpentine Gallery** (Map 3; ☎ 7402 6075, ⊖ Hyde Park Corner or Lancaster Gate), beautifully located south of the lake and just west of the main road that cuts through the park, holds temporary exhibitions and specialises in contemporary art. The gallery opens 10 am to 6 pm daily. Admission is free.

Near Marble Arch, **Speakers' Corner** (Map 3; ⊖ Marble Arch) started life in 1872 as a response to serious riots. Every Sunday anyone with a soapbox – or anything else to stand on – can hold forth on whatever subject takes their fancy. It's an entertaining experience, especially if you like nutters.

Hyde Park opens 5.30 am till midnight daily.

Marylebone & Regent's Park (Maps 2, 3 & 4)

Marylebone Rd is north of Oxford St and home to the capital's No 1 tourist trap, Madame Tussaud's. It's also close to Regent's Park, which provides a haven of peace in the city as well as being home to London Zoo.

Wallace Collection The relatively unknown Wallace Collection (Map 4; ☎ 7935 0687), Hertford House, Manchester Square W1 (⊖ Bond Street) is London's finest small gallery. It houses a treasure trove of high-quality paintings from the 17th and 18th centuries, including works by Rubens, Titian, Poussin and Rembrandt, in a splendid Italianate mansion. Still another recipient of lottery cash, parts of the house have been restored to their original splendour and new space has been created to display the entire reserve collection.

The collection opens 10 am to 5 pm daily (from 2 pm Sunday) and admission is free. Free guided tours take place daily; phone for the exact times.

Madame Tussaud's Madame Tussaud's (Map 3; ☎ 7935 6861), Marylebone Rd NW1 (☻ Baker Street), the famous collection of waxworks, lures in some 2.7 million visitors a year. In order to avoid the long queues (particularly in summer), arrive early in the morning or late in the afternoon or – better still – don't go.

Much of the modern Madame Tussaud's is made up of the **Garden Party** where you can have your picture taken alongside stars-of-the-moment (one flop movie and it's off with your head, which is kept in a cupboard until your star rises again). The **Grand Hall** is where you'll find models of world leaders past and present and the royal family.

It opens 10 am to 5.30 pm weekdays and from 9.30 am weekends. Admission costs £11/7.50. A combined ticket allowing entry to the London Planetarium (see below) as well costs £13.95/9.

London Planetarium Attached to Madame Tussaud's, the London Planetarium (Map 3) presents 30-minute spectaculars on the stars and planets livened up with special effects. Hours are the same as Madame Tussaud's. Admission costs £6.30/4.20.

Regent's Park Like many other London parks, Regent's Park (Map 2; ☻ Baker Street or Regent's Park), north of Marylebone and south-west of Camden, was once used as a royal hunting ground, subsequently farmed and then revived as a place for fun and leisure during the 18th century.

Today, the roses in **Queen Mary's Gardens** are particularly spectacular and there are performances of Shakespeare plays in the summer. Phone ☎ 7486 7905 for details.

London Zoo One of the oldest zoos in the world, London Zoo (Map 2; ☎ 7722 3333), Regent's Park NW1 (☻ Camden Town), is

– like the London Underground – a victim of its great age; it was 172 years old in 2000. The zoo is saddled with many buildings that are historically interesting but don't meet the expectations of animal-rights-minded modern visitors. After a long period in the doldrums, the zoo has now embarked on a 10-year, £21 million programme to prepare it for the third millennium. The emphasis is now firmly on conservation and education, with fewer species kept, wherever possible in breeding groups.

The zoo opens 10 am to 5.30 pm daily March to October and until 4 pm other times. Admission costs £8.50/6.

NORTH LONDON

The northern reaches of central London stretch in a broad arc from St John's Wood in the west to Islington in the east. Those two districts exemplify the great economic divide that exists in the capital: the former is all moneyed gentility, the latter the run-down opposite (albeit with pockets of gentrification) in areas around Angel, where less than 10% of the area is open public space. In between, Regent's Park and its Primrose Hill northerly extension offer the largest expanse of greenery. The Grand Union (Regent's) Canal winds round the north of the park, offering a pleasant way to avoid the traffic en route to Camden Market. North London's other main attractions include Hampstead Heath, where it's as easy to forget you're in a big city as it is to get completely lost.

Euston & King's Cross (Map 2)

Euston Rd links Euston train station to St Pancras and King's Cross stations. This is not an especially inviting area to visit although it's one that you're likely to pass through en route to or from the north of England.

British Library After 15 years and £500 million (the most expensive building in the UK after the Millennium Dome), the British Library (Map 2; ☎ 7412 7000), 96 Euston Rd NW1 (☻ King's Cross St Pancras) opened its doors in 1998. It is the nation's principal copyright library and stocks one copy of every British publication as wells as historical manuscripts, books and maps from the British Museum. Most of the complex is devoted to storage and scholarly research, but there are some public displays. Subtitled 'Treasures of the British Library', the **John Ritblat Gallery** spans almost three millennia and every continent. Important documents include the Magna Carta (1215); the Sherborne Missal (1400–07); a Gutenberg Bible (1455); Shakespeare's First Folio (1623); manuscripts by some of Britain's best-known authors (eg, Lewis Carroll, Jane Austen, George Eliot and Thomas Hardy); and *Summer Is Icumen In*, the earliest known example of poetry in English (13th century).

The British Library opens to visitors 9.30 am to 6 pm weekdays (to 8 pm Tuesday), 9.30 am to 5 pm Saturday and 11 am to 5 pm Sunday. Admission is free.

Camden (Map 2)

From Euston station you can walk up Eversholt St to Camden, a tourist mecca that is especially lively at weekends. In just over 20 years **Camden Market** has developed into London's most visited 'unticketed' tourist attraction, with some 10 million visitors a year. What started out as a collection of attractive craft stalls by Camden Lock on the Grand Union Canal now extends most of the way from Camden Town tube station to the south to Chalk Farm tube station to the north.

Hampstead

Perched on a hill 4 miles north of the City, Hampstead is an exclusive suburb, attached to an enormous, rambling heath, that just about gets away with calling itself a village.

Hampstead Heath Home to some one hundred species of bird, Hampstead Heath (Θ Hampstead; Gospel Oak or Hampstead Heath station) covers 320 hectares, most of it woods, hills and meadows. Some sections of the heath are laid out for sports such as football and cricket. Walk up Parliament Hill or the hill in North Wood, and on a clear day you'll see Canary Wharf and beyond.

Kenwood House This magnificent neoclassical mansion (☎ 8348 1286), Hampstead

Lane NW3 (Θ Archway or Golders Green, then bus No 210), on the northern side of the heath, was remodelled by Robert Adam from 1764 to 1779. Jammed with paintings by Van Dyck, Gainsborough, Reynolds, Turner, Lely, Hals and Vermeer, it's arguably the city's best small collection of European art. It opens 10 am to 6 pm daily April to September, closing at 5 pm in March and October and 4 pm the rest of the year. Admission is free.

EAST LONDON

The eastern reaches of central London are taken up by the East End – the London of old Hollywood films and Christmas pantomimes – and the sprawl of the Docklands, where the shockingly new is fast replacing the old and decaying.

East End (Maps 1 & 6)

The East End districts of Shoreditch, Hoxton, Spitalfields and Whitechapel may lie within walking distance of the City, but the change of pace and style is extraordinary. Traditionally this was working-class London, an area settled by wave upon wave of immigrants, giving it a curious mixture of Irish, French Huguenot, Bangladeshi and Jewish culture, all of which can still be felt to varying degrees today. Run-down and neglected in the early 1980s, the East End is starting to look up in places, especially where it rubs right up against the City and Liverpool Street station in Spitalfields, the *nouveau* trendy district of Hoxton, including Hoxton Square and the area around Old St.

For anyone interested in modern, multicultural London, it's well worth venturing a look at the East End.

The Docklands

The Port of London was once the world's greatest port, the hub of the British Empire and its enormous global trade. In the 16th century there were 20 cargo quays to the east of London. By the 18th and 19th centuries these were hard-pressed to cope with the quantity of cargo flowing through, and new docks were opened through the late 1880s. But after the Blitz of WWII the docks weren't able to cope with the postwar technological and political changes as the Empire evaporated. From the mid-1960s dock closures followed each other as fast as they had opened.

In 1981 the London Docklands Development Corporation (LDDC) was set up to rejuvenate the area by encouraging new office and housing development. The builders moved in and the Docklands Light Railway (DLR) was built to link the area with the rest of London.

When the recession of the early 1990s hit, the Docklands' bubble burst. Offices stood empty, people lost their jobs, flats wouldn't sell and shopping arcades emptied as trendy shops hung up 'For Sale' signs. Over it all towered the flagship development of Canary Wharf on the Isle of Dogs, bankrupted by the recession and falling property prices.

Things have turned around since then and buildings are full of tenants and more are going up. The Docklands' Achilles heel, transportation, has been largely solved through expansion of the DLR and the building of the Jubilee Line extension for the tube.

Things to See A ride on the DLR towards Greenwich will take you over and through the heart of the Docklands. **Canary Wharf** is dominated by Cesar Pelli's 500m **tower** (1991), described as a 'square prism with a pyramidal top'. **Cabot Square**, at the centre of the Canary Wharf complex, features a shopping centre and hosts arts and cultural events. Norman Foster's Jubilee Line Underground station here is very impressive.

There are plans to open a **Docklands Museum**, focusing on the history of the Thames, its port and its industries, in 2001, as well as a new visitor centre in Sugar House, a 19th-century warehouse at **West India Quay**, to the north of Canary Wharf. A project of the Museum of London, phone ☎ 7600 3699 for an update on the museum's progress.

The last DLR station on the Isle of Dogs is **Island Gardens**, from where there are exquisite views of Greenwich's architectural heritage. If you'd like to carry on south to Greenwich, take the recent DLR extension to Cutty Sark station or, alternatively, use the historic 390m-long **foot tunnel** running under the Thames.

SOUTH LONDON

Greenwich, for many, is a highlight of the lands south of the Thames. Resurgent Southwark, with the Tate Modern, is a hugely popular area. Brixton, with its colourful market, is another fine stop.

Greenwich

Packed with splendid architecture, Greenwich has strong connections with the sea, science, sovereigns and – of course – time.

Greenwich (pronounced gren-itch) lies to the south-east of central London, where the Thames widens and deepens, and there's a sense of space that is rare in the city. Quaint and village-like, and boasting the magnificent *Cutty Sark* clipper ship and the fabulous National Maritime Museum, Greenwich is a delightful place that has been on UNESCO's list of World Heritage Sites since 1997. A trip there will be one of the highlights of any visit to London, and you should certainly allow a day to do it justice.

Greenwich is home to an extraordinary interrelated cluster of classical buildings; all the great architects of the Enlightenment made their mark here, largely due to royal patronage. Henry VIII and his daughters Mary and Elizabeth were all born here. Charles II was particularly fond of the area and had Sir Christopher Wren build both the Royal Observatory and part of the Royal Naval College, which John Vanbrugh then completed in the early 17th century.

Information The TIC (☎ 8858 6376, fax 8853 4607), 46 Greenwich Church St SE10 (DLR Cutty Sark), opens 10 am to 5 pm daily.

A Greenwich Passport ticket covers admission to the three main sites – *Cutty Sark*, National Maritime Museum and Royal Observatory – for £12/2.50. It can be purchased at any of those sights. Unless indicated otherwise, most Greenwich sights are free for children.

Cutty Sark The *Cutty Sark* clipper ship (☎ 8858 3445) is in Cutty Sark Gardens at the top of King William Walk, right beside Greenwich Pier. It was the fastest ship that had ever sailed the seven seas when launched in 1869.

You can stroll on the decks, check out the progress of the ongoing restoration and then read up on the history below deck and inspect maritime prints, paintings and the world's largest collection of ship's figureheads in the hold.

It opens 10 am to 5 pm daily. Admission costs £3.50/2.50.

Old Royal Naval College If you walk south along King William Walk from the *Cutty Sark* you'll come to the entrance of the Old Royal Naval College (☎ 8858 2154) on the left. This Wren masterpiece has been largely taken over by the University of Greenwich since the Royal Navy baled out in 1998, but the buildings on the southern side allow visitors to view the fabulous Painted Hall and the Chapel. They open 10 am to 5 pm daily (from 12.30 pm Sunday) and admission costs £5.

National Maritime Museum Farther south along King William Walk, you'll come to the National Maritime Museum (☎ 8312 6565), Romney Rd SE10, a massive collection of boats, maps, charts, uniforms and marine art designed to tell the long and convoluted history of Britain as a seafaring nation.

As part of a major redevelopment, the brightly lit central courtyard, Neptune Court, has been covered with a huge single-span glass roof to provide easy access to some 16 new themed galleries on two of the museum's three levels. The galleries have interactive displays and video art that focus on such things as marine ecology and the future of the sea, the tea trade and slavery, and imperialism and white settlement. Don't miss the Nelson section, including his tunic with a hole from the bullet that killed him (they also have the bullet on display).

The museum opens 10 am to 5 pm daily. Admission is £7.50/free.

Queen's House The Palladian Queen's House (☎ 8858 4422) is attached to the National Maritime Museum on its eastern side

and has been restored to a representation of how it might have looked in the 1660s and 70s. Although Inigo Jones was commissioned to design the house in 1616, it wasn't completed until 1635. It opens 10 am to 5 pm daily. Admission costs £7.50.

Royal Observatory In 1675 Charles II had the Royal Observatory (☎ 8858 4422) built on a hill in the middle of Greenwich Park, intending that astronomy be used to establish longitude at sea. The preserved rooms are intriguing and you can see the actual timepieces described in Dava Sobel's *Longitude*, the best-selling book about the fascinating quest to measure longitude. You can place one foot either side of the meridian line and straddle the two hemispheres. It opens 10 am to 5 pm daily. Admission is £6/free.

Getting There & Away Greenwich is now most easily accessible on the DLR; Cutty Sark is the station closest to the information office and most of the sights.

There are fast, cheap trains from Charing Cross to Greenwich station via London Bridge about every 15 minutes. Maze Hill station is more convenient for most of the sights than Greenwich station.

The most pleasant way to get to/from Greenwich if the weather is fine is by boat. Westminster Passenger Services (☎ 7930 4097) operates boats between Westminster Pier (Map 4) and Greenwich. There are departures every 30 minutes to one hour daily. The one-way fare is £6.30/3.30 and the trip takes 50 minutes. Return fares cost £7.60/3.80.

Catamaran Cruisers (☎ 7987 1185) operates between Embankment Pier (Map 6) and Greenwich via Tower Pier. There are departures every 30 minutes to one hour daily and the trip lasts an hour. The return fare is £8/5.

Around Greenwich
Millennium Dome The Millennium Dome (☎ 0870 606 2000; ☯ North Greenwich), which opened on the first day of 2000, garnered almost as many column inches of

coverage in the newspapers as visitors. Hugely controversial from its opening, it cost upwards of £1 billion; an astonishing sum given that visitors to its vaguely educational displays most often rated it merely as 'enjoyable'.

A huge erection designed by Richard Rogers and with the largest roof in the world, the Dome's future was in doubt all through 2000. Just finding future investors proved a problem as every time interested parties saw the Dome's books, they ran off in fright. Whilst looking for investors, the Dome gobbled up millions more pounds of Millennium Commission cash trying to limp to the end of 2000. The final decision was that it would start a new future as a high-tech business park in 2001.

Brixton (Map 1)

After WWII, immigrants from the West Indies settled in Brixton giving it a palpable Caribbean flavour that can still be found in the exotic fruits and vegetables on sale at Brixton Market (see Shopping later). Whatever edge is left from the dark days of the 80s when there were riots has only added to the excitement of the nightlife, which itself is being tempered by ongoing gentrification.

WEST LONDON
Kew Gardens

The Royal Botanic Gardens at Kew (☎ 8332 5000, 8940 1171 for a recording), Kew Rd, Kew (⊖ Kew Gardens), is one of the most visited sights on the London tourist itinerary, which means it can get very crowded during summer, especially at weekends. Spring is probably the best time to visit, but at any time of year this 120-hectare expanse of lawns, formal gardens and greenhouses has delights to offer. Don't miss the enormous **Palm House**, a hothouse of metal and curved sheets of glass that houses all sorts of exotic tropical greenery. The stunning **Princess of Wales Conservatory** houses plants in 10 different computer-controlled climatic zones – everything from a desert to a cloud forest.

Kew Gardens opens daily at 9.30 am but closes at different times throughout the year: from 4.30 to 7.30 pm depending on the season. Admission costs £5/2.50. Kew can also be reached by Westminster Passenger Services Association river boat (☎ 7930 2062) from Westminster Pier from April to September, with reduced sailings in October. Ferries depart several times a day and take about 1½ hours. Single tickets cost £7/3 and returns £11/7.

Hampton Court Palace

Hampton Court (☎ 8781 9500; Hampton Court station) was the favourite palace of Henry VIII, who expanded it with a passion. By 1540 it was one of the grandest and most sophisticated palaces in Europe. In the late 17th century, William and Mary employed Sir Christopher Wren to build extensions. The result is a beautiful blend of Tudor and 'restrained baroque' architecture.

Today the palace is England's largest and grandest Tudor structure, knee-deep in history, and with superb gardens and a famous 300-year-old maze. You should set aside plenty of time to do it justice, bearing in mind that if you come by boat from central London the trip will have eaten up half the day already. Among the highlights: **Henry VIII's State Apartments**, including the Great Hall, the largest single room in the palace; the **Tudor Kitchens**, which could rustle up meals for a royal household of some 1200 people; the wonderful **gardens**; and the **maze**.

Hampton Court Palace opens 9.30 am (from 10.15 am Monday) to 6 pm daily, mid-March to October. It closes at 4.30 pm the rest of the year. An all-inclusive ticket costs £10.50/7.

There are trains every 30 minutes from Waterloo to Hampton Court station. The palace can also be reached by Westminster Passenger Services Association river boat (☎ 7930 2062) from Westminster Pier to Hampton Court Pier via Kew from April to September, with reduced sailings in October. Ferries depart at 10.30 am, 11.15 am and noon and take about 3½ hours. One-way tickets cost £10/4 and returns £14/7.

ORGANISED TOURS

The Original London Sightseeing Tour (☎ 8877 1722), the Big Bus Company (☎ 7233 9533) and London Pride Sightseeing (☎ 7520 2050) offer tours of the main sights on double-decker buses which allow you either to go straight round without getting off, or to hop on and off along the way. They're all expensive (around £12) and probably only worth considering if you're only going to be in London for a day or two. Most companies can sell you advance tickets to the biggest attractions to save wasting time in queues.

Convenient starting points are in Trafalgar Square in front of the National Gallery; in front of the Trocadero on Coventry St between Leicester Square and Piccadilly Circus; and in Wilton Gardens opposite Victoria Station.

London Pride Sightseeing includes Docklands and Greenwich in one of its tours, while the Original London Sightseeing Tour has an express tour for those with limited time.

River trips are always recommended; see the Greenwich, Kew and Hampton Court listings as well as the Getting Around section later in the chapter.

PLACES TO STAY

Wherever you stay in London, accommodation is going to take a great wad out of your pocket. Demand can outstrip supply – especially at the bottom end of the market – so it's worth booking at least a few nights' accommodation before arriving, particularly in July and August. Remember too that single rooms are in short supply, and places are reluctant to let a double room to one person, even during quiet periods, without charging a hefty supplement or even the full double rate.

Booking Offices

It's possible to make same-day accommodation bookings for free at most of the TICs. The telephone bookings hotline (open 8.30 am to 6 pm Monday to Friday) is ☎ 7604 2890 and costs £5 per booking. The British Hotel Reservation Centre (☎ 0800 282888), on the main concourse of Victoria train station, opens 6 am to 11.30 pm and charges £3 per booking.

The YHA operates its own central reservations system (☎ 7373 3400, fax 7373 3455, ℮ lonres@yha.org.uk). Although you still pay the individual hostel directly, the staff will know what beds are available where and when.

If you want to stay in a B&B, bookings for a minimum of three days can be made free through London Homestead Services (☎ 8949 4455, fax 8549 5492), Coombe Wood Rd, Kingston-upon-Thames KT2 7JY. London Bed & Breakfast Agency Limited (☎ 7586 2768, fax 7586 6567, ℮ stay@londonbb.com), 71 Fellows Road NW3 3JY, specialises in central London.

Places to Stay – Budget

Camping Although not a realistic option in the centre of the capital, there are a few possibilities within striking distance.

Tent City Hackney (☎ 8985 7656, Millfields Rd E5; Hackney Central station, then bus No 236 or 276). In north-east London, Tent City Hackney has a hostel tent with 90 beds and 200 tent pitches for £5 per person. It opens June to August.

Abbey Wood Caravan Park (☎ 8311 7708, fax 8311 6007, Federation Rd SE2; Abbey Wood station). South of the river and east of Greenwich, Abbey Wood has 360 pitches and opens year round. Tent/caravan pitches cost £2/8.50 plus £4/1.20 per adult/child. Electricity costs £1.50.

YHA/HI Hostels Seven hostels in the central London area are members of Hostelling International (HI), known as the Youth Hostels Association (YHA) in Britain.

The YHA hostels in central London can get very crowded in summer. All the hostels take advance credit-card bookings by phone and will hold some beds for those who show up on the day (arrive early and be prepared to queue). Most offer 24-hour access, facilities for self-catering and relatively cheap meals (eg, £3.20 for a full English or continental breakfast, £3.50 for a large packed lunch, £4.70 for a three-course evening meal).

City of London (Map 4; ☎ 7236 4965, fax 7236 7681, ℮ city@yha.org.uk, 36 Carter Lane EC4; ⊖ St Paul's). This excellent hostel (193 beds) stands in the shadow of St Paul's Cathedral. Rooms have mainly two, three or four beds, though there are a dozen rooms with five to eight beds. There's a licensed cafeteria but no kitchen. Rates are £23.50/19.90 for adults/under-18s. Remember: this part of town is pretty quiet outside working hours.

Earl's Court (Map 7; ☎ 7373 7083, fax 7835 2034, ℮ earlscourt@yha.org.uk, 38 Bolton Gardens SW5; ◑ Earl's Court). This hostel (154 beds) is a Victorian town house in a shabby, though lively, part of town. Rooms are mainly 10-bed dorms with communal showers. There's a cafe, a kitchen for self-catering and a small garden courtyard for summer barbecues. B&B rates are £18.50/16.60 for adults/under-18s.

Hampstead Heath (☎ 8458 9054, fax 8209 0546, ℮ hampstead@yha.org.uk, 4 Wellgarth Rd NW11; ◑ Golders Green). This hostel (190 beds) has a beautiful setting with a well-kept garden, although it's rather isolated. The dormitories are comfortable and each room has a washbasin. There's a licensed cafe and a kitchen. Rates are £19.90/17.70 for adults/under-18s.

Holland House (Map 3; ☎ 7937 0748, fax 7376 0667, ℮ hollandhouse@yha.org.uk, Holland Walk, Kensington W8; ◑ High Street Kensington). This hostel (201 beds) is built into the Jacobean wing of Holland House in the middle of Holland Park. It's large, very busy and rather institutional, but the position can't be beaten. There's a cafe and kitchen. Rates are £20.50/18.50 for adults/under-18s.

Oxford St (Map 5; ☎ 7734 1618, fax 7734 1657, ℮ oxfordst@yha.org.uk, 14 Noel St W1; ◑ Oxford Circus or Tottenham Court Road). This most central of the hostels (75 beds) is basic but clean and welcoming. It has a large kitchen but no meals are served apart from breakfast (£2.30). Rates are £21.50/17.50 for adults/under-18s in rooms with three or four beds and £22 per person in twin rooms, which make up the majority.

Rotherhithe (Map 1; ☎ 7232 2114, fax 7237 2919, ℮ rotherhithe@yha.org.uk, 20 Salter Rd SE16; ◑ Rotherhithe). The YHA flagship hostel (320 beds) in London was purpose-built in 1993. It's right by the River Thames and recommended, but the location is a bit remote and quiet. Most rooms have four or six beds, though there are also 22 doubles (four of them adapted for disabled visitors); all have an attached bathroom. There's a bar and restaurant as well as kitchen facilities and a laundry. B&B rates are £23.50/19.90 for adults/under-18s.

St Pancras International (Map 2; ☎ 7388 9998, fax 7388 6766, ℮ stpancras@yha.org.uk, 79–81 Euston Rd N1; ◑ King's Cross St Pancras). This central place has 152 beds. The area isn't great,

but the hostel itself is up-to-date, with kitchen, restaurant, lockers, cycle shed and lounge. Rates are £23.50/19.90 for adults/under-18s (or £25/26.50 for a twin/premium room).

Independent Hostels London's independent hostels tend to be more relaxed and cheaper than the YHA ones, though standards can be pretty low; some of the places are downright grotty.

Most hostels have at least three or four bunk beds jammed into each small room, a kitchen and some kind of lounge. Some have budget restaurants and a bar attached. Be careful with your possessions and deposit your valuables in the office safe, safe-deposit box or secure locker if provided. Check that fire escapes and stairwells are accessible.

Ashlee House (Map 2; ☎ 7833 9400, fax 7833 9677, ℮ ashleehouse@tsnxt.co.uk, 261–265 Gray's Inn Rd WC1; ◑ King's Cross St Pancras). This is a clean and well-maintained backpackers' hostel on three floors close to King's Cross station. Dorm rooms (most with bunks) can be very cramped, but there's double-glazing on the windows, a laundry and a decent-sized kitchen. Rooms with between four and 16 beds cost £15 per person in the low season and £19 in the high season. There are a few twins for £44 (£48).

Barmy Badger Backpackers (Map 7; ☎ /fax 7370 5213, ℮ barmy_badger.b@virgin.net, 17 Longridge Rd SW5; ◑ Earl's Court). This recent addition is a basic dormitory with dorm beds from £13 per person, including breakfast. Twins without/with facilities cost £32/34.

Court Hotel (Map 7; ☎ 7373 0027, fax 7912 9500, 194–196 Earl's Court Rd SW5; ◑ Earl's Court). This place is under Australasian management and has well-equipped kitchens and TVs in most rooms. Dorm beds cost £13, singles/doubles cost £30/40 a night.

The Generator (Map 2; ☎ 7388 7666, fax 7388 7644, ℮ info@the-generator.co.uk, Compton Place, 37 Tavistock Place WC1; ◑ Russell Square). The Generator in Bloomsbury is one of the grooviest budget places in central London, with futuristic decor like an updated set of Terry Gilliam's film *Brazil*. Along with 207 rooms (830 beds), it has a bar open to 2 am, a large lounge for eating, watching TV or playing pool, a room with Internet kiosks, safe-deposit boxes and a large eating area, but no kitchen. Depending on the season, a place in a dorm with seven or eight beds costs from £15 to £20 and with three to six beds £19 to £22. Singles cost £38 while twins are £45 to £48. All prices include breakfast.

International Students House (Map 2; ☎ 7631 8300, fax 7631 8315, 229 Great Portland St W1; ⊖ Great Portland Street). This Marylebone hostel feels more like a university hall of residence. The single and double rooms are ordinary but clean, and there are excellent facilities and a friendly, relaxed atmosphere. It opens year round. Prices range from £9.99 for a place in an eight-bed dorm without breakfast to £29.50 for a single with washbasin and breakfast. En suite singles/doubles cost £30/47.

Leinster Inn (Map 3; ☎ 7229 9641, fax 7229 5255, ⓔ astorhotels@msn.com, 7–12 Leinster Square W2; ⊖ Bayswater). In a large old house north-west of Bayswater tube station and close to Portobello Market, this is the largest of the Astor group hostels (100 beds). It has a bar, cafe and laundry. Rates in dorms with up to 10 beds are £17, doubles are £22 to £25 per person.

Student Accommodation

University halls of residence are let to nonstudents during the holidays, usually from the end of June to mid-September and sometimes over the Easter break. They're a bit more expensive than the hostels, but you usually get a single room (there are a few doubles) with shared facilities, plus breakfast.

University catering is usually reasonable and includes bars, self-service cafes, takeaway places and restaurants. Full-board, half-board, B&B and self-catering options are usually available.

The London School of Economics and Political Science (☎ 7955 7370), Room B508, Page Building, Houghton St, London WC2A 2AE, lets six of its halls in summer and sometimes during the Easter break.

Carr Saunders Hall (Map 4; ☎ 7323 9712, fax 7580 4718, ⓔ saunders@lse.ac.uk, 18–24 Fitzroy St; ⊖ Warren Street). Well located and recently redone, the hall charges £27/46 for singles/doubles with breakfast.

Bankside Residence (Map 6; ☎ 7633 9877, ⓔ banksidereservation@lse.ac.uk, 24 Sumner St SE1; ⊖ Blackfriars). This hall, with its enviable location near the Globe Theatre and the new Tate Modern at Bankside, has beds in four-bed rooms for £20 to £35 and entire quads for £80, including breakfast.

Other universities and colleges let out their halls of residence outside of term-time:

Goldsmid House (Map 4; ☎ 7493 8911, fax 7491 0586, 36 North Row W1; ⊖ Marble Arch). This centrally located hall has 10 singles (£16) and 120 twins (£24) available from mid-June to mid-September.

John Adams Hall (Map 2; ☎ 7387 4086, fax 7383 0164, ⓔ jah@ioe.ac.uk, 15–23 Endsleigh St WC1; ⊖ Euston). John Adams is quite a grand residence in a row of Georgian houses. It opens at Easter and from July to September. B&B costs from £24/42 for singles/doubles, depending on the time of year.

YMCAs For a list of all the YMCA hostels in the Greater London area contact YMCA England (☎ 8520 5599), 640 Forest Rd, London E17 3DZ. The main ones are:

Barbican YMCA (Map 6; ☎ 7628 0697, fax 7638 2420, ⓔ barbicanymca@aol.com, 2 Fann St EC2; ⊖ Barbican). Singles/doubles cost £25/42 with breakfast in this 240-bed YMCA.

Indian Student YMCA (Map 4; ☎ 7387 0411, fax 7383 4735, ⓔ indianymca@aol.com, 41 Fitzroy Square W1; ⊖ Warren Street). Bed plus breakfast and supper costs £33/46 for a single/double.

B&Bs, Guesthouses & Hotels This may come as a shock, but anything below £30/50 for a single/double with shared facilities and below £40/60 with private bathroom is considered 'budget' in London. In July, August and September prices can jump by 25% or more, and it's advisable to book ahead. Through the year, rates can vary widely from what is listed below depending on demand. It's always worth asking for any offers or specials. Be warned: some of the cheaper B&Bs don't accept credit cards.

Pimlico & Victoria (Map 8) Victoria may not be the most attractive part of London, but you'll be very close to the action. Pimlico is more residential, though convenient for the Tate Britain at Millbank.

Luna-Simone Hotel (☎ 7834 5897, fax 7828 2474, 47 Belgrave Rd SW1; ⊖ Victoria). If all London's budget hotels were like this central, spotlessly clean and comfortable place, we would all be happy campers (or perhaps not). Singles/doubles without bathroom start at about £35/50; a double with facilities ranges from £60 to £75. A full English breakfast is included, and there are free storage facilities if you want to leave bags while travelling. If the Luna-Simone is full, there are a lot more B&Bs on Belgrave Rd. There's a Web site at www.lunsimonehotel.com.

Brindle House Hotel (☎ 7828 0057, fax 7931 8805, 1 Warwick Place North SW1; ⊖ Victoria). This place is in a renovated old building in a quiet street; the rooms are small but clean. Singles cost £38 (shared facilities), doubles cost £50/45 (with/without bathroom), triples are £69.

Romany House Hotel (☎ 7834 5553, fax 7834 0495, ⓔ romany.hotel@virgin.net, 35 Longmore St SW1; ⊖ Victoria). Part of this hotel is built into a 15th-century cottage that boasts tales – real or imagined – of highwaymen. You'll share a bathroom, but breakfasts are good and singles/doubles cost from £28/38.

Bloomsbury (Maps 2 & 4)
Bloomsbury is very convenient, especially for the West End. There are lots of places on Gower and North Gower Sts.

Hotel Cavendish (Map 4; ☎ 7636 9079, fax 7580 3609, ⓔ hotelcavendish@virginnet.co.uk, 75 Gower St WC1; ⊖ Goodge Street). This is a clean and pleasant family run place, with singles/doubles without bath for £34/48 and with en suite facilities for £42/66, including breakfast. Its nearby sister hotel, **Jesmond Hotel** (Map 4; ☎ 7636 3199, fax 7323 4373, ⓔ reservations@jesmondhotel.org.uk, 63 Gower St WC1; ⊖ Goodge Street) is similar and charges the same rates.

Alhambra Hotel (Map 2; ☎ 7837 9575, fax 7916 2476, 17–19 Argyle St WC1; ⊖ King's Cross St Pancras). One of the better finds in this area and very convenient for King's Cross St Pancras tube and the two main-line stations, the Alhambra is a simple but spotlessly clean place with 55 rooms. Simple singles/doubles/triples cost £32/45/65; with shower they're £43/50/72. Particularly good value is the quad with shower and toilet for £90. All prices include English breakfast.

Earl's Court (Map 7)
Earl's Court is not really within walking distance of many places of interest, but Earl's Court tube station is a busy interchange, so getting around is easy. It's also an area used to lots of people in transit.

Regency Court Hotel (☎ 7244 6615, fax 01753-578279, ⓔ regencycourt@hotmail.com, 14 Penywern Rd SW5; ⊖ Earl's Court). This hotel has undergone a much needed renovation and its 15 bright rooms, all with en suite facilities,

cost £35 to £45 for singles, £50 to £60 for doubles and £65 to £75 for triples. Beds in a dormitory cost from £18.

York House Hotel (☎ 7373 7519, fax 7370 4641, ⓔ yorkhh@aol.com, 27–28 Philbeach Gardens SW5; ⊖ Earl's Court). This place is good value for what and where it is – on a quiet crescent – and the welcome is warm. The rooms are basic, although some have showers. Singles/doubles/triples without facilities cost £34/52/69; with shower and toilet they're £48/74/86.

Merlyn Court Hotel (☎ 7370 1640, fax 7370 4986, 2 Barkston Gardens SW5; ⊖ Earl's Court). This unpretentious place has a nice atmosphere and a lovely location close to the tube. Small but clean singles/doubles/triples with bathroom cost £60/70/80; without they're £35/50/65.

Bayswater & Paddington (Map 3)
Bayswater is an extremely convenient location, though some of the streets immediately to the west of Queensway, which has a decent selection of restaurants, are run down and depressing. Paddington has lots of cheap hotels and it's a good transit location; you can reach Heathrow in 15 minutes from here (see the Getting Around section later in the chapter).

Royal Hotel (☎ 7229 7225, fax 7221 8001, 43 Queensborough Terrace; ⊖ Bayswater). The dormitory accommodation here once attracted backpackers, but it's now just another budget guesthouse with affordable rates: £36/45/52 for a single/double/triple with shower.

Manor Court Hotel (☎ 7792 3361, fax 7229 2875, 7 Clanricarde Gardens W2; ⊖ Queensway). Though not a spectacular place, this hotel is in a good location just off Bayswater Rd. Singles/doubles with private shower or toilet cost from £50/60, depending on the season.

Garden Court Hotel (☎ 7229 2553, fax 7727 2749, ⓔ info@gardencourthotel.co.uk, 30–31 Kensington Gardens Square W2; ⊖ Bayswater). One of Bayswater's best options but barely in this category, the Garden Court is a well-run and -maintained family hotel cobbled from two town houses (1870), and all its 34 rooms have phone and TV. Singles/doubles without bathroom cost £36/58, with bathroom £54/86.

Norfolk Court & St David's Hotel (☎ 7723 4963, fax 7402 9061, ⓔ info@stdavidshotels.com, 16–20 Norfolk Square W2; ⊖ Paddington). Right in the centre of the action, this place with the long-winded name is clean, comfortable and friendly with the usual out-of-control decor. Basic singles/doubles/triples have washbasin,

TV and phone and cost £39/59/70; with shower and toilet £49/69/80, including a huge breakfast.
Balmoral House Hotel (☎ 7723 7445, fax 7402 0118, e balmoral@freedom2surf.co.uk, 156 & 157 Sussex Gardens W2; ⊖ Paddington). This immaculate and very comfortable hotel, with two properties directly opposite one another, is one of the better places to stay along Sussex Gardens, a street lined with small hotels but unfortunately a major traffic artery. Singles without/with bathroom cost £35/45, doubles with facilities cost £65 (breakfast included and all rooms have TVs).

Marylebone (Map 3) Marylebone is very handy for some of London's most popular sights, such as Madame Tussaud's and the London Planetarium.

Glynne Court Hotel (☎ 7262 4344, fax 7724 2071, 41 Great Cumberland Place W1; ⊖ Marble Arch). Fairly typical for this price range and location, the Glynne Court has 15 rooms. Singles cost £50 to £60 and doubles are £60 to £75. All rooms come with TV and phone.

Places to Stay – Mid-Range
The B&Bs, guesthouses and small hotels in this category offer singles/doubles from £50/70 for a single/double without private facilities and £70/90 with your own bathroom.

Pimlico & Victoria (Map 8)
Winchester Hotel (☎ 7828 2972, fax 7828 5191, 17 Belgrave Rd SW1; ⊖ Victoria). This clean, comfortable and welcoming place is also good value for the area: doubles and twins with private bathroom and TV cost £85.
Woodville House (☎ 7730 1048, fax 7730 2574, 107 Ebury St SW1; ⊖ Victoria). The Woodville has 12 simple, comfortable rooms with shared bathroom, use of a kitchen and a lovely back patio. Basic singles/doubles cost £42/62. Family rooms cost from £80 to £115. It's a friendly, good-value place.
Web site: www.woodvillehouse.co.uk
Morgan House (☎ 7730 2384, fax 7730 8842, 120 Ebury St SW1; ⊖ Victoria). This hotel is owned by the same people who run the nearby Woodville House. Singles/doubles without facilities are £42/62, those with bathroom £68/80. Family rooms cost £110. You'll find many more places to stay on this street.
Web site: www.morganhouse.co.uk

Covent Garden (Map 5) Nothing could be more central than Covent Garden but the buzz continues well into the wee hours.

Fielding Hotel (☎ 7836 8305, fax 7497 0064, e reservations@the-fielding-hotel.co.uk, 4 Broad Court, Bow St WC2; ⊖ Covent Garden). This place, on a pedestrianised street a block away from the Royal Opera House, is remarkably good value, clean and well run. All rooms have private bathroom, TV and phone. Singles/doubles start at £76/100.

Bloomsbury (Maps 2 & 4) Tucked away in leafy Cartwright Gardens (Map 2) to the north of Russell Square, within walking distance of the West End, you'll find some of London's best-value hotels. The hotels along nearby Gower St (Map 4) are also pretty good value, but not all of them have double-glazing, which is essential if you're sensitive to traffic noise.

Jenkins Hotel (Map 2; ☎ 7387 2067, fax 7383 3139, e reservations@jenkinshotel.demon.co.uk, 45 Cartwright Gardens WC1; ⊖ Russell Square). This no-smoking place has attractive, comfortable, stylish rooms with washbasin, TV, phone and fridge. Basic singles cost £52; those with private facilities are £72 and £85 for a double (all prices include breakfast). Guests get to use the tennis courts in the gardens across the road.
Crescent Hotel (Map 2; ☎ 7387 1515, fax 7383 2054, 49–50 Cartwright Gardens WC1; ⊖ Russell Square). This friendly, family owned operation, maintained at a very high standard, has basic singles from £43 to £45 and en suite singles/doubles/triples/quads from £70/82/93/102.
Arran House Hotel (Map 4; ☎ 7636 2186, fax 7436 5328, e arran@dircon.co.uk, 77–79 Gower St WC1; ⊖ Goodge Street). This welcoming place has a lovely garden and laundry facilities. Singles range from £45 with no facilities to £55 with shower, doubles from £55 to £75, triples from £73 to £93. Prices include breakfast. The front rooms are sound-proofed, and all have TV and phone.
Ridgemount Hotel (Map 4; ☎ 7636 1141, fax 7636 2558, 65–67 Gower St WC1; ⊖ Goodge Street). Readers have sent favourable comments about the old-fashioned Ridgemount. Basic singles/doubles cost £32/48; with shower and toilet they're from £43/62 (including breakfast). It also has a laundry room.
Haddon Hall (Map 4; ☎ 7636 2474, fax 7580 4527, 39 Bedford Place WC1; ⊖ Russell Square or Holborn). This hotel is well-located in an area with many places to stay. Simple singles/doubles without bathroom cost £50/65, doubles with bathroom £90.

Chelsea & South Kensington (Map 7)

Classy Chelsea and 'South Ken' offer easy access to the museums and some of London's best shops.

Annandale House Hotel (☎ 7730 5051, fax 7730 2727, ⓔ info@annandalehotel.co.uk 39 Sloane Gardens SW1; ⊖ Sloane Square). This discreet, traditional hotel just south of Sloane Square is a good choice for the noise-sensitive. Rooms, all with en suite facilities, phone and TV, cost £60 to £70 for singles and £95 to £105 for doubles.

Hotel 167 (☎ 7373 0672, fax 7373 3360, ⓔ inquiries@hotel1167.com, 167 Old Brompton Rd SW5; ⊖ Gloucester Road). This small hotel is stylish, with an unusually uncluttered and attractive decor. All 19 rooms have private bathrooms. Singles cost from £72, doubles from £90 to £99.

Swiss House Hotel (☎ 7373 2769, fax 7373 4983, ⓔ recep@swiss-hh.demon.co.uk, 171 Old Brompton Rd SW5; ⊖ Gloucester Road). The Swiss House is a clean and welcoming hotel that has something of a country feel about it. And it's good value: singles with shower start at £48, singles/doubles with shower and toilet start at £68/85, including continental breakfast.

Kensington (Map 3)

Vicarage Hotel (☎ 7229 4030, fax 7792 5989, ⓔ reception@londonvicaragehotel.com, 10 Vicarage Gate W8; ⊖ High Street Kensington). The Vicarage is pleasant and well kept, with good showers and rooms slightly larger than normal. Singles/doubles with shared facilities cost £46/76, doubles with private bathroom £99.

Abbey House (☎ 7727 2594, 11 Vicarage Gate W8; ⊖ High Street Kensington). Abbey House is a particularly good-value small hotel, with pretty decor and very high standards. Singles/doubles/triples/quads with washbasin and shared bathrooms cost £45/74/85/100, including English breakfast.

Bayswater, Paddington & Notting Hill (Map 3)

Pavilion Hotel (☎ 7262 0905, fax 7262 1324, ⓔ pavilio17@aol.com, 34–36 Sussex Gardens W2; ⊖ Paddington). This place boasts 30 individually themed rooms (Moorish, 1970s, all-red) to reflect its slogan/motto: 'Fashion, Glam & Rock 'n' Roll'. If you're feeling somewhat B-list, you might look elsewhere. Singles/doubles from £60/90 include breakfast.

Inverness Court Hotel (☎ 7229 1444, fax 7706 4240, ⓔ info@cdhotels.com, Inverness Terrace W2; ⊖ Queensway). This impressive hotel was commissioned by Edward VII for his 'confidante'

(ie, mistress), the actress Lillie Langtry, and comes complete with a private theatre, now the cocktail bar. The panelled walls, stained glass and huge open fires of the public areas give it a Gothic feel but most of the 183 rooms – some of which overlook Hyde Park – are modern and pretty ordinary. Singles/doubles cost £84/108.

Gate Hotel (☎ 7221 0707, fax 7221 9128, ⓔ gatehotel@thegate.globalnet.co.uk, 6 Portobello Rd W11; ⊖ Notting Hill Gate). The rooms in this old town house with classic frilly English decor and lovely floral window boxes all have private facilities and cost £55 to £70 for singles and £80 to £90 for doubles, including continental breakfast.

Marylebone (Map 3)

Edward Lear Hotel (☎ 7402 5401, fax 7706 3766, 28–30 Seymour St W1; ⊖ Marble Arch). Former home of the eponymous Victorian poet and painter, this small, comfortable place has rooms with satellite TV and phone. Singles/doubles without bathroom go from £48/68, with bathroom £75/93.

Bryanston Court Hotel (☎ 7262 3141, fax 7262 7248, ⓔ hotel@bryanstonhotel.com, 56–60 Great Cumberland Place W1; ⊖ Marble Arch). This place has something of a club atmosphere, with leather armchairs, sepia-toned lighting and a formal feel (though it's a Best Western hotel). All rooms have private bathroom, TV and phone and singles/doubles cost £95/120.

Places to Stay – Top End

In this section you'll find more elegant hotels, where doubles cost from £150 – and more. Of course, in this category you can always count on a private bath/shower and toilet.

Victoria (Map 8) The following place is (probably) as close as you'll ever get to staying with the Queen.

Rubens at the Palace (☎ 7834 6600, fax 7233 6037, ⓔ reservations@rubens.redcarnationhotels.com, 39 Buckingham Palace Rd SW1; ⊖ Victoria). This branch of the Rubens chain has a brilliant position overlooking the walls of the Royal Mews and Buckingham Palace. Singles/doubles start at £135/150 without breakfast. It's popular with groups.

The West End & Covent Garden (Map 5)

Hazlitt's (☎ 7434 1771, fax 7439 1524, ⓔ reservations@hazlitts.co.uk, 6 Frith St W1; ⊖ Tottenham Court Road). Built in 1718 and comprising three original Georgian houses, this is one of central London's finest hotels, with efficient personal service. All 23 rooms are named after former residents or visitors to the house and are individually decorated with antique furniture and prints. Singles/doubles start at £140/175. Booking is advisable – especially since Bill Bryson let the cat out of the bag and introduced it to the world in his best-selling *Notes from a Small Island*.

Strand Palace (☎ 7836 8080, fax 7836 2077, Ⓔ *res.strand@forte-hotls.com, Strand WC2; ⊖ Charing Cross*). This is a monstrous place (783 rooms) helped by renovations. Its position, close to Covent Garden, is excellent and there are a number of snappy bars and restaurants. Rates start at £100/150 single/double without breakfast and there are many specials.

Clerkenwell (Map 4) This area is not blessed with a wealth of accommodation.

The Rookery (☎ 7336 0931, fax 7336 0932, Ⓔreservations@rookery.co.uk, Peter's Lane, Cowcross St EC1; ⊖ Farringdon*). This 33-room hotel has been built within a row of once derelict 18th-century Georgian houses and fitted out with period furniture (including a museum-piece collection of Victorian baths, showers and toilets), original wood panelling shipped over from Ireland and open fires. Its singles/doubles start at £170/200.

Chelsea & South Kensington (Map 7)
Gracious Chelsea and South Kensington present London at its elegant best.

Blakes Hotel (☎ 7370 6701, fax 7373 0442, Ⓔblakes@easynet.co.uk, 33 Roland Gardens SW7; ⊖ Gloucester Road*). For classic style, one of your first choices in London should be this place: five Victorian houses knocked into one and decked out with four-poster beds, rich fabrics and antiques on stripped floorboards. Singles/doubles start at £165/240.

Number Sixteen Hotel (☎ 7589 5232, fax 7584 8615, Ⓔreservations@numbersixteenhotel.co.uk, 16 Sumner Place SW7; ⊖ South Kensington*). Number Sixteen has comfortable and well-equipped rooms. It's undergoing a complete renovation and is due to reopen late summer 2001 when rooms should start at about £140/200.

Kensington & Knightsbridge (Map 3)
The Gore (☎ 7584 6601, fax 7589 8127, Ⓔreservations@gorehotel.co.uk, 189 Queen's Gate SW7; ⊖ High Street Kensington or Gloucester Road*). This splendid hotel is a veritable palace of polished mahogany, Turkish carpets, antique-style bathrooms, aspidistras and portraits and prints (some 4500 of them). The attached Bistrot 190 is a fine place for brunch. Singles/doubles cost from £140/175.

Basil St Hotel (☎ 7581 3311, fax 7581 3693, Ⓔthebasil@aol.com, Basil St SW3; ⊖ Knightsbridge*). This antique-stuffed hideaway in the heart of Knightsbridge is perfectly placed for carrying back the shopping from Harrods, Harvey Nichols or Sloane St. Its singles/doubles start at £128/190.

Bayswater & Notting Hill (Map 3) You'll get more for your pound at top-end places in these two areas than you would to the south and east.

Queen's Park Hotel (☎ 7229 8080, fax 7792 1330, Ⓔthequeensparkhotel@aol.com, 48 Queens borough Terrace W2; ⊖ Bayswater*). With 86 rooms, the Queen's Park is a somewhat functional top-end place popular with groups, but the rates are good for the location: £98/130 for singles/doubles.

Portobello (☎ 7727 2777, fax 7792 9641, 22 Stanley Gardens W11; ⊖ Notting Hill Gate*). This beautifully appointed place is in a great location and one of the most attractive hotels in London. Most people consider the £145/185 for a single/double to be money well spent. Web site: www.portobello-hotel.co.uk

East End (Map 6)
Great Eastern Hotel (☎ 7618 5010, fax 7618 5011, Ⓔsales@great-eastern-hotel.co.uk, Liverpool St EC2; ⊖ Liverpool Street*). A major addition to the East End and the City, the Great Eastern is a classic Victorian railway hotel (it adjoins Liverpool Street Station) that has received a lavish redo by the Conran organisation. It's stylish and elegant and *the* place to stay for literally miles around. Rates start at £195/225 for rooms boasting everything you could want.

Places to Stay – Deluxe
Some of central London's hotels are so luxurious and well established that they're tourist attractions in their own right. Despite their often old-world splendour, all are geared for the needs of business travellers.

Claridges (Map 4; ☎ 7629 8860, fax 7499 2210, Ⓔinfo@claridges.co.uk, Brook St W1; ⊖ Bond Street*). Claridges is one of the greatest of the five-star hotels in London, a leftover from a bygone era. Many of the Art Deco features of the public areas and suites were designed in the late 1920s and some of the 1930s-vintage furniture once graced the staterooms of the lost SS *Normandie*. Expect to pay £315/370 for a single/double.

The Ritz (Map 4; ☎ 7493 8181, fax 7493 2687, ⓔ enquire@theritzhotel.co.uk, 150 Piccadilly W1; ⊖ Green Park). What can you say about a hotel that has lent its name to the English lexicon? Arguably London's most celebrated hotel, the ritzy Ritz has a spectacular position overlooking Green Park and is the royal family's 'home away from home'. Rooms cost from £295/345 single/double. The Long Gallery and the Restaurant are decked out like a rococo boudoir.

St Martins Lane (Map 5; ☎ 7300 5500, 0800 634 5500, ⓔ stmartinslane@compuserve.com, 45 St Martin's Lane; ⊖ Leicester Square). A designer hotel, providing what it calls a 'slice of New York urban chic' just a stone's throw from Covent Garden, St Martins was created by international hotelier Ian Schrager and French designer Philippe Starck. It's the place to check into if you want to bump into supermodels in the lift and have great views of the pulsating West End. Indulging in its late-90s minimalism costs from £245/265 for a single/double.

The Savoy (Map 5; ☎ 7836 4343, fax 7240 6040, ⓔ info@the-savoy.co.uk, Strand WC2; ⊖ Charing Cross). This hotel stands on the site of the old Savoy Palace, which was burned down during the Peasants' Revolt of 1381. The 207 rooms are so comfortable and have such great views that some people have been known to take up permanent residence. Singles/doubles start at £290/340. The forecourt is the only street in the British Isles where motorists drive on the right.

Serviced Apartments

Families or groups may prefer to rent a flat rather than stay in a hotel or B&B. Several agencies can help track something down. Holiday Serviced Apartments (☎ 7373 4477, fax 7373 4282, ⓔ reservations@holidayapartments.co.uk), 273 Old Brompton Rd SW5 (⊖ Gloucester Road), and Aston's Budget & Designer Studios (☎ 7590 6000, fax 7590 6060, ⓔ sales@astons-apartments.com), 39 Rosary Gardens SW7 (⊖ Gloucester Road), have a range of holiday flats on their books.

PLACES TO EAT

London is the Britain's undisputed culinary capital, and the growth in the number of restaurants and cafes – some 8500 at the last count, representing 70 different cuisines – has made the city much more international. No matter what you fancy eating, there's bound to be a restaurant serving it.

Restaurants and other eateries in London have extremely varied opening hours. Many in Soho are closed on Sunday, for example, and in the City the entire weekend. We have tried to note when restaurants stray from the standard 'open daily for lunch and dinner', but it's always safest to call and check. Also note that many of the pubs listed in the Entertainment section serve food.

Trafalgar Square (Map 5)

You won't find a tremendous number of eateries directly on the square, but there are a couple of cafes within striking distance and the brasserie (☎ 747 2885) on the 1st floor of the National Gallery's Sainsbury Wing gets good reviews.

Café in the Crypt (☎ 7839 4342, St Martin-in-the-Fields, Duncannon St WC2; ⊖ Charing Cross). The food in this atmospheric crypt is good, with plenty of offerings for vegetarians, but the place can be hectic and noisy at lunch time. Most main dishes cost from £5 to £6 and there are 'quick meals' from £3.95. It opens from 10 am to 8 pm (to 6 pm Sunday).

ICA Café (Map 4; ☎ 7930 8619, ICA, The Mall SW1; ⊖ Charing Cross). You can lunch at this bohemian magnet for less than £10 but for considerably more in the evening (£36 for two with wine). It's no-smoking, there are lots of vegetarian dishes, and it's licensed to serve alcohol until 1 am.

Westminster & Pimlico (Map 8)

We wonder where all those MPs lunch, given the dearth of restaurants in Westminster, but Pimlico has a wide assortment.

Jenny Lo's Tea House (☎ 7259 0399, 14 Eccleston St SW1; ⊖ Victoria). This simple Asian place has soup and fried noodles from £3.50 to £6.50 and rice dishes from £4.50.

O Sole Mio (☎ 7976 6887, 39 Churton St SW1; ⊖ Victoria). This standard, decent-value Italian restaurant has pizzas and pastas for around £6.

UNo 1 (☎ *7834 1001, 1 Denbigh St SW1; ✛ Victoria*). Pastas cost from £5.50 to £8 in this cheery dining room decorated in reds and yellows.

St James's & Mayfair (Maps 4 & 5)

This is an expensive part of London and not well stocked with budget places to eat.

Hard Rock Café (Map 4; ☎ *7629 0382, 150 Old Park Lane W1; ✛ Hyde Park Corner)*. This, the original Hard Rock Café, has been here since 1971 and is as popular as ever – just check out the queues that form every day of the year (no bookings taken). It serves a tried and tested diet of burgers and fries (from £7.25). The rock memorabilia is memorable.

Rasa W1 (Map 4; ☎ *7629 1346, 6 Dering St W1; ✛ Bond Street)*. This South Indian vegetarian restaurant has wonderful food and should cost about £10 per person.

The West End: Piccadilly, Soho & Chinatown (Map 5)

These days Soho is London's gastronomic heart with numerous restaurants and cuisines to choose from. The liveliest streets tend to be Greek, Frith, Old Compton and Dean Sts. Gerrard and Lisle Sts are chock-a-block with Chinese eateries of every description.

Chinese If you're with several people and want a proper sit-down meal in Chinatown (✛ Leicester Square) but are overwhelmed by the choice, consider any of the following three. They've been tested again and again and have always come up trumps:

Fung Shing (☎ *7437 1539, 15 Lisle St WC2)*
Gerrard's Corner (☎ *7437 0984, 30 Wardour St WC2)*
Mr Kong (☎ *7437 7341, 21 Lisle St WC2)*

A particularly good way to sample the best of Chinese cuisine is to try Cantonese dim sum where you select numerous small dishes and wash them down with a pot of jasmine tea.

Chuen Cheng Ku (☎ *7437 1398, 17 Wardour St W1)*. This place is ideal for the uninitiated as all the dishes (dumplings, noodles, paper-wrapped prawns, etc) are trundled around on trolleys.
Wong Kei (☎ *7437 3071, 41–43 Wardour St W1)*. Wong Kei is famous for the rudeness of its waiters. Some find this adds to the experience, but even if you don't – like us – you might be tempted by the cheap Cantonese food (main dishes from £4.50 to £7.50, rice dishes from £3, set menus from £6).

Asian All is not Chinese. There are many other fine Asian choices.

Tokyo Diner (☎ *7287 8777, 2 Newport Place WC2; ✛ Leicester Square)*. The Tokyo Diner is a good-value place to stop for a quick bowl of

---

Tea for Two or More

Given the important role that tea has always played in English culture and society, it should be no surprise that going out for 'afternoon tea' is something dear to the heart of many Londoners.
   The following are three of the best places to go for afternoon tea:

Brown's Hotel (Map 7; ☎ 7493 6020, 30 Albemarle St W1; ✛ Green Park) dispenses tea in the Drawing Room 3 to 6 pm daily, with a pianist to soothe away any lingering stress from the bustling streets outside. A sizeable tea will set you back £17.95 a head.
The celebrated **Fortnum & Mason** (Map 7; ☎ 7734 8040, 181 Piccadilly W1; ✛ Piccadilly Circus) serves afternoon tea for £13.50 and high teas for £16.50 and £18.50 (with champagne) between 3 and 5 pm Monday to Saturday.
The graceful **Orangery** (Map 5; ☎ 7376 0239; ✛ High Street Kensington or Queensway) in Kensington Gardens is a superb place to have a relatively affordable set tea; prices range from £6.50 with cucumber sandwiches or scones to £12.50 with champagne. It opens 10 am to 6 pm daily, April to September (to 4 pm the rest of the year).

noodles or a plate of sushi before the cinema or theatre. A meal is likely to cost from £8 to £10, although their set bento boxes start at £10.50.

Soba (☎ 7734 6400, 38 Poland St W1; ⊖ Oxford Circus). Soba is always our first choice for an easy (and cheap) bowl of Japanese noodles for around £5.

Yo! Sushi (☎ 7287 0443, 52–53 Poland St W1; ⊖ Oxford Circus). Yo! Sushi is one of London's livelier sushi bars, where diners sit around the bar and the dishes come to them on a 60m-long conveyor belt (drinks, on the other hand, arrive on a robotic trolley). Sushi costs from £1.50 to £3.50; you should be able to get away with around £10 a head.

Melati (☎ 7437 2745, 21 Great Windmill St W1; ⊖ Piccadilly Circus). This Indonesian/Malaysian/Singaporean restaurant has good food and a respectable range of vegetarian options. Various noodle and rice dishes cost from £6 to £8 and the fish in chilli sauce (£7.25) is excellent.

Cam Phat (☎ 7437 5598, 12 Macclesfield St W1; ⊖ Leicester Square). Cam Phat is a cheap and cheerful Vietnamese place that serves well-prepared dishes such as roast pork with vermicelli noodles (£4.50) and *pho* (£3.50), the Vietnamese soup staple of beef and noodles in a stock flavoured with lemon grass.

Other

Franx Snack Bar (☎ 7836 7989, 192 Shaftesbury Ave WC2; ⊖ Tottenham Court Road). Franx is as authentic a London 'caff' as you'll find in these parts, with eggs and bacon and other one-plate specials for around £3.

Gaby's (☎ 7836 4233, 30 Charing Cross Rd WC2; ⊖ Leicester Square). This Middle Eastern snack bar beside Wyndham's theatre has been here forever and attracts queues for staples such as *hummus* and felafel (£3.20) and *couscous royale* (£7.50).

Mildred's (☎ 7494 1634, 58 Greek St W1; ⊖ Tottenham Court Road). Mildred's is so small (and popular) that you may have to share a table. It's worth it, however, because the vegetarian food – including stir-fried vegetables and bean-burgers – is both good and well priced (from £5 to £7 for a large main course).

Pollo (☎ 7734 5456, 20 Old Compton St W1; ⊖ Leicester Square). This Italian cheapie attracts a student crowd with its pastas, *risottos*, pizzas and chicken dishes for under £4.

Spiga (☎ 7734 3444, 84–86 Wardour St W1; ⊖ Tottenham Court Road). This is where to head if you want authentic pizza (from £6), pasta or an Italian main dish in sleek, pleasant surroundings but don't want to pay the earth for it.

Garlic & Shots (☎ 7734 9505, 14 Frith St W1; ⊖ Leicester Square). Whether or not you'll want to risk eating at this place depends on your tolerance for garlic – and your plans for later in the evening. Everything, including the cheesecake, ice cream and vodka, is spiked with the stuff. Main courses clock in at £9 to £13. It opens daily for dinner only.

Gopal's of Soho (☎ 7434 0840, 12 Bateman St W1; ⊖ Tottenham Court Road). Gopal's is cramped and run-down but it offers reasonably authentic Indian food at affordable prices. *Thalis* (set meals served on circular metal trays) are good value: £11.75 for vegetarian and £1 more for the meat equivalent.

Rasa Samudra (☎ 7637 0222, 5 Charlotte St W1; ⊖ Goodge Street). This place just north of Oxford St is one of many restaurants on this street, but its emphasis on excellent southern Indian vegetarian cuisine and seafood sets it apart. Think about £15 per person.

L'Odéon (☎ 7287 1400, 65 Regent St W1; ⊖ Piccadilly Circus). This upmarket French restaurant is worth a visit just for the views of Regent St from its lofty windows. The food also comes in for good reports, especially if you go for the £15.50/19.50 two/three-course set lunch or dinner (from 5.30 to 7 pm only).

Cafes Soho's cafes are great for whiling away the hours inside or – depending on the weather – outside.

Pâtisserie Valerie (☎ 7437 3466, 44 Old Compton St W1; ⊖ Tottenham Court Road or Leicester Square). You can't beat this Soho institution for coffee or tea and something sweet (calorie-crunching cakes around £2.50), though you'll be lucky to get a seat. It also does filled croissants and club sandwiches (from £4 to £5.50).

Maison Bertaux (☎ 7437 6007, 28 Greek St W1; ⊖ Tottenham Court Road). Bertaux has been turning out confections for 130 years, and they're still as exquisite as ever.

Bar Italia (☎ 7437 4520, 22 Frith St W1; ⊖ Leicester Square). This great favourite opens round the clock and has a wonderful 1950s decor. It's always packed and buzzing (from the caffeine, no doubt); your best chance for a seat might be sometime after 1 am.

The Strand & Covent Garden (Map 5)

Right beside Soho and technically part of the West End, Covent Garden is also densely packed with places to eat. The following are all accessible from Covent Garden tube station unless indicated otherwise.

Restaurants

Rock & Sole Plaice (☎ 7836 3785, 47 Endell St WC2). This no-nonsense fish and chips shop has basic Formica tables and delicious cod or haddock in batter (£3.50 or £4.50 with chips). It's unlicensed but you can bring your own (BYO).

Food for Thought (☎ 7836 0239, 31 Neal St WC2). This tiny, no-smoking vegetarian cafe features spicy dishes for under £4.

Calabash (☎ 7836 1973, 38 King St WC2). This simple eatery in the Africa Centre serves food from all over Africa and has a menu for the uninitiated describing each dish. Typical dishes are *egusi* (£6.95), a Nigerian meat stew with tomatoes and spices, and *yassa* (£6.50), chicken marinated with lemon juice and peppers, hailing from Senegal.

Café Pacifico (☎ 7379 7728, 5 Langley St WC2). Pacifico serves Mexican food in a cheerful dining room, with main courses for about £7.50 and great margaritas.

Belgo Centraal (☎ 7813 2233, 50 Earlham St WC2). Taking the lift down to the basement and walking through the kitchens is all part of the fun at Belgo, where the waiters dress up as 16th-century monks. This being a Belgian restaurant, *moules et frites* (mussels and chips/French fries) and spit roasts are the specialities, and beer (100 different flavoured Pilsners, including banana, peach and cherry) is the drink. There's a set lunch menu for £5; a set dinner of a starter, mussels and chips and a beer costs £13.95.

Café des Amis du Vin (☎ 7379 3444, 11–14 Hanover Place WC2). This brasserie is handy for pre- or post-theatre meals with good, affordable French fare. Starters cost from £4.95 to £6.50, main courses from £10 to £13.50 and set lunches of two/three courses £9.95/12.50.

Orso (☎ 7240 5269, 27 Wellington St WC2). An established Italian eatery popular with media types, Orso is relatively expensive for dinner (about £25 per head) but does a cheaper two-/three-course lunch for £14/16 including – as any journalist would expect – a Bloody Mary or a glass of champagne.

Simpson's-in-the-Strand (☎ 7836 9112, 100 Strand WC2). For traditional English roasts, Simpson's is where to go – it's been dishing up hot meats in a fine panelled dining room since 1848. Mains average £15.

The Admiralty (Map 4; ☎ 7845 4646, Somerset House, The Strand WC2; ✆ Covent Garden or Temple). The flagship restaurant of the restored Somerset House has a traditional interior and

Modern French food. Expect to pay at least £22 each. There's a lovely outside area overlooking the Thames.

Cafes There's a cluster of enjoyable New Age cafes – some of them vegetarian – in Neal's Yard, including the two listed below. All offer a similar diet of wholesome dishes such as cheese breads and home-made noodles in pleasing surroundings, but space fills up quickly. Lunch in any of these places should cost about £5 to £6 if you choose carefully.

World Food Café (☎ 7379 0298, 14 Neal's Yard WC2)

Neal's Yard Salad Bar (☎ 7836 3233, 2 Neal's Yard WC2)

Bloomsbury (Maps 2, 4 & 5)

If you're visiting the British Museum it's worth knowing that Museum St (Map 5; ✆ Tottenham Court Road) is packed with cafes and simple lunch places where you'll get better value for your money than in the museum cafe.

Ruskins Café (Map 5; ☎ 7405 1450, 41 Museum St WC1). This place does soup and filled jacket potatoes from £2.95.

North Sea Fish Restaurant (Map 2; ☎ 7387 5892, 7–8 Leigh St WC1; ✆ Russell Square). The North Sea sets out to cook fresh fish and potatoes – a simple ambition in which it succeeds admirably. Cod, haddock and plaice, deep-fried or grilled, and a huge serving of chips will cost you between £6.95 and £7.95.

Coffee Gallery (Map 5; ☎ 7436 0455, 23 Museum St WC1). This vastly popular place serves pasta dishes and main courses (lots under £7) such as grilled sardines and salad in a bright, cheerful room with modern paintings on the walls.

Mille Pini (Map 4; ☎ 7242 2434, 33 Boswell St WC1; ✆ Russell Square or Holborn). This well-regarded place is a true, old-fashioned Italian restaurant and pizzeria with reasonable prices. You'll waddle out, but will only have spent about £6/10 for a two-course lunch/dinner.

Mandeer (Map 5; ☎ 7405 3211, 8 Bloomsbury Way WC1; ✆ Holborn). Food purists will rejoice at Mandeer, where meat, fish, preservatives and colourings are not used in the food. This Ayurvedic (an Indian holistic tradition) restaurant has numerous vegetarian and vegan meals for about £6. It opens daily except Sunday.

Holborn & Clerkenwell (Maps 2 & 4)

Holborn has a few restaurants and night spots to recommend it but is generally dead after dark. On the other hand, Clerkenwell has well and truly arrived on the eating-out map. These places are mostly accessible from Farringdon tube station.

The Greenery (Map 4; ☎ 7490 4870, 5 Cowcross St EC1). This small vegetarian cafe, hanging on for the moment amid all the gentrification of Clerkenwell, has salad platters for £3.95 and chickpea and coriander *chapatis* for £1.80.

St John (Map 4; ☎ 7251 0848, 26 St John St EC1). St John is the place to come if you fancy sampling old-fashioned British staples in new guises, such as tripe and sausage soup (£5), pigeon and Jerusalem artichoke (£11.80) and sweetbreads, peas and broad beans (£12.80). While there are some fish dishes, this place is all about meat, and offal in particular (after all, it is right next to Smithfield Market).

Gaudí (Map 4; ☎ 7608 3220, 63 Clerkenwell Rd EC1). This restaurant takes its cue from the Catalan architect's designs to provide a backdrop for a classy restaurant specialising in what has been dubbed New Spanish cuisine. Fish plays a big role, and first courses start at about £6, main courses at £14. Set lunch midweek costs £12.50/15 for two/three courses. It's got a good Spanish wine list.

Cicada (Map 2; ☎ 7608 1550, 132–136 St John St EC1). Cicada is a lovely, modern restaurant that mingles Asian tastes and flavours with great success. Starters cost from about £5, main dishes from £6 to £10.

Club Gascon (Map 4; ☎ 7253 5853, 57 West Smithfield EC1). Right next to glorious St Bartholomew's-the-Great (of *Four Weddings and a Funeral* fame), Club Gascon serves the food of south-western France. Book well in advance and expect to pay at least £30 each.

The City (Maps 4 & 6)

The City can be an irritating place in which to try to find a decent, affordable restaurant that stays open after office hours. The following are the pick of the crop.

Ye Olde Cheshire Cheese (Map 4; ☎ 7353 6170, Wine Office Court EC4; ✚ Blackfriars). Rebuilt six years after the Great Fire and popular with Dr Johnson, Thackeray, Dickens and visitor Mark Twain, the Cheshire Cheese is touristy but always atmospheric and enjoyable for a pub meal (£6).

Dim Sum (Map 4; ☎ 7236 1114, 5–6 Deans Court EC4; ✚ St Paul's). A budget traveller's delight and convenient for St Paul's and the City of London YHA hostel, Dim Sum serves Peking and Sichuan dishes for £3 to £6, but the best deal is the £9.99 all-you-can-eat buffet (minimum four people) available weekdays from 6 to 10.30 pm.

Wine Library (Map 6; ☎ 7481 0415, 43 Trinity Square EC3; ✚ Tower Hill). This is a great place to go if you want a light but boozy lunch. Buy a bottle of wine retail (no mark-up; £2 corkage fee) from the large selection on offer and then snack on patés, cheeses and salads for £9.95. The shop opens 10 am to 6 pm weekdays and for lunch from 11.30 am to 3 pm.

Da Vinci (Map 4; ☎ 7236 3938, 42–44 Carter Lane EC4; ✚ St Paul's). Here's a rare bird indeed: an affordable neighbourhood Italian place in the City. Starters cost from £3.95 to £6.95, pastas £3.80 to £5.95 and main courses £8.50 to £14. A two-course set lunch is £11.50 and there's a 'cheap lunch' for £4.50 available from 11.30 am to 1 pm.

Café Spice Namaste (Map 6; ☎ 7488 9242, 16 Prescot St E1; ✚ Tower Hill). One of our favourite Indian restaurants in London, the Namaste serves Goan and Keralan cuisine (with South-East Asian hints) in an old courthouse that has been decorated in 'carnival' colours. Try *frango piri-piri* (£7.75), a fiery hot chicken *tikka* marinated in red *masala*.

Sweeting's (Map 6; ☎ 7248 3062, 39 Queen Victoria St EC4; ✚ Mansion House). Sweeting's is an old-fashioned place, with a mosaic floor and waiters in white aprons standing behind narrow counters serving up all sorts of traditional fishy delights. Something such as wild smoked salmon costs £8.50; main courses run from £8 to £19.

Bermondsey (Map 1 & 6)

This area's culinary highlights include Terence Conran's gastronomic palaces at Shad Thames.

Blue Print Café (Map 1; ☎ 7378 7031, Design Museum, Butlers Wharf SE1; ✚ Tower Hill). Modern European cooking is the order of the day at this flagship Conran restaurant, with starters from £5 to £6.50 and main courses from £11 to £16.50. There are spectacular views of the river from here.

Cantina del Ponte (Map 6; ☎ 7403 5403, Butlers Wharf Building, 36c Shad Thames SE1; ✚ Tower Hill). This is a more affordable riverside Conran restaurant serving Italian/Mediterranean food. Starters are from £5, main courses from £13, with pizzas about £7 and pastas from £7.50 to £12.50. At lunch during the week and at dinner on Sunday there's a two-/three-course meal for £12/15. There's fabulous outside seating in warm weather.

Southwark (Map 6)

Options in this part of town should grow thanks in no small part to the Tate Modern.

Manze's (☎ 7407 2985, *87 Tower Bridge Rd SE1;* ✪ *London Bridge*). This pie shop, the oldest still trading in London, has been going strong for over a century and is handy for Bermondsey Market. In its pleasantly tiled interior jellied eels cost £2, pie and mash £2.20, and pie and liquor £1.50.

Fish! (☎ 7836 3236, *Cathedral St SE1;* ✪ *London Bridge*). Situated in an all-glass Victorian pavilion overlooking Borough Market and Southwark Cathedral, Fish! serves fresher-than-fresh fish and seafood prepared simply: steamed or grilled swordfish, cod, skate, squid (or whatever is ticked off on the placemat) served with one of five sauces. Expect to pay anything from £8.50 to £15.95 for a main course.

Waterloo & Lambeth (Map 4)

This part of south London is not immediately attractive as a place for eating out, although the cafes and restaurants in the Festival Hall, the Royal National Theatre and the National Film Theatre are popular places to meet, with reasonable food.

Konditor & Cook (☎ 7620 2700, *66 The Cut SE1;* ✪ *Waterloo*). This cafe at the Young Vic Theatre serves meals Monday to Friday from 8.30 am to 11 pm and on Saturday from 10.30 am, but we come here for the pastries and cakes made by Konditor & Cook, arguably the best bakery in London.

Mesón Don Felipe (☎ 7928 3237, *53 The Cut SE1;* ✪ *Waterloo*). This tapas place gets recommended more often than most for its wide choice, affordability (£3 to £4 per dish) and attractive surroundings.

Tas (☎ 7928 1444, *33 The Cut SE1;* ✪ *Southwark*). This is an excellent Turkish place with plush surroundings and fine food. The *choban kavurma* lamb casserole (£6.95) has many fans.

Oxo Tower Restaurant & Brasserie (☎ 7803 3888, *Barge House St SE1;* ✪ *Waterloo*). The conversion of the old Oxo Tower on the South Bank into housing with this restaurant on the 8th floor helped spur much of the restaurant renaissance south of the river. The food – a bit Mediterranean, a bit French, some Pacific Rim – is quite good. Starters cost from £5.50 to

£13.50, main courses average £18 and there's a three-course set lunch for £24.50.

Pizzeria Castello (*Map 1;* ☎ 7703 2556, *20 Walworth Rd SE1;* ✪ *Elephant & Castle*). Ask any south Londoner to direct you to the best pizzeria on this side of the Thames and you'll find yourself here. Castello has been going for years, is family owned, very friendly and prices are low (under £6). Book or count on a long wait for a table.

Brixton (Map 1)

If you're coming to Brixton for its market (✪ Brixton), don't restrict yourself to the eateries in the covered market itself. The surrounding streets (eg, Atlantic Rd, Coldharbour Lane) have a number of excellent places.

Eco Brixton (☎ 7738 3021, *4 Market Row SW9*). This restaurant has arguably the best pizzas (from £5.50), antipasto (£7.50) and cappuccino in south London. It opens to 5 pm daily (to 4 pm Wednesday and closed Sunday).

El Pilon Quindiano (☎ 7326 4316, *Granville Arcade SW9*). This Colombian cafe serves such authentic delicacies as *arepa* (small maize pancakes with various fillings), yucca and *empañadas* for around £3. A full lunch costs £6. This is the place to come if you want to try cheap South American dishes.

Satay Bar (☎ 7326 5001, *447–450 Coldharbour Lane SW9*). One of our favourite Asian eateries, the Satay Bar serves surprisingly authentic Indonesian food: *rendang ayam* (£5.95), laksa (£5.25), mixed satays (£5.95) and *mee goreng* (£4.25). *Rijsttafel* is £11.95 per person. Even more authentic are all the doors that open on to the busy street – you could easily be in a *warung* in Yogyakarta.

Bah Humbug (☎ 7738 3184, *St Matthew's Peace Garden, Brixton Hill SW2*). In the crypt of St Matthew's Methodist Church, Bah Humbug is one of the best vegetarian restaurants in London with quite a global range – from Thai vegetable fritters (£3) to Cantonese mock duck and masala curry (under £6.50).

Chelsea, South Kensington & Earl's Court (Map 7)

These three areas boast an incredible array of eateries – from Michelin-starred restaurants to trendy noodle bars to French patisseries – to suit all budgets.

Benjy's (☎ 7373 0245, *157 Earl's Court Rd SW5;* ✪ *Earl's Court*). Though Benjy's is nothing more than a fairly traditional cafe, it's always busy and the food is cheap and filling. Serious breakfasts, with as much tea or coffee as you can drink, are around £3.50, while lunch is £4.95.

Krungtap (☎ 7259 2314, 227 Old Brompton Rd SW10; ☻ Earl's Court). Krungtap (the Thai name for Bangkok) is a busy, friendly cafe open for dinner only. Most dishes are in the £3.50 to £5 range.

Blanco's (☎ 7370 3101, 314 Earl's Court Rd SW5; ☻ Earl's Court). Blanco's is a lively, authentic tapas (from £2.25 to £4.95) bar with good Spanish beer. It stays open until midnight.

Oriel (☎ 7730 2804, 50–51 Sloane Square SW1; ☻ Sloane Square). With its comfortable wicker chairs and mirrors, and tables overlooking Sloane Square, the Oriel makes the perfect place to meet before going shopping in King's Rd or Sloane St. Main dishes cost from £5 to £10, lighter fare such as pasta and salads is from £6 to £8.50.

The Collection (☎ 7225 1212, 264 Brompton Rd SW3; ☻ South Kensington). The Collection has a wonderful location in a converted gallery, with the main restaurant on a balcony overlooking the bar – great for people-watching. Starters are from £3.50 to £7, main courses £11 to £14.50, and there are set meals for £10/13 for two/three courses.

Spago (☎ 7225 2407, 6 Glendower Place SW7; ☻ South Kensington). This excellent-value Italian restaurant, with a good range of pastas and pizzas from £4.50, is convenient for the South Kensington museums. It opens daily for dinner only, and there is live music on Saturday.

New Culture Revolution (☎ 7352 9281, 305 King's Rd SW3; ☻ Sloane Square). This trendy, good-value dumpling and noodle bar has main dishes at around £6.

Daphne's (☎ 7589 4257, 112 Draycott Ave SW3; ☻ South Kensington). This place, popular with celebrities and their followers, is small enough to be intimate but large enough not to be claustrophobic. It serves delicious Mediterranean-style food, with main courses from £12.50 to £19, pastas from £9.

Bibendum (☎ 7581 5817, 81 Fulham Rd SW3; ☻ South Kensington). This Conran establishment is in one of London's finest settings for a restaurant, the Art Nouveau Michelin House (1911). The popular Bibendum Oyster Bar (£3.60 to £10.20 a half-dozen) is on the ground floor, where you really feel at the heart of the architectural finery. Upstairs it's all much lighter and brighter. A full meal with wine is likely to set you back around £55 a head.

Casual French A large number of French people live in South Kensington, and you'll find a lot of French-operated businesses there, particularly along Bute St, just south-west of South Kensington tube station, including a delicatessen called *La Grande Bouchée* (☎ 7589 8346) at No 31 and the *Rôtisserie Jules* (☎ 7584 0600) at Nos 6 to 8, a simple French-style cafeteria with flame-roasted chicken (from £4.95 to £9.75) and *gigot d'agneau*.

Around the corner, *FrancoFill* (☎ 7584 0087, 1 Old Brompton Rd SW7) is a delightful cafe-restaurant serving meals for around £10.

Kensington & Knightsbridge (Maps 3 & 4)

The restaurants, cafes and bars in these posh 'villages' of west and south-west London cater for a very well-heeled clientele, but there's always something good (and affordable) off the high streets.

Pizza on the Park (Map 4; ☎ 7235 5273, 11 Knightsbridge SW5; ☻ Hyde Park Corner). This place is as popular for its nightly jazz in the basement as for its pizza. There's also a spacious restaurant upstairs and, if you're lucky, a few tables overlooking Hyde Park. Pizzas average £6.50. Breakfast is available all day from 8.15 am (£4 for continental, £4.95 for English) and afternoon tea (£6.95) at 3.15 pm.

Bellini's (Map 3; ☎ 7937 5520, 47 Kensington Court W8; ☻ High Street Kensington). This stylish restaurant with a few pavement tables and views of a flower-bedecked alley serves two/three-course lunches for £6.75/7.90.

Fifth Floor (Map 3; ☎ 7235 5250, Harvey Nichols, 109–125 Knightsbridge SW1; ☻ Knightsbridge). This restaurant, bar and cafe is the perfect place to drop after you've shopped. It's expensive, averaging £30 per head at dinner, but there's a three-course set lunch for £23.50 served weekdays between noon and 3 pm (at weekends to 3.30 pm).

Notting Hill & Bayswater (Map 3)

Notting Hill, so popular ever since *that* film, has all sorts of interesting places to eat, and there are literally dozens of places lining Queensway and Westbourne Grove, with everything from cheap takeaways to good quality restaurants.

Market Thai (☎ 7460 8320, 240 Portobello Rd; ✆ Ladbroke Grove). Fresh and delicious Thai cuisine is on offer here one floor above a bar and way above the market crowds. Specials for £5 are good value.

Geales (☎ 7727 7528, 2 Farmer St W8; ✆ Notting Hill Gate). This popular fish restaurant prices everything according to weight and season. Fish and chips costs about £8.50 and it's worth every penny.

Café Grove (☎ 7243 1094, 253a Portobello Rd; ✆ Ladbroke Grove). Head here for gigantic and imaginative breakfasts as well as cheap and cheerful vegetarian food at around £5. The large balcony overlooking the market is great for watching all the action on a weekend morning.

Mandola (☎ 7229 4734, 139–141 Westbourne Grove W2; ✆ Bayswater). Mandola offers something entirely different: vegetarian Sudanese dishes such as *tamia* (£4.50), a kind of felafel, or *fifilia* (£6.95), a vegetable curry. Meat dishes such as chicken *halla* are around £7.

Osteria Basilico (☎ 7727 9372, 29 Kensington Park Rd W11; ✆ Notting Hill Gate or Ladbroke Grove). This neighbourhood restaurant offers a good mix of Italian rustic charm and West London chic, with an authentic menu and a lively, relaxed atmosphere. The tables by the window are best, but you will need to book. Pasta (from £6) and fish dishes (from £8) are recommended.

Kalamaras Micro (☎ 7727 5082, 66 Inverness Mews W2; ✆ Bayswater). The surroundings aren't mega, but the food is macro in this Greek spot in a quiet mews off Queensway. Main courses average about £7.50 and you can BYO.

Manzara (☎ 7727 3062, 24 Pembridge Rd W11; ✆ Notting Hill Gate). This simple place offers cheap but fresh and well-prepared Turkish food for less than £10.

The Standard (☎ 7229 0600, 21–23 Westbourne Grove W2; ✆ Bayswater). A neighbour of Khan's, the Standard serves excellent and very good-value Indian food. Count on about £10 per person.

Brasserie de Marché aux Puces (☎ 8968 5828, 349 Portobello Rd; ✆ Ladbroke Grove). On a quiet stretch of street north of the market, this delightful brasserie has French classics at good prices (most under £12) and tables outside should the sun shine.

Inaho (☎ 7221 8495, 4 Hereford Rd W2; ✆ Bayswater). This tiny Japanese restaurant has a *tempura* set dinner comprising an appetiser, soup, mixed salad, *yakitori*, sashimi, tempura, rice and seasonal fruits for £20 and a *teriyaki* equivalent for £22. A *tonkatsu* is £7, and rice and noodle dishes cost from £4 to £6.

Bali Sugar (☎ 7221 4477, 33a All Saints Rd W11; ✆ Westbourne Park). This is a lovely restaurant that's filled with flowers and charm. The excellent food is described as 'fusion' (average £27 per person) and leans slightly on the Asian side.

Euston (Map 2)

Drummond St (✆ Euston Square or Euston) has a number of good southern Indian vegetarian restaurants. **Diwana** (☎ 7387 5556) at No 121, the first (and some say still the best) of its kind on the street, specialises in Bombay-style *bel poori* (a kind of 'party mix' snack) and *dosas* (a kind of filled pancake) and has an all-you-can-eat lunch-time buffet for £3.95. Nearby at No 124, **Chutneys** (☎ 7388 0604) has a better lunch buffet (available all day on Sunday) for £4.95.

Camden (Map 2)

Camden High St is lined with good places to eat, although to watch the Sunday daytrippers snacking on takeaway sausages and chips you'd hardly believe it.

Café Delancey (☎ 7387 1985, 3 Delancey St NW1; ✆ Camden Town). The granddaddy of French-style brasseries in London, Café Delancey offers the chance to get a decent cup of coffee with a snack or a full meal in relaxed European-style surroundings complete with newspapers. Main dishes cost from £8 to £13, wine starts at £6.90 for a half-bottle. The cramped toilets, bickering staff and Charles Aznavour crooning in the background seem suitably Parisian too.

El Parador (☎ 7387 2789, 245 Eversholt St NW1; ✆ Mornington Crescent). El Parador is a quiet Spanish place where the selection of some 15 vegetarian dishes and tapas includes *empanadillas de espinacas y queso* (a spinach and cheese dish) for £3.80, with meat and fish dishes just a little more expensive (about £5).

Bar Gansa (☎ 7267 8909, 2 Inverness St NW1; ✆ Camden Town). This arty bar/cafe has tapas for around £3 and more elaborate Spanish main courses from £6.50 to £7.95. Service is good and the Spanish staff are very friendly. Breakfast costs £3.95. It serves drinks until 12.30 am (1 am on Friday and Saturday).

Lemon Grass (☎ 7284 1116, 243 Royal College St; ✆ Camden Town). Lemon Grass is one of the better Thai eateries in Camden with authentic food and charming decor and staff. Main dishes are around £6.

Thanh Binh (☎ 7267 9820, 14 Chalk Farm Rd NW1; ✆ Camden Town). A quiet little eatery opposite Camden Market, Thanh Binh serves decent Vietnamese dishes for between £4.50 and £6.50 and there's a set lunch for £5.

Sauce (☎ 7482 0777, 214 Camden High St NW1; ⊖ Camden Town). This young and trendy place makes much of the fact that it uses organic ingredients. The food is broad ranging: from salads to burgers, and averages £6 to £11.

Lemonia (Map 1; ☎ 7586 7454, 89 Regent's Park Rd NW1; ⊖ Chalk Farm). This upmarket and very popular Greek restaurant offers good-value food and a lively atmosphere. Meze costs £13.50 per person and both the vegetarian and meat *moussakas* for £7.50 are particularly tasty. There's a set weekday lunch for £7.50.

Islington (Map 2)

Islington is an excellent place for a night out. At the last count there were more than 60 cafes and restaurants between Angel and Highbury Corner, with most of the action on Upper St.

Upper St Fish Shop (☎ 7359 1401, 324 Upper St N1; ⊖ Highbury & Islington). This legendary fishmonger's doles out classy fish and chips for £7 to £7.50 and seafood such as half a dozen Irish oysters for around £6.

Afghan Kitchen (☎ 7359 8019, 35 Islington Green N1; ⊖ Angel). This small, simple yet trendy place serves simple Afghan fare – spiced meats and vegetables – that goes well with the basmati rice. It's quick and cheap (about £5).

Lola's (☎ 7359 1932, The Mall, 359 Upper St N1; ⊖ Angel). This award-winning restaurant is celebrated for its lovely decor, changing menu and popular Sunday brunch with live jazz. Starters range from £5 to £7, main courses from £10.50 to £14.

Ravi Shankar (☎ 7833 5849, 422 St John St EC1; ⊖ Angel). This small, inexpensive restaurant has some of the best Indian vegetarian food in London.

Hampstead

Hampstead, the well-to-do 'village' southwest of Hampstead Heath, has loads of good restaurants within easy walking distance of Hampstead tube station.

Café Base (☎ 7431 3241, 70–71 Hampstead High St NW3). This bright and clean cafe has unusual *ciabatta* sandwiches and wraps for £2.60 to £4.95 and salads and pastas for £2.95 to £3.95.

La Gaffe (☎ 7794 7526, 107 Heath St NW3). This comfortable, family run Italian restaurant in an 18th-century cottage has been going forever. Everything is quite reasonable.

Giraffe (☎ 7435 0343, 46 Rosslyn Hill NW3). This delightful cafe offers breakfast in the morning (banana pancakes £4.25) and an eclectic menu the rest of the day. It's comfy and casual and great if you're checking out the village or the heath.

East End (Maps 1 & 6)

From the Indian and Bangladeshi restaurants of Brick Lane to the trendy eateries of Hoxton and Shoreditch, the East End has finally made it onto the culinary map of London. Spitalfields Market (Map 6) is home to a diverse range of casual and fun eateries.

Brick Lane Beigel Bake (Map 1; ☎ 7729 0616, 159 Brick Lane E2; ⊖ Shoreditch). More of a delicatessen than a cafe, the Beigel Bake is at the Bethnal Green Rd end of Brick Lane and opens 24 hours. You won't find fresher or cheaper bagels anywhere in London. Filled bagels are a snip at 45p to 65p (the salmon and cream cheese version is a whopping 95p).

Mesón Los Barriles (Map 6; ☎ 7375 3136, 8a Lamb St E1; ⊖ Liverpool Street). This tapas bar and restaurant inside Spitalfields Market has an excellent selection of fish and seafood. Tapas range from £2 to £4.90, main courses average £6.50.

Viet Hoa (Map 1; ☎ 7729 8293, 70–72 Kingsland Rd E2; bus No 67 or 149). This simple canteen-style eatery serves excellent and authentic Vietnamese dishes. A full meal should cost you less than £10 and it's always full.

Indian Brick Lane (Map 1; ⊖ Aldgate East or Shoreditch) is lined wall-to-wall with cheap Indian and Bangladeshi restaurants – not all of them very good. *Aladin* (☎ 7247 8210) at No 132, a favourite of many, and *Nazrul* (☎ 7247 2505) at No 130 may be worth a try; both are unlicensed but you can BYO and should eat for around £8. More upmarket are *Le Taj* (☎ 7247 4210) at No 134 and *Sheraz* (☎ 7247 5755) at No 13.

Greenwich

Beautiful Greenwich has both old-style eateries and trendy new restaurants from which to choose. And don't forget the market from Friday to Sunday. The Cutty Sark DLR station is convenient for all.

Greenwich Church St has a few decent

and inexpensive cafes, including *Peter de Wit's* (☎ 8305 0048) at No 21 with cream teas for about £4.

Goddards Ye Olde Pie Shop (☎ 8692 3601, 45 Greenwich Church St SE10). Goddards is truly a step back into the past: a real London caff with wooden benches and things such as steak and kidney pie with liquor and mash, and shepherd's pie with beans and a rich brown gravy (all under £2.50). Sweet pies are from 50p. It opens 11 am to 3 or 4 pm most days except Monday.

Vietnam (☎ 8858 0871, 18 King William Walk SE10). Vietnam has inexpensive lunch plates such as spring rolls with noodles or rice (£3.95) available from noon to 5 pm.

Beachcomber (☎ 8853 0055, 34 Greenwich Church St SE10). This old stalwart festooned with flower baskets and potted plants does set two-/three-/four-course lunches for £5.90/7.95/9.90 and full breakfasts for £3.90. It's a very pleasant place on a sunny afternoon.

Fulham (Maps 1 & 7)

Fulham Rd is a good place for a meal and a night out.

Chelsea Bun (Map 7; ☎ 7352 3635, 9a Lamont Rd SW10; ⊖ Fulham Broadway or Earl's Court). This London version of an American diner is a great-value place in the area known as World's End. Breakfast is served all day, and there's seating on an upstairs veranda. Main dishes cost between £4 and £7.

The Gate (Map 1; ☎ 8748 6932, 51 Queen Caroline St W6; ⊖ Hammersmith). This may be the place to convert your carnivorous counterparts to the kinder, gentler world of vegetarianism. The beautifully presented, unusual main courses go for around £8.50; the dining room with its high ceilings and wall of glass is equally fine.

The Blue Elephant (Map 7; ☎ 7385 6595, 4–6 Fulham Broadway SW6; ⊖ Fulham Broadway). This Fulham institution serves upmarket (and very pricey) Thai food in jungle-like surroundings – you can't see the trees for the forest. The best time to come is from noon to 2.30 pm on Sunday when they do a fab Sunday set brunch for £16.75.

The River Café (Map 1; ☎ 7381 8824, Thames Wharf, Rainville Rd W6; ⊖ Hammersmith). The very buzzy, see-and-be-seen River Café owes its fame as much to its former chef, TV's Jamie Oliver, as to the food actually served here, but it does have the best Modern Italian cuisine in London. Main dishes start at £16.50 and you're unlikely to have much change from £40 once you've added a starter or dessert and wine.

Kew

A short distance north of Victoria Gate, the main entrance to Kew Gardens, is a historic cafe.

Newens Maids of Honour (☎ 8940 2752, 288 Kew Rd; ⊖ Kew Gardens). This old-fashioned tearoom that wouldn't seem out of place in a Cotswold village owes its fame to a special dessert supposedly concocted by Henry VIII's second wife, the ill-fated Anne Boleyn, from puff pastry, lemon, almonds and curd cheese. A 'maid of honour' will cost you £1.40, but don't plan on sampling it on Monday afternoon or Sunday when the tearoom is closed (otherwise it opens 9.30 am to 6 pm). Set teas (£4.65) are served from 2.30 to 5.30 pm.

ENTERTAINMENT
Pubs & Bars

Sampling a range of pubs and bars is part of the fun of visiting London. The following list includes most of our favourites, but there's no substitute for individual research. Many of the pubs listed below serve good food.

Sherlock Holmes (Map 5; 10 Northumberland St WC2; ⊖ Charing Cross). Tucked away just off Northumberland Ave, this pub filled with Holmes memorabilia doesn't get quite as busy as it otherwise might and is never touristy.

Westminster Arms (Map 4; 3 Storey's Gate SW1; ⊖ Westminster). This pleasant, atmospheric place is great for a quick one after a tiring tour of Westminster Abbey, which is a two-minute walk away. Think of the convenience.

O Bar (Map 5; 83–85 Wardour St W1; ⊖ Piccadilly Circus). This upbeat bar has two main drinking floors with a DJ downstairs nightly (£5 cover charge). It also serves half-price pitchers of cocktails till 8 pm (till closing on Monday, to midnight on Wednesday).

Lamb & Flag (Map 5; 33 Rose St WC2; ⊖ Covent Garden). Everyone's 'find' in Covent Garden and therefore always jammed, the pleasantly unchanged Lamb & Flag was once known as the Bucket of Blood.

The Queen's Larder (Map 4; 1 Queen Square WC1; ⊖ Russell Square). In a lovely square south-east of Russell Square, the Queen is a handy retreat, with outside benches and pub grub.

Museum Tavern (Map 5; 49 Great Russell St WC1; ⊖ Tottenham Court Road). After a hard day's work in the British Museum Reading Room, Karl Marx used to repair to this capacious pub, where you too can sup your pint.

Ye Olde Mitre (Map 4; 1 Ely Court EC1; ✪ Chancery Lane). One of our absolute favourites, the Mitre is one of London's oldest and most historic pubs, although the 18th-century-sized rooms can be a bit tight for late-20th-century punters like us.

Cock Tavern (Map 4; East Poultry Ave EC1; ✪ Farringdon). This legendary pub will serve you a pint between 6.30 and 10.30 am when it feeds and waters the workers from Smithfield Market.

Cantaloupe (Map 1; 35–43 Charlotte Rd EC2; ✪ Old Street or Liverpool Street). This cool pub manages to feel arty enough without being overwhelming. There's a decent restaurant (main courses from £7 to £14) at the back.

George Inn (Map 6; Talbot Yard, 77 Borough High St SE1; ✪ London Bridge or Borough). The George is London's last surviving galleried coaching inn, dates from 1676 and is mentioned in Charles Dickens' *Little Dorrit*. Here too is the site of the Tabard Inn (thus the Talbot Yard address), where the pilgrims gathered in Chaucer's *Canterbury Tales* before setting out.

The Anchor (Map 6; 34 Park St SE1; ✪ London Bridge). This 18th-century place just east of the Globe Theatre has superb views across the Thames from its terrace.

The Fire Station (Map 4; 150 Waterloo Rd SE1; ✪ Waterloo). This immensely popular gastropub (from £7 to £10 for main courses) is in a part of town that was once a culinary desert but is now always jammed. Jazz on Sunday afternoon.

Trafalgar Tavern (Park Row SE10; DLR Cutty Sark). This cavernous pub with big windows looking onto the Thames and the Millennium Dome has a lot of history. It stands above the site of the old Placentia Palace where Henry VIII was born.

King's Head & Eight Bells (Map 7; 50 Cheyne Walk SW3; ✪ Sloane Square). This attractive corner pub, pleasantly hung with flower baskets in summer, has a wide range of beers and was a favourite of the painter Whistler and the writer Carlyle.

The Churchill Arms (Map 3; 119 Kensington Church St W8; ✪ Notting Hill Gate). This traditional English pub is renowned for its Winston memorabilia, chamber pots suspended from a great height and excellent-value Thai food (around £6) served in a lovely conservatory in the back.

Windsor Castle (Map 3; 114 Campden Hill Rd W11; ✪ Notting Hill Gate). The Windsor has one of the nicest walled gardens (with heaters in winter) of any pub in London.

The Market Bar (Map 3; 240a Portobello Rd W11; ✪ Ladbroke Grove). Convenient for the market, this place has an interesting, eclectic decor and an entertaining crowd.

Oh! Bar There's good music at this large and lively place *(Map 2; ☎ 7383 0330, 111–113 Camden High St NW1; ✪ Camden Town).*

Crown & Goose (Map 2; 100 Arlington Rd NW1; ✪ Camden Town). This is a new-style pub attracting a youngish crowd with decent, no-nonsense food.

Clubs

Though the majority of London's pubs still close at 11 pm, there are clubs where you can carry on partying. Admission costs vary from £10 to £15 for most clubs, plus at least £3 per drink. The most happening clubs don't kick off until after midnight and stay open until 4 or 5 am; some are all-nighters. Dress can be smart (no suits) or casual; the more outrageous you look – within reason – the better the chance you have of getting in.

Bagley's Studios (Map 2; ☎ 7278 2777, King's Cross Freight Depot, York Way N1; ✪ King's Cross St Pancras). A huge, converted warehouse with five dance floors, four bars and an outside area in the summer.

The End (Map 5; ☎ 7419 9199, 16a West Central St WC1; ✪ Holborn). Modern industrial decor with a free water-fountain. For serious clubbers who like their music underground.

Fabric (Map 4, ☎ 7490 0444, 77a Charterhouse St EC1; ✪ Farringdon). This latest feather in Clerkenwell's well-plumed cap boasts three dance floors in a converted meat cold-store.

Ministry of Sound (Map 6; ☎ 7378 6528, 103 Gaunt St SE1; ✪ Elephant & Castle). This cavernous place, arguably London's most famous club, attracts hard-core clubbers as well as people who just want to chill out. It opens until 9 am.

Velvet Room (Map 5; ☎ 7439 4655, 143 Charing Cross Rd WC2; ✪ Tottenham Court Road). An intimate, friendly club swathed in red velvet.

Gay & Lesbian London

The best starting point is to pick up the free *Pink Paper* (very serious, politically correct) or *Boyz* (more geared towards entertainment) available from most gay cafes, bars and clubs. The four-page gay section of *Time Out* is another excellent source of information. The Lesbian & Gay Switchboard (☎ 7837 7324) answers calls 24 hours.

London's bars and clubs cater for every predilection, but there's a growing trend towards mixed gay and straight clubs.

In the 'gay village' of Soho (⊖ Tottenham Court Road or Piccadilly Circus) – particularly along Old Compton St – bars and cafes are thick on the ground. All the establishments in this section except the last one can be found on Map 5.

The *Old Compton Café* (☎ *7439 3309*) at No 34 on this street is a friendly, sometimes frantic, 24-hour place while *Balans* (☎ *7437 5212*), at No 60, is a popular, moderately priced, continental-style cafe.

Near Tottenham Court Road tube station, the long-established, friendly *First Out* (☎ *7240 8042, 52 St Giles High St WC2*) is a mixed lesbian-gay cafe that serves vegetarian food and has rotating exhibitions. Close by, the *Astoria* (☎ *7434 9592, 157–165 Charing Cross Rd WC2*) is a dark, sweaty and atmospheric club with a gay night, G.A.Y. There are good views of the stage and a huge dance floor.

Retro Bar (☎ *7321 2811, 2 George Court WC2*) is a friendly bar, tucked away down a small lane off the Strand, with a host of theme nights in the upstairs bar during the week.

The *Black Cap* (*Map 2;* ☎ *7428 2721, 171 Camden High St NW1;* ⊖ *Camden Town*) is a late-night bar famous for its drag shows.

Live Music

London's music scene is so vibrant that we can only scratch the surface with the following recommendations. Check the press to see what's on.

Rock & Pop Some great venues include:

Brixton Academy (*Map 1;* ☎ *7771 2000, 211 Stockwell Rd SW9;* ⊖ *Brixton*). Enormous and very popular venue with a good atmosphere.

Garage (*Map 2;* ☎ *7607 1818, 20–22 Highbury Corner N5;* ⊖ *Highbury & Islington*). Good venue for rock, industrial and punk.

Borderline (*Map 5;* ☎ *7734 2095, Orange Yard W1;* ⊖ *Tottenham Court Road*). Small, relaxed venue with a reputation for big-name bands playing under pseudonyms.

Underworld (*Map 2;* ☎ *7482 1932, 174 Camden High St NW1;* ⊖ *Camden Town*). Beneath the huge World's End pub, a small venue featuring new bands.

Jazz The jazz scene is diverse and spread through the city.

Jazz Café (*Map 2;* ☎ *7344 0044, 5 Parkway NW1;* ⊖ *Camden Town*). Very trendy restaurant venue; it is best to book a table. Acts cost between £8 and £15 at the door, cheaper in advance.

100 Club (*Map 5;* ☎ *7636 0933, 100 Oxford St W1;* ⊖ *Oxford Circus*). Legendary London venue, once showcasing the Stones and at the centre of the punk revolution and now concentrating on jazz (tickets from £6 to £10).

Classical Music London is Europe's classical music capital, with several symphony orchestras, various smaller outfits, brilliant venues, reasonable prices and high standards of performance. Prices can run anywhere from £5 to £50.

The *Royal Festival Hall*, *Queen Elizabeth Hall* and *Purcell Room* (*Map 4;* ☎ *7960 4242;* ⊖ *Waterloo*) are three of London's premier venues for classical concerts. All are located in the South Bank.

The *Barbican* (*Map 6;* ☎ *7638 8891, Silk St EC2;* ⊖ *Barbican*) is home to the London Symphony Orchestra.

Cinema

Leicester Square is where British films are premiered. However you'll find cinemas throughout London. Besides scores of multiplexes showing the latest Hollywood output (although Americans will wonder why films are shown here three months later), there are also scores of cinemas around showing off-beat, artistic, classic, non-English and all other manner of films. This is one category where you really do need *Time Out*.

The following two places are worth special note:

National Film Theatre (*Map 6;* ☎ *7928 3232, South Bank Centre;* ⊖ *Waterloo*). This film-lover's heaven screens an impressive range of films.

BFI London IMAX Cinema (*Map 4;* ☎ *7902 1234, Tenison Way SE1;* ⊖ *Waterloo*). A stunning structure houses Europe's largest IMAX screen. Film showings begin at noon daily and cost from £6.75/4.75.

Theatre

London is one of the world's great centres for theatre-lovers, and there's a lot more here than just *Cats*, *Art* and *Chicago*. With tickets so plentiful and reasonably priced, it would be a shame not to take in at least one or two of the best productions.

On the day of performance you can buy half-price tickets for West End productions (for cash only) from the Leicester Square Half-Price Ticket Booth, on the southern side of Leicester Square (Map 5; ☻ Leicester Square). The booth is the one with the clock tower – beware of imitations that may rip you off. It opens noon to 6.30 pm daily and charges £2 commission for each ticket.

Among the venues of note are:

Royal National Theatre (Map 4; ☎ 7452 3000, South Bank; ☻ Waterloo). This large facility has three auditoriums: the Olivier, the Lyttleton and the Cottesloe. It showcases classics and contemporary plays, and hosts appearances by the world's best companies.

Barbican (Map 6; ☎ 7638 8891, Silk St EC2; ☻ Barbican). The London home of the Royal Shakespeare Company has two auditoriums – the Barbican Theatre and the smaller Pit.

Globe Theatre (Map 6; ☎ 7401 9919, 21 New Globe Walk SE1; ☻ London Bridge). There's more than just the works of the Bard on this stage. See Central London – South of the Thames earlier for further information.

Opera & Dance

Culture at this level can cost anywhere from £5 to £100 and more.

Following a £213 million redevelopment, the *Royal Opera House* (Map 5; ☎ 7304 4000, Covent Garden WC2; ☻ Covent Garden) has welcomed home the peripatetic Royal Opera and Royal Ballet.

The home of the English National Opera, the *Coliseum* (Map 5; ☎ 7632 8300, St Martin's Lane WC1; ☻ Leicester Square) presents opera in English.

Spectator Sports

Football Tickets for Premier League football matches start at around £15 (but don't expect to find any). Some of the big teams worth watching include:

Arsenal (☎ 7704 4040, Avenell Rd N5; ☻ Arsenal).
Tottenham Hotspur (☎ 8365 5000, White Hart Lane N17; White Hart Lane station).
West Ham United (☎ 8548 2748, Green St E13; ☻ Upton Park).

The legendary **Wembley Stadium** (☎ 8900 1234, ☻ Wembley Park), ground zero for many an English football fan, is undergoing a major reconstruction lasting through 2003.

Rugby *Twickenham Rugby Stadium* (☎ 8892 2000, Rugby Rd, Twickenham; ☻ Hounslow East, then bus No 281; Twickenham station) is the shrine of English rugby union. Tickets cost around £30. The ground also boasts a Museum of Rugby (£5). It opens 10 am to 5 pm Tuesday to Saturday (from 2 pm Sunday).

Cricket Despite the dismal fortunes of the England team, cricket continues to flourish. Test matches take place at two cricket grounds: *Lord's* (Map 1; ☎ 7289 1300, St John's Wood Rd NW8; ☻ St John's Wood) and *The Oval* (Map 1; ☎ 7582 6660, Kennington Oval SE11; ☻ Oval). Tickets are expensive (from £15 to £45).

SHOPPING

London is a mecca for shopaholics from around the UK and continental Europe, and if you can't find it here, it probably doesn't exist.

If you're looking for something with a British 'brand' on it, eschew the Union Jack-emblazoned kitsch of Carnaby and Oxford Sts and go for things that the Brits themselves know are of good quality, sometimes stylish and always solid: Dr Marten boots and shoes, Burberry raincoats and umbrellas, tailor-made shirts from Jermyn St and costume jewellery (be it for the finger, wrist, nose, eyebrow or navel).

Books

General For those who read the book or saw the film *84 Charing Cross Road*, Charing Cross Rd (Map 5; ☻ Tottenham Court Road or Leicester Square) will need no introduction. This is where to go when you want reading material old or new.

Foyle's (☎ 7437 5660), 113–119 Charing Cross Rd WC2, is the biggest and by far the most confusing bookshop in London, but it often stocks titles you may not find elsewhere. Much better organised is Waterstone's (☎ 7434 4291), 121–129 Charing Cross Rd WC2, a chain that has transformed book buying for Londoners with its knowledgeable staff. Its mega-branch (Map 5; ☎ 7851 2400), the biggest bookshop in Europe, is at 203–206 Piccadilly W1 (✆ Piccadilly Circus). Blackwell's (☎ 7292 5100), 100 Charing Cross Rd WC2, has a lot of academic titles but stocks general books as well.

One of the best places for half-price second-hand books is the book market on the South Bank under the arches of Waterloo Bridge (Map 4). It opens 10 am to 5 pm at weekends, though a few stalls open throughout the week.

Travel The major chains are adequate sources of guidebooks and maps, but there are also several specialist travel bookshops:

Daunt Books (Map 4; ☎ 7224 2295), 83 Marylebone High St W1 (✆ Baker Street). Daunt has a wide selection of travel guides and books on other subjects in a beautiful old sky-lit shop.
Stanford's (Map 5; ☎ 7836 1321), 12–14 Long Acre WC2 (✆ Covent Garden). Stanford's has one of the largest selections of maps, guides and travel literature in the world.
Travel Bookshop (Map 3; ☎ 7229 5260), 13 Blenheim Crescent W11 (✆ Ladbroke Grove). This is London's best 'boutique' travel bookshop and was apparently the inspiration for the shop in *Notting Hill*. It has all the new guides, plus out-of-print and antiquarian gems.

Travel Gear
The YHA Adventure Shop (Map 5; ☎ 7836 8541), 14 Southampton St WC2 (✆ Covent Garden), is an excellent place to stock up on all sorts of camping and walking gear.

Music
For the largest collections of CDs and tapes in London check out any of the following three Goliath-sized music shops, all in the West End (Map 5):

HMV (☎ 7631 3423), 150 Oxford St W1 (✆ Oxford Circus). Open 9.30 am to 8 pm weekdays, 9 am to 7.30 pm Saturday, and noon to 6 pm Sunday.
Tower Records (☎ 7439 2500), 1 Piccadilly Circus W1 (✆ Piccadilly Circus). Open 9 am to midnight Monday to Saturday, and noon to 6 pm Sunday.
Virgin Megastore (☎ 7631 1234), 14–30 Oxford St W1 (✆ Tottenham Court Road). Open 9 am to 9 pm Monday to Saturday, and noon to 6 pm Sunday.

London also has a wide range of excellent music-shops specialising in everything from jazz and big band to world music. Worth trying are (Map 5):

Black Market Records (☎ 7437 0478), 25 D'Arblay St W1 (✆ Oxford Circus)
Trax (☎ 7734 0795), 55 Greek St W1 (✆ Tottenham Court Road)

For second-hand and rare vinyl try either of the following (both Map 5):

Division One (☎ 7637 7734), 36 Hanway St W1 (✆ Tottenham Court Road)
On the Beat (☎ 7637 8934), 22 Hanway St W1 (✆ Tottenham Court Road)

Where To Shop
Although most things can be bought throughout London, there are also streets known for their own specialities. Tottenham Court Rd, for example, is full of electronics and computer shops. Cecil Court has antiquarian bookshops, while Denmark St has musical instruments, sheet music and books about music. All these streets are on Map 5.

Some shopping streets rest on their laurels, their claim to fame having more to do with their past than what they have to offer today (eg, Carnaby Street). The twee shops and stalls inside the old market building at Covent Garden (Map 5) in the centre tend to be pricey and tourist-oriented, but the streets running off it remain a happy hunting-ground for shoppers, with Neal St and Neal's Yard in particular offering an interesting range.

Oxford St (Map 5) can be a great disappointment. Selfridges is up there with

Harrods as a place to visit. But the farther east you go, the tackier and less interesting it gets. Regent St is much more upmarket. Kensington High St (Map 3) is a good alternative to Oxford St. In the City check out some of the lovely boutiques in Bow Lane (Map 6), which runs from Cheapside to Cannon St.

Many tourist attractions have shops selling good-quality souvenirs: war books and videos at the Imperial War Museum, excellent art books at the National Gallery, tube merchandise at the London Transport Museum (we know someone who loves the 'Mind the Gap' ✆-shirts) and so on.

Department Stores London's main department stores have a variety of cafes, bars and more. They are great places to pause for afternoon tea.

Harrods (Map 3; ☎ 7730 1234), 87 Brompton Rd SW1 (✆ Knightsbridge), is always crowded, there are more rules than at an army boot camp and it's hard to find what you're looking for, but tourists flock here like lemmings. Items bearing the logo seem to be proliferating.

Harvey Nichols (Map 3; ☎ 7235 5000), 109–125 Knightsbridge SW1 (✆ Knightsbridge), is the city's heart of high fashion. It has a great food hall on the 5th floor, an extravagant perfume department and jewellery worth saving up for.

Fortnum & Mason (Map 5; ☎ 7734 8040), 181 Piccadilly W1 (✆ Piccadilly Circus), is noted for its exotic, old-world food hall on the ground floor, but it also carries plenty of fashion wear on the next four floors.

Selfridges (Map 4; ☎ 7629 1234), 400 Oxford St W1 (✆ Bond Street), is arguably the grandest shop on Oxford St and the one with the longest history. It's what Harrods was before it became a self-parody.

Liberty (Map 5; ☎ 7734 1234), 214–220 Regent St W1 (✆ Oxford Circus), has high fashion, a wonderful luxury-fabrics department and those inimitable Liberty silk scarves.

Markets Believe it or not, London has more than 350 markets selling everything from antiques and curios to flowers and fish. Some, such as Camden and Portobello Rd, are well known to visitors. But others exist just for the locals, who find everything from dinner to underwear for sale in the stalls.

The following is a highly selective list of the more noteworthy markets (note that they only operate certain days). The larger ones can occupy an entire day of browsing, snacking and strolling.

Bermondsey Market (Map 6; ☎ 7351 5353), Bermondsey Square SE1 (✆ Borough), is the place to come if you're after old opera glasses, bowling balls, hatpins, costume jewellery, porcelain or any other 'antique'. The main market on Friday (4 am to 2 pm) takes place outdoors on the square although adjacent warehouses shelter the more vulnerable furnishings and bric-a-brac.

Brick Lane Market (Map 1), Brick Lane E1 (✆ Shoreditch or Aldgate East), is fun. Activity kicks off on Sunday at around 8 am and spreads out along Bethnal Green Rd to the north. By 2 pm it's all over. There's a mix of stalls selling clothes, fruit and vegetables, household goods, paintings and bric-a-brac.

Brixton Market (Map 1; ✆ Brixton) is a cosmopolitan treat that mixes everything from the Body Shop and reggae to slick Muslim preachers, South American butcher shops and exotic fruits. On Electric Ave and in the covered Granville Arcade you can buy wigs, unusual foods and spices and homeopathic root cures. The market opens 8 am to 5.30 pm Monday to Saturday (to 1 pm only Wednesday).

Camden Market (Map 2) stretches north from Camden Town tube station to Chalk Farm Rd. It's busiest at weekends between 10 am and 6 pm, although there'll be a few stalls up and running most days. Here you'll find 1960s clothes, army-surplus goods, ceramics, furniture, oriental rugs, musical instruments, designer clothes and so on. The bridge over the old Grand Union Canal and Camden Lock offers great views.

Petticoat Lane (Map 6; ✆ Aldgate, Aldgate East or Liverpool Street) is east London's long-established Sunday market (from 8 am to 2 pm) on Middlesex St, on the border between the City and Whitechapel. These days, however, it's full of run-of-the-mill junk and tourists.

Portobello Rd (Map 3; ☎ 7727 7684; ✆ Notting Hill Gate, Ladbroke Grove or Westbourne Park) is London's most famous (and crowded) street market. Starting near the Sun in Splendour pub in Notting Hill, it wends its way northwards to just past the Westway flyover. Antiques, handmade jewellery, paintings and ethnic stuff are concentrated at the Notting Hill Gate end of Portobello Rd (roughly from Chepstow Villas as far as Elgin Crescent to the west and Colville Terrace to the east). The stalls dip downmarket as you move north (fruit and veg, second-hand clothing, cheap household goods, bric-a-brac).

GETTING THERE & AWAY

London is the major gateway to Britain, so further transport information can be found in the Getting There & Away and Getting Around chapters.

Airports

Heathrow Fifteen miles west of central London, Heathrow (LHR) is the world's busiest commercial airport, handling upwards of 60 million passengers a year. It now has four terminals. The tube and Heathrow Express each have two stations serving Heathrow: one each for Terminals 1, 2, 3 and one each for Terminal 4. Make certain you know which terminal your flight is departing from as airlines and flights can shift around the airport.

Heathrow is chaotic, overcrowded and remarkably ugly. BAA, the company that operates the airport, seems to have decided to run a third-rate shopping centre instead of a world-class travel facility. Where there were once peaceful public spaces where you could wait for your flight, now there are all manner of shops. One of the worst offenders is the departure area of Terminal 3; passengers are trapped in a windowless and smoky area surrounded by brightly lit stores. Even more cynical has been the installation of shops between the luggage belts and the outside world, delaying your escape that much longer. The petty annoyances build as well. The high-profit liquor and perfume counters are jammed with assistants and have short queues, while the low-profit newsstands may have one or two clerks serving long queues. The pubs, bars and restaurants are of minimal quality.

On the plus side, each terminal has competitive currency-exchange facilities, ATMs, information counters and accommodation desks.

There are several large international hotels – none particularly cheap or noteworthy – at or near Heathrow, should you be leaving or arriving at a peculiarly early or late hour. To reach them you must take the Heathrow Hotel Hoppa bus (☎ 01293-507099) costing £2 (in most other airports, such shuttles are free). The buses run between 6 am and 11 pm, with a service every 10 minutes at peak times, every 15 minutes otherwise, for the first three terminals. Services from Terminal 4 run every 30 minutes.

There are left-luggage facilities at Terminal 1 (☎ 8745 5301); Terminal 2 (☎ 8745 4599); Terminal 3 (☎ 8759 3344); and Terminal 4 (☎ 8745 7460). They are usually open at least 6 am to 10 pm. The charge is £3 per item for the first 12 hours and £3.50 per item for up to 24 hours. All can forward baggage.

For general enquiries and flight information phone ☎ 0870 000 0123. Beware of the touted BAA information number (☎ 0870 544 4000); it gets you a sales pitch for – you guessed it – 'the wonderful world of shopping at BAA airports'. The Hotel Reservation Service (☎ 8564 8808) is useful if you need a room near the airport.

Gatwick Although large, Gatwick (LGW) is a much smaller airport than Heathrow and in many ways easier and more pleasant to use. The northern and southern terminals are linked by an efficient monorail service; check which terminal you will use. There are all the predictable BAA stores, and several eating and drinking areas.

The left-luggage office at the North Terminal (☎ 01293-502013) opens 6 am to 10 pm daily, the one in the South Terminal (☎ 01293-502014) round the clock.

For flight (except British Airways; BA) and airport information, phone ☎ 01293-535353. For BA, phone ☎ 0870 000 0123.

Stansted Some 35 miles north-east of central London, Stansted (STN), London's third international gateway, handles many of the discount airlines such as Buzz, Go and Ryan Air. The futuristic terminal building was designed by Sir Norman Foster (although he can't be blamed for the obstructing gaggle of BAA shops just past security). There's a single number (☎ 01279-680500) for general enquiries, hotel reservations and rail information.

Luton The other major airport for the discount airlines, including easyJet, Luton

(LTN; ☎ 01582-405100 for general enquiries, hotel reservations and car-park information) is 35 miles north of the city. Recently Luton opened an airy new terminal.

London City Six miles east of central London, London City (LCY) airport (☎ 7646 0088) is in the Docklands by the Thames. Seen as a businessperson's airport and under-utilised until recently, London City now has flights to numerous British Isles and continental European destinations.

Airline Offices

See the Getting There & Away chapter for a list of airline telephone numbers for flight, booking enquiries and office information.

Bus

Most long-distance express buses (usually referred to as coaches in the UK) leave London from Victoria Coach Station (Map 8; ☎ 7730 3466 for information), an attractive 1930s-style building at 164 Buckingham Palace Rd SW1 (◉ Victoria, about 10 minutes' walk south of Victoria train and tube stations). The arrivals terminal is in a separate building across Elizabeth St from the main coach station.

Train

London has 10 main-line terminals, all linked by the tube. Each serves a different geographical area of the UK:

Charing Cross (Map 5)
   South-eastern England
Euston (Map 2)
   Northern and north-western England, Scotland
King's Cross (Map 2)
   North London, Hertfordshire, Cambridgeshire, northern and north-eastern England, Scotland
Liverpool Street (Map 6)
   East and north-east London, Stansted airport, East Anglia
London Bridge (Map 6)
   South-eastern England
Marylebone (Map 3)
   North-west London, the Chilterns
Paddington (Map 3)
   South Wales, western and south-western England, southern Midlands, Heathrow airport
St Pancras (Map 2)
   The East Midlands, southern Yorkshire

Victoria (Map 8)
   Southern and south-eastern England, Gatwick airport, Channel ferry ports
Waterloo (Map 4)
   South-west London, southern and south-western England, Brussels and Paris from the adjoining Waterloo International Eurostar terminal

In recent years a lot of work has been done to make the terminals more attractive and efficient. Liverpool Street station has been restored to its Victorian splendour, while Brunel's Paddington station is getting a much needed overhaul.

Most stations now have left-luggage facilities and lockers, toilets (20p) with showers (around £3), newsstands and bookshops, and a range of eating and drinking outlets. Victoria and Liverpool Street stations have shopping centres attached.

Car

See the Getting Around chapter for the reservations numbers for major car rental firms, all of which have airport and multiple city locations.

GETTING AROUND

Transport for London (TfL), a new organisation under control of London's mayor, is responsible for much of London's public transit. It is set to take over responsibility for the tube in 2001.

To/From the Airports

Transport to and from London's five airports is as follows (bear in mind that some airlines offer their passengers special deals and that return tickets are often cheaper than two singles):

Heathrow The airport is accessible by bus, the Underground (between 5 am and 11 pm) and main-line train.

The Heathrow Express (☎ 0845 600 1515) rail link whisks passengers from Paddington station to Heathrow in just 15 minutes. Tickets cost an exorbitant £12 each way. Trains leave every 15 minutes from around 5 am to 10.30 pm. Many airlines have advance check-in desks at Paddington.

The Underground station for Terminals 1,

2 and 3 is directly linked to the terminus buildings; there's a separate station for Terminal 4. Check which terminal your flight uses when you reconfirm. The adult single fare is £3.50, or you can use an All Zone travelcard which is £4.70. The journey time from central London is about an hour.

The Airbus (☎ 7222 1234) services are prone to traffic congestion. There are two routes: the A1, which runs along Cromwell Rd to Victoria; and the A2, which runs along Notting Hill Gate and Bayswater Rd to Russell Square. Buses run every half-hour and cost £7.

A minicab to and from central London will cost from around £25; a metered black cab around £35.

Gatwick The Gatwick Express train (☎ 0870 530 1530) runs non-stop between the main terminal and Victoria train station 24 hours daily. Singles cost £10.20 and the journey takes about 30 minutes. The Connex South-Central service to Victoria takes a little longer and costs £8.20.

Thameslink trains travel through the City via London Bridge, Blackfriars, City Thameslink and King's Cross. These trains take 30 to 45 minutes.

Jetlink 777 buses (☎ 8668 7261) from Victoria coach station cost £8 but take 90 minutes to get there.

Gatwick's northern and southern terminals are linked by a monorail; check which terminal your flight uses. Some airlines have check-in desks at Victoria.

A minicab to or from central London will cost around £35; a metered black cab around £50.

Stansted The airport is served by the Stansted Express (☎ 0845 748 4950) from Liverpool Street station which costs £11 and takes 45 minutes. The trains depart every 15 to 30 minutes.

Luton The airport (☎ 01582 405100) is connected by frequent shuttle bus to the Luton Airport Parkway station. Several trains (☎ 0845 748 4950) an hour go to/from London through the King's Cross

Thameslink station. Fares cost £9 and the journey takes about 35 minutes.

London City The airport (☎ 7646 0000) is two minutes' walk from the Silvertown & City Airport train station which is linked by train to Stratford. A frequent shuttle bus also connects the airport with the Canning Town tube, DLR and train station. The Airbus connects the airport with Liverpool Street station (£5; 30 minutes) and Canary Wharf (£2; 10 minutes).

London Underground

The London Underground, or 'tube', first opened in 1863 (it was then essentially a roofed-in trench) and sometimes it feels like not a whole lot has changed since then; it is slow, unreliable and, as the ageing system has suffered from decades of underfunding, breakdowns are common.

Still, the tube is normally the quickest and easiest way of getting round London; an estimated 2.5 million tube journeys are made every day.

Information The TfL and the tube operate information centres that sell tickets and provide free maps. There are centres at all four Heathrow terminals and at Victoria, Piccadilly Circus, Oxford Circus, St James's Park, Liverpool Street, Euston and King's Cross tube and main-line train stations. There are also information offices at Hammersmith and West Croydon stations. For general information on the tube, buses, the DLR or trains within London ring ☎ 7222 1234 or visit the TfL Web site at www.londontransport.co.uk.

Network Greater London is served by 12 tube lines, along with the independent (though linked) and privately owned DLR and an interconnected railway network (see the later DLR & Train section). The first tube train is at around 5.30 am Monday to Saturday and around 7 am on Sunday; the last train leaves between 11.30 pm and 12.30 am depending on the day, the station and the line.

Remember that any train heading from left to right on the map is designated as eastbound, any train heading from top to bottom is southbound. If your two stations are not on the same line, you need to note the nearest station where the two lines intersect, where you must change trains (transfer).

The biggest change to the tube in recent years was the completion of the 10-mile Jubilee Line extension in 1999, from Westminster to Stratford via Canary Wharf. The 11 new Jubilee Line stations were all designed by different architects and many are ultramodern works of art in themselves.

If you're caught on the Underground without a valid ticket (and that includes crossing into a zone that your ticket doesn't cover) you're liable for an on-the-spot £10 fine. If you do get nabbed, do us all a favour: shut up and pay up. The inspectors – and your fellow passengers – hear the same stories every day of the year.

Fares TfL divides London into six concentric zones. The basic fare for adults/those aged under 16 years for Zone 1 is £1.50/60p, for Zones 1 & 2 £1.80/80p, for three zones £2.10/1, for four zones £2.60/1.20, for five zones £3.20/1.40 and for all six zones (eg to/from Heathrow) £3.50/1.50. But if you're travelling through a couple of zones or several times in one day, consider a travel pass or some other discounted fare.

Travel Passes & Discount Fares A Travelcard valid all day offers the cheapest way of getting about in London and can be used after 9.30 am on weekdays and all day at weekends on all forms of transport in London: the tube, suburban trains, the DLR and buses (but *not* night buses). Most visitors will find that a Zones 1 & 2 card (£3.90) will be sufficient. A card to cover all six zones costs £4.70, just £1.20 more than a one-journey all-zone ticket – and you get to use it all day. A one-day Travelcard for those aged five to 15 costs £2 regardless of how many zones it covers, but those aged 14 and 15 need a Child Rate Photocard to travel on this fare. You can buy travelcards several days ahead but not on buses.

If you plan to start moving before 9.30 am on a weekday, you can buy a Zones

1 & 2 LT Card for £5/2.50 (£7.50/3.30 for all six zones), valid on the tube, the DLR and buses (but *not* suburban trains) for one day with no time restrictions.

Weekly Travelcards are also available but require an identification card with a passport-sized photo. A Zone 1 card for adults/those aged five to 15 costs £15.30/6.50 and Zones 1 & 2 £18.20/7.50. These allow you to travel at any time of day and on night buses as well.

At £5.80 for Zones 1 & 2, Weekend Travelcards valid on Saturday and Sunday are 25% cheaper than two separate one-day cards. Family Travelcards are also available for one or two adults and up to four children aged under 16 (who need not be related to them); they start at £2.60 per adult and 80p per child for Zones 1 & 2.

If you will be making a lot of journeys within Zone 1 *only*, you can buy a carnet of 10 tickets for £11, a saving of £4.

Bus

If you're not in much of a hurry, travelling round London by double-decker bus can be more enjoyable than using the tube. The All London bus map, available free from most TfL information centres, is an essential planning tool. For short journeys in London, it's often more efficient to take a bus than to struggle with the tube for a couple of stops.

Useful Routes The following are two examples of scenic bus routes where the ride can be an attraction itself. The buses run in both directions.

No 24
Beginning at South End Green in Hampstead Heath, it travels through Camden and along Gower St to Tottenham Court Rd. From there it goes down Charing Cross Rd, past Leicester Square to Trafalgar Square, then along Whitehall, past the Palace of Westminster, Westminster Abbey and Westminster Cathedral. It reaches Victoria station and then carries on to Pimlico, which is handy for the Tate Britain.

No 8
From Bow in east London, it goes along Bethnal Green Rd and passes the markets at Spitalfields and Petticoat Lane, Liverpool Street station, the City, the Guildhall and the Old Bailey. It then

crosses Holborn and enters Oxford St, travelling past Oxford Circus, Bond St, Selfridges and the flagship Marks & Spencer store at Marble Arch before terminating at Victoria.

The wheelchair-accessible Stationlink buses, which have a ramp operated by the driver, follow a similar route to that of the Underground Circle Line, joining up all the mainline stations. People with mobility problems and those with heavy luggage may find this easier to use than the tube, although it only runs once an hour. From Paddington there are services clockwise (designated the SL1) from 8.15 am to 7.15 pm, and anticlockwise (the SL2) from 8.40 am to 6.40 pm.

Trafalgar Square is the focus for all but six of TfL's network of 50 night buses (prefixed with the letter 'N'). They run from about midnight to 7 am, but services can be infrequent. TfL publishes a free credit-card-sized timetable that lists all the routes. Only Travelcards valid for a week or longer are valid on night buses; everyone else pays.

Fares London's bus fares are simple. Bus Zone 1 is the same as the tube Zone 1, the rest of London is covered by Bus Zone 2. Travel within Zone 1 or in both zones costs £1. Travel only in Zone 2 costs 70p. Children pay 40p no matter where they ride. Night buses cost £1.50. Travelcards and other tube passes are good on buses.

DLR & Train
The independent, driverless Docklands Light Railway (DLR) links the City at Bank and Tower Gateway with Canary Wharf, Greenwich and Stratford. It provides good views of development at this end of town. The fares operate like those on the tube.

Several rail companies operate the thicket of suburban rail services in and around London. These are especially important south of the river where there are few tube lines. Once again, fares operate like those on the tube.

Car & Motorcycle
By all means, avoid bringing a car into London. The roads are horribly clogged, drivers are aggressive in the extreme and parking space is at a premium. There are car parks, but they can cost £12 or more per day.

Traffic wardens and wheel clampers operate with extreme efficiency, and if your vehicle is towed away you won't see much change from £100 to get it back. If you do get clamped, ring the 24-hour Clamping & Vehicle Section hotline on ☎ 7747 4747.

Taxi London's famous black cabs (☎ 7272 0272) are excellent, but not cheap. A cab is available for hire when the yellow sign is lit. Fares are metered and a 10% tip is expected. They can carry five people.

Minicabs can carry four people and are cheap, freelance competitors to the black cabs. Anyone with a car can work and, although they can supposedly only be hired by phone, hawkers abound in busy places such as Soho. Beware. Some have a very limited idea of how to get around efficiently (and safely). Also, they don't have meters, so it's essential to get a quote before you start. Women are advised to use black cabs.

Small minicab companies are based in particular areas. Ask a local for the name of a reputable company, or phone one of the large 24-hour operations (☎ 7272 2612, ☎ 8340 2450 or ☎ 8567 1111). Women could phone Lady Cabs (☎ 7254 3501). Gays and lesbians can choose Freedom Cars (☎ 7734 1313).

Bicycle
Cycling around London is one way of cutting transport costs, but it can be a grim business, with heavy traffic and fumes detracting from the pleasure of getting a little exercise. It's advisable to wear a helmet and increasingly Londoners wear face-masks to filter out pollution.

Bikepark (Map 5; ☎ 7430 0083), 11 Macklin St WC2 (✆ Holborn), rents bikes and has bicycle parking. The minimum charge is £10 for the first day, £5 for the second day and £3 for subsequent days.

Dial-a-Bike (Map 8; ☎ 7828 4040), 18 Gillingham St SW1 (✆ Victoria), rents bikes from £6.99 per day and £29.90 per week.

LONDON

Boat

There is a myriad of boat services on the Thames, with more being announced all the time. By boat you avoid traffic while enjoying great views.

From Westminster Pier (Map 4), City Cruises (☎ 7930 9033) operates a popular service to/from the Tower of London. The adult fare is £4.80/6 single/return and the child fare is £2.40/3. The journeys take 30 minutes and operate several times an hour from April to October, less often other times.

Crown River Cruises (☎ 7936 2033) runs a circular cruise from Westminster Pier that calls at piers at London Bridge and St Katherine's. A ticket costs £5.80/3 and is good all-day so you can hop on and hop off. Boats run through the year, usually once an hour.

South-Eastern England

A significant chunk of London's workforce lives in the towns and villages of the counties covered in this chapter – Berkshire, Surrey, Kent, East and West Sussex, Hampshire, Buckinghamshire, Hertfordshire and Essex. Apart from providing peace and solitude away from the capital, the south-east is a region exceptionally rich in beauty and history. It provides those unshakeable traditional images of England – picturesque villages with welcoming old pubs, spectacular coastline, impressive castles, magnificent historic houses, crafted gardens, great cathedrals and kitsch seaside resorts. For this reason, and because everything is so close to London, tourist sights in the south-east are some of the country's most popular. The crowds of holiday-makers during late spring and summer can be exhausting. Be prepared also for relatively high prices with regards to accommodation, food and admission costs, particularly south of London.

ORIENTATION & INFORMATION

South of London, chalk country runs along two hilly east–west ridges, or downs. The North Downs curve from Guildford, across the Kent countryside to Dover where they stop at the famous white cliffs. The South Downs run from north of Portsmouth and end spectacularly at Beachy Head, near Eastbourne. Lying between the two is the Weald, once an enormous stretch of forest, now orchards and market gardens.

North-west of London, the hilly countryside known as the Chilterns is home to the stunning Ridgeway path and remains forested and largely unspoilt. Moving eastwards towards the coast, the forests of Essex give way to flatter and less remarkable countryside, with networks of motorways the prominent feature until you reach the coast.

Being such a heavily visited region, the south-east has plenty of tourist information centres (TICs) offering brochures, maps and B&B booking services (although usu-

Highlights

- The fairy-tale Hever Castle in Kent
- Brighton's unstoppable nightlife
- A tour of HMS *Victory* in Portsmouth
- A guided walk around the battlefield of 1066 at Battle in East Sussex
- The eerie ruins of Waverley Abbey in Surrey
- St Albans Cathedral

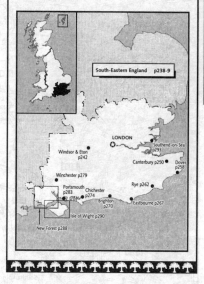

ally for a fee). There are youth hostels in most of the larger towns and cities and the many universities rent out rooms during summer. Booking ahead is advised.

GETTING AROUND

All the places mentioned in this chapter are quite easy to reach by train or bus, and each town or village could possibly be visited in a day trip from London. For information on all public transport options in Kent, ring ☎ 0870 608 2608.

237

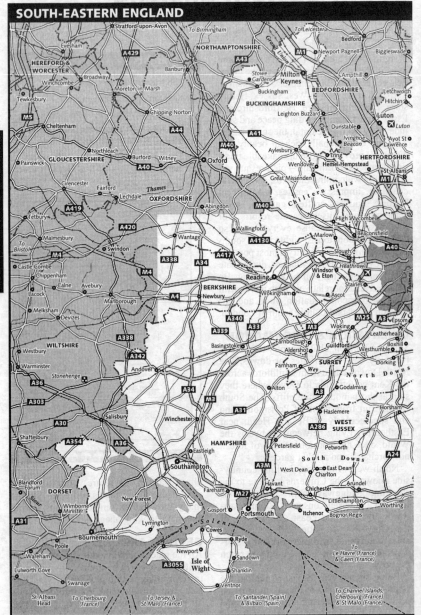

SOUTH-EASTERN ENGLAND

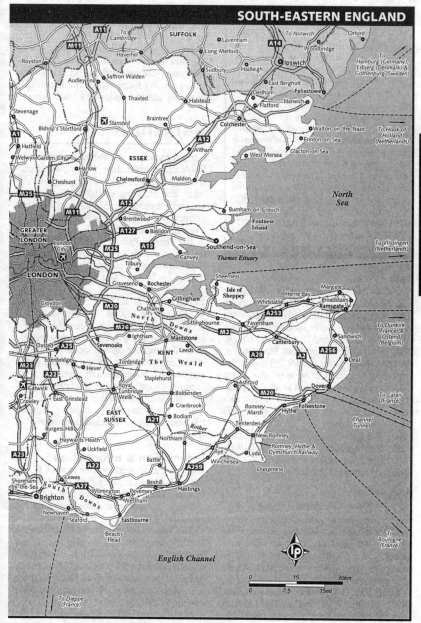

SOUTH-EASTERN ENGLAND

The North Downs Way

The North Downs Way is a walking trail that begins near Dorking in Surrey and ends near Dover in Kent. It runs along chalk ridges, through woodlands and valleys. The entire route covers 153 miles and some sections are suitable for cyclists and horse riders. Much of the North Downs trail follows the Pilgrims Way, mentioned by Chaucer in his *Canterbury Tales*, and in use for over 2000 years.

The *North Downs Way Practical Handbook* costs £1.95 and is available from most TICs in the region. It details routes, distances and places to stay and eat. There are a number of free leaflets detailing smaller sections of the North Downs Way, also available from TICs. For more information contact the North Downs Way National Trail Office on ☎ 01622-696185, ⓔ jim.walker@kent.gov.uk.

Bus

A number of companies operate fast, regular bus services from London. Explorer tickets (£6/4 for adults/children), giving unlimited travel for the day, can be used on most buses throughout the region. They can be bought from the bus drivers or from bus stations. Country Rover tickets (£5/2.50) cover the same counties and can be used after 9 am from Monday to Friday and all day at weekends. Diamond Rover Rickets (£7/5) can also be used on most Arriva (☎ 01279-426349) buses in Buckinghamshire, Hertfordshire and Essex. Tickets allowing one week's unlimited travel on Stagecoach Coastline (☎ 01903-237661) and Sussex Bus Services cost £12.50 each and can be purchased on buses.

Train

For rail information call ☎ 0345 484950. If you're considering extensive rail travel, a Network SouthEast Card (£20, allowing 33% off) is a good idea. It lasts for one year though you can only travel after 10 am on weekdays (any time at weekends). It allows accompanying children up to the age of 15 to travel for £1. A BritRail SouthEast Pass allows unlimited rail travel for three or four days out of seven, or eight days out of 15,

but they must be purchased outside the UK. See the introductory Getting Around chapter for more information.

Travelling by public transport in the counties north of London (Essex, Hertfordshire and Buckinghamshire) is not so simple as the towns of interest are not necessarily linked by rail to London or to each other.

Berkshire

Long regarded as the stomping ground for England's conservative 'old money', Berkshire does indeed have some gorgeous villages and stunning countryside, although industrial towns like Slough and the very ordinary Reading (the county's administrative centre) leave a lot to be desired.

The Thames Path (see the Activities chapter earlier) wends its way through the Berkshire Downs in the county's northern region, passing by Windsor and Reading.

WINDSOR & ETON
☎ 01753 • pop 31,000

Pretty Windsor has long been Berkshire's greatest tourist draw, but these days people make the trek out from London as much to visit Legoland as to see the famous castle and nearby college town of Eton.

Since it's only 20 miles from central London, and easily accessible by rail and road, it crawls with tourists for most of the year. If possible avoid weekends, especially in summer.

Orientation & Information

Windsor Castle overlooks the town of Windsor, which spreads along the River Thames. Eton is a small village, linked to Windsor by a pedestrian bridge, and dominated by the exclusive public school, Eton College.

The TIC (☎ 743900, fax 743904, ⓔ windsor.tic@rbwm.gov.uk), 24 High St, opens 9.30 am to 6 pm daily (from 10 am Sunday), closing at 4.30 pm from November to March. From late March to October, there are guided bus tours of Windsor and Eton costing £6.50/2.50.

Both the post office in Peascod St and the

TIC have bureaux de change. There are plenty of ATMs along High and Thames Sts. You can use the Internet at Tower Express, the CD shop, Peascod St. On-line time costs £1 for 20 minutes.

There are public toilets near the entrance to the castle (you have to buy a ticket first) and others near the tennis courts off River St.

Windsor Castle

Standing on chalk bluffs overlooking the Thames, Windsor Castle (☎ 831118) has been home to British royalty for over 900 years and is one of the greatest surviving medieval castles in Britain. It started life as a wooden motte and bailey in 1070 but was rebuilt in stone in 1165 and then successively extended and rebuilt right through to the 19th century.

It opens 10 am to 5 pm (last admission 4 pm) March to October; 10 am to 4 pm the rest of the year. In summer, weather and other events permitting, the changing of the guard takes place at 11 am daily except Sunday. The State Apartments are closed when the royal family is in residence. The Union Jack flying over the castle doesn't mean the Queen's at home; instead look for the Royal Standard flying from the Round Tower.

Admission to the castle costs £10.50/5 and £8 for over-60s. St George's Chapel and the Albert Memorial Chapel close Sunday. Guided tours of the State Apartments take about 45 minutes and leave at various times during the day; ask at the ticket office.

St George's Chapel One of Britain's finest examples of Gothic architecture, this chapel was commenced by Edward IV in 1475 but not completed until 1528.

The nave is a superb example of perpendicular architecture, with beautiful fan vaulting arching out from the pillars. The chapel is packed with the **tombs of royalty** including George V (ruled 1910–36) and Queen Mary, George VI (1936–52), and Edward IV (1461–83). The **wooden oriel window** was built for Catherine of Aragon by Henry VIII. The **garter stalls** dating back to 1478–85 are the chapel's equivalent of choir stalls. The banner, helm and crest above each stall indi-

cate the current occupant. Plates carry the names of knights who occupied the stalls right back to the 14th century.

In between the garter stalls, the **Royal Vault** is the burial place of George III (1760–1820), George IV (1820–30) and William IV (1830–37). Another **vault** between the stalls contains Henry VIII (1509–47), his favourite wife Jane Seymour, and Charles I (1625–49), reunited with his head after it was chopped off during the Civil War.

The gigantic **battle sword** of Edward III, founder of the Order of the Garter, hangs on the wall near the tombs of Henry VI (1422–61 and 1470) and Edward VII (1901–10) and Queen Alexandra.

Albert Memorial Chapel After leaving St George's Chapel, don't miss the fantastically elaborate Albert Memorial Chapel. It was built in 1240 and dedicated to Edward the Confessor. It became the original chapel of the Order of the Garter in 1350, falling into disuse when St George's Chapel was built. It was completely restored after the death of Prince Albert in 1861. A major feature of the restoration is the magnificent vaulted roof whose mosaic pieces were crafted in Venice. There's a monument to the prince, although he's actually buried with Queen Victoria in the Frogmore Royal Mausoleum in the castle grounds. A detailed guide to the chapel can be bought for £1.

State Apartments The State Apartments are a combination of formal rooms and museum-style exhibits. In 1992, a disastrous fire destroyed St George's Hall and the adjacent Grand Reception Room. Restoration work has now been finished and a rather cramped exhibition describes the process. Stop to think about which was more destructive, the fire or the restoration. In all, 350 oak trees died to rebuild the damaged rooms.

The magnificent collection of paintings inside are by such masters as Canaletto, Gainsborough, Rubens, Van Dyck, Holbein, Rembrandt and Dürer. There are only three surviving ceiling paintings by Verrio, and you'll see plenty of woodcarvings by Grinling Gibbons.

SOUTH-EASTERN ENGLAND

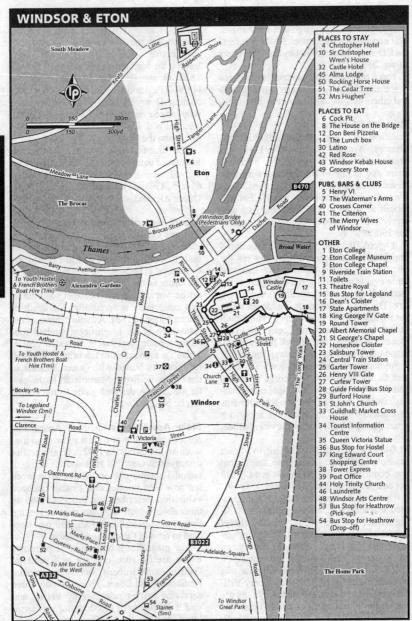

WINDSOR & ETON

PLACES TO STAY
4 Christopher Hotel
10 Sir Christopher Wren's House
32 Castle Hotel
45 Alma Lodge
50 Rocking Horse House
51 The Cedar Tree
52 Mrs Hughes'

PLACES TO EAT
6 Cock Pit
8 The House on the Bridge
12 Don Beni Pizzeria
14 The Lunch box
30 Latino
42 Red Rose
43 Windsor Kebab House
49 Grocery Store

PUBS, BARS & CLUBS
5 Henry VI
7 The Waterman's Arms
40 Crosses Corner
41 The Criterion
47 The Merry Wives of Windsor

OTHER
1 Eton College
2 Eton College Museum
3 Eton College Chapel
9 Riverside Train Station
11 Toilets
13 Theatre Royal
15 Bus Stop for Legoland
16 Dean's Cloister
17 State Apartments
18 King George IV Gate
19 Round Tower
20 Albert Memorial Chapel
21 St George's Chapel
22 Horseshoe Cloister
23 Salisbury Tower
24 Central Train Station
25 Garter Tower
26 Henry VIII Gate
27 Curfew Tower
28 Guide Friday Bus Stop
29 Burford House
31 St John's Church
33 Guildhall; Market Cross House
34 Tourist Information Centre
35 Queen Victoria Statue
36 Bus Stop for Hostel
37 King Edward Court Shopping Centre
38 Tower Express
39 Post Office
44 Holy Trinity Church
46 Laundrette
48 Windsor Arts Centre
53 Bus Stop for Heathrow (Pick-up)
54 Bus Stop for Heathrow (Drop-off)

Queen Mary's Dolls' House The work of architect Sir Edwin Lutyens, the dolls' house was built in 1923 on a 1:12 scale with the aim of raising money for children's charities. There are occasional special exhibitions here, such as displays of the Queen's childhood toys.

Windsor Great Park Stretching behind Windsor Castle almost all the way to Ascot, Windsor Great Park covers about 40 sq miles. There is a lake, walking tracks, bridleway and gardens. The Savill Garden (☎ 860222), open 10 am to 6 pm daily (to 4 pm November to February), is particularly lovely.

Around Town

Windsor's fine **Guildhall** stands on High St. It was built between 1687 and 1689, the construction completed under the supervision of Sir Christopher Wren. The council insisted that central columns were required to support the 1st floor even though Wren thought them unnecessary. The few centimetres of clear air proved him right.

The visibly leaning **Market Cross House** of 1768 is right next to the Guildhall. Charles II kept Nell Gwyn, his favourite mistress, in **Burford House** on Church St.

The **Long Walk** is a three-mile walk along a tree-lined path from King George IV Gate to the Copper Horse statue (of George III) on Snow Hill, the highest point of the park. There are some great views of the castle along here. The walk is signposted from the town centre.

Eton College

Cross the Thames by the pedestrian Windsor Bridge to arrive at another enduring symbol of Britain's class system: Eton College, a famous public (meaning private) school that was founded by Henry VI in the mid-15th century. It has educated no fewer than 18 prime ministers and counts Prince William among its former pupils.

The college (☎ 671177) opens April to September (from 2 to 4.30 pm during term and from 10.30 am during the holidays). Admission costs £2.50/2. One-hour guided tours at 2.15 and 3.15 pm cost £3.50/3. If you're thinking of sending your offspring to join the 1200 to 1300 pupils at Eton, be prepared to set aside around £14,000 per year for the basic fees.

Legoland Windsor

Visitors with children are unlikely to escape from Windsor without a trip to this elaborate mix of model masterpieces and pink-knuckle rides. The idea is family fun with the emphasis on the two to 12 age group. But you'll have to dig deep into your pockets to entertain everyone. Tickets cost a ridiculous £17.50, or £14.50 for children aged three to 15. If you prebook (☎ 0990 040404) it costs a whole £1 less per ticket.

Buses run from Thames St to Legoland between 10 am and 6.15 pm. It opens 10 am to 6 pm daily, mid-March to October (to 8 pm mid-July to August).

Places to Stay

Windsor is one of the most popular tourist destinations year round, so try to book your accommodation in advance.

Hostels A mile west of the Riverside train station is *Windsor Youth Hostel* (☎ 861710, fax 832100, ☉ yhawindsor@compuserve .com, Edgworth House, Mill Lane). Catch bus No 50A/B from outside Barclays Bank on Thames St or follow Arthur Rd or Barry Ave (along the riverbank) from the centre. It charges £11.00/7.75 for adults/under-18s. The hostel closes for one week over the new year period.

B&Bs & Hotels The Windsor TIC charges £3 to make accommodation bookings. The cheaper B&Bs can be found in the area south of Clarence Rd, between Alma and St Leonards Rds.

Mrs Hughes' (☎ 866036, 62 Queens Rd) B&B has one single room with kitchenette for £30, a double for £45 and a family room that sleeps six for £20/10 per adult/child. All rooms have fridges and bathrooms en suite.

The Cedar Tree (☎ 860362, 90 St Leonards Rd) is clean and cosy and done up in a cottage style. It costs £18/36 for singles/doubles and £40 for the double en suite.

SOUTH-EASTERN ENGLAND

Rocking Horse House (☎ 853984, 88 St Leonards Rd) next door is better value for two people than for single travellers as singles/doubles cost £38/44.

Beautifully decorated double rooms at *Alma Lodge* (☎ 854550, fax 855620, 58 Alma Rd) cost £55. Singles are negotiable but you may be out of luck in high season. The *Castle Hotel* (☎ 852359, 10 High St) is popular with well-to-do American tourists; rooms cost £150/175.

Built by Wren in 1676, *Sir Christopher Wren's House* (☎ 861354, fax 860172, Thames St) is one of the more upmarket hotels in town. Rooms cost £145/185.

Across the river in Eton, the *Christopher Hotel* (☎ 852359, 10 High St) dates from 1511 and has rooms for £98/108 plus £9.95 for a cooked breakfast. Rooms in the old building have more character than those in the newer motel-style building.

Places to Eat

With such a steady flow of visitors it's hardly surprising that Windsor is chock-a-block with eateries, though they tend to be pricey and disappointing.

Cosy and friendly *Latino* (☎ 857711, 3 Church Lane) is a Greek/continental restaurant with live music on Friday and Saturday nights.

The lively *Don Beni Pizzeria* (☎ 622042, 28 Thames St) is loud and always full of people which can only mean that the food is great. Book or be early if you want a table here.

Red Rose (☎ 620180, 69 Victoria St) is an Indian restaurant with main courses for £5 to £8 and side dishes for £2.25. A newspaper article in the window claims that orders are regularly picked up by members of the royal household.

Along Eton High St, places to eat jostle shoulders with antique shops. The rickety *Cock Pit* (☎ 860944, 47–49 High St, Eton) dates back to 1420 and serves good, simple Italian food. The fireplaces and exposed beams give this place a cosy atmosphere. *The House on the Bridge* (☎ 790197, 67 High St, Eton) is an elegant and pricey restaurant, overlooking the river and the castle. The food is modern French and Spanish, and the set menu costs £29.95 for three courses.

Windsor Kebab House (☎ 622022, 67 Victoria St) is a cheaper alternative and has doner kebabs for £2.80 and burgers from £1.80.

The Lunch Box (☎ 833323, 48 Thames St) is a takeaway lunch shop; fresh sandwiches cost from £1.30 to £1.95.

There's a *grocery store (St Leonards Rd)* and a *supermarket (King Edward Court Shopping Centre)* in the centre.

Entertainment

Windsor and Eton are simply packed with pubs, though only a few offer live entertainment. *The Merry Wives of Windsor* (☎ 861860, 65 St Leonards Rd) has long been a favourite with both locals and visitors. *The Criterion* (☎ 866139, 72 Peascod St) is more of a blokey pub while *Crosses Corner* (☎ 862867, 73 Peascod St) is frequented by the upwardly mobile set.

The Waterman's Arms (☎ 861006, Brocas St, Eton) is a small and intimate pub tucked away behind Eton High St and popular with rowers. *Henry VI* (☎ 866051, 37 High St, Eton) has an outdoor terrace and live music in the evenings from Thursday to Sunday.

The *Windsor Arts Centre* (☎ 859336, corner of St Leonards and St Marks Rds) contains a bar, theatre and live music venue. The *Theatre Royal* (☎ 853888, Thames St) is the town's main theatre.

Getting There & Away

Windsor is 20 miles from central London and only about 15 minutes by car from Heathrow airport.

Bus Greenline (☎ 020-8668 7261) bus Nos 700 (express service) and 702 depart for Windsor and Legoland from London Victoria coach station hourly (£7/3.50, 65 minutes, or 50 minutes express).

Bus Nos 192 (Monday to Saturday), 190 and 191 (Sunday) connect Windsor with Heathrow airport. For further details phone ☎ 524144.

Train There are two Windsor and Eton train stations – Central station on Thames St, opposite Windsor Castle, and Riverside station near the bridge to Eton.

From London Waterloo, trains run to Riverside station every half-hour (hourly on Sunday). Services from London Paddington to Central station require a change at Slough, five minutes from Windsor, but take about the same time (£6, 50 minutes).

Getting Around
Guide Friday's open-top double-decker bus tours of the town cost £6.50/2. From Easter to October, French Brothers (☎ 851900), Clewer Court Rd, operates 35-minute riverboat trips along the Thames. Tickets cost £3.80/1.90. The TIC has details.

Surrey

It's said that if Kent is the 'Garden of England' then Surrey is the patio. But among the sprawling dormitory towns for London commuters this much-derided county has some lovely corners that are easy to reach on a day out from the capital. It's also home to the Epsom Downs Racecourse which hosts the Derby, one of Britain's premier horse races.

GUILDFORD
☎ 01483 • pop 130,000
The administrative centre of Surrey, Guildford lies on the high ridge of the North Downs. It is an affluent town, being a haven for London commuters, though it is decidedly ugly at first glance. A bit of exploration will reveal an attractive old town which can easily be covered on foot in a day or even half a day.

The TIC (☎ 444333, e tourism@guildford.gov.uk), 14 Tunsgate, opens 9 am to 6 pm Monday to Saturday, and 10 am to 5 pm Sunday, May to September; and 9.30 am to 5.30 pm Monday to Saturday, the rest of the year. Free guided walks of the town depart from Tunsgate Arch on High St at 2.30 pm Sunday, Monday and Wednesday from May to September.

Things to See & Do
On High St near the TIC is the landmark **town hall**, a Tudor building with a 17th-century facade. It opens for guided tours at 2, 3 and 4 pm Tuesday and Thursday. Admission is free. On the other side of the street is a **medieval undercroft** (☎ 444750) which sits under 72 High St. It opens 2 to 4 pm Tuesday and Thursday, and noon to 4 pm on Saturday, May to September. Admission is free.

To the south of High St, set within landscaped gardens, is the **castle keep** which is believed to have been built by William I soon after his great victory. The keep never saw much defensive action and its main role was as the administrative centre of Guildford. Walk to the south-eastern corner of the gardens to see the remains of Guildford Palace which dates from the late 12th century.

Guildford Museum (☎ 444750) on Quarry St, which runs off High St, has a special display on Lewis Carrol who spent a lot of time in Guildford. It opens 11 am to 5 pm Monday to Saturday. Admission is free.

About 2½ miles north-west of the centre, atop Stag Hill, is the remarkable Guildford Cathedral (☎ 565287) whose construction began in 1935, was interrupted by WWII, and was completed in 1961. The interior is a combination of Gothic austerity and 1960s minimalism. It opens from 8.30 am until after Evensong. Services are at 9 am and 5.30 pm and on Sunday at 8, 9.45 and 11.30 am and 6.30 pm.

Getting There & Away
Tellings Golden Miller (☎ 020-8897 6131) bus No 740 leaves regularly from the Greenline bus station at London Victoria for Guildford (£4.60, 1 hour). Stagecoach Hampshire bus No X64 runs from Guildford bus station to Farnham (£2.75, 30 minutes) and on to Winchester hourly (£4.30, 1 hour 50 minutes).

The main train station is on Guildford Park Rd, a few minutes' walk from the centre. There are services from London Waterloo to Guildford every 15 minutes (£8, 35 minutes). Trains go to Farnham twice hourly (£3.70, 22 minutes) and to Portsmouth three times an hour (£11.80; 50 minutes).

FARNHAM
☎ 01252 • pop 38,000

Farnham is an attractive Georgian market town nestled in the valley of the River Wey, on the border with Hampshire. At first glance it seems a conservative place, populated mainly by well-to-do London commuters, but dig a little deeper and you'll find an interesting, artistic town. This may have something to do with the fact that it's home to the West Surrey College of Art & Design.

Farnham's favourite son is William Cobbett (1762–1835), the farmer turned radical social commentator who was the first person to publish parliamentary debates (now done by Hansard).

Orientation & Information
The centre of town can be explored easily on foot. The Borough is the main shopping street and the train station is on South St.

Staff at the TIC (☎ 715109, fax 725083, ⓔ info@waverley.gov.uk) in the council offices building on South St are very helpful. They have an excellent booklet detailing B&Bs in the area, and the free *Farnham Heritage Trail*. It opens 9.30 am to 5.15 pm Monday to Thursday, until 4.45 pm Friday and until noon Saturday.

You'll find an ATM on The Borough, near the corner of Castle St. The post office and a bureau de change are on West St, which is the continuation of The Borough. There are public toilets in the car park on The Hard, which runs off West St, near the post office.

Farnham Castle
Run by English Heritage (EH), Farnham Castle (☎ 713393) consists of a castle keep and a residential palace house. The **palace house** was built in the 13th century for the bishops of Winchester as a place to stop on their travels to London. It was used as such until 1926. From then until the 1950s it was used by the bishops of Guildford. It is now a Centre for International Briefing, holding courses for people going to live abroad. It's for this reason that you can only see the place by guided tour.

The house has been changed and altered on a massive scale over the centuries, with most of the changes undertaken by Bishop Morley in the 1660s. Admission costs £1.50/80p. It only opens between 2 and 4 pm Wednesday.

The **castle keep** was built in 1138 by Henri de Blois, the grandson of William the Conqueror (also responsible for the founding of Wolvesley Castle and St Cross Hospital in Winchester.) The keep has fallen into ruin over the centuries but it is possible to get to the top for some great views. It opens 10 am to 6 pm daily, April to October. Admission costs £2/1. The castle and keep can be reached by steps at the end of Castle St.

Other Things to See & Do
Any further exploration of Farnham should begin at historical Castle St. Among the Georgian frontages you'll find the **almshouses**, recognisable by their blue doors. They were built in 1619 by Andrew Windsor 'for the habitation and relief of eight poor honest old impotent persons'.

Take a stroll around the cobbled Middle, Lower and Upper Church Lanes where you'll see a string of 15th- and 16th-century **timber-framed houses**. Their original facades are hidden behind 18th-century brickwork.

The excellent **Museum of Farnham** (☎ 715094), 38 West St, has a special exhibit on the architect Falkner. It also covers the history of Farnham from prehistory, through Roman, Saxon and Norman times and up to the present. Its pride and joy is a nightcap belonging to Charles I, who stopped overnight at Vernon House (now the Library) on his way to trial in the Tower of London in 1498. He made a gift of the cap to the innkeeper.

If you walk along Castle St, past Farnham Castle for about half a mile, you will come to **Farnham Park** which spreads itself over 128 hectares. It was once a deer park for the bishops. As well as offering some great walks, the park contains a golf course, cricket pitch, football ground and children's playground.

Places to Stay
The hotels in the centre are all very expensive and most of Farnham's cheaper B&Bs are 10 to 15 minutes' walk from the centre. A few reasonable and central B&Bs are

listed here but you will need to book ahead, especially at weekends.

Mrs Burland's B&B (☎ *723047, 15 Vicarage Lane)* is great value but it's 1½ miles from the centre. If you can manage the distance then you are in for a treat. Large, comfortable en-suite rooms with views over the valley cost £18 per person (£16 if you stay for more than one night). There are a few short walks around the country lanes in this area – just ask Mrs Burland.

About the same distance from town (15–20 minutes' walk) is *Sandiway* (☎ *710721, 24 Shortheath Rd)*, where very comfortable and clean rooms cost just £20 per person.

Mrs Williams' B&B (☎ *715430, 'Wingate', 8 Trebor Ave)* is more expensive at £30 for a single en suite and £35 for a double with shared bathroom, but it's only a few minutes' walk from the centre.

The Bishop's Table (☎ *710222, fax 733494, 27 West St)* is a nice old Georgian hotel and, at £90/110 for singles/doubles, is a bit more affordable than others in the centre.

Places to Eat

Downing St is home to a number of excellent eateries. *The Banaras* (☎ *734081, 40 Downing St)* is an Indian restaurant with a very good reputation locally. The lamb tikka masala (£7.95) is supposed to be excellent.

The Stirling Sandwich Shop (☎ *711602, 49a Downing St)* makes generous sandwiches for £1.30 to £2. This place is very popular and at lunch time the queue stretches the length of Downing St.

The Traditional Plaice (☎ *718009, 50 Downing St)* is a fish and chip shop with a restaurant out the back. A seafood meal for two with a bottle of wine can be had for under £20.

The Nelson Arms (☎ *716078, 50 Castle St)* is an old timber-framed pub with an open fireplace. It escaped a brick makeover but was stuccoed instead. Meals here cost around £5.

Across the road from the museum, *Caffè Piccolo* (☎ *723277, 84 West St)* is a casual Italian restaurant in an atmospheric timber-framed building. Excellent pasta and pizza dishes cost around £7.

For self-caterers, there's a *Sainsbury's (South St)* near the corner of East St.

Getting There & Away

Stagecoach (☎ 01256-464501) bus No 64 runs between Winchester and Guildford via Farnham (twice hourly). It takes one hour and 10 minutes from Winchester (£4.20) and 30 minutes from Guildford (£2.75). The Stagecoach stop is on The Borough. National Express (☎ 0990 808080) has a service from London Victoria. They drop off at South St and pick up from The Borough.

The train station is at the end of South St, on the other side of the A31 from the old town centre. Half-hourly services run from London Waterloo (£9.50, 50 minutes) and Guildford (£3.80, 36 minutes) via Woking.

WAVERLEY ABBEY

This Cistercian abbey was the first to be built in England and dates from 1128. Like Beaulieu Abbey in the New Forest, Hampshire, Waverley was based on a parent abbey at Citeaux in France. It's easy to see why these beautiful ruins, sitting sadly on the banks of the River Wey, inspired Walter Scott's novel, *Waverley Abbey*.

The Cistercian monks believed in a simple and hardworking life. They tilled the land and carried out all kinds of manual labour, something which was greatly appreciated by the local community. Waverley suffered the same fate as many other ecclesiastical institutions in the country at the hands of Henry VIII in 1536. Although many of the buildings were destroyed, the ruins are still in a remarkable condition and it's a really beautiful spot to wander around. The abbey is off the B3001, 2 miles southeast of Farnham.

BOX HILL

This hill on the North Downs, 2½ miles north of Dorking, was famous as a beauty spot long before Jane Austen's *Emma* came here for her disastrous picnic. For everyone else it's an excellent place for a long walk, with 20-mile views from the top of the hill. Great stretches of sloping grassland are interspersed with heavily wooded areas. This is also a good area to come for mountain biking, and there are a number of bridleways.

On top of the hill is a visitor information centre where you'll find trail maps, as well as a kiosk. Behind them are the remains of a fort and arsenal, built in 1899 as one of 13 immobilisation centres in case of attack by the French. There are hourly trains between London Victoria and Boxhill & Westhumble station (£6.30, 49 minutes).

Kent

Kent is one of the most diverse and attractive counties of the region. It is the opinion of many that the character of most coastal towns was spoiled by the arrival of the railway and mass tourism in the 19th century, not to mention the kitsch video arcades and amusement parks of the 20th. It could be argued, however, that this metamorphosis has only endowed these towns with a new character – more modern perhaps, definitely tackier in some cases, but still very unique.

The inland area has some stunning countryside and some of the most English of England's villages. Probably the most distinctive feature of the fertile, rolling hills of inland Kent are the white, cone-shaped roofs of oast houses (see the boxed text 'Oast Houses').

GETTING AROUND
Reflecting the fact that it is both densely populated and home to many London commuters, Kent has a good network of public transport. The county council has a public transport information line (☎ 0345 696996).

Bus & Train
Stagecoach East Kent (☎ 01227-472082) has a good network around the region. Its Kent Compass 100 bus runs hourly (less frequently on Sunday) on a circuit taking in Canterbury, Dover, Deal, Sandwich, Ramsgate, Broadstairs, Margate, Herne Bay, Whitstable and back to Canterbury. The 200 bus does the same circuit in the opposite direction. Arriva Kent & Sussex (☎ 01634-281100) also operates a number of services in the western and northern parts of Kent.

All the main towns and cities are served several times daily by direct trains to London.

Bicycle
A marked cycle route wends its way from Dover to Deal, Sandwich, Whitstable and Canterbury. The countryside is mostly flat and there are plenty of quiet country lanes. Depending on how circuitous the route, it's about a 40-mile ride. TICs stock a good map (£6) detailing cycling routes in Kent.

CANTERBURY
☎ 01227 • pop 38,670
The city of Canterbury was severely damaged by bombing during WWII and parts, especially south of the cathedral, have been rebuilt insensitively. The atmospheric old town is very attractive but it crawls with tourists and there's not much chance of escaping queues in summer.

Canterbury's greatest treasure is its magnificent cathedral, the successor to the church St Augustine built after he began converting the English to Christianity in 597. After the

---

Oast Houses

Oast houses were basically giant, housed kilns for drying hops, used to brew beer. They sprang up in the early 15th century when beer was introduced to the region. The reason oast houses are so common in Kent is that the soil here was ideal for growing hops. Surrey and Hampshire were also successful hop-growing regions.

An oast house is made up of four rooms: the kiln (oven), the drying room (located above the kiln), the cooling room, and the storage room where hops was pressed and baled, ready to go to the local inn brewery. The cone-shaped roof was necessary to create a draught for the fire. The bits sticking out from the top of the cone are cowls. They could be moved to regulate the airflow to the fire.

Many oast houses have been converted into homes now (some are B&Bs), and are becoming more and more sought after as prime real estate.

martyrdom of Archbishop Thomas Becket in 1170, the cathedral became the centre of one of the most important medieval pilgrimages in Europe, immortalised by Geoffrey Chaucer in *The Canterbury Tales* (see the boxed text 'Chaucer's Canterbury Tales').

Canterbury can easily be visited on a day trip from London. It also makes an ideal stopover on the way to or from Dover or the Cinque Ports farther north.

Orientation & Information

The old town of Canterbury is enclosed by a medieval city wall and a modern ring road. It's easy to get around on foot, which is really the only mode of transport available as cars are not permitted to enter the Old Town.

The TIC (☎ 766567, fax 459840, e can terburyinformation@canterbury.gov.uk), 34 St Margaret's St, opens 9.30 am to 5 pm daily (to 4 pm on Wednesday). It has a free booking service for B&Bs (available until half an hour before closing time).

There's a bureau de change at 28 St Margaret's St and you'll find all the major banks and ATMs on High St, near the corner of St Margaret's St. The post office is on the corner of St Peter's and Stour Sts.

There is a laundrette at 36 St Peter's St and there are public toilets inside the cathedral grounds.

The library at the Royal Museum on High St has free Internet access for up to one hour but you'll need to book ahead on ☎ 463608.

Canterbury Cathedral

Touring the complex can easily absorb half a day. There are treasures tucked away in corners and a trove of associated stories, so a tour is strongly recommended. They take place at 10.30 am, noon and 2 pm for £3.50, or you can take a Walkman tour for £2.95 (30 minutes). Admission costs £3/2; free for those aged under five. The cathedral opens 9 am to 7 pm Monday to Saturday, Easter to September; and 9 am to 5 pm the rest of the year. It opens 12.30 to 2.30 pm and 4.30 to 5.30 pm on Sunday. Evensong is at 5.30 pm weekdays, 3.15 pm weekends. In July the cathedral closes for two days for university graduation.

Chaucer's Canterbury Tales

Geoffrey Chaucer (b. 1340) is considered to be one of the first and greatest of English writers. For many, English literature begins with Chaucer. His writing marks the triumph of the English language over the Latin of the Church – which had dominated all areas of learning – and French, which had been the language of the Normans and their court.

The Canterbury Tales, his most popular work, consists of a collection of some 24 stories told by a party of pilgrims on their journey to the shrine of Thomas Becket at Canterbury. Chaucer paints a lively, ironic picture of the pilgrims and, although the world has changed, the personalities he describes are still easily recognisable. Most 21st-century readers will find a modern translation a good deal more enjoyable to deal with than the original, however.

Canterbury Cathedral (☎ 762862) evolved in stages over many years and it reflects a number of architectural styles. St Augustine's original cathedral burnt down in 1067. Construction of a new cathedral by the first Norman archbishop began in 1070 but only fragments of this remain today. In 1174, most of the eastern half of the building was destroyed by fire but the magnificent crypt beneath the choir survived.

The fire presented the opportunity to create something in keeping with the cathedral's new status as the most important pilgrimage site in England. In response, William of Sens created the first major Gothic construction in England, a style now described as Early English. Most of the cathedral east of Bell Harry tower dates from this period.

In 1391, work began on the western half of the building, replacing the south-western and north-western transepts and nave. The new perpendicular style was used, and work continued for over 100 years, culminating with the completion of Bell Harry in 1500. Subsequently, more has been subtracted than added, although the exterior has not changed substantially.

CANTERBURY

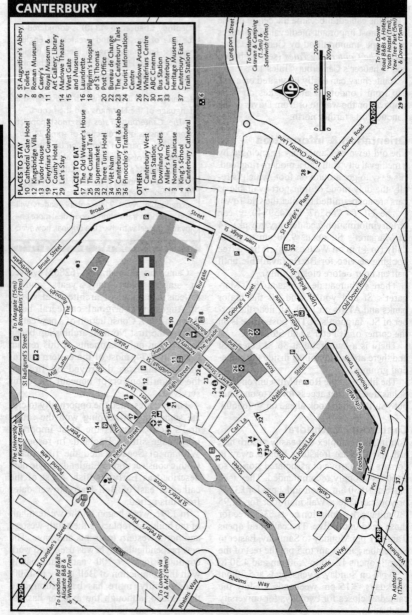

PLACES TO STAY
10 Cathedral Gate Hotel
12 Kingsbridge Villa
13 Tudor House
19 Greyfriars Guesthouse
21 County Hotel
29 Let's Stay

PLACES TO EAT
17 The Old Weaver's House
25 The Custard Tart
28 Supermarket
32 Three Tuns Hotel
35 Việt Nam
36 Canterbury Grill & Kebab
36 Pinocchio's Trattoria

6 St Augustine's Abbey
7 Toilets
8 Roman Museum
9 Casey's
11 Royal Museum &
   Art Gallery; Library
14 Marlowe Theatre
15 West Gate
   and Museum
16 Laundrette
18 Pilgrim's Hospital
   of St Thomas
20 Post Office
22 Bureau de Change
23 The Canterbury Tales
24 Tourist Information
   Centre
26 Marlowe Arcade
27 Whitefriars Centre
30 ABC Cinema
31 Bus Station
33 Canterbury
   Heritage Museum
37 Canterbury East
   Train Station

OTHER
1 Canterbury West
  Train Station;
  Downland Cycles
2 Miller's Arms
4 Norman Staircase
4 King's School
5 Canterbury Cathedral

The Canterbury Tales

The Canterbury Tales (☎ 479227), St Margaret's St, provides an entertaining introduction to Chaucer's classic tales. The general concept, however, is strange: jerky, hydraulic puppets seem an inefficient way to recreate history. Perhaps the promoters feel they need something in three dimensions to justify the £5.50/4.60 ticket. The centre opens 9 am to 5.30 pm daily (to 4.30 pm from November to March) and is usually crammed with school children.

Museums

The **Royal Museum & Art Gallery** (☎ 452747), High St, has military memorabilia and works by local artists. It opens 10 am to 5pm Monday to Saturday. Admission is free but the city's three other museums can all be visited with one passport ticket costing £4/2. Individual admission costs are given below.

The **West Gate and Museum** dates from the 14th century and is the only remaining city gate. It's now a small museum featuring arms and armour. It opens 11 am to 12.30 pm and 1.30 to 3.30 pm Monday to Saturday, year round. Admission costs £1/50p.

The **Canterbury Heritage Museum** (☎ 452747), Stour St, is in a converted 12th- and 13th-century building. It gives good, although rather dry, coverage of the city's history and local characters. It opens 10.30 am to 5 pm Monday to Saturday (last admission 4 pm) year round, plus 1.30 to 5 pm Sunday, June to October. Admission costs £2.40/1.20.

At the interesting **Roman Museum** (☎ 785575), built underground around the remains of a Roman town house in Butchery Lane, you get to visit the marketplace, smell the odours of a Roman kitchen and handle artefacts. Also on display are large sections of a mosaic floor from a Roman town house, discovered in 1946 during a clean up after WWII bombing. Much of the house is still buried under buildings in Butchery Lane. There's a lot to see here and a visit is a must. It opens 10 am to 5 pm Monday to Saturday, year round; plus 1.30 to 5 pm Sunday, June to October (last admission 4 pm). Admission costs £2.40/1.20.

St Augustine's Abbey

Henry VIII acted with thoroughness when St Augustine's Abbey (☎ 778000; EH) was demolished in 1538 – only its foundations remain. It opens 10 am to 6 pm April to October and 10 am to 4 pm November to March. Admission costs £2.50/1.30, which includes an audio tour.

Pilgrim's Hospital of St Thomas

Founded in 1180, the Pilgrim's Hospital (☎ 471688), St Peter's St, is well worth a visit. Originally built as a hospice for pilgrims to Becket's shrine in the cathedral, it is still used today to house elderly folk (they live behind the doors marked 'Private'). You will see here a Norman undercroft, a refectory hall and, on the upper level, the Pilgrims' Chapel. The building was extensively restored in the 16th century and again in the 20th century but the roof of the chapel is original and dates from the 13th century. The hospice opens 10 am to 5 pm Monday to Saturday. Admission costs £1/50p.

Organised Tours

There are guided walks from the TIC at 2 pm daily from April to October and also at 11.30 am Monday to Saturday in July and August. The walks take 1½ hours and explore the cathedral and museum precincts, King's School and the town's medieval centre. They cost £3.50/3. There is also a range of specialist tours available covering themes such as architecture, literature and pilgrimage.

Ghost Tours are proving to be more and more popular. At 6.30 pm every Friday, Saturday and Sunday during April, June, July and August you can attend a frightening guided walk around the Old Town. For bookings call ☎ 454888.

From May to September there are chauffeured punt trips (☎ 0585 318301) on the River Stour at 10 am from the West Gate Bridge. It costs £18 for four adults and two children.

You can also take a rowing-boat tour from behind The Old Weaver's House (see Places to Eat later) during summer. Tours cost £4 per person.

Places to Stay

Most Canterbury accommodation is quite expensive, particularly in July and August. In some cases prices almost double; ring ahead to avoid nasty surprises.

Camping Just under 2 miles from the centre, off the A257, is *Canterbury Caravan & Camping* (☎ 463216, *Bekesbourne Lane*). It charges from £9 for two people and a tent.

Yew Tree Park (☎ 700306, *Stone St, Petham*) is 5 miles south of Canterbury off the B2068; take New Dover Rd out of the centre and turn right just after the youth hostel. It opens April to October and charges £4 for one adult and a tent, £6 for two. A bus from Canterbury to Petham village (a half-mile walk to the camp site) leaves hourly.

Hostels In an old Victorian villa, the *youth hostel* (☎ 462911, *54 New Dover Rd*) is just under a mile east of the centre. It closes from late December to the end of January. Beds are £11.00/7.75 for adults/under-18s and there is one twin room for £28.

More homely and better value than the youth hostel is *Let's Stay* (☎ 463628, *26 New Dover Rd*). The friendly owner charges £10 per person in four-bed dorms with a cooked breakfast. Men and women are accommodated separately. Couples and families may be accommodated but you'll need to call ahead to check on availability.

The University of Kent (☎ 828000, *Tanglewood*) is 20 minutes' walk north-eastwards from the centre and open only when students are away (in April and from July to September). B&B costs from £14.50 per person.

B&Bs & Hotels Quiet and comfortable *Kingsbridge Villa* (☎ 766415, *15 Best Lane*) is a B&B in the centre of town, just off High St. There are no single rooms; doubles cost £42 with shared bathroom and from £45 to £50 with en-suite bathroom. Parking is available.

Also central and very good value is *Tudor House* (☎ 765650, *6 Best Lane*). This quaint (and slightly eccentric) 450-year-old building has singles/doubles for £18/36. They

have canoes and boats which guests can hire for £10 per day.

Greyfriars Guesthouse (☎ 456255, *6 Stour St*) is right in the heart of the centre and offers large en-suite singles/doubles from £25/£45. *Alicante B&B* (☎/fax 766277, *4 Roper Rd*) is not quite in the centre but just a minute's walk from Canterbury West station. Big double rooms cost £40; singles are negotiable. There are thoughtful touches here, such as hairdryers in each room.

The London Rd B&Bs are 10 minutes' walk from the centre. *Acacia Lodge* and *Tanglewood B&B* (☎ 769955, *39 London Rd*) are actually the same place. Cute, cottage-style, very tidy singles/doubles cost £26/38.

There's a string of decent B&Bs along New Dover Rd, all five or 10 minutes' walk to the centre. *Charnwood Lodge B&B* (☎/fax 451712, *64 New Dover Rd*), the sign out front just says 'B&B', is the best value in town and we can highly recommend it. For £35 you get a clean self-contained flat that can sleep up to three people. Breakfast is included though you are welcome to cook it yourself if you prefer.

Hampton House (☎ 464912, *40 New Dover Rd*) is run by a friendly couple who have a strict nonsmoking policy. Rooms offer a touch of luxury and cost £28/40 with shared bathroom or £45 for an en-suite double. In winter the rates drop to £20/40.

In the heart of the city, *Cathedral Gate Hotel* (☎ 464381, *fax 462800*, @ cgate@cgate.demon.co.uk, *36 Burgate*) has rooms with shared bathroom from £23/44 and en-suite rooms for £52.50/79. Although the walls are on the thin side and some of the floors slope alarmingly, the rooms are comfortable and the views of the cathedral are magnificent.

Also centrally located, *County Hotel* (☎ 766266, *30 High St*) offers true English olde-worlde charm with its 15th-century bar and 12th-century cellars. Singles/doubles cost £90/106 and breakfast will set you back £7.50 per person for continental, £10.50 for cooked.

A few cheaper hotels can be found on New Dover Rd. *The Ebury Hotel* (☎ 768433, *fax 459187*, @ info@ebury-hotel.co.uk, *65–67*

New Dover Rd) has the feel of an upmarket B&B minus the familiarity or warmth. There is an indoor heated pool here and rooms cost £45 to £50 for singles and £65 to £75 for doubles, depending on their size.

The *Canterbury Hotel* (☎ *450551, fax 780145,* ✉ *canterbury.hotel@btinternet .com, 71 New Dover Rd*) has a jovial atmosphere and helpful staff but the rooms are not quite as good as those at the Ebury. Singles/doubles/triples cost £55/75/95. The French restaurant here is excellent (see Places to Eat).

Places to Eat

The crowds of visitors and students ensure that there's a good range of reasonably priced eating places in Canterbury. Bookings are recommended, especially at weekends.

Built around 1500, *The Old Weaver's House* (☎ *464660, 1 St Peter's St*) is very cosy and serves everything from salads and pies to fish and chips and curries. Starters cost from £2.25 to £3.95 and mains go for £6.75 to £9.95. There is an outdoor terrace overlooking the River Stour, which is lovely in spring and summer.

You'll find a great variety of cuisines for various budgets along Castle St. *Viêt Nam* (☎ *760022, 72 Castle St*) has a modern South-East Asian menu. Prawns with French beans and garlic costs £5.95. The very tempting Vietnamese tapas menu features dishes costing from £2.75 to £3.50. Nearby *Pinocchio's Trattoria* (☎ *457538, 64 Castle St*) is a little more expensive but it's cheerful with a superb Italian wine selection and a terrace out the back. Pasta dishes cost from £5.60 to £8.95 and pizzas go for £4.70 to £7.30.

Standing on the site of a Roman theatre, *Three Tuns Hotel* (☎ *456391, 24 Watling St*) serves good-value pub meals from around £4. The hotel itself dates from the 16th century.

Canterbury Hotel (☎ *450551, 71 New Dover Rd*) has an excellent French restaurant, though the atmosphere might be a little quiet and stiff for some. Starters cost from £7 to £8.50 and main courses cost £12 to £16.

Canterbury Grill & Kebab (☎ *765458, 66 Castle St*) is where you can sample that wonderful British contribution to world cuisine, the chip butty (French fries sandwich) for £1.30. Kebabs cost from £3 and burgers from £2.20.

The Custard Tart (☎ *785178, 35a St Margaret's St*) is extremely popular and serves delicious baguettes from £2.30 and cream teas for £2.95. The downstairs takeaway counter is excellent value with sausage rolls for £1 and sandwiches for £1.30. Get in before the 1 pm lunch rush.

There's a *Safeway supermarket* on the corner of New Dover and Lower Chantry Rds, just south-east of the centre.

Entertainment

The free leaflet, *What & Where When*, gives details of what's on in Canterbury. It's available from the TIC.

Marlowe Theatre (☎ *787787, fax 479622,* ✉ *boxoffice@canterbury.gov.uk, The Friars*) puts on a variety of plays, dances, concerts and musicals year round. The box office opens 10 am to 8 pm Monday to Saturday.

ABC Cinema (☎ *453577, corner of Upper Bridge St and St George's Place*) shows the latest mainstream movies.

Being a university town and favourite tourist haunt, Canterbury has a number of lively pubs. The *Miller's Arms* (☎ *456057, Mill Lane*) is a classic student hang-out while *Casey's* (☎ *463252, 5 Butchery Lane*), near the main gate to the cathedral, has a large selection of Irish ales and stouts.

Getting There & Away

Canterbury is 58 miles from London and approximately 15 miles from Margate and Dover.

Bus The bus station is just within the city walls at the eastern end of High St.

National Express buses to Canterbury leave every half-hour from London Victoria (£7/9 one-way/return, 1 hour 50 minutes). Stagecoach East Kent (☎ *472082*) has a good network around the region (see Getting Around in the Kent section earlier in the chapter). Buses also run between Canterbury and Dover (£2.50/3.50 one-way/return, 30 minutes).

Train There are two train stations: Canterbury East (for the youth hostel), accessible from London Victoria; and Canterbury West, accessible from London's Charing Cross and Waterloo stations. Trains run frequently between London and Canterbury (£14.80 return, £19.99 for two adults, 1½ hours). There are also regular trains between Canterbury East and Dover Priory (£4.50, 45 minutes).

Getting Around

Taxi Try Laser Taxis (☎ 464422) or Cabwise (☎ 712929).

Bicycle Downland Cycles (☎ 479643) is based at Canterbury West station. Mountain bikes cost £10 per day or £50 per week with a £25 deposit. They have maps for the 21-mile ride to Dover or the 7-mile ride north to the coastal town of Whitstable.

Car Cars are not permitted to enter the centre of town. There are car parks at various points along and just within the ring road.

MARGATE
☎ 01843 • pop 38,535

Margate, Broadstairs and Ramsgate sit on a peninsula known as the Isle of Thanet. This is the spot where St Augustine landed in 596 to spread the good word. At this time the area sat about a mile from the mainland, separated by the Watsun Channel. The channel is still there, though these days it's barely navigable.

Margate was one of the earliest and most popular seaside resorts in England and, even though it's become shabby over the years, the town does have a unique historical appeal. You can almost picture the well-to-do Victorians promenading with their parasols or lunching on the large terraces that line the esplanade. The Old Town makes for a pleasant stroll with its interesting old houses, antique shops, museum, pubs and cafes, not to mention the Margate **caves** on Northdown Rd and the slightly disappointing **shell grotto** on Grotto Hill.

At the time of writing a huge casino was under construction on the esplanade. Hopefully, the money derived from this dubious endeavour will result in the cleaning up of Margate's much maligned sea frontage and restore the town with some of its well-deserved glory.

There's a TIC (☎ 220241, fax 230099), Marine Drive, four doors down from the sex shop. It opens 9 am to 5 pm daily (to 4 pm at weekends).

The well-run *youth hostel (☎/fax 221616, ℮ margate@yha.org.uk, The Beachcomber, 3–4 Royal Esplanade)* charges £11.00/7.75. It closes November to mid-April. Among the many B&Bs and hotels along the esplanade is *Malvern Private Hotel (☎ 290192, Eastern Espanade, Cliftonville)*. It could do with a little sprucing up but it is friendly and perfectly adequate at £21 to £23 per person.

For a taste of some local seafood try *Newbys Wine Bar (☎ 292888, Market Place)*. Snacks cost around £4 while a main dish of scampi costs £8.90 and whole sea bass is £12.25.

Getting There & Away

National Express bus No 22 runs from London Victoria to Margate and on to Broadstairs and Ramsgate (£9/14 one-way/return or £10 day return, 2¼ hours, five daily). Stagecoach East Kent (☎ 01227-472082) has a service from Canterbury to Margate and on to Broadstairs and Ramsgate. Connex (☎ 0845 748 4950) train services run hourly from London Victoria or Charing Cross to Margate (£18.20, two hours).

BROADSTAIRS
☎ 01843 • pop 23,691

Broadstairs developed later than Margate (in late-Regency/early-Victorian times) and has managed to preserve itself much better. The old part of town, by the sea, is small and intricate and still has the peculiar fascination of a real English resort that has remained unaffected by time.

The TIC (☎ 862242, fax 865650), 6b High St, opens 9 am to 5 pm weekdays.

Charles Dickens had a series of holiday homes here and he's the town's claim to fame these days. There's even an annual week-long Dickens Festival in June which culminates in a ball in Victorian dress.

Between 1837 and 1859 he wrote parts of

Bleak House and *David Copperfield* in the house on top of the cliff above the pier. It's now a museum, aptly called **Bleak House** (☎ 862224), and is well worth a visit. There are several rooms arranged as they would have been in Dickens' time, a display on local shipwrecks and, in the cellars, an entertaining display about local smuggling. If the Kentish Giant looked anything like his mannequin here he must have been absolutely terrifying! The museum opens 10 am to 6 pm daily, March to November (to 9 pm in July and August). Admission costs £3/2.

The **Dickens House Museum** (☎ 862853), 2 Victoria Parade, wasn't actually his house but the home of Mary Pearson Strong, on whom he based Betsey Trotwood. Dickensiana on display includes personal possessions and letters. It opens 2 to 5 pm daily, April to October. Admission costs £1.20/60p.

Places to Stay & Eat

There are a few nice places to stay in Broadstairs, all a stone's throw from the beach.

Broadstairs Youth Hostel (☎ 604121, fax 604121, e broadstairs@yha.org.uk, Thistle Lodge, 3 Osborne Rd) is run by helpful people who charge £10.00/6.90 for singles/doubles. From the station, turn right under the railway and continue for 30 yards to a crossroads with traffic lights, then turn left into The Broadway.

For decent, reasonably priced B&Bs with sea views head for Eastern Esplanade.

The **Bay Tree Hotel** (☎ 862502, fax 860589, 12 Eastern Esplanade) has lovely rooms for £24 per person or £26 with a sea view.

East of the High St and set back from the beach, **Sunnydene Hotel** (☎/fax 863347, 10 Chandos Rd) is good value at £19 to £21 per person.

There's a wide range of places to eat. *Sea Chef* (☎ 867964, 17 Albion St) serves good fish and chips for £2.50 or a portion of fried scampi for £2.

If seafood isn't your thing the place to go is *Amigos* (☎ 862651, 36 Albion St), a Mexican restaurant. A huge plate of spicy chicken, rice and salad costs £6.95.

The *York Gate Cafe* (☎ 862408, Harbour St), near the beach, is a wonderful traditional seaside cafe where you can get an egg and bacon sandwich or a cream tea for £2.

Getting There & Away

Stagecoach bus Nos 100, 101, 200 and 201 all run hourly from Broadstairs to Margate, Ramsgate, Sandwich, Deal and Dover. Bus Nos 100 and 200 also go to Canterbury. A bus guide to the area is available from the TIC.

Connex (☎ 0845 748 4950) train services run from London Victoria, London Bridge or Charing Cross to Broadstairs, but you may have to change trains at Ramsgate (£18.20, 2½ hours, hourly).

SANDWICH
☎ 01304 • pop 6000

Sandwich is literally a backwater, but a beautiful one, on the southern bank of the River Stour. Once a thriving Cinque Port on the sheltered Watsun Channel, it has been deserted by the sea and is now a sleepy, medieval village. The very exclusive Royal St George, perhaps the finest golf course in England, is just outside the town.

Everything of interest is within easy walking distance. You'll find a useful town map on the notice board in the car park opposite the Bell Hotel. It's also available from the TIC (☎/fax 613565) on the New St side of the Guildhall. It opens 11 am to 3 pm daily, May to September. They also have an information pack detailing seven walks near the area. Guided tours of the town can be arranged by contacting Frank Andrews on ☎ 01304-611925 (evenings only).

Strand St is said to have more half-timbered houses than any other in England. Elsewhere, a number of buildings have Dutch or Flemish characteristics (note the stepped gables in some buildings), the legacy of Protestant Flemish refugees who settled in the town in the 16th century. The impressive **Barbican** is a tollgate dating from the 16th century.

The exterior of the **Guildhall** (☎ 617197) was substantially altered in 1910 but the interior remains little changed since the 16th century. It's now home to a museum which proudly tells a detailed history of Sandwich.

Admission costs £1/50p; its opening hours are erratic.

The **Church of St Clement** has one of the finest surviving Norman towers in England. **St Peter's Church**, King St, is the earliest of Sandwich's churches though its tower was rebuilt in 1661.

There are very few cheap B&Bs but you could try the **New Inn** (☎ 612335, fax 619133, 2 Harnet St), near the Guildhall, which has rooms with private shower for £25 per person.

Getting There & Away

Stagecoach East Kent's (☎ 01227-472082) bus Nos 111 and 211 services connect Sandwich to Dover (£3.30, 45 minutes, hourly), Deal and Canterbury. Bus No 93 runs between Sandwich and Dover and No 94 runs from Ramsgate to Dover via Sandwich.

Connex (☎ 0845 748 4950) trains have a half-hourly service from Dover Priory (£4, 25 minutes) or from London Charing Cross to Deal, from where a bus takes you to Sandwich (£18.20, two hours).

AROUND SANDWICH

One and a half miles north of Sandwich, off the A256, are the remains of **Richborough Castle** (☎ 612013), a Roman hilltop fort with vast and imposing walls. The fort was built around 275 but the site was an important town well before this. In 43, the Roman army landed at Richborough and established a military supply base. Some of the relics found here are on display in the Guildhall Museum in Sandwich.

It opens 10 am to 6 pm daily, April to September, to 5 pm in October, to 4 pm from Wednesday to Sunday in November and March, and weekends only from December to February. The area is exposed and it gets very windy up here, even in the warmer months. The Stour River Bus to Richborough, which runs from the northern side of the toll bridge in Sandwich, operates erratically. Phone ☎ 820171 for details.

The nearby town of **Deal** was the place where Julius Caesar and his armies landed in 55 BC. It's a peaceful town with a great stretch of beach and an unusual circular cas-

Cinque Ports

Due to their proximity to Europe, the coastal towns of the south-east were the frontline against Viking raids and invasions during Anglo-Saxon times. In the absence of a professional army and navy, these towns were frequently called upon to defend themselves, and the kingdom, at land and sea.

In 1278, King Edward I formalised this already ancient arrangement by legally defining the Confederation of Cinque (pronounced sink and meaning 'five') Ports. The five head ports – Sandwich, Dover, Hythe, Romney (now New Romney) and Hastings – were granted numerous privileges in exchange for providing the king with ships. The number of Cinque Ports gradually expanded to include about 30 coastal towns and villages.

By the end of the 15th century most of the Cinque Ports' harbours had become largely unusable thanks to the shifting coastline, and a professional navy was based at Portsmouth.

As is often the case in Britain, while real importance and power has evaporated, the pomp and ceremony remains. The Lord Warden of the Cinque Ports is a prestigious post now given to faithful servants of the Crown – they get an apartment at Walmer Castle in Deal and a chance to wear funny clothes and a big, gold chain. The current warden is the Queen Mother, but among the previous incumbents were the Duke of Wellington, Sir Winston Churchill and Sir Robert Menzies, former prime minister of Australia.

tle – another link in Henry VIII's chain of defence on the south coast. Also here is **Walmer Castle**, the official residence of the warden of the Cinque Ports (see the boxed text 'Cinque Ports').

DOVER
☎ 01304 • pop 37,826

Dover may be England's 'Gateway to Europe' but the place has just two things going for it: a spectacular medieval castle and the famous white cliffs.

There is evidence of an Iron Age settlement, and the Romans identified the strategic importance of the site. Dubrae, as Dover was known, was a fortified port in the chain of defences along the Saxon shore. The Normans, needless to say, immediately built a castle.

The foreshore of Dover is basically an enormous, complicated (though well-signposted) and unattractive vehicle ramp for the ferries. The town itself was badly damaged during WWII and today, under siege from heavy traffic, has no charm. The feeling that everyone is en route to somewhere much more interesting – as quickly as possible – doesn't help. Maybe they've all read Bill Bryson's account of a rather gruelling visit to Dover in the early 1970s, in his hilarious *Notes from a Small Island*.

Orientation & Information

Dover is dominated by Henry VIII's enormous castle which sits on a hill top to the east of the centre. The town itself runs back from the sea along a valley formed by the unimpressive River Dour (in Roman times, this formed a navigable estuary). The train station is a short walk to the west of the town centre. The bus station is in the centre on Pencester Rd.

The TIC (☎ 205108, fax 225498, ℮ tic @doveruk.com), Townwall St, is near the seafront and opens 9 am to 6 pm daily. It has an accommodation and ferry-booking service. There is a bureau de change next door which also opens daily.

The Mangle laundrette, Worthington St, is near the Riveria Coffee House. It opens 8 am to 8 pm daily.

The library (☎ 204241), High St, offers language courses for adults and, if you book ahead, free Internet access for up to one hour.

All the major banks are located on Market Square, the post office is on Pencester Road and there are toilets in Pencester Gardens.

Dover Castle

There are spectacular views across the English Channel and the town from up here. Interestingly, there are the remains of a **Roman lighthouse**, within the fortifications, which dates from AD 50 and is possibly the oldest standing building in England. There is also a restored **Saxon church**. The **keep** was built on the orders of Henry II between 1181 and 1187 and its walls are seven metres thick in places. The castle survived sieges from rebellious barons in 1216 and the French in 1295, was captured by Parliamentarians in 1642, was the headquarters for operations against German submarines in WWI, and served as the command post for the evacuation of Dunkirk in 1940.

The excellent tour of **Hellfire Corner** covers the castle's role during WWII, and takes you along tunnels beneath the castle.

Dover Castle (☎ 211067; EH) opens 10 am to 6 pm daily (to 4 pm November to March). Admission costs £6.90/3.50. The price includes a 55-minute guided tour of Hellfire Corner. You can take Stagecoach bus No 90 from Dover Priory station to the castle.

Dover Museum & White Cliffs Experience

The Dover Museum is one of the best around and definitely shouldn't be missed. The displays are well designed and absorbing. The pride of the museum is a perfectly preserved Bronze Age boat, discovered off the Dover coast in 1992. At 3,600 years old it's the oldest known seagoing vessel in the world and measures 9.5m by 2.4m.

The White Cliffs Experience is perfect if you have kids in tow. Robots, dioramas, actors and light-and-sound shows present two periods of Dover's history – Roman times and 1940s Dover.

The Experience (☎ 210101) and museum (☎ 201066) open 10 am to 5.30 pm daily (last admission 5 pm), April to October. Admission costs £5.75/3.95 for both or £1.80/90p for the museum only. You'll find them between Market Square and York St.

Other Things to See & Do

Guided tours of the cells and Victorian court room at the **Old Town Gaol** (☎ 242766), High St, take 30 minutes and leave on the half-hour. Located in the town hall, it opens 10 am to 4.30 pm Tuesday to Saturday and 2 to 4.30 pm on Sunday. Admission costs £3.50/2.10.

Next door is the **Maison Dieu** which was

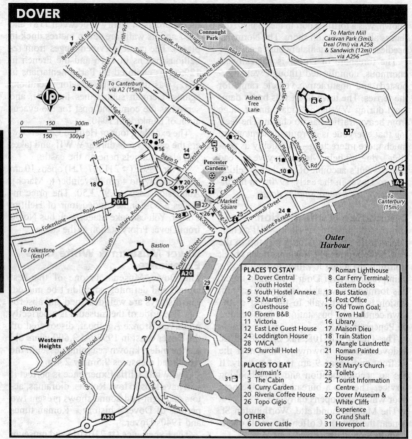

DOVER

PLACES TO STAY
2 Dover Central Youth Hostel
9 St Martin's Guesthouse
10 Florern B&B
11 Victoria
12 East Lee Guest House
24 Loddington House
28 YMCA
29 Churchill Hotel

PLACES TO EAT
1 Jermain's
3 The Cabin
4 Curry Garden
20 Riveria Coffee House
26 Topo Gigio

OTHER
6 Dover Castle
7 Roman Lighthouse
8 Car Ferry Terminal; Eastern Docks
13 Bus Station
14 Post Office
15 Old Town Goal; Town Hall
16 Library
17 Maison Dieu
18 Train Station
19 Mangle Laundrette
21 Roman Painted House
22 St Mary's Church
23 Toilets
25 Tourist Information Centre
27 Dover Museum & White Cliffs Experience
30 Grand Shaft
31 Hoverport

built as a hospice for pilgrims and wounded soldiers in 1203. It now contains a collection of arms, armour, portraits of England's kings and dignitaries, and a magnificent stained-glass window depicting events in England's history. It opens from 10 am most days of the year. Admission is free.

The **Roman Painted House** (☎ 203279), New St, is home to 1800-year-old wall paintings. It opens 10 am to 5 pm daily, April to September. Admission costs £2/80p.

Beginning at Snargate St, the **Grand Shaft** is a 43m triple staircase which was cut into the white cliffs as a short cut to town for troops stationed on the Western Heights during the Napoleonic Wars. According to popular tradition, one staircase was for officers and their ladies, the second for the NCOs and their wives, and the third for soldiers and their women!

Places to Stay

Most accommodation in Dover is nothing to write home about so it's worth looking around a bit. Finding any accommodation at all can be tough in high summer, so booking is advisable. For information on what's available call ☎ 401571.

Camping The *Martin Mill Caravan Park* (☎ *852658, Hawthorn Farm)* is 3 miles north-east of Dover, off the A258. It opens March to November and charges £6/7 for one/two people with a tent and £7/9 if you have a car too.

Hostels The *Dover Central Youth Hostel* (☎ *201314, 306 London Rd)* also has a convenient annexe *(Godwyne Rd)*; beds at both cost £11.00/£7.75 for adults/under-18s.

At the time of writing the *YMCA* (☎ *225500, 4 Leyburne Rd)* was closed for refurbishment, phone ahead to check if it has reopened.

B&Bs & Hotels Most B&Bs are along Castle St and Maison Dieu Rd, but there are others along Folkestone Rd.

St Martin's Guesthouse (☎ *205938, fax 208229, 17 Castle Hill Rd)* is highly recommended. The landlady is helpful and friendly and rooms are spotless and cosy. It costs £45 for two (singles vary). From November to March this rate can drop as low as £30.

Florern B&B (☎ *206408, 8 Castle Hill Rd)* is shabby and basic but rooms with showers are cheap at around £18 per person.

Friendly and luxurious *East Lee Guest House* (☎ *210176, 108 Maison Dieu Rd)* charges from £24/48 for singles/doubles.

Victoria (☎ *205140, 3 Laureston Place)* is an attractive Victorian home with lots of stairs. Rooms cost £22 per person (£18 in the quieter months).

Most of the B&Bs along Marine Parade are grotty and run down, and they aren't even super cheap to make up for it. *Loddington House* (☎/fax *201947, 14 East Cliff, Marine Parade)* is an exception and rooms cost £45/52–56.

One of the best-value places on the waterfront, and popular with business travellers, *Churchill Hotel* (☎ *203633, The Waterfront)* charges from £37.50 to £50.50 per person.

Places to Eat

Despite its size, Dover is short on decent places to eat – although there are plenty of pubs around Market Square offering decent meals.

Topo Gigio (☎ *201048, 1–2 King St)* is an Italian place with pasta from £3.45 and pizzas from £5.20.

For a cheap Indian restaurant with plush decor, try *Curry Garden* (☎ *206357, 24 High St)*. You can get a prawn korma for £4.20 or daal for only £1.95.

Jermain's (☎ *205956, Beaconsfield Rd)* is a clean, efficient eatery near the hostel. It has a range of good-value traditional fare, such as roast beef for £5 and pudding for £1.

One of the few offerings for gourmets, *The Cabin* (☎ *206118, 91 High St)* is a small but cosy restaurant specialising in traditional English and game dishes; vegetarians are catered for too though. Haunch of wild boar with red wine and fresh herbs costs £11.70 while haggis in whisky sauce costs £2.95 as a starter.

Riveria Coffee House (☎ *201766, 9311 Worthington St)* is very good value. Cream teas cost £1.80 and sandwiches and light meals cost from £1.20.

Getting There & Away

Dover is 75 miles from London and 15 miles from Canterbury.

Bus Stagecoach East Kent has an office on Pencester Rd (☎ 240024). They have a Canterbury to Dover service (£2.50, 30 minutes). National Express coaches leave hourly from London Victoria (£9/11 one-way/return, two hours 20 minutes).

There's an hourly bus to Brighton but you'll need to change at Eastbourne. Later in the evenings it's a direct service. An Explorer ticket for £6 is the best value on this route. Stagecoach South Coast (☎ 01424-433711) bus No 711 will take you to Hastings (£4.50). Bus Nos 111 and 211 go to Canterbury via Sandwich and Deal.

Train There are over 40 trains daily from London Victoria and Charing Cross stations to Dover Priory via Ashford and Sevenoaks (£18.20, 1½ hours).

Boat Ferries depart from the Eastern Docks (accessible by bus; see Getting Around later) below the castle, but the Hoverport is below

SOUTH-EASTERN ENGLAND

the Western Heights. P&O Stena ferries leave for Calais every 45 minutes (£24/48 one-way/return, £56 for a car and five passengers, 1¼ hours). Seafrance ferries leave every 1½ hours (£15/30, 1¼ hours). The hourly Hover-speed to Ostende costs £19.50/39 and, if you want to take your car on the Eurotunnel, the Shuttle costs £29/59 (see the introductory Getting There & Away chapter).

Call ☎ 401575 for information on day trips to France and special offers.

Getting Around

Fortunately, the ferry companies run complimentary buses between the docks and the train station as they're a long walk apart. On local buses a trip from one side of town to the other costs about £1.50.

Central Taxis (☎ 240441) and Heritage (☎ 204420) both have 24-hour services. You could also try Star Taxis on ☎ 228822. A one-way trip to Deal costs about £8; to Sandwich it's about £12.

ROMNEY MARSH & AROUND

Romney Marsh is a flat, fertile plain that was once under water. Parts of it are still below sea level. It is, somehow, a landscape in microcosm, which makes it an appropriate location for the world's smallest public railway. The **Romney, Hythe & Dymchurch Railway** (☎ 01797-362353) runs 13½ miles from Hythe to Dungeness lighthouse, from Easter to September (weekends only in March and October).

Hythe, once a Cinque Port, is a low-key seaside resort with an attractive Old Town. In the crypt of St Leonard's Church is a ghoulish attraction – 8000 thigh bones and 2000 skulls, some arranged on shelves like pots of jam in a supermarket.

Dungeness is a low shingle spit dominated by a nuclear power station and a lighthouse. There's a strange magic here that transcends the apocalyptic bleakness. The area supports the largest seabird colony in the south-east. There's a Royal Society for the Protection of Birds (RSPB) Nature Reserve visitor centre (☎ 01797-320588) open 9 am to sunset daily.

The Romney Marsh Countryside Project (☎ 01304-241806) arranges guided walks and bicycle rides around the area. Pick up a pamphlet from the RSPB Nature Reserve visitor centre in Dungeness.

Getting There & Away

Stagecoach East Kent bus No 558 runs from Canterbury to Hythe roughly every two hours from Monday to Saturday (1 hour) and South Coast bus No 711 passes through Hythe hourly (every two hours on Sunday) en route between Eastbourne and Dover.

HEVER

Idyllic Hever Castle (☎ 01732-861702) near Edenbridge, a few miles west of Tonbridge, was the childhood home of Anne Boleyn, mistress to Henry VIII and then his doomed queen. Walking through the main gate into the courtyard of Hever is like stepping onto the set of a period film. It's a truly fairy-tale place and one of the highlights of the area.

The moated castle was built in the 13th and 15th centuries and restored by the American, William Waldorf Astor who acquired the house in 1903. The exterior is unchanged from Tudor times, but the interior now has superb Edwardian carved wooden panelling.

The lower level of the gatehouse is home to a horrifying collection of torture and execution instruments. Our particular favourite – the flesh gouger!

The castle is surrounded by a garden, again the creation of the Astors, that incorporates a number of different styles, including a formal Italian garden with classical sculptures.

Hever opens 11 am to 5 pm daily, March to November. Admission to the castle and gardens costs £7.80/4.20; to gardens only costs £6.10/4. From London Victoria trains go to Hever (change at Oxted), a mile's walk from the castle (£7.10, 52 minutes). Alternatively, you could take the train to Edenbridge, from where it's a 4-mile taxi ride. A nice idea is to hire a bicycle in Edenbridge and ride to Hever. From Edenbridge High St the route to Hever is signposted.

IGHTHAM MOTE

For six and a half centuries, Ightham (pronounced eye-tam) has survived wars, storms and generation after generation of occupants. This is all the more remarkable since it is not an aristocratic mansion full of priceless treasures, just a small medieval manor house surrounded by a moat.

Although parts date from around 1340, the building today is an architectural jigsaw puzzle, and you need a detailed guide to unravel which bit belongs to which century. Some of the additions and alterations seem haphazard, but the materials (wood, stone, clay), the building's scale and the frame of water create a harmonious whole.

Run by the National Trust (NT), Ightham Mote (☎ 01732-811145) is 6 miles east of Sevenoaks off the A25, and 2½ miles south of Ightham off the A227. There are six daily buses from Sevenoaks to Ivy Hatch which is one mile from Ightham Mote. It opens 11 am to 5.30 pm daily except Tuesday and Saturday, April to October. Admission costs £5/2.

LEEDS CASTLE

Just east of Maidstone, Leeds Castle (☎ 01622-765400) is one of the most famous and most visited castles in the world. It stands on two small islands in a lake surrounded by a huge estate which contains woodlands, an aviary and a really weird grotto that can only be entered once you've successfully negotiated your way through a hedge maze.

The building dates from the 9th century. Henry VIII transformed it from a fortress into a palace, and it was privately owned until 1974 when Lady Baillie, the castle's last owner, died. Paintings, furniture and other decor in the castle date from the last eight centuries.

A private trust now manages the property and, as part of a requirement that the castle serve a function other than that of a tourist attraction, some of the rooms are used for conferences and other events. This creates a problem for the visitor in that some of the rooms are closed to the public quite regularly. If you want to be sure you can see all the rooms and get your money's worth, ring ahead. Another problem is the sheer number of people to be negotiated – at weekends it's the families, during the week it's the school groups.

It opens 10 am to 5 pm daily, March to October (to 3 pm November to February). Admission is exorbitant at £9.50/6. National Express runs one direct bus daily from London Victoria coach station, leaving at 9 am and returning at 3.50 pm (1¼ hours). It must be pre-booked and price combines admission and travel (£12.50/9.50). Greenline (☎ 020-8668 7261) buses have the same deal (£13/7, 9.35 am from London Victoria, return 4 pm).

East Sussex

East Sussex has some superb countryside along the spine of the South Downs, and some great coastal areas. Although they are touristy, Rye and Battle have a certain magic. Eastbourne and Brighton are two of England's most entertaining seaside towns, but with its extraordinary mix of tackiness and pure groove, Brighton is the main attraction.

RYE

☎ 01797 • pop 5400

The medieval town of Rye, once a Cinque Port, is the epitome of Ye Cute Olde Englishe Village. It's a desperately picturesque town with half-timbered buildings, winding cobbled streets, abundant flowerpots and a number of literary associations. The buildings, a mixture of Tudor and Georgian styles, snuggle cosily into each other.

Rye is claimed by many to be the most beautiful town in Britain and, as a result, is full of tourists. Because it is so popular and perfect it can seem strangely unreal – almost as if no-one actually lives here. If you do visit – and you should – avoid summer weekends.

Orientation & Information

Rye is small, so it can easily be covered on foot. The TIC (☎ 226696, fax 223460, ⓔ rye tic@rother.gov.uk) is on Strand Quay and opens 9 am to 5.30 pm daily, June to August; and 10 am to 4 pm the rest of the year. *Rye Town Walk* gives a detailed history of the town's buildings and costs £1. There's also an audio tour costing £2/1. For guided walks around town phone ☎ 01424-882343.

SOUTH-EASTERN ENGLAND

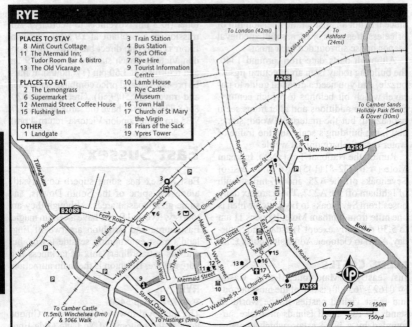

RYE

PLACES TO STAY		3	Train Station
8	Mint Court Cottage	4	Bus Station
11	The Mermaid Inn;	5	Post Office
	Tudor Room Bar & Bistro	7	Rye Hire
13	The Old Vicarage	9	Tourist Information
			Centre
PLACES TO EAT		10	Lamb House
2	The Lemongrass	14	Rye Castle
6	Supermarket		Museum
12	Mermaid Street Coffee House	16	Town Hall
15	Flushing Inn	17	Church of St Mary
			the Virgin
OTHER		18	Friars of the Sack
1	Landgate	19	Ypres Tower

To London (42mi)
To Ashford (24mi)
A268
To Camber Sands Holiday Park (5mi) & Dover (30mi)
New Road   A259
Military Road
Rope Walk
Tower St
Landgate
Fishmarket Rd
B2089
Ferry Road
Crown Fields
Ginque Ports Street
Conduit Hill
Hilder's Cliff
Tillingham
Udimore Road
Mill Lane
Wish Street
The Mint
Wish Ward
Market Rd
High Street
East Street
Lion St
Market Street
Fishmarket Road
Rother
A259
To Camber Castle (1.5mi), Winchelsea (3mi) & 1066 Walk
Strand Quay
Mermaid Street
Watchbell St
Church Sq
South Undercliff
To Hastings (9mi)
0   75   150m
0   75   150yd

The town celebrates its medieval heritage with a two-day festival each August, and in September there is the two-week Festival of Music and the Arts.

Things to See & Do

You can start your tour of the town at the TIC's **Rye Town Model Sound & Light Show** which gives a half-hour theatrical introduction to the town's history. It opens daily and admission costs £2/1.

Around the corner from the TIC, in Strand Quay, are a number of **antique shops** selling all kinds of wonderful junk. From here walk up cobbled **Mermaid St**, one of the most famous streets in England, with timber-framed houses dating from the 15th century. The Mermaid Inn was a notorious smugglers' haunt and in the 18th century the Hawkhurst Gang, one of the most feared mobs in the country, used the pub to openly celebrate successful runs.

Turn right at the T-junction for the Geor-gian **Lamb House** (☎ 224982; NT), West St, mostly dating from 1722. It was the home of American writer Henry James from 1898 to 1916, and EF Benson, author of the Mapp & Lucia stories, from 1919 to 1940. It opens 2 to 6 pm Tuesday and Saturday, April to October. Admission costs £2.50/1.25.

Continue around the dogleg until you come out at Church Square. It's surrounded by a variety of attractive houses, including the **Friars of the Sack** on the southern side at No 40. Now a private residence, it was once part of a 13th-century Augustinian friary. The **Church of St Mary the Virgin** is on the highest point in Rye and incorporates a mixture of ecclesiastical styles. The church actually dates from the 12th century but was rebuilt in the 15th. The turret clock is the oldest in England (1561) and still works with its original pendulum mechanism. There are great views from the church tower.

Turn right at the eastern corner of the square for **Ypres Tower** (pronounced wipers), part of the 13th-century fort that survived French raids. It now houses one part of the **Rye Castle Museum** (☎ 226728). The main museum on 3 East St opens 10.30 am to 5.30 pm daily, Easter to October (to 4.30 pm weekends only, November to March). Admission only to Ypres Tower costs £2/75p, and to both costs £3/1.

At the north-eastern edge of the village is **Landgate**. Built in 1329 to fortify the town, it's the only remaining gate out of four that were originally built in the 14th century.

Places to Stay & Eat
Most accommodation is not cheap, but then Rye is one place where it's really worth spending a bit more and staying somewhere special.

Running alongside a marvellously remote and rugged stretch of beach is *Camber Sands Holiday Park* (☎ 225555, fax 225756, New Lydd Rd, Camber), 5½ miles east of Rye. It opens March to October and rates vary from week to week so call ahead for costs.

Mint Court Cottage (☎ 227780, The Mint) behind the Bell Inn has one converted attic room plus a private sitting room downstairs for £25 per person or £23 from November to March.

The Mermaid Inn (☎ 223065, fax 225069, Mermaid St) has been around since 1420. Visited by royalty and proud of its resident ghost, the hotel charges from £68 per person for bed and breakfast.

Next to St Mary's Church, *The Old Vicarage* (☎ 222119, fax 227466, 66 Church Square) is very quaint with a lovely garden. Rooms cost £64 for a double or £22 per person for a three- or four-bed room.

The only Thai restaurant in town is *The Lemongrass* (☎ 222327, 1 Tower St) where curries cost £6.50.

At the dearer end of the scale, *Flushing Inn* (☎ 223292, 4 Market St) offers a '1066 Maritime Menu' and local wines. Mains range from £8.80 to £13.50.

At the Mermaid Inn, the *Tudor Room Bar & Bistro* (☎ 223065, Mermaid St) is a

The 1066 Country Walk

The 1066 Country Walk links Rye to Pevensey and passes through 31 miles of East Sussex's countryside and joins the South Downs Way. From Rye it's 3 miles to the village of Winchelsea, which is almost as attractive as Rye yet without the tourists. The path is an excellent way to reach Battle (15 miles). There are links to Hastings (about 15 miles from Rye). Another good walk from Rye is to Camber Castle (1½ miles).

A leaflet showing the route of the 1066 Country Walk and listing places to stay along the way is available free from TICs in Rye, Battle, Hastings and Pevensey.

tiny, low-ceilinged, half-timbered pub with an outdoor terrace. Baguettes cost around £5 or you can have something more substantial, such as baked local fish pie with smoked cheese for £7.50.

For a smorgasbord of coffee and snacks try *Mermaid Street Coffee House* (☎ 224858, corner of Mermaid and West Sts). Cake and coffee costs £2.90.

Self-caterers should head to the *Budgens supermarket* near the train station.

Getting There & Away
Stagecoach East Kent (☎ 01227-472082) bus No 711 runs hourly between Dover and Brighton via Rye, Hastings and Eastbourne. Local Rider No 344/345 links Rye with Hastings, and Rambler Coaches bus No 44 runs twice hourly (not at weekends) from Hastings to Rye.

Rye is only 1½ hours from London Charing Cross, via Ashford. Trains run hourly from Monday to Saturday and there are five services on Sunday. The service continues to Hastings (£17.60, 1¾ hours).

Getting Around
Try Rye Motors Taxis (☎ 223176) or Rother (☎ 224554).

Alternatively, you can rent bikes from £9 per day from Rye Hire (☎ 223033), Cyprus Place. A cycling map of East Sussex is available from the TIC.

SOUTH-EASTERN ENGLAND

HASTINGS
☎ 01424 • pop 80,820

Despite the fact that the seafront, with its tacky amusement parks and guesthouses, is run down, the sorry-looking pier has been closed, and the new town centre is grey and depressing, Hastings still attracts around 3½ million holiday-makers each year. In all fairness, the old town of Hastings could be described as atmospheric (in a decaying sort of way) with its half-timbered buildings and antique shops, and the nightlife here is much better than in Eastbourne farther down the coast. Still, we are unconvinced that the town actually has any real appeal.

The TIC (☎ 781111, fax 781133, ⓔ hic_info@hastings.gov.uk), beside the town hall on Priory Meadow, opens 9.30 am to 5 pm daily (from 10 am on Sunday). There's another branch on the foreshore near the Stade. The post office is on Cambridge Road.

It is believed William I erected a prefabricated wooden castle here before the Battle of Hastings, but the surviving fragmentary remains of **Hastings Castle** (☎ 781112) date from after the battle. Admission costs £3/2. You can get to the castle via the **West Hill Lift** cliff railway (80p/40p). The **Stade**, at the eastern end of town, is a hive of fishing activity, and there's a lot to see in the cramped but well-presented **Old Town Hall Museum** (☎ 781166), High St.

Places to Stay & Eat
The cheapest B&Bs can be found along Cambridge Gardens.

The Apollo (☎ 444394, 25 Cambridge Gardens) is recommended; rooms cost £20 per person from June to August, £15 the rest of the year. *Senlac B&B* (☎ 430080, ⓔ senlac@1066-country.com, 47 Cambridge Gardens) also gets a big tick and charges £16 per person and £18 for rooms with bathrooms en suite.

In the Old Town, the *Jenny Lind Hotel* (☎ 421392, 69 High St) has double rooms with bathroom for £30/45, which includes breakfast.

Fresh seafood is the most appropriate choice, and there are plenty of places selling fish and chips, particularly in the Old Town.

Gannets (☎ 439678, 45 High St) opens for breakfast, lunch and afternoon tea. A roast lunch costs £5.25, spaghetti bolognese with salad is £5.50 and puddings cost from £1.75 to £2.50.

Getting There & Away
Stagecoach South Coast (☎ 01424-433711) bus No 711 runs from Dover to Brighton via Hastings (£4.50, hourly, less frequently on Sunday). There are regular trains to/from London Charing Cross (£17.60 return, 1½ hours) via Battle and to/from Ashford via Rye. Every 15 minutes, trains head west around the Sussex coast from Hastings to Portsmouth (£20, 2½ hours) via Brighton (£8.60, 1 hour).

BATTLE
☎ 01424 • pop 5732

1066 and all that...Battle, 6 miles north of Hastings, is built around the site where Duke William of Normandy defeated Harold II in the last successful invasion of Britain. The highlight of any visit is the 1½ mile walk around the battlefield.

The train station is a short walk from High St, and is well signposted. The TIC (☎ 773721, fax 773436), 88 High St, opens 10 am to 6 pm daily (to 4 pm in winter).

Battlefield & Battle Abbey
The guided walk around the battlefield is a really pleasant way to spend a couple of hours. The audio tour gives blow-by-blow descriptions of the famous battle between King Harold and William the Conqueror in 1066 (see the boxed text 'The Battle' later). You can't help but be totally absorbed in the event as you wander the field and imagine the carnage that took place.

Construction of the abbey began in 1070. It was occupied by Benedictines until the Dissolution in 1539. Only the foundations of the church can now be seen and the altar's position is marked by a plaque, but quite a few monastic buildings survive and the scene is very painterly.

Battle Abbey and Battlefield (☎ 773792; EH) open 10 am to 6 pm daily (to 4 pm from November to March). Admission costs £4/2.

The Battle

Harold's army arrived first on the scene of the Battle of Hastings on 14th October 1066. They occupied a strong defensive position with archers, then cavalry, then infantry at the rear. Altogether, there were around 7000 soldiers making one of the most formidable armies of the time.

Hearing of Harold's arrival, William marched north from Hastings and took up a position about 400m south of the English. His army also numbered around 7000 men, but included 2000 to 3000 cavalry.

After several unsuccessful uphill attacks against the English shield wall, William's knights feigned retreat, drawing many English after them. This was a disastrous move for the English, as the rift in the wall of soldiers left them vulnerable to attack. Amongst the English casualties was King Harold who, according to events depicted in the Bayeux Tapestry, was struck in or near the eye. While he tried to pull the arrow from his head he was struck down by Norman knights. At the news of his death the last of the English resistance collapsed.

Places to Stay & Eat

There are not many cheap places to stay within easy walking distance, so it may be preferable to use Hastings as a base.

Opposite the abbey entrance is *Clematis Cottage* (☎ 774261, 3 High St) where singles/doubles cost £35/45 or £40/50 with en suite. *Abbey View* (☎ 775513, Caldbec Hill, Mount St)* is five minutes' walk to High St and one of the cheaper options. There are also lovely views over the surrounding countryside. Rooms cost £30 per person from May to October, £25 the rest of the year.

The King's Head (☎ 772317, corner of Mount and High Sts)* claims to be Battle's oldest pub and is a small and intimate place for a quiet beer. Alternatively, *Pilgrim's Rest* (☎ 772314, 1 High St)* is a home-style restaurant opposite the abbey with hearty English meals for around £5.

Getting There & Away

National Express bus No 067 from London to Hastings passes through Battle, and Eastbourne Buses (☎ 01323-416416) No 22 service runs from Eastbourne to Battle on weekdays (three daily). From Battle you can reach Pevensey (45 minutes) and Bodiam (20 minutes) on Eastbourne Buses' irregular No 19 service. Local Rider bus No 4/5 runs hourly to Hastings.

A cheap day return from London Charing Cross costs £15.40. From Hastings the fare is £2.30 and the trip takes 15 minutes.

PEVENSEY CASTLE

William the Conqueror's first stronghold, Pevensey Castle, is 5 miles east of Eastbourne, off the A259. The Norman castle sits within a Roman defensive wall and on the site of a Roman fort which was built between 280 and 340. In 1066, William landed here and occupied the abandoned fort for 17 days before his victory at Battle. At this time the site would have been much closer to the sea. The castle is mostly in ruins now but enough is left standing to indicate what each part of the castle was used for. It opens 10 am to 6 pm Wednesday to Sunday for most of the year, and 11 am to 4 pm November to March. Admission costs £2.50/1.30.

The Mint House, just across the road from the castle, dates from 1342 and is absolutely bursting with one of the biggest and weirdest collections of antiques and bits and pieces you may ever see. The atmosphere is decidedly nutty and admission costs £1/50p.

Regular train services between London and Hastings via Eastbourne stop at Westham, half a mile from Pevensey. Eastbourne Buses No 18 stops at Westham and Nos 7 and 19 stop at Pevensey.

EASTBOURNE

☎ 01323 • pop 81,395

Relaxed and slightly eccentric Eastbourne makes a nice change from some of the tackier seaside resorts in Sussex. Never mind that it's gained a reputation as the foremost holiday spot for octogenarians, it still has plenty of youthful character with its student hangouts, bars and amusements for kids. The beaches are clean, gardens and parks are dotted throughout the town and there are plenty of places to stay, though you will need to book well ahead. Large groups tend to fill up most of the hotels and B&Bs.

Orientation & Information

The town centre is just north of the pier, while the few interesting old buildings and couple of antique shops that make up the Old Town lie about a mile north-west of the new town centre. To the east of the centre, along the beachfront, are a number of amusement parks for kids. To the west the stunning chalk cliffs steer the way to Beachy Head, just a 3-mile walk.

The TIC (☎ 411400, fax 649574. Eeast bournetic@btclick.com), Cornfield Rd, has a number of helpful leaflets. It opens 9 am to 5.30 Monday to Saturday and 10 am to 1 pm on Sunday (closed Sundays in winter). A 3-D map of the town costing £1 is available from an automatic dispenser outside.

Internet access is available from Wired Cafe (☎ 646436, 2d Pevensey Rd) for 7p per minute with a minimum charge of £1. The post office is on Langney Rd.

Rainbows Laundrette is at 47 Seaside Rd.

Things to See & Do

Eastbourne's **pier** is home to an amusement arcade, trinket shops, a bar, a disco and lots of bird droppings. It's a nice place to watch the sun set over the water though. And you can hire fishing rods for £2 from the end of the pier.

Eastbourne Heritage Centre (☎ 411189), Carlisle Rd, west of the centre, explores the development of the town from 1800 to the present day. It opens 2 to 5 pm daily, May to September and bank holidays. Admission costs £1/50p.

If it doesn't scare the pants off you, **Wishtower Puppet Museum** (☎ 417776) on King Edward's Parade would be a great place to take the kids. They have a collection of traditional puppets from all over the world, including Punch and Judy. It opens

10.30 am to 5 pm daily Easter to November. Admission costs £1.80/1.25.

The **Museum of Shops** (☎ 737143), 20 Cornfield Terrace, has an enormous collection of Victorian and early-20th-century memorabilia – antiques, books, toys, you name it. It opens 10 am to 5.30 pm daily but may close a little earlier in winter. The admission costs are a little steep at £3/2.

Set inside beautiful **Manor Gardens** is the **Towner Art Gallery & Local History Museum** (☎ 411688), about a mile's walk from the centre. It has a great collection of 20th-century British art as well as diverse temporary exhibitions. It opens noon to 5 pm Tuesday to Saturday, and 2 to 5 pm Sunday and bank holidays (closes an hour earlier November to March). Admission is free but there's a charge for special exhibitions.

Places to Stay

Accommodation is difficult to find in Eastbourne unless you book ahead.

The best choice of places around here is *Lindau Lodge* (☎ 640792, 71 Royal Parade), five minutes' walk from the centre. B&B costs £19 per person and a three-course evening meal costs £8.

A stone's throw from the pier is *The Royal Hotel* (☎ 724027, 8–9 Marine Parade) on the waterfront. If money is your main concern then you won't do better than this. Somewhat grotty rooms with seaviews cost just £15 per person with breakfast.

The friendly *Belle Vue Hotel* (☎ 649544, 2–4 Grand Parade) is in a nice old building. It too is very close to the action and rooms cost £25 per person (£20 from November to March). At weekends during summer the rates may be higher.

The *Queen's Hotel* (☎ 722822, fax 731056, corner of Marine Parade and Seaside Rd) is very good value with elegant rooms for £26 per person. You will need to book ahead as this place fills up quickly.

There are several lovely B&Bs and hotels just west of the centre. *Arundel Private Hotel* (☎ 639481, fax 431683, 43–47 Carlisle Rd) is very reasonably priced at £25 per person for its huge rooms. The place is bright and airy; there's a great lounge and bar area too.

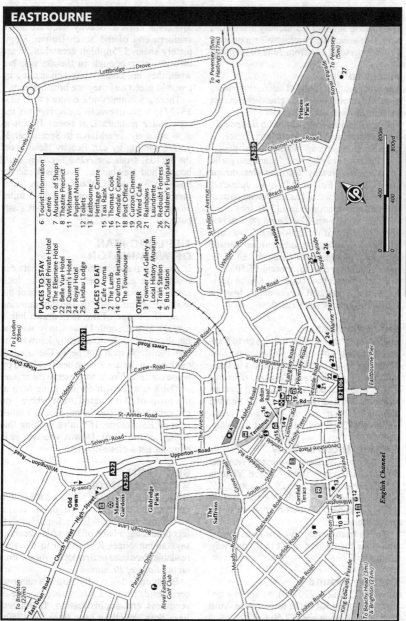

EASTBOURNE

PLACES TO STAY
9 Arundel Private Hotel
10 The Ellesmere Hotel
22 Belle Vue Hotel
23 Queen's Hotel
24 Royal Hotel
25 Lindau Lodge

PLACES TO EAT
1 Cafe Aroma
2 The Lamb
14 Dartons Restaurant;
   The Townhouse

OTHER
3 Towner Art Gallery &
   Local History Museum
4 Train Station
5 Bus Station
6 Tourist Information
   Centre
7 Museum of Shops
8 Theatre Precinct
11 Wishtower
   Puppet Museum
12 Toilets
13 Eastbourne
   Heritage Centre
15 Taxi Rank
16 Thomas Cook
17 Arndale Centre
18 Post Office
19 Curzon Cinema
20 Wired Cafe
21 Rainbows
   Laundrette
26 Redoubt Fortress
27 Children's Funparks

SOUTH-EASTERN ENGLAND

The Ellesmere Hotel (☎ 731463, 11 *Wilmington Square)* is a friendly place in an attractive area. Big, comfortable rooms cost £20 per person (£23 from June to August).

Places to Eat

The town centre has lots of interesting places to eat but there is not much elsewhere, except for unexciting hotel restaurants.

The Townhouse (☎ 734900, 6 *Bolton Rd),* a bar/restaurant with an outdoor terrace, is frequented mainly by students and under-25s. Panfried crayfish with lemon and garlic costs £6.95. Nearby *Oartons Restaurant* (☎ 731053, 4 *Bolton Rd)* is an upmarket French restaurant and has a set menu costing £13.95 for two courses or £15.95 for three.

In the Old Town, *The Lamb* (☎ 720545, *corner of High St & Ocklynge Rd)* is a half-timbered pub with traditional bar meals, such as a ploughman's lunch for £4.95 or more modern meals for around £7.50.

Cafe Aroma (☎ 640263, 54 *Crown St)* is in the Old Town and serves cream teas for £2.10 and snacks from £2.40.

Entertainment

For the latest mainstream movies go to *Curzon Cinema* (☎ 731441, *Langney Rd).* There are also a number of theatres in Eastbourne – the *Congress Theatre, (Carlisle Rd)* is just west of the centre, and *Devonshire Park Theatre (Compton St)* and the *Winter Garden* are on the same street. Phone ☎ 412000 to find out what's playing.

Getting There & Away

There are two National Express services per day to Eastbourne from London Victoria (£8/13 one-way/return or £9 day return, 2½ hours). Stagecoach South Coast (☎ 01424-433711) bus No 711 runs hourly from Dover to Eastbourne.

Trains from London Victoria leave every half-hour for Eastbourne (£16.90 one way, 1½ hours).

Getting Around

Try T&C Taxi (☎ 720720). There is a taxi rank on Bolton Rd in the town centre. Most trips around town cost £2.50 to £3.

BEACHY HEAD

The chalk cliffs at Beachy Head are at the southern end of the South Downs. Completely sheer, 175m-high coastal cliffs are awe-inspiring enough in themselves, but when they are chalk white and backed by emerald green turf they are breathtaking.

There's a countryside centre (☎ 01323-737273) with interactive displays on the area and a restaurant. It opens 10 am to 5.30 pm daily, late March to September. If you're coming by car, Beachy Head is off the B2103, from the A259 between Eastbourne and Newhaven. There is a regular bus (No 3) from Eastbourne during summer. Better still, why not walk the 3 miles along the South Downs Way from Eastbourne?

THE LONG MAN OF WILMINGTON

If you're travelling along the A27 between Eastbourne and Lewes, be sure to look southwards out the window, just east of the town of Wilmington, to see this amazing sight. The image of this man drawn into a hillside of the South Downs may well be familiar to you. No-one really knows how this 70m-high man got here. The original markings in the grass have been replaced by white concrete blocks to preserve the image.

There is a turn-off for the Long Man at the town of Wilmington from where you can get a better view. Wilmington is 7 miles west of Eastbourne. If you're walking this section of the South Downs you will pass him and get a close-up view.

BRIGHTON

☎ 01273 • pop 188,000

'How did England ever produce a town with the fizz and craziness of Brighton? It is a marvellous mystery – like a family of duffers producing a babe of Mozartian genius,' says author Nigel Richardson in his very readable *Breakfast in Brighton – Adventures on the Edge of Britain.*

Brighton is deservedly Britain's number-one seaside town – a fascinating mixture of seediness and sophistication. Londoners have been travelling here since the 1750s, when a shrewd doctor suggested that bathing in, and drinking, the local sea water was good for them. It's still fine to swim here, though a little on the cool side, but drinking the sea water is definitely not recommended.

The essential flavour of the town dates from the 1780s when the dissolute, music-loving Prince Regent (later George IV) built his outrageous summer palace for lavish parties by the sea. Brighton still has some of the hottest clubs and venues outside London, including the largest gay club on the south coast. There's a vibrant population of students and travellers, excellent shopping, a thriving arts scene and countless restaurants, pubs and cafes.

Orientation & Information

Old Steine (pronounced steen) is the major road running from the pier to the city centre. Brighton train station is half a mile or 15 minutes' walk north of the beach. The tiny bus station is tucked away in Poole Valley. West of Brighton, and now part of the same administrative unit, is slightly snobbish Hove. It's jokingly referred to as 'Hove Actually' in Brighton because most Hove residents when asked where they live will reply 'Hove, actually', to emphasise that they don't live in Brighton!

The TIC (☎ 292599, e tourism@brighton .co.uk), 10 Bartholomew Square, opens 9 am to 6 pm Monday to Friday, 10 am to 5 pm on Saturday and 10 am to 4 pm on Sunday, June to August; and 9 am to 5 pm Monday to Saturday, the rest of the year. Copies of Brighton's listings magazines, *The Brighton Latest* (30p), *Brighton & Hove Scene* (25p) and *New Insight* (45p) are available from the TIC. *Brighton Town Centre Map-Guide* costs £1. Guided tours covering a range of interests such as Regency Brighton, architecture, gardens and so on, can be booked through the TIC. The walks usually cost around £3 and take about one hour. For information on everything from shopping to clubs to eating out in Brighton go to the Web site at www.brighton.co.uk.

For Internet access check out Riki Tik (☎ 683844), 18a Bond St.

Post offices can be found on Ship St and Western Rd.

Bubbles Laundrette is at 75 Preston St.

Royal Pavilion

The Royal Pavilion (☎ 290900) is an absolute must and a highlight of any trip to southern England. It's an extraordinarily lavish fantasy: completely over-the-top and so 'un-English'! It was the fanciful idea of Prince George who used to come to Brighton to hang out with his wayward uncle, the Duke of Cumberland. He fell in love with the seaside and decided that Brighton was the perfect place to party.

In 1787, he commissioned Henry Holland to build a simple neoclassical villa which became known as the Marine Pavilion. It wasn't until 1802, when everything Eastern became the rage, that the current creation began to take shape. The final Indian-inspired exterior was designed by architect John Nash (also responsible for Regent's Park and its flanking buildings) and built between 1815 and 1822. The pavilion was also used by Queen Victoria, although it's difficult to imagine the conservative queen in these surroundings.

A free visitors guide is available which takes you through the place, room by room. It opens 10 am to 6 pm daily June to September (to 5 pm October to May). Admission costs £4.50/2.75. A combined ticket for rail travel from London and admission is available through Connex (☎ 0345 484950) for £17.75/3.75.

Brighton Museum & Art Gallery

The Brighton Museum & Art Gallery (☎ 290900), Church St, was undergoing a £10-million redevelopment programme at the time of writing. It's sure to continue housing its collection of Art Deco and Art Nouveau furniture, archaeological finds, surrealist paintings and costumes. We hope that Salvador Dali's sofa in the shape of lips will still be here.

Other Things to See & Do

Open daily and with free admission, the **Palace Pier** is the very image of Brighton.

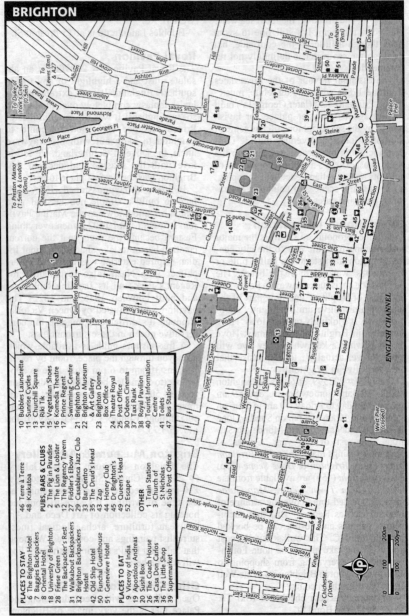

BRIGHTON

SOUTH-EASTERN ENGLAND

ENGLISH CHANNEL

To Newhaven (9mi)

Palace Pier

West Pier (closed)

To Chichester (30mi)

0   100   200m
0   100   200yd

PLACES TO STAY
6   The Brighton Hotel
7   The Ibis Backpackers
8   Baggies Backpackers
18 University of Brighton
5   Friese Green –
12 The Backpacker's Rest
31 Walkabout Backpackers
32 Brighton Backpackers Hostel
42 Old Ship Hotel
50 Funchal Guesthouse
51 Genevieve Hotel

PLACES TO EAT
9   Viceroy of India
19 Apostolos Andreas
20 Sushi Box
26 The Coach House
34 Casa Don Carlos
36 The Little Shop
39 Supermarket

46 Terre à Terre
48 Krakatoa

PUBS, BARS & CLUBS
2   The Pig in Paradise
5   The Lion & Lobster
12 The Regency Tavern
27 Fiddler's Elbow
29 Casablanca Jazz Club
33 Bar Centro
35 The Druid's Head
43 Zap
44 Honey Club
45 Dr Brighton's
49 Queen's Head
52 Escape

OTHER
1   Train Station
3   Church of St Nicholas
4   Sub Post Office

10 Bubbles Laundrette
11 Sunrise Cycles
13 Churchill Square
14 Riki Tik
15 Vegetarian Shoes
16 Komedia Theatre
17 Prince Regent Swimming Centre
21 Brighton Dome
22 Brighton Museum & Art Gallery
23 Brighton Dome Box Office
24 Theatre Royal
25 Post Office
30 Odeon Cinema
37 Taxi Rank
38 Royal Pavilion
40 Tourist Information Centre
41 Toilets
47 Bus Station

Amusement rides, takeaway food and various machines with flashing lights all drain your pocket. The famous Brighton Rock candy can be purchased here and you might want to take a ride on the helter-skelter, the inspiration for the now infamous Beatles song.

Filled up to the brim with paintings, ornaments and antiques, **Preston Manor** (☎ 290900), London Rd, is a typical Edwardian upper-class home, 2½ miles northwards from the centre. It was originally built around 1600 but was rebuilt in 1738, which is why the exterior is so understated. The guided tour of the kitchen and servants quarters is particularly interesting. The place is small and you may have to contend with school groups on weekdays so call ahead if you want to be sure of a bit of space. It opens 10 am to 5 pm Tuesday to Saturday, 1 to 5 pm Monday and 2 to 5 pm Sunday. Admission costs £3.10/1.95. You can get there on bus No 5 or 5A from the centre.

Special Events
Running for three weeks every May, Brighton Festival (☎ 292961) is the largest arts festival outside Edinburgh. Check out the Web site at www.brighton-festival.org.uk. Though it's mostly mainstream, there are fringe events too.

Places to Stay
There's plenty of accommodation in Brighton to suit all budgets. You should book ahead for weekends in summer and during the Brighton Festival in May.

Hostels Brighton independent hostels provide a more relaxed alternative to the inconveniently located YHA hostel.

The friendly *Baggies Backpackers* (☎ 733740, 33 Oriental Place) is a homely place with beds for £10 per night (plus a £5 deposit for a room key) and double rooms for £25. There are two lounges, a communal kitchen and a laundry. It's well situated in a quiet area close to the seafront and plenty of cheap restaurants.

Brighton Backpackers Hostel (☎ 777717, fax 887778, ⓔ stay@brightonbackpackers .com, 75–6 Middle St) seems to be trying very hard to cultivate a lackadaisical atmosphere. Rates are £10 per night (or £11 in the seafront annexe). The rate is very cheap if you stay for a week (£55/60 for singles/doubles). Travellers have painted the murals here. At No 20 on the same street, *Friese Green – The Backpacker's Rest* (☎ 747551) charges £9 for a bed and £30 for a double room.

It might seem like it but *Walkabout Backpackers* (☎ 770232, 79–81 West St) is not exclusively for Australians and New Zealanders. Beds in ordinary, bland dorms cost £10 or it's £12 in a double room. This place does not take reservations so it's first in best dressed.

The *University of Brighton* (☎ 643167, fax 642610, Grand Parade) has flats for two to eight people available in various locations from July to September. Prices start at £60 per person per week.

B&Bs & Hotels The biggest cluster of cheap B&Bs is east of Palace Pier. Cross the Old Steine roundabout and walk up St James St.

Funchal Guesthouse (☎/fax 603975, 17 Madeira Place) tries very hard to please with cosy, clean rooms that are serviced daily. Prices begin at £20 per person but these rates may go up a few pounds in summer. Nearby *Genevieve Hotel* (☎ 681653, 18 Madeira Place) is clean and rooms cost £20 to £25 per person, with continental breakfast.

For a real breath of fresh air among B&Bs try the *Oriental Hotel* (☎ 205050, fax 821096, ⓔ info@orientalhotel.co.uk, 9 Oriental Place). Decorated with bright colours, home-made furniture and cool decor, it's very funky. Doubles go for £54/70 weekdays/weekends. There are no single occupancy rates.

The ultimate doyen of Brighton's hotels is the *Old Ship Hotel* (☎ 329001, fax 820718, Kings Rd). In the 1830s, Thackeray stayed there whilst writing *Vanity Fair*. Singles/doubles cost from £75/99.

The Brighton Hotel (☎ 820555, fax 821555, 145 Kings Rd) is better than most that are in the same price range along this stretch. Rooms cost from £60/80.

Places to Eat

Brighton has it all as far as food goes. Wander around The Lanes or head down to Preston St which runs back from the seafront near West Pier, and you'll turn up all sorts of interesting, affordable possibilities. Vegetarians, vegans and health-foodies won't be left out in the cold either.

Serious food lovers should try *Krakatoa* (☎ 719009, *7 Poole Valley*), near the bus station. It's a small, casual restaurant with a modern Oriental fusion menu.

Terre à Terre (☎ 729051, *71 East St*) is an expensive vegetarian restaurant with a huge menu. Starters cost around £5 and mains cost about £9.50. This place is very popular so book ahead, especially at weekends.

The *Viceroy of India* (☎ 324733, *13 Preston St*) is one of the best value Indian restaurants along this street and serves a range of cuisines – kashmir, madras, ceylon, balti and tandoori. Main courses cost from £3 to £3.50.

Close to the university is the *Sushi Box* (☎ 818040, *181 Edward St*) which charges £3 to £4 for a takeaway lunch box of sashimi or California rolls.

Apostolos Andreas (☎ 687935, *George St*) is a Greek coffee house with English-style food. It's extremely popular with students because it's such good value. If you can get a seat in this tiny place you will pay about 65p for a coffee, 95p to £1.45 for a sandwich and from £1.35 for a hot meal.

The intimate *Casa Don Carlos* (☎ 327177 or 303274, *5 Union St, The Lanes*) is a Spanish tapas house and restaurant with a large selection of Spanish plonk. A large serving of paella costs £4.25 and a Spanish omelette is £3.10.

The Little Shop (☎ 325594, *48a Market St, The Lanes*) has apparently won awards for its sandwiches. They *are* delicious, and very chunky, and cost from £2.25.

The Coach House (☎ 719000, *59a Middle St*) is a relaxed cafe-bar with a student atmosphere and live music on Friday. The Thai curry with crispy noodles for £7 is absolutely delicious.

There's a *Safeway supermarket* on St James St.

Entertainment

Ever since the 1960s, Brighton has had a reputation as the club and party capital of the south, if not the whole country. In the late 1970s this reputation was enshrined in the cult movie *Quadrophenia*. For those who don't remember those good old days, maybe Fat Boy Slim rings a bell. He hails from Brighton and guest DJs quite regularly at various places around town. Pubs, bars and clubs are constantly opening, closing and changing their themes – check out *The Brighton Latest*, *New Insight* and bar and cafe walls for places of the moment. There is a huge gay scene in Brighton and most of the gay bars and clubs can be found around St James St and the Old Steine. Go to the Web site at www.gay.brighton.co.uk or www.tourism.brighton.co.uk for information about Brighton's gay scene.

Pubs & Bars The *Druid's Head* (☎ 325490, *9 Brighton Place*), decorated with skulls and votive offerings, is good for a pint. *The Lion & Lobster* (☎ 776961, *24 Sillwood St*) has live music most nights.

Fiddler's Elbow (☎ 325850, *Boyces St*) is an Irish pub with live music on Friday evenings.

Gay pubs include *Dr Brighton's* (*King's Rd*) and the *Queen's Head*, on a small side street off Marine Parade. Recognise the bloke on the pub sign here?

No pub could be more Brighton than *The Regency Tavern* (☎ 325652, *32 Russell Square*) – very plain outside, inside it's pure Regency, like an extension of the Pavilion with its striped green wallpaper and painted cameos.

Clubs All clubs open until at least 2 am, some as late as 5 am. Door charges range from £4 to £10. Some of the long-standing clubs worth investigating include *Zap* (☎ 821588, *Kings Rd Arches*) which is midway between the two piers. *Honey Club* (☎ 07000-446639, *214 Kings Rd Arches*) plays 1970s' and 80s' disco classics on Monday and Thursday. Admission costs £4. It also has guest DJs on Saturday when admission costs £12.

Bar Centro (☎ 206580, 6 Ship St) is a drum 'n' bass club and admission is free. Sunday night is for members only.

The punters at *Casablanca Jazz Club (9 Middle St)* are mainly aged 25 to 35. There's no live music but a DJ plays a range of stuff from 9 pm to 2 am, Tuesday to Saturday. Admission costs £5.

The Pig in Paradise (☎ 779411, Queens Rd) has live music every night, mostly alternative and experimental stuff with some jazz and blues thrown in. Admission costs £2 to £3. There's also *Escape* (☎ 606906, 10 Marine Parade), a laid-back place.

Theatre & Cinema There are a number of theatres in Brighton. The Art Deco *Brighton Dome* (☎ 709709, @ tickets@brighton-dome.org.uk, 29 New Rd), next to the Royal Pavilion, was once the stables and exercise yard of King George IV and is the largest theatre complex in Brighton. The box office is on New Rd.

Other major theatres are *Theatre Royal* (☎ 328488, New Rd), which hosts plays, musicals and operas, and *Komedia Theatre* (☎ 647101, Gardner St, North Laine), which is home to comedy and cabaret as well as fringe theatre.

The enormous *Odeon Cinema* (☎ 207977, corner of King's Rd and West St) shows mainstream films. The *Duke of York's Cinema* (☎ 602503, Preston Circus), about a mile north of North Rd, is the home of art-house films.

Shopping

Just south of North St (and north of the TIC) you'll find **The Lanes**, a maze of narrow alleyways crammed with jewellery, antiques and clothes shops. Some of the best restaurants and bars are around here too.

For second-hand clothes, records and CDs, bong shops, local craft and new age places (and a slightly less touristy feel), explore **North Laine**, a series of streets northwest of The Lanes, including Bond, Gardner, Kensington and Sydney Sts. On Gardner St visit Vegetarian Shoes for animal-friendly footwear. Check out the flea market on Upper Gardner St on Saturday mornings.

Getting There & Away

Brighton is 53 miles from London and bus and train services are fast and frequent.

Bus National Express has an office at the bus station and tickets can also be bought at the TIC. Coaches leave hourly from London Victoria to Brighton (£7 or £5 after 9.30 am).

Stagecoach East Kent (☎ 01227-472082) bus No 711 runs between Brighton and Dover via Hastings and Rye. Stagecoach Coastline (☎ 01903-237661) buses operate along the south coast from Brighton to Portsmouth and Southampton. Tickets for Stagecoach buses can be purchased from the drivers.

Airlinks is a daily coach service to/from all London airports (☎ 020-8844 0824).

Train There are twice-hourly services to Brighton from London Victoria and King's Cross stations (£13.70/14.60 one-way/return, 50 minutes). For £1 on top of the rail fare you can have unlimited travel on Brighton & Hove (☎ 886200) buses for the day. There are hourly services between Brighton and Portsmouth (£11.70, 1 hour 20 minutes) and frequent services to Eastbourne, Hastings, Canterbury and Dover.

Getting Around

Brighton is large and spread out though you'll be able to cover all the sights mentioned in this book on foot if you enjoy walking.

Bus The local bus company is Brighton & Hove (☎ 886200). A day ticket costs £2.60 from the driver. Guide Friday open-top buses (☎ 746205) stop on either side of the pier and take you around the main sights of Brighton. You can hop on and off as much as you like. Tickets are available from the driver and cost £6.50/2.50.

Car All we can say is – don't bother. Parking is a nightmare and driving is even more difficult due to the one-way and pedestrian-only systems. If you decide to bring you car be prepared to pay plenty for parking. To park in any street space you will need a voucher. They can be purchased from garages and various shops around town marked with a tick. It usually costs about £1 per hour but prices do vary.

Taxi Brighton Streamline Taxis (☎ 747474), Yellow Cab Company (☎ 884488) or Radio Cars (☎ 414141) are all worth a try. There is a taxi rank on the junction of East and Market Sts.

Bicycle You can hire from Sunrise Cycles (☎ 748881) by West Pier. Rates start at £10 per day. There are cycle routes along the seafront and throughout the city centre, but traffic is very unpredictable so be careful. For more information on cycling in and around Brighton call ☎ 292475.

West Sussex

West Sussex doesn't offer as many picturesque villages, castles and great houses as East Sussex and Kent. Chichester makes a good base for exploring the rolling hills and the small villages that are tucked away within them.

CHICHESTER
☎ 01243 • pop 28,000

Chichester is the thriving administrative centre for West Sussex and was founded soon after the Roman invasion of AD 43. It lies on the flat meadows between the South Downs and the sea and was once a port.

The foundations for an enormous Roman villa and its beautiful mosaics, survive at Fishbourne on the town outskirts. The Norman castle has long disappeared but the cathedral survives. The City Cross at the centre of town dates from 1501 (built by Bishop Story for the 'comfort of the poore people there'). A substantial part of the town centre is dominated by classic Georgian architecture.

Orientation & Information

Much like Canterbury and Winchester, there's a ring road outside the old city walls and the centre is easily covered on foot.

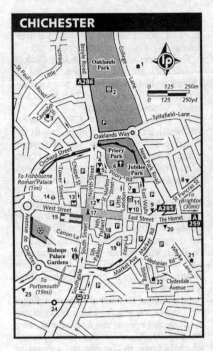

The TIC (☎ 775888, fax 539449, **e** helpline@chichester.gov.uk), 29a South St, opens 9.30 am to 5.30 pm Monday to Saturday, year round; plus 10 am to 4 pm Sundays, Easter to October. The post office is on the corner of Chapel and West Sts.

There are a few public toilets in the centre – next to the Guildhall Museum in Priory Park, off West St near the corner of Tower St and on Friary Lane.

Chichester Cathedral

Work began on the cathedral in 1075 and it has evolved over 900 years. It remains substantially Norman, or Romanesque, and is more harmonious in appearance than most other churches of similar antiquity. Artworks inside range from Norman stone carvings to 20th-century paintings. The building's story is best revealed by an expert: guided tours operate at 11 am and 2.15 pm Monday to Saturday, Easter to October.

Chichester Cathedral (☎ 782595) opens

CHICHESTER

PLACES TO STAY
1 Chichester Institute
3 11 Cavendish Street
5 Ship Hotel
7 Suffolk House Hotel
   & Restaurant
21 Whyke House
22 Encore

PLACES TO EAT
4 Clinches

8 Cafe Metro Brasserie
9 The Nag's Head
10 Little London Indian Tandoori;
    Shepherd's Tea Rooms
12 St Martin's Tea Room
20 Home Bake Cafe
25 Supermarket

OTHER
2 Festival Theatre
6 Church of the Greyfriars

11 Chichester District
    Museum
13 Post Office
14 Toilets
15 Chichester Cathedral
16 Tourist Information Centre
17 City Cross
18 Pallant House
19 Toilets
23 Bus Station
24 Train Station

SOUTH-EASTERN ENGLAND

7 am to 7 pm daily, June to August (to 6.30 pm the rest of the year). It has a fine choir, which sings daily at evensong (5.30 pm Monday to Saturday, 3.30 pm Sunday). Admission to the cathedral is free but there is a suggested donation of £2/1.

Pallant House
Of the many fine Georgian houses in town, Pallant House (☎ 774557), 9 North Pallant, is outstanding. It was built by a wealthy wine merchant who spared no expense. It has since been carefully restored and now houses an excellent collection of 20th-century, mainly British art in the form of paintings, furniture, sculpture and porcelain. Among them are works by Picasso, Moore, Sutherland and Cezanne. There are also a lot of works by a German artist named Feibusch who escaped the Nazis in Germany in 1933. He died in London in 1998 and left the contents of his studio to Pallant House. It opens 10 am to 5 pm Tuesday to Saturday, and noon to 5 pm Sunday. Admission costs £4/free.

Church of the Greyfriars
The Franciscans established a church here in 1269 on the old site of the castle – now Priory Park – in the eastern corner of the town. The simple but quite beautiful building that remains was their choir and now overlooks the local cricket pitch. After dissolution in 1538 the building became the guildhall and later a court of law, where William Blake was tried for sedition in 1804. It opens noon to 4 pm Saturdays, June to September but visits at other times can be made by arrangement (☎ 784683). Admission is free.

Chichester District Museum
Here we learn of the history and the people of West Sussex. The museum (☎ 784683), 29 Little London, opens 10 am to 5.30 pm Tuesday to Saturday. Admission is free.

Special Events
Chichester's Festival Theatre (☎ 781312, e box-office@cft.org.uk), built in 1962, is a striking modern building in parkland to the north of the ring road. Sir Laurence Olivier was the theatre's first director and other famous names to have played here include Ingrid Bergman, Sir John Gielgud, Maggie Smith and Sir Anthony Hopkins. It is now at the centre of an important arts festival, the Chichester Festivities (☎ 780192, e info@chifest.org.uk), held every July.

Places to Stay
Accommodation in Chichester is very expensive for some reason. It pays to look around a bit.

Chichester Institute (☎ 816070, College Lane) rents out rooms from July to September for £23 per person or £32 with bathroom en suite. There are 218 single rooms.

A short walk from the centre, *Encore* (☎ 528271, 11 Clydesdale Ave) charges from £20 per person for a double room with shared bathroom. Singles are not usually taken in.

11 Cavendish St (☎ 527387) is a non-smoking B&B, with one double and one single at £17 per person.

Whyke House (☎ 788767, 13 Whyke Lane) is run by a helpful couple who charge £45 per night for a minimum of two nights in a self-contained flat. Breakfast isn't included.

The attractive *Ship Hotel* (☎/fax 778000, *North St*) dates from the 18th century. It has a good restaurant and is convenient for the theatre. Singles/doubles cost £75/114.

The *Suffolk House Hotel & Restaurant* (☎ 778899, fax 787282, @ suffolkshotel .demon.co.uk, *3 East Row*) is a Georgian house in the heart of Chichester It has a range of comfortable rooms with prices starting at £59/89.

Places to Eat

With its large and varied menu, *The Nag's Head* (☎ 785823, *3 St Pancras St*) is a great place for a meal. There's also an outdoor seating area.

The best curry house in town is the *Little London Indian Tandoori* (☎ 537550, *38 Little London*). Chicken tikka masala costs £8.95 and a vegetarian dish such as sag paneer costs £2.95.

Clinches (☎ 789915, *4 Guildhall St*) is a coffee shop and restaurant and is reasonably close to the theatre. Main courses cost from £6 to £8.

The best place for a cheap feed is *Home Bake Cafe* (☎ 533785, *The Hornet*). Its *yorkie* (Yorkshire pudding), sausage, mash and beans dish is great value at £3.70.

Cafe Metro Brasserie (☎ 788771, *St Pancras St*) does set lunches for £4.50 and there's live jazz on Tuesday evening.

St Martin's Tea Room (☎ 786715, *3 St Martin's St*) and *Shepherd's Tea Rooms* (☎ 774761, *35 Little London*) both serve tea and cakes in comfortable surroundings.

There's a *Waitrose supermarket* near the train station.

Getting There & Away

Chichester is 60 miles from London and 18 miles from Portsmouth.

Bus Chichester is served by Stagecoach Coastline (☎ 01903-237661) bus No 700/701 which runs between Brighton (£3.25, two hours) and Portsmouth (1 hour, half-hourly Monday to Saturday, hourly on Sunday). National Express has a rather protracted daily service from London Victoria (£10.50/£14 one-way/return, three hours).

Train Chichester can be reached easily from London Victoria (£16, 1¾ hours, hourly) via Gatwick airport and Arundel. It's also on the coastline between Brighton (£7.60, 45 minutes) and Portsmouth (£4.50, 25 minutes).

AROUND CHICHESTER

To the south of Chichester lies the popular Chichester Harbour which has been declared an Area of Outstanding Natural Beauty. To the north of the harbour lie the beautiful South Downs, and several unspoilt villages – like East and West Dean and Charlton (6 miles from Chichester).

From Itchenor, you can take a 1½-hour cruise around the harbour with Chichester Harbour Water Tours (☎ 786418). Tours cost £5/2 and include refreshments. To get to Itchenor you could take a 4-mile canal tour from Chichester or you could just enjoy the walk along the towpath. Phone ☎ 771363 or 671051 for details.

Fishbourne Roman Palace & Museum

Discovered in 1960, the palace at Fishbourne (☎ 01243-785859), Salthill Rd, is the largest known Roman residence in Britain. It is believed to have been built around AD 75 for a local king who allied himself to the Romans. It was spectacular in size and luxury – its bathing facilities would still put most contemporary British arrangements to shame. Although all that survives are foundations and some extraordinary mosaic floors and hypocausts, the ruins still convey a vision of 'modern' style and comfort.

The pavilion that shelters the site is an ugly creation, but there are some excellent reconstructions and the garden has been replanted as it would have been in the 1st century. The museum opens year round, with variable hours – 10 am to 5 pm May to September (to 6 pm in August). Admission costs £4.40/2.30.

Bus Nos 11 and 700 leave hourly Monday to Saturday (No 56 on Sunday) from outside Chichester Cathedral and stop at the bottom of Salthill Rd (five minutes' walk away). The museum is 10 minutes' walk from Fishbourne train station, on the line between Chichester and Portsmouth.

Petworth House & Park

Twelve miles north-east of Chichester, Petworth House dates primarily from 1688. The architecture is impressive (especially the western front), but the art collection is extraordinary. JMW Turner was a regular visitor and the house is still home to the largest collection (20) of his paintings outside the Tate Gallery. There are also many paintings by Van Dyck, Reynolds, Gainsborough, Titian and Blake. Petworth is, however, most famous for its park, which is regarded as the supreme achievement of Lancelot (Capability) Brown's natural landscape theory. It's also home to herds of deer.

The house (☎ 01798-342207; NT) opens 1 to 5.30 pm (last admission 4.30 pm) Saturday to Wednesday, April to October. Admission costs £5/2.50. The car park and Pleasure Ground (part of the landscaped grounds which feature a number of classical follies) open noon to 6 pm. The park opens 8 am to sunset throughout the year. Admission is free.

Petworth is 6 miles from the train station at Pulborough. There's a limited bus service (No 1/1A) from the station to Petworth Square (Monday to Saturday).

ARUNDEL
☎ 01903 • pop 4000

Arundel is a lovely little tourist trap that sits on the River Arun at the foot of a romantic-looking castle. Despite its ancient appearance and history, however, most of the town dates from Victorian times. It can easily be explored on foot and you really only need half a day to do so.

The TIC (☎ 882268, fax 882419), 61 High St, opens 9 am to 5 pm weekdays and 10 am to 5 pm weekends, Easter to October; and 10 am to 3 pm daily the rest of the year. *A Walk Around Arundel* is available from here for 25p, although everything to see in the town is pretty well signposted. Next door is **The Museum & Heritage Centre** with a small exhibition showing the history of Arundel.

Arundel Castle (☎ 882173) has been the ancestral home of the dukes of Norfolk for over 700 years. Originally built at the end of the 11th century, it sits at the top of a hill and overlooks the town and the River Arun. It opens noon to 5 pm (last admission 4 pm) Sunday to Friday, April to October. Admission costs £7/4.50.

Set within 10 hectares, the **Waterfowl Park** (☎ 883355), Mill Rd, a mile from the centre, is a nice place to visit for those keen on a spot of bird-watching; others may find it a little lacklustre for the price. It opens 9.30 am to 5.30 pm (to 4.30 in winter) daily. Admission costs £5/3.

Arundel Cathedral (☎ 882297) is a Roman Catholic church built around 1870 in the French Gothic style. It's a stunning piece of architecture and was commissioned by Henry, the 15th duke of Norfolk. It opens 9 am to dusk, daily.

Getting There & Away

Rail is the most efficient way of getting to/from Arundel; it's 55 miles from London, 20 miles from Brighton and 11 miles from Chichester.

Hampshire

Hampshire has plenty to slow down visitors on their way to the West Country. First there's Winchester with its important cathedral; then, the important maritime centres of Portsmouth and Southampton; and, finally, the beautiful New Forest – the largest remaining relict (still original) area of forest in England.

The *Public Transport Map of Hampshire* is very useful and stocked by TICs. Solent Blue Line (01703-226235) buses cover various routes around the county, as do Wilts & Dorset (☎ 01202-673555) buses. For information on all public transport in the county phone ☎ 01962-846992.

WINCHESTER
☎ 01962 • pop 96,000

Winchester is a beautiful cathedral city on the River Itchen, interspersed with water meadows. It has played an important role in the history of England, being both the capital of Saxon England and the seat of the powerful bishops of Winchester from 670. In modern times it's most famous for the magnificent Winchester Cathedral.

The Romans built Venta Bulgarum on the present-day site; part of their defensive wall can still be seen incorporated into a later medieval defence. Alfred the Great and many of his successors, including Canute and the Danish kings, made Winchester their capital, and William the Conqueror came to the city to claim the crown of England. The Domesday Book was also written here. However, much of the present day city dates from the 18th century, by which time Winchester had settled down as a prosperous market centre.

Orientation & Information

Winchester can be covered in a day trip from London. The city centre is compact and easily negotiated on foot. The train station is five minutes' walk north-westwards from the city centre while the bus and coach station is right in the centre, directly opposite the Guildhall and TIC. High St, partly pedestrianised, is the main shopping street. Jewry St borders the western side of the centre and was once part of the city's Jewish quarter.

The TIC (☎ 840500, fax 850348, ℮ tour ism@winchester.gov.uk), the Guildhall on Broadway, opens 10 am to 6 pm Monday to Saturday, year round; plus 11 am to 2 pm Sunday, June to September. Regular guided walking tours cost £3/50p. They operate daily April to October, and on Saturday only between November and March.

The post office is on Middle Brook St and there's a smaller one on Kingsgate St, near the college.

Winchester Cathedral

Winchester's first church, the Old Minster, was built by King Kenwahl in 648. By around 1000, it was one of England's largest Saxon churches, but the Norman Conquest in 1066 brought sweeping changes and the foundations for a new cathedral were laid in 1079. The New Minster was also demolished, around 1110. The completed cathedral was the longest in Britain at the time but it faced problems, in part due to the soggy ground upon which its inadequate foundations were laid.

The Priory of St Swithun was demolished at the time of the dissolution of the monasteries. The cathedral also suffered some damage at the hands of Cromwell's armies during the Reformation. You can still see sword and axe marks on walls and statues and some stained-glass windows were replaced in the 19th century.

Near the entrance in the northern aisle is the **grave of Jane Austen**, who died a stone's throw from the cathedral in 1817. The transepts are the most original part of the cathedral. Note the early Norman rounded arches and painted wooden ceiling.

Crypt tours normally commence from the northern transept but are often suspended if the crypt is flooded. You can get access to the first part of the crypt where a spooky modern sculpture is displayed.

At the end of the presbytery is the magnificent **Great Screen**, built around 1470. During the Reformation the figures in the screen were removed and broken up. The current figures are 1890 replacements, which is how Queen Victoria (2nd level, 3rd row from right of minor figures) has managed to sneak in among the Saxon royalty. **Mortuary chests**, high up under the arches on both sides of the presbytery, contain the bones of Saxon royalty (including King Canute) and bishops.

The retrochoir has a number of **chantry chapels** – small chapels each devoted to one person. Note the unusual skeletal effigies of Bishop Gardiner and, on the other side of the cathedral, Bishop Fox (the godfather of Henry VIII). They wanted their images to be preserved like this to remind onlookers of their own human mortality and frailty.

The **wavy floor** each side of the retrochoir is a reminder of the subsidence problems the cathedral faced.

The southern transept **library** and **Triforium Gallery** house a display of cathedral treasures including damaged figures from the Great Screen and the illuminated 12th-century Winchester Bible. Opening hours are somewhat variable. Admission costs £1/50p.

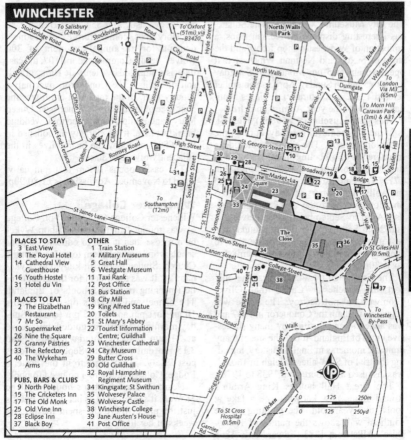

WINCHESTER

SOUTH-EASTERN ENGLAND

PLACES TO STAY
3 East View
8 The Royal Hotel
14 Cathedral View Guesthouse
16 Youth Hostel
31 Hotel du Vin

PLACES TO EAT
2 The Elizabethan Restaurant
7 Mr So
10 Supermarket
26 Nine the Square
27 Granny Pastries
33 The Refectory
40 The Wykeham Arms

PUBS, BARS & CLUBS
9 North Pole
15 The Cricketers Inn
17 The Old Monk
25 Old Vine Inn
28 Eclipse Inn
37 Black Boy

OTHER
1 Train Station
4 Military Museums
5 Great Hall
6 Westgate Museum
11 Taxi Rank
12 Post Office
13 Bus Station
18 City Mill
19 King Alfred Statue
20 Toilets
21 St Mary's Abbey
22 Tourist Information Centre; Guildhall
23 Winchester Cathedral
24 City Museum
29 Butter Cross
30 Old Guildhall
32 Royal Hampshire Regiment Museum
34 Kingsgate; St Swithun
35 Wolvesey Palace
36 Wolvesey Castle
38 Winchester College
39 Jane Austen's House
41 Post Office

Tours of Winchester Cathedral are run by enthusiastic local volunteers at 11 am and 2 pm daily, except Sunday. Sunday services take place at 8, 10 and 11.15 am and Evensong is at 3.30 pm. Evensong is at 5.30 pm, Monday to Saturday. There are tower tours at 2.15 pm on Wednesday, and 11.30 am and 2.15 pm on Saturday. These tours cost £1.50. Crypt tours begin at 10.30 am and 2.30 pm daily, except Sunday. The cathedral (☎ 853137) opens 7.30 am to 6.30 pm daily. It's free to enter but a £2.50/50p donation is requested. Photography is permitted inside.

City Mill
The City Mill (☎ 870057; NT), on the riverbank, was built in 1743 and once ground grain for the local bakers, although there was also a mill on this site in medieval times. The water wheel has been recently restored and there are some pretty gardens out the back. It opens weekends only in March, and 11 am to 4.30 pm Wednesday to Sunday, April to October. Admission costs £1/50p. The building is shared by the youth hostel and when the doors shut the Mill House doubles as the hostel dining room.

Museums

The **City Museum** (☎ 863064), The Square, has interesting displays on Roman ruins, a collection of Winchester shop fronts and the story of Saxon and Norman Winchester. It opens 10 am to 5 pm Monday to Saturday and 2 to 5 pm on Sunday, April to September (closed 1 to 2 pm Saturday). It closes Monday the rest of the year. Admission is free.

Westgate Museum (☎ 869864), High St, is in the old medieval gateway, at one time a debtors' prison. The displays include a macabre set of gibbeting irons, last used to display the body of an executed criminal in 1777. You can also see graffiti carved into the walls by prisoners. It opens 10 am to 5 pm Monday to Saturday and 2 to 5 pm Sunday, April to September (closed between 1 and 2 pm Saturday). It closes Monday the rest of the year, apart from November to January when it closes all week. Admission costs 30p/20p.

The **Great Hall** (☎ 845610) was the only part of Winchester Castle that Oliver Cromwell did not destroy. The castle was begun by William the Conqueror in 1067 and was added to and fortified by many successive kings of England. It was the site of many dramatic moments in English history, including the trial of Sir Walter Raleigh in 1603. It was last used as a court from 1938 to 1978.

The Great Hall houses King Arthur's Round Table, now known to be a fake at 'only' 600 years old. The painting on the southern wall shows the names of Hampshire's MPs from 1283 (Edward I) to 1868 (Queen Victoria). The wonderful steel gates were made in 1981 to commemorate the wedding of Charles and Diana. It opens 10 am to 5 pm daily (to 4 pm at weekends in winter). Admission is free. Part of the Roman wall, built around 200, can be seen in an enclosure near the entrance to the Great Hall.

There are also a number of military museums open to the public: the **Green Jackets Museum** (☎ 828549), the **Royal Hussars Museum** (☎ 828541), the **Light Infantry Museum** (☎ 828550), the **Royal Hampshire Regiment Museum** (☎ 863658) and the **Gurkha Museum** (☎ 828536). Opening hours vary and admission prices range from free to £2.

Wolvesey Castle & Palace

Wolvesey Castle's (☎ 854766; EH) name, so the story goes, comes from a Saxon king's demand for an annual payment of 300 wolves' heads. Commenced in 1107, the castle was completed by Henry de Blois, grandson of William the Conqueror, over half a century later. In the medieval era it was the residence of the bishop of Winchester. Queen Mary I and Philip of Spain had their wedding breakfast here. It was largely demolished in the 1680s and today the bishop lives in the adjacent Wolvesey Palace.

The castle opens 10 am to 6 pm daily, April to November. Admission is £1.80/90p.

Winchester College

Winchester College (☎ 621217) on College St was founded in 1382 by Bishop Wykeham whose idea it was to educate 70 poor scholars and prepare them for a career in the Church. Students are still known as Wykehamists. It was the model for the great public (meaning private) schools of England. The chapel and cloisters open to visitors 10 am to 1 pm and 2 to 5 pm (except Sunday morning). One-hour guided tours leave at 11 am (except Sunday) and 2 and 3.15 pm daily, April to September. Tours cost £2.50/2. They start from the Porter's Lodge, College St; there's no need to book.

Nearby is **Jane Austen's house**, College St. Well, it's referred to as her house, but it's just the place where she spent the last six weeks of her life.

St Cross Hospital

The St Cross Hospital (☎ 851375) was founded in 1132, also by Henry du Blois. It was to provide sustenance and a bed for pilgrims, the poor and the crusaders, who prayed and ate here before taking off to conquer the heathens. The hospital is the oldest charitable institution in the country and is still home to 25 brothers and continues to provide alms. Within the complex you can see the church, the brethren hall, the kitchen and the master's garden. Take the one-mile Water Meadows Walk to get here. It opens 9.30 am to 5 pm Monday to Saturday, April to October; and 10.30 am to 3.30 pm the rest of the year. Admission costs £2/50p which entitles you to the Wayfarer's Dole (a crust of bread and horn of ale).

St Mary's Abbey

Despite consisting of just a few relics in an enclosure off High St, this place has an interesting history. The nunnery was founded by Alfred the Great's wife in 903. In its heyday it was one of the foremost centres of learning in the country. It was rebuilt after the Norman Conquest and lasted well into the 16th century, at which time it was demolished by Henry VIII.

Walking

From the Wolvesley Castle entrance, the **Water Meadows Walk** goes for one mile to the St Cross Hospital. The **Riverside Walk** runs from the castle along the bank of the River Itchen to High St. The walk up to **St Giles Hill** is rewarded by great views over the city. It's at the top of East Hill, half a mile from the castle, and is signposted.

There are also **guided walks** around Winchester's main sights at 11 am and 2.30 pm Monday to Saturday, and 11.30 am Sunday, May to September; 11 am Saturday, November to March; and 2.30 pm Monday to Friday and 11 am and 2.30 pm Saturday, October and April. Tours leave from the TIC and are £2.50/free.

If you prefer you can take the **Phantasm Ghostwalk,** which leaves from outside the cathedral at sunset each day and lasts for one hour. You'll need to book ahead on ☎ 07990-876217.

Places to Stay

B&Bs in Winchester tend not to hang signs out the front. You'll have to get a list from the TIC.

Camping The *Morn Hill Caravan Club* (☎ 869877, *Morn Hill)* site is 3 miles east of the city centre off the A31. There are tent sites for £2.50 plus £3.90 per person.

Hostel The *youth hostel* (☎ 853723, *City Mill, 1 Water Lane)* is in the beautiful 18th-century water mill. It's on the other side of the river from the mill entrance. The nightly cost is £9.25/6.50 for adults/under-18s. The dining room is actually part of the City Mill.

B&Bs & Hotels There are plenty of small B&Bs, most with only one or two rooms.

The friendly *Cathedral View Guesthouse* (☎ 863802, *9a Magdalen Hill)* has nice rooms, a lounge and a sunny breakfast-room conservatory. Singles/doubles cost £30/40 with shared bathroom and £40/50 with bathrooms en suite.

The conveniently located *East View* (☎ 862986, *16 Clifton Hill)* has three small but comfortable en-suite rooms from £35/45.

The *Wykeham Arms* (☎ 853834, *fax 854411, 75 Kingsgate St)*, near the college, has some fine en-suite rooms from £70/80.

You'll find *The Royal Hotel* (☎ 840840, *fax 841582, St Peter St)* right in the heart of the city, down a quiet side street. The interiors are lovely and there's an attractive garden. Rooms cost from £82.50/89.50 but they also have special weekend deals outside summer for two nights including dinner, bed and breakfast.

Hotel du Vin (☎ 841414, *fax 842458,* e *admin@winchester.hotelduvin.co.uk, Southgate St)* is very luxurious and rather decadent – each room has a minibar, VCR and CD player, and costs from £90 to £125. Rooms are sponsored by a French wine house which is why their numbers have been replaced by names such as Courvoisier.

Places to Eat

In a Tudor-style house dating from 1509, *The Elizabethan Restaurant* (☎ 853566, *18 Jewry St)* has a traditional English and French menu and a set three-course dinner costs £10.50.

The bistro at the *Hotel du Vin* (see Places to Stay earlier) has a very good reputation and a main course, such as roast cod with a pea pancake and sauce ravigote, will set you back about £13.50.

The *Wykeham Arms* (see Places to Stay earlier) looks authentically olde Englishe with school desks as tables and tankards hanging from the ceiling. This is an excellent place to eat (and drink), with restaurant dishes from £9 to £13 and a cheaper bar menu; no food is served on Sunday.

For a more formal wine bar and restaurant try *Nine the Square* (☎ *864004, 8 Great Minster St)*. There's excellent homemade pasta for around £6 and interesting dishes, such as roast guinea fowl with garlic and rosemary, for around £14.

Mr So (☎ *861234, 3 Jewry St)* specialises in Peking, Szechuan and Cantonese food and mains cost from £6 to £7.50.

The deservedly popular *Granny Pastries* (☎ *878370, The Square)* sells pies to die for. Try a Thai green curry chicken pie or a Stilton and celery pastie. They also do huge baguettes with all kinds of exotic fillings for around £2.

The Refectory, near the entrance to the cathedral, is recommended. Sandwiches cost from £1.70 and a cream tea is £3.45.

There are several *supermarkets* in the centre of the town. The best is *Sainsbury's* on Middle Brook St.

Entertainment

On the other side of the river from *The Wykeham Arms*, the *Black Boy* (☎ *861754, 1 Wharf Hill)* has the atmosphere of an arthouse pub, if there is such a thing. Bookshelves line the wall and there is an outdoor terrace. A Sunday roast here costs £5.

The Cricketers Inn (☎ *862603, 5 Bridge St)* is dedicated to the game and no matter how hard you try not to talk about cricket, that's just the way the conversation seems to go in this place.

The Old Monk (☎ *855111, 1 High St)* has a pleasant outside seating area overlooking the river and the food is excellent.

Close to the City Museum there's the minute but atmospheric *Eclipse Inn* (☎ *865676, The Square)* and the popular *Old Vine Inn* (☎ *854616, 8 Great Minster St)*.

The small *North Pole* (☎ *878315, 9a Parchment St)* bar is popular with students and has live music on Wednesday, Friday and Saturday evenings.

Getting There & Away

Winchester is 65 miles from London and 15 miles from Southampton.

Bus National Express bus No 32 leaves every two hours from London Victoria via Heathrow (£7/9, two hours), and there are less frequent services to/from Oxford.

Solent Blue Line (01703-226235) bus No 47 runs from Southampton to Winchester (£1.95/3.30, 30 minutes). Stagecoach Hampshire (☎ 01256-464501) has a good network of services linking Salisbury, Southampton, Portsmouth and Brighton. Explorer tickets (£6/4) are good on most Wilts & Dorset (☎ 01202-673555) buses, which serve the region farther to the west, including the New Forest.

Train There are fast links with London Waterloo, the south coast and the Midlands. Trains depart about every 15 minutes from London (£17.30, 1 hour), Southampton (£3.60, 18 minutes) and Portsmouth (£6.70, 1 hour).

Getting Around

Your feet are the best form of transport. There's plenty of day parking within five minutes' walk of the centre or you can use the Park and Ride service which costs £1.50.

If you want a taxi try the rank outside Sainsbury's on Middle Brook St or phone Wintax Taxis on ☎ 854838 or 866208, or Wessex Cars on ☎ 853000.

PORTSMOUTH

☎ 023 • pop 190,000

For much of British history, Portsmouth has been the home of the Royal Navy and it is littered with reminders that this was, for hundreds of years, a force that shaped the world. Portsmouth's major attractions are the historic ships in the Naval Heritage Area but it is still a busy naval base and the sleek, grey killing machines of recent times are also here.

Largely due to bombing during WWII, the city is not a particularly attractive place but Old Portsmouth has some interesting spots, and the adjoining suburb of Southsea is a lively seaside resort.

Orientation

The bus station, Portsmouth Harbour train station and the passenger ferry terminal for

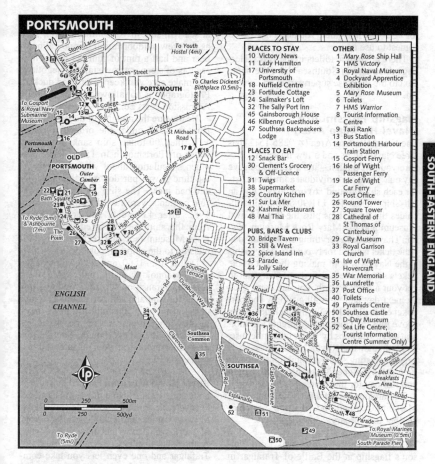

PORTSMOUTH

PLACES TO STAY	OTHER
10 Victory News	1 *Mary Rose* Ship Hall
11 Lady Hamilton	2 HMS *Victory*
17 University of	3 Royal Naval Museum
Portsmouth	4 Dockyard Apprentice
18 Nuffield Centre	Exhibition
23 Fortitude Cottage	5 *Mary Rose* Museum
24 Sailmaker's Loft	6 Toilets
32 The Sally Port Inn	7 HMS *Warrior*
45 Gainsborough House	8 Tourist Information
46 Kilbenny Guesthouse	Centre
47 Southsea Backpackers	9 Taxi Rank
Lodge	13 Bus Station
	14 Portsmouth Harbour
PLACES TO EAT	Train Station
12 Snack Bar	15 Gosport Ferry
30 Clement's Grocery	16 Isle of Wight
& Off-Licence	Passenger Ferry
31 Twigs	19 Isle of Wight
38 Supermarket	Car Ferry
39 Country Kitchen	25 Post Office
41 Sur La Mer	26 Round Tower
42 Kashmir Restaurant	27 Square Tower
48 Mai Thai	28 Cathedral of
	St Thomas of
PUBS, BARS & CLUBS	Canterbury
20 Bridge Tavern	29 City Museum
21 Still & West	33 Royal Garrison
22 Spice Island Inn	Church
43 Parade	34 Isle of Wight
44 Jolly Sailor	Hovercraft
	35 War Memorial
	36 Laundrette
	37 Post Office
	40 Toilets
	49 Pyramids Centre
	50 Southsea Castle
	51 D-Day Museum
	52 Sea Life Centre;
	Tourist Information
	Centre (Summer Only)

the Isle of Wight are conveniently grouped together, a stone's throw from the Naval Heritage Area and the TIC. The quay here is known as The Hard.

Southsea, where the beaches are, as well as most of the accommodation and restaurants, is about 2 miles south of Portsmouth Harbour. Old Portsmouth is on the old harbour known as the Camber, half a mile south of Portsmouth Harbour.

There is not really anything to see in the rest of Portsmouth, so most of your sightseeing and activities are likely to be concentrated along the water's edge.

Information

The TIC (☎ 9282 6722, fax 9282 2693, 🖃 tic@portsmouthcc.gov.uk), The Hard, provides guided tours and an accommodation service. It opens 9.30 am to 5.45 pm daily, June to August. There is another, open during summer only, next to the Sea Life Centre on Clarence Esplanade in Southsea (☎ 9283 2464, fax 9283 7519).

There's a post office, 42 Broad St, in Old Portsmouth and another in Southsea, Palmerston Rd. There are ATMs on Osbourne Rd, Southsea, as well as a laundrette.

Internet access is available at Southsea

Backpackers Lodge (see Places to Stay later) for £2.50 per half-hour. You don't have to be a guest to use it.

There are public toilets in the Naval Heritage Area and in Southsea there are some next to the Waitrose supermarket on Lennox Rd.

Flagship Portsmouth (Naval Heritage Area)

The Naval Heritage Area (☎ 9286 1512) has three classic ships and a few museums. Prepare yourself though – it's a very expensive day out. There are individual admission costs for each ship (around £6) or you can buy an All-Ships ticket for £11.90/8.90 which includes the three ships plus the Royal Naval Museum and the Mary Rose Museum. You don't have to see everything on the same day – the ticket is valid for two years. Maybe this is the Navy's way of making the cost of the tickets seem more justified – if you want to get your money's worth, you can come back the next day and do it all again. A Passport ticket costs £14.90/10.90 and includes all the above plus the Dockyard Apprentice exhibition and a Warships by Water harbour cruise. Even though the Royal Naval Museum is very interesting, the real highlight is HMS *Victory*, so if money's a problem, we suggest you just pay for this tour.

The area opens 10 am to 5.30 pm daily, March to October; and 10 am to 5 pm November to February.

The Ships HMS *Victory* was Lord Nelson's flagship at the Battle of Trafalgar in 1805. Nelson died on board during the battle. The ship carried 850 crew and her greatest speed was 10mph. She was still afloat, though in tatty condition, when she was converted to a museum in 1922.

Exploring HMS *Victory*, and walking in the footsteps of Lord Nelson and his multicultural crew of ruffians and gentlemen, is about as close as you can get to time travel – an extraordinary experience. Admission is by 45-minute guided tour with a timed ticket. The tours are conducted at high speed, though with considerable humour, and none of the gory details of life on the

ship are left out. Astounding facts about life at sea will stay in your mind forever, such as the crew's liquor ration of one gallon of beer and half a pint of rum per day! There are lots of steep, narrow stairs to negotiate, and make sure you keep your head ducked. Photography is not allowed inside the ship. Admission costs £6.50.

Nearby are the remains of the *Mary Rose*. Built in 1509 under the orders of Henry VIII, the 700-tonne ship sank in shallow water off Portsmouth in 1545. There was much speculation about why she sank. At the time it was put down to 'human folly and bad luck'. The ship and her time-capsule contents were raised to the surface in 1982, after 437 years underwater. Finds from the ship are displayed in the Mary Rose Museum (see that section later). Admission to the ship hall costs £5.95.

Dating from 1860, and at the cutting edge of the technology of the time, HMS *Warrior* was a transition ship, as wood was forsaken for iron and sail for steam. The four decks of the ship illustrate life in the navy in the Victorian era. It's not nearly as impressive as the others though. You are free to wander around at your leisure. Admission costs £5.95.

Royal Naval Museum Housed in five separate galleries, this huge museum has an extensive collection of ship models, dioramas of naval battles, and exhibits on the history of the Royal Navy, medals and paintings. Audiovisual displays recreate the Battle of Trafalgar and one even lets you take command of a battleship – see if you can cure the scurvy and avoid mutiny and execution. One gallery is entirely devoted to Lord Nelson and, among many other things, there are personal items from his private ship quarters – life at sea must have been pretty tough for the officers, who had their own wine coolers! Admission costs £6.50.

Mary Rose Museum This is an excellent museum where you can find out about the discovery of the *Mary Rose* and the successful salvage mission through exhibits, audiovisuals and great sound effects. It also recounts the failed salvage attempt made in the late 16th century by two hopeful Venetians and the massive underwater excavation mission of 1965. Considering the length of time the ship was at the bottom of the ocean, it's surprising just how many artefacts were recovered. A 15-minute film about the raising of the *Mary Rose* is shown every half-hour. Admission costs £5.95.

Dockyard Apprentice Exhibition This museum covers everything to do with shipbuilding and dockyard work. Admission (not included with the All-Ships ticket) costs £2.50.

Waterships by Water Cruises To be able to see all the ships, old and new, from a different angle you can take a 40-minute guided cruise around the harbour for £3.50/2. If you have a Passport ticket the cruise is included.

Old Portsmouth to Southsea

On a sunny day it's very pleasant to sit at **The Point**, along the cobbled streets of Old Portsmouth, and sip a pint at one of the pubs while watching the ferries and navy ships go in and out of the harbour.

Only fragments of the original 1180 **Cathedral of St Thomas of Canterbury** in Old Portsmouth remain. The nave and tower were rebuilt around 1690 and more additions and extensions were made in 1703 and between 1938 and 1939. Immediately south of Old Portsmouth is the **Round Tower**, originally built by Henry V, a stretch of old fort walls and the **Square Tower** of 1494.

At the Southsea end of the waterfront there's a cluster of attractions at Clarence Esplanade. The **Sea Life Centre** (☎ 875222) has aquarium displays and opens 10 am to 5 pm daily (11 am to 3 pm November to February). Admission costs £5.50/3.50.

Portsmouth was a major departure point for the Allied D-Day forces in 1944 and the **D-Day Museum** (☎ 827261), Clarence Esplanade, recounts the story of the Normandy landing with the 83m Overlord Embroidery (inspired by the Bayeux Tapestry) and other exhibits. It opens 10 am to 5 pm daily. Admission costs £4.75/2.85.

Southsea Castle (☎ 9282 7261) was built by Henry VIII to protect the town against French invasion. It was altered in the early 19th century to accommodate more guns and soldiers, and a tunnel under the moat. It's said that Henry VIII watched the *Mary Rose* sink from the castle. It opens 10 am to 5.30 pm daily. Admission costs £2/1.20.

The **Pyramids Centre** is a pool and waterslide complex. **South Parade Pier** is a typical British seaside pier with amusements.

Other Things to See & Do

The **Royal Navy Submarine Museum** (☎ 9252 9217) is across the water in Gosport (see Getting Around later). It opens 10 am to 5.30 pm April to October, to 4.30 pm November to March. Admission costs £3.75/2.50. A joint ticket for the **Royal Marines Museum** (☎ 9281 9385) on Barracks Rd (in Portsmouth) costs £4/2.25.

On Museum Rd is the **City Museum** (☎ 9282 7261) which tells the history of Portsmouth through audiovisual displays, reconstructions of various rooms in typical houses from the 17th century to the 1950s, and other exhibits. It opens 10 am to 5.30 pm daily. Admission is free.

Charles Dickens' Birthplace (☎ 9282 7261), 393 Old Commercial Rd, is furnished in a style appropriate to 1812, the year of Dickens' birth, but the only genuine piece of Dickens' furniture is the couch on which he died in 1870! The house opens 10 am to 5.30 pm April to October. Admission is £2/1.20.

Places to Stay

The biggest concentration of cheap B&Bs is in Southsea but the most pleasant area to stay in is The Point in Old Portsmouth. There are lovely views, a historical atmosphere and it's just five minutes' walk to the ships. Unfortunately rooms fill up quickly so book well ahead if you want to be sure of a room.

Hostels The *youth hostel* (☎ 9237 5661, Old Wymering Lane, Cosham) is about 4 miles north of the main sights. The nightly cost is £6.90/10.00 for singles/doubles. Bus Nos 12 and 12A operate to Cosham from the harbour bus station.

Far more convenient is **Southsea Backpackers Lodge** (☎ 9283 2495, 4 Florence Rd, Southsea), which charges £10 for a bed in a dorm and £15/£22 for singles/doubles. The owners are very friendly and have worked at making the place homely and comfortable.

In July and August, the **University of Portsmouth** (☎ 9284 3178) offers B&B accommodation overlooking Southsea Common from £16.75 per person. They also have six-person flats at the Nuffield Centre, St Michael's Rd.

B&Bs & Hotels We can highly recommend the tasteful **Sailmaker's Loft** (☎ 9282 3045, fax 9229 5961, 5 Bath Square). The place is run by a retired merchant seaman who can tell you a lot about Portsmouth. He charges £20/22 per person for rooms with shared bathroom/en-suite bathroom. There are great views across the harbour and one room has its own balcony.

Around the corner, **Fortitude Cottage** (☎ 9282 3748, 51 Broad St) has rooms for £23 per person (with bathroom en suite). **The Sally Port Inn** (☎ 9282 1860, fax 9282 1293, High St) is a well-run 16th-century place with sloping floors. Singles/doubles cost £37/55; there are no en-suite facilities but doubles have showers in the room.

Lady Hamilton (☎ 9287 0505, fax 9283 7366, 21 The Hard) is right by the bus station and Naval Heritage Area, and B&B costs £18/32 or £25/38 for rooms with bathrooms en suite.

Your cheapest bet is **Victory News** (☎ 9282 5158, 11 The Hard) where rooms are £14/24.

In Southsea we can recommend **Gainsborough House** (☎ 9282 2322, 9 Malvern Rd) – very good value at £17 per person (no en suites). **Kilbenny Guesthouse** (☎ 9286 1347, 2 Malvern Rd) is very similar in standard and costs £16/35 for clean, large rooms. Rooms with bathrooms en suite are a few pounds dearer.

Places to Eat
Osborne Rd and Palmerston Rd are the main restaurant strips in Southsea. **Kashmir Restaurant** (☎ 9282 2013, 91 Palmerston Rd) is relatively cheap and you can get a prawn vindaloo for £4.30, chicken tikka for £5.75 and chapati for 75p. **Sur La Mer** (☎ 9287 6678, 69 Palmerston Rd) is a French bistro/cafe with snacks from £2.95 to £3.50 and mains from £9.20 to £13.

Country Kitchen (☎ 9281 1425, 59a Marmion Rd) is a wholefood restaurant, open during the day from Monday to Saturday. A two-course lunch with a soft drink costs £4.95.

For a good Thai restaurant try **Mai Thai** (☎ 9273 2322, 27a Burgoyne Rd), just off South Parade. A four-course meal is £11, chicken coconut curry costs £4.95.

The **Lady Hamilton** (see Places to Stay earlier) is a large pub that serves roast lunch for £4.95.

Twigs (☎ 9282 8316, 39 High St) is a small coffee shop with sandwiches, baguettes and baps from £1.80 to £3.30.

The **Snack Bar** (The Hard), near the bus station, has tasty, greasy morsels from 80p.

In Old Portsmouth there's **Clement's Grocery & Off-Licence** (High St) and a **Waitrose supermarket** (Marmion Rd) in Southsea.

Entertainment
On a warm summer's evening there can be no better place for a drink than outside the **Still & West** (☎ 9282 1567, 2 Bath Square) or the **Spice Island Inn** (☎ 9287 0543, 65 Broad St) on The Point. **Bridge Tavern** (☎ 9275 2992, 54 East St), overlooking the Camber, is a real old salts' hangout and is also very popular.

Along Clarence Parade in Southsea there's a variety of seedy discos, clubs and pubs, such as the **Parade** (☎ 9282 4838) and the **Jolly Sailor** (☎ 9282 6139), both overlooking the common.

Getting There & Away
Portsmouth is 75 miles south-west of London.

Bus There are numerous National Express buses from London, some via Heathrow airport (£9/11 one-way/return, 2½ hours). There's also a daily service between Brighton and Portsmouth (£6.75). One bus a day heads westwards as far as Penzance in Cornwall, via Plymouth (£30 and £35 on Saturdays in July and August, 11 hours).

Stagecoach Coastline (☎ 01903-237661) bus No 700 also runs between Brighton and Portsmouth (£3.20) and on to Southampton via Chichester (every 30 minutes Monday to Saturday, hourly on Sunday). Stagecoach No 69 runs to Winchester (every two hours on Sunday).

Train There are over 40 trains daily from London Victoria and Waterloo station (£17.80, 1½ hours). There are hourly services to Brighton (£11.70, one hour 20 minutes), and to Winchester (£6.70, one hour). There are also trains to Chichester (£4.50, 25 minutes, three hourly).

For the ships at Flagship Portsmouth get off at the final stop, Portsmouth Harbour.

Boat There are a number of ways of getting to the Isle of Wight from Portsmouth. For information see Isle of Wight later in the chapter.

Condor Ferries (☎ 0105-761555) runs a car-and-passenger service from Portsmouth to Jersey and Guernsey (five hours) but these trips are very expensive. It costs around £76/38 (adult/child) return. Don't even consider taking your car. P&O Ferries (☎ 0870 242 4999) sails twice a week to Bilbao in Spain and daily to Cherbourg (five to six hours, two hours longer at night) and Le Havre in France. Brittany Ferries (☎ 0870 901 2400) has overnight services to St Malo, Caen (six hours) and Cherbourg in France. For more information, look at the Web site at www.brittanyferries.co.uk. The continental Ferryport is north of Flagship Portsmouth.

Getting Around

Local bus No 6 operates between the Portsmouth Harbour bus station, right beside the train station, and South Parade Pier in Southsea. Bus Nos 17 or 6 will take you from the station to Old Portsmouth.

Ferries shuttle back and forth between The Hard and Gosport (£1.10, bicycles travel free). For a taxi try MPS Taxis in Southsea on ☎ 8261 1111.

NEW FOREST
☎ 023 • pop 160,456

The New Forest is not a national park, but it has been designated an Area of Outstanding Natural Beauty. Outside the Highlands of Scotland this is the largest area of relatively natural vegetation in Britain. It's been that way since 1079 when William the Conqueror founded the area as a royal hunting ground.

The New Forest covers 145 sq miles, of which 105 sq miles is forest and heathland. The rest is occupied by villages and farmland. It's a pretty area to drive through but even better when you get off the roads and onto the cycling and walking tracks.

Information

The Lyndhurst TIC (☎ 8068 9000, fax 8028 4404), High St, next to the main car park, opens 10 am to 6 pm daily (to 5 pm November to February). It sells a wide variety of information on the New Forest including cycling maps ranging from £2 to £3.50, a map of the area showing walking tracks for

New Forest Ponies

One of the first things you will notice as you travel into the New Forest are the ponies. While much of the rest of England was being fenced off and ploughed to grow crops and graze livestock, the New Forest area remained relatively untouched due to the unsuitability of the soil for agriculture. The ponies were effectively forced into the area. Even though they are wild, each one of the 3000-odd ponies is owned by a *commoner* who has the right to graze their stock on the open forest. The Agisters, as these people are known, pay for grazing rights.

Visitors are requested not to feed the ponies; they are wild animals and feeding will attract them onto the roads. To protect the ponies, as well as cyclists and walkers, there is a 40mph speed limit on unfenced roads. If you come across an injured pony phone Lyndhurst Police on ☎ 023-8028 2813 and state the location and, if possible, the registration number of any vehicle involved in an accident. You should try to stay with the animal (but don't touch it) to protect it from further injury.

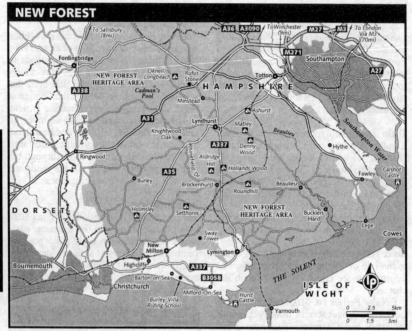

NEW FOREST

£1.50, a more comprehensive Collins map for £5.99 and a free camping and caravanning guide. It also sells the Ordnance Survey (OS) map (No 22, £5.95) which covers the area in greatest detail.

Places to Stay

You cannot simply camp anywhere you like, but there are a number of commercial camp sites detailed in a free brochure from the TIC.

There are numerous B&Bs in New Forest towns but we recommend you use Lyndhurst as a base. The Lyndhurst TIC makes free bookings. We can highly recommend *South View B&B* (☎ 8028 2224, Gosport Lane, Lyndhurst), with its friendly atmosphere and lovely dog, for £22 per person. *The Fox & Hounds* (☎ 8028 2098, 22 High St, Lyndhurst) is a 400-year-old coaching inn. Double rooms go for £50 per night, with breakfast. It's a nice place for a beer and a game of pool too.

Getting There & Away

Southampton and Bournemouth bracket the New Forest and there are regular bus services from both to New Forest towns. Wilts & Dorset (☎ 01202-673555) bus Nos 56 and 56a run twice hourly from Monday to Saturday from Southampton to Lyndhurst (£2.50/4.25 one-way/return).

Trains run every half-hour from London Waterloo station via Brockenhurst (£22.70, 1½ hours) to Bournemouth, Poole and Weymouth. There is a Brockenhurst–Lymington connection known as the Lymington Flyer.

White Horse Ferries (☎ 8084 0722) operates a service from Southampton to Hythe every half-hour (£3.60 return, 12 minutes).

Getting Around

The New Forest can be explored in a variety of ways.

Bus Busabout tickets offer unlimited travel on main bus lines for seven days and cost

£19/10. The Solent Blueline (☎ 8022 6235) X1 service goes through New Forest taking the Bournemouth–Burley–Lyndhurst–Southampton route. Wilts & Dorset (☎ 01202-673555) bus No 56 links Lyndhurst, Brockenhurst and Lymington.

Bicycle The New Forest is a great place to cycle and there are several rental shops. AA Bike Hire (☎ 8028 3349) is at Fern Glen, Gosport Lane in Lyndhurst, and charges £8/42 per day/week. Rentabike in Brockenhurst (☎ 01590-681876) offers free local delivery from 8 am to 8 pm and charges £9 per day. The New Forest Cycle Experience (☎ 01590-624204), 2–4 Brookley Rd, Brockenhurst, charges £9.50/53.20. You can pick up cycle route maps from TICs and bicycle shops.

Horse This is a nice way to explore the New Forest but we're not talking about saddling up one of the wild ponies here. There are a couple of trail riding set-ups where you can arrange a one- or two-hour ride. Sandy Balls (honestly!) is at Godshill in Fordingbridge (☎ 01425-654114), and the Burley-Villa School of Riding (☎ 01425-610278) is off the B3058, just south of New Milton. Both places welcome beginners.

Beaulieu & National Motor Museum

If you go to New Forest, a visit to Beaulieu (pronounced bew-lee) is a must. Beaulieu Abbey was another victim of Henry VIII's great monastic land-grab in the mid-16th century. The king sold the 3200 hectare estate to the ancestors of the Montague family around 1538.

It is Lord Montague's collection of 250 vehicles which makes the **Motor Museum** one of the biggest tourist attractions in the country. There are cars, motorbikes and buses, as well as a number of land-speed record-holders, such as the jet-powered Bluebird which broke the land-speed record (403mph) in 1964. This is not just a place for rev heads.

The **Palace House** was once the abbey gatehouse and is an odd combination of 14th-century Gothic and 19th-century Scottish Baronial architecture, as converted by Baron Montague in the 1860s. Unlike other manor homes you might visit, this place really feels like a home and therefore exudes a certain warmth.

The **abbey** was founded in 1204 when King John gave the land to the Cistercian monks. It was one of the first buildings in England to incorporate Gothic pointed arches. In keeping with the Cistercian credo, there are no elaborate decorative elements, such as stained glass, and the interiors are austere and cold. There is an excellent exhibit on everyday life in the monastery, and a plaque in the courtyard tells us that the European Resistance Movement used the abbey as a training camp during WWII.

Beaulieu (☎ 01590-612345) opens 10 am to 6 pm daily, Easter to September (to 5 pm the rest of the year). The Palace House opens at 11 am. Admission to the whole complex is pretty expensive at £9.25/6.75 (or £29.50 for a family of four), but it's definitely worth it.

Getting There & Away Stagecoach Hampshire (☎ 01256-464501) bus No 66/X66 runs to Beaulieu from Winchester via Lyndhurst. You can also get here from Southampton by taking a ferry to Hythe and catching bus No 112 or X9. Solent Blue Line (☎ 01703-226235) buses also run here from various towns in New Forest.

Isle of Wight

☎ 01983 • pop 125,466

Lying only a couple of miles off the Hampshire coast, the Isle of Wight makes a popular day trip from the mainland (try to avoid summer weekends) although there's enough of interest to justify a stay of more than a day. The coastal towns are full of character and the fish and chips down this way are second to none. Over a third of the island has been designated an Area of Outstanding Natural Beauty and there are 25 miles of clean and unspoiled beaches. The best way to see the island is on foot or by bicycle.

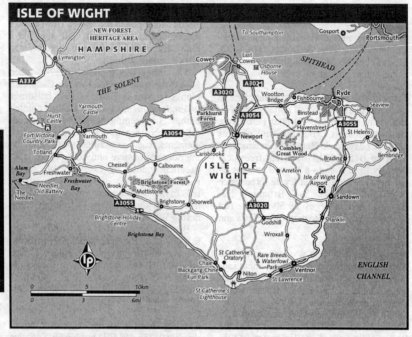

ISLE OF WIGHT

There is a 62-mile cycleway and 500 miles of walking paths. You can pick up the *Official Pocket Guide* to the island from TICs.

COWES & OSBORNE HOUSE

Located at the northern tip of the island, Cowes is a hilly, Georgian harbour town. This is a major yachting centre and the late-July/early-August Cowes Week is an important international yachting event. Naturally, the town has a maritime museum.

Since its appearance in the film *Mrs Brown*, **Osborne House** (☎ 200022) has become English Heritage's most visited attraction. The house was built between 1845 and 1851 and Queen Victoria died here in 1901. Osborne House has an antipodean connection: Victoria's Government House near Melbourne's Botanic Gardens is a copy, built in 1872. The house is in East Cowes which is separated from the rest of the town by the River Medina, and linked by a chain ferry. It opens 10 am to 5 pm daily, mid-March to

October. At other times it opens from 10 am to 2.30 pm Sunday, Monday, Wednesday and Thursday for guided tours only (£5/3). Admission costs £6.90/3.50.

RYDE

Victorian Ryde is the most important entry point to the island and the busiest of the resort towns. There is a TIC (☎ 562905, fax 567610) on Western Esplanade. At **St Cecilia's Abbey**, Appley Rise, you can hear Gregorian chants by Benedictine nuns during Mass at 9.15 am daily (at 10 am Sunday).

About 5 miles from Ryde, at the easternmost tip of the island, is **Bembridge**. There's a Shipwreck Centre & Maritime Museum (☎ 872223) open 10 am to 5 pm daily, April to October. Admission costs £2.50/1.35. The only **windmill** on the island (☎ 873945; NT), dating from 1700, can also be seen here. The three-storey windmill exhibits artefacts. Opening hours are 10 am to 5 pm (last admission 4.30 pm) Sunday to Friday,

April to October, and daily in July and August. Admission costs £1.50/75p. A fine five-mile coastal walk leads from Bembridge to Sandown.

VENTNOR

Ventnor is a typical fishing town that doesn't try too hard, nor does it need to. There is a real peace here which is very appealing. One mile south of the town, off the A3055, is the **Rare Breeds & Waterfowl Park** (☎ 852582) which is home to a large array of rare and not so rare farm animals, including llamas, African cattle and Falabella miniature horses. It opens 10 am to 5.30 pm daily from late March to late October. Admission costs £3.70/2.20 but is free for under-5s. Bus Nos 7, 7A and 31 will get you there from Ryde or Ventnor.

SOUTH COAST

The south coast of the Isle of Wight, from Ventnor to Alum Bay, is the quietest stretch of the island circuit. The southernmost point of the island is marked by **St Catherine's Lighthouse** which was built between 1837 and 1840. Looking like a stone rocket ship, **St Catherine's Oratory** is a lighthouse dating from 1314 and marks the highest point on the island. A couple of miles farther west from here is the **Blackgang Chine Fun Park** which is worth stopping at if you have a couple of kids in tow.

WEST WIGHT

Henry VIII's last great fortress was **Yarmouth Castle** (☎ 760678). Its facade, which is all that's left of it now, dates from 1547. It opens 10 am to 6 pm April to September (to 6 pm in October). Admission costs £2.10/1.10.

One mile west of Yarmouth off the A3054 is **Fort Victoria Country Park** which is home to an aquarium, a marine museum, a planetarium and the Sunken History Exhibition. Admission costs £1.50/80p to each, but only the exhibitions warrant this fee.

The **Needles**, at the western tip of the island, are three towering rocks which rise out of the sea to form the postcard symbol of the island. At one time there was another rock,

a 37m-high spire which really was needle-like, but it collapsed into the sea in 1764.

The road and bus service to this end of the island ends at **Alum Bay**, where there's a few unappealing souvenir shops and a chair lift down to the beach. A walking path leads a mile to the **Needles Old Battery** (☎ 754772; EH), a fort established in 1862 and used as an observation post during WWII. There's a 60m tunnel leading down through the cliff to a searchlight lookout. The fort opens 10.30 am to 5 pm Sunday to Thursday, April to October, and daily during July and August. Admission costs £2.50/1.60. Buses run between Alum Bay and the battery hourly (every half-hour in peak season).

PLACES TO STAY

There are numerous camp sites and accommodation listings available from TICs, or phone the TIC booking service (☎ 813813). For something different you might want to stay at the *Xoron Floatel* (☎ 874596, *Embankment Rd*) in Bembridge. This houseboat is very clean and surprisingly roomy. En-suite rooms cost £20 per person.

We can highly recommend *The Spy Glass Inn* (☎ 855338, *The Esplanade*) in Ventnor, situated above the beach with great views of the town. Accommodation is in self-contained flats above the hotel and costs £50 for two people (no kids, no dogs). The atmosphere in the pub downstairs is charged and friendly, and there's live music most nights.

The most scenic place to stay is *Brighstone Holiday Centre* (☎/fax 740244) which is on the A3055, 6 miles east of Freshwater. This caravan park and B&B, perched high on the cliffs overlooking the island's most stunning stretch of coastline, is also close to walking trails. Tents cost £5 per night, caravans are £10, self-catering cabins cost from £126 per week for two people and B&B (continental breakfast) is £18 per person.

The only really cheap place to stay around West Wight is the *Totland Bay Youth Hostel* (☎ 752165, *Hirst Hill*) which charges £11.00/7.75 per night.

GETTING THERE & AWAY

Wightlink (☎ 0990 827744) operates a passenger ferry from The Hard in Portsmouth to Ryde pier (15 minutes) and a car-and-passenger ferry (35 minutes) to Fishbourne. They run about every half-hour (£7.40 day return). Car fares start at £46.30 for a day return. Check out the Wightlink Web site at www.wightlink.co.uk.

Hovertravel (☎ 023-9281 1000) hovercrafts zoom back and forth between Southsea (near Portsmouth) and Ryde (£8.60 day return, 10 minutes).

Red Funnel (☎ 023-8033 4010) operates car ferries between Southampton and East Cowes (£7 return, from £46 with car, 55 minutes) and high-speed passenger ferries between Southampton and West Cowes (£7/12 one-way/return, 10 minutes). The Wightlink car ferry between Lymington (in the New Forest) and Yarmouth costs £6.80 for passengers and £46.30 for a cars. The trip takes 30 minutes and ferries run every half-hour. Children travel for half-price on all these services.

GETTING AROUND
Bus & Train

Southern Vectis (☎ 827005) operates a comprehensive bus service around the island. They have an office in Cowes, 32 High St. Buses circumnavigate the island hourly, and run between the towns on the eastern side of the island about every 30 minutes. Trains run twice hourly from Ryde to Shanklin and the Isle of Wight Steam Railway branches off from this line at Havenstreet and goes to Wootton.

Rover Tickets give you unlimited use of buses and trains for £6.25 for a day, £9.95 for two days and £25.50 for a week.

Bicycle

Bicycles can be rented in Cowes, Freshwater Bay, Ryde, Sandown, Shanklin, Ventnor and Yarmouth. Offshore Sports (☎ 866269), 19 Orchard Leigh Rd, Shanklin, charges £5 for five hours, £9 for a day; there are branches in Cowes (☎ 290514) and Sandown (☎ 401515). Wavells (☎ 760219) in The Square, Yarmouth, charges £10 for a day.

Essex

Despite being one of the largest counties in England, Essex lacks any vital sights. It boasts a long coastline, a number of seaside resorts and the oldest recorded town in England but it doesn't attract the tourist numbers of other south-eastern counties. If you find yourself in Essex (which will happen if you arrive at Stansted Airport or Harwich ferry terminal) you should certainly try to visit the medieval villages of Thaxted and Saffron Walden, and the countryside around Dedham, which inspired the painter Constable. If you want to explore a typical, tacky English seaside resort then head for Southend-on-Sea.

The good thing about Essex is that, compared to the rest of south-eastern England, it's very cheap. For travel information phone ☎ 0345 000333.

SOUTHEND-ON-SEA
☎ 01702 • pop 172,300

Spreading itself along the Thames Estuary, Southend is not only the most popular seaside resort in Essex, it's also the county's largest town. At just under 50 miles from central London, it's an appealing holiday spot for many of London's East Enders. It has the longest pleasure pier in the world and there's a major focus on entertainment, though this usually translates into fun parks, amusement arcades, tattoo parlours and sleazy nightspots. Southend does have more cerebral attractions however and there's a busy programme of plays and concerts throughout the year.

More recently Southend has taken on the task of housing many Eastern European refugees. What this means for the visitor is that a large number of guesthouses and a few seafront hotels are now boarding houses, so don't be surprised if you're turned away from a few places.

Orientation & Information

Southend is large and spread out. The central shopping and business district is on and around High St. East of the pier is Marine Parade which leads to Thorpe Bay where you'll find the quieter and cleaner stretches of sandy

SOUTH-EASTERN ENGLAND

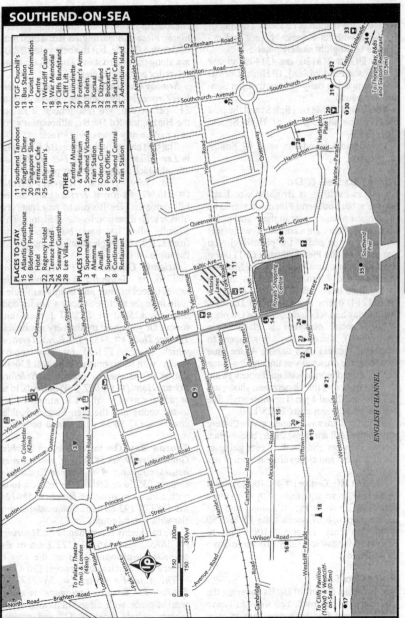

SOUTHEND-ON-SEA

PLACES TO STAY
15 Atlantis Guesthouse
16 Bideford Private
   Hotel
22 Regency Hotel
24 Terrace Hotel
26 Seaway Guesthouse
28 Lee Villas

PLACES TO EAT
3 Supermarket
4 Mamma
   Amalfi
7 Supermarket
8 Continental
   Restaurant

11 Southend Tandoori
12 Kingfisher Diner
20 Singapore Sling
23 Terrace Cafe
25 Fisherman's
   Wharf

OTHER
1 Central Museum
   & Planetarium
2 Southend Victoria
   Train Station
5 Odeon Cinema
6 Post Office
9 Southend Central
   Train Station

10 TGF Churchill's
13 Bus Station
14 Tourist Information
   Centre
17 Westcliff Casino
18 War Memorial
19 Cliffs Bandstand
21 Cliff Lift
27 Laundrette
29 Forester's Arms
30 Toilets
31 Kursaal
32 Dizzyland
33 Brockett's
34 Sea Life Centre
35 Adventure Island

Cheltenham—Road

Honiton—Road

Southchurch—Avenue

Southchurch—Avenue

Woodgrange Drive

Ambleside Drive

Kilworth Avenue

York—Road

Queensway

Pleasant—Road

Hartington—Road

Hartington
Place

Marine—Parade

Eastern Esplanade

To Thorpe Bay B&Bs
and Stassons Restaurant
(0.5mi)

Queensway

Herbert—Grove

Chancellor—Road

Royals Shopping Centre

Victoria
Lanes

Baltic Ave

York Road

Heygate Ave

Terrace

Southend Pier

ENGLISH CHANNEL

Whitegate—Road

Tylers Avenue

Chichester—Road

Warrior Square South

Queensway

Essex—Street

Southchurch—Road

High—Street

Royal

Weston—Road

Clarence Street

Cliftown—Road

Cliftown—Parade

Western—Esplanade

To Colchester
(42mi)

Victoria Avenue

Baxter—Avenue

Queensway

London—Road

Boston—Avenue

Princess—Street

Queens—Road

Cordon—Place

Ashburnham—Road

Cambridge—Road

Alexandra—Road

Clifftown—Parade

Park—Street

Hamlet—Road

Wilson—Road

Westcliff—Parade

To Palace Theatre
(1mi) & London
(48mi)

London—Road

Park—Terrace

Park—Road

North—Road

Brighten—Road

A13

To Cliffs Pavilion
(100yd) & Westcliff-
on-Sea (0.5mi)

0   150   300m
0   150   300yd

beach. Sitting atop the hill west of the pier is Westcliff, the upmarket residential district of Southend with its Regency homes and expensive but slightly shabby hotels.

The TIC (☎ 215120, fax 431449, ⓔ marketing@southend.gov.uk), 19 High St, opens 9.30 am to 5 pm daily (11 am to 4 pm Sunday in August).

You'll find ATMs on High St and the post office is on the corner of High St and Queens Rd.

Launderama laundrette is at 87 Southchurch Ave.

Things to See & Do

It's not as exciting as Brighton's or Eastbourne's, but **Southend Pier** can claim to be the longest pleasure pier in the world at 1.3 miles long. There are a couple of restaurants and a bar at the end of the pier which you can reach on the **Pier Railway** (£2/1) or on foot. The pier opens 8 am to 5 pm Monday to Friday (to 7 pm at weekends and to 10 pm June to August). The **Pier Museum** (☎ 611214) opens 11 am to 5 pm Tuesday, Wednesday and weekends, May to October.

The **Central Museum & Planetarium** (☎ 215640), Victoria Ave, is adjacent to Southend Victoria train station. At the time of writing the museum was undergoing some expansion and reorganisation. It opens 10 am to 5 pm daily and the planetarium shows are at 11 am and 2 and 4 pm. The museum is free but the planetarium costs £2.25/1.60.

Victorian Lanes is an open market where stallholders sell antiques, shoes, bric-a-brac, clothes, flowers and food. It gets going at about 9.30 am and closes around 5 pm (4 pm in winter).

The **Sea Life Centre** (☎ 462400), Eastern Esplanade, is an aquarium with everything from starfish to sharks. It's small and not exciting enough to warrant the £5.25/3.50 admission cost. It opens 10.30 am to 3.30 pm Monday to Friday (10 am to 5 pm at weekends).

Places to Stay

Southend has dozens of B&Bs covering the entire area of the town. You shouldn't have any problems finding somewhere to stay, though weekends in summer are busy. The cheaper B&Bs are concentrated along Hartington Place and Hartington Rd, which runs off Marine Parade, but the best value B&Bs are along the seafront in Thorpe Bay, about 1½ miles east of the pier.

Seaway Guesthouse (☎ 615901, *15 Herbert Grove*) is clean and very good value at £15 per person. We recommend it before the Hartington Rd B&Bs, although it's not in a particularly interesting street.

The best choice of the cheap B&Bs around is *Lee Villas* (☎ 317214, *1–2 Hartington Place*) which charges £15 per person.

The very central *Regency Hotel* (☎ 340747, *18 Royal Terrace*) sits on the hill above the pier. It's run by an expat New Yorker with a passion for naval history. This friendly place has basic but large rooms from £20/35 for singles/doubles and £55 for the triple en-suite room.

Atlantis Guesthouse (☎ 332538, *fax 392736, 63 Alexandra Rd*) is one of the newer places in town and is only a minute's walk from the station. Spacious singles/doubles are £25/40 or £25/50 for en-suite rooms. Or you could try the very reasonable *Terrace Hotel* (☎ 348143, *8 Royal Terrace*) which charges £21/34 for nice rooms. Rooms with bathrooms en suite cost £30/40.

One of the cheaper options is *Bideford Private Hotel* (☎ 345007, *7 Wilson Rd*), in an attractive part of town; it's 10 minutes' walk to the centre and the pier. Singles/doubles cost from £17.50/35 with shared bathroom.

Thorpe Bay The tasteful, clean *Pebbles Guesthouse* (☎/fax 582329, ⓔ *pebbles.guesthouse@virgin.net, 190 Eastern Esplanade*) charges £35/50 or £60 for the seaview room with a balcony. *Beaches Hotel* (☎ 586124, *fax 588377, 192 Eastern Esplanade*) is similar with tasteful rooms for £25/50.

We can highly recommend *The Moorings* (☎ 587575, *fax 586791, 172 Eastern Esplanade*), a pleasant B&B on the way to Thorpe Bay. Singles/doubles cost £30/42.50.

The Camelia Hotel (☎ 587917, *fax 585704, 178 Eastern Esplanade*) is an upmarket place with clean, luxurious rooms which include satellite TV and phones.

Singles/doubles cost £46/60, less for a stay of two nights or more.

Places to Eat

Southend has lots of cafes, fish and chip shops and little Italian restaurants. You'll find most of these places in the sidestreets off High St and along the seafront.

Mamma Amalfi (☎ 341353, 5–6 London Rd) is a modern, sophisticated Italian restaurant where Chardonnay is consumed in great quantities. The two-course lunch is good value at £6.25.

Continental Restaurant (☎ 330175, 75 Queens Rd) is a rather odd place; or maybe it's just that it's very old fashioned. The menu covers Spanish, Italian and German dishes and the lacy curtains and table clothes give the place a homely feel. Dishes are very good value at around £5, or £8 for steaks.

The modern-looking *Singapore Sling (☎ 431313, 12 Clifftown Parade)* is a restaurant and bar serving Chinese, Japanese, Malaysian and Thai food. Prices vary depending upon the cuisine but most main courses cost under £7.

Southend Tandoori (☎ 463182, 36 York Rd) is an Indian restaurant with curries from £3.50 and Malayan prawns for £4.50. Their three-course lunch for £4.25 is amazing value.

Slassors (☎ 614880, 145 Eastern Esplanade) has won various food awards and is very well known locally. It serves mainly seafood dishes in its maritime, gingham-decked surroundings. Starters cost from £2.95 to £5 and mains are £8.50 to £11. You can bring your own (BYO) wine.

Good food at very good prices is served at the *Kingfisher Diner (☎ 610306, 34 York Rd)*. Burgers at this greasy spoon cost £2.40, fish and chips cost £3.50 and kids meals only cost £1.70.

Fisherman's Wharf (☎ 346773, Western Esplanade) claims to have the best fish and chips in town, and they're not wrong. Huge fillets of juicy, delicate fish, chips, salad and a variety of condiments will cost you about £7. There's an extensive seafood menu and it's licensed.

Popular and reasonably priced, *Terrace Cafe (☎ 344158, 15 Royal Terrace)* has an alfresco feel. Bagels and baguettes cost £1.75, omelette and salad £4.25, and fish and chips £4.

There is a Sainsbury's supermarket *(London Rd)* and a Tesco *(High St)*.

Entertainment

Kids will probably want to go to *Adventure Island (☎ 468023)* on either side of the pier. Admission is free but you pay for each ride. There's also *Dizzyland*, an amusement park on the corner of Southchurch Ave and Eastern Esplanade, and *Kursaal (☎ 322322)*, across the road, a rather disappointing amusement arcade with 10-pin bowling (£3.70 per game), bars and restaurants. For a movie try the *Odeon Cinema (☎ 0870 5050007, corner of London Rd and High St)*.

The huge and rather rowdy *TGF Churchills (☎ 617866, Tylers Ave)* has a number of different bars as well as a nightclub, but the place does feel a bit like a meatmarket. For night owls there's the rundown *Brockett's (☎ 559137, Eastern Esplanade)* opposite the Sea Life Centre. DJs play mainly 50s, 60s and 70s music, and there's the occasional live act. *Forester's Arms (☎ 467927, 65 Marine Parade)*, behind Dizzyland, has a DJ and jazz is the call of the day.

The *Cliffs Bandstand* on Clifftown Parade has concerts from time to time. Phone ☎ 343605 for information or ask at the TIC. You can catch the Cliff Lift up to Clifftown Parade from Western Esplanade. The *Cliffs Pavilion (☎ 351135, Westcliff Parade)* presents concerts, plays and musicals, as does the *Palace Theatre (☎ 342564, London Rd)*.

You can try your luck at the *Westcliff Casino (☎ 352919)* on Western Esplanade.

Getting There & Away

From London, Greenline (☎ 020-8668 7261) bus No 721 runs half-hourly from Bulleid Way, opposite Victoria coach station to York Rd bus station in Southend (£4.50 return, two hours 40 minutes).

There are several trains each hour from either London Liverpool St to Southend Victoria station or from London Fenchurch St to Southend Central station.

Getting Around

Distances are quite large in Southend and it's difficult to cover everything on foot. Local bus companies are Arriva (☎ 442444) and First Thamesway (☎ 01245-262828) which are both based at the bus station on York Rd. The Southend Day Rover ticket gives you unlimited travel in and around Southend on First Thamesway or First Eastern National Buses (☎ 01245-256159) for £2.75/1.80.

If you need a taxi try Southend Taxis (☎ 334455) or ARC Taxis (611611).

COLCHESTER

☎ 01206 • pop 142,000

Britain's oldest recorded town, Colchester, was founded by the Roman emperor Claudius in AD 49. It was the capital of Roman Britain when London was just a minor trading post. It's a fairly interesting place with a castle, several museums and the remains of Roman walls, but a half-day is all you'll need to explore the sights.

Orientation & Information

There are two train stations – most services stop at North station, about half a mile north of the town centre. The bus/coach station (☎ 282645) is in the centre of town, near the TIC and the castle.

The TIC (☎ 282920, fax 282924), 1 Queen St, opens 9.30 am to 6 pm Monday to Saturday (10 am to 5 pm on Sundays and weekdays during winter). There are guided walking tours (£2.50/1.25) of the town at 11 am daily, June to September, but times may vary so phone first. You can also take an open-top bus tour from mid-July to September for £4.95/2.95 (get tickets at the TIC).

There's a post office on North Hill and another on Longe Wyre St. Banks and ATMs can be found on Culver St West.

Things to See & Do

Historical **Colchester Castle** (☎ 282939) was built by William I on the foundations of a Roman fort. Construction began in 1076 and was completed in 1125. It boasts the largest castle keep in Europe – bigger than the keep at the Tower of London. During the 14th century it was used mainly as a

prison. The museum contains Roman mosaics and statues. It opens 10 am to 5 pm Monday to Saturday (1 to 5 pm Sunday); last admission is at 4.30 pm. Admission costs £3.80/2.50. For another £1.20/70p you can take a guided tour of the Roman vaults, the Norman chapel on the roof of the castle and the top of the castle walls.

In Tymperleys – a magnificent, restored, 15th-century building – is the **Clock Museum**. It opens Tuesday to Saturday. It's also interesting to walk around the **Dutch Quarter**, just north of High St, established in the 16th century by Protestant refugee weavers from Holland.

Opposite the castle, the **Natural History Museum** (☎ 282931), High St, was closed at the time of writing. When it opens again the hours should be 10 am to 5 pm Tuesday to Saturday and 1 to 5 pm Sunday.

Places to Stay

Colchester doesn't have a great number of B&Bs, though there are plenty of small hotels with reasonable prices.

Colchester Camping (☎ 545551, Cymberline Way, Lexden) is 30 minutes' walk from the city centre, or you can catch bus No 5 from the bus station (twice hourly). It costs £6.90 for one person and a tent.

A few minutes' walk from the centre, *The Old Manse (☎ 545154, fax 545153, 15 Roman Rd)* offers comfortable accommodation for non-smokers. It's in a quiet square beside Castle Park and part of the Roman wall is at the bottom of the garden. Singles/doubles with shared bathroom cost £30/42.

Scheregate Hotel (☎ 573037, 36 Osborne St) offers adequate rooms right in the town centre. Singles/doubles cost £22/34 or £30/42 with en-suite bathroom. Also conveniently located, the *Peveril Hotel (☎ 574001, 51 North Hill)*, on the road to the train station, has 17 rooms, mostly without bathroom, from £25/36.

The *Rose & Crown Hotel (☎ 866677, East St)* is probably the best place to stay. There are 30 rooms – all doubles have a bathroom – from £62.50 to £99. There are cheaper deals for weekend stays.

Places to Eat

There are plenty of places to eat in Colchester, though fast-food places seem to outnumber just about anything else.

The Lemon Tree (☎ 767337, 48 St John's St) is very good value and offers an enticing menu. Provençal potato salad with seared fillet of mackerel costs only £3.95 as a starter. Vegetarians are well catered for here.

The *Forresters Arms (☎ 542646, Castle Rd)*, off Roman Rd, is a nice old pub in a quiet part of town behind the castle. It has seating outside in the warmer months.

Akash (☎ 578791, 40 St Botolph's St) is an Indian restaurant serving very good food and is recommended by locals. Lamb vindaloo costs £4.10 while the special balti chicken makhani is £7.95.

The colourful and casual cafe *Picasso's (☎ 561080, 2 St John's St)* must offer the best value in town; sandwiches cost from £1.70, burgers from £1.40 and hot main meals for around £4.

Getting There & Away

Colchester is 62 miles from London. There are daily National Express buses from London (£7.50/£8.50 one-way/return) and rail services every 15 minutes or so from London Liverpool St (£9.90, 55 minutes).

DEDHAM VALE

'I love every stile and stump and lane...these scenes made me a painter'

John Constable

If Dedham Vale in the Stour Valley, near the border with Suffolk, looks strangely familiar it's because you've probably already seen the romantic, bucolic images on the canvases of early-19th-century painter John Constable. Constable County, as it's known, centres on the villages of Dedham, East Bergholt (where the painter was born) and Flatford. The area is best explored in your own car but there are bus and train services.

Flatford Mill (not the original) was once owned by Constable's father but is now owned by the National Trust and used as a Field Studies Centre. You can even take an art course here (call ☎ 01206-298283 for information). **Bridge Cottage** (☎ 01206-298260; NT) features in some Constable landscapes and now houses a display about the famous painter. It opens 10 am to 5.30 pm daily, April to September; Tuesday, Thursday and Saturday in March; and weekends only the rest of the year. Guided tours operate three times daily, May to September. Admission (with a tour) costs £1.80 (free for children). **Willy Lott's House**, of *Haywain* fame, is nearby. Willy was a neighbour and friend of Constable's.

Several bus companies operate services from Colchester to East Bergholt, three-quarters of a mile from Bridge Cottage. It's better to come by train (get off at Manningtree), as you get a nice 1¾ mile walk along footpaths through Constable country. If you are in Manningtree, make a quick diversion and walk up the hill to the town of Mistly for a wonderful view over the estuary of the River Stour. The TIC in Colchester sells cycling maps of Dedham Vale.

SAFFRON WALDEN
☎ 01799 • pop 14,300

Saffron Walden was the biggest market town in the area from the 15th century until the first half of the 20th century. It is named after the saffron crocus which was cultivated in the surrounding fields. The town is a treasure trove for antiques lovers. Try also to visit the nearby village of Thaxted.

The TIC (☎ 01799-510444, fax 510445), 1 Market Place, sells a useful town trail leaflet. You can use the Internet (£1.25 for 15 minutes) at AS1 (☎ 528045), Lime Tree Court, in the centre.

The **museum** (☎ 510333) has a wealth of material and is well worth a visit. It includes a very interesting exhibit on local history and has an odd collection of objects from all over the world, including a mummy from Thebes. It opens 10 am to 5 pm Monday to Saturday (2 to 5 pm Sunday). Admission costs £1/50p. The ruins of **Walden Castle Keep**, built around 1125, are next to the museum.

The **Church of St Mary the Virgin**, off Museum St, dates mainly from 1450–1525, when the town was at the height of its prosperity. It's one of the largest in the county and has some very impressive Gothic arches, decorative wooden ceilings and a 60m spire which was added in 1832. On the eastern side of the town is an ancient earthen **maze**; a path circles for almost a mile, taking you to the centre if you follow the right route.

Places to Stay & Eat

Most of the B&Bs are in tiny houses and have only one or two rooms but there aren't too many tourists and you shouldn't have any problems finding somewhere to stay.

Saffron Walden Youth Hostel (☎ 01799-523117, corner of Myddylton Place and Bridge St) is in the best preserved 15th-century building in town. Beds cost £9.25/6.50 for adults/under-18s.

Both *The Sun Inn* and the *Queen Elizabeth Inn (☎ 520065 or 5214894, 23 Fairycroft Rd)* are recommended. Singles/doubles cost £20/38 and can be noisy on Friday and Saturday nights, but only until 11 pm.

Mrs Skipper (☎ 527857, 53–55 Castle St) has two double rooms for £20 per person in her tiny house.

The *Archway Guesthouse (☎ 501500, 11 Church St)* is an odd place, with an unusual mix of decor and a huge collection of 'stuff'. The rooms are lovely and cost £30/50.

For delicious, fresh pastries and sandwiches try *Dorringtons (☎ 522093, 9 Cross St)* the bakery. Sandwiches cost from 70p to £1.40.

There are some lovely old pubs around town including the 16th-century *Eight Bells (☎ 522790, 18 Bridge St)*, about three minutes' walk from the centre.

Getting There & Away

Stagecoach Cambus (☎ 01223-423554) bus No 102 runs hourly between Cambridge and Saffron Walden. Biss Brothers' (☎ 681155) commuter bus No 38 leaves London Victoria coach station at 5 pm each weekday, and returns from Saffron Walden at 6.55 am (£7.35, two hours).

The nearest train station is Audley End, 2½ miles to the west. Trains leave from London Liverpool St every 20 minutes (£10.70, 1 hour).

AUDLEY END HOUSE

Built in the early 17th century, this Jacobean mansion was used as a royal palace by Charles II, and was described by James I as 'too large for a king'. The 30 rooms on display house a fine collection of painting, silverware and furniture. It's set in a magnificent landscaped park, the handiwork of Capability Brown.

One mile west of Saffron Walden on the B1383, Audley End House (☎ 01799-522399; EH) opens 1 to 6 pm (last admission 5 pm) Wednesday to Sunday, April to September. The gardens open at 11 am. Admission costs £6.50/3.30. Audley End train station is 1¼ miles from the house. Stagecoach Cambus (☎ 01223-423554) bus No 102 from Cambridge to Saffron Walden stops here.

Hertfordshire

The small county of Hertfordshire isn't the most exciting of places, with its mixture of commuter-belt housing estates in the south and rolling farmland in the north. The highlight of a visit is the predominantly Georgian town of St Albans which dates back to Roman times and has a magnificent cathedral well worth seeing. About 6 miles east of St Albans is Hatfield House, one of Britain's most important stately homes and Hertfordshire's top attraction.

ST ALBANS
☎ 01727 • pop 120,700

Just 25 minutes by train from central London, the cathedral city of St Albans makes a pleasant day trip from London. To the Romans, St Albans was Verulamium, and their theatre and parts of the ancient wall can still be seen to the south-west of the city. There's also lots you can't see, buried under farmland on the town's outskirts.

St Albans is an attractive and cheerful place with some beautiful old Georgian houses, although many of the buildings here actually date back to the 15th century. There are lots of antiques shops and furniture crafters here. On Wednesday and Saturday mornings the central marketplace really comes alive.

Orientation & Information

St Peter's St, 10 minutes' walk west of the train station, is the focus of the town. St Peter's St becomes Chequer St and then Holywell Hill as it heads southwards. The marketplace is at the other end of St Peter's St, near the TIC. The cathedral lies to the west, off High St, with the ruins of Verulamium even farther to the west on St Michael's St.

The TIC (☎ 864511, fax 863533, e tic@relaxion.co.uk), in the grand town hall, Market Place, opens 9.30 am to 5.30 pm Monday to Saturday, Easter to October (10.30 am to 4 pm Sundays, July to mid-September). It opens 10 am to 4 pm Monday to Saturday, November to Easter. It sells the useful *Discover St Albans* town trail (95p). The *Official Visitors Guide* is free and features a detailed town walk that covers all the sights. There are free guided walks of the town at 11.15 am and 3 pm Sundays, Easter to September. Meet at the Clocktower on High St.

The post office and a number of ATMs are on St Peter's St, near the TIC.

There's a laundrette at 13 Catherine St, off St Peter's St.

The Alban Way is a 6½ mile path running from St Albans to Hatfield where you can visit the Jacobean Hatfield House (see Hatfield House later).

St Albans Cathedral

In 209, a Roman citizen named Alban was beheaded for his Christian beliefs, becoming Britain's first Christian martyr. In the 8th century King Offa of Mercia founded an abbey for the Benedictine monks on the site of his martyrdom. The first Norman abbot, Paul, rebuilt the church in 1077, incorporating parts of the Saxon building. You can see remnants of a Saxon archway in the southern aisle alongside the presbytery. Many Roman bricks were also used and they sit conspicuously in the central tower. Considerable restoration took place in 1877.

As you enter the cathedral you will notice the **murals** that decorate the Norman columns. They were painted by monks in the 13th century. One mural depicts Thomas Becket (southern side of the two pillars closest to the entrance) and above him is St Christopher. These paintings were hidden by whitewash after the Reformation and were not rediscovered until 1862.

The painted wooden panels of the choir ceiling date from the 15th century. The **Tower ceiling** is decorated with the red and white roses of the houses of Lancaster and York. The altar screen is mainly 16th-century although some statues were added in the 19th century.

In the heart of the cathedral is **St Alban's shrine**, immediately behind the presbytery and overlooked by a beautifully carved oak **Watching Chamber**, dating from 1400. This is where monks would stand guard to ensure pilgrims didn't pilfer relics. As you leave the shrine, turn to your left to see a marble slab embedded with marine fossils which was once an ancient altarpiece.

The cathedral (☎ 860780) opens 9 am to 5.45 pm. Admission is free but a donation of £2.50 is requested. There are guided tours at 11.30 am and 2.30 pm. In the southern aisle you can watch an audiovisual account of the cathedral's history. There are screenings from 11 am to 4 pm Monday to Saturday (with the last showing at 3.30 pm Saturday) and 2 to 5 pm on Sunday. Screenings cost £1.50/1.

Verulamium Museum & Roman Ruins

Britain's best museum (☎ 819339) of everyday life under the Romans, in St Michael's St, displays wonderful mosaic pavements and murals. There are lots of interactive displays, audiovisuals and re-creations of how rooms would have looked in a Roman house, including models of craftsmen working and women cooking. You can even hear the citizens of Verulamium talking about their lives. It opens 10 am to 5.30 pm daily (2 to 5.30 pm Sunday). Tickets cost £3.05/1.75 and allow you a return visit on the same day. You can take a free guided walk of the city of Verulamium, that is of the area it once stood, from the museum at 3 pm every Sunday.

In adjacent **Verulamium Park** you can inspect remains of a basilica, bathhouse and parts of the city wall. Across the busy A4174 are the remains of a **Roman theatre** which appear to be just a collection of grassy ditches and mounds and a few ruins. They open 10 am to 5 pm daily. Admission costs £1.50/50p, but they're probably only worth it if you're seriously keen on the Romans.

Museum of St Albans

The museum (☎ 819340), Hatfield Rd, begins with an exhibition of tools used between 1700 and 1950 by English tradesmen – coopers, wheelwrights, blacksmiths, lumberjacks and cabinet makers. It gives a rundown of the city's market and trade history and has good displays of Victorian memorabilia. It opens 10 am to 5 pm Monday to Saturday (2 to 5 pm Sunday). Admission is free.

Other Things to See & Do

The medieval **clocktower**, High St, was built between 1403 and 1412. It's the only medieval belfry in England and the original bell is still there. You can climb to the top for great views over the town between 10.30 am and 5 pm at weekends and bank holidays from Easter to October.

The **Kingsbury Water Mill**, St Michael's St, was used for milling grain until 1936. It dates back to Saxon times but the current mill buildings are actually Elizabethan with a Georgian facade. There is a small museum here and a lovely coffee shop with home-cooking and outdoor seating. It opens 11 am to 6 pm Tuesday to Saturday (to 5 pm in winter, noon to 6 pm Sunday). Admission costs £1.10/60p.

With about 30,000 specimens, the **Gardens of the Rose** (☎ 850461), 3 miles south-west of St Albans, contain the world's largest rose collection. It opens 9 am to 5 pm Monday to Saturday, mid-June to mid-October. Admission is £4/free.

Places to Stay

The following are all within five minutes' walk of the centre.

Mrs Jameson's (☎ 865498, fax 854136, 7 Marlborough Gate), off Upper Lattimore

Rd, is convenient for the train station and charges £18 per person for a basic room with shared bathroom.

The highly recommended *Mrs Thomas* (☎ 858939, 8 Hall Place Gardens) has lovely, spacious singles/doubles with garden views for £25/40, with shared bathroom. *Avona* (☎ 842216, fax 0956-857353, 478 Hatfield Rd) is good value at £20/40 or £50 for the double room with en-suite bathroom.

The White Hart (☎ 853624, fax 840237, 25 Holywell Hill), an old half-timbered hotel with exposed beams and creaky floors, is just a couple of minutes' walk from the centre. En-suite singles/doubles cost £54/70 (cheaper at weekends) and breakfast is £5 extra.

St Michael's Manor (☎ 864444, fax 848909, ⓔ smmanor@globalnet.co.uk, Fishpool St) is St Albans' swankiest hotel. It's peaceful and elegant with beautiful gardens. Singles/doubles start at £110/145 and go up to £225/295. Weekend deals including dinner and champagne are available.

Places to Eat

St Albans has no shortage of places to eat, and they all offer pretty good grub.

The fun Italian *Claudius* (☎ 850527, 116 London Rd) restaurant is covered from floor to roof with the owner's football memorabilia collection. Be sure to ask him to show you a card trick. Meals are simple and delicious and cost around £6.

Atmospheric *Kyriakos* (☎ 832841, 3 Holywell Hill) is a Greek restaurant with starters from £3 and mains from £8.95.

Claude's Creperie (☎ 846424, 15 Holywell Hill), with its rustic interior, has a huge menu combining French and Italian regional cooking. Mains cost from £6 to £8.50.

Thai Rack (☎ 850055, 13 George St) has a peaceful, leafy interior and the three-course lunch costs £9.50. A la carte main courses cost around £6.20.

Just a few minutes' walk from the town centre, *The Goat* (☎ 833934, 37 Sopwell Lane) is a nice old pub in a Tudor-style building. It has live jazz from 12.30 to 3 pm Sundays.

The Rose & Crown (☎ 851903, 10 St Michaels St) and, a little farther along, *The Six Bells* (☎ 856945, 16–18 St Michael's St), are both popular and cosy pubs with exposed beams, low ceilings and open fireplaces. Both offer traditional pub grub as well as more modern fare.

Abigail's Tearooms (☎ 856939, 7 High St), with its lacy curtains, cream teas and elderly clientele, is in the Village Arcade.

Getting There & Away

Rail is the most direct way to get to St Albans, although if you are coming from Heathrow you can catch Greenline bus No 724 which leaves hourly (£4.20, 1 hour). St Albans station is on Stanhope Rd, a 10-minute walk east of St Peter's St. Thameslink trains depart every 15 minutes from London King's Cross to St Albans station (£6.20, 23 minutes).

HATFIELD HOUSE

Hatfield House (☎ 01707-262823) is England's most impressive Jacobean house. This red-brick and stone mansion, built between 1607 and 1611 for Robert Cecil, 1st earl of Salisbury and secretary of state to both Elizabeth I and James I, is full of treasures. It was modelled on an earlier Tudor palace, built around 1497, where Elizabeth I spent much of her childhood. Only one wing of the royal palace survives and it can be seen in the gardens.

Inside, the house is extremely grand with a wonderful marble hall and famous portraits of Elizabeth and numerous English kings. The oak grand staircase is decorated with carved figures, including one of John Tradescant, the 17th-century botanist responsible for the gardens.

Five-course Elizabethan banquets, complete with minstrels and court jesters, are held in the great hall at 7.45 pm on Tuesday (£31.50 per head), Friday (£33) and Saturday (£35.50). Book on ☎ 01707-262055.

The house opens 1 to 4 pm at weekends and bank holidays. It opens noon to 4 pm Tuesday to Thursday for guided tours only. Admission costs £6.20/3.10; for the park only it's £1.80/90p. Hatfield House is 21

miles from London and 8 miles from St Albans. It's opposite Hatfield train station, and there are numerous trains from London King's Cross station (£6.30 day return, 25 minutes). Greenline (☎ 020-8668 7261) bus No 797 runs from London to Hatfield hourly and Greenline bus No 724 runs between St Albans and Hatfield every hour.

SHAW'S CORNER

This Victorian villa, in Ayot St Lawrence, is where the playwright George Bernard Shaw died in 1950. It has been preserved much as he left it. In the garden is the revolving summerhouse (revolving to catch the sun) where he wrote several works including *Pygmalion*, the play on which the film *My Fair Lady* was based.

Shaw's Corner (☎ 01438-820307; NT) opens 1 to 5 pm Wednesday to Saturday and bank holiday Mondays, April to October. Admission costs £3.50/1.75.

Bus No 304 from St Albans drops you at Gustardwood, 1¼ miles from Ayot St Lawrence.

Buckinghamshire

Buckinghamshire is uneventful commuter country, a pleasant mix of urban and rural landscapes. Among the many commuters drawn here were the influential Rothschilds, who constructed several impressive houses around Aylesbury. Other well-known figures who have lived in Buckinghamshire include the poets John Milton (in Chalfont St Giles, where his cottage is open to the public), TS Eliot and PB Shelley (Marlow), and Robert Frost (Beaconsfield).

Stretching across the south of Buckinghamshire, the Chilterns are a range of chalk hills famous for their beech woods. The countryside is particularly attractive in autumn. The 85-mile Ridgeway path follows the Chiltern hills to Ivinghoe Beacon in the east of the county. There are forest trails in the Chilterns and along the Grand Union Canal which cuts across the county's north-eastern edge on its way from London to Birmingham.

AYLESBURY

☎ 01296 • pop 52,000

Affluent Aylesbury has been the county town since 1725. Yet apart from being a transport hub with half-hourly trains to/from London Marylebone (£8.60, 54 minutes), it has very little to offer the visitor. The TIC, however, (☎/fax 330559), 8 Bourbon St, can provide general information on Buckinghamshire. It opens 9.30 am to 5 pm daily, Easter to October and 10 am to 4.30 pm the rest of the year.

AROUND AYLESBURY
Waddesdon Manor

Designed by a French architect for Baron Ferdinand de Rothschild, Waddesdon Manor (☎ 01296-651282; NT) was completed in 1889 in French Renaissance style to house the baron's art collection, Sèvres porcelain and French furniture. There are several paintings by Gainsborough and Reynolds as well as some by 17th-century Dutch masters. The family's wine cellar is open for viewing but unfortunately tastings are out of the question. An aviary houses a collection of exotic birds.

It opens 11 am to 4 pm Thursday to Sunday, April to October; plus Wednesday in July and August. Admission costs £6. The grounds open 10 am to 5 pm Wednesday to Sunday, March to mid-December. Admission costs £3/1.50 by timed ticket. You can book in advance but must pay a £2.50 booking fee.

The chateau is 6 miles north-west of Aylesbury. From Aylesbury bus station, take Aylesbury bus Nos 16 or 17. The trip takes 15 minutes.

Claydon House

The decoration of Claydon's grand rooms is said to be England's finest example of the light, decorative rococo style that developed from the more ponderous baroque in early-18th-century France. Florence Nightingale lived here for several years and a museum houses mementoes of her Crimean stay. Some scenes from the 1995 film *Emma* with Gwyneth Paltrow were filmed here.

Claydon House (☎ 01296-730349; NT) opens 1 to 5 pm Saturday to Wednesday, April to October. Admission costs £4.20. It's 13 miles north-west of Aylesbury; buses drop you in Middle Claydon, 2 miles from the house.

STOWE LANDSCAPE GARDENS

About 4 miles north of the pleasant town of Buckingham, Stowe is the sort of private school so exclusive that its driveway is half a mile long. The greatest British landscape gardeners, Charles Bridgeman, William Kent and Capability Brown, all worked on the grounds.

The Georgian gardens (☎ 01280-822850; NT) cover 400 hectares. They are known for their 32 temples, created in the 18th century by the wealthy owner Sir Richard Temple (no kidding), whose family motto was *Templa Quam Delecta* (How Delightful are your Temples). There are also arches, lakes and a Palladian bridge among other buildings.

The gardens open to the public from 10 am to 5 pm (last admission 4 pm) Wednesday to Sunday, April to October. They open daily except Monday in July and August. Admission costs £4.60/2.30. There are no buses that go past the gardens. It's a 4-mile walk or a £6 taxi ride from nearby Buckingham.

WENDOVER WOODS

About one mile north-east of the town of Wendover (off the B4009) are the Wendover Woods (☎ 01296-625825 for the forest ranger), 325 hectares of beechwood and conifer forest lining the northern edge of the Chiltern Hills. There are a number of walks you can do, ranging from the half-mile walk to the top of Coombe Hill, the highest point in the Chilterns at 260m, to the 2-mile firecrest trail. There are cycling routes and bridleways but if you don't want to be too active you can just come to this peaceful spot for a picnic.

The TIC (☎ 01296-696759, fax 622460) in the clocktower on High St, Wendover, has information on the Chilterns, the Ridgeway path and the Wendover Woods. It opens 10 am to 4 pm daily. You can pick up a walking map from the information stand at the woods themselves.

There are half-hourly train services to Wendover from London Marylebone (£7.30, 45 minutes). Aylesbury bus No 54 goes to Wendover every half-hour (15 minutes).

South-Western England

The counties of Dorset, Wiltshire, Somerset, Devon and Cornwall include some of the most beautiful countryside and spectacular coastline in Britain. They are littered with the evidence of successive cultures and kingdoms that have been swept away by one invader after another.

The region can be divided between Devon and Cornwall, out on a limb to the far west, and Wiltshire, Dorset and Somerset in the east, which are more central and so more easily accessible.

Devon and particularly Cornwall were once Britain's Wild West and rife with smuggling. Cornwall even had its own language although the last Cornish speaker died in the 1770s. The weather in this part of England is milder than elsewhere and some of the beaches boast golden sand and surfable waves. Despite the competition from cheap holidays abroad, the 'English Riviera' still seethes with sunburned suburbanites every summer. It's wise to steer clear of the coastal towns in July and August, not least because the narrow streets are choked with traffic.

Some people find Cornwall disappointing. You'll certainly feel cheated if you expect the extreme south-western tip of the island to be full of untouched, undiscovered hideaways. Thanks to thoughtless development, Land's End – a veritable icon – has been reduced to a commercially minded tourist trap, and inland much of the peninsula has been devastated by generations of tin and china-clay mining. However, many of the coastal villages retain their charm, especially out of season.

The South West Coast Path (see that section under Walking in the Activities chapter), a long-distance walking route, follows the coastline from Minehead in Somerset, around the peninsula to Poole, near Bournemouth in Dorset, giving spectacular access to the best and most untouched sections of the coastline. The Dartmoor and Exmoor national parks are equally popular with walkers.

Highlights

- Taking a stroll around Georgian Bath
- Exploring Avebury and Stonehenge
- Wandering around the Tate Gallery at St Ives
- Doing a day trip to remote Lundy Island
- Having a night on the town in Bristol
- Braving the surf in Newquay

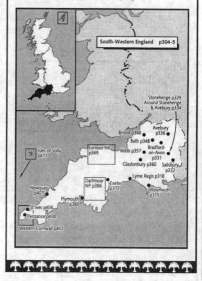

Farther east, some truly great monuments fly the flag for English civilisation: the Stone Age left Stonehenge and spellbinding Avebury; Iron Age Britons created Maiden Castle, just outside Dorchester; the Romans (and the later Georgians) developed Bath; the legendary King Arthur is supposedly buried at Glastonbury; the Middle Ages left the great cathedrals at Exeter, Salisbury and Wells; and the landed gentry of the 16th and 17th centuries left great houses like Montacute and Wilton. The east is densely packed with things to see, and the countryside,

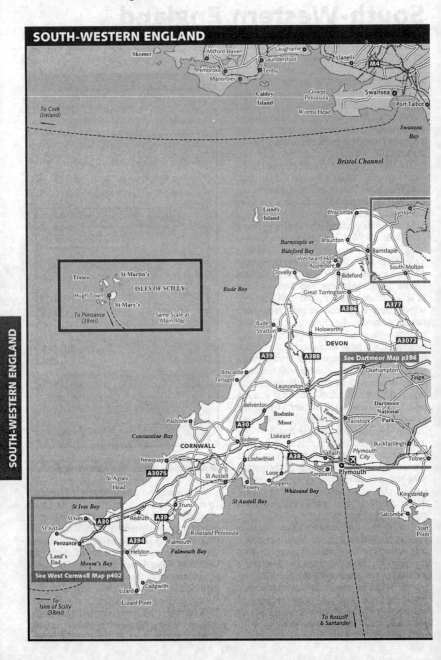

SOUTH-WESTERN ENGLAND

Skomer

Milford Haven
Pembroke
Manorbier

Laugharne
Saundersfoot
Tenby

Llanelli

M4

Swansea

Port Talbot

Caldey
Island

Gower
Peninsula

Worms Head

Swansea
Bay

To Cork
(Ireland)

Bristol Channel

Lundy
Island

Ilfracombe

Lynton

Barnstaple or
Bideford Bay

Braunton

Westward Ho!
Appledore

Clovelly

Bideford

Barnstaple

South Molton

Tresco

St Martin's

St Mary's

Hugh Town

ISLES OF SCILLY

Bude Bay

Great Torrington

A386

A377

A3072

To Penzance
(38mi)

Same Scale as
Main Map

Bude
Stratton

Holsworthy

DEVON

A39

A388

See Dartmoor Map p386

Boscastle
Tintagel

Launceston

Okehampton

Teign

Belventor

Bodmin
Moor

Tamar

Dartmoor
National
Park

Padstow

A30

Constantine Bay

CORNWALL

Bodmin

Liskeard

Tavistock

Buckfastleigh

Newquay

A3075

Lostwithiel

A38

Saltash

Plymouth
City

Totnes

St Austell

Looe

Torpoint

Plymouth

St Agnes
Head

St Austell Bay

Fowey

Polperro

Whitsand Bay

Kingsbridge

St Ives Bay

St Ives

A30

Redruth

Truro

A39

Roseland Peninsula

Salcombe

St Just

Penzance

A394

Falmouth

Start
Point

Land's
End

Helston

Falmouth Bay

Mount's Bay

See West Cornwall Map p402

Lizard

Cadgwith

To
Isles of Scilly
(38mi)

Lizard Point

To Roscoff
& Santander

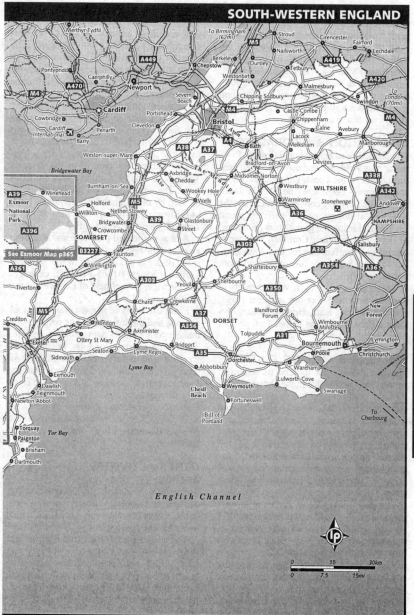

SOUTH-WESTERN ENGLAND

though varied, is a classic English patchwork of hedgerows, stone churches, thatched cottages, great estates and emerald green fields.

Cities such as Bath and Salisbury are honey-pot tourist attractions on every first-time visitor's hit list. The charms of Dorset, Somerset and North Devon are more low-key, and you can happily wander around without too many plans and without stumbling over too many people.

ORIENTATION & INFORMATION

The chalk downs centred on Salisbury Plain run across Wiltshire and down through central Dorset to the coast. Granitic Dartmoor and Exmoor dominate the Devon landscape. The railways converge on Exeter, the west's most important city, then run round the coast, skirting the granite tors (outcrops) of Dartmoor, to Truro, Cornwall's uninspiring administrative centre, and Penzance. Bristol and Salisbury are other important transport hubs.

There are several YHA youth hostels in the Dartmoor and Exmoor national parks, and at Salisbury, Bath, Bristol, Exeter, Plymouth, Penzance, Land's End, Tintagel and Ilfracombe.

WALKING & CYCLING ROUTES

The south-west has plenty of beautiful countryside, and walks in the Dartmoor and Exmoor national parks, and round the coastline, are well known. The barren, open wilderness of Dartmoor can be an acquired taste, but Exmoor boasts some of the most stunning scenery in England, and the coastal stretch from Ilfracombe to Minehead is particularly spectacular. See the sections on Dartmoor and Exmoor later in the chapter.

The South West Coast Path, the longest national trail, is not a wilderness walk – villages with food, beer and accommodation are generally within easy reach. It follows truly magnificent coastline. Completing a section of the path should be considered by any keen walker; if possible, avoid busy summer weekends.

The South West Way Association (☎ 01364-73859, ✉ coastpath.swcpa@virgin .net), 25 Clobells, South Brent, Devon, TQ10 9JW publishes an accommodation guide, as well as detailed route descriptions. The association's Web site is at www.swcp.org. The official Countryside Commission/Aurum Press guides cover Minehead to Padstow, Padstow to Falmouth, Falmouth to Exmouth and Exmouth to Poole.

Another famous walk, the Ridgeway Path, starts near Avebury and runs northeast for 85 miles to Ivinghoe Beacon near Aylesbury. Much of it follows ancient roads over the high, open ridge of the chalk downs before descending to the Thames Valley and finally climbing into the Chilterns. The western section (to Streatley) can be used by mountain bikes and horses (and, unfortunately, 4WDs). The best guide is *The Ridgeway* by Neil Curtis.

A range of useful publications, including an excellent *Information and Accommodation Guide*, is available from the National Trails Office (☎ 01865-810224), Countryside Service, Department of Leisure & Arts, Holton, Oxford OX33 1QQ.

Bikes can be hired in most major regional centres, and the infrequent bus connections make cycling more than usually sensible. There's no shortage of hills, but the mild weather and quiet backroads make this great cycling country. The West Country Way, recently opened by Sustrans (see Cycling in the Activities chapter), runs from Penzance, St Ives and Padstow in Cornwall to Bristol, via Bodmin Moor and Exmoor. It follows disused railway tracks and quiet back roads.

OTHER ACTIVITIES
Surfing

The capital of British surfing is Newquay on the north-west Cornish coast which comes complete with surf shops, bleached hair and Kombis.

The surfable coast runs from Porthleven (near Helston) in Cornwall, west around Land's End and north to Ilfracombe. The most famous reef breaks are at Porthleven, Lynmouth and Millbrook; though good, they are inconsistent and it's bloody cold in winter!

GETTING AROUND
Bus
National Express buses (☎ 0870 580 8080) provide reasonable connections between the main towns, particularly in the east, but the farther west you go the more dire the situation becomes. Transport around Dartmoor and Exmoor is very difficult in summer, and nigh on impossible at any other time. This is territory that favours those with their own transport.

Phone numbers for regional timetables include Bristol and Bath ☎ 0117-955 5111, Somerset ☎ 01823-358299, Wiltshire ☎ 0845 709 0899, Dorset ☎ 01305-224535, Devon ☎ 01392-382800 and Cornwall ☎ 01872-322142.

There are a number of one-day Explorer passes for around £5; it's always worth asking about them. For example, the Wiltshire Day Rover (£5) gives unlimited travel in Wiltshire (Salisbury, Avebury, Bradford-on-Avon and so on), and also includes Bath.

The Wilts & Dorset Explorer pass (☎ 01202-673555) gives one day's unlimited travel on Wilts & Dorset, Stagecoach Hampshire Bus, Damory Coaches, and Solent Blue Line buses for £5/2.50. This pass will take you from Portsmouth, Winchester or Southampton in the east all the way through the New Forest to Dorchester and Weymouth in the west. From the south coast, it will take you north through Salisbury to Bath, Devizes, Swindon or Newbury. A seven-day Busabout pass costs £22/11 adult/child; one passport photo is required.

Train
Train services in the east are reasonably comprehensive, linking Bristol, Bath, Salisbury, Weymouth and Exeter. Beyond Exeter, a single line follows the south coast as far as Penzance, with spurs to Barnstaple, Gunnislake, Looe, Falmouth, St Ives and Newquay. The line from Exeter to Penzance is one of Britain's most beautiful. For more information phone ☎ 0845 748 4950.

Several regional rail passes are available, such as the Freedom of the South West Rover. Over 15 days it allows eight days unlimited travel west of a line drawn through (and including) Salisbury, Bath, Bristol and Weymouth (£71.50 in summer, £61 in winter).

Dorset

Despite its natural beauty and attractive towns and villages, most of Dorset manages to avoid inundation by tourists. The impressively varied coast includes the large resort towns of Bournemouth and Weymouth, as well as Lyme Regis, a particularly attractive spot with famous literary connections. The Dorset Coast Path, part of the longer 613-mile South West Coast Path, runs for most of the length of the coast.

Inland is Dorchester, the heart of Thomas Hardy's fictional Wessex. Dorset also boasts famous earthworks (Maiden Castle), castles (Corfe Castle), stately homes (particularly Kingston Lacy), a string of Lawrence of Arabia connections, some fine churches (Christchurch Priory, Wimborne Minster and Sherborne Abbey) and one of England's best-known chalk hill figures (the Cerne Giant).

ORIENTATION & INFORMATION
Dorchester makes a good base for exploring the best of Dorset, but Lyme Regis, Bridport and Weymouth will suit those who prefer the coast. One of the reasons for Dorset's backwater status is that no major transport routes cross it. A rail loop runs west from Southampton to Dorchester, then north to Yeovil, and the main westbound InterCity trains stop at Axminster (Eastern Devon).

BOURNEMOUTH & POOLE
☎ 01202 • pop 265,000
Technically two separate towns, Bournemouth and Poole are, however, virtually continuous.

With 7 miles of clean sand, Bournemouth has been a popular beach resort since the mid-19th century and continues to exude an air of Victorian seaside prosperity, yet it also attracts a younger crowd with nightlife to rival that of Brighton (East Sussex). An artificial reef is currently under construction which could see Bournemouth become a destination for surfers.

In a recent survey by a well-known condom manufacturer, Bournemouth beach was voted the most popular place in Britain for open-air sex.

The medieval port of Poole is now a container dock and yachting centre.

Orientation & Information

Bournemouth's Tourist Information Centre (TIC; ☎ 451700) is on Westover Rd. Poole's TIC (☎ 253253) is at the Quay.

Things to See & Do

Bournemouth is noted for its beautiful chines (sharp-sided valleys running down to the sea). The wonderful **Russell-Cotes Art Gallery & Museum** (☎ 451800) looks out to sea from Russell-Cotes Rd in Bournemouth and has a varied collection, much of it garnered from its namesake's travels, including an exquisite Japanese collection.

In Shelley Park, Beechwood Ave, in Boscombe, the **Shelley Rooms** (☎ 303571) house a collection of Shelley memorabilia. They open 2 to 5 pm Tuesday to Sunday and admission is free. *Frankenstein* author Mary Shelley is buried at St Peter's.

Compton Acres (☎ 700778) is a cluster of gardens in a sheltered cliff chine. They open 10 am to 5.15 pm daily, March to October. Admission costs £5.45/2.45. Bus Nos 150 and 151 go there from the centres of Poole and Bournemouth.

Poole Old Town has attractive 18th-century buildings, including a wonderful Customs House. The **Waterfront Museum** (☎ 683138) recounts the town's history, including the prosperity brought by its Newfoundland fishing trade. It opens 10 am to 5 pm Monday to Saturday, and noon to 5 pm Sunday. Admission costs £2/1.35, except in August when the £4/2.85 charge also includes nearby **Scaplen's Court Museum**. Open for the rest of the year to school parties only, this museum is in a medieval merchant's house. **Poole Pottery** (☎ 666200) draws huge numbers of visitors and the complex includes a gift shop with seconds – a whole lot more affordable than collectable Poole in antique shops throughout Britain.

Brownsea Island is a National Trust (NT) nature reserve at the mouth of Poole Harbour where the first Boy Scout camp was held in 1907. Between April and October boats from Sandbanks (on the peninsula between Bournemouth and Poole) cost £3/2 return, plus a landing fee of £2.60/1.30. During winter the Royal Society for the Protection of Birds (RSPB) operates sporadic Birdboats to watch the harbour bird life; phone ☎ 666226 for boat information.

Places to Stay & Eat

Bournemouth and Poole are full of places to stay and the TICs make free bookings. There are also plenty of camp sites around the towns.

Bournemouth Backpackers (☎ 299491, ℮ *bournemouth.backpackers@virgin.net, 3 Frances Rd*) has a good location near the station and beds start from £12.

Still in Bournemouth, *Cartrefle Guest House* (☎ 297856, 45 St Michael's Rd) has B&B from £17 per person, £25 with ensuite facilities. *Denbry Hotel* (☎ 558700, 179 Holdenhurst Rd) has similar accommodation from £18/20 per person.

Parklands Hotel (☎ 552529, 4 Rushton Crescent) has singles/doubles for £28/50, more with a four-poster bed.

Amid the fish and chip shops are some interesting, if pricier, places to eat. Try *Sala Pepe* (☎ 291019, 43 Charminster Rd, Bournemouth). Fresh fish dishes here include monkfish with crabmeat and prawns. *Corkers* (☎ 681393, 1 High St, The Quay, Poole) opens as a cafe-bar all day, and as a restaurant for lunch and dinner. Other well-regarded restaurants include *Mr Pang's* (☎ 553748, 234 Holdenhurst Rd) for fine Chinese food in Bournemouth and *Storm* (☎ 674970, 16 High St) and *John B's* (☎ 672440, High St) for seafood with flair in Poole.

Entertainment

Liquids at the Landsdowne Hotel is getting a good reputation as somewhere to warm-up for Bournemouth's clubbing scene. For clubbing in Bournemouth, the best-known place is *Urban* and, upstairs pre-club bar *Slam* both in the same building (☎ 555129) on Firvale Rd. The *Opera House* (☎ 399922) is an incredible converted theatre, Bournemouth's answer to the super club if you like that sort of thing.

Getting There & Away
Trains take about two hours from London Waterloo. There are also regular bus links, including National Express (☎ 0870 580 8080). A ferry shuttles across from Sandbanks to Studland. This is a short cut from Poole to Swanage, Wareham and the west Dorset coast, but summer queues can be horrendous.

AROUND BOURNEMOUTH & POOLE
Christchurch
☎ 01202 • pop 30,000
Five miles east of Bournemouth is Christchurch, a small attractive town that might make a pleasant alternative base to Bournemouth. The TIC (☎ 471780) is at 23 High St.

The magnificent **Christchurch Priory** (☎ 485804) stands between the Avon and Stour rivers. The Norman nave had a new choir added to it in the 15th century, when the tower was also built. Among the wonderful misericords in the choir, look for a carving of Richard III and another of a fox 'friar' preaching to a flock of geese. In summer you can climb the tower for views and learn about priory life in **St Michael's Loft Museum**. Visitors are asked for a £1 donation.

Opposite the Priory is the **Red House Museum & Gardens** (☎ 482860), a workhouse now accommodating a local history museum. It opens 10 am to 5 pm Tuesday to Saturday, and 2 to 5 pm Sunday. Admission costs £1.50/80p.

Wimborne
☎ 01202 • pop 14,000
Wimborne is centred around its interesting old minster (church). The TIC (☎ 886116) is on High St, near the minster.

Wimborne Minster Founded around 1050, the minster was considerably enlarged in Decorated style in the 14th century and became the parish church in 1537 when Henry VIII began attacking monasteries. It's notable for its twin towers and for the varied colours of its stonework. The mid-15th-century perpendicular-style west tower was added when there were fears for the strength of the simpler Norman-style 12th-century central tower. Those fears were realised when the crossing spire fell down in 1600.

Inside, the nave columns, the piers of the central tower and the northern and southern transepts are the main Norman survivors. Traces of 13th- to 15th-century painted murals can be seen in a Norman altar recess in the northern transept. In the presbytery is a 1440 brass of King Ethelred who was killed in battle in 871, the only brass commemorating a king in England.

In Holy Trinity Chapel is the tomb of Ettricke, the 'man in the wall'. A local eccentric (but obviously one with some influence), he refused to be buried in the church or in the village and was interred in the church wall. Confidently expecting to die in 1693, Ettricke also had his memorial engraved. When he survived his prediction by 10 years, the 1693 was rechiselled to 1703.

Above the choir vestry is a **chained library** established in 1686.

Priest's House Museum Near the minster is the 16th-century Priest's House Museum (☎ 882533), an interesting local history museum with a series of reconstructed period rooms. It opens 10.30 am to 5 pm Monday to Saturday, April to October, and 2 to 5 pm Sunday, June to September. Admission costs £2.20/1.

Kingston Lacy
Two miles north of Wimborne is Kingston Lacy (☎ 842913; NT), a fine 17th-century house with 18th-century landscaped gardens. It's unusual in that it didn't decline into genteel poverty and then have to be completely refurnished. The last occupant lived in the house until 1981 without selling a thing, so the house is dense with furniture and art, much of it collected by William Bankes, who was responsible for major renovations in the 1830s.

The house opens noon to 5.30 pm Saturday to Wednesday, April to October. Admission costs £6/3; grounds only £2.50/1.25.

SOUTH-EASTERN DORSET

The south-eastern corner of Dorset – the Purbeck peninsula – is crowded with pretty thatched villages and crumbling ruins. The Dorset Coast Path, part of the 613-mile South West Coast Path, runs through wonderful scenery along this stretch. There are plenty of camp sites around and B&Bs in almost every village.

Tolpuddle

Tolpuddle, on the A35, played a historic role in the development of trade unions. In 1833, a group of farm workers met to discuss a cut in their wages and were promptly arrested, convicted of holding an illegal meeting (striking was not illegal) and sentenced to transportation to Australia. Public support for the 'Tolpuddle Martyrs' resulted in their pardon in 1836.

A memorial stands by a tree under which they probably gathered. A small museum on the western outskirts recounts the tale. It opens Tuesday to Sunday; admission is free.

Wareham

☎ 01929 • pop 2800

The pretty village of Wareham forms a neat square, bounded by the River Frome on its southern side and by a remarkably intact Saxon wall on the other three sides. To complete the pattern, North, East, South and West Sts run in the four cardinal directions from The Cross in the centre. The village was badly damaged by a succession of fires, most disastrously in 1762, after which thatched buildings were banned. Purbeck TIC (☎ 552740), in Holy Trinity Church, South St, stocks an excellent guide and walking-tour map (free).

The recently refurbished **Wareham Museum** (☎ 553448), on East St, adjacent to the town hall, opens 11 am to 1 pm and 2 to 4 pm daily, Easter to mid-October. A Lawrence of Arabia collection supplements the usual local items.

You can rent rowing boats from **Abbots Quay**, once a busy port on the River Frome. The sturdy **earth banks** around the town were built after a Viking attack in 876. A stretch on the West Wall is known as Bloody Bank, after Monmouth rebels were executed here in 1685 following the Bloody Assizes (see the boxed text 'The Bloody Assizes' under Dorchester later in the chapter).

Standing on the wall beside North St is the Saxon **St Martin's Church**, which dates from about 1020. Although the porch and bell tower are later additions, and larger windows have been added over the centuries, the basic structure is unchanged. Inside, there's a 12th-century wall painting on the northern wall and a marble effigy of Lawrence of Arabia.

Places to Stay & Eat Several camp sites can be found around Wareham. Convenient B&Bs include *Belle Vue* (☎ 552056, West St), right on top of West Wall, which costs from £42 for doubles.

Black Bear Hotel (☎ 553339, 14 South St) is fronted by a life-size figure of a bear. Singles/doubles with bathroom cost from £25/40. The picturesque *Old Granary* (☎ 552010, The Quay) charges £45 for a room and has a good restaurant. The nearby *Quay Inn* is a popular local pub with food.

Bovington Camp Tank Museum

Six miles from Wareham, the Tank Museum (☎ 405096) houses an extensive collection from the earliest WWI prototypes, through to WWII tanks from both sides, and on to examples from Cold War days. From more recent times, there's also a collection of Iraqi tanks from the Gulf War. It opens 10 am to 5 pm daily and admission costs £6.90/4.50. Lawrence of Arabia was stationed here in 1923 and there's a small museum in the shop.

Clouds Hill

The former home of Lawrence of Arabia (☎ 405616; NT) opens noon to 5 pm Wednesday to Friday, and Sunday, April to October. Admission to the tiny house costs £2.30.

Corfe Castle

Corfe Castle's magnificent ruins tower above the pretty stone village, offering wonderful views over the surrounding countryside. Even by English standards, the 1000-year-old castle had a dramatic history. In 978,

Lawrence of Arabia

The green fields and pretty villages of Dorset are a long way from the sandy wastes of Arabia but there are numerous Lawrence connections to this area. The Tourist Information Centre (TIC) in Wareham even produces *The Lawrence of Arabia Trail* leaflet.

Born in 1888 in Wales, TE Lawrence was the son of Sir Thomas Chapman, who had abandoned his first wife and their daughters in Ireland to run off with the girls' governess. As Mr and Mrs Lawrence they had five boys; Thomas Edward was the second. Lawrence studied history at Oxford University, specialising in the Middle East. He travelled extensively in the region between 1909 and 1914 and his expertise led to a Cairo army posting at the outbreak of WWI.

Turkey, still known as the Ottoman Empire at the time, was allied with Germany and, as Arab unrest began to develop, Lawrence led a brilliant guerrilla campaign against the Ottoman forces, culminating in the capture of Aqaba in mid-1917. After the war, he was disgusted to find his Arab visions discarded at the bargaining table as the old Ottoman Empire was carved up between Britain and France. Refusing military honours, he spent several years shuttling between Europe and the Middle East, while at the same time revelations of his dramatic exploits earned him the epithet 'Lawrence of Arabia'.

Lawrence was always an enigmatic character and in 1922 he clandestinely joined the Royal Air Force as a low-ranking enlisted man under the assumed name of John Hume Ross. At the same time he published, in a very limited edition, his immense work *Seven Pillars of Wisdom*. Newspapers soon broke the story of his RAF hideaway but a year later he joined the army as Private TE Shaw, a name he later assumed legally. He was stationed at Bovington Camp in Dorset and bought Clouds Hill, a nearby cottage. In 1925 he transferred to the RAF and spent the next 10 years in India and England before his discharge in 1935. Retiring to Clouds Hill at the age of 46, he was killed two months later in a motorbike accident.

Lawrence connections in Dorset include Bovington Camp, where the tank museum has a small Lawrence display. He died at Bovington Military Hospital six days after his accident, which took place between the camp and Clouds Hill, only a mile away. His grave is in the cemetery of St Nicholas Church, Moreton. Wareham Museum houses more Lawrence memorabilia and the small Saxon church in Wareham has a stone effigy of Lawrence.

17-year-old King Edward was greeted at the castle gate by his stepmother, Queen Elfrida, proffering a glass of poisoned wine; even before the poison could take effect he was stabbed to death. His half-brother, Ethelred the Unready, succeeded him, as the wicked queen had planned, but the martyred boy king was canonised as St Edward in 1001.

The castle (☎ 481294; NT) was besieged twice during the Civil War, being reduced to the present picturesque ruin after the second assault, in 1646. It opens 10 am to 5.30 pm, February to October (to 4.30 pm in March); and 11 am to 3.30 pm the rest of the year. Admission costs £4/2.

Places to Stay & Eat The village has several pubs and B&Bs, and there are camp sites nearby. The *Greyhound* is a good pub by the castle moat, with a pleasant garden, while the *Fox Inn* is a homely local pub.

The Blue Pool

The location may not be as stunning as the multi-coloured lakes of Keli Mutu on Flores, Indonesia, but the principle is the same: the water in the Blue Pool has a chameleon-like tendency to change colour. Admission to this popular local beauty spot, signposted from the A351, costs £3/1.50.

Swanage

In Victorian times local quarryman John Mowlem made a fortune supplying stone from Swanage for the huge rebuilding projects in booming London. The firm bearing his name is still a major building contractor. He also judiciously chose buildings in

London which were due for demolition and shipped material back to Swanage. As a result, there are City of London bollards dotted around town, the town hall has a grandiose stone front removed from the Wren-influenced Cheapside Mercers Company building and the Wellington Clock Tower was rescued from London Bridge and stands on the pier.

The TIC (☎ 422885) is on Shore Rd. Centrally located *Swanage Youth Hostel* (☎ *422113, Cluny Crescent*) has beds for £10.85/7.40 for adults/under-18s, and the large number of B&Bs confirm Swanage's popularity as a beach resort.

Lulworth Cove & the Coast

The lovely Dorset coast is at its most spectacular (and crowded) between Lulworth Cove and Durdle Door. Lulworth Cove is almost perfectly circular and nearly enclosed by towering cliffs. Durdle Door has a fine beach, a dramatic cove and an impressive natural archway. It's about a mile west of Lulworth Cove with fine cliff-top walks in both directions.

Places to Stay The *Durdle Door Caravan Park* (☎ *400200*) on the fields above the cliffs has tent sites costing £15 for the tent and car. There are a number of places to stay in Lulworth Cove and more just back from the coast in West Lulworth. *Lulworth Cove Youth Hostel* (☎ *01929-400564, School Lane, West Lulworth*) costs £9.80/6.75 for adults/under-18s.

DORCHESTER

☎ 01305 • pop 14,000

Famous as the home of novelist Thomas Hardy, Dorset's administrative centre is, however, a sleepy place and lively Weymouth or pretty Cerne Abbas would make equally good bases for exploring the local attractions.

Orientation & Information

Most of Dorchester's action takes place along South St which runs into pedestrianised Cornhill and then emerges in High St, divided into East and West parts at St Peter's church. The TIC (☎ 267992) is in

Trinity St alongside the Antelope Walk shopping arcade. It sells the *Historical Guide – Dorchester* with interesting walks around town, and lots of Hardy literature including a set of leaflets which retrace the scenes of individual novels.

Things to See & Do

Dorset County Museum (☎ 262735), on High West St, houses the study where Hardy did his writing. There are also sections on the archaeological excavations at Maiden Castle, fossil finds from Lyme Regis and a rural craft collection. It opens 10 am to 5 pm Monday to Saturday (on Sunday too in July and August) and admission costs £3.30/1.50.

The **Tutankhamun Exhibit** (☎ 269571) in High West St may seem out of place in Dorset but it's nevertheless an interesting place to visit. The discovery of the tomb and its contents have been recreated in montages complete with sounds and smells. It opens 9.30 am to 5.30 pm. Admission costs £4.50/2.95.

The **Keep Military Museum** (☎ 264066), beyond the Bridport Rd roundabout, traces Dorset military valour overseas. There's also a small **Dinosaur Museum** (☎ 269880), Icen Way.

The **Barclays Bank building** at No 10 South St provided the fictional home for Hardy's *Mayor of Casterbridge*. Hardy

---

The Bloody Assizes

In 1685 the duke of Monmouth, illegitimate son of Charles II, landed at Lyme Regis intending to overthrow James II and become king. His rebellion ended in defeat at the Battle of Sedgemoor in Somerset, and the duke was beheaded in the Tower of London – it took four swings of the axe to sever his head. Judge Jeffreys, the chief justice, tried the rebels in Dorchester in a barbaric trial known as the Bloody Assizes. Over 300 rebels were hanged and their gruesome drawn-and-quartered remains were displayed in towns and villages all over the region. Nearly 1000 more rebels were transported to Barbados and many more were imprisoned, fined or flogged.

himself worked for a time in an architect's office at No 62. A **statue** of Hardy watches the traffic from a seat by West Gate roundabout.

Places to Stay

The cheaper B&Bs in Dorchester have only a few rooms. *Hillfort View* (☎ 268476, 10 Hillfort Close) has a single for £18 and a double for £36. *Maumbury Cottage* (☎ 266726, 9 Maumbury Rd) is convenient for the stations and charges £34 for a double. *Mountain Ash* (☎ 264811, 30 Mountain Ash Rd) charges £20/36 for a single/double.

Casterbridge Hotel (☎ 264043, 49 High East St) is a small but luxurious hotel where B&B costs £42/72 in summer. On High St West, *Westwood House Hotel* (☎ 268018) at No 29 and *Wessex Royale Hotel* (☎ 262660) at No 32 are fine Georgian hotels charging around £49/69.

Places to Eat

An atmospheric place to take tea or a bigger meal, provided you're not squeamish about the gruesome historical associations, is the half-timbered *Judge Jeffreys' Lodgings* (☎ 264369, 6 High West St). Main dishes cost £7 to £10.

Allow around £20 a head for a three-course meal at *Mock Turtle* (☎ 264011, High West St). *The Old Tea House* across the road serves cream teas and light meals.

The *Kings Arms* (☎ 265353, High East St) has associations with Hardy's *Mayor of Casterbridge*. It offers good pub grub and has a coffee shop. The *Royal Oak (High West St)* and the nearby *Old Ship Inn* (the oldest pub in town) are also atmospheric places for a meal or drink.

Getting There & Away

There are two train stations, Dorchester South and unstaffed Dorchester West, both south-west of the town centre. Dorchester South is linked seven times daily to London's Waterloo (£32.40, three hours) via Bournemouth (£7.10) and Southampton (£14.60). There are numerous services to Weymouth (£2.50, 10 minutes). Dorchester West has links to Bath (£10.30, two hours) and Bristol.

Bus connections tend to be much slower –

buses from London take four hours. Local bus operators include Southern National (☎ 783645) for Lyme Regis and Taunton, Wilts & Dorset (☎ 01202-673555) for Salisbury, and Dorchester Coachways (☎ 262992) for Weymouth.

Getting Around

Dorchester Cycles (☎ 268787), at 31b Great Western Rd, rents bikes for £10 a day (£50 a week).

AROUND DORCHESTER
Maiden Castle

One and a half miles south-west of Dorchester, the earthwork ramparts of Maiden Castle stretch for 3 miles and enclose nearly 20 hectares. The site has been inhabited since Neolithic times but the first fort was built here around 800 BC. It was subsequently abandoned, then rebuilt around 500 BC. The earth walls were later extended and enlarged in 250 and 150 BC. Despite the addition of more defences, the Romans still captured it in AD 43, finally abandoning it

---

Charlieville

Taking shape on Dorchester's western outskirts is Poundbury, a model town designed to immortalise Prince Charles' conservative ideals and known locally as Charlieville. The estate will eventually house 5000 people. The buildings are all based on traditional designs but with modern conveniences such as double glazing and central heating.

Central to the prince's concept of a modern town is that different social groups should be mixed, living on the same street, rather than separated onto different parts of the estate. Another idea was to make the town as pedestrian-friendly as possible. Planning controls are strict, however. Window surrounds may only be painted white, and telephone wires, TV aerials and satellite dishes must be kept out of sight.

Although the project has had many critics, it's quite obviously a success. Houses are sold as quickly as they are put up and property prices have increased dramatically.

in the 4th century. The sheer size of the walls and ditches and the area they enclose is stunning, and there are wonderful views. Dorset County Museum (see Things to See & Do under Dorchester earlier in the chapter) displays finds from the site.

Hardy's Cottage

The cottage (☎ 262366) where Thomas Hardy was born and where he wrote *Far from the Madding Crowd* is at Higher Bockhampton, about 3 miles north-east of Dorchester and reached by a 10-minute walk from the car park. Despite the absence of Hardy memorabilia, the cottage is a popular attraction. It opens 11 am to 5 pm Sunday to Thursday, April to October. Admission costs £2.60.

Cerne Abbas & the Cerne Giant

Eight miles north of Dorchester, delightful Cerne Abbas has several fine 16th-century houses and a medieval church. The much rebuilt abbey house is now a private residence, although the ruins behind the house can be visited. The Abbot's Porch (1509) was once the entrance to the whole complex.

Just north of the village is the Cerne Giant, one of Britain's best-known chalk figures. The giant stands 55m tall and wields a 37m-long club. He's estimated to be anything between a few hundred and a couple of thousand years old. One thing is obvious – this old man has no need of Viagra!

With several B&Bs, Cerne Abbas would make a good alternative to staying in Dorchester (20 minutes by bus). There's good pub food at the *Red Lion* and *Royal Oak*, both on Long St.

WEYMOUTH

☎ 01305 • pop 40,000

This bustling, endearing seaside resort is an alternative to Dorchester as a base for exploring Hardy country – Weymouth was 'Budmouth' in the novels.

It was George III's experimental dip in Weymouth waters in 1789 that sparked the British passion for the seaside. Despite the shock of emerging from his 'bathing machine' to hear a band strike up in his honour, the king revisited Weymouth 13 times.

Orientation & Information

Central Weymouth, between the beach and the Inner Harbour, is only a few blocks wide. The Esplanade is the main walk along the beach, but each block of the road has a different secondary name. St Mary St is the pedestrianised shopping centre but Hope Square, on the southern side of the pretty Old Harbour, is more inviting. The TIC (☎ 785747) is on The Esplanade.

Esplanade & Old Harbour

Weymouth is a fine example of the archetypal English seaside resort and a summer walk along The Esplanade will reveal garish beach-equipment stands, deck chairs for hire, donkey rides and Punch & Judy shows. Look for the brightly painted Jubilee Memorial Clock of 1888 and the equally vivid statue of King George III, patron saint of Weymouth tourism.

The less brash Old Harbour inlet is lined with attractive old buildings used as shops, restaurants and pubs, and packed with fishing trawlers and fancy yachts from around the world.

Deep Sea Adventure

The Deep Sea Adventure (☎ 760690), in an old grainstore at 9 Custom House Quay, traces the history of diving, with exhibits on local shipwrecks, the *Titanic* and the £40 million gold recovery from HMS *Edinburgh*, sunk while part of a convoy from Russia. William Walker, the diver who spent five years shoring up the submerged footings of Winchester Cathedral earlier this century plays his part, as does the intriguing story of John Lethbridge and his pioneering 'diving engine' of 1715. The exhibit opens 9.30 am to 6.30 pm (to 8 pm in July and August). Last entry is 1½ hours before closing time. Admission costs £3.75/2.75.

Brewers Quay & the Timewalk

Brewers Quay on Hope Square has a shopping centre and plentiful attractions, including the Timewalk (☎ 777622) that takes you through the town's early history as a trading port, the disaster of the Black Death plague years, the drama of the Spanish Armada and

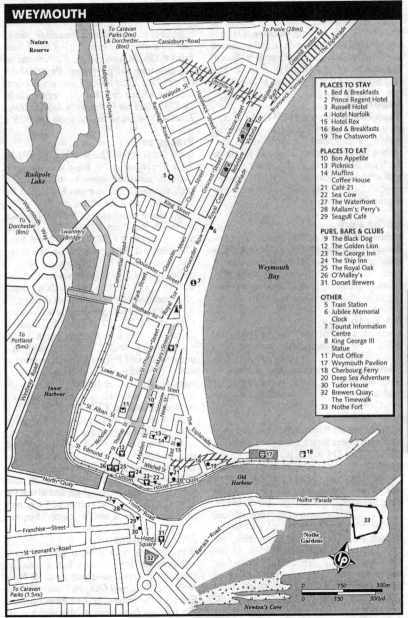

WEYMOUTH

PLACES TO STAY
1 Bed & Breakfasts
2 Prince Regent Hotel
3 Russell Hotel
4 Hotel Norfolk
15 Hotel Rex
16 Bed & Breakfasts
19 The Chatsworth

PLACES TO EAT
10 Bon Appetite
13 Picnics
14 Muffins
   Coffee House
21 Café 21
22 Sea Cow
27 The Waterfront
28 Mallam's; Perry's
29 Seagull Café

PUBS, BARS & CLUBS
9 The Black Dog
12 The Golden Lion
23 The George Inn
24 The Ship Inn
25 The Royal Oak
26 O'Malley's
31 Dorset Brewers

OTHER
5 Train Station
6 Jubilee Memorial
   Clock
7 Tourist Information
   Centre
8 King George III
   Statue
11 Post Office
17 Weymouth Pavilion
18 Cherbourg Ferry
20 Deep Sea Adventure
30 Tudor House
32 Brewers Quay;
   The Timewalk
33 Nothe Fort

SOUTH-WESTERN ENGLAND

its development as a resort. You even see a figure of the portly George III emerging from his famous bathing machine. This excellent Timewalk tour ends with the story of the Devenish brewery, in which it is housed. It opens 10 am to 5.30 pm (to 9 pm in July and August). Admission costs £4.25/3.

Tudor House

When Tudor House (☎ 812341) at 3 Trinity St was built around 1600, the waterfront would have lapped the front door. Furnished in Tudor style, it opens 11 am to 3.45 pm Tuesday to Friday, June to September; first Sunday afternoon of the month only, October to May. Admission, including a guided tour, costs £2/50p.

Nothe Fort

Perched on the end of the promontory, 19th-century Nothe Fort (☎ 787243) houses a museum on Britain's coastal defence system. It opens 10.30 am to 5.30 pm daily, early May to late September (from 2 pm only on Sunday in winter). Admission is £3/free.

Places to Stay

There is a freephone number (☎ 0800 765223) for accommodation bookings.

Camping There are caravan parks between Overcombe and Preston, north along the road to Dorchester and south near Sandsfoot Castle and Chesil Beach.

B&Bs & Hotels Weymouth has an awesome number of places to stay. Cheaper B&Bs, typically costing £14 to £18 per person, can be found all over town. Good hunting grounds include Brunswick Terrace, on the northern part of The Esplanade. The pretty B&Bs along this stretch look straight over the beach.

Lennox St, just north of the train station, and Waterloo Place, the stretch of The Esplanade from the Lennox St junction, are both packed with cheaper B&Bs. At the other end of The Esplanade, just before Weymouth Quay, there are also ranks of B&Bs from Nos 1 to 34.

The Chatsworth (☎ 785012), at No 14, looks out to sea in one direction and across the Old Harbour in the other. Rooms with bathroom start from £25 per person.

Most of the places along the central part of The Esplanade are expensive but *Hotel Norfolk* (☎ 786734) at Nos 125–6 is reasonable, charging from £30 per person. *Russell Hotel* (☎ 786059) at Nos 135–8 has singles/doubles for £32/64 and *Prince Regent Hotel* (☎ 771313) at No 139 charges £55/85. *Hotel Rex* (☎ 760400), at No 29, costs £54.50/96.

Places to Eat

In the Old Harbour, *The Sea Cow* (☎ 783524, 7 Custom House Quay) has a good range of seafood, including more exotic local fish such as John Dory. Count on £15 to £25 for a three-course meal with wine.

On the southern side of the Old Harbour on Trinity Rd, *Perry's* (☎ 785799) at No 4, and *Mallam's* (☎ 776757) at No 5 both have a la carte and fixed price menus and make imaginative use of local seafood. At Perry's, dishes on the a la carte menu range from £12.50 to £22.50 (lobster). Mallam's fixed price menu costs £18.90 for two courses.

Good places for takeaways are *Bon Appetite* (☎ 777375, 32 St Mary St), offering filled baguettes and gourmet pizza slices, and *Picknics* (☎ 761317, 31 Maiden St), north of the Old Harbour, which prepares a variety of takeaway sandwiches and filled rolls. *Muffins Coffee House* (St Alban St) is popular for lunches, with specials chalked on boards outside. *Café 21* (East St) is a funky little vegetarian place with healthy, tasty food and low prices.

Weymouth is a good place to sample that most British of fast foods – fish and chips. On the southern side of the harbour, *The Waterfront* (☎ 781237, 14 Trinity Rd) does takeaway cod, haddock, skate and plaice for around £3. Round the corner at 10 Trinity St, *Seagull Café* is another cheap chippie.

Entertainment

Weymouth is packed with pubs. *Dorset Brewers* on Hope Square has a nautical theme and serves good pub grub. *O'Malley's* and *The Royal Oak*, on Custom House Quay by the bridge, or *The Ship Inn* and the *George Inn*, towards the sea, are all popular. Back from the harbour, there's *The Golden Lion*, on the corner of St Mary and St Edmund Sts. *The Black Dog*, on pedestrianised St Mary St, is said to be the oldest pub in town and is named after the first black Labrador brought into England on a ship from Newfoundland.

Weymouth Pavilion (☎ 783225), on the quay, has a busy schedule of events year round. It's pretty highbrow stuff – highlights have included Australian male strippers and Ronnie Corbett.

Getting There & Away

Bus Buses stop along The Esplanade. Phone ☎ 224535 for local bus information. Dorchester Coachways (☎ 262992) has daily buses to London. Wilts & Dorset operates to Dorchester, Salisbury, Lyme Regis, Taunton, Poole and Bournemouth.

Train Weymouth station is conveniently located at the junction of Ranelagh Rd and King St. There are hourly services to London (£33.70, 3½ hours) via Bournemouth (£8.80) and Southampton. Services to other centres in the south-west include nearby Dorchester (£2.50, 12 minutes).

Boat Condor (☎ 761551) high-speed catamaran car ferries whiz across to Cherbourg in France in 4¼ hours. A day trip costs £29.90 return. Condor also runs ferries to Jersey and Guernsey.

WEYMOUTH TO LYME REGIS
Portland

South of Weymouth, Portland is joined to the mainland by the long sweep of Chesil Beach. Many famous buildings have been made from locally quarried Portland stone. **Portland Castle** (☎ 01305-820539) is one of the finest examples of the defensive castles constructed during Henry VIII's castle-building spree, spurred by fear of an attack from France. The castle is owned by the English Heritage (EH; see Historic Organisations in the Facts for the Visitor chapter). Admission costs £2.80/1.40.

There are superb views from the lighthouse, which houses the TIC (☎ 01305-861233), at the end of **Portland Bill**. It's £2/1.50 to climb the 41m-high tower. An earlier, smaller lighthouse now acts as a bird observatory.

Chesil Beach

Chesil Beach is a long curving sandbank (except that it's made of pebbles rather than sand) stretching along the coast for 10 miles from Portland to Abbotsbury. The bank encloses the slightly stagnant waters of the Fleet Lagoon, a haven for water birds, including the famed Abbotsbury swans. The stones vary from pebble size at Abbotsbury in the west to around 15cm in diameter at Portland in the east; local fishermen can supposedly tell their position along the bank by gauging the size of the stones. In places, the stone bank reaches 15m high. Although winter storms can wash right over the top, it has never been broken up. The bank is accessible at the Portland end and from just west of Abbotsbury.

Abbotsbury
☎ 01305

Pretty, little Abbotsbury boasts several attractions. The huge **tithe barn** (☎ 871817), at one time a communal storage site for farm produce, is 83m long and was used for a harvest supper scene in Polanski's *Far from the Madding Crowd*. It houses an interesting country museum and recent exhibits include a partial recreation of the terracotta army from Xian, China. It opens 10 am to 6 pm daily, April to October; on Sunday only the rest of the year. Admission costs £4/3.

On the coast, and offering fine views of the Fleet Lagoon, is **Abbotsbury Swannery** (☎ 871130). Swans have been nesting here for 600 years and the colony can number up to 600, plus cygnets. The walk through the swannery and reed beds will tell you all you ever wanted to know about swans. Come in May for the nests, in late May and June for the cygnets. It opens 10 am to 6 pm (to dusk in winter) and admission costs £5/3.

The swannery was founded by Abbotsbury's Benedictine monastery, which was destroyed in 1541. Traces of the monastery remain by the tithe barn. The energetic can

SOUTH-WESTERN ENGLAND

walk up to 14th-century **St Catherine's Chapel**, overlooking the swannery, the village and Chesil Beach.

Places to Stay & Eat Abbotsbury has several B&Bs and places to eat. The old *Ilchester Arms* (☎ 871243), right in the village, has interesting pub food such as Dorset sausage baguette, and a restaurant. It is also a hotel with double rooms from £45.50 excluding breakfast.

Chesil House (☎ 871324) is a friendly place with rooms from £22.50 per person.

Getting There & Away Abbotsbury is 9 miles north-west of Weymouth on the B3157 and regular buses run this route during summer.

LYME REGIS
☎ 01297 • pop 4600

The attractive, delicate seaside town of Lyme Regis marks the end of Dorset –

Devon begins just beyond the pier known as the Cobb. The Cobb is a famous literary spot: not only did Louisa Musgrove's accident in Jane Austen's novel *Persuasion* take place here, but it was also where *The French Lieutenant's Woman* stood and stared out to sea in John Fowles' novel (and where Meryl Streep stood in the film).

The town's other claim to fame is prehistoric. The limestone cliffs on either side of town are some of Britain's richest sources of fossils and the first dinosaur skeletons were discovered here.

In 1685, the duke of Monmouth landed on Monmouth Beach, west of the town, to start his abortive rebellion against James II. See the boxed text 'The Bloody Assizes' in the Dorchester section earlier in the chapter.

Orientation & Information
The A3052 drops precipitously into Lyme Regis from one side and climbs equally

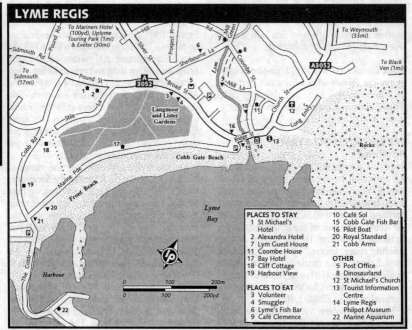

LYME REGIS

PLACES TO STAY
1 St Michael's Hotel
2 Alexandra Hotel
7 Lym Guest House
11 Coombe House
17 Bay Hotel
18 Cliff Cottage
19 Harbour View

PLACES TO EAT
3 Volunteer
4 Smuggler
6 Lyme's Fish Bar
9 Café Clemence

10 Café Sol
15 Cobb Gate Fish Bar
16 Pilot Boat
20 Royal Standard
21 Cobb Arms

OTHER
5 Post Office
8 Dinosaurland
12 St Michael's Church
13 Tourist Information Centre
14 Lyme Regis Philpot Museum
22 Marine Aquarium

steeply out on the other. From Bridge St, where the A3052 meets the coast, Marine Parade runs west to the harbour. The TIC (☎ 442138) is situated where Church St becomes Bridge St.

Museums

Lyme Regis Philpot Museum (☎ 443370), in Bridge St, has displays of fossils and local history. The cliffs west of the harbour and Monmouth Beach are still prone to fossil-exposing landslips; the museum has details of the Dowlands Landslip on Christmas Day 1839, when a stretch of cliff top three quarters of a mile long slid away, taking with it farms and houses. It opens 10 am to 5 pm (closed noon to 2.30 pm Sunday). Admission costs £1/40p.

Dinosaurland (☎ 443541), on Coombe St, is an eclectic mix of science, fossils and local folklore. It opens 10 am to 5 pm, Easter to November. Admission costs £3.20/1.90.

The Cobb

The Cobb is a 183m-long stone jetty-cum-breakwater. The small **Marine Aquarium** (☎ 443678) has interesting displays of local marine life. It opens 10 am to 5 pm (later in peak season), April to October. Admission costs £1.40/90p.

From Cobb Gate towards East Cliff runs **Gun Cliff Walk**. The superstructure ingeniously conceals the town's sewage system.

Places to Stay

Lyme Regis has plenty of hotels, guesthouses and B&Bs.

Two people with a tent can camp at **Uplyme Touring Park** (☎ 442801, Hook Farm, Uplyme) for £9 in summer. To get there, walk up Silver St/Uplyme Rd (towards Exeter) for about 15 minutes.

Lym Guest House (☎ 442164, 1 Mill Green), at the junction of Hill Rd and Sherborne Lane, has B&B from £22 per person. **Coombe House** (☎ 443849, 41 Coombe St) costs £16 for rooms with bathroom.

On Cobb Rd, up from the harbour, there is **Harbour View** (☎ 443910) which charges £17 (bed only, no breakfast), and **Cliff**

Cottage (☎ 443334) with doubles for £38 including breakfast. Both have great views.

St Michael's Hotel (☎ 442503, Pound St) has nice views and costs £35 for rooms with bathroom, £30 without the sea view. Nearby is **Alexandra Hotel** (☎ 442010), one of the town's finest hotels, which charges £50/85 for singles/doubles.

The 17th-century **Mariners Hotel** (☎ 442753, Silver St) is full of history and atmosphere, with rooms from £42 a head. **Bay Hotel** (☎ 442059, Marine Parade) has a seafront location and costs from £45 per person.

Places to Eat

Many of the pubs do food – try the **Cobb Arms** or **Royal Standard**, both on Marine Parade by the Cobb. Other possibilities include the **Volunteer** (Broad St) and **Pilot Boat** (Bridge St).

Café Sol on Coombe St has a varied and light menu for any time of day and a welcoming vibe. Around the corner in the old mill complex is popular **Café Clemence**. The **Smuggler** (Broad St) does all-day breakfasts, lunches, cream teas and early suppers, till 8 pm.

For fish and chips try **Lyme's Fish Bar** (34 Sherborne Lane) or **Cobb Gate Fish Bar** on the waterfront.

Getting There & Away

Lyme Regis makes a convenient midway point between Dorchester or Weymouth and Exeter. National Express buses connect with Exeter, a 1¾-hour trip. Southern National Bus No 31 links Lyme Regis to Taunton and Weymouth via Axminster.

AROUND LYME REGIS
Parnham House

Parnham House (☎ 01308-862204) is both a home and a showroom for owner John Makepeace's contemporary furniture. You might pick up a chair for £600 but most pieces are in the £3000 to £10,000 range. It's near Beaminster, 5 miles north of Bridport, and opens 10 am to 5 pm Tuesday to Thursday, and on Sunday, April to October. Admission costs £5/2.

SOUTH-WESTERN ENGLAND

Forde Abbey

Set in 12 hectares of magnificent gardens, Forde Abbey (☎ 01460-220231) is a monastery converted into a private home. It's 6 miles north-east of Axminster and opens 1 to 4.30 pm on Wednesday and Sunday, April to October. Admission is £5/free, which includes entry to the gardens. The gardens open 10 am to 4.30 pm and admission is £4/free.

SHERBORNE

☎ 01935 • pop 7500

Sherborne has a wonderful abbey church with a colourful history. On the edge of town, remains of the Old and New Castles face each other across Sherborne Lake. The TIC (☎ 815341) is at 3 Tilton Court, Digby Rd, opposite the abbey entrance.

Sherborne Abbey

The abbey started life as a small Saxon church early in the 8th century and became a Benedictine abbey in 998. After further expansion and decoration, it was seized by the Crown in 1539 whereupon the townsfolk clubbed together and bought it as their parish church.

Simmering unrest between monastery and town flared up in 1437. At that time, the monks used the chancel of the church while the townspeople used the nave. When the monks attempted to narrow a doorway between the abbey and the connected All Hallows Church (now gone), a pitched battle broke out and a flaming arrow shot across the church from town end to monastery end and set the roof alight.

The abbey is entered via a Norman porch built in 1180. Immediately on the left is the Norman door, built in 1140, which was the cause of the 1437 riots and fire. The remains of All Hallows are to the west of the Saxon wall; a Saxon doorway from 1050 survives. The superb fan vault above the choir dates from the early 15th century and is the oldest ceiling of this type and size in the country. The similar vault over the nave is from later in the century. Solid Saxon-Norman piers support the abbey's soaring central tower.

The monks' choir stalls date from the mid-15th century and are carved with amusing figures.

Other Abbey Sights The abbey has a cathedral-like close where you'll find the 1437 **St John's Almshouses**, open 2 to 4 pm on Tuesday, and Thursday to Saturday, May to September. Admission costs £1. The **museum** (☎ 812252) in Half Moon St has a model of the Old Castle before it was slighted. It opens 10.30 am to 4.30 pm Tuesday to Saturday, and 2.30 to 4.30 pm Sunday, April to October. Admission is £1/free. **Sherborne School**, a private school, dates back to 1550 and occupies various buildings from the monastery.

Old Castle

East of the town centre stand the ruins of the Old Castle (☎ 812730; EH), originally constructed from 1107. In the late 16th century, Sir Walter Raleigh took a fancy to the castle, and Queen Elizabeth I negotiated its purchase for him. Before Sir Walter could move in, he incurred the queen's displeasure by marrying one of her ladies-in-waiting and Sir Walter and his new bride paid a short visit to the Tower of London. Later he spent large sums of money modernising the castle, before deciding it wasn't worth the effort and moving across the River Yeo to start work on a new castle.

Cromwell destroyed the castle after a 16-day siege in 1645. 'A malicious and mischievous castle, like its owner [the earl of Bristol],' he thundered. The castle opens 10 am to 6 pm daily. Admission costs £1.60/80p.

Sherborne Castle

Sir Walter Raleigh commenced his New Castle (☎ 813182) in 1594 but by 1608 he was back in prison, this time at the hands of James I. The king first gave the castle away, then took it back, and in 1617 sold it to Sir John Digby, earl of Bristol. It's been the Digby family residence ever since. The castle opens 12.30 to 4.30 pm on Thursday, Saturday and Sunday, Easter to September. Admission costs £5/2.50.

Places to Stay
There are few budget B&B places in Sherborne. **Britannia Inn** (☎ *813300, Westbury St)* charges from £20 per person in the week, £25 at the weekend.

Clatcombe Grange (☎ *814355, Bristol Rd)* has comfortable accommodation in a converted barn and charges £25/50. **Antelope Hotel** (☎ *812077, Greenhill)* charges £44/65.

In Milborne Port, 2 miles from Sherborne, is *The Old Vicarage* (☎ *01963-251117, Sherborne Rd)*. B&B costs from £25 to £45 per person, depending on the room. There are weekend breaks also including dinner, from £41 to £63 per person. It's a listed building in an attractive country setting.

Places to Eat
For light meals try *Three Wishes* (78 Cheap St). *Cross Keys Hotel* (☎ 812492), at the junction of Cheap and Long Sts, right by the abbey, has an extensive pub-food menu. Also near the abbey is *Digby Tap*, a pub offering a wide range of ales and good-sized portions of traditional fare.

SHAFTESBURY
☎ 01747 • pop 4900
Situated on a 240m-high ridge, **Shaftesbury Abbey** (☎ 852910) was founded in 888 by Alfred the Great and was at one time England's richest nunnery. Today, only scant signs of the foundations remain, situated off Park Walk with fine views over the surrounding countryside. St Edward (see Corfe Castle under South-Eastern Dorset earlier) was said to have been buried here, and King Canute died at the abbey in 1035. It opens 10 am to 5 pm, April to October. Admission costs £1.50/60p.

The picturesquely steep cobbled street known as **Gold Hill** tumbles down the ridge from beside the abbey ruins. **Shaftesbury Museum** (☎ 852157), at the top of the hill, opens 10.30 am to 4.30 pm Easter to October. Admission is £1.20/free.

The TIC (☎ 853514) at 8 Bell St has a board outside listing local accommodation. *The Ship Inn* and *King's Arms*, by the central car park, have pub food, or try *The Salt Cellar*, a cosy cafe at the top of Gold Hill.

Wiltshire

Wiltshire boasts wonderful rolling chalk downs, Britain's most important prehistoric sites at Stonehenge and Avebury, a fine cathedral at Salisbury and a number of the stateliest of stately homes at Wilton, Stourhead and Longleat. The Ridgeway Path, taking walkers along a crest of the downs, has its western end in Wiltshire.

ACTIVITIES
The **Wiltshire Cycleway** comprises six circular routes ranging from 70 to 160 miles. TICs stock the *Wiltshire Cycleway* brochure that details the routes and lists cycle shops and rental outlets. *Wiltshire Cycleway Campsites* lists camp sites along the routes.

Stretching from Bristol to Reading, the 87-mile **Kennet & Avon Canal** was reopened in 1990 after standing derelict for 40 years. Built by the brilliant engineer John Rennie between 1794 and 1810, it's now used by narrow boats and has some fine stretches of towpath. The stretch from Bath to Bradford-on-Avon passes a notable aqueduct. The flight of 29 locks just outside Devizes is an engineering marvel. The Kennet & Avon Canal Museum (☎ 01380-721279) on the wharf in Devizes has information on the canal.

SALISBURY
☎ 01722 • pop 37,000
Salisbury is justly famous for its cathedral and its close, but it's still very much a bustling market town, not just a tourist trap. Markets have been held in the town centre twice weekly for over 600 years and the jumble of stalls still draws a cheery crowd. The town's architecture mixes every style since the Middle Ages and includes some beautiful, half-timbered, black-and-white buildings.

Salisbury makes a good base for visiting attractions throughout Wiltshire and for excursions to the coast.

Orientation & Information
The city centre is a 10-minute walk to the east of the train station or just a couple of minutes

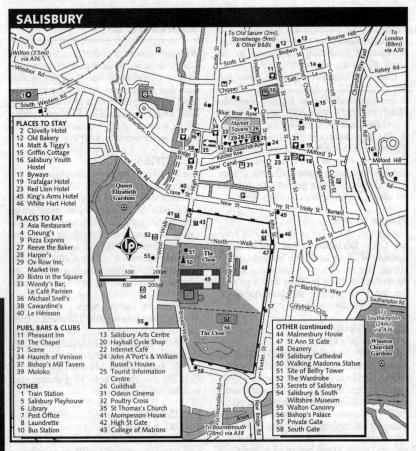

SALISBURY

PLACES TO STAY
2 Clovelly Hotel
12 Old Bakery
14 Matt & Tiggy's
15 Griffin Cottage
16 Salisbury Youth
   Hostel
17 Byways
19 Trafalgar Hotel
23 Red Lion Hotel
45 King's Arms Hotel
46 White Hart Hotel

PLACES TO EAT
3 Asia Restaurant
4 Cheung's
9 Pizza Express
27 Reeve the Baker
29 Ox Row Inn;
   Market Inn
30 Bistro in the Square
33 Woody's Bar;
   Le Café Parisien
36 Michael Snell's
38 Cawardine's
40 Le Hérisson

PUBS, BARS & CLUBS
11 Pheasant Inn
18 The Chapel
21 Scene
34 Haunch of Venison
37 Bishop's Mill Tavern
39 Moloko

OTHER
1 Train Station
5 Salisbury Playhouse
6 Library
7 Post Office
8 Laundrette
10 Bus Station

13 Salisbury Arts Centre
20 Hayball Cycle Shop
22 Internet Café
24 John A'Port's & William
   Russel's Houses
25 Tourist Information
   Centre
26 Guildhall
31 Odeon Cinema
32 Poultry Cross
35 St Thomas's Church
41 Mompesson House
42 High St Gate
43 College of Matrons

OTHER (continued)
44 Malmesbury House
47 St Ann St Gate
48 Deanery
49 Salisbury Cathedral
50 Walking Madonna Statue
51 Site of Belfry Tower
52 The Wardrobe
53 Secrets of Salisbury
54 Salisbury & South
   Wiltshire Museum
55 Walton Canonry
56 Bishop's Palace
57 Private Gate
58 South Gate

south of the bus station. Everything is within easy walking distance of Market Square, the city centre, with its impressive Guildhall.

Directly behind the Guildhall, on Fish Row, the TIC (☎ 334956) opens 9.30 am to 5 pm Monday to Saturday, and 10.30 am to 5 pm Sunday in summer. It sells *Seeing Salisbury*, a useful pamphlet which outlines walks around the town and across the water meadows for classic views of the cathedral.

Excellent one-hour walking tours of Salisbury (£2.50/1) leave from the TIC at 11 am and 6 pm, May to September. On Friday, an 8 pm ghost walk replaces the 6 pm tour.

Internet Cafe on Milford St is a swish little Internet centre with iMacs only.

Salisbury Cathedral

The Cathedral Church of the Blessed Virgin Mary (☎ 555100) is one of the most beautiful and cohesive in Britain, an inspiration to the artist John Constable who painted it from across the water meadows. It was built in uniform Early English (or early pointed) Gothic, a style characterised by the first pointed arches and flying buttresses and a feeling of austerity. The uniformity is a result of the speed with which the cathedral was built between 1220 and 1258 and that it has not subsequently undergone major rebuilding. The sole exception is the magnificent spire, at 123m the highest in Britain, an afterthought added between 1285 and 1315.

Salisbury Cathedral had its origins 2 miles farther north with a Norman cathedral at Old Sarum (see Old Sarum under Around Salisbury later in the chapter). In 1217, Bishop Poore petitioned the pope for permission to move the cathedral to a better location, complaining that the water supply on the hilltop was inadequate, the wind drowned out the singing, the weather gave the monks rheumatism, the crowded site meant the housing was inadequate and, worst of all, the soldiers were rude. His request was granted and in 1220 a new cathedral was constructed on the plains, conveniently close to three rivers.

Starting at the eastern end, **Trinity Chapel** was completed by 1225, the main part of the church by 1258 and the whole thing by 1266. The cloisters were added at about the same time and a few years later it was decided to add the magnificent tower and spire. Because this had not featured in the original plans the four central piers of the building were expected to carry an unexpected extra 6400 tons. Some fast thinking was required to enable them to do this.

The highly decorative West Screen was the last part of the cathedral to be completed and provides a fine view from across the close. The cathedral is entered via the cloister passage and the **south-west door**. The 70m-long nave, with its beautiful Purbeck marble piers, was 'tidied up' by James Wyatt between 1789 and 1792; among other things he lined up the tombs in the nave neatly. At the south-western end of the nave is the **grave slab of Bishop Joscelyn** (1141–1184), at one time thought to be the tomb of Bishop Roger, who completed the final cathedral at Old Sarum where he was bishop from 1107 to 1139. A **model** in the southern aisle shows the cathedral's construction.

The **Shrine of St Osmund** was installed in 1226, a year after Trinity Chapel was completed. St Osmund had completed the original cathedral at Old Sarum in 1092 and was canonised in 1457. His actual grave remains

in Trinity Chapel. The **Tomb of William Longespée** was the first new tomb in the cathedral, following his death in 1226. A son of Henry II, he was present at the signing of the Magna Carta and also laid one of the cathedral's foundation stones.

The soaring spire is the cathedral's most impressive feature. In 1668, Sir Christopher Wren, creator of St Paul's in London, surveyed the cathedral and calculated that the spire was leaning sideways by 75 centimetres. In 1737, a **brass plate** was inserted in the floor of the nave, directly under the centre of the spire, and the lean was recorded. It had not shifted at all since Wren's measurement, nor had it moved any farther when re-recorded in 1951 and 1970.

Other parts of the cathedral clearly show the strain, however. The tower and spire are supported by four **piers**, each nearly 2m square, but the additional weight has bent these massive stone columns. If you look up from the bottom, the curve is quite visible, particularly on the eastern piers. Flying buttresses were later added to the outside of the building to support the four corners of the original tower. More buttresses were added internally and the openings to the eastern transepts were reinforced with **scissor arches**, as in Wells cathedral. Reinforcement work on the notoriously 'wonky spire' continues to this day.

Not everything in the cathedral requires looking upwards. The **tomb of Sir Richard Mompesson**, who died in 1627, and his wife Catherine, is a brilliantly colourful work. The grandiose **tomb of Edward Seymour** (1539–1621) and **Lady Catherine Grey**, sister of Lady Jane Grey, is at the eastern end of the ambulatory. The first part of the cathedral to be built, **Trinity Chapel**, at the eastern end, has fine Purbeck marble pillars; the vivid blue **Prisoners of Conscience** stained-glass window was installed in 1980.

The Sudan chapel contains a magnificent 14th-century **memorial brass** to Bishop Robert Wyvil showing him praying in Sherborne Castle, and a **prism memorial** to artist Rex Whistler who lived in The Close. The **clock** displayed in the northern aisle is the oldest in England and one of the oldest in the world. It was certainly in existence in 1386 when funds were provided for maintenance of a 'clocke'. Restored in 1956, it continues to operate, maintaining the 600-year-old tradition of having a clock in this position.

The cloisters lead to the beautiful Gothic **Chapter House** of 1263–84 which houses one of the four surviving original versions of the **Magna Carta**, the agreement made between King John and his barons in 1215. The delicate fan-vaulted ceiling is supported by a single central column. A frieze around the room recounts Old Testament tales.

The cathedral opens 8 am to 6.30 pm; a donation of £3/1 is requested. The Chapter House opens 9.30 am to 4.45 pm Monday to Saturday, and 1 to 4.45 pm Sunday. Monday to Saturday there are tower tours (£3/2) at 11 am, 2 pm, 3 pm and 6.30 pm; 4.30 pm only on Sunday. The tour offers a unique opportunity to come to grips with medieval building practices and is highly recommended.

The Close

Salisbury Cathedral has England's largest, and arguably most beautiful, cathedral close. Many of the buildings were constructed at the same time as the cathedral although it owes most of its present appearance to Wyatt's late 18th-century clean-up of the cathedral. The Close was actually walled in, physically separating it from the town, in 1333, using the previous cathedral at Old Sarum as a source of building material. To this day it remains an elite enclave, with the gates in the wall still locked every night. Residents have their own gate keys. The most famous current resident is former prime minister Edward Heath.

Wyatt also cleared The Close of gravestones and demolished the late 13th-century **external belfry**, by then in a ruinous condition. Striding across the lawns of The Close on the western side of the cathedral is Elizabeth Frink's **Walking Madonna** (1981).

The Close has several museums and houses open for inspection, most of them with cafe facilities. **Salisbury & South Wiltshire Museum** (☎ 332151) in King's House has exhibits on local prehistory, including

Stonehenge and Old Sarum. It opens 10 am to 5 pm Monday to Saturday; and 2 to 5 pm Sunday in July and August. Admission costs £3/75p. A half-hour audiovisual performance, **'Secrets of Salisbury'**, is on show in the Medieval Hall (☎ 412472) which opens 11 am to 5 pm daily, for £1.50/1. **The Wardrobe** (☎ 414536) opens 10 am to 4.30 pm, April to October, and shows military paraphernalia. It opens on weekdays only in November, February and March. Admission costs £2.50/50p.

Built in 1701, **Mompesson House** (☎ 335659; NT) is a fine Queen Anne house with a walled garden. It opens noon to 5.30 pm Saturday to Wednesday, April to October. Admission costs £3.40/1.70.

Malmesbury House (☎ 327027) was originally a 13th-century canonry and later the residence of the earls of Malmesbury. It can be visited by guided tour (£5). Phone ahead for times.

From High St, The Close is entered by the narrow High St Gate. Just inside is the **College of Matrons**, founded in 1682 for the widows and unmarried daughters of clergymen. South of the cathedral is the **Bishop's Palace**, now the Cathedral School, parts of which date back to 1220. The **Deanery** on Bishop's Walk mainly dates from the 13th century. Izaak Walton, patron saint of fishermen, lived for a time in the **Walton Canonry**, and no doubt dropped a line in the nearby Avon.

St Thomas's Church

Were it not for Salisbury Cathedral, splendid St Thomas's Church would attract much more attention. The light, airy edifice dates mainly from the 15th century and its principal attraction is the superb 'doom', or judgement-day painting which spreads up and over the chancel arch. Painted around 1475, it was whitewashed over during the Reformation and uncovered again in 1881. In the centre, Christ sits in judgment astride a rainbow with scenes of heaven on the left and hell on the right; hell is supervised by a hairy devil whose foot pokes out onto the chancel arch. On the hell side look out for a bishop and two kings, naked except for their mitre and crowns, and for a miser with his money-bags and a female alehouse owner, the only person allowed to hang on to her clothes.

Market Square

Markets were first held here in 1219 and since 1361 have been held every Tuesday and Saturday. The market once spread much farther than the present car-park area and street names like Oatmeal Row, Fish Row or Silver St indicate their medieval specialities. The square is dominated by the late 18th-century Guildhall.

Facing towards the Guildhall are two **medieval houses**: John A'Port's of 1425 and William Russel's of 1306. Russel's looks newer because of a false front, but inside its age is revealed. The present shop owners, Watson's of Salisbury, are used to sightseers and produce a leaflet about what is probably the town's oldest house.

Immediately behind Market Square look out for Fish Row, with some fine old houses, and for the 15th-century **Poultry Cross**.

Places to Stay

Camping The *Coombe Nurseries Park* (☎ 328451) is about 3 miles west of Salisbury at Netherhampton. A tent site for two costs £9. There are other sites in the vicinity.

Hostels In an attractive old building in large gardens, *Salisbury Youth Hostel* (☎ 327572, *Milford Hill*) is an easy 10-minute walk along Milford St from the centre of Salisbury, just beyond the ring road. The nightly cost is £10.85/7.40 adults/under-18s.

Close to the bus station, *Matt & Tiggy's* (☎ 327443, 51 Salt Lane) is an independent hostel-like guesthouse with several houses around town. A bed costs £10 including a light breakfast and they can hook you up with Internet access, bike hire and the such.

B&Bs & Hotels Castle Rd, the A345 continuation of Castle St north from Salisbury, has a wide choice of B&Bs between the ring road and Old Sarum. *Leena's Guesthouse* (☎ 335419) at No 50 has six singles/doubles from £25/46. *Castlewood* (☎ 421494) at No 45 is similarly priced.

The *Edwardian Lodge* (☎ 413329) at No 59 charges £30/45 for singles/doubles with bathroom, less in the low season.

Follow Milford St out of the centre and, just beyond the ring road turn right to *Byways* (☎ 328364, 31 Fowlers Rd). Rooms cost from £35/55, almost all of them with bathroom. This is a pleasantly quiet area but only a short walk from the centre of town.

On the other side of the centre, near the train station, *Clovelly Hotel* (☎ 322055, 17–19 Mill Rd) has singles/doubles for £38/58, most with bathroom.

The *Old Bakery* (☎ 320100, 35 Bedwin St) is a small B&B in a 16th-century house with singles/doubles from £18/38. It is a convivial and comfortable place.

Another B&B that has been recommended is 17th-century *Griffin Cottage* (☎ 328259, 10 St Edmund's Church St), a small comfortable place where even the bread is home-baked. There are just two doubles at £38.

Red Lion Hotel (☎ 323334, Milford St), with singles/doubles from £84/104, is very comfortable and of great historical interest. Dating from 1230, it's said to be the oldest purpose-built hotel in Britain.

The characterful *King's Arms Hotel* (☎ 327629, 9–11 St John St) has singles/doubles from £50/75. Five hundred years old, *Trafalgar Hotel* (☎ 338686, 33 Milford St) has 18 rooms, all with bathroom, costing from £55/65 (breakfast is extra).

Concealed behind a grand portico near the cathedral close is Salisbury's top hotel, *White Hart Hotel* (☎ 327476, 1 St John St). There are 68 rooms at £95/135; breakfast is extra. Cheaper B&B deals are available at the weekend.

Places to Eat

Restaurants In Market Square in the centre, *Reeve the Baker* has an upstairs tearoom, popular for lunch and snacks. *Michael Snell's*, near St Thomas's Church, does light lunches and teas. *Cawardine's* is an immensely popular cafe with local residents.

Upstairs on Market Square, *Harper's* (☎ 333118) has reasonably priced set lunches at under £10 for three courses. Also open for dinner, the a la carte menu includes dishes such as roast Barbary duck with plum and ginger sauce and salmon with fennel. Nearby are *Bistro in the Square* (☎ 328923), which offers breakfasts, light meals, soups and filled baguettes, and French-run *Le Café Parisien* (☎ 412356, Oatmeal Row). Also very centrally located is a branch of *Pizza Express* (☎ 415191, 50 Blue Boar Row).

Le Hérisson (☎ 333471, Crane St) is a thriving deli and restaurant business that draws people with flamboyant food at unflamboyant prices. Modern British main courses are around £8.

Fisherton St, between the centre and the station, features a choice of reasonably priced ethnic restaurants. *Cheung's* (☎ 327375), at No 60, is a popular Chinese restaurant, while *Asia Restaurant* (☎ 327628), at No 90, is good for spicy Indian food.

Pubs The *Haunch of Venison* (☎ 322024, 1–5 Minster St) is an atmospheric old pub with panelled walls and oak beams. There's an interesting range of pub food and more than a hundred malt whiskies on offer. Finish your meal *before* asking to see the 200-year-old mummified hand of the card player.

Pheasant Inn (☎ 327069), an old pub on the corner of Salt Lane and Rollestone St, attracts a young crowd and serves lunches from around £5. There's a good vegetarian menu. Also atmospheric is the 14th-century *Cross Keys*, complete with beams and good pub food.

Entertainment

Trendy *Moloko* (☎ 507050, 5 Bridge St) and *Woody's Bar* (12 Minster St) are both lively hang-outs, and Moloko often has a late licence. *Ox Row Inn* and *Market Inn* are dead central on Market Square, while *Bishop's Mill Tavern* has an outdoor area with river views. *Scene*, on lively Milford St, is a minimalist cafe-bar that's an 'in' place right now. *The Chapel* is a tacky sort of pub-club that has cheap drinks during the week and a cover charge at the weekend.

There is often interesting live entertainment including high-quality contemporary music and performances in the *Salisbury Arts Centre* (☎ 321744), a converted church

in Bedwin St. It opens 10 am to 4 pm Tuesday to Saturday.

The *Salisbury Playhouse* (☎ 320333) is on Malthouse Lane. The *Odeon Cinema* on New Canal must be one of the few cinemas in the world with a medieval foyer.

Getting There & Away

See the fares tables in the Getting Around chapter at the start of the book. Salisbury is 88 miles west of London, 52 miles east of Bristol and 24 miles from Southampton.

There are excellent walking and cycling routes to and from Salisbury; Hayball Cycle Shop (see Getting Around) has the useful *Cycling Around Salisbury* (free). The Clarendon Way is a 26-mile walking route to Winchester.

Bus Three National Express (☎ 0870 580 8080) buses a day run from London via Heathrow to Salisbury (£12, three hours). National Express has a daily Portsmouth-Salisbury-Bath-Bristol service, but it's more expensive than local operators Wilts & Dorset (☎ 336855). Salisbury-Bath costs £6.25 with National Express, just £3.90 with the local operator. There are roughly hourly services to Bath (and Bristol) via Wilton and Bradford-on-Avon (two hours, hourly, X4), to Bournemouth and Poole (1½ hours, X3) and to Southampton (1¼ hours, hourly, X7).

Wilts & Dorset operates bus No 3 to Stonehenge; Nos 5 (Monday to Saturday) and No 6 (Sunday only) to Avebury, Marlborough and Swindon; and No 184 (and X84 in summer) to Dorchester. Hampshire Bus operates X68 to Winchester.

Train Salisbury is linked by rail to Portsmouth (£11.10, 1¼ hours, numerous), Bath (£9.80, two hours, numerous) and Exeter (£20.10, two hours, 10 daily). There are 30 trains a day from London's Waterloo station (£21.80, 1½ hours). To get to Winchester (£9.50) requires a change at Basingstoke or Southampton.

Getting Around

Bikes can be hired from Hayball Cycle Shop (☎ 411378) on Winchester St for £9 per day.

AROUND SALISBURY
Old Sarum

Once an Iron-Age hillfort, Old Sarum (☎ 01722-335398; EH) became a town with its own cathedral in the Middle Ages. Today, the 22-hectare site consists of impressive earthworks offering fine views of Salisbury, with ruins of the Norman fortifications and the foundations of the old cathedral nestling inside.

Bishop Osmund completed the first 53m-long cathedral in 1092 but it was immediately struck by lightning and badly damaged. Around 1130, it was rebuilt and extended but this cathedral was abandoned with the shift to Salisbury and finally demolished in 1331 to provide building material for the walls of the cathedral close.

By 1540 the last house had disappeared but Old Sarum continued to elect two members to parliament until 1833 – a classic example of the sort of 'rotten borough' the 1832 Reform Act was designed to abolish.

Old Sarum is 2 miles north of Salisbury, and there are up to four buses an hour Monday to Saturday. It opens 10 am to 6 pm and admission costs £2/1 (more if a special event is taking place).

Wilton House

Henry VIII gave Wilton House (☎ 01722-746720) to William Herbert in 1541. Herbert became the earl of Pembroke in 1551, a title the colourful family has held since. After a fire destroyed most of the house it was redesigned by Inigo Jones and completed when the fifth earl took over. The present Earl of Pembroke is the seventeenth.

A visit to Wilton House and its 8 hectares of grounds starts with a video, followed by a tour of the kitchen and laundry. The hall has a statue of Shakespeare, who dedicated the first folio edition of his plays to the third earl. Inigo Jones was responsible for the Single and Double Cube Rooms, with their magnificent painted ceilings, elaborate plaster work and paintings by Van Dyck.

Wilton House is 2½ miles west of Salisbury on the A30 and buses depart up to six times hourly. It opens 10.30 am to 4.30 pm, April to October. Admission to the house costs £6.75/4. Bus Nos 60/61 pass this way.

Chalk Figures

Wiltshire's rolling fields are a green cloak over a chalk substructure and the practice of cutting pictures into the hillsides has a long history. The technique is simple: mark out your picture and cut away the green grass and topsoil to reveal the white chalk below. The picture will need periodic maintenance, but not much – some of the chalk figures may date back to prehistoric times, though the history of the oldest figures is uncertain. Although Wiltshire has more chalk figures than any other county, the best are probably the 55m-tall Cerne Giant (with his even more notable 12m penis) in Dorset and the 110m-long Uffington White Horse in Oxfordshire (which really requires a helicopter or hot-air balloon for proper inspection).

Horses were particularly popular subjects for chalk figures in the 18th century and noteworthy ones can be seen in Wiltshire at Cherhill near Calne, Alton Barnes and Hackpen, and at Osmington near Weymouth in Dorset.

During WWI a series of regimental badges were cut into a hillside outside Fovant in Wiltshire. A New Zealand WWI regiment left a gigantic kiwi on a hillside at Bulford, near Amesbury in Wiltshire. Get a copy of Kate Bergamar's *Discovering Hill Figures* (Shire Publications) for the complete lowdown on England's chalk figures.

JANE SMITH

Britain's most famous chalk figure: Uffington's White Horse

While in Wilton, carpet fanciers might like to visit the **Wilton Carpet Factory** (☎ 01722-744919) in King St which opens 9 am to 5 pm Monday to Saturday and 11 am to 5 pm Sunday year-round (except for 10 days over Christmas and the New Year). Admission costs £4/2.50.

Old Wardour Castle

Just north of the A30 between Salisbury and Shaftesbury, the Old Castle (☎ 01747-870487; EH) was built around 1393 and suffered severe damage during the Civil War. Admission to the picturesquely sited ruins costs £2/1. It opens 10 am to 5.30 pm.

STONEHENGE

Stonehenge (☎ 01980-624715; EH/NT) is Europe's most famous prehistoric site. It consists of a ring of enormous stones (some of which were brought from Wales), built in stages beginning 5000 years ago. Reactions vary, some feeling that the car park, gift shop and crowds of tourists swamp the monument, and that the two roads surging past rob it of atmosphere. Avebury, 19 miles to the north, is more isolated and recommended for those who would like to commune with the ley lines in relative peace (see Avebury later in the chapter).

The Site

Stonehenge was built and rebuilt over a 1500-year period. Construction started around 3000 BC when the outer circular bank and ditch were constructed. An inner circle of granite stones, known as blue-stones from their original colouring, was erected 1000 years later. The stones weighed up to 4 tons each and were brought from the Preseli Mountains in Southern Wales, nearly 250 miles away.

Around 1500 BC, the huge stones which make Stonehenge instantly recognisable were dragged to the site, erected in a circle and topped by equally massive lintels to make the sarsen (the type of sandstone) trilithons (the formation of vertical and horizontal stones). The sarsens were cut from an extremely hard rock found on the Marlborough Downs about 20 miles from the site.

The Battle for Stonehenge

Despite its World Heritage Site status, the last 100 hundred years haven't been kind to Stonehenge, which is hemmed in by the busy A303 to the south and the A344 to the north. Instead of being encouraged to let their imaginations rip, visitors have to put up with being funnelled through a tunnel under the A344 and then staring at the stones from behind a barbed-wire barricade with a constant backdrop of roaring traffic.

For a relatively small site, Stonehenge has always received a daunting number of visitors...over 700,000 at the last count. To make matters worse, in the 1980s latter-day Druids and New Age travellers began to descend en masse on Stonehenge for the summer solstice, often lingering for weeks afterwards. Archaeologists claimed that they would damage not just the stone circle but the lesser monuments in the surrounding fields as well. The ensuing police clampdown on solstice visits turned into an annual stand-off, culminating in the infamous Battle of the Beanfield when television viewers were treated to pictures of women and children being tipped out of a motley assortment of ancient vehicles in a none too gentle fashion. The barbed wire is one legacy of the clash; the 1994 Criminal Justice and Public Order Act, aimed at making it harder for convoys to assemble, is another.

'A national disgrace' is how the Public Accounts Committee of the House of Commons described the situation at Stonehenge back in 1992. But what hope for a brighter future? Ideally English Heritage (EH) and the National Trust (NT) would like to see both roads moved back from the site, and the A303 rerouted through a tunnel – at a cost of £300 million.

The EH and NT have plans for a Stonehenge Millennium Park which would at least see the A344 closed and the visitor centre repositioned a mile away to give the site back some of its mystique in the future.

It's still not clear where the money's coming from but Culture Secretary Chris Smith announced that Stonehenge would be restored to its natural setting before the next election.

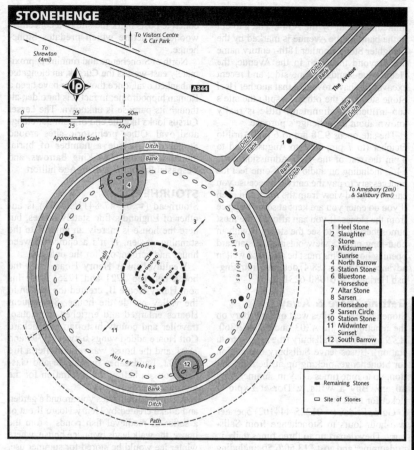

STONEHENGE

To Visitors Centre & Car Park

To Shrewton (4mi)

A344

Ditch
Bank
Ditch
Bank

The Avenue

Ditch
Bank

To Amesbury (2mi) & Salisbury (9mi)

Ditch
Bank

Path

Path

Aubrey Holes

Aubrey Holes

Approximate Scale

0 25 50m
0 25 50yd

1 Heel Stone
2 Slaughter Stone
3 Midsummer Sunrise
4 North Barrow
5 Station Stone
6 Bluestone Horseshoe
7 Altar Stone
8 Sarsen Horseshoe
9 Sarsen Circle
10 Station Stone
11 Midwinter Sunset
12 South Barrow

■ Remaining Stones
□ Site of Stones

It's estimated that dragging one of these 50-ton stones across the countryside to Stonehenge would require about 600 people.

Also around this time, the bluestones from 500 years earlier were rearranged as an inner horseshoe. In the centre of this horseshoe went the altar stone, a name given for no scientific reason in the 18th century. Around the bluestone horseshoe was a sarsen horseshoe of five trilithons. Three of these trilithons are intact, the other two have just a single upright. Then came the major circle of 30 massive vertical stones, of which 17 uprights and six lintels remain.

Farther out was another circle delineated by the 58 Aubrey Holes, named after John Aubrey who discovered them in the 1600s. Only a handful of the stones remain in this circle. In the same circle are the South Barrow and North Barrow, each originally topped by a stone. Between them are two other stones, though not quite on the east-west axis. Outside the Aubrey Holes circle was the bank and then the ditch.

The inner horseshoes are aligned along the sun's axis on rising in midsummer and setting in midwinter. From the midsummer axis, approximately NNE, the Avenue leads out from Stonehenge and today is almost immediately cut by the A344. The gap cut in the bank by the Avenue is marked by the Slaughter Stone, another 18th-century name tag. Beyond the ditch in the Avenue, the Heel Stone stands on one side, and recent excavations have revealed that another Heel Stone stood on the other. Despite the site's sun-influenced alignment, little is really known about Stonehenge's purpose.

The site opens 9.30 am to 6 pm, April to October (to 7 pm, June to August); and to 4 pm the rest of the year. Admission costs £4/2, including an audio tour. Some feel it's unnecessary to pay the entry fee because you can get a good view from the road, and even if you do enter you are kept at some distance from the stones. If you can afford it the most atmospheric way to see the stones is with an hour-long private view outside the standard opening hours. This must be arranged well in advance and a pass (£8/4) obtained from English Heritage (☎ 01980-623108).

Getting There & Away

Stonehenge is 2 miles west of Amesbury on the junction of the A303 and A344/A360. It's 9 miles from Salisbury (the nearest train station). Buses leave Salisbury bus station for Stonehenge, picking up at the train station, up to nine times a day in summer from 10 am. Buy a Wilts & Dorset Explorer ticket for £5/2.50.

Guide Friday (☎ 01225-444102) operates two-hour tours to Stonehenge from Salisbury. They depart up to three times daily in midsummer and cost £13.50/6.50, including admission to the site and this is a way to avoid the queues in peak season. There are various minibus tours to Stonehenge, including some that also go to Avebury.

AROUND STONEHENGE

Stonehenge is surrounded by a collection of mysterious prehistoric sites, several of them only recently revealed by aerial surveys. Only the sites within the NT boundaries are open to the public; others are on private property. The *Stonehenge Estate Archaeological Walks* leaflet details walks around these sites.

Three miles east of Stonehenge and just north of Amesbury is **Woodhenge**, where concrete posts mark the site of a concentric wooden structure which predates Stonehenge.

North of Stonehenge and running approximately east-west is the **Cursus**, an elongated embanked oval, once thought to have been a Roman hippodrome; in fact it is far older, although its purpose is unknown. The **Lesser Cursus** looks like the end of a similar elongated oval. Other prehistoric sites around Stonehenge include a number of burial mounds, like the **New King Barrows**, and **Vespasian's Camp**, an Iron-Age hillfort.

STOURHEAD

Stourhead (☎ 01747-841152; NT) is another of England's fine stately homes, but here the house is merely an adjunct to the stunning garden. If it's a choice between house and garden, opt for the outdoors.

Wealthy banker Henry Hoare built the house between 1721 and 1725, while his son, Henry Hoare II, created the garden in the valley beside the house. Subsequent Hoares enlarged and enriched the house: traveller and county historian Sir Richard Colt Hoare added wings between 1790 and 1804, and the house was rebuilt after a fire in 1902. Landscapes by Claude and Gaspard Poussin betray the inspiration for the Stourhead gardens.

A 2-mile circuit takes you around a garden and a lake created by Henry Hoare II out of a series of medieval fish ponds. From the house, the walk leads by an **ice house**, where winter ice would be stored for summer use. At the **Temple of Flora** it continues around the lake edge, through a **grotto** and past a **Gothic cottage** to the **Pantheon**. There's a climb up to the **Temple of Apollo**, copied from a temple at Baalbek in Lebanon, which has fine views down the length of the lake. From the temple, you descend to the 15th-century **Bristol Cross**, acquired from the city of Bristol in 1765, past **St Peter's Church** and the **Spread Eagle Inn** back to the starting point. From near the Pantheon, a 3½-mile side trip can be made to **King Alfred's Tower**, a 50m-high folly overlooking Wiltshire, Somerset and Dorset.

The garden opens 9 am to 7 pm (or sunset). The house opens noon to 5.30 pm Saturday to Wednesday, April to October. Admission to the house costs £4.60/2.60 and another £4.60/2.60 for the garden (£3.30/1.50 in winter). A combined house and garden ticket costs £8/3.80. King Alfred's Tower is another £1.50/70p.

LONGLEAT

Longleat (☎ 01985-844400) is the English stately home turned circus act. Following Henry VIII's monastic land grab, Sir John Thynne picked up the priory ruins and Longleat's 360 hectares for the princely sum of £53 in 1541. Having acquired the 13th-century Augustinian priory, he turned 16th-century architecture on its head to produce a house that looked out onto its magnificent park rather than in towards its courtyards. It was still under construction when he died in 1580 but although its external appearance hasn't changed since, there have been many internal alterations. The rooms are sumptuously furnished and feature seven libraries with 40,000 books. Capability Brown landscaped the surrounding park between 1757 and 1762, planting woods and creating the Half Mile Pond.

After WWII, taxation started to nibble away at the English nobility's fortunes, just as maintenance costs skyrocketed and servants became scarce and expensive. The sixth Marquess of Bath responded by pioneering the stately home business at Longleat, going on to add new, less serious attractions in the grounds. These days Longleat boasts a pub, a narrow-gauge railway, a Dr Who exhibit, a pets' corner, a butterfly garden and a safari park with lions, as well as the magnificent old house. The eccentric seventh Marquess has even added a series of murals, some depicting his numerous 'wifelets', in his private apartments.

Longleat House opens 11 am to 4 pm (to 5.30 pm, Easter to September). The safari park opens 11 am to 5.30 pm, mid-March to October; the other attractions open an hour later. Admission to the grounds costs £2/1, to the house £6/4, to the safari park £6/5, and there are entry charges to 13 other features.

An all-inclusive ticket costs £13/11. A Lion Link bus departs Warminster station at 11.10 am daily for the safari park's entrance gate, a 2½-mile walk from Longleat House through marvellous grounds.

BRADFORD-ON-AVON
☎ 01225 • pop 9000

Bradford-on-Avon is a beautiful old town with fine stone houses and factories rising like a series of terraced paddy fields from the river. Bath, with a much wider range of accommodation and eating options, is only 8 miles away, making a day trip a good

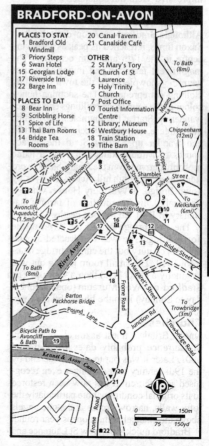

BRADFORD-ON-AVON

PLACES TO STAY
1 Bradford Old Windmill
3 Priory Steps
6 Swan Hotel
15 Georgian Lodge
17 Riverside Inn
22 Barge Inn

PLACES TO EAT
8 Bear Inn
9 Scribbling Horse
11 Spice of Life
13 Thai Barn Rooms
14 Bridge Tea Rooms

20 Canal Tavern
21 Canalside Café

OTHER
2 St Mary's Tory
4 Church of St Laurence
5 Holy Trinity Church
7 Post Office
10 Tourist Information Centre
12 Library; Museum
16 Westbury House
18 Train Station
19 Tithe Barn

SOUTH-WESTERN ENGLAND

alternative to staying here. Sadly, the extension of the Bath bypass has had the effect of displacing unwanted excess traffic into little Bradford.

Orientation & Information

Town Bridge is Bradford's most important landmark. The crowded buildings rise up from the river on the northern side. The TIC (☎ 865797) is across the bridge from the train station. The Kennet and Avon Canal passes through Bradford-on-Avon, and there's a pleasant 1½-mile walk or cycle ride along it to neighbouring Avoncliff, with its impressive Victorian aqueduct.

Around Town

Although Bradford-on-Avon dates back to Saxon times, it reached its peak as a weaving centre in the 17th and 18th centuries. The magnificent factories and imposing houses were the showpieces of the town's wealthy clothing entrepreneurs. The soothing honey colour of the solid stone buildings encourages wandering. Start at the **Shambles**, the original marketplace, inspect adjacent **Coppice Hill** and wander up Market St to the terrace houses of **Middle Rank** and **Tory**, a name probably derived from the Anglo-Saxon word 'tor', meaning a high hill. Across the river, by **Town Bridge**, is **Westbury House**, where a riot against the introduction of factory machinery in 1791 led to three deaths.

The first bridge across the Avon at the Town Bridge site was constructed around the 12th century but the current bridge dates from 1610. The small room jutting out was originally a chapel and then a **lock-up**. The **Bradford-on-Avon Museum** (open Wednesday to Sunday) is in the library by the river.

Churches

One of Britain's finest Saxon churches, tiny **St Laurence** probably dates from around 1001. Later it was put to secular use and by the 19th century was no longer even recognised as a church. It has now been restored to its original condition; note particularly the lofty walls, narrow arches and stone angels above the chancel arch. It opens year round.

Bradford quickly outgrew St Laurence and

the new **Holy Trinity Church** was completed in 1150. The original church is virtually submerged beneath 14th-century extensions, and 15th- and 19th-century rebuilding. Higher up the hill **St Mary's Tory** was built as a hermitage chapel about 1480. Used as a cloth factory in the 18th century, it has now been restored.

Tithe Barn

A pleasant short walk along the river bank leads from the town centre to the tithe barn used to store tithes (taxes in kind) in the Middle Ages. The imposing 50m-long structure was built in 1341 with 100 tons of stone tiles to roof it.

Places to Stay

The **Barge Inn** (☎ 863403, 17 Frome Rd) beyond the canal, has singles/doubles for £25/35.

If you can afford more, this is a good town for a splurge. **Priory Steps** (☎ 862230) at Newtown, is only a few minutes walk from the town centre but has wonderful views from its hillside position. Singles/doubles, all with a bathroom, are from £58/78.

Swan Hotel (☎ 868686, 1 Church St), right in the town centre, has singles for £50, doubles for £80. Close to the bridge, **Riverside Inn** (☎ 863526, 49 St Margaret's St) has a pleasant riverside setting and simple singles/doubles with a bathroom for £35/47.50. **Georgian Lodge** (☎ 862268) on Frome Rd has rooms with bathroom for £30/68, including breakfast.

Bradford Old Windmill (☎ 866842, 4 Masons Lane) is beautifully converted. It overlooks the town with luxury rooms from £79/89/99, £10 less for single occupancy.

Places to Eat

In the centre, **Swan Hotel** does bar food for under a fiver and has a restaurant with set meals. Other pub food possibilities include the **Bear Inn** (26 Silver St) and **Canal Tavern** (49 Frome Rd). **Georgian Lodge** beside Town Bridge is definitely flashier with dishes such as oak-smoked salmon with capers and lime for around £10.

For something more exotic, try **Thai Barn**

(☎ *866433, 24 Bridge St)* with an authentic Siamese feel and a varied menu.

The olde-worlde *Bridge Tea Rooms* beside Town Bridge serves excellent lunches and teas, including wholesome soups and popular cream teas. Other possibilities for lunch or tea include the tiny *Spice of Life* behind the TIC and *Scribbling Horse* beside it. The *Canalside Café* in Lock Inn Cottage, near where Frome Rd crosses the canal, does a good range of snacks at reasonable prices.

Getting There & Away
A day return by train from Bath costs £3.60 but there are also hourly buses (£3.40 return, No X4) which continue to Salisbury. Once a week there are also buses to Devizes; phone ☎ 0845 709 0899 for details.

Getting Around
Bicycles can be hired for £12 a day from Lock Inn Cottage (☎ 868068), 48 Frome Rd, by the canal. Canoes can also be hired here.

CHIPPENHAM & AROUND
☎ 01249 • pop 22,000
Chippenham is an unexceptional market town with a pedestrianised centre. The town makes a good touring base for several nearby attractions.

The TIC (☎ 657733) stocks a town trail map and can advise on accommodation costing from £15 a head. The museum in the 15th-century **Yelde Hall** opens 10 am to 12.30 pm and 2 to 4.30 pm daily except Sunday, March to October. While waiting for a bus you could pop into the delightfully old-fashioned *Waverley Restaurant*, opposite the Bear Hotel, for a cheap cuppa.

Castle Combe
A Cotswold village that's strayed, Castle Combe is as close to the dream English village as you can get. There's a 13th-century market cross and a packbridge with weavers' cottages reflected in a pool, and the main street is lined with flower-covered stone cottages, pubs and tasteful shops. Pretty, medieval St Andrew's Church also contains a remarkable 13th-century monument of Sir Walter de Dunstananville.

Gates Tea Shop (☎ *782111),* by the market cross, has two double rooms costing £45 or £55 depending on the style of bed. During the day cream teas are served.

At the opposite end of the price spectrum, the cheapest bed at the grand *Manor House Inn* (☎ *782206)* is £145. Both the *Castle Inn* and the *White Hart* do pub lunches.

Bus No 35 leaves Chippenham train station for Castle Combe every two hours – it is easiest visited with a car.

Corsham Court
An Elizabethan mansion dating from 1582, Corsham Court (☎ 01249-701610) was enlarged and renovated in the 18th century to house an art collection accumulated by Paul Methuen and his descendants. The house is 3 miles south-west of Chippenham and opens 11 am to 5 pm Tuesday to Sunday, Easter to October; phone for details of opening times for the rest of the year. Admission costs £4.50/2.50.

Lacock
☎ 01249
Exquisitely attractive Lacock lays claim to being the birthplace of photography and has many buildings from an extensive medieval monastic complex. The village dates back to the Saxon era, well before the foundation of Lacock Abbey. Many of the buildings date from medieval times and are owned by the NT; few were built after the 18th century.

The NT's free *Lacock Village* leaflet plots a route round the most interesting buildings. King John's **Hunting Lodge** dates in part from the 13th century, while the adjacent **St Cyriac's Church** is mainly late 15th century; note the brass in the southern transept to Robert and Elizabeth Baynard and their 18 children (1501). The **At the Sign of the Angel** hotel dates from 1480 (see Places to Stay). WH Fox Talbot of Lacock Abbey founded the village **primary school** in High St in 1824. His **grave** is in the village cemetery. Also check out the 14th-century **tithe barn & lock-up**.

Lacock provided the setting for many scenes in the BBC's acclaimed production of Jane Austen's *Pride and Prejudice*.

SOUTH-WESTERN ENGLAND

Lacock Abbey & The Fox Talbot Museum of Photography Lacock Abbey (☎ 730459) was established as a nunnery in 1232, then sold to Sir William Sharington by Henry VIII in 1539. Sharington converted the nunnery into a home, demolished the church, tacked a tower onto the corner of the abbey building and added a brewery, while retaining the abbey cloister and other medieval features. Despite his three marriages he died childless and the house passed to the Talbot family, who bequeathed the whole village to the NT in 1944.

In the early 19th century, William Henry Fox Talbot, a prolific inventor, conducted crucial experiments in the development of photography here. Inside the entrance to the abbey a museum (☎ 730459) details his pioneering photographic work in the 1830s, when Louis Daguerre was also working in France. Fox Talbot's particular contribution was the photographic negative, from which further positive images could be produced. Before that a photograph was a one time, one image process. A picture of the abbey's oriel window may be the first photograph ever taken.

The abbey and museum open 11 am to 5.30 pm Wednesday to Monday, April to October. Admission costs £5.80/3.20, though if you just want to see the cloister, museum and grounds it's £3.70/2.20.

Places to Stay & Eat Lacock makes a wonderful place to stay though accommodation is both limited and relatively pricey. *King John's Hunting Lodge* (☎ 730313, 21 Church St) has two lovely rooms with exposed beams costing £32.50 per person for B&B. It also houses a weekend and summer-season tearoom.

At 1 The Tanyard, atmospheric *Lacock Pottery* (☎ 730266) offers rooms for £37/59, with good healthy breakfasts and the chance to sign up for a pottery course thrown in.

Pricier but highly atmospheric are rooms in the 15th-century *At the Sign of the Angel* (☎ 730230); beds beneath exposed beams cost from £68/99, more on a Saturday night.

All three village pubs do food. At *At the Sign of the Angel* a dinner costs around

£20 to £25. The *George Inn* is cheaper and hugely popular, a great local. The *Carpenters Arms* is the most reasonably priced and spacious. In season teas are served in *The Stables* opposite the abbey.

Getting There & Away Bus No 234 operates a roughly hourly service from Chippenham (15 minutes), Monday to Saturday.

DEVIZES
☎ 01380 • pop 12,500
An attractive market town, Devizes was once an important coaching stop and several old

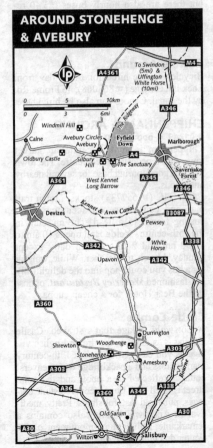

coaching inns survive in the market square. The TIC (☎ 729408) is at 39 St John's St, right by the square. Interesting buildings nearby include the **Corn Exchange**, topped by a figure of Ceres, goddess of agriculture, and the **Old Town Hall** of 1750–52.

Just beyond the TIC, **St John's Alley** has a wonderful collection of Elizabethan houses, their upper storeys cantilevered over the street. The new **town hall**, dating from 1806, is at this end of St John's St.

St John's Church displays elements of its original Norman construction, particularly in the solid crossing tower. The **Wiltshire Heritage Museum** (☎ 727369) at 41 Long St, has interesting displays on the development of Avebury and Stonehenge, a section on Roman history and an upstairs social history room. It opens 10 am to 5 pm Monday to Saturday. Admission costs £3/75p (free on Monday).

The **Kennet & Avon Canal Exhibition** (☎ 729489) in the wharf just north of the town centre, opens 10 am to 5 pm (to 4 pm in winter). Admission costs £1.50/50p. The **Caen Hill** flight of 29 successive locks raises the water level 72m in 2½ miles on the western outskirts of Devizes.

Places to Stay & Eat

At *Lower Foxhangers Farm* (☎ 828254) camping is offered for £6 a pitch plus £1 for electricity. The farm is conveniently near the canal for walkers and cyclists, but public transport is a non-starter.

In Market Place, the 17th-century *Bear Hotel* (☎ 722444) charges £59/86 while the 18th-century *Black Swan Hotel* (☎ 723259) costs £50/70. *Castle Hotel* (☎ 729300, *New Park St*) has rooms for £50/70.

The very popular *Wiltshire Kitchen* (☎ 724840, *11/12 St John's St*) does light lunches. A cellar restaurant also opens on Tuesday to Saturday from 7 pm. Otherwise the pubs around Market Place are your best bet for reasonably priced fare, especially on market days.

Getting There & Away

Bus Nos 33/X33 run from Chippenham, a limited service is operated on Sunday.

AVEBURY
☎ 01672

Avebury stone circle stands at the hub of a prehistoric complex of ceremonial sites, ancient avenues and burial chambers. It's a bigger site and less visited than Stonehenge and many find it more atmospheric and impressive. The impact of Neolithic people on the environment is so dramatic you can almost feel them breathing down your neck. Avebury itself is a pretty village where even the church walls are thatched. Silbury Hill and West Kennet Long Barrow are close by, and the Ridgeway Path ends here.

Orientation & Information

The Avebury stones encircle much of the village, but don't drive into it as the car park on the A4361 is only a short stroll from the circle. The TIC (☎ 539425) is in the late-17th-century Great Barn.

Stone Circle

The stone circle dates from around 2600 to 2100 BC, between the first and second phase of construction at Stonehenge. With a diameter of about 348m, it's one of the largest stone circles in Britain. The site originally consisted of an outer circle of 98 standing stones from three to six metres in length, many weighing up to 20 tons. These were selected for their size and shape, but were not worked to shape like those at Stonehenge. The stones were surrounded by another circle formed by a 5½m-high earth bank and a six to 9m-deep ditch. Inside were smaller stone circles to the north (27 stones) and south (29 stones).

The circles remained largely intact through the Roman period. A Saxon settlement grew up inside the circle from around 600 but in medieval times, when the church's power was strong and fear of paganism even stronger, many of the stones were deliberately buried. As the village expanded in the late 17th and early 18th century, the stones were broken up for building material. Fortunately, William Stukeley (1687–1765) surveyed the site around this time so some record survives of what had existed.

AVEBURY

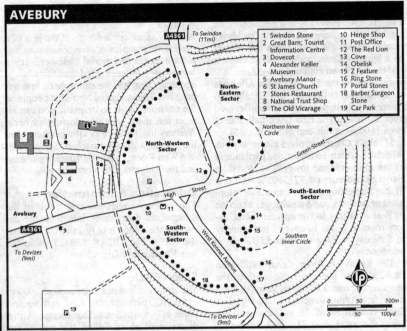

1 Swindon Stone	10 Henge Shop
2 Great Barn; Tourist	11 Post Office
Information Centre	12 The Red Lion
3 Dovecot	13 Cove
4 Alexander Keiller	14 Obelisk
Museum	15 Z Feature
5 Avebury Manor	16 Ring Stone
6 St James Church	17 Portal Stones
7 Stones Restaurant	18 Barber Surgeon
8 National Trust Shop	Stone
9 The Old Vicarage	19 Car Park

In 1934, Alexander Keiller supervised the re-erection of the buried stones and the placing of markers to indicate those that had disappeared. The wealthy Keiller eventually bought Avebury in order to restore 'the outstanding archaeological disgrace of Britain'.

Modern roads into Avebury neatly dissect the circle into four sectors. Start from High St, near the Henge Shop, and walk round the circle in an anti-clockwise direction. There are 21 standing stones in the south-western sector, one of them known as the **Barber Surgeon Stone**, after the skeleton of a man found under it; the equipment buried with him suggested he was a medieval travelling barber-surgeon, killed when a stone accidentally fell on him.

The south-eastern sector starts with the huge **portal stones** marking the entry to the circle from West Kennet Ave. The **southern inner circle** stood in this sector and within this circle was the **Obelisk** and a group of stones known as the **Z Feature**. Just outside

this smaller circle, only the base of the **Ring Stone** remains. Few stones, standing or fallen, are to be seen around the rest of the south-eastern or north-eastern sectors. Most of the northern inner circle was in the north-eastern sector. The **Cove**, made up of three of the largest stones, marked the centre of this smaller circle.

The north-western sector has the most complete collection of standing stones, including the massive 65-ton **Swindon Stone**, the first stone encountered and one of the few never to have been toppled.

Alexander Keiller Museum

Alexander Keiller, who made his fortune out of Dundee marmalade, not only bought the Avebury Circle but most of the village, West Kennet Ave, Windmill Hill and virtually everything else that was up for sale.

In the former stables of Avebury Manor, the Alexander Keiller Museum (☎ 539250) explains the history of the Avebury Circle and houses finds from the sites. It opens 10 am to 6 pm (to 4 pm in winter). Admission costs £1.80/80p.

The Village

St James Church contains round Saxon windows, a Norman font and a rare surviving rood (cross) loft. The National Trust plan to develop a new museum in the thatched **Great Barn**. It will exhibit information on the local landscape and the rediscovery of the stone circle. Note the 16th-century circular **dovecot** close by.

Graceful **Avebury Manor** (☎ 539388; NT) dates back to the 16th century but was altered in the early 18th century. It opens 2 to 5 pm on Tuesday, Wednesday and Sunday, April to October. Admission costs £3.20/1.60. The gardens (£2.25/1) open 11 am to 5 pm daily except Monday and Thursday.

Places to Stay & Eat

B&B is available at *The Old Vicarage* (☎ 539362) from £22 a head, or at *The Red Lion* (☎ 539266) where doubles cost £30 per person.

Beside the Great Barn, the popular *Stones Restaurant* offers 'megaliths' (hot dishes) for around £6.

Getting There & Away

Avebury is just off the A4 between Calne and Marlborough, and can be reached easily by Wilts & Dorset Bus No 5 which operates Salisbury-Marlborough-Avebury-Swindon three times daily. Tour buses also operate from Salisbury.

Coming from Bath, you'll have to change at Devizes; check connections with the county enquiry line (☎ 0845 709 0899). Thamesdown (☎ 01793-428428) operates from Swindon to Avebury regularly Monday to Saturday, less frequently on Sunday. Its buses also link Avebury to Marlborough and Devizes on weekdays.

AROUND AVEBURY

Several excellent walks link the important sites around Avebury, starting with a stroll across the fields to Silbury Hill and West Kennet Long Barrow. The Ridgeway Path starts near Avebury and runs northwards across Fyfield Down, where many of the sarsen stones at Avebury (and Stonehenge) were collected.

Windmill Hill

The earliest site around Avebury, Windmill Hill was a Neolithic enclosure or 'camp' dating from about 3700 BC. Ditches confirm its shape.

The Avenue & The Sanctuary

The 1½-mile-long West Kennet Ave, lined by 100 pairs of stones, connects The Sanctuary with Avebury Circle. Today, the B4003 road follows the same route and at its southern end the A4 virtually overrides the avenue. The stone shapes along the avenue alternate between column-like stones and triangular-shaped ones; Keiller thought they might have been intended to signify male and female.

Only the site of The Sanctuary remains, although the post and stone holes indicate there was a wooden building surrounded by a stone circle. The possible route of Beckhampton Ave, a similar 'avenue' into Avebury from the south-west, is mainly guesswork.

Silbury Hill

Rising abruptly from the surrounding fields, Silbury Hill is one of the largest artificial hills in Europe, similar in size to the smaller Egyptian pyramids. Like a truncated cone, its 40m-high summit ends in a flat top measuring 30m across. It was constructed in stages from around 2500 BC but its purpose is a mystery. Certainly no one seems to have been buried here.

West Kennet Long Barrow

Across the fields south of Silbury Hill stands West Kennet Long Barrow, England's finest burial mound, dating from around 3500 BC and measuring 104m by 23m. Its entrance is guarded by huge sarsens, massive stones like those at Stonehenge, and its roof is constructed of gigantic overlapping capstones. About 50 skeletons were found when it was excavated. The finds are displayed in Wiltshire Heritage Museum.

MARLBOROUGH

☎ 01672 • pop 5400

Marlborough started life as a Saxon settlement at The Green, and the main street extended westwards from there to an 18m-high prehistoric mound where the Normans later erected a motte and bailey fortification. To make more room for a market as the town grew, the houses along High St were pushed back until the road reached its present extraordinary width.

Today's High St makes an interesting stroll, particularly on Wednesday and Saturday, which are market days. The 17th-century **Merchant's House** at No 132 (☎ 511491) is now a museum. The exclusive Marlborough College now occupies the site of the **old Norman castle**. Just to the west is a small white horse cut into the hillside by schoolboys in 1804.

The TIC (☎ 513989) is in George Lane car park off High St. There's plenty of accommodation along High St and George Lane. The best of the teashops is *Harpers*, across the road from St Peter's church, although service may be quicker at the *Tudor* and *Polly Tea Rooms* in the High St. *Options*, behind Ivy House Hotel, has some vegetarian dishes on its menu. Pubs with good food along High St include the *Green Dragon*, the 15th-century *Sun Inn* and the *Wellington Arms*.

MALMESBURY

☎ 01666 • pop 4300

Perched on top of a hill, Malmesbury has a superb semi-ruined abbey church, a late-15th-century market cross and several pleasant pubs and restaurants. The well-stocked TIC (☎ 823748) is in the town hall on Market Lane. It's round the corner from the small **Athelstan Museum** and car park.

Malmesbury Abbey

Malmesbury Abbey is a wonderful blend of ruin and living church. Construction began in the 12th century and by the 14th it was a massive edifice 100m long with a tower at the western end and a tower and spire at the crossing. In 1479, a storm brought the tower and spire crashing down; its fall destroyed the crossing and the eastern end of the church.

When the monastery was suppressed in 1539, the abbey was sold to a local clothier who initially moved looms into the nave. Later he changed his mind and gave it to the town to replace the ruinous parish church of St Paul's. In about 1662, the western tower fell, destroying three of the western bays of the nave. Today's church consists of the remaining six bays – about a third of the original church – framed by ruins at either end.

The church is entered via the magnificent southern porch, its doorway a Norman work with stone sculpture illustrating Bible stories. The huge carved Apostles on each side of the porch are some of the finest Romanesque carvings in Britain. Looking out over the nave from the southern side is a watching loft whose purpose is obscure. In the north-eastern corner of the church is a medieval cenotaph (empty tomb) commemorating Athelstan, king of England from 925 to 939 and grandson of Alfred the Great.

Steps lead up to the parvise, a small room above the porch, which contains a collection of books, including a four-volume illuminated manuscript Bible dating from 1407. A window at the western end of the church shows Elmer the Flying Monk. In 1010, he strapped on wings and jumped from the tower. Remarkably, he survived, and blamed his crash-landing on aerodynamic problems.

In the churchyard, the 14th-century steeple of St Paul's, the original parish church, now serves as the belfry. Towards the south-eastern corner of the churchyard is the **gravestone of Hannah Twynnoy** who died in 1703, aged 33. Her headstone reads: 'For tyger fierce, Took life away, And here she lies, In a bed of clay'. The tiger belonged to a visiting circus and she was killed in the White Lion pub where she was a serving maid.

The abbey opens 10 am to 5 pm. Donations are appreciated.

Places to Stay & Eat

A 10-minute walk along the river leads to *Burton Hill Camping Park* (☎ 826880). It has sites at £5 for one person, £7.50 for two.

King's Arms Hotel (☎ 823383, High St) is a charming old coaching inn with singles/doubles for £30/50.

Bremilham House (☎ *822680, Bremilham Rd*) is an easy walk from the town centre and costs £19.50/34 for singles/doubles.

The historic *Old Bell Inn* (☎ *822344, Abbey Row*) by the abbey, charges from £75/95 for luxurious singles/doubles.

The cheerful *Whole Hog* (☎ *825845*) wine bar is right behind the market cross and serves hogburgers (vegetarian version available) and pigwitch sandwiches!

SWINDON
☎ 01793 • pop 182,000

Swindon has a proud place in the history of railways in Britain, providing a home to the massive Great Western Railway works for a century and a half until its closure in 1986. These days it's a fast-growing town with a burgeoning IT sector, but hardly the most inspiring place in the south-west. It is quite well-placed, however, for forays into the Cotswolds and Britain's pre-history around Wiltshire. The TIC (☎ 530328) can be located at 37 Regent St.

STEAM – Museum of the Great Western Railway (☎ 466646, Kemble Drive) is a new museum telling the story of the Great Western Railway and Swindon's place in its success. It opens 10 am to 6 pm. Admission costs £4.80/3.

Bristol

☎ 0117 • pop 414,000

Bristol is by far and away south-western England's largest and coolest city, home to Portishead, Tricky, Massive Attack, and Wallace and Gromit. Unfortunately WWII bombing raids destroyed much of the centre, which was rebuilt with scant regard for aesthetics in the 1950s and 60s. The city does, however, have pockets of magnificent architecture, docks and warehouses that have been rescued from ruin, and plenty of pubs and restaurants. Charming Clifton is every bit the equal of Bath when it comes to Georgian grandeur.

Although it's 6 miles from the Severn estuary, Bristol is most famous as a port. However, by the late 19th century changing trading needs had rendered the docks obsolete and they were relocated from the city centre to nearby Avonmouth and Portishead. Work has finally started on restoring the last pocket of dereliction around the old Floating Harbour and new developments include an Imax cinema.

The mainly Afro-Caribbean suburb of St Paul's, just north-east of the centre, remains a run-down, occasionally tense part of town with a heavy drug scene, best not visited alone at night.

Bristol is an important transport hub, with connections north to the Cotswolds and the Midlands, south-west to Devon and Cornwall, and east to Bath (an easy day trip). South Wales is linked to Bristol across the Severn Bridge and the unimaginatively named Second Severn Crossing.

HISTORY

Little is known about Bristol until the 10th century, but in the Middle Ages a town grew up around a castle near what is now Bristol Bridge. The centre of town was then around Wine, High, Broad and Corn Sts.

Several religious houses were established on high ground above the marshes, commemorated in the name of Temple Meads train station. The importance of choosing high ground is shown by a look at Bristol's own leaning tower, attached to Temple Church in Victoria St.

Soon Bristol's wealth was dependent on the triangular trade in slaves, cocoa, sugar, tobacco and manufactured goods with Africa and the New World. William Canynges, a wealthy merchant, paid for the original church on the site of St Mary Redcliffe and it was from Bristol that John Cabot sailed to discover Newfoundland in 1497.

By the 18th century, the city was suffering from competition from Liverpool in particular, and the Avon Gorge made it hard for large ships to reach the city-centre docks. By the 1870s, when new docks were opened at Avonmouth and Portishead, Britain's economic focus had shifted northwards.

ORIENTATION

The city centre, to the north of the Floating Harbour, is easy to get around on foot but

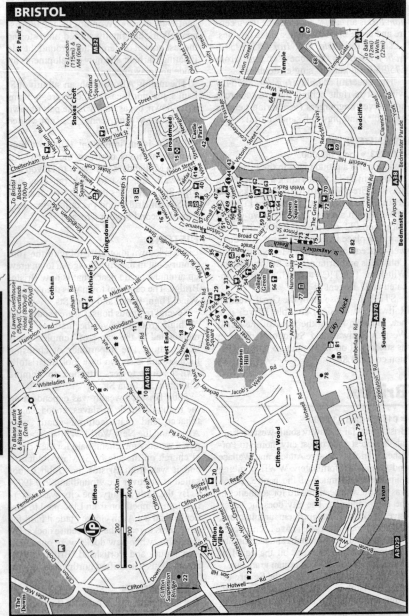

BRISTOL

very hilly. Glorious Clifton lies to the north-west, accessible by bus from the centre. Bristol's main shopping centre is the under-cover Galleries shopping centre in Broad-mead, but the shops lining Park St, Queen's Rd and Whiteladies Rd, and those in Clifton, are more interesting.

The main train station is Bristol Temple Meads, a mile south-east of the centre and linked to it by regular buses. Some trains use Bristol Parkway, 5 miles to the north, just off the M4 and accessible from the centre by bus and train. A taxi costs about £8.

The bus station on Marlborough St to the north of the city centre serves National Express coaches and Badgerline buses to surrounding towns and villages.

INFORMATION

The TIC (☎ 926 0767 or ☎ 915 7338 at the weekend) is housed in St Nicholas Church, St Nicholas St, which has a magnificent 18th-century altarpiece by William Hogarth. The comprehensive *Visitors Guide* is worth buy-ing, as are the booklets describing the *Bristol Heritage Trail* and the *Slave Trade Trail*.

Net Gates on Broad St is a sophisticated Internet cafe with more to offer than just terminals, including music, drinks and cakes. The fortnightly listings magazine *Venue* is the *Time Out* of Bristol. Bristol Books (☎ 924 5458), 180b Cheltenham Rd, is excellent for second-hand books.

BRISTOL CATHEDRAL

Originally founded as the church of an Au-gustinian monastery in 1140, Bristol Cathe-dral (☎ 926 4879) on College Green gained cathedral status in 1542. One of its most striking features is its Norman chapter

BRISTOL

PLACES TO STAY
8   Tyndales Park Hotel
9   Oakfield Hotel
10 Washington Hotel
11 The Hawthorns (University)
16 Hotel du Vin
23 Avon Gorge Hotel
39 Grand Thistle Hotel
51 Bristol Backpackers
57 Marriot Royal Hotel
66 City Inn
73 Jurys
74 Youth Hostel
79 Baltic Wharf Caravan Club

PLACES TO EAT
3   Thai Classic; Cartier Vert
18 Brown's
26 The Boston Tea Party
27 Vincenzo's
28 Melbourne's
30 Le Chateau
31 Pastificio
33 Woode's Café
37 Arc
45 The Glass Boat
47 St Nicholas Market
48 Via Vita; All Bar One
49 San Carlo
54 Harvey's Restaurant; Wine Museum
62 Aqua

65 Belgo
70 Riverstation; severnshed
72 Mud Dock

PUBS, BARS & CLUBS
4   Maze
5   Lakota
7   The Highbury Vaults
20 The Albion
21 Coronation Tap
29 All in One; Brasserie Pierre
32 Queenshilling; Silent Peach
40 Bierkeller
46 Fez Club; Las Iguanas
50 Tantric Jazz
59 Renato's Taverna
61 The Old Duke
63 Llandoger Trow
64 The Famous Royal Navy Volunteer
71 Thekla
76 Evolution

OTHER
1   Bristol Zoo
2   Train Station (Parkway)
6   Arts Cinema
12 Bristol Royal Infirmary Casualty
13 Bus & Coach Station
14 John Wesley's New Room
15 Galleries Shopping Centre

17 City Museum & Art Gallery
19 STA Travel
22 Observatory; Camera Obscura
24 Georgian House
25 St George's
34 Red Lodge
35 Colston Hall
36 Bus Stop
38 Net Gates
41 Bakers Dolphin Travel
42 Floating Harbour
43 Bristol Bridge
44 Tourist Information Centre; St Nicholas Church
52 Hippodrome
53 Taxi Rank
55 Lord Mayor's Chapel
56 Bristol Cathedral
58 Watershed Media Centre
60 Old Vic (Theatre Royal & New Vic)
67 Train Station (Temple Meads)
68 Bristol Old Station
69 St Mary Redcliffe
75 Arnolfini Arts Centre
77 @Bristol; Wildscreen
78 SS Great Britain
80 Maritime Heritage Centre
81 SS Waverley
82 Industrial Museum

house. The choir dates back to the 14th century but much of the nave and the western towers were designed by George Street in 1868. The southern transept shelters a rare Saxon carving of the 'Harrowing of Hell'.

MUSEUMS

The **City Museum & Art Gallery** (☎ 922 3571) on Queen's road, houses a mixed bag of exhibits, ranging from Egyptian mummies through natural history and local history to fine art. It opens 10 am to 5 pm. Admission is free.

Those interested in Bristol's links with the aerospace industry should head for the **Industrial Museum** (☎ 925 1470) at Princes Wharf in the docks. It opens 10 am to 5 pm Saturday to Wednesday, April to October (at the weekend only in winter). Admission is free.

Just behind the cathedral, **@Bristol** (☎ 915 5000), Anchor Road, is the city's latest interactive science museum. Admission costs £6.50/4.50.

SS *GREAT BRITAIN*

Bristol was home to the Victorian engineering genius Isambard Kingdom Brunel (1806–59), best known for the Clifton Suspension Bridge. In 1843, he designed the first ocean-going iron ship, the SS *Great Britain*, the first large ship to be driven by a screw propeller.

For 43 years the ship served as a cargo vessel and a liner, carrying passengers as far as Australia. Then in 1886 it was badly damaged passing Cape Horn. The cost of repairs was judged too high, so it was sold for storage. In 1970, it was returned to Bristol and since then has been undergoing restoration in the dry dock where it was originally built.

The ship (☎ 926 0680) is off City Dock and opens 10 am to 5.30 pm (to 4.30 pm in winter). Admission costs £6.25/3.75. Nearby is a replica of John Cabot's ship *Matthew* which undertook the journey from Bristol to Newfoundland in 1497.

Entrance is via the **Maritime Heritage Centre**, which celebrates Bristol's shipbuilding past (same opening hours as the ship). Admission is free.

CLIFTON & THE SUSPENSION BRIDGE

The northern suburb of Clifton boasts some splendid Georgian architecture, including Cornwallis and Royal York crescents, as well as some of Bristol's most attractive shopping streets. In many ways Clifton is as grand as Bath, but, thankfully, lacks the tourists. Bus Nos 8/9 and 508/9 run to Clifton from the city centre.

The spectacular 75m-high **Clifton Suspension Bridge**, designed by Brunel, spans a dramatic stretch of the Avon Gorge. Work on the bridge began in 1836 but wasn't completed until 1864, after Brunel's death. The bridge is an inevitable magnet for stunt artists. More poignantly, it's also a favoured suicide spot. A famous story relates how Sarah Ann Hedley jumped from the bridge in 1885 after a lovers' tiff. Her voluminous petticoats parachuted her safely to earth and she lived to be 85. More recently the car of Richey James Edwards from the Manic Street Preachers was found abandoned near here before his disappearance, but his body has never been found. The visitors centre opens 10 am to 6 pm. Admission costs £1.50/1.

On Durdham Downs, overlooking the bridge, an **observatory** houses a fascinating camera obscura (admission costs £1/50p), which offers a fascinating insight into what folks did for entertainment in the days before television and some incredible views of the suspension bridge. Nearby is **Bristol Zoo** (☎ 970 6176), open 9 am to 5.30 pm (to 4.30 pm in winter). Admission costs £8.20/4.60.

GEORGIAN HOUSE & RED LODGE

The Georgian House (☎ 921 1362) at 7 Great George St was home to 18th-century sugar merchant John Pinney and retains complete period fixtures and fittings.

The Elizabethan Red Lodge (☎ 921 1360) with a walled garden in Perry Rd, was much altered in the 18th century. One room is preserved as a memorial to Mary Carpenter who set up the first women's reformatory here in 1854.

Both houses open 10 am to 5 pm Saturday to Wednesday. Admission is free.

BRISTOL OLD STATION

Before rushing for their train, visitors to Temple Meads station should pause to look at what is the oldest surviving major railway terminus in the world, built to yet another Brunel design between 1839 and 1840. The original terminus stands to the left of the modern one; the Great Train Shed, with its mock hammerbeam roof, last saw a train in 1966 – try the door of the **Brunel Centre** and you may be able to look round.

CHURCHES & CHAPELS

Described as 'the fairest, goodliest and most famous parish church in England' by Queen Elizabeth I in 1574, **St Mary Redcliffe** (☎ 929 1487) is a stunning piece of perpendicular architecture with a grand hexagonal porch which easily outdoes the cathedral in splendour. It opens 8 am to 8 pm (to 5.30 pm in winter).

Once the chapel of St Mark's Hospital, the **Lord Mayor's Chapel** (☎ 929 4350) in Park St is a medieval gem squeezed in between shops opposite the cathedral and packed with stained-glass windows, medieval monuments and ancient tiles. The church-loving poet John Betjeman dubbed it 'for its size one of the very best churches in England'. It opens 10 am to noon and 1 to 4 pm daily except Monday.

Tucked away in Galleries Shopping Centre, the **New Room** (☎ 926 4740) was the world's first Methodist chapel when it opened in 1739. John Wesley, whose equestrian statue stands in the courtyard, preached from its double-decker pulpit. Upstairs, visit the old living quarters, with rooms for John and Charles Wesley and Francis Asbury.

Admission to the chapel is free and it opens 10 am to 4 pm daily except Sunday (and Wednesday in winter).

BLAISE CASTLE HOUSE MUSEUM

In the northern suburb of Henbury lies Blaise Castle (☎ 950 6789), a late 18th-century house which contains a fine museum of West Country rural and urban life. Admission is free and it opens 10 am to 5 pm Saturday to Wednesday.

On a hill stands a mock castle, in grounds laid out by Humphrey Repton. Across the road is **Blaise Hamlet**, a cluster of thatched cottages designed for estate servants in 1811 by John Nash; with its neatly-kept green and flower-filled gardens, it's everyone's fantasy of a 'medieval' English village.

Bus Nos 1/501 pass this way from the city centre.

ORGANISED TOURS

From June to the end of September, hop-on hop-off open-top bus tours circle 14 points in Bristol every day except Saturday. Tickets (£7/5) can be bought on board the bus or from the TIC. Pick up the bus in St Augustine's Parade, outside the Hippodrome.

SPECIAL EVENTS

St Paul's Carnival, a smaller version of London's Notting Hill Carnival, livens up the first Saturday of July. There's a regatta in the harbour in July, and not-to-be-missed hot-air balloon and kite festivals in Ashton Court, across Clifton Suspension Bridge, in August and September.

PLACES TO STAY
Camping

The *Baltic Wharf Caravan Club* site (☎ 926 8030, Cumberland Rd), 1½ miles from the centre, charges £2 a pitch and £4 a person. It's near the A370, A369, A4 and A3029 junctions. They no longer take bookings so arrive early at the weekend as there are just three pitches.

Hostels

Bristol has very little cheap accommodation, but the 129-bed *Bristol Youth Hostel* (☎ 922 1659, 14 Narrow Quay St) in a converted warehouse, five minutes from the town centre, is an excellent place to stay. The nightly charge is £11.90/8.20 for adults/under-18s.

Near the bus station, *Bristol Backpackers* (☎ 925 7900, 17 St Stephen's St) is a new place in a charming, old house with beds for £12.50 a night.

Outside term times, the university also lets out rooms, most centrally in *The Hawthorns* (☎ 954 5900, Woodland Rd, Clifton) which charges from £25/38 a single/double, including a continental breakfast.

B&Bs & Hotels

The *Lawns Guest House (☎ 973 8459, 91 Hampton Rd)* in the leafy suburb of Redland, offers singles/doubles for £24/40.

Most of the other cheap B&Bs tend to be a fair distance from the centre. Clifton, 1½ miles from the centre, is a very attractive suburb and a good place to stay, but most of the B&Bs here cost at least £25 per person. On Oakfield Rd (off Whiteladies Rd), the attractive *Oakfield Hotel (☎ 973 5556)* has rooms for £28.50/38.50. In Tyndalls Park Rd, *Alandale (☎ 973 5407)* charges from £40/50.

Washington Hotel (☎ 973 3980, St Paul's Rd) is midway between the city centre and Clifton Suspension Bridge. During the week, rooms are £53 or £67 with bathroom, £36/46 at the weekend.

About a mile north of the centre, *Courtlands Hotel (☎ 942 4432, 1 Redland Court Rd, Redland)* is a family-run place with a bar and restaurant. There are 25 rooms, most with bathroom, for £50/60.

Most of the city centre hotels bag their profits from their business clientele midweek and then slash prices at the weekend. *City Inn (☎ 925 1001, Temple Way)* is cheap throughout the week with comfortable if characterless rooms from around £51.50 anytime. In a classic location, *Avon Gorge Hotel (☎ 973 8955, Sion Hill, Clifton)* has a terrace overlooking the suspension bridge. It's expensive (£99/109) during the week, but prices drop to £44 a head for B&B, provided you stay two nights, at the weekend.

Grand Thistle Hotel (☎ 929 1645, Broad St) is a Victorian hotel in the heart of the city. During the week, rooms cost £84/93 without breakfast. At the weekend, B&B costs £94 per room. *Jurys (☎ 923 0333, Prince St)* has a splendid position overlooking the Floating Harbour but charges £120 for a room midweek, falling to £54/69 at the weekend.

Hotel du Vin (☎ 925 5577, Narrow Lewins Mead) is the new kid on the block and has sumptuous rooms in a former warehouse complex. Rooms are £99/125 (excluding breakfast) and the bistro here is very well regarded. Fanciest of the lot is the 19th-century *Marriot Royal Hotel (☎ 925 5100, College Green)* beside the cathedral. B&B costs £129/139 during the week, £89/110 at the weekend.

PLACES TO EAT

If you're dining on a shoestring, one of the cheapest places to eat in the city centre is inside *St Nicholas Market* where classics such as bangers and beans, jacket spuds and toasties are all available very cheaply. Nearby 27 Broad St is home to *Arc (☎ 922 6456)*, a cool little cafe that has tasty soups, bargain pizzas and main dishes for £4 such as Thai curry. At night it's a bar and club.

Other popular lunch spots include the cafe-bars in the *Watershed Media Centre (☎ 921 4135)* and the *Arnolfini Arts Centre (☎ 937 9191)*, both arts complexes overlooking the waterfront; quick, tasty meals in either cost around £5. Not far away *Mud Dock (☎ 934 9734, 40 The Grove)* above a bike shop, is a bit pricier but very popular, with more water views.

The nearby *Riverstation (☎ 914 4434)* has excellent food (scrumptious desserts) that costs less downstairs than upstairs. Next door is *severnshed (☎ 925 1212)*, a light, bright cafe-bar specialising in organic Middle Eastern cuisine in Tapas-type portions or mezzes for around £7. At night, expect Belgian beers, live jazz and higher prices.

Sticking with the waterfront area, *Aqua (☎ 915 6060)* is *the* place for Bristol's city slickers on the business schmooze with an excellent menu and a nice ambience. Figure on £10 and up for the experience. Nearby is a branch of *Belgo*, the place for mussel lovers and bountiful Belgian beers.

Heading towards Clifton, Park St is lined with reasonably priced pizzerias: try *Pastificio* or *Vincenzo's*. *Woode's Café*, at the bottom of Park St, sells excellent sandwiches, while *Le Chateau (☎ 929 7298)* at No 64 doles out reasonably priced French food and wine with a licence until 2 am. Hottest spot of all, *The Boston Tea Party (☎ 929 8601)* at No 75 has good lunches and there's a larger branch in Lewins Mead. *Melbourne's (☎ 922 6996, 74 Park St)* keeps prices down with BYO and is popular with Cliftonites. **Brown's** (☎ *930 4777, 38 Queens Rd*) serves excellent food in the classy surroundings of the neo-Venetian ex-university refectory and is consistently busy.

Heading even farther out up Whiteladies Rd are several interesting options. **Thai Classic** (☎ *973 8930*) has a balanced menu of Thai and Malaysian food and offers a good lunchtime deal of two courses for £6.50. Neighbour **Cartier Vert** is an impeccable modern French restaurant and a good lunch will cost around £15, more come the evening.

Recently the grand old bank buildings along Corn St have been given new life as pubs, cafe-bars and restaurants. There are branches of **All Bar One** and **Via Vita**, while **San Carlo** does sound pizzas.

For a splurge, the place to go is **Harvey's Restaurant** (☎ *927 5034, 12 Denmark St*) above Harvey's Wine Museum; four-course dinners cost around £30. In a prettier setting is **The Glass Boat** (☎ *929 0704*), a converted barge on Welsh Back, where dinner will cost around £20.

ENTERTAINMENT
Venue magazine (£1.90) gives details of theatre, music, gigs – the works basically.

Pubs, Bars & Clubs
Most pubs in and around St Augustine's Parade (the city centre) are best avoided, especially at the weekend. Instead, head down King St to **Llandoger Trow** or the excellent **The Old Duke** which hosts nightly jazz sessions.

Popular student hang-outs include **The Albion**, in Boyces Ave, Clifton, and **The Highbury Vaults** on St Michael's Hill, which has a courtyard for alfresco tippling. Cider-lovers shouldn't miss **The Coronation Tap** in Sion Place, Clifton. The rash of Irish pubs between Baldwin St and Corn St are cheerful enough but no more 'Irish' than those with fewer shamrocks on display.

Liberal late licences are a fresh feature in Bristol. **Riverstation**, **severnshed** and **Arc** all play late. **All in One** and **Brasserie Pierre** masquerade as restaurants, but are primarily tacky late night boozers on Park St. **Las**

Iguanas by St Nicholas Market has a healthy range of Latino tunes, and beers to accompany them. By far the best late-night drinking haunt is **Renato's Taverna dell Artista** next door to the Old Vic Theatre. It may look like an Italian restaurant, but don't be misled as this is the place to get a drink after the witching hour and the atmosphere is great. Opposite is the **Famous Royal Navy Volunteer**, an ale pub once favoured by pressgangs that dragged young men off to sea – recruitment tactics are more professional these days so we can drink freely without fear of waking up in Sierra Leone or East Timor.

The legendary **Bierkeller** (☎ *926 8514, All Saints St*) has played host to plenty of rock luminaries and still has regular world music nights. Admission costs £1 to £12 depending on the night of the week and who's playing. **Tantric Jazz** on St Nicholas St has live jazz most nights of the week.

Queenshilling, on Unity St, is arguably the city's most popular gay bar and opposite is a happening little club, the **Silent Peach** which draws a mixed crowd with low cover charges.

Trendy nightspots come and go with alarming frequency. The popular **Lakota** (☎ *942 6208, 2 Upper York St*) stays open until 6 am, whereupon you can move on to **Club Loco** (☎ *942 6208, Hepburn Rd*) off Stokes Croft, which has a 24-hour licence. Other happening clubs right now include chilled out **Fez Club** on St Nicholas St, **Maze** on Hepburn Rd, **Thekla** (*The Grove*) with big beats and house and infinitely tacky **Evolution** down by the docks.

Theatre, Cinema & Concerts
Of the theatres, the **Hippodrome** (☎ *0870 607 7500, St Augustine's Parade*) hosts ballet, musicals and pantomimes, while the **Old Vic** (☎ *926 4388, King St*) sticks with straight drama. **Colston Hall** (☎ *922 3686, Colston St*) stages everything from wrestling bouts to concerts. **St George's** (☎ *923 0359, Great George St*) is an incredible old converted church which plays host to regular classical concerts and has a cafe set in the crypt below.

Most interesting cinema programs tend to be at the **Watershed Media Centre** (☎ *925 3845*), the **Arnolfini Arts Centre** (☎ *929*

9191) and the King's Square *Arts Cinema* (☎ *942 0195)*.

GETTING THERE & AWAY

See the fares tables in the Getting Around chapter. Bristol is 115 miles from London, 75 from Exeter and 50 from Cardiff.

Air

Bristol International Airport (☎ 01275-474444) is 8 miles south-west of town, off the A38. There are buses to the airport from Marlborough St bus station and less frequently from Temple Meads train station.

Bus

Every 1½ hours National Express (☎ 0870 580 8080) has services to Heathrow airport (£24, 2½ hours) and Gatwick airport (£28, three hours). Services into central London are equally regular (£11, 2½ hours). Bakers Dolphin (☎ 972 8000) has cheaper tickets to London (£10 one way, £18 period return) – visit the Bakers Dolphin travel agencies around town.

National Express has frequent buses to Cardiff (£5, 1¼ hours). There are a couple of buses a day to Barnstaple (£14, 2¾ hours) and regular buses south to Truro in Cornwall (£25.75, 4½ hours), Exeter in Devon (£9.75, 1¾ hours), Oxford (£12.75, 2½ hours) and Stratford-upon-Avon (£13, 2½ hours).

Local Badgerline buses (☎ 955 3231) also operate out of Marlborough St bus station. There are frequent services to Bath, Wells and Glastonbury. Hourly buses to Bath can also be picked up outside Temple Meads train station. There are also hourly services to Salisbury (X4) and north to Gloucester. Day Rambler tickets (£5.30/3.75) let you use Badgerline and City Line buses all day.

Train

Bristol is an important rail hub, with regular connections to London Paddington (1½ hours). Most trains (except those to the south) use both the Temple Meads and Parkway stations.

Only 20 minutes away from Bristol, Bath

makes an easy day trip (£4.80 day return). There are frequent links to Cardiff (£6.90, ¾ hour), Exeter (£15.60, one hour), Fishguard (£21.50, 3½ hours), Oxford (£9.90, 1½ hours) and Birmingham (£19, 1½ hours).

Boat

Between July and October you can travel by boat along the Bristol Channel from Bristol to Clevedon, Penarth, Ilfracombe, Barry and Lundy Island. Sailings are on the SS *Balmoral* or the SS *Waverley*, the world's last seagoing paddle steamer. Prices start at £12.95 to Clevedon. Ring Waverley Excursions on ☎ 01446-720656 for full details.

GETTING AROUND

Bus

City Line (☎ 955 3231) bus fares aren't cheap, but Dayrider tickets available on the bus after 9 am Monday to Friday and at any time at the weekend, allow multiple journeys for a discount.

Clifton is a long walk from the city centre. Catch bus Nos 8/9 (508/509 at the weekend) from bus stop 'Cu' on Colston Ave, or from Temple Meads train station. In summer, half-hourly bus No 511 loops from Baltic Wharf to Broadmead, through Clifton Triangle and Hotwells, and back to Baltic Wharf, linking many of the major attractions and shopping centres.

Taxi

The taxi rank on St Augustine's Parade is central but not a good place to hang around late at night. To call a cab free, ring Premier Taxis on ☎ 0800 716777. A taxi to the airport costs around £13.

Boat

The nicest way to get around is to use the ferry which, from April to September, plies the Floating Harbour daily (winter weekends), stopping at the SS *Great Britain*, Hotwells, Baltic Wharf, the Centre, Bristol Bridge (for Galleries Shopping Centre) and Castle Park. The ferry (☎ 927 3416) runs every 20 minutes. A short hop costs £1/60p, a complete circuit £3/1.50.

Bath

☎ 01225 • pop 84,400

One would have to travel far and wide to find a city so grand as Bath. For more than 2000 years, the city's fortune has revolved around its hot springs and the tourism linked to it. It was the Romans who first developed a complex of baths and a temple to the goddess Sulis-Minerva on the site of what they called Aquae Sulis. Today, however, Bath is just as famous for the glorious Georgian architecture that has won it World Heritage Site status from UNESCO.

Throughout the 18th century, Bath was the fashionable haunt of English society. Aristocrats flocked here to gossip, gamble and flirt. Fortunately, they had the good sense and fortune to employ the brilliant architects who designed the Palladian terraced housing, the circles, crescents and squares, that dominate the city.

Like Florence in Italy, Bath is an architectural gem. It too has a shop-lined, much-photographed bridge. Like Florence, it can also seem at times like little more than an upmarket shopping centre for wealthy tourists. However, when sunlight brightens the honey-coloured stone, and buskers and strollers fill the streets and line the river, only the most churlish would deny its charm. Head up some of the steep hills and you can even find pockets of Georgiana that only the residents seem to appreciate.

Bath looks wealthier than Bristol, in part because its beauty attracts moneyed residents, in part because the sheer crush of visitors ensures the good life to those involved in tourism. The best-known sites in and around Abbey Courtyard receive too many visitors for their own good. Away from the centre, however, smaller museums fight for the droppings from their more famous neighbours' tables and are genuinely pleased to see those who trouble to seek them out. Inevitably, Bath also has its share of residents for whom affluence is somebody else's success story. For all the glitzy shops, you will still see beggars on the streets.

The big news in Bath is that at long last the city is to have a spa again. A grant from the Millennium Fund is overseeing the restoration of the old Hot and Cross Baths and the building of a brand-new spa complex designed by Nicholas Grimshaw, the architect behind the Eurostar Terminal at Waterloo. It is due for completion by the end of 2001.

HISTORY

Prehistoric camps on the hills around Bath indicate settlement before the Romans arrived, and legend records King Bladud founding the town after being cured of leprosy by a bath in the muddy swamps. The Romans established the town of Aquae Sulis (named after the Celtic goddess Sul) in AD 44 and it was already a spa, with an extensive baths complex, by the reign of Agricola (78–84).

When the Romans left, the town declined and was captured by the Anglo-Saxons in 577. In 944, a monastery was set up on the site of the present abbey and there are still traces of the medieval town wall in Borough Walls St. Throughout the Middle Ages, Bath served as an ecclesiastical centre and a wool-trading town. However, it wasn't until the 18th century that it really came into its own, when the idea of taking spa water as a cure for assorted ailments led to the creation of the beautiful city visitors see today. Those were the days when Ralph Allen developed the quarries at Coombe Down and employed the two John Woods (father and son) to create the glorious crescents and terraces; when Dr William Oliver established the Bath General Hospital for the poor and gave his name to the Bath Oliver biscuit; and when the gambler Richard 'Beau' Nash became the arbiter of fashionable taste.

By the mid-19th century, sea bathing had become more popular than spa visiting and Bath fell out of fashion. Curiously, even in the 1960s, few people appreciated its architecture and many houses were pulled down to make way for modern replacements before legislation was introduced to protect what remains.

BATH

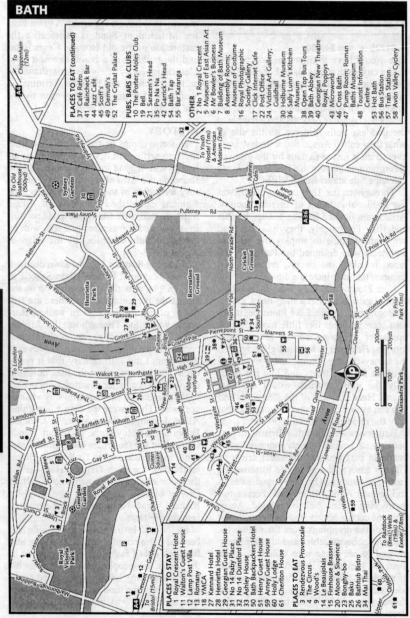

ORIENTATION

Although hemmed in by seven hills, Bath still manages to sprawl quite a way (as visitors discover if they stay at the youth hostel). Fortunately, the centre is compact and easy to get around on foot.

The train and bus stations are both south of the TIC at the end of Manvers St. The most obvious landmark is the abbey, across from the Roman Baths and Pump Room. Open-top bus tours leave from Terrace Walk nearby.

INFORMATION

From mid-June to mid-September, the TIC (☎ 477101), Abbey Chambers, Abbey Courtyard, opens 9.30 am to 7 pm Monday to Saturday, and 10 am to 6 pm Sunday. The rest of the year it closes at 5 pm (at 4 pm on Sunday). Free walking tours (highly recommended) leave from outside the pump room daily – see Organised Tours later in the section. Bath's hilly terrain makes life difficult for disabled visitors but the TIC supplies a free guide with helpful information. Bath's comprehensive Internet site can be found at www.visitbath.co.uk.

Bath has a bad traffic problem and parking space is hard to find. In the city centre, you must display a parking disc in your windscreen. It will cost you 50p for quarter of an hour and can be bought from local shops. Sainsbury's and Homebase have a huge free car park (two hours) near Charles St and the River Avon.

From mid-May to early June the Bath Festival is in full swing with events in all the town's venues, including the abbey. *Venue*, the Bristol and Bath listings magazine, publishes full program details, although popular events are booked up well in advance. Details are available from the Festival Box Office (☎ 462231), Linley House, 1 Pierrepont Place, from February each year. Accommodation is particularly hard to find during the festival.

Much of the city centre, including the maze of passageways just north of Abbey Courtyard, and Shire's Yard off Milsom St, is given over to shops of the pricey 'novelty' kind, but the Saturday and Sunday morning flea market (antiques and clothes) in Walcot St, near the YMCA, is popular with bargain hunters. The covered Guildhall Market in High St has excellent second-hand bookstalls.

Click (☎ 337711, 19 Broad St) is a handy Internet cafe with abundant terminals and cheap international telephone calls.

WALKING TOUR

Bath was designed for leisurely exploration – you need at least a day to take in the highlights.

The best starting point is the **abbey**, conveniently situated diagonally across from the **Roman Baths** and **Pump Room**. Ahead of it, you'll see a colonnade – walk under it and turn left into Stall St. On the right, Bath St has arcading so bathers could walk between the town's three sets of baths without getting rained on.

Walk down Bath St. At the end stands the **Cross Bath** where Mary of Modena, wife of James II, erected a cross in gratitude for her pregnancy in 1688. Opposite is the **Hot Bath**, the third bath built over Bath's hot springs. Turn right and walk down the alley in front of the cinema into Westgate St. Turn left and follow the road round into Barton St and past the Georgian **New Theatre Royal** and **Popjoys Restaurant**, in the house where Beau Nash lived with his mistress Juliana Popjoy. At the end of Barton St is **Queen Square**, designed by John Wood the Elder (1704–54); the northern side, where seven houses form one cohesive unit, is especially attractive.

Walk round the square and exit by the north-western corner which leads into Royal Avenue. On the right is Queen's Parade Place; the two small, stone kiosks on the right-hand side of the road were where sedan chair carriers, the Georgian equivalent of taxi drivers, used to wait for custom. Royal Avenue continues northwards into Royal Victoria Park; a path skirting the eastern side runs past the **Georgian Garden**, where you can see what a garden in Bath would have looked like during the town's 18th-century heyday, with gravel taking the place of grass to protect women's long dresses from staining. Follow the path round the perimeter and you'll emerge on the lawn in front of the famous **Royal Crescent**, designed by John Wood the Younger (1728–1801).

After inspecting the Crescent's superb architecture, turn right along Brock St and walk down to **The Circus**, a circle of 30 houses designed by John Wood the Elder. Plaques on the houses commemorate famous residents such as Thomas Gainsborough, Clive of India and David Livingstone. A left turn out of The Circus will take you down Bennett St to the **Assembly Rooms** and **Museum of Costume**. Walk in front of the museum into Alfred St, where houses retain fine 18th-century metal fittings, including snuffers to put out footmen's torches. Continue along Alfred St and turn right into Bartlett St, then right into George St and left down Milsom St, Bath's main shopping drag. About halfway down you'll pass the **Royal Photographic Society Gallery** in what was once the Octagon Chapel.

At the bottom of Milsom St, cross over into New Bond St until you reach the grand colonnaded post office. Cross the road and turn right along busy Northgate St, then left along Bridge St (passing the **Victoria Art Gallery** on the right), to the River Avon and **Pulteney Bridge**, designed by Robert Adam in 1774. From the bridge, there are views over terraced Pulteney Weir.

Continue straight ahead across Laura Place and along Great Pulteney St. At the far end is the **Holburne Museum**. A plaque opposite, at No 4 Sydney Place, commemorates Jane Austen, the author who lived here for three not particularly happy years. She wrote *Persuasion* and *Northanger Abbey* in Bath and both vividly describe fashionable life in the city around 1800. Walking back along Great Pulteney St, take any turning on the right to get to Henrietta Park, the perfect place for a rest.

ROMAN BATHS MUSEUM

Between the 1st and 4th centuries, the Romans built a bath and temple complex over one of Bath's three natural hot springs. In the Middle Ages, the baths crumbled and it wasn't until the 17th century that anyone paid the spring much more heed. However,

by the end of the century, Mary of Modena was only one of a growing number of visitors coming to 'take the cure' in Bath. In 1702 the visit of Queen Anne set the seal on the trend and the town began to expand.

Nowadays, a raised walkway gives visitors their first glimpse of the **Great Bath**, complete with Roman paving and lead base and surrounded by 19th-century arcading. A series of excavated passages and chambers beneath street level lead off in several directions and let you inspect the remains of other smaller baths and hypocaust (heating) systems. One of the most picturesque corners of the complex is the 12th-century **King's Bath**, built around the original sacred spring; through a window there are views of the pool, complete with niches for bathers and rings for them to hold on to; 1.5 million litres of hot water still pour into the pool every day. The museum outlines the history of the baths and exhibits finds made during excavations, including the fine gorgon head discovered on the site of the temple of Sul and the gilt bronze head from the cult statue.

The Roman Baths (☎ 477791), Abbey Courtyard, are one of England's most popular attractions and can be uncomfortably congested in summer, when the museum's enclosed corridors can also feel very claustrophobic. Visit early on a midweek morning and you'll probably have a much better time. The baths open 9 am to 6 pm (to 9 pm in August, to 5 pm in winter and on Sunday); allow an hour to fully appreciate it. Admission costs £6.90/4.00, but a combined ticket giving entry to the Museum of Costume as well costs £8.90/5.30.

PUMP ROOM

The elegant 18th-century Pump Room is attached to the Roman Baths Museum and a fountain from the King's Bath dispenses tepid spa water which is on sale in the classy restaurant. Since Georgian times, diners have been serenaded by a Palm Court trio, a tradition that continues today. Pictures on the wall depict Georgian luminaries, including Sir Robert Walpole and Ralph Allen, whose quarries at Coombe Down provided much of the Bath stone used to build the town's squares and crescents. There's also a statue of Beau Nash (1674–1761), the uncrowned 'king' of Georgian Bath, a gambler who laid down the rules of etiquette for the town's fashionable visitors. The Pump Room opens for stylish dining from 9.30 am to 10 pm (see Places to Eat later).

Bath Abbey

Edgar, the first king of united England, was crowned in a church in Abbey Courtyard in 973, but the present abbey, more glass than stone, was built between 1499 and 1616, making it the last great medieval church raised in England. The nave's wonderful fan vaulting was erected in the 19th century.

The most striking feature of the abbey's exterior is the western facade, where angels climb up and down stone ladders, commemorating a dream of the founder, Bishop Oliver King. The abbey boasts 640 wall monuments, the second-largest collection after Westminster Abbey; among those buried here are the Reverend Thomas Malthus, the Victorian philosopher famous for his views on population control; Sir Isaac Pitman, who devised the Pitman method of shorthand; and Beau Nash, who is buried at the eastern end of the southern aisle.

Bath Abbey (☎ 422462) opens 9 am to 6 pm (to 4 pm in winter) Monday to Saturday, and 2 to 6 pm Sunday; a donation of £2 is requested.

On the abbey's southern side, steps lead down to a vault in which a small **museum** describes the abbey's history and its links with the baths and fashionable Georgian society. It opens 10 am to 4 pm Monday to Saturday. Admission is £2/free.

ASSEMBLY ROOMS & MUSEUM OF COSTUME

In the 18th century, fashionable Bath visitors gathered to play cards, dance and listen to music in the Assembly Rooms in Bennett St. Nowadays, the basement museum displays costumes worn from the 16th to late 20th centuries, including alarming crinolines that would have forced women to approach doorways side on.

The museum (☎ 477789) opens 10 am to 5 pm (from 11 am Sunday). Admission costs £4/2.90. Combined tickets with the Roman Baths Museum are cheaper.

NO 1 ROYAL CRESCENT

Superbly restored to the minutest detail of its 1770 magnificence, this grand Palladian town house (☎ 428126) in the Royal Crescent is well worth visiting to see how people lived during Bath's glory days.

It opens 10.30 am to 5 pm Tuesday to Sunday, March to October (to 4 pm in November). Admission costs £4/3.

JANE AUSTEN CENTRE

In a Georgian town house on Gay St, the Jane Austen Centre (☎ 443000) is a fitting tribute to one of the city's most famous residents. The displays include period pieces and personal items. The centre opens 10 am to 5 pm. Admission costs £3.95/2.95.

BUILDING OF BATH MUSEUM

Housed in the 18th-century chapel of the Countess of Huntingdon in The Paragon, the Building of Bath Museum (☎ 333895) details how Bath's Georgian splendour came into being, a more interesting story than you might imagine. It opens 10.30 am to 5 pm Tuesday to Sunday, March to November. Admission costs £3.50/1.50.

HOLBURNE MUSEUM

The fine 18th-century Holburne Museum on Sydney Place (☎ 466669) was originally designed as the Sydney Hotel. It now houses a collection of porcelain, antiques, and paintings by great 18th-century artists such as Gainsborough and Stubbs. It opens 11 am to 5 pm Monday to Saturday, and 2.30 to 5.30 pm Sunday, Easter to mid-December. Admission costs £3.50/1.50.

MR BOWLER'S BUSINESS

Tucked away in Julian Rd, Mr Bowler's Business (☎ 318348) is Bath's industrial heritage centre housed in what was originally an 18th-century 'real' tennis court. Most of the fittings belonged to Jonathan Burdett Bowler's 19th- and 20th-century mineral-water bottling plant and brass foundry. It opens 10 am to 5 pm (at the weekend only November to Easter). Admission costs £3.50/2.50.

SALLY LUNN'S KITCHEN MUSEUM

Round the corner from the abbey in North Parade Passage, Sally Lunn's Kitchen Museum (☎ 461634) consists mainly of exposed foundation stones, but a commentary describes how Sally Lunn, a 17th-century Huguenot refugee, used to bake buns. Similar buns are still sold in the cafe upstairs. It opens 10 am to 6 pm Monday to Saturday, and noon to 6 pm Sunday. Admission costs 30p.

VICTORIA ART GALLERY

Opposite Pulteney Bridge, the Victoria Art Gallery (☎ 477772) contains two Thomas Rowlandson cartoons belonging to a series entitled *The Comforts of Bath*. It also has paintings by Walter Sickert who lived nearby. Admission is free and it opens 10 am to 5.30 pm (to 5 pm on Saturday and from 2 pm on Sunday).

ROYAL PHOTOGRAPHIC SOCIETY GALLERY

On Milsom St, the Royal Photographic Society Gallery (☎ 462841) contains exhibits illustrating the history of photography, a bookshop and the excellent In Focus cafe (see Places to Eat). It opens 9.30 am to 5.30 pm. Admission is £4/free.

MUSEUM OF EAST ASIAN ART

The Museum of East Asian Art (☎ 464640), 12 Bennett St, contains more than 500 jade, bamboo, porcelain and bronze objects from China, Korea, Cambodia, Thailand and Japan. It opens 10 am to 5 pm daily except Monday (from noon on Sunday; fewer hours in winter). Admission costs £3.50/2.50.

MICROWORLD

This unlikely museum (☎ 333033), 4 Monmouth St, houses a collection of microscopic sculptures, such as Tower Bridge in the eye of a needle and Mount Rushmore in a match head. The exhibition opens 10 am to 6 pm and admission costs £3.95/1.9.

ORGANISED TOURS

Free two-hour walking tours of Bath leave from outside the Pump Room at 10.30 am and 2 am from Sunday to Friday; 10.30 am and 7 pm Saturday, May to September. There are additional 7 pm tours on Tuesday and Friday during summer; phone ☎ 477786 for details.

Guide Friday (☎ 444102) runs open-top, hop-on hop-off bus tours daily from 9.15 am to 5.25 pm, Easter to October; fewer hours the rest of the year. The buses pass Terrace Walk behind the abbey, and Bath bus station. Tickets cost £8.50/3.

Two-hour ghost walks (☎ 463618) depart from Nash Bar in the Garrick's Head pub, off Saw Close, at 8 pm Monday to Friday, May to October; on Friday only in winter (£4). Bizarre Bath comedy walks (☎ 335124) leave nightly at 8 pm from the Huntsman Inn in North Parade Passage (£4.50).

PLACES TO STAY

Finding somewhere to stay during busy periods can be tough and you might want to pay the TIC's £2.50 booking fee for its help. Bath Visitor Call can fax you an accommodation list; call ☎ 0891 194601 (calls cost at least 45p a minute).

Camping

About 3 miles west of Bath, at Newton St Loe, the *Newton Mill Touring Centre* (☎ *333909*) charges £11.50 for a tent and two people. It opens year round. To reach it, take the B3310 off the A4.

Hostels

The wonderfully decorated, 52-bed *Bath Backpackers Hotel* (☎ *446787, 13 Pierrepoint St*) is Bath's most convenient budget accommodation, less than 10-minutes walk from the bus and train stations. B&B in nonsmoking dorm rooms with up to eight beds costs £12. There's a lounge, cooking facilities and Internet access.

Also central, *YMCA International House* (☎ *460471*) takes men and women and has no curfew, but is often full, especially in summer. Approaching from the south along Walcot St, look out for an archway and steps on the left about 180m past the post office on New Bond St. Singles/doubles with continental breakfast are £15/28, dorm beds £11.

The 117-bed **Bath Youth Hostel** (☎ 465674, Bathwick Hill) is out towards the University of Bath, a good 25-minute walk, or catch Badgerline bus No 18 from the bus station. There are compensatory views and the building is magnificent. It opens all day, all year, and charges £10.85/7.40 for adults/under-18s.

B&Bs & Hotels

Staying in Bath doesn't come cheap. In summer, most places charge at least £17/35 for singles/doubles. The main areas are along Newbridge Rd to the west, Wells Rd to the south, and around Pulteney Rd in the east. Bath is a popular place to spend the weekend and prices reflect this.

Considering its location, just a few minutes walk from the bus and train stations, **Henry Guest House** (☎ 424052, 6 Henry St) is reasonable at £22 per person. The eight rooms all have shared baths.

Romany (☎ 424193, 9 Charlotte St) is also dead central, and reasonable value from £40 for a double.

There are numerous B&Bs on and around Pulteney Rd. **Ashley House** (☎ 425027, 8 Pulteney Gardens) has eight rooms, some with a shower, for £26.50/50.

The nonsmoking **No 14 Raby Place** (☎ 465120) off Bathwick Hill just after you turn off Pulteney Rd, charges from £25/42.

There are several places along Henrietta St, near Henrietta Park. At No 34, the handsome **Georgian Guest House** (☎ 424103) has a range of rooms from £38/55 a single/double. **Henrietta Hotel** (☎ 447779), next door, charges from £30/50; at the weekend the price rises to £50/75! Across the road, the classy **Kennard Hotel** (☎ 310472) at No 11, has rooms with bathroom from £48/88.

In an idyllic location beside the River Avon, the **Old Boathouse** (☎ 466407, Forester Rd) is an Edwardian boating station within walking distance of the centre. Comfortable nonsmoking rooms with bathroom cost £55.

The B&Bs west of the centre along Upper Bristol Rd (A4), near The Crescent, mostly cost at least £25 a head, more if you're travelling alone. On Crescent Gardens, try **Lamp Post Villa** (☎ 331221) at No 3, or **Walton's Guest House** (☎ 426528) at No 17.

Wells Rd (A367) also harbours B&Bs. At No 99, **Arney Guest House** (☎ 310020) has three rooms and charges from £25/45 with shared bathroom. There are numerous other places nearby.

Holly Lodge (☎ 424042, 8 Upper Oldfield), a 10-minute walk from the centre, has views over the city. Rooms in this non-smoking award-winning hotel are from £48/97. Readers have also recommended **Cheriton House** (☎ 429862), across the road, with big rooms from £42/64.

Bath's top place to stay is on the grandest of grand crescents. **Royal Crescent Hotel** (☎ 739955, 16 Royal Crescent) has 46 rooms in the two central houses. There's a garden behind the hotel and an excellent restaurant. Decorated with period furnishings, rooms officially cost from £195, but if it's low season and mid-week you can usually negotiate a lower price. Similarly exclusive is the five star **Bath Spa Hotel** (☎ 444424, Sydney Rd) which has elegant rooms from £140/224, excluding breakfast!

If you can afford prices like that and have a car it's worth considering staying outside Bath at **Ston Easton Park** (☎ 01761-241631), a stunning Georgian mansion in landscaped grounds with wonderful rooms for £155/320. The village of Ston Easton is 10 miles south-west of Bath.

PLACES TO EAT

Bath has a range of eateries to suit every wallet or purse. Self-catering is covered by the Guildhall Market and local supermarkets; pubs and cafes offer value dining, while those who are flush can find plenty of top-class restaurants.

Good French restaurants include **Le Beaujolais** (☎ 423417, 5 Chapel Row), with express three-course lunches for £8.50 and a selection of regional favourites, and **Rendezvous Provencal** (☎ 310064, Upper Church St) with a similar lunchtime deal, cosy atmosphere and good location near

Royal Crescent. *The Circus* (☎ 318918, Brock St) has a good reputation, but is a step up in price.

Near the abbey, wannabee retro *Café Retro* (☎ 339347, York St) does three-course meals for around £10, though light bites are much less. Just east of Pulteney Bridge in Argyle St is *Baku* (☎ 444440), a small, cosy diner offering gourmet sandwiches and the like. Nearby, at 2 Grove St, the good-value *Bathtub Bistro* (☎ 460593) serves interesting dishes like spinach, lentil and apricot filo parcel.

Crystal Palace (☎ 423944, Abbey Green), south of Abbey Courtyard, has a beer garden, traditional ale and standard pub fare. The pleasant *Moon & Sixpence* (☎ 460962, 6 Broad St) offers two-course eat-all-you-can lunches for £5. Pubs are also the best bet for cheap evening meals, too.

Bonghy-bo, on Upper Borough Walls, is a small cafe with an eclectic mix of Asian dishes and the prices are pretty sensible, even if the name provokes a smirk. *Mai Thai* (☎ 445557, Manvers St) is a good Thai restaurant with some excellent lunchtime offers including two courses for £7.

Firehouse Brasserie (☎ 482070, Queen St) offers expensive Mediterranean food (pizzas for £10), but the prices don't stop the local business set from congregating here. *Wood's* (☎ 314812, 9 Alfred St) is more reasonable, prices for two-course lunches start at around £5.

Demuth's (☎ 446059, North Parade Passage) serves delicious vegetarian and vegan food and has two-course specials for £6.95. Good cakes are on offer in the *In Focus* cafe in the Royal Photographic Society Gallery on Milsom St. *Jazz Café* near Westgate has no music but a great selection of traditional greasy-spoon fare.

The Raincheck Bar on Westgate is a popular cafe-bar with good food, an intimate ambience and some streetside tables.

The best place for cream teas is the *Pump Room*. Here one sips one's tea and heaps one's scones with jam and cream while being serenaded by the Pump Room Trio. At £5.95, it's hardly cheap but is very much part of the Bath experience. Alternatively, pop into *Sally Lunn's* (above the Kitchen Museum), which has been baking buns for over 300 years.

ENTERTAINMENT
Pubs, Bars & Clubs
Bath has lots of atmospheric pubs and, thanks to a healthy student population, some reasonable clubs. Pubs worth a drink include the intimate *Coeur de Lion* (17 Northumberland Place), off the High St, *The Bell* (Walcot St) or the *Saracen's Head*, the city's oldest pub, on Broad St.

The *Bath Tap* on St James Parade is the most popular place among Bath's gay community. Pre-club hotspots include *The Porter*, a pub-bar with a cool atmosphere just above the popular *Moles* club, and *Bar Karanga* on Manvers St, a trendy little spot named in honour of the city's most popular club night that rocks on at *Babylon*, close to the bus station. *Po Na Na* is a popular bar club on North Parade that hits 2 am at the weekend.

To work up a thirst, follow the canal north-east 1½ miles out of Bath to the village of Bathampton, where the *George* is beside the towpath.

Theatre
The sumptuous *Theatre Royal* (☎ 448844, Barton St) often features shows on their pre-London run. *Bath Abbey* has a regular program of lunchtime recitals; the price depends on who is appearing. There's also a *Puppet Theatre* under Pulteney Bridge.

GETTING THERE & AWAY
See the fares tables in the Getting Around chapter. Bath is 106 miles from London, 19 miles from Wells and only 12 from Bristol.

Bus
There are National Express (☎ 0870 580 8080) buses every two hours from London (£11.50, three hours).

There is an hourly bus (X4) between Bristol and Salisbury via Bath (£3.90). There's also a link with Oxford (£9.75, two hours), and Stratford-upon-Avon via Bristol (£15.75, 2½ hours).

Some excellent map-timetables are available from the bus station (☎ 464446). The Badgerline Day Rambler (£5.30/3.75 adult/child) gives you access to a good network of buses in Bristol, Somerset (Wells, Glastonbury), Gloucestershire (Gloucester) and Wiltshire (Lacock, Bradford-on-Avon, Salisbury).

Train
There are numerous trains from London Paddington (£30, 1¾ hours). There are also plenty of trains to Bristol for onward travel to Cardiff, Exeter or the north. Hourly trains link Portsmouth and Bristol via Salisbury and Bath. A single ticket from Bath to Salisbury costs £10. A day return to Bristol costs £4.60.

GETTING AROUND
Car
Clamping is big business in Bath and release fees are around £110. Take care about where you park.

Bicycle
Bikes can be hired from Avon Valley Cyclery (☎ 461880), behind the train station, for £14 per day. Cyclists can use the 12-mile Bristol and Bath Railway Path that follows a disused railway line.

Boat
Passenger boats sail hourly from beneath Pulteney Bridge to Bathampton, April to October. Alternatively, you can hire canoes, punts or rowing boats to propel yourself along the Avon from £4.50 an hour (£1.50 for additional hours); try Bath Boating station (☎ 466407) on Forester Rd.

AROUND BATH
Prior Park
This recently restored, beautiful 18th-century park (☎ 833422; NT) with spectacular views of Bath was created for Ralph Allen by Capability Brown. It's on Ralph Allen Drive, accessible only by bus No 2, 4 or 733, or on foot. Admission costs £3.80/1.90 (£1 refund if you show your bus ticket) and it opens noon to 5.30 pm daily except Tuesday.

American Museum
Three miles south-east of Bath, Claverton Manor (☎ 460503) is an 1820s mansion housing re-created 17th- to 19th-century American home interiors, a collection of quilts and other American memorabilia.

Bus No 18 to the university drops you half a mile from the entrance. The house opens 2 to 5 pm daily except Monday, March to October; the grounds open 1 to 6 pm. Admission costs £5.50/3, although you can buy a grounds-only ticket for £3/2.

Dyrham Park
Eight miles north of Bath on the A46, Dyrham Park is a 105-hectare deer park encircling the fine 17th-century house of William Blathwayt, secretary of state to William III.

The house (☎ 01179-372501; NT) opens noon to 5.30 pm Friday to Tuesday, April to October. Admission is £7.50/3.70. The park can be visited noon to 5.30 pm year round. Admission costs £1.80/90p. On Friday and Saturday Ryans Coaches connect Dyrham with Bath; phone ☎ 424157 for times.

Somerset

A largely agricultural county, Somerset is known for its cider-making, cricket club and Cheddar cheese. The most interesting towns are Wells, with its superb cathedral, and mystical Glastonbury, a magnet for druids and New Age hippies.

Somerset offers good walking country. The Mendip Hills are cut by gorges where caves were inhabited from prehistoric times. The Quantocks to the west are less cultivated, while to the far west of the county, the wilder Exmoor National Park (see Exmoor National Park later in the chapter) spans the border with Devon.

GETTING AROUND
The Somerset transport enquiry line is on ☎ 01823-358299 but you can also phone the bus companies direct: the region is roughly split between Badgerline (☎ 0117-955 3231) north of Bridgwater, and Southern National (☎ 01823-272033) to the south.

The 613-mile South West Coast Path begins in Minehead and follows the West Country coast round to Poole in Dorset. TICs stock the free *Cycle Round South Somerset* describing an 80-mile cycle route, and *The Somerset Cycle Guide*.

WELLS
☎ 01749 • pop 9400
Taking its name from three springs that emerged near the medieval Bishop's Palace, Wells is England's smallest cathedral city. It has managed to hang on to much of its medieval character and the cathedral is one of England's most beautiful, with one of the best surviving examples of a full cathedral complex.

Wells is 22 miles south-west of Bath. As well as being a good base for touring the Mendip Hills, it's within easy reach of Cheddar, Wookey Hole and Glastonbury.

Orientation & Information
The city centre is compact and easy to get around. The TIC (☎ 672552) is in the town hall in picturesque Market Place near the cathedral. Bike City (☎ 343111, 91 Broad St) has bikes for hire from £8 per day and there are lots of interesting walking and cycling routes nearby; the TIC has details. Markets are held in Market Place on Wednesday and Saturday.

Wells Cathedral
The cathedral (☎ 674483) was built in stages between 1180 and 1508 and incorporates several Gothic styles. Its most famous feature is the wonderful **western front**, an immense sculpture gallery with over 300 figures, that was built between 1230 and 1250 and restored to its original splendour in 1986. Apart from the figure of Christ, installed in 1985 in the uppermost niche, all the other figures are original.

Inside, the most striking feature is the pair of **scissor arches**, separating the nave from the choir, a brilliant solution to the problem posed by the subsidence of the central tower; they were added in the 14th century, shortly after the tower's completion. Just before the hour, make sure you're

---

Wells Cathedral Clock

High up in the northern transept is a wonderful mechanical clock dating from 1392, the second oldest surviving in England after the one in Salisbury Cathedral.

The complex-looking dial shows the hours in two sets of 12 on the outer circle, with the sun rotating round the earth to mark the hours. The minutes are shown on the inner circle, each indicated by a rotating star.

The clock also shows the position of the planets and the phases of the moon, but it's the entertaining cabaret act performed above it by jousting knights on horseback that draws a small crowd on the hour (the quarter-hour in summer).

Quarterjacks in the shape of 15th-century knights use poleaxes to hit a bell to mark the time on the clock's exterior face.

---

standing in front of the intriguing **mechanical clock** in the northern transept.

Among other things to look out for in the cathedral are the elegant **Lady Chapel** at the eastern end; the seven **effigies** of Anglo-Saxon bishops ringing the choir; and the **chained library** upstairs from the southern transept. The library opens 2.30 to 4.30 pm Tuesday to Saturday, April to October. Admission costs 50p.

Reached by worn steps leading off the northern transept is the glorious mid-13th-century **Chapter House**, the ceiling ribs of which sprout like a palm from a central column.

Externally, look out for the **Chain Bridge** built from the northern side of the cathedral to Vicars' Close to enable clerics to reach the cathedral without getting their robes wet. The **cloisters** on the southern side surround a pretty courtyard.

The cathedral opens 7 am to 7 pm (to 8.30 pm in July and August); visitors are asked to donate £4/1. Guided tours are free.

Bishop's Palace
Beyond the cathedral is the moated Bishop's Palace (☎ 678691), a private residence dating back to the 13th century that

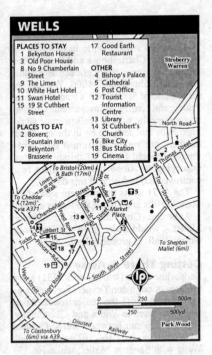

WELLS

PLACES TO STAY
1 Bekynton House
3 Old Poor House
8 No 9 Chamberlain
  Street
9 The Limes
10 White Hart Hotel
11 Swan Hotel
15 19 St Cuthbert
  Street

PLACES TO EAT
2 Boxers;
  Fountain Inn
7 Bekynton
  Brasserie

17 Good Earth
   Restaurant

OTHER
4 Bishop's Palace
5 Cathedral
6 Post Office
12 Tourist
   Information
   Centre
13 Library
14 St Cuthbert's
   Church
16 Bike City
18 Bus Station
19 Cinema

Stroberry Warren

North Road

To Bristol (20mi) & Bath (17mi)

To Cheddar (12mi), via A371

To Shepton Mallet (6mi)

South Silver Street

To Glastonbury (6mi) via A39

Disused Railway

Park Wood

0   250   500m
0   250   500yd

has beautiful gardens. It opens 11 am to 6 pm Tuesday to Friday and on bank holidays; 2 to 6 pm Sunday and daily in August. Admission is £3/free.

After a decade when no swans knew the trick, a new generation of birds has now learned to ring a bell outside one of the windows when they want to be fed.

Cathedral Close

Wells Cathedral is the focal point of a cluster of buildings whose history is inextricably linked to its own. Facing the western front, on the left are the 15th-century **Old Deanery** and a salmon-coloured building housing **Wells Museum** (☎ 673477), with exhibits about caving in the Mendips, local life and the cathedral architecture. The museum opens 10 am to 5.30 pm April to October (to 8 pm in July and August); and 11 am to 4 pm Wednesday to Sunday, November to April. Admission costs £2/1.

Farther along on the left, **Vicars' Close** is

a cobbled street of houses dating back to the 14th century with a chapel at the end; members of the cathedral choir still live here. Passing under the Chain Bridge, inspect the outside of the Lady Chapel and a lovely medieval house called **The Rib**, before emerging at a main road called The Liberty. In the Middle Ages, this marked the boundary of the cathedral precincts within which a refugee could take sanctuary.

St Cuthbert's Church

Wells Cathedral is such a major draw that many visitors never venture beyond its beautiful close. However, it's worth dropping by **St Cuthbert's Church** in Cuthbert St, to admire its splendid 15th-century perpendicular tower and brilliantly coloured nave roof. Look out for the boss of a sow suckling five piglets in the southern porch.

Places to Stay

There are plenty of B&Bs but most have only a few rooms so advance booking is advised. *9 Chamberlain St* (☎ 672270) is near the cathedral and charges £22/38.

At 29 Chamberlain St is *The Limes* (☎ 675716), with two rooms. For the four-poster bed, B&B costs £20 per person; in the twin room it's £18. Singles cost £30.

The B&B at *19 Cuthbert St* (☎ 673166) overlooks the cathedral and is in a quiet part of town; it charges from £16.50 per person. The *Old Poor House* (☎ 675052, 7a St Andrew St) is a comfortable 14th-century cottage just outside the cathedral precincts. The nightly charge is £25 per person. Slightly farther out, at 7 St Thomas St, *Bekynton House* (☎ 672222) charges £36/52.

There's a cluster of hotels in Sadler St near the cathedral. The *White Hart Hotel* (☎ 672056) has single/double rooms for £57.50/75 with bathrooms. The *Star Hotel* (☎ 670500, 18 High St) has triple rooms for £65 which is good value.

The *Swan Hotel* (☎ 678877, Sadler St) is a fine 15th-century inn with some four-poster beds; some of the rooms look straight onto the cathedral's western front. Room prices are £75/95 for singles/doubles but ask about special deals.

Places to Eat

The town's best restaurant is probably *Boxers* (☎ 672317, 1 St Thomas St) upstairs in the *Fountain Inn*; expect to pay about £20 for a three-course meal and drinks.

Near the bus station is the *Good Earth Restaurant* (☎ 678600, 4 Priory Rd), an excellent vegetarian place. The courgette and stilton lasagne is recommended and the soups are a bargain. *Bekynton Brasserie (Sadler St)* is a good place for standard lunch fare. *City Arms* (☎ 673916, 69 High St) serves enjoyable pub grub and also has a restaurant open in the evening. Part of the pub used to be a jail in Tudor times.

The most atmospheric place to eat is the *Refectory* in the cathedral cloisters where you can lunch on soup and a roll or sandwiches, overlooked by 18th-century monuments; it opens daily for lunch and afternoon tea.

Katie's Tea Room, opposite the White Hart Hotel, does a good cream tea.

Entertainment

A year-round program of lunch-time recitals and evening concerts offers the chance to hear the historic cathedral choir in full voice. For details, phone ☎ 674483.

Getting There & Away

Badgerline (☎ 0117-955 3231) operates buses hourly from Bristol and Bath. No 163 runs from Wells to Glastonbury and Street. Bus Nos 161/2 travel via Shepton Mallet to Frome. Heading for the coast, bus Nos 126 and 826 travel to Weston-super-Mare via Cheddar. There's no train station in Wells; the nearest is 15 miles away at Castle Cary.

MENDIP HILLS

The Mendip Hills are a ridge of limestone hills about 25 miles long and 5 miles wide in northern Somerset. These are not lofty hills – their highest point is Black Down (326m) to the north-west – but they stand out in an area that is otherwise very flat, giving way in the south to the Somerset Levels where roads often run on causeways above flood level.

Nowadays, the Mendip Hills form a densely cultivated agricultural area, but in the past they were more famous for coal mining, traces of which can be seen around Radstock and Midsomer Norton to the east. The Romans are known to have mined for lead around Charterhouse and Priddy; lead mining continued throughout the Middle Ages and right up until 1900. You can see the remains of St Cuthbert's lead mines near Priddy, and scruffy hollows around Charterhouse mark the sites of shallow mine workings. Pubs that seem to be in the middle of nowhere are survivors from a time when mining brought plenty of thirsty drinkers. Quarrying for stone is an important (and controversial) industry to this day.

The A371 skirts the southern side of the Mendip Hills and any of the towns along it – Axbridge, Cheddar, Wells or Shepton Mallet – would make good touring bases, though Wells is probably best.

Getting There & Away

Badgerline buses (☎ 0117-955 3231) serve this area, though don't expect services to be very frequent off the major roads. Apart from the buses to Wells and Glastonbury, Nos 126/826 run between Wells, Cheddar and Axbridge. Nos 160/162 regularly link Wells with Shepton Mallet, while No 173 runs between Bath, Radstock, Midsomer Norton and Wells.

Coming by car, the Mendip Hills are squeezed in between the A38 Bristol to Burnham-on-Sea and A37 Bristol to Wells.

Wookey Hole

Wookey Hole (☎ 01749-672243), the site of a sequence of caves carved out by the River Axe, one of them containing a spectacular lake, is just 2 miles east of Wells. The striking shape of one particular stalagmite gave rise to the legend of the Witch of Wookey. Nowadays, the caves are the focal point of a series of other attractions, including an ancient handmade-paper mill, an Edwardian fairground, a maze of mirrors and an arcade of vintage amusement machines.

The Wookey Hole attractions open 10 am to 5 pm, April to September (10.30 am to 4.30 pm in winter). Admission is £7.20/4.20. Bus No 171 offers an hourly service between Wells and Wookey Hole (£1.20/1.60 one way/return, 10 minutes). A 3-mile walk to Wookey is signposted from New St in Wells.

Cheddar Gorge

The Mendips' most dramatic scenery can be found along its southern side where the Cheddar Gorge cuts a mile swathe through the landscape, exposing great sweeps of 138m-high grey stone cliff. Approaching on foot from the north or walking along the cliff-top paths, it's possible to imagine how wild and spectacular Cheddar must have been before the stalactite and stalagmite-filled Cox's and Gough's caves started to suck in the crowds; the area immediately around the caves can be very off-putting in summer when the place heaves with visitors. It's probably best to visit out of season, bearing in mind that most of the teashops and fish and chip shops open only at the weekend in winter.

The **Cheddar Showcaves** (☎ 01934-742343) open 10 am to 5 pm, Easter to September; and 10.30 am to 4.30 pm in winter. Admission costs £7.50/5 which covers

Cheddar Cheese

The country's most famous cheese only began to become widely known when people started visiting Cheddar Gorge and taking home some of the local cheese. Cheddar was just one of many Somerset villages that produced this type of cheese.

Over the years, and with mass production not only all over Britain but in several other countries as well, Cheddar has become a generic name for any pale yellow, medium-hard cheese. The name covers a wide range of qualities, from soapy supermarket Cheddar to the delicious farmhouse variety, which is mature and tangy.

If you're interested in the process of making genuine Cheddar Cheese, the Cheddar Gorge Cheese Company (☎ 01934-742810) opens daily. You can watch the cheese-maker at work and on the hour there's a short talk. It's part of the Rural Village (just off the B3135) that also includes demonstrations of lace-making, pottery, fudge-making and spinning. Admission to the village costs £1.50/1.

entry to the heritage centre, lookout tower and cliff-top walk.

The TIC (☎ 01934-744071) in the gorge opens daily Easter to October, and on Sunday only the rest of the year.

Cheddar village, to the south-west of the gorge, has an elegant church and an ancient market cross but is otherwise disappointing. *Cheddar Youth Hostel* (☎ 01934-742494) is a mile from the caves on Hillfield, a road off The Hayes on the western side of the village. The nightly charge is £10.85/7.40.

Badgerline bus Nos 126/826 run between Wells (9 miles) and Weston-super-Mare via Cheddar (20 minutes, £2.45/3.40 one way /return), hourly from Monday to Saturday and every two hours on Sunday.

Axbridge

☎ 01934

Just 1½ miles from Cheddar, the pretty village of Axbridge is light years away from Cheddar's tackiness and makes a much nicer, albeit pricier, place to stay. One corner of the central square is dominated by the striking half-timbered **King John's Hunting Lodge** (☎ 732012; NT), a Tudor merchant's house now housing the local museum. It opens 2 to 5 pm, Easter to September. Another corner is occupied by the huge late-Gothic church of St John with a 17th-century plaster ceiling. The rest of the square is ringed with hotels and restaurants.

For somewhere to stay, try *The Lamb* (☎ 732253, e lambinn@axbridge.org.uk) where rooms cost £40/50 with bathroom, or *The Oak House* (☎ 732444) where it's £45/65 for a single/double.

To eat, choose between the *Spinning Wheel Restaurant* (☎ 732476) where a three-course dinner midweek costs £17.95 or the 15th-century *Almshouse Bistro* (☎ 732493).

You can walk or cycle to Axbridge from Cheddar. Badgerline bus No 126 from Cheddar to Burnham-on-Sea also passes through the centre.

Mendip Villages

The Mendip villages are not renowned for particularly striking buildings, although you might be interested in the 19th-century

SOUTH-WESTERN ENGLAND

Downside Abbey, established by English monks driven from France by the French Revolution. Downside is now a famous Roman Catholic boys' school.

Otherwise, many of the villages are pretty, in a low-key way, and several have fine perpendicular church towers. Especially impressive is that at **Chewton Mendip** (on the A37 from Bristol to Wells), where there's an attractive medieval churchyard cross. The village of **Compton Martin** has a Norman church with a 15th-century tower. A mile to the east, **West Harptree** is a prettier village with two 17th-century former manor houses. Near **East Harptree** are the remains of Norman Richmont Castle, captured from supporters of Matilda by those of King Stephen in 12th-century skirmishing.

GLASTONBURY
☎ 01458 • pop 6900

Although it's little more than an extended village, Glastonbury is England's unofficial New Age capital – the place to come if you want your runes read, to find out about English paganism or to buy crystals, candles and incense sticks. The juxtaposition of Somerset's gentrified classes, white witches and the soap-dodgers brigade makes for a pretty heady mix.

Myths and legends about Glastonbury abound. One story tells how Jesus came here with his great-uncle Joseph of Arimathea, while another reports Joseph bringing the chalice from the Last Supper with him. Later legends also made Glastonbury the burial place of King Arthur and Queen Guinevere, and the tor (the nearby hill), the Isle of Avalon. Finally, the tor was thought to guard a gateway to the underworld. Over time, these different tales have become entangled with each other in a potent mixture that has left Glastonbury important to Christians and atheists alike, as a glimpse at the various bookshops confirms.

Whatever you choose to believe, Glastonbury has the ruins of a 14th-century abbey, a couple of museums, mystic springs and superb views from the tor to make it well worth a visit.

Orientation & Information

The main bus stop is opposite the town hall in Magdalene St, within sight of the Market Cross and the abbey ruins.

The TIC (☎ 832954), in the Tribunal,

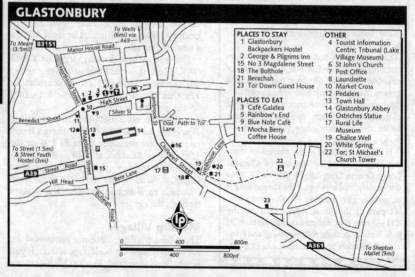

GLASTONBURY

To Wells (6mi) via A39

To Meare (3.5mi)

Manor House Road

To Street (1.5mi) & Street Youth Hostel (3mi)

Northload Street

High Street

Silver St

Benedict Street

Magdalene Street

Lambrook St

Dod Lane Path to Tor

Chilkwell Street

Bere Lane

Butleigh Road

Wellhouse Lane

Hill Head

Street Road

A39

To Shepton Mallet (9mi)

A361

PLACES TO STAY
1 Glastonbury Backpackers Hostel
2 George & Pilgrims Inn
15 No 3 Magdalene Street
18 The Bolthole
21 Berachah
23 Tor Down Guest House

PLACES TO EAT
3 Café Galatea
5 Rainbow's End
9 Blue Note Café
11 Mocha Berry Coffee House

OTHER
4 Tourist Information Centre; Tribunal (Lake Village Museum)
6 St John's Church
7 Post Office
8 Laundrette
10 Market Cross
12 Pedalers
13 Town Hall
14 Glastonbury Abbey
16 Ostriches Statue
17 Rural Life Museum
19 Chalice Well
20 White Spring
22 Tor; St Michael's Church Tower

0   400   800m
0   400   800yd

SOUTH-WESTERN ENGLAND

9 High St, stocks free maps and accommodation lists, and sells leaflets describing local walks and village trails. From Easter to October you can hire bikes for £7/30 a day/week at Pedalers (☎ 834562). There's a market on Tuesday.

There is Internet access at Café Galatea (see Places to Eat later).

Glastonbury Abbey

Legend suggests that there has been a church on this site since the 1st century, but the first definite traces date back to the 7th century when King Ine gave a charter to a monastery here. The first abbey church seems to have reached the height of its importance under the abbacy of St Dunstan, later an archbishop of Canterbury. During his time in office, King Edgar, the first king of a united England, died and was buried at Glastonbury.

In 1184, the old church was destroyed by fire; reconstruction began in the reign of Henry II. In 1191, monks claimed to have had visions confirming hints in old manuscripts that the 6th-century warrior King Arthur and his wife Guinevere were buried in the grounds. Excavations to the south of the old church uncovered what was said to be their tomb, and a lead cross recording that fact, which has since disappeared. The couple were reinterred in front of the high altar of the new church in 1278 and the tomb survived until 1539 when Henry VIII dissolved the monasteries.

The last abbot was hanged, drawn and quartered on the tor. After that, the abbey complex gradually collapsed, its component parts scavenged to provide building materials. It wasn't until the 19th century that Romanticism brought renewed interest in King Arthur and the sites associated with him.

The ruins you see at Glastonbury today are mainly of the church built after the 1184 fire. They include a **Lady Chapel**, built, unusually, at the western end of the church; some nave walls; parts of the crossing arches which may have been scissor-shaped like those in Wells Cathedral; some **medieval tiles**; and remains of the choir. The site of the supposed **tomb of Arthur and Guinevere** is marked in the grass. A little to the side of the main site, don't miss

the flagstone-floored **Abbot's Kitchen** with its soaring chimney; later use as a Quaker meeting house allowed it to survive intact.

An excellent **Visitors Centre** describes the history of the site and contains a model showing what the ruins would have looked like in their heyday. Behind it, and easy to overlook, are tiny **St Patrick's Chapel** and a **thorn tree** supposedly grown from the original which sprouted on Wearyall Hill when Joseph of Arimathea stuck his staff into the ground. It flowers in spring and at Christmas.

The site (☎ 832267) opens 9.30 am (9 am June to August) to 5.30 pm or dusk. Admission costs £3/2.50.

Lake Village Museum

A small museum (☎ 832949; EH) devoted to the prehistoric village that flourished near Glastonbury when the surrounding lowlands had not yet been drained is upstairs in the Tribunal, the medieval courthouse which dates back to 1400 and now houses the TIC. Wet conditions have allowed an unusually large quantity of wooden artefacts to survive – even a dugout canoe (in a separate room at the back). The museum opens 10 am to 5 pm Sunday to Thursday, April to September (to 5.30 pm Friday and Saturday); to 4.30 pm, October to March). Admission costs £2/1.

St John's Church

Set back from the High St is this stunning open-plan perpendicular church that has a spectacular 15th-century wooden roof and pillars so thin it's hard to believe they can support the weight of the walls. Look out for the egg-timer attached to the pulpit to guard against overlong sermons. Vandalism means the church must be kept locked when there's no one to supervise visitors. You're most likely to find it open on market day.

Glastonbury Tor

Tor is a Celtic word used to describe a hill shaped like a triangular wedge of cheese, and Glastonbury Tor opens to walkers year round. On the 160m-high summit stands a tower, all that remains of the medieval church of St Michael, a saint frequently associated with high places. You can see a carving of St Michael weighing the souls of the dead in a giant scale on the tower front.

It takes 45 minutes to walk up and down the tor and there are short-stay car parks at the bottom of both paths. Between May and September a Tor Bus runs to the tor every 20 minutes from Magdalene St (£1/50p).

White Spring

This spring flows out into a cave at the foot of the tor in Wellhouse Lane and has been dressed up with a cafe and mock medieval and Tudor house facades; atmospheric or Disneyfied depending on your mood and the number of other visitors.

Chalice Well

The Chalice Well has become entwined in Glastonbury myths and legends, although its name probably relates to its site in Chilkwell St rather than to real links with the Holy Grail. The well has a long association with traditions of healing and you can drink from it as the water pours out through a lion's head spout. It then runs through brick channels into the gardens below, eventually cascading down a series of ceramic dishes into two interlocking basins surrounded by flowers. It's a beautiful, peaceful spot to spend a few hours and opens 10 am to 5 pm. Admission costs £2.75/1.

Rural Life Museum

Partially housed in a fine late-14th-century tithe barn in Bere Lane, the Rural Life Museum (☎ 831197) exhibits artefacts associated with farming, cider-making, cheese-making and other aspects of country life in Somerset. In the grounds, you can see rare breeds of sheep and chicken, and apple trees. Upstairs, don't miss the three-seater toilet, with holes for Mum, Dad and child.

The barn has fine carvings on the gables and porch and an impressive timber roof; it now houses a collection of old agricultural machinery. The museum opens 10 am to 5 pm Tuesday to Friday, Easter to October, and 2 to 6 pm at the weekend; 10 am to 3 pm Tuesday to Saturday the rest of the year. Admission costs £2.50/1.

Glastonbury Festival

In the Glastonbury Festival, the spirit of Woodstock lives on. This three-day summer extravaganza of music, theatre, circus, mime, natural healing and so on, is a massive affair with more than 1000 acts, which doesn't always go down too well with the locals. It takes place at Worthy Farm, Pilton, 8 miles from Glastonbury. Admission is by advance ticket only (around £80 for the whole festival), but many opt to jump the fence, a pastime that is likely to be considerably tougher with new high-security fences promised. Phone ☎ 832020 for details.

Places to Stay

In the Crown Hotel, *Glastonbury Backpackers Hostel* (☎ 833353, 4 Market Place) has dorm beds for £10 and there are also a few doubles (£26), and even a bridal suite, well en suite anyhow (£30). There's a kitchen, TV room and popular cafe downstairs.

The nearest HI hostel is *Street Youth Hostel* (☎ 442961), about 3 miles south. Beds cost £9/6.20 for adults/under-18s. Bus No 376 from Glastonbury stops at Marshalls Elm, from where the hostel is a 500m walk.

There are several camp sites in and around Glastonbury. *Isle of Avalon* (☎ 833618, fax 833618, Godney Road) is a 10-minute walk from the centre, off the B3151. A tent site costs from £5.95, plus £1.90 per person.

Glastonbury has B&Bs from around £20 a night and many establishments offer aromatherapy, muesli breakfasts, vegetarian meals and so on. The TIC has a complete list.

Tor Down Guest House (☎ 832287, 5 Ashwell Lane) has singles/doubles that cost from £20/42 (nonsmoking). *The Bolthole* (☎ 832800, 32 Chilkwell St) is near the foot of the tor and has two doubles and a twin, for £19 per person. There are a couple of similar B&Bs nearby in the same street.

Berachah (☎ 834214, Wellhouse Lane) is convenient for the tor and the wells and has beds for £25 per person.

The *George & Pilgrims Inn* (☎ 831146, 1 High St) has a history dating back to the reign of Edward III. Singles/doubles cost from £45/70 but two-night special breaks including dinner offer better value.

Travellers with cash to spend may be interested in peaceful *No 3 Magdalene St* (☎ *832129*) whose owners have seen a bit of the world themselves, hence the Indian fabrics and wall hangings. Comfortable rooms with private bathrooms attached cost £55/75.

Places to Eat

A three-course lunch at the *George & Pilgrims Inn* (☎ *831146, 1 High St*) costs around £10.

Rainbow's End (17a High St) has delicious leek and mushroom pie and huge chunks of chocolate cake. It's in an alley with shops selling second-hand books and shoes and opens 10 am to 5 pm.

If you've ever considered becoming a vegetarian, Glastonbury would be an ideal place to start since it's one of the few places in England where nut roasts are more common than pot roasts.

A good place for a coffee is *Mocha Berry Coffee House*, near the Market Cross. *Blue Note Café (4a High St)* has tables in a courtyard and a plentiful selection of light lunches. Across the street, at 5a, *Café Galatea* does nutritious salads and wholesome main dishes. It's also a sculpture gallery and cybercafe.

Getting There & Away

There's a daily National Express bus to London (£19.50, 4¼ hours), and also to Bath. Badgerline runs buses from Bristol (No 376) to Wells, Glastonbury and Street. Glastonbury is only 6 miles from Wells – a 15-minute bus journey on No 163. Bus No 376 continues to Ilchester and Yeovil.

QUANTOCK HILLS

The Quantocks, in western Somerset, are a ridge of red sandstone hills, 12 miles long, not much more than 3 miles wide and running down to the sea at Quantoxhead. Like the Mendips, these are lowly hills – just 385m high at their highest point – but they're less cultivated and can look much more bleak. The narrow country lanes and woody dells make this enjoyable walking country.

Some of the most attractive country is owned by the NT, including the Beacon and Bicknoller hills that offer views of the Bristol Channel and Exmoor to the north-west. In 1861, red deer were introduced to these hills from Exmoor and there's a thriving local tradition of stag hunting.

A road runs across the bleaker part of the Quantocks from Over Stowey to Crowcombe, and there's a walkers' track as well. At Broomfield, 6 miles north of Taunton, Fyne Court houses a visitors centre (☎ 01823-451587), open 9 am to 6 pm, where you can pick up information.

Bridgwater or Taunton would make passable bases for exploring the Quantocks, but it's more atmospheric to stay in one of the villages.

Getting There & Away

To appreciate the lanes and woods of the Quantocks at their peaceful best, aim to arrive on a weekday when the Bridgwater and Taunton weekend visitors are back at their desks. Coming by car, the M5 linking Bristol and Exeter skirts the eastern edge of the Quantocks. The A358 then runs along the western side of the hills, linking Taunton to Williton in the north.

Trains from Bristol, Bath and Exeter call at Taunton and Bridgwater, and infrequent Southern National (☎ 01823-272033) buses serve the main roads. Its No 28 bus runs along the southern edge from Minehead to Taunton. Southern National also operates one service a day (No 23) between Taunton and Nether Stowey. No 15 runs between Minehead and Bridgwater. No 29 from Bristol continues to Bridgwater and Taunton after Wells and Glastonbury on Sunday and bank holidays only.

Nether Stowey & Holford

One of the Quantocks' most famous residents was the poet Samuel Taylor Coleridge, who lived in **Nether Stowey** from 1769 to 1796. You can visit **Coleridge Cottage** (☎ 01278-732662; NT) where he wrote *The Rime of the Ancient Mariner*; it opens 2 to 5 pm Tuesday to Thursday and on Sunday, April to October. Admission costs £2.60/1. Some of the rooms have been recently restored to their original bright colours.

Coleridge's friend William Wordsworth, and Wordsworth's sister Dorothy, spent 1797 at nearby Alfoxden House in **Holford** – a pretty village near a wooded valley. *Lyrical Ballads*, published in 1798, was the joint product of Coleridge's and Wordsworth's stays.

Two miles west of Holford is *Quantock Hills Youth Hostel* (☎ *01278-741224*) set in a wooded area. It opens daily in July and August, and daily except Sunday, April to June; the nightly charge is £8.10/5.65 for adults/under-18s. Southern National bus No 15 from Bridgwater gets you to Nether Stowey, No 28 from Taunton or Minehead will drop you at Williton; in either case it's then a 3½-mile walk.

West Somerset Railway

Trains on Britain's longest privately run railway steam between Bishops Lydeard and Minehead, a seaside town 20 miles away. There are stops along the line at Crowcombe, Doniford Beach, Stogumber, Williton, Watchet, Washford, Blue Anchor and Dunster.

Trains run daily May to September, and at the weekend only in winter. A ticket from Bishops Lydeard to Minehead costs £6.20/9.10 for an adult single/return; children are half-price. Phone ☎ 01643-707650 for a 24-hour talking timetable, ☎ 01643-704996 for other information.

Southern National bus Nos 28 and 28a from Taunton and Minehead pass through Bishops Lydeard.

Crowcombe

One of the prettiest Quantock villages, Crowcombe still has cottages built of stone and cob (a mixture of mud and straw), many with thatched roofs. There's a pleasant church with 16th-century bench ends, and part of its spire still in the churchyard where it fell when struck by lightning in 1725. The 16th-century Church House has mullioned windows and a Tudor door. Crowcombe Court is a fine Georgian house.

Crowcombe Heathfield Youth Hostel (☎ *01984-667249, Denzel House*) is 2 miles from the village and half a mile from Crowcombe station on the West Somerset Railway. It's a 7-mile hike over the Quantocks from the hostel in Holford. You can also get here on bus No 28C from Taunton station, getting off at Triscombe Cross and walking almost a mile. The hostel opens daily April to August (but closes on Thursday in May and June). Beds cost £9/6.20 for adults/under-18s.

TAUNTON
☎ 01823 • pop 35,000

Coming to the Quantocks by bus or train you're likely to arrive in Taunton, Somerset's disappointing administrative centre. The TIC (☎ 336344) is by the library in Paul St.

Somerset County Museum (☎ 355455) in part of the castle, opens 10 am to 5 pm Tuesday to Saturday. Admission costs £2.50/1. The **Church of St Mary Magdalene** has one of Somerset's finest towers and an impressive oak Tudor roof in the nave.

Taunton is on a main National Express coach route, with services to London (£11, 3½ hours), Bristol (£5, 1¼ hours), Bridgwater (20 minutes) and Exeter. It's also on the main West Country rail line.

MONTACUTE HOUSE

Twenty-two miles south-east of Taunton, and 4 miles west of the market town of Yeovil, Montacute House (☎ 01935-823289; NT) is an impressive Elizabethan mansion built in the 1590s for Sir Edward Phelips, a speaker of the House of Commons. The Long Gallery displays Tudor and Jacobean portraits on loan from London's National Portrait Gallery. Formal gardens and a landscaped park surround the house. Visitor numbers have shot up since it was used as a major location in *Sense and Sensibility* starring Kate Winslet and Alan Rickman, so anticipate crowds at the weekend.

It opens noon to 5 pm daily except Tuesday, April to October. Admission costs £5.50/2.80.

Exmoor National Park

Covering parts of West Somerset and North Devon, Exmoor is a small national park (265 sq miles) enclosing a wide variety of beautiful landscapes. Along the coast, the scenery is particularly breathtaking with humpbacked headlands giving superb views across the Bristol Channel. Exmoor's cliffs are the highest in England, rising in places to 366m.

A high plateau rises steeply behind the coast, but is cut by steep, fast-flowing streams. The bare hills of heather and grass run parallel to the coast; the highest point is Dunkery Beacon at 519m. On the southern side the two main rivers, the Exe and Barle, wind their way along wooded valleys.

Horned sheep, Exmoor ponies (descended from ancient hill stock) and England's last wild red deer still roam the moors. The symbol of the park is the antlered head of a stag, and depending on the season you may see people hunting. Although the sport is supported by local farmers, who see the deer as a pest, it's equally strongly opposed by others, including the National Trust, causing conflict in the hunting season.

There are several particularly attractive villages: Lynton and Lynmouth, joined by a water-operated railway; Porlock, on the edge of the moor in a beautiful valley; Dunster, dominated by its partly-medieval castle; and Selworthy, with traditional thatched cottages.

Arguably the most dramatic section of the South West Coast Path runs from Minehead in the park to Padstow in Cornwall.

ORIENTATION

From west to east the park measures only about 21 miles and north to south just 12 miles. It's accessible from the west through Barnstaple, from the south through Tiverton, and from the east through Minehead.

Within the park boundaries, the main centres are Dulverton on the southern edge; Exford in the centre; Dunster in the east; and Porlock, Lynton and Lynmouth on the coast.

There are over 600 miles of public footpaths and bridleways (a path that can be used by walkers, horse riders and cyclists), most of them waymarked.

SOUTH-WESTERN ENGLAND

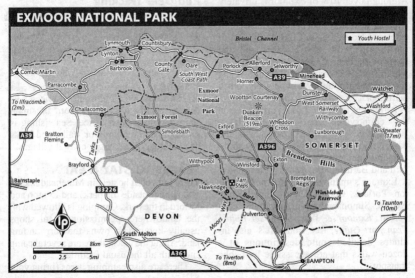

EXMOOR NATIONAL PARK

INFORMATION

The National Park Authority (NPA) has five information centres in and around the park, but it's also possible to get information in the TICs at Barnstaple, Ilfracombe, Lynton and Minehead. The NPA centres at Dunster (☎ 01643-821835), Lynmouth (☎ 01598-752509), County Gate (☎ 01598-741321), and Combe Martin (☎ 01271-883319) open daily from the end of March to October. For the rest of the year, some of these offices are closed or operate limited opening hours. The main visitor centre and the Exmoor NPA headquarters (☎ 01398-323841) in Dulverton opens year round but for limited hours only in winter.

Exmoor Visitor is a free newspaper listing useful addresses, accommodation and a program of guided walks and bike rides from the villages offered by the NPA and local organisations. Most walks are in the summer but there are some throughout the year.

The visitor centres and TICs stock a wide range of walking guides and Ordnance Survey maps.

WALKING

Although over 70% of Exmoor is privately owned, there are numerous waymarked paths. The best known routes are the Somerset and North Devon Coast Path (part of the South West Coast Path) and the Exmoor section of the Two Moors Way, which starts in Lynmouth and follows the River Barle through Withypool and on to Dartmoor.

Part of the 180-mile Tarka Trail (based on the countryside that inspired Henry Williamson's *Tarka the Otter*) is in the park. Join it in Combe Martin and walk to Lynton/Lynmouth, and then inland to Brayford and Barnstaple.

Exmoor's main walking centres are Lynton, Porlock, County Gate, Oare, Horner, Exford, Simonsbath, Withypool and Dulverton. *Exmoor & West Somerset Public Transport Guide*, free from TICs, also includes detailed route descriptions of a dozen walks that are accessible by public transport.

CYCLING ROUTES

Cyclists are not allowed on public footpaths or the open moor, and horse riders and walkers have priority on public bridleways and roads used as public paths. The visitors centres can advise on regulations.

Official places for cyclists include a coastal route – along the old Barnstaple railway line, parts of the Tarka Trail, the Brendon Hills and Crown Estate woodland. The West Country Way runs through Exmoor from Padstow to Bristol.

OTHER ACTIVITIES
Pony Trekking & Horse Riding

Exmoor is popular riding country and stables scattered round the park offer ponies and horses for all abilities for rides from a few hours to a full day. Wet weather gear is recommended – it can turn cold and rainy very quickly. Charges are from about £9 per hour.

Contact Pine Lodge Riding & Holidays (☎ 01398-323559), Higher Chilcott Farm, Dulverton; Doone Valley Riding Stables (☎ 01598-741278), Cloud Farm, Lynton; or Burrowhayes Farm (☎ 01643-862463), West Luccombe, Porlock.

Red Deer Tracking

Several companies offer Exmoor safaris – tracking wild red deer. Moorland Wildlife Safaris (bookings phone ☎ 01398-323699) charge from £10 per person for three-hour excursions.

Fishing

To fish for salmon and trout, you need a licence, usually obtainable from the main shop or village post office. Sea fishing is possible from the harbour walls, and boats can be hired in the larger coastal villages.

PLACES TO STAY & EAT

There are youth hostels in Minehead and Ilfracombe (outside the park) and Lynton and Exford in the park. Camping is allowed with the landowner's permission; local shops usually know who owns the surrounding land. Along the coast, there are several camp sites with all the usual facilities.

There are also camping barns (bring your

own sleeping bag) at Woodadvent Farm (£3.75), Roadwater, and Northcombe (£4.50), a mile from Dulverton. For bookings phone ☎ 01200-428366.

There's no shortage of B&Bs and hotels in this holiday area. There are plenty of places to eat in Exmoor – old country pubs with low beams to hit your head on and log fires in the winter, little shops serving cream teas, as well as more upmarket restaurants.

GETTING THERE & AWAY

Bus
National Express coaches go from London to Barnstaple (5 hours) and Ilfracombe (5½ hours) daily. There are also buses from Plymouth and Bristol to Barnstaple.

Red Bus (☎ 01271-345444) and Southern National (☎ 01823-272033) run buses from Minehead, Barnstaple, Ilfracombe, Dunster and Williton. You could also do part of this journey on the privately run West Somerset Railway (see West Somerset Railway under Quantock Hills earlier in the chapter). W Ridler (☎ 01398-323398) has a daily bus from Dulverton to Taunton and back.

Train
From London Paddington, intercity services stop at Taunton (2¼ hours), Tiverton Parkway (2½ hours) and Exeter (2¾ hours). These places can also be reached from Bristol (on the Bristol-Plymouth line). From Exeter, the scenic Tarka Line runs to Barnstaple; the journey takes about 1½ hours and there are about four trains a day.

GETTING AROUND
It's easiest to get around with your own transport, on foot or horseback, because bus services are limited. Some services are based on school runs, some are operated by volunteer drivers, most are seasonal and few operate on Sunday. On the other hand, the narrow streets of Exmoor villages quickly clog up in peak season and parking can be tricky.

Bus
The *Exmoor & West Somerset Public Transport Guide*, free from TICs, is invaluable. It also includes information on day hikes.

The Exmoor Bus Service's three-day ticket (£9.50/6.50) gives unlimited travel on Red Bus and Southern National services.

Bicycle
Tarka Trail Cycle Hire (☎ 01271-324202), Train Station, Barnstaple, has all kinds of bikes for hire. Charges start from £6.50 per day for tourers, £8.50 for mountain bikes.

DULVERTON
☎ 01398 • pop 1300
This attractive village, south of the moor in the Barle Valley, is the local 'capital' and home to the park's head office. The Exmoor National Park Visitors Centre (☎ 323841) is at 7–9 Fore St.

Dulverton's narrow streets get choked with traffic in summer so try to visit out of season.

Walking
The four-hour circular walk along the river from Dulverton to Tarr Steps – an ancient stone clapper bridge across the River Barle – is recommended. Add another three or four hours to the walk by continuing from Tarr Steps up Winsford Hill for distant views over Devon.

Places to Stay & Eat
There's a camping barn (£4.50 per night) at Northcombe, a mile from Dulverton. Phone ☎ 01200-428366 for bookings.

You get breakfast in bed at atmospheric *Town Mills* (☎ 323124) from £19 per person and log fires for heating. The driveway is just off the High St.

Springfield Farm (☎ 323722) is 4 miles from Dulverton on the Exford road; and just 1½ miles from Tarr Steps. B&B costs £22.50 per person, or £26 in rooms with a bathroom. Evening meals are served but only from mid-May when the lambing season is over.

Right on the edge of the moor, award-winning *Highercombe Farm* (☎ 323616) is 3 miles north of Dulverton at the end of a no-through road. B&B in rooms with a bathroom costs from £22.

Crispins Restaurant (☎ 323397, 26 High St) serves decent vegetarian food and also has a few meaty choices. *The Lion Hotel* in

Bank Square has generous servings of good bar food.

Getting There & Away

Devon Bus No 398 runs from Minehead to Tiverton via Dulverton eight times a day (except Sunday). Change in Tiverton for the No 55 on to Exeter. Devon Bus No 307 links Dulverton to Barnstaple and Taunton every couple of hours (except on Sunday).

DUNSTER

☎ 01643 • pop 800

Possibly the most attractive Exmoor village, Dunster can be packed with people in summer. The main attraction is the castle but there's also St George's Church, a working water mill, an old packhorse bridge, the nearby beach and the 17th-century octagonal Yarn Market – a relic of a time when the people of Dunster made their living from weaving, rather than tourism.

An Exmoor National Park Visitors Centre (☎ 821835) is on Dunster Steep.

Dunster Castle

Heavily restored to the Victorian ideal of how castles should look – turrets, crenellations and all – Dunster Castle (☎ 821314; NT) dates back to Norman times, although only the 13th-century gateway of the original structure survives. Inside are Tudor furnishings and portraits of the Luttrell family, including a bizarre 16th-century portrait of Sir John skinny-dipping.

It opens 10.30 am to 4.40 pm Saturday to Wednesday, April to October (to 4 pm October). Admission costs £5.50/3. The surrounding garden and park open most of the year. It's a short, steep walk up from the village.

Places to Stay

The nearest youth hostel is 2 miles away at Minehead (see that section later in the chapter).

Woodville House (☎ 821228, West St) charges from £19 for B&B. *The Old Priory* (☎ 821540) is a medieval house in walled gardens opposite the dovecote. It opens year round and charges from £27.50 per person for B&B (£50 for a room with a four-poster bed).

Dollons House (☎ 821880, Church St) does luxury B&B from £27.50 in non-smoking rooms, all with bathroom. *Exmoor House Hotel* (☎ 821268, 12 West St) is a very comfortable, nonsmoking hotel which charges £25/45 for B&B in rooms with a bathroom.

Places to Eat

The *café* (☎ 821759) at Dunster Watermill, Mill Lane, is a good place to go for lunch or tea in summer; for £2.10/1.10 you can watch flour being ground in the mill.

The Tea Shoppe (☎ 821304, 3 High St) does morning coffee, lunches and cream teas in its 15th-century tearooms. If it's full there are several other places along the High St, including *Willow Tearooms* and *Locks* complete with staff in period costume.

The Luttrell Arms (☎ 821555) opposite the Yarn Market does good bar snacks including filled baguettes and main dishes for around £5.

Getting There & Away

Devon Bus No 398 runs from Minehead to Dunster and on to Dulverton eight times a day. First Southern National runs an hourly service (No 928) between Minehead and Dunster on Sunday and public holidays – there are just six buses. You can also get here on the West Somerset Railway (see West Somerset Railway under Quantock Hills earlier in the chapter).

MINEHEAD

☎ 01643 • pop 8500

Somerset's largest seaside resort is just outside the park's eastern border. In summer, it's packed with British holiday-makers, many of them escapees from Somerwestworld, a vast holiday camp. Visit in May, however, and the town still enacts medieval May Day ceremonies with a Hobby Horse performing a fertility dance through the streets.

The TIC (☎ 702624) at 17 Friday St has a list of B&Bs if you want to stay. Two miles south of Minehead, in a secluded spot, is *Minehead Youth Hostel* (☎ 702595) at Alcombe Combe. It opens daily in July and August; daily except Monday, April to June;

and daily except Monday and Tuesday in September and October. The nightly charge is £9.80/6.75 for adults/under-18s.

From Minehead, Southern National operates service No 28 to Taunton (hourly, 1¼ hours), No 38 to Porlock Weir and No 300 to Lynton. Minehead is the northern terminus for the West Somerset Railway.

EXFORD
☎ 01643

This tiny village in the centre of the park makes a good base for walks, especially to Dunkery Beacon, the highest point on Exmoor, 4 miles from Exford.

Places to Stay & Eat

In the village centre, *Exford Youth Hostel* (☎ 831288) is in a Victorian house by the River Exe. A bed costs £9.80/6.75 for adults/under-18s, and the hostel opens daily in July and August; daily except Sunday in April, May and June. Phone for details of opening hours for the rest of the year.

Just outside Exford, off the Porlock road, *Westermill Farm Campsite* (☎ 831238) opens April to October and charges £6 for tents. There are also cottages to rent.

Exford House Hotel (☎ 831304, *Chapel St)* does B&B from £25/50 for a single/double. *White Horse Inn* (☎ 831229), a 16th-century inn right by the bridge, does B&B from £35 per person for rooms with a bathroom. There's bar food during the week and a carvery on Sunday.

Getting There & Away

Over the moor, it's a 7-mile walk to Exford from Porlock, 10 from Minehead Youth Hostel, 12 from Dunster and 15 from Lynton. During summer, Bus No 285 (☎ 01823-358232) links Porlock, Minehead and Exford – Bus No 985 on Sunday. Bus No 398 operates year round (except Sunday).

PORLOCK
☎ 01643 • pop 1500

This attractive village of thatched cottages lies in a deep valley, reached by a steep lane. Two miles farther west is the charming harbour, Porlock Weir.

The picturesque NT-owned village of **Selworthy** is 2½ miles east of Porlock. Its cream-painted cob and thatch cottages make this a popular movie location; Thomas Hardy's *The Return of the Native* was filmed here.

Places to Stay & Eat

Well-signposted and in the centre of Porlock is *Sparkhayes Farm Campsite* (☎ 862470). Charges are £3.50 per person.

Most places to stay are on the High St. For B&B, cosy, thatched *Myrtle Cottage* (☎ 862978) charges from £30/43 for rooms with a bath. It opens year round. *Lorna Doone Hotel* (☎ 862404) charges £25/50 for a single/double with bathroom, with reductions for stays of three or more days.

The Ship Inn (☎ 862507) is a 13th-century thatched hostelry mentioned in *Lorna Doone*. B&B starts at £25 per person and the pub serves meals. Try the inn's country wines – damson is good.

Open every evening, *Piggy in the Middle* (☎ 862647) does good steak and seafood. A salmon steak costs less than £10, the seafood platter more like £20. There are several tea-rooms in the High St which serve lunch as well. *The Ship Inn* is a charming thatched pub overlooking the harbour with crab sandwiches and pub classics on the menu.

Getting There & Away

Southern National (☎ 01823-272033) runs service No 300 along the coast from Barnstaple through Lynton and Porlock to Minehead and Bridgwater. Bus No 38 runs to Minehead.

LYNTON & LYNMOUTH
☎ 01598 • pop 2075

Lynmouth has the looks, Lynton the height, but an incredible water-operated cliff railway links the villages so it is easy to commute between them. The picturesque, steeply wooded gorge of the West Lyn River, which meets the sea at Lynmouth, can be delightful out of season. This is a good base for walks along the coast and in the northern part of the park.

In 1952, storms caused the East and West

SOUTH-WESTERN ENGLAND

Lyn rivers to flood, destroying 98 houses and claiming the lives of 34 people. The disaster is recorded at the **Lyn and Exmoor Museum** (☎ 752317), in haunted St Vincent's Cottage, Market St, Lynton. From late March to late October, the museum opens daily, except Saturday (afternoon only on Sunday) but closes 12.30 to 2 pm for lunch.

The **cliff railway** is a simple piece of environmentally friendly Victorian engineering. Two cars linked by a steel cable descend or ascend the slope according to the amount of water in their tanks. For £1/50p it's the best way to get between the two villages between Easter and November.

There's a TIC (☎ 752225) in Lynton Town Hall and a National Park Visitors Centre (☎ 752509) by Lynmouth harbour.

Walking

Lynton TIC and Lynmouth Visitors Centre have information about the many local walks. The South West Coast Path and the Tarka Trail pass through the villages, and the Two Moors Way, linking Exmoor with Dartmoor, starts in Lynmouth.

Leaving Lynmouth look out for signs to **Glen Lyn Gorge** which opens year round and has a small exhibition centre, open in summer only. It costs £2/1 to walk along the gorge.

The **Valley of the Rocks**, which is believed to be where the River Lyn originally flowed, was described by the poet Robert Southey as 'rock reeling upon rock, stone piled upon stone, a huge terrifying reeling mass'. It's just over a mile west of Lynton and makes a pleasant walk along the coastal footpath. East of Lynmouth, the lighthouse at **Foreland Point** is another good focus for a walk.

Watersmeet, 2 miles along the river from Lynmouth, makes another popular hike. The old hunting lodge houses a NT teashop.

Places to Stay & Eat

At Lynbridge, roughly a mile outside Lynton, *Lynton Youth Hostel* (☎ 753237) is in a Victorian house in the gorge, open daily in July and August; phone for details of opening times for the rest of the year. The nightly charge is £9.80/6.75 for adults/under-18s.

Orchard House Hotel (☎ 753247, *Waters-meet Rd, Lynmouth*) charges from £24, as does *Oakleigh* (☎ 752220, *4 Tors Rd, Lynmouth*). In Lynbridge Rd, *Valley House* (☎ 752285) charges £24/40.

The *Rising Sun* (☎ 753223) is a 14th-century inn beside Lynmouth harbour. The poet Shelley brought his 16-year-old bride here for their honeymoon and you can stay in their rose-clad cottage for £70/140 (singles/doubles). Cheaper rooms cost from £52 per person, and there are also two-night packages including dinner. This is an excellent place for a pub lunch or evening meal.

Getting There & Away

Red Bus (☎ 01271-345444) service No 310 runs five times a day between Barnstaple and Lynton (one hour), Monday to Saturday.

Southern National's service No 300 runs from Lynton to Barnstaple or Minehead.

Lyn Valley Bus (☎ 01598-752225) runs a Tuesday service from Lynton to Taunton.

Driving from Porlock, note that Porlock Hill is notoriously steep; look out for the old AA box at the top where motorists could phone to report overheated radiators. There are two alternative toll roads (£1), both of them scenic and both of them less steep.

Devon

Devon's tourist attractions are no secret. For the British, the county has long been a popular place for a traditional family holiday by the seaside and the coastal resorts are still crowded in summer.

The county's history is inextricably bound up with the sea; from Plymouth, Drake set out to fight the Spanish Armada and the Pilgrim Fathers sailed to America. Little country lanes lead to idyllic villages of thatched cottages; tearooms serve traditional cream teas and you can buy rough cider from local farms. Inland, there's superb walking country in two national parks – wild Dartmoor in the centre and Exmoor in the north, which extends into Somerset (see Dartmoor National Park later in the chapter, and Exmoor National Park under Somerset earlier in the chapter).

GETTING AROUND

Contact Devon County Public Transport Help Line (☎ 01392-382800), weekdays 9 am to 5 pm, for information. They can send you the invaluable *Devon Public Transport Map* and the useful *Dartmoor Bus Services Timetable*.

Devon's rail network skirts along the south coast through Exeter and Plymouth to Cornwall. There are some picturesque stretches where the line travels right beside the sea. Two branch lines run north – the 39-mile Tarka Line from Exeter to Barnstaple, and the 15-mile Tamar Valley Line from Plymouth to Gunnislake.

Away from the main roads, Devon is good cycling country. TICs have a free leaflet, *Making Tracks!*, which gives details of the main routes. Sustrans' West Country Way route crosses North Devon through Barnstaple and continues via Taunton to Bristol. The award-winning bike bus operates during summer between Ilfracombe in the north and Exeter in the south, and it's just 10p for the bike (more for you).

EXETER

☎ 01392 • pop 89,000

The West Country's heart and soul, home to one of the finest medieval cathedrals in the region, Exeter is the main transport hub for Devon and Cornwall, and a good starting point for Dartmoor.

Many of the older buildings were destroyed in the air raids of WWII and much of Exeter is modern and architecturally uninspiring. It is, however, a thoroughly liveable university city with a thriving nightlife.

Until the 19th century, Exeter was an important port, and the waterfront is slowly being restored.

History

Exeter was founded by the Romans in about AD 50 to serve as the administrative capital for the Dumnonii of Devon and Cornwall. There was, however, a settlement on the banks of the River Exe long before the arrival of the Romans.

By the 3rd century, the city was surrounded by a thick wall, parts of which can still be seen although most of it has either been buried or incorporated into buildings.

The fortifications were battered by Danish invaders and then by the Normans in the 11th century. In 1068, William the Conqueror took 18 days to break through the walls. He appointed a Norman seigneur (feudal lord) to construct a castle, the ruins of which can still be seen in Rougemont Park.

Exeter was a major trading port until Isabel, Countess of Devon built a weir across the river, halting river traffic. It was not until 1563, when the first ship canal in Britain was dug to bypass the weir, that the city began to re-establish itself as a trading centre.

Exeter has been closely involved in many of England's greatest battles. Three of the ships sent to face the Spanish Armada were built here and some of the greatest sea captains of the time, Drake, Raleigh and Frobisher, lived in the area for part of their lives. In 1942 heavy air raids reduced large areas of Exeter to rubble.

Orientation

The old Roman walls enclose a hill in a bend of the River Exe, and the cathedral's great square towers dominate the skyline. Most of the sights are accessible on foot; long-stay car parks are well signposted. There are two main train stations (Central and St David's); most long-distance trains use St David's, a 20-minute walk west of the city centre.

Information

The TIC (☎ 265700), Civic Centre, Paris St, is just across the road from the bus station (which may be redeveloped some day soon). It opens 9 am to 5 pm Monday to Saturday; also 10 am to 4 pm Sunday, May to September only.

Free guided tours led by the volunteer Exeter 'Redcoats' are well worth joining. They last 1½ to two hours and cover a range of subjects, from a standard walking tour (daily) to a ghost walk (7 pm Tuesday). Tours leave from outside Royal Clarence Hotel or from Quay House. Ask at the TIC for details.

For Internet access visit Hyperactive in Central Station Crescent. There are several supermarkets, including a Tesco, on Sidwell

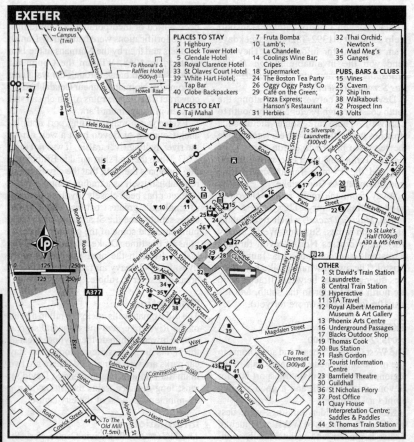

EXETER

PLACES TO STAY
3 Highbury
4 Clock Tower Hotel
5 Glendale Hotel
28 Royal Clarence Hotel
33 St Olaves Court Hotel
39 White Hart Hotel;
Tap Bar
40 Globe Backpackers

PLACES TO EAT
6 Taj Mahal
7 Fruta Bomba
10 Lamb's;
La Chandelle
14 Coolings Wine Bar;
Cripes
18 Supermarket
24 The Boston Tea Party
26 Oggy Oggy Pasty Co
29 Café on the Green;
Pizza Express;
Hanson's Restaurant
31 Herbies

32 Thai Orchid;
Newton's
34 Mad Meg's
35 Ganges

PUBS, BARS & CLUBS
15 Vines
25 Cavern
27 Ship Inn
38 Walkabout
42 Prospect Inn
43 Volts

OTHER
1 St David's Train Station
2 Laundrette
8 Central Train Station
9 Hyperactive
11 STA Travel
12 Royal Albert Memorial
Museum & Art Gallery
13 Phoenix Arts Centre
16 Underground Passages
17 Blacks Outdoor Shop
19 Thomas Cook
20 Bus Station
21 Flash Gordon
22 Tourist Information
Centre
23 Barnfield Theatre
30 Guildhall
36 St Nicholas Priory
37 Post Office
41 Quay House
Interpretation Centre;
Saddles & Paddles
44 St Thomas Train Station

St. Convenient laundrettes include Soaps beside St David's train station and Silverspin on Blackboy Rd.

Exeter Cathedral

Exeter's jewel is the Cathedral Church of St Mary and St Peter (☎ 255573), a magnificent building that has stood largely unchanged for the last 600 years. Unlike many of the cathedrals in the country, it was built within a relatively short time, which accounts for its pleasing architectural unity.

There's been a church on this spot since 932. In 1050, the Saxon church was granted cathedral status and Leofric was enthroned as the first bishop of Exeter. Between 1112 and 1133, a Norman cathedral was built in place of the original church. The two transept towers were built at this time – an unusual design for English cathedrals of the period. In 1270, Bishop Bronescombe instigated the remodelling of the whole building, a process that took about 90 years and resulted in a mix of Early English and Decorated Gothic styles.

You enter through the impressive Great West Front, with the largest surviving collection of 14th-century sculpture in England. The niches around the three doors are filled with statues of Christ and the Apostles surrounded by saints and angels, kings and queens.

Inside, the cathedral is light and airy, roofed with the world's longest single expanse of Gothic vaulting. It might have been even brighter if a controversial plan to clean all the stonework and repaint the ceiling bosses in their original bright colours hadn't been stopped. Looking up, you can see where restoration was brought to a halt by those who thought the scheme over the top even though much of the medieval cathedral would have been brightly painted.

Walking clockwise around the building, you pass the **astronomical clock** in the northern tower, which shows the phases of the moon as well as the time. The dial dates from the 15th century but the works are modern. Opposite is the **minstrels' gallery**, used by the choir at Christmas and Easter.

The **Great Screen** was erected in 1325. Behind is the choir, which features some interesting misericords including the earliest representation of an elephant in England. The **Bishop's Throne** was carved in 1312.

In the Lady Chapel, at the eastern end, are the **tombs** of bishops Bronescombe and Leofric, and a memorial to the author of *Lorna Doone*, RD Blackmore. Cathedral staff will point out the famous sculpture of the **lady with two left feet**.

The cathedral opens 8.30 am to 6.30 pm, and a £2.50 donation is requested from visitors. There are guided tours (free) at 11 am and 2.30 pm (on Saturday at 3 pm only) Monday to Friday, April to October; these last 45 minutes and are highly recommended. It's also worth attending a service – evensong is at 5 pm.

Underground Passages

The medieval maintenance passages for the lead water pipes that were laid under the city in the 14th century still survive. They're dark, narrow and definitely not for claustrophobes but the guided tours (☎ 265887) are surprisingly interesting. They take place from 2 to 4.30 pm Tuesday to Friday and from 10 am to 4.30 pm Saturday. The passages are open longer and on Monday in July and August. Admission costs £3.50/2.50 in July and August, £2.50/1.50 the rest of the year. The entrance is beside Boots in the High St.

Royal Albert Memorial Museum & Art Gallery

Most of the galleries in this large museum (☎ 265858) are laid out in classic Victorian style with crowded display cases and lots of dusty hunting trophies. The history of the city is covered in a series of exhibitions from prehistory, through Roman Exeter to modern times. The gallery upstairs includes works by Devon artists from the 18th and 19th centuries. It opens 10 am to 5 pm Monday to Saturday. Aadmission is free. The cafe is good value, too.

Guildhall

Parts of the Guildhall (☎ 265500) date from 1160, making it the oldest municipal building in the country that is still in use. It was, however, mainly built in the 14th century and the impressive portico that extends over the pavement was added at the end of the 16th century. Inside, the city's silver and regalia are on display. It opens (as long as there are no functions) 10.30 am to 1 pm and 2 to 4 pm Monday to Friday, morning only on Saturday. There's no admission charge.

St Nicholas Priory

Originally built as accommodation for overnight visitors to the Benedictine priory, St Nicholas Priory (☎ 265858), off Fore St, became the house of a wealthy Elizabethan merchant. It's now preserved, with period furniture and plaster ceilings, as it might have looked when lived in by the merchant and his family. It opens 3 to 4.30 pm Monday, Wednesday and Saturday, Easter to October. Admission costs 50p.

Quay House Interpretation Centre

Down by the river, this display and audiovisual presentation offers a painless resumé of the city's history and its commercial reliance on the river. There's no charge and it opens 10 am to 5 pm, Easter to October.

Walking & Cycling Routes

The 11-mile walk to *Steps Bridge Youth Hostel* on Dartmoor follows country lanes through Shillingford St George and Doddiscombleigh (stop at the *Nobody Inn*, one of the south-west's best pubs). A 30-mile cycle tour of Dartmoor takes you from Exeter through Doddiscombleigh and Bovey Tracey to Widecombe-in-the-Moor and back to Exeter.

Places to Stay

Hostels In a large house overlooking the River Exe, *Exeter Youth Hostel* (☎ 873329, 47 Countess Wear Rd) is 2 miles south-east of the city towards Topsham. It opens year round and the nightly charge is £10.85/7.40 for adults/under-18s. From High St, catch minibuses J, K or T (10 minutes) and ask for Countess Wear post office. Bus No 57 will get you there from the bus station.

Globe Backpackers (☎ 215521, 71 Holloway St) is a thankful addition to the budget scene and has beds for £11, a good vibe and Internet access. One of the best-value accommodation options is the university's *St Luke's Hall* (☎ 211500), which costs from just £13.50/22.50 a single/double including breakfast. The catch is that it's available only during college holidays.

B&Bs & Hotels The cheapest B&Bs are on the outskirts of the city. The *Old Mill* (☎ 259977, Mill Lane, Alphington) is in a quiet residential suburb and has B&B for £12.50 a person. It's easy to reach by bus.

Most B&Bs and cheaper hotels lie in the area east of St David's station and north of Central station. There are several reasonable B&Bs on St David's Hill. *Highbury* (☎ 434737, 85 St David's Hill) is good value from £20/35. *Glendale Hotel* (☎ 274350) at No 8, has rooms from £20 per head, some with showers.

Clock Tower Hotel (☎ 424545, 16 New North Rd) has a few singles from £30, doubles from £45. There are several other places along this road and more on Blackall Rd and Howell Rd. *Rhona's* (☎ 277791, 15 Blackall Rd) has rooms from £15/29 each. *Raffles Hotel* (☎ 270200, 11 Blackall Rd) is more upmarket; all rooms have a bathroom and charges are £34/48.

Claremont (☎ 274699) is a comfortable B&B for non-smokers at 36 Wonford Rd, quite a drive out on the eastern side of the city. Rooms are £34/44 with bathrooms.

White Hart Hotel (☎ 279897, South St) is an old coaching inn and the cobbled courtyard through which the coachmen drove their horses is still the focal point. It's an interesting place to stay; rooms with a bathroom cost from £49/64 at the weekend, £61/94 during the week. The centrally located *St Olaves Court Hotel* (☎ 217736, Mary Arches St) has 15 comfortable rooms each with a bathroom. Prices are from £65/90 at the weekend, £75/100 during the week. Some rooms come with a Jacuzzi.

Dating back to the 14th century, *Royal Clarence Hotel* (☎ 319955) has the best location of all, right in Cathedral Yard. Its weekend B&B deals are good value at £65 a head for two nights; pay the extra £10 for a front room with a superb view of the cathedral. During the week, these rooms cost £99/125; breakfast is extra. Former guests include Tsar Nicholas I and Lord Nelson.

Places to Eat

Raved about by locals, *Herbies* (☎ 258473, 15 North St) is an excellent vegetarian restaurant. Its home-made soups, chilli dishes and apple pie are highly recommended. Not far away on Queen St is *Oggy Oggy Pasty Co* with a great range of pasties from vegetarian to beef and stilton.

Fruta Bomba (☎ 412233) on Queen St has an impressive array of Latin American food. Lunch and a drink costs about £6; by night it's a popular cocktail bar. In the alley off Queen St is *The Boston Tea Party* open daily from 8 am and in the evenings from Thursday to Saturday. All meals are under £5.

In Cathedral Close there are several places to choose from. *Café on the Green* (☎ 310130) has a jolly menu that includes a British Buttie (soda bun with bacon, fried egg and lashings of HP sauce). There are also salads, pasta, pizzas and steaks. Also in Cathedral Close is a branch of *Pizza Express*, and *Hanson's Restaurant* for a cream tea or traditional lunch.

On the other side of the cathedral green is *Thai Orchid* (☎ *214215)*, which does good set lunches for £8.50 and is also open for dinner. Next door is sophisticated *Newtons* (☎ *411200)* with a more expensive modern British menu.

There are several bistro-style places around Gandy St. *Coolings Wine Bar* (☎ *434184)*, at No 11, has a good range of main dishes and an extensive wine list. *Cripes* (☎ *491411)* at No 21 specialises in sweet and savoury Brittany pancakes.

Ganges (☎ *272630, Fore St)* is reputed to be the best of the Indian restaurants, but the *Taj Mahal* (☎ *258129, 50 Queen St)* is also good value and does an all-you-can-eat Sunday buffet for £6.95.

Said to have terrorised the kitchens of the Sheriff of Exeter, Mad Meg now lends her name to a Middle Ages theme restaurant with long wooden tables and bare flagstones. *Mad Meg's* (☎ *221225, Fore St)* serves English baronial fare steaks – ribs, pheasant, rabbit and the like. Main courses range from £6 to £16.

The city's top restaurants include *Lamb's* (☎ *254269, 15 Lower North St)* under the old iron bridge. The three-course set dinner costs about £20. A couple of doors down is *La Chandelle* (☎ *435953)* where the set menu is more like £15. The restaurant at *St Olaves Court Hotel* is also popular: two courses cost £11.50, three courses are £14.50.

Entertainment

Pubs, Bars & Clubs Sir Francis Drake's favourite local is said to have been the *Ship Inn* (☎ *270891)* in Martin's Lane – the alley between the High St and the cathedral. The place trades heavily on its famous customer, but it's convenient and the food's good value. The *Tap Bar* at the White Hart Hotel feels more authentic with sawdust on the floor and jugs of real ale. *Vines* is a heaving place on Gandy St with live music on Sunday nights.

The *Prospect Inn* is a cosy pub down on the redeveloped Quay. The *Double Locks* (☎ *256947)* is a popular pub right beside the Exeter Shipping Canal, with good food,

great puddings and daily barbecues in summer. It's a 20-minute walk south along the canal from the The Quay.

Walkabout on Fore St might send Ozzies weak at the knees. There's live music or DJs each night in the excellent subterranean *Cavern* (☎ *495370, 83 Queen St)*. Most nights have a nominal admission fee.

Nightclubs come and go. Down on The Quay, *Volts* is remarkably popular with students.

Theatre The *Phoenix Arts Centre* (☎ *667080, Gandy St)* stages dance, theatre, film and music events and opens daily except Sunday. It's currently under renovation. There are two theatres: the *Northcott* (☎ *493493)*, on the university campus, and the smaller *Barnfield* (☎ *270891, Barnfield Rd)*, that features programs from touring companies and local groups.

Getting There & Away

See the fares tables in the Getting Around chapter. Exeter is 172 miles from London, 75 from Bristol, 45 from Plymouth and 120 from Land's End. If you're driving down from London, follow the M3 and then the A303. Alternatively take the M4 to Bristol and then the M5 south to Exeter.

Air Scheduled services operate between Exeter Airport (☎ *367433)* and Ireland, Birmingham, the Channel Islands and the Isles of Scilly.

Bus The booking office at the bus station opens 7.45 am to 6.30 pm.

National Express runs coaches between Exeter and numerous towns in Britain, including London (£16.50, four hours) via Heathrow airport (three hours), Bath (£12.50, 2¾ hours), Bristol (£9.75, 1½ hours), Salisbury (£12.50, two hours) and Penzance (£16, five hours).

There's a daily south-coast service between Brighton and Penzance (via Portsmouth, Weymouth, Dorchester, Bridport, Exeter and Plymouth) departing Exeter for Brighton (£22.50, seven hours).

Stagecoach Devon (☎ *427711)* runs the No

X38 hourly to Plymouth (1¼ hours). Western National (☎ 01752-222666) has buses to Okehampton (one hour) and Torquay.

Stagecoach Devon produces a useful *Smugglers' Trail* leaflet with details of walks accessible by bus. The area includes Sidmouth, Exeter, Torquay and Dartmouth. An Explorer ticket costs £5.65/14.30/24.20 for one/three/seven days of unlimited bus travel.

Train The fastest trains between London and Exeter use London Paddington and take 2½ to three hours (£38.30, hourly). Trains from London's Waterloo also leave hourly but take three hours, following a more scenic route via Salisbury.

Exeter is at the hub of lines running from Bristol (£15.60, 1½ hours), Salisbury (£20.10, two hours) and Penzance (£18.60, three hours).

The 39-mile branch line to Barnstaple (£9.70, 1½ hours) is promoted as the Tarka Line, following the river valleys of the Yeo and Taw and giving good views of traditional Devon countryside with its characteristic, deep-sunken lanes. There are 11 trains a day, Monday to Friday, nine on Saturday and four on Sunday. A reduced service operates during the winter. Most intercity trains use St David's station.

Getting Around

Bus Exeter is well served by public transport. A one-day Freedom ticket on the Exeter bus system might be useful. Bus N links St David's station with Central station and passes near the bus station.

Taxi There are taxi ranks outside the train stations, or try Capital Taxis (☎ 433433).

Bicycles & Canoes At 15 Clifton Rd, Flash Gordon (☎ 424246), rents bicycles (as well as camping equipment and canoes). Three-speeds cost £5/20 a day/week, mountain bikes cost £12 and a tandem £25.

Saddles & Paddles (☎ 424241), on The Quay, rents bikes (£12/9 per day) and Canadian canoes (from £8 per hour or £27 per day). It also organises nightly paddling parties, with a barbecue at Double Locks Hotel.

AROUND EXETER
Powderham Castle

The castle (☎ 01626-890243) is on the estuary of the River Exe, 8 miles from Exeter. It dates from the 14th century but was considerably altered in the 18th and 19th centuries. The home of the Courtenay family, it contains collections of French china and Stuart and Regency furniture and features some garish rococo ceilings. It opens 10 am to 5.30 pm daily except Saturday, April to September. Admission costs £5.85/2.95.

A la Ronde

Jane and Mary Parminter planned to combine the magnificence of the Church of San Vitale, which they'd visited in Ravenna, with the homeliness of a country cottage, to create the perfect dwelling place. The result is an intriguing 16-sided house (☎ 01395-265514; NT) whose bizarre interior decor includes a shell-encrusted room, a frieze of feathers and sand and seaweed collages.

It opens 11 am to 5.30 pm Sunday to Thursday, April to October. Admission costs £3.20/1.60. It's 2 miles north of Exmouth on the A376; Stagecoach Devon bus No 57 runs close by en route to Exeter.

SOUTH DEVON COAST

Devon's south coast is dotted with traditional seaside resorts, which are crowded in summer. They are linked by the South West Coast Path which follows the length of the coast.

Sidmouth

☎ 01395 • pop 11,000

A busy fishing port in the Middle Ages, Sidmouth became a fashionable holiday resort when the future Queen Victoria visited with her parents in 1819. The town still retains a certain grandeur, with many gracious Regency buildings. To the east, a steep path climbs Salcombe Hill, with superb views from the top.

Sidmouth is best known for its folk festival which has grown from a small gathering to a major event on the international folk scene. The festival takes over the town for a week in late July or early August. Tickets for all the events cost £140/84, plus £40/16 to camp for adults/children; a day's ticket costs £29/19 plus £8 if you're camping. Phone ☎ 01296-433669 for information.

The TIC (☎ 516441) shares a home with the public swimming pool in Ham Lane.

The nearest hostel is **Beer Youth Hostel** (☎ 01297-20296, Bovey Combe, Townsend) in a large house half a mile west of the village of Beer. It opens daily in July and August; daily except Sunday, April to June, September and October. The nightly charge in summer is £10.85/7.40.

There are two buses an hour from Exeter (£3.15, 45 minutes) to Sidmouth. Axe Valley (☎ 01297-625959) runs the X53 to Beer village.

Torbay Resorts
☎ 01803

The three towns set around Torbay – Torquay, Paignton and Brixham – describe themselves as the English Riviera, and while it's true that the climate here is impressive for England, if you're expecting Cannes, forget it.

Torquay, with a population of over 60,000, is the largest and boldest of the three. There's a long seaside promenade, hung with coloured lights at night, and streets of hotels and cheap B&Bs, all trying to vanquish the ghost of *Fawlty Towers* that took Torquay as its location. The TIC (☎ 297428) is on Vaughan Parade, near the harbour.

Agatha Christie was born here and **Torquay Museum** (☎ 293975, 529 Babbacombe Rd) has a display on the author. In summer it opens 10 am to 4.45 pm Monday to Saturday, and from 1.30 pm Sunday; weekdays only in winter. Admission costs £2/1.25. **Torre Abbey** (☎ 293593), in the park set back from the beach, was a monastery converted into a country house. It now houses a collection of furniture, glassware and more Agatha Christie mementos. It opens 9.30 am to 5 pm, April to October. Admission costs £2.75/1.50.

Torquay Backpackers (☎ 299924, 119 Abbey Rd) charges £8 per night or £48 per week and is near the town centre and the beach. There are literally hundreds of B&Bs and hotels in the Torquay area.

The **Tudor Rose** (14 Victoria Parade) is a good place for light lunches and teas. For something more substantial, **Capers** (☎ 291177, 7 Lisburne Square) has a fine array of international food with the emphasis on French; expect to spend £10 and up.

To the south around the bay, Torquay merges into **Paignton**, that promotes itself as a seaside resort for the family. Roundham Head separates the two main beaches. The TIC (☎ 558383) is on the Esplanade.

Riviera Backpackers (☎ 550160, 6 Manor Rd, Preston Sands) is a short walk from the beach. Dorm beds cost £8. Call from the train station and they'll meet you. B&Bs and hotels are here in force.

The Natural Break (☎ 526220, 41 Torquay Rd) is an excellent vegetarian restaurant open all day. **Thai Paradise** (☎ 551166, 4a Parkside Rd) is a reliable Thai restaurant.

Brixham is a fishing town crowded round a small harbour. In the middle of the 19th century, this was the country's busiest fishing port and is still the place to come for a fishing expedition. Kiosks line the harbour touting boat trips. It costs around £20 to fish for conger, ling and coalfish around the wrecks in the bay, less to fish for mackerel. Before parting with your money, it's worth asking whether there are any mackerel shoals about. To arrange a trip, contact the skippers directly – **Boy Richard** (☎ 521986) or **Our Jenny** (☎ 854444). The TIC (☎ 852861) is on the quay.

Four miles from Brixham and across the water from Dartmouth, the attractively located **Maypool Youth Hostel** (☎ 01803-842444) is a mile south-west of Galmpton. Beds cost £9/6.20 for adults/under-18s and it opens daily April to August. Stagecoach Devon bus No 12 stops at Churston Pottery, a mile away beside Churston train station.

Getting There & Away The No X46 bus service runs hourly from Exeter to Torquay (£4.10, one hour). Service No 12 operates five times an hour along the coast from Torquay to Paignton and Brixham.

A branch rail line runs from Newton Abbot, via Torquay to Paignton. The Paignton & Dartmouth Steam Railway (☎ 01803-555872) runs from Paignton along the coast on the scenic 7-mile trip to Kingswear on the River Dart, linked by ferry (six minutes) to Dartmouth. A combined rail/ferry ticket to Dartmouth costs £5.50/3.70 for an adult/child, one way; £7.50/5 return.

Dartmouth
☎ 01803 • pop 5300

On the River Dart estuary, Dartmouth is an attractive port with a long history. The deep natural harbour has sheltered trading vessels since Norman times, fishing boats for many more centuries, the Pilgrim Fathers in 1620 on their way to Plymouth, and D-Day landing craft bound for France in 1944. Today, it's filled with yachts, but naval associations continue with the Royal Navy's officers' training college on the edge of town.

Narrow streets wind through the town. In the centre, the Butterwalk is a row of timber-framed houses built in the 17th century, with a museum featuring a large collection of model boats. **Dartmouth Castle** (☎ 833588; EH), three-quarters of a mile outside the town, dates from the 15th century and was designed so that a chain could be placed to the companion castle at Kingswear to block off the estuary. The castle opens 10 am to 6 pm daily in summer (to 4 pm Tuesday to Saturday in winter). Admission costs £2.90/1.50. There's a ferry to the castle from the town every 15 minutes (£1).

The TIC (☎ 834224) is on Mayor's Ave or visit www.dartmouth-tourism.co.uk.

Places to Stay The youth hostel (see Brixham under Torbay Resorts earlier in the chapter) is across the river at Maypool, about 5 miles away.

There are cheap B&Bs along Victoria Rd. *Galleons Reach* (☎ 834339) at No 77 costs £16 per person, or £20 in a room with a bath. Near the waterfront is the *Captain's House* (☎ 832133, 18 Clarence St) with rooms from £22.50 per person.

The Little Admiral Hotel (☎ 832572, 29 Victoria Rd) offers a luxurious base with impeccable rooms from £45/90.

Places to Eat The town has something of a reputation for gourmet dining. *Royal Cas-*

tle Hotel (☎ 833033) on The Quay, has a popular restaurant, but better known is the *Carved Angel* (☎ 832465) on South Embankment, where a memorable feast will cost £48 for three courses. Run by the same people but with a cheaper menu, *Carved Angel Café* (☎ 834842, 7 Foss St) offers bistro-style main courses from £7.50; fish is a speciality. *Hooked* (☎ 832022, 5 Higher St) is another well-known fish restaurant: think £25 a head and up.

Cherub Inn (☎ 832571), also in Higher St, claims to be the town's oldest building and is a good place for a pint or a bar meal.

At the castle, *Dartmouth Castle Tea Rooms*, does cream teas and light lunches, and offers excellent views over the water. *Dartmouth Bakery* has an exceptional range of cakes and pies.

Getting There & Away The best way to approach Dartmouth is by boat, either on the ferries across from Kingswear (£2 for a car and four people, 50p for a foot passenger, six minutes) or downstream from Totnes (£5.20/£6.90 single/return, 1¼ hours). River Dart Cruises (☎ 832109) is one operator. From Exeter, take a train to Totnes and a boat from there.

Totnes
☎ 01803 • pop 7500

Nine miles inland from Torquay and 10 miles upriver from Dartmouth, Totnes was once one of the most prosperous towns in Britain, a centre for the tin and wool industry. It's now a trendy market town ('the Glastonbury of the west') with a thriving arts community.

This is a pleasant place to wander around, with interesting shops, numerous Elizabethan buildings and a busy quay. There are cruises on the river with frequent departures to Dartmouth in summer.

Totnes Museum is in a Tudor building on Fore St. It opens Monday to Saturday. A £3 ticket also covers the **Guildhall** and the **Museum of Period Costume**. **Totnes Castle** (☎ 864406; EH) opens 10 am to 6 pm in summer. Admission costs £1.60/80p.

The TIC (☎ 863168) is on The Plains.

Places to Stay & Eat The *Dartington Youth Hostel* (☎ 862303), Lownard, is 2 miles from Totnes off the A385 near Week. It opens daily in July and August, daily except Monday April to June, and daily except Monday and Tuesday in September and October; the nightly charge is £9/6.20 for adults/under-18s. Western National bus No X80 from Torquay to Plymouth via Totnes passes close by.

At 3 Plymouth Rd, just off the High St, *Alison Fenwick* (☎ 866917) offers B&B from £15 to £19 per person, and can arrange private tours of Dartmoor.

A couple of minutes' walk from Totnes train station, there's comfortable B&B at *No 4* (☎ 867365, 4 Queen's Terrace) for £25/40 for singles/doubles including a vegetarian breakfast.

The 600-year-old *Old Forge* (☎ 862174, Seymour Place) is more atmospheric and even has its own old lock-up. Rooms cost from £54.

The *Willow Vegetarian Restaurant* (☎ 862605, 87 High St) does main dishes from about £4 and has a nice garden. *Tolivers Vegetarian Bistro* (65 Fore St) is more expensive but has live music at the weekend and good food at all times. Totnes High St is lined with interesting places to eat. *Munchmania* is an organic juice bar. *Anne of Cleves Tearoom* has some mouth-watering cakes.

Getting There & Away Buses run only a few times a week to Exeter, but National Express coaches stop here. There are frequent rail connections to Exeter (£7.10, 45 minutes) and Plymouth (£5.50, 25 minutes). The train station is a 15-minute walk from the town centre.

A short walk from Totnes train station, the private South Devon Railway (☎ 01364-642338) runs to Buckfastleigh (£6.50/4 return; £6/3.50 if you book at the TIC, 25 minutes) on the edge of Dartmoor.

PLYMOUTH
☎ 01752 • pop 239,000

Plymouth was renowned as a maritime centre long before Sir Francis Drake's famous game of bowls on Plymouth Hoe in 1588, but this history is difficult to appreciate as you approach through the extensive modern suburbs of Devon's largest city. Devastated by WWII bombing raids, most of Plymouth has been rebuilt, although the Barbican (the old quarter by the harbour where the Pilgrim Fathers set sail for the New World) has been preserved.

History

Plymouth really began to expand in the 15th century with the development of larger ships; Plymouth Sound provided a perfect anchorage for warships.

The seafarer most commonly associated with Plymouth is Sir Francis Drake who achieved his knighthood through an epic voyage around the world; setting out from Plymouth in 1577 in the *Golden Hind*, he returned three years later.

In 1588, Drake played a prominent part in the defeat of the Spanish Armada, the fleet sent to invade England by Philip II who wanted to restore Catholicism to this country. On the way home from a Caribbean raid in 1586, Drake had taunted the Spanish king with an attack on some ships in Cadiz harbour.

Whether Drake really was playing bowls on the Hoe at the time is debatable, but the English fleet certainly did set sail from here. Drake was vice admiral and John Hawkins (who had sailed with him on the 1586 raid) was rear admiral. The Armada was chased up the English Channel to Calais, where the troops they were supposed to collect for the planned invasion of Britain failed to arrive. The English then attacked the fleet with fire ships. Many of the Spanish vessels escaped but were blown off course and wrecked off Scotland. Losses were England nil, Spain 51.

Thirty-two years later, the Pilgrim Fathers' two ships, the *Mayflower* and the *Speedwell*, put into Plymouth. Because the second ship was badly damaged, only the *Mayflower* set sail for America on 16 September 1620. Some of the 102 passengers and crew spent their last night on English soil in Island House, now the TIC. Another famous Plymouth mariner is Captain James Cook, who

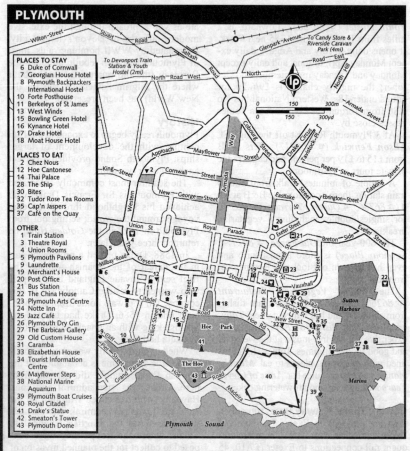

PLYMOUTH

PLACES TO STAY
6 Duke of Cornwall
7 Georgian House Hotel
8 Plymouth Backpackers
   International Hostel
10 Forte Posthouse
11 Berkeleys of St James
13 West Winds
15 Bowling Green Hotel
16 Kynance Hotel
17 Drake Hotel
18 Moat House Hotel

PLACES TO EAT
2 Chez Nous
12 Hoe Cantonese
14 Thai Palace
28 The Ship
30 Bites
32 Tudor Rose Tea Rooms
35 Cap'n Jaspers
37 Café on the Quay

OTHER
1 Train Station
3 Theatre Royal
4 Union Rooms
5 Plymouth Pavilions
9 Laundrette
19 Merchant's House
20 Post Office
21 Bus Station
22 The China House
23 Plymouth Arts Centre
24 Notte Inn
25 Jazz Café
26 Plymouth Dry Gin
27 The Barbican Gallery
29 Old Custom House
31 Caramba
33 Elizabethan House
34 Tourist Information
   Centre
36 Mayflower Steps
38 National Marine
   Aquarium
39 Plymouth Boat Cruises
40 Royal Citadel
41 Drake's Statue
42 Smeaton's Tower
43 Plymouth Dome

set out from The Barbican in 1768 in search
of a southern continent.

The royal dockyard was established at
Devonport beside the River Tamar in 1690,
and there's still a large naval base here.

Orientation & Information

The train station is about a mile north of
Plymouth Hoe, the grassy park overlooking
the sea. Between them is the pedestrianised
city centre, with shopping streets branching
off Armada Way, and the bus station. To the
east of The Hoe is the Barbican, the interesting old quarter, by Sutton Harbour.

The TIC (☎ 264849) is in Island House,
9 The Barbican. It opens from 9 am to 5 pm
Monday to Saturday and 10 am to 4 pm on
summer Sundays. If you're driving into
Plymouth from Exeter there's another TIC
(☎ 266030) next to Sainsbury's supermarket at Marshall's roundabout (off the A38).

Bicycle hire is available from conveniently located Caramba (☎ 201544) at 9
Quay Rd for £10 a day or £60 a week.

Plymouth Boat Cruises (☎ 822797) offers
a number of boat trips ranging from an hour-
long, daily harbour cruise (£4/2) to irregular
four-hour cruises up the Tamar (£6.50/3).

SOUTH-WESTERN ENGLAND

The cruise to Calstock can be combined with a rail trip on the Tamar Line. Boats leave from Phoenix Wharf, along The Barbican (below the Royal Citadel).

There are laundrettes on Notte St and Pier St.

Plymouth Hoe

This famous park gives wonderful, breezy views over Plymouth Sound. In one corner there's even a bowling green; the one on which Drake finished his game was probably where his statue now stands.

The Hoe's most obvious landmark is the red-and-white-striped **Smeaton's Tower**, originally the Eddystone Lighthouse but rebuilt here in 1882. This may look like just another lighthouse but it's actually the first scientifically-designed jointed masonry lighthouse in the world. Open in summer, it costs 75p to climb the 93 steps.

Plymouth Dome (☎ 603300), below Smeaton's Tower, details Plymouth's history through high-tech audiovisual shows. There's also a Tudor street with rowdy locals to liven things up, and a harbour observation deck with interactive computers and radar. It opens 9 am to 5 pm (to 4 pm in winter). Admission costs £4.10/2.60.

East of the Hoe is the **Royal Citadel**, built by Charles II in 1670 and still in military use. There are guided tours of parts of the fortress including the chapel at 2.30 pm, May to September. Tickets (£3/2, free for EH members) can be purchased at Plymouth Dome or at the TIC.

The Barbican

To get an idea of what Plymouth was like before the Luftwaffe redesigned it, visit The Barbican with its Tudor and Jacobean buildings and busy Victorian fish market. Americans will want to make a pilgrimage to the **Mayflower Steps** where a sign listing the passengers marks the spot.

The narrow streets contain interesting galleries and craft shops. One famous local artist to look out for is Beryl Cook, whose naughty, plump figures fetch high prices. The Barbican Gallery (☎ 661052), 15 The Parade, sells prints of her work.

The **Elizabethan House** (☎ 253871), 32 New St, is the former residence of an Elizabethan sea captain. It opens 10 am to 5 pm Wednesday to Sunday, April to October. Admission costs £1/50p.

At 60 Southside St, **Plymouth Dry Gin** (☎ 665292) has seven tours of the distillery between 10.30 am and 3.45 pm daily except Sunday, April to December; tickets cost £2.75/2.50.

Between The Barbican and the city centre is the **Merchant's House** (☎ 264878), 33 St Andrews St, a museum of social history, open the same times as the Elizabethan House. Admission costs £2/1.

National Marine Aquarium

Opened in 1998 in an impressive building opposite The Barbican, the aquarium is a non-profit making venture designed to educate as well as amuse. Following a route along ramps winding through the building, visitors can examine aquatic life in a range of habitats – moorland stream, river estuary, shore and shallow sea, and deep reef. There's also the mandatory shark pool but Jaws gets good press here. You're more likely to die from a coconut dropping on your head than from being savaged by a shark, we're told.

The aquarium (☎ 220084) is well worth visiting. It opens 9 am to 5 pm. Admission costs £6.50/4.

Places to Stay

Camping The nearest camp site is *Riverside Caravan Park* (☎ 344122), which is 4 miles from the centre on Longbridge Rd (off Plympton Rd). It costs £7 for a tent in summer.

Hostels Two miles from the centre, *Plymouth Youth Hostel* (☎ 562189, Belmont Place, Stoke) is in a Grecian-style mansion. In summer, beds cost £10.85/7.40 for adults/under-18s. The hostel opens daily, January to Christmas. Western National bus Nos 15 and 81 and Citybus Nos 33/4 pass this way from the city centre. Devonport train station is a quarter of a mile from the hostel.

Plymouth Backpackers International Hostel (☎ 225158) is a friendly place at 172

Citadel Rd, The Hoe. There are beds in dorms from £8.50 a night, with cheaper weekly rates. There are also some double rooms (£20). Showers are free (baths cost £1.50) and there's a laundry service.

B&Bs & Hotels B&Bs and hotels cluster round the north-western corner of The Hoe. Citadel Rd is lined with places to stay. *West Winds* (☎ 601777, 99 Citadel Rd) charges £20/40 for singles/doubles; the doubles have showers.

The large and friendly *Kynance Hotel* (☎ 266821, 107 Citadel Rd) has rooms from £25/40 with a bath. A continental breakfast is provided if you're leaving early on the ferry. Slightly more upmarket is *Georgian House Hotel* (☎ 663237, 51 Citadel Rd) where rooms with a bath cost from £24/38. In winter prices drop to £21/36.

Berkeleys of St James (☎ 221654, 4 St James Place East) is a comfortable, non-smoking guesthouse charging from £25/40 for rooms with a bathroom.

Bowling Green Hotel (☎ 667485, 9 Os-borne Place, Lockyer St) is, as the name suggests, right beside The Hoe bowling green. It's a small, comfortable place run by friendly people. Rooms with a shower cost from £38/50. Also on Lockyer St is *Drake Hotel* (☎ 229730, 1 Windsor Villas) with rooms for £42/52 with a bathroom.

The *Forte Posthouse* (☎ 662828), Cliff Rd, The Hoe, charges £89 for a double at the weekend. It has good views over Plymouth Sound. *Plymouth Hoe Moat House* (☎ 639988, Armada Way) charges £115/130.

The *Duke of Cornwall* (☎ 266256, Mill-bay Rd) is an impressive Victorian Gothic hotel situated between The Hoe and the ferry terminal. Room only starts from £84.50/99.50.

Places to Eat

The Barbican area makes the best hunting ground for interesting places to eat, especially along Southside St and New St behind the TIC. The *Tudor Rose Tea Rooms* (☎ 255502, New St) have a pleasant garden at the back where teas and lunches are available. Beef and Guinness pie is tasty.

The city's top restaurant is the predominantly French *Chez Nous* (☎ 266793, 13 Frankfort Gate), a short walk from the Theatre Royal. Seafood is a speciality and main courses cost around £18; a three-course set lunch or dinner is £30. Booking is advisable.

There are few restaurants in the Lockyer and Citadel Rds area, but *Hoe Cantonese* (☎ 661895, Athenaeum St) and *Thai Palace* (☎ 255770, Elliot St) are good exceptions – Hoe stays open late.

For a takeaway sandwich or baguette visit *Bites* on Quay Rd. *Cap'n Jasper's* is a popular snack stand, near the Mayflower Steps, that does breakfasts and burgers. Half a yard of hot dog is available for junk-food junkies. *The Ship* (☎ 667604), beside the marina in the Barbican, offers good value carvery meals.

Café on the Quay by the National Aquarium has light lunches including a baked potato filled with tuna – dolphin friendly, of course.

Entertainment

Pubs, Bars & Clubs The Barbican is a good place to drink in the evening; the *Dolphin*, on Southside St, and *The Ship*, on The Barbican, are both popular. *Union Rooms* has the cheapest drinks, but no music, while *Notte Inn* is part pub, part restaurant with a touch of history.

The China House (☎ 260930, Marrow-bone Slip, off Exeter St), overlooking Sutton Harbour, is a popular pub in a converted warehouse. There's live jazz on Sunday at lunch time and bands on Friday and Saturday evening. *Jazz Café* on Southside St dabbles in all sorts of music and has jazz, bands or DJs most nights. *Candy Store* and *Club Fandango* are lively clubs, while *Dance Academy* is the big one.

Theatre Plymouth's *Theatre Royal* (☎ 267222, Royal Parade) attracts surprisingly big names for a regional theatre. *Plymouth Arts Centre* (☎ 206114, 38 Looe St) has a cinema, art galleries and a vegetarian restaurant. The *Pavilions* (☎ 229922, Millbay Rd) hosts everything from Tom Jones to the Bolshoi Ballet.

Getting There & Away

Plymouth is 211 miles from London, 90 from Land's End and 46 from Exeter.

Bus First Western National (☎ 01752-402060) runs three buses an hour to Yelverton (35 minutes), with an hourly service on Sunday and bank holidays. Explorer tickets for one/three/seven days cost £5.50/13.40/22.65. Stagecoach bus X38 runs to Exeter every 90 minutes (1¼ hours).

National Express (☎ 0870 580 8080) has direct connections to numerous cities including London (£20.50, 4½ hours) and Bristol (£18, 2½ hours). Stagecoach runs the cheapest buses to/from Exeter (£5.45, ¾ hour).

Train The fastest way to get to London is by train (£44, 3½ hours). There are also direct services to Bristol (£29, 1½ hours) and Penzance (£10.30, two hours).

There's a scenic route to Exeter (£10, one hour) – the line follows the River Exe estuary, running beside the sea for part of the way. The Tamar Valley Line, through Bere Ferrers, Bere Alston and Calstock to Gunnislake, is another scenic route. In summer, it's possible to travel to Calstock by train (£3.90) and return by boat (see Orientation & Information earlier).

Boat Brittany Ferries (☎ 0870 536 0360) sails from Millbay Docks to Roscoff in France (£13 to £29 return, six hours, up to three departures a day in summer), and Santander in Spain (£47 to £149 return, 24 hours, Monday and Wednesday in summer).

AROUND PLYMOUTH
Mount Edgcumbe

The 400-year-old home of the earls of Mount Edgcumbe lies across the water in Cornwall. Although the house opens to the public and is filled with 18th-century furniture, it's the French, Italian and English gardens that draw visitors. The gardens open daily and admission is free. The house opens 11 am to 4.30 pm Wednesday to Sunday, April to September. Admission costs £4.50/2.25. You get to them from Plymouth on the Cremyll foot ferry.

Buckland Abbey

Eleven miles north of Plymouth, Buckland Abbey (☎ 01822-853607; NT) was a Cistercian monastery, transformed into a family residence by Sir Richard Grenville and bought in 1581 by Sir Francis Drake. Among the memorabilia is Drake's Drum, used to summon sailors onto the deck of the *Revenge* before battle with the Armada. When Britain is in danger of being invaded, the drum is said to beat by itself.

It opens 10.30 am to 5.30 pm daily except Thursday, April to October; and 2 to 5 pm at the weekend in winter. Admission costs £4.50/2.20. Bus Nos 83/84 from Plymouth connect with the No 55 from Yelverton.

NORTHERN DEVON
Barnstaple
☎ 01271 • pop 24,500

Barnstaple is a large town and transport hub – a good starting point for North Devon and Exmoor (see Exmoor National Park earlier in the chapter). However, apart from **The Museum of North Devon** (☎ 346747) in The Square, there's little reason to stay. See the TIC (☎ 388583), 36 Boutport St, for B&Bs.

Barnstaple is at the north-western end of the Tarka Line from Exeter and connects with a number of bus services around the coast. Red Bus (☎ 345444) No 310 runs every two hours to Lynton, but the most interesting option is the excellent No 300 scenic service that crosses Exmoor from Barnstaple, through Lynton to Minehead and Bridgwater.

Mountain bikes are available from Tarka Trail (☎ 324202) at the train station from £6.50 per day, £8.50 for mountain bikes.

Ilfracombe
☎ 01271 • pop 10,471

Rising above its little harbour, Ilfracombe is North Devon's largest seaside resort, although the best beaches are 5 miles west at Woolacombe, and at Croyde Bay, 2 miles beyond. Both are popular with surfers.

In 1998, the striking Ilfracombe Pavilion opened, comprising the 500-seat Landmark Theatre and a circular ballroom. They're housed in two white brick cones that look a bit like enormous lampshades.

The TIC (☎ 863001) is on the Promenade, and the town is packed with B&Bs. *Ilfracombe Youth Hostel (☎ 865337, 1 Hillsborough Terrace)* stands above the town, overlooking the harbour. The nightly charge is £9.80/6.75 for adults/under-18s and it opens daily except Sunday, April to September (every day in July and August).

Ocean Backpackers (☎ 867835, 29 St James Place) is a fine, friendly hostel with lively food, good tunes and beds for £9 for the first night, £8 thereafter.

Red Bus operates frequent services between Ilfracombe and Barnstaple.

Lundy Island

Ten miles out in the Bristol Channel, Lundy is a granite mass, 3 miles long, half a mile wide and up to 122m high. There's a resident population of just 19 people, one pub *(Marisco Tavern)*, one church and no roads.

People come to climb the cliffs, watch the birds, dive in the marine nature reserve or escape from the world in one of the 23 holiday homes.

Interesting properties that can be rented include the lighthouse and the castle but they need to be reserved months in advance. You can also camp from £4 to £7 per person depending on the season. For information, phone ☎ 01237-431831.

Otherwise you can day trip from Ilfracombe or Bideford (£25/12.50 for adults/children, two hours). There are between two and five sailings a week from these ports during the summer season. For bookings, phone ☎ 01237-470422 or visit www.lundyisland.co.uk.

Bideford
☎ 01237 • pop 14,000

Charles Kingsley based his epic novel *Westward Ho!* on the town of Bideford, not on the nearby tacky resort of the same name – the resort was actually named after the book. Bideford's a pleasant-enough place but there's no need to stay here. Several useful bus services pass through the town, though, and the boat to Lundy Island leaves from the quay.

The TIC (☎ 477676) is by Victoria Park. Bicycles can be hired from Bideford Bicycle Hire (☎ 424123), Torrington St for £7 a half day, £9.50 all day.

There are frequent buses to Barnstaple (30 minutes). Service No 2A runs to Appledore (15 minutes).

Appledore

This attractive little town with its narrow streets and olde-worlde charm is the complete antithesis of terribly tacky Westward Ho! nearby. Appledore was long associated with boat-building, but the industry declined in the early part of the 20th century. Revived in 1963, it has managed to continue through the recession. The North Devon Maritime Museum (☎ 01237-422064) tells the story of local boat-building, shipwrecks and smuggling and opens 11 am to 5 pm (closed 1 to 2 pm), Easter to October. Admission costs £1/30p (free on Sunday).

Seagate Hotel (☎ 01237-472589) is a friendly waterside pub that does B&B for £29/50.

King George IV's seaside palace, the Brighton Royal Pavilion

Window shopping in Rye

A fine young filly: a day at Ascot races involves people-watching as much as horse-racing.

Dover's famous white cliffs

A coaching inn, St Albans, tempts punters in for ye olde pint.

How did they get here and what are they for? Ponder ancient mysteries at Stonehenge.

The river runs through it: Bath city centre

Sunny St Mawes on the southern Cornish coast

A thick carpet of bluebells heralds the start of spring in a beech wood, Dorset.

Clovelly
☎ 01237

Looking for all the world like an oil painting, Clovelly has turned itself into a living gallery and charges visitors £2.50 to visit, although technically this is for the visitors centre (☎ 431781) and the car park above. Clinging to a steep slope above a picturesque harbour, it has to be Devon's most photographed village. From Easter to October, Land Rovers ferry visitors up the slope between 9.30 am and 5.30 pm.

The tiny village, with its one cobbled street (flat shoes advisable), is certainly attractive and the best way to appreciate it is to stay here. Several places do B&B. *Temple Bar (☎ 431438)* charges £19 per person and has a fine location above the harbour.

Mrs Golding's (☎ 431565, 104 High St) is the cheapest at £15 per person. *Donkey Shoe Cottage (☎ 431601, 21 High St)* is a homely B&B charging £18 per person.

Right by the harbour, *Red Lion Hotel (☎ 431237)* charges £83 for a double.

There are three departures a day on Red Bus (☎ 01271-345444) service No 319 to Bideford (40 minutes).

Dartmoor National Park

Although the park is only about 365 square miles in area, it encloses some of the wildest, bleakest country in England – suitable terrain for the Hound of the Baskervilles (one of Sherlock Holmes' more notorious foes). The landscape and weather (mist, rain and snow) can make this an eerie place – try not to think of the opening scenes of *American Werewolf in London* on a dark, misty evening.

Dartmoor lies within the county of Devon and is named after the River Dart, which has its source here; the West and East Dart rivers merge at Dartmeet. The park covers a granite plateau punctuated by distinctive tors, which can look uncannily like ruined castles, and is cut by deep valleys, or combes, and fast-flowing rivers and streams. Some tors, such as Vixen Tor, are almost 30m high. The moorland is covered by gorse and heather, and is grazed by sheep, cattle and semi-wild Dartmoor ponies. The countryside in the south-east is more conventionally beautiful, with wooded valleys and thatched villages.

There are plenty of prehistoric remains – Grimspound is possibly the most complete Bronze Age village site in England and the many cairns and tumuli mark the burial places of ancient chieftains.

The area was once rich in minerals such as tin, copper, silver, lead and china clay and the remains of old mines and quarries are scattered about. Most of Dartmoor's prehistoric monuments are built of rough grey local granite. The quarries at Haytor produced stone for Nelson's Column, London Bridge and many other monuments. The wealth generated by these enterprises has left the moor's small communities with attractive churches and buildings. Dartmoor's best-known building, however, is the high-security prison at Princetown.

Most of the park is around 600m high. The highest spot is High Willhays at 621m, near Okehampton. About 40% of Dartmoor is common land but 15% of the park (the north-western section, including High Willhays and Yes Tor) is leased to the Ministry of Defence (MOD) and is closed for firing practice for part of the year.

This is wonderful hiking country, but you'll be far from alone in summer on the most popular routes. It's still essential to have a good map since it's easy to get lost, particularly if the mist comes down.

ORIENTATION

Dartmoor is ringed by a number of small market towns and villages, including Ashburton, Buckfastleigh, Tavistock and Okehampton. It's 10 miles from Exeter and seven from Plymouth. Buses link these towns with Princetown, Postbridge and Moretonhampstead on the moor itself. The two main roads across the moor meet near Princetown, the only village of any size on Dartmoor.

Two Bridges, with its medieval clapper bridge, is the focal point for car and coach visitors, and can be extremely crowded in summer. Most of the places to see are on the

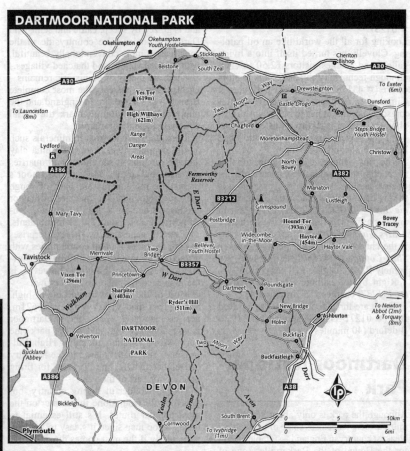

DARTMOOR NATIONAL PARK

eastern side; the western side is for serious walkers.

INFORMATION

You can get information about Dartmoor at the TICs in Exeter and Plymouth, and there are other visitors centres in and around the park. The NPA's High Moorland Visitors Centre (☎ 01822-890414), Old Duchy Hotel, Princetown, opens year round.

The other visitors centres generally open 10 am to 5 pm, April to October, and are at Haytor (☎ 01364-661520); Postbridge (☎ 01822-880272); New Bridge (☎ 01364-631303); Okehampton (☎ 01837-53020); Ivybridge (☎ 01752-897035); and Tavistock (☎ 01822-612938). Also try the website, www.dartmoor-guide.co.uk.

These information centres have useful publications, including *Dartmoor Visitor*, free and updated annually. They also stock walking guides and Ordnance Survey maps. The *Dartmoor Public Transport Guide* gives information on walks accessible by bus.

Guided walks focusing on local wildlife, birdwatching, archaeology or legends and folklore are arranged between April and October. Charges are from £2 for two hours to

£4 for six hours. Details appear in *Dartmoor Visitor*. If you arrive at the start of the walk by bus you can join it free of charge.

Don't feed the Dartmoor ponies because this encourages them to move dangerously near to the roads.

WARNING

Access to the north-western Ministry of Defence (MOD) training area, where there's good walking and some of the highest tors, is restricted when there's live firing. The areas are marked by red-and-white posts and notice boards at the main approaches. When firing is in progress, there are red flags (red lights at night) in position.

Always check the firing schedules with the MOD (☎ 0800 458 4868) or the TIC.

WALKING

Dartmoor offers excellent walking country. Postbridge, Princetown and Chagford are all good centres, and south of Okehampton is a high, wild area around Yes Tor and High Willhays (but this is within the MOD firing range). Haytor is also a popular hiking destination.

There are several waymarked routes. The Abbot's Way runs along an ancient 14-mile route from Buckfast to Princetown. The West Devon Way is a 14-mile walk between Tavistock and Okehampton along old tracks and through pretty villages on the western edge of Dartmoor. You can always take a bus for part of this route since the walk runs parallel to the No 187 bus route.

Youth hostels are conveniently placed a day's walk apart across the moor, so a five-day circuit from Exeter is possible.

The Templer Way is an 18-mile hike from Teignmouth (on the south coast) to Haytor, following the route originally designed to transport Dartmoor granite down to the docks.

The Two Moors Way runs from Ivybridge, on the southern edge of the moor, 103 miles north to Lynmouth in Exmoor. The *Two Moors Way* (£3.70 inc. postage) is available from the Ramblers' Association (☎ 020-7339 8500), 1 Wandsworth Rd, London SW8 2XX.

The Tarka Trail (see Walking under Exmoor National Park earlier in the chapter) circles north Devon and links with Dartmoor, south of Okehampton.

It's always wise to carry a map, compass and rain gear since the weather can change very quickly and not all walks are waymarked. The Ordnance Survey's *Dartmoor Map* shows the park boundaries as well as the MOD firing-range areas.

CYCLING ROUTES

Cycling is only allowed on public roads, byways open to all traffic, public bridlepaths and Forestry Commission roads.

Plym Valley Cycle Way follows the disused Great Western Railway between Plymouth and Yelverton, on the edge of the moor. Other cycle routes include a 3-mile stretch of forest tracks from Bellever; the 26-mile West Devon Tavistock Cycle Route, along country lanes; and the 30-mile Sticklepath Cycle Route, also on lanes.

Bikes can be hired in Exeter (see Bicycles & Canoes under Getting Around in the Exeter section earlier in the chapter), and also from Tavistock Cycles (☎ 01822-617630), Paddons Row, Brook St, Tavistock, and Mountain Bike Hire (☎ 01364-631505) beside the pub in Poundsgate.

OTHER ACTIVITIES
Pony Trekking & Horse Riding

There are riding stables all over the park. Lydford House Riding Stables (☎ 01822-820321), Lydford House Hotel, Lydford, charges from £10/18 for one/two hours.

Near Widecombe-in-the-Moor, Babery Farm Stables (☎ 01364-631296) offers half-day rides and pub rides (three hours riding, one hour in the pub) from £20.

Climbing

Rock climbing can only be done where there is a right of access – on private land you must ask the owner's permission first. Popular climbing areas are at Haytor, owned by the NPA, and Dewerstone, owned by the NT. Groups need to book in advance. Ask at a visitors centre or TIC for details.

SOUTH-WESTERN ENGLAND

Fishing

You can fish on certain stretches of the Rivers East and West Dart (with a Duchy of Cornwall permit), on the Rivers Tavy, Walkham, Plym, Meavy and Teign, as well as on seven reservoirs in the park. A permit is usually needed; phone the Environment Agency (☎ 01392-444000, fisheries department) for information.

PLACES TO STAY & EAT

If you're backpacking, the authorities and owners of unenclosed moorland don't usually object to campers who keep to a simple code: don't camp on moorland enclosed by walls or within sight of roads or houses; don't stay on one site for more than two nights; don't light fires; and leave the site as you found it. With large tents, however, you can only camp in designated camp sites. There are several camping and caravan parks around the area, many on farms.

There are youth hostels at Postbridge (Bellever), bang in the middle of the moor, and at Steps Bridge, near Dunsford (between Moretonhampstead and Exeter), as well as at Okehampton, Exeter, Plymouth and Dartington.

There are youth hostel camping barns at Manaton (Great Houndtor), Postbridge (Runnage), Sticklepath (Sticklepath Halt), Cornwood (Watercombe), Bridestowe (Fox & Hounds), and Lopwell (Lopwell Dam). These are 'stone tents' which sleep up to about 15 people. Cooking and shower facilities and a wood burner are provided. You sleep on the floor or on a bunk bed; bring your own bedding. Charges are from £3.75 per person. For more information and central bookings, phone ☎ 01200-428366. There are also some independent barns and bunkhouses.

The larger towns on the edge of the park (like Okehampton and Tavistock) have plentiful supplies of B&B and hotel accommodation. Within the park itself, accommodation is sometimes limited, so it is wise to book ahead in summer. There are also several comfortable country-house hotels in the park.

The Dartmoor Tourist Association (☎ 01822-890567) produces an accommodation guide; there's a service charge of £2.75 if you book rooms through any of the National Park Visitors Centres. TICs have details of farm B&Bs.

The old pubs and inns provide a focus for local communities and are sometimes the only places you can get anything to eat in small villages.

GETTING THERE & AWAY

Exeter or Plymouth are the best starting points for the park, but Exeter has the better transport connections to the rest of the country. Totnes, Exeter, Newton Abbot and Plymouth all have train services to London, Bristol and the Midlands. National Express has coach services between London and Exeter, Newton Abbot, Okehampton and Plymouth.

In 1997 Okehampton train station was reopened and there's now a Sunday service six times a day to Exeter (40 minutes). The only other train stations near the park are at Ivybridge and South Brent on the Exeter/Plymouth line. Ivybridge is useful for people who want to walk the Two Moors Way. The return fare from Exeter is £9.60 (40 minutes).

The most useful bus that actually crosses Dartmoor is DevonBus No 82, the Transmoor Link, running between Exeter and Plymouth via Steps Bridge, Moretonhampstead, Warren House Inn, Postbridge, Princetown, Sharpitor and Yelverton. It runs daily in summer (late May to late September), but there are only three buses each way, five on a Sunday. For more information phone ☎ 01752-402060.

DevonBus No 359 runs regularly from Exeter through Steps Bridge to Moretonhampstead (Monday to Saturday). No 173 is a regular service through Drewsteignton to Chagford. The No X39 (operated by Stagecoach Devon) goes along the A38 between Plymouth and Exeter, stopping at Buckfastleigh and Ashburton. First Western National Nos 83/84 operates from Plymouth via Yelverton to Tavistock every 20 minutes.

The summer-only Dartmoor Sunday Rover ticket (£5/3) entitles you to unlimited travel on most bus routes within the area and to rail travel on the Tamar Valley Line from Plymouth to Gunnislake.

On summer Sundays, DevonBus No 187 loops round from Plymouth, through Gunnislake, Tavistock, Mary Tavy, Lydford to Okehampton; you could do part of this journey on the Tamar Valley Line or even by boat (see Orientation & Information under Plymouth earlier in the chapter).

Since buses are infrequent and subject to change, it's best to work out what you want to do, then contact Devon County Public Transport Help Line (☎ 01392-382800), 8.30 am to 5 pm on weekdays. They will send you the *Dartmoor Public Transport Guide* with suggestions for walks connected to bus routes.

PRINCETOWN
☎ 01822

At 420m, Princetown is England's highest settlement and Dartmoor's largest community. With the infamous prison located here, it's not Dartmoor's most beautiful town but is close to excellent walking country.

The town was created in the late 18th century by Thomas Tyrwhitt, who wanted to convert large areas of the moorland into arable farmland. When this failed, he came up with another plan to create employment for the people who had moved into the area, suggesting that a prison be built to house prisoners of war. In the first half of the 19th century, the prison housed both French and American POWs. When hostilities with those countries ceased, British prisoners were transferred here. There are now about 600 inmates in the maximum-security prison.

The High Moorland Visitors Centre (☎ 890414) was once the Duchy Hotel. It has displays on Dartmoor and an information centre which stocks maps.

Places to Stay & Eat

The *Plume of Feathers Inn* (☎ 890240), Princetown's oldest building, is a pub near the visitors centre, with all sorts of cheap accommodation. The camp site (from £2.50 per person) opens year round, the stone tent costs from £3.50 and there's bunkhouse accommodation from £5.50 (including rooms

for two and four people). You need to book well in advance. There's also B&B from £15.50 per person.

The *Railway Inn* (☎ 890232, *Two Bridges Rd*), across from the visitors centre, is a pub offering B&B for £20/35.

Getting There & Away

DevonBus No 82 (Transmoor Link) runs here from either Exeter or Plymouth (both 50 minutes). The service operates daily between July and late September, and on Saturday, Sunday and bank holidays in May and June. A £5/3 Sunday Rover ticket allows a day's travel on the system. The No 98 links Princetown with Tavistock.

POSTBRIDGE
☎ 01822

Right in the middle of the park, Postbridge makes a popular starting point for local walks. It's known for its granite clapper bridge which crosses the East Dart River. Clapper bridges date from the 13th century and are made of large slabs of granite supported at each end by short, stone pillars.

Local legend tells of the landlady of an 18th-century temperance house who took to serving alcohol – much to the horror of her husband who poured it into the river. A dog which paused to quench its thirst was driven mad by the potent mixture and died. Its tormented spirit is still said to haunt Dartmoor, one version of the story that gave Conan Doyle the idea for *The Hound of the Baskervilles*.

From April to October, there's a NPA Visitors Centre in the car park. There's also a post office and shop in the village.

Places to Stay & Eat

The *Bellever Youth Hostel* (☎ 880207) is a mile south-east of Postbridge on the western bank of the river. It opens daily in July and August, daily except Sunday April to June, and also except Monday in September and October. A bed costs £9.80/6.75 for adults/under-18s.

Runnage Farm (☎ 880222) has a camping barn – the nightly charge is £4 per person. To reach the farm, take the small road off the

SOUTH-WESTERN ENGLAND

B3212 just before you reach Postbridge coming from the Moretonhampstead side.

East Dart Hotel (☎ *880213*) is 100m from the clapper bridge and has B&B from £26/48. ***Lydgate House Hotel*** (☎ *880209*) is a quarter of a mile from the village centre in an attractive, sheltered valley. It's an excellent place to stay with beds from £30.50 per person; a good three-course dinner is also available.

Headland Warren Farm (☎ *880206*) is an ancient farm on the moor, 5 miles from Postbridge. B&B is from £25 per person for the first night (£20 for additional nights) and it's convenient for walkers since it's by the Two Moors Way.

Two miles north-east of Postbridge, along the B3212 towards Moretonhampstead, is the ***Warren House Inn*** (☎ *880208*). It's a good place to come after a walk, and you can warm yourself by a fire they claim has been burning continuously since 1845. There's real ale and pub food including home-made rabbit pie.

Getting There & Away

The Transmoor Link (DevonBus No 82) runs through Postbridge between Plymouth and Exeter.

BUCKFASTLEIGH
☎ 01364

On the park's south-eastern edge, Buckfastleigh is an old market town near the Upper Dart Valley. Nearby is Buckfast Abbey, Britain's last working monastery.

For centuries, Buckfastleigh was a centre for the manufacture of woollen cloth. Above the town is the parish church, and in the graveyard in a heavy tomb built by villagers to ensure he could not come back to life, lies Sir Richard Cabell, the most hated man in Dartmoor. When this evil landowner died in the 17th century, it's said that black phantom hounds were seen speeding across the moor to howl beside his grave.

Buckfast Abbey

Buckfast Abbey (☎ 645500), 2 miles north of Buckfastleigh, was founded in 1016 and flourished in the Middle Ages through its involvement in the wool trade. With the Dissolution, it was abandoned in 1539. In 1806, the ruins were levelled and a mock-Gothic mansion erected; the house was purchased in 1882 by a group of exiled French Benedictine monks. The abbey church was built between 1906 and 1932 by the monks, and an impressive, modern stained-glass figure of Christ dominates the eastern end chapel.

The abbey is a popular tourist attraction. Admission is free. The monks augment their income by keeping bees and making tonic wine.

Places to Stay & Eat

About 3 miles north-west of Buckfastleigh, in Holne, there's budget accommodation in a stone barn at ***Holne Court Farm*** (☎ *631271*) from £3.50 per person.

Furzeleigh Mill Hotel (☎ *643476, Old Ashburton Rd, Dartbridge*) has rooms for £33.75/57.50 singles/doubles. ***Dartbridge Inn*** (☎ *642214, Totnes Rd*) offers B&B from £45/60 for a single/double with a bath.

The restaurant and tearooms at ***Buckfast Abbey*** are good for lunch or tea.

Getting There & Away

First Western National No 88 runs between Plymouth and Buckfastleigh three times a day, Monday to Saturday (one hour). It continues to Newton Abbot (30 minutes). Bus No X39 runs from Buckfastleigh to Exeter (one hour).

The South Devon Railway (☎ 01364-642336) links Totnes and Buckfastleigh (£6.50/4.00 adult/under 18 return, 25 minutes, every 1½ hours) with a 7-mile journey beside the River Dart on a steam-operated country branch line. The service operates daily, mid-May to September. In April and October, trains run on Wednesday, Saturday and Sunday, and in early May every day except Monday, Thursday and Friday.

WIDECOMBE-IN-THE-MOOR
☎ 01364

Uncle Tom Cobbleigh and all still flock to this popular little Dartmoor village, and not just on the second Tuesday of September when the fair, commemorated in the famous folk song, takes place. The fine 14th-century granite church, known as the Cathedral in the Moor, was funded by prosperous tin miners and has a 37m-high tower.

There's a Visitor Information Point at Sexton's Cottage, adjacent to Church House. Built in 1537 as a brewhouse, the Church House is now the village hall.

Five miles from Ashburton is *Cockingford Farm Campsite* (☎ 621258), 1½ miles south of Widecombe. It costs £2.50 per person to camp here. On the edge of Widecombe, there's B&B at *Sheena Tower* (☎ 621308) for £17 per person, £18 in a room with a bath.

MORETONHAMPSTEAD & STEPS BRIDGE

Moretonhampstead, a market town at the junction of the B3212 and the A382, is on the Transmoor Link bus route, 14 miles from Princetown.

Just inside the park's north-eastern border, 4½ miles east of Moretonhampstead, along the B3212, is *Steps Bridge Youth Hostel* (☎ 01647-252435). Beds cost £7.20/4.95 for adults/under-18s and it opens daily, April to September. It's a 10-mile walk from here to the hostel in Exeter.

You can camp at *Clifford Bridge Park* (☎ 01647-24226, *Clifford*) Easter to September, from £3.50 for a person and tent. The site is by the River Teign, 3 miles west of Steps Bridge, and there's even a heated swimming pool.

CHAGFORD

☎ 01647 • pop 1500

This delightful country town by the River Teign makes a more attractive base for the park's north-eastern area than nearby Moretonhampstead. In the 14th century, it was a Stannary town where the tin mined on the moor was weighed and checked, and the taxes paid. It's an excellent walking and riding centre.

Places to Stay & Eat

At *Glendarah House* (☎ 433270) rooms cost £26 per person with a bath, including the single room. *Lawn House* (☎ 433329, *Mill St*) offers B&B from £20 per person.

Opposite the church, the pretty *Three Crowns Hotel* (☎ 433444, *High St*), dates from the 13th century. Beds here cost from £32.50.

Evelyn Waugh stayed at *Easton Court Hotel* (☎ 433469) while writing *Brideshead Revisited*. It's a lovely thatched 15th-century building, just off the A382 at Easton, on the opposite side from the turning to Chagford. B&B costs from £78/136.

Getting There & Away

From Exeter (one hour), No 173 goes via Moretonhampstead. From Okehampton, No 179 provides a daily service.

CASTLE DROGO

Just over a mile from Chagford is **Castle Drogo** (☎ 01647-433306; NT), a medieval-looking granite fortification that was designed by Sir Edwin Lutyens, and constructed between 1910 and 1930 for a wealthy businessman, Julius Drewe, who died shortly after moving in. It overlooks the wooded gorge of the River Teign with fine views of Dartmoor.

Once you've been round what must be the most comfortable castle in the kingdom, you can rent croquet sets for a game on the lawn. It opens 11 am to 5.30 pm daily except Friday, April to October. Admission costs £5.40/2.70.

OKEHAMPTON

☎ 01837 • pop 4200

The A30, the main route to Cornwall, divides bustling Okehampton from Dartmoor. Some of the wildest walking on the moor lies south of Okehampton, but since it's within the MOD's firing area, you should phone in advance to check that it's open. The part of the park that is south of Belstone is also good, and is outside the MOD zone.

Okehampton has several attractions to delay hikers. The ruined **castle** (☎ 52844; EH) above the town charges £2.30/1.20 for admission. The **Museum of Dartmoor Life** (☎ 52295), West St, has interactive exhibits, displays and photographs about the moor and its inhabitants. It opens 10 am to 5 pm daily, June to September, phone ahead for

SOUTH-WESTERN ENGLAND

details of other opening times. Admission costs £2/1.

It's a pleasant three- to four-hour walk along part of the Tarka Trail from Okehampton to Sticklepath, where the Finch Foundry (☎ 840046; NT) has three working water wheels. It opens 11 am to 5.30 pm daily except Tuesday, April to October. Admission costs £2.80. The *Two Museums Walk* leaflet has information on this hike. Bus No X10 (daily) links Sticklepath with Okehampton and Exeter.

The TIC (☎ 53020) is at 3 West St, by the museum.

Places to Stay & Eat
At the train station, in a newly-converted goods shed is *Okehampton Youth Hostel* (☎ 53916). It has 64 beds in small dormitories and the nightly charge is £10.85/7.40 for adults/under-18s. There's also a kitchen and laundry.

Yertiz Caravan & Camping Park (☎ 52281) is three-quarters of a mile east of Okehampton on the B3260. The charge is £4 for one person and a tent in summer, £5 for two.

Olditch Caravan & Camping Park (☎ 840734) is on the edge of Sticklepath, 4 miles east of Okehampton and charges £5 for one person and a tent year round, £7/9 for two depending on the season.

Fountain Hotel (☎ 53900, Fore St) charges £16 per person for rooms with shared bathrooms. *Heathfield House* (☎ 54211, Klondyke Rd) does B&B with a bathroom from £35/50 per person, including facilities.

The *Coffee Pot* (14 St James St) does teas and lunches.

Getting There & Away
Okehampton is 23 miles west of Exeter, 29 miles north of Plymouth. There's a daily National Express bus from London via Heathrow.

First Western National Bus Nos X9 (hourly) and X10 run between Exeter and Okehampton (one hour). There are fewer buses on Sunday. Bus No 86 runs every two hours between Plymouth and Okehampton (1½ hours).

In 1997, Okehampton train station was reopened and there is now a Sunday service six times a day to Exeter (40 minutes).

The Tarka Trail passes through Okehampton and Sticklepath on a 180-mile route through north Devon.

LYDFORD
☎ 01822 • 1800
This picturesque village on the western edge of the moor is best known for the 1½-mile **Lydford Gorge**.

An attractive but strenuous riverside walk leads to the 28m-high White Lady waterfall and past a series of bubbling whirlpools, including the Devil's Cauldron. It is owned by the NT and opens 10 am to 5.30 pm, April to October (10.30 am to 3 pm in winter). Admission costs £3.50.

There's evidence of both Celtic and Saxon settlements here, and the ruins of a Norman castle. Lydford was the administrative centre for the Stannary towns (see Chagford earlier in the chapter). Courts trying recalcitrant tin workers were particularly harsh; it was said that perpetrators of offences punishable by death would be hanged in the morning and tried in the afternoon.

Places to Stay & Eat
The 16th-century *Castle Inn* (☎ 820242) was featured in *The Hound of the Baskervilles* and is right beside the castle and half a mile from Lydford Gorge. It is a good place to stay, as well as a truly atmospheric place for a pint and an excellent place to eat, offering seasonal dishes such as venison and juniper berry pie and wild boar, as well as bar snacks that are considerably better than the average pub's. The B&B charge is £35/62 for singles/doubles with bathroom.

Lydford House Hotel (☎ 820347), on the edge of the village, offers B&B from £39.50 per person. There's a riding stable in the grounds (£10 per hour, or two hours from £18).

By the main entrance to the White Lady waterfall, *Manor Farm Tea Rooms* serves cream teas and light lunches.

Letterboxing

If you see a walker acting furtively and slipping an old Tupperware box into a tree stump or under a rock, you may be witnessing someone in the act of letterboxing. This wacky pastime has more than 10,000 addicts and involves a never-ending treasure hunt for several thousand 'letterboxes' hidden all over Dartmoor.

In 1844 the railway line reached Exeter, and Dartmoor started to receive visitors, for whom this was a chance to imagine themselves as great explorers. One guide for these intrepid Victorian gentlefolk was James Perrott of Chagford. In 1854, he had the idea of getting them to leave their calling cards in a glass jar at Cranmere Pool – the most remote part of the moor accessible at that time. It was not until 1938 that the second 'box' was established and the idea really took off after WWII. Originally, people left their card with a stamped addressed envelope in a box and if someone else found it they would send it back.

There are now about 4000 boxes, each with a visitors book for you to sign and a stamp and ink pad (if they haven't been stolen) to stamp your record book. Although it's technically illegal to leave a 'letterbox' because in effect you're leaving rubbish on the moor without the landowner's permission, as long as the boxes are unobtrusive, most landowners tolerate them. Now there are even German, French, Belgian and American boxes, not to mention 'mobile boxes', odd characters who wander the moors waiting for a fellow letterboxer to approach them with the words 'Are you a travelling stamp?'!

Once you've collected 100 stamps, you can apply to join the '100 Club' whereupon you'll be sent a clue book with map references for other boxes. Contact Godfrey Swinscow (☎ 015488-21325), Cross Farm, Diptford, Totnes, Devon TQ9 7NU, for more information.

Inevitably, as more people go letterboxing, a downside (other than general nerdiness) has been identified. A code of conduct now prohibits letterboxers from disturbing rocks, vegetation or archaeological sites in their zeal. Even so there have been mutterings about the disturbance caused to nesting golden plovers and ring ouzels.

Getting There & Away

First Western National DevonBus No 86 crosses Devon from Barnstaple to Plymouth via Lydford, every two hours, Monday to Saturday. Service No 187 operates between Exeter and Tavistock via Lydford six times a day on Sunday in the summer.

TAVISTOCK
☎ 01822 • pop 8700

Tavistock's glory days were in the late 19th century. Then it was one of the world's largest copper producers. Until the Dissolution, Tavistock Abbey controlled huge areas of Devon and Cornwall; only slight ruins remain.

On the outskirts of town is a statue of **Sir Francis Drake**, who was born in Crowndale, just over a mile from Tavistock. **Buckland Abbey**, the mansion he bought after circumnavigating the globe, can be visited (see Buckland Abbey under Around Plymouth earlier in the chapter).

There's a TIC (☎ 612938) underneath the town hall. Bikes can be rented from Tavistock Cycles (☎ 617630), Paddons Row, opposite Goodes Café, Brook St, for £12 for the first day, £8 for further days.

First Western National bus Nos 83, 84 and 86 run up to three times an hour, between Tavistock and Plymouth (50 minutes). The Sunday No 187 service links Okehampton and Tavistock with Gunnislake train station for Plymouth. Sunday service No 23 links Tavistock to Exeter via Princetown, Postbridge, Chagford and Moretonhampstead.

Cornwall

At the country's extreme south-western tip, Cornwall has been described as a beautiful frame around a plain picture. The metaphor is a good one, for the coastline is wonderful – a mix of high, jagged cliffs and pretty inlets sheltering little fishing villages. The interior, however, is much less attractive, even desolate in places.

Cornwall likes to emphasise its separateness from the rest of the country and the county's cultural roots are indeed different, for this was the Celts' last bastion in England after they were driven back by the Saxons. The Cornish language survived until the late 18th century. Efforts are being made to revive it, but Cornish mainly lives on in place names – every other village name seems to be prefixed with *tre-* (meaning settlement).

In the 18th and 19th centuries Cornwall dominated the world's tin and copper markets. Most of the mines have now shut but the industrial past has left scars on the landscape. China clay is still mined around St Austell but tourism has largely replaced the mining industry. Unfortunately though, it offers mainly low-paid, seasonal work and Cornwall is now one of Britain's poorest areas.

In summer, Cornwall's seaside resorts are packed but don't let this put you off, since the holiday-makers tend to congregate around the larger resorts of Bude, Newquay, Falmouth, Penzance and St Ives, and even at the height of the season some of these towns are still worth a visit. Newquay is Britain's surfing capital and one can't fail to be impressed by beautiful St Ives.

Cornish churches lack the splendour of those in Devon and Somerset and even Truro Cathedral is a relative newcomer. However, the names of the churches speak loudly of Cornwall's separateness. Where else would you cross paths with St Non, St Cleer, St Keyne and the many others whose lives are detailed in *The Cornish Saints* by Peter Berresford Ellis?

WALKING & CYCLING ROUTES

The Cornwall Coast Path is the most scenic section of the long-distance South West Coast Path. The Saints' Way is a 26-mile waymarked trail that runs from Fowey across the centre of the county to Padstow on the north coast. It was used in the 6th century as a route for Celtic missionaries between Brittany (France) and Wales or Ireland, saving a long sea trip around Land's End.

Youth hostels are well placed along the coast for stops on a walk or cycle ride around Cornwall. In the north, the 17-mile Camel Trail follows an old railway line from Padstow through Wadebridge to Bodmin along the River Camel. Bikes can be rented from Pedals (☎ 01736-360600) in Penzance, Bridge Bike Hire (☎ 01208-813050) in Wadebridge or Padstow Bicycle Hire (☎ 01841-533533).

GETTING AROUND

For information about buses, there's an efficient helpline (☎ 01872-322142). The main bus operator is First Western National (☎ 01209-719988); an Explorer ticket gives a day's travel on its system for £6/3.50 and there are several other passes.

The main rail route from London terminates in Penzance, but there are branch lines to St Ives, Falmouth, Newquay and Looe. A Cornish Regional Rover ticket costs £39 for eight days travel in a 15-day period, or £24.50 for three days in seven. Plymouth is included in this ticket.

TICs stock the county council's annual *Public Transport Timetable* (with a map), listing all the air, bus, rail and ferry options in Cornwall.

SOUTH-EASTERN CORNWALL

Southern Cornwall is very different in character from the wild north and central parts of the county. This is a more gentle area of farms, wooded inlets and pretty fishing villages – some overrun by tourists in the summer but worth visiting at quieter times.

The mild climate favours many plants that thrive nowhere else in Britain and there are several gardens worth visiting, with rhododendron trees growing almost as tall as in their natural Himalayan habitat. TICs stock the free *Gardens of Cornwall* map and guide with full details.

The best gardens in the area are **Heligan** (☎ 01726-845100), 4 miles south of St Austell (admission costs £5.50/2.50), and **Trelissick Garden** (☎ 01872-862090; NT), 4 miles south of Truro, beside King Harry's Ferry. Trelissick opens 10.30 am to 5 pm (from 12.30 pm Sunday and closing at 5 pm in winter). Admission costs £4.30/2.10. The **Eden Project** (see the boxed text 'The Garden of Eden' later in the chapter) is a new garden opening in 2001.

Cotehele

Seven miles south-west of Tavistock, on the west bank of the Tamar, the river that forms the boundary between Devon and Cornwall, the Cotehele estate comprises a small stately home with splendid garden, a quay with a museum, and a working water mill.

One of Britain's finest Tudor manor houses, Cotehele has been the Edgcumbe family home for centuries. The hall is particularly impressive and many rooms are hung with great tapestries; because of their fragility, there's no electric lighting. Visitor numbers are limited, so you may have to wait. Pick up a timed ticket when you arrive.

Cotehele Quay is part of the National Maritime Museum and has a small museum with displays on local boat-building and river trade. The *Shamrock*, the last surviving River Tamar barge, is moored nearby.

Cotehele Mill is a 15-minute walk away and can be seen in operation; there's also an adjoining cider press.

The estate (☎ 01579-351346; NT) opens 11 am to 5.30 pm daily except Friday, April to October. Admission costs £6/3; £3.20/1.60 for the garden and mill only. You can get here by bus from Tavistock to Calstock, a mile from Cotehele, on First Western National bus No 79.

Looe
☎ 01503

A bridge connects the twin towns of West and East Looe, on either side of the river. They make up the county's second largest fishing port, the place to come if you're into shark fishing. Contact the Tackle Shop (☎ 265444) for day trips (around £25, depending on numbers and the quarry).

East Looe is the main part of town, with narrow streets and little cottages; the wide, sandy beach is to the east. Boat trips are run from the quay to tiny Looe Island, a nature reserve, and to Fowey and Polperro. The TIC (☎ 262072) is in the Guildhall on Fore St.

Trains travel the scenic Looe Valley Line from Liskeard (£2.40, 30 minutes), on the main London-Penzance line, at least six times a day.

Walking An excellent 5-mile walk links Looe to the nearby village of Polperro via beaches, cliffs and the old smuggling village of Talland. You should allow around two hours; buses connect the villages every day in summer.

Polperro

Much prettier than Looe, Polperro is an ancient fishing village around a tiny harbour, best approached along the coastal path from Looe or Talland. Unfortunately, it's very popular with day-trippers so you should try to visit in the evening or during low season.

The village is a picturesque jumble of narrow lanes and fishing cottages, and was once heavily involved in pilchard fishing by day and smuggling by night – there's a small smugglers' museum in the centre. There's no TIC.

Fowey
☎ 01726 • pop 2600

Pronounced foy, unspoilt Fowey lies on the estuary of the same name. The town has a long maritime history and in the 14th century conducted its own raids on coastal towns in France and Spain. This led to the Spanish launching an attack on Fowey in 1380. The town later prospered by shipping Cornish china clay, which it still does, although yachts mainly fill its harbour today. Although there are no specific sights (apart from a small museum and aquarium), Fowey is a good base for walks around the estuary. The TIC (☎ 833616) is in the post office, 4 Custom House Hill.

Walking Fowey is at the southern end of The Saints' Way (see Walking & Cycling Routes under Cornwall earlier in the chapter). Ferries operate across the river to Bodinnick to access the 4-mile Hall Walk to Polruan. You can catch a ferry from Polruan back to Fowey.

When did Cornish Die?

A Celtic language akin to Welsh, Cornish was spoken west of the Tamar until the 19th century. Written evidence indicates that it was still widely spoken at the time of the Reformation, but after a Cornish rising against the English in 1548 the language was suppressed. By the 17th century only a few people living in the peninsula's remote western reaches still spoke nothing but Cornish.

Towards the end of the 18th century linguistic scholars foresaw the death of Cornish and fanned out round the peninsula in search of people who still spoke it. One such scholar, Daines Barrington, visited Mousehole in 1768 and recorded an elderly woman called Dolly Pentreath abusing him in Cornish for presuming she couldn't speak her own language.

Dolly died in 1769 and has gone down in history as the last native speaker of Cornish. However, Barrington knew of other people who continued to speak it into the 1790s, and an 1891 tombstone in Zennor commemorates one John Davey as 'the last to possess any traditional considerable knowledge of the Cornish language'.

Recently efforts have been made to revive the language. Unfortunately there are now three conflicting varieties of 'Cornish' – Unified, Phonemic and Traditional – and no sign that it can regain its former importance.

Places to Stay & Eat Four miles north of Fowey in Golant is *Golant Youth Hostel* (☎ 833507, Penquite House). It opens daily February to September, and daily except Friday, October to early November. The nightly charge is £10.85/7.40 for adults/under-18s. Western National's bus No 24 from St Austell to Fowey stops in Castle Dore, 1½ miles from the hostel.

The delightful *Marina Hotel* (☎ 833315) is right on the waterfront on the Esplanade. Rooms with sea view, bathroom and breakfast are £84. It has an excellent restaurant too.

The Old Ferry Inn (☎ 870237) is near the slipway at Bodinnick. There are rooms with river views and bathrooms; charges range from £20 to £35 per person for B&B.

Other recommended pubs in Fowey include the big *King of Prussia*, on the quay, and the *Ship* and the *Lugger*, back from the water on Lostwithiel St.

Getting There & Away There are frequent departures from St Austell (50 minutes) on First Western National's service No 24, which also passes Par, the closest train station to Fowey.

Lanhydrock House

Amid parkland above the Fowey River, 2½ miles south-east of Bodmin, this grand country house (☎ 01208-73320; NT) was rebuilt after a fire in 1881. The impressive gallery, with its fine plaster ceiling, survived the fire, but the house is mainly of interest for its portrayal of the 'Upstairs Downstairs' divisions of life in Victorian England. The kitchens are particularly interesting, complete with all the gadgets that were mod cons a hundred years ago.

The house opens 11 am to 5 pm daily except Monday, April to October. Admission costs £6.60; £3.60 for the gardens only. The garden opens year round and admission is free in winter. Bodmin Parkway train station is 1¾ miles from the house.

Charlestown

Despite its size, St Austell is not particularly exciting and most people will pass straight through. However, it's worth making a detour south to visit the port of Charlestown, a marvellously picturesque village and harbour built by Charles Rashleigh between 1790 and 1815. On the best days the harbour will be filled with magnificent square-rig ships. However, these are sometimes away taking part in worldwide film assignments. The film of Daphne du Maurier's *Frenchman's Creek* was partly shot here.

The **Shipwreck and Heritage Centre** (☎ 01726-69897) has exhibits on many aspects of Cornish sea life, with animated models illustrating 19th-century village life. It opens 10 am to 5 pm, March to October (to 6 pm in the high season) and is £4.45/free. The attached *Bosun's Bistro* does teas, coffees and lunches.

If you'd like to stay, *T'Gallants* (☎ *01726-70203*) is a fine Georgian house doing B&B for £30/45. Alternatively, *Pier House Hotel* (☎ *01726-67955*) right on the quayside charges £40/63 including breakfast.

TRURO
☎ 01872 • pop 18,000

Truro was once the distribution centre for Cornwall's tin mines and its prosperity dates from this time. Lemon St has some fine Georgian architecture, and the cathedral is worth a visit if you're passing through, even though it only dates back to the late 19th century. Built in neo-Gothic style, it was the first new cathedral to be built in Britain since St Paul's in London.

The TIC (☎ 274555) is in the municipal buildings on Boscawen St, near the covered market. The **Royal Cornwall Museum** (☎ 272205) in River St has exhibits on Cornish history, archaeology and mineralogy. It opens 10 am to 5 pm daily except Sunday and admission is £3/free.

Places to Stay & Eat

There's no hostel but cheap B&Bs near the train station can be found on Treyew Rd. *The Fieldings* (☎ 262783) at No 35, charges from £18/32 for singles/doubles.

The *Royal Hotel* (☎ 270345, Lemon St) is a fine Georgian building convenient for the cathedral. Rooms cost from £35/55 at the weekend, a heftier £67/90 in the week.

Charlotte's Tea House in the old coinage hall building is an institution among Truro folk, popular for its delicious cakes and period costume. The *Old Ale House* is a decent pub on Quay St. Pub grub includes generous-sized sandwiches and main dishes served in a choice of portions. *Saffron*, on Key St, is a bistroesque restaurant with a good looking menu. The *Wig & Pen* near the museum is a lively spot by night.

Getting There & Away

Truro is 246 miles from London, 26 from St Ives and 18 from Newquay.

National Express has buses to numerous destinations, sometimes requiring a change at Plymouth. There are four direct daily ser-

---

The Garden of Eden

Construction is well under way in a disused china clay pit near St Austell to create the most spectacular botanical gardens of the new millennium. The Eden Project is a scientific foundation which aims to educate visitors about the human race's dependency on plant life.

Masterminded by Tim Smit, the man responsible for the gardens at Heligan, the project will comprise a vast geodesic dome structure 1km long and 60m high. This will be heated to 35°C and filled with 10,000 species of plants from around the world. The structure is designed by Nicholas Grimshaw, architect of the Eurostar terminal at London's Waterloo Station. Trees such as teak and mahogany will have enough space to grow to their full size, although this will take up to 50 years.

Project Eden should be fully open by 2001, and although the plants may not have had time to grow much by then, the structure is sure to impress.

---

vices to London (£27.50, 6½ hours), St Ives (£3, one hour) and Penzance (£3.25, 1½ hours). First Western National (☎ 01209-719988) covers many local bus routes.

Truro is on the main rail line between London Paddington (£53, 4¾ hours) and Penzance (£6.10, 45 minutes). There's a branch line from here to Falmouth (£2.60, 20 minutes) and to St Ives (£6, change trains at St Erth).

ROSELAND PENINSULA

South-west of Truro, the Roseland peninsula gets its intriguing name not from flowers (although there are plenty of them) but from the Cornish word *ros*, meaning promontory. Villages worth visiting include **Portloe**, a wreckers' hang-out on the Coastal Path, **Veryan** which is awash with daffodils in spring, **St Mawes** with a castle (☎ 01326-270526; EH) built by Henry VIII to guard the Fal estuary, and **St Just-in-Roseland** that boasts what must be one of the most beautiful churchyards in the country, full of flowers and tumbling down to a creek with boats and wading birds.

SOUTH-WESTERN CORNWALL
Falmouth
☎ 01326 • pop 18,000

Falmouth has a refreshing real feel as tourism is not its only industry. It has an interesting castle with a youth hostel in its grounds. There are also several worthwhile boat trips from the pier. The art college here attracts students from all over the country so Falmouth feels a little more sophisticated than many other parts of the county.

The port came to prominence in the 17th century as the terminal for the Post Office Packet boats which took mail to America. The dockyard is still important for ship repairs and building.

Pendennis Castle (☎ 316594; EH), on the end of the promontory, is Cornwall's largest fort, worth visiting for the displays inside and the superb views from the ramparts. It was an operations centre in WWII. It opens 10 am to 6 pm (to 4 pm in winter). Admission costs £3.80/1.90.

The TIC (☎ 312300) is at 28 Killigrew St, by the bus station in the town centre. From the Prince of Wales pier, there are ferries to St Mawes. In summer, boat trips run to Truro (£5 return) and there are excursions to a 500-year-old Smuggler's Cottage upriver. For more information, contact Enterprise Boats (☎ 374241) or St Mawes Ferries (☎ 313201).

Places to Stay & Eat The *Pendennis Castle Youth Hostel* (☎ 311435) is at the castle, three-quarters of a mile from Falmouth train station. It opens daily mid-February to September, and daily except Sunday and Monday in October and November; a bed costs £9.80/6.75 for adults/under-18s.

There are B&Bs and small hotels lining Melvill Rd, convenient for the train station. Try *Ivanhoe* (☎ 319083) at No 7 with B&B for £22 per person or *Tudor Court Hotel* (☎ 312807) at No 55 from £21 per person.

De Wynn's in pretty cobbled Church St is a 19th-century tearoom with dainty cakes and seafood pies. Nearby *Citrus* is a bright cafe-gallery with tasty snacks, opposite the parish church. *No 33* (☎ 211914, High St) is a very popular restaurant with lots of fancy fish on the menu, but anticipate £20

a head; opposite is *Thai Orchid*. The only fix you'll get at *Smack Alley's* is late night fish and chips – it opens until at least 1 am most nights.

Good local pubs include the *Mason Arms* for St Austell ales and the *Chain Locker* for that genuine fisherman feel. *Finn M'Couls* is one of those 'Irish pubs' but certainly the most popular in town and full of art students. Nearby *Paradox* is Falmouth's nightclub and the paradox is clear – how can such a small town produce such a lively little late night spot that's both friendly and cheap?

Getting There & Away National Express has buses from Falmouth to numerous destinations, including London (£27.50, 6¼ hours). There are two-hourly buses to Penzance (one hour). For St Ives, you must change at Penzance or Truro; this also applies to Newquay (except on Sunday).

Falmouth is at the end of the branch line from Truro (£2.60, 20 minutes). In summer, you can also travel by boat to Truro (£2.50, one hour); at low tide, when boats can only get as far as Malpas, there's a bus service to Truro.

The Lizard
The Lizard peninsula is Britain's most southerly point and good walking country since much of the coastline is owned by the National Trust. The mild climate guarantees that several rare plant species flourish, and there are stretches of unusual red-green serpentine rock.

In 1901 Marconi transmitted the first transatlantic radio signals from Poldhu. The Lizard is still associated with telecommunications and the centre is dominated by the white satellite dishes of the Goonhilly Earth Station (☎ 0800 679593). Overseas visitors can rest assured that every call home they make goes through Goonhilly, the largest satellite station on earth. It opens to visitors 10 am to 5 pm daily and costs £4/2.50.

Across the north of the Lizard is the beautiful **Helford River**, lined with ancient oak trees and hidden inlets – the perfect smugglers' hideaway. Daphne du Maurier's

Frenchman's Cove can be reached on foot from the car park in **Helford** village.

On the northern bank of the river is **Trebah Garden** (☎ 01326-250448), dramatically situated in a steep ravine filled with giant rhododendrons, huge Brazilian rhubarb plants and Monterey pines. It opens 10.30 am to 5 pm. Admission costs £3.50/1.75. Near Gweek, at the western end of the river, is the **National Seal Sanctuary** (☎ 01326-221361), which treats injured marine animals and opens 9 am to 4 pm. Admission is £6.50/4.25.

Cadgwith is the quintessential Cornish fishing village, with thatched, whitewashed cottages and a small harbour. *Cadgwith Cove Inn* serves delicious crab sandwiches. Lizard Point is a 3½-mile walk along the coast path. It's about 8 miles in the opposite direction to *Coverack Youth Hostel* (☎ 01326-280687) which opens April to October and costs £9.80/6.75 for adults/under-18s.

The Lizard's transportation hub is Helston which is served by Truronian buses (☎ 01872-273453). Bus No T1 runs from Truro via Helston to the village of Lizard (£2.75/3.45 one way/return, 1½ hours); there are four buses daily, Monday to Saturday. It's just under a mile from the village to Lizard Point.

St Michael's Mount

In 1070 St Michael's Mount was granted to the same monks who built Mont St Michel off Normandy. Though not in such a dramatic location as the French model, St Michael's Mount is still impressive. High tide cuts the island off from the mainland, and the priory buildings (☎ 01736-710507; NT) rise loftily above the crags.

St Michael's Mount was an important place of medieval pilgrimage. Since 1659 the St Aubyn family has lived in the ex-priory buildings.

At low tide, you can walk across from Marazion, but at high tide in summer a ferry (☎ 01736-710265; £1/50p) lets you save your legs for the stiff climb up to the house. The best way to appreciate the house is to use the Walkman tour. The house opens 10.30 am to 5.30 pm (last admission 4.45 pm) Monday to Friday, April to Octo-

ber. Admission costs £4.40/2.20. Phone for other opening times. The *Fire Engine Inn* in Marazion, for those feeling thirsty, has great views across to the mount.

First Western National's bus No 2 passes Marazion from Penzance and continues to Falmouth.

PENZANCE
☎ 01736 ● pop 19,000
At the end of the line from London, Penzance is a pleasant enough small town in which to linger (and shop) with a curious mix of seaside holiday-makers, locals, artists and New Age hippies. Newlyn, on the western edge of Penzance, was the centre of a community of artists in the late 19th century; some of their handiwork can be inspected in **Newlyn Museum and Art Gallery**, New Rd.

Orientation & Information

The harbour spreads along Mount's Bay, with the ferry terminal to the east, the train and bus stations just to the north and the main beach to the south. The town itself spreads uphill towards the domed Lloyds Bank building with a statue of local man, Humphrey Davy, inventor of the miner's lamp, in front. Part of the bank now houses craft shops.

The TIC (☎ 362207) is in the car park by the train and bus stations. There's a laundrette opposite the train station.

Pedals (☎ 360600), on the dockside of Wharfside Shopping Centre, hires out mountain bikes for £7.50 a day, £10.50 for 24 hours, including helmets and tool kits.

Things to See & Do

Penzance has some attractive Georgian and Regency houses in the older part of town around Chapel St, where you'll also find the exuberant early 19th-century **Egyptian House**. Farther down towards the harbour is the **Maritime Museum** by Georgian House Hotel.

Trinity House National Lighthouse Museum (☎ 360077), Wharf Rd, relates the history of the lighthouses that have helped keep ships off this dangerous coast. It opens 10.30 am to 4.30 pm, March to October. Admission costs £2.50/1.50. Some examples of

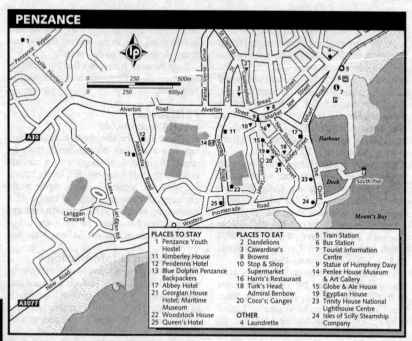

PENZANCE

PLACES TO STAY
1 Penzance Youth Hostel
11 Kimberley House
12 Pendennis Hotel
13 Blue Dolphin Penzance Backpackers
17 Abbey Hotel
21 Georgian House Hotel; Maritime Museum
22 Woodstock House
25 Queen's Hotel

PLACES TO EAT
2 Dandelions
3 Cawardine's
8 Browns
10 Stop & Shop Supermarket
16 Harris's Restaurant
18 Turk's Head; Admiral Benbow
20 Coco's; Ganges

OTHER
4 Laundrette

5 Train Station
6 Bus Station
7 Tourist Information Centre
9 Statue of Humphrey Davy
14 Penlee House Museum & Art Gallery
15 Globe & Ale House
19 Egyptian House
23 Trinity House National Lighthouse Centre
24 Isles of Scilly Steamship Company

the Newlyn school of painting are exhibited in the **Penlee House Museum & Art Gallery** (☎ 363625), on Morrab Rd. It opens daily except Sunday. Admission is £2 (free on Saturday).

Walking

The 25-mile section of the Coast Path around Land's End to/from St Ives is one of the most scenic parts of the whole route. It can be broken at the youth hostel at St Just (near Land's End), and there are plenty of other cheap farm B&Bs along the way.

Places to Stay

The **Penzance Youth Hostel** (☎ 362666, *Castle Horneck, Alverton)* is an 18th-century mansion on the outskirts of town. Bus Nos 5B, 6B or 10B run from the train station to the Pirate Inn, from where it's a 500m walk. The nightly charge is £10.85/7.40 for adults/under-18s.

Friendly *Blue Dolphin Penzance Back-*

packers (☎ 363836, *Alexandra Rd)* has 30 bunk beds for £10 each, and there are two doubles at £22. You can use the kitchen and washing machine (£3). It's all spotlessly clean – 'the bed sheets smell great', wrote one reader!

Penzance has lots of B&Bs and hotels, especially along the Promenade, Alexandra Rd and Morrab Rd. *Pendennis Hotel* (☎ 363823, *Alexandra Rd)* charges from £15 to £21 depending on the season, while *Kimberley House* (☎ 362727, *10 Morrab Rd)* has rooms from £16 to £18 per person. Friendly *Woodstock House* (☎ 369049, *29 Morrab Rd)* charges from £18 to £24.50 a head for rooms with a shower or bath.

In the older part of Penzance, *Georgian House Hotel* (☎ 365664, *20 Chapel St)* has beds from £21 with a bathroom or from £18 without. Noble *Queen's Hotel* (☎ 362371) on Western Promenade Rd charges £54 per person with sea view, £48 without.

Abbey Hotel (☎ 366906, *Abbey St)* is

owned by 1960s' supermodel Jean Shrimpton and is the top place to stay. Singles/doubles cost from £75/100.

You could rent a floor of the *Egyptian House* (see Things to See & Do earlier) from the Landmark Trust (☎ *01628 825925*). Costs range from around £123 (a four-day winter break) to £419 (a week in summer).

There's excellent farmhouse accommodation at *Ennys* (☎ *740262, St Hilary*) about 5 miles east of Penzance, near Marazion. Rooms have a bath or shower and B&B costs from £30 to £40 per person. There's a heated swimming-pool.

Places to Eat

For a splurge, head for *Harris's Restaurant* (☎ *364408*) at 46 New St, a narrow, cobbled street opposite Lloyds Bank. Smoked salmon cornets with fresh crab or venison should sate the appetite.

Dandelions, nearby at 39a Causeway Head, is a small vegetarian cafe and takeaway with fine fare. *Browns* in Bread St is similar and also has an art gallery attached.

Chapel St has several cheap places to eat as well as two well known pubs: the kitsch *Admiral Benbow* (☎ *363448*), and the *Turk's Head* (☎ *363093*) with a good reputation for its food. Across the road is *Coco's* (☎ *363540*), a flamboyant Spanish restaurant suggesting an 'if you can't beat them, join them' approach to the tourism challenge from Costa del Sol. Nearby is *Ganges*, a well-respected Indian restaurant.

A range of speciality teas and coffees are offered at *Cawardine's*, 10 Causeway Head, as well as some good value meals. A crispy bacon and melted cheese baguette or cod and chips cost around £3 to £4.

Getting There & Away

See the fares tables in the Getting Around chapter. Penzance is 281 miles from London, nine from Land's End and eight from St Ives.

There are five buses a day from Penzance to London (£27.50, five hours) and Heathrow airport, one direct bus a day to Exeter (£16, two hours) and three buses a day to Bristol via Truro and Plymouth. To St Ives (20 minutes) there are at least two services an hour. There are daily First Western National services to Land's End on bus No 1 (one hour), hourly during the week, less frequent at the weekend.

The train offers an enjoyable if pricey way to get to Penzance from London. There are five trains a day from London Paddington (£54, five hours). There are frequent trains from Penzance to St Ives between 7 am and 8 pm (£2.90, 20 minutes).

For ferries to the Scilly Isles, see Boat under Getting There & Away in the Isles of Scilly section later in the chapter.

WESTERN CORNWALL
Mousehole

Mousehole (pronounced mow-sel) is another idyllic fishing village that's well worth seeing outside the height of the season. It was once a pilchard-fishing port and tiny cottages cluster round the edge of the harbour. Like St Ives, the village attracts artists and there are several interesting craft shops.

The excellent *Ship* (☎ *01736-731234*) does good seafood and fresh fish; beds are £35/50, views are free. The *Old Coastguard Hotel* (☎ *01736-731222*) has singles from £32 and doubles for £36 per person. *Annie's Eating House* serves delicious cream teas.

Infrequent buses run the 20-minute journey to Penzance.

Minack Theatre

Probably the world's most spectacularly located open-air theatre (☎ 01736-810181), Minack perches on the edge of the cliffs overlooking the bay. It was built by Rowena Cade, an indomitable local woman who did much of the construction herself, until her death in 1983. The idea came to her when her family provided the local theatre group with an open-air venue for a production of *The Tempest*. The place was so well suited that annual performances were instituted.

There are performances at the theatre late May to late September; tickets cost £6.50/3.25. Seats are hard, so bring a cushion or hire one there. There's also an exhibition centre open 9.30 am to 5.30 pm, Easter to September (it's sometimes closed if there's a performance on). Admission is £2.50/free.

WESTERN CORNWALL

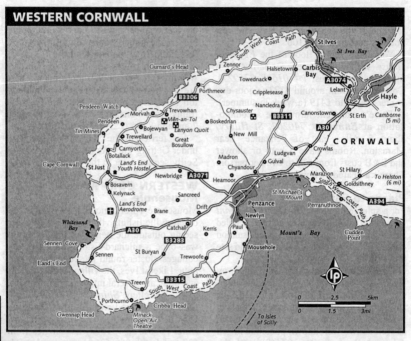

The theatre lies just below the village of Porthcurno, 3 miles from Land's End and 9 miles from Penzance. First Western National's bus No 1 from Penzance to Land's End stops at Porthcurno, from Monday to Saturday.

Land's End
☎ 01736

The coast on either side of Land's End is some of the most spectacular in Britain, but the theme park development (☎ 01736-871501) is a Thatcherite monument to the triumph of crass commerce over culture. Peter de Savary was the man who outbid the National Trust to inflict this monstrosity on Britain's most westerly point. He's long since cashed in and moved on but the damage is done. There are five separate exhibits to visit including the Air-Sea Rescue film in a mild motion cinema and Miles of Memories commemorating the various methods of transport used to get between Land's End

and John o'Groats. Admission to each costs £2.50/1.50 or there are inclusive tickets for £8. Tackiness aside, the complex does provide 250 jobs in an unemployment black spot. If you walk from Sennen Cove, less than half an hour away, you escape the car-parking charge (£3).

In summer, the place is extremely crowded, with stands selling everything from burgers to strawberry and clotted cream crêpes. To have your picture taken by the signboard listing your home town and its distance from this famous spot costs £5.

Places to Stay & Eat Despite its name, *Land's End Youth Hostel* is at St Just (see St Just later in the chapter), 5 miles from Land's End.

The comfortable *Land's End Hotel* (☎ 871844), the 'first and last hotel in England', is part of the complex and is the only place to stay right at Land's End. Staying the night gives you the chance to stroll around the headland in the evening after the crowds have gone. B&B costs from £46 per person (£10 single supplement). You can eat here too, in the *Atlantic Restaurant* or in the bar.

Just over a mile north of Land's End, Sennen Cove boasts a beautiful, sandy beach. There are good pub lunches at the *Old Success Inn* (☎ 871232), where rooms cost from £26 for the single to £39 per person in doubles with a bath. Friendly *Myrtle Cottage* (☎ 871698) serves cream teas and light lunches: B&B costs £20 per person, and there's also a fish and chip shop nearby.

Getting There & Away Land's End is 3147 miles from New York, 886 miles from John o'Groats and 9 miles from Penzance. There are open top buses (No 15) along the coast to St Ives, Sunday to Friday; and daily buses to Penzance.

Westward Airways (☎ 788771) offers flights over Land's End in Cessnas; a seven-minute hop costs £19/17.

St Just

Although there are no specific sights in remote St Just, it makes a good base for walks west to Cape Cornwall or south along the Coast Path to Land's End.

In Victorian times St Just was a centre for local tin and copper mining. **Geevor Tin Mine** (☎ 01736-788662), at Pendeen, north of St Just, finally closed in 1990 and now opens to visitors 10.30 am to 5 pm daily except Saturday. Admission costs £5/2.50.

Alongside the abandoned engine houses from old tin and copper mines, the area between St Just and St Ives is littered with standing stones and other mysterious ancient remains. If prehistory's your thing, it's worth tracking down **Lanyon Quoit**, the **Mên-an-Tol** and **Chysauster Iron Age Village**.

Land's End St Just Youth Hostel (☎ 01736-788437) is about half a mile south of the village at Letcha Vean. It opens daily April to October; phone for details of opening times the rest of the year. The nightly charge is £9.80/6.75 for adults/under-18s. You can also stay at the independent *White-sands Lodge* (☎ 01736-871776) backpackers

End to End Records

The craze for covering the route between the two extremities of Britain in as short a time as possible was started in 1875 by an American, Eliuh Burritt, who walked from John o'Groats to Land's End in 'several weeks'. Times are now measured a little more accurately and the walking record for the 886¾ miles is currently held by Malcolm Barnish, who did it in 12 days, three hours and 45 minutes. The cycling record is held by Andy Wilkinson, who in 1990 covered an 847-mile route in a mere one day, 21 hours, two minutes and 19 seconds.

Recently, people have been devising ever more offbeat ways of doing the End to End. It's been done with a wheelbarrow in 30 days, in a battery-powered Sinclair C5 in 80 hours, on a tricycle in 5½ days and on roller skates in 9½ days. In 1990, it was run in 26 days and seven hours by Arvind Pandya – no great record in itself, apart from the fact that he was running backwards!

hostel in Sennen village; dorm beds cost £10 (£4 for breakfast). There's also a double for £29 excluding breakfast.

At *Kelynack Caravan & Camping Park* (☎ 01736-787633), a mile south of St Just, a bed in the bunk barn costs £6, camping is £3 per person.

At Botallack, there's comfortable farmhouse accommodation at *Manor Farm* (☎ 01736-788525). B&B costs for £23 per person.

Zennor

There's a superb four-hour walk along the coast path from St Ives to the little village of Zennor, where DH Lawrence wrote part of *Women in Love*. The interesting church has a mermaid carved on one of its bench ends, and there's a small museum.

There are beds for £10 at *Old Chapel Backpackers Hostel* (☎ 01736-798307), a full breakfast costs £4, continental £2.50. *Tinners Arms* serves good food and cream teas.

At least four buses a day run to Zennor from St Ives.

ST IVES

☎ 01736 • pop 9500

St Ives is the ideal to which other seaside towns can only aspire. The omnipresent sea, the extraordinary brightness of the light, the harbour, the beautiful sandy beaches, the narrow alleyways, steep slopes and hidden corners are all captivating. Artists have been coming here since Turner visited in 1811, and in 1993 a branch of London's Tate Gallery opened here. These days countless galleries and craft shops line its narrow streets.

Unfortunately in summer St Ives is un-believably crowded – avoid July and August weekends.

Orientation

The area above St Ives' harbour is very built up and merges into Carbis Bay. Fore St, the main shopping street, is set back from the wharf and crammed with eating places. The north-facing section of the town, overlooking Porthmeor Beach, comprises the Tate Gallery and many guesthouses. The train station is by Porthminster Beach, with the bus station nearby, up Station Hill.

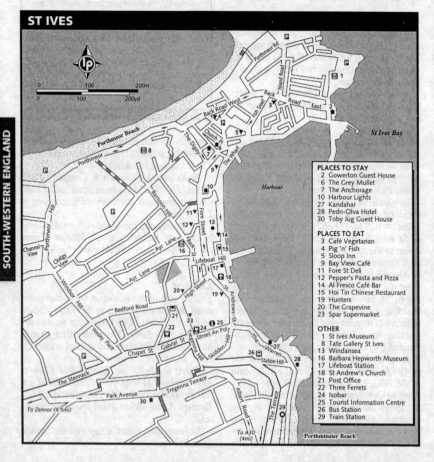

ST IVES

St Ives Bay

Porthmeor Beach

Harbour

Porthminster Beach

PLACES TO STAY
2 Gowerton Guest House
6 The Grey Mullet
7 The Anchorage
10 Harbour Lights
27 Kandahar
28 Pedn-Olva Hotel
30 Toby Jug Guest House

PLACES TO EAT
3 Café Vegetarian
4 Pig 'n' Fish
5 Sloop Inn
9 Bay View Café
11 Fore St Deli
12 Pepper's Pasta and Pizza
14 Al Fresco Café Bar
15 Hoi Tin Chinese Restaurant
19 Hunters
20 The Grapevine
23 Spar Supermarket

OTHER
1 St Ives Museum
8 Tate Gallery St Ives
13 Windansea
16 Barbara Hepworth Museum
17 Lifeboat Station
18 St Andrew's Church
21 Post Office
22 Three Ferrets
24 Isobar
25 Tourist Information Centre
26 Bus Station
29 Train Station

To Zennor (4.5mi)
To A30 (4mi)

Information
The TIC (☎ 796297) is in the Guildhall in Street-an-Pol.

In summer, a Park & Ride service operates from the Park Avenue car park above the town. Windansea (☎ 794830) on Fore St, rents wet suits and seven-foot boards (£5 per day).

Tate St Ives
Opened in 1993 in a £3 million building designed by Evans and Shalev (architects of the award-winning Truro Law Courts), the Tate is a showcase for the St Ives school of art. The impressive building (☎ 796226) replaced an old gasworks and has wide central windows framing the surfing scene on Porthmeor Beach below. The collection has annual exhibitions of modern art that is, in some way, associated to Cornwall.

The gallery opens 10.30 am to 5.30 pm Tuesday to Sunday year round, daily in July and August. Admission costs £3.95; a £6.50 ticket includes admission to the Barbara Hepworth Museum & Sculpture Garden. The cafe on the roof is almost as popular as the gallery itself.

Barbara Hepworth Museum & Sculpture Garden
Barbara Hepworth was one of the 20th-century's greatest sculptors. In the 1930s, with Henry Moore and Ben Nicholson (her then husband), she was part of the leading group of artists with an interest in abstraction. While Moore's sculpture remains close to the human form, Hepworth avoided representational works.

She moved to Cornwall in 1939 and lived here from 1949 until her death in a fire in 1975. The beautiful garden forms a perfect backdrop for some of her larger works. The museum (☎ 796226) is on Ayr Lane, near the Tate, and opens the same times with the same charges.

Leach Pottery
Bernard Leach travelled to Japan in 1909 to teach etching, but soon discovered a talent for pottery. When he returned in 1920 his Japanese-inspired work had a profound influence on British ceramics. He died in 1979 but the pottery he established is still used by several craftspeople, (including his wife, Janet Leach, until her death in 1997). The showroom (☎ 796398) opens 10 am to 5 pm on weekdays and on Saturday in summer. It's along the road to Zennor, on the outskirts of St Ives.

Beaches
There are several excellent, clean beaches in the area. **Porthmeor** is the surfing beach to the north of the town, below the Tate. Just east is the tiny, sandy cove of **Porth-gwidden**, with a car park nearby.

There are sandy areas in the sheltered harbour, but most families head south to **Porthminster**, which has half a mile of sand and a convenient car park. **Carbis Bay**, to the south-west, is also good for children. **Porthkidney Sands**, the next beach along, is only safe for swimming between the flags. It's dangerous to swim in the Hayle estuary.

Places to Stay
The *St Ives International Backpackers* (☎ 799444, *Lower Stennack*) is in a converted chapel with a range of excellent facilities and beds from £12 a night. The nearest youth hostel is in Zennor. There's no camp site by the beach, but *Ayr Holiday Park* (☎ 795855) is only half a mile above the town in Higher Ayr. It costs £12.30 for a tent.

The main road into St Ives from Penzance, above Carbis Bay, is lined with B&Bs in the £15 to £18 bracket, but the closer you are to the town centre the better.

Toby Jug Guest House (☎ 794250), convenient for the bus station at 1 Park Ave, is good value with B&B for £15 per person. There are 10 rooms, each with a toby jug as a teapot.

On Sea View Place, in an excellent location right by the sea, is *Gowerton* (☎ 796805) at No 6, for around £17 per person. There's B&B at the *Sloop Inn* (☎ 796584) by the harbour, although this location could be noisy in summer. B&B costs from £34 per person.

The Grey Mullet (☎ 796635, *2 Bunkers Hill*) is an excellent guesthouse in the old part of town, close to the harbour. Rooms cost from £20 to £24 per person, with a bath. Opposite is an attractive cottage called *The Anchorage* (☎ 797135) with similar B&B prices.

Harbour Lights (☎ 795525, *Court Cocking*) is right in the centre. B&B costs around £21 per person in summer.

Kandahar (☎ 796183, 11 The Warren) is right on the rocks by the water. It charges £21 to £28 per person It's ideally located for the bus and train stations.

Nearby is the more upmarket *Pedn-Olva Hotel* (☎ 796222, *Porthminster Beach*) which has a similar waterside location. Beds cost from £45 for B&B to £60 half board and there's a small swimming pool and sun deck.

To the south, overlooking Porthminster Beach, is the comfortable *Longships Hotel* (☎ 798180, *Talland Rd*) where rooms with sea views and bathrooms cost from £27 per person.

Places to Eat

The top place to eat is the *Pig'n'Fish* (☎ 794204, *Norway Lane*) which is renowned for its seafood. Main dishes range from about £11 to £17, with turbot, monkfish, bass, red mullet and mussels usually featuring on the menu.

Fish and chips is an obvious choice and a favourite with local seagulls who have learnt to divebomb anyone eating outdoors. It's fun to watch – less fun if it's your grub they're making off with.

Café Vegetarian is a small restaurant just off Back Rd East with an impressive array of wholesome dishes. The *Fore St Deli* is a useful stop for self caterers.

For a pizza, *Pepper's Pasta and Pizza* just off Fore St is good. *Hunters* (☎ 797074, *St Andrews St*) is a seafood and game restaurant. Nearby is *Wilbur's* (☎ 796663) serving lobster and local fish. *The Grapevine* (☎ 794030) on the nearby High St is an informal bistro with speciality seafood and a basement bar.

Best of the pubs is the 14th-century *Sloop Inn* next to the harbour where the bar is hung with paintings by local artists. Its seafood is very popular; fresh fish (cod,

sole, plaice) costs £6 to £9. There are several other places to eat along the Wharf, including *Hoi Tin Chinese Restaurant* and the *Bay View Café*.

Places to be seen in St Ives include the Italian *Alfresco Café Bar* (☎ 793737) on the Wharf, offering a Mediterranean-style menu, and *Isobar* on Tregenna Hill. Isobar is a cafe-bar with a nightclub open until 1 am. This is about as happening as St Ives gets. For a no nonsense local pub, try the *Three Ferrets* where you can even bring along your own food.

Getting There & Away

See the fares tables in the Getting Around chapter. St Ives is 277 miles from London and eight from Penzance. National Express has three buses a day to London (£27.50, 7½ hours). There are also buses to Newquay (1¼ hours), Truro (one hour) and Plymouth (three hours). For Exeter, change at Plymouth.

There's a bus service from St Ives to Land's End via Zennor, St Just-in-Penwith and Sennen Cove every day in summer, open top if the weather allows. There are three buses a day and an Explorer ticket allowing a day's travel on the route costs £6/3.50. In winter, you must go via Penzance.

St Ives is easily accessible by train from Penzance and London via St Erth.

NEWQUAY

☎ 01637 • pop 14,000

The original Costa del Cornwall, this brash and brazen town was drawing them in long before the British learnt how to say Torremolinos. Today it is a confused, if most enjoyable blend of surf town, family beach resort and testosterone-driven lad hell. Until they moved to Seignosse in France in 1998, the World Surfing Championships were held here each summer.

Little that predates the 19th century survives in Newquay, but on the cliff north of Towan Beach stands the whitewashed Huer's House, where a watch was kept for approaching pilchard shoals. Every Cornish fishing village had a watchtower like this and the netting operation was directed by the huer. Until they were fished out early in

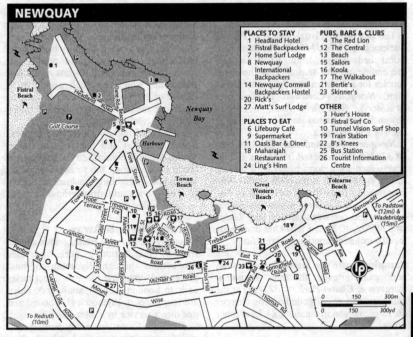

NEWQUAY

PLACES TO STAY
1 Headland Hotel
2 Fistral Backpackers
7 Home Surf Lodge
8 Newquay International Backpackers
14 Newquay Cornwall Backpackers Hostel
20 Rick's
27 Matt's Surf Lodge

PLACES TO EAT
6 Lifebuoy Café
9 Supermarket
11 Oasis Bar & Diner
18 Maharajah Restaurant
24 Ling's Hinn

PUBS, BARS & CLUBS
4 The Red Lion
12 The Central
13 Beach
15 Sailors
16 Koola
17 The Walkabout
21 Bertie's
23 Skinner's

OTHER
3 Huer's House
5 Fistral Surf Co
10 Tunnel Vision Surf Shop
19 Train Station
22 B's Knees
25 Bus Station
26 Tourist Information Centre

SOUTH-WESTERN ENGLAND

the 20th century, these shoals were enormous – one St Ives catch of 1868 netted a record 16.5 million fish.

Orientation & Information

The TIC (☎ 871345) is on Marcus Hill near the bus station in the town centre.

The surf shops all hire fibreglass boards and wet suits for around £5 each per day. Try Fistral Surf Co on Beacon Rd, or Tunnel Vision Surf Shop opposite the Somerfield supermarket on Alma Place. If you don't know how to surf, contact Offshore Surfing (☎ 877083), on Tolcarne Beach, for an all-inclusive, half-day beginner's lesson (around £20) or Winter Brothers' Surf School (☎ 879696), also £20 a time. The Sunset Surf Shop (☎ 877624) at 106 Fore St also runs in-shop 'soft' tuition.

If you don't have a tattoo, at least get yourself a temporary one before hitting the beach. Cut Snake on Fore St have a range and they'll last for up to four weeks.

Cyber Surf, 2 Broad St, has Internet access. There's a laundrette on Beach Rd.

Beaches

Fistral Beach, to the west of the town round Towan Head, is the most famous British surfing beach. There are fast hollow waves, particularly at low tide, and good tubing sections when there's a south-easterly wind.

Watergate Bay is a 2-mile-long sandy beach on the eastern side of Newquay Bay. At low tide it's a good place to learn to surf. A mile south of Newquay, **Crantock** is a small north-west-facing sheltered beach, where the waves are best at mid to high tide.

Places to Stay

Hostels Several independent hostels cater for surfers in particular. Newcomer *Home Surf Lodge* (☎ 873387, 18 Tower Rd, e home.surflodge@btinternet.com) is a great place to stay. Facilities include free

Internet access and beds start from £10 so book ahead during summer.

The nearest to Fistral Beach is *Fistral Backpackers* (☎ 873146, *18 Headland Rd*). Dorm beds range from £5.50 to £10 (depending on the season) and there are doubles for £18. In an excellent central position, *Newquay Cornwall Backpackers* (☎ 874668, *Beachfield Ave*), overlooks Towan Beach and has dorm beds for £7 a night or £39 per week.

Newquay International Backpackers (☎ 879366, *69 Tower Rd*) charges £12 in peak season for a dorm bed, £7 off season. *Rick's* (☎ 851143, *8 Springfield Rd*) only does weekly rents in summer (£70 in August). Outside the peak season it's £6 per night or £30 per week. *Matt's Surf Lodge* (☎ 874651, *110 Mount Wise*) has dorm beds for £10 including continental breakfast.

Camping There are several large caravan parks/camp sites in the area. *Trenance Caravan & Chalet Park* (☎ 873447) at the southern end of Edgcumbe Ave charges £6.75 per person in summer, £4.75 at other times.

B&Bs & Hotels Newquay is so crammed with cheap B&Bs that it makes little sense to recommend some above others. Definitely book ahead in July and August. Trebarwith Crescent, Mount Wise, Dane Rd, Tower Rd, Cliff Rd and Narrowcliffe are all packed with places to stay and the TIC has full details.

The huge *Headland Hotel* (☎ 872211) is the best located of Newquay's large hotels. As the name suggests it's out on the headland above Fistral Beach. Rooms cost £76 per person during peak season.

Places to Eat

The top Indian place is *Maharajah* (☎ 877377, *39 Cliff Rd*) and the most popular Chinese is *Ling's Hinn* (☎ 877439, *Cliff Rd*). At the junction of Fore St and Beacon Rd, *Lifebuoy Café* does good cheap breakfasts and meals. *Oasis Bar & Diner*, Fore St, does all-day breakfasts and burgers.

Entertainment

Newquay is crammed with local pubs and dodgy clubs making it a great place for a night out. *The Central* is a busy bar on Central Square. The *Red Lion* pub is *the* surfers' hang out: catch re-runs of the *Big Wednesday* and see which nightclub is flavour of the month. *Skinner's* is a pub to check out some local Cornish beers rather than the faceless imports.

Established nightclubs include *Sailors*, *Bertie's*, *Beach* and the slightly cooler *Koola*. All have nominal cover charges and cheap drinks during the week. Newcomer, *Walkabout* is grabbing business as there's live music and useful drink promotions, but no cover charge.

Getting There & Away

Newquay is 252 miles from London and 32 from St Ives. National Express provides connections through Plymouth to most places in Britain and has two direct buses daily to London (£27.50, six hours). There are four buses to Plymouth (1¼ hours) and one direct service to Exeter.

There are four trains a day between Par and Newquay on the main London to Penzance line.

NORTHERN CORNWALL

Some of Britain's best beaches face the Atlantic along the North Cornwall coast but getting around this area without your own transport can be tricky. From Newquay, the coastal road passes **Bedruthan Steps**, a series of rock stacks along a sandy beach. There's a NT teashop here. At **Constantine Bay**, there's a wide, sandy beach, good for surfing.

Padstow

☎ 01841 • pop 2300

On the Camel River estuary, Padstow is an attractive fishing village best known for its **May Day Hobby Horse**, a man dressed up in an enormous tent-like dress and mask. As he dances through the streets, he is taunted by the local women; if he catches one, he pulls her under the tent, and pinches her – to ensure future motherhood, of course.

The poet John Betjeman is buried at St Enodoc Church, across the water and north of Rock. Above the village is **Prideaux Place** (☎ 532411), built in 1592 by the Prideaux-Brune family. It opens 1.30 to 5 pm Sunday to Thursday, Easter to September. Admission costs £4/1.50.

The TIC (☎ 533449) is on the North Quay.

Padstow has several restaurants worth a gastronomic detour, but most famous is television chef Rick Stein's *Seafood Restaurant* (☎ 532485) on the harbour front which serves all manner of fish dishes; expect to pay at least £28 a head. When it's closed on Sunday you can eat bistro-style at 4 New St, *St Petroc's House* (same telephone number). Rick Stein is now so well known in Britain that you'll need to book months in advance.

Tintagel & Boscastle
☎ 01840 • pop 1750

Tintagel has sold its soul to tourism and adopted King Arthur and the Knights of the Round Table to keep the punters coming. That said, even the summer crowds and the grossly commercialised village can't entirely destroy the surf-battered grandeur of Tintagel Head. The scanty ruins are not King Arthur's castle, since they mainly date from the 13th century, but there's no reason to disbelieve the theory that he was born here in the late 5th century. The ruins (☎ 770328; EH) open 10 am to 7 pm, April to October (to 4 pm in winter). Admission costs £2.90/1.50. There are exhilarating walks along the cliffs.

Back in the village, **Tintagel Old Post Office** (☎ 770024; NT) is a higgledy-piggledy 14th-century house turned post office. It opens 11 am to 5.30 pm, April to October. Admission costs £2.20/1.10.

A couple of miles along the coast, **Boscastle** can also get overcrowded but is still absurdly picturesque. In particular, hunt out Minster church in a wonderful wooded valley. There's a well-stocked visitors centre in the car park (☎ 250010).

Places to Stay In a spectacular setting on the Coast Path, *Tintagel Youth Hostel* (☎ 770334) is three-quarters of a mile west of the village. It opens daily April to September; beds cost £9.80/6.75 for adults/under-18s. Alternatively, *Boscastle Harbour Youth Hostel* (☎ 250287) opens mid-May to mid-September (phone for details of opening times the rest of the year) for the same price. It's perfectly positioned right on the edge of the harbour.

The *Cornishman Inn* (☎ 770238) in the centre of Tintagel charges from £25 a head in rooms with bathroom. Or if it's kitsch you crave, try *King Arthur's Castle Hotel* (☎ 770202), overlooking Tintagel head, a pseudo-castle with rooms B&B from £39 per person.

With a car, you might prefer to follow the signs to Trebarwith to stay in the *Old Mill-floor* (☎ 770234), a B&B in a delightful setting charging from £18 per person. Or there's *Sunnyside* (☎ 250453) right beside Boscastle harbour, with beds from £17 without bath, £21 with.

Getting There & Away First Western National's bus No 122 runs from Wadebridge, and the X4 comes from Bude. There are occasional buses from Plymouth.

Bodmin Moor

Cornwall's 'roof' is a high heath pock-marked with bogs and with giant tors like those on Dartmoor rising above the wild landscape – Brown Willy (419m) and Rough Tor (400m) are the highest.

The A30 cuts across the centre of the moor from **Launceston**, which has a castle perched above it like the cherry on a cake (☎ 01566-772365; EH) and a granite church completely covered in carvings. At **Bolventor** is *Jamaica Inn* (☎ 01566-86250), made famous by Daphne du Maurier's novel of the same name. Stop for a drink on a misty winter's night and the place still feels atmospheric. In summer, it's full of day-trippers queuing to view the author's desk and the bizarre Mr Potter's **Museum of Curiosity**, a collection of stuffed kittens and rabbits in the best of Victorian bad taste. Bolventor is a good base for walks on Bodmin. About a mile to the south is **Dozmary Pool**, said to have been where Arthur's

SOUTH-WESTERN ENGLAND

The Daphne du Maurier Trail

Daphne du Maurier, author of a number of best-selling thriller romances set in Cornwall, has probably done more to publicise the county than anyone else. For many years she lived on the Fowey estuary, originally in Ferryside (a house in Bodinnick) and later in Menabilly.

Her first big success was *Jamaica Inn*, an entertaining tale of a smuggling ring based at the famous inn. The idea for the story is said to have come when she and a friend got lost in the mists of Bodmin Moor, eventually stumbling upon the inn. The local vicar entertained them with gripping yarns of Cornish smugglers. Jamaica Inn has a small display about the author. The vicar was from nearby Altarnun, where the church receives a steady flow of du Maurier fans.

The author's next book was *Rebecca*, written in 1938. Manderley, the house in the book, was based on Menabilly, where the author lived – it's not open to the public. *Frenchman's Creek* was set around the inlet of the same name on the Helford River. Lanhydrock House and Falmouth's Pendennis Castle both feature in *The King's General*.

The West Country Tourist Board produces a useful *Daphne du Maurier in Cornwall* leaflet. The Daphne du Maurier Festival of Arts & Literature (☎ 01726-74324) takes place in May.

sword, Excalibur, was thrown after his death. It's a 4-mile walk north of Jamaica Inn to Brown Willy.

Bude

☎ 01288 • pop 2700

Five miles from Devon, Bude is another resort that attracts both families and surfers. Crooklets Beach is the main surfing area, just north of the town. Nearby Sandymouth is good for beginners, and Duckpool is also popular. Summerleaze Beach, in the centre of Bude, is a family beach.

Bude TIC (☎ 354240) on The Crescent has lists of B&Bs.

Bude is well served by buses, including a daily National Express coach to London (£31, 6½ hours).

ISLES OF SCILLY

☎ 01720 • pop 2000

Twenty-eight miles south-west of Land's End, the Scilly Isles comprise a group of 140 rocky islands with an extremely mild climate caused by the warm Gulf Stream that allows plants and trees that grow nowhere else in Britain to flourish. One of the main objectives for visitors is the subtropical garden at Tresco Abbey. Growing flowers for the mainland is an important industry.

St Mary's, Tresco, St Martin's, St Agnes and Bryher are inhabited. St Mary's is the largest (3 miles by two) and has most of the population. Most of the islands have white, sandy beaches and gin-clear water that attracts divers. The pace of life is slow and gentle – forget any idea of Newquay nightlife.

Information

The Isles of Scilly Tourist Board (☎ 422536) is in the Wesleyan Chapel, St Mary's. The *Standard Guidebook, Isles of Scilly* is the best in-depth guide to the isles.

Accommodation should be booked in advance, particularly in summer, and tends to be more expensive than on the mainland. Many places close between November and March.

All the islands except Tresco have camp sites that charge from £3 to £6 per person. The TIC can mail an accommodation list.

Every Friday evening and on some Wednesdays in summer you can watch gig racing – traditional six-oar boats (some over 100 years old) originally used to race out to wrecked ships.

St Mary's

The capital is Hugh Town, on an isthmus that separates the Garrison area from the main part of the town, where boats from the mainland dock and it feels like a Britain of a bygone era. The TIC and most of the places to stay are here.

There are several enjoyable walks on St Mary's. The hour-long Garrison Walk offers good views of the other islands and you pass Star Castle, once an Elizabethan fort, now a hotel. There's a two-hour walk to Peninnis Head, where numerous ships have been wrecked, and a three-hour Telegraph Walk via assorted ancient historical sites and burial chambers. The TIC has details.

The *camp site* (☎ 422670) is at Garrison Farm and charges £6 per person. Cheaper B&Bs in Hugh Town include *Lyonnesse Guest House* (☎ 422458), which costs £25 for B&B or £36 for half board, and *The Wheelhouse* (☎ 422719) from £42 for half board.

Atlantic Hotel (☎ 422417) is right by the water in Hugh Town, and has a good restaurant. It costs £82.50 per person with sea view or £70 without, including B&B and dinner.

The top place to stay on St Mary's is *Star Castle Hotel* (☎ 422317). Luxuries include a heated swimming pool and four-poster beds. Rooms are from £72 to £105 per person for B&B and dinner.

Tresco

The second largest island is best known for the Abbey Garden, laid out in 1834 on the site of a 10th-century Benedictine abbey. There are more than 5000 subtropical plants and a display of figureheads from the many ships that have been wrecked off these islands.

There's no camp site or budget accommodation on the island, just the *New Inn* (☎ 422844), which charges £80 to £92 per person including dinner, and the upmarket *Island Hotel* (☎ 422883), from £90 to £130 per person in the low season, £120 to £230 in summer. There's a heated swimming-pool.

Bryher

The smallest of the inhabited islands is wild and rugged; Hell Bay in an Atlantic gale is a powerful sight. There are good views over the islands from the top of Watch Hill. From

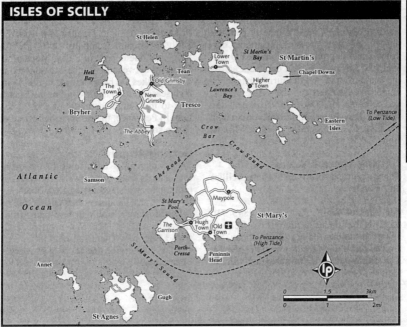

ISLES OF SCILLY

the quay, occasional boats cross to deserted Samson Island.

There's a *camp site* (☎ *422886)* in Jenford charging £5 per night, and very comfortable accommodation at *Hell Bay Hotel* (☎ *422947)* from £59 to £94 per person including dinner.

St Martin's

Known for its beautiful beaches, St Martin's is the most northerly island. There's cliff scenery along the northern shore, a good walk on Chapel Downs up to the Day Mark and long stretches of sand on both north and south coasts.

The *camp site* (☎ *422888)* is near Lawrence's Bay. B&Bs on the island include *Polreath* (☎ *422046)*, which has rooms from £28 to £39.50 per person, dinner, bed and breakfast. The only hotel is the posh *St Martin's on the Isle* (☎ *422092)* on Tean Sound where half-board costs from £85 to £135 per person. It has an excellent seafood restaurant.

St Agnes

A disused lighthouse overlooks the bulb fields of Britain's most southerly community. To the west are striking granite outcrops, including one that resembles Queen Victoria. At low tide, you can walk across the sand to the neighbouring island of Gugh. The islanders call themselves Turks.

The *camp site* (☎ *422360)* is near the beach at Troy Town Farm. B&B and evening meals at *Covean Cottage* (☎ *422620)* cost from £36.50 to £39.50 per person.

Getting There & Away

There's no transport to or from the Scillies on a Sunday.

Air Isles of Scilly Skybus (☎ 0845 710 5555) is the islands' airline. It has frequent flights in summer (daily except Sunday) between Land's End aerodrome and St Mary's. The flight takes 15 minutes and for an adult/child costs £49/25 one way (£36/18 stand-by), £57/28 for a day return and £68/34 for a short break of one to three nights. There's free parking at Land's End aerodrome, or a free shuttle bus from Penzance train station (book in advance). There are flights from Exeter and Newquay (both Monday to Saturday), Plymouth (Monday, Wednesday and Friday), Bristol (Monday, Tuesday, Thursday and Friday) and Southampton (Monday and Friday).

Scotia Helicopter Services (☎ 01736-363871) operates flights, Monday to Saturday, year round, from Penzance heliport. The journey takes 20 minutes and costs £47/23.50 in each direction, £62/31 for a day return, £69/34.50 for a five-day excursion and £62/31 for a late saver return for a one- to three-night stay (you can book only one day in advance). There are also flights to Tresco (for the gardens), Monday to Saturday, from Penzance; prices are the same as those for St Mary's. It costs £2 per day to leave your car at the heliport and there's a bus link to Penzance train station.

Boat From April to October, the Isles of Scilly Steamship Company (☎ 0845 710 5555) has one departure a day, Monday to Saturday, between Penzance and St Mary's. The trip takes 2¾ hours and costs £72/36 in high season for an adult/child return ticket. One to three-night breaks cost £52/26 return. In Penzance, the reservations office is by the south pier.

Getting Around

There are regular departures to the other four islands from St Mary's harbour. A return trip to any island costs £5.60. Boat trips to see the seals and sea birds cost £5.60.

On St Mary's, you can hire bikes from Buccabu Hire (☎ 422289), near the TIC, from £5 per day. There's also an infrequent circular bus service and tours of St Mary's by minibus.

Central England

The heart of England covers a vast swathe of land that includes some of the highs and lows of England. Many of the areas around the M1 corridor can look pretty miserable on a wet and windy day, but some of the region's liveliest cities, such as Nottingham, Leicester, Coventry and Birmingham, are here. What it lacks in prettiness, it makes up for in personality, and there is a real atmosphere to the East Midlands that isn't always found in the tourist meccas of the Cotswolds and the Peak District.

To the south-west, Oxford remains extremely beautiful and a gateway to the Cotswolds, which embody the popular image of the English countryside. The prettiness can seem artificial and few of the villages are strangers to mass tourism, but there will be moments when you'll be transfixed by the combination of golden stone, flower-draped cottages, church spires, towering chestnuts and oaks, rolling hills and emerald green fields.

The Cotswolds Way follows the western escarpment overlooking the Bristol Channel for 100 miles from Chipping Campden to Bath, but it's quite feasible to tackle a smaller section.

In the south-west the Bristol Channel and the wide Severn Valley form a natural border with agricultural Herefordshire, Worcestershire and the region known as the Welsh Marches. This is great touring country as it boasts the beauty without the numbers.

The southern Midlands is home to some of England's most popular tourist sites including Blenheim Palace, Warwick Castle and Stratford-upon-Avon, a place of pilgrimage for Shakespeare lovers from around the world.

In contrast, the northern Midlands is often dismissed as England's industrial backyard. The dense motorway network gives forewarning of the claustrophobic development and the continuing economic importance of the region, despite the decline of some traditional industries. In a

Highlights

- Seeing the honey-stone villages of the Cotswolds in spring

- Picking a favourite Oxford college

- Visiting Warwick Castle and Chatsworth

- Admiring Gloucester Cathedral and Tewkesbury Abbey

- Delving into the Peak District caverns

- Checking out the pubs and clubs of Nottingham

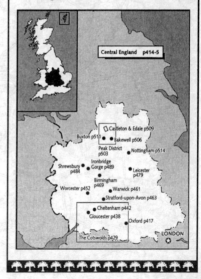

very real sense this is England's working-class heartland, with a wide gap in living standards between these northern cities and those south of Birmingham.

There are, nonetheless, some places well worth visiting, including attractive Shrewsbury and the fascinating Ironbridge Gorge Museum. Shropshire offers some beautiful, little-visited countryside, while in the centre there's the wonderful Peak District National Park, with villages every bit the equal of the

CENTRAL ENGLAND

413

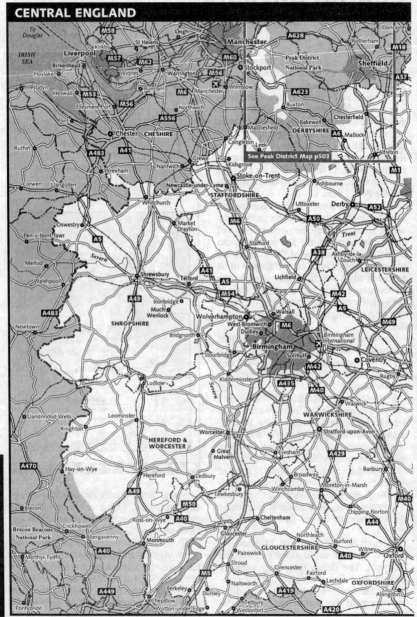

CENTRAL ENGLAND

See Peak District Map p503

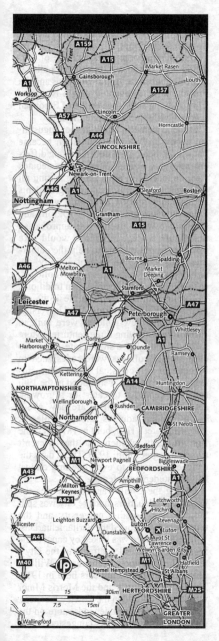

Cotswolds and some of the wildest countryside in England. Those keen on fine bone china will also want to brave the wastes of Stoke-on-Trent in search of the big-name producers. And Nottingham continues to win friends with some of the best nightlife between London and Manchester.

Oxfordshire

Oxfordshire is famous worldwide for the university town of Oxford, a mecca for tourists who come to admire the lovely honey-coloured colleges and riverside views.

The surrounding countryside has the gentle, unspectacular charm of middle England. Major features are the River Thames, which flows through the centre and south of the county; the chalk Chilterns, a wooded ridge running across the south-eastern corner of the county; and the limestone Cotswolds, extending from the west across Gloucestershire.

As well as the colleges, museums and gardens of Britain's oldest university, no one should miss Blenheim Palace, the spectacular birthplace of Sir Winston Churchill. There are good walks in the hills, and many pretty villages whose character stems from the use of local building materials.

WALKING & CYCLING ROUTES

Oxfordshire is crossed by three long-distance paths. The ancient track known as the Ridgeway runs along the county's southern border. If you want to walk it look out for either the *Ridgeway National Trail Information & Accommodation* leaflet or for the Countryside Commission official guide.

The Oxfordshire Way is a 65-mile waymarked trail connecting the Cotswolds with the Chilterns and runs from Bourton-on-the-Water to Henley-on-Thames. The leaflet *Oxfordshire Way* divides the route into 16 walks of between 2 and 8 miles in length.

The Thames Path follows the river from its mouth near the Thames Barrier in London, 175 miles west across the centre of Oxfordshire to its source at the Thames Head in Gloucestershire. Look out for the *Thames Path National Trail Information &*

Accommodation leaflet or the Countryside Commission official guide.

Oxfordshire is also good cycling country. There are few extreme gradients and Oxford offers cheap bike hire. The *Oxfordshire Cycleway* map covers Woodstock, Burford and Henley.

GETTING AROUND

Oxfordshire has a reasonable rail network, with Oxford and Banbury the main stations. There are services on the Cotswolds and Malvern line between London Paddington and Hereford, and between London Euston and Birmingham. Call National Rail Enquiries on ☎ 0845 748 4950 for details.

Oxford is the hub of a fairly comprehensive bus service. Tourist Information Centres (TICs) stock a useful free *Bus & Rail Map* showing routes and giving contact numbers for each operator. The main companies are Stagecoach (☎ 01865-772250) and Oxford Bus Company (☎ 01865-785400).

OXFORD

☎ 01865 • pop 115,000

The poet Matthew Arnold described Oxford as 'that sweet city with her dreaming spires', a phrase that still has much resonance today – provided the open-top tourist buses that ply the city's streets aren't constantly obscuring the view.

For some, Oxford University is synonymous with academic excellence, for others it's an elitist club whose members unfairly dominate many aspects of British life to the detriment of unmanufactured talent. That sense of elitism is taking on new life as the colleges, sinking under the weight of mass tourism, increasingly close themselves off from would-be sightseers.

These days the dreaming spires coexist with a flourishing commercial city that has some typical Midlands social problems. But for visitors the superb architecture and unique atmosphere of the colleges, courtyards and gardens remain major drawcards.

History

Oxford is strategically located at the point where the River Cherwell meets the Thames.

Already an important town in Saxon times, it was fortified by Alfred the Great in the battle against the Danes.

Oxford's importance as a centre of academia grew out of a 12th-century political quarrel between the Anglo-Normans and the French, which prevented Anglo-Normans from studying at the then centre of European scholastic life, the Sorbonne in Paris.

Students came to study at the Augustinian abbey in Oxford, which soon became known for theological debate among different religious orders. When such debates were conducted in an academic setting all was well, but discussions among students occasionally spilled over into violence. Eventually the universities at Oxford and Cambridge were given royal approval so that future student rebellions would take place far from London. To help the authorities keep an eye on student activity, the university was broken up into colleges, each of which developed its own traditions.

The first colleges, built in the 13th century, were Balliol, Merton and University. At least three new colleges were built in each of the following three centuries. More followed, though at a slower rate, and some of the older colleges were redesigned in baroque or neo-classical style. New colleges, such as Keble, were added in the 19th and 20th centuries to cater for a growing student population. There are now about 14,500 undergraduates and 36 colleges. Lady Margaret's Hall, built in 1878, was the first to admit women but they weren't awarded degrees until 1920. These days the colleges are open to everyone and almost half the students are female.

During the Civil War, Oxford was the Royalist headquarters, and the city was split between the Royalist university and the town, which supported the Parliamentarians.

In 1790 Oxford was linked by canal to the Midlands' industrial centres, but the city's real industrial boom came when William Morris began producing cars here in 1912. The Bullnose Morris and the Morris Minor were both produced in the Cowley factories.·

These days Oxford depends more on the service industries, but its congested centre

The green, green grass of the Peak District National Park

A bit of a balancing act: punting on the River Cherwell, Oxford

A frosty church of England

The eighteenth-century Radcliffe Camera lends itself well to Oxford University's private library.

It's hard to see straight when walking the streets of Lavenham in Suffolk.

An 18th-century windmill on the Norfolk Coast

English country gardens: a rural idyll in Suffolk

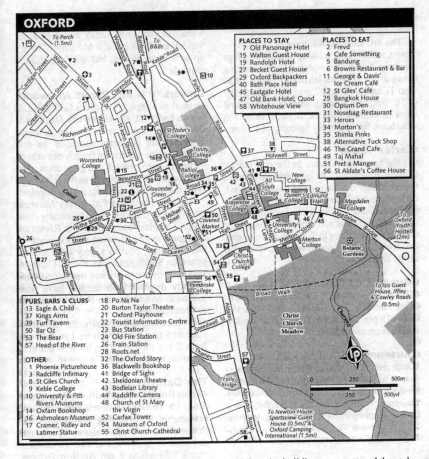

OXFORD

PLACES TO STAY	PLACES TO EAT
7 Old Parsonage Hotel	2 Frevd
15 Walton Guest House	4 Cafe Something
19 Randolph Hotel	5 Bandung
27 Becket Guest House	6 Browns Restaurant & Bar
29 Oxford Backpackers	11 George & Davis'
40 Bath Place Hotel	Ice Cream Café
45 Eastgate Hotel	12 St Giles' Café
47 Old Bank Hotel; Quod	25 Bangkok House
58 Whitehouse View	30 Opium Den
	31 Nosebag Restaurant
	33 Heroes
	34 Morton's
	35 Shimla Pinks
	38 Alternative Tuck Shop
	46 The Grand Cafe
	49 Taj Mahal
	51 Pret a Manger
	56 St Aldate's Coffee House

PUBS, BARS & CLUBS
13 Eagle & Child
37 Kings Arms
39 Turf Tavern
50 Bar Oz
53 The Bear
57 Head of the River

18 Po Na Na
20 Burton Taylor Theatre
21 Oxford Playhouse
22 Tourist Information Centre
23 Bus Station
24 Old Fire Station
26 Train Station
28 Roots.net
32 The Oxford Story
36 Blackwells Bookshop
41 Bridge of Sighs
42 Sheldonian Theatre
43 Bodleian Library
44 Radcliffe Camera
48 Church of St Mary the Virgin
52 Carfax Tower
54 Museum of Oxford
55 Christ Church Cathedral

OTHER
1 Phoenix Picturehouse
3 Radcliffe Infirmary
8 St Giles Church
9 Keble College
10 University & Pitt Rivers Museums
14 Oxfam Bookshop
16 Ashmolean Museum
17 Cramer, Ridley and Latimer Statue

and sprawling suburbs and housing estates are the legacy of its manufacturing past.

Orientation

The city centre is surrounded by rivers and streams to the south, east and west and can easily be covered on foot. Carfax Tower, at the junction of Queen and Cornmarket St/ St Aldates, makes a useful central landmark.

There are frequent buses to Carfax Tower from the train station to the west. Alternatively, turn left into Park End St and it's a 15-minute walk. The bus station is nearer the centre, off green-less Gloucester Green.

University buildings are scattered throughout the city, with the most important and architecturally interesting in the centre. It takes more than a day to do justice to them all but if pushed for time, try to visit Christ Church, New and Magdalen colleges.

Information

The TIC (☎ 726871) in Gloucester Green can be pretty hectic in summer. It opens 9.30 am to 5 pm Monday to Saturday, and 10 am to 3.30 pm on summer Sundays.

College opening hours are increasingly restrictive; some don't open at all, some only accept guided groups, many close in the morning and others charge for admission.

The TIC stocks a *Welcome to Oxford* brochure, which has a walking tour with college opening times. Two-hour guided walking tours of the colleges leave the TIC at 10.30 and 11 am and 1 and 2 pm; they cost £4.50/2.50. Inspector Morse tours (£5/3), around sites associated with the fictional detective, also leave the TIC every Saturday at 1.30 pm.

Carfax Tower

At the top of St Aldates in the city centre, Carfax Tower, with its quarterjacks (figures who hammer out the quarter hours on bells), is the sole reminder of medieval St Martin's Church. There's a fine view from the top of the tower which is good for orientating yourself. It opens 10 am to 5.30 pm daily, Easter to October (to 3.30 pm in winter). Admission costs £1.20/60p.

Museum of Oxford

This museum (☎ 815559), St Aldates, introduces the city's history. It opens 10 am to 4 pm (5 pm Saturday), Tuesday to Sunday. Admission costs £2.

Museum of Modern Art

Once described by the *Independent* newspaper as one of Europe's most influential museums, the focus is on 20th-century painting, sculpture and photography, with a healthy emphasis on other cultures. It opens 11 am to 6 pm Tuesday to Sunday. Admission is £2.50/free.

Ashmolean Museum

Established in 1683, the Ashmolean is the country's oldest museum, based on the collections of the gardening Tradescant family and Dr Elias Ashmole who presented their possessions to the university.

The Beaumont St building is one of Britain's best examples of neo-Grecian architecture and dates from 1845. It houses extensive displays of European art (including works by Raphael and Michelangelo) and Middle Eastern antiquities. Other exhibits include a unique Saxon enamel portrait of Alfred the Great and Guy Fawkes' lantern.

The museum (☎ 278000) opens 10 am to 5 pm Tuesday to Saturday and 2 to 5 pm Sunday and bank holiday Mondays. There's no admission charge, but a £3 donation is requested.

University & Pitt Rivers Museums

Housed in a superb Victorian Gothic building on Parks Rd, the **University Museum** is devoted to natural science. The dinosaur skeletons are perfectly suited to the surroundings, the patterns of their bones echoed in the delicate ironwork and glass above. The dodo relics, along the wall to the left as you enter the museum, are particularly popular.

You can reach the **Pitt Rivers Museum** (☎ 270949) through the University Museum. The glass cases at the Pitt Rivers are crammed to overflowing with everything from a sailing boat to a gory collection of shrunken South American heads. There are said to be over one million items, and some (mainly musical instruments) have been moved to an annexe, the Balfour Building, on Banbury Rd.

Both museums open daily: the University noon to 5 pm, the Pitt Rivers 1 to 4.30 pm, from 2 pm Sunday. They're free but a £2 donation is requested.

The Oxford Story

Across Broad St from Balliol is The Oxford Story (☎ 790055), a much-publicised and reasonably entertaining 40-minute ride through the university's history in carriages designed to look like old college desks. It opens 9.30 am to 5 pm April to October; 10 am to 4.30 pm the rest of the year. Admission costs £5.70/4.70.

Punting

There's no better way to soak up Oxford's atmosphere than to take to the river in a punt. The secret to propelling these flat-bottomed boats is to push gently on the pole to get the punt moving and then to use it as a rudder to keep on course.

Punts are available from Easter to September and hold five people, including the punter. Both the Thames and the Cherwell are shallow enough for punts, but the best

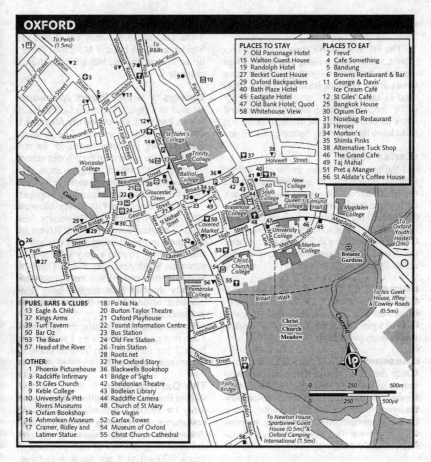

OXFORD

PLACES TO STAY
7 Old Parsonage Hotel
15 Walton Guest House
19 Randolph Hotel
27 Becket Guest House
29 Oxford Backpackers
40 Bath Place Hotel
45 Eastgate Hotel
47 Old Bank Hotel; Quod
58 Whitehouse View

PLACES TO EAT
2 Frevd
4 Cafe Something
5 Bandung
6 Browns Restaurant & Bar
11 George & Davis'
   Ice Cream Café
12 St Giles' Café
25 Bangkok House
30 Opium Den
31 Nosebag Restaurant
33 Heroes
34 Morton's
35 Shimla Pinks
38 Alternative Tuck Shop
46 The Grand Cafe
49 Taj Mahal
51 Pret a Manger
56 St Aldate's Coffee House

PUBS, BARS & CLUBS
13 Eagle & Child
37 Kings Arms
39 Turf Tavern
50 Bar Oz
53 The Bear
57 Head of the River

OTHER
1 Phoenix Picturehouse
3 Radcliffe Infirmary
8 St Giles Church
9 Keble College
10 University & Pitt
   Rivers Museums
14 Oxfam Bookshop
16 Ashmolean Museum
17 Cramer, Ridley and
   Latimer Statue
18 Po Na Na
20 Burton Taylor Theatre
21 Oxford Playhouse
22 Tourist Information Centre
23 Bus Station
24 Old Fire Station
26 Train Station
28 Roots.net
32 The Oxford Story
36 Blackwells Bookshop
41 Bridge of Sighs
42 Sheldonian Theatre
43 Bodleian Library
44 Radcliffe Camera
48 Church of St Mary
   the Virgin
52 Carfax Tower
54 Museum of Oxford
55 Christ Church Cathedral

and sprawling suburbs and housing estates are the legacy of its manufacturing past.

Orientation

The city centre is surrounded by rivers and streams to the south, east and west and can easily be covered on foot. Carfax Tower, at the junction of Queen and Cornmarket St/ St Aldates, makes a useful central landmark.

There are frequent buses to Carfax Tower from the train station to the west. Alternatively, turn left into Park End St and it's a 15-minute walk. The bus station is nearer the centre, off green-less Gloucester Green.

University buildings are scattered throughout the city, with the most important and architecturally interesting in the centre. It takes more than a day to do justice to them all but if pushed for time, try to visit Christ Church, New and Magdalen colleges.

Information

The TIC (☎ 726871) in Gloucester Green can be pretty hectic in summer. It opens 9.30 am to 5 pm Monday to Saturday, and 10 am to 3.30 pm on summer Sundays.

College opening hours are increasingly restrictive; some don't open at all, some only accept guided groups, many close in the morning and others charge for admission.

The TIC stocks a *Welcome to Oxford* brochure, which has a walking tour with college opening times. Two-hour guided walking tours of the colleges leave the TIC at 10.30 and 11 am and 1 and 2 pm; they cost £4.50/2.50. Inspector Morse tours (£5/3), around sites associated with the fictional detective, also leave the TIC every Saturday at 1.30 pm.

Carfax Tower

At the top of St Aldates in the city centre, Carfax Tower, with its quarterjacks (figures who hammer out the quarter hours on bells), is the sole reminder of medieval St Martin's Church. There's a fine view from the top of the tower which is good for orientating yourself. It opens 10 am to 5.30 pm daily, Easter to October (to 3.30 pm in winter). Admission costs £1.20/60p.

Museum of Oxford

This museum (☎ 815559), St Aldates, introduces the city's history. It opens 10 am to 4 pm (5 pm Saturday), Tuesday to Sunday. Admission costs £2.

Museum of Modern Art

Once described by the *Independent* newspaper as one of Europe's most influential museums, the focus is on 20th-century painting, sculpture and photography, with a healthy emphasis on other cultures. It opens 11 am to 6 pm Tuesday to Sunday. Admission is £2.50/free.

Ashmolean Museum

Established in 1683, the Ashmolean is the country's oldest museum, based on the collections of the gardening Tradescant family and Dr Elias Ashmole who presented their possessions to the university.

The Beaumont St building is one of Britain's best examples of neo-Grecian architecture and dates from 1845. It houses extensive displays of European art (including works by Raphael and Michelangelo) and Middle Eastern antiquities. Other exhibits include a unique Saxon enamel portrait of Alfred the Great and Guy Fawkes' lantern.

The museum (☎ 278000) opens 10 am to 5 pm Tuesday to Saturday and 2 to 5 pm Sunday and bank holiday Mondays. There's no admission charge, but a £3 donation is requested.

University & Pitt Rivers Museums

Housed in a superb Victorian Gothic building on Parks Rd, the **University Museum** is devoted to natural science. The dinosaur skeletons are perfectly suited to the surroundings, the patterns of their bones echoed in the delicate ironwork and glass above. The dodo relics, along the wall to the left as you enter the museum, are particularly popular.

You can reach the **Pitt Rivers Museum** (☎ 270949) through the University Museum. The glass cases at the Pitt Rivers are crammed to overflowing with everything from a sailing boat to a gory collection of shrunken South American heads. There are said to be over one million items, and some (mainly musical instruments) have been moved to an annexe, the Balfour Building, on Banbury Rd.

Both museums open daily: the University noon to 5 pm, the Pitt Rivers 1 to 4.30 pm, from 2 pm Sunday. They're free but a £2 donation is requested.

The Oxford Story

Across Broad St from Balliol is The Oxford Story (☎ 790055), a much-publicised and reasonably entertaining 40-minute ride through the university's history in carriages designed to look like old college desks. It opens 9.30 am to 5 pm April to October; 10 am to 4.30 pm the rest of the year. Admission costs £5.70/4.70.

Punting

There's no better way to soak up Oxford's atmosphere than to take to the river in a punt. The secret to propelling these flat-bottomed boats is to push gently on the pole to get the punt moving and then to use it as a rudder to keep on course.

Punts are available from Easter to September and hold five people, including the punter. Both the Thames and the Cherwell are shallow enough for punts, but the best advice is to bring a picnic and head upstream along the Cherwell. You can rent a punt from C Howard & Sons (☎ 761586), by Magdalen Bridge, for £7 per hour (£20 deposit) or from the Cherwell Boat House (☎ 515978), farther upstream at the end of Bardwell Rd, for £8 per hour (£40 deposit) weekdays, £10 (and £50 deposit) at weekends.

Alternatively, follow the Cherwell downstream from Magdalen Bridge for views of the colleges across the Botanic Gardens and Christ Church Meadow.

University Buildings & Colleges

Pembroke College (☎ 276444), on St Aldates, was founded in 1624. The dictionary-writer Dr Samuel Johnson was a student here and Sir Roger Bannister, the first man to run a mile in under four minutes, was a master.

Opposite Pembroke is **Christ Church** (☎ 276150), the grandest of all Oxford colleges. It was founded in 1525 by Cardinal Thomas Wolsey and refounded by Henry VIII in 1546. Illustrious former students include John Wesley, William Penn, WH Auden and Lewis Carroll.

The main entrance is below Tom Tower, so called because it is dedicated to St Thomas of Canterbury. The upper part of the tower, designed by Sir Christopher Wren in 1682, rests on a Tudor base. Great Tom, the tower bell, chimes 101 times each evening at 9.05 pm, the time when the original 101 students were called in. Since Oxford is five minutes west of Greenwich, this is actually 9 pm Oxford time.

The visitor entrance is farther down St Aldates, via the Memorial Gardens. The college opens 9.30 am to 5.30 pm (from 1 pm on Sunday). The Great Hall is closed between noon and 2 pm, the cathedral closes at 4.45 pm and the Chapterhouse at 5 pm. Admission costs £3/2.

The cloisters lead to **Christ Church Cathedral**, the smallest cathedral in the country, which has been Oxford's Anglican cathedral since the reign of Henry VIII. It was founded on the site of the nunnery of St Frideswide, whose shrine was a focus of pilgrimage until it was partly destroyed on Henry VIII's orders. The shrine was reconstructed in the 19th century. Beside it is a **Watching Loft** for the guard, who made sure no one walked off with the saint's relics. The Lady and Latin chapels boast some particularly fine windows.

From the cathedral, you enter **Tom Quad**, whose central pond served as a water reservoir in case the college caught fire. To the south side is the **Hall**, the college's grand dining room, with an impressive hammer-beam roof. You can also explore another two quadrangles (quads) and the **Picture Gallery**.

Merton College (☎ 276310), Merton St, was one of the original three colleges founded in 1264 and represents the earliest form of collegiate planning. The 14th-century **Mob Quad** was the first of the college quads. The **library** leading off it is the oldest medieval library still in use, with some books still chained up, an ancient anti-theft device. The library owns several 15th-century astrological instruments, and an astrolabe that may have been used by Chaucer. Former students include TS Eliot and Kris Kristofferson.

Magdalen College (pronounced mawd-len) is on High St, near the handsome Magdalen Bridge over the River Cherwell. One of Oxford's richest colleges, it has the most extensive and beautiful grounds, including a deer park, river walk and superb lawns. It's also a popular location for movie-makers and part of *Shadowlands*, the story of CS Lewis, was filmed here.

The college was founded in 1458 by William of Waynflete, the bishop of Winchester. The chapel, with its 43m-high bell tower, dates from the late 15th-century. At 6 am each year, the college choir ushers in May Day by singing a hymn from the top of the tower to the crowds below. Pubs open before breakfast, ensuring that this is a well-supported tradition.

Former Magdalen students include Oscar Wilde, Sir John Betjeman and Dudley Moore. The college (☎ 276000) opens noon to 6 pm daily. Admission costs £2/1 from April to September.

Opposite Magdalen is the **Botanic Gardens** (☎ 276920), founded in 1621 by Henry Danvers for the study of medicinal plants. It opens 9 am to 4.30 pm daily.

St Edmund Hall (☎ 279000), Queen's Lane, is where the Mohawk chief, Oronhyatekha, studied in 1862. Its small chapel was decorated by William Morris and Edward Burne-Jones.

Queen's College (☎ 279121), High St, was founded in 1341 but the current buildings are all in classical style. Like most colleges, Queen's preserves some idiosyncratic traditions: students are summoned to meals with a trumpet call and at Christmas a boar's head is served to commemorate a time when a scholar fought off an attacking boar by thrusting a volume of Aristotle down its throat! How appropriate, then, that Rowan Atkinson, also known as (aka) Mr Bean, once studied here. To visit the college, you must join an official tour.

University College (☎ 276602), High St, has acquired new fame as the college where Bill Clinton didn't inhale noxious substances. Despite claims that King Alfred founded it, the college actually started life in 1249. A romantic memorial commemorates the poet Percy Bysshe Shelley, who was sent down (expelled) for publishing *The Necessity of Atheism* in 1811. You need a private invitation to visit this college.

All Souls College (☎ 279379), High St, was founded in 1438, the souls in question being those of soldiers who died in the Hundred Years' War. The 100-years theme is repeated in the tradition of 'All Souls Mallard', which is re-enacted on 14 January when the warden leads a procession to look for a mythical duck that appeared when the college foundations were being dug. No undergraduates are admitted to All Souls, a small college of just 70 fellows. The college chapel, open 2 to 4 pm weekdays, is worth seeing.

At the junction of High and Catte Sts, the **Church of St Mary the Virgin** has a 14th-century tower offering splendid views. It opens 9 am to 7 pm daily in July and August (5 pm for the rest of the year). Admission costs £1.60/80p.

The **Radcliffe Camera** is a spectacular circular library ('camera' means room) built in 1748 in the Palladian style. It's not open to the public.

Dating from the 16th century, **Brasenose College** (☎ 277830) is entered from Radcliffe Square and takes its name from an 11th-century snout-like door knocker that now graces the dining room. It opens 10 to 11.30 am and 2 to 4.30 pm daily.

To reach **New College** (☎ 279555), turn down New College Lane under the **Bridge of Sighs**, a 1914 copy of the famous bridge in Venice. New College was founded in 1379 by William of Wykeham, bishop of Winchester, and its buildings are fine examples of the perpendicular style. Don't miss the chapel, which has superb stained glass, much of it from the 14th century. The west window is a design by Sir Joshua Reynolds, and Sir Jacob Epstein's disturbing statue of Lazarus is also here. The gardens contain a section of Oxford's medieval wall.

A former college warden was William Spooner, whose habit of transposing the first consonants of words made his name part of the English language – a spoonerism. It's claimed that he once reprimanded a student with the words, 'You have deliberately tasted two worms and can leave Oxford by the town drain.' The college opens 11 am to 5 pm daily Easter to October (2 to 4 pm in winter). Admission costs £2 in summer, free in winter.

In Broad St stands the **Sheldonian Theatre** (☎ 277299), the university's main public building. Commissioned by Gilbert Sheldon, archbishop of Canterbury, this was Wren's first major work and was built in 1667 when he was Professor of Astronomy. It opens 10 am to 12 pm and 2 to 4.30 pm (3.30 pm in winter) Monday to Saturday. Admission costs £1.50/1.

Britain's second most important copyright library, the **Bodleian Library**, is off the Jacobean-period **Old Schools Quadrangle**. Library tours (☎ 277000) take place at 10.30 and 11.30 am, and 2 and 3 pm, daily and show off Duke Humfrey's library (1488). They book up fast and cost £3.50 (no children under 14). Also not to be missed is the **Divinity School**, with its superb vaulted ceiling. Renowned as a masterpiece of 15th-century English Gothic architecture, it opens 9 am to 5 pm weekdays and on Saturday until 12.30 pm.

Trinity College (☎ 279900), Broad St, was founded in 1555, but the existing buildings mostly date from the 17th century. It opens 10.30 am to noon and 2 to 4 pm daily and admission costs £1.

Balliol College (☎ 277777), Broad St, was founded in 1263, but most of the buildings date from the 19th century. The wooden doors between the inner and outer quads still bear scorch marks from when Protestant martyrs were burned at the stake in the mid-16th century. It opens 2 to 5 pm daily. Admission costs £1.

Organised Tours

Guide Friday (☎ 790522) runs a hop-on, hop-off city bus tour every 15 minutes from 9.30 am to 7 pm in summer, less frequently in winter. It leaves from the train station and tickets cost £8.50/2.50.

Cotswold Roaming (☎ 250640) runs guided bus tours to several places around Oxford, including Blenheim Palace, Bath and the Cotswolds.

Places to Stay

Finding a place to stay in summer can be difficult; arrange things in advance or join the queues in the TIC and pay £2.75 for help.

Camping Conveniently located by the Park & Ride car park 1½ miles south of the city centre is *Oxford Camping International* (☎ 244088, 426 Abingdon Rd). Charges are £5.30 per person and £4.30 per pitch.

Hostels The most convenient hostel is *Oxford Backpackers* (☎ 721761, 9A Hythe Bridge St), which is a short walk from the train station. There are 80 beds, mostly in dorms, and good cooking facilities. From April to September you need to book a week in advance and leave a deposit. Beds in dorms cost £11 each.

Oxford Youth Hostel (☎ 762997, 32 Jack Straw's Lane) gets booked up quickly in summer although it's hardly central. Get there on bus No 14 or 14A from outside the post office just down the hill from the TIC. It opens all year and beds cost £11/7.75 for adults/under-18s.

University Accommodation Over the holidays it is possible to find a room in empty student accommodation.

From July to September, St Edmund Hall turns into the *Isis Guest House* (☎ 248894, 45–53 Iffley Rd), offering student digs as superior B&B accommodation. Rooms cost £26 per person with a bathroom, £24 per person without.

Otherwise try the *Old Mitre Rooms* (☎ 279821, 4B Turl St), which lets singles/doubles at £25/46 in July and August only.

B&Bs & Hotels – Central In the peak season, figure on around £20 per person for a room in a B&B. The main areas are on Abingdon Rd to the south, Cowley and Iffley Rds to the east, and Banbury Rd to the north. All are on bus routes, but Cowley Rd has the best selection of places to eat.

The fairly basic *Becket Guest House* (☎ 724675, 5 Becket St) is near the train station and has singles/doubles from £30/45. West of the station, the small *River Hotel* (☎ 243475, 17 Botley Rd) by Osney Bridge is a popular business hotel with rooms from £60/70. The *Westgate Hotel* (☎ 726721, 1 Botley Rd) charges £36/48 for a room, £39/56 with a bathroom.

St Michael's Guest House (☎ 242101, 26 St Michael's St), just off Cornmarket St, couldn't be more central. Rooms with shared bathroom are £32/48; you need to book weeks in advance. The closest B&B to the bus station is the basic *Walton Guest House* (☎ 552137, 169 Walton St). Rooms without bathroom cost £18 per person.

Oxford's choicest accommodation is also centrally located. Forte's *Randolph Hotel* (☎ 0870 400 8200, Beaumont St), opposite the Ashmolean Museum, was built in 1864 in neogothic style; rooms cost from £140/170 but there are reductions at weekends. The delightful *Old Parsonage Hotel* (☎ 310210, 1 Banbury Rd) has well-equipped rooms for £130/165.

Bath Place Hotel (☎ 791812, 4 & 5 Bath Place) is a luxurious, 10-room retreat in which all rooms have different styles, and some have four-poster beds. Rooms cost from £90/140.

The *Old Bank Hotel* (☎ 799599, 92 High St) brings the designer hotel to Oxford at designer prices. Plush, lush rooms start from £135/155, excluding (!) breakfast.

B&Bs & Hotels – East East of the centre there are several B&Bs in the student area on Cowley Rd and numerous others along Iffley Rd to the south. Another cluster lies to the north, along Headington Rd.

Farther out, the *Bravalla Guest House* (☎ 241326, 242 Iffley Rd) charges £35 for en-suite rooms. The *Athena Guest House* (☎ 243124, 253 Cowley Rd) is within walking distance of shops and restaurants and has beds for £18 a head. A bit farther out, the comfortable *Earlmont* (☎ 240236) has rooms from £35/50.

B&Bs & Hotels – North There are several B&Bs along Banbury Rd, north of the centre. *Cotswold House* (☎ 310558, 363 Banbury Rd) is very comfortable; rooms with bathroom cost from £41/66. *Burren Guest House* (☎ 513513, 374 Banbury Rd) is more basic and offers B&B from £33/48.

B&Bs & Hotels – South Closest to the city centre is the good-value *Whitehouse View* (☎ 721626, 9 Whitehouse Rd), on a side road off Abingdon Rd, with rooms from £18/34.

There are numerous other places along Abingdon Rd. *Newton House* (☎ 240561, 82 Abingdon Rd) is quite large, with rooms from £46/48. The *Sportsview Guest House* (☎ 244268, 106 Abingdon Rd) has rooms from £30/52, £35/60 with bathroom.

Places to Eat
Many Oxford eateries are aimed at the wallets of wealthy parents and tourists. To eat cheaply, track down the places that get the student trade.

Shimla Pinks (☎ 244944, 16 Turl St) is a particularly good Indian restaurant, part of a growing nationwide chain, with buffets from around £6. Out towards the station, *Bangkok House* (☎ 200705, 42A Hythe Bridge St) does set Thai meals for £15.50, assuming two diners, with cheaper options at lunchtime. Sticking to South-East Asia, *Bandung*

(☎ 511668, 124 Walton St) offers Malaysian and Indonesian cuisine with daily specials for £7. *The Opium Den* (☎ 248680, 79 George St) is considered one of the best Chinese restaurants in town and offers a series of set menus for those who like to pick and mix.

Quod (☎ 202505, 92 High St) is incredibly popular with the local set for stylish Italian cuisine in comfortable surroundings. It is best to book ahead, and reckon on £10 per head and up.

On High St, *The Grand Café* (☎ 204463), in suitably grand surroundings, offers luxury sandwiches and salads amid pillars and mirrors. Just as inviting is *Frevd* (☎ 311171, Walton St), a cafe-bar inside an old church with an impressive neo-classical facade. There is Latin dancing here on Sunday evenings. Stylish *Browns* (☎ 511995, 5 Woodstock Rd) looks more expensive than it is and offers a good selection of dishes from Europe and beyond. *Café Something* (☎ 559782) is a trendy little place specialising in pizzas and some delicious desserts.

The nonsmoking *Nosebag Restaurant* (☎ 721033, St Michael's St) does good soups and has a fine selection of cakes. Light lunches, teas and coffees are available in the *Convocation Coffee House* attached to the Church of St Mary the Virgin. If you're at the TIC around lunchtime the adjoining *Old School* pub does snack meals such as filled baguettes at reasonable prices.

There are some excellent sandwich bars throughout the centre and many a student debate has centred on which is best. *Morton's*, on Broad St, can't be faulted for its tasty baguettes and attractive garden; nearby *Heroes* builds to order with a fine selection of fillings; and *St Aldate's Coffee House* is a favourite with students.

Self-caterers should visit the *covered market*, on the northern side of High St at the Carfax Tower end, for snacks, fruit and vegetables. Among the stalls, *Palm's Delicatessen* offers a good range of pates and cheeses. *Brown's Café* has cheap fodder of the sausage and beans variety. Otherwise, the *Alternative Tuck Shop* (Holywell St) does excellent filled rolls and sandwiches at lunchtime. A popular place for snacks is *St*

Giles' Café (St Giles') with cheap fry-ups and toasted sandwiches. The popular *George & Davis' Ice Cream Café (Little Clarendon St)* serves light meals (bagels from £1) as well as delicious home-made ice cream.

Entertainment

Pubs, Bars & Clubs Oxford has some excellent city centre pubs as well as others within stumbling distance along the Thames.

The *Head of the River,* ideally situated by Folly Bridge, is very popular. Less prominent is the tiny *Turf Tavern,* a perennial student favourite, which is hidden down a city centre alley (Bath Place) and has been featured in the *Inspector Morse* TV series based on Colin Dexter's books.

Academics loosen up in the 17th-century *Eagle & Child*, St Giles', where JRR Tolkein and CS Lewis used to meet for readings from *The Hobbit* and *The Chronicles of Narnia*. Just off High St, *The Bear* is thought to be the oldest pub in the city and has a snug, intimate atmosphere thanks to its tiny size.

The *Kings Arms* is a crowded student pub in the heart of the city, opposite the Sheldonian Theatre. Most weekends see bands playing at the *Bullingdon Arms (162 Cowley Rd)*, a lively Irish local with live jazz/blues on Wednesday evening. Homesick antipodeans might seek solace in *Bar Oz*, although it's still pints and halves rather than schooners and midis.

The *Isis Tavern*, a 1½-mile walk along the towpath from Folly Bridge, is the perfect place to go on a sunny day provided you don't mind the crowds. The thatch-roofed *Perch*, by the river in Binsey, is a 25-minute walk from the city centre; from Walton St, take Walton Well Rd and cross Port Meadow.

Roots.net has a great selection of tunes from around the world and the complex includes a bar and club with live performances most nights. *Po Na Na* is probably the best of Oxford's unimpressive clubs, more a bar where people start shaking their stuff in the early hours.

Theatre & Cinema The *Oxford Playhouse* (☎ 798600, *Beaumont St)* puts on a mixed bag of theatre, music and dance. The *Old Fire Station* (☎ 794490, *George St)* stages mainly classical plays, while *Burton Taylor Theatre* (☎ 798600, *Gloucester St)* goes for more offbeat productions.

The most interesting films tend to get a screening at the *Phoenix Picturehouse* (☎ 554909, *Walton St)*.

Getting There & Away

Oxford is 57 miles from London, 74 miles from Bristol and 33 miles from Cheltenham.

Bus Several bus lines compete for business on the route to London. The Oxford Tube (☎ 772250) goes to London's Victoria coach station but also stops at Marble Arch, Notting Hill Gate and Shepherd's Bush. An overnight return to Victoria costs £7.50; the journey takes around 1½ hours and the service operates 24 hours a day. The Oxford Tube also stops on St Clements St, near Cowley Rd.

National Express (☎ 0870 580 8080) has numerous buses to central London and Heathrow airport. There are three buses a day to Cambridge (£14, three hours), two or three services to Bath (£9.75, two hours) and Bristol (£12.75, 2¼ hours), and two to Gloucester (£8, 1½ hours) and Cheltenham (£7.75, one hour).

The Oxford Bus Company (☎ 785400) is the third major operator with frequent departures to London, Heathrow, Gatwick, Birmingham and Stratford-upon-Avon.

Train Oxford has a snazzy modern station with frequent services to London Paddington (£13, 1½ hours).

There are regular trains north to Coventry and Birmingham, the main hub for transport further north, and north-west to Worcester and Hereford via Moreton-in-Marsh (for the Cotswolds).

To connect with trains to the south-west you have to change at Didcot Parkway (15 minutes). There are plenty of connections to Bath (1½ hours). Change at Swindon for another line running into the Cotswolds (Kemble, Stroud and Gloucester).

Car & Motorcycle The M40 provides fast access from London but Oxford has a serious

CENTRAL ENGLAND

traffic problem and finding anywhere to park can be difficult. It's best to use the Park & Ride system; as you approach The city follow the signs for the four car parks. Parking is free but the buses to the city centre cost £1 return. They leave every 10 minutes throughout the day, Monday to Saturday.

Getting Around

Bus Oxford was one of the world's first cities to introduce battery-operated electric buses. They run every 12 minutes from the train station into the city centre from 8 am to 6 pm Monday to Saturday for a flat fare of 30p.

The city has fallen victim to the worst excesses of bus deregulation, with so many competing buses plying Cornmarket St that it can be difficult to cross the road. The biggest companies are Citylink (☎ 785410) and Stagecoach (☎ 772250). Citylink bus No 4 serves Iffley Rd and No 5 serves Cowley Rd. The information office in the bus station has full details.

Car For car hire, Budget (☎ 724884) is near the station on Hythe Bridge St.

Taxi There are taxis outside the train station and near the bus station. A taxi to Blenheim Palace will cost around £15.

Bicycle Students have always espoused pedal power and there are cycle lanes along several streets. The *Cycle into Oxford* map shows all the local cycle routes.

Beeline Bikes (☎ 246615) rent bikes for £9/£15 per day/week (£50 deposit).

Boat Salter Bros (☎ 243421) offers several interesting boat trips from Folly Bridge from May to September, including a two-hour trip to Abingdon (£6.80/10.40 for one way/return). See Punting earlier in the chapter.

WOODSTOCK & BLENHEIM PALACE
☎ 01235

The village of Woodstock owes its fame and prosperity to glove-making and the Churchill family. Although people usually come here en route to Blenheim Palace, there's also a

fine collection of 17th- and 18th-century buildings, particularly the Bear Hotel and the town hall, built at the duke of Marlborough's expense in 1766. The church has an 18th-century tower tacked onto a medieval interior. Opposite the church, Fletcher's House accommodates **Oxfordshire County Museum** (closed on Monday).

The TIC (☎ 01993-813276) is on Hensington Rd.

Blenheim Palace

One of Europe's largest palaces, Blenheim was a gift to John Churchill, duke of Marlborough, from Queen Anne and the parliament as a reward for his role in defeating Louis XIV. A vast baroque fantasy, it was built by Sir John Vanbrugh and Nicholas Hawksmoor between 1704 and 1722. It's now a Unesco World Heritage site.

You enter the house through the great hall where the 20m-ceiling is decorated with a painting by Sir James Thornhill showing the duke of Marlborough presenting Britannia with his plan for the Battle of Blenheim. West of the great hall, apartments once used by the domestic chaplain now house the Churchill Exhibition; in the room where Winston Churchill was born you can view the great prime minister's slippers and a lock of his hair.

The windows of the sumptuous state dining room offer a glimpse of the tower of Bladon Church where Churchill and his parents are buried. Between the saloon and library are three state rooms, hung with tapestries commemorating Marlborough's campaigns.

You can also visit the chapel and grounds, which cover over 800 hectares, some of it parkland landscaped by Capability Brown. Blenheim Park railway leads to the herb garden, the butterfly house and a large maze. A separate ticket lets you look round the current duke and duchess's private apartments.

Just south-west of Woodstock, Blenheim Palace (☎ 811325) opens 10.30 am to 5 pm mid-March to October. Admission costs £9/4. The park opens from 9 am daily year round.

Places to Stay & Eat

Plane Tree House (☎ 813075, 15 High St) is an upmarket B&B, rooms cost £60. The best places in town are the *Feathers Hotel (☎ 812291, Market St)*, with luxurious singles/doubles for £88/105, and the *Bear Hotel (☎ 0870 400 8202)*, a 13th-century coaching inn with rooms from £115/140.

Harriet's Tearooms is a nice little teashop with some of the best French pastries this side of Calais. *Brotherton's Brasserie* has a fair range of Mediterranean favourites, plus a healthy wine list. Bar food at popular *Black Prince* includes Mexican dishes and pizzas.

Getting There & Away

From Oxford, catch Stagecoach bus No 20/A from Oxford bus station. Cotswold Roaming (☎ 308300) offers organised excursions to Blenheim from Oxford.

OXFORDSHIRE COTSWOLDS

For all the details on Oxfordshire's share of the beautiful Cotswolds, see Gloucestershire & the Cotswolds later in the chapter.

SOUTH OF OXFORD
Abingdon
☎ 01235 • pop 30,000

Pretty Abingdon is a market town 6 miles south of Oxford. The TIC (☎ 522711) is in Abbey Close, near the river.

The impressive **County Hall** building was designed in 1678 by Christopher Kempster, who worked on St Paul's Cathedral in London. It now houses a local museum. Wider than it is long, **St Helen's Church** is a fine example of perpendicular architecture.

On St Helens Wharf, overlooking the Thames, is the *Old Anchor Inn,* a friendly pub that also serves meals.

The nicest way to reach Abingdon from Oxford is by boat (see Oxford earlier in the chapter). Alternatively, Stagecoach bus No 31 links Abingdon, Oxford and Wantage.

Dorchester-on-Thames

A street of old coaching-inns and a magnificent medieval church are more or less all there is of Dorchester-on-Thames, although in Saxon times there was a cathedral here.

In the 12th century an abbey was founded on the site. Following the Reformation it became the parish church of Sts Peter and Paul, and it's worth stepping inside to see the rare Norman lead font with figures of the apostles; a wonderful Jesse window with carved figures and stained glass tracing Christ's ancestry; and a 13th-century monument of a knight. There's a small museum and cafe in the *Abbey Guest House,* which also dates back to the Middle Ages.

Thames Travel (☎ 01491-874216) bus No X39 connects Dorchester with Oxford and Abingdon.

Wantage
☎ 01235 • pop 9700

Wantage lies at the foot of the Downs, 15 miles south-west of Oxford. Alfred the Great was born here in 849, and his statue dominates the main square. The Ridgeway is less than 3 miles to the south.

The TIC (☎ 760176) in the museum keeps the same hours. The **Vale & Downland Museum Centre** (☎ 771447), in a converted 16th-century cloth merchant's house in Church St, has information about King Alfred and life around the Ridgeway. It opens 10 am to 4.30 pm Monday to Saturday and 2.30 to 5 pm Sundays. Admission is £1.50/1.

Places to Stay & Eat About 2 miles south of Wantage, *Ridgeway Youth Hostel (☎ 760253, Court Hill)* was created out of several old barns set round a courtyard. It opens daily, May to early September (phone for further details). The nightly charge is £9.25/6.50 for adults/under-18s.

The Chalet (☎ 769262, 21 Challow Rd) has beds from £16 per person. The *Bell Inn (☎ 763718, Market Square)* is pricier at £22.50/45 per single/double or £55 for an en-suite double.

You can get bar meals in *The Shears (Mill St).* The *Flying Teapot,* beside the church, does snacks such as jacket potatoes.

Getting There & Away

Stagecoach (☎ 01865-772250) operates regular buses to Didcot and Swindon. A Sunday Rover ticket lets you travel throughout the area for £5.

The White Horse

About 6 miles west of Wantage, a stylised image of a horse cut into the hillside is probably the most famous chalk figure in Europe. Why this mysterious figure (114m long and 49m wide) was carved into the turf about 2000 years ago is unclear. How the artist managed to get the lines and perspective exact when the whole horse can only be seen from a distance is a mystery.

Above the chalk figure are the grass-covered earthworks of Uffington Castle. From the Ridgeway Youth Hostel, near Wantage, a wonderful 5-mile walk leads along the Ridgeway to the White Horse.

Thomas Hughes, author of *Tom Brown's Schooldays,* was born in Uffington village. His house is now a museum. *The Craven* (☎ 01367-820449) is a thatched farmhouse offering B&B with singles/doubles from £25/48.

HENLEY-ON-THAMES

☎ 01491 • pop 11,000

Henley is world famous for its rowing regatta, one of those oar-fully English occasions of boaters and blazers, strawberries and cream, which these days tend to be commandeered by the high ranks of the corporate entertainers.

The TIC (☎ 578034) is in the basement of the town hall on Market Place. In summer there's also a booth in Mill Meadows.

Stately High St is dominated by **St Mary's Church**, which dates back to the 13th century. Above the arches of Henley Bridge, built in 1786, are sculptures of Isis and Father Thames. Two fine coaching inns, the Red Lion and the Angel, stand sentinel at the High St end of the bridge. Both predate their 18th-century heyday and have played host to many eminent people, from the duke of Wellington to James Boswell.

Henley Royal Regatta

In 1829, the first Oxford and Cambridge boat race took place between Hambledon Lock and Henley Bridge. Ten years later the regatta was developed to enhance Henley's growing reputation.

Each year, in the first week of July, the regatta still plays host to the beau monde. Despite its peculiar mix of pomposity and eccentricity, it's a serious event that attracts rowers of the highest calibre.

There are two main areas for spectators – the stewards' enclosure and the public enclosure – although most people appear to take little interest in what's happening on the water. Epicurean picnics are consumed, large quantities of Pimm's (an alcoholic fruit drink) and champagne are drunk, and it's still an important fixture in the social calendar. Those with contacts in the rowing or corporate worlds can get tickets to the stewards' enclosure; others pay £6 for a day ticket to the public enclosure on Wednesday and Thursday, or £10 on Friday and at the weekend.

River & Rowing Museum

Henley recently acquired a purpose-built museum, designed by minimalist architect David Chipperfield, in which to display paintings and artefacts associated with the history of Henley and with the River Thames and rowing. Like all the best modern museums, the River & Rowing Museum (☎ 415600) harnesses modern technology to liven up its story. The views from the building are lovely and there is, of course, a cafe and a shop.

It opens 10 am to 6 pm daily (from 10.30 am Sunday). Admission costs £4.95/3.75. The museum is in Mill Meadows and has its own car park.

Places to Stay

If you want to stay anywhere near Henley during the regatta you need to book weeks in advance. Even at quiet times B&Bs are relatively pricey.

Camping A quarter of a mile out of Henley on the Marlow Rd is the *Swiss Farm International Camping* (☎ 573419) site. Camping costs £4 per adult and £1 for the pitch.

B&Bs & Guesthouses Well located *No 4 Riverside* (☎ 571133, *4 River Terrace*) has singles/doubles facing the river from £40/50. Or try *Alftrudis* (☎ 573099, *8 Norman Ave*), a friendly B&B about a five-minute walk from the centre; rooms cost from £40 to £55 with bathroom. *Avalon (☎ 577829, 36 Queen St)* charges from £25/40.

Lenwade (☎ 573468, 3 Western Rd) has three double rooms from £55 (from £45 for single occupancy!). *Abbotsleigh (☎ 572982, 107 St Marks Rd)* has doubles with a bathroom for £56.

Places to Eat

Several pubs offer reasonably priced food. Near the TIC, the *Three Tuns (5 Market Place)* does good bar meals, including Sunday lunch. *The Angel* is a pub with a view next to Henley Bridge, but is expensive whether for food or drink.

There are also branches of *Café Rouge (☎ 411733)* and *Caffe Uno (☎ 411099)* facing one other in High St, and nearby is *Pizza Express (35 Market Place)*. *Henley Tea Rooms* faces onto the river on River Terrace, and you can get high tea with all the trimmings at the *Old Rope Walk (High St)*.

Getting There & Away

Henley is 21 miles south-east of Oxford on the A423 and 40 miles west of London. Thames Travel (☎ 01491-874216) bus No X39 links Henley with Oxford and Abingdon hourly.

To get from Henley to Oxford by train you must change at Twyford or Reading. Henley to London Paddington takes about one hour and costs £7.20.

Getting Around

Henley is the perfect place to indulge in a bit of messing about on the river, and plenty of boat companies near the bridge are ready to help you enjoy yourself. On summer Sundays Hobbs & Son (☎ 572035) organises cruises from £20 a head. Shorter trips to Hambledon Lock and back cost about £4/3. To hire a five seater rowing boat costs £10 an hour, or for a four seater motor boat it's £18.

AROUND HENLEY-ON-THAMES
Stonor Park

Stonor Park (☎ 01491-638587) has been occupied by the Stonor family, an unrepentant Catholic family that has suffered much indignity since the Reformation, for more than 800 years. The house has a fine collection of paintings, including works by Tintoretto and Caracci.

Stonor Park is 5 miles north of Henley. You need your own transport to get here. It opens 2 to 5.30 pm on Sunday in April; Wednesday and Sunday, May to September; plus Thursday in July and August; and Saturday in August. Admission costs £4.50.

Gloucestershire & the Cotswolds

Straddling the River Severn to the west, Gloucestershire is the source of the traditional picture of rustic, rosy-cheeked England typified by the Cotswolds, the limestone escarpment overlooking the Severn Vale between Bath and Chipping Campden. It's a region of stunningly pretty, honey-coloured stone villages and remarkable views. Some of the villages are extremely popular; the best way to escape the commercialism is to explore on foot or by bike.

Accommodation can be pricey, with few hostels or camping grounds.

The Severn Vale nurtures Cheltenham (one of Britain's best preserved Regency towns), Tewkesbury (with a beautiful abbey) and Gloucester (the capital of the county, with a historic cathedral) as well as Berkeley Castle and Slimbridge Wildfowl Trust. To the west, and geographically part of Wales, are the Forest of Dean, and the beautiful Wye Valley bordering Wales (see the South Wales chapter).

WALKING & CYCLING ROUTES

Gloucestershire and the Cotswolds are perfect for walking and cycling, with plenty of quiet roads, mild but rewarding gradients and fine pubs.

The 100-mile Cotswold Way (see Cotswold Way in the Activities chapter) runs from Bath to Chipping Campden. TICs stock walking guides and a useful pack of *Cycle Touring Routes in Gloucestershire*. Bartholomew's *Cycling in the Cotswolds* (£8.99) provides the full details. Campus Holidays (☎ 01242-250642) organises mountain-bike tours of the region, starting from Cheltenham, while Cotswold Country Cycles (☎ 01386-438706) rents out bikes for £10 a day from Chipping Campden.

Several companies offer guided or unguided walking tours; try Cotswold Walking Holidays (☎ 01242-254353, ⓔ walking @star.co.uk), 10 Royal Parade, Bayshill Rd, Cheltenham.

GETTING AROUND

Some TICs stock local bus timetables, or you can phone the Gloucestershire public transport enquiry line for details (☎ 01452-425543). Limited as it is, the Cotswolds bus service is still more comprehensive than the rail network, which skims the northern and southern borders.

NORTHERN COTSWOLDS

The northern Cotswolds are characterised by charming villages of soft, mellow stone, built in folds between the rolling wolds. Although they owe their existence to the medieval wool industry, most now rely on tourism for a living. A handful have been overwhelmed, but even these are worth a look.

Burford
☎ 01993

One of the loveliest Cotswold villages, Burford has one long street of handsome stone houses and attracts crowds of tourists in summer. Once an important coaching town, it boasts fine 14th- to 16th-century houses and a medieval bridge over the River Windrush. The TIC (☎ 823558) is by the Lamb Inn on Sheep St.

The 16th-century **Tolsey Museum** (Toll House), on High St, houses a small summer-only museum. Admission costs 50p.

Just outside Burford is the **Cotswold Wildlife Park** (☎ 823006), a long-established zoo in the grounds of a Gothic mansion. It opens 10 am to 5 pm (4 pm in winter) daily. Admission costs £6/4.

Places to Stay & Eat Burford is no place for those on a tight budget; most cheaper accommodation is 4 miles north-east at Leafield.

In Burford, *Priory Tearooms* has five rooms with bargain B&B at just £15 per person. *Chevrons* (☎ 823416) has singles/doubles with bathroom from £25/35.

Burford's oldest pub, the 15th-century *Lamb Inn* (☎ 823155, *Sheep St*), is now a very comfy place to stay, with beamed ceilings and creaking stairs. Rooms with bathrooms cost from £52.50 per person during the week, £57.50 at weekends. Short breaks are better value.

Burford has several other good pubs. On High St, the characterful *Mermaid* and the *Golden Pheasant* do bar snacks and full meals. In Witney St, the *Angel* is popular not only for its real ale but also for its award-winning food. The restaurant is expensive but meals in the bar are reasonably priced.

High St has several tearooms; *Huffkins* has the most incredible selection of cakes and is always busy, while *Priory Tea Rooms* has tables outside during the summer.

Getting There & Away From Oxford, Swanbrook (☎ 01452-712386) runs four buses a day (two on Sunday) to Burford via Witney.

Witney
☎ 01993 • pop 22,000

Ten miles west of Oxford, Witney is a gateway to the Cotswolds. Since 1669, the town has specialised in the production of blankets. Sheep on the Cotswolds and the local downs provided the wool, while the River Windrush provided the water. High-quality blankets continue to be made here; the Queen still orders hers from Early's of Witney.

The TIC (☎ 775802) is in the 18th-century town hall in Market Square.

Although the town has grown to absorb the demands of Oxford commuters and light industry, the centre retains some character. On High St, blankets were formerly weighed and measured in the 18th-century Baroque-style Blanket Hall. In Market Place stands the 17th-century Buttercross, originally a covered market.

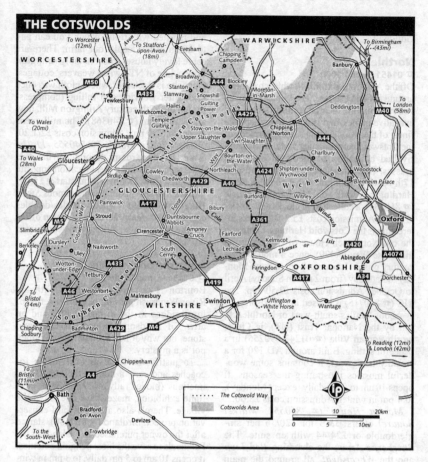

THE COTSWOLDS

The Cotswold Way

Cotswolds Area

0   10   20km

0   5   10mi

Cogges Manor Farm Museum

Clearly signposted in the suburbs of Witney is Cogges Museum (☎ 772602), where domestic farm animals roam the grounds of a 13th-century manor house, which was drastically altered in the 17th and 18th centuries. Here you can sample cakes and scones freshly baked on the old range. It opens 10.30 am to 4.30 pm Tuesday to Friday (from noon at weekends) late March to October. Admission costs £4/2. Jump off the Oxford to Witney bus (see Burford) at the Griffin Pub and walk down Church Lane.

Chipping Norton
☎ 01608

Chipping Norton is an attractive market town, the highest in Oxfordshire, which makes a useful base for touring nearby villages. Like its neighbours, its wealth was built on the backs of sheep – tweed took over where wool left off by the 19th century. The **Church of St Mary** is a classic example of the wool churches seen throughout the Cotswolds, while the old glove factory off the road to Moreton-in-Marsh is a striking monument to the industrial architecture of the 19th century.

The TIC (☎ 644379) is located in the Guildhall.

Northleach
☎ 01451 • pop 1000

Off the A40 from Oxford, Northleach clusters around a market square. The village is a marvellous mixture of architectural styles and evocative names, and is home to perhaps the finest of the wool churches, a masterpiece of the Cotswold perpendicular style, with an unrivalled collection of medieval memorial brasses. Near the square is Oak House, a 17th-century wool house that contains **Keith Harding's World of Mechanical Music** (☎ 860181), a collection of clocks and musical boxes. Admission costs £5/2.50. Just as interesting is the **Cotswold Heritage Centre,** in the old Northleach House of Correction on the Fosse Way (A429), once a model 19th-century prison. It opens 10 am to 5 pm Monday to Saturday (from 2 pm on Sunday) April to October. Admission costs £2.50/80p. The TIC (☎ 860715) is housed in the prison.

About 4 miles south-west of Northleach, run by the National Trust (NT), is **Chedworth Roman Villa** (☎ 01242-890256) in a peaceful setting. Built around AD 120 for a wealthy landowner, it contains some wonderful mosaics illustrating the seasons. It opens 10 am to 5 pm daily (except Monday), to 4 pm in winter. Admission costs £3.60.

Market House (☎ 860557, Market Square) offers B&B for £20/36 per single/double or £24/44 with en suite. The *Sherborne Arms*, the charming *Red Lion* and the *Wheatsheaf*, all around the main square, are the readiest sources of sustenance, solid or liquid.

Northleach is 9 miles from Burford and 13 miles from Cheltenham. Swanbrook (☎ 01452-712386) runs several buses a day between Cheltenham and Oxford via Northleach.

Bibury
☎ 01285 • pop 500

Described by William Morris as 'the most beautiful village in England', Bibury is a delightful place that manages to retain some dignity despite the hordes of visitors.

The River Coln flows alongside the road and is filled with trout, which you can pay to fatten at the local trout farm. There are some lovely houses, most notably **Arlington Row**, a line of NT-owned weavers' cottages. Opposite is Rack Isle, where cloth was once dried after weaving and fulling (compressing) in the 17th-century **Arlington Mill**, now a folk museum (☎ 740368). The mill opens 10 am to 5.30 pm. Admission costs £2/1.20.

The *William Morris* (☎ 740555, 11 The Street) has three rooms decorated in the style of its namesake and a great location opposite Arlington Row. Double rooms start at £55. If you want to splash out, try the famous *Swan Hotel* (☎ 740695) where singles/doubles cost £99/180. *Jenny Wren's Tearoom* offers an afternoon tea so filling you won't need dinner.

Bourton-on-the-Water
☎ 01451 • pop 2600

Bourton is certainly attractive, with the River Windrush passing beneath a series of low bridges in the village centre and an array of handsome houses in Cotswold stone, but why it has become such a honey pot is a mystery.

To justify the large area set aside for coaches and cars, a number of specific attractions (model railway and village, perfume exhibition, maze) have opened in the village. There's also a serious bird conservation project, **Birdland** (☎ 820480), started after the owner purchased two islands in the Falklands to save the local penguin colonies. It opens 10 am to 5 pm daily, to 3 pm in winter. Admission costs £4.25/2.50.

Tearooms and restaurants line the main street. The best times to see Bourton are summer evenings after the coaches have left, or in winter.

The Slaughters

Along with Bourton-on-the-Water, the Slaughters, Upper and Lower, are the most famously picturesque villages of the Cotswolds. Their repellent name is actually a corruption of a Saxon word meaning 'place of sloe trees'.

The best way to enjoy the Slaughters is to

spend an hour walking to them from Bourton. Following part of the Warden's Way will take you across the Fosse Way from Bourton, over a meadow and along a path into Lower Slaughter. Continuing past the Victorian flour mill, the route crosses meadows and goes behind the Manor House into Upper Slaughter. The mill opens 10 am to 6 pm daily March to October. Admission costs £1.50/75p.

Stow-on-the-Wold
☎ 01451 • pop 2000

At almost 240m, Stow-on-the-Wold is the highest town in the Cotswolds, the windswept meeting point of eight routes and the site of the last Civil War battle. The pretty main square resembles an Italian piazza. The Royalist Hotel, established in 947, claims to be England's oldest inn; some of its timbers have been carbon dated to the 10th century (see Places to Stay & Eat later).

The TIC (☎ 831082), Hollis House, is on the square.

Places to Stay & Eat On the eastern side of Market Square, *Stow-on-the-Wold Youth Hostel (☎ 830497, The Square)* charges £12.50/8.50 for adults/under-18s and opens daily from April to early September. Phone for opening times the rest of the year.

Otherwise, cheap accommodation is scarce. The *White Hart Inn (☎ 830674, The Square)* charges from £22 per person, while the attractive *Gate Lodge (☎ 832103, Stow Hill)*, half a mile out of the centre, charges £27/40 for singles/doubles. Another good option, charging from £40 to £52 per double, is delightful *Number Nine (☎ 870333, 9 Park St)*. The *Royalist Hotel (☎ 830670, Digbeth St)* has rooms for £45/95.

Peggums (☎ 830102, Church St) is a tiny tea shop with real character.

Getting There & Away Pulhams Coaches (☎ 01451-820369) operates daily services linking Stow with Moreton-in-Marsh (15 minutes), and a Monday to Saturday service to Cheltenham (45 minutes).

The nearest train stations are 4 miles away at Kingham and Moreton-in-Marsh.

Moreton-in-Marsh
☎ 01608 • pop 2600

Straddling the Fosse Way, Moreton may not be the most attractive Cotswold town but has some of the best transport connections. It's nowhere near a marsh (a corruption of march, meaning boundary) and grew first as a staging post and then as a railway town. Its Tuesday market, an old-fashioned affair with over 200 stalls, is worth a look.

About 2 miles west of Moreton is spectacular, Moghul-style **Sezincote House,** built in 1805 by Charles Cockerell of the East India Company and thought to have inspired Brighton Pavilion. There are tours of the house on Thursday and Friday afternoons in May, June, July and September. Admission costs £5 for the house (no children) and garden, £3.50/1 for the garden only. The garden opens 2 to 6 pm on the same days, January to November.

Places to Stay & Eat The nearest hostel is in Stow-on-the-Wold, 4 miles south. B&Bs in Moreton include *Treetops (☎ 651036, London Rd)*, which has singles/doubles with bathroom for £30/42. *Moreton House (☎ 650747, High St)* has a restaurant and a range of rooms from £24/44, or £62 with a four-poster bed.

Manor House Hotel (☎ 650501, High St) has luxurious rooms from £70/98.

Pubs include the atmospheric *White Hart Royal* and the *Black Bear,* known for its excellent hot beef sandwiches.

Getting There & Away Pulhams Coaches (☎ 01451-820369) operates a daily service (limited on Sunday) between Moreton and Cheltenham (one hour) via Stow-on-the-Wold (15 minutes) and Bourton-on-the-Water. Many surrounding villages put on market-day buses. Stratford Blue (☎ 01789-292085) bus No 569 runs hourly to Stratford via Broadway or Chipping Campden alternately.

There are trains roughly every two hours to Moreton from Oxford (£7.20, 35 minutes), Charlbury (£4.10, 20 minutes), Worcester (£7.60, 30 minutes) and Hereford (£10.40, one hour).

CENTRAL ENGLAND

Chipping Campden
☎ 01386 • pop 2000

In an area filled with exquisite villages, Chipping Campden, with its thatched roofs, neatly clipped hedges and gorgeous gardens, is one of the prettiest. The unspoilt main street is flanked by a succession of golden-hued terraced cottages, each subtly different from the next.

The TIC (☎ 841206) is in Noel Arms Courtyard, off High St. Across the road, the gabled Market Hall dates from 1627. At the western end is **St James**, a very fine Cotswold wool church with some splendid 17th-century monuments. Nearby are the Jacobean lodges and gateways of the vanished manor house, and opposite is a remarkable row of **almshouses**.

Above the town, **Dover's Hill** is named after Robert Dover, who instigated the 17th-century Cotswold Olimpick Games, recently reinstated. The games take place on Spring Bank Holiday and include sports such as slippery pole climbing and welly wanging, culminating in a torch-lit procession and dancing in the square. Transport is available from Campden Square.

About 4 miles north-east of Chipping Campden, in secluded Hidcote Bartrim, **Hidcote Manor Gardens** (☎ 438333; NT), a series of six lovely gardens designed to complement each other. The gardens open 11 am to 7 pm daily except Tuesday and Friday, April to September. Admission is £5.60/2.80.

Places to Stay & Eat None of the numerous B&Bs is cheap. *Sparlings* (☎ 840505, Leysbourne) has two rooms with bathroom for £50/53 per double/twin.

The fifteenth-century *Badgers Hall* (☎ 840839, High St) offers singles/doubles for £45/50. Readers of this guide have enjoyed staying at award-winning *Marnic* (☎ 840014) in nearby Broad Campden. Rooms cost from £36/44.

The *Eight Bells* in Church St does delicious dishes such as braised lamb in a caper dressing. *Badger Bistro* (☎ 840520, The Square) does Sunday lunch for under £6, while *Joel's Restaurant* (☎ 840598, High St) has a selection of pastas and a modern British menu. For a cream tea try *Badgers Hall* in High St.

Getting There & Away Stratford Blue (☎ 01789-292085) bus No 569 runs hourly to Stratford or Moreton. On Tuesday the market bus runs from Moreton, otherwise a taxi will cost about £8.

Getting Around You can hire a bike from Cotswold Country Cycles (☎ 438706), Longlands Farm Cottage, for £10/60 per day/week.

Broadway
☎ 01386 • pop 2000

Just over the border in Worcestershire, this well-known and much-visited village is strung out along a broad street, beneath the crest of an escarpment. Undeniably handsome, and largely unspoilt despite its fame, it has inspired writers, artists and composers, from JM Barrie to Edward Elgar. A new bypass has brought some relief from through traffic, but coaches still manage to cause maximum chaos in high summer.

The TIC (☎ 852937) is at 1 Cotswold Court, alongside some interesting shops.

The most striking house is the Lygon Arms, now a famous hotel. The unspoilt medieval **Church of St Eadburgha** is signposted from the town, a 30-minute walk away. For a longer walk, take the footpath opposite the church that leads up to **Broadway Tower** (☎ 852390), a crenellated, 18th-century folly that stands above the town with a small William Morris exhibition on one floor. On a clear day you can see 12 counties from the top. It opens 10.30 am to 5 pm daily (later on Sunday). Admission costs £3/2.20.

Places to Stay & Eat Broadway has lots of high-quality accommodation but the luxury is inevitably pricey. The excellent *Cinnibar Cottage* (☎ 858623, 45 Bury End) is about half a mile from the centre and charges £40 for its one room. The *Olive Branch Guest House* (☎ 853440, 78 High St) has singles/doubles from £35/55.

The best place to stay is the *Lygon Arms* (☎ 852255, High St) – if your budget will stretch to £99/159. Its restaurant, *Olivers*, has dishes such as fish cakes in sorrel sauce. For cheaper meals try *Roberto's Coffee House*, one of the few places open on Sunday.

Getting There & Away Broadway is 6 miles from Evesham (see Herefordshire & Worcestershire later in the chapter) and 9 miles from Moreton-in-Marsh. Castleways (☎ 01242-602949) runs bus No 559 to Evesham and No 606 to Cheltenham.

Snowshill

About 3 miles south of Broadway, **Snowshill Manor** (☎ 01386-852410; NT) is furnished with an extraordinarily eclectic collection of items, from Japanese armour to Victorian perambulators, gathered by the eccentric Charles Paget Wade. The walled gardens are particularly delightful and the restaurant has wonderful views. It opens 12 to 5 pm Wednesday to Sunday April to October; timed tickets are issued for the cramped house. Admission costs £6/3. It's an uphill walk to get here from Broadway.

Hailes

About 3 miles north-east of Winchcombe along the Cotswold Way, this former Cistercian abbey, now a romantic ruin, was once an important place of pilgrimage – people came from all over Europe to see the phial of Christ's blood kept here. After the dissolution of the monasteries, the blood was exposed as a mixture of honey and saffron. Run by English Heritage (EH) and the NT, **Hailes Abbey** (☎ 01242-602398) opens 10 am to 6 pm daily Easter to October; weekends only the rest of the year. Admission costs £2.60/1.30.

The small neighbouring **church**, with medieval stained glass, murals and heraldic tiles, is delightful. A short walk away are the organic Hayles Fruit Farm (good cider) and Orchard Tea Room.

Winchcombe
☎ 01242 • pop 5000

Saxon Winchcombe was the capital of its own county and the seat of Mercian royalty. Its Benedictine abbey was one of the country's main pilgrimage centres.

These days its main attraction is **Sudeley Castle** (☎ 604357), where the chapel houses the tomb of Catherine Parr, Henry VIII's last wife. Parts of the original building have been left in ruins, but the rest was restored in the 19th century. It opens 10.30 am to 5.30 pm daily, Easter to October. Admission costs £6.20/3.20. The gardens are especially beautiful.

In the village proper, splendid **St Peter's Church** is noted for its fine gargoyles, including one that looks like Lewis Carroll's Mad Hatter. The TIC (☎ 602925), in High St, has information about other local walks.

An excellent 2½-mile hike along the Cotswold Way leads to **Belas Knap**, a false-entrance burial chamber built about 5000 years ago.

Places to Stay & Eat The *Courtyard House* (☎ 602441, High St) has two double rooms for £45, while half-timbered *Wesley House* (☎ 602366, High St) charges £48/70 for a single/double (dinner in the excellent restaurant is from £15.50). Farther out, friendly *Blair House* (☎ 603626, 41 Gretton Rd) has beds from £25/42.50.

Wincelcumbe Tearooms (☎ 603578, 7 Hailes St) does soup with tasty rosemary and raisin bread, and classic cream teas for about £3.

Poachers Restaurant (☎ 604566, 6 North St), round the corner from the TIC, has main dishes from £8 to £11.

The *Old White Lion* in North St is an inviting 15th-century pub. The *Plaisterers Arms*, near the church, does good meals and real ales.

Getting There & Away Castleways Coaches (☎ 01242-602949) runs several buses, Monday to Saturday, from Winchcombe to Cheltenham or Broadway.

Guiting Power & Temple Guiting

The Guitings lie about 4 miles east of Winchcombe. Set around a green, Guiting Power is particularly attractive, with a shop, post office and two pubs. It even has its own music festival in July, and a remarkable Norman doorway to its church. Nearby, the **Cotswold**

Farm Park (☎ 01451-850307) preserves endangered species of farm animals such as the Gloucester old spot pig. It opens 10.30 am to 5 pm daily (to 6 pm on Sunday), April to October. Admission costs £4.50/2.30.

SOUTHERN COTSWOLDS

The southern Cotswolds are quite different in character to the northern area: the stone is more soberly coloured, the valleys are steeper and the area is less reliant on tourism. If you want to get away from the Cotswold honey pots, it's worth exploring some of these villages.

Painswick

☎ 01452 • pop 2800

Sometimes called the 'Queen of the Cotswolds', Painswick is a picture-perfect Cotswold village. **St Mary's Church** is particularly interesting, its graveyard bristling with the table-top tombs of rich wool merchants who made the town prosperous from the 17th century. The yew trees are said to be uncountable but certainly number no more than 99; if the 100th should grow, legend claims the devil will shrivel it. The church tower still has cannonball scars from the Civil War.

The streets behind the church are lined with handsome merchants' houses. Bisley St, with several 14th-century houses, was the original thoroughfare, while New St is a medieval addition. Rare, iron-spectacle stocks stand in the street just south of the church.

Painswick Rococo Garden The gardens of Painswick House (☎ 813204), half a mile north of the town, open 11 am to 5 pm daily in summer; Wednesday to Sunday, October to May; and close in December. They're best visited in February or March for the spectacular snowdrop displays. Admission costs £3.30/1.75.

Places to Stay & Eat The pleasant *Hambutts Mynd* (☎ 812352, *Edge Rd*) caters especially for Cotswold Way walkers, with doubles for £45.

Centrally positioned, *Cardynham House* (☎ 814006, *The Cross*) has nine rooms from

£36/46 per single/double; it dates back to the 15th century. Sixteenth-century *Thorne* (☎ 812476, *Friday St*) has two doubles for £50. *Painswick Hotel* (☎ 812160, *Kemps Lane*) is the best hotel, with luxurious rooms from £85/110, many with views over the valley.

The *Royal Oak* (☎ 813129, *St Mary's St*) is a popular local, as is the *Falcon*. The *Country Elephant* (☎ 813564, *New St*) does great food but think £25 per head for dinner. *Bertram's Café-Bistro*, opposite the church, is cheaper, with ploughman's lunches.

Getting There & Around Bus No 46 connects Cheltenham and Stroud with Painswick hourly. Swanbrook (☎ 01452-712386) has a better service for Gloucester. Those with their own vehicles watch out – the streets are extremely narrow.

Stroud

☎ 01453 • pop 37,800

The narrow, steep-sided Stroud Valley stands out from the rest of the southern Cotswolds and was the scene of the Cotswold wool industry's final fling.

Stroud is built around a spur above the River Frome. Although Stroudwater scarlet used to be famous throughout the world, very little cloth is produced today. Many of the old mill buildings remain, though most now have new uses. A walk around Stroud's hilly streets should take in the old Shambles market (Wednesday, Friday and Saturday), the Tudor town hall and the Stroud Museum. The Stroud Subscription Rooms on George St house the TIC (☎ 765768).

Places to Stay & Eat Opposite the town centre car park, *London Hotel* (☎ 759992) does B&B with singles/doubles from £29/42 or £39/50 with bathroom.

Fern Rock House (☎ 757307, *72 Middle St*) charges £20/35, while the nonsmoking *Deben House* (☎ 766573), off the London Rd, charges from £20/45.

In Union St, the *Pelican* serves pub lunches and there are several cafes in the pedestrianised High St, behind the TIC. Try *Woodruff's Organic Café* or *Mills Café*, which is down an alley and has a few outdoor tables.

Getting There & Away Stagecoach Stroud Valleys (☎ 763421) is the main local operator; bus No 46 runs hourly to Painswick and Cheltenham. No 93 operates half-hourly to Gloucester.

Slimbridge

Eleven miles south-west of Gloucester, the **Slimbridge Wildfowl & Wetlands Trust** (☎ 01453-891900) was established in 1946 by the late Sir Peter Scott as a breeding ground for wildfowl, notably geese and swans. Open 9.30 am to 5 pm daily, the centre is as interesting in winter (when it closes at 4 pm), when Arctic 'visitors' arrive, as it is in summer. Admission costs £5.75/3.50 and is discounted if you stay the night before at *Slimbridge Youth Hostel (☎ 01453-890275)*, half a mile south across the Sharpness Canal. The hostel opens from March to August; phone for other times. The nightly charge is £10/6.90 for adults/under-18s.

Badgerline's (☎ 0117-955 5111) bus No 308 links Bristol with Gloucester and passes by the Slimbridge crossroads, 2 miles from the centre. On Sunday, Stagecoach operates three buses to and from the sanctuary; phone ☎ 01452-527516 for exact times.

Berkeley
☎ 01453

This quiet Georgian town is best known as the place where Edward II met his grisly end in **Berkeley Castle** (☎ 810332). His last days must have been as awful as his death (supposedly impaled on a red-hot poker); the ventilation shaft in the murder room was connected to a pit in which the rotting carcasses of dead animals were kept.

The beautiful medieval castle is set in terraced Elizabethan gardens surrounded by lawns. It opens 11 am to 5 pm daily (from 2 pm on Sunday), June to September; opening hours are more restricted the rest of the year. Admission costs £5.40/2.90, or £2/1 just for the grounds. The **Butterfly Farm** across the car park opens one hour after the castle. Admission costs £2/1.

A path winds through **St Mary's** churchyard, with its unusual detached bell tower, to the **Jenner Museum** (☎ 810631), in the house where Edward Jenner performed the first smallpox vaccination in 1796. Opening hours are similar to the castle's, but it closes Mondays. Admission costs £2.50/1.

Berkeley is 6 miles south-west of Slimbridge. Badgerline's No 308 bus from Bristol to Gloucester passes this way.

Tetbury
☎ 01666 • pop 4500

On the A433, Tetbury has an interesting 18th-century Gothic church with a graceful spire and wonderful interior. The 17th-century Market House was used for wool trading. The TIC (☎ 503552) is at Old Court House in Long St.

Westonbirt (☎ 880220), a huge arboretum with a magnificent selection of temperate trees, is 2½ miles south-west of Tetbury. Walks through the trees are particularly stunning in spring and autumn. It opens 10 am to dusk daily. Admission costs £4/1.

Lechlade
☎ 01367

At the highest navigable point of the River Thames, Lechlade is graced by the spire of **St Lawrence's Church**, described as an 'aerial pile' by Shelley in his 1815 poem *A Summer Evening Churchyard, Lechlade, Gloucestershire*. A wool church, it was rededicated to the Spanish saint by Catherine of Aragon, who held the manor in the 16th century.

About 3 miles east of Lechlade off the Faringdon road, **Kelmscot Manor** (☎ 252486) was home to William Morris, the poet, artist and founder of the Arts and Crafts Movement. It opens 11 am to 1 pm and 2 to 5 pm on Wednesday only, plus occasional summer Saturdays, April to September. Admission costs £6/3. The Memorial Cottages nearby feature a beautiful carving of Morris seated under a tree.

Fairford

About 3 miles west of Lechlade, Fairford's claim to fame is **St Mary's Church**, which houses Britain's only complete set of medieval stained-glass windows. The gift of wealthy wool merchant John Tame, who also rebuilt the church, the windows are thought to be by Barnard Flower, master glass painter to Henry VII. Tiddles, the church cat, is buried in the churchyard. The high street largely consists of graceful 18th-century houses.

CIRENCESTER
☎ 01285 • pop 13,500

Cirencester was founded as a military base at the junction of the Roman Akeman St, Fosse Way and Ermin Way, starting life as Corinium, the second largest Roman town after London. Eventually it was one of the principal towns of north-western Europe. The 2nd-century amphitheatre, on Cotswold Ave, is mostly grassed over, but was one of the largest in the country. The Saxons destroyed the town in the 6th century and built smaller settlements outside the town walls, renaming it Cirencester. It only really regained its status in the Middle Ages when it became the most important Cotswold wool town.

These days it's an affluent medium-sized town with several worthwhile sights.

The centre clusters round the parish church on the Market Square, where you'll also find the TIC (☎ 654180), in the Corn Hall. Weekly markets still take place every Monday and Friday.

Church of St John the Baptist
One of England's largest churches, St John's seems more like a cathedral. It has a magnificent perpendicular-style tower, built with the reward given by Henry IV to a group of earls who foiled a rebellion. The highlight of the exterior, however, is the three storey south porch, which faces the square. Built as an office by late-15th-century abbots, it subsequently became the medieval town hall.

Inside the church several memorial brasses record the matrimonial histories of important wool merchants. A 15th-century painted stone pulpit comes complete with hourglass and the east window contains fine medieval stained glass. A wall safe displays the Boleyn Cup, made for Anne Boleyn,

second wife of Henry VIII, in 1535. The church is also notable for the oldest 12-bell peal in the country and continues to observe the ringing of the 'pancake bell' on Shrove Tuesday and the celebration of the Restoration on 29 May.

Corinium Museum
This museum (☎ 655611), in Park St, shows local Roman finds in tableaux complete with impressive mosaics. It opens 10 am to 5 pm daily (from 2 pm on Sunday); it closes on Monday in winter. Admission costs £2.50/80p.

Cirencester Park
On the western edge of town, this park features magnificent geometrical landscaping, designed with the help of the poet Alexander Pope. The Broad Ride makes an excellent short walk.

The house was built by the first Earl Bathurst between 1714 and 1718 and hides behind one of the world's highest yew hedges. It's not open to the public.

Places to Stay
Camping If you're prepared to swap lack of facilities for a cheap stay, there's camping space for £1 per person on bicycles, £2 by car, at *Abbey Home Farm* (☎ 652808, 656969), an organic farm a mile north of Cirencester on the Northleach road.

Hostels In a Victorian vicarage 5 miles north-west of Cirencester is *Duntisbourne Abbots Youth Hostel* (☎ 821682). It opens Monday to Saturday, April to October. The nightly charge is £8.50/5.75 for adults/under-18s and the hostel is renowned for its good food. You need your own transport to get here.

B&Bs & Hotels Victoria Rd has several B&Bs and guesthouses. *Apsley Villa Guest House* (☎ 653489, 16 Victoria Rd) as five rooms from £25/40 for a single/double. *Wimborne House* (☎ 653890, 91 Victoria Rd), which is nonsmoking, has rooms with bathroom from £30/40.

The *White Lion Inn* (☎ 654053, 8 Glou-

cester St) is a 17th-century coaching inn five minutes' walk from the town centre. Rooms with bathroom are from £39.50/47. The *Golden Cross* (☎ 652137, *Black Jack St)* has good value rooms from £20/30.

The comfortable *Kings Head Hotel* (☎ 653303, *Market Place)* is opposite the church. Rooms cost £65/85, less for two days or more.

During college holidays, rooms are available at the *Royal Agricultural College* (☎ 652531), on the northern outskirts. Singles/doubles cost from £24.50/45.

Places to Eat

Cirencester has plenty of good places to eat, especially in Castle St where the *Rajdoot Tandoori* (☎ 652651) has Sunday eat-all-you-can lunches for £6.95 (£4.95 vegetarian), and *Tatyans* (☎ 653529) does the sort of Chinese that makes the pages of the good food guides.

For lighter lunches try *The Café-Bar (Brewers Courtyard)*, off Cricklade St, which has a range of filled baguettes and ciabatta rolls. There's another *cafe* (☎ 657181) inside the Brewery Arts Centre opposite. Both are closed on Sunday.

Black Jack Coffee House in Black Jack St is a good place to pause for refreshment, while the *Swan Yard Café (6 Swan Yard)* does mouth-watering cakes. For putting together a picnic you can hardly better *Jeroboams*, beside the church, where they claim to 'build' sandwiches rather than make them.

The *Mad Hatter Wine Bar* and *MacKenzie* in Castle St serve cafe-bar-style lunches. *Somewhere Else* on Castle St has global food and a good courtyard for summer. There's real ale at the very local *Twelve Bells* out on Lewis Lane, and good pub food at *The Black Horse* in Castle St.

Getting There & Away

National Express (☎ 0870 580 8080) buses run from Cirencester to London (£9.75, 2¼ hours).

Stagecoach (☎ 01242-522021) bus No 51 runs to Cheltenham, 12 miles to the north. The less frequent No 52 runs to Gloucester.

GLOUCESTER
☎ 01452 • pop 106,600

The county capital Gloucester (pronounced glo-ster) is less than the sum of its past and these days finds itself in the shadow of its more glamorous neighbour Cheltenham. Approaching the city, its physical location is impressive, nestled in the vale beneath the Cotswold escarpment and beside the River Severn. The city suffered greatly from WWII bombing but is still well worth visiting, particularly for its wonderful Gothic cathedral and the cluster of museums in the restored docks. It also has some of the cheapest accommodation around, making it a good base for exploring the surrounding area.

History

To the Romans, Gloucester was Glevum, founded as a retirement home for Cirencester's centurions. It remained important to the Saxons as a garrison town at the junction of the kingdoms of Mercia and Wessex and grew to become a major monastic centre.

When Ethelred, Alfred the Great's brother, was buried in the Saxon royal palace near the cathedral, Gloucester equalled Winchester in importance; it remained so to the Normans.

In 1216, Henry III's coronation took place here in St Peter's Abbey. After murdered Edward II was buried here, Gloucester became an important place of pilgrimage, which helped develop its commercial importance.

During the Civil War, the city was a Puritan stronghold and withstood a 26-day siege. In the 18th century Gloucester flourished on the back of the Forest of Dean's iron, coal and timber industries. Throughout the 20th century it was an industrial centre, producing at various times railway rolling stock, aircraft and motorcycles.

Orientation & Information

The city centre is based around Northgate, Southgate, Eastgate and Westgate Sts, which all converge on The Cross. The TIC (☎ 421188) is now located in a handsome building at 28 Southgate St and sells the *Via Sacra* town trail and a leaflet outlining the route of the 26-mile Glevum Way round the city outskirts.

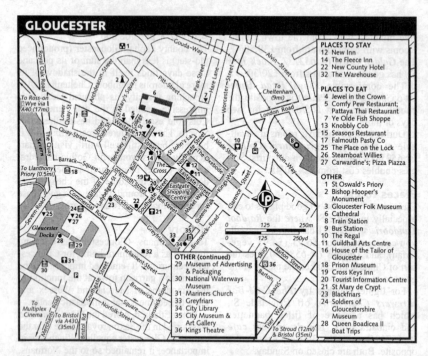

GLOUCESTER

PLACES TO STAY
12 New Inn
14 The Fleece Inn
22 New County Hotel
32 The Warehouse

PLACES TO EAT
4 Jewel in the Crown
5 Comfy Pew Restaurant;
   Pattaya Thai Restaurant
7 Ye Olde Fish Shoppe
13 Knobbly Cob
15 Seasons Restaurant
17 Falmouth Pasty Co
25 The Place on the Lock
26 Steamboat Willies
27 Carwardine's; Pizza Piazza

OTHER
1 St Oswald's Priory
2 Bishop Hooper's
   Monument
3 Gloucester Folk Museum
6 Cathedral
8 Train Station
9 Bus Station
10 The Regal
11 Guildhall Arts Centre
16 House of the Tailor of
   Gloucester
18 Prison Museum
19 Cross Keys Inn
20 Tourist Information Centre
21 St Mary de Crypt
23 Blackfriars
24 Soldiers of
   Gloucestershire
   Museum
28 Queen Boadicea II
   Boat Trips

OTHER (continued)
29 Museum of Advertising
   & Packaging
30 National Waterways
   Museum
31 Mariners Church
33 Greyfriars
34 City Library
35 City Museum &
   Art Gallery
36 Kings Theatre

Gloucester Cathedral

The city's focal point is still the gorgeous Gothic cathedral, one of the earliest examples of the English perpendicular style. Built as part of St Peter's Abbey, the cathedral's foundation stone was laid in 1089. When the abbey was dissolved in 1541, the church became the centre of the new Gloucester diocese. The nave has some wonderful Norman arcading, with the last two bays at the western end rebuilt in perpendicular style in 1420. Note how the south wall of the south aisle leans out of true because of the defensive ditch of the Roman town beneath.

The magnificent 69m-high tower was constructed from 1450 to replace the 13th-century spire.

The newly restored eastern window, made in 1349 to commemorate local participation in the Battle of Crecy, is the largest in England, while the wooden choir stalls date from 1350. Above them soars wonderfully

elaborate lierne vaulting. The late-15th-century Lady Chapel represents the final flowering of the perpendicular style.

In the southern ambulatory is an effigy of Robert, William the Conqueror's eldest son. Edward II's magnificent tomb, surmounted by an alabaster effigy, is in the northern ambulatory.

The northern transept, containing a 13th-century reliquary, leads into the treasury and also gives access to the tribune gallery, where there is an exhibition on the cathedral's history (summer only). In the northern aisle is a memorial to John Stafford Smith, a Gloucester composer who wrote the tune for the US national anthem.

At the western end stands a statue of Edward Jenner (1749–1823), who discovered how to vaccinate people against smallpox at nearby Berkeley.

The Great Cloister has the country's oldest fan vaulting, dating from the 14th century. Don't miss the stone basin for the monks to wash at, with niches for their towels across the way.

The cathedral (☎ 528095) opens 8 am to 6 pm daily. Donations of £2.50 are requested. Guided tours are available by arrangement.

Every third year Gloucester Cathedral hosts the Three Choirs Festival. It will be Gloucester's turn in 2001 and 2004.

Gloucester Docks

The present quay was first recorded in 1390. Direct trade with foreign ports started in 1580 and by 1780 some 600 ships a year were docking at Gloucester, although large ships generally only got as far as Bristol. The 15 warehouses in the dock area were built for the 19th-century corn trade. Now redundant, they've been refurbished and most house museums, offices and restaurants.

Llanthony, the largest warehouse, houses the excellent **National Waterways Museum** (☎ 318054), which has a varied collection of historic vessels and imaginative displays. It opens 10 am to 5 pm daily. Admission costs £4.75/3.75.

The Albert Warehouse, part of the Victoria Dock, which specialised in salt transshipment, houses the **Museum of Advertising & Packaging** (☎ 302309), Robert Opie's nostalgia-provoking collection of packaging ephemera. It opens 10 am to 6 pm daily. Admission costs £3.50/1.25.

In the old Custom House, the **Soldiers of Gloucestershire Museum** (☎ 522682) is live-

lier than most military museums. It opens 10 am to 5 pm daily. Admission costs £4/2.

In Hempsted Lane, across Llanthony Bridge from the dock area, are the remains of **Llanthony Priory**, one of the richest Augustinian houses in England when it was dissolved in 1538.

Other Things to See & Do

The **Gloucester Folk Museum** (☎ 526467), 99 Westgate St, is in a 16th-century former clothier's house. Displays include a dairy, an ironmonger's shop and a Victorian schoolroom. It opens 10 am to 5 pm (to 4 pm on Sunday). Admission is £2/free. **St Nicholas House**, next door, was the family home of the Whittingtons of pantomime fame, and one of those places where Elizabeth I slept. Nearby are the remains of **St Oswald's Priory** and **St Mary de Lode**, Gloucester's oldest church.

At 5 Southgate St, an Edwardian shop boasts a curious mechanical clock, with figures to represent the four countries making up the United Kingdom. **Blackfriars**, Ladybellgate St, is Britain's finest surviving example of a Dominican friary. It opens daily and admission is free.

Along Eastgate St are 15th-century St Michael's Tower, Eastgate Market (pop inside to inspect the Beatrix Potter clock), and the remains of the East Gate itself. The **City Museum & Art Gallery** (☎ 524131), on Brunswick Rd, opens 10 am to 5 pm (to 4 pm

---

Surfing the Severn Bore

A 'bore' is a tidal phenomenon that occurs when flood-tides pour into the wide mouth of an estuary in greater volume than can easily flow along the normal channel of the river. The incoming tide then sweeps over the slower river flow and pushes upstream, flooding the riverbanks as it goes.

In Britain the most striking bore occurs on the River Severn, the country's longest river. At its deepest point the Severn Bore can be 2.75m deep, although in October 1966 a bore measuring 2.82m and travelling at 13 miles an hour was recorded.

In recent years a new sport of bore-surfing has developed, with surfers, body-boarders and canoeists lining up to catch the wave. If they time it right they can ride for 1½ miles upriver, much to the irritation of traditionalists who think they're spoiling a great natural phenomenon.

The best places to see the Severn Bore are between Awre, where the estuary narrows, and Gloucester. Gloucester TIC will be able to tell you the dates to go bore-watching. Wear wellies, as the water floods the surrounding roads.

CENTRAL ENGLAND

on Sunday). Admission is £2/free. It's worth dropping by to see the beautiful Birdlip Mirror dating back to the 1st century AD.

Fans of Beatrix Potter will love the **House of the Tailor of Gloucester** (☎ 422856), off Westgate St, established in the shop that inspired the story of the same name. It opens 10 am to 5 pm, Monday to Saturday. Admission is £1/free. The exhibition includes a very popular gift shop.

Places to Stay

Many people prefer to day-trip from nearby Cheltenham. A dependable B&B is *Bienvenue* (☎ 523284, 54 Central Road), which starts at £18 a person, but gets cheaper the longer guests stay.

Much nearer the centre and situated in a charming listed property is *The Albert Hotel* (☎ 502081, 56–58 Worcester St), which charges £37/54 for singles/doubles.

The historic *New Inn* (☎ 522177 Northgate St), reckoned to have been in the hospitality business for more than 500 years, offers good value for such a central location with singles/doubles-family rooms at £29.95/49.95/59.95 and some romantic suites with four-poster beds for £79.95. Similarly olde worlde is *The Fleece Inn* (☎ 522762, Westgate St), which has rooms from £26/33 including breakfast, £35/40 including en-suite facilities.

The *New County Hotel* (☎ 307000, 44 Southgate St) is a clean, comfortable and characterful three-star hotel a five-minute walk from the centre, which has doubles with en-suite facilities from £65.

Places to Eat

The cathedral *Undercroft*, in part of the former monastery great hall, is a good place for lunch or tea. Also near the cathedral are the *Comfy Pew Restaurant* (☎ 415648), which does teas and cakes, light lunches and a la carte dinners, and *Pattaya Thai Restaurant* (☎ 520739) with set lunches for about £5 – both restaurants are housed in beautiful old timbered buildings. Opposite the Beatrix Potter shop is the *Seasons Restaurant* (☎ 307060), which does a two-course lunch for £5.95.

The Tailor of Gloucester

Beatrix Potter's own favourite story was apparently *The Tailor of Gloucester*, the famous children's story she wrote and illustrated in 1901 as a Christmas present for a friend.

While visiting some cousins at Harescombe Grange, near Stroud, she heard a story about a real-life tailor, John Prichard of Gloucester. As in her tale, he'd been asked to make a waistcoat for the city's mayor. So busy was he that the Saturday before the Monday when the garment was due, he had only reached the cutting stage. But when he returned to the shop on Monday, he found it complete, bar a single buttonhole. A note pinned to it read, 'No more twist'.

Mystified (but commercially minded), he placed an advert in his window imploring people to come to Prichard's where the 'waistcoats are made at night by the fairies'. Later it transpired that the tailor's assistants had finished the waistcoat after sleeping in the shop because they'd stayed out too late to get home.

John Prichard died in 1934 and his tombstone at Haresfield records that he was the Tailor of Gloucester. In Potter's version, the young tailor became an old one, and the fairies became mice. She spent hours sketching on the streets of Gloucester and in local cottages. The house in Gloucester's College Court, which she chose as the tailor's fictional premises, is now a gift shop-cum-museum.

For an Indian meal, consider the *Jewel in the Crown* (☎ 310666, Westgate St), which has all the popular subcontinent standards for around £5.

Gloucester Docks has several good places to eat. *The Place on the Lock* (☎ 330253), on the 1st floor of the Gloucester Docks Antiques Centre, is cheap. *Steamboat Willies* (☎ 300990) has Tex Mex dishes and pasta from £5.95 but feels a bit 1980s, like much of Gloucester. *Pizza Piazza* (☎ 311951), overlooking the water in Merchants Quay shopping centre, does pizzas. There's also a *Carwardine's* coffee shop here.

The Regal, on St Aldate St, is one of Gloucester's cheapest pubs, but for something with more character try the *Cross Keys Inn*.

For fish and chips, go to *Ye Olde Fish Shoppe* (☎ 522502, Hare Lane), just east of the cathedral; prices are relatively high for the national dish, but it has held a licence since 1535 so inflation has played its part. The *Falmouth Pasty Co* rustles up fresh pasties. Another cheap option on Westgate St for sandwiches on the run is the *Knobbly Cob*.

Getting There & Away
Gloucester is 105 miles from London, 49 miles from Oxford, 45 miles from Bath and 16 miles from Cirencester. National Express has all the usual connections, and buses every two hours to London (£11, 3½ hours). Stagecoach operates most local bus services; phone ☎ 01242-522021 for details. An Explorer ticket to use the Gloucestershire bus network for a day costs £4.50/3. There are buses every 15 minutes to Cheltenham, but the quickest way to get there is by train.

CHELTENHAM
☎ 01242 • pop 88,000
Cheltenham is, like its more illustrious sibling Bath, one of England's definitive spa towns. These days, it is not so much known for its waters as for its racecourse and its public school, Cheltenham Ladies' College. The planners haven't been quite as kind to what is essentially a Regency town as they have to Bath, but it nonetheless exudes a certain culture and class. The town's handsome squares, colourful public gardens and elegant early-19th-century architecture are interspersed with obtrusive and incongruous slabs of modernity.

With plenty of restaurants and accommodation, Cheltenham makes an ideal base for exploring the western Cotswolds. It's also the scene of four important festivals: the National Hunt Meeting in March, during which the Cheltenham Gold Cup is run; the Music and Cricket festivals in July; and the Literature Festival in October. At these times, the odds on finding a room are worse than winning the National Lottery.

History
As a village midway between Gloucester and Tewkesbury, and on the road to Winchcombe and Oxford, Cheltenham received its market charter in 1226, when it was little more than a row of houses each side of the current High St. It remained important after the Civil War when the area of the southern Cotswolds became associated, briefly, with tobacco production, but really started to flourish after 1788 when George III visited to take the waters.

In 1716, pigeons pecking in a field under what is now the Ladies' College turned out to be eating salt crystals from a spring. Following fashion, the owner's son-in-law built a substantial pump room and opened it to the public. The king's visit sealed the spa's future and several new wells were built, as well as houses to accommodate the hordes of visitors, among them Handel and Jane Austen.

Modern visitors usually find the architecture more interesting than the waters. The elegant Regency style is evident around town in beautifully proportioned terraces, mostly creamy white and decorated with wrought-iron balconies and railings. Believe it or not, many of these attractive, imposing terraces were the pre-fabs of the early 19th century, built by property speculators with an eye for a quick buck. By the 1960s, many were sinking under their own weight and millions of pounds have been spent just to keep them standing.

Orientation
Cheltenham train station is out on a limb to the west; bus F or G will run you to the centre for 65p. The bus station is more conveniently positioned immediately behind The Promenade in the town centre.

Central Cheltenham is eminently walkable. High St runs roughly east-west and south from it is The Promenade, the most elegant shopping area ('the Bond St of the West'). The Promenade extends into Montpellier, a 19th-century shopping precinct, beyond which lie Suffolk Square and Lansdown Crescent. Pittville Park and the old Pump Room are a mile north of High St.

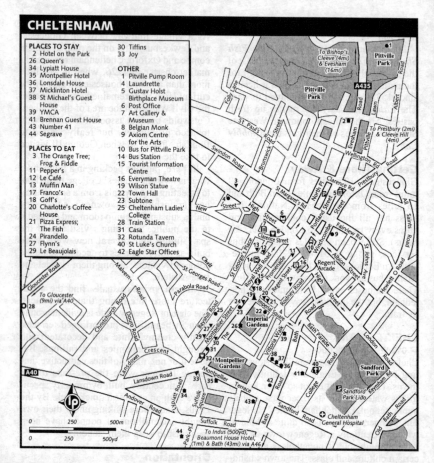

CHELTENHAM

PLACES TO STAY
2 Hotel on the Park
26 Queen's
34 Lypiatt House
35 Montpellier Hotel
36 Lonsdale House
37 Micklinton Hotel
38 St Michael's Guest House
39 YMCA
41 Brennan Guest House
43 Number 41
44 Segrave

PLACES TO EAT
3 The Orange Tree; Frog & Fiddle
11 Pepper's
12 Le Café
13 Muffin Man
17 Franco's
18 Goff's
20 Charlotte's Coffee House
21 Pizza Express; The Fish
27 Flynn's
29 Le Beaujolais

30 Tiffins
33 Joy

OTHER
1 Pitville Pump Room
4 Laundrette
5 Gustav Holst Birthplace Museum
6 Post Office
7 Art Gallery & Museum
8 Belgian Monk
9 Axiom Centre for the Arts
10 Bus for Pittville Park
14 Bus Station
15 Tourist Information Centre
16 Everyman Theatre
19 Wilson Statue
22 Town Hall
23 Subtone
25 Cheltenham Ladies' College
28 Train Station
31 Casa
32 Rotunda Tavern
40 St Luke's Church
42 Eagle Star Offices

Information

The helpful TIC (☎ 522878) is on The Promenade and sells all sorts of Cotswold walking and cycling guides, as well as *The Romantic Road,* a guide to a 30-mile circular driving tour of the southern Cotswolds. It also stocks a leaflet listing public transport options to the most popular tourist destinations around Cheltenham.

The Promenade

The Promenade is the heart of Cheltenham and is at its best in summer, when its hanging baskets are full of flowers.

The **Municipal Offices**, built as private residences in 1825, are among the best features of one of Britain's most beautiful thoroughfares. In front of the offices stands a **statue of Edward Wilson** (1872–1912), a Cheltenham man who went on Captain Scott's ill-fated second expedition (1910–12) to the South Pole and died in Antarctica.

Following The Promenade towards Montpellier, you come to the **Imperial Gardens,** originally built to service the Imperial Spa but covered by the Winter Gardens in 1902. The iron and glass structure was dismantled during WWII in case its reflection attracted German bombers.

Pittville Pump Room

Set in a delightful area of villas and park a mile from the town centre, the Pump Room is the town's finest Regency-style building. Built between 1825 and 1830, it was constructed as a spa and social centre for Joseph Pitt's new estate. Upstairs, there are occasional art exhibitions in the former library and billiard rooms. It opens daily (except Tuesday), but times vary. Admission is free. Downstairs (where you can still try the spa water), the former ballroom is used for concerts. The park itself is also used for concerts ('Pittville on Sunday') throughout the summer.

Art Gallery & Museum

Cheltenham's history is imaginatively displayed at the Art Gallery & Museum (☎ 237431) in Clarence St, which has excellent sections covering Edward Wilson, William Morris and the Arts and Crafts Movement and Dutch and British art. There's a temporary exhibition gallery on the ground floor and a cafe on the first floor. The gallery and museum open 10 am to 5.20 pm Monday to Saturday. Admission is free.

Gustav Holst Birthplace Museum

The Victorian house (☎ 524846) at 4 Clarence Rd where composer Gustav Holst (1874-1934) was born, displays Holst memorabilia alongside descriptions of life 'below stairs' at the turn of the century. You get to listen to music as you go round too (*The Planets*, usually). It opens 10 am to 4.15 pm Tuesday to Saturday. Admission costs £2.50/1.25.

Cleeve Hill

About 4 miles north of Cheltenham, Cleeve Hill, at 325m, is the highest point of the Cotswolds and lowland England, and offers fine views over Cheltenham. On weekdays, Castleways (☎ 603715) runs buses up the hill roughly once an hour from the town centre.

Cheltenham Racecourse

On Cheltenham's northern outskirts, Prestbury is reputedly Britain's most haunted village and home to the Cheltenham racecourse, one of the country's top courses. The Hall of Fame museum (☎ 513014), dedicated to its history, opens 8.30 am to 5.30 pm on weekdays. Admission is free.

Places to Stay

Hostels Often fully booked up, the *YMCA* (*☎ 524024, 6 Vittoria Walk*) has some singles for £15. Over the Easter and summer holidays *Cheltenham and Gloucester College* (*☎ 532774*) also lets rooms at its three sites; a single costs from £25.

B&Bs & Hotels There are several places in the Montpellier area, just south-west of the centre. *Segrave* (*☎ 523606, 7 Park Place*) is a small B&B charging £16/35 per single/double, set in a sturdy regency property with secure parking. Along the same road, *32 Park Place* (*☎ 582889*) offers a similar deal.

On Montpellier Drive, *Lonsdale House* (*☎ 232379*) is a comfortable B&B set in a charming town-house and has well-appointed rooms from £21/42. *St Michael's Guest House* (*☎ 513587, 4 Montpellier Drive*) is smaller but equally popular, and charges £28/40 for homely rooms.

Number 91 (*☎ 579441, 91 Montpellier Terrace*), where Wilson of the doomed 1912 Antarctic expedition was born (see The Promenade section earlier), has lovely rooms for £26/50. At sophisticated *Lypiatt House* (*☎ 224994, Lypiatt Rd*) rooms cost from £55/65. Also centrally located, the friendly *Brennan Guest House* (*☎ 525904, 21 St Lukes Rd*) has six rooms with shared bathroom from £22/40.

Beaumont House Hotel (*☎ 245986, 56 Shurdington Rd*) has rooms with bathroom from £42/60, and a couple with opulent four-poster beds for £78.

Between the town centre and Pittville Park, the luxurious Regency *Hotel on the Park* (*☎ 518898, 38 Evesham Rd*) has a good restaurant and well-appointed rooms from £78.50/96.50.

The gracious Victorian *Queen's* hotel

(☎ 514724, The Promenade) has rooms from £100/135, some with fine views across Imperial Gardens. Edward VII, Elgar and Arthur Conan Doyle all stayed here.

Places to Eat

There is some fine dining to be had in Cheltenham and two of the finest places are Le Beaujolais (☎ 525230) and Le Petit Blanc (☎ 266800). The former is a small, slick French restaurant offering sumptuous set menus for £15.95 for lunch and £18.95 for dinner, while the latter is a not-so-poor-man's introduction to the sort of food the other half eat at Raymond Blanc's famed Manoir de Quatre Saisons – it has fantastic entry level three-course meals for £15.00 but hearty eaters will not find the portions up to the presentation.

The excellent Indus (☎ 516676, 226 Bath Rd) is possibly the best of the town's Indian restaurants, but for a central location classy Joy Indian Restaurant (☎ 522888) is hard to beat, overlooking Montpellier Park.

Franco's (☎ 224880, 49 Rodney Rd) is a traditional Italian restaurant where three courses cost about £15. Another new Italian is Pirandello (☎ 234599). Pizza Express (☎ 253896, Imperial Square), inside Belgrave House, has live jazz on Wednesday evenings. Pepper's (☎ 573488, Regent St) is a brasserie with an outdoor area for summer drinks.

Cheap cafes litter the streets near the bus station; try Muffin Man (3 Crescent Terrace) or Le Café (1 Royal Well Rd). For a good, reasonably priced lunch in a central position try Café Museum in the Clarence St art gallery; soup, a roll and a cake will cost under £4. Another popular place with moving and shaking locals is Tiffins, on The Promenade, where a dazzling array of sandwiches to eat in or take away are available. If cakes alone are in order, Charlotte's can deliver. The Orange Tree (☎ 234232, 317 High St) is an inviting vegetarian restaurant. Axiom Centre for the Arts (see Theatre & Music under Entertainment later) has a vegetarian cafe (☎ 253183) serving vegie shepherd's pie.

Entertainment

Pubs, Bars & Clubs Casa, on Montpellier Walk, is a sophisticated cafe-bar where some of Cheltenham's bright, young things like to gather. The Fish is a pretty funky little place tucked away next to Pizza Express that plays some good tunes. For those more worried about beer than atmosphere, the Belgian Monk, on Clarence St, has an excellent array of strong stuff, while the Rotunda Tavern is more like the pub visitors expect from England. One last place worth a stop is the Frog & Fiddle down at the architecturally challenged end of High St, an up and coming part of town.

Dedicated clubbers might find Cheltenham lacking, but Subtone, on The Promenade, gets a steady crowd and draws occasional big-name DJs in from London.

Theatre & Music The Everyman theatre (☎ 572573, Regent St) stages anything from comedy and panto to Shakespeare. Pittville Pump Room often hosts classical music concerts, while the Town Hall (☎ 227979, Imperial Square) offers the more popular stuff. The Axiom Centre for the Arts (☎ 690243, 57 Winchcombe St) has a regular program of less mainstream theatrical events and music.

Getting There & Away

Cheltenham is 100 miles from London, 43 miles from Oxford, 40 miles from Bristol and 9 miles from Gloucester.

Bus National Express runs buses between Cheltenham and London (£11, 2¾ hours), Oxford (£7.75, 1¼ hours) and all other places on the National Express network. Swanbrook Coaches (☎ 01452-712386) also has buses to Oxford (£5, 1½ hours).

Stagecoach (☎ 522021) runs buses every 10 minutes to Gloucester (30 minutes). Monday to Saturday it has buses every two hours to Cirencester (30 minutes).

Pulhams Coaches (☎ 01451-820369) runs daily buses to Moreton (one hour) via Bourton and Stow. Castleways Coaches (☎ 602949) operates regularly Monday to Saturday, between Cheltenham and Broadway (45 minutes) via Winchcombe.

Train Cheltenham is on the Bristol to Birmingham line, with hourly trains to London (£31.50, 2½ hours), Bristol (£7.20, 45 minutes) and Bath (£11.20, one hour), and frequent departures for Gloucester (£2.30, 10 minutes).

Getting Around

Bicycle Compass Holidays (☎ 250642) have bicycles for hire for £11 per day at Cheltenham train station.

TEWKESBURY

☎ 01684 • pop 9500

Tewkesbury is a delightful small town liberally endowed with timber-framed buildings and dominated by its magnificent, partly Norman, abbey church. It's well worth wandering in and out of the narrow alleys and courts, down one of which you'll find an old Baptist chapel in a building dating from the 15th century. Church St, Mill St and Mill Bank are particularly worth exploring. During the summer, daily cruises (☎ 294088) along the Severn and Avon rivers depart from Riverside Walk. It is just 8 miles north-west of Cheltenham.

The TIC (☎ 295027) is in the museum (75p) on Barton St. The **John Moore Countryside Museum** (☎ 297174), 41 Church St, opens 10 am to 1 pm and 2 to 5 pm Tuesday to Saturday, April to October. Admission costs £1/50p.

Tewkesbury Abbey

The town's focal point is the church of the former Benedictine abbey, the last of the monasteries to be dissolved by Henry VIII. Stone to build it was brought by sea and river from Normandy in the 12th century. Tewkesbury's fortunes depended on the wool industry because the abbey owned land and sheep all over the Cotswolds. When the abbey was dissolved, the church survived because the townspeople bought it.

One of Britain's largest churches, with a 40m-high tower, it has some spectacular Norman pillars lining the nave, 14th-century stained glass above the choir and an organ dating from 1631. Don't miss the tombs of Edward, Baron Le Despenser, who fought at Poitiers in 1356 and John Wakeman, the last abbot, who is shown as a vermin-ridden skeleton.

A new visitors centre by the gate houses the Abbey Refectory, which does tea, coffee and lunches. Abbey visitors are asked for donations of £2.

Places to Stay

The nicest places to stay are all near the abbey in Church St. Cheapest is the *Crescent Guest House* (☎ 293395, 30 Church St), which charges £19 per person.

The *Abbey Hotel* (☎ 294247, 67 Church St) charges from £45/60 for singles/doubles. Opposite the abbey entrance, the *Bell Hotel* (☎ 293293) has rooms with bathroom from £75 a double. The attractive *Jessop House Hotel* (☎ 292017, 65 Church St) charges £45/75.

There are a couple of cheaper places in Barton Rd, east of the TIC. The *Barton House* (☎ 292049, 5 Barton Rd) charges £18 per person in a double and *Hanbury House* (☎ 299911, Barton Rd) from £36 a double, but the setting is less inviting.

Places to Eat

My Great Grandfather's (☎ 292687, 85 Church St) is a homely restaurant and tearoom. Cream teas are under £3 and there's roast beef, pork or lamb for weekday lunches. The *Hen & Chickens Eating House* (☎ 292703, 73 Church St) does dishes such as smoked fish and seafood crumble. Nearby, the *Abbey Tea Rooms* (☎ 292215, 59 Church St) does roasts for around £5. *Aubergine* (☎ 292703, 73 Church St) is an elegant cafe with a fresh menu.

Le Bistrot André (☎ 290357, 78 Church St) is a reasonably priced French restaurant. Starters are around £3; main dishes range from £8 to £13. For those wanting cuisine from further afield, *New World* (☎ 292225, 61 High St) is a superb Vietnamese restaurant run by a former resident of Hanoi – the food is very authentic and reasonably priced. For Aussies feeling homesick, *Woody's* (☎ 298102, Barton St) is an Australian bistro with shark, 'roo and boar on the menu; diners can get by with about £15 per head.

The *Royal Hop Pole (Church St)*, mentioned in Dickens' *Pickwick Papers,* is a popular pub, restaurant and hotel. Alternatively, try the incredibly old *Berkeley Arms (Church St)* or the historic *Ye Olde Black Bear* for a drink.

Getting There & Away
The easiest way to get to Tewkesbury is on Stagecoach's hourly bus No 41 from Clarence St in Cheltenham. Stagecoach also has weekday bus services to Tewkesbury from Gloucester and Worcester; phone ☎ 01242-522021 for details.

You can also get from Cheltenham to Tewkesbury by train, but Ashchurch station is about three miles out of town.

THE FOREST OF DEAN
Formerly a royal hunting ground, the Forest of Dean occupies a triangular plateau between Gloucester, Ross-on-Wye and Chepstow, and comprises an area of 42 sq miles (including 28 sq miles of woodland) subject to ancient forest law.

Few tourists make it to the forest even though it's an excellent area for walking or cycling. The main TIC (☎ 01594-836307) on Coleford's High St stocks walking and cycling guides. Imposing, moated *St Briavels Castle Youth Hostel (☎ 530272, Lydney)* was once a hunting lodge used by King John. It's west of the forest above the Wye Valley and charges £11/7.75 for adults/under-18s.

Miners of the Forest of Dean

From before Roman times the Forest of Dean was an important source of timber, iron and stone. A coal seam covering thousands of acres also runs under the Forest. By a curious anomaly, for the past 700 years a select band of Foresters from St Briavels have retained the right to mine this coal, a right won by their forefathers as a reward for their skill in tunnelling under castle fortifications. Although many men could still lay theoretical claim to this right after working for a year and a day in a mine, only two full-time 'free mines' are still in operation and they are one-man operations.

The **Clearwell Caves** (☎ 832535), near Coleford, have been mined for iron since the Iron Age, and you can wander through nine dank, spooky caves and inspect the paraphernalia of the mine workings alongside pools and rock formations. Every Halloween something akin to an underground rave takes place in Barbecue Churn, the largest cave; you need to book ahead to get in. The caves open 10 am to 5 pm daily, March to October. Admission costs £3/2.20. The *Tudor Farmhouse (☎ 833046),* in Clearwell village, has excellent doubles with bathroom from £65.

Less than 3 miles away is the pretty village of **Newland**, dominated by All Saints, the so-called 'Cathedral of the Forest'. In the Greyndour Chantry look for the brass depicting a free miner with a *nelly,* or tallow candle, in his mouth, a pick in his hand and a *billy,* or backpack, on his back. *Scatterford Farm (☎ 836562)* has comfortable B&B for £27/44 for singles/doubles. *Cherry Orchard Farm (☎ 832212)* has B&B from £20 per person.

At the Beechenhurst Enclosure near Cinderford you can follow the easy Forest of Dean **sculpture trail**.

The **Dean Heritage Centre** (☎ 822170), in an old mill at Soudley, near Cinderford, recounts the history of the forest and the free miners. It opens 10 am to 6 pm daily, April to September; 10 am to 5 pm in February, March and October. Admission costs £3.50/2. The *Dean Heritage Kitchen* does lunches and teas.

Getting There & Away
Buses run from Gloucester and Monmouth to Coleford and the smaller villages. Trains also run to Lydney Junction. On Wednesday, Thursday, Saturday and Sunday from April to September steam trains run on the Dean Forest Railway from Lydney to Norchard Tickets cost £4.20/2.20. For details phone ☎ 01594-845840.

NEWENT
☎ 01531 • pop 5160
The unspoilt small town of Newent has some attractive architecture and the **Shambles Museum of Victorian Life** (☎ 822144), with assorted Victorian-style shopfronts

around a tearoom. It opens 10 am to 6 pm Tuesday to Sunday, Easter to December. Admission costs £3.50/1.95.

At the **National Birds of Prey Centre** (☎ 820286), on the outskirts of Newent, you can watch hawks and owls in free flight during daily displays. It opens 10.30 am to 5.30 pm daily, February to November. Admission costs £5.50/3.25.

The TIC (☎ 822468) is at 7 Church St, almost opposite the museum. Good food with English wine can be sampled in the *restaurant* at the Three Choirs Vineyard (☎ 890223), where self-guided tours are available for £2.50/1.50.

Stagecoach bus No 32 runs here from Gloucester.

Herefordshire & Worcestershire

Bounded by the Malverns in the east and Wales to the west, Herefordshire is a sleepy county of fields and hedgerows, virtually untainted by tourism. Worcestershire comprises the flattish plains of the Severn Vale and the Vale of Evesham, but is surrounded by rolling hills, with the Malverns to the west and the Cotswolds to the south. The Rivers Wye, Severn and Avon flow through, and the county has many attractive market towns.

WALKING
Two long-distance paths pass through this area. Offa's Dyke Path runs along the western border with Wales; the 107-mile Wye Valley Walk begins in Chepstow (Wales) and follows the river's course upstream into England through Herefordshire and Worcestershire and back into Wales to Rhayader.

GETTING AROUND
First Midland Red (☎ 01905-763888) is the region's biggest bus company. A Day Rover pass costs £4.60/3.60 and allows travel anywhere on its system and routes run by most other smaller companies. For general bus information, phone ☎ 0845 712 5436. There are rail links to Hereford and Worcester.

HEREFORD
☎ 01432 • pop 48,400
Hereford, at first appearance, might feel like the back of beyond, but stay a while and it is a town of warmth and spirit, home to one of the world's most famous maps, a potent if patched-together cathedral and some fine, old architecture.

Hereford owes its importance to its position on the River Wye on the border of Wales, where it became a garrison protecting the Saxons from the Welsh tribes. It was the capital of the Saxon kingdom of Mercia, and has been a cathedral city since the beginning of the 8th century.

Orientation & Information
The High Town shopping centre is the heart of the city on the north bank of the River Wye, with the cathedral a few blocks south along Church St. The bus station lies to the north-east, off Commercial Rd, with the train station a little further out, behind the Safeway supermarket.

The ever-helpful TIC (☎ 268430) is at 1 King St, near the cathedral. There are guided walking tours (☎ 266867) at 10.30 am Monday to Saturday and 2.30 pm Sunday, June to September. Tickets cost £2/1. There is an excellent internet cafe at 17 King St.

Hereford Cathedral
The purple-red cathedral (☎ 374200) is less aesthetically satisfying than many of the great English cathedrals, partly because of the reconstruction after the western tower collapsed into the nave in 1786 and partly because the stonework is a bit too frilly.

Although parts of the cathedral date back to the 11th century and the 50m-high central sandstone tower was built in the 14th century, the west front is less than 100 years old. Inside the cathedral, much of the Norman nave, with its arches, remains. In the choir is the 14th-century Bishop's throne and King Stephen's chair, said to have been used by the king himself. In the northern transept is the shrine of St Thomas Cantilupe, a 13th-century Hereford bishop whose tomb became an object of veneration and pilgrimage. The southern transept contains three tapestries

CENTRAL ENGLAND

showing the Tree of Life designed by John Piper in 1976.

The cathedral is best known for two ancient treasures: the 13th-century Mappa Mundi and the chained library of 1500 volumes, some of them dating back from the 8th century. To house them, an impressive 'high-tech medieval building' has been erected to the south-western side of the cathedral. It opens 10 am to 4.15 pm Monday to Saturday, and 11 am to 3.15 pm Sunday; 11 am to 3.15 pm daily (except Sunday) in winter. Admission costs £4/3.

The cathedral will host the Three Choirs Festival in 2003.

Old House
Stranded in pedestrianised High Town, the Old House (☎ 260694) is a marvellous black and white three-storey wooden house built in 1621 and fitted with 17th-century wooden furnishings. Note the murals of the Muses on the 1st floor. It opens 10 am to 5 pm Tuesday to Saturday (to 4 pm on Sunday and bank holiday Mondays), April to September. Admission is free.

Other Things to See
Near the cathedral, the Bishop's Palace contains one of England's oldest timber halls. East of the cathedral is the ancient Cathedral School and Castle Green, site of a castle that was pulled down in 1652. Narrow streets and alleys lead from Cathedral Close to the shopping area.

The Museum & Art Gallery (☎ 260692), above the Broad St library, contains Roman antiquities, English watercolours and traditional farming implements. It opens 10 am to 5 pm Tuesday to Saturday, to 4 pm on Sunday. In High St, All Saints Church has a slightly bent, 65m-high tower surmounted by England's largest weathercock. More unusually, it also contains a medieval carving of a man mooning and exposing himself; it's on a beam immediately above the cafe.

Cider Factory Tours
Just off the A438 to Brecon, the Cider Museum & King Offa Distillery (☎ 354207) is in Pomona Place in a former cider works. In 1984 production of cider brandy recommenced after a 250-year gap. The museum and distillery open 10 am to 5.30 pm daily, April to October; 11 am to 3 pm Tuesday to Sunday in winter. Admission is £2.40/1.90.

Bulmers Cider Mill (☎ 352000) offers two-hour factory tours Monday to Friday. Telephone a week ahead to make a booking. Tickets cost £3.95/2.

Places to Stay
Bowes Guest House (☎ 267202, 23 St Martin's St), just north of the Wye Bridge, has singles/doubles from £18.50/34.

Merton Hotel (☎ 265925, Commercial Rd), convenient for the station, charges £45/60. Just off the main street, across from the train station, the comfortable Aylestone Court Hotel (☎ 341891, Aylestone Hill) has rooms with a bathroom from £55/85.

Castle House (☎ 356321, Church St), close to the cathedral, was once the bishop's residence and has undergone a significant upgrade so large, well-equipped rooms with bathrooms are a severe £90/165.

Comfort is more affordable at the Green Dragon (☎ 272506, Broad St) where rates start from £56/84 in a handsome, neoclassical building in the centre of town.

Places to Eat
The most atmospheric place to eat is Café@All Saints tastefully set in the western end of beautiful All Saints Church – a novel way to revive declining attendance. The menu is wholesome and vegetarians are well-catered for. Lunches are good value.

Cherries (2 Bridge St) offers a wide selection of breakfasts starting at 99p. For something a little more sophisticated, Elgar's has teas and coffees from all over the globe, cream teas and a small selection of hot food.

There are no less than two Thai restaurants in Hereford. Aroon Rai (☎ 279971, Widemarsh St) has a wide range of authentic Siamese dishes for around £7. Located in a characterful building on East St is Orchid House and locals rave about the food. For Indian specialities, The Taste of the Raj (☎ 351076, St Owen's) has a reliable reputation for good subcontinental food.

The best restaurant in town is the happening *Doodies* (☎ *269974, St Owen's)*, which has a wide range of dishes from around the world starting at £10, but with veggies on top it's likely to be £20 a head. There is a little cafe next door with lighter, cheaper meals available and a popular bar.

To put together a picnic, head straight for the covered *Butter Market,* which dates back to 1860, in the High Town.

Entertainment

The Barrels, on St Owen's, is a must for any visitor to Hereford. It is home to the Wye Valley Brewery and some welcoming locals as permanent as the wallpaper. Leading brews include *Butty Back* and *Dorothy Goodbodys,* all prepared out the back in former stables. Of the other town-centre pubs, the *Spread Eagle*, in King St, is a popular watering hole; the *Queen's Arms*, on Broad St, has an older gang of regulars; while *The Exchange*, on Widemarsh St, is noteworthy as a medieval interior with Victorian cladding.

Hereford's most prominent nightclub is *The Crystal Rooms* (☎ *267378, Bridge St)*, which sees its share of good DJs on a Friday night, but don't come expecting Cream. For live music from local bands, try *The Jailhouse* (☎ *344354, 1 Gaol St)*.

The *Courtyard Centre for the Arts* (☎ *359252, off Edgar St)* offers a theatre, two cinemas, a gallery and the usual bar and cafe.

Getting There & Away

Hereford is 140 miles from London, 25 miles from Worcester and 38 miles from Brecon in Wales.

Bus National Express (☎ 0870 580 8080) operates three services a day from London (£14.50, four hours) via Heathrow, Cirencester, Cheltenham, Gloucester, Newent and Ross-on-Wye.

First Midland Red (☎ 01905-763888) connects Hereford to Worcester (No 419 or 420) and Ludlow (No 192).

Train Hereford is linked by hourly train to London (£33, three hours), usually via Newport or Worcester. From Hereford, there are

also rail services to Worcester (£5.20, one hour).

AROUND HEREFORD

Ledbury is a handsome market town with a reputation for antiques. Many of its buildings are antiquities themselves and include a beautiful 17th-century black and white timber-framed market hall and its very own Feathers Hotel, every bit as charming as its more famous namesake in Ludlow. Church Lane is the best area to concentrate on for architectural heritage. The TIC (☎ 01531 636147) at 3 The Homend opens 10 to 4 pm.

The Golden Valley, set in a remote corner of the county bordering Wales, has been made famous by the author CS Lewis and the Hollywood adaptation of his childhood, *Shadowlands*. Following the meandering River Dore, this is one of the least-visited corners of Britain, yet offers some stunning scenery.

Herefordshire's black and white architecture is a big attraction for some visitors and the TICs promote a trail that can be followed through the most popular villages. **Eardisland** is the most picturesque, but all of them offer something that is hard to find during peak season in the Cotswolds these days – peace and tranquillity.

Of the historic properties found within the county limits, **Eastnor Castle** (☎ 01531 633160) looks like something out of El Cid, but is much more modern, dating from the 18th century, and has recently undergone much restoration work to improve the interior. The extensive grounds include a deer park and arboretum. It opens 11 am to 5 pm on Sunday, late April to early October; daily (except Saturday) in July and August. Admission costs £4.75/2.50 for the castle and £2.75/1.50 for the grounds only. It is a short distance from Junction 2 of the M50 and just a couple of miles outside Ledbury.

Croft Castle (☎ 01568 780246; NT) is near the Shropshire border and dates from the 14th century. Much of the interior was refitted in the 18th century, including a sweeping gothic stairway. A short walk away are the remains of the Iron-Age fort of **Croft Ambrey**. Ring ahead to check opening hours as they are restricted. Admission costs £3.80/1.90.

ROSS-ON-WYE
☎ 01989 • pop 8300

Winding through a landscape of woods and meadows past Ross-on-Wye, Symonds Yat and then along the border with Wales, the River Wye empties into the Bristol Channel beneath the Severn Bridge. Built on a dramatic sandstone bluff, Ross makes a good base for exploring the **Wye Valley**, the most scenic part of the river.

There are fine views of the valley and ruined Wilton Castle from the **Prospect**, a cliff-top public garden designed by 17th-century town planner John Kyrle, the 'Man of Ross', who also laid out some of the streets. His philanthropic works were much praised by Pope in *Of the Use of Riches*. Kyrle is buried in the parish church, where the Plague Cross records the burial of 315 victims of the 1637 plague.

A small **Heritage Centre** is on the 1st floor of the stilted Market House.

The TIC (☎ 562768) is in Edde Cross St. Bikes can be rented from Revolutions (☎ 562639), 48 Broad St, from £10 a day.

Places to Stay
The nearest hostel is 6 miles south of Ross at Welsh Bicknor (see Around Ross-on-Wye).

In Ross, the Georgian *Vaga House* (☎ 563024, *Wye St*) is in a pretty street near the TIC and does B&B from £19 per person, £23 with a bathroom. Next door is the *Radcliffe Guesthouse* (☎ 563895) which charges £25/44 for singles/doubles.

Nonsmoking *Linden House* (☎ 565373, *14 Church St*), opposite the church, charges £25/42 per room or £36/50 en suite and can do veggie breakfasts on request.

The comfortable *King's Head Hotel* (☎ 763174, *8 High St*) charges from £43.50/75. The smartest place to stay is the beautifully positioned *Royal* (☎ 565105, *Palace Pound*), where rooms cost £50 per person.

Places to Eat
For a night out, *Pheasants Restaurant* (☎ 565751, *52 Edde Cross St*) does fine

English cuisine Tuesday to Saturday; main courses cost around £12. Alternatively, head for *Meaders* (☎ 562803, *1 Copse Cross St*), where traditional Hungarian dishes start at about £8.50. Opposite, *Cloisters* wine bar (☎ 567717) has fish specials such as rainbow trout with lime and almonds for £8.50.

Oat Cuisine (☎ 566271, *47 Broad St*), one of the greatest names to have come out of the wholefood revolution, does inexpensive vegetarian lunches, while *Yaks n Yetis* (☎ 564963) has an extensive list of Mexican dishes, so clearly no relation of the Yak n Yeti Hotel in Kathmandu.

Ross' High St is full of tea shops, the most interesting being the *Antique Teashop* (*40 High St*), where a cream tea taken on antique chairs costs £3.65. The *Priory Coffee House* (*45 High St*) serves toasties, while *Poppy's Bistro* (*9 High St*) does hot dishes of the day for £4.95.

Ross is not known for its nightlife, but the *King Charles II* is an atmospheric enough pub, and the *Hope & Anchor Inn*, down by the river, is busy throughout the day for dining or drinking.

Getting There & Away
Ross is 14 miles from Hereford and 16 miles from Gloucester, with bus links to London via Cheltenham and Cirencester. Stagecoach (☎ 485118) operates a daily bus service between Hereford and Gloucester via Ross (No 38), and a Monday to Saturday service (No 34) from Ross to Monmouth (for Goodrich and Symonds Yat).

AROUND ROSS-ON-WYE
Goodrich
Goodrich Castle (☎ 01600-890538) is a red-sandstone castle dating from the 12th century. A Royalist stronghold during the Civil War, it fell to the Roundheads after a siege lasting 4½ months and was destroyed by Cromwell. Run by English Heritage (EH), it opens 10 am to 6 pm daily. Admission costs £3.20/1.60.

Just under 2 miles from Goodrich is *Welsh Bicknor Youth Hostel* (☎ 01594-860300), a Victorian rectory standing in 10-hectare grounds by the river. Beds cost

£11/7.75 for adults/under-18s. It opens daily, April to October; phone for other times.

Symonds Yat

Symonds Yat, 2½ miles south of Goodrich, is a popular beauty spot overlooking the Wye. It's crowded in summer but worth visiting at quieter times. There are good views from Yat Rock (Symonds Yat East), and rare peregrine falcons nest in the rock-face. Telescopes enable you to watch them from April to August.

This area is renowned for canoeing and climbing, among other activities, and the Wyedean Canoe Centre (☎ 0800 3281235) has a solid reputation for organising kayaking and white water trips.

WORCESTER
☎ 01905 • pop 75,500

Known for centuries as the faithful city after it remained staunchly Royalist during the civil war, Worcester (pronounced 'woo-ster') hasn't always been faithful to its heritage, tearing down the Elgar family's Victorian music shop in an extended moment of ill-considered town planning. World famous for its bone china and its sauce, it also has an impressive cathedral where King John of Magna Carta fame is buried. It's a disjointed town, not always immediately inviting, but some streets boast the half-timbered buildings more usually associated with Stratford-upon-Avon and it has far fewer tourists than Shakespeare's birthplace.

Orientation & Information

The main part of the city lies on the east bank of the River Severn, with the cathedral rising above it. The High St, just to the north, runs through a bewildering number of name changes as it heads north: The Cross, The Foregate, Foregate and The Tything.

The TIC (☎ 726311) is in the Guildhall, in High St. Walking tours leave from here at 11 am and 2.30 pm on summer Wednesdays. Tickets cost £3/1.50.

Worcester Cathedral

The present cathedral was begun in 1084 by Bishop – later saint – Wulfstan and the atmospheric crypt dates back to this period.

The choir and Lady Chapel were built in 13th-century Early English style, while the Norman nave was given a make-over in 14th-century Decorated style. Take a look at the carvings in the ambulatory and transepts and you'll see scenes of judgement and hell as well as of the nativity.

Wicked King John, whose treachery towards brother Richard left the country in turmoil at his death, is buried in the choir. Knowing he stood only a slim chance of making it past the Pearly Gates, the dying king is said to have asked to be buried disguised as a monk. When the tomb was opened in 1797, shreds of a monk's cowl were found over his skull.

An ornate chantry chapel south of the high altar commemorates Prince Arthur, Henry VIII's elder brother, who died while honeymooning with Catherine of Aragon.

The cathedral (☎ 28854) opens 7.30 am to 6 pm daily. A £2 donation is requested. The cathedral choir sings evensong at 5.30 pm daily (except Thursday) and at 4 pm Sundays.

Commandery Civil War Centre

Beside Sidbury Lock, south-east of the cathedral, the Commandery (☎ 361821) is in a splendid Tudor building used as Charles II's headquarters during the Battle of Worcester. This battle brought the Civil War to an end in 1651 and the centre details the ins and outs of this and many other battles that raged in 17th century England. It opens 10 am to 5 pm daily (afternoon only on Sunday). Admission costs £3.70/2.60.

Royal Worcester Porcelain Works

Worcester has been manufacturing ornate bone china since 1751, the longest continuous production of any British porcelain company. In 1789, the company was granted a royal warrant, and Worcester remains the Queen's preferred crockery.

The Royal Worcester Porcelain Works (☎ 21247) was moved to its current Severn St site in 1840. It now boasts an entire visitors complex, with shops, restaurant and museum, open 9 am to 5.30 pm Monday to Saturday, and 11 am to 5 pm Sunday.

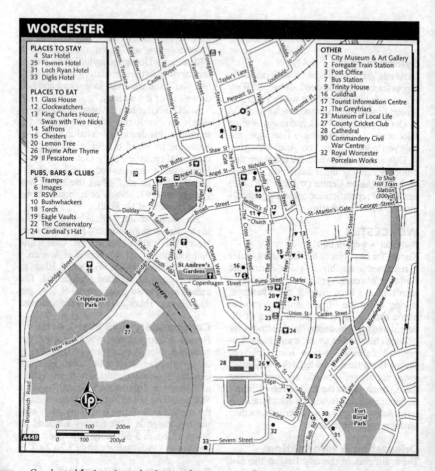

WORCESTER

PLACES TO STAY
4 Star Hotel
25 Fownes Hotel
31 Loch Ryan Hotel
33 Diglis Hotel

PLACES TO EAT
11 Glass House
12 Clockwatchers
13 King Charles House;
    Swan with Two Nicks
14 Saffrons
15 Chesters
20 Lemon Tree
26 Thyme After Thyme
29 Il Pescatore

PUBS, BARS & CLUBS
5 Tramps
6 Images
8 RSVP
10 Bushwhackers
18 Torch
19 Eagle Vaults
22 The Conservatory
24 Cardinal's Hat

OTHER
1 City Museum & Art Gallery
2 Foregate Train Station
3 Post Office
7 Bus Station
9 Trinity House
16 Guildhall
17 Tourist Information Centre
21 The Greyfriars
23 Museum of Local Life
27 County Cricket Club
28 Cathedral
30 Commandery Civil
    War Centre
32 Royal Worcester
    Porcelain Works

Conducted **factory tours** lasting one hour run Monday to Friday. They cost £5 and should be booked in advance. The **Visitors Centre** lets you see what a turn-of-the-century potter's life was like, while a film tells the story of the pottery. Admission costs £2.25/1.75.

The **gift shop** sells everything from a 23-piece 'best' dinner service for nearly £1000 to single seconds for just a few pounds.

The newly updated **Museum of Worcester Porcelain** tells the factory's story and houses the world's largest collection of Worcester porcelain, including some of the very first pieces. It opens 9.30 am to 5 pm Monday to Saturday (from 10 am on Saturday). Admission costs £3/2.25.

Other Things to See

The splendid **Guildhall**, in High St, is a Queen Anne building of 1722, designed by a pupil of Wren. Look out for the stone carving of Oliver Cromwell with his ears pinned back, just above the main entrance.

Half-timbered **Trinity House** (on The Trinity, just off The Cross) once belonged to the Guild of the Holy Trinity. After the Battle of Worcester Charles II is supposed to have hidden in what was later named **King Charles House**, 29 New St, which is now a restaurant (see Places to Eat).

Friar St is lined with fine Tudor and Elizabethan buildings. Built in 1480, **The Greyfriars** (☎ 23571; NT) has been painstakingly restored and is full of textiles and furnishings. It opens 2 to 5 pm on Wednesday, Thursday and bank holiday Mondays, Easter to October. Admission costs £2.60. The **Museum of Local Life** (☎ 722349) evokes Worcester's past with reconstructed Victorian shops, displays of toys and costumes, and details of daily life during WWII. It opens 10.30 am to 5 pm daily, except Thursday and Sunday. Admission is free.

Worcester City Museum and Art Gallery (☎ 25371), Foregate St, has exhibits about the River Severn and opens 9.30 am to 5.30 pm daily, except Sunday. Admission is free.

Away from museums and historic buildings, cricket fans will no doubt like to check out Worcestershire County Cricket Club.

Places to Stay

The nearest hostel is in Malvern Wells, 8 miles away. About 3 miles north of Worcester is the *Mill House Caravan & Camping Site* (☎ 451283), which charges £5.50 for all tents.

Barbourne Rd, north of the centre, has several B&Bs. The *Shrubbery Guest House* (☎ 24871, 38 Barbourne Rd) has a small single with shared facilities for £20 and ensuite singles/doubles for £35/45.

Another popular B&B is *Osborne House* (☎ 22296, 17 Chestnut Walk) and while not quite as flash as Queen Victoria's pad on the Isle of Wight, it is very homely with ensuite rooms from £36.

Loch Ryan Hotel (☎ 351143, 119 Sidbury), near the cathedral, has rooms from £45/60. Slap bang in the centre of town, right near the station, is the *Star Hotel* (☎ 24308, Foregate St), which offers well-appointed rooms from £65/80.

One of the best-situated hotels in town is the *Diglis House* (☎ 353518, Severn St), located on the banks of the River Severn. Rooms start at £60/75, but be sure to try and get one with a river view. The huge *Fownes Hotel* (☎ 613151, City Walls Rd), in a converted glove factory, is a popular business hotel. Midweek prices of £85 per room drop to £55 at weekends.

Places to Eat

The Guildhall's elaborate *Assembly Room Restaurant* is open Monday to Saturday for lunch and snacks. *Glass House* (☎ 611120) also has an impressive location in an old church and has a menu to suit all budgets. For those in a hurry to see their sights or explore the nearby charity shops, *Clockwatchers* (☎ 611662, 21 Mealcheapen St) is the city's most popular sandwich bar. For those with time to linger, the upstairs is a crooked old house, a real contrast with unassuming exterior, and there is a garden for warm days.

The 16th-century *King Charles House* (☎ 22449, 29 New St) offers traditional three-course lunches for £9.95 and is a good place to dine for those of an historical bent. Next door is the cheap and cheerful *Swan with Two Nicks* (☎ 28190) offering a steady diet of traditional pub food. *Saffrons* (☎ 610505, 15 New St) offers everything from Thai to modern British, a global tour, but high prices may deter some – about £25 per head all-in. Nearby *Chesters* (☎ 611638, 51 New St) concentrates on Mexican food.

The *Lemon Tree* (☎ 27770, 12 Friar St) offers modern British cooking with a distinctly international flavour in intimate surroundings: the menu makes you salivate just looking at it. Ten pounds should cover lunch and a drink, more like £20 for a full dinner.

Il Pescatore (☎ 21444, 34 Sidbury), near the cathedral, is a popular Italian restaurant offering light lunch dishes for about £5. *Thyme After Thyme* (☎ 611786, 27 College St) offers a range of teasing tasters to go with salads, baguettes or potatoes in jackets at lunch, all at around £4. At night they turn on the style and prices rise considerably.

Entertainment

RSVP (☎ 723035, The Cross) leads the way in church conversions with the original pulpit as the staircase and the font in the thick of things. As well as a popular bar at night, it is a lively lunch spot.

The popular *Farrier's Arms (Fish St)*, near the cathedral, has some outdoor seating, while Worcester's oldest pub, the *Cardinal's Hat (Friar St)* has open fires in winter. The *Eagle Vaults* is an original Victorian boozer complete with ornate tiling and elaborate interior. For cheap drinks and zany promotions, *The Conservatory* is worth a shot.

Bushwhackers (Trinity St) is an Ozzie pub that draws the crowds at night. Many of the clubs in town have the sort of names that make you wonder if the 1980s are back (perhaps they never left Worcester?) such as *Tramps* and *Images*. *Torch* is possibly the sanest bet, although a train to Birmingham might be wiser still.

Music by Elgar is always a highlight of the Three Choirs Festival, hosted by Worcester Cathedral (☎ 616211) every third year. It will be Worcester's turn in 2002.

Getting There & Away

Worcester is 113 miles from London, 57 miles from Oxford, 26 miles from Stratford-upon-Avon and 25 miles from Hereford.

Bus National Express runs at least one coach daily between Worcester, Heathrow and London (£14.50, 3½ hours). Another service links Aberdare and Great Yarmouth via Worcester, Great Malvern and Hereford.

First Midland Red (☎ 763888) operates services to Hereford, Tewkesbury and Evesham. A Day Rover ticket costs £4.60/3.

Cambridge Coach Services (☎ 01223-423900) has a weekday service linking Worcester with Cambridge via Stratford-upon-Avon and Warwick.

Train Worcester Foregate station (for trains to Birmingham and Hereford) is more central than Worcester Shrub Hill, which offers regular trains to London Paddington (£22.80, 2¼ hours). Shrub Hill is a dismal 15-minute walk from the centre. Bus No 30 passes nearby.

Getting Around

Peddlers (☎ 24238), 46 Barbourne Rd, hires out bicycles for £8/30 per day/week.

AROUND WORCESTER

There are many pleasant towns in the area including beautiful Broadway (see the Cotswolds earlier in the chapter) and Georgian Pershore. There are also many industrialised towns on the approach to Birmingham, notably **Redditch** with its incredible **needle mill** and **Droitwich Spa**, the country's active spa centre, at least until Bath's millennium baths open.

Elgar's Birthplace Museum

About 3 miles west of Worcester is Broadheath, birthplace of Sir Edward Elgar (1857–1934). The cottage itself (☎ 01905-333224) is now a museum of Elgar memorabilia. Admission costs £3/50p. Phone ahead for opening times. See also the boxed text 'On the Elgar Trail'.

Severn Valley Railway

A 20-minute ride from Worcester Forest Hill to **Kidderminster**, once known as the carpet capital of Britain, lets you link up with the Severn Valley Railway (☎ 01299-403816). For details, see Bridgnorth later in the chapter.

On the Elgar Trail

Sir Edward Elgar, composer of Britain's almost-national anthem 'Land of Hope and Glory', was born in Broadheath, three miles west of Worcester, in 1857 and died in Worcester in 1934. He lived in Hereford for eight years and drew much of the inspiration for music such as the Pomp and Circumstance marches and the Enigma Variations from the nearby Malvern Hills. The Hereford, Worcester and Malvern TICs stock a leaflet detailing a signposted 'Elgar Route' that takes you through places associated with his life. He is buried in St Wulstan's church in Little Malvern, just south of Great Malvern.

Elgar Birthplace Museum (☎ 01905-66224), in Lower Broadheath, opens from 10.30 am to 6 pm Thursday to Tuesday, May to September; 1.30 to 4.30 pm during most of winter; and is closed 16 January to 15 February.

Witley Court

Arguably the most venerable and romantic ruin in England, this mighty house was once one of the most extravagant private homes in Britain. However, a massive fire gutted the interior leaving the immense skeleton that stands today. The gardens, originally designed by William Nesfield, have been fully restored, as have the famous fountains, including that of Perseus and Andromeda that once fired water more than 30m into the air.

The adjacent **Great Witley Church** is widely considered to be one of the finest Baroque churches in Britain, including exquisite paintings by Antonio Bellucci and some exceptionally ornate carving and glasswork. All in all it feels more like a music hall than a church and regular classical concerts are held throughout the summer; phone ☎ 01299-896437 for details.

Witley Court (☎ 01299-896636; EH) opens 10 to 5 pm daily, April to October; 10 to 4 pm Wednesday to Friday, November to March. Admission costs £3.50/1.80.

It is 10 miles north-west of Worcester on the A443 and the nearest station is at Droitwich Spa, about 8 miles away. Buses travelling from Worcester to Tenbury Wells pass this way infrequently.

GREAT MALVERN

☎ 01684 • pop 30,000

The Malvern Hills form a dramatic backdrop for Great Malvern, the biggest and best known of a cluster of settlements all invoking the name of the illustrious hills that overshadow them. Famous for mineral water, a summer music festival (late May), a public school and Morgan motorcars, Great Malvern looks a bit like one of the central Welsh spa towns with a mini version of Gloucester Cathedral and lots of cedars, pines and monkey puzzle trees. Turner was inspired to paint it, before the grand Victorian piles started to straddle the hills, of course! As it is built into the side of a hill, there are some very steep streets in Great Malvern, so watch out with heavy bags.

The TIC (☎ 892289), 21 Church St, sells an access guide for disabled visitors (£1), although just getting up the hill to buy it could be a problem. It also stocks a leaflet describing six cycle routes round the Malvern Hills.

The newly restored Malvern Festival Theatre (☎ 892277) is based in the Winter Gardens Complex in Grange Rd.

Great Malvern Priory

The Priory Church, with Norman pillars lining the nave, is famous for its stained glass and tiles. Of particular note are the 15th-century western window, the clerestory windows of the choir, and the window in the Jesus Chapel in the northern transept, which shows the Joys of Mary. The choir is decorated with 1200 medieval tiles, the oldest and finest such collection in the country.

Walks in the Malvern Hills

Cut up St Ann's Rd for a short, steep walk to the summit of Worcestershire Beacon (419m) offering tremendous views. Herefordshire Beacon (334m), south of Great Malvern, is the site of the British Camp, an Iron-Age fort. There's a superb walk along the path that meanders across the summits of the Malverns.

The Malvern Hills provided Elgar with the inspiration for his 'Enigma Variations' and the 'Pomp and Circumstance' marches (see the boxed text 'On the Elgar Trail').

The TIC stocks *Malvern Map Sets*, three maps covering the chain of hills.

Places to Stay & Eat

Although there's plenty of accommodation, much of it very pleasant, this is an upmarket area with prices to match. *Malvern Hills Youth Hostel* (☎ 569131, 18 Peachfield Rd) is in Malvern Wells, 1½ miles south of Great Malvern. Take bus No 675 to British Camp. It opens from mid-February to October and charges £10/6.90 for adults/under-18s.

Great Malvern Hotel (☎ 563411, 7 Graham Rd) is very central, with singles/doubles with bathrooms for £55/80. The *Cottage in the Wood* (☎ 575859, Holywell Rd), 3 miles away near Malvern Wells, boasts spectacular views. Rooms cost from

£75/95. Dinner in its excellent restaurant costs around £30.

Church St hosts frilly *Victorias*, where you can get tea or a jacket potato from £2. Round the corner from the TIC the *Blue Bird Tearooms* serves cream teas for £2.50.

Lady Foley's Tearoom (☎ 893033, *Imperial Rd*) serves lunches and teas in the splendid Victorian train station. From 7 to 9 pm on Friday and Saturday night the station also hosts *Passionata*, serving more elaborate dishes.

The Indian *Baazi Blue Restaurant* (☎ 575744, *Church St*) is popular. The *Red Lion* (☎ 564787, *St Ann's Rd*) includes a traditional pub and modern restaurant with an excellent menu of contemporary cuisine.

Getting There & Away

Great Malvern is 8 miles from Worcester and 15 miles from Hereford. The quickest way to get there is by train from Worcester or Hereford. There are connections to London and Birmingham. National Express has a daily bus between Great Malvern and London (£12.50, four hours) via Worcester and Pershore.

VALE OF EVESHAM

Worcestershire's south-eastern corner looks particularly splendid in spring when its myriad fruit trees are in blossom. The Vale's two principal towns are Evesham itself and Pershore.

Evesham
☎ 01386 • pop 15,000

A quiet market town on the River Avon, Evesham was the scene of the battle where Prince Edward, son of Henry III, defeated Simon de Montfort in 1265. The TIC (☎ 446944), in the picturesque Almonry Centre on the southern side of town, houses a small heritage centre. Admission is £2/free.

The river flows close to the 16th-century bell tower of the lost Benedictine abbey, which makes a fine grouping with the twin medieval churches of All Saints and St Lawrence. Look out for the beautiful fan vaulting of the Lichfield Chantry in All Saints.

Places to Stay & Eat For nonsmokers only, *Berryfield House* (☎ 48214, *172 Pershore Rd, Hampton*) does B&B from £15. *Park View Hotel* (☎ 442639, *Waterside*) has singles/doubles from £23/41.

Readers have enjoyed staying at *Brookside Guest House* (☎ 443116, *Mill St*), which is three-quarters of a mile along the river from the centre in Hampton, with rooms from £18 per person. Comfortable *Evesham Hotel* (☎ 765566, *Cooper's Lane*) has rooms for £63/98.

The best place for a snack is the *Gateway Cake Shop*, beside the abbey.

The *Vine Wine Bar* (☎ 446799, *16 Vine St*) offers delicacies such as swordfish steak.

Getting There & Away The hourly First Midland Red (☎ 01905-763888) bus No 550 service operates to Pershore and Worcester, Monday to Saturday. Bus No 28 runs to Stratford-upon-Avon, Monday to Saturday.

There are frequent trains to Worcester (20 minutes), and to London (two hours) via Oxford (one hour).

Pershore
☎ 01386 • pop 6900

A backwater town of graceful Georgian houses, Pershore is chiefly noted for its abbey, which was founded in 689. The TIC (☎ 554262) is inside a travel agency at 19 High St.

A good spot for morning tea or coffee or a lunch before launching deeper into Worcestershire is *Whistlers* which has a fine range of sandwiches and salads.

Pershore Abbey When Henry VIII's henchmen moved in to dissolve Pershore Abbey the townsfolk bought the austere Early English choir to serve as their parish church. That, and the earlier southern transept, parts of which may predate the Norman Conquest, are all that remain of the abbey.

About 8 miles from Worcester, and 7 miles from Evesham, Pershore is best reached by bus from either place. The train station is 1½ miles north of town.

Warwickshire & Coventry

Warwickshire is home to two of England's biggest tourist attractions: Stratford-upon-Avon, with its Shakespearean connections, and Warwick, with its popular castle. The ruined castle at Kenilworth is also worth a look, as is the modern cathedral in Coventry. Elsewhere, the county has plenty of museums, castles, market towns, canals and pleasant countryside.

For bus information throughout the area phone ☎ 01926-414140.

COVENTRY
☎ 024 • pop 318,800

Coventry was once one of Britain's most important towns, a centre for the wool industry in medieval times and more recently a dynamic manufacturing centre for the motor car. However, between the aerial bombshells of the Luftwaffe and the architectural bombshells of the planners, much of historic Coventry disappeared under a mountain of concrete – although it should be remembered that the pedestrianised areas were among the first in the country.

It is easy to get to from Birmingham or Stratford-upon-Avon and fans of modern architecture will want to drop by to see the new cathedral built beside the bombed-out ruins of the medieval one. Nearby are some fine Georgian townhouses and medieval cottages, small clues to the city's beauty before its destruction. Coventry is also an escape from the tourist merry-go-round during the summer months.

By the 14th century Coventry was one of the four largest towns in England outside London, its fortune made on the back of sheep, literally. Then decline set in and Coventry was still essentially a medieval town when the Industrial Revolution hit it in the 19th century.

Coventry was one of the most inventive of the Victorian industrial centres and claims to be the birthplace of the modern bicycle. The first car made in Britain was a Daimler built in Coventry in 1896, and in the early years of the 20th century Coventry was Britain's motor manufacturing capital as well as a major aircraft manufacturing centre. But steady growth switched to headlong decline in the 1970s and 80s as Sunbeam, Hillman, Singer, Humber and Triumph cars all disappeared. Now only Jaguar cars remain of the home-grown models, although French Peugeots are also assembled in Coventry.

Coventry is probably best known for Lady Godiva, a medieval member of the elite that took all her clothes off to help the poor, a sort of 'Stripping Hood'.

Orientation & Information

Central Coventry is encircled by a ring road with most points of interest tucked inside. Medieval Spon St features several half-timbered buildings relocated from elsewhere in the city.

The TIC (☎ 7683 2303) is in Bayley Lane beside the University of Coventry and facing the two cathedrals.

Cathedrals

Founded in the 12th century and rebuilt from 1373, St Michael's was one of England's largest parish churches when it became a cathedral in 1918, its spire topped only by those of Salisbury and Norwich cathedrals. Then on 14 November 1940, a Luftwaffe raid gutted the cathedral, leaving only the outer walls and the spire standing amid the smoking ruins.

After the war, the ruins were left as a reminder. The new St Michael's Cathedral (☎ 7622 7597) was built beside it. Designed by Sir Basil Spence and built between 1955 and 1962, the cathedral is one of the few examples of post-war British architecture to inspire popular affection. It's noted for the soaring etched-glass screen wall at the western end, for the Graham Sutherland tapestry above the altar, for Piper's lovely stained glass and for Epstein's sculpture of St Michael subduing the devil beside the entrance steps.

The visitors centre screens an audio-visual presentation on the destruction of the old cathedral and the birth of its replacement

CENTRAL ENGLAND

for £2/1 (Monday to Saturday). Visitors to the new cathedral are asked for a £2 donation. The old cathedral spire still looks down on the ruins and its 180 steps lead up to magnificent views. Admission costs £1.

Museum of British Road Transport

This museum (☎ 7683 2425), in Hales St, has a huge collection of bicycles, motorcycles, racing cars, rally cars and even Thrust 2 (once the world's fastest car), alongside traditional British family cars. It's a sobering reminder of how to turn a good industry bad when you look at the dazzling array of glamorous models churned out in the 1950s and 1960s and the sort of skips on wheels that came out of British Leyland by the late 70s. It opens 10 am to 4.30 pm daily. Admission is free.

Other Things to See

The **statue of Lady Godiva**, at the edge of the Precinct, is a Coventry meeting spot handily overlooked by the Coventry Clock. A figure of the naked lady parades from the clock each hour, while Peeping Tom peers out from above. Godiva appears again, this time with husband Leofric, on the fairy-tale facade of the Council House in High St.

The **Herbert Art Gallery & Museum** (☎ 7683 2386), in Jordan Well, provides a quick run through Coventry's history. The upstairs art gallery has paintings of the Lady Godiva legend and the original sketches for Sutherland's cathedral tapestry. It opens 10 am to 5.30 pm Monday to Saturday, and noon to 5 pm on Sunday. Admission is free.

Other buildings that have survived Coventry's misfortune include **St Mary's Guildhall**, an elaborate, rambling civic building dating from medieval times – it is possible to visit April to October, but check with the TIC first as it is sometimes used for civic functions. **Holy Trinity Church** dates from the 12th century and its 67m-spire has long been a landmark of the city. It is home to a rare medieval painting located above the chancel arch. Smaller **St John's Church** is famous for giving the world the expression 'sent to Coventry', meaning that someone is shunned by those around them. Royalist

prisoners of war were interned here during the civil war, out of touch with their friends and family, hence sent to Coventry.

Places to Stay

The TIC makes bookings free of charge (☎ 0800 243748), although many places are uncomfortably close to the noisy ring road.

There's no hostel, but in July and August the **Priory Halls of Residence** (☎ 7688 8318, Priory St) at Coventry University offer accommodation from £15 per person.

The **Crest Guest House** (☎ 7622 7822, 39 Friars Rd) offers a good standard of comfort for £26.50 per person. Just around the corner is homely **Abigail Guesthouse** (☎ 7622 1378), with rooms starting from a very reasonable £18.50.

The **Ibis Hotel** (☎ 7625 0500) is a stone's throw from the station and offers its standard en-suite rooms for £39.95.

Places to Eat

Browns (☎ 7622 1100, Earl St) has long been a Coventry institution and should not be missed. It has a huge menu of huge dishes for £4.50 each – no-one leaves hungry. It is a popular bar by night and DJs ply their trade at the weekend.

Near the cathedral, pedestrianised Hay Lane has a branch of **Pizza Express**, but for individualised Italian, **Etna Restaurant** (☎ 7622 3183, 57 Hertford St) is hard to beat with a vast selection of southern European favourites.

Bunty's, on Hay Lane, is a pleasant tearoom serving filled bagels and excellent hot chocolate. **Ginger's**, on pedestrianised Hertford St, is a popular place for cheap sandwiches, filled spuds and hearty breakfasts. **Java Joe's** (50 Corporation St) is a great little coffee bar with the full range of international fixes.

Old-world Spon St has several eateries, including the elegant **Bastille's** (☎ 7622 9274) in a gorgeous old house, which has excellent-value two-course lunches for £5 and an extensive dinner menu for around £15 to £20 all said. Nearby **Tête à Tête** (☎ 7655 0938) scoops the afternoon tea trade.

Entertainment

Pubs, Bars & Clubs With two universities, Coventry has a thriving nightlife. The *Golden Cross* is home to 'food, drink and scruffy people', rare in this day of burly bouncers on the door. Nestled beneath the cathedrals in Hay Lane, it is one of Coventry's oldest pubs, dating from the 16th century. For the ultimate student pub, try *The Campbell* on Gosford St, which now, dangerously for some, boasts a 2 am close.

Spon St offers the pleasantly quiet *Old Windmill*, the popular *Rising Sun*, the psychedelic *Flares* and the *Shakespeare*. Other popular pubs and bars include *The Courtyard* with a nice courtyard for the sunshine, and *Red Square Vodka Bar*, although outside of weekends it has more flavours than customers.

When it comes to live music and clubs, *The Dog & Trumpet* is only really worth a go on Friday night for its alternative music, *The Coliseum* in Hillfields is rated for up and coming bands and the new *Skydome* has a couple of nightclubs.

Theatre & Cinema The University of Warwick, 4 miles south of the city, has the largest *Arts Centre (☎ 524524)* outside London, with a regular program of events and a popular cinema. *Belgrade Theatre (☎ 553055)* is in Corporation St.

Getting There & Away

Birmingham International airport (☎ 0121-767 5511) is actually closer to Coventry than Birmingham.

The train station is just across the ring road, south of the centre. Coventry is on the main rail route to London (£19.50, 1½ hours). Birmingham is £2.80 by rail.

Pool Meadow bus station is in Fairfax St. West Midlands bus services are coordinated by Centro (☎ 7655 9559). National Express tickets (☎ 0870 580 8080) cost £10.50 to London, £8 to Oxford and £16.50 to Bath. Foxhound offers hourly buses to Leicester (one hour).

Stagecoach (☎ 01788-535555) has Explorer tickets for £4.50/2.50, allowing one day's bus travel to Birmingham, Evesham, Kenilworth, Leamington, Northampton, Oxford, Stratford and Warwick.

Getting Around

Phone ☎ 7655 9559 for local bus service information; a Daytripper ticket gives you a day's use of local bus and train services.

WARWICK

☎ 01926 • pop 22,000

Warwickshire's pleasantly sedate county town is home to Warwick Castle, one of England's major tourist attractions. It's also a handy base for visits to Stratford-upon-Avon.

Orientation & Information

Warwick is simple to navigate; the A429 runs right through the centre with Westgate at one end and Eastgate at the other. The old town centre lies just north of this axis, the castle just south. The TIC (☎ 492212) is in Jury St, near the junction with Castle St.

Warwick Castle

Warwick Castle, one of England's finest medieval castles, is owned by Madame Tussaud's and can easily take up half a day to explore in depth.

Warwick was first fortified in Saxon times, but the first real castle was constructed on the banks of the River Avon in 1068, soon after the Norman Conquest. The castle's external appearance principally dates from the 14th and 15th centuries, but the interiors are from the late-17th to late-19th centuries, when the castle changed from a military stronghold to a grand residence. Capability Brown landscaped the magnificent grounds in 1753.

The castle is entered through a gatehouse beside the armoury and the dungeon and torture chamber. Just inside, a sign points to the 'Kingmaker' exhibition. The most powerful of all the castle's powerful owners was Warwick the Kingmaker, Richard Neville, the 16th earl (1428–71). Having replaced the ineffectual Henry VI with the king's son Edward IV in 1461, Neville then fell out with Edward IV and brought Henry VI back in 1470, only to be defeated and killed by Edward IV less than a year later. At one time, he had Henry VI under lock and key in the Tower of London while Edward IV was his prisoner at Warwick. The 'Kingmaker' exhibit uses models to show preparations for one of his many battles.

The Tussaud influence is most strongly felt in the private apartments which are furnished as they would have been in 1898, with a series of waxwork figures attending a weekend house party. As you walk round you bump into various members of the nobility, their servants and attendants as well as historic figures such as the young Churchill and the Prince of Wales, later Edward VII.

The castle opens 10 am to 6 pm daily, closing an hour earlier in winter. Admission costs £10.95/6.50. Phone ☎ 406600 for details of medieval banquets in the castle.

Collegiate Church of St Mary

Originally constructed in 1123, this church (☎ 403940) was badly damaged by a fire in 1694 and rebuilt in a mishmash of styles. The remarkable perpendicular Beauchamp Chapel was built between 1442 and 1460 at a cost of £2400, a huge sum for the time. Luckily it survived the fire.

The gilded bronze effigy of Richard Beauchamp, 13th earl of Warwick, sits in the centre of the chapel; Richard Neville is the sinister-looking figure on the corner of the tomb.

The church opens 10 am to 6 pm daily (to 4 pm November to March). A £1 donation is requested. Don't miss the 12th-century crypt with remnants of a medieval ducking stool, used to drench scolding wives.

Lord Leycester Hospital

At the Westgate end of the town, the road cuts through a sandstone cliff. In 1571 Robert Dudley, earl of Leicester, founded the impressive Lord Leycester Hospital (☎ 491422) above it as an almshouse.

It has a beautiful courtyard, a 14th-century chapel and a guildhall built by Neville containing a military museum. The hospital opens 10 am to 5 pm Tuesday to Sunday, April to September (to 4 pm in winter). Admission is £3/free or £1 for the garden only.

Museums

Warwickshire Museum (☎ 412500) in the 17th-century market building has displays on natural history and archaeology. The museum opens 10 am to 5.30 pm Monday to Saturday, year round; 11 am to 5 pm on Sunday, May to September. Admission is free.

In Castle St, the **Doll Museum** (☎ 412500), in the half-timbered medieval Oken's House. It opens 10 am to 5 pm daily, Easter to September. Admission costs £1/70p. **St John's House** (☎ 410410), a Jacobean mansion on St John's, has exhibits on the county's social history. It opens 10 am to 5.30 pm Tuesday to Saturday year round; 2.30 pm to 5 pm on Sunday, May to September. Admission is free.

Places to Stay

The nearest hostel is in Stratford-upon-Avon (see Stratford-upon-Avon later in the chapter).

The centre of Warwick is woefully short of budget-priced B&Bs. To stay overnight without paying through the nose you'll probably have to stay in Emscote Rd, the eastern end of the main road through Warwick. The *Avon Guest House* (☎ 491367, 7 Emscote Rd), close to the town centre, has rooms from £20 per person. *Park House* (☎ 494359, 17 Emscote Rd), is another popular place with all en-suite rooms from £25/40.

The *Warwick Arms Hotel* (☎ 492759, 17 High St) has rooms with bathroom from £40/50, £55/65 during the week. The *Lord Leycester Hotel* (☎ 491481, 17 Jury St) oozes history and offers a reasonable deal with rooms from £55/65 per person.

Charter House (☎ 496965, 87 West St) is outstanding, but doesn't come cheap. The characterful, period rooms include four poster beds and start from £49.50/75.

Places to Eat

Pizza Piazza (☎ 491641, 33–35 Jury St) does reasonable pizzas at reasonable prices. Further east, *Piccolino's* (☎ 491020, 31 Smith St) is deservedly popular, serving delicious seafood pasta.

For something Indian, try the popular, bring your own (BYO) *Castle Balti*

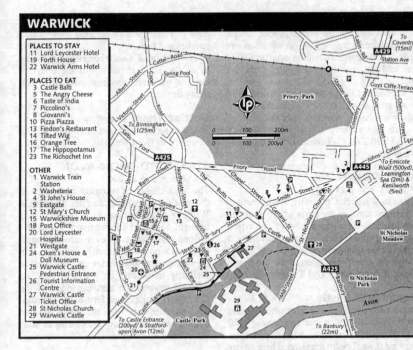

WARWICK

PLACES TO STAY
11 Lord Leycester Hotel
19 Forth House
22 Warwick Arms Hotel

PLACES TO EAT
3 Castle Balti
5 The Angry Cheese
6 Taste of India
7 Piccolino's
8 Giovanni's
9 Pizza Piazza
13 Findon's Restaurant
14 Tilted Wig
16 Orange Tree
17 The Hippopotamus
23 The Richochet Inn

OTHER
1 Warwick Train
  Station
2 Washeteria
4 St John's House
10 Eastgate
12 St Mary's Church
15 Warwickshire Museum
18 Post Office
20 Lord Leycester
  Hospital
21 Westgate
24 Oken's House &
  Doll Museum
25 Warwick Castle
  Pedestrian Entrance
26 Tourist Information
  Centre
27 Warwick Castle
  Ticket Office
28 St Nicholas Church
29 Warwick Castle

(☎ 493007, 11 St John's) or *Taste of India* (☎ 492151, 35 Smith St), which has 'traditional' Sunday buffets for £6.75.

There are a few alternatives to pasta or curry. The *Angry Cheese* (☎ 400411, St Nicholas Church St) is a wine bar-cum-bistro specialising in Mexican food. The *Tilted Wig* (☎ 410466, 11 Market Place) has a lengthy bar menu and a pleasant outdoor area for a summer's day. *The Hippopotamus* (☎ 439504, 48 Brook St) looks like a cafe by day, but by night it serves up a daring array of African and Caribbean specialities – three courses cost £12.

Across from St Mary's, *Findon's Restaurant* (☎ 411755) does romantic, candlelit two-course dinners for £15.95. *The Ricochet Inn* (☎ 491232, Castle Lane) has a sturdy menu of modern British cuisine at around £10 to £12 a main.

Nightlife is low key, to put it politely, but the *Orange Tree* is a trendy bar, by Warwick's standards.

Getting There & Away

Trains run to Birmingham, Stratford-upon-Avon and London, but there are better links to Warwick from nearby Leamington Spa. Stagecoach buses (☎ 01788-535555) stop in Market Place; a bus to Coventry takes one hour. National Express buses operate from Old Square.

AROUND WARWICK

Leamington Spa (pop 57,000) more or less runs into Warwick. Although there's not much to detain tourists, the town has some fine Regency architecture and classy shops. It is also a useful base during peak season when places such as Stratford and Warwick are overrun. The old Pump Rooms now house an interesting local Museum & Art Gallery. *Sacher's*, at the top of The Parade, is an excellent cafe and restaurant. At the opposite end of town are several super-cheap balti restaurants, exiles from Balsall Heath in Birmingham so the food is good.

CENTRAL ENGLAND

The industrial town of **Rugby** (pop 60,000) is famous only for the public school, which provided the setting for *Tom Brown's School-days*. It was here that a pupil picked up a football and ran with it, thereby inventing the sport of rugby.

Baddesley Clinton (☎ 01564-783294; NT) is an enchanting, medieval moated house, which has hardly changed since the death of Squire Henry Ferrers in 1633. Admission costs £5.20/2.60. Call ahead to confirm opening hours.

KENILWORTH
☎ 01926 • pop 21,000

Close to Warwick University, Kenilworth is a pleasant town in the parts where planners haven't left their mark and is gentrified commuterville for neighbouring Coventry, 4 miles to the north-east. Old and new Kenilworth are some way apart, with the castle closer to picturesque Old Kenilworth.

Kenilworth Castle

Dramatic, red-sandstone Kenilworth Castle (☎ 852078; EH) was founded around 1120 and enlarged in the 14th and 16th centuries. Edward II was briefly imprisoned here before being transferred to Berkeley Castle and murdered. In 1563, Elizabeth I granted the castle to her favourite, Robert Dudley, earl of Leicester. Between 1565 and 1575 she visited him at Kenilworth on four occasions and the theatrical pageants he arranged for her in 1575 were immortalised in Sir Walter Scott's 1821 work *Kenilworth*. The castle was deliberately ruined in 1644, after the Civil War. The castle opens 10 am to 6 pm daily (to 4 pm October to March). Admission is £3.50/1.80.

Places to Stay & Eat

Abbey Guest House (☎ 512707, 41 Station Rd) has singles/doubles for £26/45, while *Priory Guest House* (☎ 856173, 58 Priory Rd) charges £25/40. *The Peacock Hotel* (☎ 851156, 149 Warwick Rd) has an ugly exterior but a smart interior and charges from £65/75.

Opposite the castle on Castle Hill, the *Clarendon Arms* is renowned for serving good food. More or less next door, *Harring-*

tons (☎ 852074) is more upmarket. Next door is *Time for Tea* offering inexpensive lunches and teas.

The Virgins & Castle, on High St, claims to be the farthest pub from the coast in Britain, so street surfing only after too many drinks.

Getting There & Away

To get to Kenilworth take bus No X18 from Coventry or from Warwick.

STRATFORD-UPON-AVON
☎ 01789 • pop 22,000

The freak chance of being the birthplace of the world famous Elizabethan playwright William Shakespeare (1564–1616) has brought Stratford international fame and fortune and tourists in ever-growing numbers – it's now second only to London in popularity. The town today devotes itself to furiously marketing its favourite son. Its position beyond the northern edge of the Cotswolds makes Stratford a handy stopover en route to or from the north. It's also a good base for visiting the castles at Warwick and Kenilworth.

Orientation & Information

Arriving by coach or train, you'll find yourself within walking distance of the town centre, which is easy to explore on foot. Transport is only really essential for visiting Mary Arden's House.

The TIC (☎ 293127), close to the river on Bridgefoot, has plenty of information but gets frantically busy in summer. It opens 9 am to 6 pm Monday to Saturday and 11 am to 5 pm on Sunday; it closes an hour earlier and all day on Sunday November to March.

Every Thursday and Saturday two-hour guided walks depart from outside the Swan Theatre at 10.30 am. Tickets cost £5/4. Phone ☎ 412602 for details.

The Shakespeare Properties

The Shakespeare Birthplace Trust (☎ 204 016, ⓔ info@shakespeare.org.uk) looks after five buildings associated with Shakespeare. During summer the crowds can be

STRATFORD-UPON-AVON

PLACES TO STAY
3 Dukes
4 Payton Hotel
27 Alcester Road B&Bs
28 Backpacker's Hostel
38 Swan's Nest Hotel
41 Arden Thistle Hotel
44 The Shakespeare
48 Falcon Hotel
56 Main B&B Centre

PLACES TO EAT
5 Greek Connection
12 Lemon Tree
13 Restaurant Margaux
19 De:alto
21 café
22 Wholefood Café
23 Raj Tandoori Balti
24 Lalbagh Balti Restaurant
33 Vintner Wine Bar
34 Lambs
35 Opposition
36 Glory Hole
37 Boathouse Bar & Restaurant
46 Edward Moon's

PUBS, BARS & CLUBS
14 Slug & Lettuce
16 The Pen & Parchment
25 Bar M
32 Garrick Inn
51 Dirty Duck
55 Windmill Inn

OTHER
1 Bus Station
2 Stratford Leisure & Visitor Centre
6 The Shakespeare Centre
7 Shakespeare Bookshop
8 Cinema
9 Shakespeare's Birthplace
10 Library
11 Post Office
15 Guide Friday Bus Stop
17 Tourist Information Centre

OTHER (continued)
18 Gower Memorial
20 Taxi Rank
26 Train Station
29 American Fountain
30 Bus to Anne Hathaway's Cottage
31 Harvard House
39 Royal Shakespeare Theatre
40 Swan Theatre
42 New Place & Knot Garden
43 Nash's House
45 Midland Bank Building
47 Police Station
49 King Edward VI School
50 Guild Chapel
52 Almshouses
53 The Other Place
54 Hall's Croft
57 Sparklean Laundrette
58 Holy Trinity Church

horrendous and none of the houses was designed to accommodate such a squash; visit out of season if possible. Note that wheelchair access to the properties is very restricted.

Three of the houses are centrally located, one is a short bus ride away, and the fifth a drive or bike ride out of town. A £12/6 ticket offers access to all five properties, or £8.50/4.20 for just the three town houses. To pay for each place individually would cost nearly twice as much. More information is available from the trust's Web site at www.shakespeare.org.uk.

Shakespeare's Birthplace The premier Shakespeare attraction, in Henley St, has been so extensively rebuilt over the centuries that Will might have trouble recognising it despite having been born here. It has been a tourist attraction for three centuries; you'll see the evidence of famous 19th-century visitor-vandals who scratched their names on one of the windows. It opens 9 am to 5 pm daily (from 9.30 am on Sunday), March to October; slightly shorter hours the rest of the year. A ticket costing £5.50/2.50 includes admission to the adjacent Shakespeare Centre, which has the lowdown on its famous son.

CENTRAL ENGLAND

Across the road, the **Shakespeare Bookshop** (☎ 292176) sells the complete works in a multitude of formats.

New Place & Nash's House In retirement, the wealthy Shakespeare bought a fine home at New Place, on the corner of Chapel St and Chapel Lane. The house was demolished in 1759 and only the site and grounds remain. An Elizabethan knot garden has been laid out on part of the New Place grounds. The adjacent Nash's House, where his granddaughter lived, tells the town's history and contains an interesting picture of what the house looked like in 1876 and after a complete face-lift in 1911. It opens 9.30 am to 5 pm daily (from 10 am on Sunday), March to October; slightly shorter hours the rest of the year. Admission costs £3.50/1.70.

Hall's Croft Shakespeare's daughter Susanna married the eminent doctor John Hall and their fine Elizabethan town house stands near Holy Trinity Church. Displays explain medical practice in Shakespeare's time. Opening hours are as New Place & Nash's House (see earlier). Admission costs £3.50/1.70. There's a cafe right next door.

Anne Hathaway's Cottage Before their marriage, Shakespeare's wife lived in Shottery, a mile west of Stratford, in a pretty thatched farmhouse with a garden and orchard. The nearby Tree Garden has samples of all the trees mentioned in Shakespeare's plays. A footpath (no bikes allowed) leads to Shottery from Evesham Place, or catch a bus from Wood St. Opening hours are as Shakespeare's Birthplace (see earlier). Admission costs £4.20/1.70.

Mary Arden's House The home of William's mother now houses the Shakespeare Countryside Museum with exhibits tracing local country life over the last four centuries. Since there's also a collection of rare farm animals and a turn-of-the-century farmhouse, you'll probably need more time here than at the other properties. Opening hours are as New Place & Nash's House (see earlier). Admission costs £5/2.50.

Mary Arden's House is at Wilmcote, 3 miles west of Stratford. If you cycle there via Anne Hathaway's Cottage, follow the Stratford-upon-Avon Canal towpath to Wilmcote rather than retracing your route or riding back along the busy A3400.

Holy Trinity Church
Holy Trinity Church (☎ 266316) has transepts from the mid-13th century, when it was greatly enlarged. It has had frequent later additions; the spire dates from 1763. In the chancel, there are photocopies of Shakespeare's baptism and burial records, his grave and that of his wife, and a bust that was erected seven years after Shakespeare's death but before his wife's and thus assumed to be a good likeness. The church opens 8.30 am to 6 pm Monday to Saturday, and 2 to 5 pm Sunday in summer. Admission to see these legacies costs £1/50p.

Harvard House
Exuberantly carved Harvard House, on High St, was home to the mother of John Harvard, who founded Harvard University in the USA in the late-16th century. It now houses a collection of pewter. It opens 10 am to 4 pm Tuesday to Saturday (from 10.30 am on Sunday), May to late October. Admission is free.

Next door is the historic timber-framed **Garrick Inn**, while across the road the **Midland Bank Building** has reliefs illustrating scenes from Shakespeare's plays.

Other Things to See & Do
Erected in 1881, the **Gower Memorial** features a statue of Shakespeare surrounded by four of his characters – Falstaff, Hamlet, Lady Macbeth and Prince Hal. It overlooks the canal basin, where the Stratford-upon-Avon Canal meets the Avon River, a popular place to see narrowboats 'working the lock'.

The **Guild Chapel**, at the junction of Chapel Lane and Church St, dates from 1269, although it was rebuilt in the 15th century. Next door is **King Edward VI School**, which Shakespeare probably attended; it was originally the Guildhall.

The **Royal Shakespeare Company Gallery** (RSC; ☎ 296655) inside the Swan Theatre

CENTRAL ENGLAND

The Old Bard, William Shakespeare

Probably the greatest dramatist of all time, William Shakespeare was born in Stratford-upon-Avon in 1564, the son of a local glove maker. At the age of 18 he married Anne Hathaway, eight years his senior, and their first daughter, Susanna, was born about six months later. Boy and girl twins, Hamnet and Judith, followed two years later, but the son died at the age of 11.

Around the time of the twins' birth, Shakespeare moved to London and began to write for the Lord Chamberlain's Company. This successful company enjoyed the finest theatre (the Globe) and the best actors. It wasn't until the 1590s that Shakespeare's name appeared on his plays. Before that, the company's name was regarded as more important than the dramatist's.

Shakespeare's 37 plays made novel and inventive use of the English language, but also boasted superb plot structures and deep insights into human nature – characteristics that have ensured not only the plays' survival over the centuries but also their popularity in other languages. His earliest writings included comedies such as Comedy of Errors, historical accounts, including Henry VI and Richard III and the tragedy Romeo and Juliet. The new century saw his great tragedies, first Hamlet and then Othello, King Lear and Macbeth.

Around 1610 he retired, moved back to Stratford-upon-Avon and lived in comfortable circumstances until his death in 1616. He was buried in the parish church. His wife outlived him by seven years.

Despite Shakespeare's prodigious output of plays, no letters or other personal writing have survived and the little that is known about him and his family has been pieced together from birth, death and marriage files and other official records (including the will in which he left his wife his 'second-best bed'!). This paucity of information has bred wild theories that Shakespeare didn't actually write the plays. Since none have survived in manuscript form, there's no handwriten evidence to prove they're his. Nonbelievers speculate that Shakespeare's origins and education were too humble to have provided the background, experience and knowledge to write the plays. Their favourites for the 'real' Shakespeare are the earl of Derby or the earl of Oxford who, they claim, may have had reasons for wanting to remain anonymous.

Shakespeare's star-crossed lovers: Romeo & Juliet

---

exhibits the RSC's collection of props, costumes and theatrical paraphernalia. It opens 9.30 am to 5 pm Monday to Saturday, and noon to 4.30 pm Sunday; 11 am to 3.30 pm on Sunday in winter. Admission costs £1.50/1. Theatre tours (☎ 412602) operate at 1.30 and 5.30 pm Monday to Friday (except matinee days) and at 12.30, 1.45, 2.45 and 3.45 pm Sunday (one hour earlier in winter). Tours plus admission to the RSC collection cost £4/3.

Places to Stay

Camping There are two camp sites on Stratford's western outskirts. **Dodwell Park** (☎ 204957), Evesham Rd, charges £9 for a tent and £1.50 per person. From Easter to September two people can camp at **Stratford Racecourse** (☎ 267949, Luddington Rd) from £7.

Hostels Bad news for the YHA, **Backpackers Hostel** (☎ 263838, ⓔ stratford@hostels .demon.co.uk, 33 Greenhill St) has finally brought much needed centrally sited budget accommodation to Stratford. Beds are £11 in the dorms, £15 in twin rooms, and it is wise to book well ahead in the summer months.

The **Stratford-upon-Avon Youth Hostel** (☎ 297093, Hemmingford House, Alveston) is 1½ miles from the town centre. From the TIC, walk across Clopton Bridge and turn left along Tiddington Rd (B4086). Bus No 18 runs to Alveston from Bridge St. The hostel opens early-January to mid-December and charges £15.50/11.50 for adults/under-18s.

B&Bs During summer, B&Bs can be expensive and hard to find. If it's all too much, Leamington Spa or Warwick are worthwhile alternatives. Prime hunting grounds for cheaper places are Evesham Place, Grove Rd and Broad Walk, only a couple of minutes' walk south of the town centre. If you're stuck, the TIC charges £3 plus a 10% deposit to help you find something. South Warwickshire Tourism also has a hotline (☎ 415061) for credit card bookings. It operates 9 am to 5 pm Monday to Friday.

Possibilities in Evesham Place include the cheerful *Grosvenor Villa* (☎ 266192, 9 *Evesham Place*) at £22 a single, or £48 for an en-suite double; the *Dylan Guest House* (☎ 204819, 10 Evesham Place) for £24 per person with its period fireplaces; the good-value, nonsmoking *Clomendy* (☎ 266957, 157 Evesham Place), also £24 per person; and the cheaper *Arrandale* (☎ 267112, 208 Evesham Place) at £15.50 per person.

Virginia Lodge (☎ 292157, 12 Evesham Place) has some attractive themed rooms for £24.

Friendly *Aberfoyle* (☎ 295703, 3 Evesham Place) charges £21 per person, *Carlton Guest House* (☎ 293548, 22 Evesham Place) charges £40/48 for doubles without/with bathroom, while the welcoming *Quilts & Croissants* (267629, 33 Evesham Place) charges from £20/35 for singles/doubles – no prizes for guessing the bedding and breakfast.

Up a price bracket but rather nice is *Twelfth Night* (☎ 414595, 13 Evesham Place), charging from £27 to £31 per person. *Woodstock Guest House* (☎ 299881, 30 Grove Rd) is a highly rated, friendly B&B with en-suite rooms from £30/56.

There are several places on Alcester Rd, near the train station. *Hunters Moon Guest House* (☎ 292888, 150 Alcester Rd) has rooms with bathroom from £30/48, while the *Moonlight Bed & Breakfast* (☎ 298213, 144 Alcester Rd) is cheap from £15 per person, £17.50 en suite.

Rooms with bathrooms at attractive *Moonraker House* (☎ 299346, 40 Alcester Rd) cost from £45/49, with four-poster bed suites for £75.

Hotels Numerous pricey hotels cater to international package tours. Theatre-goers could hardly do better than stay at the *Arden Thistle Hotel* (☎ 294949), immediately across the road from the Swan Theatre, but singles/doubles start at £69/82. In Chapel St, *The Shakespeare* (☎ 0870 400 8182), with its beautiful historic buildings, has rooms from £105/210, while the charming *Falcon Hotel* (☎ 279953) has rooms from £80/115.

Smaller, more reasonably priced hotels include charming *Dukes* (☎ 269300, Payton St), which backs onto the canal and has rooms with bathroom from £56/69.50 and the much smaller *Payton Hotel* (☎ 266442, e info@payton.co.uk, 6 John St), across the road, which charges from £28 per person.

Places to Eat

Sheep St is wall-to-wall with restaurants. The *Glory Hole* (☎ 293546, 21 Sheep St) has olde worlde English food and furnishings. The other restaurants have a very similar cafe vibe and include *Opposition* (☎ 269980, 13 Sheep St) with good pasta, *Lambs* (☎ 292554, 12 Sheep St) with an oriental influence and *Vintner Wine Bar* (☎ 297259, 5 Sheep St) with lively vegetarian options.

Edward Moon's (☎ 267069, 9 Chapel St) has a tasty menu from around the globe, mains start at about £8 in these stylish surroundings. For plate-smashing fun, try the *Greek Connection* (☎ 292214), on the corner of Birmingham Rd and Shakespeare St; expect to pay from around £15 a head.

Asian restaurants include *Lalbagh Balti Restaurant* (☎ 293563, 3 Greenhill St) and the excellent *Raj Tandoori Balti* (☎ 267067, 7 Greenhill St). Nearby, *Wholefood Café* does pleasant soups and salads at lunchtime, while *Jave Café* (☎ 263400, 98 Greenhill St) offers internet access with snacks. Other excellent cafes worth a stop include *Lemon Tree* on Union St with a happy, breezy feel, and *café*, an elegant spot on Meer St, leaving nothing to the imagination.

De:alto is a trendy, popular Italian restaurant on Waterside, while *Restaurant Margaux* (☎ 269106), on Union St, has a fine variety of expensive French-influenced food – be prepared to spend £20 and up.

Entertainment

Pubs A pint at the *Dirty Duck* (aka the Black Swan), close to the river in Waterside, is an essential Stratford experience for thespians and theatre-goers alike. The *Slug & Lettuce (38 Guild St)* and the *Cask & Barrel* remain popular. The *Windmill Inn (Church St)* is reputed to be the oldest pub in town and draws a lively, young crowd most nights. The *Falcon Hotel (Chapel St)* is another bar stooped in history. *Bar M*, on Greenhill St, has a late licence most nights.

Theatre Seeing a Royal Shakespeare Company production (☎ 295623) is a must. Performances take place in the main **Royal Shakespeare Theatre**, the adjacent **Swan Theatre** or, nearby, **The Other Place**. Tickets cost from £12 to £40 and the box office in the Royal Shakespeare Theatre opens 9.30 am to 8 pm Monday to Friday. Stand-by tickets are available to students, under-19s and over-60s on the day of the performance (£13 or £16.50); over-60s also qualify for £14 tickets for weekday matinees and Wednesday evening shows, provided they book 24 hours in advance. Standing room tickets may be available up to the last moment for just £5.

Getting There & Away

Stratford is 93 miles from London, 40 miles from Oxford and 8 miles from Warwick. Bus connections are better than train connections to most parts of the country.

Bus National Express buses link Birmingham, Stratford, Warwick, Oxford, Heathrow and London several times daily. Singles from Stratford include Birmingham (£4.75) and Heathrow/London's Victoria coach station (£11). The National Express stop is on Bridge St, opposite McDonald's.

Stagecoach Midland Red (☎ 01788-535555) bus serves Warwick (20 minutes),

Coventry (1¼ hours), Birmingham (one hour) and Oxford (1½ hours). The useful Cotswold Shuttle offers three daily services (except Sunday) to Broadway, Moreton-in-Marsh, Stow-on-the-Wold and Bourton-on-the-Water. With a £4.50 Day Explorer ticket you could choose to stop off at Broadway and then continue on the same day to one of the other Cotswold towns. There is also a weekday service to Chipping Campden.

Train Stratford station is on Station Rd, a few minutes' walk west of the centre. There are only a couple of daily services direct from London Paddington (£20, 2½ hours).

Coming from the north, it's sometimes easier to transfer at Leamington Spa, sometimes at Birmingham. Services from Birmingham depart from Moor St station (£3.50, 50 minutes).

Getting Around

Call Busline (☎ 01788-535555) for local bus information. Bus No X18 operates via the Alveston hostel to Warwick and Leamington Spa, hourly Monday to Saturday.

Guide Friday (☎ 294466) operates open-top buses that do circuits past the five Shakespeare properties every 15 minutes during peak summer months for £8.50/2.50. You can pick them up outside the TIC.

Stratford is small enough to explore on foot, but a bicycle is good for getting out to the surrounding country or the rural Shakespeare properties. The canal towpath offers a fine route to Wilmcote. Punts, canoes and rowing boats are available from the boathouse by Clopton Bridge.

AROUND STRATFORD-UPON-AVON

Stratford-upon-Avon is ringed by pretty villages, atmospheric pubs and stately homes. The popular Cotswold villages of Chipping Campden and Broadway are only a short distance south, and Warwick, Coventry and Birmingham are within day-tripping distance. It is possible to walk or cycle to Birmingham along the Stratford-upon-Avon Canal towpath.

CENTRAL ENGLAND

Charlecote Park

Around 5 miles east of Stratford-upon-Avon, Sir Thomas Lucy is said to have caught the young Shakespeare poaching deer in the grounds of Charlecote Park (☎ 01789-470277; NT). The park, which was landscaped by Capability Brown, still has deer. The house was built in the 1550s and rebuilt in the 1830s. It opens 12 to 5 pm Friday to Tuesday, April to October. Admission costs £5.40/2.70. Bus Nos 19 and X18 go there from Stratford-upon-Avon.

Ragley Hall

Ragley Hall (☎ 01789-762090) is a Palladian house a couple of miles south-west of Alcester. The house was built between 1679 and 1683, but the over-the-top plaster ceilings and huge portico were added later. The intriguing South Staircase Hall, with its murals and ceiling painting, was painted between 1968 and 1982. The house opens 12.30 to 5 pm Thursday to Sunday (11 am to 3.30 pm on Saturday), April to September. Admission costs £5/3.50.

Birmingham

☎ 0121 • pop 1,014,000

Birmingham is Britain's second-largest city, culturally vibrant, socially dynamic but aesthetically challenged. Birmingham remains a major manufacturing centre, a city of fierce pride and boundless vitality. Although there are no essential sights and the city centre is chopped to pieces by ring roads, there are still some interesting corners, especially in Brindleyplace, the award-winning waterfront development around the old canal network.

The city was one of the great centres of the Industrial Revolution, home to inventors such as steam pioneers James Watt (1736–1819) and Matthew Boulton (1728–1809), gas lighting whizz kid William Murdock (1754–1839), printer John Baskerville (1706–75) and chemist Joseph Priestley (1733–1804). But by the mid-19th century, the 'workshop of the world' exemplified everything that was bad about industrial development. Under enlightened mayors such as Joseph Chamberlain (1869–1940), father of the unfortunate Neville, the city became a trendsetter in civic development, but WWII air raids undid the good work; post-war town planners completed the vandalism by designing the ring roads and motorways that virtually obliterated the old city centre. The connection between the M5, M6 and M42 is such a mess that it's commonly known as Spaghetti Junction.

The Birmingham accent is consistently rated England's most unattractive. Locally, the city is known as Brum, the inhabitants as Brummies and the dialect as Brummie.

Orientation

The endless ring roads, roundabouts and underpasses make Birmingham a confusing city to navigate, particularly for motorists.

The city centre is the pedestrian precinct in front of the huge Council House. Head west from here to Centenary Square, the Convention Centre and Symphony Hall, and the Gas St Basin/Brindleyplace development. Head north-west for the Jewellery Quarter.

South-east of the Council House, most of Birmingham's shops can be found along pedestrianised New St and in the modern City Plaza, Pallasades and Pavilions shopping centres; the latter is overlooked by the landmark Rotunda office block.

After dark the underpasses linking New St station to Digbeth coach station can seem very alarming especially for lone women. The good news is that work is currently underway that will see the whole ghastly Bull Ring mess razed to the ground.

Information

The most useful TIC (☎ 693 6300) is the one at 130 Colmore Row, on Victoria Square. There's another TIC at 2 City Arcade (☎ 643 2514) and a third in the National Exhibition Centre (☎ 780 4321), roughly midway between Birmingham and Coventry and near Birmingham airport.

Town Centre

The central pedestrian precinct of Victoria and Chamberlain squares features a statue

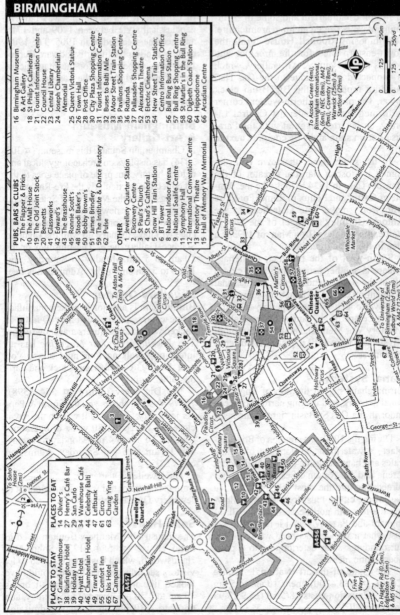

BIRMINGHAM

PLACES TO STAY
17 Grand Moathouse
38 Burlington Hotel
39 Holiday Inn
40 Hyatt Hotel
46 Chamberlain Hotel
49 Travel Inn
55 Comfort Inn
65 Ibis Hotel
67 Campanile

PLACES TO EAT
14 Olivier's
27 Henry's Café Bar
29 San Carlo
34 Warehouse Café
44 Celebrity Balti
47 Leftbank
61 Circo
63 Chung Ying Garden

PUBS, BARS & CLUBS
7 The Flapper & Firkin
10 The Malt House
19 The Old Joint Stock
20 Bennetts
41 Classworks
42 Edward's
43 The Brasshouse
45 Ronnie Scott's
48 Stood Baker's
50 Bobby Brown's
51 James Brindley
59 The Institute & Dance Factory
62 Pulse

OTHER
1 Jewellery Quarter Station
2 Discovery Centre
3 St Paul's Church
4 St Chad's Cathedral
6 BT Tower
8 Snow Hill Train Station
9 National Indoor Arena
11 National Sealife Centre
12 Symphony Hall
13 International Convention Centre
15 Repertory Theatre
16 Hall of Memory War Memorial

16 Birmingham Museum & Art Gallery
18 St Philip's Cathedral
21 Tourist Information Centre
22 Council House
23 Central Library
24 Joseph Chamberlain Memorial
25 Queen Victoria Statue
26 Town Hall
28 Post Office
30 City Plaza Shopping Centre
31 Tourist Information Centre
32 Buses to Balti Mile
33 Moor Street Train Station
35 Rotunda
36 Pavilions Shopping Centre
37 Pallasades Shopping Centre
52 Alexandra Theatre
53 Electric Cinema
54 New Street Train Station; Centro Information Office
56 Bull Ring Bus Station
57 Bull Ring Shopping Centre
58 St Martin's in the Bull Ring
60 Digbeth Coach Station
64 Hippodrome
66 Arcadian Centre

of Queen Victoria, a fountain, a memorial to Joseph Chamberlain and some of Birmingham's most eye-catching architecture. The imposing **Council House** forms the north-eastern face for the precinct and houses the Museum & Art Gallery, which is connected by a bridge to the Gas Hall building topped by the Big Brum clock tower. The precinct's north-western corner is formed by the modernist Central Library, an inverted ziggurat with the Paradise Forum shop and cafe complex next to it.

To the south stands the **town hall**, designed by Joseph Hansom (creator of the Hansom Cab) in 1834 to look like the Temple of Castor and Pollux in Rome. For those who won't make it to Gateshead to see Antony Gormley's 'Angel of the North' statue, his wingless 'Iron Man' of 1993 is a step in the same direction.

South-west of the precinct, Centenary Square is another pedestrian square closed off at the eastern end by the International Convention Centre and the Symphony Hall, and overlooked by the Repertory Theatre. In the centre of the square is the Hall of Memory War Memorial and a curious modern statue ('Forward') depicting a cluster of Brummies.

Canal System

Birmingham sits on the hub of England's canal network, and visiting narrowboats can moor in the Gas St Basin right in the heart of the city.

During the 1990s the creation of **Brindleyplace**, a waterfront development of trendy cafes and bars alongside the National Indoor Arena and the National Sealife Centre, has turned this into the most vibrant, attractive part of the city, a must for visitors. Following the towpath north-east along the Birmingham and Fazeley Canal it is easy to see just what a wonder has been worked – the surroundings soon deteriorate into a postapocalyptic mess.

The state-of-the-art **National Sealife Centre** (☎ 633 4700) opens 10 am to 5 pm daily. Admission costs £8/5.50 (£5.95/3.95 from the TIC).

St Philip's Cathedral

In Colmore Row, St Philip's was built in neoclassical style between 1709 and 1715 and became a cathedral in 1905. The 19th-century Pre-Raphaelite artist Edward Burne-Jones was responsible for the magnificent stained-glass windows: the Last Judgement at the western end, the Nativity, Crucifixion and Ascension at the eastern end.

Birmingham Museum & Art Gallery

In Chamberlain Square, this museum (☎ 303 2834) has displays on archaeology, local and natural history, but pride of place goes to the art collection, particularly the Pre-Raphaelite paintings. Until the Museum of Science and Industry finds a new home in the Millennium Point development, people keen on science will have to make do with the Light on Science Gallery here. The museum opens 10 am to 5 pm Monday to Saturday, and 12.30 to 5 pm on Sunday. Admission is free.

Jewellery Quarter

Birmingham is a major jewellery manufacturing centre and the Jewellery Quarter is packed with manufacturers and showrooms. The *Jewellery Quarter Magazine* has an interesting walking tour map taking you past the 1903 Chamberlain Clock and various other sights.

The Discovery Centre (☎ 554 3598), 75–79 Vyse St, shows you the Smith & Pepper jewellery factory, as it was on the day it closed in 1981 after 80 years of operation. It opens 10 am to 4 pm Monday to Friday, and 11 am to 5 pm Saturday. Admission costs £2.50/2.

The Jewellery Quarter is a 15-minute walk from the centre or trains run from Moor St to Jewellery Quarter station.

Soho House

The industrialist Matthew Boulton lived in Soho House (☎ 554 9122), Soho Ave, Handsworth, which has been restored to let visitors see what such a house would have looked like in the 18th century. It opens 10 am to 4.30 pm Tuesday to Saturday, and noon to 4.30 pm on Sunday. Admission

The Pre-Raphaelites & the Arts and Crafts Movement

The Pre-Raphaelite Brotherhood was formed in 1848 by three young British artists: Dante Gabriel Rossetti, William Holman Hunt and John Everett Millais. Four other artists soon joined them in their rejection of contemporary English art and reverence in favour of the directness of art prior to the High Renaissance, especially the work of Raphael.

Often unashamedly romantic in its view of the past, their work was characterised by almost photographic attention to detail, a combination of hyper-realism and brilliant colours that ensured the movement's popularity to this day.

Birmingham Museum & Art Gallery has one of the best collections of works by the Pre-Raphaelites. If you get the bug, there are more fine paintings in the Lady Lever Art Gallery at Port Sunlight near Liverpool.

The Arts and Crafts Movement followed Pre-Raphaelitism in its rejection of contemporary standards and its yearning for an earlier, purer and more naturalistic style. The socialist William Morris, the movement's leading light, had worked with Rossetti and projected the same ideals into tapestries, jewellery, stained glass and textile prints. Cheltenham Art Gallery & Museum has a fine display of Arts and Crafts furniture, as does Arlington Mill in Bibury, Gloucestershire.

costs £2.50/2. It is in walking distance from the Jewellery Quarter, or bus Nos 70, 74, 78 and 79 pass by.

Aston Hall

Built between 1618 and 1635, this Jacobean mansion (☎ 327 0062) with a fine long gallery, is in Aston Park on Trinity Rd, Aston, about 3 miles north of the city centre. It opens 2 to 5 pm daily, Easter to October. Admission is free. Get there on bus No 65 or 104, or take a train to Aston station.

Other Galleries

The small collection of old masters at the **Barber Institute of Fine Arts** (☎ 472 0962) is at the University of Birmingham, 2½ miles south of the city centre (get off at University train station). The **Ikon Gallery** (☎ 248 0708), Oozells Square, Brindleyplace, features changing exhibitions of modern art, often impressive, often utter nonsense, depending on one's taste.

Organised Tours

From May to September Guide Friday operates seven daily 90-minute bus tours for £8.50/2.50 a head. Phone the TIC (☎ 693 6300) for details of ghost and graveyard tours (£4.50/4) as well as more conventional walking tours of the city centre.

Canal boat trips can be arranged from the Gas St Basin or the Convention Centre quay (☎ 507 0477) for around £5/2.50 per person.

Places to Stay

Birmingham has no YHA hostel. Most accommodation in the centre is aimed at business visitors, and over weekends or during summer it may be worth asking at the TIC in case there are special deals to fill surplus beds. Day-tripping into Birmingham is an option but means missing out on the nightlife, something to savour these days. Stratford-upon-Avon and Coventry are short train rides away.

Although one reader of this guide recommended the 92-room *YWCA* (☎ 454 8134, Alexandra House, 27 Norfolk Rd, Edgbaston), which has dorm beds for £9 a night, the hostel is clear that 'our priority is to provide accommodation for those people without homes'.

Popular areas for B&Bs include Edgbaston (to the south-west) and Acocks Green (to the south-east). The friendly *Ashdale House Hotel* (☎ 706 3598, 39 Broad Rd, Acocks Green) has singles from £22 or £28 with bathroom, and doubles from £42. Vegetarian breakfasts can be arranged.

Birmingham has a full set of mid-range chain hotels – perfectly comfortable although lacking in character. Closest to New St station is the **Comfort Inn** (☎ 643 1134, Station St), with singles/doubles for £45/65. The centrally located **Ibis Hotel** (☎ 622 6010, Arcadian Centre, Ladywell Walk) has double rooms from £39 (breakfast is extra). The **Travel Inn** (☎ 644 5266, 230 Broad St) is ideally placed for exploring the Brindleyplace nightlife. Rooms cost a flat £49.95. Nearby is the more upmarket **Chamberlain Hotel** (☎ 606 9000), with plush rooms for £55, making them good value.

The **Burlington Hotel** (☎ 643 9191, 6 Burlington Arcade) is one of the most pleasant centrally located hotels and has rooms from £135/157 during the week, a more sensible £65/80 at weekends. Nicest of the posh places is the **Grand Moathouse** (☎ 607 9988, Colmore Row), overlooking the cathedral, but a room sets you back £110/130.

Places to Eat

Birmingham's contribution to world cuisine is the Balti, a uniquely Midlands version of Indian food. England is now engulfed with Balti houses but Birmingham remains their homeland. The most down-to-earth prices are in the Birmingham Balti Mile of Sparkbrook, Sparkhill and Balsall Heath, 2 miles south of the centre, where 54 restaurants are squeezed into just three streets. Pick up a complete listings leaflet in the TIC and head out on bus No 4, 5 or 6 from Corporation St.

Luckily there are also a few goodies in the city centre. The **Celebrity Balti** (☎ 632 6074, 44 Broad St) is much glossier than average, but the food is delicious. Baltis range from around £6 to £9.

Dine in classier surroundings in the **Edwardian Tea Room** in the Museum & Art Gallery (see Birmingham Museum & Art Gallery earlier); there are hot meals, as well as sandwiches and cakes.

Big, busy **Henry's Café Bar** (☎ 631 3827, Hill St) serves everything from burgers to cashew nut paella.

In the same building as Friends of the Earth, the **Warehouse Café** (☎ 633 0261, 54 Allison St, Digbeth) specialises in vegan food and opens Monday to Saturday until 9 pm.

In the Arcadian Centre in Hurst St, the **Green Room** serves a popular pre-theatre menu to Hippodrome punters; specials are around £5. Excellent Cantonese cuisine can be had nearby at **Chung Ying Garden** (☎ 666 6622, 17 Thorpe St), which wheels out 70 varieties of dim sum and main courses from £6.50. **Circo** (☎ 643 1400, 6 Holloway Circus) is a popular tapas bar offering a £5 lunchtime special of mussels, French fries, salad and mayonnaise.

San Carlo (☎ 633 0251, 4 Temple St) has a lengthy Italian menu, well worth sampling. **Olivier's** (☎ 644 6464), the Repertory Theatre's restaurant, comes in for plenty of praise; try the pre-theatre menu for under £10 or go a la carte and pay more like £15 – the Balti duck is said to be delicious. Brindleyplace offers wall-to-wall eateries, with many of the big chains represented. More one-off is **Tin Tin** (☎ 633 0888), a classy Chinese restaurant where fish dishes are particularly good. **Bank** (☎ 633 4466) has a classy feel and draws the punters with pre-concert meals for £15.50 for three courses. **Le Petit Blanc** offers entry level haute cuisine at almost sensible prices. Best value is the set menu at £15 for three courses.

Leftbank (☎ 643 4464) takes expensive dining to new heights, but is renowned for well prepared, well presented food. Think £30 and up.

Entertainment

What's On (free at the TIC, otherwise 80p) is a fortnightly listings guide to entertainment in and around Birmingham.

Pubs, Bars & Clubs Pleasant, canal-side pubs include the **James Brindley** (Gas St Basin), which is named after the canal pioneer, and the trendy **Glassworks** (Gas St Basin). Facing each other across the canal in Broad St are **The Brasshouse** and **Edward's**, while the **Flapper & Firkin**, a little farther along at Cambrian Wharf, is decorated in canal style. **The Malt House** has a great position near the National Indoor Arena. Also in this area is **Stoodi Baker's**, a trendy bar and club that is popular with students.

Birmingham has several impressive banks turned bars. *Bennetts* (☎ 643 9293, *Bennetts Hill*) serves up tasty food to accompany the drinks in grand surroundings. Alternatively, try *The Old Joint Stock* (*Temple Row*), facing the cathedral, which serves up fine Fuller's ales.

The *Institute & Dance Factory* (☎ 643 7788, *Digbeth High St*) is a large nightclub that often has live music. The busy *Steering Wheel* (☎ 622 5700, *Wrottesley St, Chinatown*) has three dance floors, or there's *Pulse* (☎ 643 4715, *Hurst St*), which serves up something different every night of the week. The *Que Club* (☎ 472 0777, *Corporation St*) is an incredible venue housed in a former Methodist church. Club nights and gigs are held here, including some of the big boys from London such as Return to the Source.

The *Glee Club* (☎ 693 2248, *Hurst St*) hosts stand-up comedians four nights a week.

Music *Ronnie Scott's* famous jazz club (☎ 643 4525, *Broad St*) charges £11 to £16 admission depending on the night. The City of Birmingham Symphony Orchestra plays in the ultramodern *Symphony Hall* (☎ 780 3333), Major rock and pop acts appear at the *National Exhibition Centre* (☎ 780 4133).

Theatre & Cinema The Victoria Square TIC has a ticket shop (☎ 643 2514) where, from 11 am daily, you can buy half-price theatre tickets. Theatres include the *Hippodrome* (☎ 622 7437), home of the Birmingham Royal Ballet; the *Alexandra Theatre* (☎ 643 1231); and the *Repertory Theatre* (☎ 236 4455)

The fantastically decorated *Electric Cinema* (☎ 643 7277, *Station Rd*) often shows cult movies; double bills are just £4.30.

Getting There & Away

Birmingham is a major train and coach interchange. It also boasts an increasingly busy international airport (☎ 767 7000) with flights to numerous European destinations and to New York.

Bus National Express has links to most parts of Britain from dreary Digbeth coach station.

A single ticket costs £10 to London (3½ hours), £8.75 to Oxford and £9.75 to Manchester. Local buses operate from the Bull Ring bus station. Bus No X93 goes to Kidderminster for the Severn Valley Railway.

Train New St station, one of England's busiest rail interchanges, is underneath the Pallasades shopping centre, which in turn is linked with the Bull Ring bus station and Bull Ring shopping centre. For the National Exhibition Centre or Birmingham airport get off at Birmingham International station.

Getting Around

For rail and bus services in and around Birmingham, the Centro phone number is ☎ 200 2700. A Daytripper ticket gives all-day travel on buses and trains after 9.30 am. Local trains, including the Stratford-upon-Avon service, operate from Moor St station, which is only a few minutes' walk from New St – follow the red line on the pavement. Other handy stations are at Snow Hill and the Jewellery Quarter.

AROUND BIRMINGHAM
Cadbury World & Bournville Village

Chocoholics should make a beeline for Cadbury World, where you can find out the story behind a creme egg and visit the chocolate packaging plant where around 800 bars a minute are wrapped and dispatched. Not surprisingly, this place is packed over weekends and school holidays when it's best to book ahead by phoning ☎ 0121-451 4159. Opening hours vary throughout the year but are generally 10 am to 5.30 pm daily. Admission costs £6.50/4.50.

To get to Cadbury World take a train to Bournville station from Birmingham New St. In summer Guide Friday tours drop off at Cadbury World.

Before returning, follow the signs to pretty Bournville village, designed for early-20th-century factory workers by the Cadbury family, with large houses set around a green. It's also well worth visiting **Selly Manor** (☎ 0121-472 0199), the sort of half-timbered medieval-cum-Elizabethan

CENTRAL ENGLAND

house you see in Stratford but without the crowds. It opens 10 am to 5 pm Tuesday to Friday and 2 to 5 pm on Sunday. Admission costs £2.50/50p. The manor also stocks the excellent *Bournville Trail Guide*.

Black Country Museum

The area stretching west of Birmingham and out to Wolverhampton was traditionally known as the Black Country because of the smoke and dust generated by the local coal and iron industries. The 10½ hectare Black Country Museum (☎ 0121-557 9643) features a re-created coal mine, village and fairground on the banks of the Dudley Canal at Tipton in Dudley. It's a great place for a day out, with a full program of mine trips, Charlie Chaplin films and chances to watch glass cutters and sweet makers in action.

From March to October you can also take a 40-minute boat ride through the Dudley Canal Tunnel to explore assorted caverns. Tickets cost £2.90/2.50.

The museum opens 10 am to 5 pm daily, March to October; 10 am to 4 pm Wednesday to Sunday, in winter. Admission costs £7.95/4.75. The *Stables Restaurant* offers pretty mundane on-site meals, or there's the excellent re-created *fish and chip shop*. The *Bottle & Glass Inn* can help you wash it down.

To get there from Birmingham city centre, take the No 126 bus from Corporation Rd and ask to be put off at Tipton Rd. It's a 10-minute walk along Tipton Rd to the museum, or you can catch bus No 311 or 313. A day ticket will cover the entire journey.

Northamptonshire

Northampton itself has just a handful of buildings of interest, but the surrounding area has two of England's finest surviving Saxon churches, a fine canal monument, Britain's most important motor racing circuit and the shrine to the late Princess Diana in the grounds of Althorp House. American visitors also derive a certain fascination from Sulgrave Manor, built by one of George Washington's early ancestors. There are the ruins of several castles and the sites of several battles throughout the area, attesting to its strategic importance in times gone by.

For local bus information phone ☎ 01604-620077.

NORTHAMPTON
☎ 01604 • pop 154,000

Lacking any major attractions, Northampton doesn't see a whole lot of tourists, although that can be a blessing for those tired of the frilly feel to nearby places such as Stratford and Warwick. Although nothing significant remains of it, Thomas à Becket was tried for fraud in Northampton Castle in 1164. A fire in 1675 left few other reminders of the medieval town. The Industrial Revolution made the town a shoe-manufacturing centre and the **Central Museum & Art Gallery** (☎ 39415), Guildhall St, has a collection of shoes to make foot fetishists drool. In and around town are numerous factory shops knocking out cheap Docs from the all-conquering Dr Martens factory, or for serious gentlemen, Churches also has some bespoke outlets.

Holy Sepulchre Church has curiosity value as one of only four round churches in the country. out of town on the London Rd, is the Elanor Cross, one of three originally erected to mark the places at which the funeral procession of Queen Elanor (wife of Edward I) camped on the long journey from Lincoln to Westminster Abbey following her death in 1290. The most famous of these stands in the village of **Geddington**, a short distance from Kettering on the A43.

Australian visitors might like to know that buried in the Billing Rd cemetery is Caroline Chisholm, forever known as the immigrant's friend for her work with refugees and once immortalised on the A$5 note.

The helpful TIC (☎ 22677) is at 10 Giles Square, opposite the Guildhall, and has a huge amount of information about surrounding attractions. Look out for the *Historic Town Trail* leaflet packed full of surprises.

Places to Stay & Eat

There is not exactly an abundance of accommodation in Northampton. In the cheaper range, the *Aarandale Regent Hotel* (☎ *631096, 8 Royal Terrace, Barrack Rd)* is a family-run place with a homely atmosphere where singles/doubles cost £30/44.

The *Coach House Hotel* (☎ *250981, 10 East Park Parade)* is set in a row of converted Victorian houses near the racecourse and has well-equipped singles/doubles from £55/65.

For the discerning traveller, the *Lime Trees Hotel* (☎ *632188, 8 Langham Place)* is a fine option found in a Georgian House about half a mile from the centre of town. Rooms here are £65/77 with discounts over the weekend.

Pumpernickels is a sandwich bar for those in a hurry to move on. Coffee fiends can find a fix at *Cafe Moriandi* on Gold St, which has some speciality drinks such as Espresso with Cornish ice cream. Near the main square, *Laurence's Coffee House* has a good selection of snacks and light meals. For something more fulfilling, *The Vineyard Restaurant* on Derngate has a good selection of seafood and offers two-course, pre-theatre meals for £10.

Nightlife has a very provincial feel to it in Northampton. Real ale quaffers will enjoy *The Malt Shovel*, a pub that comes recommended by none other than CAMRA. *Cuba Libre* has beer from a little farther afield, mainly Latin America, while *Bar Soviet*, on Bridge St, has a cool, intimate vibe to it.

Getting There & Away
Northampton has excellent rail links with Birmingham and London Euston with regular services throughout the day. The train station is about half a mile west of town along Gold St. The bus station is on Lady's Lane, near the Grosvenor shopping centre.

AROUND NORTHAMPTON
Althorp
With the late Diana, Princess of Wales, continuing to attract the public's attention from beyond the grave, the memorial and museum in the grounds of her ancestral home, Althorp Park, off the A428 north-west of

Northampton, is a popular tourist attraction. But the park only opens in July and August and tickets cost £10/5 (profits go to her Memorial Fund). The limited number of tickets must be booked in advance (☎ 01604-592020). Incidentally, Althorp should be pronounced altrup!

Stoke Bruerne Canal Museum
On a pretty stretch of the Grand Union Canal at Stoke Bruerne, 8 miles south of Northampton, the excellent Canal Museum (☎ 01604-862229) explains the development of English canals and displays models of pioneering canal engineering. It opens 10 am to 5 pm daily, Easter to September; 10 am to 4 pm Tuesday to Sunday in winter. Admission costs £3/2.

There are several pleasant pubs serving food on the banks of the canal, as well as the stylish *Old Chapel* restaurant (☎ *863284)*, which stays open until 9 pm. *Wharf Cottage* (☎ *862174)* offers B&B overlooking the canal.

Silverstone
The British Grand Prix motor race is held in July at Silverstone (☎ 01327-857271), just south of the A43. It's still one of the fastest racing circuits in Europe, with a lap record of more than 140 mph, despite the extra corners added in to slow cars down.

All Saints, Brixworth
About 8 miles north of Northampton, off the A508, All Saints (☎ 01604-880286) is England's largest relatively intact Saxon church. Built on a basilica plan around 680, it incorporates Roman tiles from an earlier building. The tower and stair turret were added after 9th-century Viking raids, the spire around 1350. It usually opens 10 am to 6 pm (to 4 pm in winter). Stagecoach bus Nos X7 and 62 from Northampton stop here.

All Saints, Earls Barton
About 8 miles east of Northampton, the church at Earls Barton is notable for its solid Saxon tower with patterns seemingly imitating earlier wooden models. It was

probably built during the reign of Edgar the Peaceful (959–95) and the 1st floor door may have offered access to the tower during Viking raids. Around 1100, the Norman nave was added to the original tower; other features were added in subsequent centuries. Stagecoach bus Nos 46, 47 and 48 come here from Northampton.

Sulgrave Manor

Sold to Lawrence Washington by Henry VIII in 1539, Sulgrave Manor (☎ 01295-760205) would probably be just another handsome country house were it not for the fact that 250 years later a certain family descendant named George Washington became first President of the USA. Today American tourists throng here in numbers for guided tours of this historic property and no doubt find it very quaint. Telephone ahead for opening hours as they vary widely throughout the year. Admission costs £4/2 and includes the tour.

Rushton Triangular Lodge

Northampton's most famous folly is a tribute to the Catholic fervour of one man, Sir Thomas Trensham, who designed a number of buildings in the area to express his beliefs – beliefs which landed him in prison on more than one occasion. The Triangular Lodge (☎ 01536-710761; EH) has three of everything, from sides to floors to gables and is Trensham's enduring symbol of the trinity. Built at the end of the 16th century, today it opens 10 am to 6 pm daily, April to October (to 5 pm in October). Admission costs £1.50/80p. Stagecoach bus Nos 46, 47 and 48 from Northampton stop here.

Fotheringhay

Famous for the birth of a notorious king and the death of a notorious queen, Fotheringhay Castle is today little more than a small hillock. Richard III, an infamous victim of the Tudor spin doctors and their literary wizard William Shakespeare, was born here in 1452, while Mary, Queen of Scots was executed here on the wishes of her cousin Elizabeth I in 1587.

Bedfordshire

Bedfordshire is compact, peaceful and predominantly agricultural. The River Great Ouse winds across the fields of the north and through Bedford; the M1 motorway roars across the uninteresting semi-industrial south.

The county town of Bedford is best known to tourists as the home of John Bunyan (1628–88), the 17th-century Nonconformist preacher and author of *Pilgrim's Progress*. South-east of Bedford lies the much-publicised stately home of Woburn Abbey.

GETTING AROUND

For information on buses around the county, phone the enquiry line (☎ 01234-228337). Stagecoach (☎ 01604-620077), the main regional bus company, has an Explorer ticket allowing one day's travel anywhere on its routes for £5/3.50.

BEDFORD

☎ 01234 • pop 77,000

Most visitors to Bedford are on a pilgrimage of their own to follow in the footsteps of Bedford's most famous preacher. Most places with links to John Bunyan are in and around the town, which boasts an attractive riverside setting and an impressive art gallery.

Information

The TIC (☎ 215226) is just off High St at 10 St Paul's Square. It stocks *John Bunyan's Bedford,* a free guide to places with a Bunyan connection.

The Bunyan Meeting

The **Bunyan Meeting** (☎ 358870), Mill St, was built in 1849 on the site of the barn where Bunyan preached from 1671 to 1678. The church's bronze doors, inspired by Ghiberti's doors for the Baptistry in Florence, show scenes from *Pilgrim's Progress*. One famous stained-glass window shows Bunyan in jail. The church opens 10 am to 4 pm Tuesday to Saturday, April to October. Admission is free. At the time of writing the small museum of Bunyan memorabilia opens 11 am to 4 pm

John Bunyan & Pilgrim's Progress

The son of a tinker, John Bunyan was born in 1628 at Elstow, near Bedford. He joined a Nonconformist church and became an accomplished preacher. In 1660, when the monarchy was restored, the government tried to restrain Nonconformist sects by forbidding preaching. Bunyan was arrested and spent the next 12 years in jail.

The allegorical work he started in prison, The Pilgrim's Progress from this world to that which is to come, became one of the most widely read books ever written.

An immediate success when it was published in 1678, its popularity stems from the fact that it's a gripping adventure story as well as a religious text. The pilgrim Christian, with his knapsack full of sins, embarks on a journey to paradise, via the Slough of Despond and Hill of Difficulty. On the way he is tempted by Vanity Fair and imprisoned in a giant's castle but, triumphing over these difficulties, he finally reaches the Celestial City.

Pilgrim's Progress has been translated into over 200 languages. The TIC produces a leaflet listing places associated with Bunyan in and around Bedford.

Tuesday to Saturday, March to October; once the new visitors centre is completed the opening hours should be extended so more people can admire some 169 editions of *Pilgrim's Progress* from around the world.

Cecil Higgins Art Gallery

The **Cecil Higgins Art Gallery** (☎ 353323), Castle Close, houses a splendid collection of glass, porcelain and colourful Victorian furniture. **Bedford Museum**, with archaeological and historical exhibits, is next door. Both open 1 am to 5 pm Tuesday to Saturday, and 2 to 5 pm on Sunday. Admission is £2/free.

Places to Stay & Eat

Bedford makes an easy day trip from London, but if you want to stay overnight there are several hotels and B&Bs along leafy De Pary's Ave, which leads north from High St to Bedford Park.

Bedford Park House (☎ 215100, 59 De Pary's Ave) has singles/doubles for £22/40. *De Pary's Guest House* (☎ 261982, 48 De Pary's Ave) has nine singles and six doubles. En-suite rooms cost from £29.50/37. *De Pary's Hotel* (☎ 352121, 45 De Pary's Ave) is a cut above the other places on this road and charges from £47.50/57.50.

Park View (☎ 341376, 11 Shaftesbury Ave) is very good value, although a little way out of town. Rooms are £17.50 per person. The historic *Swan Hotel* (☎ 346565),

right beside the river, has business rates of £76/84.50, but prices drop to £57.50 per person for half board at weekends.

The Orchid (☎ 266766), on St Paul's Square, is a Charles Wells pub turned Thai restaurant. The food is authentic and the price around £6 a plate. For good Italian food, look no further than *Santaniello's* on Mill St, whose Italian owners knock out some of the best pizzas in the area. Sticking to Euro flavours, *Vol au Vent* is a well-regarded French restaurant with some good deals during the week, including a three-course meal with coffee for around £10.

Many of Bedford's pubs do cheap meals, including *Hobgoblin,* cheapest of the lot thanks to a mainly student crowd. *Fleur de Lis* is more famous for its beer and has been a real-ale stalwart for many a year.

The *Bunyan Meeting* serves tea and coffee in its foyer or in summer you can snack alfresco on filled potatoes or sandwiches in the *Piazza* immediately behind St Paul's Church. *Green Cuisine* (☎ 305080, 41 St Cuthbert's St) is a real treat for vegetarians with a wide selection of inexpensive, wholesome food. For coffees from Colombia to Kenya, *Caffe Crema* hits the spot and has some fine pastries on the side.

Getting There & Away

Bedford is 50 miles north of London and 30 miles west of Cambridge. There are frequent trains from London's King's Cross Thameslink (£16 day return, one hour) to Midland station, a well-signposted 10-minute walk west of High St.

National Express has direct links between Bedford and London, Cambridge and Coventry. The bus station is half a mile west of High St.

WOBURN ABBEY & SAFARI PARK

Not an abbey but a grand, stately home built on the site of a Cistercian abbey, **Woburn Abbey** (☎ 01525-290666) has been the seat of the dukes of Bedford for the last 350 years. The house dates mainly from the 18th century, when it was enlarged and remodelled into a vast country mansion. Although half the building was demolished in 1950 because of dry rot, it remains well-worth visiting and is stuffed with furniture, porcelain and paintings.

The 1200-hectare park is home to the largest breeding herd of Père David's deer, extinct in their native China for a century (although a small herd was returned to Beijing in 1985).

It opens 11 am to 4 pm daily, late-March to October; weekends only January to March and in October. Admission costs £7.50/3 (free to under-12s). Although it's easily accessible by car off the M1 motorway, trains from King's Cross Thameslink only run to Flitwick, leaving you to take a taxi for the last 5 miles to the abbey.

A mile from the house is **Woburn Safari Park** (☎ 01525-290407), the country's largest drive-through animal reserve. It opens daily from late March to October; weekends only in winter. Admission costs £12/9.50. If you visit the abbey first you qualify for a 50% discount.

WHIPSNADE
Whipsnade Wild Animal Park

This park (☎ 01582-872171) is an offshoot of London Zoo that was originally established to breed endangered species in captivity; it claims to release 50 animals into the wild for every one captured. The 2500 animals in the 240-hectare site can be viewed by car, or the park's railway, or on foot. It opens 10 am to 6 pm daily (to 4 pm November to March). Admission costs £9.90/7.50, plus £8 for a car if you want to drive round.

In summer you can get to Whipsnade by Green Line bus from Buckingham Palace Rd near London's Victoria coach station (☎ 0870 608 7261).

Leicestershire & Rutland

Leicestershire is often overlooked by tourists as they rush between London and the Lakes or Peaks, but it has several interesting towns and historic sites. For general bus information phone ☎ 0116-251 1411. Rutland recently gained its 'independence' and is easy to get around due to its tiny size, although it lacks any major attractions.

LEICESTER
☎ 0116 • pop 320,000

Leicester (pronounced les-ter, most definitely not lie-cester!) is another Midlands centre that has suffered the triple disasters of wartime damage, uninspired post-war development and catastrophic industrial decline, but it has reacted to it better than most, reinventing itself as an environmentally progressive, ethnic entrepot of a city that could teach other, bigger cities a thing or two about multiculturalism. The modern town has a large and vibrant Asian community and there are Hindu, Moslem, Jain and Sikh temples as well as some excellent Indian, Bangladeshi and Pakistani restaurants. Many of the city's most interesting events are staged around festivals such as Holi, Diwali and Eid-ul-Fitr.

The city's history dates back to Roman times. Later, it was one of the five Danelaw towns and was the traditional home of Shakespeare's tragic King Lear. In 1239 Simon de Montfort, earl of Leicester, captured the castle. Medieval Leicester became a centre for manufacturing stockings, but remained a small town until the rapid industrial growth of the 19th century. Leicester

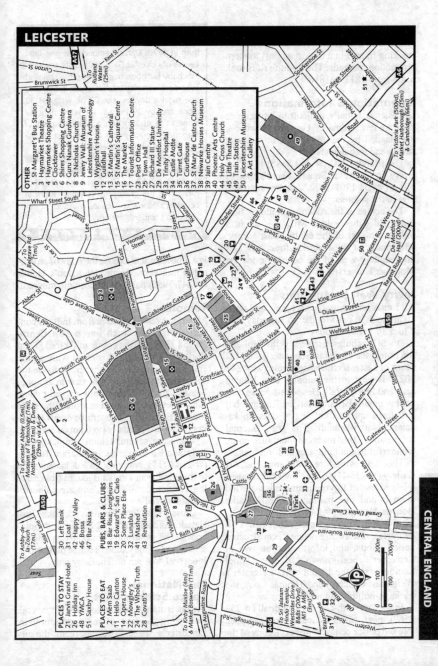

LEICESTER

OTHER
1 St Margaret's Bus Station
3 Haymarket Theatre
4 Haymarket Shopping Centre
5 Clocktower
6 Shires Shopping Centre
7 Guru Nanak Gurdwara
8 St Nicholas Church
9 Jewry Wall: Museum of
   Leicestershire Archaeology
10 Wygston's House
12 Guildhall
13 St Martin's Cathedral
15 St Martin's Square Centre
16 The Market
17 Tourist Information Centre
23 Post Office
25 Town Hall
27 Richard III Statue
29 De Montfort University
33 Trinity Hospital
34 Castle Motte
35 Turret Gate
36 Courthouse
37 St Mary de Castro Church
38 Newarke Houses Museum
39 Jain Centre
40 Phoenix Arts Centre
44 Holy Cross Church
45 Little Theatre
49 Train Station
50 Leicestershire Museum
   & Art Gallery

PLACES TO STAY
21 Jarvis Grand Hotel
26 Holiday Inn
48 YMCA
51 Saxby House

PLACES TO EAT
2 Mem Saab
11 Hello Canton
14 Opera House
24 Mowgley's
28 Covati's

30 Left Bank
31 Loaf
42 Happy Valley
46 Bossa
47 Bar Nasa

PUBS, BARS & CLUBS
18 Bar Risa; Jongleurs
19 Edward's; San Carlo
20 Some Place Else
32 Lunablu
41 Mashed
43 Revolution

24 The Whole Truth

bequeathed the word 'Luddite' to the language, after apprentice Nedd Ludd smashed stocking frames in a protest against modern production methods. The Luddite riots took place from 1811 to 1816.

Orientation & Information

Leicester is initially difficult to navigate as there are few landmarks. For those on wheels, it's plagued by the usual maze of one-way streets and forbidden turns.

The friendly TIC (☎ 299 8888) is at 7–9 Every St, Town Hall Square. There's another office (☎ 251 1301) in St Margaret's bus station in the summer.

The centre of the Asian community, Belgrave Rd ('the Golden Mile'), is about a mile north-east of the centre. Castle Park, with many of the historic attractions, lies immediately west of the centre, beside De Montfort University.

Jewry Wall & Museums

All Leicester's museums are free, and open 10 am to 5.30 pm Monday to Saturday, and 2 to 5.30 pm on Sunday.

On St Nicholas Circle, by the Holiday Inn hotel (see Places to Stay later), the **Museum of Leicestershire Archaeology** (☎ 247 3021) is next to the remains of a Roman bath and **Jewry Wall**. Despite its name, this wall is one of Britain's largest Roman civil structures and has nothing to do with Judaism. Notwithstanding its grim external appearance, the museum contains some wonderful Roman mosaics and frescoes.

The **Leicestershire Museum & Art Gallery** (☎ 255 4100), in New Walk, houses a mixed bag of Egyptian mummies, stuffed animals and fine paintings. The **Newarke Houses Museum** (☎ 247 3222) is in buildings dating from the early-16th and 17th centuries. There are some reconstructed period shops, and information on two of Leicester's best-known citizens: Daniel Lambert (see the boxed text 'Leicester's Weightiest Citizen') and Thomas Cook, the package-holiday pioneer.

In the late-14th-century **Guildhall** (☎ 253 2569), next to the cathedral, you can peep into old police cells and inspect a copy of the

Leicester's Weightiest Citizen

Born in 1770, Daniel Lambert, the one-time keeper of Leicester Gaol, started life as a normal baby but soon began to tip the scales at ever more alarming totals. Despite eating only one meal a day, by age 23 he weighed 32 stone and by 39 he was an astounding 52 stone 11 lb, making him, as the *Dictionary of National Biography* puts it, 'the most corpulent man of whom authentic record exists'.

When he died in Stamford in 1809 one wall of the house had to be dismantled to remove the coffin, and 20 pallbearers were needed to carry it to the graveyard. A whole room in Leicester's Newarke Houses Museum is devoted to Lambert's memory.

last gibbet used to expose the body of an executed murderer. Nearby **Wygston's House** (☎ 247 3056) has a small costume museum.

Temples

Materials were shipped in from India to convert a disused church into a **Jain Centre** (☎ 254 3091), on the corner of Oxford St and York Rd. The building is faced with marble and inside, the temple (the first outside the subcontinent and the only one in Europe) boasts a forest of beautifully carved pillars. Jainism evolved in India at around the same time as Buddhism. The temple opens to visitors 9 am to 5 pm daily (to 6 pm on Sunday).

There are several Hindu temples in the Belgrave Rd area. The **Sri Jalaram Temple** (☎ 254 0117), Narborough Rd, is dedicated to the Hindu saint Pujya Bapa. Marble carvings depict his life and there are colourful murals of Vedic scriptures.

Close to the Jewry Wall is the Sikh **Guru Nanak Gurdwara** (☎ 262 8606), at 9 Holybones. The small museum holds an impressive model of the Golden Temple in Amritsar. It opens 1 to 4 pm on Thursday only.

The National Space Science Centre

This is Britain's answer to Cape Canaveral. Reflecting the years of hard work put in by Leicester's Space Research Team, the city was chosen as the location for this centre, which is expected to be not only educational and entertaining but also to become a centre of excellence in studying space as it is the first Challenger Learning Centre outside the USA. It is due to have opened by spring 2001, a case of watch this space; for further details, contact ☎ 253 0811 or ℮ info@nssc.co.uk.

Great Central Railway

The Great Central Railway (☎ 01509-230726) operates steam locomotives from Leicester North to Loughborough Central, the 8-mile route along which Thomas Cook ran his original package tour in 1841. Trains run every weekend year round and daily from June to September. The round trip costs £9.50/6.50.

Festivals

The Asian community in Leicester celebrates Diwali during autumn, and the celebration, the largest of its kind outside India, draws visitors from all over the world. During August, the city is also host to the biggest Caribbean party outside London's Notting Hill Festival. A more recent addition to the festival calendar is the Comedy Festival in February, now the largest in the country, drawing names such as Eddie Izzard and Jo Brand.

Places to Stay

The TIC charges £2 to make bookings but apart from expensive hotels there's little in the centre.

The *Copt Oak Youth Hostel* (☎ 01530-242661, *Whitwick Rd, Copt Oak*) is 8 miles north-west of the centre, near junction 22 on the M1. It opens daily from May to September, phone for details the rest of the year. Beds cost £8.50/5.75 for adults/under-18s.

Richard's Backpacker's & Student Hostel (☎ 267 3107, *157 Wanlip Lane*) has beds for those aged 26 and under for just £8.50 (£45 a week), including a basic breakfast. Tent space costs £3.

The *YMCA* (☎ 255 6507, *7 East St*) is just across from the train station and has a few single rooms at £12 (£44.79 a week). There

are some cheap places on Saxby St, off London Rd just south of the train station, although this may not be the best area for lone women. Friendly but basic *Saxby House* (☎ 254 0504), at No 24, is just £13 per person, and there are other cheapies nearby.

Try Westcotes Drive, off Narborough Rd, for B&Bs. The *Scotia Hotel* (☎ 254 9200), at No 10, has singles/doubles for £21/42, a little more with en-suite facilities. The *Cumbria Guest House* (☎ 254 8459), at No 16, is slightly cheaper with rooms from £18/32.

The centrally located, venerable *Jarvis Grand Hotel* (☎ 255 5599, *Granby St*) has rooms from £92/114 during the week, almost half that at weekends. Rooms at the *Holiday Inn* (☎ 253 1161, *St Nicholas Circle*) drop from £130 during the week to £75 with breakfast at weekends.

Places to Eat

The Belgrave Rd area, to the north of the centre (bus is best), is noted for its fine Indian cuisine and excellent vegetarian food. Award-winning but budget-priced *Friends Tandoori* (☎ 266 8809, *41–43 Belgrave Rd*) serves excellent northern-Indian food, but no baltis as the word means bucket. Other popular vegetarian choices include *Sayonara* (☎ 266 5888) at No 49, *Sharmilee* (☎ 261 0503) at No 71–73, where a thali costs £7.50, and *Bobby's* (☎ 266 0106) at No 154, where delicious southern-Indian food is the speciality. The ringroad location of *Mem Saab* (☎ 253 0243, *Vaughan Way*) may not be memorable, but the food is and the weekday banquets for £10.75 will leave a glow for days.

For stylish Italian dining, head for *Covati's* (☎ 251 8251, *Westbridge Place*), a well-designed restaurant, accessible by footbridge from Castle Gardens, with main courses from £6. *Bar Nasa* (☎ 255 4667, *153 Granby St*) is a bargain Italian and a good place to linger over drinks after a meal.

Happy Valley (☎ 255 7700, *New Walk*) does Chinese business lunches for £5.50. In Guildhall Lane, the big *Hello Canton* (☎ 262 9029) offers set meals from £10.

For budget dining, *The Whole Truth (19 Belvoir St)* is a lively vegetarian cafe with a creative menu. Just up the road, *Mowgley's* is a sandwich bar to help those on the move survive the urban jungle. *Bossa*, on Granby St, has cheap toasted sarnies in a cheerful atmosphere.

Opera House (☎ 223 6666), near the cathedral, is very well-regarded by Leicester residents. The menu is a mix of French and modern British and lunch is pretty good value at £8.70/10.25 for two/three courses.

The Left Bank of the canal is a fast rising area of town, although not quite its Parisien namesake just yet, and there are a couple of gastro cafe-bars on Braunstone Gate. *Left Bank* (☎ 255 2422) was first to venture this way and has a fine menu of contemporary cuisine. *Loaf* (☎ 299 9424) has a dangerously addictive menu and the immortal motto 'it is better to have loafed and lost, than never to have loafed at all'.

Entertainment

Leicester has a thriving nightlife and places go in and out of fashion by the month. Some of the most popular at the time of writing include *Revolution* and *Mashed* in the laid back New Walk area, both of which have DJs and a chilled out atmosphere at any time. Over on Left Bank are the aforementioned *Loaf* and the rather stylish *Lunablu*, complete with games area and funky furniture. For the more traditionally-minded, the *Phoenix Arts Centre* (☎ 255 4854, *Newarke St*) hosts films, plays and dance events. Plays are also staged at the *Little Theatre* (☎ 255 1302, *Dover St*) and sometimes at the *Haymarket Theatre* (☎ 253 9797). Classical concerts are performed at the *De Montfort Hall* (☎ 233 3111, *Granville Rd*).

The *Jongleurs Comedy Club* (☎ 0800 783 9933, 30 Granby St) hosts comedians at the weekend.

Getting There & Away

Leicester is 105 miles from London, 40 miles from Birmingham, and 25 miles from Coventry and Nottingham.

Bus National Express (☎ 0870 580 8080) operates from St Margaret's bus station in Gravel St, north of the centre, which has left-luggage facilities. There are hourly services to London. The Stagecoach Express service No 777 runs to Nottingham hourly (one hour). The Busline (☎ 251 1411) offers general bus information.

Train A statue of Thomas Cook stands outside the train station on London Rd, southeast of the centre. Trains from London St Pancras arrive every half-hour; the fastest take just over one hour. There are hourly services between Birmingham and Cambridge or Norwich via Leicester.

AROUND LEICESTER
Bosworth Battlefield

South-west of Leicester at Sutton Cheny, 2 miles from Market Bosworth, Richard III was defeated by the future Henry VII in 1485, ending the Wars of the Roses. 'A horse...a horse...my kingdom for a horse', was his famous death cry. Richard III may be a villain to most for his supposed role in the murder of his young nephews, the 'princes in the tower', but Leicester has adopted him as something of a folkhero, not the hunchback of Shakespearean spin. History will never be certain who had the young princes killed, but most historians would tend to side with the victorious Tudors and blame Richard III. The visitors centre (☎ 01455-290429) opens 11 to 5 pm daily, April to October. Admission costs £3/1.90.

Ashby-de-la-Zouch

Driving from Leicester to Derby it's easy to divert via this pleasant little town with its castle (☎ 01530-413343; EH). Built in Norman times, and owned by the Zouch family until 1399, it was extended in the 14th and 15th centuries and then reduced to its present picturesque ruined state in 1648 after the Civil War. Bring a torch to explore the underground passageway that connects the tower with the kitchen. The castle opens 10 am to 4 pm daily (to 6 pm in summer). Admission costs £2.60/1.30.

Melton Mowbray
☎ 01684

Something of a culinary capital, Melton Mowbray not only gave the world pork pies, but more recently Stilton cheese. This unassuming Leicestershire town is also the fox-hunting capital of Britain, until such time as legislation is passed to outlaw this most controversial of pastimes.

The TIC (☎ 480992) is in the **Melton Carnegie Museum**.

Donington Park

The Donington Park motor-racing circuit at Castle Donington, 20 miles north-west of Leicester, hosts the annual British Motorcycle Grand Prix. It also features the **Donington Collection** (☎ 01332-811027) of racing cars (including probably the world's best collection of Formula 1 racing cars) and motorcycles. It opens 10 am to 4 pm daily. Admission costs £7/2.50. Metal fans will know it more for the Monsters of Rock festival held here each year.

Belvoir Castle

North-east of Leicester, Belvoir (pronounced bee-ver) Castle (☎ 01476-870262) is 6 miles from Grantham, off the A1. This baroque and Gothic fantasy was rebuilt in the 19th century after suffering serious damage during the Civil War. It opens 11 am to 5 pm Tuesday to Thursday and at the weekend, April to September; Sunday only in October. Admission costs £5.25/3.

RUTLAND

Rutland finally threw off the colonial yoke once more in the late-1990s, after many years of being part of Leicestershire. It is England's smallest county, formed largely by Rutland Water, a vast and beautiful reservoir supplying much of the East Midland's water. The county town of **Oakham** is pleasant if not compelling and there are many opportunities for water sports on Rutland Water. Oakham's TIC (☎ 01572-724329) is at 34 High St.

Shropshire

Covering the rolling hills between Birmingham and the Welsh border, Shropshire is a large county with a relatively small population centred on the attractive regional capital of Shrewsbury and the new town of Telford. Just outside Telford is Ironbridge, where a series of remarkable museums commemorate the birthplace of the Industrial Revolution.

Shropshire is bisected by the River Severn, which flows west to east through Shrewsbury. To the north the countryside is largely flat and uninteresting, but to the south lie the Shropshire Hills, the 'blue remembered hills' of local poet AE Housman, author of *A Shropshire Lad*. The best known of a series of ridges are Wenlock Edge, the Long Mynd and the Stiperstones. Mostly below 500m, this is excellent walking country that sees relatively few hikers.

With such an array of attractions on offer, it can only be a matter of time before Shropshire draws visitors in coachloads, but for now its ends-of-the-earth (well, England at least) location has tended to protect it from the shock troops of mass tourism.

CYCLING

Starting from Shrewsbury, a good 100-mile five- or six-day cycle route takes you round the most scenic parts of Shropshire. You can rent bikes in Church Stretton and Ludlow.

The route goes from Shrewsbury via Wroxeter to Ironbridge (14 miles), Ironbridge to Much Wenlock (only 5 miles but there's a lot to see in Ironbridge), Much Wenlock to Ludlow (20 miles), Ludlow to Clun (an easy 17-mile ride), Clun to Church Stretton (15 miles), and Church Stretton to Shrewsbury (16 miles, along side roads parallel to the busy A49).

GETTING AROUND

Public transport between Shropshire's main towns isn't bad, with railway lines and most bus routes radiating from Shrewsbury. Getting to country areas without a car is less easy but the county council has a useful phone line (☎ 0845 705 6785) for bus and rail information. The invaluable *Shropshire Bus & Train Map*, available free from TICs, shows all the bus routes.

CENTRAL ENGLAND

SHREWSBURY
☎ 01743 • pop 60,000

When Charles Dickens was staying at the Lion Hotel in Shrewsbury, he wrote, 'I am lodged in the strangest little rooms, the ceilings of which I can touch with my hands. From the windows I can look all downhill and slantwise at the crookedest black and white houses, of all many shapes except straight shapes.'

The county's capital can still claim to be the finest Tudor town in Britain, famous for its higgledy-piggledy half-timbered buildings and winding medieval streets, criss-crossed with shuts and passages. There are no vitally important sights here, which has saved Shrewsbury from inundation by tourists, but there is undoubtedly a wonderful atmosphere to much of the town, which makes it a good base for exploring Shropshire and a convenient stop en route to Wales.

History
Strategically positioned within a defensible loop of the River Severn, Shrewsbury has been important since the 5th century; the Saxon town of Scrobbesbyrig was established on the two hills here. After the Norman

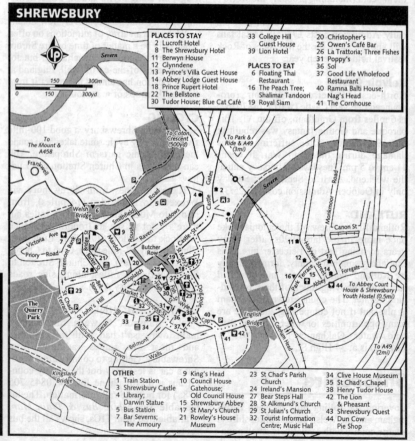

SHREWSBURY

Scale: 0 – 150 – 300m / 0 – 150 – 300yd

PLACES TO STAY
2 Lucroft Hotel
8 The Shrewsbury Hotel
11 Berwyn House
12 Glynndene
13 Prynce's Villa Guest House
14 Abbey Lodge Guest House
18 Prince Rupert Hotel
22 The Bellstone
30 Tudor House; Blue Cat Café
33 College Hill Guest House
39 Lion Hotel

PLACES TO EAT
6 Floating Thai Restaurant
16 The Peach Tree; Shalimar Tandoori
19 Royal Siam
20 Christopher's
25 Owen's Café Bar
26 La Trattoria; Three Fishes
31 Poppy's
36 Sol
37 Good Life Wholefood Restaurant
40 Ramna Balti House; Nag's Head
41 The Cornhouse

OTHER
1 Train Station
2 Shrewsbury Castle
4 Library; Darwin Statue
5 Bus Station
7 Bar Severns; The Armoury
9 King's Head
10 Council House Gatehouse; Old Council House
15 Shrewsbury Abbey
17 St Mary's Church
21 Rowley's House Museum
23 St Chad's Parish Church
24 Ireland's Mansion
27 Bear Steps Hall
28 St Alkmund's Church
29 St Julian's Church
32 Tourist Information Centre; Music Hall
34 Clive House Museum
35 St Chad's Chapel
38 Henry Tudor House
42 The Lion & Pheasant
43 Shrewsbury Quest
44 Dun Cow Pie Shop

Conquest, the town came under the control of Roger de Montgomery, who built the castle. The Benedictine abbey was founded in 1083.

For many centuries Shrewsbury played an important part in the control of the Welsh, and in 1283 the Welsh prince David III was executed here after a parliament convened in the abbey chapterhouse. Despite problems with its unruly neighbours, the town prospered from the wool trade with the Welsh hill farmers. Many of the beautiful Tudor buildings were built by wealthy wool merchants in the days when the Severn was navigable all the way from Bristol. Even as the river silted up, the town remained an important transit town on the coach route between London and Dublin, via Holyhead.

The town's best-known former resident, Charles Darwin, was born here in 1809 and educated at Shrewsbury's famous public school. His statue stands outside the library. The town has also done him the questionable honour of naming the shopping mall after him.

Orientation & Information

Housman described Shrewsbury as 'islanded in Severn stream'. The train station now lies across the narrow land bridge formed by the loop of the River Severn, a five-minute walk north of the town centre. The bus station is central and the whole town is well signposted. Many of the old winding streets still have names that reflect the occupations of their former inhabitants – Butcher Row, Fish St, Milk St.

The TIC (☎ 281200), in The Square, opens 10 am to 6 pm daily (to 4 pm on Sunday), May to September. Guided 1½-hour walking tours leave the TIC at 2.30 pm daily May to October. Tickets cost £2/1. Ring ahead for winter times.

Combined tickets for the castle, Rowley's House and Clive House cost £6/2.50.

Walking Tour

Start from the TIC, which is in the old **Music Hall** of 1839. Opposite, in the square, is the **Market Hall**, an open-sided building erected in 1595. Until the mid-19th century trade was carried on in this square and, on

the insides of the pillars at the northern end, you can still see holes for the markers used to record the numbers of fleeces sold.

Walk across the square into High St and there is a statue to Robert Clive, who laid the foundations for British control of India and was mayor of Shrewsbury in 1762. On your left is the 16th-century **Ireland's Mansion**, most impressive of the town's timber-framed buildings.

Head back along High St and turn left into narrow Grope Lane with its overhanging buildings. Cross Fish St and go up the steps into St Alkmund's Place, the original town square. The medieval tower aside, **St Alkmund's Church** was completely remodelled at the end of the 18th century. The restored 14th-century **Bear Steps Hall** opens between 10 am and 4 pm and is well worth a visit. Nearby **St Julian's Church** now houses a craft centre. There are several black and white houses along **Butcher Row**, including the Abbot's House, built in 1450.

The 'cathedral' of the Churches Conservation Trust, magnificent **St Mary's Church** is no longer used for worship but is worth visiting for its beautiful, 15th-century angel roof and stained glass. Best of all is the great Jesse window made from rare, mid-14th-century English glass. The spire collapsed in 1894 – because the townsfolk were planning a memorial to Darwin (according to the vicar).

Opposite the northern side of the church, past 17th-century St Mary's Cottage, St Mary's Water Lane leads back down into Castle St. At the far end of the street is **Shrewsbury Castle** which houses the **Shropshire Regimental Museum** (☎ 358516). It opens 10 am to 4.30 pm Tuesday to Saturday, year round; and Sunday in summer. Admission costs £2/1 but there's no charge to walk round the grounds. The entrance gate is Norman but much of the castle was remodelled by Edward I. The Scottish engineer Thomas Telford added Laura's Tower in 1780.

Down the alley near the entrance to the castle is the Jacobean-style **Council House Gatehouse** dating from 1620. Beyond it is the **Old Council House** where the Council of the Welsh Marches used to meet to administer the area.

Across the road from the castle is the library, surely one of the grandest in the land, with a **statue of Charles Darwin** outside. Returning to St Mary's St, follow it down Dogpole. At the end of Dogpole, turn right onto Wyle Cop, which is Welsh for 'hilltop'. The **Lion Hotel** was where Dickens stayed on his visit to Shrewsbury; a 200-year-old gilded lion marks its entrance. Henry VII is said to have stayed in the **Henry Tudor House**, on the other side of Barracks Passage, before the Battle of Bosworth.

Walk right down Wyle Cop and bear left for the graceful 18th-century **English Bridge**, widened and reconstructed in 1927 and offering magnificent views of the Shrewsbury skyline.

Head back up Wyle Cop and turn left along Barracks Passage. Then turn right up Belmont Bank to **St Chad's Chapel**, all that remains of the medieval church. Turn right again into College Hill and it's a short walk back to the TIC.

Rowley's House Museum

Shrewsbury's main museum (☎ 361196), on Barker St, is housed in a restored 16th-century timber-framed building and an adjoining 17th-century mansion built by a wealthy merchant.

The museum displays some of the finds from the nearby Roman town of Wroxeter (including a particularly beautiful mirror) and has a good section on medieval Shrewsbury, as well as exhibits on costume and local wildlife. It opens 10 am to 5 pm Tuesday to Saturday, year round; and 10 am to 4 pm on Sunday and Monday, mid-May to September. Admission is free.

Shrewsbury Abbey

This huge, red-sandstone church in Abbey Foregate is virtually all that remains of the Benedictine monastery founded by Roger de Montgomery in 1083. The abbey has been drawing tourists since medieval times as St Winifred's bones were brought here from Wales. Inside, the architecture is part pure-Norman and part-Victorian copy. In the vestry don't miss the photo of men rowing in the choir after a flood! The church-

yard contains a memorial to Wilfred Owen, one of the best known of the WWI poets, killed just a week before the war ended. In the car park opposite, a stranded stone pulpit also survives from the abbey.

Shrewsbury Quest

Across the street from the abbey, the Shrewsbury Quest (☎ 243324) stands on the site of some of the old abbey buildings. It was inspired by the Brother Cadfael medieval detective stories. Visitors look for clues to solve a medieval murder as they wander around displays relating to 12th-century monastery life and a pleasant herb garden. Fans of the Ellis Peters books will love it. Open 10 am to 6.30 pm daily (to 5.30 pm November to March). Admission costs £4.50/2.95. There's a good cafe on-site.

Places to Stay

Camping Four miles north of Shrewsbury, at Montford Bridge on the B4380, *Severn House* (☎ 850229) has a riverside site where you can camp for £5.50 a tent, including showers.

Hostels A mile from the train and bus stations, just off the roundabout by Lord Hill's Column, is *Shrewsbury Youth Hostel* (☎ 360179, Abbey Foregate). It opens daily February to October, Friday and Saturday only from November to Christmas. It's a great place to stay for £9.25/6.20 for adults/under-18s.

B&Bs & Hotels While most hotels are in the town centre (some of them in appropriately historic timber-framed buildings), B&Bs are mainly concentrated in and around Abbey Foregate, to the north up Coton Hill, and to the west along the A458 and A488. As ever, there's a shortage of decent single rooms.

In the Abbey Foregate area, friendly *Glynndene* (☎ 352488), overlooking the abbey in Park Terrace, has rooms from £20 per person. Nearby is *Berwyn House* (☎ 354858, 14 Holywell St), a comfortable family house with B&B from £20/40 for a single/double. *Prynce's Villa Guest House*

(☎ 356217, 15 Monkmoor Rd), off Abbey Foregate, is a slightly cheaper option with rooms from £18/32.

Abbey Court House (☎ 364416, 134 Abbey Foregate) is a step up in comfort and has rooms with bathroom from £20 per person, £22 with bathroom. Farther along, **Abbey Lodge Guest House** (☎ 235832), at No 68, charges from £18 a head, £20 with en-suite facilities. About a 10-minute walk north of the train station, the Coton Hill area harbours another group of B&Bs and hotels. In Coton Crescent, **Bancroft Guest House** (☎ 231746), at No 17, charges from £18 to £22 a person, and **The Stiperstones Guest House** (☎ 246720), at No 18, has rooms for £22/37.

Lucroft Hotel (☎ 362421, Castle Gates), on the way into town from the train station, has clean if unexciting rooms for £20/34, including breakfast.

College Hill Guest House (☎ 365744, 11 College Hill) has an excellent location near the centre of town and has cosy rooms for £21/42.

Dating from 1460, quaint **Tudor House** (☎ 351735, 2 Fish St) is centrally located on a quiet, medieval street. Beds in pretty beamed rooms with no straight lines and a filling breakfast cost from £21 per person. Another historic lodging is the **Golden Cross Hotel** (☎ 362507, Princess St), one of the oldest pubs in town, where rooms cost from £20/35.

A couple of affordable mid-range places have emerged: **The Shrewsbury Hotel** (☎ 236203, Bridge Place) is a Wetherlodge, a new breed of McHotels looking set for big things with large, clean rooms from £32, regardless of numbers. Arguably offering a bit more character and a little less chain is **The Bellstone** (☎ 242103, Bellstone), where all rooms cost £37.50 and are very comfortable.

The **Lion Hotel** (☎ 353107, Wyle Cop) has well-appointed rooms from £70/90. Two-night bed, breakfast and dinner deals offer better value from around £40 a head in the low season. Rooms at the luxurious **Prince Rupert Hotel** (☎ 499955, Butcher Row) cost £75/85, including access to the Jacuzzi and sauna.

Places to Eat

Shrewsbury has plenty of reasonably priced places to eat during the day but in the evening many of the cheaper places close. On a tight budget, it is best to make for a pub (any excuse).

Sol (☎ 340560, 82 Wyle Cop) is a splash-out option where three-course meals costing £25 a head are served in classy, colourful surroundings. At the bottom of the hill, **The Cornhouse** (☎ 231991) serves beautifully presented modern British cuisine in the £7 to £10 range. At weekends they have a recovery brunch menu for those that played too hard the night before.

The Peach Tree (☎ 355055, 21 Abbey Foregate) also specialises in good modern British cuisine and has had a cool makeover in recent times. Expect to pay around £15 per head at the restaurant, considerably less downstairs in the cafe-bar. If that all sounds too much, have a beer and be one of the beautiful set on the cheap. A meal at the **Shalimar Tandoori** (☎ 344440), two doors down the road, is a cheaper option; another good option for curry heads is **Ramna Balti House** (☎ 363170, Wyle Cop), which is not only BYO, but also offers inexpensive set meals.

For good Italian food try **La Trattoria** (☎ 249490, Fish St) – although it only opens Tuesday to Saturday.

Popular with the local crowd, **Owens Café-Bar** (☎ 363633, Butcher Row) has a wide range of wines, bottled and draught beers and interesting dishes such as mixed tapas. Opposite in the 14th-century timber-framed **Royal Siam** (☎ 353117), fans of Thai food can get an atmospheric taste of all the favourites. However, for the ultimate Thai experience in ultimately strange surroundings, try the **Floating Thai Restaurant** (☎ 243123, Welsh Bridge), which has tasty, authentic food at sensible prices. The Severn is not quite the Chao Praya, but then Shrewsbury is thankfully not Bangkok.

The **Good Life Wholefood Restaurant** (☎ 350455), in restaurant-lined Barracks Passage off Wyle Cop, is a fantastic place for lunch with huge portions of righteous food, all at absurdly reasonable prices.

For light lunches on the run, *Christopher's* is a swish sandwich-bar on Mardol. *The Blue Cat Café*, on Fish St, is a newish place that draws the locals in droves and has a huge range of sandwiches, ciabattas and tortillas, and some tempting desserts such as rhubarb and ginger crumble. Another delightful summer spot for a snack is the little *coffee shop* tucked away in Bear Steps.

Entertainment

City centre pubs worth trying include *The Loggerhead Tap House* for its selection of ales, *The Nag's Head* for the young crowd out and about or for those that like a bit of history in the surroundings, the nonsmoking *Three Fishes (Fish St)* or the genuinely yokel local, *The King's Head* on Mardol. Farther out in Abbey Foregate the *Dun Cow Pie Shop* is full of clutter but manages to be extremely cosy. Sports fans may like to catch some live action at the vast *Bar Severns*, on Victoria Ave, while next door is *The Armoury*, a huge theme pub that may satisfy some.

In the old Music Hall that houses the TIC, a small *cinema* (☎ 281281) shows recent releases, classics and foreign films to small audiences. The small *theatre* has the same booking office.

Getting There & Away

Shrewsbury is 150 miles from London, 68 miles from Manchester, 43 miles from Chester and 27 miles from Ludlow.

Bus National Express (☎ 0870 580 8080) has three buses daily to/from London (five hours) via Telford and Birmingham.

For information on transport in Shropshire, call the county help line (☎ 0845 705 6785). Bus No X5 (☎ 01952-200005) runs between Shrewsbury and Telford via Ironbridge regularly. Bus No 420 connects Shrewsbury with Birmingham twice daily. Arriva (☎ 01543-466123) runs Shropshire Link bus No 435 to Ludlow via Church Stretton and Craven Arms (for Stokesay Castle).

Train Two fascinating small railways terminate at Shrewsbury, in addition to plenty of main-line connections. It's possible to do an excellent rail loop from Shrewsbury around northern Wales to Chester. Although it can be done in a day if the connections are smooth, it's much better to allow a couple of days as there are plenty of interesting places to visit along the way (see the North Wales chapter). The North & Central-Wales Flexi Rover ticket, allowing travel on three days out of seven, is the most economical way of covering this route (£26.30/17.35).

From Shrewsbury you head due west across Wales to Dovey Junction (1¾ hours), to connect with the Cambrian Coast Line, which hugs the beautiful coast on its way north to Porthmadog (1½ hours). Here you can pick up the Ffestiniog Railway, a superbly restored narrow-gauge steam train that winds up into Snowdonia National Park to the slate-mining town of Blaenau Ffestiniog (1¼ hours). From Blaenau another small railway carves its way through the mountains and down the beautiful Conwy Valley to Llandudno (1¼ hours) and Conwy. From there it's a short trip to Chester.

Another famous line, promoted as the Heart of Wales Line (☎ 0845 702 3641), runs south-west to Swansea (four hours), connecting with the main line from Cardiff to Fishguard.

There's one direct train a day to/from London Euston (£55, three hours), and regular links to Chester (£5.80, one hour). There are also regular trains from Cardiff to Manchester via Bristol, Ludlow and Shrewsbury. Telford Central costs £3.20.

AROUND SHREWSBURY
Attingham Park

This elegant late-18th-century neoclassical house (☎ 01743-708162; NT) is 4 miles south-east of Shrewsbury on the B4380. Set in a 92-hectare deer park, it's the grandest of Shropshire's stately homes. It features magnificent state rooms with decorated ceilings, a 300-piece collection of Regency silver, and a picture gallery designed by John Nash.

Attingham Park opens 1.30 to 5 pm Friday to Tuesday, late-March to October; the grounds open daily in daylight hours. Admission to house and park costs £4.20/2.10.

Bus No X5 stops in Atcham at the end of the lengthy drive.

Wroxeter Roman City

In Roman times Wroxeter was the fourth largest British city, after London, Colchester and Verulamium (St Albans). Much of the site lies under farmland but visitors can explore the extensive remains of the baths. Admission to the ruins (☎ 01743-761330; EH) costs £3.20/1.60.

A short walk along a country lane leads to **Wroxeter church** where a huge font was created out of a column from the Roman site. The church has some fine 17th- and 18th-century woodwork and 17th-century monuments.

Bus No X96 runs to Wroxeter.

Hawkstone Historic Park & Follies

This restored 40-hectare park (☎ 01939-200611) is an 18th-century fantasia of follies, caves and cliffs, mostly artificially created. A 3-hour walking tour takes you up the White Tower (from which a dozen counties are said to be visible), over the Swiss Bridge, into the Hermit's Cave and rhododendron jungle, and through a rocky chasm. Bizarre as it is, fans of Disneyland will probably find it tame.

Hawkstone Park is about 10 miles north of Shrewsbury off the A49, and you need your own transport to get here. It opens 10.30 am to 5 pm daily, April to September; Wednesday to Sunday in winter. Admission costs £4.50/2.50, £5/3 at weekends. Disabled access is limited to the tearoom, gift shop and picnic area.

IRONBRIDGE GORGE
☎ 01952

The Silicon Valley of the 18th century, Ironbridge is blessed not just with a beautiful setting but with a wealth of important industrial relics. Not far from the eminently forgettable

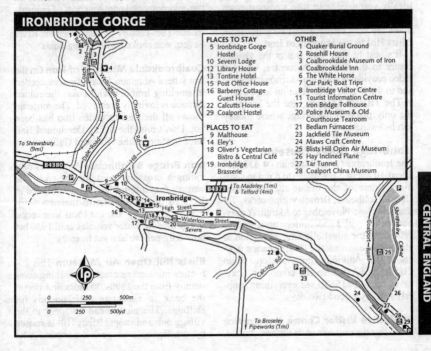

IRONBRIDGE GORGE

PLACES TO STAY
5 Ironbridge Gorge Hostel
10 Severn Lodge
12 Library House
13 Tontine Hotel
15 Post Office House
16 Barberry Cottage Guest House
22 Calcutts House
29 Coalport Hostel

PLACES TO EAT
9 Malthouse
4 Eley's
18 Oliver's Vegetarian Bistro & Central Café
19 Ironbridge Brasserie

OTHER
1 Quaker Burial Ground
2 Rosehill House
3 Coalbrookdale Museum of Iron
4 Coalbrookdale Inn
6 The White Horse
7 Car Park; Boat Trips
8 Ironbridge Visitor Centre
11 Tourist Information Centre
17 Iron Bridge Tollhouse
20 Police Museum & Old Courthouse Tearoom
21 Bedlam Furnaces
23 Jackfield Tile Museum
24 Maws Craft Centre
25 Blists Hill Open Air Museum
26 Hay Inclined Plane
27 Tar Tunnel
28 Coalport China Museum

To Shrewsbury (9mi)

To Madeley (1mi) & Telford (4mi)

To Broseley Pipeworks (1mi)

0 250 500m
0 250 500yd

CENTRAL ENGLAND

Telford, Ironbridge is a UNESCO World Heritage List site and an enduring monument to the Industrial Revolution. In 1709 it was here that Abraham Darby pioneered the technique of smelting iron ore with coke that led to the production of the first iron wheels, the first iron rails, the first steam locomotive and the first iron bridge. Readily accessible deposits of iron ore and coal and easy transportation on the River Severn soon made Ironbridge the dynamo driving industrial progress in the 18th century, but by 1810 its glory days were already over as action shifted to Birmingham, Sheffield and Manchester.

The Ironbridge Gorge Museum is Britain's best industrial archaeology complex, with seven museums and several smaller sites spread over 6 sq miles around the beautiful old iron bridge. It's well worth visiting even if industrial archaeology may not seem the most obvious drawcard.

Orientation & Information

Ideally you need your own transport since the museum sites are so spread out and buses are very infrequent. It's 3 miles from Blists Hill to the Museum of Iron.

It's best to start your trip at the visitors centre to the west of the centre, where a video provides a good introduction to the site and to the Industrial Revolution in general.

The TIC (☎ 432166) near the bridge is the only place in Ironbridge where money can be exchanged.

Ironbridge Gorge Museum

The Ironbridge Gorge Museum (☎ 433522) opens 10 am to 5 pm daily (to 6 pm in summer). Some of the minor sites (Rosehill House, Tollhouse, Broseley Pipeworks, Tar Tunnel) close November to March. A passport ticket (valid indefinitely until you've visited all the sites) allowing admission to all the museums costs £10/6. Separate tickets to the individual museums cost from £1/50p to £7.50/5 so the combined ticket saves around £15. To see everything properly it takes a good two days.

Ironbridge Visitor Centre An interesting video sets the museum in its historic context,

JANE SMITH

The world's first cast-iron bridge, from which the town of Ironbridge got its name

but otherwise the centre mainly focuses on the environmental consequences of industrialisation. A useful model shows the gorge in its late-18th-century heyday when the River Severn was choked with sailing boats.

Coalbrookdale Museum of Iron On the site where Abraham Darby first succeeded in smelting iron ore with coke, the ruined furnace is lovingly preserved. The museum shows all the uses to which iron has been put. Don't miss the 812kg Deerhound Hall table upstairs in the Glynwed Gallery.

Iron Bridge & Tollhouse As well as providing a crossing point for the river, the world's first iron bridge was constructed in 1779 to draw attention to the new iron-based technology and the local ironworks. It was used by motor vehicles until 1930 but now only pedestrians get to cross.

Blists Hill Open Air Museum This 20-hectare museum re-creates a working community from the 1890s. Visitors first stop at the bank to exchange their pounds for shillings. The money can be spent in the village pub and shops. Blists Hill is staffed by craftspeople in period costume who demonstrate the old skills. You can visit the foundry, sweetshop, church, doctor's surgery, butcher's, candle maker's and carpenter's. On certain days, the only wrought ironworks still operating in the western world is also set in motion. Allow at least half a day for a visit.

Coalport China Museum By the early-19th century, iron-making skills had spread to other parts of the world and Ironbridge went into a steep decline, slowed only by the development of the porcelain and decorative tile industries around Coalport and Jackfield. Fine Coalport china was made here until the company moved to Staffordshire in 1926. The museum exhibits all sorts of elaborate pottery, but also describes the life of the factory workers and how they carried out their tasks.

Jackfield Tile Museum A footbridge leads across the river to an abandoned factory where you can see displays of the decorative tiles produced here until the 1960s.

Other Things to See & Do About 90m up the hill from the Museum of Iron, 18th-century **Rosehill House** was built by the Darbys but is maintained as it was when it was home to an early-19th-century ironmaster. There's a **Quaker burial ground** nearby.

The small **Police Museum** (☎ 433838) in Waterloo St shows off original police cells and a birching stool.

Near the China Museum is the astonishing **Hay Inclined Plane**, designed to transport boats between the River Severn and the Shropshire Canal. Also nearby is the **Tar Tunnel**, a natural source of bitumen discovered in 1785.

Across the river the **Broseley Pipeworks** contains a museum devoted to the clay pipe-making industry.

The newest addition to the many museums of Ironbridge is the **Open Air Museum of Steel Sculpture** (☎ 433152), which has 60 contemporary sculptures set in landscaped gardens. It opens 10 am to 5 pm daily (except Monday), March to November. Admission costs £2/1.50.

Places to Stay
There's camping at **Severn Gorge Caravan Park** (☎ 684789, Bridgnorth Rd, Tweedale), three-quarters of a mile north of Blists Hill. The charge is £3 per adult.

Ironbridge has two youth hostels. The **Ironbridge Gorge Hostel** (☎ 588755) is in Coalbrookdale, near the Museum of Iron, while the **Coalport Hostel** (also ☎ 588755) is near the China Museum. Lots of school groups visit during term time, but both tend to be quieter in the holidays. Both open from February to November and beds cost £11/7.75 for adults/under-18s.

Overlooking the famous bridge, **Post Office House** (☎ 433201, 6 The Square) has three rooms, one with a bathroom, costing from £30/40 for a single/double. The historic **Tontine Hotel** (☎ 432127), also with a bird's eye view of the bridge, has rooms for £22/40 without bathroom, or £36/56 with bathroom.

Across the river is the comfortable, friendly **Barberry Cottage Guest House** (☎ 882110, 71 Bower Yard) with rooms for £22/38. Also this side of the river is **Calcutts House** (☎ 882631), a Georgian ironmaster's house, with rooms from £29/39 in the coach house and £49/59 en suite in the main house.

Other accommodation in Ironbridge tends to be pricey. The salubrious Georgian **Library House** (☎ 432299, ✉ libhouse@enta.net, 11 Severn Bank), right in the centre of Ironbridge, has rooms for £45/55. A short walk above the river is the delightful, award-winning **Severn Lodge** (☎ 432148, New Road), an attractive Georgian house with a secluded garden. There are two doubles and a twin room, all with bathroom, for £45/59 per room.

Places to Eat
The **Ironbridge Brasserie** (☎ 432716), on High St, goes for modern British cuisine with prices and decor to match, and for the summer months it has a garden area overlooking the bridge. The **Malthouse** (☎ 433712) has a fine menu of contemporary cooking, and a three-course meal can be had for around £15. It opens daily, handy for those Monday blues when everywhere else seems to close, and

speaking of blues, they host regular live jazz performances.

The Old Courthouse (☎ 433838) above the Police Museum in Waterloo St, is the most interesting of the *tea shops*, where you sip your drink in what was a Victorian courtroom.

Oliver's Vegetarian Bistro (☎ 433086, 33 High St) opens for lunch and dinner from Tuesday to Saturday and has been dishing up top tastes for years; starters are around £3, main courses more like £6. Nearby, the cheap and cheerful *Central Café* serves anything with chips,

One reader wrote in to rate the *Coalbrookdale Inn (☎ 433953)*, near the Ironbridge hostel, the best pub in the world. It would take some research to verify that claim but the real ale and pub grub (not Sunday) certainly go down a treat. Another decent pub worth a pint is the *Bird in Hand Inn* with a large garden with views across the gorge.

There are *cafes* at the Museum of Iron, the China Museum, Blists Hill (and a pub too) and Rosehill House, as well as in the Maws Craft Centre. For a snack or a picnic, *Eley's* on the square does an excellent, really porky pork pie, among other pies and pasties.

Getting There & Away

Ironbridge is 14 miles from Shrewsbury. Coming from the other direction, it's well signposted from the M54. See Getting There & Away under Shrewsbury earlier in the chapter for bus information. The nearest train station is at Telford and there are fairly frequent buses (£1.15) to Ironbridge from there.

BRIDGNORTH

Clinging to a sandstone bluff, Bridgnorth has a dramatic location above the River Severn and is the northern terminus of the **Severn Valley Railway**. To negotiate the cliffs, the town has one of Britain's oldest funicular railways dating from 1892, or for the bold or virtuous there are a series of steep stairways. The town has plenty of good accommodation; for more details contact the TIC (☎ 763358) on Listley St.

The Severn Valley Railway is one of Britain's most popular steam lines connecting Bridgnorth to Kidderminster (Worcestershire), via the pretty village of Bewdley. A return ticket costs £9.60/3.50. Bus Nos 436 and 437 run to Shrewsbury via Much Wenlock. Bus No 141 heads to Ludlow and No 297 to Kidderminster.

WENLOCK EDGE

There are great walks along this steep escarpment that stretches 15 miles from Ironbridge Gorge to Craven Arms, with superb views across to the Long Mynd to the west. It's geologically famous, in particular for its ancient coral reef exposures. Wenlock limestone was formed 400 million years ago when this area was under the sea.

The *Wilderhope Manor Youth Hostel (☎ 01694-771363)*, 7 miles south of Much Wenlock, is open February to October for £11/7.75 for adults/under-18s.

For walkers, there are several trails, including one west along the top of Wenlock Edge. There are infrequent buses from Ludlow; you really need your own transport.

MUCH WENLOCK
☎ 01952

Much Wenlock is a rather idyllic village, home to the ruins of 13th-century **Much Wenlock Priory** (☎ 727466; EH) and an informative little town museum. Believe it or not, it also has a strong claim to be the birthplace of the modern-day Olympic Games, thanks to Dr Brooks and the Wenlock Olympian Games. Mountain bikes are available from Wenlock Bike Hire (☎ 727089) for £10 a day.

Walton House (☎ 727139) has a warm atmosphere and a great price from £15, but only opens from April to October. *The Old Police Station (☎ 727056)* has got to be a secure base for exploring the area and has comfortable rooms for £42 an en-suite double. For those in search of a meal, *The George & Dragon Inn* offers classic pub food and good ales. *The Talbot Inn* has a more sophisticated menu and a wonderful atmosphere, with colossal beams and cavernous fireplaces – great on a cold or wet day, and there are many of those in Shropshire.

Much Wenlock is about 7 miles north-west of Bridgnorth. Bus Nos 436 and 437 running between Shrewsbury and Bridgnorth stop here.

THE LONG MYND & CHURCH STRETTON
☎ 01694

The Long Mynd is probably the best-known of Shropshire's hills – an excellent area for walking. Mynd is an abbreviation of the Welsh *mynydd* (mountain), but since these hills are below 550m they can hardly be called mountains. Nevertheless, there are superb views from the top of the ridges. **The Portway** is an ancient track that runs the full length of the Long Mynd.

The village of Church Stretton makes a good base for walks on the Long Mynd. The Victorians called the area Little Switzerland, bottled the local spring water and promoted Church Stretton as a health resort.

From Monday to Saturday, Easter to September, you can get walking information and leaflets from the Shropshire Hills Information Centre (☎ 723133), beside the library in Church St. At other times, enquire in the library itself. Mountain bikes (£10) and tandems can be rented from Terry in All Stretton; phone ☎ 01694-723302.

Walking

Just a 10-minute walk from Church Stretton Market Place, the **Carding Mill Valley** trail leads up to the 517m-high summit of the Long Mynd, with views of the Stiperstones to the east. You can drive part of the way and in summer a National Trust information centre and tea shop opens in the valley. On the other side of the A49, the walk up **Caer Caradoc** to an ancient fort is less busy. The 5-mile trip should take about 2½ hours.

Places to Stay

The *Bridges Long Mynd Youth Hostel* (☎ 01588-650656) is 5 miles from Church Stretton in an old village school at Ratlinghope, in the valley between the Long Mynd and the Stiperstones. It opens year round (book ahead in winter). Beds cost £8.50/7.75 for adults/under-18s. The walk

from Church Stretton train station takes a couple of hours.

Just inside the grounds of the Long Mynd, *Dalesford* (☎ 723228) has blissfully quiet rooms for £20 per person. *Brookfields Guest House* (☎ 722314, Watling St North) charges £45 for very comfortable rooms with a bathroom.

The excellent 16th-century *Jinlye Guest House* (☎ 723243) is on Castle Hill on the Long Mynd, just outside All Stretton and 2 miles north of Church Stretton. Rooms with views and showers cost from £27 per person.

Longmynd Hotel (☎ 722244, Cunnery Rd) stands above Church Stretton and boasts a heated swimming pool, sauna and solarium. Singles/doubles are from £55/100.

Getting There & Away

Shropshire Link bus No 435 takes 45 minutes from Shrewsbury, or 35 minutes from Ludlow. Trains are more than twice as fast, but Church Stretton station is unstaffed.

BISHOP'S CASTLE

This is real Shropshire, wild borderlands country, not the emigre Shropshire of Ludlow. The main reason for visiting Bishop's Castle in the south-western corner of Shropshire is not the castle (which no longer exists) but the *Three Tuns* (☎ 01588-638797), in Salop St, a locally famous pub and brewery that still makes its own beer. The food here is also very good for those passing through at lunchtime.

Tourist information is available from Old Time (☎ 01588-638467) at 29 High St. There are good local walks. Eight miles to the north, the **Stiperstones** are an inhospitable group of ridges topped with rough rocks. When the mist comes down and Satan settles into The Devil's Chair, it can seem a pretty sinister place.

Bus No 745 runs to Ludlow via Clun and Craven Arms.

CLUN
☎ 01588

About 6 miles south of Bishop's Castle is the village of Clun, with a wonderful ruined castle and more good walking country; it's

CENTRAL ENGLAND

just a few miles east of Offa's Dyke. Despite the current shortage of trees, this area is known as Clun Forest because it was once a royal hunting ground.

Beds at the *Clun Mill Youth Hostel* (☎ 640582), in an old water mill on the outskirts of the village, cost £9.25/6.50 for adults/under-18s. It opens daily from mid-July to August. Phone to confirm other opening times. *Clun Farm* (☎ 640432, High St) does B&B from £15 per person.

Bus 745 runs this way from Ludlow.

LUDLOW
☎ 01584 • pop 7500

Ludlow positively oozes charm and culture from every nook and cranny. Unfortunately, during the high season (Ludlow Festival) it can also appear to ooze tourists from the very same nooks and crannies – although, take heart, it hasn't yet attained Cotswoldesque proportions.

The centre, especially along Broad St, boasts fine Georgian town houses interspersed with occasional half-timbered black and white buildings. A rambling ruined castle rises above the River Teme.

Ludlow developed around its 11th-century castle. Involved in the medieval wool trade, it prospered from the sale of fleeces and the manufacture of woollen cloth. The town was also an important administrative centre and until 1689 the Council of the Welsh Marches was based here.

The TIC (☎ 875053), in the 19th-century Assembly Rooms in Castle St, has a small museum attached with some diverting exhibits, such as the world's oldest known spider (dead, not alive). Admission costs £1/50p. Guided tours leave from outside the castle entrance at 2.30 pm on summer weekends and cost just £1.50 for adults.

Pearce Engineering (☎ 876016), Fishmore Rd, about a mile north-east of the centre, rents out mountain bikes for £12.

Ludlow Castle

Built around 1090 by Roger de Lacy to control the Welsh – something that took years to achieve as Tony Blair should have noted before trying to appoint his man to run the Welsh Assembly – this impressive castle consists of a huge fortification with a large outer courtyard where the townspeople could shelter if attacked, and a solid keep of generous proportions. Note the unusual ruins of a 12th-century circular chapel. In the 14th century, the castle was turned into a palace by Roger Mortimer, whose mistress was Queen Isabella, wife of Edward II. In the 16th century the Judges' Lodgings were added to accommodate the March administrators.

The castle (☎ 873355) opens 10 am to 5 pm daily, May to September; to 4 pm in winter. Admission costs £3/1.50.

Other Things to See

The large, mainly Early English and Decorated-style **Church of St Laurence** has some fine medieval misericords, including one showing a mermaid admiring herself in a mirror. On the outside wall by the northern entrance is a simple memorial to Housman. Note the unusual hexagonal porch.

Near the castle, the partially half-timbered **Castle Lodge** dates back to the 14th century, although most of what you'll see inside is mainly Elizabethan or later. During its life, it has been a prison and home to the officials of the Council of the Marches, who presided over the borderlands after the demise of an independent Wales. Inside is some particularly fine plasterwork. Ring the bell for admission, which costs £2.

The waymarked 30-mile **Mortimer's Trail** to Knighton starts just outside the castle entrance. Phone ☎ 797052 for details.

Special Events

During June and July the town plays host to the Ludlow Festival, an annual arts bash that includes a Shakespearean epic performed in the castle ruins, an amazing experience for those able to time their visit and find a ticket. Phone ☎ 872150 for full details.

Places to Stay

The youth hostel has closed, so budget options are limited.

Ludlow's B&Bs tend to be expensive but about a mile from the centre, *Cecil Guest*

House (☎ 872442, *Sheet Rd*) has 10 rooms from £20 per person or £25 en suite. *The Globe* (☎ 874212) is a town centre pub by day and night, but also a cheap B&B with rooms at £20 per person. Another attractively located pub with good value lodgings is *The Charlton Arms* (☎ 872813), above Ludford Bridge overlooking the river, where rooms run from £30/45.

Best of the cheaper B&Bs is *Hen and Chickens Guesthouse* (☎ 874318, *103 Old St*), which has a good location, ample parking and a homely atmosphere, all from £20 per person. Those with wheels can enjoy the comforts of medieval *Lower House Farm* (☎ 823648, *Cleedownton*), about 5 miles outside Ludlow, where B&B is £24 per person.

For those that can afford it, the timber-framed Jacobean *Feathers Hotel* (☎ 875261, *Bull Ring*) has charm and character in abundance. Some rooms have four-poster beds and staying in this beautiful building is a delight. Rooms normally cost from £65/85, but it's worth asking about cheaper leisure breaks. Right beside the castle, the Georgian *Dinham Mill Hotel* (☎ 876464) is equally pricey, with rooms at £65/110.

Places to Eat

Ludlow has emerged as the gastronomic capital of rural England with three Michelin-starred restaurants in walking distance of the centre.

For teas and coffees, head for the old-fashioned *De Grey's Café* (*Broad St*). *Organza* is a good lunch-time stop-off for those in a hurry with wholesome sandwiches and cheap soups. *The Olive Branch* (☎ 874314, *2 Old St*) is undoubtedly the place to go for lunch, an excellent vegetarian restaurant with plenty of salads and a positively dangerous selection of desserts, although it heaves with diners during the high season.

For anything more substantial the classy *Ego Café-Bar* (☎ 878000, *Quality Square*), off Castle Square, does exquisite contemporary cuisine at prices a whole lot more accessible than the Michelin mob. Speaking of which, these high flying restaurants deserve a mention, although in the company

of Michelin and AA it may be best to say little more than check your bank balance first. *Merchant House* (☎ 875438, *Lower Corve St*) is perhaps the best-known. *Oaks* (☎ 872325, *17 Corve St*) and *Mr Underhill's* (☎ 874431, *Dinham Weir*) are also very highly rated by those in the know.

Ludlow Fish Bar hasn't got a Michelin star, but does very passable fish and chips for the staunch traditionalists that just can't get their heads around nouvelle cuisine.

There are several good pubs in Ludlow including the *Blue Boar Inn*, an atmospheric tavern popular with the festival crowd on Mill St; the *Unicorn Inn* on Lower Corve St, with a good local crowd most nights; and *The Globe*, which gets a younger crowd at weekends.

Getting There & Away

Ludlow is 29 miles from Shrewsbury and 24 miles from Hereford. From Ludlow train station there are direct services to Shrewsbury (£6.80, 30 minutes), Church Stretton (£3.70, 15 minutes), Hereford (£5.30, 25 minutes), Cardiff, Liverpool and Manchester.

For information on First Midland Red buses to Hereford, Birmingham, Kidderminster and Shrewsbury, phone ☎ 01905-763888. For specific transport information on southern Shropshire, call ☎ 877717.

STOKESAY CASTLE

Seven miles north-west of Ludlow, Stokesay Castle (☎ 01588-672544; EH) is one of the most picturesque 13th-century fortified manor houses in England. The grouping of stout stone walls, the half-timbered 17th-century gateway and the church tower is one to set a thousand camera shutters clicking – as it does on sunny summer days. It opens 10 am to 6 pm, April to September (to 4 pm in winter). Admission costs £3.50/1.80.

Shropshire Link bus No 435 runs to Stokesay from Shrewsbury and Ludlow; drivers will drop you at the bottom of the lane leading to the castle. It's often quicker to take a train to Craven Arms and walk a mile south to the site. Teas and light lunches are available in the castle grounds themselves or *Pottery Cottage* beside the car park;

or there's food and accommodation back in lovely Ludlow or uninspiring Craven Arms.

Staffordshire

Most visitors pass straight through Staffordshire, which stretches from the northern edge of Birmingham nearly to the southern fringes of Manchester. It's worth a stop to see Lichfield's wonderful cathedral, to sample the beer in Burton-upon-Trent or for an adrenaline rush at Alton Towers, Europe's most famous theme park. Lovers of fine porcelain will also want to break their journey in Stoke-on-Trent, heart of the famous Potteries district. To the north-east the Staffordshire moorlands blend into the Peak District National Park.

For information on Staffordshire buses, call the Busline on ☎ 01782-206608.

LICHFIELD
☎ 01543 • pop 25,000

Lichfield, with its justly famous cathedral, is a small, handsome market town of cobbled streets and attractive gardens. It was also home to the famous 18th-century diarist and wit Samuel Johnson.

The TIC (☎ 308209), on Market Square, organises guided city walks throughout the summer. Tickets cost £1.50/1.25.

Lichfield Cathedral
The fine, red-brick cathedral is famous for its three spires although it also has a fine western front adorned with exquisitely carved statues of the kings of England from Edgar through to Henry I. Most of what you see dates from the various rebuildings of the Norman cathedral during the Middle Ages. St Chad, the first bishop of Lichfield, was laid to rest in each building in turn. His gold-leafed skull was once kept in St Chad's Head Chapel, just to the west of the southern transept.

The Lichfield Gospels, a superb illuminated manuscript from 730, is displayed in the beautifully vaulted mid-13th-century chapterhouse. Don't miss the effigy of George Augustus Selwyn, who became the first bishop of New Zealand in 1841, in the Lady Chapel, or the poignant memorial to the two daughters of a cathedral prebendary at the eastern end of the southern aisle. A donation of £3 is requested.

Once finished in the cathedral, it's worth walking around the **cathedral close** which is ringed with imposing 17th- and 18th-century houses.

Other Things To See & Do
Samuel Johnson was born here in 1709. His pioneering dictionary, together with the biography written by his close friend James Boswell *(The Life of Samuel Johnson)*, established him as one of the great scholars, critics and wits of the English language. Statues of Johnson and Boswell adorn the Market Square. The **Samuel Johnson Birthplace Museum** (☎ 264972), on the square, opens 10.30 am to 4.15 pm daily. Admission costs £2/1.10p. You can inspect the famous diary on computer in the bookshop in the lobby.

The **Heritage & Treasury Exhibition** (☎ 256611), also on the square, opens 10 am to 4 pm daily. Admission costs £2/1.50p. It is possible to climb the tower for fine views of the city.

The **Erasmus Darwin Centre** (☎ 306260) commemorates Erasmus Darwin, grandfather of the more famous Charles, and is located in the house where he lived from 1756 to 1781 in Beacon St. It opens 10 am and 4.30 pm (last entry 3.45 pm) Tuesday to Saturday, noon to 4.30 pm on Sunday. Admission costs £2.50/2.

Places to Stay & Eat
There are several B&Bs charging £17 to £20 a head in Beacon St, round the corner from the cathedral close. For a little more, you can stay in the Close itself; there are three rooms at the excellent *No 8* (☎ 418483), singles/doubles are £22/44 with shared bathroom, or £26/52 with a bathroom and great view of the cathedral.

The *Angel Croft Hotel* (☎ 258737, Beacon St) has comfortable rooms for £62/75, or £51/62 at weekends.

The *Cathedral Coffee Shop*, set in a charming 18th-century house, does soup and sandwich lunches for around £3.50. Another popular local spot for coffee is the **Rendezvous Coffee House** on Market St. For atmospheric surroundings, **Tudor of Lichfield** is hard to beat, a real teashop in a Tudor building.

The Eastern Eye (☎ 262697) and **The Lal Bagh** (☎ 262697) are two highly rated Bangladeshi restaurants on Bird St. For a splash-out, try **Colleys Yard** (☎ 416606, 26 Bird St), where a modern British dinner costs from £15 to £20. **Chandlers Grande Brasserie** (☎ 416688) is locally renowned for continental cuisine and a fine ambience in the old Corn Exchange – but bank on little change from £20 at night.

The Sozzled Sausage is a lively pub on Church St that has gone well beyond alcopops to bring us alcoholic sausages. Another pub worth a jar is **The King's Head** on Bird St.

Getting There & Away
Lichfield is an easy 30 minutes' ride from Birmingham New St station and trains leave every 15 minutes (£3.30 day return).

STOKE-ON-TRENT
☎ 01782
Stoke-on-Trent is not known as Britain's most glamorous town. Nevertheless, it is home to some of Britain's most glamorous porcelain and the famous factories continue to draw large numbers of visitors, the most famous of all is arguably Wedgwood. Factory tours generally need to be booked in advance and don't run during factory holiday periods, but the Wedgwood, Spode and Royal Doulton visitor centres are permanently open, as well as the Gladstone and The Potteries museums where it is safe to browse without the temptation to buy.

Arnold Bennett left memorable descriptions of the area in its industrial heyday in his novels *Clayhangar* and *Anna of the Five Towns* – something of a misnomer since Stoke actually consists of six towns!

Orientation & Information
Stoke-on-Trent comprises Tunstall, Burslem, Hanley, Stoke, Fenton and Longton – which,

together, are often called The Potteries. Hanley is the official 'city centre'. Stoke-on-Trent train station is south-west of the city centre, but buses from outside the main entrance will run you to the centre in minutes. The bus station is right in the city centre.

The various visitor centres, factories and showrooms are widely scattered about, but the TIC (☎ 236000) in Quadrant Rd, Hanley, stocks maps with their locations. Last admission for all is one hour before closing time.

Royal Doulton Visitor Centre
The Royal Doulton Visitor Centre (☎ 292434), on Nile St, Burslem, opens 9.30 am to 5 pm Monday to Saturday, and 10.30 am to 4.30 pm on Sunday. Admission costs £3/2.25. Factory tours take place at 10.30 am and 1.15 and 2.45 pm Monday to Thursday (10.30 am and 1.30 pm Friday) for an extra £3.50/2.75.

Spode Museum & Visitor Centre
The Spode Museum & Visitor Centre (☎ 744011) is conveniently situated near the train station in Church St, Stoke. It opens 9 am to 5 pm Monday to Saturday, and 10 am to 4 pm Sunday. Admission costs £2.75/2.25. Factory tours take place at 10 am and 1.30 pm Monday to Thursday, and 10 am on Friday, costing an extra £2/1.50.

Wedgwood Visitor Centre
Wedgwood Visitor Centre (☎ 204218), in Barlaston, open 9 am to 5 pm daily, opening at 10 am at weekends. Admission costs £4.95/3.95. Factory tours are self-guided so have no fixed times.

Potteries Museum
This large museum and art gallery (☎ 232323), on Bethesda St, Hanley, opens 10 am to 5 pm daily (from 2 pm on Sunday). Admission is free. Come here to discover the history of The Potteries and to inspect a miscellaneous collection of ceramics.

Gladstone Pottery Museum
Constructed around Stoke's last remaining bottle kiln and its yard, this wonderful museum (☎ 319232), Uttoxeter Rd, Longton, is

Josiah Wedgwood

Born in 1730, Josiah Wedgwood was the twelfth child of parents who were already turning out pots. When he was nine his father died and Josiah went to work in the family business inherited by his older brother Thomas. After a lengthy apprenticeship, he jumped ship and went into partnership with Thomas Whieldon who had a pottery in Fenton. It was there that he started the experiments that eventually led to his own distinctive wares.

Although Wedgwood is best known for his blue and white jasper, and black basalt wares, his first success was in creating a green glaze that could be used to finish off the then fashionable pots and jugs in the shape of vegetables.

Five years after joining Whieldon, Wedgwood was confident enough to branch out on his own, opening the Ivy House Works in Burslem. In 1765 he was allowed to name his distinctive cream-coloured pottery Queen's Ware after Queen Charlotte, wife of George III. Five years later he completed an order for Catherine II of Russia.

Wedgwood perfected his technique for producing black basalt pottery in 1768, but the distinctive blue and white jasper ware didn't put in an appearance until 1775.

Wedgwood was more than just a master potter. A supporter of the French and American Revolutions, he also worked for the abolition of slavery, finding time to devise new machinery for his business at the same time. When he died in 1795, he left a business well on its way to the international success it enjoys today.

great on evoking the hot, unhappy working life of those who worked in The Potteries until the Clean Air Acts of the 1950s changed everything beyond recognition. Particularly fun is the gallery devoted to Victorian sanitaryware – toilet bowls more flowery than you would think possible. It opens 10 am to 5 pm daily. Admission costs £3.95/ 2.50. Make sure you try a Staffordshire oatcake (actually a pancake) in the pleasant cafe.

Etruria Industrial Museum
On the site of the original canalside Wedgwood factory, Stoke's newest museum (☎ 233144), Lower Bedford St, Etruria, incorporates a steam-powered bone and flint mill and a blacksmith's forge, as well as a visitors centre. It opens 10 am to 4 pm Wednesday to Sunday. Admission costs £1.50/1.

Places to Stay & Eat
It takes more than a day to see all Stoke's sights properly which is a shame since decent accommodation is thin on the ground. Two places in Leek Rd convenient for the train station are *L. Beez Guest House* (☎ 846727) and *Rhodes Hotel* (☎ 416320); to find them, come out of the station, turn

right and walk along Station Rd to the junction with Leek Rd, where you'll see them on the left, past a couple of pubs. Both offer B&B for £20/35 for singles/doubles.

Cafe-bars and gastro pubs haven't really hit Stoke in a big way, but this is good news for those who worry more about cost than class. It is probably best to eat at the cafes attached to the museums and visitor centres, particularly those at Wedgwood and Spode, although food at the *North Stafford Hotel* (☎ 744477), opposite the station, is said to be good.

Getting There & Away
There are regular trains to Stoke-on-Trent from Birmingham New Street and from Manchester Piccadilly. National Express (☎ 0870 580 8080) buses do day returns from London to The Potteries for £14, if you think you can squeeze everything in six hours.

Getting Around
The Wedgwood Express no longer operates. Bus Nos 6, 7 and 8 serve Wedgwood and Gladstone and Nos 20, 21 and 22 serve Doulton and Spode. The Potteries Museum is within walking distance of the centre.

AROUND STOKE-ON-TRENT
Biddulph Grange Gardens

The National Trust has recently restored these gorgeous Victorian gardens (☎ 01782-517999), with their Chinese and Egyptian corners. Seven miles north of Stoke, they open noon to 6 pm Wednesday to Friday, 11 am to 6pm at weekends, April to October. Admission costs £4.40/2.30, but if you also visit Little Moreton Hall (see next section), 6 miles to the east, a joint ticket costs £6.75/3.30.

Little Moreton Hall

Off the A34 south of Congleton, Little Moreton Hall (☎ 01260-272018; NT) is England's most spectacular black and white timber-framed house, dating back to the 15th century. It opens noon to 5.30 pm Wednesday to Sunday, late-March to October (from 11 am in August). Admission costs £4.40/2.30.

Shugborough

This regal, neoclassical mansion is the ancestral home of Lord Lichfield, although he's more famous for his photographs than his house. Construction began in 1693, but it was only with considerable work during the 18th and 19th centuries that the house reached its present immense proportions. The estate is famous for the monuments within its grounds, including a Chinese House, Doric Temple and the Triumphal Arch, and for a fine collection of Louis XV and XVI furniture. There is also a museum and a farm to investigate. Shugborough (☎ 01889-881388) opens 11 am to 5 pm Monday to Saturday, late-March to late-September. Admission to the house or museum costs £4/3, or a family ticket including the museum and farm is just £18.

Burton-upon-Trent

Burton-upon-Trent has been a brewing centre for centuries and the **Bass Museum & Visitor Centre** (☎ 01283-511000) tells the full story. Founded in 1777, Bass is now Britain's biggest brewer. The centre opens 10 am to 4 pm daily. Admission costs £4.50 and includes the obligatory free Bass beer.

Alton Towers

Alton Towers (☎ 0870 520 4060) is Britain's most popular theme park and a must for white knuckle fiends everywhere. There are over 100 rides, including Oblivion, the world's first vertical drop roller-coaster that blows the mind. Located between Stoke-on-Trent and Ashbourne, it opens 9.30 am to 7 pm daily, late-March to October. Admission costs £19.95/15.95 (high season). There is an expensive hotel within the park, but most visitors opt to stay in nearby villages such as Alton.

Derbyshire

Derbyshire is all about the Peak District, most of which falls within the county boundaries (see the Peak District section later in the chapter), one of the most wild, beautiful areas in England. It also has the industrial town of Derby and some wonderful stately homes, including unforgettable Chatsworth.

The Derbyshire Wayfarer ticket covers buses and trains throughout the county and beyond to link up with Sheffield, Macclesfield and Burton-on-Trent. It costs £7.25 or £12 for a family. For general bus information phone ☎ 01332-292200.

DERBY
☎ 01332 • pop 220,000

There is something of an intense rivalry between Derby and Nottingham, and Derby often comes out second best on most counts. The Industrial Revolution transformed sleepy Derby (pronounced dar-by) first into a pioneering silk production centre, then into a major railway centre. In the 20th century it became famous as the home of Rolls-Royce aircraft engines. Although there are no major tourist attractions, the town makes a peaceful base for exploring the surrounding area.

The TIC (☎ 255802) is in the Assembly Rooms in the Market Place.

Derby's 18th-century **cathedral** boasts a 64m tower and some magnificent ironwork. Look out for the tomb of Bess of Hardwick (see Hardwick Hall in the Around Chesterfield section later in the chapter) in the southern aisle.

A short walk from the cathedral, in Full St, **Derby Industrial Museum** (☎ 255308) recounts Derby's industrial history with pride of place going, of course, to Rolls-Royce aircraft engines. Other possibilities include the **Museum & Art Gallery** (☎ 716659) in The Strand, and **Pickford's House Museum** (☎ 255363), 41 Friar Gate, a museum of Georgian life. All these museums open 10 am to 5 pm daily (afternoons only on Sunday) and are free.

Tours of the **Royal Crown Derby** china factory, at 194 Osmaston Rd, take place at 10.30 am and 1.45 pm Monday to Thursday, 1.15 pm on Friday. Phone ☎ 712841 for more information.

Places to Stay & Eat
Crompton St is central and has a number of standard B&Bs such as the recently reopened **Wayfarer** (☎ 348350), at No 27, with singles/doubles for £18/32 and **Chuckles** (☎ 367193), at No 48, where they're £19/34.

The large, modern **International Hotel** (☎ 369321, 288 Burton Rd), just south of the centre, charges £62.50/72 but prices drop at weekends.

Old Blacksmith's Yard is in an attractive area of town and houses several popular restaurants, including the cafe-bar **Farriers** with a lively little menu and **Steliana's and Sapho's Greek Tavern** (☎ 385200), a local favourite. Huge **Arkwright's** is a popular cafe-bar on the square by the TIC – the building is hideous, but it's pleasant in the summer when tables are put out the front.

For good Indian food, head south down Normanton Rd, where there's a large Asian community. Nearer the centre on Curzon St are **Balti Towers** (☎ 200443) and **Curry Mania** (☎ 344786), both inexpensive, unpretentious curry houses.

Chai Yo Thai (360207, 8 Bold Lane) has great value Thai food at lunchtime – under £5 for a main course and two courses plus coffee for £6.30.

Entertainment
Pubs, Bars & Clubs For cheap pub grub, **Ye Olde Dolphin Inne**, on Queen St, does the business, as does **Ryan's Bar** under the shadow of St Peter's. Other pubs worth a call include **The Standing Order** for its cheap drinks, **The Wardwick**, a handsome traditional pub, and **The Victoria Inn** near the train station, probably the best live music venue in Derby. If a pub doesn't cut the mustard, **Casa** is a trendy bar, while **Boom Club** is the liveliest choice for clubbers. However, Nottingham has more to offer.

Getting There & Away
Derby is 130 miles from London, 60 miles from Manchester, 40 miles from Birmingham and 30 miles from Leicester.

The dismal bus station is close to the centre. The TransPeak TP service operates from Manchester through the Peak District to Derby, taking just 30 minutes to continue onto Nottingham.

Trains link Derby with London in just under two hours.

AROUND DERBY
Kedleston Hall
Construction of this superb, neoclassical mansion (☎ 01332-842191; NT) with its Palladian front was started in 1758 by a trio of architects. The Curzon family has lived at Kedleston since the 12th century and Sir Nathaniel Curzon tore down an earlier house in order to construct this stunning masterpiece. He also moved Kedleston village a mile down the road so it wouldn't interfere with the landscaping! Only the medieval village church beside the house remains.

The entrance to the Marble Hall, with its statues of Greek and Roman deities, is breathtaking. The 20 alabaster-columns were originally plain but from 1776 to 1777 it was decided that the room was too austere and fluting was chiselled into the columns *in situ*. The circular saloon, with its domed roof, was modelled on the Pantheon in Rome.

The whole house is lavishly decorated and includes the Indian Museum, displaying a later Lord Curzon's oriental collection. From 1898 to 1905 he was the viceroy of India; a century earlier, Government House in Calcutta (now Raj Bhavan) was modelled on Kedleston Hall. The adjacent church houses a collection of family memorials, their increasing magnificence indicating the Curzons' escalating fortunes.

Kedleston Hall is 5 miles north-west of Derby. It opens 12 to 4 pm daily, except Thursday and Friday, Easter to October. Admission costs £5/2.50.

Calke Abbey

Ten miles south of Derby in Ticknall is captivating Calke Abbey (☎ 01332-863822; NT), which was built between 1701 and 1703 but had been left untouched since the last baronet died in 1924. It contains a treasure-trove ranging from natural history to a caricature room. Admission is by timed ticket; at busy periods it's wise to phone ahead and check that you'll be able to get in.

The house opens 1 to 5.30 pm daily, except Thursday and Friday, April to October. Admission costs £5.10/2.50.

CHESTERFIELD
☎ 01246 • pop 70,000

Chesterfield is justly famous for its Leaning Tower of Jesus, the famous twisted spire of **St Mary's & All Saints Church** in Church Way. The 68m-high spire leans nearly 3m to one side and performs a painful-looking twist, the result of heavy lead tiles over a poorly seasoned timber frame. It opens to climb on bank holiday Mondays for £2.50/1.

Located on the eastern edge of the Peak District, nearer to Sheffield than Derby, the town is pleasant enough for a detour but lacks enough to justify a night. The TIC (☎ 207777) is on Low Pavement. The **Museum & Art Gallery**, in St Mary's Gate, opens 10 am to 4 pm daily, except Wednesday and Sunday. A market is held on Monday, Friday and Saturday.

Buses run from Chesterfield to Sheffield, Derby or Nottingham.

AROUND CHESTERFIELD
Hardwick Hall

Hardwick Hall (☎ 01246-850430; NT) was Bess of Hardwick's crowning achievement and the ES initials on the walls loudly trumpet her ownership as Elizabeth, countess of Shrewsbury. Separated from her fourth husband, the earl of Shrewsbury, Bess moved to Hardwick after buying it from her bankrupt brother in 1583. Lacking the means to build a home commensurate with her high opinion of herself, she initially settled for rebuilding Hardwick Old Hall. But as soon as her husband died in 1590, and she got her hands on his fortune, work started on Hardwick Hall.

The house features the very best of late-16th-century design, including vast amounts of glass, a considerable status symbol at the time. It's notable for its many late-16th- to early-17th-century tapestries and for a remarkably thorough inventory taken in 1601; many items from that inventory still exist. Over the centuries the house managed to escape both modernisation and neglect so it retains a wonderfully ancient feel. Despite its airy appearance – 'more glass than wall' – it remains rather austere.

The house opens 12.30 to 5 pm (or sunset if earlier) on Wednesday, Thursday, Saturday and Sunday, April to October. Admission costs £6/3. The adjacent ruins of Hardwick Old Hall (EH) open 10 am to 6 pm. Admission costs £2.60/1.30, a joint ticket to both properties costs £8/4. Hardwick Hall is about 10 miles south-east of Chesterfield, just off the M1 between junctions 28 and 29.

Peak District

Although the Peak District is principally in Derbyshire it spills over into five adjoining counties. It's a remarkable region – smack bang in the middle of one of the most densely populated, industrialised parts of England is one of the country's best loved national parks. So loved is it in fact that it's the busiest in Europe. Dotted with pretty villages, historic sites and fascinating limestone caves, the Peak District also encompasses some of England's most wild and beautiful scenery.

ORIENTATION

Although it's squeezed between Manchester and Sheffield, with the industrial towns of Yorkshire to the north and the northern Midlands to the south, there are no large towns within the Peak District National Park.

Nor are there any actual peaks in the Peak District, just endless rolling hills; the name comes from the ancient people who once inhabited the region. The 555 sq miles of the national park are divided into two areas: the harsher, wilder Dark Peak to the north, and the more pastoral, 'prettier' White Peak to the south. Both areas are limestone, but the higher Dark Peak moorlands are on coarse gritstone, while the green fields of the White Peak are patterned with dry-stone walls, much like Ireland, and divided by deep-cut dales.

INFORMATION

There are TICs or National Park Information Offices in Bakewell, Castleton, Edale and other locations. Information for disabled visitors is available by calling ☎ 01629-816200. The Ordnance Survey (OS) *Peak District* map (1:63,360) will be adequate for most users, but there are also separate maps of the White and Dark Peaks.

Pick up a copy of the free *Peak District* from TICs. It lists all sorts of walks guided by National Park rangers.

WALKING & CYCLING ROUTES

The Pennine Way has its southern end at Edale in the Peak District. See the Activities chapter for more information on this classic British long-distance walk and for essential preparations and precautions. There are many other shorter walks within the park, but those intending to explore the Dark Peak or engage in the local practice of 'bog trotting' should be prepared for the often vicious changeable weather; a map and compass, wet weather gear and emergency food supplies are essential. TICs stock the handy *Walks Around...* and *Walks About...* guides.

The High Peak and Tissington trails are equally popular with walkers and cyclists. There are several Peak Cycle Hire centres, including the Parsley Hay centre near the junction of the Tissington and High Peak trails. A leaflet details the centres, their opening times and rental charges (£9/6 for one day, £20 deposit and ID required).

TICs also stock the *Peak Park Cycle Route* booklets produced by the national park authorities.

Limestone Way

The 26-mile Limestone Way winds through the White Peak from Castleton to Matlock via Peak Forest, Miller's Dale, Taddington, Flagg, Monyash, Youlgreave, Winster and Bonsall. There are youth hostels at both ends and at Ravenstor (near Miller's Dale), Youlgreave and Elton (near Winster). Camping barns and camp sites are dotted about, and there are B&Bs in most of the villages as well as an ample supply of pubs. The walk is signposted with fingerposts, yellow arrows and the walk's Derbyshire Ram logo. TICs and the Bakewell National Park Office have a detailed walk leaflet.

High Peak & Tissington Trails

The 17½-mile High Peak Trail follows the pioneering **High Peak & Cromford Railway line**. This was originally envisaged as a canal but when the engineering problems proved insurmountable the developers decided to build a railway line instead. They applied canal thinking to the new technology, labelling the stations as wharves and ending up with a line which surmounted hills by going up them steeply, like a flight of canal locks. As a result the line never worked very well; railway engineers soon discovered that trains worked best on long, gentle inclines rather than short, steep ones. Opened in 1830, the line actually predated the general use of steam locomotives and at first the carriages were hauled by horses and pulled up the steep inclines by stationary engines installed at the tops of the hills.

When the line finally closed in 1967 the tracks were torn up and it was made into a walking and cycling track. The wide, well-surfaced trail is ideal for cycling and makes a pleasant day out in rolling White Peak country. The 1-in-14 Hopton Incline was the steepest gradient worked by locomotives in

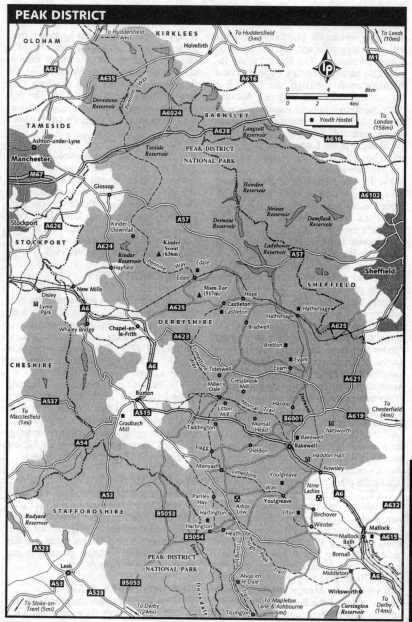

PEAK DISTRICT

OLDHAM

To Huddersfield (4mi)

KIRKLEES

To Huddersfield (3mi)

To Leeds (10mi)

Holmfirth

A62

A635

A6024

BARNSLEY

Dovestone Reservoir

Pennine Way

A628

Langsett Reservoir

A616

To London (158mi)

TAMESIDE

Ashton-under-Lyne

Torside Reservoir

PEAK DISTRICT NATIONAL PARK

Howden Reservoir

Strines Reservoir

Damflask Reservoir

Manchester

M67

Glossop

Derwent Reservoir

A6102

Stockport

A626

STOCKPORT

Kinder Downfall

A57

Kinder Scout (636m)

Ladybower Reservoir

A57

Sheffield

A624

Kinder Reservoir

Hayfield

Pennine Way

Edale

Edale

Mam Tor (517m)

Hope

Castleton

Castleton

Hathersage

SHEFFIELD

Disley

New Mills

A6

A625

Bradwell

Hathersage

A625

Lyme Park

DERBYSHIRE

Bretton

Whaley Bridge

Chapel-en-le-Frith

A623

Eyam

Eyam

CHESHIRE

A6

Limestone Way

Tideswell

Cressbrook Mill

A621

Miller's Dale

Hassop

Derwent

To Macclesfield (1mi)

A537

Buxton

Litton Mill

Monsal Trail

B6001

A619

To Chesterfield (4mi)

A515

Monsal Head

Gradbach Mill

Taddington

Chatsworth

A54

Flagg

Sheldon

Bakewell

Bakewell

Monyash

Limestone

Haddon Hall

Rowsley

Way

Youlgreave

Nine Ladies

A6

A632

Parsley Hay

Arbor Low

Youlgreave

Elton

Birchover

STAFFORDSHIRE

B5053

Hartington

Winster

Matlock

Rudyard Reservoir

Hartington

Heathcote

Tissington Trail

High Peak Trail

Matlock Bath

A615

Bonsall

A53

B5054

PEAK DISTRICT NATIONAL PARK

Middleton

A6

A523

Leek

Dovedale

Alsop en le Dale

Wirksworth

To Derby (14mi)

A53

A523

B5053

To Stoke-on-Trent (5mi)

To Derby (24mi)

Tissington

To Mapleton Lane & Ashbourne (6mi)

Carsington Reservoir

★ Youth Hostel

0   4   8km
0   2   4mi

CENTRAL ENGLAND

the British Isles. At Middleton Top, the 1829 steam-winding engine which used to haul trains up the 1-in-8¾ Middleton Incline is still in working order and jolts into action on Sunday in summer. The Sheep Pasture Incline also required winding engines to haul the trains up. At the High Peak Junction at the southern end of the trail, near Matlock Bath, the former railway workshop is now used as a visitor centre and museum. Goods were transferred to boats on the Cromford Canal at this point. Later it took trains up to seven hours to cover the distance a cyclist can now ride in just a couple.

The 13-mile Tissington Trail was a much later line, opened in 1899, but it never proved economically feasible and, as the High Peak Trail, was closed in 1967. The two trails meet just south of Parsley Hay and continue farther north, although not all the way to Buxton.

Bicycles can be hired on the trails at Parsley Hay (☎ 01298-84493), at Middleton Top (☎ 01629-823204), towards the southern end of the High Peak Trail, or at Ashbourne (☎ 01335-343156), at the southern end of the Tissington Trail. If you've got time it's a pleasant, 40-mile round trip from Parsley Hay down the High Peak Trail and up the Tissington Trail, linking the two trails by the B5053 from Matlock Bath to Ashbourne. The B5053 section undulates a lot so make sure you allow plenty of time.

Monsal Trail

Like the High Peak and Tissington trails, the Monsal Trail, along the deep valley of the River Wye, follows a disused railway line. It's used by walkers more than cyclists (unlike the other two).

The 8½-mile trail starts from the Coombs Rd Viaduct, just east of Bakewell, but there's no view of the viaduct from the trail. You can also walk from Rowsley on the A6 to the beginning of the trail. The old train station at Hassop near Bakewell has been converted into the Country Bookstore. At Monsal Head there's a pub, B&B and a superb view of the **Monsal Viaduct**, a man-made wonder of the Peak District and the subject of considerable controversy when it

was first built. **Cressbrook Mill** opened as a water-powered cotton mill in 1783 and continued to operate, powered by steam, from 1890 until 1965. **Litton Mill** opened in 1782 and was infamous for its owner's exploitation of child labourers. Walking west, the final tunnel requires what can be a very muddy, slippery and wet detour. The trail ends at Blackwell Mill Junction, a short walk from the A6, 3 miles east of Buxton.

Other Walks

The Peak District is crisscrossed with good walks and the TICs are packed with information. Castleton and Bakewell in the White Peak make particularly good centres for short walks. From Edale you can walk in either direction: north to the Dark Peak and nearby Kinder Scout, or south towards Castleton. Hayfield is another good starting point for walks into the Dark Peak.

OTHER ACTIVITIES

The Peak District limestone is riddled with caves including 'showcaves' open to the public in Castleton, Buxton and Matlock Bath. For information on caving trips and courses contact Derbyshire Caving Association (☎ 01629-534775). *The Caves of Derbyshire* by TD Ford has extensive information on the county's caves.

The Peak District has been a training ground for some of Britain's best-known mountaineers, and cliff faces such as High Tor, overlooking Matlock Bath, are still popular. Jumping off the cliff faces on hanggliders is becoming equally popular. Fishing on most Peak District rivers is private.

PLACES TO STAY

Walkers may appreciate the *camping barns* (☎ *01629-825850*) that offer a roof over your head from £3.50 per person per night. A leaflet shows the locations of the barns and explains how to book a place. Another brochure details camping grounds in and around the Peak District.

GETTING THERE & AWAY

The Peak District authorities are trying hard to wean visitors off their cars, and TICs stock the excellent *Peak District Timetable* covering all local bus and train services.

There are train services from Derby to Matlock, at the southern edge of the Peak District, or from Sheffield across the northern part of the district through Edale to New Mills and on to Manchester. There's also a Manchester-New Mills-Buxton service.

The convenient TransPeak TP bus operates right across the Peak District, linking Nottingham, Derby, Matlock, Bakewell, Buxton, New Mills and Manchester (3½ hours); Matlock to Buxton takes about an hour. Yorkshire Traction has services from Barnsley into the district from the north and down to Castleton and Buxton.

A Derbyshire Wayfarer ticket costs £7.25 (including one child or dog), £12 for a family, for one day's unlimited travel on most train and bus services into and around the Peak District. An Explorer ticket also gives you all-day travel on Trent and Barton buses including the TransPeak TP service. It costs £5 and includes one child. The Busline information service can be contacted on ☎ 01298-23098.

BAKEWELL
☎ 01629 • pop 3900

Famous more for its tarts than the original puddings, this picture-postcard village is the largest population centre within the Peak District National Park boundaries and a notorious traffic bottleneck on summer weekends. The village found its way into the cookbooks as a result of the accidental invention of the Bakewell pudding.

Information
The TIC (☎ 813227), in the 17th-century Market Hall on Bridge St, has an informative display about the national park. There's a market on Mondays.

Things to See
All Saints Church has Norman features and a fine octagonal spire. There's a Saxon cross from around 800 in the graveyard. The **Old House Museum**, in Cunningham Place near the church, has a local collection housed in a 1534 building, but only opens on summer afternoons. Admission costs £2.50/1.

The pretty, five-arched **bridge** over the River Wye dates from medieval times. The popular **Monsal Trail** walking and cycling track starts just outside Bakewell, but there are many other good walking routes around the village, including trails to Magpie Mine, Haddon Hall and Chatsworth House.

Places to Stay
Hostels On Fly Hill, *Bakewell Youth Hostel* (☎ 812313) costs £10/6.90 for adults/under-18s. It opens daily except Sunday, April to October; on Friday and Saturday only the rest of the year.

B&Bs & Hotels The historic *Castle Inn* (☎ 812103, Bridge St) charges £39.50 for rooms accommodating up to four people, good value for those that like it cosy. *Bridge House* (☎ 812867, Bridge St) is not just a fine building, but has a fine location and charges from £17.50 per head for a room

Which Bakewell Pudding?

Bakewell blundered into the cookbooks around 1860 when a cook at the Rutland Arms Hotel misread the strawberry tart recipe and spread the egg mixture on top of the jam instead of stirring it into the pastry, thus creating the Bakewell pudding (pudding, mark you, not tart). It features regularly on local dessert menus and is certainly worth sampling.

Bakewell establishments are locked in battle over whose is the original recipe, a dispute so serious it may finally be settled by the European Court in Brussels. Bloomers (☎ 813724), Water St, insists it created 'the first and only Bakewell puddings' and swiftly converted its name to a registered trademark. But the Old Original Bakewell Pudding Shop (☎ 812193) is adamant that its recipe is older, and it pulls more trade thanks to its position on the main thoroughfare.

In a blind tasting, this author preferred Bloomers' version. The pastry was thicker, and the egg mixture less heavy. It also cost 65p as opposed to 99p.

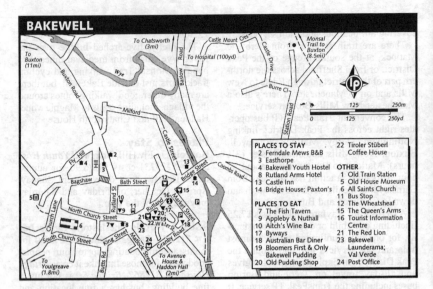

BAKEWELL

PLACES TO STAY
2 Ferndale Mews B&B
3 Easthorpe
4 Bakewell Youth Hostel
8 Rutland Arms Hotel
13 Castle Inn
14 Bridge House; Paxton's

PLACES TO EAT
7 The Fish Tavern
9 Appleby & Nuthall
10 Aitch's Wine Bar
17 Byways
18 Australian Bar Diner
19 Bloomers First & Only
   Bakewell Pudding
20 Old Pudding Shop

22 Tiroler Stüberl
   Coffee House

OTHER
1 Old Train Station
5 Old House Museum
6 All Saints Church
11 Bus Stop
12 The Wheatsheaf
15 The Queen's Arms
16 Tourist Information
   Centre
21 The Red Lion
23 Bakewell
   Launderama;
   Val Verde
24 Post Office

and continental breakfast, from £20 with full English breakfast.

Buxton Rd is home to a cluster of good B&Bs, including the gothic *Easthorpe* (☎ 814929) with bed and breakfast from £23 per person.

The accidentally gastronomically pioneering (see the earlier boxed text 'Which Bakewell Pudding?') *Rutland Arms Hotel* (☎ 812812) is a fine establishment right on the main square in town, with singles/doubles from £47/79. Front rooms can be a bit noisy.

Places to Eat

There are a few restaurants. In Granby Rd, the *Australian Bar Diner* (☎ 814909) has roast meals for around £5 and all sorts of snacks. *Aitch's Wine Bar* (☎ 813895, Rutland St) has the most imaginative menu, 'around the world in eighty dishes' type of thing, while at weekends *Paxtons* (☎ 814336, Bridge St)*, by the river, turns from a tearoom into a romantic restaurant. *Val Verde* (☎ 814404) is an Italian restaurant with live music on Friday.

The Red Lion and the *Queen's Arms* serve standard pub food; the food at the *Castle Inn* is especially good. *The Fish Tavern*, North Church St, is the place to be for fish and chips.

Bakewell has lots of tea and coffee shops, most invoking the name of England's most famous tart. The most imaginative is the *Tiroler Stüberl Coffee House* attached to *Bloomers First & Only Bakewell Pudding shop*. *Byways* is a nice spot for afternoon tea.

For a picnic it's worth dropping in on *Appleby & Nuthall* in Buxton Rd, which has a wide range of wholesome supplies.

Getting There & Away

The TransPeak TP bus services the Buxton-Bakewell-Matlock route. Bus No 170 runs to Over Haddon and on to Chesterfield, bus No 171 to Youlgreave. For details of all local buses phone ☎ 01246-250450.

AROUND BAKEWELL
Chatsworth

More than two-thirds of sumptuous Chatsworth (☎ 01246-582204), the 'Palace of the Peak', is still occupied by the duke of Devonshire's family.

The original Elizabethan house was started in 1551 by the inimitable Bess of

Hardwick (see Around Chesterfield earlier in the chapter) and her second husband. Mary Queen of Scots was imprisoned here several times between 1570 and 1581 at the behest of her cousin Elizabeth I. Mary's jailer, the earl of Shrewsbury, was Bess' fourth husband, but her suspicion that the 'knave, fool and beast' was rather more than just a jailer led to their separation. The house was extensively altered between 1686 and 1707 and then enlarged in the 1820s.

The amazing baroque ceiling paintings are among the house's prime attractions, but all the rooms are a treasure-trove of splendid furniture and magnificent artworks.

The house is surrounded by 40 hectares of gardens, beyond which stretch another 400 hectares of parkland landscaped by Capability Brown.

Chatsworth is about 3 miles north-east of Bakewell. The house opens 11 am to 4.30 pm daily, Easter to October. Admission costs £6.75/3 for the house and garden, plus £1 to park. It costs another £3.50 per head for the **farmyard and adventure playground**.

On Sunday in summer bus No 210 (☎ 01709-566360) leaves Sheffield Interchange for Chatsworth at 9.15 am, returning at 5.40 pm.

Haddon Hall

Although there's been a house on the site from much earlier, beautiful Haddon Hall (☎ 01629-812855) dates mainly from Tudor times. The site was originally owned by William Peveril (see Castleton later in the chapter). The house was abandoned right through the 18th and 19th centuries, hence the minor changes in that period. Highlights include the 14th-century chapel and the medieval kitchens and great hall. Visitor numbers have risen significantly since some scenes from the popular film *Elizabeth* were shot here.

Outside, terraced gardens step down to the River Wye near an old stone packhorse bridge. The house is 2 miles south of Bakewell on the A6 and opens 10.30 am to 5 pm daily, April to September. Admission costs £5.75/3.

Dovedale

The steep-sided valley of the **River Dove** is one of the most beautiful – and so most crowded – of the Derbyshire Dales. The river flows beneath natural features such as Thorpe Cloud, Dovedale Castle, Lovers' Leap, the Twelve Apostles, Tissington Spires, Reynard's Kitchen and Ilam Rock. **Beresford Dale**, upstream from Dovedale, was a favourite haunt of Izaak Walton, author of *The Compleat Angler*. The 17th-century Fishing Temple is a memorial to him.

Tideswell
☎ 01298

The huge church at Tideswell is sometimes described as the 'cathedral of the Peaks' and is worth visiting to see its brasses, woodwork and fine ceilings.

Poppies (☎ 871083, *Bank Square*) has B&B (closed January) from £17.50. The *George Hotel* (☎ 871382), beside the church does good pub food and has rooms from around £25 per person.

EYAM
☎ 01433 • pop 900

The small village of Eyam (pronounced eeem) is famous for a dreadful incident in 1665 when a consignment of cloth from London delivered to a local tailor brought with it the Black Death. As the dreaded disease spread through Eyam, the village rector, William Mompesson, convinced the villagers that rather than risk spreading it to other villages Eyam should quarantine itself. By the time the plague burnt itself out in late 1666, more than 250 of the village's 350-strong population were dead, including the rector's wife. The *Eyam History Trail* details all the sites associated with the plague.

The **Church of St Lawrence** dates from Saxon times and has many reminders of the events of 1665 and 1666, including a cupboard said to have been made from the wooden box that carried the infected cloth to Eyam. The plague register records the names of those who died during the outbreak. The church also has a leaflet describing some of the monuments and headstones in the churchyard, which has an

8th-century **Celtic cross**, one of the finest in the country. Many of the plague victims were buried in the churchyard, but apart from that of Catherine Mompesson, the rector's wife, only one other headstone relating to the plague has survived. Other victims were buried around the village – at the Riley graves, Mrs Hancock buried all seven members of her family one by one.

Next to Eyam's church are the **plague cottages** where the tailor lived. A walk up Water Lane from the village square, or a drive towards Grindleford from Hawkhill Rd, will bring you to **Mompesson's Well**. Food and other supplies were left here by friends from other villages. Back in Eyam, the 17th-century **Eyam Hall** (☎ 631976) opens 11 am to 4 pm on Wednesday, Thursday and Sunday, Easter to October. Admission costs £4/3.

Places to Stay & Eat
Eyam Youth Hostel (☎ 630335, Hawkhill Rd) charges £11/7.75 for adults/under-18s. *Delf View House* (☎ 631533, Church St) offers courteous, comfortable B&B in a Georgian house with singles for £25/35 and en-suite doubles for £32 per person.

The *Eyam Tearooms* offer the quintessential cream tea, but gets busy at weekends. The *Miner's Arms* on the square, which dates from 1630, turns out good sandwiches and refreshing beers.

Getting There & Away
There are daily buses from Tideswell to Eyam (No 65 or 66).

CASTLETON
☎ 01433 • pop 900
Overshadowed by 517m-high Mam Tor, this tiny village is a popular base for exploring the Peaks and features caves and a castle. It's also the northern terminus of the Limestone Way. Mam Tor is the boundary between the limestone of the White Peak and the gritstone of the Dark Peak.

Orientation & Information
Castleton nestles at the western end of the Hope Valley. Mam Tor's unstable condition undermined the A625 road through Castle-

ton and it's now bypassed by the spectacular Winnats Pass road, which goes through a steep-sided dale. Castle St is home to the church, pubs, B&Bs and the youth hostel.

The National Park Information Centre (☎ 620679) in Castle St opens 10 am to 5.30 pm daily, Easter to October; weekends only in winter.

Peveril Castle
Castleton is overlooked by the ruins of Peveril Castle (☎ 620613; EH), built by William Peveril, son of William the Conqueror. The keep, which is about all that remains, was added by Henry II in 1176. The castle sits more or less on top of Peak Cavern. From it there are superb views north to Mam Tor and the Dark Peak and south over pretty Cave Dale, directly behind the castle. Admission costs £2.20/1.10.

Walking
Start the 26-mile Limestone Way by taking the narrow, rocky entrance into beautiful Cave Dale behind the castle. There are many other excellent walks around Castleton. A fine day walk (see the Castleton & Edale map) of about 7 miles can be taken by going south along the Cave Dale track to a road where you turn right, and right again to pass by Rowter Farm and meet the Buxton Rd just beyond Winnats Pass. The route then climbs up to Mam Tor where ditches marking a pre-Roman fort can be distinguished on the top. The trail follows the ridge to Back Tor, but just before reaching that high point there's a path down from the ridge directly into Castleton along Hollowford Lane and Mill Bridge. Another pleasant day walk makes a 7-mile round trip via Edale, starting point of the Pennine Way.

Caves
The area around Castleton is riddled with caves, four of which are open to the public. Although most of them are natural, the area has also been extensively mined for Blue John, a reddish-pink form of fluorspar, as well as lead, silver and other minerals. Miners often broke into natural chambers during the course of their excavations.

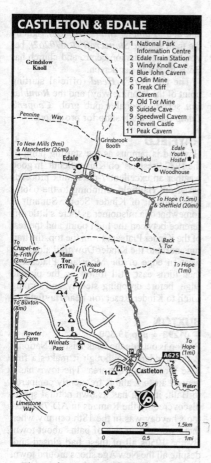

CASTLETON & EDALE

1 National Park
   Information Centre
2 Edale Train Station
3 Windy Knoll Cave
4 Blue John Cavern
5 Odin Mine
6 Treak Cliff
   Cavern
7 Old Tor Mine
8 Suicide Cave
9 Speedwell Cavern
10 Peveril Castle
11 Peak Cavern

Grindslow
Knoll

Pennine   Way

To New Mills (9mi)
& Manchester (26mi)

Grinsbrook
Booth

Edale   Cotefield   Edale
                              Youth
                              Hostel
            Woodhouse

To Hope (1.5mi)
& Sheffield (20mi)

To
Chapel-en-
le-Frith
(2mi)

Mam
Tor
(517m)   Road
          Closed

Back
Tor

To Hope
(1mi)

To Buxton
(8mi)

Rowter
Farm

Winnats
Pass

To
Hope
(1mi)

A625

Castleton

Peakhole

Water

Cave   Dale

Limestone
Way

0   0.75   1.5km

0   0.5   1mi

The **Peak Cavern** (☎ 620285), popularly known as the Devil's Arse, is reached by a pretty stream-side walk from the village centre. Unfortunately the ugly wall erected to stop you sneaking a free peek into the yawning 18 by 30m chasm detracts from the natural beauty. Rope was made here until 1974 and rope-makers' houses used to stand just inside the cave entrance. The cave opens 10 am to 4 pm daily, Easter to October, weekends only in winter. Admission costs £4.75/2.75.

The small, stalactite-filled **Treak Cliff Cavern** (☎ 620571) opens 10 am to 5.30 pm

year round (to 4 pm November to February). Admission costs £5/3.

Speedwell Cavern (☎ 620512) contains a long, artificially flooded tunnel along which you travel by electric boat to the 'bottomless' pit at the end; before electrification the boatman would propel the boat along the tunnel by 'walking' it with his feet on the tunnel roof. It opens 10 am to 4.30 pm daily. Admission costs £5.25/3.25.

On the other side of the closed section of road by Mam Tor is the impressive **Blue John Cavern** (☎ 620638) where it's thought that Blue John may have been mined in Roman times. One of the cave's chambers has a collection of 19th-century mining equipment. It opens 9.45 am to 5 pm daily (dusk in winter). Admission costs £6/3.

Experienced potholers can explore other caves, including the **Odin Mine** below Mam Tor, and the **Suicide Cave** and **Old Tor Mine** on Winnats Pass. The remains of prehistoric animals have been found in **Windy Knoll Cave**.

Places to Stay

Large and impressive *Castleton Youth Hostel* (☎ 620235, Castle St), opposite the church charges £11/7.75 for adults/under-18s.

Of the B&Bs, handsome *Cryer House* (☎ 620244), also in Castle St, costs from £21 – there is a highly popular tearoom downstairs. *Rambler's Rest* (☎ 620125, Mill Bridge), set in a 17th-century cottage, charges from £17.50 or £22 en suite.

Bargate Cottage (☎ 620201, Market Place) is full of character. You'll pay from £21.50, or £23.50 with a four-poster bed, and be prepared for convivial breakfasts.

The slightly pricier *Swiss House Hotel* (☎ 621098), on the main road on the Hope side of the village, offers pleasant rooms with bathroom for £35/45 per single/double. For a splash, *The Castle* (☎ 620578) has rooms with four-poster beds and jacuzzis for £65 during the week.

Places to Eat

The most obvious places to eat are the pubs. The *Castle Hotel* probably does the best meals, but the *George* and *Ye Olde Cheshire*

Cheese are also popular. Otherwise, there's a *fish and chip shop* round the corner from the hostel, or *Hilary Beth's Tea Room* in Market Place and *Rose Cottage* beside the Blue John Craft Shop for teas and coffees.

Ye Olde Nag's Head Hotel (☎ 620451) does romantic candlelit suppers for £17.95 and Sunday lunches for £12.95.

Getting There & Away

There's a train station at Hope, 2 miles east of Castleton.

Trent and South Yorkshire PTE buses run to Castleton. Mainline buses run to Sheffield.

EDALE

☎ 01433 • pop 350

Tiny Edale, the southern terminus of the 250-mile Pennine Way, is easily accessible by train from Sheffield to Manchester. It makes a good starting point for short walks, whether north to Kinder Scout or south to Mam Tor, the ridge overlooking Castleton.

Edale stretches from the main road and train station up to the Old Nag's Head pub. The National Park Information Centre (☎ 670207) opens 9 am to 5.30 pm daily.

Walking

There are several pleasant short walks from Edale up to the ridge between Mam Tor and Back Tor, overlooking Castleton. Alternatively you can walk north onto the Kinder Plateau; Jacob's Ladder offers the easiest route onto Kinder. If the weather is cooperative, a fine 6-mile walk takes you from the information office, past the youth hostel and up onto the moors along the southern edge of Kinder before dropping back down to Edale.

Places to Stay & Eat

Edale Youth Hostel (☎ 670302), at Rowland Cote, Nether Booth, about a mile east of the village, charges £11/7.75 for adults/under-18s.

The small *Fieldhead Camp Site* (☎ 670386) charges £3.25 per person and is right by the information centre. Showers cost 50p, cars £1.20. To the north of the village, *Cooper's Camp* (☎ 670372) charges £2.75 per person, 50p for cars.

B&B for £32/52 per single/double is available at the *Rambler Inn* (☎ 670268), right by the train station. *Stonecroft* (☎ 670262), beyond the information centre and church has B&B from £26 per person.

The *Old Nag's Head* (official starting point of the Pennine Way) and the *Rambler Inn* serve reasonable pub grub. *Cooper's Camp* has a small shop for provisions.

HAYFIELD

Hayfield is famous as the starting point of the 1932 'trespass' on Kinder Scout. In good weather an excellent 7-mile walk proceeds east from Hayfield, climbing to the 636m-high summit of Kinder Scout. Summit is somewhat of a misnomer as there's little difference between the high point and the rest of the Kinder Plateau. From the top, the trail runs north to the Kinder Downfall along the western edge of the Moorland Plateau. It then turns east, still following the plateau edge, before dropping steeply and turning south to Kinder Reservoir near Hayfield.

BUXTON

☎ 01298 • pop 19,500

Buxton is outside the Peak District National Park boundaries, although it makes a fine base for visiting the area. The town has a genteel air to it and is frequently compared to Bath; it even has its own natural spring discovered by the Romans in AD 78. Buxton's heyday was in the 18th century when there were seven sets of baths about town. By the 1950s all of these had closed and, despite all the New Age shops around town, it seems unlikely they will reopen.

Orientation & Information

The TIC (☎ 25106) is beside the Crescent, slowly but surely being restored.

Those coming by train arrive near pedestrianised Spring Gardens and the Spring Gardens shopping centre. Those arriving by bus are dropped in the Market Place where most of Buxton's eating choices can be found.

The Opera House is the focus for the annual late-July to early-August Buxton Festival (☎ 70395).

Things to See & Do

Renovation of the graceful **Crescent** (1784–88), which was modelled on the Royal Crescent in Bath, is well under way, although no obvious new use has been found for the building as yet. Across from it, the **Pump Room**, which dispensed Buxton's spring water for nearly a century, now hosts temporary art exhibitions. Fill your water bottle with delicious warm mineral water from **St Ann's Well**, next to the Pump Room.

Across the road, the TIC is housed in the old **Natural Mineral Baths** building where you can still see the spa water source; a side room tells the full story. On the corner of the Square and the Crescent is the **Old Hall Hotel** where Mary Queen of Scots stayed while visiting to take the waters; the hotel was rebuilt a century later in 1670. Buxton's fine **Opera House** opened in 1903 and stands in a corner of Pavilion Gardens. Behind it is the glassy **Pavilion** of 1871 and the **Pavilion Gardens Concert Hall** of 1876. The **Museum**, in Terrace Rd, round the corner from the town hall, opens 9.30 am to 5.30 pm Tuesday to Friday, to 5 pm on Saturday and from 10.30 am on Sunday. Admission costs £1/50p.

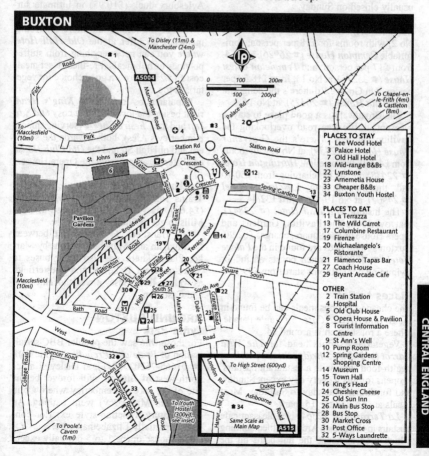

BUXTON

To Disley (11mi) & Manchester (24mi)

To Macclesfield (10mi)

To Chapel-en-le-Frith (4mi) & Castleton (8mi)

To Macclesfield (10mi)

Pavilion Gardens

To Poole's Cavern (1mi)

To High Street (600yd)

To Youth Hostel (300yd, see inset)

Dukes Drive

Ashbourne Road

Same Scale as Main Map

A515

PLACES TO STAY
1 Lee Wood Hotel
3 Palace Hotel
7 Old Hall Hotel
18 Mid-range B&Bs
22 Lynstone
23 Arnemetia House
33 Cheaper B&Bs
34 Buxton Youth Hostel

PLACES TO EAT
11 La Terrazza
13 The Wild Carrot
17 Columbine Restaurant
19 Firenze
20 Michaelangelo's Ristorante
21 Flamenco Tapas Bar
27 Coach House
29 Bryant Arcade Cafe

OTHER
2 Train Station
4 Hospital
5 Old Club House
6 Opera House & Pavilion
8 Tourist Information Centre
9 St Ann's Well
10 Pump Room
12 Spring Gardens Shopping Centre
14 Museum
15 Town Hall
16 King's Head
24 Cheshire Cheese
25 Old Sun Inn
26 Main Bus Stop
28 Bus Stop
30 Market Cross
31 Post Office
32 5-Ways Laundrette

CENTRAL ENGLAND

Poole's Cavern (☎ 26978), less than a mile from the centre, is a stalactite- and stalagmite-filled cave known since Neolithic times. It opens 10 am to 5 pm daily, March to October. Admission costs £4.75/2.50. A 20-minute walk leads from the cave through Grin Low Wood to **Solomon's Temple** (Grin Low Tower), an 1896 folly with fine views over the town.

Places to Stay

Buxton Youth Hostel (☎ 22287, Sherbrook Lodge, Harpur Hill Rd), south of the centre, charges £8.50/5.75 for adults/under-18s. It's usually closed on Sunday.

Places to try on Compton Rd include gastronomic *Griff Guest House (☎ 23628)*, at No 2, with rooms for £18 per person; comfortable *Compton House (☎ 26926)*, at No 4, from £17 per person; and *Templeton Guest House (☎ 25275)*, at No 13, from £18.50 per person. On Grange Rd there's the delightful *Arnemetia House (☎ 26125)*, at No 14.

The Broadwalk is a good place to stay; a pleasant, traffic-free road overlooking the Pavilion Gardens. There's the *Grosvenor House Hotel (☎ 72439)*, at No 1, with rooms from £45/50, the excellent *Hartington Hotel (☎ 22638)*, at No 18, charging from £50/70 and the nonsmoking *Roseleigh Hotel (☎ 24904)*, at No 19, from just £32/44.

The historic *Old Hall Hotel (☎ 22841)*, that overlooks the Pavilion Gardens and Opera House on the Square, charges £62/90. Buxton's finest beds are found in the *Palace Hotel (☎ 22001)*, which boasts an indoor swimming pool. Rooms start from £99/114.

Places to Eat

The cheapest serious meals can be found in the *Bryant Arcade Café,* off Eagle Parade, where a roast lunch is around £4.

Vegetarians should head for *The Wild Carrot (☎ 22843, 5 Bridge St)*, an excellent health-food store with a restaurant upstairs. It opens for lunch every day except Sunday, and for dinner Thursday to Saturday. Most meals are around the £5 mark.

La Terrazza (☎ 72364) is a pleasant cafe upstairs in Cavendish Arcade, a tiled building which used to house the hot baths on the Crescent. Market Place, in front of the town hall, has several places. Among the possibilities here are *Michaelangelo's Ristorante (☎ 26640)*, which goes for meaty dishes, rather than the pizzas and pastas on offer at the popular *Firenze (☎ 72203)* across the road. Behind it, on Hardwick Square South, the *Flamenco Tapas Bar (☎ 27392)* has a range of tapas for around £2.50 each. Back on Market Square, the *Coach House* is a popular local fish and chippie but closes by 7 pm.

Turn down Hall Bank behind the town hall for the *Columbine Restaurant (☎ 78752)*, which offers traditional English fare such as Aylesbury duck (£10.95) in intimate surroundings.

One of the longer and more interesting menus is on offer at the *Old Hall Hotel* where you can get everything from stuffed potatoes to full meals. Pre-theatre set meals cost £15.25. There's a good choice for vegetarians too.

Popular pubs include the *King's Head*, right beside the town hall, the cosy *Old Sun Inn* and the *Chesire Cheese* (serving smooth Kimberley's Ales), both towards the southern end of High St, and the *Old Club House* on Water St, across from the Opera House.

Getting There & Away

Trains run from Buxton to Manchester (£4.60) via New Mills. Change at New Mills to get to Sheffield via Edale.

The TransPeak TP bus service between Nottingham and Manchester stops by Market Place. There are also daily buses to Stoke-on-Trent, Bakewell and Chesterfield, as well as three buses a week to Tideswell and Castleton.

AROUND BUXTON
Lyme Park

For those who saw the popular BBC serialisation of *Pride and Prejudice*, Lyme Park (☎ 01663-762023; NT), at Disley, 9 miles north-west of Buxton, will forever be the site of the lake at Pemberley where Colin Firth (aka Mr Darcy) went bathing. An 18th-century Venetian-style exterior conceals a partially Elizabethan core.

The house opens 1 to 5 pm daily except

Wednesday and Thursday, April to October; the park keeps longer hours. Admission costs £4.50/2.25 and £3.50 for a car.

MATLOCK & MATLOCK BATH
☎ 01629

Located on the south-eastern edge of the Peak District are the twin towns of Matlock and Matlock Bath.

Despite its spectacular setting, squeezed into the narrow valley of the River Derwent, Matlock Bath feels more like a displaced seaside resort than a country town. You might want to come here to visit the **Peak District Mining Museum and Temple Mine** (☎ 583834) where you can have a go at panning for gold. It opens 10 am to 5 pm daily. Admission costs £2.50/1.50, or £4/2.50 including the mine. Alternatively, cable cars carry visitors up to the **Heights of Abraham** (☎ 582365) and its mixture of nature trails and family attractions. It opens 10 am to 5 pm daily, Easter to October. Admission costs £6.50/4.50.

The helpful TIC (☎ 55082), in the pavilion on Grand Parade, can suggest B&Bs. *LettinGo* (☎ 580686, ℮ *n&j@lettingo.free serve.co.uk, 1 Bounswood Rd*) is a great new backpackers pad near the station with beds from £11.50 a person.

Matlock, a couple of miles beyond, has more shops, restaurants and *Matlock Youth Hostel* (☎ 582983, 40 Bank Rd), with beds for £11/7.75 for adults/under-18s. Over weekends (and daily during August) you can travel by steam train through lovely scenery on the restored **Peak Railway** from Matlock Riverside station to Rowsley South. For timetable details phone ☎ 01629-580381. Return fares cost £6/3.

Trains and buses run to Manchester and Derby.

AROUND MATLOCK
The National Tramway Museum, Crich

Trams were a major feature of British life until a disastrous policy decision saw them wiped off the landscape of cities throughout the country. Today they are making a comeback from Sheffield to Croydon, but here in Crich they never went away. This living museum has a dramatic location in an old quarry and provides a home to more than 40 trams of all ages. It opens 10 am to 5.30 pm daily, April to October, 10.30 am to 4.30 pm Sunday and Monday in winter. Admission costs £6.70/3.30.

Nottinghamshire

Nottinghamshire is most famous for a man in tights, and Robin Hood, his merry men and the Sheriff of Nottingham have been roped into a variety of amusement parks, pubs and restaurants, although there's not actually much left of Sherwood Forest these days. Nevertheless, the city of Nottingham is undoubtedly one of the most happening cities in the Midlands and there are several other worthwhile places around the county.

NOTTINGHAM
☎ 0115 • pop 275,000

Nottingham is the happening heart of the East Midlands, home to a vibrant fashion, music and sporting scene that competes with the best in Britain. Paul Smith has picked up where lace left off to keep the city on the clothing map of Britain; the clubs and bars are some of the liveliest outside London; and while Nottingham Forest and Notts County may no longer be setting the football world alight, Trent Bridge remains a major draw for cricket fans.

The Saxon city bore the less than charming name of Snotingham, but modern Nottingham had its moment of glory in the 19th century when the lace industry transformed the city centre. Nottingham was a centre for the Luddite riots of 1811 to 1816. Lace-making declined during the 1890s and was virtually killed off by WWI, although the tourist industry supports some small-scale lace production. The city remains an industrial centre and is home to Raleigh bicycles.

Nottingham's famed Goose Fair dates back to the Middle Ages but these days it's just an outsize funfair which takes place in the Forest Recreation Ground on the first Thursday, Friday and Saturday of October.

NOTTINGHAM

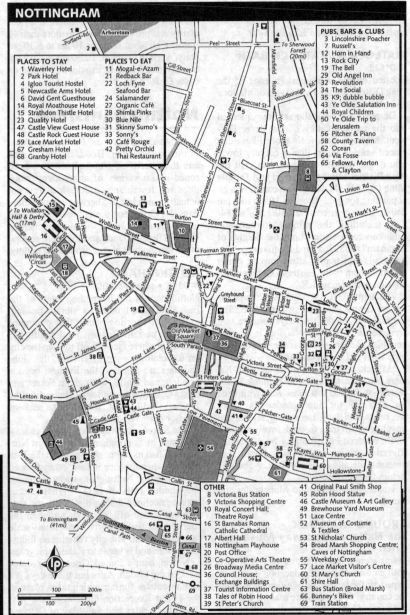

PLACES TO STAY
1 Waverley Hotel
2 Park Hotel
4 Igloo Tourist Hostel
5 Newcastle Arms Hotel
6 David Gent Guesthouse
14 Royal Moathouse Hotel
15 Strathdon Thistle Hotel
23 Quality Hotel
47 Castle View Guest House
48 Castle Rock Guest House
59 Lace Market Hotel
67 Gresham Hotel
68 Granby Hotel

PLACES TO EAT
11 Mogal-e-Azam
21 Redback Bar
22 Loch Fyne Seafood Bar
24 Salamander
27 Organic Café
28 Shimla Pinks
30 Blue Nile
31 Skinny Sumo's
33 Sonny's
40 Café Rouge
42 Pretty Orchid Thai Restaurant

PUBS, BARS & CLUBS
3 Lincolnshire Poacher
7 Russell's
12 Horn in Hand
13 Rock City
19 The Bell
29 Old Angel Inn
32 Revolution
34 The Social
35 K9; dubble bubble
43 Ye Olde Salutation Inn
44 Royal Children
50 Ye Olde Trip to Jerusalem
56 Pitcher & Piano
58 County Tavern
64 Ocean
64 Via Fosse
65 Fellows, Morton & Clayton

OTHER
8 Victoria Bus Station
9 Victoria Shopping Centre
10 Royal Concert Hall; Theatre Royal
16 St Barnabas Roman Catholic Cathedral
17 Albert Hall
18 Nottingham Playhouse
20 Post Office
25 Co-Operative Arts Theatre
26 Broadway Media Centre
36 Council House; Exchange Buildings
37 Tourist Information Centre
38 Tales of Robin Hood
39 St Peter's Church
41 Original Paul Smith Shop
45 Robin Hood Statue
46 Castle Museum & Art Gallery
49 Brewhouse Yard Museum
51 Lace Centre
52 Museum of Costume & Textiles
53 St Nicholas' Church
54 Broad Marsh Shopping Centre; Caves of Nottingham
55 Weekday Cross
57 Lace Market Visitor's Centre
60 St Mary's Church
61 Shire Hall
63 Bus Station (Broad Marsh)
66 Bunney's Bikes
69 Train Station

The city is also noted for its peculiar Midlands dialect. If someone greets you with a hearty 'eyupmeduck', a suitable response is 'hello'.

Orientation & Information
Like other Midlands cities, Nottingham is chopped in pieces by an inner ring road. The train station is south of the canal on the southern edge of the centre. There are two bus stations: Victoria bus station is hidden away behind the Victoria shopping centre, just north of the city centre, while Broad Marsh bus station is behind Broad Marsh shopping centre to the south.

The TIC (☎ 947 0661), in the Council House, opens daily in summer.

Nottingham Castle Museum, the Brewhouse Yard Museum, the Costume Museum and Wollaton Hall are all free during the week but have admission charges at the weekend. Anyone planning to visit the Caves of Nottingham, the Tales of Robin Hood and the Galleries of Justice should consider buying an Explorer Pass (£15.95/9.95), which also covers the other museums at weekends. Passes are available from all the attractions they cover.

Nottingham Castle Museum & Art Gallery
Nottingham Castle was demolished after the Civil War and replaced with a mansion in 1674. This was, in turn, burned out during the Reform Bill Riots of 1831, but a museum was opened inside the shell in 1875. The museum (☎ 915 3651) describes Nottingham's history and houses some of the alabaster carvings for which Nottingham was noted between 1350 and 1550. Upstairs there's also an art gallery. The castle opens 10 am to 5 pm daily. At weekends admission costs £1.50/80p. Tours of Mortimer's Hole beneath the castle take place at 2 and 3 pm Monday to Friday for £2/1. There's also a stylish cafe and an excellent shop.

Caves of Nottingham
Nottingham stands on a plug of Sherwood sandstone which is riddled with man-made caves dating back to medieval times. Rather surprisingly you need to go inside Broad Marsh shopping centre to find the entrance to the most fascinating, readily accessible caves (☎ 924 1424). These contain an air-raid shelter, a medieval underground tannery, several pub cellars and a mock-up of a Victorian slum dwelling. They open 10 am to 4.15 pm Monday to Saturday, and from 11 am Sunday. Admission costs £3.25/2.25.

The Tales of Robin Hood
The Tales of Robin Hood (☎ 948 3284), at 30–38 Maid Marian Way, is a modern tourist attraction that takes you through models of Nottingham Castle and Sherwood Forest in the days when Robin Hood was battling it out with the Sheriff. Afterwards you have time to find out more about the reality behind the legend, or to watch clips from the various film versions in the cafe.

It opens 10 am to 4.30 pm daily. Admission costs £4.95/3.95. Medieval banquets take place here, too, but are best booked in advance.

Wollaton Hall
Built in 1588 by Sir Francis Willoughby, land and coal-mine owner, Wollaton Hall (☎ 915 3900) is a fine example of Tudor architecture at its most extravagant. Architect Robert Smythson was also responsible for the equally avant-garde Longleat (see Longleat in the South-Western England chapter). Wollaton Hall now houses the **Nottingham Natural History Museum**.

The **Industrial Museum**, in the estate buildings, has lace-making equipment, Raleigh bicycles, a gigantic 1858 beam engine and oddities such as a locally invented, 1963 video recorder which never got off the ground. Opening hours for both museums are 10 am to 5 pm Monday to Saturday, 1.30 pm Sunday, April to September. The Industrial Museum opens Thursday to Sunday only October to March. Combined admission costs £1.50/1. Wollaton Hall is on the western edge of the city, 2½ miles from the centre; get there on a No 25 bus.

CENTRAL ENGLAND

The Legend of Robin Hood

In the Middle Ages most of Nottinghamshire was covered in forest. It was here that Robin Hood and his band of merry men were said to have waged their private war on the wicked sheriff of Nottingham while Richard I was away crusading.

The Robin Hood story has generated many films, the most recent and successful was *Robin Hood Prince of Thieves*, with Kevin Costner following in the footsteps of Errol Flynn as Robin and Alan Rickman as the Sheriff. Burnham Beeches in Buckinghamshire stood in for Sherwood Forest, while other scenes were filmed in the church of St Bartholomew-the-Great in London, Peckforton Castle in Preston, Lancashire, and in France.

Nottinghamshire is littered with sites associated with Robin. Nottingham Castle obviously played a key role, as did St Mary's Church. Robin is said to have married Maid Marian in Edinstowe church, while Fountaindale, near Blidworth, is the supposed site of his battle with Friar Tuck.

But did Robin ever really exist? As long ago as 1377 William Langland made fleeting reference to him in his poem Piers Plowman, but it was only in the early 16th century that the story began to be fleshed out, most notably in the ballad 'A Geste of Robyn Hoode'. In 1795 Joseph Ritson collected all the known accounts of Robin into one volume, since when innumerable authors (including Scott and Tennyson) have turned them into torrid novels and poems.

In spite of all this, researchers have failed to turn up any hard evidence that the outlaw actually existed. He is, for example, said to have been born in Lockesley in Yorkshire or Nottinghamshire, but no such place appears on any map. Optimists point to a Loxley in Staffordshire where Hood's father supposedly owned land. But it may be that 'Robin' is no more than a jumbled memory of ancient ideas about forest fairies, or a character made up to give voice to medieval resentments.

Other Things to See

The **Brewhouse Yard Museum** (☎ 915 3600) is housed in five 17th-century cottages on Castle Boulevard virtually below the castle. It re-creates everyday life in 19th-century Nottingham with particularly good displays of traditional shops. An underground passageway known as Mortimer's Hole leads from the castle to Brewhouse Yard. Roger Mortimer, who arranged Edward II's murder, is said to have been captured by supporters of Edward III who entered via this passage. It opens 10 am to 4 pm daily. Admission is free during the week, £1.50/80p at weekends.

The **Museum of Costume & Textiles** (☎ 915 3500), on Castle Gate, has displays of costumes from 1790 to the mid-20th century arranged in period rooms, as well as tapestries and lace. Opening times are the same as the Brewhouse. Across from the castle a small **Lace Centre** (☎ 941 3539) is housed in the medieval Severns building in Castle Rd.

In the impressive **Shire Hall** building on High Pavement, the **Galleries of Justice** (☎ 952 0558) has been redeveloped as a **National Museum of Law**. The interactive Police Galleries let you visit a pretend crime scene and assess the available evidence, while the Crime & Punishment Galleries look at how offences were handled in Victorian times. It opens 10 am to 5 pm Tuesday to Sunday and bank holiday Mondays. Admission costs £7.95/4.95.

Places to Stay

The cheapest accommodation is at the *Igloo Tourist Hostel* (☎ 947 5250, ⓔ reception@ igloohostel.co.uk, 110 Mansfield Rd), a short walk north of Victoria bus station. A bunk bed in a dorm is £11. A little closer to town is the *Newcastle Arms Hotel* (☎ 947 4616, 68 North Sherwood St), with rooms from £17 per person including breakfast, and a host of inexpensive B&Bs on the Mansfield Rd as it enters Sherwood.

Just south of the castle on Castle Boulevard, the *Castle View Guest House* (☎ 950 0022), at No 85, charges £19/30 for a single/ double including breakfast and the *Castle*

Rock Guest House (☎ *948 2116)*, at No 79, starts from £18 a head.

South of the centre there are some cheap B&Bs near the train station. The *Granby Hotel* (☎ *958 2158, 19 Station St)* has rooms from £20 per night and the *Gresham Hotel* (☎ *950 1234, 109 Carrington St)* has rooms from around £22/36 per night.

Pricier places, north of the centre, include the *Park Hotel* (☎ *978 6299, 5–7 Waverley St)* right across from the arboretum. Prices start at £48/68. Just off Waverley St, the *Waverley Hotel* (☎ *978 6707, 107 Portland Rd)* is cheaper at £27/55. It's also worth considering the *Quality Hotel* (☎ *947 5641, George St)* that charges £71/83.

Over weekends and throughout August, Nottingham's business hotels often offer a special discounted 'Robin Hood Rate' at hotels such as the *Holiday Inn* (☎ *993 5000, Castle Marina Park)* and *Rutland Square Hotel* (☎ *941 1114, St James St)*. Otherwise avoid them as prices are huge!

The *Lace Market Hotel* (☎ *852 3232, 31 High Pavement)* is extremely nice and costs £89/99 during the week, £65/75 at weekends.

Places to Eat

The Hockley area, around Carlton St to the east of the centre, is a good place to start looking for something to eat. There's good vegetarian food on Goose Gate where *Organic Café* is a vegan/vegetarian cafe above the Hiziki wholefood store. Moroccan stew is tasty.

Nearby, classy *Sonny's* (☎ *947 3041, 3 Carlton St)* has a bright and imaginative menu, with main dishes (modern British) from around £10. *Skinny Sumo's* (☎ *952 0188, 11 Carlton St)* offers sushi on a conveyor belt and cheap speciality nights during the week – mains are £6. In Broad St, the *Broadway Media Centre* (☎ *952 6611)* has a good, if smoky, cafe where you can get soup, a baguette and endless coffee for £4.50 at lunchtime. The *Blue Nile* (☎ *941 0976, upstairs, 5 Heathcoate St)* is an Egyptian restaurant with vegetarian dishes and belly dancing. Down on Goose Gate is one of the city centre's best Indian restaurants, *Shimla Pinks* (☎ *958 9899)*.

Beside the Theatre Royal, the *Mogal-e-Azam* (☎ *947 2911, 7 Goldsmith St)* is an acclaimed Indian restaurant.

The *Loch Fyne Seafood Bar* (☎ *950 8481, 17 King St)* is a branch of the excellent Scottish oyster and smoked seafood company. Half a dozen oysters cost £5. Round the corner, the *Redback Bar* (☎ *953 1531, Queen St)* offers good beer and company, plus rooburgers and outback soup.

Bridlesmith Gate is a lively cut-through, with a branch of *Café Rouge*. Just off it, the *Pretty Orchid Thai Restaurant* (☎ *958 8344)* does lunches for £4.50, but dinner will cost more like £15.

Entertainment

Pubs, Bars & Clubs Tucked into the cliff below the castle, *Ye Olde Trip to Jerusalem* is one of Britain's best; the upstairs bar is actually cut into the rock. Crusaders are said to have gathered here before setting off to the Holy Land and today pub crawlers follow in their footsteps before setting out to conquer Nottingham. Just over the ringroad, *Ye Olde Salutation Inn* is now part of the Hogshead chain, but has decent beers and some caves beneath.

Real ale fiends should get to the *Lincolnshire Poacher*, a brilliant pub on the Mansfield Rd with well-kept beer. Just up the hill is the *Forest Tavern* which has a dangerous selection of Belgian beers; the happening, little *Maze Club* is in the same spot. Another great ale pub to look out for is *Bunkers Hill* at the bottom of Goose Gate in Hockley.

Fellows, Morton & Clayton is an excellent pub overlooking the canalside. Neighbouring *Via Fosse* is one of *the* places to go in town and heaves during summer. The *Old Angel Inn* in Hockley is a popular student pub, as is the *County Tavern* on High Pavement, near the incredible *Pitcher & Piano*, a spectacular church conversion that draws a faithful crowd. *The Social* (☎ *950 5078, 23 Pelham St)* is a remarkably trendy bar and has DJs and live guests. *Revolution* *(Broad St)* remains a cool place to wind down. *Gatsby's (Huntingdon St)* is a busy gay bar, as is the *Admiral Duncan*.

CENTRAL ENGLAND

Rock City (☎ *941 2544, Talbot St*) is a popular rock venue with a £4 to £12 admission charge. Nearby are a host of popular student pubs such as *Russell's* and the *Horn in Hand*.

K9 is a retro cafe-bar that is always rammed and downstairs is *dubble bubble* which is one of the city's better clubs. *Ocean* is a large townie type of club.

Theatre, Cinema & Classical Music

The *Broadway* (☎ *952 6611, Broad St*) cinema is the city's art-house movie centre. Theatrical venues include the *Co-operative Arts Theatre* (☎ *947 6096, George St*) and the *Nottingham Playhouse* (☎ *941 9419, Wellington Circus*). The *Royal Concert Hall* and *Theatre Royal* share a booking office (☎ *948 2626*) and an imposing building close to the centre.

Getting There & Away

Nottingham is 135 miles from London, around 75 miles from Manchester and Leeds, and 50 miles from Birmingham.

Bus National Express (☎ 0870 580 8080) buses operate from the Broad Marsh bus station. A single to London costs £12.25.

For local bus information phone the Buses Hotline on ☎ 924 0000. Sherwood Forester buses (☎ 977 4268) operate services to tourist attractions all over Nottinghamshire in summer. An unlimited travel Ranger Ticket for £4.50/2.50 gives discounted admission to some attractions. Rainbow Route services by Trent & Barton Buses (☎ 01773-712265) operate to Derby and continue through the Peak District to Manchester (TransPeak). They operate from both bus stations and a one-day Explorer Ticket costs £5.95; one child goes free.

Train Nottingham is not on the main railway routes through the Midlands but regular services to London St Pancras take 1¾ hours.

Getting Around

A Day Rider ticket gives you unlimited travel for one day for £2.20.

Bunney's Bikes (☎ 947 2713), at 97 Carrington St, near the train station, has bicycles from £8.50 per day (£100 deposit!).

AROUND NOTTINGHAM
Newstead Abbey

Converted into a home after the dissolution of the monasteries in 1539, Newstead Abbey (☎ 01623-455900) is chiefly notable for being the home of Lord Byron (1788–1824), but the Byronic connections are sparse.

The facade of the ruined priory church is next to the house, which was already in bad shape when Byron inherited it from his great-uncle. The continuing decline of the family fortune forced him to sell it in 1817. The poet used to hold shooting sessions indoors and a friend commented that a visit was so pleasant it 'made one forget that one was domiciled in the wing of an extensive ruin'.

The house opens noon to 4 pm daily, April to September; the garden opens year round. Admission to house and garden costs £4/1.50. The house is 12 miles north of Nottingham, off the A60. The Sherwood Forester bus runs right there on summer Sundays; otherwise take bus Nos 737 and 747 and walk a mile from the abbey gates.

Southwell Minster

To judge by its magnificent minster, medieval Southwell must have had an importance the modern town just doesn't. For those who love Britain's Gothic architecture but loathe the crowds, Southwell Minster (☎ 01636-812649) will come as a great relief. The highlight of the building is the lovely Decorated chapterhouse which is filled with naturalistic carvings of leaves, pigs, dogs and rabbits. Children will also enjoy looking for wooden mice carved by Yorkshire's famous woodcarver Robert Thompson, for whom they acted as a 'signature'.

Admission is free, but a donation of £2/1 is suggested. You can get to Southwell on regular bus No 61 from Nottingham.

DH Lawrence Birthplace Museum

The birthplace (☎ 01773-763312) of DH Lawrence (1885–1930), Nottingham's controversial author, is at 8a Victoria St in Eastwood, about 10 miles north-west of the city. It's now a museum, open 10 am to 5 pm daily, April to October; to 4 pm in winter. Admission costs £3.50/1.50.

Sherwood Forest

Only tiny fragments of Robin Hood's mighty forest remain but a quarter of a million people visit the 180-hectare Sherwood Forest Country Park near the village of Edinstowe every year. At least the hokey Sherwood Forest Visitor Centre (☎ 01623-824490) keeps some of the crowds out of the real woods where Robin is supposed to have hidden in the Major Oak. Speaking of the oak, if ever there was a case for euthanasia for plantlife, this is it as the tree almost has more supports than branches these days. It opens 10.30 am to 5 pm daily (to 4.30 pm November to March). Admission costs £1.50.

Sherwood Forester buses run the 20 miles to the park from Nottingham.

Newark-upon-Trent
☎ 01636

This proud market town has many buildings of distinction, including the ruins of **Newark Castle**, one of the few castles to hold out against Cromwell's men during the civil war. Charles I commanded Lord Bellasis to surrender and soon after the castle was rubble. An impressive Norman gate remains and the castle opens 10 am to 3 pm Wednesday, Friday and Sunday. Admission is free. The town has a large, cobbled square overlooked by the medieval White Hart Inn and the Clinton Arms Hotel from where Gladstone made his first political speech and where Lord Byron stayed while his first book of poems was published.

The TIC (☎ 655765) is in the Gilstrap Centre, Castelgate, and has good accommodation listings. There are regular buses to Nottingham.

Eastern England

With the exception of Cambridgeshire, most of the eastern counties included in this chapter – Suffolk, Norfolk, Cambridgeshire and Lincolnshire – have been overlooked by tourists, who have preferred York over Lincoln, Bath over Bury St Edmunds, Canterbury over Ely. The part of this region known as East Anglia (Norfolk, Suffolk and east Cambridgeshire) has always been distinct, separated from the rest of England by the fens (reclaimed marshlands) and the Essex forests.

Motorways, bus routes and train lines have rendered this separation less tangible in modern times but still the caravans of tour buses keep their distance – hence your reason for going. Here you will find a softer England where picturesque medieval market towns straddle a gently undulating landscape, criss-crossed by waterways and marshland and bordered by some stunning coastlines. It is difficult to believe that this pastoral idyll was once the epicentre of economic power in England but in the region's more important towns – Cambridge, Norwich, Ely, Bury St Edmunds, King's Lynn and Lincoln – you will find enough evidence of its busy medieval past.

To the east of the fens, Norfolk and Suffolk have unspectacular scenery that can still be very beautiful. Norfolk's county seat, Norwich, has long been dismissed as 'quiet' (read 'boring') but an impressive program of urban rejuvenation and the presence of a university has given it a new lease of life. Cambridgeshire is home to one of the finest university towns in the world but Cambridge has been more than just a host to dozens of Nobel Prize winners and an academic tradition with few rivals in the world. Its mix of fine architecture and large tracts of parkland straddling a bend in the River Cam make this one of the most attractive towns in southern England.

The distinctive architectural character of the region was determined by the lack of suitable building stone. Stone was occasionally

Highlights

- Reliving the past in medieval Lavenham
- Boating on the beautiful Norfolk Broads
- Dreaming of being a Nobel laureate while strolling around the University of Cambridge
- Trying to punt on the River Cam
- Hiking up Steep Hill to Lincoln's superb cathedral

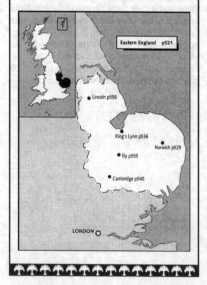

imported for important buildings but for humble churches and houses three local materials were used: flint, clay bricks and oak. The most unusual of the three, flint, can be chipped into a usable shape but a single stone is rarely larger than a fist. Often the flint is used in combination with dressed stone or bricks to form decorative patterns.

More than any other part of England, East Anglia has close links with northern Europe. In the 6th and 7th centuries it was overrun by the Norsemen. From the late Middle Ages,

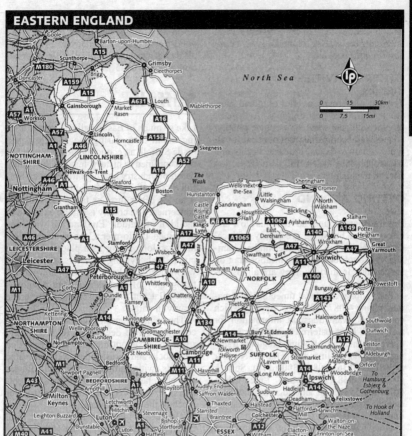

Suffolk and Norfolk grew rich trading wool and cloth with the Flemish; this wealth built scores of churches and helped subsidise the development of Cambridge. The windmills, the long, straight drainage canals and even the architecture (especially in King's Lynn) call the Low Countries to mind.

ORIENTATION & INFORMATION

Norwich, King's Lynn, Cambridge and Lincoln are all easily accessible from London by train and bus. Ely, Peterborough and King's Lynn are on a direct train line from Cambridge. The East of England Tourist

Board (☎ 01473-822922, ⓔ eastofengland touristboard@compuserve.com) can provide further information. Its Web site is at www.visitbritain.com/east-of-england.

WALKING & CYCLING ROUTES

The Peddars Way and Norfolk Coast Path link to form a 94-mile walking track which crosses the middle of Norfolk to Holme-next-the-Sea and follows the coastline south to Cromer. See the Activities chapter for more information.

This is ideal cycling country. Where there are hills, they're gentle. Bicycles can be hired cheaply in Cambridge and the Tourist Information Centres (TICs) can suggest several interesting routes. Ask for the *England's Cycling Country* booklet.

OTHER ACTIVITIES
Boating
The Norfolk Broads, a series of inland lakes (ancient, flooded peat diggings) to the east of Norwich, constitute a popular boating area. Several companies rent out boats of all types – narrow boats, cruisers, yachts and houseboats. See the Norfolk Broads section later in the chapter.

GETTING AROUND
Bus
Bus transport around the region is slow and disorganised but there are plenty of local companies linking all but the smallest hamlets. Although bus trips invariably drag on longer than train rides, they are almost always cheaper.

For national and local timetable information, phone ☎ 0870 608 2608. Specify which county you want transport information for and you'll be transferred to the appropriate operator. There are also direct regional transport information lines in operation: Norfolk (☎ 01603-613613/0845 300 6116), Suffolk (☎ 0845 958 3358) and Lincolnshire (☎ 01522-553135). Cambridgeshire operates an expensive 0891 number (calls are 50p per minute) – ☎ 0891 910910.

A new Web site set up by the Southern Vectis Company (☎ 01983-522456) was not up and running at the time of writing but should be operational by the time you read this. Its address is www.xephos.com and it promises comprehensive and detailed information on all bus travel in the area, including fares, timetables and connections for all bus companies large and small.

Train
From Norwich you can catch trains to the Norfolk coast and Sheringham but there's an unfortunate gap between Sheringham and King's Lynn (you could take the bus) which prevents a rail loop back to Cambridge. It may be worth considering an Anglia Plus pass which offers travel for three days out of seven for £18, one day for £8.50. These are valid from 8.45 am Monday to Friday and all day at weekends. For all train information phone ☎ 0845 748 4950.

Suffolk

Like so much of East Anglia, the great trading boom that, during the Middle Ages, made Suffolk an economic powerhouse has been confined to history, leaving the county bereft of industry and big cities. Today Suffolk is something of a rural backwater, and is all the better for it as far as the visitor is concerned. The county is a good example of the idyll of 'middle England'. It was once described by former Conservative prime minister John Major as a place where one might find 'cycling spinsters, cricket and warm beer'. In keeping with the general topography of East Anglia, the county is pretty flat but the landscape has a serene beauty in parts.

The painter Constable enthused about the county's 'gentle declivities, its woods and rivers, its luxuriant meadow flats sprinkled with flocks and herds, and its well-cultivated uplands, with numerous scattered villages and churches, farms and picturesque cottages'. The description still holds true for much of the county today.

The region's economic boom as a wool trading centre lasted until the 16th century and has left the county with its magnificently endowed 'wool' churches, many built to support much larger populations than live here now. Some of the villages have changed little since then and Suffolk buildings are famous for their *pargeting* – decorative stucco plasterwork.

IPSWICH
☎ 01473 • pop 129,600
Suffolk's county town was a principal player in the Saxon world and, while today it barely registers on the list of Britain's most important towns, it's still an important commercial and shopping centre. Aesthetics were largely ignored when developers sought to kick-start

the town's commercial fortunes over the last 30 years, however, and the town is hardly inspiring. The notable exception is the recently renovated Wet Dock quayside, a testament to more thoughtful modern development and a pleasant spot to while away a couple of hours.

As Ipswich is a transport hub for the region, you might end up here anyway; if so, make an effort to check out the town's beautiful examples of the Tudor style, Ancient House and Christchurch Mansion.

The TIC (☎ 258070, fax 432017,ⓔ tourist @ipswich.gov.uk@ipswich.gov.uk) is in St Stephen's Church, off St Stephen's Lane, near the bus station and Ancient House. It opens 9 am to 5 pm Monday to Saturday. The TIC organises 90-minute guided tours (£1.75/ 1.25 per adult/child) of the town at 2.15 pm every Tuesday and Thursday. The train station is a 15-minute walk south-west of the TIC along Princes St and across the roundabout.

Things to See & Do

The 17th-century **Ancient House** (☎ 214144), 40 Buttermarket, is now a branch of Lakelands kitchen outfitters, and you can wander in to take a look at the exquisite hammerbeam roof on the first floor. The external decor, done around 1670, is an extravagant example of the Restoration style, with plenty of stucco and some of the finest examples of pargeting in the country. The store opens 9 am to 5.30 pm Monday to Saturday. The house is about 50 yards north of the TIC, just off St Stephen's Lane.

At the **Ipswich Museum**, on High St, there's a replica of the Sutton Hoo ship burial found near Woodbridge, east of Ipswich, in 1939. It was the richest archaeological discovery in the country; the original artefacts are now in the British Museum.

Set in a 65-acre park about 300 yards north of town on Soane St, **Christchurch Mansion** (☎ 433554) is a fine Tudor mansion built between 1548 and 1550. The exterior is awash with Dutch-style gables, while the enormous interior is decorated with period furniture and the walls are adorned with a pretty extensive collection of

works by Constable and Gainsborough. The Wolsey Art Gallery hosts contemporary art exhibitions. The mansion and gallery opens 10 am to 5 pm Tuesday to Saturday (to 4 pm October to February), and 2.30 to 4.30 pm on Sunday. Admission is free. To get there, walk north from the TIC along St Stephen's Lane, which becomes Tower St. Turn right onto St Margaret's St and then take a left at the fork onto Soane St.

Places to Stay & Eat

Dickens used the *Great White Horse Hotel* (☎ 256558, fax 253396, ⓔ gwh@keme.co .uk, Tavern St) in *Pickwick Papers*. The 'mouldy, ill-lighted rooms' were recently renovated (no more mould and plenty of light); singles/doubles cost £45/55.

Cliffden Guest House (☎ 252689, fax 461077, ⓔ cliffden@btinternet.com, 21 London Rd) is a 10-minute walk west of the TIC along Tavern St. Rooms cost from £20/34.

There's also very comfortable farmhouse accommodation from £18/42 at *College Farm* (☎/fax 652253, ⓔ bryce1@agripro .co.uk, Hintlesham), 6 miles west of Ipswich, just off the A1071 to Hadleigh.

There are some good places to eat by the Wet Dock. We recommend *Il Punto* (☎ 289748), located aboard a pleasure boat docked along the quayside. The food is French and you can eat well for around £15.

Getting There & Away

National Express (☎ 0870 580 8080) runs daily coaches to Ipswich from a number of destinations, including London (£8.50, 2¾ hours) and Cambridge (£6.75, 1½ hours). The largest of the several local bus companies is First Eastern Counties (☎ 0845 602 0121). It runs eight buses daily, Monday to Friday, to Sudbury (£2.40, one hour). Beestons (☎ 823243) also runs about 10 buses daily, Monday to Saturday (£1.35 return) between the two towns. On Sunday, Chambers (☎ 01787-227233) runs five buses (£2.40).

There are half-hourly trains to London's Liverpool St station (£18.40, 1¼ hours) and Norwich (£11.50, 50 minutes); 12 trains daily to Bury St Edmunds (£4, 30 minutes); and six daily to Lowestoft (£8.40, 1½ hours).

STOUR VALLEY

Running along the border between Suffolk and Essex, the River Stour flows through a soft, pastoral landscape that has inspired numerous painters, of which the most famous are Constable and Gainsborough. For Dedham Vale, the area known as Constable country, see the Essex section in the South-Eastern England chapter.

Long Melford
☎ 01787 • pop 2800

Known for its long High St (the longest in England, the locals like to claim) and the lovely timber-framed buildings that line it, Long Melford has a magnificent church with some fine stained-glass windows, two stately homes and the obligatory antique shops.

Built in 1578, **Melford Hall** (☎ 880286) is a turreted Tudor mansion in the centre of the village. There's an 18th century drawing room, a Regency library, a Victorian bedroom and a display of paintings by Beatrix Potter, who was a relative of the Parker family, owners of the house from 1786 to 1960, when it passed into the hands of the Treasury. Run by the National Trust (NT), it opens 2 to 5.30 pm Wednesday to Sunday, May to September; 2 to 5.30 pm Saturday and Sunday, April and October; phone for other times. Admission costs £4.30/2.15.

On the edge of the village, down a tree-lined avenue, lies **Kentwell Hall** (☎ 310207), another red-brick Tudor mansion but one that's privately owned and makes much more of its Tudor origins. Between mid-June and mid-July, over 200 Tudor enthusiasts abandon their contemporary cynicism and descend on Kentwell Hall to recreate and live out a certain year in the Tudor calendar. The house is surrounded by a moat and there's a brick-paved Tudor Rose maze and a rare-breeds farm. The house and grounds open noon to 5 pm daily, April to October. Admission costs £4.90/2.90, more expensive during the historical re-enactment period.

The Great Church of the Holy Trinity has lunchtime recitals at 1.10 pm every Wednesday mid-May to mid-September. For details of what's on, contact Mrs Jilly Cooper on ☎ 281836.

Getting There & Away Chambers Buses (☎ 227233) runs 13 buses from Monday to Saturday between Long Melford and Bury St Edmunds (£2, one hour) calling at Sudbury (£1, five minutes). It also runs a circular bus route between Long Melford and Sudbury (£1, 10 minutes) at 10 and 40 minutes past the hour from Monday to Saturday.

Sudbury
☎ 01787 • pop 17,800

Sudbury's prosperity was founded on the cloth industry and it continues to produce silk to this day, although on a much smaller scale than before. The TIC (☎ 881320, fax 374314) is in the town hall. It opens 10 am to 4.45 pm Monday to Saturday, Easter to October (shorter hours the rest of the year). Its Web site is at www.babergh-south-suffolk.gov.uk.

The painter Thomas Gainsborough (1727–88) was born in Sudbury and **Gainsborough's House** (☎ 372958), 46 Gainsborough St, is preserved as a shrine; it has the largest collection of his work in the country. It opens 10 am to 4 pm Tuesday to Saturday, and 2 to 4 pm on Sunday. Admission costs £3/1.50.

Places to Stay If you plan to stay, *The Old Bull Hotel* (☎ 374120, fax 379044, Church St) is a family-run hotel in a 16th-century building with nine rooms, all decorated differently. Singles/doubles start at £38/52.

Equally priced is the *Boathouse Hotel* (☎/fax 379090, Ballingdon Bridge) – rooms start at £34/52. But it's on the water and the hotel rents out rowing boats.

Getting There & Away Bus travel in and out of Sudbury is quite tricky. See Getting There & Away in the Long Melford section for details of Chambers Bus services. Beestons (☎ 01473-823243) runs nine buses daily, Monday to Friday (seven on Saturday), to Ipswich (£2.70, one hour). To get most anywhere else involves a few changes. For Cambridge, you first have to get to Haverhill; Beestons has nine buses per day Monday to Friday (£1.70, 45 minutes), seven on Saturday and five on Sunday. From Haverhill, Stagecoach Cambus (☎ 01223-423554) runs buses roughly every 30 minutes to Cambridge (£2.40, one hour) from Monday to Saturday and every two hours on Sunday.

Sudbury also has a train station with an hourly service to London (£15.90, 1¼ hours).

LAVENHAM
☎ 01787 • pop 1700

A tourist honey pot, Lavenham can get crowded with bus tours but it's nevertheless worth seeing. It's a beautifully preserved example of a medieval wool town, with over 300 listed buildings. Some are timber-framed, others decorated with pargeting. There are cosy, pink, thatched cottages, crooked houses, antique shops and art galleries, quaint tea-rooms and ancient inns. When the wool industry moved to the west and north of England in the late 16th century, none of Lavenham's inhabitants could afford to build anything more modern. Today, as long as there aren't too many tourists around, you can feel as if you're in a time warp while walking through parts of the village.

The TIC (☎ 248207), Lady St, has lists of places to stay. It opens 10 am to 5.30 pm daily.

Market Place, off High St, is dominated by the handsome **Guildhall** (☎ 247646; NT), a superb example of a close-studded, timber-framed building, dating back to the early 16th century. It's now a local history museum with displays on the wool trade and is open 11 am to 5 pm daily, April to October (11 am to 4 pm weekends only, March to November). Admission costs £3.

Little Hall, which has soft ochre plastering and grey timber, is a private house that can be visited. It opens 2 to 5.30 pm Wednesday, Thursday and at weekends, April to October. Admission costs £1.75/1.

At the southern end of the village, opposite the car park, is the **Church of St Peter and St Paul**. Its soaring steeple is visible for miles around. The church bears witness to Lavenham's past prosperity at the centre of the local wool trade.

One of the most attractive places to stay is *Lavenham Priory* (☎ 247404, fax 248472, e mail@lavenhampriory.co.uk, Water St). Once the home of Benedictine monks, then medieval cloth merchants, upmarket B&B is now offered here for £39 to £59 per person. It's a beautiful place but you cannot visit it unless you are a guest. You can, however, get a virtual tour of the building through the Web site at www.lavenhampriory.co.uk.

Most people come just for the day and there are numerous *teashops* offering light lunches.

Chambers Buses (☎ 227233) connect Lavenham with Bury St Edmunds (£1.60, 30 minutes) and Sudbury (£1.60, 20 minutes) with an hourly bus (until 6 pm Monday to Saturday, no service on Sunday) from Bury St Edmunds to Colchester via Sudbury and Lavenham. There are no direct buses from Cambridge; you must go via Sudbury, also the location of the nearest train station (see that section earlier in the chapter).

BURY ST EDMUNDS
☎ 01284 • pop 30,500

This is easily Suffolk's most attractive large town, straddling the Lark and Linnet Rivers amid gently rolling farmland. The town has a distinct Georgian flavour, with street upon street of handsome, 18th-century facades that hark back to a period of great prosperity. It's now a busy agricultural centre and cattle, vegetable and fruit markets are held every Wednesday and Saturday. Greene King, the famous Suffolk brewer, is based here.

Centrally placed, Bury is a convenient point from which to explore western Suffolk. Worth seeing is the ruined abbey, set in a beautiful garden. There's also a fascinating clock museum, and recommended guided tours of the brewery.

History

Bury's motto 'Shrine of a King, Cradle of the Law' recalls the two most memorable events in its history. The Danes decapitated Edmund, a Christian prince from Saxony who was destined to be the last king of East Anglia, in 856 and his body was brought here for reburial in 903. The shrine to this saint became the focal point of a new Benedictine monastery called St Edmundsbury, around which the town grew. The abbey, now ruined, became one of the most famous pilgrimage centres in the country and, until the dissolution of the monasteries in 1537, was the wealthiest in the country; for many years St Edmund was patron saint of England.

The second memorable episode in Bury's early history took place at the abbey. In 1214, at St Edmund's Altar, the English barons drew up the petition that formed the basis of the Magna Carta.

Orientation & Information

Bury is an easy place to find your way around because it has preserved Abbot Baldwin's 11th-century grid layout.

The train station is a quarter of a mile north of the town centre; there are regular bus connections to the centre (50p). The bus station is in the heart of town. The TIC (☎ 764667, fax 757084, ⓔ eloise.appleby@burybo.stedsbc.gov.uk), 6 Angel Hill, opens 9 am to 5.30 pm daily from Easter to October and daily except Sunday the rest of the year. Phone for information and times of the guided walking tours (£3/free) which start from here.

There are tours of the Greene King Brewery (☎ 763222), Crown St, at 2.30 pm Monday to Thursday. Tickets cost £6; tours are popular, so you'll need to book ahead.

Walking Tour

Outside the TIC on Angel Hill there are many fine Georgian buildings such as the 18th-century Angel Hotel, which is covered in thick Virginia creeper.

The Abbey & Park Although the abbey is very much a ruin, it's a spectacular one set in a beautiful garden. After the dissolution of the monasteries, the townspeople made off with much of the stone – even St Edmund's grave and bones have disappeared.

To reach the abbey, walk right along Angel Hill until you're opposite the second Abbey Gate, which is still as impressive in its austere regality as it was in Norman times. Cross over and walk round the green, home to Elizabeth Frink's statue of St Edmund (1976). From here, you can see the remains of part of the western front and Samson Tower, which have houses built into them.

The abbey opens daily until sunset. Admission is free. A visitor's centre is housed in Samson's Tower (once part of the western side of the abbey), where an excellent 45-minute audio tour (£1.50) is available. Alternatively, you can guide yourself around the ruins using the information boards, which help to show how large a community this must have been, with its chapels and priory, its chapter house and treasury, abbot's palace and garden. The huge church dominated everything in the vicinity. It was built in the shape of a cross, and contains a crypt and St Edmund's Altar, near which is the plaque commemorating the barons' pledge of 1214.

Walk down to the river, past the old dovecote, before turning back to head for the superb formal gardens. Leave by the Gothic Gate and turn left to reach the cathedral.

St Edmundsbury Cathedral The cathedral dates from the 16th century but the eastern end was added between 1945 and 1960 and the northern side was not completed until 1990. It was made a cathedral in 1914. The interior is light and lofty with a painted hammer-beam roof. It opens 8.30 am to 8 pm daily, April to October (until 7 pm the rest of the year). The cathedral was recently granted £10-million of National Lottery funds by the Millenium Commission, which will go toward the cathedral's restoration; the project is expected to last until 2004.

St Mary's Church From the cathedral, turn left out of the western door and walk past the Norman Tower to reach St Mary's. Built around 1430, it contains the tomb of Mary Tudor (Henry VIII's sister and one-time queen of France). A curfew bell is still rung, as it was in the Middle Ages.

Manor House Museum At 5 Honey Hill, near St Mary's, is this magnificent museum of horology, art and costume, housed in a Georgian building. It is worth being here around noon, when all the clocks strike. Manor House (☎ 757072) opens 10 am to 5 pm Tuesday to Sunday. Admission costs £2.85/1.85.

Art Gallery & Moyse's Hall Retrace your steps on Honey Hill and Crown St, then turn left up Churchgate St, turning right at the end onto Guildhall St. Up the street, on the right, is Market Cross, remodelled in 1774 by Robert Adam as a theatre and now the Art Gallery (☎ 762081). It opens 10.30 am to 5 pm Tuesday to Sunday. Admission costs 50p. Turn right by the Corn Exchange and continue to the Buttermarket where Moyse's Hall, dating from the 12th century, is probably East Anglia's oldest domestic building. It's now a local museum (☎ 757488); it's closed for refurbishment until October 2001; call for details.

Places to Stay

B&B at *Hilltop* (☎ 767066, @ bandb@hill top22br.freeserve.co.uk, 22 Bronyon Close), off Flemyng Rd, costs £16 per person. *Sheila Keeley Oak Cottage B&B* (☎ 762745, fax 762745, 54 Guildhall St) is a centrally located place with rooms for the same price.

Ounce House (☎ 761779, fax 768315, @ pott@globalnet.co.uk, Northgate St) is very comfortable, central and nonsmoking. Singles/doubles with bathroom start at £55/75; ask for a room with a garden view.

Charles Dickens stayed at the *Angel Hotel* (☎ 753926, fax 750092, @ sales@theangel .co.uk, 3 Angel Hill) in the centre of Bury. It's an upmarket place with prices to match, starting at £69/84 (breakfast extra). Weekend breaks are cheaper at £54 per person for B&B or £67 including dinner.

Places to Eat

Maison Bleue (☎ 760623, 31 Churchgate St) is a highly recommended seafood restaurant. Main dishes (brill, sea bass, monkfish and so on) range from £9 to £14.50, and there's a set menu for £19. It closes on Sunday.

Holland & Barrett (☎ 706677, 6 Brentgovel St) is a vegetarian restaurant and cafe; most dishes are around £3. It opens until 4.30 pm Monday to Saturday.

Next to the TIC is the *Scandinavia Coffee House* (☎ 700853, 30 Abbeygate). A smoked-salmon open Danish sandwich is a good lunch for £5.25. The *Refectory* at the cathedral also does teas and light lunches.

The best-known pub in Bury is the *Nutshell* (☎ 764867, The Traverse), also the smallest pub in the country. It's off Abbeygate.

Getting There & Away

Bury is 75 miles from London, 35 miles from Norwich and 28 miles from Cambridge.

There's a daily National Express bus to London (£12.25, two hours and 20 minutes). From Cambridge, Stagecoach Cambus (☎ 01233-423554) runs buses to Bury (£4.20 for a day return, 35 minutes) every two hours from Monday to Saturday; the last bus back to Cambridge leaves at 5.05 pm.

Bury is on the Ipswich to Ely railway line so trains to London (£23.50, 1¾ hours) go via these towns. From Cambridge, there are trains every two hours to Bury (£5.30, 45 minutes).

AROUND BURY ST EDMUNDS
Ickworth House & Park

Three miles south-west of Bury on the A143, Ickworth House (☎ 01284-735270; NT) is the eccentric creation of the earl of Bristol. It's an amazing structure, with an immense oval rotunda dating back to 1795. It contains a fine collection of furniture, silver and paintings (by Titian, Gainsborough and Velasquez). Outside, there's an unusual Italian garden and a park designed by Capability Brown, with waymarked trails, a deer enclosure and a hide.

Ickworth House opens 1 to 5 pm daily, mid-March to October. The park opens 7 am to 7 pm daily, year round. Admission costs £5.50/2.40 for the house and park, £2.40/80p for the park alone.

First Eastern Counties (☎ 0845-602 0121) runs a twice-daily bus service at 12.35 and 4.10 pm (£1.25) bound for Garboldisham (No 304), leaving from outside Bury train station.

SUFFOLK COAST

This is a coast of great contrasts with traditional seaside resorts such as Lowestoft in the north, the busy port of Felixstowe (now freight only – passenger ferries all go from Harwich) in the south, and some of the least-visited sections of coastline in Britain in-between. It's a coastline that's being gradually whittled away by the sea – the old section of the village of Dunwich now lies underwater. One of the reasons that it's not well visited is that public transport along the coast is non-existent in places.

Aldeburgh
☎ 01728 • pop 2800
The sea is closing in on Aldeburgh, where the beach is now only yards from the village. The place is best known for the Aldeburgh Festival, an annual program of music and the arts that was instigated in 1948 by Benjamin Britten and Peter Pears. It takes place each June in venues around Aldeburgh and at Snape Maltings, 3 miles up the river. It's the most important festival in Eastern England. For information and bookings, phone the box office on ☎ 453543.

The TIC (☎/fax 453637, ⓔ atic@suffolk coastal.gov.uk), on High St, opens 9 am to 5.15 pm daily, Easter to October; 10 am to 4 pm Monday to Saturday the rest of the year.

Blaxhall Youth Hostel (☎ 688206) is 4½ miles from Aldeburgh, near Snape Maltings; beds cost £11/7.75 for adults/under-18s. First Eastern Counties (☎ 0845 602 0121) runs hourly buses between Ipswich and Aldeburgh (£3, one hour and 20 minutes).

Orford
Few visitors get to this little village, 6 miles south of Snape Maltings, but there are several worthwhile attractions. The ruins of **Orford Castle** (☎ 01394-450472) date from the 12th century; only the keep has survived. Run by English Heritage (EH), it opens 10 am to 5 pm daily (shorter hours between November and March). Admission costs £2.50/1.30.

The other draw is gastronomic. From Orford Quay, *MV Lady Florence* (☎ 0831 698298) takes diners on all-inclusive, 2½-hour brunch cruises (9 to 11.30 am) or four-hour lunch or dinner cruises, year round. The brunch cruise costs £18.25 all-inclusive (the menu is fixed), while the lunch and dinner cruises cost £10 per person for the boat plus whatever you choose from the menu: mains cost from £6.95 to £8.75.

Norfolk

The inhabitants of Norfolk have long endured a reputation for living in a dull county, a view popularised by Noel Coward's oft-quoted quip that 'Norfolk is very flat'. For 'dull', though, read 'sleepy', and it is precisely the lack of frenetic activity that makes Norfolk a favourite among those looking for a relaxing holiday. Bird-watchers and their binoculars are attracted by its several nature reserves, while its superb, unspoilt coastlines draw a limited number of tourists eager to escape the cheesy, 'holiday-by-the-sea' feel that has afflicted so many of Britain's beaches. If you're looking for a happening night out on the town you've probably come to the wrong place. Although nightlife has become a lot livelier in Norwich in recent years, it's still not Monte Carlo and that's what's nice about it.

Once a busy wool-producing and trading area, making use of the ports of King's Lynn and Great Yarmouth, Norfolk is now much quieter and less populated than it was in the Middle Ages. Norwich, the county town, is a very pleasant place with an interesting castle and cathedral, as well as the best nightlife in the whole region (bar Cambridge) – due for the most part to the presence of the university, which means that the town is overrun by students. The Norfolk Broads is a network of inland waterways that have long been popular for boating holidays, and King's Lynn is a historic port on the River Ouse, which has several very well-preserved buildings along the waterfront – even though the newer part of town is best described as 'soulless'. The whole area is easily accessible from Cambridge.

WALKING & CYCLING ROUTES
Several waymarked walking trails cross the county, the best known being the Peddars Way (see the Activities chapter earlier). The Weavers Way is a 57-mile walk from Cromer to Great Yarmouth via Blickling and Stalham. The Angles Way follows the valleys of the Waveney and the Little Ouse for 70 miles. The Around Norfolk Walk is a 220-mile trail

linking the Peddars Way, the Norfolk Coast Path, the Weavers Way and the Angles Way. TICs have information leaflets on these walks and on cycle routes. See the Web site at www.visitnorfolk.co.uk.

GETTING AROUND

The county public transport phone line (☎ 01603-613613, ☎ 0845 300 6116) has information on bus routes; there are several operators, the largest being First Eastern Counties (☎ 0845 602 0121).

Norwich, King's Lynn, Cromer and Great Yarmouth are accessible by rail.

NORWICH
☎ 01603 • pop 170,000

Norfolk's county town (pronounced 'nor-ridge') has come a long way since the Middle Ages, when it was bigger than London. Historians and economists may ruefully study the town's golden epoch, when its prosperity was based on trade with the Low Countries, and wonder what exactly went wrong, but to our minds the town seems to have got much of it just right. Although hardly a metropolis (and who needs another metropolis?), there is enough hustle and bustle to give the city an air of genuine

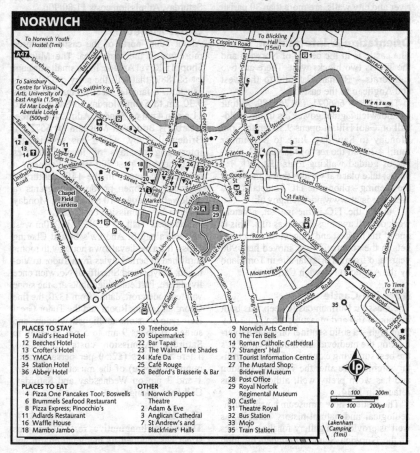

NORWICH

PLACES TO STAY
5 Maid's Head Hotel
12 Beeches Hotel
13 Crofter's Hotel
15 YMCA
34 Station Hotel
36 Abbey Hotel

PLACES TO EAT
4 Pizza One Pancakes Too!; Boswells
6 Brummels Seafood Restaurant
8 Pizza Express; Pinocchio's
11 Adlards Restaurant
16 Waffle House
18 Mambo Jambo

19 Treehouse
20 Supermarket
22 Bar Tapas
23 The Walnut Tree Shades
24 Kafe Da
25 Café Rouge
26 Bedford's Brasserie & Bar

OTHER
1 Norwich Puppet Theatre
2 Adam & Eve
3 Anglican Cathedral
7 St Andrew's and Blackfriars' Halls

9 Norwich Arts Centre
10 The Ten Bells
14 Roman Catholic Cathedral
17 Strangers' Hall
21 Tourist Information Centre
27 The Mustard Shop; Bridewell Museum
28 Post Office
29 Royal Norfolk Regimental Museum
30 Castle
31 Theatre Royal
32 Bus Station
33 Mojo
35 Train Station

prosperity without quite losing its provincial, large-town feel. A healthy dose of visible commercial activity plays its part and the presence of the University of East Anglia on its western outskirts has flooded the city with students, giving it a youthful, vibrant air.

The East Angles had a fortified centre at Norwich that was burnt down twice by marauding Danes. The Normans built the splendid castle keep, now the best-preserved example in the country. Below the castle lies what has been described as the most complete medieval English city. Clustered round the castle and cathedral, within the circle of river and city walls, are more than 30 parish churches.

Orientation & Information

The castle is in the centre of Norwich and the TIC is two blocks west. There are two cathedrals – Roman Catholic to the west and Anglican to the east.

The TIC (☎ 666071, fax 765389, ⊜ tour ism.norwich@gtnet.gov.uk) is in the guildhall on Gaol Hill. It opens 9.30 am to 5 pm Monday to Saturday, June to September (until 4.30 pm the rest of the year). A number of guided walking tours (£2.50/1, 1½ hours) take place at various times, including the evening – phone the TIC for details. The Web site is at www.norwich.gov.uk.

Outside the TIC is the market, a patchwork of stall awnings known as tilts. This is one of the biggest and longest-running markets in the country. It was moved here 900 years ago from its original site in Tombland by the Anglican Norwich Cathedral.

Norwich Castle

The massive Norman castle keep was built in about 1160 and measures 28m square by 21m high – a solid sentinel on the hill overlooking the medieval and modern cities. It's the best surviving example of Norman military architecture after the Tower of London and has worn pretty well, although it was refaced in 1834.

The castle is now a museum housing archaeological and natural-history exhibits, as well as providing a gallery for the paintings of the Norwich School. Founded by John

Crome in the early 19th century, this group, which included John Cotman, painted local landscapes and won acclaim throughout Europe. Also on the premises, in the Shirehall (entrance opposite the Anglia TV station), is the **Royal Norfolk Regimental Museum**, detailing the history of the local regiment since 1830. At the time of writing, Norwich Castle Museum (☎ 493624) is undergoing a substantial refurbishment, courtesy of funds provided by the Millennium Commission, and is due to reopen in the spring of 2001. Call for details. The regimental museum (☎ 493649) opens 10 am to 5 pm Monday to Saturday. Admission costs £1.80/90p.

Other Museums

About 200m north of the castle are three museums in the same area. **The Mustard Shop**, 15 Royal Arcade, has a small museum (☎ 627889) that tells the story of Colman's Mustard, a famous local product. It opens 9.30 am to 5 pm Monday to Saturday and 11 am to 4 pm on Sunday. Admission is free. Nearby is **Bridewell Museum** (☎ 667227), Bridewell Alley, which has surprisingly interesting displays of local industries throughout the past 200 years. Formerly a merchant's house, in the 14th century it served as an open prison for vagrants (a bridewell). It opens 10 am to 5 pm Monday to Saturday. Admission costs £2/1.

Strangers' Hall (☎ 629127) is 250m west of here, along St Andrew's St and Charing Cross. It's a medieval town house with rooms furnished in period styles from Tudor to Victorian. Mayors and Sheriffs of Norwich once lived here. Particular highlights are the stone vaulted undercroft, dating from 1320, the fine Georgian Dining Room and the Tudor Great Hall with its stone-mullioned window and screen. It opens 9 am to 5 pm Monday to Saturday. Admission costs £2.50/1.50. There are tours (£2.50 per person, maximum 15 people) of the museum at 11 am, 1 and 3 pm on Wednesday and Saturday. Call for bookings.

Elm Hill

Thanks to imaginative restoration, this street has retained its medieval charm and atmosphere and is, appropriately enough, the centre of the local antique business. It's one of the most attractive parts of the city. From here walk down Wensum St to Tombland, where the market was originally located. 'Tomb' is an old Norse word for 'empty' – hence space for a market.

Norwich Cathedral

The focal point of the city, the Anglican cathedral has retained the appearance and characteristics of a great Anglo-Norman abbey church more than any other English cathedral except Durham.

The foundation stone was laid in 1096, and the building took 40 years to complete. In 1463 it was made fireproof by means of a magnificent stone lierne vault (a kind of inside roof) which, with its sculpted bosses, is one of the finest achievements of English medieval masonry.

As you enter the cathedral through the western door, the first thing that strikes you is the length of the nave. Its 14 bays are constructed in yellow-beige stone. Above, on the amazing vault, stories from the Old and New Testament are carved into the bosses. Beyond the tower, which is richly patterned, is probably the most beautiful part of the cathedral – the eastern section.

At the eastern end, outside the War Memorial Chapel, is the grave of Edith Cavell, a Norfolk nurse who was shot by the Germans in Belgium during WWI for helping POWs to escape. Her famous last words were, 'I realise patriotism is not enough. I must have no hatred or bitterness towards anyone.'

The cathedral close contains some handsome houses and the old chapel of the King Edward VI School (where Nelson was educated). Its current students make up the choir, which usually performs in at least one of the three services held daily here.

The cathedral (☎ 764385) opens 7.30 am to 7 pm daily (to 6 pm October to April). Admission is free.

Sainsbury Centre for Visual Arts

To the west of the city, on the university campus (a 20-minute bus trip from Castle Meadow), this gallery is remarkable both for the building itself and the art it contains. It was designed by Norman Foster and filled with an eclectic collection of works by Picasso, Moore, Bacon and Giacometti, displayed beside art from Africa, the Pacific and the Americas. It opens 11 am to 5 pm Tuesday to Sunday. Admission costs £2.50/1.25.

Places to Stay

Camping One mile south of the centre by the A146 on Martineau Lane is *Lakenham Camping* (☎ 620060), which charges £4.80 per person (plus £4.30 if you're not a Camping & Caravanning Club member). It opens from Easter through October.

Hostels Two miles from the train station on the western edge of the city is *Norwich Youth Hostel* (☎ 627647, fax 629075, ⓔ norwich@yha.org.uk, 112 Turner Rd). It opens daily from April to October; the rest of the year they run the Rent-a-hostel scheme, which caters to large groups only; phone for information. The nightly charge is £10/6.90 for adults/under-18s, and there are some family rooms with two to six beds.

The *YMCA* (☎ 620269, fax 762151, 48 St Giles St) is in a better location. Singles cost £13.50; dorm beds cost £9. Breakfast is included.

B&Bs & Hotels Most of the B&Bs and cheaper hotels are outside the ring road, along Earlham and Unthank Rds to the west, and around the train station.

The B&Bs along Earlham Rd become more expensive the closer they are to the centre. *Aberdale Lodge* (☎ 502100), at No 211, charges £17 per person in a room with shared bathroom. *EdMar Lodge* (☎ 615599, fax 495599, ⓔ edmar@cwcom.net, 64 Earlham Rd) is an excellent place, with singles/doubles from £26/£34, all with shower.

Still on Earlham Rd, in the shadow of the Roman Catholic cathedral, *Crofter's Hotel* (☎ 613287), at No 2, has 15 rooms for £44.50/59.50, all with bathroom. Next door, at No 4–6, is the comfortable *Beeches Hotel* (☎ 621167, fax 620151, ⓔ reception @beeches.co.uk). Rooms cost from £59/76 to £64/88; there's a lovely garden.

In the train station area, the *Abbey Hotel* (℡/fax 612915, 16 Stracey Rd) charges £19/ 38 with shared bathroom. There are several other places in this area, including the *Station Hotel* (℡ 611064, fax 615161, e station_hotel@norwich.netkonect.co.uk, 5–7 Riverside Rd), with rooms for £30/54.

In the centre is the comfortable and historic *Maid's Head Hotel* (℡ 209955, fax 613688, Tombland), a 700-year-old former coaching inn. Room charges are £91.75/ 120.50 (including breakfast) during the week, £46 per person including breakfast at weekends (minimum two-night stay).

Places to Eat

The large student population ensures that there's a good range of places to eat in town.

For a splurge, there's *Adlard's Restaurant* (℡ 633522, 79 Upper St Giles St) offering classic French cuisine. It opens on Monday for dinner and from Tuesday to Saturday for lunch and dinner; dinner costs £35 for four courses. Alternatively, *Brummels Seafood Restaurant* (℡ 625555, 7 Magdalen St) operates on the 'eat fish, live longer' premise – the catch is always fresh and the prices discreet. There's a two-course menu for £21.95 – pricey but worth it.

In the city centre, *The Walnut Tree Shades* (℡ 620166, Old Post Office Court) is a fabulous little restaurant that is one of Norwich's best-kept secrets; the steak Diane (£11.95) will have carnivores drooling.

There's a branch of *Café Rouge* (℡ 624230, 31 Exchange St) and an excellent *Pizza Express* on St Benedict's St. Almost next door is *Pinocchio's* (℡ 613318), a good Italian place. *Pizza One Pancakes Too!* (℡ 621583, 24 Tombland) is near the Anglican cathedral and does as its name says.

Treehouse (℡ 763258, 14 Dove St), above a health food shop, is an excellent vegetarian restaurant serving such delicacies as nut and moonbeam pate. Main courses come in two sizes – £4.60 and £6.10. It's closed on Sunday.

Bar Tapas (℡ 764077, 18 Exchange St) describes itself as 'the rhythm of South America and the taste of Spain'. Tapas range from £3 to £6; a jug of sangria is £12.50. Two

streets west is the Mexican-Cajun *Mambo Jambo* (℡ 666802, 14–16 Lower Goat Lane). A Jambo Dog with chilli, cheese and coleslaw is £5.95.

The *Waffle House* (℡ 612790, 39 St Giles St) specialises in savoury and sweet Belgian waffles. They range in price from £2.50 to £7 and there's a wide selection of fillings. On some nights a classical guitarist entertains diners.

Kafe Da (℡ 622836, 18 Bedford St) is a trendy new cafe themed around international espionage: the subs are named after Bond movies, the sandwiches after Russian leaders, and everything costs between £4 and £6. Almost opposite is *Bedford's Brasserie & Bar* (℡ 666869, 1 Old Post Office Yard). On the menu are sauteed king prawns with chilli jam and a light puff pastry (£6) – not run-of-the-mill pub grub!

There's a convenient *Tesco Metro* supermarket by the TIC for self-catering.

Entertainment

ArtEast is a useful, free Norfolk listings magazine published bimonthly. You can pick it up in the TIC and in most cafes.

Pubs The wine bar *Boswells* (℡ 629099), on Tombland, has live jazz or blues most nights. Serious beer drinkers should head for the *Adam & Eve* (℡ 667423) on Bishopgate. *The Ten Bells* (℡ 667833, 76 St Benedict's St) is popular with students.

Nightclubs Norwich's club scene is the only one to rival Cambridge in East Anglia. *Mojo* (℡ 622533, 62 Prince of Wales Rd) features soul, breaks, hip hop and R'n'B. It opens until 2 am. Admission costs £3.50. The biggest club in town is the 1700-capacity *Time* (℡ 767649, Norwich Riverside Development) about 1 mile west of town on the Yare. The music is hard house and other dance anthems. It stays open until 2 am and admission between £2 and £5, depending on the night. Trainers, jeans and dressing down are no-nos.

Theatre & Concerts The *Theatre Royal* (℡ 630000, Theatre St) features programs by touring drama and ballet companies. *Norwich Arts Centre (☎ 660352, Reeves Yard, St Benedict's St)* features a wide-ranging program of drama, concerts, dance, cabaret and jazz.

On St George's St, *St Andrew's and Blackfriars' Halls*, once home to Dominican Blackfriars, now serve as an impressive civic centre where concerts, antique and craft markets, the Music and Arts Festival, and even the annual beer festival are held; there's also a cafe in the crypt.

The *Norwich Puppet Theatre (☎ 629921, St James, Whitefriars)* is popular, particularly with children. Tickets cost around £6/4.

Getting There & Away

Cambridge Coach Services (☎ 01223-423900) has four buses per day to Cambridge (£7 single, £8 day return, two hours), and National Express (☎ 0870 580 8080) has a daily bus to Cambridge (£8, two hours) and London (£12.50, three hours). First Eastern Counties runs hourly buses to King's Lynn (£4.70, 1½ hours) and Peterborough (£4.90, two hours 40 minutes); and half-hourly buses to Cromer (£1.90, one hour). There's no bus service to Ely, and for Bury St Edmunds you must change in Diss.

By train, there is a half-hourly service to London (£28.20, two hours); hourly trains to Cambridge (£10.50, two hours), Ely (£9.70, 1¼ hours) and Great Yarmouth (£3.30, ½ hour); and six daily to Cromer (£3.40, 50 minutes).

AROUND NORWICH
Blickling Hall

Anne Boleyn, one of Henry VIII's unfortunate wives, lived in the original Blickling Hall. It's said that on the anniversary of her execution a coach drives up to the house – drawn by headless horses, driven by headless coachmen and containing the queen with her head on her lap.

The current house dates from the early 17th century and is filled with Georgian furniture, pictures and tapestries. There's an impressive Jacobean plaster ceiling in the long gallery. The house is surrounded by parkland offering good walks.

Blickling Hall (☎ 01263-733084; NT) is 15 miles north of Norwich, and opens 1 to 4.30 pm Wednesday to Sunday (plus Tuesday in August), Easter to October. Admission costs £6/3. The gardens open 10.30 am to 5.30 pm Wednesday to Sunday, Easter to October, shorter hours the rest of the year.

Saunder's Coaches (☎ 01692-406020) runs hourly buses here from Norwich from June through the end of August (£1.20, 20 minutes). Aylsham is the nearest train station, 1¾ miles away.

NORFOLK BROADS

The Norfolk Broads is an area of rivers, lakes, marshland, nature reserves and bird sanctuaries in eastern Norfolk. The area, measuring some 117 sq miles, has 'national protected status', which is equivalent to being a national park. Just to make doubly sure that everyone recognises its national value, the government announced in May 2000 that the area is one of a number of protected 'Areas of Outstanding National Beauty'.

A broad is a large piece of water formed by the widening of a river. The main river is the Bure, which enters the Broads at Wroxham and is then joined by several other rivers, including the Ant and the Thurne. The Waveney joins the Yare to meet the Bure at Great Yarmouth, where this large network of rivers flows into the sea. What makes this area special is that all these lakes, rivers and their tributaries are navigable. In all, there are 125 miles of lock-free waterways.

There's little variety of scenery but the ecology of the area means that it's a wonderful place for nature lovers and for people who like being on or near the water. The habitat includes freshwater lakes, slow-moving rivers, water meadows, fens, bogs and saltwater marshes, and the many kinds of birds, butterflies and water-loving plants that inhabit them.

How Hill, a mere 12m above sea level, is the highest place in the Broads. Since there's nothing to impede the path of sea breezes, this is a good area for wind power. Many wind pumps (which look like windmills) were built to drain the marshland and to return the water to the rivers.

The Origin of the Broads

For many years the origin of the Norfolk Broads was unclear. The rivers were undoubtedly natural and many thought the lakes were too – it's hard to believe they're not when you see them – but no one could explain how they could have formed.

The mystery was solved when records were discovered in the remains of St Benet's Abbey (on the River Bure). They showed that from the 12th century certain parts of land in Hoveton Parish were used for peat digging. The area had little woodland and the only source of fuel was peat. Since East Anglia was well populated and prosperous, peat digging became a major industry.

Over a period of about 200 years, approximately 1040 hectares were dug up. However, water gradually seeped through causing marshes, and later lakes, to develop. The first broad to be mentioned in records is Ranworth Broad in 1275. Eventually, the amount of water made it extremely difficult for the diggers and the peat-cutting industry died out. In no other area of Britain has human effort changed the natural landscape so dramatically.

Orientation

The Broads form a triangle with Norwich-Cromer road, the Norwich-Lowestoft road and the coastline as the three sides.

Wroxham, on the A1151 from Norwich, and Potter Heigham, on the A1062 from Wroxham, are the main centres. Along the way there are plenty of waterside pubs, villages and market towns where you can stock up on provisions, and stretches of river where you can feel you are the only person around.

Information

The Broads Authority (☎ 01603-610734), Thomas Harvey House, 18 Colegate, Norwich NR3 1BQ, can give details on conservation centres and RSPB bird-watching hides at Berney Marshes, Ranworth, Bure Marshes, Cockshoot Broad, Hickling Broad, Horsey Mere, How Hill, Strumpshaw Fen and Surlingham Church Marsh.

You can also get information about the Broads from the Norwich TIC. *The Broadcaster* is a visitors' magazine, published annually.

Getting Around

Two companies that operate boating holidays are Blakes (☎ 01603-782911) and Hoseasons (☎ 01502-501010). Costs depend on the boat size, the facilities on the boat, the time of year and the length of the holiday. A boat for two to four people costs £500 to £800 for a week including fuel and insurance. Short breaks (three to four days) during the off season are much cheaper.

Many boat yards (particularly in the Wroxham and Potter Heigham areas) have a variety of boats for hire by the hour, half-day or full day. Charges still vary according to the season and the size of the boat but they start from £10 for one hour, £28 for four hours and £45 for one day.

No previous experience is necessary but remember to stay on the right side of the river, that the rivers are tidal, and to stick to the speed limit – you can get prosecuted for speeding. If you don't feel like piloting your own boat, Broads Tours runs 1½-hour pleasure trips from April to September, with a commentary, for £5.20/3.95 per person. Broads Tours has two bases: The Bridge, Wroxham (☎ 01603-782207), and Herbert Woods, Potter Heigham (☎ 01692-670711).

NORFOLK COAST
Great Yarmouth
☎ 01493 • pop 54,800

One of Britain's more popular seaside resorts, this town has gone the way of so many others and is overrun by tacky amusement arcades, greasy spoon cafes and cheap B&Bs. It's also an important port for the North Sea oil and gas industries.

Despite the dubious attractions of industry and cheesy seaside development, Great Yarmouth does have a couple of genuine lures: a wide, sandy beach and a number of interesting buildings in the old town.

The TIC (☎ 846345, fax 846221) is in the town hall in the centre of town. It opens 9 am to 5 pm Monday to Friday, throughout the year. From Easter to the end of September a second office (☎ 842195) opens on Marine Parade 9.30 am to 5.30 pm daily.

The **Elizabethan House Museum** (☎ 745526), South Quay, was a merchant's house and now contains a display of 19th-century domestic life. It opens 10 am to 5 pm daily except Saturday. Admission is £2/1.50. The **Old Merchant's House** (☎ 857900), Row 111, South Quay, is a group of typical 17th-century town houses. It opens 10 am to 1 pm and 2 to 5 pm daily, April 1 to October 1. Admission costs £1.85/1.40. The **Tolhouse Museum** (☎ 858900), Tolhouse St, was once the town's courthouse and jail; prison cells can be seen and there's a display covering the town's history. The museum (☎ 858900) opens 10 am to 5 pm Monday to Friday and 1.15 to 5 pm at weekends. Admission costs £1.10/90p. There's also a small **maritime museum** on Marine Parade near the TIC. It has the same opening hours and admission prices as the Tollhouse.

There are numerous **B&Bs**, and **Great Yarmouth Youth Hostel** (☎ 843991, 2 Sandown Rd) is three-quarters of a mile from the train station, near the beach. Charges are £9.25/6.50 for adults/under-18s. **Tunstall Camping Barn** (☎ 700279, Manor Farm, Tunstall, Halvergate) is an independent hostel with 20 sleeping platforms in a barn which charges £4 per person. It's about 6 miles from Great Yarmouth, on the Norwich road.

Great Yarmouth has bus and rail routes to Norwich. First Eastern Counties runs an hourly service between Norwich and Great Yarmouth (£2.65, 40 minutes). Wherry Lines runs trains roughly every half hour to Norwich (£4, 25 minutes) every day except Sunday, when there are hourly departures between 8.20 am and 5.20 pm only.

Cromer
☎ 01263 • pop 4500

In the late Victorian and Edwardian eras, Cromer was transformed into the most fashionable resort on the coast. It's now somewhat run-down, but with its elevated seafront, long sandy beach and scenic coastal walks, it's still worth visiting. Cromer has long been famous for its crabs,

and they're still caught and sold here. The TIC (☎ 512497, fax 513613) is by the bus station, and opens 9.30 am to 6 pm Monday to Saturday (until 5 pm on Sunday), July 18 to August 31; 10 am to 5 pm Monday to Saturday, the rest of the year.

Two miles south-west of Cromer, **Felbrigg Hall** (☎ 837444; NT) is one of the finest 17th-century houses in Norfolk. It contains a collection of 18th-century furniture; outside is a walled garden, orangery and landscaped park. It opens 1 to 5 pm daily except Thursday and Friday, Easter to October. Admission costs £5.40/2.10.

Cromer is one of the few coastal resorts with a train station linked to Norwich. There are 13 trains daily Monday to Saturday and six on Sunday (£3.40, 45 minutes).

Cley Marshes
Between Cromer and Wells, Cley Marshes (☎ 740008) is one of the top birdwatching places in Britain, with over 300 species recorded. There's a visitors centre built on high ground to give good views over the area.

Wells-next-the-Sea
☎ 01328 • pop 2400

Set back from the sea, Wells is both a holiday town and a fishing port. It's a pleasant place, with streets of attractive Georgian houses, flint cottages and interesting shops. The TIC (☎ 710885, fax 711405) is on Staithe St. It opens 10 am to 5 pm Monday to Saturday (to 4 pm on Sunday), Easter to mid-July and September to October; and 9.30 am to 6 pm Monday to Saturday (to 5 pm on Sunday), mid-July to the end of August.

Holkham Hall (☎ 710227) is a most impressive Palladian mansion situated in a 1200-hectare deer park 2 miles from Wells. The grounds were designed by Capability Brown. The house opens 1 to 5 pm daily, except Friday and Saturday, from late May to September. Admission is £6/3 and includes the Bygones Museum (a small museum of local folklore and artefacts) and the park.

A narrow-gauge steam railway runs 5 miles to **Little Walsingham**, where there's a Catholic shrine that has been an object of pilgrimage for almost 1000 years.

KING'S LYNN
☎ 01553 • pop 37,500

Only 3 miles from the sea on the River Great Ouse, Lynn (as the locals call it) was one of England's chief ports in the Middle Ages. It was also a natural base for fishing fleets and their crews, and home to a number of religious foundations. The old town is a fascinating mixture of these three elements and Lynn is still a port today, though much less busy than it once was. Away from the port, the modern town is sadly sterile, with the main streets clogged with chain stores and bland architecture.

Orientation & Information
The old town lies along the eastern bank of the river. The train station is on the eastern side of the town. Modern Lynn and the bus station are between them.

The TIC (☎ 763044, fax 777281, e kings-lynn.tic@west-norfolk.gov.uk) is in the Custom House on Purfleet Quay. It opens 9.15 am to 5 pm Monday to Saturday and 10 am to 5 pm on Sunday, April to October; 10.30 am to 4 pm daily the rest of the year.

There are three market days a week – Tuesday (the major market, with everything from clothing to bric-a-brac and fish), Friday (a recent addition with a limited selection of flowers and vegetables) and Saturday (a food market selling fish, fruit, flowers and vegetables). The Tuesday market takes place in the apposity named Tuesday Market Place, while the Friday and Saturday markets are held in Saturday Market Place, in front of St Margaret's Church. The markets are up and running by 8.30 am and usually go on until 4 pm, depending on the weather. In July, there's the popular King's Lynn Festival of Music and the Arts (see that section later).

Walking Tour
This walk takes around 2½ hours. Start in the Saturday Market Place at **St Margaret's** parish church, founded in 1100 with a

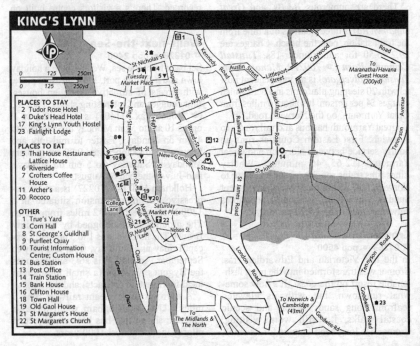

KING'S LYNN

PLACES TO STAY
2 Tudor Rose Hotel
4 Duke's Head Hotel
17 King's Lynn Youth Hostel
23 Fairlight Lodge

PLACES TO EAT
5 Thai House Restaurant;
   Lattice House
6 Riverside
7 Crofters Coffee
   House
11 Archer's
20 Rococo

OTHER
1 True's Yard
3 Corn Hall
8 St George's Guildhall
9 Purfleet Quay
10 Tourist Information
   Centre; Custom House
12 Bus Station
13 Post Office
14 Train Station
15 Bank House
16 Clifton House
18 Town Hall
19 Old Gaol House
21 St Margaret's House
22 St Margaret's Church

To Maranatha/Havana Guest House (200yd)

To Norwich & Cambridge (43mi)

To The Midlands & The North

Benedictine priory. Little remains of the original buildings but the church is impressive for its size (72m long) and contains two Flemish brasses which are among the best examples in the country. By the west door there are flood-level marks – 1976 was the highest but the 1953 flood claimed more lives.

Walk south down Nelson St to see a fine collection of domestic and industrial buildings. Their frontages are 17th and 18th century but their interiors are much older. On the corner of St Margaret's Lane, and dating back to the 15th century, is a restored building that was once the warehouse or 'steelyard' of the Hanseatic League (the Northern European merchants' group). Now known as **St Margaret's House**, it is home to a number of civic offices, including the Education League, the Weights & Measures department and the town registrar. In theory access is restricted to those offices alone, but you can wander in and have a look at the interior. If there's a group of you, you're better off seeking permission by calling ☎ 669200 (the Education League).

Continue north-west on Margaret Plain to College Lane and the former Thoresby College, which was founded in 1508 to house priests and is now the youth hostel (see Places to Stay later). Across Queen St is the **town hall**, dating back to 1421. Next to it, at 45 Queen St, is the **Town House Museum** (☎ 773450). Inside you will find exhibits charting life in the town from the middle ages up to the 1950s. It opens 10 am to 5 pm Monday to Saturday (from 2 pm on Sunday), May to October and 10 am to 4 pm Monday to Saturday the rest of the year. Admission costs £1.80/1.40.

Next door, the **Old Gaol House** (☎ 774297) has been converted into a tourist attraction with self-guided audio tours. The town's priceless civic treasures, including the 650-year-old King John Cup, can be seen in the basement. It opens 10 am to 5 pm daily (last entry at 4.15 pm), Easter to October (same hours, Friday to Tuesday the rest of the year). Admission costs £2.40/1.75.

Continuing down Queen St you pass **Clifton House**, with its quirky barley-sugar columns and waterfront tower, which was used by merchants scanning the river for returning ships. Its interior is in dire need of restoration so access is restricted to groups organised by the TIC. Walk down the lane to the river past the sturdy, red floodgates. The stately Bank House is on your right. Opposite the square is **Purfleet Quay**, in its heyday the principal harbour. The quaint building with the lantern tower is the **Custom House** (housing the TIC), which dates back to 1683.

Turn into King St, where the second medieval town begins. It was planned in the latter half of the 12th century and had its own church, guildhall, market and friary. There are many interesting buildings in King St, especially on the left-hand (western) side, where the wealthier merchants built their homes and warehouses on reclaimed land. **St George's Guildhall** (☎ 767557; NT) is the largest surviving 15th-century guildhall in England. It has served as a warehouse, theatre, courthouse and armoury (during the Civil War), and now contains art galleries, a theatre, restaurant and coffee house. This is the focal point of the annual King's Lynn festival.

At the end of King St is the spacious **Tuesday Market Place**, which fulfils its original role once a week. It's bordered with old buildings, including the Corn Hall (1854) and the Duke's Head Hotel (1689).

Walk diagonally across the Tuesday Market Place and turn right into St Nicholas St to reach the **Tudor Rose Hotel**, a late-15th-century house with some very interesting features, including the original main door. North of here, on the corner of St Ann's St, is **True's Yard**, where the two remaining cottages of the 19th-century fishing community that used to be here have been restored and now house a folk museum (☎ 770479) detailing the life of a shellfish fisherman around 1850. It opens 9.30 am to 3.45 pm daily (closed for Christmas week). Admission costs £1.90/1.50.

Return to Chapel St and on the corner of Market Lane is an attractive building known as **Lattice House** – dating from the 15th century, it now houses a restaurant and is a good place to stop.

King's Lynn Festival of Music & the Arts

Celebrating its 50th anniversary in 2000, the King's Lynn Festival (the brainchild of Lady Ruth Fermoy) offers a diverse program of concerts and recitals of all kinds of music, from medieval ballads to Jamaican Jazz. It usually takes place in the last week of July. For details of programmed events, call the administrative office at ☎ 767557 (fax 767688, ⓔ enquiries@kl-festival.freeserve.co.uk) or the box office at ☎ 764864. There is a Web site at www.kl-festival.freeserve.co.uk.

Places to Stay

Excellently located, *King's Lynn Youth Hostel (☎ 772461, Thoresby College, College Lane)* is open fully from 1 July to 31 August and haphazardly outside that time – call for details. A bed costs £9.25/6.50 for adults/under-18s.

Maranatha/Havana Guest House (☎ 774596, fax 763747, 115–117 Gaywood Rd) are two former guest houses now joined into one under the same proprietors. It offers budget accommodation from £15 per person, while a double room costs £36 (£40 with a bathroom).

Fairlight Lodge (☎ 762234, fax 770280, 79 Goodwins Rd) is a comfortable guesthouse with seven rooms, four with a bathroom, which charges £25/40 for a single/double with bathroom and £20/34 without.

Tudor Rose Hotel (☎ 762824, fax 764894, ⓔ kltudorrose@aol.com, St Nicholas St) is a 15th-century house. B&B costs from £35/60.

The town's top hotel is *Duke's Head Hotel (☎ 774996, fax 763556, Tuesday Market Place)*, a fine classical building overlooking the market. Rooms cost £79/95; there are also special weekend deals at £42 per person, per night including breakfast, £52 including dinner.

Places to Eat

Pub grub at *Tudor Rose Hotel* (see Places to Stay earlier) is good value. At the *Thai House Restaurant (☎ 767397)*, in Lattice House at the corner of Chapel St and Market Lane, you'll get a good selection of Thai dishes. It is also a popular pub.

If you're looking for something more up-market there are two very good options. *Riverside (☎ 773134)* is right by the river, near the undercroft. Main courses range from £6.50 to £18. Opposite St Margaret's Church is the excellent *Rococo (☎ 771483, 11 Saturday Market Place)*. A two-course lunch costs £9.95 and set dinners range from £22.50 to £32.50.

Archer's (☎ 769177, Purfleet St), open Monday to Saturday, is a pleasant, friendly place; many dishes are between £4 and £5.50 and there's a good range of coffees.

There are several places for teas or light meals. *Crofters Coffee House (King St)*, in the guildhall undercroft at the Arts Centre, is recommended. It opens 9.30 am to 5 pm Monday to Saturday.

Getting There & Away

King's Lynn is 43 miles north of Cambridge on the A10.

First Eastern Counties runs an hourly bus service to Norwich (£4.35, 1½ hours) Monday to Saturday; on Sundays the service runs every two hours from 8.25 am with the last bus at 6.55 pm.

There are hourly trains from Cambridge (£6.90, 50 minutes).

AROUND KING'S LYNN
Rising Castle

The amazingly well-preserved 12th-century keep of this castle (☎ 01553-631330; EH) is set in the middle of a massive earthwork. It was once the home of Queen Isabella, who arranged the murder of her husband Edward II. It opens 10 am to 6 pm daily (4 pm November to March). Admission costs £3.25/1.60. First Eastern Counties (☎ 0845 602 0121) bus No 411 runs here (£1.40, 19 minutes) every hour from King's Lynn bus station, 6 miles to the south.

Sandringham

The Queen's country pile is set in 25 hectares of landscaped gardens and lakes, and it's open to the hoi polloi when the court is not in residence. The house was bought by Queen Victoria in 1862 and the royal family still spends three weeks here from mid-July to early August. The museum contains a collection of vintage cars and other royal trinkets.

Sandringham (☎ 01553-772675) opens 11 am to 4.45 pm daily, April to September (except when the royal family is here). Admission costs £5.50/3.50 (£4.50/3 if you only want to see the grounds and museum). First Eastern Counties bus No 411 (which also goes to Castle Rising Castle) run here from King's Lynn bus station (£1.80, 25 minutes), 10 miles south-west.

Houghton Hall

Built for Sir Robert Walpole in 1730, Houghton Hall (☎ 01485-528569) in the Palladian style is worth seeing for the ornate state rooms alone. It's 14 miles northeast of King's Lynn and opens 1 to 5.30 pm Thursday and Sunday only (last admission 5 pm), Easter to September. Admission costs £6/3.

Unfortunately, the house is not served by public transportation; if you don't have your own wheels you'll have to get here from King's Lynn by taxi, which should cost between £10 and £12. A reputable service in King's Lynn is Ken's Taxis (☎ 01553-766166).

Cambridgeshire

For most visitors, there is only one reason to come to Cambridgeshire: to walk and poke around the hallowed cobbled streets of one of the world's most famous university towns. In the south of the county, Cambridge sits on a bend in the River Cam at the edge of the fens – the flat, fertile, once-submerged region that covers the rest of the county.

The lack of hills makes this excellent cycling country. A towpath winds all the way from Cambridge to Ely (15 miles) where the superb cathedral, on ground slightly higher than the surrounding plain, is known as the 'ship of the fens'. In the north of the county there's another fine cathedral at Peterborough, which carries the questionable title of England's shopping capital.

GETTING AROUND

Public transport centres on Cambridge. Rather than phoning the costly council transport helpline (☎ 0891-910910, 50p per minute), get the useful *Cambridgeshire and Peterborough Passenger Transport Map* and contact the bus companies directly.

The main bus companies operating in the area are Stagecoach Cambus (☎ 01223-423554) between Cambridge, Ely and Bury St Edmunds; Cambridge Coach Services (☎ 01223-423900) from Cambridge to Norwich; and Stagecoach United Counties (☎ 01604-620077) from Cambridge to Huntingdon and Peterborough.

Cambridge is only 55 minutes by rail from London. This line continues north through Ely to terminate at King's Lynn in Norfolk. From Ely, branch lines run east through Norwich, and south-east into Suffolk.

CAMBRIDGE

☎ 01223 • pop 88,000

Writing in praise of Oxford, 19th-century essayist (and Oxford graduate) William Hazlitt wrote that 'Cambridge lies out of the way, on one side of the world'. When you consider that this town only 55 minutes from London, is home to unquestionably one of the great universities of the world, Hazlitt's comment speaks volumes about the rivalry that exists between the two universities, even though today the public rivalry is largely restricted to an annual boat race on the Thames. Cambridge is an extraordinary place: with over 60 Nobel prizewinners, it is at the top of the research league in British universities; it owns a prestigious publishing firm and a world-renowned examination syndicate; it is the leading centre for astronomy in Britain; its Fitzwilliam Museum contains an outstanding art collection; and its library is used by scholars from around the world.

It is hardly surprising that there is a fierce rivalry between the two cities and the two universities, and a futile debate over which is best and most beautiful. If you can, visit both. Oxford is bigger, busier and draws more tourists, so if you only have time for one, choose Cambridge. Its trump card is the choir

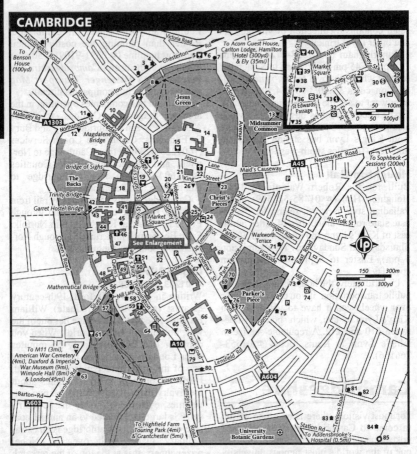

CAMBRIDGE

and chapel of King's College, which should not be missed by any visitor to Britain.

Cambridge's position and lack of heavy industry gives it a rural flavour, but Cambridge is hardly rustic. A busy market town brimming with history and antiquity, Cambridge is in the process of upgrading itself for the 21st century. Its streets are lined with elegant designer shops and fancy boutiques and there is no shortage of overpriced continental-style cafes and trendy restaurants, all clamouring for a share of Cool Britannia's bulging wallet. Yet it is Cambridge's tranquil, ageless appearance which is hardest to match, and which the visitor will remember best.

History

Neolithic tools and weapons (circa 3000 BC), and ancient burial grounds have been found around Cambridge. There is also an Iron Age fort, Wandlebury, in the Gog Magog hills nearby. In AD 43, when the Romans needed a road from Colchester to Godmanchester, the River Cam was forded just below Magdalene Bridge and a fort was built on the small hill overlooking it.

The camp became a town, and trading took

CAMBRIDGE

PLACES TO STAY
1 Antony's Guest House
2 Belle Vue Guest House
3 Arundel House Hotel
4 Aaron House
58 Garden House (Moat Hotel)
69 University Arms Hotel
71 Warkworth House
75 YMCA
80 Lensfield Hotel
81 Cambridge Youth Hostel; Six Steps Guest House
83 Tenison Towers Guest House
84 Sleeperz

PLACES TO EAT
6 Twenty-two
12 Michel's Brasserie
13 Midsummer House
23 Efe's Restaurant
26 Clowns
27 Tatties
35 No 1 King's Parade; The Eagle Pub
36 Rainbow
37 Nadia's (King's Parade)
54 Fitzbillies
56 Nadia's (Silver St)
62 Choices Café
65 Browns

67 The Dôme
70 Hobb's Pavilion
76 The Depot
78 Shalimar Restaurant

PUBS, BARS & CLUBS
5 Boathouse
9 Rat & Parrot
15 Po Na Na
19 Fez
28 Fifth Avenue
40 Bar Ha! Ha!
61 Granta (& Punt Hire)

OTHER
7 Laundrette
8 Cambridge River Cruises
10 Magdalene College
11 Kettle's Yard
14 Jesus College
16 Round Church
17 St John's College
18 Trinity College
20 American Express
21 Westcott
22 All Saints Church
24 Bus Station (Drummer Street)
25 Christ's College
29 Abbey National (Bank)
30 Thomas Cook
31 Post Office
32 International Telecom Centre

33 Tourist Information Centre
34 Arts Theatre
38 Heffers Bookshop
39 Great St Mary's Church
41 Gonville & Caius College
42 Trinity Punts
43 Trinity Hall College
44 Clare College
45 Senate House
46 King's College Chapel
47 King's College
48 Queens' College
49 St Catherine's College
50 Corpus Christi College
51 St Benet's Church
52 Corn Exchange
53 Pembroke College
55 Ben Hayward Cycles
57 Scudamore's Punt Hire
59 Little St Mary's Church
60 Peterhouse College
63 Cambridge Recycles
64 Fitzwilliam Museum
66 Downing College
68 Emmanuel College
72 Police Station
73 Mike's Bikes
74 CB1
77 HSBC (Bank)
79 Sub Post Office
82 Geoff's Bike Hire
85 Train Station

place by road and river. In the 5th century the Romans withdrew and there followed a series of invasions from Europe – first by the Anglo-Saxons, who didn't do much to develop the town: Ely monks in the 7th century described it as 'desolate'. It was kick-started back into life in the 9th century by the Norse/Danish invaders, who were great traders.

Next, in 1066, came the Normans who replaced the fort with a castle (now a mere mound on Castle Hill) in order to campaign against the bold Saxon leader Hereward the Wake, who lurked in the marshy fens round Ely. The 1086 *Domesday Book* records 400 'burgesses' (full citizens) in Cambridge.

In 1209 the university town of Oxford exploded in a riot between scholars and townspeople, with the result that three students were hanged. A number of them decided

enough was enough, packed their books and arrived in Cambridge to found the nucleus of a new university. The facts surrounding the foundation are a little hazy, undoubtedly due to another riot in 1261 between 'town and gown', when the university records were burnt. At the rioters' trial, the judges ruled in favour of the students, setting a precedent that would last for centuries. The new university had found favour with the law and began to establish a firm footing within the town.

The collegiate system, unique to Oxford and Cambridge, came into being gradually with the first college, Peterhouse, founded in 1284 by Hugh de Balsham (later bishop of Ely). The plan was for tutors and students to live together in a community, much as they would in a monastery.

From the 14th century onwards, a series

of colleges was founded by royalty, nobility, leading church figures, statesmen, academics and trade guilds – all for men only. In 1869 and 1871, however, women were finally accorded the right to study here with the founding of women-only Girton and Newnham colleges – although they had to wait until 1948 before they were allowed to graduate. Gender integration has come a long way since then, today 29 of the 31 colleges are co-educational with two choosing to maintain their 'women-only' status.

Orientation

The colleges and university buildings comprise the centre of the city – like Oxford, Cambridge has no campus. The central area, lying in a wide bend of the River Cam, is easy to get around on foot or by bike. The best-known section of the Cam is the Backs, which combines lush river scenery with superb views of six colleges, including King's College Chapel. The other 25 colleges are scattered throughout the city.

The bus station is in the centre on Drummer St, but the train station is a 20-minute walk to the south. Sidney St – which becomes St Andrew's St to the south and Bridge and Magdalene Sts to the north – is the main shopping street.

Information

The TIC (☎ 322640, fax 457588, ℮ tourism@cambridge.gov.uk), Wheeler St, opens 10 am to 6 pm Monday to Friday, to 5 pm on Saturday and 11 am to 4 pm on Sunday, April to October, and 10 am to 5.30 pm Monday to Saturday, the rest of the year. It organises walking tours (☎ 457574 for information) at 1.30 pm every day, year round, with more from May to September. Group sizes are limited so buy your ticket in advance. Tours costs £7 and include King's College; £6 if King's College is closed, in which case the tour includes St John's College. The TIC's Web site is at www.cambridge.gov.uk.

The University of Cambridge The university has three eight-week terms: Michaelmas (October to December), Lent (mid-January to mid-March) and Easter (mid-April to mid-June). Exams are held from mid-May to mid-June. There's general mayhem for the 168 hours following exams – the so-called May Week. Most colleges are closed to visitors for the Easter term and all are closed for exams. Precise details of opening hours vary from college to college and year to year, so contact the TIC for up-to-date information. Five colleges (King's, Queen's, Clare, Trinity and St John's) charge admission to tourists (£1.20 to £3.50). You may, however, find that tourists are now denied admission at some of the colleges described in this section. Each year more colleges decide that the tourist bandwagon is just too disruptive. For all university-related enquiries, call the university's central office at ☎ 337733.

Post & Communications The main post office (☎ 323325) is at 9–11 St Andrew's St. It opens 9 am to 5.30 pm Monday to Saturday. To collect email or make cheap international phone calls go to the International Telecom Centre (☎ 357358) directly opposite the TIC. It opens 9 am to 10 pm daily. CB1 (☎ 576306), 32 Mill Rd, is an internet cafe with nine terminals and walls are stacked with second-hand books. Access costs £3 per hour. It opens 10 am to 8 pm daily.

Money There are plenty of banks with ATMs around the city centre. Abbey National (☎ 350495) has a branch at 60 St Andrew's St and HSBC (☎ 314822) is at 75 Regent St. American Express (☎ 345203) is at 25 Sidney St. It opens 9 am to 5.30 pm Monday to Friday (to 5 pm on Saturday). Thomas Cook (☎ 543100) is at 8 St Andrew's St. It is open 9 am to 5.30 pm Monday to Saturday except Wednesday, when it opens at 10 am.

Laundry The Cleanomat Dry Cleaners (☎ 464719) is at 10 Victoria Ave, just north of the bridge and near Chesterton Rd. You can drop off your laundry or do it yourself.

Walking Tour One

This three-hour walk visits King's College Chapel and the most central colleges, and includes a stretch along the river.

From the TIC, walk west to King's Parade, turn right and continue north to **Great St Mary's Church** (☎ 741716) on Senate House Hill. This university church, built between 1478 and 1519 in the late-Gothic perpendicular style, has a feeling of space and light inside thanks to its clerestory, wide arch and wood carving. The traditional termly university sermons are preached here. To get your bearings, climb the 123 steps of the tower (£1.75) for a good view of the city. The building across King's Parade, on the right-hand side of the square, is the **Senate House**, designed in 1730 by James Gibbs. It's the most beautiful example of pure classical architecture in the city; graduations are held here.

Gonville & Caius Now walk onto Trinity St, head north, and turn left into the first gateway to reach this fascinating old college (☎ 332400). It was founded twice, first by a priest called Gonville, in 1347, and then again by Dr Caius (pronounced keys), a brilliant physician and scholar, in 1557. Of special interest here are the three gates: Virtue, Humility and Honour. They symbolise the progress of the good student, since the third gate (the *Porta Honoris*, a fascinating confection with a quirky dome and sundials) leads to the Senate House and thus graduation. Walk through the gate, turn right, then left, to reach King's College Chapel.

King's College Chapel All the college chapels are individually remarkable but King's College Chapel is supreme in its grandeur. It's one of the finest examples of Gothic architecture in England and is comparable with Chartres.

The chapel was conceived as an act of piety by the young Henry VI and dedicated to the Virgin Mary. Its foundation stone was laid by the king in 1446 and building was completed around 1516. Henry VI's successors, notably Henry VIII, glorified the interior (and themselves in doing so). Services are led by its choir, originally choristers from Eton College, another of Henry VI's foundations. The choir's Festival of the Nine Lessons and Carols on Christmas Eve is heard all over the world.

Enter through the southern porch. Despite the original stained-glass windows, the atmosphere inside is light. Cromwell's soldiers destroyed many church windows in East Anglia but it is believed that, having been a Cambridge student, their leader spared King's.

The stunning interior of 12 bays is about 11m wide, 22m high and 80m long. This vast expanse is the largest in the world canopied by fan vaulting. It's the work of John Wastell, and is a miracle of beauty and skill. Upon seeing it, Christopher Wren reputedly stated that he could have built it but only if someone had shown him where to set the first stone.

The elaborate carvings, both in wood and stone, include royal coats of arms, intertwined initials, the royal beasts of heraldry, and flowers that were the emblems of Tudor monarchs and related families. Among the Yorkist roses on the western wall is one containing the figure of a woman. Some claim she is Elizabeth of York but it's more likely that she's the Virgin Mary.

The antechapel and the choir are divided by the superbly carved **wooden screen**, another gift from Henry VIII. Designed and executed by the king's master carver Peter Stockton, the screen bears Henry's initials entwined with those of Anne Boleyn, who supposedly inspired Henry's act of generosity. Almost concealed by the mythical beasts and symbolic flowers is one angry human face: perhaps it is Stockton's jest for posterity?

Originally constructed between 1686 and 1688, the magnificent organ has been rebuilt and developed over the years, and its pipes now top the screen on which they rest.

The **choir stalls** were made by the same craftsman who worked on the screen but the canopies are Carolingian. Despite the dark wood, the impression is still of lightness as one approaches the **high altar**, which is framed by Rubens' *Adoration of the Magi* and the magnificent east window.

The excellent **Chapel Exhibition** is in the northern side chapels, to the left of the altar. Here, you can see the stages and methods of building the chapel set against the historical panorama from inception to completion. On display are costumes, paintings, illuminated manuscripts and books, plans, tools and scale models, including a full-size model showing how the fan vaulting was constructed.

Admission costs £3.50/2.25. The vergers are helpful with information and there are occasional guided tours at the weekend. Weekday tours can be arranged at the TIC. King's College Chapel (☎ 331100) comes alive when the choir sings; even the most pagan heavy-metal fan will find **Choral Evensong** an extraordinary experience. Evensong is at 5.30 pm, Tuesday to Saturday (men's voices only on Wednesday, a capella on Friday) and there are two services on Sunday, at 10.30 am and 3.30 pm. There are services from mid-January to mid-March, mid-April to mid-June, mid-July to late July, early October to early December and on 24 and 25 December.

Trinity College From King's College Chapel, return to King's Parade and follow it north into Trinity St; the entrance to Trinity College (☎ 338400) is on the left opposite Heffers bookshop. Henry VIII founded Trinity in 1546 but it was left to Dr Nevile, Master of Trinity (1593–1615) in Elizabeth's reign, to fulfil his wishes, as Henry died six weeks later.

As you walk through the impressive brick gateway (1535), have a look at the statue of Henry that adorns it. His left hand holds a golden orb, while his right grips a table leg, put there by students who removed the golden sceptre years ago. As you enter the **Great Court**, scholastic humour gives way to a gaping sense of awe, for it is the largest of its kind in the world. The place is literally dripping with history: to the right of the entrance is a small tree, planted in the 1950s and reputed to be a descendant of the apple tree made famous by Trinity alum Sir Isaac Newton.

The square is also the scene of the run made famous by the film *Chariots of Fire* – 380 yds in 43 seconds (the time it takes the clock to strike 12). Although plenty of students have a go, Harold Abrahams (the hero of the film) never actually attempted it and

his fictional run wasn't even filmed here. If you fancy your chances remember that you'll need Olympian speed to even come close to making it in time (we tried and failed miserably!).

The Gothic antechapel to the right of the gate is full of huge statues of famous Trinity men, such as Tennyson and Newton. The vast hall has a hammerbeam roof and lantern. Beyond the hall are the cloisters of Nevile's Court and the dignified **Wren Library**, complete with 55,000 books printed before 1820 and over 2500 manuscripts, including AA Milne's original *Winnie the Pooh*. Both he and his son Christopher Robin were graduates. The library opens to visitors noon till 2 pm Monday to Friday and (during term) 10.30 am to 12.30 pm on Saturday. It is certainly worth visiting, though you may have to queue. Admission to the college costs £1.75.

Along the Backs Walk out of the cloisters and turn right to look at St John's New Court on the western bank. It's a 19th-century residence block connected with the rest of **St John's College** by two bridges: Kitchen Bridge and the **Bridge of Sighs** (built in 1831, a replica of the original in Venice). Cross Trinity Bridge and turn left, following the footpath until you come to Garret Hostel Bridge. Pause on top to watch the punts below and look upstream to the bridge at **Clare College**. It's ornamented with decorative balls and is the oldest (1639), most interesting bridge on the Backs. Its architect was paid the grand total of 15p for his design so, feeling aggrieved at such a measly fee, he cut a slice out of one of the balls adorning the balustrade (the next to last one on the left) thus ensuring that the bridge would never be 'complete'. Or so the story goes. Walk on, then turn right into Trinity Hall.

Trinity Hall This is a delightfully small college (☎ 332500), wedged among the great and the famous. Despite the name, it has nothing to do with Trinity College. It was founded in 1350 as a refuge for lawyers and clerics escaping the ravages of the

When I was a Student...

Admittance to any of Cambridge's colleges carries with it a heavy burden of responsibility. The academic standards are among the highest in the world, and every achievement by modern-day students struggles to escape the long shadows cast by the luminaries of yesteryear. In addition, students must strike a precarious balance between their studies and the other great responsibility of one's college years: having a good time, getting drunk and getting to as many good parties as possible.

Yet it was not always so. In the 15th century the life of a student was far less hedonistic, even bordering on the monastic. A typical day began at 4.45 am and was followed by prayers for the health and welfare of the monarch. By 5 am the all-male student body was expected in the college chapel for morning worship; lectures began at 6 am with the 'explanation of texts' delivered by a senior academic. At 9 am there was a 'disputation', whereby two students would debate a prepared topic using logic. Lunch was at 11 am, after which students studied until 6 pm. After dinner, they were allowed one hour of free time and were in bed by 8 pm, but only after praying once more for the king (or queen).

Rules were strictly enforced. Students were not permitted to go to town unsupervised, nor were they allowed into taverns. They couldn't play games, keep a pet, or attend the theatre. If they broke any rules, they were punished by no food, beatings and – in extreme cases – expulsion. On the bright side, education was free (but then again, so is prison).

Black Death, thus earning it the nickname of the 'Lawyers' College'. You enter through the newest court, which overlooks the river on one side and has a lovely Fellows' garden on another. Walking into the next court, you pass the 16th-century library, which has original Jacobean reading desks and books chained to the shelves to prevent their permanent removal – the 16th century's equivalent of electronic bar codes.

Old Schools As you walk out of the first court, you'll see a tall, historic gate, which receives little attention. It's the entry to Old Schools, the administrative centre of the university. The lower part dates back to 1441 and the upper section was added in the 1860s. You are now back in the heart of the university.

Walking Tour Two

This walk visits Christ's College, Jesus College, the Round Church and Magdalene College. The walk should take about two hours and you could continue afterwards to see the Kettle's Yard art gallery. Start outside Christ's, on the corner of St Andrew's and Hobson Sts. Christ's only opens to visitors 10.30 am to 12.30 pm and 2 to 4 pm, so plan your walk accordingly.

Christ's College Christ's (☎ 334900) was founded in 1505 by that pious and generous benefactress, Lady Margaret Beaufort, who also founded St John's. It has an impressive entrance gate emblazoned with heraldic carving. The figure of the founder stands in a niche, hovering over all like a guiding spirit. Note the stout oak door leading into First Court, which has an unusual circular lawn, magnolias and wisteria creepers. The court is a mixture of original buildings and 18th-century facings and windows. The hall was rebuilt in neo-Gothic style last century and the chapel's early sections include an oriel window which enabled the founder to join in services from her 1st-floor room.

The Second Court has an interesting Fellows' building, dating back to 1643. Its gate leads into a Fellows' garden, which contains a mulberry tree under which Milton (who came up to the college in 1628) reputedly wrote *Lycidas*. Continuing through Iris Court you're confronted by the stark, grey, modern students' block, which seems totally out of place. Look at the little theatre tucked into the right-hand corner, then walk out past New Christ's into Hobson St; turn right, then left and right into Jesus Lane. You'll pass Westcott, another theological college (not part of the university), then All Saints

Church – dubbed St Op's (St Opposite) by Jesus students. Charles Darwin studied here.

Jesus College The approach to Jesus (☎ 339339), founded 1496, via the long 'chimney' is impressive, as is the main gate, which is under a rebus of the founder, Bishop Alcock. A rebus is a heraldic device suggesting the name of its owner: the bishop's consists of several cockerels. The spacious First Court, with its red-brick ranges, is open on the western side – an unusual feature.

The best parts of Jesus are the tiny, intimate cloister court to your right and the chapel, which dates back to the St Radegund nunnery. The bishop closed the nunnery, expelled the nuns for misbehaving and founded the new college in its place.

The chapel is inspiring and reflects Jesus' development over the centuries. It has a Norman arched gallery from the nunnery building, a 13th-century chancel and beautiful restoration work and Art Nouveau by Pugin, Morris (ceilings), Burne-Jones (stained glass) and Madox Brown.

The other buildings in Jesus are rather an anticlimax but the extensive grounds, which include a cricket pitch, are pleasant to walk through.

Round Church Turn right out of Jesus College, go up Jesus Lane, turn right into Park St and left into Round Church St. At the top of this street is the amazing Round Church, or Church of the Holy Sepulchre (☎ 518219). It was built in 1130 to commemorate its namesake in Jerusalem and is one of only four in England. It's strikingly unusual, with chunky, round Norman pillars that encircle the small nave. The rest of the church was added later in a different style; the conical roof dates from just the 19th century. No longer a parish church, it's now a brass-rubbing centre. Depending on the size of the brasses, this costs from £4 to £22. The Brass Rubbing Centre (☎ 07831 839261) opens 10 am to 6pm daily in summer, 1 to 4 pm daily in winter.

Magdalene College Turn right down Bridge St. It was around Magdalene Bridge that the Romans built the bridge that marked the origins of Cambridge. Boats laden with cargo tied up and unloaded where the block of flats now stands on the river bank. Facing you across the river is Magdalene (pronounced 'mawd-lin'), which you enter from Magdalene St.

Originally a Benedictine hostel, the college (☎ 332100) was refounded in 1542 by Lord Audley. It has the dubious honour of being the last college to allow women students; when they were finally admitted in 1988, male students wore black armbands and flew the college flag at half-mast.

Its river setting gives it a certain appeal but its greatest asset is the Pepys Library, housing the magnificent collection of books the famous diarist bequeathed to his old college – he was a student here 1650–53.

Walking Tour Three

Taking in the colleges just to the south of the centre, including Corpus Christi, Queen's and Emmanuel, this walk takes about two and a half hours.

Corpus Christi From King's Parade, turn into Bene't (short for Benedict) St to see the oldest structure in Cambridgeshire – the Saxon tower of the Franciscan Church of St Bene't (☎ 353903), built in 1025. The rest of the church is newer but full of interesting features. The round holes above the belfry windows were designed to offer owls nesting privileges; their services were valued as mice-killers. It was here in 1670 that parish clerk Fabian Stedman invented change-ringing (the ringing of bells with different peals in a sequential order). The church also has a bible that belonged to Thomas Hobson, owner of a nearby livery stable who insisted that customers renting a horse take the one nearest the door because that had rested longest – hence the term 'Hobson's choice', meaning no choice at all.

The church served as chapel to Corpus Christi (☎ 338000), next door, until the 16th century when the college built its own. There's an entrance to the college leading into Old Court, which has been retained in its medieval form and still exudes a monastic atmosphere. The door to the chapel is flanked by two statues; on the right is Matthew Parker, who was college Master in 1544 and archbishop of Canterbury for much of the reign of Elizabeth I. A pretty bright lad, Mr Parker was known for his curiosity, and his endless questioning gave us the term 'nosy parker'. Christopher Marlowe was a Corpus man, as a plaque, next to a fascinating sundial, bears out. New Court, beyond, is a 19th-century creation.

The college library has the finest collection of Anglo-Saxon manuscripts in the world which, with other valuable books, were preserved from destruction at the time of Henry VIII's dissolution of the monasteries.

Queens' College Queens, one of the Backs' colleges, was the first Cambridge college to charge admission – now £1.20. This was initiated to pay for soundproofing its vulnerable site on this busy street. It takes its name from the two queens who founded it – Margaret of Anjou (wife of Henry VI) and Elizabeth of Woodville (wife of Edward IV), in 1448 and 1465 respectively – yet it was a conscientious rector of St Botolph's Church who was its real creator.

The college's (☎ 335511) main entrance is off Queens' Lane. The red-brick gate tower and Old Court, which immediately capture your attention, are part of the medieval college. So is Cloister Court, the next court, with its impressive cloister and picturesque, half-timbered President's Lodge (President is the name for the Master). The famous Dutch scholar and reformer Erasmus lodged in the tower from 1510 to 1514. He wasn't particularly enamoured of Cambridge: he thought the wine tasted like vinegar, the beer was slop and the place was too expensive, but he did write that the local women were good kissers. The Cam is outside Cloister Court, and is crossed by the wooden Mathematical Bridge which brings you into the 20th-century Cripps Court.

Peterhouse College Founded in 1284 by Hugh de Balsham, later Bishop of Ely, this is the oldest and smallest of the colleges (☎ 338200). It stands to the west of Trump-

ington St, just south of the Church of St Mary the Less (better known as Little St Mary's). St Peter's-without-Trumpington-Gate was the church's original odd-sounding name (because it stood outside, or 'without', the old gate) and it gave the college its name. Inside is a memorial to Godfrey Washington, an alum of the college and a great-uncle of George Washington. His family coat of arms was the stars and stripes, the inspiration for the US flag. A walk through Peterhouse gives you a clear picture of the 'community' structure of a Cambridge college though, unusually, the Master's house is opposite the college, not within it. The college's list of notable alumni includes the poet Thomas Grey, who came up in 1742, and Henry Cavendish, the first person to measure the density of water. He also calculated the weight of the planet: if you must know, Earth weighs six thousand million million tonnes.

First Court, the oldest, is small, neat and bright, with hanging baskets and window boxes. The 17th-century chapel is on the right, built in a mixture of styles which blend well. Inside, the luminous 19th-century stained-glass windows contrast with the older eastern window.

The Burrough range, on the right, is 18th century and the hall, on the left, a restored, late-13th-century gem. Beyond the hall are sweeping grounds extending to the Fitzwilliam Museum. Bearing right, you enter a court with an octagonal lawn, beyond which are the library, theatre and First Court.

Pembroke College Pembroke (☎ 338100) has several courts linked by lovely gardens and lawns. It was founded in 1347 by Marie de St Pol de Valence, the widowed countess of Pembroke. At 17 she had married the 50-year-old earl, but he was killed in a joust on their wedding day, making her 'maid, wife and widow all in one day'. As usual, the oldest court is at the entrance. It still retains some medieval corner sections. The chapel, on the extreme right, is an early Wren creation (1665): his uncle Mathew Wren, bishop of Ely, had spent 18 years imprisoned in the Tower of London courtesy of Oliver Cromwell, and had promised that if he was released he would build a chapel in his old college.

Crossing Old Court diagonally, walk past the handsome Victorian dining hall and into charming Ivy Court. Walk through and round the corner to see a sweeping lawn with an impressive statue of Pitt the Younger (prime minister in the 18th century) outside the ornate library clock tower.

Continue through the garden past the green where students play croquet after exams in summer, and out, right, into Pembroke St.

Emmanuel College Founded in 1584, this is a medium-sized college (☎ 334200), on St Andrew's St, comprising a community of some 600 people.

If you stand in Front Court, one of the architectural gems of Cambridge faces you – the Wren chapel, cloister and gallery, completed in 1677. To the left is the hall; inside, the refectory-type tables are set at right angles to the high table.

The next court, New Court, is round the corner. It has a quaint herb garden reminiscent of the old Dominican priory which preceded the college. There are a few remnants of the priory in the *clunch* (chalk) core of the walls of the Old Library. Turn right to re-enter Front Court and go into the chapel. It has interesting windows, a high ceiling and a painting by Jacopo Amigoni. Near the side door is a plaque to a famous scholar, John Harvard (BA 1632), who was among 30 Emmanuel men who settled in New England. He left money to found the university that bears his name in the Massachusetts town of Cambridge. His portrait also features in one of the stained-glass windows but, as the artist had no likeness of Harvard from which to work, he used the face of John Milton, a contemporary of Harvard's at the college.

Fitzwilliam Museum

This massive neoclassical edifice with its vast portico takes its name from the seventh Viscount Fitzwilliam, who bequeathed his fabulous art treasures to his old university in 1816. The building in which they are stored was begun by George Basevi in 1837, but he did not live to see its comple-

tion in 1848: while working on Ely Cathedral he stepped back to admire his handiwork, slipped and fell to his death. It was one of the first public art museums in Britain and has been called the 'finest small museum in Europe'.

In the lower galleries are ancient Egyptian sarcophagi and Greek and Roman art, as well as Chinese ceramics, English glass and illuminated manuscripts. The upper galleries contain a wide range of paintings, including works by Titian, Rubens, the French Impressionists, Gainsborough, Stubbs and Constable, right up to Cézanne and Picasso. It also has fine antique furniture.

The museum (☎ 332900) opens from 10 am to 5 pm Tuesday to Saturday and 2.15 to 5 pm on Sunday. There are guided tours at 2.30 pm on Sunday. Admission is free. Its Web site is at www.fitzmuseum.cam.ac.uk.

Kettle's Yard

Situated on the corner of Northampton and Castle Sts, this gallery was the home of HS 'Jim' Ede, a former assistant keeper at the Tate Gallery in London, and his wife Helen. In 1957 they opened their home to young artists with a view toward creating 'a home and a welcome, a refuge of peace and order, of the visual arts and of music.' Their efforts resulted in a beautiful collection of 20th-century art, furniture, ceramics and glass by such artists as Henry Moore, Henri Gaudier-Brzeska and a host of others Britons. In 1966 they donated their home and collection to the university, who opened it as a museum but didn't touch the arrangement of the pieces. In the adjoining exhibition gallery (opened 1970) there are temporary exhibits of contemporary art.

Kettle's Yard museum (☎ 352124) opens 2 to 4 pm Tuesday to Sunday; the gallery opens 12.30 am to 5.30 pm Tuesday to Saturday and 2 to 5.30pm Sunday. Admission is free. Its Web site is at www.kettles yard.co.uk.

Punting

Taking a punt along the Backs is sublime, but it can also be a wet and hectic experience, especially on a busy weekend. Look

How to Punt

Punting looks pretty straightforward but, believe us, it is not. No sooner had we dried off and hung our clothes on the line, we thought it was a good idea to offer a couple of tips on how to move the boat and stay dry.

1. Standing at the end of the punt, lift the pole out of the water at the side of the punt.

2. Let the pole slide through your hands to touch the bottom of the river.

3. Tilt the pole forward (that is, in the direction of travel of the punt) and push down to propel the punt forward.

4. Twist the pole to free the end from the mud at the bottom of the river, and let it float up and trail behind the punt. You can then use it as a rudder to steer with.

5. If you've not yet fallen in, raise the pole out of the water and into the vertical position to begin the cycle again.

JANE SMITH

Experience the pole thing on board a punt on the River Cam

before you leap. If you do wimp out, the Backs are also perfect for a walk or a picnic.

Rental prices vary considerably. Cheapest, but not always available, are those at Trinity Punts (☎ 338483) behind Trinity College. They charge £6 per hour (plus £25 deposit). Next is the punt hire at the Granta pub (see Entertainment) for £7 per hour with a £30 deposit. Punts hired by Magdalene Bridge or outside the nearby Rat & Parrot pub (see Entertainment later) cost the same. Down by Silver St, Scudamore's (☎ 359750) charges £10 per hour plus £50 deposit or a credit card imprint. If you don't feel confident about your abilities in a punt, consider renting one with a chauffeur; it costs £35 per punt and the trip lasts 45 minutes. Due to the traffic on the Cam, between 1 and 6 pm the punts carry a maximum of 12 people; at other times they can carry up to 18.

Punting the 3 miles up the river to the idyllic village of Grantchester makes a great day out.

Walking & Cycling Routes

The best outing in the area is to Grantchester, 3 miles along the towpath. You can go on foot, by bike or in a punt. For longer walks, the TIC stocks a number of guides, including *Walks in South Cambridgeshire*.

If you're a lazy cyclist, the flat topography makes for ideal biking country, although the scenery can get a little monotonous. The TIC also stocks *Cycle Routes and the Cambridge Green Belt Area* and the *Cambridge Cycle Route Map*, which are useful guides. For further information on cycling in the area, contact the Cyclists' Touring Club (☎ 563414).

Organised Tours

Guide Friday (☎ 362444) runs hop-on hop-off tour buses round the city, calling at the train station. Tours are daily, year round. Tickets cost £8.50/2.50.

Cambridge River Cruises (☎ 300100) run 90-minute cruises from the river near Jesus Green for £7/5. From April to September there's at least one departure daily at 1 pm, with more frequent departures in mid-season.

Places to Stay

Camping Four miles south-west of Cambridge is *Highfield Farm Touring Park* (☎/fax 262308, Long Rd, Comberton). From July to August it charges £8.75 for a two-person tent (£7.25 at other times). It opens April to October only.

Hostels *Cambridge Youth Hostel* (☎ 354601, fax 312780, 97 Tenison Rd) has small dormitories and a restaurant near the train station. Beds costs £12.50/8.50 for adult/under-18 YHA members; non-members pay an extra £2. It's very popular – book ahead.

B&Bs There are numerous B&Bs to choose from at any time of the year, even more during university holidays from late June to late September.

YMCA (☎ 356998, fax 312749, Gonville Place) charges £22.65/37 per single/double. It's a bargain for weekly stays (£127.50/224).

There are several B&Bs on Tenison Rd, including *Tenison Towers Guest House* (☎ 363924), at No 148, which charges from £22 to £27 per person. *Six Steps Guest House* (☎ 353968, fax 356788), at No 93, costs from £25 per person. One reader eulogised about the food here: 'the only good bread I tasted in the UK'.

Just off Parkside is *Warkworth House* (☎ 363682, fax 369655, Warkworth Terrace), a lovely Victorian terraced house with comfortable singles/doubles from £35/55. The breakfast is delicious and the owner is extremely friendly. It is popular with students from overseas.

The other B&B area is in the north of the city around Chesterton Rd. *Antony's Guest House* (☎ 357444, 4 Huntingdon Rd) is spacious and comfortable, with four singles, four doubles and three triples at £15 to £22 per person. Similarly priced but a bit farther out, *Benson House* (☎/fax 311594, 24 Huntingdon Rd) has well-equipped doubles with showers – and a friendly cat. It is strictly nonsmoking.

Closer to the city centre on Chesterton Rd, *Belle Vue Guest House* (☎ 351859), at No 33, has comfortable doubles for £40. *Aaron House* (☎ 314723), at No 71, is a small place with singles from £27 to £29 and doubles from £44 to £56. All are en suite.

Farther east along Chesterton Rd, at No 154, is *Acorn Guest House* (☎ 353888, fax 350527) with well-appointed rooms from £25/40 to £45/58, all with bathroom. Vegetarians are catered for; smokers are not. *Carlton Lodge* (☎ 367792, fax 566877, e info@carltonlodge.co.uk, 245 Chesterton Rd) is run by widely travelled, friendly people. Rooms cost £19/38 and smoking is strictly prohibited.

Hotels Right outside the train station is *Sleeperz* (☎ 304050, fax 357286, e info@sleeperz.com, Station Rd), an attractively converted railway warehouse with single/twin rooms with shower for £35/45 including breakfast. Rooms with a double bed are larger and cost £55. It's nonsmoking and there's wheelchair access to some rooms.

On Chesterton Rd, *Arundel House Hotel* (☎ 367701, fax 367721) at No 53, is in a large Victorian building overlooking the Cam. There are 42 single rooms ranging from £53 to £72.50, and 60 doubles from £69 to £96; all are en suite. *Hamilton Hotel* (☎ 365664, fax 314866, e enquiries@hamiltoncambridge.co.uk, 156 Chesterton Rd) has 25 rooms for £22/50 to £40/65, mostly en suite.

In the south, near the Fitzwilliam Museum, the *Lensfield Hotel* (☎ 355017, fax 312022, e enquiries@lensfieldhotel.co.uk, 53 Lensfield Rd) has 32 rooms and charges from £55/70 for a single to £80 for a double. Pricey, but the rooms are very well-appointed.

The posh *Garden House (Moat House)* (☎ 259988, fax 316605, Granta Place, Mill Lane) is in the centre right on the Cam and has its own private garden. There are 117 luxurious bedrooms with prices to match – £140/245 (not including breakfast). There are serious discounts on weekend rates.

The *University Arms Hotel* (☎ 351241, fax 461319, e devere.uniarms@airtime.co.uk, Regent St), overlooking Parker's Piece, is the other top place in town, a huge Victorian mansion charging £110/135.

Places to Eat
Cambridge may be a university town but tourism is an enormous cash cow, a fact reflected in food prices. There are, however, a number of reasonably priced restaurants, some of which give student discounts.

The city's best cuisine is served overlooking the river on Midsummer Common at *Midsummer House* (☎ 369299). It's a smart, sophisticated place, said to have one of the most comprehensive wine lists outside Paris. There are set lunch menus at around £27.50 and set dinners at £42. It opens for lunch Tuesday to Friday and on Sunday; for dinner Tuesday to Saturday. You may need to book several weeks in advance.

Near the Boathouse pub (see Entertainment later), *Twenty-two* (☎ 351880, 22 Chesterton Rd) may look like just another house among the hotels and B&Bs on this road, but inside it's a gourmet restaurant. A set dinner costs £25.

Across the road from King's College is *Rainbow* (☎ 321551, 9 King's Parade), a good vegetarian restaurant. Couscous is £6. *No 1 King's Parade* (☎ 359506) is a cellar bar-restaurant opposite King's College. An express two-course lunch costs £6.95. Wild boar and apple sausages are £8.25.

Clowns (☎ 355711, 54 King St) is popular with students and serves good-value light meals. Just up the street at No 78 is *Efe's Restaurant* (☎ 350491), a good-value Turkish restaurant where mains cost between £6 and £7. It opens noon to 2.30 pm and 6 to 11 pm Monday to Saturday and noon to 11 pm on Sunday.

There's a number of reasonably priced restaurants on Regent St. *The Depot* (☎ 566966, 41 Regent St) is stylish yet good value, offering an interesting international menu based around starters (around £4.50 each). *Shalimar Restaurant* (☎ 355378, 84 Regent St) is an Indian place offering discounts to students.

One of the most pleasant and central dining options is *The Dôme* (☎ 313818, 33–34 St Andrew's St), a French-style brasserie with friendly staff, a small garden at the back and a fabulous steak sandwich for £9. There are a few vegetarian options too.

Browns (☎ 461655, 23 Trumpington St) is part of the chain that has branches in several university towns. It's not as expensive as it looks. *Michel's Brasserie* (☎ 353110, 21 Northampton St) has set lunches from £7.25 and more expensive a la carte dinners.

Bar Ha! Ha! is a trendy cafe-bar with a good selection of salads and sandwiches from £3 to £6. See also Entertainment later.

Hobb's Pavilion (☎ 367480, Park Terrace) occupies the old cricket pavilion and specialises in filled pancakes. It opens Tuesday to Saturday.

Fitzbillies (☎ 352500, 52 Trumpington St) is a brilliant bakery/restaurant. The Chelsea buns (80p) are an outrageous experience and so is the chocolate cake beloved by generations of students, but there are many other temptations in addition to the usual sandwiches and pies – stock up before you go punting. Cakes and buns are also available by mail order.

Tatties (☎ 323399, 11 Sussex St) has long been a budget favourite. It specialises not only in baked potatoes stuffed with a variety of tempting fillings but also in breakfasts, filled baguettes, salads and cakes. The delicious Breakfast Baguette (hot Cambridge sausages) costs £2.50.

Nadia's is a small chain of bakeries that are excellent value (for example, bacon sandwich and coffee for 95p before 10.30 am). A smoked ham and Emmental cheese baguette is £1.05. There are branches on King's Parade and Silver St.

Choices Café (☎ 360211, Newnham Rd) will make up picnic hampers for punters for about £4 per person.

Entertainment

Pubs & Bars Punting is a big part of the Cambridge tourist experience and there are a number of pubs where you can enjoy a half (or ten) of ale before or after you hit the water. *Rat & Parrot* (☎ 311701, Thompson's La) is by the river north of Magdalene Bridge; punts are available from here. *Granta* (☎ 505016, Newnham Rd) is another pub with punt hire beside it. *Boathouse* (14 Chesterton Rd) can be visited by punt and even has its own mooring place.

Nobel-prizewinning scientists Crick and Watson spent equal time in the laboratory and *The Eagle* (☎ 505020, Bene't St), so perhaps Greene King, the Suffolk brewers, played a part in the discovery of the structure of DNA. This 16th-century pub was also popular with American airmen in WWII; they left their signatures on the ceiling.

If you're looking for bars with a more contemporary feel, there has been a spate of new openings. *Bar Ha! Ha! (☎ 305089, 17 Trinity St)* is popular with the trendy young things (see also Places to Eat earlier).

The oddly named *Sophbeck Sessions (☎ 569100, 14 Tredgold La)* is a Cajun-style bar, in the north-east of town, that is fast gaining in popularity among students and visitors alike as a good place to have a drink and enjoy some jazz and soul.

Clubs If clubbing is your thing, then *Fez (☎ 519224, 15 Market Passage)* is the place to go: there are queues most nights and the music is loud and thumping. Admission costs between £2 and £7, depending on the night – it opens 8 pm to 2 pm Monday to Saturday. Admission is free before 9 pm on Monday and Wednesday.

Po Na Na (☎ 323880, 7b Jesus La) is a terrific new bar and club in the basement of a neoclassical building. The style is Moroccan casbah, and the DJs spin a mix of Latin, House and other funky rhythms. Admission costs £1.50 and it opens until 2 am.

Fifth Avenue (☎ 364222, Heidelburg Gardens, Lion Yard) is also popular; it's a bit of a meat market but shopping can be good fun. With nights called 'Desire', 'Hustle' and 'A Kick up the 90s' it is Cambridge's own version of 'Ibiza Uncovered'. Admission costs around £7.

Theatre Near the TIC, *Corn Exchange (☎ 357851)* is the city's main centre for arts and entertainment, with shows as diverse as the English National Ballet and Sesame Street Live! The restored *Arts Theatre (☎ 503333)* is at 6 St Edward's Passage. The King's College Choir is unique to Cambridge – don't miss it. See King's College Chapel in the Walking Tour One section earlier.

Getting There & Away

Cambridge can easily be visited as a day trip from London (although it's worth staying at least a night) or en route north. It's well served by trains, though not so well by bus.

Bus For bus information, phone ☎ 317740. National Express (☎ 0870 580 8080) has hourly buses to London (£8, 2½ hours), and four buses per day to/from Bristol (£25.75, six hours). Unfortunately, connections to the north aren't straightforward. To get to Lincoln or York you'll have to change at Peterborough or Nottingham, respectively. King's Lynn is also only accessible via Peterborough – it's easier to take a train.

Cambridge Coach Services (☎ 423900) runs the Inter-Varsity Link via Stansted airport to Oxford (£8, three hours, six per day). It also runs buses to Heathrow (£15.50) and Gatwick (£18.50) airports.

Train There are trains every 30 minutes from London's King's Cross and Liverpool St stations (£14.50, 55 minutes). Network Railcards are valid. If you catch the train at King's Cross you travel via Hatfield and Stevenage. There are also hourly connections to Bury St Edmunds (£5.30, 45 minutes), Ely (£2.90, 15 minutes) and King's Lynn (£6.90, 50 minutes). You can connect at Peterborough with the main northbound trains to Lincoln, York and Edinburgh. If you want to head west to Oxford or Bath you'll have to return to London first. Phone ☎ 0845 748 4650 for details.

Getting Around

Most vehicles are now banned from the centre of Cambridge. It's best to use the well-signposted Park & Ride car parks (£1.25).

Bus A free, gas-powered shuttle stops at Emmanuel St in the centre. Cambus (☎ 423554) also runs numerous buses (50p) around town from Drummer St, including bus No 1 from the train station to the town centre.

Taxi For a taxi, phone Cabco (☎ 312444). Unless you have a lot of luggage, it's not really worth taking one from the train station to the centre. It costs between £3 and £3.60 and takes about 10 minutes (longer in rush hour); you can walk it in about 25 minutes.

Bicycle It's easy enough to get around Cambridge on foot but, if you're staying out of the centre, or plan to explore the fens, a bicycle can be useful. You don't need a flash mountain bike because there are few hills; most places rent three-speeds. Ben Hayward Cycles (☎ 35229), 69 Trumpington St, rents bikes for £10 per day from mid-May to mid-October. You can book on-line at www.ben haywardcycles.com. Geoff's Bike Hire (☎ 365629), 65 Devonshire Rd, near the youth hostel, charges £7 per day and around £15 per week but gives a 10% discount to YHA members. Cambridge Recycles (☎ 506035), 61 Newnham Rd, charges £6 to £10 per day. Mike's Bikes (☎ 312591), Mill Rd, is cheapest at £5 per day or £8 per week (plus £25 deposit) for a bike with no gears.

AROUND CAMBRIDGE
Grantchester

Three miles from Cambridge, Grantchester is a delightful village of thatched cottages and flower-filled meadows beside the Granta River (as the Cam was once known and is still known here). Its quintessential Englishness was recognised by the poet Rupert Brooke, who was a student at King's before WWI, in the immortal lines: 'Stands the church clock still at 10 to three, And is there honey still for tea?' Grantchester's most famous resident is the novelist Jeffrey Archer, who lives in the Old Vicarage.

There are teashops, some attractive pubs and the *Orchard Tea-garden*, where cream teas are served under apple trees. The best of the pubs is the *Red Lion*, near the river, which has a very pleasant garden.

Walk here via the towpath or hire a punt.

American War Cemetery

Four miles west of Cambridge, at Madingley, is a very moving cemetery with neat rows of white-marble crosses stretching down the sloping site to commemorate 3811 Americans killed in battle while based in Britain. The latest soldier to be buried here died during the Gulf War in 1991. The cemetery (☎ 01954-210350) opens 8 am to 5.30 pm daily, April 16 to September 30 (until 5 pm the rest of the year).

You can visit the cemetery as part of a Guide Friday tour (see Organised Tours under Cambridge earlier).

The Fens

The fens were strange marshlands that stretched from Cambridge north to The Wash and beyond into Lincolnshire. They were home to people who led an isolated existence fishing, hunting and farming scraps of arable land among a maze of waterways. In the 17th century, however, the Duke of Bedford and a group of speculators brought in Dutch engineer Cornelius Vermuyden to drain the fens and the flat, open plains with their rich, black soil were created. The region is the setting for Graham Swift's excellent novel *Waterland*.

As the world's weather pattern changes and the sea level rises, the fens are beginning to disappear underwater again. It's estimated that by the year 2030 up to 400,000 hectares could be lost.

Imperial War Museum

Military hardware enthusiasts should head for this war museum (☎ 01223-835000) in Duxford, 9 miles south of Cambridge right by the motorway. The museum is housed in an airfield that played a significant role in WWII, especially during the Battle of Britain. It was the home of the famous Dambuster squadron of Lancasters, and today is home to the Royal Airforce's Red Arrows squadron, which performs all kinds of celestial trickery at air shows throughout the world.

Here you'll find Europe's biggest collection of historic aircraft, ranging from WWI biplanes to jets, including Concorde. The new American Air Museum, designed by Norman Foster, is also on the site. It has the largest collection of American civil and military aircraft outside of the United States. Air shows are frequently held here and battlefield scenes are displayed in the land warfare hall, where you can check out WWII tanks and artillery. Kids will enjoy the adventure playground and the flight simulator. In 1998 the museum was awarded the Stirling Prize, Britain's most coveted architecture award.

Opening hours are 10 am to 6 pm daily, July to August; to 4 pm the rest of the year. Admission costs £7.40/3.70. The museum runs courtesy buses – the price of the journey is included in the admission – from Cambridge train station every 40 to 50 minutes between 9.40 am and 4.40 pm (until 2.20 pm September to June); they also stop outside the Crowne Plaza Hotel by the Lionyard.

Wimpole Hall

A large, gracious, 18th-century mansion set in 140 hectares of beautiful parkland, Wimpole Hall (☎ 01223-207257; NT) was the home of Rudyard Kipling's daughter until her death in 1976. Wimpole Home Farm, next to it, was established in 1794 as a model farm; today, it preserves and shows rare breeds.

Wimpole Hall is 8 miles south of Cambridge on the A603. Admission costs £5.90/2.95, or £8.50/4.25 including the Home Farm. There's no charge to just walk in the park. The farm opens 10.30 am to 4 pm daily except Monday and Friday, March to November; until 5 pm in July and August. The hall opens 1 to 5 pm daily except Monday and Friday; these hours are currently under review. Please call for details.

Whippet service No 175 passes this way from Cambridge. Alternatively, you could try walking the Wimpole Way, a 13-mile waymarked trail from Cambridge. A leaflet is available from the TIC.

ELY

☎ 01353 • pop 9000

Ely (pronounced 'ee-lee') is an unspoilt market town with neat Georgian houses, a river port and one of the country's great cathedrals. It stands in the centre of the fens. Ely used to be an island and derived its name from the eels that frequented the surrounding waters.

Ely is an easy day trip from Cambridge. The TIC (☎ 662062, fax 668518) is in Oliver Cromwell's House. It opens 10 am to 5.30 pm daily, April to September; 10 am to 5 pm Monday to Saturday and 11 am to 4 pm on Sunday the rest of the year.

A joint ticket, the 'passport to Ely', is available for £9 (£7 for students) for the main sights – Ely Cathedral, the stained glass museum, Ely Museum and Oliver Cromwell's House.

Ely Cathedral

The cathedral's origins stem from a remarkable queen of Northumbria, Etheldreda. She had married twice but was determined to pursue her vocation to become a nun. She founded an abbey in 673 and, for her good works, was canonised after her death. The abbey soon became a pilgrimage centre.

It was a Norman bishop, Simeon, who began the task of building the cathedral. It was completed in 1189 and remains a splendid example of the Norman Romanesque style. In 1322 – after the collapse of the central tower – the octagon and lantern, for which the cathedral is famous, were built. They have fan vaulting and intricate detail.

Other features of special interest include the Lady Chapel, the largest of its kind in England, which was added in the 14th century. The niches were rifled by iconoclasts but the delicate tracery and carving remain intact. There's an amazing view from just inside the western door – right down the nave, through the choir stalls and on to the glorious eastern window – no clutter, just a sublime sense of space, light and spirituality.

Ely was the first cathedral in the country to charge admission (now £4) and, with funds gathered since 1986, it has managed to restore the octagon and lantern tower. There are free guided tours of the cathedral and also an octagon and roof tour. There's a stained glass museum (£3.50) in the south triforium. The cathedral (☎ 667735) opens 7 am to 7 pm daily (to 5 pm from September to Easter). Choral Sunday service is at 10.30 am and evensong is at 3.45 pm.

Other Attractions

The area round the cathedral is historically and architecturally interesting. There's the Bishop's Palace, now a nursing home, and King's School, which supplies the cathedral with choristers.

Oliver Cromwell's House (☎ 662062) stands to the west, across St Mary's Green. Cromwell lived with his family in this attractive, half-timbered, 14th-century house from 1636–46, when he was the tithe collector of Ely. The TIC, occupying the front room in the house, offers an audiovisual

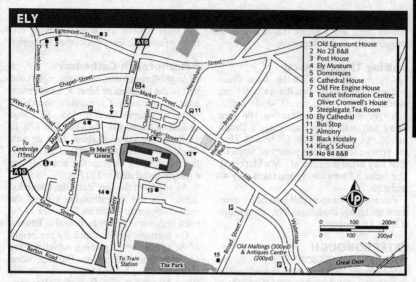

ELY

1 Old Egremont House
2 No 23 B&B
3 Post House
4 Ely Museum
5 Dominiques
6 Cathedral House
7 Old Fire Engine House
8 Tourist Information Centre;
  Oliver Cromwell's House
9 Steeplegate Tea Room
10 Ely Cathedral
11 Bus Stop
12 Almonry
13 Black Hostelry
14 King's School
15 No 84 B&B

presentation and an interesting tour of the rooms (£3/2.40).

The history of the town is told in **Ely Museum** (☎ 666655), in the Old Gaol House. It opens 10.30 am to 5.30 pm daily (to 4.30 pm November to April). Admission is £2/1.25.

It's worth walking down to the river by following the signs. There is an interesting **antiques centre** near the river. The **Old Maltings** (☎ 662633) on Ship Lane, which stages exhibitions and has a cafe (the Waterfront Brasserie) is nearby.

River Great Ouse is a busy thoroughfare – swans and ducks compete with boats for river space. The towpath winds up and downstream; for a quiet walk, turn left, turn right for the pub and tea garden. If you continue along this path you'll see the fens stretching to the horizon.

Places to Stay

There are few budget options in Ely. There are several B&Bs on Egremont St. At No 31, **Old Egremont House** (☎ 663118, fax 666968) offers comfortable B&B for £40/46 for singles/doubles in an attractive house with a large garden. At **No 23** (☎ 664557), B&B costs £25/40.

The Post House (☎ 667184), at 12a, is unmissable with the Union flag raised outside. Rooms cost £19/38.

On Broad St, **No 84** (☎ 666862) has just one double room for £18/32.

Cathedral House (☎/fax 662124, ℮ farm dale@cathedralhouse.co.uk, 17 St Mary's St) offers very comfortable B&B for £40/50.

Places to Eat

Eels are a local delicacy served in several of the restaurants. A good place to try them is at Ely's best restaurant, **Old Fire Engine House** (☎ 662582, St Mary's St). It seems more like the comfortable house of a friend than a restaurant but the food is excellent. Main dishes are all about £12. It opens daily except Sunday.

Dominiques (☎ 665011, St Mary's St) serves cream teas, as well as lunches and set dinners (£18). It's closed on Monday and Tuesday. Totally nonsmoking, it has good vegetarian choices.

Steeplegate Tea Room (☎ 664731, 16 High St) is right beside the cathedral. Light lunches and baked potatoes from £2.50 are available. Close by, virtually in the grounds of the cathedral, is an attractive garden restaurant, the *Almonry* (☎ 666360), to the left of the Lady Chapel. There's a wide range of teas and coffees here.

Getting There & Away

Ely is on the A10, 15 miles from Cambridge. Following the Fen Rivers Way (map available from TICs); it's a 17-mile walk.

Stagecoach Cambus bus No 106 runs every half hour from Cambridge's Drummer St bus station (£3.10, 1¼ hours). They are pretty slow, making plenty of stops on their way to the terminus at Ely's Market St. The faster X8 runs hourly and takes only 40 minutes.

Faster (and cheaper) still is to go by train: there are hourly departures from Cambridge (£2.90, 15 minutes).

PETERBOROUGH

☎ 01733 • pop 156,600

Peterborough likes to advertise itself as the capital city of shopping and, while this may do wonders for the retail trade, it does precious little for tourism, especially the kind that is familiar with British shopping centres and high-street chain stores. It is undoubtedly an industrious place, a product of having been part of the 1960s 'New Towns' program – which lead to a substantial urban renewal, including the construction of new residential townships and a number of dual carriageways – but aside from a few central sites of historic importance it is a little grim. Construction continues to this day, with the last of the four planned townships – Hampton – being expanded on the city's southern side. Yet Peterborough is home to a wonderful cathedral that is worth making the trip for, but only just. Luckily, it's an easy day trip from Cambridge.

Orientation & Information

The cathedral precinct is an extension of the busy Cowgate, Bridge St and Queensgate. The TIC (☎ 452336, fax 452353, ⓔ tic@ peterborough.gov.uk), 45 Bridge St, is nearby. It opens 8.45 am to 5 pm Monday to Friday (from 10 am on Thursday) and 10 am to 4 pm on Saturday. There is good online information about shopping and the cath-

edral at www.peterborough.gov.uk. The bus and train stations are within walking distance of the TIC, just west of the city centre.

Peterborough Cathedral

In Anglo-Saxon times, when the region was part of the kingdom of Mercia, King Peada, a recent convert to Christianity, founded a monastic church here in 655. This was sacked and gutted by the Danes in 870. In 1118, the Benedictine abbot John de Sais founded the present cathedral as the monastic church of the Benedictine abbey. It was finally consecrated in 1237.

As you enter the precinct from Cathedral Square you get a breathtaking view of the early-13th-century western front, one of the most impressive of any cathedral in Britain.

On entering you're struck by the height of the nave and the lightness, which derives not only from the mellow Barnack stone (quarried close by and transported via the River Nene) but also from the clerestory windows. The nave, with its three storeys, is an impressive example of Norman architecture. Its unique timber ceiling is one of the earliest of its kind in England (possibly in Europe) and its original painted decoration has been preserved.

The Gothic tower replaced the original Norman one, but had to be taken down and carefully reconstructed after it began to crack in the late 19th century.

In the northern choir aisle is the tombstone of Henry VIII's first wife, the tragic Catherine of Aragon, buried here in 1536. Her divorce, engineered by the king because she could not produce a male heir, led to the Reformation in England. Her only child (a daughter) was not even allowed to attend her funeral. Directly opposite, in the southern aisle, two standards mark what was the grave of Mary Queen of Scots. On the accession of her son, James, to the throne, her body was moved to Westminster Abbey.

The eastern end of the cathedral, known as the New Building, was added in the 15th century. It has superb fan vaulting, probably the work of master mason John Wastell, who worked on King's College Chapel in Cambridge.

The cathedral (☎ 343342) opens from 8.30 am to 5.15 pm daily. Admission is free (but a 'donation' of £3 is encouraged). Every January 29 there is a procession in the cathedral to mark the death of Catherine.

Getting There & Away
Peterborough is 37 miles north of Cambridge. Stagecoach United Counties (☎ 01604-620077) and National Express run buses from Cambridge (£7, one hour); some services require a change in Huntingdon. There are hourly trains from Cambridge (£8.60, 55 minutes).

Lincolnshire

Sneering southerners who've never visited tend to think of Lincolnshire as flat and boring. Although far from Alpine, the county is made up of several diverse landscapes, from the hilly countryside of the western county to the flat marshlands of the east. It's easy cycling and walking country, but has a number of other attractions that make a visit worthwhile. The unspoiled nature of some of the Lincolnshire towns – cobbled streets, solid stone-built houses with red-tiled roofs has attracted a number of film companies looking for an 'olde Englande' setting for their films. One of the finest Gothic buildings in Europe and the country, Lincoln Cathedral, along with many beautiful parish churches, was built on the proceeds of the flourishing wool trade.

The Lincolnshire Wolds, to the north and east of Lincoln, are comprised of low rolling hills and small market towns. To the southeast, the flat Lincolnshire Fens is fertile agricultural land reclaimed from the sea. The whole area is crisscrossed by a network of rivers and dykes, while the coastline to the east is marked by wide sandy beaches as well as salt marshes, dunes and pools.

GETTING AROUND
Regional transport is poor but the main routes are well enough served by train or bus. The Lincolnshire timetable hotline (☎ 01522-553135) has details of bus and rail times for the county; it operates 8 am to 4.45 pm Monday to Friday.

The Viking Way is a 140-mile way-marked trail that runs from the Humber Bridge, through the Lincolnshire Wolds, to Oakham in Leicestershire.

Renting a bike in Lincoln, or bringing one with you, is an excellent idea. TICs stock sets of *Lincolnshire Cycle Trails*.

LINCOLN
☎ 01522 • pop 81,500
Tougher to get to than other cities in the region (namely York), many visitors give Lincoln a miss and rush to marvel at its great rival's wonderful cathedral instead. Unfortunately, they are losing out on Lincoln's own 900-year-old cathedral, the third largest in Britain and one of the finest examples of Early English architecture in the country. Lincoln's unattractive and depressing suburbs don't do the city's tourist authorities any favours, but hidden inside the bland outskirts is a compact medieval centre with some wonderful Tudor architecture and one of the steepest urban climbs this side of San Francisco. The people, largely spared the tourist hordes, are particularly friendly, while the presence of a university means that there are plenty of young people around.

History
For the last 2000 years, most of Britain's invaders have recognised the potential of this site and made their mark. Lincoln's hill was of immense strategic importance, giving views for miles across the surrounding plain. Communications were found to be excellent – below it is the River Witham, navigable to the sea.

The Romans established a garrison and a town they called Lindum. In AD 96 it was given the status of a colonia, or chartered town – Lindum Colonia, hence Lincoln. Gracious public buildings were constructed and it became a popular place for old soldiers past their prime to spend their twilight years.

The Normans began work on the castle in 1068 and the cathedral in 1072. In the 12th century the wool trade developed and wealthy merchants established themselves.

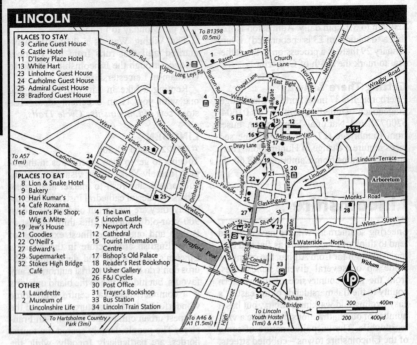

LINCOLN

PLACES TO STAY
3 Carline Guest House
6 Castle Hotel
11 D'Isney Place Hotel
13 White Hart
23 Linholme Guest House
24 Carholme Guest House
25 Admiral Guest House
28 Bradford Guest House

PLACES TO EAT
8 Lion & Snake Hotel
9 Bakery
10 Hari Kumar's
14 Café Roxanna
16 Brown's Pie Shop;
   Wig & Mitre
19 Jew's House
21 Goodies
22 O'Neill's
27 Edward's
29 Supermarket
32 Stokes High Bridge
   Café

OTHER
1 Laundrette
2 Museum of
  Lincolnshire Life
4 The Lawn
5 Lincoln Castle
7 Newport Arch
12 Cathedral
15 Tourist Information
   Centre
17 Bishop's Old Palace
18 Reader's Rest Bookshop
20 Usher Gallery
26 F&J Cycles
30 Post Office
31 Trayer's Bookshop
33 Bus Station
34 Lincoln Train Station

The city was famous for the cloth known as Lincoln green, said to have been worn by Robin Hood. Many of the wealthiest merchants were Jews but, following the murder of a nine-year-old boy in 1255 for which one of their number was accused, they were mercilessly persecuted, many being driven out.

During the Civil War the city passed from Royalist to Parliamentarian and back again, but it began to prosper as an agricultural centre in the 18th century. In the following century, after the arrival of the railway, Lincoln's engineering industry was established. Heavy machinery produced here included the world's first tank, which saw action in WWI.

Orientation & Information

The cathedral sits on top of the hill in the centre of the old part of the city, with the castle and most of the other attractions conveniently nearby. Three-quarters of a mile down from the cathedral (a 15-minute walk) lies the new town, and the bus and train stations. These two parts of Lincoln are connected by the appropriately named Steep Hill.

The TIC (☎ 529828, fax 564506) is in the old black-and-white building at 9 Castle Hill. It opens 9 am to 5.30 pm Monday to Thursday (to 5 pm on Friday and at weekends).

Guided walking tours (£3/2) from the TIC take place at 11 am and 2 pm daily June to September, and at weekends in June, September and October. There are also Guide Friday bus tours (☎ 01789-294466) daily from April to September (£5.50/2).

You can check email at Trayer's Bookshop (☎ 511156), 211 High St, down a flight of stairs behind Stokes High Bridge Café (see Places to Eat later). There's only one terminal, but you get a free cup of coffee. Charges are £1 for 15 minutes. It opens 10 am to 5.30 pm Tuesday to Friday, 9 am to 5 pm on Saturday and 11 am to 4 pm on Sunday.

There's a laundrette on Rasen Lane.

Cathedral

This superb cathedral is the county's greatest attraction. Its three great towers dominate the city and can be seen from miles around. The central tower stands 81m high, which makes it the second-highest in the country after Salisbury Cathedral. While this is impressive enough, imagine it twice as high, which it was until toppled by a storm in 1547.

Lincoln Cathedral was built on the orders of William the Conqueror and construction began in 1072. It took only 20 years to complete the original building, which was 99m long with two western towers, but in 1185 an earthquake caused severe damage. Only the western front of the old cathedral survived. Rebuilding began under Bishop Hugh of Avalon (St Hugh) and most of the current building dates from the late 12th to late 13th centuries, in the Early English style.

The entrance is below the famous mid-12th-century frieze on the **western front**. Unfortunately, the frieze is currently hidden behind the scaffolding of a long-term restoration project. Emerging into the **nave**, most people are surprised to find a substantial part of the cathedral empty, but this is actually how it would have looked back in 1250 when it was completed. Medieval cathedrals and churches, like mosques and Hindu temples today, did not have pews. This open area is now used for concerts and plays; services take place in St Hugh's choir. The stained glass in the nave is mostly Victorian, but the **Belgian marble font** dates back to the 11th century.

There are interesting stained-glass windows at each end of the transepts. The **Dean's Eye** contains glass that has been here since the 13th century; the glass in the **Bishop's Eye** dates from the 14th century. High above in the central tower, Great Tom is a 270kg bell that still sounds the hours.

St Hugh's Choir was the first section of the church to be rebuilt. The vaulting above is arranged at odd angles, but the canopied stalls of the choir are beautifully carved and over 600 years old.

The **Angel Choir**, named after the 28 angels carved high up the walls under the highest windows, was built as a shrine to St Hugh. Modern pilgrims search for the famous **Lincoln Imp**, a stonemason's joke that has become the city's emblem. The legend goes that this malevolent being was caught trying to chat up one of the 28 angels and was turned to stone.

There are free, one-hour tours of the cathedral at 11 am, 1 and 3 pm daily; there's also a tour of the roof (one hour; maximum 14 people) beginning at 2 pm.

The cathedral (☎ 544544) opens 7.15 am to 8 pm Monday to Saturday (to 6 pm on Sunday), June to August; 7.15 am to 6 pm Monday to Saturday (to 5 pm on Sunday), the rest of the year. Admission costs £3.50/3. There's evensong daily except Wednesday at 5.15 pm (3.45 pm on Sunday), and sung Eucharist at 9.30 am on Sunday.

Lincoln Castle

Begun in 1068, just four years before the cathedral, the castle was built over the original Roman town and incorporates some of the old Roman walls. As well as the usual views from the battlements that one expects from a castle, the old prison is particularly interesting. Public executions used to draw crowds of up to 20,000 people, taking place in front of Cobb Hall, a horseshoe-shaped tower in the north-eastern corner that served as the city's prison for centuries. The red-brick building on the eastern side replaced it and was used until 1878.

In the same building as the chapel, Lincoln's copy of the Magna Carta is on display.

Lincoln Castle (☎ 511068) opens 9.30 am to 5.30 pm Monday to Saturday (from 11 am on Sunday), April to September; to 4 pm daily the rest of the year. Admission costs £2.50/1.50; there are free tours of the castle at 11 am and 2 pm daily, April to September.

Walking Tour

After looking round the cathedral and the castle, leave by the castle's western exit. Across the road is **The Lawn** (☎ 560306), a former lunatic asylum that now houses a concert hall and several exhibition areas. The **Sir Joseph Banks Conservatory**, in this complex, is a tropical glasshouse containing descendants of some of the plants brought back by this Lincoln explorer who accompanied Captain Cook to Australia. The Lawn opens 9 am to 5 pm Monday to Friday and 10 am to 5.30 pm at the weekend, year round (shorter hours in winter).

A short walk up Burton Rd is the **Museum of Lincolnshire Life** (☎ 528448). It's a fairly interesting museum of local social history – displays include everything from an Edwardian nursery to a WWI tank built here. It opens daily 10 am to 5.30 pm. Admission costs £2/60p.

Return to Westgate and continue east to Bailgate. Turn left to see the **Newport Arch**. Built by the Romans, this is the oldest arch in Britain that still has traffic passing through it. Walk back along Bailgate and continue past the TIC down **Steep Hill**. There are several shops to tempt the tourist, including second-hand bookshops (the Reader's Rest is good) and teashops.

As well as the black-and-white Tudor buildings on Steep Hill, **Jew's House** is of particular interest, being one of the best examples of 12th-century domestic architecture in Britain. It's now an upmarket restaurant (see Places to Eat later). A few doors down is **Goodies** (☎ 525307), a traditional sweet shop that has 300 varieties in stock – bull's eyes, pear drops, sherbet lemons and humbugs. (Goodies is Lincs dialect for sweets/chocolate.)

Located one block east of Jew's House on Lindum Rd is the **Usher Gallery** (☎ 527980), the city's art gallery. It opens 10 am to 5.30 pm Monday to Saturday and 2.30 to 5 pm on Sunday. Admission costs £2/30p.

Places to Stay

Camping About three miles south-west of the train station is *Hartsholme Country Park* (☎ 873577, *Skellingthorpe Rd*). It opens from March 31 to October 31; a tent and two people costs £4.40. To get here, take the R66 bus from the main bus station in the direction of Birchwood Estate; ask the driver to drop you off (it's about a 20-minute ride).

Hostels Providing good budget accommodation in various size rooms is *Lincoln Youth Hostel* (☎ 522076, fax 567424, 77 South Park Ave). A double costs £18, a five-bed dorm room £42.50 and the daily rate for adults/under-18s is £10/6.90. It opens daily February through October, and on Friday and Saturday in November and December.

B&Bs & Hotels There's a good group of B&Bs on West Parade, west of the modern centre of Lincoln. *Linholme Guest House* (☎ 522930), at No 116, is small with two twins and a double at £18 per person. It's a pleasant place to stay and two rooms have a bathroom.

Parallel to and just south of West Parade is Carholme Rd, with numerous B&Bs. *Carholme Guest House* (☎ 531059, fax 511590), at No 175, has five rooms – all en suite – and charges from £20/38 for a single/double.

Admiral Guest House (☎/fax 544467, 16–18 Nelson St), a lovely 100-year-old house just off Carholme Rd, charges £22/36 for a single/double.

Bradford Guest House (☎ 523947, 67 Monks Rd) is good value at £20/35. The neat and tidy rooms all have showers.

More upmarket is *Carline Guest House* (☎/fax 530422, 1 Carline Rd). The 12 rooms have been individually appointed and all have private bathroom. Rooms are £30/42. It's vehemently nonsmoking.

D'Isney Place Hotel (☎ 538881, fax 511321, e info@disney-place.freespace.co .uk, Eastgate) is small and comfortable, with rooms from £61.50/79 including breakfast in bed.

Castle Hotel (☎ 538801, fax 575547, Westgate), directly across from the TIC, is in a restored 19th-century building with rooms for £62/79. It's fancy and comfortable.

Lincoln's top hotel is the *White Hart Hotel* (☎ 526222, fax 531798, e heritagehotels-lincoln.white-hart@forte-hotels.com), on Bailgate by the cathedral. It's a luxurious place with doubles going for £114.

Places to Eat

As one might expect in a city of this size, there's a reasonable range of places to eat, some of them particularly good value.

Lincoln's top restaurant is the *Jew's House* (☎ 524851, Steep Hill), occupying a 12th-century building that's an attraction in its own right. A three-course set dinner costs £28; set lunches are £13.95.

The *Lion & Snake Hotel* (☎ 523770) was founded in 1640, which makes it Lincoln's oldest pub. Situated on the Bailgate, it's probably better known for its real ale and good-value, home-made bar food.

Hari Kumar's (☎ 537000, 80 Bailgate) is a stylish restaurant serving Indian and English food. Saffron breast of chicken is £6.95.

Across the road is *Café Roxanna* (☎ 546464) where you can choose between a set meal at £8 or an international 'game fayre platter' of wild boar, alligator, pheasant, pigeon, kangaroo and ostrich for a mere £75.50 (24 hours' notice required).

Brown's Pie Shop (☎ 527330, 33 Steep Hill) is close to the cathedral and popular with tourists. It's still worth eating here since pies are a Lincolnshire speciality. Rabbit pie with Dorset scrumpy costs £8.95 but there are cheaper options.

The *Wig & Mitre* (☎ 535190, 29 Steep Hill) is near Brown's Pie Shop. It's a pub with a restaurant, open daily.

A branch of *O'Neill's* (☎ 556011) dominates the northern end of High St, but a cooler place to hang out is *Edward's* (☎ 519144, 238 High St), one block south. At this stylish bar-brasserie you can get everything from a coffee or a beer to a full meal.

Stokes High Bridge Cafe (☎ 513825, 207 High St) is popular with tourists since it's in a 16th-century timbered building right on the bridge over the River Witham. You can get lunches and teas. It opens 9 am to 5 pm Monday to Saturday.

There's a *Co-op supermarket* on Silver St and a good *bakery* on the corner of Westgate and Bailgate.

Entertainment

Pubs Every guided tour makes a stop at (or at least acknowledges) the *Victoria* (☎ 536048, 6 Union Rd). Lincoln's most famous public house doesn't disappoint: it's a terrific bar with a huge selection of beers.

Dog & Bone (☎ 522403, 10 John St) is a distinctive bar with a fine selection of ales east of High St, just off Monks Rd.

George & Dragon (☎ 520924, 100 High St) is one of the more popular pubs in town, and what it lacks in original character it more than makes up for in friendly ambience – though it can get very crowded at weekends.

Clubs With three clubs in one *Pulse-Ritzy-Jumpin Jaks* (☎ 522314, Silver St) aims to grab as much of the younger, student crowd as it can, and it does. Pulse (open 10 pm to 2 am Tuesday, Friday and Saturday) is the more hardcore venue, featuring the heavy sound of speed garage. Ritzy (open 10 pm to 2 am daily except Monday and Wednesday) is more commercial, an uptempo dance club where you'll bop to mostly commercial stuff. Jumpin Jaks (open 8 pm to 2 am Wednesday to Sunday) is more of a bar than a club, but the music is loud and drawn from a mixed bag. Admission to all three varies from £3 to £7, depending on the night, but there are discount fliers handed out throughout many of the city's bars.

Getting There & Away

Lincoln is 132 miles from London, 85 miles from Cambridge and 75 miles from York.

Bus National Express operates a daily direct service (at 7.55 am) between Lincoln and London (£19.25, 4½ hours), via Stamford (£8.75, 1½ hours). There are direct services to Birmingham (£10.75, 2¾ hours) and Glasgow (£32.50, nine hours). For Cambridge (£15.25, three hours) you must change at Peterborough, which usually involves a lengthy wait.

The main local bus company is Lincolnshire Roadcar (☎ 532424). It runs hourly buses between Lincoln and Grantham (£2.60, 1¼ hours), Monday to Saturday. Stamford is also served by Kimes Coaches (☎ 01529-497251), albeit on Saturday only with a departure at 4 pm (£3 return, 1½ hours). From Lincoln to Boston (£3.15, 1¾ hours) there are nine buses, Monday to Saturday only, run by Brylaine Travel (☎ 01205-364087).

Train To get to and from Lincoln usually involves a change. Hourly trains to Boston (£7.20, 1¼ hours) and Skegness (£9.80, two hours) include a change at Sleaford. For Cambridge (£20.80, 2½ hours), you must change at Peterborough (£13.40, 1½ hours) and Ely (£19.10, two hours 20 minutes) and sometimes also at Newark, although there are a handful of trains that include only a stop at Peterborough. There are hourly departures throughout the day. Grantham (£6.40, 40 minutes) is on the main London to Glasgow line, so you'll need to change at Newark; there are about 20 trains per day.

Getting Around

Bus The city bus service is efficient. From the bus and train stations, bus No 51 runs past the youth hostel and Nos 7 and 8 link the cathedral area with the lower town. Fares are 50p.

Bicycle You can rent everything from a three-speed to a mountain bike from F&J Cycles (☎ 545311), 41 Hungate, but 21 speeds are hardly an essential requirement for cycling in this flat county. Rent an 18-speed from £6 to £8 per day, and up to £25 per week.

GRANTHAM
☎ 01476 • pop 31,000

Anyone old enough to remember the eventful reign of Lady Margaret Thatcher (1925–), who served as British prime minister from 1979 to 1990, will find a good example of her vision for Britain in the pleasant red-brick town where she was born. Lady Thatcher lived at 2 North Parade, above her father's grocer shop; today it is a chiropractor's clinic. The only other noteworthy inhabitant was Sir Isaac Newton, who received his early education here. There's a statue of him in front of the guildhall – a statue of the former Conservative prime minister might eventually grace the town but this book will have gone through several more editions before it does.

For the time being, Lady Thatcher will have to content herself with a section devoted to her in the town's **museum**, St Peter's Hill. Another section is devoted to Newton and frankly, unless you really want to see the famous handbag with which Lady Thatcher saluted the press after her 1979 electoral victory, it is by far the more interesting. The museum opens 10 am to 5 pm Monday to Saturday. Admission is free.

The TIC (☎/fax 406166) is by the Guildhall on Avenue Rd. It opens 9.30 am to 5 pm Monday to Saturday.

The town has an interesting parish church, **St Wulfram's**, with a 85m-high spire, the sixth-highest in England. It dates from the late 13th century.

Three miles north-east of Grantham on the A607 is **Belton House** (☎ 566116; NT), one of the finest examples of Restoration country-house architecture. Built in 1688 for Sir John Brownlow, the house is known for its ornate plasterwork ceilings and wood carvings attributed to the Dutch carver Grinling Gibbons. Set in a 400-hectare park, it opens 1 to 5 pm Wednesday to Sunday, April to October. Admission costs £5.20. Bus Nos 601 and 609 pass this way.

Places to Stay & Eat

In a listed Georgian building in the town centre, *Red House* (☎ 579869, fax 401597, 74 North Parade) has three en-suite rooms; singles/doubles cost £21/43.

Just outside Belton House, *The Coach House* (☎/fax 573636, ⓔ coachhousenn@ cwcom.net) is a listed building with rooms for £22.50 per person including breakfast. Smokers will have to exercise their lungs in the large garden – it's a smoke-free joint.

Beehive (☎ 404554, Castlegate) is best known for its pub sign – a real beehive full of live South African bees! The bees have been here since 1830, which makes them one of the oldest populations of bees in the world. Good, cheap lunches are available, and the bees stay away from the customers.

Getting There & Away

Grantham is 25 miles south of Lincoln. Lincolnshire Roadcar (☎ 01522-532424) runs buses every hour between these two towns, Monday to Saturday, and four on Sunday (£2.60, one hour 10 minutes). It also runs a service (four daily, Monday to Saturday) to Stamford (£2.25, 1½ hours); National Express runs one bus daily, Monday to Saturday.

By train (£6.40, 40 minutes), you'll need to change at Newark to get to Lincoln. There is at least one train per hour throughout the day. Direct trains run from London Kings Cross to Grantham (£18.90, one hour).

STAMFORD
☎ 01780 • pop 16,000

This beautiful town of stone buildings and cobbled streets was made a conservation area in 1967 and is one of the finest stone towns in the country. The TIC (☎/fax 755611) is in the Stamford Arts Centre at 27 St Mary's St. It opens 9.30 am to 5 pm Monday to Saturday (and 10 am to 3 pm on Sunday, April to October).

It's best just to simply wander round the town's winding streets of medieval and Georgian houses, but the **Stamford Museum** (☎ 766317), Broad St, is certainly worth visiting. As well as displays charting the history of the town, there's a clothed model of local heavyweight Daniel Lambert, who tipped the scales at 336kg before his death in 1809. After his death his suits were displayed in a local pub where Charles Stratton, better known as Tom Thumb, would put on a show by fitting into the suit's armholes. Hilarious, apparently. It opens 10 am to 5 pm daily (2 to 5 pm on Sunday, April to September).

Places to Stay & Eat
There's B&B from around £18 per person at *St Peter's Rectory* (☎ 753999, fax 766667, 8 St Peter's Hill), which has rooms for £18/36.

St George's B&B (☎ 482099, 16 St George's Sq), not to be confused with the George hotel (see below) is a gorgeous 19th-century house decorated with Victorian fireplaces and antiques. It also has a private garden. Singles/doubles cost £22/35.

Martin's (☎ 752106, fax 482691, 20 St Martin's Rd) is another great B&B, just beyond the bridge over the Welland River, only a couple of minutes walk from the centre of town. Room cost £30/50.

There are a number of historic pubs that also offer accommodation. The *Bull & Swann Inn* (☎ 763558, High St) does good meals and has rooms with a bathroom for £35/45 for singles/doubles.

Across the street, the *George* (☎ 750750, fax 750701, ✉ georgehotelofstamford@btinternet.com, 71 St Martin's St) is the top place to stay. It's a wonderful old coaching inn, parts of the building date back a thousand years. There's a cobbled courtyard and luxurious rooms from £78/100. There's also an excellent restaurant which also serves upmarket pub grub: if you want anything fancier expect to fork out at least £20.

Getting There & Away
Stamford is 46 miles from Lincoln and 21 miles south of Grantham.

National Express serves Stamford from London (£8.50, 2¾ hours) via Lincoln (£7.50, 1½ hours). Lincolnshire Roadcar (☎ 01522-532424) operates four buses daily, Monday to Saturday only, between Stamford and Grantham (£2.25, 1½ hours). National Express also runs one bus daily.

There are 16 trains daily to Cambridge (£11.90, 1¼ hours) and Ely (£7.90, 55 minutes). Norwich (£13.50, one hour 50 minutes) is on the same line, but there are fewer direct trains; you will most likely have to change at Ely.

AROUND STAMFORD
Burghley House
Just one mile south of Stamford, this immensely grand Tudor mansion (pronounced 'Bur-lee') is the home of the Cecil family. It was built between 1565 and 1587 by William Cecil, Queen Elizabeth's adviser.

It's an impressive place with 18 magnificent state rooms. The Heaven Room was painted by Antonio Verrio in the 17th century and features floor-to-ceiling gods and goddesses disporting among the columns. There are over 300 paintings, including works by Gainsborough and Brueghel; state bedchambers, including the four-poster Queen Victoria slept in; and cavernous Tudor kitchens.

The house (☎ 01780-752451) opens 11 am to 4.30 pm daily, April to early October.

Admission costs £6.50/3.20; one child is admitted free per paying adult. It's a pleasant 15-minute walk through the park from Stamford train station. The Burghley Horse Trials take place here over three days in early September and are of international significance.

BOSTON
☎ 01205 • pop 34,000

A major port in the Middle Ages, Boston lies near the mouth of the River Witham, in the bay known as The Wash. By the end of the 13th century the town was one of the most important wool traders in the country, exporting the fleeces of three million sheep annually. In keeping with its high-flying status, the town ordered the construction of an impressive church in 1309, the result of which was **St Botolph's** (☎ 362864) and its 88-metre tower – known as the Boston Stump – the tallest in the country. The fenland on which it is built was not solid enough to support a thin spire, hence the more solid-looking tower. You can climb the 365 steps to the top from where, on a clear day, you can see Lincoln, 30 miles away. It opens 9 am to 4.30 pm Monday to Saturday, and also on Sunday between services. Admission to the tower costs £2/1, admission to the church is free.

It was from Boston that the Pilgrim Fathers made their first break for the freedom of the New World in 1607. They were imprisoned in the **Guildhall** (☎ 365954), where the cells that held them are now a tourist attraction. By 1630 the vicar of St Botolph's, John Cotton, was encouraging his parishioners to follow in the footsteps of the first pilgrims, and many embarked for America where they founded the namesake town in the colony of Massachussetts. Cotton was renowned for his two-hour sermons, which he delivered from the magnificent pulpit inside the church. The Guildhall opens 10 am to 5 pm Monday to Saturday (1.30 to 5pm on Sunday, summer only). Admission costs £1.25.

The TIC (☎/fax 356656) is under the Assembly Rooms on Market Place. It opens 9 am to 5 pm Monday to Saturday, year round. Market days are Wednesday and Saturday; you can buy pretty much everything from a fish to a bicycle.

Places to Stay & Eat
A five-minute walk from the marketplace, *Park Lea* (☎/fax 356309, 85 Norfolk St) has singles/doubles for £24/36 with bathroom; there's also a double without bathroom for £32.

An old 18th-century farmhouse, *Bramley House* (☎/fax 354538 @ bramleyhouse @ic24.net, 267 Sleaford Rd) is about half a mile west of town along the Sleaford road. It has nine comfortable rooms for £20/37.50.

The *White Hart* (☎ 364877, fax 355974, Bridge Foot) has 21 rooms with bathroom at £40/65, breakfast included. It also does good pub grub.

Getting There & Away
From Lincoln it's easier to get to Boston by train than by bus, but even that involves a change at Sleaford. Trains run from Lincoln hourly (£7.20, 1¼ hours).

SKEGNESS
☎ 01754 • pop 18,000

'Skeggy' is a classic English seaside resort, the Blackpool of the east coast. There are rows of jolly B&Bs, bingo every evening and donkeys on the six miles of beach. Danny La Rue, Chas 'n' Dave and a host of Abba tribute bands appear throughout the year at the Embassy Centre (☎ 768333), shows usually kick off at 7.30 pm, and the whole place twinkles with 25,000 light bulbs every night from July to October during the Skegness Illuminations. It's the kind of place the English middle and upper classes wouldn't be seen dead in.

The TIC (☎/fax 764821), in the Embassy Centre on Grand Parade, has all the information on B&Bs. They can be cheap, from £15 per person. Opening hours are 9 to 5.30 pm Monday to Saturday; until 6 pm April to September.

Skegness is pretty easy to get to by either bus or train. From Boston, Lincolnshire Roadcar runs five buses daily, Monday to Saturday (£2.40, 1¼ hours). Brylaine Travel (☎ 01205-364087) runs three daily along the same route. Tickets, however, are only valid on the service provided by the issuing company. From Lincoln, Lincolnshire Roadcar buses run hourly, Monday to Saturday, and five on Sunday (£3.35, 1¾ hours).

There are 15 trains daily, Monday to Saturday, and eight on Sunday, between Skegness and Boston (£4.20, 35 minutes). Although there is a train link between Skegness and Lincoln, it involves a change at Sleaford; you're better off getting the bus.

North-Western England

North-western England is a mixture of densely populated urban centres and rolling hills of quintessential English countryside, with the jam-packed, overdeveloped conurbation that takes in Manchester and Liverpool sandwiched between the diversity of Lancashire to the north and prosperous Cheshire to the south.

First-time visitors may not want to linger in the cities, but both Manchester and Liverpool have pockets of great vitality and interesting old buildings and museums. The walled city of Chester is often used as a staging post for getting from the southern Midlands to the Lake District and Scotland, or to North Wales.

If you want to experience the tacky taste that is a British seaside resort, big, brash Blackpool fits the bill perfectly. Afterwards you can stop off in Lancaster, a manageably small town with a dominating castle and not too much tourist traffic.

Manchester

☎ 0161 • pop 460,000

Probably best known around the world for its football team, the modern city that produced Oasis, Take That, Simply Red and the distinctive 'Manchester Sound' is also a monument to England's industrial history. In the 19th century, Friedrich Engels (coauthor of the *Communist Manifesto*) used Manchester to illustrate the evils of capitalism; perhaps someone making a similar study today might uncover echoes behind the sometimes glitzy facade.

The 1990s saw a gradual transformation of parts of the city centre, a process given added impetus by the IRA bomb blast of 1996 that devastated much of the area round the Arndale Shopping Centre. If every cloud has a silver lining, then the 1996 bombing that ripped the heart out of Manchester has allowed the city to create some wonderful public spaces and stunning mod-

Highlights

- Sampling the vibrant Manchester nightlife
- Seeing the industrial past brought to life at Quarry Bank Mill
- Walking Chester's city walls
- Taking Liverpool's ferry across the Mersey
- Enjoying the peacefulness of Port Sunlight
- Delving into the quirky and beautiful world of the Isle of Man
- Riding Europe's tallest and fastest roller coaster at Blackpool Pleasure Beach

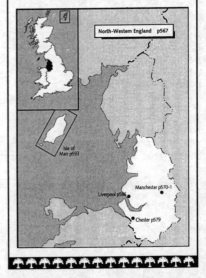

ern architecture. More money has been poured into the city's development as it gets set to host the 2002 Commonwealth Games, the biggest multi-sport event to be seen in Britain.

There are still areas where empty warehouses and factories rub shoulders with stunning Victorian Gothic buildings; rusting train tracks and motorway flyovers with flashy bars and nightclubs. But things are

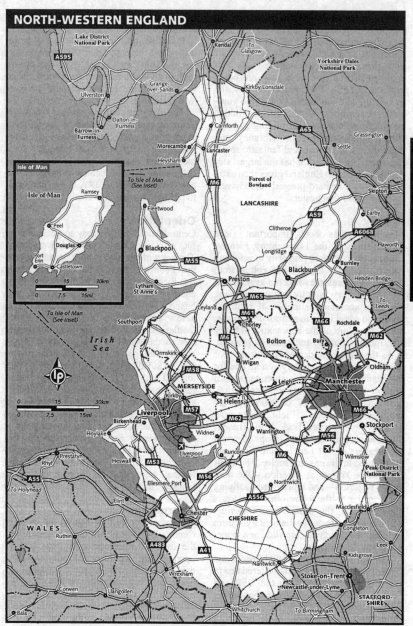

NORTH-WESTERN ENGLAND

improving as warehouses are given new life as upmarket apartment blocks.

You're unlikely to fall in love with Manchester at first sight, especially if one of your first encounters is with the ugly Piccadilly Gardens (but even they are being given a facelift). The longer you stay, the greater the likelihood that you'll find yourself succumbing to the city's hidden charms. Not many cities in England can rival Manchester for its vibrancy and nightlife, its gay scene and fantastic sports facilities. The fact that it has the largest student population in England gives it an extra spark – you'd be hard-pressed not to have a good time in Manchester.

History

Manchester has been important since Roman times. In the 14th century, Flemish weavers (who worked primarily in wool and linen) settled the area. When cotton from the American colonies became available in the 18th century the city, with its weaving tradition, accessible supplies of coal and water and canal links to surrounding towns, became the hub of the new textile industry and, in effect, of the Industrial Revolution.

As the city grew, demands increased for reform of the parliamentary system and for free trade; the artificial protection of corn prices by the Corn Law tariffs was particularly unpopular. In 1819, 60,000 people assembled in St Peter's Field, a site now occupied by the Free Trade Hall. The authorities ordered mounted troops to arrest the speakers and 11 people were killed and 400 injured in the ensuing melee. The affair came to be known as Peterloo – the poor man's Waterloo – and it provided a rallying point in the battle for reform. Two years after Peterloo, the *Manchester Guardian* was founded to foster parliamentary reform and free trade; today's *Guardian* newspaper is a direct descendent.

The late 19th century brought economic depression as textile exports suffered due to growing competition from the USA and Europe. Rather than re-equip themselves with modern machines, the mill owners exploited the captive markets of the Empire, a process that continued into the 20th century and led to the industry's final decline.

In an attempt to reduce the loss of its industry to Liverpool and its reliance on cotton, the Ship Canal to the River Mersey was built in 1894. Manchester briefly flourished as Britain's third-largest port until its post-WWII decline.

The city was badly damaged by WWII bombing and then battered by the postwar decline in manufacturing industries. It remains one of Britain's most important commercial and financial centres, with a thriving cultural life. In 1996, central Manchester was badly damaged by an IRA bomb, and work to put right the damage is still going on.

Orientation

Central Manchester is easy to get round on foot or by the excellent Metrolink tramway. The heart of the city, if only because all the buses converge on it, is the hideous, gardenless Piccadilly Gardens. Canal St and Manchester's famous Gay Village (see the later boxed text 'Gay & Lesbian Manchester') lie a few streets south of the Gardens, the Castlefield Urban Heritage Park a little farther to the west. The University of Manchester lies south of the city centre (on Oxford St/Rd). Continue south along Wilmslow Rd and you'll reach the cheap Indian restaurants of Rusholme and the student area. West of the university is Moss Side, a ghetto with high unemployment and a thriving drug trade controlled by violent gangs – don't go near it. Farther west again, near the Bridgewater Canal, is Old Trafford, home to Manchester United, England's most famous football team, and to Lancashire County Cricket Club's oval.

Information

The extremely helpful Tourist Information Centre (TIC; ☎ 234 3157, fax 236 9900), in the town hall extension off St Peter Square, opens 10 am to 5.30 pm Monday to Saturday and 11 am to 4 pm Sunday. Castlefield has its own visitors centre (☎ 834 4026, fax 839 8747, @ enquiries@castlefield.org.uk), 101 Liverpool Rd, also open daily. There are two information desks at the airport (☎ 489

6412) and a 24-hour Phone Guide service (☎ 0891 8715533) with accommodation details and so on. Calls cost 60p a minute.

The TIC sells tickets for guided walks on themes such as 'Canals Under the City Streets' and 'Death on the Doorstep (Cholera)' – how inviting! These operate most weekends and almost daily all year round. They cost £4/3 for an adult/child.

The post office on Lincoln Square opens 9 am to 5.30 pm Monday to Friday.

Keep in touch with friends and family at the Internet cafe Cyberia at the northern end of Oxford St.

Manchester's Web site at www.manchester .gov.uk/24hrcity/ offers information on a range of subjects.

City Centre

Dominating Albert Square is the enormous Victorian Gothic **town hall**, designed by Albert Waterhouse (of London's Natural History Museum fame) in 1876, with an 85m-high tower. The interior is rich in sculpture and baroque decoration; ask the TIC about the very informative tours.

The distinctive circular building on St Peter's Square houses the **Central Library** and the **Library Theatre**. On Peter St, the **Free Trade Hall** is the third to be built on the site of the Peterloo massacre.

Farther west on Deansgate, the gorgeous **John Rylands Library** (☎ 834 5343), built in memory of the wealthy cotton manufacturer, is another good example of Victorian Gothic. It has a fine collection of early printed books (including a Gutenberg Bible, several Caxtons and manuscripts dating back to 2000 BC). It opens 10 am to 5.30 pm Monday to Friday and 10 am to 1 pm Saturday. Admission is free. Tours every Wednesday at noon cost £1.

The **Pumphouse People's History Museum** (☎ 839 6061), Bridge St, focuses on social history and the Labour movement. The pumphouse itself is an Edwardian pumping station that provided hydraulic power to the city from 1909 to 1972. It opens 11 am to 4.30 pm daily except Monday. Admission costs £1 (free on Friday).

The area around King St and St Ann's Square is Manchester's **West End**. It's the most attractive part of the city centre and the pedestrianised streets are lined with classy shops.

On the north-western side of St Ann's Square is the beautiful glass-roofed **Barton Arcade**. It was built in 1871 and unfortunately is now largely bereft of shops. On the eastern side of St Ann's Square is the imposing **Royal Exchange**, originally at the hub of the city's commerce. Trading boards still show the exact price of raw cotton around the world on the day the building closed. It's now home to shops, a cafe-bar and a theatre.

Opposite, and in stark contrast, stands the hideous monstrosity of the **Arndale Centre**, at 10 hectares it's one of the largest (and surely ugliest) covered shopping areas in Europe. Improvements are still going on after the bomb blast but the structure is now complete. Farther up Deansgate, the 15th-century perpendicular **cathedral** was the focal point of medieval Manchester. It was substantially restored after bomb damage in WWII. Across Fennel St from the cathedral is **Chetham's Hospital School & Library**, a medieval manor house, now a national school for young musicians.

The **City Art Gallery** on the corner of Princess and Mosley Sts was designed by Sir Charles Barry (architect for the Houses of Parliament) in 1824. It is currently undergoing a £25 million expansion scheme, which includes the refurbishment of current galleries, the creation of new galleries and an education centre and the provision of full access for disabled persons. Its impressive collection covers everything from early Italian, Dutch and Flemish painters to Gainsborough, Blake, Constable and the Pre-Raphaelites. It's expected to reopen late 2001; check with the TIC for daily opening times.

Castlefield Urban Heritage Park

In AD 79, Castlefield was at the heart of Manchester's fortunes when a Roman fort was built here. It starred again from 1761 when the opening of the Bridgewater Canal put it at the centre of a revolutionary transport network. In 1830 the world's first passenger train station opened in Liverpool Rd.

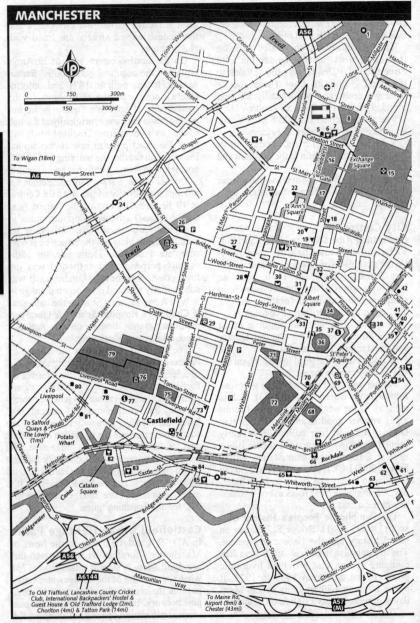

MANCHESTER

NORTH-WESTERN ENGLAND

To Wigan (18mi)

Castlefield

To Liverpool

To Salford Quays & The Lowry (1mi)

Catalan Square

To Old Trafford, Lancashire County Cricket Club, International Backpackers' Hostel & Guest House & Old Trafford Lodge (2mi), Chorlton (4mi) & Tatton Park (14mi)

To Maine Rd, Airport (9mi) & Chester (43mi)

MANCHESTER

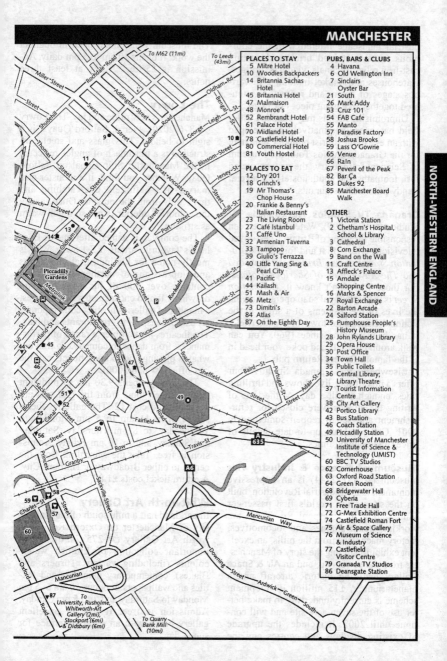

PLACES TO STAY
5 Mitre Hotel
10 Woodies Backpackers
14 Britannia Sachas Hotel
45 Britannia Hotel
47 Malmaison
48 Monroe's
52 Rembrandt Hotel
61 Palace Hotel
70 Midland Hotel
78 Castlefield Hotel
80 Commercial Hotel
81 Youth Hostel

PLACES TO EAT
12 Dry 201
18 Grinch's
19 Mr Thomas's Chop House
20 Frankie & Benny's Italian Restaurant
23 The Living Room
27 Café Istanbul
31 Caffé Uno
32 Armenian Taverna
33 Tampopo
39 Giulio's Terrazza
40 Little Yang Sing & Pearl City
41 Pacific
44 Kailash
51 Mash & Air
56 Metz
73 Dimitri's
84 Atlas
87 On the Eighth Day

PUBS, BARS & CLUBS
4 Havana
6 Old Wellington Inn
7 Sinclairs Oyster Bar
21 South
26 Mark Addy
53 Cruz 101
55 FAB Cafe
55 Manto
57 Paradise Factory
58 Joshua Brooks
59 Lass O'Gowrie
65 Venue
66 Rain
67 Peveril of the Peak
82 Bar Ça
83 Dukes 92
85 Manchester Board Walk

OTHER
1 Victoria Station
2 Chetham's Hospital, School & Library
3 Cathedral
8 Corn Exchange
9 Band on the Wall
11 Craft Centre
13 Affleck's Palace
15 Arndale Shopping Centre
16 Marks & Spencer
17 Royal Exchange
22 Barton Arcade
24 Salford Station
25 Pumphouse People's History Museum
28 John Rylands Library
29 Opera House
30 Post Office
34 Town Hall
35 Public Toilets
36 Central Library; Library Theatre
37 Tourist Information Centre
38 City Art Gallery
42 Portico Library
43 Bus Station
46 Coach Station
49 Piccadilly Station
50 University of Manchester Institute of Science & Technology (UMIST)
60 BBC TV Studios
62 Cornerhouse
63 Oxford Road Station
64 Green Room
68 Bridgewater Hall
69 Cyberia
71 Free Trade Hall
72 G-Mex Exhibition Centre
74 Castlefield Roman Fort
75 Air & Space Gallery
76 Museum of Science & Industry
77 Castlefield Visitor Centre
79 Granada TV Studios
86 Deansgate Station

NORTH-WESTERN ENGLAND

The legacy of all this is an extraordinary industrial landscape littered with the enormous weather-stained brick and rusting cast-iron relics of canals, viaducts, bridges, warehouses and market buildings, in various stages of decay and renovation, tumbled together like giant pieces of Lego.

Unpromising as this may sound, Castlefield has been imaginatively redeveloped with an eye to the tourist pound. Come here for the Granada Studios Tour, the Museum of Science & Industry, the reconstructed fort, footpaths, the youth hostel and several trendy pubs and restaurants.

Granada TV Studios The Granada TV Studios (☎ 832 4999), Water St, have been responsible for many of Britain's best-loved television series – first and foremost *Coronation Street* but also *Brideshead Revisited* and *The Adventures of Sherlock Holmes*. For those who don't know it, *Coronation Street* is the archetypal soap opera, showing the lives of the residents of a street in the fictional Lancashire town of Weatherfield. It has been running since 1960. You can walk around the sets and poke your head in at the famous **Rovers Return** pub.

Elsewhere, the Granada Studios Tour offers a mix of sets, live shows and thrilling rides, enough to fill a day. At the time of writing the studios were closed for refurbishment and set to reopen sometime in 2001. Call to obtain up-to-date details of prices and opening times.

Museum of Science & Industry This museum (☎ 832 2244) is an impressive monument to the Industrial Revolution, built on the site of the world's first passenger train station in Liverpool Rd. There are working steam engines and locomotives, factory machinery from the mills, an excellent exhibition telling the story of Manchester from the sewers up, and an **Air & Space Gallery** featuring historic aircraft and a planetarium. A £15 million development scheme is currently underway to make better use of the seven-acre site and will continue until 2002. It includes the upgrade of existing displays and centres and the creation of interactive exhibits and galleries. The museum will remain open throughout the work. It opens 10 am to 5 pm daily. Admission is £5/free. Allow at least three hours.

The Lowry

Manchester's new pride and joy, The Lowry (☎ 876 2020), Pier 8, Salford Quays, is a sight to behold. This glass and steel construction is a mishmash of angles reflected in the Manchester Ship Canal on Salford Quay. Whether you think it a monster or a marvel, it's definitely eye-catching and that's only from the outside. Once inside, the colourful interior is not so much warm as striking.

The complex is named after one of England's favourite artists, LS Lowry, who is mostly noted for his industrial landscapes and impressions of northern towns, and contains over 300 of his paintings and drawings. It also encapsulates two theatres, a number of galleries hosting contemporary art exhibitions, shops, restaurants and bars. The theatres host a diverse range of performances, from dance to comedy. To find out what is playing and to book tickets call the box office (☎ 876 2000).

The Lowry opens 9.30 am to midnight daily. Guided tours from the galleries are available and cost £2. The galleries themselves open 11 am to 5 pm Monday to Wednesday, to 8 pm Thursday, Saturday and Sunday, and to 10 pm Friday. Admission is free. Take the Metrolink from the centre to either Broadway or Harbour City. A return ticket costs £1.80.

Whitworth Art Gallery

In parkland half a mile south of the University of Manchester on Oxford Rd, Whitworth Art Gallery (☎ 275 7450) has an important collection of English watercolours (including various Turners and Blakes), contemporary paintings and textiles and wallpapers. It opens 10 am to 5 pm Monday to Saturday and 2 to 5 pm Sunday. Admission is free. It has an excellent gallery bistro with an outdoor terrace for sunny days.

Places to Stay

There's a reasonable range of places to stay but most cheap options are some way from the centre. The big central hotels cater to businesspeople during the week and often offer excellent weekend rates. The TIC charges £2.50 to make bookings so try ringing round yourself first.

Note that beds fill up quickly whenever Manchester United are playing at home.

Hostels The stunning *Manchester Youth Hostel* (☎ 839 9960, fax 835 2054, @ *manchester@yha.org.uk, Potato Wharf)*, near the Museum of Science & Industry in the Castlefield area, has comfortable four-bed dorms for £18/13.50 for adults/under-18s. From mid-June to mid-September, the University of Manchester lets student rooms to visitors from around £12.25 per person, £8 if you're a student. Contact *St Anselm Hall* (☎ 224 7327, 14 Victoria Park) or *Woolaton Hall* (☎ 224 7244).

Two miles south of the centre, Stretford has a good private hostel. The *International Backpackers' Hostel & Guest House* (☎ 872 3499, 41 Greatstone Rd) has beds from £10, cooking facilities and a TV lounge. The closest Metrolink stop is Old Trafford.

The newly opened *Woodies Backpackers* (☎ 228 3456, @ *backpackers@woodiesuk .freeserve.co.uk, 19 Blossom St)*, 10 minutes' walk north-east of Piccadilly Gardens, is modern and comfortable and offers Internet access. Dorm beds cost £12 per night.

B&Bs & Hotels – Central Liverpool Rd in Castlefield offers two good accommodation options. The *Commercial Hotel* (☎ 834 3504, 125 Liverpool Rd) is a traditional pub close to the museum with singles/doubles for £25/40. Rather pricier is the modern *Castlefield Hotel* (☎ 832 7073, fax 837 3534, 3 Liverpool Rd)* with rooms for £49/59 at weekends, including use of its sports facilities.

The warm and welcoming *Mitre Hotel* (☎ 834 4128, fax 839 1646, Cathedral Gates)* is well placed near Victoria Station. Rooms without bathroom can cost as little as £20 per person; ask for one with views of the cathedral.

Opposite Manchester Piccadilly train station, *Monroe's* (☎ 236 0564, 38 London Rd)*, popular with a gay clientele, offers rooms for £25/36. Another popular gay hotel and hangout is the *Rembrandt Hotel* (☎ 236 1311, fax 236 4257 @ *therembrandt hotel@aol.com, 1 Sackville St)* in the heart of the Gay Village on Canal St. Rooms cost £35/50 with bathroom.

Once a cotton warehouse, the *Britannia Hotel* (☎ 228 2288, @ *sales@britannia-man.itsnet.co.uk, Portland St)* has been converted into a luxury four-star hotel. Singles cost £39.50 to £60, doubles costs £65 to £105. The *Britannia Sachas Hotel* (☎ 228 1234, fax 236 9202 @ *brit-sachas@connect free.co.uk, Tib St)*, which looks run down but is actually quite nice inside, has rooms from £45/65 at weekends.

Palace Hotel (☎ 288 1111, fax 288 2222, Oxford St)*, near Oxford Rd station, is in a converted 19th-century insurance company building. Rooms, some more interesting than others, cost from £99/£126 at weekends; cheaper deals exist if there's availability.

The sumptuous Edwardian *Midland Hotel* (☎ 236 3333, fax 932 4100, @ *sales@mhccl .demon.co.uk, Peter St)*, opposite the G-Mex Exhibition Centre, is where Mr Rolls and Mr Royce supposedly met. Weekend rates start from £99 for a double, a standard double on weekdays costs £139.

Across the road from Piccadilly station is the luxurious *Malmaison* (☎ 278 1000, fax 278 1002, @ *manchester@malmaison.com, Joshua Hoyle Building Auburn St)* with rooms for a flat-rate £110 and a French brasserie.

B&Bs & Hotels – Suburbs Didsbury, 4 miles from central Manchester, is an attractive southern suburb, with good local pubs and frequent buses into the city. Wilmslow and Palatine Rds have many hotels in converted Victorian houses.

The comfortable *Elm Grange Hotel* (☎/fax 445 3336, @ *elmgrange.hotel@tvc .org.uk, 561 Wilmslow Rd)* has singles/doubles from £31/48. *Fernbank Guest House* (☎ 01625-523729, fax 539515, Wilmslow Rd)* is 12 miles from the centre but only 10 minutes from the airport. It is comfortable, pleasant and similarly priced.

Cricket fans can stay at the **Old Trafford Lodge** (☎ 874 3333, 📧 sales.lancs@ecb.co .uk, Talbot Rd) which has modern rooms overlooking the Lancashire cricket ground. At weekends rooms cost £42; book ahead when there's a match on.

Chorlton, 2½ miles from the centre, also has plenty of B&Bs that are reasonably convenient for Old Trafford to the south-west of the city centre.

Places to Eat

Restaurants The most distinctive restaurant zones are Chinatown in the city centre and Rusholme in the south. The restaurants listed here are just the tip of the iceberg.

Chinatown, bounded by Charlotte, Portland, Oxford and Mosley Sts, has lots of restaurants. Many, but not all, are Chinese and most are not particularly cheap. Highly acclaimed is the **Little Yang Sing** (☎ 228 7722, 17 George St), specialising in Cantonese cuisine. During the day there is a set menu for £8.95 but expect to pay twice that in the evening. **Pacific** (☎ 228 6668, 58 George St) is a highly rated Thai/Chinese restaurant serving up fantastic food. Readers of this guide rate **Pearl City** (☎ 228 7683, 23 George St) where the house banquet for two costs £19.50 per person.

Rusholme, on Wilmslow Rd, the extension of Oxford St/Rd, is more commonly known as Curry Mile and has a concentration of Indian/Pakistani restaurants unsurpassed in Europe. Try **Sanam Sweet House & Restaurant** (☎ 224 8824, 145 Wilmslow Rd), which does Karachi chicken for £5.50 as well as an array of mouth-watering sweets. **Darbar** (☎ 224 4392, 65–67 Wilmslow Rd) is not only cheap (student discounts are available) but exceptionally good. Most main courses cost between £6.50 and £6.90. Bring your own booze. More central, the deservedly popular **Kailash** (☎ 236 1085, 34 Charlotte St) serves Nepalese and Indian dishes – four-course lunches cost £5.80.

Grinch's (☎ 907 3210, Chapel Walks) serves chilled crispy duck wrap for £5.25 in arty surroundings. The name may not be

inviting, but the food at **Mr Thomas's Chop House** is. It's probably the best pub food in town and they pour great real ale; dishes start at £6.50.

Albert Square is gradually filling up with places to eat. In addition to **Caffé Uno**, look out for **Tampopo** (☎ 819 1966), a minimalist noodle bar where mee goreng costs £6.25.

More unusual is the basement **Armenian Taverna** (☎ 934 9025, 3–5 Princess St) which will do you a cous cous bidaoui for £7.90 or a Tbilisi kebab for £7.95. It closes on Monday. Farther west is the colourful **Café Istanbul** (☎ 833 9942, Bridge St), serving up a nice range of dishes including Istanbul chicken for £8.60. **Giulio's Terrazza** (☎ 236 4033, 14 Nicholas St) dishes up business lunches for £6.50. **Frankie & Benny's Italian Restaurant** (☎ 835 2479, 36 St Ann St) does spaghetti ragu bolognese for £5.45.

Vegetarians could try **On the Eighth Day** (☎ 273 4878, 111 Oxford Rd) next to the Metropolitan University or the pleasant **Dimitri's** (☎ 839 3319, Campfield Arcade) which serves up a mixture of Greek, Italian and Spanish food. A quick lunch will cost £3.

Cafes Cafe-bars, like many places, are big in Manchester. The first, **Dry 201** (☎ 236 5920, 28 Oldham St), is still among the best and coolest. **Atlas** (☎ 834 2124, 376 Deansgate), wedged beneath the railway line and a couple of busy streets, is a funky place serving up good Italian food. If you want to catch a glimpse of the Manchester United players, try the ultra-trendy **The Living Room** (Deansgate).

Entertainment

In keeping with its old 'Madchester' reputation, Manchester comes into its own at night, offering all sorts of high-quality entertainment. City Life, an invaluable, fortnightly what's-on magazine, has the details.

Pubs & Bars There are plenty of places to go if all you're looking for is a pint. The **Lass O'Gowrie** (☎ 273 6932, 36 Charles St), off Oxford St, is a popular student hangout, with an excellent small brewery on the premises and good-value bar meals.

Two historic pubs that required a lot of repair after the 1996 bomb are the *Old Wellington Inn* (☎ *830 1440, 4 Cathedral Gates)* and *Sinclairs Oyster Bar* at the top of New Cathedral St. Both are great for a quiet pint or for soaking up the sun outdoors. *Peveril of the Peak* (☎ *236 6364, 127 Great Bridgewater St)* is another unpretentious pub with wonderful Victorian glazed tilework outside. Opposite is *Ra¡n* (☎ *235 6500, 80 Great Bridgewater St)*, a relaxed drinkers joint with a huge balcony out back.

There are several popular places to drink in Castlefield, including *Bar Ça* (☎ *839 7099, Catalan Square)* which is owned by Mick Hucknall of Simply Red and has outdoor seating for sunny days. Another option is *Dukes 92*, (☎ *839 8646, 2 Castle St)* a popular canalside pub. For more waterside views, try *Joshua Brooks* (☎ *274 4059, Charles St)* with a canalside balcony, or *Mark Addy* (☎ *832 4080, Stanley St)*, one of the few places perched on the River Irwell.

Clubs The clubbing scene in Manchester is London's biggest challenger for the clubbing crown in Britain, and the following is but a small selection of the choice in Manchester. Clubs host a forever-changing mixture of dance nights, so check *City Life* for what's on when you're in town. Both Dry 201 (see Cafes earlier) and Joshua Brooks (see Pubs & Bars earlier) hold regular club nights.

South (☎ *831 7756, 4A King St)* is a popular club, especially on Saturdays nights when funk and disco fill the airwaves.

If you're a big fan of *Thunderbirds* check out *FAB Cafe* (☎ *236 2019, 111 Portland St)*. The music is loud but best of all are the Thunderbirds models and puppets decorating the club. FAB Virgil!

For Latino groves head to *Havana* (☎ *832 8900, 42 Blackfriars St)*, with the occasional free dance lesson given early in the evening.

Gay nightlife is centred on Canal St and has had a resurgence since the groundbreaking TV series *Queer as Folk* was screened on British television (see the boxed text 'Gay & Lesbian Manchester'). The likes of the *Rembrandt Hotel* (see Places to Stay earlier) and the ever-popular *Manto* (☎ *236 2667, 46 Canal St)* are but a few of

NORTH-WESTERN ENGLAND

Gay & Lesbian Manchester

Apart from London, Manchester has the best gay scene in Britain, and the scene has been boosted by the *Queer as Folk* series which was screened on primetime British television in 1999 and 2000. Following the lives and loves of three young men in and around the 'Gay Village', it attracted first criticism then acclaim, and focused the spotlight on Manchester's gay life.

The TIC stocks the useful *Gay & Lesbian Village Guide* that lists numerous gay bars, clubs, galleries and groups, including the Manchester Gay Centre (☎ 274 3814) on Sydney St. The Lesbian & Gay Switchboard (☎ 274 3999) operates 4 to 10 pm daily. *All Points North* is a good free monthly paper covering the north of England and Scotland.

The centre of Manchester's vibrant gay nightlife scene is Canal St. There are said to be over 30 bars and clubs in the so-called 'Gay Village'. The ground-breaker was the Manto Bar (☎ 236 2667, 46 Canal St), which has been copied around the world. Across the canal is Metz (☎ 237 9852), another cafe bar, currently more fashionable than Manto. There are several more traditional pubs nearby, including the New Union (☎ 228 1492). On Friday there's a women-only night at the upstairs bar at the Rembrandt Hotel (☎ 236 1311, 33 Sackville St).

The club scene changes so quickly it's difficult to make recommendations but the Paradise Factory (see Clubs above) is usually popular. Nearby is Cruz 101 (☎ 237 1554, 101 Princess St), the largest gay nightclub in the city.

Britain's biggest gay and lesbian arts festival, It's Queer Up North (IQUP), takes place every two years – next in spring 2002. The Manchester Mardi Gras kicks off around the end of August each year and attracts around 500,000 people.

the lively spots. *Paradise Factory* (☎ 273 5422, 112 Princess St) is a cutting edge club, with gay nights at the weekend.

Live Music The famous music scene that spawned The Smiths, Joy Division, New Order, and the 'Manchester Sound' of the Stone Roses, The Charlatans and the Happy Mondays continues, although it's more subdued than at its peak. One of the best live music venues is *Band on the Wall* (☎ 832 6625, Swan St) which hosts everything from jazz to blues, folk and pop. *Manchester Board Walk* (☎ 228 3555, Little Peter St) and the *Venue* (☎ 236 0026, Whitworth St West) are also good venues. Many of the cafes mentioned in the Places to Eat section hold regular club nights.

Classical Music Manchester is home to two world-famous symphony orchestras, the cash-strapped Halle and the BBC Philharmonic. The enormous and impressive *Bridgewater Hall* (☎ 907 9000, Lower Mosley St), home to the Halle, was completed in 1996 at a cost of £42 million. Another large venue is the *Opera House* (☎ 242 2509, Quay St).

Theatre, Cinema & Exhibitions The *Green Room* (☎ 236 1677, 54 Whitworth St West) is the premiere fringe venue and also has a good cafe-bar. There's nearly always something interesting on at the *Royal Exchange* (☎ 833 9833, St Ann's Square) or the *Library Theatre* (☎ 236 7110, St Peter's Square).

The *Cornerhouse* (☎ 228 2463, 70 Oxford St) has a decent cinema, gallery and cafe.

Opposite the Bridgewater Hall, the *G-Mex Exhibition Centre* (☎ 834 2700), cleverly converted from the derelict Central train station, hosts exhibitions, concerts and indoor sporting events.

Spectator Sports

Manchester United Many regard Manchester United's Old Trafford stadium as holy ground – almost every week supporters demonstrate this literally by asking to have their ashes scattered on the pitch (and they are – behind the goals, where it doesn't matter if it damages the grass).

There are tours (☎ 868 8631), every 10 minutes, 9.30 am to 4.30 pm daily (except match days). The museum opens 9.30 am to 5 pm daily. Admission to the museum and the tour costs £8/5.50; the museum only costs £5/3.50. Tickets to games are as scarce as hens' teeth, even if Manchester United are playing a friendly against Scunthorpe United. A return Metrolink ticket to Old Trafford costs £1.80 from the centre.

Manchester City Manchester's second premiership club (some would say the first) is enjoying a resurgence in its fortune at present; over the last few years it's tumbled from the premiership to the second division and back again. The club enjoys a fanatical following so tickets will be just as hard to come by at Maine Road (the club ground in the heart of Moss Side) as at Old Trafford, but you can try on ☎ 226 2224. There's also a tour of the ground (☎ 226 1782), which costs £3. If you plan to talk footy while in town, whatever you do don't mix up the teams!

Lancashire County Cricket Club The Lancashire Club (☎ 282 4000), Warwick Rd, hosts county matches throughout the summer, and international test matches. Admission to county games costs £8 to £10.

Shopping

In Oldham St, to the north of Piccadilly Gardens, **Affleck's Palace** is a restored warehouse full of stalls, shops and cafes selling clubbing gear from young designers, secondhand clothes, crystals, leather gear, records – you name it. A thriving, buzzy place with a great atmosphere, it opens 10 am to 5.30 pm Monday to Saturday. Don't miss it.

The world's largest **Marks & Spencer**, covers an enormous 23,000 sq metres of newly built shopping heaven. The building itself is a commanding state-of-the-art construction. A handy walkway connects with the Arndale Centre.

One hundred metres north of Affleck's Palace is Manchester's impressive **Craft**

Centre (☎ 832 4274), housed in the old fish and poultry market building. It opens 10 am to 5.30 pm Monday to Saturday.

All your regular high street shops can be found at the northern end of Deansgate.

Getting There & Away

Manchester is about 200 miles (three hours) from London, 250 miles from Glasgow (3½ hours), 60 miles from York (two hours) and 35 miles (half an hour) from Liverpool by road.

Air Manchester airport (☎ 489 3000) is the largest outside London, serving 35 countries. It's convenient if you're heading to/from the north or the Lake District. A train to the airport costs £2.70, a coach £2. The excellent TIC at the airport can recommend nearby B&Bs, some of which will pick you up and drop you off.

Bus National Express (☎ 0870 580 8080) offers numerous coach links with the rest of the country from Chorlton St coach station in the city centre. Buses leave almost hourly from Manchester to Liverpool (£4, one hour) and Leeds (£7, 80 minutes). A coach to London costs £15 (4¾ hours).

Train Manchester Piccadilly is the main station for trains to and from the rest of the country, although Victoria station serves Halifax and Bradford. The two stations are linked by Metrolink. Trains run to Liverpool Lime St (£6.95, one hour) but are slower now than in Victorian times! Numerous trains serve the following destinations: London (£44, three hours), Glasgow (£38.90, three hours) and Newcastle (£32.50, three hours).

Getting Around

Day Saver tickets allow one day's travel throughout the Greater Manchester area and cover a range of transport combinations: bus only (£3), bus and train (£3.50), bus and Metrolink (£4.50) train and Metrolink (£5) and all three (£6.50). For enquiries about local transport, including night buses, phone ☎ 228 7811 (8 am to 8 pm daily).

Bus Centreline bus No 4 provides a free service around the heart of Manchester every 10 minutes. Pick up a route map from the TIC. Most local buses start from Piccadilly Gardens where the downside of bus deregulation is obvious in the crush of multi-coloured vehicles, all touting different fares to move you about the city. The central Travelshop (at the TIC) has timetables but no fares, forcing you to consult each bus driver individually.

Metrolink The Metrolink trams operate on a mixture of disused rail tracks and tracks laid along the city-centre streets. There are frequent links between Victoria and Piccadilly train stations and G-Mex (for Castlefield). Buy tickets at the machines on the platforms. For information phone ☎ 205 2000. A return to the Lowry Centre or Old Trafford is £1.70.

Train Castlefield is served by Deansgate station with rail links to Piccadilly, Oxford Rd and Salford Crescent stations.

AROUND MANCHESTER
Quarry Bank Mill

In Wilmslow, 10 miles south of Manchester, you can visit an 18th-century cotton mill in beautiful Styal Country Park. Not only can you see the old waterwheel that used to power the mill and some of the old machinery, but costumed guides in the **Apprentice House** will give you a depressing insight into the life of some of the mill's younger workers – a life of shared beds, and brimstone and treacle cures. Owned by the National Trust (NT), the mill (☎ 01625-527468) opens 11 am to 6 pm, April to September, closing at 5 pm and on Monday during the rest of the year. The Apprentice House opens 2 to 4.30 pm Tuesday to Friday and 11.30 am to 6 pm weekends. Admission costs £6/3.70 for both. To get there take a train (except Sunday) to Styal station and walk for half a mile, or catch the free No 200 bus from Manchester airport. The car park costs £2.

Wigan Pier Heritage Centre

Home to the now defunct band The Verve and one of Britain's top rugby league teams, Wigan is otherwise a dreary Midlands town, famous mainly because George Orwell used it as the basis for his book, *The Road to Wigan Pier*. But forget any thought of fortune-telling booths and kiss-me-quick hats – this pier was never more exciting than a contraption used for tipping coal into barges on the Leeds & Liverpool Canal.

Nevertheless, the site has been used to create a fine heritage centre that attempts to bring to life what it was like to work in a mine in the late 1800s. You can also see inside an old textile mill, whose machinery can still be set working for visitors, and Opies museum, housing a collection of memorabilia from the 1900s to the present day.

The Heritage Centre (☎ 01942-323666) opens 10 am to 5 pm Monday to Thursday and from 11 am at weekends. Admission to all the attractions costs £6.95/5.25. There's also a TIC (☎ 01942-825677) in the mill building that provides an accommodation service. To get there, take bus No 32 from Cannon St in Manchester city centre (1¼ hours), or take a train to Wigan station from Victoria station (Manchester) or Liverpool.

Tatton Park

Three and a half miles north of Knutsford, the huge Tatton Park estate (☎ 01625-534435; NT) is set around 19th-century Wyatt House. There's a medieval great hall, a 1930s-style working farm and a series of gardens. Wyatt House opens noon to 4 pm daily (except Monday), April to October, although the park opens 10 am to 7 pm daily. Only the house and gardens are free to NT members. Admission to the mansion costs £3/2, the farm £2.50/1.50 and the old hall 2.50/1.50. Tickets to any two of the Tatton attractions is £4.50/2.50. Car admission to the park costs £3.50.

On Sunday, bus No X2 links Tatton Park with Chester (one hour). Attractive, upmarket Knutsford has a good choice of places to stay and eat.

Cheshire

You can scan the stars with the gigantic radio telescope at Jodrell Bank, investigate the canals at the wonderful waterways museum at Ellesmere Port, or return your Roller to its birthplace at Crewe, but when it comes down to it, Cheshire is all about Chester.

CHESTER
☎ 01244 • pop 80,000

Despite steady streams of tourists Chester remains a beautiful town, ringed by an almost continuous red sandstone wall that dates back to the Roman times. However, appearances can be deceptive – many of the medieval-looking buildings in the centre are actually Victorian.

History

Roman Chester was the fortress city of Deva, a bulwark against the fierce Welsh tribes. It was not completely abandoned when the Romans withdrew in the 5th century, but the Welsh border is only a stone's throw west of Chester and the Welsh remained a threat long after the Romans had gone. It was only in the 14th century that the danger subsided and the regulations which banned the Welsh from the town after dark and stipulated that they couldn't bear arms, hold meetings or enter pubs were withdrawn.

Medieval Chester became the largest port in the north-west but in the Civil War the city took the Royalist side and was besieged for 18 months (1645–46) by Cromwell's forces. It wasn't until the next century that the walls were repaired and took on a new role as a tourist attraction. The first guidebook to Chester was published in 1781!

Orientation

Nestling in a bow formed by the River Dee, the walled centre is now surrounded by suburbs. Most places of interest are inside the walls where the Roman street pattern is relatively intact. From the High Cross (the stone pillar which marks the town centre), four roads fan out to the four principal gates. A nasty ring road, which cuts through the city walls, also encircles the centre.

Information

The TIC (☎ 402111, ⓔ tourism@chester .org), Northgate St, is in the town hall opposite the cathedral. It opens 9 am to 5.30 pm

CHESTER

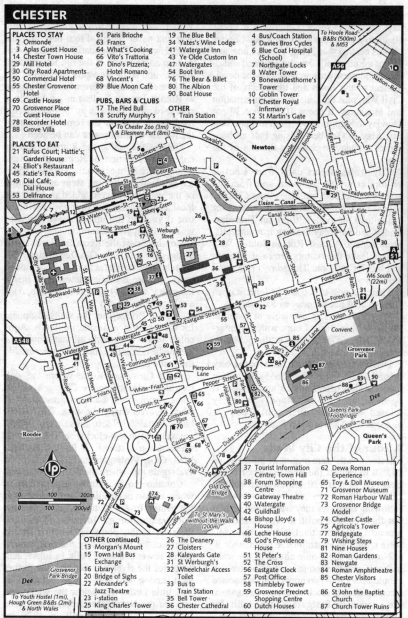

PLACES TO STAY
2 Ormonde
3 Aplas Guest House
14 Chester Town House
29 Mill Hotel
30 City Road Apartments
50 Commercial Hotel
55 Chester Grosvenor Hotel
69 Castle House
70 Grosvenor Place Guest House
78 Recorder Hotel
88 Grove Villa

PLACES TO EAT
21 Rufus Court; Hattie's; Garden House
24 Elliot's Restaurant
45 Katie's Tea Rooms
49 Dial Café; Dial House
53 Delifrance
61 Paris Brioche
63 Francs
64 What's Cooking
66 Vito's Trattoria
67 Dino's Pizzeria; Hotel Romano
68 Vincent's
89 Blue Moon Café

PUBS, BARS & CLUBS
17 The Pied Bull
18 Scruffy Murphy's
19 The Blue Bell
34 Yates's Wine Lodge
41 Watergate Inn
43 Ye Olde Custom Inn
47 Watergates
54 Boot Inn
76 The Bear & Billet
80 The Albion
90 Boat House

OTHER
1 Train Station
4 Bus/Coach Station
5 Davies Bros Cycles
6 Blue Coat Hospital (School)
7 Northgate Locks
8 Water Tower
9 Bonewaldesthorne's Tower
10 Goblin Tower
11 Chester Royal Infirmary
12 St Martin's Gate

OTHER (continued)
13 Morgan's Mount
15 Town Hall Bus Exchange
16 Library
20 Bridge of Sighs
22 Alexander's Jazz Theatre
23 i-station
25 King Charles' Tower
26 The Deanery
27 Cloisters
28 Kaleyards Gate
31 St Werburgh's
32 Wheelchair Access Toilet
33 Bus to Train Station
35 Bell Tower
36 Chester Cathedral
37 Tourist Information Centre; Town Hall
38 Forum Shopping Centre
39 Gateway Theatre
40 Watergate
42 Guildhall
44 Bishop Lloyd's House
46 Leche House
48 God's Providence House
51 St Peter's
52 The Cross
56 Eastgate Clock
57 Post Office
58 Thimbleby Tower
59 Grosvenor Precinct Shopping Centre
60 Dutch Houses
62 Dewa Roman Experience
65 Toy & Doll Museum
71 Grosvenor Museum
72 Roman Harbour Wall
73 Grosvenor Bridge Model
74 Chester Castle
75 Agricola's Tower
77 Bridgegate
79 Wishing Steps
81 Nine Houses
82 Roman Gardens
83 Newgate
84 Roman Amphitheatre
85 Chester Visitors Centre
86 St John the Baptist Church
87 Church Tower Ruins

NORTH-WESTERN ENGLAND

Monday to Saturday and 10 am to 4 pm Sunday, May to October. Otherwise it opens 10 am to 5 pm Monday to Saturday. Chester visitors centre (☎ 402111), Vicar's Lane, just east of the city walls, has displays and audiovisuals on the town's architecture, the development of the Rows and the events of the Civil War, plus the usual tourist information and brochures. It opens 10 am to 5.30 pm Monday to Saturday and 10 am to 4 pm Sunday, May to October, closing half an hour earlier Monday to Saturday the rest of the year.

City walks depart daily from Chester visitors centre at 10.30 am and from the town hall at 10.45 am. They cost £3/2.30. From June to September, Ghosthunter Trails take place at 7.30 pm on Thursday, Friday and Saturday, leaving from the TIC. From June to August, Roman Soldier Wall Patrols leave the visitors centre at 1.45 pm and the TIC at 2 pm Thursday, Friday and Saturday.

There's a post office at 2 St John St open 9 am to 5.30 pm Monday to Saturday.

Internet access is available at *i*-station (☎ 401680) in Rufus Court, which is entered off Abbey Gardens, or in the public library next to the TIC.

Disabled visitors should head for the very helpful Dial House (☎ 345655), Hamilton Place, which offers advice and a cafe. It opens 10 am to 4 pm Monday to Friday (closed Wednesday afternoon). The cafe also opens 10 am to 3 pm Saturday.

A Tour of the City Walls

Chester's walls were originally built around AD 70 to protect the Roman fort of Deva. Between 90 and 120 they were rebuilt in stone by the Roman 20th Legion. Over the following centuries they were often altered but their present position was established around 1200. After the Civil War the walls were rebuilt as a fashionable promenade.

Nowadays the 2-mile circuit of the walls makes a great introduction to Chester and should take 1½ to two hours. This suggested circuit proceeds clockwise from **Eastgate** at the prominent **Eastgate Clock**, built for Queen Victoria's Diamond Jubilee in 1897.

The **Thimbleby Tower**, also known as the Wolf Tower, was destroyed during the Civil War and never rebuilt. From here you can look down on the foundations of the southeastern angle tower of the old Roman fort. Just beyond is the **Newgate**, added in 1938 but in medieval style. From here the original Roman fortress walls ran westwards, a course roughly followed by the modern ring road. From Newgate the remains of part of the **Roman Amphitheatre** can be seen.

Outside the walls, the **Roman Gardens** contain a collection of Roman stonework brought here from excavations around Chester. Descend the **wishing steps** at the corner of the wall. They were added in 1785 and local legend claims that your wish will come true if you can run up and down the steps while holding your breath.

Continue past the Recorder Hotel to the **Bridgegate** beside the **Old Dee Bridge**. This oft-rebuilt bridge dates from 1387, although parts of it are centuries newer. Just inside the gate is the 1664 **Bear & Billet** pub, once a tollgate into the city.

Beyond Bridgegate, the walls disappear for a short stretch. Inside the walls, **Agricola's Tower** is virtually all that remains of the medieval castle. Turn the corner beside the castle ruins.

Cross Grosvenor Rd to where the wall runs alongside the **Roodee**, Chester's ancient horse racing track built on grassland left when the river changed course. The Roodee hosts Britain's oldest horse race which, uniquely, is run anti-clockwise. The city wall stands a-top a stretch of **Roman Harbour Wall**. Cross **Watergate** and look left to the **Watergate Inn**, where the river once passed.

Continue to the north-western corner, where a short peninsula of wall leads out to the **Water Tower**. Actually on the corner, **Bonewaldesthorne's Tower** once guarded the river at this point but when it shifted course in the 14th century the extension to Water Tower had to be built. In subsequent centuries the river has moved even farther west leaving both towers high and dry.

A little farther on, below the walls, you can see the **Northgate Locks**, a short but steep series of locks built in 1779 by

Thomas Telford, the pioneering canal engineer. Continue past **Morgan's Mount** where a Captain Morgan defended the city during the Civil War. Across the canal is the **Blue Coat Hospital (School)**, now closed.

From **Northgate** the walls tower above the **Shropshire Union Canal** which runs in what was once a moat-like ditch constructed by the Romans outside the walls. From **King Charles' Tower** at the corner, Charles I looked out to see his defeated army straggling back from battle in 1645.

Cross the 1275 **Kaleyards Gate** through which monks would go to work in their vegetable gardens outside the walls; it's still ceremonially locked every night at 9 pm. Traces of the original Roman wall are still visible from outside the walls just south of Kaleyards Gate. Continue past **Chester Cathedral** and the **Bell Tower** and you'll be back at the Eastgate Clock.

Chester Cathedral

A Saxon church dedicated to St Werburgh was built here in the 10th century but in 1092 it became a Benedictine abbey and a Norman church replaced the earlier construction. The abbey was closed in 1540 with Henry VIII's dissolution of the monasteries and a year later the building became a cathedral. The 12th-century cloister and its surrounding buildings are essentially unaltered and retain much of the early monastic structure.

The present cathedral (☎ 324756) was built between 1250 and 1540 but there were later alterations and a lot of Victorian reconstruction. It opens 7.30 am to 6.30 pm daily. Visitors are asked to donate £2.

The Rows

Chester's eye-catching two-level shopping streets probably date back to the post-Roman period. As the Roman walls slowly crumbled into rubble, medieval traders may have built their shops against the rubble banks, while later arrivals built theirs on top of the banks. Whatever their origins, the Rows make a convenient rainproof shopping promenade along the four ancient streets fanning out from the Cross.

Dewa Roman Experience

On Pierpoint Lane, off Bridge St, this museum (☎ 343407) aims to show what life was like in Roman times. Your tour begins in a reconstructed galley after which you move into a Roman street and watch an entertaining audiovisual presentation. After that you can wander at your own pace past the Roman castle foundations and medieval rubbish pits, and through the interesting museum and finds' room. It opens 9 am to 5 pm daily. Admission costs £3.95/2.25.

Museums

This **Grosvenor Museum** (☎ 402008), Grosvenor St, has the usual hotchpotch of paintings and silver but the displays on Roman Chester, and particularly the Roman tombstones, are very good, as is the new Chester Timeline Gallery spelling out the city's past. The Stuart, mid-Georgian and Victorian period rooms are also worth seeing. It opens 10.30 am to 5 pm Monday to Saturday and 2 to 5 pm Sunday. Admission is free.

'All things toys' is the idea behind the **Toy & Doll Museum** (☎ 346297) on Lower Bridge St, which displays an eclectic array of antique toys and dolls and opens 10 am to 5 pm Monday to Saturday and 11 am to 5 pm Sunday. Admission costs £2/1.

St John the Baptist Church

Directly opposite the visitors centre in Vicars Lane stands St John the Baptist Church, built on the site of an older Saxon church in 1075. It started out as a cathedral of Mercia before being rebuilt by the Normans. The foundations could not have been too sound as the north-western tower has collapsed twice in its history, in 1573 and 1881. The eastern end of the church, abandoned in 1581 when St John's became a parish, now lies in peaceful ruin and includes the remains of a Norman choir and medieval chapels. The church opens 9.15 am to 6 pm daily.

Along the River

Beyond the city walls, The Groves is a popular riverside promenade leading to Grosvenor Park. You can hire rowing boats (£4 per hour), pedal boats (£4 per half-hour) or motor boats (£4 per half-hour), or take a short cruise (£2.50/1.50 per half-hour).

Chester Zoo

Chester is home to England's largest zoo (☎ 380280), noted for its pleasant garden setting. It opens 10 am daily. Admission costs £9.50/7.

The zoo is on the A41, 3 miles north of the city centre. Bus Nos 11C and 12C run between the Town Hall Bus Exchange and zoo (£1.80 return, every 15 minutes Monday to Saturday, twice-hourly on Sundays).

Places to Stay

Although Chester has numerous places to stay, late arrivals without a reservation may have to do some searching in summer. Most places are outside the city walls but within easy walking distance of the centre. Both the TIC and the visitors centre can arrange accommodation, but charge £3 for the service.

Hostels A mile from the city centre across Grosvenor Park Bridge is the *Chester Youth Hostel* (☎ 680056, fax 681204 ⓔ *chester@ yha.org.uk, 40 Hough Green)*. The nightly cost is £11/7.75 for adults/under-18s.

If you just want a bed try *City Rd Apartments* (☎ 813125, ⓔ *cityroad@lineone.net, 18 City Rd)*. It's close to the city centre with basic beds for £10 per person, sharing a shower.

B&Bs & Hotels – Outside the Walls Brook St near the train station has a couple of good-value B&Bs from around £17 per person. The friendly and accommodating *Ormonde* (☎ 328816, 126 Brook St) and the comfortable *Aplas Guest House* (☎ 312401, 106 Brook St)* are both less than five minutes' walk from the train station.

Hoole Rd, a 10–15 minute walk from the centre and leading beyond the railway tracks to the M53/M56, is lined with low- to mid-price B&Bs . *Bawn Park Hotel* (☎ 324971, fax 310951, 10 Hoole Rd)* is cosy, with B&B starting at £17 per person. The *Ba Ba Guest House* (☎ 315047, ⓔ *reservations@baba guesthouse.freeserve.co.uk, 65 Hoole Rd)* is worth the extra few pounds with rooms from

£20 per person. The attractive, small *Glann Hotel* (☎ 344800, 2 Stone Place),* with a friendly cat, is off the Hoole Rd and charges from £26 per person.

The Victorian *Grove Villa* (☎ 349713, ⓔ *grove.villa@tesco.net, 18 The Groves)*, with views of the River Dee, is one of the better B&Bs in town and has beautiful rooms with bathroom for £20 per person. The larger *Mill Hotel* (☎ 350035, fax 345635, ⓔ *reservations@millhotel.com, Milton St)* on either side of the canal, boasts a health club, swimming pool and canal cruises with singles/doubles from £49/65.

B&Bs & Hotels – Inside the Walls Centrally situated *Grosvenor Place Guest House* (☎ 324455, fax 400225, 2–4 Grosvenor Place)* has singles/doubles for £36/44 with bathroom. The nearby *Castle House* (☎ 350354, 23 Castle St)*, dating from the 16th century, has comfortable rooms (some with bathroom) from £23 per person.

You can't get more central than the *Commercial Hotel* (☎ 320749, fax 348318, St Peter's Churchyard)* which has rooms from £35 per person.

The eager-to-please *Recorder Hotel* (☎ 326580, ⓔ *ebbs@compuserve.com, 19 City Walls)* is just off Lower Bridge St, right on the walls and near the river. The newly refurbished rooms are lovely and cost from £35 per person. The *Chester Town House* (☎ 350021, ⓔ *davidbellis@chestertown house.co.uk, 23 King St)* in its quiet, pleasantly old-world surroundings, dates from 1680. Rooms with a bathroom cost £35/50. At *Hotel Romano* (☎ 320841, Lower Bridge St),* above Dino's Pizzeria (see Places to Eat later), rooms cost £45/65.

If you're pushing the boat out, the *Chester Grosvenor Hotel* (☎ 324024, ⓔ *chesgrove@ chestergrosvenor.co.uk, 58 Eastgate St)* has an unmatchable location in Eastgate. Expect to pay £130/165 in off-peak season.

Places to Eat

Chester has the usual selection of international fast-food outlets, plus a few centrally located fish and chip places, particularly in Lower Bridge St.

Every day the deservedly popular *Francs*
(*☎ 317952, 14 Cuppin St)* serves traditional
French food. Nearby *What's Cooking*
(*☎ 346512, 14–16 Grosvenor St)*, on the
corner of Cuppin St, offers burgers and
other American-style food. *Vito's Trattoria*
(*☎ 317330, 25 Lower Bridge St)* is a standard pizza and pasta specialist. A little farther
down, *Dino's Pizzeria* (*☎ 325091, 51
Lower Bridge St)* has similar fare while
colourful *Vincent's* (*☎ 310854, 58-60
Lower Bridge St)* has Caribbean cuisine;
blue marlin costs £12.95.

The *Garden House* (*☎ 320004, Rufus
Court)* serves English food and has some
vegetarian choices. *Elliot's Restaurant*
(*☎ 329932, 2 Abbey Garden)* also serves
English food. Check the board for the day's
specials.

Pubs serving good, basic food at reasonable prices include Chester's original
coaching inn *The Pied Bull* (*☎ 325829,
Northgate St)* and *Ye Olde Custom Inn*
(*Watergate St)*. *The Blue Bell* (*☎ 317758,
Northgate St)* serves up better quality food;
escalope of calves livers costs £12.95.
Watergates (*☎ 320515, 11 Watergate St)*, a
moody restaurant/bar set in an old crypt,
does a great hot lemon chicken salad for
£5.95. *The Albion* (*☎ 340345, 4 Albion St)*,
a fine Edwardian pub, serves reliable English food, without chips or fry-ups, and the
best real ale in town.

Paris Brioche (*☎ 348708, 39 Bridge St)*
and *Delifrance* (*☎ 322024, 30 Northgate
St)* both turn out good sandwiches and
baguettes to eat in or take away.

The gorgeous *cathedral refectory*
(*☎ 313156, Abbey Square)* serves soup of
the day for £1.95 but the stone-walled
Katie's Tea Rooms (*☎ 400322, Watergate
St)*, spread over three floors of an historic
building, gives it a run for its money as the
best place for a light lunch. Cheaper is *Hattie's* teashop (*☎ 345173, Rufus Court)*,
near the Northgate. The 1950s-style *Blue
Moon Café* is a good spot for a bite to eat
by the river. The *Dial Café* (*☎ 345655,
Hamilton Place)* offers disabled access in a
town that is decidedly difficult for wheelchair users.

Entertainment

Pubs The pubs mentioned under Places to
Eat are all equally good for a pint or two.

Overlooking the river, the *Boat House*
(*The Groves)* is a good spot, as is the *Boot
Inn* (*Eastgate Row)*, where 14 Roundheads
were killed. If you're looking for live music
try *Yates's Wine Lodge* (*☎ 344813, Frodsham St)* which attracts a noisy, young
crowd at night, or *Scruffy Murphy's*
(*☎ 321750, Northgate St)*.

Theatre & Music *Alexander's Jazz Theatre* (*☎ 340005, Rufus Court)* is a combination of wine bar, coffee bar and tapas bar.
Admission is sometimes free before 10 pm
otherwise it costs £2 to £7.50, depending on
who's performing.

The *Gateway Theatre* (*☎ 340392, Hamilton Place)* is beside the Forum Shopping
Centre.

Getting There & Away

Chester is 188 miles from London, 85 miles
from Birmingham, 40 miles from Manchester and 18 miles from Liverpool. It has
excellent transport connections, especially
with North Wales.

Bus Just north of the city walls inside the ring
road is the National Express (*☎ 0870 580
8080)* bus station. It has numerous services to
Glasgow (£22.50, six hours, one daily), Manchester (£4.50, 1¼ hours, three daily), Bristol
(£17.50, four hours, three daily), Llandudno
(£5.50, 1¾ hours, two daily), Liverpool (£5,
one hour, four daily), Birmingham (£8.25,
2½ hours, five daily) and London (£15, 5½
hours, five daily).

For information on local bus services,
ring the Cheshire Bus Line (*☎ 602666)*.
Local buses leave from the Town Hall Bus
Exchange. On Sunday and bank holidays a
Sunday Adventurer ticket gives you unlim-
ited travel in Cheshire for £3/2.

Train The train station is a 15-minute walk
from the city centre via Foregate St and
City Rd, or Brook St. City-Rail Link buses
are free to people with rail tickets, and stops
outside the station and on Frodsham St.

There are numerous trains to Shrewsbury (£5.80, one hour), Manchester (£8.50, 1½ hours), Liverpool (£3, 40 minutes), London Euston (£44, three hours) and Holyhead (£16.15, two hours), via the North Wales coast, for Ireland.

Getting Around
Much of the city centre is closed to traffic from 10.30 am to 4.30 pm so a car is likely to be a hindrance. Anyway, the walled city is easy to walk around and most places of interest are close to the wall.

City buses depart from the Town Hall Bus Exchange. Call ☎ 602666 for details. Guide Friday (☎ 347457) offers open-top bus tours of the city; an all-day ticket costs £6.50/2 (£8/2.50 if you want a half-hour river cruise included).

Davies Bros Cycles (☎ 371341), 5 Delamere St, has mountain bikes for hire at £10 per day.

AROUND CHESTER
Ellesmere Port
The superb Boat Museum (☎ 0151-355 5017), 8 miles north of Chester on the Shropshire Union Canal, has a large collection of canal boats as well as indoor exhibits. It opens 10 am to 5 pm daily, April to October; 11 am to 4 pm Saturday to Wednesday, the rest of the year. Admission costs £5.50/3.70.

Take Bus No 4 from the Town Hall Bus Exchange in Chester (45 minutes) or it's a 10-minute walk from Ellesmere Port train station.

Liverpool

☎ 0151 • pop 510,000

Of all the north-western cities, Liverpool has perhaps the strongest sense of its own identity, which is closely tied up – as you'll discover on even the shortest visit – with the totems of The Beatles, the Liverpool and Everton football teams, and the Grand National, run at Aintree since 1839.

The city has a dramatic site, rising on a series of steps above the broad River Mersey estuary with its shifting light, its fogs, its gulls

and its mournful emptiness. You're bound to be struck by the contrast between the grandeur and the decay, between the decrepit streets and boarded-up windows and the massive cathedrals and imperious buildings.

Liverpool's economic collapse has been even more dramatic than Manchester's and gives the whole city a sharp edge you'd do well not to explore. When people party, they seem to do so with a touch of desperation, certainly with plenty of abandonment. At weekends the city centre vibrates to music from countless pubs and clubs.

It's well worth setting aside time to explore Liverpool properly. The Albert Dock, the Western Approaches Museum, the twin cathedrals and the city streets themselves offer vivid testimony to the city's rugged history and the perverse exhilaration of its present-day decline.

History
Like Bristol, 18th-century Liverpool prospered on the back of the triangular trading of slaves for raw materials. From 1700, ships carried cotton goods and hardware from Liverpool to West Africa, where they were exchanged for slaves. The slaves were, in turn, carried to the West Indies and Virginia, where they were exchanged for sugar, rum, tobacco and raw cotton, a story retold in an excellent gallery in the Merseyside Maritime Museum (see Albert Dock later).

As a great port, the city attracted thousands of immigrants from Ireland and Scotland and its Celtic influences are still apparent. However, between 1830 and 1930 nine million emigrants – mainly English, Scots and Irish, but also Swedes, Norwegians and Russian Jews – sailed from Liverpool for the New World.

The start of WWII led to a resurgence in Liverpool's importance. Over one million American GIs disembarked here before D-Day and the port was, once again, hugely important as the western gateway for transatlantic supplies. The city also accommodated the Combined Headquarters of the Western Approaches, which coordinated the transatlantic convoys and the battle against German U-boats.

Liverpool has a long history of left-wing radicalism. The outrageous excesses of 19th-century capitalism led to bitter and violent confrontations with increasingly well-organised labour organisations. More recently, unemployment and housing problems have dragged the city down. In the early 1980s racial tensions led to rioting in Toxteth, a run-down suburb just south of the city centre.

As elsewhere, the previous Conservative government saw tourism as a way out of Liverpool's problems and money was poured into the redevelopment of the Albert Dock, which includes an offshoot of the Tate Gallery, several museums and a range of shops and restaurants.

Orientation

Liverpool stretches north–south along the River Mersey estuary for more than 13 miles. The main visitor attraction is the Albert Dock on the waterfront west of the city centre. The centre, including the two cathedrals to the east, is quite compact and easy to explore on foot.

Lime St, the main train station, is just to the east of the city centre. The National Express coach station is 300m north on the corner of Norton and Islington Sts. The bus station is in the centre on Paradise St.

Information

The main TIC (☎ 709 5111, ⓔ askme@ visitliverpool.com), in the Queen Square Centre, opens 9 am to 5.30 pm Monday to Saturday and 10.30 am to 4.30 pm Sunday, while the branch in the Albert Dock (☎ 708 8854) opens 10 am to 5.30 pm daily. Both can book accommodation.

Look for the excellent **Liverpool Heritage Walk**, an illustrated guide to the city's landmarks, identified by numbered metal markers set in the footpath.

Both TICs sell tickets for city bus tours. The hop-on hop-off bus tour has 11 stops and costs £6/4.50. There's also a highly recommended 2¼-hour Beatles tour (see the later boxed text 'Doing The Beatles to Death').

The post office at 1 Bold St opens 9 am to 5.30 pm Monday to Saturday.

Planet Electra (☎ 708 0303), 36 London Rd, doubles as a regular and Internet cafe.

If you're planning on visiting several museums make sure to spend £3/1.50 on an NMGM Eight Pass, covering admission to six city centre attractions – Liverpool Museum, Walker Art Gallery, Merseyside Maritime Museum, HM Customs & Excise National Museum, Museum of Liverpool Life and the Conservation Centre – as well as to the Lady Lever Art Gallery in Port Sunlight and to Sudley House (☎ 724 3245) in Aigburth. It's valid for 12 months and is on sale at all the museums.

Check out www.visitliverpool.com for online information on Liverpool.

City Centre

The **town hall**, at the end of Castle St, was designed by John Wood the Elder of Bath and completed in 1754. Both the dome and the impressive portico and balcony, where The Beatles were received by the Lord Mayor in 1964, were added later.

The confusing **Clayton Square** is a modern shopping centre opposite the Central station. **Bold St**, south of Central station, was once a ropewalk used in the manufacture of ropes for visiting ships.

Once considered one of the world's most luxurious hotels, the **Britannia Adelphi Hotel** on Lime St was completed in 1912 to serve wealthy passengers staying overnight before or after the Atlantic crossing. Farther north along the road is the superb Edwardian pub **Vines**, with its luxurious interior (built in 1907), and the welcoming **American Bar**, favoured by the US forces during WWII. In the 19th century, Lime St was famous for prostitution and was immortalised in the song 'Maggie May'.

A group of Liverpool's most impressive buildings are clustered together opposite Lime St station, although traffic funnelling into the city and the entrance of the Queensway Mersey Tunnel makes it difficult to appreciate them. Built as a concert hall in 1854, **St George's Hall** is considered one of the world's greatest neoclassical buildings; its exterior is Grecian, its interior Roman. Admission costs £2 and tours take

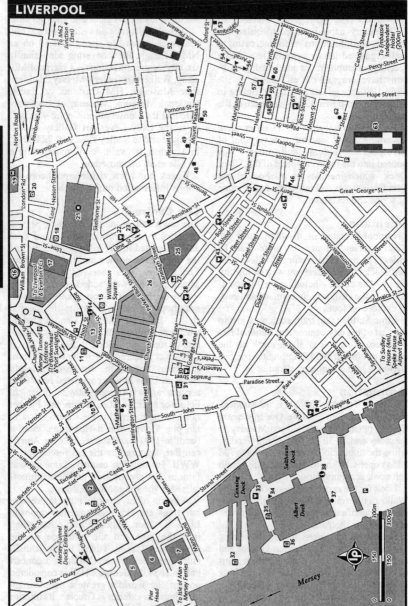

LIVERPOOL

LIVERPOOL

PLACES TO STAY		33	Pumphouse Inn	17	St George's Hall
4	Tower Thistle	41	The Baltic Fleet	18	The Empire
24	Britannia Adelphi Hotel	42	Cream	19	National Express
39	Campanile Hotel	43	RSVP		Coach Station
40	Youth Hostel	44	Mardi Gras	20	Planet Electra
48	YMCA	45	Blue Angel	21	Lime Street Train Station
49	Belvedere; Aachen Hotel	57	Philharmonic Dining Room	25	Central Train Station
50	Selhal	59	Flying Picket	26	Clayton Square
51	Feathers Hotel	61	Ye Cracke		Shopping Centre
53	University of Liverpool,			27	Post Office
	Mulberry Court	**OTHER**		29	Bluecoat Arts Centre
		1	Moorfields Train Station	31	Bus Station & Parking
PLACES TO EAT		2	Town Hall	32	Museum of
10	Casa Bella	3	Western Approaches Museum		Liverpool Life
34	Blue	5	Royal Liver Building	35	Merseyside
46	Far East	6	Cunard Building		Maritime Museum
47	Cafe Tabac	7	Port of Liverpool Building	36	Tate Gallery Liverpool
54	Everyman Bistro & Theatre	8	James Street Train Station	37	The Beatles Story
55	El Macho	9	Cavern Club	38	Tourist Information Centre
56	Becker's Brook	11	Conservation Centre		(Albert Dock)
		12	Queen Square Bus Stops	52	Metropolitan Cathedral
PUBS, BARS & CLUBS		13	Queen Square Centre	58	Unity Theatre
22	American Bar	14	Tourist Information Centre	60	Philharmonic Hall
23	Vines	15	Liverpool Playhouse	62	Institute for
28	Krazy Bar	16	Liverpool Museum; Walker		Performing Arts
30	The Escape		Art Gallery	63	Anglican Cathedral

NORTH-WESTERN ENGLAND

place daily, except Sunday, from mid-July to August for £1.50.

Liverpool Museum & Walker Art Gallery

Liverpool Museum (☎ 478 4399), William Brown St, is a traditional museum covering everything from archaeology to natural history, which also has a planetarium and hosts interesting temporary exhibitions. As well as its renowned collection of Pre-Raphaelite art, the Walker Art Gallery (☎ 478 4199) has an important collection of Italian and Flemish paintings and some interesting impressionists and post-impressionists, including a Degas, Cézanne and Matisse. There's a pleasant cafe on the ground floor.

The museum and gallery are side by side and open 10 am to 5 pm Monday to Saturday, noon to 5 pm on Sunday. Admission to each costs £3/1.50.

Western Approaches Museum

The Combined Headquarters of the Western Approaches (☎ 227 2008), the secret command centre for the Battle of the Atlantic, was buried under yards of concrete beneath an undistinguished building behind the town hall in Rumford Square. At the end of the war the bunker was abandoned with virtually everything left intact. You can look round it from 10.30 am to 4.30 pm daily except Friday and Sunday, March to October. Admission costs £4.75/3.45.

Conservation Centre

The Conservation Centre (☎ 478 4999), in the disused Midland Railway Goods Depot in Old Haymarket, is a state-of-the-art exhibition telling the story behind the conservation of the items on display in local museums and art galleries. Hand-held wands allow you to tune into different stories as you walk around and you'll probably be surprised to discover how much fun it all is. Did you know, for example, that a stuffed toucan's bill must be repainted after death? The Conservation Centre opens 10 am to 5 pm Monday to Saturday and noon to 5 pm Sunday. Admission costs £3/1.50.

The Cathedrals

As you walk along Hope St, you can see Liverpool's twin cathedrals looming at either end, vying for dominance, the Roman Catholic version to the north, the Anglican to the south.

Metropolitan Cathedral According to Sir Edwin Lutyens' original plans, Liverpool's Roman Catholic cathedral would have been larger than St Peter's in Rome. Unfortunately, the war and Liverpool's decline forced the priests to lower their sights. The present church-in-the-round (locally referred to as 'Paddy's Wigwam') was completed in 1967 and incorporates Lutyens' crypt. The soaring exterior is strikingly successful and the interior space impressive, although opinions on the modern decorations vary. The cathedral (☎ 709 9222) opens 8 am to 6 pm daily (5 pm in winter).

Anglican Cathedral Work on the red sandstone, neo-Gothic Anglican cathedral started in 1902 and was finally completed in 1978, by which time it was only exceeded in size by St Peter's and the cathedrals of Milan and Seville. Almost everything about the place is larger than life, including the central bell, which is the world's third largest. The cathedral was the life work of Sir Giles Gilbert Scott (1880–1960). Scott was also responsible for the design of the old red telephone booth, which explains why one of these is tucked away upstairs.

Even those who don't usually care for neo-Gothic are likely to be awed by this great, austere sea of space. The best views of Liverpool are from the top of the 101m tower. The cathedral (☎ 709 6271) opens 7.30 am to 6 pm daily and a donation of £2 is requested. The tower opens 11 am to 3 pm Monday to Saturday, as does the exhibition of ecclesiastical embroidery. Admission is £2.50/1.50. The excellent refectory opens 11 am to 4 pm.

Beside the porch steps, look out for a **memorial** to the 96 Liverpool football fans who died in the crush at Hillsborough Stadium in 1989. The imitation Greek temple nearby is the Oratory, designed in 1929 and open to visitors from Easter to September.

Albert Dock

Built between 1841 and 1848, the Albert Dock was one of the earliest enclosed docks in the world. Now 2¾ hectares of water are ringed by a colonnade of enormous cast-iron columns and impressive five-storey warehouses.

In the 1980s, the warehouses were restored and now house several outstanding museums, numerous shops and restaurants, offices, studios for Granada TV, a branch of the TIC and several tacky tourist attractions. The site could easily absorb four hours and that's without exploring the impressive buildings north along the waterfront. The Waterfront Pass costs £9.99/6.99 and saves you money on The Beatles Story, Merseyside Maritime Museum and a cruise on a Mersey Ferry.

Merseyside Maritime Museum This museum (☎ 478 4499) has a large range of imaginatively developed exhibits. Major displays are Emigrants to a New World, the WWII Battle of the Atlantic, and Builders of Great Ships. The latest addition is the new gallery dedicated to merchant ships and their crew. There is also an absorbing Transatlantic Slave Gallery which describes the shameful trade and its repercussions in the form of modern racism. Anything to Declare? is a gallery devoted to the history of HM Customs & Excise – sounds pretty dry but gives you the chance to find out whether you could catch a smuggler.

The museum opens 10 am to 5 pm daily. Admission costs £3/1.50.

Museum of Liverpool Life This museum (☎ 478 4080) looks at four main themes: Mersey Culture, especially entertainers; Making a Living, showing regional trades; Demanding a Voice, about the growth of unionism and democracy; and A Healthy Place to Live?, a look at Liverpool's record on public health. It opens 10 am to 5 pm daily. Admission costs £3/1.50.

Tate Gallery Liverpool It's particularly appropriate that Liverpool should have been chosen as home to this extension of the London Tate Gallery – Henry Tate, benefactor of the original gallery, co-founded the famous Tate & Lyle sugar business here. The newly refurbished Albert Dock Gallery (☎ 702 7400) hosts high-quality changing exhibitions. The Tate and the Albert Dock Gallery, which is the special exhibition part of the Tate, both open 10 am to 6 pm Tuesday to Sunday. Admission is free.

The Beatles Story Despite its promising name this attraction (☎ 709 1963) fails to capitalise on its subject's potential – fanatics won't discover anything they don't already know and, aside from some old TV clips there's little to kindle excitement for later generations. It opens 10 am to 6 pm daily. Admission is pricey at £6.95/4.95. A Beatles Combo ticket costing £15 gets you into the exhibition and a seat on the Magical Mystery Tour (see the boxed text 'Doing The Beatles to Death').

North of Albert Dock The area to the north of Albert Dock is known as **Pier Head**, after a stone pier built in the 1760s. This is still the departure point for ferries across the River Mersey (see Getting Around later), and was, for millions of migrants, their final contact with European soil.

Today this area is dominated by a trio of

Doing The Beatles to Death

A Victorian warehouse in Mathew St was once home to a music venue called the Cavern Club. Between March 1961 and August 1963, The Beatles played here a staggering 275 times. Other bands, such as Gerry and the Pacemakers who helped define 'beat' music and the 'Mersey sound', were also regulars. Cilla Black was in charge of the cloakroom.

Turn down Mathew St today and you're hardly able to move for businesses cashing in on The Beatles phenomenon. There's an Abbey Rd Oyster Bar, an Abbey Rd Shop, a Lucy in the Sky With Diamonds cafe and a Lennon Bar...and that's before you stumble on Cavern Court and the Cavern Walks shopping mall.

The irony is, of course, that the original Cavern Club where the Fab Four started their career was closed in 1973 and the site ruthlessly redeveloped in 1980. A statue of Lennon in his Hamburg period may slouch against the wall of the memorabilia-crammed Cavern Pub (☎ 236 1957) but the present day Cavern Club (☎ 236 1964) at 2 Mathew St only opened in 1984. You may well find it hosting a disco or closed for a private party.

Serious Beatles fans might prefer to head off in search of other Liverpool sites associated with the mopheads. Both TICs sell tickets to the Magical Mystery Tour (☎ 709 3285), a 2¼-hour bus trip taking in Penny Lane, Strawberry Fields and many other landmarks. It departs from opposite the Pumphouse pub in Albert Dock at 2.20 pm and from the main TIC at 2.30 pm daily. In July and August, there are also Saturday tours at 11.50 am. Tickets cost £10.95. Better value is the Beatles Combo ticket at £15, which covers admission to The Beatles Story (☎ 709 1963) and a seat on the Magical Mystery Tour.

If you'd rather do it yourself, the TICs also stock the *Discover Lennon's Liverpool* guide and map, and Robin Jones' *Beatles Liverpool*.

JANE SMITH

They just couldn't stand still: The Beatles giving it the 'hippy hippy shake'

self-important buildings dating from the days when Liverpool's star was still ascending. The southernmost, with the dome mimicking St Paul's Cathedral, is the **Port of Liverpool Building**, completed in 1907. Next to it is the **Cunard Building**, in the style of an Italian palazzo, once HQ to the Cunard Steamship Line. Finally, the **Royal Liver Building** (pronounced lie-ver) was opened in 1911 as the head office of the Royal Liver Friendly Society. It's crowned by the famous 5.5m copper Liver Birds, Liverpool's symbol. Tours of the building are free but must be pre-booked (☎ 236 2748). Liverpool's original seal depicted an eagle, but over time artists' representations came to look more like a seagull or cormorant!

Football Club Tours
Fans of Everton Football Club will want to head out to Goodison Park to tour the club grounds and find out more about its history. Tours take place at 11 am and 2 pm Monday, Wednesday, Friday and Sunday except on match days, but you must book in advance (☎ 330 2266). They cost £5/3.30 per person.

Fans of Liverpool FC should head for Anfield Rd where a similar experience is available (☎ 260 6677). To visit the museum and take a tour costs £8.50/5.50.

Places to Stay
Note that beds can be hard to find when Liverpool or Everton football clubs are playing at home. You'll also be lucky to find anything if you haven't booked ahead for the third week of August when The Beatles annual convention comes to town. The TIC offers a free accommodation service.

Hostels The excellent and welcoming *Embassie Independent Hostel (☎ 707 1089, fax 707 8289, 1 Falkner Square)* is to the east of the Anglican cathedral but still within walking distance of the centre. Dorm beds cost £11.50, including tea and coffee, and facilities include a laundry and TV lounge.

The new *Liverpool Youth Hostel (☎ 248 5647, fax 709 0417, ᴇ liverpool@yha.org .uk, 25 Tabley St)*, across the road from Albert Dock, is 600m south of James Street

station. Beds cost £18/13.50 for adults/under-18s, including breakfast.

Spartan *Selhal (☎ 709 7791, 1 Rodney St)* is off Mount Pleasant where the YWCA used to be and charges £12 per night. The *YMCA (☎ 709 9516, 56 Mount Pleasant)* offers B&B for £14.50 per person.

The *University of Liverpool (☎ 794 3298, fax 794 3816)* has self-catering rooms at *Mulberry Court (Oxford St)*, near the Metropolitan Cathedral, for £16 per head. It also has a *B&B (☎ 794 6440, Greenbank Lane)* over Easter and from mid-April to mid-May and mid-June to mid-September from £15.50.

B&Bs & Hotels There's a handy group of hotels on Mount Pleasant, between the city centre and the Metropolitan Cathedral. The cheapest option is the *Belvedere (☎ 709 2356, 83 Mount Pleasant)* with beds from £18.50.

Feathers Hotel (☎ 709 9655, fax 709 3838 ᴇ feathershotel@feathers.uk.com, 117–125 Mount Pleasant) is a good mid-range hotel. The 75 rooms boast a variety of facilities. Singles/doubles (some very small) start at £29/44. The award-winning *Aachen Hotel (☎ 709 3477, fax 709 1126, 89 Mount Pleasant)* has well-equipped rooms, most with showers, for £34/40.

Close to Albert Dock, the modern *Campanile Hotel (☎ 709 8104, fax 709 8725, Chaloner St)* offers rooms for £39.50.

The five-star *Tower Thistle (☎ 227 4444, fax 236 3973, Chapel St)* is virtually beside the Royal Liver Building and is a modern multistorey hotel with good views over the River Mersey. Rooms start from £80/90 but good-value weekend breaks are available.

When it was completed in 1912, the 391-room *Britannia Adelphi Hotel (☎ 709 7200, fax 708 0743, Ranelagh Place)* was considered one of the world's most luxurious hotels. Some readers have commented on poor service but it's in a wonderfully central location and charges £45/60.

Places to Eat
The area around Slater and Bold Sts is worth trying for a reasonable choice of places to

eat. *Cafe Tabac* (☎ 709 3735, Bold St) is a relaxed place that attracts a young crowd. Roasts on Sunday cost around £4.25.

The *Everyman Bistro* (☎ 708 9545, 5 Hope St), underneath the Everyman Theatre, is highly recommended as a place to tuck into cheap, good food (pizza slices for less than £2 and delicious desserts). *El Macho* (☎ 708 6644, 23 Hope St) has a cheerful atmosphere and enormous servings of spicy Mexican food. Most main dishes cost around £9 but the lunch menu is cheaper, including nachos for £3. *Becher's Brook* (☎ 707 0005, 29A Hope St), a few doors south, does classy modern British cookery and is one of the better restaurants in town.

Liverpool's Chinatown has declined since its glory days, but there are still several Chinese restaurants around Berry St and it does have the largest Chinese gate in Europe. One of the most popular is *Far East* (☎ 709 3141, 27 Berry St), above a Chinese supermarket. Set menus start at £15.50, but you could eat for less – plenty of dishes cost around £8.

Casa Bella (☎ 258 1800, 25 Victoria St) is a good, cheap Italian serving pizza and pasta from £6.30.

The Albert Dock is also a good place to look for something to eat. Enjoy the comfortable couches and the view of the dock at *Blue* (☎ 709 7097, 17 Edward Pavilion). Main courses cost around £8.

The *refectory* (☎ 707 1722, St James Mount) in the Anglican cathedral serves great-value hot lunches for around £4. There are also excellent *cafes* in the Walker Art Gallery and the Conservation Centre.

Entertainment

To find out what's on where, look out for the free monthly entertainment guide *In Touch*.

Pubs, Bars & Clubs Liverpool has a thriving, and changeable, nightlife. Wander around Mathew St and south-east to Bold, Seel and Slater Sts and you'll stumble upon an amazing array of pubs and clubs catering to every imaginable taste.

On the corner of Hope and Hardman Sts, the *Philharmonic Dining Room* (☎ 709 1163, 36 Hope St), built in 1900, is one of Britain's most extraordinary pubs. The interior is resplendent with etched glass, stained glass, wrought iron, mosaics and ceramic tiling – and if you think that's good, just wait until you see inside the toilets. A little more ordinary but still wonderful is *The Baltic Fleet*, (☎ 709 3116, 33 Wapping) next to the youth hostel (see Places to Stay earlier), which pours a superb traditional ale.

Ye Cracke (☎ 709 4171, 13 Rice St) has long been favoured by students from the nearby College of Art. John Lennon and Cynthia Powell were regular customers. *Garands* (Eberle St) and *The Escape* (☎ 708 8909, Fifth Ave, Paradise St) are popular gay hang-outs.

Best known of the clubs is *Cream* (☎ 709 1693, off Parr St), which rings the changes between jazz, samba and techno. The *Blue Angel* (☎ 428 1213, 108 Seel St) is popular with students, as is the downstairs bar at *Casablanca* (Hope St).

Other clubs worth checking out include *Mardi Gras* (Bold St) and colourful *Krazy House* (☎ 708 5016, 16 Wood St). For indie rock try the *Flying Picket* (☎ 708 5318, 24 Hardman St). The *Irish Centre* (☎ 709 4120) often has live bands and *RSVP* (☎ 707 6470, Wood St) is a cavernous place pulling in the punters. *Revolution* (☎ 707 2727, Wood St) is also popular and specialises in vodka.

Theatre & Classical Music The *Everyman Theatre* (☎ 709 4776, Hope St) is one of Britain's most famous repertory theatres and has featured the works of local playwright Alan Bleasdale, among others. The *Liverpool Playhouse* (☎ 709 8363, Williamson Square) or *The Empire* (☎ 709 1555, Lime St) could be staging anything from straight plays to musicals. The *Bluecoat Arts Centre* (☎ 709 5279, School Lane) and the *Unity Theatre* (☎ 709 4988, Hope Place) host innovative, small-scale companies.

The Royal Liverpool Philharmonic Orchestra plays in the *Philharmonic Hall* (☎ 709 3789, Hope St).

Getting There & Away

Liverpool is 210 miles from London, 100 miles from Birmingham, 75 miles from Leeds and 35 miles from Manchester.

Air Liverpool airport (☎ 288 4000), 8 miles to the south of the city centre, has flights to Belfast, Dublin, the Isle of Man and a number of destinations in continental Europe. Bus No 80A or 180 departs from Paradise St Station every 20 minutes.

Bus National Express services link Liverpool to most major towns. There are regular services from London (£15, five hours). To get to the town centre from the coach station, turn right up Seymour St and then right again along London Rd. To get to Chester catch bus No X8 from Queen Square in the city centre.

Train Numerous services run to Lime St station, including trains from Wigan (£3.55, 50 minutes), Chester (£3, 40 minutes), Manchester (£6.95, one hour) and London (£44, three hours).

Boat The Isle of Man Steam Packet Company (☎ 0870 552 3523) operates a service between Douglas and Liverpool (Pier Head) every weekend throughout the year and more frequently during the summer months. The journey time is 4¼ hours by ferry or 2½ hours by catamaran. Foot passenger fares start at £25 single but are cheaper at off-peak times. Bicycles are transported free but a car will cost from £72 each way.

Getting Around

Local public transport is coordinated by Merseytravel (☎ 236 7676). Various zonal tickets are also sold at post offices. An all-zone all-day ticket for bus, train and ferry (except cruises) costs £4.30.

Bus Most local buses leave from Queen Square to the east of St George's Hall. Smart Bus Nos 1 and 5 link Albert Dock with the city centre and the university every 20 minutes.

Train If you don't fancy the ferry across the Mersey (see Ferry), the local train network will take you under the river. As well as Lime St, trains call at Central Station – as the name suggests, it's a useful stop for the central shops and bars.

Taxi Mersey Cabs (☎ 298 2222) operates tourist taxi services and has some cabs adapted for disabled visitors.

Ferry The famous ferry across the River Mersey (£1.05/80p), started 800 years ago by Benedictine monks but immortalised by Gerry & the Pacemakers, still offers one of the best views of Liverpool. Boats for Woodside and Seacombe depart from Pier Head Ferry Terminal, next to the Liver Building to the north of Albert Dock. Special one-hour commentary cruises depart hourly, 10 am to 3 pm on weekdays and until 6 pm at weekends year round and cost £3/50/1.80. Phone ☎ 639 0609 for more information.

AROUND LIVERPOOL
Port Sunlight

South-east of Liverpool across the River Mersey on the Wirral peninsula, Port Sunlight is a picturesque 19th-century village created by the philanthropic Lever family to house workers in its soap factory. It's a surprise to find such a peaceful place in the hustle and bustle of the Merseyside area. The main reason to come here is the wonderful **Lady Lever Art Gallery** (☎ 478 4136) where you can see some of the greatest works of the Pre-Raphaelite Brotherhood, as well as some fine Wedgwood pottery. It opens 10 am to 5 pm Monday to Saturday and from noon on Sunday. Admission costs £3/1.50.

Also in the village is the **Heritage Centre** (☎ 644 6466), 95 Greendale Rd, which tells the story of the creation of Port Sunlight. It opens 10 am to 4 pm daily (from 11 am at weekends in winter). Admission is 60/30p.

Trains run from Lime St station to Port Sunlight.

Speke Hall & 20 Forthlin Rd

Six miles south of Liverpool is Speke Hall (☎ 427 7231; NT), a marvellous black and white half-timbered hall with several priest's holes where Roman Catholic priests could hide in the 16th century when they were forbidden to hold Masses. The hall opens 1 to 5.30 pm daily, except Monday, April to October, and 1 to 4.30 pm weekends only the rest of the year. Admission costs £4.20/2.10.

Bus No 80 or 82 from Lime St station will drop you within a mile of Speke Hall. Visitors to Speke Hall can also go by minibus to 20 Forthlin Rd, Liverpool, once home to Beatle Paul McCartney. It's been restored to its 1950s' appearance although there's little directly linked to the great Macca. Tours leave Speke Hall at 3.10 and 4 pm Wednesday to Saturday, from Easter to October. A combined ticket with Speke Hall costs £5.10/2.60. It's advisable to pre-book by phoning ☎ 0151-486 4006. Tours also run from outside The Beatles Story at Albert Dock.

Isle of Man

☎ 01624 • pop 70,000

Ask an English person about the Isle of Man and more often than not the answer will be 'weird place, full of inbreeds'! And yet the majority of mainlanders have never set foot on the Isle. It's a pity because the Isle of Man has much to offer the visitor. Lush valleys, barren hills and rugged coastlines make for great walks, cycling trails and drives, and the isle's rich history is well told in castles and museums.

But it does have to be said, the Isle of Man is a quirky world of its own. The number one industry is tax avoidance – wealthy Brits can shelter their loot here without having to move to Monte Carlo or the Cayman Islands. And the Isle of Man is a motorcyclist's Mecca: each year's May–June Tourist Trophy (TT) races add 45,000 to the island's small population. Home to the world's oldest continuous parliament, the Isle of Man enjoys special status in Britain, and its annual parliamentary ceremony honours the 1000-year history of the Tynwald (a Scandinavian word meaning 'meeting field'). Unfortunately, Douglas, the capital, is a run-down relic of Victorian tourism with fading B&Bs. The tailless Manx

cat and the four-horned loghtan sheep are unique to the Isles.

ORIENTATION & INFORMATION

Situated in the Irish Sea, equidistant from Liverpool, Dublin and Belfast, the Isle of Man is about 30 miles long by 10 miles wide. Ferries arrive at Douglas, the port and main town on the south-east coast. Flights come in to Ronaldsway airport, 10 miles south of Douglas. Most of the island's historic sites are operated by Manx National Heritage, which offers free admission to NT or English Heritage (EH) members. Unless otherwise

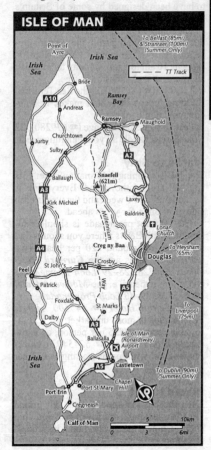

ISLE OF MAN

NORTH-WESTERN ENGLAND

indicated, Manx Heritage (MH) sites open 10 am to 5 pm daily, Easter to October. The phone number for all enquiries is ☎ 648000.

The Millennium Way traverses the island north-east to south-west, following the route of a medieval highway.

DOUGLAS
☎ 01624 • pop 20,000

Looking across the Irish Sea towards Blackpool, Douglas is not particularly endearing. Half the Victorian seafront terraces look ready for demolition, renovation or a good coat of paint. More modern buildings look to have been designed by some of Britain's least inspired architects on their off days.

The Manx Museum (MH) gives an introduction to everything from the island's prehistoric past to the latest TT race winners. It opens 10 am to 5 pm Monday to Saturday all year round. Admission is free.

The TIC (☎ 686766), in the Sea Terminal Building, opens daily and makes free accommodation bookings.

Feegan's Internet Lounge (☎ 679280), 22 Duke St, can handle all your emailing needs.

Places to Stay
The TIC's camping information sheet lists sites all around the island. Everything is booked out for TT week and the weeks each side of it, often for years ahead.

The seafront promenade is shoulder-to-shoulder with B&Bs where you should find something for around £20 per head. Two reasonable places are the *Curnard Hotel* (*☎/fax 676728, 28–29 Loch Promenade*) and, more expensive, the *Modwena Hotel* (*☎ 675728, 39–40 Loch Promenade*).

The *Sefton Hotel* (*☎ 645500, Harris Promenade*) is more upmarket, with comfortable rooms at £35 per person, as is the *Castle Mona Hotel* (*☎ 624540, Central Promenade*) with rooms starting at £33 per person.

Places to Eat
Even the big fast-food outlets skip round Douglas, leaving a choice of fish and chip shops, Chinese takeaways and a handful of restaurants.

Scott's Bistro (*☎ 623764, John St*) is pleasant and moderately priced with Manx trout for £9.95. Set in a lovely stone building overlooking the quay, *Blazer's* (*☎ 673222, North Quay*), on the corner of North Quay and Bridge St, is a wine bar with pub-style food. Underneath is the pricey *Waterfront* restaurant.

L'Expérience (*☎ 623103, Summerhill*), at the bottom of Summerhill, is a smart French restaurant that serves *queenies* (local scallops).

There are a few good pubs around, including the popular local hang-out *Tramshunter* on the promenade and the originally named *Rovers Return* (*☎ 676459, 11 Church St*) specialising in the local brew Bushy Ales.

AROUND THE ISLE OF MAN
Petrol-heads are likely to start their island circuit with motorcycling's **Mountain Circuit**. At 50mph some of the long sweeping bends are a delight, at 150mph they must be terrifying. Fortunately for the unconverted, the island has other attractions, including the 90-mile **Raad ny Foillan**, or Road of the Gull, a coastal walking path which makes a complete circuit of the island.

Castletown to Port Erin
At the southern end of the island is Castletown, a quiet harbour town which was originally the capital of the Isle of Man. The town is dominated by the impressive 13th-century **Castle Rushen** (MH). The flagtower affords fine views of the town and coast. Admission costs £4/2. There's also a small **Nautical Museum** (MH) displaying, among other things, its pride and joy *Peggy*, a boat built in 1791 and still housed in its original boathouse. Admission costs £2.50/1.50. A school dating back to 1570 in **St Mary's church** (MH) is located behind the castle. Admission is free.

Between Castletown and Cregneash, the Iron-Age hillfort at **Chapel Hill** encloses a Viking ship burial site.

On the southern tip of the island, the **Cregneash Village Folk Museum** (MH) recalls traditional Manx rural life. Admission costs £2.75/1.50. The **Calf of Man**, the small island just off Cregneash, is a bird sanctuary. Calf Island Cruises (☎ 832339) run between the islands regularly during the summer. Visits cost £10/5 from Port Erin.

Port Erin, another Victorian seaside resort, plays host to the small **Railway Museum** depicting the history of steam railway on the island. It opens daily April to October. Admission costs £1/50p.

Places to Stay & Eat Port Erin has a good range of accommodation, as does Port St Mary. *Aaron House (☎ 835702, ⒺE aaron _house_iom@yahoo.com, on the Promenade)*, in Port St Mary, is a splendid Victorian-style B&B with sea views. Rooms cost £25 per person.

Port Erin makes a good stop for a bite to eat. The *Whistle Stop Coffee Shop (☎ 833802)* in the railway station makes filling sandwiches for around £2 and lovely home-made cakes.

Peel

Dating from the 11th century, **Peel Castle** (MH), with its long curtain wall, is stunningly positioned atop St Patrick's Island, joined to Peel by a causeway. Admission costs £3/1.50. The excellent **House of Manannan** (MH) museum uses interactive displays to explain Manx history and its seafaring traditions. It opens year round and costs £5/2.50. A combined ticket for both costs £7/3.50.

Three miles east of Peel is **Tynwald Hill** at St John's where the annual parliamentary ceremony takes place on 5 July.

Peel has several B&Bs including the *Fernleigh Hotel (☎ 842435, Marine Parade)*. Rooms start at £17 per person. Opposite the House of Manannam is the *Creek Inn (☎ 842216 fax 843359, East Quay)*, offering self-catering rooms from £30. It is also popular for food, serving Manx queenies for £6.95.

Ramsey to Douglas

You can follow the TT course up and over the mountain or wind around the coast. The mountain route takes you close to the summit of **Snaefell** (621m), the island's highest point. It's an easy walk up to the summit or

JANE SMITH

When the first TT race was held in 1907, the winner's average speed was just 38.22 mph.

you can take the electric tram from Laxey on the coast. The tram stops by the road where **Murray's Motorcycle Museum** displays motorcycles and TT memorabilia.

On the edge of Ramsey is the **Grove Rural Life Museum** (MH). Admission costs £2.75/1.50. The church in the small village of **Maughold** is on the site of an ancient monastery; a small shelter houses quite a good selection of stone crosses and ancient inscriptions.

Describing the **Laxey Wheel** (MH), built in 1854 to pump water from a mine, as a 'great' wheel is no exaggeration; it measures 22m across and can draw 250 gallons of water per minute from a depth of 1800 feet. Admission costs £2.75/1.50. The wheel-headed cross at **Lonan Old Church** is the island's most impressive early Christian cross.

GETTING THERE & AWAY
Air

Manx Airlines (☎ 0845 725 6256) has frequent connections with much of Britain and Ireland, as does Jersey European (☎ 0870 567 6676) but there are also other smaller operators. Weekend return flights from London generally cost £140 but can be as low as £59 from Liverpool.

Boat

The Isle of Man Steam Packet (☎ 0870 552 3523) operates regular car ferries and high-speed SeaCat catamarans to Douglas from Dublin, Belfast, Heysham, Fleetwood,

Liverpool and Ardrossan. Foot passenger fares start at £25 single but you'll have to pay from £72 to take a car across. At times it can be cheaper to fly and hire a car on arrival. The crossing from Liverpool takes 2½ hours by SeaCat or four hours by ferry. From time to time you can get special fares so its worth calling ahead or checking out their Web site at www.steam-packet.com.

GETTING AROUND

A taxi from the airport into Douglas will cost about £15 compared with £1.50 by bus. There are several car rental operators at the airport and in Douglas, charging from £26 upwards for a day's rental. The Isle also has a comprehensive bus service; the TIC in Douglas has timetables and fares. In Douglas, bicycles can be hired at Eurocycles (☎ 624909), 8A Victoria Rd. The charge is £10 for the first day, £9 per day for three-day hire and £8 per day for five-day hire. The whole of the island is good for cycling.

There are several interesting rail services (☎ 663366) that operate from Easter to September. These include the Douglas-Laxey-Ramsey electric tramway; a steam train operating Douglas-Castletown-Port Erin; the Snaefell Mountain Railway; and the narrow-gauge Groudle Glen Railway. A ticket covering rides on all these trains for three days in seven costs £19.90.

Lancashire

Lancashire is bordered by the River Mersey in the south, the sea in the west, the Pennines in the east and the Lake District in the north. Manchester and Liverpool, the region's great port, are administered separately.

Business and commerce have gravitated towards the industrial towns of Preston (a major transport interchange), Blackburn, Accrington and Burnley in southern Lancashire, once famous for its coal and cotton industries. Unfortunately, there's not much to draw you here, unless to use the towns as a base for exploring the rest of the county.

Of the traditional seaside resorts serving Manchester and Liverpool, Blackpool lives

splendidly, if tackily, on, but Morecambe is in sad decline, worth visiting only to see the Art Deco Midland Hotel crumbling away on the seafront.

LANCASTER
☎ 01524 • pop 46,300

The historic city of Lancaster is certainly worth a visit. Standing on the banks of the River Lune, it dates back to Roman times and has a wealth of fine Georgian architecture.

The TIC (☎ 32878, fax 382849, ⓔ devt@lancaster.gov.uk), 28 Castle Hill, stocks a comprehensive free guide to Lancaster and Morecambe. It opens 10 am to 5 pm daily and makes accommodation bookings.

Internet access is available in the City Library on Market Square.

Lancaster Castle & Priory

Lancaster's imposing castle (☎ 64998), part of which is still a prison, was originally built in the 11th century but what you see now is much newer. Regular tours take in the courtroom and Hadrian's Tower with its display of instruments of torture and the dungeons. One famous trial that took place here was of the so-called Pendle Witches in 1612. It opens 10 am to 5 pm daily from mid-March to mid-December. A full tour costs £4/2.50, less at times when court sittings curtail the tours.

Immediately next to the castle is the equally fine **priory church** (☎ 65338), founded in 1094 but extensively remodelled later in the Middle Ages. It opens 9.30 am to 5 pm. Admission is free.

Other Things to See

The **Maritime Museum** (☎ 64637), St George's Quay, in the 18th-century Custom House, recalls the days when Lancaster was a flourishing port at the centre of the slave trade. It opens 11 am to 5 pm daily (12.30 to 4 pm November to Easter). Admission costs £2/1.

The **City Museum** (☎ 64637), Market Square, has a mixed bag of local historical and archaeological exhibits. It opens 10 am to 5 pm Monday to Saturday. Admission is free.

The **Judges' Lodgings** (☎ 32808), off China St, is a 17th-century townhouse containing a Museum of Childhood and some fine furnishings. Admission costs £2/1. The **Cottage Museum** (☎ 64637), 15 Castle Hill, has been furnished to show life in an artisan's house in the early 19th century and opens 2 to 5 pm daily April to September. Admission costs 75/25p.

Places to Stay & Eat

Lancaster lacks a youth hostel but over Easter and in summer 400 beds are available for B&B at £18.80 per head in the *accommodation block* at the *University College of St Martin* (☎ 384460) on Bowerham Rd.

St Mary's Parade on Castle Hill has two good B&Bs. The *Castle Hill* (☎ 849137, 27 St Mary's Parade) is a lovely refurbished Victorian town house charging £25/40 for singles/doubles. *The Priory* (☎ 845711, 15 St Mary's Parade) is equally beautiful and charges slightly more. Next to the Maritime Museum, the *Wagon & Horses* (☎ 846094, 27 St Georges Quay) is a relaxed pub offering rooms with river views for £25/43.

Pizza Margherita (☎ 36333, 2 Moor Lane) is a relaxed place with great pizzas at a reasonable price, including Calzone Mexicana for £5.95. Next to the Maritime Museum, *Simply French* (☎ 843199, 27A St Georges Quay) serves a filling two-course lunch for £5 and jugs of Sangria for £5.95 to liven up the place. *Folly Cafe* (☎ 388540, 27 Castle Park) serves dishes such as Morecombe Bay potted shrimps (£4.95) in a building that doubles as a small art gallery. From Easter to October, teas and lunches are available in the *Priory Refectory* (☎ 65338, Priory Church).

A reasonable student population makes Lancaster a relatively lively place during term. The *White Witch Pub* (Aldcliffe Rd) has a good spot on the canal on while the *Friary & Firkin* (St Leonardgate), originally a church, has enough room to accommodate the regular mobs and live music.

Getting There & Away

Lancaster is on the main west-coast railway line and on the Cumbrian Coast Line. Trains serve Kendal (£5.40, 30 minutes),

Windermere (£7.45, one hour) and Carlisle (£17, 3½ hours). There are also National Express links with most local towns.

BLACKPOOL
☎ 01253 • pop 147,000

The king of the tacky and brazen English seaside resort is Blackpool, which attracts over eight million visitors a year – all making the journey to let their hair down by the sea. Even though Blackpool is well past its use-by date, it has to be seen to be believed, so if you're planning on visiting a seaside resort, make sure this is the one.

Blackpool is famous for its tower, its three piers, its Pleasure Beach and its **Illuminations**, a successful ploy to extend the brief summer holiday season. From early September to early November, 5 miles of the Promenade are illuminated with thousands of electric and neon lights.

Orientation & Information

Blackpool is surprisingly spread out but can still be managed easily without a car – trams run the entire 7-mile length of the seafront Promenade.

'Amusement' arcades with slot machines and bingo games stretch all the way along the Golden Mile from the South Pier to the Central and North piers. South Pier, the least impressive, is alongside Blackpool Pleasure Beach and The Sandcastle, an enormous indoor pool complex. The town centre and Blackpool Tower lie between the Central and North Piers.

The helpful TIC (☎ 478222, fax 478210, ⓔ tourism@blackpool.gov.uk), 1 Clifton St, books local accommodation for free. There's a branch in the Pleasure Beach (☎ 403223) and by the North Pier (summer only).

For online information check out the Web site www.blackpooltourism.com.

Blackpool Tower

Built in 1894, this metal tower (☎ 622242) was the second of its kind in Europe and is now Blackpool's best-known symbol. It's over 150m high and houses a vast entertainment complex, as well as a laser show and indoor circus.

The highlight is the magnificent, rococo **ballroom**, with extraordinary sculptured and gilded plasterwork, murals and chandeliers. Couples still glide across the floor to the melodramatic tones of a huge Wurlitzer organ from 2 to 11 pm every day. *Saturday Night Fever* might never have happened.

The Tower opens 10 am to 11 pm daily from Easter. Admission costs £10/5.

Blackpool Pleasure Beach & The Sandcastle

The UK's most visited outdoor attraction, Blackpool Pleasure Beach (☎ 0870 444 5566) is a 16-hectare funfair packed with rides and shows. The most interesting of rides are the historic wooden roller coasters, particularly the brilliant Grand National and Wild Mouse. But the most stomach churning is the Pepsi Max Big One, the tallest and fastest roller coaster in Europe, and the newest of them all, Playstation, with an adrenaline pumping vertical ascent/descent at 80mph.

Admission to the park is free. Rides are divided into categories and you can buy tickets for individual categories or for a mixture of them all. An unlimited ticket to all rides costs £25. It opens from 10 am daily, April to early November, and weekends the rest of the year. There are no set times for closing, it depends on how busy they are.

Across the road is **The Sandcastle** (☎ 343602), an indoor water complex complete with its own rides, open 10 am daily, May to October, and weekends the rest of the year. Admission costs £4.80, £3.70 after 2 pm.

Sea Life Centre

Close to Tower World in New Bonny St is this state-of-the-art aquarium (☎ 622445). It opens 10 am to 8 pm daily. Admission costs £6.99/4.99.

Places to Stay

Reputedly, Blackpool has over 2500 hotels, B&Bs and self-catering units, showing just how popular a holiday destination it is. Even with so many places to stay, it is worth booking ahead during the illuminations.

Competition is fierce so you should have no trouble finding somewhere to stay for less than £18 a head, except at the height of summer. The TIC produces an accommodation guide specifically for gay and lesbian holiday-makers, reflecting Blackpool's popularity as a gay and lesbian holiday destination.

Good places to start looking are Albert and Hornby Rds, 300m back from the sea but close to the tower, pubs and discos. B&Bs, in Albert Rd, charging around £20 a head include *Boltonia Hotel* (☎ 620248, fax 299064, 124 Albert Rd) and *Royal Albert Hotel* (☎ 623667, 41 Albert Rd). Nearby, the pleasant *Hotel Bambi* (☎ 343756, Bright St) charges £17.50 per person.

Quiet Gynn Ave, about half a mile north of North Pier is lined with B&Bs charging around £18 per person. Possibilities include the *Bramleigh Hotel* (☎ 351568, 15 Gynn Ave), the *Haldene Private Hotel* (☎ 353763, 4 Gynn Ave) or *The Austen* (☎ 351784, 6 Gynn Ave).

At the base of the North Pier with superb sea views is the more upmarket *Clifton Hotel* (☎ 621481) charging £35 per person at the weekend, £30 during the week.

Places to Eat

Forget gourmet meals – the Blackpool experience is all about stuffing your face with burgers, hot dogs, doughnuts, and fish and chips. Most people eat at their hotels where roast and three vegetables often costs just £3 a head.

There are a few restaurants around Talbot Square (near the TIC) on Queen St, Talbot Rd and Clifton St. The most interesting possibility is the Afro-Caribbean *Lagoonda* (☎ 293837, 37 Queen St) where starters average £4, main meals £9. *Giannini* (☎ 28926, 2 Queen St) does pizza and pasta for around £4.90 to £5.90.

Entertainment

There are plenty of pubs and clubs up and down the length of Blackpool so you'll not have to search long and hard to find one or the other. *Yates' Wine Lodge* (☎ 752443, Talbot Square) is a popular drinking hole, as is its counterpart by the Central Pier. *Bar Me*

(Clifton St) is a colourful, cavernous place and like most places has gorillas on the door.

Both *Insomnia* (☎ 292923, Topping St) and *Heaven and Hell* (☎ 625118, Bank Hey St) are popular clubs with the masses. Blackpool's thriving gay scene has produced its own form of entertainment in *Funny Girls* (☎ 291144, Queen St), a pub with drag shows.

For information on theatre and shows check with the main TIC.

Getting There & Away
Blackpool is approximately 50 miles from both Liverpool and Manchester and 250 miles from London.

Bus One interesting possibility is Primrose Coaches' (☎ 0191-232 5567) daily service to/from Newcastle, leaving at 8.45 am, via Kirkby Stephen, Raby Castle, Barnard Castle and Durham (Bus No 352, £16, 4½ hours).

National Express has services to most major towns in Britain. The central coach station is on Talbot Rd, near the town centre.

Train To get to Blackpool you often have to change in Preston (£4.85, 30 minutes). Trains also run from London (£49.50, four hours).

Getting Around
To get into the swing of things, hop on and off the vintage trams that run up and down the Promenade. The buses are marginally cheaper but nothing like as much fun. A one day travel card covering trams and buses costs £4.50/4. With more than 14,000 car parking spaces in Blackpool you'll have no problem finding a space.

Yorkshire

In the 9th century the Danes made York their capital and ruled the Danelaw – all of England north and east of a line between Chester and London. Later, their Norman cousin William the Conqueror found the north rebellious and difficult, and he responded with brutal thoroughness. After 500 knights were massacred at Durham, he burnt York and Durham and devastated the surrounding countryside. Seventeen years later, when the royal commissioners arrived to record the tax capacity of Yorkshire (for the *Domesday Book*), they recorded the simple, but frighteningly eloquent, 'waste' beside many parish names. It took the north generations to recover.

The region again prospered on the medieval wool trade, which sponsored the great cathedral at York and enormous monastic communities, the remains of which can be seen at Rievaulx and Fountains. Leeds, Bradford and Sheffield later became powerhouses during the Industrial Revolution.

The countryside is a grand backdrop to this human drama, containing two of England's best national parks and some spectacular coastline. The Yorkshire Dales is the best known and arguably the most beautiful of the parks, but the North York Moors has a great variety of landscapes and includes a superb coastline. Parts of both parks can be very crowded in summer but it's easier to escape the masses in the North York Moors National Park.

The Danish heritage survives today, especially in the language but also, some would argue, in the independent spirit of the people. Place names ending in *thorp*, *kirk* and *by* all have a Danish origin.

ORIENTATION & INFORMATION
The Pennine Hills are the dominant geological feature forming a north–south spine through the Yorkshire Dales National Park. The major transport routes – the M1/A1 highways and the main London to Edinburgh railway line – basically run east of this spine.

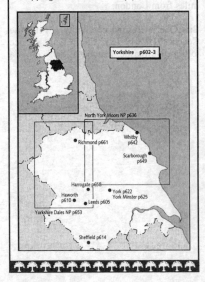

Highlights

- Riding the railways of the North Yorkshire Moors
- Hiking in the stunning Yorkshire Dales
- Absorbing the history of York Minster
- Munching fish and chips in Whitby
- Walking the windswept coast north of Scarborough
- Sipping an ale in a country pub

Yorkshire p602-3

North York Moors NP p636

Richmond p661
Whitby p642
Scarborough p649

Harrogate p658
Haworth p610
Leeds p605
York p622
York Minster p625
Yorkshire Dales NP p653

Sheffield p614

The Yorkshire Tourist Board (☎ 01904-707961, fax 701414, ✆ info@ytb.org.uk), 312 Tadcasrer Rd, York YO24 1GS, has plenty of information. Its Web site (www .ytb.org.uk) has a good accommodation-finding feature.

WALKING
There are several great walks in this region. The most famous is the Pennine Way, which stretches 250 miles from Edale in the Peak District to Kirk Yetholm near Kelso in

Scotland. It cuts a neat path right through the Dales. Unfortunately, its popularity means that long sections turn into unpleasant bogs, so it's worth considering quieter alternatives.

For example, it's possible to walk sections of the difficult 190-mile Coast to Coast Walk which crosses eastward from the Lake District, through the Yorkshire Dales and North York Moors.

The Yorkshire Dales and the North York Moors also have numerous walks. See the Activities chapter for information on the beautiful Cleveland Way and the often overlooked Wolds Way. In the Dales, consider the relatively easy, but still interesting, Dales Way, which runs 81 miles from Ilkley to Windermere in the Lake District, linking two national parks.

CYCLING

Cycling is a great way to see this part of England; the only disadvantages are the weather, the hills and the fact that, at weekends, even some of the minor B-roads can be very crowded. On the whole, however, all you need is a good map and some imagination, and you'll have a great time.

One route worth considering is the 130-mile Dales Way (see Yorkshire Dales National Park later in the chapter). It mostly follows the rivers but there are still some steep climbs.

Following the rugged coast between Whitby and Scarborough is made easier by a disused railway line which now serves as a bike path.

GETTING THERE & AROUND
Bus

Bus transport around the region can be difficult, particularly around the national parks. Fortunately, the national travel information service (☎ 0870 608 2608) now covers all of Yorkshire (and includes trains). National Express (☎ 0870 580 8080) has services to most British cities.

There are a myriad of one-day Rover tickets available from the various bus operators in the region. But note that many are only worthwhile if you plan on spending all day on the bus (if this sounds like a good idea, the money might be better spent on mental therapy). It's always worth asking the driver what the best ticketing option is for your intended journey.

Train

The main-line routes from London run north to Edinburgh via York and west to Carlisle through the Dales. Travelling to/from the south, it may be necessary to make connections at Leeds. Phone the national enquiry line (☎ 0345 484950) for all train enquiries.

Boat

P&O North Sea Ferries (☎ 01482-377 177) runs nightly ferries from Hull to Rotterdam in the Netherlands and Zeebrugge in Belgium. The journeys take about 13 hours. See the Web site (www.ponsf.com) for details.

West Yorkshire

For hundreds of years the prosperity of West Yorkshire depended on wool and cloth manufacturing. The industry flourished through the Middle Ages and was given an added boost by the advent of improved machinery during the Industrial Revolution. A cottage industry that traditionally employed women spinning downstairs while their men wove away upstairs quickly gave way to factories.

By the beginning of the 20th century West Yorkshire, and particularly Leeds and Bradford, dominated the wool industry. Although the industry has almost completely disappeared since WWII, large parts of the landscape are still dominated by reminders of it. Long rows of weavers' cottages (with 2nd-storey windows to provide light for the loom) and workers' houses built along the ridges overlook multistorey mills with towering chimneys in the valleys below. These industrial towns and valleys are separated by the wild stretches of moors so vividly described by the Brontë sisters who lived at nearby Haworth.

The Leeds/Bradford conurbation is one of the biggest in the country, virtually running into the industrial towns of Halifax, Huddersfield and Wakefield.

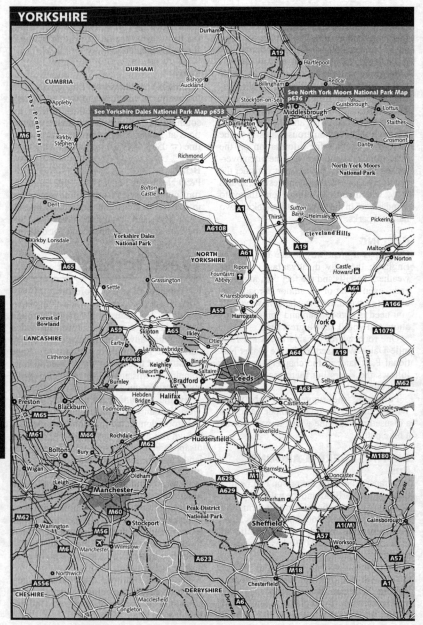

YORKSHIRE

YORKSHIRE

Durham

A19 Hartlepool

DURHAM

CUMBRIA

The Pennines

Appleby

Kirkby Stephen

Tees

Bishop Auckland

Billingham

Redcar

Stockton-on-Sea

See North York Moors National Park Map p636

Middlesbrough

Guisborough

Loftus

Staithes

M6

See Yorkshire Dales National Park Map p653

A66

Darlington

Danby

Grosmont

Dent

Richmond

Bolton Castle

Northallerton

A1

North York Moors National Park

Kirkby Lonsdale

Yorkshire Dales National Park

A6108

Thirsk

Sutton Bank

Helmsley

Pickering

A65

NORTH YORKSHIRE

A61

Cleveland Hills

A19

Malton

Settle

Grassington

Ripon

Fountains Abbey

Castle Howard

Norton

Forest of Bowland

Knaresborough

A64

A166

LANCASHIRE

Clitheroe

A59

Harrogate

York

A1079

A59

Skipton

A65

Ilkley

Otley

A64

A19

Ouse

Derwent

A6068

Earby

Laneshawbridge

Keighley

Bingley

Saltaire

A63

Selby

M62

Burnley

Haworth

Bradford

Leeds

Preston

Hebden Bridge

Halifax

Castleford

Goole

Blackburn

Todmorden

M65

M66

Rochdale

M62

Huddersfield

Wakefield

M61

Bolton

Bury

M180

Wigan

Oldham

A628

Barnsley

M1

Doncaster

Leigh

A629

Manchester

Rotherham

M62

M60

Stockport

Peak District National Park

Sheffield

Gainsborough

Warrington

M56

A1(M)

M6

Manchester

Wilmslow

A57

Worksop

A57

Northwich

A623

Derwent

Trent

M18

A556

CHESHIRE

Macclesfield

DERBYSHIRE

Chesterfield

A1

Congleton

A6

GETTING AROUND

The Metro public transport network, based in Leeds and Bradford, has won awards for its effective integrated bus and rail services. The area is particularly well served by rail with most towns in this section accessible by frequent trains. For extensive travel in West Yorkshire, buy the Metro DayRover passes (£4.50), good for travel after 9.30 am on weekdays and all day at weekends. There is also a thicket of additional Day-Rovers covering just buses and/or trains.

Metroline (☎ 0113-245 7676) answers phone enquiries on all public transport in West Yorkshire from 8 am to 7 pm on weekdays and 9 am to 5.30 pm on Saturday. It also publishes useful maps and timetables, most available in the Tourist Information Centres (TICs). Note that the Metroline number is due to be superseded by the national public transit enquiries number (☎ 0870 608 2608).

LEEDS

☎ 0113 • pop 455,000

Of all Britain's big cities, Leeds is certainly one of the most inviting. Not for nothing has it been dubbed the 'Knightsbridge of the North'; indeed, there are so many shops and shopping centres you could be forgiven for assuming that every single resident of Leeds is in the business of selling fancy frocks and household goods to other Leeds residents. There are over 1000 shops in the compact, pedestrianised centre.

Many of the fine Victorian buildings in the city centre have already been given a facelift and others are being smartened up as you read this. A large student population ensures a thriving nightlife.

The main tourist attraction is the purpose-built Royal Armouries, along the restored waterfront. Leeds also makes a good base for excursions to Haworth, Hebden Bridge and Bradford.

Orientation

The city is strung out along the northern bank of the River Aire and the Leeds–Liverpool Canal. The train and bus stations are centrally located but most affordable hotels are a bus ride away. If you are arriving

YORKSHIRE

by car, your best bet is to ditch it in one of the many parking lots that ring the centre and make your explorations on foot. The University of Leeds (☎ 243 1751) and Leeds Metropolitan University (☎ 283 2600) are both just north-west of the centre.

Information

Tourist Offices The Gateway to Yorkshire TIC (☎ 242 5242, fax 246 8246, e tour info@leeds.gov.uk), in the train station, opens 9.30 am to 6 pm Monday to Saturday, and 10 am to 4 pm Sunday.

Post & Communications The main post office (☎ 237 2849), right on City Square, opens 8 am to 5.30 pm Monday to Saturday.

The tiny WHSmith bookshop across from the TIC in the train station has free Internet access. It opens 7 am to 7.30 pm weekdays, 10 am to 6 pm Saturday, and 10 am to 4 pm Sunday.

Bookshops All the major chains can be found in Leeds. Waterstone's (☎ 244 4588), 97 Albion St, is one of the larger stores and has a good selection of maps.

Medical Services Leeds General Infirmary (☎ 243 2799) is the huge local hospital. It is west of Calverley St in the city centre.

Royal Armouries

Leeds' pride and joy is the spectacular building created to house the Royal Armouries (☎ 220 1996), on Armouries Drive, on the banks of the Leeds–Liverpool Canal. This grey-and-white edifice looks remarkably like a fortress and finding the way in if you've walked along the canal to get there can seem as tricky as trying to penetrate the defences of a medieval castle. Once inside, however, you'll find four floors of exhibits centred on the themes of war, tournaments, self-defence, hunting and the Orient. The displays are all modern and well done. They deserve credit for showing the realities of war. There are numerous demonstrations throughout the day so be sure to pick up a schedule when you arrive.

Outside you can see displays of jousting

and falconry from Easter to October. The Menagerie Court shows off the animals who take part in the displays, while the Craft Court allows you to see gun-makers, armourers and leather-workers in action. Perhaps the most controversial thing about the armouries is that they are in Leeds. When the weapons were on display in the Tower of London, they attracted far more visitors.

The Armouries open 10.30 am to 5 pm daily. Admission costs £4.90/3.90 per adult/child (a reduction from past years). If you don't want to walk (about 15 minutes from the TIC) you can get there by bus No 95 from Park Row near City Square (direction: Clarence Dock).

Other Things to See & Do

Star attraction of the **City Art Gallery** (☎ 247 8248) on The Headrow is the Henry Moore Collection, to the right inside the front entrance. One of the century's greatest sculptors, Henry Moore (1898–1986) was a graduate of Leeds School of Art. There is also a notable collection of French post-impressionist art. It opens 10 am to 5 pm daily, opening at 1 pm on Sunday and closing at 8 pm on Wednesday. Admission is free.

The adjoining **Henry Moore Institute** (☎ 246 7467) stages periodic exhibitions of 20th-century sculpture. Beneath the gallery there's a separate **Craft & Design Gallery**.

Sadly, the **City Museum**, homeless since WWII, has been sent packing – literally – from its temporary location in the library. Call ☎ 214 6526 for details on where the many displays may have found a new home.

Tucked away off northern Briggate is the redundant **St John's Church**, a one-off masterpiece of 17th-century design full of elaborate box-pews and with a wonderful screen resplendent with huge carvings of the arms of James I and of Charles I as Prince of Wales.

Places to Stay

The TIC books accommodation and has numerous special offers. Weekend packages aimed at clubbers start from £32 per person per night in fairly swank hotels.

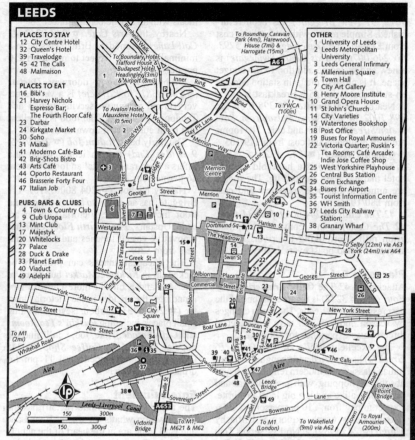

LEEDS

PLACES TO STAY
12 City Centre Hotel
32 Queen's Hotel
39 Travelodge
45 42 The Calls
48 Malmaison

PLACES TO EAT
16 Bibi's
21 Harvey Nichols
   Espresso Bar;
   The Fourth Floor Café
23 Darbar
24 Kirkgate Market
30 Soho
31 Maitai
41 Moderno Café-Bar
42 Brig-Shots Bistro
43 Arts Café
44 Oporto Restaurant
46 Brasserie Forty Four
47 Italian Job

PUBS, BARS & CLUBS
4 Town & Country Club
9 Club Uropa
13 Mint Club
17 Majestyk
20 Whitelocks
26 Palace
28 Duck & Drake
33 Planet Earth
40 Viaduct
49 Adelphi

OTHER
1 University of Leeds
2 Leeds Metropolitan
   University
3 Leeds General Infirmary
5 Millennium Square
6 Town Hall
7 City Art Gallery
8 Henry Moore Institute
10 Grand Opera House
11 St John's Church
14 City Varieties
15 Waterstones Bookshop
18 Post Office
19 Buses for Royal Armouries
22 Victoria Quarter; Ruskin's
   Tea Rooms; Café Arcade;
   Indie Jose Coffee Shop
25 West Yorkshire Playhouse
27 Central Bus Station
29 Corn Exchange
34 Buses for Airport
35 Tourist Information Centre
36 WH Smith
37 Leeds City Railway
   Station;
38 Granary Wharf

YORKSHIRE

Camping The most convenient camp site is the *Roundhay Caravan Site* (☎ 265 2354, fax 237 0077), 4 miles out in Elmete Lane, Roundhay. From March to November it has pitches for £4.10 per person. Bus Nos 2, 10 and 19 all pass the site.

Hostels There are no youth hostels in Leeds; the nearest are in Haworth and York.

B&Bs There's a group of B&Bs behind the University of Leeds on Woodsley Rd but you pay for the (relative) convenience. The *Avalon Hotel* (☎ 243 2545, fax 242 0649),

at No 132, has reasonable decor and is well run and comfortable. Most rooms have a private bathroom and singles/doubles start at £23/34. The *Manxdene Hotel* (☎ 243 2586), at No 154, is similar and charges from £24/36, which includes parking.

Another batch of B&Bs on Cardigan Rd, Headingley, have rates around £25/35. The *Boundary Hotel* (☎/fax 275 7700) at No 42 welcomes children and has cable TV in every room. Unusually named *Trafford House & Budapest Hotel* (☎ 275 2034, fax 274 2422, e trafford @fsbdial.co.uk) at No 16 is spread over three Victorian homes and has parking.

Hotels The *City Centre Hotel* (☎ 242 9019, 51 New Briggate) has been refurbished. Simple rooms without facilities cost from £25/40. The *Travelodge* (☎ 244 5793, fax 246 0076, Blayds Court, Swinegate) is a new and welcome addition to the budget scene. It is close to the train station and has en-suite rooms for £50. Breakfast is extra.

Nearby, the *Malmaison* (☎ 398 1000, fax 398 1002, ℮ leeds@malmaison.com, Sovereign Street) is stylish and chic. The rooms are well equipped and cost from £79/105.

Queen's Hotel (☎ 243 1323, fax 242 5154, City Square) is a huge old railway hotel that has been spruced up. The rooms are aimed at business travellers and cost from £80/105.

42 The Calls (☎ 244 0099, fax 234 4100, 42 The Calls) is in a converted Victorian grain mill overlooking the river. Rooms start at £98 and boast every luxury.

Places to Eat

Attached to 42 The Calls, *Brasserie Forty Four* (☎ 234 3232) is regarded as one of the best restaurants in Leeds. The menu changes by season and you can have a wonderful three-course experience for about £22.

The excellent *Bibi's* (☎ 243 0905, 16 Greek St) has a varied and changing menu of Italian classics and modern renditions. It gets absolutely hopping with pre-clubbers and older folks alike and is a big local favourite. Expect to pay from £10 per person.

Briggate is worth exploring. Unflashy *Maitai* (☎ 243 1989), at No 159, serves Thai dishes for around £6. *Moderno Café-Bar* (☎ 234 0301) at No 165 has music (from 8 to 11 pm) to go with its sandwiches and pizzas. At No 169, greenery-filled *Brig-Shots Bistro* (☎ 242 5629) has a pre-theatre menu for £10.50 until 7 pm. Its modern-European menu is long and interesting.

The streets between the Corn Exchange and 42 The Calls (see Places to Stay earlier) contain all sorts of glitzy bars and restaurants. In Call Lane you'll find the extremely popular *Oporto Restaurant* (☎ 243 4008) at No 31–33 where vegetarian meals are under £8; cheaper bites are available in the adjoining bar. Across the road at No 35, *Soho* (☎ 242 9009) has both meaty and vegetarian meals with an artistic bent for under £6.

Nearby, the *Arts Café* (☎ 243 8243, 42 Call Lane) has modern British cuisine in a minimalist setting. Expect to pay from £10 per person.

Despite the modest doorway, *Darbar* (☎ 246 0381, 16 Kirkgate) is a very large, very grand restaurant serving Indian and Tandoori specialities. The food is excellent and most curries cost upwards of £6.50.

The fairly basic *Italian Job* (☎ 242 0185, 9 Bridge End) has an iconic name and offers a good range of Italian food for about £6 per person.

Harvey Nichols (☎ 204 8000), 107–111 Briggate, has an *espresso bar* on the ground floor facing into the Victoria Quarter arcade. Upstairs, *The Fourth Floor Café* has innovative casual lunches and formal dinners from £20.

The cheapest snacks can probably be picked up in *Kirkgate Market* but if you're after tea and a bite in more cheerful surroundings, the arcades in the Victoria Quarter (☎ 245 5333) harbour several inviting small places, including *Ruskin's Tea Rooms* and *Café Arcade*. Here, too, you'll find the popular *Indie Joze Coffee Shop* (☎ 245 0569) which stays open until 11 pm for drinks and sandwiches.

Entertainment

The monthly *Leeds Guide* (£1.50) has the low-down on what's on where. Boar Lane and Call Lane are at the heart of the action, with lots of overdressed people wandering from bar to pub to club.

Pubs Perhaps the most famous Leeds pub is *Whitelocks* (☎ 245 3950) in Turk's Head Yard, a small alley off Briggate. It's a classic Edwardian pub with outside tables and traditional pub food such as Yorkshire pudding (£1.50).

The ornate Edwardian *Adelphi* (☎ 245 6377, 3–5 Hunslet Rd) boasts wood panelling, tiles and engraved glass, and attracts a varied clientele. Considered the home pub for the Carlsberg-Tetley Brewery, it is an attraction itself.

Duck & Drake (☎ 246 5806, 43 Kirkgate) has a good range of real ales and live music several nights a week. In winter it has large fireplaces to bake out the damp.

Possibly the widest choice of ales can be found at *Palace* (☎ 244 5882, Kirkgate) which has one large room dating from the 1930s. It's popular for its long list of lunch specials and has a good beer garden.

Viaduct (☎ 246 9178, 11 Lower Briggate) is a classic old pub that's had a sensible updating and now includes amenities such as a nonsmoking room and facilities for the disabled. The beer garden is another winner and it's busy at lunchtime.

Clubs Leeds has a tremendous club scene that attracts people from many miles around in addition to the scores of local students. At the weekends you'll see lots of well-dressed young people cavorting in the centre before a night of club-hopping. In winter, lots of people brave the cold wearing next to nothing to avoid cloakroom hassles. The weekend admission charges average £5.

The following clubs all have hugely varied line-ups of music and themes. *Club Uropa* (☎ 242 2224, 54 New Briggate) is one of the most popular and attracts top DJs. *Majestyk* (☎ 242 4333) and *Planet Earth* (☎ 243 4733) are both on City Square. Most people try to shuttle between both.

The *Town & Country Club* (☎ 280 0100, 55 Cookridge St) has both live rock and disco nights. The *Mint Club* (☎ 244 3168, 8 Harrison St) changes constantly. It also has very popular women-only nights every week.

Theatre Chaplin and Houdini both performed at *City Varieties* (☎ 243 0808, Swan St), one of Britain's last old-fashioned music halls.

West Yorkshire Playhouse (☎ 244 2111, Quarry Hill Mount) has a good reputation for live drama. Many local works are performed on its two stages. *Grand Opera House* (☎ 222 6222, 46 New Briggate) where tickets for a wide variety of performances (not just opera) cost from £8.

Spectator Sports

For many people, Leeds means Headingley and Headingley means cricket. The first cricket match played here was in 1890, and it's still a venue for Test matches and home ground to the Yorkshire County Cricket Club.

To get to the cricket ground, take bus No 74 or 75 from Park Row or catch a train to Burley Park station, a short walk from the ground. For match bookings (from £18 for a Test match) phone ☎ 278 7394.

Shopping

There are scores of places to shop in Leeds. **Granary Wharf** (☎ 244 6570), behind the train station, is reached via the Dark Arches. It's a cobbled area under vaulted arches at the meeting point of the canal and the river, with art and craft shops, free entertainment and markets selling local, hand-made goods on Friday, Saturday and Sunday.

A highlight of any visit is a stroll round the magnificent **Victoria Quarter** (☎ 245 5333) arcades on Briggate which are roofed with a stained-glass canopy, paved with mosaics and decorated with marble. The shops are suitably upmarket and intimidating, all the more so since **Harvey Nichols** (☎ 204 8000) opened its first store outside London here.

Just as much fun in a more down-to-earth way is the **Kirkgate Market** (☎ 214 5162), once home of Marks, who later joined Spencer. Here, in Europe's largest covered market, arcades of wrought-iron and ceramic tiles surround stalls piled high with fresh produce and cheap baked goods – ideal for stocking up for a picnic. The market is open from Monday to Saturday, closing at 1 pm on Wednesday. The adjoining open-air markets function on Tuesday, Friday and Saturday.

The wonderful circular **Corn Exchange** (☎ 234 0363), built in 1865, is the place to come if you're into one-off clothes shops and specialities such as stencilling. It opens daily.

Getting There & Away

Air Leeds-Bradford airport (☎ 250 9696), 8 miles north of the city via the A65, offers both domestic and international flights to a few major European cities. The Airlink 757 bus operates hourly from the airport to Leeds City Square, next to the train station (£1.50, 25 minutes). A taxi will cost around £15.

Bus The Central Bus Station is a 10-minute walk east of the train station, off St Peter's St. National Express has services to most British cities including nine coaches daily to/from London (£12, 3 hours).

Yorkshire Coastliner (☎ 0870 608 2608) has a useful service linking Leeds, York, Castle Howard, Goathland and Whitby (Nos 840 and 842). Many other services link Leeds, York and Scarborough.

Train Leeds City station is large and busy, with hourly services to London King's Cross (£56) that take as little as two hours. It's also the starting point for the famous Leeds-Settle-Carlisle (LSC) line. There are frequent services to both Sheffield (£4.90, 30 minutes) and York (£6.20, 30 minutes).

Getting Around
You can get a Metro bus to most parts of the city and to the suburbs from the Central Bus Station. Most also serve a stop on or near City Square. Ask the TIC or bus drivers about the various Metro DayRover passes which cover trains and/or buses and can be used to get to Bradford, Haworth and Hebden Bridge as well as around the city.

HAREWOOD HOUSE
Harewood is one of Britain's most beautiful stately homes but it's also extremely popular at peak periods. The building is great, the interiors are over the top and the surrounding park is glorious, but some may find the perfection and commercialisation rather 'cold'.

Harewood has been home to the Lascelles family since it was built between 1759 and 1772. No expense was spared – Capability Brown was responsible for the grounds, Thomas Chippendale for the furniture, and Italy was raided to create an appropriate art collection (including works by Tintoretto, Titian, Bellini and many others).

In addition to the house, there's the Stables Gallery, the Bird Garden and a children's adventure playground. The stables house a pleasant cafe. Enjoyable walks take you round Harewood Lake and to 15th-century **Harewood Church** which is no longer in use (the village it originally served was moved when the house was constructed!) but contains some fascinating tombs and monuments.

The house (☎ 0113-218 1010) is 7 miles north of Leeds on the A61 to Harrogate. Bus Nos 36, 36A, 36C and 781 will get you there from Leeds. It opens 11 am to 4.30 pm daily, April to October. Admission is £6.95/4.75.

BRADFORD
☎ 01274 • pop 296,000
The centre of Bradford is 9 miles west of Leeds but the two cities are virtually continuous. Until WWII Bradford was the uncontested capital of the world wool trade. After that the industry collapsed, leaving the city struggling to find a new role. Since the 1960s over 60,000 Indians and Pakistanis have settled here and helped reinvigorate the city.

Some people come to Bradford for its famous curry houses and others for the National Museum of Photography, Film & Television. However, most are passing through on their way to Saltaire, Haworth or the Dales.

Orientation & Information
Central Bradford is compact. The Bradford Interchange, the combined bus and rail terminal, is right in the centre of town along Bridge St.

The TIC (☎ 753678, fax 739067, ⓔ bradford@ytbtic.co.uk) is in the Central Library on Prince's Way. It opens 9 am to 5.30 pm on weekdays, and until 4 pm on Saturday. They have the usual wealth of information on the area including useful accommodation and eating guides.

The library (☎ 753600) has free Internet access. There is parking behind the complex.

Things to See & Do
The **National Museum of Photography, Film & Television** (☎ 202030) is a large and well-funded operation right next to the library and TIC on Prince's Way. This is a

great place where, as well as learning about the history of photography, you can try out lots of video and graphics technology and play at being a TV newsreader or cameraperson. There are a range of special exhibitions through the year. The museum houses an IMAX cinema and there are other movie theatres where off-beat, historical and even mainstream films are shown. The exhibits are open 10 am to 6 pm (closed Monday except for bank holidays) and are free. The cinemas are open through the evening and there are varying charges for films.

The **Colour Museum** (☎ 390955), 82 Grattan Rd, the home of the Society of Dyers and Colourists, is more interesting than you might expect. It draws on Bradford's woollen past to show how clothes are given their colours. It also has a good section showing how different species sense colour in different ways (what's blue to you isn't blue to Fido). The museum is 10 minutes from the Bradford Interchange. It opens 10 am to 4 pm Tuesday to Saturday. Admission costs £1.50/1.

The **Bradford Industrial Museum** (☎ 631756), Moorside Rd, is in an old spinning mill dating from 1875. Exhibits give an idea of what life was like at the peak of the industrial revolution. It opens 10 am to 5 pm (from noon Sunday, closed Monday). Admission is free.

The wonderful **Undercliffe Cemetery** (☎ 642276), between Undercliffe Lane and Otley Rd, has Britain's best collection of Victorian funerary art. It's open daily during daylight hours and is free.

Places to Stay & Eat

The TIC will be very happy to find you accommodation.

The *Castle Hotel* (☎ 393166, 20 Grattan Rd) is near the centre. It has simple singles/doubles which cost from £26/36 without breakfast.

Top choice is the *Quality Victoria Hotel* (☎ 728706, fax 736358, Bridge St) which has been restored to its heyday of 1875, when it was built. Rooms are opulent and there's a health club and more. Rooms start at £75 and there are weekend specials.

There's a lot of argument about where Britain's ubiquitous – and most home-grown – chicken tikka masala was first served, although it may well have been Bradford. Top among the local curry places is *Kashmir* (☎ 726513, 27 Morley St), which is in the centre and has excellent curries for around £4. It opens until 2 am.

Bombay Brasserie (☎ 737564, Simes Gate, Westgate) is a high-end Indian place with food to match the lovely interior. Here you might pay £6 for a main dish.

Karrotz Cafe Bar (☎ 201787, 1 Petergate) is an organic vegetarian cafe and a bar. It's open for lunch during the week and dinner from Thursday to Saturday. Meals cost under £7 and much less at lunch.

Getting There & Away

Bradford's main station is Bradford Interchange although some trains go from Forster Square on Cheapside, which is a bit less convenient.

There are frequent trains to Bradford from Leeds (£1.80, 20 minutes, every 15 minutes) and York (£7.80, one hour, hourly).

SALTAIRE

Well worth a visit is the **Saltaire** suburb, some 3 miles north of Bradford. It was built in 1851 by wool-baron Titus Salt, who wanted a company village and factory that contributed to the health of its inhabitants and workers. Care was taken to provide for good light, ventilation, heating and other services. If nothing else, Salt created a gem of a village, which is built from the local honey-coloured stone to neo-Italianate designs. **Salt's Mill** (☎ 531163) is the key building and was the largest factory building in the world when it was completed. The entire village has been nominated for UNESCO World Heritage Site status. One main feature today is the **1853 Gallery** (☎ 531185), dedicated to Bradford-born artist David Hockney.

The TIC (☎ 774993, fax 774464), 2 Victoria Rd, runs guided walks through the year and can book beds in local B&Bs. It opens 10 am to 5 pm daily. Most sites in Saltaire open 10 am to 6 pm daily and are free.

From Bradford, there's a frequent Metro train service from Forster Square Station. From Bradford Interchange, take bus No 679.

At nearby **Bingley** you can see a series of five 18th-century canal locks which raise the Leeds–Liverpool Canal 18m.

HAWORTH
☎ 01535 • pop 5100

As the village that was home to the Brontë family, Haworth rivals Stratford-upon-Avon as England's most important literary shrine. The surrounding countryside seems haunted both by the sisters and their literary creations. Even without this, the old part of the village would still draw tourists; the cobblestoned Main St running steeply down to Bridgehouse Beck (stream) from the parish church provides a quintessential Yorkshire view. In fact one local told us: 'Lots of those people on the coach tours don't even know why they're here. They just want to buy something.' Certainly, retail opportunities abound and you can buy anything imaginable and more bearing the Brontë name or likeness.

Patrick Brontë and his family moved to the Parsonage in 1820. It was not a healthy move. His wife Maria died of cancer at 38;

his daughters Maria and Elizabeth died as children. His son Branwell lasted until he was 31, spending many of his final years in pubs.

Emily, who wrote *Wuthering Heights*, died in 1848 at age 30 after catching a 'chill'. Anne, who penned *Agnes Grey* using the name Acton Bell, died at age 29 in 1849. Of all the siblings, Charlotte held on the longest. She wrote *Jane Eyre* and even married. However, she died shortly afterwards at age 38 in 1855.

Only Patrick survived to old age, dying in the Parsonage at the age of 84. The Parsonage museum gives a fascinating insight into their lives. Away from the maddening crowds, the West Yorkshire countryside will immediately seem familiar to fans of the sisters' books.

Orientation & Information
Haworth's development parallels that of the textile industry. The old village, with its cottage-based weavers and spinners, grew up along the ridge above the valley. Then in the 19th century the outworkers were replaced by factories.

The TIC (☎ 642329, fax 647721, ⓔ haworth@ytbtic.co.uk), 2–4 West Lane, opens

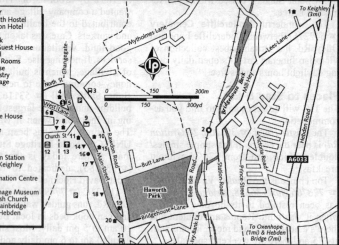

HAWORTH

PLACES TO STAY
1 Haworth Youth Hostel
4 Old White Lion Hotel
6 Weaver's
8 Rookery Nook
10 Apothecary Guest House
11 The Black Bull
15 Haworth Tea Rooms
   & Guest House
19 The Old Registry
20 Heather Cottage
   Guest House

PLACES TO EAT
7 King's Arms
14 Villette Coffee House
   & Bakery
17 Copper Kettle
18 Fleece Inn

OTHER
2 Haworth Train Station
3 Bus Stop for Keighley
   & Bradford
5 Tourist Information Centre
9 Post Office
12 Brontë Parsonage Museum
13 Haworth Parish Church
16 Venables & Bainbridge
21 Bus Stop for Hebden
   Bridge

9 am to 5 pm daily (until 5.30 pm April to September) and has an excellent supply of information on the Brontë family.

The post office is at 98 Main St and opens 9 am to 5.30 pm Monday to Friday, and until 12.30 on Saturday.

Venables & Bainbridge, 111 Main St, sells used books, including many vintage Brontë volumes.

Brontë Parsonage

Set in a pretty garden, the Parsonage is a Georgian house overlooking the cemetery. The core of the house is furnished and decorated as it would have been when the Brontës lived there. Some of the furnishings are original and there are many personal possessions on display. The museum section houses lots of material, including the fascinating miniature books the children wrote.

The museum is operated by the Brontë Society, a group which was in the news during 2000 as internal divisions threatened to sink the entire operation. The Parsonage (☎ 642323) opens 10 am to 5.30 pm daily, April to September; from 11 am the rest of the year. Admission costs £4.50/1.40.

Keighley & Worth Valley Railway

The K&WV Railway (☎ 645214) is a favourite movie location with film crews, as much for the six restored stations as for the classic steam engines.

Especially at summer weekends when Haworth can be jam-packed, it's worth parking at Keighley and catching the train to the village. Better yet, you can avoid the drive entirely by taking a regular train to Keighley, which is on the Leeds-Settle-Carlisle line, then changing for the K&WV Railway. The Brontë Parsonage is a 10-minute walk uphill from the station.

Trains operate virtually hourly at weekends year round. Over school holiday periods there's a daily service too. A one-day Rover ticket costs £8/4, a return is £6/3 and the ride from Keighley takes 15 minutes.

Walking

The TIC has information on lots of interesting walks that take in sights associated with the Brontë family. It sells a walking brochure (30p) that shows a 6½-mile course which traces many key scenes in *Wuthering Heights*. Some of the other walks can be worked in around the K&WV Railway, the Brontë Way (which links Haworth with Bradford and Colne) and the two routes to Hebden Bridge (see that section later in the chapter). Haworth is just east of the Pennine Way.

Brontë Way by Marje Wilson describes 11 circular walks that cover the entire route of the Way. Particularly interesting is the fairly strenuous 9-mile walk from the Parsonage to Colne/Laneshawbridge via Top Withens (Wuthering Heights), Ponden Hall (Thrushcross Grange) and Wycoller Hall (Ferndean Manor). From Laneshawbridge you can catch a bus to Keighley and complete the loop by catching the K&WV Railway back to Haworth.

Places to Stay

Hostel A half-mile walk east from the train station is *Haworth Youth Hostel* (☎ 642234, fax 643023, ✉ haworth@yha.org.uk, Longlands Drive, Lees Lane). Beds cost £10/6.90 for adults/under-18s; it is closed on Sunday in November and December. You can get any of the buses to/from Keighley to stop at Longlands Drive.

B&Bs & Hotels Although there are lots of places to stay, it's still worth booking ahead in summer. The TIC books rooms.

Main St, the most atmospheric part of town, has lots of accommodation but can feel a bit oppressive in high season. *Heather Cottage Guest House* (☎ 644511, 25/27 Main St) has singles/doubles from £15/30.

The *Old Registry* (☎ 646503, 2–4 Main St) across the road has en-suite rooms for £25/42. Lone travellers can't be accommodated on Saturdays.

Farther up the hill at the top of Main St is *Black Bull* (☎ 642249, **119 Main St)**, famous for being Branwell Brontë's local. It has two rooms with private bathroom for £29/49.

Opposite the Black Bull, the popular *Apothecary Guest House* (☎/fax 643642, 86 Main St) has a range of rooms, most with bathroom, from £19/38.

Haworth Tea Rooms & Guest House (☎ 644278, 68 Main St) has standard but nice rooms from £25/40.

The simple *Rookery Nook* (☎ 643374, 6 Church St) is right across from Haworth Parish Church. Rooms cost £20 per person and you can have dinner for £5.

Old White Lion Hotel (☎ 642313, fax 646222, 6 West Lane) is the main hotel in the village. It is almost 300 years old and has a bar and a restaurant. Rooms vary in size but the average price is about £44/70.

Also on West Lane, the very comfortable *Weavers* (☎/fax 643822), No 15, has singles/doubles for £50/75. Some of the rooms are quite romantic.

Places to Eat

Main St and West Lane are lined with tearooms and restaurants, many of which are noted above in Places to Stay.

Weaver's easily has the best food in town. Its restaurant (closed Sunday and Monday) serves complete meals that feature local specialities and game. Expect to pay at least £20 per person for three courses. The wine list is also good.

King's Arms (☎ 643146) is slightly down Church St, off Main St; turn off at the Black Bull. It has a good beer garden and fine dinners of steaks and the like for about £10.

Fleece Inn (☎ 642172, 51 Main St) has a good range of real ales and fine pub lunches for under £5. *The Black Bull* wins plaudits for its dinners.

Copper Kettle (☎ 642809, 81 Main St) has meals for under £3.50. You can find the usual array of sandwiches and jacket potatoes here.

The friendly *Villette Coffee House & Bakery* (☎ 644967, 115 Main St) is particularly good value with all-day breakfasts for £2.80 and wonderful Yorkshire curd tarts (very sweet, rich and filling) for 75p. They also have veggie burgers.

Getting There & Away

Keighley & District buses Nos 663, 664, and 665 link Haworth with Keighley at least three times an hour (20 minutes). The same company runs a few buses daily direct to Bradford (one hour). In summer, bus No 500

offers a service four times a day between Todmorden, Hebden Bridge, Haworth and Keighley (Wednesday and Sunday in winter).

The previously mentioned K&WV Railway is a good link from Haworth to Keighley and the national rail network.

HEBDEN BRIDGE & HEPTONSTALL
☎ 01422

Heptonstall, with its hill-top location, was settled before Hebden Bridge down in the valley. However, the latter was able to take advantage of its riverside location to build mills and it soon eclipsed its elevated neighbour.

Heptonstall consists of typical grey-stone weavers' cottages. The Cloth Hall on the main street is Yorkshire's oldest, dating back to 1554. When steam power arrived, mills were set up in the valley along the River Calder, and the Rochdale Canal was built to provide transport. The mills have closed and Hebden Bridge seems to huddle apologetically in a valley now given over to tourism. The late Ted Hughes grew up near Hebden Bridge and wrote many poems about the area. His wife Sylvia Plath is buried in the Wesleyan chapel graveyard at Heptonstall.

Orientation & Information

It's easy to get around Hebden Bridge on foot but the steep half-mile walk up to Heptonstall is a killer. Better to hang on for a bus unless you're feeling energetic.

The TIC (☎ 843831, fax 845266, e hebdenbridge@ytbtic.co.uk), 1 Bridge Gate, opens 10 am to 5 pm daily.

Things to See & Do

Wandering the streets and hills is the chief attraction here. The **Heptonstall Museum** (☎ 843738), Church Bottom, is in a 17th-century school building and has items covering local history. Its limited hours are 1 to 3 pm weekends, April to October. Admission costs £1/50p.

Hardcastle Crags (☎ 844518), run by the National Trust (NT) is an unspoilt wooded valley complete with waterfalls, 1½ miles north-west of town off the A6033. There are numerous walks around here, some of which link to the Pennine Way. Those odd hills you see are made by the valley's often-studied residents, hairy wood ants.

Perhaps it's the honey exhibition that draws tourists to **Walkley Clogs** (☎ 842061) in a manner not unlike flies to... There's all manner of knick-knackery for sale and you can see clog-making amid a clutter of competing attractions. It's one mile west of Hebden Bridge on Burnley Rd (A646). A ticket covering everything costs £4/2.

At **Calder Valley Cruising** (☎ 845557), The Marina on New Rd offers horse-drawn cruises along the Rochdale Canal. The trips last from 20 minutes to two hours and run from 10 am to 5 pm daily, April to October.

Places to Stay

Camping At High Greenwood House, Heptonshall, *Pennine Camp Site (☎ 842287)* has 50 tent pitches and charges £3 per person.

Hostels In an ancient manor house in a typical Yorkshire village, *Mankinholes Youth Hostel (☎/fax 01706-812340)* is near Todmorden, 4 miles south-west of Hebden Bridge, south of the A646 to/from Rochdale, and half a mile from the Pennine Way. From mid-April to October it's usually open daily except Sunday and possibly Monday. It is worth calling in advance to check. Beds cost £10/6.90 for adults/under-18s. Trains from Leeds to Manchester stop at Todmorden, 2 miles from the hostel.

B&Bs & Hotels The friendly *Royd Well (☎ 845304, 35 Royd Terrace)* is a three-minute walk from town; rooms with shared bathroom cost from £14 per person.

Redacre Mill (☎/fax 885563, Mytholmroyd) is in a canalside mill surrounded by gardens. Rooms cost from £39.

Robin Hood Inn (☎ 842593, fax 844938), 2 steep miles out at Pecket Well on the Keighley Rd, has four beautifully decorated rooms with nice views (from £21 per person).

White Lion Hotel (☎ 842197, fax 846619, Bridge Gate) has 10 rooms in a fine riverside location and dates from 1656. Rooms start at £22.50 per person.

Places to Eat

Hebdens Pizzeria (☎ 843745, Hanginroyd Lane) is a bistro in Hebden Bridge where pizzas cost around £5.

Otherwise the inns mentioned in the Places to Stay section are probably your best bet. If you have a car, it's worth driving out to *Robin Hood Inn* on the Keighley Road. *White Lion Hotel* has a fine pub with good beer and food.

Getting There & Away

Hebden Bridge is within the Leeds Metro area. The rail service runs from Leeds and Bradford to Hebden Bridge and Todmorden (for the youth hostel), then continues to Manchester Victoria. Some services run right through from York to Liverpool.

The buses are slower and less frequent than the trains, but in summer, Keighley & District's bus No 500 offers a handy four times a day service between Todmorden, Hebden Bridge, Haworth and Keighley.

Sheffield & Around

Until recently, Sheffield didn't feature on tourist itineraries but in 1997 the smash-hit film *The Full Monty*, the tale of a group of unemployed steelworkers who turned to stripping for a living, sparked interest in this old industrial town.

Today's visitors find a city working hard to reinvent itself. Galleries and parks are being spiffed up in the centre and attractions pegged to the industrial past are well worth a visit.

Sheffield makes a good base for exploring West Yorkshire, including the Brontë area. The Peak District brushes up against its western outskirts and Chesterfield, with its twisted spire, is just a train hop away (see The Midlands chapter).

SHEFFIELD

☎ 0114 • pop 475,000

Five hundred years ago Sheffield was already renowned for its cutlery production and the words 'Sheffield steel' still have a familiar ring to them. Nowadays the industry employs far fewer people than in the

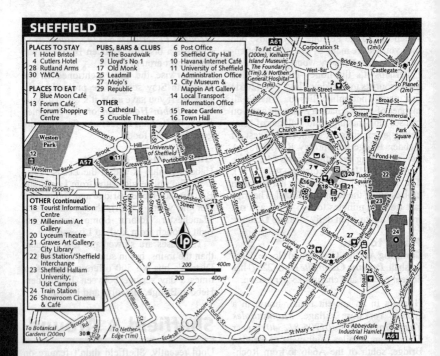

SHEFFIELD

PLACES TO STAY
1 Hotel Bristol
4 Cutlers Hotel
28 Rutland Arms
30 YMCA

PLACES TO EAT
7 Blue Moon Café
13 Forum Café;
Forum Shopping
Centre

PUBS, BARS & CLUBS
2 The Boardwalk
9 Lloyd's No 1
17 Old Monk
25 Leadmill
27 Mojo's
29 Republic

OTHER
3 Cathedral
5 Crucible Theatre

6 Post Office
8 Sheffield City Hall
10 Havana Internet Café
11 University of Sheffield
Administration Office
12 City Museum &
Mappin Art Gallery
14 Local Transport
Information Office
15 Peace Gardens
16 Town Hall

OTHER (continued)
18 Tourist Information
Centre
19 Millennium Art
Gallery
20 Lyceum Theatre
21 Graves Art Gallery;
City Library
22 Bus Station/Sheffield
Interchange
23 Sheffield Hallam
University;
Usit Campus
24 Train Station
26 Showroom Cinema
& Café

past but they turn out more knives and forks than ever before.

Victorian Sheffield with its grim factories and mills is synonymous with the worst industrial exploitation. Many buildings were damaged in WWII and post-war rebuilding added little to be admired. Despite this, England's fourth largest city is a lively place. It has an exuberant student population and a much-trumpeted recent survey of British students showed that Sheffield ranked first in terms of 'good times'. The survey avoided discussing what impact this might have on academic achievement.

Orientation

If you arrive by bus you'll find yourself at the vast Sheffield Interchange on Pond St which is ringed with roads and high-rises. The train station is clearly signed, three minutes south of the bus stands.

Sheffield's main street changes its name from Glossop Rd to West St to Church St to High St as it proceeds from west to east. Immediately south of West St is the area known as the Devonshire Quarter (Devonshire St, Division St and Barker's Pool) where there are trendy shops and bars. Just west, the Broomhill area and Ecclesall Rd are lined with shops, cafes and pubs.

The two major universities are the University of Sheffield (☎ 222 2000), west of Upper Hanover, and Sheffield Hallam University (☎ 225 5555), near the train station.

Information

Tourist Offices The very friendly TIC (☎ 221 1900, fax 201 1020, ⓔ info@destinationsheffield.org.uk) is at 1 Tudor Square on Surrey St. It opens 9.30 am to 5.15 pm on weekdays, and until 4.15 pm on Saturday.

Post & Communications There is a post office on Norfolk Row that opens 8 am to 5.30 pm on weekdays, and until 12.30 pm on Saturday.

Havana Internet Café (☎ 249 5453), 32–34 Division St, charges £1.25 for 15 minutes access. It opens from at least 10 am to 6 pm daily.

Travel Agencies Usit Campus (☎ 275 8366) is right across from the train station on Pond St in the Sheffield Hallam University student union.

Medical Services Northern General Hospital (☎ 243 4343) is north of the centre on the corner of Herries and Barnsley Roads.

Museums & Art Galleries
In 2001, the major new **Millennium Art Gallery** will open on Surrey St. It will have travelling exhibits from the Victoria & Albert Museum in London and will also be the new home to the city's eclectic **Ruskin Gallery** (☎ 278 2600). The collection was established by the Victorian critic and Gothic-revivalist John Ruskin in 1875 in an attempt to meld art and industry.

The **Peace Gardens** in front of the grand Town Hall are a recent addition to the city centre. Fountains and a range of sculpture enliven what had been a pretty dead spot.

The nearby **Graves Art Gallery** (☎ 278 2600) displays contemporary British and European art atop the City Library on Surrey St. Matisse, Spencer and Nash are some of the artists featured. The space has been refurbished and it is also the site of major touring shows. It opens 10 am to 5 pm Monday to Saturday. Admission is free.

One mile west of the centre in pleasant Weston Park, the **City Museum & Mappin Art Gallery** (☎ 278 2600) has exhibits on local archaeology and the history of the cutlery industry, as well as a varied collection of art works. It opens 10 am to 5 pm Tuesday to Saturday, and from 11 am Sunday. Admission is free.

One mile north of the centre, the excellent **Kelham Island Museum** (☎ 272 2106) covers not just cutlery but the city's wider industrial heritage. One of the main exhibits is the still-operational River Don Steam Engine, a house-sized, steam-powered metal press once used to make armour plate for battleships. It opens 10 am to 4 pm Monday to Thursday, and 11 am to 4.45 pm on Sunday. Admission costs £3.50/2.50.

Abbeydale Industrial Hamlet (☎ 236 7731), 4 miles south-west on the A621, is a restored industrial hamlet from the 18th century. Here you can see what the steel industry was like when it was literally a cottage industry. It opens 10 am to 4 pm Monday to Thursday, and 11 am to 4.45 pm on Sunday from mid-April to late October. Admission costs £3/2.

Other Things to See
In 1914 the 15th-century church of Sts Peter and Paul on West St was upgraded to **cathedral** status. Note, at the western end, the memorial to the crew of the HMS *Sheffield* lost during the Falklands conflict.

Foremost among Sheffield's many parks, the **Botanical Gardens** (☎ 250 0500) on Clarkehouse Rd, one mile south-west of the city-centre, cover 18 acres and contain three restored glasshouses by the Victorian designer Paxton. It opens 7.30 am (from 10 am at weekends) to dusk. Admission is free.

Climbing
Sheffield's proximity to the Peak District has helped it become a centre for British mountain-climbing training. The **Foundry Climbing Centre** (☎ 279 6331), 45 Mowbray St, is one of several climbing centres in the area. It has over 10,000 sq feet of climbing walls, some of which are 40 feet tall. There are instructors as well as a climbing shop. It opens 10 am to 10 pm weekdays (to 6 pm weekends). Admission costs £5.30/3.50.

Places to Stay
The TIC books rooms and has a special reservation line (☎ 201 1011).

During the summer holidays rooms are available in various dorms at the *University of Sheffield* (☎ 222 0260, fax 222 0288). The housing office is at 12 Claremont Crescent and arrangements are hotel-style. The minimum stay is two nights and the cost is £8.90 per person. There are laundry facilities.

The big, slightly Spartan *YMCA* (☎ 268 4807, 20 Victoria Rd) caters for both sexes with rooms for £16/26 but it's a fair walk south-west of the centre.

Scores of B&Bs are concentrated on the western side of town, in Nether Edge and along Ecclesall Rd. Take bus No 22 to Nether Edge and bus Nos 81, 82 and 83 to Ecclesall Rd. *Gulliver's B&B* (☎ 262 0729, 167 Ecclesall Rd) is a simple but comfy place with singles/doubles from £17/32. *Abbey House* (☎ 266 7426, 484 Ecclesall Rd) has similar accommodation and charges £20/38.

In Nether Edge, *Lindum Hotel* (☎ 255 2356, fax 249 4746, 91 Montgomery Rd) charges £20/33 for very basic rooms. More upmarket, the *Nether Edge Hotel* (☎ 255 4363, fax 255 4737, ☎ rec@nether-edge-hotel.co.uk, 21–23 Montgomery Rd) has en-suite rooms from £30/40.

The *Rutland Arms* (☎ 272 9003, fax 273 1425, 86 Brown St) is a lovely pub near the train station and has numerous rooms from £24/37; many are en suite.

Another good choice in the centre is *Cutlers Hotel* (☎ 273 9939, fax 276 8332, ☎ en quiries@cutlershotel.co.uk, George St). The fairly simple but comfortable rooms all have bathrooms and start at £49/60.

The *Hotel Bristol* (☎ 200 4000, fax 220 3900, ☎ sheffield@bhg.co.uk, Blonk St) is another one of those stylish, modern places happily cropping up throughout Britain. Rooms cost from £60.

Places to Eat

When it comes to eating you can't go wrong by heading for the Devonshire Quarter. *Forum Café* (☎ 276 6544) in the designer-clothes-filled Forum Shopping Centre (at the junction of Division St and Eldon St) attracts a young and trendy crowd. Lunch will run to about £5.

There are scores of places on Ecclesall Rd. One of the best is *Nonna's* (☎ 268 6166, No 539–541) which is an Italian cafe and bar. The food is fresh and you can have a great meal for £12.

Up in Broomhill, *UK Mama* (☎ 268 7807, 257 Fulwood Rd) is a funky Afro-Caribbean restaurant where, if you're lucky, they'll let you play with the drums. Expect to pay under £8 for dinner. Across the street,

Balti King (☎ 266 6655, 216 Fulwood Rd) is an especially fine Indian place that is open most nights until 3 am. Dinner and drinks will cost about £8 per person.

The excellent *Blue Moon Café* (☎ 276 3443, Norfolk Row) caters for vegetarians; soup and good bread cost just £1.80. Locals rave about the place but note that it's open for lunch only. The excellent *cafe* at the Showroom Cinema (see Entertainment later) has fresh, reasonably priced food until late.

Entertainment

To keep up with Sheffield's vibrant music scene, check out the weekly *Sheffield Telegraph* newspaper (50p) which comes out every Friday.

Pubs In a sad sign of the times, what was once the Division St HQ of the National Union of Mineworkers (when Arthur Scargill ruled the roost in the early 1980s) is now a branch of *Lloyds No 1* (276 5076). It's at the corner of Division St with Holly St. There are many more chain bars and pubs nearby. Near the TIC, the old TSB Bank is now a particularly grand branch of *Old Monk* (☎ 257 2526, Norfolk St).

One of Sheffield's finest pubs is easily the *Fat Cat* (☎ 249 4801, 23 Alma St), near the Kelham Island Museum. Not only do they brew their own beer but they also have a wide range of real ales from all over Yorkshire plus a fine collection of Belgian products. The interior is delightfully unreconstructed and there's a fascinating exhibit on local sanitation in the men's toilets (really!).

Clubs & Venues For live music and DJs check out *Leadmill* (☎ 275 4500, 6–7 Leadmill Rd), although *Republic* (☎ 276 6777, 112 Arundel St) is known for the best DJs. *Planet* (☎ 244 9033, 429 Effingham Rd) is a lively gay club.

Sheffield City Hall (☎ 278 9789) is a grand old performance venue at Division St and Barkers Pool. *The Boardwalk* (☎ 279 9090, Snig Hill) is a good place to see top local bands.

At the corner of Paternoster Row and

Charles St you'll see a striking stainless building. An unintentional monument to Britain's Millennium excess, it was built to house the National Centre for Popular Music. The centre lasted a mere 16 months before it was closed, having attracted few visitors. The fact that few of the displays were actually connected with pop music seemed to play a big role in its flop. Meanwhile, the ground-floor venue *Mojo's* (☎ 249 8885) has live music on many nights.

Theatre & Cinema The *Crucible* and *Lyceum* theatres face each other across Tudor Square and share the same box office (☎ 276 9922). Both are home to some excellent regional drama.

Showroom Cinema (☎ 275 7727, 7 Paternoster Row) shows off-beat and interesting films. It also has a good bar and cafe.

Getting There & Away
Bus Sheffield is 160 miles from London, just off the M1. National Express services link Sheffield with London (£9.50, four hours) and other major centres in the north. There is a frequent bus service to/from Leeds (£3, 1½ hours). Bus No X18 serves Bakewell and the Peak District to the west.

There are luggage lockers at the Sheffield Interchange bus station.

Train Sheffield's grimy train station is the hub for services throughout the north. There are regular services to Leeds (£4.90, 30 minutes), Manchester Piccadilly (£10.40, one hour), Manchester Airport (£14.05, 70 minutes), York (£11.90, 80 minutes) and Hull (£13.20, 1½ hours).

There are frequent trains from London St Pancras via Leicester and Nottingham or Derby (£44). Sheffield is also a jumping-off point for the Peak District. The Hope Valley railway line that cuts through the northern Peak District via Edale runs between Sheffield in the east and New Mills and Manchester in the west. The scenery is gorgeous.

Getting Around
Sheffield's privatised buses are a muddle of competing lines and services. Call ☎ 01709-515151 for information on all services in South Yorkshire. There is a useful information centre across from the Town Hall on Pinstone St. It sells tickets and passes and opens 9 am to 5 pm Monday to Saturday.

First Mainline offers a fare of 20p on its buses within the city centre. Aside from the bus services, Sheffield also boasts a modern Supertram which trundles through the city centre. Fares start at 70p.

The Travelmaster ticket (£4.95) is valid for one day of travel on all of the buses, trams and trains of South Yorkshire.

AROUND SHEFFIELD
Only 10 miles north-east of the failed National Centre for Popular Music lies another Millennium Commission-funded attraction, **Earth Centre** (☎ 01709-513933), a vast 'green' exhibition in an abandoned colliery. Originally planned as a sort of theme park for ecologists, Earth Centre combines numerous displays showing how sustainable agriculture and technology can lead to a better future. Unfortunately all the high-minded rhetoric resulted in low visitor numbers. In 2000, the centre partially closed while more Millennium Commission money was shovelled in to make it more 'educational'. Due to reopen in 2001 (in 2000 only specially arranged group tours could visit) the organisers hope to profit from corporate events and from visitors who will snap up locally produced products such as organic cotton and the like.

Call for the latest opening times (if any) and prices. The Earth Centre is off the A6023 near Conisbrough. It's adjacent to the Conisbrough train station, which is on the line linking Sheffield and Dorchester.

East Riding of Yorkshire

The word Riding comes from the Danish *treding*, meaning 'third', dating back to the 9th century when the conquering Danes divided Yorkshire into administrative regions.

The county is mostly flat, although the rolling, attractive Wolds extend northwards in a narrow spine from Lincolnshire. The 79-mile Wolds Way National Trail runs from near Hull north across the low hills to Filey on the coast where it joins meets Cleveland Way. See the Activities chapter for details.

The Wolds are the northernmost of the chalk downs that originate in Wiltshire and end at Flamborough Head. The rest of the county was once largely marshland, which has been drained and is now intensively (and rather unattractively) farmed.

Hull, or Kingston-upon-Hull as it is officially known, is a large port and university town, with ferries to Zeebrugge (Belgium) and Rotterdam (Netherlands). Ten miles north, on the edge of the Wolds, is the small, unspoilt market town of Beverley, with two superb churches.

GETTING AROUND

Hull is easily reached by rail from Leeds and York, and from there a line runs north to Beverley, Filey and Scarborough. Hull is also a hub for regional bus services.

HULL (KINGSTON-UPON-HULL)

☎ 01482 • pop 331,200

Fortunately, only pedants call Hull by its unwieldy official name. Historically, this north-eastern town was a major port, and so it remains today. Hull was hard hit during WWII and initial impressions are not encouraging. But persevere and you'll be rewarded with a range of diversions.

Orientation & Information

The Old Town of Hull is the most interesting. It is bordered by the Rivers Humber and Hull as well as Ferensway and Freetown Way. The **Princes Quay Shopping Centre** (☎ 586622), an imposing glass building set in a moat facing the modern marina, is filled with chain stores of every kind. It has a commodious parking lot.

The TIC (☎ 223559, fax 613959, ℮ hull paragon@ytbtic.co.uk) on Carr Lane is surrounded by the imposing buildings of Register Square. It opens 9 am to 6 pm Monday to Saturday, and 11 am to 3 pm on Sunday.

City Museums

Hull has a remarkable collection of free, city-run museums (☎ 613902 for all). They open 10 am to 5 pm Monday to Saturday, and 1.30 to 4.30 pm on Sunday. All are free unless otherwise stated.

Queen Victoria Square is the focus of historic Hull. It is flanked by the **Ferens Art Gallery** and **Maritime Museum**, both in impressive Victorian buildings. The former has a decent selection of European art, while the latter celebrates Hull's long maritime traditions.

A few streets east, High St has three more interesting museums. Near Drypool Bridge and the water, **Wilberforce House** was the birthplace in 1759 of the anti-slavery crusader William Wilberforce. It was built in 1639 and the museum, which covers the history of slavery and the campaign against it, overflows into several attractive Georgian houses. Next door is the **Streetlife Transport Museum** which is just what its name implies and which has a very pleasant garden. South past Chapel Lane Staith, the **Hull & East Riding Museum** is a fairly entertaining place that traces local history from Roman times to the present.

Other Sights

At the heart of the Old Town, a church typifies Hull's importance at early stages of its history. **Holy Trinity Church** (☎ 446757) is a magnificent medieval building with a striking central tower. It opens daily.

Lovely, pedestrianised **Parliament St** suggests what much of 18th-century Hull must have looked like.

Sometime late in 2001, a huge new lottery-funded aquarium called **The Deep** is due to open on the marina. Check with the TIC for the latest developments.

Midway between the Old Town and ferry docks along the A1033, **Fort Paull** (☎ 893339) is a lavishly restored fort that for centuries protected the entrance to the Humber. Wax figures recall moments dating back to the time of Cromwell. It opens 10 am to 6 pm daily, April to October. Admission costs £4.50/3.

Walking Tours

The TIC sells a brochure called *The Seven Seas Fish Pavement Trail* (40p) which is pegged to a highly entertaining self-guiding tour of the Old Town. Fish shapes embedded in the pavement lead visitors on a delightful and historic tour. Kids love it.

Guided walks leave from the TIC daily (except Tuesday and Sunday) at 2 pm and cost £2.50/1.

Places to Stay & Eat

The TIC has lists of B&Bs, most of which are at least one mile from the centre.

Clyde House Hotel (☎ 214981, 13 John St) is the best budget choice near the Old Town. Simple singles/doubles start at £24/40.

Forte Posthouse Marina (☎ 0870 400 9043, fax 213299, Castle St) is the obvious choice if you want to be right on the water. The well-equipped rooms cost £95 midweek and £65 at weekends.

There are several old pubs in the Old Town that have good food. *Ye Olde White Hart* (☎ 326363, 25 Silver St) dates from the 1700s and has a good range of beer and food (served from noon to 8 pm daily).

Jaz Cafe Bar (☎ 228063, 41 Lowgate) has live jazz and an interesting menu with many vegetarian options for around £6. The kitchen opens 11 am to 11 pm daily (from 7 pm Sunday).

Getting There & Away

The bus station is on Ferensway, just north of the train station. National Express has several trips a day to/from London (£17, 5½ hours).

The train station is west of Queen Victoria Square, in the centre of town. Hull is on a branch line off the London King's Cross to Edinburgh line and has good rail links north and south, and west to York (£10, one hour, hourly) and Leeds (£11.90, one hour, hourly).

The ferry port is just east of the centre at King George Dock. There are shuttle buses between the port and the train station. P&O North Sea Ferries (☎ 01482-377177) has daily ferries to/from Rotterdam (13 hours) and Zeebrugge (13½ hours) and Hull. The fares on both routes cost £81/136. The P&O Web site is at www.ponsf.com.

BEVERLEY

☎ 01482 • pop 21,900

At the centre of a rich agricultural region, Beverley, once the capital of the East Riding, is a gem of an 18th-century market town hardly marred by modern development. It's dominated by beautiful Beverley Minster, formerly a monastic church and still the equal of many cathedrals in magnificence.

Information

Beverley TIC (☎ 867430, fax 885237, @ bev erley@ytbtic.co.uk), 34 Butcher Row, opens 9.30 am to 5.30 pm weekdays, until 5 pm on Saturday (June to August), and 10 am to 2 pm on Sunday.

Beverley Minster

The first church on the site was built in the 7th century. The present building dates from 1220 but construction continued for two centuries, spanning the Early English, Decorated and perpendicular periods. The end product is best known for its magnificent Gothic perpendicular western front (1420) with its twin towers and wonderful sculpture.

Inside, extraordinary medieval faces and demons peer down from every possible vantage point, while stone angels play a variety of silent instruments. Note particularly a 10th-century Frith Stool (or sanctuary chair) the canopy of the Percy Tomb (to the north of the altar); and the 68 medieval misericords (support ledges for choristers).

The minster opens 9 am to 5 pm Monday to Saturday, and noon to 5 pm Sunday. It sometimes open later from June to August. Donations of £1 are requested.

St Mary's Church

Stately St Mary's church would attract all the attention if it were anywhere else but Beverley. Here it inevitably plays second fiddle to the minster. Still, if you like medieval churches, this is a particularly fine example, built in stages between 1120 and 1530. In the ambulatory look out for a carving thought to have inspired Lewis Carroll's White Rabbit. Its hours are similar to the minster.

YORKSHIRE

Markets

General markets are still held on Wednesday and Saturday. A 400-year-old cattle and pig market is held to the north of the town centre every Tuesday and Wednesday (Wednesday is the big day; selling starts at 10.30 am and finishes by 1 pm).

Places to Stay

The TIC has a lengthy list of B&Bs.

Friary Youth Hostel (☎ 881751, fax 880118), in a beautifully restored 14th-century Dominican friary on Friar's Lane, is open daily (except Sunday) from mid-April to October. Beds cost £8.50/5.75 for adults/under-18s.

Most of the cheaper B&Bs are a short walk south of the minster. *Eastgate Guest House* (☎ 868464, fax 871899, 7 Eastgate) has singles/doubles from £21/34. It is close to the train station.

Market Cross Hotel (☎ 679029, 12–14 Lairgate) is another central place that charges from £23 per person. It's recently been refurbished.

The *Beverley Arms Hotel* (☎ 869241, fax 870907, North Bar Within) is a dignified old Georgian mansion. It has singles/doubles from £48/85.

Places to Eat

Stylish *Wednesdays* (☎ 869727, 8 Wednesday Market) is much acclaimed. The menu melds Europe with Asia and the wine list is excellent. Three courses cost under £20.

White House (☎ 861973, Hengate) is an atmospheric old pub that serves excellent pub lunches for less than £4.

There are several teashops on Highgate between the minster and Wednesday Market; *The Tea Cosy* (☎ 868577, 37 Highgate) serves hot lunch dishes for under £5.

Getting There & Away

The train station lies just east of the town centre; the bus station is north on Sow Hill.

Bus East Yorkshire bus No X46 links Beverley with York (70 minutes, hourly). Buses Nos 121, 122 246 and X46 run to/from Hull at least twice an hour (30 minutes).

Train There are regular trains to/from Scarborough via Filey (£7.10, one hour, twenty minutes). Trains to/from Hull (£3.10, 15 minutes) run at least hourly.

North Yorkshire

North Yorkshire is one of Britain's largest counties, containing some of the finest monuments, most beautiful countryside and most spectacular coastline in the country. It includes two national parks (the Yorkshire Dales and North York Moors), the medieval city of York, the great monastic ruins of Rievaulx and Fountains abbeys, the classical beauty of Castle Howard, and the grim castles of Richmond and Bolton.

Medieval Guilds

In medieval and Tudor times, craftsmen and tradesmen formed themselves into guilds, which were basically a form of trade union or professional association. Crafts and trades were restricted to the members of an appropriate guild except at markets (which were usually weekly) or fairs (which were usually annual).

The guilds checked the quality of the work done, investigated complaints and regulated prices. While those first two activities may have actually served their customers, the regulation of prices was at the heart of the guilds' existence. Prices were fixed at levels that allowed for comfortable margins and a basic fat and happy existence. If there's any doubt about the profits these monopolistic practices allowed, just look at some of the surviving guild halls in England such as York's Merchant Adventurers' Hall.

Competition among guild members was only allowed in terms of quality and service. Admission was restricted to those who had served a seven-year apprenticeship and paid a fee. An apprentice was completely bound to his master and received little more than food and board. He couldn't do anything without explicit permission – this included having any relations with the opposite sex. Imagine: 'Excuse me master, I've met this wench...'

Most of North Yorkshire was untouched by the Industrial Revolution and, to a large extent, the accompanying agricultural revolution. The winter climate is harsh and much of the countryside lends itself to sheep grazing, an activity largely unchanged from medieval times. Great fortunes – private and monastic – were founded on wool.

In the west the Pennines, including the peaks of Ingleborough (723m) and Pen-y-ghent (694m), dominate the beautiful dales, whose flanks are defined by snaking stone walls and overlooked by wild, heather-clad plateaus. In the east, stone villages shelter at the foot of bleak and beautiful moors. These stretch to the high cliffs of the east coast, with its fishing villages and the holiday resorts of Whitby and Scarborough.

GETTING THERE & AROUND

A spider's web of buses and trains connect places in North Yorkshire. Call ☎ 0870 608 2608 for all Yorkshire bus and train information. There are various explorer passes covering the North Yorkshire Moors. Individual bus and train companies also offer their own schemes, so it's always worth asking for advice on the best deal when you buy your ticket.

YORK

☎ 01904 • pop 123,000

For nearly 2000 years York has been the capital of the north. Its city walls, built during the 13th century, are among the most impressive surviving medieval fortifications in Europe. They encompass a thriving, fascinating centre with medieval streets, grand Georgian town houses, riverside pubs and modern shops. The crowning glory is the minster, England's largest Gothic cathedral, but there's a bewildering array of things to see and do. If you arrive by car on the B1363 from the north, you'll be treated to a sudden view of the minster, across fields, that has been unchanged for centuries. As you take in the view, imagine how it must have affected pilgrims hundreds of years ago.

York attracts millions of visitors, and the July and August crowds can get you down; try to visit out of season if you can.

History

The Brigantes probably had a settlement at the meeting point of the Rivers Foss and Ouse before the Romans arrived to set up a walled garrison called Eboracum in AD 71.

Eboracum was strategically important, hence the visits of several emperors: Hadrian used it as a base in 121; Septimius Severus used it to hold Imperial Court in 211; and in 306 Constantius Chlorus died here. He was succeeded by his son Constantine, the first Christian emperor and founder of Constantinople (Istanbul), who was probably proclaimed emperor on the site of the cathedral.

The Anglo-Saxons founded the cathedral city of Eoforwic on the Roman ruins. Eoforwic was the capital of the independent kingdom of Northumbria which, like that of the Brigantes, stretched from the Humber to the Firth of Forth.

In 625 Christianity was brought by Paulinus, a Roman priest who had joined Augustine's Canterbury mission. He succeeded in converting the Saxon king of Northumbria, King Edwin, and his nobles. The first wooden church was built in 627 and became a centre of learning that attracted students from around Europe.

The Danish Vikings captured and burnt the city in 867 but then made it their capital, Jorvik, for nearly 100 years. Under their rule it became an important trading port. Not until 954 did the kings of Wessex succeed in reuniting the Danelaw with the south but their control remained tenuous. King Harold was forced to tackle a Norwegian invasion-cum-uprising at Stamford Bridge, east of York, immediately before the Battle of Hastings.

William the Conqueror was also faced with rebellion. After the north's second uprising in 1070, he burnt York and Durham and laid waste the countryside – the 'harrying of the North'. Afterwards, the Normans rebuilt the walls and erected two castles and a new cathedral. York once again became an important port and the centre of the profitable new trade in wool.

In the 15th century the city declined, losing influence and power to London. During

YORKSHIRE

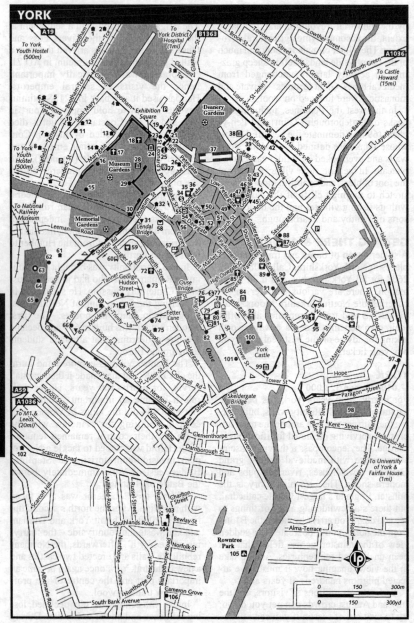

YORK

PLACES TO STAY
1 Gables Guest House
2 Brontë House
3 Claremont Guest House
4 Hudson's Hotel
5 Elliotts Hotel
6 Alcuin Lodge
7 Martins Guest House
8 Briar Lea Guest House
9 Riverside Walk B&B;
   Abbey Guest House
10 Crook Lodge
11 23 St Mary's
12 Treetops Guest House
13 Coach House Hotel
14 Jorvik Hotel
26 Dean Court Hotel
32 Judges Lodging Hostel
41 Monkbar Hotel
61 Royal York Hotel
69 York Backpackers
75 York Youth Hotel
95 St Denys Hotel
102 Wheatlands Lodge
103 Nunmill House
104 Acorn Guest House
105 Rowntree Park Camping

PLACES TO EAT
20 Café No 8
22 Juice Up
31 Pizza Express
33 Ask; Grand
   Assembly Rooms
36 Taylor's
43 La Piazza
44 Lime House
45 Siam House
46 Coffee Espress
49 Scott's of York

50 Oscar's Wine Bar & Bistro
51 Victor J's
54 Rubicon
56 Betty's
67 Jinnah
68 Blake Head Bookshop & Café
83 Fiesta Mexicana
90 Blue Bicycle
94 Loucedes Tapas

PUBS, BARS & CLUBS
35 Ye Olde Starre
48 Old White Swan
59 Maltings
71 Ziggy's
76 King's Arms
79 Lowther Arms
86 Blue Bell
87 Fibbers
96 Spread Eagle

OTHER
15 Gatehall; Hospitium
16 St Mary's Lodge
17 St Olave's Church
18 St Mary's Abbey
19 Kaos
21 Bootham Tower
23 Bootham Bar
24 York City Art Gallery
25 Tourist Information Centre
27 York Theatre Royal
28 Yorkshire Museum
29 Multangular Tower
30 Yorkboat River Trips
34 American Express
37 York Minster
38 Treasurer's House
39 St William's College &
   Restaurant

40 Bob Trotter Bike Hire
42 Monk Bar;
   Richard III Museum
47 Holy Trinity, Goodramgate
52 Nevisport
53 Borders
55 Internet Exchange
57 City Screen
58 Post Office
60 Bus Stops (Rougier Street)
62 York Model Railway
63 York Train Station
64 Hertz
65 Europcar
66 York Brewery
70 Wildcat Records; Ken
   Spellman Booksellers
72 All Saints,
   North Street Church
73 Bus Information Office
74 Practical Car & Van Rental
77 Thomas Cook
78 Grand Opera House
80 York Dungeon
81 Riding Lights Theatre
82 Yorkboat River Trips
84 Jorvik Viking Centre
85 All Saints, Pavement
88 Archaeological Resource
   Centre
89 Jack Duncan Books
91 Merchant Adventurers' Hall
92 Fairfax House
93 St Denys Church
97 Walmgate Bar
98 York Barbican Centre
99 York Castle Museum
100 Clifford's Tower
101 Eddie Brown Tours
106 The Washeteria

YORKSHIRE

the Civil War, York twice came under siege from the Parliamentarian army. The first siege was lifted after two months by the arrival of an army under the command of King Charles' nephew Prince Rupert. In the war's bloodiest battle, Prince Rupert chased the retreating Parliamentarians to Marston Moor where they turned on him and cut his army to pieces, killing 4000 men. The siege was resumed, and the city finally fell in July 1642. Fortunately, the commander of the Parliamentarian forces, Sir Thomas Fairfax, a local man, prevented the troops pillaging the minster.

The coming of the railway in 1839 once again placed York at the hub of the north-east.

Orientation

Although the centre is relatively small, York's streets are a confusing medieval tangle. Remember that, in York, *gate* means street and *bar* means gate.

The city is circled by a ring road. There are five major landmarks in the centre: the wall that encloses the city centre; the minster at the northern corner; Clifford's Tower, a 13th-century castle and mound at the southern end; the River Ouse that cuts the centre in two; and the enormous train station just outside the western corner.

Information

Tourist Offices The main TIC (☎ 621756, fax 551801, ☐ tic@york-tourism.co.uk), is in De Grey Rooms, Exhibition Square, north of the river near Bootham Bar. It opens daily from 9 am to 6 pm (10 am to 4 pm Sunday). There's also a small TIC at the train station. It opens 9 am to 6 pm daily (until 5 pm Sunday and until 7 pm, June to August). The TIC sells the useful *York Map & Guide* (80p).

Money American Express (☎ 676501), 6 Stonegate, has an exchange service open 9 am to 5.30 pm (closed Sunday).

Post & Communications The post office is at 22 Lendal and opens 9 am to 5.30 pm Monday to Saturday.

The Internet Exchange (☎ 638808), 13 Stonegate, has a minimum charge of £1 and an additional fee of 10p per minute for Web surfing.

Travel Agencies The Thomas Cook (☎ 653626) at 4 Nessgate is a full-service travel agent.

Bookshops All the usual high street bookshops can be found in York. The largest is Borders (☎ 653300), 1–5 Davygate, which occupies part of a 19th-century chapel. It opens 8 am to 10 pm (11 am to 5 pm Sunday). There is a wealth of used and antiquarian bookshops. See the Shopping section later for details.

Laundry The Washeteria (☎ 656145), 148 Bishopthorpe Rd, is about a 10-minute walk south of the centre.

Medical Services York District Hospital (☎ 631313) is just north of the centre on Wiggington Rd.

York Minster

York Minster (☎ 624426), or the Cathedral & Metropolitan Church of St Peter, is Europe's largest medieval cathedral and one of

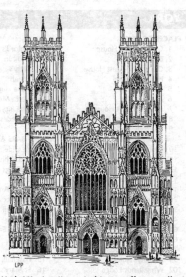

LPP

York Minster: its central tower offers excellent views over the city

the world's most inspiring buildings. The word 'minster' suggests that one of the previous buildings was once connected with a monastery. The minster is the seat of the archbishop of York, who holds the title of Primate of England and is second only in importance to the archbishop of Canterbury, the Primate of All England.

The minster, a time capsule incorporating the remains of seven buildings, is most famous for its extensive medieval stained-glass, particularly in the enormous Great East Window (1405–8).

The first church on the site was a wooden chapel built for Paulinus's baptism of King Edwin on Easter Day 627; its site is marked in the crypt. This church was built near the site of a Roman basilica, a vast assembly hall at the heart of Roman military headquarters; parts can be seen in the foundations. A stone church was started but fell into disrepair after Edwin's death. St Wilfred built the next church but this was destroyed as part of William's brutal response to a northern rebellion. The first Norman church was built in stages from 1060 to

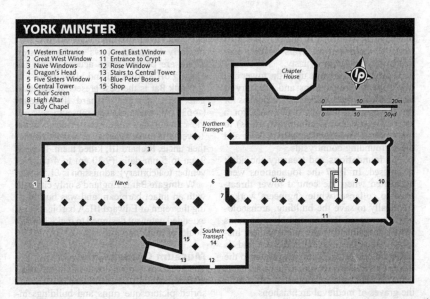

YORK MINSTER

1 Western Entrance
2 Great West Window
3 Nave Windows
4 Dragon's Head
5 Five Sisters Window
6 Central Tower
7 Choir Screen
8 High Altar
9 Lady Chapel
10 Great East Window
11 Entrance to Crypt
12 Rose Window
13 Stairs to Central Tower
14 Blue Peter Bosses
15 Shop

Chapter House

Northern Transept

Nave

Choir

Southern Transept

1080; you can see surviving fragments in the foundations and crypt.

The present building, built mainly from 1220 to 1480, incorporates several architectural styles. The northern transept was built in Early English style between 1241 and 1260; the nave, choir and octagonal Chapter House were built in Decorated style between 1260 and 1405; and the central, or lantern, tower was the last addition, built in perpendicular style from 1460 to 1480.

You enter from the western end. The nave is unusually tall and wide; although the aisles (to the side) are roofed in stone, the central roof is wood painted to look like stone. On both sides of the nave are the shields of nobles who met Edward II at a parliament in York. Also note the **dragon's head** projecting from the gallery – it's a crane believed to have been used to lift a font cover. There are several fine **windows** dating from the early 14th century, but the most dominating is the **Great West Window**, from 1338, with beautiful stone tracery.

The transepts are the oldest part of the building above ground and the **Five Sisters Window**, with five lancets over 15m high, is the minster's oldest complete window; most

of it is from around 1260. In 1984 the south transept was destroyed in a fire. Six of the **bosses** in the new roof were designed by children who won a competition sponsored by the popular TV program *Blue Peter*.

The **chapter house** is a magnificent example of the Decorated style. Superb stonework decorated with tiny individual stone heads surrounds a wonderful space uninterrupted by a central column.

The heart of the church is dominated by the awesome **central tower**. The 15th-century **choir screen** depicts the 15 kings from William I to Henry VI.

The **lady chapel** behind the **high altar** is dominated by the **Great East Window**, the largest intact stained-glass medieval window in the world. Created between 1405 and 1408, it illustrates the beginning and end of the world as described in Genesis and the Book of Revelation.

Entered from the southern choir aisle, the **crypt** contains fragments from the Norman cathedral. The font shows King Edwin's baptism and marks the site of Paulinus' original wooden chapel.

In the southern transept, the **Rose Window** commemorates the union of the royal houses of Lancaster and York, through the marriage of Henry VII and Elizabeth of York, which ended the Wars of the Roses and began the Tudor dynasty.

The entry to the stairs up to the tower and down to the Foundations and Treasury is also in the southern transept. The queues for the tower are long but the reward for a steep, claustrophobic climb (275 steps) to the top is an excellent view over York and the surrounding countryside.

The **foundations** and **treasury** shouldn't be missed. In 1967 the foundations were excavated when the central tower threatened to collapse; while engineers worked frantically to save the building, archaeologists uncovered Roman and Norman ruins which now illustrate the site's ancient history – one of the most extraordinary finds is a Roman culvert, still carrying water to the River Ouse. The Treasury houses artefacts from the 11th century, including relics from the graves of medieval archbishops.

To see everything could easily absorb the best part of a day. The minster opens 7 am to 6 pm daily (from 1 pm Sunday) and has extended hours June to September. Admission is free, but a £2 donation is requested. There are charges for access to the following: the crypt, foundations and treasury (£3/1), the chapter house (£1) and the tower (£3/1). The worthwhile guided tours are free.

Around the Minster

Owned by the minster since the 15th century, **St William's College** (☎ 637134), College St, is an attractive half-timbered Tudor building housing an excellent restaurant (see Places to Eat later).

The **Treasurer's House** (☎ 624247; NT), Minster Yard, was home to the minster's medieval treasurers. Substantially rebuilt in the 17th and 18th centuries, it now houses a fine collection of 18th-century furniture and gives a good insight to life at that time. It opens daily 10.30 am to 5 pm (closed Fridays), April to October. Admission is £3.50/1.75.

City Walls

You can get onto the walls, built in the 13th century, via steps by **Bootham Bar** (on the site of a Roman gate) and follow them clockwise to Monk Bar, a walk offering particularly beautiful views of the minster. There are oodles more access points including off Station Rd and Monkgate.

Monk Bar is the best preserved medieval gate, with a small **Richard III Museum** (☎ 634191) upstairs. The museum sets out the case of the murdered 'Princes in the Tower' and invites visitors to decide whether their uncle, Richard III, killed them. It opens 9 am to 5 pm daily (9.30 am to 4 pm November to February); admission is £1.50/50p.

Walmgate Bar is England's only city gate with an intact barbican, and was built during the reign of Edward III. A barbican is an extended gateway designed to make life difficult for uninvited guests.

Museum Gardens

The Museum Gardens (open daily to dusk) make a peaceful 10-acre city-centre oasis. Assorted picturesque ruins and buildings include the **Museum Gardens Lodge** (Victorian Gothic Revival, 1874) and a 19th-century working **observatory**. The **Multangular-Tower** was the western tower of the Roman garrison's defensive wall. The small Roman stones at the bottom have been built up with 13th-century additions.

The **Yorkshire Museum** (☎ 629745), in a classical building completed in 1829, has some interesting Roman, Anglo-Saxon, Viking and medieval exhibits and is worth visiting if there's a good temporary exhibition. It opens 10 am to 5 pm daily. Admission costs £3.95/2.50.

The **Gatehall** was the main entry to **St Mary's Abbey**, a Benedictine monastery founded in 1080 with a later Early-English-style church. The ruined 15th-century gateway provided access from the abbey to the river. The adjacent **Hospitium** dates from the 14th century, although the timber-framed upper storey is a much-restored survivor from the 15th century; it was used as the abbey guesthouse. **St Mary's Lodge** was built around 1470 to provide VIP accommodation.

St Olave's Church dates from the 15th century, but there has been a church dedicated to the patron saint of Norway on this site since at least 1050.

Merchant Adventurers' Hall

Built in the mid-14th century, the Merchant Adventurers' Hall (☎ 654818) on Fossgate (access also from Piccadilly) testifies to the power of the medieval guilds. They controlled all foreign trade into and out of York – a handy little monopoly. The Guild Hall with its massive oak timbers is outstanding.

The hall is open from 9.30 am to 5 pm daily (noon to 4 pm Sunday), April to mid-November; 9.30 am to 3.30 pm (closed Sunday), the rest of the year. Admission costs £2/70p.

Jorvik Viking Centre

From 1976 to 1981 excavations in Coppergate uncovered Jorvik, the 9th-century Viking settlement that preceded modern York. Jorvik Viking Centre (☎ 643211), Coppergate, is one of York's most popular attractions and you may have to queue for up to 30 minutes. You travel in a 'time car' to a smells-and-all recreation of what the Viking town probably looked like, complete with fibreglass figures speaking a language derived from modern Icelandic. At the end of the ride there's a chance to inspect finds from the site. It's all less hokey than it sounds and well worth a visit.

It opens 9 am to 5.30 pm daily, April to October. There are shorter hours the rest of the year. Admission costs £5.65/4.25.

The Jorvik people also run the **Archaeological Resource Centre** (ARC; ☎ 653000) in the old church at St Saviourgate. It has various programs that allow for hands-on exploration of archaeology. Call for details.

Clifford's Tower

After laying waste to the north as punishment for its rebellion, William the Conqueror built two mottes (mounds) crowned with wooden towers. The original one on this site was destroyed by fire during anti-Jewish riots in 1190; 150 Jews sheltering in the castle took their own lives. It was then rebuilt into the keep for York Castle using the highly unusual figure-eight design. There's actually not much to see inside (☎ 646940) but the views over the city are excellent. Run by English Heritage (EH), it opens 10 am to 6 pm daily, April to October (9.30 am to 7 pm July and August) and 10 am to 4 pm, the rest of the year. Admission costs £1.80/90p.

York Castle Museum

One of Britain's most popular museums, York Castle Museum (☎ 653611) contains displays of everyday life, complete with Victorian and Edwardian streets and fascinating reconstructions of domestic interiors. An extraordinary collection of everyday objects from the past 400 years includes old TVs, radios, washing machines, vacuum cleaners and gadgets guaranteed to bring childhood memories flooding back for any Brit. Others may find it comparable to an extended stray into the attic of a keen hoarder.

The museum opens 9.30 am to 5 pm daily, April to October (until 4 pm the rest of the year). Admission costs £5.25/3.50 and you should allow about two hours for a visit.

National Railway Museum

This museum (☎ 621261), Leeman Rd, is one of the world's biggest railway museums. It focuses on the all-too-distant past when Britain was a leader in railway technology. This legacy is traced via an impressive collection of carriages (including Queen Victoria's saloon) and locomotives (including the speed-record-breaking *Mallard*). A vast annexe includes the restoration shops which you can visit. Allow two hours to do it justice. It opens 10 am to 6 pm daily. Admission is an enlightened £6.50 for adults and is free for those aged 16 and under.

Medieval Churches

Of York's 41 pre-16th-century churches, 20 still survive, often with their stained glass intact. The finest is **All Saints, North St** (☎ 728122), which John Betjeman dubbed 'the best reconstruction of a medieval interior'. It has wonderful 14th-century glass including one bit depicting a man wearing glasses. It's easily spotted by the octagon rising above its tower. It's only open, however, from 1.30 to 3.30 pm on Thursday.

YORKSHIRE

Just as atmospheric, if more homely, is **Holy Trinity, Goodramgate** (☎ 613451), tucked away in a churchyard popular with lunching shopworkers off Goodramgate. Inside, box pews surround an 18th-century two-tier pulpit and there's never a straight line in view. It opens 9.30 am to 5.30 pm Tuesday to Saturday.

On a busy corner, **All Saints, Pavement**, between High Ousegate and Coppergate has a fine lantern tower and 14th-century stained glass. It opens 9.30 am to 4 pm daily.

Quiet **St Denys Church** is on Walmgate. It has the oldest glass in York and a Norman porch. It opens 10 am to 4.30 pm daily April to October.

Other Things to See & Do

On Castlegate, **Fairfax House** (☎ 655543) is a beautiful Georgian house with a renowned collection of 18th-century furniture and clocks. It's one of many buildings that have been restored by the York Trust, a local preservation group. It opens 11 am to 5 pm Monday to Thursday and Saturday, and 1.30 to 5 pm on Sunday, March to December. Admission costs £4/1.50.

Opposite the TIC, **York City Art Gallery** (☎ 551861), Exhibition Square, has a range of paintings including works by Lely, Hogarth, Reynolds, Nash and Lowry. It opens 10 am to 5 pm daily. Admission costs £2/1.50.

York Brewery (☎ 621162), 12 Toft Green, has tours of its small plant and the all-important tastings throughout the day year round. The cost is £4.25/3.

York Dungeon (☎ 632599), 12 Clifford St, is what you'd expect – a series of gruesome historical reconstructions, intended to scare those who find the Chamber of Horrors tame. For the especially hardened there's a lovely bit on the plague. It opens 10 am to 5.30 pm daily (until 4.30 pm, October to March) and costs £6.50/4.95.

In the heart of York, the quaintly cobbled **Shambles** hints at what a medieval street might have looked like if it was over-run with people told they have to buy something silly and be back on the tour bus in 15 minutes. It takes its curious name from the Saxon word *shamel*, meaning slaughterhouse.

If modern British train technology has failed you and you have time to kill at the station, you might find the **York Model Railway** (☎ 630169) diverting. It's right next to the station entrance and comprises a huge set-up where, at least in this miniature world, the trains always run on time. It opens 9.30 am to 6 pm daily, March to October (10.30 am to 5 pm the rest of the year). Admission costs £2.95/1.95.

Organised Tours

Bus For a good overall introduction you might consider one of the open-top buses that trundle about town. Tours leave from outside the main TIC. First York (☎ 622992) runs guided double-decker bus tours which circle the city calling at the main sites; you can get on and off where you please (buses run every 20 minutes) and tickets are valid all day. The main starting point is Exhibition Square, near Bootham Tower opposite the TIC.

Guide Friday (☎ 640896) operates essentially the same service. Competition between the two is fierce and frequent price wars mean that the usual fare of £7.50/2.50 is often heavily discounted.

Eddie Brown (☎ 640760), 8 Tower St, runs a range of good-value day bus tours into the surrounding countryside. These include Castle Howard for £6.50, North York Moors Railway and Moorland for £15.95, and Yorkshire Dales and Herriot Country for £22.50. Prices don't include admission charges. Children under 14 travel free on most tours.

Boat Yorkboat River Trips (☎ 628324), Lendal Bridge, runs cruises along the River Ouse. One-hour round trips depart from King's Staith (behind the fire station) and Lendal Bridge (next to the Guildhall) from 10.30 am daily. The frequency varies with the season and the cost is £4/2. From April to October, there's the obligatory ghost cruise at 7 pm daily from King's Staith (£5.50/2.75).

Walking Yorkwalk (☎ 622303) offers a series of two-hour themed walks on Roman York, medieval York, the snickelways (alleys) of York, saints and sinners of York and many more, including one on Jewish

York. Each walk costs £4.50/1 and walkers get a £1 discount off Guide Friday tours. Walks depart from Museum Gardens Gate.

The Association of Voluntary Guides (☎ 640780) has free walking tours of the city from Exhibition Square in front of York City Art Gallery at 10.15 am daily year round. There is also a 2.15 pm tour from April to October and a 7 pm tour from June to August.

The Complete York Tour (☎ 706643) is a detailed and scholarly walk. Call for details.

York has many companies offering ghost walks that are heavy on drama and light on facts. The following are the bare bones: the Original Ghost Walk of York (☎ 01759-373090) leaves the King's Arms at 8 pm daily; the Ghost Hunt of York (☎ 608700) leaves the Shambles at 7.30 pm daily; Mad Alice Ghost Tours (☎ 425071) leaves from Clifford Tower at 7.30 pm daily; and the Haunted Walk of York (☎ 621003) leaves from the front of York City Art Gallery at 8 pm daily. All cost £3/2; phone first to make certain that the guides haven't given up the ghost and taken a day off.

Places to Stay

Despite the existence of hundreds of hotels and B&Bs, it can be difficult to find a bed in midsummer. Prices also jump significantly in the high season. The TIC has an efficient accommodation booking service that charges £4.

Camping There are a dozen camp sites and caravan parks around York but most are at least 4 miles from the centre. The closest is *Rowntree Park Camping (☎ 658997, Terry Ave)* which is a 20-minute walk south-east of the station in a park by the river. They are a few sites for backpackers at £10 for two adults. There's little grass on the sites so, although tents are allowed, you'd need something soft to sleep on.

Hostels Open year round is *York Youth Hostel (☎ 653147, fax 651230, e york@yha .org.uk, Water End, Clifton)*. Adults/under-18s pay £15.50/11.50, including breakfast. It's a large but very busy YHA hostel so book ahead. The hostel is about 1 mile north-west

of the TIC: turn left into Bootham, which becomes Clifton (the A19), then left into Water End. Alternatively, there's a riverside footpath from Lendal Bridge.

Equally popular, particularly with school and student parties, is the *York Youth Hotel (☎ 625904, fax 612494, e info@yorkyouth hotel.demon.co.uk, 11 Bishophill Senior)*. There's a range of rooms, from 20-bed dorms (£11) to twin bunk rooms (£15 per person).

York Backpackers (☎ 627720, fax 339350, e yorkbackpackers@cwcom.net, 88–90 Micklegate) is a friendly place in a 1752 Georgian building. Beds in the large dorms cost £11; doubles are £30.

The University of York offers accommodation in its halls of residence during holiday times. *Fairfax House (☎ 432095, e aeg2@ york.ac.uk, 99 Heslington Rd)* is a 20-minute walk south-east of the city. It has single rooms with washbasins for £20 per person.

B&Bs – North-West There are lots of B&Bs and hotels in the streets north and south of Bootham (the A19 to Thirsk) to the north-west of the city. Running along the railway line, Bootham Terrace (south of Bootham), Bootham Crescent and Grosvenor Terrace (both north of Bootham) are virtually lined with B&Bs. Most are standard but the position is central. Marygate is a good street as it's quiet and the road leads right down to the river. Longfield Terrace is quiet and can be easily reached from the river path.

Martins Guest House (☎ 634551, fax 339063, e martinsbb@aol.com, 5 Longfield Terrace) is one of several B&Bs in a long Victorian row. The standard rooms with bathroom cost from £18 per person.

Claremont Guest House (☎ 625158, e claremont.york@dial.pipex.com, 18 Claremont Terrace) charges from £18 per person for its two double rooms.

Sycamore Place, off Bootham Terrace, has several places to stay including the *Alcuin Lodge (☎ 632222, fax 626630, e al cuinlodge@aol.com, 15 Sycamore Place)*, which has decent en-suite doubles from £35.

Briar Lea Guest House (☎ 635061, fax 330356, e briargh8l@aol.com, 8 Longfield

Terrace) is in a Victorian building. The rooms are all en suite and cost from £25/36.

With a central position beside the river, *Abbey Guest House* (☎ 627782, fax 671743, ⓔ abbey@rsummers.cix.co.uk, 14 Earlsborough Terrace) is a standard B&B with rooms starting at £20 per person.

Gables Guest House (☎ 624381, fax 624381, 50 Bootham Crescent) is a basic place that charges from £20 per person.

The comfortable *Riverside Walk B&B* (☎ 620769, fax 646249, ⓔ julie@riverside walkbb.demon.co.uk, 9 Earlsborough Terrace) has rooms with bathroom from £24 per head.

Treetops Guest House (☎ 658053, 21 St Mary's) is a basic place that is entirely nonsmoking. Rooms cost from £24 per person.

Pleasant *Brontë House* (☎ 621066, fax 653434, ⓔ bronte_guest_house@compu serve.com, 22 Grosvenor Terrace) has ensuite singles/doubles from £35/46.

Crook Lodge (☎ 655614, fax 655614, 26 St Mary's) has comfortable double rooms starting at £48 and parking for guests.

23 St Mary's (☎ 6226378, fax 628802, 23 St Mary's) has fully equipped singles/ doubles from £32/54. It is surrounded by flowers and has many little touches such as a rocking horse in the drawing room.

B&Bs – South-West There are many B&Bs clustered around Scarcroft Rd, Southlands Rd and Bishopthorpe Rd, the continuation of Bishopgate which takes off from the southern corner of the wall after Skeldergate Bridge.

Acorn Guest House (☎ 620081, 1 Southlands Rd) is a decent guesthouse with ensuite rooms that cost from £18 per person.

Nunmill House (☎ 634047, fax 655879, ⓔ b&b@nunmill.co.uk, 85 Bishopthorpe Rd) is a good place with en-suite rooms from £25 per person.

Wheatlands Lodge (☎ 654318, fax 654318, ⓔ wheatlodge@aol.com, 75 Scarcroft Rd) takes up a whole row of attractive, listed Victorian villas. Most of the 60 rooms are sunny and rates start at £28/40.

Hotels – North-West At 2–4 Sycamore Place, *Elliotts Hotel* (☎ 623333, fax 654908, ⓔ elliottsht@aol.com), is a small hotel where good singles/doubles with private facilities cost £35/52.

Coach House Hotel (☎ 652780, fax 679943, 20/22 Marygate) has 12 rooms in a quiet spot across from the city walls. There is a small restaurant with meals for under £10. Rooms cost from £31/56.

Jorvik Hotel (☎ 653511, fax 627009, 50 Marygate) has a walled garden and 23 comfortable rooms with bathroom. Doubles cost from £50 to £70 and there's a single for £32.

Hudson's Hotel (☎ 621267, fax 654719, 60 Bootham) has 30 well-equipped rooms in a modern annexe, and a restaurant and bar in a Georgian town house. Rooms cost from £65/105 single.

Hotels – Centre Prices are a bit higher in the centre of York and you don't have the leafy charms of the less central streets above.

St Denys Hotel (☎ 622207, fax 624800, ⓔ thestdenys@aol.com, St Denys Rd) has a good location opposite the church of the same name. En-suite rooms cost from £45/55.

Judges Lodging Hotel (☎ 638733, fax 679947, 9 Lendal) is a classy place in a Georgian mansion. Well-equipped rooms go for £75/100.

Dean Court Hotel (☎ 625082, fax 620305, ⓔ deancourt@btconnect.com, Duncombe Place) has a commanding position across from the minster. The rooms are very comfortable and cost from £80/95.

Monkbar Hotel (☎ 638086, fax 629195, St Maurice's Rd) is a full-service hotel just outside the gate. The rooms have air-con and there is parking and a central garden. Prices start at £74/120.

The *Royal York Hotel* (☎ 653681, fax 623503, Station Rd) is a huge grand Victorian railway hotel adjoining the station. There are three acres of gardens and a new health spa. Most of the rooms have been lavishly redone and cost from £90/110.

Places to Eat

There's a huge range of eateries with all styles of food in York. All budgets are catered for. See the listings in the Entertainment section later for pubs that serve food.

Restaurants There's a funky burger joint, *Victor J's* (☎ *673788, 1 Finkle St)*, that's open until 7 pm weekdays and later at weekends. It's very central and it has a bar. The burgers cost £3.50.

Pizza Express (☎ *672904, 17 Museum St)* serves the usual range of good pizzas (about £5) in the elegant setting of what was once a gentlemen's club overlooking the Ouse.

Fiesta Mexicana (☎ *610243, 14 Clifford St)* is popular with students for its cheap burritos (£3) and strong margaritas. It can get delightfully rowdy.

La Piazza (☎ *642641, 51 Goodramgate)* has excellent Italian food, including pizzas from £5.30.

Atmospheric *Oscar's Wine Bar & Bistro* (☎ *652002, 8 Little Stonegate)* has an outdoor area and a wide range of interesting dishes (including vegetarian meals). Most dishes on the broad menu cost £5 to £8.

Siam House (☎ *624677, 63a Goodramgate)* has fresh Thai food in a lovely upstairs dining room. The menu is endless and most dishes cost £4 to £5.

The Rubicon (☎ *676076, 5 Little Stonegate)* is an airy vegetarian restaurant offering two-course lunches for £5 and three-course meals for £7.

Jinnah (☎ *659999, 105–107 Micklegate)* is a fine Indian restaurant that's a few cuts above average. The dishes average £7 and are carefully prepared and creatively served. Its opens until midnight.

Café No 8 (☎ *653074, 8 Gillygate)* serves lunch, teas and dinner. It has a fine modern British menu. Most items under £10. It's closed Sunday.

Loucedes Tapas (☎ *674848, 48 Walmgate)* is run by two local women who cook up a good array of Spanish tapas treats that cost about £4 each.

The gorgeous Grand Assembly Rooms are home to *Ask* (☎ *637254, Blake St)*, a good Italian place for lunch and dinner (about £11).

Lime House (☎ *632734, 55 Goodramgate)* is busy, especially at the weekends (closed Monday and Tuesday). The speciality is steak (£12) and it also offers vegetarian dishes (£8.50).

St William's Restaurant (☎ *634830)*, off College St, is a great spot to relax after exploring the minster. It opens from 10 am to 10 pm. Lunch includes soups for £3.25 and two-course dinners are £12.95. There is a beautiful cobbled courtyard.

Blue Bicycle (☎ *673990, 34 Fossgate)* is a popular place with locals who love the romantic, candle-lit atmosphere and tasty French seafood dishes. Expect to pay at least £15 per person.

Cafes At 60 Goodramgate, *Coffee Espress* has a range of coffees and free Internet access for its customers. It opens from at least 8 am to 10 pm daily.

Betty's (☎ *659142)* is a very popular, extremely elegant bakery and tea-room on St Helen's Square. Depending on your mood, you can choose to relax in the spacious, airy upstairs or the wood-panelled no-smoking downstairs. A pot of tea is £2 and sandwiches are about £4. Betty's opens from 9 am to 9 pm; a pianist plays from 6 pm.

There's more tea on offer upstairs in *Taylor's* (☎ *622865, 46 Stonegate)*, where queues are as likely as at Betty's. A traditional Yorkshire high tea here costs £9 and would set you up for a week.

The best vegetarian eatery in York is the *Blake Head Bookshop & Café* (☎ *623767, 104 Micklegate)*. The emphasis is on simple but imaginative cooking. It opens daily for lunch; soup costs £2.50, a three-course meal £7.50.

Other There are often queues down the road for *Scott's of York* (☎ *622972, 81 Petergate)*, a pork shop where you can buy pork pies to make the taste buds weep from £1.85.

Juice Up (☎ *677732, 3 Bootham)* has a healthy range of fresh juices and sandwiches (under £3). It has a few stools at a counter but is mostly a take-away.

Entertainment
York Music is a monthly flyer that's a guide to the local music scene. You can find it at the TICs and in many pubs.

YORKSHIRE

Pubs & Clubs Although it's in tourist central, *Ye Olde Starre (☎ 623063, 40 Stonegate)* is a popular place with locals. It has decent ales and lots of tables outside its hidden location.

Old White Swan (☎ 540911, 80 Goodramgate) has a range of live music, from jazz to polka to rock.

King's Arms (☎ 659435, King's Staith) does lunch (£5) and has tables overlooking the river on the south-eastern side of the Ouse Bridge (the middle of the three main bridges).

Lowther Arms (☎ 622987, 8 Cumberland St) has bar meals for under £4 but its chief charm seems to be that it opens until midnight.

Maltings (☎ 655387), on Tanners Moat below Lendal Bridge, has a great beer selection, a fine atmosphere and good lunch specials.

Spread Eagle (☎ 635868, 98 Walmgate) is a popular pub with locals who enjoy the good beer selection and decent menu of typical bar chow. There's a garden out back.

Blue Bell (☎ 654907, 53 Fossgate) first opened in 1798 and seems little changed since. Certainly the characters found in the small front and back bars are timeless.

You should visit *Fibbers (☎ 625250, 8-12 The Stonebow)* after dark so you can't see its hideous building. However, this is a place for the ears, with regular offerings of local music.

Ziggy's (☎ 620602, 53–55 Micklegate) is a relaxed club with theme nights ranging from Goth to disco.

Theatres & Venues On St Leonard's Place, *York Theatre Royal (☎ 623568)* stages well-regarded productions of theatre, opera and dance.

Despite its name, the *Grand Opera House (☎ 671818, Clifford St)* puts on a wide range of productions.

Riding Lights Theatre (☎ 0845-961 3000, Lower Friargate) stages serious drama.

For big-name concerts head for *York Barbican Centre (☎ 656688)* in an interesting, partly pyramidal modern building on Barbican Rd.

Cinema There's a big multiplex, *City Screen (☎ 541144)*, off Coney St on the Ouse. It has first-run movies and a big bar overlooking the river.

Shopping

Coney St is the hub of York shopping and stores can be found on all the adjoining streets.

Nevisport (☎ 639567), 8 St Sampson Square, is a large sporting-goods shop with walking and camping gear as well as maps and guides.

Kaos (☎ 611532), 5 Gillygate, has all sorts of trendy and stylish clothes for parties and clubbing. There are many other interesting and unusual shops on this bit of Gillygate.

Wildcat Records (☎ 625456), 76 Micklegate, has an off-beat selection of used and new CDs and LPs.

York has many bookshops selling used and antiquarian books. They are clustered in two main areas, Micklegate and Fossgate. Ken Spellman Booksellers (☎ 624414), 70 Micklegate, stocks rare books covering fine arts and literature. Jack Duncan Books (☎ 641389), 36 Fossgate, sells cheap paperbacks and more unusual books. It also has a rotating exhibition of cartoons.

Getting There & Away

Bus The main bus stops are along Rougier St (off Station Rd, inside the city walls on the western side of Lendal Bridge) but some local and regional buses leave from outside the train station.

There is a very useful Bus Information Office (☎ 551400), 20 George Hudson St, that has complete schedule information. It also sells local, regional and National Express tickets. It opens 8.30 am to 5 pm weekdays, and 9 am to 12.30 pm on Saturday.

National Express buses leave from Rougier St. There are at least three services daily to London (£18, 5 hours), two daily to Birmingham (£17, 3 hours) and one to Edinburgh (£21.75, 6 hours).

For information on regional buses (to Castle Howard, Helmsley, Scarborough, Whitby, Leeds and so on), call the Yorkshire bus and train line or the Bus Information Office. The services are operated by a score of companies, some of which offer their own passes.

Train When York's railway station opened in 1877 it was the largest in the world and the city is still well-served by rail. The station has numerous food outlets and you can leave luggage at the Europcar office by platform 1.

There are numerous trains from London's King's Cross station (£59, two hours) and on to Edinburgh (£47, 2½ hours). North–south trains also connect with Peterborough (£33, 1½ hours) for Cambridge and East Anglia. There are good connections with southern England including Oxford via Birmingham (£25.50, 2½ hours).

Local trains to/from Scarborough take 45 minutes (£9.10). For Whitby it's best to get a bus from Scarborough.

Car & Motorcycle By road York is about 200 miles from London and Edinburgh and 25 miles from Leeds and Helmsley.

Europcar (☎ 656161) is right by platform 1 in the station. Besides a full range of cars, it rents bikes and stores luggage. Hertz (☎ 612586) is near platform 3 in the station.

Practical Car & Van Rental (☎ 624848), 10 Fetter Lane, is a five-minute walk from the station and often has good deals.

Getting Around

York is easily walked on foot. You're never really more than 20 minutes from any of the major sights or areas.

Bus The local bus service is provided by First York, which sells a day pass valid on all of its local buses after 9.30 am, for £1.70. The Bus Information Office has service details (see the listing under Bus in the Getting There & Away section earlier).

Car & Motorcycle York gets as congested as most British cities in summer and car parking in the centre can be expensive (up to £8 for a day).

Taxi Try Station Taxis (☎ 623332), which has a kiosk by the train station, ABC Blue Circle (☎ 638787) or Ace Taxis (☎ 638888).

Bicycle You can hire bikes for £9.50 a day from Bob Trotter (☎ 622868) at 13 Lord Mayor's Walk outside Monk Bar. Europcar in the train station rents bikes for the same price.

The Bus Information Office has a useful free map showing York's bike routes.

If you're energetic you could do an interesting loop out to Castle Howard (15½ miles), Helmsley and Rievaulx Abbey (12½ miles) and Thirsk (another 12½ miles), where you could catch a train back to York. There's also a Trans-Pennine Trail cycle path section from Bishopthorpe in York to Selby (15 miles) along the old railway line. The TICs have maps.

CASTLE HOWARD

There are few buildings in the world that are so perfect that their visual impact is almost a physical blow – Castle Howard (☎ 01653-648333), of *Brideshead Revisited* fame, is one. It has a picturesque setting in the rolling Howardian Hills and is surrounded by superb terraces and landscaped grounds dotted with monumental follies.

Not surprisingly, Castle Howard is a major tourist attraction and draws enormous crowds. Outside weekends, however, it's surprisingly easy to find the space to appreciate this extraordinary marriage of art, architecture, landscaping and natural beauty. Wandering about the grounds, views open up over the hills, the Temple of the Four Winds and the Mausoleum, but the great baroque house with its magnificent central cupola is an irresistible visual magnet.

In 1699 the earl of Carlisle made an audacious choice when he picked a successful playwright and army captain, Sir John Vanbrugh, as architect. Vanbrugh in turn chose Nicholas Hawksmoor, who had worked for Christopher Wren, as his clerk of works. This successful collaboration was subsequently repeated at Blenheim Palace.

The house is full of treasures and the grounds include a superb walled rose garden.

Castle Howard is 15 miles north-east of York, 4 miles off the A64. It opens 10 am (grounds) or 11 am (house) to 4.30 pm daily, mid-March to October. Admission to the house and garden costs £7/4. All in all, it could absorb the best part of a day; take a picnic.

Getting There & Away

The castle can be reached by several tours from York. Check with the TIC for up-to-date schedules. Yorkshire Coastliner has a useful service that links Leeds, York, Castle Howard, Pickering, and Whitby (Nos 840 and 842). A Freedom ticket good for unlimited rides all day costs £8.60.

THIRSK

☎ 01845 • pop 6800

Thirsk is a small market town outside the western edge of the North York Moors National Park, below the Hambleton Hills in the Vale of Mowbray. It's the fictional 'Darrowby' of James Herriot's stories of life as a Yorkshire vet. Although it's known locally for its large market square (markets held Monday and Saturday), the opening of the flashy World of James Herriot attraction is drawing the tourist hordes.

The TIC (☎ 01845-522755, fax 526230, ⓔ thirsk@ytbtic.co.uk) is in the Herriot centre at 23 Kirkgate and opens 10 am to 5:30 pm daily.

World of James Herriot

His name was Alfred Wright but to millions of fans he's James Herriot, the wry Yorkshire veterinarian whose adventures were recorded in a series of books – *All Creatures Great and Small* and so on – and in a much-loved 1970s–80s TV show. The building where the real Dr Wright lived, worked and wrote his books has been lavishly turned into the World of James Herriot (☎ 524234). It has been restored to its 1940s appearance, complete with vintage copies of trade journals such as *Tail-Wagger* lying about.

But there's much more here than just artefacts from Wright's life (he used a pen-name because his professional organisation said that writing of his practice under his real name would be 'marketing'). There's a video documentary on his life and a recreation of the sets used on the TV show. It's all quite well done and you'll be in the company of true fans, many of whom have that

look of pilgrimage on their faces. It opens 10 am to 6 pm daily (to 5 pm from November to February). Admission costs £4/3. Note that although animals are celebrated inside, they're required to stay outside.

Thirsk Museum

Housed in the home where Thomas Lord (of Lord's Cricket Ground fame) was born in 1755, the tiny Thirsk Museum (☎ 527707), 14–16 Kirkgate, has a small collection of items from Neolithic times to the Herriot era. It opens 10 am to 4 pm (closed Thursday and Sunday). Admission costs £1/50p.

Places to Stay & Eat

The TIC books B&Bs. There are several pubs offering accommodation around the Market Place. The first, of what may prove to be many, ice-cream/fudge shops has also opened.

Three Tuns Hotel (☎ *523124, fax 526126, Market Place)* has decent singles/doubles from £35/55. Meals start at £5 and there are vegetarian options.

The *Golden Fleece* (☎ *523108, fax 523996, Market Place)* has quite nice rooms starting at £60/80. The food is also fairly creative and dishes cost from £7.

Getting There & Away

There are two buses daily (none on Sunday) between Thirsk and Helmsley on Stephenson's bus No 57.

Thirsk is well served by trains on the line between York and Middlesbrough. However the train station is 1½ miles west of town and the only way to cover that distance is by foot or cab (☎ 522473).

North York Moors National Park

Only Exmoor and the Lake District rival the North York Moors National Park for natural beauty but the North York Moors are less crowded than the Lake District and more expansive than Exmoor. The coast is superb, with high cliffs backing onto

Heather & Grouse

The North York Moors have the largest expanse of heather moorland in England. You can see three species: ling is the most widespread, has a pinkish-purple flower and is most spectacular in late summer; bell heather is deep purple; and cross-leaved (or bog) heather prefers wet ground, unlike the first two, and tends to flower earlier. Wet, boggy areas also feature cotton grass, sphagnum moss and insect-eating sundew plants.

The moors have traditionally been managed to provide an ideal habitat for the red grouse – a famous game bird. The shooting season lasts from the 'Glorious Twelfth' of August to 10 December. The heather is periodically burned, giving managed moorland a patchwork effect. The grouse nests in mature growth but feeds on the tender shoots of new growth – that is, until someone comes along and blasts it out of existence.

beautiful countryside. From the ridge-top roads and open moors there are wonderful views, and the dales shelter abbeys, castles and small stone villages.

One of the principal glories of the moors is the vast expanse of heather. From July to early September it flowers in an explosion of purple. Outside the flowering season its browns-tending-to-purple on the hills – in vivid contrast to the green of the dales – give the park its characteristic and moody appearance.

ORIENTATION

The park covers 553 sq miles. The western boundary is a steep escarpment formed by the Hambleton and Cleveland hills; the moors run east–west to the coast between Scarborough and Staithes. Rainwater escapes from the moors down deep, parallel dales – to the Rivers Rye and Derwent in the south and the Esk in the north.

After the open space of the moors, the dales form a gentler, greener landscape, sometimes wooded, often with a beautiful stone village or two.

The coastline is as impressive as any in

Britain, and considerably less spoilt than most; Scarborough and Whitby are both popular resorts, but Whitby retains more of its charm. Helmsley (near Rievaulx, pronounced ree-voh) is the centre for the western part of the park.

INFORMATION

There are visitors centres at Sutton Bank, Danby and Robin Hood's Bay. The TICs in Whitby, Pickering and Helmsley are open most of the year. A very useful tabloid visitors guide (50p) is widely available. The park's Web site is www.northyorkmoors-npa.gov.uk

WALKING

There are a huge number of walks in the park. The Cleveland Way (see the Activities chapter) covers a good cross-section of the park and the spectacular coastline.

With a little imagination, it's possible to put together some interesting itineraries that make the most of the varied scenery and the limited, but interesting, railway lines. One possible itinerary starting in York involves taking a bus to Castle Howard, a bus to Pickering, the North York Moors Railway (NYMR) to Grosmont and the Esk Valley line to Whitby, then walking to Scarborough and taking a bus to Helmsley, then another back to York.

If you're feeling a bit more energetic, take a bus to Pickering, the NYMR to Grosmont and the Esk Valley line to Kildale. From there, walk along the Cleveland Way north-east to Saltburn-by-the-Sea, then south to Whitby and Scarborough, from where you can catch a bus to Helmsley.

PLACES TO STAY

The park is ringed with small villages, all of which have a good range of accommodation. Most of the rural pubs have a few rooms. There's a reasonable sprinkling of youth hostels that provide good walking bases at Boggle Hole, Robin Hood's Bay, Helmsley, Lockton (north of Pickering), Scarborough, Wheeldale (near Goathland) and Whitby.

Another possibility is the network of camping barns, which are particularly useful

YORKSHIRE

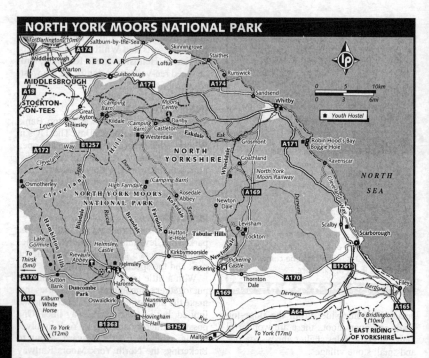

NORTH YORK MOORS NATIONAL PARK

for walkers equipped to cope with basic accommodation. The barns basically provide a roof over your head, a sleeping platform (you bring your own foam pad and sleeping bag), a toilet and running water. They cost £3.60 per person. The barns are administered by the YHA but you don't have to be a member.

The barns are *Farndale Barn (☎ 01751-433053, High Farndale)*, *Kildale Barn (☎ 01642-722135, Kildale)* and *Westerdale Farm (☎ 01287-660259, Westerdale)*.

To check availability and make reservations, contact the Camping Barns Reservations Office (☎ 01200-420102, fax 420103, @ campbarnsyha@enterprise.net) 6 King St, Clitheroe, Lancashire, BB7 2EP.

GETTING THERE & AROUND

From the south, York is the usual jumping-off point for the North York Moors. From there, buses run to Helmsley, Pickering and Scarborough. There's a frequent bus service

between Scarborough and Whitby. From the north, Darlington, on the main east-coast railway line, and Middlesbrough, at the western end of the beautiful Esk Valley line to Whitby, are good starting points. Call ☎ 0870 608 2608 for all bus and train information.

There is a highly useful Moorsbus network (☎ 01845-597426) that is aimed at park-users and hikers. It operates on Sunday from May to October and daily from mid-July to August. The network of routes covers most destinations within the Moors and connects with the regular trains and buses.

The private North York Moors Railway (NYMR) cuts across an interesting section of the park from Pickering to Grosmont on the Esk Valley line.

The Moorslink ticket allows unlimited travel on the Esk Valley line as well as the NYMR and the Moorsbus network. It costs £12.50/6.25 and is a good deal if you plan to really make a day of it.

SUTTON BANK

On the A170 between Thirsk and Helmsley, Sutton Bank is the western escarpment of the Hambleton Hills, with magnificent views across the Vale of Mowbray to the Pennines and Yorkshire Dales. From the car park at the top there are walks to Lake Gormire and the Kilburn White Horse, and along the Cleveland Way.

The National Park Visitors Centre (☎ 01845-597426), off the A170 right at Sutton Bank, is an excellent resource centre with exhibitions on the Moors and more. It opens daily 10 am to 5 pm, April to October (until 5.30 pm in August). The rest of the year it is open 11 am to 4 pm daily (weekends only January and February).

HELMSLEY

☎ 01439 • pop 1540

Helmsley is a classic Yorkshire market town, built around the expansive Market Place that still hosts a busy Friday market. Narrow Etton Gill runs west of Market Place before joining the River Rye in the south and there are some fascinating cottages along its banks, many built traditionally in grey-yellow limestone with red pantile roofs.

Almost all elements of the Moors' history and architecture come together in and around Helmsley: the ruins of a 12th-century Norman castle stand south-west of Market Place; the superb 12th-century ruins of the Cistercians' Rievaulx Abbey shelter in Ryedale, 3½ miles to the west; a 16th-century manor house, Nunnington Hall, is 4½ miles south-east; a grand 18th-century country house, Duncombe Park, lies beyond the castle; and there's the vernacular architecture of the town itself.

Helmsley makes an ideal base for exploring the North York Moors. There are numerous short walks in the surrounding countryside that take in the aforementioned sights and, for the more ambitious, Helmsley is a starting point for the Cleveland Way (see the Activities chapter).

Orientation & Information

Everything radiates out from the central Market Place – the parish church is to the north-west and the castle and Duncombe Park are to the south-west.

The TIC (☎ 770173, fax 771881, ⓔ helmsley@ytbtic.co.uk) is on the Market Place. It opens 9.30 am to 6 pm daily, April to October; 10 am to 4 pm Friday to Sunday, the rest of the year.

Helmsley Castle

The castle (☎ 770442; EH) is most famous for its extensive surrounding earthworks – huge earthen banks and ditches – but parts of the curtain wall, the keep and a 16th-century residential wing survive. Begun in the early 12th century, various additions were made through to the Civil War when, after a three-month siege in 1644, it surrendered.

A retired London banker, Thomas Duncombe, bought the castle in 1689 and later built neighbouring Duncombe Park. Once the castle was no longer used as a residence it fell into disrepair but it still makes a picturesque sight. It opens 10 am to 6 pm daily, April to October; until 4 pm Wednesday to Sunday the rest of the year. Admission costs £2.30/1.20.

Duncombe Park

Duncombe Park (☎ 770213) dates from 1713 and was built for Thomas Duncombe by William Wakefield, a friend of Vanbrugh. It was restored in the 1980s after 60 years as a girls' school. The building is neo-classical and is beautifully located in 600 acres of landscaped parkland. There are enormous lawns and terraces with views across the moors and surrounding countryside (see Rievaulx Terrace & Temples under Around Helmsley later); the park has a number of walks.

The entrance to the house is signposted from the A170 from Thirsk. It opens 10.30 to 6 pm daily, April to October. Tickets for the house and grounds cost £6/3. Admission to the grounds only costs £4/2.

Places to Stay

Two miles south-east of town and off the A170, *Foxholme Caravan Park* (☎ 770416, *Harome*) has 60 individual pitches among trees, costing from £7 per day.

Helmsley Youth Hostel (☎ 770433, fax 770433, Carlton Lane) is a purpose-built place a quarter of a mile east of Market Place. To get there, take Bondgate from the north-eastern corner of the place and turn left at Carlton Rd. It opens daily April to August, closed Sunday and Monday in September and October. Rates are £9.25/6.50 for adults/under-18s.

There are several B&Bs on Ashdale Rd; leave Market Place at the north-eastern corner along Bondgate, and Ashdale Rd is the second street on the right. *Ashberry (☎ 770488, 41 Ashdale)* is a traditional B&B with shared facilities costing from £17 per person.

Several places look onto Market Place. *Feathers (☎ 770275, Market Place)* is a soft-spoken pub with nice rooms for £30 per person. *Black Swan Hotel (☎ 770466, fax 770174, Market Place)* has upscale rooms that overlook the lovely back gardens. Singles/doubles start at £80/110.

Places to Eat
Feathers serves good steaks (from £8) and the *Black Swan Hotel* has a fine restaurant offering lunch, tea and dinner (for around £15).

Just south of Market Place, *Gepetto's (☎ 770479, 8 Bridge St)* is a great Italian restaurant with an open kitchen, good smells and pizzas for £6.

An ideal place to stock up for a picnic is *Nicholson's (☎ 770249, Market Place)*, which has a large deli.

Getting There & Away
Stephenson's bus No 57 runs twice daily between York and Helmsley (1½ hours) via Thirsk. Scarborough & District bus No 128 has an hourly service between Helmsley and Scarborough (1½ hours) via Pickering (40 minutes). There are only four buses on Sunday.

Getting Around
Ring A&R (☎ 771040) for a taxi. Footloose (☎ 770886), on Borogate just off Market Place, hires bicycles for £7.50 per day. Booking is advisable.

AROUND HELMSLEY
Rievaulx Abbey
An enjoyable 3½ mile uphill walk from Helmsley, following the first section of the Cleveland Way, leads to the remains of the 13th-century Rievaulx Abbey (☎ 798228; EH), arguably the most beautiful monastic ruin in England. Although it doesn't have the same overwhelming grandeur as Fountains Abbey, the site is incomparable. It lies in a secluded, wooded valley beside a small village and the River Rye.

When the site was granted to a group of 12 Cistercians in 1132, Ryedale was a complete wilderness but the monks proved to have extraordinary energy and skills. The enormous profits from the 'agribusiness' they developed (which included fishing, sheep rearing and textiles) allowed them to build quickly on an impressive scale.

By 1170 there were 150 monks, more than 250 lay brothers and 250 hired workmen. By the end of the century most of the building was complete (the nave is Norman, the transepts are transitional and the choir is Early English). By the dissolution in 1539, however, there were only about 20 monks. Many of the surrounding buildings, including much of pretty Rievaulx village, were constructed from stone pillaged from the ruins.

Rievaulx Abbey, off the B1257 to Stokesley, opens 10 am to 6 pm daily, April to September (9.30 am to 7 pm in July and August); 10 am to 4 pm the rest of the year. Admission costs £3.40/1.70 and includes an audio tour.

Rievaulx Terrace & Temples
In the 1750s Duncombe Park was landscaped to create a romantic series of views overlooking Rievaulx Abbey, Ryedale and the Hambleton Hills. Rievaulx Terrace & Temples (☎ 798340; NT) consists of a half-mile-long grass-covered terrace with carefully planned openings into the surrounding woods. There's no access to the abbey from the terrace. The terrace, which includes a new historic exhibition in the Ionic Temple, opens 10.30 am to 5 pm from April to late-October. Admission costs £3/1.50.

Nunnington Hall

Nunnington Hall (☎ 748283; NT) is an attractive manor house on the banks of the River Rye, about 4½ miles south-east of Helmsley off the B1257. It includes sections from the 16th century but most of the building dates from the 17th. There's a tearoom and an attractive garden. It opens 1.30 to 5 pm Wednesday to Sunday, May to September, until 4.30 pm in April and October. Admission costs £4/2.

PICKERING

☎ 01751 • pop 5315

Once you get away from the traffic along the A170, Pickering is a surprisingly attractive little town. As the main starting point for trips on the NYMR, it also draws an enormous number of tourists.

Orientation & Information

Most of the town is within a five-minute walk of the Market Place, a long narrow rectangle.

The TIC (☎ 473791, fax 473487, ⓔ pickering@ytbtic.co.uk) is in the Ropery across from the main car park. It opens 9.30 am to 5.30 pm daily, March to October; until 4.30 pm (closed Sunday) the rest of the year.

Pickering Castle

The main attraction, Pickering Castle (☎ 474989; EH), was founded by William the Conqueror but the remaining ruins date from a later period. Some of the curtain walls with towers, and part of the keep on a 40-foot-high motte, survive. It's a beautiful site with good views over the town. It opens 10 am to 6 pm April to September; until 4 pm the rest of the year. Admission costs £2.30/1.20.

Places to Stay & Eat

The nearest youth hostel is the *Old School Youth Hostel* (☎ 460376, fax 460376, Lockton), about 4 miles north on the A169 between Pickering and Whitby. It's about 2 miles from the NYMR station at Levisham and is passed by Yorkshire Coastliner's bus No 840 between Leeds/York and Whitby. The hostel makes a good walking base. It opens daily in July and August, and Monday to Saturday from mid-April to June and

in September. Rates are £7.50/5.25 for adults/under-18s.

Black Swan (☎ 472286, fax 472926, 18 Birdgate) is a popular pub. B&B starts at £22.50 per person.

White Swan Hotel (☎ 472288, fax 475554, ⓔ welcome@white-swan.co.uk, Market Place) is a highly acclaimed small inn. Rooms cost from £30 to £45 per person. The pub has fine ales and the food is drawn from local produce. A three-course meal will run to about £20.

The hospitable *Rose* (☎ 475366) pub is near the NYMR station on Bridge St. Bar meals cost less than £5.

Getting There & Away

Scarborough & District bus No 128 has an hourly service between Helmsley (40 minutes) and Scarborough (50 minutes) via Pickering. There are only four on Sunday. Yorkshire Coastliner bus No 840 and 842 link Pickering with Goathland and Whitby to the east and with York and Leeds to the west. See Getting There & Around earlier for contact details.

NORTH YORKSHIRE MOORS RAILWAY

Aside from appealing to railway enthusiasts with some magnificent restored engines and carriages, the NYMR cuts across an interesting section of the moors and opens up some excellent day walks. And it can still fulfil its original function of providing a link to Whitby.

History

The line from Pickering to Whitby was the third passenger line to open in Yorkshire, coming 10 years after the Stockton-Darlington Railway. For the first 10 years, carriages on the Pickering-Whitby line were pulled by horses, except at Beck Hole, where the 1:15 incline was conquered by a balancing system of water-filled tanks, and on downhill stretches where the horses were put in a carriage and the train freewheeled! The first steam locomotive was used in 1847.

In the 1950s government policy went against common sense and the railways;

after 1965 only the Esk Valley line remained in operation. Thousands of locals opposed the 'rationalisation' however, and in 1967 a volunteer preservation society was formed to restore and operate the Grosmont-Pickering line. Today the NYMR carries 310,000 passengers a year.

Orientation & Information

The NYMR runs north–south and links Grosmont (on Northern Spirit's Esk Valley line between Whitby and Middlesbrough) with Pickering. It's 18 miles long; the full journey takes an hour and costs £9.50/4.80.

The main station is at Pickering (☎ 01751-472508). At all stations there's information about waymarked walks, designed as family strolls lasting between one and four hours. The railway, Pickering and the surrounding countryside can easily absorb a day. Look for the *Walks from the Train* booklet (80p).

From May to September several special dining trains operate. Call Pickering Station for details.

The timetable is too complicated to repeat here but there's a recorded timetable (☎ 01751-473535). Roughly speaking, there are five to eight trains daily between April and early November.

The Journey

From Pickering the line follows Pickering Beck. The first stop is **Levisham station**, 1½ miles west of beautiful **Levisham** village, which faces **Lockton** across a steep valley. Lockton, off the A169 between Whitby and Pickering, has the *Old School Youth Hostel* (see Pickering earlier).

Goathland is a picturesque village 152m above sea level among the heather-clad moors. Most passengers get off here to view the village because it's used in the British TV series *Heartbeat*. There are several good walks from the station. You can camp at *Abbott's House Farm* (☎ 01947-896270) for £6 and at *Brow House Farm* (☎ 01947-896274) for £5. *Heatherdene Hotel* (☎/fax 896334) is in the Old Vicarage. It's a licensed place with good meals (under £7) and rooms from £29 per person. There are many more B&Bs.

The sleepy, little village of **Grosmont** (pronounced grow-mont) has accommodation at *Hazelwood House* (☎ 01947-895292) which charges upwards of £19 per person. There's also one pub, the *Station Tavern (895060)*, and that's about it.

Getting There & Away

Most passengers begin their journey at Pickering. A good day would feature a triangular tour combining the NYMR, the Esk Valley Line to Whitby and the Yorkshire Coastliner bus to Pickering. Check the schedules carefully in advance and you should be able to complete the triangle and have several stops along the way.

There are usually five trains daily on the Esk Valley line between Middlesborough and Whitby that stop at Grosmont.

DANBY
☎ 01287 • pop 400

Danby (sometimes referred to as Danby-in-Cleveland) is at the head of Eskdale, and the surrounding countryside is particularly beautiful. Fourteenth-century Danby Castle can be seen from the road; Danby Beacon, 2 miles to the north-east, has great views; and Duck Bridge, downstream from the village, is a 14th-century packhorse bridge.

The Moors Centre (☎ 660654), the main headquarters for the national park, is in Danby, half a mile from the village proper. There are displays, information, an accommodation-booking service and tea-rooms in an 18th-century manor house. The centre opens 10 am to 5 pm daily, April to October; 11 am to 4 pm daily, the rest of the year (weekends only in January and February). There are several short circular walks from the centre.

Places to Stay & Eat

Some local farms offer good-value B&B, costing around £18 per person. One example is *Crag Farm* (☎ 660279).

Fox & Hounds (☎ 660218, fax 660030, e ajbfox@globalnet.co.uk) near the train station has good views and rooms from £27 per person. It also has a good restaurant and a pub.

A tight squeeze: narrowboating, Rochdale Canal

Old news: a traditional town crier in Manchester

A church has stood on the site of the grand old minster of York since the year 627.

Golden at sunset, the River Wharfe wends its silent way through the rolling Yorkshire Dales.

Chewing the cud in Kildale, North Yorkshire

The green dales of Yorkshire

Robin Hood's Bay, Yorkshire, was once a haven for smugglers.

Getting There & Away

There are five trains daily on the Esk Valley line. Whitby is 20 minutes east (£2.50); Middlesbrough one hour west (£4.50).

STAITHES

Tucked beneath high cliffs and running back along the steep banks of a small river, the old fishing village of Staithes is one of the most picturesque on the English coast. The idyll is somewhat spoiled, though, by the large potash mine in the hills behind.

In some ways, the village seems untouched by the 20th century, focusing still on its centuries-old battle with the sea. James Cook served as an apprentice grocer in a shop that has since been reclaimed by the sea; the shop and the street have been recreated in the **Capt Cook & Staithes Heritage Centre** (☎ 841454). Legend says that fishermen's tales of the high seas and bad treatment by his master led him to steal a shilling from the till and run away to

Whitby and the sea. The centre opens 10 am to 5.30 pm daily. Admission costs £2.25/1.

The TIC in Whitby handles bookings and information for Staithes. There's accommodation in the two pubs and in a couple of guesthouses. *Springfields* (*☎ 01947–841011, 42 Staithes Lane*) is a Victorian house with good views, which charges £15 per person.

WHITBY

☎ 01947 • pop 15,200

Somehow Whitby transcends the amusement arcades, fish and chip shops, and coaches – the imposing ruins of an abbey loom over red-brick houses that spill down a headland to a beautiful estuary harbour. This small town has had a disproportionate impact on world history, both as the site for the Synod of Whitby (which determined the nature of the medieval English church; see the boxed text 'Christianity & the Synod of Whitby' for details) and as the starting point

---

Christianity & the Synod of Whitby

When the Romans withdrew from Britain at the beginning of the 5th century, they left behind the Christian faith. Although the Angles and Saxons who arrived next weren't Christians, the Celts kept the religion alive, especially in Cornwall, Wales and Ireland.

Pope Gregory's missions to the Angles, led by Augustine in Kent (597) and Paulinus in Northumberland (627), gained tenuous footholds but lasted only six years in the case of Paulinus. His Northumbrian patron, King Edwin, was defeated and killed by Welsh and Mercian invaders. However, Edwin's heir, Oswald, was exiled on the island of Iona, a Celtic Christian outpost. When he won back power in 635 he appealed to the Iona monks to help him restore Christianity.

The saintly Aidan met this request and succeeded in planting Christianity so deeply in the north that it was never again challenged. The conversion of the Mercian kingdoms of the Midlands began and the forgotten arts of writing and keeping records were re-established. A great monastery was founded on Lindisfarne and St Hilda, a Northumbrian princess, established a monastery at Streoneshalh (Whitby's name before the Danish Viking invasions) in 657.

In 664, the Celtic and Roman churches met at Streoneshalh to resolve their differences. Most importantly, the Roman church, under the leadership of the pope, was intent on establishing a centralised organisation transcending the tribal distinctions that had left much of Europe in an almost continuous state of war since the collapse of the Roman Empire. Matters of ritual also differed – the churches celebrated Easter on different days, for instance – and Celtic priests and monks preferred a system that allowed them to follow their individual consciences rather than an autocratic rule.

Eventually, the synod decided in favour of the Roman church's rites and organisation, although the decision wasn't entirely unanimous. The Roman archbishop of Canterbury, Theodore, allowed a number of Celtic practices to continue, including divorce and remarriage in certain cases and the private confession of sins rather than confession in front of a congregation.

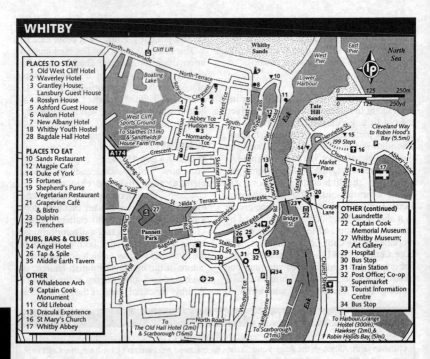

WHITBY

PLACES TO STAY
1 Old West Cliff Hotel
2 Waverley Hotel
3 Grantley House;
  Lansbury Guest House
4 Rosslyn House
5 Ashford Guest House
6 Avalon Hotel
7 New Albany Hotel
18 Whitby Youth Hostel
28 Bagdale Hall Hotel

PLACES TO EAT
10 Sands Restaurant
12 Magpie Café
14 Duke of York
15 Fortunes
19 Shepherd's Purse
   Vegetarian Restaurant
21 Grapevine Café
   & Bistro
23 Dolphin
25 Trenchers

PUBS, BARS & CLUBS
24 Angel Hotel
26 Tap & Spile
35 Middle Earth Tavern

OTHER
8 Whalebone Arch
9 Captain Cook
  Monument
11 Old Lifeboat
13 Dracula Experience
16 St Mary's Church
17 Whitby Abbey

OTHER (continued)
20 Laundrette
22 Captain Cook
   Memorial Museum
27 Whitby Museum;
   Art Gallery
29 Hospital
30 Bus Stop
31 Train Station
32 Post Office; Co-op
   Supermarket
33 Tourist Information
   Centre
34 Bus Stop

for the maritime career of one of the world's greatest explorers, Captain James Cook.

Whitby is one of the most interesting and attractive towns on the British coast and among the highlights of a trip to the north. It's the perfect base from which to explore the nearby cliffs, coves, fishing villages and beaches, which are among the most spectacular on this island. Watch for the salmon that come up the River Esk in the spawning season and the seals that follow and feed on them.

The town itself combines the colour of a working harbour (on the estuary of the Esk), a muddle of medieval streets with a range of restaurants and pubs, the silhouette of the abbey which seems to float over the town, and the paraphernalia of a seaside resort. It attracts a diverse group of people – not just retirees and young families.

The past is powerfully evoked, particularly when mists roll up the Esk valley but also when Whitby is at its sunniest and loveliest.

And you'll never have any doubt that you're close to the water, thanks to the shrieks of seagulls and the smells from the sea.

History
The Romans had a signal station on the high cliffs east of town. Over 200 years after their departure, Celtic Christianity was firmly established in the kingdom of Northumbria by St Aidan. In 635 he founded the great Lindisfarne monastery (see Holy Island in the North-Eastern England chapter). In 657 St Hilda, a Northumbrian princess, established a monastery at Streoneshalh (as Whitby was known before the Danish Viking invasions). In 664 the Celtic and Roman churches met at the abbey to resolve their differences. Eventually, the grand bishops, monks and nuns of the Whitby Synod (or council) on their windy headland decided the future of the English church in favour of Rome and its organisation based at Canterbury.

The Danish destroyed the abbey in 867 but they recognised Whitby's potential as a port. The abbey was refounded by Benedictines in 1078 and flourished until the Dissolution in 1539 – the Benedictine ruins survive today.

From the Middle Ages, the importance of Whitby as a maritime centre increased; Whitby-built and Whitby-crewed ships were to serve generations of Whitby traders, whalers, fishermen and explorers. In 1746, the 18-year-old James Cook arrived in the town as an apprentice to a local shipowner. For nine years Cook worked on Whitby cats – unique Whitby-built colliers that carried coal south from the Durham coalfields to London. These sturdy flat-bottomed vessels were specially designed to allow them to be beached for loading and off-loading.

In 1755 Cook joined the navy, and in 1768 he began the first of three voyages of discovery. On all three voyages the ships he chose to use, including the *Endeavour*, were Whitby cats.

Orientation

Old Whitby grew up along the steep sides of the Esk estuary. Until the 18th century the eastern bank was the most important, but in the 19th century a new town with terraced crescents grew up on the western side, catering to the new tourist industry. This is also where most 20th-century development has occurred.

To confuse matters, one street sometimes has two names: for example, the southern side of one street is Hudson St, while the northern side is Abbey Terrace.

Information

The TIC (☎ 602674, fax 606137), Langborne Rd, near the train station, opens 9.30 am to 6 pm daily, May to September; 10 am to 4.30 pm daily October to April. It has a wealth of information on this part of the moors and the coast.

The post office is across from the TIC on Endeavour Wharf inside the Co-op Supermarket. It opens 8.30 am to 5.30 pm Monday to Saturday.

There's a laundrette at 72 Church St.

Whitby Abbey & St Mary's Church

Nothing survives of the Saxon abbey founded by St Hilda; it lay a little to the north of the existing ruins. A Benedictine abbey was re-established on the site in 1078 and the remains visible today are of the Benedictine church built in the 13th and 14th centuries (mainly in the Early English style).

In many ways, the nearby St Mary's Church is more interesting than the abbey ruins. It's a lovely medieval church with a low Norman tower and an atmospheric, extraordinary interior full of skewwhiff Georgian galleries and box pews. The nautical term 'crow's nest' may have come from the name given to the high pulpit from which the priest, dressed in black, gave his sermon. The climb of 199 steps up the side of the cliff is worth it just for the view.

The abbey (☎ 603568; EH) opens 10 am to 6 pm daily, April to September; until 4 pm the rest of the year. Admission costs £1.70/90. The church (☎ 603421) opens 10 am to 5 pm daily (until 4 pm November to March) and admission is free. Parking costs £1.50.

Captain Cook Memorial Museum

The museum (☎ 601900) is in the harbourside house, below the abbey, once owned by John Walker, the Quaker captain to whom Cook was apprenticed. Cook sometimes lodged in the attic. It's well worth a visit for the house itself and for the interesting displays on Cook's life and voyages.

The museum opens 9.45 am to 5 pm daily, April to October. In March it opens 11 am to 3 pm at weekends only. Admission costs £2.80/2.

Whitby Museum

Whitby Museum (☎ 602908), Pannett Park, was founded in 1823. It's a traditional place full of dusty glass cabinets displaying fascinating stuff. It has a good collection of fossils, including a crocodile and a dinosaur, both found locally. There is also a fine collection of ship models. It's surrounded by a beautiful, steep garden with views (partly marred by an ugly block of modern flats) that give you another perspective on the town.

The museum opens 9.30 am to 5.30 pm on weekdays and 2 to 5 pm Sunday, May to September; 10 am to 1 pm Tuesday, 10 am to 4 pm Wednesday to Saturday and 2 to 4 pm Sunday, October to April. Admission costs £2/1. There's also a small art gallery open the same hours, which is free.

Dracula Experience

Always looking for a way to sink their teeth into tourists, local promoters have scored big with the Dracula Experience (☎ 601923) at 9 Marine Parade. With lots of lights and mirrors, it puts on a show loosely based on the Bram Stoker novel, parts of which are set in Whitby (see the boxed text 'Dracula' for details). It opens 10 am to 10 pm daily, May to September before retiring to the modest hours of noon to 5 pm, weekends only, the rest of the year. Admission costs £1.95/1.50.

Monuments

At the top of the cliff near East Terrace, there is a **Captain Cook Monument** that shows him looking out to sea. Not far away, the **Whalebone Arch** is just that. It's made from the huge jawbones of whales once caught by Whitby's long-defunct whaling industry.

Tours

Several companies along the eastern bank of the estuary offer boat and fishing trips. Get a list of operators from the TIC. You can also haggle for rides with the operators of the old lifeboat (☎ 821553) docked along Pier Rd.

The wonderfully named Heritage Harry (☎ 821734) offers walking tours of the town that depart from the TIC at 11.30 am on Tuesday and Thursday from July to September. The cost is £3/1. Harry also offers tours at other times as well as Dracula and ghost tours.

The Whitby Tour (☎ 0191-521 0202) uses an open-top bus that prowls the city daily from the Co-op Supermarket. The fare is £4.50/3.

Walking

The 5½-mile cliff-top walk south to Robin Hood's Bay is a real treat. If you don't want to make it a round-trip, call ☎ 0870 608

Dracula

Bram Stoker wrote the story of Dracula in 1897 while staying at a B&B in Whitby. And indeed the seashore resort plays a crucial role in three chapters. If you are familiar with the book – as opposed to the lurid Hollywood versions which spend much of their time in deepest, darkest Transylvania – then you will recognise some of the following sites.

The car park in front of Whitby train station was once sidings for freight cars. It's here that Dracula left Whitby for London in one of his boxes of dirt. Over at the Lower Harbour, look for the stone jetty out into the water. This is where the Russian boat chartered by Dracula was wrecked as it flew into the harbour ahead of a huge storm. Onlookers found the ship deserted except for a huge and ill-tempered black dog that jumped off and took flight. This scene from the book has its basis in the wreck of an actual Russian boat in 1885, although this one had a crew and not a dog with unusual tastes.

You can climb the same 199 stone steps that the heroine Mina ran up when trying to save her friend Lucy, who met a fellow not-unrelated to the big black dog… the steps lead to St Mary's Church, the moody, medieval house of worship where Mina first saw Lucy sitting on a bench with a suspicious black being next to her. By that time, of course, it was too late.

There are many other important Dracula sites in Whitby; the TIC sells an excellent walking tour leaflet for 30p.

JANE SMITH

A sinister creature of the night: Bram Stoker's Dracula

2608 to check on return trips. Alternatively, there are also some beautiful, small fishing villages, such as Staithes, to the north.

Cycling

The **Whitby–Scarborough Coastal Cycle Trail** follows the 20-mile route of the old railway line and is an excellent trip. Trailways (☎ 820207) is a bike rental firm based in the Old Railway Station in Hawkser, two miles south of Whitby towards Robin Hood's Bay. Prices start at £5 per day and the company will pick you up at Whitby train station or deliver your bike to you there.

Places to Stay

There are plenty of places to stay, but beware the Easter weekend, Whitby Festival (mid-June) and Whitby Regatta (August), when the place can be booked out.

Camping From £7 per night, *Sandfield House Farm* (☎ 602660, fax 606274), on Sandsend Rd (the A174), has five tent sites and 50 touring pitches. Take the No X56 bus in the direction of Middlesbrough.

Hostels Beside the abbey, *Whitby Youth Hostel* (☎ 602878, fax 825146, East Cliff), at the top of the 199 steps, has great views over the town. It opens daily from late May to early September but closes during the day until 5 pm. Call for the complex hours for the rest of the year. Beds cost £10/6.90 for adults/under-18s.

The alternative is the well-designed and well-positioned *Harbour Grange Hostel* (☎ 600817, ℮ backpackers@harbourgrange .onyxnet.co.uk, Spital Bridge) on the eastern side 10 minutes' walk from the TIC. It opens year round and during the day. There are family rooms, parking, and beds cost £8 (£1 for linen).

B&Bs A number of places in the centre of the medieval town (on the eastern side of the river) offer B&B. There is accommodation above the *Shepherd's Purse Vegetarian Restaurant* (☎ 820228, 95 Church St) with pleasant rooms, including a vegetarian breakfast, from £17 per person.

Most accommodation, however, is on the western side, the part of town that developed in Victorian times. A walk along Royal Crescent, Crescent Ave, Hudson St/Abbey Terrace and East Terrace will turn up many decent possibilities.

Ashford Guest House (☎ 602138, fax 821734, ℮ fcoll@globalnet.co.uk, 8 Royal Crescent) is an unspoilt place with sea views and a range of rooms from £20 per person, all nonsmoking.

Waverley Hotel (☎/fax 604389, 17 Crescent Ave) has doubles from £20 per person. It also has a small bar in the basement.

In a nice old Victorian building, the *Old West Cliff Hotel* (☎ 603292, fax 821180, 42 Crescent Ave) has six rooms with bathroom from £25 per person.

The *New Albany Hotel* (☎ 603711, 3 Royal Crescent) has decent rooms with sea views from £25 per person.

Possibilities on Hudson St/Abbey Terrace include *Lansbury Guest House* (☎/fax 604821, 29 Hudson St), with comfortable singles and doubles from £20 per person, and *Grantley House* (☎ 600895, 26 Hudson St) where rooms with numerous amenities cost from £20 per person. *Rosslyn House* (☎/fax 604086, 11 Abbey Terrace) has eight rooms, each with TV, that cost from £16 per person.

Hotels In a Jacobean house built in 1603, overlooking the Esk Valley, is *The Old Hall Hotel* (☎/fax 602801, High St, Ruswarp). There's quite a range of rooms, some with bathroom, from £22 to £33 per person.

Avalon Hotel (☎ 820313, fax 602349, ℮ avalon@avalonhotel.freeserve.co.uk, 13–14 Royal Crescent) has good singles/ doubles with great views from £30/40.

Bagdale Hall Hotel (☎ 602958, fax 820714, 1 Bagdale) has very comfortable rooms and good service. It costs from £39 per person and there are also simple lodge rooms in a nearby building available for £39 a night. These sleep up to five.

Places to Eat

There are plenty of reasonable eating places in Whitby, with a predictable emphasis on seafood.

Restaurants On the eastern side of the river, the *Shepherd's Purse Vegetarian Restaurant* (☎ 820228, 95 Church St) is at the back of the wholefood shop opposite Market Place. It has starters such as stilton and onion soup (£2.50) and mains such as stuffed avocado (£5.95). Takeaways are available and it also has an outside courtyard – and pleasant rooms (see Places to Stay).

A delightful addition nearby is the *Grapevine Café & Bistro* (☎ 820275, 2 Grape Lane). Lunch baguettes with interesting fillings cost £3.25. At dinner, Mediterranean tapas dishes are around £5 each. The food is excellent and you'd best book for dinner.

Pubs At the end of Church St and overlooking the harbour, the *Duke of York* (☎ 600324, Church St) is a good place to try the local crab, either in a salad (£5.95) or a sandwich.

The *Dolphin* (☎ 602197, Bridge St) has comfortable tables inside or picnic tables outside. The cod and chips are succulent (£5.95) and there are more complex seafood dishes as well.

Fish & Chips It's claimed that the *Magpie Café* (☎ 602058, 14 Pier Rd) does the best fish and chips in the world but unfortunately most of the world knows, so there are often long queues. Staff will fry, grill or poach the fish of your choice (from £6 to £10); there are also some vegetarian meals. It opens from 11.30 am to 9 pm.

Trenchers (☎ 603212, New Quay Rd), near the train station, is also highly regarded for its fish – it can get busy. A recent expansion means that it's better equipped for the mobs.

There are numerous other fish and chips places in town, costing a little less – just take your pick.

Overlooking the sea, *Sands Restaurant* (☎ 603500, Khyber Pass) is on the cutting that links the western cliffs and the old town. It is a spic-and-span, efficient operation with vegetarian meals for £5.95 and cod, chips, peas and tea for £5.75.

Although you can't eat, one of the most famous contributors to English cuisine is *Fortunes* (☎ 601659, 20 Henrietta St), a

small family company that has produced and sold kippers since 1872. Kippers are fish (traditionally herring) that have been salted and smoked.

Entertainment
There are several quite lively pubs that are good for music. Check the *Whitby Gazette*, which comes out on Tuesday and Friday, to see what's on.

The *Angel Hotel* (☎ 602943, New Quay Rd) has live music and a young and boisterous crowd. The *Tap & Spile* (☎ 603937, New Quay Rd), opposite the train station, is similar.

For a quieter pint away from the crowds try *Middle Earth Tavern* (☎ 606014, 26 Church St). It often has folk music.

Shopping
Jet (black fossilised wood) is found around Whitby. In Victorian times over 200 workshops produced jet jewellery; only a few still do so today. Some shops around town sell it.

Getting There & Away
Whitby is 230 miles from London, 45 miles from York and 20 miles from Scarborough.

Bus North East has a number of services in the Whitby area. There are regular buses, Nos 93 and 93A (via Robin Hood's Bay), to/from Scarborough (£2.70, one hour). Yorkshire Coastliner has useful services (bus Nos 840 and 842) between Whitby and Leeds (£8.10) via Goathland, Pickering and York. Note that, in another privatisation nightmare, the bus companies have stopped using the coach station and now stop near the old station or past the TIC on Langborne Rd.

Train Although it's not, in some ways, particularly efficient, you can get to Whitby by train. The Esk Valley line from Middlesbrough (£6.60) is one of the most attractive in the country – even more interesting scenically than the much-promoted NYMR (see the North Yorkshire Moors Railway section earlier).

En route, it's possible to connect with the northern terminal of the NYMR at Grosmont (to visit Danby) and Kildale (a possible starting or finishing point for the Cleveland Way). However, the Esk Valley line is only really efficient if you are coming from the north. There are only four trains a day and you have to change at Middlesbrough. If you are travelling from London and the south, it is much quicker to get a train to Scarborough from York, then a bus from Scarborough.

Getting Around

Whitby is a compact place and there's those 199 steps to help you burn off the fish and chips. The cliff lift to/from Whitby Sands operates May to September.

Taxi The main taxi rank is beside the TIC, opposite the train and bus station. Harrison Taxis (☎ 600606) is one of the main operators. The minimum fare is £1.50 and you can get to most places around Whitby for less than £3.

COOK COUNTRY WALK

Explorer and navigator Captain James Cook was born and raised in the north of this area, and there are a number of museums and monuments commemorating his life. The Cook Country Walk, a 40-mile hike, links the most important sites of Cook's early years. The first half basically follows the northern flanks of the Cleveland Hills east from Marton (near Middlesbrough), then the superb coast south from Staithes to Whitby. It's designed to be broken into three easy days. The TICs in the region all have maps and leaflets.

ROBIN HOOD'S BAY

☎ 01947 • pop 1200

Bay, or Baytown as the locals call it, probably has a lot more to do with smugglers than with the Sherwood Forest hero but it's a picturesque haven. A steep road drops from the coastal plateau down to the sea. There's compulsory parking at the top — don't even think about cheating and driving down, because there's hardly even room to turn at the bottom.

The village is a honeycomb of cobbled alleys and impossibly small houses that seem to hide in secret passages. There are a few gift shops and a trail of pubs (start from the bottom and work your way up) but really this is a place to just sit and watch the world go by, preferably out of season.

The NT opened a major new visitors centre in October 2000 in conjunction with the North York Moors National Park Authority. Housed in the restored 19th-century Old Coastguard Station next to the slipway on the bay, exhibits look at the life and ecology of the Moors and coast. Call ☎ 01947-885900 for opening details and hours.

Unless you book, or are prepared to walk a mile (along the beach at low tide or the cliff at high tide) to the popular *Boggle Hole Youth Hostel* (☎ 880352, fax 880987, ⓔ bogglehole@yha.org.uk, Mill Beck, Fylingthorpe), don't plan on staying. Beds cost £10/6.90 for adults/under-18s.

The *Victoria Hotel* (☎ 880205, fax 881170, Station Rd), across from the parking lot at the entrance to the village, has a commanding view. Singles/doubles with bathrooms cost from £40/58.

The Olde Dolphin (☎ 880337), accessed from King St, has huge bar meals (from £5) which feature seafood and vegetarian choices.

North East bus Nos 93 and 93A offer an hourly service between Whitby and Scarborough via the Bay.

SCARBOROUGH

☎ 01723 • pop 39,300

Scarborough is a large, often kitsch, seaside resort. Unlike Blackpool (and many other places of that ilk), however, it has a long history and, most importantly, a spectacular site. These, combined with the traditional trappings of an English seaside holiday resort, make it an appealing and enjoyable place.

Although some parts are a bit run-down, Scarborough, for the most part, survived the 20th century and the impact of cheap package holidays to the Mediterranean. It remains a classic resort, with two beautiful bays separated by a castle-crowned headland, and is popular with young families and pensioners from all round the north. In 1998 it got a new dose of fame from the delightful movie

YORKSHIRE

Little Voice, which was shot in Scarborough and starred Michael Caine and Jane Horrocks.

History

The headland that separates the North and South bays has an impressive defensive position and has been occupied since Celtic times. A fishing village was, according to tradition, established by Vikings in the 9th century around what is now known as the Old Harbour. The Normans built their castle in around 1130 and it survived until 1648 when it was heavily damaged by the Parliamentarians. It was also bombarded by a German battleship in 1914.

The medieval fishing and market town grew up around the Old Harbour. Mineral springs were discovered in 1620 and it was transformed into a fashionable spa town. It became one of the first places in Britain where sea bathing was popular and since the mid-18th century it has been a successful seaside resort. It therefore has a legacy of fine Georgian, Victorian and Edwardian architecture.

Orientation

Modern suburbs sprawl west of the town centre, which is above the old town and the South Bay. The town is on a plateau above the beaches; three cliff lifts, steep streets and footpaths provide the links. The Victorian development to the south is separated from the town centre by a steep valley, which has been landscaped and is crossed by high bridges.

The main shopping street is Westborough which has a dramatic view of the castle rising in the distance. The North Bay is home to all the tawdry seashore amusements; the South Bay is more genteel. The old town lies between St Mary's Church and the castle and the Old Harbour.

The railway station is conveniently central with the bus station behind it. However, note that buses may also leave from the east side of Brunswick Centre.

Information

The busy TIC (☎ 373333, fax 363785, @ dtls@scarborough.gov.uk) is right at the corner of Westborough and Valley Bridge Rd. It opens 9.30 am to 6 pm daily, May to September; 10 am to 4.30 pm daily, the rest of the year.

The post office is at 11–15 Aberdeen Walk. It opens 9 am to 5.30 pm Monday to Friday and until 12.30 pm on Saturday.

Complete Computing (☎ 500990), 14 Northway, offers Internet access for £1.50 for 15 minutes.

Waterstone's (☎ 500414) has a good-sized shop at 97–98 Westborough.

There's a handy laundrette (☎ 375763) at 48 North Marine Road.

Things to See & Do

Well it's a beach resort, innit? So there are all the things the British do at beaches, plus some bonuses.

Scarborough Castle (☎ 372451; EH), approached via a 13th-century barbican, survives, as do the curtain walls dating from around 1130 and the shell of a keep built around 1160. There are excellent views. It opens 10 am to 6 pm daily, April to September; 10 am to 4 pm Wednesday to Sunday, the rest of the year. Admission costs £2.30/1.20, which includes an audio guide.

Below the castle is **St Mary's Church** (☎ 354555) dating from 1180 and rebuilt in the 15th and 17th centuries, with some interesting 14th-century chapels. Anne Brontë is buried in the churchyard. It opens 10 am to 4.30 pm weekdays (2 to 4 pm Sunday), May to September.

The **Church of St Martin-on-the-Hill** (☎ 360437) is on Albion Rd south of the centre. It was built in 1863 to a very high standard and has some Pre-Raphaelite stained-glass windows. The doors are open 7.30 am to 5.30 pm daily. Nearby along the shore, the grand old **Spa Complex** hints at Scarborough's roots as a fashionable resort. Nowadays it is a venue for conferences (☎ 376 774).

The **Rotunda Museum** (☎ 374839) on Vernon Rd traces local history from prehistoric times right up to the present. It opens 10 am to 5 pm (closed Monday) at Easter and from late May to late October. Admission costs £2/1.

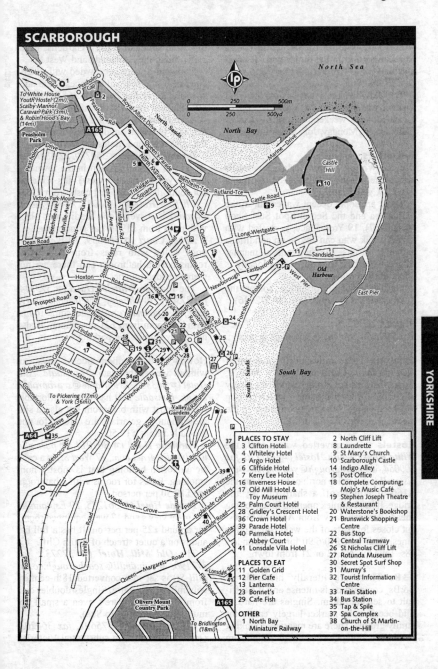

SCARBOROUGH

PLACES TO STAY
3 Clifton Hotel
4 Whiteley Hotel
5 Argo Hotel
6 Cliffside Hotel
7 Kerry Lee Hotel
16 Inverness House
17 Old Mill Hotel &
   Toy Museum
25 Palm Court Hotel
28 Gridley's Crescent Hotel
36 Crown Hotel
39 Parade Hotel
40 Parmelia Hotel;
   Abbey Court
41 Lonsdale Villa Hotel

PLACES TO EAT
11 Golden Grid
12 Pier Cafe
23 Lanterna
23 Bonnet's
29 Cafe Fish

OTHER
1 North Bay
  Miniature Railway

2 North Cliff Lift
8 Laundrette
9 St Mary's Church
10 Scarborough Castle
14 Indigo Alley
15 Post Office
18 Complete Computing;
   Mojo's Music Café
19 Stephen Joseph Theatre
   & Restaurant
20 Waterstone's Bookshop
21 Brunswick Shopping
   Centre
22 Bus Stop
24 Central Tramway
26 St Nicholas Cliff Lift
27 Rotunda Museum
30 Secret Spot Surf Shop
31 Murray's
32 Tourist Information
   Centre
33 Train Station
34 Bus Station
35 Tap & Spile
38 Church of St Martin-
   on-the-Hill

YORKSHIRE

The **North Bay Miniature Railway** (☎ 381344) is north of the centre across Burniston Rd from Peasholm Park. It operates daily mid-April to October and rides cost £1.40/80p.

The Old Mill Hotel (see Places to Stay) has a small **toy museum** (☎ 372735), opens 10 am to 4 pm weekends, April to October (daily except Monday, July and August).

Activities

See the Whitby section earlier for details about the 20-mile Whitby–Scarborough Coastal Cycle Trail.

There are some decent waves out in the North Sea and the Secret Spot Surf Shop (☎ 500467), 19 York Place, is staffed with friendly folk who can advise on conditions and offer lessons. The shop rents all manner of gear. The best time for waves locally is September to May.

For local diving information, contact the Scarborough Sub Aqua Club (☎ 372036).

Places to Stay

The TIC will only make bookings in person.

Camping Three miles north of town is *Scalby Manor Caravan Park* (☎ 366212, *Burniston Rd*). It's a large park with plenty of pitches for vans and tents, which cost up to £9 for a site. There are good views of the moors. Take bus No 12 or 21.

Hostels In a converted water mill, the *White House Youth Hostel* (☎ 361176, fax 500054, @ scarborough@yha.org.uk, Burniston Rd) is 2 miles north of town along the A166 to Whitby off a sharp turn by the bridge. It has complex opening times so ring ahead. It opens daily from April to August but closes for parts of the weekend at other times. Beds cost £10/6.90 for adults/under-18s. Take bus No 12 or 21 from town.

B&Bs There are literally hundreds of B&Bs, competition is intense and it's difficult to separate them. Singles are hard to find because the market largely caters for family groups. There are many overlooking North Bay along Queens Parade, Blenheim

Terrace and North Marine Rd, and another big zone south of Valley Gardens, especially along the Esplanade and West St.

Trafalgar Square is crowded with B&Bs and one of the best value places is the non-smoking *Kerry Lee Hotel* (☎ 363845) at No 60. Standard rooms start at £12 per person.

Argo Hotel (☎ 375745, 134 North Marine Rd) is a pleasant, small B&B overlooking the cricket ground. Rates are from £14.

Inverness House (☎ 369770, 22 Aberdeen Walk) has a great position in the town (although you sacrifice a view). It's a classic but comfortable place that costs from £16.

Cliffside Hotel (☎ 361087, 79-81 Queens Parade) is a well-kept, traditional place with rates from £19. It has good views.

Abbey Court (☎ 360659, 19 West St) is good value with rates from £20. Most rooms have a bathroom and there are numerous added touches.

The 10-room *Whiteley Hotel* (☎ 373514, fax 373007, @ whiteley_hotel@compuserve.com, 99 Queens Parade) has some rooms with bathroom from £21 per person. It also has a few singles and parking.

Hotels On the southern side of town, but without views, the stately *Lonsdale Villa Hotel* (☎ 363383, @ lonsdale@scarborough.co.uk, Lonsdale Rd) has nine comfortable rooms, most with bathroom but also a single without. Vegetarians are catered for and the daily rate is £19.50.

Parmelia Hotel (☎ 361914, @ parmelia hotel@btinternet.com, 17 West St) is a classic Victorian building that is mostly non-smoking. Rates for rooms with a bathroom are £19.50 per person.

Parade Hotel (☎ 361285, 29 Esplanade) has great views and 17 well-equipped rooms for around £25 per person. It has a full bar and is on a quiet stretch of South Cliff.

The *Old Mill Hotel* (☎ 372735, fax 377190, @ windmill@scarborough.co.uk, Mill St) is set in a converted 18th-century windmill in the centre. Singles/doubles cost from £33/48 and there's even a small toy museum (see Things to See).

Clifton Hotel (☎ 375691, fax 364203, Queen's Parade) is a substantial Victorian building with great views over North Bay. It has a ballroom with frequent tea dances. Rooms start at £35/50

Palm Court Hotel (☎ 368161, fax 371547, *St Nicholas Cliff*) has well-equipped rooms and an indoor pool. Rooms cost from £40/60.

Gridley's Crescent Hotel (☎ 360929, fax 354126, *The Crescent*) has a fine position near the centre and South Bay. It has two restaurants and is located on a small park. Rooms cost from £43/75.

The grand *Crown Hotel* (☎ 373491, fax 362271, *Esplanade*) has views of the castle and South Bay. Rooms start at £65/85.

Places to Eat
There's a bunch of traditional fish and chip places on Foreshore Rd. In general, though, the possibilities aren't immense so most people either eat at their hotels – many B&Bs do evening meals and some have alcohol licences – or stay in self-catering flats.

Lanterna (☎ 363616, 33 Queen St) is a splendid Italian dinner spot that specialises in fresh local seafood. The salmon-filled ravioli and various risottos are tops. Expect to pay upwards of £25 each. Booking is advised and it's closed on Sunday.

At *Cafe Fish* (☎ 500301, 19 York Place) you select your fresh fish from a case, specify how you would like it prepared and then pay based on its weight (usually £10 to £15 per person).

In the Stephen Joseph Theatre (see Entertainment) the *Restaurant* (☎ 368463) has interesting and fresh fare. Lunch is a bargain, with sandwiches under £2, while a three-course dinner from the changing menu costs £14.50.

Golden Grid (☎ 360922, 4 Sandside), on the foreshore, has been selling fish and chips since 1883. It's bright, popular and across from the fishing fleet, so there's a good chance the fish is fresh; cod costs from £4. There's also a vegetarian menu.

Nearby, *Pier Cafe* sells simple, honest fare such as Yorkshire pudding with gravy (£1.50).

Bonnet's (☎ 361033, 38–40 Huntriss Row) is an excellent tea room with fine cakes and a serene courtyard. It also has an upstairs restaurant open Thursday to Saturday evenings where fresh fish costs around £11. It sells delicious hand-made chocolate too.

Mojo's Music Café (☎ 351983, 18-20 Northway) combines a funky CD shop with a diner. It opens 10 am to 6 pm (closed Sunday) and serves fresh soups, salads and sandwiches for less than £4.

Entertainment
Indigo Alley (☎ 375823, North Marine Rd) is a welcome addition to local nightlife. It has a good range of beers and live jazz and blues.

Murray's (☎ 503170, Westborough) is right next to the TIC. Local rock bands perform several nights a week.

The *Tap & Spile* (☎ 363837, 94 Falsgrave Rd) is a relaxed pub with a good selection of Yorkshire ales. It has folk music on many nights.

The *Stephen Joseph Theatre* (☎ 370541, Westborough) is in an imposing building by the train station. It stages a good range of drama, including original works by local playwright Alan Ayckbourn. It also has a fine restaurant (see Places to Eat).

Getting There & Away
Scarborough is a good transport hub. It's 230 miles from London, 70 miles from Leeds, 16 miles from Pickering and 20 miles from Whitby.

Bus There are reasonably frequent Scarborough & District buses along the A170 to Pickering and Helmsley (No 128, 1½ hours). They leave from Westborough.

There are regular buses, Nos 93 and 93A (via Robin Hood's Bay), to/from Whitby (£2.70, one hour). Yorkshire Coastliner has a frequent service between Leeds and Scarborough (No 843) via York (£8.40).

Train Scarborough is connected by regular trains with Leeds (£15.40, 1½ hours) via Harrogate. There's a service to/from York (£9.50, 45 minutes) every 30 minutes. Trains also serve Kingston-upon-Hull via Beverley. The journey from Leeds shows a good cross section of Yorkshire.

YORKSHIRE

Getting Around

Bus Local buses leave from the western end of Westborough and outside the train station.

Taxi There's a taxi rank outside the train station or contact Station Taxis (☎ 361009 or 366366), a 24 hour service; £3 should get you to most places.

Yorkshire Dales National Park

Austere stone villages with simple, functional architecture; streams and rivers cutting through the hills; wide, empty moors and endless stone walls snaking over the slopes – this is the region made famous by James Herriot and the TV series *All Creatures Great and Small* (even if he lived in Thirsk outside the park to the east).

The landscape is completely different from that of the Lake District – the overwhelming impression is of space and openness. The high tops of the limestone hills are exposed moorland, and the sheltered dales between them range from Swaledale, which is narrow and sinuous, and Wensleydale and Wharfedale, which are broad and open, to Littondale and Ribblesdale, which are more rugged.

The Yorkshire Dales are very beautiful but in summer, as with the Lake District, they are extremely crowded. Avoid weekends and the peak summer period, or try to get off the beaten track. The famous Pennine Way runs to the area and can be unbelievably busy while other local footpaths are deserted.

ORIENTATION

The 683 sq miles of the Yorkshire Dales can be broken into northern and southern halves. In the north, the two main dales run parallel and east–west. Swaledale, the northernmost, is particularly beautiful. If you have your own transport, the B6270 from Kirkby Stephen to Richmond is highly recommended. Parallel and to the south is broad Wensleydale.

In the south, Ribblesdale runs north–south and is the route taken by the Leeds-Settle-Carlisle railway line, which provides access to a series of attractive towns. Wharfedale is roughly parallel and to the east.

Skipton is the most important transport hub for the Dales but apart from its castle it's not very interesting. Richmond, handy for the north, is a beautiful town. If you don' have your own transport, the best bets are the places accessible on the Leeds-Settle-Carlisle line: Kirkby Stephen, Dent and Settle.

INFORMATION

The main National Park Visitors Centre (☎/fax 01756-752774) is in Grassington, 6 miles north of Skipton. It opens 9.30 am to 5 pm daily from April to October but much less at other times; call for details. Among the other visitors centres is a useful one in Malham (see that section).

The centres have stacks of the useful *Visitor* newspaper which, among other things, has a good listing of the myriad of events occurring within the confines of the park. They also have a huge range of publications, including an excellent series about the park's flora, fauna and history. The Web site is at www.yorkshiredales.org.uk.

WALKING

There's a huge range of walks from easy strolls to extremely challenging hikes; the TICs are good places to get information on day walks.

The Pennine Way crosses the park; it's a demanding and deservedly popular walk through the rugged western half. Another possibility is the Dales Way, which begins in Ilkley, follows the Rivers Wharfe and Dee to the heart of the Dales, and finishes at Bowness-on-Windermere in the Lake District. If you started at Grassington, it would be an easy five day, 60-mile walk. See the Activities chapter for details of both of these walks.

The Yorkshire Dales Walking Company (☎ 01969-624699) runs a huge range of guided walks, from 5 to 11 miles in length, through the year. Fees start at £4 depending on the walk. See the Web site at www.ydwc.co.uk for details.

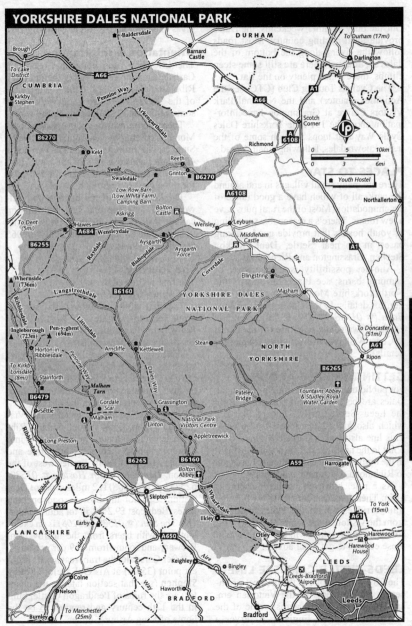

YORKSHIRE DALES NATIONAL PARK

CYCLING ROUTES

Outside busy summer weekends, the Dales provide ideal cycling country. Most roads follow the rivers along the bottom of the dales so, although there are still some steep climbs, there's also plenty on the flat.

The Cyclists Touring Club (CTC; see the Activities chapter) and the National Park Visitors Centre at Grassington have information about the 131-mile Yorkshire Dales Cycle Way that loops through some of the lesser known dales, following small B-roads.

PLACES TO STAY

There are many small villages in and around the park, all of which have a good range of accommodation. Most of the rural pubs have a few rooms. There's a reasonable sprinkling of youth hostels that provide good walking bases in or near Settle, Dent, Kirkby Stephen, Grassington and Richmond.

Another possibility is the network of camping barns; see Places to Stay in the North Yorkshire Moors National Park section for details. In the Dales, the *Low Row Barn* (☎ *01748-884430*) is on Low Whita Farm in Swaledale, one mile off the Coast to Coast Walk (see the Activities chapter for details).

GETTING THERE & AROUND

For public-transport users from the south, the Dales are best accessed from Leeds using the Leeds-Settle-Carlisle line to Skipton, which also gives good access to the west. This line also makes Carlisle a jumping-off point in the north-west. Life is more difficult in the north-east and east, although buses run to Richmond, Harrogate and Ripon.

As a rule, however, public transport is grim. There is a free timetable for bus and train services within the Dales available from the visitor centres and TICs. Your best source of information will be to call one of these centres to get local advice.

LEEDS-SETTLE-CARLISLE LINE

The LSC line was one of the greatest engineering achievements of the Victorian era, and it takes passengers across some of the best countryside in England. It serves a number of attractive market towns and gives excellent access to the western dales.

Orientation & Information

The LSC line runs between Leeds and Carlisle, along the Aire Valley then through Ribblesdale, Dentdale and the western edge of the Dales. There are good walks from some of the small stations along the way.

There are trains roughly every two hours Monday to Saturday year round, and five on Sunday. The entire journey takes two hours 40 minutes and costs £17.90 one way. There is a Freedom of the Line ticket for £30 valid for three days of unlimited travel.

The line is part of the national rail network and schedule and fare information calling ☎ 0845 748 4950. Various special trains operate through the year; call ☎ 09065 660607 for details.

The Journey

The first section of the journey is along the Aire Valley from Leeds.

The first stop is **Keighley,** the starting point for the Keighley & Worth Valley Railway to Haworth (of Brontë fame). See Haworth earlier for details.

Skipton is considered the gateway to the southern dales. After Skipton the railway crosses the moors to Ribblesdale and the attractive market town of **Settle**. Both of these towns are covered later in the chapter.

Next is the spectacular Ribbleshead Viaduct and Blea Moor Tunnel, linking Ribblesdale with Dentdale. The line crosses into Cumbria, where there's the attractive and popular village of **Dent**, 4 miles west of the station. *Dentdale Youth Hostel* (☎ *01539-625251, fax 625068*) is 2 miles south of Dent station. Call for the hostel's odd opening times. Beds cost £9.25/6.50 for adults/under-18s. The *Sun* (☎ *01539-625208*) is an excellent pub with beers from the nearby Dent Brewery and rooms from £19 per person.

After **Garsdale**, the train reaches its highest point (356m) at Ais Gill. Before **Kirkby Stephen** (see that section later in the chapter) are the ruins of Pendragon Castle, built in the 12th century and reputed to be the home of King Arthur's father.

Appleby is home to the famous Gipsy Horse Fair, held on the second Wednesday of June. After Appleby and to the east is Cross Fell, at 893m, the highest point on the Pennines. **Langwathby** is just north-west of Penrith, a jumping-off point for the Lakes. Armathwaite Viaduct is above the village and castle of **Combe Eden**, after which you reach **Carlisle** (see the Cumbria chapter).

Getting There & Away

For information about connecting services, see Leeds earlier in the chapter and Carlisle in the Cumbria chapter.

SKIPTON

☎ 01756 • pop 13,000

Skipton is a popular gateway to the Dales and a market town, so it can get very busy on summer weekends. The TIC (☎ 792809, fax 797528, e skipton@ytbtic.org.uk), 9 Sheep St, opens 10 am to 5 pm Monday to Friday and from 9 am on Saturday.

Skipton Castle (☎ 792442), at the top of High St, is considered to be one of the best-preserved medieval castles in Britain. You can tour from the dungeon to the look-out points. It opens 10 am to 6 pm daily (from noon on Sunday). Admission costs £4/2.

Most accommodation is on Keighley Rd, which is convenient for the train station. *Craven House (☎/fax 794657)* at No 56 has rooms with shared bathroom for £19 per person. *Highfield Hotel (☎/fax 793182)* at No 58 has rooms for £19 per person, all with bathroom.

Napier's Restaurant (☎ 799688, fax 798111, Chapel Hill) is lovely old 18th-century farmhouse near the centre of Skipton. The rooms cost from £33.50 per person and, as the name implies, it's also a restaurant, and a good one at that (£20 per head).

By the canal, *Bizzie Lizzies (☎ 793189, 36 Swadford St)* is a modern, large restaurant and takeaway, locally celebrated for the quality of its fish and chips (£4.50).

The train station is about half a mile out of town on Swadford Rd (A59). Skipton is on the famous LSC line and is only three stops north of Keighley; change for the Keighley & Worth Valley Railway (☎ 01535-645214) to Haworth. It is also the last stop on the Metro network out of Leeds and trains are frequent.

GRASSINGTON

☎ 01756 • pop 1200

Grassington is an attractive village that makes a good base for exploring the Dales, especially Upper Wharfedale.

See Information in the Yorkshire Dales National Park section for details of National Park visitors centre, which can book accommodation.

Linton Youth Hostel (☎ 752400, fax 753159, Linton) is three-quarters of a mile south of Grassington, in the adjoining hamlet of Linton. It opens Monday to Saturday from April to September, daily from June to August; telephone for its complicated opening schedule the rest of the year. Rates are £10/6.90 for adults/under-18s.

Raines Close (☎ 01756-752678, e raines close@yorks.net, 13 Station Rd) has comfortable doubles and twins from £21 per person.

The *Black Horse Hotel (☎ 752770, fax 753425, Garrs Lane)* is a good pub that was an old coaching inn. Rooms start at £30 per person.

From Skipton train station, Pride of the Dales bus Nos 71 and 72 depart about every two hours Monday to Saturday and four times a day on Sunday.

SETTLE & AROUND

☎ 01729 • pop 2500

Settle is a pleasant market town in Ribblesdale, on the edge of the geological fault that delineates the limestone to the north and the gritstone to the south. A wander round the village makes a good stroll but you really want to head up into the hills for the scenery and the views. Market day is Tuesday.

The TIC (☎ 825192, fax 824381, e set tle@ytbtic.co.uk) in the town hall opens 10 am to 5 pm daily, April to September, and closes at 4 pm the rest of the year.

The Three Peaks

The countryside to the north is dominated by the well known Three Peaks, which are part of a challenging 26-mile circuit involving 1500m of ascent. Beginning at Horton-in-Ribblesdale, you follow the Pennine Way to **Pen-y-ghent** (693m), with a distinctive sphinx-like shape.

Next is **Whernside** (736m), the northernmost peak, then finally **Ingleborough** (723m), which has a distinctive flat top of gritstone and was the site of a Celtic settlement – hut circles and parts of a defensive wall can still be seen.

Places to Stay & Eat
Knight Stainforth Hall (☎ *822200, Stackhouse Lane)*, opposite the high school, is about 3 miles from Settle; tent sites start at £8.75.

Stainforth Youth Hostel (☎ *823577, fax 825404,* e *stainforth@yha.org.uk, Stainforth)* is 2 miles north of Settle on the B6479 to Horton-in-Ribblesdale. It opens every Friday and Saturday night. The rest of the year, the openings are pegged to school holidays. Call for details. Beds cost £11/7.75 for adults/under-18s.

The *Golden Lion Hotel (* ☎ *822203, fax 824103, Duke St)* is central and has nice rooms from £24.50 per person. It also has a deservedly popular pub.

The *Royal Oak (* ☎ *822561, fax 823102, Market Place)* is a good pub with bar meals starting at around £5, including plenty of vegetarian dishes and salads; it also offers B&B from £28.50 per person.

Getting There & Away
Settle supplies the S on the LSC line. The train station is close to the centre.

MALHAM
☎ 01729 • pop 350

This pretty little village is a great 6-mile hike over the hills east from Settle. It gets crowded, not only for its charm but also for the natural wonders that are nearby. The 4½-mile-long **Malham Landscape Trail** circles Malham Cove, a huge natural amphitheatre. It also covers **Gordale Scar**, a deep limestone canyon with waterfalls and the remains of an Iron Age settlement. The hiking possibilities are many: the Pennine Way

passes right through town and you can follow an 11-mile path east to Grassington.

There's a National Park Visitors Centre (☎/fax 830363) open 10 am to 4 pm daily from April to October; weekends only at other times. It has the usual wealth of information and maps and can also book accommodation.

Malham Youth Hostel (☎ *01729-830321, fax 830551,* e *malham@yha.org.uk)* is right in the village centre. It opens daily and charges £11/7.75 for adults/under-18s.

The *Lister Arms Hotel (* ☎ *830330, fax 830323)* is a 17th-century coaching in that has an excellent pub, restaurant and gardens. Rooms cost from £22 per person.

If you don't want to hike, you'll probably have to drive as public transport here is woeful. The surrounding villages are lovely, one was the home of American writer Bill Bryson for many years.

KIRKBY LONSDALE
Kirkby Lonsdale is actually in Cumbria. It's outside the park borders but essentially a Dales town, both in appearance and as a useful touring centre. It has all the usual stores.

The TIC (☎/fax 015242-71437), 24 Main St, opens 9.30 am to 5 pm daily (10.30 am to 4.30 pm Sunday), April to October and 10.30 am to 4.30 pm Thursday to Sunday the rest of the year. It can find accommodation in the area, a useful service when towns inside the Dales are booked.

Kirkby Lonsdale is 17 miles from Settle and 15 miles from Windermere; the nearest railway connection is at Oxenholme (12 miles). Bus connections are not good at all.

KIRKBY STEPHEN
☎ 017683 • pop 1800

Kirkby Stephen is a classic market town with stone Georgian-style houses flanking an attractive High St. There's nothing very remarkable about the place but, like its Cumbrian colleague Kirkby Lonsdale, it can be a useful base for Dales explorations, especially during busy times. The market day is Monday.

The TIC (☎ 71199, fax 72728), Market St, opens 9.30 am to 5.30 pm daily (10 am to 4 pm Sunday), April to October; 10 am to noon and 2 to 4 pm Monday to Saturday, the rest of the year. It can find accommodation.

Kirkby Stephen is the central point on the **Coast to Coast Walk**, which runs from St Bees Head on the west coast to Robin Hood's Bay on the east (see the Activities chapter).

Kirkby Stephen Youth Hostel (☎/fax 71793, Market St) is in a converted chapel in the centre of town, south of Market Square. It opens Thursday to Monday, April to June; daily in July and August; and Wednesday to Monday in September and October. Beds cost £10/£6.90 for adults/under-18s.

The *Old Court House (☎/fax 71061, ☻ hilary-claxton@hotmail.com, High St)* has excellent accommodation and, yes, it's in the Old Court House. Rooms cost £17.50 per person.

Kirkby Stephen is on the LSC line.

HARROGATE

☎ 01423 • pop 65,800

After the grimy cities of the Midlands and parts of Yorkshire, Harrogate is reminiscent of the more prosperous south. Primarily built in the 19th century as a fashionable spa town, it has managed to remain affluent although its original excuse for existence – the health-giving effects of the mineral springs – doesn't really hold water anymore.

The town is famous for its spring and summer floral displays but the extensive gardens flanked by stately Victorian terraces are beautiful at any time of year. There are numerous high-quality hotels, B&Bs and restaurants which help to make Harrogate a restorative stop, especially if you've been busy tackling the Dales.

Orientation & Information

Harrogate is actually outside and south-east of the national park but makes an excellent touring base. The town is almost surrounded by gardens including the 200-acre Stray in the south.

The main shopping streets – Oxford St and Cambridge St – are lined with smart shops and malls and are mostly pedestrianised. The Conference Centre (☎ 500500) is on Kings Rd.

The TIC (☎ 537300, fax 537305, ☻ tic@harrogate.gov.uk), in the Royal Baths Assembly Rooms on Crescent Rd, opens 9 am to 6 pm Monday to Saturday and noon to 3 pm Sunday, April to September; 9 am to 5 pm weekdays and until 4 pm on Saturday the rest of the year.

The post office, 11 Cambridge Rd, opens 9 am to 5.30 pm Monday to Saturday.

The Waters

A visit should start at the ornate **Royal Pump Room Museum** (☎ 503340), Crown Place, built in 1842 over the most famous of the sulphur springs. It gives quite a curious insight into the phenomenon. It opens 10 am to 5 pm daily (from 2 pm Sunday), April to October. The rest of the year it closes at 4 pm. Admission costs £2/1.25. There are frequent special exhibitions.

You can experience the waters first-hand at the **Turkish Baths** (☎ 556746) in the Royal Baths Assembly Rooms. The entrance is on Parliament St around the corner from the TIC. The restored facility offers a full range of watery delights and a visit should last at least two hours. Start in the steam room, then plunge into the cold pool, recover your senses in the tepid pool and sympathise with lobsters in the hot pool. You can repeat this process as often as you like before relaxing in the Frigidarium, where you can drink beverages and read magazines.

Of course you enjoy the waters naked and (this being England and all) this means that there's a complicated schedule of opening hours that are at turns men-only and women-only – call for details on your sex. Overall the baths open 9 am to 9 pm daily and admission costs £9.50. There are a range of massages and other therapies for an extra cost that you can pre-book.

Mercer Art Gallery

The **Mercer Art Gallery** (☎ 556188), Swan Rd, is home to locally produced works of art and visiting shows. It also has a collection of local archaeological finds. It opens 10 am to 5 pm Tuesday to Saturday (from 2 pm on Sunday) and admission is free.

HARROGATE

PLACES TO STAY
1 The Alexander
2 Daryl House Hotel
3 Dragon House
4 Franklin Hotel
6 Old Swan Hotel
7 St George Hotel
10 Harrogate Brasserie & Hotel
21 Cavendish Hotel
26 The Imperial
28 Ashbrooke House

PLACES TO EAT
9 Oliver's 24
11 Graveley's
14 Rajput
15 Fino's Tapas Bar
23 Drum & Monkey
27 Betty's

OTHER
5 Conference Centre
8 Jimmy's
12 Bus Station
13 Harrogate Theatre
16 Turkish Baths
17 Tourist Information Centre
18 Mercer Art Gallery
19 Hales
20 Sun Pavilion
22 Royal Pump Room Museum
24 Post Office
25 Train Station

Gardens

The **Valley Gardens** are quite beautiful. Their crown jewel is the **Sun Pavilion** (☎ 522588), a vast and ornate glass-covered shelter that was built in 1933. Recently restored, it is the scene of concerts on Sunday afternoons from June to August.

The **West Park Stray** is another fine garden and park, south of the centre.

Tours

There are free historical walking tours offered daily from late-April to October. Times vary; check with the TIC for details.

Special Events

The Harrogate Flower Show is held in April. It is predictably immense.

The Great Yorkshire Show (☎ 541000) is the major annual exhibition staged each July by the Yorkshire Agricultural Society. It's a real treat, with all manner of farm critters competing for prizes and last year's losers served up in a variety of ways at innumerable food stands.

Places to Stay

Camping Two miles north of town, *Bilton Park* (☎ 863121, ⓔ tony@bilton-park*

.swinternet.co.uk, Village Farm, Bilton) has sites for £8. It opens late-April to October.

B&Bs Standards of accommodation in Harrogate are high and even at the cheapest places you can expect every room to be en suite and have a colour TV.

Franklin Hotel (☎ 569028, ⓔ *flack @frantel74.freeserve.uk, 25 Franklin Rd)* has simple singles/doubles for £17/36.

Dragon House (☎ 569888, *6 Dragon Parade)* has six basic rooms which cost £18/36.

Daryl House Hotel (☎ 502775, *fax 502775, 42 Dragon Parade)* has a pretty and quiet location and charges £19/38.

The Alexander (☎ 503348 *fax 540230, 88 Franklin Rd)* is a fully restored Victorian mansion that is entirely nonsmoking. The comfortable rooms cost £24/46.

Ashbrooke House (☎/fax 564478, *140 Valley Dr)* is close to Valley Gardens and has fine rooms that cost £27/50.

Cavendish Hotel (☎ 509637, *fax 504434, 3 Valley Dr)* has very comfortable rooms and can cater for vegetarians. Rates start at £32/50.

Hotels The *Harrogate Brasserie & Hotel* (☎ 505041, *fax 722300,* ⓔ *harrogate.bras serie@zoom.co.uk, 28–30 Cheltenham Parade)* has 14 rooms, each with its own stylish decor, costing from £45/65 for a single/ double. It has an excellent restaurant and frequent live jazz.

The Imperial (☎ 565071, *fax 500082, Prospect Place)* is a grand hotel in the centre of town with good views of the Stray. The ornate rooms start at £95/109.

The *St George Hotel* (☎ 561431, *fax 530037, 1 Ripon Rd)* has a commanding position across from the TIC. The rooms are posh and there is an indoor pool, health club and more. Rates start at £95/120. The hotel was recently bought by the Marriott organisation.

The *Old Swan Hotel* (☎ 500055, *fax 501154, Swan Rd)* is an ivy-clad 18th-century coaching house set in 5 acres of gardens. This is where Agatha Christie chose to hide from the world when she did a runner in 1926. Rooms cost from £105/120.

Places to Eat

Harrogate Brasserie & Hotel (see Places to Stay) has a French dinner menu with many vegetarian options. There's a good wine list and you can have three courses for £15.

The *Drum & Monkey* (☎ 502650, *5 Montpellier Gardens)* is a hugely popular, traditional seafood restaurant that fairly reeks of garlic butter. The changing menu always reflects what's fresh. Expect to pay £20 and up per person. It's closed on Sunday.

Fino's Tapas Bar (☎ 565806, *31 Cheltenham Parade)* is bright and cheerful, not unlike the food. The long list of small dishes average about £4.

Rajput (☎ 562113, *9–11 Cheltenham Parade)* has very good Indian food for £4 to £6. It opens until 11 pm.

Oliver's 24 (☎ 568600, *24 King's Rd)* is a light and airy cafe set in an old Victorian house. Very good Modern British meals cost £10.50/13.95 for two/three courses.

Betty's (☎ 502746, *1 Parliament St)* is a classic Yorkshire tea-room dating from 1919. It has a large variety of teas, coffees and teacakes, and reasonably priced soups, sandwiches and main meals (under £7). It opens 9 am (for breakfast) to 9 pm. A pianist plays from 6 pm.

Graveley's (☎ 507093, *8–10 Cheltenham Parade)* serves tasty fish and chips (£5.50) from its takeaway operation. There are outside tables. The main restaurant has a long and varied menu with many fish items for £5 to £8.

Harrogate Theatre (see Entertainment) has a grand old cafe that's popular at lunch.

Entertainment

Hales (☎ 725571, *1 Crescent Rd)* is a traditional pub serving meals. A highlight of the wooden interior is the vintage gas lighting.

There's nothing traditional about *Jimmy's* (☎ 544100, *16 Kings Rd)*, which is a raucous nightclub popular with a young crowd.

Harrogate Theatre (☎ 502116, *Oxford St)* stages serious drama through the year.

Getting There & Away

Harrogate is roughly between Leeds (15 miles) and York (22 miles) and is best reached by train. It is on the line that runs between Leeds (£4.10, 38 minutes, every 30 minutes) and York (£4.10, 40 minutes, hourly). The modern train station has lockers.

Getting Around

Harrogate is easily walkable (and a healthy stroll is in keeping with local traditions).

Spa Cycles (☎ 887003), 1 Wedderburn Rd, about 10 minutes south-east of the train station, rents bikes from £10 per day.

RICHMOND

☎ 01748 • pop 8000

Richmond is one of the most beautiful towns in England – and surprisingly few people know. A ruined castle perches high on a rocky outcrop overlooking a rushing stream, and looms over the steeply sloping Market Square, which is surrounded by Georgian buildings. Cobbled streets, closely lined with stone cottages, radiate from the square and run down to the river, providing exhilarating glimpses of the surrounding hills and moors.

The town is just north of Catterick Garrison, one of the most important British Army bases.

Orientation & Information

Richmond is to the east of the actual national park but it makes an excellent touring base for the park and is definitely in the Yorkshire Dales. Market day on the square is Saturday.

The TIC (☎ 850252, fax 825994, ⓔ richmond@ytbtic.co.uk) Friary Gardens, Victoria Rd, opens 9.30 am to 5.30 pm daily, April to October, and 9.30 am to 4.30 pm Monday to Saturday, the rest of the year. It has good brochures (from 40p to 90p) showing walks around the town and surrounding countryside, including one to Easby Abbey.

Free walking tours leave from the TIC at 2.15 pm every Sunday from May to September. The self-guiding *Richmond Town Trail* (£1) is an excellent historical booklet sold by the TIC.

The post office, 6 Queen's Rd, opens 9 am to 5.30 pm weekdays and until 12.30 pm on Saturday.

Richmond Castle

Begun in 1071, Richmond Castle (☎ 822493; EH) was built by William the Conquerer to help subdue the rebellious north. It was one of the first in England to be built out of stone and was so stout that it was never successfully besieged. It has had a myriad of uses through the years, including a stint as a prison for conscientious objectors during WWI.

The castle features surviving 11th-century curtain walls, a gatehouse, a chapel and what is believed to be the oldest surviving Norman great hall (Scollard's Hall). The impressive 30m-high keep (1171), beside the gatehouse, is in remarkably good condition. It has been refloored and reroofed to give an idea of what it was like in medieval times.

It's a dramatic ruin so it's not surprising that legends (however unlikely) cling to it like moss: some say an underground tunnel links it to Easby Abbey, and that King Arthur and his knights are in a magical sleep here and will wake when the country needs them.

It opens 10 am to 6 pm daily, April to September; and 10 am to 4 pm the rest of the year. Admission costs £2.60/1.30.

Museums

The **Richmondshire Museum** (☎ 825611), Ryder's Wynd, is a small but interesting local history museum. It has displays on the lead mining industry which forever altered the local landscape. It opens 11 am to 5 pm daily, Good Friday to late-October. Admission costs £1.50/1.

Green Howards Museum (☎ 822133), Market Place, shows the history of the Green Howards, a famous Yorkshire regiment that fought battles from the Crimean War to WWII. It opens 9.30 am to 4.30 pm Monday to Saturday and from 2 pm on Sunday, April to October; and 10 am to 4.30 pm Monday to Friday in February, March and November. Admission costs £3/2.

Georgian Theatre Royal

Built in 1788, the Georgian Theatre Royal (☎ 823021), Victoria Rd, this is the oldest theatre in the UK surviving in its original form. It opens for guided tours 10.30 am to 3.45 pm Monday to Saturday (11 am to

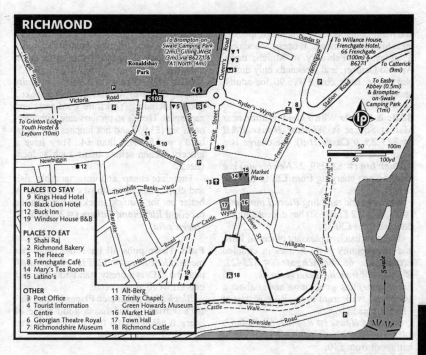

RICHMOND

PLACES TO STAY
9 Kings Head Hotel
10 Black Lion Hotel
12 Buck Inn
19 Windsor House B&B

PLACES TO EAT
1 Shahi Raj
2 Richmond Bakery
5 The Fleece
8 Frenchgate Café
14 Mary's Tea Room
15 Latino's

OTHER
3 Post Office
4 Tourist Information Centre
6 Georgian Theatre Royal
7 Richmondshire Museum
11 Alt-Berg
13 Trinity Chapel; Green Howards Museum
16 Market Hall
17 Town Hall
18 Richmond Castle

YORKSHIRE

1.15 pm on Sunday), April to October. Admission costs £1.50/1. There are local dramatic productions staged at various times through the year.

Market Place

Staid **Trinity Chapel** dominates Market Place, a classic market square that dates back at least 900 years. It was once the outer bailey of the castle, which accounts for its horseshoe shape. Bits of the chapel once formed the castle's church and in the intervening years it has had a number of uses, including as prison, warehouse and school.

The **Town Hall** is classically Georgian and dates from 1756. The **Market Hall** has a similar pedigree.

Cycling Routes

Cycling on the narrow Dales roads isn't fun on a busy summer weekend; that point aside, this is great cycling country.

One cycle route to consider is a 20-mile

trip to Barnard Castle along the edge of the Cleveland Plain. Take the B6271 to Gilling West, then the B-roads south of the A66 through Whashton, Kirby Hill, Gayles, Dalton, Newsham, Barningham and Greta Bridge. Turn right onto the A66 for a short section, then left for Barnard Castle (a steep climb).

Another possibility is the 33-mile trip to Kirkby Stephen along beautiful Swaledale.

Places to Stay

Camping Offering tent sites (from £3.60) along the River Swale is *Brompton on Swale Camping Park* (☎ 824629, fax 826383). There's a riverside path all the way to Richmond. To reach the camp by road, take the B6271 east from where it branches off from the A6108 just north of Richmond.

Hostels The nearest is *Grinton Lodge Youth Hostel* (☎ 884206, fax 884876, ⓔ grinton@yha.org.uk, Grinton), 10 miles to the west, and south of the B6270 between Richmond and Reeth. Built as a shooting lodge, the hostel is high on the moors. It opens Monday to Saturday, mid-February to March; daily, April to October; and weekends only during November. Beds cost £10/6.90 for adults/under-18s.

B&Bs & Hotels With a great position near Market Square is *Windsor House B&B* (☎ 823285, 9 Castle Hill); the charge is a reasonable £18.

Buck Inn (☎ 822259, 27 Newbiggin) is a nice old pub charging from £22 to £26 per person.

The large and rambling *Black Lion Hotel* (☎ 823121, 12 Finkle St) has decent singles/doubles from £20/35.

There's a batch of pleasant places in 17th- and 18th-century town houses in cobbled Frenchgate. *66 Frenchgate* (☎ 823421, ⓔ paul@66french.freeserve.co.uk, 66 Frenchgate) has good views and is about a 10-minute walk from town. Rooms start at £18 per person.

Willance House (☎ 824467, fax 824467, 24 Frenchgate) has doubles with TV and bathroom from £40.

More upmarket, the *Frenchgate Hotel* (☎ 822087, fax 823596, 59–61 Frenchgate) has comfortable rooms costing between £60 to £78. It has a bar, gardens and parking.

Kings Head Hotel (☎ 850220, fax 850635, ⓔ res@khead.demon.co.uk, Market Place) overlooks the central square and has comfortable rooms and a range of services. There's some nice touches, such as the school photos of the owners' kids scattered about. Rooms cost from £50/70.

Places to Eat

Restaurants & Cafes The *Shahi Raj* (☎ 826070, 8 Queen's Rd) has a classic Indian curry house menu with most items from £5 to £8.

Frenchgate Café (☎ 824949, 29 Frenchgate) is open late for coffees and espresso. They have good sandwiches at lunch for less than £3. Dinner is served until 9 pm and you can have a two-course modern British treat for less than £12.

Latino's (☎ 825008, 2 Trinity Church Square) is up a flight of stairs and serves an extensive range of fresh pastas and other mains costing £8 to £15. It has an excellent wine list.

Mary's Tea Room (☎ 824052, 5 Trinity Church Square) offers delicious baked goods, including Yorkshire curd tarts and game pies. There's an upstairs cafe with afternoon tea (£3.95) and hot lunches like shepherd's pie for less than £4. They have a grocery section selling items such as local cheese.

There are cheap, and unremarkable, fish and chips places on almost every block. A better bet for a quick snack or lunch is the excellent *Richmond Bakery* (☎ 850625, 10 Queen's Rd).

Pubs These pubs all have the usual bar meals. *The Fleece* (☎ 825733, Victoria Rd), near the TIC, is a pretty standard place that gets crowded at weekends.

Black Lion Hotel (see Places to Stay earlier) is friendly and has a good range of beers. It has several different bars scattered about its historic interior.

Shopping

Finkle St, off Market Square, has some interesting shops. Alt-Berg (☎ 850615) at No 14 sells a wide range of outdoor gear. They have their own line of boots, rent all manner of walking gear and sell maps.

Getting There & Away

North East bus company runs numerous regular services (bus Nos 27, X27 and 28) to/from Darlington (30 to 50 minutes), which has a major train station at the junction of several lines (including the main east-coast line from London's King's Cross to Edinburgh).

FOUNTAINS ABBEY & STUDLEY ROYAL WATER GARDEN

Sheltered in a secluded valley, with a number of monumental buildings surrounded by extensive parkland and gardens, this complex in the narrow valley of the River Skell is the only World Heritage Site in Yorkshire.

It includes the magnificent ruins of Fountains Abbey, a 12th-century Cistercian abbey; Fountains Hall (1610), a five-storey Jacobean mansion; St Mary's Church, a sumptuous Victorian church built in the 1870s; and a number of 18th-century follies. These are all set within a beautiful, 18th-century, 800-acre, landscaped park built around a series of artificial lakes and designed to feature the abbey ruins.

History

Fountains Abbey began as a small breakaway group of 13 monks from the Benedictine abbey of St Mary's in York. In 1132 the Archbishop of York granted them land in what was virtual wilderness. Lacking assistance from any established abbey or order, they turned to the Cistercian order for help.

The Cistercians were often called the White Monks because they wore a habit of undyed wool, reflecting the austerity and simplicity of their order. They were committed to long periods of silence and eight daily services. Clearly, this didn't leave much time for practical matters. So the Cistercians ordained lay brothers who lived within the monastery but pursued the abbey's ever-growing business interests – wool, lead mining, quarrying, animal breeding and so on.

Sadly, the idealism and purity didn't last long. After economic collapse in the 14th century, the monks rented their lands to tenant farmers and replaced lay brothers with servants. By the beginning of the 16th century the vast abbey had a population of only 30 monks.

After the dissolution the estate was sold into private hands and between 1598 and 1611 Fountains Hall was built with stone from the abbey ruins. The hall passed through several families until it and the ruins were united with the Studley Royal Estate in 1768.

The main house of Studley Royal burnt down in 1946 but the superb landscaping survives virtually unchanged from the 18th century. Studley Royal was owned by John Aislabie, who spent 20 years creating an extensive park. Major engineering works were required to create the lakes and to control the flow of the river.

Orientation & Information

Fountains Abbey lies 4 miles west of Ripon off the B6265. There are two entrances, one leaving the B road 1½ miles from Ripon, for the Canal Gates entrance, and one 3 miles from Ripon, for the impressive visitor centre (☎ 01765-608888; NT).

The abbey, hall, water garden and visitor centre open 10 am to 7 pm daily, April to September and until 5 pm the rest of the year. The deer park opens daily during daylight hours. St Mary's Church was undergoing restoration in 2000; phone for its reopening date.

Admission to the abbey, hall and garden costs £4.30/2.10; the deer park is free.

There are free one-hour guided tours at 2.30 pm daily, April to October; and at 11 am and 3.30 pm, May to September. There's almost no public transport, call the abbey for details of any buses that might be running.

Cumbria

Much of Cumbria is a scenic feast, with the Lake District National Park at its heart. The mountains, valleys and lakes are beautiful, although ever since they were popularised by the early-19th-century Romantics they've been the centre of a major tourism industry. Nonetheless, if you avoid summer weekends and the main roads and do some walking, it's still possible, like Wordsworth, to wander 'lonely as a cloud'.

The M6 and west-coast railway cut the county into an eastern third, which runs into the Yorkshire Dales and Pennine Hills, and a western two-thirds that includes the Lake District National Park and England's highest mountains. Not surprisingly, the western area draws the largest crowds, although bits of the east, particularly the Eden Valley, are also very beautiful.

WALKING

Cumbria offers some of the best walks in Britain. See the Activities chapter for information on the Cumbria Way, and the Lake District National Park later in the chapter. For more details, see Lonely Planet's *Walking in Britain*.

CYCLING ROUTES

This is also a good area for cycling. Keen cyclists should consider the waymarked 259-mile circular Cumbria Cycle Way. It can be done in five days, but a full week is better. For more details look for *The Cumbria Cycle Way* by Roy Walker and Ron Jarvis. Carlisle's tourist information centre (TIC) also stocks plenty of information.

Another possibility is the 140-mile Sea To Sea (C2C) route from Whitehaven or Workington to Newcastle or Sunderland. Most people will need five days to complete this cross-country route. The *National Cycleway Network Guide* provides all the details.

If you're planning to cycle along Hadrian's Wall, TICs sell the *Hadrian's Wall Country Cycle Map* (£2.50).

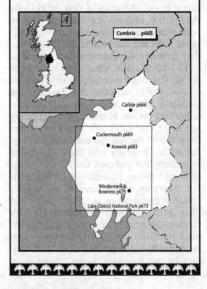

GETTING AROUND

Cumbria Journey Planner (☎ 01228-606000) provides information on all local bus, boat and train services. It opens 9 am to 5 pm Monday to Friday, 9 am to noon on Saturday.

Bus

The main operator is Stagecoach (☎ 0870 608 2608). Its Explorer tickets give unlimited travel on all services, including the No 685 to Newcastle upon Tyne and Stagecoach Ribble buses in Lancashire, and half-price travel on bus No 682 running along

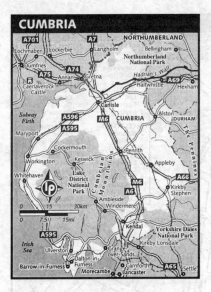

CUMBRIA

Hadrian's Wall. They cost £5.75/4.25 (adult/child) for one day or £13.60/9.50 for four days, but check carefully that you're doing enough travelling to save on the deal. One-day tickets can be bought on any bus and four-day tickets are on sale at TICs.

Tours

Mountain Goat offers half-day (around £14) and full-day (around £24) escorted minivan tours of Cumbria and the Lake District. If you don't have your own transport this offers a good way of getting to some of the more remote areas, especially out of season. Mountain Goat is at Victoria St, Windermere (☎ 015394-45161, ⓔ mountain-goat@lakes-pages.co.uk) and Central Car Park Rd, Keswick (☎ 017687-73962), but has lots of other pick-up points and can pick up from hotels.

CARLISLE

☎ 01228 • pop 72,000

Modern Carlisle may be sleepy and small now, but its location as a border town made peace impossible for 1600 years as it defended the north of England, or the south of Scotland depending on who was winning. Although its character was spoilt to some extent by 19th-century industrialisation, it's an interesting town and its strategic location can be exploited by visitors to Northumberland, Hadrian's Wall, Dumfries & Galloway, the beautiful Scottish Borders, as well as the Lake District. It's also a hub for five excellent rail journeys.

History

Carlisle's history has been dominated by warfare and it seems miraculous that it could be peaceful today. The Romans under Agricola built a military station here, probably on the site of a Celtic camp or *caer* (preserved in the modern name of Carlisle).

Later, Hadrian's Wall was built a little to the north, and Carlisle became the Roman administrative centre for the north-west. But even the mighty Roman Empire was hard-pressed to maintain control and the Picts sacked the town in AD 181 and 367.

Carlisle survived into Saxon times, but was under constant pressure from the Scots and was sacked by Danish Vikings in 875. The Normans seized it from the Scots in 1092 and William Rufus began construction of the castle and town walls, but the Scots gained control again between 1136 and 1157. Forty years later the city withstood a siege by the Scottish King William. Sixty years later it managed to repulse William Wallace during the Scottish War of Independence.

The Scottish Borders, or the Debateable Lands as they were known, were virtually ungovernable from the late 13th century to the middle of the 17th century. The great families with their complex blood feuds fought and robbed the English, the Scots and each other. The city's walls, Courts (two rotund structures to the south of the centre) and the great gates that slammed shut every night served a very real purpose.

During the Civil War, Carlisle was Royalist, and was eventually taken by the Scottish army after a nine-month siege from 1644 to 1645. In 1745 it also surrendered to Bonnie Prince Charlie, who proclaimed his father king at the market cross.

After the Restoration, peace came at last to Carlisle. So, eventually, did industry, cotton mills and railways.

CUMBRIA

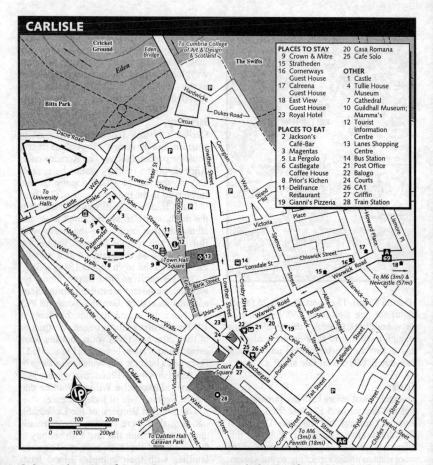

CARLISLE

PLACES TO STAY
9 Crown & Mitre
15 Stratheden
16 Cornerways
   Guest House
17 Calreena
   Guest House
18 East View
   Guest House
23 Royal Hotel

PLACES TO EAT
2 Jackson's
   Café-Bar
3 Magentas
5 La Pergolo
6 Castlegate
   Coffee House
8 Prior's Kichen
11 Delifrance
   Restaurant
19 Gianni's Pizzeria

20 Casa Romana
25 Cafe Solo

OTHER
1 Castle
4 Tullie House
   Museum
7 Cathedral
10 Guildhall Museum;
   Mamma's
12 Tourist
   Information
   Centre
13 Lanes Shopping
   Centre
14 Bus Station
21 Post Office
22 Balogo
24 Courts
26 CA1
27 Griffin
28 Train Station

Orientation & Information

The train station is south of the city centre, a 10-minute walk from Town Hall Square and the TIC. You will find the bus station on Lowther St, one block east of the square.

The TIC (☎ 625600, fax 625604, ⓔ tour ism@carlisle-city.gov.uk) in Town Hall Square stocks an enormous quantity of literature and opens 9.30 am to 5 pm Monday to Saturday (to 6 pm July and August) and 10.30 am to 4 pm on Sunday, May to September; and 10 am to 4 pm Monday to Saturday, November to February.

Carlisle Castle

Probably built on the site of British and Roman fortresses, brooding Carlisle Castle (☎ 591922), run by English Heritage (EH), is well worth exploring. The fine Norman keep was built in 1092 by William Rufus, and Mary Queen of Scots was briefly imprisoned here in 1568 after she was abdicated from the Scottish throne. There is a maze of passages and chambers and great views from the ramparts. It opens 9.30 am to 6 pm daily, April to September (to 5 pm in October and 4 pm from November to March). Admission costs £3/1.50.

Carlisle Cathedral

The small, red sandstone cathedral was originally constructed as a priory church in 1123
but became a cathedral in 1133. During the
1644–45 siege, two-thirds of the nave was
torn down to provide stone for repairing the
city wall and castle. Serious restoration
didn't begin until 1853 but a surprising
amount survives, including the eastern window and part of the original Norman nave.

Features to look out for include the 15th-
century misericords, including one with a
mermaid; the lovely Brougham Triptych (a
16th-century carved Flemish altarpiece)
from Antwerp in the northern transept; and
the treasury at the western end. The cathedral opens 7.30 am to 6.15 pm Monday to
Saturday, and to 5 pm on Sunday. Visitors
are asked to donate £2.

Surrounding the cathedral are other relics
of the priory, including the 16th-century
Fratry (housing the Prior's Kitchen Restaurant) and the **Prior's Tower**.

Tullie House Museum

The excellent Tullie House Museum is particularly strong on Roman Carlisle, with lots
of information on Hadrian's Wall. A lively
section is devoted to the Border Reivers (see
the boxed text 'The Border Reivers' later in
the chapter). The museum (☎ 534781) opens
10 am to 5 pm Monday to Saturday and noon
to 5 pm on Sunday year round. Admission
costs £3.75/2.50. The separate Georgian
house outside has a gallery of childhood
open noon to 4 pm. Admission is free. It's
worth dropping into the Garden Restaurant
and the small art gallery afterwards.

Guildhall Museum

The small Guildhall Museum (☎ 532781)
was built as a townhouse in the 15th century, but was later occupied by Carlisle's
trade guilds. It opens as a local history museum noon to 4.30 pm Thursday to Sunday,
from Easter to October.

Places to Stay

Camping The *Dalston Hall Caravan Park*
(☎ 710165), just off the B5299 to the south
of the city, has caravan and tent sites from £6.

Hostels The University halls double as the
Carlisle Youth Hostel (☎ 597352, @ dee.car
ruthers@unn.ac.uk), from early July to early
September, in the Old Brewery Residences
on Bridge Lane. A bed costs £12.50/8.75 for
adults/under 18s.

B&Bs & Hotels With plenty of comfortable B&Bs within walking distance of the
city centre, you shouldn't have to pay more
than £16.

The small and friendly *Stratheden*
(☎ 520192, 93 Warwick Rd) has pleasingly
decorated rooms for £16 to £20 per head.
Cornerways Guest House (☎ 521733, 107
Warwick Rd) is larger and does B&B from
£16. *East View Guesthouse* (☎ 522112, 110
Warwick Rd) has single/double rooms with
bath costing £20/34. *Calreena Guest House*
(☎ 525020, 123 Warwick Rd) charges from
£15 to £16.

Two minutes from the train station, the
Royal Hotel (☎ 522103, fax 523904, 9
Lowther St) has a range of rooms from
£17.50/42. Moving upmarket, the Victorian
Crown & Mitre (☎ 525491, fax 514553,
English St), overlooking Town Hall Square,
has been refurbished to provide modern
rooms from £54.50.

Places to Eat

If you like Italian food, you'll do well in
Carlisle where many places have happy
hours from 5.30 to 7 pm with meals for
around £3.50. *La Pergolo* (☎ 34084, 28
Castle St), *Gianni's Pizzeria* (☎ 521093,
Cecil St) and *Casa Romana* (☎ 591969, 44
Warwick St) are all popular places to tuck
into pizza and pasta.

If Italian is not your thing, *Cafe Solo*
(☎ 631600, The Crescent), near the train station, is a popular place serving international-
style food such as nachos grande for £3.95.

For something a bit more upmarket, try
Magentas (☎ 546363, 18 Fisher St) with a
set menu costing £18 per person.

The *Prior's Kitchen Restaurant* in the
old Fratry beside the cathedral provides an
atmospheric vaulted room in which to eat
light lunches. Nearby, *Castlegate Coffee
House* (☎ 592353, Castle Court, Castle St)

offers an old-fashioned ambience in which to take tea.

There's a branch of **Delifrance** *(☎ 591323, 35 Fisher St)* with great sandwiches, behind the TIC. **Jackson's Café-Bar** *(☎ 596868, 4 Fisher St)* stays open until 2 am and doubles as a club at the weekend.

Entertainment
Bar hopping and 'getting lashed' are common practices in much of northern England, and Carlisle is no exception to the rule. It's hard to find a pub not jam-packed and blaring out music on a Saturday night. Much of the action is centred just south of the city centre near the train station. **Balogo** *(Warwick Rd)* and **CA1** *(☎ 530460, Botchergate)* are the flavours of the month for the young and trendy and you'd be hard pressed to find a more buzzing place than the cavernous **Griffin** *(Botchergate)*.

Getting There & Away
Carlisle is 299 miles from London, 98 miles from Edinburgh, 95 miles from Glasgow, 115 miles from York and Manchester and 58 miles from Newcastle upon Tyne.

Bus Numerous National Express connections can be booked at the TIC. There are five buses to/from London (£22, 6½ hours) and many to Glasgow (£12.75, two hours). Six buses a day run to Manchester (£16, three hours).

For information on Stagecoach buses, phone ☎ 0870 608 2608. The Lakeslink 555 passes through Keswick, Grasmere, Ambleside, Windermere and Kendal on its way to Lancaster. No 104 connects Carlisle with Penrith where the X4/5 connects with Keswick, Cockermouth and Workington.

A Rail Link coach service runs from the train station to Hawick, Selkirk and Galashiels in the Scottish Borders.

The Hadrian's Wall Bus No 682/685 connects Carlisle with Haltwhistle, Hexham and Newcastle.

Train Fifteen trains a day link Carlisle with London Euston station (from £26, four hours).

Carlisle is the terminus for five famous scenic railways; phone ☎ 0845 748 4950 for information on day Ranger tickets (offering unlimited travel) and timetable details.

Leeds-Settle-Carlisle Line cuts across the Yorkshire Dales south-eastwards through beautiful, unspoilt countryside (£17.90, 2¾ hours).

Lakes Line branches off the main north–south Preston and Carlisle line at Oxenholme, just outside Kendal, for Windermere; there are plenty of trains daily (£2.95, 20 minutes).

Tyne Valley Line follows Hadrian's Wall to/from Newcastle upon Tyne. See Newcastle upon Tyne and Hadrian's Wall in the North-Eastern England chapter (£9.10, 1½ hours).

Cumbrian Coast Line (see that section later in the chapter) follows the coast in a great arc around to Lancaster, with views over the Irish Sea, and back to the Lake District (£17, one hour).

Glasgow-Carlisle Line is the main route north to Glasgow and gives you a taste of the spectacular Scottish landscape. Most trains make a few stops (from £10.80, 1½ hours).

COCKERMOUTH
☎ 01900 • pop 7000
Lying outside the Lake District National Park, Cockermouth is an attractive small town, well placed for exploring the less populous north-west (especially beautiful Crummock Water and Buttermere). In fact, being outside the park has saved it from the worst excesses of Lakes tourism. It may have been discovered but so far it hasn't been spoilt.

Information
The TIC (☎ 822634), in the town hall, opens 9.30 am to 4.30 pm Monday to Saturday (until 5 pm from July to September). Fellside Sports (☎ 823071) on Main St stocks outdoor gear.

Wordsworth House
This Georgian country house (☎ 824805), built in 1745 and run by the National Trust (NT), was the birthplace and childhood home of William Wordsworth and his sister Dorothy. It's furnished in 18th-century style and contains some Wordsworth memorabilia. It opens 10.30 am to 4.30 pm weekdays late March to October, and on summer Saturdays. Admission costs £3/1.50.

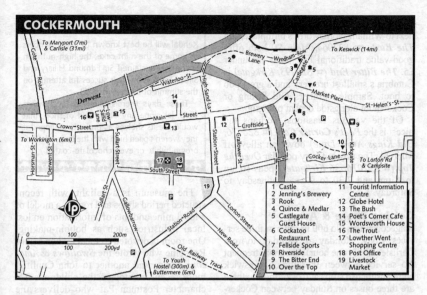

COCKERMOUTH

To Maryport (7mi) & Carlisle (31mi)
Cote Road
Derwent
To Workington (6mi)
Crown Street
Sullart Street
Derwent St
Horsman St
Waterloo St
Main Street
Low Lane
Brewery Lane
Wyndham Row
High Sand Lane
Castlegate
Market Place
St Helen's St
Croftside
Station Street
Crallower St
Cocker Lane
Kirkgate
South Street
Sullart St
Gallowbarrow
Lorton Street
Station Road
New Road
Old Railway Track
To Youth Hostel (300m) & Buttermere (6mi)
To Keswick (14mi)
To Lorton Rd & Campsite

0   100   200m
0   100   200yd

1 Castle	11 Tourist Information
2 Jenning's Brewery	Centre
3 Rook	12 Globe Hotel
4 Quince & Medlar	13 The Bush
5 Castlegate	14 Poet's Corner Cafe
Guest House	15 Wordsworth House
6 Cockatoo	16 The Trout
Restaurant	17 Lowther Went
7 Fellside Sports	Shopping Centre
8 Riverside	18 Post Office
9 The Bitter End	19 Livestock
10 Over the Top	Market

Jenning's Brewery

If you appreciate decent beer, you'll very quickly find yourself enjoying Mr Jenning's traditionally brewed products, particularly the Dark Mild and Bitter, brewed here for over 170 years. From mid-February to October, the brewery (☎ 821011) alongside the River Cocker offers 1½-hour tours (£3/1.50) at 11 am and 2 pm Monday to Friday, with 12.30 pm tours in July and August, and at 11 am and 2 pm on Saturday and Sunday from April to September. Children aged under 12 are not admitted.

Places to Stay

Camping Nearest is *Violet Bank Holiday Home Park* (☎ 822169, *Simonscales Lane*), off Lorton Rd. Tent pitches cost from £5.

Hostels The *Cockermouth Youth Hostel* (☎ 822561, *Double Mills*) is on the southern edge of town in a 17th-century water mill. From Main St follow Station St, then Station Rd. Keep left after the war memorial, then left into Fern Bank Rd. Take the track at the end of Fern Bank. The hostel opens daily mid-April to October. Beds cost £8.50/5.75 for adults/under-18s.

B&Bs & Hotels In a beautiful Georgian town house, B&B at *Castlegate Guest House* (☎ 826749, *6 Castlegate*) costs from £17.50 to £20 per person and serves packed lunches for £3.50. It's opposite the Quince & Medlar restaurant (see Places to Eat). Readers have also recommended the similarly priced *Rook* (☎ 828496, *9 Castlegate*) across the road. By the time you read this, the *Riverside* (☎ 827504, *12 Market St*), next to the TIC, should have opened. It's well placed on the river in a quiet corner.

The Globe Hotel (☎ 822126, *Main St*) has singles/doubles costing £25/48. Robert Louis Stephenson stayed here when he visited Cockermouth in 1871.

Places to Eat

The *Quince & Medlar* (☎ 823579, *12 Castlegate*) is one of the country's best vegetarian restaurants and booking is advisable. The menu features main dishes such as celery and stilton strudel for £8.45, with starters costing around £4.50. It opens evenings Tuesday to Saturday. The exuberant *Cockatoo Restaurant* (☎ 826205, *Market Place*) around the corner also does vegetarian and vegan food, such as Chinese mushrooms for £9.99.

The *Trout Hotel (☎ 823591, Crown St)*, next to William Wordsworth's birthplace, and *The Bush (☎ 822064, Main St)* both offer good-value traditional bar meals for under £5. *The Bitter End (☎ 828993, Kirkgate)* is Cumbria's smallest brewery and a great pub to boot. Sample Skinners Old Strong or Cockersnoot alongside decent pub grub.

Of the various teashops, perhaps the nicest is the *Poet's Corner Café (☎ 828676, Old Kings Arms Lane)* down an alley off Main St. The tiny but very popular *Over the Top (☎ 827016, 36 Kirkgate)* opens 10 am to 4 pm and 7.30 to 9 pm Wednesday to Saturday.

Getting There & Away

Stagecoach Bus No 600 has two or three services a day, Monday to Saturday, to/from Carlisle (£3.05, one hour). The more frequent X5 service between Workington, Keswick and Penrith also stops at Cockermouth; there are three buses on Sunday between Cockermouth and Keswick (£2.40, 30 minutes).

KENDAL

☎ 01539 • pop 23,400

On the eastern outskirts of the Lake District National Park, Kendal is a lively town that has had a market since the 12th century. While it's not particularly beautiful and central to the Lakes, it does have several interesting museums, including the Museum of Lakeland Life, which more than justifies a visit.

The TIC (☎ 725758), in the town hall in Highgate, opens 9 am to 5 pm Monday to Saturday (to 6 pm in summer) and 10 am to 4 pm on Sunday from April to October. As well as the museums and art gallery, you can clamber up to the ruins of Kendal Castle, just to the west of the river, where Henry VIII's last wife Catherine Parr is believed to have lived.

Museums & Galleries

To the south of town, in the grounds of Abbott Hall on the banks of the River Kent, you'll find the **Museum of Lakeland Life** and the **Abbot Hall Art Gallery** (☎ 722464, fax 722494).

The Climbers' Friend

Kendal will be best known to many climbers as home of the mint cake, the high-nutrition snack that sustained Sir Edmund Hillary and Sirdar Tensing on their successful attempt on the summit of Everest in 1953.

These days there's barely a local sweet shop, let alone any other kind of shop, that would see its shelves as properly equipped if they weren't piled high with the bars, whether brown, white or even chocolate-coated.

The museum is a delight, with reconstructed period shops and rooms, a model of a local mine and lots of information on lost local industries such as bobbin-making. One room is devoted to local author Arthur Ransome who wrote the *Swallows & Amazons* books, and another to John Cunliffe, more recent creator of the children's TV character Postman Pat who delivers the mail in Greendale (aka Longsleddale).

The Abbot Hall Art Gallery also makes much of local artist George Romney (1734–1802), many of whose portraits and drawings are on display. The temporary exhibitions on the 1st floor can be particularly worthwhile.

The **Kendal Museum** (☎ 721374) in Station Rd has collections on natural history and archaeology.

All three museums open 10.30 am to 5 pm daily from mid-February until Christmas, but close at 4 pm February, March, November and December. Admission to each costs £3/1.50, although once you've visited one you can see the others for £1.

Places to Stay & Eat

Beds at *Kendal Youth Hostel (☎ 724066, fax 724906, 118 Highgate)* cost £12.80/9.65 for adults/under-18s. It opens daily from mid-April to August, closing on Sunday and Monday from September to October and mid-February to mid-April, and open Friday and Saturday from November to mid-February.

Fortywinx (☎ 720576, ⓔ fortywinxken dal@hotmail.com, 22 Gillingate), a new backpackers hostel, is a good alternative; dorm beds start at £10 with breakfast.

Martindales (☎ 724028, 9–11 Sandes Ave) is about five minutes' walk from the railway station; rooms with bathroom cost £28/44. The listed *Highgate Hotel* (☎/fax 724229, ⓔ highgatehotel@kendal-hotels.co.uk, 128 Highgate) is centrally located with comfortable rooms starting at £29 per person.

Right next door to the Highgate Hotel is the *Brewery* (☎ 725133, Highgate), one of those wonderful arts complexes that manages to be all things to all people, with a theatre and cinema, and an excellent bar-bistro. The menu changes every fortnight and prices are reasonable with soup of the day costing £2.95 and dishes such as seared tuna with salsa verde for £8.25.

Other possibilities for light meals include *Castle Dairy* (☎ 721170), a lovely 14th-century house on Stramongate, and the *coffee shop* attached to the Abbot Hall Art Gallery. The *Olde Fleece* on Highgate is a well-refurbished pub serving up fine food and good ale. The sweet toothed should head for the *1657 Chocolate House* (☎ 740702, Branthwaite Brow), which serves up all manner of things chocolate.

Getting There & Away

Kendal is on the branch train line from Windermere to Oxenholme, with connections north to Carlisle (£13.20, one hour) and south to Lancaster (£5.40, 30 minutes) and

Barrow-in-Furness (£11, two hours). Stagecoach also runs a reasonably frequent service from Windermere to Barrow via Kendal.

Getting Around

If you're sick of steep hills it's possible to hire an electrically driven bike. Velosolex Cumbria (☎ 822452) at 4 Staveley Mill Yard, Staveley Village, rents out imaginatively named Powabykes or Electropeds for £17 per day or £11 per half-day.

AROUND KENDAL
Sizergh Castle

Signposted 3½ miles south of Kendal off the A590 is Sizergh Castle (☎ 60070). Set in a water cattle meadow, the castle has been the home of the Strickland family for over 700 years. Central to its construction is what was thought to be a 14th-century *pele* (fortified) tower, but may in fact be a solar tower with foundations dating back even earlier. Much of the interior is Elizabethan, with some stunning carved wooden chimney-pieces. The pride and joy of the castle is the newly fitted Elizabethan inlaid chamber panelling, returned by the Victoria & Albert Museum in London after 100 years.

The castle opens 1.30 to 5.30 pm Sunday to Thursday, Easter to October; the garden opens one hour earlier. Admission costs £4.60/2.30, or £2.30/1.20 for the garden only. Bus No 555 from Kendal runs nearby.

The Border Reivers

People who fret about the modern-day crime wave should thank their lucky stars they didn't live in the Border Lands during the 400 years when the rapacious Reivers were king.

The Reivers were brigands whose backgrounds differed, but who had in common a complete disregard for the governments of England and Scotland. For the Reivers, sheep rustling and burning the homes of their enemies were a way of life. As a result, northern Cumbria and Northumberland, the southern Scottish Borders and Dumfries & Galloway are littered with minor castles and towerhouses, as people struggled to protect themselves.

It wasn't until James VI of Scotland succeeded Elizabeth I of England and united the two countries that order was finally reasserted. The Reivers are credited with giving the words 'blackmail' and 'bereaved' to the English language. And if your surname is Armstrong, Carruthers, Dixon, Elliot, Henderson, Johnstone, Maxwell, Nixon, Scott, Taylor, Wilson or Young, genealogists would have us believe you could be descended from a Reiver.

Levens Hall

Another 2 miles south of Sizergh castle is Levens Hall (☎ 60321), an Elizabethan mansion built around a 13th-century pele tower. The house is beautifully kept and contains some wonderful 17th- and 18th-century furniture; it also has a good collection of paintings. The topiary garden is worth the stop alone and dates from the 1690s.

The house opens noon to 5 pm (the gardens are open from 10 am) Sunday to Thursday, April to early October. Admission to the house and gardens costs £5.50/2.80, or £4/2.10 for the gardens only. It's best to catch bus No 555 or 556 from Kendal or Lancaster, which stop outside Levens Hall once per hour.

Lake District National Park

I wandered lonely as a cloud
That floats on high o'er dales and hills
When all at once I saw a crowd...
William Wordsworth

The Lake District is one of England's most beautiful corners, a magical mix of dainty green dales, stark, rocky mountains and the eponymous lakes. It manages to look beautiful even on the murkiest days – which is just as well since few visitors to the Lakes escape without a soaking! The Cumbrian Mountains are not particularly high – none reach 1000 metres – but they're much more dramatic than their height would suggest.

Unfortunately, an estimated 14 million people pour into the Lakes every year. After London, it's the second most visited part of Britain. The crowds can be so dense and the traffic jams so long that it's debatable whether it's worth visiting on any weekend between May and October, or any time at all from mid-July to the end of August. Stick with weekdays in May and June, or in September to October to make the most of the scenery without having to queue. Fortunately, the NT owns a quarter of the total area. This is partly thanks to the author Beatrix Potter

who sold the NT half of her large estate at cost and bequeathed the rest.

ORIENTATION

The two main bases for the Lakes are Keswick in the north (particularly for walkers) and Windermere and Bowness in the south (two contiguous tourist traps). Coniston is a less hectic alternative and also good for walkers. All these towns have youth hostels, plus numerous B&Bs and places to eat.

Ullswater, Grasmere, Windermere, Coniston Water and Derwent Water are often considered to be the most beautiful lakes, but they also teem with boats. Wast Water (one of the remotest), Crummock Water and Buttermere are equally spectacular but much less crowded.

In general, the mob stays on the A-roads, and the crowds are much thinner west of a line drawn from Keswick to Coniston.

INFORMATION

The TICs stock a frightening number of guidebooks and brochures about the Lakes. The Windermere and Keswick TICs are good places to start exploring the Lake District; both have lots of information and free local booking services. The national park runs nine TICs in the area, plus a visitors centre (☎ 015394-46601) at Brockhole, on the A591 between Windermere and Ambleside. Altogether there are about 30 dotted around.

If you're staying several days, consider buying a copy of *National Park Walks in the Countryside*, which has 40 walks of all grades, even for kids. *A Walk Round the Lakes* by Hunter Davies will fill in some of the background details. The classic walking guides are the seven hand-written, hand-drawn volumes of Alfred Wainwright's *Pictorial Guide to the Lakeland Fells*, still useful despite their age and cost. Many of the TICs sell cheap leaflets covering local walks of the area and are a good alternative to lugging around a book.

The numerous walking and climbing shops, particularly in Ambleside and Keswick, are also good sources of local information.

The hills around Keswick look bleak under threatening clouds.

GLENN BEANLAND

A glimpse of the Lake District

HUGH WATTS

Don't miss the boat, hire one instead on Lake Windermere.

DAVID ELSE

Ain't no mountain high enough? Try conquering a few Cumbrian ones in the Lake District.

DAVID ELSE

A surviving stretch of Hadrian's Wall, Northumberland, follows a precarious course.

Men in white: cricket alongside Warkworth Castle

Lock, stock and a smoking grouse, Newcastle

The 200-ton Angel of the North near Newcastle

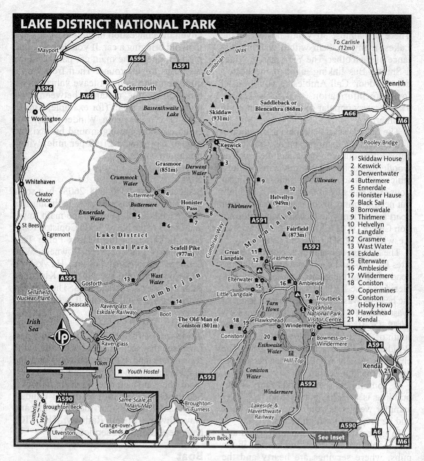

LAKE DISTRICT NATIONAL PARK

Map legend:
1 Skiddaw House
2 Keswick
3 Derwentwater
4 Buttermere
5 Ennerdale
6 Honister Hause
7 Black Sail
8 Borrowdale
9 Thirlmere
10 Helvellyn
11 Langdale
12 Grasmere
13 Wast Water
14 Eskdale
15 Elterwater
16 Ambleside
17 Windermere
18 Coniston Coppermines
19 Coniston (Holly How)
20 Hawkshead
21 Kendal

WALKING & CYCLING ROUTES

Walking or cycling are the best ways of getting around, but bear in mind that mountain weather conditions prevail – changeable and potentially treacherous – and the going can be very, very steep. Off-road mountain biking is popular, but there are also some good touring routes. See Getting Around in the Windermere & Bowness section later in the chapter for mountain-bike hire details.

Several outdoor shops and centres hire boots, tents and hiking equipment. Phone the Weatherline on ☎ 017687-75757 before setting out on ambitious excursions. TICs stock free leaflets with basic information on safety in the fells and on the water.

See the Activities chapter at the beginning of the book for details on the Cumbria Way. The Cumbria section has information on the Cumbrian and Sea To Sea Cycle Ways.

Guided walks of a number of towns in South Lakeland are organised from June to August, mainly leaving from the TICs. A single walk costs £2.30/1.10 and a multi-ticket – five walks – costs £7/3. Pick up a brochure from the TICs.

CUMBRIA

PLACES TO STAY & EAT

There are almost six youth hostels in the Lakes, many of them within walking distance of each other. The YHA also provides a Shuttle Bus linking eight of the hostels door-to-door. Call Ambleside youth hostel for more information (☎ 015394-32304). They're very popular so book well ahead in summer.

The Lake District National Park Authority administers 12 camping barns (traditional barns kitted out with basic facilities such as wooden sleeping platforms, taps, toilets, tables and benches) all in picturesque locations. You can stay in them for £3.50 a night but need to bring all the usual camping gear apart from a tent. Contact Keswick Information Centre (☎ 017687-72645), 31 Lake Rd, Keswick CA12 5DQ, for full details.

The NT also operates three excellent camp sites for tents and cars (not caravans): at the head of Great Langdale, 8 miles from Ambleside on the B5343 (☎ 015394-37668); at the head of Wasdale, on the western shore of Wast Water (☎ 019467-26620); and at Low Wray (☎ 015394-32810) nearly 2 miles south of Ambleside on the western shore of Windermere, access from the B5286. The charge is usually £3.50/1.50 per person per night in the high season.

It sometimes seems that every other building is a B&B, but despite this, over summer weekends you're advised to book and be prepared for high prices.

In general, food is reasonably good and reasonably priced. Prices are keenest in the pubs, where servings are hearty and the menus often surprisingly imaginative (even for vegetarians).

GETTING THERE & AWAY

There's a direct rail link from Manchester airport to Barrow-in-Furness (2½ hours) and Windermere (2¼ hours). Carlisle has several bus services to Keswick, the heart of the northern lakes.

Windermere has a train station and good road links, and is the main centre for the southern lakes. To both Windermere and Carlisle, coaches from London take about 6½ hours, trains 3½ hours.

GETTING AROUND

Given the congestion in the Lakes, it's best to avoid bringing a car. If you do bring one, put it in one of the main car parks and use the buses to get around. Theft from cars is quite common so don't leave valuables behind. Since the distance between most points is quite small (for example, Ambleside is 3 miles from Windermere), you could consider getting around by taxi; expect to pay around £1.50 per mile, with a minimum charge of £2.

Bus

Stagecoach (☎ 0870 608 2608) has some excellent local bus services, including the No 555 Lakeslink between the main towns and Carlisle; the No 505/506 Coniston Rambler minibuses on the Beatrix Potter Trail with hourly links between Bowness, Windermere, Ambleside, Hilltop, Hawkshead and Coniston; and the No 517 Kirkstone Rambler over Kirkstone Pass. The free *Explorer* leaflet, available at TICs, has details.

Train

Aside from British Rail's Cumbrian Coast Line (see that section later for details of the Ravenglass and Eskdale railway) and the branch line from Oxenholme to Windermere, there are a number of steam railways. See the Other Activities section of Windermere and Bowness for the Lakeside and Haverthwaite Steam Railway. The TICs have details of other services.

Boat

Windermere, Coniston Water, Ullswater and Derwent Water are all plied by ferries, often providing time-saving links for walkers. See Windermere & Bowness, Coniston and Keswick later in the chapter for details. For information on the Ullswater, Glenridding to Pooley Bridge service phone ☎ 017684-82229.

WINDERMERE & BOWNESS
☎ 015394 • pop 8300

Windermere was originally the name of England's largest lake. The town of the same name is a reasonably modern development

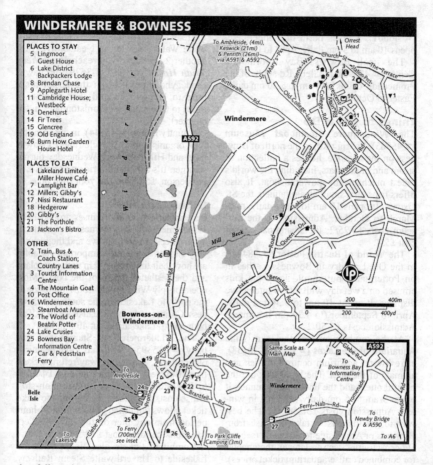

WINDERMERE & BOWNESS

PLACES TO STAY
5 Lingmoor Guest House
6 Lake District Backpackers Lodge
8 Brendan Chase
9 Applegarth Hotel
11 Cambridge House; Westbeck
13 Denehurst
14 Fir Trees
15 Glencree
19 Old England
26 Burn How Garden House Hotel

PLACES TO EAT
1 Lakeland Limited; Miller Howe Café
7 Lamplight Bar
12 Millers; Gibby's
17 Nissi Restaurant
18 Hedgerow
20 Gibby's
21 The Porthole
23 Jackson's Bistro

OTHER
2 Train, Bus & Coach Station; Country Lanes
3 Tourist Information Centre
4 The Mountain Goat
10 Post Office
16 Windermere Steamboat Museum
22 The World of Beatrix Potter
24 Lake Crusies
25 Bowness Bay Information Centre
27 Car & Pedestrian Ferry

that followed on the heels of the railway in 1847. The Windermere and Bowness conglomerate quickly grew to become the Lake District's largest tourist centre. At times it feels like a seaside resort, thanks to the crowds and the tat, and gives Oxford St in London a run for its money for the build up of exhaust fumes.

Orientation

It's 1½ miles downhill along Main Rd, New Rd, Lake Rd, Crag Brow and The Promenade from Windermere station to Bowness Pier; a taxi will run you there for around £2.50. All the way along you'll see B&Bs and hotels. Buses and coaches all leave from outside the train station. Most of the places to eat are concentrated in Bowness, which is the livelier place to be in the evening.

Information

Windermere TIC (☎ 46499) in Victoria St is excellent and visitors can even send and receive faxes at reasonable cost. It also provides an accommodation booking service free of charge covering most of the Lake District. It opens 9 am to 6 pm daily (to 7.30 pm in summer, 5 pm in winter). The

Brockhole National Park Visitor Centre (☎ 46601), 3 miles north of Windermere, opens 10 am to 5 pm daily, April to October.

The small Bowness Bay Information Centre (☎ 42895), in Glebe Rd south of the Promenade, opens 9.30 am to 5.30 pm daily, Easter to October.

Things to See & Do

The **Windermere Steamboat Museum** (☎ 45565), Rayrigg Rd, to the north of Bowness on the lakeside, houses a collection of steam and motorboats, including the world's oldest mechanically powered boat. It also offers trips on a small steam launch, the SL *Osprey*. It opens 10 am to 5 pm daily, mid-March to October. Admission to the museum costs £3.25/2; the steamboat cruises cost £5/4.

The **World of Beatrix Potter** (☎ 88444), in the Old Laundry in Bowness, cashes in on Pottermania but should keep the kids amused on a wet day with lots of interactive displays. It opens 10 am to 5.30 pm daily, April to September (to 4.30 pm in winter). Admission costs £3.50/2.

At the southern end of the lake is the **Aquarium of the Lakes** (☎ 015395-30153), a freshwater aquarium centred on fish and animals of the area. The highlights are the playful otters and the under-water tunnel. It opens 9 am to 6 pm daily (to 5 pm in winter). Admission costs £5.25/3.95. The best way to get there is to take a cruise from Bowness or Ambleside to Lakeside (see the Other Activities section later in the chapter for combined cruise/aquarium ticket prices).

Walking & Cycling Routes

Across the main road from the train station, Orrest Head, offering one of the classic Lakeland views, is just 1½ miles away, although it's a steep climb to get there. Another good viewpoint is Brant Fell, 2 miles from the Bowness ferry terminal. It's another steep climb but the views of Bowness and Lake Windermere are worth the effort.

Beatrix Potter's cottage at Hill Top and the village of Hawkshead are easily accessible to walkers. Catch the ferry across Windermere, and it's a 2-mile walk to Hill Top (see Hill Top later in the chapter). Follow the road around to the western side of Esthwaite Water (turn left at Near Sawrey) for another 2 miles and you reach **Hawkshead Youth Hostel** (☎ 015394-36293, e hawkshead@yha.org.uk). From the hostel it's a mile to Hawkshead and then another 5 miles to Coniston (see Coniston later in the chapter).

Country Lanes (☎ 44544), in the train station, organises guided cycle rides to Hawkshead and Hill Top every Wednesday during summer. It's a 17½-mile ride and costs £17 per person, £5 if you use your own bike.

Other Activities

Several companies run cruises around Lake Windermere from Bowness Promenade. Their prices are competitive and their routes very similar, so the most important variables are how their timetables fit in with your plans and the aesthetic appeal of the boats. Most operators ply Windermere from Ambleside in the north to Lakeside in the south, via Bowness. Cruises to Ambleside take about half an hour and to Lakeside about 40 minutes.

The Windermere Iron Steamboat Company (☎ 015395-31188) has three beautiful old cruisers. Adult one-way/return tickets from Bowness to Ambleside cost £4/5.80; to Lakeside £4/6. A 45-minute non-stop cruise costs £4.50. A Freedom of the Lake ticket allows unlimited cruises for a 24-hour period from any pier on the Lake. Tickets for adults/children cost £10/5.

Combined tickets also tie in with the Lakeside to Haverthwaite Steam Railway (☎ 015395-31594) which runs from Easter to November. Returns cost £9.20 from Bowness and £12.40 from Ambleside. A ticket for the railway alone costs £2.20/1.45. It's also possible to purchase a combined ticket for a cruise and admission to the Aquarium of the Lakes; a return ticket from Bowness costs £10, from Ambleside it costs £13.20.

Rowing boats can be hired at the lake.

Places to Stay

Camping With all mod cons and 180 pitches on grass, *Park Cliffe* (☎ *015395-31344,* e *parkcliffe@btinternet.com, Birks Rd*) has great views. It costs £9.60 per two person tent. It is located 3 miles south of Bowness and bus No 618 from Windermere passes by.

Hostels Within spitting distance of the train station is the *Lake District Backpackers Lodge* (☎ 46374, High St) which offers beds in small dormitories for £11, and breakfast for £3.50. Guests have access to a kitchen, lounge and washing machine.

Windermere Youth Hostel (☎ 43543, [e] windermere@yha.org.uk, High Cross, Bridge Lane, Troutbeck) may be larger but is 2 miles from the station. Leave Windermere on the A591 to Ambleside and turn right up Bridge Lane at Troutbeck Bridge, a mile north of Windermere. Numerous buses run past Troutbeck Bridge and in summer the hostel sends a minibus to meet trains. It opens daily from mid-February to early October, and Friday and Saturday the rest of the year. Beds cost £11/7.75 for adults/under-18s.

B&Bs & Hotels – Budget to Mid-Range Lovely slate stone *Brendan Chase* (☎ 45638, 1 and 3 College Rd, Windermere) has eight rooms priced from £12.50 to £25 per person; farther along, *Applegarth Hotel* (☎ 43206, College Rd) has 18 rooms ranging from £20 to £45 per head. Readers have enjoyed staying at *Denehurst* (☎ 44710, 40 Queens Drive) where beds cost from £19 to £25.

Lingmoor Guest House (☎ 44947, [e] lindsfarne@clara.net, 7 High St) has seven rooms costing from £16 to £24; it is non-smoking. *Cambridge House* (☎ 43846, [e] mbdfear@aol.com, 9 Oak St) rises to vegetarian breakfasts and charges £16 to £20 per person.

Lake Rd, which runs down to Bowness, is packed solid with hotels. Most have rooms from around £20 a night; many show prices and vacancies at the front. Cheaper places sometimes lurk down side streets.

Heading down to Bowness, *Fir Trees* (☎ 42272) is a lovely Victorian hotel with eight rooms with private bathroom at £22 to £32 per head. Across the road, *Glencree* (☎ 45822) overlooks woodland and has beds from £20 to £30.

B&Bs & Hotels – Top End In the heart of Bowness overlooking the lake, the elegant *Old England* (☎ 0870 400 8130, Church St) is a Georgian country mansion with an open-air heated pool. Rooms are £75 per person at weekends, but ask about short-break deals.

Holbeck Ghyll Country House Hotel (☎ 32375, Holbeck Lane) is overlooking the lake in a 19th-century hunting lodge. Singles/doubles start from £65/75 and increase depending on the view and the plushness of the rooms.

Two minutes from the lake, with a mixture of motel-style chalets and rooms and a restaurant in a large Victorian house, *Burn How Garden House Hotel* (☎ 46226, [e] burnhowhotel@btinternet.com, Back Belsfield Rd) has rooms starting from £38/44.

Places to Eat

At first sight neither Bowness nor Windermere offers much in the way of gourmet cuisine, although the restaurants at the *Burn How* and *Holbeck Ghyll* hotels (see Places to Stay earlier) offer top-class, expensive cuisine.

Millers (☎ 43877, 31 Crescent Rd) in Windermere offers a standard, cheapish tourist menu. *Gibby's* (☎ 43267, 43 Crescent Rd), a few doors down, is cheap and filling, with home-made chicken and mushroom pie for £4.60. The *Lamplight Bar* (Oakthorpe Hotel, High St) is popular with the locals and occasionally has live folk music. The menu ranges from Mexican chilli for £7.50 to whole grilled plaice for £9.75.

In the evening, Bowness is more promising. A good place to start looking is pedestrianised Ash St which has Italian and Indian restaurants. Here you'll also find *The Porthole* (☎ 42793, 3 Ash St), a wine buff's paradise with relatively pricey Italian and modern British dishes from £6 to £16. Immediately across the street is another branch of *Gibby's* (☎ 43060, Ash St), open in the evening and serving a set three-course menu for £7.15.

Just up the road, the *Nissi Restaurant* (☎ 45055, Crag Brow) is a Greek place selling lobster soup for £3.25, kebabs for £7.50 and vegetarian dishes for £6.95.

CUMBRIA

Jackson's Bistro (☎ 46264, West End) is pleasant and reasonable with a three-course dinner costing £11.95.

Few of the teashops are particularly inspiring, but you could drop into the *Old England* (see Places to Stay earlier) for a cuppa with a lake view. Alternatively, try the *Hedgerow Teashop*, above a bookshop on Crag Brow, serving light lunches for around £4. In Windermere, surprisingly nice cakes can be had in the *Miller Howe Café (☎ 46732, Station Precinct)* in the unlikely surrounds of the Lakeland Limited factory shop behind the train station.

Getting There & Away

Windermere is 265 miles from London, 55 miles from Blackpool, 45 miles from Carlisle and 5 miles from Ambleside.

Bus There are two National Express buses a day from Manchester via Preston (£14, three hours) and on to Keswick (£17, 4½ hours). There's also a service from London (£24, 7½ hours) and on to Keswick (£24, 8½ hours).

Stagecoach (☎ 0870 608 2608) has several useful services, including the No 555 Lakeslink, which links Lancaster with Keswick, via Kendal, Windermere (train station, Troutbeck Bridge and Brockhole), Ambleside, Grasmere and Carlisle. The No 618 runs between Ambleside and Barrow-in-Furness, passing through Windermere, Newby Bridge, Haverthwaite and Ulverston. No 505/506 links Kendal to Coniston via the Steamboat Museum, Brockhole and Ambleside. The No 599 service runs between Grasmere, Ambleside, Brockhole, Bowness, Windermere train station and Kendal. A Round Robin Ticket allows five breaks of journey between Bowness and Grasmere for £5.

Train Windermere is at the end of a spur line from Oxenholme which connects with the main line from London Euston to Glasgow. There are 10 trains a day from London Euston station (£60.70, £26 if booked 14 days in advance, 3½ hours). You need to change at Oxenholme for the connecting service to Windermere (20 minutes, hourly).

Boat See Other Activities earlier in this section. The Windermere ferry plies across the lake from Bowness to Far Sawrey every 20 minutes from around 7 am to 10 pm. A single ticket costs 40p.

Getting Around

Country Lanes Cycle Centre (☎ 44544), at the train station, rents out bikes for £14 a day.

AROUND BOWNESS
Hill Top

Beatrix Potter wrote many of her famous children's stories in the 17th-century farmhouse at Near Sawrey (☎ 36269; NT), 2 miles south of Hawkshead, which is packed with visitors in summer. The place is a shoebox so you may have to wait to get inside during school holidays. It opens 10.30 am to 5 pm Saturday to Wednesday, June to August; 11 am to 4.30 pm March to May and September and October. Admission costs £4/2. See Walking & Cycling Routes in the Windermere & Bowness section for details of how to get there, or catch Bus No 505 from Ambleside or Coniston.

AMBLESIDE
☎ 015394 • pop 4400

The pretty little town of Ambleside is a major centre for climbers and walkers and makes a good base for the southern lakes. But although it has an attractive position half a mile north of the lake, its narrow streets can barely cope with the numbers of walkers in fluorescent outdoor gear who regularly descend on it. Inevitably it's choked with B&Bs, teashops and outdoor equipment shops. If you're looking for advice on where to go, the TIC (☎ 32582, ⓔ ambleside-tic@telinco.co.uk), on the corner of Market Cross and Rydal Rd, opens 9 am to 5.30 pm daily.

Compston Rd is particularly full of equipment shops, with branches of Rohan (☎ 32946), Hawkshead (☎ 35255) and the YHA Adventure Shop. The vast Climber's Shop (☎ 32297) also hires out camping gear, boots and waterproofs.

The one specific attraction is **The Armitt** (☎ 31212), Rydal Rd, a lavish, if rather specialist exhibition about Lakeland's less-famous literary characters. It opens 10 am to 5 pm daily. Admission costs £2.50/1.80.

Walks head off in every direction. The TIC provides plenty of information on walks in the area and whether you can complete them or not! The Loughrigg circuit (7 miles), running from the Rydal Rd car park to Grasmere Lake and back, is a good combination of woods, farmland, steep hills and great views. For a shorter walk (2 miles) but still taking in the views, head for Stockghyll Force, east of Ambleside. You can either head back to Ambleside through farmland or push on to the village of Troutbeck, returning via Jenkyn's Crag, a rocky outcrop offering superb views of Lake Windermere. The circuit is 7 miles and good boots are required.

Places to Stay

One mile south of the village on the A591 on Lake Windermere, *Ambleside Youth Hostel* (☎ 32304, 🖃 ambleside@yha.org.uk, Windermere Rd) has Internet access and is open year round; beds cost £13.50/9.50 for adults/under-18s. The free YHA shuttle bus meets trains at Windermere station from spring to autumn. *Low Wray* (☎ 32810), a NT camp site, is 3 miles south of Ambleside on the western shore of Windermere (access from the B5286). It opens Easter to October and charges £3.50 per person per night plus £2 for a car.

B&Bs worth considering include *3 Cambridge Villas* (☎ 32307, Church St), a classic B&B with rooms from £16 to £20 per person, and the welcoming *Melrose Hotel* (☎ 32500, Church St), charging £14 to £25 per person. *Compston House Hotel* (☎ 32305, 🖃 compston@globalnet.co.uk, Compston Rd) has views and comfortable rooms with bathroom from £25 to £29 per person. *Mill Cottage* (☎ 34830, Rydal Rd), above a centrally positioned teashop, has beds for £21 to £30.

Places to Eat

Two great eateries are *Lynchristies* (☎ 33332, Kelsick Old Hall), serving international food with a Cumbrian twist – Winnsboro bean rarebit costs £3.95 – and the lively *Lucy's on a Plate* (☎ 31191, Church St) with more European-style food; a Greek salad is £3.95.

Tuck into pizza at *Zeffirelli's Wholefood Pizzeria* (☎ 33845, Compston Rd) before adjourning to the attached cinema; the £15.50 'double feature' menu covers a three-course dinner and cinema ticket.

Another stylish addition to the eating scene is *The Glass House* (☎ 32137, Rydal Rd), attached to the glass-blowing studio. It opens for teas, lunches and evening meals, serving a mix of Mediterranean and British food. Popular with walkers are the *Golden Rule* (☎ 32257, Smithy Brow), a welcoming pub away from the buzz of tourists, which pours a fine pint of ale.

Getting There & Around

The bus stop is one block south of Church St. Bus Nos 555 and 599 run to Windermere, Grasmere and Keswick, and No 505 runs to Coniston. Bike Treks (☎ 31505, Compston Rd) hires out bikes for £14 per day.

GRASMERE & WORDSWORTH COUNTRY

☎ 015394 ● pop 2700

Grasmere is a picture-postcard village and a lovely place to stay out of season. In summer, its good looks together with its associations with the poet Wordsworth ensure it's overrun with tourists. Most of the buildings date from the 19th and 20th centuries, but the village is actually ancient. St Oswald's Church, with its complicated raftered roof, dates from the 13th century. Wordsworth is buried in the churchyard with his wife Mary and sister Dorothy. The TIC (☎ 35245, Red Bank Rd) has a helpful visual display on walks around Grasmere, and opens 9.30 am to 5.30 pm daily.

Dove Cottage & Wordsworth Museum

Dove Cottage, just off the A591 on the outskirts of Grasmere, is the main Wordsworth shrine, where he wrote his greatest poems. Once a public house, it has flagstone floors, panelled walls and fine lake views, but it is far too small for the crush of people who want to see it – do yourself a favour and visit out of season. The half-hour guided tours are particularly worthwhile.

The Wordsworth Museum houses manuscripts and paintings along with personal possessions.

The complex (☎ 35544) opens 9.30 am to 5.30 pm daily, except early January to early February. Present your ticket at Rydal Mount for a 15% discount on admission there.

Rydal Mount

Following his marriage, Wordsworth lived at Rydal Mount from 1813 to 1850. Even then, as many as 100 fans a day would visit in the hope of catching a glimpse of the only Poet Laureate who never wrote a line of official verse. Rydal Mount is a 16th-century farmhouse with 18th-century additions set in 1¾ hectares of gardens originally landscaped by Wordsworth. It contains some of his furniture as well as manuscripts and possessions.

The house (☎ 33002) is still owned by one of Wordsworth's descendants. It opens 9.30 am to 5 pm daily, March to October, and 10 am to 4 pm in winter (except Tuesday and for most of January). Admission costs £3.75/3, although you can visit the grounds for £1.75/1.25.

In spring it's worth diverting through the churchyard below the Mount to see **Dora's Field**, planted with daffodils in memory of Wordsworth's daughter.

Places to Stay

Grasmere has two youth hostels, one close to the village, the other a mile away in an old farmhouse. *Butterlip How Youth Hostel* (☎ 35316, fax 35798, ℮ grasmere@yha.org .uk) is just north of the village; follow the road to Easedale for 150 yards, then turn right. It opens daily mid-February to October, Friday and Saturday from November to mid-December, and Thursday to Monday the rest of the year. Overnight charges are £12.50/8.50 for adults/under-18s. *Thorney How Youth Hostel* (same contact details as Butterlip How), farther out on Easedale Rd, opens April to October and is a little cheaper.

About 10 minutes' walk west of the centre is the friendly *Glenthorne Quaker Guest House* (☎ 35389, ℮ gthorn@global net.co.uk, Easedale Rd). It's well set up for

walkers, being on the Cumbrian Way, with good drying facilities and offering dinner. B&B costs £19 per person, and full board costs £39 per person. The Wordsworth Trust owns *How Foot Lodge* (☎ 35366), literally yards from Dove Cottage, where rooms start at £23 per person.

The Travellers Rest Inn (☎ 35604, ℮ travellers@lakelandsheart.demon.co.uk) has it all – comfortable rooms, excellent pub food, and a warm, welcoming bar – except for the A591 running past its door. Rooms start at £29 per person, but cost more at the weekend. It's just north of Grasmere and Bus No 555 stops outside.

Places to Eat

The *Dove Cottage Tea Rooms & Restaurant* (☎ 35268) is an impressive modern vegetarian enterprise offering pasties and pies from £3.30, as well as a range of cakes and sandwiches. The restaurant opens Tuesday to Saturday night and the tearooms 10 am to 5 pm daily.

In the village itself, *Baldry's Tea Room (Red Lion Square)* is a wholefood place serving hot lunches for around £5.50 and mouth-watering home-made bread and butter pudding for £2.95.

As you leave the churchyard follow your nose to find *Sarah Nelson's Gingerbread Shop* (☎ 35428, Church Stile) which has been trading on the same spot for more than 130 years.

Getting There & Away

Stagecoach Bus No 555 runs from Ambleside to Grasmere, stopping at Rydal church and outside Dove Cottage. A 2½-mile walk links Grasmere and the two Wordsworth shrines.

AROUND GRASMERE
Elterwater

Elterwater is superbly located at the end of a small lake, tucked in under the Langdales. It's on the Cumbria Way with good walks around and about. There's a wonderful view from Loughrigg Terrace at the southern end of Grasmere, looking northwards over the lake and the village. Follow the road to

High Close Youth Hostel and continue to the east, taking a footpath to the right off the road. It's approximately 3 miles return to Elterwater. The Maple Tree Corner Store, on the central green, can handle most of your consumer needs.

There's a nice slate hostel in town, over the bridge. *Elterwater Youth Hostel (☎ 37245)* opens daily April to September, Monday to Friday at other times except January, when it only opens Friday and Saturday. Beds cost £9.25/6.50 for adults/under-18s. On the hills to the east, a mile from the village, *Langdale High Close Youth Hostel (☎ 37313, ℮ keswick@yha.org.uk)* is a rambling Victorian mansion in extensive gardens with great views. Generally it opens daily from April to October, but it closes at irregular times; phone ahead to be sure it's open. Beds cost £10/6.90.

Barnhowe (☎ 37346), 90m from the village centre, has two doubles and a single costing from £17 per person. The friendly *Britannia Inn (☎ 37210)* has a pleasant patio overlooking the 'main' street and good-value food and guest ales; the home-grown local speciality, Herdwick Lamb, costs around £7. It also has cosy rooms from £27 to £35 per person.

Elterwater is 3½ miles from Ambleside (take Bus No 516) and 5 miles from Coniston.

CONISTON
☎ 015394 • pop 1800

John Ruskin, the famous Victorian art critic, thought Coniston Water 'more beautiful than anything I had ever seen to my remembrance in gladness and infinitude of light'. And you'd be hard pressed not to agree. Coniston itself has the manicured look of a classic Lake District tourist town, but magnificent craggy hills glower over it and there are refreshingly few tourist shops. Needless to say, there are a number of superb walks in the neighbouring countryside, in particular the walk up the Old Man of Coniston (801m). On a clear day the breathtaking view from the top takes in the Cumbrian Coast and across to Lake Windermere.

Information
The well-equipped TIC (☎ 41533, ℮ conistontic@lake-district.gov.uk), on the road to Hawkshead, displays a useful topographical map of the area. It opens 9.30 am to 5.30 pm daily, Easter to October, and 10 am to 3.30 pm at the weekend in winter.

Summitreks (☎ 41212, ℮ info@summitreks.co.uk), 14 Yewdale Rd, offers a range of adventure activities, hires out walking and climbing gear, and is also the base for Coniston Mountain Bikes, which rents out bikes for £13 per day.

Ruskin Museum
The recently renovated and expanded Ruskin Museum (☎ 41164) not only delves into the life and times of John Ruskin but also covers the story of Coniston itself. Interactive screens provide a good introduction to Ruskin and his work and there are a few of his watercolours and drawings on display. The rest of the museum is a mixed bag of local industry, such as Ruskin Lace, the farming of Herdwick, the local breed of sheep and the uses of Coniston Copper and Slate. There's also a shrine to the late great speed demon Donald Campbell, the only person in the world to hold both water and land speed records in the same year. Tragically, he died in 1967 in his *Bluebird K7* boat on Coniston Water whilst breaking the 300mph barrier. The museum opens 10 am to 5.30 pm daily, April to early November. Admission costs £3/1.75.

Boat Trips
Now owned by the NT, the unique and beautiful steam yacht *Gondola*, with its luxurious saloons, was launched on Coniston Water in 1859. The *Illustrated London News* described it as 'a perfect combination of the Venetian gondola and the English steam yacht'.

The *Gondola* (☎/fax 63856) sails daily from April to October and services Brantwood and Park-a-Mor on the eastern side of Coniston. A round trip costs £4.70/2.80, although you can also take shorter hops.

The motorised *Coniston Launch* (☎/fax 36216) is another option to cruise the lake

CUMBRIA

and visit Brantwood. The North Lake sailing calls at four jettys, including Brantwood, for £3.60 return (£7.10/2.80 including admission to Brantwood House). The South Lake cruise sails as far as Lake Bank at the southern end of the lake, and also calls at Brantwood. Return tickets are £5.80. It's possible to break your journey and catch the later ferry, or walk to the next jetty.

It's also possible to hire boats at the Coniston Boating Centre (☎ 41366, Coniston Jetty), ranging from motor boats at £10 per hour, to the more exhausting canoes for £18 per day.

Brantwood

Brantwood, the house created by John Ruskin, has a beautiful site overlooking Coniston Water with the Old Man of Coniston behind.

It opens 11 am to 5.30 pm daily, mid-March to mid-November; and 11 am to 4 pm Wednesday to Sunday in winter. The best way to get there is by the *Gondola* or *Coniston Launch* (see Boat Trips earlier). Admission costs £4/1 and there's a good teashop.

Places to Stay

Camping There are plenty of tent sites at *Coniston Hall Camp Site* (☎ 41223) beside the lake. It costs £3.50 per person and £8.50 for a car and two people. Turn left opposite the Catholic church and keep left down to the lake.

Hostels A few minutes' walk from the town centre, *Holly How Youth Hostel* (☎ 41323, e conistonhh@yha.org.uk) is just off Ambleside Rd (the A593). It's open over Easter, from late June to late September, and weekends at other times. Beds cost £10/6.90 for adults/under-18s.

Coppermines Youth Hostel (☎ 41261) has a spectacular mountain setting but is only just over a mile from Coniston; take the minor road between the Black Bull and the Co-op. Don't try to drive there, the road is quite bad. It opens daily, late May to August, and Tuesday to Saturday, April, May, September and October. Beds cost £9.25/6.50.

B&Bs & Hotels The *Beech Tree* (☎ 41717, Yewdale Rd), formerly the Old Vicarage, offers vegetarian cooking and has eight rooms, some with bathroom, from £18 to £25 per person. Nearby is *Oaklands* (☎ 41245, Yewdale Rd), a small, nonsmoking place with rates from £18 to £20; and *Orchard Cottage* (☎ 41373, 18 Yewdale Rd), with rooms with private bathroom from £19 to £22.

East of town, *Lakeland House* (☎ 41303, Tiberthwaite Ave) has nine rooms with beds costing from £16 to £40 per person; *Shepherds Villa* (☎ 41337, Tilberthwaite Ave) has rooms with private bathroom costing from £18 to £24 per person.

The highly rated *Coniston Lodge Hotel* (☎ 41201, Station Rd) has six rooms with private bathroom from £29.50 to £45.50 per person.

Places to Eat

The *Sun Hotel* (☎ 41248, fax 41219) is worth the effort of finding it; walk out of town towards Ulverston, cross the bridge and turn right up the hill. Specials include dishes such as vegetable peanut roast and homemade pies. It also has rooms with views from £30 per person. The *Blue Café* (☎ 41649, Lake Rd), down by the ferry landings, serves filling jacket potatoes for £3. For a local pint, head to the *Black Bull* (☎ 41335, Yewdale Rd), which brews its own Bluebird beer.

Getting There & Around

Stagecoach's No 505/506 Coniston Rambler service runs from Bowness Pier to Brockhole, Ambleside and Coniston. In summer there are half a dozen services a day and three on Sunday; and in winter only two services on Saturday and none on Sunday.

KESWICK
☎ 017687 • pop 5000

As the northern centre for the Lakes, Keswick has been on the tourist map for over 100 years and is very busy indeed. An important walking base on the Cumbria Way, it lies between the great rounded peak of Skiddaw and Derwent Water, although the town is cut off from the lake shore by a busy main road. Controversy rages over

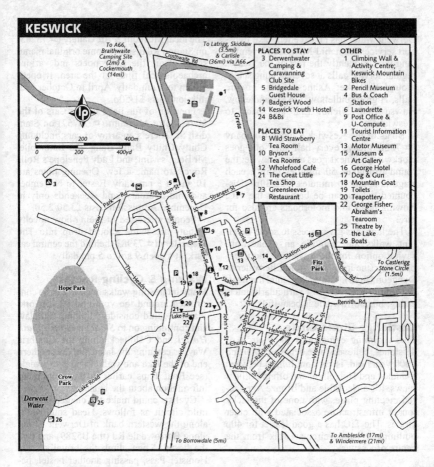

KESWICK

To A66,
Braithwaite
Camping Site
(2mi) &
Cockermouth
(14mi)

To Latrigg, Skiddaw
(3.5mi)
& Carlisle
(36mi) via A66

Crosthwaite Rd

Greta

0   200   400m
0   200   400yd

Park   Rd

Tithebarn St

Crow

Heads Rd

Main St

Stranger St

The Heads

Market Rd

Derwent

Cl

Victoria St

Station St

Station Road

Brundholme Rd

Fitz
Park

To Castlerigg
Stone Circle
(1.5mi)

Hope Park

Station

Penrith Rd

Lake Rd

Blencathra St

Southey St

St John's St

Wordsworth St

Helvellyn St

Eskin St

Ratcliffe Pl

Church St

Acorn St

Borrowdale Rd

Heads Rd

Lake Road

Crow
Park

Derwent
Water

Ambleside
Road

To Borrowdale (5mi)

To Ambleside (17mi)
& Windermere (21mi)

PLACES TO STAY
3 Derwentwater
  Camping &
  Caravanning
  Club Site
5 Bridgedale
  Guest House
7 Badgers Wood
14 Keswick Youth Hostel
24 B&Bs

PLACES TO EAT
8 Wild Strawberry
  Tea Room
10 Bryson's
  Tea Rooms
12 Wholefood Café
21 The Great Little
  Tea Shop
23 Greensleeves
  Restaurant

OTHER
1 Climbing Wall &
  Activity Centre;
  Keswick Mountain
  Bikes
2 Pencil Museum
4 Bus & Coach
  Station
6 Laundrette
9 Post Office &
  U-Compute
11 Tourist Information
  Centre
13 Motor Museum
15 Museum &
  Art Gallery
16 George Hotel
17 Dog & Gun
18 Mountain Goat
19 Toilets
20 Teapottery
22 George Fisher;
  Abraham's
  Tearoom
25 Theatre by
  the Lake
26 Boats

whether Derwent Water, Ullswater or
Crummock Water is the most beautiful lake,
but Derwent Water is certainly the most accessible for those without private transport.
An old market town, Keswick became the
centre of a mining industry in the 16th century. These days you can't move for tearooms, B&Bs and outdoor equipment
shops.

Information
The busy but helpful TIC (☎ 72645,
ⓔ keswicktic@lake-district.gov.uk), Moot
Hall, Market Place, opens 9.30 am to 4.30 pm

daily, year round (to 5.30 pm in summer). A
free accommodation service is provided and
the TIC staff are a great source of information
on local walks.

George Fisher (☎ 72178), 2 Borrowdale
Rd, is an enormous outdoor equipment shop
with gear for hire. Various outdoor activities
and courses, such as canoeing, abseiling and
cycling, are organised by the knowledgeable
and friendly Climbing Wall & Activity
Centre (☎ 72000), behind the Pencil Museum. Log onto the Internet at U-Compute
(☎ 75127), above the post office on Market
Place.

CUMBRIA

Boat Trips

Derwent Water has an excellent lake transport service. From mid-March to November (and less frequently the rest of the year) a regular service calls at seven landing stages around the lake: Ashness Gate, Lodore Falls, High Brandlehow, Low Brandlehow, Hawse End, Nichol End and back to Keswick.

Boats of the Keswick Launch Company (☎ 72263) leave every half-hour, one goes clockwise, the next goes anticlockwise; the round trip takes 50 minutes (£5/2); each stage is about 10 minutes (75p/30p). Discounted tickets can be bought at the TIC. Rowing boats and motorboats are also for hire.

The launches give access to some excellent walks and provide an exhaustion-saving option for those walking the Cumbria Way (the long walk from Elterwater or Dungeon Ghyll). The walk around the western side of the lake isn't particularly interesting, but Borrowdale is beautiful.

Castlerigg Stone Circle

This charming egg-shaped stone circle of 48 stones, believed to be between 3000 and 4000 years old, is set on a hilltop between Skiddaw and Helvellyn, and offers brilliant views. It's a Neolithic and Bronze Age sacred meeting place, with none of the tacky tourist infrastructure associated with other circles. The TIC has a good leaflet for 40p outlining a 4-mile circular walk from the centre of Keswick.

Cumberland Pencil Museum

In the 16th century, graphite was discovered in Borrowdale, leading to the creation of a pencil-making industry that is still going strong even though the components are now imported from as far afield as Sri Lanka and California. The museum attached to the Derwent Watercolour pencil factory tells the whole story with the help of a video. You get to see the world's largest pencil too. The museum and pencil shop (☎ 73626, e museum @pencils.co.uk) open 9.30 am to 4 pm daily, but hours may be extended at peak times. Admission costs £2.50/1.25.

Other Things to See & Do

The local Museum & Art Gallery (☎ 73263) on Station Rd displays some original manuscripts from the Lake poets and various archaeological finds of the area. It opens 10 am to 4 pm daily, April to October. Admission costs £1/50p.

For a bit of fun head for the Cars of the Stars Motor Museum (☎ 73757) on Standish St. There's an array of cars, including Chitty Chitty Bang Bang, the Batmobile, Mr Bean's Mini, and Lady Penelope's Rolls Royce, to name a few. Opening times are 10 am to 5 pm daily, Easter to November and mid-February, and weekends only in December. Admission costs £3.50/2.50.

People interested in seeing how novelty teapots are made should drop into The Teapottery (☎ 73983) behind the central car park. It's open 9 am to 5 pm daily.

Walking & Cycling Routes

Many interesting walks or rides can be constructed around the youth hostel network. Walkers could consider climbing Skiddaw and continuing on to *Skiddaw House Youth Hostel* and Caldbeck along the Cumbria Way, or catching the launch to the southern end of the lake and walking up Borrowdale (see Boat Trips earlier in this section for information about the launches).

Cyclists could make the challenging 30-mile circuit as follows. Head southwards along the western bank of Derwent Water, along Borrowdale Rd (the B5289) and past the hostel. Then climb the brutally steep Honister Pass, passing another hostel, before running down to beautiful Buttermere (and another hostel) and Crummock Water. From Buttermere you could finish the loop by returning below Knott Rigg along the Keskadale Beck past Stair. Alternatively, you could continue on to Cockermouth and return via the B5292.

Places to Stay

Camping There are tent pitches at *Braithwaite Camping Site (☎ 78343)*, just off the A66 on the B5292, from £3.10 per person. The *Derwentwater Camping & Caravanning Club Site (☎ 72392)*, on the lake shore a few minutes' walk from town, has caravan sites and tent pitches from £3 per person.

Hostels A short walk down Station Rd from the TIC is *Keswick Youth Hostel (☎ 72484, fax 74129, ⓔ keswick@yha.org.uk, Station Rd)*; turn left on the walkway by the river. It opens daily from mid-February to December. Beds cost £11/7.75 for adults/under-18s.

B&Bs & Hotels One of the best-value B&Bs in the Lake District, the *Bridgedale Guest House (☎ 73914, 101 Main St)* has a range of rooms, some with private showers, for just £16 per person. Without breakfast this drops to £12, which is only slightly more than the youth hostel. You can leave your bags here for £2 if you're just passing through on the bus. *Badgers Wood (☎ 72621, 30 Stranger St)*, close to the centre, is friendly and welcoming, with comfortable rooms starting at £17.50 without bathroom.

To the east of the town centre, along Southey, Blencathra, Helvellyn and Eskin Sts, virtually every house is a B&B. Prices are competitive and standards high. Unless otherwise stated, rooms have private bathroom and the price is per person per night.

Nonsmoking *Allerdale House (☎ 73891, 1 Eskin St)* has excellent rooms from £24 per person, while *Charnwood (☎ 74111, 6 Eskin St)* has comfortable beds from £19 to £26. Both *Clarence House (☎ 73186, 14 Eskin St)* and *Braemar (☎ 73743, ⓔ braemar@kencomp.net, 21 Eskin St)* have single rooms available in a similar price range.

Bluestones (☎ 74237, ⓔ bluestoneskeswick@cwcom.net, 7 Southey St) has beds from £15 to £19; *Glendene (☎ 73548, 8 Southey St)* from £15; and *Edwardene (☎ 73586, 26 Southey St)* from £25.

The Derwentdale (☎ 74187, 8 Blencathra St) has a good range of rooms with beds from £17.50 to £20.50, while the small *Blencathra (☎ 71435, 48 Blencathra St)* has two family rooms for £16.50 per person.

Places to Eat

In the evening, pubs are a good bet. The *Dog & Gun (2 Lake Rd)* is good value with homemade lamb curry for £5.75. The *George Hotel (☎ 72076, 3 St John's St)* serves pub grub for around £6–8 and the establishment is welcoming and friendly.

Greensleeves Restaurant (☎ 72932, 26 St John's St) is a large 'tourist' restaurant, but it has a good-value menu with pasta from around £5.30 and dishes such as supreme of salmon for £8.50. Serving a good range of evening meals, and a separate vegetarian menu, is *The Great Little Tea Shop (☎ 73545, 26 Lake Road)*. Mains start at £6.95, including vegetable Thai curry.

For teas and light lunches *Bryson's Tea Room (38 Main St)* is an excellent bakery, exporting its cakes as far afield as the USA. It also serves meals during the day. *Abraham's Tearoom*, tucked into the rafters of the enormous George Fisher outdoor-equipment shop (see the Information section earlier) offers great views and light meals such as Cumberland rarebit for £3.95. There's also the inviting *Wholefood Café (Hendersons Yard, off Market Square)* or *The Wild Strawberry Tea Room (54 Main St)*.

Getting There & Away

Keswick is 285 miles from London, 31 miles from Carlisle and 15 miles from Penrith.

Bus See Windermere & Bowness earlier in the chapter for information on National Express and Stagecoach buses and connections to Keswick.

In summer, Keswick is also accessible from Penrith train station (one to two services Monday to Saturday, one on Sunday) with Wright Brothers' (☎ 01434-381200) No 888 service. This bus continues cross country to Langwathby, on the Leeds-Settle-Carlisle line, to Hexham and Corbridge, on Hadrian's Wall, and finally to Newcastle upon Tyne.

Stagecoach's Lakeslink (No 555) runs from Carlisle to Lancaster via Keswick, Ambleside, Windermere and Kendal. There are frequent services between Keswick and Kendal. Three a day go on to Carlisle from Monday to Saturday.

Getting Around

Behind the Pencil Museum on Southey Hill, two places hire out bikes. Keswick Mountain

Bikes (☎ 75202) has bikes for hire from £13/10 per day/half-day, while the Keswick Climbing Wall & Activity Centre (☎ 72000) rents them out for £14/8.50.

AROUND KESWICK
Places to Stay

There's an excellent network of youth hostels around Keswick, most linked by mountain paths. For information on walks connecting the hostels, consult the Keswick TIC, pick up the handy walk route maps produced by the YHA at the hostels, or call ☎ 0870 870 8808.

Derwentwater Youth Hostel (☎ 77246, fax 77396, ℮ derwentwater@yha.org.uk, Barrow House, Borrowdale) is on the eastern side of the lake, 2 miles from Keswick, 5 miles from Thirlmere and 11 miles from Grasmere. It opens daily mid-February to early November, and Friday and Saturday for much of the rest of the year. Price: £11/7.75 for adults/under-18s.

Borrowdale Youth Hostel (☎ 77257, fax 77393 ℮ borrowdale@yha.org.uk, Longthwaite, Borrowdale) is at the head of beautiful Borrowdale, 2 miles from Honister, 5 miles from Derwent Water and 7 miles from Buttermere. Price: £11/7.75.

Thirlmere Youth Hostel (☎/fax 73224, Old School, Stanah Cross) is at the head of Thirlmere on the A591 to Ambleside, 5 miles from Keswick, 6 miles from Longthwaite, 7 miles from Grasmere and 9 miles from Skiddaw House. Price: £6.75/4.75.

Honister Hause Youth Hostel (☎/fax 77267, Seatoller, Keswick) is at the summit of Honister Pass, 3 miles from Black Sail, 2 miles from Longthwaite and 4 miles from Buttermere. Price: £9.25/6.50.

Buttermere Youth Hostel (☎ 70245, fax 70231, ℮ buttermere@yha.org.uk, Buttermere, Cockermouth) overlooks Buttermere and is 4 miles from Honister, 7 miles from Longthwaite and 9 miles from Keswick. Price: £11/7.75.

Ennerdale Youth Hostel (☎ 01946-861237, Cat Crag, Ennerdale) is in a remote location at the head of Ennerdale, 5 miles from Ennerdale Bridge and 2½ miles from Bowness Knott car park. Price: £9.25/6.50.

Black Sail (☎ 0411-108450, fax 159472, Black Sail Hut, Ennerdale) is in a quiet wooded valley 2½ miles from the Honister pass and only accessible by foot. Price: £9.25/6.50.

Skiddaw House Youth Hostel (book by post, or call Carrock Fell Hostel ☎ 016974-78325, fax 78325, Bassenthwaite, Keswick CA12 4QX) is in a remote location behind Skiddaw, 6 miles from Keswick and 8 miles from Carrock Fell, and can only be reached on foot. Price: £7.50/5.25.

CUMBRIAN COAST LINE

The Cumbrian Coast railway line, serving the industrial towns and ports of the Cumbrian coast, loops 120 miles around the Cumbrian coast from Carlisle to Lancaster (both cities are on the main line between London Euston and Glasgow). For most of the way it skirts the coast and although parts are beautiful – especially between Ravenglass and Barrow-in-Furness – it also passes some depressing industrial towns in terminal decline and the eyesore of Sellafield Nuclear Power Plant.

Although most of it lies outside the park boundary, the line provides useful access points for the western lakes. It's also a potential return link for walkers on the Cumbria Way who've left their vehicles at Carlisle, and walkers on the Coast to Coast Walk who've left their cars at St Bees.

There are about two trains per hour Monday to Saturday, and one train per hour on Sunday, running between Lancaster and Carlisle. A one-way ticket booked a week ahead costs £15. Phone ☎ 0845 748 4950 for full details.

At Ravenglass you can swap to the private narrow-gauge **Ravenglass to Eskdale** railway, originally built to carry iron ore. The beautiful 7-mile journey costs £6.80/3.40 return. Phone ☎ 01229-717171 for timetable details.

Note that Carnforth station was the one immortalised in the Trevor Howard/Celia Johnson classic film *Brief Encounter*, although these days it looks more like an air-raid shelter.

ULVERSTON
☎ 01229 • pop 12,000

Time seems to have passed Ulverston by – if you're looking for an antidote to the tourist tat of the Lake District towns, this could fit the bill nicely. It's also the starting point for the Cumbria Way.

The helpful TIC (☎ 587120, ℮ ulvtic@tel

inco.co.uk), in Coronation Hall, County Square, can help with making bookings for accommodation along the Cumbria Way. It opens 9 am to 5 pm Monday to Saturday.

Things to See & Do
Comedian Stan Laurel was born at 3 Argyle St and fans of Laurel & Hardy will want to make the pilgrimage to the museum at 4c Upper Brook St. The **Laurel & Hardy Museum** (☎ 582292) is floor to ceiling with memorabilia. Admission costs £2/1, which lets you sit in on some of the old movies too. It opens 10 am to 4.30 pm daily, except in January.

The small **Heritage Centre** (☎ 580820) in Lower Brook St tells the story of the days before rail and road, when getting to Ulverston from Lancaster involved a treacherous journey across the Leven or Kent Sands. It opens 9.30 am to 4.30 pm Monday to Saturday (closed Wednesdays from January to April). Admission costs £2/1.

Coming into town by train you'll see a tower on top of Hoad Hill. This commemorates Sir John Barrow (1764–1848), a local explorer.

Cartmel Priory
Between Grange-over-Sands and Ulverston stands the magnificent 12th-century Cartmel Priory (☎ 015395-36261). The church was not demolished during the Dissolution and survives as one of the finest in the northwest, and dominates the pretty town of Cartmel. It opens 9 am to 5.30 pm daily (to 3.30 pm in winter), with guided tours at 11 am and 2 pm on summer Wednesdays.

Places to Stay
The friendly and welcoming **Walkers Hostel** (☎ 585588, ✉ povey@walkershostel

.freeserve.co.uk, Oubas Hill) is 10 minutes' walk from the town centre on the A590 to Kendal. B&B in dorm rooms costs £10 (£16 with evening meals). Right in the centre, **Church Walk House** (☎ 582211, Church Walk) is opposite Stables furniture shop and has rooms with bath from £20 per person. **Rock House** (☎ 586879, 1 Alexander Rd) has three large family rooms and a single costing £20 per head. The **Trinity House Hotel** (☎ 587639, Princes St) has six rooms costing £22.50 to £37.50 per person. Best of all is **The Whitehouse** (☎ 583340, Market St), a superbly renovated 300-year-old cottage, a bargain for £25/40.

Places to Eat
The recommended **Ugly Duckling Restaurant** (☎ 581573), in the Buxton Place car park, serves tasty dishes in the evening only from Tuesday to Saturday; breast of duck costs £11.95. In the town centre the **Rose & Crown** (☎ 583094, King St) is a classic pub with excellent food, enormous servings and reasonable prices. The **Farmers Arms** (☎ 861277, Lowick Garden), overlooking Market Place, has a few outdoor tables good for sunny days. For a lunchtime snack, the **Hot Mango Cafe** (☎ 584866, 27 King St) makes great cold sandwiches for £4, or hot for £5.

Getting There & Away
The Cumbrian Coast Line train from Lancaster (£5.20, 30 minutes) drops you at Ulverston station, five minutes' walk south of the town centre. Alternatively, Stagecoach has services linking it to Barrow-in-Furness and to Ambleside, via Windermere (except Sunday). Monday to Friday you can also get to Cartmel from Ulverston by bus (30 minutes).

North-Eastern England

North-eastern England is quite different from the rest of the country, although it's misleading to think of it as a single entity. Collectively known as Northumbria, the major sections are County Durham in the south and Northumberland in the north, with the latter area bordering Scotland. The metropolis of Newcastle is squeezed between the two.

As a rule, the countryside here is harder and more rugged than in southern England, and it's as if history reflects this because every inch has been fought over. The central conflict was the long struggle between north and south, with the battle lines shifting over the centuries.

In the years before the Roman invasion, the area from the River Humber to the Firth of Forth was ruled by a confederation of Celtic tribes known as the Brigantes. The Romans were the first to attempt to delineate a border: Hadrian's Wall, stretching 73 miles from Newcastle to Bowness-on-Solway near Carlisle, was the northern frontier of the empire for almost 300 years. It was abandoned around AD 410, but enough remains to bring the past dramatically alive.

The struggle for dominance of the area didn't end until the 18th century. Saxon rule, Viking raids and the uncontrollable Reivers kept the local populace in constant fear; the plethora of *pele* (fortified) towers and castles testify to the war-like times. The Norman kings attempted to bring peace to the land and left a legacy of spectacular fortresses and the marvellous Durham Cathedral.

County Durham is rich in the history of the prince bishops who, due to the fierce nature of the area, ruled it almost as a separate kingdom. Picturesque valleys lie to the west, while unsightly industrial towns spread eastwards to the coast.

Newcastle is the natural hub of the northeast. Situated near the mouth of the River Tyne, it was not surprising that it became rich and prosperous on the back of coal exporting and shipbuilding. Economic depression hit

Highlights

- Being awestruck by Durham Cathedral
- Partying with the Geordies in Newcastle
- Exploring the Coastal Castles – especially Alnwick and Bamburgh
- Strolling along the robust city walls of Berwick
- Getting away from it all in Northumberland National Park
- Walking the windswept Hadrian's Wall

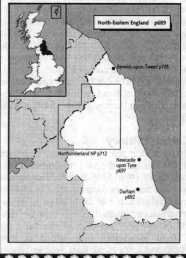

North-Eastern England p689

Berwick-upon-Tweed p705

Northumberland NP p712

Newcastle upon Tyne p697

Durham p692

hard after the decline of industry in the area, but today Newcastle is very much alive and kicking and well worth exploring.

Visitors seeking seclusion should opt for Northumberland National Park, which lies north of Hadrian's Wall and incorporates the open, sparsely populated Cheviot Hills. Walks through the National Park cross some of the loneliest parts of England and can be challenging. The most interesting part of Hadrian's Wall is also included (along the southern boundary) – see the Hadrian's Wall section later in the chapter.

ORIENTATION & INFORMATION

The Pennines are the dominant geological feature that form a north–south spine dividing the region from Cumbria and Lancashire in the west and providing the source of major rivers such as the Tees and the Tyne.

The major transport routes basically run east of this spine: from Durham northwards to Newcastle and Edinburgh. Newcastle is an important ferry port for Scandinavia.

WALKING

There are many great hikes in this region. The most famous is the Pennine Way, which stretches 250 miles from Edale in the Peak District to end at Kirk Yetholm near Kelso in Scotland. Unfortunately, its popularity means that long sections turn into unpleasant bogs, so it is worth considering quieter alternatives. For example, it's possible to walk sections of Hadrian's Wall, or to hike in the remote Cheviot Hills of Northumberland National Park.

CYCLING

Cycling is a great way to see this part of England; the only disadvantages are the weather, the hills and the fact that, at the weekend, even some of the B-roads can be very crowded. On the whole, however, all you need is a good map and some imagination, and you'll have a great time.

There's an 88-mile Sea to Sea cycle route from Whitehaven on the western coast to Sunderland or Newcastle on the eastern coast cutting through the Lake District and Northumberland National Park. A good map and accommodation guide costing £5.99 is available from Sustrans (☎ 0117-926 8893), 35 King St, Bristol BS1 4DZ.

GETTING THERE & AROUND

Air

Teesside Airport (☎ 01325-332811) is an option if you are flying from Continental Europe or Dublin to the north. Newcastle International Airport (☎ 286 0966) has direct services to Aberdeen, London, Cardiff,

NORTH-EASTERN ENGLAND

Dublin, Belfast, Oslo, Amsterdam, Paris and Brussels.

Bus

Bus transport around the region can be difficult, particularly around the remoter parts of Northumbria in the west. For all your transport needs in the north-east call ☎ 0870 608 2608 for information on connections, timetables and prices.

There are several one-day Explorer tickets; always ask if one might be appropriate. The Explorer North East is particularly interesting as it covers all of north-eastern England and other parts of the country, including northern Yorkshire, Hawes (in the Yorkshire Dales) and Carlisle. The major operator in the scheme is Arriva (☎ 0191-212 3000), which can help plan an itinerary. Unlimited travel for one day costs £5.25/4.25 for adults/under-18s, and there are also numerous admission discounts for holders of Explorer tickets (available on buses).

Train

Main-line routes run northwards to Edinburgh via Durham, Newcastle and Berwick; and westwards to Carlisle from Newcastle roughly following Hadrian's Wall. Travelling to/from the south, it may be necessary to make connections at Leeds and York. Phone ☎ 0845 748 4950 for all train enquiries.

There are numerous Rover tickets, for one-day travel and for longer periods, so ask if one might be appropriate. For example, the North Country Flexi Rover allows unlimited travel throughout the north (not including Northumberland) for any four days out of eight for £55.

Boat

Color Line (☎ 0191-296 1313) operates two ferries a week from Newcastle to Stavanger, Haugesund and Bergen in Norway.

See the introductory Getting There & Away chapter at the beginning of the book.

County Durham

The Durham area includes some of the most beautiful parts of the northern Pennines, one of the greatest Christian buildings in the world, and an ancient mining heritage that has left a legacy of uninspiring half-towns.

Although its history isn't as turbulent as that of neighbouring Northumberland (which actually formed Durham's defensive buffer), Durham has known its fair share of bloodshed. In the Middle Ages it was still sufficiently wild to warrant the prince bishops of Durham having virtually limitless power. They combined lay and religious responsibilities as the rulers of a palatinate (a kingdom within a kingdom). The prince bishop (aka the count palatine) had the right to have his own army, nobility, coinage and courts. His great cathedral and castle was once described by Sir Walter Scott as, 'Half church of God, half castle 'gainst the Scot.'

The prince bishops did bring peace to Durham, and this allowed the county to develop long before Northumberland, a fact reflected in the higher population density

and the neat hedges and stone-walled fields. The western half of the county is dominated by the heather-covered hills of the northern Pennines, while the eastern half was, from the 18th century, the centre for a major coal-mining industry which has now largely disappeared.

GETTING AROUND

The transport enquiry line (☎ 0870 608 2608), open 7 am to 8 pm daily, covers all your needs. The Explorer North East ticket (see Bus under Getting There & Around earlier in the chapter) is valid on many services in the county.

DURHAM

☎ 0191 • pop 83,000

Durham is the most dramatic cathedral city in Britain, with a massive Norman cathedral dominating a wooded promontory high above a bend in the River Wear. Other cathedrals are more refined but none has more impact – it's an extraordinary structure built to survive, with utter confidence in the enduring qualities of faith and stone. It is impressive from a distance and simply astounding up close.

The story of Durham begins with the monks of Holy Island (Lindisfarne) fleeing from Viking raiders with their most precious treasures, St Cuthbert's body and the illuminated *Lindisfarne Gospels*. The Lindisfarne monastery had thrived for 240 years, but in 875 the monks began a search for a safer site. Finally, in 995 they found a perfect, easily defended position above the River Wear. The current cathedral is the third to be built on the site; its foundation stone was laid on 12 August 1093.

The prince bishops reached the peak of their power in the 14th century, and although they survived with great pomp and ceremony into the 19th century, their real influence ebbed away. In 1836 the last privileges were returned to the Crown and the last count palatine gave the castle to the newly founded Durham University (1832), the third-oldest university in England. Durham is still the centre for local government in the county.

Orientation

Durham is surprisingly small. The centre of town is limited by the space available on the teardrop-shaped peninsula, and although the city, especially the university, has now overflowed to some extent, everything is within easy walking distance.

Market Place, the tourist information centre (TIC), the castle and cathedral are all on the peninsula surrounded by the River Wear. The train station is north-west of the cathedral and on the other side of the river. The bus station is also on the western side of the city. Using the cathedral as your landmark, you can't really go wrong.

Information

The TIC (☎ 384 3720, ℮ tic@durhamtic .demon.co.uk), Market Place, a short walk north of the castle and cathedral, opens 10 am to 5 pm Monday to Saturday. There's also a Thomas Cook office on Market Place.

Internet access is available at Reality X (☎ 384 5700) 2nd Floor, 1 Framwelgate Bridge, west of Market Place on the way to the bus station.

Durham Cathedral

Built as the shrine for St Cuthbert, Durham Cathedral dates almost entirely from the 12th century and is the most complete and spectacular example of Norman architecture. The Romanesque style as developed by the Normans had a monumental simplicity, characterised by great scale, round arches, enormous columns and zigzag chevron ornament – all shown at their best in Durham. The cathedral's vast interior is like a cave that is only partly artificial, its exterior like time-worn cliffs.

A number of places give good views of the exterior; perhaps the two most famous are from Framwelgate Bridge and Prebend's Bridge, although the approach across Palace Green is also impressive.

History The choir, transepts and nave of the cathedral were built between 1093 and 1133 and still survive in uncompromised Romanesque form. There have been four major additions, all successful: the beautiful Galilee Chapel, with its slim pillars of Purbeck marble at the western end, built between 1170 and 1175; the western towers, built between 1217 and 1226; the Chapel of Nine Altars, with the pointed arches and carved capitals of the Early English style, built between 1242 and 1280; and the central tower, which was rebuilt between 1465 and 1490.

Information The cathedral (☎ 386 4266) opens 9.30 am to 8 pm Monday to Saturday, and 12.30 to 8 pm on Sunday, late May to September; 9.30 am to 6 pm Monday to Saturday, and 12.30 to 5 pm on Sunday, October to April. A donation is requested. It is open for private prayer only from 7.30 to 9.30 am Monday to Saturday, and 7.45 am to 12.30 pm on Sunday, year round.

Guided tours (£3/free for under-16s) start at 10.30 am and 2 pm Monday to Saturday, late May to September; also at 11.30 am in August. Evensong is at 5.15 pm Tuesday to Saturday (Evening Prayer on Monday) and at 3.30 pm on Sunday.

Inside the Cathedral The main entry is through the **north door**. Note the great bronze knocker. This was a sanctuary knocker and was used by people escaping from the rough justice of the Middle Ages and seeking the protection of the church. They would bang the knocker to attract the attention of two watchmen who slept in a room above the door and were then allowed to choose between trial and voluntary exile.

The nave is dominated by massive carved piers, every second one is round and carved in geometric designs; the round piers have an equal height and circumference of 6.6m. Durham was the first European cathedral to be roofed with stone-ribbed vaulting and has the earliest pointed transverse arches in England.

The **Galilee Chapel** is one of the most beautiful parts of the cathedral. The **paintings** on the northern side are among the few surviving examples of 12th-century wall painting and probably feature St Cuthbert and St Oswald. The chapel also contains the **tomb of the Venerable Bede**, author of the *Ecclesiastical History of the English People*. Bede was

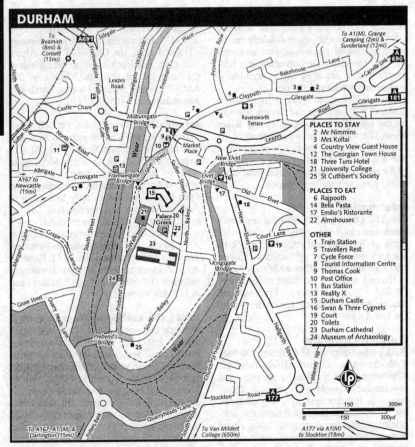

DURHAM

PLACES TO STAY
2 Mr Nimmins
3 Mrs Koltai
4 Country View Guest House
12 The Georgian Town House
18 Three Tuns Hotel
21 University College
25 St Cuthbert's Society

PLACES TO EAT
6 Rajpooth
14 Bella Pasta
17 Emilio's Ristorante
22 Almshouses

OTHER
1 Train Station
5 Travellers Rest
7 Cycle Force
8 Tourist Information Centre
9 Thomas Cook
10 Post Office
11 Bus Station
13 Reality X
15 Durham Castle
16 Swan & Three Cygnets
19 Court
20 Toilets
23 Durham Cathedral
24 Museum of Archaeology

an 8th-century Northumbrian monk, a great historian and polymath whose work held a pre-eminent role in Latin literature for four centuries and is still the prime source of information on the development of early Christian society and institutions in Britain. Among other things, he began the practice of dating years from the birth of Jesus.

The Lords of Raby, the great Neville family, were the first lay people to be buried in the cathedral (in the late 14th century), but their **tombs** and a later chantry were badly damaged by Scots prisoners taking revenge on their traditional enemy.

The only wooden item in the cathedral to survive the anger of the Scots was **Prior Castell's Clock**, a much-restored clock dating from the late 15th century – it possibly survived because of the Scots thistle towards the top of the case.

The **Bishop's throne**, set over the tomb of Bishop Thomas Hatfield, dates from the mid-14th century, and Hatfield's effigy is the only one to have survived. The **high altar** is separated from **St Cuthbert's tomb** by the beautiful stone **Neville Screen**, made around 1375.

St Cuthbert was originally a shepherd but he became an inspirational leader of the northern church and he was also widely loved by the northern peasants. At times he would meditate for days without food and it is said that eider ducks would nestle in his clothing. He died in 687 and when the Viking raids made Lindisfarne untenable, the monks carried his miraculously preserved body with them. His reputation attracted many pilgrims to Durham.

The Chapel of the Nine Altars actually did once have nine altars – in order to facilitate giving Mass to all the monks!

Cloisters The monastic buildings are centred on the cloisters. They were heavily rebuilt in 1828. The cloisters' western door is particularly famous for its 12th-century ironwork. On the western side is a monastic dormitory, now a library, and an undercroft which now houses the Treasury and restaurant.

Treasury Museum The recently refurbished Treasury Museum is definitely worth visiting as it includes relics of St Cuthbert from the 7th century and a collection of illuminated manuscripts and cathedral 'paraphernalia'. It opens 10 am to 4.30 pm Monday to Saturday, and 2 to 4.30 pm on Sunday. Admission costs £2/1.50.

Durham Castle

The castle was begun in 1072 and served as the home for Durham's prince bishops. It has been substantially rebuilt over the years, but still preserves the fundamental layout of a Norman motte-and-bailey castle. It is now a residential college for the university, and it is possible to stay here during summer holidays (see Places to Stay later). There are 40-minutes guided tours every half-hour from 10 am to 12.30 pm and 2 to 4 pm Monday to Saturday, 10 am to noon and 2 to 4 pm on Sunday, late March to early October; 2 to 4 pm on Monday, Wednesday, Saturday and Sunday the rest of the year. Admission costs £3/2.

Museum of Archaeology

In an old fulling mill on the banks of the Wear between Framwelgate and Prebend's bridges, the Museum of Archaeology (☎ 374 3623) has a collection illustrating the history of the city. It opens 11 am to 4 pm April to October; 11.30 am to 3.30 pm Friday to Monday November to March. Admission costs £1/50p.

Walks

There are superb views back to the cathedral and castle from the outer bank of the river; walk around the bend between Elvet and Framwelgate bridges, or hire a boat at Elvet Bridge.

Bluebadge 1½-hour guided walks of the city (£3/free) leave from outside the TIC at 2 pm on Wednesday and at the weekend, June to September.

Cruises

The Prince Bishop River Cruiser (☎ 386 9525), Elvet Bridge, offers one-hour cruises along the river. Trips run at 2 and 3 pm June to September and cost £3.50/1.50.

Rowing boats can be hired for £2.50 per person per hour from Browns Boathouse (☎ 386 3779), below Elvet Bridge.

Places to Stay

The TIC makes local bookings free, which is useful since convenient B&Bs aren't numerous; the situation is particularly grim during graduation week in late June.

Camping Two miles north-east of the city centre, *Grange Camping & Caravan Site* (☎ *384 4778, Meadow Lane)* charges from £8.40 for a car, two people and a tent.

B&Bs & Hotels Several colleges let their rooms out during the university holidays (particularly July to September). The Web site at www.dur.ac.uk/conference_tourism /colleges.htm provides information and links to all the university accommodation available. The most exciting possibility is *University College* (☎ *374 3863,* e *Durham .castle@durham.ac.uk),* in the grounds of Durham Castle, which has B&B singles/doubles for £20.50 per person. The cheapest university accommodation is at *St Cuthbert's Society* (☎ *374 3364),* south of the Cathedral, which charges £19 per person.

There are a few unpretentious B&Bs starting at around £16 per person on Claypath and Gilesgate. Leave Market Place from its northern end and cross over the A690 onto Claypath, where you'll find *Country View Guest House* (☎ 386 1436) with rooms for £20/34. Claypath becomes Gilesgate, where *Mrs Koltai* (☎ 386 2026), at No 10, has three rooms at £16 per person; and *Mr Nimmins* (☎ 384 6485, e bb@nimmins.co.uk), at No 14, has four adequate rooms from £17.

More upmarket and comfortable is *The Georgian Town House* (☎ 386 8070) where breakfast is served in the garden, weather permitting. Singles/doubles start at £45.50/60, some with cathedral views. In the city centre, *Three Tuns Hotel* (☎ 386 4326, *New Elvet*) is a historic hotel with luxury facilities and rooms from £65/75.

Places to Eat

Most of the eating possibilities are within a short walk of the market square. *Emilio's Ristorante* (☎ 384 0096), just over Elvet Bridge, is good value with pizzas and pastas from £5.45. On the other side of the peninsula, *Bella Pasta*, on the eastern side of Framwelgate Bridge, has good views over the river; between 5 and 7 pm two courses cost £5.95.

Almshouses (☎ 386 1054, *Palace Green*) serves up an imaginative and satisfying selection of vegetarian and meat dishes. It opens 9 am to 5 pm; to 8 pm April to September. Choices include spinach pie (£4.60) and celery soup with roll (£2.75).

Rajpooth (☎ 386 1496, *80 Claypath*) has a good reputation for Indian food; main courses start at £5.95.

Entertainment

It's worth checking what's going on; a half-hour walk will give you an idea and the TIC has a *What's On* guide. There are a couple of pubs on Claypath, including the pleasant *Travellers Rest*. The *Swan & Three Cygnets (Elvet Bridge)* is a bright riverside pub with tables overlooking the river and good bar food and the *Court (Court Lane)* has a good mix of students and professionals.

Getting There & Away

Durham is 260 miles from London, 75 miles from Leeds and 15 miles from Newcastle.

Bus There are six National Express (☎ 0870 580 8080) buses a day to London (£20, 6½ hours), one to Edinburgh (£17.50, 4½ hours), and numerous buses to/from Birmingham (£26.50, 6¾ hours,) and Newcastle (£2.75, 30 minutes). There's one bus a day (No 383) between Durham and Edinburgh via Jedburgh and Melrose in the Scottish Borders.

Primrose Coaches (☎ 232 5567) has a daily service (No 352) between Newcastle and Blackpool via Durham, Barnard Castle, Raby Castle and Kirkby Stephen. It leaves Durham from the Sutton St bus stop.

Train There are numerous trains to York (£13.90, one hour), many of which continue to London (£68, £23 if booked seven days in advance, three hours) via Peterborough (for Cambridge). Newcastle is only 15 minutes away (£3.10) and frequent trains from London continue through to Edinburgh (£32.50, two hours).

Getting Around

Taxi Pratt's Taxis (☎ 386 0700) charge a minimum of about £1.80.

Bicycle Cycle Force (☎ 384 0319) at 29 Claypath charges £15 per day for mountain bike hire.

BEAMISH OPEN-AIR MUSEUM

Beamish (☎ 01207-231811) was founded on the ruins of Durham's coal industry; overheard from a grizzled ex-miner sitting in the sun at the entrance waiting for his grandchildren to return, 'Spent half my life down a pit. No way am I going to pay seven quid to go down one again!'

Visitors can go underground, and explore mine heads, a working farm, cottages, a school, a pub and shops.

Beamish opens 10 am to 5 pm April to October; to 4 pm the rest of the year. Allow a minimum of two hours to do the place justice. Ticket prices range from £3 in winter to £10/7 in summer.

Beamish is about 8 miles north-west of Durham; it's signposted from the A1(M) motorway (take the A691 west at junction 63). Bus No 709 from Newcastle, 720 from Durham and 775/778 from Sunderland run to the museum.

BARNARD CASTLE
☎ 01833 • pop 6070

Barnard Castle is an attractive market town, and it makes a good base for exploring Teesdale and the northern Pennines. The TIC (☎ 630272, 690909, e tourism@tees dale.co.uk), Flats Rd, opens 10 am to 6 pm daily April to October and 11 am to 4 pm in winter.

The ruins of Barnard Castle (☎ 638212), run by English Heritage (EH), on the banks of the Tees, cover almost two and a half hectares and testify to its importance; it was founded by Guy de Bailleul and rebuilt by his nephew around 1150. Admission costs £2.30/1.70.

The completely out-of-place but impressive 19th-century French chateau, 1½ miles west of town, houses the **Bowes Museum** (☎ 690606). The chateau, built by local businessman John Bowes and his French wife to exhibit their art collection, is quite magnificent and includes paintings by El Greco and Goya. A prime exhibit is the 18th-century mechanical silver swan in the hall; ask when you can see it in operation. The museum opens 11 am to 5 pm. Admission costs £3.90/2.90.

Accommodation can be hard to find in summer, so the TIC's booking service can be particularly useful. Galgate, which heads north-east from the castle, is a good place to look for accommodation. At No 98, *Marwood House* (☎ 637493, e john@kilgar riff.demon.co.uk) is good value at £20 per person and serves evening meals. *Old Well* pub (☎ 690130, 21 The Bank), downhill from Market Cross, has good, filling pub food, and comfortable doubles with bathroom for £60. There are not a lot of options for a bite to eat but *Hayloft* off Horsemarket is nicely tucked away from the busy main street and serves sandwiches and light meals.

Primrose Coaches (☎ 0191-232 5567) has a daily service between Newcastle and Blackpool via Durham, Barnard Castle, Raby Castle and Kirkby Stephen (No 352). Arriva bus No 75 runs frequently between Durham and Barnard Castle, and No 76 runs from Darlington.

AROUND BARNARD CASTLE

The ruins of **Egglestone Abbey**, open dawn until dusk, are on a lovely bend of the Tees, a pleasant mile's walk south of Barnard Castle. Otherwise it's a five-minute drive.

The countryside around Barnard Castle is beautiful, especially **Teesdale** to the north-west. **High Force** waterfall, where the River Tees jumps 14.7m, is considered one of the best in Britain. It's a surprise to have to pay £1 to see it, but walkers on the Pennine Way on the left-hand bank can view for free. The car park costs an additional £1.50. There are a number of popular walks, including several sections of the Pennine Way.

Raby Castle

Raby Castle (☎ 660202) is a romantic-looking 14th-century castle, a stronghold of the Neville family until the Rising of the North. Most of the interior has been substantially altered, but the exterior remains true to the original design, built around a

---

The Rising of the North

Barnard Castle played its most important role in 1569 during the reign of Elizabeth I. The Percys (Earls of Northumberland) and the Nevilles (Earls of Westmoreland) plotted at nearby Raby Castle to release Mary Queen of Scots from Bolton Castle in Wensleydale, where she was imprisoned, place her on the throne and restore Roman Catholicism.

Sir George Bowes remained loyal to Elizabeth, however, and he and other loyalists held Barnard Castle. On 2 December, 5000 rebels besieged Barnard. On 8 December, the walls were breached and Bowes retreated to the Inner Ward. On 12 December, Bowes was finally forced to surrender, but the delay had allowed the Earl of Sussex to assemble his forces at York and the rebels were defeated.

courtyard and surrounded by a moat. The castle and its beautiful grounds open 1 to 5 pm on Wednesday and Sunday in May and September; 1 to 5 pm Sunday to Friday, June to August. Admission costs £5/2. It's 6 miles north-east of Barnard Castle off the A688. Bus No 8 runs from Barnard Castle (15 minutes, at least six daily).

Newcastle upon Tyne

☎ 0191 • pop 210,000

Newcastle is the largest city in the north-east. It grew famous as a coal-exporting port, and in the 19th century became an important steel, shipbuilding and engineering centre – all industries that went into serious decline after WWII. It had a dour struggle to survive, but retains some 19th-century grandeur, and the famous six bridges across the Tyne are an arresting sight.

Newcastle is currently undergoing a substantial face-lift to boost its image as a major city in Britain. Geordies, as the locals are known, are fiercely proud of their city so they would say Newcastle already is. Money is being poured into the city and is especially apparent around the Quayside area. The brand-new International Centre for Life, and the revamping of the Baltic Flour Mill, on the southern side of the quays, as a contemporary visual arts centre (due to open in late 2001) testify to the headway Newcastle is making.

Plan to stay at least one night; the exuberance with which Geordies let their hair down is well worth experiencing.

Orientation

Although Newcastle is dauntingly large, the city centre is easy to get around on foot, and the Metro (convenient for the hostel and B&Bs) is cheap, efficient and pleasant to use.

The Central Station is on Neville St, just to the south of the city centre. The coach station is on Gallowgate. Local buses, and buses for Beamish, leave from Eldon Square and buses for the north leave from Haymarket.

Information

The convenient TIC (☎ 277 8000), in the train station, opens 10 am to 5 pm Monday to Friday, October to May and to 8 pm, June to September; 9 am to 5 pm Saturday, year round. The well-stocked main office (☎ 277 8000, ☻ tourist.info@newcastle.gov.uk), Grainger St, opens 9.30 am to 5.30 pm Monday to Saturday (until 7.30 pm on Thursday) year round; 10 am to 4 pm on Sunday, June to September. There is also a desk at the airport. They all have a free map, guide and accommodation list, and booking service. A helpful interactive information booth is located at the southern end of Northumberland St.

Thomas Cook (☎ 219 8000) has an office on the corner of Northumberland St and New Bridge. Blacks (☎ 261 8613), the outdoor equipment chain, has a shop at 81–83 Grainger St and The Newcastle Map Centre (☎ 261 5622), 55 Grey St, has a good supply of maps and guides.

You can eat and surf the Net at McNulty's Internet Café (☎ 232 0922) on Market St, behind the main TIC.

International Centre for Life

The big new attraction for the city is the colourful and brash Life Interactive World (☎ 243 8210), next to Central Station, on Scotswood Rd. It is actually part of the International Centre for Life, a complex costing £70 million devoted to the study of DNA. The centre brings together a number of institutes under one roof – the Institute of Human Genetics, the Reproductive Medicine Centre, the Bioscience Centre, and the Policy, Ethics and Life Science Research Institute.

Interactive is the right word to describe the experience of visiting the centre as almost everything is set up for a bit of hands-on fun. A planned route allows all the attractions to be taken in; these range from the amazing 3-D film following the beginnings of Jack as a fertilised egg to a newborn baby to the Secret of Life show incorporating live actors and mostly reluctant audience participation. Kids will love the place, and so will you if you want to be a kid again.

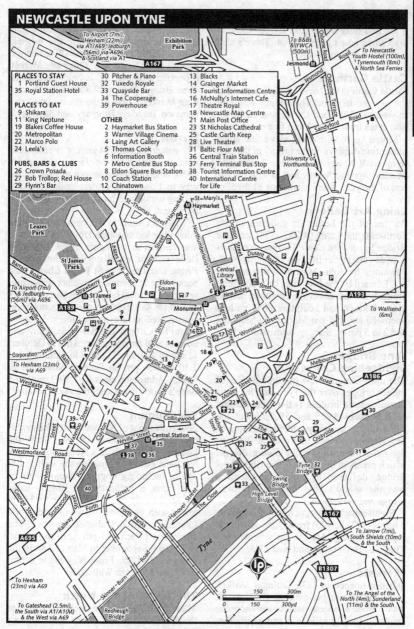

NEWCASTLE UPON TYNE

PLACES TO STAY
1 Portland Guest House
35 Royal Station Hotel

PLACES TO EAT
9 Shikara
11 King Neptune
19 Blakes Coffee House
20 Metropolitan
22 Marco Polo
24 Leela's

PUBS, BARS & CLUBS
26 Crown Posada
27 Bob Trollop; Red House
29 Flynn's Bar

30 Pitcher & Piano
32 Tuxedo Royale
33 Quayside Bar
34 The Cooperage
39 Powerhouse

OTHER
2 Haymarket Bus Station
3 Warner Village Cinema
4 Laing Art Gallery
5 Thomas Cook
6 Information Booth
7 Metro Centre Bus Stop
8 Eldon Square Bus Station
10 Coach Station
12 Chinatown

13 Blacks
14 Grainger Market
15 Tourist Information Centre
16 McNulty's Internet Cafe
17 Theatre Royal
18 Newcastle Map Centre
21 Main Post Office
23 St Nicholas Cathedral
25 Castle Garth Keep
28 Live Theatre
31 Baltic Flour Mill
36 Central Train Station
37 Ferry Terminal Bus Stop
38 Tourist Information Centre
40 International Centre
for Life

Life Interactive World opens 10 am to 5 pm and tickets cost £6.95/4.50; allow at least three hours to get round. There's also a cafe and a shop on site.

Castle Garth Keep

Castle Garth is the 'new' castle from which the city gets its name. The original was built in wood in 1080 and the current construction dates from 1168. It is a fine example of a square keep, with good views and some interesting displays on the history of the city. It opens 9.30 am to 5.30 pm Tuesday to Sunday, April to September; to 4.30 pm the rest of the year. Admission costs £1.50/50p.

Laing Art Gallery

As one of the better art galleries in the north-east, the Laing (☎ 232 7734), on New Bridge St near the Central Library, contains a wide-ranging collection under its roof. Paintings by John Martin, William Hunt and Edward Burne Jones can be found here, along with art covering costume, silver, glass, pottery and sculpture. The gallery opens 10 am to 5 pm Monday to Saturday and 2 to 5 pm on Sunday. Admission is free.

Tyne Bridges & Sightseeing Cruises

The most famous view in Newcastle is of the six bridges over the Tyne, and the most famous of the bridges is the **Tyne Bridge**, built between 1925 and 1928, about the same time as, and very reminiscent of, Sydney Harbour Bridge in Australia. Perhaps the most interesting is the **Swing Bridge**, which pivots in the middle. The **High Level Bridge**, designed by Robert Stephenson, was the world's first road and railway bridge and was opened in 1849.

Sightseeing cruises are run by River Tyne Cruises (☎ 251 5920) from Quayside pier at 2 pm on Sunday, May to early September. They last three hours and cost £7/5.

Markets

When it opened in 1835 **Grainger Market**, in a magnificent building on Grainger St, was Europe's largest undercover shopping centre. It mainly sells fruit and vegetables,

but there are other interesting stalls, including the Marks & Spencer Original Penny Bazaar where unfortunately the original motto of 'Don't ask the price – it's a penny!' doesn't count these days. **Quayside Market**, a popular flea market, is held beneath the Tyne Bridge 9 am to 2.30 pm on Sunday. **Bigg Market** is held in the street of the same name on Tuesday, Thursday and Saturday.

Jarrow

The eastern suburb of Jarrow is embedded in labour history for the 'Jarrow Crusade' in 1936, when 200 men set out to walk all the way to London to protest against the appalling conditions brought about by unemployment.

Today's visitors to this grim district might think little has changed. However, Jarrow is also famous as the home of the Venerable Bede (author of *History of the English People*), and parts of St Paul's Church date back to the 7th century. Together with a museum and Jarrow Hall, it forms part of **Bede's World** (☎ 489 2106), a park with many reconstructed medieval buildings. It opens 10 am to 5.30 pm Tuesday to Saturday, and noon to 5.30 pm on Sunday April to October; 11 am to 4.30 pm Tuesday to Saturday, and 2.30 to 5.30 pm on Sunday, November to March. Admission costs £3/1.50. Jarrow and Bede's World are accessible via the Metro.

Segedunum

Four miles east of Newcastle at Wallsend is the site of Segedunum (☎ 295 5757), the last outpost of Hadrian's Wall. A lot of work has been put in to bringing the wall to life again, including ongoing excavations of fort ruins, a reconstructed Roman bathhouse, the only one in Britain, and a 34.5m tower with views of the whole site. Good interactive displays also do the trick. The site opens 10 am to 5 pm April to August; to 3.30 pm September to March. Admission costs £2.95/1.95. From Newcastle centre catch the Metro to Wallsend.

The Angel of the North

Made from 200 tons of steel, The Angel of the North (a human frame with wings), created by sculptor Antony Gormley, is the largest sculpture in Britain at 19.5m high and a wingspan wider than a Boeing 767. It towers over the A1(M) 5 miles south of Newcastle, and is hard to miss heading north or south. It's best to make your own mind up over the mass of steel – controversy rages over whether it's a total waste of money or a spectacular creation attracting attention to the north.

Places to Stay

Camping The nearest sites are in South Shields: *Sandhaven* (☎ 454 5594, *Bents Park Rd*), charges £9.50 for two people and a car and *Lizard Lane* (☎ 454 4982, *Marsden*), where a site for a two-person tent and car costs £7.20.

Hostels North-east of the city centre, *Newcastle Youth Hostel* (☎ 281 2570, e *Newcastle@yha.org.uk, 107 Jesmond Rd*) opens February to November (Friday to Sunday only, the rest of the year). Dorm beds cost £11/7.75 for adults/under-18s. Call in advance, as it can be busy. Jesmond is the closest Metro station.

North East YWCA (☎ 281 1233, *Jesmond House, Clayton Rd*) accepts male and female guests at £16 per person. Turn left on Osborne Rd from Jesmond station and take the second street on the right.

B&Bs & Hotels For its size, Newcastle is a little sparse on cheap accommodation in the centre of town. Most of it is concentrated in the suburb of Jesmond, north-east of the city. There are quite a number of B&Bs along Osborne Rd and the best way to get there from the city centre is to catch the Metro to West Jesmond station, or catch bus No 33 from Central Station, Grainger St, or the corner of New Bridge and Pilgrim St.

Portland Guest House (☎ 232 7868, *134 Sandyford Rd*) is about the closest and cheapest B&B to the centre of town. A room without bathroom starts at £18/36.

Mere mortals hunting on Osborne Rd should consider *Gresham Hotel* (☎ 281 4341), at No 92, a medium-sized, comfortable hotel from £29/39, although at that price

in Newcastle you still share a bathroom. *Minerva Hotel* (☎ 281 0190), at No 105, is a small place with decent prices; rooms cost £22.50/35. The friendly *George Hotel* (☎ 281 4442, e *georgehotel@dial.pipex.com*) at No 88 has clean and comfortable rooms for £35/46.

Fern Ave is the fifth street on the right if you head down Osborne Rd from Jesmond station. *Adelphi Hotel* (☎ 281 3109), at No 63, is an attractive terraced house with rooms at £29.50/49.50. *Westland Hotel* (☎ 281 0412, *27 Osborne Ave, off Osborne Rd*) has 15 rooms starting from £22/40 per single/double.

Beside Central Station, the impressive *Royal Station Hotel* (☎ 232 0781, *Neville St*) has rooms from £60/72.50, as well as cheaper weekend deals.

Places to Eat

Newcastle has a most un-English attitude to food. Geordies believe in going out to eat and they believe the food should be cheap. As a result, Newcastle has numerous restaurants to choose from. It's best to eat early in the evening, as many places have 'happy hours' when you can often get cheap specials.

Restaurants are widely scattered. There are some at the northern end of town (handy for the university, the youth hostel and the B&Bs on Osborne Rd), and Chinatown is on Stowell St to the south-west of Eldon Square. Perhaps the most interesting zone to explore, however, is the southern part of the city centre. Walk southwards down Grey St (lined with beautiful Georgian and Victorian offices), which becomes Dean St and takes you down to the River Tyne and Quayside.

On Grey St itself, *Blakes Coffee House* (☎ 261 1235) at No 53 is good for a coffee and a bite to eat but for a fuller meal try *Metropolitan*, No 35, a local favourite serving up sandwiches and English-style food. Dean St offers up a number of restaurants, the best being *Leela's* (☎ 230 1261) at No 20. Exceptionally good southern Indian dishes can be had for around £10. If you're looking for a cheap meal, *Marco Polo* (☎ 232 5533) at No 33 has pizzas and pastas for as little as £2.95.

There are a number of interesting pubs at the bottom of the hill. *Flynn's (63 Quayside)* has a beer garden and cheap food and drink, but check out *Bob Trollop* (voted best vegetarian pub 2000) and *Red House* which have pub meals for about £3.

One of the most acclaimed restaurants is *Shikara (☎ 233 0005, 52 St Andrew's St)*, serving excellent Indian food; it's cheap for lunch, most main courses in the evening cost £6 to £10. *King Neptune (☎ 261 6657, 34 Stowell St)* is one of the better Chinese restaurants specialising in seafood and Peking dishes. Set menus start at £14.80 per person.

For something a little different check *The Valley Restaurant* entry under Places to Stay & Eat in Corbridge later in the chapter if you like train rides.

Entertainment

Newcastle caters to most tastes, with high culture and low. At the weekend young people come from other parts of the country to enjoy Newcastle's nightlife. There are a number of guides to what's on: *Paint it Red* and *The Crack* (free), and the *Evening Chronicle* on Wednesday.

The Bigg Market area is notorious for the crowds of young people it attracts – especially on Friday nights when groups of scantily clad young women and increasingly drunken young men circulate the street ogling each other. Be prepared for queues, thick-necked bouncers and infuriating dress codes in some bars and clubs – places may turn people away for wearing trainers, others may insist on a collar and tie (no one wears jackets, even on the coldest days!).

The pubs and clubs around Quayside are more relaxed. *Quayside Bar (35 The Close, Quayside)* is a well-restored warehouse with a great spot right on the river and a quiet courtyard. If real ale and unspoilt pubs are your thing, head for *Crown Posada (31 The Side)*. Long and narrow, it's a wonderful place full of character and serves one of the better pints in town. *The Cooperage (☎ 232 8286, 32 The Close, Quayside)* is a popular pub with a wide-ranging clientele, and doubles as a club after 9 pm on Friday and Saturday. Its timbers are supposedly

from ships sunk in the Tyne. Considering it's part of a bar chain, *Pitcher & Piano (108 Quayside)* is actually worth going to! It's a beautiful modern construction, with huge plate-glass walls and a prime spot overlooking the Tyne across to the Baltic Flour Mill. One of the more unusually located and popular clubs is *Tuxedo Royale (☎ 477 8899, Hillgate Quay)*, on the Tuxedo Princess ship under Tyne Bridge. Tuesday is a big student night. In Waterloo St, *Powerhouse Nightclub (☎ 261 4507)* is a gay and lesbian venue.

The Royal Shakespeare Company is a regular visitor to the superb *Theatre Royal (☎ 232 0997, 100 Grey St)* but there are also fringe companies such as *Live Theatre (☎ 232 1232, 27 Broad Chare, Quayside)*.

Warner Village Cinema (☎ 221 0222, Manors) is one of the better cinemas in town.

Spectator Sports

Football St James Park (☎ 201 8400), on Strawberry Place west of Eldon Square, is holy ground to Geordies who follow the local football team Newcastle United. Tours of the ground are available but it's advisable to book in advance; tours cost £5/3. And like for all teams that play in the most popular football league in the world, it's almost impossible to get a ticket to a game, but you can try on ☎ 261 1571.

Shopping

Shopaholics might be tempted by the MetroCentre at Gateshead, an enormous shopping centre – one of the largest in Europe – with 360 shops, 50 places to eat (mostly fast food) and fairground rides. A free bus runs to the centre from Metro Centre bus stop in town.

Eldon Square, in the heart of Newcastle, is Britain's largest city-centre shopping complex and is another enormous modern shrine to consumerism. Needless to say, markets such as old Grainger Market have *much* more character.

Getting There & Away

Newcastle is 275 miles from London (about five hours by car), 105 miles from Edinburgh (about 2½ hours), 57 miles from Carlisle, 35 miles from Alnwick and 15 miles from Durham. It's a major transport hub, so travellers have many options, including air and sea links.

Air Newcastle International Airport (☎ 286 0966) is 7 miles north of the city, linked by the Metro, and 20 minutes by car off the A696. There are direct scheduled services to Aberdeen, London, Cardiff, Dublin, Belfast, Oslo, Amsterdam, Paris and Brussels.

Bus There are numerous National Express connections with virtually every major city in the country. There are buses every two hours to London (£15, 5¼ hours) and Edinburgh (£7.50, 3¼ hours), and a number of buses each day from York (£12, 2¼ hours).

For local buses around the north-east, don't forget the excellent-value Explorer North East ticket, valid on most services for £5.25. Arriva (☎ 212 3000) operates services to Berwick (No 505) and along Hadrian's Wall (No 685); see the appropriate sections later in the chapter.

Between April and September, Keswick can be reached with Wright Brothers' (☎ 01434-381200) daily No 888 service.

Train Newcastle is on the main London-Edinburgh line so there are numerous trains; Edinburgh (£31.50, 1¾ hours), London's King's Cross (£74, £23 if booked seven days in advance, three hours), York (£11.30, one hour). Berwick (£10.30, 1¾ hours) and Alnmouth (£5.70, 30 minutes), for connections to Alnwick, are north on this line.

There's also the interesting, scenic Tyne Valley Line west to Carlisle. See the Hadrian's Wall section later in the chapter.

Boat See the Getting There & Away chapter, at the beginning of the book, for details of ferry links to Stavanger and Bergen in Norway, Gothenburg (Sweden) and Amsterdam (The Netherlands).

Getting Around
To/From the Airport The airport is linked to town by the excellent Metro system.

There are frequent services daily, and the fare is £1.70.

To/From the Ferry Terminal Bus No 327 links the ferry (at Tyne Commission Quay), the Central Station and Jesmond Rd (for the youth hostel and B&Bs). It leaves the train station 2½ and 1¼ hours before each sailing; the fare is £3.

There's a taxi rank at the terminal; £12 to the city centre.

Bus, Metro & Car There's a large bus network but the best means of getting around is the excellent, cheap, underground railway known as the Metro, with fares from 55p. A DaySaver ticket costs £3 or you can get a day Network Travel Ticket, covering all modes of transport in the Tyne & Wear county, for £3.50. For advice and information ring the travel line (☎ 232 5325). The TIC can supply you with route plans for the bus and Metro networks.

Driving in and around Newcastle isn't fun thanks to the web of roads, the bridges and the one-way streets in the centre – avoid peak hours. Saying that, there are plenty of car parks.

Taxi Late at night at the weekend, taxis can be hard to come by; try Noda Taxis (☎ 222 1888), which has a kiosk outside the entrance to Central Station.

Northumberland Coast

Taking its name from the Anglo-Saxon kingdom of Northumbria (north of the River Humber), Northumberland is one of the wildest, least spoilt of England's counties. There are probably more castles and battlefield sites here than anywhere else in England, testifying to the long, bloody struggle with the Scots.

After the arrival of the Normans, large numbers of castles and fortified houses were built. Many changed hands several times as the Scottish border was pushed back and forth for the next 700 years. Most have now lapsed into peaceful ruin, but others, like Bamburgh and Alnwick, were converted into great houses, which can be visited today. The scenic Coastal Route drive is well signposted but should be renamed the Castle Route considering the amount of castles and ruins it passes.

Some of the most remote beaches can be found along this stretch of coastline and they make for great walks. Swimming, on the other hand, is a cold affair – only for the extremely warm-blooded or the insane.

GETTING AROUND

The excellent *Northumberland Public Transport Guide* is available from local TICs or from the Section Manager Public Transport (☎ 01670-533128), Northumberland County Council, County Hall, Morpeth NE61 2EF. Transport options are good, with a train line (☎ 0845 748 4950) running along the coast from Newcastle to Berwick and on to Edinburgh. The principal bus operator is Arriva (☎ 0191-212 3000), but there are many other smaller operators.

WARKWORTH
☎ 01665 • pop 1600
Warkworth is a small, quaint village beneath the formidable remains of a 14th-century castle and set in a loop of the River Cocquet. Of interest are the impressive ruins of **Warkworth Castle** (☎ 711423; EH), immortalised in Shakespeare's *Henry IV*, and the tiny **Warkworth Hermitage**, a short boat trip up river from the castle. The castle opens year round but the hermitage only opens 11 am to 5 pm on Wednesday and Sunday, April to September. Admission to the castle costs £2.40/1.20; £1.60/80p for the hermitage.

The village has a number of B&Bs, including *Bide a While* (☎ 711753, 4 Beal Croft), where rooms cost from £16 per person. The more upmarket *Sun Hotel* (☎ 711259) has views of both the castle and the river, with rooms starting at £49/75. *The Green House*, in the centre of the village, makes great coffee and snacks.

Warkworth is served by Arriva (☎ 0191-212 3000), bus No X18 links Newcastle,

Warkworth, Alnmouth and Alnwick. There's a train station on the main east-coast line, about 1½ miles west of town.

ALNWICK
☎ 01665 • pop 7000
Alnwick (pronounced annick) is a charming market town that has grown up in the shadow of magnificent Alnwick Castle. The old town still has a medieval feel with narrow, cobbled streets and a market square.

The castle is on the northern side of town and overlooks the River Aln. The TIC (☎ 510665, ℮ alnwick@northumberland .gov.uk), at The Shambles, the traditional location for butchers' stalls, adjacent to the market, opens 9 am to 5 pm Monday to Saturday, 10 am to 4 pm on Sunday.

Internet access is available at Barter Books, on the road heading towards Newcastle. It's one of the largest second-hand bookshops in Britain and in a lovely Victorian railway station.

Alnwick Castle
Outwardly the castle hasn't changed much since the 14th century, but the interior has been substantially altered, most recently in the 19th century. If you enjoy castles, don't miss this one and for a taster check out the Web site www.alnwickcastle.com.

The six rooms open to the public – state rooms, dining room, guard chamber and library – have an incredible display of Italian paintings, including 11 Canalettos and Titian's *Ecce Homo*. There are also some fascinating curiosities, including Oliver Cromwell's camp pillow and night cap, and a hairnet used by Mary Queen of Scots which is actually made from her hair!

The castle (☎ 510777) opens 11 am to 5 pm Easter to October; admission costs £6.25/3.50. For a great view back to the castle, looking up the River Aln, take the B1340 towards the coast.

Places to Stay & Eat
Situated near the roundabout, *Aln House* (☎ 602265, ℮ alyn@alnhouse.freeserve.co .uk, South Rd, the A1 Newcastle road) is an Edwardian house with rooms at £20 per head.

Bondgate Without, just outside the town's medieval gateway, has several accommodation options. The small *Lindisfarne Guest House* (☎ 603430), at No 6, has rooms for £16 with a vegetarian breakfast option. For something a bit different, make an effort to see the dining room of the *Olympic*, sister ship to the *Titanic*, in **White Swan Hotel** (☎ 602109, *Bondgate Within*). The original panelling, ceiling and stained-glass windows from the ship were used to set up this unique room. Rooms at the hotel start at £30/42.

Half wine shop, half cafe, *Wine Cellar Café Bar (Bondgate Within)* is pleasant and relaxed, with a fine selection of bloomers (sandwiches) and baguettes for £2.95. The pubs present the best options for a meal; wander around town before making a choice. *Market Tavern (Fenkle St)*, near the market square, is friendly and the food is good and portions generous; a giant beef stottie costs £4.50.

Getting There & Away

Alnwick has reasonable transport links since it's on the A1 between Newcastle and Edinburgh. Arriva (☎ 0191-212 3000) has a number of services linking Newcastle and Berwick. Bus No X18 has services to the attractive towns of Warkworth and Alnmouth (also stopping at the train station there, which is the nearest to Alnwick).

FARNE ISLANDS

Owned and managed by the National Trust (NT), the Farne Islands lie 3 to 4 miles offshore from Seahouses. Despite being basically bare rock, they provide a home for 18 species of nesting sea birds, including puffins, kittiwakes, Arctic terns, eider ducks, cormorants and gulls. There are also colonies of grey seals. There are few places in the world where you can get so close to nesting sea birds. It's an extraordinary experience.

St Cuthbert, of Lindisfarne fame, died on the islands in 687, and there's a tiny chapel to him on Inner Farne, where it's possible to land. The best time to go is in the breeding season (roughly May to July), when you can see chicks being fed by their parents.

Crossings can be rough – and may not be possible at all in bad weather. Tours take between two and three hours; inexplicably, they use open boats with no proper cabin, so make sure you've got warm, waterproof clothing if there's a chance of rain.

There are various tours and tour operators. There's really nothing to separate the operators, but it's definitely worth landing on one of the islands – preferably Inner Farne. Tours start at 10 am April to September. A three-hour tour around the islands and a landing on Inner Farne costs £7/5; there's an additional £4/2 fee payable to the NT (if you're not a member) for landing. The TIC (☎ 01655-721099), close to the pier, can provide more information.

Tickets are available from booths beside the pier in Seahouses, a couple of miles along the coast from Bamburgh. Operators include Billy Shiel (☎ 01665-720308) and Hanvey & Sons (☎ 01665-720388).

There isn't much to Seahouses but if you need a place to stay the *Olde Ship Hotel* (☎ 01665-720200, ✉ theoldeship@seahouses.co.uk, Main St) offers all you need; fine food, good ale and comfortable rooms starting at £33.

BAMBURGH
☎ 01668 • pop 440

Bamburgh is an unspoilt hamlet just inland from miles of magnificent sandy beaches and dominated by the romantic profile of a stunning castle.

Bamburgh Castle

This fortress, impressive-looking by day but even more so by night, sits on a basalt crag rising from the sea and dominates the coast for miles. The site has been occupied since prehistoric times, but the current castle is largely a 19th-century construction, the passion of the first Lord Armstrong, and is still the home of the Armstrong family. The castle (☎ 214515) opens 11 am to 5 pm April to October. Admission costs £4/1.50.

Places to Stay

Grass pitches and all mod cons, including showers and laundrette, are provided at *Bradford Caims Caravan Park (☎ 213432)*.

The cost of a pitch starts from £7. The caravan park is north of Bamburgh on the B1341 towards Lucker. *Greengates* (☎ 214535, 34 Front St) opens year round and offers B&B for £19 per person.

Getting There & Away

Arriva bus No 501 runs from Alnwick to Berwick via Seahouses and Bamburgh; Monday to Saturday there are services every 1–2 hours. Bus No 401 from Alnwick four stops in Seahouses and Bamburgh.

HOLY ISLAND (LINDISFARNE)

The drive from the mainland over a causeway crossing 3 miles of muddy flats is worth the trip to Holy Island (or Lindisfarne as it was once known) alone. And there's always the chance of getting caught midway by the incoming tide, an occurrence that happens all too frequently despite the warnings. Even in the low season, the windswept 2-mile square island is full of tourists but seems to have few facilities for them.

St Aidan founded a monastery here in 635, and it became a major centre of Christianity and learning. The exquisitely illustrated *Lindisfarne Gospels*, which originated here, can be seen in the British Library. St Cuthbert lived on Lindisfarne for a while, but even he didn't like it and went to the Farne Islands after a couple of years.

Lindisfarne Priory (☎ 01289-389200; EH) consists of the remains of the priory's church and the later 13th-century St Mary the Virgin Church. The museum next to these shows the remains of the first monastery and how monks used to live. It opens 10 am to 6 pm April to September, to 5 pm in October and to 4 pm during the winter. Admission costs £2.80/1.40.

Lindisfarne Castle (☎ 01289-389244; NT) was built in 1550, and restored and converted by Sir Edward Lutyens in 1903. Note that it is half a mile from the village and there's no toilet. It always opens noon to 3 pm but, depending on the tide, these hours may be extended, April to October. Admission costs £4.

It's possible to stay on the island, but try to book. Probably the best bet is *The Ship*

(☎ 01289-389311, Marygate) with three comfortable rooms staring at £22 per person, and serving up good local seafood in the bar. *Britannia House* (☎ 01289-389218, near the town green), a traditional B&B, has rooms from £20 per person.

Lindisfarne can be reached by bus No 477 from Berwick and is 14 miles from Berwick train station. People taking cars across are requested to park just outside the village and to walk into town; parking costs £2 per day. The sea covers the causeway and cuts the island off from the mainland for about five hours each day. Tide times are printed in local papers and at each side of the crossing.

BERWICK-UPON-TWEED

☎ 01289 • pop 13,000

The stone-built town of Berwick, the northernmost town in England, has a dramatic site flanking the estuary of the River Tweed. The river, often graced with flotillas of swans, is crossed by a low stone bridge (built in 1634), the soaring arches of the railway bridge (1850) and a concrete span for road traffic (1928).

Between the 12th and 15th centuries, Berwick changed hands between the Scots and the English no less than 13 times. This merry-go-round ceased prior to the construction of massive Elizabethan ramparts that still enclose the town centre – although, reflecting geographical realities, the football team still plays in the Scottish League!

Berwick is a great place to explore on foot. There are several small museums, but there's nothing, apart from the walls, that must be seen.

Orientation & Information

The fortified town of Berwick proper is on the northern side of the Tweed; the three bridges link with the suburbs of Tweedmouth, Spittal and Eastcliffe. The town centre is compact and easy to walk around, but some B&Bs are quite far-flung.

The TIC (☎ 330733, ⓔ tourism@berwick -upon-tweed.gov.uk), 106 Marygate, opens 10 am to 7 pm July to September, to 6 pm Easter to June; to 4 pm Monday to Saturday the rest of the year.

Internet access is available at Business Link on Anderson Court (off Hide Hill), open 8.30 am to 5 pm Monday to Friday.

The Walls

Berwick has had two sets of walls: little remains of the first which were built during the reign of Edward II; the ones guarding the town today were begun in 1558 and are still intact. They represented the most advanced military technology of the day and were designed both to house the increasingly effective artillery (in arrow-head-shaped bastions) and to withstand it (the walls are low and massively thick, but it's still a long way to fall!).

It's possible to walk virtually the entire length of the walls and this is a must for visitors. There are some wonderful views and the entire circuit takes about 1½ hours. The TIC has a brochure describing the main sights. Between Easter and October there are recommended guided tours, at 11.15 am Monday to Saturday, 2.30 pm on Sunday (£2.50/free).

Places to Stay

If you have no luck finding accommodation around the centre of town, there are plenty of cheap B&Bs south of the river in Tweedmouth, Spittal and Eastcliffe; fortunately there are frequent buses. The B1 runs from the main bus station on Golden Square (Bridget St) across the bridge to Tweedmouth, before turning off and heading to Spittal. The TIC provides an accommodation booking service.

There's a group of places on North Rd: *Dervaig* (☎ 307378, 🅴 dervaig@btinternet .com), at No 1, has two double rooms with bathroom from £20 per person; the friendly, nonsmoking *Four North Road* (☎ 306146, 🅴 sandra@thorntonfour.freeserve.co.uk) at No 4, has clean rooms from £16 per person and large breakfasts.

It's preferable to stay in the centre of town, but it can be hard to find a room. *Mansergh House* (☎ 302297, 86 Church St) is clean and comfortable with rooms from £18 per person. Similarly priced is *Wallace House* (☎ 306539, 1 Wallace Green).

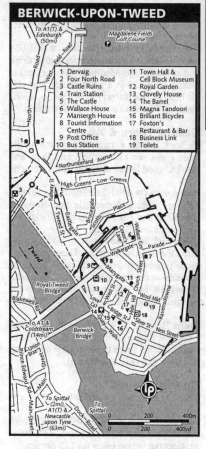

BERWICK-UPON-TWEED

1	Dervaig	11	Town Hall &
2	Four North Road		Cell Block Museum
3	Castle Ruins	12	Royal Garden
4	Train Station	13	Clovelly House
5	The Castle	14	The Barrel
6	Wallace House	15	Magna Tandoori
7	Mansergh House	16	Brilliant Bicycles
8	Tourist Information	17	Foxton's
	Centre		Restaurant & Bar
9	Post Office	18	Business Link
10	Bus Station	19	Toilets

Clovelly House (☎ 302052, 🅴 vivroc @clovelly53.freeserve.co.uk, at 58 West St) has to be one of the best B&Bs in town with great breakfasts and comfy, warm rooms from £17.50 per person.

If a pub stay is preferable, *The Castle* (☎ 307900, 103 Castlegate) is good value at £20 per person.

Places to Eat

Probably the best Indian restaurant in town is *Magna Tandoori* (☎ 302736, 39 Bridge St). Most main courses cost £5.50 to £10 and are good quality. For Chinese food, head to

Royal Garden (☎ 303939) on Marygate, where a filling three-course lunch costs £4.90.

Foxton's Restaurant & Bar (☎ 303939) on Hide Hill is a great place for both a drink and a meal. The Mediterranean vegetable quiche for £5.20 is a good choice. For real ale head to *The Barrel* (56 Bridge St), a welcoming place with occasional live music.

Getting There & Away
Berwick is quite a transport hub; it's on the main east-coast railway line and road, and also has good links into the Scottish Borders.

Bus Arriva (☎ 0191-212 3000) has several services linking Newcastle and Berwick (No 505). Bus No 501 runs to Alnwick via Seahouses and Bamburgh.

Berwick is a good starting point to explore the Scottish Borders. There are buses on to Edinburgh around the coast via Dunbar and west to Coldstream, Kelso and Galashiels. For information on buses in the Scottish borders phone ☎ 01835-824000.

Train Berwick is on the main east-coast London-Edinburgh line, and there are numerous trains south to Newcastle and north to Edinburgh (£12 day return).

Getting Around
Taxi Try Blue Star (☎ 305660).

Bicycle Brilliant Bicycles (☎ 331476 ⓔ com ments@brilliantbicycles.co.uk), 17 Bridge St, hires out hybrid bikes for £15 per day.

Hadrian's Wall

Hadrian's Wall was the most monumental attempt in the island's history to divide the north from the south. It cuts 73 miles across the narrow neck of the country, from Solway Firth in the west, virtually to the mouth of the Tyne in the east, through beautiful, varied countryside. It is a World Heritage Site, and although mainly foundations survive, the ruins and their beautiful locations are extraordinarily evocative.

The wall was the greatest single engineering project undertaken by the Roman Empire – it involved moving two million cubic yards of soil and took over six years (from 122) to build.

The section from Newcastle to the River Irthing was built of stone, turf blocks were used on the section to Solway – roughly 3m thick and 4.5m high. A 3m-deep, 9m-wide ditch and mound were excavated immediately in front (except where there were natural defences). Every Roman mile (1620 yards) there was a gateway guarded by a small fort (milecastle) and between each milecastle were two observation turrets. Milecastles are numbered right across the country, starting with Milecastle 0 at Wallsend and ending with Milecastle 80 at Bowness-on-Solway. The intermediate turrets are tagged A and B, so Milecastle 37 (quite a good one) will be followed by Turret 37A, Turret 37B and then Milecastle 38. A second ditch (the vallum) and a military road were built between 60 and 150m to the south.

A series of forts were developed as bases some distance south (and may actually predate the wall), and 16 actually lay astride it. The prime remaining forts on the wall are Cilurnum (Chesters), Vercovicium (Housestead) and Banna (Birdoswald). The best forts behind the wall are Corstopitum, at Corbridge, and Vindolanda, at Chesterholm.

Today it's possible to visit a number of picturesque surviving sections of the wall, milecastles, forts and turrets, and some excellent museums. Several small, attractive towns make good touring bases.

HISTORY
By building the wall, Emperor Hadrian intended simultaneously to establish control over a clearly delineated frontier and reduce the demand on manpower. He came to Britain in 122 to see it started, and the actual building was undertaken by Roman legions. The wall was primarily a means of controlling the movement of people across the frontier – it could easily have been breached by a determined attack at any single point – and of preventing low-level border raiding.

No one knows when the troops finally abandoned their posts; it's most likely that around 400 Britain was simply set adrift as the Roman Empire fragmented. When pay stopped arriving the soldiers remaining on the wall would simply have left for greener pastures.

ORIENTATION

Hadrian's Wall crosses beautiful, varied country. Starting in the lowlands of the Solway coast, it crosses the lush hills east of Carlisle to the ridge of basalt rock known as Whin Sill (which is bleak and windy, still) overlooking Northumberland National Park, and ends in the urban sprawl of Newcastle. The most spectacular section is between Brampton and Corbridge.

Carlisle, in the west, and Newcastle, in the east, are good starting points, but Brampton, Haltwhistle, Hexham and Corbridge all make good bases.

The B6318 basically follows the course of the wall from the outskirts of Newcastle to Birdoswald; from Birdoswald to Carlisle it pays to have a detailed map. The main A69 road and the railway line follow 3 or 4 miles to the south.

INFORMATION

The TICs in Carlisle and Newcastle are good places to start gathering information, but there are also TICs in Hexham and Haltwhistle open all year, and in Corbridge and Brampton open seasonally. The extremely helpful Northumberland National Park Visitor Centre (☎ 01434-344396) off the B6318 at Once Brewed, opens 9.30 am to 5 pm March to October.

See the Activities chapter for information on walking Hadrian's Wall.

PLACES TO STAY & EAT

Brampton and Corbridge are the most attractive small towns close to the wall, but Haltwhistle is also convenient, and bustling Hexham is another good possibility. All have plentiful B&Bs. There are also a few well-placed lodgings along the wall itself and three usefully placed youth hostels (book in summer): Greenhead, Once Brewed and

Acomb. See also Places to Stay under Newcastle earlier in the chapter and under Carlisle in the Cumbria chapter.

GETTING THERE & AROUND
Bus

West of Hexham the wall runs parallel to the A69, between Carlisle and Newcastle. Bus No 685, operated jointly by Arriva (☎ 0191-212 3000) and Stagecoach Cumberland (☎ 0870 608 2608), runs hourly between those cities on the A69. It passes relatively near the youth hostels and 2 to 3 miles south of the main sites.

Late May to September the special hail-and-ride Hadrian's Wall Bus (No 682) runs between Hexham and Carlisle via Haltwhistle train station, connecting with trains. It follows the B6318, which runs close to the wall, calling at the main sites, the Northumberland National Park Visitor Centre and youth hostel at Once Brewed. This puts the youth hostels at Acomb and Greenhead within easy reach. A Day Rover ticket costs £5/3 and is half price to holders of Explorer North East bus tickets or Stagecoach Cumberland Explorer tickets. It's also possible to purchase a Rover ticket that allows you two days travel in a three-day period. For further information contact Hexham TIC (☎ 01434-605225), or pick up a timetable at any of the Hadrian's Wall TICs.

Train

The Tyne Valley railway line between Newcastle and Carlisle has stations at Corbridge, Hexham, Haydon Bridge, Bardon Mill, Haltwhistle and Brampton. This service runs daily but not all trains stop at all stations.

Taxi

Sproul's (☎ 01434-321064) in Haltwhistle charges around £15 to Hexham.

CORBRIDGE
☎ 01434 • pop 3500

Corbridge is one of the more picturesque towns near the wall. It's on the banks of a beautiful stretch of the River Tyne, 17 miles west of Newcastle, and has attractive stone houses (some very old) lining tree-shaded cobbled streets. It has an ancient history beginning with the Romans. An Anglo-Saxon monastery followed and the town thrived despite being burned three times in border clashes.

St Andrew's Church, mostly rebuilt in the 13th century but with some Anglo-Saxon features, also has a fascinating 14th-century pele tower in its grounds. The TIC (☎ 632815), Hill St, opens 10 am to 1 pm and 2 to 6 pm, Monday to Saturday, and 1 to 5 pm on Sunday, April to October.

Corbridge Roman Site & Museum

Corbridge (or Corstopitum to the Romans) was a garrison town. There were a succession of forts and supply depots, and a surrounding civil settlement. It lies south of the wall on what was the main road from York to Scotland.

The site (☎ 632349; EH) is half a mile west of Corbridge off Trinity Terrace (just over a mile from Corbridge train station). It opens 10 am to 6 pm April to September, 10 am to 5 pm in October; 10 am to 1 pm and 2 to 4 pm Wednesday to Sunday, November to March. Admission costs £2.80/1.40.

Places to Stay & Eat

There are several attractive hotels, most with rooms and bar meals. On the main street, the 17th-century *Angel Inn* (☎ 632119) has comfortable rooms with bathroom for £42 per person while the *Riverside Guest House* (☎ 632942), opposite, has rooms starting at £22 per person. *Holmlea* (☎ 632486, *Station Rd*) near the station, is a terraced house with a comfortable double and a family room from £20 per person. *Town Barns* (☎ 633345), off Trinity Terrace, offers a single, a double and a family room for £24 per person.

The pubs are probably your best bet for food. *Angel Inn* serves good, quite adventurous food. The *Golden Lion (Hill St)* has filling meals for less than £4. You could also try *Corbridge Tandoori*, on the central square, where main courses cost £5.75 to £14.95. Above the train station *The Valley Restaurant* (☎ 633434) supplies delicious

Indian food as well as providing a unique service. A group of 10 or more diners from Newcastle can catch the train to Corbridge accompanied by a waiter, who will supply snacks and phone ahead to have the meal ready when the train arrives.

Getting There & Away

Bus No 685 between Newcastle and Carlisle comes through Corbridge, as does bus No 602 from Newcastle's Eldon Square to Hexham. The town is also on the Newcastle-Carlisle railway line.

HEXHAM

☎ 01434 • pop 11,300

Hexham is quite an interesting town, but is rather marred by being a busy shopping centre. The TIC (☎ 605225), in Safeways' car park north-east of the town centre, opens 9 am to 6 pm Monday to Saturday, and 10 am to 5 pm on Sunday, Easter to September; 9 am to 5 pm daily the rest of the year.

Hexham Abbey, surrounded by a park, is considered a fine example of Early English architecture. The crypt survives from St Wilfrid's Church, which was built in 674, and inscribed stones from Corstopitum can be seen in its walls. Opening hours are 9 am to 7 pm May to September, 9 am to 5 pm October to April.

The Old Gaol (☎ 652349), completed in 1333 as England's first purpose-built prison, is the setting for the Border History Museum. The history of the Border Reivers (see the boxed text 'The Border Reivers' in the Cumbria chapter) is retold along with the punishments handed out in the prison. It opens 10 am to 4.30 pm April to October and Monday, Tuesday and Saturday in February, March and November.

Hexham's size means it's a good place near the wall for accommodation and places to eat. The TIC can book accommodation for you. *West Close House* (☎ 603307, *Hextol Terrace*), off Allendale Rd (the B6305), has a range of comfortable rooms from £18 per person. *Beaumont Hotel* (☎ 602331, ⓔ beaumont.hotel@btinternet.com, Beaumont St) overlooks the abbey and has high-quality accommodation from £45 per person.

There are several bakeries on Fore St and, if you turn left into the quaintly named Priestpopple near the bus station, you'll find some decent restaurants. Possibilities include *Restaurant Fortini*, where pizza and pasta cost around £6, and next door, the *Coach & Horses*, a pleasant pub with a beer garden and bar meals. Across the road, *Diwan-E-Am Tandoori* serves all the traditional Indian dishes.

Bus No 685 between Newcastle and Carlisle comes through Hexham, and the town is also on the Newcastle-Carlisle railway line.

HEXHAM TO HALTWHISTLE
Chesters Roman Fort & Museum
Chesters (☎ 01434-681379; EH) is even more extensive and better preserved than Housesteads, but although the surroundings are attractive, they're not as dramatic as the latter's. The remains are of a Roman cavalry fort and include part of a bridge (very complex and beautifully constructed) across the River North Tyne, an extraordinary bathhouse and a well-preserved under-floor heating system. The museum has an extensive collection of Roman sculpture and stone inscriptions. It opens 10 am to 6 pm April to September, to 5 pm in October and to 4 pm November to March. Admission costs £2.80/2.10.

Brunton Water Mill (☎ 01434-681002, @ pesarra@bruntonmill.freeserve.co.uk, Chollerford) is just a stone's throw from Chollerford bridge and B&B costs from £20 per person. At the much pricier but pleasant *George Hotel (☎ 01434-681611)*, beside the bridge, B&B costs from £85. The Chesters fort site has an excellent small cafe, *Lucullus Larder*, and the restaurant in George Hotel has a good reputation.

Chesters is half a mile west of Chollerford on the B6318, 5½ miles from Hexham and on the route of bus No 682.

Housesteads Roman Fort & Museum
Perched high on a ridge overlooking the moors of Northumberland National Park, Housesteads (☎ 01434-344363; EH) is one of the best known, best preserved and most

dramatic of the sites on the wall. The fort covers two hectares, and the remains of many buildings, including granaries, barracks, latrines and a hospital, can be seen. This is the starting point for some excellent walks and the one to Steel Rigg is considered the most spectacular section of the entire wall.

Housesteads is 2½ miles north of Bardon Mill on the B6318, and about 3 miles from Once Brewed. It's popular, so try to visit outside summer weekends. Opening times are the same as the Chesters Roman Fort & Museum. Admission costs £2.80/2.10.

Vindolanda Roman Fort & Museum
Vindolanda (☎ 01434-344277), 1½ miles north of Bardon Mill between the A69 and B6318 and a mile from Once Brewed, is an extensively excavated fort (excavations are still continuing) with accompanying civil buildings. There are reconstructions of the stone wall with a turret, a length of turf wall and a timber milecastle gate. The museum has some extraordinary relics, including a leather shoe and a fragment of a letter on a wooden writing tablet that talks of socks and underclothes being sent to a soldier on the wall. Nothing has changed: in this climate you can never have too many.

It's managed by the Vindolanda Trust and opens at 10 am mid-February to mid-November but closes at different times during the year: at 4 pm in February and November, 5 pm in March and October, 6 pm in May and June and 6.30 pm in July and August. Admission costs £3.80/2.80 or £5.60/4.10 with a joint ticket for the Roman Army Museum (see Haltwhistle to Brampton later in the chapter).

Places to Stay
Hostels The *Once Brewed Youth Hostel* (☎ 01434-344360, @ oncebrewed@yha.org .uk, Military Rd, Bardon Mill) is modern, well equipped, and central for both Housesteads Fort (3 miles) and Vindolanda (1 mile). Northumbria bus No 685 (which you can catch at Hexham or Haltwhistle train stations) will drop you at Henshaw, 2 miles south, or you could leave the train at Bardon

Mill 2½ miles south-east. The Hadrian's Wall bus drops you at the door (see Getting There & Around under Hadrian's Wall earlier in the chapter). It opens late March to October, Monday to Saturday in February and March and Friday and Saturday only in November. Dorm beds cost £11/7.75 adults/under-18s.

Acomb Youth Hostel (☎ 01434-602864, Main St) is on the edge of Acomb village about 2½ miles north of Hexham and 2 miles south of the wall. Hexham can be reached by bus or train. It opens Friday and Saturday January to March, Wednesday to Sunday in April, May, September and October, Tuesday to Sunday in June and daily from mid-July to August. Dorm beds cost £6.75/4.75.

Set in 18 hectares of countryside, *Hadrian's Wall Backpackers (☎ 01434-688688, North Rd, Haydon Bridge)* is just north of the A69, and is accessible by bus or train. Dorm beds cost £8, or £12.50 with breakfast. It opens April to October.

HALTWHISTLE
☎ 01434 • pop 3750

Haltwhistle, just north of the A69, is a small market town that straggles some distance along Main St. It's a pleasant-enough place, but doesn't have quite the charm of either Brampton or Corbridge.

The TIC (☎ 322002), in the train station, opens 10 am to 1 pm and 2 to 6 pm Monday to Saturday and 1 to 5 pm on Sunday Easter to October; 10 am to 12.30 pm and 1 to 3.30 pm Thursday to Tuesday the rest of the year.

Ashcroft (☎ 320213, Lanty's Lonnen) is an attractive B&B with rooms from £22.50 to £30 per person. *Manor House Hotel (☎ 322588, Main St)* is central, very friendly and has good pub food; B&B starts at £16.50 per person and goes up to £25.

Bus No 685 between Newcastle and Carlisle comes through Haltwhistle, as does Hadrian's Wall bus No 682. Bus No 681 heads south to Alston. The town is also on the Newcastle–Carlisle railway line. Local taxi services include Turnbull's (☎ 320105) and Sproul's (☎ 321064).

HALTWHISTLE TO BRAMPTON
Roman Army Museum

One mile north-west of Greenhead near Walltown, the museum (☎ 016977-47485) has models and reconstructions featuring the Roman army and the troops that garrisoned the wall. Children will enjoy it. It opens the same hours as Vindolanda Fort & Museum. Admission costs £3/2.10, or £5.60/4.10 if you have a joint ticket with Vindolanda.

Birdoswald Roman Fort

Birdoswald (☎ 016977-47602; EH) is one of the most interesting ruins along the wall, with a well-preserved fort on an escarpment overlooking the beautiful Irthing Gorge. The Willowford bridge abutment, across the river, is worth seeing. There's also a good stretch of wall and the exhibition centre displays how life must have been for the Roman soldiers and local people. It's on a minor road off the B6318 about 3 miles west of Greenhead. It opens 10 am to 5.30 pm late March to November. Admission costs £2.50/1.50.

Places to Stay

The cheapest accommodation around is very close to Banks East Turret at *Bankshead Camping Barn (☎ 01200-420102, @ campbarnsyha@enterprise.net)*. It's basic but adequate, with shower and cooking facilities provided and a dry space for 10 people to sleep; a dorm bed costs £3.60 per person. The Hadrian's Wall bus drops you outside.

Greenhead and nearby Gilsland have pubs and B&Bs. *Greenhead Youth Hostel (☎ 016977-47401)* is in a converted Methodist chapel 3 miles west of Haltwhistle train station. It's also served by Northumbria's bus No 685 (see Getting There & Around under Hadrian's Wall earlier in the chapter for details of this and other transport possibilities). It opens Monday to Saturday April to June, daily in July and August, Friday to Monday September to October (also other times). Dorm beds cost £9.25/6.50 adults/under-18s. For your own bedroom in a lovely old farmhouse, try the *Holmhead Guest House (☎ 016977-47402, @ holmhead@hadrians wall.freeserve.co.uk)*, up behind the youth hostel. Rooms start at £26 per person.

BRAMPTON
☎ 016977 ● pop 5000

Brampton is a charming market town built in red Cumbrian sandstone and surrounded by beautiful countryside. The town is particularly interesting on market day (Wednesday). It would make a great base for exploring Hadrian's Wall, and it's on the Cumbrian Cycle Way.

The TIC (☎ 3433) opens 10 am to 5 pm, Monday to Saturday, Easter to October.

The 17th-century *White Lion Hotel* (*☎ 2338, High Cross St*) is one of several pubs serving good bar meals from around £5; gammon steak here is £5.95. It also has comfortable rooms with bathroom from £17.50 to £31.50 per person. *Cobblelane Cottage* (*☎ 3676*, ⓔ kate@footlights.demon .co.uk), behind St Mary's church, is lovely and charges £25 per person, but opens only May to October. *Capon Tree Café* is small and cosy and serves a good selection of snacks.

Bus No 685 between Newcastle and Carlisle comes through Brampton, and the town is also on the Newcastle-Carlisle railway line.

Northumberland National Park

Northumberland National Park covers 398 sq miles of some of the emptiest countryside in the British Isles. The landscape is characterised by windswept grassy hills cut by streams and is almost empty of human habitation.

After the Romans left, the region remained a contested zone between Scotland and England, and home to warring clans and families. Few buildings constructed prior to the 18th century survive, partly because few were built. The cattle-farming families lived in simple structures of turf that could be built quickly and cheaply, and be equally quickly abandoned. Peace came in the 18th century, but coincided with new farming practices, so the tenant farmers were dispossessed, leaving large estates. Unlike the rest of England, this area has no scattering of villages, few stone walls and few small farms. Scenically, it has a bleak grandeur, with wide horizons and vast skies.

ORIENTATION & INFORMATION
The park runs from Hadrian's Wall in the south, takes in the Simonside Hills in the east and runs into the Cheviot Hills along the Scottish border. There are few roads.

For more information, contact the Information Officer (☎ 01434-605555), Eastburn, South Park, Hexham, Northumberland NE46 1BS.

There are several visitor centres: Ingram (☎ 01665-578248), for the Cheviots, opens April to September and at the weekend only in October; Rothbury (☎ 01669-620887) for the central area, opens mid-March to October and at the weekend only the rest of the year; and Once Brewed (☎ 01434-344396) for the Hadrian's Wall area, opens mid-March to October and at the weekend only the rest of the year. There's also a centre (☎ 01434-344525), in partnership with the National Trust, at Housesteads on Hadrian's Wall (see Housesteads Roman Fort & Museum earlier in the chapter), open April to October and at the weekend over winter. All handle accommodation bookings.

WALKING & CYCLING
Walkers are attracted to the **Pennine Way**, which enters the park at its south-eastern corner on Hadrian's Wall, continues to Bellingham, crosses The Cheviot (801m high), and leaves the park near Kirk Yetholm. This is a demanding walk and should be undertaken only if you're properly equipped to deal with tough conditions.

In preparation for opening in 2002 is the 81-mile **Hadrian's Wall Path** from Bowness-on-Solway in Cumbria to Wallsend in Newcastle which will pass through the southern part of the park.

Though at times strenuous, cycling in the park would be a pleasure; the roads are good and the traffic is light. There's off-road cycling in Border Forest Park.

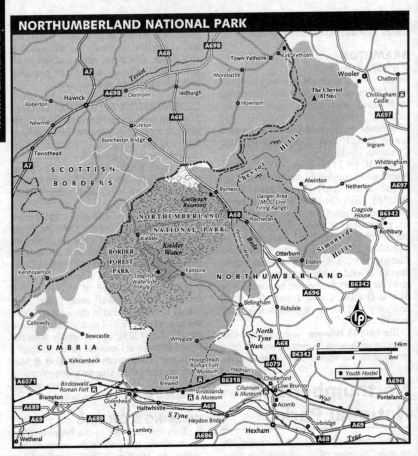

NORTHUMBERLAND NATIONAL PARK

PLACES TO STAY

There's plenty of accommodation in the south around Hadrian's Wall, but the possibilities further north are extremely limited. There are a few B&Bs in Bellingham and Otterburn, and hostels in Bellingham and Byrness (on the Pennine Way). *Byrness Youth Hostel (☎ 01830-520425)* opens April to September. Dorm beds cost £6.75/4.75 (adults/under-18s).

GETTING THERE & AROUND

Public-transport options are also extremely limited, aside from buses on the A69. Bus

No 808 operates 2–3 times a day Monday to Saturday between Otterburn and Newcastle. Postbus No 815, operated by the Royal Mail (☎ 01325-38112, Darlington) runs twice daily on weekdays between Hexham and Bellingham, as does Arriva bus No 880.

National Express operates two services a day between Newcastle and Edinburgh via Otterburn, Byrness, Jedburgh, Melrose and Galashiels. See Getting There & Around under Hadrian's Wall earlier in the chapter for details of access to the south.

BELLINGHAM
☎ 01434 • pop 900

There is not much in Bellingham, but it's surrounded by beautiful countryside, particularly south towards Hadrian's Wall, and makes a good base for day trips in the park. The TIC (☎ 220616), Main St, opens 10 am to 1 pm and 2 to 6 pm Monday to Saturday, and 1 to 5 pm on Sunday Easter to October; 2 to 5 pm Monday to Friday November to March. The 12th-century **St Cuthbert's Church** is unique to the area because of its roof. Made of stone rather than wood like most buildings of the time, it was a place of refuge during the Border wars and the Reivers prominence due to the fact that it wouldn't burn down!

Bellingham Youth Hostel (☎ *220313, Woodburn Rd*) is fairly spartan but cosy and opens Monday to Saturday mid-April to June, September and October, and daily in July and August. Dorm beds cost £8.50/5.75 adults/under-18s. The lovely *Westfield House* (☎ *220340*) has five rooms, all with private bathroom, which cost from £25 per person. The friendly *Lyndale Guest House* (☎ *220361*) is a home away from home with B&B from £20 per person. The more up-market *Riverdale Hall Hotel* (☎ *220254,* e *iben@riverdalehall.demon.co.uk*) has great rooms starting from £69 per person and an excellent restaurant. Bellingham is on the Pennine Way so it's advisable to book ahead in summer.

ROTHBURY
☎ 01669 • pop 1700

Rothbury is a traditional market town situated on the Coquet River at the foot of the Cheviot Hills. It's a quaint place centred on the parallel Front and High streets and the Market Place. There's a TIC and visitors centre (☎ 620887) on Church St, open 10 am to 5 pm late March to October (to 6 pm in summer).

The real reason to head for Rothbury is **Cragside House, Garden and Estate** (☎ 620333; NT), one mile north of the town on the B6341. Built by the first Lord Armstrong as his Victorian countryside retreat, he had a system developed in 1878 using man-made lakes and underground piping to supply the house with hydroelectricity, making it the first house in the world to be lit by such power. The Victorian mansion and gardens are quite stunning and are well worth exploring. Around the house is one of the world's largest rock gardens and a 19th-century Clock Tower, still chiming out the passing hours. There's also a visitors centre, restaurant and shop in the grounds.

Cragside House opens 1 to 5.30 pm Tuesday to Sunday April to October, while the estate and gardens open 10.30 am to 7 pm. Admission to all three costs £6.50/3.25, for the estate and gardens only £4/2. There is no public transport to the front gates from Rothbury; try Rothbury Motors (☎ 620516) for a taxi.

High St is a good place to look for accommodation. *Alexander House* (☎ *621463*) offers B&B from £19 per person, as does the comfortable *Katerina's Guest House* (☎ *602334*) from £23 per person. A few of the pubs do meals, or you could try *Rothbury Bakery*, on the High St, for fresh pies and sandwiches.

Bus No 416 from Morpeth leaves every two hours Monday to Saturday and three times on Sunday. On Sundays and public holidays, late May to September, Arriva bus No 508 runs to Rothbury from Newcastle Central Station. The bus leaves at 10.30 am and arrives at noon (returning at 4.35 pm).

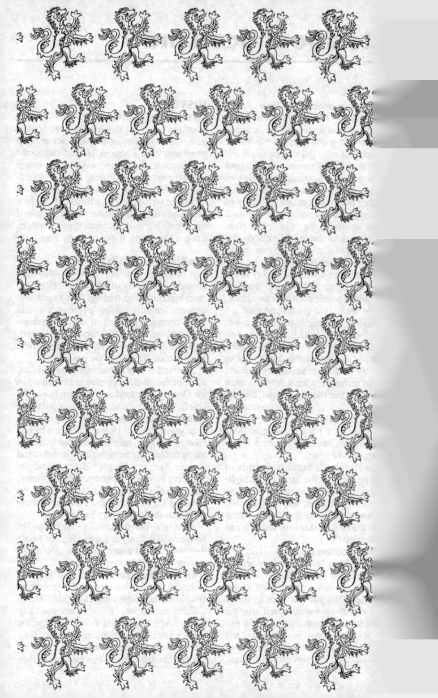

Facts about Scotland

Scotland is hardly a secret but, for a country with an interesting history and some of the world's most dramatic scenery, it's curiously underappreciated and unknown. No visitor to Britain should miss the chance to see it.

Despite its official union with England and Wales in 1707, Scotland maintains an independent national identity that extends much further than the occasional display of kilts and bagpipes. It is also very beautiful and suffers less from the poor urban planning that blights so much of England. The wild Highlands, in particular, are extraordinary. There's a combination of exhilarating open space and a rain-washed quality to the light that illuminates a wonderful range of colours – subtle purples, browns and blues, interspersed with vivid greens and gold.

The weather is sometimes harsh, but 'bad' weather, with scudding clouds and water spilling from storm-wrapped mountains and hills, can be spectacular. It's not an easy country and even Scottish engineers and modern technology have failed to tame it completely. When the winds howl, the rain lashes and the dark grey clouds descend, a human being can still feel extremely vulnerable. At times, it's hard to imagine how human settlement has survived here for so many thousands of years.

But then the clouds break and shafts of sunlight play across the landscape, highlighting snowcapped mountains, heather-covered hills, vast lochs and fast-running streams. And then come the balmy, sunny days when the countryside is as seductive as anywhere on earth.

Traditional Scottish culture survives particularly strongly in the countryside and on the islands but the urban centres are also unique: Edinburgh is one of the world's most beautiful cities; Glasgow is a vibrant cultural centre, vigorously reinventing itself after the collapse of its traditional industries; St Andrews is a lovely coastal university town, and prosperous Aberdeen surveys the North Sea (and its oilfields) with proprietorial interest.

HISTORY
First Immigrants

Scotland's earliest inhabitants were hunter-gatherers who began arriving about 6000 years ago from England, Ireland and northern Europe. Over the next few thousand years these colonisers came in waves to different parts of the country. There are indications of Baltic cultures in eastern Scotland and Irish cultures on the islands of the west. Mesolithic flints from northern France have been found at many sites.

Prehistoric Civilisations

The Neolithic era, beginning in 4000 BC, brought a new way of life, with agriculture, stockbreeding and trading. The result was unprecedentedly large populations and more complex patterns of social organisation evolved to control them. With organised groups of workers, more ambitious construction projects were possible.

Scotland is rich in Neolithic sites; in fact, some of the most impressive in Europe are in the Orkney, Shetland and Western Isles. The chiefs who led these growing populations built elaborate tombs such as the great passage grave at Maes Howe, Orkney, which is constructed from carefully dressed boulders. Stone circles date from the late Neolithic and Bronze Age; the Ring of Brodgar and the Standing Stones of Stenness, both in Orkney, are magnificent examples. At Callanish, on Lewis in the Hebrides, there's a stone circle similar to that at Avebury in England.

Neolithic people usually built wooden houses, and it's only in treeless regions where they were forced to use stone that their architecture has survived. The northern islands contain rare examples of Neolithic domestic architecture; there's an entire village at Skara Brae in Orkney dating from around 3100 BC.

Between the late Neolithic and the early Bronze Age, the Beaker People reached the British Isles from mainland Europe. They were so named because of the shape of the earthenware drinking vessels that they

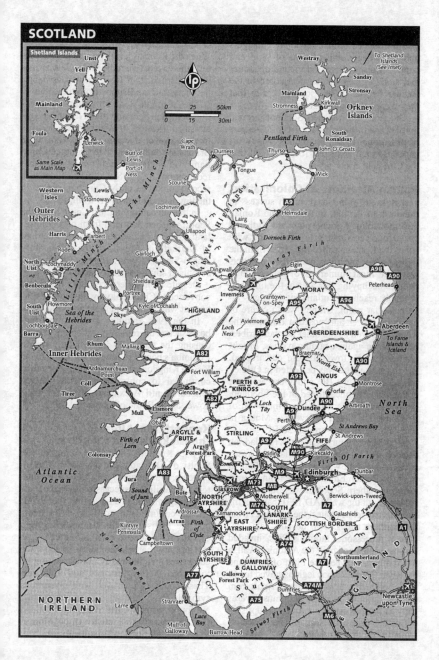

customarily buried with their dead. They also introduced bronze for knives, daggers and arrowheads and articles of gold and copper. Many of Scotland's standing stones and stone circles can be accredited to the Beaker People. Some sources claim that they were the original Celts.

The Iron Age reached Scotland around 500 BC, with the arrival of Celtic settlers from Europe. In the Highlands, which escaped Roman influence, it lasted well into the Christian era.

Roman Attempts at Colonisation

The Romans didn't have much success in the north of Britain. In AD 80, the Roman governor Julius Agricola marched north and spent four years trying to subdue the wild tribes the Romans called the Picts (from the Latin *pictus*, meaning painted). The Picts were the most numerous of many Celtic peoples occupying this area at the time and probably reached Scotland via Orkney.

In the far north, Orkney was a centre of maritime power and posed a threat to the Romans as well as the other northern tribes. For defence against raiding parties, *brochs* (fortified stone towers) were constructed. Broch architecture was perfected in Orkney in the 1st century BC and there are over 500 examples concentrated in the Shetland, Orkney and Western Isles and the north of Scotland. The best preserved, at Mousa in Shetland, dates from around 50 BC.

By the 2nd century AD, Emperor Hadrian decided that this inhospitable land of mists, bogs, midges and warring tribes had little to offer the Roman Empire so the Roman presence in southern Scotland was pulled back. Hadrian built the wall (AD 123) that took his name as a defence against the pressures from the northern tribes. Two decades later Hadrian's successor, Antoninus Pius, invaded Scotland again and built the Antonine Wall, a turf rampart, between the Firth of Forth and the River Clyde. Roman legions stayed for 40 years before they again withdrew. Apart from one final brief incursion by Septimus Severus early in the 3rd century to quell an uprising of Scottish tribes, the Romans abandoned attempts to subdue Scotland.

Feuding Celtic Tribes & Christianity

When the Romans left Britain in the 4th century, there were two indigenous Celtic tribes in northern Britain (then known as Alba): the Picts, and the Britons from the south.

The historian Bede attributes Christianity's arrival in Scotland to St Ninian who established a centre in Whithorn in 397. It's likely, however, that some of the Romanised Britons in southern Scotland adopted Christianity after the religion was given State recognition in 313. St Columba founded a second important early Christian centre on the tiny island of Iona, off Mull, in 563.

In the 6th century a third Celtic tribe, the Scotti, reached Scotland from northern Ireland (Scotia) and established the kingdom of Dalriada in Argyll. In the 7th century Anglo-Saxons from north-eastern England colonised south-eastern Scotland.

Despite their difference, these tribes had converted to Christianity by the late 8th century, at which time a new invader appeared.

In the 790s, raiding Norsemen in longboats sacked the religious settlement at Iona, causing the monks to flee inland (with St Columba's bones) to found a cathedral in the Pictish Kingdom at Dunkeld. The Norsemen continued to control the entire western seaboard until Alexander III broke their power at the Battle of Largs in 1263.

Kenneth MacAlpin & the Makings of a Kingdom

In 843 Kenneth MacAlpin, king of the Scotti of Dalriada and son of a Pictish princess, took advantage of the Pictish custom of matrilineal succession to make himself king of Alba. Thereafter the Scotti gained cultural and political ascendancy and the Pictish culture disappeared. Alba eventually became known as Scotia.

The only material evidence of the Picts comprises their unique symbol stones set up to record Pictish lineages and alliances. These boulders, engraved with mysterious symbols of an otherwise unknown people, are found in many parts of eastern Scotland (see the boxed text 'Pictish Symbol Stones' in the Central Scotland chapter).

Canmore Dynasty

Shakespeare's Malcolm was Malcolm III, a Canmore, who killed Macbeth at Lumphanan in 1057. With his English queen, Margaret, he founded a dynasty of able Scottish rulers.

They introduced Anglo-Norman systems of government and religious foundations, and David I (1124–53) increased his influence by adopting the Norman feudal system, granting land to great Norman families in return for their acting as what amounted to a government police force. By 1212, Walter of Coventry remarked that the Scottish court was 'French in race and manner of life, in speech and in culture'.

Clans & Feudalism

The old society was based on ties of kinship between everyone in the tribe, or clan, and its head. Unlike a feudal lord, a chief might still command the loyalty of his clan whether he was a landowner or not. The feudal system, despite its initial bloody reception, was eventually grafted onto the old system. It created families and clans who were enormously powerful in terms of land ownership and loyal fighting men.

Highlands & Lowlands

Inaccessible in their glens, the Highland clans remained a law unto themselves for another 600 years. A cultural and linguistic divide grew up between Gaelic-speaking Highlanders and the Lowland Scots, who

Tanistry: Finding a King

Unlike the matrilineal Picts, the Scots preferred tanistry – the selection of a suitable male heir from anyone in the family who could claim a king as great-grandfather. The chosen successor was known as the tanist. As Shakespeare demonstrated to great effect in Macbeth, this had dire consequences for Scottish history with many successions decided by the murder of one's predecessor. While the play isn't historically or geographically accurate, it certainly manages to evoke the dark deeds, bloodshed and warring factions of the period.

spoke Lallans, a language made up of English, Norse and Gaelic constituents.

In the Lowlands, small commercial centres such as Berwick, Roxburgh, Stirling, Edinburgh and Forfar grew up through the trading activities of Angles, Scandinavians and Flemings. These centres later became independent, self-governing burghs, trading wool from the monasteries of the Borders for Flemish cloth or wine from Burgundy. Most of the population, however, eked out a subsistence from the land. Until the 20th century, the rural Scots' diet consisted largely of oatmeal, barley, milk, cheese, herrings, rabbits, grouse and kail (cabbage).

Wars of Independence

Two centuries of the Canmore dynasty effectively ended in 1286 when Alexander III fell to his death into the Firth of Forth at Kinghorn, Fife. He was succeeded by his four-year-old granddaughter, Margaret (the Maid of Norway), who was engaged to the son of England's Edward I, but she died in 1290.

There followed a dispute over the succession to the throne for which there were no less than 13 'tanists' or contestants, but in the end it came down to two: Robert Bruce of Annandale and John Balliol. Edward, as the greatest feudal baron in Britain, was asked to arbitrate and he chose Balliol.

Instead of withdrawing, Edward I sought to formalise his feudal overlordship and travelled the country forcing clan leaders to sign a declaration of allegiance to him. Balliol allied with France in 1295, thus beginning the enduring Auld Alliance.

In a final blow to Scottish pride, Edward removed the Stone of Destiny, the coronation stone on which the kings of Scotland had been invested for centuries, and sent it from Scone to London (see the boxed text 'The Stone of Destiny' in the Edinburgh chapter). Resistance broke out throughout the country, some of it serious, and Edward's response earned him the title 'Hammer of the Scots'. In 1296 he laid siege to and captured Berwick.

In 1297, William Wallace's forces defeated the English at the Battle of Stirling Bridge. After further skirmishes he was

Scotland's hero:
Sir William 'Braveheart' Wallace of Ellerslie

JANE SMITH

betrayed, captured and executed – hanged, drawn, emasculated, burnt and quartered – at Smithfield in London in 1305. He's still remembered as the epitome of patriotism and a great hero of the resistance movement.

Robert the Bruce (grandson of Robert Bruce of Annandale) emerged as a contender for the throne. Early in 1306 he murdered his rival John Comyn (also known as Red Comyn) and crowned himself king of Scotland.

That same year Bruce's forces were defeated in battle at Methven and Dalry. According to myth, while Bruce was on the run he was inspired to renew his own efforts by a spider's persistence in spinning its web. He later went on to defeat the English at the Battle of Bannockburn in 1314, a turning point in Scotland's fight for independence from England.

After his death, the country was ravaged by endless civil disputes and plague epidemics. The Wars of Independence strengthened links with France and Europe; the Auld Alliance was constantly renewed up to 1492.

The Stewarts & the Barons

Bruce's son became David II of Scotland. He was soon caught up in battles with Scots disaffected by his father and aided by England's Edward III. He suffered exile and imprisonment but was released after agreeing to pay a huge ransom. He appointed Edward's son as his heir; when David II died in 1371, however, the Scots quickly crowned Robert Stewart (Robert the Bruce's grandson), the first of the Stewart dynasty.

The early Stewart kings were ruthless in their attempts to break the power of the magnates. These were not peaceful years. Time and again the king met with an untimely death and clans like the Douglases and the Donalds (Lords of the Isles after the Norsemen were driven from the Hebrides in 1266) grew to wield almost regal power.

James IV & the Renaissance

In 1503, James IV married the daughter of Henry VII of England, the first of the Tudor monarchs, thereby linking the two families. However, this didn't prevent the French from persuading James to go to war against his in-laws. He was killed at the battle of Flodden Hill in 1513, along with 10,000 of his subjects.

Renaissance ideas flourished in Scotland during James's reign. Scottish poetry thrived. The rigorous intellectual climate was fertile ground for the ideas of the Reformation, which criticised the medieval Catholic Church, and the rise of Protestantism.

Much graceful Scottish architecture dates from this time; examples of the Renaissance style can be seen in alterations made to the palaces at Holyrood, Stirling, Linlithgow and Falkland. The building of collegiate churches and universities brought opportunity for education in Scotland, along French lines. St Andrews University was founded in 1410, Glasgow in 1451 and Aberdeen in 1495.

Mary Queen of Scots & the Reformation

In 1542, James V died – broken-hearted, it is said, after his defeat by the English at

Solway Moss. His baby daughter, Mary, became queen of Scots.

At first the country was ruled by regents, who rejected Henry VIII's plan that Mary should marry his son and sent her to France instead. Henry was furious and his armies ravaged the Borders and sacked Edinburgh in a failed attempt to force agreement – the Rough Wooing, as it was called. Aged 15, Mary married the French dauphin, thereby becoming queen of France as well as Scotland, and claimed England on the grounds that her Protestant cousin, Elizabeth I, was illegitimate.

While Mary, a devout Catholic, was in France, the Reformation of the Scottish Church was under way. The wealthy Catholic Church was riddled with corruption, and the preachings of John Knox, pupil of the Swiss reformer Calvin, found sympathetic ears. In 1560 the Scottish Parliament created a Protestant church that was independent of Rome and the monarchy. The Latin Mass was abolished and the pope's authority denied.

Following her husband's death, Mary returned to Scotland. Still only 18 and a stunning beauty, she was a headstrong Catholic and her conduct did nothing to endear her to the Protestants. She married Henry Darnley and gave birth to a son. However, domestic bliss was short-lived and, in a scarcely believable train of events, Darnley was involved in the murder of Mary's Italian secretary Rizzio (rumoured to be her lover). Then Darnley himself was murdered, presumably by Mary and the earl of Bothwell, her lover and future husband.

Forced to abdicate in favour of her son, James VI, Mary was imprisoned in the castle in the middle of Loch Leven but escaped to England and became the Protestant Elizabeth I. Since Mary had claims to the English throne and Elizabeth had no heir, she was seen as a security risk and Elizabeth kept her locked in the Tower of London. It took her 19 years to agree to sign the warrant for Mary's execution. When the childless Elizabeth died in 1603, James VI of Scotland united the crowns by also becoming James I of England.

Religious Wars of the 17th Century

Religious differences led to civil war in Scotland and England. The fortunes of the Stuarts (spelt the French way following Mary's Gallic association) were thereafter bound with the Church's struggle to establish independence from Rome. To complicate matters, religious reform in Scotland was divided between Presbyterians, who shunned all ritual and hierarchy, and less extreme Protestants who were more like the Anglicans south of the border. The question of episcopacy (rule of the bishops) was particularly divisive.

Earning himself the nickname of the Wisest Fool in Christendom, James VI pursued a moderate policy despite the reformers' fervour. But he also insisted that his authority came directly from God (the Divine Right of Kings) and was therefore incontestable, and encouraged the paranoia which led to witchhunts – many innocent people, set up as scapegoats, suffering appalling deaths by torture and burning as a consequence.

In 1625 James was succeeded by his son, Charles I, a devout Anglican who attempted to impose a High Anglican form of worship on the Church in Scotland.

Twelve years later the dean of St Giles Cathedral in Edinburgh was reading from the English prayer book (a symbol of episcopacy) when he was floored by a stool thrown by Jenny Geddes, an Edinburgh greengrocer. The common people wanted a common religion and riots ensued which ended with the creation of a document known as the National Covenant. The Covenanters sought freedom from Rome and from royal interference in church government, the abolition of bishops and simpler church rituals.

The dispute developed into civil war between moderate royalists and radical Covenanters. The marquis of Montrose is still recalled as a dashing hero who, though originally a Covenanter, eventually held out for the king. Betrayed to the English Republicans while hiding at Ardvreck Castle in Loch Assynt, he was executed as a traitor in 1650.

In the meantime, civil war raged in England. Charles I was defeated by Oliver Cromwell and beheaded in 1649. His exiled son, Charles, was offered the crown in Scotland as long as he signed the Covenant. He was crowned in 1650 but soon forced into exile by Cromwell.

After Charles II's restoration in 1660, episcopacy was reinstated. Many of the clergy rejected the bishops' authority and started holding outdoor services, or conventicles. Charles II's successor, James II, a Catholic, appeared to set out determinedly to lose his kingdom. Among other poor decisions, he made worshipping as a Covenanter a capital offence.

The prospect of another Catholic king was too much for the English Protestants so they invited William of Orange, a Dutchman who was James' nephew and married to his oldest Protestant daughter, to take power. In 1689 he landed with a small army; James broke down and fled to France. In the same year, episcopacy was abolished.

Union with England in 1707

The wars left the country and economy ruined. During the 1690s, famine killed up to a third of the population in some areas.

Anti-English feeling ran high. The Jacobite Graham of Claverhouse (Bonnie Dundee) raised a band of Highlanders and routed the English troops at Killiecrankie (1689), near Pitlochry. The situation was exacerbated by the Darien Disaster, the failure of an investment venture in Panama set up by the Bank of England to boost the economy, which resulted in widespread bankruptcy in Scotland.

In 1692, people were horrified by the treacherous massacre, on English government orders, of the MacDonalds by the Campbells in Glen Coe, for failing to swear allegiance to William. The massacre became Jacobite (Stuart) propaganda that still resonates today.

In this atmosphere, the lure of trade concessions to boost the economy and the preservation of the Scottish church and legal system (along with financial inducements) persuaded the Scottish Parliament to agree to the 1707 Act of Union. This act united the two countries under a single parliament but such a union was unpopular with most ordinary Scots (and ordinary English people had no say in it either).

The Jacobites

The Jacobite rebellions, most notably of 1715 and 1745, were attempts to replace the Hanoverian monarchy (chosen by parliament to succeed the house of Orange) with Catholic Stuarts. Despite Scottish disenchantment with the Act of Union, however, there was never much support for the Jacobite cause outside the Highlands, owing to the fear that it would invite Catholicism back into Scotland.

James Edward Stuart, the Old Pretender, was the son of the exiled James VII. With support from the Highland clans he made several attempts to regain the throne but fled to France after the unsuccessful 1715 rebellion. In an effort to impose control on the Highlanders, General Wade and the English military (the Redcoats) were sent to construct roads into the previously inaccessible glens.

In 1745, James's son, Charles Edward Stuart (Bonnie Prince Charlie, the Young Pretender), landed in Scotland to claim the crown for his father. He was successful initially, getting as far south into England as Derby; back in Scotland after retreating north, however, the prince and his Highland supporters suffered catastrophic defeat at Culloden in 1746. Dressed as a woman, he escaped via the Western Isles assisted by Flora MacDonald.

After 'the '45' (as it became known), the government banned private armies, wearing the kilt and playing the pipes. Many Jacobites were transported or executed or died in prison; others forfeited their lands.

Beginnings of the Industrial Revolution

From about 1750 onwards, Lowland factories began to draw workers out of the glens. The tobacco trade with America boomed before the American War of Independence (1776–83) and then gave way to the textile industry. People came to work in the cotton and linen mills in Glasgow and Lanarkshire. Established in 1759, the Carron ironworks became the largest ironworks in Britain. The jute trade developed in Dundee and shipyards opened on the Clyde in the early 19th century.

Scottish Enlightenment

In the flowering of intellectual life, known as the Scottish Enlightenment, of the 18th century, the philosophers David Hume and Adam Smith emerged as influential thinkers nourished on generations of theological discussion.

After the bloodshed and fervent religious debate of the Reformation, people applied themselves with the same energy and piety to the making of money and the enjoyment of leisure. There was a revival of interest in vernacular literature, reflected in Robert Fergusson's satires and Alexander MacDonald's Gaelic poetry. The poetry of Robert Burns, a man of the people, achieved lasting popularity. Sir Walter Scott, the prolific poet and novelist, was an ardent patriot.

Highland Clearances & the 19th Century

With the banning of private armies, the relationship of chief to clansman in the late 18th and early 19th centuries became one of economic, not military, consideration. The kelp industry (the production of soda ash from seaweed) was developed and Highland populations continued to grow.

By the mid-19th century, overpopulation, the collapse of the kelp industry and the potato famine of the 1840s led to the Highland Clearances. People were forced off the land and shipped or tricked into emigrating to North America, Australia and New Zealand. Those who remained were moved to smallholdings, known as crofts. Rents were extortionate and life for the crofters was extremely precarious. Common grazing ground was confiscated for sheep or deer runs. In 1886, however, the Crofters Commission was set up to ensure security of tenure and to fix fair rent for smallholders (see also the boxed text 'Crofting & the Clearances' in the Highlands & Northern Islands chapter).

In the 19th century, it became fashionable for wealthy southerners to holiday in the Highlands to shoot deer and grouse. Queen Victoria built Balmoral Castle (1848) in Aberdeenshire and spent a great deal of time there after Prince Albert died, disguising herself as a simple Scotswoman and promenading in the company of her Scots servant, John Brown.

Elsewhere, the new urban society saw a growing bourgeoisie take precedence in politics over the still-powerful landed aristocracy. Political life was more closely linked with England. Two Scotsmen had a significant impact on British politics. The popular Liberal, William Gladstone, was prime minister four times and Keir Hardie was the first leader of the British Labour Party.

There was much constitutional and parliamentary reform throughout the Victorian era. Legislation to improve the education system was connected with reform and dissension in the Church. Desire for betterment might send a farmer's child, barefoot and with a sack of oatmeal on their back, to university. The education system remains distinct from England's.

In the great industrial cities, conditions among the working classes were hard. In the notorious Glasgow Gorbals, where typhoid epidemics were rife, people lived in overcrowded tenements on barely subsistence wages. Despite prosperity from the thriving shipyards, coal mines, steelworks and textile mills, Glasgow and Clydeside still harboured many unemployed, unskilled immigrants from Ireland and the Highlands.

The Economy in the 20th & 21st Centuries

Industry thrived through WWI, with Clydeside as a munitions centre. The postwar slump wasn't felt in Scotland until the 1920s but the Great Depression of the 1930s hit so hard that heavy industry never recovered. In fact, the seeds of Scotland's 20th-century economic failure could be said to lie in the success of the preceding industrial era.

The discovery of oil and gas in the North Sea in the 1970s brought prosperity to Aberdeen and the surrounding area and to the Shetland Islands. However, most of the oil revenue was siphoned off to England. This, along with takeovers of Scottish companies by English ones (which then closed the Scottish operations, stripped them of their assets and transferred the jobs to England), fuelled increasing nationalist sentiment in Scotland.

Light engineering and high-tech electronics companies have replaced the defunct coal mines and steelworks of the Central Lowlands but many are foreign owned. The fishing industry, profitable until Britain joined the European Union (EU), is in decline, crippled by fishing quotas imposed from Brussels and by over-fishing.

Depopulation of the rural areas continues despite grant schemes that subsidise new business initiatives over the more traditional industries of agriculture and fishing.

Self-Rule

From 1979 to 1997, Scotland was ruled by a Conservative government in London for which the majority of Scots hadn't voted. Nationalist feelings, always present, grew stronger. In 1967 the Scottish National Party (SNP) had won its first seat, and support for it grew during this period.

Both the Labour Party and the Conservatives had toyed with the idea of offering Scotland devolution, or a degree of self-government. In 1979 Scots voted in a referendum on whether to establish a directly elected Scottish assembly, but the necessary majority wasn't obtained.

Following the landslide victory of the British Labour Party in May 1997, another referendum was held over the creation of a Scottish parliament. This time voters were overwhelmingly in favour. Two years later, using a system of proportional representation, the people elected members to sit in Scotland's first parliament since 1707. It was officially opened in Edinburgh by the Queen on July 1 1999, from which date devolution took effect.

The Labour Party, under the leadership of Donald Dewar (1937–2000), who became the first minister, formed a government in coalition with the Liberal Democrats. The SNP, with about 30% of the vote, became the second largest party and de facto opposition. Although devolution has occurred

within the UK, the prospect of a totally independent Scotland doesn't seem as unlikely as it once did.

GEOGRAPHY & GEOLOGY

Scotland covers 30,414 sq miles, about half England's size. It can be divided into three areas: Southern Uplands, Central Lowlands, and northern Highlands and Islands.

South of Edinburgh and Glasgow are the Southern Uplands, with fertile coastal plains and ranges of hills bordering England. The Central Lowlands comprise a triangular slice from Edinburgh and Dundee in the east to Glasgow in the west and contain the industrial belt and most of the population.

The Highland Boundary Fault, a geographical division, runs north-east from Helensburgh (west of Glasgow) to Stonehaven (south of Aberdeen) on the east coast. North of it are the Highlands and Islands, roughly two-thirds of the country and an area that includes mountain ranges of sandstone, granite and metamorphic rock. Mountains over 914m – there are almost 300 of them in Scotland – are known as Munros, after the man who first listed them (see the boxed text 'Munros & Munro Bagging' in the Highlands & Northern Islands chapter). Some rise directly from the steep sea fjords (usually referred to as lochs) of the west coast. Ben Nevis, in the western Grampians, is Britain's highest mountain at 1343m.

The main Highlands watershed is near the west coast, resulting in long river valleys running east, many of which contain freshwater lochs and some arable areas. The Great Glen, a fault line running from Fort William north-east to Inverness, contains a chain of freshwater lochs (including Loch Ness) connected by the Caledonian Canal.

Of Scotland's 790 islands, 130 are inhabited. The Western Isles comprise the Inner Hebrides and the Outer Hebrides. To the north are two other island groups, Orkney and Shetland, the northernmost reaches of the British Isles.

Edinburgh is the capital and financial centre, Glasgow the industrial centre and Aberdeen and Dundee the two largest regional centres.

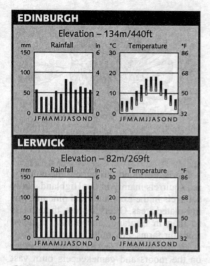

EDINBURGH

Elevation – 134m/440ft

LERWICK

Elevation – 82m/269ft

CLIMATE

'Varied' is a vague but accurate way to describe the many moods of Scotland's cool temperate climate. The weather changes quickly – a rainy day is often followed by a sunny one. There are also wide variations over small distances; while one glen broods under a cloud, the next may be basking in sunshine. May and June are generally the driest months, but expect rain at any time.

Considering how far north the country lies (Edinburgh is on the same line of latitude as Moscow), you might expect a colder climate, but the winds from the Atlantic are warmed by the Gulf Stream. The east and west coasts have relatively mild climates. The east coast tends to be cool and dry – rainfall averages around 650mm and winter temperatures rarely drop below 0°C, although winds off the North Sea can rattle your teeth. The west coast is milder and wetter, with over 1500mm of rain and average summer highs of 19°C.

In the Highlands, rainfall levels can reach 3000mm; the average summer high is 18°C.

ECOLOGY & ENVIRONMENT

Though much of Scotland's beautiful, wild, open countryside looks natural, it isn't. It's almost entirely 'spoilt', in as much as 99% of the original forest has gone. Parts remain, however, and there are now attempts to conserve and increase the abundance of indigenous species such as Scots pine.

In many areas you'll notice thick coniferous plantations. The Thatcher government encouraged landowners to plant these fast-growing trees despite serious ecological drawbacks. As well as ruining wildlife habitat, conifers increase acidity in soil and, in the far north, bog land has been destroyed.

Eye-catching scenery there is a-plenty, but the visitor to Scotland will also see a land pockmarked by litter and graffiti, especially at entry points to the country. For those coming by train from the south to Glasgow, for example, the corridor between Motherwell and Central station offers a particularly ugly vista. Scotland also has some of the most littered beaches in the UK.

The Scottish environment faces other challenges including a legacy of derelict and contaminated land (such as discharge from abandoned mines) as a result of more than two and a half centuries of industrialism; an increasing use of chemicals; and fossil fuel extraction, especially oil. Oil accounts for about 30% of the pollution of Scottish marine environment.

On a positive note the Scottish government (together with EU- and UK-wide legislation) is tightening the regulations on businesses and individuals in relation to the environment.

Conservation organisations preserving and providing access to the natural environment include:

The Scottish Environmental Protection Agency
(☎ 01786-457794) Erskine Court, The Castle Business Park, Stirling FK9 4TR. It also has an emergency number to call if you see a pollution incident: ☎ 0800-807060. Web site: www.sepa.org.uk
John Muir Trust
(☎ 0131-554 0114) 12 Wellington Place, Leith, Edinburgh EH6 7EQ
Web site: www.jmt.org
National Trust for Scotland (NTS)
(☎ 0131-226 5922) 28 Charlotte Square, Edinburgh EH2 4ET
Web site: www.nts.org.uk

Royal Society for the Protection of Birds (RSPB)
(☎ 0131-311 6500) Dunedin House, 25 Ravelston Terrace, Edinburgh EH4 3TP
Web site: www.rspb.org.uk

Scottish National Heritage (SNH)
(☎ 0131-447 4784) 12 Hope Terrace, Edinburgh EH9 2AS
Web site: www.snh.org.uk

Scottish Wildlife Trust
(☎ 0131-312 7765) Cramond House, 16 Cramond Glebe Rd, Edinburgh EH4 6NS
Web site: www.wildlifetrust.org.uk

JANE SMITH

One of the most prized of game birds: the capercaillie

FLORA & FAUNA

Flora

Although much of the country was once covered by the Caledonian forest – a mix of Scots pine, oak, silver birch, willow, alder and rowan, with heather underfoot – deforestation has reduced this mighty forest to a few small pockets of indigenous trees.

Almost three-quarters of the country is uncultivated bog, rock and heather. In mountainous areas such as the Cairngorms, Alpine plants thrive, while in the far north are lichens and mosses found nowhere else in Britain. Acidic peat covers almost two million acres, most notably in the Flow Country of Caithness and Sutherland, a conservation area.

Although the thistle is commonly associated with Scotland, the national flower is the harebell or bluebell. Yellow flag, wild thyme and yarrow abound in the summer. Purple-coloured heather is probably the most noticeable of Scottish flowering plants.

Fauna

Red deer are found in large numbers but the beaver, auroch (wild ox) and wolf became extinct well before the 19th century. Native reindeer died out in the Middle Ages but a herd introduced from Sweden now roams the Cairngorms. Once extinct, wild boars were reintroduced in the south-west and there are still some wildcats but, along with wild goats, they're rarely seen.

Sheep graze the grass-covered hills, and much of the Lowlands is given over to agriculture. The Shetland pony and hairy Highland cattle are well adapted to survive the cold; take care in approaching the latter – those diminutive bovines have foul tempers.

Foxes are found throughout the country, red squirrels mainly in the Highlands, grey squirrels in the Lowlands and pine martens in isolated areas. Otters are rare, though less so than in England, and minks, escaped from fur farms, are multiplying.

Large numbers of grouse graze the heather on the moors and gamekeepers burn vast areas to encourage the new shoots that attract this small game bird. In heavily forested areas you may be lucky enough to see a capercaillie, a black, turkey-like bird, which is the largest member of the grouse family. Birds of prey such as the eagle, osprey, peregrine falcon and hen harrier are protected. Millions of greylag geese winter on the lowland stubble fields.

Scotland has a long indented coastline so it's not surprising to find millions of sea birds here. Trips to see whales, dolphins and porpoises follow more substantial photographic prey, and seals are frequently visible. The major rivers attract anglers from around the world to fish for the famed Scottish wild salmon.

Endangered Species

Scotland is home to many animals and birds that are rare elsewhere in the UK but they too are constantly threatened by the changing environment. The habitat of the once common corncrake, for example, has been almost completely destroyed by modern farming methods. Farmers now receive a subsidy for mowing in corncrake-friendly fashion. Other threats don't even have an economic justification: osprey nests, such as the one at Boat of Garten in the Cairngorms, have to be closely watched to prevent so-called 'collectors' from stealing the eggs.

Rare species once threatened with extinction are protected by law; these include the golden eagle, buzzard, pine marten, polecat and wildcat. Many of these are a natural enemy of game birds and some unscrupulous estate owners and gamekeepers poison birds such as the golden eagle to preserve game birds for sporting shooters.

Scottish Natural Heritage (SNH), a government agency, has established a Species Action Programme to restore populations of endangered species.

Conservation Areas

Scotland's first national park, Loch Lomond & the Trossachs National Park, is due to open in April 2001 (although, at the time of writing it looked as if new legislations would cause delays), straddling the borders of Argyll and Stirling in Central Scotland.

The Monarch of the Glen

The red deer, the Monarch of the Glen, is causing a serious environmental problem in Scotland. Unlike many other species, it isn't hurtling towards extinction but multiplying rapidly. In spite of an increase in culling, around 350,000 now roam the Highlands causing damage to natural and commercial forests by grazing on the shoots of young trees.

Fencing off woodland isn't the answer as it reduces the territory of the deer and leads to even heavier grazing of these areas. In some parts of Scotland, no new trees have been able to grow since deer populations started to increase about 300 years ago.

The balance of nature was upset when the natural predator of the red deer, the wolf, was eradicated in the 17th century. Recently, Scottish National Heritage (SNH) considered re-establishing controlled colonies of wolves but abandoned the proposal when sheep farmers protested. However, some zoologists consider the reintroduction of wolves as the most effective way of resolving this enormous ecological issue.

Other large areas under protection are various designated National Scenic Areas (NSAs), especially in the Highlands, and National Nature Reserves (NNRs). Sites of Special Scientific Interest (SSSIs) are significant for their geology, flora, fauna or habitats or combinations thereof. There are also Local Nature Reserves (LNRs), sites of local-conservation interest for public use; Regional Parks, areas of countryside set aside for public use; and Country Parks, smaller and usually closer to towns.

GOVERNMENT & POLITICS

As part of the process of devolution from London, the first Scottish parliament in nearly 300 years began sitting in May 1999. The single-chamber parliament has 129 members (MSPs – Members of the Scottish Parliament), sits for four-year terms and is responsible for levying income taxes, education, health and other domestic affairs. Westminster still reserves control over areas such as defence, foreign affairs and social security. Elections are held under a mix of first past the post (73 seats) and proportional representation (56 seats).

The Scottish Parliament is temporarily housed in the Assembly Rooms of the Church of Scotland in Edinburgh until construction of its permanent home near the Palace of Holyroodhouse is completed.

The government is called the Scottish Executive, which is headed by the First Minister who appoints the executive's members, known as Scottish Ministers. The Secretary of State for Scotland isn't part of the Scottish Executive but a member of the UK government and, as a result of devolution, only represents Scotland on issues such as defence, social security and foreign affairs.

There are currently 72 Scottish MPs in the House of Commons at Westminster but this may be reduced in the future as the Scottish and UK parliaments work out their constitutional relationship. Scottish peers have a seat in the House of Lords.

There are 32 administrative regions, which roughly correspond to the old counties (such as Argyll, Perthshire and so on) that existed prior to the 1974 reforms.

Radical Politics

The radical Scottish tradition that produced John Knox and other church reformers also generated some later influential political thinkers.

The trade unions produced James Keir Hardie, who helped form the Scottish Labour Party (1888), the Independent Labour Party for Great Britain (1893) and the Labour Representative Committee (1900), forerunner of the British Labour Party. Scottish statesman Ramsey MacDonald became Britain's first Labour prime minister in 1924 but later moved to the centre politically.

The economic distress of the 1930s pushed Scottish political opinion further to the left and several major players in the Communist Party of Great Britain were Scots.

The formation in 1934 of the Scottish National Party (SNP) was initiated by several distinguished men of letters – Hugh MacDiarmid, Eric Linklater, Sir Compton Mackenzie, Neil Gunn and Lewis Grassic Gibbon. This party achieved political success only relatively recently, traditionally most Scots being Labour supporters. Following elections to the Scottish Parliament, it had the second largest number of MSPs (Members of the Scottish Parliament). It sees the new parliament as only a stepping stone to complete independence, for which it has a target date of 2007 – the 300th anniversary of the Act of Union.

The main political parties are the same as for the rest of Britain with the addition of the Scottish Nationalist Party (SNP). Following the 1999 election to the Scottish Parliament, the Labour Party, led by Donald Dewar who became the First Minister, formed government. (Dewar died the following year as the result of a brain haemorrhage and was replaced by Henry McLeish.) The Labour Party, however, could only form a government in coalition with the Liberal Democrats whose leader, Jim Wallace, was made deputy. The SNP, led by Alex Salmond, garnered nearly 30% of the vote, making it the second largest party and effective opposition. The Conservatives won 18 seats, thereby regaining a toehold in Scottish politics – in the 1997 British general election, they had won no seats in Scotland.

The biggest test facing the Labour/Liberal Democrat government is to prove that Scottish solutions to Scottish issues can be made within the constitutional framework of the UK. Like Labour and the Liberal Democrats, the aim of the Conservative party (which had opposed devolution) is to maintain Scotland's position within the union. On the other hand, the SNP believes that the issues facing the country can only be resolved by full political independence.

ECONOMY

Scotland's economy is in a process of transition. The coal-mining and steel industries have contracted considerably. Oil and gas are still extracted from North Sea and North Atlantic platforms but the oil-boom days are over. The old heavy industries are being replaced by less labour-intensive high-tech engineering projects, electronics (including computers and telecommunications), finance and service industries.

Some traditional industries survive and thrive, however. Woollens, tweeds and tartans from Harris (Outer Hebrides) and the Scottish Borders are world-renowned, as are the whisky distilleries. Tourism is Scotland's largest industry and continues to grow, while Edinburgh is an important international finance centre.

In the Highlands some sheep and cattle farming continues, although the grouse moors, deer forests and salmon rivers are more important economically. The fertile lowland plains support barley, oats, wheat, potatoes, turnips, cattle and sheep. EU policy, however, requires farmers to put around 15% of arable land out of production. Scotland catches over two-thirds of UK fish and shellfish even with EU fishing quotas.

Unemployment is generally higher than the UK average, though employment grew by 12% between 1984 and 1998 in line with the rest of the UK – largely as a result of the expansion of part-time female employment.

POPULATION & PEOPLE

Scotland has just over five million people, nearly 9% of the UK's total population. Glasgow is the largest city with 611,500 people, Edinburgh follows with 409,000, Aberdeen with 217,260 and Dundee with 177,540. Scotland has the lowest population density in the UK and the Highland region is Britain's most sparsely populated administrative area, with an average of 20 people per sq mile. Throughout the 20th century, the net population of Scotland declined through emigration.

Early history describes a belligerent people of mixed origin. Invading Romans, raiding Vikings, avaricious English kings and clan warfare never gave them a chance to settle down. Centuries-old disagreements between clans are remembered and even today a Colquhoun won't sit with a MacGregor because of the massacre of Colquhouns by Rob Roy and a band of MacGregors 300 years ago. Religious differences also play a part (see Religion later in the chapter).

Influences from different parts of Europe have created a country of people who are far from homogeneous. The 'hurdy-gurdy' accent of Shetlanders and Orcadians betrays their Scandinavian roots. Gaelic is still spoken in parts of the Highlands and Islands, and Highland society is very different to the anglicised Lowlands. In the 20th century, immigrants, including Irish, Italians, Jews, Poles and other Eastern Europeans, Africans and Asians, have settled mostly in the larger towns.

EDUCATION

As a by-product of the Church, Reformation Scotland developed one of the best education systems in the world. Education was controlled by the Church for a long time and the great universities were set up to provide a source of educated churchmen. By the 17th century there was a school in every parish and standards continued to rise until the Industrial Revolution, when the use of child labour increased. Basic education became compulsory in 1872.

The 1962 Education Act introduced a uniform system preserving the broader-based Scottish system from erosion by anglicisation. Schools today are run by the Scottish Executive Education Department and follow a curriculum and examination system different from England's. Management and content of curriculum is the responsibility of local education authorities

Scots Abroad

'The Scotsman is never at home but when he's abroad' goes the saying. This reflects the fact that the Scots' sense of Scottishness and national identity is often more keenly felt when they're away from the land of their birth.

Scots have emigrated to all corners of the globe for hundreds of years and there are now about 90 million people outside the country who claim some form of Scottish ancestry, compared to just over five million within it.

Evicted Highlanders were sent to Canada, Free Church supporters went to Dunedin in New Zealand, others joined the Hudson's Bay Company and the East India Company. Large numbers of Scots were among those who colonised the countries of the British Empire, well prepared by the hardship of existence in Scotland for the pioneering life. The missionary zeal of the Presbyterians was great in Africa: Dr Livingstone, explorer of the source of the Nile, is one example of many. Some Scots, such as Andrew Carnegie in the USA, had a disproportionate influence on their adopted country.

One of Scotland's greatest exports has been its intellect. Alexander Graham Bell was living and working in the United States when he invented the telephone and most of the country's Nobel Prize winners received the award for their achievements outside Scotland.

and school principals. A new system of courses and qualifications above Standard Grade (age 16) is being introduced.

There are many independent, fee-paying schools run along English lines. At tertiary level, there are 13 universities, the most prestigious being Aberdeen, St Andrews, Dundee, Edinburgh, Glasgow and Stirling.

Many young people leave school without qualifications but educational standards aren't really falling as some claim, rather the educational results of other countries are improving.

SCIENCE & PHILOSOPHY

It's hard to imagine the modern world without the enormous contribution of Scottish scientists. Some of the greats include John Napier, the inventor of logarithms; Lord Kelvin, who invented the absolute temperature scale which bears his name, revealed the second law of thermodynamics and pioneered transatlantic telegraphy; and James Clerk Maxwell, who described the laws of electromagnetism. James Hutton is considered the founder of modern geology.

Among the technologists were James Watt, who revolutionised steam power, and John Dunlop, inventor of the pneumatic wheel. John McAdam developed the road surface that bears his name (though spelt differently) and Charles Mackintosh invented waterproof material. Alexander Graham Bell invented the telephone, John Logie Baird TV, Sir Robert Watson Watt radar, the list goes on...

In medicine, doctors John and William Hunter were pioneers in anatomy, Sir Joseph Lister led the use of antiseptics and Alexander Fleming co-discovered penicillin.

Among Scotland's philosophers and thinkers were David Hume, whose works included *A Treatise of Human Nature* (1740), and Adam Smith, author of the influential *The Wealth of Nations* (1776) and advocate of free trade.

Many reasons have been given for this extraordinary roll call but one is the long tradition of high-quality education, which can be traced back as far as the earliest monastic institutions. Another perhaps is the weather, which has caused thinking

Scots to remain indoors to ponder life, the universe and all that's within it.

ARTS

Between them, Edinburgh and Glasgow dominate the arts in Scotland. Both have an energetic cultural scene, partly reflected by their respective festivals, which showcase an extraordinary range of performers and artists. Historically, however, although the Scots have had a disproportionate impact on science, technology, medicine and philosophy, they are – with the notable exception of literature – under-represented in the worlds of art and music.

The arts never seem to have caught the Scottish popular imagination – or at least not in a form recognised by modern culture vultures. Perhaps the need for creative expression took different, less elitist paths – in the *ceilidh* (see Society & Conduct later in the chapter), oral poetry, and folk music, dance and stories.

Literature

Scotland's literary heritage is so rich that most parts of the country have a piece of writing that captures its spirit.

Sir Walter Scott's prodigious output did much to romanticise Scotland and its historical figures. *Rob Roy* portrays the cattle rustler/blackmailer rather rosily but the descriptions of the Trossachs, in which the MacGregor family operated, are more accurate.

Several Robert Louis Stevenson novels have Scottish settings. *Kidnapped*, set in Edinburgh and remote parts of the Highlands and Islands, including the island of Mull and Rannoch Moor, captures the country vividly. Originally published in 1886 with many Scottish words and phrases deleted by its publisher, a new edition is now available as Stevenson wrote it, in the full vernacular.

Sir Compton Mackenzie's *Whisky Galore* is required reading for long Hebridean ferry rides; it's the witty, true-life tale of what happened when a cargo of whisky runs aground on one of the islands during WWII. (The TV series *Monarch of the Glen* is adapted from his novels.) Derek Cooper's more serious *Hebridean Connection* is also recommended.

Visitors to the Orkneys should read at least one of George Mackay Brown's novels, which perfectly evoke the special mood of these islands. *Greenvoe* is a wonderfully poetic description of an Orkney community and his short-story collection *A Calendar of Love* is delightful.

Lewis Grassic Gibbon's trilogy, *A Scot's Quair*, evocatively recaptures early-20th-century rural life in Aberdeenshire. His *Sunset Song* is a literary classic. Neil Munro's *Para Handy,* about a steamship captain, gives an insight into early-20th-century Gaelic life in the north-west.

Muriel Spark's *The Prime of Miss Jean Brodie* is a shrewd portrait of 1930s' Edinburgh. In sharp contrast, Irvine Welsh's *Trainspotting* and other novels take the reader on a tour of the modern city's underworld of drugs, drink and despair. Sometimes compared to Welsh is Alan Warner whose novels, *The Morvern Callar* and *These Demented Lands*, cover similar themes but are set in the Highlands.

The grim realities of contemporary Glasgow are vividly recounted in James Kelman's short-story collection, *Not Not while the Giro*. Kelman won the 1994 Booker Prize with the controversial *How Late It Was, How Late*. Alisdair Gray's acclaimed *Lanark* is also set in a run-down city based on modern Glasgow; Duncan McLean's *Bucket of Tongues* is an equally disturbing short-story collection is set in assorted depressed urban locations.

Journalist Isla Dewar's novels are spirited accounts of small-town life in modern Scotland. Titles include *Women Talking Dirty* (now a film) and *Giving up on Ordinary*.

Nigel Tranter is a prolific historical novelist whose books are set in Scotland. Recent novels include *High Kings and Vikings* and *The Lion's Whelp*, which is about young James II of Scotland.

Other writers to look out for are Des Dillon, Laura Hird, John Hodge, AL Kennedy and Elizabeth McNeill.

Collections of ballads and poems by the popular national bard (poet) Robert Burns are widely available. Other 18th-century poets were Robert Fergusson, friend of Burns and possibly Edinburgh's greatest poet, and Alexander MacDonald who wrote in Gaelic. Sorley MacLean and Norman Mc-Caig were also exceptional poets. Scotland's finest modern poet is Hugh MacDiarmid. Perhaps the worst is William MacGonagall, who is celebrated for the sheer awfulness of his rhymes. His *Poetic Gems* offers a taster.

Painting

There are few internationally known Scottish figures in the visual arts, although the National Gallery of Scotland in Edinburgh and the galleries in Glasgow, Aberdeen, Perth and Dundee have important Scottish collections.

Scottish painting emerged in the mid-17th century with portraits by George Jameson and John Wright. Scottish portraiture peaked during the Scottish Enlightenment in the figures of Alan Ramsay and Henry Raeburn. Enlightenment landscape painter Alexander Nasmyth had immense influence on 19th-century painters, most notable of whom was William MacTaggart.

Since the end of the 19th century, Glasgow has dominated the Scottish art scene, partly thanks to the Glasgow School of Art, which has produced several outstanding artists. These included Charles Rennie Mackintosh and Maude Armour.

In the 1890s, the Glasgow Boys, among them James Guthrie and EA Walton, were stylistically influenced by French impressionism. They were succeeded by the Scottish Colourists whose striking paintings drew upon post-impressionism and Fauvism. In the same period there emerged the Glasgow Girls, exponents of decorative arts and design.

The Edinburgh School of the 1930s were modernist painters who depicted the Scottish landscape. Following WWII, artists such as Alan Davie and Eduardo Paolozzi gained international reputations in abstract expressionism and pop art. Today's new wave of painters include the New Glasgow Boys whose work is characterised by concern for social issues.

Scotland on Film

Scotland has been the setting for many films. Some early adaptations from Scottish novels were *The Prime of Miss Jean Brodie* (1969) and *Kidnapped* (1972). For a time the film most closely associated with Scotland was probably *Local Hero* (1983), Bill Forsyth's gentle story of an oil magnate turned conservationist for love of the scenery. His other great success was *Gregory's Girl* (1980), about an awkward Glasgow schoolboy's romantic exploits. He followed this up with a sequel 20 years later, *Gregory's Two Girls* (2000), in which the awkward schoolboy becomes an awkward schoolteacher.

When *Braveheart*, the Mel Gibson spin on the William Wallace saga, won an Oscar in 1996, the Scottish Tourist Board (STB) cheered, anticipating a boom in tourists lured by the glorious scenery in the background. What the STB wasn't shouting about, however, was that though it was partly filmed around Fort William, most of *Braveheart* was shot in Ireland which had been wooing Hollywood film-makers with tax breaks.

The same year saw the release of *Loch Ness*, a romantic comedy focussing on the monster myth, following fast on *Trainspotting*, the grim filmic rendition of Irvine Welsh's novel set in Edinburgh. All this, when memories of *Rob Roy*, the 1995 interpretation of the outlaw's tale, starring Liam Neeson and Jessica Lange with wonky Scottish accents, were only just fading. Billy Connolly's accent was real enough when he played John Brown, Queen Victoria's Scottish servant in *Mrs Brown* (1997).

Following the success of Irvine Welsh, journalist Isla Dewar's novel *Women Talking Dirty*, an account of small-town life in modern Scotland, was adapted for the screen, starring Helena Bonham Carter and released in 2000. Hollywood, seeing the potential, has now begun to tap into the rich mine of modern Scottish writers and we can expect more adaptations of Scottish fiction in the future.

Music

In the 1950s and 60s many people's idea of Scottish music was represented by Kenneth McKellar and Andy Stewart, who sang mostly sentimental ballads often accompanied by the accordian and sometimes the bagpipes. But Scotland has always had a strong folk tradition and in the 60s and 70s Robin Hall and Jimmy McGregor, the Corries, and the talented Ewan McColl plied their trade in the pubs and clubs of Britain. The Boys of the Lough were one of the first to successfully blend Scottish (and Irish) folk music with pop/rock music and they've been followed by the Battlefield Band, Runrig (who write songs in Gaelic), Alba, Capercaillie and others.

In the 1980s and 90s rock musicians such as Simple Minds and the Pogues borrowed from Scottish themes. And the last two decades have seen an outpouring of Scottish talent in popular music, especially from Glasgow. Just a few of the names include Gerry Rafferty, Annie Lennox, Nazareth, Aztec Camera, Tears for Fears, Wet Wet Wet, Texas and the latest young guns, Idlewild.

Architecture

Scottish architecture can be divided into six periods: Celtic (to the 11th century), Anglo-Norman (to the 16th century), post-Reformation or Renaissance (to the 17th century), Georgian (18th century), Victorian Baronial (19th century) and modern (20th century onwards) which so far evades simple characterisation.

Interesting buildings can be seen throughout Scotland but Edinburgh has a particularly remarkable heritage of superb architecture from the 12th century to the present day.

Celtic Few Celtic buildings survive although the Islands have some of the best remaining examples in Europe. The best known are the stone villages of Skara Brae (from 3100 BC) in Orkney, Jarlshof (from 1500 BC) in Shetland, and the characteristic brochs, probably built by chieftains, that can be seen in some places, including Carloway in Lewis and Mousa in Shetland.

The crofters' blackhouses of the Highlands and Islands were probably little changed from Celtic times through to the early 20th century but only a few remain. Originally they were circular but at some point they came to be long, low rectangular buildings. They had thick dry-stone walls and thatched roofs, sometimes augmented with skins and canvas, tied down with ropes and nets. There were no chimneys so smoke from a central peat fire simply leaked through the thatch (although enough soot remained to cover the walls, hence their name). The kitchen and communal area was in the centre; the family slept to one side, the animals to the other.

Anglo-Norman The Normans were great builders and their Romanesque style, with its characteristic round arches, can still be seen in David I's church (1128) at Dunfermline and the beautiful 12th-century church at Leuchars.

Military architecture was also influenced by the Normans in castles such as Caerlaverock (1290) and, later, at Stirling (1496). Most feudal lords, however, built more modest tower, or peel, houses such as Threave and Smailholm (14th century). These had a single small entrance, massively thick stone walls and a single room at each of about five levels.

As the Gothic style developed in England and Europe, it was brought to Scotland and adapted by religious orders. The characteristic pointed arches and stone vaulting can be seen in Glasgow Cathedral (13th century) and the ruins of great border abbeys such as Jedburgh (1138).

Post-Reformation After the Reformation most churches were modified to suit the new religion, which frowned on ceremony and ornament. In some areas, tower houses and castles became less relevant because of the increasing effectiveness of artillery. The gentry therefore had the luxury of expanding their houses and at the same time making them more decorative. Features such as turrets, conical roofs, garrets and gables became popular in buildings such as Castle Fraser (1636) in Aberdeenshire & Moray, and Thirlestane Castle (12th century) in the Scottish Borders.

Georgian The greatest exponent of the austere, symmetrical Georgian style in Scotland was the Adam family, in particular Robert Adam. Among other buildings he designed in the mid-18th century were Hopetoun House near Edinburgh, Mellerstain House near Kelso in the Scottish Borders and Culzean Castle south of Ayr.

Victorian Baronial As the Scottish identity was reaffirmed by writers such as Burns and Scott, architects turned to the towers and turrets of the past for inspiration. Fanciful buildings such as Balmoral in Aberdeenshire, Scone Palace (north of Perth) and Abbotsford (home of Sir Walter Scott) in the Scottish Borders were created. The fashion is also exhibited in many civic buildings.

Modern Scotland's most famous 20th-century architect and designer is Charles Rennie Mackintosh of Glasgow, one of the most influential exponents of Art Nouveau. His best known work is the Glasgow School of Art, which still looks modern nearly a century after it was built.

In general, the quality of modern building has been poor, although there are notable exceptions such as the impressive gallery housing the Burrell Collection in Glasgow. The larger towns and cities have suffered badly under the onslaught of the motor car and the unsympathetic impact of large-scale, shoddy council housing. Traditional houses badly affected by dampness have been demolished in large numbers, but many remain.

SOCIETY & CONDUCT
Outside Scotland, Scots are often portrayed as a tight-fisted bunch but nothing could be further from the truth – most are in fact extremely generous. Scots may appear reserved but are passionate in their beliefs whether it's politics, religion or football. They generally treat visitors courteously and the class distinctions that so bedevil England are less prevalent. The influence of religion is declining but sectarian tension between Protestants and Catholics occasionally erupts in violence and in the Highlands and Islands religion still closely affects daily life.

Traditional Culture

Bagpipes One of the oldest musical instruments still used today is the bagpipe. Although no piece of film footage on Scotland is complete without the sound of the pipes, their origin probably lies outside the country. The Romans used bagpipes in their armies and modern versions can be heard as far from the Highland glens as India and Russia.

The Highland bagpipe is the type most commonly played in Scotland. It comprises a leather bag inflated by a blowpipe and held under the arm; the piper controls the flow of air through the pipes by squeezing the bag. Three pipes, appropriately known as 'drones', play all the time without being touched by the piper. The fourth, the chanter, is the one on which tunes are played.

Ceilidh The Gaelic word 'ceilidh' (pronounced kay-lee) means 'visit' – a ceilidh was originally a social gathering in the house after the day's work was over. A local bard presided over the telling of folk stories and legends; there was also music and song. Today, a ceilidh is an evening of entertainment including music, song and dance.

Clans A clan is a group of people who claim descent from a common ancestor. In the Highlands and Islands, where the Scottish clan system evolved between the 11th and 16th centuries, many unrelated families joined clans to be under the clan chief's protection. So, although they may share the same name, not all clan members are related by blood. Clan members united in raiding the more prosperous Lowlands or neighbouring glens to steal other clans' cattle.

After the 18th-century Jacobite rebellions the suppression of Highland culture brought the forced breakdown of the clan system, but the spirit of clan loyalty remains strong, especially among the 25 million Scots living abroad. Each clan still has its own chief, (now merely a figurehead) and its own tartan (see Tartans later in the chapter).

Crofting In the Highlands and Islands, a few acres of land supporting some sheep or cows or a small market garden is known as a croft. Crofting has always been a precarious way of life. In the 19th-century crofters were regularly forced off the land by landlords demanding extortionately high rents. In the 20th century, unrealistic demands upon the land by agricultural economists almost killed off the crofting tradition.

Now, however, there's increased interest in crofting and some communities support more people than they have done since the mid-19th century. (See the boxed text 'Crofting & the Clearances' in the Highlands & Northern Islands chapter.)

Highland Games These games take place throughout the summer and not just in the Highlands. Assorted sporting events with piping and dancing competitions attract locals and tourists alike.

The original games were organised by clan chiefs and kings who recruited the strongest competitors for their armies and as bodyguards. Even today the Queen unfailing attends the Braemar Gathering, the best known and most crowded of all Highland Games, in September.

Some events are peculiarly Scottish, particularly those that involve the heavies in bouts of strength testing. The apparatus used can be primitive – tossing the caber involves heaving a tree trunk into the air. Other popular events in which the heavies take part are throwing the hammer and putting the stone.

Tartans Tartan, popular the world over, is a patterned woollen material which today is made into everything from kilts to key-fobs. The oldest surviving piece dates back to the Roman period.

The *plaid* is the traditional dress, with a long length of tartan wrapped around the body and over the shoulder. Particular *setts* (patterns) didn't come to be associated with certain clans until the 17th century, although today every clan, indeed every football team, has a distinctive tartan.

The wearing of Highland dress was banned after the Jacobite rebellions but revived under royal patronage in the following century. For their visit in 1822, George IV and his English courtiers donned kilts.

Sir Walter Scott, novelist, poet and dedicated patriot, did much to rekindle interest in Scottish ways. By then, however, many of the old setts had been forgotten – some tartans are actually Victorian creations. The modern kilt only appeared in the 18th century, reputedly invented by Thomas Rawlinson – an Englishman!

Dos & Don'ts

Though using the term British is fine, the Scots don't like being called English (see the boxed text 'What's in a Name?' in the Facts for the Visitor chapter), especially in the Highlands and Islands where Scottish nationalism is strongest.

The mixture of religion and football creates intense rivalry particularly between Protestant Glasgow Rangers and Catholic Glasgow Celtic. Whenever subjects like religion, football or Scottish nationalism come up, as a visitor it's probably a good time for you to practise your listening skills.

RELIGION

About 22% of Scotland's people are active members of a religion, of whom 91% are members of Christian churches.

Christianity reached Scotland in the 4th century although in some places vestiges of older worship survived. As recently as the 18th century, Hebridean fishing communities conducted superstitious rites to ensure a good catch. With the Reformation, the Scottish Church rejected the pope's authority. A schism later developed among Scottish Protestants – the Presbyterians favoured a more simplified church hierarchy, without bishops, than the Episcopalians.

About 200,000 Scots belong to the Presbyterian Church (or Kirk) of Scotland. There are two Presbyterian minorities: the Free Church of Scotland (known as the Wee Frees) and the United Free Presbyterians, found mainly in the Highlands and Islands where strict adherence to the scriptures means that ferries aren't always allowed to operate on Sunday. The Episcopal (Anglican) Church of Scotland, once widespread north of the Tay, now has only about 20,000 members, many of them from the landed gentry.

There are about 284,000 Catholics, mainly around Glasgow, many descended from 19th-century Irish immigrants. Some islands, such as Barra, and areas of Aberdeenshire and Lochaber, were converted to Roman Catholicism as a result of secret missionary activity after the Reformation. Sectarian tensions can be felt in Glasgow, especially when the Protestant Rangers and Catholic Celtic football teams play and during the Orange marching season (which climaxes on 12 July).

About 1% of the population adheres to other religions including Buddhism, Hinduism, Islam, Judaism and Sikhism.

LANGUAGE

Ancient Picts spoke a language that may have been of non Indo-European origin. It survives mainly in place names prefixed by 'Pit' (for example, Pitlochry). With the coming of Gaelic-speaking Celts (Gaels or Scotti, later called Scots) from northern Ireland between the 4th and 6th centuries, Gaelic became the language spoken in most of Scotland. This predominance lasted until the 9th or 11th centuries when Anglo-Saxons arrived in the Lowlands. Gaelic then went into a long period of decline and it has only been making a comeback since the 1970s.

Lallans or Lowland Scots evolved from Anglo-Saxon and has Dutch, French, Gaelic, German and Scandinavian influences. It's the language of Robert Burns and Sir Walter Scott and it too is undergoing a revival. And then there's English. Aye, but the Scots accent can make English almost impenetrable to the *Sassenach* (an English person or a Lowland Scot) and other foreigners, and there are numerous Gaelic and Lallan words that linger in everyday English speech. Ye ken?

Edinburgh

☎ 0131 • pop 409,000

Edinburgh has an incomparable location, studded with volcanic hills, on the southern edge of the Firth of Forth. Its superb architecture ranges from extraordinary 16th-century tenements to monumental Georgian and Victorian masterpieces – all dominated by a castle on a precipitous crag in the city's heart. Sixteen thousand buildings are listed as architecturally or historically important in this city, which is a World Heritage Site.

The geology and architecture combine to create an extraordinary symphony in stone. The Old Town, with its crowded tenements, stands in contrast to the orderly grid of New Town with its disciplined Georgian buildings. There are vistas from every street – sudden views of the Firth of Forth, the castle, the Pentland Hills, Calton Hill with its memorials, and rugged Arthur's Seat.

All the great dramas of Scottish history have played at least one act in Edinburgh, the royal capital since the 11th century. Even after the union of 1707 it remained the centre for government administration (now the Scottish Executive), the separate Scottish legal system and the Presbyterian Church of Scotland. With devolution and the location of the Scottish Parliament in Edinburgh, the city once again wields real political power.

In some ways, however, it's the least Scottish of Scotland's cities, partly because of the impact of tourism, partly because of its closeness to England and partly because of its multicultural, sophisticated population. Edinburgh has a reputation for being civilised and reserved, especially in comparison with intense, gregarious Glasgow. Nevertheless, the vibrant pub scene, large student population and series of festivals make Edinburgh a lively city.

On the down side, life is grim for many living in the bleak council housing estates surrounding the city; there's also a thriving drug scene, prostitution and a distressing AIDS problem.

Highlights

- Walking up to Arthur's Seat or the Salisbury Crags to savour the views of Edinburgh
- Cycling in Holyrood Park or following one of the many cycle paths into the surrounding countryside
- Treating yourself to performances at the Fringe Festival
- Letting yourself be guided through the city's underground passages in search of ghosts
- Taking a cruise on the Firth of Forth from South Queensferry to Inchcolm Island
- Exploring the vibrant pub and bar scene

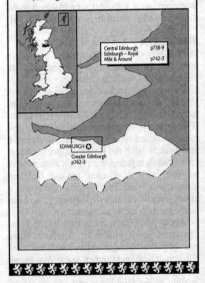

Central Edinburgh p738-9
Edinburgh – Royal Mile & Around p742-3

EDINBURGH ✪
Greater Edinburgh p762-3

HISTORY

Castle Rock, a volcanic crag with three vertical sides, dominates the city centre. This natural defensive position was probably what first attracted settlers; the earliest signs of habitation date back to 850 BC.

Northumbrian Angles captured Lothian in the 6th century, rebuilding a fortress, known as Dun Eadain, on Castle Rock. This served as the Scots' southern outpost until 1018 when Malcolm II established a frontier at the River Tweed. Nonetheless, the English sacked the city seven times.

Edinburgh began to grow in the 11th century when markets developed at the foot of the fortress, and from 1124 David I held court at the castle and founded the abbey at Holyrood.

The first effective town wall was constructed around 1450 and circled the Old Town and the area around Grassmarket. This restricted, defensible zone became a medieval Manhattan, forcing its densely packed inhabitants to build tenements that soared to 12 storeys.

A golden era that saw the foundation of the College of Surgeons and the introduction of printing ended with the death of James IV at the Battle of Flodden in 1513. England's Henry VIII attempted to force a marriage between Mary (James V's daughter) and his son but the Scots sent the infant Mary to France to marry the dauphin. The city was sacked by the English and the Scots turned to the French for support.

The Scots were increasingly sympathetic to the ideas of the Reformation and when John Knox returned from exile in 1555 he found fertile ground for his Calvinist message.

When James VI of Scotland succeeded to the English crown in 1603, he moved the court to London and, for the most part, the Stuarts ignored Edinburgh. When Charles I tried to introduce episcopacy (the rule of the bishops) in 1633 he provoked the National Covenant (see Greyfriars Kirk & Kirkyard later in the chapter) and more religious turmoil which finally ended in triumph for Presbyterianism.

The Act of Union in 1707 further reduced Edinburgh's importance but cultural and intellectual life flourished. In the second half of the 18th century a new city was created across the ravine to the north. The population was expanding, defence was no longer vital and the thinkers of the Scottish

The Flodden Wall

In 1513 the English defeated the Scots at the Battle of Flodden, and King James IV and 10,000 of his followers were killed. The citizens of Edinburgh were thrown into such despair by this episode that they decided to separate their city from the outside world altogether. To that end they built the Flodden Wall across High St between what are now the World's End and The Tass pubs. Part of the wall can still be seen in the basement of the World's End.

Enlightenment planned to distance themselves from Edinburgh's Jacobite past.

The population exploded in the 19th century – Edinburgh quadrupled in size to 400,000, close to today's figure – and the Old Town's tenements were taken over by refugees from the Irish famines. A new ring of crescents and circuses was built south of New Town and grey Victorian terraces sprung up. In the 20th century the slum dwellers were moved into new housing estates farther out that now foster severe social problems.

Edinburgh entered a new era following the 1997 referendum in favour of an independent Scottish Parliament, which began functioning in July 1999. The parliament is temporarily housed in the Church of Scotland Assembly Rooms in the Old Town while a modern Parliament building is under construction (despite some controversy and a blowout in costs) at the eastern end of the Royal Mile across from Holyroodhouse.

ORIENTATION

The most important landmark is Arthur's Seat, the 251m-high rocky peak south-east of the city centre. The Old and New Towns are separated by Princes St Gardens, with the castle dominating both of them.

The main shopping street, Princes St, runs along the northern side of the gardens. Buildings are restricted to its northern side, which has the usual high-street shops. At the eastern end, Calton Hill is crowned by several monuments. The Royal Mile (Lawnmarket,

EDINBURGH

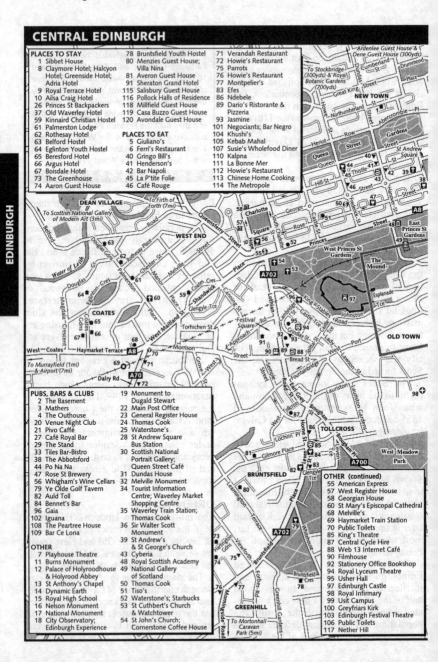

CENTRAL EDINBURGH

PLACES TO STAY
1 Sibbet House
8 Claymore Hotel; Halcyon Hotel; Greenside Hotel; Adria Hotel
9 Royal Terrace Hotel
10 Ailsa Craig Hotel
26 Princes St Backpackers
37 Old Waverley Hotel
59 Kinnaird Christian Hostel
61 Palmerston Lodge
62 Rothesay Hotel
63 Belford Hostel
64 Eglinton Youth Hostel
65 Beresford Hotel
66 Argus Hotel
67 Boisdale Hotel
73 The Greenhouse
74 Aaron Guest House
78 Bruntsfield Youth Hostel
80 Menzies Guest House; Villa Nina
81 Averon Guest House
91 Sheraton Grand Hotel
115 Salisbury Guest House
116 Pollock Halls of Residence
118 Millfield Guest House
119 Casa Buzzo Guest House
120 Avondale Guest House

PLACES TO EAT
5 Giuliano's
6 Ferri's Restaurant
40 Gringo Bill's
41 Henderson's
42 Bar Napoli
45 La P'tite Folie
46 Café Rouge
71 Verandah Restaurant
72 Howie's Restaurant
75 Parrots
76 Howie's Restaurant
77 Montpelier's
83 Efes
86 Ndebele
89 Dario's Ristorante & Pizzeria
93 Jasmine
101 Negociants; Bar Negro
104 Khushi's
105 Kebab Mahal
107 Susie's Wholefood Diner
110 Kalpna
111 La Bonne Mer
112 Howie's Restaurant
113 Chinese Home Cooking
114 The Metropole

PUBS, BARS & CLUBS
2 The Basement
3 Mathers
4 The Outhouse
20 Venue Night Club
21 Pivo Caffé
27 Café Royal Bar
29 The Stand
33 Tiles Bar-Bistro
38 The Abbotsford
44 Po Na Na
47 Rose St Brewery
56 Whigham's Wine Cellars
79 Ye Olde Golf Tavern
84 Auld Toll
84 Bennet's Bar
96 Gaia
102 Iguana
108 The Peartree House
109 Bar Ce Lona

OTHER
7 Playhouse Theatre
11 Burns Monument
12 Palace of Holyroodhouse & Holyrood Abbey
13 St Anthony's Chapel
14 Dynamic Earth
15 Royal High School
16 Nelson Monument
17 National Monument
18 City Observatory; Edinburgh Experience
19 Monument to Dugald Stewart
22 Main Post Office
23 General Register House
24 Thomas Cook
25 Waterstone's
28 St Andrew Square Bus Station
30 Scottish National Portrait Gallery; Queen Street Café
31 Dundas House
32 Melville Monument
34 Tourist Information Centre; Waverley Market Shopping Centre
35 Waverley Train Station; Thomas Cook
36 Sir Walter Scott Monument
39 St Andrew's & St George's Church
43 Cyberia
48 Royal Scottish Academy
49 National Gallery of Scotland
50 Thomas Cook
51 Tiso's
52 Waterstone's; Starbucks
53 St Cuthbert's Church & Watchtower
54 St John's Church; Cornerstone Coffee House
55 American Express
57 West Register House
58 Georgian House
60 St Mary's Episcopal Cathedral
68 Melville's
69 Haymarket Train Station
70 Public Toilets
85 King's Theatre
87 Central Cycle Hire
88 Web 13 Internet Café
90 Filmhouse
92 Stationery Office Bookshop
94 Royal Lyceum Theatre
95 Usher Hall
97 Edinburgh Castle
99 Royal Infirmary
99 Usit Campus
100 Greyfriars Kirk
103 Edinburgh Festival Theatre
106 Public Toilets
117 Nether Hill

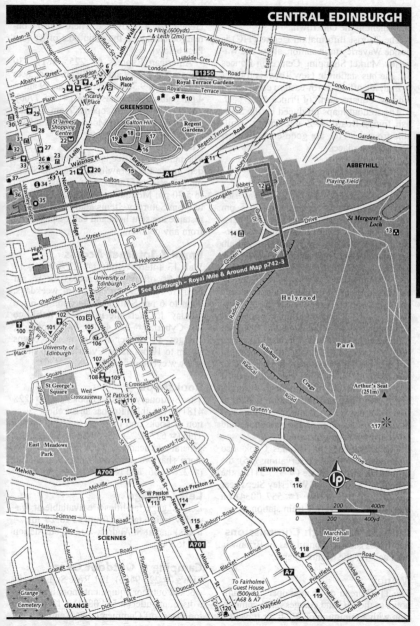

CENTRAL EDINBURGH

EDINBURGH

High St and Canongate) is the parallel equivalent in the Old Town.

The Tourist Information Centre (TIC) is beside Waverley train station, above the Waverley Market Shopping Centre on Princes St. The bus station in New Town is trickier to find; it's off the north-eastern corner of St Andrew Square, north of Princes St.

The foldout maps produced by the Scottish Tourist Board, A–Z and Collins, available from the TIC, are good enough to get you to most places.

INFORMATION
Tourist Offices
The busy main TIC (☎ 557 1700), Waverley Market, Princes St, opens 9 am to 5 pm Monday to Wednesday, 9 am to 6 pm Thursday to Saturday, 10 to 5 pm Sunday, October to April; 9 am to 7 pm daily (from 11 am Sunday) in May, June and September; and 9 am to 8 pm daily, July and August. There's also a branch (☎ 333 2167), where credit card bookings are possible, at Edinburgh airport. The Web site is at www.edinburgh.org.

The TIC has information about all of Scotland, and sells the *Essential Guide to Edinburgh* (£1). Its accommodation service charges a steep £3 and only books one night in advance. This is useless if you need to forward plan for busy periods but handy if you find yourself in Edinburgh during a major event and accommodation is hard to find. Alternatively, get the free *Edinburgh & Lothians* accommodation brochure and do your own ringing round.

Three branches of Thomas Cook also make accommodation reservations (£5): the Edinburgh airport office (☎ 333 5119), the office (☎ 557 0905) on Waverley Steps near the TIC, and the office (☎ 557 0034) on Platform 1 of Waverley train station.

Consulates & High Commissions
See Embassies & Consulates in Britain in the Facts for the Visitor chapter.

Money
The TIC bureau de change opens the same hours as the TIC and charges 2.5% commission with a minimum of £2.50 for travellers cheques, or 4% with a minimum of £4 for a credit card cash advance. There's also a bureau de change at the main post office (see Post below).

American Express (☎ 225 7881), 139 Princes St, opens 9 am to 5.30 pm Monday to Friday (from 9.30 on Thursday) and 9 am to 4 pm Saturday. Thomas Cook (☎ 465 7700), 26–28 Frederick St, opens 9 am (10 am Thursday) to 5.30 pm Monday to Saturday.

Post
The main post office is inconveniently hidden inside the sprawling St James' Shopping Centre, off Leith St. It opens 8.30 am to 5.30 pm Monday to Friday and 8.30 am to 6 pm Saturday. Items addressed to poste restante are sent here and can be picked up from any counter.

Email & Internet Access
Web 13 Internet Café (☎ 229 8883), 13 Bread St, offers online access for £5 per hour. It opens 9 am to 10 pm weekdays, 9 am to 6 pm Saturday and noon to 6 pm Sunday. Its Web site is at www.web13.co.uk. Cyberia (☎ 220 4403), 88 Hanover St, charges £2.50 per half-hour and opens 10 am to 10 pm daily. Cyberia's Web site is at www.cybersurf.co.uk.

Bookshops
The Stationery Office Bookshop (☎ 228 4181), 71 Lothian Rd, has an excellent selection of books and maps on Scotland. James Thin (☎ 622 8222), 53–59 South Bridge, is a general and academic bookshop and Waterstone's has two stores on Princes St at No 128 (☎ 226 2666) and Nos 13–14 (☎ 556 3304).

Left Luggage
Left-luggage facilities are available at Waverley train station (from £3 to £5 for 24 hours) and at St Andrew Square bus station (£2 to £4).

Camping & Outdoor Gear
Tiso's (☎ 225 9486), 121 Rose St, is a well-stocked outdoor equipment shop; it also has a discount outlet (☎ 554 0804) at 13 Wellington Place, off Commercial St, Leith.

Emergency

The free emergency numbers are ☎ 999 and ☎ 112.

EDINBURGH CASTLE

Edinburgh Castle (☎ 225 9846) dominates the city centre. It sits astride the core of an extinct volcano, its three sides scoured almost vertical by glacial action. There was a settlement here as early as 850 BC, although the first historical references date from the 6th century when the Northumbrian King Edwin rebuilt a fortress here as a defence against the Picts.

A favoured royal residence from the 11th to the 16th centuries, Edinburgh only became Scotland's capital at the end of the Middle Ages. The oldest surviving part of the castle is St Margaret's Chapel, a simple stone edifice probably built by David I around 1130 in memory of his mother.

Although it looks impregnable, the castle often changed hands between the Scots and English. It last saw action in 1745 when Bonnie Prince Charlie's army tried, but failed, to breach its walls.

During the Wars of Independence (1174–1356), the English captured it several times. In 1313 it was demolished by the Scots as part of Robert the Bruce's scorched earth policies and wasn't rebuilt until 1371 (by David II). Little of this work survives, however, as the castle was strengthened and renovated in the 16th, 17th and 18th centuries.

The Stone of Destiny

Alleged to have accompanied the Scots in all their mythical journeys, the original Stone of Destiny (the Fatal Stone) was a carved block of sandstone brought to Scotland by missionaries from Ireland. In 838 it was eventually placed in the abbey at Scone, a couple of miles north of Perth, where for the next four and a half centuries Scottish monarchs placed their feet upon it as part of the coronation ceremony.

Stolen by Edward I in 1296, this venerable talisman was incorporated into the Coronation Chair, used by all English (and later British) monarchs, in London's Westminster Abbey. Apart from being taken to Gloucester during the air raids in WWII, the Stone lay undisturbed for centuries.

On Christmas Eve 1950, however, a plucky band of Scottish students drove down from Glasgow, jemmied the door of Westminster Abbey and made off with the Stone. English officialdom was outraged. The border roads had roadblocks on them for the first time in 400 years; but while Scots living in London jeered the English police as they searched the Serpentine Lake in Hyde Park and the River Thames, the Stone was being smuggled back to Scotland.

King George VI was 'sorely troubled about the loss', but the students issued a petition affirming their loyalty to him, stating that they would give back the Stone as long as it could remain on Scottish soil. The authorities refused to negotiate and, three months after it was stolen, the Stone turned up on the altar of the ruined Arbroath Abbey, where, in 1320, the Arbroath Declaration had been signed, reaffirming the right of Scots to self-rule and independence from England. Before the public were aware that the Stone had even been found, it was back in London. No charges were brought and Ian Hamilton, the student who led this jolly caper, published his story in *The Taking of the Stone of Destiny*.

Then in 1996 the Scottish Secretary and Conservative MP Michael Forsyth arranged for the return of the sandstone block to Scotland, but not to the site of the abbey in Scone where Scone Palace now sits. Instead it went to Edinburgh Castle. If it was an attempt to boost his flagging political standing, it failed dismally: Forsyth lost his seat in the House of Commons in the May 1997 general election.

Many Scots, however, hold that the original Stone is safely hidden somewhere in Scotland and that Edward I was fobbed off with an imitation. This is possibly true, for descriptions of the original state that it was decorated with intricate carvings not that it was a block of plain sandstone. But given that Scottish nationalism is running high, this powerful symbol of Scotland would surely have been brought out by now.

From the 16th century, the royal family built more comfortable domestic accommodation at places such as Holyrood and the castle developed as a seat of government and military power. However, in 1566 Mary Queen of Scots underlined its continuing symbolic importance when she chose to give birth to her son in the castle. In 1573 much of it was destroyed when loyalists attempted to hold it for Mary; the oldest substantial work, including the Half Moon Battery and Portcullis Gate, survives from the subsequent rebuilding. The castle was then taken in turn by the Covenanters (in 1640), Cromwell (in 1650) and King William and Queen Mary (the last true siege, in 1689). In 1715 and 1745 the Stuarts tried unsuccessfully to recapture it. In the gaps between sieges more defences were added, and by the mid-18th century the castle looked much as it does today.

Partly thanks to Sir Walter Scott (who promoted all things Scottish), in the 19th century the castle began to recover its importance as a Scottish symbol. Efforts were made to improve its appearance and to restore important buildings, including St Margaret's Chapel, then in use as a powder magazine.

Visitors enter from the **Esplanade**, a parade ground where the Military Tattoo takes place each August. The changing of the guard also takes place here on the hour. Inside the castle, the most important sights are the **Stone of Destiny**, **St Margaret's Chapel** (the oldest building in Edinburgh), the **Mons Meg** (a 500-year-old siege cannon), the **Palace** (including the Scottish crown jewels and the room where Mary gave birth to James) and the **Scottish National War Memorial**, added to the complex in the 1920s.

The castle crawls with tourists and, although the views are great, you may decide it's more impressive from the outside. It opens 9.30 am to 6 pm daily, April to September; and 9.30 am to 5 pm October to March. The admission price of £7/2 includes provision of an audiotape commentary.

ROYAL MILE

Following a ridge that runs from Edinburgh Castle to the Palace of Holyroodhouse, the Royal Mile is one of the world's most fascinating streets. From the western end you can look past craggy Arthur's Seat and over the waters of the Firth of Forth, with

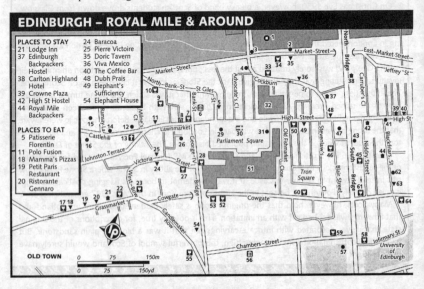

EDINBURGH – ROYAL MILE & AROUND

PLACES TO STAY		PLACES TO EAT
21 Lodge Inn	24 Baracoa	5 Patisserie
37 Edinburgh	25 Pierre Victoire	Florentin
Backpackers	35 Doric Tavern	11 Polo Fusion
Hostel	36 Viva Mexico	18 Mamma's Pizzas
38 Carlton Highland	40 The Coffee Bar	19 Petit Paris
Hotel	48 Dubh Prais	Restaurant
39 Crowne Plaza	49 Elephant's	20 Ristorante
42 High St Hostel	Sufficiency	Gennaro
44 Royal Mile	54 Elephant House	
Backpackers		

OLD TOWN
0   75   150m
0   75   150yd

tantalising glimpses of the Old and New Towns through the *closes* (entrances) and *wynds* (lanes) on either side. Although there are shops stuffed with tacky Scottish souvenirs and tourists aplenty, the street still feels a real part of a thriving city. It's lined with extraordinary buildings, including multistoreyed *lands* (apartment buildings) dating from the 15th century.

To see all the sites would take several days but, even with limited time, it's worth ducking through a *pend* (arched gateway) or *close* to explore the narrow wynds and courts beyond.

Scotch Whisky Heritage Centre

If time doesn't allow you the chance to tour a real whisky distillery in Scotland and you'd like to know how whisky is manufactured, the Scotch Whisky Heritage Centre (☎ 220 0441), Castlehill, is worth exploring. It offers a tour with audiovisual presentations followed by a ride in a car past a tableau explaining the history of the 'water of life', with a taster at the end. The centre opens 10 am to 5.30 pm daily. The full experience costs £5.50/2.75. If you don't want to do the tour you could put the money towards the purchase of one (or more) of the hundreds of different brands of whisky sold in the shop.

Outlook Tower & Camera Obscura

On the corner of Ramsay Lane, Camera Obscura (☎ 226 3709) offers great views over the city from *inside* the Outlook Tower. The 'camera' is a curious device (originally dating from the 1850s, although improved in 1945) a bit like a periscope, using lenses and mirrors to throw a 'live' image onto a large interior bowl. The accompanying commentary is entertaining and the whole exercise has a quirky charm. You can also get good views from the rooftop's external balcony.

Camera Obscura opens 9.30 am to 6 pm daily, April to October; and 10 am to 5 pm daily, November to March. Admission costs £4.25/2.10.

Highland Tolbooth Kirk

With the tallest spire (73m) on one of Edinburgh's highest points, the Highland Tolbooth Kirk, at the bottom of Castlehill, is an important feature of the skyline. It was built

EDINBURGH – ROYAL MILE & AROUND

PLACES TO EAT (continued)	45 The Vaults	4 Traveline	43 James Thin
63 Black Bo's	46 City Café	6 The Writers' Museum;	47 Tron Kirk; Visitor Centre
66 Netherbow Theatre Café	50 EH169	Lady Stair's House	51 Parliament House
70 The Reform Restaurant	52 The Three Sisters	8 Gladstone's Land	56 Royal Museum of Scotland;
73 Bramble's Tearoom	53 The Subway	12 Church of Scotland General	Museum of Scotland;
76 Clarinda's Tea Room	55 Greyfriars Bobby's Bar	Assembly Rooms Hall (Temporary	The Lumière
	58 Oxygen Bar & Grill;	Scottish Parliament)	57 Old College (University
PUBS, BARS & CLUBS	O2 Club	13 Highland Tolbooth Kirk; The Hub	of Edinburgh)
7 Deacon Brodie's	59 Number One Brasserie	& Edinburgh Festival Office	62 Edinburgh Cycle Hire
9 Jolly Judge	60 Siglo	14 Outlook Tower & Camera Obscura	65 John Knox House
10 The Car Wash	61 Bannerman's	15 Ramsay Garden	67 Museum of Childhood
17 Beehive Inn;	64 Wilkie House	16 Scotch Whisky Heritage Centre	69 Netherbow Port
Literary Pub Tour	68 World's End	26 Brodie's Close	72 The People's Story
22 The Last Drop	71 The Bongo Club	29 Heart of Midlothian	74 Huntly House Museum
23 Bow Bar		30 St Giles Cathedral;	75 Canongate Kirk
27 Espionage	OTHER	Lower Aisle Restaurant	77 Scottish Parliament
28 Bar Kohl	1 Train Station	31 Mercat Cross	(Under Construction)
33 Malt Shovel Inn	2 Edinburgh Tattoo Office	32 Edinburgh City Chambers	78 Abbey Lairds
34 Hebrides Bar	3 LRT Travel Shop	41 Haggis Backpacker Travel Shop	79 Queen Mary's Bath House

in the 1840s by James Graham and Augustus Pugin (one of the architects of London's Houses of Parliament). It now contains **The Hub**, which is the home of the Edinburgh Festival office. There's a visitor centre, ticket office and shops. The office opens 9.30 am to 11 pm daily (8 am to 1 am during the festival).

Across from the *kirk* (church) is the **Church of Scotland General Assembly Hall**, temporary home of the Scottish Parliament until its permanent residence is built.

Ramsay Garden

Constructed around the mid-18th-century home of the painter and poet Alan Ramsay, the attractive apartments here overlook the Esplanade and the small garden from which they get their name. They were designed in the 1890s by an early town planner, Patrick Geddes, in an attempt to revitalise the Old Town. They're now very expensive, very wonderful, private apartments.

Gladstone's Land

Owned by the National Trust for Scotland (NTS), Gladstone's Land (☎ 226 5856), 477 Lawnmarket, gives visitors a fascinating glimpse of the past. The narrow, six-storey house was built in the mid-16th century and extended around 1617 by wealthy merchant Thomas Gledstanes. Its comfortable interior contains fine painted walls and ceilings and some splendid furniture. It opens 10 am to 5 pm Monday to Saturday and 2 to 5 pm Sunday (last admission 4.30 pm), April to October. Admission costs £3.50/1.

The Writers' Museum

The Writers' Museum (☎ 529 4901), on Lady Stair's Close, is housed in **Lady Stair's House**, built in 1622, and contains manuscripts and memorabilia belonging to Robert Burns, Sir Walter Scott and Robert Louis Stevenson. The static displays will probably only interest enthusiasts of these three greats, but there are also temporary exhibitions featuring other writers. It opens 10 am to 5 pm Monday to Saturday and, during the Edinburgh Festival, 2 to 5 pm Sunday. Admission is free.

Brodie's Close

Brodie's Close is named after the father of the notorious William Brodie – a deacon and respected citizen by day, a burglar by night. Brodie was the inspiration for Robert Louis Stevenson's *The Strange Case of Dr Jekyll and Mr Hyde* and, some would say, a dramatic reflection of Edinburgh's schizophrenic undercurrents. He met his end on the gallows in 1788.

Parliament Square

Lawnmarket ends at the crossroads of Bank St and George IV Bridge; at the south-eastern corner of the intersection, brass strips set in the road mark the site of the scaffold where public hangings took place until 1864. From here the Royal Mile continues as High St.

Parliament Square, largely filled by St Giles Cathedral, is on the southern side. This was the heart of Edinburgh until the 18th century, and a cobblestoned **Heart of Midlothian** is set in the ground. Passers-by traditionally spit on it for luck. This was the site of the entrance to the Tolbooth, originally built to collect tolls but subsequently a meeting place for parliament, the town council and the General Assembly of the Reformed Kirk, then law courts and, finally, a prison and place of execution.

The 19th-century **Mercat Cross** took the place of the original 1365 cross and marks the spot where merchants and traders met to transact business, and royal proclamations were read.

The square's southern side is flanked by **Parliament House**, which was the meeting place of the Scottish Parliament from 1639; its neoclassical facade was added in the early 19th century. After the Act of Union in 1707 the building became the centre for the Scottish legal system – the Court of Session and High Court – which retained its independence. The most interesting feature is **Parliament Hall**, where the parliament actually met, which is now used by lawyers and their clients as a meeting place.

St Giles Cathedral

There has been a church on this site since the 9th century. A Norman-style church was built in 1126 but this was burnt by the English in 1385; the only substantial remains are the central piers that support the tower. The present church was then built in stages, with the crown spire completed in 1495.

Inside, near the entrance, is a life-size statue of John Knox, minister from 1559 to 1572; he preached his uncompromising Calvinist message and launched the Scottish Reformation from here. The new austerity this ushered in led to changes in the building's interior – decorations, stained glass, altars and the relics of St Giles were thrown into the Nor Loch.

St Giles (the High Kirk of Edinburgh) was at the heart of Edinburgh's struggle against episcopacy. A tablet marks the spot where, in 1637, Jenny Geddes threw a stool at the dean who was using the English prayer book (a symbol of episcopacy). According to popular belief this led to the signing of the National Covenant at Greyfriars the following year; a copy is displayed on the wall.

One of the most interesting corners of the church is the **Thistle Chapel** built between 1909 and 1911 for the Knights of the Most Ancient & Most Noble Order of the Thistle. The carved Gothic-style stalls have canopies topped with the helms and arms of the 16 knights.

St Giles opens 9 am to 7pm weekdays, to 5 pm Saturday and 1 to 5 pm Sunday, Easter to September; and 9 am to 5 pm Monday to Saturday and 1 to 5 pm Sunday, the rest of the year. Admission to the church is free but a £1 donation is requested; there's a good cafe here.

Edinburgh City Chambers

The City Chambers were originally built by John Adam (brother of Robert) in 1761 to replace the Mercat Cross and serve as a Royal Exchange but the merchants continued to prefer the street. The building was eventually occupied by the town council in 1811, which has been there ever since.

Tron Kirk

At the south-western corner of the intersection with South Bridge, Tron Kirk owes its name to a salt *tron* or public weighbridge

that stood on the site. It was built in 1637 on top of Marlin's Wynd, which has been excavated to reveal a cobbled street with cellars and shops on either side. Traditionally, Hogmanay revellers gather at the church, which also acts as a visitor centre for the Old Town. It opens 10 am to 5 pm (closed 1 to 2 pm) Thursday to Monday, Easter to May; and 10 am to 7 pm daily, June to early September.

John Knox House

Perhaps the most extraordinary building on the Royal Mile, John Knox House (☎ 556 9579) dates from 1490. The outside staircase, overhanging upper floors and crow-stepped gables are typical of a 15th-century town house. John Knox is thought to have occupied the 2nd floor from 1561 to 1572. The labyrinthine interior reveals the original walls, fireplaces and painted ceiling. An interesting display on his life includes a record of his interview with Mary Queen of Scots, whose mother was a target of his diatribe *First Blast of the Trumpet Against the Monstrous Regiment of Women*. It opens 10 am to 4.30 pm Monday to Saturday (plus Sunday afternoon to 5 pm in July and August). Admission costs £2.25/75p.

Museum of Childhood

This museum (☎ 529 4142), 42 High St, covers the serious issues of childhood – health, education, upbringing and so on – but more enjoyable is the enormous collection of toys, dolls, games and books which fascinates children and revives adults' childhood memories. The museum opens 10 am to 5 pm Monday to Saturday (plus 2 to 5 pm on Sunday during the Edinburgh Festival). Admission is free.

Netherbow Port

High St ends at the intersection with St Mary's and Jeffrey Sts. The city's eastern gate, Netherbow Port, no longer exists, although it's marked by brass strips set in the road. The next stretch of the Mile, Canongate, takes its name from the canons (priests) of Holyrood Abbey. From the 16th century, it was home to aristocrats attracted to the Palace of Holyroodhouse. Originally governed by the canons, it remained an independent burgh until 1856.

The People's Story

Canongate Tolbooth, with its picturesque turrets and projecting clock, is an interesting example of 16th-century architecture. Built in 1591, it served in turn as a collection point for tolls (taxes), a council house, a courtroom and a jail. It now houses a fascinating museum (☎ 331 5545) telling the story of the life, work and pastimes of ordinary Edinburgh folk from the late-18th century to modern times. It opens 10 am to 5 pm Monday to Saturday (plus 2 to 5 pm on Sunday during the Edinburgh Festival). Admission is free.

Huntly House Museum

Huntly House, built in 1570, is a good example of the luxurious accommodation that aristocrats built for themselves along Canongate; the projecting upper floors of plastered timber are typical of the time. The house contains a local history museum (☎ 529 4143) with some interesting displays, including a copy of the National Covenant of 1638, and collections of glass, pottery and silver. It opens the same hours as The People's Story. Admission is free.

Canongate Kirk

Attractive Canongate Kirk was built in 1688 and Prince Charles Stuart (the Young Pretender) used it in 1745 to hold prisoners taken at the Battle of Prestonpans. The royal family attends services here when in residence at Holyroodhouse. Several famous people are buried in the churchyard, including the economist Adam Smith, author of *The Wealth of Nations*, who lived nearby in Panmure Close.

Scottish Parliament

Close to Holyroodhouse, construction is well under way for the modern, purpose-built Scottish Parliament, scheduled for completion in 2002.

Abbey Lairds

On the northern side of Abbey Strand, flanking the entrance to the Palace of Holyroodhouse, the Abbey Lairds provided sanctuary for aristocratic debtors from 1128 to 1880. They could avoid prison as long as they remained within the palace and Holyrood Park, although they were allowed out on Sunday.

Queen Mary's Bath House

Farther north is this small, 16th-century turreted lodge where, according to legend, Queen Mary used to bathe in white wine and goat's milk – as frequently as twice a year! It's more likely to have been a summer house or dovecote.

PALACE OF HOLYROODHOUSE & HOLYROOD ABBEY

The Palace of Holyroodhouse developed from a guesthouse attached to medieval Holyrood Abbey. It was a royal residence at various times from the 16th century and is still the monarch's official residence in Scotland, so access is very restricted. You can only view a few apartments, walk around part of the grounds and visit the abbey ruins.

The abbey, founded by David I in 1128, was probably named after a fragment of the cross (*rood* is an old word for cross) said to have belonged to his mother St Margaret. As it lay outside the city walls it was particularly vulnerable to English attacks but the church was always rebuilt and survived as Canongate parish church until it collapsed in 1768. Most of the surviving ruins date from the 12th and 13th centuries, although a doorway in the far south-eastern corner survives from the original Norman church.

James IV extended the abbey guesthouse in 1501 to create more comfortable living quarters than in bleak, windy Edinburgh Castle; the oldest surviving section of the building, the north-western tower, was built in 1529 as a royal apartment. Mary Queen of Scots spent 16 eventful years living in the tower. During this time she married Darnley (in the abbey) and Bothwell (in what is now the Picture Gallery), and this is where she debated with John Knox and witnessed the murder of her secretary Rizzio.

Although Holyroodhouse was never again a permanent royal residence after Mary's son

James VI departed for London, it was extended further during Charles II's reign.

Although you're carefully shepherded through a limited part of the palace, there's a certain fascination in following in Mary's footsteps and seeing the room where Rizzio was cut down.

Opening hours are 9.30 am to 6 pm (last admission at 5.15 pm) daily, April to October; and 9.30 am to 4.30 pm (last admission at 3.45 pm) daily, November to March. Admission costs £6/3. However, the complex sometimes closes for State functions or when the Queen is in residence, usually in mid-May and mid-June to around 7 July; phone ☎ 556 1096 to check.

HOLYROOD PARK

Edinburgh is blessed in having a real wilderness on its doorstep. Holyrood Park covers 260 hectares of varied landscape, including mountains, moorland, lochs and fields, and contains some rare plants and insects. The highest point is the 251m-high extinct volcano, Arthur's Seat.

You can circumnavigate the park by car or bike and it has several excellent walks. Opposite the palace's southern gate, a footpath named Radical Rd runs along the base of the **Salisbury Crags** but is partly blocked because of danger from falling rocks. An easy half-hour walk leads from Dunsapie Loch to the summit of **Arthur's Seat**, with magnificent views. **Duddingstone Loch**, the one natural lake, is a bird sanctuary and home to some otters.

DYNAMIC EARTH

Looking rather like a giant, white crustacean from the outside, this modern, interactive museum (☎ 550 7800) sits between Holyrood Rd and Queen's Drive in the shadow of the Salisbury Crags. Using computers, video screens and special effects its galleries recreate and explore the planet's geology, geography and natural history, beginning with a trip in a 'time machine' back to the start of the universe. Children love it. It opens 10 am to 6 pm daily, Easter to October; and 10 am to 5 pm Wednesday to Sunday, November to Easter. Admission costs £6.95/3.95.

SOUTH OF THE ROYAL MILE

The area south of the Royal Mile contains some of the oldest, most crowded and most atmospheric parts of the Old Town at the foot of Castle Rock and the Mile. Around the university and the beautiful Meadow Park it opens up to run south into sturdy Victorian suburbs such as Bruntsfield, Marchmont and Grange.

One of the city's main traffic arteries (carrying traffic to/from the A68 and A7), with many shops, restaurants and guesthouses, runs along the eastern side – beginning as North Bridge and becoming successively South Bridge, Nicolson St, Clerk St, Newington Rd, Minto St, Mayfield Gardens and Craigmillar Park.

Grassmarket & Around

Grassmarket, one of Edinburgh's nightlife centres with numerous restaurants and pubs, has had a seamy history. The site of a market from at least 1477 to the start of the 20th century, Grassmarket was always a focal point for the Old Town. Riots frequently occurred here. This was the main place for public executions and over 100 hanged Covenanters are commemorated with a cross at the eastern end. The notorious murderers William Burke and William Hare operated from a now vanished close off the western end. In around 1827 they enticed at least 18 victims here, suffocated them and sold the bodies to Edinburgh's medical schools.

Grassmarket, an open area hedged by tall tenements and dominated by the looming castle, can be approached from George IV Bridge via **Victoria St**, an unusual two-tiered street clinging to the ridge below the Royal Mile, with some excellent shops. Leading off the south-eastern corner, **Candlemaker Row** climbs back up to George IV Bridge and Greyfriars Kirk.

Cowgate, the street which runs parallel to the Royal Mile off the eastern end of Grassmarket, has the feel of a bleak tunnel, thanks to the bridges built over it. Once a fashionable place to live, it now has a couple of Fringe Festival venues and one or two good pubs.

Greyfriars Kirk & Kirkyard

At the bottom of a stone canyon made up of tenements, churches, volcanic cliffs and the castle, Greyfriars Kirkyard is one of Edinburgh's most evocative spots – a peaceful oasis dotted with memorials and surrounded by Edinburgh's dramatic skyline.

The church was built on the site of a Franciscan friary and opened for worship on Christmas Day in 1620. The National Covenant was signed here in 1638, rejecting Charles I's attempts to reintroduce episcopacy and a new English prayer book and affirming the independence of the Scottish Church. Many of those who signed were later executed in Grassmarket and, in 1679, 1200 Covenanters were held prisoner in terrible conditions in an enclosure in the yard.

Tour groups, however, come to pay homage to a tiny statue of **Greyfriars Bobby** (in front of the nearby pub, Greyfriars Bobby's Bar). Bobby was a Skye terrier who maintained a vigil over the grave of his master from 1858 to 1872, a story immortalised in a novel by Eleanor Atkinson in 1912 and later turned into a film by Walt Disney. Inside the kirk you can buy *Greyfriars Bobby – The Real Story at Last*, Forbes Macgregor's debunking of some of the myths.

University of Edinburgh

The University of Edinburgh is one of Britain's oldest, biggest and best universities. Founded in 1583, it has nearly 18,000 undergraduates. The students make a major contribution to the lively atmosphere of Grassmarket, Cowgate and the nearby restaurants and pubs. The university sprawls for some distance but the centre is the **Old College** (also called the Old Quad), at the junction of South Bridge and Chambers St, a Robert Adam masterpiece designed in 1789.

Royal Museum of Scotland & Museum of Scotland

These are part of the network of museums collectively known as the National Museums of Scotland.

The Royal Museum of Scotland (☎ 247 4219), Chambers St, is a Victorian building housing a comprehensive collection covering geology and fossils; Egyptology; Chinese, Islamic and European decorative art; and even technology. One section features one of the world's oldest steam locomotives, the *Wylam Dilly* (1813). Next door, the superb, modern, sandstone Museum of Scotland (☎ 247 4422) explores the history of Scotland in chronological order starting with the country's earliest history in the basement and finishing with the most recent on the top floor.

The museums open 10 am to 5 pm Monday to Saturday (to 8 pm Tuesday) and noon to 5 pm on Sunday, and free guided tours are available. Admission is £3/free, and free for everyone after 4.30 pm on Tuesday.

CALTON HILL & AROUND

Calton Hill, at the eastern end of Princes St, is another distinctive component of Edinburgh's skyline, 100m high and scattered with grandiose memorials mostly dating from the first half of the 19th century. Here you get one of the best views of Edinburgh, taking in the entire panorama – the castle, Holyrood Park, Arthur's Seat, the Firth of Forth, New Town and Princes St.

Approaching from Waterloo Place, you pass the imposing **Royal High School**, Regent Rd, dating from 1829 and modelled on the Temple of Theseus in Athens. Former pupils include Robert Adam, Alexander Graham Bell and Sir Walter Scott. Now called St Andrew's House, it's home to the Scottish Executive. Farther up Regent Rd is the **Burns Monument** (1830), a small round temple commemorating the Scottish bard.

The largest structure on Calton Hill is the **National Monument**, an over-ambitious attempt to replicate the Parthenon, in honour of Scotland's dead in the Napoleonic Wars. Construction began in 1822, but funds ran dry when only 12 columns were complete.

The **City Observatory** (1818) houses the **Edinburgh Experience** (☎ 556 4365), a 20-minute, 3-D portrayal of Edinburgh's history. It opens 10 am to 5 pm daily, April to October. Admission costs £2/1.20.

Looking like an upturned telescope, the **Nelson Monument** (☎ 556 2716) was built after Nelson's death at Trafalgar. It opens (for great views) 1 to 6 pm Monday and 10 am to 6 pm Tuesday to Saturday, April to September; and 10 am to 3 pm Monday to Saturday, October to March. Admission costs £2.

There's also the small, circular **Monument to Dugald Stewart** (1753–1828), an obscure professor of philosophy.

NEW TOWN

New Town, dating from the 18th century, lies north of the Old Town, separated from it by Princes St Gardens and occupying a ridge that runs below, but parallel to, the Royal Mile. It's in complete contrast to the tangle of streets and buildings that evolved in the Old Town, and typifies the values of the Scottish Enlightenment.

Despite being confined behind city walls, the Old Town was still periodically sacked by the English or torn by civil wars and disputes. The overcrowding and non-existent sanitation gave it its nickname, Auld Reekie. So when the Act of Union (1707) brought the prospect of long-term stability, aristocrats were keen to find healthier, more spacious surroundings. Cowgate was bridged to open up the south; Nor Loch, at the northern foot of Castle Rock, was drained and the North Bridge was constructed.

In 1767, 23-year-old James Craig won a competition to design New Town. His plan was brilliant in its simplicity. George St followed the line of the ridge between Charlotte and St Andrew Squares. Building was restricted to one side of Princes St and Queen St only, so the town opened onto the Firth of Forth to the north, and to the castle and Old Town to the south.

New Town continued to sprout squares, circuses, parks and terraces, and some of its finest neoclassical architecture was designed by Robert Adam. Today, New Town is the world's most complete, unspoilt example of Georgian town planning and architecture.

Princes St

Princes St was originally envisaged as the rear of New Town, as it was literally and figuratively turning its back on the Jacobite past. However, the transport links and stunning outlook soon led to its development as Edinburgh's principal thoroughfare.

The main train station at the eastern end is overshadowed by the uninspiring **Waverley Market shopping centre**, with the entrance to the main TIC via the street level piazza.

The street's northern side is lined with standard high-street shops; few 18th- century buildings survive. One exception is the beautiful **General Register House** (1788), designed by Robert Adam to hold Scotland's national archives, opposite North Bridge. About midway, the massive Gothic spire of the **Sir Walter Scott Monument**, built by public subscription after his death in 1832, testifies to a popularity largely inspired by his role in rebuilding pride in Scottish identity. You enter via Princes St Gardens and climb 287 steps up a narrow winding staircase. From the top there are good views of the city. The monument opens 9 am to 6 pm daily, October to May; and 9 am to 8 pm Monday to Saturday and 10 am to 6 pm Sunday, June to September. Admission costs £2.50.

Princes St Gardens are cut by **The Mound**, a mound of earth dumped during the construction of New Town which provides a road link between the Old and New Towns. The Royal Scottish Academy and the National Gallery of Scotland are also here (see those two sections below).

St John's Church, at the western end of Princes St, stands above some interesting shops and the Cornerstone Coffee House. **St Cuthbert's Church**, round the corner, has a watchtower in the graveyard – a reminder of the Burke and Hare days when graves were guarded against robbers.

Royal Scottish Academy (RSA)

The Grecian style RSA (☎ 225 6671), built in 1826, hosts regular exhibitions of contemporary art throughout the year. It opens 10 am to 5 pm Monday to Saturday and 2 to 5 pm Sunday. Admission is free (although there are charges for some exhibitions).

National Gallery of Scotland

The national gallery (☎ 556 8921), behind the RSA, is an imposing classical building dating from the 1850s. The gallery houses an important collection of European art from 15th-century Renaissance to 19th-century post-impressionism. There are paintings by Tintoretto, Titian, Holbein, Rubens, El Greco, Poussin, Rembrandt, Constable, Gainsborough, Turner, Monet, Pissaro, Gauguin and Cézanne, but perhaps the most interesting section shows specifically Scottish art in the basement.

Antonio Canova's statue of the *Three Graces* is owned jointly with London's Victoria & Albert Museum where it's currently on display. It's due to return here in 2006.

The gallery opens 10 am to 5 pm Monday to Saturday and noon to 5 pm Sunday. Admission is free. A free shuttle bus takes you from here to several other galleries around Edinburgh.

George St & St Andrew Square

George St was originally envisaged as the main thoroughfare of residential New Town. It's now home to highly successful Scottish financial institutions which between then control billions of pounds. **St Andrew's & St George's Church**, built in 1784, boasts a wonderful oval plaster ceiling.

St Andrew Square, dominated by the **Melville Monument** in the central park (not open to the public), isn't architecturally distinguished. However, the Royal Bank of Scotland is in the impressive **Dundas House**, which has a spectacular dome, visible from inside, and frieze.

Charlotte Square & the Georgian House

At the western end of George St, Charlotte Square was designed in 1791 by Robert Adam and is regarded as the jewel of New Town. The Church of St George is now **West Register House**, an annexe to General Register House in Princes St and home to Scottish archives and occasional exhibitions.

On the northern side is one of Robert Adam's masterpieces. Number 7, the **Georgian House** (☎ 225 2160; NTS), has been beautifully restored and refurnished to show how Edinburgh's elite lived at the end of the 18th century. A 35-minute video brings it to life quite well. It opens 10 am to 5 pm

Monday to Saturday and 2 to 5 pm Sunday, April to October. Admission costs £5/1.

Scottish National Portrait Gallery

The gallery (☎ 556 8921), in a large Italian-Gothic building dating from 1882 (at the junction of St Andrew and Queen Sts), records Scottish history through portraits and sculptures of its most significant protagonists. The hall is decorated with a frieze showing the main participants while the balcony is displayed with frescos, painted by William Hole in 1897, of important moments in Scottish history. The subjects themselves are probably the main source of interest but some portraits are also excellent paintings.

The gallery opens 10 am to 5 pm Monday to Saturday and 2 to 5 pm Sunday. Admission is free.

WEST END

The last part to be built, the West End is an extension of New Town. Huge **St Mary's Episcopal Cathedral**, Palmerston Place, built in the 1870s, was Sir Gilbert Scott's last major work.

Alongside the Water of Leith, **Dean Village** is an odd corner of Edinburgh – once a milling community, it has now been colonised by young professionals. A pleasant walk begins on the left bank of the Water of Leith at Belford Bridge. The footpath takes you up onto the Dean Path, then onto Dean Bridge, from where you can look down on the village. You continue on the right bank of the Leith, through Stockbridge, and can then detour to the Royal Botanical Garden.

Scottish National Gallery of Modern Art

Just beyond the West End and Dean Village, the Scottish National Gallery of Modern Art (☎ 556 8921), Belford Rd, repays the effort of getting there (take bus No 13 from George St). It's housed in an impressive classical building surrounded by a sculpture park. The collection concentrates on 20th-century art, with work by Matisse, Picasso, Miro, Kirchner, Magritte, Mondrian, Giacometti and Henry Moore. It's small enough not to overwhelm and opens

10 am to 5 pm Monday to Saturday and 2 to 5 pm Sunday. Admission is free.

NORTH OF NEW TOWN

New Town's Georgian architecture extends north to Stockbridge and the Water of Leith, a rewarding area to explore since it's well off the tourist trail. **Stockbridge** is a trendy area with its own distinct identity, some interesting shops and a good choice of pubs and restaurants.

North of Stockbridge is the lovely **Royal Botanic Garden** (☎ 552 7171), 20a Inverleith Row. It's worth visiting for its exotic plants, rhododendron collection and the different perspective you get on the Edinburgh skyline from *The Terrace Café*. The garden opens 9.30 am to 7 pm daily, April to August; to 6 pm in March and September; to 5 pm in February and October; to 4 pm November to January. Admission is free. Bus Nos 8, 19, 23, 27 and 37 get you there.

ORGANISED TOURS

There are lots of walking tours of Edinburgh, including the popular McEwan's 80/- Literary Pub Tour (☎ 226 6665/7) in which actors give you a light-hearted lesson in Scottish literature while taking you to pubs frequented by literary figures. Tours leave from the Beehive Inn on Grassmarket at 7.30 pm and cost £7.

Open-topped buses depart from Waverley Bridge, outside the train station, and offer hop-on, hop-off tours of the main sights. Guide Friday (☎ 556 2244) charges £8.50, while Lothian Regional Transport's (LRT) Edinburgh Classic Tour (☎ 553 6363) costs £7.50. They're a good way of getting your bearings – although with a bus map and a Day Saver bus ticket (£2.40) you could do the same thing, minus the commentary.

PLACES TO STAY

Edinburgh has masses of accommodation but the city still fills up quickly over the New Year, at Easter, between mid-May and mid-September (particularly while the festivals are in full swing) or when there's a major event in the sporting calendar. Book in advance if possible or use an accommodation booking service (see Information earlier in the chapter).

Camping

Mortonhall Caravan Park (☎ 664 1533, 38 Mortonhall Gate), off Frogston Rd East 5 miles south-east of the centre, opens March to October. Tent sites cost £8.25 to £12.75. Take bus No 11 from Princes St.

Hostels & Colleges

Edinburgh has two SYHA hostels and lots of independent backpacker abodes.

The two good SYHA hostels both open year round; their rates increase by £1 in July and August. *Eglinton Youth Hostel* (☎ 337 1120, 18 Eglinton Crescent) is near Haymarket train station. Beds cost £12.75/11.25 for adults/under-18s. *Bruntsfield Youth Hostel* (☎ 447 2994, 7 Bruntsfield Crescent) is trickier to get to but has an attractive location overlooking Bruntsfield Links about 2½ miles south-west of Waverley train station. Rates are £11.75/10.50. Catch bus No 11 or 16 from the garden side of Princes St and alight at Forbes Rd just after the gardens on the left.

The long-established, well-equipped *High St Hostel* (☎ 556 2981, 8 Blackfriars St) has received some good reviews from travellers. Beds cost £10.50 per night in a 10-bed dorm, plus £1.60 for breakfast.

Just up from John Knox House is *Royal Mile Backpackers* (☎ 557 6120, 105 High St) which charges from £11.50 to £13 for one of its dorm beds and also organises walking and coach tours.

Princes St Backpackers (☎ 556 6894, 5 West Register St) is also well positioned, behind Princes St and close to the bus station. Entry is next to the Guildford Arms pub and you have to negotiate 77 exhausting steps to reach reception. Dorm beds cost £9.50, doubles £24 (7th night free). Breakfast costs £2, and Sunday night dinner is free! It also has a jobs noticeboard and Internet access.

Belford Hostel (☎ 225 6209, 6–8 Douglas Gardens), in a converted church, is well run and cheerful with good facilities and no curfew. Dorm beds cost from £11.50 to £13.50 depending on the season, and there are several doubles from £33.

Special Events

Festivals and other special events take place in Edinburgh throughout the year, but August is the climactic month.

The two-week **Edinburgh International Festival** is the world's largest, most important arts festival, with the best performers playing to capacity audiences. Lasting three weeks, the **Edinburgh Fringe Festival** grew in tandem to showcase would-be stars and claims to be the largest such event in the world – there are over 500 amateur and professional groups presenting every possible kind of avant-garde performance. A separate, major attraction is the **Edinburgh Military Tattoo**, an extravaganza of regimental posturing, held over three weeks in the same period on the Esplanade of Edinburgh Castle.

If you want to attend the International Festival, it's best to book well ahead; the program is published in April and is available from the Edinburgh Festival Office (☎ 473 2000), The Hub, Castlehill, Royal Mile, EH1 2NE. Its Web site is at www.eif.co.uk. Prices are generally reasonable and you can buy any unsold tickets for half-price on the day of the performance. Unsold tickets are available from The Hub from 1 to 5 pm and from the venue one hour before the performance starts.

The Fringe is less formal and not at all elitist. In most cases the performers and front of house people are friendly and relaxed, they're grateful to have an audience, so there's no need to feel intimidated. Just be prepared to take the bad with the good…many performances have empty seats left at the last moment but it's still worth booking for well-known names or if the production has good reviews. Programs are available, from June, from the Festival Fringe Society (☎ 226 5257,), 180 High St, EH1 1QS. Its Web site is at www.edfringe.com.

To book for the Military Tattoo contact the Tattoo Office (☎ 225 1188) 32 Market St, EH1 1QS. Its Web site is at www.edintattoo.co.uk.

To make sure that every hotel room and B&B for 40 miles around is full, several other festivals take place at roughly the same time. The nine-day **Edinburgh International Jazz & Blues Festival** (☎ 25 2202) attracts top musicians from around the world. Its Web site is at www.jazzmusic.co.uk

The two-week **Edinburgh International Film Festival** (☎ 229 2550) is the world's oldest film festival. Its Web site is at www.edfilmfest.org.uk. Authors and literary enthusiasts gather in Charlotte Square for the **Edinburgh Book Festival** (☎ 225 5444), also two weeks. Its Web site is at www.edbookfest.co.uk.

It's a great time to be in Edinburgh and the city is at its best, but booking accommodation months ahead is strongly advised.

Hogmanay, the Scottish celebration of the New Year, is another major fixture in Edinburgh's festival calendar, with street parties and events in various venues around town. For details contact the TIC (☎ 557 1700).

Quiet *Palmerston Lodge* (☎ 220 5141, 25 *Palmerston Place*), on the corner of Chester St, is in a listed building, once a boarding school. Rates, with continental breakfast, start at £12 for a dorm bed; singles/doubles with bathroom are £30/40. All rooms have colour TV and tea/coffee-making facilities.

Women, married couples and families are welcome at *Kinnaird Christian Hostel* (☎ 225 3608, 13–14 Coates Crescent) where dorm beds in a Georgian house cost from £14, singles/doubles from £20/34.

During university holidays *Pollock Halls of Residence* (☎ 667 0662, 18 Holyrood Park Rd) has modern singles/doubles for £25/48, including a full breakfast.

B&Bs & Guesthouses

If you are on a tight budget the best bet is a private house; get the TIC's free accommodation guide and phone around. Outside festival time you should get something for about £20, although it'll be a bus ride away in the suburbs. Places in the centre aren't always good value if you have a car since parking is severely restricted; find out about parking facilities when you book.

Guesthouses are generally two or three pounds more expensive than B&Bs and for a room with a private bathroom you'll pay about £25 to £30. The main concentrations are around Pilrig St, Pilrig; Minto St (a southern continuation of North Bridge), Newington; and Gilmore Place and Leamington Terrace, Bruntsfield.

There are a couple of good places on Eyre Place, north of New Town near Stockbridge and the Water of Leith, a mile from the centre. Elegant *Ardenlee Guest House* (☎ 556 2838), No 9, has comfortable beds from £26 per person, while nearby *Dene Guest House* (☎ 556 2700), No 7, does B&B in relaxed surroundings from £19.50.

Pilrig St, left off Leith Walk, has lots of guesthouses within easy reach of the centre. *Balmoral Guest House* (☎ 554 1857), No 32, is a terraced Georgian house with beds from £20 to £30 per person. Similar is *Barrosa* (☎ 554 3700), No 21, with doubles only for £22/32 per person without/with bathroom. The attractive, detached, *Balquhidder Guest House* (☎ 554 3377), No 94, has rooms with bathroom from £20 to £40 per person.

There are lots of guesthouses on and around Minto St/Mayfield Gardens in Newington, south of the centre, accessed by plenty of buses. The best places are in the streets on either side of the main road.

Salisbury Guest House (☎ 667 1264, 45 Salisbury Rd), east of Newington and 10 minutes south from the centre by bus, is a quiet, genteel Georgian place with fluted columns beside its entrance. Rooms with bathroom cost from £25/48. It is nonsmoking and is closed in January. The welcoming *Avondale Guest House* (☎ 667 6779, 10 South Gray St), west of Minto St, is a comfortable, traditional B&B in a quiet neighbourhood with singles/doubles from £20/36. Open year round, *Fairholme Guest House* (☎ 667 8645, 13 Moston Terrace), east of Mayfield Gardens, is a pleasant Victorian villa with free parking. The range of rooms includes a single from £18.

Nonsmoking *Casa Buzzo Guest House* (☎ 667 8998, 8 Kilmaurs Rd), east of Dalkeith Rd, is quite a way out and has doubles only from £20 per person. *Millfield Guest House* (☎ 667 4428, 12 Marchhall Rd), also east of Dalkeith Rd past Pollock Halls of Residence, is a pleasant, two-storey, nonsmoking Victorian house with rooms from £20/36.

In Bruntsfield, busy *Averon Guest House* (☎ 229 9932, 44 Gilmore Place) is within walking distance of Princes St, and has rooms from £20/36. Using the same bus stop as for Bruntsfield Youth Hostel, you can get to *Menzies Guest House* (☎ 229 4629), down Leamington Terrace at No 33. It's reasonably clean, well run and has rooms from £20/28 to £40/60. Up the street, *Villa Nina* (☎ 229 2644), No 39, is cheaper, but only has doubles (from £34 to £50 per room) and closes in December and January.

There are several quiet guesthouses in Hartington Gardens, off Viewforth, itself off Bruntsfield Place. *Aaron Guest House* (☎ 229 6459) is handy for drivers since it has a private car park. Comfortable en-suite rooms start at £25/40. Vegetarians/vegans will enjoy *The Greenhouse* (☎ 622 7634, 14 Hartington Gardens), where even the shampoo and soaps in the bathrooms are free of animal products. Breakfasts are huge, and the proprietors, Suzanne and Hugh, endeavour to keep the food GM-free. The rooms, homely and finely furnished, cost from £25/30 per person without/with bathroom.

Hotels

The international hotels in the centre are expensive, although there can be good deals outside summer, especially at weekends.

There's a handy batch of mid-range places on Coates Gardens, off Haymarket Terrace near Haymarket train station. Comfortable *Boisdale Hotel* (☎ 337 1134), No 9, has rooms with bathroom from £30 to £45 per person. Other possibilities include *Argus Hotel* (☎ 337 6159), No 14, and *Beresford Hotel* (☎ 337 0850) at No 32.

Rothesay Hotel (☎ 225 4125, ✉ info@rothesay-hotel.demon.co.uk, 8 Rothesay Place) is in a quiet, central street in the West End and has pleasantly spacious rooms, most with bathroom, from £45 to £80 per person.

Royal Terrace has a great position on the northern side of Calton Hill. *Ailsa Craig Hotel* (☎ *556 1022*), No 24, is a refurbished Georgian building. Singles/doubles, most with bathroom, cost £55/90 in the peak season. *Claymore Hotel* (☎ *556 2693*), No 6, *Halcyon Hotel* (☎ *556 1032*), No 8, *Greenside Hotel* (☎ *557 0022*, e *greensidehotel@ednet.co.uk*), No 9, and *Adria Hotel* (☎ *556 7875*), No 11, are similar. Also on Royal Terrace, and the biggest of the lot, is the thoroughly swish *Royal Terrace Hotel* (☎ *557 3222*) with rooms from £95/160.

Lodge Inn (☎ *220 2299, 94 Grassmarket*) is in the heart of the Old Town in one of the city's nightlife centres. Rooms with bathroom and TV cost from £44.95. The entrance is next to Biddy Mulligan's pub and every floor is accessible by lift.

Old Waverley Hotel (☎ *556 4648,* e *owh@scottishhighlandhotels.co.uk, 43 Princes St*) has a prime, central site and its front rooms have views of Princes St Gardens and the castle. Rooms with bathroom cost from £99/218.

Crowne Plaza (☎ *557 9797*, e *sales@crowneplazaed.co.uk, 80 High St*) is a purpose-built hotel whose exterior mimics the Royal Mile's 16th-century architecture. The interior, with its 238 en-suite rooms, is as modern as you could wish. Rates are from £155/180.

The *Sheraton Grand Hotel* (☎ *229 9131,* e *rachel_williamson@sheraton.com, 1 Festival Square*) is off Lothian Rd, west of the castle. You pay for, and get, luxury. Rooms cost from £240/280.

More personal is the beguiling, beautifully furnished *Sibbet House* (☎ *556 1078,* e *sibbet.house@zetnet.co.uk, 26 Northumberland St*) where rooms cost from £90 to £110 and your host may give you an impromptu bagpipe recital.

PLACES TO EAT

There are good-value restaurants scattered all round the city. For cheap eats, the best areas are Union Place, near the Playhouse Theatre; around Grassmarket, south of the

castle; near the university around Nicolson St, the extension of North/South Bridge; and in Bruntsfield. Most restaurants offer cheap set menus at lunchtime. Many close on Sunday evening, so ring ahead.

Royal Mile & Around

Despite being a tourist Mecca, the Royal Mile area has lots of good-value, enjoyable eating oases.

Restaurants The excellent, small *Polo Fusion* (☎ *622 7722, 503 Lawnmarket*) is reasonably priced by Edinburgh standards and offers an interesting menu that blends a variety of international dishes, using Scottish produce, with an emphasis on seafood. Lunchtime main courses cost from £4.50 to £6.50. It opens noon to 2 pm and 6 to 10 pm daily.

Viva Mexico (☎ *226 5145, 41 Cockburn St*) is a cheerful, atmospheric restaurant and the food is great. Burritos cost from £8.95. Some tables have views of New Town. It opens noon to 2.30 pm and 6.30 to 10.30 pm Monday to Saturday (Sunday 6.30 to 10 pm).

Doric Tavern (☎ *225 1084, 15 Market St*) is a cosy upstairs bistro offering classic Scottish dishes. A three-course set dinner costs £19.50. For sweets try the chocolate and whisky mousse. It opens noon to 1 am Monday to Saturday and 12.30 pm till late Sunday.

Unpretentious *Black Bo's* (☎ *557 6136, 57–61 Blackfriars St*) offers an imaginative vegetarian menu in candle-lit surroundings. Main courses, such as mushroom and olive roulade, cost around £9.95. It opens noon to 2 pm and 6 to 10.30 pm Monday to Saturday (evenings only on Sunday).

You can sample an array of traditional Scottish dishes at the stylish *The Reform Restaurant* (☎ *558 9992, 267 Canongate*) where delicious two-course lunch specials with wine cost under £8. It opens daily. Popular with locals and tourists, the basement *Dubh Prais* (☎ *557 5732, 123b High St*) is one of the best places to try Scottish cuisine. The menu features starters such as fried haggis in whisky sauce for £3 and main courses such as venison in thyme

Scotland's National Dish

A popular rhyme, penned by an English poet, goes:

> For the land of Burns
> The only snag is
> The haggis

Scotland's national dish is sometimes ridiculed by foreigners because its ingredients don't sound too mouthwatering. However, once you get over any delicate sensibilities towards tucking into chopped lungs, heart and liver mixed with oatmeal and boiled in a sheep's stomach, with the accompanying glass of whisky it can taste surprisingly good.

Haggis should be served with *tatties* and *neeps* (mashed potatoes and turnips, with a generous dollop of butter and a good sprinkling of black pepper).

Although it's eaten year round, haggis is central to the celebrations of 25 January in honour of Scotland's national poet, Robert Burns. Scots worldwide unite on Burns Night to revel in their Scottishness. A piper announces the arrival of the haggis and Burns' poem *Address to a Haggis* (otherwise known as the *Selkirk Grace*) is recited to this 'Great chieftan o' the puddin-race'. The bulging stomach is then lanced with a *dirk* (dagger) to reveal the steaming offal within.

Vegetarians (and quite a few carnivores, no doubt) will be relieved to know that vegie haggis is available in some restaurants in Scotland.

sauce for £15. It opens noon to 2 pm and 6.30 to 10.30 pm Tuesday to Saturday.

Cafes Attracting a mix of students, young professionals and tourists is *Patisserie Florentin (8 St Giles St)*. It has excellent light meals and pastries; sandwiches cost £3.80 and good coffee £1.20. There's a small dining area at street level and a larger room upstairs. It opens 7 am to 9 pm Sunday to Friday, to 10 pm on Saturday, and stays open till the wee small hours during the festival.

The *Lower Aisle Restaurant*, beneath St Giles Cathedral in Parliament Square, is peaceful outside peak lunchtimes. Baked potatoes cost from £1.90. It opens 9.30 am to 4.30 pm Monday to Friday and 9 am to 2 pm Sunday.

Open daily, the central *Elephant's Sufficiency (☎ 220 0666, 170 High St)* is a bustling breakfast and lunch spot that uses good-quality Scottish produce. Try the Orkney burger for £4.75.

The enormously popular *Elephant House (☎ 220 5355, 21 George IV Bridge)* is an atmospheric cafe with newspapers, light meals, delicious pastries, some of the best coffee (from £1.20) in Edinburgh and elephants in all shapes and sizes.

The Coffee Bar (☎ 558 3083, 105 High St), next to the Royal Mile Backpackers hostel, is a simple cafe serving good coffee and baguettes from £1.25. The *Netherbow Theatre Café* on Canongate, entered through John Knox House, serves cheap breakfasts from 9.30 am to 11.30 pm and lunches (big portions) which include salads and baked potatoes from £2.75 to £3.75.

Two traditional, busy tearooms lurk at the Holyrood end of the Mile. *Clarinda's Tea Room (69 Canongate)* sells a variety of teas from 55p and delicious cakes from 98p. Opposite the People's Story, *Bramble's Tearoom* does soup and a roll for £1.50 and sandwiches for £2.15. Both open daily.

Grassmarket & Around

Grassmarket is a good starting point for a night out and its lively pubs and restaurants on the northern side cater to a mixed crowd.

The casual *Ristorante Gennaro (☎ 226 3706)*, No 64, has standard but good Italian fare with savoury antipasti from £3.20 to £5.95 and pizzas from £4.80 to £6.95. It opens noon to midnight daily. Popular, informal *Mamma's Pizzas (☎ 225 6464)*, No 30, does excellent pizzas with imaginative toppings (from £3.95 to £9.95) and opens noon till late daily.

The busy *Petit Paris Restaurant (☎ 226 2442, 38–40 Grassmarket)* recreates a little bit of Paris in Edinburgh with its good-value food combining Scottish produce and French cuisine. Main courses cost from £8 to £14.80.

EDINBURGH

It opens for lunch and dinner daily and you can bring your own (BYO) wine. More exotic is *Baracoa* (☎ 225 5846, *7 Victoria St*), a Cuban restaurant and bar decorated with Latin memorabilia, serving tasty, filling main courses for under £10. It opens 11 am to 1 am daily and has music most nights.

Pierre Victoire (☎ 225 1721, *10 Victoria St*) serves authentic, good-value French cuisine in a lively, informal setting. Main courses cost from £9 to £12.45. It opens 11 am to 1 pm and 5.30 to 11 pm daily.

New Town

New Town is neither particularly well endowed with eating places nor a particularly interesting part of town at night, but there are some reasonable options, especially in Hanover St.

Henderson's (☎ 225 2131), downstairs at No 94, is an Edinburgh institution which has been churning out vegetarian food for more than 30 years. Hot dishes start at £3.50, sweets from £2.30. It opens 8 am to 10.45 pm Monday to Saturday. The offbeat *Gringo Bill's* (☎ 220 1205), No 110, with its bright yellow entrance, does filling Tex-Mex meals from £7.20 to £11.50 plus lunchtime specials for £6. It opens for lunch and dinner daily. There are several Italian restaurants clustered together including the cheerful *Bar Napoli* (☎ 225 2600), downstairs at No 75, which serves pasta and pizza for under £6. Its three-course lunch is a bargain at £3.95. It opens noon to 2 pm Monday to Thursday and Sunday, noon to 4 am Friday and Saturday.

La P'tite Folie (☎ 225 7893, *61 Frederick St*), with its decor of French memorabilia, offers reasonably priced, good-quality French food. Most main courses cost under £10. It opens noon to 3 pm and 6 to 11 pm daily. In the same French vein there's a branch of the popular *Café Rouge* (☎ 225 4515) chain nearby.

Midway along Princes St, on the 2nd floor of the huge Waterstone's bookshop near the corner of South Charlotte St, is a branch of *Starbucks*. Here you can read quietly, enjoy the view through the bow window overlooking Princes St and drink some good coffee.

Queen Street Café, in the Scottish National Portrait Gallery, serves delicious home-baked cooking from 10 am to 4.30 pm Monday to Saturday and to 2 pm Sunday.

Leith Walk

Several places on Leith Walk, including some Italian options, pitch for Playhouse Theatre-goers. Pick of the bunch is friendly, informal *Giuliano's* (☎ 556 6590, *18 Union Place*) opposite the theatre. It opens noon to 2.30 am daily, serving pastas and pizzas for under £6. *Ferri's Restaurant* (☎ 556 5592, *1 Antigua St*), a trattoria on the corner of Union Place, also dishes up tasty pasta and pizza at similar prices, with a good vegetarian selection. It opens noon to 2.30 pm and 5 pm to midnight Monday to Thursday, noon to 2.30 am Friday and Saturday, and 5 pm to midnight Sunday.

Dalry Rd (West End)

A few places on busy Dalry Rd are convenient for those staying in or near the West End.

The well-established, informal *Howie's Restaurant* (☎ 313 3334, *63 Dalry Rd*), a popular Scottish restaurant, opens daily; advance booking is wise. Main dishes include wildboar sausages, and a house speciality for desert is banoffi pie. Its two-course lunch is a bargain at £7 and you can BYO booze.

At the northern end of Dalry Rd, the *Verandah Restaurant* (☎ 337 5828), No 17, is an excellent tandoori restaurant often frequented by celebrities. A three-course lunch costs only £5.95; its evening meals are more expensive. It also has a good range of vegetarian meals and opens till midnight daily.

Stockbridge

Village-like Stockbridge is popular with the young and affluent, and has some enjoyable pubs and restaurants. With the 'American Wild West' as its theme, *Buffalo Grill* (☎ 332 3864, *1 Raeburn Place*), at the junction of Dean St, is a carnivore's delight. Dishes are mainly beef (burgers start at £7.95) but there are also chicken, fish and even vegetarian options. It opens daily.

Patisserie Florentin (☎ 220 0225, 5 North West Circus Place) is a smaller version of its sister cafe off the Royal Mile and has excellent baguettes, pastries and coffee. Another *Howie's Restaurant (☎ 225 5553)* is on the corner of Glanville Place and Hamilton Place.

Lothian Rd & Around

A few places around the southern end of Lothian Rd and on Grindlay St cater for the Royal Lyceum Theatre's clientele. Big, jolly *Dario's Ristorante & Pizzeria (☎ 229 9625, 85 Lothian Rd)* opens until 5 am daily. Its three-course set lunches cost £4.25 and, in the evening, pasta and pizzas cost from £5 to £6. Opposite the theatre's entrance, *Jasmine (☎ 229 5757, 32 Grindlay St)* has excellent Chinese cooking, especially seafood. You'll be able to eat well for under £15 and its weekday three-course lunch costs only £6.

Bruntsfield

A batch of moderately priced restaurants line Home and Leven Sts (which lead to Bruntsfield Place), but some more interesting places are farther south around the junction of Bruntsfield Place, Montpelier Park and Murchison Place.

Named after a tribe in southern Africa, the friendly *Ndebele (☎ 221 1141, 57 Home St)* is a good-value African-style cafe and sandwich deli. It's cheaper to take away but if you eat in, hot dishes from around Africa cost £4.

Parrots (☎ 229 3252, 3 Viewforth), off Bruntsfield Place, is a popular nonsmoking restaurant selling excellent-value evening meals in pleasant parrot-themed surroundings. The extensive menu offers everything from chicken rigatoni (£4.95) to vegetable stroganoff (£5.95). Reservations are recommended. It's even possible to eat alone here without feeling like a leper. It opens daily except Sunday and Monday. Farther south, *Montpelier's (☎ 229 3115, 159 Bruntsfield Place)* serves excellent Scottish and vegetarian breakfasts all day for £6.55 and has an interesting dinner menu.

Nearby is a branch of *Howie's Restaurant (☎ 221 1777, 208 Bruntsfield Place)* in a former bank (see Dalry Rd earlier).

University

There are lots of places near the university. Many student favourites are between Nicolson St and Bristo Place at the end of George IV Bridge.

Kebab Mahal (☎ 667 5214, 7 Nicolson Square) is a legendary source of cheap sustenance with excellent kebabs from £2.95 and curries from £3.25. All dishes are halal and it opens till late daily.

Vegetarians will enjoy *Susie's Wholefood Diner (☎ 667 8729, 51 West Nicolson St)* where good, inexpensive main courses cost from £3.75 to £4.95. There's live music and a belly dancer for entertainment in the evenings. It opens 9 am to 8 or 9 pm Monday to Saturday and 12.30 to 8 pm Sunday.

Negociants (☎ 225 6313, 45–7 Lothian St) is a hip cafe and music venue with good-value food – main courses start from £6.75. It offers a wide selection of beers and has tables outside in fine weather. It opens 9 am till late daily.

Spartan, atmospheric *Khushi's (☎ 556 8996, 16 Drummond St)* is the original Edinburgh curry house and not much has changed since it opened in 1947. Lamb bhuna at £4.95 is said to be the local favourite; you can BYO booze. It takes cash only and opens daily except Sunday.

Kalpna (☎ 667 9890, 2 St Patrick's Square) is a highly acclaimed, reasonably priced Gujarati (Indian) vegetarian restaurant. On Wednesday nights it lays on a gourmet buffet (£8.95) of 20 dishes from one region of India – the region varies each week. During the week it offers lunch buffets for £5.

Newington & Around

If you're staying in Minto St or Mayfield Gardens, you need to head towards the centre to find several good choices.

The Metropole, on the corner of East Newington Place, is a large cafe with a wide choice of coffees and teas from 90p and good pies and pastries. It also serves light meals for £6 to £9 and is a good place to relax with a newspaper or book.

Chinese Home Cooking (☎ 668 4946, 34 West Preston St) is a real bargain BYO restaurant with simple decor but filling, tasty food. Main courses cost from £4 to £9 but its three-course lunch is a bargain at £4.50. It opens daily but for dinner only on Sunday.

Another branch of *Howie's Restaurant* (☎ 668 2917, 75 St Leonard's St) is near the corner of Montague St (see Dalry Rd earlier).

La Bonne Mer (☎ 622 9111, 113 Buccleuch St) is an elegant, popular restaurant specialising in seafood with a French twist but also offering steak dishes. A three-course meal costs £17.95. Open for dinner only, it's closed Sunday and Monday.

ENTERTAINMENT

For full coverage buy *The List* (£1.95), Edinburgh's and Glasgow's fortnightly events guide. The magazine's annual *Edinburgh & Glasgow Eating & Drinking guide* (£3.95) gives detailed descriptions of restaurants, pubs, bars and cafes. Also look for the free *city live*, a monthly magazine listing Edinburgh's live music scene.

Pubs & Bars

Edinburgh has over 700 drinking holes which are as varied as the population – everything from lavish Victorian palaces to modern, swish bars to earthy, rough, drinking holes.

Royal Mile & Around The pubs on the Royal Mile aren't very inspiring, although there are some classics along the side streets. The intimate *Jolly Judge* (7a James Court) offers a taste of old Edinburgh, retaining its distinctive 17th-century character; it also has live music and, in cold weather, a cheering fire. The *Malt Shovel Inn* (13 Cockburn St) serves a good selection of beers and whiskies, offers jazz on Tuesday nights and has tables outside on fine days.

Another traditional pub with a large range of beers and whiskies is *Deacon Brodie's*, on the corner of Lawnmarket and High Sts, named after the burglar William Brodie (see Brodie's Close earlier in the chapter). It also serves reasonably priced food. The *Hebrides Bar* (17 Market St) provides a mix of Scottish and Irish folk music on Friday and Saturday nights (when it can get very busy), while on Sunday afternoon anyone is invited to come along and play.

The trend to theme and modern, stylish bars has hit Edinburgh. *The Car Wash* (11–13 North Bank St) is a bright mix of kitsch and 1970s retro and specialises in jugs of cocktails; happy hour is 5 to 8 pm daily. *EH1* (997 High St) is a bar/cafe with DJs playing most Friday and Saturday evenings. Food is served until 7 pm. For serious vodka drinking try *Bar Kohl* (54 George IV Bridge) which offers an incredible 250 imported vodkas and 54 home-made specialities including the potent Red Hot Chilli Pepper.

Grassmarket & Around Despite its picturesque name, *The Last Drop* (74 Grassmarket) actually commemorates the hangings that used to take place nearby. As well as good beer it serves reasonably priced food. The *Beehive Inn*, No 18, is another popular watering hole and the starting point for the McEwan's 80/- Literary Pub Tour.

The popular, blue-painted *Bow Bar* (80 West Bow) serves a variety of real ales and a huge selection of whiskies. The Cuban bar *Baracoa* (see Places to Eat earlier) features DJs playing salsa and Latino grooves.

On Cowgate, running off the south-eastern corner of Grassmarket, is the cheerful, friendly *Bannerman's*, No 212, which serves cask-conditioned beers and attracts a mix of students, locals and backpackers; there's often live music or a disco. Also on Cowgate is *Siglo*, No 184, a trendy, modern bar serving Mexican food and a range of cocktails. On Tuesday night there are Salsa dance lessons.

You can't miss *The Three Sisters* on Cowgate, a huge, popular pub/club with five bars and a capacity of almost 900; despite this you'll have to queue if you arrive after 9 pm. It closes early for a club, at 1am.

Farther south, *Greyfriars Bobby's Bar* (Candlemaker Row), named after the statue out the front, is a popular student haunt serving reasonable food.

University Area The lively *Iguana* (☎ 220 4288, 41 Lothian St) attracts students and young professionals with its extensive cocktail list, good food and DJs from Wednesday to Sunday nights. *Oxygen Bar & Grill* (2–5

Infirmary St) is a trendy, stylish bar which sold canisters of oxygen until the fire service stopped the practice. Downstairs the *O2 Club* has DJs on Friday and Saturday nights. If it's late and you're looking for somewhere to go, *Number One Brasserie*, Chamber St, stays open until 3 am Wednesday to Saturday, and has a varied, inexpensive menu plus live jazz every Friday.

To enjoy the long summer evenings, *The Peartree House (38 West Nicolson St)* has a large outdoor courtyard popular with students, while *Bar Ce Lona (2–8 West Crosscauseway)* sets out pavement tables when weather permits.

New Town Rose St may have lots of pubs but they're not all worth frequenting. Two exceptions are the *Abbotsford*, No 3, which has authentic Victorian decor, and the *Rose St Brewery*, No 55, which has a good range of real ales, including some brewed on the premises.

It's worth sticking your nose through the door of the *Café Royal Bar (17 West Register St)* to see its amazing stained-glass windows, Victorian interior and ceramic portraits of famous people. Nearby on Andrew St, *Tiles Bar-Bistro* is similarly lavish and serves good food.

Pivo Caffé (☎ 557 2925, 2–6 Calton Rd) is a fantastic Czech bar offering over 15 types of lager at £2.50 a bottle, plus a pre-club lineup of DJs on weekends. *The Stand (5 York Place)* is one of the few bars with a comedy club; admission charges vary but Sunday lunchtime it's free with drinks or a meal.

Broughton St has a plethora of pubs and bars. *The Basement*, No 10a, is always packed with a young, noisy crowd and serves good Mexican food until 10 pm at weekends. In sharp contrast *Mathers*, No 25, is a traditional pub good for a quiet drink; it serves inexpensive real ales and a huge selection of malts. *The Outhouse*, down Broughton St Lane, is a simple, stylish bar with a pool table upstairs and a beer garden that is often the venue for free barbecues on Saturday and Sunday nights.

At New Town's western end, between Princes St and Charlotte Square, *Whigham's*

Wine Cellars (Hope St) is an old (and pricey) wine bar in atmospheric cellars.

Bruntsfield Beside the King's Theatre, *Bennet's Bar (8 Leven St)* is a Victorian pub serving traditional beer; its chief feature is the large curved mirrors with tiled surrounds. Nearby, the *Auld Toll (39 Leven St)* is an old, unpretentious pub good for a quiet drink. *Ye Olde Golf Tavern (30 Wright's Houses)*, overlooking Bruntsfield Links, is decorated with golfing memorabilia and has a good selection of whiskies and cask-conditioned ales.

Clubs

Edinburgh offers a variety of venues with club nights ranging from seriously cool to pure cheese. There are some interesting music/club venues in old vaults under the George IV and South Bridges. *The Vaults (☎ 558 9052, 15 Niddry St)*, under South Bridge, has a variety of reliable club nights offering house, techno, reggae and R&B in its two rooms. It opens 10.30 pm to 3 am Thursday to Saturday.

The *City Café (☎ 220 0125, 19 Blair St)* is a cool, 1950s' US-style bar and diner, with pool tables, meals, snacks and all-day breakfasts (£5.45). Downstairs there's a dance floor, *City Café 2*, where DJs entertain the hip crowd on Thursday, Friday and Saturday nights.

Worth checking out is the *Venue Night Club (☎ 557 3073, 17 Calton Rd)* which has dance music on three floors. Its fortnightly Disco Inferno, from 10.30 pm to 3 am on Saturday, is a popular session with disco, funk and soul music. Admission costs £7.

The Bongo Club (☎ 556 5204, 14 New St) has a wide variety of nights ranging from hip hop to drum'n'bass, plus Al's All Night Jokeshop, a bizarre monthly mix of DJs, live music, interactive videos and comedy. Admission costs £8, or £5 before 9 pm.

Wilkie House (☎ 225 2935, Cowgate) hosts a number of club nights including the monthly, predominantly gay, dance night Joy.

A few places offer free club nights. *Po Na Na (☎ 226 2224, 26 Frederick St)* is a favourite post-pub venue with a Middle

Eastern theme. Admission is free Monday to Friday and before 11 pm at weekends. Other free venues include *Bar Negro* at *Nego-ciants* (see Places to Eat earlier), which plays funk, dance, house and techno, attracting a large student following; and *Espionage* (☎ 477 7007, 4 India Buildings, Victoria St), with over five floors of mainstream music – go early to avoid the queues.

If you're after chart and party music with a door price rarely over £4, head to *Gaia* 229 9438, King Stables Rd) or *The Subway* (☎ 225 6766, 69 Cowgate).

Concerts, Theatre & Cinema

Partly because of the frantic festival activity, Edinburgh has more than its fair share of theatres. The *Edinburgh Festival Theatre* (☎ 529 6000, 13–29 Nicolson St) stages everything from ballet to folk music from around the world. The *Royal Lyceum Theatre* (☎ 229 9697, 30 Grindlay St), opposite Festival Square, regularly hosts concerts, ballet and children's shows. Next door, *Usher Hall* (☎ 228 1155) puts on classical and popular concerts (but was closed at the time of research for refurbishment).

The voluminous *Playhouse Theatre* (☎ 0870 606 3424, 18–22 Greenside Place), on Leith Walk east of the centre, stages folk and pop concerts, musicals and dance and children's shows.

Filmhouse (☎ 228 2688, 88 Lothian Rd) shows arthouse as well as mainstream films on its three screens, puts on regular film festivals and has a good cafe-bar. Entered via the rear of the Royal Museum of Scotland on Lothian St, *The Lumiére* (☎ 247 4219) shows classic and cult films, Friday to Sunday only.

Scottish Evenings

Several places offer an evening of eating, singing and dancing. Early May to mid-September, *Carlton Highland Hotel* (☎ 472 3000, North Bridge) has a Hail Caledonia night for £39.50 which includes five courses, entertainment and a nip of whisky. The action kicks off at 7.30 pm and ends around 10.30 pm, depending on how much the audience gets into the swing of things.

GETTING THERE & AWAY

Edinburgh is 378 miles from London, 46 miles from Glasgow, 105 miles from Newcastle upon Tyne, and 194 miles from York. See also the Getting There & Away and Getting Around chapters.

Air

Edinburgh airport (☎ 333 1000), 7 miles west of the city in Turnhouse, has domestic services and a growing number of international services. Aer Lingus, British Airways, British Midland, easyJet and Virgin all have regular flights.

Bus

There are frequent daily links with many cities in England and Wales, with National Express (☎ 0870 580 8080) and Scottish Citylink (☎ 0870 550 5050) the main operators. Bus fares from London are competitive and you may be able to get cheap promotional tickets. The journey time is 9½ to 11¼ hours depending on the route; the fare is £22 one way. Other cities include Newcastle (2¾ hours, £8) and York (5½ hours, £21.75).

Buses and coaches leave from the St Andrew Square bus station where Scottish Citylink has an enquiry and ticket counter. Scottish Citylink has buses to virtually every major town in Scotland. Most west-coast towns are reached via Glasgow to which there are buses every 15 to 20 minutes (£5 return); there are also regular services to St Andrew, Aberdeen and Inverness.

Train

The main train station is Waverley in the heart of the city, although most trains also stop at Haymarket station, which is convenient for the West End.

There are up to 20 trains daily from London's King's Cross; apart from Saver fares (which must be booked in advance), tickets are expensive (see the Getting Around chapter), but they're also quicker and more comfortable than buses.

ScotRail has two northern lines from Edinburgh: one cuts north across the Grampians to Inverness (£29.90, 3½ hours) and on to

Thurso; the other follows the coast north around to Aberdeen (£33.10, three hours) and on to Inverness. All services are non-smoking. There are trains every 15 minutes to Glasgow (50 minutes, £7.30 one way).

For rail enquiries, phone ☎ 0845 748 4950.

Car Rental
In addition to the big national operators, the TIC has details of reputable local car rental companies. One is Melville's (☎ 0870 160 9999), 9 Clifton Terrace, which charges £19 per day (plus mileage if under four days, and insurance) for a small car.

GETTING AROUND
To/From the Airport
Between 5 am and midnight Lothian Regional Transport's (LRT) frequent Airlink buses run from Waverley Bridge near the train station to the airport, taking 35 minutes and costing £3.30/5 for one way/return. A taxi costs around £15 one way.

Bus
The two main companies, LRT (☎ 555 6363) and First Edinburgh (☎ 663 9233), provide frequent, cheap services. You can buy tickets when you board buses but you must have the exact change. For short trips, fares cost from 50p to £1. A Day Saver ticket (£2.40, or £1.40 after 9.30 am), available from bus drivers when you board, covers a whole day's travel and all weekend. After midnight there are special night buses. The free *Edinburgh Travelmap* shows the most important services and is available from the TIC, or contact Traveline (☎ 225 3858, 0800 232323) at 2 Cockburn St, weekdays only.

Train
Trains heading west and north link Waverley station with Haymarket but it's cheaper to catch a bus down Princes St. Eastward to North Berwick the first stop is Musselburgh. Call ☎ 08457-484950 for information.

Taxi
There are numerous central taxi ranks; costs are reasonable and £7 gets you almost anywhere around the centre. Local companies include Capital Taxis (☎ 228 2555), Central Radio Taxis (☎ 229 2468) and City Cabs (☎ 228 1211).

Bicycle
Although there are plenty of steep hills to negotiate, Edinburgh is ideal for cycling – nothing is more than half an hour away, the traffic is fairly tolerable and scenic Holyrood Park is close by.

Open daily, Edinburgh Cycle Hire (☎ 556 5560, ⓔ info@cyclescotland.co.uk), 29 Blackfriars St, hires out mountain and hybrid bikes for £10 to £15 per day, or from £35 per week. It hires out tents and camping equipment from £3 to £5 per night and arranges cycling tours of the city from £15 for half a day. It also organises tours of Scotland and sells used bikes and buys them back, the price depending on the condition in which they're returned.

Central Cycle Hire (☎ 2287 6333), Lochrin Place off Home St, near Tollcross, operates from the Bike Trax shop and has touring/mountain bikes for £10/15 per day.

Greater Edinburgh

NORTH & NORTH-WEST
Leith
Leith is and was Edinburgh's main port, although it remained an independent burgh until the 1920s. It's still among Britain's busiest ports but in the 1960s and 70s it fell into a sad state – abandoned to council housing, a prey to drug dealers, and blighted by AIDS. A revival began in the 1980s and the area is now home to the royal yacht *Britannia* and is noted for its interesting eateries and pubs.

Parts of this neighbourhood are still a little rough – as are sections of Leith Walk, the main approach – but it's a distinctive corner of Edinburgh. The most interesting parts are bounded by North/Great Junction, Commercial and Constitution Sts, but the prettiest area is around The Shore, where the Water of Leith path south-west to Balerno starts.

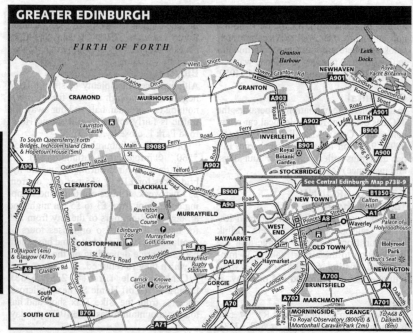

GREATER EDINBURGH

Royal Yacht Britannia The former royal yacht *Britannia* (☎ 555 5566) is moored in Leith harbour, just off Ocean Drive (though it is scheduled to move to the new Ocean Terminal, also in Leith). The visitor centre alongside the yacht gives you an insight into its history; then, with a handset to guide you, you head off to explore the yacht itself. Allow at least 1½ hours to look around and note that the use of cameras on board is prohibited.

Britannia opens 10.30 am to 6 pm (last admission 4.30 pm) daily. Admission to the visitors centre and the ship costs £7.75/3.75/20 for adults/children/families. Tickets should be reserved in advance by telephone or purchased from the Edinburgh Tattoo Office, 32 Market St.

Places to Stay & Eat In a 19th-century sailor's home, *Malmaison Hotel* (☎ 468 5000, 1 Tower Place) is a beautifully designed and furnished, stylish hotel with rooms from £105. It has both a cafe-bar and a brasserie where good-value main courses, including plenty of vegetarian options, cost from £8.50 to £16.50. A two-course lunch costs £9.50.

Nearby, two good eateries specialise in seafood. At *Fishers Bistro* (☎ 554 5666, 1 The Shore), in a 17th-century signal tower, main courses (from £9.50 to £14.50) include chargrilled swordfish on coriander. *The Shore* (☎ 553 5080, 3–4 The Shore) has live traditional music from 9 pm on Tuesday, Wednesday and Saturday, and main courses for under £13. Its delicious bread and butter pudding costs £3.75. Both open daily.

Bar meals and real ales are available in two historic pubs, the *Malt & Hops,* the oldest in Leith, and *King's Wark*.

Getting There & Away Take bus No 87, 88 or 88A from St Andrew Square, or bus X50 from Waverley Bridge to *Britannia*.

19th-century baronial style and contains a collection of fine furniture and antiques.

There are 40-minute guided tours from 11 am to 1 pm and 2 to 5 pm Saturday to Thursday, April to October; and 2 to 4 pm weekends only, November to March. Admission costs £4.50/3. Take bus Nos 29A and 40 from the centre.

South Queensferry & the Forth Bridges

South Queensferry lies on the southern bank of the Firth of Forth, at its narrowest point. From early times it was a ferry port, but not anymore – it's now overshadowed by two bridges.

The magnificent Forth Rail Bridge is one of the finest Victorian engineering achievements. Completed in 1890 after seven years' work and the deaths of 58 men, it's over a mile long and the 50,000 tons of girders take three years to paint. The Forth Road Bridge, completed in 1964, is a graceful suspension bridge.

In picturesque High St there are several places to eat and the small **Queensferry Museum** (☎ 331 5545) at 33 High St contains some interesting background information on the bridges. The prize exhibit is a model of the Furry Man; on the first Friday of August, some hapless male still has to spend nine hours roaming the streets covered from head to toe in burrs and clutching two floral staves in memory of a medieval tradition. It opens 10 am to 1 pm and 2.15 to 5 pm Monday and Thursday to Saturday and noon to 5 pm Sunday. Admission is free.

The *Maid of the Forth* (☎ 0131 331 4857) leaves from Hawes Pier and cruises under the bridges to Inchcolm Island (see Inchcolm Island & Abbey later) and **Deep Sea World** (☎ 01383-411880), the huge aquarium across the firth in North Queensferry. Weather permitting, there are daily sailings from mid-July to early September (weekends only from April to June and October). In summer there are evening music cruises for £10 per person.

Frequent trains run to South Queensferry's Dalmeny station (15 minutes). There

Newhaven

Once a small, distinct fishing community, Newhaven is now part of the Edinburgh conurbation. The old fish-market building houses **Newhaven Heritage Museum** (☎ 551 4165), 24 Pier Place, which is worth a visit. A 15-minute video reveals the astonishingly tribal lifestyle that survived here until the 1950s when overfishing ended the traditional source of income. The museum opens noon to 5 pm daily. Admission is free.

Next to the centre you can taste the delights of the enormously popular *Harry Ramsden's* (☎ 551 5566), purveyor of fish and chips, open from noon daily. Take bus No 7 or 11 from Princes St.

Lauriston Castle

Three miles north-west of the centre, Lauriston Castle (☎ 336 2060), Cramond Rd South, overlooks the Firth of Forth. It started life in the 16th century but was 'modernised' in are also numerous buses from St Andrew Square, including Nos 43, 47, X47 and 47A.

Inchcolm Island & Abbey

Inchcolm Island has one of Scotland's best preserved medieval abbeys (☎ 331 4857), which was founded for Augustinian priors in 1123. In well-tended grounds stand remains of a 13th-century church and a remarkably well-preserved octagonal chapter house with stone roof.

Unless you take your own boat, the only way to the island is on the *Maid of the Forth* (see South Queensferry & the Forth Bridges). The journey takes 30 minutes and you're allowed 1½ hours ashore. The abbey is owned by Historic Scotland (HS) and the admission cost of £2.50/1 is included in the £7.50/3.60 ferry cost (HS members should show their cards for a reduction). Non-landing tickets cost £5/2.60 and allow you to see the island's grey seals, puffins and other seabirds.

Hopetoun House

Two miles west of South Queensferry, Hopetoun House (☎ 331 2451), one of Scotland's finest stately homes, has a superb location in lovely grounds beside the Firth of Forth. There are two parts, the older built between 1699 and 1702 to Sir William Bruce's plans and dominated by a splendid stairwell, the newer designed between 1720 and 1750 by William Adam and his sons, Robert and John. The rooms have splendid furnishings, and staff make sure you don't miss details such as the revolving oyster stand for two people to share.

The Hope family supplied a viceroy of India and a governor-general of Australia so the upstairs museum displays interesting reminders of the colonial life of the ruling class. Even farther up there's a viewing point on the roof, ideal for photos.

The house opens 10 am to 5.30 pm daily, April to September; same hours weekends only in October. Admission costs £5.30/2.70.

You can reach Hopetoun House from South Queensferry or from Edinburgh – turn off the A90 onto the A904 just before the Forth Bridge Toll and follow the signs.

WEST & SOUTH
Edinburgh Zoo

To provide relief from museums, parents of young children will be relieved to know there's a zoo (☎ 334 9171), on Corstorphine Hill 3 miles west of the centre on the A8 road to Glasgow. It has the world's largest collection of captive penguins who parade at 2 pm daily, April to September. The zoo opens 9 am to 6 pm daily April to September (to 4.30 pm October and March). Admission costs £7/4. Bus Nos 12, 26, 26A and 31 pass by.

Craigmillar Castle

Edinburgh's suburbs surround the castle and the approach road, Craigmillar Castle Rd, runs through a poor housing area. Nevertheless, massive Craigmillar Castle (☎ 244 3101; HS), about 2½ miles south of the city centre off the A68 to Dalkeith, is still impressive.

Dating from the 15th century, the tower house rises above two sets of walls that enclose a 0.6-hectare area. Mary Queen of Scots took refuge here after the murder of Rizzio, her secretary; plans to murder her husband Darnley were laid here too. Look for the prison cell complete with built-in sanitation. It opens 9.30 am to 6.30 pm daily, April to September; 9.30 am to 4.30 pm Monday to Saturday (closed Thursday morning and Friday) and 2 to 4.30 pm on Sunday, October to March. Admission costs £2/75p. Bus Nos 2, 14, 21, 32, 42, 46 and 52 pass by.

Royal Observatory

The Royal Observatory (☎ 668 8405) sits atop Blackford Hill south of the city centre. The interactive displays and computers are magnets for kids, though some displays are rather dated. You can see the observatory's telescopes and there are panoramic views of Edinburgh from the external gallery. The visitor centre opens 10 am to 5 pm Monday to Saturday and noon to 5 pm on Sunday. Admission costs £3.50/2.50. From The Mound take bus No 40 or 41 to Blackford Ave, then walk up Observatory Rd.

Southern Scotland

Southern Scotland is a large, sometimes breathtakingly beautiful region interspersed with some ugly urban development. It's something of a transitional, indeterminate area. Historically, it was the buffer between the rambunctious, imperialist English and the equally unruly Scots. Although today's inhabitants are proudly and indisputably Scottish they are unique – like but unlike Scots to the north, like but unlike the northern English to the south. This duality perhaps isn't incompatible with the fact that this region was home to the two men – Robert Burns and Sir Walter Scott – who, in the late 18th and early 19th centuries, did most to reinvent, reinvigorate and popularise Scottishness.

The Romans attempted to draw a clean line across the map first with Hadrian's Wall (AD 123) in northern England, then with the Antonine Wall (142) in southern Scotland itself, leaving the Celtic Picts to their own devices. The great Anglo-Saxon kingdoms of Bernicia and Northumbria, however, dominated the east and the south-west and succeeded in driving many Celts farther north. Another wave of Anglo-Saxons arrived from northern England after 1066, bringing with them a language that evolved into Lowlands Scots – like but unlike English, as Burns so vividly illustrated.

The Norman invasion of England led to war with the Scots, although in times of peace, especially in the south, the aristocracy intermarried, leading to complicated land holdings on both sides of the border. The wars of Scottish independence from the late 13th to the late 14th century took a terrible toll on southern Scotland. Although the Scots succeeded in consolidating their independence and great monastic estates were established, the south was still periodically trampled by opposing armies.

Worse still, large parts of today's Scottish Borders and Dumfries & Galloway regions were abandoned – neither the English nor the Scottish had any real interest in bringing

Highlights

- Enjoying the bucolic beauty of the Tweed Valley
- Strolling amongst the heather in the picturesque Eildon Hills around Melrose
- Taking in Glasgow's Burrell Collection, a unique exhibition of artwork
- Revelling till the wee hours in Glasgow's pubs, bars and clubs
- Exploring the lochs, mountains and pine forests of the remote Galloway Hills
- Experiencing the captivating atmosphere of Traquair House

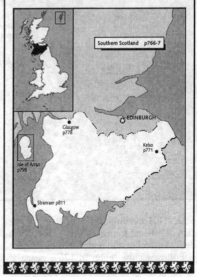

stability to their enemy's border. There were periods of relative calm when great monasteries were constructed, but the Debateable Lands, as they were known, were virtually ungoverned and ungovernable from the late 13th to the mid-17th century. The great families with their complex blood feuds fought and robbed the English, the Scots and each

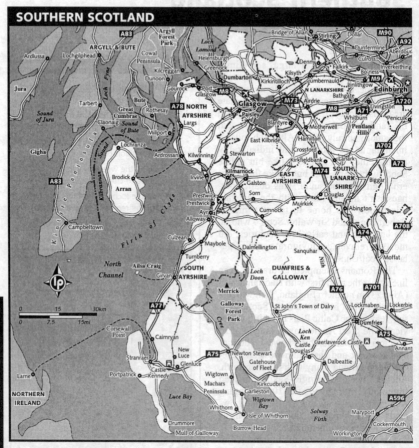

SOUTHERN SCOTLAND

other. This continuous state of guerrilla warfare, it's been argued by some, had an indelible effect on the region and its people.

Following the union in 1707, peace allowed a new surge of development. The Scottish Borders, partly thanks to the abbeys, had traditionally been an important woolgrowing and -processing region, and during the 19th century the knitting and weaving industries that survive today were created.

The region is transitional in another sense. Although not undiscovered by tourists, many only pass through quickly on their way north or south. Yet a lingering sojourn is well re-

warded. In the east, the countryside varies from gentle, flat open fields to beautiful wooded hills flanking the River Tweed. In the west are the high, remote Glenken and Galloway hills. Away from the main roads there's little traffic, particularly in the southwest, which makes for good walking and cycling.

ORIENTATION

Southern Scotland can be divided into four regions. The north-west is made up of North and South Lanarkshire, and North, South and East Ayrshire, plus smaller unitary authorities

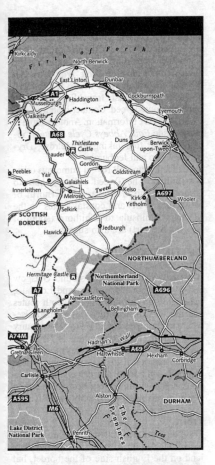

approach the grandeur of the north. The Scottish Borders have beautiful country-side, particularly around the River Tweed, and pleasant towns built around monastic ruins. The Lothians, most of which are easily accessible on day trips from Edinburgh, have some wild, bleak hills and a beautiful coastline to the east.

INFORMATION

Small towns have excellent tourist information centres (TICs) with a range of brochures, a free local accommodation booking service and onward accommodation booking (Book-A-Bed-Ahead) for £3. In northern England, Southwaite TIC (☎ 01697-473445/6), about 5 miles south-east of Carlisle on the M6, has a lot of information on southern Scotland. It opens 10 am to 6 pm daily April to September; 10 am to 5 pm Monday to Friday, and 10 am to 2 pm on Saturday, October to March. There's another useful TIC, the Gretna Gateway to Scotland (☎ 01461-338500), at Gretna services inside the border on the A74.

The TICs have information on car touring routes, including the Burns Trail, starting from near Ayr where Burns was born to Dumfries where he died; the Solway Coast Heritage Trail, from Gretna Green around the beautiful coast to Ayr; and the Scottish Borders Woollen Trail, taking in the mills and mill shops.

SYHA hostels are scarce and, in general, not very accessible unless you have a car. The exceptions are the ones at Melrose, Minnigaff (near Newton Stewart) and Ayr.

WALKING ROUTES

In the Tweed Valley especially, there are numerous circular walks around the small towns; TICs have information.

The most famous is the **Southern Upland Way**, Britain's first official coast-to-coast footpath. It runs 212 miles from Portpatrick on the south-west coast (near Stranraer) to Cockburnspath on the east coast.

The route includes some long, extremely demanding stretches, so walkers tackling its entire length must be fit and experienced. Parts are sparsely populated, with shelter and

around Glasgow. In the north-east, linked to Edinburgh, are the Lothians (East Lothian, Midlothian and West Lothian). The Scottish Borders, in the south-east, also looks to Edinburgh, and there are good bus links with that city. Dumfries & Galloway is in the south-west and is quite isolated (except for the main routes to Stranraer for ferries to Northern Ireland).

Ayrshire was the birthplace of Scotland's national poet, Burns, but is the least spectacular part of southern Scotland, despite being an area of fertile farmland. In Dumfries & Galloway the coast and mountains transport virtually nonexistent. Proper equipment is essential; in summer you can expect to experience everything from snow to a heat wave. Although the route is waymarked, walkers must be able to navigate with map and compass when visibility is bad. Walkers are advised to walk from west to east. The walk could take anything between 10 and 20 days, although 14 is a fair guess. The route incorporates cliff-top paths, old Roman roads, hill ridges and droving trails. It passes over high hilltops and wide moors, through valleys, forests, farms and villages.

The official guide to the walk, *Southern Upland Way*, is published by the government Stationery Office and comes with two 1:50,000 OS route maps. It's available from bookshops, TICs and Stationery Office bookshops in London and Edinburgh.

Accommodation is difficult to find in some parts and many walkers use tents. Book accommodation in advance, especially in the busy summer months. Local TICs can help, and supply a free accommodation leaflet.

Shorter, less demanding sections of the walk can be undertaken. Two possibilities are Portpatrick to New Luce (23 miles) and Yair (west of Galashiels) to Melrose (7½ miles).

Another long-distance walk is the 100-mile **St Cuthbert's Way**, inspired by the travels of St Cuthbert, which runs from Melrose in the Scottish Borders, eastwards to Lindisfarne in Northumberland. A shorter walk is **The Pilgrims Way**, 25-miles long between Glenluce and the Isle of Whithorn in Galloway.

CYCLING ROUTES

With the exception of the main north–south A-roads and the A75 to Stranraer, traffic is sparse, which, along with the beauty of the countryside, makes this ideal cycling country. Remember the prevailing winds are from the south-west. Local TICs have information on possible routes.

The **Tweed Cycle Way** is a waymarked route running 62 miles along the beautiful Tweed Valley following minor roads from Biggar to Peebles (13 miles) and onwards to Melrose (16 miles), Coldstream (19 miles) and Berwick-upon-Tweed (14 miles). Jedburgh TIC (☎ 01835-863435), Murray's Green, Jedburgh TD8 6BE, has information.

Another interesting route is outlined in the guide *Scottish Border Cycle Way*, although this isn't a waymarked route. It runs 210 miles coast-to-coast from Portpatrick to Berwick-upon-Tweed. Contact Jedburgh TIC (☎ 863435) for information. Another route is in the guide *Four Abbeys Cycle Route*, a 55-mile circular tour taking in Melrose, Dryburgh, Kelso and Jedburgh.

A decent map will reveal numerous other possibilities. The Tweed Valley is hard to ignore, but the Galloway Hills (north of Newton Stewart) and coastal routes on the Machars Peninsula to Whithorn (south of Newton Stewart) are also superb.

GETTING AROUND
Bus

Bus transport is excellent around Glasgow and Ayrshire, in the Borders and Lothians, reasonable on the main north–south routes and the A75 to Stranraer, but limited elsewhere in Dumfries & Galloway. The enquiry lines and the telephone numbers for major operators are given in the relevant sections. Various explorer tickets are available. These can be bought from bus drivers or bus stations, and are usually your best-value option if you're travelling reasonably extensively.

Train

Train services are limited. There are stations at Berwick-upon-Tweed (in Northumberland on the English side of the border, but the natural jumping-off point for the Tweed Valley) on the main east-coast line; at Dumfries on the main west-coast line; and at Stranraer, which is linked to Glasgow. For enquiries call ☎ 0845 748 4950.

Scottish Borders

There's a tendency to think that the 'real' Scotland doesn't start until you're north of Perth, but the castles, forests and glens of the Scottish Borders have a romance and beauty of their own. The region survived centuries of war and plunder and was romantically portrayed by Burns and Scott.

Although areas, especially to the west, are wild and empty, the fertile Tweed Valley has been a wealthy region for over 1000 years. The population was largely concentrated in a small number of *burghs* (towns, from *burh*, meaning a defensive ring of forts), which also supported large and wealthy monastic communities. These provided an irresistible magnet during the border wars and were destroyed and rebuilt numerous times.

The monasteries met their final fiery end in the mid-16th century, burned by the English yet again, but this time English fire combined with the Scottish Reformation and they were never rebuilt. The towns thrived once peace arrived and the traditional weavers provided the foundation for a major textile industry, which still survives.

If you pause here on your way north, you'll find the lovely valley of the Tweed, rolling hills, castles, ruined abbeys and sheltered towns. This is excellent cycling and walking country. Walking possibilities are the challenging coast-to-coast Southern Upland Way, St Cuthbert's Way and Borders Abbeys Way. For cyclists there's the Tweed Cycleway among others (see Walking Routes and Cycling Routes earlier).

The Scottish Borders region lies between the Cheviot Hills along the English border, and the Pentland, Moorfoot and Lammermuir Hills, which form the border with Lothian and overlook the Firth of Forth. The most interesting country surrounds the River Tweed and its tributaries.

GETTING AROUND

For general information about public transport in the Borders contact the Scottish Borders Council (☎ 01835-825200).

Bus

There's a good network of local buses. For those coming from the south-west, McEwan's Coaches (☎ 01387-710357), in Dumfries, operates a Rail Link coach service between Carlisle in north-western Cumbria and Galashiels; there are up to eight a day

Monday to Saturday, three on Sunday (£5 one way, two hours).

First Edinburgh (☎ 01896-752237), in Galashiels, has numerous buses between Edinburgh and Galashiels, and frequent buses between Galashiels and Melrose. Regular First Edinburgh buses run between Berwick-upon-Tweed and Galashiels via Coldstream, Melrose and Kelso. Another useful, frequent service links Jedburgh, Melrose and Galashiels. First Edinburgh's Waverley Wanderer ticket allows a day (£11.50) or week (£33.50) of unlimited travel around the Scottish Borders and to Edinburgh.

National Express (☎ 0870 580 8080) bus No 383 runs twice a day between Chester and Edinburgh, stopping at Manchester, Leeds, Newcastle, Jedburgh and Melrose.

Munro's of Jedburgh (☎ 01835-862253), Oakvale Garage, Bongate, Jedburgh, is a small local bus company.

Train

The main line north from Carlisle skirts the west of the region, the line north from Berwick-upon-Tweed skirts the east on the coast. In between, buses are the only option.

COLDSTREAM

☎ 01890 • pop 1750

Coldstream, a small, relatively uninspiring town on the banks of the River Tweed, is best known as the birthplace in 1650 of the Coldstream Guards, (see the boxed text 'Coldstream Guards' later). The TIC (☎ 882607), Town Hall, opens daily April to September; Monday to Saturday in October.

The history of the regiment is covered in the **Coldstream Museum** (☎ 882630), off High St in Market Square, which is open April to September. Admission costs £1/50p for adults/children. There's a short, pleasant trail beside the river called **Nuns' Walk**.

Coldstream Caravan & Camping Site (☎ 883376) has a beautiful grassy location beside the river and charges £4 per site (£6 for two persons). The Georgian *Crown Hotel* (☎ 882558, Market Square), opposite the museum, is a family-run hotel with singles/doubles for £18/35 (£26/46 with bathrooms) and good-value bar meals.

Coldstream Guards

The Coldstream Guards were formed in 1650 in Berwick-upon-Tweed for duty in Scotland as part of Oliver Cromwell's New Model Army and were originally known as Colonel Monck's Regiment of Foot. The regiment took its present name from the town where it was stationed in 1659. Its full title is the Coldstream Regiment of Foot Guards.

The regiment played a significant part in the restoration of the monarchy in 1660. It saw service at Waterloo against Napoleon, at Sebastopol during the Crimean War, in the Boer War, at the Somme and Ypres in WWI, and at Dunkirk and Tobruk in WWII.

It remains the oldest regiment in continuous existence in the British army and is the only one directly descended from the New Model Army. The regiment's emblem is the Star of the Order of the Garter, its regimental motto is *nulli secundus* (second to none) and its colonel-in-chief is the British monarch.

First Edinburgh (☎ 01896-752237) runs up to seven buses a day (Monday to Saturday) from Berwick-upon-Tweed to Kelso via Coldstream, as well as services to Edinburgh.

KELSO
☎ 01573 • pop 6045
Kelso is a prosperous market town with a broad cobbled square, flanked by Georgian buildings, at the hub of narrow cobbled streets. There's an interesting mix of architecture and the town has a lovely position at the junction of the Rivers Tweed and Teviot. Kelso Bridge was used as the model for the old London Bridge. Kelso is busy during the day, but dies completely in the evening. It's a real town, however, not a tourist trap.

The TIC (☎ 223464), Town House, The Square, opens daily April to October. Opening times are complex but its core hours are 10 am to 5 pm Monday to Saturday, and 10 am to 1 pm on Sunday, extended in July and August.

Kelso Library, Bowmont St, offers Internet access for £2.50 per half-hour and opens Monday to Saturday.

Kelso Abbey
Kelso Abbey was built by Tironensians, an order founded at Tiron in Picardy and brought to the Scottish Borders around 1113 by David I. Once one of the richest abbeys in southern Scotland, English raids in the 16th century reduced it to ruins. Today there's little to see, although the abbey precincts are attractive and the nearby octagonal **Kelso Old Parish Church** (1773) is intriguing. The abbey opens 9.30 am to 6 pm Monday to Saturday, and 2 to 6 pm on Sunday, April to September; it closes at 4 pm October to March. Admission is free.

Floors Castle
Grandiose Floors Castle (☎ 223333), Scotland's largest inhabited house, overlooks the Tweed about a mile north-west of Kelso. Built by William Adam in the 1720s, the original Georgian simplicity was 'improved' during the 1840s with the addition of rather ridiculous battlements and turrets. Although the Roxburgh family still lives here, Floors is in the tourism business and there's little sense that this is a real home – visitors are restricted to 10 rooms and a busy restaurant.

Floors Castle opens 10 am to 4.30 pm daily from Easter to late October. Admission costs £5/3. You can follow the Cobby Riverside Walk to reach the castle grounds' entrance, though you have to rejoin Roxburgh St to gain admission.

Walking Routes
The **Pennine Way**, which starts its long journey at Edale in the Lake District, ends at Kirk Yetholm Youth Hostel, about 6 miles south-east of Kelso on the B6352. Less ambitious walkers should leave The Square by Roxburgh St, and take the signposted alley to **The Cobby Riverside Walk**, a pleasant ramble along the river (past some expensive fishing spots) to Floors Castle.

Places to Stay
Accommodation can be difficult to find during local festivals and markets held late June to mid-September so book ahead.

Open March to October, *Springwood Caravan Park* (☎ 224596), about a mile

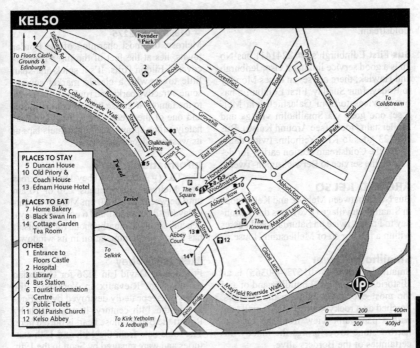

KELSO

To Floors Castle
Grounds &
Edinburgh

Poynder
Park

To
Coldstream

The Cobby Riverside Walk

Tweed

Teviot

To
Selkirk

Abbey
Court

To Kirk Yetholm
& Jedburgh

To
Coldstream

Chalkheugh
Terrace

The Square

The Knowes

Mayfield Riverside Walk

Kelso Bridge

PLACES TO STAY
5 Duncan House
10 Old Priory &
   Coach House
13 Ednam House Hotel

PLACES TO EAT
7 Home Bakery
8 Black Swan Inn
14 Cottage Garden
   Tea Room

OTHER
1 Entrance to
   Floors Castle
2 Hospital
3 Library
4 Bus Station
6 Tourist Information
   Centre
9 Public Toilets
11 Old Parish Church
12 Kelso Abbey

0   200   400m
0   200   400yd

south on the A699, has tent sites for £9. *Kirk Yetholm Youth Hostel* (☎ 420631) is in a Georgian mansion 6 miles south-east of Kelso. It opens March to October and dorm beds for adults/under-18s cost £8.25/7.25. Bus No 81 runs to/from Kelso up to six times daily Monday to Saturday.

In Kelso, *Duncan House* (☎ 225682, *Chalkheugh Terrace*) is an old house near the town centre, but with a view over the Rivers Tweed and Teviot. There's a double, twin and family room and private bathrooms, with rates from £17 per person. The attractively decorated, central *Old Priory & Coach House* (☎ 223030, *12 Abbey Row*) also has an entrance on Woodmarket. Its eight rooms have bathrooms and go for £32.50/45 for singles/doubles.

The top place is the elegant *Ednam House Hotel* (☎ 224168, *Bridge St*), a Georgian house with fine gardens overlooking the river. It has a range of rooms, all with bathrooms; B&B costs from £38/58.

Places to Eat

The *Black Swan Inn* (☎ 224563, *Horsemarket*) has decent, generous bar meals from £5.25 to £10; it doesn't look too prepossessing outside but it's comfortable inside. It also has B&B for £27/40.

Bar lunches at *Ednam House Hotel* (see Places to Stay earlier) are well priced with open sandwiches and salad for £4.50 and hot dishes for £6.45. Set dinners aren't bad either with a main dish, dessert and coffee or tea for £11.50. It opens daily for lunch and dinner.

For takeaway, the *Home Bakery* (*Horsemarket*), behind the TIC, sells delicious quiches, pies and filled rolls. The *Cottage Garden Tea Room* (*7 Abbey Court*), in a quiet corner near the abbey, serves tea, coffee and light lunches (from £4). It has some outdoor seating in fine weather.

Getting There & Away

Kelso is 340 miles from London, 44 miles from Edinburgh, 18 miles from Galashiels,

11 miles from Jedburgh and 9 miles from Coldstream.

Bus First Edinburgh's (☎ 224141) bus No 20 is a good service linking Kelso, Jedburgh and Hawick; there are seven buses Monday to Friday, four Sunday. First Edinburgh has two services to/from Galashiels via Melrose; one goes via Smailholm village and Mellerstain House (see Around Kelso). Bus No 223 goes to Kirk Yetholm, twice daily.

See the Coldstream section earlier for details on the service to Berwick-upon-Tweed.

AROUND KELSO

Bus No 65 between Melrose and Kelso stops in Smailholm village (five times daily Monday to Friday, twice on Saturday) and passes within a mile or so of Mellerstain House.

Smailholm Tower

Smailholm Tower (☎ 01573-460365) is an Historic Scotland (HS) building and one of the most evocative sights in the Borders. Perched on a rocky knoll above a small lake with a panoramic view from the top, the narrow stone tower brings the bloody uncertainties of the Borders alive.

The nearby farm, Sandyknowe, was owned by Sir Walter Scott's grandfather. Scott's imagination was fired by the ballads and stories he heard at Sandyknowe as a child, and by the ruined tower of his ancestors a stone's throw away. You pass through the farmyard to get to the tower.

The tower is 6 miles west of Kelso, a mile south of Smailholm village on the B6397. It opens standard HS hours. Admission costs £2/75p.

Mellerstain House

Mellerstain House (☎ 01573-410225), considered Scotland's finest Robert Adam designed mansion, is famous for its ornate interiors and plaster ceilings. Completed in 1778, it has a classically elegant style. It opens 12.30 to 5 pm Sunday to Friday, Easter to September. Admission costs £4.50/2. It's about 10 miles north-west of Kelso near Gordon. Take the A698 north from Kelso, then turn left onto the A6089.

MELROSE
☎ 01896 • pop 2275

Melrose, the most charming of the Border towns, lies at the feet of the three heather-covered Eildon Hills. It's a spick-and-span little town, with a classic market square, some attractive parks and rugby ovals (home to the famous Melrose Sevens competition), and one of the great abbey ruins. Unfortunately, urban sprawl from Galashiels laps at its western edges.

Information

The TIC (☎ 822555), Abbey House, across from Melrose Abbey, opens 9.30 or 10 am until between 5 and 6.30 pm Monday to Saturday (until between 1 and 6 pm on Sunday), depending on the month; phone for details. It has a list of accommodation in its window.

Melrose Abbey

Founded by David I in 1136 for Cistercian monks from Rievaulx in Yorkshire, the abbey was repeatedly destroyed by the English in the 14th century. It was rebuilt by Robert the Bruce whose heart is buried here. The ruins date from the 14th and 15th centuries and were repaired by Scott in the 19th. They're pure Gothic and are famous for their decorative stonework. The adjoining museum was closed at the time of research.

The abbey (☎ 822562; HS) opens 9.30 am to 6.30 pm daily, April to September; 9.30 am to 4.30 pm Monday to Saturday and 2 to 4.30 pm on Sunday, October to March. Admission costs £3/1.

Next to the abbey are National Trust Scotland's (NTS) walled **Priorwood Gardens** (☎ 822493), featuring plants used for dried flower arrangements (£1 donation requested). It opens daily year round.

Activities

There are attractive walks in the surrounding Eildon Hills, and St Cuthbert's Way, the coast-to-coast Southern Upland Way and the Tweed Cycleway pass through Melrose.

Places to Stay

Hostels The *Melrose Youth Hostel* (☎ 822521) is in a large Georgian mansion on the edge of town. From Market Square, follow the signposts for the A68. It opens Easter to September; dorm beds cost £11.25/10 (adults/under-18s).

B&Bs & Hotels Melrose B&Bs and hotels aren't cheap by Scottish standards, but are of a high standard – this wouldn't be a bad place to treat yourself. There aren't that many, so consider booking ahead.

Friendly *Birch House* (☎ 822391, High St) is a large, open place with a double and a twin for £18 per person; breakfasts are substantial and include a choice of fresh fruit. Near the abbey, *Braidwood* (☎ 822488, Buccleuch St) is an excellent B&B with high-quality facilities and a warm welcome. Its three doubles and one family room cost from £19 per person.

The 18th-century *Burt's Hotel* (☎ 822285, Market Square) offers upmarket B&B for £50/88. Opposite, *Bon Accord Hotel* (☎ 822645, Market Square) is a small comfortable hotel where singles/doubles cost £43/70 with bathroom.

Places to Eat

The acclaimed *Melrose Station Bar & Bistro* (☎ 822546, Palma Place), in a former railway station, opens 9 am till late Monday to Saturday. Book for evening meals. Mains cost £8 to £14 and the chef does a vegetarian meal of the day for £6.95.

The pubs have excellent food and offer lunch and dinner daily. The *Kings Arms* (☎ 822143, High St) has substantial mains, such as giant Yorkshire pudding and beef, for £5.95 to £10. In Market Square, *Burt's Hotel* has good food (mains cost £7 to £13), as does the *Bon Accord Hotel* (☎ 822645) opposite, where beef pie costs £7. All provide vegetarian meals.

Getting There & Away

Melrose is 340 miles from London, 38 miles from Edinburgh and 12 miles from Kelso and Jedburgh.

First Edinburgh (☎ 01896-752237) provides bus links every five to 15 minutes to Galashiels, Kelso and Jedburgh. Bus No 62 runs regularly to Peebles and Edinburgh,

while bus No 65 to Kelso travels via Smailholm and close to Mellerstain House (see Around Kelso earlier in the chapter).

AROUND MELROSE
Dryburgh Abbey

The most beautiful, most complete Borders abbey is Dryburgh, partly because the neighbouring town of Dryburgh no longer exists (another victim of the wars), and partly because it's in a lovely, sheltered valley by the River Tweed. The abbey belonged to the Premonstratensians, a religious order founded in France, and dates from about 1150. The pink-hued stone ruins were chosen as the burial place for Scott and later for Earl Haig, the WWI Allied commander. There are some beautiful picnic spots here.

The abbey (☎ 01835-822381; HS) is 5 miles south-east of Melrose on the B6404, which passes famous Scott's View overlooking the valley. It opens 9.30 am to 6.30 pm daily April to September; 9.30 am to 4.30 pm Monday to Saturday, and 2 to 4.30 pm on Sunday, October to March. Admission costs £2.50/1. Bus No 67 passes nearby.

Abbotsford

The fascinating home of Sir Walter Scott isn't an architectural masterpiece but it's in a beautiful setting. There's an extraordinary collection of the great man's library and other possessions, which make it well worth visiting. It opens 10 am to 5 pm Monday to Saturday, and 2 to 5 pm on Sunday, mid-March to October (from 10 am on Sunday June to September). Admission costs £3.80/1.90.

The house (☎ 01896-752043) is about 2 miles west of Melrose between the River Tweed and B6360. Frequent buses run between Galashiels and Melrose; alight at the Tweedbank traffic island and follow the signposts (it's a 15-minute walk).

Thirlestane Castle

Thirlestane (☎ 01578-722430), 10 miles north of Melrose, near Lauder off the A68, is one of Scotland's most appealing castles. The massive original keep was built in the 13th century but refashioned and extended in the 16th century with fairytale turrets and towers – achieved without compromising the scale and integrity of the building. It's still very much a family home and as a visitor you feel almost as if you're prying.

It opens 11 am to 4.15 pm Sunday to Friday, Easter to October. Admission costs £5. Bus Nos 29 and 30 go to Lauder.

GALASHIELS
☎ 01896 • pop 13,765

Galashiels is a busy, unprepossessing mill town strung along the A6091, 3 miles east of Melrose, and is an important transport hub for the Scottish Borders. There's quite a bit of accommodation but little reason to stay. It has a confusing one-way traffic system, and the town virtually closes down by 6 pm.

The TIC (☎ 755551), 3 St John St, opens 10 am until between 4 and 6 pm Monday to Saturday (from 1 or 2 pm on Sunday), depending on the month; phone for details.

First Edinburgh (☎ 01896-752237) is the main operator with frequent buses to/from Edinburgh and Borders towns. Bus Nos 62 and 95 run almost hourly Monday to Saturday (every two hours Sunday) to Melrose.

SELKIRK
☎ 01750 • pop 5950

Selkirk is an unusual little town that climbs a steep ridge above Ettrick Water, a tributary of the River Tweed. Mills came to the area in the early 1800s, but it's now a quiet place (much quieter than Galashiels or the textile centre of Hawick). The TIC (☎ 720054), Halliwell's House, off Market Place, opens 10 am to 5 pm Monday to Saturday, and 2 to 4 pm on Sunday, April to October (extended hours in July and August). The adjoining Halliwell's House Museum has an interesting display on local history.

County Hotel (☎ 721233, 3–5 High St), near Market Place, has en-suite accommodation for £32.50/54 and good bar meals for around £5.

First Edinburgh (☎ 01896-752237) bus Nos 73 and 95 run half-hourly Monday to Friday (hourly on Saturday) between Hawick, Selkirk, Galashiels and Edinburgh.

JEDBURGH
☎ 01835 • pop 4090

Jedburgh, the most visited of the Borders towns, has some interesting sites on which it has capitalised effectively. It's an attractive town, and many old buildings and *wynds* (narrow alleys) have been intelligently restored.

The large, efficient TIC (☎ 863435), Murray's Green, has a bureau de change and offers Internet access. It opens between 9 and 10 am (between 10 am and noon on Sunday) until between 4.30 and 8 pm daily, depending on the month; phone for details.

Jedburgh Abbey

Jedburgh Abbey dominates the town. Founded in 1138 by David I as a priory for Augustinian canons, it was the site for a royal wedding and a coronation, but suffered the usual cycle of sacking and rebuilding. The red sandstone ruins are roofless but comparatively complete.

The abbey (☎ 863925; HS) opens 9.30 am to 6.30 pm daily April to September; 9.30 am to 4.30 pm Monday to Saturday (from 2 pm on Sunday) October to March. Admission costs £3/1.

Mary Queen of Scots House

Mary stayed here in 1566 after her famous ride to Hermitage Castle to visit the injured earl of Bothwell, her future husband. It's a beautiful 16th-century tower house and worth a visit – the sparse displays are interesting and evoke the sad saga of Mary's life. The house (☎ 863331) is signposted from the car park behind the TIC and from the town square. It opens 10 or 10.30 am until between 3.30 and 5 pm Monday to Saturday (from noon or 1 pm on Sunday), depending on the month; phone for details. Admission costs £2/1.

Special Events

Every two years the town hosts a food fair the third weekend in April. It's enormously popular, but Jedburgh doesn't have enough parking space for all the vehicles so there's often gridlock. The next fair is in 2002.

Places to Stay

Camping About a mile north of the town centre is *Elliot Park Camping & Caravanning Club Park* (☎ 863393, Edinburgh Rd), opposite Jedburgh Woollen Mill. It is set back from the main road and so is quiet. Tent sites cost £4.60/8.60 for members/ nonmembers, though the £4 difference is usually waived for backpackers.

B&Bs & Hotels On the corner of Abbey Close, *Castlegate Restaurant* (☎ 862552, 23 Castlegate) has two large clean rooms from a reasonable £16 per person.

Kenmore Bank (☎ 862369, Oxnam Rd) overlooks the abbey and is good value. All the singles/doubles have bathrooms and cost £29/37. Rooms at the very comfortable *Glenfriar's Hotel* (☎ 862000, Friarsgate) all have bathrooms and cost from £35 per person.

Places to Eat

Castlegate Restaurant serves a traditional Scottish menu; haggis in whisky cream sauce costs £5.60. It's a good place for either a full meal (you can bring your own wine) or just a cup of tea. The *Pheasant Lounge Bar* (☎ 862708, 61 High St) has a good range of tasty offerings with bar meals from around £5 to £9.

Getting There & Away

Jedburgh is 330 miles from London, 45 miles from Edinburgh, 17 miles from Galashiels and Selkirk and 11 miles from Kelso.

Bus Jedburgh has good bus connections around the Borders. First Edinburgh (☎ 01896-752237) is the main operator and the bus stop can be found in the car park behind the TIC. There are many connections to Hawick, Galashiels and Kelso. Bus No 23 runs to and from Berwick-upon-Tweed via Kelso and Coldstream. Bus Nos 29 and 30 run six times daily between Edinburgh and Jedburgh in each direction.

Munro's of Jedburgh (☎ 01835-862253) bus No 115 runs to the towns of Selkirk and Melrose.

PEEBLES

☎ 01721 • pop 7080

Peebles is a prosperous little town set among rolling wooded hills on the banks of the River Tweed. There's little of note in the town itself, but it's a pleasant place to stay. There's a broad, attractive High St and the interesting local **Tweeddale Museum** (☎ 724820).

The TIC (☎ 720138), High St, opens between 9 and 10 am until between 4 and 8 pm daily (closes between 12.30 and 1.30 pm and on Sunday, November to March, and at 2 pm on Sunday in April, May and October). Opening times depend on the month so it's advisable to phone for details.

Places to Stay & Eat

Set in 27 acres, 2½ miles west of Peebles on the A72, *Rosetta Caravan Park* (☎ 720770) has tent sites for £7.

In town, *Rowanbrae* (☎ 720630, Northgate) has only two rooms but it's a pleasant B&B, with rates from £17 to £19.50 per person. *Green Tree Hotel* (☎ 720582, 41 Eastgate) is a well-organised, tidy hotel. There's a range of rooms, including singles (most with bathrooms) for £28.50 per person. *The County Hotel* (☎ 720595, 35 High St) is a downbeat but good pub, often with live music in the evening. It has B&B (£19 per person), decent bar meals for around £5, and a more expensive restaurant.

About 2½ miles north on the A703, *Cringletie House* (☎ 730233) is a comfortable country house hotel with an excellent restaurant. Rooms start at £75 per person. There are set lunches for £17 and set dinners for £29.50.

Getting There & Away

Bus The bus stop is beside the post office on Eastgate. First Edinburgh (☎ 01896-752237) bus No 62 runs hourly to Edinburgh, Galashiels and Melrose.

Bicycle April to October, Scottish Border Trails (☎ 720336), Glentress, organises bicycle tours – both on- and off-road. It also hires touring/mountain bikes from £16/10 per day. Prebooking is recommended; bikes are delivered to you free in the Peebles area.

SOUTHERN SCOTLAND

AROUND PEEBLES
Neidpath Castle

Neidpath Castle is a 14th-century tower house perched on a bluff above the River Tweed, a mile west of Peebles on the A72. Although there's not much to see inside, it's a lovely spot. The castle (☎ 01721-720333) opens 11 am to 5 pm Monday to Saturday, and 1 to 5 pm on Sunday, Easter week and July to September. Admission costs £3/1.

Traquair House

Traquair (pronounced trakweer) is one of Britain's great houses; others may be more aesthetically pleasing but this one has a powerful, atmospheric beauty – and exploring it is like time-travelling. Parts are believed to have been constructed long before the first official record of its existence in 1107. The massive tower house was gradually expanded over the next 500 years, but has remained virtually unchanged since 1642.

Since the 15th century, the house has belonged to various branches of the Stuart family whose unwavering Catholicism and loyalty to the Stuart cause is largely why development ceased when it did. The family's estate, wealth and influence was gradually whittled away after the Reformation and there was neither the opportunity nor, one suspects, the will to make any changes.

One of the most fascinating rooms is the concealed room where priests secretly lived and gave Mass – up to the passing of the 1829 Catholic Emancipation Act. Other beautiful timeworn rooms hold fascinating relics, including the cradle used by Mary Queen of Scots for her son, James VI of Scotland (James I of England), and many letters written by the Stuart pretenders to their supporters.

In addition, there's a maze, an art gallery, a small brewery producing Bear Ale and an active craft community.

Traquair House (☎ 01896-830323) is 1½ miles south of Innerleithen, about 6 miles south-east of Peebles. It opens 12.30 am to 5.30 pm daily Easter to October (from 10.30 am June to August). Admission costs £5.20/2.60.

HERMITAGE CASTLE

Hermitage Castle is a massive collection of stone with a heavy cubist beauty, and sits isolated beside a rushing stream surrounded by bleak, empty moorland. Dating from the 13th century, but substantially rebuilt in the 15th, it embodies the brutal history of the Scottish Borders; the stones themselves almost speak of the past. It was Scott's favourite castle.

It's probably best known as the home of the earl of Bothwell, and the spot where Mary Queen of Scots rode in 1566 to see him after he had been wounded in a border raid. It's also where, in 1338, Sir William Douglas imprisoned his enemy Sir Alexander Ramsay and deliberately starved him to death. Ramsay survived for 17 days by eating grain that trickled into his pit (which can still be seen) from the granary above.

The castle (☎ 013873-76222; HS) is 5½ miles north-east of Newcastleton off the B6339. It opens 9.30 am to 6.30 pm daily April to September; 9.30 am to 4.30 pm Monday to Saturday, and 2 to 4.30 pm on Sunday, October and November. Admission costs £1.80/75p.

Glasgow

☎ 0141 • pop 611,500

Although lacking the instantly inspiring beauty of Edinburgh, Glasgow is one of Britain's largest, liveliest and most interesting cities with a legacy of appealing Georgian and Victorian architecture and several distinguished suburbs of terraced squares and crescents. At the same time, however, the city is pockmarked by ugly housing estates and its heart is scarred by the invasive surgery of the M8 motorway, dissecting the city centre from the West End.

Although influenced by thousands of Irish immigrants, Glasgow is the most Scottish of cities, with a unique blend of friendliness, urban chaos, black humour and energy. The city also boasts excellent art galleries and museums, most of them free, including the famous Burrell Collection, as well as numerous good-value restaurants, countless pubs, bars and clubs and a lively arts scene.

That said, arguably Glasgow's greatest asset is its proximity to some of the world's great scenery – Loch Lomond, the Trossachs and the Highlands to the north, the islands of the Hebrides to the west and the rolling hills of southern Scotland to the south.

History

Glasgow grew around the cathedral founded by St Kertigan, later to become St Mungo, in the 6th century. In 1451, it became the site of the University of Glasgow, the second university in Scotland. Unfortunately, with the exception of the cathedral, virtually nothing of the medieval city remains. It was swept away by the energetic people of a new age – the age of capitalism, the Industrial Revolution, and the British Empire.

In the 18th century, much of the tobacco trade between Europe and the USA was routed through Glasgow and provided a great source of wealth. Other New World imports included rum and sugar. Even after the tobacco trade declined in the 19th century, the city continued to prosper as a centre of textile manufacturing, shipbuilding and the coal and steel industries.

The new industries created a huge demand for labour and peasants poured in from Ireland and the Highlands to crowd the city's tenements. In the mid-18th century the population was 17,500 and by the end of the century it had risen to 100,000. After 20 years that figure had doubled and by 1860 it was home to 400,000 people. The outward appearance of prosperity, however, was tempered by the dire working conditions in the factories, particularly for women and children. In the second half of the 19th century the city experienced four major cholera outbreaks and the average life expectancy was a mere 30 years.

While the workers suffered, the textile barons and shipping magnates prospered, and Glasgow could justifiably call itself the second city of the Empire. Grand Victorian public buildings were constructed and some of the wealthier citizens spent their fortunes on amassing the large collections of art that now form the basis of the city's superb galleries.

In the first half of the 20th century, Glasgow was the centre of Britain's munitions industry, supplying arms and ships for the two world wars. After those boom years, however, the port and heavy industries began to decline and by the early 1970s, the city looked doomed. Glasgow has always been proud of its predominantly working-class nature, but unlike middle-class Edinburgh with its varied service industries, it had few alternatives when recession hit and unemployment spiralled.

In that period, the name Glasgow became synonymous with unemployment, economic depression and urban violence. It was known for bloody confrontations between rival supporters of Protestant Rangers and Catholic Celtic football teams. Over the following years, however, the city reinvented itself, rediscovering its rich cultural roots and proclaiming a new pride through a well-orchestrated publicity campaign. By 1990, it was elected European City of Culture and in 1999 served as the UK's City of Architecture & Design.

As well as the blossoming of the comic genius Billy Connolly, the 1980s and 1990s saw an incredible outburst of musical talent, producing such groups as Simple Minds, Tears for Fears, Deacon Blue, Aztec Camera, Wet Wet Wet, Texas and the latest pop sensation, Travis.

Certainly there's renewed confidence in the city, but behind the optimism the standard of living remains low for Britain and life continues to be tough for those affected by relatively high unemployment, inadequate housing and generally poor diet.

Orientation

Glasgow's tourist sights are spread over a wide area. The city centre is built on a grid system north of the River Clyde. The two train stations (Glasgow Central and Queen Street), Buchanan Street bus station and the TIC are all within a couple of blocks of George Square, the main city square. Running east–west along a ridge in the northern part of the city, Sauchiehall St (first syllable

GLASGOW

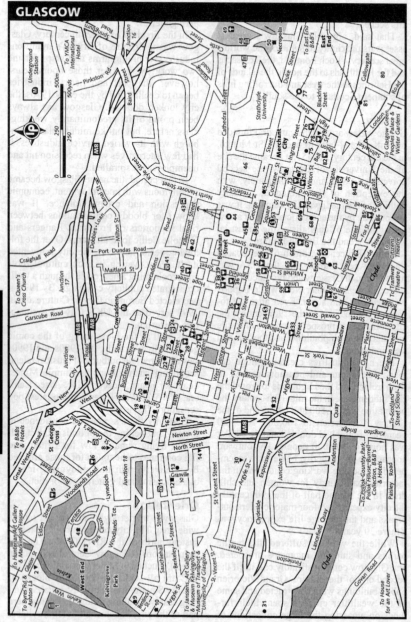

GLASGOW

PLACES TO STAY			
3	Glasgow Youth Hostel	28	Brunswick Cellars
4	Glasgow Backpackers Hostel	33	Waterloo Bar
9	Alamo Guest House	35	Buddha
10	Smith's Hotel	36	Bar Censsa
12	Berkeley Globetrotters	37	MacLachlan's Brew Bar
15	Lodge Inn	39	Nomad
17	Baird Hall	40	Victoria's Nightclub
18	McLay Guest House	45	Sadie Frost's
20	Willow Hotel;	57	Drum & Monkey
	Hampton Court Hotel	58	The Horse Shoe Bar
21	The Victorian House	59	The Underworld
32	Glasgow Marriott	61	MacSorleys
46	University of Strathclyde	65	Bar 10
50	Cathedral House Hotel	67	The Bank
		70	Polo Lounge, Del Monica's;
PLACES TO EAT			Café Latte
2	Shalimar	71	Court Bar
8	Insomnia Café	73	Bennet's Nightclub
14	Mitchell's Bistro & Bon Accord	76	Babbity Bowster
16	Ristoro Ciao Italia; Loon Fung	78	Bargo
25	Willow Tearoom	82	Blackfriars
29	Bradford's	84	The 13th Note Club
30	The Buttery; The Belfry	85	Scotia Bar
38	Modern India	86	Riverside Club
55	The Jenny		
62	The Granary	OTHER	
79	Café Gandolfi	1	Hunterian Museum
		7	Surfin' Internet Café
		11	Internet Café
PUBS, BARS & CLUBS		13	Mitchell Library
5	Uisge Beatha	19	The Tenement House
6	Halt Bar	22	Glasgow School of Art
26	Spy Bar	23	Centre for Contemporary
27	Bar Gaudi		Arts

24	Glasgow Film Theatre	
31	Scottish Exhibition &	
	Conference Centre	
34	American Express	
41	Theatre Royal	
42	Glasgow Royal Concert Hall	
43	Buchanan Street Bus Station	
44	Glasgow Queen Street	
	Train Station	
47	Provand's Lordship	
48	St Mungo's Museum of	
	Religious Life & Art	
49	Glasgow Cathedral	
51	City Chambers	
52	Bank of Scotland	
53	Tourist Information Centre	
54	Gallery of Modern Art	
56	Post Office	
60	Glasgow Central	
	Train Station	
63	St Enoch Square	
	Travel Centre	
66	St Enoch Shopping Centre	
66	Princes Square	
	Shopping Centre	
68	Tobacco Exchange	
69	Trades House	
72	Sheriff Court House	
74	Hutchesons' Hall	
75	City Halls	
77	High Street Train Station	
80	The Barras Flea Market	
81	Barrowland Dance Hall	
83	Tron Theatre	

pronounced soch as in loch) has a pedestrian mall with numerous High St shops at its eastern end, and pubs and restaurants at the western end. Merchant City is the commercial district, east of George Square.

The SYHA and University of Glasgow hostels are near Kelvingrove Park, northwest of the city centre in the West End. Pollok Country Park and the Burrell Collection are in South Side, south-west of the centre.

Motorways bore through the suburbs and the M8 slices through the western and northern edges of the centre. Glasgow airport lies 10 miles west of the centre.

Information

Tourist Offices The main TIC (☎ 204 4400), 11 George Square, has a £2 accommodation booking service. It opens 9 am to 6 pm Monday to Saturday, 9 am to 7 pm in June and September, and 9 am to 8 pm in July and August. It also opens 10 am to 6 pm Sunday, Easter to September. There's another branch (☎ 848 4440) at Glasgow airport. Visit on-line at www.seeglasgow.com.

Money The TIC and the post office, on the corner of Buchanan and St Vincent Sts, both have bureaux de change.

Email & Internet Access You can access the Internet at the Internet Cafe (☎ 564 1052), 569 Sauchiehall St, for £2/3/5 for 15/30/60 minutes. It opens 9 am to 11 pm Monday to Thursday, 10 am to 7 pm Saturday, and noon to 7 pm Sunday. Alternatively, insomniacs and Web junkies can try the 24-hour Surfin' Internet Cafe (☎ 332 0404), 81

St George's Rd. The cheapest time is 5 am to noon when you can surf for 3p a minute (minimum of 15 minutes) or £1 per hour.

Emergency Like the rest of Britain, the free emergency numbers are ☎ 999 or ☎ 112.

George Square

The TIC is on George Square, a good starting point for exploring the city. The square is surrounded by imposing Victorian architecture, including the post office, the Bank of Scotland and the City Chambers. There are statues of Burns, James Watt, Lord Clyde and, atop a 24m-high Doric column, Sir Walter Scott.

The grand City Chambers (☎ 221 9600), the seat of local government, was built in the 1880s at the high point of the city's wealth. The interior is even more extravagant than the exterior, and the chambers have sometimes been used as a movie location to represent the Kremlin or the Vatican. There are free, 45-minute tours (☎ 287 4017) from the main entrance, 10.30 am and 2.30 pm Monday to Friday.

A Walk Through Merchant City

An interesting hour-long walk can be taken from George Square to Glasgow Cathedral through Merchant City, a planned, 18th-century civic development. The Tobacco Lords were entrepreneurs who opened up European trade with the Americas, importing tobacco, rum and sugar in the 18th century, and their profits went to build these warehouses, offices and gracious homes. Redevelopment has turned the warehouses into apartments for Glaswegian yuppies, and stylish shopping malls such as the Italian Centre have sprung up to serve their retail needs.

Once you've seen the City Chambers, cross George Square and walk one block south down Queen St to the **Gallery of Modern Art** (1827). This four-storey colonnaded building was originally the Royal Exchange, where business transactions were negotiated.

The gallery faces Ingram St, which you follow east for two blocks. To the right, down Garth St, is **Trades House**, designed

by renowned Scottish architect Robert Adam in 1791 to house the trades guild. A further two blocks east along Ingram St brings you to the elegant **Hutchesons' Hall** (NTS), built in 1805 to a design by David Hamilton. It opens 10 am to 5 pm Monday to Saturday year round.

Retrace your steps one block and continue southwards down Glassford St, turn right into Wilson St and first left along Virginia St, lined with the old warehouses of the Tobacco Lords. The **Tobacco Exchange** became the Sugar Exchange in 1820 and many of the old warehouses have been converted into flats.

Back on Wilson St, the bulky **Sheriff Court** fills a whole block. It was built in 1842 as Glasgow's town hall and merchants' house. Continue eastwards past **Ingram Square**, another warehouse development, to the **City Halls**, now used for concerts. The city's markets were once held here. Turn right from Albion St into Blackfriars St. Emerging onto High St, turn left and follow the street up to Glasgow Cathedral.

Glasgow Cathedral

Glasgow Cathedral (☎ 552 6891; HS) is a shining example of pre-Reformation Gothic architecture and the only mainland Scottish cathedral to survive the Reformation. Most of the current building dates from the 15th century – only the western towers were destroyed in the turmoil.

This has been hallowed ground for over 1500 years. The site was blessed for Christian burial in 397 by St Ninian. In the following century St Mungo accompanied the body of a holy man from Stirlingshire to be buried here. He stayed to found a monastic community and built a simple church. The first building was consecrated in 1136, in the presence of King David I, but it burned in 1197 and was rebuilt as the lower church. In the 13th century, the city grew up around Glasgow Cathedral, east of the modern centre.

Entry is through a side door into the **nave**, hung with regimental colours. The wooden roof above has been restored many times since its original construction, but some of the timber dates from the 14th century.

Much of the cathedral's stained glass is modern – to your left, you'll see Francis Spear's 1958 work *The Creation*, which fills the western window.

The cathedral is divided by a late-15th-century stone choir screen, decorated with seven pairs of figures representing the Seven Deadly Sins. Beyond is the **choir**. Also by Francis Spear, the four stained-glass panels of the eastern window depicting the apostles are particularly effective. At the north-eastern corner is the entrance to the 15th-century **upper chapter house**, where the University of Glasgow was founded. It's now used as a sacristy.

The **lower church** is the most interesting part of the cathedral and is reached by a stairway. Its forest of pillars creates a powerful atmosphere around St Mungo's tomb, the focus of a famous medieval pilgrimage that was believed to be as meritorious as a visit to Rome. Edward I paid three visits to the shrine in 1301.

Behind the cathedral, the crumbling tombs of the city's rich and famous crowd the renovated **Necropolis** (originally opened in 1833), from the top of which there are good city views.

The cathedral opens to visitors 9.30 am to 6.30 pm Monday to Saturday, and 2 to 6.30 pm on Sunday, April to September; it closes at 4.30 pm daily the rest of the year. Sunday services are held at 11 am and 6.30 pm.

It takes about 15 to 20 minutes to walk from George Square but numerous buses pass by. Bus Nos 11, 12, 38 and 51 follow Cathedral St; bus No 2 runs from Argyle St via High St.

St Mungo's Museum of Religious Life & Art

This award-winning museum (☎ 553 2557), near the cathedral, is named after the patron saint of Glasgow. It's understandably challenging to select works of art representative of the world's main religions – but the result is well worth a look and is small enough not to be overwhelming.

The building may look like a restored antiquity, but it is in fact a £6.5 million reconstruction of the bishop's palace that once stood here, and only dates from the early 1990s. A 10-minute video provides an overall view before you delve into the exhibits. There are three galleries representing religion as art, religious life and, on the top floor, religion in Scotland. In the main gallery, Dali's *Christ of St John of the Cross* hangs beside statues of the Buddha and Hindu deities. Outside, you'll find Britain's only Zen Buddhist garden.

There's a good restaurant downstairs serving vegetarian and meat dishes. The museum opens 10 am to 5 pm Monday to Saturday (from 11 am on Sunday). Admission is free.

Provand's Lordship

Across the road from St Mungo's Museum, Provand's Lordship (☎ 552 8819) is the oldest house in Glasgow. Built in 1471, as a manse for the chaplain of St Nicholas Hospital, it's said to have been visited by Mary Queen of Scots, James II and James IV. It's now a museum of various period displays connected with the house. These are as diverse as a 20th-century sweet shop and the room of one of the chaplains who lived here in the 16th century. At the time of writing it was closed for structural repairs but it should be open by the time you read this.

Burrell Collection

Glasgow's top attraction, the Burrell Collection (☎ 649 7151), was amassed by wealthy industrialist Sir William Burrell before it was donated to the city. It's now housed in a prize-winning museum in **Pollok Country Park**, 3 miles south of the city centre. This idiosyncratic collection includes everything from Chinese porcelain and medieval furniture to paintings by Renoir and Cézanne. It isn't so big as to be overwhelming, and the stamp of the collector creates an intriguing coherence.

The building from the outside seems somewhat of a hybrid, but the spectacular interior provides a fitting setting for an exquisite collection of tapestries, Oriental porcelain, paintings and European stained glass. Floor-to-ceiling windows admit a flood of natural light, and the trees and landscape outside enhance the effect created by the exhibits.

Carpeted floors mean silence to contemplate the beautifully displayed treasures. Carved-stone Romanesque doorways are incorporated into the structure so visitors actually walk through them. Some galleries are reconstructions of rooms from Hutton Castle, the Burrell residence. Even the public seating is of superb design and production quality.

The light and airy cafe on the lower ground floor includes the same floor-to-ceiling windows, hung with heraldic glass medallions.

The Burrell Collection opens 10 am to 5 pm Monday to Saturday, and 11 am to 5 pm on Sunday, April to September; 10 am to 5pm Monday to Thursday and Saturday, and 11 am to 5 pm Friday and Sunday, October to March. Admission is free, but parking your car costs a hefty £1.50. There are occasional guided tours.

Numerous buses pass the gates (including bus Nos 45, 48A and 57 from the centre) and there's a twice-hourly bus service between the gallery and the gates (a pleasant 10-minute walk). Alternatively, catch a train from Central station to Pollokshaws West (the second station on the light blue line south, trains for East Kilbride or Kilmarnock, three per hour).

Pollok House

Also in Pollok Country Park, and a 10-minute walk from the Burrell Collection, is Pollok House (☎ 616 6410; NTS), built about 1740. It contains a fine collection of Spanish paintings, including works by El Greco and Goya. Parts of this Georgian house have been redecorated with historically correct colour schemes. There's a tearoom in the old kitchens. The house opens 10 am to 5 pm daily, April to October; 11 am to 4 pm daily, November to March. Admission is £4/free.

Mackintosh Buildings

There are some superb Art Nouveau buildings designed by the Scottish architect and designer, Charles Rennie Mackintosh (CRM). From mid-May to October there are weekend tours of these buildings (once or twice a month); the cost is £100, including

Charles Rennie Mackintosh

The quirky, linear and geometric designs of this famous Scottish architect and designer have had almost as much influence on the city as have Gaudí's on Barcelona. Many of the buildings Mackintosh designed in Glasgow are now open to the public, and you'll see his tall, thin, Art Nouveau typeface repeatedly reproduced.

Born in 1868, he studied at the Glasgow School of Art. In 1896, when he was aged only 27, his design won a competition for the School of Art's new building on Renfrew St. The first part was opened in 1899 and is considered to be the earliest example of Art Nouveau in Britain, and Mackintosh's supreme architectural achievement. This building demonstrates his skill in combining function and style.

Mackintosh applied himself to every facet of design, from whole facades to the smallest window fastener. As a furniture designer and decorative artist, he designed the interiors for Kate Cranston's chain of Glasgow tearooms between 1896 and 1911, including the Willow Tearoom, 217 Sauchiehall St.

Although Mackintosh's genius was quickly recognised on the Continent (he contributed to a number of exhibitions in France, Germany and Austria), he didn't receive the same encouragement in Scotland. His architectural career here lasted only until 1914 when he moved to England to concentrate on furniture design. He died in 1928, but it was only in the last decades of the 20th century that Mackintosh's genius became widely recognised. If you want to know more about the man and his work, contact the Charles Rennie Mackintosh Society (☎ 0141-946 6600, fax 0141-945 2321, @ info@crmsociety.com), Queen's Cross Church, 870 Garscube Rd, Glasgow, G20 7EL. Its Web site is at www.crmsociety.com.

B&B for two nights and admission to the Mackintosh buildings. Contact the CRM Society for details (see Queen's Cross Church later).

Glasgow School of Art Widely recognised as Mackintosh's greatest building, the Glasgow School of Art (☎ 353 4526), 167 Renfrew St, still houses the educational institution. It's hard not to be impressed by the thoroughness of the design – the architect's pencil seems to have shaped everything inside and outside the building. The interior design is austere, with simple colour combinations (often just black and cream) and those uncomfortable-looking, high-backed chairs for which he is famous. The library, designed as an addition in 1907, is a masterpiece of rectangular pillars, horizontal beams and Mackintosh's characteristic linear style.

There are guided tours at 11 am and 2 pm Monday to Friday and at 10.30 and 11.30 am on Saturday (plus 1 pm on Saturday and 10.30, 11.30 am and 1 pm on Sunday in July and August). Admission costs £5/3. Parts of the school may be closed to visitors if they're in use.

Willow Tearoom The Willow Tearoom (☎ 332 0521), 217 Sauchiehall St, is more Mockintosh than Mackintosh – a reconstruction of the tearoom Mackintosh designed and furnished in 1904 for restaurateur Kate Cranston. The restaurant closed in 1926 and the premises were occupied by a series of retail businesses. Reconstruction took two years and the Willow opened as a tearoom again in 1980. Sauchiehall means 'lane of willows', hence the choice of a stylised willow motif.

Queues for light meals and tea (see Places to Eat later) often extend into the gift shop and jeweller's downstairs.

Queen's Cross Church Now the headquarters of the CRM Society, Queen's Cross Church (☎ 946 6600), 870 Garscube Rd, on the corner of Maryhill Rd north of the centre, is the only one of Mackintosh's church designs to be built (1896). The simplicity of the design is particularly inspiring. There's an information centre, a small display and a gift shop. The church opens 10 am to 5 pm Monday to Friday, 10 am to 2 pm on Saturday and 2 to 5 pm on Sunday. Admission is free but a donation is suggested.

Other Mackintoshiana The **Scotland Street School** (☎ 429 1202), 225 Scotland St, an impressive Mackintosh building dominated by two glass-stair towers, is now a museum of education from Victorian times to WWII; it may sound dull but is actually quite fascinating. It opens 10 am to 5 pm Monday to Saturday and 2 to 5 pm on Sunday. Admission is free.

Although designed in 1901 as an entry in a competition run by a German magazine, the **House for an Art Lover** (☎ 353 4770), Bellahouston Park, Drumbreck Rd south of the river, was only completed in 1996. It's part of the Glasgow School of Art and has permanent Mackintosh displays. It's about 2½ miles from the centre and opens 10 am to 4 pm Saturday to Thursday, April to September; 10 am to 4 pm daily, October to March. Admission costs £3.50/2.50. It operates a postgraduate study centre and sometimes restricts access; call ahead before visiting.

Twenty-three miles north-west of Glasgow at Upper Colquhoun St in Helensburgh is **Hill House** (☎ 01436-673900; NTS), Mackintosh's domestic masterpiece, which he designed for Glasgow publisher, Walter Blackie. It opens 1.30 to 5.30 pm daily, April to October. Admission costs £6/4.

Finally, the principal rooms from Mackintosh's house have been reconstructed as the **Mackintosh House** at the Hunterian Art Gallery (see later in the chapter), while the Art Gallery & Museum, Kelvingrove, houses a display of Mackintosh paintings, furniture and decorative art.

Tenement House

An extraordinary time capsule experience, the small apartment in the Tenement House (☎ 333 0183; NTS), 145 Buccleuch St, gives a vivid insight into middle-class city life at the turn of the 20th century. With its box-beds, original kitchen range and all the fixtures and fittings of the Toward family who lived here for more than 50 years, it's interesting but probably cleaner and more orderly than the family would have kept it.

Despite the additional exhibition area in the ground-floor flat, the restricted hours means that it can get crowded. The flat opens 2 to 5 pm daily (last admission 4.30 pm) March to October. Admission costs £3.50/1.

West End

In the West End you'll find the University of Glasgow, several museums and galleries, lots of restaurants and the extensive Kelvingrove Park. The area swarms with students during term time but is quieter during holidays.

Hunterian Museum & Art Gallery Part of the university, and now housed in two separate buildings on either side of University Ave, the Hunterian was opened in 1807 as Scotland's first public museum. It houses the collection of William Hunter (1718–83), famous physician, medical teacher and one-time student of the university.

The Hunterian Museum (☎ 330 4221), in the university building, comprises a disparate collection of artefacts including a notable coin collection, fossils and minerals, dinosaur eggs, Romano-British stone slabs and carvings, a display detailing the archaeological history of Scotland, and some of Captain Cook's curios from his voyages to the South Seas.

From the medieval cloisters of the museum, head to the modern concrete building housing the Hunterian Art Gallery (☎ 330 5431), nearby at 82 Hillhead St. The collection lies behind a pair of imposing cast-aluminium doors created by Edinburgh-born Paolozzi. The Scottish colourists (Peploe, JD Fergusson, Cadell) are well represented, and include McTaggart's Impressionistic Scottish landscapes and a gem by Thomas Millie Dow. There's a special collection of James McNeill Whistler's limpid prints, drawings and paintings. Some of his furniture and household goods are also here, and it's interesting to compare them to the contents of the Mackintosh House, the final section in the gallery.

Set up as a reconstruction of the architect Mackintosh's demolished Glasgow home, the style of the Mackintosh House is quite startling even today. You ascend from the gallery's gloomy ground floor into the cool, white austere drawing room. There's something otherworldly about the mannered style of the beaten silver panels, the long-backed chairs, and the surface decorations echoing Celtic manuscript illuminations. The North-ampton guest bedroom is impossibly elegant and dazzling in blue and white stripes.

The Hunterian opens 9.30 am to 5 pm Monday to Saturday; Mackintosh House closes from 12.30 to 1.30 pm. Admission is free. Bus Nos 44 and 59 pass this way from the city centre (Hope St).

Art Gallery & Museum, Kelvingrove Opened in 1902, this grand Victorian cathedral of culture (☎ 357 3929) shouldn't be missed, particularly for its excellent collection of Scottish and European art.

The impressive central hall is dominated at one end by organ pipes; recitals are an integral part of the museum programme. An authentic museum smell emanates from the natural history of Scotland section, popular with school tours. Downstairs there's a rather dowdy presentation of some interesting artefacts, including archaeological finds of prehistoric Scotland, European arms and armour, and silver.

The art gallery upstairs houses the city's art collection of 19th- and 20th-century works. Scottish painters of luminous landscapes and still lifes are comprehensively represented – Melville, McTaggart, Cadell, Crawhall; and, among the moderns, Paolozzi, Bruce McLean, Hockney and Jasper Johns. Other paintings include Rembrandt's wonderful *Man in Armour* and works by Botticelli, Monet, Van Gogh and Picasso.

Grandly set back from the road in Kelvingrove Park, west of Kelvin Way, the art gallery and museum open 10 am to 5 pm daily (from 11 am on Sunday). Admission is free. Any bus for Dumbarton Rd (such as No 6, 6A, 57, 64 or 64A) passes this way. Kelvin Hall is the nearest underground station.

Museum of Transport Across Argyle St from the Art Gallery & Museum is the surprisingly interesting and comprehensive Museum of Transport (☎ 287 2720), 1 Bunhouse Rd. Exhibits include a reproduction of a 1938 Glasgow street scene (Kelvin St), a display of cars made in Scotland, plus assorted railway locomotives, trams, bikes and model ships. One of the model ships is the unique turbot-shaped *Livadia*, at the rear of the Clyde Room. The museum opens 10 am to 5 pm daily (from 11 am on Sunday), April to September; 10 am to 5 pm Monday to Thursday and Saturday (from 11 am on Friday and Sunday), October to March. Admission is free.

Other Attractions

On Glasgow Green, the city's oldest park, **The People's Palace** (☎ 554 0223) was built in the late 19th century as a cultural centre for Glasgow's East End. It's now a splendid museum of social history, telling the story of the city from 1750 to the present. The **Winter Gardens**, in the glasshouse behind the palace, are also worth seeing. The museum and gardens open 10 am to 5 pm Monday to Saturday and from 11 am on Sunday. Admission is free.

The Barras, Glasgow's flea market on Gallowgate, shouldn't be missed. There are almost 1000 stalls and many people come to wander as much as to shop, which gives the place a holiday air. It takes place only on Saturday and Sunday. The Barras is known for copycat designer gear, so don't expect the real thing! And watch out for pickpockets.

Walking & Cycling Routes

There are numerous green spaces within the city. **Pollok Country Park** surrounds the Burrell Collection with many woodland trails. Nearer the centre, the **Kelvin Walkway** follows the River Kelvin through Kelvingrove Park, the Botanic Gardens and on to Dawsholm Park.

There are also several long-distance walking/cycling routes that originate in Glasgow and follow off-road routes for most of the distance. The TIC has a range of maps and leaflets detailing these routes, many of which start from Bell's Bridge (by the Scottish Exhibition & Conference Centre, or SECC, beside the river). For further information on routes in Glasgow contact Glasgow City Council (☎ 287 9171). For the latest information on the expanding National Cycle Network, call the Sustrans Information Hotline (☎ 0117 929 0888). Visit online at www.sustrans.co.uk.

The **Glasgow to Loch Lomond Route** traverses residential and industrial areas following a disused train line to Clydebank, the Forth and Clyde canal towpath to Bowling, and then a disused train line to Dumbarton. It reaches Loch Lomond via the towpath by the River Leven. There's an extension to this route all the way to Inverness, from Balloch via Aberfoyle, Loch Vennacher, Callander and Strathclyde to link with the Glen Ogle Trail, Killin, Pitlochry and Aviemore.

The **Glasgow to Greenock Route** runs via Paisley, the first section mainly on roads. From Johnstone to Greenock the route follows a disused train line; the final section runs from Greenock to nearby Gourock. Sculptures from the Sustrans' public arts project brighten parts of the way.

The **Glasgow to Irvine/Ardrossan and West Kilbride Cycle Way** runs via Paisley, then off-road as far as Glengarnock. From there to Kilwinning it follows minor roads, then the route is partly off-road to Ardrossan from which ferries leave for the Isle of Arran, popular with cyclists.

The long-distance footpath, the **West Highland Way**, begins in Milngavie, 8 miles north of Glasgow, and runs for 95 miles to Fort William (see the introductory Activities chapter).

Organised Tours

March to October, Scotguide Glasgow Tour (☎ 204 0444) runs daily hop-on hop-off, open-top tourist buses every 30 minutes along the main sightseeing routes; the full circuit takes about 40 minutes and fares cost £7/2.50 for a day ticket. Guide Friday's (☎ 556 2244) Discover Glasgow tour is similar and runs from April to October.

Special Events

Like Edinburgh, Glasgow has developed several festivals of its own, starting with a two-week Celtic Connections (☎ 332 6633) music festival from mid-January. The West End Festival (☎ 341 0844) of music and the arts runs for two weeks in mid-June and is Glasgow's biggest festival. The excellent International Jazz Festival (☎ 400 5000) is held in early July.

Other festivals include the Royal Scottish

National Orchestra Proms (☎ 332 6633), a two-week series of classical music concerts in mid-June, and the World Pipe Band Championships (☎ 221 5414) in mid-August, with over 100 pipe bands competing.

Places to Stay

Finding somewhere decent to stay in July and August can be difficult – for a B&B get into town reasonably early and use the TIC's booking service. Unfortunately, Glasgow's B&Bs are expensive by Scottish standards – you may have to pay up to £25. However, at weekends many expensive business hotels slash prices by up to 50%, making them great value for tourists.

Camping The *Craigendmuir Caravan Park (☎ 779 4159, Campsie View)*, 4 miles north-east of the city in Stepps, is the nearest, but it's still a 15-minute walk from Stepps station (on the Cumbernauld rail line from Queen Street station). It takes cars and tents for £8.50 (two people).

Hostels & Colleges On a hill overlooking the city, *Glasgow Youth Hostel (☎ 332 3004, 7 Park Terrace)* has 144 beds and many rooms have en-suite facilities; book ahead in summer. It opens all day and costs £13.25/ 11.75 (adults/under-18s), including continental breakfast. From Central station take bus No 44 or 59 and ask for the first stop on Woodlands Rd.

Berkeley Globetrotters (☎ 221 7880, 63 Berkeley St) has beds from £8.50 to £10.50 in dorms, £12.50 in twin rooms. Phone ahead for bookings; the reception is at No 56 opposite the hostel. Berkeley St is a western continuation of Bath St (one block south of Sauchiehall St). The hostel's just past Mitchell Library Theatre.

Near the SYHA hostel, the very popular *Glasgow Backpackers Hostel (☎ 332 5412, Maclay Hall, 17 Park Terrace)* is in one of the university's halls of residence, and only opens July to September. Beds cost £10 to £12.50.

Mid-March to mid-April and July to September the *University of Glasgow (☎ 330 5385, 3 The Square)* has self-catering,

hostel-style accommodation from £13.50/ 81 per day/week, and a range of B&B accommodation from £30 per room. From the centre head west along St Vincent St then north-west along Argyle St.

The *University of Strathclyde (☎ 553 4148, Cathedral St)* also opens its halls of residence to tourists mid-June to September. Its *Campus Village (☎ 552 0626)*, opposite Glasgow Cathedral, opens 24 hours and offers hostel accommodation on a weekly basis (£43 per week, sleeping bag required). If you don't mind staying farther out of town, the university's cheapest B&B accommodation is at *Jordanhill Campus (76 Southbrae Drive)*. Comfortable rooms are £20.50/30, and bus No 44 from Central station goes to the college gates. The university's impressive Art Deco *Baird Hall (460 Sauchiehall St)* offers some B&B accommodation in a central location year round. It has singles/doubles from £19/33.

The *YMCA International Hotel (☎ 558 6166, David Naismith Court, 33 Petershill Drive, Springburn)* is a characterless tower block north of the M8. With continental breakfast the nightly charge is £17/28 or £107.10/176.40 per week.

B&Bs & Hotels – City Centre The places along Renfrew St just above Sauchiehall St are in a great central location. However, it's a narrow, one-way street and parking is limited.

McLay Guest House (☎ 332 4796, 264 Renfrew St) is labyrinthine, but considering the position, you can't quibble at £21/27 for a single room without/with bathroom; doubles cost £38/46.

If you can't get in there try *The Victorian House (☎ 332 0129, 212 Renfrew St)* – down from the School of Art. It's a large guesthouse; prices are £23/38 (singles/doubles) with shared bathroom, £29/48 with private bathroom. There are several other similarly priced places along this street, including the *Willow Hotel (☎ 332 2332)*, No 228, where rooms start at £24/44, all en suite. *Hampton Court Hotel (☎ 332 6623)*, No 230, is slightly cheaper: singles without bathroom are £17; rooms with bathroom cost £25/40.

In a building whose design is attributed to

Robert Adam, *Babbity Bowster* (☎ 552 5055, 16 Blackfriars St) is a lively pub/restaurant (see Entertainment later) with six bedrooms on the 1st floor. Rates start at £50 per person. It's a great place to stay, but not if you like to turn in early with a cup of cocoa.

Owned by Scottish & Newcastle brewery, *Lodge Inn* (☎ 221 1000, 10 Elmbank Gardens), in the tower above Charing Cross train station, offers room-only rates of £44.95.

Glasgow Marriott (☎ 226 5577, fax 221 7676, 500 Argyle St) is a comfortable city-centre hotel where rooms including breakfast start at £61/144; rates are cheaper at the weekend.

B&Bs & Hotels – East There's a batch of reasonable-value B&Bs east of the Necropolis. *Campsie Guest House* (☎ 554 6797, 2 Onslow Drive) has decent rooms with shared bath from £18 per person and opens year round. Alternatively there's *Craigpark Guest House* (☎ 554 4160, 33 Circus Drive) with rooms from £16/28 and the circa 1850 *Seton Guest House* (☎ 556 7654, 6 Seton Terrace) for £18/31.

One of the best places is the small *Cathedral House Hotel* (☎ 552 3519, fax 552 2444, 28 Cathedral Square). Housed in a Victorian baronial-style building complete with turrets, it's close to the cathedral and easily accessible from the M8. There's a pleasant cafe bar and an Icelandic restaurant where diners cook at the table on hot rocks. The well-appointed rooms cost from £49/60, all with bathroom.

B&Bs & Hotels – West End Many places in this area are on or around Great Western Rd. There are several B&Bs on Hillhead St (south of Great Western Rd and near Byres Rd), including *Chez Nous Guest House* (☎ 334 2977), No 33, with rooms from £20 per person, and *Iona Guest House* (☎ 334 2346), No 39, which is smaller with singles/doubles from £22/36.

Amadeus Guest House (☎ 339 8257, 411 North Woodside Rd) is north of Great Western Rd and the M8 and about a mile from the centre. Its eight rooms (five with bathrooms) cost from £18. Nearby is the 16-room *Albion Hotel* (☎ 339 8620), No 405–7, with singles/doubles with bathroom from £39/48.

The highly recommended *Kirklee Hotel* (☎ 334 5555, 11 Kensington Gate) is more upmarket and you'll probably be treated as carefully as the plants in the window boxes. Rooms with shower/bath cost £48/64. Off Great Western Rd, a little nearer the city centre, is the comfortable *Terrace House Hotel* (☎ 337 3377, fax 337 3377, 14 Belhaven Terrace), which charges £39/58. There are 13 rooms, all with bathrooms. In the same area, *The Town House* (☎ 357 0862, 4 Hughenden Terrace), is similar to these last two, very well run and an excellent choice. Rooms cost from £58/68.

There are other places closer to the centre just south of Kelvingrove Park. *Alamo Guest House* (☎ 339 2395, 46 Gray St) is good value with rooms from £20/34. *Smith's Hotel* (☎ 339 6363, 963 Sauchiehall St) charges £20/36 for its budget rooms.

Probably Glasgow's best hotel is *One Devonshire Gardens* (☎ 339 2001, ⓔ one devonshire@btconnect.com), address the same, off Great Western Rd. Sumptuously decorated and occupying three classical terrace houses, the atmosphere is that of a luxurious country house. There are 27 well-appointed rooms at £140/156. There's also an excellent restaurant.

B&Bs & Hotels – South of the Clyde If you're in town for the football you might want to stay at *Holly House* (☎ 427 5609, 54 Ibrox Terrace), near Ibrox Park Stadium, Glasgow Rangers' home ground. Rooms start at £18 per person.

On and around Pollokshaws Rd, on the way to Pollok Country Park, there are several places in this quiet suburb. *Reidholm Guest House* (☎ 423 1855, 36 Regent Park Square) has B&B accommodation in seven rooms from £20 per person with shared bathroom.

On the other side of Pollokshaws Rd, south of Queen's Park, *Boswell Hotel* (☎ 632 9812, 27 Mansionhouse Rd), off Langside Ave, can be an entertaining place to stay. The Boswell is better known as a watering hole, with three bars, real ales and live jazz or R&B

on occasion. All rooms have baths/showers and cost £42.50/60 during the week, £30/50 at weekends; the price includes breakfast.

North of Pollok Country Park, in the Bellahouston area between the M8 and M77, there's *Mr Bristow's* (☎ 427 0129, 56 Dumbreck Rd), which charges from £25/34 and opens year round.

Places to Eat

Glasgow not only has an excellent range of places to eat but many are also moderately priced. The West End probably has the greatest range of restaurants – everything from Glasgow's most famous place to eat, the upmarket Ubiquitous Chip, to cheap cafes where chips really are served with everything. In the city centre, however, and along Sauchiehall St there's also no shortage of eateries. If you're on a budget, have your main meal at lunchtime – the set lunches offered by many restaurants are usually very good value at around £3 to £5.

West End Some of Glasgow's top restaurants are on Ashton Lane. *The Ubiquitous Chip* (☎ 334 5007), No 12, has earned a solid reputation for its excellent Scottish cuisine, fresh seafood and game, and for the length of its wine list. A two-course dinner with coffee and sweetmeats costs £27.95. This is an excellent place for a night out. There's a cheaper restaurant here, *Upstairs at the Chip*, where most mains cost around £7 to £15, including the popular vegetarian haggis with *neeps* (turnip) and *tatties* (potatoes). It opens noon to 11 pm Monday to Saturday and from 12.30 pm on Sunday. Open for dinner only, *Mitchells* (☎ 339 2220), No 35, is a cosy, informal bistro with excellent Scottish dishes. Mains range from £8 to £12 (you can bring your own wine).

On the western side of Byres Rd, directly across from Ashton Lane, is Ruthven Lane, with a couple of interesting eateries among the wacky shops. The affordable, candle-lit *Back Alley* (☎ 334 7165, 8 Ruthven Lane) has a wide-ranging menu from fajitas to fish and chips (£6 to £8) and includes vegetarian options. It opens daily. The intimate *Puppet Theatre* (☎ 339 8444), No 11, is a classy,

expensive place featuring Scottish cuisine but with some international influences. Dinner mains cost £9.50 to £19.50, lunch mains £4 to £7. It closes Monday.

In the Kelvingrove Park area you'll find a scattering of restaurants on and around Gibson St and Great Western Rd. *Shalimar* (☎ 339 6453, 25 Gibson St) is a large Pakistani restaurant that offers a four-course buffet dinner from 6 to 9 pm for £8.95 (Sunday to Thursday) or £9.95 (Friday and Saturday). It opens until midnight daily.

East of Byres Rd, the vegan and vegetarian *Bay Tree Cafe* (☎ 334 5898, 403 Great Western Rd) has plain decor but is excellent value. Filling mains (mostly Middle Eastern) cost less than £5, salads are generous, and there's a good range of hot drinks. It opens 9.30 am to 9 pm Monday to Saturday and 10 am to 8 pm on Sunday. It also serves takeaway. Closer to the city centre, the 24-hour *Insomnia Cafe* (☎ 332 5500, 38 Woodland Rd) has never closed since it first opened in October 1995. Soup and a roll costs £1.55 and there's a wide range of meals (mains cost £5 to £6.25), herbal teas and coffees.

Back towards the west near the Art Gallery & Museum, Kelvingrove, Dutch-run *Janssens* (☎ 334 9682, 1355 Argyle St) brings a touch of Amsterdam to Glasgow. It serves good lunches, from interesting sandwiches to a variety of full meals. Mains cost £6 to £11; Dutch beef stew is £9.60.

The main restaurant/pub area in the West End is about three-quarters of a mile west of the youth hostel, around Byres Rd. The nearest underground station is Hillhead.

The University Cafe (☎ 339 5217, 87 Byres Rd) is a university institution. It's cheap with all meals under £4 and there's superb home-made ice cream.

Off the eastern side of Byres Rd, cobble-stoned Ashton Lane is packed with places to eat. A popular student hang-out is the *Grosvenor Cafe* (☎ 339 1848), No 31, where you can get soup, filled rolls (around £2.50) and hot meals all day.

City Centre Although surrounded by grim, grey, tower-block flats, *The Buttery* (☎ 221 8188, 652 Argyle St), just west of the M8, is a top, Victorian-era restaurant. The menu is a combination of Scottish produce and Mediterranean cuisine; its three-course lunches cost £16.85. Beside it is the traditional *Belfry* (☎ 221 0630), a cheaper but popular bistro; reservations are advised. A two-/three-course pre-theatre dinner (5 to 7 pm) costs £9.50/11.95. Both places close on Sunday.

There are some good choices on Sauchiehall St. *Ristoro Ciao Italia* (☎ 332 4565), No 441, is an efficient Italian restaurant where you can get a filling three-course lunch (£6.50) or pre-theatre three-course dinner (£8.95), both with a glass of wine. It closes Sunday. A little east, *Loon Fung* (☎ 332 1240), No 417, is one of the best Cantonese places in town, with a good selection of chicken, seafood and vegetarian dishes. A three-course lunch costs £6.30, or on Thursday to Saturday nights you could try the all-you-can-eat special banquet (£13.95). It opens daily to 11.30 pm.

The *Centre for Contemporary Arts* (☎ 332 7521, 346–50 Sauchiehall St) has a well-regarded cafe, but it was closed for renovations at the time of research. At the main branch of Glasgow's best-known bakery chain, *Bradford's* (245 Sauchiehall St), there's a good upstairs tearoom where light meals are available (£3.85 to £5.25).

The *Willow Tearoom* (☎ 332 0521, 217 Sauchiehall St), above a jewellery shop, was designed as a tearoom by Mackintosh in 1904 (see under Mackintosh Buildings earlier) and its menu is mostly Scottish. At lunch and tea the queues can be long: avoid them by arriving when it opens at 9.30 am (noon on Sunday) and splash out on a superior breakfast (served all day) for £5.30. It closes at 4.30 pm daily.

Using fresh ingredients, the welcoming *Modern India* (☎ 331 1980, 51 West Regent St) combines traditional tandoori Indian dishes with more experimental, modern ones. It's good value with daily three-course lunches for £5.95 and a pre-theatre set menu for only £6.95. It opens daily to 11.30 pm.

Princes Square is the stylish shopping centre at 48 Buchanan St (over the entrance is an imposing, metal sculpture of a peacock). Here, the top floor is given over to food stalls ranging from Mexican to Chinese and a few more-upmarket restaurants. *Ming's* (☎ 248 6330) serves a variety of Asian food and offers a two-course lunch for £6.50.

Nearby, *The Jenny* (☎ 204 4988, 18–20 Royal Exchange Square), a congenial tearoom and bistro with a pavement cafe in summer, is highly recommended and specialises in Scottish cuisine. Try the savoury buns (from £4.75) or partake of afternoon tea (cake and a pot of tea) for £3.25. It opens 8 am to 6.30 pm Monday to Saturday, and to 6 pm Sunday.

The Granary (☎ 226 3770, 82 Howard St), near St Enoch Shopping Centre, is relaxed, inexpensive and serves nourishing, mainly vegetarian food but with a few non-veggie choices. Mains are £3.50 to £4.50. It opens daily.

In the Merchant City, near the City Halls, *Cafe Gandolfi* (☎ 552 6813, 64 Albion St), once part of the old cheese market, is very much a place to be seen. It's an excellent bistro and upmarket coffee shop whose menu combines Scottish and French cuisine. Black pudding with mushrooms and pancakes costs £4.50. It closes Sunday.

Mitchell's (☎ 204 4312, 157 North St), near the Mitchell Library, is an excellent bistro with an eclectic menu, and its desserts are worth leaving some room for. Lunch mains cost £5 to £13. It closes Sunday.

Entertainment

Some of Scotland's best nightlife is found in the pubs, bars and clubs of Glasgow. Most pubs and bars also do food, although many stop serving at around 8 pm. *The List* (£1.95) is an invaluable fortnightly events guide and its annual *Edinburgh & Glasgow Eating & Drinking Guide* (£3.95) is worth buying if you're staying for an extended period. Also look out for the monthly *Go!* (£1.90), a Glasgow events magazine, and the free *City Live*, a monthly listing of the city's live music.

The centre is where the pre-club and club action is focused, but the West End offers a cool nightlife alternative for the post-college crowd. West Regent St and Bath St have a plethora of small, subterranean hangouts; Merchant City is full of larger, hip joints, but there's no shortage of fun places to drink anywhere. Glasgow has its chain bars but, like New York City, London and rival Edinburgh, it also has its own style movers and shakers who keep coming up with original environments. The best thing about Glasgow is that it has maintained an unpretentious and welcoming atmosphere while keeping up with the funky beat of fashion.

Pubs & Bars – West End There are numerous pubs on or around Byres Rd. *Curlers* (☎ *334 1284*), No 256, is popular with students who come for the bargain food (the kitchen closes at 7 pm) and stay for the comedy club on Wednesday night, or the DJs Thursday to Sunday. There's also *Cul de Sac* (☎ *334 4749, 44 Ashton Lane*), which serves French food and attracts a student and arty crowd to its upstairs bar, The Attic. *The Ubiquitous Chip* (☎ *334 5007, 12 Ashton Lane*) also has an upstairs bar.

Jinty McGuinty's (☎ *339 0747, 23–29 Ashton Lane*) is a popular Irish theme pub. It has plenty of space in the summer in its beer garden and there's often an overspill into secluded Ashton Lane.

The *Halt Bar* (☎ *564 1527, 160 Woodlands Rd*) is a popular university pub that hasn't been tarted up. There's a great atmosphere and free live music most nights; Wednesday is 'open stage' night and any performer gets a free pint. It opens until midnight on Friday and Saturday (until 11 pm other nights).

Farther along Woodlands Rd, *Uisge Beatha* (☎ *564 1598*), No 232–246, keeps the same hours. It's friendly, with eclectic decor including church pews and four bar areas. The name's Gaelic for whisky (literally, water of life) of which it sells a huge range.

Bar Oz (☎ *334 0884, 499 Great Western Rd*), on the corner of Bank St, is an Australian theme pub offering 'Aussie tucker' and a good range of antipodean bottled beers, lagers and wines.

Pubs & Bars – City Centre The basement *Underworld* (☎ *221 5020*), by the Union St exit of Central station, is quirky and stylish, but not too pretentious. Security staff guard the entrance and inside there's loud music, a dance floor and a restaurant area serving Tex-Mex food.

In a converted warehouse, *Bar 10* (☎ *572 1448, 10 Mitchell Lane*), between Mitchell and Buchanan Sts, is a stylish, popular cafe bar open until midnight daily and with DJs at the weekend. It's great in the evening if you're dressed up and ready to club. During the day it excels at continental cafe culture and has a good selection of vegetarian food. *Brunswick Cellars* (☎ *572 0016, 239 Sauchiehall St*) is a popular, smoky, candle-lit, subterranean bar that's popular with a younger crowd who come to hear some of Glasgow's lesser known bands play live. It does excellent value, simple bar food (around £5) and between 3 and 8 pm serves a pint of Miller's for a mere £1.20.

Opened in 1792, the *Scotia Bar* (☎ *552 8681, 112 Stockwell St*) lays claim to being Glasgow's oldest pub and is home to the Glasgow Folk Club. There's live music most nights and poetry readings on Sunday. It's a 'free house' serving real ales and bar lunches, and opens till midnight daily. It's a bit of a walk from the centre though, and attracts a male-dominated crowd.

Babbity Bowster (*16–18 Blackfriars St*) is a restored, 18th-century Merchant City pub with a good range of real ales and excellent pub grub from £1.75 to £6.50. There's also a small hotel (see Places to Stay earlier) and restaurant noted for its Scottish cuisine. It's a good place for refreshments during the day or if you're looking for a quiet evening out.

A former warehouse in Merchant City now houses *Bargo* (☎ *553 4771, 80 Albion St*), an upmarket, 20-something hang-out decked out in metallic that gives it a 21st-century industrial feel. The food is cheap, it's really spacious and the abundance of tiny designer chairs and tables make it easy to get a seat. It fills up in the evening, especially when the atmosphere is notched up by the weekend DJs.

A popular meeting place, *The Horse Shoe Bar* (☎ 229 5711, 17 Drury Lane) dates from the late 19th century and remains largely unchanged. It may have the longest continuous bar in the UK, but its main attraction is what's served over it – real ale and excellent-value food. Upstairs in the lounge there are nightly karaoke sessions.

By Mitchell's Bistro is the traditional *Bon Accord* (☎ 248 4427, 153 North St) with real ales, including a rotating menu of guest ales, and a selection of malt whiskies. There's also great pub grub – doorsteps (large toasted sandwiches) cost £2.65.

Lots of city-centre pubs do live music, including *The Bank* (☎ 248 4455, 35 Queen St), *Blackfriars* (☎ 552 5924, 36 Bell St), on the corner of Albion St; *Drum & Monkey* (☎ 221 6636, 93 St Vincent St), on the corner of Renfield St; and *MacSorley's* (☎ 248 8581, 42 Jamaica St).

Buddha (☎ 243 2212, 142a St Vincent St) is a hip, Moroccan-style bar that provides an intimate, chilled-out atmosphere that many of Glasgow's minimalist trendy places can't. It's full of low-to-the-ground furnishings and has plenty of space. It's ideal as a pre-club venue with upbeat, cool, background music – it has a club upstairs if you don't feel like going very far!

Bar Censsa (☎ 353 1022, 140 West George St) is *huge*. At night it has a great party atmosphere and attracts people of all ages and ranges. The mezzanine level has numerous bars so you don't wait long to be served and there's a walkway over the bar below that clearly raises the sexual energy of the men beneath it. There's an occasional free buffet to showcase the interesting Mediterranean menu.

MacLachlan's Brew Bar (☎ 332 0595, 57 West Regent St) is a contemporary Scottish bar that has interesting candelabras, rich green walls and few of the national stereotypes. It attracts an unpretentious, 30+ crowd who arrive early to get seated. It's renowned for its home-brewed, organic, GM-free beer and overwhelming selection of whisky. The prices are reasonable and you can purchase bottles of the home-brew to take away.

Next to MacLachlan's is the contrasting *Nomad* (☎ 572 0007, 53 West Regent St). It has a designer North African feel, with bold decor and scene-setting watercolours on the walls. After a day on your feet it's ideal for relaxing, with comfy sofas and groovy music. The space is used well, each table being suitably private so you feel right at home. It really picks up at night when in the dim light you're less likely to notice the slightly grubby state of the upholstery.

Definitely worth a perusal if you're suited, booted and cashed up, the *Spy Bar* (☎ 221 7711, 153 Bath St) is one of the more spacious subterranean places on Bath St. Decked out in silver and red, it's more millennium-esque than cosy, but has a welcoming, varied crowd. A selection of DJs provide music on Tuesday, Friday and Saturday nights and on Sunday all drinks cost £1.50.

Bar Gaudi (☎ 572 0834, 118a Blythswood St) is a tribute to the Spanish architect in style and name. It's the size of a small cafe but is so stylish you feel privileged to spend time there. It's suitably intimate for romancing couples or a good chat with friends and so welcoming you wouldn't feel out of place there on your own. The music is whatever the bar staff feel like playing.

Clubs Glasgow's club scene rivals London's and Manchester's, and is continually changing. Check *The List* and *Go!* and ask around for the latest places. Glaswegians usually hit the clubs after the pubs have closed, so many clubs offer discounted admission and cheaper drinks if you go before 10 or 11 pm. Most also give discounts for students. Owing to an unusual law in Glasgow you may not be allowed admission to a club after 1 am; check the current regulations. Don't arrive in trainers or you'll be turned away from most places.

Off Jamaica St and under Central station, *The Arches* (☎ 221 4001, 30 Midland St) doubles as a theatre showing contemporary, avant-garde productions and, on Friday and Saturday nights, a club with superb DJs mixing techno, trance and other beats on different floors until 3 or 4 am.

The Tunnel (☎ 204 1000, 84 Mitchell St),

east of Central station, is a stylish city club that pounds out house and garage music. The gents loos are famous for their designer waterworks: one Glasgow attraction women might have to miss!

The 13th Note Club (☎ 553 1638, 50–60 King St) is a well-established restaurant, bar and music venue that's getting a name as a club. It provides an alternative hard rock night unique in Glasgow as well as a more 1970s-sounding, dance-floor classics night on Thursday.

Victoria's (☎ 332 1444, 98 Sauchiehall St) is a large, glitzy nightclub with two discos (music from the 1960s to the 1990s), a 2nd-floor piano bar with a resident cabaret, and a cabaret room featuring Scotland's foremost artistes. The club opens Wednesday to Sunday and the Sunday disco is free before 11.30 pm; cabaret and buffet costs £15.95.

Gay & Lesbian Venues Glasgow has a lively, well-established scene of gay pubs, cafes and clubs, while some straight clubs do crossover gay nights.

The traditional *Waterloo Bar* (☎ 221 7359, 306 Argyle St), on the corner of Wellington St, is Scotland's oldest gay bar that mainly caters to mature male customers. Other pubs include the friendly, unobtrusive *Court Bar* (☎ 552 3103, 69 Hutcheson St) and *Sadie Frost's* (☎ 332 8005, 8 West George St), at the north-western corner of George Square, which has a cafe, restaurant and weekend disco.

The *Polo Lounge* (☎ 553 1221, 84 Wilson St) is a splendiferous bar and nightclub popular with women, and the funky *Del Monica's* (☎ 552 4803, 68 Virginia St) attracts a sybaritic following.

The relaxed *Cafe Latte* (☎ 553 2553, 63 Virginia St) caters to a mixed crowd and opens 9 to 1 am Monday to Thursday, and to 3 am Friday to Sunday. Renovated *Bennet's Nightclub* (☎ 552 5761, 80 Glassford St) is the city's oldest gay club, popular with mostly young males.

Concerts, Theatre & Cinema For tickets contact the Ticket Centre (☎ 287 5511),

City Hall, Candleriggs, east of the centre. The office opens 10.30 am to 6.30 pm Monday to Saturday (the phone line closes at 9 pm), noon to 5 pm Sunday.

The *Theatre Royal* (☎ 332 9000, 282 Hope St) is the home of Scottish Opera, and the Scottish Ballet often performs there. The Royal Scottish National Orchestra's home is the modern *Glasgow Royal Concert Hall* (☎ 227 5511, 2 Sauchiehall St), but rock and pop musicians also perform there.

Rock and pop bands on the international circuit often play at the large *Scottish Exhibition & Conference Centre* (SECC; ☎ 248 3000, Finnieston Quay), by the river, sometimes called the 'Armadillo' because of its shape.

Some bands choose the *Barrowland* (☎ 552 4601, 244 Gallowgate), a vast dance hall in the East End that's far funkier. West of Gallowgate, the *Tron Theatre* (☎ 552 4267, 63 Trongate) stages contemporary Scottish and international performances. The *Citizens' Theatre* (☎ 429 0022, 119 Gorbals St) is one of the most highly regarded theatres in Scotland and it's well worth trying to catch a performance here.

The *Centre for Contemporary Arts* (☎ 332 7521, 346–50 Sauchiehall St) is an interesting venue for the visual and performing arts. It's temporarily housed at *MacLellan Galleries*, No 270, while the centre is being refurbished. Off Sauchiehall St, *Glasgow Film Theatre* (☎ 332 8128, 12 Rose St) screens new releases, classics and popular reruns.

The *Tramway* (☎ 287 3900, 25 Albert Drive) theatre and exhibition space has been extensively redeveloped and attracts cutting-edge theatre groups and varied artistic exhibitions.

Ceilidh If it's a wee bit of Scottish dancing you're after, go to the *Riverside Club* (☎ 248 3144, Fox St), off Clyde St down by the river, on Friday or Saturday evening for the *ceilidh* (pronounced kaylee; informal evening entertainment and dance). Doors open at 7.30 pm and the band starts at 9 pm. It's good clean fun for £6.

Getting There & Away

Glasgow is 405 miles from London, 97 miles from Carlisle, 42 miles from Edinburgh and 166 miles from Inverness.

Air Glasgow international airport (☎ 887 1111), 8 miles west of the city near Paisley, handles domestic traffic and international flights to continental Europe and North America.

Bus Long-distance buses arrive and depart from Buchanan Street bus station. Bus fares from London are competitive. Silver Choice (☎ 332 7133) offers the cheapest deal at £19/24 for a one-way/return. Departures are at 10 pm daily from Victoria coach station, London, and Buchanan Street bus station in Glasgow; the run takes 8½ hours. The service is popular so you'll need to book.

National Express also leaves from both Victoria and Buchanan Street and has up to four daily services from £20/30. Try to catch the 8.15 am bus from London so that you arrive in good time to organise accommodation. There are also three daily direct buses from Heathrow airport.

There are numerous links with other English cities. National Express services include: three or four daily buses from Birmingham (5½ hours); two from Cambridge (nine hours); seven from Carlisle (two hours); two from Newcastle (four hours); and one from York (6½ hours).

Scottish Citylink (☎ 0870 550 5050) has buses to most major towns in Scotland. There are buses to Edinburgh every 15 to 25 minutes during the day (£4.50 one way, £5/7 off-peak/peak returns, 1¼ hours). Around 18 buses run daily to Stirling (45 minutes), 12 to Inverness (from 3½ hours), four to Oban (three hours), 21 to Aberdeen (3¼ to six hours), four to Fort William (three hours) and four to Portree on Skye (6¼ to seven hours).

Stagecoach Western (☎ 01387-253496) runs hourly buses to Stranraer (£7.50, three hours) from where there are ferries to Larne in Northern Ireland.

Stagecoach Fife (☎ 01592-642394) operates services to Anstruthers (three hours, six per day), St Andrews (2¼ hours, hourly)

and Dundee (2¼ hours, hourly) via Glenrothes; the return fare to all costs £12.50.

Walkers should check out First Edinburgh (☎ 01324-613777), which runs hourly buses to Milngavie (£2.10 one way, 30 minutes), the starting point of the West Highland Way.

Train As a general rule, Central station serves southern Scotland, England and Wales, and Queen Street serves the north and east. There are buses every 10 minutes between the two (50p or free with a through train ticket). There are up to 10 direct trains daily from London's Euston station; they're not cheap, but they're much quicker (five to six hours) and more comfortable than the bus. There are also up to nine direct services from London King's Cross.

ScotRail operates the West Highland line north to Oban and Fort William (see Oban & Around in the Central Scotland chapter and Fort William in the Highlands & Northern Islands chapter) and direct links to Dundee, Aberdeen and Inverness. There are trains every 15 minutes to Edinburgh (£7.30 one way, 50 minutes).

For rail enquiries call ☎ 0845 748 4950.

Car There are numerous car rental companies; the big names have offices at the airport. Melville's (☎ 0870 160 9999), 192–4 Battlefield Rd, charges £19 per day (plus mileage if under four days, and insurance) for a small car.

Getting Around

At the St Enoch Square Travel Centre (☎ 226 4826), in the centre of St Enoch Square, Strathclyde Passenger Transport (STP) provides information on all transport in the Glasgow region. It opens 8.30 am to 5.30 pm Monday to Saturday. Here you can get a copy of the *Guide to Getting Around Glasgow* (free) which includes a map.

The Roundabout Glasgow ticket (£3.50/1.75) covers all public transport in the city for a day; it also entitles you to a £1.50 discount on city bus tours.

To/From the Airport Between Glasgow international airport and Buchanan Street bus

SOUTHERN SCOTLAND

station (£2.70, 25 minutes) there are buses every 15 minutes Monday to Friday, every 30 minutes at weekends. A taxi costs £12 to £15.

Bus Bus services are frequent. You can buy tickets when you board buses, but on most you must have exact change. For short trips in the city, fares are 70p. After midnight there are limited night buses from George Square.

Train Glasgow has an extensive suburban rail network; tickets should be bought before travel if the station is staffed, or from the conductor if it isn't. The network connects with the Underground at Buchanan Street station. The circular Underground line serves 15 stations in the city's centre and western side (north and south of the river) for 80/40p one way. A Discovery Pass (£2.50) gives unlimited travel after 9.30 am on the system for a day.

You'll see signs at some train stations for 'Low Level Trains': these are part of the suburban network not the Underground.

Car The city centre's complex one-way system, dead-end streets and restricted parking make driving an unattractive proposition, though street parking is easier in the West End. The presence of the motorway (M8) can add to your difficulties: if you miss your turning, you could find yourself several miles out of the centre before you reach the first exit.

Taxi There's no shortage of taxis and you can hail them from the street. If you order a taxi from Glasgow Wide Taxis (☎ 332 6666) by phone you can pay by credit card.

Bicycle West End Cycles (☎ 357 1344), 16 Chancellor St, just off the southern end of Byres Rd, rents out 24-speed mountain bikes for £12/50 per day/week. You'll need two IDs, or credit card or £50 deposit.

Around Glasgow

Glasgow is surrounded by a grim hinterland of post-industrial communities. Industrial archaeologists could have a field day

here and some might see a perverse beauty in the endless suburbs of grey councilhouse architecture. It's here, possibly, that the Glasgow area's gritty, black humour is engendered, partly as a way of coping with the dreary surroundings and realities of life.

PAISLEY
☎ 0141 • pop 78,000

Now really a suburb west of Glasgow, this town gave its name to the well-known fabric design of swirling stylised teardrops or pine cones called the Paisley Pattern. The famous design was, in fact, copied from shawls brought back from India.

The helpful TIC (☎ 889 0711), 9a Gilmour St, just down from the Cross, opens year round. There's no need to stay in Paisley overnight but, should you wish to, the TIC has the usual accommodation lists.

Paisley grew up around **Paisley Abbey** which was founded here in 1163 and heavily 'restored' by the Victorians. It opens 10 am to 3.30 pm Monday to Saturday. By the 19th century the town was a major producer of printed cotton and woollen cloth. At one time, Paisley was the largest producer of cotton thread in the world; the Coats family of thread-makers have enjoyed a long association with the town.

The history of the Paisley Pattern is outlined in an interesting exhibition at the **Museum & Art Galleries** (☎ 889 3151), on High St, with a large display of Paisley shawls. It opens 10 am to 5 pm Monday to Saturday. Admission is free.

Trains leave Glasgow's Central station every 15 minutes for Paisley's Gilmour Street station; there are also frequent buses (about every 10 minutes).

FIRTH OF CLYDE

The ghosts of once great shipyards still line the southern banks of the Clyde west of Glasgow, which are connected to the northern side by the impressive Erskine Bridge, 10 miles downstream. The only place of any interest along the coast west of here is Greenock, although in the otherwise unprepossessing town of **Port Glasgow** you could stop to see the replica of the *Comet*,

Greenock Rd, Europe's first commercial, seagoing paddle steamer (the original was built in 1812, this version in 1962).

GREENOCK
☎ 01475 • pop 57,325

James Watt, who perfected the steam engine, was born in this large town, 27 miles from Glasgow. The **Custom House Museum** (☎ 726331), on the quay north of Greenock Central train station, traces the history of the Customs & Excise service. Burns and Adam Smith were former employees. Worth a visit, it's open 10 am to 12.30 pm and 1.30 to 4 pm Monday to Friday. Admission is free. In the **Mclean Museum & Art Gallery** (☎ 723741), 15 Kelly St, west of the town centre, displays chart the history of steam power and Clyde shipping. The museum opens 10 am to 5 pm Monday to Saturday. Admission is free.

There are three trains an hour from Glasgow Central (£4.30 return) and hourly buses. The Glasgow to Greenock walking/cycling route follows an old train track for 10 miles (see Walking & Cycling Routes in the earlier Glasgow section).

GOUROCK
☎ 01475 • pop 11,000

Gourock is a seaside resort 3 miles west of Greenock, though urban sprawl connects the two. From near the train station CalMac (☎ 650100) ferries leave daily every 30 minutes for Dunoon (£2.65, 20 minutes) on Argyll & Bute's Cowal peninsula. Nearby, Clyde Marine (☎ 721281) runs a passenger-only service to Kilcreggan (£1.60, 12 minutes, 13 per day) and Helensburgh (£1.60, 40 minutes, four per day), Monday to Saturday.

Further west on the edge of Gourock, Western Ferries (☎ 650626) operates car and passenger ferries to Dunoon.

Lanarkshire

South and east of Glasgow are the large satellite towns of East Kilbride, Hamilton, Motherwell, Coatbridge and Airdrie. Farther upstream, the Clyde passes through central Lanarkshire, once an important coal-mining

district and still important for its fruit farms. Plums from the area around Crossford and strawberries from Kirkfieldbank are particularly tasty.

BLANTYRE
☎ 01698 • pop 18,531

This town's most famous son was David Livingstone, epitome of the Victorian missionary-explorer, who opened up central Africa to Europe. Born in the one-roomed tenement that now forms part of the David Livingstone Centre, he worked by day in the local cotton mill from the age of 10, educated himself at night, and qualified with a medical degree in 1840 before setting off for Africa.

The **David Livingstone Centre** (☎ 823 140), 165 Station Rd, tells the story of his life from a youngster in Blantyre to his later days as missionary and explorer in Africa, his battle against slave traders, and his famous meeting with Stanley. It's by the River Clyde and opens 10 am to 5 pm Monday to Saturday, and from 12.30 pm on Sunday, April to September; 10.30 am to 4 pm Monday to Saturday, and from 12.30 pm on Sunday, October to March. Admission costs £3/2.

It's a 20- to 30-minute walk over the nearby footbridge, down along the river then uphill to **Bothwell Castle** (☎ 816894; HS), Uddingston. It was much fought over during the Wars of Independence and is regarded as the finest 13th-century castle in Scotland. Built of red sandstone, the substantial ruins include a massive circular keep standing above the river. It opens standard HS hours April to September and closes Thursday afternoon, Friday and Sunday morning between October and March. Admission costs £2/75p.

Buses stop on Main St, a 15-minute walk from the David Livingstone Centre, but it's best to come by train from Glasgow Central (£2.50 off-peak return, 20 minutes) as Blantyre station is close to the centre.

LANARK & NEW LANARK
☎ 01555 • pop 9000

Below the market town of Lanark, in an attractive gorge by the River Clyde, are the excellent restored mill buildings and warehouses of New Lanark, a World Heritage Site. Once the largest cotton-spinning complex in Britain, it was better known for the pioneering social experiments of Robert Owen, who managed the mill from 1800. An enlightened capitalist, he provided his workers with housing, a cooperative store (that was the inspiration for the modern cooperative movement), the world's first nursery school for children, a school with adult education classes, a sick-pay fund for workers and a social centre he called the New Institute for the Formation of Character.

The mills operated from 1785 to 1968 and restoration began in the early 1970s.

Orientation & Information

The TIC (☎ 661661), Horsemarket, Ladyacre Rd in Lanark, opens 10 am to 5 pm Monday to Saturday year round. The bus and train stations are nearby. New Lanark is about a mile downhill (signposted from the TIC).

Things to See & Do

Probably the best way to get the feel of this impressive place is to wander round the outside of the buildings, then go to the **Visitor Centre** (☎ 661345). Here you need to purchase a ticket (£3.75/2.50) to enter the main attractions. These include **Robert Owen's home**, a restored millworkers' house, the **Annie McLeod Experience** (a high-tech, audiovisual ride where the spirit of a 10-year-old mill girl describes life here in 1820) and the 1920s-style village store. The visitor centre and attractions open 11 am to 5 pm daily. There are craft shops in the restored buildings and good-value woollens on sale. Visit on-line at www.newlanark.org.

After you've seen New Lanark you can then walk up to the **Falls of Clyde** through the nature reserve which is managed by the Scottish Wildlife Trust, who also run the **Falls of Clyde Wildlife Centre** (☎ 665262) by the river in New Lanark. It opens 10 am to 5 pm daily, April to September (to 6 pm in July and August). Admission to the centre costs £1/50p but the reserve is free. Walk for a couple of miles to the hydroelectric power station, then half a mile to the beautiful **Cora Linn** (waterfalls that inspired both Turner and Wordsworth) and beyond them, **Bonnington Linn**.

Places to Stay & Eat

At *New Lanark Youth Hostel* (☎ 666710, *Wee Row*), pleasantly positioned by the River Clyde, beds cost £11.25/10 (adults/under-18s) with continental breakfast; it closes November and December. Nearby, *New Lanark Mill Hotel* (☎ 667200) has singles/doubles from £55/65, all with bathrooms.

If you want to stay in Lanark, the TIC has a free accommodation list for the area. There are numerous B&Bs, including the friendly, clean *St Catherine's B&B* (☎ 662295, *1 Kenilworth Rd*), where you're served big breakfasts and there are extra nibbles in the room; it costs £20 per person with shared bathroom. Others worth trying are *Mrs Buchanan's* (☎ 661002, *5 Hardacres*), who charges from £17/32, and *Mrs Allen's* (☎ 662540, *9 Cleghorn Rd*), with rooms from £22/40.

The highly regarded *Crown Tavern* (☎ 662465, *17 Hope St*), off the main street, does good bar meals with mains for £4.75 to £13. In the New Lanark Visitor Centre the *Mill Pantry* serves sandwiches (from £1.35), snacks and light meals. For something more substantial try the bar or restaurant in the *New Lanark Mill Hotel*.

In Lanark, self-caterers can stock up at the large *Somerfield supermarket* behind the TIC.

Getting There & Around

Lanark is 25 miles south-east of Glasgow. Hourly trains run daily from Glasgow Central to Lanark (£6.40 return, 50 minutes).

The 20-minute walk down to the valley to New Lanark is worth it for the views, but bus Nos 35 and 335 run hourly (daily) from the train station. Returning to Lanark, the last bus leaves New Lanark at 6.57 pm.

Ayrshire

The rolling hills and rich farmland of Ayrshire are best known as the birthplace and home of poet Robbie Burns. These fertile pastures were once also famous for the

Ayrshire breed of dairy cattle, now largely replaced by Friesians. Parts of the coast comprise attractive sandy beaches and low cliffs overlooking the mountainous island of Arran.

There are famous golf courses at Troon and Turnberry. It was at Prestwick Golf Club that the major golf tournament, the British Open Championship, was initiated in 1860.

NORTH AYRSHIRE
Isle of Great Cumbrae (Argyll & Bute)
☎ 01475 • pop 1200
Although part of Argyll & Bute, Great Cumbrae is included here because it's reached from North Ayrshire. The island is in fact only 4 miles long, but it's called 'great' because it's bigger than the privately owned Little Cumbrae island just south.

Millport is the main town, where you'll find the TIC (☎ 530753), 28 Stuart St (on the waterfront), open April to September. Millport has two sandy beaches and boasts Europe's smallest cathedral, **Cumbrae Cathedral** (☎ 530353), also called the Cathedral of the Diocese of the Isles, which opens daily. The interesting **Robertson Museum & Aquarium** (☎ 530581) is on the edge of town towards the ferry pier. Admission costs £1.50/75p.

A frequent 15-minute CalMac ferry links the town of Largs on the mainland with Great Cumbrae (£3.50). Island buses meet the ferries for the 3½-mile journey to Millport.

Several places in Millport hire out bikes, including Mapes (☎ 530444), 3 Guildford St (£2.40/3.60 for two/three hours).

Ardrossan
☎ 01294 • pop 11,000
The main reason for coming here is to catch a CalMac ferry to Arran. Trains leave Glasgow Central (£4.30, one hour, five daily) to connect with ferries (see the Isle of Arran). If you need a B&B, try *Edenmore Guest House* (*☎ 462306, 47 Parkhouse Rd*) off the main A78 road. Rooms cost from £18 per person.

ISLE OF ARRAN
☎ 01770 • pop 4800
'Scotland in miniature' they call it, and parts of this island certainly are suggestive of the country as a whole. There are challenging walks in the mountainous northern part of the island, often compared to the Highlands. The landscape in the south is gentler, similar to the rest of southern Scotland.

Since Arran is easily accessible from Glasgow and the south of the country, being less than an hour's ferry ride from Ardrossan, it's very popular. Despite this popularity, the 20-mile long island seems to be big enough to absorb everyone. The bucket-and-spade brigade fills the southern resorts, cyclists take to the island's circular road and hikers tackle the hills, the highest being Goat Fell (874m). With seven golf courses, Arran is also popular with golfers.

Orientation & Information
The ferry from Ardrossan docks at Brodick, the island's main town. To the south, Lamlash is actually the capital, and, like Whiting Bay farther south, a popular seaside resort. From the village of Lochranza in the north there's a summer ferry link to Claonaig on the Kintyre peninsula.

Near Brodick pier, the TIC (☎ 302140) opens 9 am to 7.30 pm Monday to Saturday, and 10 am to 5 pm on Sunday, May to September; and 9 am to 5 pm Monday to Saturday, October to April.

Things to See & Do
The town of **Brodick** isn't particularly interesting, but it's in a pleasant location on a long curving bay. Taking the road 1½ miles north you come to the small **Heritage Museum** (☎ 302636), open 11 am to 4 pm daily, April, May, September and October; and 10 am to 5 pm Monday to Saturday, 11 am to 4 pm on Sunday, June to August. Admission costs £2.25/1.

Brodick Castle (☎ 302202; NTS), 2½ miles north of town, was the ancient seat of the dukes of Hamilton. It's an interesting stately home, with rather more of a lived-in feel than some NTS properties. The kitchens

SOUTHERN SCOTLAND

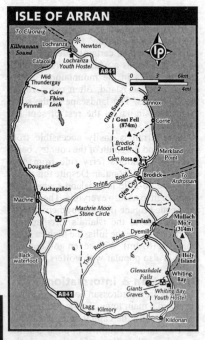

ISLE OF ARRAN

here. There's also a youth hostel, camp site and several B&Bs. On a promontory stand the ruins of the 13th-century **Lochranza Castle** (HS), said to be the inspiration for the castle in *The Black Island*, a Hergés Tintin adventure. Also in Lochranza is Isle of Arran Distillers (☎ 830264). Tours run 10 am to 6 pm daily, April to October and cost £3.50. Two miles beyond Lochranza in **Catacol**, a group of whitewashed terraced cottages known as the 'Twelve Apostles' stare out across Kilbrannan Sound.

On the western side of the island, reached by String Rd across the centre (or the coast road), are the **Machrie Moor Stone Circle**. It's an eerie place, and these are the most impressive standing-stone circles on the island. Others are nearby at **Machrie** and **Auchagallon**.

Blackwaterfoot is the largest village on the west coast. From here, you can walk down to the **King's Cave** via Drumadoon Farm – Arran is one of several islands that lays claim to a cave where Robert the Bruce, on the run after his defeat at the Battle of Glentrool, was inspired by a spider's persistence in spinning its web. Myth has it that this small act spurred him on to future success including the defeat of the English at Bannockburn. The walk could be combined with a visit to the Machrie standing stones.

The landscape in the southern part of the island is much gentler; the road drops into little wooded valleys, and it's particularly lovely around **Lagg**. At **Kildonan** there are pleasant sandy beaches and the ruin of an ivy-clad castle.

North of Whiting Bay is **Holy Island**, owned by the Samyé Ling Tibetan Centre (based in Dumfriesshire) and used as a retreat, though it does allow day visits. One ferry runs from Whiting Bay (☎ 700382, £6/4, 15 minutes, three daily, May to September), the other goes from Lamlash (☎ 0860 235086, £6/4, 30 minutes, seven daily). No dogs, alcohol or fires are allowed on the island. There's a good walk to the top of **Mulloch Mór** (314m), a two- to three-hour round trip from the ferry terminal.

Lamlash is a sailing centre.

and scullery, complete with displays of peculiar kitchen devices, are well worth a look. The grounds, now a country park with various trails among the rhododendrons, have an attractive walled garden. The house opens 11 am to 4.30 pm April to October. The park opens 9 am to sunset year round. Admission to the castle and park costs £6/1 and to the park only £2.50/1.

As you go round Brodick Bay, look out for seals, which are often seen on the rocks around **Merkland Point**. Two types live in these waters – the Atlantic grey and the common seal. They're actually quite easy to tell apart – the Atlantic grey has a Roman nose; the common seal has a face like a dog.

The road follows the coast to the small village of **Corrie**, and one of the tracks to Goat Fell starts here. After **Sannox**, where there's a sandy beach, the road cuts inland. **Lochranza** is a village in a small bay at the north of the island. In summer there's a ferry link to the Kintyre peninsula from

Walking & Cycling Routes

The walk up **Goat Fell** takes five to six hours for the round trip and, if the weather is good, there are superb views from the summit. It can, however, be very cold and windy so come well prepared. There are paths from Brodick Castle and Corrie. Another good walk on a marked path goes up to **Coire Fhionn Lochan** from Mid Thundergay; it takes about 1½ hours to reach the loch.

More moderate walks include the trail through **Glen Sannox** from the village of Sannox up the *burn* (creek), a two-hour return trip. From Whiting Bay Youth Hostel there are easy one-hour walks through the forest to the **Giant's Graves** and **Glenashdale Falls** and back.

The 50-mile circuit on the coastal road is popular with cyclists and has few serious hills – more in the south than the north. Traffic isn't bad, except at the height of the season.

Special Events

The week-long Arran Folk Festival (☎ 302 623) takes place in early June.

Places to Stay

It's a good idea to book, especially at weekends, even outside the busy summer months.

Camping Without the permission of the land owner, camping isn't allowed, but there are several camp sites (open April to October). When choosing a site note that midges (similar to mosquitoes) can be a major nuisance in sheltered spots.

Two miles north-west of Brodick, you can camp at *Glen Rosa Farm* (☎ 302380) from £4 for a tent and two people. In Kildonan, *Breadalbane Caravan & Camping Park* (☎ 820210) charges campers £3.50 each; it's located by the shore and the breeze here keeps the midges away. *Lochranza Golf Caravan & Camping Site* (☎ 830273, Lochranza) charges from £8 for a tent and two people.

Hostels In the north of the island, the excellent, self-catering *Lochranza Youth Hostel* (☎ 830631) opens February to October and charges £9.25/8 (adults/under-18s). In

the south there's *Whiting Bay Youth Hostel* (☎ 700339) which charges £9.25/7.25. It opens April to October.

B&Bs & Hotels – Brodick You get a better feel for the island if you get out into the smaller villages, although Brodick does have numerous places to stay.

The *Douglas Hotel* (☎ 302155), near the pier, charges from £25 to £30 per person and is convenient if you're catching an early ferry. Some rooms have bathrooms. *Tigh-na-Mara* (☎ 302538, Shore Rd), on the front, and *Belvedere* (☎ 302397, Alma Rd) both charge from £18 per person. Half a mile from the centre of Brodick *Rosaburn Lodge* (☎ 302383) is a comfortable B&B surrounded by gardens and woodland, with three rooms for £24 to £28, all with bathrooms.

B&Bs & Hotels – Glen Coy The island's best hotel, the *Kilmichael Country House Hotel* (☎ 302219, Glen Coy), 2½ miles west of Brodick, is also its oldest building. It's a small, elegant hotel with B&B from £45 to £70 per person. There's also an excellent restaurant here.

B&Bs & Hotels – Corrie There are good views across to Bute and Cumbrae from the seafront *Blackrock Guest House* (☎ 810282). It opens March to October and offers B&B from £17 per person in rooms with shared bathrooms. *Corrie Hotel* (☎ 810273), open April to October, has rooms from £21/42 with shared bathroom, £26/52 with bathroom.

B&Bs & Hotels – Lochranza This village is a great place to stay. In the centre beside the water, *Castlekirk* (☎ 830202) is a converted 19th-century church retaining many original features with two rooms for £18 per person. Tudor-style *Kincardine Lodge Guest House* (☎ 830267) charges £20 to £22 per person and some rooms have baths. You'll be well looked after in very comfortable surroundings at *Apple Lodge* (☎ 830229); its three double rooms cost £29 per person.

B&Bs & Hotels – Whiting Bay Like Brodick, Whiting Bay has plenty of options. The central *Norwood* (☎ 700536) is a B&B with two comfortable double rooms (shared bathroom) from £17 per person; it opens March to October. Open the same months, *The Royal* (☎ 700286) is a guesthouse with six rooms, each with bath/shower, from £23 per person. The larger, Edwardian *Burlington Hotel* (☎ 700255) faces the beach, has singles/doubles from £25/48 and opens Easter to October.

Hotels – Kildonan This is a peaceful spot down a steep road. The friendly *Breadalbane Hotel* (☎ 820284) has holiday flats with bedrooms, bathroom and kitchen, sleeping four to six people. It charges from £80 to £200 per week depending on the season; outside the high season it may let a flat for less per week, depending on demand. It also has singles/doubles with bathroom from £20 per person.

Places to Eat

The award-winning, bistro-style *Creelers Seafood Restaurant* (☎ 302810), 1½ miles north of Brodick by the Arran Aromatics shopping centre, opens Tuesday to Sunday mid-March to October (closed in August). The produce is fresh with main dishes from £6 to £17. There's also a shop here selling seafood and smoked foods. You can stock up on local cheeses from the cheese shop opposite.

Back in Brodick, *Stalkers Eating House* (☎ 302579) along the waterfront does good-value meals. Its mostly seafood mains cost £5.50, and there are solid British puddings such as fruit crumble and sherry trifle. *Duncan's Bar* at the Kingsley Hotel, on Shore Rd, does good pub grub (£4.20 to £6.65) and serves real ales. *Ormidale Hotel* (☎ 302293, Glen Cloy) is similar with dinner mains for £6 to £7, and occasional live music.

Two miles from Lochranza, the bar at *Catacol Bay Hotel* (☎ 830231) does excellent bar food, with mains from £5 to £7. It opens 11 am until late daily. In summer there are often *ceilidhs* and live music.

In Kildonan, the *Breadalbane Hotel* (☎ 820284) does great home-made bar food such as Yorkshire pudding and sausage casserole; main courses cost from £3.25 to £9. The licensed *Carraig Mhor* (☎ 600453, Shore Rd), Lamlash, is recommended for its excellent seafood, though it does other dishes as well. Vegetarians need to give 24-hours' notice. A two-course meal costs £18. It only opens 7 to 9 pm Thursday, Friday and Saturday so you'll need to book.

Shopping

Arran is known for its local cheeses; Arran mustard is also worth buying. Watch out for the woollens though. Real Aran (one 'r') sweaters come from the Irish island of Aran, not this one.

Getting There & Away

CalMac (☎ 302140) runs a daily car ferry between Ardrossan and Brodick (£4.25, 55 minutes, four to six daily); it operates a service between Claonaig and Lochranza, April to September (£3.90, 30 minutes, 10 daily).

If you're going to visit several islands it's worth planning your route in advance. CalMac has a wide range of tickets including Island Hopscotch fares that work out cheaper than buying several single tickets.

Getting Around

The island's efficient bus services are operated by Stagecoach Western (☎ 302000) and Royal Mail (☎ 01246-546329). There are about four to six buses a day from Brodick Pier to Lochranza (£1.70, 40 minutes). An Arran Rural Daycard costs £3 (buy it on the bus). For a taxi, phone ☎ 302274 in Brodick or ☎ 600725 in Lamlash.

In Brodick several places rent bikes, including Mini Golf Cycle Hire (☎ 302272), Shore Rd, with bikes from £9/30 per day/week.

SOUTH AYRSHIRE
Ayr
☎ 01292 • pop 49,500

Ayr's long sandy beach has made it a popular family seaside resort since Victorian times. It's also known for its racecourse – the top course in Scotland, with more racing

One of many monuments crowning Calton Hill, Edinburgh

A bare-chested bagpipe recital

Fit for commoners too: the Royal Mile is one of Edinburgh's most majestic streets.

Princes St at dusk, Edinburgh

Wake up and smell the coffee in Edinburgh's Old Town.

Water wheel immobilised by nature, Angus

Feast on fresh lobster and shellfish in Crail.

If lost, find an Isle of Mull mile marker.

Building castles in the air, South Ayrshire

days than any other in Britain. Ayr, with its many Georgian and Victorian buildings, is the largest town on this coast and makes a convenient base for a tour of Burns territory.

Information The TIC (☎ 288688) is opposite the train station on Burns Statue Square, but is scheduled to move. It opens 9.15 am to 5 pm Monday to Saturday, October to May; 9.15 am to 6 pm Monday to Saturday, and 10 am to 5 pm on Sunday, June to August.

The CyberCentre in the Carnegie Library (☎ 618492), 12 Main St, offers Internet access for £3 per hour. The library opens 10 am to 7.30 pm Tuesday, Thursday and Friday; 10 am to 5 pm Wednesday and Saturday. To get there go down High St, turn right and cross over the bridge; the library is on the corner.

Things to See Apart from the **beach**, attractions in Ayr are mainly Burns-related. The bard was baptised in the **Auld Kirk** (old church) off High St. Several of his poems are set in Ayr. In his *Twa Brigs*, Ayr's old and new bridges argue with one another. The **Auld Brig**, near the bottom of High St, was built in 1491 and spans the river just

---

Robert Burns

Best remembered for penning the words of *Auld Lang Syne*, Robert Burns is Scotland's most famous poet, and a popular hero whose birthday (25 January) is celebrated as Burns Night by Scots around the world.

He was born in 1759 in Alloway. Although his mother was illiterate and his parents poor farmers, they sent him to the local school where he soon showed an aptitude for literature and a fondness for the folk song. He began to write his own songs and satires, some of which he distributed privately. When the problems of his arduous farming life were compounded by the threat of prosecution from the father of Jean Armour, with whom he'd had an affair, he decided to emigrate to Jamaica. He gave up his share of the family farm and published his poems to raise money for the journey.

The poems were so well reviewed in Edinburgh that Burns decided to remain in Scotland and devote himself to writing. He went to Edinburgh in 1787 to publish a second edition, but the financial rewards were not enough to live on and he had to take a job as a customs officer in Dumfriesshire. He contributed many songs to collections published by Johnson & Thomson in Edinburgh, and a third edition of his poems was published in 1793. Burns died in Dumfries in 1796, aged 37, after a heart attack.

While some dispute Burns' claim to true literary genius, he was certainly an accomplished poet and songwriter, and has been compared to Chaucer for his verse tale *Tam o'Shanter*. Burns wrote in Lallans, the Scottish Lowland dialect of English that isn't very accessible to the foreigner. Perhaps this is part of his appeal. He was also very much a man of the people, satirising the upper classes and the Church for their hypocrisy.

Many of the local landmarks mentioned in *Tam o'Shanter* can still be visited in Alloway. Farmer Tam, riding home after a hard night's drinking in a pub in Ayr, sees witches dancing in Alloway churchyard. He calls out to the one pretty witch, but is pursued by them all and has to reach the other side of the River Doon to be safe. He just manages to cross the Brig o'Doon, but his mare loses her tail to the witches.

The Burns connection in southern Scotland is milked for all it's worth and TICs have a Burns Heritage Trail leaflet leading you to every place that can claim some link with the bard.

If you're a Burns fan have a look at www.robertburns.org.

National poet Robert Burns, who wrote his verse in Scottish dialect

down from the church. In Burns' poem *Tam o'Shanter*, Tam spends a boozy evening in the pub at 230 High St that now bears his name.

Cycling Routes With few steep hills, the area is well suited to cyclists. See Walking & Cycling Routes in the earlier Glasgow section for the cycle way from that city. The TIC has a useful leaflet.

From Ayr, you could cycle to Alloway and spend a couple of hours seeing the Burns sights before continuing via Maybole to Culzean. You could either camp at Culzean after seeing the castle and park, or cycle back along the coastal road to Ayr, a round trip of about 22 miles.

In Ayr, AMG Cycles (☎ 287580), 55 Dalblair Rd, rents bikes for £10 per day (24 hours).

Places to Stay Five miles south of Ayr on the A719, *Heads of Ayr Caravan Park* (☎ 442269) charges from £7.50 for a small tent and two people. *Ayr Youth Hostel* (☎ 262322, 5 Craigweil Rd) is in a magnificent turreted mansion by the beach and is less than a mile south of the train and bus stations. It opens February to October; the nightly charge is £9.25/8 (adults/under-18s).

There are numerous B&Bs and hotels. Georgian *Eglinton Guest House* (☎ 264623, 23 Eglinton Terrace) is a short walk west of the bus station towards the sea and has singles/doubles for £18/34.

A five- to 10-minute walk south from the station past Wellington Square brings you to a crescent of upmarket Victorian B&Bs and small hotels. On Park Circus, *Belmont Guest House* (☎ 265588), at No 15, has en-suite rooms for £20/36. *Lochinver Hotel* (☎ 265 086), at No 32, is a homely sort of place and costs from £16 per person. *Richmond Hotel* (☎ 265153), at No 38, is a small, friendly and efficient place with rooms from £25/40.

Park Circus continues into Bellevue Crescent where there are more places to stay.

Places to Eat The best place is *Fouters Bistro Restaurant* (☎ 261391, 2a Academy St)*, on the corner of New Bridge St, opposite the town hall. It specialises in Ayrshire produce and local seafood cooked Mediterranean style. Mains cost £11 to £14, and there's a cheaper bistro menu. It opens Tuesday to Saturday for lunch and dinner, Sunday for dinner only.

The Hunny Pot (☎ 263239, 37 Beresford Terrace), with its Winnie the Pooh theme, is a short walk from the TIC. It's a pleasant place serving good teas and light meals (£4.50 to £5), 9 am to 10 pm Monday to Saturday and 10.30 am to 9 pm on Sunday. Nearer the TIC, the *Ayrshire & Galloway Hotel* (☎ 262626, 1 Killoch Place), facing Burns Statue Square, does good-value lunchtime pub meals for £4.95.

Getting There & Away There are at least two trains an hour from Glasgow Central to Ayr (£4.90, 50 minutes) and some trains continue south to Stranraer (£10.20, 1½ hours from Ayr). The main bus operator is Stagecoach Western (☎ 613500) – its hourly X77 service from Glasgow to Girvan/Stranraer via Ayr costs £3.20.

AROUND AYR
Alloway

Three miles south of Ayr, Alloway is where Burns was born on 25 January 1759. Even if you're not a fan it's still worth a visit, since the Burns-related exhibitions give a good impression of life in Ayrshire in the late 18th century. The sights are within easy walking distance of each other and come under the umbrella title of **Burns National Heritage Park**.

Burns Cottage & Museum (☎ 01292-441215) stands by the main road from Ayr. Born in the little box bed in this cramped thatched cottage, the poet spent the first seven years of his life here. There's a good museum of Burnsiana by the cottage, exhibiting everything from his writing compendium to a piece of wood from his coffin. Light meals are available in the tearoom. The museum opens 9 am to 6 pm daily, April to October; 10 am to 4 pm daily, November to March. Admission costs £2.80/1.40; the ticket also permits entry to the Burns Monument & Gardens.

From here you can visit the ruins of **Alloway Auld Kirk**, the setting for the witches' dance in *Tam o'Shanter*. Burns' father, William Burnes (his son dropped the 'e' from his name) is buried in the *kirkyard* (churchyard).

The nearby **Tam o'Shanter Experience** (☎ 01292-443700) has audiovisual displays (£2.80/1.40) and a book/gift shop. It opens 9 am to 6 pm daily, April to October (9 am to 5 pm the rest of the year). The restaurant does excellent home-made soups. The **Burns Monument & Gardens** (opening hours as for the Burns Cottage) are nearby. The monument was built in 1823 and affords a view of the 13th-century **Brig o'Doon** (now a hotel). There are also statues of Burns' drinking cronies in the gardens.

Brig O'Doon House Hotel (☎ 01292-442466) has a brasserie serving three-course dinners for around £15. Conveniently located, its rooms cost £75/100. *Northpark House Hotel* (☎ 01292-442336), off the road to Ayr, is a small, luxurious hotel with a fine restaurant; rooms cost from £60/80.

Stagecoach Western (☎ 613500) bus Nos 57 and A1 each run up to nine times daily Monday to Saturday between Alloway and Ayr; on Sunday bus No A10 runs four times (£1.70 return). Otherwise, rent a bike in Ayr and cycle here.

Culzean Castle & Country Park

Well worth seeing, Culzean (pronounced cul-lane), 12 miles south of Ayr, is one of the most impressive of Scotland's great stately homes. Perched dramatically on the edge of the cliffs, this 18th-century mansion was designed by Robert Adam to replace the castle built here in the 16th century.

The original castle belonged to the Kennedy clan, who, after a feud in the 16th century, divided into the Kennedys of Culzean and Cassillis, and the Kennedys of Bargany. Because of the American connection (Eisenhower was a frequent visitor) most people wrongly assume that the Culzean Kennedys are closely related to JFK. Culzean Castle was given to the NTS in 1945.

Robert Adam was the most influential architect of his time, renowned for his meticulous attention to detail and the elegant classical embellishments with which he decorated his ceilings and fireplaces. The beautiful oval staircase here is regarded as one of his finest achievements.

On the 1st floor, the opulence of the circular saloon contrasts splendidly with the views of the wild sea below. The other rooms on this floor are also interesting and Lord Cassillis' bedroom is said to be haunted by a lady in green, mourning for a lost baby. Even the bathrooms are palatial, the dressing room beside the state bedroom being equipped with a state-of-the-art shower that directs jets of water from almost every angle.

Set in a 563-acre park combining woodland, coast and gardens, there's much more to see than just the castle. An interesting exhibition in the Gas House explains how gas was produced for the castle. There's also a visitors centre, ice house, swan pond and aviary.

Culzean Castle (☎ 01655-760269) is the NTS's most visited property and gets crowded at summer weekends. It opens 10.30 am to 5.30 pm April to October. The park opens 9.30 am to sunset year round. Admission to the park and castle costs £7/5, or £3.50/2.50 if you want to visit the park only.

It's possible to stay in the castle from April to October, but gracious living doesn't come cheap. A night for two in the exclusive Eisenhower apartment costs from £140 to £265. If you're not in that league there's a *Camping & Caravanning Club* (☎ 01655-760627) in the park. Tent sites cost £4.60/8.60 per person for members/nonmembers.

Maybole is the nearest train station, but since it's 4 miles away it's best to come by bus No 58 or 60 from Ayr (£4.05 return, 30 minutes, 11 per day, Monday to Saturday). Buses pass the park gates, but it's still a 20-minute walk through the grounds from the gates to the castle.

Turnberry

To play the world-famous golf course here visitors usually stay at the luxurious *Turnberry Hotel* (☎ 01655-331000, Ⓔ *Turnberry @westin.com*), where they're able to land their private aircraft or helicopter. Singles/doubles cost from £155/270. If you can afford that, dinner mains in the award-winning restaurant are a snip at £24.50 to £35. Lesser mortals can opt for the smaller but gracious *Malin Court Hotel* (☎ 01655-331457, e info@malincourt.co.uk), whose well-maintained rooms cost a mere £65/104.

Ailsa Craig

From much of the southern Ayrshire coastline, you can see curiously shaped Ailsa Craig, looking rather like a giant bread roll floating on the sea. Granite rock quarried from here is used for *curling* (a game played on ice) stones. Ailsa Craig is also a bird sanctuary. From **Girvan** on the mainland the MFV *Glorious* (☎ 01465-713219) will take you onto this 340m-high rocky outcrop to see the gannets that crowd it.

Dumfries & Galloway

The tourist board bills this region as Scotland's surprising south-west, but it's only surprising if you expect beautiful mountain and coastal scenery to be confined to the Highlands. The local architecture may disappoint, but otherwise it has many of the features for which Scotland is renowned – mountains (which reach over 600m), rolling hills, lochs and a rugged coastline. This is, though, one of the forgotten corners of Britain, and beyond the main transport routes to Stranraer, traffic and people are sparse.

Dumfries & Galloway lies south of the Southern Uplands. Warmed by the Gulf Stream, this is the mildest corner of Scotland, a phenomenon that has allowed the development of some famous gardens. This is excellent cycling and walking country, and it's crossed by the coast-to-coast Southern Upland Way (see Walking and Cycling Routes at the start of the chapter).

Notable historic and prehistoric attractions are linked by the Solway Coast Heritage Trail (information is available from TICs). Caerlaverock Castle, Threave Castle and Whithorn Cathedral & Priory are just three of many. Kirkcudbright is a beautiful town, and makes a good base. Stranraer in the far west is the ferry port to Larne in Northern Ireland, the shortest link between Britain and Ireland.

For information check out the tourist board Web site at www.galloway.co.uk.

GETTING THERE & AROUND

The regional council has a travel information line (☎ 0845 709 0510) open 9 am to 5 pm Monday to Friday.

Bus

National Express has coaches from London, Birmingham (via Manchester and Carlisle), and Glasgow/Edinburgh to Stranraer. These service the main towns and villages along the A75 (including Dumfries, Kirkcudbright and Newton Stewart). Stagecoach Western (☎ 01387-253496) and MacEwan's (☎ 01387-710357) provide a variety of local bus services. Sometimes bus companies' services along the same route charge different prices, so ring the travel information line for more info.

The Day Discoverer (£5/2) is a useful day ticket that can be used on all buses in the region and on Stagecoach Cumberland in Cumbria.

Train

Two lines from Carlisle to Glasgow cross the region, via Dumfries and Moffat respectively. The line from Glasgow to Stranraer runs via Ayr. Call ☎ 0845 748 4950 for details.

DUMFRIES

☎ 01387 • pop 31,000

Dumfries is a large town with a strategic position that placed it smack in the path of vengeful English armies. As a result, although it has existed since Roman times, the oldest standing building dates from the 17th century.

It has escaped modern mass tourism, although it was the home of Burns from 1791 to his death in 1796, and there are several important Burns-related museums. It also makes a good base from which to explore the

Solway coast. The centre is rather uninspiring, but there are some pleasant 19th-century suburbs built in the area's characteristic red sandstone.

Orientation & Information

The main bus station is beside the River Nith at one end of the car park; the train station is a 10-minute walk north-east.

The TIC (☎ 253862, ℯ info@dgtb.oss ian.net), 64 Whitesands, opposite the car park by the river, opens 10 am (between 10 am and noon on Sunday) until between 4 and 5.30 pm daily, depending on the month; phone for details. Early closing day is Thursday. You can book National Express/ Citylink buses here.

Burnsiana

The **Robert Burns Centre** (☎ 264808), Mill Rd, is an award-winning museum in an old mill on the banks of the River Nith across from the TIC. It tells the story of Burns and Dumfries in the 1790s. There's also a cafe/gallery. It opens 10 am to 8 pm Monday to Saturday, and 2 to 5 pm on Sunday, April to September; 10 am to 1 pm and 2 to 5 pm Tuesday to Saturday, October to March. Admission is free but the audio-visual presentation costs £1.50/75p.

On Burns St, the red sandstone **Burns House** (☎ 255297) is a place of pilgrimage for Burns' enthusiasts. Here the poet spent the last years of his life and there are some interesting relics and original letters and manuscripts. It opens 10 am to 5 pm Monday to Saturday, and 2 to 5 pm on Sunday, April to September; 10 am to 1 pm and 2 to 5 pm Tuesday to Saturday, October to March. Admission is free. Nearby, Burns' **mausoleum** is in the graveyard at St Michael's Kirk. Back in the centre at the top of High St is a **statue** of the bard.

Places to Stay

There are some good-value B&Bs in a quiet, pleasant suburb near the train station. *Cairndoon (☎ 256991, 14 Newall Terrace)* has spacious, comfortable rooms with TVs and a warm welcome for £20 per person. On Lovers Walk, you could try the *Fulwood*

Hotel (☎ 252262), No 30, with singles/doubles for £20/34, or *Torbay Lodge Guest House (☎ 253922)*, where rooms cost from £18/34.

You'll find several accommodation options on Lauriknowe, including *Edenbank Hotel (☎ 252759)*, No 17, a short walk from the centre on the other side of the river. It's a small, family-run, renovated hotel with a bar, restaurant and a range of rooms including two singles, all with bathrooms, for £39.75/55.

Places to Eat

Open daily, *Olivers*, a bakery on the High St mall, has a range of good-value takeaway baked goods, sandwiches and rolls, and a self-serve coffee shop at the back. The two-course set lunch menu at *Pierre (☎ 265888, 113 Queensbury Rd)*, above the Tam o'Shanter pub, is excellent value at £4.50. In the evening mains cost £5.90 to £12. It has a good wine list and opens Monday to Saturday.

Open daily, the popular Italian restaurant *Bruno's (☎ 255757, 3 Balmoral Rd)* is one of the best places to eat. Lasagne della casa costs £5.50. Next door is the highly recommended *Balmoral Fish & Chicken Bar*, run by the same family, where you can buy takeaways.

The *Globe Inn (56 High St)*, a traditional pub said to be Burns' favourite watering hole, has good bar meals and a restaurant.

Entertainment

The *Hole in the Wa' Inn (High St)*, also frequented by Burns, has music most nights, including the occasional traditional Scottish music session.

Getting There & Away

Dumfries is 330 miles from London, 75 miles from Edinburgh, Glasgow and Stranraer and 35 miles from Carlisle.

Bus National Express bus No 920 runs three times daily between London and Belfast, via Birmingham, Manchester, Carlisle, Dumfries, the towns along the A75, and Stranraer. Local buses run regularly to

Kirkcudbright and towns along the A75 to Stranraer (£4.50, three hours). Stagecoach Western (☎ 253496) has two buses daily (No 100) to/from Edinburgh.

Train Dumfries is on a line that leaves the main west-coast line at Gretna Green, and from Dumfries runs north-westwards along Nithsdale to join the Glasgow-Stranraer line at Kilmarnock. You can join the service at Carlisle or Glasgow. Monday to Saturday there are seven trains daily (five on Sunday) between Carlisle and Dumfries (£6.20, 35 minutes), and six daily between Dumfries and Glasgow (£9.20, 1½ hours). For enquiries call ☎ 0845 748 4950.

Getting Around
Grierson & Graham (☎ 259483), 10 Academy St, and Nithsdale Cycle Centre (☎ 254 870), 46 Brooms Rd, hire bikes from £7 per three hours.

AROUND DUMFRIES
Caerlaverock Castle
The ruins of Caerlaverock Castle (☎ 01387-770244; HS), on a beautiful stretch of the Solway coast, are among the loveliest in Britain. Surrounded by a moat, lawns and stands of trees, the unusual pink-hued, triangular, stone castle looks impregnable – in fact it fell several times. The present castle dates from the late 13th century. Inside, there's an extraordinary Scottish Renaissance facade to apartments that were built in 1634.

It opens 9.30 am to 6.30 pm daily, April to September; 9.30 am to 4.30 pm Monday to Saturday, and 2 to 4.30 pm on Sunday, October to March. Admission costs £2.50/1.90. Monday to Saturday, the castle can be reached from Dumfries by Stagecoach Western's (☎ 01387-253496) bus No 371.

Caerlaverock Wildfowl & Wetlands Trust Centre
You can combine a visit to the castle with one to the centre (☎ 01387-770539), which is about a mile east past the village of Shearington. Here you can see whooper geese and many other birds from hides and observatories. The centre opens 10 am to 5 pm daily. Admission costs £3.50/2.25.

The centre is connected to the **Caerlaverock National Nature Reserve**. It consists of nearly 8000 acres of saltmarsh (merse) and mudflats which stretch along the coast from here westwards past the castle. It's famous for the Svalbard barnacle geese that winter here and is also home to the most northerly natterjack toads in Britain. About a mile west of Caerlaverock Castle you can join a trail that leads through woods beside the reserve.

NEW GALLOWAY & AROUND
☎ 01644 ● pop 290
New Galloway is a quaint little hill town surrounded by beautiful countryside. There's nothing much to bring you here, except to get away from it all. Tourist information is available from The Smithy teashop at the bottom of High St.

South-west is **Galloway Forest Park**, with great whale-backed, heather-covered mountains (although clear-felling on the lower slopes by the Forestry Commission mars the aesthetic appeal a little). The countryside to the south-east and north is particularly beautiful and unusual. You feel as if you're on a high plateau, surrounded by tumbling short-pitched hills. There's a sense of space unusual in Britain.

On High St, the family-run *Leamington Hotel* (☎ 420327) has rooms with bathrooms from £18.50 to £20 per person.

MacEwan's (☎ 01387-710357) bus No 521 runs twice a week (Wednesday and Saturday) to Dumfries; bus No 520 runs seven times daily Monday to Saturday (once on Sunday) to Castle Douglas.

CASTLE DOUGLAS & AROUND
☎ 01556 ● pop 3500
Castle Douglas is an open, attractive little town that was laid out along King St, the main street, in the 18th century by Sir William Douglas, who had made a fortune in the Americas. Beside the town is the small but beautiful **Carlingwark Loch**. The TIC (☎ 502611), in a small park at the top of King St, opens 10 am to 5 pm Monday to Saturday, April to mid-September (plus

11 am to 4.30 pm Sunday mid-June to mid-September).

Threave Garden & Estate
About 1 mile west of town off the A75, Threave Garden & Estate (☎ 502575; NTS) is particularly beautiful in springtime. The garden opens daily year round but the visitor centre only opens 9.30 am to 5.30 pm daily, April to October. Admission costs £3/1.50.

Threave Castle
A farther 2 miles west off the A75 is Threave Castle (☎ 0411-223101; HS), an impressively grim tower on a small island in the middle of the lovely River Dee. It's only a shell, but it's a romantic ruin nonetheless. Built in the late 14th century it became a principal stronghold for the Douglases.

It's a 10-minute walk from the car park to pick up the ferry (a small open boat) across to the island. The castle opens 9.30 am to 6.30 pm daily, April to September. Admission costs £2/75p, including the ferry ride.

Places to Stay
Lochside Caravan & Camping Site (☎ 502949), an attractive spot alongside Carlingwark Loch, has sites for cars and tents from £7.75. On the shore of Loch Ken, north of Parton village (where James Clark Maxwell, the physicist, is buried), *Galloway Sailing Centre* (☎ 420625) offers outdoor activities and backpacker accommodation year round; dorm beds cost £9.50. Bus No 520 from Castle Douglas stops in Parton.

Craigvar House (☎ 503515, 60 St Andrew St) is a comfortable B&B with rooms from £20 per person. *Douglas Arms Hotel* (☎ 502231, King St) has good food and a range of comfortable rooms with bathrooms from £33.75 per person.

Getting There & Around
MacEwan's (☎ 01387-710357) bus No 501 between Dumfries and Kirkcudbright stops in Castle Douglas nine times daily Monday to Friday, and five times on Sunday. Ace Cycles (☎ 504542), 11 Church St, hires mountain bikes for £10 per 24 hours.

KIRKCUDBRIGHT
☎ 01557 • pop 3500
Situated on the River Dee, Kirkcudbright (pronounced kirkoobree), with its dignified streets of 17th- and 18th-century merchants' houses and its interesting harbour, is the ideal base to explore the beautiful south coast. The lovely surrounding countryside has distinctive hummocky hills covered in gorse.

Orientation & Information
Everything is within easy walking distance. The TIC (☎ 330494), Harbour Square, opens 10.30 am to 4.30 pm daily, Easter to October. Early closing day is Thursday. There are some useful brochures outlining walks and driving tours in the surrounding district.

Things to See & Do
Kirkcudbright's modest sights have charm and provide an excuse for exploring the town. **McLellan's Castle**, near the harbour and TIC, is a large ruin, built in 1577. Nearby, the 17th-century Broughton House contains **Hornel Art Gallery**, a reminder of the town's 19th-century artist's colony, featuring paintings by Australian-born EA Hornel and a beautiful Japanese garden. **Tolbooth Arts Centre** caters to today's local artists, and the **Stewartry Museum** is particularly interesting; admission to each costs £1.50/75p.

Places to Stay & Eat
Silvercraigs Caravan & Camping Site (☎ 330123) overlooks the town and has great views. It has sites from £7.75.

Parkview (☎ 330056, 22 Millburn St), off St Cuthbert St, is a small, blue-painted B&B charging £17/32 per single/double. *Gladstone House* (☎ 331734, 48 High St) offers upmarket B&B to non-smokers from £39/60 in an attractively decorated Georgian house.

The large, well-run *Royal Hotel* (☎ 331 213, St Cuthbert St) offers B&B in rooms with bathrooms for £22.50/38. It has good-value bar meals, including an all-you-can-eat lunchtime buffet for £4.95, noon to 2.30 pm Monday to Saturday. The *Selkirk Arms Hotel* (☎ 330402, High St) has well-equipped rooms, all with bathrooms, for

£60/90. It also has good bar meals, plus a more expensive dining room.

The best place to eat is the *Auld Alliance* (☎ 330569, 5 Castle St), which opens nightly for dinner, plus lunch on Sunday, Easter to October. Its name refers to the political alliance between Scotland and France, but here alludes to its combination of local fresh Scots produce (such as small scallops known as queenies) and French cooking and wine. Main dishes range from £6.50 to £15; booking is advised.

Getting There & Away

Kirkcudbright is 25 miles from Dumfries and 50 miles from Stranraer. MacEwan's (☎ 01387-710357) bus Nos 501 and 503 run frequently to Dumfries (£2.50, 70 minutes), and bus Nos 500 and X75 run twice daily to Dumfries and Stranraer (£3.50, 1½ hours).

GATEHOUSE OF FLEET
☎ 01557 • pop 900

Gatehouse of Fleet is an attractive little town stretched along one main sloping street, in the middle of which is an unusual-looking, castellated clocktower. The town lies on the banks of the Water of Fleet and is surrounded by partly wooded hills – completely off the beaten track. The TIC (☎ 814212), High St, opens 10 am to 5 pm Monday to Saturday, April to mid-September (plus 11 am to 4.30 pm on Sunday, mid-June to mid-September).

A mile south-west on the A75, **Cardoness Castle** (☎ 814427; HS) is a classic 15th-century tower house with good views (£2/75p). The *Bank O' Fleet Hotel* (☎ 814302, 47 High St) has B&B from £30/47 per single/double (with bathroom) and good bar meals for around £6.

MacEwan's (☎ 01387-710357) bus No 500 runs up to five times daily to Dumfries and Stranraer. Bus No X75 runs once daily, Monday to Saturday.

NEWTON STEWART
☎ 01672 • pop 3200

Surrounded by beautiful countryside and set on the banks of the River Cree, Newton Stewart is a centre for hikers and anglers.

Most accommodation is in Minnigaff, a village just across the bridge. The TIC (☎ 402 431), Dashwood Square off the top of High St, opens 10 am to 4.30 pm daily, April and October; 10 am to 5 pm May, June and September; and 10 am to 6 pm July and August.

Many walkers head for Glen Trool in the Galloway Hills in **Galloway Forest Park**, which consists of 300 sq miles of lochs, mountains and forest. In the park, Merrick (843m) is the highest peak in south-western Scotland. If you're interested in renting fishing gear, contact Creebridge House Hotel (see Places to Stay & Eat). About 4 miles north of Newtown Stewart, past the youth hostel, is the 680-acre **Wood of Cree Nature Reserve**, which contains a variety of habitats, including marshes, and over 400 acres of oak woodland.

Places to Stay & Eat

In Minnigaff, the small *Creebridge Caravan Park* (☎ 402324), about 300 yards from the bridge, charges from £3 for a tent, £9 with a car. *Minnigaff Youth Hostel* (☎ 402211), in a former school, opens from April to September; dorm beds cost £8.25/7.25 (adults/under-18s).

On the banks of the River Cree, five minutes from town, is the friendly, nonsmoking *Flowerbank Guest House* (☎ 402629, Millcroft Rd, Minnigaff). B&B starts from £20/37 (singles/doubles). It also does evening meals and caters for vegetarians.

Creebridge House Hotel (☎ 402121) is a magnificent 18th-century mansion built for the Earl of Galloway. The hotel organises huntin', shootin' and fishin' trips and has an excellent restaurant. The rooms, all with bathrooms, are tastefully decorated; B&B costs £59/78.

Getting There & Around

Newton Stewart is served by buses running between Stranraer and Dumfries, including bus No 920 (National Express) and bus Nos 500 and X75. Bus No 431 runs twice daily (no Sunday service) to Kirkcudbright. The town is also a starting point for buses south to Wigtown and Whithorn.

At the time of research, the Central Cafe

(☎ 402656), High St, was getting set up to hire out mountain bikes.

MACHARS PENINSULA

South of Newtown Stewart, the Galloway Hills give way to the serene, rolling pastures of the Machars peninsula, which is ideal for walking and cycling. The south has many early Christian sites and the 25-mile **Pilgrims Way**.

From Newtown Stewart, Stagecoach Western (☎ 01387-253496) bus No 415 runs six times daily Monday to Saturday, (four on Sunday) to the towns and villages on the peninsula.

WIGTOWN

☎ 01988 • pop 1000

Overlooking Wigtown Bay and the Galloway Hills, Wigtown has expansive views and is surrounded by attractive rolling countryside. For a long time economically run down, the town's revival began in 1998 when it became Scotland's 'National Book Town'; this was endorsed by the Scottish Parliament the following year. There are now around 17 bookshops, offering the widest selection of books in Scotland. For information contact Ian Barr, Book Town Development Officer (☎ 403036, e booktown@wigit.btinternet.com), at 26 South Main St, Wigtown DG8 9EH.

Glaisnock House (☎ 402249, South Main St), in the town centre, has a range of rooms, three of which are en suite. B&B costs from £16.50 per person. It has a licensed restaurant open for lunch and dinner Tuesday to Sunday; roast beef costs £4.50. *County Hotel*, also on South Main St, serves bar meals.

WHITHORN

☎ 01988 • pop 1000

Whithorn has a broad, attractive High St virtually closed at both ends; it was designed originally to enclose a medieval market. Although economic hard times have hit the town and there are few facilities, it's worth visiting because of its fascinating history.

In 397, while the Romans were still in Britain, St Ninian established the first Christian mission beyond Hadrian's Wall in Whithorn (predating St Columba on Iona by

166 years). The modest ruins of Whithorn Cathedral Priory, once the focus of an important medieval pilgrimage, are now the centre point for the **Whithorn Dig** (☎ 500508; HS). The substantial remains of the old monastic settlement are being excavated and there are exhibitions and an audiovisual display. There's also a museum with some important early-Christian stone sculptures. It opens 10.30 am to 5 pm daily, Easter to October. Admission costs £2.70/1.50.

ISLE OF WHITHORN

☎ 01988 • pop 300

The Isle of Whithorn – once an island but now part of a peninsula – is a small, raggedy fishing village with an attractive harbour. In 1998 a shipwreck killed seven local fishermen, a tragedy that devastated the small community. **St Ninian's Chapel**, probably built for pilgrims who landed nearby, is sited on the windswept, rocky headland.

The 300-year-old *Dunbar House (☎ 500 336, Tonderghie Rd)*, overlooking the harbour, has B&B in large rooms for £18/30 per single/double. On the quayside, the *Steam Packet Inn Hotel (☎ 500334)* has popular, excellent-value bar meals, serving everything from green pea soup to fresh lobster; most mains cost under £5. There's also B&B in rooms with bathrooms from £22.50 per person.

PORTPATRICK

☎ 01776 • pop 600

Portpatrick is a charming port on a rugged stretch of coast. Until the mid-19th century it was the main port for Northern Ireland, so it's quite substantial. It's now a lifeboat station, a quiet resort and the starting point for the Southern Upland Way.

It's possible to follow the Southern Upland Way virtually to Stranraer (9 miles). It's a cliff-top walk, followed by sections of farmland and heather moor. Start at the Way's information shelter at the northern end of the harbour. The walk is marked until a half-mile south of Stranraer, where you get the first good views of the town. The route then continues south-eastwards.

SOUTHERN SCOTLAND

Places to Stay

There are lots of places to stay on North Crescent, which curves around the harbour. *Knowe Guest House & Tea Room (☎ 810 441)*, No 1, is a charming place overlooking the harbour; B&B with private bathroom costs £17/32 per single/double. *Ard Choille Guest House (☎ 810313, 1 Blair Terrace)* has doubles, including one with a private bathroom, from £15 per person.

Formerly the customs house, *Harbour House Hotel (☎ 810456, 53 Main St)* is a popular pub with a range of rooms, some with bathrooms, from £25 per person. It serves bar meals at lunch and dinner and tea/coffee all day.

Getting There & Away

McCulloch (☎ 01776-830236) bus No 367 runs to Stranraer up to nine times daily Monday to Saturday (three times on Sunday).

STRANRAER & CAIRNRYAN
☎ 01776 • pop 10,000

Although a little run down, Stranraer is more pleasant than the average ferry port, but there's no reason to stay unless you're catching or coming off a ferry. Make for the south coast (maybe nearby Portpatrick) or Glasgow.

To join the Southern Upland Way, walk westwards along High St, turn left into Glebe St and follow the Portpatrick road (look for a road-sign pointing right). Shortly after passing the second rise at the top of the hill, you'll see a waymarker with a yellow arrow pointing to the right.

Orientation & Information

In Stranraer, the bus and train stations, accommodation and TIC are close to the Stena Sealink and SeaCat terminals. The friendly TIC (☎ 702595), 28 Harbour St, opens between 9.30 and 10.30 am until between 4 and 5.30 pm Monday to Saturday (10 am to 5 pm on Sunday, mid-June to mid-September). Opening times depend on the month so it's advisable to phone for details. Early closing day is Wednesday. You can also book National Express/Citylink buses here.

Places to Stay

Aird Donald Caravan Park (☎ 702025, London Rd), one mile east of the centre, is the nearest camp site that takes tents. Sites cost £3.70, or £6.70 with a car. It's open year round. Nearby is *Balyett Farm Hostel (☎ 703395, Cairnryan Rd)*, on a working farm overlooking Loch Ryan. It accommodates six people and has a kitchen/living area, shower and toilet. If you call ahead they'll pick you up.

Harbour Guest House (☎ 704626, Market St), on the front near the SeaCat terminal, has B&B for £17 to £20 per person. There's a string of standard places along Agnew Crescent facing the harbour, including the low-key *Aislie View Guest House (☎ 705792)*, No 8, which is run by Anne Laurie (no relation to the singer), has good views of Loch Ryan and B&B from £15 per person with shared bathroom.

Jan-Da-Mar Guest House (☎ 706194, 1 Ivy Place, London Rd) is conveniently located and has a range of rooms (some with bathrooms). Singles/doubles start at £18/34. The owners speak German, Dutch, French and Spanish. The most luxurious hotel in Stranraer is *North West Castle Hotel (☎ 704 413, Portrodie)*, though the front could do with a coat of paint. Formerly the home of Arctic explorer Sir John Ross, it's expensive but good, with rooms from £55/77.

If you fancy a night in a lighthouse, *Corsewall Lighthouse Hotel (☎ 853220, ℮ Jim-Neilson@msn.com)*, dating from 1815, is 10 miles north of Stranraer at Corsewall Point. The rooms, with great views, cost from £80/100 to £120/200; one room is specially equipped for disabled travellers. It also has a highly regarded restaurant.

Places to Eat

There are reasonable pizzas and other fast food at two places in George/Charlotte St. *Petrucci Pizzeria* has pizzas from £2.50, and *Romano's* does breakfasts (£3.75) until noon and a fish and chips special for £4.95. Another option is the flower-filled *Star Fish Restaurant (14 Charlotte St)*, with its varied menu: beef curry costs £5, pizzas from £2.50. It opens 9 am to 11 pm daily.

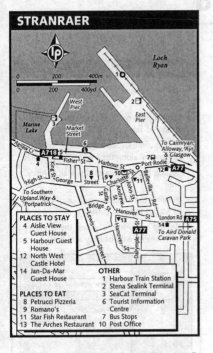

STRANRAER

Loch Ryan

West Pier

Marine Lake

Market Street

East Pier

To Cairnryan, Alloway, 'Ayr & Glasgow

Agnew Cr · A718

Fisher St · Harbour St · Port Rodie · A77

High St · George

King St · Charlotte St

Castle St · Andrews St · John's St · Belleville Rd

Bridge St · Lewis St

Hanover St · London Rd

Hanover St · A77 · A75

To Aird Donald Caravan Park

To Southern Upland Way & Portpatrick

Hanover Sq

PLACES TO STAY
4 Aislie View Guest House
5 Harbour Guest House
12 North West Castle Hotel
14 Jan-Da-Mar Guest House

PLACES TO EAT
8 Petrucci Pizzeria
9 Romano's
11 Star Fish Restaurant
13 The Arches Restaurant

OTHER
1 Harbour Train Station
2 Stena Sealink Terminal
3 SeaCat Terminal
6 Tourist Information Centre
7 Bus Stops
10 Post Office

There are several eateries on Hanover St including *The Arches Restaurant,* a bright, popular cafe with hot meals for £4 to £5.25. The most prestigious restaurant is the *Regency Dining Room* at North West Castle Hotel (☎ 704413). Expect to pay around £20 for a three-course meal.

Getting There & Away
Stranraer is 390 miles from London, 120 miles from Edinburgh, 80 miles from Glasgow and 75 miles from Dumfries.

Sea See the introductory Getting There & Away chapter for details on services to Northern Ireland. There are three alternatives: P&O (☎ 0870 242 4666) ferries from Cairnryan to Larne; Stena Line (☎ 0870 570 7070) ferries from Stranraer to Larne and Belfast; and fast SeaCat (☎ 0870 552 3523) catamarans from Stranraer to Belfast.

The Cairnryan to Larne service is used mainly by motorists and hauliers. Cairnryan is 5 miles north of Stranraer, on the northern side of Loch Ryan. From George St in Stranraer, Stagecoach Western (☎ 01387-253496) bus Nos 58 and 60 together run to Cairnryan post office 10 times daily Monday to Saturday (four times on Sunday). For a taxi (£4) contact McLean's Taxis (☎ 703 348, 24 hours), just up from the TIC.

Stena Line ferries for Larne connect directly with rail and bus services. The train station is on the ferry pier. The SeaCat terminal is south of the ferry pier.

Bus National Express runs three daily services between London and Belfast, via Birmingham, Manchester, Carlisle, Dumfries, the towns along the A75, and Stranraer. Stagecoach Western (☎ 01387-253496) runs hourly buses to Glasgow (£7.50, three hours). Bus No 500 runs three times daily to Kirkcudbright (£3.50, 1½ hours) and Dumfries (£4.50, two hours); and bus No 416 runs three times daily, Monday to Saturday to Newtown Stewart (£2.50, 1¾ hours).

Train There are up to four trains daily between Stranraer and Belfast Port (nine hours), and regular services to Glasgow (£15.30, 2½ hours). For enquiries you can call ☎ 0845 748 4950.

AROUND STRANRAER
Castle Kennedy Gardens
Magnificent Castle Kennedy Gardens (☎ 01776-702024), several miles east of Stranraer off the A75, are among the most famous in Scotland. They cover 75 acres and are set on a peninsula between two lochs and two castles: Castle Kennedy, burnt in 1716, and Lochinch Castle, built in 1864. The landscaping was undertaken in 1730 by the earl of Stair, who used unoccupied soldiers to do the work. The gardens open 10 am to 5 pm daily, April to September. Admission costs £3/1. MacEwan's (☎ 01387-710357) bus Nos 500 and X75 stop here.

Central Scotland

The Highland line, the massive geological fault that divides the Highlands from the Lowlands, runs across the centre of Scotland, making this possibly the most scenically varied region in Britain. South of the fault line are gently undulating hills and agricultural plains; to the north, the dramatic, bare Highland peaks.

The town of Stirling, 26 miles north-east of Glasgow, has witnessed most of the great battles in the Scottish struggle against English domination. Its spectacular castle, perched high on a rock as is Edinburgh's castle, was of paramount strategic importance for centuries, controlling the main routes in the area.

Less than 20 miles north-west of Glasgow are the famous 'bonnie, bonnie banks' of Loch Lomond, straddling the Highland line. Tourists have been visiting this area and the Trossachs (the lochs and hills east of Loch Lomond) for over 150 years – Queen Victoria among them. She had set her heart on adding a Highland residence to her list of royal properties and eventually purchased the Balmoral estate in Aberdeenshire.

In the south-east, Fife was for centuries an independent kingdom. The attractive seaside town of St Andrews, its capital, was once the ecclesiastical centre of the country, but is now known for its university and as the home of golf.

Perth is on the direct route from Edinburgh and Glasgow to Inverness or Aberdeen. Now just a busy town, it was once the capital of Scotland. Dunkeld and Pitlochry, to the north, are appealing (if touristy) villages, and useful as walking bases. Frequent buses and trains service this route.

Following the coast to Aberdeen from Perth or St Andrews, you quickly reach Dundee, one of Scotland's largest cities. Despite its excellent location, it's only now recovering from poor modern development and the loss of its jute and shipbuilding industries. It's worth pausing in Dundee to visit Captain Scott's Antarctic ship, *Discovery*, near the Tay Bridge.

Highlights

- Visiting Scotland's grandest castle at Stirling
- Strolling the medieval streetscapes and hallowed fairways of St Andrews
- Seeing some of Scotland's most spectacular scenery along the West Highland Way
- Tasting the delights of the Malt Whisky Trail
- Viewing the scenic splendour of the isles of Mull, Iona and Staffa
- Getting away from it all on the wonderfully remote isles of Islay and Jura

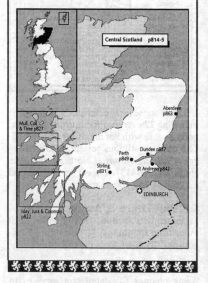

To the west is Argyll & Bute and the western coastline, indented by long inlets and sea lochs forged by glaciers thousands of years ago. Off this coast are the popular islands of the Inner Hebrides. Accessible from the town of Oban, Mull receives the most tourists, but is large enough to absorb them. There are some wonderful mountain walks up Mull's challenging 900m peaks. Off the south-western tip of Mull is the Isle of Iona, where St Columba, after sailing from Ireland, came to build his Christian foundation. West of Mull lie Coll and Tiree – long, low islands, seen from the ferry on a summer's day as a blue haze tinged with the silver of their sandy beaches. South-west of Oban are the isles of Colonsay, Islay and Jura. The latter's breast-shaped mountains are known as the Paps of Jura, and are visible from far away on a clear day. Islay is more agricultural and is famous for its whisky distilleries.

The eastern Highlands is a great elbow of land jutting into the North Sea between Perth and the Firth of Tay in the south, and Inverness and Moray Firth in the north. There are excellent hill walks in the Grampians, and the Cairngorm plateaus are as bleak and demanding as any Scottish mountains. The coastline, especially from Stonehaven north round to Buckie (east of Elgin), is particularly attractive. The valley of the Dee – the Royal Dee thanks to the Queen's residence at Balmoral – has sublime scenery. Braemar is surrounded by good walking country, and every September hosts Scotland's most important Highland Games, the Braemar Gathering.

The largest city in the north-east is prosperous Aberdeen, a lively, attractive place fattened on the proceeds of a long history of sea trade and, currently, the North Sea oil industry, for which it's the onshore base.

Few people visit the small fishing villages along the north coast, but some are very pretty. Farther west along this coast, experiments with alternative lifestyles continue at the Findhorn Foundation, an international spiritual community that welcomes outsiders. Spiritual nourishment of a different order is provided in neighbouring Speyside, where whisky distilleries welcome visitors with tours and free drams.

ORIENTATION & INFORMATION

This central section of the country comprises the administrative regions of Fife, Stirling, Perthshire & Kinross, Angus, Aberdeenshire, Moray, and Argyll & Bute.

The main mountain range is the Grampians, rising to over 1060m; the Cairngorms (1220m) border the Highland region. Off the west coast, the islands of the southern Inner Hebrides – Islay, Jura, Colonsay, Mull, Iona, Coll and Tiree – are accessible from Oban. (For the northern Inner Hebridean islands, including Skye, see the Highlands & Northern Islands chapter.)

There are Tourist Information Centres (TICs) in all the main tourist centres, many open daily late June to early September. Smaller TICs close from October to Easter. Most TICs charge for booking local accommodation, usually around £1 or £2; most ask only for a 10% advance.

WALKING & CYCLING ROUTES

The **West Highland Way**, possibly the finest long-distance walk in Britain, cuts across the centre of this region from Milngavie (near Glasgow) to Fort William. See the Activities chapter for details.

There are some superb hill walks in the Highland areas of central Scotland; Braemar is one of a number of good bases – there's a challenging walk from here through the Cairngorms to Aviemore. The isles of Mull and Jura have wild, mountainous areas and are excellent for walking holidays. When completed, the **Fife Coastal Path** will run for 60 miles between the Forth Bridges and the Tay Bridge (it's currently complete from North Queensferry below the Forth Rail Bridge to Crail, a distance of 46 miles).

The side roads away from the busy A9 are refreshingly free of traffic and excellent for cycling. There's an official cycle trail – the **Glasgow, Loch Lomond & Killin Cycle Way** – which follows forest trails, small roads and disused rail routes.

GETTING AROUND

Although the larger towns are easily reached by bus and train, travel into the Grampians and other interesting walking areas is often difficult without your own transport. The division between the eastern and western Highlands reflects the transport realities – there are few coast-to-coast links across central Scotland. But you can hire cars in the larger towns (see Rental under Car & Motorcycle in the Getting Around chapter).

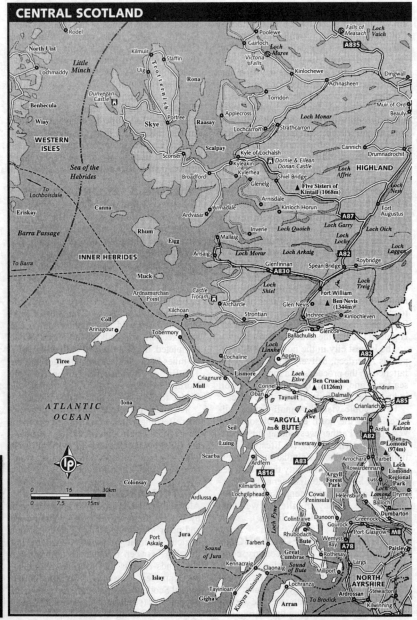

CENTRAL SCOTLAND

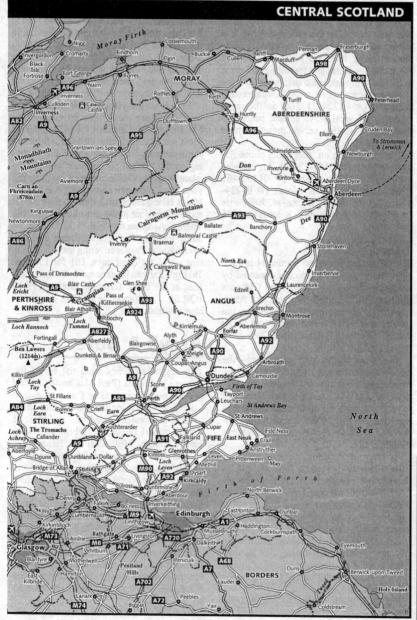

CENTRAL SCOTLAND

Bus

Scottish Citylink (☎ 0870 550 5050) links the main towns in the area and Perth is a major hub for its services. As already mentioned, away from the population centres there are few buses and travelling east-west is difficult, though bus transport around the north-east coast is reasonable. Stagecoach Bluebird (☎ 01224-212266) is the main operator of local services and postbuses (☎ 01246-546329) serve many remote communities.

For information on local buses phone Argyll & Bute (☎ 0141-226 4826); Dundee (☎ 01382-433125); Angus (☎ 01307-461 775); Aberdeenshire & Moray (☎ 01224-664581); Stirling (☎ 01786-442707); Fife (☎ 01592-416060); Perth & Kinross (☎ 0845 301 1130).

Train

The rail system in central Scotland has three lines running north to south, connected by a fourth running north-east from Glasgow through Stirling, Perth, Dundee and Aberdeen. It's a reasonably efficient service, but has one major flaw – east-west travel across central Scotland is impossible. You must travel via Glasgow.

The West Highland line, possibly the most spectacular train journey in Britain, runs north-west from Glasgow to Fort William and Mallaig. A branch line west from Crianlarich connects Oban to the system, and overnight trains run between London and Oban for ferries to the Hebridean islands.

Another scenic train journey runs north from Perth to Inverness and includes a beautiful climb through the Cairngorms from Dunkeld to Aviemore.

ScotRail's regional Rover tickets cover parts of the system. The Central Scotland Rover (£29), valid for three days out of seven, allows travel between Edinburgh, Glasgow, Falkirk and Stirling. See also the Highland Rover ticket information under Getting Around at the start of the Highlands & Northern Islands chapter.

For rail information telephone ☎ 0845 748 4950.

Boat

From Aberdeen, P&O (☎ 01224-572615) has departures Monday to Friday leaving in the evening for Lerwick (Shetland). May to September, there are departures at noon on Tuesday and Saturday to Lerwick via Stromness (Orkney). See the Aberdeen section later in the chapter for more information.

Ferries to the Hebridean islands off the west coast are mostly run by Caledonian MacBrayne, or 'CalMac' (☎ 01475-650100). Most routes depart from Oban, but there are some services from Kennacraig and Claonaig on the Kintyre peninsula. If you plan to island hop, you'll save money by planning your trip in advance and buying one of CalMac's Island Hopscotch tickets covering set routes. See Boat in the introductory Getting There & Away section in the Highlands & Islands chapter for details. There are also Island Rover Passes covering the whole system – £42 for eight days, £61 for 15 days. Taking a car can be expensive. Contact CalMac at the Ferry Terminal, Gourock PA19 1QP, for a free timetable and fare structure – also available from TICs.

Argyll & Bute

This region stretches from the tip of the Kintyre peninsula (Paul McCartney's *Mull of Kintyre*) almost to Glen Coe, and east to Loch Lomond. It includes the Isle of Bute, parts of the Western Highlands, and some of the islands of the Inner Hebrides – Islay, Jura, Colonsay, Mull, Coll and Tiree.

This area is centred on the ancient kingdom of Dalriada, named by the Irish settlers (known as the Scots) who claimed it around the 5th century. From their headquarters at Dunadd, in the Moine Mhor (great bog) near Kilmartin, they gained ascendancy over the Picts and established the Kingdom of Alba, which eventually became Scotland.

Just 20 miles north of Glasgow, Loch Lomond is a popular destination. Its western bank, where most tourist activity takes place, lies in Argyll & Bute; the eastern bank is in Stirling.

The Firth of Clyde, to the south, lies a

complex system of long, deep fjords, or sea lochs, such as Loch Long and Loch Fyne. This pattern of glacial valleys, drowned by the incoming sea, continues north along the west coast of Scotland, creating hundreds of miles of indented coastline. The area records some of the highest rainfall in Britain.

Most people heading for the islands pass through the pleasant town of Oban, the only place of any size in the area. Ferries leave for the popular Isle of Mull (nothing to do with the Mull of Kintyre). It's a great place to hike, with peaks over 900m. There are two interesting castles, Torosay and Duart, near the eastern port of Craignure, and a narrow-gauge railway. The pretty fishing port of Tobermory is in the north of the island.

A five minute ferry trip to the west of Mull is the tiny Isle of Iona, where St Columba arrived from Ireland in the 6th century. Boat trips leave for the uninhabited Isle of Staffa, where the incredible fluted pillars of Fingal's Cave inspired Felix Mendelssohn to compose the *Hebridean Overture*.

Ferries continue from Tobermory to the islands of Coll and Tiree. Southbound ferries from Oban link Colonsay and Islay. The latter is the most southerly island in the Hebrides and is famous for its whisky distilleries, which produce wonderfully peaty single malts. West of Islay is the wild Isle of Jura, where George Orwell wrote *1984*. There are ferry links from Islay to the Kintyre peninsula and the mainland.

For additional information contact Argyll, the Isles, Loch Lomond, Stirling & Trossachs Tourist Board (☎ 01631-566606, ℮ info@scottish.heartlands.org). Check out their Web site at www.scottish.heartlands.org.

GETTING AROUND

The main bus companies in the area are Scottish Citylink (☎ 0870 550 5050), Oban & District Buses (☎ 01631-562856) and West Coast Motor Service (☎ 01586-552319), Campbeltown, which runs buses throughout Kintyre, mid-Argyll.

There's only one railway line: the scenic branch line off the West Highland line between Crianlarich and Oban.

CalMac (☎ 01631-566688) runs most of the ferries to the islands. Its Island Hopscotch tickets, based on 20 route combinations, are better value than single tickets, but require advance planning. For example the ticket that combines Wemyss Bay (in Inverclyde on the mainland), Rothesay (Isle of Bute), Rhubodach (Isle of Bute) to Colintraive (Cowal Peninsula) or vice versa costs £3.75 (£17.30 for a car), a saving of 9% on regular fares. Bicycles are carried free with a Hopscotch ticket.

The Argyll Tourist Route is a driving route marked with brown signposts. It runs from Tarbet on Loch Lomond through Inveraray, Lochgilphead, Oban, Connel and Balachulish (in Glen Coe) to Fort William.

ISLE OF BUTE
☎ 01700

The island lies south of the Cowal Peninsula, and the resort of Rothesay is its only town. The TIC (☎ 502151), 15 Victoria St, Rothesay, opens year round and has lists of B&Bs and hotels, of which there are plenty, especially along the seafront.

Rothesay was built around the substantial ruins of 13th-century **Rothesay Castle** (☎ 502691). The castle is owned by Historic Scotland (HS; see Historic Organisations under Useful Organisations in the Facts for the Visitor chapter for details). Victorian mock-Gothic **Mount Stuart House** (☎ 503 877), the Marquess of Bute's house set in 300 acres, is worth seeing. The house opens 11 am to 4.30 pm Friday to Monday and Wednesday, May to September. Admission costs £6/2.50 per adult/child. The main beach is in the south by **Kilchattan Bay**.

Bute's popular International Folk Festival & World Ceilidh Championships (☎ 831 614) takes place over four days in late July.

The small *Bute Backpackers* (☎ 504446), on the Esplanade in Rothesay, opens year round and has beds for £7 to £9.50.

CalMac (☎ 502707) ferries ply daily (two per hour) between Wemyss Bay and Rothesay (£3.15, 35 minutes). Another CalMac ferry crosses between Rhubodach in the north of Bute and Colintraive (95p, five minutes) on the Cowal Peninsula.

LOCH LOMOND

After Loch Ness, this is perhaps the most famous of Scotland's lochs. Measuring almost 27½ sq miles, Loch Lomond is the largest single inland waterway in Britain and forms part of a new national park that includes the Trossachs in Stirling. Its proximity to Glasgow means that parts of the loch get crowded in summer. The main tourist focus has always been on the west coast, along the A82, and the southern end, around Balloch, which can be a nightmare of jet skis and motorboats. The east coast north of Rowardennan, which the West Highland Way follows, receives few visitors.

The loch, formed by the action of glaciers, lay at the junction of the three ancient Scottish kingdoms of Strathclyde, Dalriada and Pictland. Some of the 37 islands in the loch made perfect retreats for early Christians. The missionary St Mirrin spent some time on Inchmurrin, the largest island, which is named after him.

The loch straddles the Highland fault line separating lowland and highland Scotland, and its character changes distinctly as you move north to south, with the most dramatic scenery in the north. The loch's highest mountain is Ben Lomond (974m) on the east coast.

Orientation & Information

Loch Lomond is 22 miles long and up to 5 miles wide. The A82, a major route north, follows the west coast through Tarbet and on to Crianlarich. The east coast's main thoroughfare is just a walking trail, the West Highland Way, but it's reached by road from Drymen and Aberfoyle.

There are TICs at Balloch (☎ 01389-753533), Balloch Rd, open April to October; Drymen (☎ 01360-660068), in the library on the square, open late May to August; and Tarbet (☎ 01301-702260), at the A82/83 junction, open early April to mid-October.

Walking & Cycling Routes

The big walk is the **West Highland Way** but it's easy to access parts of the trail for shorter walks (see under Walking in the Activities chapter). From Rowardennan you can tackle **Ben Lomond** (974m), a popular five to six hour round trip. The route begins from the car park by the Rowardennan Hotel, and you can return via Ptarmigan (731m) for good views of the loch.

The main cycle route is the **Glasgow, Loch Lomond & Killin Cycle Way**, which reaches the loch at Balloch and Inversnaid. Most of the route is set back to the east of the loch, through the Queen Elizabeth Forest Park. Along the west coast, the A82 is very busy in summer, but sections of the old road beside it are quieter.

Boat Trips

The main centre for boat trips is Balloch, where Sweeney's Cruises (☎ 01389-752 376) offers a wide range of trips from £4.80/2.50 an hour. There is a 2½ hour cruise (£6.80/3.50) to the village of Luss, allowing 30 minutes ashore. The twee village is popular with Scottish visitors hoping to catch a glimpse of the stars of the TV soap *Take the High Road*, though the large car park built to accommodate visitors now detracts from its charm.

Cruise Loch Lomond (☎ 01301-702356) operates from Tarbet, and MacFarlane & Son (☎ 01360-870214) from Balmaha.

Places to Stay

Camping The popular, well positioned *Forestry Commission Cashel Campsite* (☎ *01360-870234*), on the eastern shore, costs £8.40 per site; *Ardlui Caravan Park* (☎ *01301-704243*), open year round, charges £10 per site; and *Tullichewan Holiday Park* (☎ *01389-759475, Old Luss Rd*), Balloch, has full facilities and costs from £8.50 per tent (two people).

Hostels Reputedly haunted but very impressive, the *Loch Lomond Youth Hostel* (☎ *01389-850226*), is in an imposing building set in beautiful grounds 2 miles north of Balloch, near Arden. It's open all year and charges £12.25/10.75 for adults/under-18s. Book ahead in summer.

Rowardennan Youth Hostel (☎ *01360-870259*), across the loch halfway up the east coast by the water, opens late January to the end of October. Beds are £9.25/8. It's also an activity centre, organising walking trips, fishing and canoeing, and is the perfect base for climbing Ben Lomond.

B&Bs & Hotels There are numerous B&Bs, centred on Balloch, Luss, Inverbeg and Tarbet. And there's one pub you shouldn't miss. The *Drover's Inn* (☎ *01301-704234*), in Inverarnan at the northern end of the loch, has smoke-blackened walls, bare wooden floors, a grand hall filled with moth-eaten stuffed animals, and wee drams served by barmen in kilts. It's a great place for serious drinking and you can stay here for £22 per person B&B.

Getting There & Away
Several Scottish Citylink buses (Nos 915/16/35) daily link Glasgow with Balloch (40 minutes, £4.50); other services continue up the west coast to Luss (55 minutes), Tarbet (65 minutes), Ardlui (1¼ hours) and, north of the loch, Crianlarich (50 minutes).

There are two railway lines. From Glasgow, one serves Balloch (35 minutes, £3); the other is the West Highland Line to Oban and Fort William (three daily), which follows the loch from Tarbet to Ardlui.

Getting Around
Small private operators run ferry services between Midross (a mile north of Arden) and Inchmurrin Island; Balmaha and the nature reserve on Inchcailloch Island; Inveruglas and Inversnaid; and Inverbeg and Rowardennan.

Balloch Mobile Bike Hire (☎ 07947-584288, 07773-416717), in Balloch, rents out bikes for £8/15 for a half/full day.

INVERARAY
☎ 01499 • pop 700

On the shores of Loch Fyne, Inveraray is a picturesque, small town with some interesting attractions. It's a planned town, built by the Duke of Argyll when he revamped his nearby castle in the 18th century. The TIC (☎ 302063), on Front St beside the loch, opens year round.

Inveraray Castle
Well worth visiting, Inveraray Castle (☎ 302203) has been the seat of the chiefs of Clan Campbell, the dukes of Argyll, since the 15th century. The current 18th century building includes whimsical turrets and fake battlements. Inside is the impressive armoury hall, whose walls are patterned with more than 1000 pole arms, dirks, muskets and Lochaber axes. The dining and drawing rooms have ornate ceilings and there's a large collection of porcelain. Near the castle, the **Combined Operations Museum** (☎ 500218) relates the town's role in the training of Allied troops for the D-day landings. The castle opens early April to mid-October, Saturday to Thursday (but open Friday in July and August) from 10 am to 5.45 pm (Sunday from 1 pm); admission costs £4.50/2.50.

Inveraray Jail
The Georgian jail and courthouse, in the centre of Inveraray, have been converted into an entertaining tourist attraction, where you sit in on a trial, try out a cell, and discover the meaning of 'picking oakum'. Chatty warders and attendants in 19th-century costume accost visitors. The jail (☎ 302 381) opens April to October, daily from 9.30 am to 6 pm and November to March from 10 am to 5 pm (last entry an hour before closing); admission costs £4.75/2.30.

Inveraray Maritime Museum
The *Arctic Penguin*, a three-masted schooner built in 1911 and one of the world's last iron sailing ships, is now a 'unique maritime experience'. There are displays on the maritime history of the Clyde, piracy and the Highland Clearances, archive videos, and activities for children. It opens April to September daily from 10 am to 6 pm (5 pm October to March); admission costs £3/1.50.

Places to Stay & Eat
The modern, large *Inveraray Youth Hostel* (☎ *302454, Dalmally Rd*) opens April to September and charges £8.25/7.25 for adults/under-18s.

There are several good B&Bs. The cosy *Breagh Lodge* (☎ *302061, The Avenue*), on the southern side of town, charges from £16 per person. Open year round, the larger *Old Rectory* (☎ *302280*) faces the loch and has nine rooms from £18 per person. Breakfast is in the conservatory overlooking the garden. B&B costs £40/64 a single/double at the *Argyll Hotel* (☎ *302466, Front St*), which offers views of the loch and pub meals from £4.95.

Overlooking the loch and open daily, *Loch Fyne Oyster Bar* (☎ *600236*), 6 miles north of Inveraray on the A83 near Clachan, serves excellent seafood and smoked fish. A dozen oysters cost £8.90. Cheaper fish and other food are sold in the attached shop.

Getting There & Away
There are six Scottish Citylink buses a day (three on Sunday) from Glasgow (1¾ hours, £6.60). There are also buses to Oban (1¼ hours, £5.40). Buses arrive and depart on Main St.

KILMARTIN GLEN
This magical glen is the centre of one of the most concentrated areas of prehistoric sites in Scotland. The Irish invaders founded Dalriada and formed the kingdom of Alba here, which eventually united a large part of the country, so this part of mid-Argyll is seen as the cradle of modern Scotland.

There are some 10th-century Celtic crosses in Kilmartin churchyard. Beside the church, the **Museum of Ancient Culture** (☎ 01546-510278) is an interesting centre for archaeology and landscape interpretation with artefacts from the sites, reconstructions, interactive displays and guided tours. The project was partly funded by midges – the curator exposed himself in Temple Wood on a warm summer's evening and was sponsored per midge bite! It opens year round, daily from 10 am to 5.30 pm; admission costs £3.90/1.20.

About 8 miles south of Kilmartin in **Lochgilphead**, the glen's TIC (☎ 01546-602344), 27 Lochnell St, is open daily April to October, and has a bureau de change.

The oldest monuments date from around 5000 years ago and comprise a linear cemetary of burial cairns, running south of Kilmartin village for 1½ miles. There are also two stone circles at **Temple Wood**, three-quarters of a mile south-west of Kilmartin. Three miles north of Lochgilphead, at **Kilmichael Glassary**, elaborate designs are cut into rock faces; their purpose is unknown.

The hill fort of **Dunadd**, 4 miles north of Lochgilphead, was the royal residence of the first kings of Dalriada, and was probably where the Stone of Destiny, used in the investiture ceremony, was located. The faint rock carvings – an ogham inscription (ancient script), a wild boar and two footprints – were probably used in some kind of inauguration ceremony. The fort overlooks the boggy plain that is now the **Moine Mhor Nature Reserve**.

Places to Stay & Eat
Near Temple Wood, opposite the standing stones on the A816, the charming *Dunchraigaig House* (☎ 01546-605209), set in two acres, offers B&B for £20/36 a single/double. *Kilmartin Hotel* (☎ 01546-510250) charges £23 per person (£30 with bathroom) and has a restaurant and bar; there's folk music here some weekends. *Cairn Restaurant* (☎ 01546-510254), nearby, does good lunches and dinners (with dinner mains costing £11 to £15, lunch mains about half that).

At Ardfern, adjacent to Craobh Haven and in an idyllic, peaceful location overlooking the Isles of Shuna and Luing, is *Lunga* (☎ 01852-500237), a grand 17th century mansion, 10 miles north of Kilmartin. The hospitable laird offers B&B from £17 to £20 per person. There are also self-catering apartments on this 1200 hectare coastal estate.

Getting There & Away
Between Lochgilphead and Kilmartin there are up to five buses daily Monday to Saturday (15 minutes, £1.80). Oban to Kilmartin, there's one daily Monday to Saturday (1¼ hours, £3.75), leaving at 1.45 pm.

KINTYRE
Forty miles long and 8 miles wide, the Kintyre peninsula is almost an island, with only a narrow strand connecting it to the wooded hills of Knapdale at Tarbert.

Magnus Barefoot the Viking, who was allowed to claim any island he circumnavigated, made his men drag their longship across this strand to validate his claim.

Tarbert, in the peninsula's north, is the gateway to Kintyre and a busy fishing village that also attracts members of the yachting community. The TIC (☎ 01880-820429), open April to October, is by the harbour. Above Tarbert is a small, crumbling **castle** built by Robert the Bruce.

Apart from Scots, who pack the B&Bs and camping grounds of **Machrihanish** in the south-west, few other tourists venture here and public transport is limited. There are CalMac ferry terminals at **Kennacraig** (☎ 01880-730253) for Port Askaig on Islay, and at **Claonaig** (no tel) for Lochranza on the north of Arran.

From **Tayinloan** on the west coast, there are hourly ferries (20 minutes, £4.60 return) to the **Isle of Gigha** (pronounced **ghee**-a), a flat island 7 miles long by about one mile wide. It's known for its sandy beaches and the subtropical gardens of Achamore House (☎ 01583-505254), open daily from 9 am to dusk; admission costs £2/1. It's about 1½ miles south of Ardminish. There are island walks and bikes can be rented from the post office. Several places do reasonable B&B. *Post Office House* (☎ *01583-505251*) charges from £20 per person and the *Gigha Hotel* (☎ *01583-505254*) has rooms from £50/76 a single/double, plus a good restaurant and bar. Gigha cheese is sold in many parts of Argyll and is recommended, though not cheap.

Also noted for its cheeses, **Campbeltown** was in its prime in the late 19th century. Despite its isolated position the ferry to Northern Ireland helps bring in the tourists. The TIC (☎ 01586-552056), in McKinnon House by the pier, opens year round. A narrow, winding road leads to the **Mull of Kintyre**, popularised by Paul McCartney's song of the same name – and the mist does indeed roll in. A lighthouse marks the spot closest to Ireland, 12 miles across the water. Campbeltown is linked daily by up to seven Scottish Citylink (☎ 0870 550 5050) buses to Glasgow (£10.50, 4½ hours).

ISLE OF ISLAY
☎ 01496 • pop 4000

The most southerly of the islands of the Inner Hebrides, Islay (pronounced **eye**-lah) is best known for its single malt whiskies, which have a highly distinctive, smoky flavour. Islay receives fewer visitors than Arran or Mull since it is farther from the coast and services are limited, but it's equally worth the trip.

Orientation & Information

Port Askaig is the ferry terminal opposite Jura and, to the south, Port Ellen is larger, with three distilleries nearby. Bowmore, 10 miles from both Port Askaig and Port Ellen on the island's western coast, is the island's capital. Across Loch Indaal is the attractive village of Port Charlotte.

The TIC (☎ 810254), The Square, Bowmore, opens year round.

Things to See & Do

The island's long history is related in the **Museum of Islay Life** (☎ 850358) in Port Charlotte. It opens 10 am to 5 pm, Monday to Saturday, 2 to 5 pm Sunday, Easter to October. Admission costs £2/1. Islay was an early focus for Christianity. The exceptional 8th century **Kildaton Cross**, at Kildaton Chapel, 5 miles north-east of Port Ellen, is the only remaining Celtic High Cross in Scotland. The island was also a seat of secular power for the Hebrides, and the meeting place of the Lords of the Isles during the 14th century. At **Finlaggan**, near Port Askaig, are the ruins of the castle from which the powerful MacDonald Lords of the Isles administered their considerable island territories. At Bowmore, the **Round Church** was built in 1767 in this unusual shape to ensure that the devil had no corners to hide in.

Seven **whisky distilleries** welcome visitors for guided tours – Ardbeg, Bowmore, Bunnahabhainn, Bruichladdich, Caol Ila, Lagavulin and Laphroaig.

With over 250 recorded bird species, Islay is wonderful for **birdwatching**. It's an important wintering ground for white-fronted and barnacle geese. There are also miles of sandy **beaches** and good **walks**.

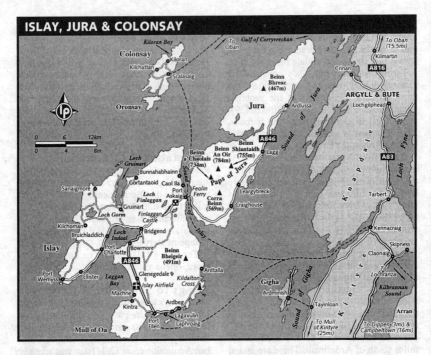

ISLAY, JURA & COLONSAY

Places to Stay & Eat

In Port Charlotte, *Islay Youth Hostel* (☎ 850 385) opens April to September and has beds for £8.75/7.75 for adults/under-18s. There are also several B&Bs and the four-star, renovated *Port Charlotte Hotel* (☎ 850360) beside the beach; singles/doubles with bathroom cost from £49/57.

About 3 miles north-west of Port Ellen on Laggan Bay, *Kintra Bunk Barns Hostel* (☎ 302051) has 23 beds for £6.50 to £8.50 per person; it's self-catering but June to August it also runs a restaurant. You can also camp here. In Port Ellen itself, the pleasant *Trout Fly Guest House* (☎ 302204, 8 Charlotte St), near the ferry terminal, has rooms from £16.50 to £22.50 per person; evening meals are £12.50 (residents only). Opposite the Museum of Islay Life, the *Croft Kitchen* (☎ 850230) is a casual bistro with delicious baked goods, soup and snacks during the day and full meals in the evening, including vegetarian options. It opens mid-March to October, daily 10 am to 8.30 pm.

In Bowmore, the friendly *Tiree* (☎ 810 633, Jamieson St) offers B&B from £17. The refurbished *Harbour Inn* (☎ 810990), overlooking Loch Indaal, offers B&B for £37.50/55 in comfortable singles/doubles. It has a good seafood restaurant.

Getting There & Away

CalMac (☎ 302209) has a ferry from Kennacraig to Port Ellen (2¼ hours, £6.85) and another to Port Askaig (two hours, £6.85). They operate daily but on Wednesday there's only a ferry to Port Askaig, and on Sunday there's only a ferry to Port Ellen. June to mid-September, on Wednesday there's a ferry between Colonsay and Port Askaig (1¼ hours, £3.45).

Getting Around

Islay Coaches (☎ 840273) operates buses up to four times daily between Port Ellen,

Bowmore and Port Askaig. Also, 10-seater postbuses (☎ 01246-546329) run once daily Monday to Saturday from Port Askaig to Ardbeg via Bowmore and Port Ellen.

Islay's size makes it ideal to explore by bike and Bowmore post office (☎ 810366) hires out mountain bikes for £10/50 per day/week.

ISLE OF JURA
☎ 01496 • pop 200

Jura is a magnificently wild, lonely island and one can understand why George Orwell chose it as a retreat. He spent several months at Barnhill, a house in the north. It is a wonderful place to walk – in fact, there is little else to do, apart from visiting the Craighouse Distillery (☎ 820420) in the island's only village. The mountain scenery is superb and the distinctive shapes of the Paps of Jura are visible from miles around.

North of the island, between Scarba and Jura, is the epicentre of a great tidal race known as the Corryvreckan Whirlpool. Caused by the tide running out more slowly on the landward side of the islands, it can be heard roaring on a still day. Although stags have been known to swim it, and quite small boats to slip through, it has claimed many victims who didn't calculate the tides properly. It's most impressive an hour after low tide.

Walks

The Paps of Jura provide a tough hill walk that requires good navigational skills and takes eight hours, although the record for the Paps of Jura fell race is just three hours! Look out for adders – the island is infested with them, but they're shy snakes that'll move away as you approach.

A good place to start is by the bridge over the River Corran, north of Leargybreck. The first pap you reach is Beinn a'Chaolais (734m, 2407 feet), then Beinn an Oir (784m, 2572 feet) and finally Beinn Shiantaidh (755m, 2477 feet). Most people also climb Corra Bheinn (569m, 1866 feet), before joining the path that crosses the island to descend to the road.

Places to Stay & Eat

Gwen Boardman (☎ 820379, 7 Woodside), in Craighouse, provides comfortable B&B for £19 per person. The family run Jura Hotel (☎ 820243) is a great place to stay and the place for a drink on Jura. It charges from £32 per person; try to get a room at the front for the views. There's good pub grub using local produce and full set meals for £18.

Getting There & Away

The only access to Jura is via Islay. Western Ferries (☎ 840681) shuttles between Port Askaig and Feolin roughly hourly, Monday to Saturday, six times on Sunday (85p, five minutes). The ferry also takes cars.

ISLE OF COLONSAY
☎ 01951 • pop 110

North of Islay is remote Colonsay, an unspoilt island of varied landscapes and flora with a good sunshine record, receiving only half the rainfall of the Argyll mainland. As well as cliffs and a rocky coastline, there are several white-sand beaches, the most spectacular being Kiloran Bay.

The island is particularly interesting to ornithologists, with more than 150 species of birds recorded, including golden eagles. Botanists will appreciate the subtropical gardens of Colonsay House, in Kiloran, known for their rhododendrons. The gardens are open year round but the best time to visit is April to June. There is no admission charge. Grey seals are often seen around the coast and wild goats inhabit some of the neighbouring islets.

At low tide you can walk across the strand to the small Isle of Oronsay, to the south, where the ruins of the priory date from the 14th century.

Places to Stay & Eat

Camping isn't allowed and there are few places to stay (none of them cheap). For B&B, there's the friendly Seaview (☎ 200 315), a croft house in Kilchattan on the rugged western coast, charging £23 per person. The 18th-century Isle of Colonsay Hotel (☎ 200316), in Scalasaig, opens March to October. Most people stay on a

B&B and dinner basis with rates from £60 per person, including bicycle hire.

Getting There & Away

CalMac (☎ 200308) has ferries Sunday, Wednesday and Friday to Scalasaig from Oban (£9.85, 2¼ hours), and Wednesday from Islay's Port Askaig (1¼ hours, £3.45) and from Kennacraig on the Kintyre peninsula (3½ hours, £9.85).

OBAN & AROUND
☎ 01631 • pop 8500

As the most important ferry port on the west coast, Oban gets inundated by visitors, but it's on a beautiful bay and the harbour is interesting. By Highlands standards, it is quite large, but you can easily get around on foot. There isn't a great deal to see or do in town, but there are some good coastal and hill walks in the vicinity.

Orientation

The bus, train and ferry terminals are together beside the harbour, on the southern edge of the bay. Argyll Square is one block east of the train station, and George St leads north past the North Pier. From the pier, Corran Esplanade runs round the northern edge of the bay.

From Inveraray, the A85 brings you into the northern end of town.

Information

Oban's busy TIC (☎ 563122) is on Argyll Square, next to the site of the Tolerable Inn, where Johnson and Boswell stayed on 22 October 1773 on their travels through the Western Isles. The TIC opens 9 am to 9 pm Monday to Saturday (7 pm Sunday), July and August; until 5.30 pm May, June, September and October (4 pm Sunday); 9.30 am to 5 pm Monday to Saturday (weekends noon to 4 pm), November to March.

Things to See

Crowning the hill above the town is Mc-Caig's Tower, built at the end of the 19th century. Intended to be an art gallery, it wasn't completed and now looks like an ugly, smaller version of Rome's Colosseum.

There are, however, good views over the bay from beside this peculiar structure. It's always open and admission is free. There's an even better view from **Pulpit Hill**, south of the town.

Oban Distillery (☎ 572004), Stafford St in the town centre, has been producing Oban single malt whisky since 1794. There are tours 9.30 am to 5 pm Monday to Friday, February to November (to 8.30 pm plus 9.30 am to 5 pm Saturday, July to September); afternoons only in December and January. Tours cost £3. Even if you don't want the tour or the whisky, it's worth visiting the distillery for the small exhibition in the foyer.

Walking & Cycling Routes

It's a pleasant 20 minute walk north from the youth hostel along the coast to **Dunollie Castle**, built by the MacDougalls of Lorne in the 15th century. It's open all the time and very much a ruin. You could continue along this road to the beach at **Ganavan Sands**, 2½ miles from Oban.

A TIC leaflet lists local bike rides. They include a 7 mile Gallanach circular tour, a 16 mile route to Seil Island, and routes to Connel, Glenlonan and Kilmore.

Organised Tours

A number of tour operators offer day trips from Oban to Iona, Mull, Staffa and other islands, some using CalMac ferries (☎ 566 688). Gordon Grant (☎ 0800 783 8470) has a Mull and Iona tour for £19/10; a Mull, Staffa and Iona tour for £30/15; and, for bird lovers, a tour to the Threshnish Isles for £35/17.50. Bowman & MacDougall's (☎ 563221), 3 Stafford St, has similar tours.

CalMac itself has day trips to Colonsay, Coll and Tiree (£20).

Places to Stay

Camping The nearest camp site is *Oban Caravan & Camping Park* (☎ 562425, *Gallanachmore Farm*), by the sea 2½ miles south of Oban on the road to Gallanach. It costs around £8 per site.

Hostels The popular, friendly *Oban Backpackers Lodge* (☎ 562107, *Breadalbane St*) has a communal kitchen and charges from £9.50 to £11 (including sheets). Breakfast costs £1.60. From the train station and ferry terminal walk north to the end of George St, past the cinema, and veer right into Breadalbane St.

The Victorian-era **Oban Youth Hostel** (☎ 562025, Corran Esplanade), north of town across the bay from the terminals, opens year round and charges £12.25/10.75 (£13.25/11.75 in its modern annexe) for adults/under-18s which includes continental breakfast.

Jeremy Inglis Hostel (☎ 565065, 21 Airds Crescent) is across the square from the TIC. Jeremy Inglis (who also runs McTavish's Kitchens) charges £6.50 to £7 per person – including continental breakfast – so gets booked up quickly. There are some double and family rooms.

B&Bs & Hotels Near the ferry terminal, **Maridon Guest House** (☎ 562670, Dunuaran Rd) is a large blue house with eight rooms, all with private bathroom. B&B ranges from £16 to £20 per person. Book in advance in summer.

The main area for guesthouses and B&Bs is at the northern end of George St, along Dunollie Terrace and Breadalbane St. **Sand Villa Guest House** (☎ 562803, Breadalbane St) is an efficient place with 15 rooms, charging from £14 to £22 per person.

North of the town, Corran Esplanade is lined with more expensive guesthouses and small hotels, all facing seaward and most offering rooms with bathrooms. The expansive **Glenrigh Guest House** (☎ 562991) offers B&B from £25/46 a single/double. Rooms here all have bathrooms as do those at the excellent **Kilchrenan House** (☎ 562663), near the youth hostel, which charges £24 to £32 per person. At the far end of Corran Esplanade is the highly recommended **Barriemore Hotel** (☎ 566356) with B&B from £25 to £32 per person. It does an excellent dinner.

A number of B&Bs sit below McCaig's Tower. In a quiet location, **Crathie Guest House** (☎ 562619, Duncraggan Rd) has seven rooms priced from £15 per person.

There are good views from **Invercloy Guest House** (☎ 562058, Ardconnel Terrace) which offers B&B in its five rooms for £15 to £20 per person.

In the centre with good views across the harbour, **Palace Hotel** (☎ 562294, George St) has B&B in en-suite rooms for £20 per person. The **Regent Hotel** (☎ 562341, Corran Esplanade), just north of the North Pier, is Oban's attempt at Art Deco. B&B in a room with bathroom costs £28 per person; dinner costs £10.

Also highly recommended is **Heatherfield House** (see Places to Eat) which has been described as a restaurant with rooms. B&B costs £25 to £35 per person, and here you may well be treated to the finest breakfast you'll ever eat! The top hotel is **Manor House** (☎ 562087, fax 563053, Gallanach Rd), south round the bay. Built in 1780, this house was originally part of the estate of the Duke of Argyll. It's worth eating in the hotel's restaurant if you're staying here. B&B and dinner ranges from £52 to £85 per person.

Places to Eat

There's no shortage of eateries in Oban. Most are along the bay between the train station and the North Pier, and along George St.

You can't miss the highly publicised, central **McTavish's Kitchens** (☎ 563064, 34 George St). There's a self-service cafe offering standard but eatable food (burgers cost £3.25), and a Scottish show in the restaurant each night (see Entertainment).

Opposite Oban Distillery, the **China Restaurant** (☎ 563575, 39 Stafford St) does takeaways and table service, with most dishes under £8. It opens daily.

Studio Restaurant (☎ 562030, Craigard Rd), off George St, continues to deserve its good reputation. Local cuisine includes paté and oatcakes, roast Angus beef, Scottish cheeses and fresh fish. A three course dinner costs £11.25 between 5 and 6.30 pm, £13.95 until 10 pm.

North of the North Pier, along Corran Esplanade, is **Coasters Pub**, a popular place with inexpensive food; pizzas cost from £5.95.

CENTRAL SCOTLAND

The *Waterfront Restaurant* (☎ *563110, 1 Railway Pier*) is an excellent place for seafood, where you can view the chef preparing it. Lunch time mains are good value at £5.95 to £7.25. It opens daily mid-March to Christmas.

The best place to eat is *Heatherfield House* (☎ *562681, Albert Rd*); the owners bake their own bread, cure their own hams and all seafood is locally caught. However, the restaurant was closed at the time of research, so call to see if it has reopened.

Entertainment
The nightly Scottish show at *McTavish's Kitchens* (see Places to Eat) packs 'em in. Shows are staged May to September nightly at 8.30 pm, with dancing, a live band and a piper. It costs £3.50/1.75 or £1.75/1 if you eat here; there are also set meals starting at £8.50, including the show.

The *Gathering Restaurant & O'Donnell's Pub* (☎ *564849, Breadalbane St*) has live entertainment most nights. O'Donnell's opens from noon to 1 am, the restaurant from 5 pm to midnight. The restaurant specialises in Scottish cuisine.

The best pub is the *Oban Inn*, which dates from 1790 and overlooks the harbour by the North Pier. It's a lively place with a good range of single malt whiskies, and serves bar meals in its upstairs lounge until 10 pm.

Getting There & Away
Oban is 504 miles from London, 123 from Edinburgh, 115 from Inverness, 93 from Glasgow and 50 from Fort William.

Bus Scottish Citylink runs two to four buses a day to Oban from Glasgow (£10, three hours). Oban to Inveraray is a 1¼ hour journey (£5.50). Another service follows the coast via Appin to Fort William (£6.20, 1¾ hours) to Inverness.

Train Oban is at the end of a scenic branch line that leaves the West Highland line at Crianlarich. Up to three trains a day leave Glasgow for Oban (£15, three hours). To get to other parts of Scotland from Oban, the

train isn't much use. To reach Fort William requires a trip via Crianlarich – it's better to take the bus.

Boat Numerous CalMac (☎ 566688) boats link Oban with the Inner and Outer Hebrides. There are services to Mull (up to seven a day), Colonsay (three times a week), Coll and Tiree (Monday to Wednesday, Friday and Saturday), Barra and South Uist (one daily). See the island entries for details.

There are also up to two daily services Monday to Saturday to Achranoish on the Isle of Lismore (£2.35/3.95 single/return, 50 minutes).

Getting Around
Oban & District (☎ 562856), the local bus company, has services up to McCaig's Tower and to the beach at Ganavan Sands.

Hazelbank Motors (☎ 566476), Lynn Rd near Tesco supermarket, rents out mountain bikes for £4 per hour and cars.

ISLE OF MULL
pop 2678
It's easy to see why Mull is so popular with tourists. As well as having superb mountain scenery, two castles, a narrow-gauge railway and accessibility – being on the route to the holy isle of Iona – it's also a charmingly endearing place. Where else would you find a police station that uses gerbils to shred documents (really), or a stately home where notices encourage you to sit on the chairs? And there can be few places left where the locals seldom lock their doors. Despite the numbers of visitors, the island seems large enough to absorb them, and many pass through, sticking to the well-travelled route from Craignure to Iona, returning to Oban in the evening.

Orientation & Information
Two-thirds of Mull's population is centred on Tobermory, in the north. Craignure, on the eastern coast where most people arrive, is very small.

There are TICs at Craignure (☎ 01680-812377), opposite the quay and open year round, and at Tobermory (☎ 01688-302182), Main St, open April to October.

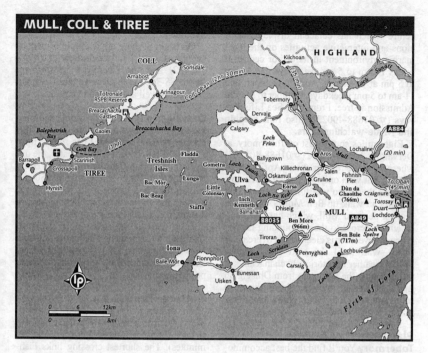

MULL, COLL & TIRE

Things to See & Do

There's little to keep you in **Craignure**, except to catch the Mull Rail (☎ 01680-812494) narrow-gauge, miniature steam train that takes passengers 1½ miles south to **Torosay Castle** (£3.30/2.20 return, 10 minutes). The castle (☎ 01680-812421) is a Victorian mansion in the Scottish Baronial style set in a beautiful garden. 'Take your time but not our spoons' advises the sign, and you're left to wander at will. The house opens 10.30 am to 5 pm daily, Easter to mid-October. Admission costs £4.50/1.50.

A 40 minute walk (about 2 miles) southeast of Torosay is **Duart Castle** (☎ 01680-812309), a formidable fortress dominating the Sound of Mull. The seat of the Maclean clan, this is one of the oldest inhabited castles in Scotland. The keep was built in 1360 and the castle was lost to the Campbells in 1745. In 1911, Sir Fitzroy Maclean bought and restored the castle. It has damp dungeons, vast halls and bathrooms with ancient fittings. In the excellent tearoom you can try one of Lady Maclean's Chocolate Specials. The castle opens 10.30 am to 6 pm daily, May to mid-October. Admission costs £3.50/1.75.

In the island's north is the beautiful little fishing port of **Tobermory**, Mull's capital. The brightly painted houses, reflected in the water, make this one of the most picturesque villages in Scotland. Somewhere out in the bay is the wreck of a ship that was part of the Armada, sunk here in 1588. No one is sure if the ship was the *Florida*, the *San Juan* or the *Santa Maria*, but rumours of a cargo of gold have kept treasure hunters looking ever since.

There are a few things to see in Tobermory. There's the small **Mull Museum** (☎ 01688-302208), open 10.30 am to 4 pm Monday to Friday, 10 am to 1 pm Saturday, Easter to mid-October. Admission is £1/10p. The tiny **Tobermory Distillery** (☎ 01688-302645), opens 10 am to 5 pm weekdays, Easter to October. Admission is £2.50/free. The **Hebridean Whale & Dolphin Trust**

(☎ 01688-302620), 28 Main St, is a research centre which has cetacean displays, skeletons and interactive activities on the local marine environment in its visitor centre. It opens 10 am to 5 pm weekdays and 11 am to 5 pm at weekends, April to October; and 11 am to 5 pm weekdays, October to March. Admission is free. From here Sea Life Surveys (☎ 01688-400223) also runs **dolphin and whale-watching tours**.

Eight miles south-west of Tobermory, at Dervaig, is **Mull Theatre** (☎ 01688-400245) where there are regular shows April to September, but with only 43 seats it's Britain's smallest theatre so you'll need to book.

You can walk up **Ben More** (966m), the highest peak on Mull, which has spectacular views across to the surrounding islands when the weather is clear. If it's overcast or misty, wait until the next day because Mull's weather is notoriously changeable. A trail leads up the mountain from Dhiseig on Loch na Keal's southern shore about 10 miles south-west of Salen. Allow five to six hours for the round trip.

Places to Stay & Eat

Tobermory You'll find the best accommodation choices at Tobermory. *Tobermory Youth Hostel (☎ 01688-302481, Main St)* opens early-March to October but has only eight beds, which cost £8.75/7.95 for adults/under-18s.

The Cedars (☎ 01688-302096), on Old Dervaig Rd, offers B&B from £16/30 a single/double with shared bathroom. Mrs Harper has a couple of rooms at *2 Victoria St (☎ 01688-302263)* for £15 to £18 per person, also with shared bathroom. The central *Failte Guest House (☎ 01688-302495, Main St)*, overlooking the bay, has seven rooms costing from £25/40, all with bathroom.

One of Mull's top hotels is the *Western Isles Hotel (☎ 01688-302012)*, on the hillside overlooking the village and with superb views across the bay. Well-appointed rooms cost from £38 to £87 per person. You can eat either in its restaurant or conservatory/bar.

Mishnish Hotel (☎ 01688-302009, Main St) is *the* place to drink. The food's good

value (mains £4.75 to £13) and there's often live music.

On Main St there are a couple of upmarket places. *Back Brae Restaurant (☎ 01688-302422)* and the *Lochinvar Restaurant (☎ 01688-302253)* both serve locally caught seafood as well as steak and venison.

Dervaig In a 19th-century former shooting lodge with views of Loch Cuin, *Cuin Lodge (☎ 01688-400346)* has rooms from £10 to £17.50. Beside Mull Theatre, the upmarket, Victorian *Druimard Country Hotel (☎ 01688-400345)* charges from £60 per person for a bed in one of its seven rooms, all with bathroom. In its excellent restaurant a three course set meal costs £28.50.

Craignure Conveniently positioned *Linnhe View (☎ 01680-812423)*, close to the ferry terminal, provides B&B year round for £20 per person.

Getting There & Away

There are up to seven CalMac (☎ 01680-812343) ferries a day from Oban to Craignure (£3.45/23.95 for a passenger/small car, 45 minutes). The shortest crossing links Fishnish, 6 miles north-west of Craignure, with the mainland at Lochaline (£2.05, 20 minutes) on the Morvern peninsula; boats run every 15 minutes Monday to Saturday, hourly on Sunday. From Tobermory a service runs to Kilchoan (£3.30, 35 minutes) on the Ardnamurchan peninsula.

Tour operators in Oban have trips out to Mull (see Organised Tours under Oban).

Getting Around

Several bus companies operate on the island connecting the ferry points and main villages. The Craignure to Tobermory service (£3, one hour) goes up to eight times a day Monday to Saturday (once on Sunday). The Craignure to Fionnphort service (£3.45, 1¼ hours) is equally frequent.

Cycling is a good way to get around and you can rent bikes from a number of places. In Craignure try Mull Travel & Crafts (☎ 01680-812487), near the ferry terminal, which rents bikes for £7/12 per half/full day.

In Tobermory, contact Mrs MacLean at Tom-A-Mhuillin (☎ 01688-302164), Salen Rd.

AROUND MULL
Isle of Iona
☎ 01681 • pop 150

St Columba landed on Iona from Ireland in 563 before setting out to convert Scotland. A monastery was established, where the *Book of Kells* – the prize attraction of Dublin's Trinity College – is believed to have been transcribed. The book was taken to Kells in Ireland when Viking raids drove the monks from Iona.

The monks returned and the monastery prospered until its destruction in the Reformation. The ruins were given to the Church of Scotland in 1899, and by 1910 the **Iona Abbey** was reconstructed by priests who established the Iona Community (☎ 700404). It's still a flourishing spiritual community holding regular courses and retreats.

Iona is indeed a special place, but the hordes that pile off the tour buses make it difficult to appreciate. It's best to stay overnight. After the crowds have gone, you can walk to the top of the hill, go to an evening service or look around the ancient graveyard where 48 of Scotland's early kings, including Macbeth, are buried. The grave of former Labour leader John Smith is also here, and is a focus for tour groups.

For B&B try *Bishop's House* (☎ 700800), complete with chapel, opposite the ferry landing, for £18 per person. The comfortable *Argyll Hotel* (☎ 700334) is the island's best; it opens April to October and charges from £39 per person.

From Fionnphort on the south-western tip of Mull a five minute CalMac (☎ 01681-700559) ferry ride brings you to Baile Mor on Iona (£3.20 return)

Isle of Staffa

This uninhabited island is a truly magnificent sight, and once there you'll understand why it inspired Mendelssohn to write *Hebridean Overture*. It forms the eastern end of that geological phenomenon – made up of huge, many-sided basalt pillars – which begins in Northern Ireland where it's known as the Giant's Causeway. Here the pillars are called the Colonnade and form the sides and line the walls of the cathedral-like **Fingal's Cave**, which you can walk into at low tide. Staffa is also visited by a sizeable **puffin colony**. The TIC on Mull books tickets for boat trips (£10 return, 2¼ hours), most of which leave from Fionnphort.

ISLE OF COLL
☎ 01879 • pop 150

This little island, 7 miles west of Mull, has a good sunshine record but the wind can be strong and on the western coast has formed **sand dunes** 30m high. There's a good walking trail round the island, and the **Totronald RSPB Reserve** protects a corncrake colony. There are also two castles, both known as **Breacachacha Castle** and both built by the Macleans.

On Breacachacha Bay, near the castles and 4½ miles from the ferry dock at Arinagour, *Garden House* (☎ 230374, *Castle Gardens*) offers B&B from £18/32 a single/double, plus £12 for the evening meal. *Coll Hotel* (☎ 230334, *Arinagour*) has rooms for £25 per person and a good restaurant specialising in seafood. A set dinner costs £25.

CalMac (☎ 230347) ferries run Monday to Wednesday, Friday and Saturday to Tiree (£2.80, one hour) and Oban (£11.10, 2½ hours).

You can hire mountain bikes from Tammie Hedderwick (☎ 230382), Coll Ceramics, Arinagour, for £7.50 per day.

ISLE OF TIREE
☎ 01879 • pop 800

A low-lying island with some beautiful, sandy beaches, Tiree has one of the best sunshine records in Britain, particularly during early summer. It also gets fairly breezy making it the **windsurfing** centre of Scotland – there are competitions during the Tiree Wave Classic each October. Call the windsurfing school (☎ 220399) for information.

If you want to camp, make sure to get the landowner's permission first. *The Shieling* (☎ 220503), in Crossapol near the airport 4 miles west of Scarinish, does B&B for £18 per person. The *Tiree Lodge Hotel*

(☎ 220368), about 1 mile east of Scarinish beside the white, sandy beach of Gott Bay, has singles/doubles from £26/46, most with private bathroom.

From Tiree airport (☎ 220309) British Airways/Loganair (☎ 0845 773 3377) flies to Glasgow, the Highlands and other islands. CalMac (☎ 230347) ferries from Oban arrive via Coll (see the preceding section).

Stirling & Around

The administrative area of Stirling includes country either side of the Highland fault line: agricultural and industrial Lowlands to the south, and the bare peaks of the Highlands to the north. Stirling was formerly known as Central region, a name appropriate not only for its location, but also for the pivotal role it has played in Scotland's history.

The capital, also called Stirling, at the head of the Firth of Forth and the main route into the Highlands, is the most strategically important spot in the country and has a superb castle.

Loch Lomond lies on the western edge of the region (see that section under Argyll & Bute earlier in the chapter). The Trossachs, a scenic area in the west, is Rob Roy country, and a busy tourist destination. The mountainous north of Stirling gets fewer visitors; public transport here is patchy in some parts, nonexistent in others.

For additional information, contact Argyll, the Isles, Loch Lomond, Stirling & Trossachs Tourist Board (☎ 01631-566606, Ⓔe info@scottish.heartlands.org). It has a Web site at www.scottish.heartlands.org.

GETTING AROUND

For local transport information in the Stirling administrative region, phone ☎ 01786-442707.

The main bus operator is First Edinburgh (☎ 01324-613777). May to September, the vintage Trossachs Trundler is a useful bus service circling Aberfoyle, Callander and Trossachs Pier on Loch Katrine (from where you catch SS *Sir Walter Scott*). Check with the TIC in Callander (see that section later in the chapter). First Edinburgh buses connect with the Trundler in Callander. Alternatively, postbus (☎ 01246-546329) No 24 does the same circuit twice daily Monday to Friday (once on Saturday) via Port of Mentieth and Brig o'Turk.

Stirling town is the rail hub, but the lines only skirt the region, so you'll be relying on buses if you don't have your own transport.

The **West Highland Way** cuts along the western region from Glasgow to Fort William (see Walking in the Activities chapter). There are numerous other walks in the area. Bartholomew's *Walk Loch Lomond & the Trossachs* is a useful guidebook available from TICs.

The **Glasgow, Loch Lomond & Killin Cycle Way** crosses the region from the centre of Glasgow via Balloch on the southern tip of Loch Lomond, Aberfoyle and Callander in the Trossachs, Loch Earn, Killin and Loch Tay. There are detours through Queen Elizabeth Forest Park and round Loch Katrine. It's a good route for walkers as well as cyclists because it follows forest trails, old train routes and canal towpaths. A brochure showing the route is available from TICs.

STIRLING
☎ 01786 • pop 37,000

Stirling is such a strategic site that there's been a fortress here since prehistoric times. It was said that whoever held Stirling controlled the country, and Stirling has witnessed many of the struggles between the Scots and the English. The castle is perched high on a rock and dominates the town. It's one of the most interesting castles in the country, better even than Edinburgh Castle.

Two miles north of Stirling, and visible for miles around, the Wallace Monument commemorates William Wallace. Mel Gibson's movie *Braveheart* revived interest in this hero of the wars of independence against England. You can climb this Victorian tower for a panoramic view of seven battle grounds – one of them at Stirling Bridge, where Wallace beat the English in 1297.

A more famous battlefield is 2 miles south of Stirling at Bannockburn where, in 1314, Robert the Bruce and his small army

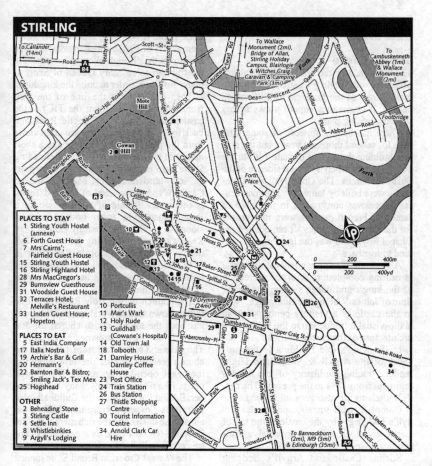

STIRLING

PLACES TO STAY
1 Stirling Youth Hostel
   (annexe)
6 Forth Guest House
7 Mrs Cairns';
   Fairfield Guest House
15 Stirling Youth Hostel
16 Stirling Highland Hotel
28 Mrs MacGregor's
29 Burnsview Guesthouse
31 Woodside Guest House
32 Terraces Hotel;
   Melville's Restaurant
33 Linden Guest House;
   Hopeton

PLACES TO EAT
5 East India Company
17 Italia Nostra
19 Archie's Bar & Grill
20 Hermann's
22 Barnton Bar & Bistro;
   Smiling Jack's Tex Mex
25 Hogshead

OTHER
2 Beheading Stone
3 Stirling Castle
4 Settle Inn
8 Whistlebinkies
9 Argyll's Lodging

10 Portcullis
11 Mar's Wark
12 Holy Rude
13 Guildhall
   (Cowane's Hospital)
14 Old Town Jail
18 Tolbooth
21 Darnley House;
   Darnley Coffee
   House
23 Post Office
24 Train Station
26 Bus Station
27 Thistle Shopping
   Centre
30 Tourist Information
   Centre
34 Arnold Clark Car
   Hire

0   200   400m
0   200   400yd

of determined Scots (outnumbered four to one) put Edward II's English force to flight and reclaimed Stirling Castle. In the long struggle against the threat of English domination, this victory turned the tide of fortune sufficiently to favour the Scots for the following 400 years.

Although you can fit the main sights of Stirling into a day trip from Edinburgh or Glasgow, it's a very pleasant place to stay. There's an excellent youth hostel near the castle, and the town lays on enjoyable medieval markets and numerous other activities in summer.

Orientation & Information

The town centre lies west of the River Forth. The largely pedestrianised old town slopes up from the train station and nearby bus station to the castle in the north-west, which sits 75m above the plain atop the plug of an extinct volcano. Stirling University's modern campus is to the north, by Bridge of Allan.

The TIC (☎ 475019), 41 Dumbarton Rd, opens 9 am to 7.30 pm daily (to 6.30 pm Sunday), July and August; 9 am to 6 pm Monday to Saturday, June and September; 10 am to 4 pm Sunday; and shorter hours Monday to Saturday the rest of the year. The post office, 84–86 Murray Place, has a bureau de change.

Stirling Castle

The location, architecture and historical significance of Stirling Castle combine to make it one of the grandest of all Scottish castles. It commands superb views across the surrounding plains.

There has been a fortress of some kind here for several thousand years, but the current building dates from the late 14th to the 16th centuries, when it was a residence of the Stuart monarchs. The Great Hall and Gatehouse were built by James IV. The spectacular palace was constructed in the reign of James V; French masons were responsible for the stonework. James VI remodelled the Chapel Royal and was the last king of Scotland to live here.

A program of improvements at the castle is nearing completion, with the recreation of the king's and queen's chambers in the time of James V being the final stage. Next to the castle is a visitors centre with an audio-visual introduction to the history and architecture of the castle.

In the King's Old Building is the **museum** of the Argyll & Sutherland Highlanders, tracing the history of this famous regiment from 1794 to the present. The castle's kitchens are also very interesting.

Complete with turrets, spectacular **Argyll's Lodging** – by the castle at the top of Castle Wynd – is the most impressive 17th-century town house in Scotland.

Stirling Castle and Argyll's Lodging (☎ 450000; HS) open 9.30 am to 5.15 pm (last entry) daily, April to October; to 4.15 pm November to March. Admission to both costs £6/1.50. There's a car park next to the castle (£2 for three hours).

Old Town

Below the castle is the Old Town, which grew from the time that Stirling became a royal burgh, around 1124. In the 15th and 16th centuries, when the Stuart monarchs held court in Stirling, rich merchants built their houses here.

Stirling has the best surviving **town wall** in Scotland and it can be followed on the **Back Walk**. It was built around 1547 when Henry VIII of England began what became known as the 'Rough Wooing' – attacking the town to force Mary Queen of Scots to marry his son in order to unite the kingdoms.

The walk follows the line of the wall from Dumbarton Rd (near the TIC) to the castle, continuing round Castle Rock and back to the Old Town. There are great views from the path, and you could make a short detour to Gowan Hill to see the **Beheading Stone**, now encased in iron bars to keep ritual axe murderers away. **Mar's Wark**, on Castle Wynd at the head of the Old Town, is the ornate facade of what was once a Renaissance-style town house commissioned in 1569 by the wealthy Earl of Mar, Regent of Scotland during James VI's minority. During the Jacobite Rebellion in 1715, the Earl chose the losing side and his house became the town's barracks, eventually falling into ruin.

The **Church of the Holy Rude** is a little farther down Castle Wynd, on St John St. It has been the town's parish church for 500 years. James VI was crowned here in 1567. The nave and tower date from 1456 and the church features one of the few surviving medieval open-timber roofs. The church opens 10 am to 5 pm daily, May to September. Behind the church is the **Guildhall** (also known as Cowane's Hospital), built as an almshouse in 1637 by the rich merchant John Cowane. It's now used as a genealogy centre and for ceilidhs, banquets and concerts.

The **Mercat Cross**, in Broad St, is topped with a unicorn and was once surrounded by a bustling market. Nearby is the **Tolbooth**, built in 1705 as the town's administrative centre. A courthouse and jail were added in the following century. The **Old Town Jail** opens 9.30 am to 6 pm daily, April to September; until 5 pm during October; and until 4 pm November to March. Admission costs £3.30/2.45. There are displays on prison life, 'living history' performances, and a good view from the roof. At the end of Broad St is **Darnley House**, where Mary Queen of Scots' second husband, Lord Darnley, is said to have stayed.

Where does the sky end and Skye begin? The Black Cullin mirrored in the waters of a small lochan

All metal and masts: the colourful boats of Ullapool anchored at the end of a day's work, Wester Ross

The crude landscape of the Cromarty Firth is illuminated by the rays of the setting sun.

'Wherever I wander, wherever I roam/ The hills of the Highlands for ever I love': Robert Burns

In dire need of a trim: Highland cattle in Scourie

Turning pink over Loch Scavaig, Isle of Skye

Wallace Monument

Two miles north of Stirling is Scotland's Victorian monument to Sir William Wallace, who was hung, drawn and quartered by the English in 1305. The view from the top is as breathtaking as the climb up, and the monument contains interesting displays including a parade of other Scottish heroes and Wallace's mighty two-handed sword. Clearly the man was no weakling.

The Wallace Monument (☎ 472140) is open from 10 am to 5 pm daily, March to May (and October); 10 am to 6 pm June and September; 9.30 am to 6.30 pm July and August; and 10 am to 4 pm November to February. Admission costs £3.30/2.30. June to September, an open-top tour bus links the monument with Stirling Castle, but you could also walk (see Walking & Cycling Routes).

Bannockburn

On 24 June 1314 the greatest victory in Scotland's struggle to remain independent took place at the Battle of Bannockburn. At the Bannockburn Heritage Centre (☎ 812664), owned by the National Trust for Scotland (NTS; see Historic Organisations under Useful Organisations in the Facts for the Visitor chapter for details) the story is told with audiovisual displays. Outside is the Borestone site, said to be Robert the Bruce's command post before the battle. There's also his grim-looking statue, dressed in full battle gear and mounted on a charger.

The site, 2 miles south of Stirling, never closes but the heritage centre opens 10 am to 5.30 pm daily, April to October; the last audiovisual show is at 5 pm; in March, November and December, it opens daily from 11 am to 3 pm. Admission is free.

Cambuskenneth Abbey

The only substantial remnant of this Augustinian abbey, founded in 1147, is the belfry. In medieval times, Cambuskenneth became one of the richest abbeys in the country, and its high status is supported by the fact that Robert the Bruce held his parliament here in 1326, and James III and his queen are both buried here. The abbey is a

mile east of Stirling Castle and opens at all times. There is no admission charge.

Walking & Cycling Routes

The best way to reach the Wallace Monument is on foot (1½ miles from the town centre) or by bike. Cross the railway line on Seaforth Place, continue straight ahead into Shore Road and Abbey Rd. There's a footbridge over the River Forth to Cambuskenneth, where you should visit the ruins of the abbey. The Wallace Monument is a mile north of here; follow Ladysneuk Rd and turn left at the junction with Alloa Rd.

Organised Tours

Popular guided ghost walks leave at 8.30 pm Tuesday to Saturday, May to September, from the Old Town Jail (£5/3). The TIC has details.

From May to early October Guide Friday's (☎ 0131-556 2244) open-top, hop-on hop-off bus tour runs hourly from the castle, through the city to the Wallace Monument; there are two buses every hour. A day ticket costs £6/2.

Special Events

The town puts on an entertaining program of events in summer, including ceilidhs at the Guildhall (Cowane's Hospital) on Monday and Saturday evening, pipe bands on Tuesday and Saturday, and medieval markets. There are also 'living history' plays performed in and around the castle.

Places to Stay

Camping Scenic *Witches Craig Caravan & Camping Park* (☎ 474947), Blairlogie, on the edge of the Ochil Hills, 3 miles east of Stirling by the A91, costs £9.50 per site (two people).

Hostels The facade of a 19th-century church conceals the *Stirling Youth Hostel* (☎ 473442, St John St), in a perfect location in the old part of town. Open year-round, it's a superb modern hostel with 126 beds in small dorms; the £11.50/9.95 charge for adults/under-18s includes a continental breakfast. The hostel has a less attractive but comfortable annexe in Union St, open June to September only.

On the landscaped *Stirling Holiday Campus* (☎ 467141), near Bridge of Allan, 3 miles north of town, student rooms are let from June to August for £20 and there's a pub, golf course and cinema here. Take bus Nos 53 or 58 from Stirling.

B&Bs & Hotels There's a clutch of B&Bs on Linden Ave (just off Burghmuir Rd), which is fairly close to the bus station and less than half a mile from the train station. *Linden Guest House* (☎ 448850), No 22, has double rooms from £20 per person. *Hopeton* (☎ 473418), No 28, charges £20/36 a single/double for its three ground-floor rooms.

Across from the TIC is the pleasant *Woodside Guest House* (☎ 475470, 4 Back Walk), where B&B costs from £18/32 with bathroom. Equally close to the TIC, *Burnsview Guesthouse* (☎ 451002, 1 Albert Place) has three rooms and charges from £20 per person. Conveniently central *Mrs MacGregor's* (☎ 471082, 27 King St) does B&B from £20/32; dinner is £7 extra.

A short walk north of the train station is the excellent *Forth Guest House* (☎ 471 020, 23 Forth Place), just off Seaforth Rd. It's a small Georgian terrace house with a tiny rose-filled front garden and three comfortable rooms, all with bathroom. B&B costs from £25/39.

Central *Mrs Cairns'* (☎ 479228, 12 Princes St) is an easy walk from the train station. B&B costs from £18/20 per person, without/with bathroom. *Fairfield Guest House* (☎ 472685, 14 Princes St) has five rooms, all with bathroom, from £23/40 a single/double, plus a varied choice for breakfast.

Friendly, efficient *Terraces Hotel* (☎ 472 268, ℮ terraceshotel@compuserve.com, 4 Melville Terrace) is popular with businesspeople during the week, and rooms cost £68/80. It also serves good food and real ales.

The town's smartest hotel is *Stirling Highland Hotel* (☎ 475444, ℮ andrews@scottish highlandhotels.co.uk, Spittal St), a sympathetic refurbishment of the old high school. B&B costs £116.50/165 in summer, but there are less-expensive, special offers available.

Places to Eat

There are good views from the *Overport Café* at Stirling Castle but it's rather overpriced. Down the hill from the castle, at the end of Broad St *Darnley Coffee House* (☎ 474468), in Darnley House, does good coffee and tea and is a convenient pit stop as you walk around the Old Town.

Barnton Bar & Bistro (312 Barnton St), opposite the main post office, is a popular student hangout serving excellent all-day breakfasts. Open daily and until 1 am at weekends, it's a great place to eat or drink. Nearby, the licensed *Smiling Jack's Tex Mex* (☎ 462809, 17 Barnton St) does quesadillas from £6. It opens daily for lunch and dinner.

Italia Nostra (☎ 473208, 25 Baker St) is a busy Italian place that also serves gelati and does takeaways; pasta dishes cost £6.20 to £8.50. The *Hogshead*, on the corner of Baker and Friars Sts, does good bar meals including a varied vegetarian selection, for around £5.

The basement *East India Company* (☎ 471330, 7 Viewfield Place) is a good Indian restaurant and takeaway.

Close to the castle, *Archie's Bar & Grill* (☎ 473929, 39 Broad St) was formerly the town's bathhouse. It now serves contemporary Scottish cuisine (mains £8 to £20) and specialist ales and wines. It opens for dinner 6 to 9 pm daily (9.30 pm Friday and Saturday), for lunch Wednesday to Sunday noon to 2.30 pm.

Hermann's (☎ 450632, 58 Broad St) is an excellent Scottish-Austrian restaurant with a two course set lunch for £8.95 and a more expensive dinner menu. It opens noon to 2.30 pm and 6 to 9 pm Monday to Friday; and noon to 10 pm at weekends. Popular *Melville's* (☎ 472268), at the Terraces Hotel (see Places to Stay), has good bar meals from £7 to £13.50.

Entertainment

Portcullis (☎ 472290, Castle Wynd), below the castle, serves a good range of malt whiskies and pub meals all day. There are two pubs farther down St Mary's Wynd: *Whistlebinkies* and the very popular *Settle*

Inn – the oldest pub in Stirling, dating from 1773. *Barnton Bar & Bistro* (see Places to Eat) is another popular place for a drink.

Getting There & Away
Stirling is 26 miles north of Glasgow, 35 from Edinburgh and 420 from London.

Bus Scottish Citylink has a number of services, usually hourly, from Glasgow (£3.20, 45 minutes). Some buses continue to Aberdeen via Perth and Dundee. Stirling to Aberdeen takes 3½ hours and costs £13.20; you'll probably need to change at Perth. Local services are operated by First Midland Bluebird (☎ 01324-613777) and First Edinburgh (same phone number).

Train ScotRail runs services to Edinburgh (£5, 50 minutes) twice an hour most of the day, Monday to Saturday, hourly on Sunday. Not all services are direct. There are hourly trains from Glasgow (£4.20, 40 minutes) and frequent services to Perth (£7.40, 35 minutes), Dundee (one hour, £11.30) and Aberdeen (£30, 2¼ hours). For rail information call ☎ 0845 748 4950.

Car Arnold Clark (☎ 478686), Kerse Rd, provides rental cars; cheapest are Fiats at £16 per day including insurance and 250 free miles.

Getting Around
It's easy to walk around the town centre. From the train station to the castle is about three-quarters of a mile uphill. Woodside Taxis (☎ 450005) can organise sightseeing trips for up to four people at around £18 per hour.

AROUND STIRLING
Dunblane
Dunblane, 5 miles north-west of Stirling, will for many years be associated with the horrific massacre that took place in the primary school in 1996. The TIC (☎ 01786-824428), Stirling Rd, is open from May to mid-September.

The main interest is **Dunblane Cathedral**. Beloved of Ruskin, it's a simple, elegant,

sandstone building – a superb example of the Gothic style. The lower parts of the walls date from Norman times; the rest is mainly 13th to 15th century. The roof of the nave collapsed in the 16th century, but the cathedral was saved from ruin by a major restoration project in the 1890s. It opens 9.30 am to 6.30 pm Monday to Saturday, 2 to 6 pm Sunday, April to September; 9.30 am to 4 pm Monday to Saturday, 2 to 4 pm Sunday, October to March.

Opposite, the small **Cathedral Museum**, on the square, relates the history of both cathedral and town. It opens 10 am to 12.30 pm and 2 to 4.30 pm Monday to Saturday, May to October. You can walk to the small town of **Bridge of Allan** from Dunblane along the Darn Rd, an ancient path used by the monks; alternatively, there are frequent buses from Stirling.

First Midland Bluebird (☎ 01324-613777) runs buses hourly to Dunblane from Stirling. Trains from Stirling run every 15 to 30 minutes.

Doune
Seven miles north-west of Stirling, Doune is now a quiet rural town. It was once the capital of the ancient kingdom of Menteith, and was later a famous centre for the manufacture of sporrans and pistols.

Doune Castle (☎ 01786-841742) is one of the best preserved 14th-century castles in Scotland, having remained largely unchanged since it was built for the Duke of Albany. It was a favourite royal hunting lodge, but was also of great strategic importance because it controlled the route between the Lowlands and Highlands. Mary Queen of Scots stayed here, as did Bonnie Prince Charlie – the first as a guest, the second as a prisoner. There are great views from the castle walls and the lofty gatehouse is impressive, rising nearly 30m. The castle opens standard HS hours (but October to March it's closed Thursday afternoon, Friday and Sunday mornings). Admission costs £2.50/1.

Monday to Saturday, there are First Midland Bluebird (☎ 01324-613777) buses every hour or so to Doune from Stirling (£2.40).

CENTRAL SCOTLAND

Dollar

About 11 miles east of Stirling, in the foothills of the Ochil Hills that run east into Perthshire, is the small town of Dollar. **Castle Campbell** (☎ 01259-742408) is a 20-minute walk into the hills above the town. It's a spooky old stronghold of the dukes of Argyll and stands between two ravines; you can clearly see why it was known as Castle Gloom. There's been a fortress of some kind on this site from the 11th century, but the present structure dates from the 15th century. Opening hours and charges are as for Doune Castle.

There are buses to Dollar from Stirling (hourly Monday to Saturday) and Alloa (every two hours, Monday to Saturday). From Kinross, bus No 204 runs twice a day Monday to Friday.

THE TROSSACHS

The narrow glen between Loch Katrine and Loch Achray is named the Trossachs, but it's also used to describe a wider scenic area around the southern border of the Highlands. It's now part of a national park that includes Loch Lomond in Argyll.

As the tourist literature repeatedly informs you, this is Rob Roy country. Rob Roy Macgregor (1671–1734) was the wild leader of the wildest of Scotland's clans, Clan Gregor. Although he claimed direct descent from a 10th-century king of the Scots and rights to the lands the clan occupied, these Macgregor lands stood between powerful neighbours. Rob Roy became notorious for his daring raids into the Lowlands to carry off cattle and sheep, but these escapades led to the outlawing of the clan – hence their sobriquet 'Children of the Mist'. He also achieved a reputation as a champion of the poor. He lies buried in the churchyard at Balquhidder, by Loch Voil.

Walter Scott's historical novel *Rob Roy* brought tourists to the region in the 19th century. Loch Katrine was the inspiration for Scott's *Lady of the Lake* and, since the beginning of the 20th century, the SS *Sir Walter Scott* has been taking visitors across Loch Katrine. The main centres in the area are Aberfoyle and Callander. Postbuses and,

May to September the Trossachs Trundler, link these two places with Loch Katrine.

Aberfoyle

☎ 01877 • pop 600

Known as the southern gateway to the Trossachs, Aberfoyle is on the eastern edge of the Queen Elizabeth Forest Park, which stretches across to the hills beside Loch Lomond. The large TIC (☎ 382352), Main St, opens daily April to October, weekends only November to March.

Four miles east off the A81 is one of Scotland's two lakes, **Lake Menteith**. The substantial ruins of Inchmahome Priory (☎ 385 294; HS) where Mary Queen of Scots was kept safe as a child, during Henry VIII's 'Rough Wooing' (see under Old Town in the Stirling section), are on Inchmahome Island. A ferry takes visitors from the village to the priory. It opens 9.30 am to 6.30 pm daily (last sailing 5.15 pm), April to September; 9.30 am to 4.30 pm Monday to Saturday, and 2 to 4.30 pm Sunday (last sailing 3.15 pm), October. Admission costs £3/1 including the ferry.

On a hill, about half a mile north of Aberfoyle, on the A821, is the **Queen Elizabeth Forest Park Visitors Centre** (☎ 382258), which has information about the numerous walks and cycle routes in and around the park. There are good views from the centre.

Walking & Cycling Routes Waymarked trails start from the visitors centre on the hills above the town.

An excellent 20 mile circular cycle route links with the ferry (☎ 385294) across Loch Katrine. From Aberfoyle, join the Glasgow, Loch Lomond & Killin Cycle Way on the forest trail, or take the A821 over Duke's Pass. Following the southern shore of Loch Achray, you reach the pier on Loch Katrine. The ferry should drop you at Stronachlachar, on the western shore (note that afternoon sailings don't stop here). From Stronachlachar, follow the B829 via Loch Ard to Aberfoyle.

Places to Stay & Eat Off the A81, 2 miles south of Aberfoyle, *Cobleland Caravan & Camping Site* (☎ 382392) charges £7.50 for sites. In Aberfoyle, *Mrs Phillips* (☎ 382696, *Forth House, Lochard Rd*) offers B&B for £20 per person, with bathroom.

In the middle of the village, the *Forth Inn* (☎ 382372, *Main St*) does B&B from £17.50/35 to £27.50/46 in singles/doubles all with bathroom, though you'll have to put up with some noise from the bar. Pub meals are available all day.

Getting There & Away First Edinburgh (☎ 01324-613777) has up to five buses a day from Stirling. For the Trossachs Trundler see Getting There & Away in the Callander section.

Callander
☎ 01877 • pop 3000

Callander, 14 miles north of Stirling, is a large tourist town that bills itself as the eastern gateway to the Trossachs. It has been pulling in the tourists for over 150 years, and tartan shops and cafes line the long main drag.

The **Rob Roy & Trossachs Visitor Centre** (☎ 330342) is also the TIC, open year round. A Rob Roy audiovisual is shown 9.30 am to 6 pm, June; 9 am to 10 pm, July and August; 10 am to 6 pm, September; 10 am to 5 pm, March to May and October to December; 11 am to 4.30 pm weekends only, January and February. Admission costs £2.75/1.25.

Places to Stay Accommodation is plentiful. Purpose-built *Trossachs Backpackers* (☎ 331200) is in a beautifully isolated spot; take Bridge St off Main St, then turn right onto Invertrossachs Rd and follow the road, which runs on the southern side of the river draining Loch Vennachar, for a mile. All rooms have their own bathroom and family rooms have their own kitchen. Beds are £12.50 to £15, including sheets and breakfast. If you ring they'll pick you up from the TIC or bus stop.

Greenbank Guest House (☎ 330296, *143 Main St*), in a two-storey terraced house, charges £15 per person. North of town, *Arden House* (☎ 330235, *Bracklinn Rd*) is an excellent place and was used as the setting for the TV series *Doctor Finlay's Casebook*.

B&B is £27.50/50 a single/double. Upmarket *Roman Camp Hotel* (☎ 330003), beautifully located by the river, dates from 1625 and has a good restaurant. Rooms cost from £75/95.

Getting There & Away First Edinburgh (☎ 01324-613777) operates buses hourly from Stirling (£2.90, 45 minutes). The Trossachs Trundler calls here on its circuit which includes Aberfoyle, Port of Lentieth and Trossachs Pier on Loch Katrine (35 minutes from Callander). The bus operates five times a day Sunday to Friday, May to September; the full trip takes 1½ hours and costs £5.50/3.50.

Getting Around Callander Cycling Centre (☎ 331100), based at Trossachs Backpackers (see Places to Stay), hires out bikes for £7.50/12.50 a half/full day.

Loch Katrine & Loch Achray

This rugged area, 6 miles north of Aberfoyle and 10 miles west of Callander, is the heart of the Trossachs. From April to October, SS *Sir Walter Scott* (☎ 01877-376316) sails Loch Katrine from Trossachs Pier at the eastern tip of the loch; tickets cost £5.50/3.60.

NORTH CENTRAL REGION
Crianlarich & Tyndrum

These villages (combined population 350) are little more than service junctions on the main A82 road, although they're both in good hiking country and on the **West Highland Way**. Tyndrum has a TIC (☎ 01838-400246), open April to October, across from the Invervey Hotel which serves food.

With good views, *Crianlarich Youth Hostel* (☎ 01838-300260, *Station Rd*), near the train station, has dorm beds for £9.25/8 for adults/under-18s; it opens February to December.

There are buses from Killin, once a day on Tuesday, Thursday and Saturday, plus daily rail connections from Fort William, Oban, Edinburgh and Glasgow.

Killin

In the north-eastern corner of the region, just west of Loch Tay, Killin (population

700) is a pleasant village to use as a base for exploring the hills and glens of the surrounding area. The TIC (☎ 01567-820254), in the Breadalbane Folklore Centre, Main St, opens daily March to October, weekends in February. Killin is a popular destination for tour buses that bring people to see the pretty **Falls of Dochart** in the centre of the village.

Walking & Cycling Routes Killin is at the northern end of the cycle way from Glasgow (see Getting Around at the start of the Stirling & Around section).

Five miles north-west of Killin and rising above Loch Tay is Ben Lawers (1214m, 3984 feet). There's a NTS visitor centre and trails lead to the summit (see West Perthshire under Perthshire & Kinross later in the chapter).

Places to Stay & Eat Pleasant *Killin Youth Hostel (☎ 01567-820546)*, open daily March to October (Friday and Saturday only the rest of the year), charges £8.75/7.75 for adults/under-18s.

There are numerous B&Bs and hotels. At the 17th-century *Falls of Dochart Cottage (☎ 01567-820363)*, in the middle of the village, there's comfy B&B from £17 per person. *Clachaig Hotel (☎ 01567-820270)* overlooks the falls; all rooms have bathrooms and cost from £22/40 a single/double.

Getting There & Away First Edinburgh (☎ 01324-613777) operates a service five times daily Monday to Friday (twice on Saturday) from Stirling (£4.75, 1¼ hours) via Callander. There's no bus from Pitlochry to Killin, but Monday to Friday there's a postbus service (No 202) between Aberfeldy and Killin (three hours).

Fife

This region, lying between the Firths of Forth and Tay, refers to itself as the Kingdom of Fife – it was home to Scottish kings for 500 years.

Despite its integration with the rest of Scotland it has managed to maintain an individual Lowland identity, separate from the rest of the country. As they still say outside the region, 'It takes a long spoon to sup with a Fifer'.

In the west, the Lomond Hills rise to over 500m; the eastern section is much flatter. Apart from a few notable exceptions inland, Fife's main attractions are around the coast. For most visitors, the focus of the region is undoubtedly St Andrews – an ancient university town and ecclesiastical centre that's also world famous as the home of golf. In the south, along the indented coastline of East Neuk, are picturesque fishing villages. This coast is pleasant walking country, and the **Fife Coastal Path** runs 46 miles between North Queensferry and Crail. At Anstruther there's the interesting Scottish Fisheries Museum.

For information contact the Fife Tourist Board (☎ 01592 750066, ℮ fife.tourism@ kftb.ossian.net) or you can visit its Web site at standrews.rroom.net/fife/fifehome.htm.

GETTING AROUND

Fife Council produces a useful transport map, *Getting Around Fife*, available from TICs, bus and train stations and has a Public Transport Information Line (☎ 01592-416060). Fife Scottish (☎ 01334-474238) is the main bus operator.

Trains are less useful in Fife than in some regions as the tracks don't run along the coast or to St Andrews: the nearest station is at Leuchars, 5 miles to the north-west.

If you're driving from the Forth Road Bridge to St Andrews, a slower but much more scenic route than the M90/A91 is along the signposted Fife Coastal Tourist Route.

WESTERN FIFE
Culross
☎ 01383 • pop 460
Around the 17th century, Culross (pronounced coo-ross), 12 miles west of the Forth Rd Bridge off the A985, was a busy little community trading in salt and coal. Now it's the best preserved example of a Scottish burgh and the NTS owns 20 of the buildings, including the palace. It's a picturesque village with small, red-tiled, white-washed buildings lining the cobbled streets.

Culross has a long history. As the birthplace of St Mungo, the patron saint of Glasgow, Culross was an important religious centre from the 6th century. The burgh developed as a trading centre under the businesslike laird George Bruce (a descendant of Robert the Bruce), whose mining techniques involved digging long tunnels under the sea to reach coal. A vigorous sea trade developed between Culross and the Forth ports and Holland. From the proceeds Bruce built the palace, completed in 1611. When a storm flooded the tunnels and mining became impossible the town switched to making linen and shoes.

The NTS Visitors Centre (☎ 880359), in the lower part of the Town House, has an exhibition on the history of Culross. You can visit **Culross Palace**, more a large house than a palace, which features decorative, painted woodwork and an interior largely unchanged since the early 17th century. The **Town House** and the **Study**, also early 17th century, are open to the public, but the other NTS properties can only be viewed from the outside. The opening hours for buildings are 1 to 5 pm daily, April, May and September; 10 am to 5 pm daily, June to August; and 1 to 5 pm October weekends. Admission costs £5/1.

On the hill, the grand, ruined **Culross Abbey** (HS), founded by the Cistercians in 1217, is open daily; the choir of the abbey church is now the parish church.

Stagecoach Fife (☎ 01592-642394) bus Nos 14/14A run hourly, every day, between Glasgow, Stirling, Culross and Dunfermline.

Dunfermline
☎ 01383 • pop 52,000

Six Scottish kings, including Robert the Bruce, are buried at Dunfermline Abbey. Once the country's capital, Dunfermline is now a large regional centre surrounded by suburbs that aren't particularly attractive, but the abbey's worth a visit.

Orientation & Information The train station is 600m west of the town centre and the bus station is in the centre; both are within walking distance of the abbey. The TIC (☎ 720999), 13 Maygate, opens 9.30 to

5.30 pm Monday to Saturday, year round; and 11 am to 4 pm Sunday, April to September.

Things to See In the 12th century David I built **Dunfermline Abbey** (HS) on the hill here as a Benedictine monastery. It grew into a major religious centre, eclipsing the island of Iona (off Mull) as the favourite royal burial ground. The large intact building you see today is actually made up of two connected halves. There's the original 12th century half, with its external buttresses, which is closed to visitors; a church was added to it in the early 19th century and it's here that Robert the Bruce is buried under the pulpit. You can visit the church April to September, weekdays from 9.30 am to 6 pm, 2 to 6 pm Sunday (October to March it closes at 4 pm).

Next to the abbey are the ruins of **Dunfermline Palace** (☎ 739026; HS) rebuilt from the abbey guesthouse in the 16th century for James VI. It was the birthplace of Charles I, the last Scottish king born on Scottish soil. The palace is open standard HS hours. Admission costs £2/75p.

Dunfermline's most famous former inhabitant was Andrew Carnegie, born in a weaver's cottage, now a museum, in 1835. He emigrated to America in 1848 and by the late 19th century had accumulated enormous wealth, US$350 million of which he gave away. Dunfermline benefited by his purchase of Pittencrieff Park, beside the palace, which he opened to the public. **Carnegie Birthplace Museum** (☎ 724302), Moodie St, opens 11 am to 5 pm Monday to Saturday, 2 to 5 pm Sunday, April to October; 2 to 4 pm daily November to March. Admission is £1.50/free.

Dunfermline is a major transport hub, with buses hourly to Glasgow, Edinburgh, Stirling and Dundee. It's a half hour train ride from Edinburgh, and there's at least one direct train an hour, Monday to Saturday, two an hour on Sunday.

SOUTH COAST
Aberdour
☎ 01383 • pop 1800

It's worth pausing in this popular seaside town to see **Aberdour Castle** (☎ 860519; HS). It was built by the Douglas family in

1342 and the original tower was extended in the 16th and 17th centuries. By the 18th century it was partly in ruins and abandoned by its owners. The east wing is still in use, however. An impressive feature of the castle is its attractive walled garden. There's a fine circular dovecote (called a doocot in Scotland), shaped like a beehive, dating from the 16th century. **St Fillan's Chapel**, in the grounds, dates from the 12th century. The castle opens standard HS hours (but closes Thursday afternoon, Friday and Sunday morning, October to March). Admission costs £2/75p.

Stagecoach Fife (☎ 01592-642394) bus No 57 runs every two hours to Edinburgh, daily; bus No 7 runs twice an hour to Dunfermline and Kirkcaldy, Monday to Saturday (hourly on Sunday).

Kirkcaldy
☎ 01592 • pop 49,570
Kirkcaldy (pronounced **kir**-koddy) stretches along the edge of the sea for several miles and has an attractive promenade, an interesting museum and an art gallery. In the second half of the 19th century it was the world's largest manufacturer of linoleum. The TIC (☎ 267775), 19 Whytecauseway, opens 10 am to 5 pm Monday to Saturday, year round.

Kirkcaldy Museum & Art Gallery (☎ 412 860) is beside the train station and a short walk from the bus station. As well as covering the town's history, the museum has a small display on the political economist Adam Smith, who was born in Kirkcaldy; the gallery houses an impressive collection of Scottish and English paintings from the 18th and 19th centuries. The gallery and museum open 10.30 am to 5 pm Monday to Saturday, 2 to 5 pm Sunday. Admission is free.

After looking around the museum, you could walk along the Esplanade to ruined **Ravenscraig Castle**, in the park by the sea. Two miles north of Kirkcaldy, in Dysart, the **John MacDouall Stuart Museum** (☎ 260732), the birthplace of the engineer and explorer who in 1862 became the first person to cross Australia from the south coast to the north. It opens 2 to 5 pm daily, June to August. Admission is free. Bus Nos X26 and X27 from Kirkcaldy centre pass this way every hour.

If you're staying, **Invertiel House** (☎ 264 849, 21 Pratt St), just south of the centre by Beveridge Park, is a comfortable Victorian place with B&B from £24/40 a single/double.

Kirkcaldy is a major transport hub and from Hill St bus station (☎ 642394), two blocks inland from the Esplanade, there are numerous buses including hourly buses to Edinburgh and Glasgow and three per hour to Dunfermline. The town is on the main Edinburgh/Glasgow to Dundee/Aberdeen rail line. There are two trains an hour to Edinburgh (£5, 30 minutes).

CENTRAL FIFE
Falkland
☎ 01337 • pop 1120
Below the soft ridges of the Lomond Hills in the centre of Fife is the attractive village of Falkland, surrounded by rich farmland and with many buildings of architectural or historical importance. A pleasant place to stay, it's known for its superb 16th-century **Falkland Palace** (☎ 857397; NTS), a country residence of the Stuart monarchs. Mary Queen of Scots is said to have spent the happiest days of her life 'playing the country girl in the woods and parks' at Falkland.

French and Scottish craftspeople were employed to create this masterpiece of Scottish Gothic architecture, built between 1501 and 1541 to replace a castle dating from the 12th century. The chapel, which has a beautiful painted ceiling, and the king's bedchamber have both been restored; you can also look around the keeper's apartments in the gatehouse.

The wild boar that the royals hunted, and the Fife forest that was their hunting ground, have now disappeared. One feature of this royal leisure centre still exists: the oldest royal tennis court in Britain, built in 1539 for James V, is in the grounds and still in use. Although the palace still belongs to the Queen, it's administered by the NTS.

Falkland Palace opens 11 am to 5.30 pm Monday to Saturday, 1.30 to 5.30 pm Sunday, April to October. Admission is £5/free.

Places to Stay & Eat Though usually open mid-March to early October, *Falkland*

Backpackers (☎ 858367, Back Wynd) was closed at the time of research for renovations; call for rates. Opposite the palace, there's the *Hunting Lodge Hotel (☎ 857226, High St)* offering B&B (with one en-suite room) from £20 per person. It also serves bar meals (from around £7) at lunch and dinner, plus snacks during the day.

Getting There & Away Falkland is 11 miles north of Kirkcaldy. There are three Stagecoach Fife (☎ 01592-642394) buses a day Monday to Saturday to Kinross (see the Perthshire & Kinross section later in the chapter), and buses roughly every two hours from Perth and Cupar. The nearest train station is 5 miles away at Markinch, on the Edinburgh-Dundee line.

Cupar & Around
☎ 01334 • pop 7610

Cupar is a pleasant market town and the capital of the region. The main reason to visit is to see the **Hill of Tarvit Mansion House** (☎ 653127; NTS), off the A916 half a mile south of town. It was rebuilt for Frederick Sharp in the late 1800s by Scottish architect Robert Lorimer. Sharp was a wealthy Dundee jute manufacturer who bought the house as a showcase for his valuable collection of furniture, Dutch paintings, Flemish tapestries and Chinese porcelain. A 15 minute walk takes you to the top of the Hill of Tarvit, which has an excellent panoramic view. The house opens 1.30 to 5.30 pm daily, Easter to June and September; 11 am to 5.30 pm daily, July and August. Admission is £4/free. The grounds open 9.30 am to 9 pm daily, April to September.

Cupar is a busy transport centre with direct daily Stagecoach Fife (☎ 01592-642394) bus services hourly to St Andrews, Dundee and Edinburgh. It's also on the rail line between Edinburgh (one hour) and Dundee (20 minutes), one per hour.

ST ANDREWS
☎ 01334 • pop 13,900

St Andrews is a beautiful, unusual seaside town – a concoction of medieval ruins, obsessed golfers, windy coastal scenery, tourist kitsch and an ancient university where wealthy English undergraduates rub shoulders with Scottish theology students.

Although St Andrews was once the ecclesiastical capital of Scotland, both its cathedral and castle are now in ruins. For most people the town is the home of golf. It's the headquarters of the game's governing body, the Royal & Ancient Golf Club, and the location of the world's most famous golf course, the Old Course.

History

St Andrews is said to have been founded by the Greek monk St Regulus in the 4th century. He brought important relics from Greece, including some of the bones of St Andrew, who became Scotland's patron saint.

The town soon grew into a major pilgrimage centre for the shrine of the saint. The Church of St Regulus was built in 1130 (only the tower remains); the adjacent cathedral was built in 1160. St Andrews developed into an ecclesiastical centre and, around 1200, the castle (part fortress, part residence) was constructed for the bishop.

The university was founded in 1410, the first in Scotland. James I received part of his education here, as did James III. By the mid-16th century there were three colleges: St Salvator's, St Leonard's School and St Mary's.

Although golf was being played here by the 15th century, the Old Course dates from the following century. The Royal & Ancient Golf Club was founded in 1754 and the imposing clubhouse was built a hundred years later. The British Open Championship, which was first held in 1860 in Prestwick, on the west coast near Glasgow, has taken place regularly at St Andrews since 1873.

Orientation

St Andrews preserves its medieval plan of parallel streets with small closes leading off them. The most important parts of the old town, lying east of the bus station, are easily explored on foot. The main commercial streets are Market and South Sts, running east-west. Like Cambridge and Oxford, St Andrews has no campus – the university

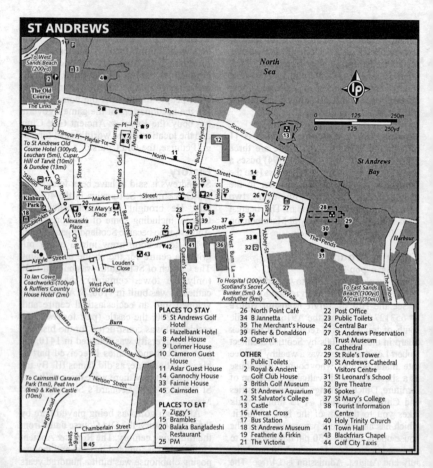

ST ANDREWS

PLACES TO STAY
5 St Andrews Golf Hotel
6 Hazelbank Hotel
8 Aedel House
9 Lorimer House
10 Cameron Guest House
11 Aslar Guest House
14 Gannochy House
33 Fairnie House
45 Cairnsden

PLACES TO EAT
7 Ziggy's
15 Brambles
20 Balaka Bangladeshi Restaurant
25 PM

26 North Point Café
34 B Jannetta
35 The Merchant's House
39 Fisher & Donaldson
42 Ogston's

OTHER
1 Public Toilets
2 Royal & Ancient Golf Club House
3 British Golf Museum
4 St Andrews Aquarium
12 St Salvator's College
13 Castle
16 Mercat Cross
17 Bus Station
18 St Andrews Museum
19 Featherie & Firkin
21 The Victoria

22 Post Office
23 Public Toilets
24 Central Bar
27 St Andrews Preservation Trust Museum
28 Cathedral
29 St Rule's Tower
30 St Andrews Cathedral Visitors Centre
31 St Leonard's School
32 Byre Theatre
36 Spokes
37 St Mary's College
38 Tourist Information Centre
40 Holy Trinity Church
41 Town Hall
43 Blackfriars Chapel
44 Golf City Taxis

buildings are integrated into the central part of the town. There's a small harbour near the cathedral and two sandy beaches: East Sands extends south from the harbour and the wider West Sands is north of town.

Information

The TIC (☎ 472021), 70 Market St, makes theatre and Edinburgh Military Tattoo bookings and sells NTS passes. It opens 9.30 am to 6 pm Monday to Saturday, 11 am to 4 pm Sunday, April and May; 9.30 am to 7 pm Monday to Saturday, 11 am to 6 pm Sunday, June and September to mid-October; 9.30 am

to 8 pm Monday to Saturday, 11 am to 6 pm Sunday, July and August; and 9.30 am to 5 pm Monday to Saturday the rest of the year.

The post office is at 127 South St. It opens 9 am to 5.30 pm Monday to Friday, 9 am to 12.30 pm Saturday.

Half-day closing is on Thursday, but in summer many shops stay open. Parking requires a voucher, on sale in the TIC and many shops.

Walking Tour

A good place to start a walking tour is **St Andrews Museum** (☎ 477706), Doubledykes

Rd, near the bus station. Displays chart the history of the town from its founding by St Regulus through its growth as an ecclesiastical, academic and sporting centre. More interesting than some local history museums, it opens 10 am to 5 pm daily, April to September; 10.30 am to 4 pm Monday to Friday, 12.30 to 5 pm Saturday and Sunday, October to March. Admission is free.

Turn left out of the museum driveway and follow Doubledykes Rd back to the roundabout. Turn right, then left into South St. You pass through **West Port**, formerly Southgait Port, the main entrance to the old city. It was remodelled in 1589 on Netherbow Port in Edinburgh. Walking down South St, you pass **Louden's Close** on the right, a good example of the closes built according to the city's medieval street plan. Continuing along South St, the apse of the 16th-century **Blackfriars Chapel** stands in front of Madras College.

Opposite the Victorian town hall is **Holy Trinity**, the town's parish church, built in 1410. On the same side of the street as the town hall is **St Mary's College**, founded in 1537; beside it is the university library. The oak in the courtyard is over 250 years old.

Cross over to cobbled Market St – parallel (one street north) to South St – via Church St. Street markets are held around **Mercat Cross**, although the cross is now a fountain. The TIC is nearby, at No 70. At the TIC, follow Market St down to the junction with South Castle St, turn left, and then right into North St. On the right is **St Andrews Preservation Trust Museum** (☎ 477629), an old merchant's house and a museum of local social history. The museum is open 10 am to 5 pm daily, June to October. Admission is free.

It's interesting to note that St Andrews didn't retain its medieval character by accident. In the mid-19th century, the provost (mayor) Hugh Lyon Playfair implemented plans for sympathetic civic improvements making sure that they didn't involve the destruction of old buildings.

St Andrews Cathedral At the eastern end of North St is the ruined western end of St Andrews cathedral, once the largest and one of the most magnificent cathedrals in the country. Although it was founded in 1160, it wasn't consecrated until 1318. It stood as the focus of this important pilgrimage centre until 1559, when it was pillaged during the Reformation. Many of the town's buildings are constructed from the stones of the cathedral.

St Andrew's bones lay under the high altar; until the cathedral was built, they had been enshrined in the nearby Church of St Regulus (St Rule). All that remains is **St Rule's Tower**, well worth the climb for the view across St Andrews and a great place for taking photographs. In the same area are parts of the ruined 13th-century **priory**. The visitors centre includes the calefactory, the only room where the monks could warm themselves by a fire; masons' marks on the red sandstone blocks, identifying who shaped each block, can still be seen clearly. There's also a collection of Celtic crosses and gravestones found on the site.

The cathedral site opens standard HS hours; tickets are £3.75/1.25 including admission to the castle. If you only want to visit the cathedral, it's £2/75p.

St Andrews Castle Round from the cathedral, above the sea, St Andrews castle was founded around 1200 as the fortified home of the bishop. In the 1450s the young king James II often stayed here. A visitors centre gives a good audiovisual introduction and has a small collection of Pictish stones.

In 1654 part of the castle was pulled down to provide building materials for the harbour wall. Enough survives to give you an idea of what each of the chambers was used for. After the execution of Protestant reformers in 1545, other reformers retaliated by murdering Cardinal Beaton and taking over the castle. The cardinal's body was hung from a window in the Fore Tower before being tossed into the bottle-shaped dungeon. The reformers then spent almost a year besieged in the castle; one of the most interesting things to see is the complex of **siege tunnels**, said to be the best surviving example of siege engineering in Europe. You can walk along the damp, mossy tunnels, lit by electric lights.

Playing the Old Course

Golf has been played at St Andrews since the 15th century and by 1457 was apparently so popular that James II had to place a ban on it because it was interfering with his troops' archery practice. Everyone knows that St Andrews is the home of golf, but few people realise that anyone can play on the Old Course, the world's most famous golf course. Although it lies beside the exclusive, all-male Royal & Ancient Golf Club, the Old Course is a public course and is not owned by the club.

However, getting a tee-off time is something of a lottery. Unless you book months in advance, the only chance you have of playing here is by entering a ballot before 2 pm on the day before you wish to play. Be warned that applications by ballot are normally heavily oversubscribed, and green fees are a mere £80. There's no play allowed on Sunday. You must present a handicap certificate or letter of introduction from your club to the St Andrews Links Trust (☎ 01334-466666). If you want to make a booking yourself, write a year in advance (for summer and autumn reservations) to The Secretary, St Andrews Links Trust, Pilmour Cottage, St Andrews, Fife, KY16 9SF. You can book through the Internet at www.golfagent.com.

If your number doesn't come up, there are five other public courses in the area, none with quite the cachet of the Old Course but all of them significantly cheaper. Their fees are: New £40, Jubilee £35, Eden £25, Strathtyrum £17 and Balgove £7.

JANE SMITH

The Open Championship was first played at the Old Course, St Andrews, in 1873.

The castle opens standard HS hours and admission costs either £2.50/1, or £3.75/1.25 as part of the combined cathedral ticket.

The Scores From the castle, follow The Scores west past St Salvator's College. At the western end is **St Andrews Aquarium** (☎ 474786), which has the usual displays of marine life and opens 10 am to 6 pm daily (9 am to 7 pm in July and August). Admission costs £4.50/3.50.

Nearby, the **British Golf Museum** (☎ 478 880) is an interesting, modern museum with audiovisual displays and touch screens, as well as golf memorabilia. It opens 9.30 am to 5.30 pm daily, April to mid-October; 11 am to 3 pm Thursday to Monday, mid-October to March. The admission price is £3.75/1.50.

Opposite the museum is the **club house** of the Royal & Ancient. Outside the club is the **Old Course**, and beside it stretch the sands of the beach made famous by the film *Chariots of Fire*.

Walking & Cycling Routes

The TIC has a list of local walks and sells OS maps. You could walk from St Andrews to Crail along the coast but it's about 15 miles and you'd have to take care not to get caught by the tide. There are some excellent shorter walks along the southern part of the East Neuk coast (see that section later in the chapter).

Since there are few steep hills in eastern Fife, cycling is pleasant and there are some good rides along the quiet side roads. Kellie Castle (see under Around St Andrews later in the chapter) and Hill of Tarvit mansion are both approximately 10 miles away. We don't advise cycling the narrow, busy coastal road from St Andrews to Crail due to dangerous bends and no verges in places.

Organised Tours

There are guided walks in summer (the University Tour, ☎ 476161) or all year (the Witches Tour, ☎ 655057).

Places to Stay

Camping & University Accommodation

From April to October you can camp at *Cairnsmill Caravan Park* (☎ 473604, *Largo Rd*), one mile south of St Andrews on the A915, for £10.50 per site plus two people.

There's no hostel, but there is a bunkhouse 9 miles south-east near Anstruther (see that section later in the chapter). Between June and August, however, you can stay for £10 in one of the dorms at the university's *Gannochy House* (☎ 464870, *North St*), next to Younger Hall, but there's no kitchen. You must check-in between 9 and 10 am and 2 and 6 pm.

B&Bs

One of the cheaper ones is *Cairnsden* (☎ 476326, *2 King St*), south of the centre, with a single/double for £20/36. It opens year round. In the centre, *Fairnie House* (☎ 474 094, *10 Abbey St*) is a little bigger with one single and two twin rooms. It's near the Byre Theatre, and charges £15 to £30 per person.

Almost every house on Murray Park and Murray Place is a B&B. The area couldn't be more convenient but prices are on the high side – most places charge from around £22 per person. Most rooms have bathrooms. During summer you need to book in advance, but at other times it's probably best to knock on a few doors and pick what you like. *Lorimer House* (☎ 476599, *19 Murray Park*) opens year round and charges from £18 to £30 per person. *Cameron Guest House* (☎ 472306, *11 Murray Park*) offers B&B from £24 to £30 per person in comfortable rooms. In Murray Place *Aedel House* (☎ 472315), No 12, has seven rooms all with bathroom, for £18 to £28 per person.

Aslar Guest House (☎ 473460, e enquiries@aslar.com, *120 North St*) is an elegant, Georgian terraced house with rooms for £25 to £30 per person.

Hotels

Facing the bay, more expensive hotels line The Scores. At No 28, *Hazelbank Hotel* (☎ 472466, e bookings@hazelbank .com) is a Victorian townhouse with rooms from £30 to £60 per person. *St Andrews Golf Hotel* (☎ 472611, e thegolfhotel@ standrews.co.uk, *40 The Scores*) is an excellent upmarket hotel 200m from the Old Course. Prices are £72.50 to £92.50 per person. There are also cheaper two-night breaks. The hotel has a bar and excellent restaurant.

Under 2 miles west of the town centre, *Rufflets Country House Hotel* (☎ 472594, e reservations@rufflets.co.uk, *Strathkinness Low Rd*) is a top class hotel with a recommended restaurant. B&B and dinner costs from £105 per person.

If money's no object, stay at *St Andrews Old Course Hotel* (☎ 474371, e info@old coursehotel.co.uk), the imposing building by the golf course at the western end of town. Rooms at this luxurious establishment range from £165/190 to £315. There are resident golf pros, a team of therapists and beauticians providing massage for both body and ego.

Places to Eat

If you're on a tight budget, *PM*, on the corner of Market and Union Sts, does breakfast, burgers and fish and chips from £1.95. For more upmarket snacks, try *Fisher & Donaldson* (Church Street), which sells Selkirk bannocks (rich fruit bread), cream cakes and a wonderful range of pies and pastries.

Close to the cathedral and castle, *North Point Café* (24 North St) is a good place for coffee, cream tea or a light lunch; soup and a roll costs £2. One of the busiest places at lunchtime is *Brambles* (5 College St), which has excellent soups, salads and vegetarian dishes. It's not open in the evening. *The Merchant's House* (☎ 472595, *49 South St*), in a venerable building, serves a delicious three-course lunch for £8.95 but is closed on Monday.

Balaka Bangladeshi Restaurant (☎ 474 825, *St Mary's Place*) is recommended for curries and none other than Sean Connery has eaten here. It uses herbs grown in its own garden. A three-course lunch costs £5.95. It opens daily for lunch and dinner.

Ziggy's (☎ 473686, *6 Murray Place*) is popular with students and has burgers from £3.95 and a range of Mexican, vegetarian and seafood dishes. *Ogston's* (☎ 473473, *116 South St*) is a trendy but reasonably priced bar and bistro; mains are £4.50 to £5.50.

Apart from the pricey *Road Hole Grill* (☎ 474371) at St Andrews Old Course Hotel (see Places to Stay), you need a car to reach the top restaurants in the area. The recommended *Peat Inn* (☎ 840206), south-west of St Andrews on the B940 (turn right off the A915) towards Cupar, offers four-course set lunches for £19.50 per person; set dinners, including excellent fresh seafood, cost £28 per person, plus wine. It opens Tuesday to Saturday for lunch and dinner.

Finally, don't leave town without sampling one of the 52 varieties of ice cream from *B Jannetta (31 South St)*. This is a St Andrews institution. Most popular flavour? Vanilla. Weirdest? Irn Bru!

Entertainment

In July and August the Royal Scottish Country Dance Society holds dances and will show novices the steps. Contact the TIC for information. There are also other country dances in summer.

The *Byre Theatre* (☎ 476288, Abbey St) is being completely rebuilt and should have reopened by the time you read this.

St Andrews has a good supply of pubs, reflecting its varied population. The *Central Bar (Market St)* is all polished brass and polished accents, with a mix of students from south of the border, tourists and locals. The *Featherie & Firkin (5 Alexandra Place)* has occasional live music and real ales. *The Victoria (St Mary's Place)* is a bistro and bar popular with students.

Getting There & Away

St Andrews is 55 miles north of Edinburgh and 16 miles south of Dundee.

Bus Stagecoach Fife (☎ 01592-642394) has a half-hourly bus service from St Andrew Square, Edinburgh, to St Andrews (£5.70, two hours) and on to Dundee (£2.40, 30 minutes).

Train The nearest station to St Andrews is Leuchars (pronounced lew-**kars**), 5 miles away on the Edinburgh (£8.10, one hour), Dundee, Aberdeen, Inverness coastal line. There are three direct trains to London each day. From Leuchars, bus Nos X59 and X60 leave every half-hour Monday to Saturday to St Andrews, Sunday hourly.

Car Ian Cowe Coachworks (☎ 472543), 76-78 Argyle St, rents Fiats from £23 per day with unlimited mileage.

Getting Around

Try Golf City Taxis (☎ 477788), 23 Argyle St. A taxi from the train station at Leuchars to the town centre costs around £7.

You can rent bikes at Spokes (☎ 477835), 77 South St; mountain bikes and hybrids cost from £9.50 per day.

AROUND ST ANDREWS
Kellie Castle

A magnificent example of Lowland Scottish domestic architecture, Kellie Castle (☎ 01333-720217; NTS) is well worth a trip. It's set in a beautiful garden and many rooms contain superb plasterwork. The original part of the building dates from 1360; it was enlarged to its present dimensions around 1606. Robert Lorimer worked on the castle in the late 1800s, when it wasn't in good shape. It was bought by the NTS in 1970.

Kellie Castle is 3 miles north-west of Pittenweem on the B9171. It opens 1.30 to 5.30 pm daily, Easter to June and September; from 11 am daily, July and August. Admission is £4/free. The garden and grounds open year round from 9.30 am to sunset.

Stagecoach Fife (☎ 01592-642394) runs bus Nos 61A and 61B from St Andrews to Arncroach, past the castle gates, four times daily Monday to Saturday (one hour).

Scotland's Secret Bunker

The grim bunker (☎ 01333-310301), at Troy Wood by the B9131 about 5 miles south of St Andrews, was earmarked to be one of Britain's underground command centres and a home for Scots leaders in the event of nuclear war. Hidden 30m underground and surrounded by reinforced concrete are the austere operation rooms, communication centre and dormitories. An audiovisual display explains how it would have been used.

It opens 10 am to 5.30 pm daily, April to October. Admission costs £6.45/3.45.

Stagecoach Fife (☎ 01592-642394) runs nine buses daily Monday to Saturday between St Andrews and Arncroach, Earlsferry or Leven, via Troy Wood and Anstruther.

EAST NEUK

The section of the southern Fife coast that stretches from Leven east to the point at Fife Ness is known as East Neuk. There are several picturesque fishing villages and some good coastal walks in the area.

Crail
☎ 01333 • pop 1290

One of the prettiest of the East Neuk villages, Crail, 10 miles south-east of St Andrews, has a much-photographed harbour surrounded by white cottages with red-tiled roofs. There are fewer fishing boats in the harbour now than there once were, but you can still buy fresh lobster and shellfish.

The TIC (☎ 450869), 62 Marketgait, opens Easter to September. The village's history and involvement with the fishing industry are outlined in the **Crail Museum** (☎ 450310), in the same building as the TIC. The museum opens 10 am to 1 pm, 2 to 5 pm Monday to Saturday, 2 to 5 pm Sunday, Easter week and June to September; 2 to 5 pm weekends only, April and May.

The congenial *Caiplie House (☎ 450564, 53 High St North)*, in the village centre, has comfortable singles/doubles from £18/34 with shared bathroom, and filling breakfasts.

Stagecoach Fife bus No 95 runs hourly to Dundee.

Anstruther
☎ 01333 • pop 3270

Anstruther is a large former fishing village 9 miles south of St Andrews. The helpful TIC (☎ 311073), 70 Market St, by the harbour, opens 9.30 am to 5 pm Monday to Saturday, April to September.

The village is worth visiting for the **Scottish Fisheries Museum** (☎ 310628), beside the TIC. Displays include a cottage belonging to a fishing family and the history of the herring and whaling industries that once formed the mainstay of the local economy. It opens 10 am to 5.30 pm Monday to Saturday, 11 am to 5 pm Sunday, April to October; 10 am to 4.30 pm Monday to Saturday, noon to 4.30 pm Sunday, November to March. Admission costs £3.50/2.50.

From the harbour you can take a five hour excursion (☎ 310103) to the **Isle of May**, a nature reserve, for £12.50/5.50; the crossing takes just under an hour. April to July, the cliffs are packed with breeding kittiwakes, razorbills, guillemots, shags and puffins. Inland are the remains of **St Adrian's Chapel**, a 12th-century monastery.

Places to Stay & Eat At the friendly *Bunkhouse (☎ 310768, West Pitkierie)*, 1½ miles out of Anstruther on the B9131, beds cost £7.50; book ahead in summer.

Just uphill from the museum (follow Haddfoot Wynd), the agreeable *Mayview House (☎ 310677, Ladywalk)* offers B&B for £15/20 per person without/with bathroom. *Spindrift (☎ 310573, Pittenweem Rd)* is a very comfortable guesthouse a short walk south from the village centre. All rooms have bathrooms and cost from £26.50 per person.

As well as several simple cafes, Anstruther boasts one of Scotland's top places to eat. *The Cellar Restaurant (☎ 310378, 24 East Green)*, behind the museum, is famous for its variety of seafood. Advance bookings are essential. Lunch mains cost £5.50 to £8.95 (try the baked quiche of lobster and smoked salmon) and there's a three-course set dinner for £28.50.

Getting There & Away The hourly Stagecoach Fife (☎ 01592-642394) bus No 95 runs daily from Dundee to Leven via St Andrews, Crail, Anstruther (harbour), St Monans and Elie.

Pittenweem
☎ 01333 • pop 1640

This is now the main fishing port on the East Neuk coast, and there are lively fish sales in the early morning at the harbour. The village name means 'place of the cave', referring to the cave in Cove Wynd which was used as a chapel by the 7th-century missionary St Fillan. He was a saint who possessed miraculous powers – when he wrote his sermons in the dark cave his arm would illuminate his work by emitting a luminous glow.

Perthshire & Kinross

This area contains in miniature as many variations in terrain as Scotland itself: from the bleak expanse of Rannoch Moor in the west, to the rich farmland of the Carse of Gowrie between Perth and Dundee. At its heart is the River Tay and its tributaries.

It has also been an important region historically. From 838, Scotland's monarchs were crowned at Scone. Robert the Bruce signed a declaration of independence from England at Arbroath Abbey in 1320. Mary Queen of Scots was imprisoned in Lochleven Castle, and at Killiecrankie the Jacobites repelled the government forces.

The county town of Perth, built on the banks of the Tay, has a medieval church and many fine Georgian buildings. West of Perth there's attractive Strathearn, with small towns and villages including the wealthy former resort of Crieff. Blairgowrie lies north of Perth, in an area known for fruit growing.

The Highland line traverses this region – in the north and north-west are the rounded, heathery Grampians. North of Blairgowrie, the twisty road to Braemar follows Glen Shee and crosses the Cairnwell Pass, Britain's highest main road pass.

Flowing out of Loch Tay, in Western Perthshire, the River Tay runs eastwards through hills and woods towards Dunkeld, where there's a cathedral on the riverbank. Queen Victoria, when looking for a place to buy, was quite taken by the Pitlochry area, particularly the view over Loch Tummel. North of Pitlochry, at Blair Atholl, is Blair Castle, ancestral seat of the dukes of Atholl.

For information on accommodation, attractions etc check out the Perthshire Tourist Board Web site at www.perthshire.co.uk.

GETTING AROUND

Perth is a major transport hub; phone Perth & Kinross Council's Public Transport Traveline on ☎ 0845 301 1130. The main bus operators in the area include: Scottish Citylink (☎ 0870 550 5050), Stagecoach Perth (☎ 01738-629339), Fife Scottish (☎ 01334-474238) and Strathtay Scottish (☎ 01382-228345).

Trains run alongside the A9, destined for Aviemore and Inverness. The other main line connects Perth with Stirling (in the south) and Dundee and Arbroath (in the east).

The A9, Scotland's busiest road, cuts across the centre of this region through Perth and Pitlochry. It's the fast route into the Highlands and to Inverness – watch out for speed traps.

KINROSS & LOCH LEVEN
☎ 01577 • pop 4032
Kinross lies in the extreme south of Perthshire & Kinross region, on the western shore of Loch Leven. It's the largest loch in the lowlands, known for its extensive bird life.

The helpful Kinross Services TIC (☎ 863 680), by Junction 6 of the M90, opens daily year round.

Loch Leven Castle (☎ 01786-450000; HS), on an island in the loch, served as a fortress and prison from the late 14th century. Its most famous captive was Mary Queen of Scots, who spent almost a year incarcerated there from 1567. Her infamous charms bewitched Willie Douglas, who managed to get hold of the cell keys to release her then row her across to the shore. The castle is now roofless but basically intact. It opens standard HS hours, April to September only. Admission costs £3/1, including the ferry trip from Kinross.

Gallowhill Farm Caravan Park (☎ 862 364), open April to October, is 2 miles from Kinross, near the A91. Camping charges start at £5. There's basic B&B at the *Roxburghe Guest House* (☎ 862498, 126 High St) from £16 to £22 per person. Four miles from the M90 (Junction 6), near Milnathort, there's comfortable *Warroch Lodge* (☎ 863 779) where B&B costs £20 per person and it opens year round.

Scottish Citylink and Stagecoach Fife

(☎ 01592-642394) have hourly services Monday to Saturday between Perth and Kinross (£2.70, 30 minutes).

PERTH
☎ 01738 • pop 43,000

In *The Fair Maid of Perth*, Sir Walter Scott extolled the virtues of this county town. 'Perth, so eminent for the beauty of its situation, is a place of great antiquity', he wrote, and this is still true.

Perth's rise in importance derives from Scone (pronounced scoon), 2 miles north of town. In 838, Kenneth MacAlpin became the first king of a united Scotland and brought the Stone of Destiny, on which all kings were ceremonially invested, to Scone. An important abbey was built on the site. From then on all Scottish kings were invested here, even after Edward I of England carted the sacred talisman off to Westminster Abbey. In 1996 the stone was returned to Scotland, but it went to Edinburgh Castle rather than Scone.

Built on the banks of the River Tay, Perth grew into a major trading centre, known for weaving, dyeing and glove-making. It was originally called St John's Toun, hence the name of the local football team, St Johnstone. From the 12th century Perth was Scotland's capital, and in 1437 James I was murdered here. There were four important monasteries in the area and the town was a target for the Reformation movement in Scotland.

Perth is now a busy market town and centre of service industries. It's the focal point for this agricultural region and there are world famous cattle auctions of the valuable Aberdeen Angus breed. The bull sales in February draw international buyers.

The top attraction is Scone Palace, but the town itself has a number of interesting things to see, including an excellent art gallery, housing the work of local artist JD Fergusson.

Orientation & Information
Most of the town lies on the western bank

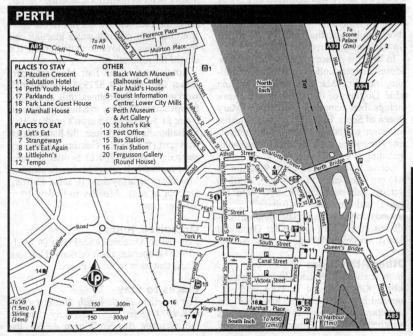

of the Tay; Scone Palace and some of the B&Bs are on the eastern bank. There are two large parks: North Inch, the scene of the infamous battle of the clans in 1396, and South Inch. The bus and train stations are near to each other, near the north-western corner of South Inch.

The TIC (☎ 450600), West Mills St, is in the same building as Lower City Mills (see below). It opens 9 am to 8 pm Monday to Saturday, 11 am to 6 pm Sunday, July and August; it closes two hours earlier April to June and in September and October; 9 am to 5 pm Monday to Saturday, November to March.

Parking of cars is limited and carefully controlled; just about every bit of street space is either metered or has double yellow lines.

Scone Palace

Two miles north of Perth, Scone Palace (☎ 552300), home of the Earl and Countess of Mansfield, shouldn't be missed. It was built in 1580 in the grounds of a former abbey; the abbey was destroyed in 1559 by a crowd inflamed by John Knox's sermon in St John's Kirk. With the destruction of the abbey buildings, the land passed to the Gowrie family, then to the Murrays.

In 1803 the palace was enlarged, and now houses a superb collection of French furniture, including Marie Antoinette's writing table. Displays of 16th-century needlework include bed hangings worked by Mary Queen of Scots. In the library is a valuable collection of 18th-and 19th-century porcelain. The palace is surrounded by parkland, including rare pine trees.

Scone Palace opens daily 9.30 am to 5.15 pm (last entry at 4.45 pm), April to October. Admission costs £5.60/3.30 for the house and grounds, half-price for the grounds only. Guide Friday's hop-on hop-off bus comes here (see under Organised Tours), as does the Blairgowrie bus (No 57).

Other Attractions

From High St, walk one block south to St John's Kirk. Founded in 1126, and surrounded by cobbled streets, this is still the centrepiece of the town. In 1559, John Knox preached a powerful sermon here that helped begin the Reformation and the resulting destruction of monasteries, including the one at Scone. The kirk was restored in the 1920s.

Four blocks south of High St is the Round House, the old waterworks building on the edge of South Inch that now houses the **Fergusson Gallery** (☎ 441944). JD Fergusson, a Perthshire artist and one of the Scottish Colourists, was noticeably influenced by French styles after spending much of his life in France in the early part of the 20th century. The gallery is well worth seeing; it opens 10 am to 5 pm Monday to Saturday. Admission is free.

A block north of High St is **Perth Museum & Art Gallery** (☎ 632488), which charts local history and is one of the oldest museums in Britain. There are displays of Perth art glass, an impressive silver collection and natural history displays. It opens the same hours as the Fergusson Gallery.

Nearby, on Curfew Row, stands the **Fair Maid's House**, the house chosen by Sir Walter Scott as home for Catherine Glover, the novel's romantic heroine. The novel was set in the 14th century, but this house dates from the 16th, when it was a meeting hall for the town's glove manufacturers. It's closed for restoration.

South-west of the Fair Maid's House, **Lower City Mills** (☎ 627958) is a restored, working, Victorian, oatmeal mill, open April to November, Monday to Saturday, 10 am to 5 pm; £1.50/75p. In the town's north on Hay St, Balhousie Castle houses the **Black Watch Museum** (☎ 621281), charting the military campaigns since 1740 of Scotland's foremost regiment. It opens May to September, Monday to Saturday from 10 am to 4.30 pm; October to April, Monday to Friday, 10 to 3.30 pm; free.

Organised Tours

May to early October, Guide Friday (☎ 0131-556 2244) operates a hop-on hop-off bus tour (£6/2) that takes in Scone Palace.

Places to Stay

The excellent *Perth Youth Hostel (☎ 623 658, 107 Glasgow Rd)* opens early March to late October. Bus No 7 from outside the office on South St stop right outside. Beds cost £9.25/8 for adults/under-18s.

The main B&B areas are along Glasgow Rd, Dunkeld Rd, Dundee Rd and Pitcullen Crescent. *Iona Guest House* (☎ 627261, 2 Pitcullen Crescent) charges from £18 per person; rooms have private showers and the breakfasts are good. Also on Pitcullen Crescent is the similar *Achnacarry Guest House* (☎ 621421), No 3; charges are from £23/42 per single/double. Nearby, the larger *The Darroch Guest House* (☎ 636893), No 9, charges from £16/18 per person without/ with bathroom. At *Pitcullen Guest House* (☎ 626506), No 17, all rooms are en-suite and cost from £26/44 a single/double.

Closer to the centre, there are several places along Marshall Place where the Georgian terraced houses overlook South Inch. *Marshall House* (☎ 442886), No 6, has three rooms with private showers and charges £17.50 per person. The very comfortable, whitewashed *Park Lane Guest House* (☎ 637218), No 17, offers B&B from £23 per person.

Salutation Hotel (☎ 630066, fax 633598, 34 South St) dates from 1699 and was reputedly used as a headquarters by Bonnie Prince Charlie during the 1745 rebellion. It has been modernised since then and its well-appointed singles/doubles cost from £67/86, but there are often special deals at weekends.

Small but luxurious, *Parklands* (☎ 622 451, fax 622046, St Leonards Bank) is one of the top hotels and all its 14 rooms have baths, one with a spa. B&B starts at £77.50/80.

Places to Eat

At Scone Palace there's the *Coffee Shop* for snacks and the *Old Kitchen* restaurant for more substantial meals. In Perth there are plenty of daytime cafes along High St.

Open daily till late, *Littlejohn's* (☎ 639 888, 24 St John's St) provides the same standard menu it offers at other branches. Mains include pizzas (£6.95), burgers (£4.95) and several vegetarian options. *Tempo's* (☎ 633334, 47 South St) international menu includes baked aubergine (£7.95) and pastas (£4.50 and under) and meals are occasionally accompanied by live music. It closes Sunday.

Strangeways (☎ 628866, 24 George St), a trendy cafe/bar that opens daily, is a good place to have a drink in the evening, but it stops serving food at 5 pm.

Over the road, is the relaxed bistro *Let's Eat Again* (☎ 633771, 33 George St) which endeavours to serve genetically modified-free food. Mains like penne pasta cost £7.50 to £14.75, but save room for the mango and lemon steam pudding (£3.95). It has a sister restaurant, *Let's Eat* (☎ 643377), on Kinnoull St.

Getting There & Away

Scottish Citylink operates one to two buses per hour from Perth to Glasgow (£7, 1½ hours), Edinburgh (£4.70, one to 1½ hours), Dundee (£3.20, 35 minutes), Aberdeen (£9.50, 2½ hours) and Inverness (£9.20, 2½ hours).

There's an hourly train service Monday to Saturday (every two hours on Sunday) from Glasgow's Queen St (£11.40, one hour), two-hourly on Sunday, and hourly trains from Edinburgh (£9.30, 1½ hours). See also the fares tables in the Getting Around chapter.

STRATHEARN

West of Perth, the wide *strath* (valley) of the River Earn was once a great forest where medieval kings hunted. The Earn, named after a Celtic goddess, runs east from St Fillans (named after the mystic who lived on an island in Loch Earn), through Comrie and Crieff and eventually into the Firth of Tay near Bridge of Earn. The whole area is known as Strathearn, an attractive region of undulating farmland, hills and lochs. The Highlands begin in the western section of Strathearn and the Highland line runs through Comrie and Crieff, and through Kirriemuir and Edzell east to Stonehaven.

Crieff & Around

☎ 01764 • pop 6360

Attractively located on the edge of the Highlands, Crieff has been a popular resort town since Victorian times. Until 1770 it was the scene of a large cattle fair; some vendors would come from as far away as

Skye – swimming the cattle across to the mainland. There's a TIC (☎ 652578) on the High St, open year round; its core hours are 9.30 am to 5 pm Monday to Friday, 9.30 am to 2.30 pm Saturday, with extended hours and Sunday opening Easter to October.

The main attraction these days is **Glenturret Distillery** (☎ 656565), about a mile north-west of the centre of town. Its visitors centre opens 9.30 am to 6 pm (from noon Sunday), the last tour is at 4.30 pm, Monday to Saturday, February to December. It's all fairly touristy but a free dram is included in the price of £3.50.

Braincroft Bunkhouse (☎ 670140), 5 miles west of Crieff on the A85, has basic accommodation in small rooms for £8.50 per person.

Stagecoach Perth (☎ 01738-629339) operates up to four buses a day Monday to Friday, two on Saturday, to Crieff from Perth.

Auchterarder
☎ 01764 • pop 3000
In the south of Strathearn, this small town stands in the centre of a rich agricultural area. Overlooking town are the Ochil Hills, which run north-east into the Sidlaws. The friendly TIC (☎ 663450), 90 High St, opens year round (daily April to October) and houses an interesting, free heritage centre upstairs.

The town is probably best known for the internationally famous hotel on its outskirts. Splendid *Gleneagles Hotel* (☎ 662231, 0800 704705, e *resort.sales@gleneagles.com*) has four golf courses (one of which is a championship course), a swimming pool, jacuzzi, sauna, gym, and tennis and squash courts. Room charges, including full use of the leisure facilities, range from £190/280 a single/double to £1350 for the Royal Lochnagar Suite (complete with antiques, silk-lined walls and hand-woven carpets). It's served by Gleneagles train station (£9/9.50 single/cheap day return, 50 minutes from Glasgow), and there's complimentary transport between the station and hotel.

PERTH TO AVIEMORE
There are several major sights strung out along the A9, the main route north to Aviemore in the Highlands. Frequent buses and trains run along this route; most stop at the places described in this section.

Dunkeld & Birnam
☎ 01350 • pop 1050
Fifteen miles north of Perth, Dunkeld is an attractive town on the Highland line. There are some excellent walks in the surrounding wooded area. Dunkeld TIC (☎ 727688), The Cross, opens 10 am to 4 pm daily, mid-April to September; Tuesday to Saturday the rest of the year.

Dunkeld Cathedral must be among the most beautifully sited cathedrals in the country. Half is still in use as a church, the rest is in ruins. The oldest part of the original church is the choir, completed in 1350. The 15th-century tower is also still standing and contains a small museum. The cathedral was damaged during the Reformation and burnt in the battle of Dunkeld in 1689.

On High and Cathedral Sts is a collection of 20 **artisans' houses** restored by the NTS; one of them is an NTS shop. Across Telford Bridge, named after Thomas Telford, is Birnam, made famous by Shakespeare's *Macbeth*. There's not much left of Birnam Wood, but there's a small Beatrix Potter Park (the author spent childhood holidays in the area).

Good local walks include the **Hermitage Woodland Walk** from the car park, a mile west of Dunkeld. The well marked trail follows the River Braan to the Black Linn Falls, where the Duke of Atholl built a folly, **Ossian's Hall**, in 1758.

Scottish Citylink buses between Glasgow/ Edinburgh and Inverness stop at Dunkeld & Birnam train station (beside the A9 just outside Birnam) up to five times daily. Monday to Saturday there are five Stagecoach Perth (☎ 01738-629339) buses daily to Pitlochry, 11 to Aberfeldy.

There are three trains daily Monday to Saturday to Glasgow (1½ hours) and Inverness (two hours), two on Sunday.

Pitlochry
☎ 01796 • pop 2440
Despite the tourist shops, Pitlochry is a pleasant town and makes a useful base for explor-

ing the area. There are good transport connections if you don't have your own wheels.

The TIC (☎ 472215), 22 Atholl Rd, opens 9 am to 6 pm Monday to Saturday, noon to 6 pm Sunday, April to mid-May and October; 9 am to 8 pm daily, mid-May to September; 9 am to 5 pm Monday to Friday, 9.30 am to 1 pm Saturday the rest of the year. It has a currency exchange facility.

Pitlochry has two whisky distilleries which both offer tours. **Bell's Blair Athol Distillery** (☎ 472234), at the southern end of town, charges £3, while a tour of **The Edradour** (☎ 472095), Scotland's smallest distillery, 2½ miles east of Pitlochry, is free.

When the power station was built on the River Tummel, a **fish ladder** was constructed to allow the salmon to swim up to their spawning grounds. It's at the north-eastern end of town, and you can walk up from the Pitlochry Festival Theatre to watch the fish from the viewing chamber of the visitor centre (☎ 473152), 10 am to 5.30 pm daily, April to October. Admission costs £2/1. May and June are the best months.

Walking & Cycling Routes The TIC sells the useful *Pitlochry Walks*, which lists four short and four long local walks.

The Edradour walk (2 miles) goes past the distillery and the Black Spout waterfall. An 8½ mile walk goes round Loch Faskally, past the theatre and fish ladder, and up to the Pass of Killiecrankie. A 7 mile walk takes you to Blair Castle; you could catch the bus back, but check times with the TIC before you go. There's a steep, 3 mile round trip to 400m-high Craigower, a viewpoint above Pitlochry. For a more spectacular view, tackle Ben Vrackie (841m), a steep, 6 mile walk from Moulin (on the A924).

Places to Stay & Eat Pitlochry is packed with places to stay, but anything central tends to be pricey. *Pitlochry Youth Hostel* (☎ 472308, Knockard Rd) overlooks the town centre and has great views. It opens year round and beds cost £11.25/10 for adults/under-18s.

The cheapest B&Bs are in Moulin, just over a mile to the north on the A924. At

Lavalette (☎ 472364, Manse Rd) B&B costs from £15 per person; it has three rooms, two with bathrooms. In Pitlochry, Lower Oakfield has several B&Bs and guesthouses. Purpose-built *Derrybeg Guest House (☎ 472070)*, No 18, has en-suite rooms and apartments from £18 per person.

There are plenty of places along Atholl Rd, which runs through the town centre. *Number Ten (☎ 472346)*, at No 10, is a small, family run hotel charging from £22 per person. The luxurious *Acarsaid Hotel (☎ 472389)*, No 8, has 19 rooms, all with bathroom, and charges £29 to £37 per person. It opens March to December.

The cafe at the *Festival Theatre* has been recommended, but at the time of research the theatre was closed for renovations. Lots of eateries line the Atholl Rd. The *Old Smithy (☎ 472356, 154 Atholl Rd)* is good. It opens daily from 10 am for snacks and light meals such as jacket potatoes with salad (£4.95). It also does full meals, including vegetarian options, and offers a two-course lunch for £5.

Getting There & Away Scottish Citylink runs buses approximately hourly between Inverness and Glasgow/Edinburgh. Journey times and prices to destinations from Pitlochry are: Inverness (£7.20, two hours), Aviemore (£5.50, 1¼ hours), Perth (£4.50, 40 minutes), Edinburgh (£6.50, 2¾ hours) and Glasgow (£7, 2¼ hours).

Pitlochry is on the main rail line from Perth to Inverness. There are eight trains daily Monday to Saturday from Perth (£4.90, 30 minutes), three on Sunday.

Pass of Killiecrankie

The first skirmish of the Jacobite Rebellion took place in 1689 in this beautiful, rugged gorge 3½ miles north of Pitlochry (on the B8079). Highland soldiers led by Bonnie Dundee routed government troops led by General Mackay. As the government troops fled, one of the soldiers is said to have jumped across the gap now known as Soldier's Leap to evade capture. An NTS visitor centre (☎ 01796-473233), open 10 am to 5.30 pm daily, April to October, has a display on the battle. It's only accessible by private transport (it's on the B8079, three miles north of Pitlochry).

Blair Castle & Blair Atholl

One of the most popular tourist attractions in Scotland, Blair Castle (☎ 01796-481207), and its 28,000 hectares, is the seat of the Duke of Atholl. Outside this impressive, white castle, set beneath forested slopes above the River Garry, a piper pipes in the crowds each day and every May there's a parade of the Atholl Highlanders, the only (legal) private army in Britain. The original tower was built in 1269, but the castle has undergone significant remodelling since then. In 1746, it was besieged by the Jacobites, the last castle in Britain to be subjected to siege.

Thirty-two rooms are open to the public and they're packed with paintings, arms and armour, china, lace, and embroidery, presenting a wonderful picture of upper-class Highland life from the 1500s to the late 20th century. One of the most impressive rooms is the ballroom, which has a wooden roof and walls covered in antlers.

Blair Castle is 7 miles north of Pitlochry, and a mile from Blair Atholl village. It opens 10 am to 6 pm (last entry 5 pm) daily, April to October; tickets to the castle and grounds cost £6/4, just the grounds £2/1.

Other attractions in Blair Atholl village include a working **water mill** (☎ 01796-481321), open daily Easter to October.

The Gothic *Atholl Arms Hotel* (☎ *01796-481205*), a pub near the train station, provides B&B for £60/80 but also does special deals.

Elizabeth Yule Buses (☎ 01796-472290) runs a service two to four times daily between Pitlochry and Blair (£2.35 return, 20 minutes). There are up to seven trains a day to Perth (30 minutes) and three to Glasgow (1¾ hours).

You can hire bikes from Atholl Mountain Bikes (☎ 01796-481646) for £6/10 a half/full day. It has a leaflet listing cycle routes in the area, including a 16 mile ride along an estate road up Glen Tilt, a 12 mile ride around Bruar Falls and Old Struan, or a 6 mile ride to Killiecrankie Pass and back.

For a continuation of this route, see Aviemore in the Highlands & Northern Islands chapter.

WEST PERTHSHIRE

The lochs and hills of this remote area can be reached by public transport, but buses are usually once-a-day postal services.

From the A9, south of Pitlochry, the A827 heads west to Crianlarich and the west coast. At **Aberfeldy** there's a TIC (☎ 01887-820 276), The Square, open year round. **Castle Menzies** (☎ 01887-820982), 1½ miles west of town, is the seat of the Chief of the Clan Menzies; it opens 10 am to 6 pm Saturday to Thursday (plus Friday in July and August), April to mid-October. Admission costs £3/1.50. West of Aberfeldy, the pretty village of **Fortingall** is famous as the birthplace of Pontius Pilate and possibly the world's oldest tree.

The bulk of **Ben Lawers** (1214m) rises above **Loch Tay**. Ben Lawers, part of a National Nature Reserve that includes the nearby Tarmachan range, is in the care of the NTS, which has a visitor centre (open 10 am to 5 pm daily, April to September) on the slopes of the mountain. The rich limestone soil and rocks have created a rare diversity of wildlife. A trail leads to the summit from the centre, but a more interesting, seven hour route is up Lawers Burn from Machuim Farm, just north of Lawers village. You can walk around the ridges via Meall Garbh to the summit, but you should take a good map (OS Landranger sheet No 51).

At the western end of Loch Tay is the village of **Killin** (see that section under Stirling & Around earlier in the chapter).

Dundee & Angus

Dundee and Angus are two separate unitary authorities. Dundee was once a thriving centre for jute, whaling and shipbuilding, but when these industries declined in the second half of the 20th century so did the city. However, in recent years Dundee has begun to revive and for visitors there are several interesting attractions.

Pictish Symbol Stones

The Romans permanently occupied only the southern half of Britain up to 410. Caledonia, the section north of Edinburgh and Glasgow, was mostly left alone, especially after the mysterious disappearance of the Ninth Legion. Caledonia was the homeland of the Picts, a Celtic race, about whom little is known. It was the Romans who gave them the name Picts, which means 'painted people'.

In the mid-9th century they were culturally absorbed by the Scots (who had originally come from Ireland), leaving only a few archaeological remains and a scattering of Pictish place names beginning with Pit-. However, there are hundreds of mysterious standing stones decorated with intricate symbols, mainly in the north-east. The capital of the ancient Southern Pictish kingdom is said to have been at Forteviot in Strathearn, and Pictish symbol stones can be found throughout this area and all the way up the east coast of Scotland into Sutherland and Caithness.

It's believed that the stones were set up to record Pictish lineages and alliances, but no-one is yet quite sure exactly how the system worked. The stones fall into three groups. Class I, the earliest, are rough blocks of stone, carved with any combination from a basic set of 28 symbols. Class II are decorated with a Celtic cross as well as with symbols. Class III, dating from the end of the Pictish era (790–840), have only figures and a cross.

With your own transport, it's possible to follow a number of symbol-stone trails in the area.

Starting at Dundee (visit the McManus Galleries first), drive northeast to Arbroath. On the outskirts of Arbroath is **St Vigeans Museum** which contains several interesting stones. Continue north along the A92 to **Montrose**, where there are more stones in the local museum. Along the A935, in **Brechin Cathedral**, is a good example of a Class III stone. In Brechin Castle, **Pictavia** (☎ 01307-461460) is an interesting exhibition on Pictish stones and the Picts' way of life. From Brechin, take the B9134 to **Aberlemno**, where there are excellent examples of all three classes. Along the A94, at **Meigle**, there's a museum with one of the best collections of stones in the country.

For more information, it's worth getting a copy of *The Pictish Trail* (Orkney Press) by Anthony Jackson, which lists 11 driving tours, or his more detailed *Symbol Stones of Scotland*, both available in Tourist Information Centres.

One of hundreds of carved standing stones erected by the Picts

---

Angus is an attractive county of peaceful glens running down to the sea. The area was part of the Pictish kingdom in the 7th and 8th centuries, and there are interesting Pictish symbol stones at **Aberlemno**, but the main draw is Glamis Castle of *Macbeth* fame.

For information contact the Angus & Dundee Tourist Board (☎ 01382-527527, e enquiries@angusanddundee.co.uk), 21 Castle St, Dundee DD1 3AA, or check its Web site at www.angusanddundee.co.uk.

GETTING AROUND

Angus Council (☎ 01307-461775) publishes an annual *Public Transport Map & Guide*, available from TICs. Strathtay Scottish (☎ 01382-228345) is the main bus operator between Dundee and places in Angus. Trains run along the scenic coastline from Dundee east to Arbroath and Montrose.

DUNDEE

☎ 01382 • pop 177,540

In its 19th-century heyday this merchant city boasted elegant streets, dignified stores and more millionaires per head than anywhere else in Britain. When the industries declined or disappeared during the 20th century

CENTRAL SCOTLAND

Dundee's unemployment soared, the streets turned grubby and many of the shops vanished. Poor town planning in the 1960s and 70s compounded its problems leaving ugly blocks of flats and office buildings, and traffic congestion brought by the Tay Road Bridge.

In spite of this legacy, the dour, desolate Dundee of legend is fading. Tourism has been encouraged with the development of Discovery Point and Victoria Dock. The establishment of the Dundee Contemporary Arts centre is a declaration of the city's cultural vigour and ambition. And the more sensitive design of the new glass and sandstone Westgate shopping centre demonstrates the city's attempt to learn from past architectural mistakes.

But Dundee's real asset is its people. Dundonians are among the friendliest, most welcoming and most entertaining people you'll meet anywhere in the country.

It's worth staying here awhile. The hotels and restaurants are good value, there are some great drinking places and 4 miles east of the city is the Victorian seaside suburb of Broughty Ferry.

History

Dundee first began to grow in importance as a result of trade links with Flanders and the Baltic ports. It was awarded the first of its royal charters by King William in the late 12th century.

In its chequered history, Dundee was captured by Edward I, besieged by Henry VIII and destroyed by Cromwellian forces in the 17th century. It went on to become the second most important trading city in Scotland (after Edinburgh).

In the 19th century, Dundee was a major player in the shipbuilding and railway engineering industries. Linen and wool gave way to jute and, since whale oil was used in the production of jute, whaling developed alongside. At one time there were as many as 43,000 people employed in the textile industry, and as the jute workers became redundant, light engineering, electronics and food processing provided employment.

Dundee was once called the city of the three 'Js' – jute, jam and journalism. No jute is produced here any more, and when the famous Keiller jam factory was taken over in 1988 production was transferred to England. There's still journalism, and DC Thomson, best known for its comics (such as the *Beano*), is still one of the city's largest employers.

Orientation

Most people approach the city from the Tay Road Bridge or along the A90 from Perth; both routes take you into the centre. The train station and Captain Scott's ship *Discovery* are near the bridge; the bus station is a short walk to the north, just off Seagate. Four miles east of Dundee is Broughty Ferry, Dundee's seaside resort. It's connected by regular buses and is a pleasant place to stay.

Information

The very helpful TIC (☎ 434664), 21 Castle St, opens 9 am to 6 pm Monday to Saturday, 10 am to 4 pm Sunday, May to September; 9 am to 5 pm Monday to Saturday, October to April. As well as the usual bed booking facility (£1 for local bookings), it sells Scottish Citylink and National Express tickets. Pick up a copy of *What's On* for listings.

The post office, 4 Meadowside, opens 9 am to 5.30 pm Monday to Friday, 9 am to 7 pm Saturday. You can access the Internet and send emails at Intercafé on the 1st floor of Debenham's department store in the Overgate shopping centre; it costs £2.50 for half an hour.

Dundee Royal Infirmary (☎ 660111) is on Barrack Road.

Discovery Point

Make an effort to see this impressive visitor attraction, centred on Captain Scott's famous polar expedition vessel, the research ship *Discovery* (☎ 201245). The ship was constructed here in 1900 with a hull more than half a metre thick to survive the Antarctic pack ice. Scott sailed for the Antarctic in 1901 and, in a not uneventful voyage, spent two winters trapped in the ice.

After viewing the interesting exhibitions and audiovisual displays in the main build-

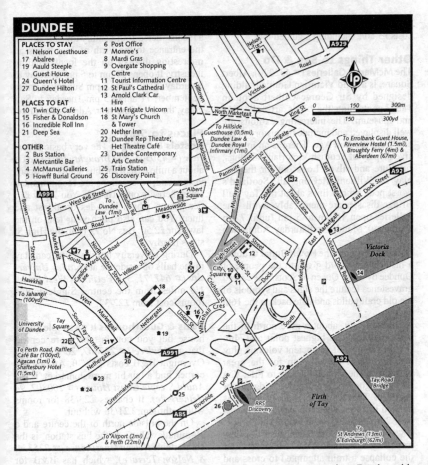

DUNDEE

PLACES TO STAY
1 Nelson Guesthouse
17 Abalree
19 Aauld Steeple
   Guest House
24 Queen's Hotel
27 Dundee Hilton

PLACES TO EAT
10 Twin City Café
15 Fisher & Donaldson
16 Incredible Roll Inn
21 Deep Sea

OTHER
2 Bus Station
3 Mercantile Bar
4 McManus Galleries
5 Howff Burial Ground
6 Post Office
7 Monroe's
8 Mardi Gras
9 Overgate Shopping
   Centre
11 Tourist Information Centre
12 St Paul's Cathedral
13 Arnold Clark Car
   Hire
14 HM Frigate Unicorn
18 St Mary's Church
   & Tower
20 Nether Inn
22 Dundee Rep Theatre;
   Het Theatre Café
23 Dundee Contemporary
   Arts Centre
25 Train Station
26 Discovery Point

ing, go on board the ship to see the cabins used by Scott and his crew. The complex is on the bank of the Firth of Tay, near the Tay Road Bridge. It opens 10 am to 5 pm Monday to Saturday, from 11 am Sunday, April to October; until 4 pm November to March. Admission costs £5/4.15.

HM Frigate Unicorn

Unlike the *Discovery*, Dundee's other floating tourist sight retains the atmosphere of an old sailing ship. Built as a warship in 1824, the *Unicorn* (☎ 200900) is the oldest British-built warship still afloat – perhaps because it never saw action. By the mid-19th century, sailing ships were outclassed by steam and the *Unicorn* instead served as storage for gunpowder, then later as a training vessel. When it was proposed to break up the historic ship for scrap in the 1960s a preservation society was formed.

Wandering around the four decks gives you an excellent impression of what it must have been like for the 300-strong crew to live in such cramped conditions. The *Unicorn* is berthed in Victoria Dock, east of the Tay Bridge. It opens daily 10 am to 5 pm, mid-March to October; 10 am to 4 pm weekdays

CENTRAL SCOTLAND

November to mid-March only. Admission costs £3.50/2 including a guided tour.

Other Things to See & Do

The **McManus Galleries** (☎ 432020), Albert Square, is a solid Victorian Gothic building designed by Sir George Gilbert Scott in 1867, containing the city's art collection and museum. The interesting exhibits are well displayed and include the history of the city from the Iron Age. There is an impressive display of Scottish Victorian paintings, furniture and silver. Look out for the display on William McGonagall, Scotland's worst poet, whose lines about the Tay Rail Bridge disaster are memorably awful. The galleries open 10 am to 5 pm (until 7 pm Thursday), Monday to Saturday. Admission is free.

Over the road is the **Howff Burial Ground**, a historic graveyard given to the people of Dundee by Mary Queen of Scots. The carved gravestones feature the signs and symbols of the old craft guilds and date back to the 16th century.

Dundee Law, about a mile north of the centre is the city's highest point at 174m. It's the remains of an ancient volcanic plug and it's worth the hike up for the great views over the city and across to Fife. You also get a good view of the two bridges over the Tay. The 1½ mile road bridge was opened in 1966. The railway bridge, at just over 2 miles long, is the longest in Europe. It was built in 1887, replacing a section destroyed by a storm in 1879. Moments after the collapse a train attempted to cross and plunged into the firth, killing 75 people.

Broughty Ferry

This pleasant suburb is 4 miles east of Dundee. There's a long, sandy beach (though not exactly litter free) and a number of good places to eat and drink.

Claypotts Castle (☎ 01786-450000), north of town, was built in the late 16th century. Looking like a house perched on top of a castle, it's actually one of the most complete Z-plan tower houses in Scotland. It opens 9.30 am to 6 pm weekends only, July to September. Admission costs £2.50.

Broughty Castle Museum (☎ 776121) is a reconstructed 16th-century tower guarding the entrance to the Firth of Tay. It has an interesting display on the local whaling industry. It opens 11 am to 5 pm Monday to Saturday, 12.30 am to 4 pm Sunday, April to September; 11 am to 5 pm Tuesday to Saturday, the rest of the year. Admission is free.

Places to Stay

Hostels & Colleges The very basic *Riverview* (☎ 450565, 127 Broughty Ferry Rd) is about a mile east of the bus station. It opens year round; reservations are recommended since there are only 10 beds. You'll pay £10 per person which includes breakfast and linen. You can also pitch your tent on the lawn for £2.50. Bus No 75 from the High St stops nearby.

During university holidays you can stay in the halls of residence at *Dundee University* (☎ 647171, 319 Perth Rd, West Park), 1½ miles from the centre. Single/double rooms cost from £22/32.

B&Bs & Guesthouses It's a simple guesthouse but you couldn't be more central than at *Abalree* (☎ 223867, 20 Union St). Overnight B&B costs £18/30. Around the corner, and a fair bit more upmarket, is the *Aauld Steeple Guest House* (☎ 200302, 94 Nethergate). It charges £23/38 for rooms with bathroom, £21/36 without.

On the hillside north of the centre and a 10-minute walk from the bus station, is the comfortable *Nelson Guesthouse* (☎ 225354, 8 Nelson Terrace), which has B&B for £17/32. The roomy Victorian *Hillside Guest House* (☎ 223443, 43 Constitution St), off Constitution Rd, charges £24/42.

In the east near the river, *Errolbank Guest House* (☎ 462118, 9 Dalgleish Rd) charges £17/32.

There's a good range of accommodation in Broughty Ferry. *Auchenean* (☎ 774782, 177 Hamilton St), in a quiet cul-de-sac, charges £19 per person. It's a pleasant place five minutes' walk from the beach. *Hollies Orchard* (☎ 776403, 12 Castle Roy Rd) has two rooms, both with bathrooms, and does B&B from £25 per person.

Hotels The *Shaftesbury Hotel* (☎ 669216, e reservations@shaftesbury-hotel.co.uk, 1 Hyndford St) is in Dundee's west, just off Perth Rd and about 1½ miles from the city centre. It's a former jute baron's mansion, and an excellent place, popular with businesspeople. B&B costs from £49.50/72, but there are bargain midweek and weekend rates available.

The two main business hotels in the centre are the *Queen's Hotel* (☎ 322515, 160 Nethergate), a grand Victorian hotel with B&B from £40/60, and the waterfront *Dundee Hilton* (☎ 229271), by the Tay Bridge, which charges £115/135 on weekends (more during the week).

Places to Eat

There's a number of interesting eateries in Dundee and prices are competitive. For a takeaway snack, the *Incredible Roll Inn*, Whitehall Crescent, is a good sandwich shop with a wonderful range of hot and cold filled rolls from £1.

The *Deep Sea (81 Nethergate)* is the oldest fish and chip shop in Dundee, and opens 9.30 am to 6.40 pm Monday to Saturday; lemon sole is £6.50. More upmarket, *Fisher & Donaldson*, at 12 Whitehall St, is an excellent bakery/patisserie with a small cafe attached.

The *Het Theatre Café* (☎ 200813, Tay Square), at the Dundee Rep Theatre, is a European-style coffee bar, open till late Monday to Saturday, and a great place for a coffee, drink or snack (toasties £1.50). Downstairs is a more formal restaurant open for lunch and dinner. *Twin City Café* (☎ 223662, 4 City Square), a trendy modern cafe overlooking City Square, is good for coffee, snacks or meals (pastas under £7) and delicious ice cream.

It's worth going to *Jahangir* (☎ 202022, 1 Session St) for the decor alone. This extraordinary Indian restaurant looks like a nightclub from the outside; inside, it's pure Moghul Hollywood, with an over-the-top tent and fountain. The food's good and it also does takeaways. Chicken curries start at £4.50. It opens until 1 am at the weekend, midnight during the week.

There are lots of interesting places along Perth Rd, though some are a fair walk from the centre. One of the liveliest places, *Raffles Café Bar* (☎ 226344, 18 Perth Rd), isn't far and mains such as chicken curry are good value at £4.85 to £8.25; it also does pizzas and pasta. The most interesting restaurant is the colourful *Agacan* (☎ 644227, 113 Perth Rd), part Turkish restaurant, part art gallery, and a great place to spend an evening. Mains are £7.50 to £10.40.

In Broughty Ferry, *Visocchi's (Gray St)* is an Italian ice-cream shop and cafe that's an institution. Ice creams cost from £1, pizza from £4.50. It's closed Monday. *Gulistan Balti & Tandoori Restaurant* (☎ 738844, Queen St), near the railway bridge and the corner of Fort St in an old church hall, serves tasty food Sunday to Thursday from 5 pm to midnight, Friday and Saturday to 1 am.

Entertainment

The excellent *Dundee Rep Theatre* (☎ 223 530, Tay Square) hosts touring companies as well as staging local productions. Some of the Dundee Jazz & Blues Festival (June) is held here. The city's cultural life took a leap forwards with the opening of the *Dundee Contemporary Arts* (☎ 432000, 152 Nethergate) centre, housing two galleries, a two-screen cinema showing mainstream and arthouse films, and a cafe-bar which has become a cool place to hang-out.

The *Nether Inn* (☎ 202658, 134 Nethergate) is a large, stylish pub popular with students. There's live jazz Saturday afternoon. The *Mercantile Bar* (☎ 225500, 100 Commercial St) is a lively city centre pub. Dundee has several popular nightclubs including *Monroe's* (☎ 228181, South Ward Rd) and the nearby, large *Mardi Gras* (☎ 205551).

In Broughty Ferry, the *Fisherman's Tavern (12 Fort St)* serves good cask ales and around the corner on the seafront the *Ship Inn (121 Fisher St)* offers views across the Tay. Both do good pub grub.

Getting There & Away

Dundee is 472 miles from London, 83 from Glasgow, 62 from Edinburgh, 67 from Aberdeen and 21 from Perth. If you're driving over the Tay Road Bridge from Fife, it's toll-free in that direction only. See the fares tables in the Getting Around chapter.

Air The airport (☎ 643242), Riverside Drive, is about 1½ miles west of the centre; it has flights to Aberdeen, London, Manchester and Denmark.

Bus Scottish Citylink has hourly buses from Edinburgh (£6.50, two hours) and Glasgow (£7, 2¼ hours). On some services, you may have to change in Perth. There are also hourly services to Perth (£3.20, 35 minutes) and Aberdeen (£6.70, 2 hours).

Getting to the west coast is a major pain – you must go via Glasgow to reach Fort William or Oban.

Train From Edinburgh (£14.60, 1¼ hours) and Glasgow (£19.20, 1½ hours), trains run at least once an hour, Monday to Saturday; hourly on Sunday to Edinburgh, every two hours on Sunday to Glasgow. For Aberdeen (£17, 1¼ hours), trains run via Arbroath and Stonehaven. There are two trains an hour, fewer on Sunday.

Car The branch of Arnold Clark (☎ 225382) car dealers on East Marketgait rents out cars.

Getting Around
For information on buses within the Dundee and Broughty Ferry area phone Travel Dundee (☎ 01382-201121). Most city centre buses pass along the High St, stopping by St Mary's Church. It's possible to catch a train to Broughty Ferry, but buses (80p, 15 minutes) from the bus station are more frequent. There are taxis outside the train station; alternatively phone Tele Taxis (☎ 889333).

GLAMIS CASTLE
Looking every bit a Scottish castle, with turrets and battlements, Glamis Castle (pronounced glarms) was the legendary setting for Shakespeare's *Macbeth*. The Grampians and an extensive park provide a spectacular backdrop for this family home of the Earls of Strathmore and Kinghorne. Glamis (☎ 01307-840242) has been a royal residence

since 1372; the Queen Mother (née Elizabeth Bowes-Lyon) spent her childhood here and Princess Margaret (the Queen's younger sister) was born here.

The five-storey, L-shaped castle was given to the Lyon family in 1372, but was significantly altered in the 17th century. The most impressive room is the drawing room, with its arched plasterwork ceiling. There's a display of armour and weaponry in the crypt (haunted) and frescoes in the chapel (also haunted). Duncan's Hall is where King Duncan was murdered in *Macbeth*. You can also look round the royal apartments, including the Queen Mother's bedroom.

Glamis Castle is 12 miles north of Dundee. It opens 10.30 am to 5.30 pm daily April to October, from 10 am (last entry 4.45 pm) in July and August. You're escorted on an hour-long tour which leaves every 15 minutes. Tickets to the castle and grounds are £6/3; to the grounds only, they're £3/free.

There are up to five Strathtay Scottish (☎ 01382-228345) buses a day from Dundee (£2.10, 35 minutes).

ARBROATH
☎ 01241 • pop 23,530
Source of the famous Arbroath smokie (smoked haddock), this fishing port was established in the 12th century. Nowadays, the town is impoverished and unemployment high, but it's no less interesting for all that. The TIC (☎ 872609), Market Place, opens Monday to Saturday year round, plus Sunday June to August.

The settlement grew up around **Arbroath Abbey** (☎ 878756; HS), founded in 1178 by King William the Lion, who is buried here. It was at the abbey that Robert the Bruce signed Scotland's famous declaration of independence from England in 1320. Closed following the Dissolution, the fortified abbey fell into ruin but enough survives to make this an impressive sight. There's a tall gable in the south transept, with a circular window once home to a shipping beacon. Parts of the nave and sacristy are intact. The abbey is open standard HS times. Admission costs £2/1.50.

For **sea fishing trips**, contact the skipper of the *Girl Katherine* (☎ 874510).

If you want to stay *Harbour House Guest House* (☎ *878047)* has decent rooms for £16 to £20 per person.

Strathtay Scottish (☎ 01382-228345) has frequent buses from Dundee (as does Scottish Citylink from Edinburgh). However, it's better to go by train because it's a scenic trip along the coast from Dundee (£3.10, 20 minutes, up to three per hour).

Aberdeenshire & Moray

This beautiful area is bound to the west and south by the Grampian Mountains, to the north and east by the North Sea. The largest urban centre is prosperous Aberdeen, a tidy city of impressive granite architecture, still benefiting from the North Sea oil industry.

Aberdeenshire incorporates the valley of the grand River Dee, Royal Deeside – royal because Queen Victoria liked it so much that she bought Balmoral. The royal family still spends part of every summer here, appearing at the Braemar Gathering, the best known of the Highland Games.

Around the coast are the fertile plains, immortalised by Lewis Grassic Gibbon in his trilogy the *Scots Quair*, which was based on the life of a farming community early in the 20th century. The east coasters, and particularly the Aberdonians, have always had a reputation for being hard-working and thrifty. Certainly anyone living near, or making a living from, the North Sea would have to be tough.

There is a vigorous culture in the northeast quite separate from the rest of Scotland. Much of it is expressed in lively anecdotal or poetic form (in dialect). The *both y* ballads and bands which provided home entertainment among the workers on the big farms still get high billing on local radio and TV.

Along the northern coast of Banff and Moray are small fishing ports which have neat, little streets looking out to sea, with nothing between them and Scandinavia to the north. This sandy coastline gets a lot of

sun and not much rainfall, and the unspoilt, small towns have a brisk, no-nonsense feel.

There are many castles in the characteristic Scottish baronial style in this area. In the north-west, and across the border in the Highlands, the biggest industry is the distilling of whisky – many distilleries offer tours followed by drams.

GETTING AROUND

For information on buses around Aberdeen phone ☎ 01224-664581. Stagecoach Bluebird (☎ 01224-212266) is the main bus company in the area. Its Bluebird Rover day ticket (£9) covers all Stagecoach Bluebird and Stagecoach Inverness services.

The only railway line runs from the south to Aberdeen and continues through Inverurie, Huntly and Elgin to Inverness.

There are some superb walks in the mountains in the south-western part of this region and TICs sell the useful *Hillwalking in Grampian Highlands*.

ABERDEEN
☎ 01224 • pop 217,260

Aberdeen is an extraordinary symphony in grey. Almost everything in the city centre is built of grey granite, including the roads, which are paved with crushed granite. In the sunlight, especially after a shower of rain, the stone turns silver and shines like a fairytale, but with low, grey clouds and rain scudding in off the North Sea it can be a bit depressing.

Aberdeen was a prosperous North Sea trading and fishing port centuries before oil was considered a valuable commodity. After the townspeople supported Robert the Bruce against the English at the Battle of Bannockburn in 1314, the king rewarded the town with land for which he had previously received rent. The money was diverted into the Common Good Fund, to be spent on town amenities, as it still is today. It finances the regimented floral ranks that have won the city numerous awards, and helps keep the place spotless. As a result, the inhabitants have been inculcated with a strong sense of civic pride.

The name Aberdeen is a combination of two Pictish-Gaelic words, *aber* and *devana*, meaning the meeting of two waters. The area was known to the Romans and was raided by the Vikings when it was an increasingly important port, with trade conducted in wool, fish, hides and fur. By the 18th century, paper and rope-making, whaling and textile manufacture were the main industries; in the following century it was a major herring port.

Since the 1970s, Aberdeen has become the main onshore service port for one of the largest oilfields in the world. Unemployment rates, once among the highest in the country, dropped dramatically, but have since fluctuated with the rise and fall of the price of oil.

Aberdeen is certainly worth a visit. It is a very lively city – there are more bars than would seem even remotely viable. Start with over 200,000 Scots, then add multinational oil workers and a large student population – the result: a thriving nightlife.

Orientation

Aberdeen is built on a ridge that runs east-west between the River Dee and River Don. Union St, the main commercial street, follows the line of the ridge. South of Union St, the bus and train stations are next to each other, off Guild St. East of the bus and train stations is the ferry quay, off Market St.

Old Aberdeen and the university are about 1½ miles north of Union St. To the east lies a couple of miles of clean, sandy beach; at its southern end is Footdee (pronounced fitt-ee), a fishing community at the mouth of the River Dee.

Information

The TIC (☎ 632727), St Nicholas House, Broad St, opens 9 am to 5 pm daily, May to September (extended hours July and August); Monday to Saturday October to May. There's the usual bed-booking facility and currency exchange. The post office, St Nicholas Centre, Upperkirkgate, opens 9 am to 5.30 pm Monday to Saturday.

On Rousemount Viaduct, the Central Library (☎ 652500) has self-service, coin-operated Internet terminals in the 1st floor reference section for £1 for the first 15 minutes (closed Sunday).

The Harbour

The harbour has always been a busy place. From dawn until about 8 am the fish market operates as it has for centuries.

Maritime Museum Situated in Provost Ross's House, the oldest building in the city, the Maritime Museum (☎ 585788) explains Aberdeen's relationship (almost exclusively commercial) with the sea. There are some interesting displays about shipbuilding and the whaling and fishing industries. Speedy Aberdeen clippers were a 19th-century shipyard speciality which were attractive to British tea merchants in China for the transportation of emigrants to Australia and, on return, the importation of tea, wool and exotic goods (opium, for instance). It opens 10 am to 5 pm Monday to Saturday (noon to 3 pm Sunday). Admission is free.

The City

Union St is the main thoroughfare in the city, lined with solid granite buildings, many of them Victorian. The oldest area is **Castlegate**, at the eastern end, where the castle stood. When it was captured from the English for Robert the Bruce, the password used by the townspeople was 'Bon Accord'. A street and shopping centre commemorate the password.

Provost Skene's House About 50m behind the TIC, surrounded by ugly concrete and glass office blocks, is a late medieval, turreted town house (☎ 641086) occupied in the 17th century by the provost (the Scots equivalent of a mayor) Sir George Skene. It was commandeered by the Duke of Cumberland and his English redcoat soldiers, and later it became a dosshouse. It would have been demolished in the 1940s but for a successful, long-running campaign to save it, supported by the present-day Queen Mother, which led to its opening as a museum in 1953.

Typical of its kind, the house has intimate, panelled rooms. The 1622 tempera-painted ceiling, with its Catholic symbolism, is unusual for having survived the depredation of the Reformation. It is a gem of its time, featuring earnest looking angels,

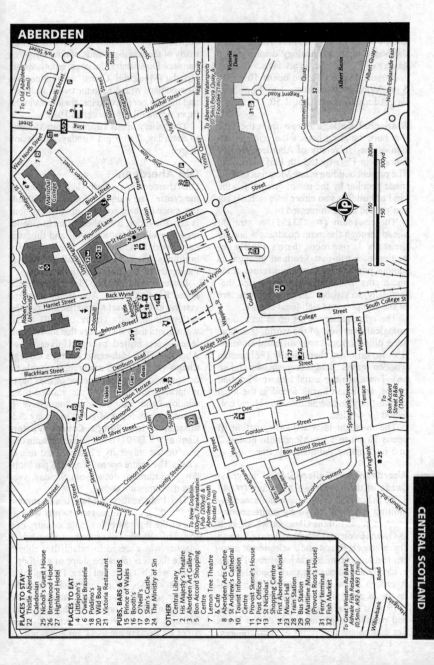

ABERDEEN

PLACES TO STAY
22 Thistle Aberdeen Caledonian
25 Nicholl's Guest House
26 Brentwood Hotel
27 Highland Hotel

PLACES TO EAT
4   Littlejohn's
6   Owlies Brasserie
18 Poldino's
20 Wild Boar
21 Victoria Restaurant

PUBS, BARS & CLUBS
15 Prince of Wales
16 Booth's
17 O'Neill's
19 Slain's Castle
24 The Ministry of Sin

OTHER
1   Central Library
2   His Majesty's Theatre
3   Aberdeen Art Gallery
5   Bon Accord Shopping Centre
7   Lemon Tree Theatre & Cafe
8   Aberdeen Arts Centre
9   St Andrew's Cathedral
10 Tourist Information Centre
11 Provost Skene's House
12 Post Office
13 St Nicholas
14 First Aberdeen Kiosk
23 Shopping Centre
28 Music Hall
29 Train Station
30 Bus Station
31 Maritime Museum (Provost Ross's House)
32 Fish Market

St Peter with cockerels crowing, and Cromwellian-looking soldiers. At the top of the house is an archaeology display and a gallery of local domestic artefacts.

Provost Skene's House opens 10 am to 5 pm Monday to Saturday, 1 to 4 pm Sunday. Admission costs 2.50/1.50.

Marischal College Across from the TIC, this huge building houses the science section of the University of Aberdeen. It was founded in 1593 by the 5th Earl Marischal. The present building is late Victorian Gothic, made peculiar by the use of granite. It's the kind of building you either love or hate, but can't avoid being impressed by.

The **museum** (☎ 273131) is straight ahead through the main quadrangle and up the stairs. In one room, there's a lively depiction of north-east Scotland through its famous people, customs, architecture, trade and myths. The displays are organised thematically, so visitors can get a good picture of the complex and rich local culture.

The other gallery is set up as an anthropological overview of the world, incorporating objects from vastly different cultures. It's also arranged thematically (Polynesian wooden masks alongside gasmasks and so on). There are the usual bizarre Victorian curios, an Indian kayak found in the local river estuary and some Eskimo objects collected by whalers.

The museum is well worth visiting. It opens 10 am to 5 pm Monday to Friday, 2 to 5 pm Sunday. Admission is free.

Aberdeen Art Gallery Behind the grand façade of the Aberdeen Art Gallery (☎ 646 333), Schoolhill, is a cool, white space exhibiting the work of young contemporary painters, mostly of the Glasgow School, such as Gwen Hardie and Stephen Conroy. There's also a Francis Bacon and a selection of modern textiles, ceramics and jewellery. There's evidently a vigorous school of applied arts in Aberdeen. There are also several Joan Eardley landscapes; she lived in a cottage on the cliffs near Stonehaven in the 1950s and 60s and painted tempestuous oils of the North Sea and poignant portraits of slum children.

Among the Pre-Raphaelites upstairs is a collection of 92 small portraits of artists, many of them self-portraits of now forgotten painters. Downstairs, the large, empty, white, circular Memorial Court, commemorates Aberdonians who died in the two world wars and the 165 people who lost their lives in the Piper Alpha oil rig disaster in 1988.

The gallery opens 10 am to 5 pm Monday to Saturday, 2 to 5 pm Sunday. Admission is free.

Old Aberdeen

Old Aberdeen is a suburb 1½ miles north of the centre. The name is somewhat misleading, since the area south around the harbour is actually older; it's called Alton in Gaelic, meaning village by the pool, and this was anglicised to Old Town. The university buildings and St Machar's Cathedral are at the centre of this peaceful, urban oasis.

It was here that Bishop Elphinstone established King's College, Aberdeen's first university, in 1495. Earl Marischal founded the college in the city centre in 1593 but it wasn't until the 19th century that the two colleges were united as the University of Aberdeen. The 16th-century **King's College Chapel** (☎ 272137) is easily recognisable by its crowned spire. The interior of the chapel is largely unchanged – the stained-glass windows and choir stalls are impressive. It opens 9 am to 5 pm Monday to Friday. Admission is free. **King's College Visitors Centre** (☎ 273702) houses a multimedia display on the university's history; next to it is a cafe. The centre opens 10 am to 5 pm Monday to Saturday, from 2 pm Sunday, year round. Admission is free.

The 15th century **St Machar's Cathedral** (☎ 485988), with its massive twin towers, is one of the few examples in the country of a fortified cathedral. According to legend, St Machar was ordered to establish a church where the river takes the shape of a bishop's crook, which it does just here. The cathedral is best known for its impressive heraldic ceiling, dating from 1520, which has 48 shields of kings, nobles, archbishops and bishops. It opens 9 am to 5 pm daily; services on Sunday are at 11 am and 6 pm.

Scuba Diving

If you're willing to brave the waters of the North Sea then PADI-approved Aberdeen Watersports (☎ 581313), 79 Waterloo Quay, will take you out.

Places to Stay

Hostels A mile west of the train station, *Aberdeen Youth Hostel (☎ 646988, 8 Queen's Rd)* is open year round, and charges £12.25/10.75 for adults/under-18s in small dormitories (£1 surcharge in July and August). Walk west along Union St and take the right fork along Albyn Place until you reach a roundabout; Queen's Rd continues on the western side.

During university holidays some colleges let rooms to visitors. The list of colleges offering accommodation changes from year to year – check with the TIC. The *University of Aberdeen (☎ 272644, Crombie Johnston Hall)* has en-suite rooms from £24.20 to £35.55 per person; dinner is available. The *Scottish Agricultural College (☎ 711195, Craibstone Estate, Bucksburn)*, 5 miles north-west of Aberdeen, offers functional rooms from £20 to £36 per person.

B&Bs & Hotels Clusters of B&Bs line Bon Accord St and Springbank Terrace (both close to the centre) and Great Western Road (the A93, about a mile). They're all much the same occupying two or three-storey terraced houses, and are more expensive than is usual in Scotland. With all the oil industry workers here, single rooms are at a premium, but prices tend to be lower at the weekend.

The more expensive guesthouses are at the city end of Bon Accord St. At No 154, the nonsmoking and efficient *Applewood Guest House (☎ 580617)* charges from £20 to £26 per person for B&B, with shared bathroom. *Crynoch Guest House (☎ 582743, 164 Bon Accord St)* has singles/doubles from £20/34. The two guesthouses next door are both similarly priced: *Denmore Guest House (☎ 587751)*, No 166, and *Dunrovin Guest House (☎ 586081)*, No 168.

Nearby, *Nicholl's Guest House (☎ 572 867, 63 Springbank Terrace)* is a recommended, friendly place with rooms at

around £20/32 (£30/44 with bathroom). There are plenty of other alternatives in the area.

There are numerous places along Great Western Rd. *Penny Meadow Private Hotel (☎ 588037)*, No 189, is a small, friendly place where rooms with bathroom cost from £34/48. The *Corner House Hotel (☎ 313 063)*, No 385, is a solid, turreted building with off-street parking and evening meals if required. It charges from £38/50 for en-suite rooms. For nonsmokers only, *Strathisla Guest House (☎ 321026)* at No 408 provides comfortable rooms all with bathroom and charges from £27/40. The genteel *Kildonan Guest House (☎ 316115)*, No 410, charges from £25/40. *Aurora Guest House (☎ 311602)* at No 429 is another small, family-run B&B. There are five rooms, ranging from £21/32 to £22/36, all with shared bathroom.

Back in the centre of Aberdeen, the friendly *Brentwood Hotel (☎ 595440, 101 Crown St)* is comfy, but often full during the week. Rooms cost from £35/50 to £70/80; less at weekends. The hotel has a good bar and restaurant.

Atholl Hotel (☎ 323505, ℮ info@atholl -aberdeen.co.uk, 54 Kings Gate), an elegant granite building on the western edge of the town, has an excellent reputation. Luxurious rooms range from £51/59 at weekends to £81/89 during the week. A fine hotel in the town centre is the *Thistle Aberdeen Caledonian (☎ 640233, ℮ aberdeen.cale donian@thistle.co.uk, Union Terrace)*, with 80 rooms. Its published tariff starts from £115/135 but cheaper rates are available.

Places to Eat

Aberdeen has an excellent range of places to eat, from branches of the big-name, fast-food chains to expensive gourmet restaurants.

For cheap eats there's the food court on the 1st floor of the *Bon Accord Shopping Centre* with stalls offering sandwiches, pastries, pastas and pizzas.

The *New Dolphin (3 Chapel St)*, just off Union St, isn't a Chinese take-away but an excellent fish and chip shop with a sit-in section. Haddock and chips costs £3.95. It

CENTRAL SCOTLAND

opens from 11.45 am till late Monday to Saturday, from 4 pm Sunday. *Ashvale Fish Restaurant* (☎ 596981, 46 Great Western Rd) is a popular fish and chip restaurant and takeaway that's well known outside the city, having won several awards. Mushy peas with haddock and chips (from £6.25) don't taste as bad as they sound. It opens 11 am to 11 pm daily.

The cafe at the *Lemon Tree* (☎ 642230, 5 West North St) does excellent coffee, meals and cakes. It opens noon to 3 pm Wednesday to Sunday (see also under Entertainment).

The 1st floor *Victoria Restaurant* (☎ 621 381, 140 Union St), beside a jewellery store, does good-quality snacks and sandwiches from £3.50, and more substantial meals from £4.25. It's closed Sunday. Just around the corner, the *Wild Boar* (☎ 625357, 19 Belmont St) is a popular, stylish bistro. Main courses range from £4.50 to £11, with vegetarian choices. Cake fanatics will have a great time here. It opens daily noon till late.

Poldino's (☎ 647777, 7 Little Belmont St) is an upmarket Italian restaurant serving pizza and pasta for £6.90 to £7.80. It opens noon to 2.30 pm, 6 to 10.45 pm Monday to Saturday.

The highly recommended *Owlies Brasserie* (☎ 649267, Littlejohn St) is good value and very popular. It produces tasty food with unusual flavours, including a good range of vegetarian and vegan food – try the couscous de legumes (£7.60). It's closed Sunday and Monday.

There's a branch of the chain *Littlejohn's* (☎ 635666, 46 School Hill), with all the usual diversions including the toy train. The service is good if a little slick. There are burgers from £4.95, and other mains (such as chargrilled chicken) from £7.25 to £8.55.

For a splurge, you have a few choices. *Silver Darling Restaurant* (☎ 576229), at the southern end of the Beach Esplanade on Pocra Quay in Footdee, east of the centre, is renowned for its French cuisine, seafood and superb location overlooking the port entrance. Mains cost £13.50 to £18.50.

Four miles south-west of the centre in the pretty suburb of Cults is the excellent *Faradays Restaurant* (☎ 869666, 2 Kirk Brae).

The cuisine is a combination of traditional Scottish and French, with lots of fresh, local ingredients. On Friday and Saturday nights it offers a three course dinner for £18.50. It opens noon to 2 pm, and 7.30 to 9.30 pm Tuesday to Saturday.

Entertainment

To find out about current listings check *What's on in Aberdeen*, available from the TIC, or the bimonthly *Aberdeen Arts & Recreation Listings*. You can book tickets for most plays and concerts on the Aberdeen Box Office line (☎ 641122).

Theatre & Music The city's main theatre is *His Majesty's* (☎ 637788, Rosemount Viaduct), which hosts everything from ballet and opera to musicals and pantomimes. The *Music Hall* (☎ 632080, Union St) is the main venue for classical music concerts. The *Aberdeen Arts Centre* (☎ 635208, King St) stages exhibitions at its gallery and drama in its theatre.

The *Lemon Tree* (☎ 642230, 5 West North St) usually has an interesting program of dance, music or drama. It hosts festivals and often has rock, jazz and folk bands playing.

Pubs & Nightclubs Aberdeen is a great city for a pub crawl – it's more of a question of knowing where to stop than where to start. Note that many pubs don't serve food in the evening.

The *Prince of Wales* (☎ 640597, 7 St Nicholas Lane) is possibly the best-known Aberdeen pub. Down an alley off Union St, it boasts the longest counter in the city, a great range of real ales and good-value pub grub at lunchtime. It can also get very crowded. Nearby, on Back Wynd, *Booth's* is a better place for a pub lunch. It has a good range of traditional pies as well as ales and malts.

Frankenstein (☎ 626720, 504 Union St), a pub with a suitably 'horrific' decor and mood lighting, is a popular spot for young people. Also popular with the young set is *Slain's Castle* (☎ 624642, Belmont St), in a deconsecrated church; here the theme is ghosts and vampires. Its cocktail list is named after the seven deadly sins: 'Greed' is a concoction of vodka, kahlua, cola and cream.

There are numerous nightclubs but most won't let you in if you're wearing trainers and some will turn you away if you're wearing jeans. *The Ministry of Sin* (☎ 211661, Dee St), in a deconsecrated church, attracts young clubbers from near and far. One of the wildest clubs is upstairs at *O'Neill's* pub (☎ 621 456, 9 Back Wynd), open nighty until 2 am, while downstairs there's live music.

Getting There & Away

Aberdeen is 507 miles from London, 129 from Edinburgh and 105 from Inverness. See the fares tables in the Getting Around chapter.

Air Aberdeen airport (for information phone ☎ 722331) is about 7 miles north-west of the city centre. The oil industry ensures that there are flights to numerous cities in the UK, including Orkney and Shetland, and international flights to the Netherlands and Norway.

Bus Scottish Citylink runs direct services to Dundee (£6.70, two hours), Perth (£9.50, 2½ hours), Stirling (£13.20, 3½ hours, Edinburgh (£13.50, four hours) and Glasgow (£13.50, 4¼ hours). National Express (☎ 0870 580 8080) runs buses daily from London, but it's a tedious 12 hour trip (£28 one way).

Stagecoach Bluebird (☎ 212266) is the major regional operator.

Train There are numerous trains from London's King's Cross station, taking an acceptable seven hours, although they are considerably more expensive than buses. Other destinations served from Aberdeen by rail include Edinburgh (£33.10, 2¾ hours), Glasgow (£36.40, 2¾ hours), Perth (£20.20, 1¾ hours), Stirling (£30, 2¼ hours), Dundee (£17, 1¼ hours) and Inverness (£17.80, 2¼ hours).

Car There are several car rental companies in Aberdeen. Arnold Clark (☎ 249159), Girdleness Rd, has competitive rates starting at £16 per day for a small Fiat. Melville's (☎ 0870 160 9999), 16 Broomhill Rd,

charges £19 per day (plus mileage if under four days, and insurance) for a small car.

Boat The passenger terminal is a short walk east of the train and bus stations. P&O (☎ 572 615) has daily evening departures from Monday to Friday leaving for Lerwick (Shetland). The trip takes approximately 14 hours (20 hours via Orkney). A reclining seat costs £52/58 in the low/high season, one way.

Mid-April to mid-December there are weekly Saturday (plus Tuesday from June to August), departures to Stromness (Orkney). The journey costs £39/42 and takes 10 hours.

Getting Around

To/From the Airport Bus Nos 27/27A run from the city centre to the airport, taking about 35 minutes (£1.30). A taxi to the airport costs around £7.

Bus The *Aberdeen Passport* is available from the TIC and gives basic details of city bus services. For local bus information phone the Grampian Busline (☎ 650000). The two main operators are First Aberdeen (☎ 650065) and Stagecoach Bluebird (☎ 212266).

The most useful services are First Aberdeen's bus Nos 18, 19 and 24 from Union St to Great Western Rd, No 27 from the bus station to the youth hostel, and Nos 20 and 26 for Old Aberdeen. If you're using the buses frequently, get a prepaid farecard (£5) from the First Aberdeen kiosk on St Nicholas St near St Nicholas' Shopping Centre.

Taxi There are taxis at the train station or you could phone Mair's (☎ 724040).

Bicycle Mountain bikes can be rented from Alpine Bikes (☎ 211455), 64 Holburn St. It opens daily and charges £8/12 per half/full day during the week, £24 for the weekend (Friday evening to Monday morning).

DEESIDE & DONSIDE

The region around the Rivers Dee and Don, eastwards from Braemar to the coast, is castle country and includes the Queen's residence at Balmoral. There are more fanciful examples of Scottish baronial architecture here than anywhere else in Scotland. The TICs have information on a Castle Trail, but you really need private transport to follow it.

The River Dee, flowing through the southern part of this area, has its source in the Cairngorm mountains, to the west. The River Don follows a shorter, but almost parallel, course. The best walking country is around Braemar and Ballater, in upper Deeside.

Ballater
☎ 013397 • pop 1260

This small town supplies nearby Balmoral Castle with provisions, hence the shops sporting 'By Royal Appointment' crests. The TIC (☎ 55306), Station Square, opens 10 to 1 pm and 2 to 5 pm Monday to Saturday, Easter to October, 1 to 5 pm Sunday.

The place has been famous for its spring water since the 19th century. There are no great sights, but there are some pleasant walks in the surrounding hills and the TIC has details. The woodland walk up Craigendarroch (400m) takes just over an hour, but it's quite steep. Morven (872m) is a more serious prospect, taking around six hours, but has good views from the top.

B&Bs include the cosy *Celicall* (☎ 55699, 3 Braemar Rd), from £22/36 a single/double. The *Alexandra Hotel* (☎ 55376, 12 Bridge Square) is a friendly, comfortable hotel offering B&B from £24 to £30 per person.

Stagecoach Bluebird (☎ 55422) runs buses almost every hour from Aberdeen (£6.70, 1¾ hours); every two hours on Sunday. The service continues to Braemar.

Balmoral Castle

Eight miles west of Ballater, Balmoral Castle (☎ 013397-42334) was built for Queen Victoria in 1855 as a private residence for the royal family. The grounds and an exhibition of paintings and other royal trinkets in the ballroom are open; the rest of the castle is closed to the prying eyes of the public. On the edge of the estate is Crathie Church, which the royals use when they're here.

Balmoral opens 10 am to 5 pm daily, Easter to early August (closed on Sunday in April), and attracts large numbers of visitors. Admission costs £4/1. It's just off the A93

(where there's a TIC) near the village of Crathie and can be reached on the Aberdeen-Braemar bus (see the Braemar section).

Braemar
☎ 013397 • pop 410

Braemar is an attractive village surrounded by mountains; it makes an excellent walking base. There's a helpful TIC (☎ 41600), The Mews, Mar Rd, which opens daily year round and has lots of useful information on walks in the area.

Things to See & Do North of the village, turreted **Braemar Castle** (☎ 41219) dates from 1628, and was a garrison post after the 1745 Jacobite Rebellion. It opens 10 am to 6 pm Saturday to Thursday, Easter to October. Admission is £3/free.

An easy walk from Braemar is up **Creag Choinnich** (538m), a hill to the east above the A93. There are route markers and the walk takes about 1½ hours. For a longer walk (three hours) and superb views of the Cairngorms, climb **Morrone** (859m), the mountain south of Braemar.

Special Events On the first Saturday in September, Braemar is invaded by 20,000 people, including the royal family, for the Braemar Gathering (Highland Games); bookings are essential.

Places to Stay & Eat South of the centre, *Braemar Youth Hostel* (☎ 41659, 21) Glenshee Rd) is open all year and charges £9.25/ 8 for adults/under-18s. *Braemar Bunkhouse* (☎ 41242, 15 Mar Rd) has dorm accommodation for £7 to £8.50 and opens year round.

Craiglea (☎ 41641, Hillside Dr) is a homely B&B with singles/doubles from £17/ 35, while *Wilderbank* (☎ 41651, Kindrochit Drive) has two en-suite doubles for £18 per person. *Callater Lodge Hotel* (☎ 41275, 9 Glenshee Rd) is a small hotel set in its own grounds; most rooms have baths and cost £23 per person. Evening meals are available. The top place to stay is *Braemar Lodge* (☎ 416 27, Glenshee Rd), a restored Victorian shooting lodge on the outskirts of the town. B&B costs from £20 to £40 per person.

The pubs are the best places for food and entertainment: *Fife Arms Hotel* serves bar meals at lunch and dinner and snacks from 9 am to 5 pm; *Invercauld Arms Hotel* also serves food and a decent pint.

Getting There & Away It's a beautiful drive between Perth and Braemar but public transport is limited. From Aberdeen to Braemar (2¼ hours, £6.50) up to six buses a day, operated by Stagecoach Bluebird (☎ 01224-212266), travel along the beautiful valley of the River Dee.

Inverey

Five miles west of Braemar is the little settlement of Inverey. Numerous mountain walks start from here, including the adventurous Lairig Ghru walk – 21 miles over the pass to Aviemore. The Cairngorm peaks of Cairn Gorm and Ben Macdui (see under Aviemore in the Highlands & Northern Islands chapter) are actually just this side of the regional border.

Inverey Youth Hostel (☎ 013397-41969) opens mid-May to early October; beds cost £6.75/6 for adults/under-18s. Postbus (☎ 012 46-546329) No 072 leaves Braemar at 12.30 pm Monday to Saturday for the hostel (1½ hours) and Linn of Dee.

Glenshee

Glenshee is Scotland's largest skiing area, where the borders of Perthshire and Aberdeenshire meet. The A93 ploughs through the middle of the resort. **Blairgowrie** is the main accommodation centre for Glenshee, although there's a small settlement 5 miles south of the ski runs at **Spittal of Glenshee**. The TIC (☎ 01250-872960) at Blairgowrie, 26 Wellmeadow, opens year round.

Places to Stay & Eat As well as the accommodation centres of Braemar and Blairgowrie, places to stay are strung out along the A93 around Glenshee. Just south of the Spittal of Glenshee the friendly *Compass Christian Centre* (☎ 01250-885209, *Glenshee Lodge*) is an activity centre, and welcomes all comers. It charges £15 per person for room only, and £5 more for lunch.

The *Spittal of Glenshee Hotel* (☎ 01250-885215) offers B&B in rooms with bathroom from £24.75/33.50 a single/double; it also has a rear bunkhouse where dorm beds cost £11 to £12.50. Grand *Dalmunzie House Hotel* (☎ 01250-885224, *Glenshee*) boasts the highest nine hole golf course in Britain, and is set in a 2400-hectare estate 1½ miles off the main road. B&B costs from £37/60.

Getting There & Away Strathtay Scottish (☎ 01382-228345) operates a service from Perth to Blairgowrie (50 minutes, £2.10), hourly Monday to Saturday, six times a day on Sunday. The only service from Blairgowrie to the Glenshee area is the once daily Monday to Saturday postbus (☎ 01246-546329) No 216 to Spittal of Glenshee.

INLAND ABERDEENSHIRE & MORAY

The direct, inland rail and road route from Aberdeen to Inverness cuts across rolling agricultural country that, thanks to a mild climate, produces everything from grain to flower bulbs. The grain is turned into that magical liquid known as malt whisky. You may be tempted by the **Malt Whisky Trail**, a 70 mile signposted tour which gives you an inside look and complimentary tastings at a number of famous distilleries (including Cardhu, Glenfiddich and The Glenlivet). TICs stock a leaflet covering the tour.

Castle Fraser (☎ 01330-833463; NTS), 3 miles south of Kemnay, looks rather like a French chateau and dates from the 16th century. **Haddo House** (☎ 01651-851440; NTS), 19 miles north of Aberdeen, was designed by William Adam in 1732. It's best described as a classic English stately home transplanted to Scotland. **Fyvie Castle** (☎ 01651-891266; NTS), 8 miles south of Turriff, is a magnificent example of Scottish baronial architecture. There are numerous other castles in various states of preservation.

Huntly

☎ 01466 • pop 4150

This small town, with an impressive ruined castle, is in a strategically important position

The Malt Whisky Trail

Around 40 Scottish whisky distilleries open to the public and you should certainly try to visit one while you're in Scotland.

In some, showing tourists around has become a slick marketing operation, complete with promotional videos, free drams, gift shops that rival the distillery in size and an entry charge of around £3. In Aberdeenshire & Moray, seven Speyside distillers – Cardhu, Dallas Dhu, Glenfarclas, Glenfiddich, Glen Grant, The Glenlivet and Strathisla – and Speyside Cooperage (where oak casks are made) promote themselves in the Malt Whisky Trail, a pleasant drive around Speyside. Check out the trail online at www.maltwhiskytrail.com.

You could also create your own malt whisky trail on the Isle of Islay (Inner Hebrides) where six distilleries are open to visitors – Ardbeg, Bunnahabhainn, Bowmore, Caol Ila, Laphroaig and Lagavulin.

The process of making malt whisky begins with malting. Barley is soaked in water and allowed to germinate so that enzymes are produced to convert the starch in the barley to fermentable sugar. The barley is then dried in a malt kiln over the peat fire that gives malt whisky its distinctive taste. Since most distilleries now buy in their malted barley, tourists rarely see this part of the process.

The malt is milled, mixed with hot water and left in a large tank, the *mash tun*. The starch is converted into sugar and this liquid, or 'wort', is drawn off into another large tank, the washback, for fermentation.

This weak alcoholic solution, or wash, is distilled twice in large copper-pot stills. The process is controlled by the stillman, who collects only the middle portion of the second distillation to mature in oak barrels. The spirit remains in the barrels for at least three years, often much longer. During bottling, water is added to reduce its strength.

Some recommended distillery tours include: Glenfiddich, The Glenlivet and Strathisla on Speyside; any of the Isle of Islay distilleries; and Highland Park on Orkney, one of the few distilleries where you still see the barley malting process.

on a low-lying plain, along the main route from Aberdeen into the Strathspey and Moray regions. The TIC (☎ 792255), 7a The Square, opens daily from early April to late October.

On the northern edge of town, **Huntly Castle** (☎ 793191; HS), the former stronghold of the Gordons, is on the banks of the River Deveron. Over the main door is a superb carving that includes the royal arms and the figures of Christ and St Michael. The castle opens standard HS hours. Admission costs £2.50/1.

Stagecoach Bluebird (☎ 01224-212266) bus No 10 (Aberdeen to Inverness) passes through Huntly hourly each day. The town is also on the rail line that follows the same route.

Dufftown
☎ 01340 • pop 1700

Founded only in 1817 by James Duff, 4th Earl of Fife, Dufftown is 14 miles west of Huntly. It's a good place to start the Malt Whisky Trail – there are seven working distilleries in Dufftown alone! The TIC (☎ 820 501), 9a The Square in the clock tower, opens Monday to Saturday, April to October, plus Sunday June to August.

North of town is **Glenfiddich Distillery Visitors Centre** (☎ 820373). Visitors are guided through the process of distilling, and can also see whisky being bottled – the only Highland distillery where this is done on the premises. It opens 9.30 am to 4.30 pm Monday to Saturday, year round; noon to 4.30 pm Sunday, Easter to mid-October. There's no admission charge – your free dram really is free.

Stagecoach Bluebird (☎ 01224-212266) links Dufftown to Elgin hourly (no Sunday service).

GRAMPIAN COAST

The Grampians meet the sea at Stonehaven, home to spectacular Dunnottar Castle. Continuing north around the coast from Aberdeen, there are long stretches of sand and, on the north coast, some magical fishing villages – like Pennan, where the film *Local Hero* was shot.

Stonehaven

☎ 01569 • pop 9310

Originally a small fishing village, 'Stanehyve' became the county town of Kincardineshire in 1600 and is now a low-key, seaside resort. The TIC (☎ 762806), 66 Allardice St, opens 10 am to 7 pm Monday to Saturday, 1 to 7 pm Sunday, July and August; 10 am to 1 pm and 2 to 5 pm Monday to Saturday, April, May and October; until 6 pm June and September.

The most pleasant way to reach **Dunnottar Castle** (☎ 762173), 1½ miles south, is on foot; the TIC has a walking leaflet. The castle ruins are spread out across a flat rock rising 45m above the sea – as dramatic a film set as any director could wish for. It was last used for Zeffirelli's *Hamlet*, starring Mel Gibson. The original fortress was built in the 9th century; the keep is the most substantial remnant, but the Drawing Room is more interesting. The castle supported quite a large community, judging from the extent of the ruins.

It opens 9 am to 6 pm Monday to Saturday, 2 to 5 pm Sunday, Easter to September; 9 am to sundown Monday to Friday, 2 pm to sundown Sunday, November to March, last admission is half an hour before closing. Admission costs £3.50/1.

The TIC has a list of B&Bs or you can try the welcoming *Seaview* (☎ 766673, 59 Ann St), uphill from the centre, which has two rooms with shared bathroom for £20 per person, and gives you the option of a traditional or vegetarian/vegan breakfast.

Scottish Citylink (☎ 0870 550 5050) and Stagecoach Bluebird (☎ 01261-833533) buses stop in Stonehaven travelling between Dundee and Aberdeen, as do trains following the same route.

Aberdeen to Fraserburgh

There are attractive **beaches** at Cruden Bay and Newburgh along this section of the coast, but little to hold the visitor. The remains of a once-great fishing industry are now based in Peterhead.

At Fraserburgh, **Scotland's Lighthouse Museum** (☎ 01346-511022) is worth a look if you're in the area. There are guided tours to the top of Kinnaird Head lighthouse (originally a castle). It opens April to October, Monday to Saturday from 10 am to 6 pm, Sunday noon to 4 pm; November to March, Monday to Saturday 10 am to 4 pm, Sunday noon to 4 pm; £2.50/2. Kinnaird Head is a clear landmark, a fact recognised as early as AD 140 by the ancient geographer, Ptolemy. Fraserburgh could be an attractive little town, but there's vandalism and neglect here.

Stagecoach Bluebird (☎ 01261-833533) bus No 251 runs once a day Monday to Saturday, between Fraserburgh and Aberdeen.

Banff & Macduff

☎ 01261 • pop 8170 (combined)

A popular seaside resort, the twin towns of Banff and Macduff are separated by Banff Bridge. Interesting Banff is a fairly attractive little town and nearby Macduff is a busy fishing port. The helpful TIC (☎ 812419), High St, Banff, opens Monday to Saturday, April to September, plus Sunday in July and August, and has a Walkman tour (£1) to encourage you to look around the town.

Completed in 1749, **Duff House** (☎ 818 181), in Banff upstream from the bridge and across from the TIC, is an impressive Georgian baroque mansion designed by William Adam. It's been a hotel, hospital and POW camp and is now an art gallery housing a collection of paintings from the National Gallery of Scotland. It opens 11 am to 5 pm daily, April to September; 11 am to 4 pm Thursday to Sunday, October to March. Admission costs £3/2.

Stagecoach Bluebird (☎ 833533) runs hourly buses to Aberdeen and Elgin, and a twice daily service to Fraserburgh.

Elgin

☎ 01343 • pop 20,000

At the heart of Moray, Elgin has been the provincial capital since the 13th century. The TIC (☎ 542666), 17 High St, opens daily April to September, weekdays only October to March.

In medieval times, Elgin was of greater importance than it is now. The great **Elgin Cathedral** (☎ 547171; HS), known as the 'lantern of the north', was consecrated in 1224. In 1390 it was burnt down by the infamous Wolf of Badenach, the illegitimate son of Robert II, following his excommunication by the bishop. It was rebuilt, but ruined once more in the Reformation. It opens 9.30 am to 6.30 pm Monday to Saturday, 2 to 6.30 pm Sunday, April to September; until 4.30 pm Sunday and closed Thursday afternoon and Friday the rest of the year. Admission costs £3/1.20.

Places to Stay A few minutes walk from the centre of the town, *Bellville (☎ 541515, 14 South College St)* opens year round and has singles/doubles from £17/34, with bathroom. *Southbank Guest House (☎ 547132, 36 Academy St)* has 11 rooms (all with shower or bath) and charges from £23/38. Just west of the centre, *Rosemount (☎ 542 907, 3 Mayne Rd)* offers comfortable B&B in two en-suite rooms for £25/40.

Getting There & Away Stagecoach Bluebird (☎ 544222) runs services hourly along the coast to Banff and Macduff, south to Dufftown, and half-hourly west to Inverness, and south-east to Aberdeen. Trains run six to 10 times daily from Elgin to Aberdeen and Inverness.

Findhorn & Forres

Old and new hippies should check out the Findhorn Foundation (☎ 01309-690311), Forres IV36 0RD. The Foundation is an international spiritual community founded in 1962. There are about 150 members and many more sympathetic souls who have moved into the vicinity. With no formal creed, the community is dedicated to creating 'a deeper sense of the sacred in everyday life, and to dealing with work, relationships and our environment in new and more fulfilling ways'. In many ways it's very impressive. Find out more on their Web site at www.findhorn.org.

There are daily tours at 2 pm in summer. The area it occupies isn't particularly attractive itself – it started life in the Findhorn Bay Caravan Park and still occupies one end of the site. Far more attractive are the nearby fishing village of Findhorn (1 mile north) and the town of Forres (2½ miles). It's possible to stay in *Findhorn Bay Caravan Park (☎ 01309-690203)*, which has camping from £6.50. There are also week-long residential programs from £240 to £495, including food and accommodation. Findhorn is 4 miles north of Forres, which is on the main bus and rail route between Inverness and Elgin and has a few eateries.

Highlands & Northern Islands

Forget castles, forget towns, forget villages. The Highlands and northern islands are all about mountains, sea, heather, moors, lochs – and wide, empty, exhilarating space. This is one of Europe's last great wildernesses and it's more beautiful than you can imagine. The east coast is dramatic, but it's the north and west, where the mountains and sea collide, that exhaust superlatives. Some of the most beautiful areas can only be reached by many miles of single-track road, by boat or on foot. Make the effort and you'll be rewarded!

The Highlands is an imprecise term for the upland area that covers the far west and northern half of mainland Scotland. This chapter covers the administrative region known as Highland, the Isle of Skye and the islands of the northern Inner Hebrides, the Outer Hebrides (Western Isles), Orkney and Shetland.

ORIENTATION & INFORMATION

The Great Glen, with its series of deep, narrow lochs (including mysterious Loch Ness) cuts across the country south-west to north-east, from Fort William to Inverness, neatly dividing the southern Highlands from the north. East of Loch Ness are the Monadhliath and Cairngorm Mountains' Arctic plateaus, with Aviemore as the main tourist resort. Ben Nevis dominates the town of Fort William in the west.

Most population centres in the rugged, wild Highlands are dotted around the coast. Several island groups are linked to the Highlands. The Orkney Islands are off the north-eastern corner, and farther north are the remote Shetland Islands. West are the Outer Hebrides, while closer, between the Outer Hebrides and the mainland, the beautiful Isle of Skye (part of the Inner Hebrides) is a stone's throw from the mainland coast – to which it's connected by a bridge. For the Isle of Mull and other Inner Hebridean islands to the south, see the Central Scotland chapter.

There are Tourist Information Centres (TICs) in the major towns in the Highlands

Highlights

- Marvelling at the soaring mountain peaks of Glen Shiel
- Seeing how many munros you can bag in the Cuillin Hills on Skye
- Taking one of the world's great railway journeys along the West Highland line from Fort William to Mallaig
- Cycling the scenic Great Glen from Fort William to Inverness
- Enjoying the coastal walks of Hoy and Yesneby in the Orkneys
- Viewing the many thousands of birds in the Shetlands

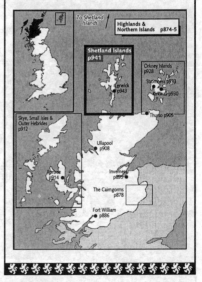

and northern islands, but many smaller offices close during the low season, usually October to March or April; and those that open year round have shorter low-season opening hours.

Almost all TICs charge £1 to £2 for accommodation bookings. The regional tourist

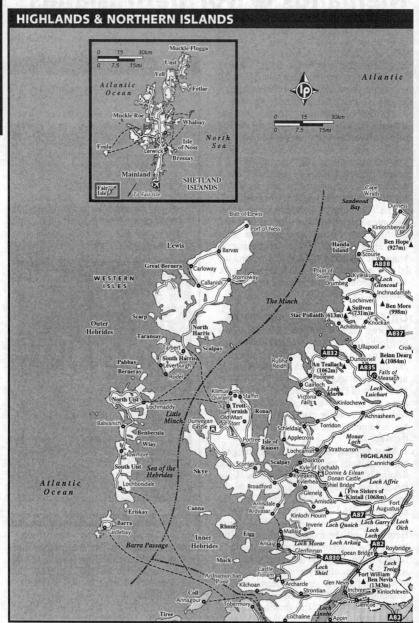

HIGHLANDS & NORTHERN ISLANDS

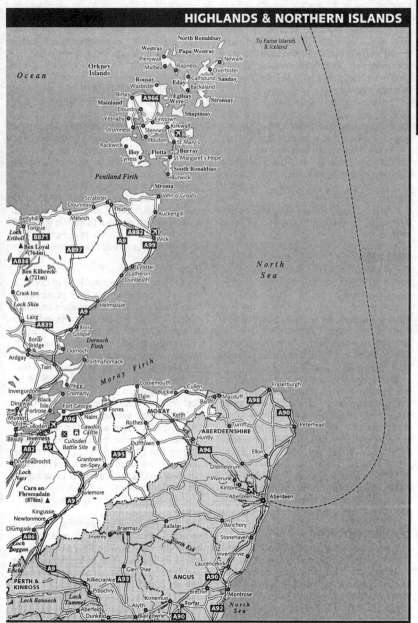

boards all publish annual accommodation guides, usually available for free. The guide from the Highlands of Scotland Tourist Board (☎ 01997-421160, ℮ admin@host.co .uk) covers the Highlands north of Glencoe (and includes the Isle of Skye). Its Web site is at www.host.co.uk.

The Western Isles Tourist Board (☎ 01851-703088) does the same for the Western Isles. Its Web site is at www.witb.co.uk. There are also separate tourist boards for Orkney (☎ 01856-872856, ℮ info@otb.ossian.net) and Shetland (☎ 01595-693434, ℮ shetland .tourism@zetnet.co.uk). Their Web sites are at www.orkney.com and www.shetland-tour ism.co.uk, respectively.

A Web site of local information, including maps, is available at www.cali.co.uk /highexp.

WALKING

The Highlands offer some of Scotland's (and Britain's) finest walking country, whether along the coast, or up to inland peaks and ridges such as the Aonach Eagach, the Five Sisters of Kintail, An Teallach, Stac Pollaidh, Suilven (the Sugar Loaf) or Ben Hope – Britain's most northerly 'Munro', a mountain of 900m or higher. See the later boxed text 'Munros & Munro Bagging'.

The mountains can be treacherous and every year a number of walkers need rescuing; some even die. The weather can change quickly. Mountaincall is a telephone weather-report service – call ☎ 0891 500441 for western Scotland or ☎ 0891 500442 for eastern Scotland (both 50p per minute). Avalanche information is available free on ☎ 0800 987 988. The leaflet, *Enjoy the Scottish Hills in Safety*, published by the Mountaineering Council of Scotland, offers basic safety tips and is available at outdoor equipment shops.

OTHER ACTIVITIES

Fishing is a popular Highlands activity, but it's strictly regulated and some of the famous salmon fishing beats can be very expensive. Fishing for brown trout in the trout lochs is more affordable. Local TICs can suggest the best locations and advise on permits and equipment.

Cycling, bird-watching, pony trekking and golf are other popular Highland activities, and surfing is gaining in adherents: Thurso, on the north coast, has some of Europe's best surf.

GETTING AROUND

Aviemore, Inverness, Fort William, Mallaig and Oban are easily accessible by bus and train. Buses and trains also provide regular connections from Inverness up the east coast to Wick and Thurso, and from Inverness across the Highlands to Kyle of Lochalsh and Ullapool. Postbuses (☎ 01246-546329) serve many remote communities. Although you can make your way around the north and west coasts from Thurso to Ullapool and on to Kyle of Lochalsh by public transport, consider hiring a car in Inverness or Fort William to visit more remote areas.

Bus

Wick, Thurso, Ullapool and Kyle of Lochalsh can all be reached by bus from Inverness, or from Edinburgh and Glasgow via Inverness or Fort William. See the Inverness and North & West Coast sections later for information.

There are several bus services specifically aimed at backpackers. Go Blue Banana (☎ 0131-556 2000) operates a hostel-to-hostel loop around Scotland with stops at Inverness, Kyleakin on the Isle of Skye and Fort William. Haggis Backpackers (☎ 0131-557 9393) has a similar service that includes Oban (see the introductory Getting Around chapter under Backpackers Buses). The Orkney Bus (☎ 01955-611353) operates an east-coast link from Inverness bus station to Kirkwall on Orkney via John o'Groats daily, May to September.

Train

The two Highland railway lines from Inverness – north along the east coast to Wick and Thurso, and west to Kyle of Lochalsh – are justly famous. The West Highland line also follows a spectacular route from Glasgow to Fort William and Mallaig (for the Isle of Skye and the Small Isles).

ScotRail's Highland Rover ticket gives unlimited travel for four days in eight (£49) on

Munros & Munro Bagging

The Scottish Highlands cover the most extensive tract of hill country in the British Isles, but Scottish mountains are relatively modest in height, with Ben Nevis – the highest – reaching only 1343m above sea level. In addition to their appeal to scenery seekers, they present many challenges for hill-walkers, rock, snow and ice climbers and mountaineers. Unpredictable weather conditions any time of year and often remote summits, together with few opportunities for shelter, mean that those who venture into the hills should be properly equipped and aware of their own capabilities.

At the end of the 19th century, Sir Hugh Munro compiled a list of summits over 3000 feet with nearly 300 gaining the status of 'Munros'. Since then, after various revisions to the list, which is maintained by the Scottish Mountaineering Club (SMC), there are now 284 Munros in the eponymous tables.

'Munro bagging' is a popular leisure activity, not to say obsession. Sir Hugh himself narrowly failed to complete the full round; the first person to succeed in this monumental task was the Reverend AE Robertson in 1901, a Scottish Gaelic-speaking minister of the church. Since then, his feat has been matched by about 2000 others and the number continues to increase.

Munro bagging has created a boom in books devoted to walking and climbing in the Scottish mountains, so there's no shortage of advice on the subject.

To the uninitiated, it may seem curious that Munro baggers see a day (or longer) plodding around to the point of exhaustion in the mist, cloud and driving rain as time well spent. However, for those who can add one or more ticks to their list, the vagaries of the weather are part of the enjoyment – at least in retrospect. Munro bagging is, of course, more than merely ticking off names on a list. It takes you to some of the wildest, most beautiful parts of Scotland and, for many, provides years of healthy enjoyment and spiritual reward.

Visitors to Scotland may wish to experience something of the magic of the Scottish mountains, and there's no reason why any reasonably fit person shouldn't bag a few, but, with limited time, choices must be made. All parts of the Highlands and Islands have their own devotees and there are many Munros within easy reach of Scotland's major cities.

Some areas are outstanding for their own particular reasons. These include the Torridon Hills in Wester Ross, ancient mountains rising steeply from sea level; Ben Nevis and Glencoe, offering an infinite variety of walks and climbs as well as the highest peak and biggest cliffs in Britain; and the Cairngorms, a sub-arctic wilderness of stoney plateau far from public roads. The traverse of the Cuillin Hills on the Isle of Skye provides the finest mountaineering challenge of all, taking in seven Munros with serious rock climbing punctuating the route. Completion of the traverse in a day is a considerable achievement, but is really only possible in good, settled weather.

The weather is the key. When the sun shines, it's easy to understand the lure of the Scottish mountains, but wind, rain, and even snow are likely at any time of year. Skill and judgement are then at a premium in deciding whether to carry on, to turn back or even not to set out at all. On such occasions it's worth reminding yourself that the hills will be there for another day.

Hugh Gore

the lines from Inverness to Wick and Thurso, Kyle of Lochalsh, Aberdeen and Aviemore; on the West Highland line between Glasgow, Oban, Fort William and Mallaig; free travel on Scottish Citylink buses between Oban/ Fort William and Inverness; and a return ticket for the price of a single on Caledonian MacBrayne ferries between Oban and Mull and between Mallaig and the Isle of Skye.

For rail information call ☎ 0845 748 4950.

Boat

Ferries connect the mainland with the islands off the west and north coasts. Caledonian MacBrayne or 'CalMac' (☎ 0870 565 0000 for reservations, ☎ 01475-650100 for enquiries, e reservations@calmac.co.uk), The Ferry Terminal, Gourock PA19 1QP, is the main operator off the west coast. Its Web site is at www.calmac.co.uk.

P&O (☎ 01224-572615, ✉ passenger@po scottishferries.co.uk), PO Box 5, Jamieson's Quay, Aberdeen AB11 5NP, operates from the north coast to the Orkneys and Shetlands. Its Web site is at www.poscottishferries.co .uk. John o'Groats Ferries (☎ 01955-611353) has a ferry from John o'Groats to South Ronaldsay in the Orkneys.

The Cairngorms

The magnificent Cairngorms, Britain's highest mountain range and most popular skiing area, soar above forests of regenerating native Caledonian pine in the upper reaches of Strathspey (Speyside). More attractive than the regimented Forestry Commission conifer plantations, these native woodlands are home to rare animals such as pine martens and wildcats. Red squirrels, ospreys and ca-

percaillie survive here, as does Britain's only herd of reindeer.

The Cairngorm summits provide Britain's only Arctic tundra vegetation, inhabited by birds such as snow buntings, ptarmigans and dotterels. What's more, even nonhikers can reach the high peaks, as the Cairngorm chair lift operates year round (a funicular railway is being built to replace it).

Aviemore, popular with skiers, hikers and cyclists, is the main resort town. The top hiking routes include the 24-mile Lairig Ghru trail through the peaks and right down to Braemar in the Grampians. If you prefer to avoid the crowds, the lovely but less dramatic Monadhliath (pronounced mona-lee-a) range, west of the River Spey, sees fewer tourists.

The 100-mile River Spey, one of Scotland's top salmon rivers, attracts anglers from all over the world. Pure mountain water from its tributaries provides a basic ingredient for whisky production, and some distilleries are open to visitors (see Aberdeenshire

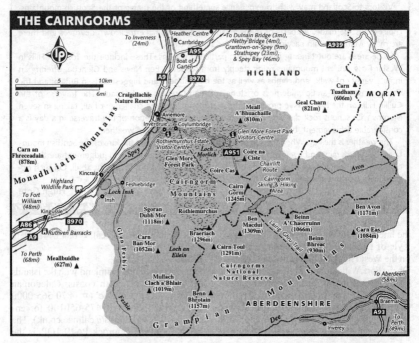

THE CAIRNGORMS

& Moray in the Central Scotland chapter). The **Speyside Way** is a waymarked trail that follows the river for 70 miles from Spey Bay on the east coast south to Aviemore. North of Grantown-on-Spey, the River Spey joins the River Avon (pronounced ahn) and continues out of the Cairngorms into Morayshire.

AVIEMORE
☎ 01479 • pop 2421

In the early 1960s, Aviemore was a sleepy Highland village of 200 inhabitants, but today it looks more like a downmarket resort in the Rockies that can't quite reinvent itself in the swank image to which it aspires. Fortunately, winter visitors are spared the appalling summer kitsch, and even then you can avoid it by heading for the hills.

Orientation & Information
Aviemore is just off the A9 bypass. With all the kitsch along Grampian Rd you can hardly get lost. The train station, banks and eateries are on this road. The Cairngorm skiing/hiking area is 8 miles south-east of Aviemore at the end of the Ski Rd (B970/A951) which runs through two large forest estates: Rothiemurchus and Glen More.

The busy TIC (☎ 810363), 500m south of the centre on Grampian Rd, opens daily year round, with extended hours in July and August (9 am to 7 pm Monday to Saturday, until 6 pm Sunday). Accommodation bookings through the TIC cost £1.50. There's a bureau de change here too. It sells a good range of books and maps, including the yellow Ordnance Survey (OS) Outdoor Leisure Map No 3 *The Cairngorms, Aviemore & Glen Avon* which covers the whole area, while its *Cairngorm Walks*, part of the Pathfinder series, describes the main hikes.

Of the outdoor-equipment shops along Grampian Rd, try Ellis Brigham (☎ 810175) at No 9 near the train station, which organises equipment hire and ski lessons.

Rothiemurchus Estate
The Rothiemurchus Estate, which takes in the villages of Inverdruie and Coylumbridge, extends from near Aviemore to the Cairngorm tops. It's owned by a single fam-

ily, the Grants (no connection with the whisky family), who manage the extensive Caledonian pine forest here, and lay on facilities for visitors. It features in the BBC TV series *Monarch of the Glen*. There's free access to 50 miles of footpaths, including some particularly attractive trails through the forests and around Loch an Eilein. Visitors can also opt for ranger-guided walks, clay pigeon shooting instruction, Land Rover tours, and fishing for rainbow trout at the estate's fish farm or in the River Spey.

The Rothiemurchus Estate Visitor Centre (☎ 810858), a mile from Aviemore along Ski Rd, opens 9.30 am to 5.30 pm daily. Pick up the free *Visitor Guide & Footpath Map*.

Glen More Forest Park
Farther along, Ski Rd passes through 2000 hectares of pine and spruce that make up Glen More Forest Park around Loch Morlich, 7 miles from Aviemore. The visitor centre (☎ 861220) near the loch has the *Glen More Forest Guide Map* detailing local walks.

As well as walks, attractions include a pleasant sandy beach and the popular **Loch Morlich Watersports Centre** (☎ 861221) offering canoeing, windsurfing, sailing and fishing. At the **Cairngorm Reindeer Centre** (☎ 861228), beside the visitor centre, the warden will take you to see and feed the reindeer. Walks leave daily at 11 am (and 2.30 pm in summer) and cost £4/3 per adult/child.

Activities
Walking To get straight to the best views, take the chair lift (☎ 861261) to the Cairngorm plateau. It starts from the car park at the end of Ski Rd and ascends in two sections to the 1097m level. It operates from 9.15 am to 5.15 pm daily and costs £6/3.60 return. After much controversy over its environmental impact, a funicular railway is being built to replace the chair lift and is planned to begin operating in late 2001.

From the top station, it's a relatively short climb to the summit of **Cairn Gorm** (1245m). You can continue south to climb **Ben Macdui** (1309m), but this can take six to eight hours, including the chair lift ride up.

The **Lairig Ghru** trail, which can take up to eight hours, is a demanding 24-mile route from Aviemore over the Lairig Ghru Pass to Braemar. If you're not doing the full route, it's still worth hiking the six-hour return trip up to the pass.

Hikers will need lunch, plenty of liquids, a map, a compass and a windproof jacket. The weather can change almost instantly and snow, even in midsummer, isn't unknown.

Skiing Aviemore isn't Aspen or Val d'Isère, but with 28 runs it's Britain's biggest ski area, and when the snow is optimum and the sun's shining, you can close your eyes and imagine you're in the Alps. The season runs from January until the snow melts, which can be at the end of April.

The ski area is about 8 miles south-east of Aviemore and lifts start from the main Coire Cas car park, and are connected to the more distant Coire na Ciste car park by free shuttle bus. A Cairngorm Day Ticket costs £20/10. The TIC distributes the free *Cairngorm Piste Map* leaflet with advice for safe skiing and snowboarding.

During the ski season the TIC displays relevant avalanche warnings. Call the Ski Hotline (☎ 0891 654655) or tune into Ski FM on 96.6MHz FM for reports on snow conditions.

As well as downhill skiing, there are also several cross-country routes. For more information on skiing see the Activities chapter.

Fishing This is a major sport, both on the River Spey and in most of the lochs. Ask the TIC for information on beats and permits. At local shops, fishing permits for salmon cost from £25 to £33 per day, while trout permits cost £15. Rothiemurchus Estate Visitor Estate (☎ 810703) hires rods for £5 per day.

Places to Stay

Camping The nearest camp site is *Rothiemurchus Camping & Caravan Park* (☎ 812800, Coylumbridge), 1½ miles along Ski Rd. It charges from £9 per tent. *Glenmore Camping & Caravan Park* (☎ 861 271), 5 miles farther along the road near Loch Morlich, charges £8.50 per site.

Hostels Upmarket hostelling in a refurbished building is offered by *Aviemore Youth Hostel* (☎ 810345, 25 Grampian Rd) from late December to mid-November. It's near the TIC and the start of Ski Rd; beds cost £12.25/10.75 for adults/under 18s (with a £1 surcharge in July and August).

In Glen More Forest Park, 7 miles from Aviemore, the popular *Loch Morlich Youth Hostel* (☎ 861238) has a great location, but prebooking is essential. It opens year round and charges £9.25/8. North of Loch Morlich and a mile from Ski Rd, *Badaguish Outdoor Centre* (☎ 861285) has dormitory accommodation from £5 to £10 and camping from £2.50.

B&Bs & Hotels – Aviemore Just off Grampian Rd on Craig na Gower Ave, 350m north of the train station, there's an enclave of B&Bs. Most offer single/double rooms with private bathrooms for around £18/35. Try *Karn House* (☎ 810849) which charges £18/32 or *Mrs Sheffield's* (☎ 810 698, Dunroamin Cottage) which is a bit dearer with three rooms all with private bathroom costing £25/36. On the main drag near Tesco supermarket is *Kila* (☎ 810573, Grampian Rd), open year round, where comfortable en-suite rooms cost £18/32.

On the other side of the railway line there are two larger guesthouses. Modern *Kinapol Guest House* (☎ 810513, Dalfaber Rd) charges from £16/30, while *Ardlogie Guest House* (☎ 810747, Dalfaber Rd) has five rooms all with bathroom for £17 to £19 per person.

In the centre is the recommended *Cairngorm Hotel* (☎ 810233, Grampian Rd), otherwise known as the Cairn, which charges £25 per person for B&B. Meals are served in the bar from noon to 9.30 pm.

One mile from Aviemore is an excellent small country-house hotel, *Lynwilg House* (☎ 811685, Lynwilg Rd). B&B is £28 to £38 per person, or £45 to £60 for B&B and a dinner to write home about. It's closed January and February.

B&Bs & Hotels – Ski Rd In Inverdruie, the small *Avondruie Guest House* (☎ 810267) charges £19/35 for rooms with bathroom, while *Mrs McIntyre* (☎ 810153) asks from £25/40 for her three en-suite rooms.

Just beyond Inverdruie are several B&Bs including *Junipers* (☎ 810405, 5 Dell Mhor), which has three rooms all with bathroom for £17/30.

The excellent *Corrour House Hotel* (☎ 810220, fax 811500, Inverdruie), 1½ miles from Aviemore off Ski Rd, offers splendid views of the Lairig Ghru Pass. It opens December to October and charges £25 to £37.50 per person for rooms with bathroom.

Perhaps the finest of the resort hotels is *Stakis Coylumbridge* (☎ 811811, @ reservations@stakis.co.uk), which enjoys an excellent, woodland location just outside Aviemore. Rates start at £55/70.

Places to Eat
In Aviemore itself, there's no shortage of places to eat, but few are particularly inviting.

For spicy curries visit *Aviemore Tandoori Restaurant* (☎ 811199, 43 Grampian Rd), near the TIC, which serves chicken tandoori for £6.75, tasty vegetarian dishes from £6.95 and takeaways. The plain *Smiffy's Fish & Chip Restaurant*, nearer the station, does takeaways and a reasonable fry-up, with cod and chips at £2.30. At the nearby, trendy *Café Mambo* (☎ 811670) bar meals start at £7 in colourful surroundings; it opens 9 am to 11 pm daily.

Farther north along Grampian Rd, opposite the police station, a branch of *Littlejohn's* (☎ 811633) serves steaks, pizzas and burgers in slightly offbeat surroundings. Main dishes cost from £4.25 to £12.95 and it opens 10 am to 11 pm daily. Over the road at No 9, carnivores can try the *Ski-ing Doo* (☎ 810392), which serves a range of steaks, including 285g sirloins (£13). The *Winking Owl* (☎ 810646) has a reasonable choice of pub food and specialises in steaks (from £7.95) but also does fish and pasta. It opens 11 am to midnight Monday to Saturday, and 12.30 to 11 pm Sunday.

The highly recommended, traditional *Old Bridge Inn* (☎ 811137, Dalfaber Rd), across from the TIC (follow the road that goes under the railway line from Grampian Rd), does an excellent barbecued salmon in dill mayonnaise (£8.50).

You'll find Britain's highest cafe, the *Ptarmigan*, at the top of the Cairngorm chair lift, but it'll be replaced by a restaurant when the funicular railway begins operating. The visitor centres at Rothiemurchus Estate and Glen More Forest Park both have cafes serving snacks and light meals. For smoked trout, venison, paté and other delicacies visit the Rothiemurchus Estate farm shop at the visitor centre.

If you prefer to self-cater, Aviemore has an enormous *Tesco supermarket*.

Entertainment
Aviemore Mountain Resort, a large leisure complex, has been demolished and is being completely rebuilt. For real ales there's the *Old Bridge Inn* and *Winking Owl*, while *Café Mambo* attracts a younger, cooler crowd. *Littlejohn's* has live music on Saturday nights (see Places to Eat).

Getting There & Away
Aviemore is 33 miles from Inverness, 62 miles from Fort William, 127 miles from Edinburgh and 505 miles from London.

Bus Buses stop on Grampian Rd; you can make bookings at the TIC.

Scottish Citylink (☎ 0870 550 5050) connects Aviemore with Inverness to the north (£4.20, 45 minutes); and to the south to Kincraig (10 minutes), Kingussie (20 minutes), Newtonmore (30 minutes), Dalwhinnie (45 minutes), Pitlochry (1¼ hours), Perth (two hours), Glasgow (3½ hours) and Edinburgh (3½ hours). For Aberdeen, change to a Stagecoach Bluebird (☎ 01463-239292) bus at Inverness.

There's one direct daytime service to London's Victoria coach station (£28, 11 hours), an overnight service and an early morning service requiring a change in Glasgow. There are also overnight services to Heathrow and Gatwick airports.

Train There are direct train services to London (£90.50 standard single, 7½ hours),

Glasgow/Edinburgh (£28, three hours) and Inverness (£9, 40 minutes).

March to October and around Christmas, the Strathspey Steam Railway (☎ 810725) operates between Aviemore, Boat of Garten and Nethy Bridge (work is continuing on an extension to Grantown-on-Spey). The station is over the tracks from the main train station.

Car MacDonald's Self Drive (☎ 811444), 13 Muirton, rents cars out from £34 per day and will deliver to/collect from your hotel.

Getting Around

Highland Country's Snowlink (☎ 811211) buses link Aviemore and Cairngorm, four to six times daily from late October to April (£2.50/1.25).

Several places in central Aviemore hire out mountain bikes. You can also hire bikes in Rothiemurchus Estate and Glen More Forest Park. Most places charge around £8/14 per half/full day. Bothy Bikes (☎ 811007) on Grampian Rd near the train station organises guided bike tours.

AROUND AVIEMORE
Kincraig & Around

Kincraig, 7 miles south-west of Aviemore, is another good Cairngorm base. Run by the Royal Zoological Society of Scotland, **Highland Wildlife Park** (☎ 01540-651270), about 1½ miles south of the village, features breeding stocks of local wildlife. There's a drive-through safari park, then several woodland walks offering most people their best opportunity to come face-to-face with an elusive wildcat or furiously displaying male capercaillie. It opens 10 am to 6 pm daily, April to October (to 7 pm June to August); and 10 am to 4 pm the rest of the year. Admission costs £6.50/4.35.

At Kincraig, the River Spey widens into **Loch Insh**, home of the Loch Insh Watersports Centre (☎ 01540-651272) which offers canoeing, windsurfing, sailing, bike hire and fishing. There's also B&B accommodation from £17.50 per head in comfortable rooms with bathrooms. Food here is good, especially after 6.30 pm when the lochside cafe transforms into a restaurant.

Glen Feshie extends south into the Cairngorms. About 5 miles from Kincraig, *Glen Feshie Hostel* (☎ 01540-651323) is a friendly, independent 14-bed hostel that's popular with hikers. The nightly charge of £8 includes bed linen and a steaming bowl of porridge to start the day. They may be able to pick you up from Aviemore if you ring ahead.

Scottish Citylink (☎ 0870 550 5050) connects Kincraig with Aviemore (10 minutes).

Carrbridge
☎ 01479 • pop 543

At pretty Carrbridge, 7 miles north-east of Aviemore, the **Landmark Highland Heritage Centre** (☎ 841614), set in a forest of Scots pines, offers a few novel and worthwhile attractions, such as the raised Treetop Trail, which allows you to view red squirrels, crossbills and crested tits. Some of it, however, seems rather tacky: the 'Wild Water Coaster' has less to do with heritage and more to do with keeping the kids amused. The centre opens daily year round, with extended hours in summer. Admission costs £5.95/4.20.

You'll find the ultimate in humpback bridges in the village centre. Built in 1717, it now looks decidedly unsafe and isn't used, but remains impressive.

In September, the village hosts a Celtic music festival (☎ 841242 for details) and a series of *ceilidhs* (evenings of entertainment).

Highland Country (☎ 811211) bus No 336 runs to Aviemore up to four times daily.

Boat of Garten

Near Carrbridge, Boat of Garten is known as the Osprey Village, since these rare birds of prey nest at the RSPB **Loch Garten Osprey Centre** (☎ 01479-831694) in Abernethy Forest Reserve. RSPB volunteers guard the site throughout the nesting season to deter egg collectors. The hide opens to visitors 10 am to 6 pm daily, April to August. Admission for nonmembers costs £2.50/50p. The centre is a distance of about 2 miles from the village and is signposted.

The best way to get here is on the Strathspey Steam Railway (☎ 01479-810725). It runs at least five times daily from Aviemore – a ticket in 3rd class costs £5.40 return.

Dulnain Bridge & Skye of Curr

At the **Heather Centre** (☎ 851359) in Skye of Curr off the A9, 2 miles south-west of Dulnain Bridge, you'll learn about the innumerable uses of heather over the centuries. After strolling around the garden centre, you can sample one of 21 recipes for Scottish dumpling (rich fruit cake steamed in a *cloot* or muslin cloth) in the adjacent *Clootie Dumpling Tearoom*; the 'Heather Centre Special' is hot dumpling with cream, ice cream, heather cream liqueur, chopped nuts and blackcherry preserve for £3.20.

Buses operated by Highland Country (☎ 811211) run three times a day Monday to Friday from Grantown-on-Spey to Dulnain Bridge.

GRANTOWN-ON-SPEY
☎ 01479 • pop 2000

This Georgian town on the River Spey, which attracts throngs of coach tourists in summer, lies amid an angler's paradise. Most hotels can either kit you out for a day of fishing or put you in touch with someone who can. The TIC (☎ 872773), 54 High St, opens 9.30 am to 5 pm Monday to Friday, and 10 am to 5 pm Saturday, April to October.

Places to Stay & Eat

Grantown's accommodation reflects its clientele, with plenty of comfortable upmarket hotels notable for their food, although there are some budget options.

Grantown-on-Spey Caravan Park (☎ 872 474), signposted half a mile west from the centre, charges from £7 to £9.50 per pitch. *Scotpackers* (☎ 873514, 16 The Square), also known as the Stopover, has dorm beds for £8.50 to £11 per person, but you'll need your own sleeping bag.

Open year round, *Crann Tara Guest House* (☎ 872197, High St) has comfortable singles and doubles from £16 per person with shared bathroom, while the sturdy, spacious *Bank House* (☎ 873256, 1 The Square), in a former Bank of Scotland, does B&B from £17 to £19 per person.

Highly commended *Ardconnel House* (☎ 872104, Woodlands Terrace) is a Victorian villa known for its French/Scottish cuisine and elegant atmosphere. Dinner and B&B costs from £48/86 per single/double, and all rooms have private bathrooms. Similarly deluxe *Ravenscourt House Hotel* (☎ 872286, Seafield Ave), in beautiful gardens near The Square, has en-suite accommodation from £35/60.

Getting There & Away

Highland Country (☎ 01463-233371) runs up to five buses between Grantown and Aviemore Monday to Saturday (£3.40, 35 minutes). Highland Country runs buses to/from Inverness Monday to Saturday (£3.75, 1¼ hours, two or three a day).

KINGUSSIE
☎ 01540 • pop 1461

The tranquil Speyside town of Kingussie (pronounced king-yewsie) is best known as the home of one of Scotland's finest folk museums. The TIC (☎ 661297), just off High St in Duke St, opens daily, April to September.

Highland Folk Museum

Kingussie's Highland Folk Museum (☎ 661 307), Duke St, comprises a collection of historical buildings and relics revealing all facets of Highland culture and lifestyles. The 18th-century Pitmain Lodge holds displays of *ceilidh* musical instruments, costumes and washing utensils. The village-like grounds also include a traditional thatch-roofed Isle of Lewis blackhouse, a water mill, a 19th-century corrugated iron shed for smoking salmon, and assorted farm implements. In summer, you can watch spinning, woodcarving and peat-fire baking demonstrations. It opens 10.30 am to 5.30 pm Monday to Saturday, and 1 to 5 pm Sunday, mid-April to August. Admission costs £4/2.

Ruthven Barracks

Built in 1719 on the site of an earlier 13th-century castle, Ruthven Barracks (pronounced rivven) was one of four fortresses constructed after the first Jacobite rebellion of 1715 as part of a Hanoverian scheme to take control of the Highlands. Given the long-range views, the location makes perfect sense. The barracks were last occupied by Jacobite troops awaiting the return of Bonnie Prince Charlie after the Battle of Culloden. Learning of his defeat and subsequent flight, they destroyed the barracks before taking to the glens. The ruins are the property of Historic Scotland (HS; see Historic Organisations, under Useful Organisations in the Facts for the Visitor chapter). Admission is free and the ruins are floodlit at night. Follow Ruthven Rd off High St.

Walking Routes

The **Monadhliath Range**, north-west of Kingussie, attracts fewer hikers than the nearby Cairngorms, and makes an ideal destination for walkers seeking peace and solitude. However, during the deer-stalking season (August to October), you'll need to check with the TIC before setting out.

The recommended six-hour circular walk to the summit of **Carn an Fhreceadain** (878m) above Kingussie begins north of the village. It continues to Pitmain Lodge and along the River Allt Mór before climbing to the cairn on the summit. You can then follow the ridge east to the twin summits of **Beinn Bhreac** before returning to Kingussie via a more easterly track.

Places to Stay & Eat

At *Lairds Bothy Hostel (☎ 661334, 66 High St)*, behind the Tipsy Laird pub in the town centre, there are four family rooms and several simple eight-bed dorms with beds costing £8 per person.

On the western outskirts friendly *Homewood Lodge (☎ 661507, Newtonmore Rd)* does B&B for £15 to £20 per person and has good views from outside the front, as does the elegant *St Helens (☎ 661430, Ardbroilach Rd)*, closer to town, where singles/doubles cost from £36/40. The *Osprey Hotel (☎ 661510, Ruthven Rd)* charges from £25 per person for B&B in a comfortable Victorian house with good home cooking.

If you're feeling flush, *The Cross (☎ 661 166, Tweed Mill Brae, Ardbroilach Rd)* is one of the Highlands' top hotel-restaurants (closed Tuesday). Dinner and B&B costs from £95 per person. Rather cheaper are pub meals at the *Tipsy Laird (66 High St)* for

£4.50. The most promising of High St cafes is *La Cafetière*, which does soup and homemade seed bread or herb scone and butter for £1.45, and toasties from £2.10.

Getting There & Away

Kingussie is 120 miles from Edinburgh, 75 miles from Perth and 40 miles from Inverness. It's on the main Edinburgh/Glasgow to Inverness route, so all trains and most Scottish Citylink (☎ 0870 550 5050) buses stop here, as do Highland Country (☎ 01463-233371) buses. Scottish Citylink has five buses to Inverness daily and two to Aviemore. From the train station at the southern end of town, there are at least five trains to Edinburgh, Glasgow and Inverness daily. For rail information call ☎ 0845 748 4950.

KINGUSSIE TO FORT WILLIAM

Just north of Kingussie there's a choice of routes south. The A9 continues to Perth, leaving the Highland region via the bleak Pass of Drumochter. You could detour to visit **Dalwhinnie Distillery** (☎ 01528-522 208) which claims to be Scotland's highest distillery (326m, 1073ft). It opens 9.30 am to 4.30 pm Monday to Friday, October to May (plus Saturday from June to September, and from 11.30 am Sunday in July and August). Tours cost £3.

The A86 to Fort William leaves the A9 at Kingussie, continuing through Newtonmore to run along Loch Laggan and **Loch Moy**, a particularly fine stretch of water, with views of Ben Nevis.

The railway joins the road at Tulloch station and follows Glen Spean to the Great Glen, through **Roybridge** and **Spean Bridge**. In Roybridge, the independent hostel *Grey Corrie Lodge (☎ 01397-712236, Roybridge Inn)* charges from £9 per night. Two miles away at Auchluachrach is a recommended hostel, *Aite Cruinnichidh (☎ 01397-712 315)*, with beds for £8. Both open year round.

About 7 miles north-east of Fort William, the **Nevis Range Ski Area** (☎ 01397-705825) skirts the slopes of Aonach Mór (1221m). The gondola cable car (655m) operates year round (£6.75/4.15 return), except mid-November to Christmas, to the top station where the **Snow Goose Restaurant** does hearty inexpensive meals. There are several walking routes from the Snow Goose and through nearby **Leanachan Forest**. At the base station there's a cafe and you can rent bikes for £8.50/12.50 for a half/full day.

The Great Glen

The Great Glen is a natural fault line running across Scotland from Fort William to Inverness as a series of lochs – Linnhe, Lochy, Oich and Ness – linked by the Caledonian Canal. It has always been a communication (and invasion) route and General George Wade built a military road along the southern side of Loch Ness from 1724. The modern A82 road along the northern side was completed in 1933.

The 80-mile **Great Glen Cycle Route** from Fort William to Inverness via Fort Augustus follows canal towpaths and gravel tracks through forests to avoid busy roads where possible. The *Cycling in the Forest* leaflet, available from TICs or the Forestry Commission, provides details.

Scottish Citylink (☎ 0870 550 5050) and Highland Country (☎ 01463-222244) collectively operate several bus services along the Great Glen between Fort William and Inverness (£6.50, two hours, up to six daily).

FORT WILLIAM & AROUND
☎ 01397 • pop 10,774

Fort William, which lies beside Loch Linnhe amid some of Britain's most magnificent mountain landscapes, has one of the finest settings in the country. Although insensitive civic planning compromised its appeal for many years, the conversion of the high street to a pedestrian mall and the determination of its people have turned it into a rather attractive little town. As a major tourist centre, it's easily accessed by rail and bus, and makes a great base for exploring the mountains and glens of Lochaber.

Magical Glen Nevis begins near the northern end of the town and extends west below the slopes of Ben Nevis. 'The Ben' – Britain's highest mountain at 1343m – and

neighbouring mountains are a magnet for hikers and climbers. The glen is also popular with movie-makers – parts of *Braveheart*, *Rob Roy* and *Local Hero* were filmed here.

Orientation & Information
The town meanders along the edge of Loch Linnhe for several miles. The centre, with its small selection of shops, cafes and pubs, is easy to get around on foot unless you're booked into a far-flung B&B.

The busy TIC (☎ 703781) at Cameron Square opens year round and has a good range of books and maps. For local walks, its leaflet series of *Great Walks* – incorporating a map and basic information – are handy, but you'll need an OS map for more adventurous hikes such as Ben Nevis. More information is available from the Glen Nevis (Ionad Nibheis) Visitor Centre, 2 miles south-east along the glen from town. It opens 9 am to 5 pm daily, Easter to October. Admission is free.

As you'd expect, Fort William has wellstocked outdoor-equipment shops. Nevisport (☎ 704921), near the train station, has a marvellous range of books and maps for mountaineers. West Coast Outdoor Leisure (☎ 705777) is at the other end of High St.

West Highland Museum
This museum (☎ 702169) is packed with Highland memorabilia. Of particular interest is the secret portrait of Bonnie Prince Charlie. After the Jacobite rebellions, all things Highland were banned, including pictures of the exiled leader. This picture looks like nothing more than a smear of paint until placed next to a curved mirror, when it reflects a likeness of the prince. The museum opens 10 am to 4 pm Monday to Saturday year round (to 5 pm from May to September) and 2 to 5 pm Sunday in July and August. Admission costs £2/50p.

Other Things to See & Do
There's little left of the original **Fort William** from which the town takes its name, as it was pulled down in the 19th century to make way for the railway. It was originally built by General Monk in 1635 to control the Highlands, but the surviving ruins are from

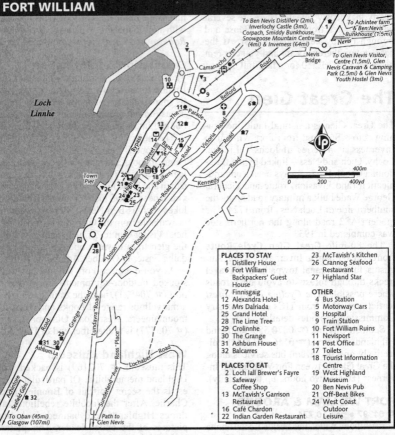

FORT WILLIAM

Loch Linnhe

To Ben Nevis Distillery (2mi),
Inverlochy Castle (3mi),
Corpach, Smiddy Bunkhouse,
Snowgoose Mountain Centre
(4mi) & Inverness (64mi)

To Achintee farm
& Ben Nevis
Bunkhouse (1.5mi)

To Glen Nevis Visitor,
Centre (1.5mi), Glen
Nevis Caravan & Camping
Park (2.5mi) & Glen Nevis
Youth Hostel (3mi)

Town Pier

To Oban (45mi)
Glasgow (107mi)

Path to
Glen Nevis

PLACES TO STAY
1 Distillery House
6 Fort William
  Backpackers' Guest
  House
7 Finnisgaig
12 Alexandra Hotel
15 Mrs Dalriada
25 Grand Hotel
28 The Lime Tree
29 Crolinnhe
30 The Grange
31 Ashburn House
32 Balcarres

PLACES TO EAT
2 Loch Iall Brewer's Fayre
3 Safeway
  Coffee Shop
13 McTavish's Garrison
  Restaurant
16 Café Chardon
22 Indian Garden Restaurant

23 McTavish's Kitchen
26 Crannog Seafood
  Restaurant
27 Highland Star

OTHER
4 Bus Station
5 Motorway Cars
8 Hospital
9 Train Station
10 Fort William Ruins
11 Nevisport
14 Post Office
17 Toilets
18 Tourist Information
  Centre
19 West Highland
  Museum
20 Ben Nevis Pub
21 Off-Beat Bikes
24 West Coast
  Outdoor
  Leisure

0   200   400m
0   200   400yd

a fort built in the 1690s by General MacKay
and named after the king, William III.

The local **Ben Nevis Distillery** (☎ 702476),
Lochy Bridge, has a visitors centre open 9 am
to 5 pm weekdays, and until 12.30 pm on
Saturday, all year. A tour and tasting costs £2.

Walking & Cycling Routes

The most obvious hike, up **Ben Nevis**, should
not be undertaken lightly. The weather at the
top is more often bad (thick mist) than good.
Be prepared for the worst, even if it's sunny
when you set off. Bring warm clothes, food
and something to drink, and a detailed map.

The path begins in Glen Nevis, either
from the car park by Achintee Farm (on the
northern side of the river and reached by the
road through Claggan), or from the youth
hostel on the road up the glen. These two
trails join after less than a mile, then follow
the Red Burn before zigzagging up to the
summit and the ruins of the old observatory.
It can take three to five hours to reach the
top and 2½ to four hours to get down again.

You can walk for miles on the ridges of
the **Mamores**. One of the best hill walks in
the area starts at the Lower Falls in Glen
Nevis (at Achriabhach) and goes south-

wards up the glen between **Sgurr a'Mhaim** and **Stob Ban**. A good path takes you to the tiny loch below the **Devil's Ridge**, zigzags up the steep slope north-east of the loch and turns left along the spectacular ridge for Sgurr a'Mhaim (1099m). The round trip takes about six hours.

There are pleasant (far less strenuous) walks along Glen Nevis through the gorge at the eastern end to beautiful **Steall Meadows**. You could also walk part of the **West Highland Way** from Fort William to Kinlochleven via Glen Nevis (14 miles) or even to Glencoe (21 miles to the junction with the A82).

The 80-mile **Great Glen Cycle Route** links Fort William and Inverness. The Forestry Commission's free leaflet gives details of this mainly off-road route.

Organised Tours

Whistle Stop Tours (☎ 702804) does three-hour, 35-mile tours in seven-seater buses to Neptune's Staircase, Spean Bridge and Glen Nevis for £7.50. Tours can be booked at the TIC.

From April to October there are also 1½-hour boat trips on the loch with Seal Island Cruises (☎ 703919) – it operates from the pier, where there's a booking kiosk. There are four trips during the day, plus an evening cruise at 7.45 pm on summer weekdays (£6/3).

Places to Stay

Fort William has numerous B&Bs and hotels but you should still book ahead in summer, even for hostels.

Camping The large *Glen Nevis Caravan & Camping Park* (☎ 702191), 2½ miles northeast of Fort William, opens March to October and charges £7 to £10.30 for two-person tents depending on the season. The few seasonal camp sites at Nevis Bridge are little more than fields with basic facilities.

Hostels The popular, 38-bed *Fort William Backpackers' Guest House* (☎ 700711, *Alma Rd*) is a short walk from the train station and charges from £10 a night.

Three miles from Fort William, by the

start of the path up Ben Nevis in Glen Nevis, the large *Glen Nevis Youth Hostel* (☎ 702 336) opens year round. The charge is £12.25/10.75 for adults/under-18s and includes breakfast. Across the river, *Ben Nevis Bunkhouse* (☎ 702240, *Achintee Farm*) is a good alternative (£9).

In Corpach, 4 miles along the Mallaig road north of Fort William, the *Smiddy Bunkhouse* (☎ 772467, *Station Rd*) is a restful, snug hostel charging from £7 to £8.50. The attached Snowgoose Mountain Centre (☎ 772752) organises mountaineering, kayaking and sailing trips.

B&Bs & Hotels The B&Bs in and around Fassifern Rd are closest to the train and bus stations. Try *Finnisgaig* (☎ 702453, *Alma Rd)*, which charges from £16 for a double, or the nonsmoking *Mrs Dalriada* (☎ 702533, *2 Caberfeidh, Fassifern Rd*), where comfy B&B costs £28/32 per single/double, though the 'do' and 'do not' signs around the place can be a bit irritating.

Achintore Rd, which runs south along the loch, is packed with B&Bs and hotels, but some seem large and characterless. More interesting is the B&B-cum-art gallery at *The Lime Tree* (☎ 701806), which has beds for £15 to £20 per person. The very comfortable *Ashburn House* (☎ 706000) has rooms with bathroom for £30 to £40 per person. Several B&Bs just off Achintore Rd offer panoramic loch views, including *Balcarres* (☎ 702377, *Seafield Gardens)*, which costs from £25/36.

On Grange Rd, parallel to Achintore Rd, there are two congenial guesthouses whose owners' attention to detail has earned them the top tourist-board rating. The excellent three room *The Grange* (☎ 705516, *Grange Rd)* and the *Crolinnhe* (☎ 702709, *Grange Rd)* next door charge from £37.50 per person (double).

The *Alexandra Hotel* (☎ 702241, e *sales@miltonhotels.com, The Parade)* is a large, traditional hotel with commodious rooms with bathroom from £49/79. The less-expensive, but agreeable *Grand Hotel* (☎ 702928, e *thegrandhotel@compuserve.com, Gordon Square)* is the other large, central hotel, with rooms from £25/44.

Distillery House (☎ *702980, North Rd*), in the old Glenlochy Distillery opposite the road into Glen Nevis, is thoroughly recommended. Rooms with bathrooms cost £20 to £35 per person.

The wonderfully grand, five-star *Inverlochy Castle* (☎ *702177*, ⓔ *info@inverlochy .co.uk*), in 200-hectare grounds 3 miles north of Fort William, is an opulent Victorian creation completed in 1865. It has everything you'd expect to find in a castle – crenellated battlements, stags' heads, log fires and a wide staircase. Its luxurious rooms cost from £90 to £225. Reservations are requisite.

Glen Nevis offers several more places to stay, including *Achintee Farm* (☎ *702240*), which, as well as the bunkhouse (see Hostels earlier), has self-catering accommodation sleeping up to five people for £280 to £380 per week.

Places to Eat

With the honourable exception of the Crannog Seafood Restaurant, Fort William is pretty much a culinary desert.

You can shop, eat and drink at *Nevisport Bar & Restaurant* (☎ *704921*), in the outdoor-equipment shop near the train station, where its cheap meals include vegetarian options; but it closes at 7.30 pm Monday to Saturday, and 5.30 pm Sunday. Its breakfast special costs £1.99.

Most other eateries line High St. *McTavish's Kitchen* (☎ *702406, High St*) has the same menu and floor show (see Entertainment) as the Oban branch (see the Central Scotland chapter). A busy self-service restaurant downstairs, open 9 am to 4 pm daily, dishes up honest, no-frills food at reasonable prices; beef casserole costs £4.75. On High St, *McTavish's Garrison Restaurant* (same phone number) has food only, to 5 pm daily.

Indian Garden Restaurant (☎ *705011, 88 High St*) is popular and not too expensive. It does a two-course lunch for £5.95 and takeaways from £5 to £9 from noon to 2 pm and 5.30 to 11 pm daily. You can also get takeaways from the Chinese restaurant, *Highland Star* (☎ *703905, 155 High St*), which has a good reputation and where chicken and pork dishes cost under £7.50.

The best restaurant is the elegant *Crannog Seafood Restaurant* (☎ *705589*), on the pier, giving diners an uninterrupted view over the loch. Main courses, including baked trout, cost from £9.95 to £18.

For those on a tight budget, the *Safeway Coffee Shop* near the bus and train stations is good value – filled jacket potatoes cost from £1.99. It opens until 8 or 9 pm weekdays, 6 pm at the weekend. Across the road, *Loch Iall Brewer's Fayre* (☎ *703707*) does a range of main courses from £4.99, including steak and kidney pie, and has facilities for kids.

For a snack try *Café Chardon*, upstairs in P Maclennan's store on High St, where tasty toasted sandwiches cost £1.95 and filling focaccia costs £3.40.

Entertainment

McTavish's Kitchen (☎ *702406*) takes the pile 'em high, sell 'em cheap approach to Scottish cuisine and culture, but the music's good and it can be fun if you get into the spirit of things. Shows are staged at 8.30 pm nightly, May to September, with dancing, a live band and a piper. It costs £1.75/1 (adult/child) with a meal, £3.50/1.75 without; set meals start at £8.50, including the show.

On the opposite side of High St, the Jacobite Bar in the *Ben Nevis* pub is a popular music venue and a good place for a cask-conditioned ale or inexpensive bar meals. The *Nevisport Bar*, in the Nevisport complex, beckons walkers and climbers.

Getting There & Away

Fort William is 597 miles from London, 146 miles from Edinburgh, 104 miles from Glasgow and 66 miles from Inverness. If you have a spare week the best way to get here is on foot, along the 95 mile West Highland Way from just north of Glasgow (see the Activities chapter).

Bus Scottish Citylink (☎ 0870 550 5050) has buses to Glasgow (£10.50, three hours, four or five daily) via Glencoe, with connections to London. There are also direct Citylink buses between Fort William and Kyle of Lochalsh (£9.50, two hours, three daily) and between Fort William and Oban (£6.20, 1¾ hours, two or three daily). There are several services daily along Loch Ness to Inverness (£6.50, two hours) and two or three daily except Sunday to and from Mallaig (£4.50, 1½ hours), via Glenfinnan. Another useful Monday to Saturday service runs to Glencoe (£1.40, 30 minutes).

Highland Country Buses (☎ 702373) operates services to Kinlochleven (£2.10, 45 minutes, six daily) via Glencoe.

Train The spectacular West Highland line runs from Glasgow via Fort William to Mallaig. There's a particularly wonderful wild section across bleak Rannoch Moor. There's no direct rail connection between Oban and Fort William; use the Scottish Citylink bus services to avoid backtracking to Crianlarich.

There are trains from Glasgow to Fort William (£22.70, 3¼ hours, two or three daily), and one to four trains between Fort William and Mallaig (£7.40, 1¼ hours). The Highland Rover ticket (£49) allows unlimited travel for four days in an eight-day period.

An overnight train connects Fort William and London Euston (from £79 including the sleeper) but you'll miss the views.

Car The TIC has a leaflet listing car hire places. Try Motorway Cars (☎ 702030), in the service station on Camanachd Crescent.

Getting Around
Bus Highland Country Buses run from the bus station up Glen Nevis to the youth hostel (£1.10, 10 minutes), leaving roughly hourly from 8 am to 11 pm Monday to Saturday, June to September. Buses to Corpach (15 minutes) are more frequent.

Bicycle Off-Beat Bikes (☎ 704008), 117 High St and also at the Nevis Range base station, rents out mountain bikes for £8.50/12.50 for a half/full day.

FORT WILLIAM TO GLEN COE
South of Fort William, the A82 follows Loch Linnhe for 8 miles as far as **Inchree**. Here you'll find *Inchree Bunkhouse (☎ 01855-821287)*, with beds from £7 to £10; facilities

include a pub and bistro on the site. It's easy to get to by bus, as this is the main route between Fort William and Glasgow or Oban. For something more stylish, there's the *Lodge on the Loch (☎ 01855-821237)* in nearby **Onich**, with luxurious singles/doubles from £33 to £56 per person and a good restaurant.

At North Ballachulish you can either cross the bridge and continue along the A82 into Glencoe village or take the side road that runs up Loch Leven to Kinlochleven and back to Glencoe along the southern shore.

GLEN COE
Scotland's most famous glen is also one of its most beautiful, with steeply sloping and narrow-sided valleys that once provided cattle-rustling Highlanders with the perfect place to hide their stock. The glen is dominated by three massive, brooding spurs, known as the Three Sisters of Glen Coe. There are wonderful walks in this moodily atmospheric glen, much of which is owned by the National Trust for Scotland (NTS; see Useful Organisations in the Facts for the Visitor chapter), and some excellent accommodation.

Glen Coe was written into the history books in 1692 when the MacDonalds were murdered by the Campbells in what became known as the Massacre of Glen Coe (see the boxed text 'The Glen Coe Massacre' later).

Glencoe Village
☎ 01855 • pop 360
Standing by Loch Leven, at the entrance to the glen, the village is 16 miles from Fort William on the main Glasgow road. The small thatched **Glencoe Folk Museum** aside, there's little to see in the village. About 1½ miles from the village along the road into the glen is an NTS visitors centre (☎ 811307, 811729). It opens 9.30 am to 5.30 pm daily, May to August; and 10 am to 5 pm daily in March, April, September and October. It's worth paying the 50/30p admission fee to see the 14-minute video on the history of the glen including the Glencoe Massacre.

The Glen Coe Massacre

The brutal murders that took place here in 1692 were particularly shameful, perpetrated as they were by one Highland clan on another (with whom they were lodging as guests).

In an attempt to quash remaining Jacobite loyalties among the Highland clans, William III had ordered that all chiefs take an oath of loyalty to him by the end of the year (1691). Maclain, the elderly chief of the MacDonalds of Glen Coe, was late in setting out to fulfil the king's demand, and going first to Fort William rather than Inverary made him later still. He thus missed the deadline.

The Secretary of State for Scotland, Sir John Dalrymple, declared the MacDonalds should be punished as an example to other Highland clans, some of whom had not bothered to even take the oath. A company of 120 soldiers, mainly of the Campbell clan, was sent to the glen. Since their leader was related by marriage to Maclain, the troops were billeted in MacDonald homes. It was a long-standing tradition for clans to provide hospitality to passing travellers.

After they'd been guests for 12 days, the order came for the soldiers to put to death all MacDonalds under the age of 70. Some Campbells alerted the MacDonalds to their intended fate, while others turned on their hosts at 5 am on 13 February, shooting Maclain and 37 other men, women and children. Some died before they knew what was happening, while 300 others fled into the snow, where some died of exposure.

The ruthless brutality of the incident caused a public uproar and after an enquiry several years later, Dalrymple lost his job. There's a monument to Maclain in Glencoe village and members of the MacDonald clan still gather here on 13 February each year.

Interestingly, several MacDonalds were involved in making the video at the NTS visitor centre in Glen Coe, but no Campbells.

Places to Stay & Eat You can pitch a tent at *Invercoe Caravans* (☎ 811210) where sites cost from £8 to £12 per night, or you can rent a caravan by the week.

Glencoe Youth Hostel (☎ 811219), a 1½-mile walk from the village on the northern side of the River Coe, is popular, particularly with climbers, so you'll need to book ahead. Open year round, it charges £9.25/8 for adults/under-18s. Nearby, *Leacantuim Farm Bunkhouse* (☎ 811256) has basic bunkhouse accommodation for £7.50, or £6.50 in the Alpine Barn. It also runs *Red Squirrel Campsite*, charging campers £3.50 each.

On the village outskirts and scenically positioned beside the river, *Glencoe Guest House* (☎ 811244, Strathlachan) charges £17 to £24 per person. Two and a half miles east of the village is the old-world *Clachaig Inn* (☎ 811252) offering B&B in rooms with private bathroom from £25 to £35 per head. There's also a bar here with real ale, good food and live music several times a week.

Getting There & Away Scottish Citylink (☎ 0870 550 5050) buses run to Glasgow (£9.20, 2½ hours), while Highland Country (☎ 01463-222244) operates between Fort William and Glencoe (30 minutes).

Kingshouse Hotel

Scotland's oldest established inn, this isolated hotel (☎ 851259) has been a landmark for so long that it now appears on maps, marked simply as 'Hotel'. It's on the West Highland Way at the eastern end of the glen, and hikers stop here to tuck into a plate of haggis, *tatties* (potatoes) and *neeps* (turnips) and a refreshing drink in the bar. It's a good, busy place to stay, with rooms from £24.50/48 (shared bathroom) plus £7 for a full breakfast.

Glen Coe Ski Centre

About 1½ miles east from Kingshouse Hotel, on the other side of the A82, is the car park and base station for this ski centre, where commercial skiing in Scotland first started in 1956. At the base station, the **Museum of Scottish Skiing & Climbing** (☎ 851226), open 8.30 am to 5 pm daily, has among its relics the ice axe Chris Bonington used to climb Mt Everest.

The chair lift (☎ 851226), which operates from 9.30 am to 4.45 pm year round, is the easiest way to get to the dramatic 640m-high viewpoint and several good walks. It costs £3.75/2.50 return.

Walking Routes

This is serious walking country and you'll need maps, warm clothes, and food and water. The NTS visitor centre (☎ 811307, 811729), in the glen, opens year round and stocks lots of useful information.

A great six-hour hike leads through the Lost Valley to the top of **Bidean nam Bian** (1141m). Cross the footbridge below Allt-na-Reigh and follow the gorge up into the Lost Valley, continuing up to the rim, then along it to the right, to the summit. You need to be very careful crossing to Stob Coire nan Lochan as there are steep scree slopes. Descend the western side of this ridge and round into Coire nan Lochan, where a path heads back to the road.

For something less strenuous, hike this route as far as the **Lost Valley**, a hidden mountain sanctuary. Allow three hours for the return trip.

Aonach Eagach, the glen's northern wall, is said to be the best ridge walk on the Scottish mainland, but it's difficult in places and you need a good head for heights. Some parts could almost be graded a rock climb. It's best done from east to west, and there's a path up the hillside north of Allt-na-Reigh and down from Sgor nam Fiannaidh towards Loch Achtriochtan. The more direct gully that leads to Clachaig Inn isn't a safe way down. It takes six to eight hours.

FORT WILLIAM TO FORT AUGUSTUS

From Fort William to Fort Augustus it's only 33 miles along the A82, but it's worth taking the slightly longer B8004 route at first to see **Neptune's Staircase**, a flight of eight locks that raises the water in the Caledonian Canal by 19.5m. Scottish engineer Thomas Telford's canal was built from 1803 to 1822

to connect the east and west coasts of Scotland, from Inverness to Fort William. The lochs, of which there are 29, make up 38 miles of the canal's total 60 miles.

This side trip rejoins the A82 at the **Commando Memorial** to the WWII military force that trained here. The road then runs along the south-eastern shore of **Loch Lochy** before crossing the canal by the Laggan Locks to run along the northern shore of narrow **Loch Oich**. At the head of Loch Oich, the **Well of the Heads** details the summary justice handed out to seven 16th-century murderers by their victims' aggrieved family.

FORT AUGUSTUS
☎ 01320 • pop 600

Fort Augustus, at the junction of four of General Wade's military roads, was the headquarters for his road-building operations from 1724. Between 1729 and 1742, as part of his plan to pacify the Highlands, General Wade built a fort where the River Tarff joined Loch Ness. Although it was captured and later damaged by the retreating Jacobites, it remained occupied until 1854. In 1876, Benedictine monks took over the building and founded Fort Augustus Abbey. The adjoining Catholic boys' school was closed in 1994, then the abbey closed in 1998; there is no public access.

The TIC (☎ 366367) in the central car park opens 9 am to 5.30 pm Monday to Saturday, April to October. It charges £2 for local accommodation bookings and provides currency exchange.

Things to See & Do

At Fort Augustus, boats using the **Caledonian Canal** are raised and lowered 13m by **five locks**. When the swing bridge is opened, however, it can cause long delays on the busy A82. The promontory between the canal and the River Oich affords a fine view over Loch Ness. Tiny **Cherry Island**, on the Inverness side of Fort Augustus, was originally a *crannog* or artificial island settlement. Fort Augustus is also on the **Great Glen Cycle Route**.

Cruises on Loch Ness on the *Royal Scot* (☎ 366221) operate daily, April to October. The 50-minute trip costs £5.50/2.50.

Places to Stay & Eat

There's a good choice of B&Bs for £15 to £20 per person, including *Appin* (☎ *366541, Inverness Rd*), a bungalow with three rooms open April to September, and the aptly named *Greystone's* (☎ *366736, Station Rd*), open year round.

The *Scots Kitchen*, opposite the car park, offers cafe-style food, but with some interesting dishes such as steak and ale pie for £5.95. Near the canal the *Jac-O-Bite* tearoom deserves a visit for its name alone; simple meals such as steak and kidney pie cost around £3.

The *Bothy Restaurant & Bar* (☎ *366710*), beside the canal, is an alternative lunch spot with canal views; most mains cost under £7. Nearby, *The Loch Inn* (☎ *366302*) serves great bar meals, such as baked sea trout (£9.50) and Caribbean fruit and vegetable curry (£6.25), but you should definitely save room for one of the delicious sweets such as banana and toffee pudding covered in cream (£3.50).

Getting There & Away

Scottish Citylink (☎ 0870 550 5050) runs five or six buses daily between Inverness and Fort William, stopping at Fort Augustus en route. To get to either town takes an hour and costs £6.

LOCH NESS

Dark, deep and narrow Loch Ness stretches 23 miles from Fort Augustus at its southern end nearly as far as Inverness. Its bitterly cold waters have been extensively explored for Nessie, the elusive Loch Ness monster, and although some visitors get lucky, most see only a cardboard cut-out form. Along the north-western shore runs the congested A82, while the more tranquil and extremely picturesque B862 follows the south-eastern shore. A complete circuit of the loch is about 70 miles, and you'll have the best views travelling anticlockwise.

Drumnadrochit

☎ 01456 • pop 600

Exploitation of poor Nessie reaches fever pitch at Drumnadrochit where two 'Monster' exhibitions vie for the tourist dollar. The villages of Milton, Lewiston and Strone are adjacent to Drumnadrochit while Urquhart Castle is immediately south.

Monster Exhibitions

The prominent **Official Loch Ness Monster Exhibition Centre** (☎ 450573) is the better of the two Nessie theme exhibitions. It features a 40-minute audiovisual presentation with lasers, digital projection systems and special effects plus exhibits of equipment used in underwater monster hunts. It opens 9.30 am to 5.30 pm daily, April to June; 9 am to 8 pm July and August; 9 am to 6.30 pm September and October; and 10 am to 4 pm the rest of the year. Admission costs £5.95/3.50.

The nearby **Original Loch Ness Monster Centre** (☎ 450342) shows a marginal 30-minute Loch Ness video (with multilingual headsets), next to its gift shop, the centre's real focus. It opens 10 am to 5.30 pm daily from April to June, September and October; 9 am to 8 pm daily, July and August; and 10 am to 4 pm the rest of the year. Admission costs £3.50/2.75.

Urquhart Castle

Urquhart Castle (☎ 450551; HS), one of Scotland's best-known castles, was taken and lost by Edward I, held by Robert the Bruce against Edward III and fought over by everyone who passed this way. Not only was the castle repeatedly sacked, damaged and rebuilt over the centuries, but the unfortunate inhabitants of the Great Glen were also regularly pillaged and robbed in the process.

Destruction and reconstruction occurred so often that it's hard to trace the full story of the castle's development. By the 1600s it had become redundant, superseded by more palatial residences and more powerful fortresses at Fort William and Inverness. It was finally blown up in 1692 to prevent Jacobites using it and its remains perch dramatically on the edge of the loch, approached by a steep path from the roadside car park.

The castle was entered by a drawbridge that led into the gatehouse. The summit of the upper bailey (outermost wall) at the southern end was probably used as a hillfort

Nessie

There's a tale of St Columba meeting 'Nessie' (the Loch Ness Monster) in the 6th century, but the craze only really developed after 1933, when the A82 road was completed along the northern banks of the loch.

The classic photograph of a dinosaur-like creature's long neck emerging from the water was taken in 1934, from which time the monster hunt gathered pace. In recent years there have been sonar hunts, underwater cameras and computer studies, but no monster has yet been spotted. The loch is very deep and very murky, so the Nessie tourist business has to pedal hard to make a go of it. Keep your camera handy though, you might be the one to prove incontrovertibly that Nessie exists.

If you want to find out more before you leave, check out the official Nessie Web site at www.lochness.co.uk.

JANE SMITH

over 1000 years ago, but by the 15th century, the nether bailey at the northern end had become the focus of fortifications. The five-storey tower house at the extreme northern end is the most impressive remaining fragment and offers wonderful loch views.

It opens 9.30 am to 6.30 pm daily, April to September (to 4.30 pm October to March). Admission costs £3.80/1.20.

Places to Stay & Eat

The smart *Loch Ness Backpackers* (☎ 450 807, East Lewiston) is in a farmhouse within walking distance of Drumnadrochit (signposted) and Urquhart Castle. Dorm beds cost from £8.50 to £9. *Loch Ness Youth Hostel* (☎ 01320-351274), 13 miles down the western side of the loch at Glenmoriston, costs

£8.25/7.25 for adults/under-18s and opens mid-March to October. Buses from Inverness stop nearby. There are numerous B&Bs in Drumnadrochit but single rooms are in short supply. If you're driving, try the welcoming *Drumbuie Farm* (☎ 450634), on the right as you enter Drumnadrochit from Inverness. It has comfortable single/double rooms for £22/36.

Near the village green are the pleasant *Glen Café Bar* (☎ 450282), open till late daily, and the more expensive, nonsmoking *Fiddler's Café Bar* (☎ 450678) with traditional Scottish fare and a non-GM food policy; try its whisky-glazed grilled salmon for £11.95. The restaurant at the *Drumnadrochit Hotel* (☎ 450218) is noted for its fine cuisine (using local produce) and service.

HIGHLANDS & NTH ISLANDS

B&B in well-appointed rooms costs from £17.50 to £40 per person.

Getting There & Away
Scottish Citylink (☎ 0870 550 5050) has up to six services daily along Loch Ness between Fort William and Inverness, via Drumnadrochit.

INVERNESS
☎ 01463 • pop 41,800
Inverness has a great location on the Moray Firth at the northern end of the Great Glen. The town was probably founded by David I in the 12th century and is now the capital and transportation hub of the Highlands. In summer it's full of visitors intent upon monster-hunting at nearby Loch Ness. However, it's worth spending some time strolling and bird-watching along the fast-flowing, picturesque River Ness or cruising on the Moray Firth in search of its 100 or so bottlenose dolphins.

Orientation & Information
The River Ness, which links Loch Ness and the Moray Firth, flows through the heart of town. The bus and train stations and hostels are east of the river, within 10 minutes' walk of each other. The TIC (☎ 234353), beside the museum on Castle Wynd just off Bridge St, opens daily June to September except Sunday between October and May. It has a currency exchange, as does the post office in Queensgate.

The reference section of Inverness Public Library (☎ 236436), near the bus station, offers free Internet access including email, but you need to book a time. It opens daily except Sunday.

The Laundrette at 17 Young St just over the bridge, opens daily.

Inverness Museum & Art Gallery
The Inverness Museum & Art Gallery (☎ 237114) contains wildlife dioramas, geological displays, period rooms with historic weapons, Pictish stones and a modest art gallery. It's entered through Castle Wynd off Bridge St and opens 9 am to 5 pm Monday to Saturday. Admission is free.

Inverness Castle
In the 11th century a timber castle probably stood to the east of the present castle site. In the 12th century it was replaced with a stone castle, which was then rebuilt in the 15th century. It was repaired in 1718 and expanded in 1725, only to be taken by the Jacobites in 1746 and blown up. The present rose-coloured structure was constructed between 1837 and 1847.

Today it serves as the local Sheriff's Court and most of the youths hanging around outside are waiting for their cases to be heard. In front stands a statue of the Highland heroine Flora MacDonald, who helped the escaping Bonnie Prince Charlie. The Drum Tower now houses the **Castle Garrison Encounter** (☎ 243363), where for £3/2 you meet actors representing characters from the Hanoverian army of 1746. It opens 10.30 am to 5.30 pm Monday to Saturday, Easter to late November (and Sunday in July and August).

Other Things to See & Do
Thanks to Inverness' often violent history, few buildings of real age or historical significance have survived, and much of the town dates from the completion of Telford's Caledonian Canal in 1822. Medieval structures line Church St including the 1593 **Abertarff House**. Inverness' **Mercat Cross** stands in front of the ornate **Town House**, the Gothic-style town hall on Bridge St.

Across the river and south along the river bank lies **St Andrew's Cathedral**, dating from 1866–9, and the **Eden Court Theatre** which hosts regular art exhibits. It's also worth strolling to the **Ness Islands**, about half a mile south of the centre and connected to the river banks by footbridges.

Organised Tours
Walking Tours Guided walking tours, exploring the history of the town, leave from outside the TIC. They take 1¼ hours and cost £4/2; the TIC can provide times.

Bus Tours Over Easter and from May to early October, Guide Friday (☎ 224000) runs open-top, hop-on hop-off bus tours of

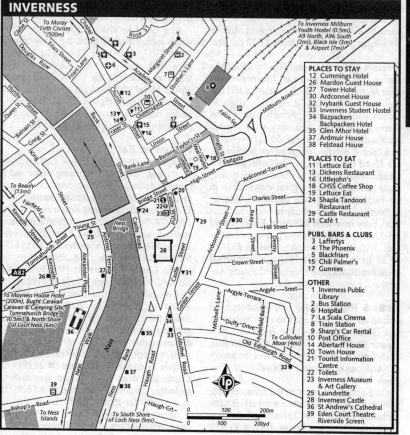

INVERNESS

Inverness and the Culloden battlefield. An all-day ticket costs £6.50/5.

Ken White's (☎ 223168) and Peter Forbes (☎ 236719) both do tours to Loch Ness from the TIC at 10.30 am and 2.30 pm daily and take in Urquhart Castle (admission fee extra). Tours take around four hours and cost £7.50/6.50.

Cruises From Tomnahurich Bridge, the *Jacobite Queen* (☎ 233999) cruises Loch Ness for £9.50/7.50 to £13.50/10 per adult/child. A one-way trip to Urquhart Castle, including admission, costs £10/8.

Moray Firth Cruises (☎ 717900) offers 1½ hour wildlife cruises to see dolphins, seals and bird life. Sightings aren't guaranteed but it's still enjoyable, especially on fine days. Follow signs to Shore St Quay from the far end of Chapel St. Trips cost £10/5 and leave between 10.30 am and 4.30 pm daily March to October (6 pm in July and August). Buses leave the TIC 15 minutes before sailings.

Places to Stay
In the peak season, either prebook your accommodation or start looking early. The TIC charges £1.50 for local bookings.

Camping *Bught Caravan & Camping Site* (☎ *236920, Glenurquhart Rd)*, half a mile south by the A82 on the river's west bank, is well-equipped and costs from £3.10 per site.

Hostels A 10-minute walk up from the train station, just past the castle, *Inverness Student Hostel* (☎ *236556, 8 Culduthel Rd)* has the same owner as Edinburgh's High St Hostel – you can make phone bookings from there. It's friendly and cosy with a great view and charges £9 to £10.50 in five- to 10-bed dorms. Nearby, *Bazpackers Backpackers Hotel* (☎ *717663, 4 Culduthel Rd)* is a clean building with a wood-burning fire, small garden and more great views. Beds in six-bed dorms cost from £7.50, with linen.

Possibly the best-equipped hostel in Scotland, busy *Inverness Millburn Youth Hostel* (☎ *231771, Victoria Drive)*, about 15 minutes' walk from the centre, charges £12.75/11.25 for adults/under-18s with continental breakfast. Rates are £1 higher in July and August and booking is essential.

B&Bs & Hotels Along Old Edinburgh Rd and on Ardconnel St are lots of guesthouses and B&Bs. Heritage-listed *Ivybank Guest House* (☎ *232796, 28 Old Edinburgh Rd)*, costs from £20 per person as does the graceful *Ardconnel House* (☎ *240455, 21 Ardconnel St)*.

On Kenneth St, west of the river, and adjoining Fairfield Rd, there are several B&Bs, including *Mardon* (☎ *231005, 37 Kenneth St)*, a five-room guest house charging £15/28 per single/double (£21/40 with bathroom).

For a few pounds more it's possible to get a river view in Ardross Terrace/Ness Walk, on the western side of the river, or Ness Bank, along the eastern side. Family-run, Georgian *Ardmuir House* (☎ *231151, 16 Ness Bank)* has rooms from £33.50/55, all with private bathroom. Unpretentious *Felstead House* (☎ *231634, 18 Ness Bank)* is cheaper and has rooms with and without bathroom from £25 per person. The grand *Glen Mhor Hotel* (☎ *234308, 10 Ness Bank)* has en-suite rooms from £45/58 and two restaurants.

In the city centre, the four-star, rambling *Cummings Hotel* (☎ *232531, Church St)* has rooms, most with bathroom, from £45/75. It has changed hands, however, and may close.

In a quiet location across the river towards Eden Court Theatre, the *Tower Hotel* (☎ *232765, 4 Ardross Terrace)* has well-appointed rooms from £30/52. Also west of the river, and just off the A82, *Moyness House Hotel* (☎ *233836, 6 Bruce Gardens)* is an elegantly furnished Victorian villa offering B&B with bathroom for £31 to £35 per person and exceptional meals for £20.

Places to Eat

Littlejohn's (☎ *713005, 28–30 Church St)* is bright and noisy, with amusing decor and a highly descriptive pasta-Mexican-burger menu. Its volcanic vegetarian burrito costs £7.95. Upmarket *Dickens Restaurant* (☎ *713 111, 77–79 Church St)* has a good reputation and specialises in seafood, international cuisine and vegetarian dishes from £6.80 to £13. It opens daily for lunch and dinner.

The *Castle Restaurant* (☎ *230925, 41 Castle St)* is a traditional cafe that prides itself on plain plentiful food at low prices; mains cost from £4.20 to £8.20. Down the street, the classier *Café 1* (☎ *226200)* does good-value, two-course lunches for £5.95; dinner mains cost £7.50 to £14. It opens daily except Sunday. The recommended *Shapla Tandoori Restaurant* (☎ *241919, 2 Castle Rd)* does spicy Indian specialities, including chicken tikka masala for £6.95. It opens daily for lunch and dinner.

Inverness Museum has a small *coffee shop*, open 10 am to 4 pm Monday to Saturday, that does light meals at lunchtime. The busy, intimate *CHSS Coffee Shop* (5 Mealmarket Close)* offers cheap nourishing, healthy food in a relaxed atmosphere. Baguettes cost £1.65. It opens 10 am to 4 pm Monday to Saturday. For takeaway sandwiches from 75p to £1.85, try *Lettuce Eat* (☎ *715064, 7 Lombard St)*, which only opens during the day.

Entertainment

Blackfriars and *The Phoenix* are popular real ale pubs on Academy St near *Laffertys*, an Irish theme pub with music at the weekend. *Gunnies (Union St)* also has live bands from Tuesday to Saturday. *Chili Palmer's*, on the corner of Church St and Queensgate, is a cool, cavernous pub popular with young people.

Eden Court Theatre (☎ 234234, Ness Walk) provides regular musical and theatre performances, while *Riverside Screen*, at the same location, is Inverness' art-house cinema. *La Scala (Strother's Lane)* shows mainstream films.

Getting There & Away

Inverness is 155 miles from Edinburgh, 110 miles from Aberdeen and 135 miles from Dundee.

Air Inverness airport (☎ 232471), 7 miles east at Dalcross, offers flights to Glasgow, Edinburgh, Stornoway and other centres. Discount airline easyJet (☎ 0870 600 6000) also has flights between London Luton and Inverness.

Bus For the Inverness bus station phone ☎ 233371. Scottish Citylink (☎ 0870 550 5050) has connections with major centres in England, including London (£28, 13 hours) via Perth and Glasgow. There are numerous buses daily to/from Glasgow (£12, 3½ hours), Edinburgh via Perth (£12.50, four hours) and Aberdeen (£10, three hours).

There are buses to Ullapool Monday to Saturday (£5, 1½ hours, two daily), connecting with the CalMac ferry to Stornoway on Lewis.

Buses run via Wick to Thurso and Scrabster (£9, from three hours, three or four daily) for ferries to Orkney. The Scottish Citylink bus leaving Inverness at 1.30 pm connects at Wick with a Highland Country bus service to John o'Groats. There are connecting ferries and buses from John o'Groats to Burwick and Kirkwall in the Orkney Islands. It also runs regular daily services along Loch Ness to Fort William (£6.50, two hours).

Citylink/Skyeways (☎ 01599-534328) runs three buses a day (two on Sunday) from Inverness to Kyle of Lochalsh and Portree, on the Isle of Skye (£7.50, three hours).

It's possible to head to the north-west through Lairg. Stagecoach Inverness (☎ 239

292) has a Monday to Saturday service to Lairg (Sunday also in summer). In summer, daily buses run through to Durness. There's also a Monday to Saturday postbus service (☎ 01246-546329), travelling Lairg-Tongue-Durness.

Train The standard single fare from London to Inverness costs £90.50 and the journey takes about eight hours. There are direct trains from Aberdeen (£17.80), Edinburgh and Glasgow (£29.90).

The onward line from Inverness to Kyle of Lochalsh (£14.70, 2½ hours) offers one of the greatest scenic journeys in Britain. The line to Thurso (£12.50, 3½ hours) connects with the ferry to Orkney. There are three trains a day Monday to Saturday on both lines.

Car The TIC has a handy *Car Hire* leaflet. As well as the big boys there's Sharp's Car Rental (☎ 236694), 1st floor, Highland Rail House, Station Square, where rates start from £24 per day (plus tax).

Getting Around

To/From the Airport The twice-daily airport bus connects with Stornoway and London flights (£2.50, 20 minutes). A taxi costs between £9 and £10.

Bus Stagecoach Inverness (☎ 239292) and Highland Country (☎ 222244) operate buses to places around Inverness including Nairn, Forres, the Culloden battlefield, Beauly, Dingwall and Lairg. A Stagecoach Inverness Day Rover Highland ticket costs £9/4.50. The Highland Country return fare to Culloden costs £2.10; to Cawdor it costs £8.50.

Bicycle There are great cycling opportunities out of Inverness and several rental outlets, including Inverness Student Hostel (☎ 236556), 8 Culduthel Rd, where bikes cost £6/12 for a half/full day.

AROUND INVERNESS

Unless otherwise stated Highland Country (☎ 01463-233371) buses service the sights mentioned in this section.

Beauly

☎ 01463 • pop 1800

In 1584, Mary Queen of Scots is said to have given this village its name when she exclaimed, in French: '*Quel beau lieu!*' (What a beautiful place!) Founded in 1230, the red-sandstone **Beauly Priory** is now an impressive ruin. Admission costs £1.20/75p (get the key from the Priory Hotel).

Stagecoach Inverness (☎ 239292) operates hourly services Monday to Saturday from Dingwall and Inverness (six run on Sunday).

Black Isle & Cromarty

Actually a peninsula rather than an island, Black Isle can be reached from Inverness by a short cut across the **Kessock Bridge**. You'll find the vaulted crypt of a 13th-century chapterhouse and sacristy, and ruinous 14th-century southern aisle and chapel, at **Fortrose Cathedral**. In Rosemarkie, the **Groam House Museum** (☎ 01381-620961) has a superb collection of Pictish stones incised with designs such as those on Celtic Irish stones. It opens 10 am to 5 pm Monday to Saturday and 2 to 4.30 pm Sunday, Easter and May to September; and 2 to 4 pm at weekends only, October. Admission costs £1.50/50p.

The Cromarty Firth is famous for the huge offshore oil rigs which are built at Nigg before being towed out to the North Sea.

At the peninsula's north-eastern end, the pretty village of Cromarty has many fascinating 18th-century stone houses. In Church St, **Cromarty Courthouse** (☎ 01381-600418) has a thoroughly interesting local history museum, open 10 am to 5 pm daily, April to October (shorter hours in winter). Admission costs £3/2 and includes headsets for a recorded tour of Cromarty's other historic buildings. Two doors down from the courthouse is **Hugh Miller's Cottage** (☎ 01381-600245; NTS). This well-known author's thatched-roof home opens 11 am to 1 pm and 2 to 5 pm daily, May to September (afternoon only on Sunday). Admission costs £2.50/1.

From Cromarty Harbour, Dolphin Ecosse (☎ 01381-600323) runs boat trips along Cromarty Firth to see bottlenose dolphins and other wildlife. The trips cost £15 and last 2½ hours. Check out the Web site at www.dolphinecosse.co.uk.

Several places offer B&B from £16 per head including **Mrs Robertson** (☎ 01381-600488, 7 Church St), which also hires out bikes. For something to eat the pleasant **Country Kitchen** tearoom on the corner of Church St and Forsyth Place opens daily except Monday, or try **The Cromarty Arms** (☎ 01381-600230, Church St), opposite the courthouse, a good pub with bar meals and live music.

Highland Country (☎ 01463-233371) runs buses from Inverness to Fortrose and Rosemarkie Monday to Saturday. Some continue on to Cromarty (£4.70, 55 minutes).

Cawdor

Cawdor Castle (☎ 01667-404615), 14th-century home of the Thanes of Cawdor, was reputedly the castle of Shakespeare's Macbeth and location of Duncan's murder. The central tower dates from the 14th century, but the wings are 17th-century additions. It opens 10 am to 5 pm daily, May to October. Admission costs £5.60/3.

Cawdor Tavern (☎ 01667-404777) in the nearby village is worth a stop, although deciding what to drink can be difficult as it stocks over 100 varieties of whisky. There's also reasonable pub grub, with most specials under £8, and live music at weekends.

Culloden

Culloden is about 6 miles east of Inverness. The Battle of Culloden in 1746, the last fought on British soil, saw the defeat of Bonnie Prince Charlie and the slaughter of over 1200 Highlanders in a 68-minute rout. The duke of Cumberland won the label Butcher Cumberland for his brutal treatment of the defeated Scottish forces. The battle sounded the death knell of the old clan system, and the horrors of the Clearances soon followed (see the boxed text 'Crofting & the Clearances' later in the chapter). The sombre 49-hectare moor where the conflict took place has scarcely changed to this day. The site, with its many markers and memorials, is always open.

The visitors centre (☎ 01463-790607; NTS) offers a 15-minute audiovisual presentation on the battle. It opens 9 am to 6 pm daily, April to October; and 10 am to 4 pm the rest of the year. It's closed completely in January. Admission costs £3.50/free.

Clava Cairns

Clearly signposted 1½ miles east of Culloden, the Clava Cairns are a picturesque group of cairns and stone circles dating from the late Neolithic period (from around 4000 to 2000 BC). There's a superb railway viaduct nearby.

Fort George

Off the A96 about 11 miles north-east of Inverness and covering much of the headland is a virtually unaltered 18th-century artillery fortification, one of the best examples of its kind in Europe. It was completed in 1769 as a base for George II's army. The mile-plus walk around the ramparts offers fine views out to sea and back to the Great Glen. Given its size, you'll need several hours to look around. The visitors centre (☎ 01667-462777; HS) is open standard Historic Scotland hours. Admission costs £4/1.50.

Brodie Castle

The castle (☎ 01309-641371; NTS) is 8 miles east of the small town of Nairn, set in 70 hectares of parkland. Although the Brodies have lived here since 1160, the present structure dates from the 16th century. You can look around several rooms, some with extravagant ceilings, and there's a large collection of paintings and furniture. Don't miss the huge Victorian kitchen. There are also woodland walks in the parkland and an observation hide by the pond.

The castle opens 11 am to 5.30 pm Monday to Saturday and 1.30 to 5.30 pm Sunday, April to September. Admission is £5/free. Stagecoach Bluebird (☎ 01463-239292) bus No 10 runs every half-hour, taking 45 minutes to reach Brodie from Inverness via Culloden.

East Coast

The east coast starts to get interesting once you leave behind Invergordon's industrial development. Beyond this, great heather-covered hills heave themselves out of the wild North Sea, with pleasant little towns moored precariously at their edge. It's well served by buses, and trains follow the coast up to Wick then across to Thurso (up to seven daily).

DINGWALL TO BONAR BRIDGE

Located at the head of Cromarty Firth, **Dingwall** (population 5000) is the legendary birthplace of Macbeth. Local military hero Sir Hector MacDonald features in the **Dingwall Museum** (☎ 01349-865366), High St, and in a monument overlooking the town. It opens 10 am to 5 pm Monday to Saturday.

Sir Hector Munro, another military hero, commemorated his most notable victory, the capture of the Indian town of Negapatam in 1781, by erecting the Fyrish Monument, a replica of the town's gateway, high above nearby **Evanton**. Turn towards Boath off the B9176; from the car park it's a 45-minute walk along the Jubilee Path.

Invergordon is the main centre for repairing North Sea oil rigs in the Cromarty Firth.

Tain was a centre for the management of the Clearances and has a curious 16th-century tollbooth in the town centre. St Duthac was born in Tain around 1000 (died in Armagh, Northern Ireland, in 1065) and is commemorated by the 11th- to 12th-century ruins of St Duthac's Chapel, as well as by St Duthus Church, now part of the **Tain Through Time** heritage centre (☎/fax 01862-894089), Tower St. It opens 10 am to 6 pm daily, April to October; and noon to 4 pm in November, December and March. Admission costs £3.50/2.

The A9 crosses Dornoch Firth. Alternatively, from Ardgay at the head of Dornoch Firth, a small road leads 10 miles up Strathcarron to **Croick**, scene of notorious evictions during the 1845 Clearances. Refugee crofters from Glencalvie scratched their sad messages on the eastern windows of Croick Church.

Another detour from Ardgay along the Kyle of Sutherland leads after 4½ miles to **Carbisdale Castle** (dating from 1914), which now houses *Carbisdale Castle Youth Hostel* (☎ *01549-421232*), Scotland's largest. It opens March to October and charges £12.75/11.25 for adults/under-18s. The sweeping **Bonar Bridge** then crosses the head of the firth to rejoin the A9 just before Dornoch.

DORNOCH
☎ 01862 • pop 1000
On the coast, 2 miles off the A9, Dornoch is a picturesque seaside town clustered around **Dornoch Cathedral**. The original building was destroyed in 1570 during a clan feud and, despite some patching up, it wasn't completely rebuilt until 1835–7.

The TIC (☎ 810400), in the main square, opens daily mid-April to October (weekdays only the rest of the year).

Dornoch has several camping grounds and plenty of B&Bs. If you want to stay in grand *Dornoch Castle* (☎ *810216*), the 16th-century former Bishop's Palace on the square, you'll pay from £40.50/72 per single/double. It opens April to October. You can also dine in style here. Its grilled monkfish costs £7.95. *Sutherland House* (☎ *811023, Argyll St*), just off the square, has reasonably priced pub-style food (steak and kidney pie costs £5.95).

South of Dornoch, seals are often visible on the sand bars of **Dornoch Firth**. North of Dornoch the A9 crosses the head of **Loch Fleet** on the Mound, an embankment built by Telford from 1815 to 1816.

DUNROBIN CASTLE
One mile north of **Golspie** (☎ 01408-633177), the largest house in the Highlands (187 rooms, but visitors only see about 17), dates back to around 1275. Additions were made in the mid-1600s and late-1700s, but most of what you see today was built in French style between 1845 and 1850. One of the homes of the earls and dukes of Sutherland, it's richly furnished and offers an insight into their opulent lifestyle.

Judging by the numerous hunting trophies and animal skins, much family energy went into hunting. The house also displays innumerable gifts from farm tenants (probably grateful that they weren't evicted as part of the Sutherlands' Clearance). Behind the house, formal gardens – where falconry demonstrations are given – slope down to the sea. Beside them, a museum (once a summerhouse) offers an eclectic mix of archaeological finds, natural history exhibits and, what really strikes you when you first walk in, a huge number of big-game trophies.

The castle opens 10.30 am to 4.30 pm Monday to Saturday and from noon to 4.30 pm Sunday, April to October; and 10.30 am to 5.30 pm daily, June to September. Admission costs £5.50/4.

BRORA & HELMSDALE
Brora, at the mouth of a river famed for its salmon, has a fine beach and plenty of B&Bs. Three miles south towards Dunrobin is the **Carn Liath Broch**, a well-preserved Iron Age fort.

Farther north, Helmsdale, with its pretty harbour and salmon river, is busy in summer. The TIC (☎ 01431-821640) is in the **Timespan Heritage Centre** (☎ 01431-821327), Dunrobin St. The heritage centre has details of the 1869 Strath of Kildonan gold rush and a model of Dame Barbara Cartland, the late queen of pulp romance novelists. It opens 9.30 am to 5 pm Monday to Saturday and 2 to 5 pm Sunday, April to mid-October (to 6 pm daily, July and August). Admission costs £3.50/1.75.

There are several B&Bs (a list is posted on the heritage centre door), or you can enjoy a simple bed at *Helmsdale Youth Hostel* (☎ *01431-821577*) for £6.75/6 for adults/under-18s. It opens mid-May to September, but book well ahead for July or August.

Cartland holidayed in Helmsdale for over 60 years and Nancy Sinclair, proprietor of *La Mirage (Dunrobin St)* fish and chip shop, looks very much like her – they shared the same hairdresser. Nancy's fish and chips aren't bad either.

Crofting & the Clearances

Many Highland settlements are described as crofting communities. The word croft comes from the Gaelic *croitean*, meaning a small enclosed field.

Highland land was generally owned by clan chiefs until the early 19th century, and their tenants farmed land on the 'run-rig' system. That is, the land was divided into strips which were shared among the tenants. The strips were periodically shuffled around so no tenant was stuck with bad land or always enjoyed the good land. Unfortunately, it also meant they might end up with several widely scattered strips and there was no incentive to improve them because tenants knew they would soon lose them. Accordingly, the system was changed and the land rented out to the tenants as small 'crofts', averaging about 1.2 hectares. Each tenant then built their own house on their croft and the former tight cluster of homes became spread out. Crofters could also graze their animals on the common grazings, land which was jointly held by all the local crofters.

Crofting remained a precarious lifestyle. The small patch of land barely provided a living and each year the tenancy could be terminated and the crofter lose not only the croft but the house they had built on it. During the Highland Clearances, that was precisely what happened. Following the ban on private armies, clan chiefs no longer needed large numbers of tenants and many decided sheep farming was more profitable than collecting rent from poverty-stricken crofters. The guidebook to Dunrobin Castle, seat of the Sutherland family, blithely notes that they 'proceeded to make large-scale improvements to Sutherland's communications, land and townships which involved the clearance of some 5000 people from their ancestral dwellings'.

Despite the Clearances, a number of crofters remained, and when the economic depression of the late 19th century hit, many couldn't pay their rent. This time, however, they resisted expulsion, instead forming the Highland Land Reform Association and their own political party. Their resistance led to several of their demands being acceded to by the government, including security of tenure, fair rents and eventually the supply of land for new crofts. Crofting tenancies still exist today and complex regulations now protect the crofters.

HELMSDALE TO LATHERON

North of Helmsdale, the road climbs to a fine viewpoint at the **Ord of Caithness**. About 7 miles north of Helmsdale, a 15-minute walk from the A9 takes you to **Badbea**, where the ruins of crofts are perched on the cliff top. In early summer puffin colonies inhabit the shoreline near Berriedale. Just north of Dunbeath, **Laidhay Croft Museum** (☎ 01593-731244) re-creates crofting life from the mid-1800s to WWII. It opens 10 am to 5 pm daily, April to October. Admission costs £1/50p.

At **Clan Gunn Heritage Centre & Museum** (☎ 01593-731370) in Latheron you learn that it was really a Scot, not Christopher Columbus, who discovered America. It opens 11 am to 5 pm Monday to Saturday, June to September plus 2 to 5 pm Sunday in July and August. Admission costs £1.50/75p.

CELTIC SITES

Several Celtic sites are signposted off the A9 between Dunbeath and Wick. Turn north on the A895 at Latheron, and at Achavanich, wedged between Loch Rangag and Loch Stemster, double back on the road to Lybster to the 40 or so **Achavanich Standing Stones**.

Just beyond Lybster, a turn-off leads to the **Grey Cairns of Camster**, 5 miles north of the A9. Dating from between 4000 and 2500 BC, the burial chambers are hidden in long, low mounds rising from an evocatively desolate stretch of moor. The Long Cairn is 61m by 21m. You can enter the main chamber but you must crawl into the well-preserved Round Cairn. Afterwards, continue 7 miles north on this remote road to approach Wick on the A882.

The **Hill o'Many Stanes** just beyond the Camster turn-off is a curious, fan-shaped arrangement of 22 rows of small stones probably dating from around 2000 BC. Nearer to Wick at Ulbster, the **Cairn o'Get** is a quarter-mile off the A9, and then a 2-mile walk. Steps lead down to a small, picturesque harbour, directly opposite the Cairn o'Get.

WICK
☎ 01955 • pop 8000
Wick, with its boarded-up buildings and polluted river, wasn't always so grim. Around the turn of the 20th century, it was the world's largest herring fishing port, its harbour crammed with fishing boats and larger ships to carry barrels of salted herring abroad, and thousands of seasonal workers streaming into town to pack the catch. After WWI the herring began to disappear and by WWII the town had died.

Wick's massive harbour was the work of Telford, who designed Pulteneytown, the model town commissioned by the engagingly named British Society for Extending the Fisheries & Improving the Sea Coasts of the Kingdom. A failed attempt to add a breakwater was the work of Thomas Stevenson, father of author Robert Louis Stevenson.

Information
The TIC (☎ 602596) is off High St in Whitechapel Rd, which leads down to the Safeway supermarket car park. It opens daily, mid-April to October (weekdays only the rest of the year).

Wick Heritage Centre
This award-winning local museum (☎ 605 393), Bank Row, tracking the rise and fall of the herring industry, deserves all the praise it has received.

It displays everything from fishing equipment to complete herring fishing boats. The Johnston photographic collection is the museum's star exhibit. From 1863 to 1977, three generations of Johnstons photographed everything that happened around Wick, and the 70,000 photographs are an amazing portrait of the town's life. The museum even displays the Johnstons' photo studio; prints of superb early photos are for sale. It opens 10 am to 5 pm Monday to Saturday, June to September. Admission costs £2/50p.

Other Things to See
A path leads a mile south of town to the 12th-century ruins of **Old Wick Castle**, with the spectacular rock formations of the **Brough** and the **Brig**, or **Gote o'Trams**, just to the south. In good weather, it's a fine coastal walk to the castle.

Just past the turn-off to Wick airport, on the northern side of town, you can watch the glass-blowing operations in **Caithness Glass Visitors Centre** (☎ 602286). Opening hours are 9 am to 4.30 pm Monday to Friday. The shop stays open until 5 pm daily (opening at 11 am Sunday, April to December).

Places to Stay
Close to the town centre, *Riverside Caravan Club Site* (☎ 605420, *Riverside Drive*) charges from £4 to £11 per tent and opens May to September.

For a central B&B, try *Wellington Guest House* (☎ 603287, *41 High St*), behind the TIC, which has decent singles/doubles with bathroom for £25/40 and opens March to October. By the A9 at the southern edge of town, another recommended B&B is *The Clachan* (☎ 605384, *South Rd*) which charges from £25/40. The *Nethercliffe Hotel* (☎ 603344, *Louisburgh St*), signposted off the main drag, is better than its pebble-dashed exterior might suggest. B&B costs from £25 to £35 per person.

Places to Eat
There's not a lot of choice but prices are reasonable. Most places are along High St and its continuation, The Shore. One exception is the *Harbour Chip Shop*, Harbour Quay, which has a 1st-floor restaurant with views of the harbour.

Standard pub food is available at *Carter's Bar* (☎ 603700, *2 The Shore*) from 11 am to 9 pm daily. Mains cost from £3 to £4.20. On High St, the *Home Bakery & Café* does very reasonably priced hot snacks, such as scrambled egg on toast for under a £1 and baked potatoes for £1 to £1.50. The old-style *Cabrelli's Café* (*134 High St*), near the harbour, does good pasta from £3.70 and fish meals from £4.10.

Getting There & Away

Wick is 280 miles from Edinburgh and 125 miles from Inverness.

GillAir (☎ 01955-603914) and British Airways (BA; ☎ 0845 773 3377) fly to Wick from Aberdeen, Edinburgh, Orkney and Shetland. There are regular bus and train services from Inverness to Wick and on to Thurso (see the Inverness section earlier in the chapter). Highland Country (☎ 01847-893123) runs the connecting bus service from Wick to John o'Groats for the passenger ferry to Burwick, Orkney.

JOHN O'GROATS
☎ 01955

Disappointingly, the coast at the country's north-eastern tip isn't particularly dramatic, and modern John o'Groats is little more than a ramshackle car park and tourist trap. Its name comes from Jan de Groot, one of three brothers commissioned by James IV to operate a ferry service to Orkney in 1496 for just four pence.

The TIC (☎ 611373), beside the car park, opens 10 am to 5 pm Monday to Saturday, April to October. There are also shops and a crafts complex.

Two miles east of John o'Groats is **Duncansby Head**, home to many seabirds at the start of summer. A path leads to **Duncansby Stacks**, a spectacular natural rock formation soaring over 60m above the sea. There is a series of narrow inlets and deep coves on this wonderful stretch of coast.

Places to Stay & Eat

On the headland *John o'Groats Caravan & Camping Site* (☎ 611329) has 90 sites from £7 per tent and opens April to October. Three miles west of John o'Groats at Canisbay, the neat *John o'Groats Youth Hostel* (☎ 611424) opens from late March to September and charges £8.25/7.25 for adults/under-18s. In Canisbay there are also several B&Bs.

The big *John o'Groats House Hotel* (☎ 611203) has a reasonable restaurant, but was closed at the time of writing for full refurbishment. The adjoining *Groats Inn* serves bar meals but closes Monday and

Tuesday. There is a coffee shop at the *John o'Groats Knitwear* store.

Getting There & Away

Highland Country (☎ 01847-893123) runs up to seven buses daily to John o'Groats from Wick or Thurso from Monday to Saturday, and Sunday from mid-May. Harrold Coaches (☎ 631295) runs from Thurso to John o'Groats up to six times daily, Monday to Saturday. The fare is £2.50.

From May to September, MV *Pentland Venture* (☎ 611353) shuttles daily across to Orkney. The single fare to Burwick is £16/8 and day tours around Orkney cost £32/16.

See the Inverness section earlier for details on connecting buses from there to ferries to the islands. See the Orkney Islands section later for ferry details.

DUNNET HEAD

Contrary to popular belief, John o'Groats isn't the mainland's most northerly point, an honour which goes to the more dramatic Dunnet Head, a few miles west. The final stretch is along a narrow road across blanket bog. The head is marked by a lighthouse (built by Robert Stevenson, grandfather of Robert Louis Stevenson) that dates from 1832. The tricky Pentland Firth, the strait between Orkney and the mainland, stretches from Duncansby Head to Dunnet Head. *Dunnet Head Tearoom* (☎ 01847-851774) offers inexpensive food including meals for vegetarians, and B&B from £15 per head.

Just past Dunnet Head and a magnificent stretch of sandy beach, there's a turning to the tiny harbour at **Castlehill** where a heritage trail explains the evolution of the local flagstone industry.

North & West Coast

From just west of Thurso, the coast round to Ullapool is mind-blowing. Everything is massive – vast, empty spaces, enormous lochs and snowcapped mountains. Ullapool is the most northerly town of any significance and there's more brilliant coast south round to Gairloch, along the incomparable Loch Maree and down to Kyle of Lochalsh (a short hop from the Isle of Skye).

Farther south from there you're back in the land of the tour bus; civilisation (and main roads) can be quite a shock after all the empty space.

Local tourist offices have an excellent series of information leaflets about the coast route. Look for *Scotland's North Coast* (John o'Groats to Durness), *West Sutherland Coastal Route* (Durness to Elphin, just before Ullapool) and *Wester Ross Coastal Route* (Elphin to Kyle of Lochalsh). Others worth getting are *North-West Sutherland*, *Mid & East Sutherland* and *Caithness & North Coast Sutherland*.

Banks and petrol stations are few and far between in this corner of Scotland, so check your funds and fuel before setting out.

GETTING AROUND

Public transport in the north-west is very patchy. Getting to Thurso or Kyle of Lochalsh by bus or train is easy, but it can be difficult to follow the coast between these places.

In July and August, Highland Country (☎ 01463-222244) runs a once-daily bus (N59) from Thurso to Durness. At other times of the year, Highland Country and Rapson's (same telephone number) have services (N60) from Thurso to Bettyhill Monday to Saturday. There's also a postbus (☎ 01246-546329) from Tongue to Cape Wrath once daily from Monday to Saturday.

The alternative is to come north from Inverness via Lairg. There are trains daily to Lairg, from where Highland Country bus No 64 runs north to Durness daily, Monday to Saturday. The N70 runs west from Lairg to Lochinver on the west coast. From Durness bus No N67 travels south along the west coast to Lochinver and Ullapool before heading inland to Inverness.

Monday to Saturday postbus services operate the Lairg-Talmine-Tongue (No 134) and Lairg-Kinlochbervie-Durness (No 104) routes. There are also services around the coast from Elphin to Scourie, Drumbeg to

Lochinver, Shieldaig to Kishorn via Applecross, and Shieldaig to Torridon and Strathcarron, but always with gaps between towns.

There are frequent Highland Country and Scottish Citylink (☎ 0870 550 5050) bus services between Inverness and Ullapool.

Off the main routes, renting a car or hitching are perhaps better options.

THURSO & SCRABSTER
☎ 01847 • pop 9000

The most northerly town on the mainland, Thurso is a fairly large, fairly bleak place looking across Pentland Firth to Hoy in Orkney. Medieval Thurso was Scotland's major port for trade with Scandinavia. Today, ferries cross from Scrabster, 2½ miles west of Thurso, to Orkney. The ferry aside, Scrabster is little more than a collection of BP oil storage containers.

Information

The TIC (☎ 892371), Riverside Rd, opens from April to October, daily from late May.

Things to See & Do

Worth a visit is the small **Thurso Heritage Museum** (☎ 892459) in Thurso Town Hall. It opens 10 am to 1 pm and 2 to 5 pm Monday to Saturday, June to September. Admission costs 50p. The ruins of **Old St Peter's Kirk** date mainly from the 17th century, but the original church on the site was founded around 1220. The small, round, stone building over the **Meadow Well** marks the site of a former well.

Thurso is an unlikely **surfing** centre, but the nearby coast has arguably the best, most regular surf in Britain. There's an excellent right-hand reef break on the eastern side of town, directly in front of Lord Caithness' castle, and another shallow reef break 5 miles west at Brimms Ness.

North of Scrabster harbour, there's a fine cliff walk along **Holborn Head**. Take care in windy weather.

Places to Stay

By the coast on the edge of Thurso towards Scrabster, *Thurso Camping Site* (☎ 607 771) charges from £8 per tent. A few minutes' walk from the train station, ***Thurso Hostel*** (*☎ 896888, Ormlie Rd*), otherwise known as Ormlie Lodge, has 25 beds, opens year round and charges £6/8 for dorm beds without/with sheets. In July and August ***Thurso Youth Club Hostel*** (*☎ 892964, Old Mill, Millbank*), near the river, has basic dorm accommodation for £8 including linen and breakfast; phone ahead to check availability.

Thurso has many moderately priced B&Bs; the TIC charges £1.50 for local bookings. ***Waterside*** (*☎ 894751, 3 Janet St*) is a comfy guesthouse costing £16 per person, with another £1 to use the spa bath. Also central is the large ***Pentland Hotel*** (*☎ 893202, Princes St*), with rooms from £25 to £35 per person. The bigger, more up-market ***Royal Hotel*** (*☎ 893191, Traill St*) offers B&B from £30/50 per single/double.

Places to Eat
For a cheap, filling bar meal, try the ***Central Hotel*** (*☎ 893129, Traill St*), where mains cost from £6.20 to £10.95. Simple cafes include ***Reid's Bakery*** in the pedestrian mall and ***Johnston of Thurso (10 Traill St)***, while the ***Stewart Pavilion*** out at the camp site does excellent-value meals.

Getting There & Away
Thurso is 290 miles from Edinburgh, 130 miles from Inverness and 21 miles from Wick. From Inverness, Scottish Citylink buses operate via Wick to Thurso (£9.40, 3½ hours). Highland Country (*☎ 893123*) operates the Wick-Thurso-Dounreay bus route.

Monday to Saturday there are train services from Inverness (£12.50, 3½ hours, up to three daily), but space for bicycles is limited so book ahead.

Getting Around
It's a 2-mile walk from Thurso train station to the ferry port at Scrabster, or there are buses for £1. Wheels Cycle Shop (*☎ 896124*), The Arcade, 34 High St, rents out mountain bikes from £10 per day. Park Lane Motors (*☎ 894622*) near the bridge rents out cars for £35 per day.

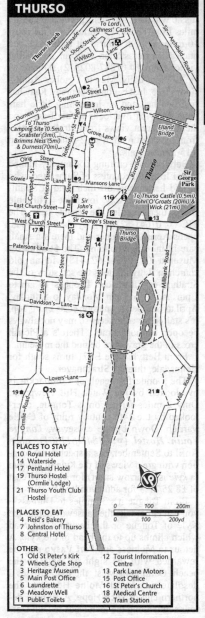

PLACES TO STAY
10 Royal Hotel
14 Waterside
17 Pentland Hotel
19 Thurso Hostel (Ormlie Lodge)
21 Thurso Youth Club Hostel

PLACES TO EAT
4 Reid's Bakery
7 Johnston of Thurso
8 Central Hotel

OTHER
1 Old St Peter's Kirk
2 Wheels Cycle Shop
3 Heritage Museum
5 Main Post Office
9 Meadow Well
11 Public Toilets
12 Tourist Information Centre
13 Park Lane Motors
15 Post Office
16 St Peter's Church
18 Medical Centre
20 Train Station

THURSO TO DURNESS

It's 80 winding and often spectacular coastal miles from Thurso to Durness. On the coast 10 miles west of Thurso, at **Dounreay**, is a nuclear power station with an interesting visitor centre (☎ 01847-802572). It opens 10 am to 4 pm daily, May to October. Admission is free. Just beyond Dounreay, **Reay** has fine beaches and an interesting little harbour. **Melvich** overlooks a fine beach and there are great views from **Strathy Point** – from the coast road, it's a 2-mile drive, then a 15-minute walk.

Bettyhill is a crofting community named after Elizabeth, countess of Sutherland, who kicked her tenants off their land at Strathnaver to make way for more profitable sheep, then resettled the tenants here. The TIC (☎ 01641-521342), by the main road, opens April to October and there's a small cafe in the same building. The **Strathnaver Museum** (☎ 01641-521418), in an old church in Bettyhill, tells the sad story of the Strathnaver Clearances. It opens 10 am to 1 pm and 2 to 5 pm Monday to Saturday, April to October. Admission costs £1.90/50p. It's staffed by volunteers so may not always be open at those times. There's a Pictish cross in the graveyard behind the museum.

From Bettyhill the B871 turns south for Helmsdale, through **Strathnaver**.

The wonderful beach at **Coldbackie** is overlooked by the Watch Hill viewpoint. Only 2 miles farther on is **Tongue**, overlooked by the 14th-century ruins of Castle Varrich. Down by the causeway, **Tongue Youth Hostel** (☎ 01847-611301), open April to September, has a spectacular location with great views of the **Kyle of Tongue** (a *kyle* is a narrow strait) for a nightly cost of £8.25/7.25 for adults/under-18s.

From Tongue it's 30 miles to Durness – you can either take the causeway across the Kyle of Tongue or the beautiful old road which climbs up to the head of the kyle. A detour to **Melness** and **Port Vasgo** may be rewarded with the sight of seals on the beach. Continuing west, the road crosses a desolate moor past **Moine House** to the northern end of **Loch Hope**. A 10-mile detour south along the loch leads to **Dun Dor-**naigil, a preserved **broch** (defensive tower) in the shadow of **Ben Hope** (927m). If you'd like to bag this Munro it's a three- to four-hour round trip along the route from the car park, which is 2 miles before the broch. Beyond Loch Hope, **Heilam** has stunning views out over **Loch Eriboll**, Britain's deepest sea inlet.

DURNESS

☎ 01971 • pop 300

The scattered village of Durness is in a great location, backed by the rocky hills of Sutherland. The TIC (☎ 511259) opens April to October, and has guided walks in summer.

Things to See

There's a path down to **Smoo Cave**, a mile east of the TIC. The vast cave entrance stands at the end of an inlet, or *geo*, and after heavy rain a river cascades through its roof and then flows out to sea. At low tide you can walk into the cave. Durness has several beautiful **beaches**, starting at Rispond to the east, and the sea offers some superb scuba-diving sites complete with wrecks, caves, seals and whales. At **Balnakeil**, less than a mile beyond Durness, a scruffy craft village occupies what was once a radar station. A walk along the beach to the north leads to **Faraid Head**, where you can see puffin colonies in early summer.

Places to Stay & Eat

By the beach and near the TIC, *Sango Sands Caravan Park* (☎ 511222) has tent sites costing £4 per person. *Durness Youth Hostel* (☎ 511244), at Smoo on the eastern side of the village in buildings resembling army barracks, opens April to September and costs £6.75/6 for adults/under-18s. Durness has several agreeable B&Bs, such as *Orcadia* (☎ 511336) or *Puffin Cottage* (☎ 511208) from £16 per person. The restaurant at *Sango Sands Oasis* bar, sandwiched between the caravan park and the TIC, is one of the few places to eat in Durness (mains cost from £4 to £9.45). Another is *Smoo Cave Hotel* (☎ 511227), which does B&B from £16.50 per person and reasonable pub grub, including a vegetarian selection.

DURNESS TO ULLAPOOL

It's 69 miles from Durness to Ullapool, with plenty of side trips and diversions to make along the way.

Cape Wrath

The cape is crowned by a lighthouse (dating from 1827) and stands close to the seabird colonies on Clo Mor Cliffs, the highest sea cliffs on the mainland. Getting to Cape Wrath involves a ferry ride (☎ 01971-511376) from Keoldale across the Kyle of Durness (£3.65 return) and a connecting minibus (☎ 01971-511287) for the 11 miles to the cape (40 minutes one way, £6.50 return). Services operate May to September daily, and up to eight times daily in July and August.

South of Cape Wrath, **Sandwood Bay** boasts one of Britain's most isolated beaches. It's about 2 miles north of the end of a track from Blairmore (approach from Kinlochbervie), or you could walk south from the cape (allow eight hours) and on to Blairmore.

Handa Island & Scourie

Boats go out to Handa Island's important seabird sanctuary from Tarbet. You may see skuas and puffins, as well as seals. You can see the **Old Man of Stoer** across Eddrachillis Bay. Scourie is a pretty crofting community with a well-known herd of Highland cattle.

Kylesku & Loch Glencoul

Cruises on Loch Glencoul pass seal colonies and the 213m drop of **Eas a'Chual Aulin**, Britain's highest waterfall. In summer, the MV *Statesman* (☎ 01571-844446) runs two-hour trips at 11 am and 2 pm from Kylesku Old Ferry Pier for £10/free. While you wait, you can have a pint and a snack or meal in *Kylesku Hotel* (☎ 01971-502231) overlooking the pier.

It's a fine three-hour, 6-mile (round trip) walk to the top of the falls, starting from beside Loch na Gainmhich at the top of the climb out of Kylesku towards Ullapool. The OS Landranger map No 15 shows the route.

The Old Man of Stoer

It's about a 30-mile detour off the main A894 out and back to the Point of Stoer and the Rhu

Stoer Lighthouse (1870). Along the coast road you need to be prepared for single-car-width roads, blind bends and summits…and sheep. The rewards are spectacular views, pretty villages and excellent beaches along the way. From the lighthouse, it's a good one-hour cliff walk to the Old Man of Stoer, a spectacular sea stack (a tower of rock rising from the sea). There are more good beaches between Stoer and Lochinver.

Lochinver & Around

☎ 01571 • pop 560

This popular little fishing port has a TIC (☎ 844330). It opens 10 am to 5 pm Monday to Saturday, April to October (plus 11 am to 4 pm Sunday, July and August). The **Hills of Assynt** near Lochinver are popular with walkers and include the peaks Suilven (731m), Quinag (808m), Ben More Assynt (998m) and Canisp (846m).

The detour to the Old Man of Stoer and Lochinver returns to the main road at **Skiag Bridge**, on the northern shore of Loch Assynt.

Places to Stay & Eat Sheltered by rocky hills, the small *Achmelvich Youth Hostel* (☎ 01571-844480), 4 miles north-west of Lochinver at Achmelvich, costs £6.75/6 for adults/under-18s and opens April to September. There are numerous B&Bs in Lochinver including the friendly *Mrs Baines* (☎ 844 443) which has two rooms with shared bathroom for £16 per person. Sprawling, waterfront *Lochinver House Travel Lodge* (☎ 844 270) is a hotel offering singles/doubles from £25/30 (breakfast extra). Interesting local food can be had at *Lochinver Larder & Riverside Bistro* (☎ 844356); the menu emphasises fish, but there's also pasta and chicken. Filleted haddock costs £10.95.

Inchnadamph Lodge (☎ 822218), at the Assynt Field Centre on the Lochinver-Lairg road (A837) in Inchnadamph is ideal for walkers and climbers. Dorm beds cost from £8.50 (£9.95 with breakfast); singles/doubles cost from £20/30.

Knockan, Inverpolly & Around

About 3 miles south of Knockan, there are geological and nature trails and a Scottish

National Heritage (SNH; see Ecology & Environment in the Facts for Scotland chapter) visitor centre (☎ 01854-666234) beside Inverpolly National Nature Reserve. The reserve has numerous glacial lochs and the three peaks of Cul Mor (849m), Stac Pollaidh (613m) and Cul Beag (769m).

At the crofting village of **Achiltibuie**, reached by a circuitous route around Loch Lurgainn (head west off the A835 at Drumrunie), the **Hydroponicum** (☎ 01854-622 202) grows tropical fruit and flowers. Tours operate on the hour from 10 am to 5 pm daily, early April to September; they cost £4/2.50.

Boat trips (☎ 01854-622200) also operate to the Summer Isles from Achiltibuie.

As you travel south, there are good views of the Isle Martin from just before Ardmair and then of the Summer Isles, Loch Broom and Ullapool.

ULLAPOOL
☎ 01854 • pop 1000

Ullapool is a pretty fishing village from where ferries sail to Stornoway on the Isle of Lewis. Small though it is, Ullapool is the biggest settlement in Wester Ross. Although it's a long way around the coast in either direction, Ullapool is only 60 miles from Inverness via the A835 along beautiful Loch Broom.

The TIC (☎ 612987), 6 Argyle St, opens year round (daily mid-April to October). The only bank is the Royal Bank of Scotland in Ladysmith St. Ullapool Bookshop (☎ 612 356), in Quay St opposite The Seaforth pub, is excellent and has lots of books on Scottish topics.

Ullapool Museum & Visitor Centre (☎ 612987), in a church in West Argyle St, opens 9.30 am to 5.30 pm Monday to Saturday, April to October; and noon to 4 pm November to March. Admission is £2/free.

Places to Stay

Five-minutes' walk west of the ferry terminal, *Broomfield Holiday Park* (☎ 612664) has camping from £5 (hiker and tent) up to £11 (car and tent). The convenient, harbourside *Ullapool Youth Hostel* (☎ 612 254) opens year round except much of January. Dorm beds cost £9.25/8 for adults/under-18s. Booking is advisable at Easter and in summer. *Ullapool Tourist Hostel* (☎ 613126, West Argyle St), also called

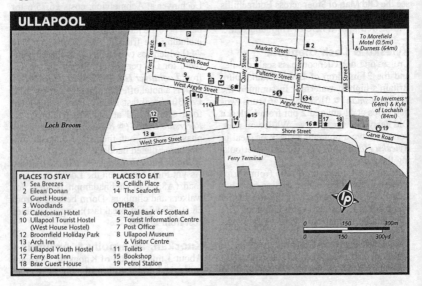

ULLAPOOL

Loch Broom

To Morefield Motel (0.5mi) & Durness (64mi)

To Inverness (64mi) & Kyle of Lochalsh (84mi)

Ferry Terminal

PLACES TO STAY	PLACES TO EAT
1 Sea Breezes	9 Ceilidh Place
2 Eilean Donan Guest House	14 The Seaforth
3 Woodlands	**OTHER**
6 Caledonian Hotel	4 Royal Bank of Scotland
10 Ullapool Tourist Hostel (West House Hostel)	5 Tourist Information Centre
12 Broomfield Holiday Park	7 Post Office
13 Arch Inn	8 Ullapool Museum & Visitor Centre
16 Ullapool Youth Hostel	11 Toilets
17 Ferry Boat Inn	15 Bookshop
18 Brae Guest House	19 Petrol Station

0   150   300m
0   150   300yd

West House Hostel, charges from £9.50 per dorm bed.

There are lots of B&Bs and guesthouses along Seaforth Rd and Pulteney St, and on Argyle St near the Quay St junction. Single rooms are as rare as gold dust, but out of season, proprietors may agree to put you in a double rather than risk leaving it empty.

Arch Inn (☎ *612454, 11 West Shore St*) has rooms with good views from £20 to £30 per person. Also right on the waterfront, *Brae Guest House* (☎ *612421, Shore St*) has rooms, including one single, with and without bathroom from £20 per person.

The friendly *Eilean Donan Guest House* (☎ *612524, 14 Market St*) does decent B&B from £18 per person. At *Woodlands* (☎ *612 701, 1a Pulteney St*) the owners make their own marmalade, jams and bread and even smoke their own fish; rooms with shared bathroom cost from £20 per person. At the welcoming *Sea Breezes* (☎ *612520, 2 West Terrace*) singles/doubles cost from £18/32.

The *Ferry Boat Inn* (☎ *612366, fax 613 299* e *reservations@ferryboat-inn.com, Shore St*) has pleasant hotel rooms with views of Loch Broom from £30 per person. The big *Caledonian Hotel* (☎ *612306, Quay St*), open March to October, offers rooms with private bathroom from £30/50.

Places to Eat

Upstairs at the junction of Quay and Shore Sts, *The Seaforth* (☎ *612122*) is a busy pub/restaurant serving good fish and chips for £4.95. *Arch Inn* and *Ferry Boat Inn* (see Places to Stay) do decent pub grub at lunchtime and early evening from around £5.50. For excellent but pricier food *Morefield Motel* (☎ *612161, North Rd*), on the northern extension of Mill St, does full menus (its seafood sampler costs £8.50) and bar meals.

The *Ceilidh Place* (☎ *612103, West Argyle St*) is a bit of a tourist mecca but it's pleasant enough. It opens 8 am to 11 pm daily, and has a daytime cafe with soup and snacks from £1.95 and a much pricier evening restaurant. It's also Ullapool's main entertainment centre, with live music most nights in summer.

Getting There & Around

Ullapool is 215 miles from Edinburgh and 60 miles from Inverness. See the Inverness section for information on bus and train links with the ferry to Stornoway on Lewis.

Bikes can be rented from Ullapool Tourist Hostel for £10 per day.

ULLAPOOL TO KYLE OF LOCHALSH

Although it's less than 50 miles as the crow flies from Ullapool to Kyle of Lochalsh, it's more like 150 miles along the circuitous coastal road, with fine views of beaches and bays backed by mountains all along the way.

Falls of Measach

The A832 doubles back to the coast from the A835, 12 miles from Ullapool. Just before the junction, the Falls of Measach ('ugly' in Gaelic; NTS) spill 45m into the spectacularly deep and narrow **Corrieshalloch Gorge**.

Inverewe Gardens

At Poolewe on Loch Ewe, the subtropical Inverewe Gardens (☎ 01445-781229; NTS) are a testament to the warming influence of the Gulf Stream. The gardens were founded by Osgood Mackenzie in 1862 – a barren, windswept peninsula was gradually transformed into a luxuriant, colourful, 26 hectare garden. They're open 9.30 am to 9 pm daily, mid-March to October; and 9.30 am to 5 pm November to mid-March. Admission costs £4.80/3.20. There's a pleasant cafeteria-style restaurant for soup and sandwiches open between 10 am and 5 pm.

Gairloch

Gairloch is a group of villages around the inner end of a loch of the same name. The TIC (☎ 01445-712130), in the car park in Auchtercairn, opens mid-April to October and has a bureau de change. **Gairloch Heritage Museum** (☎ 01445-712287) tells of life in the western Highlands, complete with a typical crofting cottage. It opens 10 am to 5 pm Monday to Saturday, April to September, and 10 am to 1.30 pm weekdays in October. Admission costs £2.50/50p.

For accommodation, there's the beautifully remote *Carn Dearg Youth Hostel* (☎ *01445-712219, Carn Dearg*), 3 miles west of Gairloch on the road to Melvaig, which costs £8.25/7.25 for adults/under-18s and opens mid-May to October. At the end of the road, 13 miles from Gairloch, you can stay at the *Rua Reidh Lighthouse* hostel (☎ *01445-771263,* e *ruareidh@netcom uk.co.uk, Melvaig*) from £7.50. In Gairloch there's plenty of B&B accommodation and bigger hotels such as the *Myrtle Bank Hotel* (☎ *01445-712004*), which has reasonable rooms with bathroom from £36 to £46 per person.

Loch Maree & Victoria Falls

The A832 runs alongside craggy Loch Maree, sprinkled with islands and with a series of peaks along the northern shore culminating in 980m-high Ben Slioch. The Victoria Falls (commemorating Queen Victoria's 1877 visit) tumble down to the loch between Slattadale and Talladale. Look for the 'Hydro Power' signs to find them.

Kinlochewe to Torridon

Small Kinlochewe is a good base for outdoor activities. From here the road follows Glen Torridon, overlooked by the multiple peaks of Beinn Eighe (1010m) and Liathach (1055m). The road hits the sea at Torridon, where the **Torridon Countryside Centre** (☎ 01445-791221; NTS) offers information on walks in this rugged area; it opens May to September. *Torridon Youth Hostel* (☎ *01445-791284, Torridon*), surrounded by great scenery, charges £9.25/8 for adults/under-18s.

Applecross & Loch Carron

A long side trip abandons the A896 to follow the coast road via the remote seaside village of Applecross. Turning inland from Applecross, the road climbs to the Bealachna Bo Pass (626m), then drops steeply to rejoin the A896. This winding, precipitous road can be closed in winter.

The A896 continues through the village of Lochcarron, then skirts Loch Carron itself.

PLOCKTON
☎ 01599 • pop 400

From Stromeferry, there are two routes to Kyle of Lochalsh, from where ferries used to cross to the Isle of Skye. The coastal route detours via idyllic Plockton, once a clearing centre for those displaced in the Clearances. This is a delightful place to stay, its main street lined with palms and whitewashed houses, each with a seagull perched on its chimney-stack gazing out at the sea. The steady throughput of visitors is augmented by viewers of the popular TV series *Hamish Macbeth* coming in search of scenes from the stories.

Leisure Marine (☎ 544306) runs seal-watching cruises for £4.50/2.50, May to September.

Places to Stay & Eat

Plockton Station Bunkhouse (☎ *544235*), a nonsmoking hostel with laundry and a TV lounge, opens year round and charges £8.50 to £10 including sheets. There are several pleasant places to stay in Harbour St; try *An Caladh* (☎ *544356, 25 Harbour St*) with beds from £18 per head, or *The Sheiling* (☎ *544282*), right by the sea, for £18/22 without/with bathroom. For self-caterers there's *Craig Highland Farm* (☎ *544205*), 3 miles east of Plockton, a delightful conservation centre with lots of animals around and cottages (holding up to six people) for £120 to £400 per week.

Plockton Hotel (☎ *544274, Harbour St*) isn't the village's prettiest building but its pub food ain't half bad; filleted sole costs £6.75. Good, home-made food is available at *Off The Rails* (☎ *544423*), at Plockton train station about half a mile inland from the harbour. During the day you can get things such as burgers for £2.85; in the evening mains cost from £6.95 to £13.95. It opens 10.30 am to 9.30 pm daily. The best food is at the *Haven Hotel* (☎ *544223, Innes St*) where delicious four-course meals cost £27.

KYLE OF LOCHALSH
☎ 01599 • pop 800

Until the Skye Bridge opened in 1995, Kyle of Lochalsh was the main jumping-off point for trips to the Isle of Skye. Now, however, its many B&B owners have to watch most of their trade whizz past without stopping.

The TIC (☎ 534276), beside the seafront car park, stocks useful information on the Isle of Skye. It opens 9 am to 5.30 pm Monday to Saturday, April to October.

The *Seagreen Restaurant & Bookshop* (☎ 534388, Plockton Rd), less than a mile from the centre of Kyle, has a wonderful wholefood cafe and restaurant. Alternatively you could try the pricier *Seafood Restaurant* (☎ 534813) in the train station, which affords views across the sea to the Isle of Skye.

Kyle can be reached by bus and train from Inverness (see Getting There & Away under Inverness earlier), and by direct Scottish Citylink buses from Glasgow (£15.30, five hours), which continue across to Kyleakin and on to Portree (£6.20, one hour) and Uig (£7.20, 1½ hours), for ferries to Tarbert on Harris and Lochmaddy on North Uist.

The 82-mile train ride between Inverness and Kyle of Lochalsh (£14.70, 2½ hours) is one of Scotland's most scenic. From May to September you can enjoy the view from the observation saloon, or the view and a meal from the dining car.

KYLE OF LOCHALSH TO THE GREAT GLEN

It's 55 miles via the A87 from Kyle to Invergarry, which is between Fort William and Fort Augustus on Loch Oich.

Eilean Donan Castle

Photogenically sited at the entrance to Loch Duich, Eilean Donan Castle (☎ 01599-85202) is Scotland's best-looking castle. It was ruined in a Jacobite uprising in 1719 and not rebuilt until 1932. Inside you get an excellent exhibition and history display for your £3.75/3. It opens 10 am to 6 pm daily, April to October.

Scottish Citylink (☎ 0870 550 5050) buses from Fort William and Inverness to Portree stop opposite the castle.

Glen Shiel & Glenelg

From Eilean Donan Castle, the A87 follows Loch Duich into the spectacular Glen Shiel valley, with 1000m peaks soaring up on both sides of the road. Turn off towards Glenelg to see two fine ruined Iron Age **brochs**, Dun Telve and Dun Troddon. From Glenelg round to **Arnisdale** the scenery becomes even more spectacular.

ROAD TO THE ISLES

The scenic, 46-mile 'Road to the Isles' (the A830) runs from Fort William via Glenfinnan to Arisaig and Mallaig. Just outside Fort William, at Banavie, is **Neptune's Staircase** (see the Fort William to Fort Augustus section earlier).

At Glenfinnan, you'll find the **Glenfinnan Monument** (☎ 01397-722250; NTS) erected in 1815 to commemorate the clansmen who died in the cause of Prince Charles Edward Stuart, or Bonnie Prince Charlie. The visitors centre recounts the story of the 1745 uprising that started here and ended nearby 14 months later when he fled to France. A lookout tower offers fine views over Loch Shiel. The centre opens 9.30 am to 6 pm daily, mid-May to August; and 10 am to 5 pm April to mid-May and September to October. Admission costs £1.50/1.

From the pier at **Arisaig**, the MV *Shearwater* (☎ 01687-450224) runs day trips to the islands of Rhum, Eigg and Muck from Wednesday to Monday. The return fares are £13 to Eigg and Muck, £17 to Rhum; trips last three to seven hours. From Arisaig, the road winds around attractive bays, and the beaches known as the **Silver Sands of Morar**. Morar village is at the entrance to **Loch Morar**, Britain's deepest body of fresh water. It's thought to contain its own monster, named Morag.

MALLAIG
☎ 01687 • pop 900

The lively fishing village of Mallaig makes a pleasant stopover between Fort William and the Isle of Skye or the Small Isles. The TIC (☎ 462170) opens Monday to Saturday, April to October, plus Sunday from June to August.

Mallaig Marine World (☎ 462292) is an informative aquarium of mainly local species. It opens 9 am to 9 pm daily, June to September; and 9.30 am to 5.30 pm Monday

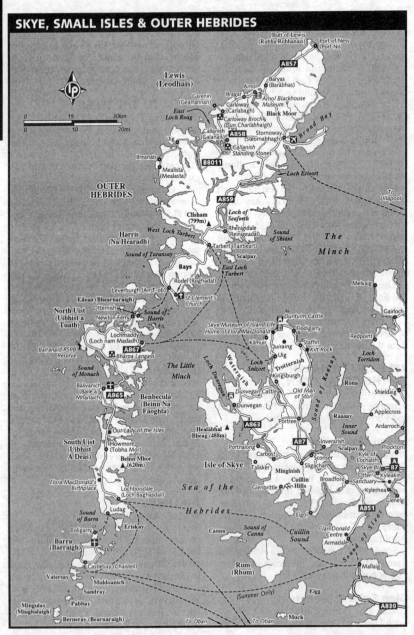

SKYE, SMALL ISLES & OUTER HEBRIDES

to Saturday and 11 am to 5 pm Sunday, the rest of the year. Admission costs £2.75/1.50. **Mallaig Heritage Centre** opens 11 am to 4 pm Monday to Saturday and from 1 pm Sunday. Admission costs £1.80/90p.

It's advisable to book ahead for the popular *Sheena's Backpacker's Lodge* (☎ 462 764, Harbour View), in the centre, which has dorm beds for £9.50 and doubles for £12 per person. There are several pleasant B&Bs. Convenient for the ferry terminal, *Anchorage* (☎ 462454, Gillies Park) has three rooms with TV and bathroom from £16 per person.

From July to September, Scottish Citylink operates buses Monday to Saturday between Fort William and Mallaig (£4.50, 1½ hours, up to three a day). The beautiful West Highland railway line between Fort William and Mallaig (£7.40, 1¼ hours) operates four times a day, Monday to Saturday, and once on Sunday, with connections to Glasgow. Mid-June to September, *The Jacobite* steam train (☎ 01524-732100) runs Monday to Friday from Fort William to Mallaig,

CalMac Ferries (☎ 462403) operates services from Mallaig to the Isle of Skye and the Small Isles year round.

The Interior

As you travel along the coast of northern Scotland it's sometimes easy to forget the interior highlands, even though their presence is always so visible. Access to this bleak but inspiring high country is provided by only a few roads, some single-track.

From June to September, just south of Lairg, at the southern end of Loch Shin, you can watch salmon leaping the **Falls of Shin** on their way upstream. From Lairg, single-track roads run north to Tongue, Laxford Bridge (between Durness and Kylesku) and Ledmore (between Kylesku and Ullapool). The A836, north from Lairg to Tongue passes **Ben Klibreck** (721m) and **Ben Loyal** (764m). Just west of Ben Loyal lies **Ben Hope** (927m), at the head of Loch Hope.

Stagecoach Inverness (☎ 01463-239292) bus No R3 runs three times daily Monday to Saturday, from Inverness to Lairg via Tain

(then north to Thurso and Wick). Postbus services (☎ 01246-546329) connect Lairg to the north-west coast; see Getting Around at the start of the North & West Coast section.

Isle of Skye

pop 8200

The Isle of Skye or 'Skye' is a rugged, convoluted island, 50 miles from end to end, connected to the mainland at Kyle of Lochalsh by the Skye Bridge. It's ringed by a beautiful coastline and dominated by the Cuillin Hills, immensely popular for the sport of Munro bagging (see the boxed text 'Munros & Munro Bagging' earlier). The island is an important centre for Gaelic culture, and nearly half of Skye's residents speak Gaelic.

Tourism is a mainstay of the economy, so you won't escape the hordes until you get off the main roads. Come prepared for changeable weather – when it's nice it's very, very nice, but it often isn't! Skye's name comes from an old Norse word for 'cloud'.

Portree and Broadford are the main population centres. Getting around the island midweek is fairly straightforward, with postbuses supplementing normal bus services. However, here, as much as in the Highlands, transport dwindles to almost nothing at the weekend, particularly in winter, and even more dramatically (so it seems) when it rains.

In spite of the bridge there are still two ways to travel 'over the sea' to Skye. From mid-July to August CalMac (☎ 01678-462 403) operates ferries from mainland Mallaig to Armadale (cars from £15.25, passengers £2.70, 30 minutes). There's also a six-car ferry from Glenelg to Kylerhea (☎ 01599-511302) service from mid-April to late October (not always on Sunday), taking 10 minutes and costing £6 for a car, driver and four passengers, 70p for foot passengers.

PORTREE (PORT RIGH)
☎ 01478 • pop 2500
Port Righ is Gaelic for King's Harbour, named after a 1540 call paid by James V to pacify local clan chieftains. Portree is Skye's biggest settlement, with a particularly pretty

harbour and most facilities such as banks, petrol stations and a post office with foreign exchange facilities.

The TIC (☎ 612137), just south of Bridge Rd, opens year round and also does foreign exchange.

On the southern edge of Portree, the **Aros Experience** (☎ 613649, fax 613775), Viewfield Rd, offers a lively introduction to Skye life. It opens 9 am to 6 pm daily (to 11 pm in July and August). Admission is £3.50/2.50.

Places to Stay

Central *Portree Independent Hostel* (☎ 613 737, The Old Post Office), near Somerled Square, offers dorm beds from £8.50, while the relaxed *Portree Backpackers Hostel* (☎ 613641, 6 Woodpark), a little farther out on Dunvegan Rd, charges from £7.50.

Portree hotels include the *Tongadale* (☎ 612115, Wentworth St), with rooms from £20 to £30 per person. The friendly *Isles Inn* (☎ 612129, Somerled Square) costs from £22/30 per single/double, while *Portree Hotel* (☎ 612511) is pricier at £35/60. *Rosedale Hotel* (☎ 613131, Beaumont Crescent), on the waterfront with good views, costs from £40/68.

Places to Eat

The *Bayfield Chip Shop* does good takeaway fish and chips for £2.95. Upmarket *Harbour View Seafood Restaurant* (☎ 612069, Bosville Terrace) serves most mains for under £15. As well as seafood it serves venison, pheasant and wild boar. There's good pub food from £5.50 to £6.95 at the *Portree* and *Tongadale* hotels (see Places to Stay) and you can even sample curry at the *Spice Hut* (☎ 612681, Bayfield Rd). The excellent, 1st-floor *Ben Tianavaig Bistro* (☎ 612152, 5 Bosville Terrace) has an extensive vegetarian and seafood menu. Evening mains cost from £8.95 to £9.50. It's closed Monday.

An Tuireann Art Centre Café (☎ 613 306) about a 20-minute walk out of town – follow Bridge Rd onto Dunvegan Rd and then left onto Struan road (the B885) – caters for vegetarians/vegans and serves sandwiches for £2.95, or a soup and sandwich combo for £4.40. It opens 10 am to

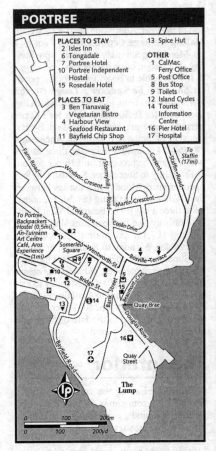

5 pm Monday to Saturday. Temporary contemporary art exhibitions are held here.

The *Pier Hotel* is a popular waterfront drinking spot.

Getting There & Away

Somerled Square is the Portree bus stop. Scottish Citylink (☎ 0870 550 5050) operates a Glasgow-Fort William-Kyle of Lochalsh-Kyleakin-Portree-Uig route three times daily, June to September, taking three hours from Fort William to Portree (£13). It also runs the Inverness to Portree service (£11, three hours, twice daily).

Getting Around

Island Cycles (☎ 613121) hires out bikes for £7.50/12 a half/full day. It opens daily except Wednesday.

KYLEAKIN (CAOL ACAIN)
☎ 01599

Even more than Kyle of Lochalsh, Kyleakin had the carpet pulled from under its feet by the opening of the Skye Bridge, but it's a pleasant enough wee place and is popular with backpackers.

From 10 am daily, **SeaCruise** (☎ 534760) charges £5.50/3.50 for a one-hour wildlife (including seals and porpoises) and history cruise on Loch Alsh.

Kyleakin Youth Hostel (☎ 534585) charges £12.25/10.75 for adults/under-18s (£1 more in July and August) and is just doors from friendly *Skye Backpackers* (☎ 534510), where beds cost from £10 to £12. Both stare out across the kyle to the mainland. Simple accommodation is available at the bothy-style *Dun Caan* (☎ 534087, Castle View) for £8.50. Nearby, *Pier Coffee House* does sandwiches and meals (under £6) and opens 9 am to 8 pm daily.

KYLERHEA (CAOL REITHE)

Kylerhea is about 4 miles south-east of Kyleakin and there's a car ferry from there to Glenelg on the mainland. Before crossing to Glenelg, you can follow a 1½ hour nature trail offering the chance to see otters from a shoreline hide (☎ 01320-366581) overlooking the pier. Even if the otters elude you, you should still see basking seals and assorted birds. Admission is free.

The ferry (☎ 01599-511302) operates 9 am to 6 pm Monday to Saturday, mid-April to late May; 9 am to 8 pm Monday to Saturday and 10 am to 6 pm Sunday, late May to early September; and 9 am to 6 pm Monday to Saturday and 10 am to 6 pm Sunday, early September to late October. A car and four passengers costs £6; a foot passenger is 70p.

ARMADALE (ARMADAL)
☎ 01471

It's still possible to arrive on Skye by boat from Mallaig. If you do that you'll wind up in remote Armadale. If you visit the **Clan Donald Centre** (☎ 844305), in the ruined Armadale Castle, a guided tour will tell you all you ever wanted to know about the MacDonald clan. It opens 9.30 am to 5.30 pm daily, late March to October. Admission costs £3.85/2.60. There's a pleasant restaurant serving home-made soup and a roll for £2.25.

It's just 350m from the Armadale ferry terminal to the scenically positioned *Armadale Youth Hostel* (☎ 844260, Ardvasar, Sleat), which opens April to September and costs £8.25/7.25 for adults/under-18s. Four miles along the road is *Hairy Coo Backpacker Hotel* (☎ 833231, fax 833393, e stotty@hairycooskye.freeserve.co.uk, Toravaig House, Knock Bay), a big, basic place with dorm beds for £10.50.

BROADFORD (AN T-ATH LEATHANN)
☎ 01471

Broadford's TIC (☎ 822361), open Monday to Saturday, April to October (and Sunday in July and August), is by the large Esso petrol station. There's nothing much to detain you in Broadford except the **Skye Serpentarium** (☎ 822209), open Easter to October, where you can see and touch all sorts of snakes, most of them illegally imported, impounded by customs and given refuge here. Admission costs £2.50/1.50.

Broadford Youth Hostel (☎ 822442), with views over the bay, opens February to October and charges £9.25/8 for adults/under-18s. The smaller *Fossil Bothy Hostel* (☎ 822644, 13 Lower Breakish), at nearby Lower Breakish, opens April to November and charges £7.50.

You can hire a bike from Fairwinds Cycle Hire (☎ 822270), near the Broadford Hotel, for £7 per day, or rent a car from Skye Car Rental (☎ 822225) at the Esso petrol station.

THE CUILLIN HILLS & MINGINISH PENINSULA
☎ 01478

The rocky Cuillin Hills, west of Broadford, provide spectacular walking and climbing country. The complete traverse of the Black Cuillin ridge requires two days and involves real climbing; make sure you're properly equipped. Sgurr Alasdair, at 993m, is the highest point.

At Carbost, the **Talisker Distillery** (☎ 640 314) opens for whisky tours from 9 am to 4.30 pm Monday to Friday, April to June and October (and Saturday from July to September); 2 to 4.30 pm Monday to Friday, November to March. The tour costs £3.

At **Sligachan (Sligeachan)**, the *Sligachan Camp Site* (☎ 650333), open Easter to October, is a popular jumping-off point for Cuillin climbers (£4 per person). There are two hostels in **Portnalong (Port nan Long)**: the simple *Croft Bunkhouse* (☎ 640254), in a converted cowshed 3 miles from Talisker Distillery, charges from £6.50 to £8 (less for campers); the larger *Skyewalker Independent Hostel* (☎ 640250, Fiskavaig Rd), at a former school, costs £7 to £8.

NORTH-WEST SKYE
☎ 01470

On the western side of the Waternish Peninsula, magnificent **Dunvegan Castle** (☎ 521 206) dates back to the 13th century, although it was restored in Romantic style in the mid-19th century. Inside, you can visit the dining room, lounge, a decidedly alarming dungeon and, next door, an excellent drawing room. The castle opens 10 am to 5.30 pm daily, mid-March to October; and 11 am to 4 pm daily, November to mid-March. Admission costs £5.50/3.

Of several possible places to stay in Dunvegan, charming *Roskhill Guest House* (☎ 521317) has singles/doubles from £32/54, while the two-star *Tables Hotel* (☎ 521404), a mile from the castle, has agreeable rooms for £25/52.

From Monday to Saturday there are four Skyeways Travel (☎ 01599-534328) buses daily to Dunvegan from Portree; one leaves at 10 am, returning from the castle at 12.52 pm (giving you two hours at the castle).

TROTTERNISH PENINSULA
☎ 01470

North of Portree, Skye's coastal scenery is at its finest in the Trotternish Peninsula. Look out in particular for the rocky spike of the **Old Man of Storr**, the spectacular **Kilt Rock** and the ruins of **Duntulm Castle**.

The biggest settlement is tiny **Staffin (Stamhain)**, about 2 miles north-west of which is the spectacular **Quiraing** offering some wonderfully dramatic hill walking. Three miles north of Staffin in even tinier **Flodigarry (Flodaigearraidh)** you can stay at historic *Flodigarry Country House Hotel* (☎ 552203), with B&B from £48 to £75 per

---

Flora MacDonald

The Isle of Skye was home to Flora MacDonald, who became famous for helping Bonnie Prince Charlie escape following his defeat at the Battle of Culloden in 1746.

Flora was born in 1722 at Milton, 5 miles south of Howmore (Thobha Mór), in South Uist; a memorial cairn marks the site of one of her early childhood homes. After her mother's abduction by Hugh MacDonald of Skye, Flora was reared by her brother and educated in the home of the Clanranald chiefs.

In June 1746 she met Bonnie Prince Charlie, who had a £30,000 price on his head. Disguising the prince as Betty Burke, her Irish maid, she helped him escape from Benbecula to Skye. Their little boat was fired on, but they managed to land safely and Flora escorted the prince to Portree where he gave her a gold locket containing his portrait before taking his leave and sailing to Raasay.

A week later Flora was arrested and imprisoned in the Tower of London. She never saw or heard from the prince again.

Released in July 1747, she returned home, marrying Allan MacDonald of Skye and going on to have seven children. Dr Samuel Johnson stayed with her in 1773 during his journey round the Western Isles, but later poverty forced her family to emigrate to North Carolina. There her husband was captured by rebels during the American War of Independence. Flora returned to Kingsburgh on Skye, followed later by her husband when he was released. She died in 1790 and was buried (thousands attended the funeral) in Kilmuir churchyard, wrapped in the sheet in which Bonnie Prince Charlie and Dr Johnson had slept.

person. The home of **Flora MacDonald** is now part of the hotel (see the boxed text 'Flora MacDonald' earlier). Nearby, *Dun Flodigarry Hostel* (☎ 552212) is more affordable at £9 per head; it has family rooms and will pick you up if you call ahead.

At the northern end of the peninsula at Kilmuir (Cille Mhoire), the **Skye Museum of Island Life** (☎ 252213) re-creates crofting life in a series of cottages overlooking marvellous scenery. It opens 10.30 am to 4 pm Monday to Saturday, April to October. Admission costs £1.75/75p.

Flora MacDonald's grave at Kilmuir indicates that she is a real victim of 'trophy' tourism. The 1955 memorial records that of the original memorial 'every fragment has been removed by tourists'.

UIG (UIGE)
☎ 01470

Uig TIC (☎ 542404), in the ferry terminal building, opens Monday to Saturday, April to October (plus Sunday, mid-July to mid-September).

Perched on the hillside, *Uig Youth Hostel* (☎ 542211) opens late March to October and costs £8.25/7.25 for adults/under-18s. There's a cluster of bungalow B&Bs with beds from around £15 or £16, including the attractive *Orasay* (☎ 542316, 14 Idrigill). The *Old Ferry Inn* (☎ 542242) is pricier at £28/50 per single/double, and the whitewashed *Uig Hotel* (☎ 542205) pricier still at £37/70, but both have fine positions overlooking the bay.

From Uig pier, CalMac (☎ 542219) has ferry services daily to Lochmaddy on North Uist (cars from £39, passengers £8.30, 1¾ hours) and Monday to Saturday to Tarbert on Harris (same times and prices).

ISLE OF RAASAY
☎ 01478 • pop 163

There are great walks on this long, narrow, quiet, rugged island off Skye's north-east coast. Forest Enterprise publishes a free leaflet with suggested walks and forest trails. There's no petrol on Raasay (Rathatsair).

Raasay Outdoor Centre (☎ 660266), Inverarish Road, provides a range of activities,

rents out bikes and offers camping (£4), dorm beds (£12) and B&B (£17 per person). The small, greystone *Raasay Youth Hostel* (☎ 660240), just north of Inverarish, opens mid-May to September and costs £6.75/6 for adults/under-18s.

CalMac (☎ 612075) ferries from Sconser on Skye (between Portree and Broadford) sail to Inverarish on Raasay, Monday to Saturday only (£2.20/9.10 for passenger/car, 15 minutes, 10 a day).

Outer Hebrides

Synonymous with remoteness, the Outer Hebrides (also called the Western Isles, or Na h-Eileanan an Lar in Gaelic) are a string of over 200 islands running in a 130-mile arc from north to south, shielding the northwest coast of Scotland. Bleak, isolated, treeless and exposed to gales that sweep in from the Atlantic, the Outer Hebrides are almost irresistibly romantic. They form one of Europe's most isolated frontiers and have a fascinating history, signposted by Neolithic standing stones, Viking place-names, empty crofts and folk memories of the Clearances.

Immediate reality can be disappointing, however. The towns are straggly, unattractive and dominated by stern, austere churches. Although the ruins of traditional blackhouses (named after the soot left on the walls by the burning peat fire in the centre) can still be seen, they've been supplanted by unattractive (though no doubt more comfortable) concrete-block bungalows. Rugged and apparently inhospitable though the islands are, they support quite a large and widely distributed population and in summer CalMac ferries disgorge a daily cargo of tourists.

The landscapes can be mournful, but they're also spectacular, with wide horizons of sky and water, dazzling white beaches, azure bays, wide peat moors and countless lochs, mountains and stony hills. These islands reward an extended stay, especially if you travel on foot or by bike: a rushed tour will be less satisfying, and when driving you have to pay too much attention to the road (often single-tracked and sheep-ridden) to appreciate the views.

The local culture isn't very accessible to outsiders, but it is distinctive. Of the 18,000 crofts registered in Scotland, 6000 are on the Outer Hebrides. Of the 66,000 Scottish Gaelic speakers, around 25,000 live on the islands. Religion still plays a central role in island life, especially in the Protestant north, where the Sunday Sabbath is strictly observed. Most shops, pubs, restaurants and service stations are closed, there's no public transport and some accommodation providers prefer guests not to arrive or depart on Sunday.

These are deeply conservative parts where a Scot from Glasgow is as much an incomer as someone from London. The European Union (EU), however, is working to reduce the islands' isolation and many roads are being upgraded courtesy of loans from the European Regional Development Fund.

Life moves very slowly, with supplies dependent on boats and planes, and inclement weather can cause supplies to dry up altogether. Often newspapers and bread are unavailable before 10 am. Accommodation is in fairly short supply so book ahead, especially in summer.

HISTORY

The first evidence of settlement dates back to around 4000 BC when Stone Age farmers settled on the islands. They constructed massive stone tombs and the mounds can still be seen (as at Barpa Langass, North Uist). Bronze Age Beaker People (named after their distinctive pottery) arrived around 1800 BC, and at about that time groups of standing stones were set up, most notably at Callanish on Lewis.

Around 1000 BC, the climate deteriorated and the peat that now blankets much of the islands – in places to depths of 6m – began to accumulate. Acidity increases when soil becomes permanently water-

The Wee Frees & Other Island Creeds

Religion plays a complex and important role in island life and priests and ministers enjoy powerful positions in the community. The split between the Protestants north of Benbecula (lying between North Uist and South Uist) and the Catholics to the south creates, or perhaps reflects, a different communal atmosphere.

Hebridean Protestants have developed a distinctive fundamentalist approach, with Sunday being devoted to religious services, prayer and Bible reading. On Lewis and Harris, virtually everything closes down. In general, social life is restricted to private homes and, as public drinking is frowned upon, pubs are mostly uninspiring.

The Protestants are further divided into three main sects, with convoluted, emotionally charged histories. The Church of Scotland, the main Scottish church, is state-recognised or 'established'. The Free Presbyterian Church of Scotland and the Free Church of Scotland (or Wee Frees) are far more conservative and restrictive, permitting no ornaments, organ music or choirs. Their ministers deliver uncompromising sermons (usually in Gaelic) from central pulpits, and precentors lead the congregation in unaccompanied, but atmospheric, psalm singing. Visitors are welcome to attend services, but due respect is essential.

The most recent split occurred in 1988 when Lord Mackay, lord chancellor and a prominent Free Presbyterian, committed the awful crime of attending a friend's Catholic requiem Mass. The church elders threatened him with expulsion, and he and his supporters responded by establishing the breakaway Associated Presbyterian Church!

The Catholic Church south of Benbecula survived the Reformation. The priests were expelled early in the 17th century but, despite several missionary attempts, Protestantism failed to take hold. The Sunday Sabbath on South Uist and Barra is more easy-going, and the attitude towards the demon drink more tolerant.

logged, creating a sterile environment where bacterial activity slows, and where dead grass, sedge, heather and moss build up in layers instead of rotting.

This spongy, nutrient-poor land wasn't good for farming, and the population was forced onto the coastal fringe. When cut and dried, however, the peat provided the islanders with fuel. Every spring, families still cut it into bricks, which are wind-dried in neat piles before being stacked outside homes.

The Iron Age Gaelic-speaking Celts arrived around 500 BC and several defensive brochs remain from this period, the most impressive at Carloway on Lewis.

Vikings settled on the islands by AD 850, and many island clans, including the Morrisons, Nicolsons, MacAulays and Macleods, are thought to have Norse backgrounds. The traditional island houses, the blackhouses that remained in common use into the 1930s, were essentially Viking longhouses. The Middle Ages saw a new influx of Gaelic-speaking Celts from mainland Scotland and Ireland, and a weakening of the links with Norway, resulting in a Gaelic-speaking Celtic-Norse population.

LANGUAGE

Scottish Gaelic is basically the same as Irish Gaelic. About 75% of the islanders speak it (as opposed to just 1.5% of the total Scottish population), and efforts are made to ensure its survival. Many Gaelic TV and radio programs are now produced.

All islanders speak English, and there's no reluctance to use it when speaking to outsiders. However, all road signs are in Gaelic, which can cause confusion. When talking to outsiders, islanders use the anglicised version of a name, but this can bear little similarity to the Gaelic on the signs. The CalMac ferry company and airlines also use anglicised names. Visitors should obtain a bilingual road map showing both names; Estate Publications' red-covered *Official Tourist Map – Western Isles* is ideal and costs £3.95.

This book uses English names where they're in common usage with the Gaelic name in brackets at the first main reference.

ORIENTATION & INFORMATION

Lewis and Harris are actually one island with a border of high hills between them. The northern half of Lewis is low and flat with miles of peat moors; southern Lewis and Harris are rugged, with some impressive stony mountains and glorious beaches. Stornoway, on Lewis, is the largest town in the Outer Hebrides, with a reasonable range of facilities.

North Uist, Benbecula and South Uist are joined by bridge and causeway. These are low, flat, green islands half-drowned by sinuous lochs and open to the sea and sky. Benbecula has a large army and air force base.

There are TICs in every ferry port. Those in Stornoway and Tarbert open year round (the others open early April to mid-October) for ferry arrivals up to midnight.

The Western Isles Tourist Board (☎ 01851-703088), 26 Cromwell St, Stornoway, Lewis HS1 2DD, produces an annual *Western Isles* brochure showing all accommodation possibilities. Its Web site is at www.witb.co.uk. *The Outer Hebrides Handbook & Guide*, written by local experts, gives lots of data on the islands' history, culture, flora and fauna.

PLACES TO STAY & EAT

Camp sites with facilities are scarce, but free camping is usually allowed, provided you get permission from the nearest house and remove all rubbish. Some landowners may ask for a small fee.

There are a few basic hostels in old crofts scattered around the islands, but most are difficult to get to without transport or a readiness to hike. Most are run by the Scottish Youth Hostel Association (SYHA) or Gatliff Hebridean Hostels Trust (GHHT), 71 Cromwell St, Stornoway, Lewis PA87 2DG, in association with the SYHA. Charges are the same as for SYHA grade 3 hostels. The GHHT hostels have bunk beds, blankets, cooking equipment, cold running water and open fires. Bring a sleeping bag and eating utensils. Local crofters look after the hostels, but they don't accept advance bookings and prefer people not to arrive or depart on a Sunday.

There are also several independent hostels which tend to be clean, modern and, consequently, more expensive than the GHHT or SYHA hostels.

B&Bs provide an otherwise rare opportunity to meet the islanders, who are famous both for their hospitality and the size of their breakfasts. Few offer private bathrooms, but they're usually comfortable and clean and offer hearty dinners as well. Most B&B hosts, especially on Lewis and Harris, appreciate guests booking ahead if they're going to stay on Sunday night.

A few B&Bs are handy for the ferry ports, but most are scattered around the countryside. The ports themselves are generally uninspiring, but always have at least one pub where meals are available. If you stay in the countryside – which is recommended – check whether there's a convenient pub, make arrangements to eat at your B&B, or take your own provisions to a hostel.

Self-catering cottages must be booked in advance.

Options for eating out centre on the pubs, which are few and far between and not particularly cheap. Most hotels manage at least one vegetarian dish.

GETTING THERE & AWAY
Air
British Regional Airlines and Loganair, part of the BA (☎ 0845 773 3377) network, fly to the islands, and there are airports at Stornoway, on Lewis, and on Benbecula and Barra. The main airport, 4 miles east of Stornoway, is served by daily flights from Glasgow and Inverness (Monday to Saturday). There are also flights to Benbecula and Barra from Glasgow Monday to Saturday, with additional Sunday flights in peak summer months.

Bus
Regular Scottish Citylink (☎ 0870 550 5050) bus services to Ullapool, Uig and Oban connect with the ferries.

Train
Spectacular train services run as far as Oban, Mallaig and Kyle of Lochalsh from Glasgow and Edinburgh. To get to Ullapool, take the train to Inverness, then a bus to Ul-

lapool. For rail information phone ☎ 0845 748 4950.

Boat
CalMac runs comfortable passenger and car ferries from Ullapool to Stornoway on Lewis (2½ hours, two or three times a day Monday to Saturday); from Uig, on the Isle of Skye, to Tarbert on Harris and Lochmaddy on North Uist (1¾ hours, once or twice a day Monday to Saturday); and from Mallaig and Oban to Castlebay on Barra (3¼ hours, daily) and Lochboisdale on South Uist (seven hours, Monday to Saturday).

The timetables are complicated and, especially from July to September, car space can fill up fast. Advance booking is essential, although foot and bicycle passengers should have no problems.

There are eight different Island Hopscotch fares for set routes in the Outer Hebrides, offering worthwhile savings. Island Rover Passes give unlimited travel on all CalMac routes for eight or 15 days; convenient certainly, but you need to use enough services to recoup the cost. For reservations and service details contact CalMac (☎ 0870 565 0000 for reservations, ☎ 01475-650100 for enquiries), The Ferry Terminal, Gourock PA19 1QP.

A one-way ticket from Stornoway to Ullapool costs £12.70 for a passenger or driver, plus £59 for a car. From Otternish to Leverburgh it costs £4.60/21.35; from Lochboisdale to Castlebay £5.15/29.50; and from Lochboisdale or Castlebay to Oban £18.25/65. For a passenger this totals £40.70, for a car £174.85 – as against £37 and £158 for the equivalent Island Hopscotch ticket. Allow at least a week to tackle this full north–south route. Bikes are carried free with an Island Hopscotch ticket (otherwise it's £1 to £2 per sailing).

GETTING AROUND
The *Skye & Western Isles Travel Guide*, available from TICs, lists all current air, bus and ferry services. Visitors without their own transport should anticipate a fair amount of hitching and walking.

Air

Flights by BA (☎ 0845 773 3377) partners, British Regional Airlines and Loganair, link Barra and Benbecula with Stornoway. At Barra the planes land on the beach at Cockle Strand, so the timetable depends on the tides.

Boat

Within the Outer Hebrides there are CalMac ferries between Leverburgh on South Harris and Otternish on North Uist; and between Lochboisdale on South Uist and Castlebay on Barra. There are also smaller ferries from Ludag at the tip of South Uist to the tiny island of Eriskay and to Eoligarry on north Barra.

Bus

Bus transport is limited, although there are enough services to allow crofters to get to the shops in the morning and return in the afternoon. No buses operate on Sunday. Contact Stornoway bus station (☎ 01851-704327) for information about Lewis and Harris services.

Car

Most roads are single-track and the main hazard is posed by sheep wandering onto the roads. Petrol stations are far apart, expensive and usually closed on Sunday.

Cars can be hired from around £20 per day at Arnol Motors (☎ 01851-710548), Arnol, Lewis; Mackinnon Self Drive (☎ 01851-702984), 18 Inaclete Rd, Stornoway, Lewis; Gaeltech Car Hire (☎ 01859-520460), Grimisdale Guest House, Leverburgh, Harris; Maclennan Brothers (☎ 01870-602191), Balivanich, Benbecula; Ask Car Hire (☎ 01870-602818), Liniclate, Benbecula; and Laing Motors (☎ 01878-700267), Lochboisdale, South Uist.

Bicycle

Cycling north to south is quite popular, but allow at least a week for the trip. The main problems are difficult weather, strong winds (you hear stories of people cycling downhill and freewheeling uphill) and sheep that believe they have right of way.

Bikes are available for hire from Alex Dan's Cycle Centre (☎ 01851-704025), 67 Kenneth St, Stornoway, Lewis; Barra Cycle Hire (☎ 01871-810284), 29 St Brendan's Rd, Castlebay, Barra; and from Rothan Cycles (☎ 01870-620283), 9 Howmore, South Uist. Booking is advisable.

Hitching

Hitching is feasible, although traffic is light and virtually non-existent on Sunday, especially on Harris and Lewis. The islanders are generally hospitable, and hitching is definitely safer here than around big cities. See Hitching in the Getting Around chapter.

LEWIS (LEODHAIS)
☎ 01851 • pop 20,160

Lewis is the northernmost of the Hebridean islands. Its ethereal, remote landscape is dominated in the low, flat northern half by the vast Black Moor, peat moorland peppered with numerous, small, freshwater lochs. The coastal fringes have some arable land and are surprisingly densely populated, though not particularly attractive.

The old blackhouses may have gone, but most holdings are crofts that follow a traditional pattern dating back to medieval times. Most are narrow strips, designed to give everyone an equal share of good and bad land. Usually they run back from the foreshore (with its valuable seaweed), across the machair (grassy sand dunes that were the best arable land) and back to the peaty grazing land.

Nowadays few crofts are economically viable, so most islanders supplement their income from the land with other jobs. Many travel away to work on oil rigs or ships, and others work in the fishing industry (including fish farming), service industries or the traditional tweed-weaving industry.

The most interesting and beautiful part of Lewis is south of Barvas and Stornoway, where the mountainous terrain is reminiscent of parts of the mainland's north-west Highland coast. Three of the Outer Hebrides' most important sights – the Arnol Blackhouse, Carloway Broch and Callanish Standing Stones – are also here.

Stornoway (Steornabhagh)

pop 8100

Stornoway lies on a beautiful natural harbour surrounded by rolling hills, but the town itself isn't very pleasant. It's the island's only sizeable town and for tourists there are adequate if limited facilities. For this reason some visitors might choose to base themselves here, but others will want to escape as quickly as possible.

Stornoway is the Outer Hebrides' administrative and commercial centre, and the base for the Western Isles Council (Comhairle nan Eilean), a hospital and the islands' Gaelic TV and radio stations. There's an airport and a ferry link with Ullapool (see Getting There & Away earlier).

The small **Museum nan Eilean** (☎ 703 773), Francis St, examines the island's history. It opens 10 am to 5.30 pm Monday to Saturday, April to September; 10 am to 5 pm Tuesday to Friday and to 1 pm Saturday, the rest of the year.

Orientation & Information Stornoway is on the east coast and compact enough to make exploring on foot easy. The ferry docks at the CalMac (☎ 702361) ferry terminal on the foreshore, beside which is the bus station. The Western Isles Tourist Board TIC (☎ 703088), 26 Cromwell St, is a short walk north-east from the ferry pier. Its Web site is at www.witb.co.uk. In theory you could use this office to book B&Bs around the islands, but in practice it's best to take the free accommodation list and make the calls yourself.

Some residential areas (and B&Bs) are a fair hike without a car, and many people commute in from communities around the island to work and shop, so there's more traffic than you might expect.

Places to Stay & Eat As well as tent sites (£6.50), *Laxdale Holiday Park* (☎ 703234, 6 Laxdale Lane), 1½ miles north of town off the A857, has a hostel-style bunkhouse for £8.50 per person. It opens April to October.

At the easy-going *Stornoway Backpackers Hostel* (☎ 703628, 47 Keith St) dorm beds cost £9 including breakfast, and there's a self-

catering kitchen. It's a five-minute walk from the ferry and bus station – head up Kenneth St then walk east along pedestrianised Point St, which becomes Francis St, pass the post office, then turn left into Keith St.

B&Bs are widely scattered. Nonsmoking *Hollsetr* (☎ 702796, 29 Urquart Gardens), is a mile north of the ferry terminal, but immaculate and welcoming, with a single, twin and family room from £17 per person. A few pleasant places line Matheson Rd, closer to the centre: *Fernlea* (☎ 702125, 19 Matheson Rd) has rooms with bathroom from £18 per head, while *Ravenswood* (☎ 702673, 12 Matheson Rd) charges from £20. *Park Guest House* (☎ 702485, James St) is a charming, Victorian home with rooms from £24 per person and a highly regarded, licensed restaurant specialising in local seafood. To find it follow the waterfront east, then veer left just past the bus station at the signpost for the A866.

The *Royal Hotel* (☎ 702109, Cromwell St), north of the TIC, has harbour views and more character than most Stornoway hotels. B&B is from £35 per person. Its pleasant bar serves meals from around £5; the hotel also has a more expensive restaurant with a seafood slant. The *Crown Hotel* (☎ 703181, Castle St) is another option for reasonable bar meals.

During the day the *An Lanntair Arts Centre* tearoom, in the town hall on South Beach St, does snacks (from £2) and light meals in agreeable surroundings. It opens 10 am to 5 pm Monday to Saturday, year round. From around £6, curries are available at *Stornoway Balti House* (☎ 706116, 24 South Beach St) which also does takeaways and opens Sunday.

Butt of Lewis (Rubha Robhanais)

Lewis' northern tip is windswept and rugged, with a lighthouse and large colonies of nesting fulmars on the high, steep cliffs. To get there, drive across the bleak expanse of Black Moor to **Barvas (Barabhas)**, then follow the densely populated west coast to the northeast. **St Moluag's Church** is an austere, barnlike structure believed to date from the 12th century, still used by the Episcopal Church.

Port of Ness (Port Nis) is an attractive harbour with a sandy beach popular with surfers.

Arnol Blackhouse Museum

This museum (☎ 710395; HS), about 1 mile south-east of Barvas off the A858, is the only authentically maintained, traditional blackhouse – a combined byre, barn and home – left on the islands. Built in 1885, it was inhabited until 1964 and now offers a wonderful insight into the old crofting way of life. It opens 9.30 am to 6.30 pm Monday to Saturday, April to September; and 9.30 am to 4.30 pm Monday to Thursday (and Saturday), October to March. Admission costs £2.50/1.

At nearby **Bragar** whale jawbones form an arch by the road, with the rusting harpoon that killed the whale dangling from the centre.

Carloway (Carlabagh)

Carloway looks across a beautiful loch to the southern mountains and has a post office and small store. At nearby **Garenin (Gearrannan)** some fascinating, ruined blackhouses are quietly mouldering alongside new concrete cottages. Also here is *Garenin Crofters' Hostel*, itself a restored blockhouse (£6.50/5 for adults/under-18s). To get to the hostel from the war memorial by the church, cross the bridge and turn left, but don't take the road under the bridge. Pass the shop, but don't turn left; continue straight on at the next junction. The hostel is half a mile farther on at the end of the road.

Carloway Broch (Dun Charlabhaigh), off the A858, is a well-preserved, 2000-year-old dry-stone defensive tower, in a beautiful position offering panoramic views. Nearby is the **Dun Carloway Centre**, with an interpretative display, open 10 am to 6 pm Monday to Saturday, April to October. Admission is free.

Callanish (Calanais)

Twelve miles west of Stornoway on a promontory overlooking Loch Roag, the **Callanish Standing Stones** form one of the most complete stone circles in Britain. It was built about 4000 years ago, predating the Pyramids by 1000 years. Its great age,

the mystery of its purpose, its impressive scale and its undeniable beauty have the effect of dislocating you from the present day. The site opens daily year round.

The **Calanais Visitor Centre** (☎ 621422), a *tour de force* of discreet design, opens 10 am to 7 pm Monday to Saturday, April to September; and 10 am to 4 pm, the rest of the year. Admission is free. Inside is a small exhibition about the stones, admission to which costs £1.50/1. The centre also provides a rare place to eat in the area as does the *Calanish Tearoom* in a converted blackhouse.

There are a couple of attractive B&Bs nearby: *Mrs Morrison* (☎ 621392) in the house by the stones (from £20), or the purpose-built *Eschol Guest House* (☎ 621357), half a mile back towards Carloway (from £29). *Tigh Mealros* (☎ 621333, Garynahine) does light lunches from about £2 and evening meals from £7.85, including local wild scallops.

Mealista (Mealasta) & Around

The road to Mealista (the B8011 south-west of Callanish, signposted to Uig) takes you through the most remote parts of Lewis. Follow the road round towards **Breanais** for some truly spectacular white-sand beaches, although the surf can make swimming treacherous. The famous 12th-century walrus-ivory Lewis chess pieces were discovered in the sand dunes here in 1831; of the 78 pieces, 67 wound up in the British Museum in London.

HARRIS (NA HEARADH)
☎ 01859 • pop 2220

Harris has the Outer Hebrides' most dramatic scenery, combining mountains, magnificent beaches, expanses of machair (grass and wildflower-covered sand dunes) and weird rocky hills and coastline.

North Harris is actually the forbidding mountainous southern tip of Lewis, beyond the peat moors south of Stornoway – the Clisham (An Cliseam) is the highest point at 799m. South Harris, across the land bridge at Tarbert, is less mountainous but has a fascinating variety of landscapes and great beaches.

Harris is famous for Harris Tweed, high-quality woollen cloth still hand-woven in islanders' homes. The industry employs about 400 millworkers and 750 independent weavers. Tarbert TIC can tell you about weavers and visitable workshops.

Tarbert (Tairbeart)
pop 500

Tarbert is a village port midway between North and South Harris with ferry connections to Uig on the Isle of Skye. Not in itself particularly inspiring, it has a spectacular location on a narrow land bridge between two lochs and overshadowed by mountains.

The TIC (☎ 502011), Pier Rd, signposted up the hill and to the right from the ferry terminal, opens 9 am to 5 pm Monday to Saturday, April to October, and for ferry arrivals. For ferry information phone CalMac (☎ 502444). Tarbert has basic facilities: a petrol station, a Bank of Scotland (no ATM) and two general stores. The Harris Tweed Shop (☎ 502493) stocks a wide range of books on the islands.

A good B&B is the cosy *Tigh na Mara* (☎ 502270), a five-minute walk from the ferry, with views of the east loch and beds from £16 to £18 per person. Closer to the ferry terminal is the congenial *Minchview House* (☎ 502140), an attractive building with three rooms, charging £17 per person.

The long-standing *Harris Hotel* (☎ 502 154) has a range of spacious rooms, some with bathroom, from £28 per head. It also serves good-value pub meals (including vegetarian options) from around £5, and a wide selection of whiskies.

The homely *First Fruits* tearoom, opposite the TIC, opens April to September, and does a few hot dishes as well as sandwiches and cakes.

North Harris

North Harris is the most mountainous region of the Outer Hebrides. Only a few roads run through it, but there are many opportunities for **climbing**, **walking** and **birdwatching**.

The small, remote village of **Rhenigidale (Reinigeadal)**, in the south-east, is accessible by road. The primitive *Rhenigidale Crofters' Hostel* can also be reached on foot (three hours and 6 miles from Tarbert). It's an excellent walk, but take all necessary supplies. From Tarbert, take the road to Kyles Scalpay for 2 miles. Just beyond Laxdale Lochs, at a bend in the road, a signposted track, marked on OS maps, veers off to the left across the hills. The hostel is a white building on the hillside above the road on the eastern side of the glen; the warden lives in the house closest to the shore. Beds cost £6.50/5 for adults/under-18s.

South Harris

Beautiful South Harris is ringed by a tortuous 45-mile road. The beaches on the west coast, backed by rolling machair and mountains, with views across to North Harris and to offshore islands, are stunning.

The ferry port of **Leverburgh (An T-ob)**, in the south, is named after Lord Leverhulme (the founder of the conglomerate Unilever). He bought Lewis and Harris in 1918 and 1919 for which he had grand plans, particularly Obbe, as Leverburgh was then known, which he wanted to be a major fishing port. It's now a sprawling, ordinary town but with a shop and several agreeable B&Bs; try *Caberfeidh House* (☎ 520276), which charges from £17 per person or *Garryknowe* (☎ 520246), where doubles go for £16/20 without/with bathroom.

A passenger ferry goes from Leverburgh to Otternish on North Uist. It runs three or four times daily Monday to Saturday, late April to late October, and once daily the rest of the year (£4.60/21.35 for a passenger/car, one hour). Tarbert TIC has information, or phone CalMac (☎ 01859-502444).

Three miles east at attractive **Rodel (Roghadal)** stands **St Clement's Church**, mainly built between the 1520s and 1550s, only to be abandoned in 1560 after the Reformation. Inside there's the fascinating tomb of Alexander MacLeod, the man responsible for the initial construction. Crude carvings show scenes of hunting, a castle, a galleon and various saints including St Clement clutching a skull.

The east, or Bays, coast is traversed by

the 'Golden Road', derisively nicknamed by national newspapers that didn't think so much money should be spent on building it. This is a strange, rocky moonscape, still dotted with numerous crofts. It's difficult to imagine how anyone could have survived in such an inhospitable environment, but they did, and still do.

NORTH UIST (UIBHIST A TUATH)
☎ 01876 • pop 1815

North Uist, half-drowned by lochs, is noted for its fishing but also has some magnificent beaches on the western side and great views north to the mountains of Harris. For birdwatchers this is an earthly paradise, with huge populations of migrant waders – oystercatchers, lapwings, curlews and redshanks at every turn. The landscape is less mountainous and less wild than Harris but it has a sleepy, subtle appeal.

Car ferries for Leverburgh, on South Harris, leave from **Otternish**, about 6 miles north of Lochmaddy near the Berneray causeway.

Lochmaddy (Loch nam Madadh)

There isn't much to keep you in tiny Lochmaddy, but it has the ferry terminal for sailings to Uig on the Isle of Skye, and there are a couple of stores, a Bank of Scotland (no ATM), petrol station, post office and a pub. The TIC (**☎** 500321) opens 9.30 am to 5.30 pm Monday to Friday and 9 am to 5 pm Saturday, April to mid-October, and for late ferry arrivals. For ferry information, phone CalMac (**☎** 500337).

The interesting **Taigh Chearsabhagh** museum and arts centre (**☎** 500293) opens 10 am to 5 pm Monday to Saturday, March to December (from 8 pm June to September). Its cafe does soups and sandwiches.

The *Uist Outdoor Centre* (**☎** 500480) has dormitory accommodation for £7 to £9, and provides a range of activities including walking, wildlife watching, climbing and diving.

The *Old Court House* (**☎** 500358) is a charming B&B with two singles, a twin and a double, all with bathroom, costing from £21 per person. The solid *Old Bank House* (**☎** 500275) starts at £18 per person. Comfortable and well presented, *Stag Lodge*

(**☎** 500364) is a pleasing whitewashed guesthouse with B&B from £25. There's also a small restaurant here. All three open year round.

If you're interested in fishing then the traditional *Lochmaddy Hotel* (**☎** 500331) is a good option. You can buy fishing permits here and there's a range of rooms (all with bathroom) from £32.50 per person including breakfast. Its restaurant serves excellent fish and seafood, or you can get bar meals (most under £6) until 8.30 pm.

Balranald RSPB Reserve

At this reserve (**☎** 510730), 18 miles west of Lochmaddy off the A865, you can watch migrant waders or the rare red-necked phalarope and listen for corncrakes. There's a visitor centre with a resident warden open April to September.

Bharpa Langass & Pobull Fhinn

The large, chambered Neolithic burial tomb of Bharpa Langass built into the side of Ben Langass is 6 miles south-west of Lochmaddy, just off the A867. It's believed to date back 5000 years. It's not safe to enter the tomb, which has collapsed, and the path up to it can be boggy.

Pobull Fhinn (Finn's People) is a stone circle of similar age, about 1 mile southeast, accessible from a path beside Langass Lodge Hotel. There are lovely views over the loch, where seals are sometimes visible.

BENBECULA (BEINN NA FAOGHLA)
☎ 01870 • pop 1803

Squeezed between North Uist and South Uist and connected to them by causeways, Benbecula is a low-lying island that's almost as much water as land. Although the number of British soldiers based here has declined, enough remain to do target practice at the Uist Army Rocket Range.

The troops and their families are quartered in the north-west around hideous **Balivanich (Baile a'Mhanaich)**, the commercial centre, where the Bank of Scotland has an ATM and the big NAAFI/Spar supermarket opens daily. Good food is available at the *Stepping*

Stone Restaurant (☎ 603377) where lunchtime mains cost under £5. There's one flight a day, Monday to Saturday, to Glasgow.

SOUTH UIST (UIBHIST A DEAS)
☎ 01878 • pop 2285

South Uist is the second largest island in the Outer Hebrides and rewards those who explore beyond the main north–south road (A865). Once again, it lacks the drama of Harris, but there's an expansiveness that has its own magic. The west coast is low, with machair backing an almost continuous sandy beach, while the east coast is quite hilly, with **Beinn Mhor** reaching 620m, and cut by four large sea lochs.

As you drive south from Benbecula, watch out for the granite statue of **Our Lady of the Isles** standing on the slopes of Ben Rueval.

Lochboisdale (Loch Baghasdail)

The ferry port of Lochboisdale in the southeast is the island's largest settlement. The TIC (☎ 700286) opens 9 am to 5 pm Monday to Saturday, Easter to mid-October, and for late ferry arrivals. There's a branch of the Royal Bank of Scotland (no ATM) and petrol supplies.

Accommodation should be booked in advance, especially if you're arriving on a night ferry. Friendly *Lochside Cottage* (☎ 700472) has B&B from £18 and will pick you up from the ferry, while *Riverside* (☎ 700250), on a working croft, starts at £14. *Bay View* (☎ 700329), near the pier, has two double rooms and charges £18/20 per person without/with bathroom. *Lochboisdale Hotel* (☎ 700332), above the ferry terminal, provides a variety of rooms, all with bathroom, for £36 to £46 per head. Its pub has good food with meals and snacks ranging from around £2.50 to £6.

CalMac (☎ 700288) has ferry links from Lochboisdale to Oban and Mallaig on the mainland and to Castlebay on Barra.

Howmore (Tobha Mor)

This attractive coastal village in the northwest, with its thatched cottages and ruined chapels, was the burial site of the Clan Ranald chiefs. Flora MacDonald was born about 6 miles to the south (see the boxed text 'Flora MacDonald' earlier). In the village, *Howmore Youth Hostel* (no telephone) opens year round with beds for £6.50/5 for adults/under-18s. To get to it, take the turn-off from the A865 to Tobha Mor – the hostel is the white building with a porch by the church at the road's end. The warden lives at Ben More House, at the junction with the main road.

The South

The southern tip of the island looks across to the islands of Eriskay and Barra. From **Ludag**, there's a car ferry (☎ 720261) to Eriskay and a passenger ferry (☎ 720238) to Eoligarry on Barra's northern tip.

BARRA (BARRAIGH)
☎ 01871 • pop 1316

Barra is a tiny island, just 12 miles around and ideal for exploring on foot. With beautiful beaches, machair, hills, Neolithic remains and a strong sense of community, it could be said to encapsulate the Outer Hebridean experience.

Castlebay (Bagh a Chaisteil) in the south is the largest village. The TIC (☎ 810336), Main St, opens early April to mid-October. The village gets its name from **Kisimul Castle** (☎ 810336), built by the MacNeil clan in the 12th century. It was sold in the 19th century and restored in the 20th century by US architect Robert MacNeil, who became clan chief. A standard flies above the castle when his son and heir is in residence.

With only about 20 B&Bs scattered around the island and some ferries arriving late in the evening, it's best to book ahead. In Castlebay, try *Tigh-na-Mara* (☎ 810858), the closest B&B to the ferry pier, with its five en-suite rooms from £22/40 per single/double, or *Faire Mhaoldonaich* (☎ 810441), 1½ miles from the pier in Nask, which costs £25/40 for singles/doubles with bathroom. The small but comfortable *Craigard Hotel* (☎ 810200) has seven rooms, all with bathroom, from £25 to £62 per person.

CalMac (☎ 8103060) ferries operate from Castlebay to Mallaig and Oban on the mainland and to Lochboisdale on South

Uist. A passenger ferry (☎ 01878-720238) from Eoligarry, in the north, links Barra with Ludag on South Uist.

Orkney Islands

Just 6 miles off the north coast of the Scottish mainland, this magical group of islands is known for its dramatic coastal scenery, ranging from 300m cliffs to white, sandy beaches; its abundant marine bird life; and for a plethora of prehistoric sites, including an entire 5000-year-old village at Skara Brae.

Sixteen of the 70 islands are inhabited. Kirkwall is the main town and Stromness is a major port – both are on the largest island, known as Mainland. The landscape is virtually treeless, but lush, cultivated and level rather than rugged. The climate, warmed by the Gulf Stream, is surprisingly moderate, with April and May being the driest months.

Over 1000 prehistoric sites have been identified on Orkney, the greatest concentration anywhere in Europe. Since there has always been a lack of wood, everything was made from stone. This explains the survival of ancient domestic architecture that includes a 5000-year-old house, Europe's oldest, on Papa Westray. The most impressive ancient monuments – the village of Skara Brae, the tomb of Maes Howe and the Ring of Brodgar – are all on Mainland.

Orkney's Pictish rulers were replaced by Norse earls in the 9th century. The Norse ruled until the mid-13th century and built the magnificent St Magnus Cathedral in Kirkwall. Even today, there are hints of those distant Scandinavian connections in the lilting accent with which Orcadians speak English.

Orkney is popular with bird-watchers and the Royal Society for the Protection of Birds (RSPB) runs several reserves. From May to mid-July, vast numbers of seabirds come to nest on the cliffs. The clear waters around the islands also attract divers, and Scapa Flow, south of Mainland, offers the most interesting wreck dive site in Europe (see the boxed text 'Scapa Flow Wrecks' later).

If you're in the area around mid-June, don't miss the St Magnus Arts Festival. Sir Peter Maxwell Davies, one of the greatest living British composers, usually contributes to the festival – he lives on Hoy. The poet and writer George Mackay Brown lived in Orkney. *Greenvoe*, or any of his other books set in Orkney, perfectly captures the special atmosphere of these islands.

GETTING THERE & AWAY
Air
There are flights to Kirkwall airport on BA/Loganair (☎ 0845 773 3377) Monday to Saturday from Aberdeen, Edinburgh, Glasgow, Inverness and Shetland, with connections to London Heathrow, Manchester and Belfast. The cheapest return tickets (which must usually be bought 14 days in advance and require at least a Saturday night stay in Orkney) cost £175 from London and £130 from Inverness.

Bus & Boat
There's a car ferry from Scrabster, near Thurso, to Stromness operated by P&O (☎ 01856-850655). The crossing can be exhilaratingly rough, a real stomach churner. There's at least one departure daily, with single fares costing £16. Scottish Citylink (☎ 0870 550 5050) has daily coaches leaving Inverness for Scrabster, at around 1.30 pm, and you can connect with this service on early morning departures from Glasgow or Edinburgh, or London on the overnight coach departing around 11 pm.

P&O also sails from Aberdeen (see the Central Scotland chapter).

John o'Groats Ferries (☎ 01955-611353) has a ferry (passengers and bicycles only) from John o'Groats to Burwick on South Ronaldsay from May to September (up to four daily). A one-way ticket costs £16, but it also offers an excellent deal to Kirkwall (£27 return). In Thurso, a free bus meets the train from Inverness at about 2.45 pm, and a bus for Kirkwall meets the ferry in Burwick (20 miles away). From June to September, it also operates the Orkney Bus, a bus/ferry/bus through service between Inverness and Kirkwall via John o'Groats.

From Lerwick (Shetland), P&O sails to Stromness on Friday year round (plus

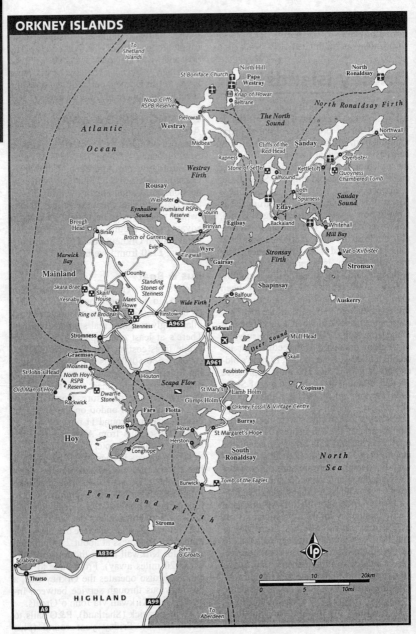

ORKNEY ISLANDS

Wednesday from June to August). It's an eight hour trip; the cheapest single ticket costs £39.

KIRKWALL
☎ 01856 • pop 6100

Orkney's capital is a bustling market town set back from the wide bay. Founded in the early 11th century by Earl Rognvald Brusson, the original part is one of the best examples of an ancient Norse town. St Magnus Cathedral, one of Scotland's finest medieval cathedrals, is certainly worth a visit and the town has a number of other things to see and do, including an above-average whisky distillery tour.

Orientation & Information

Kirkwall is fairly compact and it's easy enough to get around on foot. The cathedral and most of the shops are set back from the harbour on Broad St, which changes its name several times along its length. Ferries leave from the harbour for the northern Orkney islands.

The helpful TIC (☎ 872856), 6 Broad St near the cathedral, opens 8.30 am to 8 pm Monday to Saturday, April to September; and 9.30 am to 5 pm Monday to Saturday, October to March. It has a good range of publications on Orkney, and you can also change money. A recommended walking guide is *Walks in Orkney* by Mary Welsh. The TIC's Web site is at www.orkney.com.

The Royal Bank of Scotland, Tankerness Lane, has an ATM. Launderama opens 8.30 am to 5.30 pm Monday to Friday, and 9 am to 5 pm Saturday.

St Magnus Cathedral

Founded in 1137 and constructed from local red sandstone and yellow Eday stone, St Magnus Cathedral (☎ 874894) was built by masons who had worked on Durham Cathedral. Its interior is especially impressive and, although much smaller than the great cathedral at Durham, the same powerful atmosphere of an ancient faith pervades the place.

Earl Rognvald Kolsson commissioned the cathedral in the name of his martyred uncle, Magnus Erlendsson, who was killed by Earl Hakon Paulsson on Egilsay in 1115.

The building is the result of 300 years of construction and alteration, and includes Romanesque, transitional and Gothic styles.

The bones of Magnus are interred in one of the pillars in the cathedral. Other memorials include a statue of John Rae, the Arctic explorer, and the bell from HMS *Royal Oak*, sunk in WWII with the loss of 833 crew members.

The cathedral opens 9 am to 6 pm Monday to Saturday and 9 am to 2 pm Sunday, April to September; and 9 am to 1 pm and 2 to 5 pm Monday to Saturday, October to March. There's a Sunday service at 11.15 am.

Earl's Palace & Bishop's Palace

Near the cathedral, and on opposite sides of the street, these two ruined buildings are in the care of HS (☎ 875461). The Bishop's Palace was built in the mid-12th century to provide comfortable lodgings for Bishop William the Old. There's a good view of the cathedral from the tower, and a plaque showing the different phases of the construction of the cathedral. The Earl's Palace was once known as the finest example of French Renaissance architecture in Scotland. It was begun in 1600 by Earl Patrick Stewart, but he ran out of money and it was never completed.

They're open 9.30 am to 6.30 pm daily, April to September; and 9.30 am to 4.30 pm Monday to Saturday and from 2 pm Sunday, October to November. Admission costs £2/ 1.50, or £10/3 for a ticket that also includes Maes Howe, Skara Brae, Skaill House and the Broch of Gurness.

Tankerness House Museum

This excellent, restored merchant's house (☎ 873191) contains an interesting museum of Orkney life over the last 5000 years. The house and garden open 10.30 am to 12.30 pm and 1.30 to 5 pm daily, May to September; and afternoons only in winter. Admission is free.

Highland Park Distillery

Not only is Highland Park a fine single-malt, but the tour of the world's most northern whisky distillery (☎ 874619) is also one of the best. You'll see the whole whisky-making

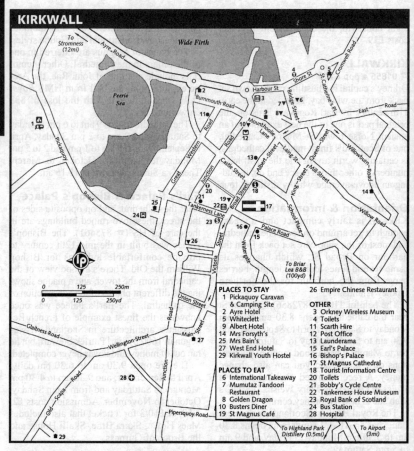

KIRKWALL

PLACES TO STAY
1 Pickaquoy Caravan & Camping Site
2 Ayre Hotel
5 Whiteclett
8 Albert Hotel
14 Mrs Forsyth's
25 Mrs Bain's
27 West End Hotel
29 Kirkwall Youth Hostel

PLACES TO EAT
6 International Takeaway
7 Mumutaz Tandoori Restaurant
8 Golden Dragon
10 Busters Diner
19 St Magnus Café

26 Empire Chinese Restaurant

OTHER
3 Orkney Wireless Museum
4 Toilets
11 Scarth Hire
12 Post Office
13 Launderama
15 Earl's Palace
16 Bishop's Palace
17 St Magnus Cathedral
18 Tourist Information Centre
20 Toilets
21 Bobby's Cycle Centre
22 Tankerness House Museum
23 Royal Bank of Scotland
24 Bus Station
28 Hospital

process – this is one of the few distilleries that still does its own barley malting.

There are tours (£3) of the distillery every half-hour from 10 am to 4 pm Monday to Friday, April to October plus noon to 4 pm at weekends in July and August. There are weekday tours at 2 pm, November to March (and by appointment). At the end of the tour you get to taste a wee dram.

Orkney Wireless Museum

This museum (☎ 874272), Junction Rd, is a fascinating jumble of communications equipment from 1930 onwards, especially relating to the Scapa Flow naval base. It opens 10 am to 4.30 pm Monday to Saturday and from 2 pm Sunday, April to September. Admission costs £2/1.

Organised Tours

Wildabout Tours Orkney (☎ 851011, ⓔ wild about@orkney.com, or book at the TIC) is a small company with tours of various archaeological and historical sights and bird-watching areas for £11.50/17 (half/full day). Orkney Guides (☎ 811777, ⓔ sales@orkney guides.co.uk) has personal guides who travel in your own vehicle or on foot and tailor tours on Orkney to your interests (£65/90 for five/nine hours). Discover Orkney Tours (☎ 872865) also tailors tours to your specific interests (from £12) and arranges trips to Westray and Papa Westray.

Places to Stay

Camping On the town's western outskirts off the A965, *Pickaquoy Centre Caravan & Camping Site* (☎ 873535, Pickaquoy Rd) operates May to September and charges £3.25 for a small tent. It's OK but would be nicer if it were beside the sea.

Hostels Whitewashed *Kirkwall Youth Hostel* (☎ 872243, Old Scapa Rd) is a 20-minute walk (signposted) from the harbour. Though no architectural gem it's large and well equipped and costs £8.75/7.75 for adults/under-18s.

B&Bs & Hotels There's a good range of cheap B&Bs, though most are small and few have rooms with private bathrooms.

With its neatly mown front lawn, central *Whiteclett* (☎ 874193, St Catherine's Place) has three doubles for £16 per person. *Mrs Forsyth's* (☎ 874020, 21 Willowburn Rd) is a small, friendly place, and costs from £16/26 per single/double. The grander *Briar Lea* (☎ 872747, 10 Dundas Crescent) is a comfortable B&B with two singles and two doubles for £18 per person. *Mrs Bain's* (☎ 872862, 6 Frasers Close) is down a quiet lane near the bus station. There are two rooms, both with bathroom, costing £14 or £15 per person.

The three-storey *West End Hotel* (☎ 872368, Main St) dates from 1824 and has rooms from £40/58, all with bathrooms. It does good bar meals. The central *Albert Hotel* (☎ 876000, Mounthoolie Lane) has a couple of lively bars. Singles/doubles cost from £35/50 to £75/100 with bathroom.

The harbourfront *Ayre Hotel* (☎ 873001, e ayre.hotel@orkney.com, Ayre Rd) is the top place to stay. It's a very comfortable town house hotel, built over 200 years ago. B&B costs from £54/80 for singles/doubles; the most pleasant rooms are those with a sea view.

Places to Eat

There are several places to eat around Bridge St, near the harbour. Open daily *Mumutaz Tandoori Restaurant* (☎ 876596, 7 Bridge St) has a wide range of mains from £5.50 to £12, and two-course lunches for £4.95. Opposite, *International Takeaway* dishes up fairly good fish and chips for £2.90. It opens daily except Sunday.

For Chinese food there are a couple of restaurants that also do takeaways. At the *Golden Dragon* (☎ 872933, 25a Bridge St) most mains cost under £6 and there's a good selection of vegetarian dishes. It opens daily except Tuesday. The *Empire Chinese Restaurant* (☎ 872300, 51 Junction Rd), opens daily for lunch and dinner. Lunchtime mains are good value at £4 to £4.50.

Licensed *Busters Diner* (☎ 876717, 1 Mounthoolie Place) is an American/Italian/Mexican place serving pizzas, burgers and hotdogs (from £3.95). It opens daily until 10 pm, and also does takeaways.

The restaurant at the *Ayre Hotel* is expensive, though it does a three-course lunch special for £7.95. *Stables Restaurant* at the Albert Hotel (see Places to Stay) offers gourmet cuisine with mains costing from £12.95 to £18.50; Orkney scallops in white wine sauce costs £12.95. Both also do bar meals.

Busy *St Magnus Café* (☎ 873354) – in the Kirkwall & St Ola Community Centre across from the cathedral – has good, cheap food such as soups (£1.30) and baked potatoes, and Orkney ice cream. It opens 9.30 am to 4 pm and 7 to 10 pm Monday to Saturday year round (plus Sunday afternoons in July and August).

Entertainment

The *Albert Hotel* serves real ale and often has live music in its 'Bothy Bar'; Thursday to Saturday there's a disco in the 'Matchmakers' bar. The *West End Hotel* (☎ 872368, Main St) is also a pleasant watering hole.

Getting There & Away

The airport (☎ 872494) is 2½ miles from the town centre. See Getting There & Away at the start of the Orkney Islands section for flight information. For flights and ferries to the northern islands, see the individual island sections.

From the bus station, Orkney Coaches (☎ 870555) runs eight buses a day on weekdays, six on Saturday, to Stromness (£2.20, 35 minutes). For Orphir and Houton (£1.40, 25 minutes), it also has at least three buses a day, Monday to Saturday. Causeway Coaches (☎ 831444) runs buses to St Margaret's Hope (£2.20), South Ronaldsay. Shalder Coaches (☎ 850809) operates the service to Tingwall and Evie. Note that no buses run on Sunday in Orkney.

Getting Around

There are several car rental places including Scarth Hire (☎ 872125), Great Western Rd, where rates are from £31 per day. Bobby's Cycle Centre (☎ 875777), Tankerness Lane, rents out mountain bikes for £10/60 per day/week.

WEST & NORTH MAINLAND
Stromness
☎ 01856 • pop 2400

P&O docks at this attractive little greystone village. As a place to stay, many visitors prefer Stromness to Kirkwall – it's smaller, it has more of the feeling of a working fishing village, and it's convenient for the island of Hoy. There are some excellent places to stay, and the winding main street has a civilised selection of shops.

Although it was officially founded in 1620, Stromness had been used as a port by the Vikings in the 12th century, as well as by earlier visitors. Its importance as a trading port grew in the 18th century, and in the 19th century it was a busy centre for the herring industry. Until the beginning of the 20th century, ships from the Hudson's Bay Company would stop to take on fresh water from Login's Well.

The TIC (☎ 850716) is in the ferry terminal and opens daily year round, staying open later when ferries dock.

Places to Stay On the headland overlooking the bay at the southern end of town is *Point of Ness Caravan & Camping Site*

(☎ 873535), although it can be a little breezy. It costs £5 for a small tent.

Stromness Youth Hostel (☎ 850589, Hellihole Rd) is a 10-minute walk up from the ferry terminal and opens mid-May to September; it costs £8.25/7.25 for adults/under-18s. Popular, independent *Brown's Hostel* (☎ 850661, 45 Victoria St) opens year round. It has 14 beds (£8 each) and no curfew.

For B&B try *Mrs Hourston's* (☎ 850642, 15 John St), close to the ferry terminal, from £15 to £20 per person with shared bathroom. Out towards the camping ground, there's *Mrs Worthington's* (☎ 850215, 2 South End) with singles/doubles from £20/36. Nonsmoking *Thira* (☎ 851181, Innertown), about 2 miles inland from the ferry, is a pleasant bungalow with good views. B&B costs £23 per person and dinner is available for an extra £10.

With good harbour views, the *Braes Hotel* (☎/fax 850495, Hellihole Rd) has rooms, some with bathroom, from £18 to £30 per person. Near the harbour, the *Ferry Inn* (☎ 850280, ℮ m&cm@ferryinn.com) has singles/doubles, all with bathrooms, from £18/34.

Places to Eat There's a good bar at the *Ferry Inn* (see Places to Stay) and a restaurant serving seafood including smoked Westray haddock from £5.90. For a pint try Orkney Dark Island or Red McGregor, two of the local brews. The bar at the *Stromness Hotel* also has seafood on its menu, as well as beef and vegetarian options from £5, and there's a large open fireplace. The most popular place to drink is the *Royal Hotel*, mainly because it serves tasty meals such as honey-glazed duck for under £8 and stays open late. The top place is the excellent *Hamnavoe Restaurant* (☎ 850606, 35 Graham Place) where you can expect to pay around £16 to £20 for a three-course meal. It closes October to March.

Also a general store *The Café* (☎ 850368, 22 Victoria St) does toasties (from £1.50), pizzas (from £2.50), baked potatoes and burgers – to eat in or take away.

Getting There & Away For information on ferries to/from Scrabster, Lerwick and

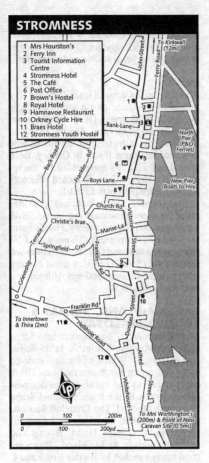

STROMNESS

1 Mrs Hourston's
2 Ferry Inn
3 Tourist Information Centre
4 Stromness Hotel
5 The Café
6 Post Office
7 Brown's Hostel
8 Royal Hotel
9 Hamnavoe Restaurant
10 Orkney Cycle Hire
11 Braes Hotel
12 Stromness Youth Hostel

To Kirkwall (12mi)
John Street
Ferry Road
Bank Lane
North Pier (P&O Ferries)
Back Road
Franklin Rd
Boys Lane
New Pier (Boats to Hoy)
Church Rd
Victoria Street
Christie's Brae
Terrace
Manse La
Springfield Cres
Franklin Rd
Grieveship
Franklin Rd
Dundas Street
Franklin Rd
To Innertown & Thira (2mi)
Hellihole Road
Alfred Street
Whitehouse Lane
To Mrs Worthington's (200m) & Point of Ness Caravan Site (0.5mi)

0   100   200m
0   100   200yd

Aberdeen, see Getting There & Away at the start of the Orkney section. For boats to Hoy, see Hoy later.

Orkney Coaches (☎ 870555) runs buses to Kirkwall (£2.20, 35 minutes), Monday to Saturday. Shalder Coaches (☎ 850809) has a bus to Birsay (£1) on Monday only.

Getting Around Orkney Cycle Hire (☎ 850255) rents out bikes for £5 per day.

Stenness

This village is little more than a petrol station (with a shop that sells outrageous hats).

A mile east, however, are some of the most interesting prehistoric monuments on Orkney. Since the road between Stromness and Kirkwall passes through, you can travel by bus, Monday to Saturday.

Maes Howe Constructed nearly 5000 years ago, Maes Howe is the finest chambered tomb in Western Europe. A long stone passage leads into a chamber in the centre of an earth-covered mound, which is over 6.7m high and 35m across. The passage is aligned with sunset in midwinter.

No remains were found when the tomb was excavated in the 19th century. It's not known how many people were originally buried here or whether they were buried with any of their worldly goods. In the 12th century, however, Vikings returning from the Crusades broke into the tomb searching for treasure. They found none, but left a wonderfully earthy collection of graffiti, carved in runes on the walls. Some of it's pretty basic – 'Thorni bedded Helgi Carved', but 'many a woman has walked stooping in here' is a little more subtle – you have to stoop to get through the passage.

Maes Howe (☎ 01856-761606; HS) opens 9.30 am to 6.30 pm Monday to Saturday and from 2 pm Sunday, April to September, and for shorter hours from October to March. Admission costs £2.50/1. There's also a combined ticket for £10/3 that includes Skara Brae, Skaill House, the Broch of Gurness, the Brough of Birsay and the Bishop's and Earl's Palaces. Get your ticket in Tormiston Mill, on the other side of the road from Maes Howe, where there's a cafe, gift shop and small exhibition.

Standing Stones of Stenness Near Maes Howe stand only four of the original 12 mighty boulders that once formed a ring. They were erected around 2500 BC; one is over 5m high. There's no admission charge.

Ring of Brodgar About a mile along the road from Stenness towards Skara Brae is a wide circle of standing stones, some over 5m tall. Thirty-six of the original 60 stones are still standing among the heather. It's an impressive sight and a powerful place. These old stones, raised skywards 4500 years ago, still attract the forces of nature – on 5 June 1980, one was struck by lightning.

Admission is free and the monument is always open.

Skara Brae

Idyllically situated by a sandy bay 8 miles north of Stromness, and predating the pyramids of Giza or Stonehenge, Skara Brae (☎ 01856-841815; HS) is northern Europe's best-preserved prehistoric village. Even the stone furniture – beds, boxes and dressers – has survived the 5000 years since a community first occupied it. It was hidden under the sand until 1850, when a severe storm blew the sand and grass away, exposing the houses underneath.

Opening times are as for Maes Howe earlier. Admission costs £4.50/1.30. It's worth buying the guidebook, which gives a guided tour involving eight viewpoints.

You need your own transport except on Monday when there's a bus to Birsay. Alternatively, it's possible to walk along the coast from Stromness via Yesnaby and the Broch of Borwick.

Yesnaby Sea Stacks

Six miles north of Stromness are some spectacular coastal walks. Less than half a mile south of the Yesnaby car park is Yesnaby Castle, a sea stack similar to the Old Man of Hoy. Watch out during the nesting season in early summer, as seabirds will dive-bomb you to scare you away from their nests.

Birsay

The small village of Birsay is 6 miles north of Skara Brae. The ruins of the **Earl's Palace** (HS) are in the centre of Birsay. The palace was built in the 16th century on an even grander scale than the palace in Kirkwall. It is always open and admission is free.

When the tide is low, you can walk out to the **Brough of Birsay**, three-quarters of a mile from the Earl's Palace. It's a Norse settlement built around the 12th-century St Peter's Church, of which the foundations remain.

Reliable B&B accommodation is available at **Primrose Cottage** (☎ 721384), overlooking Marwick Bay, for £14/34 per single/double or £38 for a double with bathroom.

Evie

About 1½ miles down a track from the tiny village of Evie, and past a sandy beach, is the **Broch of Gurness** (HS). Although not nearly as impressive as Mousa Broch in Shetland, this is the best preserved example of a fortified stone tower in Orkney. Built around 100 BC, it's surrounded by the remains of a large village. Standard HS hours apply. Admission costs £2.50/1.

Evie Hostel (no telephone) provides primitive accommodation just outside Evie for £5 per bed. Go to nearby Flaw's Farm for the key (signposted). Those with a bit more money to spend can opt for **Woodwick House** (☎ 01856-751330), a small country hotel in peaceful surroundings with singles/doubles from £30/50.

EAST MAINLAND, BURRAY & SOUTH RONALDSAY

After a German U-boat sneaked into Scapa Flow and sank the battleship HMS *Royal Oak* in 1939, Sir Winston Churchill ordered better protection for the naval base. Using concrete blocks and old ships, the channels between some of the islands around Scapa Flow were blocked. The **Churchill Barriers**, as they're known, now link the islands of Lamb Holm, Glimps Holm, Burray and South Ronaldsay to Mainland. There are good sandy beaches by Barrier Nos 3 and 4.

East Mainland is mainly agricultural. There are large colonies of nesting seabirds at Mull Head, and the shores of Deer Sound attract wildfowl.

On the island of Lamb Holm, the **Italian Chapel** (☎ 01856-781268) is all that remains of a prisoner of war (POW) camp that housed the Italian prisoners who worked on the Churchill Barriers. They built the remarkable chapel in their spare time, using two Nissen huts, scrap metal and their considerable artistic and decorative skills. One of the artists returned in 1960 to restore the paintwork. It's definitely worth seeing.

Scapa Flow Wrecks

The wrecks that litter these clear waters make Scapa Flow the best diving location in Europe. Enclosed by Mainland, Hoy and South Ronaldsay, this is one of the world's largest natural harbours and has been used by vessels as diverse as King Hakon's Viking ships in the 13th century and the NATO fleet of today.

It was from Scapa Flow that the British Home Fleet sailed to meet the German High Seas Fleet at the Battle of Jutland on 31 May 1916. After the war, 74 German ships were interned in Scapa. Conditions for the German sailors were poor and there were several mutinies as negotiations for the fate of the ships dragged on. When the terms of the armistice were agreed on 6 May 1919 with the announcement of a severely reduced German navy, Admiral von Reuter, who was in charge of the German fleet in Scapa Flow, decided to take matters into his own hands. On 21 June, a secret signal was passed from ship to ship and the British watched incredulously as every German ship began to sink.

Most of the ships were salvaged, but seven vessels remain to attract divers. There are three battleships – the *König*, the *Kronprinz Wilhelm* and the *Markgraf* – which are all over 25,000 tonnes. The first two were subjected to blasting for scrap metal, but the *Markgraf* is undamaged and considered one of the best dives in the area. Four light cruisers (4400 to 5600 tonnes) – the *Karlsruhe*, *Dresden*, *Brummer* and *Köln* – are particularly interesting as they lie on their sides and are very accessible to divers. The *Karlsruhe*, though severely damaged, is only 9m below the surface. Its twisted superstructure has now become a huge metal reef encrusted with diverse sea life.

As well as the German wrecks, numerous other ships litter the Scapa Flow sea bed. HMS *Royal Oak*, which was sunk by a German U-boat in October 1939, with the loss of 833 crew, is now an official war grave. Earlier, in 1917, the sinking of HMS *Vanguard* following an explosion claimed a thousand lives.

If you're interested in diving in Scapa Flow, the following PADI-affiliated companies offer tuition and trips: Dolphin Scuba Services (☎ 01856-731269), Garisle, Burray; or Scapa Scuba (☎ 01856-851218), 13 Ness Rd, Stromness. Scapa Scuba runs half-day courses for beginners.

JANE SMITH

British and German wrecks litter the sea bed and make Scapa Flow ideal for diving.

On Burray, the road passes the **Orkney Fossil & Vintage Centre** (☎ 01856-731255), a quirky collection of local furniture and clothes, and 360-million-year-old fish fossils. It opens 10 am to 6 pm daily, April to September (and from 10.30 am in October). Admission costs £2/1. Its tea shop is excellent.

A visit to the **Tomb of the Eagles** (☎ 01856-831339), Liddle Farm, on the southern tip of South Ronaldsay, is highly recommended. The 5000-year-old burial chamber was discovered by local farmers, the Simpsons, who now run this privately owned attraction. It's as interesting for their entertaining guided tour as for the tomb itself. After handling some of the skulls and eagles' claws found in the tomb, you walk across the fields, put on kneepads and crawl down the entrance passage. It opens 10 am to 8 pm daily, April to October; and 10 am to noon the rest of the year. It's well worth the £2.50 ticket.

The main village on South Ronaldsay is **St Margaret's Hope**, named after Margaret, the Maid of Norway, who was to have married Edward II of England but is thought to have died here in 1290 on her way to the wedding. The summer-only ferry from John o'Groats docks in **Burwick**, on the south coast of South Ronaldsay. See Getting There

& Away at the start of the Orkney Islands section.

Places to Stay & Eat

St Margaret's Hope, South Ronaldsay, is a good place to stay. On an organic farm about 1½ miles east of the village centre, **Wheems Bothy** (☎ 01856-831537, Wheems, Eastside) is a basic but delightful hostel offering bed and organic breakfast for £6.50. It opens April to September and you can camp if the hostel is full.

Bellevue Guest House (☎ 01856-831 294), just east of the village, has two comfortable rooms (one with bathroom) from £20 to £25 per person. The *Creel Inn & Restaurant* (☎ 01856-83311, Front Rd) has B&B accommodation from £30/60 per single/double, and is one of the best places to eat in Orkney. Excellent main dishes such as Orcadian fish stew cost £15.50, starters and sweets cost £5.50; try the baked lemon tart. It opens daily, April to September.

Mrs Murray & Mrs Woodward (☎ 01856-731305, Vestlaybanks) run their B&B in a scenic spot on Burray overlooking Scapa Flow. Its two rooms (one with private bathroom) go for £22 to £25 per person; dinner is an extra £10.

Getting There & Away

Between Kirkwall and St Margaret's Hope, Causeway Coaches (☎ 01856-831444) runs four buses a day on weekdays and two on Saturday (£2.20). Shalder Coaches (☎ 01856-850809) runs the Kirkwall-Burwick service that connects with the ferries.

HOY

☎ 01856 • pop 400

The highest hills in Orkney are on Hoy (the name means High Island). At 57 sq miles it is the second largest island in the group. There's spectacular cliff scenery, including some of the highest vertical cliffs in Britain at **St John's Head** (346m) on the west coast. The island is probably best known for the **Old Man of Hoy**, a 137m-high sea stack off the north-west coast that can be seen from the Scrabster-Stromness ferry.

The best scenery is in the north of the is-

land, a large part of which forms the **North Hoy RSPB Reserve**. There are some excellent walks, the most popular being to the edge of the cliffs opposite the Old Man of Hoy. Allow about seven hours for the return trip from Moaness Pier in Hoy village on the east coast where the ferries dock. There's basic hostel accommodation in Rackwick on the west coast, a two-hour walk across the island from the pier through beautiful **Rackwick Glen**. You pass the 5000-year-old **Dwarfie Stone**, the only example of a rock-cut tomb in Britain, and **Berriedale Wood**, the country's most northerly native forest.

Lyness, in the south-east, was an important naval base during both world wars, when the British Grand Fleet was based in Scapa Flow. With the dilapidated remains of buildings and an uninspiring outlook towards the Elf Oil Terminal on Flotta Island, this isn't a pretty place, but the **Scapa Flow Visitor Centre** (☎ 791300) is well worth a visit. It's a fascinating naval museum and photographic display in an old pumphouse. It opens 9 am to 4.30 pm on weekdays year round, plus Saturdays from mid-May to mid-September and 10.30 am to 3.45 pm Sunday from mid-May to June and early September (9.45 am to 6 pm in July and August). Admission costs £2/1.

Places to Stay & Eat

Affiliated with the SYHA, *Hoy Outdoor Centre* (☎ 873535) is just over a mile inland from Moaness Pier. It opens May to early September and beds cost £6.75/6 for adults/under-18s. Bring your own sleeping bag and supplies. Near the post office and the pier, *Hoy Inn* (☎ 791313) is a bar with a restaurant serving good seafood; the RSPB has a small information centre here.

In Rackwick Glen, just north of the village, *Rackwick Youth Hostel* (☎ 873535 ext 2404) opens early March to early September and has 10 beds in two dorms; bring your own sleeping bag and supplies. It charges £6.75/6 for adults/under-18s and the warden comes to collect the money each evening.

There are several good B&Bs on the island, with accommodation at around £18 per person. In Lyness, *Mrs Budge's* (☎ 791234) has two rooms with bathroom. The *Anchor Bar* (☎ 791356), also in Lyness, does bar meals and the Scapa Flow Visitor Centre *cafe* serves snacks.

Getting There & Away

Orkney Ferries (☎ 872044) runs a passenger ferry between Stromness and Moaness Pier (£2.50, 30 minutes), at 7.45 and 10 am and 4.30 pm weekdays, plus 7 and 9.30 pm on Friday, and 9.30 am and 6 pm at the weekend. There's a reduced schedule from mid-September to mid-May. In the other direction, the service departs 30 minutes after its arrival on Hoy. Boats call at Graemsay Island, Monday to Friday (on request Friday evening and weekends).

Orkney Ferries also sails to Hoy (Lyness and Longhope) and the island of Flotta from Houton on Mainland, Monday to Saturday (£2.50 one way, £7.50 for a car; up to six times a day). The more limited Sunday service runs from mid-May to mid-September. Flotta and Houton are 20 minutes and 45 minutes from Lyness, respectively.

NORTHERN ISLANDS

The group of windswept islands north of Mainland provides a refuge for migrating birds and a nesting ground for seabirds; there are several RSPB reserves. Some of the islands are also rich in archaeological sites. However, the beautiful scenery, with wonderful white-sand beaches and lime-green to azure seas, is the main attraction.

The TICs in Kirkwall and Stromness have a useful brochure, *The Islands of Orkney*, with maps and details of these islands. Note that the pronunciation of the 'ay' ending of each island name is 'ee' (for example Shapinsay is pronounced shapinsee).

Orkney Ferries (☎ 01856-872044) operates an efficient ferry service. From Kirkwall you can day-trip to many of the islands (except North Ronaldsay; see that section later) most days of the week, but it's really worth staying for at least a few nights.

Shapinsay

A short ferry trip from Kirkwall, Shapinsay is a fertile, highly cultivated, low-lying island.

Balfour Castle (1848), built in the Scottish Baronial style, is the most impressive sight and is now a hotel. There are tours on Wednesday and Sunday at 3 pm, May to September, which must be arranged in advance at the TIC in Kirkwall (£15/7.50 for combined castle admission and return ferry ticket).

Mrs Wallace (☎ *01856-711256, Girnigoe*) offers B&B for £18/34 per single/double. With home-made bread and jam, the breakfasts at this farmhouse are excellent; four-course dinners are also available. At the grander *Balfour Castle* (☎ *01856-711 282*), dinner and B&B costs £100 per person per night.

There are up to six sailings daily (except Sunday between early September and mid-May) between Kirkwall and Shapinsay (£2.50/7.50 passenger/car, 25 minutes).

Rousay

Lying close to Mainland's north-east, this hilly island, with a population of around 200 people, is known as 'the Egypt of the North' for its numerous archaeological sites. It also has the important Trumland RSPB Reserve and three lochs for trout fishing.

West of the pier are four prehistoric burial cairns – the two-storey Taversoe Tuick, the stalled cairns of Yarso and Blackhammer, and Midhowe Cairn. Holding the remains of 25 people and dating from the 3rd millennium BC, the 'Great Ship of Death', as Midhowe Cairn is called, is the longest chambered cairn in Orkney. Nearby, Midhowe Broch is the best example of a broch in Orkney.

The TICs on Mainland have a useful leaflet, *Westness Walk*, describing the archaeologically significant mile walk from Midhowe Cairn to Westness Farm.

Places to Stay & Eat On an organic farm half a mile west of the ferry, *Rousay Hostel* (☎ *01856-821252, Trumland Farm*) offers excellent dormitory accommodation from £6 (with your sleeping bag) to £8, and tent sites for £2.50. You can get bar meals at the *Pier Restaurant* (☎ *01856-821359*) by the pier.

Taversoe Hotel (☎ *01856-821325*), about 2 miles south-west of the pier, does B&B from £25 per person. There are superb views of Eynhallow Sound from its restaurant and a good selection of malt whiskies in the bar. It opens daily except Monday.

Getting There & Away A small car ferry connects Tingwall (Mainland) with Brinyan on Rousay (£2.50/7.50 for a passenger/car, 30 minutes) and the other nearby islands of Egilsay and Wyre up to six times daily. For bookings phone ☎ 01856-751360.

Getting Around Bikes can be rented for £6 per day from ABC (☎ 01856-821398), near the pier, and the island's one road makes a pleasant circuit of about 13 miles.

Egilsay & Wyre

These two small islands lie 1½ miles east of Rousay. On Egilsay, a **cenotaph** marks the spot where Earl Magnus was murdered in 1116. After his martyrdom, pilgrims flocked to the island and St Magnus Church, now roofless, was built.

Wyre is even smaller than Egilsay. In the mid-12th century it was the domain of the Viking baron Kolbein Hruga ('Cubbie Roo'). The ruins of his castle and St Mary's Chapel can be visited free.

These two islands are reached on the Rousay-Tingwall ferry (see the Rousay section), but you must ask if you wish to land.

Stronsay

In the 18th century, the major industry on this island, north-east of Shapinsay, was the collection and burning of seaweed to make kelp, which was exported for use in the production of glass, iodine and soap. In the 19th century, it was replaced by herring-curing, and Whitehall harbour became one of Scotland's major herring ports.

A peaceful and attractive island, Stronsay now attracts seals, migratory birds and tourists. There are good coastal walks and, in the east, the **Vat o'Kirbister** is the best example of a *gloup* (natural arch) in Orkney.

Places to Stay & Eat At the *Stronsay Hotel* (☎ 01857-616213), Whitehall, you can get B&B in one of its refurbished rooms from £14 per person and reasonable pub grub

in its bar from around £4.50. At *Stronsay Bird Reserve* (☎ 01857-616363), beside the sandy beach on Mill Bay, there's B&B for £15 per person; you can also camp.

Getting There & Away BA/Loganair (☎ 01856-872494, 0845 773 3377) has up to three flights per week (the days vary) from Kirkwall (£31/62 per single/return).

A ferry service links Kirkwall with Stronsay (£5, 1½ hours, twice daily), and Stronsay with Eday (£2.50, 35 minutes, once daily). There's a reduced service on Sunday.

Eday

North-west of Stronsay and only 8 miles long, Eday has a hilly centre and cultivated fields around its coast. It supplied some of the stone for St Magnus Cathedral in Kirkwall, and peat to most other northern islands. Occupied for at least the last 5000 years, Eday has numerous chambered cairns, and also one of Orkney's most impressively located standing stones, the **Stone of Setter**.

It's worth getting hold of the *Eday Heritage Walk* leaflet, which details an interesting four-hour ramble from the Community Enterprises shop, near the ferry pier, to the sandstone **Cliffs of the Red Head** in the island's north.

Places to Stay Looking like army barracks on the outside, the renovated *Eday Youth Hostel* (☎ 01857-622283) is 4 miles north of the ferry on the Bay of London. There are 24 beds for £6.75/6 for adults/under-18s and it opens April to September; bring your own sleeping bag. *Mrs Cockram's* (☎ 01857-622271), in a comfortable farmhouse at Skaill, near the church, charges £30 per person for dinner and B&B. It opens year round except during lambing in April/May.

Getting There & Away BA/Loganair (☎ 01856-872494, 0845 773 3377) flies once a week on Wednesday from Kirkwall (£31 one way) to London airport – that's London, Eday. The ferry service from Kirkwall sails via Stronsay (£5, 1¼ to two hours). There's a link between Sanday and Eday on Monday, Friday and Sunday.

Sanday

This island is aptly named, for the best **beaches** in Orkney are here – dazzling white sand of the sort you'd expect in the Caribbean. The island is 12 miles long and almost entirely flat, apart from the cliffs at **Spurness**. There are several archaeological sites, the most impressive being the **Quoyness Chambered Tomb**, similar to Maes Howe, dating from the 3rd millennium BC.

Places to Stay With permission, you can camp on the island, but there's no hostel. There's comfortable accommodation at the two-star *Belsair Hotel* (☎ *01857-600206*), which has six rooms, three with bathrooms, from £20 per person.

Getting There & Away BA/Loganair (☎ 01856-872494, 0845 773 3377) flights from Kirkwall (£31 one way) operate to Sanday and Westray twice daily Monday to Friday, once on Saturday. There's at least one ferry daily between Kirkwall and Sanday (£5, 1½ hours), mid-May to mid-September.

Getting Around Cars can be hired from Kettletoft Garage (☎ 01857-600321) and Quivals (☎ 01857-600418); the latter also hires out bikes.

Westray

This is the largest of the northern islands, with a population of around 700. It's quite a varied island, with fertile farmland, prehistoric sites, some sandy beaches, impressive cliff scenery and the ruins of 16th-century **Noltland Castle** (a fortified Z-plan house). It's also famous for the **Noup Head RSPB Reserve**, in the north-west, which attracts tens of thousands of breeding seabirds.

In the north, **Pierowall**, the main village and one of the best natural harbours in Orkney, was once an important Viking base. Ferries from Kirkwall dock at Rapness, about 7 miles south of Pierowall.

Places to Stay & Eat With permission, you can camp almost anywhere. Several places offer B&B from around £16 per person including *Sand o'Gill* (☎ 01857-

677374), which also has a six-berth caravan from £60 to £80 per week. The welcoming *Pierowall Hotel* (☎ *01857-677208*) is a popular pub with singles/doubles for £21/38.

The most comfortable place is *Cleaton House Hotel* (☎ *01857-677508*), a refurbished Victorian manse 3 miles south of Pierowall. B&B costs £30/55, all with bathroom. It serves good bar and restaurant meals.

Getting There & Away For information on flights see the Getting There & Away section for Sanday. A ferry service links Kirkwall with Rapness and Pierowall on Westray, and Papa Westray. There are up to three daily in each direction (£5, 1½ hours).

Papa Westray

This tiny island (4 miles long and a mile wide) attracts superlatives – Europe's oldest domestic building is the **Knap of Howar** (built about 5500 years ago), the world's shortest scheduled flight is the two-minute hop across Papa Sound from Westray, and the largest colony of Arctic terns in Europe is at **North Hill**. The island was also the cradle of Christianity in Orkney – restored **St Boniface Church** dates from the 12th century.

Places to Stay & Eat The excellent *Papa Westray Hostel* (☎ *01857-644267*), at Beltane just over a mile from the ferry, opens year round. There are 16 beds costing £8/7 for adults/under-18s. The community cooperative, which runs the hostel, also has four comfortable rooms with bathrooms on a B&B basis for £28/48 per single/double. It also runs a small shop and restaurant.

Getting There & Away Flying to Papa Westray or North Ronaldsay from Kirkwall is an amazing deal compared to other flights in Orkney – about twice the distance for half the price. To either island it's £30 return, with flights twice daily Monday to Saturday.

There's a passenger-only ferry from Pierowall on Westray to Papa Westray, mid-May to mid-September (£5, 30 minutes, three to six times daily). This service is operated by a private ferry company: contact Tommy

Rendall (☎ 01857-677216). On Tuesday and Friday, there's an Orkney Ferries (☎ 01856-872044) through service from Kirkwall (£5, 1¾ hours).

North Ronaldsay

Pity the poor sheep on this remote, windswept island – they're kept off the rich farmland by a wall and forced to feed mostly on seaweed, which is said to give their meat a unique flavour.

North Ronaldsay (population 50) is only 3 miles long, 1 mile wide and almost completely flat. The island is an important stopover point for migratory birds. The *North Ronaldsay Bird Observatory* (☎ 01857-633200), in the south-west, offers solar-powered accommodation and ornithological activities at £17 per person including dinner. *Garso Guest House* (☎ 01857-633244), about 3 miles west of the pier, charges £26 per head for dinner and B&B.

See Papa Westray earlier for details of flights. There's also a weekly ferry from Kirkwall each Friday, plus on Sunday from late June to early September. Phone Orkney Ferries (☎ 01856-872044) for details.

Shetland Islands

Sixty miles north of Orkney, the Shetland Islands remained under Norse rule until 1469, when they were given to Scotland as part of a Danish princess' dowry. Even today these remote, windswept, treeless islands are almost as much a part of Scandinavia as of Britain – the nearest mainland town is Bergen, Norway.

Much bleaker than Orkney, Shetland is famous for its varied bird life and teeming seabird colonies (check out the Web site www.wildlife.shetland.co.uk), for a 4000-year-old archaeological heritage that includes the ancient settlement of Jarlshof, and for its rugged, indented coastline that offers superb cliff-top walks.

Almost everything of interest is on the coast rather than inland, so you're much more aware of the presence of the sea than on Orkney's Mainland. In fact, in Shetland

it's impossible to get farther than 3 miles from the sea. There are some impressively located places to stay, and budget accommodation includes six camping *böds* (barns).

Of the 100 islands, 15 are inhabited. Mainland is by far the largest; Lerwick is the capital. Shetland is the base for the North Sea oilfields, and pipelines feed Europe's biggest oil refinery at Sullom Voe, in north Mainland. Oil has brought to the islands a certain amount of prosperity: there are well-equipped leisure centres in many villages.

GETTING THERE & AWAY

Unlike Orkney, Shetland is relatively expensive to get to from mainland Britain.

Air

The oil industry ensures that air connections are good. The main airport is at Sumburgh, 25 miles south of Lerwick. There are at least four flights daily between Sumburgh and Aberdeen (50 minutes) on BA/Logan Air (☎ 0845 773 3377). The standard fare is around £135 return. You can also fly direct from Inverness, Glasgow, Edinburgh, Belfast and London.

BA/Loganair operates a low-flying turboprop aircraft daily between Orkney and Shetland (from £76.10 return, 35 minutes).

Boat

P&O (☎ 01224-572615) runs car ferries from Lerwick to Aberdeen and Stromness (Orkney); see those sections for details. For details of the ferry link between Lerwick and Bergen (Norway) see the introductory Getting There & Away chapter.

GETTING AROUND
Bus

There are several bus operators; for information on all their services call ☎ 01595-694100.

Car

Shetland's wide roads seem like motorways after Orkney's narrower, winding lanes. It's cheaper to rent a car in Lerwick than at the airport. Try Star Rent A Car (☎ 01595-692 075), 22 Commercial Rd, opposite Lerwick

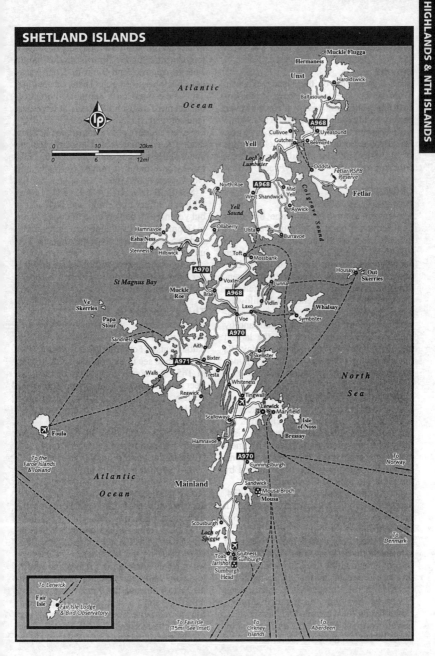

SHETLAND ISLANDS

Atlantic Ocean

Muckle Flugga
Hermaness
Unst
Haroldswick
Baltasound
A968
Cullivoe Uyeasound
Yell Gutcher Belmont
Oddsta
Loch of Fetlar RSPB
Lunbister Reserve
North Roe A968
West Shandwick Mid Yell Fetlar
Yell Aywick
Sound
Hamnavoe Ollaberry Ulsta
Esha Ness Burravoe
Stenness Hillswick Toft Mossbank
A970 Housay Out
St Magnus Bay Voxter Lunna Skerries
Muckle Brae A968 Vidlin Whalsay
Roe Laxo
Voe Symbister
Ve A970
Skerries Skellister North
Papa Aith
Stour Bixter Sea
Sandness A971 Whiteness
Walls Tresta Tingwall
Reawick Lerwick Maryfield
Scalloway Isle
of Noss
Hamnavoe Bressay
To the A970
Faroe Islands Cunningsburgh
& Iceland
Sandwick
Atlantic Mousa Broch
Ocean Mainland Mousa
Foula
Scousburgh To
Loch of Norway
Spiggie
Toab Grutness
Jarlshof Sumburgh
Sumburgh
Head To
Denmark
To Lerwick
Fair
Isle Fair Isle Lodge
& Bird Observatory
To Fair Isle To Orkney To
(15mi, See Inset) Islands Aberdeen

0 10 20km
0 6 12mi

bus station, or John Leask & Son (☎ 01595-693162), The Esplanade.

Bicycle

If it's fine, cycling on the islands' excellent roads can be an exhilarating way to experience Shetland's stark beauty. It can, however, be very windy (wind speeds of up to 194mph have been recorded!) and shelter is scarce. Eric Brown upstairs at Grantfield Garage (☎ 01595-692709), North Rd, Lerwick, hires out bikes for £7.50/45 per day/week.

LERWICK

☎ 01595 • pop 7500

A pleasant town of grey-stone buildings built around a natural harbour, Lerwick is the only place of any size in Shetland.

Although the Shetland Islands have been occupied for several thousand years, Lerwick was only established in the 17th century. Dutch herring fleets began to shelter in the harbour, in preference to Scalloway, which was then the capital. A small community grew up to trade with them and by the late 19th century this was the largest herring town in northern Europe. Today, it's the main port of entry into the Shetlands and transit point to the North Sea oil rigs.

Orientation & Information

The main ferry terminal is a 20-minute walk north of the old harbour, which forms the focus of the town and is now used by visiting yachts and pleasure cruisers. Commercial St, one block back from the waterfront, is the main shopping street, dominated by the Victorian bulk of the Grand Hotel.

On Market Cross, the TIC (☎ 693434, ⓔ shetland.tourism@zetnet.co.uk) has a bureau de change, a good range of books and maps, and brochures on everything from Shetland pony stud farms to lists of safe anchorages for yachts. The *Shetland Islands* annual guide to accommodation and services is free in the rest of Scotland but costs £1 here. However, the *Inter-Island Transport Timetable*, an invaluable publication listing local air, sea and bus services, is well worth its 80p. *Walks on Shetland* by Mary Welsh is a good walking guide.

The TIC opens 8 am to 6 pm Monday to Friday and to 4 pm Saturday, April to September (plus Sunday from 10 am to 1 pm in June to August); and 9 am to 5 pm weekdays, October to March. There's a seasonal TIC at the main ferry terminal. For information there's a useful Web site at www.shetland-tourism.co.uk.

Seven countries have consulates in Shetland. The consulates for Denmark, Iceland and Sweden can be contacted on ☎ 692533; those for Finland, France, Germany and Norway on ☎ 692556.

Shetland Library (☎ 695057), Lower Hillhead, offers free email and Web access but you need to book a time. It opens 10 am to 7 pm Monday, Wednesday and Friday, and to 5 pm on Tuesday, Thursday and Saturday.

Lerwick Laundry (☎ 698043) is on Market St but it's not do-it-yourself. It opens daily except Sunday.

Things to See & Do

Above the town, there are good views of Lerwick and the island of Bressay from the battlements of **Fort Charlotte**, though there's not much to see in the fort itself. It was built in 1653 by troops from the Cromwellian fleet and housed the town prison in the 19th century. It now provides the headquarters for the Territorial Army. It opens 9 am to 10 pm daily. Admission is free.

It's worth visiting the **Shetland Museum** (☎ 695057), above the library on Lower Hillhead, for an introduction to the island's 5000-year history. There are replicas of the St Ninian's Isle treasure, and displays detailing the fishing, whaling and knitting industries. It opens the same hours as the library. Admission is free.

The **Up Helly Aa Exhibition**, off St Sunniva St, explains the Viking fire festival that takes place on the last Tuesday in January, when locals dress up as Vikings and set fire to a ship built here. Opening hours are limited: 2 to 4 pm and 7 to 9 pm Tuesday, 7 to 9 pm Friday and 2 to 4 pm Saturday from mid-May to mid-September. Admission is £2/free.

The fortified site of **Clickimin Broch**, about a mile west of the town centre, was occupied

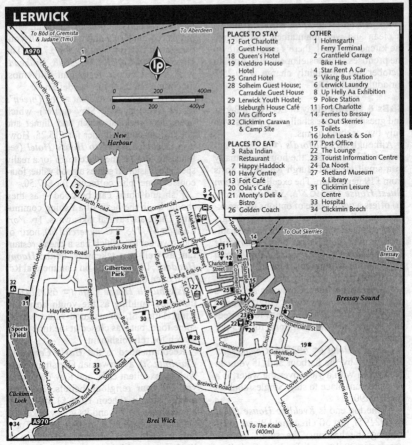

LERWICK

To Böd of Gremista
& Judane (1mi)

To Aberdeen

A970

Holmsgarth Road

North Road

New Harbour

0   200   400m
0   200   400yd

North Road

Anderson Road

St-Sunniva-Street

Gilbertson Park

North-Lochside

Gairnfield-Road

Sports Field

Clickimin Loch

A970

Commercial

Market Street

St Magnus-St

Harbour Street

King Harald Street

St Olaf Street

Burgh Road

Bell's Road

King Erik-St

Charlotte Street

Esplanade

Commercial Road

Hillhead

Union-Street

Hayfield-Lane

South-Road

Clickimin Road

South-Lochside

Scalloway Road

Breiwick Road

Clairmont Pl

Greenfield Place

Church Road

Commercial St

Lover's Loan

Knab Road

Twageos Road

Gressy Loan

Brei Wick

To The Knab
(400m)

To Out Skerries

To Bressay

Bressay Sound

PLACES TO STAY
12 Fort Charlotte Guest House
18 Queen's Hotel
19 Kveldsro House Hotel
25 Grand Hotel
28 Solheim Guest House; Carradale Guest House
29 Lerwick Youth Hostel; Isleburgh House Café
30 Mrs Gifford's
32 Clickimin Caravan & Camp Site

PLACES TO EAT
3 Raba Indian Restaurant
7 Happy Haddock
10 Havly Centre
13 Fort Café
20 Osla's Café
21 Monty's Deli & Bistro
26 Golden Coach

OTHER
1 Holmsgarth Ferry Terminal
2 Grantfield Garage Bike Hire
4 Star Rent A Car
5 Viking Bus Station
6 Lerwick Laundry
8 Up Helly Aa Exhibition
9 Police Station
11 Fort Charlotte
14 Ferries to Bressay & Out Skerries
15 Toilets
16 John Leask & Son
17 Post Office
22 The Lounge
23 Tourist Information Centre
24 Da Noost
27 Shetland Museum & Library
31 Clickimin Leisure Centre
33 Hospital
34 Clickimin Broch

---

from the 7th century BC to the 6th century AD. It's always open and admission is free.

The **Böd of Gremista**, about a mile north of the ferry terminal, was the birthplace of Arthur Anderson, one of the founders of P&O. It's been restored as an 18th-century fishing booth and there's also a small exhibition about Anderson. It opens 10 am to 1 pm and 2 to 5 pm Wednesday to Sunday, mid-September. Admission costs £2/1.50.

Special Events
It's worth being here for the Folk Festival in April/May, or the Fiddle & Accordion Fes-

tival in October. See also Up Helly Aa Exhibition under Things to See & Do earlier.

Places to Stay
Camping Behind Clickimin Leisure Centre (where you register) by the loch on the western edge of town, *Clickimin Caravan & Camp Site* (☎ 741000) is about 20 minutes' walk from the ferry. It opens late April to September and charges £6.20 for a small tent; the price includes use of the shower in the centre. A path from the camp site takes you up into the hills behind.

Hostels In the centre of town *Lerwick Youth Hostel (☎ 692114, King Harald St)* is clean and well maintained and, though the kitchen is small, there's a good cafe on the premises. The hostel opens mid-April to October and the nightly charge is £9.25/8 for adults/under-18s.

B&Bs & Hotels Many of Lerwick's B&Bs and guesthouses are small, cosy places with only two or three rooms.

Although *Mrs Gifford's (☎ 693554)* address is 12 Burgh Rd, the house is actually in a small lane off Burgh Rd. B&B costs from £19 per person. The excellent *Solheim Guest House (☎ 695275, 34 King Harald St)* offers a good range of options for breakfast including yoghurt and fruit. Large, clean single/double rooms with shared bathroom cost £20/36. Next door, *Carradale Guest House (☎ 692251, 36 King Harald St)* is similar with rooms from £20 per person; it also offers evening meals on request.

Squeezed between Commercial St and the fort, *Fort Charlotte Guest House (☎ 695956, 1 Charlotte St)* has four agreeable rooms, all with bathroom, for £25 per person.

Queen's Hotel (☎ 692826, Commercial St) is right by the harbour and, if you can get a room with a view over the water, is a very pleasant place to stay. Singles/doubles cost £65/90.

At the top end is *Kveldsro House Hotel (☎ 692195)*, just off Greenfield Place, overlooking the harbour; the small, narrow streets can make it difficult to find. Pronounced kelro, it's a very comfortable, small hotel with 17 rooms from £70/94. If it isn't busy at the weekend you may be able to negotiate a special deal.

Places to Eat

Although there's good fresh fish, Shetland is no place for gastronomes. *Restit* is the best known local dish – lumps of mutton cured with salt and made into a soupy, salty stew traditionally eaten in the long winter months. It tastes quite as awful as it sounds and consequently rarely appears on menus. *Raba Indian Restaurant (☎ 695585, 26*

Commercial Rd), near the bus station, is one of the best curry houses in Shetland. Most mains cost under £5 and it does an all-you-can-eat buffet on Sunday for £7.95. The large *Golden Coach (☎ 693848, Hillhead)* is a good Chinese restaurant with most lunchtime mains costing under £6.

There's a good restaurant at the *Queen's Hotel* (see Places to Stay earlier), which opens for breakfast, lunch and dinner and does a four-course dinner for £15.25. However, secluded *Kveldsro House Hotel* (see Places to Stay) is the place to go for a really special occasion. It serves a good value, four-course dinner plus coffee/tea for £17.50.

Fish and chips can be good – as they should be in the heart of a fishing community. There are several takeaways. Try *Fort Café (☎ 693125, 2 Commercial St)*, north of the town centre, which has a cheap restaurant as well as a takeaway, or the *Happy Haddock*, farther round on Commercial Rd. Both open daily.

Islesburgh House Café (☎ 692114), in the same building as the youth hostel on King Harald St, serves good-value, wholesome food, but was closed at the time of research for refurbishment.

Recommended is the *Havly Centre (9 Charlotte St)*, a Norwegian Christian centre with an excellent cafe, and they don't quiz you on your religious beliefs. It serves mainly snacks (bacon rolls £1.60, homemade pizzas £3.75) and its gooey cakes are heavenly. It opens 10 am to 4.45 pm Tuesday, Thursday and Saturday, and to 3 pm on Wednesday and Friday.

The colourful *Osla's Café (Mounthooly St)*, below a small art gallery, serves savoury and sweet pancakes (£2.90), a speciality of the house, as well as soup, sandwiches and cakes. It opens daily year round (except Sunday from October to April). Just down from here is *Monty's Deli & Bistro (☎ 696555)*, which dishes up interesting cheap snacks and meals during the day – spinach wraps (Greek salad in spinach bread) cost £3.50. In the evening, mains cost from £8 to £13.50. It opens 11.30 am to 2.30 pm and 6.30 to 9 pm Monday to Saturday.

Entertainment

The best place to drink is at **The Lounge** *(Mounthooly St)* near the TIC, where there's live traditional music on Wednesday and weekend evenings. *Da Noost (Commercial St)* also has traditional music nights. The Shetland Fiddlers play at a number of locations and it's worth attending their sessions – enquire at the TIC.

Shopping

Best buys are the woollen jerseys, cardigans and sweaters for which Shetland is world famous. There are numerous shops selling woollens, but for bargains you must go to the factories. One is Judane (☎ 693724), on the industrial estate north past the power station. It sells plain sweaters for £12 and patterned ones for £16. Most sought-after are real Fair Isle sweaters, which cost from £28.50. To qualify as such, they must not only have the distinctive OXOXO pattern, but must also have been made on Fair Isle.

Getting There & Away

Ferries dock at Holmsgarth terminal, a 20-minute walk from the town centre (see the introductory Getting There & Away chapter). From the main airport at Sumburgh, Leask's (☎ 693162) runs regular buses to meet flights (£1.90 one way).

AROUND LERWICK

Two islands lie across the water from Lerwick: **Bressay** (pronounced bressah), and beyond it the National Nature Reserve of the **Isle of Noss**, which is well worth visiting to see the seabirds nesting on its 180m-high cliffs.

From the dock below Fort Charlotte in Lerwick, there are hourly ferries (☎ 01426-980317) daily to Maryfield on Bressay (£1.25, five minutes). It's then a 2½ mile walk across the island; some people bring rented bikes from Lerwick.

An inflatable dinghy shuttles across the water between Bressay and the Isle of Noss (£2.50/1 return); it operates 10 am to 5 pm Tuesday, Wednesday and Friday to Sunday from late May to August. Check with the TIC before leaving Lerwick as the Noss dinghy doesn't operate in bad weather.

There's B&B accommodation on Bressay at the *Maryfield Hotel (☎ 01515-820207)*,

Bird-watching in the Shetlands

Lying on the north–south and east–west migration routes, this island group is internationally famous for its bird life, and is one of Britain's top bird-watching locations. As well as the islands being a stopover for migrating Arctic species, there are large seabird breeding colonies. Of the 24 seabird species that nest in the British Isles, 21 are found here. June is the height of the breeding season. The bird population vastly outnumbers the human population of about 22,000 – there are said to be around 30,000 gannets, 140,000 guillemots, 250,000 puffins and 300,000 fulmars.

The Royal Society for the Protection of Birds (RSPB) maintains reserves on south Mainland at **Loch of Spiggie**, which attracts wildfowl in autumn and winter; **Lumbister** on Yell, a 1600 hectare moorland reserve; and on the remote island of **Fetlar**, which supports the richest heathland bird community, known particularly for its snowy owls.

There are national nature reserves at **Hermaness**, where you can't fail to be entertained by the clownish antics of the almost tame puffins – known here as the tammy norrie – and on the **Isle of Noss**, which can be reached from Lerwick. **Fair Isle**, owned by the National Trust for Scotland (NTS), supports large seabird populations and you can stay at the bird observatory.

Lerwick Tourist Information Centre (TIC) has lots of ornithological leaflets. Take care when bird-watching, as the cliff-edge sites can be dangerous. Also watch out for skuas (bonxies) that will dive-bomb you if you go near their nests. Since they aim for the highest part of your body, it's wise to walk with a stick, pointing it above your head if they approach. And don't get too close to nesting fulmars or you'll be the target for their smelly, oily spittle!

near the ferry terminal, but you can't stay on the Isle of Noss. There are also wildlife cruises from Lerwick around the Isle of Noss from April to September with Bressaboats (☎ 693434).

Six miles west of Lerwick, **Scalloway** (pronounced scallowah), the former capital of Shetland, is a busy fishing village with the ruins of **Scalloway Castle**, built in 1600, rising above the warehouses of the port. The small **Scalloway Museum** nearby is interesting for its displays on the 'Shetland Bus', the boats that the Norwegian resistance movement operated from Scalloway during WWII. Buses run from Lerwick Monday to Saturday (95p, 20 minutes, up to five times daily).

SOUTH MAINLAND
Sandwick & Around

Opposite the small but scattered village of Sandwick is the small isle of Mousa, on which stands the impressive double-walled fortified tower **Mousa Broch**. The best preserved broch in Britain, it was built between 100 BC and AD 100. There are regular boat trips (£7/3.50 return, 15 minutes), allowing 2½ hours on the island from April to September. Phone Tom Jamieson (☎ 01950-431367) in advance for reservations. There are six buses a day, Monday to Saturday (two Sunday), between Lerwick and Sandwick (£1.30, 25 minutes).

Sumburgh

At the southern tip of Mainland, this village is the location of the international airport and **Jarlshof** (☎ 01950-460112; HS), Shetland's most impressive archaeological attraction. This large prehistoric and Norse settlement was hidden under the sand until exposed by a gale at the turn of the 20th century. You should buy the short guide which interprets the ruins from a number of vantage points. It's an interesting place, but modernity impinges with the airport and hotel so close. It opens 9.30 am to 6.30 pm daily, April to September. Admission costs £2.30/1.

Near Jarlshof you can visit **Sumburgh Head** where large colonies of kittiwakes, fulmars, guillemots and razorbills nest.

Sumburgh Hotel (☎ 01950-460201) is a large, upmarket hotel with a bar and restaurant, next to Jarlshof. Single/double rooms cost from £45/60. To get here from Lerwick take the airport bus (£1.90, 50 minutes) and get off at the second last stop.

NORTH MAINLAND

The red, basalt lava cliffs of **Eshaness**, in the north-west of Mainland, form some of the most impressive coastal scenery in Shetland; this is good walking country. *Johnnie Notions Camping Böd* is at Hamnavoe nearby. It charges £5 per night (book at Lerwick TIC)

Buses from Lerwick run (evenings only, no Sunday service) as far as **Hillswick**, 7 miles from Eshaness, where the *St Magnus Hotel* (☎ 01806-503372) offers B&B for £30 per person. *Booth Restaurant & Café* (☎ 01806-503348), Shetland's oldest pub, serves vegetarian food and has live music. It opens May to September. All proceeds go to the local wildlife sanctuary.

There's B&B accommodation at **Brae**, 11 miles along the road back to Lerwick. *Busta House Hotel* (☎ 01806-522506), just outside Brae, is a luxurious country-house hotel with singles/doubles from £55/82.50. The restaurant, considered to be the best in Shetland, offers four-course dinners for £24.50. There are also cheaper bar meals.

YELL & UNST

Yell and Unst are connected with Mainland by small car ferries between Toft and Ulsta, and Gutcher and Belmont. Each ferry costs £3 for a car and although you don't need to book in advance, from May to September traffic is constant so it's wise to do so. Call ☎ 01957-722259.

Yell is a desolate, heather-covered peat moor, but there are some good coastal and hill walks. *Windhouse Lodge* is a camping *böd* in the centre of the island below the haunted ruins of **Windhouse**. It charges £5 (book at Lerwick TIC).

Unst is the northernmost part of Britain. Fittingly, its northernmost point is a wonderfully wild and windy nature reserve, **Hermaness**, where you can sit on the cliffs, commune with the puffins and gaze across the sea into the Arctic Circle. Robert Louis Stevenson wrote *Treasure Island* while living on Unst – his uncle built the lighthouse on **Muckle Flugga** a rock near Hermaness. There's comfortable B&B accommodation at *Mrs Ritch's (☎ 01957-711323, Gerratoun, Haroldswick)*, from £15 per person, and at *Mrs Firmin's (☎ 01957-755234, Prestegaard, Uyeasound)*, from £18 per person.

Haroldswick is 55 miles from Lerwick, and if you don't have a car you must spend the night on Unst as buses only run twice daily. From Lerwick, if you catch the 8 am bus to South Yell you can make connections with ferries and other buses to reach Haroldswick before noon. It's then 2 miles to the Hermaness car park. Pause to mail a card from Britain's most northerly post office.

OTHER ISLANDS

Regular ferries connect Yell and Unst with **Fetlar**, where there's an RSPB reserve. West of Shetland is **Foula**, a windy island supporting a community of 40 people, 1500 sheep and 500,000 seabirds amid dramatic cliff scenery. It's reached by twice-weekly ferries (☎ 01595-753232) from Walls and planes (£42.60 return) from Tingwall (☎ 01595-840246).

Fair Isle is Britain's most remote, inhabited island. Known for its patterned knitwear, still produced in the island's cooperative, it's also a bird-watcher's paradise. Twenty-four miles from Sumburgh and only three by 1½ miles in size, it was given to the NTS in 1954. Accommodation must be booked in advance and includes meals. The *Fair Isle Lodge & Bird Observatory (☎ 01595-760 258)* has full-board accommodation, charging £25 in the dorm and £40/70 for singles/doubles. Locals also offer rooms with meals from around £20 per person; try *Mrs Riddiford (☎ 01595-760250)* in Schoolton.

From Tingwall (☎ 01595-840246) there are two flights a day there and back (£74.40 return, 25 minutes) on Monday, Wednesday, Friday and Saturday. A day return allows about six hours on the island (seven on Monday). A ferry sails from Grutness (near Sumburgh) to Fair Isle (£21, 2½ hours) on Tuesday, Saturday and alternate Thursdays from May to September, and from Lerwick (4½ hours) on alternate Thursdays. Book with JW Stout (☎ 01595-760222).

Facts about Wales

'Every day when I wake up I thank the Lord I'm Welsh,' run the lyrics of Catatonia's title track on their album, *International Velvet*. There's a remarkably upbeat feeling in Wales today. In 1979, the majority of the people voted against home rule; yet in the 1997 referendum they said yes to a Welsh Assembly, whose first members were elected in May 1999 and are now based in Cardiff. In the Welsh lyrics of *International Velvet*, however, Catatonia urges Wales to 'wake up...the weakness is deep'. The country has been subservient to its dominating neighbour for almost a thousand years now.

Wales, or Cymru in Welsh, has had the misfortune to be so close to England that it could not be allowed its independence, and far enough away to be conveniently forgotten. It is almost miraculous that anything Welsh should have survived the English onslaught, but the culture has proved to be remarkably enduring, and the language stubbornly refuses to die.

Wales' appeal lies in its countryside. In general, the towns and cities are not particularly inspiring. The best way to appreciate the great Welsh outdoors is by walking, cycling, canal boating or using some other form of private transport. Simply catching buses or trains from one regional hub to another is not recommended. Instead, base yourself in a small town or farm B&B, and explore the surrounding countryside for a few days. Hay-on-Wye, Brecon, St David's, Dolgellau, Llanberis and Betws-y-Coed are possibilities that come to mind.

Much of the countryside is breathtakingly beautiful and is still dotted with rustic villages that feel relatively untouched by modern influence. While the abundance of castles and stately homes will appeal to many, Wales' allure may lie, for some, in the bleak mining towns and windswept valleys, which possess a certain characteristic charm. Wales has many peculiar hidden treasures, for all tastes, that distinguish it from its perhaps more familiar neighbour.

The most attractive countryside is now protected by the Pembrokeshire Coast National Park, the Brecon Beacons National Park and the Snowdonia National Park, but the Gower peninsula and the Llŷn peninsula are also outstanding. Outside the national parks, and particularly in the north, however, miles of coastline have been ruined by shoddy bungalows and ugly caravan parks. Without much exploration though, it is still possible to come across stretches of untouched coastline, verdant valleys and dramatic mountain ranges.

Wales has an unsurpassed legacy of magnificent medieval castles. Edward I built a string of fortresses in the north-west – Caernarfon, Conwy, Beaumaris and Harlech are listed as UNESCO World Heritage Sites and should not be missed.

HISTORY
Prehistory & the Celts
Wales is among the oldest countries in the world. Some of the rocks within its borders were formed over 3000 million years ago, and evidence of human habitation stretches back nearly 200,000 years. The stone frames of *cromlechs* (burial chambers) left by Neolithic people can still be seen in several parts of the country – Pentre Ifan in Pembrokeshire, for example. The Celts arrived from Europe sometime after 600 BC. Little is known about them, although it is to their Celtic forebears that the modern Welsh attribute national characteristics such as eloquence, warmth and imagination.

The Romans
From AD 60, the region – for it was not yet Wales – was occupied by the Romans, who for the next 300 years kept close control over the tribes from the garrison towns at Chester and Caerlon. In his *Historia Britonum* (circa 800), Nennius suggests that the people revered their Roman governors. One of the Romans, Magnus Maximus, is transformed into a near mythical hero called

WALES

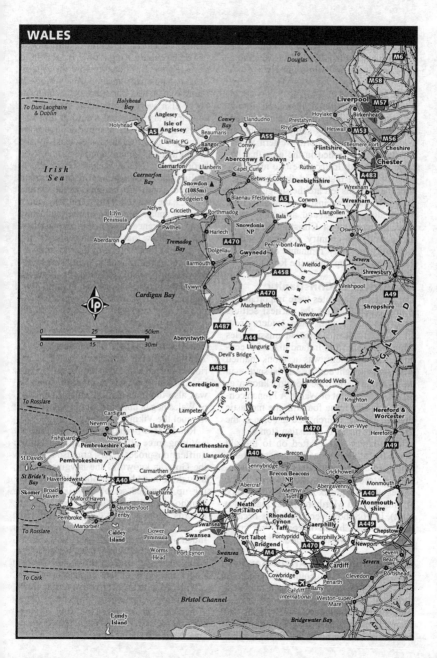

Maxen Wledig, with an elaborate genealogy. This embroidering seems so much part of Welsh history that little of it is verifiable, and fact slides readily into fantasy.

Irish Invaders

Around 400, people from the Brythonic kingdom of Gododdin in Scotland arrived, led by Cunedda. They came ostensibly to drive out the Irish in north-western Wales, but stayed and settled in the area that became Gwynedd. In fact, the two main features of Welsh history in the Dark Ages after the Romans left are the struggle of the native Brythons against these raiding Irish pirates along the coast and, around the same time, the coming of Christianity. During this period, the country was made up of kingdoms, possibly remnants of administrative units set up under the Romans.

The Arrival of Christianity

The western sea routes were important for Wales. They brought the earliest settlers from the south and, later, traders from the Mediterranean. Christian missionaries came, probably from Ireland in the 5th century. Among them was a monk named Dewi, who sought converts in the south – in the Norman period, he became known as David, patron saint of Wales. A French connection is also to be found in the monastic character of the church, and in some of the inscriptions on early Christian stones.

Christianity was grafted on to the old Celtic belief system, with its sacred wells, holy men and hermit saints in the contemplative tradition, remembered in place names with the prefix Llan (enclosed place or church) and Merthyr (burial place of a saint). In 768, however, Christians became subject to the Church of Rome, which then dominated the Western world.

King Arthur & the Anglo-Saxons

From the 5th to 11th century, the people in this region were under almost constant pressure from the Anglo-Saxon invaders of England. By the 8th century, the Brythons had been cut off by these invaders from their compatriots to the north in Cumbria, and it

is around this time that they started to call themselves Cymry or fellow countrymen.

The legendary King Arthur is thought to have led the Brythons against the Anglo-Saxons sometime during this period. It seems that he was Christian and, as many of the Welsh were, Romanised. Scarcely a contemporary historical record of him survives and yet he has inspired a huge body of poetry and literature, not least by the Welsh in *The Mabinogion*. He is said to be buried on the 'Isle of Avalon' (Glastonbury) in England. The legends of his court at Camelot, with his knights of the Round Table, have sparked many a fruitless search into the annals for more than a tantalising scrap of evidence of his historical existence.

We do know that in the 8th century, Offa, the king of Mercia (one of the most powerful of the Anglo-Saxon kingdoms in southern Britain), constructed a dyke marking the boundary between the Welsh and the Mercians. Offa's Dyke can still be seen today – in fact you can walk its length (see the Activities chapter).

Early Unification of Wales

The 9th and 10th centuries witnessed a period of savage attacks on the coasts by Danish and Norse pirates raiding the south. It was also the time that the small kingdoms of Wales began unifying, through necessity, to repel the Vikings.

Rhodri Mawr (who died in 878) defeated a Viking force off Anglesey and began the unification process. His grandson Hywel the Good is known as the lawgiver and is thought to have been responsible for drawing up a unified set of laws between the kingdoms. Although the earliest written records of these laws date from the 13th century, they probably originate in this much older society.

Ironically, as Wales was becoming a recognisable entity, so did it fall further under the aegis of the English crown. In 927, faced with the destructive onslaught of the Vikings, the Welsh kings recognised Athelstan, the Anglo-Saxon king of England, as their overlord in exchange for an alliance against the Vikings.

The Normans & Edward I

By the time the Normans arrived in England, the Welsh had returned to their warring, independent ways. To secure his new kingdom, William the Conqueror set up powerful, feudal barons along the Welsh borders at Chester, Shrewsbury and Hereford. The Lords Marcher, as they were known, developed virtually unfettered wealth and power and began to advance on the lowlands of South and Mid Wales.

Llywelyn the Great (who died in 1240) attempted to set up a state in Wales along the lines of the new feudal system in England. However, it was his grandson Llywelyn the Last who was recognised as the first Prince of Wales, by Henry III of England in 1267. The tide turned with Henry's successor, the great warrior king Edward I, who descended on the country in a bloody campaign. Wales became a dependent principality, owing fealty and allegiance under feudal rules to England. In 1302, the title of Prince of Wales was given to the monarch's eldest son, a tradition that continues today. To maintain his authority, Edward built the great castles of Conwy, Beaumaris, Caernarfon and Harlech. English boroughs, settled by colonists, were established around these, and the country was broken up into English-style counties.

Owain Glyndŵr

In 1400, driven by economic and social frustration, Owain Glyndŵr (Owen Glendower to the English) headed a rebellion. As a descendant of the princes of northern Powys and head of the royal house of Deheubarth in the south-west, he had a good claim to Wales. Although his rebellion was crushed by Henry IV, feelings were roused that rankled for many years after. Punishments were severe. The Welsh were barred from public life, the lords of the manor suffered heavy fines and loss of rents, and much farming land was devastated. Glyndŵr died an outlaw in 1416.

Acts of Union

By the time the half-Welsh Henry Tudor picked the crown of England off a battlefield in 1485 and became king, the Welsh were only too grateful to enjoy the consequences – preferential treatment at the English court and new career opportunities in English public life.

Likewise, the Acts of Union of 1536–43, under Tudor's son Henry VIII, were welcomed by an aspiring Welsh gentry, bringing as they did English law, parliamentary representation for Wales, plenty of trade opportunities and participation in government. The Welsh language, however, ceased to be recognised in the law courts.

With James I of Great Britain came the Stuart kings. James exchanged the Welsh lion, which Henry VII had incorporated into the royal coat of arms, for the Scottish unicorn. However, the Welsh did remain loyal to the monarchy throughout the Civil War of the 17th century.

Industrial Revolution & Methodism

Puritanism was not a force in Wales until the 1730s brought Methodism and the Great Awakening. They were by-products of the Industrial Revolution, and the character of modern Wales is coloured by the social and economic changes that started at this time. The great centres of Methodism were the Welsh mining valleys and the factory towns of the English Midlands.

By 1811, the Calvinistic Methodists had broken away from the Church of England, and in 1851 nonconformists accounted for 76% of the churchgoing population. By this time, copper, iron and slate were being extracted and ironworks were in operation in the Merthyr Tydfil and Monmouth areas. The 1860s saw the Rhondda valleys opened up for coal mining, and Wales soon became a major exporter of coal. By 1875, most of the world's tin plate was produced in Wales.

Economic & Political Change

The population increased phenomenally with industrialisation. What had been almost exclusively a fragmented, rural population became concentrated in the south in mining and industrial communities, with a character and toughness of their own – vigorous, close-knit, self-reliant and nonconformist. Strikes and occasional violence broke out, as did protests against low wages and bad working conditions, but it was much later that a trade union movement began to emerge.

Tension grew between the nonconformists and the Anglicised 'squirearchy', who were the traditional ruling class. The Church became a target for reform; the established Church was seen as being unrepresentative and expensive to maintain. Nonconformism began to ally itself politically with liberalism, which favoured nationalism and the disestablishment of the Church. It was not until 1920, while David Lloyd George, Welsh Liberal and champion for home rule in Wales, was prime minister of Britain, that the Church was disestablished.

From around 1900, support began to grow for the Labour Party in South Wales. Keir Hardie was elected to parliament from Merthyr Tydfil, and through the economic depression of the 1930s and after, this support increased. The severity of the Depression led to 242,000 people leaving the valleys.

Welsh Nationalism

In 1925, Plaid Cymru, the Welsh National Party, was formed by six men in a hotel room during the Royal National Eisteddfod (*eisteddfod*: cultural festival). Political independence through language and cultural differences was the goal of a small minority. The Welsh Language Society, for instance, resorted to civil disobedience to press their point, with the result that in 1942 the Welsh language was made legally acceptable.

The colleges of Aberystwyth, Cardiff and Bangor had been united in 1893 as the University of Wales, and the eisteddfod had become a focus for the preservation of Welsh language and culture. In 1955, Cardiff was made the official capital of Wales. In 1964, a Welsh minister of state was appointed with cabinet rank in the British government, and in 1966 a Welsh Nationalist was elected to parliament. By 1978, a Labour-dominated parliament passed an act to create an elected Welsh Assembly with power over some Welsh domestic affairs, but a referendum in 1979 showed the enthusiasm of the 1960s had waned, and the subject was dropped (see under Government and Politics later in the chapter for more details on the Welsh Assembly). The country finally got a Welsh-language TV channel when S4C started in 1982.

Wales Today

The 20th century, especially the 1960s, 70s and 80s, saw the coal industry and the associated steel industry collapse. Large-scale unemployment persists today, although numbers have decreased marginally, as Wales attempts to move to more high-tech and service industries. Coal is king no more – Tower Colliery, Wales' last large coal mine, closed in 1994, although it was reopened a year later as a smaller, private concern.

Tourism is now a major industry, accounting for 10% of all jobs in the country. Wales is currently experiencing something of a tourist boom with record numbers of visitors. The increased nurturing of its language and culture in recent years and Wales' greater political autonomy have helped give modern Wales its own distinct stamp.

GEOGRAPHY

Covering an area of 8017 sq miles, Wales is approximately 170 miles long and 60 miles wide. Surrounded by sea on three sides, its border to the east with England still runs roughly along Offa's Dyke, the giant earthwork constructed in the 8th century.

Wales has two major mountain systems: the Black Mountains and Brecon Beacons in the south and the mountains of Snowdonia in the north-west. At 1113m, Snowdon is the highest peak in England and Wales and more rugged than the rounded Brecon Beacons to the south. These glaciated mountain areas are deeply cut by narrow river valleys. Rolling moorlands between 180m and 600m stretch from Denbigh in the north to the Glamorgan valleys in the south, ending on the west coast in spectacular cliffs and the plains of river estuaries. The population is concentrated in the southeast, along the coast between Cardiff and Swansea and in the old mining valleys that run north into the Brecon Beacons.

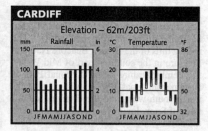

CARDIFF
Elevation – 62m/203ft

CLIMATE

Although Welsh weather is as difficult to second-guess as anywhere else in Britain, it's probably fair to say that it suffers from an excess of rainfall; it would be unwise to arrive without rainproof clothing and mud-proof footwear. Westerly and south-westerly winds can also make life pretty miserable, especially when it's raining as well. That said, the closeness of the mountains to the coast means that you can encounter very different climatic conditions within a relatively short geographical distance. It's also slightly warmer – but not so you'd notice – along the south coast.

ECOLOGY & ENVIRONMENT

Anyone returning to South Wales who'd last seen the place in its coal-mining days would scarcely recognise the valleys now. The mines have closed, many of the ugly slagheaps have been grassed over and the air is cleaner than it's been for centuries.

It's not been all good news for the environment over the past few years, though. In February 1996, Pembrokeshire hit the world news when the supertanker *Sea Empress* broke up off the Pembrokeshire Coast National Park, releasing 76,000 tonnes of light crude oil into the sea. More than 120 miles of coastline were covered with oil and although this soon dispersed, it will be decades before the ecology completely recovers. The real damage to the environment is always less obvious – a population of rare starfish was wiped out in West Angle Bay, for example. As long as there's an oil refinery at Milford Haven, in the centre of the national park, there will always be a risk of further pollution.

Wales is experiencing largely similar environment problems as the rest of Britain: the overuse of pesticides on fields, the destruction of hedgerows and an ever increasing number of vehicles on the roads. Tourism is taking its toll, too. The increased number of tourists in national parks has led to serious footpath erosion, particularly acute in Snowdonia.

One of the biggest tourist attractions in the country is the eco-friendly Centre for Alternative Technology (☎ 01654-702400, fax 702782), Machynlleth, Powys, SY20 9AZ. Its Web site is at www.cat.org.uk.

For details of several British wildlife and environmental groups see the Ecology & Environment section of the Facts About England chapter.

FLORA & FAUNA

Much of Wales was once covered by forest, mainly sessile oak, but very little remains and none of it is completely untouched. Most has long since been cleared for agriculture, or chopped down for shipbuilding, charcoal burning or construction – not least for pit props in the mines. Overgrazing also makes it hard for new oak saplings to take root; in Snowdonia the rampant spread of wild rhododendron bushes prevents them even seeding. Imported oaks, such as the Turkey oak, actually seem to fare better. Pengelli Forest in Pembrokeshire is as close as you'll get to untouched Welsh woodland nowadays.

Ash trees are also native to Wales and are common everywhere, especially along rivers and in woods and thickets in the Gower peninsula and the Brecon Beacons. In their shade grow primroses, common dog violets and several species of orchid. Hornbeams were once restricted to south-eastern Wales but are now found elsewhere, too. You'll see plenty of wild cherry trees and field maples, and churchyards often harbour yew trees, as in England. Nor could anyone miss the massed stands of sitka spruce, popular with plantation owners seeking a quick-growing source of timber, but far from ideal as habitats for native birds and mammals, the sturdy pine marten aside.

Wales' mountainous terrain has made it a

perfect breeding ground for fragile Alpine-Arctic plants, including the unique Snowdon lily, which brightens the slopes of Mt Snowdon between the end of May and the middle of June. Easier to spot are saxifrage plants and moss campion growing on the rocks. Amid the coastal sand dunes, you may find evening primroses, sea spurge, sea bindweed and marram grass, while the Gower peninsula is a good place for thrift, samphire and sea lavender. Around Tenby, you might even find the unique Tenby daffodil.

Like Scotland, Wales' lengthy coastline ensures it a sizeable seabird population. Grassholm harbours one of the world's largest gannet colonies, with 30,000 breeding pairs. Wales also has 150,000 pairs of Manx shearwaters, 30% of the world's population. The rock faces of Skomer and Skokholm islands in particular are densely filled with colonies of guillemots, razorbills, storm petrels, kittiwakes and puffins. There are also a few pairs of rare choughs on Ramsey and Bardsey islands, and passing migrants include the occasional great northern diver.

In general, the Welsh inland bird population mirrors that of England, with few notable exceptions. It does have 100 breeding pairs of red kites, mainly found in the Elan Valley of Mid Wales.

The mammal population is also similar to England's, although the greater horseshoe bat is now confined to Wales and corners of south-western England, and Skomer boasts a unique species of vole. Red squirrels are vanishing fast throughout Britain, but a few survive around Lake Vyrnwy. Otters, once very rare, are re-establishing themselves along the River Teifi and in the border area of Montgomeryshire. A colony of grey seals is breeding successfully on the west coast of Ramsey Island.

With so many fast-flowing rivers, it's hardly surprising that Wales has a wide variety of fish, including salmon (in the Usk and Wye), brown trout and char. Bala Lake also boasts a unique species, the white gwyniad, said to have been hanging around since the Ice Age. Cockles are still harvested at low tide in the Burry Inlet on the Gower peninsula and made into pies by the locals.

National Parks

The three national parks in Wales could not be more different from each other. The rolling hills of the Brecon Beacons National Park are in the southern part of Mid Wales, the Pembrokeshire Coast National Park is Britain's only coastal park and lies in the extreme south-west, and the dramatic mountains of Snowdonia National Park dominate the north.

GOVERNMENT & POLITICS

Wales is technically a principality and since 1302, when Edward I invested his son as Prince of Wales, the British sovereign's eldest son has been given the title. In 1969, Charles was formally proclaimed Prince of Wales at Caernarfon Castle. It goes without saying that few Welsh Nationalists are openly supportive of this state of affairs.

In 1997, the people of Wales voted to be governed by a Welsh Assembly, rather than from the House of Commons in London – a decision that came into effect in May 1999. Following the transfer of the devolved powers from the Secretary of State for Wales to the National Assembly, the 60-member Assembly headed by First Secretary Rhodri Morgan, now has responsibility for such national portfolios as education, health, housing and language but has no authority on international affairs or defence. Elections will be held every four years and laws passed in Westminster still apply to Wales. Plaid Cymru is the largest nationalist party in Wales and holds seventeen seats in the Assembly.

The likelihood of Wales emerging as a nation independent of the rest of the UK is currently small – certainly smaller than Scotland's, which has independent judicial and education systems.

ECONOMY

Research carried out by the Wales Tourist Board (WTB) suggests that people who have never visited Wales imagine it a grim, grey country scarred by the ugly paraphernalia and detritus of heavy industry, primarily coal mining, steel manufacture and slate quarrying. In some ways nothing could be further from the truth; although the steel industry and slate quarrying linger on around Port Talbot and Blaenau Ffestiniog, coal mining has more or less vanished, turned into little more than an adjunct of the much cleaner heritage-tourism industry. The scale of the change is typified by the Rhondda Valley, where 50 pits once employed 40,000 men. There are now no large working pits left there.

Mass unemployment and the ensuing social disruption in parts of the South Wales valleys have led some commentators to draw not altogether ridiculous comparisons with the developing world. Probably the most successful modern industry – aside from agriculture and forestry – is tourism, but unfortunately that can rarely make up for the loss of well-paid manual jobs in the areas worst affected by the 1980s and 90s pit closures. Two-thirds of Welsh jobs are now in the service industries.

In 1976, the Welsh Development Agency (WDA) was set up to help Wales make the awkward transition to new sources of employment. It's been phenomenally successful in attracting foreign investment, particularly from Japanese companies, among them Sony, National Panasonic, Aiwa and Toyota. There has also been a mini-boom in new financial businesses opening or moving to Wales, a fact confirmed by a glimpse at the name-boards going up around Cardiff Bay. Although Wales has only one-twentieth of the UK's population, since 1986 it's succeeded in attracting one-sixth of inward investment.

POPULATION & PEOPLE

Wales has a population of around 2.9 million, about 5% of the population of the UK. The largest centre of population is Cardiff, with 285,000 residents. Swansea and Newport, also in South Wales, are the other main population centres. Mid Wales is the least densely populated part of the country, although it's interesting to note that the population of Powys, the emptiest area, actually grew between 1981 and 1991, as people deserted the cities in favour of the countryside and an alternative lifestyle.

The caricature Welshman of English imagination was a coal miner who went to chapel on Sunday and spent his spare time singing or playing rugby. His wife wore long skirts with a pinafore and shawl, and a tall black top hat. The 1980s and 90s saw the mining part of this picture laid to rest, and the chapel-going, too, has died as much of a death in Wales as in England. The only places you're likely to see women in national costume nowadays are at the *eisteddfodau* or the Welsh Folk Museum. That said, the Welsh do remain a people apart, if only because of their accents and the fact that their language is still very much alive.

The long struggle of the Welsh to stay separate from England probably accounts for some of the continued sense of 'difference', not to mention the hostility some (but not many) visitors claim to experience in the Welsh-speaking enclaves of the northwest. As a foreign visitor, you're unlikely to experience any hostility, although the Welsh can sometimes be as reserved as the English when it comes to introducing themselves to strangers.

The indigenous Welsh are of Celtic stock who seem to have arrived from the European mainland around 600 BC. During the Industrial Revolution, the population makeup was drastically altered as wealthy investors moved to Wales to take advantage of its mineral wealth, recruiting in their wake a large non-Welsh working force. It was at this time that the Welsh language began a decline that has only recently been halted.

Wales has a small ethnic-minority population, mainly concentrated in Cardiff, Newport and Swansea. But you'll probably be amazed at how many English people live in Wales and, in particular, how many of them make a living out of tourism: running B&Bs, craft centres, cafes and other attractions. In fact, if you're not careful, you could spend more time talking to English incomers than to native Welsh people.

EDUCATION

In most ways, the Welsh education system mirrors the English one. However, the recent revival of interest in the Welsh language makes for some inevitable differences. There are, for example, special Welsh-medium schools where the normal curriculum is taught in Welsh, and English is treated as a second language to be introduced at about age seven. Although there are plenty of Welsh-medium primary and junior schools, many parents chicken out when it comes to secondary education. In any case, there are currently too few Welsh-medium secondary schools to accommodate all the children coming up from the elementary schools. The status of Welsh in the national curriculum, introduced in 1990, seems, like so much else, to fluctuate from year to year.

There are universities at Cardiff, Aberystwyth, Bangor, Lampeter, Swansea and Treforest.

ARTS
Music
Wales is seen as a country positively bursting at the seams with lusty male voice choirs, mysterious eisteddfodau and pretty female harpists.

Even within their national sport, rugby, a tradition of singing in the terraces has developed in its own right. But in recent years, Wales has seen a virtual pop-music explosion, with bands such as the Manic Street Preachers, bilingual-singing Super Furry Animals, alternative pop trio the Stereophonics and Catatonia enjoying considerable success on the world stage. Enduring swashbuckler Tom Jones has proven to be perennially popular, and now with an even younger audience, thanks to a hugely successful album of classic pop covers and collaborations with high-profile bands.

Literature
Welsh literature can be classified according to two periods. Early Welsh literature was dominated by the work of the bards, who were patronised by the Welsh princes until the late 13th century. The modern era began around the time of the Reformation. The nascence of contemporary Welsh literature is often attributed to the foundation of the University of Wales in the late 19th century.

The poet and prose writer Dylan Thomas,

JANE SMITH

It's not unusual for girls to throw their underwear at Welsh crooner Tom Jones.

born in Swansea in 1914, is undoubtedly the most famous of Wales' literary progeny. His personal life and reckless bouts of drinking are almost equally as well known as his work, acclaimed for its comic profusion and pathos. At 16, he left school to work as a reporter for the *South Wales Evening Post* and four years later published his first book of poems, simply titled *18 Poems*. He subsequently moved to London and, while working for the BBC, married an Irish woman Caitlin MacNamara and had two sons and a daughter. He is best known for his humorous account of Welsh life in *My Life As A Young Dog* and his widely celebrated play *Under Milk Wood*, portraying the lives of the inhabitants of a small Welsh town. He died of an alcoholic overdose in New York in 1953.

Theatre
There have been ongoing attempts to establish a Welsh national theatre but none have proven successful to date and many

campaigners have become disheartened by the controversial 'prioritising' (essentially cost-cutting) strategies towards theatre of the main funding body, the Arts Council – all at a time when audience figures for theatre across Britain are on the increase. Despite this, many small experimental groups and established regional theatre companies continue to put out acclaimed works, among them the long-standing and prolific Made in Wales and Clwyd Theatre companies. The small Mid Wales Opera company has also enjoyed considerable success for over a decade.

Painting

The country hasn't been so blessed when it comes to the visual arts, with few Welsh artists other than Augustus and Gwen John achieving real fame. Graham Sutherland did, nevertheless, settle in Wales and do much of his work at Picton Castle. As if to make up for this dearth of indigenous talent, Gwendoline and Margaret Davies ploughed the money they inherited from their father (who created Barry Docks) into amassing a stunning collection of impressionist paintings, including Monets, Manets, Sisleys and Pisarros, which are now on show at the National Museum of Wales in Cardiff.

Architecture

On the architectural front, Wales is best known for the great medieval castles in various states of ruination that ring the coasts and Marches (border areas). Ironically, most of them were built by the English to ward off Welsh nationalists of the medieval kind. The finest of all are the ones Edward I had built in North Wales, such as Caernarfon, Harlech, Conwy and Beaumaris, but wherever you go in South or North Wales there'll be a ruined castle within reasonable reach. It's also worth making a special trip to see some of the following castles: Rhuddlan, Denbigh, Cricieth, Raglan, Pembroke, Kidwelly, Chepstow and Caerphilly. Most of them are cared for by Cadw, the Welsh Historic Monuments Agency (see Useful Organisations in the Facts for the Visitor chapter).

The ruined castles aside, Wales is not noted for its wonderful architecture. Although the history of Christianity in Wales stretches back to the 5th century, medieval Wales never shared in the prosperity that led to the blossoming of splendid churches and cathedrals in England. Cadw cares for atmospheric ruined abbeys at Tintern, Neath, Strata Florida and Valle Crucis, and the cathedral at St David's is as splendid as many in England. There are also some pleasing towered churches in Pembrokeshire and Gwent, but the real boom in Welsh church building came after the Industrial Revolution as people flooded into the newly industrialising areas.

This population growth coincided with the high point of interest in nonconformist religion. Wales is scattered from end to end with Methodist, Baptist and Congregationalist chapels, and since none of these sects believed in lavish church building, their legacy is a landscape of small, plain chapels. What's more, none of these sects has gone to such lengths as the Anglican Church to conserve its redundant premises, so wherever you go in Wales you'll see chapels boarded up, crumbling or converted for some wholly irreligious new function.

There are also a few fine houses, like Tredegar outside Newport, Williams Hall at Bodelwyddan, which now houses the National Portrait Gallery's Victorian collection, and Plas Newydd, the half-timbered house once occupied by the Ladies of Llangollen (see under Llangollen in the North Wales chapter). Some of the finest houses are in the care of the National Trust for England and Wales. Cardiff also boasts two more unusual 'castles' – Cardiff Castle and Castell Coch – designed by the Victorian architect William Burges, who specialised in love-it-or-hate-it repro-Gothic.

Not surprisingly, Wales has an abundance of industrial architecture, and attitudes to this have changed enormously. The great colliery towers and winding gear once regarded as eyesores are now seen through the rose-tinted glasses of nostalgia, especially once they've been cleaned up and made presentable for their visitors. In South Wales it's well worth visiting Big Pit at Blaenafon or the Rhondda Heritage Centre, and in Mid Wales you can visit old slate-quarrying sites at Blaenau Ffestiniog.

SOCIETY & CONDUCT
Eisteddfodau

The eisteddfod is a thoroughly Welsh institution that tends to leave the non-Welsh mystified. Its precise origins are shrouded in legend, but the word means a 'gathering of bards', and the traditional eisteddfod was a contest involving poetry and music. The first recorded event seems to have taken place in Cardigan in 1176, but after the Act of Union in 1536, eisteddfodau seem to have become less frequent and less lively, a process accentuated in the 17th and 18th centuries as the dour nonconformist sects got their claws into Wales.

All this changed in the 1860s when the National Eisteddfod Society was established to revive the old traditions. There are now three major annual eisteddfodau: the International Music Eisteddfod in purpose-built premises at Llangollen every July; the Royal National Eisteddfod, which moves between North and South Wales each August; and the newer Urdd ('Youth' – under 25s only) Eisteddfod, which also alternates between sites in North and South Wales each May.

Male Voice Choirs

The Welsh male voice choir (cor meibion) is something of an institution, and most closely associated with the coal mining communities of the South Wales valleys. Perhaps surprisingly, it was the nonconformist sects, particularly Methodism, that breathed life into these choirs, so their repertoires are stronger on hymns than might be anticipated.

The collapse of the old coal-mining communities presents a threat to the survival of the choirs, but so far they're hanging in. The Wales Tourist Board booklet Welsh Male Voice Choirs lists rehearsal nights for village choirs that are happy to host visitors. There are choirs in all the main towns, but the largest concentration is in the south. As a sign of the times, some of them now boast female voices too.

For details of the International Music Eisteddfod in Llangollen, phone ☎ 01978-860236. The Royal National Eisteddfod (☎ 029-2076 3777) takes place at a different location each year.

If you'd like to see an eisteddfod but can't make any of the big competitions, it's still worth contacting the WTB for its events booklet, which also lists local contests.

Alternative Culture

In the 1980s, parts of Mid Wales in particular became popular refuges for people in search of an alternative lifestyle. At its most extreme, this has meant setting up tepee camps in remote valleys; at its most moderate, it has led to a rash of alternative bookshops and restaurants in small towns such as Llanidloes and Machynlleth.

Near Machynlleth, the Centre for Alternative Technology (CAT) has brought together many of the characteristics of this craving for something different: organic farming, wind and water power, and the recycling of virtually everything, all in a communal setting.

Dos & Don'ts

Probably the greatest insult you can give the Welsh is to refer to them as English, or tell them how much you like being 'here in England', when you mean 'here in Wales'.

RELIGION

Christianity is believed to have been introduced to Wales in the 5th century, going its own way until the time of the Reformation, when the Welsh Church was reorganised to become part of the regular Anglican Church. In 1588, Bishop Morgan translated the Bible into Welsh.

As the population grew in the 18th century, the new industrial working classes proved fertile recruiting ground for various Protestant nonconformist sects, particularly Baptists, Methodists and Congregationalists. An 1851 survey discovered that almost 80% of the population was nonconformist, and in 1920 the Anglican Church actually ceased to be the established church of Wales. The nonconformist tradition brought a puritanical strain to Welsh life that might account for the rather dour image of its people. Until recently, it wasn't just shops that stayed shut on Sunday in Wales – pubs did too.

But all that has changed, and now it would be hard to argue that Wales is any more actively religious than England. The most recent survey found 108,400 people identifying themselves as members of the Anglican Church, 60,600 as Roman Catholics and 220,300 as Methodists, Baptists and assorted other nonconformists.

LANGUAGE

The one thing that marks Wales out so distinctly from the rest of Britain is the survival of Welsh as a living language. Despite its weird and seemingly unpronounceable double ls and consecutive consonants, Welsh is an Indo-European language, from a Celtic offshoot. Its closest linguistic cousins are Cornish and Breton.

During the Roman occupation, people in positions of authority probably spoke Latin, even if everyone else spoke Welsh. Gradually, a bilingual Latin/Welsh-speaking population emerged, and the influence of Latin on Welsh is clear, as is the influence of French (from the Norman period) and English. The language as it is spoken today seems to have been more or less fully developed by the 6th century, making it one of Europe's oldest languages.

Following the Act of Union in 1536, people were forbidden to hold high office unless they spoke English as well as Welsh. Bishop Morgan's translation of the Bible in 1588 is thought to have played an important part in keeping the language alive.

During the 17th and 18th centuries, the nonconformist sects that made such headway in Wales also supported the native language. However, the Industrial Revolution brought a whole new class of industrial landlords and employers, few of whom spoke Welsh. From then on, the number of native Welsh speakers went into steep decline. At the start of the 19th century, 80% of the population probably spoke Welsh, but by 1901 this had sunk to 50%. Now, only about 20%

of the population speak Welsh. Welsh speakers are concentrated particularly in the northwestern and western parts of the country where up to 75% of the population of a given locality may speak it. In contrast, only 2.4% of people living in Monmouthshire know more than the odd word.

Reasons for the decline in the number of people speaking Welsh are not hard to find: television, better communications, emigration, mixed marriages and tourism are just some of those commonly cited. Perhaps what is more surprising is that so many people have continued to speak the language despite all these threats. Indeed, in the 1980s and 90s there was revived interest in the language, not least among incomers.

Since the 1960s the importance of Welsh has been officially recognised, and in 1967 the Welsh Language Act ensured that Welsh speakers could use their own language in court. Since then an increasing number of publications have been bilingual and it's rare nowadays to see a road sign in just one language. Radio Cymru transmits in Welsh, and roughly 400 books a year are published in the language.

In 1982, Channel 4 set up Sianel Pedwar Cymru (S4C – Channel 4 Wales), which broadcasts Welsh television programs daily and has even made the odd feature film. There have been other developments too. In 1988, a Welsh Language Board was set up to advise the secretary of state for Wales on everything to do with the language, while in 1994 a new Welsh Language Act gave equal validity to Welsh as a language for use in public-sector businesses.

If all this sounds almost too good to be true, there are those who would argue that this is indeed the case and that the cause of the Welsh language has been espoused by middle-class interlopers as a way of ensuring grants and jobs. There are also English visitors who get very hot under the collar when they visit Welsh-speaking areas and find themselves unable to understand what is being said.

For See also Welsh in the Language chapter at the back of the book.

Cardiff (Caerdydd)

☎ 029 • pop 285,000

As Glasgow did in the early 1990s, the Welsh capital is busy reinventing itself as 'the fastest growing capital city in Europe'. Much of the city is currently under redevelopment but this shouldn't put you off visiting. Cardiff has a striking city-centre castle, a world-class museum and art gallery, a renovated docks area, and pockets of beautiful architecture.

The giant freshwater marina in Cardiff Bay was completed in March 2000 and is open to visitors. However, environmentalists point out that this is at the price of losing the mud flats that have traditionally provided feeding grounds for thousands of wading birds. Another major project has been the impressive 75,000-seater Millennium Stadium built for the Rugby World Cup in November 1999. Sadly, plans for architect Zaha Hadid's opera house, designed as a dazzling 'crystal necklace' of glass, were scotched by a campaign orchestrated by the local press. A more conservative multipurpose building will take the place of the one that could have done for Cardiff what the Opera House did for Sydney.

Cardiff is a good base for visiting a few sites in the surrounding area, including the Rhondda Heritage Park, the Museum of Welsh Life at St Fagans, the castles at Caerphilly and Castell Coch and the Big Pit Mining Museum at Blaenavon. Transport links are good, with the M4 linking Cardiff to Swansea and Bristol.

HISTORY

The Romans first settled the area to the east of the River Taff, but once they pulled out of Britain the site, it seems, became abandoned until after the Norman conquest. Robert Fitzhamon was responsible for the motte and bailey castle, remains of which still stand in the grounds of the later Cardiff Castle. Throughout the Middle Ages there was a settlement at Cardiff (St John's Church in the city centre is a reminder of this period) but it was very small; even in 1801, the census figures suggest barely 1000 people lived here.

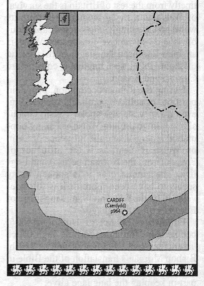

Cardiff really owes its development to coal mining in the valleys to the north. In 1839, the marquis of Bute had the first docks built in Cardiff, and the Bute family, who owned much of the land on which coal had been found, were able to insist all exported coal was traded through their ports. Cardiff boomed, and by the end of the 19th century there were probably about 170,000 people living here. However, hard times returned in the 20th century, especially during the slump of the 1930s. The city was also badly damaged by bombs during WWII, which explains some of the nastier modern development in the centre. The South Wales coal industry has now disappeared – the last mines seen off in the years since the catastrophic 1984 strike.

It was only in 1955 that Cardiff was designated the capital of Wales, a status that brought it renewed prosperity as government agencies concerned with Wales relocated their headquarters here. However, the docks couldn't recover their lost importance and it wasn't until the creation of the Cardiff Bay Development Corporation in 1987 that serious efforts were made to revive the area. With the new Welsh Assembly located by Cardiff Bay, it looks as if the revival is almost complete.

ORIENTATION

Cardiff originally grew up around Tiger Bay (now Cardiff Bay), about half an hour's uninspiring walk from town, but the city centre gradually migrated northwards as the port trade dried up.

The castle, at the northern end of the main thoroughfare (which includes St Mary and High Sts), acts as a useful landmark. Buses and trains arrive just off the southern end of the main thoroughfare. Behind the castle stretches Bute Park and opposite lies the main shopping area, where the most interesting places tend to be tucked away in the 19th- and early-20th-century arcades.

Cardiff Central train station is off Penarth Rd and the main bus terminal is right in front of it on Central Square. Some local train services leave from Cardiff Queen Street station to the east. Bute Street station is within walking distance of Cardiff Bay.

INFORMATION

The TIC (☎ 2022 7281, ⓔ enquiries@cardifftic.co.uk), Wood St, opens 9 am to 6 pm daily (10 am to 6 pm Tuesday and 10 am to 4 pm Sunday).

The TIC sells the Cardiff Card (£12), which gives two days' unlimited travel on buses and Valley Lines trains and admission to the National Gallery, Techniquest, the Big Pit and Rhondda Heritage Park. It also offers free and reduced admission to other attractions and discounts at some restaurants.

The main post office is at The Hayes, near St David's Shopping Centre.

You can leave luggage at the train station for £3 an item.

There is a branch of Campus Travel (☎ 2022 0744), 13 Castle St, inside the YHA Adventure Shop.

Buzz is a useful free bimonthly magazine with up-to-date event listings in the city; it's available from the TIC and cafes. For current gig, cinema and arts listings, check out the Web site www.virtualcardiff.co.uk.

Email and Internet Access

Free Internet access is available at Cardiff central library (☎ 2038 2116), Frederick St. It opens 9 am to 5.30 pm Monday to Saturday (until 6.30 pm on Thursday and 5 pm on Saturday); booking is advisable.

There are several Internet cafes around charging roughly the same rate. In the centre, Cardiff Internet Cafe, 15–17 Wyndham Arcade, charges £3.50 hourly and opens 9 am to 9 pm daily.

Laundry

Fabricare laundrette (☎ 2039 6556), 164 Clare Rd, opens 9 am to 5.30 pm daily.

Medical Services

Pharmacies rotate late opening hours; check local papers for details. Boots (☎ 2023 1291), 36 Queen St, opens until 8 pm on Thursday.

The University Hospital of Wales (☎ 2074 7747), Heath Park, slightly to the north of the city centre, has an accident and emergency department.

CARDIFF CASTLE

It would be hard to miss the castle, which is ringed by a low wall with sculpted bears, lions and wolves crawling all over it. Although excavations on the site indicate it was first occupied by the Romans, the first substantial remains (a motte and bailey castle) date back to Norman times. However, the present Cardiff Castle is much newer. It was designed for the third Lord Bute by the Victorian architect William Burges (1827–81),

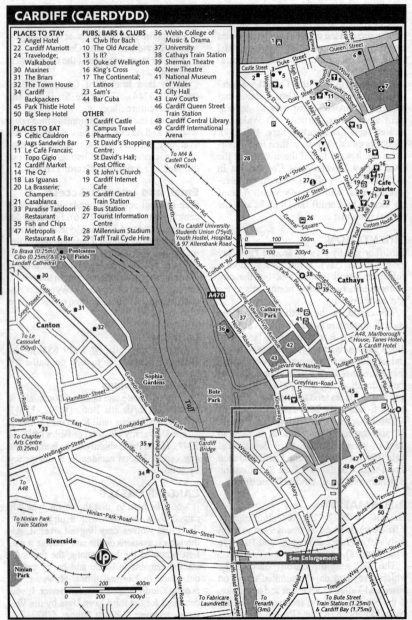

CARDIFF (CAERDYDD)

PLACES TO STAY
2 Angel Hotel
22 Cardiff Marriott
24 Travelodge;
   Walkabout
30 Maxines
31 The Briars
32 The Town House
34 Cardiff
   Backpackers
45 Park Thistle Hotel
50 Big Sleep Hotel

PLACES TO EAT
5 Celtic Cauldron
9 Jags Sandwich Bar
11 Le Café Francais;
   Topo Gigio
12 Cardiff Market
14 The Oz
18 Las Iguanas
20 La Brasserie;
   Champers
21 Casablanca
33 Paradise Tandoori
   Restaurant
35 Fish and Chips
47 Metropolis
   Restaurant & Bar

PUBS, BARS & CLUBS
4 Clwb Ifor Bach
10 The Old Arcade
13 Is It?
15 Duke of Wellington
16 King's Cross
17 The Continental;
   Latinos
23 Sam's
44 Bar Cuba

OTHER
1 Cardiff Castle
3 Campus Travel
6 Pharmacy
7 St David's Shopping
   Centre;
   St David's Hall;
   Post Office
8 St John's Church
19 Cardiff Internet
   Cafe
25 Cardiff Central
   Train Station
26 Bus Station
27 Tourist Information
   Centre
28 Millennium Stadium
29 Taff Trail Cycle Hire

36 Welsh College of
   Music & Drama
37 University
38 Cathays Train Station
39 Sherman Theatre
40 New Theatre
41 National Museum
   of Wales
42 City Hall
43 Law Courts
46 Cardiff Queen Street
   Train Station
48 Cardiff Central Library
49 Cardiff International
   Arena

who specialised in Victorian Gothic. The outrageous interior is now more Hollywood than medieval, but you'll only get to explore the Banqueting Hall, the Arab Room and the Fairytale Nursery on a guided tour.

The castle (☎ 2087 8100) opens 9.30 am to 6 pm daily, March to October, with tours at 20-minute intervals. In winter, the grounds open 9.30 am to 4.30 pm, but there are only five daily tours, the first at 10.30 am and the last at 3.15 pm. A visit and tour costs £5/3; to explore the grounds only costs £2.50/1.50.

NATIONAL MUSEUM OF WALES

In Cathays Park, the National Museum forms a pleasing turn-of-the-century grouping of grey-white buildings with the City Hall and the Law Courts. For anyone with children, this place is a must. There's also a wonderful exhibition on the evolution of Wales, complete with mammoths that wave their trunks and waggle their ears.

The natural history galleries are also excellent; in particular, look out for the rooms housing the skeleton of a young humpback whale washed up near Aberthaw in 1982 and the remains of a giant leatherback turtle found dead on the beach at Harlech in 1988.

On the 4th floor is a magnificent collection of paintings, including Gwendoline and Margaret Davies' bequest of impressionist paintings, with some Monet *Water Lilies* and works by Sisley, Pisarro, Manet and Degas. There's also a version of Rodin's *The Kiss* and an even nicer model of *The Earth and the Moon*.

The museum (☎ 2039 7951) opens 10 am to 5 pm, Tuesday to Sunday. Admission costs £4.50/2.65.

ST JOHN'S CHURCH

Jutting up incongruously from the tacky shopping precinct surrounding it is the graceful 15th-century tower of St John's Church. The church is a retreat from the bustle outside and one of the few reminders of Cardiff's pre-Victorian past.

CARDIFF BAY

The area once called Tiger Bay is now more prosaically named Cardiff Bay. The fast-developing new bay area is rather soulless, with bars and restaurants popping up in designated units almost overnight, but time will probably instil a more amenable atmosphere.

The most striking edifice is the Pierhead Building, a huge, red-brick, Victorian masterpiece. A little away from the bay itself, off James St, is Mount Stuart Square, which has some imposing Victorian architecture. It's a haven of restored grandeur amid the general drabness of Butetown. The National Assembly is also based in Cardiff Bay, although ongoing plans for an extension to the current building are in question.

Bus No 8 runs from the city centre to Cardiff Bay, or you can get a train to Bute Street station and walk.

Techniquest

The UK's largest hands-on science exhibition, Techniquest (☎ 2047 5475), is on the waterfront. It has everything from a machine that blows smoke rings to a wet area with exhibits pertaining to liquid. There's also a planetarium and science theatre.

It opens 9.30 am to 4.30 pm, Monday to Friday and 10.30 am to 5 pm at weekends. Admission costs £5.50/3.80. Visit the Web site at www.tquest.org.uk.

Cardiff Bay Visitors Centre

Little more than a way of soft-soaping visitors into buying the Cardiff Bay Development Corporation's view of things, the visitors centre is at least housed in an imaginative building (a long white tube that acts like a giant telescope overlooking the bay). Admission is free and it opens 9.30 am to 4.30 pm, Monday to Friday, and 10.30 am to 5 pm at weekends.

LLANDAFF CATHEDRAL

If Cardiff seems too busy and brash for comfort, hop on bus No 133 or 65X along Cathedral Rd to Llandaff, a peaceful, pretty northern suburb where Llandaff Cathedral sits in a dip in the landscape.

Dating from 1130, it was largely rebuilt in the 19th century, and extensively restored again after being damaged by a land mine in 1941. The west-end towers epitomise the cathedral's fragmented history: one was built in the 15th century, the other in the 19th. Nowadays, the most striking internal feature is the giant central arch carrying the organ and Jacob Epstein's striking *Majestas*. Fans of the Pre-Raphaelites will be interested in the Burne-Jones reredos in St Dyfrig's chapel and the stained glass by Rossetti and William Morris' company. Outside, the heads of the British monarchs are carved along the top of the southern aisle wall; look out for the uncrowned head of Edward VIII, who abdicated before his coronation.

ORGANISED TOURS

During the summer, hop-on hop-off, open-top bus tours, run by Guide Friday (☎ 2038 4291), circle 11 points around the city, from Llandaff in the north to Cardiff Bay in the south. Tickets cost £7/2.50 (£5.50 for students) and give you a 10% discount at Cardiff Castle. Tours leave from Cardiff Castle and if you stay on the bus for the whole tour, it takes one hour.

PLACES TO STAY
Hostels

At *Cardiff Youth Hostel* (☎ 2046 2303, 2 Wedal Rd, Roath Park) a bed costs £13.50/10.20 for adults/under-18s and includes breakfast. It opens daily, January to November. The hostel is 2 miles north of the city centre – bus Nos 78, 80 and 82 run this way from Cardiff Central train station.

Cardiff Backpackers (☎ 2034 5577, 98 Neville St, Riverside) is an independent hostel less than a mile from the train and bus stations. The cheapest beds are in small dorms (£13.50), but singles (£20), doubles (£35) and triples (£41) are also available. A light breakfast is included, and there's also a bar. 'Cleanest backpackers' place I've ever stayed in,' said one visitor. It's well run and popular so book ahead. The Backpacker Bus Company (☎ 2066 6900) is also based here.

B&Bs & Hotels

Cardiff has the usual range of B&Bs from around £18 per head; most of them can be found along Cathedral Rd, to the west, and

Newport Rd, to the east. Cathedral Rd is a leafy avenue, less than 10 minutes' walk from the city centre.

Maxines (☎ 2022 0288, 150 Cathedral Rd) does B&B from £18/38 for a single/double. Rooms at *The Briars* (☎ 2034 0881, 126 Cathedral Rd) are similarly priced.

On Newport Rd, good bets are the *Tanes Hotel* (☎ 2049 3898, 148 Newport Rd), where beds cost £18/32, or the simple but clean *Cardiff Hotel* (☎ 2049 1964, 138 Newport Rd), where basic rooms start from £21/33. Out of season, many hotels along these two roads bring their prices down – look for offers in the windows.

A quieter option is the guesthouse at *97 Allensbank Rd* (☎ 2062 1230) in Heath, to the north, where rooms cost £20/36.

Mid-range hotels are also concentrated in Cathedral and Newport Rds. *The Town House* (☎ 2023 9399, 70 Cathedral Rd) is a comfortable, friendly place to stay. All rooms have a bathroom and cost £39.50/49.50. *Marlborough House* (☎ 2049 2385, 98 Newport Rd) has rooms for £39/49 with bathroom.

The modern, new, no-frills *Big Sleep Hotel* (☎ 2063 6363, Bute Terrace), opposite the Cardiff International Arena, charges £58 per room mid-week or £45 at weekends, including light breakfast. The chain hotel *Travelodge* (☎ 2039 8697, Imperial Gate, St Mary St) charges £49.95 per room mid-week and £39.95 at weekends.

The *Cardiff Marriott* (☎ 2039 9944, Mill Lane) is centrally located by the Cafe Quarter. Rooms cost £99 during the week, £82 at weekends for doubles.

The *Angel Hotel* (☎ 2023 2633, Castle St), opposite the castle, has grand public rooms and charges £105/120. At weekends, however, B&B costs £78 for a double. The *Park Thistle Hotel* (☎ 2038 3471, Park Place), off Queen St shopping centre, is conveniently located and charges from £73/82 (breakfast costs extra).

The St David's Hotel & Spa (☎ 2045 4045, Havannah St), in the bay, is a plush, new hotel with a striking, minimalist foyer and rooms from £130/160 (breakfast costs extra). They also offer leisure breaks.

PLACES TO EAT

The best French restaurant in Cardiff is *Le Cassoulet* (☎ 2022 1905, 5 Romilly Crescent), off Llandaff Rd, in the west of the city. Start your evening with one of the excellent cocktails. Set lunches cost £12.50/15 for two/three courses. In the evening there's an a la carte menu (£13 to £18 per dish). It's open Tuesday to Saturday.

The classy bistro style *Metropolis Restaurant & Bar* (☎ 2034 4300, 60 Charles St) has an interesting menu. Seared tuna costs £12.55 and there are also two-course set lunches for £7.95.

La Brasserie and *Champers* (☎ 2037 2164, 2037 3363, 60–61 St Mary St), two informal restaurants run by the same management, offer a range of Spanish, French and Welsh food, balanced with a good choice of seafood.

New restaurants and bars seem to spring up overnight in the developing Cardiff Bay area. The main thoroughfare is the decked Mermaid Quay, overlooking the Oval Basin. *Via Fossa* (☎ 2045 0947) is a bright, open-plan Italian restaurant with pasta from £7 or steaks for £12. Adjacent to it, *De:Alto* (☎ 2049 1882) serves reasonable Mediterranean cuisine, including pizza from £5.35 which is baked in a wood-burning oven. Around the corner on Stuart St, *Wood's Brasserie* (☎ 2049 2400, Pilotage Building, Stuart St), in an old stone house, is a stylish restaurant with a terrace. Mains, such as corn-fed chicken in chilli and ginger, cost £11.95. They also do a reasonable lunch menu.

Mill Lane, in the town centre, has been dubbed Cardiff's Cafe Quarter and although it only stretches around 50m, several lively places to eat and drink there give the area a vibrant atmosphere. *Las Iguanas* (☎ 2022 6373, 8 Mill Lane) is a Mexican joint with two cocktail bars and main courses from £10 to £12. It has live music every night and opens until 2 am at weekends. *Casablanca* (☎ 2064 1441, 3 Mill Lane) is a Morroccan/Iberian restaurant with tapas for £3 or main courses from £8.

On Church St, just off High St, there are any number of eating options. Opposite St John's Church is *Le Café Francais* (☎ 2064 5188), where the baguette fillings are tasty and imaginative. The *Jags Sandwich Bar* (☎ 2022 0993, Church St) also has a good selection of baguettes, such as hot roast turkey for £2.75. Cardiff's strong Italian community guarantees plenty of pizza and pasta places to choose from. *Topo Gigio* (☎ 2034 4794, 12 Church St) is a lively spot with a traditional array of pizza and pasta from £6.95.

Immediately opposite the castle is the *Celtic Cauldron* (☎ 2038 7185, Castle Arcade), where you can sample traditional Welsh dishes including *laver bread* (seaweed), *cawl* (thick vegetable broth) and oatmeal pancakes. For good pub grub or a carnivorous all-day breakfast, try antipodean *The Oz* (☎ 2066 8008, 112 St Mary St). Lunch specials cost only £3.

Head to Cardiff's Tudor St for an unlimited selection of Chinese restaurants and Cowbridge Rd East in Canton for Indian. The reasonable *Paradise Tandoori Restaurant* (☎ 2022 7131, 207 Cowbridge Rd East) is recommended.

Just off Cathedral Rd, check out the delicious, inventive sandwiches at *Brava* (☎ 2037 1929, 71 Pontcanna St). Nearby, *Cibo* (☎ 2023 2226, 83 Pontcanna St) is an Italian cafe bar with good fresh coffee and Italian fare to eat in or take away.

Also in Cardiff Bay, the reconstructed *Norwegian Church Arts Centre* (☎ 2045 4899, Harbour Drive), near the visitors centre, has been converted from a church to an arts centre and coffee shop, doing excellent cakes, waffles and sandwiches. The author Roald Dahl was christened here.

If you're on a tight budget, head for *Cardiff Market* in The Hayes, where there are several snack bars. The market is the place to come if you're after cheese, cold meats, laver bread and rolls for a picnic. Convenient for Cardiff Backpackers, there's always *Fish and Chips* (Lower Cathedral Rd).

ENTERTAINMENT
Pubs & Bars

The local brew is Brains SA (Special Ale or Skull Attack depending on how many pints you have). There are numerous places to try it. The Wellington *(Mill Lane)* is in the centre of the so-called Cafe Quarter (otherwise known as Drunk's Alley).

The **King's Cross** (☎ 2064 9891, *Mill Lane)* is a busy gay bar. **Walkabout** (☎ 2072 7930, *65 St Mary's St)* is a cavernous Australian bar, usually thronged with students at weekends, when they have live music. The downstairs pub at the *Angel Hotel* (☎ 2023 2633, *Castle St)* is another popular student hang out. **Is It?** (☎ 2041 3600, *12 Wharton St)*, in the town centre, is a trendy cafe-style bar with mezzanine and DJs at weekends. For hectic pre-club drinks, try **Bar Cuba** (☎ 2039 7967, *The Friary)*, just off Queen St. **Bar 38** (☎ 2049 4375, *Mermaid Quay)* is a fashionable, new watering hole for Cardiff's young socialites, in the nascent bay area.

The Old Arcade (☎ 2023 1740, *Church St)* is a decent traditional pub just off Lower Cathedral Rd.

Clubs

For upcoming DJ and live events, check out *Buzz.* **Clwb Ifor Bach** (☎ 2023 2199, *11 Womanby St)* has three floors and hosts various club nights from hip-hop and house to jungle and even live rock on Monday nights. They have a Welsh-speaking bar downstairs for members and guests. **Sam's** (☎ 2034 5189, *Mill Lane)* opens until 2 am every night and has DJs Monday to Wednesday with live music on other nights. The *Cardiff University Students Union* (☎ 2038 7421, *Park Place)* holds regular live events open to non-students; ring for details. Not for the faint-hearted, *The Continental* (☎ 2064 5000, *Mill Lane)* is a noisy restaurant/bar which doubles as club *Latinos* after 9.30 pm. There is live music on Sunday nights.

Other Entertainment

Cardiff's best-known entertainment is rugby. International matches and sometimes local fixtures take place at the new *Millennium Stadium* (☎ 0990-582582, *Westgate St)*. Real enthusiasts can visit the stadium grounds and sit in the VIP box or walk from the dressing rooms, down the tunnel to the pitch for a mere £5/£2.50. Guided tours are available 9 am to 5 pm daily (from 10 am on Sunday). Visit on-line at www.millennium stadium-plc.co.uk.

If you're after something less frenetic in somewhat warmer surroundings, *St David's Hall* (☎ 2087 8444, *The Hayes)* offers a full range of theatrical and musical events, in

Welsh Rugby

Although the Welsh play conventional football, it's really rugby union that fires the soul of most sporting enthusiasts. During the 1970s, the Welsh national team was immensely successful, winning six out of 10 Five Nations Championships. Since then, however, things haven't gone quite so swimmingly, and in 1991 Wales went down to ignominious defeat (63–6) at the hands of Australia. Despite this, Wales did win the 1994 Five Nations Championship, in which Wales, England, Scotland, Ireland and France competed against each other. Perhaps Wales' fortunes will rise again (like France's did when it held the World Cup football finals in 1998) since hosting the 1999 Rugby World Cup in Cardiff, where the team reached the quarter final under then new manager Graham Henry. Indeed, a memorable victory against South Africa in June that year and a placing of fourth in the inaugural Six Nations championship will have renewed confidence in the team and Henry's abilities. And a glorious win over the Barbarians, at the Millennium Stadium in May 2000, only served to consolidate their position even more.

If you'd like to see Wales play, the team's home is the Millennium Stadium, on the grounds of the former Cardiff Arms Park, in the centre of Cardiff. Tickets for normal fixtures are easy to obtain at reasonable prices (around £10 to £25; phone ☎ 0990-582582 for details), although those for big events sell out months in advance of the match.

The most successful club sides are Cardiff, Swansea, Neath and Llanelli, and you can catch their matches between September and Easter. Most of the former mining valley towns also have their own sides.

For more information about rugby union visit the official Web site at www.wru.co.uk.

allegedly one of the best acoustic auditoriums in Europe. It hosts the Welsh proms every July. There are also two smaller theatres, the *Sherman Theatre* (☎ 2023 0451, *Senghennydd Rd, Cathays)*, which offers comedy as well as drama, and the *New Theatre* (☎ 2087 8889, *Park Place)*, currently the home of the Welsh National Opera.

Most imaginative cinema programmes tend to be shown at the *Chapter Arts Centre* (☎ 2031 1050, *Market Rd, Canton)*, popular with students. To get there catch bus No 12, 14 or 16.

Regular classical music concerts are staged at St David's Hall, with less frequent ones in Llandaff Cathedral and St John's Church. The *Cardiff International Arena* (☎ 2022 4488, *Mary Ann St)* and the new Millennium Stadium host large-scale pop concerts. Stately *Coal Exchange* (☎ 2033 0220, *Mount Stuart Square)*, in the bay, has occasional gigs.

GETTING THERE & AWAY

Cardiff is 155 miles from London, 50 miles from Bristol and 48 miles from Swansea.

Air

Cardiff airport (☎ 01446-711111) is 12 miles south-west of the centre.

Bus

National Express coaches (☎ 0990 808 080) run between London Victoria station and Cardiff (from £13 single, 3¼ hours, every two hours). There are hourly services linking Cardiff and Bristol (£5, hourly). Via Birmingham, there are services between Cardiff and Llandudno (£36.25, 7¼ hours, twice-daily) and Cardiff and Rhyl (£35.25, 6½ hours). There are frequent services to Bristol (£5) and two to Bath (£10.50).

The First Cymru Shuttle (☎ 0870 608 2608) links Cardiff with Swansea (£6.50 single/return, one hour, almost hourly). Bicycles are taken free. The Traws Cambria 701 connects Cardiff with Holyhead (£20, nine hours, daily) via Swansea, Aberystwyth, Caernarfon and Bangor. For more information, contact Arriva Cymru (☎ 0870 608 2608).

Train

Intercity trains run from London to Cardiff (£43.50 single, £20.50 booked in advance, two hours, hourly) and Cardiff to Swansea (£7.80, one hour, every 20 minutes). Regional Railways' Alphaline also has direct services between Cardiff and London Waterloo, timed to connect with international services through the Channel Tunnel.

Direct hourly train services connect Cardiff and Manchester, Liverpool (change at Crewe), Birmingham, Nottingham and the ports at Portsmouth and Southampton. Trains to Chester continue to Holyhead (£51.20) for Dun Laoghaire. There are trains connecting Cardiff and Pembroke Dock via Tenby (£13.90, four hours, four daily), Milford Haven via Haverfordwest (£13.90, three hours, six daily), and Fishguard Harbour (for Rosslare, £13.90, 2½ hours, one daily).

Cardiff Valley Lines' services (from Cardiff Central or Queen Street) link Cardiff with Merthyr Tydfil, Aberdare, Pontypridd, Treherbert, Rhymney and Coryton. The free bus map from Cardiff Bus Office includes a map of the valley rail routes.

Car & Motorcycle

The M4 loops round Cardiff, linking it to Swansea, Bristol and London. The Peripheral Distributor Rd across Cardiff Bay provides direct links to the M4, bypassing the city centre.

Boat

In summer, you can get to Penarth, 3 miles from Cardiff, on the *Balmoral* or *Waverley* ships operating from Bristol.

GETTING AROUND

Cardiff's sights are scattered around the city, so walking is only really recommended to get around the centre, parts of which are pedestrianised.

Bus

Orange and white Cardiff Bus services provide quick, cheap access to many parts of town. Most want exact fares; the only way you'll get any change is to ask for a change ticket and either use it on another service or wait two days before cashing it in at the city bus office.

Network Rider tickets (£4.50) are available all day and can be used to travel around the city centre and get to Penarth, Castell Coch, St Fagans, Llandaff and Cardiff Bay.

Cardiff Bus Office (☎ 2066 6444), Wood St, is in St David's House right in front of the bus terminal. Its excellent free map shows not just the city bus routes, but also the local train lines too.

Train

There are local train stations at Queen St, Cathays, Llandaff, Ninian Park and Bute Rd (for the bay).

Car

Parking in the centre of Cardiff is usually subject to restriction. Many places require

you to display vouchers, which you need to buy in advance from local shops. An 80p voucher lasts one hour. Car hire is available from Hertz (☎ 2022 4548).

Taxi

You can usually flag taxis on the street, or try Capital Cabs (☎ 2077 7777).

Bicycle

Cardiff is at the southern end of the Welsh National Cycle Route, Lôn Las Cymru, which runs the length of Wales to end in Holyhead, Anglesey. From Cardiff the route follows the Taff Trail (see Brecon Beacons National Park in the Mid Wales chapter).

Taff Trail Cycle Hire (☎ 2039 8362), off Cathedral Rd, is by the Cardiff Caravan Park. Bike rental costs £8 per day. It has some adapted bikes for disabled cyclists.

South Wales

Stretching from the Wye Valley on the border with England, westwards to Pembrokeshire, this area includes the capital of Wales (Cardiff), the second-largest town in Wales (Swansea) and the 230-sq-mile expanse of the Pembrokeshire Coast National Park.

The south coast from Newport to Swansea is heavily industrialised, but there are still stretches of beautiful coastline such as the Glamorgan Heritage Coast. This protected coastline stretches 14 miles from Aberthaw to Porthcawl.

The valleys running northwards into the Black Mountains and the Brecon Beacons National Park are still struggling to come to grips with the loss of the coal-mining industry. Even so, the little villages that form a continuous chain along the valleys have their own stark beauty, more attractive now that the old slag heaps are being grassed over, and the people are particularly friendly.

The Pembrokeshire Coast National Park is the only largely coastal national park in Britain – it's also the smallest. Despite many scenic attractions in the area, only the places on the milder southern part of the coastline have been developed into tourist resorts – the more exposed north coast is still virtually unspoilt and offers some of the best walking in Britain.

South-Eastern Wales

This part of the country contains over half the population and most of Wales' factories. Hidden among the urban sprawl, however, are some interesting places. There's the Wye Valley and, between the traditional market town of Monmouth and the dramatically located castle at Chepstow, there are the scenic ruins of Tintern Abbey.

To the west is Cardiff, a fast-developing city. The Welsh are proudly defensive of their capital, which has been rapidly transformed

Highlights

- Spending an afternoon at the Museum of Welsh Life at St Fagans
- Visiting the Wye Valley and Tintern Abbey
- Exploring the National Botanic Garden
- Seeing the Dylan Thomas Boathouse
- Discovering the Pembrokeshire Coast National Park
- Browsing around the town of St David's

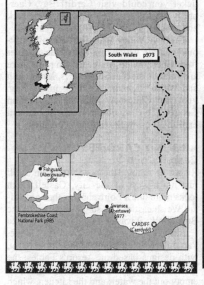

South Wales p973

Fishguard
(Abergwaun)
p996

Pembrokeshire Coast
National Park p985

Swansea
(Abertawe)
p977

CARDIFF ☉
(Caerdydd)

from a dull provincial backwater into a prosperous university city with an increasingly lively arts scene (see the Cardiff chapter).

Swansea was where the poet and writer Dylan Thomas grew up. It's the gateway to the Gower, a sparsely populated peninsula with long, sandy beaches and attractive cliff scenery.

GETTING AROUND

Bus and train services are good in this part of Wales, although the country's mountainous

SOUTH WALES

geography means that direct journeys from South to North Wales are tricky and time-consuming. For information on bus services in Wales, phone ☎ 0870 608 2608.

First Cymru's (☎ 0870 608 2608) Rover-bus Day Saver ticket costs £4.80 and is valid for a day's travel throughout South Wales. It's not valid on the Cardiff-Swansea Shuttle but you can use it on the slow X1 service between Cardiff and Swansea.

For rail information, phone ☎ 0845 748 4950. Cardiff Valley Lines has a one-day unlimited Day Ranger ticket for £5.50/2.75 for adults/children allowing rail travel in the Cardiff area and the valleys. On this ticket you could visit Cardiff Bay, Caerphilly Castle, the Rhondda Heritage Park and along the Rivers Taff and Rhymney.

The Wye Valley Walk is a 107-mile way-marked trail, which runs alongside the river from Chepstow to Rhayader. En route there are youth hostels at St Briavels, Monmouth and Welsh Bicknor. For more information visit the Chepstow Tourist Information Centre (TIC), which also has a permanent exhibition on walks in the Wye Valley.

AROUND CARDIFF
Castell Coch
Rising up among the beech trees on a hill just north-west of the city, Castell Coch looks more like a Loire chateau than a standard Welsh castle. The summer retreat of the Bute family, it was designed by Burges (like Cardiff Castle) in gaudy Victorian Gothic. Particularly interesting are the sitting room, with designs based on Aesop's Fables; the bedroom, which has a sink that swings up to empty out the water; and the kitchen, which has a fine Welsh dresser.

Castell Coch (☎ 029-2081 0101) is run by Cadw, the Welsh historic monuments agency, and opens 9.30 am to 6 pm daily in summer (to 4 pm in winter). Admission costs £2.50/2. Cardiff Bus No 26 will take you to Tong-wynlais and it's 10 minutes' walk from there.

Caerphilly Castle
Nine miles north of Cardiff, Caerphilly is a fairytale ruined medieval castle complete with moat – although its setting is somewhat

marred by the ugly development of Caerphilly itself, right on its doorstep.

The castle was built in stages between 1268 and 1277 by Gilbert de Clare, under constant threat of attack from Prince Llywelyn. It has a long external wall with a gatehouse opening onto a causeway over the moat. This leads to the keep, which stands on a platform. The castle was in a dismal state in the 19th century, when the Bute family offered funds to restore it to its present state.

Caerphilly Castle (☎ 029-2088 3143; Cadw) opens 9.30 am to 6 pm daily, Easter to October; 9.30 am to 4 pm, Monday to Saturday and 11 am to 4 pm on Sunday, in winter. Admission costs £2.50/2. Caerphilly train station is a quarter of a mile from the castle. There are frequent trains or you can get there on bus Nos 71 and 72.

Museum of Welsh Life at St Fagans
Four miles west of Cardiff along the A4232, St Fagans is a small village with a vast tourist attraction. The 40-hectare museum is a collection of 30 reconstructed buildings brought from all over the country. Among them are a tollhouse, a cockpit, a chapel and assorted houses, cottages, and a row of Victorian shops brought here from the valleys.

Craftspeople still work in many of the buildings, allowing visitors to see how clogs, barrels, cider and wooden artefacts were made. In the grounds, you can also see examples of peculiarly Welsh breeds of livestock and poultry. History is regularly brought to life here, especially on public holidays when the site can get horribly cluttered with families tucking into hot lamb sandwiches.

The museum (☎ 029-2057 3500) opens 10 am to 6 pm daily (to 5pm in winter). Admission costs £5.50/3.20. Cardiff Bus Nos 32, 32A and 32B run to St Fagans from Cardiff Central bus station.

Penarth
A relatively demure seaside resort, Penarth has a Victorian pier from which you can take

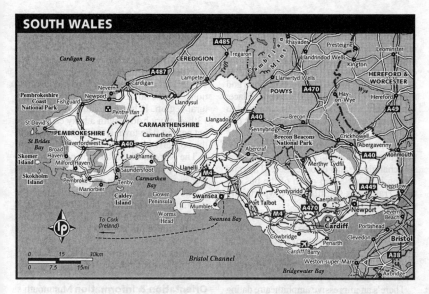

SOUTH WALES

summer boat trips across to England – to Clevedon, Minehead, Ilfracombe and many other destinations. Some trips are on the last surviving operational paddle steamer, PS *Waverley*. For details of boat departures, phone ☎ 01446-720656.

In Penarth, you can visit the **Turner House Gallery**, an offshoot of the National Museum of Wales, which displays *objets d'art* and touring exhibitions.

You can get to Penarth on Cardiff Bus Nos P1, P2, P3, P4 and P5 or by train (£1.50, 11 minutes, three per hour).

Barry
☎ 029 • pop 45,000

Eight miles west of Cardiff, Barry is an uninspiring dormitory town for commuters to the capital. If you've got children, however, Barry does boast a **Pleasure Beach** (a funfair modelled on Blackpool), a **Play Centre** and a **Quasar Centre**. Trains from Cardiff run directly to the fair (get off at Barry Island station, £2.50, 17 minutes, three per hour) and Cardiff Bus offers hourly services (No 354) from Cardiff Central station. In summer, pleasure boats link Barry with Bristol across the Bristol Channel.

Rhondda Valley & Heritage Park

If you're interested in the industrial history of the valleys, don't miss the Rhondda Heritage Park, 10 miles north-west of Cardiff, between Pontypridd and Porth. This was the centre of the coal-mining industry in South Wales; the Heritage Park is built on the site of Lewis Merthyr colliery, which closed in 1983. Here, an exhibition brings the old colliery buildings back to life and tries to explain what life was like for those who worked here and their families. You can descend in a cage to the coalface, with a retired miner as your guide.

The park (☎ 01443-682036) is a half-hour train ride north from Cardiff Central station. The site opens 10 am to 6 pm daily (except Monday from October to Easter). Admission costs £5.60/4.30.

Newport
☎ 01633 • pop 148,000

Newport is a busy industrial and commercial centre, one of the biggest in Wales.

The TIC (☎ 842962, ✉ newport-tic@tsww.com), John Frost Square, is opposite the southern end of the bus station, in the same building as the museum and art gallery.

The **town museum** has interesting displays on the Roman fortress of Caerleon and on the history of mining in the area. Also of interest is **Tredagar House**, a restored 17th-century mansion set in a park on the western outskirts of the town. The legendary pub and rock venue TJ's (☎ 216608), Clarence Place, is allegedly where Kurt Cobain proposed to Courtney Love. The Newport Centre (☎ 662 662), Kingsway, hosts big pop concerts.

The fact that Newport is a major transport junction means that you may find yourself changing trains or buses here. The train station is about 500m north of the bus station. Trains link Cardiff and Newport daily until just before midnight.

Caerleon Roman Fortress

At Caerleon, 4 miles north of Newport, is the most important Roman site in Wales. It was known as Isca in Roman times, after the River Usk that flows past the town.

There's an impressive amphitheatre dating from AD 90, fortress baths and the only legionary barracks on display in Europe. There are excellent displays in the Roman Legionary Museum (☎ 423134; Cadw). It's all very well presented and well worth a visit.

The amphitheatre is always open and is free. Joint admission to the baths and museum costs £3.30 for adults. The museum is free for children but entry to the baths costs £1.50. The museum opens 10 am to 5 pm Monday to Saturday and 2 to 5 pm Sunday.

WYE VALLEY

The River Wye flows 154 miles from its source at Plynlimon in central Wales to meet the River Severn at Chepstow. From the mossy spring where the water rises, it runs through the mountains to Rhayader, past Glasbury and Builth Wells, on through Hay-on-Wye (see Brecon Beacons National Park in the Central Wales chapter), Hereford and Ross-on-Wye (see Herefordshire & Worcestershire in the Central England chapter) and down through Monmouth, past the picturesque ruins of Tintern Abbey, to Chepstow. The Wye Valley Walk (see Getting Around earlier in the chapter) follows the river from Rhayader to Chepstow, and the section of the river from Monmouth to Chepstow is particularly attractive.

Monmouth
☎ 01600 • pop 12,000

While Monmouth is a town of few distinctions, it's the attractive centre of an agricultural region. It has a beautiful and unique 13th-century bridge with a busy cattle market nearby. The town is on the Welsh side of the border with England.

The Normans built a castle on the town's easily defended site. It was the birthplace of Henry V but was later destroyed and Great Castle House, still standing, was built from its stones. Occupied by both Royalists and Roundheads during the Civil War, Monmouth subsequently became the county town of Monmouthshire, prospering from livestock and country markets, and as the site of the regular Assize Court.

Orientation & Information Monmouth's shape is governed by its position at the confluence of the Rivers Monnow, Wye and Trothy. The town is centred on Agincourt Square. From here, Monnow St, the principal thoroughfare and lined with shops, descends to the Monnow Bridge. Above the square, along a number of smaller lanes, are bookshops and pubs. The TIC (☎ 713899, ⓔ monmouth.tic@tsww.com) is under the portico of the Shire Hall on Agincourt Square. Monmouth hosts a renowned sailing regatta at the end of May each year. Contact the TIC for information.

Things to See & Do The symbol of the town is the **Monnow Bridge**, unique in Britain as the only complete example of a late-13th-century stone-gated bridge. Built as part of the city defences, it was also a toll bridge.

The centre of the town is **Agincourt Square**, an irregularly shaped hub with the arcade of the Shire Hall, built in 1724, on one side. In front of it is the **statue of Charles Rolls**, Monmouth son and co-founder of the Rolls-Royce car and aero-engine company.

The **Nelson Museum & Local History Centre** (☎ 713519), Priory St, houses an extraordinary collection of memorabilia relating to the great admiral, even though he had only the most tenuous of connections with the town. The collection includes letters to his mistress, Emma Hamilton. It opens 10 am to 5 pm, Monday to Saturday and 2 to 5 pm on Sunday. Admission costs £1/75p.

Places to Stay & Eat Beside the river and near the bridge is *Monnow Bridge Caravan & Camping* (☎ 714004, Drybridge St). It charges from £3.50 for a tent and one person.

There are many hotels in the surrounding area, but few in the town itself. *Bob's Place* (☎ 712600), over the cafe on Church St, charges £30/45 for singles/doubles – all rooms have a bathroom. The *Riverside Hotel* (☎ 715577, Cinderhill St) is the smartest place in town. It's just over the Monnow Bridge from the centre. Rooms with bathroom cost £48/68.

There are a number of places to eat around or near Agincourt Square. The *Punch House* (☎ 713855, Agincourt Sq) is an attractive pub. *Cygnet's Kitchen* (☎ 715555, White Swan Court), just off the square, does very good home-made soups and lunchtime fare; Roquefort and apple souffle costs £4.95 and you can sit on the patio in summer. For a more expensive and sophisticated meal, try the *French Horn Brasserie* (☎ 772733, 24 Church St). They do a mid-week, two-course special for £9.95.

Getting There & Away There are regular buses to Chepstow (No R69), Lydney and Coleford.

There's no train station but buses link Monmouth with the nearest stations at Hereford and Newport (16 miles, Monday to Saturday).

Tintern Abbey

The tall walls and empty, arched windows of this 14th-century Cistercian abbey on the edge of the River Wye have been painted by Turner and lauded by Wordsworth. It's one of the most beautiful ruins in the country. As a result, the village of Tintern swarms with visitors in summer. The abbey ruins are indeed an awe-inspiring sight, though

best visited towards the end of the day after the crowds have dispersed.

This Cistercian house was founded in 1131 by Walter de Clare, but the present building dates largely from the 14th century. It lasted until the dissolution and, compared to other religious sites that were laid to waste at this time, a remarkable amount remains.

The abbey (☎ 01291-689251; Cadw) opens 9.30 am to 6 pm daily, May to late October; 9.30 am to 4 pm Monday to Saturday and 11 am to 4 pm on Sunday, November to March. Admission costs £2.40/1.90.

The town follows the course of the River Wye with the abbey ruins located on the western bank. The TIC (☎ 01291-689566) is north of the town at the old station, a long walk from the abbey.

Stagecoach Red & White (☎ 01633-266336) bus No 69 runs every two hours between Chepstow and Monmouth, Monday to Saturday only. The Wye Wanderer runs on Sunday in summer.

Raglan Castle

Seven miles west of Monmouth on the road to Abergavenny, Raglan Castle is a very impressive and atmospheric ruin. Constructed in the 15th and 16th centuries, it was the last medieval castle to be built in the country. It's particularly interesting to see how castle design had evolved by this time to include flamboyant embellishments (such as the gargoyles and heraldic stonework on the gatehouse).

The castle (☎ 01291-690228) opens 9.30 am to 5 pm daily (to 4 pm in winter). Admission costs £2.40/1.90.

CHEPSTOW
☎ 01291 • pop 11,000

Just over the border from England, Chepstow is an attractive, small town near the confluence of the Rivers Wye and Severn. It's noted for its superb castle but is also well known for its racecourse. Although a day is certainly sufficient to explore the town, Chepstow is a good base from which to delve into the area.

Essentially a Norman town, Chepstow

(from Old English *chepe* and *stowe*, meaning marketplace) was developed as a base for the Norman conquest of south-eastern Wales. It later prospered as a port for the timber and wine trades, but as river-borne commerce declined so Chepstow's importance diminished to that of a typical market town.

Orientation & Information

The centre of Chepstow tapers upwards from the river in a wedge shape, with the castle on a bluff to the west and the A48 to the east. The main streets are Bridge, High and pedestrianised St Mary Sts. The TIC (☎ 623772, ℮ chepstow-tic@tswcom.com) is at the bottom of Bridge St, in the castle car park.

Things to See & Do

The main attraction is **Chepstow Castle**, which is fairly well preserved in its dramatic location on a cliff overlooking the River Wye – best seen as a whole from the English side of the river. Construction began in 1067, making it the first stone castle in Wales, perhaps in Britain – a sure sign of its importance. Its massive fortifications were added in the 12th century, followed by mostly domestic construction in the 13th century. Towards the end of the Civil War, it was used as a prison; by 1690, when the garrison was dispersed, it had become all but an irrelevance. The castle (☎ 624065; Cadw) opens 9.30 am to 6 pm daily (to 4 pm in winter). Admission costs £3/2.

The well-preserved, 13th-century city wall – the **Port Wall**, or Customs Wall – was built more as a means of controlling entry than for defence. It can best be seen from the main car park off Welsh St or in the vicinity of the train station. The Town Gate, originally part of the Port Wall, was much restored in the 16th century.

Chepstow Museum This museum (☎ 625 981) is near the TIC in an 18th-century town house. Mostly devoted to the history of the port, it also has a collection of 18th- and 19th-century prints and drawings of the Wye Valley. It opens 10.30 am to 1 pm and 2 to 5.30 pm Monday to Saturday, and 2 to 5.30 pm on Sunday. Admission is £1/free.

The handsome Wye River Bridge, made of iron, was built in 1816.

Places to Stay

Langcroft (☎ 625569, 71 St Kingsmark Ave) is a short walk from the centre and has rooms for £15.

There are several B&Bs and hotels along Bridge St. The *Afon Gwy Hotel* (☎ 620158) has rooms, with bathroom, overlooking the river for £36/49 for singles/doubles. The restaurant is recommended. The *Castle View Hotel* (☎ 620349, Bridge St) has rooms from £36.95/50.95 (breakfast is extra).

Mrs Potts (☎ 627173, Upper Sedbury House, Sedbury) is a mile outside town and does good B&B for £21.50/37. She has an outdoor swimming pool too.

The Beaufort Hotel (☎ 622497, Beaufort Sq) is centrally located and charges from £35/45.

The top place to stay is the *George* (☎ 625 363, Moor St), next to the city gate. The George dates back to 1610 and its comfortable rooms cost £70/80. There's also a weekend B&B rate of £45 per person.

Places to Eat

The restaurant at the *Afon Gwy Hotel* (see Places to Stay) is an excellent place to eat. There's a three-course set menu for £12.95.

The *Coach & Horses* (☎ 622626, Welsh St) does excellent pub grub, and bar meals are also available from the *Three Tuns Inn* (☎ 623497, 32 Bridge St), by the castle. The *Castle View Hotel* (see Places to Stay) offers substantial meals from around £10. *The Boat Inn* (☎ 628192, The Back) is in a lovely location overlooking the Wye and does good vegetarian food.

There's a *Pizza Express* (☎ 630572, 29 High St) or the brasserie-style *Classics* (☎ 623222, Nelson St) which does pasta and bakes from £8.95. *St Mary's Tea Rooms* (5 St Mary St) does very good snacks and well-priced meals and cakes.

Getting There & Away

Chepstow has good bus connections. Stagecoach Red & White (☎ 01633-266336) and Badgerline (☎ 0117-955 3231) run buses to

Bristol (£2.70, 50 minutes, hourly) from Chepstow bus station. No 69 goes to Monmouth via Tintern. No 73 goes to Newport (£3.40, 45 minutes, hourly), Gloucester (50 minutes, hourly) and Cardiff.

There are direct trains to Cardiff (£5.20, 40 minutes), Gloucester (£5.30, 30 minutes) and Newport.

SWANSEA (ABERTAWE)
☎ 01792 • pop 285,000

Swansea is the second-largest town in Wales, and the gateway to the superb coastal scenery of the Gower Peninsula.

Dylan Thomas grew up in Swansea and later called it an 'ugly, lovely town'. It certainly is in a lovely location on the bay, but some of the concrete developments here are distinctly ugly. Among all this, though, are attractions that make it worth pausing in Swansea, including an excellent maritime museum beside the regenerated dockland area, an interesting local art galley, a literary

centre and, around the bay at Mumbles, a mile of pubs that constitute one of the best pub crawls in Britain.

The Vikings named this area Sveins Ey (Swein's Island), probably referring to the sandbank in the mouth of the river. The Normans built the castle, but Swansea's heyday didn't come until the Industrial Revolution, when it rapidly developed into a centre for copper smelting. Ore was imported first from Cornwall, easily accessible across the Bristol Channel by boat. By the 19th century, this was Copperopolis – the world centre for the nonferrous-metal's refining industry. Ore came from Chile, Cuba and the USA, while Welsh coal was sold in return.

By the 20th century, the heavy-industry base of the town had declined but the oil refinery and numerous factories were still judged a worthy target for the Luftwaffe, which devastated the centre of Swansea in 1941.

SWANSEA (ABERTAWE)

PLACES TO STAY
2 Cefn Bryn
3 Crescent Guest House
6 Oystercatcher Hotel
7 Lyndale Hotel
8 Bayswater Hotel
13 Dolphin Hotel
20 Forte Posthouse
25 Swansea Grand Hotel

PLACES TO EAT
5 Joe's Ice Cream Parlour;
   Indian Restaurants
14 Swansea Market
15 Gershwin's Coffee
   House; La Baguette
19 Cafe Mambo

23 Expresso Bar
   Restaurant
26 Cafe Gelato
27 Monkey Cafe Bar
30 Supermarket
32 Hwyrnos
34 Ask
35 Yates's Wine Lodge
36 Valentino's
37 Pitcher & Piano
38 Indigo

OTHER
1 Dylan Thomas' House
4 Laundrette
9 Bus Station
10 Tourist Information Centre

11 Swansea Grand Theatre
12 Quadrant Shopping
   Centre
16 Sanctuary
17 Escape
18 Post Office
21 Public Library
22 Glynn Vivian Art Gallery
24 Train Station
28 Swansea Castle
29 Plantasia
31 Dylan Thomas Centre
33 No Sign Bar
39 Swansea Museum
40 Dylan Thomas Theatre
41 Maritime & Industrial
   Museum

SOUTH WALES

Orientation & Information

The train station is on High St, about half a mile north of the town centre, while the bus station is at the Quadrant, in West Way. Swansea University is to the west. About 4 miles farther west around Swansea Bay is the seaside village of Oystermouth, also known as Mumbles. Its many pubs are as popular with today's students as they were with Dylan Thomas.

The TIC (☎ 468321, ⓔ swantrsm@cable ol.co.uk), Plymouth St, is in the bus station car park. It opens 9.30 am to 5.30 pm, Monday to Saturday. There's also a seasonal TIC (☎ 361302) on the seafront in Mumbles. Visit online at www.swansea.gov.uk.

Internet access is available at the public library (☎ 516757), Alexandra Rd, for £1.50 per half-hour. It opens 9 am to 7 pm, Monday to Saturday (to 5 pm on Thursday and Saturday).

The laundrette, 91 Bryn-y-Mor Rd, opens 8 am to 8 pm daily (to 6 pm at weekends).

The main post office, Kingsway, is nearly opposite Cafe Mambo (see Places to Eat).

Pharmacies rotate the late night service. Check local press, the *South Wales Evening Post* (available at newsagents), for details. Singleton Hospital (☎ 205666), Sketty Lane, has an Accident & Emergency department and is about 2 miles west of the city centre, heading towards Mumbles.

Swansea Castle

The castle, originally Norman, dates from the 14th century. The ruins, reflected in the mirrored glass of the surrounding tower blocks, are not substantial. Most of the castle was destroyed by Cromwell in 1647; what remained was converted into a prison in the 19th century. Swansea Castle opens year round. Admission is free.

Glynn Vivian Art Gallery

This gallery (☎ 655006), Alexandra Rd, rightly claims to be 'one of Britain's liveliest provincial galleries'. There are works by Welsh artists, a display of Swansea china, European ceramics and clocks, and temporary exhibitions. The gallery opens 10 am to 5 pm Tuesday to Sunday. Admission is free.

Plantasia

Eight hundred species of plants from around the world, plus attendant insects and reptiles, are housed in the three climatic zones of this striking pyramidal greenhouse. Plantasia (☎ 474555), off The Strand, opens 10 am to 5 pm daily. Admission costs £2.30/1.60.

Maritime Quarter

The area around the old docks has been converted into a marina and tourist area, with dockside apartments, two museums, the Dylan Thomas Theatre, the Dylan Thomas Centre and a rather odd-looking seated statue of the man himself.

On the north-eastern edge of the Maritime Quarter, **Swansea Museum** (☎ 653763), Victoria Rd, covers 200 centuries of local archaeology. It opens 10 am to 5 pm, Tuesday to Sunday. Admission is free.

Rather more interesting is the **Maritime & Industrial Museum** (☎ 650351), Museum Square. In the main hall is a Gilbern Invader, Wales's first contribution to the world's automotive industry. It's a sports car with a fibreglass body, powered by a Ford V6 engine. Even less successful, Clive Sinclair's C5, the plastic one-seater that he claimed would revolutionise personal transport in Britain, was built at the nearby vacuum cleaner factory. Upstairs, there's a collection of boats, including the circular Welsh coracle, and machinery from the Neuth Abbey wool mill. Moored nearby are a lightship and a steam tug. In an annexe is the restored town tram that plied between Swansea and Mumbles, on the world's first public passenger train, from 1804 to 1960. Opening hours are the same as the Swansea Museum. Admission is free.

The **Dylan Thomas Centre** (☎ 463980), the National Literature Centre for Wales, off Somerset Place, was opened by Jimmy Carter in 1995. It opens 10.30 am to 4.30 pm, Tuesday to Sunday. Facilities include a theatre, exhibition galleries, bookshops, a restaurant and bar. Should the desire take you, you can even get married here.

Oystermouth Castle

Five miles west of Swansea centre, in Mumbles, Oystermouth Castle was the stronghold of the Norman Lords of Gower, who established a wooden fort here in the 1180s. They built a stone castle in the late 13th century. It's worth walking up to the ruins for the view over Swansea Bay. It opens 11 am to 5 pm, April to September. Admission costs £1/80p.

Walking & Cycling Routes
The Swansea Bike Path is a five-mile beachfront trail that runs out to Mumbles; it's also used by walkers. The Riverside Path is another cycle trail, running northwards along the River Tawe.

Other Things to See & Do
Dylan Thomas' House, 5 Cwmdonkin Drive, opens for viewing by appointment with the Dylan Thomas Centre (☎ 463980). The centre is adding to the small amount of memorabilia to see there. A booklet called *The Dylan Thomas Trail*, outlining local sites associated with the poet, is available from the TIC for £1.50.

If you're looking for a uniquely Welsh souvenir, one of the largest stockists of lovespoons in the country is the **Lovespoon Gallery**, 492 Mumbles Rd, Oystermouth; prices range from £3 to £300.

Special Events
The annual **Swansea Festival** lasts from late September to early November, and includes six weeks of drama, opera, film, ballet, jazz, classical music and dance competitions. For information, phone ☎ 475715.

Places to Stay
Central Swansea There's no youth hostel in Swansea; the nearest is 15 miles away on the Gower Peninsula (see Gower Peninsula later in the chapter).

Conveniently situated outside the train station, *Swansea Grand Hotel* (☎ 650541, *Ivy Place*) has good-value singles/doubles for £18/25, although it's a bit shabby.

Oystermouth Rd, on the seafront, is lined with B&Bs and guesthouses. The *Bayswater Hotel* (☎ 655301, *322 Oystermouth Rd*) has rooms from £19/34. The *Lyndale Hotel* (☎ 653882, *324 Oystermouth Rd*) offers sea views from most rooms, which go for

£16/26, less for longer stays. The *Oystercatcher Hotel* (☎ 456574, *386 Oystermouth Rd*) has 14 rooms, mostly with bathroom, for £17 per person. There's also a bar here and evening meals are available.

In the rather more upmarket neighbourhood of Uplands, there's another clutch of B&Bs along Uplands Crescent and Eaton Crescent. Nonsmoking *Cefn Bryn* (☎ 466 687, *6 Uplands Crescent*) charges £27/47 for comfortable rooms with bathroom included. *Crescent Guest House* (☎ 466814, *132 Eaton Crescent*) has six rooms, all with bathroom, for £29/47.

The chain hotel *Forte Posthouse* (☎ 651 101, *39 Kingsway*) is centrally located. Double rooms cost from £65 to £79 and there's a gym and pool. If it's quiet at weekends there are sometimes special room deals. The *Dolphin Hotel* (☎ 650011, *Whitewalls*) is also central and popular with businesspeople. It charges £55/60 during the week, £45/55 at weekends.

Mumbles There are several guesthouses along Mumbles Rd, overlooking Swansea Bay. The *Coast House* (☎ 368702, *708 Mumbles Rd*) is run by a friendly family and B&B costs from £21/40 for singles/doubles. Alternatively, the *Beach House Hotel* (☎ 367650, *734 Mumbles Rd*) has rooms from £20/46, all with bathroom, some with sea views.

One of the most pleasant places to stay is the *Hillcrest Hotel* (☎ 363700, *1 Higher Lane*). It has a plain exterior but very comfortable rooms based on highly imaginative themes. Rooms cost £50/70, with bathroom. The safari room (£90) at the front is best. It comes complete with four-poster bed, an imitation leopard-skin cover and African bush decor. The hotel also has an excellent restaurant.

Places to Eat
Central Swansea Wind St is the up-and-coming cafe quarter. Overlooking the castle, above a pub, is *Yates's Wine Lodge* where two-course lunches are £5. A few doors down is *Valentino's* (☎ 644611, *66 Wind St*), a traditional Italian restaurant with pizza and pasta starting at £6.95. The stylish *Pitcher &*

Piano (☎ 464132, 59–60 Wind St) is a comfortable, airy bar with sofas and wooden floors. Daily specials for £4.95 include a drink. Across the street, *Ask* (☎ 477070, 6 Wind St) is a smart, trendy place with a good selection of pastas from £5.30. Just off Wind St, down an alley encouragingly titled Salubrious Place, is *Indigo* (☎ 463466), a popular Mediterranean bar-bistro which also does Welsh dishes from £4.95 or cheaper tapas.

Hwyrnos (☎ 641437, Green Dragon Lane), off Wind St, puts on a Welsh night some evenings, with roast lamb in honey, cider and herbs eaten to the accompaniment of live harp music and folk songs.

Monkey Cafe Bar (☎ 480822, 13 Castle St) is a funky place serving baguettes, fruit lassis or beer during the day, main courses from £5.95 and a good selection of vegetarian dishes from £3.50. The colourful Caribbean *Cafe Mambo* (☎ 456620, 46 The Kingsway) has an eclectic menu with vegetarian mains from £8.30 and meat dishes from £9.50. They also do tapas and great cocktails.

Opposite the train station is the *Expresso Bar Restaurant*, a greasy spoon serving cheap all-day breakfasts. *Cafe Gelato* (Castle St) is marginally more stylish and does more than coffee and ice cream.

There are several places close to the TIC. *Gershwin's Coffee House* (Singleton St) does breakfasts, lunches, cream teas and good coffee. Nearby, *La Baguette* offers what it says, from £1.80 to £2.80 to take away.

On the western side of town, on St Helen's Rd, is a line of Indian restaurants popular with students. The Sunday all-you-can-eat buffets (around £7) are very popular. Nearby, *Joe's Ice Cream Parlour* has been producing delicious, really creamy ice cream since 1922.

Self-caterers should head for the *Swansea Market*, which has been operating at the same site since 1830. It's interesting to wander round even if you're not buying. In the centre, stalls sell Pen-clawdd cockles along with that other local delicacy, *laver bread* (seaweed). You'll find cockles with bacon and laver bread on the menus of many hotels and restaurants, it's a delicious dish. The market opens 8.30 am to 5.30 pm Monday to Saturday.

There's a large Sainsbury's supermarket by the river.

Mumbles The *Hillcrest House Hotel Restaurant* (☎ 363700, 1 Higher Lane, Mumbles) is an excellent place to eat. They have a broad ranging menu, with dishes from £8.95 to £12.95. Also in Mumbles is *L'Amuse* (☎ 366 006, 93 Newton Rd), a good French restaurant where set lunches cost from £10.95 for two courses and set dinners cost £18.50.

Entertainment

Pubs & Bars At weekends, the students head west to the many pubs that line Mumbles Rd in Oystermouth. This is certainly the most lively place to drink. To do the Mumbles Mile you have to have a drink in all 11 pubs, between Newton Rd and Bracelet Bay, in one night. Start with the *White Rose* and work your way via the *Knab Rock* rock and roll pub to end at *Cinderella's* or *Neptune's*, the nightclubs. There are even T-shirts for those who finish. The Mumbles pub where Thomas used to drink is now called *Dylan's Tavern*, and is fairly touristy.

In town, the *No Sign Bar* (56 Wind St) is a laid-back cafe-style bar, although its claim to be the 'best pub north of Salzburg' may be stretching things. *Monkey Cafe Bar* (see Places to Eat) is a cool hangout with two floors and various DJ club nights. It opens until 11 pm, Wednesday to Saturday. Thursday is open mike night and on Saturday it turns into a reggae and dub club. *Cafe Mambo* (see Places to Eat) is where Swansea's youth go for early evening cocktails.

Clubs Check the hip *Buzz* magazine (available at the TIC or bars) for comprehensive club and live listings. *Escape* (☎ 652854, Northampton Lane) is Swansea's answer to Ibiza. This large house/garage club opens 10 pm to 4 am at weekends. Admission costs from £8 to £12. The newest club venue to open is *Sanctuary* (☎ 366511, The Kingsway). Friday and Saturday feature a mix of funk, garage and house with local and guest DJs playing two floors.

Theatre The *Dylan Thomas Theatre* (☎ 473 238, *Gloucester Place*), near his statue on Swansea Marina, often stages the works of Thomas. The *Taliesin Arts Centre* (☎ 296 883) stages a varied program of music, theatre, dance and film at Swansea University, Singleton Park, on the western side of town. *Swansea Grand Theatre* (☎ 475715, *Singleton St*) is the town's main theatre, hosting everything from pantomimes to ballet.

Getting There & Away

The Swansea-Cardiff Shuttle bus runs Monday to Saturday (£6.50 return, 55 minutes, hourly). Phone ☎ 0870 608 2608 for details.

Swansea trains run via Cardiff (£7.80, 50 minutes) and Bath on the main line to London Paddington. There are also direct trains to Fishguard for ferries to Ireland. An interesting cross-country line runs from Swansea, north-eastwards through Llandrindod, Knighton and Craven Arms, to Shrewsbury (four hours).

There are daily ferries to Cork (Ireland), except Tuesday, in summer and less frequent departures in winter. For details contact Swansea-Cork Ferries (☎ 456116). A single costs from £34 per person. With a car, it costs £95 in winter and £165 in summer. The terminal is on the opposite side of the river to the town centre. In midsummer, there are ferries to Ilfracombe in Devon.

Getting Around

Bus There's an efficient local bus service, with colour-coded routes, run by First Cymru (☎ 0870 608 2608). A Swansea multi-ride ticket offers all-day bus travel in the Swansea and Mumbles area for £3.30. Bus Nos 2, 2A and 3 run to Oystermouth and Mumbles (£1.50).

Car Street parking is metered in the city centre. Short-stay car parks charge 80p an hour, long-stay charge £2.30 per day. Car hire can be arranged locally with Avis (☎ 460939) or Europcar (☎ 650526).

Taxi For a taxi try Yellow Cabs (☎ 644446). It costs about £6.50 to Mumbles from the train station.

Cool Cymru

Even apart from the renowned institution of the male choir, the Welsh have always had a knack of producing fine singers – most people will have heard of natives Tom Jones, Shirley Bassey and Charlotte Church. The last decade, however, has seen an almost phenomenal emergence of a potent pop music culture with bands such as the Manic Street Preachers, Super Furry Animals, Stereophonics and Catatonia gaining international recognition and acclaim.

Formidable rockers, the Manics, paved the way with a series of successful albums; their seminal debut *Generation Terrorists* was released in 1992 and established them as one of the key British bands of the 1990s. The three-piece Stereophonics followed with a string of infectious singles, many derived from their Welsh roots. Bilingual-singing cult band Super Furry Animals became almost as well known for their alternative approach as their irreverent melodious songs. Going from strength to strength, Cardiff-based Catatonia, fronted by kooky female vocalist Cerys Matthews, shot to stardom after the 1998 release of their album *International Velvet* sold over 750,000 copies.

Other notables such as David Gray and Katell Keineg have been steadfastly making their mark in the singer/songwriter genre and a host of younger bands inspired by the success of their predecessors are now tuning up for the world stage.

🌺🌺🌺🌺🌺🌺🌺🌺🌺🌺🌺🌺🌺🌺

GOWER PENINSULA

Extending 15 miles east of Mumbles, the Gower Peninsula was the first part of Britain to be officially designated an Area of Outstanding Beauty, and it well deserves its title. A favourite haunt of Thomas, it has some superb sandy beaches and beautiful cliff scenery – good walking country. In summer, however, it can get very crowded.

Much of the Gower is owned by the National Trust (NT). On the south coast is **Oxwich Bay**, the first sandy beach of any size you come to. Around Oxwich Point is **Port Eynon**, which has camp sites and a youth hostel by the beach. The extreme western tip is known as **Worms Head**, an apt name for this elongated, rocky headland. You can walk out across the causeway onto the Worm only during the two-hour period either side of low tide.

Rhossili

This village is above Worms Head, and stretching northwards is 3 miles of the Gower's best and biggest beach, Rhossili Bay. Hang-gliders soar off the cliffs onto the wide expanse of sand. The **Rhossili Visitor Centre** (☎ 01792-390707, ℮ gshrho@smtp .ntrust.org.uk), at the start of the path to Worms Head, is run by the NT.

In the 18th century, smugglers landed brandy and tobacco from France on these beaches and secret coves. The seas around this area are treacherous: over 250 boats have been lost off the Gower. On Rhossili Beach, the bows of the *Helvetica*, wrecked in 1880, stick out of the sand.

You can take surfing lessons at the **Welsh Surfing Federation School** (☎ 01792-386426, ℮ surfwsf@aol.com) at The Croft, Llangennith, in the northern end of Rhossili, for £18/£28 per half/full day, including wetsuit.

Walking

A useful publication is *Circular Walks in Gower*, stocked by TICs. For a good five-hour ramble, start in the car park on the eastern side of Middleton, walk down to Worms Head and back up to the visitor centre at Rhossili. Then climb up to the beacon on Rhossili Down, walk down to Hillend and then back to Rhossili and Middleton along the beach. You can phone the visitor centre to check the tide times for crossing to Worms Head. While you're there you could have lunch or tea at the Worms Head Hotel.

Places to Stay & Eat

Hotels and guesthouses tend to be more expensive on the Gower Peninsula than in Swansea and Mumbles.

Carreglwyd Camping Site (☎ 01792-390795), Port Eynon, charges £7.50 for a tent and one person.

The *Port Eynon Youth Hostel* (☎ 01792-390706) is an old lifeboat house superbly situated right on the beach at Port Eynon, 15 miles from Swansea. It opens daily except Sunday April to October but does open Sunday on bank-holiday weekends and in midsummer. The hostel charges £9.25/6.50 for adults/under-18s.

The *Worms Head Hotel* (☎ 01792-390512) is in a splendid location overlooking Worms Head and Rhossili Bay. B&B costs £43/66 for singles/doubles with bathroom. Most rooms, and the restaurant, have sea views. There's also a bar.

Getting There & Away

From Swansea bus station, First Cymru (☎ 0870 608 2608) bus Nos 18 and 18A run daily to South Gower, Port Eynon, Rhossili (£2.45) and Horton. Nos 48 and 49 go on a tour of Gower in summer. Bus No 16 runs to North Gower, Llanrhidian and Llangennith.

CARMARTHEN (CAERFYRDDIN)

☎ 01267 • pop 15,000

It's difficult to believe that this unexciting place, Carmarthenshire's county town, was where Merlin the magician from the Arthurian legends was allegedly born. At least it's a little more Welsh than Swansea and Cardiff – you'll hear the language spoken here. There's no real reason to stop, but since it's an important transport hub, you may have to.

Carmarthen lies on the northern side of the River Towy. The TIC (☎ 231557), 113 Lammas St, is in the centre of town.

Buses stop along Blue St and the train station is across the bridge, on the southern bank. Trains run to Carmarthen from Cardiff (£10.60, two hours, six daily).

The National Botanic Garden of Wales

If you're anywhere in the area, you should not miss a visit to the impressive National Botanic Garden (☎ 01558-668768), Middleton Hall, in Llanarthne, 7 miles east of Carmarthen. The garden, set over 180 acres in a former regency estate, opened in May 2000 and is due to expand considerably over the coming years. One of the garden's most striking features is the imposing 100m-wide Great Glasshouse – one of the world's largest single-span glasshouses. Designed by architect Norman Foster, it houses plants of the Mediterranean climate, among rock pools and fountains. There's also a Zen garden, a large herbaceous border with pools and a restaurant. The garden opens 10 am to 6 pm daily year round. Admission costs £6.50/3. Visit online at www.gardenofwales.org.uk.

Getting There & Away

From Swansea, bus Nos X11 and X30 run to Carmarthen (£3.60, hourly), and you can connect with bus No 222 to Laugharne for the Dylan Thomas Boathouse.

Carmarthen is on the main train line from London Paddington that goes through Cardiff and Swansea. West of Carmarthen, the line divides: one route continues to Pembroke Dock, another to Milford Haven and a third to Fishguard.

LAUGHARNE

☎ 01994 • pop 1200

Pilgrims on the Dylan Thomas trail come to this little town on the western side of the Taff Estuary to see the house where he lived, the pub where he perfected the drinking habit that finally killed him and the churchyard where he is buried. Even if you're not particularly a fan, it's an attractive place to visit.

Dylan Thomas Boathouse

Built into the hillside, this boathouse (☎ 427 420) is five minutes' walk from town, down a leafy lane. He spent the last four years of his life here with his wife Caitlin, and the house is preserved as a shrine. There are photographs, manuscripts and recordings of the poet reading from his own works. Above the house, you can look through the window in the old wooden shed – 'The Shack', he called it – where he wrote *Under Milk Wood*. Beside the house is a tearoom on the terrace, where you can look out across the 'heron priested shore' that inspired some of Thomas' best work. It opens 10 am to 5 pm daily, Easter to October; 10.30 am to 3 pm in winter. Admission costs £2.75/1.

Laugharne is a pretty town of Georgian houses and has the remains of a 12th-century

castle. The poet's simple grave is in the churchyard of St Martin's Church.

Places to Stay & Eat

The stately *Castle House* (☎ 472616), *Market Lane)* is a pleasant B&B next to the castle and charges £30/50 for singles/doubles with bathroom. *The Stable Door Wine Bar and Brasserie* (☎ 427777, *Market Lane)* is a lovely old building with a garden looking onto the castle. Salmon in filo pastry costs £9.75 or they have a selection of vegetarian dishes for under £8. The atmospheric *Brown's Hotel* (no accommodation) was where Thomas drank, and it's still a serious drinking place – no DT cocktails here for the visitors.

Getting There & Away

Bus No 222 runs from Carmarthen (hourly, Monday to Saturday). You can get here from Swansea via Carmarthen using a Day Saver bus ticket (£4.80).

Pembrokeshire Coast National Park

Most of the coastline of the Pembrokeshire Coast National Park consists of rugged cliffs, broken up by stretches of superb sandy beaches – the best in Wales – and rocky coves. Pembrokeshire has some of the oldest rocks in the world, formed over 3000 million years ago.

The park is probably best known for the 189-mile Pembrokeshire Coast Path, which runs from Amroth in the south to Poppit Sands in the north. But as well as excellent walks, there are numerous other outdoor activities – climbing, mountain biking, bird-watching, pony trekking, surfing, sea kayaking and canoeing.

The Preseli Hills are the only upland area in the park. Ancient trade routes run through them and hill forts, standing stones and burial chambers are all evidence of the prehistoric people who once lived here.

The offshore islands of Skomer, Skokholm and Grassholm were given their names by

Viking raiders. They're now inhabited by seabird colonies – puffins, guillemots, razorbills (the emblem of the park) and gannets. Ramsey and Skomer Islands are breeding grounds for the grey seal and Caldey Island is owned and farmed by Cistercian monks. All of the islands can be visited.

Anyone who comes to Pembrokeshire should not miss St David's, where the superb cathedral, the most impressive in Wales, is a shrine to the country's patron saint.

The area's warm, sunny climate makes it a place that you can visit year round. In July and August, the main tourist areas can be very crowded. May and September are probably the best months for clear days and lack of crowds.

ORIENTATION

The park covers about 230 sq miles and includes 180 miles of rocky coastline. Within the park you're never over 10 miles from the sea. The park can be divided into four separate sections – the coastline east of Fishguard to Cardigan and inland to the Preseli Hills; the coastline west of Fishguard down to Milford Haven; the upper stretches of the Milford Haven waterway; and the coastline round the southern Pembroke peninsula. The industrial coastline around Pembroke and Milford Haven is not part of the park.

The highest point in the park is Foel Cwm Cerwyn in the Preseli Hills, which rises to 536m. The hills are now acknowledged as being the source of the blue stones that form the inner circle of Stonehenge (see the South-Western England chapter).

The southern part of Pembrokeshire is often known as 'Little England beyond Wales', because of the 50 castles built by the English invaders. The invasion continues today – resorts such as Tenby are very popular with English holiday-makers. Many of the B&Bs and guesthouses are run not by the Welsh but by incomers.

INFORMATION

The head office for the Pembrokeshire Coast National Park (☎ 01437-764636, ⓔ pcnp@pembrokeshirecoast.org.uk) is in Winch Lane, Haverfordwest.

There are National Park Information Centres, open year-round, in the TIC in St David's (☎ 01437-720392); in the TIC in Newport (☎ 01239-820912); and in the centre of Haverfordwest (☎ 01437-760136), 40 High St.

You can also get information about the park from any of the TICs in the towns and villages mentioned in this section.

Disabled travellers can hire electric wheelchairs (£3 per day) and a range of other aids in Haverfordwest for use in the park. For information phone ☎ 01437-760999.

ACTIVITIES

The National Park Authority organises a wide range of activities, including walks (along the coast and into the Preseli Hills), cycle and horse rides, island cruises, canoe trips and minibus tours. Details of all the organised activities are given in *Coast to Coast*, the useful freebie newspaper available from TICs and National Park Information Centres.

Walking

The big walk here is the Pembrokeshire Coast Path, and you should walk at least a section of this superb 189-mile trail. Pembrokeshire Walking Holidays (☎ 01437-760075) offer a luggage-carrying service for lazy walkers.

Guides that cover the whole route include Dennis Kelsall's *Pembrokeshire Coastal Path*, which follows the route from south to north – the recommended way to do it. CJ Wright's *A Guide to the Pembrokeshire Coast Path*, and the *National Trail Guide – Pembrokeshire Coast Path* both have more detailed mapping but cover the route in the opposite direction. TICs also sell local walking guides. The national park's excellent *Six Circular Walks* series cover St David's, Strumble Head, Newport, Broad Haven and Saundersfoot. National park rangers lead guided walks. A half-day walk costs from £2 and a full-day from £3.50. There is even a 14-day guided walk of the complete coast path for around £120. See the *Coast to Coast* newspaper for details.

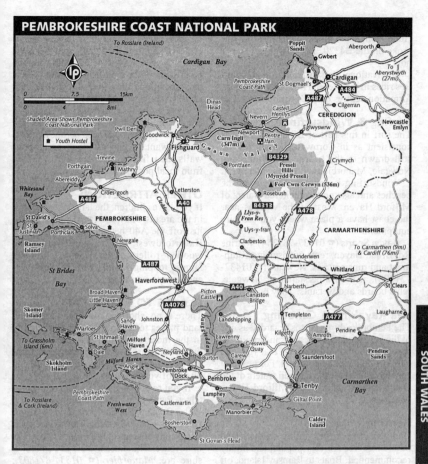

PEMBROKESHIRE COAST NATIONAL PARK

Cycling

Although bikes are not allowed on the Pembrokeshire Coast Path, the local lanes and bridleways offer excellent cycling. In the north of the country there are more difficult routes for mountain bikes. If you plan to cycle off the roads, it is best to check your route with the national park head office (☎ 01437-764636).

There are numerous places in the area – St David's and Newport among them (see those sections later in the chapter) – where you can hire touring and mountain bikes.

Pony Trekking & Horse Riding

The fact that this is an ideal area for riding is reflected in the number of stables in the area. You can ride along the beaches, across open moorland, along wooded bridleways or down quiet country lanes.

East Nolton Riding Stables (☎ 01437-710360) is 3 miles from both Broad Haven and Newgale. Rides cost £15 per hour.

Maesgwynne Riding Stables (☎ 01348-872659) charges £8 per hour. It's near Fishguard – turn off the A40 in Fishguard past the Pendre pub and it's 200m down Maesgwynne Lane. Pembrokeshire Riding Centre

(☎ 01646-682513), Pennybridge Farm, Hundleton, is 2½ miles south-west of Pembroke on the B4320. The charge is £10 per hour.

The National Park Authority also organises rides in the Preseli Hills. Contact the information centres or TICs for details.

Surfing & Windsurfing

The surf in this part of Britain is rarely as consistent as in Cornwall, but surfies are still drawn to the beaches at Whitesand, Newgale, Manorbier and Freshwater West.

Windsurfing is popular off many of the beaches and also on the sheltered waters of Milford Haven. Most of the villages near the coast have a place where you can hire equipment.

Haven Sports (☎ 01437-781354), Marine Rd, Broad Haven, rents windsurfing equipment and runs courses. Newsurf (☎ 01437-721398), at the filling station at Newgale, rents boards and wetsuits. They open daily.

Sea Kayaking & Canoeing

The Pembrokeshire coast is regarded as one of the best sea-kayaking areas in Britain, although you should be aware that rips and currents here can be powerful. For peaceful canoeing, head for the tranquil waters of the Dauggleddau Estuary (the Milford Haven waterway end).

Boating

Boat trips to see the wildlife on the island nature reserves are very popular and highly recommended. Boats to Ramsey Island, off St David's, depart from St Justinian or Whitesand Bay. Trips to Skomer, Skokholm and Grassholm Islands are also possible from St Justinian, or from Martin's Haven. Boats to Caldey Island go from Tenby. As well as trips on small ex-fishing boats, there are also excursions on high-speed, water-jet propelled inflatables.

Charges vary according to the length of the trip and the number of islands visited, but you should expect to pay £10 to £20 for a day trip. For details of the trips, see the sections on the individual islands later in the chapter.

Fishing

To fish the rivers you must have a rod licence (£2.50 to £5.50 a day) from the Environment Agency (☎ 01437-760081) and the permission of the land/fishery owner. Clubs or associations may give day tickets. On small rivers, approach local farmers.

There's good sea fishing – Newgale is one of the best beaches in Wales to fish from. However, you'll need permission first if you want to fish off dock or harbour walls. Sea fishing licences are available from local post offices.

OTHER ATTRACTIONS

If you have children, the largest theme park in the area is Oakwood (☎ 01834-891376), just off the A40 between Carmarthen and Haverfordwest, at Canaston Bridge. The wooden roller-coaster ride is Europe's largest, topping 55mph, with 11 crossovers and a maximum drop of 83ft.

PLACES TO STAY & EAT

There's no shortage of accommodation and places to eat in this area, particularly in the more developed seaside resorts on the south coast. At the cheaper end, there are camp sites (from about £3 per tent) and plenty of youth hostels.

If you're booking two or more of the hostels in Pembrokeshire, you can use the West Wales Booking Service at *St David's Youth Hostel (☎ 01437-720345)*. The service costs £2.50 and bookings must be made two weeks in advance. The other hostels in Pembrokeshire are: *Manorbier (☎ 01834-871803)*; *Lawrenny (☎ 01646-651270)*, 12 miles from Pembroke; *Marloes Sands (☎ 01646-636 667)*; *Broad Haven (☎ 01437-781688)*; *Solva (Pen-y-Cwm, ☎ 01437-720959)*; *Trevine (Trefin, ☎ 01348-831414)*; *Pwll Deri (☎ 013 48-891233)*, at a wonderful location on cliffs 2¾ miles south of Strumble Head; *Newport (☎ 01239-820080)* and *Poppit Sands (☎ 012 39-612936, St Dogmaels)*.

GETTING THERE & AWAY

There's a National Express (☎ 0870 580 80 80) bus from London to Haverfordwest (£24, twice daily).

From London Paddington there's an hourly intercity service as far as Swansea, where you may need to change to catch less frequent trains to Narberth, Kilgetty, Tenby, Penally, Saundersfoot, Manorbier, Lamphey and Pembroke. Some services from London continue beyond Swansea in summer.

Trains from Swansea also run to Haverfordwest (£8.30, seven daily but less frequently on Sunday) and Fishguard (twice daily). Trains from Swansea to Pembroke run about every two hours (£8.20, two hours).

GETTING AROUND

Bus services around Pembrokeshire are reasonably good. Timetables are available from TICs. For transport information phone ☎ 01437-764551 ext 5227.

The three main local operators are Richards Brothers (☎ 01239-613756), who run services from Haverfordwest to Newgale, St David's, Fishguard and Newport; Silcox Motor Coach Co (☎ 01646-683143), who offers services to Pembroke, Tenby and other places south of Haverfordwest; and First Cymru (phone ☎ 0870 608 2608 for details).

The West Wales Rover ticket (£4.60/3.40) allows unlimited travel for one day on services in Pembrokeshire, Carmarthenshire and Ceredigion. It can be bought on the bus. Richards Brothers also has its own Day Explorer ticket (£3.40/2.30) or Weekly Explorer (£14/9.50), only valid on those services.

Trains are less useful for getting around the area. There's no service westwards to St David's or connecting with the northern end of the coast path. You could, however, use the train to get from Tenby to Pembroke, and from Haverfordwest to Milford Haven or Fishguard. For rail enquiries, phone ☎ 0845 748 4950.

TENBY (DINBYCH Y PYSGOD)
☎ 01834 • pop 5500

The Welsh name for this genteel seaside town, built around a beautiful bay, is as charming as Tenby itself. It means Little Fort of the Fishes.

The Normans built the castle on the promontory above the two sandy beaches. The town was fortified in the 13th century

after several unsuccessful attempts by the Welsh to recapture it. It grew as a port and in the 19th century developed into a holiday resort. Unlike many other seaside resorts in Britain, Tenby has managed to avoid being overtaken by amusement arcades and fish and chip shops. It's a lively town, popular with young surfers and well-heeled tourists alike and, although it gets crowded in summer, it's nonetheless worth visiting. The coast path runs right through the town.

Orientation & Information

The town extends east of the castle on the promontory, with the harbour and North Beach on one side and South Beach on the other. The train station is on the western side, at the bottom of Warren St. The bus station is one block south of Warren St on Upper Park Rd.

The TIC (☎ 842404), in The Croft, opens 10 am to 9 pm daily in July and August; shorter hours the rest of the year.

Things to See & Do

Tall, elegant Georgian houses, most of them now hotels, rise above the pretty harbour. The most interesting building to look round is the **Tudor Merchant's House** (☎ 842279; NT), Quay Hill, a late-15th-century house that shows how a merchant lived in this time. The remains of three frescoes can be seen on the interior walls. The house opens 10 am to 5 pm daily (except Wednesday and Saturday) and 1 to 5 pm on Sunday, April to November. Admission costs £1.80/90p.

Other things to see in Tenby include the **castle ruins** (good for views over the bay) and the **Museum & Art Gallery** on Castle Hill.

Town Trails (☎ 845841) run **guided walks** of Tenby's historical sites, starting from the church on Tudor Square, at 11 am on Monday, Wednesday, Friday and Saturday in summer. The walk costs £3/2 and takes 1½ hours.

When the tide is down, you can walk across the sand to **St Catherine's Island**. The Victorian fortress here is not open to the public. A popular boat trip from Tenby harbour is across to Caldey Island (see Around Tenby later).

SOUTH WALES

Places to Stay

There's a large camp site, *Kiln Park Holiday Centre* (☎ *844121, Marsh Rd*), five minutes' walk west of town along the beach. A tent and two adults costs £11, which includes admission to two swimming pools, tennis courts and the entertainment centre.

There are no youth hostels in Tenby, but there is one about 6 miles west at Skrinkle Haven (Manorbier). See Around Tenby.

There's a good choice of cheaper B&Bs along Harding and Warren Sts, near the train and bus stations. *Weybourne* (☎ *843 641, 14 Warren St*) charges from £25/44 for a single/double in summer.

Myrtle House Hotel (☎ *842508*) is a comfortable nonsmoking hotel on St Mary's St. All rooms have a bathroom or shower and B&B costs £25 per person.

There's no shortage of places to stay along the Esplanade, above the South Beach, and on Victoria St, Picton Terrace and Sutton St, which lead off of it. Prices range from £20 to £30 per person, depending on the size of the room and whether it has a sea view.

The *Fourcroft Hotel* (☎ *842886, The Croft*) is a comfortable place that's been run by the same friendly family for over 50 years. It costs £49 per person in rooms with bathroom and sea view; without the view it's £41, and rates drop to £31 per person in winter. The hotel overlooks the bay and has a pool and private garden above the beach. *Tenby House Hotel* (☎ *842000, Tudor Sq*) offers traditional accommodation in the centre of town for £55/80.

The *Atlantic Hotel* (☎ *842881, The Esplanade*) is an excellent place, with a heated pool and a private garden leading onto the beach. B&B costs £62/86.

Places to Eat

Most of the town's restaurants and pubs can be found inside the town walls around Tudor Square.

The *Bay Tree* (*Tudor Square*) is a friendly bistro with main dishes from £6.95 to £11.50, which has live music at weekends. *Pam Pam*, just across the street, is a pub-style restaurant with seafood and steaks from £8.40 to £12.99.

The *Reef* (*Tudor Square*) is a colourful, new bistro-style restaurant with a good vegetarian selection. Interesting mains go from £5.95 to £7.50.

Plantagenate Restaurant (☎ *842350, Quay Hill*) is by the Tudor Merchant's House and claims to be the oldest house in town. As well as being an interesting building it's an excellent place to eat. Crab sandwiches cost £4.95; main dishes range from £11.25 to £15.95 and there are good vegetarian choices.

Most of the larger hotels have restaurants that are open to non-guests.

In summer, Tenby has a glut of teashops and cafes serving overpriced snacks and lunches. *Blueberry's Restaurant* (*High St*) is a pleasant cafe serving lunchtime sandwiches and baked potatoes.

The *Lifeboat Tavern* (*corner of Quay Hill and High St*) is small, lively pub, popular with young people.

Getting There & Away

Bus service No 358 or 359 runs between Haverfordwest and Tenby (£2.55, 1¼ hours, hourly Monday to Saturday). There's also a direct train service from Swansea (£8.20, 1¾ hours).

AROUND TENBY
Caldey Island

A 20-minute boat trip from Tenby is Caldey Island, home to a small community of 16 Cistercian monks, seals and sea birds. The monks make a variety of products for sale, including perfume, dairy products and chocolate – industries that now employ people from the mainland. There are guided tours of the monastery twice daily (men only), and great walks around the island, with good views from the lighthouse. Make sure you visit the old priory and St Illtyd's Church, with its oddly shaped steeple. Inside is a fascinating ogham stone, with inscriptions in this ancient Irish script.

There are regular services to the island (£7 return, including landing fee), Monday to Friday from Easter to October (and Saturday from May to September). Tickets are sold from a kiosk at the slipway in the harbour.

Saundersfoot

☎ 01834 • pop 2200

Situated 3 miles north of Tenby, the attractive village of Saundersfoot was once a fishing port and was also involved in the export of anthracite. It's now a busy seaside resort with a good beach. There's a TIC (☎ 813 672), in the harbour car park, open daily.

There are numerous B&Bs and guesthouses in the area. *Cliff House* (☎ *813931, Wogan Terrace*) is a friendly place with singles/doubles overlooking the bay from £25/40 in summer. *White Horses* (☎ *814835, Pen-y-Craig, the Glen*) is a comfortable, country house with cliff-side garden and three double rooms from £70 to £90. It's half a mile from town, just off the A478.

Bus No 351 runs to Saundersfoot from Tenby (95p, 10 minutes). The train station is a mile north of town.

Manorbier

Above this pretty village are the ruins of **Manorbier Castle**, with superb views over the sea. This 12th-century fortification was the birthplace of Giraldus Cambrensis, Gerald of Wales, one of the country's greatest scholars and tutor to both Richard the Lion-Heart and King John. 'In all the broad lands of Wales, Manorbier is the best place by far,' he wrote. In some of the castle's rooms you'll find waxworks in period costume – a job lot of rejects from Madame Tussaud's in London. Look for the two figures that were originally Prince Philip – in one room he's dressed in chain mail, and he pops up again in another, this time disguised as a 'Welsh Lady' beside a spinning wheel! The castle opens 10.30 am to 5.30 pm daily, Easter to September. Admission costs £2/1.

The impressive *Manorbier Youth Hostel* (☎ *871803*) is 200m from the sandy beach at Skrinkle Haven, on the eastern side of the village; you can also camp here. It opens daily from March to October. The nightly charge is £11/7.75 for adults/under-18s and the hostel is 2½ miles south of Manorbier train station. Bus service No 358 or 359 runs daily from Manorbier to Tenby (20 minutes) and Pembroke (20 minutes).

PEMBROKE

☎ 01646 • pop 15,400

Founded over 900 years ago, Pembroke's medieval street plan has survived along with its castle, the oldest in western Wales. Although there are other castles in the country that have more atmosphere, this one is certainly worth a visit, but Pembrokeshire's county town need not delay you for much more than half a day.

Just over 2 miles to the west of Pembroke is **Pembroke Dock**, where ferries leave for Rosslare (Ireland). The dock is on the southern bank of the Milford Haven waterway.

Pembroke grew into an important trading centre after the castle was built in 1093. In 1154, local traders gained a monopoly in the area when an Act of Incorporation was passed, making it illegal to land goods in the Milford Haven waterway at anywhere other than Pembroke. The castle was home to the early Tudors, and King Henry VII was born here. During the Civil War, it was besieged by Cromwell for 48 days before it fell.

The Pembroke Visitors Centre and TIC (☎ 622388), Commons Rd, is south of the castle. It opens 10 am to 5.30 pm daily, Easter to October; and on Tuesday, Thursday and Saturday in November and March. As well as the usual TIC services, there's an interpretive display about the town. It also stocks a *Town Trail* walking guide.

At Pembroke Dock, there's a TIC (☎ 622 246) in the restored Gun Tower, Front St.

Pembroke Castle

Pembroke's main attraction dominates the western end of town. Although a fort was established here in 1093 by Arnulph de Montgomery, the current buildings mainly date from the 12th and 13th centuries. The fort was in use until 1945, and was the home of the earls of Pembroke for over 300 years.

The massive walls enclose a large area of grass and an ugly tarmac parade ground. Passages run from tower to tower, and a plaque in one marks the birthplace (in 1456) of Harry Tudor, who defeated Richard III to become Henry VII.

In the centre of the castle grounds stands a 23m-high tower. One hundred steps lead to the top and a glorious view. If it's windy, the tower is closed.

The castle (☎ 681510) opens 9.30 am to 6 pm daily, April to September; 10 am to 5 pm in March and October; and to 4 pm, November to February. Admission costs £3/2.

Museum of the Home

The Museum of the Home (☎ 681200), 7 Westgate Hill, just across the road from the castle, is worth visiting. It has a great collection of toys and games, including Roman die and the first snakes and ladders board, as well as cooking and eating implements and other objects of past eras, in a domestic setting. There are no labels – you're shown round by the enthusiastic owners. It opens 11 am to 5 pm, Monday to Thursday, May to September. Admission costs £1.20/90p. Children under 5 are not allowed.

Places to Stay & Eat

Lovely wisteria-clad *Beech House* (☎ 683 740, 78 Main St) does B&B for £15 per person in very comfortable surroundings. Just up the road, *Merton Place House* (☎ 684 796, 3 East Back, by Main St) is another good place, with B&B from £17.50/35 for singles/doubles.

High Noon Guest House (☎ 683736, Lower Lamphey Rd) is comfortable and welcoming. Rooms, with bathroom, cost £26/42.

The Coach House Hotel (☎ 684602, Main St) is a comfortable place with rooms for £45/70 and a very good restaurant. They offer a discount on rooms when not busy.

The *Kings Arms Hotel* (☎ 683611, Main St), a traditional old county town hotel, does B&B from £32.50/45. The bar food is about the best in Pembroke.

The upmarket *Left Bank Restaurant* (☎ 622333, 63 Main St) serves a very good two-course dinner for £19.50, including Welsh lamb with couscous.

If you're not counting calories, *Brown's Snack Bar (Main St)* is the place to go for pie and chips at £3. It's an authentic 1960s diner, in all its tacky originality, complete with weighing scales at the door.

Henry's Gift & Coffee Shop (☎ 622293) is the unmissable pink building near the castle, with traditional cakes for under £1. There are several other cafes near the castle.

The *Watermans Arms*, just over the bridge and by the river, has lovely views of the castle, and the terrace is a good place for a drink. More serious drinking is done in the *Old Cross Saws (Main St)*, where accommodation costs £15.50 per person.

Getting There & Away

Bus service No 359 operates from Haverfordwest to Pembroke (£2, 40 minutes, hourly Monday to Saturday). Service No 358 also goes to Pembroke but takes longer. Both services go to Pembroke Dock and stop near the centre of Pembroke. Silcox Motors (☎ 683143) service No 333 runs to Pembroke Dock via Carmarthen and Tenby (Monday to Friday). Bus No 361 goes to Saundersfoot and Kilgetty.

Pembroke is connected to the branch train line that runs through Tenby and terminates at Pembroke Dock.

Irish Ferries (☎ 0870 517 1717) runs two ferries a day to Rosslare (Ireland) from Pembroke Dock.

AROUND PEMBROKE
Carew Castle & Tidal Mill

Looming romantically over the River Carew, with its wide, empty windows reflected in the still water, Carew Castle is an impressive sight. These rambling ruins started off as an early 12th-century castle, built by Gerald de Windsor, Henry I's constable of Pembroke. It was eventually converted into an Elizabethan country house. Abandoned in 1690, the castle is still home to a large number of bats, including the protected greater horseshoe bat. In summer a program of events is held, which includes battle re-enactments and open-air theatre performances.

On the causeway nearby is the Elizabethan Tidal Mill. It was used to grind corn until WWI and is one of three working tidal mills in Britain; it was restored using its original machinery. The rising tide fills the millpond and, when the tide falls, a head of water is released through a sluice. This turns the main millwheel, which in turn powers the machinery in the mill.

The castle and mill (☎ 01646-651782) open 10 am to 5 pm daily, Easter to October. Admission to the castle only costs £1.90/1.40; a combined ticket that includes the mill costs £2.75/1.80.

There's a fine **Celtic Cross**, dating from the 11th century, not far from the castle entrance. The nearby *Carew Inn* is a cosy pub, serving food from noon to 2 pm.

Carew is 4 miles from Pembroke and five from Tenby. Bus No 361 runs between Tenby and Pembroke Dock via Carew Cross about three times a day.

HAVERFORDWEST (HWLFFORDD)
☎ 01437 • pop 14,000

Although this market town is not within the borders of the park, it's the commercial centre of the area and a focal point for public transport.

The town was founded beside the River Western Cleddau in about 1110, as a Flemish settlement. Overpopulation in Flanders had forced some of the inhabitants to seek other land, and the Flemings who reached Wales were granted land around this river. A castle was built at the time the town was founded. The port remained important until the arrival of the railway in the mid-19th century.

There's not much to see in Haverfordwest today – the castle ruins are fairly plain. The **Castle Museum & Art Gallery** (☎ 763 087) is in the outer ward of the castle.

The TIC (☎ 763110, ✉ haverfordwest informationcentre@pembrokeshire.gov.uk) is near the bus station on Old Bridge St. The National Park Information Centre (☎ 760 136) is at 40 High St.

Places to Stay & Eat
Villa House (☎ 762977, *St Thomas Green*) has B&B from £16 per person. There are several other places in this area.

The excellent *Penrhlwllan* (☎ 769049, *Well Lane, Prendergast*) is a small B&B a short walk from the bus station. Rooms cost £21 per person with bathroom, £18 without.

The comfortable *County Hotel* (☎ 762 144, *Salutation Square*) charges £40/60 for singles/doubles, with bathroom. There are

good bar meals in the pub downstairs at *Castle Hotel* (☎ 769322, *Castle Square*) and also at the rustic *Olde Three Crowns,* on the corner of High and Quay Sts. *The Barking Shark* (*Quay St*) is popular with young people for a drink.

Getting There & Away
Haverfordwest is 249 miles from London and about 7 miles from Milford Haven. There are buses from here to many parts of Pembrokeshire. Richards Brothers (☎ 01239-613756) No 412 runs from Haverfordwest via Fishguard to Cardigan (£3.03, 1¼ hours, hourly, Monday to Saturday). Other services link Haverfordwest with St David's and Pembroke. The National Express bus service from London to Haverfordwest takes 6¾ hours.

Trains also link Swansea and Haverfordwest (£8.30, 1½ hours, seven daily, fewer on Sunday).

ST BRIDES BAY (BAE SAIN FFRAID)
St Brides Bay is at the western end of the 'landsker', the invisible boundary between the Welsh and anglicised parts of Pembrokeshire. The best beaches in Wales line this wide bay, and they're big enough to absorb the crowds of holiday-makers they attract at the height of the summer season. There are numerous camp sites, and most of the farmers will be happy to let you use one of their fields for a couple of pounds; you must ask permission first.

Skomer, Skokholm & Grassholm Islands
These islands, lying off the coast on the southern side of the bay, are nature reserves populated mainly by sea birds. The bird colonies are busiest between April and mid-August. You can see plenty of grey seals with their pups on the beaches there, during their autumnal mating season, and occasionally porpoises and dolphins in the surrounding seas. To visit the islands, book through any National Park Information Centre, or at Dale Sailing Company (☎ 01646-601636). Visits cost £12 per person.

SOUTH WALES

Easiest to reach is Skomer, and from Martin's Haven there are departures at 10 and 11 am and at noon daily except Monday. Boats return from about 3 pm, allowing several hours on the island. There's no shop or cafe so you need to bring a picnic.

Skokholm is famous for its Manx shearwaters and, with Skomer, provides shelter for 45% of the world's population of this bird. There are services to the island at 10 am on Monday only, from early-June to mid-August. The largest gannetry in the northern hemisphere is on Grassholm, a small island 10 miles offshore.

Broad Haven

This is a lively seaside village with several caravan parks and camping grounds. Also here is the modern *Broad Haven Youth Hostel* (☎ *01437-781688*), open daily from mid-February to October. The nightly charge is £11/7.75 for adults/under-18s.

Newgale

The beach, the biggest in the area, is the only reason to visit this tiny village, popular with both swimmers and surfers. At very low tides, the fossil remains of a prehistoric forest can be seen. You can hire surf skis, boards, boogie boards and wetsuits from Newsurf Hire Centre (☎ 01437-721398) at Newgale Filling Station. Body boards cost £2.50/£4.50 for one/four hours.

Places to Stay & Eat There are several excellent camp sites. *Newgale Camp Site* (☎ *01437-710253*) is across the road from the beach; it charges from £3 per person. There's a *cafe*, *pub* and *shop* nearby.

The top-notch *Penycwm Youth Hostel* (☎ *01437-720959*) is 1½ miles north of Newgale at Whitehouse. It's open year round and beds cost £11/7.75 for adults/under-18s. There's also B&B at this hostel and excellent meals are available. There's more accommodation at Solva, Simpsons Cross and Nolton.

Getting There & Away Newgale is a stop on Richards Brothers' hourly service No 411 or 412 from Haverfordwest to St David's and Fishguard. The journey from Haverfordwest

takes 25 minutes (£1.54) and it's another 20 minutes from there to St David's.

ST DAVID'S (TY-DDEWI)
☎ 01437 • pop 1800

There's something very special about St David's that even the crowds of holidaymakers in summer fail to extinguish. The magic must have worked for Dewi Sant (St David), who chose to found the first monastic community here in the 6th century only a short walk from where he was born. St David is dear to the hearts of the Welsh – he's their patron saint and his relics are kept in a casket in the cathedral.

Although St David's is no bigger than a village, with only one square and a few side roads leading off it, the cathedral's presence earns it the right to be called a city. As you approach the place you're unaware of the cathedral, which is just as its builders intended, for it was hidden in the depression below the square in the vain hope that passing Norse raiders might miss it. It's a magnificent sight, and if you visit only one cathedral in Wales, make it this one.

Information

The National Park Visitors Centre and the TIC (☎ 720392, ⓔ enquiries@stdavids.pem brokeshirecoast.org.uk) are in a purpose-built exhibition and visitor centre at the Grove, at the southern entrance to the village. It opens daily.

The St David's Arts Festival, held in the first half of August, includes open-air Shakespeare plays in the Bishop's Palace that are well worth seeing. There's a music festival centred on the cathedral in late May.

St David's Cathedral

St David's Cathedral was built in the late 12th century, but there has been a church on this site since the 6th century. Norse pirates ransacked the site at least seven times, and various bishops added to the building between the 12th and 16th centuries. In the Middle Ages, two pilgrimages to the shrine of St David's were said to equal one to Rome – thus the cathedral has seen a constant stream of visitors.

Highly strung: the Severn Estuary bridge

A new stadium for the new millennium, Cardiff

Old and new stand side by side in Swansea.

DALE BUCKTON

NEIL SETCHFIELD

BRYN THOMAS

Underneath the arches of Llanthony Priory's monastic remains, Ewyas Valley

The Cliff Railway in the university town of Aberystwyth is the longest of its kind in Britain.

Danger lurks over rugged cliffs in the Pembrokeshire Coast National Park.

Inside the cathedral, there's an atmosphere of great antiquity. The floor slopes 1m upwards and the pillars keel over drunkenly, the result of an earthquake in 1248. In the Norman nave is a superbly carved oak-ceiling, installed in the 16th century. St David's shrine is by the northern choir aisle. This cathedral is the only one in the UK in which the reigning monarch has a permanently reserved stall.

Services are held at 8 am and 6 pm on most days. On Sunday there are services throughout the morning, and a choral evensong at 6 pm. Some services are held in Welsh. Admission to the cathedral (☎ 720 202) is free, although a donation of £2/1 is suggested. There are also photography charges. Regular classical concerts are held at the cathedral; ring for details.

Bishop's Palace

Beside the cathedral are the extensive ruins of the Bishop's Palace (☎ 720517; Cadw), largely built by Henry de Gower between 1328 and 1347. Until the 16th century, this was a grand residence. It now provides a spectacular setting for the open-air plays held in the summer (see Information earlier). Most of the walls still stand – the ruins are substantial and impressive – and there are two small exhibitions on the site. It opens 9.30 am to 6 pm daily June to September; to 5 pm in April, May and October; and 4 pm daily (afternoon only on Sunday), November to March. Admission costs £2/1.50.

St Non's Bay

St David is said to have been born three-quarters of a mile south of the cathedral, beside the bay that was later named after his mother. A small spring is said to have emerged on the site just as he emerged into the world. The shrine still attracts pilgrims, and the water is believed to have curative powers. Also here are the 13th-century ruins of St Non's Chapel, a modern chapel and a building used as a retreat.

Walking & Cycling Routes

Incorporating sections of the coast path, there are some excellent two- to three-hour walks around St David's peninsula.

From St David's, you could walk south-westwards to the coast at Porthclais, follow the coast path to Caerfai Bay and return to St David's – a walk that will probably take less than two hours.

A wonderful 4½-hour walk takes you from St David's to Porthclais, where you pick up the coast path. Continue right around the western tip of the peninsula (opposite Ramsey Island) to St Justinian, where you follow the road back to St David's.

The quiet lanes that run parallel to the northern coast of Pembrokeshire are perfect for cycling. Voyages of Discovery, on the square, can give advice about routes and St David's Bookshop, at the cathedral entrance, sells booklets on local trails.

Other Things to See & Do

The **Oceanarium** (☎ 720453), 42 New St, houses large sea fish and small sharks. It opens 10 am to 5 pm daily. Admission costs £3/1.80.

Thousand Islands Expeditions (☎ 721 686), Cross Square, offers several **boat tours**. The Two Hour Spectacular on a water-jet boat costs £20/10. Boats are booked here and depart from Whitesand Bay or St Justinian.

TYF Adventure Days (☎ 721611), 1 High St, does coasteering, sea-kayaking, climbing and surfing trips. Prices start at £32/55 for a half/full day. Also here is Voyages of Discovery (☎ 721911), which runs the *Viking Voyager*, an inflatable craft fitted with underwater video cameras, enabling you to see the sea life and wrecks on a trip to Ramsey Island (see St David's to Fishguard later in the chapter). Trips cost £12/7. Visit their Web site at www.tyf.vom.

St David's Scuba Diving Centre (☎ 721 788), Caerfai Bay Rd, is a PADI and BSAC diving school.

Places to Stay

Camping Closest to St David's is *Caerfai Farm Camp Site* (☎ 720548), 20 minutes' walk away. It's 400m from the beach and charges from £3.50, including hot water.

The *Hendre Eynon Caravan & Camping Site* (☎ 720474) is 2½ miles north-east of St David's, situated between the Dowrog

Common Nature Reserve and the coast path. It opens April to September. They charge £3 per person.

You can also camp at **Pencarnan Farm Caravan & Camping Site** (☎ 720324, Porthsele), 2 miles from St David's, and at **Lleithyr Farm** (☎ 720245), near Whitesand Bay.

Hostels Near Whitesand Bay, 1½ miles north-west of St David's, is **St David's Youth Hostel** (☎ 720345). It opens daily (except Thursday) May to September (open Thursday in July and August). The charge is £8.50/5.75 for adults/under-18s.

B&Bs & Hotels A pleasant place to stay is **The Coach House** (☎ 720632, High St), with standard rooms for £15 per person, or £20 with bathroom (£5 extra in August). They also have a good cafe in the house. **Ty Olaf** (☎ 720885, Mount Gardens) is an excellent place offering very comfortable B&B from £16 (winter) to £18 (summer) per person.

The **Old Cross Hotel** (☎ 720387, Cross Square) is set back from the old market square. All rooms have a bathroom, and there's a restaurant and bar. B&B costs £41 per person or £56.50 per person including a two-course dinner.

The modern dormer-bungalow **Ramsey House** (☎ 720321, Lower Moor), half a mile from the cathedral, has seven rooms and is open year round. During high season it only does dinner, B&B deals at £46 per person. Out of season, it's cheaper.

Places to Eat

Cartref Restaurant (☎ 720422, Cross Square) is built round a 17th-century stone cottage. It has vegetarian mains for under £9. For an upmarket meal, **Morgan's Brasserie** (☎ 720508, 20 Nun St) does excellent seafood and has an imaginative Welsh menu. Main dishes, including black fillet steak, cost from £9.50 to £16.50.

There are several teashops to choose from. **The Coach House** (see Places to Stay) has a very nice cafe for light lunches, specialist breakfasts and fresh coffee. The **Pebbles Yard Gallery & Coffee Shop** (☎ 720122, The Pebbles) is a laid-back coffee shop

above a small gallery with organic baguettes (£2.75), fresh juice presses and cakes. **Dyfed Cafe** (☎ 720250, Cross Square) serves lunches and suppers and also has a fish and chip shop if you want takeaway.

The **Farmer's Arms** (Goat St) is the place to drink. It has excellent bar meals and there's a pleasant terrace.

For a pricey, high-calorie snack, you can't miss **Chapel Chocolates**, on the way down to the cathedral.

Getting There & Away

Bus service No 411 or 412 runs from Haverfordwest to St David's (£1.95, 45 minutes, hourly Monday to Saturday, twice daily on Sunday in summer), continuing to Fishguard.

Getting Around

Voyages of Discovery (☎ 721911), on the square, rents bikes for £10 per day.

ST DAVID'S TO FISHGUARD

The coast from St David's to Fishguard is far less touristy than the southern part of Pembrokeshire. The coves and beaches, if they're accessible at all, are reached by tiny, winding lanes and footpaths. If you're only going to walk part of the Pembrokeshire Coast Path, this would be an excellent section to tackle.

Two miles north of St David's is **White-sand Bay**, one of the finest beaches in Wales, and popular with surfers. It can get quite crowded but there's an excellent secluded beach at **Porthmelgan**, 15 minutes' walk northwards.

Lying off St David's Head, **Ramsey Island** is a Royal Society for the Protection of Birds (RSPB) reserve with beautiful cliff scenery and varied bird life, which includes a healthy population of choughs. Ramsey Island Pleasure Cruises (☎ 01437-720285) operates cruises around the island from April to September. They depart daily from St Justinian (3 miles from St David's), at around 10 am, 2 pm and 3.30 pm. Tickets cost £10 on the conventional boat for a 1½-hour cruise or £12 on the rigid inflatable one for an hour's trip. If you're there between late August and mid-November, you may see seal pups. Thousand Islands Expeditions (see St David's earlier) does trips that land on the island, but you'll probably see more wildlife from the boat.

Porthgain is an interesting old coastal village, former brickworks and slate centre. People now come here primarily to eat and drink. In an age of theme pubs, the *Sloop Inn* is famous for its old-fashioned ordinariness. It's a fantastic place for a pint and some pub grub and there are interesting photos showing what the village was like in its industrial heyday. Across the car park there's the more upmarket *Harbour Lights Restaurant* (☎ 013 48-831549) for light lunches or a three-course evening meal for £25 at weekends.

On the route between St David's and Fishguard are two well-located hostels, and numerous farmhouse B&Bs. *Trevine Youth Hostel* (☎ 01348-831414) is in the old school in the centre of Trevine, half a mile from the sea. It's 11 miles along the coast path from Whitesand Bay. Also in the village is the *Old Court House* (☎ 01348-837095), a vegetarian guesthouse and walking-holiday centre. There's B&B for £22.50 per person and delicious vegie dinners for £14.50 most nights.

Eight miles further east from Trevine along the path is *Pwll Deri Youth Hostel* (☎ 01348-891233), in a spectacular location overlooking the bay.

FISHGUARD (ABERGWAUN)
☎ 01348 • pop 3200

Ferry ports tend to be ugly, depressing places, but Fishguard stands out as an exception to the rule. It's on a beautiful bay, and the old part of town (Lower Fishguard) was the location for the 1971 film version of *Under Milk Wood*, which starred Richard Burton and Elizabeth Taylor.

In February 1797, a band of French mercenaries and convicts landed at Carregwastad Point near Fishguard and conducted a series of undisciplined raids on houses in the Pen Caer area.

During one particular raid, the invaders came upon large stocks of Portuguese wine, which proved their undoing. With the invaders in a state of drunkenness, the local people were soon able to round them up.

Appropriately, the surrender was signed in the Royal Oak Inn.

In 1997, the town commemorated the bicentenary of the last invasion of Britain with a 30m tapestry telling the story of the invasion. The tapestry is now on display at St Mary's Town Hall (☎ 874997), Main St. It opens 10 am to 5 pm daily (from 2 pm on Sunday). Admission costs £1.50/50p.

Orientation & Information
The train station, harbour and ferry terminal (for Stena Line ferries to Rosslare, Ireland) are at Goodwick, 20 minutes' walk down the hill from central Fishguard. Eastwards, the road winds round the picturesque harbour of Lower Fishguard.

The TIC (☎ 873484), in the town hall on Market Square, opens daily.

In late July, Fishguard stages a music festival, which includes classical and jazz musicians, some from abroad. For information, phone the festival office (☎ 873612).

You can email at Ocean Lab's Cyber Cafe (☎ 874737), by the Watersports Leisure Centre, between Fishguard and Goodwick. It costs £4 an hour.

The post office is 200 yards down West St from Annie Francis Corner Cafe.

Places to Stay
You can camp at *Fishguard Bay Caravan Park* (☎ 811415), 3 miles to the east, between Fishguard and Newport on the headland at Dinas Cross. It's well situated for the coastal path, and opens March to January. It charges £4 for one person and a tent.

Friendly *Hamilton Guest House & Backpackers Lodge* (☎ 874797, 21 Hamilton St) is near the TIC in Fishguard. It opens 24 hours, with 20 beds in small dorms for £10 per person; double rooms cost £12. There's a kitchen for self-caterers, a TV lounge and laundry. The nearest *hostel* is at Pwll Deri, 4 miles west of Goodwick.

The Beach House (☎ 872085, off Quay Road), above the train line in Goodwick, overlooks the bay and is five minutes' walk from the ferry. It's remarkably welcoming given the constant flow of visitors. B&B costs around £15 per person.

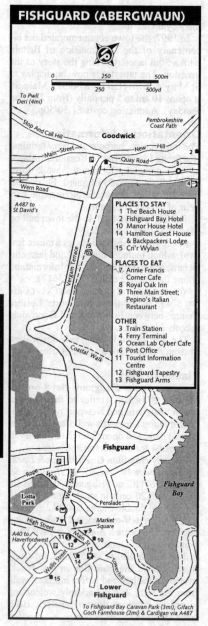

FISHGUARD (ABERGWAUN)

To Pwll Deri (4mi)

Stop And Call Hill
Goodwick
Main Street
New Hill
Quay Road
Wern Road
A487 to St David's
Pembrokeshire Coast Path

Vergam Terrace
Coastal Walk

Rope Walk
West Street
Lotta Park
High Street
A40 to Haverfordwest
Wallis Street
Penslade
Market Square
Fishguard
Fishguard Bay
Lower Fishguard

To Fishguard Bay Caravan Park (3mi), Gifach Goch Farmhouse (2mi) & Cardigan via A487

PLACES TO STAY
1 The Beach House
2 Fishguard Bay Hotel
10 Manor House Hotel
14 Hamilton Guest House & Backpackers Lodge
15 Cri'r Wylan

PLACES TO EAT
7 Annie Francis Corner Cafe
8 Royal Oak Inn
9 Three Main Street; Pepino's Italian Restaurant

OTHER
3 Train Station
4 Ferry Terminal
5 Ocean Lab Cyber Cafe
6 Post Office
11 Tourist Information Centre
12 Fishguard Tapestry
13 Fishguard Arms

SOUTH WALES

There are several other B&Bs in this area, and also the large *Fishguard Bay Hotel* (☎ 873571, Quay Rd, Goodwick), formerly the Great Western Railways Hotel. Single/ double rooms with bathroom cost £45/65.

The excellent *Gifach Goch Farmhouse* (☎ 873871), 2 miles north of Fishguard, is on the road to Cardigan – the Cardigan bus stops at its gate. The farmhouse has six rooms and a lovely garden and offers B&B for £23. It opens March to November.

Back in Fishguard, there's comfortable B&B at *Cri'r Wylan* (☎ 873398, Penwallis), a short walk from the TIC. The charge is £20 per person and it's a small place. *Manor House Hotel* (☎ 873260, Main St) has sea views from the back rooms. B&B costs from around £23 per person, £29 for a room with a view.

Nearby *Three Main Street* (☎ 874275) is recommended. It has only three doubles, all with bathroom, from £30 per person. There's a superb restaurant here.

Places to Eat

There's a good restaurant at *Manor House Hotel* (see Places to Stay earlier). *Pepino's Italian Restaurant* (☎ 875349, 5 Main St) has a good range of pasta and pizzas from £6.75 and also specialises in local seafood. *Three Main Street* (see Places to Stay) next door is one of the best restaurants in South Wales. Set dinners are £23 for two courses, £28 for three. You'll probably need to book.

Try cheap and cheerful *Annie Francis Corner Cafe (Market Square)* or the famous *Royal Oak Inn* (☎ 872514), full of invasion memorabilia.

The *Fishguard Arms (Main St)* is where the serious drinking is done.

Getting There & Away

Richards Brothers (☎ 01239-820751) operates an hourly service, Monday to Saturday, from Haverfordwest to Fishguard (£1.98, 45 minutes). It also runs buses to St David's and Cardigan.

Fishguard is the northern train terminus of a branch line that crosses southern Wales. Fishguard to London trains run twice daily (£44, five hours).

Stena Line (☎ 0990 707070) runs a ferry and catamaran to Rosslare, Ireland (several daily).

Getting Around

Bus service No 410 runs a regular circuit from Fishguard Square to Goodwick Square, Fishguard Harbour and back to Fishguard Square. It operates to coincide with ferry departures (twice hourly, Monday to Saturday).

NEWPORT (TREFDRAETH)

☎ 01239 • pop 1200

This small, attractive town grew up around the castle, and the rocky outcrop **Carn Ingli**, which dominates the town and beach. The castle is Norman but there's evidence of much earlier settlements in the area. Newport makes a very pleasant base for walks along the wild coast or into the Preseli Hills to the south. It's also a nice walk up Carn Ingli, from where there are great views over the bay. There are several beaches – **Parrog**, close to the town, and the better **Newport Sands**, across the river and around the bay.

The National Park Visitors Centre and TIC (☎ 820912), Bank Cottages, Long St, opens Monday to Saturday. Bikes can be hired for £12 per day from Newport Mountain Bikes (☎ 820008) at Llysmeddyg Guest House, East St.

Places to Stay & Eat

Two miles from Newport, is *Brithdir Mawr* (☎ 820164, Cilgwyn Rd), where bunkhouse beds cost £5. The *Morawelon Caravan & Camping Park* (☎ 820565, Parrog Beach), west of Newport, charges £4.20 per person and tent.

Trefdraeth Youth Hostel (☎ 820080, Lower St Mary's St) opens daily except Wednesday and Thursday from April to September (daily in July and August). It charges £9.25/6.50 for adults/under-18s.

Soarhill (☎ 820506, Cilgwyn Rd) is five minutes' walk from town, where rooms cost £18 per person or £22 with bathroom. *Hafan Deg* (☎ 820301, Long St) is a friendly, modern house with garden. Singles/doubles cost from £19/44.

On the outskirts of Newport, and 100m from the coast path, is the excellent *Grove Park Guesthouse* (☎ 820122, Pen-y-Bant). B&B costs around £20 per person.

There are several places you could try for accommodation and food in East St. The *Golden Lion Hotel* (☎ 820321, East St) does B&B from £20/35, and has a bar and restaurant. *Cnapan Country House* (☎ 820575, East St) has five rooms for £28 per person, and opens March to January. It also has a very good restaurant (closed on Tuesday). Set dinners cost £18.

Llysmeddyg Guest House (☎ 820008, East St) is a comfortable, efficiently run B&B in a most attractive building. It charges from £24 per person and includes bathroom. You can also rent bikes here.

The *Llwyngwair Arms* (☎ 820267, East St) is the best pub. It also has a restaurant specialising in Indian food and takeaway.

The homely *Fronlas Cafe* (☎ 820351, Market St) does good lunches – home-made paté, soups and salads; prawn and avocado salad costs £5.95. Bring your own wine from the Spar shop opposite. There are herbal teas, coffees, scones and cakes.

Cafe Fleur (☎ 820131, Market St) serves delicious savoury and sweet crepes and waffles from £2.75 and good fresh coffee.

Getting There & Away

Newport is 7 miles from Fishguard and 12 miles from Cardigan.

Richards Brothers (☎ 820751) operates an hourly service (No 412) to Haverfordwest (£2.44, 1¼ hours) and Cardigan (£1.91, 20 minutes). The service to Haverfordwest runs via Fishguard.

AROUND NEWPORT
Nevern

Situated 2 miles east of Newport, this little village, with its overgrown castle and the **Church of St Brynach**, makes an interesting excursion. St Brynach was a 5th-century Irish holy man who lived in a hut on Carn Ingli, above Newport.

The church is best known for its carved stones. The Maglocunus Stone is thought to date from the 5th century and has an inscription in *ogham* (an ancient Celtic script) and

Latin. In the idyllic churchyard are two more stones, one with another ogham inscription, and the other one of the most impressive Celtic crosses in Wales, dating from the 10th century. Some of the gravestones are interesting, and one of the yew trees is known as the 'bleeding yew', for the blood-like red sap that oozes from it.

Castell Henllys

Located 2 miles south-east of Nevern, this site was originally occupied 2500 years ago and has now been reborn as the **Castell Henllys Iron Age Settlement**.

Some of the buildings – roundhouses, animal pens, a smithy and a grain store – have been partially reconstructed. The settlement

opens 10 am to 5 pm daily, April to October. Admission costs £2.70/1.80.

To get there by bus, take the hourly No 412 from Newport towards Cardigan. Get off at the Melina Rd stop and it's a half-mile walk.

Pentre Ifan

Pentre Ifan is a 4500-year-old *cromlech* (burial chamber) in a remote site, with views across to the sea – to the south stretch the Preseli Hills. Said to be the best-preserved Neolithic burial chamber in Wales the 5m-high capstone is supported by 2m-high boulders. Situated 2 miles south of Nevern, Pentre Ifan is accessible by taking the bus to the same stop for Castell Henllys and then walking southwards down the side roads for a mile.

Central Wales

The majority of visitors to this part of Wales head for the grass-capped mountains of the Brecon Beacons National Park, leaving the quiet valleys of central Wales to the Welsh.

This is unspoilt walking country – farming land interspersed with bare, rolling hills and small lakes. The 120-mile Glyndŵr's Way is a walking trail that visits the sites associated with the Welsh hero between Knighton (on Offa's Dyke Path) and Welshpool via Machynlleth.

Aberystwyth, the only place of any size on the west coast, is a remarkably pleasant university town with good transport connections. Steam trains run through the Vale of Rheidol to Devil's Bridge, with spectacular views of the nearby waterfalls. Several of Wales' other 'Great Little Trains' (narrow-gauge railways) are found in central Wales.

Machynlleth is an attractive market town that makes a good base for exploring the region. On the outskirts of the town, the Centre for Alternative Technology experiments with green living in an interesting working community that welcomes visitors.

Highlights

- Pony trekking in the Brecon Beacons
- Drinking a cool beer at the Brecon Jazz Festival
- Browsing for books in Hay-on-Wye
- Taking the water lift at the Centre for Alternative Technology, Machynlleth
- Riding the steam train from Aberystwyth to Devil's Bridge

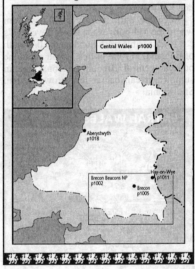

Central Wales p1000

Aberystwyth
p1018

Brecon Beacons NP
p1002

Hay-on-Wye
p1011

Brecon
p1005

Brecon Beacons National Park

Formed in 1957, 'Parc Cenedlaethol Bannau Brycheiniog' covers 522 sq miles of high, grassy ridges, including the highest mountains in southern Britain, interspersed with wooded valleys. Most of the park is privately owned and the slopes provide grazing for thousands of sheep. Pen-y-Fan, at 886m, is the highest point, and the 3200 hectares surrounding it are in the hands of the National Trust (NT).

Although they're referred to as mountains, the Brecon Beacons are hardly the Himalayas and the countryside is less dramatic than Snowdonia to the north. Nevertheless, these bare escarpments are undeniably beautiful, rising in a series of great, green waves above the plains to the north and the former mining valleys to the south. From their crests, walkers are rewarded with spectacular views.

Two long paths pass through the park: Offa's Dyke Path, along the eastern border, and the Taff Trail, south from Brecon. Most people come here to walk but the region offers numerous other outdoor activities. Lôn Las Cymru, the Welsh National Cycle Route, passes through the park on quiet minor roads and cycling paths and on through Glasbury and Builth Wells.

This is perfect pony-trekking country; you can also go fishing, mountaineering and hang-gliding and rent canoes or narrowboats on the Monmouthshire & Brecon Canal. To the south of the park, cavers are attracted to some of the deepest black holes in Britain.

On the northern edge, the eccentric town of Hay-on-Wye, where almost every other shop sells second-hand books, is well worth a visit. Just south of the park at Blaenavon is the Big Pit Mining Museum – the guided tours that venture deep into this old coal mine are highly recommended. Just north of Merthyr Tydfil, vintage steam locos still operate on a short section of the Brecon Mountain Railway.

Since the park is only 30 miles from where the M4 bridges the River Severn, it's easily accessible from London and the south of England. In spite of this, if you avoid the popular central Brecon Beacons area in summer, it can be far less crowded than Snowdonia.

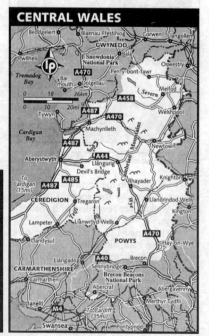

CENTRAL WALES

ORIENTATION

The park is a mere 15 miles from north to south and 45 miles from west to east, yet it comprises four mountain ranges and a variety of terrain.

In the centre is the Brecon Beacons, the range that gives the park its name; the high ridges here form the focal point for walkers. To the west is Fforest Fawr, an area of hills, valleys and, to the south, waterfalls. Farther west is the isolated Black Mountain. In the east are the confusingly named Black Mountains (plural), running north to south between Hay-on-Wye and Abergavenny.

The town of Brecon is the main urban centre within the park's boundaries and it makes a good base, though the nearest train stations are at Abergavenny and Merthyr Tydfil. The Monmouthshire & Brecon Canal follows the valley of the River Usk from Brecon through Abergavenny, which is a good base for the eastern area of the park. Hay-on-Wye, on the northern edge, has a wide range of accommodation.

INFORMATION

The National Park Visitors Centre (☎ 01874-623366, ⓔ mountain.centre@breconbeacons.org) is in open countryside near Libanus, 5 miles south-west of Brecon off the A470. It opens 9.30 am to 6 pm daily in July and August, 4.30 pm in winter and 5 pm at other times. There's also a gift shop and cafe here.

The National Park Information Centres at Brecon (☎ 01874-623156) and Abergavenny (☎ 01873-853254) may be more convenient. The centres open 9.30 am to 5.30 pm daily, April to September; 10.30 pm to 4 pm in October. Although they're only open for part of the year, they're in the same buildings as the Tourist Information Centres (TICs), which are open year round and also have information about the park.

There's an information centre at Llandovery (☎ 01550-720693), which opens 10 am to 1 pm and 1.45 to 5.30 pm daily, April to September (shorter hours the rest of the year; phone for details). There's another at Pen-y-cae (☎ 01639-730395, ⓔ cyncp@breconbeacons.org) in Craig-y-nos Country Park, which opens 10 am to 6 pm Monday to

Friday, to 7 pm at the weekend, May to August (shorter hours the rest of the year; phone for details).

A large range of publications and maps is on sale at these information centres and at TICs in the area. Harveys Superwalker maps cover the park in two 1:25,000 sheets. The park's walking booklets cover the main areas in enough detail for most people spending a few days here. The park even has an *Aircraft Crashes in the National Park* guide. Leaflets describing walks and other activities are listed in the following sections.

Check the weather forecast before setting out on a mountain hike. Take a sweater and waterproof clothing with you, even if it's a sunny day when you start, and be prepared to turn back if the mist comes down. Whatever the weather, it can be very windy on the exposed ridges. Bring something to eat with you but resist the temptation to share it with the sheep or ponies, especially in unfenced areas, as they may become attracted to cars on the roads and cause accidents.

WALKING & CYCLING

The choice of walks in the park is infinite, ranging from a strenuous mountain climb to a gentle stroll along the canal towpath.

In summer, traffic on the A-roads can make cycling hazardous, so stick to smaller roads. The Lôn Las Cymru/Taff Trail is the most interesting cycling route between Cardiff and Brecon. See the Taff Trail & Lôn Las Cymru section later.

Cycle hire is available in some towns (see Brecon, Abergavenny, Hay-on-Wye, Llanwrtyd Wells and Aberystwyth). Bicycle Beano (☎ 01982-560471) organises cycling holidays, with vegetarian wholefood catering. Brecon Cycle Centre (☎ 01874-622651) offers half-day, day and weekend tours, and can arrange accommodation. Its Web site is at www.breconcycles.enta.net.

Brecon Beacons

The classic walk in the park is to the top of the highest of these ridges, Pen-y-Fan, but this area gets crowded in the summer and at weekends. The many routes up are covered in the leaflet *Walks in the Brecon Beacons Area*.

The shortest trail is from the car park at Pont ar Daf or from the Storey Arms (no longer a pub) a mile north. They're both on the bus route along the A470 between Brecon and Merthyr Tydfil. From here it's a 2½-hour hike to the top and back. If you're starting from the Llwyn-y-Celyn Youth Hostel, allow three hours for the return trip. Walking from Brecon it will take five to six hours; follow the side road out of town to the trailhead at Cwm Gwdi.

Directly below Pen-y-Fan, in the natural amphitheatre formed 10,000 years ago during the last Ice Age, there are less strenuous walks around the small lake with the tongue-twisting name of Llyn-cwm-Llwch (pronounced hlin-coom-hlooch).

Taff Trail & Lôn Las Cymru

Linking canal towpaths, disused railways and paths, the 77-mile Taff Trail between Cardiff and Brecon forms the first section of the Lôn Las Cymru, the Welsh National Cycle Route that runs across the country to Anglesey. From Cardiff the waymarked route follows the River Taff north via Castell Coch, the market town of Pontypridd, Merthyr Tydfil, the Pontsticill Reservoir and Talybont-on-Usk to the canal at Pencelli, where there's a choice of routes into Brecon. You can either continue along the canal or follow the side road via Llanfrynach.

Usk Valley

The least demanding walks in the park are along the towpath of the Monmouthshire & Brecon Canal, which follows the valley of the River Usk. It's possible to walk the full 33-mile length of the canal between Brecon and Pontypool. Crickhowell, just north of the canal, would make an excellent overnight stop but there are numerous other villages along the route offering accommodation in B&Bs or pubs. Most walkers just hike the 20-mile Abergavenny to Brecon section.

Black Mountains

Some of the best views on the entire 168-mile length of Offa's Dyke Path are from the 17-mile section that runs through the Black Mountains from Pandy to Hay-on-Wye.

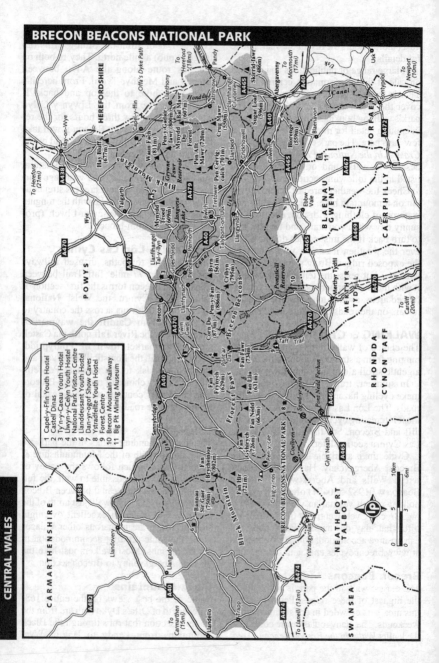

BRECON BEACONS NATIONAL PARK

1 Capel-y-Ffin Youth Hostel
2 Castell Dinas
3 Ty-n-y-Caeau Youth Hostel
4 Llwyn-y-Celyn Youth Hostel
5 National Park Visitors Centre
6 Llanddeusant Youth Hostel
7 Dan-yr-ogof Show Caves
8 Ystradfellte Youth Hostel
9 Forest Centre
10 Brecon Mountain Railway
11 Big Pit Mining Museum

Pandy is on the A465, on the bus route between Abergavenny and Hereford. The route is along a high, exposed grassy ridge that can be very windy. It's definitely worth dropping down to visit the ruins of Llanthony Priory, where the remaining buildings now house a pub and a delightfully atmospheric hotel. Farther north up the valley is the Capel-y-ffin Youth Hostel. As a less strenuous alternative to walking along the ridge, you could follow the River Honddu from Llanfihangel, lower down in the valley. TICs stock the two leaflets that cover walks in the northern and southern parts of this area.

The highest point in the Black Mountains is Waun Fach (811m). If you've got a car, it's best to drive via Patrishow (an interesting 13th-century church in an idyllic location) to the end of the track in the Mynydd Du Forest. Follow the old railway track up to Grwyne Fawr Reservoir, where a path runs up Waun Fach. Alternatively, the peak can be reached by climbing from Llanbedr up to the ridge that runs north via Pen-y-Gadair-fawr.

Around Abergavenny

There are rewarding walks up any of the three hills near Abergavenny, described in detail in *Thirty Walks in the South Black Mountains & the Abergavenny Area*, available from the TIC.

Three miles to the north is the cone-shaped Sugar Loaf (596m). It's a steep climb to the top. A couple of miles southwest of the town is Blorenge (559m), also popular as a launching pad for hang-gliders. Three miles north-east of Abergavenny is Skirrid-fawr (486m); from the top there are good views of Sugar Loaf, the Usk Valley and the Black Mountains.

Fforest Fawr & Waterfall Walks

There's a great variety of scenery in this area, which was once a Norman hunting ground. In the north there are mountain walks in terrain similar to that of the Brecon Beacons.

The youth hostel at **Ystradfellte** makes a good base, and there are a number of attractive waterfalls along the rivers and streams to the south in this wooded area. The most attractive is Sgwd-yr-eira ('the

spout of snow'), where you can actually view the falls from behind the water. It's an easy 2-mile walk south of Ystradfellte, on the River Hepste. There are other falls at Pontneddfechan and Coelbren. Look out for the leaflet on *Waterfall Walks* at the TICs.

Black Mountain

It's not surprising to find another Black Mountain in this range – when the weather is bad, any bare piece of high ground in the Brecon Beacons deserves the name. This western section of the park contains the wildest, least visited walking country. The highest point, Fan Brycheiniog (802m), can be reached from the youth hostel at Llanddeusant or along a path that leads off the side road just north of the Dan-yr-ogof Show Caves (see the next section).

OTHER ACTIVITIES

The Talybont Venture Centre (☎ 01874-676458) in Talybont-on-Usk, 5 miles southeast of Brecon, offers a range of activities, including abseiling, caving, rock climbing, mountain biking and orienteering.

For **cavers**, there are several limestone cave systems in the south of the park, including some of the longest and deepest in Britain. Pick up a copy of the *Caving* leaflet from TICs and, unless you know what you are doing, contact one of the outdoor activity centres (such as the Talybont Venture Centre). If a subterranean sound and light show with stalagmites illuminated in pretty colours is more your idea of going underground, the Dan-yr-ogof Show Caves (☎ 01639-730284) are in the south-western area of the park, 20 miles from Brecon.

Gliders are available for hire from the Black Mountains Gliding Club (☎ 01874-711463), near Talgarth, which offers introductory courses from £45.

There are good fishing rivers in this area. Just to the north of the park, and flowing through Hay-on-Wye, the River Wye is reputed to be the finest salmon river south of the border with Scotland. In the park, the River Usk is among the best waters in Wales for brown trout and salmon fishing. Many of the reservoirs, including the Usk and the

Talybont, are stocked with trout and there's coarse fishing in the canal and Llangorse Lake. You'll need a permit from the owner of the fishing rights as well as an Environment Agency licence.

Pony Trekking & Horse Riding

The open hillsides make this ideal pony-trekking country and there are numerous trekking centres. Charges are from £11 to £16 for two hours (£23 for a full day) and many of the centres are on farms which also offer B&B accommodation. Places to try include the Grange Pony Trekking Centre (☎ 01873-890215) at Capel-y-ffin, and Llangorse Riding Centre (☎ 01874-658272) near Brecon. Llangorse Riding Centre will also cater to serious riders interested in a superior mount, as will Cwmfforest Riding Centre (☎ 01874-711398) at Talgarth, which offers a range of riding holidays.

Canal Cruising

The Monmouthshire & Brecon Canal links Brecon with Pontypool in Gwent. There are only six locks along its 33-mile length and there's one lock-free section of 22 miles. Built for the iron industry in the early 19th century, it fell into disuse in the 1930s but has now been restored and opened to recreational traffic.

Traditional narrowboats can be hired for a week from Cambrian Cruisers (☎ 01874-665315), Ty Newydd, Pencelli, near Brecon, starting at around £700 for a two-berth. Dragonfly Cruises (☎ 0831 685222) in Brecon operates 2½-hour cruises at noon and 3 pm on Wednesday, Thursday (summer only), Saturday and Sunday, for £5/3 for adults/children. The 1½-hour cruises (£3.25/2.50) run by Water Folk (☎ 01874-665382), Old Storehouse, Llanfrynach, are more traditional – the boats are horse drawn.

PLACES TO STAY & EAT

There are five YHA youth hostels in the national park – Ty'n-y-Caeau (2½ miles from Brecon), Llwyn-y-Celyn (by the A470 Merthyr Tydfil to Brecon road), Capel-y-ffin (8 miles south of Hay-on-Wye, attached to a pony-trekking centre), Ystradfellte (in the

waterfall and caving district) and isolated Llanddeusant below the Black Mountain.

There are 15 independent bunkhouses in the area. Some are mentioned here but contact TICs or the Association of Bunkhouse Operators (☎ 07071-780259) for the full list.

With the permission of the farmer or landowner, it's possible to camp almost anywhere in the park, but not on NT land. TICs have lists of camp sites with full facilities.

There's a good range of B&Bs and hotels in and around the main centres of Brecon, Abergavenny and Hay-on-Wye, as well as in the villages along the Usk Valley. Some hotels offer all-inclusive activity holidays, including fishing or riding.

GETTING THERE & AROUND

It takes three to four hours to drive to the Brecon Beacons from London, via the M4 over the River Severn and along the A4024 from Newport.

Stagecoach Red & White (☎ 01633-266 336) buses run between Cardiff, Merthyr Tydfil and Abergavenny; Brecon, Hay-on-Wye and Hereford; and Brecon, Abergavenny, Pontypool and Newport. First Cymru runs buses between Swansea and Brecon. For information on First Cymru's national and local bus services, call ☎ 0870 608 2608.

There are rail services to Abergavenny (via Newport) and Merthyr Tydfil (via Cardiff) but not to Brecon. Phone ☎ 01332-387601 for information.

Between smaller villages, public transport is severely limited. Distances are not great, however, and if you're not prepared to walk it's worth considering a taxi.

Explore the Brecon Beacons is a useful free guide available from TICs. It lists bus and train timetables plus walks that can be linked to public transport routes.

BRECON (ABERHONDDU)

☎ 01874 • pop 7000

The principal centre in the national park is the attractive, historic market town of Brecon. It is an excellent base for exploring the area and has a good range of accommodation for all budgets, including a youth hostel just outside the town, as well as plenty of places to eat.

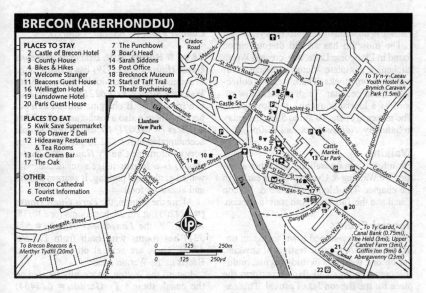

BRECON (ABERHONDDU)

PLACES TO STAY
2 Castle of Brecon Hotel
3 County House
8 Bikes & Hikes
10 Welcome Stranger
11 Beacons Guest House
16 Wellington Hotel
19 Lansdowne Hotel
20 Paris Guest House

7 The Punchbowl
9 Boar's Head
14 Sarah Siddons
15 Post Office
18 Brecknock Museum
21 Start of Taff Trail
22 Theatr Brycheiniog

PLACES TO EAT
5 Kwik Save Supermarket
8 Top Drawer 2 Deli
12 Hideaway Restaurant
   & Tea Rooms
13 Ice Cream Bar
17 The Oak

OTHER
1 Brecon Cathedral
6 Tourist Information
   Centre

*To Brecon Beacons &
Merthyr Tydfil (20mi)*

*To Ty'n-y-Caeau
Youth Hostel &
Brynich Caravan
Park (1.5mi)*

*To Ty Gardd,
Canal Bank (0.75mi),
The Held (3mi), Upper
Cantref Farm (3mi),
Griffin Inn (9mi) &
Abergavenny (23mi)*

0   125   250m
0   125   250yd

The Celtic hill forts of Pen-y-Crug and Slwch attest to the fact that the area was occupied long before the Romans arrived in AD 75. The remains of their camp at Y Gaer, 3 miles west of the town, can be visited. It was not until Norman times that Brecon began to grow. The local Welsh chieftain was overthrown by Bernard de Newmarch, the Norman lord who built the castle and church.

Orientation

Brecon is a compact town with everything within walking distance. There's no train or bus station – most buses leave and arrive at the Bulwark in the centre, close to the TIC. B&Bs are in two groups: around the Watton and across Bridge St in Llan Faes, the western area of Brecon.

Information

The TIC (☎ 622485, ⓔ brectic@powys.gov .uk), open 10 am to 6 pm daily, is in the Cattle Market car park. The National Park Information Centre (☎ 623156) shares the same office and opens daily from Easter to October; at other times, the well-stocked TIC can help with information.

For information on the Jazz Festival (see Special Events later) contact the festival office (☎ 625557). Some performances are hosted in the new Theatr Brycheiniog (☎ 611 622), by the canal on Canal Rd.

Brecon Cathedral

Built in the 11th century above the River Honddu in the north of Brecon, on the site of an earlier church, all that remains of the Norman building are parts of the walls of the nave. The tower, choir and transepts date from the 13th century. In the mid-1860s the church was restored by Sir Gilbert Scott. In the western end of the nave is a stone cresset (an ancient lighting device), the only one that exists in Wales. The 30 cups each held oil to illuminate the church lamps.

There's an exhibition about the cathedral in the heritage centre (☎ 625222), housed in the restored tithe barn on Cathedral Close. The exhibition opens 10 am to 4.30 pm Monday to Saturday, April to December. A £1 donation is requested from visitors.

Brecknock Museum

This is one of the more interesting museums of the old county of Brecknockshire of which Brecon was the county town. The district is now absorbed into Powys.

The museum has an old dugout canoe found in Llangorse Lake, a re-created Welsh kitchen, a complete Victorian assize court and the town stocks. There's also a collection of that peculiar Welsh utensil (now reborn as a tourist souvenir), the lovespoon. The museum opens 10 am to 5 pm, Monday to Saturday. Admission costs £1/50p.

Walking

For information on walking and other activities see Walking & Cycling Routes earlier in the chapter. The Monmouthshire & Brecon Canal and the Taff Trail both start in Brecon.

Special Events

This sober, grey-stoned town seems an unlikely venue for a music festival of any kind but on one weekend in mid-August, multicoloured awnings and flags transform the place for the Brecon Jazz Festival. This has become one of Europe's leading jazz festivals and it attracts thousands for what is essentially one long party. One famous jazz musician you may see in town is George Melly, who has a house nearby.

Places to Stay

Camping One and a half miles east of Brecon is *Brynich Caravan Park* (☎ 623325, *Brynich*). A caravan or tent with two people costs £8.50/9.50 in low/high season.

During the jazz festival, open areas in the town are turned into temporary camp sites.

Hostels In a large country house near the caravan park is the *Ty'n-y-Caeau Youth Hostel* (☎ 665270, *Groesfford*). Open from February to October, it closes on Sunday except on bank holiday weekends and during the middle of summer; phone for details of opening times. The nightly charge is £10/6.90 for adults/under-18s.

There are several bunkhouses in the area, all charging £7.50 to £9. Less than a mile from Brecon is *Canal Bank* (☎ 625361, *Ty Camlas, Canal Bank*). Three miles southeast of Brecon, there's *The Held* (☎ 624646, *Cantref*). There is more bunkhouse accom-

modation, and also a riding centre, at *Upper Cantref Farm* (☎ 665223, *Cantref*).

B&Bs & Hotels At 16 Bridge St, *Beacons Guest House* (☎ 623339) has a large range of rooms, with singles/doubles from £25/36. *Welcome Stranger* (☎ 622188, *7 Bridge St*) is a friendly B&B charging around £16 per person. There's also a restaurant here. *Bikes & Hikes* (☎ 610071, *10 Struet*) does simple accommodation for £12.50 per person. The very comfortable *County House* (☎ 625844, *Struet*) is a former judge's residence with walled garden and parking. It charges £35/55 and also does food.

Along the Watton, the *Paris Guest House* (☎ 624205), at No 28, has rooms for £17/38. At No 39, the *Lansdowne Hotel* (☎ 623 321) has rooms with bath from £27.50/47.50. There are several other hotels and B&Bs in the Watton area.

Just off the Watton, peacefully located on the canal, there's *Ty Gardd* (☎ 623464) where rooms cost £17/34 or £40 for the double with bath.

The *Wellington Hotel* (☎ 625225) is right in the centre of town on the Bulwark. It's a comfortable place with a good range of facilities including a pub, coffee shop and wine bar. B&B costs £35/55.

The only part of the Norman castle that you can visit has been incorporated into the *Castle of Brecon Hotel* (☎ 624611, *Castle Square*), though there's not much left of the old building. Rooms in the main hotel cost £54/69, and in the lodge nearby they're £45/59, all with bath or shower.

The *Griffin Inn* (☎ 754241) at Llyswen (about 9 miles from Brecon on the A470) is a good place to stay and an excellent place to eat. B&B costs around £35 per person. Distinctly superior pub grub includes wood pigeon, jugged hare, braised wild duck and partridge with game chips. Most main dishes cost from £9.90 to £13.85.

Places to Eat

The restaurant at the *Beacons Guest House* (see Places to Stay earlier) is open to non-residents and the food is all home-made and very good. There's a three-course dinner for

£14.85 to £17.95. The dining room at the upmarket *Castle of Brecon Hotel* is more expensive but recommended.

There are several tearooms that also do reasonably priced meals, but they close early in the evening. *Hideaway Restaurant & Tea Rooms (High St)* is the place for cream teas, light lunches and superb chocolate gateau. *The Oak (☎ 625501)*, on the Bulwark, is a little more upmarket and has a pleasant garden patio.

For self-catering, there's the *Kwik Save supermarket* opposite Mount St or the *Top Drawer 2 Deli (High St)*, which stocks a wonderful range of breads and Welsh cheeses. The *Ice Cream Bar*, in the alley opposite the TIC, is always busy. Everything is home-made and very good.

Entertainment

The town has a good selection of pubs. Locals head for the lively *Boar's Head*, Ship St, *The Punchbowl* on High St and the *Sarah Siddons*, on the Bulwark. Sarah Siddons, one of the most famous actresses of the 18th century, was born in Brecon. The bar at the *Wellington Hotel* is recommended and has live jazz some evenings.

Getting There & Away

Brecon is 167 miles from London, 45 miles from Cardiff, 48 miles from Bristol and 20 miles from Abergavenny. The nearest train stations are at Abergavenny and Merthyr Tydfil (from Cardiff). Taxis charge about £15 to Merthyr Tydfil.

National Express (☎ 0870 580 8080) has daily links to Brecon from most parts of southern Britain via Cardiff (£2.75, 1½ hours). Stagecoach Red & White (☎ 01633-266336) operates daily coaches between Brecon and Merthyr Tydfil (35 minutes), Swansea (85 minutes) and four indirect services a day to Cardiff.

Bus No 39 runs between Brecon and Hereford via Hay-on-Wye five times a day (No 40, twice on Sunday).

Getting Around

Mountain bikes can be rented from Bikes & Hikes (see Places to Stay earlier). Rates are £10/15 for a half/full day; they also arrange guided walks and other outdoor activities. There's pony trekking available at Upper Cantref Farm (see Places to Stay) for £9/£22 per hour/day. For taxis, try Brecon Taxis (☎ 623444).

BRECON TO ABERGAVENNY
Crickhowell
☎ 01873 • pop 2000

This little village on the bus route between Brecon and Abergavenny is another good walking base. An impressive 17th-century stone bridge crosses the River Usk, leading to the neighbouring village of Llangattock. The TIC (☎ 812105, @ brecon.tourism@ powys.gov.uk) is on Beaufort St by the main A40. There's no shortage of pubs in the village, most serving food, and plenty of decent accommodation in the area to suit all budgets.

There's a camp site in the village, the *Riverside Caravan Park (☎ 810397, New Rd)*; charges are £8 per tent (two adults).

The most central B&B is *Mrs Morgan's (☎ 811177, 2 Greenhill Villas, Beaufort St)* with rooms from £20/36 for a single/double. The friendly *Ty Gwyn (☎ 811625)* is a lovely house on the Brecon road and charges £42 to £45 for a double or £35 for single occupancy.

The *Bear Hotel (☎ 810408, Beaufort St)* is the best place to stay in town, and rates range from £49.50 to £94 for a single, £65 to £120 for a double. Some rooms have Jacuzzis. There's excellent bar food and a good restaurant.

Tretower Court & Castle

Three miles north-west of Crickhowell, Tretower combines a large, medieval manor house and, across the meadow, a 13th-century tower, part of a castle. The house has been considerably restored and was originally the home of the Vaughan family; the best-known member of the family was the metaphysical poet, Henry Vaughan.

Tretower Court (☎ 01874-730279) is run by Cadw, the Welsh historic monuments agency, and opens 10 am to 4.30 pm daily; it closes end of October to March. Admission costs £2.20/1.70.

CENTRAL WALES

ABERGAVENNY (Y FENNI)

☎ 01873 • pop 11,000

Standing by the eastern edge of the park, surrounded by hills, this busy market town styles itself as the 'Gateway to Wales'. It's a good base for walking in the Black Mountains, with a wide range of accommodation and, unlike Brecon, a train station.

The TIC (☎ 857588, ⓔ abergavenny-tic@tsww.com) is by the bus stand in Swan Meadow, and opens year round. In the same building is a National Park Visitors Centre (☎ 853254).

The town's history goes back 4000 years when there was a Neolithic settlement here. The Romans established Gobarium Fort nearby and stayed from AD 57 to 400, but Abergavenny only really began to grow after Hamelin de Ballon built his castle in 1090. Eventually falling into ruin, the keep was heavy-handedly restored by the Victorians and now houses a small **museum** of local history. It opens 11am to 5pm Monday to Saturday (closed for lunch) and 2pm to 5pm on Sunday. It closes at 4pm daily and all day Sunday from November to February. Admission is £1/free.

The lively weekly market on Tuesday in the original Market Hall sells food, clothing and bric-a-brac, and is worth checking out for its bargains and ambience.

Among the former visitors who have enjoyed the town's rural position was Rudolf Hess in 1941. Although he wasn't here on holiday, his wardens did allow him a weekly hike up Pen-y-Fan.

Activities

Axis Paragliding School (☎ 850910, 37 Cross St) offer one- and two-day introductory courses in **paragliding** and **hanggliding** from the Sugar Loaf, Blorenge and other mountains in the area. The course costs £84/£160 for one/ two days (including membership of the British Hang Gliding & Paragliding Association; BHPA); longer courses are also available. For more down-to-earth types, visit Sugar Loaf Vineyard (☎ 858675) where you can sip the local produce of seven varieties of grape. The visitor centre opens daily 10 am to 5 pm,

March to December; you'll find it just off the A40, about a mile from town.

Places to Stay

Two miles north of Abergavenny, in the village of Pantygelli, is the recently renovated *Smithy's Bunkhouse* (☎ 853432), down the farm track opposite the Crown Inn. There are two dormitories at this well-equipped bunkhouse (with a new bunkhouse planned for 2001); charges are around £7 per person. There's a laundry, common room and kitchen. The nearest youth hostel to Abergavenny is at Capel-y-ffin, 15 miles north on the road to Hay-on-Wye.

In the north of the town, the 200-year-old *Aenon House* (☎ 858708, 34 Pen-y-Pound) is a very pleasant place to stay. Rooms cost £18/35 for a single/double. Award-winning *Pentre House* (☎ 853435, Brecon Rd) is another good choice, with rooms for £25/34. 'Best place I stayed in,' wrote one reader.

There are several other B&Bs around the train station. On Holywell Rd, *Belchamps Guest House* (☎ 853204) charges £21/38.

Park Guest House (☎ 853715, 36 Hereford Rd) is a Georgian building with six rooms for £18/32. The *Guest House* (☎ 854 823, 2 Oxford St) is nearby, with comfortable rooms for £19.50/36 and evening meals.

The *Great George Hotel* (☎ 854230, Cross St) charges £25 including breakfast (£20 room only). The top place in town is the *Angel Hotel* (☎ 857121, Cross St). Rooms cost £55/70 and there are cheaper two-night deals at weekends.

Places to Eat

On Market St there's *Market St Fish & Chips* (☎ 855791) for takeaways. There are any number of coffee shops for lunch fare on and around Cross St. *Luigi's* on Cross St has a good selection of pasta dishes for under £5. For decent Chinese, try *The Peking Chef*, across the road.

Three miles north-east of Abergavenny at Llandewi Skirrid is the legendary *Walnut Tree Inn* (☎ 852797), opened in 1963 and reputed to be the best restaurant in Wales. The chef is Italian, the cuisine international and the ingredients, as far as possible,

Welsh. The menu might include anything from *vincigrassi* (pasta, bechamel, porcini and truffles) to bubble and squeak. It closes Sunday and Monday, and is very busy when it's open so you must book for the restaurant. They also have a bistro and do a popular lunch and evening trade. After a memorable dinner for two, including drinks and service, don't expect any change out of £80.

Getting There & Around

There's no direct National Express service from London; you must change at Hereford. Stagecoach Red & White (☎ 01633-266336) runs services to Brecon (£2.30, 1 hour) or Cardiff (£2.50, 2 hours 20 minutes).

The train station is just off Monmouth Rd, a 15-minute walk from the bus station and TIC. There are services to Cardiff every hour (£7.30) and direct trains to Manchester. London requires a change at Newport. For information phone ☎ 08457 484950.

For a taxi try Lewis Taxis (☎ 854140) or Station Taxis (☎ 857233). You can rent bikes from Access Paragliding School (see Activities earlier) for £15 per day.

AROUND ABERGAVENNY
Blaenavon

Five miles south-west of Abergavenny, Blaenavon is home to the **Big Pit Mining Museum**, created inside a real mine which ceased production in 1980 – 100 years after the first miners began work there.

You can descend 90m to the pit floor in an old mine lift and inspect the tunnels and coalfaces. Safety precautions are treated seriously so you'll be decked out in a hard hat and a heavy power pack will be attached to your waist to light your helmet lamp. Some of the guides were once miners who cut coal here. It's not a trip for the claustrophobic. As well as the mine itself, you can see the old pithead baths, the blacksmith's workshop and other colliery buildings.

The Big Pit (☎ 01495-790311) opens 9.30 am to 5 pm daily, March to November, with one-hour underground tours from 10 am (last tour 3.30 pm). It's cold at the bottom of the mine, and you should wear sturdy shoes. Admission costs £5.75/3.95.

ABERGAVENNY TO HAY-ON-WYE
Llanfihangel Crucorney

This little village, 5 miles from Abergavenny off the road between Abergavenny and Hereford, attracts lots of tourists. They mainly come to see the *Skirrid Mountain Inn* (☎ 01873-890258), which claims to be the oldest pub in Wales. From the early 12th century until the 17th century this was the courthouse, where almost 200 prisoners were hanged – the rope marks on one of the beams can still be seen.

The most pleasant place to stay nearby is wonderful *Penyclawdd Court* (☎ 01873-890719), a tastefully restored Tudor manor house below Bryn Arw mountain. B&B is £50/80 for a single/double and you must book ahead.

Llanthony

The ruins of the 13th-century Augustinian priory church and the monastic buildings of **Llanthony Priory** (Cadw) are set in a beautiful, remote location in the Ewyas Valley. There's a superb walk from the car park up onto the bare ridge above. Offa's Dyke runs along the ridge.

The *Abbey Hotel* (☎ 01873-890487) is built into some of the surviving abbey buildings. Like Penyclawdd Court in Llanfihangel Crucorney, it's recommended for its atmosphere. There's a public bar in the vaulted crypt that serves basic meals. It opens daily from Easter to October and at weekends in winter. Rooms are let only as doubles, and they're £46 during the week and £110 for a minimum two-night stay (for two people) at weekends.

Capel-y-Ffin

Farther up the valley is Llanthony Monastery, founded in 1870. It was unoccupied in the 1920s when Eric Gill, artist and typographer, started a commune in it. It's now a private residence.

Capel-y-ffin Youth Hostel (☎ 01873-890650) is a mile north of the village, by the road to Hay-on-Wye. Its opening hours are complex – phone for details – but it usually opens daily from June to August and closes in December and January. The nightly charge is £8.50/5.75 for adults/under-18s.

There's a riding school by the hostel – this is excellent pony-trekking country; bookings can be made through the hostel. Offa's Dyke Path is 1½ miles from the hostel on the ridge. The walk to Hay-on-Wye is highly recommended.

HAY-ON-WYE
☎ 01497 • pop 1500

On 1 April 1977 Hay-on-Wye declared independence from Britain – just one publicity stunt this eccentric little bookshop town has used to draw attention to itself.

Most of the publicity has been generated by bookseller Richard Booth, the colourful, self-styled King of Hay, who is largely responsible for Hay's evolution from just another market town on the Welsh/English border to the second-hand bookshop capital of the world.

A day browsing among the shops is definitely recommended. With its small centre made up of narrow sloping lanes, the town itself is also interesting and the people it attracts certainly are. On the north-eastern corner of the national park, Hay makes an excellent base for the Black Mountains.

History
Most events in the history of Hay have been connected with its location as a Marches town, on the border of Wales and England. In fact, during the Norman period the town was administered as English Hay (the town proper) and Welsh Hay (the countryside to the south and west of the town).

A castle had already stood in the town before the construction of the present one, built in about 1200 by the treacherous William Breos II (one of the Norman barons, or Lords Marcher, granted vast tracts of land on border country to consolidate conquered territory). From then until the final acquisition of Wales by the English Crown, Hay changed hands many times. It subsequently became a market town, employing a large number of people in the flannel trade during the 18th century. The first large-scale second-hand bookshop opened in 1961, the vanguard of a new industry.

The castle, complete with the Jacobean mansion built within its Norman walls, was purchased by Booth in 1971 but a fire in 1977 left it in its present dilapidated state.

Orientation & Information
Hay's compact centre contains the castle and most of the bookshops within a roughly square perimeter. The main central thoroughfare is Castle St, which links Oxford Rd with Lion St.

The TIC (☎ 820144) is on Oxford Rd, on the edge of town and just by the main car park. It opens 10 am to 5 pm daily, Easter to October, and from 11 am to 4 pm at all other times.

Most bookshops stock the useful free town plan that locates and describes all the bookshops in Hay. The annual Festival of Literature takes place in May/June and is a very popular and entertaining affair.

Canadian canoes (for two/three people) can be hired from Paddles & Pedals (☎ 820 604), Castle St, for £15 per canoe for half a day or £25 for a day.

Things to See & Do
There are now over 30 second-hand bookshops in Hay, containing literally hundreds of thousands of books – 400,000 in Richard Booth's bookshop alone. British publishers churn out more than 80,000 new titles each year, and this country has a long history of publishing. According to the experts, quantity rather than quality is what you'll find in most places in Hay.

Some of these bookshops specialise in esoteric fields – for example, **B & K Books** (☎ 820386) on Newport St boasts the world's finest stock of books on apiculture. **Rose's Books** (☎ 820013) at 14 Broad St stocks rare and out-of-print children's books. **Lion St Bookshop** (☎ 820121), 1 St John's Place, deals in militaria and anarchism. There's theology and church history at **Marches Gallery** (☎ 821451), Lion St. **Murder and Mayhem** (☎ 821613), 5 Lion St, is filled with detective fiction, true crime and horror.

Many bookshops, however, cover everything – the most famous being **Richard Booth's** (☎ 820322), 44 Lion St, and the **Hay Cinema Bookshop** (☎ 820071), Castle

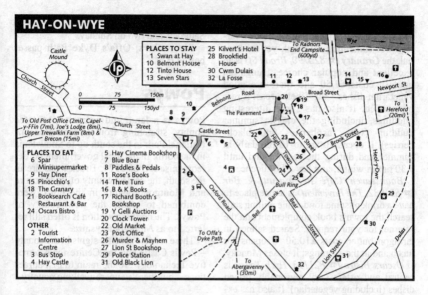

HAY-ON-WYE

PLACES TO STAY
1 Swan at Hay
10 Belmont House
12 Tinto House
13 Seven Stars
25 Kilvert's Hotel
28 Brookfield House
30 Cwm Dulais
32 La Fosse

PLACES TO EAT
6 Spar Minisupermarket
9 Hay Diner
15 Pinocchio's
18 The Granary
21 Booksearch Café Restaurant & Bar
24 Oscars Bistro
5 Hay Cinema Bookshop
7 Blue Boar
8 Paddles & Pedals
11 Rose's Books
14 Three Tuns
16 B & K Books
17 Richard Booth's Bookshop
19 Y Gelli Auctions
20 Clock Tower
22 Old Market
23 Post Office
26 Murder & Mayhem
27 Lion St Bookshop
29 Police Station
31 Old Black Lion

OTHER
2 Tourist Information Centre
3 Bus Stop
4 Hay Castle

St. Some shops will carry out searches to locate out-of-print books. **Booksearch** (Hay-on-Wye, Hereford HR3 5EA) deals only by post or through its Web site at www.booksearch-at-hay.com, but you can eat and drink here – see Places to Eat later. There are regular book auctions at **Y Gelli Auctions** (☎ 821179), Broad St.

Places to Stay
Radnors End Campsite (☎ 820780) is 600 yards from the bridge over the River Wye, on the road to Clyro. The cost is £3 per person.

Hay has a fair number of B&Bs and hotels but the nearest youth hostel is at Capel-y-Ffin, 8 miles south (see the Abergavenny to Hay-on-Wye section earlier in the chapter). To stay at **Joe's Lodge** (☎ 01874-711845, Hay Rd, Talgarth), 8 miles south-west of Hay, you need to book in advance. It's an independent hostel and B&B costs £10. Also in Talgarth, there's an upmarket B&B at **Upper Trewalkin Farm** (☎ 01874-711349, Pengenffordd) for £20 per person. Evening meals (from £13 per person) are excellent. Short-stay specials are also available.

Back in Hay, **Brookfield House** (☎ 820 518, Brook St) is a centrally located 16th-

century residence. Singles/doubles cost from £18/32. **Belmont House** (☎ 820718, Belmont Rd) is well located, with rooms for £20/32 (£38 for a double with bathroom). At the friendly and central **Cwm Dulais** (☎ 820640, Heol-y-Dwr), there's B&B for £19 per person or £25 for a single. **La Fosse** (☎ 820613, Oxford Rd) is a comfortable place charging £40 for a double room with bathroom (no singles). Popular **Kilvert's Hotel** (☎ 821042) is right in the centre on the Bull Ring, with rooms from £35/65.

The **Seven Stars** (☎ 820886, Broad St) is an excellent place to stay. As well as comfortable rooms from £22/37 (or £28/45 with bath), it even has a swimming pool and sauna. Booking ahead is advisable. Almost next door, **Tinto House** (☎ 820590) is a pleasant place with a secluded garden, which charges £30/40.

The **Swan at Hay** (☎ 821188, Church St) is more conventionally luxurious, charging £50 for singles and £65 to £100 for doubles.

Two miles from Hay, at Llanigon and near Offa's Dyke Path, is the **Old Post Office** (☎ 820008), an excellent vegetarian B&B with rooms for £17 per person with shared bathroom, £25 with private bathroom.

Places to Eat

For such a small place, there's a lot of variety. For something informal, yet substantial, the *Granary* (☎ 820790, Broad St) is an excellent and popular choice. Hungarian goulash costs £7.50 and there are good vegetarian dishes – the Tibetan roast is recommended. It also has some interesting puddings, including the classic summer pudding (with raspberries and blackberries). It opens 10 am to 10 pm daily in summer and during the festival and until 5.30 pm in winter, and has a full licence.

Booksearch Café Restaurant & Bar (☎ 821932, The Pavement) is a nice place to have a drink or some food while willing staff search the town's book complement and the Internet for your request. Seared salmon in tarragon butter costs £10.50. It opens for lunch and in the evenings; it closes Monday.

Oscars Bistro (☎ 821193, High Town) is central and offers very reasonably priced dishes (including vegetarian). It also has excellent filled baguettes for £3.50. *Pinocchio's* (☎ 821166, 2 Broad St) is a good Italian restaurant with excellent pizza.

The tiny *Three Tuns* (Broad St) is a wonderful old pub and cider house, popular with locals. The *Blue Boar* (☎ 820884, Castle St) has a wide selection of bar food, and there's upmarket pub grub at the *Old Black Lion* (Lion St). *Kilvert's Hotel* (see Places to Stay earlier) is a cosy place which has good pub food and an a la carte restaurant. The pub part can get a bit smoky if you're dining. Escalope of salmon with lemongrass costs £10.95; pizza and pastas start at £4.

Hay Diner, on Castle St, is good for a coffee, a beer or a full meal – and there's a takeaway next door. The diner opens 10 am to 10 pm daily. There's some seating in the garden. There's a *Spar minisupermarket* on Castle St for picnic material.

Getting There & Away

The nearest train station is in Hereford. There are six buses a day to Hereford (£3.40, one hour), Monday to Saturday, and three buses on Sunday. Departures are from Oxford Rd and there are also additional services from the clock tower on Broad St. For Brecon (40 minutes), there are six buses a day, Monday to Saturday, and two on Sunday.

For walkers, Offa's Dyke Path passes beside Hay.

Powys

Powys is a large and sparsely populated county, stretching from Brecon Beacons National Park in the south up to Snowdonia in the north. In the local government border reorganisation of 1974, Brecknockshire in the south, the central county of Radnorshire and Montgomeryshire in the north were combined to create the new county of Powys. The northern section is often still referred to as Montgomeryshire.

There are few specific sights in the county – Powis Castle and the Centre for Alternative Technology are the main tourist attractions – but there's superb walking country.

WALKING

The best-known walk in the area is **Offa's Dyke Path**, the 168-mile national trail that runs the length of Wales, following the eastern border of Powys. See the Activities chapter for more information.

The 120-mile **Glyndŵr's Way** passes through beautiful countryside and has the added interest of following in the footsteps of the Welsh hero Owain Glyndŵr. Contact the Planning Information Service, Powys County Council, County Hall, Llandrindod Wells, Powys LD1 6GG, for a series of leaflets covering the trail. There's also a guidebook: *Owen Glyndŵr's Way* by Richard Sale.

It takes five to nine days to walk from Knighton to Welshpool via Machynlleth. Some sections are along roads, which you could cut out by using public transport.

GETTING AROUND

Public transport in this area is limited. To visit the more remote areas, a certain amount of advance planning is necessary.

Bus

Arriva Cymru operates bus services to and from many areas in central Wales. It has daily Red Rover tickets for £4.60/2.30 which allow unlimited travel on its services in Gwynedd and Anglesey, except for the 701. They also have a one-/three-/five-day Explorer ticket for £5/10/15. You can also use this pass on Arriva Midland services across the border in England.

Train

Rail services are sparse. The Cambrian Main Line runs through Shrewsbury and Machynlleth to terminate in Aberystwyth; the Heart of Wales Line brushes across the south-eastern corner from Shrewsbury via Llandrindod Wells and Builth Wells and continues south to Swansea.

A useful ticket is the North & Mid Wales Rover, valid for seven days (£40.90) or for any three out of seven days (£26.30) on main-line services between Aberystwyth and Shrewsbury, Shrewsbury to Crewe and Crewe to Holyhead, and also on most bus services in the area. The Rover also entitles the holder to discounts on some of the private railways. However, it doesn't include services on the Shrewsbury-Llandrindod Wells-Swansea line. Phone ☎ 08457 484950 for information.

LLANWRTYD WELLS

☎ 01591 • pop 600

Llanwrtyd Wells was developed as a spa town in the 18th century when the health benefits of the local sulphur spring (still flowing) were discovered. This small attractive town (reputedly the smallest town in Britain) is surrounded by beautiful country-side, with the Cambrian Mountains to the north-west and the Mynydd Eppynt to the south-east. As well as walking, mountain biking and pony trekking, the town hosts a number of less orthodox events and pastimes – see the boxed text 'World Bog Snorkelling Championships' below.

There's a TIC (☎ 610666, ⓔ tic@celt.rural wales.org) on the square. The *Stonecroft Hostel* (☎ 610332) is a friendly self-catering guesthouse near the centre of town on Dol-y-coed Rd. It's a good place with rooms from £12.50 per person. There's a kitchen, riverside garden and TV room. The *Stonecroft Inn*, next door, is an excellent place for a pint and good pub grub. The *Neuadd Arms* (☎ 610236) on the square does B&B from £24 per person (£27 with bathroom). It rents mountain bikes for £12 per day.

LLANDRINDOD WELLS

☎ 01597 • pop 5200

Roman remains at Castell Collen nearby show that people were here long before Llandrindod Wells was reinvented as a spa town in the 18th and 19th centuries. The town's architecture – towers, balustrades, balconies – and ironwork reflect the tastes and style of that time. You can still take the water outside the Pump Room in Rock Park though no treatments are available. Once a year there's a Victorian Festival where the townspeople dress up in Victorian clothes.

The town is the administrative centre for Powys. The TIC (☎ 822600 ⓔ llantic@ powys.gov.uk) is in the Old Town Hall, Memorial Gardens, Temple St. The *Llanerch*

World Bog-Snorkelling Championships

Llanwrtyd Wells hosts numerous alternative activities. There's the Real Ale Wobble, a cycling event held in conjunction with the beer festival, and the Man vs Horse Marathon, in which runners and horses compete. In 1982, the sponsors very nearly had to hand over the £10,000 prize money to man, as horse won by only four minutes.

The most alternative of all events held here, however, must be the World Bog-Snorkelling Championships. Held over the August bank holiday, competitors must swim two lengths of a specially prepared 55m-long peat bog trench using a snorkel and fins. They may surface only twice for navigational purposes. Anyone can enter and people come from all over the world to do so. Amazingly, it's the only event of its kind in the world.

(☎ 822086, Waterloo Rd) is a traditional pub known for its good-value bar food.

KNIGHTON

On the border with England, Knighton lies on Offa's Dyke, at the junction of Offa's Dyke Path and Glyndŵr's Way.

The Offa's Dyke Centre & TIC (☎ 01547-528753, ☒ oda@offasdyke.demon.co.uk), West St, is open daily from Easter to October.

For B&B try *Pilleth Court* (☎ 01547-560272, Whitton), which charges £18 to £20 per person.

Knighton is located on the Shrewsbury-Llandrindod Wells-Swansea train line.

WELSHPOOL

☎ 01938 • pop 8000

This town, situated in the Severn Valley, was originally called Pool, but the name was changed to avoid confusion with Poole in Dorset. Really the only reason to come here is to get to Powis Castle or ride the narrow-gauge railway.

The TIC (☎ 552043, ☒ weltic@powys .gov.uk) is in the Vicarage Gardens car park. There's a livestock market every Monday, which dates back to 1263.

Things to See & Do

The **Welshpool & Llanfair Light Railway** (☎ 810441) was originally built to take local people to market with their sheep and cattle. The line was closed in 1956 but reopened by enthusiasts in 1960. It runs an 8-mile journey from Raven Square and operates between Easter and early October – but not every day (phone for timetables). The return fare for an adult costs £7.90; it's £1 for a child (or £4 if unaccompanied).

One mile south of Welshpool is **Powis Castle** (☎ 554336; NT). The castle is an impressive sight with its red walls and beautiful terraced gardens. The museum contains treasures that Clive of India brought back from India – his family married into the Herberts of Powis. The castle opens 1 to 5 pm Wednesday to Sunday, from early April to the end of October. It also opens on Tuesday in July and August. The gardens open 11 am to 6 pm on the same days. Admission to the castle and gardens costs £7.50/3.75, and to the gardens only it's £5/2.50.

Five miles south of Welshpool, at Berriew, is the **Andrew Logan Museum of Sculpture** (☎ 01686-640689), open noon to 6 pm, Wednesday to Sunday, from the end of May to August; and 2 to 4 pm at the weekend only in September and October. Admission costs £2/1. Andrew Logan is one of Britain's top modern sculptors and this wacky, slightly camp collection is highly entertaining.

Getting There & Away

Welshpool is on the Shrewsbury to Aberystwyth train line. From Shrewsbury to Welshpool takes 30 minutes (£4.30) with departures approximately every two hours Monday to Saturday, less often on Sunday.

MACHYNLLETH

☎ 01654 • pop 2000

On the western edge of Montgomeryshire, Machynlleth (pronounced mahuncliff) holds an important place in Welsh history as it was here that Glyndŵr set up his parliament. In recent years it's become better known as a centre of green living, mainly due to the influence of the Centre for Alternative Technology (CAT) on the edge of the town (see the boxed text 'The Centre for Alternative Technology' later).

Machynlleth is in the Dyfi Valley and there's good cycling in this area. The TIC is in the Canolfan Owain Glyndŵr Centre on Maengwyn St (☎ 702401, ☒ mactic@mail .powys.gov.uk). It sells a leaflet on walks on Cadair Idris, which is about 7 miles north of Machynlleth. The TIC opens 9.30 am to 5.30 pm daily, May to September; until 5 pm the rest of the year.

Internet access is available at Cyberspace on Pentrehedyn St in the town centre for £4/3 an hour during the week/weekend. There's a street market on Maengwyn St on Wednesday.

Things to See & Do

The **Glyndŵr Parliament House** (☎ 702 827) opens Monday to Saturday from April to September and has displays showing life in the Middle Ages in Wales, as well as on

The Centre for Alternative Technology

If you're anywhere in the area don't miss the Centre for Alternative Technology (CAT; ☎ 01654-702400), 3 miles north of Machynlleth. Founded in 1974 by a group of environmentalists on a 16-hectare site that was once a slate mine, it's now a self-sufficient working community. It's probably the most interesting eco-centre in Europe.

There are more than 50 exhibits: working displays of wind, water and solar power; a low-energy self-built house and an organic garden; an underground display on the world of soil (complete with giant mole); and a transport maze. The displays are interesting and fun yet also educational. There's a water-powered cliff railway (closed in winter in case of frost) to the main centre, bookshop and excellent vegetarian restaurant.

The centre opens 10 am to 5 pm daily in summer (until 4pm in winter); last entry is 4 pm or at dusk if earlier. Admission costs £6.90/3.50 for adults/children. Arrive by bike and get a 10% discount. There are also discounted tickets available when you buy rail or bus tickets – enquire on buses or at the train station.

CAT runs residential courses throughout the year. Basic accommodation and meals are provided.

Glyndŵr's fight for Welsh independence. Admission is free.

Despite the fact that the Celts have played a defining role in the culture of Europe, the first museum devoted solely to them was only opened in 1995, in Machynlleth. **Celtica** (☎ 702702), Y Plas, Aberystwyth Rd, is an interpretative centre and exhibition that highlights not only Wales' Celtic roots but also includes all the Celtic groups of Europe. The main exhibition is a multimedia entertainment (£4.95/3.80) devised by the people that created the Jorvik Centre in York. There's a Celtic settlement, magic forest and a meeting with a druid. It's actually rather more entertaining than it sounds. The interpretative centre is good and there is also a bookshop and restaurant. The centre recently added a computer resource room for people who want to research information related to Celtic life. Celtica opens 10 am to 6 pm daily (last admission is at 4.40 pm). Admission is free, except for the main exhibition.

The Tabernacle (☎ 703355) at Heol Penrallt in the centre of town is an art gallery that hosts regular exhibitions by Welsh artists and an impressive classical music festival in August each year. The gallery opens 10 am to 4 pm, Monday to Saturday.

For energetic types, **The Wynnstay Hotel** (see Places to Stay later) organises adventure activities such as white-water rafting, paragliding, pony trekking and quad biking for individuals or groups. Prices vary; ring the hotel for details.

Places to Stay

At Corris, 5 miles north of Machynlleth, the energy-efficient *Corris Youth Hostel* (☎ 761 686) is in the Old School. It opens daily from March to October and at weekends or by request at other times. The nightly charge is £9.25/6.50 for adults/under-18s.

Maenllwyd (☎ 702928, Newtown Rd) charges £38 for a double room and is a very pleasant place to stay; vegetarian breakfasts are served if required. *Pendre Guest House* (☎ 702088, Maengwyn St) has four rooms, two with a bath; it costs from £18 to £20.

Try the *Glyndŵr Hotel* (☎ 703989, 14 Doll St); B&B costs from £16 per person. *The Wynnstay Hotel* (☎ 702941, Maengwyn St) is a friendly old coaching inn right in the centre of town. Rooms with bath cost from £45/70 for a single/double and they do discounts for short stays. There's an excellent farm B&B available 5 miles out of town at *Mathafarn* (☎ 01650-511226, Llanwrin) for £20 per person. Vegetarian breakfasts are available and Mrs Hughes will collect you from the train station if required. *Plas Llwyngwern* (☎ 703970, Pantperthog), a large B&B with garden, is 250m from CAT and charges £17.50 per person. Or there's camping across the road at *Llwyngwern Farm* (☎ *702492*) for £6.50 for a tent and two adults.

Places to Eat

The earthy *Wholefood Café (Maengwyn St)* serves vegetarian food and uses organic ingredients where possible. Potato and chickpea curry costs £4.25. *Bwyty Maengwyn* (☎ *702126, 57 Maengwyn St*) uses local produce, including Welsh lamb. Lemon chicken with potatoes is good value at £3.99.

The Wynnstay Hotel offers hearty Welsh food and great desserts in its restaurant. *The Bay Tree* sandwich bar, also on Maengwyn St, does reasonable light lunches and cakes.

At the Celtica exhibition, there's a good tearoom with light lunches. Welsh leek soup and a roll costs £2.20.

Getting There & Around

Machynlleth is on the Shrewsbury to Aberystwyth train line. Services from Shrewsbury (£10.80, 1½ hours) operate almost every two hours. Arriva Cymru's bus No 32 from Aberystwyth (£3, 40 minutes) operates every two hours Monday to Saturday and twice on Sunday.

Mountain bikes can be hired from Greenstiles (☎ 703543), just beside the clock tower in the town centre, for £12 (50% off for visitors to CAT).

Ceredigion

Ceredigion (Cardiganshire) is the county that encompasses the southern coastal section of Cardigan Bay, and which extends inland to Powys. Welsh is the first language of three out of every five people who live here.

The county includes 50 miles of coastline, much of which is protected by heritage coast status. The capital is the university town and classic seaside resort of Aberystwyth, certainly the most happening place in Ceredigion.

GETTING AROUND
Bus

There are a couple of Rover tickets covering services in Ceredigion and neighbouring

counties. The West Wales Rover ticket (£4.60) includes most services in Ceredigion, Pembrokeshire and Carmarthenshire. Arriva Cymru also operates bus services in North and Mid Wales. It has a Day and Weekly Saver ticket (£4.80/16).

Train

There are few lines in Ceredigion. The only main-line service is into Aberystwyth via Machynlleth from Shrewsbury (see the Powys section earlier in the chapter). There's a popular private line, the Vale of Rheidol Railway, which takes tourists from Aberystwyth up to Devil's Bridge.

CARDIGAN (ABERTEIFI)
☎ 01239 • pop 4500

This was the county town of Cardiganshire. The Welsh name refers to the town's position at the mouth of the Teifi, an important seafaring and trading centre until the harbour silted up.

The first competitive National Eisteddfod (see Society & Conduct in the Facts about Wales chapter) was held in the castle here in 1176. A strong local interest in the arts continues and the town has a good alternative theatre and arts centre, Theatr Mwldan (☎ 621200). The TIC (☎ 613230, ⓔ cardigantic@ceredigion.gov.uk) is in the same building, on Bath House Rd. It opens 10 am to 5 pm daily in summer.

There's a country market selling local crafts and produce in the Guildhall on High St from 9.30am to 3.30pm, Thursday and Saturday in summer.

Places to Stay & Eat

The comfortable *Poppit Sands Youth Hostel* (☎ *612936, Poppit Sands*) is 4 miles from Cardigan, by the start of the Pembrokeshire Coast Path. It opens daily except some Sundays and Mondays from March to October; beds cost £9.25/6.50.

There are several good places to stay on Gwbert Rd, in the north of town. *Maes-a-Môr* (☎ *614929, Park Place, Gwbert Rd*) is opposite the King George V Park. B&B costs £20 per person in a room with a bath (cheaper off-season). Smoking is not permitted. A few doors down is **Brynhyfryd Guest House** (☎ 612861), where B&B costs £19 per person. The bus from Aberystwyth stops at the end of Gwbert Rd.

Two miles from Cardigan Bay is the very comfortable **Penbontbren Farm Hotel** (☎ 810248, Glynarthen). All rooms have a bath and cost £49/86 for a single/double. Dinner, bed and breakfast costs £58 per person.

For a light meal, the **Theatr Mwldan Café**, (☎ 614848, Bath House Rd) in the theatre building, is excellent. They serve decent and reasonable vegie food and there's outdoor seating in summer. The **Red Lion Hotel** (☎ 612482, Pwllhai St) pulls a reasonable pint and has good pub grub. **Go Mango Wholefoods** (Black Lion Mews) is a wholefood shop serving snacks to take away.

During term time at Coleg Ceredigion you can taste the catering students' experiments in the **Gordon Edwards Restaurant** (☎ 612032, Park Place). Set lunches cost around £6 and dinners cost about £11.

Getting There & Away

Cardigan is not accessible by rail. The easiest way to get there is to go to Aberystwyth and then take the hourly No 550 bus service (£3.61, two hours), Monday to Saturday. There's only one service on Sunday. The route is covered by two operators – Richards Brothers (☎ 613756) and Arriva Cymru.

Alternatively, you could go to Haverfordwest or Carmarthen and take the hourly No 412 service via Fishguard to Cardigan (£3.03, 1½ hours), which runs Monday to Saturday.

ABERYSTWYTH

☎ 01970 • pop 12,000

On the central coast of Wales, Aberystwyth combines the attractions of a traditional seaside resort with a lively university town and is well worth a visit.

Like many other towns in the area, it was founded by Edward I when he started building a castle at the mouth of the River Rheidol in Ceredigion Bay in 1277. It was captured by Glyndŵr in 1404 and destroyed by Oliver Cromwell's forces in 1649. By the beginning of the 19th century, the walls and gates had virtually disappeared. Now a pretty unimpressive ruin by day, it's quite attractive when floodlit at night.

The town developed a fishing industry, and silver- and lead-mining industries were also important in the area. With the arrival of the railway in 1864, it became a fashionable resort. In 1872 Aberystwyth was chosen as the site of the first college of the University of Wales, and in 1907 it became home to the National Library of Wales.

The TIC (☎ 612125, [e] aberyswythtic@ceredigion.gov.uk) is located at the junction of Terrace Rd and Bath St. It opens 10 am to 6 pm daily during summer; from 10 am to 5 pm in winter, excluding Sunday.

There's Internet access at Biognosis, on Pier St. On Bath St, near the TIC, there's a laundrette, open daily.

Things to See & Do

The **Cliff Railway** (☎ 617642) is the longest electric cliff railway in Britain, running from the Promenade to the top of Constitution Hill. The hill offers good views over the bay and a **Camera Obscura** (free). This is a simple optical instrument, similar to a projecting telescope, which almost gives you a peek at the inside of locals' houses. Trains depart every few minutes from 10 am to 6 pm daily, Easter to October; tickets cost £2/1 return.

The **National Library of Wales** (☎ 623 800) holds over five million books in a variety of languages and various ancient manuscripts and pictures. It also houses the oldest existing manuscript in the Welsh language, the 12th-century *Black Book of Carmarthen*. It opens 9.30 am to 6 pm, Monday to Friday and until 5 pm on Saturday.

Ceredigion Museum (☎ 617911) is in the Coliseum, a restored Edwardian music hall on Terrace Rd, next to the TIC. It has an entertaining collection of folk material based on the three main occupations of the people of Ceredigion – agriculture, seafaring and lead mining. There are also temporary exhibitions showing works by local artists. It opens 10 am to 5 pm Monday to Saturday; admission is free.

The **Vale of Rheidol Railway** (☎ 625819) runs from Aberystwyth to Devil's Bridge, a journey of 11¾ miles, and is hauled by a

CENTRAL WALES

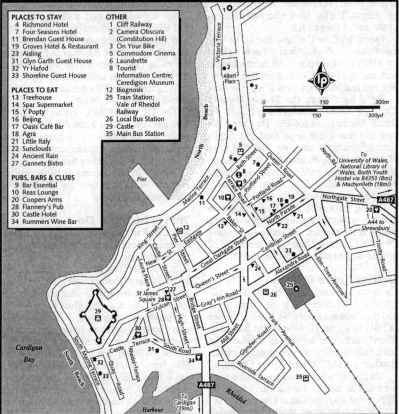

ABERYSTWYTH

PLACES TO STAY
4 Richmond Hotel
7 Four Seasons Hotel
11 Brendan Guest House
19 Groves Hotel & Restaurant
23 Aisling
31 Glyn Garth Guest House
32 Yr Hafod
33 Shoreline Guest House

PLACES TO EAT
13 Treehouse
14 Spar Supermarket
15 Y Popty
16 Beijing
17 Oasis Café Bar
18 Agra
21 Little Italy
22 Sunclouds
24 Ancient Rain
27 Gannets Bistro

PUBS, BARS & CLUBS
9 Bar Essential
10 Reas Lounge
20 Coopers Arms
28 Flannery's Pub
30 Castle Hotel
34 Rummers Wine Bar

OTHER
1 Cliff Railway
2 Camera Obscura (Constitution Hill)
3 On Your Bike
5 Commodore Cinema
6 Laundrette
8 Tourist Information Centre; Ceredigion Museum
12 Biognosis
25 Train Station; Vale of Rheidol Railway
26 Local Bus Station
29 Castle
35 Main Bus Station

To University of Wales, National Library of Wales, Borth Youth Hostel via B4353 (8mi) & Machynlleth (18mi)

A44 to Shrewsbury

To Cardigan (39mi)

narrow-gauge steam train. The railway was constructed to take the lead and timber from the Rheidol Valley, and the engines were built by the Great Western Railway in 1923.

The station is next to Aberystwyth's main-line station and the ticket office opens at 10 am. The service runs daily from Easter to October, with some exceptions; ring to check the times. Trains usually go twice a day in each direction (starting at 11 am in Aberystwyth with the last train returning from Devil's Bridge at 4.30 pm) in low season, with four trips a day on certain days in July and August. The journey takes an hour

each way. The return fare is £10.50 for adults, £1.50 each for the first two children accompanied by an adult and £5.25 per child thereafter. Have a look at its Web site at www.rheidolrailway.co.uk.

Places to Stay

Borth Youth Hostel (☎ 871498) is 8 miles to the north, near a wide sandy beach. It opens from April to November. The nightly charge is £10/6.90 for adults/under-18s.

Yr Hafod (☎ 617579, 1 South Marine Terrace) is an great little B&B costing from £18 to £25 per person. Nearby *Shoreline Guest*

House (☎ 615002, 6 South Marine Terrace) does B&B for £17 per person. There are 11 rooms, all with satellite TV. It's a good place.

Near the train station, the friendly *Aisling* (☎ 626980, 21 Alexandra Rd) has B&B for £19 per person. *Brendan Guest House* (☎ 612252), a simple, clean place on Marine Terrace, charges £18/36 for a single/double (£20/40 with bath). Most rooms have sea views. *Glyn Garth Guest House* (☎ 615050, South Rd) is a comfortable place with B&B from £20 to £26 per person.

The *Groves Hotel & Restaurant* (☎ 617 623, 44 North Parade) has rooms for £45/60, all with bathroom. The *Richmond Hotel* (☎ 612201, 44–45 Marine Terrace) has B&B for £48/70. The *Four Seasons Hotel* (☎ 612 120, 50–54 Portland St) has 14 bedrooms, all with a bath, for £55/82.

Places to Eat

The student presence ensures that there are plenty of good, cheap places to eat in town.

Gannets Bistro (☎ 617164, 7 St James Square) has evening main dishes from £5 to £10 and good-value lunches. It does tasty traditional food, such as beef Wellington (£10.95), black beef steaks and local seafood dishes. It closes on Sunday.

Treehouse (☎ 615791, 14 Baker St) is a very good organic restaurant for vegetarians or meat-eaters. It uses locally grown organic produce and is open during the day Monday to Saturday and in the evenings Thursday to Saturday. There's also a takeaway shop downstairs for snacks such as salads, soups and pizza slices. Another vegie place for lunch is *Ancient Rain* (Cambrian St).

For Chinese food, try *Beijing* (Portland Rd). The best of the several Indian restaurants is *Agra* (☎ 636999, North Parade), which specialises in balti cuisine and is open for lunch and dinner. Bring your own wine.

Oasis Café Bar (North Parade) is a trendy joint that does good filled rolls from £3.85, all-day breakfasts (a favourite of students) and hot specials. Try the spinach and mushroom lasagne (£4.75). It opens daily till late in the evening. Across the road, *Sunclouds* has a good range of coffees and does light lunches. Nearby is *Little Italy*

(☎ 625707) with a large range of pasta dishes from £6.25 and pizzas from £4.95.

Y Popty on Terrace Rd is a bakery that sells savoury snacks for under £1, baguettes from £1.45 and spit-roast chickens. The 24-hour *Spar supermarket* is just across the road.

Entertainment

Rummers Wine Bar (Bridge St) is right by the river, with seats outside. It opens 7 pm to midnight. The *Castle Hotel* (Castle Terrace) is a good traditional pub, and the *Coopers Arms* (Northgate St) has live music some nights. Irish bar *Flannery's Pub* on the corner of Vulcan St and High St has traditional Irish folk music on Wednesday nights. The hippest watering hole in town is the *Bar Essential* (Portland St). *Reas Lounge* on the corner of Terrace Rd and Eastgate is a large, lively bar with an upstairs terrace.

Aberystwyth Arts Centre (☎ 623232, Penglais Rd), at the University, holds regular music, film and theatrical events; ring for details. The small *Commodore Cinema* (☎ 612 421, Bath St) shows current releases in the evening and has a matinee at weekends.

Getting There & Away

National Express (☎ 0870 580 8080) operates one direct service a day from London (£19.25, £4 extra on Friday, seven hours).

Arriva Cymru's bus No 701 links Bangor with Bristol and passes through Aberystwyth. There are two buses a day between Aberystwyth and Cardiff (£11.35, four hours) and one a day to/from Bangor (three hours).

Service No 550 runs between Aberystwyth and Cardigan (hourly Monday to Saturday, twice on Sunday) and takes two hours. Service No 32 goes between Aberystwyth and Caernarfon (change to No 2 at Dolgellau) approximately every two hours. It's a three-hour trip and can be covered with a Rover ticket (£4.80).

Aberystwyth is at the end of the Cambrian line from Shrewsbury. There are departures every two hours (£14.10), Monday to Saturday, less frequently on Sunday.

CENTRAL WALES

Getting Around

For information on local bus services and timetables, ring the TIC (☎ 01970-612125).

On Your Bike (☎ 626996) offers cycle hire for £10/15 for a mountain bike/tandem for a day. It's based in the Old Police Yard, Queen's Rd.

AROUND ABERYSTWYTH
Devil's Bridge

Devil's Bridge is situated at the head of the Rheidol Valley in the Pumlumon Hills. The fast-flowing Rivers Mynach and Rheidol meet in a gorge below the village. The River Mynach drops 90m in a series of spectacular waterfalls.

The Mynach is also notable for the three stone bridges which have been built on top of one another. The first is believed to have been built by the Knights Templars before 1188, the second in 1753 and the last more recently.

The Rheidol Valley Steam Railway goes to Devil's Bridge (see Things to See & Do in the Aberystwyth section earlier).

Places to Stay & Eat The excellent *Mount Pleasant Guest House* (☎ 890219) is 200m from the Rheidol Steam Railway. It charges £29/42 for a single/double, with continental breakfast (£4 extra for a cooked breakfast). *Hafod Arms Hotel* (☎ 890232) is also about 200m from the railway and was originally a shooting lodge. B&B costs £35/56 with bathroom.

North Wales

North Wales is dominated by the beautiful Snowdonia Mountains, which loom over the coastline. This stretch contains some fine sandy beaches, many of which have long since been developed into traditional British holiday resorts and their associated attractions, catering mainly for families. If donkey rides and candy floss aren't your thing, you may want to venture farther west to the relatively quieter beaches of the Llŷn Peninsula.

Heading west from Chester, the country is industrialised and uninteresting until you reach Llandudno – virtually contiguous with the walled town of Conwy. From either place you can catch buses or trains into the Snowdonia National Park. The park is also accessible from the coastal market town of Porthmadog on the Ffestiniog Railway. From Porthmadog, you can loop back to Shrewsbury along the Cambrian coast.

The remote Llŷn Peninsula in the west escapes the crowds to a large extent; start from Caernarfon, with its magnificent castle, or Pwllheli. To the north is the island of Anglesey, joined to the mainland by bridges, which has one of the main ferry ports for Ireland, Holyhead. Near Porthmadog is whimsical Portmeirion, an entire village built in the Italianate style – attractive but crowded in summer.

This section of Wales includes the counties of Gwynedd, Anglesey, Conwy, Denbighshire, Flintshire and Wrexham.

GETTING AROUND

Gwynedd Public Transport Maps and Timetables is invaluable and includes the Llŷn Peninsula and all of Snowdonia. It's available from Tourist Information Centres (TICs), bus stations or the Transport Unit (☎ 01286-679535). For Anglesey, phone ☎ 01248-752 459. For the eastern half of North Wales, Flintshire County Council (☎ 01352-704035) produces bus timetables covering all the services within its area. For information on national and local bus services in Wales, call ☎ 0870 608 2608.

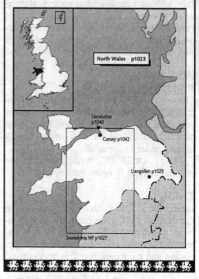

North Wales p1023

Llandudno p1040

Conwy p1042

Llangollen p1025

Snowdonia NP p1027

Rail services in North Wales include the North Wales Coast Line from Chester via Llandudno Junction, Conwy and Bangor, terminating at the ferry terminal at Holyhead. By using trains that cross Snowdonia (Conwy Valley line, Ffestiniog Railway and Cambrian Coast line), you can link with the service that runs halfway along the Llŷn Peninsula to Pwllheli. Phone ☎ 0845 748 4950 for rail enquiries.

A North & Mid Wales Day Ranger pass

(£26.30) covers most rail and bus services in this area.

See Snowdonia National Park later in the chapter for information on transport in that region.

North-Eastern Wales

Most travellers simply pass through this area of Wales to reach Snowdonia, but along the valley of the River Dee are a number of places worth stopping at. The International Musical Eisteddfod is held in Llangollen in July, although the town has enough alternative attractions to merit a visit at any time of year. However, the north coast of this section, from the English border to Colwyn Bay, has little of great interest.

WREXHAM
☎ 01978 • pop 43,000

The unappealing town of Wrexham is situated in the Clywedog Valley, near the border with England. The main reason for coming here is to see Erddig, the 17th-century stately home 2 miles to the south.

The TIC (☎ 292015, @ tic@wrexham.gov.uk) in Lambpit St opens year round.

Erddig
Erddig (☎ 355314), inhabited by the Yorke family until 1973, gives probably the best insight in Britain into the 'upstairs-downstairs' relationship that existed between the upper classes and their servants. The Yorkes lived here for more than 200 years and were known for the respect with which they treated their servants. Upstairs is a fine collection of furniture and an impressive state bed. Downstairs are photographs of servants through the ages and an interesting collection of household devices, such as the box mangle, which was filled with heavy stones and rolled over the laundry. Outside is an 800-hectare country park where there are pleasant walks.

Run by the National Trust (NT), Erddig grounds open 11 am to 6 pm daily, except Thursday and Friday, early April to late

October, the house opens 12 to 5 pm. Last admission to the house is at 4 pm. During October, the house opens noon to 4 pm (last admission 3 pm).

Because Erddig is very popular, timed admission tickets may be issued. Admission to the grounds, family rooms and below stairs costs £6/3, while admission to the grounds and below stairs only costs £4/2. A family ticket costs £15/10, depending on how much you want to see.

Places to Stay
Grove Guest House (☎ 354288, *36 Chester Rd*) has 14 rooms and charges from £17 per person for B&B. *The Yale Hostel* (☎ 355 314, Erddig), a self-catering lodge, accommodates up to 18 people in two dorms in the grounds of Erddig. The house costs £108 a night for a group, although individuals willing to work in the country park for free can stay without charge. Bring your own sleeping bag.

Getting There & Away
National Express (☎ 0990 808080) has one service a day from London (£22.25). Arriva Cymru operates service No 1 from Chester to Wrexham every 15 minutes Monday to Saturday, hourly on Sunday.

Wrexham is accessible by train from London via Shrewsbury, and also from Liverpool. There are departures every two hours from Shrewsbury (£4.40, 40 minutes).

LLANGOLLEN
☎ 01978 • pop 3500

Llangollen is famous for its International Musical Eisteddfod. The six-day music and dance festival attracts folk groups from around the world.

This attractive town makes an excellent base for outdoor activities such as walks to ruined Valle Crucis Abbey and the Horseshoe Pass, horse-drawn canal boat trips and canoeing on the River Dee.

Orientation & Information
Covering both banks of the River Dee, Llangollen is small enough to walk around. The TIC (☎ 860828, @ croeso@nwt.co.uk)

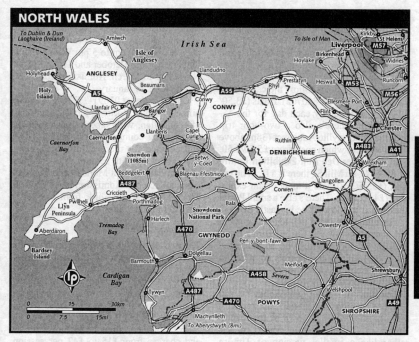

NORTH WALES

in the town hall, Castle St, opens 10 am to 6 pm daily during the summer, 9.30 am to 5 pm daily in winter. They offer a bed-booking service for £1.

There's a laundrette on Regent St.

International Musical Eisteddfod

The International Musical Eisteddfod was first held in 1947. It now takes place in a purpose-built venue by the river over six days every July. It's a massive affair, with over 12,000 performers – choirs, musicians, folk singers and dancers – and crowds of over 120,000. Phone ☎ 860236 for details. The booking office is in the centre of town.

Plas Newydd

Plas Newydd (☎ 861314) was the home of the so-called Ladies of Llangollen, Lady Eleanor Butler and Sarah Ponsonby, who lived here from 1780 to 1829. In their own words, the women were 'seized with the oak-carving mania' and they set about transform-

ing their house into a bizarre combination of Gothic and Tudor romantic styles. They added stained-glass windows and carved oak panels, and created formal gardens. The black-and-white timbering was, however, an alteration made by the next owner.

Sir Roy Strong, former director of the Victoria & Albert Museum in London, called Plas Newydd 'an early monument to architectural salvage'. It's a fascinating place. South-east of the town centre, the house opens 10 am to 5 pm daily, Easter to October; last entry is 4.15 pm and admission costs £2.50/1.25.

Other Things to See & Do

ECTARC (☎ 861514), Castle St, is the European Centre for Traditional & Regional Cultures, which stages exhibitions on the cultures of lesser-known European groupings. It opens 10 am to 6 pm daily in summer and 10 am to 5 pm in winter. Admission is free.

Llangollen Steam Railway (☎ 860979) runs over a 7-mile line via Berwyn and the Horseshoe Falls to Glyndyrfrdwy and Carrog (£7.50/3.75), from April to October and during Christmas daily, and at weekends year round.

Horse-drawn boats follow the canal from **Llangollen Wharf** (☎ 860702). Boats (£3.50/2.50) depart regularly each day for the 45-minute trip. There's also a two-hour trip over the Pontcysyllte Aqueduct (38m above the River Dee) which costs from £5.50/4.50.

In the **Lower Dee Mill Exhibition Centre** (☎ 860584), on Mill St, there is a Dr Who exhibit (£5.75/3.50) and a model train exhibition (£4.75/3.75). There's also a small Postal Museum at the post office in Castle St.

The dilapidated ruin that tops the conical hill above the town is **Castell Dinas Bran**, built by Madoc ap Gruffydd and deserted since the 16th century. There's not much to see apart from the views, but it's an exhilarating walk up from the town.

The ruins of **Valle Crucis Abbey** (☎ 860 326) are far more substantial, and stand 1½ miles north-west of the town by the road to Ruthin. In a beautiful setting, Valle Crucis is rather like a smaller version of Tintern Abbey (see the South Wales chapter). In the care of Cadw, the Welsh historic monuments agency, it opens 10 am to 5 pm daily, April to September. Admission costs £2/1.50.

Along the road out here you pass a small **Motor Museum** (☎ 860324) with a selection of vehicles from the 1920s to 1970s on display. It opens 10 am to 5 pm Wednesday to Sunday, April to October and 11 am to 5 pm November to March. Admission costs £2/1 and it closes in January.

Chirk Castle (☎ 01691-777701) is a magnificent Marcher fortress, 5 miles south-east of Llangollen, with superb views over the surrounding country. It was built in 1310 and adapted for more comfortable living from about the 16th century. It opens noon to 5 pm daily except Monday and Tuesday, April to October. Admission costs £5/2.50. There are buses to Chirk from Market St bus stop in Llangollen.

Activities

The two best walks in the area are along the canal to the Horseshoe Falls or up to Castell Dinas Bran. Hendre Holidays (☎ 861760) offers a number of guided walks of the area.

Llangollen is well known for canoeing and there are several centres. Jim Jayes (☎ 860 763), Mile End Mill, Berwyn Rd, half a mile from Llangollen, offers a range of activities and charges from £15 to £42 per session. White-water rafting costs £24 per person. There's bunkhouse accommodation here (see Canoe Inn Riverside Café & Accommodation under Places to Stay later).

The Ladies of Llangollen

Lady Eleanor Butler and the Honourable Sarah Ponsonby, the 'Ladies of Llangollen', lived in Plas Newydd from 1780 to 1829 with their maid, Mary Carryl. They fell in love in Ireland, where they were brought up in aristocratic Anglo-Irish families. Their families discouraged the relationship and, in a desperate bid to be allowed to live together, the women eloped to Wales disguised as men. They set up home in Llangollen to devote themselves to 'friendship, celibacy and the knitting of stockings'.

Their romantic friendship became well known yet respected, and they were visited by many literary and national figures of the day, including the duke of Wellington, the duke of Gloucester, Richard Brinsley Sheridan, Robert Southey, William Wordsworth and Sir Walter Scott. Wordsworth called them 'sisters in love, a love allowed to climb, even on this earth above the reach of time'. He was less accepting of Plas Newydd, which he called 'a low browed cot'.

Their relationship with their maid, Mary, was also close – most unusual for those days. She managed to buy the freehold of Plas Newydd and left it to them when she died. They erected a large monument to her in the graveyard at the Church of St Collen on Bridge St, where they are also buried. Lady Eleanor died in 1829, Sarah Ponsonby two years later.

...or Llanfair PG for short, holds the record for the longest British place name.

Snowdonia National Park

The mighty Caernarfon Castle

Not so clean slate, North Wales

Home to the Ladies of Llangollen, Anglesey

Vintage steam train bound for Mt Snowdon

The good old horse and cart still exists as a mode of transport on traffic-free Sark.

Sailing hardware at Guernsey's St Peter Port

Standing out from the neighbours on Guernsey

Jersey's financial capital, St Helier

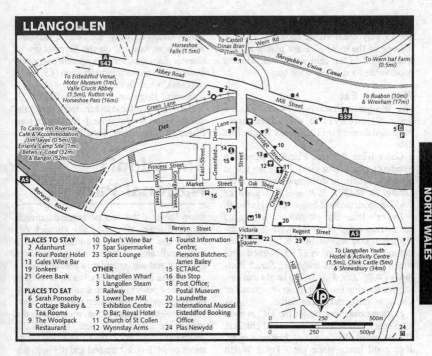

LLANGOLLEN

PLACES TO STAY	10 Dylan's Wine Bar	14 Tourist Information
2 Adanhurst	17 Spar Supermarket	Centre;
4 Four Poster Hotel	23 Spice Lounge	Piersons Butchers;
13 Gales Wine Bar		James Bailey
19 Jonkers	OTHER	15 ECTARC
21 Green Bank	1 Llangollen Wharf	16 Bus Stop
	3 Llangollen Steam	18 Post Office;
PLACES TO EAT	Railway	Postal Museum
6 Sarah Ponsonby	5 Lower Dee Mill	20 Laundrette
8 Cottage Bakery &	7 D Bar; Royal Hotel	22 International Musical
Tea Rooms	11 Church of St Collen	Eisteddfod Booking
9 The Woolpack	12 Wynnstay Arms	Office
Restaurant		24 Plas Newydd

NORTH WALES

Special Events

As well as the International Musical Eisteddfod, a hot-air balloon festival takes place yearly on the first weekend in September. Details are available from the TIC.

Places to Stay

There are plenty of places to stay but for accommodation in July around the Eisteddfod you should book long in advance. If you're coming to Llangollen for the canoeing, some of the canoe centres also offer cheap accommodation.

Eirianfa Camp Site (☎ 860919, *Berwyn Rd*) charges £6 for a tent and two people. It's about a mile from Llangollen, towards Betws-y-Coed. The camp site at *Wern Isaf Farm* (☎ 860632) is across the river and to the east, half a mile from the Dinas Barn school. Charges are £3 per person in a tent (£1.50 per child), £10 for a caravan with electric plug-in, £8 for a caravan without.

Llangollen Youth Hostel & Activity

Centre (☎ 860330) is in Tyndwr Hall, a Victorian manor house 1½ miles east of the centre. It opens year round, and the charge is £10/6.90 for adults/under-18s. *Canoe Inn Riverside Café & Accommodation* (☎ 869 589, *Mile End Mill, Berwyn Rd*), half a mile from Llangollen, charges from £7.50 per person for dormitory accommodation.

Centrally located *Green Bank* (☎ 861835, *Victoria Square*) has views of Castell Dinas Bran and offers comfortable accommodation from £17.50 per person. Mike & Annie Pearce run a friendly guesthouse, *Adanhurst* (☎ 860562, *Abbey Rd*), with one double room with bathroom for £20 per person.

In a quaint building with sloping floorboards, *Jonkers* (☎ 861158, *9 Chapel St*) is an interesting place to stay with two doubles with shared bathroom for £36, or £20 for single occupancy.

The *Four Poster Hotel* (☎ 861062, *Mill St*) specialises in four-posters, charging from £32 per person.

Gales Wine Bar (☎ 860089, 18 Bridge St) has 15 very comfortable rooms at £45/63. It's one of the most pleasant places to stay and is right in the centre of town. There's good-value food in the wine bar.

Places to Eat

The Woolpack Restaurant (☎ 860300, 13 Bridge St) is a cosy place, with a three-course early-bird dinner for £10. Sunday lunch costs £10.

Gales Wine Bar (see Places to Stay) is a wonderful place for a meal. There are baked potatoes, salads, seafood and steaks. *Spice Lounge (☎ 861877, 36 Regent St)* is good for tandoori food; the balti house special is £6.20. *Dylan's Wine Bar (☎ 869099, Bridge St)* has a wide range of well-priced dishes, including a good vegetarian selection. Poached salmon in white wine is £7.95. Named after one of the Ladies of Llangollen, *Sarah Ponsonby (☎ 861119, Mill St)* is a bright and airy bar overlooking the river. It serves snacks or a la carte lunch and dinner daily.

Piersons Butchers, beside the TIC, is good for a snack and sells hot barbecued chicken. The adjacent delicatessen, *James Bailey*, does good home-made pies. Try a Welsh Oggie (meat, potato and onion pasty). *Cottage Bakery & Tea Rooms (Castle St)* does good cream teas.

There is a *Spar supermarket* (open 8 am to 11 pm daily) on Castle St.

Entertainment

The *Wynnstay Arms* on Bridge St is good for a drink. The *D Bar* at the Royal Hotel is probably the most happening place in Llangollen, but only opens Thursday to Saturday.

Getting There & Around

Llangollen is 10 miles from Wrexham and there are frequent buses between the two. There's a daily National Express bus to London.

Bryn Melyn (☎ 860701) runs bus services from Llangollen to Ruabon, Wrexham, Oswestry and Horseshoe Falls. Public transport to Snowdonia is very limited. Bus No 94 runs to Dolgellau where you can pick up the No 701 for Aberystwyth.

The train station here only serves the Llangollen Steam Railway; the nearest mainline station is at Ruabon, on the Shrewsbury to Chester main line. Services operate every two hours from Shrewsbury to Ruabon (£5.30, 30 minutes). A taxi from Ruabon costs about £6 – contact Llangollen Taxis (☎ 861018).

Bikes are available to hire from the Llangollen Youth Hostel & Activity Centre (see Places to Stay earlier) for £12 a day.

Snowdonia National Park

Snowdonia is the second-largest national park in Britain, after the Lake District. Although the Snowdonia mountains cover a fairly small area, in the north they loom over the coast and are undeniably spectacular.

The area around Mt Snowdon, at 1085m the highest peak in Britain south of the Scottish Highlands, is the busiest part of the park. About 500,000 people climb, walk or take the train to the summit each year. This was the area where members of the first successful attempt on Mt Everest trained and it's been the training ground for many of Britain's best-known mountaineers since then.

The Welsh name for Snowdon is Yr Wyddfa, which means 'great tomb' – legend has it that a giant who was killed by King Arthur is buried at the summit. The English name is said to have been derived from an old word for snow, which crowns the peaks in winter.

As well as impressive mountains, the park contains a wide variety of other natural features – rivers, lakes, waterfalls, forests, moorlands, glacial valleys and a lovely coastline.

Despite the inhospitable nature of this rugged area, Snowdonia has provided both a home and a store of valuable natural resources for people since it was shaped by the retreating glaciers of the Ice Age. There are Stone-Age burial chambers at Dyffryn Ardudwy and Capel Garmon; Bronze-Age burial cairns at Bryn Cader Faner near Talsarnau; a hill fort at Pen-y-Gaer; Roman forts at Caerhun, Tomen-y-Mur and Caer Gai; and Welsh and Norman castles. The

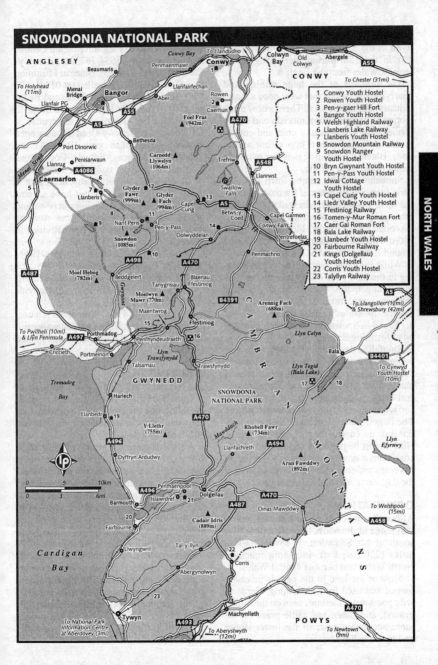

SNOWDONIA NATIONAL PARK

1 Conwy Youth Hostel
2 Rowen Youth Hostel
3 Pen-y-gaer Hill Fort
4 Bangor Youth Hostel
5 Welsh Highland Railway
6 Llanberis Lake Railway
7 Llanberis Youth Hostel
8 Snowdon Mountain Railway
9 Snowdon Ranger
   Youth Hostel
10 Bryn Gwynant Youth Hostel
11 Pen-y-Pass Youth Hostel
12 Idwal Cottage
   Youth Hostel
13 Capel Curig Youth Hostel
14 Lledr Valley Youth Hostel
15 Ffestiniog Railway
16 Tomen-y-Mur Roman Fort
17 Caer Gai Roman Fort
18 Bala Lake Railway
19 Llanbedr Youth Hostel
20 Fairbourne Railway
21 Kings (Dolgellau)
   Youth Hostel
22 Corris Youth Hostel
23 Talyllyn Railway

NORTH WALES

ANGLESEY

CONWY

To Holyhead (11mi)

To Llandudno
Conwy Bay

Beaumaris
Penmaenmawr
Conwy
Colwyn Bay
Old Colwyn
Abergele
A55

Llanfair PG
Menai Bridge
Bangor
Llanfairfechan
Rowen
Caerhun
A470
To Chester (31mi)

Menai Strait
Aber
Foel Fras (942m)

Port Dinorwic
Penisarwaun
Bethesda
Carnedd Llywelyn (1064m)
Trefriw
A548
Llanrwst

Llanrug
A4086
Caernarfon
Glyder Fawr (999m)
Glyder Fach (994m)
Swallow Falls
A5
Capel Garmon

Llanberis
Capel Curig
Betws-y-Coed
Conwy Falls
Pentrefoelas

Nant Peris
Pen-y-Pass
A5

Snowdon (1085m)
Dolwyddelan
Penmachno

A498
Beddgelert
Blaenau Ffestiniog

Moel Hebog (782m)
Tanygrisiau
Moelwyn Mawr (770m)
Arennig Fach (688m)

A487
Maentwrog
Ffestiniog
Llyn Celyn

To Pwllheli (10mi) & Llŷn Peninsula
A497
Porthmadog
Penrhyndeudraeth
Bala
B4401

Cricieth
Portmeirion
Llyn Trawsfynydd
Talsarnau
Trawsfynydd
Llyn Tegid (Bala Lake)
To Cynwyd Youth Hostel (10mi)

To Llangollen (12mi) & Shrewsbury (42mi)

Tremadog Bay
GWYNEDD
SNOWDONIA NATIONAL PARK

Harlech
Caer Gai

Llanbedr
Y Llethr (755m)
Mawddach
Rhobell Fawr (734m)
A494
Llyn Efyrnwy

A496
Dyffryn Ardudwy
Llanfachreth
Aran Fawddwy (892m)

Penmaenpool
Dolgellau
A470
To Welshpool (15mi)

Barmouth
Islawrdref
A487
Dinas Mawddwy
A458

Fairbourne
Cadair Idris (889m)
Llwyngwril
Tal-y-llyn
Corris
A493
Machynlleth
POWYS
A470

Cardigan Bay
Tywyn
Abergynolwyn

To National Park Information Centre at Aberdovey (3mi)
To Aberystwyth (12mi)
To Newtown (9mi)

0   5   10km
0   3   6mi

mountains sheltered both Llywelyn ap Gruffydd in the 13th century and Owain Glyndŵr in the 15th during their struggles to reclaim Wales from the English.

The remains of the huge mining and quarrying operations that were once a major industry can still be seen. There's now more money to be made from tourism and so the former slate quarries and gold and copper mines are being turned into visitor attractions. Blaenau Ffestiniog now has two slate mines open to the public.

Snowdon and the nearby town of Llanberis form the main target for most visitors, but there's good mountain walking in many other parts of the park. Above Dollgellau in the south, Cadair (Cader) Idris rises to almost 900m. There are hikes in the forests and hills around Betws-y-Coed in the north-east.

While the most popular reason for coming to the park is to walk, there are numerous other activities – climbing, white-water rafting, pony trekking and windsurfing. Several of Wales' 'Great Little Railways' are found in Snowdonia, including the famous Ffestiniog Railway.

Rainfall in the area is very high, with over 500mm some years. By way of comparison, the town of Leicester in England manages an annual average of only 63mm. There are several lakes in Snowdonia and some are used for water storage for hydroelectric power. The largest pumped storage scheme in Europe is on the edge of the park near Tanigrisau. Hikers must be prepared to deal with hostile conditions at any time of the year. You should never go walking without rain gear, even if the day starts with a cloudless sky.

ORIENTATION

Although it takes its name from the mountain range in the north, the park extends far south of Mt Snowdon. It covers 840 sq miles (2200 sq km), including much of North Wales and parts of central Wales.

Most of the land in the park is privately owned and used for hill farming. Herds of wild goats are sometimes seen on the higher ground, and sheep and cattle graze on the more accessible grass of the lower slopes and in the valleys.

INFORMATION

There are National Park Information Centres at Aberdovey (☎ 01654-767321), Betws-y-Coed (☎ 01690-710426), Blaenau Ffestiniog (☎ 01766-830360), Dollgellau (☎ 01341-422 888), Harlech (☎ 01766-780658) and Beddgelert (☎ 01766-890615). All open 9.30 am to 6 pm in the high season, and the centres at Dollgellau and Betws-y-Coed are also open in winter – Dollgellau opens 10 am to 5 pm Thursday to Monday, Betws-y-Coed opens 9.30 am to 4.30 pm daily. The head office (☎ 01766-770274) is at Penrhyndeudraeth.

All the information centres have accommodation lists, a bed-booking service and public transport timetables, as well as leaflets about walks and other activities in the area.

There are TICs at Barmouth (☎ 01341-280787), Tywyn (☎ 01654-710070), the Craft Centre in Corris (☎ 01654-761244), Llanberis (☎ 01286-870765) and Machynlleth (☎ 01654-702401).

Available from TICs, *Snowdonia* is a useful free newspaper, listing guided walks and other activities in the region. It's published annually.

WALKING

The National Park publishes a useful series of leaflets on many of the mountain walks, including one on each of the six routes up Snowdon. They're available from TICs and information centres.

Although there are walks of all grades, you should be aware that even some walks described as easy may follow paths that go near very steep slopes and over loose scree. Take the Pyg Path up Snowdon and you'll find yourself literally climbing parts of it. Inevitably, with so many people on the mountains, accidents happen – usually on the way down. Each year, an average of 70 serious incidents occur and about 10 people end their lives up here. Be properly equipped before setting out, with food, drink, warm clothing and waterproofs.

The National Park organises a wide variety of 5- to 6-mile guided walks at various levels of difficulty. Charges are usually £1.50/50p.

Scaling Snowdon

Despite the fact that 500,000 people tramp up Snowdon every year, it's still a worthwhile hike to the 1085m (3558 feet) high summit. Views are stupendous on a clear day, and even if it's cloudy you often find you're above the clouds – they swirl beneath your feet, occasionally clearing to give brief glimpses of the valley far below. It's probably not a great idea to choose a midsummer weekend for this walk or you may be inclined to agree with Prince Charles who, on seeing the crowds, the litter and the cafe at the summit, declared it to be the 'highest slum in Europe'.

There's a choice of seven paths to the top. The easiest are the Llanberis Path (5½ hours), which follows the train track from Llanberis, and the Snowdon Ranger Path (five hours), which starts at the Snowdon Ranger Youth Hostel (near Beddgelert).

From Pen-y-Pass there are three routes. The Miners' Track (five hours) is the easiest of them, while the Pyg Track (5½ hours) includes some easy climbing, and the Snowdon Horseshoe combines the two with a spectacular ridge walk that can take up to nine hours.

The Watkin Path (seven hours) is a tough walk from the south. The Rhyd Ddu Path (five hours) approaches Snowdon from the west, and is easier.

All these walks start from roads that are served daily by the Snowdon Sherpa bus.

CYCLING

The high level of use of bridleways for off-road cycling to the summit of Snowdon has led to erosion and fears for walkers' safety. A ban is now in place and cycling is not allowed between 10 am and 5 pm, June to September.

There are cycling routes through the following forests: Coed-y-Brenin, between Dolgellau and Ffestiniog; Gwydyr Forest near Betws-y-Coed; and Beddgelert Forest Park.

PONY TREKKING & HORSE RIDING

There are many stables offering escorted and unescorted rides. Snowdonia Riding Stables (☎ 01286-650342) is based at Waunfawr, on the western edge of the park near Caernarfon. It offers escorted rides only – one hour costs £12 and a full day £45. The stables are near the bus stop in Waunfawr, and the Snowdon Sherpa bus service (see Getting Around later) between Caernarfon and Llanberis stops here.

Meifod Isaf Riding & Trekking Centre (☎ 01341-247651), on the outskirts of Dyffryn Ardudwy, between Harlech and Barmouth, opens Easter to October (closed on Saturday in July and August) and offers rides from £9 for one hour to £17 for an afternoon.

NARROW-GAUGE RAILWAY JOURNEYS

One of the features of this area is the number of narrow-gauge railways. The Ffestiniog Railway runs from Porthmadog to Blaenau Ffestiniog; Snowdon Mountain Railway from Llanberis to the summit; and Talyllyn Railway from Tywyn to Abergynolwyn. Shorter lines include the Llanberis Lake Railway, the Fairbourne Railway, the Bala Lake Railway and the Welsh Highland Railway.

PLACES TO STAY

There are 13 youth hostels in and around the park, among them some of the best in the country.

Around Mt Snowdon, there are *hostels* at Pen-y-Pass (☎ 01286-870428), near Llanberis on the Pyg and Llyn Llydaw Miners' tracks up to the summit; Llanberis (☎ 01286-870280); Bryn Gwynant (☎ 01766-890251), Nant Gwynant, 4 miles from Beddgelert near the Watkin Path up Snowdon; Snowdon Ranger (☎ 01286-650391), 5 miles from Beddgelert at the starting point for the Ranger Path; and Idwal Cottage (☎ 01248-600225), Nant Ffrancon, near Bethesda.

There are also hostels at Capel Curig (☎ 01690-720225), 5 miles from Betws-y-Coed; Lledr Valley (☎ 01690-750202), on the main road between Betws-y-Coed and Ffestiniog; Rowen (☎ 01492-530627), 5 miles from Conwy; Conwy (☎ 01492-593 571), Sychnant; Llanbedr (☎ 01341-241 287), Plas Newydd (near Harlech); and Kings (☎ 01341-422392), Penmaenpool, near Dolgellau.

In addition to the hostels, there are bunk-houses and camp sites. To camp on a non-official site, you need to get the permission of the landowner.

Within the park, Betws-y-Coed has the most B&Bs and guesthouses; others are found in smaller villages and on farms.

GETTING THERE & AWAY
Bus
National Express runs services from London to Llandudno (seven hours, £17) and Bangor (8½ hours, £21) twice daily, and from London to Aberystwyth (seven hours, £19) once daily.

Arriva Cymru operates the Traws-Cambria service (No 701) daily from Bristol through Cardiff, Machynlleth, Dolgellau and Caernarfon to Bangor.

Train
There's a regular InterCity service from London's Euston station via Crewe (where you may have to change) to Llandudno Junction (£50, 3½ hours) and Bangor, with at least one train an hour. Change at Llandudno Junction for the Conwy Valley line, which connects Llanrwst, Betws-y-Coed, Pont-y-Pant and Blaenau Ffestiniog.

There's also an InterCity service from London via Birmingham to Shrewsbury, where you can take the line to Machynlleth (£41, 4½ hours). From there, the scenic Cambrian Coast Railway runs to Pwllheli via Harlech.

For train enquiries ring ☎ 0845 748 4950.

GETTING AROUND
Despite the reorganisation of county boundaries, bus and train information for the area continues to be produced in the useful *Gwynedd Public Transport Maps and Timetables*, available from TICs. Phone ☎ 01286-679535 for information.

Many bus companies operate services in the area and several share a route, often with one company operating during the week and another at weekends. Red Rover passes allow unlimited travel for a day on routes within the park as well as from access points such as Wrexham and Aberystwyth for £4.40.

The Snowdon Sherpa bus service operates in the area – these buses are particularly good for walkers and for people staying in youth hostels. The buses will stop on request at any safe place in the park and they follow a round-the-mountain route so that walkers can go up one path and down another. Route 95 goes from Caernarfon to Beddgelert seven times a day, and three times a day on to Llanberis, throughout the year (daily except Sunday). Route 96 goes from Llandudno to Llanberis via Llanrwst, Betws-y-Coed and Pen-y-Pass Youth Hostel. The service operates three times daily and twice on Sunday (change at Betws-y-Coed) from May to September. There is also a restricted service on Sundays. For information, call ☎ 01286-870880.

Apart from the narrow-gauge railways, there are three lines within the park that are useful for travellers – the Conwy Valley line, the Cambrian Coast line and the Ffestiniog Railway (see Getting There & Away earlier for enquiries line).

If you plan to do a lot of travelling in one day, the North & Mid Wales Day Ranger allows travel on most bus services (except the 701, which goes from Holyhead via Caernarfon, Porthmadog and Cardiff to Bristol) and most trains, including the Ffestiniog Railway, and gets discounts on many of the private railways. Only available for travel after 9 am, the ticket costs £17.30. There's also the North & Mid Wales Flexipass, with the same bus and train coverage and restrictions. This costs £40.90 for seven days' travel or £26.30 for three days within a seven-day period. Family tickets are available and offer good value.

BETWS-Y-COED
☎ 01690 • pop 700
Betws-y-Coed or Betus (as it's known and pronounced) is a tourist village that styles itself as the eastern gateway to the park. The name means Chapel (or Prayer House) in the Wood, so called because of the 14th-century church here; the village is still in an attractive woodland setting in the Gwydir Forest.

Betws-y-Coed has been Wales' most popular inland resort since the Victorian days and gets very crowded in summer. There are walks to Swallow and Conwy Falls nearby and pleasant hikes in the surrounding hills. It can make a reasonable base for walking in the Snowdon range, particularly if you have your own transport, but you may wish to stay in one of the villages closer to the mountains.

Orientation & Information

It's a little place with virtually only two roads.

The National Park Information Centre and TIC (☎ 710426) is in Royal Oak Stables, at the far end of the playing fields past the train station.

On High St, Ultimate Outdoor (☎ 710555) sells books on walking in the area.

Things to See & Do

There's little to do here except walk and take tea, which in this case is enough. There are two museums, neither of very great interest. **Betws-y-Coed Motor Museum** (☎ 710760) is a small collection near the information centre. Admission costs £1.50/1. There's also the **Conwy Valley Railway Museum** (☎ 710568), which is adjacent to the train station (£1/50p).

There's **pony trekking** at Ty Coch Farm (☎ 760248), Penmachno, 6 miles south of Betws-y-Coed. Rides through the Gwydyr Forest cost from £10 an hour. The farm also does a popular pub ride for £26, lasting around four hours.

Walking & Cycling

The information centre has details of a number of walks in the surrounding area.

The popular Bridges & Rivers walk is an easy hike that takes two to three hours and starts from outside the information centre. You pass the meeting point of the Rivers Llugwy and Conwy, the Waterloo Bridge, built in 1815 (of course) and decorated with leek, rose, shamrock and thistle. The next bridge is Pont-y-Pair – the Bridge of the Cauldron – which was built in the 15th century, and finally there's the Miners' Bridge.

Places to Stay

Betus has the largest number of beds in the park, and there are B&Bs and hotels to suit all budgets.

There are two youth hostels, both about 5 miles away. *Lledr Valley Youth Hostel* (☎ 01690-750202, Pont-y-Pant), on the A470, costs £9.25/6.50 for adults/under-18s. There's also the *Capel Curig Youth Hostel* (see Capel Curig later).

On High St, *Cross Keys Hotel & Restaurant* (☎ 710334) charges £30/40 for single/double rooms with bath. Next door is *Glan Llugwy* (☎ 710592), which is nonsmoking. The charge is £16.50 per person.

Closer to the centre, and also on High St, the *Pont-y-Pair Hotel* (☎ 710407) charges £23 to £26 per person. In the centre of town, on High St near the green, is the *Plas Dderwen Hotel & Restaurant* (☎ 710388). B&B costs £18 to £20 per person.

There are several places on Llanrwst Rd, which is off the A470 heading to Llandudno and half a mile from Waterloo Bridge. The excellent *Bron Celyn Guest House* (☎ 710 333) charges £48 for a double room with bathroom. *Bryn Bella Guest House* (☎ 710 627), also on Llanrwst Rd, charges from £20/48. The proprietors of both guesthouses will pick you up from the train station.

East of Betws-y-Coed in Capel Garmon is *Tan-y-Foes Country House* (☎ 710507). In a 16th-century stone building, it's a very comfortable nonsmoking hotel with nine rooms, some with four-poster beds. B&B costs from £70 to £90 per person.

Ty Gwyn (☎ 710383), south of the bridge in the village, is a 17th-century coaching inn where B&B costs from £17 per person, rising to £28 for a room with bathroom, or £37 per person for a four-poster bed. There's a good restaurant here.

Places to Eat

On one side of the train station entrance is *Dil's Diner* (☎ 710346), open 8.30 am until around 8 pm. It does cheap, filling meals such as fish and chips (£4.30). On the other side of the station entrance is the excellent *Alpine Coffee Shop*. Good sandwiches (on various breads including ciabatta), full meals and a range of traditionally British warming drinks such as Bovril or Ovaltine are available.

The top restaurant is at the *Ty Gwyn* (see Places to Stay). Dishes range from £7 to £14.

NORTH WALES

There are several teashops along High St. The *Pont-y-Pair Hotel* does good bar food.

Getting There & Around

Betws-y-Coed is served by rail and bus from Llandudno Junction. There are seven trains a day, Monday to Saturday, on the Conwy Valley line from Llandudno Junction (£3.40, 30 minutes).

Buses take about 10 minutes longer from Llandudno Junction to Betus. Snowdon Sherpa buses run from Llandudno to Conwy, Betws-y-Coed, Capel Curig and Pen-y-Pass (for the youth hostels), then on to Llanberis and Caernarfon.

Mountain bikes can be hired from Beics Betws (☎ 710829), beside the TIC. The charge is a hefty £16 a day.

CAPEL CURIG

Six miles west of Betws-y-Coed is a small village that is one of the oldest resorts in the area. It's a popular place with walkers, climbers and outdoor enthusiasts of all types.

The National Mountain Centre at Plas y Brenin (☎ 01690-720214) is on the edge of the village and has a bar, climbing wall and dry ski slope. It runs residential courses in canoeing and climbing, and often holds public lectures. You can rent equipment and occasionally accommodation is offered.

The *Capel Curig Youth Hostel* (☎ 01690-720225) opens daily from mid-February to mid-December. It's in the village, next to the garage. The nightly charge is £10/6.95 for adults/under-18s. The friendly *Bron Eryri* (☎ 720240) has five rooms with bathrooms and charges £21 per person.

In the evenings, everyone meets at the *Bryn Tyrch* (☎ 720223), a hotel (B&B from £20.50 per person) with a busy pub, at *Cobdens Hotel* (☎ 720243), where B&B costs £29 per person, or at the bar at Plas Y Brenin.

The Snowdon Sherpa bus passes this way between Betus and Llanberis.

LLANBERIS

☎ 01286 • pop 2000

This tourist village lies at the foot of Mt Snowdon and becomes packed with walkers and climbers. It makes an excellent base,

though accommodation can be booked out in July and August.

Orientation & Information

Llanberis is bypassed by the A4086, which also separates the village from its two lakes, Llyn Padarn and Llyn Peris. The friendly TIC (☎ 870765, e llanberis.tic@gwynedd .gov.uk) is on High St, opposite the post office. Almost all the accommodation and places to eat are strung out along this street – you can't get lost.

Snowdon Mountain Railway

Snowdon Mountain Railway (☎ 870223), Britain's only public rack-and-pinion railway, opened in 1896 and climbs more than 900m from Llanberis to the summit of Snowdon, a 5-mile journey that takes an hour.

Seven vintage steam locomotives and four modern diesel locomotives haul carriages up and down between mid-March and the end of October. Schedules are subject to the weather and queues can be long during summer, but if you can't be bothered walking to the top of Snowdon, a return ride costs £15.80/11.30. It's sometimes possible to buy a stand-by ticket down from the top for £8/5.50.

Other Things to See & Do

Across the bypass, **Electric Mountain** (☎ 870 636) adopts the Disney approach to Welsh history, with talking trees and a brief scattering of historical facts. A quite interesting tour into the underground power station starts here. Dinorwig is a quick-response power station, constructed to deal with power surges on the national grid when half the population of Britain simultaneously puts the kettle on during TV commercial breaks. The museum is free and tickets for the power station are £5/2.50; they are both open 9.30 am to 5.30 pm daily, April to September; 10.30 am to 4.30 the rest of the year.

The **Llanberis Lake Railway** (☎ 870549) runs beside Llyn Padarn between March and October. The round trip takes 45 minutes and costs £4.20/2.50. The **Welsh Slate Museum** (☎ 870630) is on the site of the old Dinorwic Quarry, on the shore of Llyn

Padarn. Visits to the old quarry workshops and demonstrations of the skills involved in splitting slate into tiles are interesting. The museum opens 10 am to 5 pm, April to October and till 4 pm the rest of the year except Saturday when it's closed. Admission is £3.50/free.

Dolbadarn Castle is a 13th-century ruin that was built to guard Llanberis Pass. It's a pleasant walk south-east of the town. It is run by Cadw, the Welsh historic monuments agency.

Activities
High Trek Snowdonia (☎ 871232) offers a variety of guided treks, gorge scrambling, night hikes and abseiling around Snowdon for adventurers. There are numerous other outdoor activities in the area. The Dolbadarn Pony Trekking Centre (☎ 870277) operates from the Dolbadarn Hotel and charges £10 per hour.

The Padarn Watersports Centre (☎ 870 556), Llyn Padarn, offers a wide range of activities (kayaking, canoeing, raft building, climbing, abseiling and mountain walking) for groups of two to four people (or more). The charge for a group of five for half a day is £18 per person whatever the activity. Menai Historical Cruises (☎ 07974 716418) run half-hour boat trips on Llyn Padarn in summer for £3.50/2; the boat leaves from the jetty near the Slate Museum car park.

Places to Stay
Camping Two miles from Llanberis, *Cae Gwyn Camp Site* (☎ 870718), at Nant Peris, charges £2.50 for a tent pitch.

Hostels There's dorm accommodation at *The Heights Hotel* (☎ 871179, 74 High St) for £9 or £12.50 with breakfast. The hotel also has singles/doubles with bathrooms for £25/40.

Surrounded by Welsh Black cattle and with a good view over the top of the slate quarry, *Llanberis Youth Hostel* (☎ 870280) was originally a quarry manager's dwelling. It's half a mile south-west of the town and opens daily from April to August. The rest of the year it opens for most of the week –

phone for details. The nightly charge is £10/6.90 for adults/under-18s. *Pen-y-Pass Youth Hostel* (☎ 870428) is superbly situated at the top of Llanberis Pass, 5½ miles from Llanberis. It was once a hotel popular with Victorian mountaineers. The hostel opens daily from January to October and over the New Year; beds cost £11/7.75 for adults/under-18s.

Snowdon House (☎ 870356, 3 Gwastadnant) is at Nant Peris, 3 miles out of Llanberis on the way to Pen-y-Pass. There's bunkhouse accommodation from £5 per person, camping for £2.50 and a cottage to let. Facilities include a coin-operated drying room, showers and cooker.

About 3 miles from Llanberis on the Bangor road, *Jesse James Bunkhouse* (☎ 870521, Penisarwaun) has been going since 1966 and is a popular walkers' base – non-smokers only. JJ is a mountain guide who also offers a range of accommodation from £7.50 to £15.

B&Bs & Hotels At the far end of High St from the station, overlooking the lake, *Beech Bank Guest House* (☎ 870414) charges £15 per person. The *Bron Y Graig* (☎ 872073, Capel Coch) is a comfortable guest house, just off High St, which charges from £18 per person. At the Caernarfon end of Llanberis is the *Alpine Lodge Hotel* (☎ 870294, 1 High St), with doubles/triples from £35/45.

At the other end of High St, *Padarn Lake Hotel* (☎ 870260, High St) charges £36/59 for singles/doubles. The *Dolbadarn Hotel* (☎ 870277, High St), opposite, has rooms for £17/34 (£40 for a double with bathroom). The hotel has a restaurant and bar, and there's a pony trekking centre beside it. Nearby, the pleasant *Y Gwynedd Hotel* (☎ 870203, High St) charges £18 to £24 per person for rooms with bathrooms.

Pen-y-Gwyrd Hotel (☎ 870211) is 7 miles from Llanberis, just beyond Pen-y-Pass on the junction of the A498 and A4086. B&B costs from £23 per person. The 1953 Everest team used the inn as a training base – you can see their signatures on the ceiling. The residents sit down together for the evening meal in the dining room; bar food is also available.

At Llanrug, 5 miles north-west of Llanberis, *Plas Tirion* (☎ 673190) is a very comfortable farmhouse that charges from £22 per person.

In Llanberis, the top place to stay is the *Royal Victoria Hotel* (☎ 870253), near the Snowdon Mountain Railway station. It has rooms with bathroom at £47.50 per person, including breakfast, or £53.50 for dinner, bed and breakfast. There may be reduced rates when business is slow. In the restaurant, there are two three-course set menus, one at £11.85 and the other at £17.25.

Places to Eat

Y Bistro (☎ 871278, 45 High St) is the place to go for a splurge – Welsh produce with a rustic French twist. It only opens in the evening and has set dinners from £19.50 to £23.

Pete's Eats (☎ 870358, 40 High St) is a warm cafe where hikers swap information over large portions of healthy food. For walking fodder, try their Big Jim – a mixed grill for £8.50. There are good vegetarian choices and a useful notice board here.

The people from *Snowdon House* (see Places to Stay) also run the cosy climber's haunt, the *Vaynol Arms* (☎ 870284, Nant Peris) which does a range of hot meals and snacks to suit all pockets.

In the evenings, climbers hang out at *The Heights Hotel* (☎ 871179) – its pub even has its own climbing wall. See Places to Stay earlier.

Getting There & Away

Llanberis is 13 miles from Bangor. From Bangor, take bus No 77 or 86 that run hourly from Monday to Saturday (£1.90, 40 minutes). From Caernarfon, take bus No 88, which runs about twice-hourly from Monday to Saturday (£1.40, 25 minutes). Some buses on this route continue to Nant Peris.

There are five No 95 Sherpa buses a day from Caernarfon (1¼ hours), Monday to Saturday, and about three daily (No 19 to Llanrwst, then change to No 96) in the high season from Llandudno (two hours).

BEDDGELERT
☎ 01766 • pop 300

This is one of the most attractive of the Snowdon villages, situated on the banks of the River Gwynant. The name means Gelert's Grave and comes from a local legend that tells of Prince Llewlyn's dog Gelert, killed by its owner after he thought it had savaged his baby son, when the dog had in fact killed a wolf that was attacking the baby.

The village has a National Park Information Centre (☎ 890615), at Canolfan Hebog, which opens 10 am to 6 pm daily, summer only.

Just outside the village is the **Sygun Copper Mine** (☎ 510100), mined from Roman times until it was turned into a tourist attraction. It opens daily in summer and admission costs £4.75/3.

Places to Stay & Eat

Beddgelert Forest Campsite (☎ 890288) is both well equipped and situated, a mile out on the Caernarfon road. Charges start at £4 per person.

The *Snowdon Ranger Youth Hostel* (☎ 01286-650391) is 5 miles north of the village, at the base of Snowdon. Open April to October, the nightly charge is £10/6.90 for adults/under-18s.

The *Bryn Gwynant Youth Hostel* (☎ 890 251) is 4 miles from Beddgelert on the A498, in an idyllic location above Llyn Gwynant. It opens daily March to October; a bed costs £10/6.90 for adults/under-18s. They also have some bedrooms with bathrooms from £26.80.

For B&B, *Plas Colwyn* (☎ 890458), in the centre of the village, charges from £18 per person. They also serve Welsh food in the restaurant downstairs. Try local Likky Pie (pork and leeks) for £7.25. *Beddgelert Bistro & Tearooms* (☎ 890543), beside the bridge, also serves local dishes from £9.95 and has three rooms from £18 per person. The *Sygun Fawr Hotel* (☎ 890258) is less than a mile from town, in an old house. Singles/doubles with bathroom cost £44.50/59.

Don't pass *Glaslyn Ices* in the village without trying one of their award-winning home-made ice creams or sorbets.

Getting There & Around

Beddgelert is on the route of the Snowdon Sherpa (☎ 01286-870880) bus. There are several services a day to Caernarfon and Llanberis.

Beics Beddgelert (☎ 890434), 2 miles from the village on the Caernarfon road, rent mountain bikes for £7.50 for two hours or £16 per day.

BLAENAU FFESTINIOG

☎ 01766 • pop 6000

Slate was the basis of Snowdonia's wealth in the 19th century and Blaenau Ffestiniog was the centre of the industry. Although slate mining continues here on a small scale, it's now a tourist town. The history of the slate industry, the Ffestiniog Railway (which has its northern terminus here) and the hydroelectric power station are the main tourist attractions.

Despite being in the centre of the park, the grey slate waste tips that surround Blaenau Ffestiniog prevented it from being officially included in the national park. The two main mines in the area are in the town. Nearby is the smaller village of Ffestiniog.

The National Park Information Centre (☎ 830360) is on the High St.

Ffestiniog Railway

A means of access as well as an attraction, the Ffestiniog Railway (☎ 512340) is a 13½-mile narrow-gauge line extending from Porthmadog on the coast and terminating in Blaenau Ffestiniog.

Construction of the line began in 1832. In 1836, horse-drawn wagons started to take the slate from the mine down to Porthmadog, from where it was shipped to Europe and America. In the 1860s, steam locomotives were introduced and the line was opened up as a passenger service.

The railway opens 9.15 am to 5 pm daily, March to November. A return trip costs £13.80 on a steam train. A 1st-class ticket allowing you to sit in the observation car or in a traditional vintage coach costs £5 extra.

Slate Mines

The Llechwedd Slate Caverns (☎ 830306) opens 10 am to 6 pm (shorter hours in the winter) year round. You can ride into the tunnels on the miners' tramway, dating from 1846, or descend into the Deep Mine on the steepest passenger railway in Britain. As you walk through vast underground chambers, a commentary explains what it was like to work down here. Tickets cost £6.95/4.80 for a single tour and £10.50/7.20 for both tours.

Places to Stay & Eat

Most of the people who visit Blaenau Ffestiniog do so on day trips on the train. If you want to stay, there's a small choice of accommodation.

Afallon (☎ 830468, Manod Rd) is a friendly place with three rooms; B&B costs £15 per person. It's only half a mile from the station but transport can be arranged.

The excellent *Ty Clwb* (☎ 762658) is a modernised 18th-century stone guesthouse in the square, offering B&B from £19 per person.

Tyddyn Du Farm (☎ 590281) is about 6 miles outside the town at Gellilydan. There are three rooms in the 17th-century farmhouse; B&B is from £22 to £28 per person, with Jacuzzis in some suites.

Five miles south of Blaenau in the village of Maentwrog is the *Old Rectory* (☎ 590 305), where upmarket B&B with bathroom costs £45/55 for a single/double in the house, £30/45 in the annexe. Also in Maentwrog is *Grapes Hotel* (☎ 590208), which charges £25 per person. It also has a pub and restaurant that does snacks and excellent meals from £5.50.

Getting There & Away

There are hourly buses from Caernarfon to Blaenau Ffestiniog (£3.60, 1½ hours) Monday to Saturday and three on Sunday. There are also services to Harlech, Barmouth and Pwll-heli. Bus No 35 goes to Dolgellau four times a day, Monday to Saturday.

The Conwy Valley line goes from Llandudno or Llandudno Junction via Betws-y-Coed to Blaenau Ffestiniog, seven times a day, Monday to Saturday (£4.40, 1 hour). From Porthmadog there's the Ffestiniog Railway.

HARLECH
☎ 01766 • pop 1300

Dramatically positioned above the plains, the ruins of Harlech Castle dominate this sleepy little town. There are superb views out to sea and some good beaches nearby.

The TIC (☎ 780658) is on High St and opens daily April to October. The train station is on the plain below the castle.

Harlech Castle

The castle (☎ 780552; Cadw) is a World Heritage Site, and rightly so. Another creation of Edward I, it was built between 1283 and 1289. The castle is rectangular with two concentric sets of walls and is constructed of local grey sandstone.

Harlech is sometimes called the Castle of Lost Causes because it has been defended so many times to no avail. It was taken in 1404 by Owain Glyndŵr and became his stronghold until 1409. He was in turn besieged here by the future Henry V. It was the last castle to fall in the Wars of the Roses – attacks on the Lancastrians by the Yorkists continued from 1461 until 1468. By Elizabethan times, the castle was in ruins except for the massive twin-towered gatehouse and the outer walls, which are still intact. They make the place seem impregnable even now.

When it was built, the sea covered the plain below and ships could sail right to the foot of the castle stairway that is still in use today. The castle opens 9.30 am to 6 pm daily, May to September; 9.30 am to 5 pm October; 9.30 am to 4 pm November to April. Admission costs £3/2.

Places to Stay & Eat

Llanbedr Youth Hostel (☎ 01341-241287, *Plas Newydd, Llanbedr*) is 3 miles south of Harlech. It opens April until October and charges £9.25/6.50 for adults/under-18s; it's closed Sunday and Monday after September.

Godre'r Graig (☎ 780905), on Ffordd-newydd or New Rd, is below the castle and charges £16 per person for B&B. On High St next to the church, *Byrdir House* (☎ 780316) does B&B for £20 per person in a double or £16 for a single.

The *Lion Hotel* (☎ 780731), near the cas-tle, charges £21 per person. There's cheap pub grub in the bar.

The *Castle Hotel* (☎ 780529, *Castle Square*) has some rooms with great views – Nos 3 and 4 are the best. Singles/doubles cost £25/40.

Nearby, *Castle Cottage* (☎ 780479, *Pen-llech*) is a very comfortable place to stay, with rooms from £40/59. It also has two singles without bathroom for £26. Set dinners cost £23.

Plas Café (☎ 780204, *High St*) boasts the finest view of any restaurant in Harlech – across to the castle and down to the sea. You can also sit outside. They do breakfast, lunch and dinner, and there are good vegetarian choices.

Yr Ogof Bistro (☎ 780888, *High St*) serves a variety of traditional Welsh and vegetarian dishes.

Getting There & Away

Trains run from Machynlleth to Harlech six times a day (£8.20, 1¼ hours). Bus No 38 operates from Barmouth to Harlech (25 minutes) nine times a day and continues to Blaenau Ffestiniog five times a day.

BARMOUTH
☎ 01341 • pop 2500

Barmouth is a pleasant seaside resort with a long sandy beach, and there are some enjoyable walks in the area. The approach road from Dolgellau along the estuary is a scenic one. You can hike up on the cliffs of Dinas Oleu above the town or across the estuary to Fairbourne.

The TIC (☎ 280787, 📧 barmouth.tic@ gwynedd.gov.uk) is on Station Rd and sells leaflets on local walks for 40p. The Fairbourne & Barmouth Railway (☎ 250362) runs 2½ miles from Fairbourne train station to Penrhyn Point, April to October. The Three Peaks Yacht Race is an annual event in June (☎ 280298). There's a small market on High St on Thursday and Sunday.

Places to Stay & Eat

There are numerous hotels and B&Bs. *The Gables* (☎ 280553, *Mynach Rd*) is a friendly place with sea views, half a mile from Barmouth. B&B starts at £18 per person. *Wavecrest Hotel* (☎ 280330, 8 Marine Parade) is a friendly sea-front hotel with comfortable accommodation from £18 to £27 per person.

Two miles north of town on the A496, *Llwyndu Farmhouse* (☎ 280144) is a 16th-century house overlooking the sea with garden. B&B costs £29 to £34 per person and it also serves food. Seafood restaurant *The Inglenook* (☎ 280807, Harbour Lane), housed in a 17th-century building off Church St, serves decent mains for under £8.

The Bistro on Church St is a cosy place, which offers evening meals from £6.75 to £9.75. Spicy Thai chicken costs £8.95 and good vegetarian meals start at £5.95. The renowned *Balti Clipper* (☎ 280252), also on Church St, offers restaurant or takeaway meals. Bring your own wine and try the fresh salmon marinated in spices for £8.50.

TYWYN

This small seaside town is best known for the **Talyllyn Railway** (☎ 01654-710472), which runs 7 miles inland to Abergynolwyn. Other than that, there's not much to detain you in town. Trains run daily in summer and are all steam-hauled; tickets cost £8/2.

There's a small **railway museum** containing narrow-gauge locomotives by the station in Tywyn. The TIC (☎ 01654-710070) is on High St. The scenic route from Tywyn to Dolgellau via the B4405 passes through the village of Abergynolwyn, from where a visit to the remains of Castell Y Bere makes a nice walk or picnic diversion. Three miles from the village, the sprawling ruin of the 13th-century castle, built by Llywelyn the Great and later seized by the English, is set against the mountainous backdrop of the Dysynni Valley. Walk 300m down the road to the quaint 12th-century St Michael's Church and graveyard. Note the leper's window, through which local lepers, in less salubrious times, were allowed to observe the sacraments.

DOLGELLAU

☎ 01341 • pop 3500

Dolgellau (pronounced doll-geth-lie) is a quiet market town that makes a good base for walks on Cadair Idris, one of the highest mountains in Snowdonia National Park (889m).

In the 15th century the town was Owain Glyndŵr's capital and his parliament was held here. The town has historical links with the Quaker movement, which established a community in the area. In the 18th century, Dolgellau was the centre of the prosperous Welsh wool industry. It's now the administrative centre for the region. The town can be seen in less than an hour.

The TIC and National Park Information Centre (☎ 422888) is in Ty Meirion, Eldon Square and offers theme walks around the various Quaker sites in the summer. The centre opens 10 am to 6 pm daily in summer; shorter hours in winter. Upstairs, the **Quaker Heritage Centre** has an interesting exhibition. Admission is free.

Walking

The information centre has leaflets (40p) on local walks, including national park descriptions of the trails up Cadair Idris. Geoff Elliott's useful booklet *Local Walks Around Dolgellau* costs £3.80 at the TIC and describes 15 local trails of varying lengths and levels of difficulty. The standard route up Cadair Idris is the Pony Track from Ty Nant, a return trip of four to five hours. It can be wild up here if the weather comes down. Francis Kilvert wrote of his 1871-trip in *Kilvert's Diary*, describing it as 'the stoniest, dreariest, most desolate mountain I was ever on...It is an awful place in a storm. I thought of Moses on Sinai.' On a sunny summer's day, however, it's glorious.

The least energetic walk is the town trail. The Precipice Walk, which sounds rather more lethal than it actually is, starts near Llanfachreth and takes in wonderful views of the Mawddach Estuary.

Other Things to See & Do

Just 3½ miles south of Dolgellau, in an idyllic setting, **Abergwynant Farm & Pony Trekking Centre** (☎ 422377) offers hourly treks through forests and along the foothills of Cadair Idris from £10. You can also fish for trout and salmon there, along the Gwynant River for £2 a day. You can hire bikes for £12 a day from **Dragons Bikes & Kites** (☎ 423008) on Smithfield St, in the town centre.

Places to Stay

According to local legend, anyone who spends the night on top of Cadair Idris will either wake as a poet or go mad. Luckily there's a wide range of accommodation in the area. There's a camping barn, camp site and tearoom at *Ty Nant* (☎ 423433, Ffordd y Gader). The stone barn sleeps 12 (£4 per person) – all you need is a foam mat and sleeping bag. Gas cookers and cooking utensils are available.

Caban Cader Idris (☎ 01248-600478) is an old schoolhouse in a secluded valley at Islawrdref, about 3 miles south-west of Dolgellau. The nightly charge is £5 per person. It's usually let to groups and sleeps 19 people.

One mile out of Dolgellau, on the old Fairbourne Rd, is *Glynn Farm* (☎ 422286) with lovely views of the Mawddach Estuary. B&B costs £15 per person, or £18 with bath. There's a small single for £14.

Nonsmoking *Tanyfron* (☎ 422638, Arran Rd) is an excellent place to stay with a pretty garden, half a mile from Dolgellau. B&B costs £22 per person and it also provides camping facilities in summer for £10 for two people.

Clifton House Hotel (☎ 422554, Smithfield Square) has double rooms for £36, or £46 with bathroom. *Ivy House* (☎ 422535) is centrally located in Finsbury Square. B&B costs from £28/37 for a single/double.

Fronoleu Farm Hotel (☎ 422361, Tabor) is an old farmhouse and restaurant about a mile from town. It has 12 rooms at £27 per person. The restaurant features live harp music on weekday nights.

Dolserau Hall Hotel (☎ 422522), 1½ miles east of Dolgellau, has 16 en-suite rooms. The hotel opens year round and charges from £45 per person for B&B. A dinner and B&B special costs from £43 to £60. It's in a peaceful location and there are excellent views from the rooms.

Penmaenuchaf Hall Hotel (☎ 422129), 2 miles from Dolgellau at Penmaenpool,

is the most luxurious hotel in the area – a peaceful retreat in 9-hectare grounds. Rooms cost from £70/100 to £110/160. The restaurant opens to non-residents and a four-course dinner costs £26.50.

Places to Eat

Dylanwad Da Restaurant (☎ 422870, 2 Ffos-y-Felin) is a good place for dinner with main dishes from about £9 to £14. Burgundy Welsh lamb with bacon and red wine costs £12.20. It opens nightly in summer except Monday. *Y Sospan*, just off Eldon Square in Queen's Square, is a lunch-time cafe that serves sandwiches and jacket potatoes.

Outside Dolgellau, in Penmaenpool, is the *George III* (☎ 422525), a pub and hotel overlooking Mawddach Estuary, which offers a wide range of bar food or full restaurant menu with mains starting at £11.50.

Getting There & Away

Arriva Cymru operates several services to Dolgellau. Bus No 2 from Caernarfon (£4.35, 1½ hours) operates six times a day, Monday to Saturday, and twice a day on Sunday; the No 94 from Barmouth (20 minutes) operates frequently, Monday to Saturday, and continues to Llangollen and Wrexham; and the No 32 from Aberystwyth/Machynlleth (35 minutes) operates five times a day Monday to Saturday, once on Sunday. Bus No 35 goes to Blaenau Ffestiniog four times a day, Monday to Saturday.

BALA

☎ 01678 • pop 2100

Bala is a small market town, on one long street, situated at the eastern end of Llyn Tegid, the largest natural lake in Wales. The lake is 4 miles long and almost three-quarters of a mile wide. It's now the centre for a wide variety of water-based activities – the main attraction of Bala. There's a TIC (☎ 521021, ℮ bala.tic@gwynedd.gov.uk) on Pensarn Rd.

The Bala Adventure & Water Sports Centre (☎ 521059) behind the TIC offers introductory sessions in mountain biking, canoeing, raft building, windsurfing, sailing, rock climbing and abseiling. Sessions cost from around £20 per person. Canolfan

Tryweryn (☎ 521083) offers a 20-minute white-water rafting trip for £10.

The well-equipped *Pen y Bont Touring & Camping Park* (☎ 520549, Llangynog Rd) is in a good spot close to the lake and charges from £5.90 for a tent to £10.45 for a caravan. It opens April to the end of October.

Cynwyd Youth Hostel (☎ 01490-412814, The Old Mill, Cynwyd) is the nearest HI hostel, 10 miles from the lake, and charges £7.50/5.25 for adults/under-18s. It opens Easter to the end of September.

Back in town, there's a licensed *Express Pizzeria* on Berwyn St that does good pizza from £3.80 to £5.95. Most of the town's pubs also serve food.

The Bala Lake Railway (☎ 540666) runs the 4½ miles from Bala station to Llanuwchllyn along the lake, April to October. A single trip takes 25 minutes and costs £3.80/2.

North-Western Wales

This section includes all of north-western Wales lying outside the Snowdonia National Park. Llandudno is a traditional seaside resort, Conwy and Caernarfon are dominated by spectacular castles, and the particularly Welsh areas of Anglesey and the Llŷn Peninsula see far fewer tourists than other parts of the country.

LLANDUDNO
☎ 01492 • pop 18,000

As the largest seaside resort in Wales, Llandudno seethes with tourists in summer and also attracts a steady staple of pensioners year round. The coastal area is known colloquially as Costa Geriatrica. It was developed as an upmarket Victorian holiday town and has retained its beautiful architecture and 19th-century atmosphere. There's a stately pier and promenade, and suitably antiquated attractions such as donkeys and Punch & Judy shows on the beach.

Llandudno is on its own peninsula, situated between two sweeping beaches, and is dominated by the spectacular limestone headland – the Great Orme – with the mountains of Snowdonia as a backdrop. The Great Orme, with its Bronze Age mine, tramway, chair lift and superb views, is quite fascinating.

In its 19th-century heyday, Llandudno's visitors included many of the famous people of the day, such as Gladstone and Disraeli. In 1861, the Liddell family, whose daughter was Lewis Carroll's model for *Alice in Wonderland*, spent the summer in the house that is now the St Tudno Hotel. The Liddells later built a house on the other side of the town; it's since become the Gogarth Abbey Hotel.

Orientation & Information

The town fills the central section of the peninsula, with the Llandudno Bay beach to the north-east and the West Shore to the south-west. Mostyn St is the main shopping street where branches of all main banks can be found. The tip of the peninsula is the Great Orme; the Little Orme is to the east.

The TIC (☎ 876413), 1–2 Chapel St, opens 9.30 am to 5 pm daily year round.

There's a laundrette at 25 Brookes St.

Things to See & Do

There are superb views from the Great Orme and the headland is home to many species of flowers, butterflies and birds. Guided walks are offered May to September, and there's a cafe and gift-shop complex at the top.

The **Great Orme Tramway** (☎ 876749), at the top of Church Walks, takes you up in original 1902 tramcars. It operates 10 am to 6 pm daily, Easter to October; tickets cost £3.80/2.60 for a return. The **Great Orme Mine** (☎ 870447) is a Bronze-Age copper mine halfway along the tramline; it opens at the same time as the tram. Admission costs £4.40/2.80. A combined ticket for the tramway and the mine is £7.25/5. There's also a **cable car** (☎ 877205) that operates, subject to the weather, from Happy Valley, above the pier. Tickets are £5/2.60 for a return.

Elegant Victorian **Llandudno Pier** reaches 670m into the sea. The pier was first built in 1857, but it collapsed in a storm two years later. The current pier was started in 1877 and its main use was as a disembarkation point for passengers from the Isle of Man

NORTH WALES

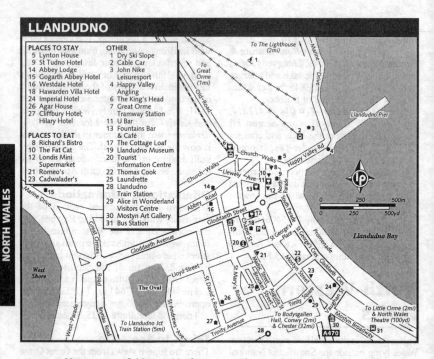

LLANDUDNO

PLACES TO STAY	OTHER
5 Lynton House	1 Dry Ski Slope
9 St Tudno Hotel	2 Cable Car
14 Abbey Lodge	3 John Nike
15 Gogarth Abbey Hotel	Leisuresport
16 Westdale Hotel	4 Happy Valley
18 Hawarden Villa Hotel	Angling
24 Imperial Hotel	6 The King's Head
26 Agar House	7 Great Orme
27 Cliffbury Hotel;	Tramway Station
Hilary Hotel	13 U Bar
	13 Fountains Bar
PLACES TO EAT	& Café
8 Richard's Bistro	17 The Cottage Loaf
10 The Fat Cat	19 Llandudno Museum
12 Londis Mini	20 Tourist
Supermarket	Information Centre
21 Romeo's	22 Thomas Cook
23 Cadwalader's	25 Laundrette
	28 Llandudno
	Train Station
	29 Alice in Wonderland
	Visitors Centre
	30 Mostyn Art Gallery
	31 Bus Station

steamers. You can rent fishing tackle from Happy Valley Angling (☎ 877678) at the pier entrance, and fish from the pier.

The **Alice in Wonderland Visitors Centre**, alias The Rabbit Hole (☎ 860082), 3 Trinity Square, makes the most of the town's Alice connection with amateurish tableaux that will excite only the most ardent fans. It opens 10 am to 5 pm daily (to 4 pm Sunday) in summer and from Monday to Saturday in winter. Admission costs £2.95/2.50.

The **Mostyn Art Gallery** (☎ 879201), 12 Vaughan St, is the leading gallery for contemporary art in North Wales. It opens Monday to Saturday and admission is free. They also run short arts workshops. Ring for details. The **North Wales Theatre** (☎ 872000), on the promenade, is one of the largest in Britain and opened in 1996. The **Llandudno Museum** (☎ 876517), 17–19 Gloddaeth St, has a few local history artefacts on view 10.30 am to 1 pm Tuesday to Saturday in summer. Admission costs £1.50/75p.

If none of these interests you, there's always the **dry ski slope** above the town. John Nike Leisuresport (☎ 874707), on Happy Valley Rd, offers daily winter skiing, snowboarding and toboggan tuition.

Places to Stay

There are 700 hotels and guesthouses here so finding a bed is rarely a problem. There are no camping facilities in the immediate area.

St David's Rd is a good place to start looking for rooms in the region of £18 to £20 per person. *Cliffbury Hotel* (☎ 877224), at No 34, is a decent non-smoking place. At No 32, the *Hilary Hotel* (☎ 875623) or *Agar House* (☎ 875572) are both simple and comfortable.

There are also some reasonable places along St Mary's Rd, one block towards the Promenade.

Hawarden Villa Hotel (☎ 860447) is almost right across from the TIC at 27 Chapel St. It is friendly and offers modest, good-value accommodation for £15 per person.

Westdale Hotel (☎ 877996, 37 Abbey Rd) is a very comfortable place. B&B costs from £18 per person and there is also a package that includes dinner from £22.50. The excellent, nonsmoking *Abbey Lodge* (☎ 878042, 14 Abbey Rd) has a pretty garden and offers B&B from £25 per person. *Lynton House* (☎ 875057, 80 Church Walks) is well placed for the pier and the tramway, and charges £24 per person; all rooms have a bathroom.

For an unusual night's rest, try *The Lighthouse* (☎ 876819, Marine Drive), in working use until 1985, situated on a 100m sheer cliff edge at the end of the Great Orme promontory. Decorated like a ship on the inside with pitch pine, there are three rooms with bathroom and binoculars from £47.50 per person. Try the Lamp Room which has panoramic sea views.

At the top end of the accommodation scale are some of the hotels along the Promenade, such as the *Imperial Hotel* (☎ 877 466, The Promenade), an elegant Victorian building where B&B costs £65/95 for a single/double. Discounts may be offered when business is slack.

The *St Tudno Hotel* (☎ 874411, North Parade) is a luxurious hotel that charges from £75 for a single to £270 for a suite. It's notable in that, out of the many awards it has won, it has several times received the accolade 'Best Hotel Loos in Great Britain'!

Gogarth Abbey Hotel (☎ 876211, West Shore), the rather old-fashioned former summer home of Alice Liddell, subject of *Alice in Wonderland*, charges from £50 per person for B&B; there are 38 rooms, all with bathroom. They also offer self-catering holiday apartments from £325 to £440 per week. One of the top hotels in Wales, *Bodysgallen Hall* (☎ 584466) is 3 miles from the town, just off the A470. It's a luxurious country-house hotel where rooms cost from £104/205. It does two-day champagne breaks for around £110 per person per night.

Places to Eat

The restaurant at the *St Tudno Hotel* (☎ 874 411, 16 North Parade) is regarded as the top place to eat in town with main courses from £14.50 to £18.50.

On Church Walks, the swanky *Richard's Bistro* (☎ 875315) opens from 5.30 pm every night and is very popular. Main dishes range from £13 to £17.

On Upper Mostyn St you will find fast-food restaurants, cafes, and fish and chip places. *Cadwalader's* is an ice-cream parlour that's part of the Welsh chain named after the brother of Owain Glyndŵr. *The Fat Cat* (☎ 871844, 149 Mostyn St) is an excellent cafe-bar where you can get anything from a drink to a full meal. They have a good selection of baguettes from around £4, all-day breakfast and vegetarian specials for under £6. It's a vibrant place with real ales and board games. *Romeo's* (☎ 877777, St Georges Place) does traditional pizzas from £5 and steaks from £10.50 to £12.50.

Many of the B&Bs and guesthouses will provide evening meals if arranged in advance. They're used to serving them early so expect to eat between 6 and 7 pm.

There is a *Londis Mini Supermarket* near the Fat Cat cafe-bar.

Entertainment

The Cottage Loaf, on Market St, and *The King's Head*, by the tramway station on Old Rd, are good places for a drink. The *U Bar* on Upper Mostyn St, beside Londis, is probably the trendiest watering hole in town, with seats outside. Opposite, *Fountains Bar & Café* (☎ 875600) has a good range of beers and serves burgers and pasta dishes for around £5.

Getting There & Away

There are two National Express buses a day from London (£19, 7½ hours). Bus No 5 runs frequently between Llandudno, Bangor and Caernarfon.

The train station at Llandudno Junction is on the main line from London's Euston, a 3½-hour journey. There are lots of trains but only two direct services a day. Services from Crewe (£13.70, 1¼ hours) and Chester (£9.80, 50 minutes) are fairly frequent throughout the year. Trains run on the Conwy Valley line from Llandudno Junction to Betws-y-Coed and Blaenau Ffestiniog.

Llandudno itself is a short train journey

(£1.30, 10 minutes) from Llandudno Junction. Trains run frequently, or you could take bus No 19 for the 8-mile journey.

CONWY
☎ 01492 • pop 3800

Conwy has been revitalised since the through traffic on the busy A55 was consigned to a tunnel that burrows under the estuary of the River Conwy and the town. It's now a picturesque and interesting little place, dominated by the superb Conwy Castle, one of the grandest of Edward I's castles and a medieval masterpiece.

The TIC (☎ 592248) is in the Conwy Castle Visitors Centre, not to be confused with the Conwy Visitors Centre by the train station. It offers a bed-booking service and opens 10 am to 4 pm, Monday to Saturday and from 11 am to 4 pm on Sundays, March to October.

Things to See & Do

Conwy Castle (☎ 592358; Cadw) looks every bit a castle, with eight massive crenellated towers. Its construction took five years, from 1282 to 1287, and its shape was largely dictated by the rock on which it's built. The best view of the castle is from across the river, with the Snowdonia Mountains providing a dramatic backdrop – on the rare occasion when they're not veiled in cloud.

Inside, the castle is largely a ruin, though there are some rooms that contain tableaux and exhibitions. The great hall is impressive, and the royal apartments and chapel are interesting. From the battlements there are good views across town and of Telford's suspension bridge, built in 1826. Reached by a bridge, the castle opens 9.30 am to 6 pm in summer and 9.30 am to 4 pm in winter. Admission costs £3.50/2.50.

Conwy's **town walls** make this one of the best examples of a medieval walled town in Europe. Still enclosing the town, they are three-quarters of a mile long, with 22 towers and three original gateways. You can walk along part of the walls.

Aberconwy House (☎ 592246) is a 14th-century timber-and-plaster house on Castle St that has been restored by the NT. There are rooms furnished in period style and an interesting audiovisual presentation. The house opens 11 am to 5 pm daily except Tuesday, April to October. Admission costs £2/1 or £5 for a family.

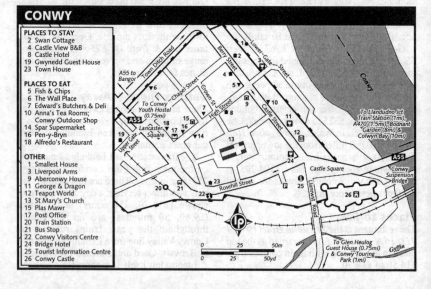

CONWY

PLACES TO STAY
2 Swan Cottage
4 Castle View B&B
8 Castle Hotel
19 Gwynedd Guest House
23 Town House

PLACES TO EAT
5 Fish & Chips
6 The Wall Place
7 Edward's Butchers & Deli
10 Anna's Tea Rooms;
    Conwy Outdoor Shop
14 Spar Supermarket
16 Pen-y-Bryn
18 Alfredo's Restaurant

OTHER
1 Smallest House
3 Liverpool Arms
9 Aberconwy House
11 George & Dragon
12 Teapot World
13 St Mary's Church
15 Plas Mawr
17 Post Office
20 Train Station
21 Bus Stop
22 Conwy Visitors Centre
24 Bridge Hotel
25 Tourist Information Centre
26 Conwy Castle

Plas Mawr (☎ 580167, Cadw), on High St, is a newly restored Tudor house that's well worth visiting. Admission costs £4/3 and includes a headphone tour. It opens 9.30 am to 5 pm daily except Monday, April and October.

The **Smallest House**, a tiny building that claims to be the smallest house in Britain, is down on the quay, but not surprisingly there's little to see for your 50/30p. There's also a teapot museum (**Teapot World**) on Castle St, which opens daily Easter to October.

A popular excursion from Conwy is to **Bodnant Garden** (☎ 650460; NT), 8 miles south, off the A470, one of the finest gardens in Britain. Admission costs £4.60/2.30 and it opens 10 am to 5 pm daily, Easter to October. Bus No 25 passes close by.

Places to Stay

Camping is possible at **Conwy Touring Park** (☎ 592856), 1½ miles south of Conwy on the B5106; tent sites cost from £7.16 to £10.76 for two people in summer.

Conwy Youth Hostel (☎ 593571, Larkhill, Sychnant Pass Rd) is in a converted hotel. Dorms are small and all have shower rooms. Open daily mid-February to mid-December, the hostel is a 10-minute walk from the town centre. The nightly charge is £12.50/8.50 for adults/under-18s.

Within the town walls there's the **Town House** (☎ 596454, 18 Rosehill St), with B&B from £16 per person in a room with shared bathroom, £38 per room with private bathroom. **Castle View B&B** (☎ 596888, 3 Berry St) charges from £14 per person.

Glan Heulog Guest House (☎ 593845) is a good place on Llanrwst Rd, to the south of the town but within walking distance. B&B costs £17 for a single and £34 to £38 for a double with bathroom.

Gwynedd Guest House (☎ 596537, 10 Upper Gate St), with four rooms, charges £16 per person in a double or £18 for a single.

Swan Cottage (☎ 596840, 18 Berry St) is a small, 16th-century house with three rooms from £15 per person.

The **Castle Hotel** (☎ 592324, High St), an old coach house, is dead central and rooms cost from £60/80 for a single/double.

Places to Eat

Alfredo's Restaurant (☎ 592381), on Lancaster square, is an Italian place open 6 to 10 pm each evening and also on Saturday for lunch. Traditional pasta and pizza dishes go from £4.95 to £5.90. There's a set three-course dinner at the **Castle Hotel** (☎ 592324) for £15.95, or they serve snacks in the bar.

The Wall Place (☎ 596326, Chapel St), a quaint, secluded cottage with garden, does excellent vegetarian food, with all dishes under £5. Try the cashew and chickpea korma with gourmet rice for £4.95. They also host exhibitions from Llandudno's renowned Mostyn Gallery.

There are several tearooms dotted about the town, of which the best is the 16th-century **Pen-y-Bryn** (☎ 596445, 28 High St), where a full cream tea includes *bara brith* (spicy fruit loaf) and cake. It also does light lunches. **Anna's Tea Rooms**, above the Conwy Outdoor shop on Castle St, is also good for traditional fare.

For great finger-licking chips, try the sensibly titled **Fish & Chips** on the corner of High and Berry Sts.

For self-caterers, there's the **Spar supermarket** on High St. A few doors down and across the road is **Edward's Butcher & Deli**, where you can get pies and hot meals to take away.

Entertainment

There are several pubs. The **Liverpool Arms**, down on the quay, is where the fishing crowd drinks. The **Bridge Hotel**, on the corner of Castle and Rosehill Sts, does good-value lunches, particularly on Sunday. The **George & Dragon** (Castle St), beside Teapot World, serves reasonable pub grub and has a small beer garden.

Getting There & Away

Situated 5 miles west of Llandudno, and a mile from Llandudno Junction, Conwy is linked to both places by several buses an hour. There are frequent buses to Bangor (£2.40, 30 minutes) from outside the train station. Other buses stop all over town, but mostly on Castle St.

NORTH WALES

Conwy's train station is now used only by regional trains. Llandudno Junction, a 15-minute walk from Conwy, is the mainline station. There are trains every hour or two between Llandudno Junction and Conwy (£1.85, three minutes).

BANGOR
☎ 01248 • pop 12,000
The town of Bangor is at its liveliest during the university terms. It's home to the University College of North Wales, which attracts students from all over Britain.

The first settlement here was probably the Celtic monastery established in 525 by St Deiniol, which would make Bangor the oldest diocese in Britain. The present **cathedral** was built in the 13th century, though much of it has been restored since. Inside is the renowned early-16th-century carved figure known as the **Mostyn Christ**. The university's main building, up on the hill, is often mistaken for the cathedral, which is not surprising since that's what it was modelled on.

The renovated **pier** is worth seeing. It was built in 1896 and stretches 450m into the Menai Strait. You get a good view of Thomas Telford's Menai Suspension Bridge, built in 1826 to link Anglesey to the mainland.

The TIC (☎ 352786, e bangor.tic@gwynedd.gov.uk) is in the Town Hall on Deniol Rd.

Places to Stay
Bangor Youth Hostel (☎ 353516, Tan-y-Bryn) is half a mile from the town centre and has good views of Penrhyn Castle. It opens daily January to November and charges £11/7.75 for adults/under-18s.

Treborth Hall Farm Caravan & Campsite (☎ 364399, Treborth Rd) is less than 2 miles from town, near the Menai Bridge. You can camp here for £4 to £7.

The *University of Bangor (☎ 388088 e holidays@bangor.ac.uk, College Rd)* lets out student rooms on a B&B basis in summer and at Easter for £35 for two nights. It has special deals for longer stays.

Y Garreg Wen (☎ 353836, 8 Deiniol Rd) offers B&B for £12.50 per person. There are only a few rooms but it's convenient for the station and is a very friendly place.

The British Hotel (☎ 364911, High St) offers B&B for £25 per person for rooms with a bathroom. A three-course dinner costs £10.50; it also serves bar meals.

Nant-Y-Fedw (☎ 351683, Trefelin, Llandygai), a mile and a half from town, is a very comfortable guest house with pleasant gardens; the nightly charge is from £23/38 for singles/doubles.

The excellent *Eryl Môr Hotel (☎ 353789, 2 Upper Garth Rd)*, overlooking the pier and the Menai Strait, costs £22 for a single or £36/52 for a single/double with bathroom.

The best place to stay is the comfortable *Menai Court Hotel (☎ 354200, Craig-y-Don)*, which has a nice garden, well-fitted-out rooms for £51/69 (all with bathrooms) and good views.

Places to Eat
The best place to eat is the *Menai Court Hotel* (see Places to Stay) with mains from £5 to £15.

Down at the pier, Italian restaurant *Pulcinella (☎ 362807)* has good views and does pizza from £4.50 or pasta from £5.50.

There are several cheap eateries along Holyhead Rd, the main student area, and on High St.

Fat Cat (☎ 370445, 161 High St) has long been a popular place with students, with its home-made burgers (£5.10) and filled baguettes (£3.65). Vegetarian choices include wild mushroom rigatoni (£6.25), and wine, beer and cocktails are available inside or at the outdoor bar.

There's a bar and nightclub, *Time*, at the university's Students' Union on Deiniol Rd. The club is closed on Tuesdays and Thursdays. The best place in the area for live music is the *Victoria Hotel*, across the bridge on Anglesey.

Getting There & Away
National Express has two services a day from London to Bangor (£21).

Arriva Cymru operates bus services from Bangor to most places in the area. Most buses leave from Garth Rd. Services from Bangor operate to the following: Caernarfon (Bus Nos 5 and 5A), every 20 minutes Monday to

Saturday and hourly on Sunday; Beaumaris (Nos 53, 57 and 58), hourly and five (No 53) on Sunday; and Llanberis (No 77), from Bangor Plaza, about five times a day.

Bangor is on the InterCity line from London's Euston (£25 if you book in advance or a whopping £53.60 otherwise). There are four trains a day direct to Bangor (3¾ hours), and many more services from Crewe to Bangor (£16.15, 1½ hours). It's also on the North Wales coast line from Chester (£12.20, 1¼ hours).

AROUND BANGOR
Penrhyn Castle
One and a half miles east of Bangor is Penrhyn Castle (☎ 01248-353084; NT). Unlike most other castles in the area, it was not built by Edward I nor is it a genuine Norman castle. It was constructed between 1820 and 1837 in the neo-Norman style, using a lot of local slate, by Thomas Hopper for Lord Penrhyn. It's certainly an impressive place, with the great hall modelled on Durham Cathedral and containing mock-Norman furniture.

The castle is in a lovely setting and is worth a visit. It opens 11 am to 5 pm daily (except Tuesday) during July and August, and noon to 5 pm April to the end of October. Admission costs £5/2.50.

CAERNARFON
☎ 01286 • pop 9500
In 1301, Edward I made his son the first Prince of Wales and installed him in the mighty castle that still dominates this town. In 1911, in a bid to involve the crown more closely with his constituency in this part of Wales, Prime Minister David Lloyd George had the investiture ceremony for the heir to the throne transferred to the castle. It was an action that did not curry favour with the local people – Caernarfon is at the heart of Welsh-nationalist Wales and is a very depressed area that the royal link has done little to help. When Prince Charles was ceremonially invested here by his mother in 1969, there was an attempt to blow up his train.

Like Conwy, Caernarfon has a magnificent attraction in its castle and comparisons between the two towns are often drawn.

While both are spectacular, Caernarfon is probably even more impressive from the outside but perhaps a little too neat and tidy within.

Further back, Caernarfon was important for the Romans, who established a fort, Segontium, in the 1st century.

Orientation & Information
The castle stands by the river and there's a large car park below it. The TIC and the market square are immediately to the north and the town walls enclose a small area four blocks wide and two deep.

The friendly TIC (☎ 672232, ⓔ caernarfon.tic@gwynedd.gov.uk) is at Castle Pitch, Oriel Pendeitsh, Castle St. It opens 10 am to 6 pm daily in summer. There's internet access at Dimensiwn 4 on Bangor St.

Caernarfon Castle
Edward I wanted Caernarfon to be the most impressive of his Welsh fortresses, and it was modelled on the 5th-century walls of Constantinople. The castle was built between 1283 and 1301 as part of Edward's series of monumental forts that were constructed to keep the Welsh under control. It's particularly attractive at night when the walls are floodlit.

Caernarfon was also designed to be a palace and Edward's son was born here. Living quarters were contained in the towers, one of which is the Queen's Tower, named after Edward's wife Eleanor. This tower contains the regimental museum of the Royal Welsh Fusiliers, a regiment that seems to have produced quite a few poets and writers – Robert Graves and Siegfried Sassoon among them. The other towers contain exhibitions on Edward I's campaigns and the royal investiture in 1969.

The castle (☎ 677617; Cadw) opens 9.30 am to 6 pm daily (from 11 am on Sunday), May to October, and until 4 pm in March and 5 pm for the rest of the year. Admission costs £4.20/3.20.

Other Things to See & Do
The castle is very much the main attraction but there's also a small **Maritime Museum**

at Victoria Dock. The museum opens daily June to September.

The foundations of the Roman fort **Segontium** (☎ 675625) are three-quarters of a mile east of the castle; there's also a small museum. In the care of Cadw, it opens 10 am to 5 pm daily, April to October, to 4 pm the rest of the year; afternoon only on Sunday. Admission costs £1.25/75p.

Places to Stay

Cadnant Valley Camping & Caravan Park (☎ 673196) is half a mile from the castle on Llanberis Rd. It opens March to October and costs from £7 to £9 for two people with tent.

Totters (☎ 672963, *Plas Porth Yr Aur, 2 High St*) offers cheap, friendly accommodation in the centre of town by the yacht club. A bed in a four- or six-bed dorm costs £10, including bedding and breakfast.

One block east of the castle at 4 Church St is *Tegfan* (☎ 673703), which charges from £20/40 for a single/double.

The *Black Boy Inn* (☎ 673604, *Northgate St*) is an attractive old pub, centrally located. There are rooms without bathroom at £20/34 and with bathroom for £23/40.

There are several guesthouses and hotels along North Rd, the road to Bangor. The *Menai Bank Hotel* (☎ 673297) is good and charges from £30/50. At 21 North Rd, there's *Gorffwysfa Guest House* (☎ 678981); B&B costs from £16.50.

Closer to the centre, North Rd becomes Bangor St. Here, the *Prince of Wales Hotel* (☎ 673367) is a former coaching inn. There are 21 bedrooms and B&B costs from £25 per person.

Ten miles from Caernarfon and Porthmadog, on the A487, *Hen Ysgol* (☎ 660701, *Bwlchderwin, Pant Glas*) is a pleasant old school with garden. Rooms cost from £17 per person with a three-course evening meal for £10.

Places to Eat

The top place to eat is *Courtenay's Bistro* (☎ 677290, *9 Segontium Terrace*), close to Castle Square. It's also surprisingly inexpensive, with most main dishes in the £7 to £10 range. Rack of lamb costs £9.20. Local produce is used as much as possible – mussels, sea trout, lamb and Welsh cheeses. It's closed on Sunday and Monday.

The main places to eat are down Hole in the Wall St. *Stone's Bistro* (☎ 671152) is a reasonable place with main dishes at around £10, including interesting vegetarian choices.

Near Stone's Bistro is a pub, *Y Goron Fach* (☎ 673338, *Hole in the Wall St*), where bar meals are available every day and evening meals from Monday to Thursday. Their big-screen TV means it can get a bit packed at match times. *The Palace Vault* near the TIC, on Castle Ditch, also does good pub lunches. Reasonable set meals can be had at the restaurant at the *Black Boy Inn* (see Places to Stay) or there is good pub grub at the bar. Another good choice, *Macsen Café & Restaurant* (☎ 676464, *11 Castle Square*) specialises in Welsh food in the upstairs restaurant, or has home-made cakes and snacks below in the airy cafe.

Getting There & Around

There are no train services to Caernarfon, but National Express has a direct coach service from London (8¾ hours). Or you could go to Bangor and pick up a bus from there. Bus Nos 5, 5A and 5B run several times an hour (hourly on Sunday) from Bangor to Caernarfon (£1.80, 30 minutes). The bus stop is at Poolside, near the castle.

Caernarfon is a focal point for bus services to Snowdonia and the Llŷn Peninsula.

Bikes are available for hire from Beics Castell on High St (☎ 677400) for £3 an hour.

ANGLESEY (YNYS MÔN)

Covering 276 sq miles, Anglesey is the largest island in Wales and England, with a population of around 71,000. It's been linked with the mainland since 1826 when Thomas Telford built the Menai Bridge, the first heavy-duty suspension bridge constructed.

It's the flattest part of Wales, though there are some rugged cliffs around the coast. It has an interesting coastline with some good sandy beaches. Most visitors, however, see little more than the countryside that surrounds the A5 on the route through to Holyhead and the ferries to Ireland.

Anglesey was a holy place to the ancient Celts and there are still many remains of ancient settlements. Inhabitants since then have relied on farming, smuggling, copper and coal mining and quarrying, as well as the sea, for their income. The land is very fertile and the island is referred to as Môn Mam Cymru – Mother of Wales – as it provides wheat, cattle and other farm produce for North Wales.

Llanfairpwllgwyngyllgogerych-wyrndrobwllllantysiliogogogoch

The tour buses pour into this little village simply because it's in the record books as having the longest name of any place in Britain, a sum total of 58 letters that are generally shortened to Llanfair PG or Llanfairpwll. The name means 'St Mary's Church in the hollow of the White Hazel near a rapid whirlpool and the Church of St Tysilio near the Red Cave' and was dreamt up in the 19th century to get the tourists in. It's a stop on the main line between Bangor and Holyhead and if you so wish you can buy a large platform ticket as a souvenir. At the TIC (☎ 01248-713177) in the knitwear shop next door, they'll teach you how to pronounce it.

Plas Newydd

This is one of the most interesting stately homes in North Wales, an 18th-century house designed in the Gothic style for the marquess of Anglesey. There are superb views across to Snowdonia from the grounds. In the cavalry museum at the house is the state-of-the-art wooden leg designed for the marquess, who was field marshal at Waterloo. The house contains a celebrated mural by Rex Whistler.

Plas Newydd (☎ 01248-714795; NT) opens 12 to 5 pm daily, April to October (closed on Thursday and Friday). The gardens open 11 am to 5.30 pm. Admission costs £4.50/2.25. It's a mile from Llanfair PG train station.

Beaumaris

☎ 01248 • pop 1500

Beaumaris used to be the principal town and chief port of Anglesey. It's now known for the castle that James of St George built here for Edward I and as a sailing and watersports centre. It's a picturesque town with narrow streets and makes a nice afternoon diversion.

Beaumaris Castle (☎ 810361; Cadw) is the last and largest of the castles built by Edward I. Construction started in 1295 on a site overlooking the Menai Strait. The flatness of the site meant the castle could be designed and built with geometrical symmetry – it's truly impressive and it's clear why it's a World Heritage Site.

The castle is surrounded by a water-filled moat, then the outer walls, then evenly spaced towers, then more walls and towers. It seems impregnable but Owain Glyndŵr did manage to conquer it. The castle last saw action in 1646 during the Civil War. It opens 9.30 am to 6 pm daily, June to September; 9.30 am to 5 pm, March to May and October; 9.30 am to 4 pm (from 11 am Sunday), November to March. Admission costs £2.20/1.70.

Other things to see here include **Beaumaris Gaol** (☎ 810921), a model prison when it opened in 1829, and the **Courthouse**. Both open 10.30 am to 5 pm in summer or by appointment. There is a **Museum of Childhood** (☎ 712498), opposite the castle.

Cruises Several operators run summer cruises from Beaumaris pier to Puffin Island (to look at the seabirds) or along the Menai Strait. Try Beaumaris Marine Services (☎ 810746), which has a kiosk on the pier. Cruises are operated from 12.30 pm daily, April to October. An hour's cruise to Puffin Island costs £4/3.

Places to Stay & Eat There's little in the way of cheap accommodation in Beaumaris. *Swn-y-Don* (☎ 810794, 7 Bulkley Terrace) opens April to November and offers B&B for £19 per person. Some rooms overlook the Menai Strait; all have bathrooms.

Ye Olde Bulls Head Inn (☎ 810329, Castle St) is the best place to stay. It has 15 rooms, all with bathrooms, for £53/83 for a single/double. The inn dates back to 1472 – it was originally the posting house of the borough. The bedrooms are named after several of Dickens' characters, in honour of the author who once stayed in the hotel. There's a set three-course meal in the restaurant for £27.50 or good baguettes and hot meals in the brasserie from £3.50 to £15.

Getting There & Away Beaumaris is 10 miles from Bangor. Bus No 57 runs almost hourly Monday to Saturday from Bangor to Beaumaris (£1.65, 25 minutes). On Sunday there are five services (No 53).

Holyhead
☎ 01407 • pop 19,000

Holyhead, perched on a promontory at the edge of Holy Island, is a typically uninspiring ferry port town whose potential has never been exploited. Though one of the main exit points to Ireland, restaurants, accommodation and recreational facilities are remarkably limited. The surrounding area on Holy Island however, which is separated from the main island by sandbanks and a narrow channel, has some impressive scenery and fine beaches to explore. The TIC (☎ 762622) is by the ferry terminal. They provide free leaflets on cycling routes and circular walks around Anglesey. If you're killing time waiting for a ferry, there's a small cinema, the Empire Theatre on Stanley St, or the Ucheldre Centre (☎ 763361), an interesting arts centre and cafe, is on Ucheldre Ave, five minutes' walk from the town centre.

Places to Stay B&Bs are used to late ferry arrivals. Closest to the terminal is *Min-y-don* (☎ 762718, *Newry Fawr*). It's pleasant and has rooms for £15 per person.

An excellent place, though it only has three rooms, is *Hendre* (☎ 762929, *Porth-y-Felin Rd*). B&B costs from £30/40 for a single/double. The *Boathouse Hotel* (☎ 762094, *Newry.Beach*) has B&B from £30 per person. About 5 miles south of Holyhead at Rhoscolyn, there's bunkhouse accommodation for £9.50 at *Outdoor Alternative* (☎ 860469, *Cerrig-yr-Adar*). It's beautifully situated, 300m from the beach.

Getting There & Away Both Irish Ferries (☎ 0870 517 1717) and Stena Line (☎ 0990 707070) run ferries to Ireland. See the

Getting There & Away chapter. If you fancy a day-trip to Dublin, Irish Ferries sometimes has special offers from as little as £9 return.

There are hourly trains east to Llandudno, Chester, Birmingham and London, via Bangor (£5.50, 40 minutes).

Arriva Cymru operates bus service No 4 from Bangor to Holyhead (£2.85, 1¼ hours) twice-hourly Monday to Saturday. Bus No 44 runs every two hours on Sunday.

LLŶN PENINSULA

This isolated peninsula is the most staunchly Welsh part of the country – in the villages you rarely hear a word of English spoken. It's a peaceful, largely undeveloped place with 70 miles of coastline, a few small fishing villages, some beautiful beaches, good walks and quiet lanes for cycling.

The best beaches are at Abersoch, 7 miles from Pwllheli; Aberdaron, from where you can catch a boat to Bardsey Island; and Nefyn, on the north coast.

Criccieth

This busy seaside town is the gateway to the Llŷn. **Criccieth Castle** dates from the early 13th century. Open 10 am to 6 pm daily April to September, it's worth a visit and there are good views over the bay. Admission costs £2.20/1.70.

The Bardsey Pilgrimage

A tiny island off the tip of the Llŷn peninsula, Bardsey was once known as the Isle of Twenty Thousand Saints. In the 6th century the obscure St Cadfan created a monastery here. At a time when journeys from Britain to Italy were long, perilous and beyond the means of most people, three pilgrimages to Bardsey came to have the same value as one to Rome. The twenty thousand were probably not so much saints as pilgrims who came here to die.

Most modern pilgrims to Bardsey are more prosaic seabird-watchers, although there are remains of a 13th-century abbey to mull over. The Bardsey Island Trust is in charge of visitor arrangements; phone ☎ 01758-730740 for more information.

Criccieth is on the train line between Porthmadog and Pwllheli and there are lots of B&Bs and hotels here, mostly on the road leading into town. Just over a mile from Criccieth on the B4411 Caernarfon road, there's bunkhouse accommodation for £5 per person at *Stone Barn* (☎ *01766-522115, Tyddyn Morthwyl)*. Book in advance. *The Lion Hotel* (☎ *01766-523075)*, in the town centre, has rooms with views of the castle and sea from £30.50/55 for singles/doubles. The *Bryn Hir Arms* on High St does good lunches and has a beer garden.

Pwllheli
☎ 01758 • pop 5000
The only place of any size on the peninsula is the market town of Pwllheli, of greatest interest to the visitor for its Welshness. It was here in 1925 that Plaid Cymru, the Welsh Nationalist Party, was formed. It's also a good spot for birdwatching in winter. In the minds of many British people, however, the town is synonymous with the Butlins Holiday Camp, which is several miles from Pwllheli and has been renamed Starcoast World.

The TIC (☎ 613000, ☐ pwllheli.tic@gwynedd.gov.uk), opposite the train station, has useful information on the Llŷn Peninsula.

Places to Stay & Eat A working organic dairy farm a mile from Pwllheli, *Gwynfryn Farm* (☎ *612536)* does B&B for £18 plus. It also has camping from £3 per tent. *Mrs Jones* (☎ *613172, 26 High St)* does B&B from £12. *Pompeii Restaurant & Pizzeria* does a good selection of pasta dishes for under £7 or pizzas for £5.90. Next door, *Jane's Sandwich Bar* on High St provides reasonable hot and cold picnic material.

Getting There & Away Pwllheli is the last stop on the train line from Shrewsbury (£16.80 or £10.50 off peak, 3½ hours).

It's also accessible by bus route No 12, operated by Clynnog & Trefor (☎ 01286-660208) hourly from Caernarfon Monday to Saturday, with only one bus on Sunday (£2.20). The other operator is Berwyn Buses (☎ 01286-660315). Their service runs hourly every day (£2, 45 minutes).

PORTHMADOG
☎ 01766 • pop 4000
People come to this former slate port today for two reasons – to catch the Ffestiniog Railway to Blaenau Ffestiniog (see the Snowdonia National Park section) and to visit the nearby village of Portmeirion. The town makes a reasonable base for both.

The friendly TIC (☎ 512981, ☐ porthmadog.tic@gwynedd.gov.uk) is on High St. One of North Wales' best beaches is at Blackrock, 3 miles from town out on the Morfa Bychan Rd.

Places to Stay & Eat
Tyddyn Llwyn Caravan Park provides camping facilities on the grounds of *Tyddyn Llywyn Hotel* (see below) for £7 to £9 per tent or caravan.

The simple B&B at *5 Glaslyn St* (☎ *514 461)* charges £17. The newly renovated *Yr Hen Fecws* (☎ *514625, 16 Lombard St)*, in a restored stone building near the harbour, is good value for money and one of the best places to stay in town. Rooms cost from £22.50 per person and good food is available from the bistro downstairs. *Tyddyn Llwyn Hotel* (☎ *513903, Morfa Bychan Rd)* is on the edge of Porthmadog in open countryside. It's a comfortable, nonsmoking place with singles/doubles for £30/47, all with bathrooms.

The top place to eat in Porthmadog is *Pond's Bistro* (☎ *512333, 47 High St)*. Cajun halibut is £9.95 and a decent range of vegetarian dishes for under £9 is served. Another good place to eat is the fish-based *Harbour Restaurant* (☎ *512471, 3 High St)*. *The Ship Inn* on Lombard St and *The Australia* on High St are good for a pint and bar food. There's a small cinema on High St, but little else by way of evening entertainment in the town.

The premium place to stay, *Hotel Portmeirion* (☎ *770000)*, is 2 miles from Porthmadog in the fantasy village of the same name (see Portmeirion later). Charges are from £135 to £220 per room in the main building or £110 to £170 for a room in one of the cottages in the village. The restaurant does set dinners at £33.

NORTH WALES

Getting There & Away

From Caernarfon, Express Motors (☎ 01286-881108) runs an hourly service (No 1) every day to Porthmadog (£2.30, 50 minutes). The service continues to Blaenau Ffestiniog.

Porthmadog is on the train line from Shrewsbury (3½ hours, £16.80 or £10.50 off peak). You usually have to change at Machynlleth. The service is not frequent but there's at least one train a day throughout the year.

PORTMEIRION

For kitsch enthusiasts, head 2 miles east of Porthmadog to Portmeirion, a somewhat bizarre, private Italianate village (even the scenery is Mediterranean) created by the Welsh architect Sir Clough Williams-Ellis. It was built between 1925 and 1927 on a secluded peninsula 5 miles from his ancestral home. Sir Clough wanted to show that architecture could be fun, intriguing and interesting, and a visit to the village certainly fulfils all of these requirements – though in summer the crowds can detract from the pleasure.

There are 50 buildings around a central piazza, some of which were brought to the site to save them from destruction elsewhere. There's also a restaurant, an ice-cream parlour, a hotel and seven shops, one of which sells seconds of the popular Portmeirion pottery line.

Noel Coward spent time writing in Portmeirion in the 1940s. The perfect film set, Portmeirion was where the cult TV series *The Prisoner* was made in the 1960s. It still draws the fans and there's even a **Prisoner Information Centre**.

The village (☎ 01766-770000) is open from 9.30 am to 5.30 pm daily and admission costs £4.50/2.25. There's a very good restaurant in the hotel here (see Porthmadog earlier in the chapter).

The Channel Islands

'Little bits of France dropped into the sea and picked up by Britain' was how the exiled French writer Victor Hugo described this small group of islands in the English Channel, just off the coast of France's Normandy. In reality, at times they seem more like a little bit of Britain that floated over to France.

There are five main islands in the group – Jersey, Guernsey, Alderney, Sark and Herm. Their separation from mainland Britain is not just geographical. Although British since 1066, the islands are not part of the UK and are administered locally. Entry formalities are as for the UK: if you're visiting via Britain you don't need to show your passport.

Low rates of tax have made them something of a tax haven, and Jersey's capital, St Helier, is part buckets-and-spades beach-holiday resort, part international finance centre. The islands issue their own currency (exchangeable at par with the British pound) and postage stamps. There is no VAT on goods. Very low income taxes mean that the islands are a true tax haven and you'll see lots of well-healed retired folk lounging about as well as many, many yachts in the harbours at St Helier and St Peter Port. Catering to this clientele are some excellent seafood restaurants. Local specialities include oysters, crabs and lobsters.

Although there are pleasant beaches, good walks and cycle rides on the islands, in reality there's not that much to see and do. However, this may be an inducement for many. Bring some good books, settle back, enjoy the tax-free prices (and the French-influenced food and drink) and r-e-l-a-x. Should you feel the need to move around a bit, there's always a minor sight worthy of a diversion.

GETTING THERE & AWAY
Air
British Airways (☎ 0345 222111) has numerous flights a day to/from Jersey and Guernsey to/from London's Heathrow and Gatwick airports as well as daily flights to Manchester and Plymouth. The Heathrow

Highlights

- Experiencing Jersey Zoo
- Exploring the Guernsey coast
- Cycling around Alderney
- Relaxing in post day-tripper Sark – Europe's last feudal state

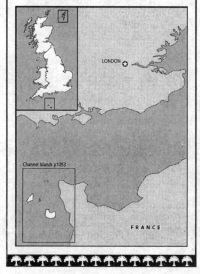

LONDON

Channel Islands p1053

FRANCE

flights are operated with jets, the rest by commuter affiliates.

British Midland (☎ 0870 607 0555) flies daily from Jersey and Guernsey to East Midlands airport. It also has summer weekend services to places such as Belfast, Edinburgh and Leeds.

British European (☎ 0870 567 6676), which used to be called Jersey European, has a frequent service from Jersey to London's Gatwick and Luton airports, Birmingham and Exeter. From Guernsey it has daily flights to London Gatwick, Birmingham, Exeter and Southampton.

Aurigny Air Services (☎ 01481-822886) flies from Guernsey to London Stansted and

Amsterdam. It also operates all Alderney flights, which go to Southampton in Britain. To France, Aurigny operates flights between Alderney, Jersey and Guernsey and Dinard.

Return air fares between Jersey/Guernsey and London on all these airlines range from around £50 up to £270. Fares to other parts of the UK as well as the Continent start at £90. The discount fares come with all the usual advance purchase and limited seats qualifiers.

Boat

Condor (☎ 01305-761551) runs daily fast ferries to/from Poole and Weymouth. The boats start and end their runs in Jersey, having travelled via Guernsey. Return fares between Britain and Jersey (3½ hours) start at around £49 for a foot passenger, £211 for a car and driver. The fare system is complex and varies by day of week and time of year. There is also a slow daily ferry from Portsmouth to Guernsey (6½ hours) and Jersey (10½ hours). There are no real savings for foot passengers, but a car and driver can go from £142 return.

Condor has daily fast ferries to St Malo in France from Guernsey (three hours) via Jersey (two hours). Return fares on this service cost from £28 for foot passengers. Strange regulations between France and Britain prevent most cars from being carried on this service; call for details.

Ferry links to France are run by Emeraude (☎ 01481-711414) with car ferry services between Guernsey/Jersey and St Malo. There are also passenger ferries from Guernsey and Alderney to Diélette as well as Jersey to Carteret, Portbail and Granville.

JERSEY
☎ 01534 • pop 83,000
Jersey is the largest of the Channel Islands, and the most popular destination for visitors. There are lots of safe, clean, sandy beaches, the best in the region. The north coast of the island is a good place for an escape; it's thinly populated.

Orientation & Information
Covering 45 sq miles, the island is roughly rectangular in shape; St Helier, the capital, is on the south coast.

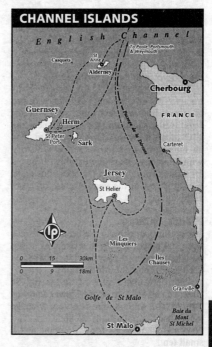

Jersey Tourism (☎ 500777, fax 500899, e info@jersey.com) is on Liberation Square, a short walk from the ferry terminal and opposite the bus station. It opens 8.30 am to 7 pm daily May to September and 8.30 am to 5.30 pm weekdays and until 1 pm Saturday the rest of the year. They sell a range of walking guides and maps.

Things to See & Do
Of universal interest is **Jersey Zoo** (☎ 860 000), Les Augres Manor, Trinity, which was started by writer and naturalist Gerald Durrell as a conservation and breeding centre for endangered species. It's a fascinating place to visit and opens 9.30 am to 6 pm daily April to October, closing at dusk other times. Admission costs £8/5.50.

Other things to see include several **castles** in various states of repair; as well as being an inspiration, they can be goals for good walks. One of the best is Mont Orgueil Castle in Gorey, which was built in the 1200s.

The **German underground hospital** (☎ 863 442) is a curious attraction and dates from WWII when the Germans occupied the islands. It is set to reopen in 2001 after a major renovation that is meant to include a new museum devoted to the occupation.

St Helier, the capital, is not particularly attractive; it's an international finance centre that even boasts a few multi-storey buildings. **Jersey Museum** (☎ 633300), near the TIC in an alley off Ordnance Yard, has an interesting display on Jersey's history with interactive maritime exhibits. It opens 10 am to 5 pm April to October, closing at 4 pm the rest of the year. Admission costs £3.50/2.50.

Places to Stay

Jersey Tourism publishes a brochure listing over 300 places to stay and operates a free booking service, Jerseylink (☎ 500888, or use the TIC contact information).

There are camp sites at St Martin, St Breezed and St Ouen. *Rose Farm Camping* (☎ 875236), at St Aubin, is a very friendly place that's popular with backpackers. The charge is £4.50 to £8 for two people and a small tent.

St Helier is home to a range of places to stay. *Corinthian* (☎/fax 878655, 18 Mulcaster St) charges £15 for simple rooms. *Woodford Guest House* (☎ 721372, fax 625251, 43 Stopford Rd) charges £14 to £17 per person for basic accommodation.

The *Royal Yacht Hotel* (☎ 720511, fax 767729, The Weighbridge) is much improved after a full renovation. It has excellent harbour views and charges from £45 per person for well-equipped rooms.

The island's top hotel is the *Longueville Manor* (☎ 725501, fax 731613), east of St Helier off the A3. It is housed in a stately mansion; parts date back to the 13th century. Everything is luxurious, right down to the hotel's own herb garden. Single/double rooms start at £165/200.

Places to Eat

There's a wide choice – everything from fish and chip shops to high-end seafood restaurants. Many have lovely patios and verandas where locals while away the hours spending their tax savings.

In St Helier, the *Typsy Toad Town House* (☎ 615000, New St) is owned by the island's brewery, Jersey Brewery. It has a long menu of burgers, sandwiches and the like (about £5) as well as a fine selection of beers at very good prices (pints £1.50) thanks to the low taxes.

The *Admiral* (☎ 730095, St James St) is a traditional pub that's popular with the young employees of the many local banks. It gets fun at night and has a simple menu with many items under £5.

If your offshore investments have matured – as it were – *Longueville Manor* (see Places to Stay), which boasts a Michelin star and exquisite set meals from £40, is one of the best places to eat on the island. Main dishes cost around £20 and there are set menus from £35 to £55.

Getting There & Away

Aurigny Air Services (☎ 01481-822886) has many flights a day each way between Jersey and Guernsey (£66, 15 minutes) and flights to Alderney.

Emeraude and Condor both link Jersey and Guernsey as part of their services to the mainlands. All services take one hour and both companies charge £28 for a foot-passenger return ticket.

Getting Around

Between the airport and St Helier there's a choice of taxi (£6 to £8) or bus (£1.40). The journey takes 15 to 45 minutes depending on traffic. Public buses cover most of the island.

Car hire is cheap – from £15 per day – but there are said to be around 55,000 cars on the island, so you may find yourself sitting in a traffic jam. Try Zebra (☎ 736556) which is opposite the TIC and rents out cars and bikes.

GUERNSEY

☎ 01481 • pop 58,000

More easy-going and peaceful than Jersey, Guernsey boasts good dramatic scenery including high cliffs on the south coast. The ruins of Castle Cornet overlook the capital and main port, St Peter Port.

Orientation & Information

Guernsey is two-thirds the size of Jersey: roughly 9 miles long by 4 miles wide.

There are TICs at both the airport and ferry terminals but the main office of Guernsey Tourism (☎ 723552, fax 714951, e inquiries@tourism.guernsey.net) is on the waterfront in St Peter Port. It opens 9 am to 5 pm weekdays, to 4 pm Saturday and 9.30 am to 12.30 pm Sunday.

Things to See & Do

There are numerous beaches. **St Peter Port** is one of the most attractive towns in the Channel Islands, looking out across the busy harbour to Sark and Herm. Victor Hugo was exiled here in 1855 and lived in St Peter Port until 1870. His home, Hauteville House (☎ 721911), still boasts the unusual decor from the time he lived there. It opens 2 to 5 pm April to September (also 10 am to noon in July and August). Admission costs £4/2.

There's a bunch of sights connected with WWII. All are generally open 10 am to 5 pm daily April to September and for shorter hours at other times. There's a **Military Museum** (☎ 722300) and **Occupation Museum** (☎ 238305) in St Peter Port and a German **underground hospital** (☎ 239100) in St Andrews.

Far removed from the celebrated military past, the **Little Chapel** in St Andrews is colourfully decorated with local shells. The door is always open.

Places to Stay

There are several camp sites. *Fauxquets Valley Farm Campsite* (☎ 255460, fax 251797, e fauxquets@campguernsey.free serve.co.uk, Castel) has a heated pool, bicycle hire and restaurant. Its charges on average £5 for one person and a small tent.

There are about 100 hotels and B&Bs. The TIC does walk-in bookings only. The following are all in St Peter Port.

Midhurst House (☎ 724391, fax 729451, Candie Rd) is an excellent small hotel with a quiet garden and good food. Rates are £26 to £36 per person.

Sunnycroft Hotel (☎ 723008, fax 712225, 5 Constitution Steps) has good views and a restful location. The en-suite rooms cost from £27 per person.

The *Old Government House Hotel* (☎ 724 921, fax 724429, e ogh@guernsey.net, St Ann Place), formerly the official residence of the Guernsey governors, is a large old hotel with good views of the harbour. Accommodation ranges from £75 to £90 per person.

Places to Eat

There's good pub grub at the *Yacht Inn* (☎ 715488, South Esplanade, St Peter Port), which is one of many places around the port catering to the nautical set.

Merchant House (☎ 728019, 38 High St) is a great nonsmoking restaurant in St Peter Port. Fantastic seafood dishes average £15.

Getting There & Away

See Getting There & Away at the start of the chapter for services to Britain and France. For inter-island services see the other islands.

Getting Around

From the airport to St Peter Port there's a choice of taxi (£7, 15 minutes) or bus (£1.30, 20 minutes). The TIC has a very useful local bus timetable and map. With outlets at the airport and harbour, Value (☎ 243547) rents cars from £12 per day. Quay Cycle Hire (☎ 714146) is on the New Jetty in St Peter Port. It rents out bikes from £6 per day.

HERM
☎ 01481 • pop 40

A 20-minute boat trip across the bay from Guernsey, Herm is a pretty island half a mile wide by 1½ miles long. No cars, motorcycles or even bicycles are allowed, making this a walkers' and day-trippers' mini-paradise.

Herm had been deserted for years when the Wood family bought a 99-year lease on the island in 1949. It's an undeniably attractive place with white-sand beaches famous for their variety of shells, clear sea and pleasant walks. The Guernsey TIC handles information enquiries.

Places to Stay & Eat

Accommodation is booked through the island's administration office (☎ 722377, fax

700334). There's a choice between a camp site (£5 site fee plus £4.20 per person) and just one hotel – the upmarket *White House Hotel* (☎ 722159, fax 710066) from £57 to £74 per person for dinner, bed and breakfast – and 18 self-catering cottages (£165 per week).

For places to eat there's the *Mermaid Tavern* (☎ 710170), the *Ship Restaurant* at the White House Hotel and two *beach kiosks*.

Getting There & Away

Trident Travel (☎ 721379) runs up to seven trips in each direction (£7/3.50 for adults/children) between St Peter Port and Herm (20 minutes). Beat the crowds in summer and take the Milk Boat (£5.10/2.50 for a return) at 8.30 am.

Getting Around

The only way to get around is on foot. It takes about two hours to walk around the island.

ALDERNEY
☎ 01481 • pop 2500

Although it's the third largest of the Channel Islands, Alderney is just 3½ miles by 1½ miles at its widest point. It's the quietest of all the Channel Islands – the day-trippers tend to head for Sark and Herm.

There are white-sand beaches, cliff walks, and coastal forts dating from the 19th century and from the 1940s when the Germans occupied the island. (However, there's no underground hospital here.) St Anne, the capital, has a small museum (☎ 823222) that opens 10 am to noon and 2 pm to 4 pm daily (£2/1). The Alderney Railway (☎ 822980) operates in the tourist season, using old carriages from the London Underground that provide 15-minute rides.

The majority of the population lives in St Anne, in the centre of the island less than a mile from the airport. Alderney Tourism (☎ 823737, fax 822436, @ tourism@alderney.net) is on Victoria St in St Anne. It opens 10 am to noon Monday to Saturday.

Places to Stay & Eat

The only place where camping is permitted is *Saye Campsite* (☎ 822556) on Saye Bay,

which is slightly over one mile away from St Anne. Sites cost from £4.

Accommodation is not cheap. There are about eight guesthouses on the island, with B&B from £20 to £35 per person. *St Anne's Guest House* (☎ 823145, 10 Le Heuret, St Anne) is friendly and charges £20 per person.

There are more than a dozen hotels. By the beach in Braye, the *Sea View* (☎ 822738, fax 823572, @ seaview@internet.alderney.gg) has B&B accommodation costing from £25 to £38 per person.

The *Georgian House* (☎ 822471, fax 822471, @ georgian-hotel@virgin.net, Victoria St, St Anne) has rooms for £35 per person. The restaurant here is known for its seafood specialities, especially the local crab (£15.50).

The popular *Divers Inn*, immediately north of St Anne at Braye Harbour, is one of many local pubs. *Harbour Lights* in quiet Newtown has a nice beer garden.

Getting There & Away

With the much-protested withdrawal of ferry services, Aurigny Air Services (☎ 822886) has a monopoly on transport. It has two flights a day to/from Alderney and Jersey (£60 return, 15 minutes) and eight a day each way to Guernsey (£60 return, 15 minutes).

Getting Around

Alderney Hire Cars (☎ 823352) rents cars and mopeds; Peddle Power (☎ 822286) rents bikes. Both are located in St Anne, the latter on Les Rocquettes.

SARK
☎ 01481 • pop 580

Traffic-free Sark is probably best known as Europe's only feudal state. The seigneur, currently Michael Beaumont, rules through a feudal constitution that dates back to Elizabethan times. Sark levies no income tax, and maintains its own government and a collection of laws that includes such anomalies as the fact that no woman is entitled to divorce.

Three miles by 1½ miles, but with a jagged coastline of over 30 miles, the island has beautiful scenery best appreciated after the crowds of day-trippers have departed.

Sark is ideal for walkers who enjoy an unhurried pint – the pubs seem to remain open all hours, Monday to Saturday.

Contact Sark Tourism (☎ 832345, fax 832483) for its island guide which gives details and prices of places to stay. It's near the ferry dock and opens 10 am to 12.15 pm and 2 to 4.45 pm weekdays. There are no ATMs, but there are two banks that open 10 am to 3 pm on weekdays.

Places to Stay & Eat

There are camp sites (both charging £4.50 per person) at La Vallette (*☎ 832066, fax 832 636)* and Pomme de Chien *(☎/fax 832316)*.

There are about 20 hotels and B&Bs. The cheapest is *Le Pellon (☎ 832289)*. It's near the centre of the island and charges from £13 to £16 per person.

La Sablonnerie (☎ 832061, fax 832408) is a very comfortable hotel in the south of the island across the isthmus on Little Sark. Charges per person range from £38 to £86.

Founiais Restaurant (☎ 832626, Harbour Hill) is a good fish restaurant. Main dishes average £10 and local lobster is a speciality. There are several cafes and the larger hotels all have restaurants.

Getting There & Away

Isle of Sark Shipping (☎ 724059) is based on Guernsey and has up to five sailings each way every day between St Peter Port and Sark (£12.50/16.50 single/day-return, 45 minutes). The company also offers cheaper half-day excursions. Emeraude (☎ 01534-66566) operates a daily catamaran service to Jersey (£24/14 for adult/child with a single ticket or a cheap-day-return, 45 minutes).

Getting Around

There are no cars on the island, a tractor and trailer being the only motorised form of transport. Luggage carriers meet all scheduled ferries. There are horse-drawn carriage rides for £5 to £7.50 per hour. Avenue Cycle Hire (☎ 832102) rents out bikes for £4/22 day/week.

Language

Scottish Gaelic

Scottish Gaelic (*Gàidhlig* – pronounced *gallic* in Scotland) is spoken by about 80,000 people in Scotland, mainly in the Highlands and Islands, and by many native speakers and learners overseas. It is a member of the Celtic branch of the Indo-European family of languages which has given us Gaelic, Irish, Manx, Welsh, Cornish and Breton.

After two centuries of decline, the language is now being encouraged through financial help from government agencies and the EU. Gaelic education is flourishing from playgroups to tertiary levels. This renaissance flows out into the field of music, literature, cultural events and broadcasting.

Grammar

The usual word order in Gaelic is verb-subject-object; English, by comparison, has a subject-verb-object word order, eg The girl (subject) reads (verb) the book (object). There are two forms of the pronoun 'you' in Gaelic: the singular *thu*, and the plural form *sibh* which is also used as a formal (ie polite) singular. We use the informal *thu* in the following phraselist.

Pronunciation

Stress usually falls on the first syllable of a word. The Gaelic alphabet has only 18 letters:

Vowels

There are five vowels: **a**, **e**, **i**, **o** and **u** – **a**, **o** and **u** are known as broad vowels, **e** and **i** are known as slender vowels. A grave accent indicates that a vowel sound is lengthened, eg *bata* (a stick), *bàta* (a boat).

Consonants

There are 12 consonants: **b**, **c**, **d**, **f**, **g**, **l**, **m**, **n**, **p**, **r**, **s** and **t** and the letter **h** (only used to change other sounds).

c	always a hard 'k' sound; never an 's' sound
d	when broad, thicker than English 'd'; when slender, as the 'j' in 'jet'
l, ll	when slender, as in 'value'
n, nn	when slender, as in 'new'
s	when slender, as 'sh'
t	when broad, thicker than English 't'; when slender, as the 'ch' in 'chin'

When consonants are followed by 'h', a change of sound occurs:

bh mh	as 'v'
ch	when broad, as in *loch* (not 'lock'!); when slender, as the German *ich*
dh gh	when broad, voiced at the back of the throat; when slender, as 'y' – there's no English equivalent
fh	silent
ph	as 'f'
sh	as 'h' if before a broad vowel
th	as 'h'

Greetings & Civilities

Good morning.
  Madainn mhath.
  madding va
Good afternoon/Good evening.
  Feasgar math.
  fesskurr ma
Good night.
  Oidhche mhath.
  uh eech uh va
Goodbye. (lit: Blessings go with you)
  Beannachd leat.
  B yan achd let
Goodbye. (The same with you)
  Mar sin leat.
  mar shin let
How are you?
  Ciamar a tha thu?
  kimmer uh ha oo?
Very well, thank you.
  Glè mhath, tapadh leat.
  gley va, tappuh let

Please.
Mas e do thoil e.
mahs eh doh hawl eh
Thank you.
Tapadh leat.
tappuh let
Many thanks.
Mòran taing.
moe ran ta eeng
You're welcome.
'Se do bheatha.
sheh doh veh huh
I beg your pardon.
B'àill leibh.
baaluv
Excuse me.
Gabh mo leisgeul.
gav mo lishk yal
I'm sorry.
Tha mi duilich.
ha mee dooleech

Useful Words & Phrases

Do you speak (have) Gaelic?
A bheil Gàidhlig agad?
uh vil ga lick ackut?
Yes, a little.
Tha, beagan.
ha, beg an
Not much.
Chan eil mòran.
chan yil moe ran
What's your name?
De an t ainm a tha ort?
jae an tannam uh ha orsht?
I'm ...
Is mise ...
is meeshuh ...
Can you tell me ...?
An innis thu dhomh ...?
un yee ish oo ghoe ...?
I want to go to ...
Tha mi ag iarraidh a dhol gu ...
ha mee ug ee urry uh gholl goo ...
How do I get to ...?
Ciamar a gheibh mi gu ...?
kimmer uh yaev mee goo ...?

by bus
air a' bhus   ir uh vuss

by train
air an trean   ir un tren
by car
ann an car   a woon un car
a hotel
taigh òsda   tuh ee awstu
a bedroom
rùm cadail   roowm caddil
a toilet
taigh beag   tuh ee beck

a cup of coffee
cupa cofaidh   coopa cawfee
a cup of tea
cupa tì   coopa tee
a glass of water
glainne uisge   glanyuh ooshkuy

Cheers!
Slàinte mhath!   slahntchuh va!
beer
leann   lyawn
whisky
uisge beatha   ooshkuy beh huh
a glass of wine
glainne fìon   glahnyuh feeuhn
red wine
fìon dearg   feeuhn jerrack
white wine
fìon geal   feeuhn gyahl

Welsh

Pronunciation

For newcomers, Welsh is not the easiest language to master. The following is a brief guide to the pronunciation.

Vowels

The Welsh vowels are **a**, **e**, **i**, **o**, **u**, **w** and **y**. All except **y** have short and long versions.

a	long, as in 'car', *tad* (father)	
a	short, as in 'ham', *mam* (mother)	
e	long, as in 'sane', *hen* (old)	
e	short, as in 'ten', *pen* (head)	
i	long, as in 'marine', *mis* (month)	
i	short, as in 'tin', *prin* (scarce)	

o	long, as in 'or', *môr* (sea)
o	short, as in 'on', *ffon* (walking stick)
w	long, as in the 'oo' in 'moon', *swn* (sound)
w	short, as the 'oo' in 'look', *gwn* (gun)
y	three possible pronunciations: as the 'ee' in 'geese', *dyn* (man); as the 'i' in 'tin', *cyn* (before); as the 'u' in 'run', *dynion* (men)
oe	as the 'oy', in 'annoy', *coed* (wood)
u	as the 'i' in 'imp', *pump* (five)

Word stress usually falls on the second-last syllable in Welsh pronunciation.

Consonants

c	as in 'cat', *cath* (cat)
ch	as in Scottish 'loch', *fach* (small)
dd	as 'th' in 'them', *mynydd* (mountain)
f	as in 'of', *fach* (small)
ff	as in 'off', *ffenestr* (window)
g	as in 'go', *gardd* (garden)
h	as in 'hat', *het* (hat)
ll	no equivalent sound in English; try putting your tongue on the roof of your mouth, near the teeth, as if to pronounce 'l', and then blow the 'l'!
th	as in 'three' *byth* (ever)

Words & Phrases

If you're feeling brave, here are a few expressions you might like to try out in the Welsh-speaking parts of the country.

Good morning.	*Bore da.*
Good afternoon.	*Prynhawn da.*
Good night.	*Nos da.*
How are you?	*Sut mae?*
Thanks.	*Diolch.*
Cheers!	*Hwyl!*
What's your name?	*Beth ydy'ch enw chi?*
How much?	*Faint?*
good	*da*
very good	*da iawn*

women	*merched*
men	*dynion*
exit	*allan*
open	*ar agor*
hotel	*gwesty*
bus	*bws*
pub	*tafarn*

1	*un*
2	*dau*
3	*tri*
4	*pedwar*
5	*pump*
6	*chwech*
7	*saith*
8	*wyth*
9	*naw*
10	*deg*
11	*un-deg-un*
12	*un-deg-dau*
13	*un-deg-tri*
20	*dau-ddeg*
21	*dau-ddeg-un*
30	*tri-deg*
40	*pedwar-deg*
50	*pum-deg*
60	*chwe-deg*
70	*saith-deg*
80	*wyth-deg*
90	*naw-deg*
100	*cant*
200	*dau cant*
500	*pum cant*
1000	*mil*

Wales is famous for having the longest place name in the world – Llanfairpwll-gwyngyllgogerychwyrndrobwllllantysiliog-ogogoch – which, translated, means 'St Mary's Church in the hollow of the White Hazel near a rapid whirlpool and the Church of St Tysilio near the Red Cave'. It can be tricky to say after a pint of Brains.

Glossary

abe – estuary (Wales)

afon – river (Wales)

agister – someone paid to care for stock

aka – also known as

almshouse – accommodation offered to the aged or needy

auld – old (Scotland)

aye – yes/always (Scotland)

BABA – Book-A-Bed-Ahead scheme

bach – small (Wales)

bailey – outermost wall of a castle

bairn – baby (Newcastle & Scotland)

banger – old, cheap car

bangers – sausages

bap – bun

bar – gate (York)

bara birth – spicy fruit loaf (Wales)

ben – mountain (Scotland)

bent – not altogether legal

bevvied – drunk

bevvy – a drink

bevvying – drinking

bill – restaurant check

billion – a million million, not a thousand million

biscuit – cookie

bitter – a type of beer

black pudding – a type of sausage made from dried blood and other ingredients (Scotland)

blatherskite – boastful or talkative person (northern England)

bloke – man

bloody – damn

bodge job – poor-quality repairs

böd – barn (Scotland)

bothy – hut or mountain shelter (Scotland)

brae – hill (Scotland)

bridleway – path that can be used by walkers, horse riders and cyclists

broch – defensive tower (Scotland)

Brummie – a native of Birmingham

bryn – hill (Wales)

BTA – British Tourist Authority

burgh – town (Scotland)

burn – creek (Scotland)

bus – local bus; *see also* coach

BYO – bring your own

cadair – stronghold/chair (Wales)

Cadw – Welsh Historic Monuments Agency

caer – fort (Wales)

caff – cheap cafe

canny – good, great (Newcastle)

capel – chapel (Wales)

car bonnet – hood

car boot – trunk

carreg – stone (Wales)

ceilidh – informal evening entertainment and dance (Scotland)

cheers – thanks; *also* a drinking toast

chemist – pharmacist

chine – valleylike fissure leading to the sea

chips – deep-fried potatoes

circus – a junction of several streets, usually circular

close – entrance (Scotland)

clun – meadow (Wales)

coach – long-distance bus; *see also* bus

coaching inn – inn along a coaching route at which horses were changed

coasteering – steering your way around the coastline by climbing, jumping, swimming or scrambling

coch – red (Wales)

coed – forest/wood (Wales)

Corbett – mountain of between 762m and 914m

couchette – sleeping berth in a train or ferry

courgette – zucchini

courts – courtyards

crack – good conversation (originally from Ireland)

crannogh – artificial island settlement

crisps – potato chips

croft – plot of land with adjoining house worked by the occupiers

cromlech – burial chamber (Wales)

cwm – valley (Wales)

de – south (Wales)

dear – expensive

din (dinas) – fort (Wales)

DIY – do-it-yourself, as in handyman shop

dolmen – chartered tomb

dosh/dough – money

downs – rolling upland, characterised by lack of trees

du – black (Wales)

duvet – doona

EH – English Heritage

eisteddfod – festival in which competitions are held in music, poetry, drama and the fine arts (Wales)

EU – European Union

evensong – daily evening service (Church of England)

fag – cigarette; *also* a boring task

fagged – exhausted

fanny – female genitals, not backside

fawr – big (Wales)

fen – drained or marshy low-lying flat land

ffordd – road (Wales)

firth – estuary (Scotland)

fiver – five-pound note

flat – apartment

flip-flops – thongs

fussock – irritating woman (from Yorkshire)

gaffer – boss or foreman

gate – street (York)

geo – inlet (Scotland)

ginnel – alleyway (Yorkshire)

glan – shore (Wales)

glas – blue (Wales)

glen – valley (Scotland)

gloup – natural arch (Scotland)

glyn – valley (Wales)

gobslutch – slovenly person (northern English)

grand – one thousand

greasy spoon – cheap cafe

gutted – very disappointed

guv, guvner – governor, term of address for owner or boss, can be used ironically

gwrydd – green (Wales)

gwyn – white (Wales)

haar – fog off the North Sea (Scotland)

hammered – drunk

hire – rent

Hogmanay – New Year's Eve (Scotland)

hosepipe – garden hose

hotel – accommodation with food and bar, not always open to passing trade

HS – Historic Scotland

Huguenots – French Protestants

inn – pub with accommodation

jam – jelly

jelly – jello

jumper – sweater

ken – know (Scotland)

kirk – church (Scotland)

kyle – narrow strait

lager lout – *see* yob

laird – estate owner (Scotland)

lands – multistorey apartment buildings (Scotland)

lass – young woman (northern England)

laver bread – seaweed fried as a breakfast food (Wales)

ley – clearing

lift – elevator

linn – waterfall (Scotland)

llan – enclosed place or church (Wales)

llyn – lake (Wales)

lock – part of a canal or river that can be closed off and the water levels changed to raise or lower boats

lolly – money; *also* candy on a stick (possibly frozen)

lorry – truck

love – term of address, not necessarily to someone likeable

machair – grass- and wildflower-covered sand dunes

mad – insane, not angry

manky – low quality (southern England)

Martello tower – small, circular tower used for coastal defence

mate – a friend of any sex, term of address

mawr – great (Wales)

merthyr – burial place of a saint (Wales)

midge – a mosquito-like insect

motorway – freeway

motte – mound on which a castle was built

Munro – mountain of 914m or higher (Scotland)

mynydd – mountain (Wales)

naff – inferior, in poor taste
nant – valley/stream (Wales)
nappies – diapers
newydd – new (Wales)
NT – National Trust
NTS – National Trust for Scotland

oast house – building containing a kiln for drying hops
off-licence (offie) – shop selling alcoholic drinks
ogof – cave (Wales)
OS – Ordnance Survey
owlers – smugglers

pavement – sidewalk
pee – pence
pele – fortified houses
pen – headland (Wales)
pend – arched gateway (Scotland)
pissed – drunk (not angry)
pissed off – angry
pistyll – waterfall (Wales)
pitch – playing field
plas – hall/mansion (Wales)
ponce – ostentatious or effeminate male
pont – bridge (Wales)
pop – fizzy drink (northern England)
postbuses – minibuses that follow postal delivery routes
pub – short for public house, a bar usually with food, sometimes with accommodation
punter – customer
pwll – pool (Wales)

queue – line
quid – pound

ramble – to go for a short walk
reiver – warrior (Scotland and Northern England)
restit – a type of stew made from mutton (Scotland)
return ticket – round-trip ticket
rhiw – slope (Wales)
rhos – moor/marsh (Wales)
roll-up – roll-your-own cigarette
rood – alternative word for cross

RSPB – Royal Society for the Protection of Birds
rubber – eraser
rubbish bin – garbage can
rugger – rugby

sacked – fired
sarnie – sandwich
Sassenach – an English person or a lowland Scot (Scotland)
sett – tartan pattern
shag – have sex
shout – to buy a group of people drinks, usually reciprocated
shut – partially covered passage
single ticket – one-way ticket
snicket – alleyway (from York)
snogging – kissing
spondulicks – money
sporran – purse (Scotland)
SSSI – Site of Special Scientific Interest
steaming – drunk
stone – 14 lb, 6.35 kg
strath – valley (Scotland)
subway – underpass
sweet – candy

ta – thanks
thwaite – clearing in a forest
TIC – Tourist Information Centre
ton – one hundred
tor – Celtic word describing a hill shaped like a triangular wedge of cheese
torch – flashlight
towpath – a path running beside a river or canal
trainers – tennis shoes/sneakers/runners
traveller – nomadic, New-Age hippy
tre – town (Wales)
tron – public weighbridge
twitchers – birdwatchers
twitten – passage, small lane
twr – tower (Wales)
tube – London's underground railway (subway)
ty – house (Wales)

underground – London's underground railway (subway)
uisge-bha – the water of life: whisky (Scotland)

VAT – value-added tax, levied on most goods and services, currently 17.5%
verderer – officer upholding law and order in the royal forests

way – a long-distance trail
wellied – drunk
wide boy – ostentatious go-getter, usually on the make
wold – open, rolling country

WTB – Wales Tourist Board
wynd – lane (Scotland)

ynys – island (Wales)
yob – hooligan
ystwyth – winding (Wales)

ziggurat – a kind of rectangular temple tower or tiered mound

Glossary of Religious Architecture

Abbey
A monastery of monks or nuns or the buildings they used. When Henry VIII dissolved the monasteries between 1536 and 1540, many English and Irish abbeys were destroyed or converted into private homes, though some survived as churches. Thus an abbey today may be a church or a home.

Aisle
Passageway or open space along either side of the nave and/or down the centre.

Alignment
Even if this doesn't conform with geography, churches are always assumed to be aligned east–west, with the altar, chancel and choir towards the eastern end and the nave towards the western end.

Ambulatory
Processional aisle at the eastern end of a cathedral, behind the altar.

Apse
Semicircular or rectangular area for clergy, at eastern end of church in traditional design.

Baptistry
Separate area of a church used for baptisms.

Barrel Vault
Semicircular arched roof.

Boss
Covering for the meeting point of the ribs in a vaulted roof (often colourfully decorated, so bring binoculars).

Brass
Type of memorial common in medieval churches consisting of a brass plate set into the floor or a tomb, usually with a depiction of the deceased but sometimes simply with text.

Buttress
Vertical support for a wall; see Flying Buttress.

Campanile
Free-standing belfry or bell tower; Chester

and Westminster Cathedrals have modern ones.

Chancel
Eastern end of the church, usually reserved for choir and clergy. The name comes from the Latin word for lattice because of the screen that once separated the two parts of the church.

Chantry
Chapel established by a donor for use in his or her name after death.

Chapel
Small, more private shrine or area of worship off the main body of the church. In some British cathedrals, chapels were established by different crafts guilds.

Chapel of Ease
Chapel built for those who lived too far away from the parish church.

Chapter House
Building in a cathedral close where the dean meets with the chapter, the clergy who run the cathedral.

Chevet
Chapels radiating out in a semicircular sweep, common in France but also found at Westminster and Canterbury.

Choir
Area in the church where the choir is seated, usually to the east of the transepts and nave; sometimes used interchangeably with chancel or presbytery.

Clerestory
Also clearstory; wall of windows above the triforium.

Cloister
Covered walkway linking the church with adjacent monastic buildings.

Close
Buildings grouped around a cathedral, also known as the precincts.

Collegiate
Church with a chapter of canons and prebendaries, but not a cathedral.

Corbel
Stone or wooden projection from a wall supporting a beam or arch.

Crossing
Intersection of the nave and transepts.

Flying Buttress
Supporting buttress in the form of one side of an open arch.

Font
Basin used for baptisms, usually towards the western end of the building, often in a separate baptistry.

Frater
Common room or dining area in a medieval monastery.

Lady Chapel
Chapel, usually at the eastern end of a cathedral, dedicated to the Virgin Mary.

Lancet
Pointed window in Early English style.

Minster
A church connected to a monastery.

Misericord
Hinged choir seat with a bracket (often elaborately carved) that can be leant against.

Nave
Main body of the church at the western end, where the congregation gather.

Piscina
Basin for priests to wash their hands.

Presbytery
Eastern area of the chancel beyond the choir, where the clergy operate.

Priory
Religious house governed by a prior, inferior to an abbey.

Pulpit
Raised box where priest gives sermon.

Quire
Medieval term for choir.

Refectory
Monastic dining room.

Reredos
Literally 'behind the back'; backdrop to an altar.

Rood Screen
A screen carrying a rood or crucifix, which separated the nave from the chancel.

Squint
Angled opening in a wall or pillar to allow a view of the altar.

Transepts
North–south projections from the nave, often added at a later date and giving the whole church a cruciform cross-shaped plan. Some medieval English cathedrals (Canterbury, Lincoln, Salisbury) feature smaller second transepts.

Triforium
Internal wall passage above the arcade and below the clerestory; behind it is the 'blind' space above the side aisle.

Undercroft
Vaulted underground room or cellar.

Vault
Roof with arched ribs, usually in a decorative pattern.

Vestry
Robing room, where the parson's clerical robes are kept, and where they put them on.

Acknowledgments

Many thanks to the travellers who used the last edition and wrote to us with helpful hints, useful advice and interesting anecdotes:

A Johnston, Adrian Lawton, AH Berry, Alasdair Brooks, Alex Castrodale, Alison Coles, Alison Tucker, Allison Marsh, Alvin T Hudec, Amanda Bresnan, Amanda Donovan, Amy Mackay, Andrew Knoza, Andrew Stark, Andy Bradshaw, Andy Hancock, Angela Herd, Angela Schacht, Ann Dolan, Ann Mione, Annacarin Skarstedt, Antonio Skliris, Ashley Eastwood, Assaf A Harlap, Axel Holewa, B van Selm, Barbara Wolf, Barry Maxwell, Batya Fromm, Belinda Coombs, Belinda Romers, Beth Bergen, Beth Smith, Bethan Morgan, Bev Bingham, Bjorn Olav, Brad Wilson, Brian & Chau Loo Smith, Brian Kovacsi, Bridie Smith, Britta Hammersley, Brooke Aldrich, Bruce Baldey, C Harris, C Mills, C Shearer, Callie Elliston, Carla Halbreich, Carmen Estermann, Carol Rudd, Carole Bennett, Carrie Lee, Cat Llewellyn, Catarina Ang, Cath Petersen, Catherine Brew, Cato Kjavvik, Celine Schranz, Charlotte Colliander Golding, Cheng Hin Saw, Chris Brown, Chris Day, Chris Fitzer, Chris Lock, Chris Truax, Christian Corkin, Christiane Thage, Christina Rizzo Adams, Christine Tiscareno, Christopher Sonne, Colin Hill, Conrad Heine, Craig X, Craig Miller, D Higbre, D&O Middleton, Dafydd Charles, Dan Morris, Daniel Cox, Dave Baldcock, David Evanoff, David Gott, David Hinds, David Hugh Smith, David Neate, David Robertson, David Roby, David Woodhead, Davould Davies, Dawn Dean, Dean Purkis, Deborah Fraser, Delphine Sifflet, Dennis Whittle, Derek Luce, Desmond Harney, Diane Yoder, Diarmuid Wilson, Dom Wilson, Dr John Kennedy, DR Williamson, Dr Wolfgang Lechleitner, E Reynar, Ed Rozmiarek, Edgar Locke, Edgar Locke, Eliane Dosker, Eliane Keith, Elinor Yeo, Elizabeth Poole, Elizabeth Ross, Elizabeth Wilder, Emanuela Tasinato, Erica Schumacher, Essi Suikkanen, Eva, Evelyn Reynar, Fiona Clarke, Fiona Gunn, Flor Espinar Maat, Fran Callinan, Frank Grenfell, GA Battrun, Gareth Roberts, Ged Major, George Peckham, Georgia King, Geraldine Perriam, Gez Collins, GF Taylor, Gillian Roberts, Giorgio Morandi, Glenn Forsyth, Goldie Church, Gordon Garraway, Gordon Woods, Greg Alford, Gregory Fields, Gwen & Dick Kiefer, H. Kuivenhoven, Hans von Tour, Heather Beswick, Heather Milne, Helen Morrison, Hortensia Chang, Ian Hall, Ian Harrison, Ian Kershaw, J Hippisley, J Ramano, Jack Fitzsimons, Jackie & Joan Staines, Jackie Lake, Jackie Lee, Jan Howard Finder, Jan Macintyre, Janet O'Shea, Janine Pike, Jean Smith, Jean-Gut Leblanc, Jeff Weeks, Jennifer Ngai, Jennifer Wolfersberger, Jeremy & Julia Holmn, Jeremy Speechley, Jill E Bell, Jimmy Patrick Haffenrichter, Jo Miklosi, Jo Rider, Jodi Lipson, Jodie Lugton, Joe Miklosi, Joe Morgado, John Green, John Lambert, John Napier, John Wren, Jonathan Fuller, JR Holder, Judson Ford, Judy Smith, Judy Whitby, Jules & Dr Rossman, Julian Bryers, Julian Luebbert, June X, Kalvin Embling, Karen X, Karen Adamson, Karen Crawford, Karen Holland, Kathryn and Peter Lepage, Kathryn Mumell, Kathy Kitao, Kay X, Kelly Alexander, Kelly Thomas, Kelvin LO, Kerrin Hardy, Kirstine Postma, Kirsty McWalter, KL Marsden, Knut Albert Solem, Krista Maciolek, Kristine Lang, Krystal Marshall, Kylie Lawrence, L Ceyne, Laura Shanner, Laurent Mousson, Leanne Drummond, Lermot Dobson, Leslie Boot, Liam Campbell, Lina Harbinson, Linda X, Linda Battin, Linda M Haston, Lonneke van der Burgt, Lorraine Spence, Luke Dolby, Luke McKean, Lynne Dunford, M Ramsay, Maggie Fifoot, Malcolm Glaister, Marcia Keenan, Margaret Micheben, Marie & Stewart Dougan, Mark Edebone, Mark Gaskell, Mark Murray, Mark Nixon, Mark Ridgwell, Mark Schiefelbein, Mark Stone, Martin Dammann, Martin Dorey, Martin Schirra, Martina Baldinger, Martti Huuskonen, Mary de Ruyter, Mary Golden, Matt Moore, Matthew Gream, Mavis & Doug Haynes, Meg Francis, Melissa Christie, Melissa Thomas, Melissa Yap,

Melissa Yap, Michael Dudley, Michael Koops, Michael Slattery, Michael Teague, Michele Seigerman, Michelle Chee, Michelle Shipworth, Mike Taylor, Mindy Nagorsky, MJ Louis, Monica & Rob Perkavac, Monica Lanier, Monito, Natalia Strachan, Nidia Lorenzana, Nigel Hamilton, Nils Andreas Thommesen, Norma Davies, Pam & Gordon Oates, Pam Davidson, Paul Greening, Paul Lucock, Paul Pedersen, Paul Raistrick, Paul Wilson, Paula Reid, Paula Thomas, Pavlina Krzovski, Pazu Yau, PD & SY Markham, Peggy Longley, Penny Smith, Penny Wyrd, Pete & Deb Meigs, Peter Cocks, Peter Schoch, Phil Bassett, Philip Bladon, Philip Haggerty, Philip Harper, Phillipa Hay, Polly Ioannou, PR Ward, Priscilla Woodward, R Johnston, Rachelle Garaland, Ramona Mapp, Randall van Someren, Ray Smith, Reeves Novak, Rene van Eijk, RF Jarrett, Rhianna Edwards, Richard, Rob Jones, Robert Thorensen-Davies, Robin Percy, Rod Miller, Rod Willard, Rose Corney, Royce Wilson, Roz Russell, Rupert Stewart, S Graham, S O'Brien, Sally Bothroyd, Sally Trerise, Sally Weigard, Sam Allen, Sandra Wehrley, Sandra Wells, Sarah Bellamy, Sarah Guy, Savita Vyas, Scott Gilmore, Scott Neilson, Sean Anderson, Sheila & John Lough, Sherri-Lynn Morissette, Silke Remmel, Simon Chambers, Simon Skerritt, Simon Wood, Simone de Wet, SP Holt, Stacey Henerey, Stephen Brady, Stephen Cross, Stephen Grove, Sterling Vorus, Steve Curwood, Steve Reid, Steven Wilson, Sue Findlay, Sue Kitchin, Sue Moss, Sue Walker, Susan Toh, Tanya Jansen, The Boyles, Thomas Buch-Andersen, Tim Oliver Eynck, Tim Wood, Tina Storm Nielsen, Tom Page, Tom Willmott, Toni Nash, Tony Carenzo, Tony Craggs, Tracy Savage, Trevor J Allcott, Trine & Bruce Macadam, Trish Morrow, Ursula Haas, V McHugh, Veronica, Veronica W Rogers, VI Quarmby, Vicki Barnes, Vickie Barnes, Victoria Steward, Wallace M Olson, Wayne Evan, Wei & Jenny Ching, Wendy Porter, Wendy Turner, Wendy Valois, Will Campbell, William Hipperson, Winifrid Ruger, WL West

LONELY PLANET

You already know that Lonely Planet publishes more than this one guidebook, but you might not be aware of the other products we have on this region. Here is a selection of titles that you may want to check out as well:

British phrasebook
ISBN 0 86442 484 1
US$5.95 • UK£3.99

Cycling Britain
ISBN 1 86450 037 9
US$19.99 • UK£12.99

Edinburgh
ISBN 0 86442 580 5
US$11.95 • UK£6.99

England
ISBN 0 86450 194 4
US$21.99 • UK£13.99

London
ISBN 0 86442 793 X
US$15.95 • UK£9.99

London City Map
ISBN 1 86450 008 5
US$5.95 • UK£3.99

London condensed
ISBN 1 86450 043 3
US$9.95 • UK£5.99

Out to Eat – London 2001
ISBN 1 86450 083 2
US$14.99 • UK£7.99

Scotland
ISBN 0 86442 592 9
US$15.95 • UK£9.99

Wales
ISBN 0 86450 126 X
US$15.99 • UK£9.99

Walking in Britain
ISBN 0 86450 280 0
US$21.99 • UK£13.99

Available wherever books are sold.

LONELY PLANET

Guides by Region

L onely Planet is known worldwide for publishing practical, reliable and no-nonsense travel information in our guides and on our Web site. The Lonely Planet list covers just about every accessible part of the world. Currently there are 16 series: Travel guides, Shoestring guides, Condensed guides, Phrasebooks, Read This First, Healthy Travel, Walking guides, Cycling guides, Watching Wildlife guides, Pisces Diving & Snorkeling guides, City Maps, Road Atlases, Out to Eat, World Food, Journeys travel literature and Pictorials.

AFRICA Africa on a shoestring • Cairo • Cairo City Map • Cape Town • Cape Town City Map • East Africa • Egypt • Egyptian Arabic phrasebook • Ethiopia, Eritrea & Djibouti • Ethiopian (Amharic) phrasebook • The Gambia & Senegal • Healthy Travel Africa • Kenya • Malawi • Morocco • Moroccan Arabic phrasebook • Mozambique • Read This First: Africa • South Africa, Lesotho & Swaziland • Southern Africa • Southern Africa Road Atlas • Swahili phrasebook • Tanzania, Zanzibar & Pemba • Trekking in East Africa • Tunisia • Watching Wildlife East Africa •   Watching Wildlife Southern Africa • West Africa • World Food Morocco • Zimbabwe, Botswana & Namibia
Travel Literature: Mali Blues: Traveling to an African Beat • The Rainbird: A Central African Journey • Songs to an African Sunset: A Zimbabwean Story

AUSTRALIA & THE PACIFIC Auckland • Australia • Australian phrasebook • Australia Road Atlas • Cycling Australia • Cycling New Zealand • Fiji • Fijian phrasebook • Healthy Travel Australia, NZ and the Pacific • Islands of Australia's Great Barrier Reef • Melbourne • Melbourne City Map • Micronesia • New Caledonia • New South Wales • New Zealand • Northern Territory • Outback Australia • Out to Eat – Melbourne • Out to Eat – Sydney • Papua New Guinea • Pidgin phrasebook • Queensland • Rarotonga & the Cook Islands • Samoa • Solomon Islands • South Australia • South Pacific • South Pacific phrasebook • Sydney • Sydney City Map • Sydney Condensed • Tahiti & French Polynesia • Tasmania • Tonga • Tramping in New Zealand • Vanuatu • Victoria • Walking in Australia • Watching Wildlife Australia • Western Australia
Travel Literature: Islands in the Clouds: Travels in the Highlands of New Guinea • Kiwi Tracks: A New Zealand Journey • Sean & David's Long Drive

CENTRAL AMERICA & THE CARIBBEAN Bahamas, Turks & Caicos • Baja California • Bermuda • Central America on a shoestring • Costa Rica • Costa Rica Spanish phrasebook • Cuba • Dominican Republic & Haiti • Eastern Caribbean • Guatemala • Guatemala, Belize & Yucatán: La Ruta Maya • Healthy Travel Central & South America • Jamaica • Mexico • Mexico City • Panama • Puerto Rico • Read This First: Central & South America • World Food Mexico • Yucatán
Travel Literature: Green Dreams: Travels in Central America

EUROPE Amsterdam • Amsterdam City Map • Amsterdam Condensed • Andalucía • Austria • Baltic States phrasebook • Barcelona • Barcelona City Map • Berlin • Berlin City Map • Britain • British phrasebook • Brussels, Bruges & Antwerp • Brussels City Map • Budapest • Budapest City Map • Canary Islands • Central Europe • Central Europe phrasebook • Corfu & the Ionians • Corsica • Crete • Crete Condensed • Croatia • Cycling Britain • Cycling France • Cyprus • Czech & Slovak Republics • Denmark • Dublin • Dublin City Map • Eastern Europe • Eastern Europe phrasebook • Edinburgh • Estonia, Latvia & Lithuania • Europe on a shoestring • Europe phrasebook • Finland • Florence • France • Frankfurt Condensed • French phrasebook • Georgia, Armenia & Azerbaijan • Germany • German phrasebook • Greece • Greek Islands • Greek phrasebook • Hungary • Iceland, Greenland & the Faroe Islands • Ireland • Italian phrasebook • Italy • Krakow • Lisbon • The Loire • London • London City Map • London Condensed • Madrid • Malta • Mediterranean Europe • Mediterranean Europe phrasebook • Moscow • Mozambique • Munich • Netherlands • Norway • Out to Eat – London • Out to Eat – Paris • Paris • Paris City Map • Paris Condensed • Poland • Portugal • Portuguese phrasebook • Prague • Prague City Map • Provence & the Côte d'Azur • Read This First: Europe • Romania & Moldova • Rome • Rome City Map • Russia, Ukraine & Belarus • Russian phrasebook • Scandinavian & Baltic Europe • Scandinavian phrasebook • Scotland • Sicily • Slovenia • South-West France • Spain • Spanish phrasebook • St Petersburg • St Petersburg City Map • Sweden • Switzerland • Tuscany • Ukrainian phrasebook • Venice • Vienna • Walking in Britain • Walking in France • Walking in Ireland • Walking in Italy • Walking in Spain • Walking in Switzerland • Western Europe • World Food France • World Food Ireland • World Food Italy • World Food Spain
Travel Literature: Love and War in the Apennines • The Olive Grove: Travels in Greece • On the Shores of the Mediterranean • Round Ireland in Low Gear • A Small Place in Italy • After Yugoslavia

LONELY PLANET

Mail Order

Lonely Planet products are distributed worldwide. They are also available by mail order from Lonely Planet, so if you have difficulty finding a title please write to us. North and South American residents should write to 150 Linden St, Oakland, CA 94607, USA; European and African residents should write to 10a Spring Place, London NW5 3BH, UK; and residents of other countries to Locked Bag 1, Footscray, Victoria 3011, Australia.

INDIAN SUBCONTINENT Bangladesh • Bengali phrasebook • Bhutan • Delhi • Goa • Healthy Travel Asia & India • Hindi & Urdu phrasebook • India • Indian Himalaya • Karakoram Highway • Kerala • Mumbai (Bombay) • Nepal • Nepali phrasebook • Pakistan • Rajasthan • Read This First: Asia & India • South India • Sri Lanka • Sri Lanka phrasebook • Tibet • Tibetan phrasebook • Trekking in the Indian Himalaya • Trekking in the Karakoram & Hindukush • Trekking in the Nepal Himalaya
Travel Literature: The Age of Kali: Indian Travels and Encounters • Hello Goodnight: A Life of Goa • In Rajasthan • A Season in Heaven: True Tales from the Road to Kathmandu • Shopping for Buddhas • A Short Walk in the Hindu Kush • Slowly Down the Ganges

ISLANDS OF THE INDIAN OCEAN Madagascar & Comoros • Maldives • Mauritius, Réunion & Seychelles

MIDDLE EAST & CENTRAL ASIA Bahrain, Kuwait & Qatar • Central Asia • Central Asia phrasebook • Dubai • Farsi (Persian) phrasebook • Hebrew phrasebook • Iran • Israel & the Palestinian Territories • Istanbul • Istanbul City Map • Istanbul to Cairo on a shoestring • Jerusalem • Jerusalem City Map • Jordan • Lebanon • Middle East • Oman & the United Arab Emirates • Syria • Turkey • Turkish phrasebook • World Food Turkey • Yemen
Travel Literature: Black on Black: Iran Revisited • The Gates of Damascus • Kingdom of the Film Stars: Journey into Jordan

NORTH AMERICA Alaska • Boston • Boston City Map • California & Nevada • California Condensed • Canada • Chicago • Chicago City Map • Deep South • Florida • Great Lakes • Hawaii • Hiking in Alaska • Hiking in the USA • Las Vegas • Los Angeles • Los Angeles City Map • Miami • Miami City Map • New England • New Orleans • New York City • New York City City Map • New York City Condensed • New York, New Jersey & Pennsylvania • Oahu • Out to Eat – San Francisco • Pacific Northwest • Rocky Mountains • San Francisco • San Francisco City Map • Seattle • Southwest • Texas • USA • USA phrasebook • Vancouver • Virginia & the Capital Region • Washington, DC • Washington, DC City Map • World Food Deep South, USA
Travel Literature: Caught Inside: A Surfer's Year on the California Coast • Drive Thru America

NORTH-EAST ASIA Beijing • Beijing City Map • Cantonese phrasebook • China • Hiking in Japan • Hong Kong • Hong Kong City Map • Hong Kong Condensed • Hong Kong, Macau & Guangzhou • Japan • Japanese phrasebook • Korea • Korean phrasebook • Kyoto • Mandarin phrasebook • Mongolia • Mongolian phrasebook • Seoul • Shanghai • South-West China • Taiwan • Tokyo
Travel Literature: In Xanadu: A Quest • Lost Japan

SOUTH AMERICA Argentina, Uruguay & Paraguay • Bolivia • Brazil • Brazilian phrasebook • Buenos Aires • Chile & Easter Island • Colombia • Ecuador & the Galapagos Islands • Healthy Travel Central & South America • Latin American Spanish phrasebook • Peru • Quechua phrasebook • Read This First: Central & South America • Rio de Janeiro • Rio de Janeiro City Map • South America on a shoestring • Trekking in the Patagonian Andes • Venezuela
Travel Literature: Full Circle: A South American Journey

SOUTH-EAST ASIA Bali & Lombok • Bangkok • Bangkok City Map • Burmese phrasebook • Cambodia • Hanoi • Healthy Travel Asia & India • Hill Tribes phrasebook • Ho Chi Minh City • Indonesia • Indonesian phrasebook • Indonesia's Eastern Islands • Java • Lao phrasebook • Laos • Malay phrasebook • Malaysia, Singapore & Brunei • Myanmar (Burma) • Philippines • Pilipino (Tagalog) phrasebook • Read This First: Asia & India • Singapore • Singapore City Map • South-East Asia on a shoestring • South-East Asia phrasebook • Thailand • Thailand's Islands & Beaches • Thailand, Vietnam, Laos & Cambodia Road Atlas • Thai phrasebook • Vietnam • Vietnamese phrasebook • World Food Thailand • World Food Vietnam

ALSO AVAILABLE: Antarctica • The Arctic • The Blue Man: Tales of Travel, Love and Coffee • Brief Encounters: Stories of Love, Sex & Travel • Chasing Rickshaws • The Last Grain Race • Lonely Planet Unpacked • Not the Only Planet: Science Fiction Travel Stories • On the Edge: Extreme Travel • Sacred India • Travel with Children • Travel Photography: A Guide to Taking Better Pictures

Mail Order

Index

Text

Bold indicates maps.

Bold indicates maps.

Bold indicates maps.

Bold indicates maps.

Boxed Text

MAP LEGEND

BOUNDARIES

—■—■—■— International
—■—■—■— Regional
— ■ — ■ — Suburb

HYDROGRAPHY

Coastline
River, Creek
Lake
Canal

ROUTES & TRANSPORT

Autoroute
Primary Road
Secondary Road
Tertiary Road
Unsealed Road
City Autoroute
City Primary Road
City Road
City Street, Lane

AREA FEATURES

Forest
Market

MAP SYMBOLS

Cathedral or Church
Cave
Cinema, Theatre
Cliff or Escarpment
Embassy
Fountain
Golf Course
Hospital
Internet Cafe
Lighthouse
Lookout
Monument
Mountain, Range
Museum
One Way Street

Note: not all symbols displayed above appear in this book

Pedestrian Area
Tunnel
Train Route & Station
Metro & Station
Tramway
Cable Car or Chairlift
Walking Track
Walking Tour
Ferry Route & Terminal

Beach
Cemetery

Park, Gardens
Urban Area, Building

LONDON .... Capital City
Bristol .... City or Large Town
Cambridge .... Town
Bideford .... Village
• .... Point of Interest
▪ .... Place to Stay
▲ .... Camp Site
🚐 .... Caravan Park
▼ .... Place to Eat
⬛ .... Pub or Bar
✈ ✝ .... Airport, Airfield
Ancient or City Wall
⑤ .... Bank
🏖 .... Beach
🐦 .... Bird Sanctuary
🚏 .... Bus Stop, Station
🏰 .... Castle or Fort

Parking
Pass
Police Station
Post Office
Ruins
Shopping Centre
Ski Field
Stately Home or Palace
Swimming Pool
Telephone
Toilet
Tomb
Tourist Information
Transport
Vineyard
Waterfall
Zoo

LONELY PLANET OFFICES

Australia
Locked Bag 1, Footscray, Victoria 3011
☎ 03 9689 4666 fax 03 9689 6833
email: talk2us@lonelyplanet.com.au

USA
150 Linden St, Oakland, CA 94607
☎ 510 893 8555 TOLL FREE: 800 275 8555
fax 510 893 8572
email: info@lonelyplanet.com

UK
10a Spring Place, London NW5 3BH
☎ 020 7428 4800 fax 020 7428 4828
email: go@lonelyplanet.co.uk

France
1 rue du Dahomey, 75011 Paris
☎ 01 55 25 33 00 fax 01 55 25 33 01
email: bip@lonelyplanet.fr
www.lonelyplanet.fr

World Wide Web: www.lonelyplanet.com *or* AOL keyword: lp
Lonely Planet Images: lpi@lonelyplanet.com.au